ROUTLEDGE LIBRARY EDITIONS:
HISTORY OF MEDICINE

Volume 8

MEDICAL OBITUARIES

MEDICAL OBITUARIES

American Physicians' Biographical Notices in Selected Medical Journals before 1907

LISABETH M. HOLLOWAY, ERNEST N. FEIND
AND GEORGE N. HOLLOWAY

LONDON AND NEW YORK

First published in 1981 by Garland Publishing, Inc.
This edition published in 1995 by Garland Publishing Inc.

This edition first published in 2019
by Routledge
2 Park Square, Milton Park, Abingdon, Oxon OX14 4RN

and by Routledge
52 Vanderbilt Avenue, New York, NY 10017

Routledge is an imprint of the Taylor & Francis Group, an informa business

British Library Cataloguing in Publication Data
A catalogue record for this book is available from the British Library

ISBN: 978-0-367-08576-6 (Set)
ISBN: 978-0-429-02312-5 (Set) (ebk)
ISBN: 978-0-367-02746-9 (Volume 8) (hbk)
ISBN: 978-0-367-02749-0 (Volume 8) (pbk)
ISBN: 978-0-429-39803-2 (Volume 8) (ebk)

Publisher's Note
The publisher has gone to great lengths to ensure the quality of this reprint but points out that some imperfections in the original copies may be apparent.

Disclaimer
The publisher has made every effort to trace copyright holders and would welcome correspondence from those they have been unable to trace.

MEDICAL OBITUARIES

American Physicians' Biographical Notices

in Selected Medical Journals before 1907

Lisabeth M. Holloway
with the assistance of
Ernest N. Feind
George N. Holloway

Reset from the 1981 edition
with minor corrections
and an additional preface . . .
Also issued on CD–ROM

Lisabeth M. Holloway
Boone, N. C.
1995

CONTENTS

ACKNOWLEDGMENTS

This work originated during the latter 1960's in the compiler's activity as cataloguer under the late Walton Brooks McDaniel, 2d, Curator of Historical Materials, College of Physicians of Philadelphia. While conducted entirely as an extra–curricular project in off–hours, and in no sense under McD's eye, this work, growing from a casual side–interest into a sometimes overwhelming hobby, derives its existence from McD's scholarly influence.

The compiler owes especial thanks to:

Francis James Dallett, Archivist of the University of Pennsylvania, who brought to our attention and allowed us to photocopy and incorporate material from the University's unique annotated copies of its 1877, 1887, and 1897 Medical School alumni catalogues, showing for the majority of graduates special biographical data;

Colin B. Burke, then Assistant Professor of History, University of Maryland, Baltimore County, who was engaged in a large–scale study of college and professional school graduates before 1862; and gave help with individual physicians;

Barbara Williams, then Archivist and Historical Librarian of Hahnemann Medical College, Philadelphia, who gave us ready access to the unique biological resources of Hahnemann in respect to homeopaths;

Angela Williams, of New York City, who graciously allowed us to incorporate entries from her unpublished index to the 800–odd medical obituaries in the *Medical Register of New York, New Jersey and Connecticut*, 1862–1895;

Edward C. Atwater, M.D, of Rochester, NY, who supplied information on many doctors of Rochester and vicinity from his extensive collections;

John B. Blake and the staff of the National Library of Medicine, who allowed us to photocopy several scarce lists of medical graduates not otherwise obtainable.

Many kindnesses and courtesies were received from staff members at these libraries: the Pennsylvania Hospital; the Van Pelt Library of the University of Pennsylvania; the Logan Clendening Library of the University of Kansas Medical Center, Kansas City; the Kansas State Historical Society, Topeka; the Kenneth Spencer Research Library, Department of Special Collections, University of Kansas, Lawrence; the Frances Carrick Thomas Library of Transylvania College, Lexington, Kentucky; and the Moody Medical Library, University of Texas Medical Branch at Galveston.

In the eleven years or so of its existence, this project grew, Topsy–like, to overflow various corners and crannies of the compiler's home in Germantown; she owes to George M. Holloway, her husband, much thanks for his tolerance of drifts of papers, photocopies, index–cards and file–boxes. James B. Holloway, her younger son, assisted in clerical aspects of the work in its earlier days. To Audrey Smith, former revisor of the compiler, she is indebted for careful proofreading.

George N. Holloway, as a student at Germantown Friends and a freshman at Kenyon, progressed from typist, file clerk and transcriber to indexer and researcher, and exhibited in all these roles his exceptional accuracy.

Lastly the compiler's father, the Reverend Dr. Ernest N. Feind, B.A., S.T.B, M.A., D.D., and C.L.U., retiring at 75 from a varied career in the ministry and in insurance, not to mention agriculture and teaching, took up this work as a retirement hobby, and contributed the bulk of the indexing and transcription. To his industry and patience the book owes much of its usefulness.

The compiler must take unto herself the innumerable errors of omission, commission (and typesetting) which will certainly be discovered in the succeeding pages. "A work," as Sir Thomas Browne observed, "of this nature is not to be performed upon one legg, and should smell of oyl, if duly and deservedly handled." We hope that this particular work, though perhaps not duly and deservedly handled, will at least smell of oyl

Lisabeth M. Holloway

Germantown, Philadelphia
July 30, 1981.

PREFACE

Biographical data for American physicians alive after 1906 is rather easy to come by. The AMA directories, beginning in 1906 and appearing thereafter every two, three, or four years, may be used in conjunction with the JAMA death-indexes to find about 85–90% of American physicians with relative ease -- except for the physical labor of handling several unwieldy volumes per search.

Before the AMA directories, no ready source exists for American medical biography *en masse*. Certainly the largest body of such biographical matter is buried in the thousands of volumes of journals and society proceedings, but their indexes are skimpy, sporadic, and sometimes even non-existent. (Some journals, like the *Medical & surgical reporter*, Philadelphia, a major source, used death-notices merely as filler, not indexing them even in the volumes in which they appeared.) *The Index-Catalogue* of the Surgeon-General's Library, although it indexed other substantive matter in detail, in Series 1 and 2, for example, lists obituaries or biographical brevia for only 52 Americans named Smith. (We have easily found 200 Smiths over roughly the same period. The largest compilation of biographical notices, Kelly & Burrage's *Dictionary of American Medical Biography*, 1928 (K & B III), runs to 2,049 persons from the 17th century to 1927. These are mostly, though not all, physicians of considerable importance and influence as teachers, innovators, founders of hospitals.

But grass-roots practitioners of medicine in the United States during the 18th and 19th centuries must have run to very substantial numbers indeed. The census for 1850 shows 40,755 physicians; for 1880, 82,000; for 1890, 100,180; and for 1900, 119,749. This present compilation lists only some 17,350 names, and by no means exhausts the possibilities, even within its limitation of eligibility. (Without doubt, another 17,000 names could be found in other periodicals like those here indexed.)

These persons -- mostly men, some women, and 22 individuals known or presumed to be black* -- must constitute below those included by Kelly & Burrage (and many appear in both groups, obviously) the next broader stratum of professional respectability** and importance. Many of those recorded here are not degree-holders (though we have hunted them quite faithfully through the extensive medical-school registers listed above). Until licensure came into force in the various states during the 1870's and 1880's -- and even afterwards among those qualifying under "grandfather clauses" -- practitioners need not have attended a medical school at all, though many had taken a course or two without paying the additional fee for the diploma. (It is this fact which makes it so difficult to estimate the numbers of the profession before licensure, since preceptorships -- the alternative source of medical education -- were almost never subject to statistical oversight, and many medical schools never published their matriculates but only their graduates.)

Usually, of course, graduates -- especially of the University of Pennsylvania, and of Jefferson (between them the largest producers of American physicians during the first three-quarters of the 19th century), of the College of Physicians & Surgeons of New York, Harvard, Rush, the Medical College of Ohio, the University of Louisville, or the good small schools of Maine, Vermont, and New Hampshire, to mention a few highly-regarded institutions -- these graduates tended to attract more patients, obtain more hospital and teaching posts, organize or hold office in their local medical societies, and generally rise higher in their profession than did their hometown brethren without degrees. And consequently, were more likely to be eulogized. So the following lists, including a high proportion of graduates, probably represent an elite group.

In at least two other respects, this compilation is skewed by the compiler's bias: first, for feelings of sentiment and obscurity, toward participants on either side in the War of the Rebellion. The Civil War surgeon has been memorialized in rather spotty

*Those identified in the obituary as Negro, or presumed so because graduates of schools limited to or designed for persons of color, are: Augusta, Alexander T.; Brown, Anthony Leopold; Coker, John H.; Conrad, Rufus; Corey, Waterman Franklin; Dismond, Samuel H.; Dorsette [Dorsat], Cornelius H.; Flores y Hernandez, Mauricio; Henderson, George Robinson; Howell, Hanry S.; Jackson, Albert Lafayette; Janney, Edgar; Johnson, Levi; Johnson, Richard H.; Key, Lucinda Davis; Purman, Willis H.; Roberts, Grace; Rolerfort, George W.; Smith, James McCune; Spackman, Mary D; Tate, R.H.; and Wimmer, James Monroe.

**Sometimes the Victorian eulogist departed from the proprieties, however, and called a spade a spade, especially in discussing drunkards and suicides.

fashion (see *The Watermark* III(2): 1–3, October, 1979 for the compiler's efforts to record some such collections), but no one, possibly excepting Strait's unindexed and unsatisfying efforts on behalf of the U.S. Commissioner of Pensions in 1882, seems even to have tried to make a comprehensive list of either Union men or Confederates. (The surviving Confed–erate records are, of course, very limited indeed.) This compilation is only a very snall step towards identifying Civil War surgeons.

Similarly, the physician–victims of the 1878 yellow–fever epidemic in Tennessee and neighbor–ing states, who came to help and died often before anybody knew who they were, have been included, though mostly unconfirmed.

This compilation is primarily based on citations in periodicals, except as indicated above for Civil War surgeons, and for physicians dying before 1850 -- a period when medical biography is sparse, editors apparently preferring matters of substantive or broad professional interest to personalities. For these two categories of persons we have included entries based on citations in medical–school or college alumni registers, without periodical citation. For all entries we have sought supporting data in biographical compendia -- K & B III, or, for homeopaths, Cleave; and Atkinson. Appropriate directories have also been searched: Butler, 1874 or 1878; Polk, 1886 and its successors; Flint, 1897.

The present compilation must be regarded as only a springboard toward further research, not in any sense a work of completeness or authority in its own right. For one thing, the obituary, on which it is based, is often written soon after the subject's death, under pressures of time and emotion, and is often full of inaccuracies. (Sometimes of course, especially for obscure personages, it may be the only surviving record.) We have discovered many discrepancies of date, place, education, and so on, in the citations here recorded; sometimes we have not attempted to reconcile them, for lack of authoritative information.

A thorough researcher will investigate also the following avenues of approach:

> Further medical literature, both contemporary (additional citations in the *Index–Catalogue*; city and state medical histories; medical society records; college and medical school histories and catalogues, etc.) and retrospective (citations in the *Bibliography of the History of Medicine in the United States and Canada, 1939–40.*
>
> Local sources (newspaper reports; city and county histories; census listings; birth and death records; tax lists; family genealogies).
>
> General bibliographical and historical sources (*National Union Catalog, Retrospective* replac–ing the *Library of Congress Catalog; National Union Catalog of Manuscript Collections; Biography Index*; publications of state and local historical societies, and the like).
>
> Special–interest sources as appropriate, for physicians as politicians, writers of belles–lettres, artists, musicians, inventors, non–medical scien–tists, or in other areas of prominence.

With all of these limitations of scope, resources, and extent, as sketched above, and all deficiencies of execution, conscious and otherwise, the compiler hopes that the work will prove useful to librarians, researchers, and persons interested in professional and personal history; and that it will encourage further and more comprehensive compilations.

PRINCIPAL SOURCES INDEXED: Journals, Society Transactions, etc., with Materials Used in Support

The following lists of journals, society proceedings, transactions, etc., indexed in the text are arranged according to their national, regional, or state and local coverage. Selected for their inclusion of biographical material -- many illustrious journals, such as the *American Journal of the Medical Sciences*, gave no space or virtually none to biography -- these journals and society publications were chiefly indexed in Philadelphia libraries, especially the College of Physicians and the University of Pennsylvania, and to some extent the Pennsylvania Hospital. Others were seen at the National Library of Medicine; at the Kansas Historical Society, Topeka; the University of Kansas Spencer Research Library at Lawrence; and the Library of the University of Texas Medical Branch at Galveston. Not every volume of every journal was found. Many other journals might have been included, and should have been; the compiler must acknowledge limitations of time, funds, energy and patience.

JOURNALS, SOCIETY TRANSACTIONS, PROCEEDINGS, etc

National

American Medical Association. *Journal (JAMA)* v.1, 1883 - v.37, 1904

American Medical Association. *Transactions (Tr AMA)* v.3, 1850 - v.33, 1882 (no obits in v.1 & 2)

Boston medical & surgical journal (Bost m&s j or *Bost med & surg j)* v.1, 1828 - v.151, 1904)

Medical & surgical reporter, Philadelphia (*Med surg rep Phila*) v.1, 1858/59 - v/61, 1889 (with some omissions)

Regional

North and Middle Atlantic

Medical register of New York, New Jersey & Connecticut (Med reg NY NJ Conn) 1862–1895.

Buffalo medical journal (Buff med jour or *Buff m j*) v.1, 1845 - v.15, 1860

Buffalo medical & surgical journal (Buff m&s j) v.1, 1861 - v.74, 1905

South

New Orleans medical & surgical journal (New Orl m&s j) v.1, 1844/45 -

Southern medical & surgical journal (So med & surg jour or *So m&s j)* v.1, 1836/7 - v.3, 1839; ns v.1–21, 1845–60; s3, v.21, 1866–67.

Southern practitioner (So pract) v.1–1879 -

West

Chicago medical journal (Chic m j) with other titles: *Illinois medical & surgical journal (Ill m&s j); Illinois & Indiana medical & surgical journal (Ill & Ind m&s j); Northwestern medical & surgical journal (NW m&s j)* (entries under above titles) v.1, 1844 - v.58, 1889 (with some omissions)

Transylvania journal of medicine and the associated sciences (Transylv j m & assoc. sci) v.1, 1828 - v.12, 1839.

Western journal of medicine & surgery (West j m&s) v.1 - 2, 1840.

State and Local

Alabama

Medical Association of the State of Alabama. *Transactions* (v.1–6 as *Proceedings*) 1847, 1850–52, 1854–55 1871–74, 1881, 1889, 1890

California

Medical Society of the State of California. *Transactions (Tr M S St Cal)* 1856–58, 1870–78, 1880–84, 1891–96

California state journal of medicine (Cal st j m) 1902 v.4, 1906.

Colorado

Colorado State Medical Society. *Transactions (Tr Colo St M S)* 1877–78, 1898–99.

Connecticut

Connecticut State Medical Society. *Proceedings (Pr Conn M S)* 1792–1829, 1832–33, 1835–42, 1844–49, 1852–55, 1857–75, 1882–1906

District of Columbia

Medical Society of the District of Columbia. *History (Hist Med Soc DC*), 1909.

Florida

Florida Medical Association. *Transactions* also *Proceedings (Tr Fl M Assn; Proc Fl M Assn)* 1887–93; 1896–99.

Illinois

Illinois State Medical Society. *Transactions* also *Proceedings* 1887–93; 1896–99

Chicago medical recorder (Chic m rec) v.1, 1890? –v. 18, 27, 28

Chicago medical review (Chic m rev) v.1, 1878? - v.6, ?

Indiana

Indiana State Medical Society. *Transactions* 1850–55 as *Proceedings (Tr Ind St M S)* 1849, 1852, 1855, 1857, 1859–61, 1863, 1865–99, 1901–06

Iowa

Iowa State Medical Society. *Transactions (Tr Ia St M S)* 1867–92, 1900, 1904

Kansas

Kansas Medical Society. *Transactions (Tr Kans St M S)* 1866–82

Kansas Medical Society. *Journal (Jour Kans M S)* v.1, 1901 – v.6, 1906

Kansas medical journal (Kans med j) v.1, 1889 – v.10, 1898.

Kentucky

Kentucky State Medical Society (later Association). *Trans actions (Tr Ky St M S)* 1851–52, 1856, 1867–69* 1870, 1884* 1892–97 [*title as *Proceedings*]

Louisiana

Louisiana State Medical Society. *Transactions (Tr La St M S)* 1898.

Maine

Maine Medical Association. *Transactions (Tr Me M Assn)* 1866–97

Maryland

Cordell, E. F. *Medical Annals of Maryland*, 1799–1899. Baltimore, 1903. *(Med ann Md)*

Baltimore medical & physical recorder (Balto med & phys rec) v.1–1808 – v.2, 1809.

Michigan

Michigan medical news (Mich m news) v.1, 1878 – v.5, 1882; afterwards as *Medical age (Med age)* v.1, 1883 – v.6, 1888

Minnesota

Minnesota State Medical Society. *Transactions (Tr Minn St M S)* 1869–81, 1883, 1885–1904

Minnesota medical monthly (Minn m mo) 1882–88

Mississippi

Mississippi State Medical Association. *Transactions (Tr Miss St M Assn)* 1873/74; 1876–89

Missouri

Missouri State Medical Association. *Transactions (Tr Mo St M Assn)* 1877–78, 1880–81, 1883–87, 1892–94

Nebraska

Nebraska State Medical Society. *Proceedings (Proc Nebr St M S)* 1896–97, 1899–1900

New Hampshire

New Hampshire Medical Society. *Transactions (Tr NH M S)* 1851–62, 1870, 1873, 1884–99

New Hampshire journal of medicine (NH j m) v.1, 1850 – v.8, 1858

New Jersey

Medical Society of New Jersey. *Transactions (Tr MS NJ)* v.1, 1766 – v.137, 1903

New York

Medical Society of the State of New York. *Transactions (Tr Med Soc St NY)* 1807–31, 1840–43, 1853–55, 1857–89, 1891–92, 1895–1905

Medical Society of the County of New York. *Minutes (Min M S Co NY)* 1806–1878

New York medical & philosophical journal and review (NY med & phil jour & rev) v.1, 1809 – v.3, 1811

New York medical journal (NY med jour) v.1, 1830 – v.2, 1831

New York medical & physical journal (NY med & phys j) v.1, 1822 – v.9, 1830

Medical record, New York *(Med rec, NY)* v.3, 1869 – v.20, 1881, with some omissions

North Carolina

Medical Society of the State of North Carolina. *Transactions (Tr NC M S)* 1849–60, 1867–81, 1891–92, 1896–97, 1900

North Carolina medical journal (NC m j) v.1, 1878 – v.55, 1906

Ohio

Ohio State Medical Society. *Transactions (Tr Ohio St M S)* 1853 – 1899

Oregon

Oregon State Medical Society. *Proceedings (Proc Ore St M S)* 1879, 1897

Pennsylvania

Pennsylvania State Medical Society. *Transactions (Tr Pa St M S)* 1856– 1896

Pennsylvania medical journal (Pa m j) v.1, 1897/98 – v.10, 1906/07

College of Physicians of Philadelphia. *Transactions* centennial volume, 1887 [unnumbered] *(Tr CPP* cent vol)

Philadelphia medical & physical journal (Phila m & phys j) v.1, 1804 – v.3, 1808

Philadelphia medical & surgical journal (Phila m & s j) v.1, 1852 – v.6, 1858

Philadelphia medical times (Phila m times) v.1, 1870/71 – v.9, 1878/79 [?]

Medical bulletin, a monthly journal of medicine and surgery (Med bull med & surg) v.4, 1882 – v.14, 1892, v.17, 1895

Lehigh Valley medical magazine (Lehigh Valley med mag) v.1, 1889 – v.11, 1900

Luzerne County [Pa] Medical Society. *Transactions (Tr Luzerne Co (Pa) M S)* 1886 – 1906

Medical reporter (West Chester, Pa) v.1, 1853 – v.3, 1856

Philadelphia medical register & directory (Phila med reg & dir)

Rhode Island

Rhode Island Medical Society. *Transactions (Tr RI M S)* v.1, 1859–77; 1906

Tennessee

Medical Society of Tennessee. *Transactions (Tr Tenn M S)* 1842–46, 1850–51, 1853, 1858, 1868–69, 1875–85, 1888

Memphis medical recorder (Memphis m rec) v.1, 1852 – v.6, 1857/58

Texas

Texas State Medical Association. *Transactions (Tr Tex St M Assoc)* 1870, 1874–78, 1883–84, 1896–1904

Galveston medical journal (Galveston m j) v.1, 1866 –

v.5, 1871, ns v.1, 1880 with some omissions

Daniel's Texas medical journal (Daniel's Tex m j) ns? v.1, 1885/86 – v.14, 1898–99

Texas medical & surgical journal (Tex m & s j) v.1, 1881 – v.3, 1883

Texas courier-record of medicine (Tex cour-rec med) v.1, 1883 – v.14, 1896/97, v.20, 1902/03, v.24, 1906/07

Texas medical news (Tex m news) v.5, ? –v. 8, 1898/99

Texas medical & surgical record (Texas m & s rec) v.1, 1881 – v.3, 1883

Texas medical practitioner (Tex m pract) v.10 – 11, 1897–98

Texas state journal of medicine

Utah

Utah State Medical Society. *Proceedings (Proc Utah St M S)* 1895 – 1896

Vermont

Vermont State Medical Society. *Transactions (Tr Vt St M S)* 1883, 1895 – 1899

Virginia

Medical Society of Virginia. *Transactions (Tr M S Va)* 1870–75, 1883–85, 1888, 1892–93, 1897, 1900–05

West Virginia

West Virginia State Medical Association. *Transactions (Tr WVa M Assn)*

Wisconsin

Wisconsin State Medical Society. *Transactions (Tr Wis St M S)* 1873–1902.

HOMEOPATHIC JOURNALS, SOCIETY TRANSACTIONS, PROCEEDINGS, etc

Names of homeopaths were obtained from:

1) "Necrological List" published in *Biographical Cyclopedia of Homeopathic Physicians & Surgeons* (Chicago, American Homeopathic Biogaphical Association, c1893), pp [119]–172; as expanded and annotated by Thomas L. Bradford in the unique copy at Hahnemann Medical College Archives and History of Medicine Collections; and
2) American Institute of Homeopathy Necrological Lists of 1895 (in its *Transactions* 1895: 1092–1101) and of 1906 (*ibid.*, 1906: 879–95).

The obituaries themselves were seen at Hahnemann Medical College Archives in T. L. Bradford's scrapbooks of biographies of American homeopaths (1916; 35 vols). Occasionally Bradford omitted to note the source of the clipping.

The thousand or so homeopaths included in the present volume include only a small number of those recorded in the necrological lists above.

American homeopathic observer (later *American observer*; both cited as *Amer hom obs*) v.1, 1864 – v.20, 1884

American homeopathic review (Amer hom rev) v.1, 1858 – v.6, 1866

American homeopath[ist], v.1, 1877 – v.27, 1901?

American Institute of Homeopathy. *Transactions (Tr Am Inst Hom)*

Clinical reporter (Clin rep) v.1, 1888 – v.8, 1895

Hahnemannian monthly (Hahn mo) v.1, 1865 – ns v.6, 1884; continued as *Hahnemannian*

Homeopathic recorder (Hom rec) v.1, 1886 – v.16, 1901

Homeopathic times, NY also *New York journal of homeopathy* and *New York medical times)* v.1, 1873 – v.22, 1894

Massachusetts Homeopathic Medical Society. *Publications* (Mass Hom M S. *Publs*) v.1, 1840 – v.11, 1888.

Medical advance (many variants of title; *Med adv*) v.1, 1873 – v.44, 1906

Medical counselor (Med couns) v.1, 1879 – v.14, 1889; v.1, 1896 – v.6, 1901

Medical current, v.3, 1886 – v.12, 1896

Medical era, v.1, 1883/84 – v.21, 1903

Medical visitor; a directory of homeopathic physicians, v.1, 1885 – v.21, 1905

New England medical gazette (New Engl med gaz) v.1, 1866 – v.41, 1906

North American journal of homeopathy (No Amer j hom) v.1, 1851 – 3s v.21, 1906

Ohio medical & surgical reporter (Ohio m & s rep) v.1 1867 – v.11, 1877

Philadelphia journal of homeopathy (Phila j hom) v.1, 1852/53 – v.4, 1855/56.

U.S. medical investigator (US m invest) v.1, 1875 – v.24, 1889.

Western homeopathic observer (West hom obs) v.1, 1863 – 1863 – v.7, 1870/71

Biographical Compilations

Cleave, E. *Biographical cyclopaedia of homeopathic physicians and surgeons*. Philadelphia, Galaxy, 1873

King, W. H. *History of homeopathy and its institutions in America....* NY, Lewis Publ Co, 1905. 4v.

MILITARY SURGEONS – CIVIL WAR

The following sources have been included for Civil War surgeons, except as indicated:

Union and Confederate

University of Pennsylvania men who served in the Civil War, Ewing Jordan, comp Dept. of Medicine, Classes 1816–1882. (Compiled from the University's *Alumni Register,* 1916–17.) Contains over 1,700 names. ca 25% of Confederate surgeons; ca 6% of Union surgeons. Cited as *UPa m alum CW,* by year of graduation.

Union

"List of physicians, now deceased, who served their country professionally, either in the army or navy, during the rebellion, with their rank, time, place and manner of death." J. M. Toner, comp. *National medical journal* 1: 289–304, 1870–71. (Cited as *Nat m j* 1: , 1870/71.

Harvard University in the War of 1861–65, a record of services rendered in the Army and Navy of the U.S. by graduates and students of Harvard College and the professional schools, by Francis H. Brown. Boston, 1886.

Hamersly, L. R. *Records of living officers of the U.S. Navy and Marine Corps....* Philadelphia, 1870. Not indexed but used for supporting data.

Heitman, F. B. *Historical register and dictionary of the U.S. Army*, from its organization Sept. 29, 1789, to March 2, 1903. Washington, 1903. Not indexed but used for supporting data.

Henry, G. V. *Military record of civilian appointments in the U.S. Army.* NY, 1873. Not indexed, but used for supporting data.

Confederate

[Virginia, University of.] *The University memorial*: biographical sketches of alumni of the University of Virginia who fell in the Confederate War. Johnson, J. L., comp. Baltimore, 1871.

Blanton, W. B. "Virginia surgeons in the Civil War" (pp. 393–420 of his *Medicine in Virginia in the 19th Century*. Richmond, 1933. (Cited as Blanton, *Va surgs CW.*) Not indexed, but used for supporting data.

"Roster of the Medical Officers of the Army of Tennessee during the Civil War." Joseph Jones, comp. *Southern Historical Society Papers*, 22:165–280, 1983. (Cited as *SHSP.*) Not indexed but used for supporting data.

MATERIALS USED FOR SUPPORTING DATA

Biographical Compilations

Kelly, H. A. & W. L. Burrage. *Dictionary of American medical biography....* NY, 1928. (Contains 2,049 sketches of deceased physicians; all entries in this volume have been checked against *K&B III* – so cited.)

________. *American medical biographies*, 1920 (Cited as *K&B II.*)

Kelly, H. A. *Cyclopedia of American biography*, 1912. (Cited, inaccurately, as *K&B I.)* The two last-named works have been cited only for entries deleted in K&B III.)

Atkinson, W. B. *The physicians and surgeons of the United States*. Philadelphia, 1878. (Includes only living persons. Cited as *Atkinson* I.)

Directories

Butler, S. W. *The medical register and directory of the United States*, systematically arranged by states: comprising names, post-office address, educational and professional status of more than 50,000 physicians... Philadelphia, 1874. (No index; degrees and military service occasionally given; unreliable as to spelling, etc. The 2d edition, 1878, adds some names, usually in a group at end of city or state. Cited as *Butler*.

Polk's medical & surgical directory of the United States. Detroit, 1886. (First national medical directory with an index; includes by code the subject's medical school and date of graduation; sometimes gives additional data; includes street address. Later editions 1890 and 1896, were updated. An important source for verification.)

Flint's medical and surgical directory of the United States and Canada, NY, 1897. Similar to Polk's directories.

Local Sources Occasionally Cited

Indiana. Kemper, G.W .H.A. *A medical history of the state of Indiana.* Chicago, 1911. (Cited as Kemper's *Indiana.*)

Iowa. Fairchild, D. S. *History of medicine in Iowa.* Des Moines, 1927. (Cited as Fairchild's *Iowa.*)

Massachusetts. Massachusetts Medical Society. *A catalogue of the officers, fellows and licentiates, 1781–1893.* Boston, 1894. (Cited as *Mass M S cat* 1894.)

New Hampshire. Conn, G.P. *History of the New Hampshire surgeons in the War of Rebellion*. Concord, N.H.

New Jersey. *History of medicine in New Jersey and its medical men....to A.D. 1800*. Newark, 1879.

Pennsylvania. Pennsylvania State Board of Health. [*Official register of physicians licensed to practise in Pennsylvania*, 1881–88.] Harrisburg, 1889? (Its Fourth annual report. Cited as *Off'l reg Pa phys* 1881–88.)

South Carolina. Waring, J.I. *A history of medicine in South Carolina*, 1670–1825. Columbia, 1964. Also, his *A history of medicine in South Carolina*, 1825–1900. Columbia, 1967. (Cited as *Waring* I and *Waring* II.)

Texas. Red, G. P. *The medicine man in Texas.* Houston, 1930. (Cited as G.P. Red.)

A CHART OF GRADUATING CLASSES
AT AMERICAN MEDICAL COLLEGES BEFORE 1907

The following chart attempts to collate the compiler's collection* of lists of graduates of American medical colleges against "Historical Matter of American Colleges" in the AMA directories -- the 1931 edition was used -- and against similar lists, numbered differently, in the Polk directories, beginning in 1886.

This collection was compiled -- reluctantly at the beginning -- as a reference tool for this work, *Medical Obituaries*, which is limited to physicians dying before 1907. (As noted above, finding data on physicians living beyond that date is rather easy: the AMA directories, beginning with 1906, can be correlated with the death notices published in *JAMA* and indexed at least twice each year.)

Begun in the crammed pamphlet–boxes of the College of Physicians of Philadelphia during the compiler's tenure there 1964–1976, and continued in host–libraries of AAHM and ALHHS convention–cities then and later, the pursuit was concluded in the vast stacks of NLM. This list with its many imperfections and uncertainties is presented in the hope that others may find new and better information.

Some difficulties result unavoidably from the discrepancies and confusions carelessly perpetrated by the schools themselves. In general, these are passed on to the reader with no more than a question–mark, as beyond the compiler's capacity to clarify. For example, AMA says that Cooper Medical College, San Francisco, graduated its first class in 1860, but Cooper's own announcement of 1881 (which he had in photocopy) names 3 graduates in 1859. Hobart–Geneva's two lists, one undated, occasionally contradict each other. So do the collective lists of Western Reserve, when compared against those of its constituents -- Wooster, Cleveland Medical, Hudson and Charity Hospital. Jefferson's very long lists are inconveniently broken up by period, without index. King's lists of homoeopathic medical college graduates, often the only ones obtainable, do not always match those lists surviving.

On the other hand, certain institutions stand out as models of completeness and clarity. Bowdoin, Dartmouth, Brown, the University of Pennsylvania, and Hahnemann of Philadelphia come to mind as truly *matres almae*, keeping track of their sons in war and peace, in life and death. F. C. Waite reconstructed the biographies of graduates of Vermont's extinct medical schools, Castleton and Woodstock, with thorough scholarship; H. J. Abrahams attempted the same for the extinct medical schools of Philadelphia with less success; J. I. Waring filled in gaps in South Carolina. One could wish that Harvard, Yale, and the big New York schools had issued biographical catalogues of their alumni as well–researched as those of Bowdoin or Brown.

One hopes that the following will be useful as it stands to librarians and others of our ilk who are importuned to identify physicians, physicians–as–authors, physicians–as–grandfathers or whatever, and to discover their medical schools, if any.

One hopes even more that others may be stimulated to pursue supplementary lists of graduates in out–of–the–way repositories in their own cities, and return their findings, so that we may in time achieve a comprehensive list, based on all discoverable records of graduates and matriculates.

The top line of each two–line entry opposite the name or names of the school, and its AMA and Polk numbers, represents the compiler's holdings, as marked by asterisk (*). The lower line, marked by plus–sign (+), represents the years when AMA or Polk asserts that classes graduated.

---

*Since the above note was written in 1980, the author's collection has been dispersed. It is our hope that a second and more extensive collection may be created and permanently preserved in electronic format, preferably as a cooperative project of Archivists and Librarians In the History of the Health Sciences.

LMH, 1995.

State/Title of school/City	AMA #	Polk #	Years of grad. classes till 1906 * used by LMH; + a/c AMA or Polk
ALABAMA			
Graffenburg Med. Inst Dadeville	Ala 1		*99 Misc names +1856–62
U Ala (Med Coll Ala), Tuscaloosa	Ala 2		*1860 1861 1869–1900 +1861, 1869–
Southern U Med Dept Greensboro	Ala 3	101	[any actual graduates?] +1872?–80?
Birmingham Med Coll Birmingham	Ala 4	101A	*1899, 1900 +1895–06
Med Coll Montezuma Univ Bessemer	Ala 5		*1898 +1897 1898
ARKANSAS			
U Ark Sch Med (Ark Indust U Med Dept) Little Rock	Ark 1	102	*1880– +1880–
CALIFORNIA			
Cooper Med Coll (U Pacif- ic Med Dept) San Francisco	Cal 1	103	*1859–64 1870–92 1893–99 1903 1905 +1860–64 1870–
U Cal Med Dept, Toland Med Coll, San Francisco	Cal 2	104	*1864–1905 +1864–
Calif Eclectic Med Coll, San Francisco, then Oakland	Cal 4		*1880–1902 +1880–
Hahnemann Med Coll of the Pacific, San Francisco	Cal 5	106	*1884–1905 +1884–
U So Calif Sch of Med Los Angeles	Cal 6	106½	*1888– +1888–
Coll of Phys & Surg of San Francisco	Cal 7	104½	*1897–1905 +1897–
Coll of Phys & Surg of Los Angeles	Cal 9		*1905 +1905
COLORADO			
Denver Coll of Medicine Denver	Colo 1	107	*1882–1902 +1882–1902
U Colo Sch Med (Colo Sch Med)	Colo 2	108	*1885–96 1900– +1885–97 1900–
Gross Med Coll (Med Dept Rocky Mtn Univ) Denver	Colo 3	108½	*1888–1901 +1888–1902
Denver Coll Phys & Surg (Den- ver Homeopathic Coll) Denver	Colo 4	108A	*1895–1905 +1895–
Denver & Gross Coll (Med Dept Univ Denver)	Colo 5	107?	*1903–05 +1903–
CONNECTICUT			
Yale Univ Sch of Med New Haven	Conn 1	109	*1814– +1814–
DISTRICT OF COLUMBIA			
Columbian Coll Med Dept (Nat	DC 1	110	*1826–34 1838–63 1866–92 94 97 99 00

State/Title of school/City	AMA #	Polk #	Years of grad. classes till 1906 * used by LMH; + a/c AMA or Polk
Med Coll; Geo Washington U)			+1826–34 1838–61 1863–
Georgetown Univ Sch Med	DC 2	111	*1852–
Washington			+1852–
Howard Univ Sch Med	DC 3	112	*1871–
Washington			+1871–
National Univ Med Dept	DC 4	113	*1885–1903
Washington			+1885–1903
Washington Homeop Med Coll	DC 5	113B	*1894–1906
(Nat'l Homeop Med Coll)	DC–5	113A	+1894–96
FLORIDA			
Tallahassee Coll of Med	Fla 1	114	*1884–86
(Univ of Fla) Tallahassee			+1884–86
GEORGIA			
Med Coll of Georgia (Univ	Ga 1		*1833–56 1858 1865–67 1885 1889 1894
of Georgia) Augusta			+1833–61 1863–
Southern Botanico–Medical Coll	Ga 2	116	*1882
(Reform Med Coll of Ga)		119	+1841–61 1868–77 1881–84
(Coll Amer Med & Surg) all Atlanta		122	
Savannah Med Col	Ga 4	118	*1857
Savannah			+?1853–61 1866–1880
Atlanta Med Coll	Ga 5	120	*1855–61 1865–98 [incl grads in 1874]
Atlanta			+1855–61 1865–73 1875–98 [none 74!]
Southern Med Coll	Ga 10	124	*1880–98
Atlanta			+1880–98
Atlanta Coll of Phys & Surg	Ga 11		*1898–
Atlanta			+1898–
Oglethorpe Med Coll	Ga 6	121	*1856–58
Savannah			+?1856–61
Women's Med Coll of Ga	Ga 16	125½	
Atlanta			+1890–
Georgia Coll M & S (Ecl)	0 AMA	123	*1878–97
			+1878–
ILLINOIS			
Rush Med Coll	Ill 1	126	*1844–95 1898 1900 1902
Chicago			+1844–
Illinois Coll Med	Ill 2	127	*1846
Chicago			+?1843–1848
Franklin Med Coll (St	Ill 3	128	
Charles Univ) St Charles)			+?1842–45
Hahnemann Med Coll	Ill 4	131	*1861–
Chicago			+1861–
Chicago Physio–Med Inst or Coll	Ill 5	137½	
(Coll Med & Surg, Physio–Med)			+1886–
Chicago Med Coll (Lind Univ Med	Ill 6	130	*1860–
Dept; Northwestern U Med Dept)			+1860–
Bennett Coll Ecl Med & Surg	Ill 8	132	*1870–1902
Chicago			+1870–
Northwestern U Woman's Med Sch	Ill 9	134	*1871 1873–85, 1896
(Woman's [Hosp] Med Coll)			1871, 1873–1902

State/Title of school/City	AMA #	Polk #	Years of grad. classes till 1906 * used by LMH; + a/c AMA or Polk
Chicago Hom Med Coll	Ill 10	135	*1877–1904
Chicago			+1877–1904
Coll of Phys & Surg of Chicago	Ill 11	136	*1883–95
(Univ Illinois Coll Med)			+1883–
Quincy Coll Med	Ill 12	137	*1884–86
(Chaddock School...) Quincy			+1883–90
Harvey Med Coll (night	Ill 13	137E	*1898
school) Chicago			+1895–1905
Nat'l Med Univ (Nat'l [Hom]	Ill–14	137A	
Med Coll) Chicago			+1892–
Hering Med Coll	Ill 15	137C	*1893–1905
Chicago			+1893–
Dunham Med Coll	Ill 18	137J	*1896–
Chicago			+1896–
Amer Missionary Med Coll	Ill 19	137K	*1904
Chicago			+1899–
INDIANA			
Indiana Med Coll (La Porte Univ	Ind 1		*1847
Med Dept) La Porte			+1845–49
Med Coll of Evansville	Ind 2		*1850–54 1873–84
Evansville			+1850–54 1873–84
Indiana Med Coll	Ind 4		
Indianapolis			+1870–78
Coll Phys & Surg	Ind 6		
Indianapolis			+1874–78
Med Coll of Indiana (Med	Ind 8	143	*1878–90
Dept, Butler U) Indianapolis			+1878–
Med Coll of Fort Wayne	Ind 7	142	*1877 1881
Fort Wayne			+1877–83
Central Coll of Phys & Surg	Ind 9	144	
Indianapolis			+1880–1905
Fort Wayne Coll of Med, Ft Wayne	Ind 10	145	
[?Med Dept Northern Ohio U?]			+1880–98 1900–05
Indiana Ecl Med Coll (absorbed	Ind 11	146	*1881–88
Beach Med Inst 1886) Indianapolis			+1881–90
Hospital Med Coll	Ind 13	147	*1883–85
Evansville			+1883–86
IOWA			
Coll Phys & Surg, Keokuk; Coll Phys	Ia 1	149	*1849–85
& Surg Upper Miss, Rock Isl, Ill; U			+1849–99
Iowa Med Dept [See also Iowa 9 & 10 below for sequence as merged]			
Keokuk Med Coll	Ia 9	155A	*1890–99
Keokuk			+1890–99
Keokuk Medical College [and]	Ia 10		*1900
Coll Phys & Surg, Keokuk			+1900–
State Univ Iowa. Coll of Med	Ia 3	151	*1871–1904
Iowa City			+1871–1904
State Univ Iowa. Coll of Hom Med	Ia 4	152	*1877–1904
Iowa City			+1877–

State/Title of school/City	AMA #	Polk #	Years of grad. classes till 1906 * used by LMH; + a/c AMA or Polk
Iowa Eclect Med Coll, Des Moines			+1882–87
also Drake Univ Med Dept	Ia 6	153	*1883–87
after 1887 Iowa Coll Phys & Surg		154	+1883–
KANSAS			
Kansas Med Coll	Kan 1	156½	
Independence			+?1873–75
Univ Kansas, Lawrence & Kans	Kan 2		*1883–
City (Columbia MC; KC MC; Med–Chir)			+1884
[Many components, grads listed together]			
Kansas Med Coll (Med Coll	Kan 3	156 A	
Washburn, Univ) Topeka			+1892–1900 1902–
KENTUCKY			
Transylvania Univ Med Dept	Ky 1	157	*1820–55
Lexington			+1817–55
Kentucky Sch of Med	Ky 1	159	*1851–83 1887 1889–93 1895 1898
Louisville			+1850–
Louisville Med Inst	Ky 2	158	*1838–62 1864–81 85 87 91–92 95 97
Univ Louisville Sch Med			+1838–62 1864–
Louisville Med Coll	Ky 4	160	*1871 73 75 77 80 82 84 93 97
Louisville			+1880
Hospital Coll Med	Ky 5	161	*?undated list 1889 1891 1893–
Central Univ Ky			+1875–
Louisville Nat'l Med Coll	Ky 7	160½	*1889–99
Louisville [Black]			+1889–
Southwestern Hom Med Coll	Ky–9	161A	*1894–
Louisville			+1894–
Kentucky Univ Med Dept	Ky 11	158	
Louisville [see also Ky–2]			+1899–
LOUISIANA			
Univ Louisiana Med Sch (Med Coll	La 1	162	*1835–62 1866–
La; Tulane) New Orleans			+1835–62 1866–
New Orleans Sch Med	La 2	163	*1855–60 1866 1870
New Orleans			+1856–70
Charity Hosp Med Coll	La 3	164	
Mew Orleans			+?1873–77?
New Orleans Univ M C			*1894
(Flint Med Coll) [Black]			+1892–95 1897
MAINE			
Bowdoin Med Sch (Med Sch Me)	Me 1		*1821–
Portland, Brunswick			+1821–
MARYLAND			
Univ Maryland Sch Med	Md 1		*1812–90 1892–97 1899
Baltimore			+?1810–
Washington Univ Sch Med	Md 2	170	*1827–51 1867–77
Balto			+1828–51 1867–77

State/Title of school/City	AMA #	Polk #	Years of grad. classes till 1906 * used by LMH; + a/c AMA or Polk
Coll of Phys & Surg	Md 3	171	*1873–78 82 85 87 89 1892–
Balto			+1873–
Baltimore Med Coll	Md 4	172	*1882–
Balto +1882–			
Woman's Med Coll	Md 5	174	*1883–98 1899–
Balto			+?1882–98 1899–
Baltimore Univ Sch Med	Md 6	173	*1885–1904
Baltimore			+1885–
Johns Hopkins Univ Sch Med	Md 7	175	*1897–
Baltimore			+1897–
Atlantic Med Coll, Balto	Md 8	175A	*1892–
(Southern Hom Med Coll)			+1892–
MASSACHUSETTS			
Harvard Univ Med Sch	Mass 1	176	*1788–
Cambridge			+1788–
Berkshire Med Institution	Mass 2	177	*1823–67
(Med Dept Williams Coll) Pittsfield			+1823–67
New England Female Med Coll	Mass 3	179	*?1854–74
Boston			+1853–74
Boston Univ Sch Med	Mass 5	180	*1874–
Boston [Homeopathic]			+1874–
Worcester Med Coll (Eclectic)	Mass 4	178	*1846 1848 1850 1852 1854 1856
(New Engl Botanico–Med Coll)			+1846–59?
College of Phys & Surg	Mass 6	181	*1882–
Boston			+1882–
Tufts Coll Med Sch	Mass 7	184B	*1894–1900
Boston			+1894–
MICHIGAN			
Univ Michigan Dept Med & Surg	Mich 1	185	*1851–1901
Ann Arbor			+1851–
Univ Michigan Hom Med Sch	Mich 5	188 A	*1877–1901
Ann Arbor			+1877–
Detroit Med Coll	Mich 2	185½	*1872–80 1882 1885
Detroit			+1869–85
Michigan Coll Med	Mich 6	189	*1882
Detroit			+1881–85
Detroit Coll Med	Mich 7	186	*1886 1888 1895–98 1900
Detroit			+1886–
Detroit Hom Med Coll	Mich 3 &	187	*1872–75 1900–05
Detroit	Mich 11		+1872–75 1900–
MINNESOTA			
St Paul Med Coll	Minn 2	192½	
St Paul			+1886–87
Minnesota Hosp Coll	Minn 3	191	*1882–?85]
Minneapolis			+1882–86 or 88?
Univ Minn Med Sch	Minn 4	192	*1889–
Minneapolis			+1889–

State/Title of school/City	AMA #	Polk #	Years of grad. classes till 1906 * used by LMH; + a/c AMA or Polk
Univ Minn Coll Hom Med &	Minn 6	190½	*1889–
Surg (Minn Hom Med Coll)			+1889–
Minneapolis Coll Phys & Surg	Minn 5	192	*1884–1901
(Hamline Univ Med Dept)			+1884–
MISSOURI			
Missouri Med Coll (Kemper; U Mo	Mo 1	193	*1841–61 1866–84 1891–97
Med Sch; "McDowell's"	Mo 3	195	+1841–61 1866–99
St Louis U Med Dept ("Pope's"	Mo 2	194	*1843–68 71–74 76 78–87 89 91–93 95
Med Sch; Washington U Med Sch) St Louis			+1843–
Humboldt Med Coll (St Louis Coll	Mo 4	196	*1867–68
Med & Phys Sci) St Louis			+1856?–69
Homeopathic Med Coll Mo	Mo 5	197	*1860–61 1865–1905
St Louis			+1860–61 1865–
St Louis Coll Hom Phys & Surg	Mo 6	199	[any graduates?]
St Louis			
St Louis Coll Phys & Surg	Mo 7	205	*1880–85 1887 1893–94
St Louis			+1870–73 1880–
Kansas City Med Coll	Mo 8	198	*1870–91 1896 1902
(Coll Phys & Surg Kansas City)			+1870–
American Med Coll, Eclectic	Mo–10	202	*1874–93
(Nat'l Univ Arts & Sci) [graduated 2 classes/yr to 83)			1874–
St Joseph Hosp Med Coll	Mo 14	203	
St Joseph			+1878–82
Coll of Physicians & Surgeons	Mo 15	204	*1881?
St Joseph			+1879–81?
Univ Med Coll of Kans City	Mo 20	209	*1882 1889–93 1897–98 1905
(Univ Kans City Med Dept)			+1882–
Kansas City Hosp Coll Med	Mo 21	211	*1885
Kansas City			+1883–88
Ensworth Med Coll (Ensworth	Mo 22	210	
Central Med Coll)			+1883–91 1893–
Kansas City Hom Med Coll	Mo 26	208½	*1889–1905
Kansas City			+1889–
Marion–Sims Coll Med (Marion–	Mo 27	196A	
Sims – Beaumont Med Coll) St Louis			+1891–
Beaumont Hosp Med Coll	Mo 24	207½	
St Louis			+1887–1901
Barnes Med Coll	Mo 28	213A	
St Louis			+1893–
Woman's Med Coll	Mo 30	213D	
Kansas City			+1896–1903
St Louis Univ Sch Med	Mo 34		
St Louis			+1902–
NEBRASKA			
Univ Nebraska Coll Med (Omaha	Neb 5	214	*1882–
Med Coll; Omaha Univ) Omaha			+1882–
Lincoln Med Coll, Eclectic	Neb 4	214A	*1891–
(Cotner Univ Med Dept) Lincoln			+1891–

State/Title of school/City	AMA #	Polk #	Years of grad. classes till 1906 * used by LMH; + a/c AMA or Polk
Creighton Univ Sch Med Omaha	Neb 6	217A	*1893– +1893–
NEW HAMPSHIRE			
Dartmouth Med Sch Hanover	NH 1	218	*1798– +1798–
NEW YORK			
College of Phys & Surg, NY (Columbia U Coll of Phys & Surg; Kings Coll 1769)	NY 1	223	*1793–1807 1810– +1793–1807 1811–
Coll Phys & Surg of Western District (Fairfield)	NY 2	224	*1816–40 +1816–40
Albany Med Coll (Union Univ Med Dept) Albany	NY 3	230	*1839–99 1901– +1839–
Geneva Med Coll (Hobart Coll Med Dept) Geneva	NY 4	229	*1835–53 1855–72 +1835–53 1855–72
Univ of the City of New York Med Coll, NYC	NY 5	231	*1842–98 +1842–98
Univ of Buffalo Sch Med Buffalo	NY 6	232	*1847– +1847–
New York Med Coll NYC	NY 7	233	*1851–64 +1851–64
Long Island Hosp Coll Med Brooklyn	NY 8	239	*1860– [index only, no dates] +1860–
New York Hom Med Coll NYC	NY 9	240	*1861– +1861–
Bellevue Hosp Med Coll NYC	NY 10		*1862–98 +1862–98
New York Med Coll & Hosp for Women			*1864– +1864–
Eclectic Med Coll of the City of New York, NYC	NY–11		*1881 1882 1884–89 1893 1898 1904–05 +1867–
Woman's Med Coll of the New York Infirmary NYC	NY 14		*1870–99 +1870–99
Syracuse Univ Coll of Med Syracuse	NY 15		*1873–93 +1873–
College of Phys & Surg of Buffalo (Homeopathic)	NY 17		 +1880–84
Niagara Univ Med Dept Buffalo	NY 18		*1886–90 1893–97 +1886–98
University and Bellevue Hosp Med Coll, NYC	NY 14		*1899– +1899–
Cornell Univ Med Coll NYC	NY 20		*1899–1905 +1899–
Rutgers (Queen's) Coll Med Faculty, NYC	NY 21		*1792–3 1812–16 1827 1830–33 1835 +1792–3 1812–16 1827 [1830–32 1835]
New York Free Med Coll for Women, NYC	NY 35		 +1873–75
NORTH CAROLINA			

State/Title of school/City	AMA #	Polk #	Years of grad. classes till 1906 * used by LMH; + a/c AMA or Polk
Univ No Carolina	NC 1	252	*1903–
Chapel Hill			+1903–
Leonard Med Sch (Shaw Univ)	NC 3	254	*1893–
Raleigh Black			+1886 1888–
No Carolina Med Coll (Davidson	NC 4	--	*1895
Sch Med) Charlotte			+1893–
OHIO			
Med Coll Ohio	O 1	255	*1819–
Cincinnati			+1819–
Cincinnati Med Coll [merged	O–27		*1836–46
1846 into above]			+1836–38
Worthington Med Coll Cincinnati	O 2	262	*1833–38 1846–1901 1903 1905
Eclectic Med Coll or Inst		256	*1833–38 1844–
Starling Med Coll, Columbus	O 3	263	*1836–
Willoughby	O 25		+1836–
Ohio Med Univ	O 28	258	+1836–
Physio–Med Coll Cincinnati	O 4	260	
(Cincinnati Lit & Sci Inst)		259	+?1846–
Botanico–Med Coll Ohio	O 5	260½	
Cincinnati			+?1838–50?
Western Reserve Univ Cleveland	O 6	261 269	*1844–85 1888–1905
(Hudson Med Coll; Wooster; Charity Hosp)			+1844–
Cleveland Univ Med & Surg (Hom)	O 7	264	*1851–97
Western Hom M C; Clev'd M C (Hom)	O 23	264A	+1851–
Cincinnati Coll M & S	O 8	265	*1852–93
(incl Women's M C Cincinnat)		279½	+1852–1902
Miami Med Coll	O 9	266	*1853–57 1866–85 1890–
Cincinnati			+1853–57 1866–
Physio–Med Inst	O 10	268	
Cincinnati			+?1860–85
Pulte Med Coll (Hom)	O 13	270	*1873–04
Cincinnati			+1873–
Columbus Med Coll	O 14	272	*1876–92
Columbus			+1876–92
Northwestern Ohio Med Coll	O 18	278	*1887?
Toledo			+1884–91
Toledo Med Coll (Toledo	O 19	277	*1883–1901
Univ Med Dept			+1883–
Woman's Med Coll	O 20	279½	*1888–95
Cincinnati			+1888–95
Laura Memorial Woman's Med	O 21	279F	*1896–1903
Coll Cincinnati			+1896–1903
Presbyterian Hosp & Woman's	O 24		*1892–95
Med Coll Cincinnati			+1892–95
OREGON			
Willamette Univ Med Dept	Ore 1	280	*1867–95 1897–
Salem & Portland			+1867–95 1897–
Univ Oregon Med Sch	Ore 2	280½	*1888–97 1899
Portland			+1888–97 1899

State/Title of school/City	AMA #	Polk #	Years of grad. classes till 1906 * used by LMH; + a/c AMA or Polk
PENNSYLVANIA			
Univ Pennsylvania Med Sch	Pa 1	281	*1768– [except grads are unknown
(College of Phila; Univ State Pa			+1768– for 1772, 1775–79]
Jefferson Med Coll	Pa 2	282	*1826–
Philadelphia			+1826–
Pennsylvania Med Coll, Phila	Pa3	285	*1840–60
(Med Dept Penna Coll {in Gettysburg}			+1840–60
Philadelphia Coll Med & Surg	Pa 4	286	*1847–59 [some classes
Phila			+1847–59 unknown]
Franklin Med Coll	Pa 5	287	*1847–52
Phila			+1847–52
Woman's Med Coll of Penna	Pa 7	284	*1852–61 1863–
Phila			+1852–61 1863–
Penn Medical Univ	Pa 8	288	*1853–67 1874–80
Phila			+1855–67 1874–81
Hahnemann Med Coll & Hosp	Pa 9	283	*1849–
(Momeop Med Coll Pa) Phila		289	+1849–
Medico–Chirurg Coll Phila	Pa 11	294½	*1882–
Phila		294	+1882–
Univ of Pittsburgh Sch Med	Pa 12	294½	*1887–
(Western Penna Sch Med)			+1887–
Temple University Sch Med	Pa 13		*1904–
Phila			+1904–
North Amer Acad of Hom Healing	Pa 15		* [some miscellanous names]
Art Allentown			+?1835–41? [no lists survive]
Eclectic Med Coll Pa	Pa 17		
Phila			+?1856–80?
RHODE ISLAND			
Brown Univ Med Sch	RI 1	295	*1812–28
Providence			+1812–28
SOUTH CAROLINA			
Medical Coll of State of So	SC 1	297	*1834–38 ?
Carolina Charleston			+1834–38 ?
Med Coll So Carolina		296	*1825–61 1866– ?
Charleston			+1825–61 1866– ?
Univ So Carolina Med			*1868–73
Dept Columbia			+1868–73
TENNESSEE			
Univ of Nashville	Tenn 1	299	*1852–85 90 95 97 1899–1902 04
			+1852–
Vanderbilt Univ	Tenn 5	299?	*1874–85 90 1895–98 1900–04
Nashville [joint list of grads w/U Nashville 1874–94]			*1874–
Memphis Med Coll (Cumberland	Tenn 2	300	*1854 1858
Univ Med Tenn)			+?1855–61? 1868–73
Shelby Med Coll	Tenn 4	300½	
Nashville			+1858–62?

State/Title of school/City	AMA #	Polk #	Years of grad. classes till 1906 * used by LMH; + a/c AMA or Polk
Univ of Tennessee	Tenn 6	301	*1877–
(Nashville Med Coll)			+1877–
Meharry Med Coll	Tenn 7	302	*1877–
Nashville Black			+1877–
Memphis Hospital Med Coll	Tenn 8	304	*1881–88
Memphis			+1881–
Chattanooga Med Coll	Tenn 9	304½	*1890–
Chattanooga			+1890–
Tenn Med Coll, Knoxville (Linc–	Tenn 10	302½	1890 1894
oln Mem Univ; Grant Univ Med Dept0			+1900–
Sewanee Med Coll (Univ of	Tenn 11	304A	*1892–
the South) Sewanee			+1893–
Knoxville Med Coll	Tenn 13	304B	
Knoxville Black			+1900–05
Univ of W Tenn Coll Med	Tenn 14	304E	*1904–
& Surg Jackson Black			+1904–
TEXAS			
Texas Med Coll & Hosp	Tex 1	305	*1866–72 1874 1880
(Galveston Med Coll)			+1866–81 1888–91
Univ of Texas Med Sch	Tex 2	305A	*1892–
Galveston			+1892–
Fort Worth Sch Med (Texas	Tex 3	305B	*1895–
Christian Univ)			+1895–
Baylor Univ Coll Med (Univ	Tex 4	305D	
(Dallas Med Dept)			+1901–
Physio–Medical Coll Texas		305C	
Dallas			+1902–
Southern Methodist Univ	Tex 6		
Med Dept Dallas			+1904–
Gate City Med Coll	Tex 7	305G	
Dallas			+1903–
Bell Med Coll (Coll Phys	Tex 8	305I	
& Surg) Dallas			+1904–
Dallas Med Coll (Trinity	Tex 10	305E	
Univ Med Dept)			+1901–
VERMONT			
Castleton Med Coll (Vermont	Vt 1	309	*1819–37 1839–61
Acad Med) Castleton			+1819–37 1839–61
Vermont Coll Med	Vt 2	307	*1823–1904
Burlington			+1823–
Vermont Med Coll	Vt 3	308	*1830–56
Woodstock			+1830–56
VIRGINIA			
Univ of Virginia Dept Med	Va 1	310	*1828–64 1866–
Charlottesville			+1828–64 1866–
Medical Sch of Valley of Va	Va 2	311	
Winchester			*1826–61

State/Title of school/City	AMA #	Polk #	Years of grad. classes till 1906 * used by LMH; + a/c AMA or Polk
Winchester Med Coll	Va 3		*1848
Winchester			+1826–29 1850–61
Med Coll of Va (Hampden–Sidney)	Va 4	312	*1839–60 66–7 74–7 80 2 84–9 94 96–9
Richmond			+1839–
Randolph–Macon Coll Med Dept	Va 5	311½	
Prince Edward CH			+1840–55
University Med Coll	Va 6	311A	*1896–1905
of Richmond			+1894–
WISCONSIN			
Wisconsin Coll Phys & Surg	Wis 2	313	*1894–
Milwaukee			+1894–
Milwaukee Med Coll	Wis 3	315	*1895–
Milwaukee			+1895–

ELEMENTS & FORMAT OF THE ENTRY

FULL NAME capitalized & in bold type
Place(s) of practice if known, or Army or Navy service, if subject made it a part of his career or died in service. American place–names include states, unless unique or very well–known
Birth date in parentheses [month numbered in Roman]
Birthplace if different from place of practice
Death date in similar format
Place of death in similar format
Medical degree(s) or further medical education if stated*
Civil War service (see below) or service in other wars**
Citations from *journals*, etc. from *biographical compendia* and from *directories.* In this edition (1995) abbreviations of journal–titles and the like have been condensed.

Example

MILLER, SAMUEL JAMES FERGUS, CW–USA; Cincinnati & Dayton, O; Milwaukee (b/III–12–1837 Pleasant Ridge, O; d/VIII–9–1893 Togus, Me) MD UPa 1862. *Bost m&s j* 129: 208, 1893. *U Pa med alum CW*: 1862. *Butler* 1878: 612.

Education

Medical school citations follow, in general, "Historical Matter of American Medical Colleges," as appearing in *AMA Directory*, 1931, though the compiler has found some discrepancies between this list and the lists published by the colleges themselves. (Of course, some colleges do not seem to have been able to list their graduates coherently or spell their names the same way twice.)

**Military Service

Civil War (CW) service has been mentioned as briefly as possible, to avoid errors of date, regiment or ship, etc., etc. Obituaries and other such matter tend to extreme unreliability in respect to military service.
CW–USA denotes Union service, known or presumed to have been in the Army
CW–USN similarly denotes service in the Union Navy
CW–US San Comm denotes service in the hospitals or hospital ships of the US Sanitary Commission
CW–CSA denotes Confederate service, known or presumed to have been in the Army
CW–CSN similarly denotes service in the Navy

ABADIE, EUGENE HILARIAN, USA (b/1810 France; d/XII-12-1874 St Louis) MD UPa 1833. *Med & surg rep Phila* 16:388-389, 1867. *Tr AMA* 187: 633-634. *Med rec* 10:8, 30, 1875.

ABBAY, ISAAC S , Paragon Mills, Tenn (b/XI-12-1847 Commerce, Miss; d/II-3-1894) MD U Nashville 1873. *Nashville jour m & s* 75:240-241, 1894. *Polk* 1890:1060.

ABBAY, SIDNEY MORSE, Centreville, La (d/II-6-1905 @ 67) MD U La 1866; AB Princeton 1856, AM 1859. CW-CSA. *JAMA* 44:562, 1905. *Polk* 1886:413.

ABBE, ALANSON, Boston (b/1796? d/IV-4-1864 @ 68) MD Yale 1821, *Bost m & s jour* 70:248, 1864.

ABBE, EDWARD PAYSON, New Bedford, Mass (d/II 25-1897 @69) MD Harvard 1852; AB Yale 1848. *Bost m & s jour* 136:217, 1897. *JAMA* 28: 569,1897.

ABBEY, DANIEL, CW-USA (d/I-28-1863) *Nat med jour* 1: 289, 1871.

ABBOT, JOHN PICKENS, Warren, RI (b/VII-26-1828; d/X-10-1886) MD Berkshire 1866; AB Bowdoin 1850. CW-USN. *Bowdoin cat* class 1850.

ABBOT, SAMUEL LEONARD, Boston (d/VII-1-1904 @ 86) Harvard 1841; AB 1838. *Bost m & s jour* 151:28, 54-55, 1904.

ABBOTT, CHARLES, Winterport, Me. (b/III-27-1824 Frankfort, Me; d/VIII-19-1879) MD UCNY 1849. CW-USA. *Med rec* 16:311, 1879. *Atkinson* I: 470.

ABBOTT, EZRA, Canton Mass (d/IV-21-1872 @63)MD Harvard 1837. *Bost m & s jour* ns 9:276, 1872.

ABBOTT, FRANK, NYC (b/IX-5-1836 Shapleigh, Me; d/IV-20-1897) MD UCNY 1871. *JAMA* 28; 860, 1897. *Polk* 1896: 1034.

ABBOTT, GEORGE, Auburn NY (d/I-23-1859 Egypt) MD U Buffalo 1847 & 1852. *Buff med jour* 14:703, 1859.

ABBOTT, JAMES BUSWELL, Loudun, NH 1827-1838; Sanbornton 1843-1870 (b/VI-24-1799 Concord; d/VII-5-1870) MD Dartmouth 1826. *Tr NH Med Soc* 1871: 106-108.

ABBOTT, JEHIEL, Westfield, Mass (b/IX-3-1795 Tolland, Conn; d/IX-23-1872) MD Yale hon 1843. *Tr AIH* 1873:512. *Am jour hom mat med* 6: 324, 1873. *NE med gaz* 8:200, 1873. Homeopath.

ABBOTT, JOEL, Lexington, Ga (b/III-17-1776; d/XI-19-1826) *Am jour med sci* 2:239-240, 1826.

ABBOTT, JOHN HAMILL, Fall River, Mass (d/XI-1-1902 @ 54) MD Jefferson 1872. *Bost m & s jour* 147:532, 1902.

ABBOTT, LILLIAN E , Concord, NH (b/VI-28- 1868 Penacock, NH; d/V-27-1901) MD Woman's Med Coll NY 1895. *Tr NH Med Soc* 1901:332.

ABBOTT, LUCY M , NYC (b/XII-14-1834; d/II- 9-1875) MD Woman's Med Coll Pa 1865. *Med reg NY NJ Conn* 1875: 195.

ABBOTT, LUTHER JEWETT, Troy, NY 1852; Irvington, Fontenelle, Fremont, Lincoln, Neb (b/IX-15-1831 Blue Hill, Me; d/II-22-1900) ng Ohio Med Coll 1849; MD Jefferson 1854. *Proc Nebr St Med Soc* 1900: 22-24. *JAMA* 34:574, 1900. *Atkinson* I: 513. *Polk* 1893: 757.

ABBOTT, OSCAR DUNREATH, Manchester, NH (b/IX-13-1824 Cornish Flat; d/I-1-1902) MD Berkshire 1850. *Boston m & s jour* 146:52, 1902. *Tr NH Med Soc* 1902: 315-316.

ABBOTT, ROBERT OSBORNE, USA (d/VI-16-1867 Brooklyn) MD UPa 1847. *Med & surg rep Phila* 16:544, 1867. *Tr AMA* 19: 419, 450-451, 1868.

ABBOTT, SAMUEL WARREN, CW-USN; Newton Centre, Mass (b/VI-12-1837 Woburn; d/X-22-1904) MD Harvard 1862; AB Brown 1858. *Boston m & s jour* 151: 478, 1904. *Tr RI Med Soc* 6:279-280, 1904-09. *Harvard in CW*: 269-270. *K & B* III:1.

ABEL, AMACEY B, Philadelphia (d/I-22-1906 @ 63) MD Jefferson 1875. *Pa med jour* 9:360, 1905-06. *Polk* 1896: 1297.

ABELL, ERASMUS DARWIN, Rindge NH 1841-52; Chicopee Mass 1852-76; Farmington, Minn 1876-99 (b/I-26-1817 Lempster, NH; d/X-2-1899) MD Dartmouth 1839. *Tr Minn St Med Soc* 1899: 191. *Polk* 1896: 786.

ABELL, IRA HILL, Antwerp. NY (b/I-1-1823 Fairfield, Vt; d/IV-29-1844) MD Vt Med Coll 1844. *Tr NY St Med Soc* 1894:741 ff. *Polk* 1890: 764.

ABELL, LUCY W , Washington, DC 1878-1882 (b/1808? d/XII-3-1893 @ 85) ng New Engl Fem Med Coll: MD Pa Med U 1860. *NE med gaz* 29: 1894. Homeopath.

ABELL, MATTHIAS, Providence, RI (b/I-1-1830, Flemington, NJ; d/V-1-1902) MD CPSNY 1857. *Tr RI Med Soc* 6:545-546, 1899. *Polk* 1890: 1026. *Atkinson* I: 383.

ABERDEIN, ROBERT, Syracuse, NY (d/X-18-1903) MD Bellevue 1867; MB U Toronto 1867. *Bost m & s jour* 149:500, 1903. *Polk* 1886: 710.

ABERNETHY, AUGUSTUS HUGGINS, Bridgeport, Conn (b/V-21-1838 Litchfield Conn; d/XI-9-1884) MD Yale 1864. *Med reg NY NJ Conn* 1885: 229. *Proc Conn Med Soc* 1885: 216. *Med & surg rep Phila* 51: 104, 1884. *Butler* 1878: 72.

ABERNETHY, GEORGE HASKELL, Augusta, Ill (b/ Harwinton, Conn; d/1844) MD Yale 1830. *Proc Conn Med Soc* ns 2: 149-150, 1882-83.

ABERNETHY, HUGH HORNER, Belvidere, NJ (d/XII-9-1891 @83) MD UPa 1830. *Med reg NY NJ Conn* 1892: 271.

ABERNETHY, JOHN JAY, USN(b/XII-26-1805 d/II-28-1880) MD CPSNY 1828; AB Yale 1825. *Bost m & s jour* 101:746. 1879. *Med reg NY NJ Conn* 1880:232. *Med & surg rep Phila* 41:462, 1879. *Med rec NY* 16:16, 1879.

ABERNETHY, SAMUEL, Rahway, NJ (b/II-22-1806 Tinicum, Pa; d/II-13-1874) MD U Pa 1830; AB Union 1827. *Tr AMA* 25: 528, 1874. *Med & surg rep Phila*

30:204, 276, 1874. *Trans Med Soc NJ* 1874: 102–104.

ABORN, ORIN, Marshfield, Ind (b/VIII–20–1826 Lincoln, Vt: d/VIII–5–1885) ng U Mich 1853–54. *Tr Ind St Med Soc* 1886: 202. *Butler* 1878:191.

ABRAHAMS, JAMES ARMISTEAD, Demopolis, Ala (d/III–15–1900) MD Med Coll Ala 1892. *JAMA* 34: 702, 1900.

ABRAHAMS, SIMEON, NYC (b/1810? d/1867) MD NY Med Coll 1852. *Tr AMA* 19:408–09, 1868. *Med & surg rep Phila* 16:368, 1867. *Med reg NY NJ Conn* 1867: 207.

ABY, THOMAS Y , New Orleans, La (d/XII–24– 1905 @ 65) MD Tulane 1866. *Bost m & s jour* 58: 683, 1906. *Polk* 1896: 418.

ACKER, EPHRAIM LEISTER, Allentown, Pa (d/V–12–1903 @ 76 Norristown) MD U Pa 1852; AB Franklin & Marshall 1846, AM 1850; LLB U Pa 1886. *Pa med jour* 7:278, 1903.

ACKER, GEORGE B Jr, Pittsburgh, Pa (d/XI–30–1903 @ 35) MD West Pa U 1897. *Pa med jour* 7: 278, 1903.

ACKLEY, HENRY, USN (b/I–29–1837 Phila; d/1865/66) MD Jefferson 1858. *Tr NJ Med Soc* 1865–67:130–33.

ACKLEY, HORACE AUSTIN, Cleveland, O (b/1813 Genesee, NY; d/IV–24–1859) MD Fairfield 1831. *Bost m & s jour* 60:288, 1859. *Tr Ohio St Med Soc* 1875: 193. *Med & surg rep Phila* ns2: 135, 1859. *K&B* III:2–3.

ACKLEY, JOHN BOLTON, USN (b/X–6–1834 Vincentown; d/IX–11–1874 Pensacola) MD UPa 1860. *U Pa med alum CW*: 1860.

ADAIR, JAMES TODD, Indiana, Pa; CW–USA (b/I–24–1836; d/V–5–1866) MD Jefferson 1859. *Med & surg rep Phila* 14:458, 1866. *Nat med jour* 1: 289, 1870.

ADAM, GEORGE, Canaan, Conn (b/1813? d/1894) MD CPSNY 1837. *JAMA* 22:97, 1894. *Polk* 1886: 542.

ADAMS, ABEL BRYANT, Lexington, Mass (d/VIII–13 1884 @73) MD Harvard 1836. *Bost m & s jour* 111:192, 1884.

ADAMS, ALBERT RISTINE, NYC (d/XI–21–1884 @ 36) MD UCNY 1878. *Med & surg rep Phila* 51: 668, 1884.

ADAMS, ARTHUR C , Washington, DC (b/IV–14–1847; d/I–1–1905) MD Columbian 1873. *Hist Med Soc DC*: 303. *Polk* 1893: 267.

ADAMS, BENJAMIN BELA, Washington, DC (b/VIII–15–1851 Havre, France; d/I–25–1897) MD Howard 1875; MD Georgetown 1876. *Hist Med Soc DC*: 112, 307. *JAMA* 28: 284, 1897. *Polk*: 1886: 211.

ADAMS, BENJAMIN FANEUIL DUNKIN, Waltham, Mass; Colorado Springs, Col 1882– ; (b/1839? d/X–28–1895 @ 56) MD Harvard 1864; AB 1860. *Bost m & s jour* 133: 480, 1895.

ADAMS, CHARLES GOLDTHWAITE, Keene, NH (b/1793? d/III–9–1856 @ 63) MD Harvard 1816; AB Dartmouth 1810. *Bost m & s jour* 54:247, 1856.

ADAMS, CHARLES WISNER, Kansas City, Mo (b/1854 Rochester, NY; d/VIII–3–1899) MD CPSNY 1879; AB Rochester. *JAMA* 33: 427, 1899. *Polk* 1896: 844.

ADAMS, CLIFFORD BURDETT, Fair Haven, Conn (b/I–8–1850 Suffield, Conn; d/VIII–19–1898 New Haven) MD Hahnemann Phila 1872. *Hahn mo* 33: 153–154, 1898. *Tr AIH* 1899: 74. *Polk* 1886: 194. Homeopath.

ADAMS, DANIEL, Keene, NH (b/1776 Lincoln, Mass; d/VIII–22–1830) MD Dartmouth 1803. *Tr NH Med Soc* 1864:4.

ADAMS, DANIEL LUCIUS, New Haven, Conn (b/XI–1–1814, Mt Vernon, NH; d/I–3–1899) MD Harvard 1838; AB Yale 1835. *JAMA* 32:145, 1899.

ADAMS, EDWARD [EDWIN?] AUSTIN, Kalamazoo, Mich (b/ V–5–1848 Lawrence, Mass; d/I–7–1882) MD U Buffalo 1876; ng Amherst 1869. *Men of Amherst*.

ADAMS, EDWIN, Boston (d/X–22–1867 @ 66) MD Harvard 1823. *Bost m & s jour* 77:280, 1867.

ADAMS, ELIZABETH S , NYC (b/1821; d/XII–14–1876) MD NY Med Coll Women 1869. *Homeop times* 4:285, 1877. *Cleave*. Homeopath.

ADAMS, ENOCH, Litchfield, Me (b/V–21–1829 Andover, Me; d/I–23–1900) MD Harvard 1851; ng Bowdoin Med Coll. *JAMA* 34:312, 1900. *Atkinson* I:304. *Polk* 1896: 637. CW–USA.

ADAMS, GEORGE A , Webster, Mass (b/New Boston, NH; d/I–15–1880) MD NY Hom Med Coll 1874. *Tr Mass Homeop Med Soc* 1880. Homeopath.

ADAMS, HENRY, Sackett's Harbor, NY 1812?–1848; Cohoes, NY 1850–1857 (b/VII–6–1787 Coxsackie, NY; d/VII–6–1857) Stud med w/father, Peter C Adams. USA–1812. *Trans AIH* 1893: 123. Homeopath.

ADAMS, HIRAM, Fabius, NY (b/1803? d/1865) MD conferred by regents NY State U 1856. *Tr AMA* 18: 315, 1867.

ADAMS, HORACE WALTER, Boston (b/XII–8–1827; d/II–7–1861) MD Harvard 1853; AB 1849. *Bost m & s jour* 64:77, 106–109, 1861. *Palmer's Necrol alum Harvard*: 379–380.

ADAMS, IRA HERBERT, West Derry, NH (b/VIII–10–1846 Pomfret, Vt; d/IX–15?–1897) MD Dartmouth 1875. *JAMA* 29: 709, 1897. *Tr NH Med Soc* 1897: 306. *Polk* 1896:918.

ADAMS, IRA R , Lowville, NY (b/1830; d/XI–19–1862) MD Hahnemann Phila 1860. *Amer homeop rev* 3:576, 1862. *Tr NY Homeop Soc* 2: , 1864.

ADAMS, JAMES BEMIS (b/I–12–1825 Lyons, NY; d/I–16– 1853 West Indies) MD CPSNY 1851; AM Harvard 1847. *Palmer's Necrol alum Harvard*: 22.

ADAMS, JAMES M , Noah, Marion, Ind (b/I–15–1820 Scott Co. Ky; d/IX–16–1894) ng Ohio Med Coll 1853. *Trans Ind St Med Soc* 1895:404. *Polk* 1886: 331.

ADAMS, JAMES M C , Frankfort, Ind (b/IV–26–1839 Hendricks Co, Ind; d/XI–23–1888) MD Rush 1869. *Trans Ind St Med Soc* 1889:213. *Polk* 1886: 319.

 Spec. educ'l status abbrev. as: ***ng*** = college verified attendance without degree;

ADAMS, JAMES WILLIAM, Des Moines, Ia (b/XII-26 1840 Hendricks Co Ind; d/IX-13-1901) MD Rush 1881; ng U Mich Med 1867. *Trans Ia St Med Soc* 20:49-50, 1902. *Polk* 1886: 356.

ADAMS, JOHN GLOVER, NYC (b/VIII-12-1807; d/ VI-19-1884 England) MD CPSNY 1830; AB Yale 1826, AM 1829. *Med reg NY NJ Conn* 1885:229. *Bost m & s jour* 111:22, 1884. *Tr Med Soc St NY* 1885:339-341. *Atkinson* I:357.

ADAMS, JOHN SMALLEY, Oakland, Cal (b/XII-24-1830 Highgate, Vt; d/VII-27-1899) MD Albany 1855. *Trans Med Soc St Calif* 1900: 548. *Atkinson* I:144.

ADAMS, JULIA A, Palos Park, Ill (d V-30-1905 @74) MD Homeop Hosp Cleveland 1871. *Ill med jour* 8:80, 1905. *Polk* 1896: 223 (Oakland, Cal). Homeopath.

ADAMS, JULIUS W , CW-USA (d/XI-15-1865 Brooklyn, NY) MD *Nat med jour* 1:289, 1870/71.

ADAMS, LUCIUS S , Stockbridge, Mass (d/III-7-1880 @ 76 St. Paul Minn) MD Berkshire 1830. *Med surg rep Phila* Phila 42: 264, 1880.

ADAMS, NEWTON H , CW-USN (d/XI-17/18-1869 @ 34) *Nat med jour* 1:289, 1870/71, *Phila med reg & dir* 1871: 302. *Tr AMA* 21:497, 1870.

ADAMS, ORION JOHN HALL, Chicago (d/II-24-1874) MD Rush 1872. *Med reg Chic* 1874-75: 345.

ADAMS, ORSON BARNES, Elgin Ill; Oakland Calif (d/ X-14-1894 @64) MD Rush 1860. *JAMA* 23: 697, 1894.

ADAMS, PETER N , Dayton, O (d/VII-17-1898 @ 44) MD Starling 1878. *JAMA* 31: 314, 1898. *Polk* 1886: 752.

ADAMS, SAMUEL, USA (b/Maine; d/IX-9-1867 Galveston) MD *Med surg rep Phila* 17: 281, 1867. *Nat med jour* 1:289, 1870/71.

ADAMS, SANFORD WILLIAM, Mt. Vernon, NY (b/V-17-1878 Westfield, Mass; d/III-7-1906) MD UCNY & Bellevue 1899. *Bost m & s jour* 154:308, 1906.

ADAMS, WILLIAM B , Montgomery, Mo (d/III-6-1900 @82) MD Mo Med Coll 1846. *JAMA* 34:702, 1900.

ADAMS, WILLIAM E, Greensboro, Ga; Farragut, Ia; Hot Springs, SD (d/IX-12-1897 Henderson Ky) MD CPS Keokuk 1876. *JAMA* 29:660,1897. *Polk* 1886:230, 358.

ADAMS, ZABDIEL BOYLSTON, Boston (b/II-19-1793 Roxbury, Mass; d/I-25-1855) MD Harvard 1816; AB 1813. *Bost m & s jour* 51: 545-546, 1854. Palmer's *Necrol Harvard alum*: 47-48.

ADAMSON, WILLIAM ROBERT, Lake George, NY (b/1852? d/ VII-6-1894) MD Bellevue 1873. *Med reg NY NJ Conn* 1895:215. *Polk* 1886: 665.

ADDISON, EDMUND BRICE, Baltimore; Washington, DC (b/X-5-1794 Oxon Hill, Md.; d/II-14-1878) MD U Pa 1815. *Hist Med Soc DC*: 219. *Med annals Md*: 298.

ADDISON, JOHN Baltimore (d/1859) MD U Md 1830. *Med annals Md*: 298.

ADDISON, ROBERT S, Chicago (d/II-21-1894) MD Chic Med Coll 1862. *JAMA* 22:313 1894. *Butler* 1878: 129.

ADDISON, SAMUEL RIDOUT, USN (d/VIII-28-1860 Naval Hosp. Chelsea, Mass) MD U Pa 1836. *Med surg rep Phila* ns4: 510, 1860. *Hamersly*.

ADKINS, CHARLES W , Langston, Ala (d/IX-4-1901 @60) MD U Louisville 1868. *JAMA* 37:790, 1901. *Polk* 1886: 135.

ADLER, JOHN MERCER, Philadelphia (b/VIII-9-1928 Georgetown DC; d/ 1904) MD Columbian Wash 1851; AB Princeton 1847, AM 1851, *Trans CPP* centennial vol: 207. *Pa med jour* 8:334, 1904/05. *Atkinson* I:237. *Butler* 1874: 657. CW-USA.

ADREON, STEPHEN W , St Louis, Mo (b/Baltimore; d/XII- 9-1867) MD U Md 1828. *Med annals Md*: 298.

ADRIAN, JAMES A , Logansport, Ind (b/I-12-1826; d/I- 29-1886) MD Cleveland Med Coll 1854. *Med reg NY NJ Conn* 1887:251.

ADY, ALBERT, Muscatine, Ia (b/II-27-1830 Harrison Co., O; d/III-20-1893) MD Starling 1867; MD Bellevue 1874. *Trans Ia St Med Soc* 11:133, 1893. *Polk* 1886: 364.

AGARD, AURELIUS HORNER, Western Star, O; Sandusky O 1856- ; Oakland, Cal 1875?- (b/X-10-1822 Wadsworth, O; d/VIII-31-1892) MD Jefferson 1849. *Tr Med Soc Calif* 23:281-282, 1893. *Atkinson* I:355.

AGARD, LAWRENCE MORE, Auburn, Cal (b/VII-1-1859 Sandusky, O; d/XII-3-1889) MD Cooper 1883. *Trans Med Soc Calif* 20:326-327, 1890. *Polk*: 1886: 163.

AGNEW, ALEXANDER W , Fayette, Ala (d/XI-12-1897) MD Transylvania 1844. *Trans Med Assn St Ala* 1898:240. *Polk* 1886: 133.

AGNEW, CORNELIUS REA, NYC (b/VIII-8-1830; d/IV-18-1888) MD CPSNY 1852; AB Columbia 1849. *Med reg NY NJ Conn* 1888:240. *JAMA* 10:539-540, 1888. *Boston m & s jour* 118:437-438, 1888; 119:640, 1888. *Atkinson* I:485-487. *K & B* III: 7-8.

AGNEW, DAVID HAYES, Philadelphia (b/XI-24-1818; d/III-22-1892) MD UPa 1838; LLD Princeton 1876. *Tr CPP* 3s15: xxix ff. *Trans Med Soc Pa* 1892:180-89. *JAMA* 18: 468-470,1892. *Atkinson* I:31-32. *K&B* III: 9.

AGNEW, HENRY, Harrisburg, Pa (d/IV-12-1868 @ 28 Easton) MD UPa 1866. *Phila med reg & dir* 1871:296. *Med & surg rep Phila* 18:442,1868.*Men of Lafayette*: 182.

AGNEW, HULBERT, Philadelphia (d/IV-6-1894 @ 32) MD UPa 1888; AB Princeton 1883, AM 1886. *JAMA* 22: 601, 1894.

AGNEW, JOHN PARKER, Philadelphia (d/II-5-1903 @ 69) MD UPa 1864. *Pa med jour* 7: 278, 1903/04.

A'HERON, TERENCE MAHONEY, Hampton Jct, NJ (b/Irel'd; d/XI-16-1906 @ 60) MD UCNY 1873. *Boston m & s jour* 155:630, 1906. *Polk* 1890: 724.

AHL, JOHN, York, Pa (d/IV-4-1902) MD Washington U Balto 1845. *Pa med jour* 6:259, 1902/03. *Polk* 1886: 840.

AIKEN, EDWARD W, Winnsboro, SC (d/VIII-3-1886 @ 31) MD SC Med Coll 1876. *New Orl m & s jour* 4s14: 317, 1886. *Polk* 1886: 858.

AIKEN, ELISHA WILBOUR, Boston, Hingham, Mass (d/IV-13-1898 @70) MD Harvard 1864. *Boston m & s jour* 138:388, 1898. *JAMA* 30:1061 1898. *Polk* 1896:691.

AIKEN, JOHN, Chester Valley, Pa (b/X-8-1838 Phila; d/II-26-1866) MD UPa 1862. CW-USA. *Med & surg rep Phila* 14:360, 1866. *Nat med jour* 1:289, 1870/1. *UPa med alum CW*: 1862.

AIKEN, WILLIAM HENRY, Malden, Mass (d/IX-16-1885 @36) MD Harvard 1871. *Bost m & s jour* 113: 312, 1885.

AIKIN, WILLIAM EDWARD AUGUSTIN, Baltimore (b/1807 NY; d/V-30-1888) MD Castleton 1834; MD UCNY 1849. *Med annals Md*: 298-299. *Polk* 1886: 435.

AILLS, WILLIAM, Steen's Creek Miss (b/I-8-1826; d/I-14- 1905) MD Tulane 1853. *So pract* 27:335, 1905. *Flint* 1897: 536.

AIMES, JOHN MARTIN, West Haven, Conn (b/VII-21 1828 NYC; d/X-27-1881) MD Yale 1858; AM Columbia 1850. *Proc Conn St Med Soc* ns2: 166-167, 1882-83. *Butler* 1878: 72. *Atkinson* I: 440.

AINSWORTH, FREDERICK SMITH, CW-USA; Boston (b/IV-17-1820 Jaffrey, NH; d/X-7-1878) MD Harvard 1844; AB Dartmouth 1840. *Harvard in CW*:231.

AITKIN, JOHN SCOTT, NYC (d/V-10-1893 @ 40) MD CPSNY 1878. *Med reg NY NJ Conn* 1893: 296. *Polk*: 1886:670.

AKERMAN, CHARLES EDWIN, Hampton Falls, NH (d/XII-27-1862 @ 31 N Andover, Mass) MD Harvard 1860. *Boston m & s jour* 67: 490, 1862.

AKERS, OSCAR J [?OWEN JAMES?] Newark, NJ (b/1823; d/IV-9-1861) MD CPSNY 1846 *Trans NJ Med Soc* 1865-67: 133-134. *Tr AMA* 14: 208, 1863.

ALBEE, JAMES E, Detroit (d/IX-1-1897) MD Mich Coll M & S 1891. *JAMA* 29: 555, 1897. *Polk* 1896: 745.

ALBEE, WILLIAM AUGUSTUS, Union, Me; Rockland (b/X-15-1840 Washington, Me; d/XI-3-1895) MD Bowdoin 1866. *Trans Me Med Assn* 1896: 425. *Atkinson* I: 78. *Butler* 1878: 303.

ALBERS, HENRY, Baltimore (b/1812 Germany; d/X-7-1882) <MD 1837 Göttingen> *Med annals Md*: 299. *Butler* 1878: 310.

ALBERT, CHARLES, Easton, Md (b/1851; d/V-30-1882) MD U Md 1872. *Med annals Md*: 299.

ALBERTSON, JOSEPH A , San Francisco (b/1826 Rush, NY; d/VII-7-1899) MD Hahnemann Chic 1862 *Tr Am Inst Homeop* 1900: 828. *Polk* 1886: 170. Homeopath.

ALCOCK, EDWARD J , Baltimore (d/XII-26-1836) MD U Md 1827. *Med annals Md*: 299.

ALCORN, ALEXANDER W , Ravenna, O (b/V-23-1835 Gatensville, Pa; d/1891) ng U Mich Med Sch 1862-63. *Trans O Med Soc* 1892: 384. *Atkinson*I: 512. *Polk* 1886: 766.

ALCORN, JAMES P , Allegheny Co, Pa (b/VIII-15-1822 Clarion Co, Pa; d/I-19-1875) MD Jefferson 1850. *Trans Med Soc Pa* II: 160-161, 1876.

ALCOTT, WILLIAM ALEXANDER, Auburndale, Mass (b/VIII-6-1798 Wolcott, Conn; d/III-29-1859) ng Yale Med Sch. *Boston m & s jour* 60:208, 1859. *Med & surg rep Phila* ns2: 29, 1859. *K&B*III:10-11.

ALDEN, EBENEZER, Randolph, Mass (b/III-17-1788; d/XII-29-1881) MB Dartmouth 1811; MD U Pa 1812; AB Harvard 1808. *Boston m & s jour* 105:623, 1881. *Tr AMA* 32: 494-495, 1881. *K&B*II: 3. *Atkinson* I:413.

ALDRICH, HENRY, Wyoming, RI (b/XII-12?/20?-1802 Hopkinton, RI; d/V-8-1886) Licensed 1828; Hon MD Yale 1855. *Tr RI Med Soc* 1883-1888: 375-376. *Butler* 1878: 745. *Atkinson* I:413.

ALDRICH, OLIVE DEWEY, Philadelphia (d/I-11-1897) MD Woman's Med Coll Pa 1874. *JAMA* 28: 328, 1897. *Polk* 1896: 1297.

ALDRICH, THOMAS R , Charleston, SC (b/IX-27-1812; d/1886) MD Med Coll SC 1833. *New Orl m & s jour* ns14:161, 1886. *Polk* 1886:852.

ALDRICH, WILLIAM DANIEL, Warrensburg, NY (b/I-15-1851, Thurman; d/VI-4-1897) MD Dartmouth 1872. *JAMA* 28:1202-1203, 1897. *Polk* 1896: 1110.

ALDRIDGE, JOHN HENRY, Baltimore (b/1832; d/III-21-1889) MD U Md 1855. *Med annals Md*: 299. *Butler* 1874: 310.

ALEXANDER, ANDREW, Dorchester, Mass (b/IV-21-1812 Edinburgh; d/IV-22-1885) MD Harvard 1835. *Boston m & s jour* 112:432, 1885. *Atkinson* I: 419.

ALEXANDER, ASHTON, Baltimore (b/1772 Arlington, Va; d/II-1855) MD U Pa 1795. *Tr AMA* 32: 495-496, 1881.*Med annals Md*: 299. *K&B*III: 11.

ALEXANDER, E H, Pine Bluff, Ark (d/IX-16-1884 @ 30) MD U La 1882. *New Orl m & s jour* ns12:415, 1884.

ALEXANDER, F V P , (d/X-1-1878, Greenville, Miss) *Tr AMA* 30:850, 1879. *Med rec. NY* 14:300, 1878.

ALEXANDER, HAMILL MARR, Marietta, Pa (d/X-13 1903 @52) MD UPa 1876. *Pa med jour* 7:80, 1903/04. *Chic med rec* 25:355, 1903. *Polk* 1896:1290.

ALEXANDER, HARVARD AUGUSTUS, Birmingham, Ala (d/V-29-1901) MD Ky Sch Med 1875. *Trans Med Assn St Ala* 1902:130. *Polk* 1893:151.

ALEXANDER, HERMAN WILLIAM, Joliet, Ill (b/XII-1-1837 St. Joseph Co, Mich; d/III-27-1889) MD Chic Med Coll 1873. *Trans Ill St Med Soc* 1890:40. *Butler* 1878:139.

ALEXANDER, JOHN LOCKE, Belmont, Mass (b/XII-21 1806 Winchester, NH; d/XI-9-1890) MD Berkshire 1835. *Men of Amherst*, 1831.

ALEXANDER, JOSEPH WEST, Canonsburg, Pa (b/IV-5-1815; d/IV-20-1892) ng Jefferson 1839, 1840. *Tr Med Soc Pa* 23:191-192, 1892. *Butler* 1878:701.

ALEXANDER, LEE M , Marshall, Mo (d/II-26-1900) MD Columbian, DC 1860. *JAMA* 34:639, 1900. *Polk* 1890:663.

 Spec. educ'l status abbrev. as: ***ng*** = college verified attendance without degree;

ALEXANDER, MATTHEW McCLUNG, Knoxville, Tenn (d/II-1/or I-26?} 1887) MD UPa 1867. *New Orl m & s jour* ns14:723, 1867. *Polk* 1886:867.

ALEXANDER, REID, Topeka, Kans (b/XI-1-1860; d/X-8 1894) MD UPa 1885. *JAMA* 23:624, 1894. *Kans med jour* 6:528-529, 540-545, 1894. *Polk* 1890:449.

ALEXANDER, SAMUEL S , CW-USA (d/XI-27-1861 of wounds rec'd Drainsville, MD) *Nat med jour* 1:289, 1870/71.

ALEXANDER, WILLIAM W , Athens, Tenn (b/VII-18-1830 Rogersville, Tenn; d/VIII-1-1876) MD UCNY 1854. CW-USA. *Med surg rep Phila*35:180, 1876.

ALISON, LOCKWOOD, Kingston, La (d/III-12-1896) MD Med Coll St SC 1828. *NC med jour* 37:214, 1896. *Polk* 1886:414.

ALISON, ROBERT HENRY, Ardmore, Pa (d/VII-161906 @59) MD UPa 1869. *Trans CPP centennial vol*:208. *Pa med jour* 9:804, 1905-06.

ALLABAND, SAMUEL COOPER, Philadelphia (d/IX 18-1905 @ 63) MD UPa 1865. *Pa med jour* 9:27, 608, 1905-06. Polk 1886:1811.

ALLABEN, ORSON M , Margaretville, NY (b/Delaware Co, NY; d/XI-27-1891) MD Woodstock 1831. *Trans NY St Med Soc* 11:741 ff. 1894. *Polk* 1890:796.

ALLAN [ALLEN], HENRY WILLIAM, Brooklyn, NY (d/II-5-1903 @ 42) MD Bellevue 1882. *Boston m & s jour* 148:194, 1903. *Polk* 1896:991.

ALLEMAN, LEVI J , Boone, Ia (b/XII-12-1841 Fayette, NY; d/VIII-26-1888) MD UCNY 1863. *Tr Ia St Med Soc* 7:525-526, 1886-89. *Polk* 1886:351.

ALLEN, ALMON NELSON, Pittsfield, Mass (b/Petersburg, NH; d/II-6-1884 @ 63) MD Albany 1845. *Bostm & s jour* 110:168, 288, 1884; 111:619, 1884. *Mass Med Soc cat.* 1894.

ALLEN, ALMON S , Brooklyn, NY (b/XI-21-1847; d/III-17-1889) MD Albany 1872. *Med reg NY NJ Conn* 1889:266. *Polk* 1886:643.

ALLEN, AMOS, Grafton, NY (d/III-8-1899 Canarsie, NY) MD Berkshire 1846. *JAMA* 32:733, 1899. *Polk* 1886:662.

ALLEN, BENJAMIN W , Morgantown, WVa (b/VI-1-1824 Preston Co, Va; d/1887) MD UVa 1848. CW-USA. *Tr Med Soc W Va* 1887: 493-494. *Atkinson* I:425. *Butler* 1878:848.

ALLEN, CARLOS, Vernon, NJ (b/IX-18-1814 Huntington, Vt; d/II-19-1903) MD Dartmouth 1838. *Tr Med Soc NJ* 1903:389-390. *Atkinson* I:437. *Polk* 1896:951.

ALLEN, CHARLES CLINCH, Chillicothe, Ill (b/Ill; d/I 23-1901) MD U Mo 1850; MD Bellevue 1872. *Ill med jour* ns11:533, 1901. *Off'l reg Ill phys* 1884:168.

ALLEN, CHARLES GILBERT, Barre, Mass (d/1896) MD Harvard 1864. CW-USA. *Harvard in CW*:284-285.

ALLEN, CHARLES LINNAEUS, Rutland, Vt (b/VI-21-1820; d/VII-2-1890) MD Castleton 1846; AB Middlebury 1842, AM 1845; MD (hon.) Rush 1873. *JAMA* 15:159, 1890. *Bost m & s jour* 123:48, 1890. *K & B* III:13.

ALLEN, CHARLES T , Minneapolis (d/XI-28-1897) MD Minnesota Hosp Med Coll 1882. *JAMA* 29:1234, 1897. *Trans Minn St Med Soc* 1899:191. *Polk* 1896:789.

ALLEN, CHARLES WARRENNE, NYC (b/XII-4-1854 Flemington, NJ; d/V-31-1906 @ Gibraltar) MD CPSNY 1878. *Bost m & s jour* 154:664, 1906.

ALLEN, CHESTER GRISWOLD, NYC (b/II-15-1838; d/IX-18-1878) MD Bellevue 1877. *Med reg NY NJ Conn* 1879:187.

ALLEN, DAVID L , Shenandoah, Ia (d/I-24-1884, Princeton, Kans) MD LICH 1874. *Med surg rep Phila* 50:255, 1884.

ALLEN, DAVIS B , Warsaw, Ky (d/III-26-1895 @ 46) MD U Louisville 1870. *JAMA* 24:497, 1895. *Butler* 1878:268.

ALLEN, E H , Oxford, Ala (d/III-23-1883) MD Med Coll SC 1849. *Tr Med Assn St Ala* 1883:243. *Butler* 1874:14.

ALLEN, EDMUND W , Shrewsbury, NJ (b/VIII-11-1788; d/V-17-1867) Lic. NJ Med Soc 1810 by examination; ng UPa Med Sch. *Tr NJ Med Soc* 1867:207-8; 1871: 91. *Tr AMA* 19:431, 1868.

ALLEN, EZRA PASCAL, Athens, Pa (b/VI-5-1821 Smithfield; d/V-21-1895) MD Berkshire 1847. *JAMA* 24:861,1895. *Atkinson* I:266, 1878.*Polk* 1886:791.

ALLEN, FRANCIS TRACY, Granby, Conn (b/V-28-1803 Norwich, Conn; d/X-8-1882) ng Yale 1825? *Proc Conn Med Soc* 1883:169-170. *Butler* 1878:72.

ALLEN, FRANKLIN HALEY, Haverhill, Mass (b/II-26 1856; d/IV-23-1905) MD Bowdoin 1877. *Boston m & s jour* 152:508, 1905. *Polk* 1896:713.

ALLEN, FREDERICK, Hallowell, Me (b/ca1811; d/1858) MD Harvard 1836; ng Amherst 1836. *Men of Amherst*, 1836. *Mass Med Soc cat* 1894.

ALLEN, GALEN, Red Wing, Minn (b/VIII-2-1833 Chelsea, Vt; d/XII-25-1900) MD Boston U 1875; AB Dartmouth 1862. *Minn homeop mag* Feb 1901. *Polk* 1886:516. Homeopath.

ALLEN, GEORGE, Middletown, Gowanda, Waterville, NY (b/IX-16-1853 Poultney, Vt; d/XI-14-1897) MD Hahnemann Phila 1877; AB URochester 1875. *Tr Am Inst Homeop* 1899:74. *No Amer jour homeop* 45:771, 1897. *Polk* 1886:714. Homeopath.

ALLEN, GEORGE OTIS, W Roxbury, Mass (b/X-25-1838 Norton, Mass; d/X-3-1887) MD Harvard 1866. *Boston m & s jour* 117:372, 636, 1887.

ALLEN, GEORGE W , Edwards, Miss (d/III-29-1886) MD U Louisville 1852. *New Orl m & s jour* ns13: 915, 1886. *Polk* 1886:527.

ALLEN, HARLAN PRESTON, Columbus, O (b/1856 Mass; d/V-2-1895 NYC) MD CPSNY 1879. *Med reg NY NJ Conn* 1895:215. *Trans Ohio Med Soc* 1895:48-49. *JAMA* 24:775-776, 1895.

ALLEN, HARRISON, Philadelphia (b/IV-17-1841; d/XI-14-1897) MD UPa 1861. *Trans CPP* 3s20:xxxix-liii, 1897. *JAMA* 29:1129, 1897. *Atkinson* I:675. *K & B* III:15. CW-USA.

ALLEN, HIRAM, Woonsocket Falls, RI (b/1803 Franklin, Mass; d/III-15-1864 [presumably; also given as III-15-1861]) MD Brown 1825. *Tr AMA* 16:617-618, 1865. *Tr RI Med Soc* 1:217-219, 1859-1877.

ALLEN, HORACE R , Chicago; Indianapolis (b/1832 Ohio; d/II-13-1900) MD Cleveland Med Coll 1858. *JAMA* 34:511, 1900. *Trans Ill St Med Soc* 1899-1906:463.

ALLEN, HORATIO GATES, Wayne, Me 1832-37; Dresden, Me 1837-82 (b/VIII-7-1807 Bath; d/III-27-1884) MD Bowdoin 1832. *Bowdoin cat. Butler* 1878:296.

ALLEN, IRA, Roxbury, Mass (d/VIII-29-1875 @ 63) MD Dartmouth 1852. *Bost m & s jour* ns16: 313, 1875.

ALLEN, JAMES A , Shiloh, Ala (d/1890) <MD Graffenburg 1853> *Trans Med Assn St Ala* 1891: 261. *Polk* 1886:139.

ALLEN, JAMES HART, NYC (d/VIII-1858) MD CPSNY 1844; AB UCNY 1839. *Trans Am Inst Homeop* 1893:123. Homeopath.

ALLEN, JOEL, Burlington, Vt (b/I-18-1850 N Hero, Vt; d/XII-6-1898) MD U Vt 1875. *JAMA* 31:1584, 1898. *Polk* 1896:1473.

ALLEN, JOHN C , Baton Rouge, La (d/IV-28-1905) MD Louisville Med Coll 1883. *New Orl m & s jour* 57:914, 1905. *Polk* 1900:756.

ALLEN, JOHN LARRABEE, Springfield, Saco, Me (b/IV-26-1814 Cornish; d/IX-4-1897) MD Bowdoin 1836 *JAMA* 29:606, 1897. *Atkinson* I:512. *Polk* 1896: 639.

ALLEN, JOHN LINN, Lafayette, NJ (b/VII-13-1820 NJ; d/I-29-1893) MD UCNY 1852. *Trans NJ Med Soc* 1893:177. *Butler* 1878:465.

ALLEN, JOHN MILTON MANN, Chester, Pa (Phila; d/IV-20-1903 @ 84?) MD UPa 1840 CW-USA. *UPa med alum CW*: 1840.

ALLEN, JONATHAN ADAMS, Middlebury, Vt (b/XI-17-1787 Holliston, Mass; d/II-2-1848) MD Dartmouth 1814; AM 1821. *Tr AMA* 3:430-432, 1850. *Bost m & s jour* 38:453-461, 1848. *K & B* III:16-18.

ALLEN, JONATHAN ADAMS, Jr, Chicago (b/I-16-1825 Middlebury, Vt; d/VIII-15-1890) MD Castleton 1846; AB Middlebury 1845, AM 1848. *JAMA* 15:303-4, 1890. *Chic med rec* 1:190, 1891. *Bost m & s jour* 123:216, 1890. *Atkinson* I:30. *K & B* III:18.

ALLEN, JONATHAN MOSES, Philadelphia (b/IV-30-1815 Princeton, Mass; d/IV-7-1867 Lowell, Mass) MD UPa 1840; ng Yale. *Med surg rep Phila* 16:367, 389, 1867. *Bost m & s jour* 76:383, 1867. *K & B* III:18.

ALLEN, JOSHUA GIBBONS, Philadelphia (b/IV-23-1832 Marple Twp, Pa; d/IX-26-1903) MD UPa 1856. *Pa med jour* 7:278, 240, 1903/04. *Atkinson* I:316.

ALLEN, MYRON OLIVER, Lowell, Mass (d VIII-1-1861 @ 30) MD Pa Med Coll 1854; AB Yale 1852. *Bost m & s jour* 65:28, 1862.

ALLEN, NATHAN, Lowell, Mass (b/IV-13 [or 25] 1813 Princeton, Mass; d/I-1-1889) MD Pa Med Coll 1841; MD (hon) Castleton 1847; AB Amherst 1836. *Bost m & s jour* 120:28, 52, 1889; 121: 644, 1889. *Atkinson* I:49. *K & B* III:18.

ALLEN, NATHANIEL N , Hempstead, Tex (d/XI- -1881) MD Jefferson 1853. *Texas med rec* 2:80, 1882.

ALLEN, PETER, Kinsman, O (b/VII-1-1787 Norwich, Conn; d/IX-1-1864) MD Jefferson 1838. *Trans O St Med Soc* 1875:193. *K & B* III:19-20.

ALLEN, RICHARD NUN, Harford Co, Md (b/1796; d/IV-27-1833) MD UMd 1817. *Med annals Md*:300.

ALLEN, SETH, Shideler, Ind (b/V-29-1845 Zanesville, O; d/III-15-1898) MD Cinc Coll Med & Surg 1879. *Trans Ind St Med Soc* 1898:386. *Flint* 1897:327.

ALLEN, THOMAS, CW-USN (d/X-10-1865 Naval Hosp Memphis) *Nat'l med jour* 1:289, 1870-71.

ALLEN, THOMAS J , Shreveport, La (d/II-16-1899 @70) MD Jefferson 1855. *JAMA* 32:506, 1899. *New Orl m & s jour* 51:528, 1899. *Polk* 1896:626.

ALLEN, THOMAS W , Fort Davis, Tex (d/V- -1897) MD Memphis Hosp Coll 1889. *Tex med news* 6:1896-97. *Texas med jour* 13:94, 1897-98. *Polk* 1890:1085.

ALLEN, TIMOTHY FIELD, NYC (b/IV-24-1837 Westminster, Vt; d/XII-6-1902) MD UCNY 1861; AB Amherst 1858. *Trans Am Inst Homeop* 1903:725-727. *Hom rec* 18:1-4, 1903. *Cleave*. *K & B* III:20. CW-USA. Homeopath.

ALLEN, WILLIAM E , Scranton, Pa (b/NJ; d/VIII-25-1903 @ 62) MD Albany 1856. *Pa med jour* 7:278, 1903/04. *Flint* 1897:834.

ALLEN, WILLIAM GEORGE, Mansfield, Mass (d/IV 5-1903 @ 69) MD Albany 1857. *Bost m & s jour* 148:408, 1903. *Polk* 1886:469.

ALLEN, WILLIAM HENRY, Orono,Me; CW-USA (b/IX-3-1806 Farmington; d/I-29-1863 Richmond Prison) MD Bowdoin 1834. *Tr AMA* 16:609-610, 1865.

ALLEN, WILLIAM HENRY, Cazenovia, NY 1833-36; Carlisle, Pa 1836-46; Brunswick, Me 1848-49; Philadelphia 1847-48, 1849-62, 1867-1882 (b/III-27-1808 Readfield, Me; d/VIII-29-1882) MD Bowdoin 1847; MD Phila Coll Med 1848 ad eundem; AB Bowdoin 1833. *Bowdoin cat* 1833.

ALLENTON, GOODWIN, Providence, RI (b/1792; d/V-12-1819) MD Brown 1817; AB 1814. *Brown hist cat* 1814.

ALLEY, JAMES T, St. Paul, Minn (b/La Grange, NY; d/IX-17-1878 @47) MD NYU 1854. *Trans Am Inst Homeop* 1879:1243. *Med advance* 6:615, 1879. *Cleave.* Homeopath.

ALLEY, JOHN BURROUGHS, Boston (d/IV-29-1862 @ 38) MD Harvard 1844; AB Yale 1840. *Bost m & s*

Spec. educ'l status abbrev. as: ***ng*** = college verified attendance without degree;

jour 66:281, 284, 1862.

ALLEY, WILLIAM BELDEN, Moravia; Nunda NY (b/1802 Sullivan Co, NY; d/I–14–1893) MD Berkshire 1848. *Med vis* 9:75, 1893. *Trans Med Soc St NY* 1891:457. *Polk* 1886: 699. Homeopath 1841– .

ALLEYNE, JEREMIAH S B, St. Louis, Mo (b/1826 Boston; d/V–2–1895) MD St Louis Med Coll 1848. *Med bull m & s* 17:235–236, 1895. *Atkinson* I:682. *Atkinson* I:682.

ALLIN, CHARLES MASON, Flushing, NY (b/X–30–1827; d/VI–19–1880) MDCPSNY 1851; AB Brown 1847. *Med reg NY NJ Conn* 1881:232. *Med rec NY* 17: 740, 1880. *Atkinson* I:316.

ALLINGHAM, JAMES JOHNSON, CW–USN (d/X–13–1865 Cherbourg, France) MD CPSNY 1859. *Med surg rep Phila* 13:374,1865. *Nat med jour* 1:289,1870/1.

ALLISON, BENJAMIN A, Decatur, Ill (d/II–6–1906 @ 89) MD Jefferson 1844. *Ill med jour* 9:228, 1906. *Polk* 1886:275.

ALLISON, GEORGE W, Beaver, Pa (b/1803 [or 1794?] Washington, Pa; d/XII [or IX?]–7–1863) att? UMd *Tr AMA* 18:327–328, 1867. *Trans Med Soc Pa* 1864:407–408.

ALLISON, HARTWELL, Shreveport or Bayou La Chute, (b/Ala; d/I–21–1897 @ ca 50) MD U Louisville 1872. *New Orl m & s jour* ns24:536–537, 1897. *Polk* 1890:485.

ALLISON, JOHN A, Statesville, NC (b/X–10–1830; d/V–17–1891) MD Jefferson 1858; ng UNC. CW–CSA. *Univ NC cat* 10. *Polk* 1886:726.

ALLISON, THOMAS HENDERSON, Kittaning, Pa (b/VI– –1820 W.Middleton, Pa; d/VI–11–1898) MD Jefferson 1854. *Pa med jour* 2:162–163, 1898. *JAMA* 30:1534, 1898. *Polk* 1896:1285.

ALLMOND, REUBEN J, Carlinsville, Ill (d/I–8–1899 @ 81) MD Jefferson 1839. *JAMA* 32:195, 1899. *Polk* 1886:292.

ALPUENTE, FRANÇOIS RUIZ, New Orleans (d/VIII–15–1876 @ 62) MD Paris 1840. *New Orl m & s jour* ns14:303, 1876. *Butler* 1874:287.

ALSENTZER, CHARLES F, Philadelphia (d/II–6–1904 @ 38) MD UPa 1893/ *Pa med jour* 8:334, 1904/05.

ALSOP, JOSEPH WRIGHT, Middletown, Conn (b/VIII 20–1838 NYC; d/6–2–1891) MD UCNY 1864. *Proc Conn Med Soc* 1892:867–869. *Bost m & s jour* 124:646, 1891. *Butler* 1878:72.

ALSTON, SOLOMON WILLIAMS, CW–CSA (b/VII–16–1839 Tusculum, NC; d/VII– –1862 Tusculum) MD UPa 1859. *UPa med alum CW*: 1859.

ALSUP [or ALSOP?] JOSEPH L, CW–CSA (d/X–28–1863) *SHSP* 22:169, 1893.

ALTHOF, HERMANN, NYC (b/VIII–8–1835 Horn, Lippe–Detmold, Germany; d/I–14–1877) MD Berlin 1857; post–grad study Europe. *Med reg NY NJ Conn* 1877:195. *Med rec* 12:48, 223, 1877. *K & B* III:23.

ALVIS, DAVID H, Kewanee, Ill (b/1845 Todd Co, Ky; d/I– –1880) MD Chic Med Coll 1871. *Trans Ill St Med Soc* 1880:210. *Butler* 1878: 139.

ALVORD, SAMUEL, Chicopee Falls, Mass (b/II–5–1812 Springfield; d/II–5–1892) MD NY Hom Med Coll 1866. *Trans Am Inst Homeop* 1893:123. *Med vis* 8:122, 1897. *Polk* 1886:464. Homeopath.

AMBROSE, JOHN KENNEDY, NYC (b/ca 1837 Ireland; d/V–17–1892) MD LICH 1873. *Med reg NY NJ Conn* 1893:296. *Polk* 1886:670.

AMEDEN, ARCHIBALD OGDEN, Ticonderoga, Glens Falls, NY (d/XI–28–1890) MD U Vt 1865. *JAMA* 16:143, 1891. *Polk* 1886:662.

AMERMAN, ALONZO, Danville, Pa (b/IV–16–1850; d/I 19–1886) MD UPa 1875. *Trans Med Soc Pa* 18:249, 1886.

AMERMAN, GEORGE K, Chicago (b/VII–10–1832 Cayuga Co NY; d/VI–20–1867) MD UCNY 1854. *Chic med jour* 24:444, 1867. *Chic med reg & dir* 1:334–5, 1872.*Med reg Chic* 1872–73:334–336.

AMERY, SAMUEL A, Cincinnati (b/1844 Charles Co Md; d/1881) MD Georgetown 1866. *Hist Med Soc DC*: 279.

AMES, ALFRED E, Minneapolis (Colchester, Vt; d/IX–23–1874) MD Rush 1845. *Tr AMA* 27:651, 1876. *Trans Ill St Med Soc* 1895:72.

AMES, CHARLES E, Cleveland,O; CW–USA (d/IV–28 1868) MD UCNY 1843. *Nat med jour* 1:289, 1871.

AMES, DELANO, Baltimore (b/1868 Springfield, O; d/III–10–1899) MD U Md 1892. *JAMA* 32:733, 1899. *Med annals Md*: 310.

AMES, LOREN JESSE, Mount Morris, NY (d/V– –1891 @ 76) MD Geneva 1843. *Trans Med Soc St NY* 1892: 428. *Polk* 1886:668.

AMICK, CHRISTOPHER C, Hayden, Ind (b/VI–17–1849 Jennings Co; d/IV–15–1901) MD Cinc Coll M & S 1876. *Trans Ind St Med Soc* 1901:480. *Flint* 1897: 315.

AMICK, JOHN HERBST BRUCE, Philadelphia (d/IX–20–1903 @ 58) MD UPa 1876. *Pa med jour* 7:178, 1903/04.

AMIRAUX, JAMES C, Paterson, NJ (b/XII–15–1832 Quebec; d/VI–25–1885) MD LICH 1872. *Trans NJ Med Soc* 1886–87:151–153. *Buler* 1878:465.

AMISS, JOHN B, Harrisonburg, Va (b/IX–20–1834 Rappahannock Co; d/I–4–1902) MD UCNY 1858. *Trans Med Soc Va* 1903:268–269. *Polk* 1900:1764.

AMISS, WILLIAM HENRY, Sperryville, Va (d/VIII–8–1903 @ 75) MD UPa 1853. *So pract* 25:588, 1903.

AMMAN, JOHN B, Scranton, Pa (d/II–27–1900 @ 57) MD "Switzerland Staats Examen 1867"; lic. by years of practice. *JAMA* 34:639, 1900. *Pa Reg Phys* 1881–1889:210. *Polk* 1896:1334.

AMMON, GEORGE WASHINGTON, Reading, Pa (d/VIII–13–1899 @ 37) MD Jefferson 1888. *JAMA* 33:620, 1899. *Polk*: 1896:1331.

AMMONS [AMMON], JACOB S , Reading, Pa (d/IX 5-1905 @ 68) MD UPa 1868. *Pa med jour* 9:28, 1905/06. *Polk* 1886:832.

AMORY, CHARLES, Boston (d/II-10-1898) MD Harvard 1832. *Bost m & s jour* 138:189, 1898.

AMOS, CORBIN, Baltimore (b/III-31-1784 Harford Co; d/VII-21-1866) MD UMd 1812. *Med annals Md*: 301.

AMSDEN, AMOS L , Sullivan, NY; St.Joseph, Mich (b/c1779 Conway, Mass; d/XI- -1848) Stud w/Dr Wm S Williams, 1800-03. *Tr AMA* 3:432-434, 1850.

AMY, CHAUNCEY WILLARD, Decorah, Ia (b/1842 Ohio; d/I-29-1900) MD Rush 1879. *JAMA* 34:446, 1900. *Polk* 1886:355.

ANAWALT, JAMES WHITE, Greensburg & Dayton, O (b/X-14-1828 Bakersville, Pa; d/VIII-26-1896) MD Jefferson 1855. *JAMA* 27:613, 1896. *Atkinson* I:678.

ANDERSON, ALEXANDER, NYC (b/IV-21-1775; d/I-17-1870) MD Columbia 1796. *Tr AMA* 21:469, 1870. *Med reg NY NJ Conn* 1870:309. *Phila med reg & dir* 1871:303. *K & B* III:25-26.

ANDERSON, ALFRED, Williamsport, Md; Ala (d/XI-29-1849) MD UPa 1830. *Med annals Md*: 301.

ANDERSON, BENJAMIN SMITH, Manoa, Pa (d/I-24 1894 @ 71) MD UPa 1846. *JAMA* 22:202, 1894. *Polk* 1886:806.

ANDERSON, CHARLES GILLET, Belmont, NY (d/XI 26-1896 @ 62) MD Geneva 1861. *JAMA* 28:92, 1897. *Polk* 1896:989.

ANDERSON, DAVID MILLER, CW-USA; Venetia, Pa (d/II-16-1903 @ 65) MD Bellevue 1866; ng U Mich Med Sch 1863-64. *Pa med jour* 7:278, 1903/04. *Polk* 1886:837.

ANDERSON, ELLA M , NYC (d/III-8-1895 on Ohio River) MD Woman's Med Coll Pa 1893. *Med reg NY NJ Conn* 1895:215. *JAMA* 24:497, 1895.

ANDERSON, ELSIE (FOWLER), Valparaiso, Ind. (d/IV-29-1895) MD U Mich 1872. *JAMA* 24:731, 1895. *Polk* 1890: 391.

ANDERSON, GEORGE BONBRIGHT, Latrobe, Pa (b/VIII-8-1853; d/X-5-1896) MD Jefferson 1877; stud. Lafayette. *JAMA* 27:878, 1896. *Polk* 1886:804.

ANDERSON, HENRY JAMES, NYC (b/II-6-1799; d/X-19-1875) MD CPSNY 1824; AB Columbia 1818. *Med reg NY NJ Conn* 1876:240.

ANDERSON, ISAAC, Philadelphia (d/VIII-25-1865) MD Jefferson 1835 [?as Isaac W] *Med surg rep Phila* 13: 166, 1865.

ANDERSON, JAMES, Harford Co, Md (d/II- -1816) MD UMd 1815. *Med annals Md*: 302.

ANDERSON, JAMES, NYC (b/II-21-1798; d/X-7-1886) MD CPSNY 1820.*Med reg NY NJ Conn* 1887:253. *Med surg rep Phila* 15:215-218, 1866. *Bost m & s jour* 115:361, 1886. *Atkinson* I:672.

ANDERSON, JAMES HENRY, NYC (b/Botterzin Ireland; d/IX-7-1866 @ 41) MD UCNY 1866. *Med reg NY NJ Conn* 1867:208.

ANDERSON, JAMES MOAT, Chester-Town, Md (b/1752; d/XII-8-1820) Stud. w/Morgan & Shippen, UPa & at Edinburgh. *Phila jour med & phys sci* 2:414-415, 1821. *Med annals Md*: 302.

ANDERSON, JAMES ROSS, Bedford, Pa (d/I-19-1873 @ 31) MD UPa 1865. *Med surg rep Phila* 28: 184, 1873.

ANDERSON, JOHN WALLACE, Hagerstown, Md (b/1802; d/1830, Liberia, Africa) MD UPa 1828. *Med annals Md*: 303.

ANDERSON, JOHN WALLACE, Rockville, Md (b/c 1805; d/VII-8-1867) MD UPa 1830. *Med annals Md*: 1803.

ANDERSON, LINNAEUS B , Charlottesville; Norfolk, Va (d/XII-5-1902) MD Med Coll Va 1844. *Trans Med Soc Va* 1903:269. *Polk* 1900:1759.

ANDERSON, OLIVER F , Wheeling, WVa (b/IV-16-1839 Clermont Co, O; d/VI-23-1883) MD Med Coll O 1873. *Trans Ind St Med Soc* 1884:210.

ANDERSON, PETER EDWARD, Rodophil, Va (d/VII-24-1905 @ 67) MD Jefferson 1859. *So pract* 27:636, 1905. *Polk* 1886:926.

ANDERSON, SAMUEL T, Bloomington Ill (d/VIII-10 1896 @ 52) MD Rush 1881. *JAMA* 27:449, 1896. *Polk* 1886:255.

ANDERSON, SANFORD MIRKLE, Mattoon, Ill (d/IV-19-1898) MD Miami Med Coll 1883. *JAMA* 30:1061, 1898. *Polk* 1886:287.

ANDERSON, WILLIAM, Indiana, Pa (b/VI-6-1825; d/III-29-1896) MD Jefferson 1852. *Trans Med Soc Pa* 27:369, 372, 1897. *JAMA* 27:108, 1896. *Atkinson* I:129.

ANDERSON, WILLIAM, Brooklyn (d/V-6-1891 @ 47) <MD Royal Coll Phys & Surg Edinb 1871> *Med reg NY NJ Conn* 1891:267. *Polk* 1886:643.

ANDERSON, WILLIAM DEXTER, New Haven, Conn (b/1841 Londonderry, NH; d/III- -1901) MD Yale 1865; AB 1862. *Hahn advocate* Apr 1901. *Polk* 1886:194. Homeopath, 1868-

ANDERSON, WILLIAM HENRY, Mobile, Ala (b/V-6-1820 Richmond, Va; d/XI-14/15-1887) MD UVa 1842, AB Wm & Mary 1841. *Trans Med Assn St Ala* 1888:31-32, 316. *New Orl m & s jour* ns15: 493, 1887. *Atkinson*I:109-110. *Polk* 1886:136.

ANDERSON, WILLIAM WATKINS, Farmville, Va (b/IX-29-1816 Dinwiddie Co, Va; d/XI-23-1900) *UPA alum reg* 19:373, 1916-17. CW-CSA.

ANDES, JOHN BELTZ, Honey Brook, Pa (b/1857 Sadsbury Twp; d/XII-16-1903 @ 46) MD UPa 1881. *Pa med jour* 7:278, 1903/04.

ANDREAS, BENJAMIN ADAM, So Bethlehem, Pa (b/XII-12-1859 Cherryville; d/X-16-1903) MD Jefferson 1888. *Pa med jour* 7:278, 392, 1903/04. *Flint* 1897:836.

ANDREWS, ALMON ETHAN, Bartlett, NH (b/V-21-1850 Biddeford, Me; d/IX- -1878) MD Bowdoin 1877; ng Bowdoin Coll. 1872-74. *Bowdoin cat* 1876.

Spec. educ'l status abbrev. as: ***ng*** = college verified attendance without degree;

ANDREWS, BENJAMIN, Brooklyn (d/VI-26-1902 @ 83) MD UCNY 1847. *Bost m & s jour* 147:30, 1902.

ANDREWS, D C, Pittsfield, Ill (d/IX-25-1902 @ 80) Lic yrs of pract. *Ill med jour* ns4:425, 1902. *Polk* 1886:285.

ANDREWS, EDGAR LEON, NYC (b/VII-7-1860; d/ III-12-1887) MD UVt 1883. *Med reg NY NJ Conn* 1887:253. *Med surg rep Phila* 56:448, 1887. *Polk* 1886:670.

ANDREWS, EDMUND, Chicago (b/IV-22-1824 [?] Putney, Vt; d/I-22-1904) MD UMich 1852; AB 1849; LLD 1881. *Chic med rec* 26:111-115, 1904. *Atkinson* I:72. *K & B* III:29. *Flint* 1897:255.

ANDREWS, FRANKLIN M , CW-USA (d/X-8-1864) MD UCNY 1861. *Nat med jour* 1: 289, 1870/71.

ANDREWS, HENRY F , Washington, Ga (d/VI-5-1892) MD UCNY 1857. CW-CSA *UCNY Cat. Polk* 1886:236.

ANDREWS, JAMES P , Colerain, Pa (d/VI-7-1875 @ 55) MD Jefferson 1845. *Phila med times* 5:624, 1875.

ANDREWS, JAMES [JOHN?] RICHARDSON, Camden, NJ; Philadelphia (d/II-19-1864 @ 46) MD Pa Med Coll 1840. *Trans Am Inst Homeop* 1867:156. Homeopath.

ANDREWS, JARVIS MUDGE, NYC (b/XI-2-1818 Huron, NY; d/I-26-1878) MD CPSNY 1845. *Med reg NY NJ Conn* 1878:178. *Butler* 1874:493.

ANDREWS, JOEL R , NYC (b/Dedham, Mass; d/VI 1-1870 @ 52 Winona, Minn) MD Berkshire 1859. *Tr Am Inst Homeop* 1870:633. *New Engl med gaz* 5: 344, 406, 1870. Homeopath.

ANDREWS, JOHN, Worcester, Mass (b/1793? d/XII-7-1872 @ 79) MD UPa 1826. *Bost m & s jour* ns10: 460, 1872.

ANDREWS, JOHN SUMMERFIELD, Brooklyn (b/1829 Bristol, Conn; d/I-3-1889) MD UCNY 1849. *Med reg NY NJ Conn* 1889:267. *Trans NY St Med Soc* XI: 741 ff. *Polk* 1886:659.

ANDREWS, JUDSON BOARDMAN, CW-USA; Buffalo (b/IV-25-1834;d/VIII-3-1894) MD Yale 1863; AB 1855, AM 1858. *Med reg NY NJ Conn* 1895:215. *JAMA* 23:248, 1894. *Buff m & s jour* 34:92, 1894. *Bost m & s jour* 131:152, 1894. *K & B* III:29-30.

ANDREWS, SARA WASSON, Chicago (b/I-17-1834 La Porte, Ind; d/II-26-1902) MD Hahnemann Chic 1882. *Med vis*, March 1902. *Trans Am Inst Homeop* 1902:884-885. *Cleave*. *Polk* 1886:283. Homeopath.

ANDREWS, SOLOMON, Perth Amboy, NJ (d/X-17-1872) MD Rutgers 1827. *Tr AMA* 24:364-365, 1873. *Med surg rep Phila* 27:416, 1872.

ANDREWS, THOMAS D , Brooklyn (b/1824; d/VII 22-1866 @ 42) MD UCNY 1847. *Med surg rep Phila* 15:132, 1866.

ANDREWS, WILLIAM CURTIS CLARK, USA (b/ 1852; d/IV-19-1877 Ft Stevens, Ore) MD Bellevue 1874; ng UMich Med Sch 1871-72; AB Marietta 1870, AM 1873. *Tr AMA* 28:641, 1877. *Med rec* 12:318, 1877.

ANDREWS, WILLIAM HARVY, Milford, Conn (d/I-24-1890) MD Bellevue 1873. *Med reg NY NJ Conn* 1890: 260.

ANDREWS, WILLIAM HENRY, Springfield, Mass (d/ V-19-1902 @ 47) MD UCNY 1882. *Bost m & s jour* 146:588, 1902. *Polk* 1896:723.

ANDROS, FREDERICK, Minneapolis (d/IV-28-1895 @92) <MD "Parsons Med Sch 1824"> ng Brown 1824. *JAMA* 24:690, 1895. *Polk* 1890:233.

ANDROS, JAMES S , Natick, RI (b/X-18-1808 Plainfield, Conn; d/XI-3-1867) MD Berkshire 1836. *Trans RI Med Soc* 1:323, 1859-1877.

ANGEAR, JOHN J M , Chicago (d/X-8-1902 @73) MD Rush 1860. *Chic med rec* 23:376, 1902. *Ill med jour* ns4: 425, 1902. *Flint* 1897:255.

ANGEL, L H , CW-USA (d/III-28-1865) *Nat med jour* 1:289, 1870/71.

ANGELL, RICHARD, Mississippi 1843; Louisville, Ky; Huntsville, Ala; New Orleans, 1845- (b/III-16-1804 London, Engl; d/VI-10-1879) MD Columbian 1826. *Homeop news* July 1879. *Cleave*. *King* 1:190. Homeopath, 1844- .

ANGELL, SAMUEL MINTER, New Orleans (b/VIII-2-1833 Jefferson Co, Miss; d/X-5-1895) MD Hahnemann Phila 1857. *Trans Am Inst Homeop* 1896:1185. *Hahn mo* 30:143-144, 1895. *King* 1:190. *Polk* 1886:415.

ANGELL, WILLIAM COOK, San Francisco (b/X-20-1839 Scituate, RI; d/V-7-1893) MD Bellevue 1868; AB Brown 1866, AM. *Brown hist. cat.* 1866. *Polk* 1886:777 (Coquille Ore.)

ANGLE, JOHN SAMUEL, Devon, Pa (b/III-28-1841 Franklin Co, Pa; d/XI-15-1905) MD Jefferson 1862; AB Dickinson, 1858. *Pa med jour* 9:220, 1905/06. *Flint* 1897:836.

ANGNEY, WILLIAM MUIR, Philadelphia (d/XI-19-1906) MD Jefferson 1878. *Pa med jour* 10:213-214, 1906/07. *Flint* 1897:813.

ANNAN, ANDREW, Emmitsburg, Md (b/IV-29-1805; d/VII-7-1896) MD UMd 1827. *Med annals Md*:303. *Butler* 1874:317.

ANNAN, ROBERT LANDALES, Emmitsburg, Md (b/ XI-22-1765 Neelytown, NY; d/VII-12-1827) Stud. w/Rush 2 yrs, certif. 1789; ng Brown 1786. *Med annals Md*: 304.

ANNAN, SAMUEL, Baltimore; CW-CSA (b/1797 Phila; d/I-19-1868) MD Edinb 1820. *Med annals Md*: 304. *K & B* III:30.

ANNIN, JONATHAN DICKENSON, Irvington; Newark, NJ (b/XI-26-1806 Liberty Corner, NJ; d/XI-26-1883) MD ng CPSNY. *Med surg rep Phila* 49:420, 1883. *Tr Am Inst Homeop* 1893:124. Allopath 30 yrs; homeopath. *Butler* 1878:451.

ANTHONY, ALBERT GALLATIN, Oakland, Cal (d/IV 3-1895 @ 50) MD UVt 1875. *JAMA* 24: 609, 1895.

Trans Med Soc Calif 25:418, 1895. *Polk* 1890:190.

ANTHONY, THEODORE V W, Fishkill, NY (d/IV 15–1868 @ 67) MD ? AB Union 1819. *Med surg rep Phila* 18:376, 1868. *Phila med reg & dir* 1871:296.

ANTHONY, WALTER EUGENE, Providence, RI (b/XII–12–1847; d/X–7–1897) MD UCNY 1867; AB Brown 1864. *JAMA* 29:867, 1897. *Trans RI Med Soc* 5: 497–498, 1894–98. *Atkinson* I:199. *Polk* 1896:1351.

ANTHONY, WILLIAM CHURCH, Princeton, Ill (b/VI–6–1806 Sherburne; d/IX–21–1890) MD Woodstock 1833. *Med vis* 7:113, 1891. *Trans Am Inst Homeop* 1893: 1092. *Polk* 1886:294. Homeopath.

ANTIS, HENRY TAYLOR, CW–USA; Geneseo, Ill (d/X–23–1899) MD LICH 1866; AB Williams 1860. *Tr Ill Med Soc* 1899; 287. *JAMA* 33:1441, 1899. *Polk* 1896:239.

ANTISELL, THOMAS, Dublin Ireland to 1848; NYC to 1854; CW–USA Washington, DC (b/Dublin I–16–1817; d/VI–14–1893) Lic RCS Lond 1839; AB Trinity (Dublin?) *JAMA* 21:58, 93–94, 1893. *Bost m & s jour* 128:660, 1893. *Hist Med Soc DC*: 261–263. *Atkinson* I:16–17. *K & B* III:31–32.

ANTONINI, ANTONIO DEGLI, NYC (d/X– –1882) <MD Padua 1858> *Med reg NY NJ Conn* 1883:218. *Butler* 1878:493.

APLINGTON, BURTON Z, LaSalle, Ill (d/IX–13–1897 @ 41) MD Chic Med Coll 1879. *JAMA* 29:660 1897. *Polk* 1886:285.

APPLEBY, DAVID JEFFERS [JEFFRIES?] Tyrone, Pa (d/VII–3–1906 @ 57) <MD Washington U Med Balto 1872> *Pa med jour* 9:805, 1905/06. *Reg Pa Phys* '81–'88:76. *Flint* 1897:838.

APPLEGATE, ANDREW JACKSON, Indianola, Ia (d/III–2–1895 @ 63) MD CPS Keokuk 1864. *JAMA* 24:422, 1895. *Trans Ia St Med Soc* 13:409, 1900. *Butler* 1878:230.

APPLEGATE, LEWIS, NYC; CW–USA (b/V–31–1840; d/XII–4–1870 NYC) MD CPSNY 1866. *Med reg NY NJ Conn* 1871:344. *Med rec* 6:94, 1871–72.

APPLETON, JOHN, Cambridge, Mass (b/1809 Salem; d/II–4–1869. MD Harvard 1833. *Bost m & s jour* 3:48, 1869; 4;27, 1869.

ARBUCKLE, J E, New Hope, Ga (b/X–27–1853 Greenbrier Co, WVa; d/II–8–1897) MD CPS Balto 1878. *Trans Med Soc Va* 1900: 320–321. *Polk* 1886:922.

ARCHER, JAMES, Mississippi (b/VIII–2–1779 Harford Co, Md; d/V–15–1815) MD UPa 1804. *Med annals Md*: 304.

ARCHER, JASON HAWES, Wrentham, Mass (b/II–10–1794; d/I–22–1861) MD Brown 1819; AB 1816. *Brown hist cat*: 1816.

ARCHER, JOHN, Sr, Harford Co, Md (b/V–5–1741 Churchville, Md; d/IX–28–1810) MD UPa 1768. *Med annals Md*: 304–305. *K & B* III:34–35.

ARCHER, JOHN, Jr, Baltimore, Md (b/X–9–1777 Harford Co, Md; d/V–21–1830) MD UPa 1798. *Med annals Md*: 305.

ARCHER, THOMAS, Harford Co, Md (b/II–23–1768; d/X–7–1821) Stud w/John Archer Jr. *Med annals Md*: 305.

ARCULARIUS, LOUIS, NYC (b/Gny; d/VII–1–1900 @ 62) MD U Giessen 1868. *Bost m & s jour* 143:48, 1900. *Polk* 1886: 670.

ARDERY, OSCAR KEMPER, Anderson, Ind (b/I–5–1859 Decatur Co, Ind; d/IX–5–1897) MD UMich 1883. *Trans Ind St Med Soc* 1898:380–381. *Flint* 1897:307.

AREY, CLARENCE OLIVER, Cleveland, O (d/VIII–11–1896) MD UPa 1894; Certif eng. Brown 1878. *JAMA* 27:449, 1896. *Polk* 1896:1170.

ARMENTROUT, JOHN C, Keokuk, Ia (d/II–7–1894) MD St U Iowa 1883. *JAMA* 22:235, 1894. *Chic med rec* 6:217, 1894. *Polk* 1890:418.

ARMISTEAD, WILLIAM HENRY, Vaiden, Miss (b/VIII–5–1820 Randolph Co, NC; d/XI–30–1878) MD U Louisville 1847. *Tr AMA* 31:1008–1009, 1880. *Trans Miss St Med Assn* 12:36, 61–63, 1878–79. *Atkinson* I:546.

ARMITAGE, AUSTIN WILSON, Solebury, Pa (d/X–31 1883 @35) *Med surg rep Phila* 49:616, 1883.

ARMITAGE, JAMES, Baltimore (b/1811; d/II–26–1896) MD UMd 1831. *Med annals Md*: 306. *Polk* 1886:435.

ARMOR, SAMUEL GLASGOW, Brooklyn (b/I–29–1819; d/X–27–1885. MD Mo Med Coll (Kemper) 1844. *JAMA* 5:503, 1885. *Med reg NY NJ Conn* 1886:241. *Med age* 3:516–517, 1885. *Butler* 1878: 528. *K & B* III:35.

ARMOR, SAMUEL GLASGOW, Brooklyn, NYC (b/V–11–1867 Millersburg, O; d/X–10–1896 or I– –1897, Kalonga–Longa, Congo) MD LICH 1891. *JAMA* 28:714, 1897.

ARMOR, THOMAS, Baltimore; Emporia, Kans (b/IX–5–1815 Newcastle Co, Del; d/I–23–1901) MD Hahnemann Phila 1851. *Hahn mo* Apr 1901. Homeopath.

ARMS, STILLMAN E, Elizabeth, NJ (b/XI–30–1803 Canaan, NY; d/VII–10–1877) MD Castleton 1844; AB Rensselaer Poly. *Trans NJ Med Soc* 1878:197. *Med rec NY* 13:455, 1878. *Butler* 1878:465.

ARMS, WILLIAM, Patagonia, Borneo, Batavia, Singapore 1833–1838; Vermont & Wisconsin 1842–1859; DuQuoin, Ill 1867–1889 (b/V–18–1802 Wilmington, Vt; d/VI–21–1889) AM Andover Theol Sem 1833; MD Dartmouth 1839; AB Amherst 1830. *Med surg rep Phila* 61:28, 1889.

ARMSBY, JAMES HARVEY, Naples, Italy; Albany, NY 1830– (b/XII–31–1809 Sutton, Mass; d/XII–3–1875) MD Castleton 1833; AM (hon) Rutgers 1839. *Tr AMA* 27:657–663, 1876. *Trans Med Soc St NY* 1876: 313–319. *Med rec* 10:832, 1875; II:428, 1876. *K & B* III:36.

ARMSTRONG, ALFRED W, Kirkwood, Ill (d/XI–19–1893) MD Rush 1849. *JAMA* 22:31, 1894. *Butler* 1878:139.

 Spec. educ'l status abbrev. as: ***ng*** = college verified attendance without degree;

ARMSTRONG, CLINTON, CW–USA; Carrollton, Ill (d/VIII–23–1893 @ 70 Eureka Springs, Ark) MD Mo Med Coll 1847. *JAMA* 21:390, 1893. *Butler* 1878:139.

ARMSTRONG, CLINTON L , Cincinnati (d/by I–7–1899) MD Cinc Coll Med & Surg 1871. *JAMA* 32:145, 1899. *Polk* 1886:740.

ARMSTRONG, ELLIS W , Flora, Ind (d/XI–23–1898) MD Med Coll Ind 1881. *JAMA* 31:1490, 1898. *Polk* 1886:313.

ARMSTRONG, F C , Eldorado, Kans; Manila, PI (d/XII–4–2899 @46) MD Columbus Med Coll 1884. *JAMA* 33:1632, 1899. *Polk* 1890:437.

ARMSTRONG, FRANK NEWELL, Richmond, Ill (d/III 13–1905 @ 38) MD Rush 1890. *Ill med jour* 7:379, 1905. *Polk* 1896:438.

ARMSTRONG, JAMES A, Camden NJ; CW–USA (b/VI 12–1835 Phila; d/XI–13–1885) MD UPa 1861. *Trans NJ Med Soc* 1886–87: 164–165. *U Pa med alum CW*: 1861.

ARMSTRONG, JAMES ADELBERT, Hellam, Pa (b/1839? Amboy, Ill; d/VII–20–1805) MD UPa 1870. *Pa med jour* 8:727, 1904/05.

ARMSTRONG, JAMES FOWKES, CW–USA; Cleveland, O (b/X–3–1840 Germantown, O; d/XII–7–1897) MD Western Reserve 1864. *JAMA* 30:106, 1898. *Atkinson* I: 254. *Polk* 1896: 1170.

ARMSTRONG, JAMES GRAY, Wilson Co, NC; CW–CSA. (b/IX–22–1836 Edgecombe Co, NC; d/II–2–1873) MD UPa 1858. *U Pa med alum CW*: 1858.

ARMSTRONG, JAMES LOUDON, Rutherford Co, Tenn (b/IV–2–1782 Greenbrier Co, Va; d/IV–5–1868 Bedford Co, Tenn) Stud w/Dudley @ Lexington, Ky. *Trans Med Soc Tenn* 1876:78. USA War of 1812.

ARMSTRONG, JAMES TITUS, Iowa; Omaha, Nebr (b/XII–28–1856, Columbiana Co, O; d/I–14–1899 Beatrice, Nebr) MD Iowa St U 1879; stud Parsons Coll, Ia. *Proc Nebr St Med Soc* 1899:22–23. *Polk* 1893:755.

ARMSTRONG, JOHN, Princeton, NJ (b/1798? d/III–7–1870 @ 71) MD ; ng Dickinson 1816. *Phila med reg & dir* 1871:304. *Tr AMA* : 23:594, 1872.

ARMSTRONG, LEWIS C , Taylorville, Ill (d/El Paso, Tex III–19–1900) MD Mo Med Coll 1883. *Trans Ill St Med Soc* 1899–1900:509. *JAMA* 34:766, 1900. *Polk* 1886:299.

ARMSTRONG, LEWIS P , Newtown, Ind (b/VI–28–1836 Montgomery Co, Ind; d/III–16–1905) MD Miami Med Coll 1873. *Trans Ind St Med Soc* 1905:439. *Flint* 1897: 323.

ARMSTRONG, R L Sr, Pleasant Hill, La (d/I–4–1899 @ 75) MD Tulane 1844. *New Orl m & s jour* 51: 453, 1899. *Polk* 1890:492.

ARMSTRONG, ROBERT, NYC (b/1789 Ireland; d/VIII–12–1873 Brooklyn) Lic Royal Coll Phys Lond [?] 1815. *Med reg NY NJ Conn* 1874–75:270.

ARMSTRONG, SAMUEL TREAT, USA (d/XII–4–1899 Philippines) MD St Louis Med Coll 1879. *JAMA* 33:1566, 1899.

ARMSTRONG, THEODORE SPENCER, Owego, NY 1861–1880; Binghamton 1880– (b/1825 Esperance, NY; d/XII–27–1891) MD Geneva 1847. *Med vis* 8:58, 1892. Homeopath.

ARMSTRONG, WILLIAM CHAMBERLAIN, Wayne, Pa (d/XII–20–1905) MD UPa 1880. *Pa med jour* 9:280, 1905/06. *Flint* 1897:839.

ARMSTRONG, WILLIAM G , Lafontaine, Ind (b/IX–10–1822 Rush Co, Ind; d/I–20–1881) MD Med Coll O 1849. *Trans Ind St Med Soc* 1881:243. *Butler* 1878:192.

ARMSTRONG, WILLIAM J , Memphis (d/IX–20–1878 yellow fever) MD U Nashville 1862. *Tr AMA* 30:850. 1879. *Trans Med Soc Tenn* 1879:19. *Butler* I.

ARMSTRONG, WILLIAM SAMUEL, Philadelphia (b/VII–13–1846; d/VI–8–1868) MD UPa 1868; AB 1865. *Med surg rep Phila* 18:542, 1868.

ARMSTRONG, WILLIAM SIMPSON, CW–CSA; Atlanta (b/X–9–1838 Wilkes Co, Ga; d/II–11–1896) MD UCNY I:353. *Polk* 1886:224.

ARNER, EDGAR WILLIAM, Fairview, NJ (d/X–13–1894) MD U Vt 1894. *Lehigh Valley med mag* 6:70, 1894–95.

ARNOLD, ABRAHAM BLUMENTHAL, Carlisle, Pa; Baltimore (b/II–4–1820 Jebenshausen, Württemberg; d/III–28–1904) MD Washington U Balto 1848. *Med annals Md*: 306. *Atkinson* I:209. *K & B* III:36–37.

ARNOLD, EDMUND ALDOUS, NYC (b/III–17–1857; d/VI–19–1885) MD Bellevue 1880. *Med reg NY NJ Conn* 1886:242.

ARNOLD, GEORGE JEROME, CW–USA; Old Orchard, Me; Roxbury, Mass (V–28–1835 Londonderry, Vt; d/X–3–1883) MD Harvard 1861. *Bost m & s jour* 109:503, 617, 1883. *Harvard in CW*: 262. *Atkinson* I:638.

ARNOLD, GEORGE MILES, NYC (d/I–25–1890 @ 38) MD UCNY 1873. *Med reg NY NJ Conn* 1890:260. *Polk* 1886:670.

ARNOLD, GLOVER CRANE, NYC (b/Charleston, SC; d/XI–29–1906 @ 57) MD Bellevue 1873. *Bost m & s jour* 155:698, 1906. *Polk* 1896:1039.

ARNOLD, JACOB WYATT, CW–CSA; Natural Bridge, Va (d/XI– 1887) MD UVa 1867; AB Washington & Lee 1861. *Trans Med Soc Va* 1888:275. *Polk* 1886:922.

ARNOLD, JOHN ALLEN, Rockland, RI (d/XII–4–1896 @ c50) MD Bellevue 1871. *Bost m & s jour* 135:610, 1896. *Polk* 1886:991.

ARNOLD, JOHN WILLIAM SCHMIDT, NYC 1872–82; Thomasville, Ga; Sewanee, Tenn (b/V–16–1846 Charleston, SC; d/X–20–1888) MD Bellevue 1871; AB Columbia 1868, AM 1871. *Med reg NY NJ Conn* 1889:267. *Bost m & s jour* 119:442, 1888. *NC med jour* 24:142–1`44, 1889. *Atkinson* I:580.

ARNOLD, LUCY MARILLA, Detroit (b/Lakeville, Mich; d/VII[? – 1900) MD New Engl Female Med Coll

1867. *Med couns* ns5: ,1900 (July). *Polk* 1886:487.

ARNOLD, RICHARD DENNIS, Savannah, Ga (b/VIII-19-1803; d/VII-10-1876) MD UPa 1830; AB Princeton 1826, AM 1829. *Trans CPP* centennial vol:277. *Tr AMA* 29:615-618, 1878. *K & B* III:37.

ARNOLD, SALMON AUGUSTUS, Providence, RI (b/VI 26-1797; d/XII-12-1878) MD CPSNY 1821; AB Brown 1816. *Bost m & s jour*99:812,1878; 100:59, 1879. *Trans RI Med Soc* 2:215-216,1877-82. *Atkinson* I:690.

ARNOUX, EDWARD F , Fort Lee, NJ (d/X-29-1884) MD NY Med Coll 1855. *Med reg NY NJ Conn* 1885:230. *Med surg rep Phila* 51:572, 1884.

ARONSON, ALEXANDER I , NYC (b/Gny; d/VI-5 1895 @ 37) <MD Jena 1879> *Med reg NY NJ Conn* 1895:216. *Bost m & s jour* 133: 50, 1895. *JAMA* 25:76, 1895.

ARONSTEIN, ADOLPH, San Francisco (d/VIII-28 1901 @ 66) <MD U Munich 1860> *JAMA* 37:710, 1901. *Polk* 1886:170.

ARRINGTON, J D , Hartsboro, Ga (d/X-16-1893) MD Georgia Coll Ecl Med & Surg 1882. *JAMA* 21:700, 1893. *Polk* 1890:267.

ARRINGTON, SAMUEL JONES, CW-CSA (b/II-6-1827; d/IV-6-1866 Brewsville, Ala) MD UPa 1853. *UPa med alum CW*: 1853.

ARROWSMITH, JOSEPH E GAR, Key Port, NJ (b/ nr Middleton; d/I-3-1906 @77) MD UCNY 1844. *Bost m & s jour* 142:76, 1900. *JAMA* 34:186, 1900. *Polk* 1896:944.

ARTHUR [ARTHURS], BIDDLE, Pittsburgh, Pa (d/IV 1906 @ 78) MD *Pa med jour* 9:672, 1905/06.

ARTHUR, CHRISTOPHER C , Portland, Ind (b/ IX-15-1832 Highland Co, O; c/X-16-1898) <MD Starling> *Trans Ind St Med Soc* 1899:395. *JAMA* 31:1066, 1898. *Polk* 1896:487.

ARTHUR, ENOCH, Jr , Frankford, Pa (d/V-27-1868 @ c1836) MD UPa 1856. *Phila med reg & dir* 1871:293. *Med surg rep Phila* 18:504, 1868.

ARTHUR, JOSHUA P, Laredo, Tex (d/VIII-19-1898 @ 58) MD UPa 1868. *JAMA* 31:551, 1898. *Polk* 1896:1438.

ARWINE, JOHN S , Columbus, Ind (b/I-4-1824 east Tenn; d/XII-2-1905) Lic Cinc O by years of practice. *Trans Ind St Med Soc* 1906:491. *Polk* 1886:314.

ASCH, JACOB H , NYC (d/V-19-1905 @ 65) MD U Berlin 1864. *Bost m & s jour* 152:620, 1905. *Polk* 1896:1039.

ASCH, MORRIS JOSEPH, NYC (b/VII-4-1833 Phila; d/X-5-1905) MD Jefferson 1855; AB UPa 1852. *Bost m & s jour* 147:447, 1902. *Nashville jour m & s* 92:181, 1902. *K & B* III-37-38.

ASH, JAMES, Philadelphia (d/IX-6-1895 Asbury Park, NJ) MD UPa 1846. *JAMA* 25:510, 1895.

ASH, JOHN, Brighton, Ill (d/I-31-1903 @84) MD Pa Med Coll 1851. *Ill med jour* ns4:665, 1903. *Polk* 1886, 256.

ASH, JOSHUA W , Delaware Co, Pa (b/VII-3-1802; d/ II-26-1879) MD UPa 1826. *Trans Med Soc Pa* 12:1879: 760-761.

ASHBRIDGE, WILLIAM, Philadelphia (b/III-15-1846; d/XII-13-1884) MD UPa 1867; ng Haverford Coll. *Trans CPP* centennial vol:208. *Med surg rep Phila* 51:732, 1884. *Atkinson* I:199.

ASHE, EDMOND FONTAINE, Wadesboro, NC (b/XI-30-1822; d/I-28-1892) MD Jefferson 1850; stud U Ala 1837. *U Ala gen cat*: 54. *Polk* 1886:727.

ASHE, WILLIAM CINCINNATUS, CW-CSA; Demopolis, Ala (b/1815; d/XII-17-1867) MD UPa 1836; stud UAla 1832. *U Ala gen cat*:33. *UPa med alum CW*: 1836.

ASHER, WILLIAM C , Atlanta (d/IX-30-1891 @ 54) MD U Nashville 1858. *Bost m & s jour* 125:392, 1891. *Polk* 1890:260.

ASHFORD, FRANCIS ASBURY, Washington, DC (b/IX 18-1841 Fairfax Co, Va; d/V-19-1882) MD Columbian 1867. *JAMA* 1:192, 1883. *Hist Med Soc DC*: 283-284. *Atkinson* I:78.

ASHHURST, FRANCIS, Mt Holly, NJ (b/I-5-1844 Phila; d/VIII-17-1885) MD UPa 1867. *Trans Med Soc NJ* 1886:157-158.

ASHHURST, JOHN, Jr, CW-USA; Philadelphia (b/ VIII-23-1839; d/VII-7-1900) MD UPa 1860; AB 1857. *Trans CPP* centennial vol:208-209; 3d ser 24:xliii ff. *So pract* 22:457, 1900. *Nashville jour m & s* 58:47 ff, 1900. *K & B* III:39.

ASHHURST, SAMUEL, Philadelphia (b/IX-14-1840; d/ XI-12-1901) MD UPa 1861; stud Amherst. CW-USA. *Pa med jour* 5:295, 314, 1901/02. *Trans CPP* centennial vol:209. *UPa med alum CW*: 1861. *Atkinson* I:207.

ASHLEY, LUCIAN, CW-USA (d/1853) MD Northwestern 1860. *Nat med jour* 1: 289, 1870/71.

ASHLEY, RUBE L , Perry, O (d/II-13-1899 @ 58) MD Cleveland Med Coll 1871. *JAMA* 32:442, 1899. *Polk* 1886:765.

ASHMEAD, THEODORE, Philadelphia (b/1799? d/XII-26/27, 1853 @ 54) MD UPa 1822. *Phila m & s jour* 2:230, 1854. *Trans Med Soc Pa* 1856:158.

ASHMEAD, WILLIAM, Philadelphia (b/VII-2-1801; d/ II-2-1888) MD UPa 1826. *Trans CPP*, centennial vol: 209.

ASHTON, ADOLPHUS H , Philadelphia (b/V-18-1826; d/II-17/18-1883) MD Hahnemann Phila 1852. *Trans Am Inst Homeop* 1893:124. *Am observer* 20:95, 1884? *Hahn mo* 18:191, 1883. *US med inv* 17:183, 1883. Homeopath.

ASHTON, ISAIAH HEYLIN, Dobbs Ferry, NY (b/Phila; d/II-16-1889) MD UPa 1870. *Trans NY St Med Soc* II:741 ff, 1894. *Polk* 1886:658.

ASHTON, LAWRENCE, Falmouth, Fredericksburg, Va; Dallas, Tex (b/King Geo Co, Va; d/III-6-1902 Branchville, NJ) MD UCNY 1885; stud Columbian, Univ Va. *Trans Med Soc Va* 1902:214-215. *Polk* 1886:1546.

ASHTON, SAMUEL KEEN, Philadelphia (b/IV-6-1822;

 Spec. educ'l status abbrev. as: ***ng*** = college verified attendance without degree;

d/II-13-1895) MD UPa 1843; AB 1841. *Med bull m & s* 17:115, 1895. *Polk* 1886:812.

ASHWIN, EDWARD HILBORNE, Brooklyn (b/1845 Engl; d/III-28-1899) MD LICH 1882; MD Bennet 1870. *JAMA* 32, 787, 1889. *Polk* 1896:991.

ASKEW, HENRY FORD, Wilmington, Del (b/VI-24-1805; d/III-5-1876) MD UPa 1826. *Tr AMA* 27:647, 1876. *Med rec m & s* 11:213, 1876. *K & B* II:43-44.

ASKREN, CORT F , Terre Haute, Ind (d/VIII-1-1901 @ 60) MD Ky Sch Med, Louisville 1883. *JAMA* 37:398, 1901. *Polk* 1886:337.

ASPINWALL, THOMAS WILLIAMS, E Providence, RI (b/IV-8-1818 Mansfield, Conn; d/XII-21-1867) MD Jefferson 1839. *Bost m & s jour* 77:552, 1867. *Trans RI Med Soc* 1865-1872:323-327.

ASSENHEIMER, HENRY, NYC (b/XI-12-1814; d/II-1-1886) <MD Würzburg 1839> *Med reg NY NJ Conn* 1886:242.

ATCHISON, THOMAS A , Nashville, Tenn (b/V--1818 Fayette Co, Ky; d/X-2-1900) MD Transylvania 1839. *Nashvl j m & s* 88:188-190, 1900. *Polk* 1886:870.

ATEN, HENRY F , Brooklyn (b/1829 Groveland, NY; d/XII-18-1892) MD Western Reserve 1856. *Trans Am Inst Homeop* 1895:1092. *Polk* 1886:643. Homeopath.

ATHERLY, JOSEPH B , CW-USA (d/VIII-12-1862 Falmouth, Va) MD U Glasgow 1851. *Trans Med Soc NY* 1864:399. *Nat med jour* 1:289, 1870/71.

ATHON, JAMES SEANDERSON, Indianapolis (b/IV-1-1811 Loudoun Co, Va; d/X-25-1875) MD U Louisville 1838. *Tr AMA* 28:613, 1877. Kemper's *Indiana*: 235-236.

ATKINSON, ALBERT S, Baltimore (d/II-24-1902) MD Hahnemann Phila 1893; ?ng UMd Med Sch. *Pa med jour* 6:259, 1902/03. *Am med mo* June, 1902. Homeopath.

ATKINSON, ARCHIBALD, Jr, Baltimore; CW-CSA; (b/II-23-1832 Smithfield, Va; d/X-29-1903) MD UPa 1854. *Med annals Med*:308. *Atkinson* I:575. *UPa med alum CW*: 1854. *Polk* 1886:435.

ATKINSON, BENJAMIN, W Amsbury, Mass (b/I-29-1806; d/X-22-1861) MD Bowdoin 1830. *Bost m & s jour* 65: 280, 1861.

ATKINSON, GEORGE H , Brooklyn (b/1851 Portland, Ore; d/XII-27-1884) MD LICH 1873; AB Dartmouth 1871. *Med reg NY NJ Conn* 1885:230. *Bost m & s jour* 126: 540, 1892. *Butler* 1878:528.

ATKINSON, ISAAC EDMONDSON, Baltimore (b/I-23 1846; d/XI-24-1906) MD UMd 1865. *Med annals Md*: 308. *Bost m & s jour* 155:660, 1906. *K & B* III:41.

ATKINSON, JOSIAH, Newburyport, Mass (b/VIII-16-1817; d/VI-21-1869) MD Berkshire 1844; AB Bowdoin 1842. *Bowdoin cat* 1841.

ATKINSON, MOSES LITTLE, Lawrence, Mass (b/VII-14-1814 Newbury; d/VII-13-1852) MD Harvard 1844; AB Dartmouth 1838. *Dartmouth cat* 1838. *Mass Med Soc cat* 1893:70.

ATKINSON, ROGER TROWBRIDGE, USN (b/1872; d/XI-10-1902 Portsmouth, Va) MD Harvard 1898; AB 1894. *Bost m & s jour* 147:578, 1902.

ATKINSON, THOMAS HANLON, Jersey City, NJ (b/VII-17-1872; d/II-5-1898) MD CPSNY 1895; AB Wesleyan 1892. *Trans NJ Med Soc* 1898:375. *JAMA* 30:448, 1898.

ATKINSON, THOMAS PLEASANTS, Staunton, Danville, Va (b/1795 Chesterfield Co; d/VIII-30-1874) MD UPa 1817. *Trans Med Soc Va* 1874:55. *Tr AMA* 26:475-476, 1875.

ATKISSON, WILLIAM, CW-USA (d/IV-9-1862) MD *Nat med jour* 1:289, 1870/71.

ATLEE, EDWIN AUGUSTUS, Cincinnati (b/XI-16-1776; d/III-8-1852) MD UPa 1804; ng Dickinson 1795. *Trans CPP* centennial vol: 209.

ATLEE, JOHN LIGHT, Sr, Lancaster, Pa (b/XI-2-1799; d/X-1-1885) MD UPa 1820. *Trans CPP* 3s8:xxxv-xliii, 1886. *Trans Med Soc Pa* 1886: 241-242. *Atkinson* I:489. *K & B* III: 42.

ATLEE, JOHN LIGHT, Lancaster, Pa (b/VI-21-1830; d/VII-18-1885) MD UPa 1853; AB Yale 1849. *Tr Med Soc Pa* 1886:243-244. *Med bull m & s* 8: 257, 1885.

ATLEE, WASHINGTON LEMUEL, Lancaster, Pa & Philadelphia (b/II-22-1808; d/IX-7-1878) MD Jefferson 1829. *Tr AMA* 30:794-805. *Trans Med Soc St Pa* 1879:831-849. *Trans CPP* centennial vol:209. *K & B* III:43.

ATLEE, WASHINGTON LEMUEL, Philadelphia (b/1842 Lancaster, Pa; d/I-14-1900) MD Jefferson, 1870. *JAMA* 34:251, 1900. *Atkinson* I:560. *Polk* 1896:1297.

ATWATER, ALBERT WARING, St.Regis Falls, NY (b/VII-24-1861 Burlington, Vt; d/I-2-1903) MD UVt 1885. *Bost m & s jour* 148:80, 1903. *Polk* 1896:1098.

ATWATER, HIRAM HAYDEN, Burlington,Vt (b/II-17 1828 Norfolk, NY; d/VIII-19-1891) MD Woodstock 1851; AB UVt 1847. *Bost m & s jour* 125:232, 1891. *Med bull* 14:38,1892. *Butler* 1878:803. *Atkinson* I:475.

ATWATER, JOHN PHELPS, Poughkeepsie, NY (b/1813 Carlisle, Pa; d/V-23-1897) MD Yale 1837; AB 1834. *Bost m & s jour* 136:527, 1897. *JAMA* 28: 1252, 1897.

ATWOOD, CHARLES FREEMAN, Winterport, Me (d/IX-6-1901 @ 45) MD Bellevue 1879. *JAMA* 37:790, 1901. *Polk* 1886:430.

ATWOOD, EUGENE SULLIVAN, Chicago (d/III-2-1906) MD Rush 1877. *Ill med jour* 9:463, 1906. *Polk* 1896:378.

ATWOOD, FRANCIS, St.Paul, Minn (b/VIII-20-1846 Franklin, Mass; d/VIII-5-1882) MD Harvard 1873; AB 1869, AM 1873. *Bost m & s jour* 107:168, 192, 1882. *Chic med rev* 6:362, 1882. *Trans Minn St Med Soc* 1882:268-269. *JAMA* 1:160, 1883.

ATWOOD, GEORGE, Fairhaven, Mass (d/I-16-1888 @

72) MD Harvard 1837. *Bost m & s jour* 119:641, 1888.

ATWOOD, JOSEPH FREEMAN, Brooklyn (b/1845 NJ; d/IX–21–1898) MD CPSNY 1870. *Amer homeop* Dec 1898. *Bost m & s jour* 139:585, 1898. Homeopath.

ATWOOD, MOSES, Francistown, NH (d/IV–28–1850 New Boston (Stud. w/Samuel Gregg, Boston. *Trans Am Inst Homeop* 1893:125. Kirby's *Am jour homeop* 5:30. Homeopath.

ATWOOD, ROBERT NUTTING, CW–USA & USN; Claremont, Vt; Brooklyn (b/VII–20–1838; d/XI–1–1876) MD U Vt 1861. *Med reg NY NJ Conn* 1877:196.

ATWOOD, SHADRACH, Franklin, Mass (d/XI–27–1888) MD Harvard 1830; Amherst ng 1829. *Polk* 1886:466. *Amherst, Men of*, 1829.

AUGUSTA, ALEXANDER T, CW–USA; Washington, DC (b/Pa; d/XII–21–1890) MD Trinity Toronto 1856. *JAMA* 16: 178, 1891. *Polk* 1886: 211. Black.

AUGUSTINE, THOMAS JEFFERSON, Pittsburgh (d/XII–25–1872 @ 38) MD Bellevue 1866. *Med surg rep Phila* 28:78, 1873.

AULICK, RALPH V, Washington, DC (b/1839; d/X–3–1872) MD UPa 1867. *Tr AMA* 24:341, 1873. *Hist Med Soc DC*: 293.

AUSTIN, ALVIN AVA, New London, Conn (d/VII–21–1889) MD Jefferson 1873. *Med bull m & s* II:262, 1889.

AUSTIN, CALEB HOPKINS, New Haven, (b/1794? d/VIII–3–1866 @ 72) Hon MD Yale 1832. *Proc Conn Med Soc* 1866: 272–274.

AUSTIN, HORACE B, Athol, Mass (d/VIII–14–1856) MD Woodstock 1831. *Bost m & s jour* 55:87, 1856.

AUSTIN, JAMES H, Bristol, Conn (b/Suffield 1824; d/III–27–1873 @ 49) MD Berkshire 1847. *Trans Am Inst Homeop* 1873:666. *New Engl med gaz* 8:344, 1873. Homeopath 1858–

AUSTIN, JAMES HERBERT, Kansas City; El Paso before 1903: Toronto (d/X–28–1905 Toronto) MD Toronto 1893; MRCS(E). *Texas st jour med* 1:220, 1905/06.

AUSTIN, JAMES MARSHALL, Washington, DC (b/Va; d/1865 Howardsville, Va) MD UPa 1832. *Hist Med Soc DC*: 245.

AUSTIN, K O, Chicago (b/1865; d/IX–7–1903) MD CPS Chic 1896; ng Bennet Med 1893–95. *JAMA* 41:736, 1903.

AUSTIN, PHILIP H, Baltimore (b/1822; d/X–28–1878) MD UMd 1845. *Med annals Md*: 308–309. *Butler* 1874:310.

AUSTIN, WILLIAM G, New Orleans (d/VI–12–1894 @ 80) <MD Wash'n U Balto 1836> *Bost m & s jour* 131:24, 1894. *JAMA* 23:86, 1894. *Polk* 1886:530.

AUSTIN, WILLIAM MORRIS, USA (b/X–5–1844 Engl; d/V–9–1868 El Paso, Tex) MD LICH 1865. *Tr AMA* 21:492, 1870. *Phila med reg & dir* 1871:296. *Med surg rep Phila* 18:504, 1868.

AVENT, BENJAMIN WARD, Murfreesboro, Tenn; CW–CSA; (b/1812 Petersburg, Va; d/IX–12–1878 Memphis, yellow fever) MD Transylvania 1834. *Tr AMA* 30:850–851, 1879. *Med rec* 14:240, 1878.

AVERILL, JAMES JUDSON, Falls Village, Conn (b/XII–20–1843 Shrewsbury, Mass; d/VI–20–1887) MD Yale 1866. *Proc Conn Med Soc* ns4:218–219, 1888. *Butler* 1878:72.

AVERY, CHARLES H, NYC (b/XII–10–1834 Perryville, NY; d/XI–2–1897) MD LICH 1865. *Bost m & s jour* 137:504–505, 1897. *JAMA* 29:1028, 1897. *Polk* 1896:1040.

AVERY, CHARLES L, Cincinnati (d/II–5–1867) MD Med Coll O 1836. *Med surg rep Phila* 16:179, 1867.

AVERY, GEORGE W, Norwich, NY (b/Earlville, NY; d/XI–1–1888) MD Albany 1850. *Trans NY St Med Soc* 11:741 ff, 1894. *Polk* 1886:699.

AVERY, GEORGE WHITEFIELD, Hartford, Conn (d/II–23–1893 @ 53) MD Yale 1861. *Bost m & s jour* 128:228, 1893. *Proc Conn Med Soc* 1893: 247–250. *Butler* 1878: 72.

AVERY, HENRY NEWELL, Morristown, NJ 1867; Poughkeepsie, NY 1868; Winona, Minn 1873; Galesville, Wis; Minneapolis 1883– (b/IV–30–1838 Clinton, NY; d/IV–30–1898) MD NY Homeop Coll 1866; AB Hamilton 1858. CW–USA. *Minn homeop mag* 7: 1898 (June). Homeopath.

AWL, WILLIAM MaCLAY, Columbus, O (b/V–24–1799 Harrisburg, Pa; d/XI–19–1876) MD Jefferson 1834; hon MD Willoughby U 1839. *Tr AMA* 31: 1009–1011, 1880. *Trans Ohio St Med Soc* 1877:69–80. *K & B* III:45.

AXFORD, SAMUEL McDONALD, Flint, Mich (d/XII–10–1873) ng U Mich Med Sch 1851–53. *Tr AMA* 33: 517, 1882.

AXSON, FOSTER A [or A FOSTER], New Orleans; MexWar–USA (b/c1816 Charleston, SC; d/IX–12–1881) MD Charleston Med Coll 1837. *New Orl m&s j* ns9:397, 629–632, 1882. *Atkinson* I: 480. *Butler* 1871: 253.

AXTELL, A J, Bloomington, Ind (b/1827, Pa; d/I–25–1900) Lic. years of practice. *JAMA* 34:380, 1900. *Polk* 1896:459.

AXTELL, JAMES C, CW–USA (d/X–18–1862 Covington, Ky) *Nat med jour* 1:269, 1870/71.

AXTELL, LUCIUS VESPASIAN, Jamestown, NY (d/IV 14–1863) MD Willoughby 1842. *Med surg rep Phila* 10:64, 1863.

AXTELL, WILLIAM HARVEY, Sheakelyville, Pa (b/Washington Co, Pa; d/IX–19–1906 @ 90) <MD Med Coll O> *Pa med jour* 10:119, 1906/07.

AXTELLE, THOMAS LINCOLN, Waterbury, Conn (b/IV–28–1852, Allegheny, Pa; d/IX–26–1904) MD Bellevue 1881. *Proc Conn Med Soc* 1905:512–514. *Flint* 1897:179.

AYDELOTT, WILLIAM R, Badger, Ind (d/IX–1–1885) MD Rush 1870. *Trans Ind St Med Soc* 1885:220.

 Spec. educ'l status abbrev. as: ***ng*** = college verified attendance without degree;

AYER, DAY FAYETTE, Haverhill, Mass (d/VI-31-1856 @ 31) MD Dartmouth 1851; ng Woodstock 1851. *Bost m & s jour* 54:427, 1856.

AYER, JAMES, Boston (b/X-4-1815 Newfield, Me; d/XII-31-1891) MD Bowdoin 1839; AB 1834. *Bost m & s jour* 126:24, 1892. *Atkinson* I:605-606.

AYER, JOSEPH CULLEN, Boston (b/VIII-24-1811 Newfield, Me; d/I-22-1846) MD Harvard 1836; AB Bowdoin 1832. *Bowdoin cat* 1832.

AYER, OTIS, CW-USA; LeSueur, Minn (b/VI-19-1817 Hampton, NH; d/I-27-1889) MD Dartmouth 1842; MD Jefferson 1842. *Trans Minn St Med Soc* 1889:239-242. *Atkinson* I:251. *Polk* 1886:513.

AYER, WASHINGTON, San Francisco (b/VI-18-1823 Haverhill, Mass; d/II-15-1899) MD Harvard 1847. *JAMA* 32: 732, 1899. *Atkinson* I:220. *Polk* 1896:230.

AYERS, JAMES NELSON, Kalamazoo, Mich (b/V-23-1821 St. Johnsville, NY; d/V-15-1899) MD Castleton 1842. *Trans Am Inst Homeop* 1899:75. Homeopath.

AYLING, GEORGE FRED, Brooklyn (b/England, d/IV-6-1877 NYC) MD LICH; lic. Apothecaries' Hall, London, 1857. *Med reg NY NJ Conn* 1877:196.

AYRES, ALEXANDER, Montgomery Co, NY (b/IV-9-1811 Oppenheim, NY; d/VIII-27-1886 Fort Plain, NY) MD Castleton 1842. *Trans NY St Med Soc* 11:741 ff, 1894. *Polk* 1886:661.

AYRES, DANIEL, E Canada Creek, NY; Amsterdam, NY (b/V-17-1787 New Braintree, Mass; d/V-25-1853) Stud w/Dr Hanchett, Salisbury, NY; lic 1816? *Trans Med Soc St NY* 10:170-174, 1855.

AYRES, DANIEL, Brooklyn (b/X-6-1822 NYC; d/I-18-1892) MD UCNY 1845; AB Princeton 1842; LLD Wesleyan 1856. *Med reg NY NJ Conn* 1892:272. *JAMA* 18:151-152, 1892. *Bost m & s jour* 126:104, 1892. *K & B* III:46.

AYRES, GEORGE BYRON, Omaha (d/VIII-19-1890) MD LICH 1876; MD U Mich Med Sch 1877. *Med & surg rec Omaha*: 181, 1890. Homeopath.

AYRES, HENRY CHRISTOPHER, Barnard, Vt (b/1823 Hartland, Vt; d/IV-5-1862) MD Vt Med Coll 1852. *Trans Vt Med Soc* 1883:103.

AYRES, HENRY P , Ft Wayne, Ind (b/IX-1-1813 Morristown, NJ; d/XII-25-1887) MD UCNY 1846. *Trans Ind St Med Soc* 1888:208. *K & B* III:46.

AYRES, ROBERT H , Baltimore (d/X-9-1868 Navissa Isle, WI @ 59) MD UMd 1835. *Phila med reg & dir* 1871:298. *Med surg rep Phila* 20:40, 1869.

AYRES, WILLIAM ORVILLE, New Haven, Conn (b/IX-11-1817; d/IV-30-1887) MD Yale 1854. *Proc Conn Med Soc* ns3:174-176, 1887.

AZBILL, OVERTON T , Big Hill, Ky (d/VI-7-1896 @ c60) MD U Louisville 1890. *JAMA* 26:1245, 1896. *Polk* 1896: 578.

BABBITT, HENRY SMITH, Dorchester, Mass (d/XII-10-1904 @ 78) MD Berkshire 1848. *Bost m & s jour* 151: 670, 1904. *Polk* 1890: 534.

BABBITT, NATHAN SNELL, N Adams, Mass (b/VIII-30-1812 Hancock, Mass; d/XI-5-1889) MD Berkshire 1833; AB Williams. *Bost m & s jour* 121: 500, 645, 1889. *Polk* 1886:470.

BABBITT, ROBERT A , W Randolph Vt; CW-USA (b/1842? d/X-17-1864 @ 22) *Bost m & s jour* 71: 408, 1864. *Nat med jour* 1: 289, 1871.

BABCOCK, BENJAMIN B , Washington, DC (b/Pa; d/I-21-1868) MD Georgetown 1867. *Hist Med Soc DC*: 289.

BABCOCK, HERMAN POTTER, Oakland, Cal 1870-(b/X-28-1840; d/XII-27-1878 Buffalo, NY) MD U Buffalo 1863. CW-USN. *Buffalo m & s jour* 18: 230, 276-277, 1879. *Atkinson* I:200. *Butler* 1878:56. *Trans Calif Med Soc* 1870:13.

BABCOCK, HORACE, Gowanda, NY; Las Vegas, NM (d/III-25-1895) MD U Buffalo 1851. *JAMA* 24:609, 1895. *Polk* 1886: 662.

BABCOCK, I L , Hallowell, Me (d/VIII-13-1874) MD NY Homeop Med Coll 1872. *New Engl med gaz* 9: 528, 1874. *Am jour homeop mat med* 8: 120, 1874? *Med surg rep Phila* 31:180, 1874. Homeopath.

BABCOCK, MOSES TREAT, Hammondsport, NY (d/III-31-1902 @77) MD Geneva 1852. *Bost m & s jour* 146:398, 1902. *Trans Med Soc St NY* 1903:[412] *Med reg NY NJ Conn* 1889-90:128. *Polk* 1886: 663.

BABCOCK, MYRON NORTHRUP, Saratoga Springs, NY (b/IX-18-1818 Sheldon, Vt; d/V-21/22-1892) MD Woodstock 1842. *Bost m & s jour* 126:540, 1892. *Butler* 1878:540.

BABCOCK, WILLIAM HENRY, USA (b/1833; d/X-2-1859 Bates' Station, Montague Co, Tex) MD UCNY 1854. *Med surg rep Phila* ns3:111, 319, 1859/60.

BABCOCK, WILLIAM ROWLAND, New London, Conn (b/IV-2-1872 Lyme, Conn; d/XII-6-1897) MD UCNY 1894. *Proc Conn Med Soc* 1898:335-336.

BACHE, BENJAMIN FRANKLIN, USN (b/II-7-1801; d/XI-2-1881, NYC) MD UPa 1823; AB Princeton 1819. *JAMA* 1:192, 1883. *Med bull m & s* 3:288, 1881. *Med rec* 20: 551, 1881. *Chic med rev* 4:520, 1881.

BACHE, FRANKLIN, Philadelphia (b/X-25-1792; d/III 19-1864) MD UPa 1814; AB 1810. USA 1814-16. *Trans Med Soc St Pa* 4s1: 1865:137-138/ *Tr AMA* 16:635 ff. 1865. *Trans CPP* centennial vol:209. *K & B* III:47.

BACHELDER, JOSIAH, Beverly, Mass (b/1775? d/II-5-1857 @ 82 Falmouth, Me) MD Harvard 1799 [as Batchelder] AB Dartmouth 1796. *Bost m & s jour* 56: 67, 1857.

BACHELER, JOSEPH HOWARD, Grand Rapids, Mich (d/XI-7-1899 @ 57) MD UMich 1872. *JAMA* 33:1441, 1899. *Polk* 1886:495.

BACHER, FRANZ, Quincy, Ill (d/X-15-1905 @ 77) MD

Heidelberg 1848. *Ill med jour* 8:430, 1905. *Polk* 1896:436.

BACHMAN, SOLOMON STERN, Philadelphia (b/XII-28-1836 Durham, Pa; d/IX/10/1906) MD LICH 1870; AB Muhlenberg 1862. *Pa med jour* 10:53, 1906/07.

BACKUS, CYRUS, Ann Arbor, Mich (b/VIII-12-1812; d/II-1-1886) MD UCNY 1850. *Med couns* 2, Feb. 1886. *Polk* 1886:482. Homeopath 1866-

BACKUS, FREDERICK FANNING, Rochester, NY (b/VI-1794 Bethlehem, Conn; d/XI-4-1858) MD Yale 1816; AB 1813. *Trans Med Soc St NY* 1860:176-180. *Tr AMA* 13:799-800, 1860. *K & B* III:46.

BACKUS, RUFUS, Harvard, Ill, 1865-1872 Racine, Wis, 1872-1877; (b/VI-3-1838 Kingsbury, Ind; d/IX-11-1877) <MD Hahnemann Chic 1865> *US med inv* 6:516, 1877. *Am homeop obs* 15:63, 1877? Homeopath.

BACON, A J, Table Grove, Ill; Gardena,Cal (b/1840? d/III-30-1900 @ 60) MD Rush 1864. *Trans Ill St Med Soc* 1899-1900:574. *JAMA* 34:957, 1900. *Polk* 1896: 215.

BACON, ALVAN, Auburn, Me (b/IV-25-1806 Scarborough, Me; d/XI-24-1860) MD Bowdoin 1833. *Trans Me Med Ass'n* 1880-1882:382-383. *Butler* 1878:303.

BACON, AMASA DURKEE, Sharon, Mass (b/VIII-20-1806 N Yarmouth; d/III-29-1881) MD Bowdoin 1837. *Bost m & s jour* 105: 1881 [XI-29-1881]

BACON, CHARLES AUSTIN, NYC to 1885/86; Washington, DC (b/IV-14-1838 NYC; d/I-9-1892 Florida) MD NY Med Coll 1863. CW-USA. *Trans Am Inst Homeop* 1893:125. Homeopath.

BACON, CYRUS, Jr USA 1861-68 (d/IX-1/2-1868) ng UMich Med Sch 1856-58. *Tr AMA* 21:492-493, 1870. *Phila med reg & dir* 1871:298. *Med surg rep Phila* 19:239, 1868. *Nat med jour* 1:289, 1871.

BACON, DAVID FRANCIS, NYC (b/XI-30-1813 Prospect, Conn; d/I-23-1865) MD Yale 1836; AB 1831. *Med surg rep Phila* 12:285, 1864/65. *K & B* III:48.

BACON, GEORGE WASHINGTON, NYC (b/IX- - 1834; d/XII-25-1874) MD CPSNY 1865; AB Columbia 1854; AM 1857; LLB 1865; att? Episc Theol Sem NY. *Med reg NY NJ Conn* 1875:195.

BACON, HENRY CLINT, Harveyville, Pa (d/VIII-15-1906 @64) MD Jefferson 1868. *Pa med jour* 10:54, 1906/07. *Flint* 1897: 805.

BACON, JAMES E, Baltimore; St Mary's Co, Md; (d/XI-23-1868 @ 40) MD UMd 1846. *Phila med reg & dir* 1871:298. *Med surg rep Phila* 20:40, 1869.

BACON, JOHN, Boston (d/ 1881) MD Harvard 1840; AB 1837. *Bost m & s jour* 105: 527, 623, 1881. *Tr AMA* 33: 518, 1882.

BACON, RICHARD SMITH, NYC (d/VII-6-1897 @ 58) MD CPSNY 1865; AB Columbia 1859; AM 1862; LLB 1862. *JAMA* 29:200, 1897.

BACON, WILLIAM, Newport, NJ (b/VI-20-1802; d/II-26-1868) MD UPa 1822. *Trans NJ Med Soc* 1871-73: 186-187. *Med surg rep Phila* 18:376, 1868.

BACON, WILLIAM CLEMENT, Darby, Pa (d/VII-27-1871) MD UPa 1860. *Trans Med Soc Pa* 9:102, 1872.

BACON, WILLIAM TURNER, Hartford, Conn (b/VIII-27-1846; d/III-15-1906) MD UCNY 1871; AB Yale 1868. *Proc Conn M S* 1906:281-283. *Flint* 1897: 174.

BADARAQUE, THOMAS Philadelphia (d/X-22-1857 Deer Island, Mass) Stud Med Inst Phila before 1847. *Bost m & s jour* 57: 267, 1857.

BADEN, JOSEPH ABELL, Baltimore (b/1833 St Mary's Co, Md; d/I-20-1902) MD UMd 1856. *Med annals Md*: 309. *Polk* 1893:557.

BADHAM, JAMES THOMAS, NYC (d/V-9-1833) MD UCNY 1875. *Med reg NY NJ Conn* 1883:218.

BAELZ, FREDERICK CLEMENS, Pittsburgh, Pa (b/XI-18-1814 Württemberg, d/IX-30-1872) MD U Zurich 1836. *Hahn mo* 8:230, 1872-73. Homeopath.

BAER, CHARLES J, Roanoke Co, Va (b/VIII-8-1823 Frederick City, Md; d/IV-30-1888) MD UMd 1845. *Med annals Md*: 309.

BAER, EMANUEL SWARR, Lancaster, Pa (b/X-29-1852 Millersville, Pa; d/V-26-1`875) MD UCNY 1875; AB Franklin & Marshall 1872. *Franklin & Marshall obit rec:* 223-224.

BAER, JACOB SHELLMAN, Frederick Co, Md (b/V-22-1783; d/IV-10-1866) MD UPa 1808. *Med annals Md*: 304.

BAER, MICHAEL SHELLMAN, Baltimore (b/1795 Md; d/VI-8-1854) MD UMd 1818. *Med annals Md*:304.

BAER, OLIVER PERRY, Ohio; Richmond, Ind 1849- (b/VIII-25-1816 Frederick City, Md; d/VIII-10-1888) MD Louisville Med Sch 1838? MD Hahnemann Phila 1867; MD Homeop Med Coll Mo 1868. *Trans Am Inst Homeop* 1889: 176. *Med vis* 4:301, 1888. *Med couns* 13:388, 1888. *Med adv* 21:384, 1888? Homeopath. Cleave.

BAETHIG, HENRY Sr, Buffalo, NY (b/Germany; d/XII-5-1871) Lic Erie Co Homeop Soc St NY. *Trans Am Inst Homeop* 1873:512. Homeopath.

BAETHIG, HENRY, Jr, Buffalo, NY (b/1850 Nuremberg; d/VII-4-1906) MD Hahnemann Phila 1870. *Tr Am Inst Homeop* 1906: 766-767. Homeopath.

BAGBY, GEORGE WILLIAM, CW-CSA; Richmond, Va (b/VIII-13-1828 Buckingham Co, Va; d/XI-29-1883) MD UPa 1849. *UPa med alum CW*: 1849.

BAGG, JOHN SULLIVAN, USN 1878-1883; W Springfield, Mass (b/XII-31-1848; d/VII-9-1887) MD UPa 1873; ng Amherst 1872. *Amherst, Men of*: 1872.

BAGG, MOSS MEARS, Utica, NY (b/VII-13-1816; d/V-2-1900) MD Geneva 1841; AB Yale 1837. *Bost m & s jour* 142:528, 1900. *JAMA* 34:1210, 1900. *Med reg NY NJ Conn* 1889/90: 147. *Trans Med Soc St NY* 1901:427-428.

BAGLEY, FILLMORE DREW, ?NYC (b/III-8-1850; d/III-10-1883) MD UCNY 1878. *Med reg NY NJ Conn* 1883: 218.

Spec. educ'l status abbrev. as: ***ng*** = college verified attendance without degree;

BAGLEY, GEORGE LEONARD, Des Moines, Ia (b/1850? d/1894 @ 44) MD Western Reserve 1885. *JAMA* 23:878, 1894. *Trans Ia St Med Soc* 14:328, 1896.

BAGLEY, HERMAN BEARDSLEY, Marshall, Mich 1865– ; Seattle, Wash 1874– (b/III–12–1845 near Auburn, NY; d/III–8–1899) MD Western Homeop Coll Cleveland 1865; <postgr Bellevue 1866> *Trans Am Inst Homeop* 1899:75; 1900:828–829. *Polk* 1886:932.

BAGULEY, DAVID, Wheeling, W Va (b/1822; d/1877) MD Phila Coll Med 1851. *Trans Med Soc W Va* 1875–82:588–589; 1884:154.

BAHAN, THOMAS S , NYC (b/New Brunswick; d/IV–6–1897 Douglaston, NY) MD UCNY 1856. *JAMA* 28:810, 1897. *Butler* 1878: 506. *Polk* 1896: 1040.

BAILEY, ABRAM, ?Philadelphia (b/IX–5–1760; d/VIII–13–1825) <ng UPa Med Sch> *Med rep* 1: 62–64, 1853.

BAILEY, ALEXANDER H , Santa Cruz, Cal (b/Hawaii? d/VIII–24–1897) MD Hosp Coll Med Louisville 1883. *JAMA* 29:555, 1897.

BAILEY, BENJAMIN, ?NYC (b/1797; d/VII–5–1879) MD Castleton 1823. *Med reg NY NJ Conn* 1880: 232. *Med surg rep Phila* 41:88, 1879.

BAILEY, CHARLES, Pittsfield, Mass (b/IX–2–1821 E Medway, Mass; d/II–9–1895) MD Berkshire 1843; AB Brown 1841. *Brown hist cat*: 1841. *Cleave*. *Polk* 1886: 471. Homeopath.

BAILEY, DAVID LELAND, Carbondale, Pa (d/IV–13–1904 @53) MD UCNY 1875. *Pa med jour* 8:334, 1904/05. *Flint* 1897: 797.

BAILEY, ELISHA P , Marlborough, NY (d/V–17–1891 @ 71) MD UCNY 1848. *Med reg NY NJ Conn* 1891: 267.

BAILEY, ELISHA WILSON, Atglen, Pa; CW–USA (b/1821? d/ XII–4–1904 @ 83) MD Jefferson 1844. *Pa med jour* 8:334, 1904/05.

BAILEY, EVELYN SAMANTHA or **SAMANTHA EVELYN?** San Diego, Cal (d/XII– –1902) MD St U Iowa Homeop Dept 1883. *Pacific Coast jour homeop* 11 [?]: 1903 (Jan) *Polk* 1886: 386 (Winfield, Kans).

BAILEY, FREDERICK KINSMAN, Knoxville (d/VI–17 1876 @ 59) MD Castleton 1837. *Med rec* 11:517–518, 1876. *Med surg rep Phila* 35:40, 1876.

BAILEY, J S , Freeport, O (b/II–2–1830 Flushing, O; d/VIII–29–1875) MD Miami Med Coll 1857. *Trans O St Med Soc* 1877:63.

BAILEY, JAMES F , Cincinnati, (d/III–16–1894 @ 55) MD Miami Med Coll 1879. *JAMA* 22:482, 1893. *Polk* 1890: 898.

BAILEY, JAMES LEWIS, NYC (d/V–29–1899 @ 45) MD UCNY 1883. *JAMA* 32:1399, 1899. *Polk* 1896:1040.

BAILEY, JAMES SPENCER, Cusseta, Ala 1853–59; Mobile; Hempstead, Tex; 186_? Albany, NY; CW–CSA (b/II–25–1830 Bethlehem, NY; d/VII–1–1883 Albany) MD Albany 1860; hon MD Soulé U, Galveston, Tex. *Trans Med Soc St NY* 1884: 388–391. *Atkinson* I: 210–211. *Butler* 1874: 525.

BAILEY, SILAS, Utica, NY to 1845; Toledo, O (b/V–9–1815; d/X–16–1879) MD Berkshire 1835; ng Fairfield Med Sch. *Trans Am Inst Homeop* 1895: 1092. *Trans NY Homeop Soc* 10:635. Homeopath.

BAILEY, THOMAS HENDRICKSON, NYC (d/III–17 1900 @ 51) MD Bellevue 1869. *Bost m & s jour* 142:316, 1900. *Polk* 1886: 970.

BAILEY, WALTER, Sr, New Orleans (b/V–12–1890) MD ULa 1855. *Med vis* 6:203, 1890. *Southern jour homeop* 8: , 1890. *Polk* 1886: 415. Homeopath.

BAILEY, WHITE J , Janelew, WVa (b/IX–30–1853 Lewis Co, WVa; d/V–8–1887) MD Bellevue 1881. *Trans Med Soc W Va* 1887:500; 188:589–590. *Polk* 1886:942.

BAILEY, WILLIAM HOWARD, Albany, NY (b/XII–28–1825 Bethlehem, NY; d/VI–24–1898) MD Albany 1853. *Buff m & s jour* 38:69–70, 1898. *JAMA* 31: 141, 1898. *Trans Med Soc St NY* 1899:437–439. *Atkinson* I:203. *Butler* 1874: 541.

BAIN, CHARLES, Murphysboro, Ill (d/IX–27–1895 @ 70) Lic. yrs pract. *JAMA* 25: 595, 1895. *Polk* 1890: 341.

BAIR, JOHN B , Elizabeth, Pa (d/XI–27–1868 @ 28) MD Jefferson 1865. *Phila med red & dir* 1871: 299. *Med surg rep Phila* 19:508, 1868.

BAIRD, DAVID, Woodland Farm, Miami Co, O (d/X–26–1866 Cincinnati) MD Med Coll O 1829. *Med surg rep Phila* 15:407, 1866.

BAIRD, EDWARD MONTESQUE, Chattanooga (b/X–17–1853 Rutherford Co, Tenn; d/X–13–1878) MD Med Coll O 1878. *Tr AMA* 30:851–852, 1879. *Trans Med Soc Tenn* 1879: 176–177.

BAIRD, GEORGE, Wheeling, WVa (b/XI–30–1829 Washington, Pa; d/III–7–1891) MD UPa 1852; stud Wash & Jeff. *Med bull m & s* 13:198, 1895. *Atkinson* I:444. *Polk* 1886:945.

BAIRD, JACOB A , Dunlo, Pa (d/II–10–1902) MD CPS Balto 1878. *Pa med jour* 6:259,1902/03. *Flint* 1897: 800.

BAIRD, OSCAR HARTWELL, CW–CSA; Waverly Station, Va (b/X–7–1833 near Petersburg, Va; d/III–4–1887) MD UPa 1856. *UPa med alum CW*: 1856. *Polk* 1886:929.

BAIRD, WILLIAM FERRIL, Lexington, Ky (d/I–1–1832) Stud Transylvania 1832. *Transylvania jour med & assoc sci* 4:595, 1831.

BAIRD, WILLIAM J B , Seattle,Wash (d/XI–30–1893) MD UPa 1892. *JAMA* 21:936, 1893. *Polk* 1893:1278.

BAISLEY, ROBERT BARFE, E Rockaway, NY (d/XII–17–1898) MD CPSNY 1842. *JAMA* 32:41, 1899. *Bost m & s jour* 140:26, 1899. *Butler* 1896:541.

BAKER, ACHBOR JEHU, Grafton, WVa (d/VI–24–1901) MD UMich 1886; AB Iowa Coll 1881; AM 1884. *JAMA* 37:43, 1901.

BAKER, ALVAH H , Cincinnati (b/XI–3–1806 Chester

Co, Pa; d/VII-30-1865) <MD Jefferson 1831> *Tr AMA* 18:346,1867. *Trans Ohio St Med Soc* 1878: 262. *Med surg rep Phila* 13:133, 1865. *K & B* III:52.

BAKER, CHARLES O , Auburn, NY (b/1852; d/VII-16-1897) MD Syracuse 1874. *JAMA* 29:297, 1897. *Polk* 1886: 641.

BAKER, CLAIBORNE HENRY, CW-CSA; Seven Mile Ford, Va (d/VIII- -1885) MD UCNY 1861. *Blanton 19th cent Va*: 393. *Polk* 1886:927.

BAKER, DAVID BRYAN, Quincy, Ill (d/X- -1884) MD Rush 1870. *Med surg rep Phila* 51:697-698, 1884.

BAKER, EDWIN O , Spokane, Wash (d/IV-18-1900 @ 70) MD Castleton 1855. *JAMA* 34:1146, 1900. *Polk* 1886:956 (Menominee, Wis).

BAKER, ELIJAH P , Aurora, NY (d/VI-4-1893 @ 74) MD Geneva 1847. *Med reg NY NJ Conn* 1894: 233. *Polk* 1886:641.

BAKER, FRANK EDWIN, Newark (d/III-1-1904 @ 48) MD CPSNY 1882. *Bost m & s jour* 150:254, 1904. *Polk* 1886: 609.

BAKER, GEORGE, Chelsea, Mass (b/VII-9-1796 Dedham; d/XII-25-1852) MD Harvard 1820; AM 1816. *Palmer's Necrol Harvard alum*: 17.

BAKER, GEORGE PIERCE, CW-USA; Providence, RI (b/I-27-1826 Rehoboth, Mass; d/VIII- -1890) MD Harvard 1851; ng Amherst 1850. *Trans RI Med Soc* 4:332-337, 1889-93. *Polk* 1886:845. CW-USA.

BAKER, GEORGE RICHARD, Wilmington, Del (d/IV-28-1862) MD UPa 1836. *Tr AMA* 14:211, 1864.

BAKER, GEORGE W , Brooklyn (b/1837; d/XII-4-1898) MD CPSNY 1864; AB Union 1861. *Bost m & s jour* 139:636, 1898. *JAMA* 31:1542, 1898.

BAKER, HENRY C , Kansas City, Mo (b/IV-25-1843 Ill; d/IV-8-1895) MD St Louis Coll Med & Surg 1870. *Trans Am Inst Homeop* 1893:1092. *JAMA* 24:609, 1895. *Cleave*. *Polk* 1890:657. Homeopath.

BAKER, J E SEYMOUR, Angel's Camp, Cal (d/I-23 1889 @ 32) MD UMd 1881. *Trans Med Soc Calif* 1889: 20-211. *Polk* 1886:163.

BAKER, JAMES ERWIN, Lancaster, Pa (b/1853? NY; d/IX-29-1905 @ 52) MD Jefferson 1882. *Pa med jour* 9: 127, 1905/06. *Flint* 1897:806.

BAKER, JAMES I , Yaphank, NY (b/II-22-1829; d/V-6-1886) MD Albany 1854. *Med reg NY NJ Conn* 1887:253.

BAKER, JOHN A P , Abingdon, Va (d/XII-21-1899) MD Jefferson 1862. *JAMA* 34:62, 1900. *Polk* 1886:1485.

BAKER, JOHN W , West York, Ill (d/I-29-1906 @ 54) MD Med Coll O 1883. *Ill med jour* 9:228, 1906.

BAKER, JOSEPH C , Concord & Keene, NH; Middleboro, Mass (b/X-12-1814 Loudon, NH; d/II-23-1865) MD Hahnemann Phila 1856. *Trans Am Inst Homeop* 1893:126. *Mass Homeop Soc* 2:395, 1890. Homeopath.

BAKER, JOSEPH H , Lafayette, Ind (d/XII-6-1893 @ 37?) MD Jefferson 1877. *JAMA* 21:982, 1893. *Trans Ind St Med Soc* 1894:223.

BAKER, JOSEPH HENRY, CW-CSA; Tarboro, NC (b/XII-25-1831 Edgecombe Co, NC; d/II-12-1902) MD UPa 1854; stud UNC. *UPa alum reg* 19: 72, 1916-17. *Atkinson* I: 625. *Polk* 1886:726.

BAKER, LEANDER H , Oak Park, Ill (d/V-4-1900) MD U Louisville 1842. *Ill med jour* 50:48, 1900. *JAMA* 34:1210, 1900. *Polk* 1886:691.

BAKER, LEWIS FREDERICK, NY; CW-USA (b/1834; d/IX-6-1864 near Washington, DC) MD UCNY 1858. *Med surg rep Phila* 12:116, 1864/65. *Nat med jour* 1:290, 1870/71.

BAKER, LUCIUS WILLARD, Baldwinsville, Mass (d/XII-7-1902 @ 50) MD UCNY 1880. *Bost m & s jour* 147:688, 1902. *Polk* 1896:691.

BAKER, MARY GREEN (CRITCHETT), Middleboro, Mass; Worcester, Mass 1869-1879 (b/VII-1-1824 Epsom, NH; d/II-19-1879 or II-17-1880) MD New Engl Female Med Coll 1862. *Trans Am Inst Homeop* 1893:126. *Mass Homeop Soc* Sept 1880. Homeopath.

BAKER, MILTON HOBART, Highland Park, Ill (b/VIII-1-1826 Miller's Corners, NY; d/X-19-1893) MD Hahnemann Chic 1868. *Trans Am Inst Homeop* 1894: 257. *Polk* 1886:282. Homeopath.

BAKER, PAUL DELACY, CW-CSA; Eufaula, Ala (d/VII-6-1883 @ 55) MD Med Coll Ga 1854. *JAMA* 1:64, 1883. *Butler* 1878: 14.

BAKER, PETER, Cincinnati 1839-41; Memphis 1841-54; Warsaw, Ill 1854-62; Monmouth, Ill 1864-67 (b/IV-6-1818 Baltimore; d/II-19-1887 Kansas City, Mo) MD Hahnemann Chic 1863. *Med adv* 18:499, 1887. *Polk* 1886:550. Botanic physician; homeopath.

BAKER, PHILIP DANIEL, Franklintown, Pa (d/III-8-1898) MD UPa 1874. *JAMA* 30:745, 1898.

BAKER, PHILIP SCHAFFNER, Clifton Hill, Mo (b/X-14-1851 Evansville, Ind; d/IX-2-1901 Asheville, NC) MD Med Coll Ind 1879. *Trans Ind St Med Soc* 1902:408. *Polk* 1886:544.

BAKER, RICHARD CARSON, Brooklyn (b/Otsego, NY; d/IV-24-1901 @ 47) MD UCNY 1874. *Bost m & s jour* 144:438, 1901. *Polk* 1896: 992.

BAKER, ROBERT F , CW-USA; Moline, Ill to 1868; Davenport, Ia (b/VII-6-1831 Jefferson, Ind; d/I-28-1890) MD Bellevue 1865; att? Cleveland Homeop Med Coll *Trans Am Inst Homeop* 1890:148. *Med vis* 6:70, 1890. *NW jour homeop* 1:373, 1890. *Polk* 1886:355.

BAKER, ROLLIN T , CW-USA (d/X-19-1864) MD UCNY 1862. *Nat med jour* 1:290, 1870/71.

BAKER, RUFUS, Middletown, Conn (b/I-7-1815 Albion, Me; d/XII-27-1891) MD Columbian DC 1842. *Proc Conn Med Soc* 1892:847-849. *Butler* 1878: 72.

BAKER, SAMUEL, Baltimore (b/X-31-1785; d/X-16-1835) MD UPa 1808. *Am jour med sci* 17:548, 1836, 18:534, 1836. *Med annals Md* 310. *K & B* III:53.

BAKER, SAMUEL GEORGE, Baltimore (b/X-2-1814;

 Spec. educ'l status abbrev. as: *ng* = college verified attendance without degree;

d/VIII-1-1841) MD UMd 1835; AB Yale 1832. *Med annals Md* 310.

BAKER, SIBELIA F , Chicago (b/1841 Terry O; d/ VIII-29-1879) MD Woman's Med Coll Pa 1870. *Chic med jour* 39:558-559, 1879. *Med surg rep Phila* 41:242, 1879. *Butler* 1878:129.

BAKER, THOMAS H B , Pekin, Ind (b/IV-3-1838 Washington Co, Ind; d/VI-1-1905) MD U Louisville 1876. *Trans Ind St Med Soc* 1905:440. *Polk* 1896:486.

BAKER, TIMOTHY H , Wooster, O (d/III-5-1871 @ 50) MD Willoughby 1846. *Med surg rep Phila* 24:262, 1871. *Trans Ohio St Med Soc* 1875:193. *Butler* 1878:618.

BAKER, W C , CW-USA (d/VII-17-1865) *Nat med jour* 1:290, 1871.

BAKER, WASHINGTON HOPKINS, Philadelphia (d/ IV-1-1904) MD UPa 1875. *Pa med jour* 8:334, 1904/05. *Trans CPP* centennial vol: 210. *Polk* 1896: 1298.

BAKER, WILLIAM D , Astoria, Ore (d/VII-1-1898 @ 53) MD Bellevue 1869; MD Willamette 1868. *JAMA* 31: 366, 1898. *Polk* 1893: 1042.

BAKER, WILLIAM H , Lynchburg, Va (d/XI-27-1898) MD UMd 1881. *JAMA* 31:1490, 1898. *Polk* 1896: 1493.

BAKER, WILLIAM NELSON, Baltimore (b/I-17-1811; d/II-16-1841) MD UMd 1832. *Med annals Md*: 311.

BALDINGER, ARTHUR F , Cleveland, O (b/I-13-1864 Ravenna, O; d/VII-2-1906) MD Cleveland Homeop 1889. *Trans Am Inst Homeop* 1906:773. Homeopath.

BALDRIDGE, ALEXANDER S , CW-CSA (d/VII-27-1863) MD Jefferson 1857. *SHSP* 22:173, 1893.

BALDWIN, ABEL SEYMOUR, Jacksonville, Fla (d/XII 8-1898 @ 87/88) MD Geneva 1838. *JAMA* 31:1584-1585. *Proc Fla Med Assoc* 1899: 37-39. *Polk* 1890:253.

BALDWIN, ABRAM VAN NEST, New Brunswick, NJ (b/XI-16-1858; d/II-14-1897) MD CPSNY 1882; AB Rutgers 1879, AM. *Trans NJ Med Soc* 1897:301-302. *JAMA* 28:419, 1897.

BALDWIN, DEXTER, Saxonville, Mass; Me (b/VII-5-1798 Antrim, NH; d/V-27-1870 Framingham, Mass) MD Dartmouth 1823. *Bost m & s jour* 5:424, 1870.

BALDWIN, EDWIN CANDEE, Dover, NJ (b/1813 Southbury, Conn; d/III-29-1901) MD UMd 1844. *Med annals Md*:311. *Polk* 1893:557.

BALDWIN, ELIJAH, Canterbury, Conn (b/X-6-1820; d/ III-7-1868) MD Harvard 1845. *Proc Conn Med Soc* ns4: 253-254, 1888-1891. *Butler* 1878: 73.

BALDWIN, FREDERIC AUGUSTUS, NYC (b/I-7-1846; d/IX-21-1905) MD Bellevue 1881. *Bost m & s jour* 153:376, 1905. *Polk* 1896:1040.

BALDWIN, GARRETT ROMYNE, CW-USA; Ft Scott, Kans (b/V-13-1840 Saugerties, NY; d/III-4-1888) MD Bellevue 1866. *Trans St Med Soc Kans* 2:522-523, 1888. *JAMA* 10:379, 1888. *Atkinson* I:269. *Butler* 1897:250.

BALDWIN, HENRY RUTGERS, New Brunswick, NJ (b/IX-18-1829 NYC; d/II-3-1902) MD CPSNY 1853; AB Rutgers 1849. *Bost m & s jour* 146:184, 1902. *Atkinson* I:283. *Polk* 1896:944.

BALDWIN, HIRAM S , San Francisco (b/Pa; d/III-21-1887 @ 68) MD Pa Med Coll 1859 ad eundem. *Tr Calif St Med Soc* 1887:394-395. *Polk* 1886:170.

BALDWIN, J MARION, Dayton, NJ (d/X-2-1883) MD Jefferson 1880. *Med bull m & s* 5:257, 1883.

BALDWIN, JAMES, Danbury, Conn (b/1802 Easton, Conn; d/ 1883) MD Yale 1825. *Proc Conn Med Soc* ns3:167, 1884-87. *Atkinson* I: 52. *Butler* 1878:72.

BALDWIN, JAMES H , Hopewell, NJ (b/1798 Monmouth Co, NJ; d/V-2-1869) Lic Bd Censors Monmouth Co, NJ; ng UPa Med Sch. *Tr AMA* 21:468, 1870. *Trans Med Soc NJ* 1871:94; 1872:211.

BALDWIN, LOUIS KIMBALL, Philadelphia (b/III-27-1836; d/ -1893) MD Jefferson 1862. *Trans CPP* centennial vol:210. *Proc Phila Co Med Soc* 15:xvii-xix, 1894. *Atkinson* I: 312. *Polk* 1886:812.

BALDWIN, MILTON, E Orange, NJ (b/X-22-1821 Newark; d/II-29-1892) MD UCNY 1843. *Tr Med Soc NJ* 1892:208-209, 293-294. *JAMA* 18:340, 1892. *Butler* 1878:462.

BALDWIN, NEILSON ABEEL, CW-USA; Brooklyn (b/II-28-1839 Flatbush, NY; d/VIII-29-1906) MD Yale 1861; AB Lafayette 1858. CW-USA. *Bost m & s jour* 155:298, 1906. *Polk* 1896:902.

BALDWIN, ROBERT FREDERICK, CW-CSA; Staunton, Va (b/ VIII-16-1829 Winchester, Va; d/XI-21-1879) MD UPa 1851. *Med surg rep Phila* 41:528, 1879. *UPa med alum CW*: 1851.

BALDWIN, WILLIAM OLIVER, Washington, DC (b/ IV-9-1827 Prince Georges Co, Md; d/XII-21-1894) MD Columbian DC 1852. *Hist Med Soc DC*: 299. *Polk* 1893:268.

BALDWIN, WILLIAM OWEN, Montgomery, Ala (b/ VIII-9-1818; d/V-30-1886) MD Transylvania 1837 *JAMA* 6:643, 1886. *Trans CPP* centennial vol: 277. *New Orl m & s jour* ns14: 74-77, 1886. *Trans Med Assoc Ala* 1887: 306. *NC med jour* 17: 389, 1886; 18: 41-43, 1886. *Atkinson* I: 630.

BALFOUR, GILBERT, CW-USN; Philadelphia (b/NJ; d/XI-29-1879 @ 36) MD UPa 1865. *Med surg rep Phila* 41:506, 1879.

BALFOUR, WILLIAM THOMAS, Vicksburg, Miss (b/ III-12-1812; d/XII-12-1877) MD UPa 1834. *Tr Miss St Med Assoc* 1878:164.

BALL, ALONZO SPAFFORD, Syracuse, NY, NYC 1835- (b/II-11-1800 Keene, NH; d/XII-17-1893) Lic Lewis Co Med Soc 1825; att? CPSNY; hon MD NY Homeop Med Coll 1876. *Trans Am Inst Homeop* 1894: 257. *No Amer jour homeop* 35:132, 1894. Homeopath.

BALL, CHARLES E , Breese, Ill (d/III-3-1893) MD Cincinnati Coll Med & Surg 1865. *Trans Ill St Med Soc*

1893:58. *Polk* 1886: 256.

BALL, CHARLES DICKENS EVANS, Wilmington, Del; Boston (d/III–29–1903 @ 44) MD UMd 1880. *Bost m & s jour* 148:382, 1903. *Polk* 1886:206.

BALL, CHARLES W, New Orleans (d/1878, Grand Junction, Tenn) MD Tulane 1875. *Tr AMA* 30:852, 1879.

BALL, COLLIN, Olympia, Ky (d/XI–17–1899 @ 37) MD U Louisville 1890. *JAMA* 33:1441, 1889. *Polk* 1896:600.

BALL, DANIEL R, Albion, Ia; Nelson, Neb (d/IV–11 1892 @ 67) MD CPS Keokuk 1857. *JAMA* 18:624, 1892. *Butler* 1878: 231.

BALL, JAMES T, Colorado City, Colo (d/VII–15–1898 @ 39 near Judson, Ind) MD Cincinnati Coll Med & Surg 1883. *JAMA* 31:257, 1898. *Polk* 1886:324.

BALL, JOHN, Brooklyn (b/V– –1818; d/IV–2–1890) MD UCNY 1846. *Med reg NY NJ Conn* 1890:260; 1891:267. *JAMA* 14:624, 1890. *Butler* 1878: 528.

BALL, JOSEPH T, Rushville, Ill (d/IV–4–1895 @ 69) MD Missouri Med Coll 1878. *JAMA* 24:609, 1895.

BALL, ROBERT RANDOLPH, Cascade,Va; USA (d/X–4–1897 Washington, DC?) MD Med Coll Va 1885. *JAMA* 29:817, 1897.

BALL, STEPHEN, Boston (d/XII–21–1871 @ 69) MD Harvard 1825. *Bost m & s jour* 8: , 1871.

BALLARD, EDGAR ABBOTT, Chicago (b/III–8–1838; d/XI–9–1881) MD Hahnemann Chic 1863. *Trans Am Inst Homeop* 1893:1092. *Med vis* 7:393, 1891. *Polk* 1886:259.

BALLARD, EDWARD, River Falls, Wis (b/XI–14–1837 Fryeburg, Me; d/VIII–8–1896) MD Bowdoin 1864. *Trans Wis St Med Soc* 31:636, 1897.

BALLARD, HORACE D, Findlay, O (d/VII–19–1872) MD Cleveland Med Coll 1860. *Trans Ohio St Med Soc* 1874: 3181; 1875:193.

BALLARD, HORATIO NELSON, , Horn Lake, Miss (b/VI–10–1827 Dudley, Mass; d/I–23–1888) MD Harvard 1854; AB Brown 1851. *Brown hist cat* 1851. *Polk* 1886: 528.

BALLARD, NATHAN HEYWOOD, Richmond, Ind (b/III–24–1849 near Goshen, O; d/XII–25–1898) MD Med Coll O 1881. *Trans Ind St Med Soc* 1899:401. *JAMA* 32:92, 1899. *lint* 1896:325.

BALLARD, SILAS H, Haubstadt, Ind (b/III–26–1856; d/II–28–1885) MD Jefferson 1877. *College and clin rec* [Jefferson] 7:22, 1886. *Trans Ind St Med Soc* 1885:218. *Butler* 1878:193.

BALLOU, A B, Burnettsville, Ind (b/VII–21–1831 Orleans Co, NY; d/XII–26–1893) MD Med Coll Ind 1874. *Trans Ind St Med Soc* 1894:224. *Butler* 1878:193.

BALLOU, ARIEL, Woonsocket, RI (b/X–25–1805 Cumberland, RI; d/VII–15–1887) MD Bowdoin 1830. *Tr RI Med Soc* 3:467–471, 1883–1888. *Butler* 1878:746.

BALLOU, LUCINDA A (BULLARD), Concord, Mass (b/1835 Rowe, Mass; d/VI–13–1889) MD Boston U 1881. *New Engl med gaz* 24:336, 1889. *Med vis* 5:262, 1889. *Polk* 1886:465.

BALLOU, NEWTON HERRICK, St Albans & Burlington, Vt; Lansingburg, NY (b/1816 Sheldon, Vt; d/IX–9–1895) MD Jefferson 1839. *JAMA* 25:510, 1895.

BALLOU, WILLIAM RICE, ?Maine (b/VII–27–1864; d/III–8–1893) MD Bellevue 1886. *Med reg NY NJ Conn* 1893:296.

BALSBAUGH, GEORGE S, Forreston, Ill (d/VIII–26–1904 @ 75) MD Jefferson 1861. *JAMA* 43:749, 1904. *Polk* 1886:279.

BALSER, HENRY, Jr, NYC (d/II–14–1902 @ 62) MD UCNY 1866. *Bost m & s jour* 146:214, 1902. *Polk* 1896:1040.

BALTZELL, FRANK EMANUEL, Baltimore (b/VIII–29–1847; d/III–16–1879) MD UMd 1871; AB Princeton 1869; AM 1872. *Med annals Md*: 311.

BALTZELL, WILLIAM HENRY, Frederick City, Md (b/1832; d/IX–12/19–1899) MD UPa 1854; AB Princeton 1851. *Med annals Md*:311. *JAMA* 33:872, 1899. *Polk* 1896:670.

BANCROFT, AMOS, Groton, Mass (d/1848) MD Harvard 1811; AB 1794. *Tr AMA* 3:434, 1850.

BANCROFT, AMOS BIGELOW, Groton, Mass (b/IV–3–1811; d/1879) MD Harvard 1834; AB 1831. *Tr AMA* 32:496–498, 1881. *Atkinson* I: 165.

BANCROFT, ERASTUS, Walcottville, Conn (b/1790 Farmington, Conn; d/XI–22–1873) MD Berkshire 1854; hon MD Yale 1855. *Proc Conn Med Soc* 4:291, 1874.

BANCROFT, JESSE PARKER, Concord, NH (b/IV–17–1815 Gardner, Mass; d/IV–30–1891) MD Dartmouth 1845; AB 1841. *Bost m & s jour* 124:474, 1891. *Trans NH Med Soc* 1891:243–246. *K & B* III:55.

BANCROFT, KIRK HENRY, Lowell, Mass (d/X–16–1869 @ 31) MD Berkshire 1863. *Bost m & s jour* ns4:216, 1869.

BANER, WILLIAM JONES, NYC (b/1821 Springborough, O; d/XI–6–1885) MD NY Med Coll 1858. *Tr Am Inst Homeop* 1886:140. *NY med times* 13:280, 1885. *Cleave*. Homeopath.

BANKS, JAMES LENOX, NYC (b/V–11–1832 d/VI–3–1883) MD CPSNY 1857 *Med reg NY NJ Conn* 1884:122. *Trans Med Soc St NY* 1884:387–388. *Atkinson* I:133.

BANKS, NEHEMIAH, Wallingford, Conn (b/XI–8–1813 Bethel, Conn; d/VI–11–1890) MD Yale 1844. *Proc Conn Med Soc* 1892:850–851. *Butler* 1878: 72.

BANKS, RICHARD, Gainesville, Ga (b/1794; d/V–6–1856) MD UPa 1821. *So m & s jour* 11:375–376, 1856.

BANNAN, DOUGLASS RIDGWAY, USN (b/III–6–1832 Schuylkill Co, Pa; d/XI–16–1871 Charlestown–Mass) MD UPa 1856; AB Yale 1852. *Bost m & s jour* ns9: 10, 1872. *UPa med alum CW*:1856.

BANTA, WESTERVELT, Buffalo, NY (d/VI–17–1901)

 Spec. educ'l status abbrev. as: ***ng*** = college verified attendance without degree;

MD Niagara U 1888. *JAMA* 37:43, 1901.

BANTON, BENSON, Waterloo, Ia (b/I-20-1828 Knox, Me; d/VII-27-1894) MD Rush 1876. *Trans Am Inst Homeop* 1895:214. *Polk* 1886: 369.

BARBEE, ANDREW RUSSELL, Jr, CW-CSA; Point Pleasant, WVa (b/XII-9-1827 Hawsburg, Va; d/VIII-5-1903 Pruntytown, WVa) MD UPa 1851. *UPa med alum CW*:1851. *Atkinson* I:454. *Polk* 1886: 943.

BARBER, HIRAM, Ossining-on-Hudson, NY (d/IV-24 1905 @ 85) MD Albany 1847. *Bost m & s jour* 152:536, 1905. *Polk* 1900:1316.

BARBER, ISAAC HENRY, Brooklyn (b/1831 Florida, NY; d/II-5-1896) MD CPSNY 1851. *Bost m & s jour* 134:477, 1896. *Polk* 1886:643.

BARBER, JOHN, CW-USA; Sharon, Pa (b/III-26-1836 Canfield, O; d/IX-27-1879 Harrisville, Pa) MD UPa 1862. *Trans Med Soc Pa* 13:427-428, 1880. *UPa med alum CW*: 1862.

BARBER, JOSEPH SNELLING, Gloucester, Mass (d/X 19-1866 @ 63) MD Bowdoin 1831. *Bost m & s jour* 75:292, 1866. *Med surg rep Phila* 15:407, 1860.

BARBER, LUCIUS ISRAEL, Simsbury, Conn (b/X-7-1806; d/II-16-1889) MD UPa 1835; AB Amherst 1826. *Amherst, Men of*, 1826.

BARBER, WILLET PECHAM, Lebanon, Conn (b/VI-3-1846 S Kingston, RI; d/IV-8-1892) MD Dartmouth 1871. *Proc Conn Med Soc* 1893:239.

BARBARIN, FRANCIS ST CLAIR, Washington, DC (b/VIII-21-1832 Newport, RI? d/III-29-1900) MD Georgetown 1856. *Hist Med Soc DC*: 274.

BARBOUR, CLEMENT CLAY, Newport, Ky (b/VIII-5 1842; d/V-5-1893) MD Georgetown 1864. *Trans Med Soc Va* 1894:186-187.

BARBOUR, JAMES EDGAR, CW-USA & USN; Norwalk, Conn (b/XI- 17-1843 NYC; d/XII-6-1879) MD CPSNY 1865. *Proc Conn Med Soc* 1880:170. *Atkinson* I: 456. *Butler* 1878: 72.

BARBOUR, JOHN FORD, Louisville, Ky (b/V-25-1861 Lexington, Mo; d/I-15-1896) MD UCNY 1885. *JAMA* 26:192, 1896. *Polk* 1890: 468.

BARBOUR, PHILIP C STANHOPE, Louisville, Ky (b/IX- -1847; d/XI-14-1898) MD Jefferson 1867. *JAMA* 31:1320, 1898. *Polk* 1896:590.

BARBOUR, THOMAS, St Louis (d/VI-18-1849) MD UPa 1830. *Tr AMA* 3:436, 1850.

BARCLAY, ALEXANDER, Jr, NJ (b/I-9-1832 Scotland; d/VI-18-1865) MD Castleton 1853. *Trans NJ Med Soc* 1872:142-143; 1866: 130.

BARCLAY, DELANCEY H , Baltimore (d/VII-9-1900) MD NY Homeop Med Coll 1876. *Hahn mo* Aug. 1900. Homeopath.

BARCLAY, JOHN O'CONNER, USN (d/XII-17-1865 at sea) MD UPa 1836. *Nat med jour* I:290, 1870/71. *Tr AMA* 18:359, 1867.

BARCLAY, PETER MOIR, Newburgh, NY (b/1834 Scotland; d/II-11-1901) MD UCNY 1856. *Bost m & s jour* 144:198, 1901. *Polk* 1896:1033.

BARD, CEPHAS LYTTLE, Ventura, Cal (b/IV-7-1843 Franklin Co, Pa; d/IV-21-1902) MD Jefferson 1866. *Calif St jour med* 1:172, 1903.

BARD, SAMUEL, NYC (b/IV-1-1742; d/V-25-1821) MD Edinburgh 1765; LLD Princeton 1816. *Amer med rec* 4: 1821. *K & B* III:58-60.

BARDEN, OLIVER PARKER, Tioga, Pa (b/X-1-1839 Benton, NY; d/I-25-1892) MD Hahnemann, Phila 1868. *Trans Am Inst Homeop* 1893:1092. *Med vis* 8:187, 1892. *Hahn Mo* 27:267, 1892. *Polk* 1886:837. Homeopath.

BARDIN, ALMON Z , Philadelphia (d/XII-2-1883 @ 63) MD UPa 1844. *Med surg rep Phila* 49:707, 1883. *Butler* 1878:658. Homeopath?

BARDWELL, GEORGE A , Dixon, Ill (b/III-3-1820 NY; d/VI-28-1885) MD Willoughby 1841. *Trans Ill St Med Soc* 1886:257-258. *Butler* 1878:140.

BARDWELL, JAMES R, Peachbottom Pa (d/V-29-1870 @ 44) MD UMd 1850. *Phila med reg & dir* 1871: 305.

BARKER, ANDREW J , Tipton, Ind (b/III-1-1840 Baxter Co, WVa; d/II-4-1883) <att? CPS Indianapolis 1879> MD Med Coll Ind 1876[?] *Trans Ind St Med Soc* 1883:273. *Butler* 1878: 193.

BARKER, ARTHUR MARTIN, Buffalo (b/1850; d/XII-6-1887 MD U Buffalo 1877. *Buff m & s jour* 27:285-286, 1898.

BARKER, BENJAMIN FORDYCE, NYC (b/V-2-1817 or V-2-1818 Wilton, Me; d/V-30-1891) MD Bowdoin 1841; AB 1837. *Trans CPP* centennial vol: 277-278. *Med surg rep Phila* 15:156-158, 1866. *Proc Conn Med Soc* 1893: 229-230. *K & B* III: 60-61.

BARKER, JOHN, Brooklyn (b/VI-2-1823 Wallingford, Conn; d/1868) MD CPSNY 1852. *US m & s jour* 3:470, 1869. *New Engl med gaz* 3:179, 1868. Homeopath.

BARKER, WILIAM CALVIN, Waukegan, Ill (b/IX-26-1812 Ballston Springs, NY; d/IX-10-1891) MD Homeop Hosp Cleveland 1860. *Trans Am Inst Homeop* 1892: 209. *Med vis* 7:298, 1891; 8:14, 1892. *Polk* 1886:301. Homeopath.

BARKER, WILLIAM REEVES, Newport, Md (d/VI-22-1901) MD UCNY 1882. *JAMA* 37:126, 1901.

BARKSDALE, JAMES G , Shelbyville, Tenn (b/IX- -1801; d/II-23-1885) ng Transylvania. *Trans Med Soc Tenn* 1885: 113-115. *Butler* 1878:764.

BARKWELL, WESLEY W , Chicago (d/I-28-1901 Tucson, Ariz) MD Detroit Med Coll 1889. *Ill med jour* ns2:533, 1901.

BARLOW, SAMUEL BANCROFT, Florida, NY 1834-41; NYC 1841- (b/1798? d/II-27-1876 @ 76) ng Yale Med Sch 1822? hon MD Berkshire 1834; hon MD Cleveland Homeopathic 1853. *Trans Am Inst Homeop* 1877: 967. *Homeop times* 3:24,1876 (March). *Cleave*. Homeopath.

BARNABY, JOHN EASOM, England; Allegheny City,

Pa (b/V-20-1821 Salop, Shropshire; d/I-5-1869 Key West, Fla) MD Hahnemann 1866. *Trans Am Inst Homeop* 1893:127. *Am homeop obs* 6:200, 1869. *Tr Homeop Med Soc Pa* 1869, 1870-71, 1873. *Cleave*. Homeopath.

BARNARD, REBECCA, Worcester, Mass (d/IX-9-1905 @ 68) MD Woman's Med Coll NY Infirmary 1878? *Bost m & s jour* 153:376, 508-509, 1905. *Polk* 1896:727.

BARNDT, SOLOMON K , Arbutus, Pa (d/XII-5-1904 @ 62) MD Jefferson 1863. *Pa med jour* 8:334, 1904/05.

BARNES, ALLEN T , Bloomington, Ill (b/VI-21-1832 Bedford, Ky; d/V-21-1901) MD Ky Sch Med 1857. *Ill med jour* ns3:91, 1901. *Atkinson* I:610. *Polk* 1886:255.

BARNES, EDWARD FORREST, Claremont, NH (b/ 1850? d/VIII-28-1883) MD Bellevue 1877. *Med surg rep Phila* 49:336, 1883. *Med bull m & s* 5:240, 1883.

BARNES, GEORGE WILLIAM, Mt Vernon, O 1851-65; Cleveland to 1869; San Diego (b/XII-9-1825 Frederick Co, Va; d/II-13-1890 @ 65) MD Cleveland Homeop 1851. *Trans Am Inst Homeop* 1892:204. *No Amer jour homeop* 38:200, 1890. Homeopath.

BARNES, HORACE B , Ionia, Mich (b/VIII-15-1834 Chandon, O; d/IX-29-1899) MD U Louisville 1859. CW-USN. *JAMA* 33:927, 1899.

BARNES, JOHN PATTERSON, Mobile, Ala; CW-CSA (b/I- -1826 Suggsville, Ala; d/XII-1-1875) MD UPa 1845. *UPa med alum in CW*: 1845.

BARNES, JOSEPH DEANE, Washington, DC; USA (b/ 1845, Ft. Jessup, La; d/V-13-1882) MD UPa 1867. *Hist Med Soc DC*:289. *UPa med alum in CW*: 1867. *Butler* 1874: 90.

BARNES, JOSEPH K , USA (b/VII-21-1817 Phila; d/ IV-5-1883 Washington, DC) MD UPa 1838. *UPa med alum CW*: 1838. *Bost m & s jour* 108: 355, 379, 477-478, 1883. *K & B* III:62-63.

BARNES, JULIUS STEELE, Southington, Conn (b/II-23-1792 Tolland, Conn; d/XI-11-1870) MD Yale 1818; AB 1815. *Proc Conn Med Soc* 3:492-494, 503 ff, 1871.

BARNES, LEWIS SHERMAN, Scranton, Pa (b/c1865 Bradford Co, Pa; d/VI-18-1902) MD Jefferson 1889. *Pa med jour* 5:547, 567-68, 1901; 6:259, 1902. *Flint* 1897:834.

BARNES, ORSON, Athens, Pa; Paterson, NJ (b/1830 Baldwinsville, NY; d/VII-23-1875) MD Albany 1852. *Tr AMA* 28:622-23, 1877. *Trans Med Soc NJ* 1876: 139-140.

BARNES, WILLIAM H , Philadelphia (d/VIII-1-1894 Hackettstown, NJ) MD Hahnemann 1878. *Hahn mo* (news & advts) 30:80, 1895. *Med vis* 10: 363, 1894. Homeopath.

BARNET, OLIVER, New Germantown, NJ (d/XII-25-1809 @ 66?) *Trans Med Soc NJ* 1872:173-174.

BARNETT, BENJAMIN NEVILLE, CW-CSA (b/VIII-23-1838 Yazoo City, Miss; d/ 1861 Vicksburg) MD UPa 1860. *UPa med alum CW*: 1860.

BARNETT, ENOCH EDWARD, Crawfordsville, Ind (d/ I-23-1873 Marysville, Cal) MD UMiami 1868; UMich ng 1865-68. *Med surg rep Phila* Phila 29:18, 1873.

BARNETT, JAMES RICHARDS, Vicksburg, Miss CW-CSA (b/1837 Yazoo City, Miss; d/V- -1879) MD UPa 1853. *Tr AMA* 35:518,1882. *UPa med alum CW*: 1853.

BARNETT, JOSEPH WILLIAM, Sharon, Ga; CW-CSA (b/V- -1834 Wilkes Co, Ga; d/XII-25-1900) MD UCity NY 1860. *UCNY alum cat*: 1860.

BARNETT, NATHANIEL P , CW-USA (d/VIII-10-1863 Georgetown, DC) *Nat med jour* 1:290, 1870/71.

BARNETT, SARAH AMELIA, NYC (b/VII-28-1814; d/XII-26-1897) MD NY Med Coll Women 1865. *Tr Am Inst Homeop* 1898:48. Homeopath.

BARNEY, CHARLES G , Richmond, Va (b/1814 NYC; d/IX-15-1894) MD CPSNY 1841. *JAMA* 23:592, 1894.

BARNEY, JOHN WILLARD, Concord, NH (b/I-19-1816 St Johnsbury, Vt; d/III-4-1883) MD Woodstock 1841; MD Dartmouth 1873. *Trans NH Med Soc* 1883: 176-177. *Atkinson* I: 409.

BARNS, WILLIAM C , Marion, Ind (b/IV-22-1850; d/ VI-20-1905) MD Ohio Med Coll 1875. *Trans Ind St Med Soc* 1906:495. *Flint* 1897: 321.

BARNUM, BOLIVAR, CW-USA; Van Buren Co, Mich (b/IV-22-1826; d/XI-6-1881) MD UMich 1854. *Tr AMA* 33:519-520, 1882.

BARNUM, DAVID ALBERT, Cassville, NY (b/1845? d/ I-1-1905 @ 60) MD Albany 1865. *Trans Med Soc St NY* 1905: [362]. *Polk* 1886: 656.

BAROSS [BARROSS?] FRANKLIN RICHARDS, Attica, NY (b/1832? d/VIII-17-1896 @ 64) MD U Mich 1853. *Buff m & s jour* 36:136-137, 1896. *Polk* 1886:641.

BARR, JOHN W , Philadelphia (d/II-14-1891 @ 41) MD Jefferson 1874. *Med bull m & s* 13:188, 1895. *Polk* 1886:812.

BARR, ROBERT, Indiana, Pa (b/VIII-3-1828; d/III-1882) MD Jefferson 1854. *Trans Med Soc Pa* 14:335-336, 1882.

BARR, ROBERT NELSON, CW-USA; Columbus, O; Chattanooga, Tenn (b/X-27-1827 Columbus; d/X-13-1878) MD Starling 1854. *Tr AMA* 30:852-853, 1879. *Trans Med Soc Tenn* 1879:177-178.

BARRATT, JOHN PERKINS, Charleston & Abbeville Dist. SC (b/1795 England; d/IX-26-1859) <MD CPSNY> *Med surg rep Phila* ns3:131, 1859/60.

BARRETT, BEVERLY A, Springfield, Mo (d/VI-1-1899 @ 73) MD Missouri Med Coll 1853. *JAMA* 32: 1460, 1899. *Polk* 1896:883.

BARRETT, CHARLES B Jr, Philadelphia; Ionia, Mich 1870- (d/VI-5-1871 @ 25) MD Hahnemann Phila 1867. *Trans Am Inst Homeop* 1893:127. *Med inv* 8:527, 1871? *Amer obs* 8:357, 1871. Homeopath.

BARRETT, EDWARD BENJAMIN, Northampton,

Mass (b/X-1-1836; d/XI-24-1865) MD CPSNY 1859; AB Amherst 1858. *Amherst, Men of*: 1858.

BARRETT, FREDERICK, Duluth, Minn (d/V-17-1895) MD Jefferson 1866. *JAMA* 24:861,1895. *Polk*1890:1167.

BARRETT, HENRY AUGUSTUS, CW-USA; Concord, Mass (d/IV-6-1889 @ 70) MD Harvard 1845; AB Amherst 1844. *Bost m & s jour* 120:376, 400, 1889. *Atkinson* I: 418.

BARRETT, JOHN, Portland, Me (b/II-21-1802 Northfield, Mass; d/IV-20-1842) AM & MD Bowdoin 1824; AB 1821. *Bowdoin cat*: 1821.

BARRETT, MOSES, Ripon, Wis (b/II-26-1816 Rowe, Mass; d/XI-9-1873) MD Berkshire 1837. *Tr AMA* 25:530,1874. *Trans Wis St Med Soc* 1874:109; 1891:356.

BARRETT, PATRICK G , Scranton, Pa (b/1846 Ballycastle, Ireland; d/XII-8-1893) <MD CPS Baltimore 1883> *JAMA* 22:31, 1894.

BARRETT, WILLIAM MARSHALL, Westborough, Mass (b/X-7-1822 Townsend, Mass; d/XI-14-1906) MD Bowdoin 1846. *Bost m & s jour* 155:630, 1906.*Polk* 1896:725.

BARRINGTON, JOHN C , CW-USA (d/XI- -1866 Chelsea, Mass) *Nat med jour* 1:290, 1870/71.

BARRINGTON, SAMUEL, USN (d/IX-4-1862 @ 60) MD UPa 1822. *Tr AMA* 14:216, 1864. *Med surg rep Phila* ns8:532, 1862. *Nat med jour* 1:290, 1870/71.

BARRON, HENRY WINSTON, Brooklyn (b/1834; d/VIII-27-1872) MD CPSNY 1857. *Med reg NY NJ Conn* 1873:335. *Med surg rep Phila* 27:188, 1872.

BARRON, JAMES F , Clinton, Ga (d/I-18-1898 @ 70) MD UCNY 1852. *JAMA* 30:279, 1898. *Polk* 1896:329.

BARROW, WILLIAM, Jackson, NC (b/I-5-1821 Scotland Neck, NC; d/IV-20-1881) MD UPa 1841; AB UNC 1858. *NC med jour* 7:318, 1881.

BARROWS, ASHBEL WARD, Hartford, Conn (b/XII-3 1816; d/I-3-1896) MD Yale 1841. *Proc Conn Med Soc* 1896:317-321. *Atkinson* I: 79. *Polk* 1890:221.

BARROWS, CHARLES, Mansfield, Conn 1817-22; Decatur, NY 1822-32; Clinton, NY (b/IX-11-1793; d/IX-2-1870) Hon MD Geneva 1843; att? Yale; lic 1817. *Trans Med Soc St NY* 1872:346-348.

BARROWS, GEORGE, Taunton, Mass (b/V-12-1815 Attleborough; d/I-18-1878) MD Hahnemann Phila 1852; MD Berkshire 1846; AB Amherst 1840. *Trans Am Inst Homeop* 1878:1114. *New Engl med gaz* 13:131-32, 1878. *Trans Mass Homeop Soc* 1878-79. *Cleave*. Homeopath.

BARROWS, GEORGE T, Mansfield, Conn (d/IV-15-1855 @ 23) MD UCNY 1855. *Bost m & s jour* 52:247, 328, 1855.

BARROWS, IRA, Pawtucket, RI to 1837; Norton, Mass (b/XI-18-1804; d/X-14-1882) MD Harvard 1827; AB Brown 1824. *Trans Am Inst Homeop* 1883:147. *Am homeop obs* 20:47, 1883. *New Engl med gaz* 17:383, 1882. *Hahn mo* 17:703, 1882. *Cleave*. Homeopath.

BARROWS, LYMAN JOSEPH, Janesville, Wis (b/IV-24-1825 Cooperstown, NY; d/I-14-1895) MD U Buffalo 1848. *Trans Wis St Med Soc* 29:539, 1895. *Polk* 1886: 954.

BARROWS, RUEL, Fryeburg, Me (b/1791? d/VII-18-1857 @ 66) Hon MD Bowdoin 1848. *Bost m & s jour* 56: 527, 1857.

BARROWS, THOMAS MANNING, Providence, RI (d/1832) Hon MD Brown 1815. *Trans RI Med Soc* 1:44, 1859-77.

BARRY, JOHN SAMUEL, Vulcan, Mich (b/I-16-1853 Dane Co, Wis; d/VI-30-1883) MD Rush 1878. *Tr Wis St Med Soc* 1883: 126.

BARRY, REDMOND DILLON, Tarboro, NC; Gallatin, Tenn (b/XII-1766 Ireland; d/II-1821) <MD Dublin> *Trans Med Soc Tenn*, 1876: 78-79.

BARRY, ROBERT ALEXANDER, Brooklyn (b/X-24-1824 Phila; d/I-7-1882) MD CPSNY 1851; AB Williams 1844. *Med reg NY NJ Conn* 1882:221. *Chic med rev* 5:80, 1882.

BARRY, WILLIAM J , Baltimore (b/Md; d/XII-15-1890 Pikesville) MD UMd 1844. USA-MexWar; CW-CSA. *Med annals Md*: 313.

BARSS, JAMES RICHMOND, Malden, Mass (b/Bermuda; d/X-25-1898 @ 49) MD Harvard 1873; AB Halifax. *Bost m & s jour* 139:432, 1898.

BARSTOW, CASPER, E Hartford, Conn (b/V-13-1853 Canterbury, Conn; d/II-22-1890) MD UVt 1878. *Proc Conn Med Soc* ns4:279, 1890. *Polk* 1886: 197.

BARSTOW, DONALD McLEAN, NYC (d/VI-9-1906 @ 39) MD CPSNY 1892; AB Yale 1889. *Bost m & s jour* 154:722, 1906. *Polk* 1896:1040.

BARSTOW, GIDEON FORRESTER, Putnam, Conn; CW-USA (b/XII-23-1815 Salem, Mass; d/VI-5-1864) MD Harvard 1837; AB 1834. *Bost m & s jour* 70:388, 1864. *Proc Conn Med Soc* 1865: 154.

BARSTOW, JULIUS SUMNER, Oxford, Mass (b/III-4-1815 Sutton, Mass; d/XII-24-1839) MD Woodstock 1838. ng Amherst 1835. *Amherst, Men of*: 1835.

BARTHOLOMEW, BRADLEY, Chariton, Ia; Danville, Ind (b/X-26-1804 Charlotte, Vt; d/VII-2-1902) MD Miami Med Coll 1857. *Trans Ind St Med Soc* 1903:332. *Polk* 1896: 463.

BARTHOLOMEW, IRA HAWLEY, Lansing,Mich (b/I-4-1828 Waddington, NY; d/X-18-1889) MD U Mich 1853. *Bost m & s jour* 121:447, 1889. *Atkinson* I:579. *Butler* 1878: 367.

BARTHOLOMEW, ORLANDO D , Nashville, Tenn (d/- -1878) MD U Nashville 1876; MD Vanderbilt 1877. *Tr AMA* 30:853, 1879.

BARTHOLOW, ROBERTS, USA; Cincinnati; Philadelphia (b/XI-18-1831 New Windsor, Md; b/V-10-1904) MD UMd 1852; AB 1848; AM 1854. *Pa med jour* 8:334, 1904/05. *Trans CPP* centennial vol: 210; ser3, 26: xliii ff.

Med annals Md:313.

BARTINE, DAVID HEDDING, Merchantville, NJ (b/XI-7-1841 Morristown; d/V-3-1901) MD UPa 1862. CW-USA. *UPa med alum in CW*: 1862. *Polk* 1886:606.

BARTLESON, SAMUEL P , Clifton Heights, Pa (b/XII-27-1830 Radnor, Pa; d/I-16-1900) MD Jefferson 1854. *Pa med jour* 3:654-55, 1900. *JAMA* 34:251, 1900. *Atkinson* I:565. *Flint* 1897: 798.

BARTLETT, ABNER R , Aurora, Ill (d/XII-26-1880) MD Cleveland Homeop 1856. *Trans Am Inst Homeop* 1881:134. *Am homeop obs* 18:104, 1880? Homeopath.

BARTLETT, BENJAMIN DIXON, Cambridge, Mass (b/IX-17-1789 Concord; d/II-7-1853) MD Harvard 1813; AM 1810. *Palmer's Necrol alum Harvard*: 16.

BARTLETT, BENJAMIN WEBBER, Rowley, Mass (b/II-11-1850 Jackson, Me; d/VIII-6-1900) MD Bowdoin 1873. *Bost m & s jour* 143:276, 1900. *Polk* 1886:721.

BARTLETT, EDWARD GRIFFEN, NYC (b/Portsmouth, NH; d/VII-23-1889 @ 65 Nantucket) MD UCNY 1850. *Trans Am Inst Homeop* 1895:1092. *NY med times* 17:164, 1889. Homeopath.

BARTLETT, ELISHA, Smithfield, RI; Lowell, Mass; Kentucky, &c (b/X-6-1804; d/VII-19-1855 Smithfield, RI) MD Brown 1826. *So m & s jour* 10:574, 1855. *Bost m & s jour* 52:507, 1855; 142:49-53, 77-82, 1900. *Med annals Md*: 314. *K & B* III:65-66.

BARTLETT, EZRA, So Berwick, Me; Exeter, NH; Brooklyn (b/IX-28-1811 Warren, NH; d/VI-16-1892) MD Dartmouth 1832. *Med reg NY NJ Conn* 1893:296. *Bost m & s jour* 126:648, 1892. *Polk* 1886:591.

BARTLETT, FRANCIS DANA, So Dartmouth, Mass; (b/IV-15-1803 Kingston, Mass; d/XI-11-1888) MD Dartmouth 1824. *Bost m & s jour* 119:544, 1888; 120:28, 1889. *Polk* 1886:473.

BARTLETT, FREDERIC WILLIAM, Buffalo (d/III-17 1897 @ 71) MD NY Coll Med 1854. *Buffalo m & s jour* 36:710-711, 1897. *JAMA* 28:620, 1897.

BARTLETT, GEORGE, Somerville, Mass (d/IX-24-1864 @ 57) MD Harvard 1830; AB 1827. *Bost m & s jour* 71:188, 1864.

BARTLETT, HENRY, Boston Highlands, Mass (d/VII 20-1872 @ 72) MD Harvard 1824; AB 1820. *Bost m & s jour* ns10:76, 1872.

BARTLETT, HOMER LYMAN, Brooklyn (b/1830 Chittenden Co, Vt; d/II-3-1905 Thomasville, Ga) MD CPSNY 1855.*Bost m & s jour* 152: 176, 1905. *Polk* 1896:992.

BARTLETT, HORACE C , Lyndon, Vt; Marblehead, Mass 1865; Lynn, Mass 1866-67 (b/1838 Lyndon, Vt; d/I-18-1884 at sea) MD Hahnemann Phila 1864. *Mass Homeop Med Soc* 1884.

BARTLETT, JOHN CALL, Chelmsford, Mass (b/X-4-1808 Charlestown, Mass; d/I-13-1878 or VII-31-1831 Boston) MD Harvard 1831; AB Bowdoin 1828. *Tr AMA* 31:1011, 1880.

BARTLETT, JOHN KNOWLTON, Milwaukee, Wis (b/II-28-1816 Portsmouth, NH; d/XI-26-1889) MD Yale 1841; AB 1838. *JAMA* 13:829, 1889. *Trans Wis St Med Soc* 1891:356. *Atkinson* I:333. *Polk* 1886:956.

BARTLETT, JOHN WILLIAM, Quincy, Ill (b/X-23-1811 Barbados, WI; d/III-5-1874) MD UPa 1835. *Med surg rep Phila* 30:300, 1874.

BARTLETT, JOSIAH, Stratham, NH (b/V-3-1803 Warren, NH; d/V-6-1853) MD Dartmouth 1824. *Bost m & s jour* 51:497-498, 1854. *Trans NH Med Soc* 1854: 51-52.

BARTLETT, LEVI, Skaneateles, NY (b/X-4-1806; d/VI-22-1892) MD Dartmouth 1837; AB 1827. *Med reg NY NJ Conn* 1893:296. *Atkinson* I:210. *Polk* 1890:850.

BARTLETT, LYMAN, New Bedford, Mass (b/1807; d/1865) MD Berkshire 1833. *Tr AMA* 16:613-614, 1865. *Bost m & s jour* 72:436, 1865.

BARTLETT, RUFUS HENRY, Chicago (d/XI-21-1905 @ 50) MD Rush 1879. *Ill med jour* 8:530, 1905. *Polk* 1896:372.

BARTLETT, SHUBAEL FITCH, USA (b/1811; d/1849 Calif) MD Yale 1839; AB 1833; lic before 1841? *Tr AMA* 3:436-437, 1850.

BARTLETT, STEPHEN CHALKER, Waterbury, Conn (b/IV-19-1839 N Guilford; d/II-3-1879) MD Yale 1866. *Atkinson* I:465. *Proc Conn Med Soc* 1879: 164-165. *Butler* 1878:72.

BARTLETT, WILLIAM REED, Chicopee, Mass (d/XII-7-1879) MD Boston U Sch Med 1877. *Mass Homeop Med Soc* 1880-83; 1890 (Sept.) Homeopath.

BARTOLETTE, CHARLES, Milford, NJ (b/IV-8-1825 or IV-3-1823; d/III-10-1866) MD Jefferson 1846. *Trans Med Soc NJ* 1872:140-141; 1867:203-205.

BARTOLETTE, THOMAS MILES, Mt Pleasant, NJ; Asbury 1864-66 (b/XI-4-1827; d/IX-29-1866) MD Jefferson 1855. *Trans Med Soc NJ* 1867:205; 1872:144.

BARTON, AMY STOKES, Philadelphia (b/X-1-1841 Camden Co, NJ; d/III-19-1900) MD Woman's Med Coll, Phila 1874. *JAMA* 34:830, 1900. *K & B* III:68.

BARTON, BENJAMIN SMITH, Philadelphia (b/1766; d/XII-15-1815) MD Kiel 18 . *The Portfolio* 1(4), 1816. *Jour hist med* 26:197-203, 1971. *K & B* III:68.

BARTON, EDWARD, Philadelphia (d/XII-27-1821 Genoa, Italy) MD UPa 1815. *Phila jour med & phys sci* 5:188-192, 1822.

BARTON, EDWARD, S Orange, Mass (b/II-5-1806; d/V-7-1880) MD Woodstock 1832. *JAMA* 10:220, 1888.

BARTON, EDWARD HALL, Columbia, SC (d/IX-20-1859) MD UPa 1817; AB Dickinson 1813; AM hon 1830.*Bost m & s jour* 61:208, 1859. *Med surg rep Phila* ns3: 36, 1859/60. *K & B* II:69.

BARTON, HENRY CLAY, Philadelphia (d/III-12-1906) MD Jefferson 1896. *Pa med jour* 9:524, 1905/06.

BARTON, JOHN RHEA, Philadelphia (b/IV- -1794 Lancaster, Pa; d/I-1-1871) MD UPa 1818. *Phila med*

 Spec. educ'l status abbrev. as: ***ng*** = college verified attendance without degree;

reg & dir 1873:303. *Phila med times* 1:163, 1871. *Med rec* 5:526, 1870/71. *Med surg rep Phila* Phila 24:46, 68, 1871.*K & B* III:69.

BARTON, LYMAN, Willsboro, NY (b/IX-19-1812 Hebron, NY; d/X-20-1899) MD Dartmouth 1839; AM UVt 1869. *Tr Med Soc St NY* 1900:431. *Polk* 1886:716.

BARTON, THOMAS JEFFERSON, Zanesville, O (b/IV-15-1848 Wooster, O; d/IV-22-1896) MD Bellevue 1876. *Trans Ohio Med Soc* 1896:394-395.

BARTON, WILLIAM H , Morris Plains, NJ (d/VI-20-1902) MD UMd 1884. *Bost m & s jour* 146:706, 1902. *Polk* 1896:1485 (Abingdon, Va).

BARTON, WILLIAM PAUL CRILLON, USN; Philadelphia, (b/XI-17-1786; d/II-27-1856) MD UPa 1808; AB Princeton 1805. *Trans CPP* centennial vol:210-211. *Phila m & s jour* 5:126, 1856. *Nashville jour m & s*: 11: 371, 1856. *K & B* III:69-70.

BARTOW, CHARLES, Astoria, NY (d/X-26-1895 @ 26) MD CPSNY 1894; AB Columbia 1891. *JAMA* 25: 911, 1895.

BARTOW, CLARENCE W , NYC (b/Orange, NJ; d/XI-26-1905) MD CPSNY 1905; AB Columbia 1901.*Bost m & s jour* 153:656, 1905.

BARTRAM, THOMAS SHIPLEY, Philadelphia (d/II-2-1885) MD Pa Med Coll 1859. *Med bull m & s* 7:90, 1885.

BARWIS, FRANK TAYLOR, NYC (d/III-9-1899 @ 38) MD CPSNY 1885. *JAMA* 32:628, 1899.

BASCOMB, MARSHALL THOMPSON, Pleasant Grove, Minn; Clark, Dakota Terr (d/I-28-1899 @ 47 Rochester) MD Western Reserve 1882. *JAMA* 32: 324, 1899. *Polk* 1886: 200.

BASKERVILL, WILLIAM O , Oxford, NC; Petersburg, Va 1896- (b/VII-25-1854 Granville Co, NC; d/XI-25-1899 Boydton, Va) MD Med Coll Va 1876; Va Mil Inst 1875. *Trans Med Soc Va* 1900:322. *Polk* 1886:725.

BASKERVILLE, CHARLES, Malone's Landing, Tenn (b/VIII-19-1846; d/III- -1883) MD Jefferson 1867; U Ala 1863. *Univ Ala cat*: 161.

BASKERVILLE, ROBERT DORTCH, CW-CSA Eureka, Va (b/IX-16-1826 Waverley, Va; d/IX-2-1891) MD UPa 1846. *Trans Med Soc Va* 1892:91. *UPa med alum CW*: 1846. *Butler* 1878:823.

BASKETTE, WILLIAM TURNER, CW-CSA; Rutherford Co, Tenn; (b/X-3-1804 Fluvanna Co, Va; d/II-27-1867) MD Med Coll Ohio 1837. *Trans Med Soc Tenn* 1876:79.

BASKIN, GEORGE W , Mercer, Pa (b/I-25-1825; d/IV-1-1853) MD Jefferson 1846; AB Lafayette 1842. *Lafayette, Men of*: 1842.

BASKIN, JAMES HILLHOUSE, Buena Vista, Miss; CW-CSA (b/IV-3-1822; d/V-7-1863 Okalona, Miss) ng U Ala 1841. *U Ala cat*: 1841.

BASS, JEPTHA DOZIER, CW-CSA; Pittsburg Tex (b/X-17-1829 Warren Co Ga; d/I-7-1905) MD UCNY 1855. *Texas st jour med*: 1:242, 1906. *Polk* 1896: 1445.

BASS, SETH, Stow, Mass (b/1780? d/XII-30-1867 @ 87) MD Dartmouth 1815. *Bost m & s jour* 77: 488, 1867.

BASS, WILLIAM MOSELEY, Dedham, Mass (d/VII-21 1905 @ 95 Dorchester) MD Berkshire 1835; AB Middlebury, 1832. *Bost m & s jour* 153:128, 1905.

BASS, ZACCHEUS, Middlebury, Vt (b/1791? d/1881) Hon MD Middlebury 1829. *Trans Vt Med Soc* 1883:103.

BASSETT, JARED, Evanston, Ill (d/V-10-1905 @ 91) MD Albany 1839. *Ill med jour* 7:611, 1905.

BASSETT, MOSES F , Quincy, Ill (d/VII-11-1901 @ 81) MD Worcester 1848. *Ill med jour* ns3:141, 1901.

BASSETT, THOMAS, Kingston, NH (b/VIII-12-1797 Deerfield, NH; d/XII-1-1889) MD Dartmouth 1824. *Bost m & s jour* 121:596, 189. *Trans NH Med Soc* 1890:141-142. *Polk* 1886: 592.

BASSETT, WILSON T , Cooperstown, NY (d/X-3-1905 @ 84) MD Albany 1844. *Bost m & s jour* 153: 430, 1905. *Polk* 1896: 1017.

BATCHELDER, DANIEL HOMER, Danversport, Mass (b/1811 Londonderry, NH; d/IX-4-1890) MD Berkshire 1840. *Bost m & s jour* 123:264, 1890. *Trans RI Med Soc* 1889-1893: 245-247.

BATCHELDER, HENRY F , Danvers, Mass (b/X-10-1860 Middletown, Conn; d/II-15-1901) MD Boston U 1883. *Trans Amer Inst Homeop* 1900: 913. *Polk* 1886:469. Homeopath.

BATCHELDER, JOHN PUTNAM, NYC (b/VIII-6-1784 Wilton, NH; d/IV-7-1868) Hon MD Berkshire Med; MD Harvard 1815; AM Middlebury 1821. *Phila med reg & dir* 1871: 296. *Tr AMA* 21:432-33, 1870. *Bost m & s jour* ns1: 192, 223, 1868. *Med reg NY NJ Conn* 1868:321. *K & B* III: 72-73.

BATCHELOR, ALBERT A , Pointe Coupee, La (b/1842? d/V-3-1905 @ 63) MD Tulane 1874. *New Orl m & s jour* 57:941, 1905.

BATCHELOR, KEMP BATTLE, Baltimore (b/VI-7-1867; d/XIII-24-1898) MD UMd 1889; <att? UNC> *JAMA* 32:41, 1899. *Med annals Md*: 314.

BATE, ARTHUR EDWIN, Philadelphia (b/Birmingham, Engl; d/I-6-1899) MD Jefferson 1891. *JAMA* 32:195, 1899. *Polk* 1896:1298.

BATEMAN, BENJAMIN RUSH, Cumberland Co, NJ (b/III-4-1807; d/VII-23-1883) <MD Jefferson 1828> *JAMA* 2:333, 1884. *Trans Med Soc NJ* 1884:163-165. *Med bull m & s* 5:24, 1883. *Med surg rep Phila* 54:168, 1883>*Atkinson* I:383. *Butler* 1878:465.

BATEMAN, ELI ELMER, Cedarville, NJ (d/VII-23-1886 @ 80) MD UPa 1833. *Med reg NY NJ Conn* 1887:254.

BATEMAN, EPHRAIM, Fairfield & Downe, NJ (b/VII-9-1780; d/I-28-1829) <ng UPa Med Sch 1802/03> *Trans Med Soc NJ* 1871-73:148-152.

BATEMAN, ROBERT MORRISON, Bridgeton, NJ (b/IX-14-1836 Cedarville, NJ; d/VI-4-1878) MD UPa

att? = college list unavailable; **< >** = obit.& college list apparently contradictory...

1859. *Trans NJ Med Soc* 1878/79: 197–199. *UPa med alum CW*:1859. *Atkinson* I:253. *Butler* 1878:466.

BATES, AARON J , Kokomo, Ind (b/1843 Howard Co, Ind; d/IV–23–1906) MD Med Coll Ind 1873. *Trans Ind St Med Soc* 1906:497. *Flint* 1897:319.

BATES, DANIEL, Northfield, Vt (b/X–27–1801 Brookfield, Vt; d/VII–21–1870) MD UVt 1828. *Trans Vt Med Soc* 1883:103.

BATES, EDWARD F , CW–USA (d/III–6–1864 Washington, DC) ng U Mich 1861–62. *Tr AMA* 16:652, 1865. *Nat med jour* 1:290, 1870/71.

BATES, FRANCIS ASBURY, Marion, Ala (b/II–14–1819 Springfield, Mass; d/IV–23/29–1889) MD ULa 1843; ng Wesleyan. *Trans Med Soc Ala* 1890:218. *Polk* 1886: 136.

BATES, FRANCIS HENRY, NYC (d/II–20–1880) MD UCNY 1879. *Med reg NY NJ Conn* 1880:232. *Med surg rep Phila* 42:220, 1880.

BATES, GEORGE, Boston (b/1783?d/IV–30–1867 @84) MD Harvard 1813. *Bost m & s jour* 76:296, 1897.

BATES, GEORGE ANSON, Worcester, Mass (d/VIII–9–1885 @ 65) MD Harvard 1844. *Bost m & s jour* 113:192, 1885. *Butler* 1878:346.

BATES, GEORGE FAIRBANKS, NYC? (b/V–2–1851; d/IV–19–1882) MD Bellevue 1872. *Med reg NY NJ Conn* 1882:222.

BATES, GEORGE W , Louisville, Ky (b/II–22–1847 Fairmount, Ky; d/IV–4–1895) MD Hosp Coll Med Louisville 1878? Cecelian Coll 1869. *JAMA* 24:609, 1895.

BATES, JAMES, Yarmouth, Me (b/IX–24–1789; d/II–25–1882) MD Harvard 1813. *Trans Me Med Assoc* 1882: 514–516. *Atkinson* I:265. *K & B* III:73.

BATES, JOHN THWING, Winthrop, Me; CW–USA (b/V–11–1834 Richmond, Me; d/IV–11–1863 Port Royal, SC) MD Bowdoin 1859. *Nat med jour* 1:291, 1870/71.

BATES, JOSEPH, Canaan Four Corners, NY to 1839; Lebanon Springs, NY (b/IX–16–1804 Hampshire Co, Mass; d/V–23–1879 Chicago) MD UVt 1832; ng Castleton. *Trans Med Soc St NY*: 1880:457–460. *Atkinson* I: 478. *Butler* 1874:527.

BATES, JOSEPH NYE, Worcester, Mass (b/III–16–1811; d/II–22–1883) MD Dartmouth 1831. *Bost m & s jour* 109:617, 1883. *Butler* 1878:346.

BATES, JULIAN, CW–USA St Louis (b/I–7–1833; d/VII–20–1902) MD UPa 1855. Pa med alum CW: 1855. *Polk* 1886:560.

BATES, WOODVILLE S , St Louis (d/VIII–2–1893 Badenweiler, Germany; MD CPS Baltimore 1884. *JAMA* 21:390, 1893. *Polk* 1890:194.

BATHGATE, JAMES, NYC (b/c1825; d/IV–27–1891) MD CPSNY 1846. *Med reg NY NJ Conn* 1891:268. *Bost m & s jour* 124:372, 1891. *Polk* 1886:871.

BATTEE, JOHN SUMMERFIELD Baltimore; USA MexWar; CW–USN (b/I–24–1824; d/XI–13–1865) MD UMd 1845; AB Dickinson 1842. *Dickinson cat*: 1842.

BATTEY, ROBERT, Rome, Ga (b/XI–26–1828 Augusta, Ga; d/XI–8–1895) MD Jefferson 1857. *Buff m & s jour* 35:426, 1895. *So pract* 17:424, 1895. *Chic med rec* 9:345, 1895. *Nashville jour m & s* 79:144–45, 1896. *K & B* III:74.

BATTLE, CAMILLUS LITTLE, Rocky Mount, NC (d/1881) MD Bellevue 1879. *NC Med Soc* 1881:24. *NC med jour* 7:400, 1881.

BATTLE, JOEL DOSSY, Chapel Hill, NC (b/III–12–1828 Franklin Co, NC; d/XI–22–1858) MD UPa 1850; AB UNC 1847. *Trans NC Med Soc* 1859:10; 1860:18.

BATTLE, THOMAS WILLIAM, Columbus, Ga (d/VI–16–1889 @ 73) MD UPa 1840. *Med surg rep Phila* 61:111, 1889. *Polk* 1886: 228.

BATTLES, WILLIAM SNOWDEN, Shreve & Wooster, O (b/–12–1827 near Phila; d/VIII–9–1895) MD Starling 1852. *Trans Ohio Med Soc* 1896:393–94. *JAMA* 25: 342, 1895. *Polk* 1890: 933.

BATTS, HENRY THOMPSON, Norfolk Va 1898– (b/VIII–28–1875 Tarboro, NC; d/VII–10–1902) MD UMd 1897; ng UNC. *Trans Med Soc Va* 1903:269. *Polk* 1900: 1769.

BATWELL, EDWARD, Ypsilanti, Mich (d/XII–27–1899 @ 71) MD RCS(E) 1859. *JAMA* 34:187, 1900. *Polk* 1890: 605.

BAUER, ADOLPH, Lynn Twp, Pa 1834–48; Cincinnati (d/X–17–1867 @ 61) <MD Allentown Acad 1840> *Tr Am Inst Homeop* 1895:1092. *King* I:152, 177. Homeopath.

BAUER, LOUIS, Prussia; London; Brooklyn; St. Louis (b/1814 Stettin, Prussia; d/XI–5–1898) MD RCS(E) 1852.*Trans Minn St Med Soc* 1899:191. *JAMA* 31:1257, 1898. *Polk* 1890:670. *K & B* III: 75.

BAUER, MODESTUS, Vincennes, Ind (b/VII–12–1830 Baden, Germany; d/VI–5–1884) MD Freiburg 1859. *Trans Ind St Med Soc* 1884:223.

BAUGHMAN, JOHN T , N English, Ia (d/VIII–29–1901) MD Starling 1851. *JAMA* 37:710, 1901. *Polk* 1886: 361.

BAUGHMAN, SAMUEL, Sibley, O (d/XII–27–1893) MD Med Coll Ohio 1876. *JAMA* 22:31, 1894.

BAUSMAN, ANDREW B , Chicago (d/X–21–1902 @ 46) MD Rush 1882. *Ill med jour* ns4:425, 1902. *Polk* 1896: 372.

BAXLEY, HENRY WILLIS, Baltimore (b/VI– –1803; d/III–13–1876) MD UMd 1824; att? St Mary's Coll, Balto. *Med annals Md*: 315. *Tr AMA* 27:649–650, 1876. *K & B* III: 75–76.

BAXLEY, J BROWN, Jr Baltimore (b/IX–5–1856; d/VII–12–1892. Md UMd 1884. *Med annals Md*: 315. *Polk* 1886: 435.

BAXTER, EDWARD KELLOGG, Sharon, Vt 1874–93 (b/II–3–1840 Barton, Vt; d/V–22–1896 Boston) MD Dartmouth 1865. *Trans Vt St Med Soc* 1896:415–418. *Polk* 1886: 907.

Spec. educ'l status abbrev. as: ***ng*** = college verified attendance without degree;

BAXTER, HENRY FLICKWIR, Philadelphia (b/VI-26-1843; d/II-1-1901) MD UPa 1864; AB Central High Sch Phila 1860; AM 1865. *Pa med jour* 5:295, 1901/02. *Trans CCPP* centennial vol: 211.

BAXTER, JEDEDIAH HYDE, USA (b/V-11-1837 Strafford, Vt; d/XII-4-1890) MD UVt 1860. *Buff m & s jour* 30:317, 1890. *JAMA* 15:879, 1890. *K & B* III:76. *Atkinson* I:181.

BAXTER, JOHN SPRINGS, Macon, Ga (b/1832; d/X-12-1896) MD Jefferson 1856; AB UGa 1853. *JAMA* 27:1021, 1896. *Butler* 1878:108.

BAXTER, JOSEPH BENJAMIN, Minneapolis (b/V-10-1837 Milton, Me; d/IV-17-1872) MD Harvard 1862. *Bost m & s jour* ns11: 662, 1873.

BAXTER, MYRON LESLIE, CW-USA Derby Line, Vt (d/I-8-1895 @ 55) MD Dartmouth 1862. *JAMA* 24:136, 1895. *Bost m & s jour* 132: 72, 1895.

BAXTER, WILLIAM, Wappinger's Falls, NY (b/II-19-1805 Delhi, NY; d/VII-3-1875) MD CPSNY 1831; AB Union 1828. *Trans Am Inst Homeop* 1877:982. Homeopath.

BAXTER, WILLIAM HENRY, Wilton Junction, Ia (b/XII-28-1828 Canonsburg, Pa; d/1887) MD Keokuk 1865. *Trans Ia St Med Soc* 18:409, 1900. *Atkinson* I:471. *Polk* 1886: 370.

BAY, WILLIAM, Albany, NY (b/X-14-1773 Albany; d/1865) MD Columbia 1797. *Tr AMA* 18: 315-316, 1867. *Trans Med Soc St NY* 1866:317 ff.

BAYARD, EDWARD, NYC (b/III-6-1806 Wilmington, Del; d/IX-28-1889) MD UCNY 1844; AB Union 1825; hon MD Cleveland U Med & Surg 1851. *Trans Am Inst Homeop* 1890:129. *No Am jour homeop* 37:813, 1889. *Med vis* 5: 408, 1889. *Homeop phys* 9:437, 1889? *Cleave*. Homeopath.

BAYER, CHARLES, Allegheny City, Pa 1841?- (b/Württemberg, Germany; d/1865) <MD Tübingen> *Tr Hom Med Soc Pa* 1870/71. *King* 1:151-152. Homeopath.

BAYLES, GEORGE, CW-USA. Orange, NJ (b/1836 NY; d/XII-20-1901) MD CPSNY 1859. *Bost m & s jour* 145:726, 1901. *Polk* 1896:945.

BAYLESS, GEORGE WOOD, Louisville, Ky (d/IX-9-1873) MD UPa 1839. *NW m & s jour* 4:197, 1873.

BAYLIS, THOMAS, Brooklyn (b/IX-1-1838; d/VI-15-1880) MD UCNY 1860. *Med reg NY NJ Conn* 1881:233.

BAYLOR, JOHN CAPRON, CW-CSA. Norfolk, Va (b/II-7-1835; d/I-13-1879 Denver, Colo) MD UPa 1859. *UPa med alum CW*: 1859.

BAYLY [BAYLEY] ALEXANDER HAMILTON, Cambridge, Md (b/III-3-1814; d/III-14-1892) MD UMd 1835; ng Trinity Coll, Hartford, Conn. *Med annals Md*: 315-316. *K & B* III:77. *Polk* 1886:441.

BAYNE, JOHN WOART, Washington, DC (b/II-9-1846 Prince Georges Co, Md; d/V-17-1905) MD U Md 1868. *Hist Med Soc DC*: 326. *Polk* 1893:268.

BAYNES, WILLIAM T , Troy, NY (b/England; d/I-22-1892) MD Albany 1871. *Trans NY St Med Soc* 11:731 ff, 1894. *Polk* 1890:853.

BAYNHAM, WILLIAM, London, Engl; Essex Co, Va (b/XII-7-1749 Va; d/XII-8-1814) MCS(L), 1781. *Am jour med sci* 4:186-203, 18__. *K & B* III:77-78.

BEACH, A M , Niles O (d/IV-20-1900 @ 52) MD Starling 1891. *JAMA* 34:1144,1900. *Polk* 1896: 1205.

BEACH, ERASMUS DARWIN, New Orleans (d/VIII-6-1902) MD Med Coll Ohio 1842. *New Orl m & s jour* 55:194, 1902. *Polk* 1896: 61.

BEACH, JAMES S , Chicago (b/II-24-1826; d/V-16-1885) MD Homeop Med Coll Cleveland 1857; ng Rush. *Am homeop obs* 21:95, 1885. *Med vis* 2:196, 285, 1886. *Butler* 1878:125. Homeopath..

BEACH, JOHN C , Springfield, Mass (d/VII-23-1901 St Louis) MD Berkshire 1845. *JAMA* 37:342, 1901.

BEACH, JOHN NOBLE, W Jefferson O (b/I-27-1829 Madison Co, O; d/VII-17-1897 Chattanooga) MD Starling 1850. *JAMA* 29:252, 349-50, 1897. *Atkinson* I:407. *Polk* 1896:1221.

BEACH, ROLLIN E , Vandalia, Ill (d/I-23-1901) MD Missouri Med Coll 1872. *Ill med jour* ns2:533, 1901. *Polk* 1886:300.

BEACH, SAMUEL, Fairfield Co, Conn (d/1853) MD Yale 1826. *Proc Conn St Med Soc* 1854: 19.

BEACH, SAMUEL E , CW-CSA (d/XI-4-1863 Nashville, Tenn) *Nat med jour* 1:290, 1870/71.

BEACH, THOMAS, CW-USA (d/III-2-1865 Dodgeville, Wis) *Nat med jour* 1:290, 1870/71.

BEACH, WILLIAM MORROW, London, O (b/V-10-1831 Amity, O; d/V-6-1887) MD Starling 1853. *Tr O Med Soc* 1877:236-37. *JAMA* 9:351-352, 1887. *Butler* 1878: 619.

BEACH, WILLIAM T , Minersville, Pa (d/IV- 18-1904 @ 64) MD Jefferson 1863. *Pa med jour* 8:334, 1904/05. *Flint* 1897:810.

BEADLE, EDWARD LANGDON, Poughkeepsie, NY (b/1808; d/IV-5-1882) MD CPSNY 1829. *Med reg NY NJ Conn* 1882: 222. *Chic med rev* 5:230, 1882.

BEAHAN, HERMAN SCOFIELD, Rochester, NY (d/X-2-1898) MD CPSNY 1882. *JAMA* 31:942, 1898. *Polk* 1896: 1093.

BEAKES, GEORGE M , CW-USA; Bloomingburg, NY (d/VI-16-1900 @ 69) MD Albany 1856. *JAMA* 34: 1645, 1676, 1900. *Polk* 1896: 990.

BEAKLEY, GEORGE, Fonda, NY (b/1817? d/III-7-1879 @ 62) MD Albany 1850; ng Fairfield 1839-40. *Tr Am Inst Homeop* 1895: 1092. *Homeop times*7:47, 1879?

BEAKLEY, JACOB, Schoharie Court House, NY to 1839; Albany to 1842; NYC to 1853 & after 1860; Phila. 1853-60 (b/Sharon Springs, NY; d/VII-6-1872 Peekskill, NY) MD Fairfield 1834. *Trans Am Inst Homeop* 1893:127. *NY jour homeop* 1:140, 1872? Homeopath.

BEAL, GEORGE W German Gulch; Butte City, Mont

(d/VI-8-1901) MD Med Coll Ohio 1863. *JAMA* 37:43, 1901. *Polk* 1886:573.

BEAL, LEVI C , Uniontown, Pa (b/Ireland; d/X-29-1902) MD Western Reserve 1884. *Pa med jour* 6:259, 1902/03. *Flint* 1897:838.

BEALE, EDMUND, Philadelphia (d/VI-1-1901 @81) MD *Pa med jour* 5:295, 1901/02. *Polk* 1896:1298.

BEALE [BEALL?], JAMES SHIELDS, Washington, DC (b/XI-14-1841; d/II-12-1884) MD Georgetown 1869. *JAMA* 2:614, 1884. *Hist Med Soc DC*: 300-301. *Butler* 1878: 92.

BEALE, JOSEPH, Jr, USN 1837-76; Philadelphia (b/XII-30-1814 Phila; d/IX-22-1889) MD UPa 1836; AB 1832. *JAMA* 13:505, 1889. *Med surg rep Phila* 61: 392,1889. *Med annals Md*: 316. *Atkinson* I:165. *UPa med alum CW*: 1836.

BEALE, PHILIP W , Camden, NJ (d/VI-7-1904 @ 47) MD Jefferson 1876. *JAMA* 43:61, 1904. *Polk* 1886: 601.

BEALE, STEPHEN T , Philadelphia (b/1814 Sussex, Engl; d/XII-14-1899) MD Jefferson 1847. *JAMA* 33:1632, 1889. *Polk* 1896: 1298.

BEALES, JOHN CHARLES, Mexico City c1830- ; NYC (b/III-20-1804 Norfolk Co, Engl; d/VII-25-1878) <MRCS(E) 1838>; lic Proto Medicato Mexico; <MD Coll Phys Madrid> *Med reg NY NJ Conn* 1879:187. *Med surg rep Phila* 16:39-21, 1867.

BEALS, HIRAM F , CW-USA (d/1864 @ 29 Dowagiac, Mich) ng UMich Med Sch 1853-54. *U Mich cat*: 616.

BEAN, BENJAMIN HURST, Cherry Valley, Ill (d/VI-18-1899) MD Rush 1877. *JAMA* 32: 1460, 1899. *Polk* 1896: 438.

BEAN, CHARLES THOMAS, Chelsea, Mass; CW-USA (b/1823 Me; d/XI-24-1890 @ 67) MD Bowdoin 1860. *JAMA* 15: 880, 1890.

BEAN, DANIEL HURD, Mendota & Chicago, Ill (d/VII-17-1901) MD Rush 1886. *Ill med jour* ns3:327, 1901. *Polk* 1896:429.

BEAN, LUTHER CUMMINGS, Waukegan, Ill (b/XII-13-1820 Sanbornton, NH; d/II-20-1905) MD Woodstock 1849; Hon MD Dartmouth 1868. *Ill med jour* 7:302, 1905. *Polk* 1896:445.

BEANE, FRANK DUDLEY, NYC (b/XI-1-1851; d/I-6-1894) MD Columbian DC 1871. *Med reg NY NJ Conn* 1894:233.

BEANE, GEORGE WASHINGTON, Bainbridge, Pa (b/II-22-1839 Hagerstown, Md; d/VII-15-1895) MD Jefferson 1866. *Trans Med Soc Pa* 27:372-73, 1897. *Butler* 1878:703.

BEANE, WILLIAM H , Middletown, Pa (d/XI-8-1899) MD Jefferson 1862. *JAMA* 33:1441, 1899. *Polk* 1896:1291.

BEARD, CORNELIUS, New Orleans; Brookline, Mass (d/V-29-1906 @ 70) MD Tulane 1849. *New Orl m & s jour* 59:86, 1906. *Polk* 1890:534.

BEARD, FERDINAND W , Vincennes, Ind (b/II-7-1835 Harrison Co; d/II-11-1891) MD Bellevue 1867; ng Rush. *Trans Ind St M S* 1891:283. *Butler* 1878: 193.

BEARD, GEORGE MILLER, NYC (b/V-8-1839; d/I-23-1883) MD CPSNY 1866; AB Yale 1862; AM 1867. *Med reg NY NJ Conn* 1883: 218. *Bost m & s jour* 108:116,325-326,1883. *Atkinson* I:138. *K & B* III:80-81.

BEARD, HENRY C , Lucasville, O (b/XII-21-1839 Middlebrook, Va; d/VIII-21-1895) MD Cincinnati Coll Med & Surg 1869. *Trans Ohio Med Soc* 1896:395-96.

BEARD, THEODORE EDWARD, New Haven, Conn (d/I-1-1906 @ 39) MD Yale 1897. *Proc Conn Med Soc* 1906:300.

BEARDSLEY, GROVE S , USN; Syracuse, NY (d/III-7-1906 Atlantic City, NJ) MD UCNY 1859. *Bost m & s jour* 154: 308, 1906.

BEARDSLEY, LUCIUS NICHOLS, Milford, Conn (b/X 8-1814 Monroe, Conn; d/XI-22-1880) MD Yale 1838. *JAMA* 2: 276-77, 1884. *Proc Conn Med Soc* 1880: 215-18. *Bost m & s jour* 103:551, 1880. *Atkinson* I: 415. *Butler* 1878:73.

BEARDSLEY, SHELDON, No Bradford, Conn (b/1803 Trumbull, Conn; d/I-26-1872) MD Yale 1831. *Proc Conn Med Soc* 4:153, 1872.

BEARDSLEY, WELLS, Litchfield Co, Conn (b/1782? d/IV-5-1860 @ 78) Hon MD Yale 1839. *Proc Conn Med Soc* 1:67 (appendix) 1860?

BEASLEY, ALFRED, Ripley, O 35 yrs (d/1868 Peoria, Ill) MD Med Coll Ohio 1826. *Phila med reg & dir* 1871: 296. *Med surg rep Phila* 18:420, 1868.

BEATTIE, ROBERT FOWLER, Brookline, Mass (d/VIII-6-1905 @ 35) MD McGill 1898. *Bost m & s jour* 153: 178, 1905. *Polk* 1900:892.

BEATTIE, STEPHENS RITTENHOUSE, Winchester, Va; Rochester, NY; Washington, DC (d/III- -1830) MD Transylvania 1828. *Transylvania jour med & assoc sci* 3:296, 1830. *Med annals Md*: 317.

BEATTY, DOUGLASS P , Tuscaloosa, Ala; Kennesaw, Ga (d/XI-26-1903) MD UCNY 1857. *UCNY med cat*: 1857. *Polk* 1886: 140.

BEATTY, GEORGE DOBBIN, Baltimore (b/XI-30-1937; d/X-19-1877) MD UMd 1863. *Med annals Md*: 316. *Butler* 1874: 310.

BEATTY, WILLIAM GIBBS, Whistler, Ala (b/I-9-1849; d/IX- -1889) MD Atlanta 1870; ng? UAla 1865. *Trans Med Soc Ala* 1890:218. *Polk* 1886: 141.

BEAUMONT, GEORGE HARRISON, Philadelphia (d/III-14-1870 @ 51) MD UPa 1843. *Phila med reg & dir* 1871: 294.

BEAUMONT, GODFREY N , Dallas & Austin, Tex (d/VIII-4-1905 @ 65 Winfield, Kans) MD U Louisville 1865. *Tex st jour med* 1:119, 1905/06. *Polk* 1886:863.

BEAUMONT, JOHN N , Joliet, Freeport, Ill 1864- (b/II 12-1818 Champlain, NY; d/II-24-1882 @ 64) MD Hahnemann, Chic 1864. *Trans Am Inst Homeop* 1893: 126. Homeopath.

 Spec. educ'l status abbrev. as: ***ng*** = college verified attendance without degree;

BEAUMONT, WILLIAM, USA; St. Louis (b/IX-21-1785 Lebanon, Conn; d/IV-25-1853) Lic 3d Med Soc Vt c1812; Hon MD Columbian, DC 1833. *Buffalo med jour* 9:191, 1853. *So m & s jour* 9:440, 1853. *Bost m & s jour* 48:388, 1853. *Memphis med rec* 2:47, 1853. *K & B* III: 82-85.

BEAUMONT, WILLIAM SHEPHERD, Jamaica Plain, Mass (d/I-7-1897 @ 31) MD Harvard 1892. *Bost m & s jour* 136:48, 1897.

BEAVER, LLEWELLYN D , Reading, Pa (d/V-2-1899 @ 84) MD Pa Med Coll 1841. *JAMA* 32:1074, 1899. *Polk* 1886:832.

BECK, CHARLES FREDERICK, Philadelphia (d/II-13 1859 Rome, Italy @ 53) MD & AM UPa 1827; AB 1823. *Med & surg rep Phila* ns2:51, 1859.

BECK, CHARLES SIDLES [SEIDLER?], Wilkes-Barre, Pa (d/XII-25-1905) MD Pa Med Coll 1853. *Pa med jour* 9:672, 1905/06.

BECK, CHARLES SIDLES, Jr, Renovo, Pa; W Superior, Wis (b/X-8-1860 Wilkes-Barre, Pa; d/IX-2-1895) MD UPa 1886. *Trans Wis St Med Soc* 30:550-52, 1896. *Polk* 1890:1012.

BECK, CHARLES THOMAS, NYC (b/XII-21-1849; d/VIII-29-1882) MD UCNY 1877. *Med reg NY NJ Conn* 1883:220.

BECK, ELIAS W H , Delphi, Ind (b/I-18-1822 Lewistown, Pa; d/X-6-1888) MD UCNY 1848. USA MexWar & CW. *Trans Ind St Med Soc* 1889:211. *Atkinson* I:136-137.

BECK, FRANK AMANDUS, NYC (b/VII-1-1851 Württemberg, Germany; d/III-23-1883) MD CPSNY 1876; Coll Pharm NY 1872. *Med reg NY NJ Conn* 1883:220.

BECK, GEORGE A , Flemington, Pa (b/VI-8-1853 Jacksonville, Pa; d/XI-14-1904) MD UPa 1875. *Pa med jour* 8:126, 334, 1904/05. *Flint* 1897: 802.

BECK, JOHN BRODHEAD, NYC (b/IX-18-1794 Schenectady; d/IV-1851 Rhinebeck, NY) MD CPSNY 1817; AB Columbia 1813. *Buff m & s jour* 6:760, 1851. *K & B* III:85-86.

BECK, JOSEPH REINMUND, Fort Wayne, Ind (b/III-19-1843; d/XII-30-1880) MD UPa 1866. *Tr AMA* 33:520, 1882. *Kemper*: 238-39. *Trans Ind St Med Soc* 1881:243. *Atkinson* I: 522-23.

BECK, THEODORE D F , ?Pa (d/XI-30-1880) MD Jefferson 1877. *Med bull m & s* 3:18, 1881.

BECK, THEODORE ROMEYN, Albany (b/VIII-11-1791 Schenectady; d/XI-19-1855) MD CPSNY 1811; AB Union 1807. *Buff med jour* 11:48, 1855. *Med & surg jour Phila* 4:191, 1855. *Bost m & s jour* 53:375, 382-387, 1856. *K & B* III:86-87.

BECKER, ALFRED NAUMAN, Schaefferstown, Pa (d/IX-22-1902) MD Jefferson 1896. *Pa med jour* 6: 259, 1902/03.

BECKES, LYMAN MARSHALL, Vincennes, Ind (b/VII 26-1862 Knox Co; d/V-26-1904) MD Med Coll Ind 1887. *Trans Ind St Med Soc* 1905:441. *Polk* 1896: 495.

BECKETT, JAMES, Chicago 1891- (b/1854 England; buried I-18-1899) MD UCNY 1883. *JAMA* 32:195, 1899.

BECKWITH, JOSIAH G , Litchfield, Conn (b/IX-12-1803 Stamford, NY; d/III-21-1871) MD Fairfield 1829.*Proc Conn Med Soc* 3:503, 1871.

BECKWITH, ROBERT MONROE, CW-CSA (d/1863 Chattanooga) MD UCNY 1860. *UCNY med cat*: 1860.

BECKWITH, SETH R , Norwalk, O 1851; Cleveland; Cincinnati 1871- (b/XI-22-1830 Huron Co; d/I-20-1905) MD Western Coll Homeop O 1853. *Trans Am Inst Homeop* 1905:840-41. *Ohio m & s rep* 5:62, 1871. Homeopath.

BECKWITH, T STANLEY, Petersburg, Va (d/VIII-22 1884 @ 71) MD Jefferson 1836. *Trans Med Soc Va* 1884:8.

BECTON, FREDERICK EDWARD, Rutherford Co, Tenn; Murfreesboro; Mississippi (b/X-7-1801 Craven Co, SC; d/VI-30-1838) MD UMd 1823; ng Transylvania Med Coll. *Trans Med Soc Tenn* 1876:79.

BEDELL, RIGMALD HEBER, NYC (b/VII-12-1847; d/III-6-1892) MD NY Hom Med Coll 1873; ng Bellevue, att? Columbia Coll. *Trans Am Inst Homeop* 1895: 1092. *Med vis* 8:187, 1891. *Polk* 1886: 671. Homeopath.

BEDFORD, FREDERICK, NYC (d/XII-28-1891 @ 54) MD UCNY 1859. *Med reg NY NJ Conn* 1892:272. *JAMA* 18:82, 1892. *Bost m & s jour* 125: 720, 1891. *Trans Med Soc St NY* 1892: 495. *Butler* 1878:506.

BEDFORD, GUNNING S , NYC (b/1806 Baltimore; d/IX-5-1870) MD Rutgers 1829; AB St Mary's Coll 1825. *Med reg NY NJ Conn* 1871: 345. *Chic med jour* 27:629, 1870. *Bost m & s jour* ns6:176, 1870. *K & B* III: 17-88.

BEDFORD, HENRY MOORE, Richfield Springs, NY (d/IX-20-1880) MD UCNY 1854; AB Columbia 1851. *Med reg NY NJ Conn* 1881: 234.

BEEBE, ARTHUR APPLETON, Boston (d/III-16-1900 @28) MD Harvard 1898; AB 1894. *Bost m & s jour* 142:316, 1900.

BEEBE, CASPER VOLNEY, Superior, Wis (d/I-8-1896 @ 54) MD U Mich 1870. *JAMA* 26:192, 1896. *Polk* 1890: 1174.

BEEBE, CLARENCE EDWIN, CW-USA, NYC (b/I-4-1839 or VI-4-1849!; d/III-1 or 14-1900) MD UCNY 1873; AB Yale 1871. *Bost m & s jour* 142: 288, 1900. *Trans Am Inst Homeop* 1900: 829. Homeopath.

BEEBE, ELEAZAR W , Elizabeth, Ill (d/VIII-25-1900) MD Northwestern 1867. *Ill med jour* ns2:237, 1900. *Polk* 1886:278.

BEEBE, ELLEN O , Chicago (d/XII-30-1904 @ 55) MD Hahnemann Chic 1879. *Ill med jour* 7:242, 1905. *Polk* 1896: 372. Homeopath.

BEEBE, FRANK D , CW-USA; Hamilton, NY (d/IV

21–1893 @ 62) MD UCNY 1854. *Trans Med Soc St NY* 1895: 369. *Polk* 1886: 663.

BEEBE, GAYLORD D , CW–USA; Chicago (b/V–28–1835 Newark, NY; d/IV–11–1877) MD Hahnemann Phila 1857; ng Albany 1855–56.*Trans Am Inst Homeop* 1895:1092. *US med invest* 5:414, 446, 1877. *Med vis* 2: 281, 1886. *Cleave*. Homeopath.

BEEBE, JAMES ADDISON, Detroit; Pierce Co, Wash (d/IX–26–1898 Tacoma) MD UMich 1880. *Trans Med Soc St Washington* 9:87, 1898. *Polk* 1886:487.

BEEBE, NELSON DUDLEY, Freeport, Ill (b/VII–26 1832 Adrian, Mich; d/XII–22–1872) MD UVt 1857; ng Castleton 1854. *Trans Am Inst Homeop* 1875:805. Homeopath.

BEEBE, RICHARD, Alford, Mass (d/X–20–1896 @ 72) MD Berkshire 1854. *JAMA* 27:1021, 1169, 1896. *Polk* 1896: 688.

BEEBE, SENECA, McDonough, NY 1845–1859; Marathon, NY 1861?– (b/V–25–1816; d/XI–10–1881) MD Geneva 1844. *Trans Med Soc St NY* 1882: 347–350.

BEECH, JOHN HENRY, Coldwater, Mich (b/IX–24–1819 Gaines, NY; d/X–17–1878) MD Albany 1841. *Tr AMA* 30:805–08, 1879. *Mich med news* 1:220, 231, 243, 1875. *Atkinson* I:55. *K & B* III:88.

BEECHER, ABRAHAM CLIFFORD WOLF, Philadelphia (b/III–26–1859? Bainbridge, Pa; d/XI–7–1893) MD Jefferson 1867. *JAMA* 21:784, 1893. *Butler* 1878:682.

BEECHER, HARRIS H , USA? (d/VII–14–1889 @ 69) MD Castleton 1846. *Med reg NY NJ Conn* 1890: 261.

BEECHER, JOSIAH HALL, New Haven, Conn (b/1825 Barkhamstead, Conn; d/III–14–1873) MD Yale 1846. *Proc Conn Med Soc* 4:225, 1873.

BEEKMAN, JOHN CULVER, NYC (d/IX–28–1906 @ 48) MD UCNY 1882. *Bost m & s jour* 155:426, 1906. *Polk* 1896:1041.

BEEMAN, PAUL, Sidney, O (d/IV–12–1899 Carysville) MD Ecl Med Inst O 1873. *JAMA* 32:956, 1899. *Polk* 1886:768.

BEERS, FRANK , Bushkill, Pa (d/X–29–1906 @ 47) MD Jefferson 1881. *Pa med jour* 10: 118, 1906/07. *Flint* 1897:797.

BEERS, GEORGE HALL, NYC (d/III–6–1903) MD CPSNY 1891. *Bost m & s jour* 148: 356, 1903. *Polk* 1896: 1023.

BEERS, JOHN E , Danby, NY (d/XII–4–1901 @ 61) MD Georgetown 1864. *Bost m & s jour* 145: 664, 1901. *Polk* 1896:1018.

BEERS, TIMOTHY PHELPS, New Haven, Conn (b/XII–25–1789; d/IX–22–1858) MD Yale 1824; AB 1808; ng UPa Med Sch. *Tr AMA* 13:797–98, 1860. *Am jour med sci* ns27: 283, 1859. *Proc Conn St Med Soc* 1859: 19, 85–89. *Bost m & s jour* 59:188, 1859.

BEESLEY, THEOPHILUS ELMER, Philadelphia (b/XII–5–1796; d/X–17–1867) MD UPa 1819. *Tr AMA* 21:458, 1870. *Trans Med Soc St Pa* 1868:164–65.

BEGEL, CHARLES EPHRAIM, Jackson, Mich (d/II–3–1901) MD UMich 1876. *Ill med jour* ns3:142, 1901.

BEHANE, JEREMIAH, Braddock, Pa (d/XI–22–1906) <MD RCS(Dublin) 1894>*Pa med jour* 10:295, 1906/07. *Flint* 1897:796.

BEIDELMAN, ABRAHAM C , Bedminster, Pa (d/I–19–1868 @ 46) MD Jefferson 1865. *Phila med reg & dir* 1871:295. *Tr AMA* 21:458, 1870. *Trans Med Soc St Pa* 1868:82.

BEIDLER, DANIEL, Bridgeport, Pa (d/XI–27–1872 @ 57) MD Pa Med Coll 1845 & 1850. *Med surg rep Phila* 27:506, 1872; 28:778, 1873.

BELCHER, CALEB, Cumberland, RI (b/II–2–1800 Wrentham, Mass; d/IV–7–1875) MD Harvard 1827; AB Brown 1823. *Brown hist cat*: 1823.

BELCHER, ELISHA R , NYC (b/1792? d/III–19–1860 @ 68) MD unknown. *Med surg rep Phila* ns3:590, 1859/60. *Med reg NY NJ Conn* 1862: 153.

BELCHER, GEORGE ELISHA, NYC; Portchester, NY (b/II–17–1818 Greenwich, Conn; d/XI–1–1890) MD CPSNY 1839. *Trans Am Inst Homeop* 1891: 86. *Med vis* 7:48, 1891. *No Amer jour homeop* 38:846, 1890; 39:60 ff, 1891. *Polk* 1886:671. *Cleave*. Homeopath.

BELDEN, BENJAMIN, NYC (b/IX–22–1797 Wilton, Conn; d/V–6–1877) MD unknown *Med reg NY NJ Conn* 1878: 178.

BELDEN, EBENEZER BANKS, NYC (b/VIII– –1820? d/VIII–20–1888) MD Yale 1847; AB 1841. *Med reg NY NJ Conn* 1889:268.

BELDEN, JAMES GRIDLEY, New Orleans; Mobile, Ala 1846–47 (b/IX–22–1822 Moscow, NY; d/VII–6–1896) MD CPSNY 1846. *Hahn mo* 31:112–13, 1891 (news & advt) *Polk* 1886: 415. Homeopath.

BELDEN, OLIVER STOUGHTON, CW–USA (b/ VI–18–1832 Salem, NJ; d/X–26–1904 Camden) MD UPa 1858; AB Princeton, 1853. *UPa med alum CW*: 1858. *Polk* 1886:601 (Camden)

BELDEN, RUFUS, Amherst, Mass (b/I–26–1809 Whately; d/IV–29–1870) MD Berkshire 1834; AB Amherst 1833. *Phila med reg & dir* 1871: 305.

BELDING, ALVIN, Ravenna, O (b/1812 Randolph, O; d/II–25–1880) Hon MD Starling 1852. *Trans O St Med Soc* 1880: 119–121.

BELFIELD, RICHARD ALEXANDER, Richmond Co, Va (b/V–1–1832; d/IV–24–1885) MD Med Coll Va 1854. *Trans Med Soc Va* 1885:280. *Butler* 1878: 823.

BELL, ALBERT WELLS, Moodus, Conn (b/IX–10–1852 Killingworth, Conn; d/II–11–1889) MD UCNY 1873. *Proc Conn Med Soc* ns4:264–265, 1888–91.

BELL, AURELIUS EATY, CW–USA; Zanesville, O (b/XI–19–1824 Middleway, Va; d/I–15–1897) MD Jefferson 1849. *Trans O St Med Soc* 1897: 419–421. *Atkinson* I:393.

BELL, CHARLES, Concord, NH (d/I–29–1856 @ 22) MD UPa 1854; AB Brown 1853. *Bost m & s jour* 54:107,

1856. *Trans NH Med Soc* 1856:7.

BELL, CYRUS, Feeding Hills, Mass (b/VI-14-1813; d/1882) MD Berkshire 1839. *JAMA* 1:160, 1883. *Bost m & s jour* 107:312, 618, 1882. *Butler* 1878:346.

BELL, EDWIN R , Ripley, O (d/II-24-1900 @ 72) MD Jefferson 1855. *JAMA* 34: 702, 1900. *Polk* 1896: 1209.

BELL, F P , Naples, NY (d/III-12-1898 @ 39) MD Cincinnati Coll Med & Surg 1889. *JAMA* 30: 745, 1898. *Polk* 1896: 1033.

BELL, HARRY ALBERT, Butler, Pa (d/IX-17/21-1902 Tucson, Ariz) MD UPa 1897. *Pa med jour* 6:27, 259, 1902/03.

BELL, HENRY W , Peekskill, NY 1857; Mt St Clemens, Mich 1862- (b/c1800; d/VII- -1863 @ c63) <ng Boston U Med Sch> *Med surg rep Phila* 10: 216, 1863. *Trans Am Inst Homeop* 1870: 634. Homeopath.

BELL, JAMES, Olathe, Kans (b/Washington, Pa; d/I-13-1893 @ 67) MD Jefferson 1864. *JAMA* 20:223-224, 1893. *Chic med rec* 5: 225, 1893.

BELL, JAMES JOHNSTON, Chicago (d/XI-4-1902 @ 41) MD Rush 1886; BS unknown. *Ill med jour* ns4:425, 1902. *Polk* 1896:372.

BELL, JOHN, Philadelphia; Cincinnati (b/1796 Ireland; d/VIII-19-1872) MD UPa 1817. *Trans CPP* cent vol: 211. *Trans Med Soc St Pa* 10:746-50, 1875. *Phila med reg & dir* 1873: 303. *Med surg rep Phila* 27:188, 217-220, 1872. *K & B* III: 89-90.

BELL, JOHN, CW-USA; Chester, NH (b/VII-19-1831; d/XI-13-1883) MD UPa 1854; AB Dartmouth 1852. *UPa med alum CW*: 1854.

BELL, JOSEPH G , USN (d/I-24-1870 Mobile, Ala) MD Jefferson 1864. *Phila med reg & dir* 1871: 303.

BELL, LUTHER VOSE, Londonderry, NH 1827-37; Boston 1837-1855; CW-USA (b/XII-20-1806 Francistown, NH; d/II-11-1862 Budd's Ferry, Va) MD Dartmouth 1826; AB Bowd 1823. *Tr AMA* : 14: 215, 1864. *Bost m&s j* 66:69-74, 91, 95, 1862. *Tr NH M S* 1862: 67. *N H j m* 4:93-99, 1855. *Nat m j* 1:291, 1870/71.

BELL, ROBERT, Medway, Mass (b/VII-4-1845 England; d/VII-4-1902 Roxbury) MD Harvard 1884. *Bost m & s jour* 147:58, 1902. *Polk* 1896:718.

BELL, SYLVESTER D , Millerstown, Pa (b/VI-30-1847 Brady's Bend, Pa; d/I-14-1902 Tucson, Ariz) MD Cleveland Med Coll 1874. *Pa med jour* 5: 276, 1901/02. *Atkinson* I: 552. *Flint* 1897: 797.

BELL, THEODORE STOUT, Louisville, Ky (b/1807 Lexington; d/XII-28-1884) MD Transylvania 1832. *New Orl m & s jour* ns12:577, 1885. *Med bull m & s* 7:25, 29, 1884. *K & B* III:91-92.

BELL, WILLIAM, Xenia, O (b/1799? d/X-11-1869 @ 70) MD Middlebury 1824 [?] *Bost m & s jour* 4:268, 1869.

BELL, WILLIAM CAMPBELL, Austerlitz, NY; Housatonic, Mass 1850-56; Middletown, Conn (b/IX-6-1806 Chester, Mass; d/VIII-12-1894 Blandford, Mass) MD Berkshire 1833; ng Woodstock. *Trans Am Inst Homeop* 1895: 214. *Polk* 1886: 193. Homeopath.

BELLAMY, CHARLES EDWARD, Marianna, Fla; Bolivar Co, Miss; CW-CSA (b/IV-5-1832; d/VII-27-1864 Ringgold, Ga) MD UPa 1854; AB UNC 1851. *SHSP* 22:174, 1893.

BELLAMY, JOHN DILLARD, Wilmington, NC (b/XI-18-1817 near Charleston, SC; d/VIII-30-1896) MD UPa 1839. *NC med jour* 38: 184-85, 1896.

BELLANGEE, JAMES BARTON, NJ; CW-USA (d/X-6-1864 Morehead City, NC) MD Jefferson 1854. *Med surg rep Phila* 12:219, 1864/65. *Nat med jour* 1:291, 1870/71.

BELLINGER, JOHN, Charleston, SC (b/IX-24-1804 St Bartholomew's Par, SC; d/VIII-13-1860) MD UPa 1826. *Med surg rep Phila* ns4:466, 1860. *Nashville jour m & s* 19:383, 1860. *K & B* II: 94.

BELLINGHAM, WILLIAM, Petersburg, Va; CW-CSA (b/Del; d/VI-20-1864) *Med & surg rep Phila* 12:18, 1864/65.

BELLOWS, HORATIO KNIGHT, Norwich, NY (b/XI-5-1823 New Berlin, NY; d/III-30-1880) MD UCNY 1847. *Tr M S St NY* 1881: 371-72. *Butler* 1874: 527.

BELLOWS, MATTHIAS B , Seneca Falls, NY (b/IV-9-1788 Hebron, NY; d/V-1-1854) Lic NY St Bd Reg 1844. *Buff med jour* 10: , 1854.

BELT, CHARLES BRADFORD, So Boston (b/IX-16-1847 Hartford, Conn; d/VIII-23-1898) MD Harvard 1871. *Bost m & s jour* 139:284, 1898. *JAMA* 31: 551, 1898. *Polk* 1896:692.

BELT, EDWARD OLIVER, Washington, DC (b/V-19-1861 Rock Hall, Md; d/XII-30-1906) MD UMd 1886. *Hist M S DC*: 334-35. *K & B* III:92-93. *Polk* 1893: 268.

BELT, RICHARD GRAFTON, Washington, DC (b/1784 Md? d/VII-31-1865. MD UMd 1821. *Med annals Md*: 318. *Med surg rep Phila* 13:102, 1865.

BELT, WALTER T , Beltsville, MD (b/c1812; d/VIII- -1872) MD UMd 1835. *Med annals Md*: 318.

BELVIN, JAMES, Va; CW-USN (d/XI-4-1893 Belgium) <MD Med Coll Va> *JAMA* 21:784. 1893.

BEMIS, CHARLES VOSE, Medford, Mass (d/XI-6-1906 @ 90) MD Harvard 1839. *Bost m & s jour* 155:562, 1906. *Polk* 1896: 717.

BEMIS, JONATHAN WHEELER, Cambridge, Mass (d/I-6-1895) MD Harvard 1834; AB 1830. *Bost m & s jour* 132:48, 1895. *JAMA* 24: 101, 1895. *Butler* 1878:377.

BEMIS, JOHN MERRICK, Worcester, Mass (b/V-6-1820 Sturbridge, Mass; c/X-3-1904) MD Castleton 1852. *Bost m & s jour* 151:394, 1904. *Polk* 1896:727.

BEMIS, NATHAN MARVIN, Wilmington, Vt; Faribault, +Minn (b/III-25-1821 Whitingham, Vt; d/I-29-1891) ng Woodstock 1840. *JAMA* 16: 320, 1891. *Butler* 1878:391.

BEMISS, JOHN, Nelson Co, Ky (b/II-16-1773; d/1851) Lic 1801; stud under Zachariah Standish. *Trans Ky Med*

Soc 1860: 14–20.

BEMISS, JOHN HARRISON, Hawaii 1878–82; New Orleans 1882– (b/1856 Louisville, Ky; d/IX-2-1897 Ocean Springs, Miss) MD ULa 1878; AB UVa 1876. *New Orl m & s jour* 50:269–303, 1897? *Trans La St Med Soc* 19:21–23, 1898. *Texas med news* 6:476, 1896–97. *JAMA* 29: 660, 816, 1897. *Polk* 1896: 489.

BEMISS, SAMUEL MERRIFIELD, CW–USA; New Orleans (b/X-15-1821 Nelson Co, Ky; d/XI-18-1884) MD UCNY 1846. *So pract* 6:596, 1884. *New Orl m & s jour* ns12:488–93, 1884. *Tex cour-rec med* 2:254, 1884. *JAMA* 3:642–643, 1884. *Atkinson* I:39.

BEMUS, WILLIAM P, Jamestown, NY (b/Chautauqua Co, NY; d/IX-19-1890) MD Berkshire 1847. *Trans NY St Med Soc* 11:741 ff, 1894. *Polk* 1886: 664.

BENBOW, JOHN B, Gilliam, Mo (d/X-17-1899 @ 48) MD Cincinnati Coll Med & Surg 1879. *JAMA* 33:1183, 1899. *Polk* 1886: 547.

BENBROOK, OTIS B, Natchez, Miss; St Joseph, La (d/VII-14-1899 @ 29) MD Tulane 1893. *JAMA* 33:302, 1899. *Polk* 1896: 813.

BENEDICT, ABIJAH G, Red Hook, NY (b/1790 Salem, NY; d/X-3-1862) Lic Dutchess Co Med Soc 1815. *Trans Med Soc St NY* 1864: 447–48. *Tr AMA* 16:625, 1865.

BENEDICT, HARRIS S, Havana, NY; Corning, NY 1864– (b/VII-12-1823 Warwick, NY; d/X-18-1869) MD Western Homeop Cleveland 1863. *Trans Am Inst Homeop* 1893: 129. *Trans NY Homeop Soc* 9:637, 1869? Homeopath.

BENEDICT, JOSEPH MOTT, Hoboken, NJ; Long Island, NY; Salt Lake City 1870– (b/IV-29-1844 So Canaan, Conn; d/VII-24-1896) MD UCNY 1867; AB 1867. *Proc Utah St Med Soc* 2:166, 1896. *JAMA* 27:337, 1896.

BENEDICT, MICHAEL DUNNING, CW–USA New Haven Conn; Skaneateles 1838–61; Syracuse 1865– (b/I-21-1814 Danbury, Conn; d/I-7-1885) MD Yale 1836. *Trans Med Soc St NY* 1886:595–601. *Butler* 1874:527.

BENEDICT, NATHAN DOW, Magnolia, Fla (d/IV-30-1871) MD UPa 1840; AB Rutgers 1837; AM 1840. *Trans CPP* centennial vol: 278. *Rutgers gen cat*: 89.

BENEDICT, THOMAS BENJAMIN, Ionia, Mich (b/III-28-1829 Orange Co, NY; d/III-1-1874) MD Homeop Med Coll Cleveland 1861) *Trans Am Inst Homeo* 1874: 655. *Amer obs* 9:236, 1872. *New Engl med gaz* 9:240, 1874. *Cleave*. Homeopath.

BENEDICT, WILLIAM CURTIS, Brooklyn (b/IV-19-1820 Schenectady, NY; d/VIII-17-1896) MD UPa 1844; AB Union 1840. *JAMA* 27:503, 1896. *Polk* 1896: 992.

BENETEAU, ALFRED F, Detroit, Mich (d/IV-3-1899) MD Detroit Med Coll 1895. *JAMA* 32: 845, 1899. *Polk* 1896: 745.

BENHAM, BENJAMIN H, Honeoye Falls, NY (d/V-31-1897 @ 38) MD UCNY 1851. *JAMA* 28:1156, 1897. *Polk* 1896:1026.

BENHAM, JOHN CASPARUS, Hudson, NY (d/II-19 1899 @ 82) MD Castleton 1837. *JAMA* 32:506, 1899. *Polk* 1896:1027.

BENJAMIN, HENRY G, Greenpoint, NY (d/IV-24-1868 @ 44) MD UCNY 1860. *Med surg rep Phila* 18:398, 1868. *Phila med reg & dir* 1871:296.

BENJAMIN, JOHN BENSON, Carmel, Me (b/VIII-3-1822 Etna, Me; d/IV-9-1884) MD Jefferson 1853; ng Bowdoin Med Coll 1852. *Bowdoin cat*: 1852 (med).

BENJAMIN, JOSEPH RITNER, Troy, NY (d/X-30-1885 @ 45) MD CPSNY 1868; AB Yale 1864; AM 1867.*Med reg NY NJ Conn* 1886:242.

BENKENDORF, EDWARD G, St Louis, Mo (b/Prussia; d/1896) MD St Louis Med Coll 1847. *JAMA* 27:776, 1896. *Polk* 1890: 670.

BENNER, IRWIN LEACH, Sellersville, Pa (d/I- 25-1903) MD UPa 1893. *Pa med jour* 7:278, 1903/04. *Flint* 1897: 835.

BENNET, GEORGE H R, Brooklyn (d/I-26-1904 @ 67) MD UCNY 1860. *Bost m & s jour* 150:138, 1904. *Polk* 1896:992.

BENNETT, ALONZO WHITE, Uxbridge, Mass (d/VII 19-1888 @ 67) MD CPSNY 1846. *Bost m & s jour* 119: 96, 1888. *Polk* 1886: 474.

BENNETT, ASAHEL M, Rochester, NY (b/VIII- -1836 Moravia, NY; d/III- -1885) <D NY Homeop Med Coll 1870. *Trans Am Inst Homeop* 1885:96. Homeopath.

BENNETT, FARNHAM O, Willimantic, Conn (b/XII-23-1832 Ashford; d/III-26-1899) MD Berkshire 1859. *Proc Conn Med Soc* 1899:352–353. *JAMA* 32:1133, 1899. *Polk* 1886:197.

BENNETT, GEORGE I, Brooklyn (d/VIII-1-1875) MD UCNY 1842. *Med reg NY NJ Conn* 1876:241.

BENNETT, HANFORD NICHOLS, Bridgeport, Conn (d/IV-21-1868) MD Yale 1838. *Phila med reg & dir* 1871:296. *Proc Conn Med Soc* 1868: 19.

BENNETT, HILEM, Rochester, NY (b/1791? d/X-28-1868 @ 77) <MD Fairfield> *Med surg rep Phila* 19:412, 1868. *Phila med reg & dir* 1871: 298. *Trans Am Inst Homeop* 1870: 635. Homeopath.

BENNETT, HOLLIS KENDALL, Hartford, NY 1862; Whitehall, NY 1866; Fitchburg, Mass 1872– (b/VII-16-1839 Warren, Vt; d/VI-19-1889) <ng UPa Med Sch c1860> *Trans Am Inst Homeop* 1889: 185. *New Engl med gaz* 24:334, 1889. *No Am jour homeop* 37:304, 1889. *Med vis* 6:137, 1890. *Cleave*. Homeopath.

BENNETT, JOHN LANG, Wollaston, Mass (b/III-19-1851; d/IX-13-1886) MD Bowdoin 1876. *Bost m & s jour* 115:292, 1886.

BENNETT, LUTHER WILLIAM, Boston (d/I-4-1888 @ 37) MD Harvard 1879. *Bost m & s jour* 119: 640, 1888. *Polk* 1886: 454.

BENNETT, NEHEMIAH KNIGHT, Brooklyn (b/IX-23

Spec. educ'l status abbrev. as: ***ng*** = college verified attendance without degree;

1831 Warwick, RI; d/X–20–1894) MD NY Homeop 1877. *Trans Am Inst Homeop* 1895: 215. Homeopath.

BENNETT, STEPHEN B , Canton, Ill (d/III–1–1901) Lic by years of practice. *Ill med jour* ns2:533, 1901. *Polk* 1898: 474.

BENNETT, WILLIAM COMSTOCK, CW–USA; Danbury, Conn (b/III–7–1836; d/VII–12–1886) MD CPSNY 1860; AB Yale 1858. *Med reg NY NJ Conn* 1887: 254. *Proc Conn Med Soc* 1887: 187. *Butler* 1878: 73.

BENNETT, WILLIAM H , West River, Md (d/XI–13–1899 @ 57) MD UMd 1866. *JAMA* 33:1440–1441, 1899.

BENNETT, WILLIAM H F , Brooklyn (d/IX–1–1898 @ 54) MD UCNY 1870. *JAMA* 31:618, 1898.

de BENNEVILLE, JAMES SEGUIN, CW–USA (b/VI–19–1824 Phila; d/IX–5–1866 Phila) MD UPa 1854. *UPa med alum CW*: 1854.

BENREUTER [BERNREUTER], EDWARD D , Mt Olive, Ill (d/XII–9–1904 @ 46) MD Missouri Med Coll 1880. *Ill med jour* 7:242, 1905. *Polk* 1886:289.

BENSCOTER, PERRY HUBLER, USA ?Pittston, Pa (d/XI–4–1898 @ 30) MD Jefferson 1894. *JAMA* 31: 1257, 1898. *Polk* 1896: 1330.

BENSON, EDWARD SCOTT, NYC? (b/VIII–24–1866 Susquehanna Co, Pa; d/X–18/19–1897) UCNY 1893. *Pa med jour* 2:41–43, 1898.

BENSON, GEORGE E , Hudson, NY (d/V–30–1896 @ 68) MD Albany 1853. *Trans Med Soc St NY* 1897: 479. *Polk* 1886:665.

BENSON, GEORGE W , Baltimore (b/IV–8–1831; d/VIII–22–1893) MD UMd 1852. *JAMA* 21:357, 1893. *Med annals Md*: 31. *Butler* 1878: 318.

BENSON, JOHN ALFRED, Chicago (b/1859 Hoboken, NJ; d/III–10–1898) MD CPSNY 1880. *Chic med rec* 16:275, 1899. *JAMA* 32:627–628, 1899. *Flint* 1897:256.

BENSON, JULIUS L , Noblesville, Ind (d/IX–8–1896) MD Med Coll Ind 1875. *JAMA* 27: 661, 1896. *Polk* 1886:331.

BENSON, PHILANDER VIRGIL, Baltimore (d/XI–10 1898 @ 60) MD UMd 1862. *JAMA* 31:1319, 1898. *Polk* 1886:435.

BENSON, PHILIP OSCAR CORNELL, Skaneateles, NY (b/VI–19–1839; d/I–27–1890) MD NY Homeop 1865. *Trans Am Inst Homeop* 1893: 1093. *No Am jour homeop* 38: 197, 1901. *Med vis* 6:137, 1890. *Cleave*. Homeopath.

BENSON, WILLIAM HENRY, Staunton, Va (b/V–10–1835; d/X–3–1888 Philadelphia) MD UMd 1861; matric U Ala 1852. *U Ala cat*: 1852.

BENTZ, JOHN AUGUST, ?NYC (d/XII–20–1886) MD UCNY 1874. *Med reg NY NJ Conn* 1887: 255.

BERDAN, DWIGHT WARREN, Cheboygan Mich (d/VII–8–1894 @ 41) MD Bellevue 1884. *JAMA* 23: 164, 1894.

BERENS, BERNARD, Philadelphia (d/V–15–1886) MD UPa 1880; PhB Yale 1877. *Trans Am Inst Homeop* 1893: 1093. *Polk* 1886: 812. Homeopath.

BERENS, JOSEPH, Philadelphia (b/XII–2–1813 Westphalia; d/XII–8–1905 @ 62) MD Pa Med Coll 1841. *Pa med jour* 9:281, 1905/06. *Trans Am Inst Homeop* 1906: 758. *Flint* 1897: 814.

BERESFORD, SAMUEL BARWICK, Hartford, Conn (b/VII–5–1806 Dutch [?] Guiana; d/X–13–1873) MD Edinburgh 1826. *Proc Conn Med Soc* 4:276–80, 293 ff, 1874. *Med surg rep Phila* 29:305, 324, 1873.

BERGEN, ABRAM WINFRED, Cornwall-on-Hudson, NY (d/I–2–1897) MD NY Homeop 1887. *No Amer jour homeop* Apr 1897. *Med vis* 13:160, 1897. Homeopath.

BERGEN, ANDREW CONOVER, Sioux City, Ia (b/II–3–1849 Franklin, Ind; d/X–3–1900) MD LICH 1870. *Trans Ia St Med Soc* 19: 440, 1901. *Polk* 1896:538–39.

BERGER, FRANÇOIS ELOI, NYC (b/1789? d/II–1–1866 @ 77) MD unknown. *Med surg rep Phila* 14:120, 1866. *Tr AMA* 18:317, 1867. *Med reg NY NJ Conn* 1867:209. *K & B* III:1226.

BERGHAUS, JULIUS MARTIN, St Louis 1851–54; NYC 1856?–72 (b/XI–11–1825 Halle, Westphalia; d/X–17–1878) <MD Erlangen> *Trans Am Inst Homeop* 1893: 1093. *Am homeop obs* 15: 63, 187_? (d/IX–20–1877? St Maurice, Switzerland). Homeopath.

BERKELÉ, ELMER FOX, Brooklyn (d/VIII– –1892 @ 27) MD CPSNY 1890; AB Yale 1887) *Med reg NY NJ Conn* 1893:297.

BERKELEY, CARTER NELSON, Philadelphia (d/IV–16–1842) MD UPa 1837. *Trans CPP* centennial vol: 212.

BERKELEY, LEWIS DARRACOTT, CW–CSA; Macon, Miss (b/IX–12–1824 Hanson Co, Va; d/I–5–1896) MD UPa 1849. *UPa med alum CW*: 1849.

BERKELEY, PEYTON RANDOLPH, CW–CSA, Worsham, Va (b/XI–23–1804 Richmond; d/V–5–1870) MD UPa 1828; AB Hampden-Sidney 1824. *UPa med alum CW*: 1828.

BERKELEY, RICHARD FARREL, CW–CSA; ?Baltimore (b/XII–24–1819 Hanover Co, Va; d/V–25–1886) MD UPa 1843. *UPa med alum CW*: 1843.

BERKELEY, THOMAS AVERETT, CW–CSA; Staunton, Va (b/VIII–13–1826; d/XII–15–1871 Stilesboro, Ga) MD UPa 1850. *UPa med alum CW*: 1850. *Tr Med Soc Va* 1872:26, 157.

BERKEMEYER, LOUIS C , Allentown, Pa (d/VIII–8 1901 @ 61) MD unknown. *Pa med jour* 5:296, 1901/02. *Polk* 1886: 804.

BERLIN, JAMES O , Bath, Pa (d/III–24–1903 @ 56) MD Jefferson 1874. *Pa med jour* 7:90, 278, 1903/04. *Flint* 1897: 795.

BERNACKI, CHARLES, NYC (b/XI–3–1812 Galicia; d/IX–17–1896 @ 84) MD U Vienna 1839. *JAMA* 27: 776, 1215, 1896. *Polk* 1896:1041.

BERNACKI, CHARLES WILLIAM, Tremont, NY (d/XII–29–1879 @ 39) MD UCNY 1866. *Med reg NY NJ Conn* 1880:233.

BERNAYS, GEORGE J , St Louis (d/XII-16-1888 @ 64) <MD Würzburg 1859> *Bost m & s jour* 120:28, 1889. *Polk* 1886:561.

BERNEY, JAMES, Hayneville, Ala (b/1812; d/VII-9-1880, Sunnyside Retreat, NY) MD UPa 1833. *Tr AMA* 33:521-23, 1882. *Trans Med Soc Ala* 1881:270.

BERNHARDT, DALLAS, Three Springs, Pa (d/III-30 1903 @ 46) MD CPS Balto 1885. *Pa med jour* 7: 278, 1903/04.

BERRY, ABRAHAM J , CW-USA; Brooklyn (b/1797? d/X-22-1865) MD CPSNY 1828. *Nat med jour* 1:291, 1870/71. *Tr AMA* 18:315, 1867. *Med surg rep Phila* 13:310, 1865.

BERRY, ANDREW JACKSON, St Louis; CW-USA (b/ 1824? d/V-4-1862 @ 38) ng UMich Med Sch 1856-57. *U Mich cat*: 620.

BERRY, CHARLES THOMAS, Pittsfield, NH (b/IV-3-1819; d/I-9-1855) MD Columbian 1843; AB Dartmouth 1839. *Trans NH Med Soc* 1855: 6.

BERRY, DAVID, Ashley, Ill (d/I-21-1906 @ 70) MD Med Coll Va 1862. *Ill med jour* 9:228, 1906. *Polk* 1896:361.

BERRY, EDWARD SWETT, Concord, NH (b/X-29-1844 Pittsfield, NH; d/I-7-1892 @ 47) MD Dartmouth 1870. *Bost m & s jour* 126:48, 1892.

BERRY, ISAAC C , Grafton WVa (b/II- -1844; d/III- -1877) ng Starling? *Trans Med Soc WVa* 1877: 315; 1884: 154. *Butler* 1878: 848.

BERRY, JAMES, Gloversville, NY (b/XII-25-1809 Mayfield, NY; d/III-8-1870) MD Castleton 1835. *Tr NY Homeop Soc* 9:635. Homeopath.

BERRY, PHILO, W Constable, NY (b/XII-16-1861) MD Vt Med Coll 1859. *Med surg rep Phila* ns7:311, 1861/62.

BERRY, WILLIAM BOGARDUS, Montclair, NJ; Los Angeles (b/III-22-1854 Syracuse, NY; d/XII-21-1896) MD CPSNY 1876; AB Rutgers 1874, AM 1877. *JAMA* 28:665, 1897. *Polk* 1896: 225.

BERRY, WILLIAM HENRY, DC (b/XII-3-1827; d/II-19-1859) MD UMd 1850; AB Princeton 1847; AM 1850. *Tr AMA* 13:814-15, 1860. *Hist Med Soc* DC: 254.

BERRY, WILLIAM ROBERT, Gallatin, Mo (d/XI-26-1893) MD UMich 1866. *JAMA* 21:936, 1893. *Butler* 1878:422.

BERTINE, LOUIS EDGAR, Mt Vernon, NY (d/V-30-1898) MD Bellevue 1881. *JAMA* 30:1481, 1898. *Polk* 1896:1033.

BERTOLET [BARTOLETT?], JONATHAN C , Reading Pa; CW-USA (d/V-15-1868) MD Jefferson 1858. *Phila med reg & dir* 1871:297. *Tr AMA* 21:459, 1870. *Trans Med Soc Pa* 1868:83-84. *Nat med jour* 1:290, 1870/71.

BERTOLET, ROBERT MORRIS, ?Santa Fe, NM (d/V-10-1882 Santa Fe) MD UPa 1868; ng Lafayette. *Tr CPP* centennial vol: 212.

BERTOLETT, DAVID KAISER, Washington, O (d/V-20-1873) MD UPa 1849. *Med surg rep Phila* 29:18, 1873.

BESHLER, J B , CW-USA (b/VIII-29-1839 Berrysburg, Pa; d/IV-8-1869) MD UPa 1861. *UPa med alum CW*: 1861.

BESSAC, HENRY BERTRAND, Oroville, Cal (d/XII-3 1904) MD UMich 1873. *Calif st jour med* 3:58, 1905. *Polk* 1886: 499 (Milan, Mich)

BETHELL, CHARLES P , Philadelphia (d/I-22-1873) MD UPa 1858. *Med surg rep Phila* 28: 166, 1873.

BETHUNE, GEORGE AMORY, Boston (d/IV-5-1886 @ 73) MD Harvard 1834; AB 1831. *Bost m & s jour* 114:336, 1886; 115:630, 1886. *Butler* 1878: 337.

BETTERLY, EMANUEL LAZARUS, USA; Wilkes Barre, Pa (b/IV-13-1832; d/XI-3-1898) MD UCNY 1882. *JAMA* 31:1257, 1898. *Rec Assn Asst Surgs USA* 1891:23. *Polk* 1896:1344.

BETTMAN, BOERNE, Chicago (b/IX-6-1856 Cincinnati; d/V-25-1906) MD U Miami 1877. *Chic med rec* 28:354, 1906. *Flint* 1897:256. *K & B* III:93-94.

BETTON, GEORGE W , Tallahassee, Fla (b/II-22-1822 Alexandria, Va; d/XI-1-1896) MD UPa 1845; AB St Johns, Md 1842. *JAMA* 27:1120, 1896. *NC med jour* 38:347, 1896. *Butler* 1878: 100.

BETTON, THOMAS FORREST, Germantown; Phila. CW-USA (b/VII-29-1809; d/V-21-1875) MD UPa 1832. *UPa med alum CW*: 1832. *Trans CPP* centennial vol: 212.

BETTS, HENRY WATSON, Albemarle, NC (b/II-2-1856; d/IV-11-1883) ng UCNY Med Sch 1878; lic NC 1881. *NC med jour* 11:375, 1883. *Trans Med Soc St NC* 1887:156.

BETTS, NATHANIEL AUGUSTUS, Brooklyn (b/ VIII-5-1854; d/III-20-1885 or 86) MD LICH 1884; LLB UCNY 1874. *Med reg NY NJ Conn* 1886: 243.

BETTS, WILLIAM ALEXANDER, Red Bank, NJ (b/ XI-1-1833 Phelps, NY; d/VIII-4-1895) MD CPSNY 1861. *JAMA* 25:298, 1895. *Trans M S NJ* 1896:368-369. *Bost m & s jour* 133:172-73, 1895. *Butler* 1878: 466.

BEVAN, BENJAMIN, Pittston, Pa (d/II-20-1903 @ 42) MD UCNY 1891. *Pa med jour* 7:278, 1903/04. *Flint* 1897: 831.

BEVAN, THOMAS, CW-USA; Chicago (b/VI-11-1830 Cincinnati; d/III-15-1880) MD Med Coll Ohio 1851 [1857?] *Tr AMA* 31:1012-13, 1880. *Trans Ill St Med Soc* 1880: 209. *Atkinson* I:430.

BEVER, JOHN C , Vincennes, Ind (b/I-29-1819 Steubenville, O; d/III-15-1903) <MD Physio-Med Coll Cincinnati 1850> *Trans Ind St Med Soc* 1903: 333. *Polk* 1886: 339.

BEVERLY, JOHN E , Winchester, Ind (b/IX-17-1816 Marlborough, SC; d/V-6-1880) MD Med Coll O 1857. *Trans Ind St Med Soc* 1889:207.

BEVERLY, P F , Columbus, O (d/IX-18-1896 @ 69)

MD Missouri Med Coll 1857. *JAMA* 27: 776, 1896. *Polk* 1886: 750.

BEVINGTON, JOSIAH S , Freedom Center, O (b/VI-14-1844 Holmes Co; d/I-3-1885) MD Western Reserve 1877. *Trans O St Med Soc* 1885:211.

BEYERLE, W GEORGE, Bernville, Pa (d/X-15-1905) MD Jefferson 1853. *Pa med jour* 9:399-400, 1905/06. *Flint* 1897: 796.

BIBB, GEORGE RICHARD, Jacksonville, Ill (b/1842; d/1874) MD Rush 1864. *Tr AMA* 26: 455-56, 1875.

BIBBINS, WILLIAM BURR, NYC (b/VIII-8-1823, Fairfield, Conn; d/I-16-1871) MD CPSNY 1849; AB Yale 1845, AM 1848. *Med reg NY NJ Conn* 1871: 348; 1889: 265. *Trans Med Soc St NY* 1872: 327-32. *Med rec* 5:552, 1870/71; 6: 39, 71-74, 1871/72. *Med surg rep Phila* 24:112, 1871.

BIBBY, EDWARD NEWENHAM, NYC (b/X-23-1791; d/XI-24-1882) Hon MD Med Soc NYC 1812; AB Columbia 1809.*Med reg NY NJ Conn* 1883: 221.

BIBIGHAUS, CHARLES H , Philadelphia (d/VII-13-1854) MD CPSNY 1834. *Trans Med Soc Pa* 1856:185.

BIBIGHAUS, JOHN, Middleburg, Pa (d/VIII-3-1860) Hon MD UMd 1846; ng Jefferson? *Med surg rep Phila* ns4:368, 1860.

BICKFORD, HEZEKIAH COOK, Woburn, Mass (d/1878 @ 61) MD Jefferson 1845. *Bost m & s jour* 99:402-04 1878.

BICKHAM, CHARLES JASPER, New Orleans (b/VII-8-1830 Covington, La; d/II-14-1898) MD ULa 1856; <AM S W Texas U 1854> *Trans La St Med Soc* 19:24-25, 1898. *JAMA* 30:507, 1898. *New Orl m & s jour* 50: 547-48, 1898. *Polk* 1890: 489.

BICKNELL, LEWIS C , Fort Atkinson, Wis (d/VIII-26-1888) MD Rush 1855. *Trans Wis St Med Soc* 1891:356. *Polk* 1886: 953.

BICKNELL, RUFUS, Philadelphia (b/New England; d/X-25-1868 @ 61) MD UPa 1837. *Phila med reg & dir* 1871: 293. *Med surg rep Phila* 19:368, 1868.

BICKNELL, SIMEON SMITH, CW-USA (d/X-29-1863 St Louis, Mo) ng U Mich Med Sch 1862-63. *U Mich cat*: 621.

BIDDLE, JOHN BARCLAY, Philadelphia (b/I-3-1815; d/I-19-1879) MD UPa 1836; AB St Mary's Coll Balto 1834. *Trans CPP* centennial vol: 212. *Tr AMA* 31: 1013-14 1880. *Phila med times* 9:219, 244, 1879. *Bost m & s jour* 132, 162-63, 1879. *Med rec* 15:94-95, 119. *K & B* III: 94-95.

BIDLACK, WILLIAM WALLACE, Milford, Pa; CW-USA (b/VII-24-1833; d/X-30-1899) MD UPa 1852. *UPa med alum CW*: 1852.

BIDWELL, EDWIN CURTIS, Vineland, NJ (d/XI-11-1905) MD Yale 1844; AB Williams 1841. *Bost m & s jour* 153:598, 1905. *Polk* 1896:950.

BIDWELL, JOHN WELCH, W Winstead, Conn 1851- (b/X-20-1824 S Tyringham, Mass; d/IV-19-1897) MD Berkshire 1846. *Proc Conn Med Soc* 1897:337-38. *Atkinson* I:383. *Flint* 1897:179.

BIEBER, LEWIS DANIEL, Easton, Pa (b/IV-6-1845 Kutztown; d/II-26-1906) MD UPa 1867. *Pa med jour* 9:523, 1905/06. *UPa med alum CW*: 1867. *Polk* 1886: 610 (Phillipsburgh, NJ)

BIERCE, FREDERICK A , Warren, O (d/V-9-1891 @ c70) Stud med in Nelson, O. *Hahn mo* 20: 20, 1892 (news & advert) *Polk* 1886:772. Homeopath.

BIGALOW, ABRAM T , Worcester, NY (d/II-8-1867 @ 65) <MD Fairfield> *Med surg rep Phila* 16: 272, 1867.

BIGELOW, BROWN A , Belleville, Pa (d/III-16-1906 @ 44) MD Jefferson 1874. *Pa med jour* 9:523, 1905/06. *Flint* 1897:796.

BIGELOW, FRANKLIN, Toledo, O 1854-65; Syracuse, NY 1853, 1865-79) b/VII-13-1827 Batavia, NY; d/III-12-1879) MD Hahnemann Phila 1853. *Trans Am Inst Homeop* 1879: 1249; 1880: 141. *Cleave*. Homeopath.

BIGELOW, GEORGE FREDERIC, Boston (d/VIII-10-1893 @ 73) MD Jefferson 1846; AB Williams 1843. *Bost m & s jour* 129:180, 1893. *Butler* 1878: 337.

BIGELOW, HENRY, Newton, Mass (d/I-21-1866 @ 48) MD Harvard 1839. *Tr AMA* 18:307-08, 1867. *Bost m & s jour* 73:528, 1865. *Med surg rep Phila* 14: 100, 1886.

BIGELOW, HENRY JACOB, Newton, Mass (b/III-11-1818; d/X-30-1890) MD Harvard 1841; AB 1837. *Boston med surg jour* 123: 450,474,480,553-54,602, 1890. *JAMA* 15:733-34,1890. *Atkinson* I:663. *K & B* III:95-97.

BIGELOW, HORACE, NYC (b/XII-18-1871 Fayetteville, NY; d/X-15-1901) MD CPSNY 1896; AB Amherst 1893. *Bost m & s jour* 145: 478, 1901.

BIGELOW, ISAAC STOVER, Buncombe, Ia (d/III-21-1900 @81) MD Rush 1881[?] *JAMA* 34:830, 1900.

BIGELOW, JACOB, Boston (b/II-27-1787; d/I-10-1879) MD UPa 1810; AB Harvard 1806. *Trans CPP* centennial vol: 278. *Bost m & s jour* 106:598, 1882. *Tr AMA* 33:524-27, 1882. *K & B* III:97-98.

BIGELOW, JAMES, NYC (b/II-25-1831 Hartford, Conn; d/X-4-1871) MD Bellevue 1866; AB Williams 1862. *Med reg NY NJ Conn* 1872: 342.

BIGELOW, JAMES K, CW-USA; Indianapolis, Ind (b/X-17-1833, Bellebrook, O; d/VI-1-1886) Stud w/Dr W L Wickersham, Anderson,Ind; ng U Louisville Med Sch 1874/5. *Trans Ind St Med Soc* 1886:218. *Polk* 1886: 322.

BIGELOW, ORVIS FURMAN, Amherst, Mass (d/II-2-1899 @ 63) MD UVt 1862. *Bost m & s jour* 140: 152, 1899. *JAMA* 32:385, 1899. *Polk* 1886: 453.

BIGELOW, SAMUEL LEE, CW-USA (d/XI-1-1862 Hagerstown, Md) MD Harvard 1848; MD U Paris 1852. *Tr AMA* 14:216, 1864. *Bost m & s jour* 67: 308, 1862. *Med surg rep Phila* ns9:164, 1862/63. *Harvard in CW*: 234. *Nat med jour* 1:290, 1870/71.

BIGELOW [BIGLOW?], URIAH G , Albany, NY (b/X 2-1821 Worcester, NY; d/II-23-1873) MD Albany Med

Coll 1843. *Med reg NY NJ Conn* 1873:335. *Buff med jour* 12:318, 1873. *Trans Med Soc St NY* 1875: 376–79.

BIGELOW, WILLIAM, Bennington, Vt (b/XI–9–1791 Middletown, Vt? d/IV–16–1863 Springfield, Mass) Hon MD Castleton 1828. *Bost m & s jour* 68:270, 1863.

BIGHAM, WILLIAM, CW–USA; Seville, O (d/X–13–1898) ng U Mich Med Sch 1861–62. *JAMA* 31:1066, 1898. *Polk* 1886: 767.

BIGLER, BERNARD EUGENE, Bethlehem, Pa; Colo Spr (b/XI–14–1878 Phila; d/II–20–1905) MD Hahnemann 1900. *Hahn mo* 40: 33, 1905 (news & advert). Homeopath.

BIGLER, D MITCHELL, York Co, Pa (d/XII–21–1869 @26) MD Jefferson 1869.*Phila med reg & dir* 1871:303.

BIGLER, GEORGE WASHINGTON, Marietta, O; Hagerstown, Md; Cincinnati 1850– (b/Harrisburg, Pa; d/IV–28–1871) MD Hahnemann 1850; ng Jefferson? *Tr Am Inst Homeop* 1895: 1093. *Am homeop obs* 8: 262, 1871. *Ohio m & s rep* 5:190, 1871? Homeopath.

BIGLER, WILLIAM HOWARD, Philadelphia (b/VI–10 –1840; d/XII–10–1904) MD Hahnemann Phila 1871; AM Moravian. *Hahn mo* 40:51–53,1905 (news & advt) *Trans Am Inst Homeop* 1904: 837. Homeopath.

BIGNEY, PETER M , Cincinnati (d/V–8–1895 @ 61) MD Miami 1866. *JAMA* 24: 776, 1895. *Polk* 1890: 898.

BIGONY, FRANKLIN W , Montgomery Square, Pa (d/ VI–23–1906 @ 80) MD Jefferson 1852. *Pa med jour* 9:805, 1905/06. *Flint* 1897: 810.

BILL, CURTIS HARVEY, CW–USA; Bridgeport, Conn (b/VII–2–1835; Albany, Vt; d/VII–4–1905) MD UCNY 1859. *Proc Conn Med Soc* 1906: 308–311. *Atkinson* I:441–42. *Flint* 1897: 173.

BILL, HARRIET P , W New Brighton, NY (d/III–7–1900 NH) MD Woman's Med Coll Pa 1893. *Bost m & s jour* 142:288, 1900. *Polk* 1896:1112.

BILLINGS, A JUDSON, Freedom, Me (d/II–7–1900 @ 74) MD Albany 1854. *Bost m & s jour* 142: 179, 1900. *JAMA* 34:511, 1900. *Polk* 1896: 635.

BILLINGS, GEORGE HENRY, Cohoes, NY (b/VI–19–1835 Claremont, NH; d/V–20–1893) MD Castleton 1857. *Trans Am Inst Homeop* 1895:1093. *Polk* 1886: 657. Homeopath.

BILLINGS, JAMES AVERY, Batavia, NY (b/1795; d/ 1858) Hon MD Willoughby 1837. *Tr AMA* 13:800, 1860. *Buff med jour* 14:275–76, 1858.

BILLINGS, LUCIUS FLAGG, Barre, Mass (d/XI–26–1893 @ 72) MD Berkshire 1845. *JAMA* 21: 982, 1893. *Bost m & s jour* 130:52, 1894.

BILLINGSLEA, JAMES CLEMENT, USA–MexWar; Augusta, Ark (b/XII–27–1826; d/XII–25–1869) MD Med Coll Ga 1853; ng U Ala 1843. *U Ala cat*: 80.

BILLINGSLEA, JAMES L , Westminster, Md (b/1804; d/X–23–1881) MD UMd 1827. *Med annals Md*: 321. *Butler* 1874:317.

BILLINGSLEA, MARTIN B , Baltimore (b/VI–10–1849 Harford Co, Md; d/XII–8–1902) MD UMd 1874. *Med annals Md*: 321. *Polk* 1886: 435.

BILLINGTON, CORNELIUS EVARTS, NYC (b/1844? d/I–9–1904 @ 60) MD UCNY 1864. *Bost m & s jour* 150:56, 1904. *Polk* 1896: 1041.

BING, JAMES PHELPS, Portsmouth, O (d/IV–8–1900 @ 78) MD Starling 1851. *JAMA* 34: 1021, 1900. *Polk* 1886: 766.

BINGHAM, EDWARD BENTON, USN (b/1845 Phila; d/II–24–1872 Oakland, Calif) MD UPa 1864. *Bost m & s jour* ns9:164, 1872. *Tr AMA* 24:391–92, 1873. *UPa med alum CW*: 1864.

BINGHAM, REGINALD HEBER, Oshkosh, Wis (b/VI–8–1829 Hampton, NY; d/VI–12–1890) MD Castleton 1849. *Trans Wis St Med Soc* 1891: 356. *Polk* 1886:959.

BINKERD, A D , CW–USA; Monterey, Pa (b/III–29–1831 Perry, Pa; d/X–27–1903) MD LICH 1865. *Pa med jour* 7:278, 1903/04. *Flint* 1897: 839.

BINNEY, AMOS ABRAM, Boston (b/X–18–1803; d/II–18–1847 Rome, Italy) MD Harvard 1826; AB Brown 1821. *Brown hist cat*: 1821.

BINNEY, BARNABAS, Franklin Co, Pa; RevWar–USA (b/1751 Boston; d/VI–21–1787) <MD UPa 1776> AM Brown 1774. *Brown hist cat*: 1774.

BIRCH, GEORGE BRIGHT, Hannibal, Mo (d/X–10 1873 @ 54 Allahabad, India) MD Cincinnati Ecl Med Coll 1856. *Trans Am Inst Homeop* 1893:129. *Med inv* 11:253, 1880 *Cleave*. Homeopath.

BIRCHETT, THEOPHILUS GILLIAM, CW–CSA; Vicksburg, Miss (b/VI–27–1835 Orange Co, Va; d/I–1–1904) MD UPa 1856. *New Orl m & s jour* 56: 632, 1904. *UPa med alum CW*: 1856. *Polk* 1886: 533.

BIRCKHEAD, LENNOX, Baltimore (b/II–27–1794 Cambridge, Md; d/IX–2–1865) MD UMd 1817. *Med annals Md*: 321.

BIRCKHEAD, SOLOMON, Baltimore (b/VII–21–1761 Cambridge, Md; d/XI–30–1836) MD UPa 1783. *Med annals Md*: 322.

BIRCKHEAD, WILLIAM HUNTER, Newport, RI (d/ IV–12–1895 @ 56) MD CPSNY 1864; AB Trinity Conn 1861, AM 1864. *JAMA* 24: 650, 1895. *Butler* 1878: 746.

BIRD, ALFRED M, Mason City, Ill (d/I–25–1905 @ 62) Cert Exam Bd. *Ill med jour* 7:242, 1905. *Polk* 1896: 429.

BIRD, FRANCIS W , Brooklyn (d/IV–15–1877 @43) MD Queen's U Ont 1859. *Med reg NY NJ Conn* 1877: 196.

BIRD, JAMES CLARK, Washington, DC (b/VII–1–1828 Del; d/XII–5–1904) MD UPa 1853. *Hist Med Soc DC*: 315. *Polk* 1893: 268.

BIRD, JOHN FRANCIS, Fox Chase, Pa (b/III–7–1816 West River, Md; d/VI–22–1904) MD UPa 1843. *Pa med jour* 8:334, 1904/05. *Atkinson* I:28. *Polk* 1896:1298.

BIRD, JOHN QUIMBY, Jersey City, NJ (b/IV–20–1845 Barnardsville, NJ; d/VI–17–1887) MD UCNY 1868. *Bost m & s jour* 116:621, 1887. *Med surg rep Phila*

 Spec. educ'l status abbrev. as: ***ng*** = college verified attendance without degree;

56:826, 1887. *Atkinson* I:510–11. *Butler* 1878: 466.

BIRD, JOHN STERLING, Hyde Park, NY (b/VIII-29-1836; d/IV-3-1900) MD CPSNY 1863. *Bost m & s jour* 142: 396, 1900. *JAMA* 34:957, 1900. *Polk* 1896:1027.

BIRD, ROBERT, Cobham, Va (b/Engl; d/X-31-1890 @ 58) MD Edinburgh 1854. *Trans Med Soc Va* 1891: 259–260.

BIRD, ROBERT MONTGOMERY, Philadelphia (b/1803 [1805?] Newcastle, Del; d/I-22-1854) MD UPa 1827. *Phila m & s jour* 2:260, 1854. *K & B* II:104.

BIRD, WILLIAM BLAND, Baltimore (d/IV-4-1898 @ 25) MD UMd 1895. *JAMA* 30:933,1898. *Polk* 1896:656.

BIRD, WILLIAM PLUMMER, South River, Md (b/VII-25-1825 Anne Arundel Co, Md; d/X-15-1884) MD UMd 1849; AB Dickinson 1846. *Med surg rep Phila* 52: 288, 1885.

BIRDSALL, ASAHEL HOUGHTON, NYC; Brooklyn (b/VIII-15-1851 Newburgh, NY; d/VIII-8-1897) MD Hahnemann Phila 1873. *Trans Am Inst Homeop* 1898: 48. *Polk* 1886: 643. Homeopath.

BIRDSALL, WILLIAM RANDALL, NYC (b/1851; d/VI-7-1892) MD UMich 1876; MD CPSNY 1877. *Med reg NY NJ Conn* 1893: 297. *JAMA* 19: 20, 1892. *Bost m & s jour* 126:620, 1892.

BIRKEY, THOMAS WILLIAM, Philadelphia; CW-USA (b/1831; d/I-10-1899) MD UPa 1851. *JAMA* 32: 195, 1899. *UPa med alum CW*: 1851. *Polk* 1896:1299.

BIRKEY, WILLIAM J A, USA; Newportville, Pa (d/XI-1-1904 @ 80) MD Phila Coll Med & Surg 1849. *Pa med jour* 8:334, 1904/05.

BIRNEY, DAVID BELL, Philadelphia (d/XI-2 or 23-1906 @ 44) MD UPa 1885; AB 1882, AM 1886. *Pa med jour* 10:213, 1906/07. *Flint* 1897: 814.

BIRNEY, SAMUEL H, Urbana, Ill (d/VII-1-1900) MD Rush 1869. *Ill med jour* ns2:141, 1900. *Polk* 1886:300.

BIRNSTILL, JOSEPH, Erie, Pa 1839; Massillon, O; Worcester, Mass; Boston 1847–49; Newton Corner, Mass (b/VIII-9-1809 Baden, Germany; d/II-16-1867) <MD Würzburg> *Trans Am Inst Homeop* 1893:129. *New Engl med gaz* 2:69, 1867. *King* I:94, 234. Homeopath.

BIRTWELL, CHARLES EBENEZER, Lawrence, Mass (d/XII-8-1904 @43, Providence, RI) MD UCNY 1884. *Bost m & s jour* 151: 726, 1904. *Polk* 1886: 468.

BISHOP, CALVIN STANHOPE, Easton, Pa; CW-USA (b/III-3-1820 Hunterdon Co, NJ; d/IX-19-1866 Phila) MD UPa 1854. *Med surg rep Phila* 15:287, 441, 1866.

BISHOP, DAVID FOWLER, Lockport, NY 1855- (b/IX-4-1828 Oneida Co, NY; d/IV-24-1885 @ 57) MD Hahnemann Phila 1854. *Trans Am Inst Homeop* 1886: 130. Homeopath.

BISHOP, DENNIS DENNETT, Chicago (d/IV-1-1896) MD Rush 1892. *Chic med rec* 10:305, 1896. *Polk* 1897: 372.

BISHOP, EBENEZER HUGGINS, New Haven, Conn (b/II-11-1807; d/X-2-1890) MD Yale 1829; AB 1826. *Med reg NY NJ Conn* 1892:272. *JAMA* 15: 916, 1890. *Proc Conn Med Soc* 1891: 302. *Bost m & s jour* 123: 360, 1890.

BISHOP, EDWIN RUBERGALL, Geneva, NY; Brantford, Ont (d/VII-24-1901 @ 44) MD Trinity Med Coll, Toronto 1888. *JAMA* 37:398, 1901.

BISHOP, ELIJAH, Smithburg, Md (b/1798 Lisbon Co; d/III-1870) MD Yale 1823; AB 1819. *Med annals Md*:322.

BISHOP, GEORGE B, Silver Creek, NY; Titusville, Pa (d/I-21-1880 @ 51) MD Buffalo 1875. *Med surg rep Phila* 42:132, 176, 1880.

BISHOP, HENRY MARTURIN, Sharon, Pa; Brentwood, Mass (b/X-13-1837 Middletown, Conn; d/III-16-1901) MD CPSNY 1869; AB Amherst 1858. *Amherst, Men of*: 1858. *Polk* 1886: 844.

BISHOP, JOHN, NYC (b/II-17-1820; d/VII-29-1878) MD UCNY 1848. *Med reg NY NJ Conn* 1879:188.

BISHOP, LEVERETT, Sauquoit, NY (b/VII-19-1791 Guilford, Conn; d/III-30-1885) MD Oneida Co Med Soc dipl. *Med adv* 16:242, 1886. *Hom phys* 5:282, 1886? *Trans NY St Homeop Soc* 10:632. Homeopath c1846–

BISHOP, PHANUEL EUCLID, CW-USA; Pawtucket, RI (b/III- 30-1844; d/IX-21-1890) ng Bowdoin & Dartmouth 1873; PhB Brown 1866. *Trans RI Med Soc* 4:244–45, 1889–93. *Polk* 1886: 844.

BISHOP, TRUMAN, Ohio (d/II- -1829) *Transylvania jour med & assoc sci* 2:298, 1829.

BISHOP, WILLIAM S, CW-USN (d/XII-28-1868 Phila) MD Jefferson 1842 *Tr AMA* 21: 494–95, 1870. *Trans Med Soc NJ* 1869:104–05. *Med surg rep Phila* 20: 20, 1869. *Nat med jour* 1: 291, 1870/71.

BISSELL, DANIEL PEREZ, Utica, NY 1846- (b/V-27 1801 Randolph, Vt; d/X-30-1874) Lic Conn St Med Soc 1826; ng Yale Med Sch 1826. *Tr AMA* 27:667–668, 1876. *Trans Med Soc St NY* 1875: 373–376. *Buff med jour* 14: 157, 1874.

BISSELL, EVELYN LYMAN, New Haven, Conn (b/IX-10-1836 Litchfield, Conn; d/XII-9-1905) MD Yale 1860. *Proc Conn Med Soc* 1906:298–99. *Flint* 1897: 176.

BISSELL, HENRY HIRAM, Erie, Pa; NYC (d/1858) MD Yale 1826. *Tr AMA* 13:800, 1860. *Buff med jour* 14: 318, 1858.

BISSELL, PHILIP, NYC (d/IV-13-1904 @ 27) MD CPSNY 1902; AB Columbia 1897. *Bost m & s jour* 150: 442, 1904.

BISSELL, WILLIAM HARRISON, Monroe Co, Ill; Springfield (b/IV-25-1811 Hartwick, NY; d/III-18-1860) MD Jefferson 1834; stud law. *Med surg rep Phila* ns4: 28, 1860. *Biogr direct Congress*.

BISSEY, HERMAN S, Philadelphia (d/II-22-1903 @ 48) MD UPa 1880. *Pa med jour* 7:278, 1903/04. *Polk* 1896: 1299.

BITELY, EUGENE, Paw Paw, Mich (b/IV-17-1824 Moreau, NY; d/III-31-1873) MD Homeop Coll Cleveland 1853. *Am homeop obs* 10:400, 1873. *Ohio m & s rep* 7:192, 1873. *Trans Am Inst Homeop* 1874:661.

BITEMEN, JAMES H , CW–USA (d/IX–25–1865 San Antonio, Tex) *Nat med jour* 1:291, 1870–71.

BITTINGER, CHARLES, Washington, DC (b/V–19–1852; d/VII–31–1879) MD Georgetown 1873. *Hist Med Soc DC*: 299.

BIXBY, GEORGE HOLMES, CW–USA; Boston (b/1837 So America; d/II–26–1901) MD Dartmouth 1858; ng Harvard 1857; ng Williams. *Bost m & s jour* 144:245, 1901. *Harvard in CW*: 247. *Atkinson* I: 317.

BIXBY, SYLVANUS NEWELL, Strawberry Point, Ia (b/V–16–1844; d/V–10–1886) MD CPS Keokuk 1877. *Trans Ia St Med Soc* 7:528, 1886–89; 14:328, 1896.

BIXLER, JACOB R , Carlisle, Pa (b/IV–15–1840 Franklin Co, Pa; d/XI–3–1904) MD Jefferson 1866; AB Dickinson 1865. *Pa med jour* 8: 334, 1904/05.

BIZZELL, W A , Elizabethtown, NC (b/1827 Johnson Co, NC; d/I–15–1880) ng UPa Med Sch 1855/56. *NC med jour* 5: 275, 1880.

BLACHLEY, L S , CW–USA (d/V–23–1863) *Nat med jour* 1:290, 1870/71.

BLACHLEY STEPHEN L , Wilkinsburg, Pa (b/XII–15–1815 Sparta, Pa; d/X–28–1903) MD Jefferson 1870. *Pa med jour* 7: 278, 1903/04. *Atkinson*: I: 447.

BLACK, CHARLES H , Turtle Creek, Pa (d/I–2–1903) MD Jefferson 1875. *Pa med jour* 7:278, 1903/04.

BLACK, CHARLES STRATTON, St Louis (d/IV–6–1898 @ 40) MD St Louis Med Coll 1879. *JAMA* 30:999, 1898. *Polk* 1896: 865.

BLACK, HARVEY, Marion, Va; CW–CSA (b/VIII–21–1827 Blacksburg, Va; d/X–18–1888) MD UVa 1849. *Trans Med Soc Va* 1888: 275. *Trans Med Soc Va* 1888: 275. *Atkinson* I:352. *Polk* 1886: 914.

BLACK, HENRY MILLER, Strasburg, Pa (b/Lancaster Co; d/II–28–1897 @ 45) MD Jefferson 1875. *JAMA* 28: 569, 1897. *Polk* 1886: 836.

BLACK, JAMES E , London, Ont (b/1837; d/V–18–1864) MD Hahnemann, Phila 1858. *Am homeop obs* 1: , 1864 (Aug). Homeopath.

BLACK, JAMES MADISON, Knoxville, Tenn (b/1867; d/IV–5–1906) MD Kentucky Sch Med 1889; AB U Louisville. *Nashville jour m & s* 98: 233–35, 1906. *Polk* 1896: 1392.

BLACK, JOSEPH NANCE, Clayton Ill (d/VI–8–1905 @ 45) MD Rush 1883. *Ill m j* 8: 80, 1905. *Polk* 1896: 414.

BLACK, NORMAN W , Selma, Ind (b/III–28–1827 Harrisburg, Pa; d/VII–30–1880) MD unknown. *Trans Ind St Med Soc* 1881:235.

BLACK, THOMAS CRUTCHER, McMinville, Tenn (b/III–15–1809 Sumner Co, Tenn; d/V–28–1878 Murfreesboro, Tenn) MD Transylvania 1831. *Trans Med Soc Tenn* 1879: 181–83. *Butler* 1878: 764.

BLACKBURN, CARY B , CW; Louisville, Ky (b/Woodford Co, Ky; d/XII–4–1895) MD Jefferson 1861. *JAMA* 25: 1010, 1895. *Butler* 1878: 264.

BLACKBURN, CHURCHILL JONES, Covington, Ky (b/1793? d/V–13–1868 @ 75) MD UPa 1814. *Phila med reg & dir* 1871: 297. *Med surg rep Phila* 18:486, 1868.

BLACKBURN, RICHARD SCOTT, Clarke Co, Va (b/III–28–1809 Prince William Co, Va; d/IX–2–1867) MD UPa 1832. *Med annals Md*: 323.

BLACKEMORE, JAMES ALEXANDER, Gallatin, Tenn (b/VIII–8–1800 Sumner Co, Tenn; d/VI–2–1863 Nashville) MD Transylvania 1823. *Trans Med Soc Tenn* 1876: 79–80.

BLACKFAN, JOHN WILKINSON, CW–USA; Lebanon, NJ (b/XII–28–1821 Solebury, Pa; d/VI–3–1881) MD UPa 1844. *UPa med alum CW*: 1844.

BLACKFORD, THOMAS THORNBERG, Luray & Lynchburg, Va (b/1794 Pine Grove Furnace, Pa; d/VII–28–1863) MD UPa 1817; AB Dickinson 1812. *Dickinson cat*: 1812.

BLACKIE, GEORGE STODART, Nashville, Tenn 1857– (b/IV–10–1834 Aberdeen, Scotland; d/V–29–1881) MD Edinburgh 1855. *So pract* 3:215–222, 1881. *Chic med rev* 4:346, 1881. *Nashville jour m & s* ns28:35, 1881. *K & B* III: 104–105.

BLACKMAN, GEORGE, Westport, Conn (b/VII– –1803; d/VIII–8–1874) Hon MD Yale 1845; lic 1826. *Proc Conn Med Soc* 4:289 ff, 1874. *Butler* 1878: 73.

BLACKMAN, GEORGE CURTIS, Cincinnati (b/IV–21–1819 Newtown, Conn; d/VII–19–1871 Avondale, O) MD CPSNY 1841. *Tr AMA* 24:370–74, 1873. *Tr Ohio St Med Soc* 1872: 259–60. *Bost m & s jour* ns8: 76, 1871. *K & B* III: 105.

BLACKMAN, MARTIN C , Davidson Co, Tenn (d/1878) MD Vanderbilt 1878. *Tr AMA* 30:854, 1879.

BLACKMER, JOHN, CW–USA; Springfield Mass (b/Plymouth; d/IV–15–1895) MD Harvard 1854. *Bost m & s jour* 132:396, 1895. *Harvard in CW*: 240.

BLACKNALL, GEORGE, USN 1828–1861; CSN 1861– (b/IX–13–1804 Granville Co, NC; d/I–20–1862 Norfolk, Va) MD UPa 1831. *UPa med alum CW*: 1831.

BLACKNALL, GEORGE WILLIAM, CW–CSA; Raleigh, NC (b/IV–21–1829 Granville Co, NC; d/XI–10–1897) MD UPa 1849. *UPa med alum CW*: 1849.

BLACKWOOD, BENJAMIN WHITALL, Haddonfield, NJ (d/I–19–1866) MD UPa 1828. *Med surg rep Phila* 14:80, 1866. *King* I:249. Homeopath 1853– .

BLACKWOOD, SAMUEL WOODWARD, CW–USA (d/X–6–1871 Callao, Peru) MD UPa 1865. *UPa med alum CW*: 1865.

BLACKWOOD, THOMAS RAKESTRAW, Camden, NJ (b/VII–30–1835 Moorestown, NJ; d/VII–30–1895) MD Hahnemann Phila 1870. *Trans Am Inst Homeop* 1896:1185. *Hahn mo* 31:103, 1896 (news & advert). *Polk* 1886: 601. Homeopath.

BLADEN, WILLIAM T , CW–USA (d/X–29–1863 Washington, DC) *Nat med jour* 1:290, 1870/71. *Med*

 Spec. educ'l status abbrev. as: ***ng*** = college verified attendance without degree;

surg rep Phila 10:398, 1863.

BLAINE, EPHRAIM McDOWELL, USA 1830–35 (b/IX–24–1796 Carlisle, Pa; d/III–13–1835 Savannah, Ga) MD UPa 1827; AB Dickinson 1814. *Dickinson cat*: 1814.

BLAIR, ALEXANDER R , York, Pa (b/1826 Lancaster Co, Pa; d/VII–16–1889) MD Jefferson 1853. *Trans Med Soc Pa* 21:300, 1889–90. *JAMA* 13:757, 1889. *Med bull m & s* 11:262, 1889. *Butler* 1878: 740.

BLAIR, ARBA, Rome, NY (b/VII–9–1781; d/VI–20–1863) Hon MD Regents, State UNY 1849. *Tr AMA* 16:626–27, 1865.

BLAIR, FRANK WEEKS, Farmington, NH (b/II–13–1875 Boothbay Harbor, Me; d/XI–19–1905 Portsmouth) MD Bowdoin 1899; AB 1895. *Trans NH Med Soc* 1906: 236. *Polk* 1900: 1120.

BLAIR, GILES TOMKINS, Westerville, O (d/XI– –1886) MD Cleveland Homeop 1868; MD Eclectic Med Inst 1859. *Med vis* 3: , 1887 (Feb). *Polk* 1886: 773. Homeopath.

BLAIR, HORACE P , Georgia, Vt (b/1799? d/VII–14–1874 @ 75) MD UVt 1824. *Bost m&s j* 91: 170, 1874.

BLAISDELL, CLARK, Marblehead, Mass (b/I–8–1809 Canaan, NH; d/III–23–1862) MD Woodstock 1835. *Bost m & s jour* 67:368, 1862.

BLAISDELL, JACOB, Keesville, NY (b/1795? d/V–3–1866 @ 71) MD Bowdoin 1829. *Med surg rep Phila* 15: 28, 1866.

BLAISDELL, WARREN O , Macomb, Ill (d/III–18–1903 @ 48) Lic by years of practice. *Ill med jour* ns4: 889, 1903. *Polk* 1896: 428. Homeopath.

BLAISDELL, WESLEY, Coeymans, NY; CW–USA (d/X–20–1864 Grand Bridge Mills, Va) *Med surg rep Phila* 12:219, 1864/65.

BLAKE, CALVIN, Hartland, Me (b/IX–5–1798 Turner, Me; d/X–8–1870) MD Bowdoin 1824. *Trans Me Med Assn* 1871–73; 189–90.

BLAKE, CHARLES EDWARD, CW–USA; Prescott, Ariz; San Francisco (b/VIII–14–1845 Holden, Me; d/I–17–1894) MD Med Coll Pacific 1873; stud law Phila; AB Yale 1865. *Trans Med Soc Calif* 1894:293–94. *Butler* 1878:53.

BLAKE, CHARLES MORRIS, San Francisco (b/XII–24 1819 Brewer, Me; d/VI–3–1893) MD U Calif 1876; AB Bowdoin 1842. *Bowdoin cat* 1842.

BLAKE, EDMUND H , Washington Co, Pa; Houston, Tex; 1855– (d/VII–8–1876 Austin, Tex) MD Hahnemann Phila 1858 [ad eundem?] *Amer homeop obs* 13?: 1876 (Oct). Homeopath 1855?– .

BLAKE, ELI WHITNEY, New Haven, Conn CW–USA (b/XII–27–1819 Whitneyville, Conn; d/XI–19–1873) MD Yale 1842; ng Harvard 1840. *Proc Conn Med Soc* 4:291 ff, 1874.

BLAKE, GEORGE T , Elizabeth, NJ; NYC (d/VIII–1861 @ 41) MD UCNY 1846. *Trans NJ Med Soc* 1871–73: 174.

BLAKE, JAMES HEIGHE, Georgetown, Md (b/VI–11–1768; d/VII–26–1819) <UPa Med Sch 1789> *Hist Med Soc DC*: 213–14.

BLAKE, JOHN B , Washington, DC (b/VIII–12–1800; d/X–26–1881) MD UMd 1824. *Hist Med Soc DC*: 224. *Butler* 1874: 90.

BLAKE, JOHN ELLIS, NYC (b/X–20–1831 Brattleboro, Vt; d/IX–27–1880) MD Harvard 1855; AB 1852. *Bost m & s jour* 103: 602–03, 1880. *Butler* 1878: 507.

BLAKE, JOSIAH MERRILL, Otisfield, Me (b/VI–1–1817; d/I–18–1859) MD Bowdoin 1841. *Tr AMA* 13: 789, 1860. *Nashville jour m & s* 16:375, 1859.

BLAKE, WARREN PERKINS, Springfield, Mass (b/VII 1–1858 Barnstead, NH; d/II–15–1906) MD Dartmouth 1884. *Bost m & s jour* 154: , 1906. *Polk* 1890: 709.

BLAKELY, WILLIAM JAMES, St Mary's, Pa; Pittsburgh (b/IV–26–1839; d/I–14–1877) MD Hahnemann Phila 1861; AB Georgetown 1857. *Trans Am Inst Homeop* 1895: 1093. *US med inv* 5: 165, 1877. *Tr Homeop Med Sc* Pa 1870–71: ; 1874–78: . Homeopath.

BLAKEMAN, RUFUS, Greenfield Hill, Conn (b/1795 Monroe, Conn; d/II–17–1870) MD CPSNY 1822; AB Union 1819. *Phila med reg & dir* 1871:304. *Proc Conn Med Soc* 3:414, 1871.

BLAKEMAN, WILLIAM NELSON, NYC (b/1805 Roxbury, Conn; d/VIII–10–1890) MD Yale 1832. *Med reg NY NJ Conn* 1891: 269. *Bost m & s jour* 123: 189, 1890. *Butler* 1878: 507.

BLAKER, GILBERT HICKS, Philadelphia; CW–USA (d/VII–18–1865 @ 47 Frankford, Phila) MD UPa 1851. *Nat med jour* 1:290, 1870/71.

BLAKESLEE, CHARLES LEWIS, S Windsor, Conn (d/V–2–1897 @ 34) MD UCNY 1890. *JAMA* 28:1045, 1897. *Polk* 1896: 278.

BLANC, HENRY WILLIAM, New Orleans (d/VII–25–1896 @ 35 Asheville, NC) MD Tulane 1885. *New Orl m & s jour* ns24: 175–76, 1896. *Med bull m & s* 18:392, 1897. *Polk* 1890: 489.

BLANCHARD, ANDREW DELAVAL, Melrose, Mass (b/Medford; d/VI– –1906 @ 83) MD Harvard 1846; AB 1842. *Bost m & s jour* 154: 722, 1906.

BLANCHARD, FERDINAND, Peacham, NH (b/XI–8–1851 W Windsor, Vt; d/XII–22–1892) MD Dartmouth 1878; AB 1874. *Polk* 1886: 906.

BLANCHARD, GEORGE ANDERSON, Scranton, Pa (b/Hudson, NH; d/VII–19–901 @ 35) MD UPa 1895. *Pa med jour* 4:828, 1900/01; 5:295, 1901/02.

BLANCHARD, HENRY, Dorchester, Mass (d/II–10–1897 @ 85) MD Harvard 1840. *Bost m & s jour* 137: 172, 263, 690, 1897. *Polk* 1886: 485.

BLANCHARD, JAMES AUGUSTUS, Brooklyn (b/Norwich, Conn; d/I–8–1896 @ 55) MD CPSNY 1867. *JAMA* 26:243, 1896. *Polk* 1896: 922.

BLANCHARD, SAMUEL B , Washington, DC (b/1817

Mass; d/VIII–21–1877) MD Columbian DC 1850. *Tr AMA* 29:618, 1878. *Hist Med Soc DC*: 245.

BLANCHARD, SAMUEL WOODBURY, Searsport, Me 1845–48; Yarmouth, Me 1848–57 (b/IV–15–1818; d/XII–23–1857) MD Jefferson 1844; AB Bowdoin 1841. *Bowdoin cat*: 1841.

BLAND, DANIEL WEBSTER, CW–USA; Pottsville, Pa (b/I–28–1837; d/III–28–1899) MD Pa Coll Med Dept 1857. *Pa med jour* 3:107, 1899/1900. *Lehigh Valley med mag* 10:22–23, 1899. *JAMA* 32:845, 1899. *Polk* 1896: 1330.

BLAND, ELBERT, ?SC; CW–USA (d/IX–19–1863) MD UCNY 1844. *UCNY – Bellevue alum cat*: 5.

BLAND, WILLIAM JOHN, Clarksburg, WVa (b/XI–10–1816 Kingwood, Va; d/II–20–1897) MD Jefferson 1849; MD Louisville Med Col 1842. *JAMA* 28:476, 1897. *Atkinson* I: 310. *Butler* 1878: 848.

BLANDING, WILLIAM, Rehoboth, Mass (b/II–7–1773; d/X–12–1857) MD Brown 1821; AB 1801. *Bost m & s jour* 57: 247, 295–96, 1857.

BLANDY, THOMAS ROBERT, CW–CSA; Huntingdon, Pa (b/X–30–1828 Newark, Del; d/IV–21–1885) MD UPa 1851; AM Del Coll 1848. *UPa med alum CW*: 1851. *Reg lic Pa phys* 1881–85: 774.

BLANE, JOHN, Perryville, NJ (b/VII–7–1802 New Brunswick, NJ; d/VI–18–1885) Lic Bd Censors Somerset Co NJ 1827; ng CPSNY & Rutgers 1824–1827. *Trans Med Soc NJ* 1886: 147–51. *Butler* 1878: 466.

BLANEY, JAMES VAN ZANDT, Chicago; CW–USA (b/V–1–1820 Newcastle, Del; d/XII–11–1874) MD UPa 1842; AB Princeton 1838, AM 1841. *Tr AMA* 26: 456–60, 1875. *UPa Med alum CW*: 1842. *Trans Ill Med Soc* 1875: 229–32. *Chic med jour* 32:3–8, 1874. *K & B* III:112.

BLANKENSHIP, JOHN S , Rushville, Ill (d/XII–2–1896) Lic by years of practice. *JAMA* 28:92, 1897. *Polk* 1886: 256.

BLANKS, JOHN HARRISON, Meridian, Miss (d/X–19–1906 New Orleans) MD Columbia 1876; MD Ala Med Coll 1874. *New Orl m & s jour* 59:480, 1906. *Polk* 1890:1058.

BLANTON, CARTER, Hickman,Ky (d/1878) MD Jefferson 1864. *Tr AMA* 30:854,1879. *Med rec* 14:240, 1878.

BLATCHFORD, THOMAS WINDEATT, Troy, NY (b/VII–20–1794 Topham, Engl; d/I–7–1866) MD CPSNY 1817; Hon AB Union 1815. *Tr AMA* 18:316–17, 1867. *Buffalo m & s jour* 5:251–52, 1866. *Bost m & s jour* 73:508, 1865; 74:27–28, 1866. *Trans Med Soc St NY* 1866: 322 ff. *K & B* III:112–13.

BLAUVELT, CHARLES C , Hightstown, NJ (b/VIII–20–1806; d/III–28–1855) <ng UVa Med Sch>; Hon AB Rutgers 1828; Hon AM 1831. *Trans Med Soc NJ* 1871–73: 87–88.

BLAUVELT, JAMES F , NYC; CW–USA (d/V–17–1884 @ 60) MD CPSNY 1851. *Med surg rep Phila* 50: 704, 1884.

BLAUVELT, WILBUR A , Newark, NJ (d/II–18–1903 @ 27) MD NY Homeop Med Coll 1900. *No Amer jour homeop* 51: , 1903 (May). Homeopath.

BLEECKER, EDWARD, Whitestone, NY (b/I–9–1844 Albany NY; d/XI–5–1899) MD CPSNY 1865. *Bost m & s jour* 141: 508, 1899. *JAMA* 33:1308, 1899. *Polk* 1896: 1112.

BLENNERHASSETT, JOHN, Brooklyn (b/1791? Ireland; d/II–12–1877 @ 66) <MD Dublin> *Med reg NY NJ Conn* 1877: 196.

BLICHFELDT, M , Chattanooga, Tenn (d/X–12–1878 Vicksburg, Miss) *Tr AMA* 30:854, 1879. *Med rec* 14:240, 1878.

BLICKHAHN, WALTER LOUIS, St Joseph, Mo; St Louis (d/V–20–1895 @ 33) MD St Louis Med Coll 1882. *JAMA* 24:861, 1895. *Polk* 1890:671.

BLINN, ODELIA, Chicago (b/1845? d/I–20–1905 @ 60) MD Woman's Med Coll Pa 1868. *Chic med rec* 27:157, 1905. *Ill med jour* 7:242, 1905. *Flint* 1897: 256.

BLISS, ABNER FRANKLIN, Wardsboro, Vt (b/VII–30–1829 Alstead, NH; d/VIII–13–1901) MD Castleton 1851. *JAMA* 37:710, 1901. *Polk* 1886: 907.

BLISS, CHARLES, NYC (d/I–23–1889 @ 48) MD Berkshire 1865. *Med reg NY NJ Conn* 1889:268. *Polk* 1886: 672.

BLISS, DOCTOR [sic] **WILLARD**, Washington, DC (b/VIII–18–1825 Auburn, NY; d/II–24–1889) MD Western Reserve 1849. *Bost m & s jour* 120:228, 1889. *Hist Med Soc DC*: 277. *Med bull m & s* 11:125, 1889. *Butler* 1878: 93.

BLISS, ELA D [or L], CW–USA (d/VIII–23–1865 @ 26) MD Rush 1863. *Nat med jour* 1:290, 1870/71. *Med surg rep Phila* 13:166, 1865.

BLISS, HENRY DWIGHT, Holley, NY (d/IV–13–1900 @ 46 Rochester) MD UPa 1883; BS unknown. *JAMA* 34:1084, 1900. *Polk* 1896:992.

BLISS, JAMES COTTON, NYC (d/VII–30–1854) MD CPSNY 1815. *NW m & s jour* 4: 438, 1854.

BLISS, WILLIAM W , ?Orange, NJ (d/IX–5–1873 @ 51) MD UPa 1844. *Med surg rep Phila* 29:216, 1873.

BLISS, ZENAS ELLIOTT, Grand Rapids, Mich; CW–USA (d/IV–23–1877) MD U Mich 1855. *Med rec* 15: 617, 1879.

BLIVEN, GEORGE FREMONT, Providence, RI (b/I–17–1857 Pawtucket; d/IX–28–1893) MD UCNY 1881. *Trans RI Med Soc* 4:626–627, 1889–93. *Polk* 1890: 1029.

BLIVEN, JEREMIAH PARKER, NYC (d/VII–12–1887) MD Yale 1835. *Med reg NY NJ Conn* 1888:242.

BLOCH, ALBERT J , Denver (d/VI–7–1901 @ 33) MD Tulane 1892. *New Orl m & s jour* 54: 59, 1901. *Polk* 1896: 619.

BLODGETT, CHARLES, Holyoke,Mass (d/VI–25–1903 @ 75 Grass Valley, Calif) MD Berkshire 1859. *Bost m &*

	Spec. educ'l status abbrev. as: ***ng*** = college verified attendance without degree;

s jour 149:114, 1903. *Polk* 1886: 467.

BLODGETT, GEORGE W , NYC (d/XI-28-1887) MD NY Homeop Med Coll 1877. *No Amer jour homeop* 36: 141, 1888. *Med couns* 12:576, 1887/88. *Polk* 1886:672. Homeopath.

BLODGETT, JOSHUA, Stafford, Conn (b/VIII-10-1801; d/1881) MD Berkshire 1825. *Proc Conn Med Soc* ns2: 180-83, 1882-83. *Butler* 1878: 73.

BLOMER, GEORGE DAVIS, Philadelphia (b/IV-16-1864; d/XII-1-1902 @ 38) MD Jefferson 1890. *Pa med jour* 6:153, 259, 1902/03. *Flint* 1897: 814.

BLONDELL, EUGENE, NYC (d/II-1-1885 @ 37) MD CPSNY 1877; AB Coll City NY 1867. *Med reg NY NJ Conn* 1885:230.

BLOOD, HENRY S , CW-CSA (d/II-27-1862) *Nat med jour* 1:290, 1870/71.

BLOOD, JOSIAH MARK, Ashby, Mass (d/XI-19-1898) MD UCNY 1857. *Bost m & s jour* 139:560, 1898. *Polk* 1896: 691.

BLOOD, OLIVER HUNTER, Worcester, Mass (b/V-31-1800; d/IV-8-1858 @ 57) MD Harvard 1826; AB 1821. *Bost m & s jour* 58: 227, 1858. *Necrol alum Harvard*: 193 ff.

BLOOD, SOLOMON, Rochester, Wis; Steele Co. Minn (b/II-16-1810 Hollis, NH; d/XII-3-1881 Owatonna, Minn) MD Woodstock 1838. *Tr AMA* 33:527-29, 1882. *Trans Minn St Med Soc* 1882: 264-67; 1888: 272. *Atkinson* I:412.

BLOOD, WARREN HOME, Oakland, Calif (d/IX-12-1903 @ 39) MD Cooper 1885. *Calif st jour med* 1:323, 1903. *Polk* 1886: 164.

BLOODGOOD, ABRAHAM, Flushing, NY (d/II-8-1880 @ 69) MD CPSNY 1833; AB Union 1829. *Med surg rep Phila* 42: 198, 1880. *Butler* 1878: 528.

BLOODGOOD, WILLIAM EDWARD, NYC (d/X-10-1897 @ 74) MD CPSNY 1847; AB UCNY 1845. *Bost m & s jour* 137: 430, 1897.

BLOOMFIELD, OGDEN, Syracuse; NYC (b/1841? d/IV-4-1891 @ 50) MD unknown *Med reg NY NJ Conn* 1891: 269. *Polk* 1896: 660.

BLOOMFIELD, THOMAS BLANCH, Westbrook, Conn (b/XI-17-1846 NYC; d/II-7-1905) MD CPSNY 1876; ng Rutgers 1864/65. *Proc Conn Med Soc* 1905: 501-02. *Flint* 1897: 179.

BLOSS, GEORGE ALVIN, Eddyville, Pa (d/X-15-1904 @ 49) MD Jefferson 1883. *Pa med jour* 8:334, 1904/05. *Flint* 1897: 801.

BLOSS, RICHARD, E Bethel & Royalton, Vt; Troy, NY 1846- (b/IV-13-1798 Royalton; d/IX-3-1863) MD Dartmouth 1823. *Trans Am Inst Homeop* 1867: 156. Homeopath 1843- .

BLOUNT, CYRUS N , Kokomo, Ind (b/VIII-26-1832 Highland Co; d/XII-28-1887) MD Jefferson 1865. *Polk* 1886: 320. *Trans Ind St Med Soc* 1888: 209.

BLOUSE, JOHN ANDREW, York, Pa (d/VIII-27-1896 @ 28) MD UPa 1891. *JAMA* 27: 613, 1896.

BLUE, JOHN H , Montgomery, Ala (d/I-8-1894) MD Washington U Sch Med Balto 1870. *Med reg NY NJ Conn* 1894: 234. *JAMA* 22: 97, 1894.

BLUMBERG, ALBERT, Pittsburgh, Pa (d/XII-1-1903 @ 54) MD Würzburg 1873. *Pa med jour* 7:209, 278, 1903/04. *Polk* 1896: 1323.

BLUMENTHAL, CHARLES EDWARD, NYC (b/Hamburg; d/X-11-1883 @ 69 or 80?) MD unknown. *Amer homeop obs* 20: 383, 1884. *Med adv* 14: 278, 1884. *Med couns* 8:576, 1884. *Med surg rep Phila* 49: 476, 1883.

BLUMENTHAL, OLIVER A , Syracuse, NY (d/XII-21-1905 @ 35) MD Syracuse 1893. *Bost m & s jour* 153: 737, 1905. *Polk* 1896: 1102.

BLUNDEN, BOYLE N , Philadelphia (d/IV-3-1885 @ 27) MD Jefferson 1879. *Med surg rep Phila* 52: 512, 1885.

BLUNT, MARK SHERBURNE, Mt Vernon, Ind (b/VII-28-1826 Norridgewalk, Me; d/X-2-1881) MD Bowdoin 1851. *Trans Ind St Med Soc* 1882: 198. *Butler* 1878: 194.

BLUTHARDT, THEODORE J , Chicago (d/I-15-1906 @ 68 Germany) MD Chic Med Coll 1861. *Ill med jour* 9:131, 1906. *Polk* 1896:374.

BLYTHE, SMITH GREEN, Nora Springs, Ia (b/XI-6-1841 Cranbury, NJ; d/VIII-10-1899) MD Bellevue 1878; att? Lafayette. *JAMA* 33:620, 1899. *Polk* 1896: 534.

BOAL, CLIFFORD DOYLE, Baden, Pa (d/XII-20-1903 @ 24) MD U So Calif 1901. *Pa med jour* 7: 278, 1903/04.

BOARDMAN, HORACE E , Monroe, Wis; Larned, Kans (b/V-15-1835 W Rutland, Vt; d/II-26-1888) MD Hahnemann Chic 1867; AB Middlebury 1856. *Trans Am Inst Homeop* 1888: 28. *Med inv* 3: 1887 (Dec.) *Polk* 1886: 958. Homeopath.

BOARDMAN, JOHN, Buffalo (b/VI-4-1828 Watertown, NY; d/VII-9-1898 @ 70) MD UPa 1853; ng Buffalo Med Coll. *Buff m & s jour* 38: 67-68, 1898. *JAMA* 31:198, 1898. *Butler* 1878: 536.

BOARDMAN, JOSEPH CANFIELD, Trenton, NJ (b/V-4-1813 Wethersfield, Conn; d/VII-26-1896) MD UPa 1844. *Trans Am Inst Homeop* 1897:63. *No Amer jour homeop* 44:662, 1896. *Polk* 1886:611. Homeopath.

BOARDMAN, WALTER, Lancaster, Pa (d/XII-16-1899) MD Jefferson 1885. *JAMA* 34: 61, 1900. *Polk* 1896: 1286.

BOARMAN, CHARLES S , Boonville, Mo (d/III-15-1898 @ 72) MD UMd 1837. *JAMA* 30:745, 1898. *Polk* 1896: 833.

BOARMAN, CHARLES VERNON, Washington, DC (b/III-2-1851 DC; d/XI-2-1901) MD Georgetown 1871. *Hist Med Soc DC*: 297. *Polk* 1983: 268.

BOAS, MERRITT L , St Louis (d/IV-28-1899 @ 46) MD Central CPS, Ind 1881. *JAMA* 32: 1074, 1899. *Polk* 1886: 312 (Brownstown, Ind).

BOATNER, ELIAS S , Victoria, Tex (d/VIII-1-1896)

MD Tulane 1891. *JAMA* 27: 503, 1896. *Polk* 1896:1454.

BOAZ, CRISPIN DAVID, Fulton, Ky (d/IX-21-1878) MD U Louisville 1852; MD UPa 1857. *Tr AMA* 30: 854-55, 1879.

BOBBS, JOHN STOUGH, CW-USA; Indianapolis (b/ XII-28-1809 Greenvillage, Pa; d/V-1-1870) Stud w/ preceptor; <ng Jefferson>. *Phila med reg & dir* 1871: 305. *Trans Ind St Med Soc* 1870: 158. *Kemper's Ind*: 240. *K & B* III:114-115.

BOBO [BOBA?], BURWELL A , Ga (d/1878 Memphis) MD Med Coll SC 1858. *Tr AMA* 30:855, 1879.

BOCKEE, JACOB, Poughkeepsie, NY; CW-USA (b/ (Northeast, NY; d/XI-26-1885) MD UPa 1838; AB Union 1836. *UPa med alum CW*: 1838.

BODAMER, GEORGE A , Philadelphia (d/VIII-20-1902 @ 43) MD UPa 1884. *Pa med jour*5:663, 1901/02; 6:259, 1902/03. *Flint* 1897: 814.

BODENHAMER, WILLIAM, New Rochelle NY (b/1808 E Berlin Pa; d/III-31-1905) MD Worthington 1839. *Bost m & s jour* 152: 416,1905. *K & B* III:115.

BODENIUS, FRANCIS H , Madison, Wis (b/VII-21-1845 Baden, Germany; d/VII-21-1898 @ 53 Baltimore) <MD Heidelberg 1869> *JAMA* 31: 257, 1898. *Trans Wis St Med Soc* 1898: 553. *Polk* 1896: 1553.

BODGE, JAMES HENRY, Newton Centre, Mass (b/VI-26-1841; d/X-9-1893) MD Harvard 1867; AB Dartmouth 1865; AM. *JAMA* 21:700, 1893. *Bost m & s jour* 129: 432, 1893.

BODINE, JOSEPH LAMB, Trenton, NJ (b/VI-26-1839 Pemberton, NJ; d/I-2-1888 or 1889) MD UPa 1865; AB Princeton 1860, AM 1863. *Med reg NY NJ Conn* 1890: 261. *Trans NJ Med Soc* 1889:173. *Butler* 1878: 466.

BODKIN, DOMINICK G , Brooklyn, NY (b/1833 Ireland; d/I-26-1902) MD UCNY 1866. *Bost m & s jour* 146: 156, 1902. *Polk* 1896: 992.

BODLEY, RACHEL L , Philadelphia (b/XII-7-1831 Cincinnati; d/1888) Hon MD Woman's Med Col Pa 1879. *Med bull m & s* 10:264, 1888. *K & B* III:116-17. *Polk* 1886: 813.

BOEHME, J D , NYC (b/Gny; d/XI-21-1877 @ 47) MD Zurich 1864. *Med reg NY NJ Conn* 1878: 179. *Butler* 1874: 507.

BOERICKE, FRANCIS EDMUND, Philadelphia (b/VI-3-1826 Glauchau, Gny; d/XII-17-1901) MD Hahnemann Phila 1863. *Trans Amer Inst Homeop* 1902: 837 ff.

BOERSTLER, GEORGE W , Lancaster, O (b/X-19-1792 Funkstown, Md; d/XI-11-1871) MB UMd 1820; Hon MD UMd 1834. *Tr AMA* 31: 1014-16, 1880. *Trans Ohio St Med Soc* 1872: 268-71. *Med annals Md*: 324. *K & B* II:117.

BOGAN, MARTIN VAN BUREN, Washington, DC (b/IX-16-1820 Woodstock, Va; d/IV-19-1898) MD Columbian DC 1851. *JAMA* 30: 1125, 1898. *Hist Med Soc* DC: 244. *Polk* 1896: 301.

BOGERT, CORNELIUS ROBERT, ?NYC (d/1877) MD CPSNY 1824; AB Yale 1820. *Med reg NY NJ Conn* 1878: 179.

BOGERT, STEPHEN VAN RENSSELAER, Staten Isl, NY (b/III-14-1804 Albany; d/I-10-1896) MD Fairfield 1825. *JAMA* 26: 192, 1896. *Bost m & s jour* 134: 98, 1896. *Polk* 1886: 669.

BOGGS, JOSIAH N , Allegheny, Pa; CW-CSA (d/V-31 1900 @ 71 St Louis, Mo) MD Atlanta Med Coll 1861. *JAMA* 34:1574, 1900. *Polk* 1886: 789.

BOGGS, SETH D , Brooklyn, NY (b/1852; d/VIII-10-1895) *Bost m & s jour* 153: 206, 1905. *Polk* 1896: 992.

BOGLE, R L , Raymond, Miss (d/VII-13-1888) MD Jefferson 1858. *New Orl m & s jour* ns 16: 159, 1888. *Polk* 1886: 531.

BOGMAN, EDWARD YOUNG, Providence, RI; Atlanta, Ga (b/II-24-1849 Boston; d/III-5-1900) MD Harvard 1876; AB Brown 1873. *Brown hist cat*: 1873. Homeopath [?].

BOGUE, ROSWELL GRISWOLD, CW-USA; Chicago (b/V-3-1832 Louisville, NY; d/XII-8-1893) MD CPSNY 1857. *Chic med rec* 5: 457, 1893. *JAMA* 21: 936, 1893. *Trans Ill St Med Soc* 1894: 54-56.

BOHANNAN, RICHARD LAFON, Richmond, Va (b/1787 Essex Co, Va; d/VII-15-1855) MD UPa 1811; AB Wm & Mary. *Phila m & s jour* 4: 96, 1855. *Tr AMA* 31: 1016-18. 1880.

BOHN, H ROBERSON, Biloxi, Miss (d/XI-8-1901) MD Tulane 1893. *New Orl m & s jour* 54: 410, 1901. *Polk* 1896: 619.

BOHRER, BENJAMIN SCHENKMYER, Washington, DC (b/ ; d/) MD UPa 1810. *Tr AMA* 31: 1018-19, 1880. *Hist Med Soc DC*: 217.

BOISLINIERE, LOUIS CHARLES, St Louis, Mo (b/ IX-2-1816 Guadeloupe, WI; d/I-13-1896) MD St Louis Med Coll 1848. *Buff m & s jour* 35: 596-97, 1896. *JAMA* 26: 192, 1896. *Med bull m & s* 18: 114, 1896. *K & B* III: 118.

BOISNOT, JAMES MONROE, CW-USA; Philadelphia (b/VII-20-1836 Somerset Co, NJ; d/X-30-1879) MD UPa 1858. *Trans Med Soc Pa* 13: 381-85, 1880. *Med surg rep Phila* 41: 440, 1897. *UPa med alum CW*: 1858. *Atkinson* I: 178.

BOKER, CHARLES STEWART, Philadelphia (b/X-22-1828; d/XII-30-1894) MD UPa 1852; AB Princeton 1849, AM 1852, *Trans CPP* centennial vol: 213. *Atkinson* I: 365.

BOLDEMANN, ALBERT, NYC (b/X-14-1823; d/I-11-1870) <MD Göttingen> *Med reg NY NJ Conn* 1870:313.

BOLING, WILLIAM M , Montgomery, Ala (b/VII-14-1811 Baltimore Co, Md; d/III-4-1858 or 1859) MD Jefferson 1838. *New Orl m & s jour* 16: 757-59, 1859. *Nashville jour m & s* 16: 475, 1859. *Proc Ala Med Soc* 1870: 233-234.

BOLL, WILLIAM, Castroville, Tex (d/V-8-1891) MD St Louis Med Coll 1878. *Daniel's Tex med jour* 6: 527,

Spec. educ'l status abbrev. as: ***ng*** = college verified attendance without degree;

1890–91. *Polk* 1896: 1072.

BOLLES, EDGAR, Macomb, Ill (b/I–12–1837 Clyde, O; d/V–14–1900) MD Detroit Med Coll 1869. *JAMA* 34: 1356, 1900. *Ill med jour* ns2:48, 140, 1900.

BOLLES, JOHN CALVIN, Montville, Conn (b/IX–18–1816; d/IX–11–1847) MD Woodstock 1840. *Proc Conn Med Soc* 1898: 337–38. *JAMA* 29:660, 1897. *Bost m & s jour* 137: 304, 1897. *Flint* 1897: 176.

BOLLES, LUCIUS STILLMAN, CW–USA; Philadelphia (b/IV–21–1837 Boston; d/VIII–15–1873) MD UPa 1862; AB Brown 1859. *Trans CPP* centennial vol: 213. *U Pa med alum CW*: 1862. *Trans Med Soc St Pa* 10: 750–55, 1875.

BOLLES, RICHARD MONTGOMERY, Delhi, NY; NYC (b/IV–16–1797 Hudson, NY; d/VIII–9–1865) Lic Med Soc Columbia Co, NY; Hon MD Berkshire 1832. *Trans Am Inst Homeop* 1870: 637. *New Engl med gaz* 6: 191, 1871. *Med surg rep Phila* 13: 133, 1865.

BOLLING, ROBERT Jr, Philadelphia (b/XII–11–1832 Petersburg, Va; d/V–12–1901) MD UPa 1855; AB UVa. *Trans CPP* centennial vol: 213. *Pa med jour* 5: 295, 1901/02. *Atkinson* I: 63.

BOLLING, WILLIAM HOLT, Louisville, Ky (d/V–5–1891 @ 51) MD UPa 1867. *Bost m & s jour* 124:498, 1891 *Polk* 1886: 399.

BOLTER, ALFRED, Ovid, NY (b/VII–4–1811; d/VII–12–1880) MD Geneva 1838. *Trans Med Soc St NY* 1881: 379–81.

BOLTON, CHARLES, Whitemarsh, Pa (d/I–24–1840) MD UPa 1840. *Med surg rep Phila* 30: 180, 1874.

BOLTON, JACKSON, NYC (b/III–31–1814; d/II–16–1866) MD U Paris 1838; AB Columbia 1833. *Med reg NY NJ Conn* 1867: 209; 1869: 228/ *Tr AMA* 21: 434–35, 1870.

BOLTON, JAMES, Richmond, Va (b/1812; d/1869) MD CPSNY 1836; AB Columbia 1831; AM 1835. *Tr AMA* 31:1019–21, 1880.*K & B* I:95.

BOLTON, JOSEPH PEEKY, Philadelphia (b/XII–31–1839; d/II–24–1906) MD Jefferson 1890. *Jeffersonian* 7: 122, 1906. *Pa med jour* 9:430. 1905/06. *Flint* 1897: 814.

BOMAR, NATHANIEL T , Gainesville, Tex (d/X–9–1898) Lic by years of practice. *JAMA* 31: 1066, 1898. *Polk* 1896: 1430.

BOMBAUGH, CHARLES CARROLL, CW–USA; Baltimore (b/II–10–1828 Harrisburg, Pa; d/1906) MD Jefferson 1853; AB Harvard 1850. *Med annals Md*: 324–25. *Harvard in CW*: 45. *Polk* 1886: 435.

BOND, ARTHUR GRANT, Austin, Ill (d/IX–11–1898 @ 60) MD Rush 1878. *Chic med rec* 15: 192, 1898. *Flint* 1897: 252.

BOND, ELNATHAN J , Ord, Nebr; Loogootee, Ill (d/VII 17–1901 @ 73) MD Rush 1865. *Ill med jour* ns3:189, 1901. *JAMA* 35:342, 1901.

BOND, FRANK, Brooklyn (b/1827 Erie Co, Pa; d/II–10–1901) MD UCNY 1857; AB Williams 1854. *Bost m & s jour* 144:198, 1901. *Polk* 1896: 992.

BOND, HENRY, Philadelphia (b/III–21–1790 Watertown, Mass; d/V–4–1859. MD Dartmouth 1817; AB 1813. *Bost m & s jour* 63:251–58, 1861. *Trans Med Soc St Pa* 1860: 154–67. *Trans CPP* centennial vol: 213. *K & B* III: 119.

BOND, HENRY D , Buenos Aires (b/Md; d/1831) MD UMd 1817. *Med annals Md*: 325.

BOND, RICHARD CLAYTON, Aurora, Ind (b/III–22–1822 Wood Co, WVa; d/VI–30–1904) MD Miami 1857. *Trans Ind St Med Soc* 1905: 442. *Polk* 1896: 458.

BOND, ROBERT, Knowlton, NJ (b/I–12–1853 Phila; d/II–20–1891) MD UPa 1876; AB 1873, AM 1876. *Tr Med Soc NJ* 1892: 193–94.

BOND, SAMUEL SUPER, Washington, DC (b/VII–18–1834 Upper Darby, Pa; d/VII–4–1899) MD Georgetown 1865. *Hist Med Soc DC*: 275. *Polk* 1886: 211.

BOND, T W, Brownsville,Tenn (d/IV–16–1878 Memphis) *Tr AMA* 30: 855,1879. *Med rec* 14:240, 1878.

BOND, THOMAS EMERSON, War 1812–USA; Baltimore (b/II–1782; d/ III–14–1856) <Stud UPa Med Sch> *Med annals Md*: 325–26.

BOND, THOMAS EMERSON, Jr, Baltimore (b/XI– –1813 Harford Co, Md; d/VIII–19–1872) MD UMd 1834. *Med annals Md*: 326. *K & B* III:121.

BOND, THOMAS HOLDSWORTH, Calvert Co, Md (b/XII–15–1807; d/VIII–11–1838) MD Washington Med Coll Balto 1830. *Med annals Md*: 326.

BOND, THOMAS SHELDON, Evanston, Ill (b/XII–14–1842 Lee, Mass; d/XII–4–1895) MD Chicago Med Coll 1867; AB Amherst 1863. *Amherst, Men of*: 1863. *Polk* 1886: 278.

BONE, ROBERT D , Larissa, Tex (d/II–24–1892) MD U Nashville 1858. *Tex courier rec of med* 9: 191, 1892. *Polk* 1886: 889.

BONER, KARL [CHARLES] ALBERT, Brooklyn (d/X 15–1879 @ 34) MD Harvard 1868. *Med reg NY NJ Conn* 1879: 189.

BONFILS, SAUVEUR FRANÇOIS, Nashville, Tenn; Trenton; St Louis (d/VI–15–1855 @ 35) MD Transylvania 1840; ng U Ala 1836. *Bost m & s jour* 52: 487, 1855.

BONN, LOUIS E , Chicago (d/VI–25–1900) MD Northwestern 1893. *Ill med jour* ns2: 141, 1900.

BONNELL, CHARLES LEWIS, Brooklyn (b/X–15–1846; d/I–15–1902) MD Hahnemann Phila 1871; ng CPSNY; ng Wesleyan U. *Trans Am Inst Homeop* 1902: 845. Homeopath.

BONNER, SAMUEL LAFAYETTE, Reform, Ala; Merange, La (b/IV–7–1835; d/VI–4–1894) MD ULa 1860, stud UAla 1854. *U Ala cat*: 123. *Polk* 1886: 139.

BONNER, SAMUEL R , Camden, Ala (d/XII–24–1890) MD CPS Balto 1887. *Trans Med Assn St Ala* 1891:262.

BONNER, STEPHEN P , Cincinnati (d/III–5–1876) MD Ohio Med Coll 1858. *Trans O St Med Soc* 1877: 66. *Butler* 1878: 609.

BONNER, THOMAS HAMILTON, Orrville, Ala (b/III-23-1827 Troup Co, Ga; d/XI-14-1880) MD Ala St Bd Med Exam 1878. *Trans Med Assn St Ala* 1881: 270. *Butler* 1874: 15.

BONNEY, CALVIN F, Manchester, NH (b/Winthrop, Me; d/V-12-1886 @ 68) MD CPSNY 1868. *Trans NH Med Soc* 1886: 145-48. *Polk* 1886: 592.

BONNEY, E T, Bellville, Tex; CW-CSA (b/1832 Boston; d/VIII-6-1869) MD U Iowa 1855; <St Louis Med Coll 1856> *Proc Tex St Med Assn* 1870: [38].

BONSALL, JESSE KERSEY, Manila, PI; Chester, Pa 1842- (b/1797? d/XI-7-1858 @ 61) MD UPa 1828. *Med surg rep Phila* ns1: 124, 1858/59.

BONSTEEL, ALMON SPENCER, Corry, Pa (b/VII-17-1838 Ellicottville, NY; d/X-22-1887) MD Bellevue 1872. *JAMA* 9:831, 1887. *Butler* 1878: 705.

BONYNGE, FRANCIS G, Chicago (d/XII-26-1899 @ 50) <Lic RCS (Ireland) 1879> *Trans Ill St Med Soc* 1899-1900: 352. *Polk* 1896: 375.

BOON, JACOB, Glenolden, Pa (d/VII-17-1898 @ 61) MD Jefferson 1867 *JAMA* 31:257,1898. *Polk* 1896:1280.

BOONE, SAMUEL H, Denver, Colo (d/1877) MD U Louisville 1857. *Trans Colo St Med Soc* 1898-99: 508.

BOONE [BOON?], WILLIAM HENRY, Gap, Pa (b/VIII-9-1826 Chester Co, Pa; d/1859?) MD UMd 1850. *Trans Pa St Med Soc* 5: 107-08, 1860.

BOOR, WALTER AXLINE, New Castle, Ind (b/I-27-1849; d/V-24-1897) MD UMich 1872. *Trans Ind St Med Soc* 1898:375. *JAMA* 28:1092,1897. *Polk* 1896:484.

BOORAEM, AUGUSTUS C, NYC (b/1826; d/XII-2-1871 MD UCNY 1846. *Med reg NY NJ Conn* 1872: 342.

BOOTH, AUGUSTINE R, US Marine Hosp Serv (d/XII-27-1900 @ Shreveport, La) MD U Louisville 1874. *Bost m & s jour* 149: 54, 1901. *Polk* 1874: 626.

BOOTH, CHAUNCEY Jr, Somerville, Mass (b/1816 Coventry, Conn; d/I-12-1858) MD Berkshire 1839; ng Woodstock 1839; ng Amherst 1837. *Bost m & s jour* 57:514-15, 1857.

BOOTH, DAVID WINFIELD, Vicksburg, Miss (b/VII-17-1840; d/VIII-27-1878) MD ULa 1861. *Tr AMA* 30:808, 1879. *Trans Miss St Med Assn* 1879: 36-37, 58. *Med rec NY* 14:220, 1878. *Atkinson* I: 519.

BOOTH, FRANKLIN, Newtown & Long Island City, NY (b/Windsorville, Conn; d/VIII-19-1900) MD Bellevue 1864; PhB Yale 1859. *Bost m & s jour* 143: 223, 1900. *Polk* 1886: 669.

BOOTH, JAMES WEBB, Hartford, Conn (d/XII-23 1898 @ 54) <MD St Thomas' Hosp London 1866> *JAMA* 32:92, 1899. *Polk* 1886: 192.

BOOTH, JOSEPH ARTHUR, NYC (b/Balto, Md; d/II-26-1902 @ 62) MD CPSNY 1882; AB Columbia 1878. *Bost m & s jour* 146:270, 1902. *Polk* 1896: 1042.

BOOTH, WILBUR HIRAM, Utica, NY (d/IX-25-1897 NYC) MD Yale 1874. *JAMA* 29:761, 1897. *Polk* 1896: 1108.

BOOTHBY, ALONZO, Boston (d/II-9-1902) MD Georgetown 1863. *Trans Am Inst Homeop* 1902:838-39. *Polk* 1886:454. Homeopath.

BOOTT, FRANCIS, Boston (d/XII-25-1863 England) MD Edinburgh 1824; AB Harvard 1810. *Bost m & s jour* 69:508, 1863.

BOOZE [BOOZ?], WILLIAM, Carthage, Ill (d/II-20-1901)MD CPS Keokuk 1877. *Ill med jour* ns2:533, 1901.

BOPP, LOUIS, NYC (d/II-22-1885 @ 45) MD Würzburg 1866. *Med reg NY NJ Conn* 1885:230. *Butler* 1878: 494.

BORDE, JOACHIM F, New Orleans (b/1830 St John the Baptist, La; d/V-6-1888) <MD Paris Fac Med 1855 or 1858> *New Orl m & s jour* ns15: 914, 1888. *Polk* 1886: 415.

BORDE, ROBERT V, New Orleans (d/XII-27-1893 @ 27) MD ULa 1888. *New Orl m & s jour* ns21: 552, 1894. *Polk* 1890: 489.

BORDLEY, JAMES, Centreville, Md & Baltimore (b/XII-8-1808; d/XII-6-1870) MD UMd 1829; AM Washington Coll, Chestertown. *Tr AMA* 23:588, 1872. *Med annals Md*: 327.

BORDLEY, WILLIAM H, Queen Anne's Co, Md (b/IX-18-1741[?] d/I-9-1813) MD unknown. *Med annals Md*: 328.

BORG, JOSEPH N, Jackson, Miss (d/X-15-1887) MD ULa 1883. *New Orl m & s jour* ns15:413, 1887. *Polk* 1886: 414.

BORLAND, ANDREW JACKSON, Washington, DC (b/XI-19-1825 York, Pa; d/XII-5-1880) MD Columbian 1861. *Hist Med Soc DC*: 265. *Butler* 1874: 90.

BORLAND, JOHN NELSON, Boston (b/I-14-1828; d/VIII-10-1890) MD Harvard 1851; AB Yale 1848. *JAMA* 15:555, 1890. *Bost m & s jour* 123:168, 1890. *Atkinson* I: 347. *Polk* 1890: 224.

BORROWE, SAMUEL, NYC (d/III-8-1828) MD Columbia 1793. *New York med & phys jour* 7:165, 1828.

BORROWS, JOSEPH, Washington, DC (b/I-20-1807; d/V-30-1889) MD Columbian 1828. *Hist Med Soc DC*: 227. *Polk* 1886: 211.

BORST, ELMAN HILTS, Newburgh, NY (b/Cobbleskill; d/XI-8-1895 @32) MD CPSNY 1889. *JAMA* 25: 1009-10, 1895.

BORTREE, THOMAS WASHINGTON, Wynnewood, Pa (d/III-4-1906 @ 47) MD Jefferson 1890. *Pa med jour* 9:429, 1905/06; 10:167, 1906/07.

BOSANKO, SAMUEL ARTHUR, Leadville, Colo (d/XI 23-1895 @ 39) MD U Toronto 1881. *Trans Colo St Med Soc* 1898-99: 509. *Polk* 1893: 240.

BOSBYSHELL, CHARLES BARRINGTON, Glenwood, Ia (b/VII-18-1833 Port Carbon, Pa; d/I-16-1900) MD Jefferson 1854. *JAMA* 34: 312, 1900. *Trans Ia St Med Soc* 18: 391, 1900. *Polk* 1896: 525.

BOSCH, JOHN ALEXANDER, ?NYC (d/VI-6-1890)

 Spec. educ'l status abbrev. as: ***ng*** = college verified attendance without degree;

MD CPSNY 1885. *Med surg rep Phila* 1891: 269.

BOSCOW, CHARLES S , Lincoln, Calif (b/XI-2-1860 Warsaw, Ill; d/I-23-1888) MD CPS Keokuk 1884. *Trans Calif St Med Soc* 1888: 299-300.

BOSLER, JACOB, Dayton, O (d/XI-21-1868 @ 66) Hon MD Cleveland U Med & Surg 1868. *Med surg rep Phila* 19:468, 1868. *Phila med reg & dir* 1871:298. Homeopath.

BOSLEY, GEORGE HENRY, NYC, CW-USA (d/XII-3 1892 @ 51) MD Albany 1864; MD CPSNY 1868. *Med reg NY NJ Conn* 1893: 297. *Bost m & s jour* 127: 564, 1892.

BOSLEY, GRAFTON MARSH, Towson, Md (b/III-8-1825; d/I-25-1901) MD UMd 1847; ng Dickinson 1844. *Med annals Md*: 328. *Butler* 1874: 310.

BOSSERT, CHARLES, NYC (b/1830 Gny; d/XII-19-1886) MD NY Homeop Coll 1872. *Trans Am Inst Homeop* 1887: 214. *Polk* 1886: 672. Homeopath.

BOSTWICK, DAVID E , Litchfield, Conn (b/II-22-1821 New Milford, Conn; d/III-17-1872) MD Albany 1872. *Proc Conn Med Soc* 4: 153, 1872.

BOSTWICK, H P , CW-USN (d/XII-31-1862) *Nat med jour* 1: 291, 1870/71.

BOSWELL, JOSEPH, Lexington, Ky (d/VI-10-1833) MD UPa 1815. *Transylvania jour med & assoc sci* 6:305, 1833.

BOSWELL, E V B , Washington, DC (b/V-31-1839 Montgomery Co, Md; d/XII-9-1878) MD Georgetown 1865. *Hist Med Soc DC*: 275.

BOSWORTH, GEORGE G , Trenton,NY (b/I-16-1873 @29) MD Albany 1869. *Med reg NY NJ Conn* 1873:335.

BOTSFORD, ALLAN B, CW-USA; Owen Ky; Franklin La; Albion NY; Grand Rapids Mich 1875- (b/IX-1 1823 Arcade NY; d/III-17-1895) MD Cleveland Homeop 1872. *Med current* 11: ,1885. *Polk* 1886:493. Homeopath.

BOTSWORTH, GIDEON, Greenville, NY (b/VI-5-1811; d/IX-17-1880) MD Fairfield 1832. *Trans Med Soc St NY* 1885: 303-04. *Butler* 1874: 529.

BOTTOME, FRANK ARCHER, NYC (b/1865 Bridgeport, Conn; d/XII-20-1898) MD CPSNY 1889. *Bost m & s jour* 140:26, 1899. *JAMA* 32:41, 1899. *Polk* 1896: 223.

BOTTOMLEY, SAMUEL H , Chicago; CW-USA (b/ Engl; d/VII-26-1896 @ 51) MD Northwestern 1863. *JAMA* 27: 279, 1896. *Polk* 1886: 260.

BOUCHELLE, EZRA F , Baligee, Ala (b/1816; d/1874) MD Transylvania 1837; stud U Ala 1832. *U Ala cat*: 41.

BOUCHER, GUSTAVE, Brooklyn (b/Naples, It; d/V-21 1903 @ 67) <MD U Naples 1864> *Bost m & s jour* 148: 600, 1903.

BOUCHER, JAMES H , Iowa City, Ia (b/IX-7-1827 Columbia Co, NY; d/IV-22-1874 San Francisco) MD Jefferson 1856. *Trans Ia St Med Soc* 1872-76: 215; 1877-78: 64-66.

BOUDE, JOHN KNOX, CW-USA; Ocean Grove, NJ (b/ XII-5-1832 Felicity, O; d/IX-8-1901 Washington, DC) MD UPa 1857; AB Miami 1852. *JAMA* 37: 847, 1901. *U Pa med alum CW*: 1857.

BOUDRIAS, LOUIS, Cohoes NY (d/VII-23-1894) <MD U Victoria, Coburg, Ont 1848> *Trans Med Soc St NY* 1895: 369. *Polk* 1886: 657.

BOUGHNER, ABRAHAM LEWIS, Chester, Pa (d/I-16 1900 @ 40) MD U Mich 1885. *JAMA* 34: 312, 1900. *Polk* 1896: 1340.

BOULDEN, JAMES E P , Baltimore (b/VII-8-1825 Cecil Co, Md; d/VII-18-1880) MD UMd 1850. *Med annals Md*: 329. *Butler* 1874: 310.

BOUNELL, MATTHEW H , Lebanon, Ind (b/X-14-1822 Butler Co, O; d/III-23-1896) MD Rush 1857. *Trans Ind St Med Soc* 1896: 271. *Butler* 1878: 194.

BOULWARE, JEPTHA RICHARDS, CW-USA; Albany, NY (b/ X-14-1820 Frankfort, Ky; d/X-17-1887) MD Albany 1859. *Trans Med Soc St NY* 1888: 548-53. *Butler* 1874: 529.

BOURNE, THOMAS PERKINS, Lubec & Calais, Me; Newcastle, NB (b/XII-27-1798 Kennebunk, Me; d/V-1863) MD Bowdoin 1823; AB 1819. *Bowdoin cat* 1819.

BOURNONVILLE, ANTOINE [ANTHONY] Philadelphia (b/VIII-6-1797 Denmark; d/II-27-1863) <MD Copenhagen 1818> Hon MD Jefferson 1848. *Tr AMA* 16:637-39, 1865. *Trans Med Soc St Pa* 1864:530-33. (See also Bournonville, Auguste, *My theatre life*, 1979: 658n.)

BOURNONVILLE, AUGUSTUS CASPAR HILARIAN, CW-USA; Philadelphia (b/III-10-1827 Norfolk, Va; d/XII-3 1906) MD Jefferson 1847; AB UPa 1846. *Pa med jour* 10:294, 1906/07. *Atkinson* I:116.

BOURNS [BOURNES], JOHN FRANCIS, Norristown, Pa (d/XII-21-1899 @ 89) MD UPa 1849. *JAMA* 34: 187, 1900. *Polk* 1896: 1299.

BOUTELLE, NATHANIEL R , Waterville, Me (b/I-1821; d/XII-27-1890) MD Jefferson 1847. *JAMA* 16: 321, 1891. *Butler* 1878: 304.

BOUTELLE, THOMAS RICHARDSON, Fitchburg, Mass (b/VI-9-1795; d/VII-13-1869) MD Yale 1819. *Bost m & s jour* 5:19, 1870.

BOUTON, GEORGE BERIAH, Westport, Conn (b/IV-27-1828; d/XI-6-1905) MD Yale 1856; MD NY Med Coll 1856. *Proc Conn Med Soc* 1906: 312-13. *Atkinson* I:324. *Flint* 1897: 179.

BOWDITCH, HENRY INGERSOLL, Boston (b/VIII-9 1808 Salem; d/I-14-1892) MD Harvard 1832; AB 1828. *JAMA* 18: 151, 1892. *Proc Conn Med Soc* 1893: 230-31. *Bost m & s jour* 126: 67-70, 226, 402, 1892. *K & B* III: 127-131.

BOWEN, AURELIUS, No Ill; Kans; Nebraska City, Nebr 1856- (b/I-30-1817 Reading, Vt; d/VIII-5-1895) MD Castleton 1856. *Proc Nebr St Med Soc* 1896: 22-23. *Atkinson* I: 447. *Polk* 1893: 760.

BOWEN, CHARLES Ap ARTHUR, St Catharines, Canada West; Geneva, NY (b/1832? d/I-20-1860) MD Buffalo 1853. *Med surg rep Phila* ns3: 442, 1859/60.

BOWEN, CHARLES HENRY, Washington, DC (b/V 30-1838; d/III-12-1901) MD Columbian DC 1862. *Ill med jour* ns3: 142, 1901. *Hist Med Soc DC*: 276. *Polk* 1896: 301.

BOWEN, GEORGE W, Philadelphia (d/IX-30-1903 @ 56) MD UPa 1872. *Pa m j* 7: , 1903/04. *Polk* 1896: 1299.

BOWEN, HENRY CHARLES, Springfield, Mass; USA (b/1868 Castle Creek, NY; d/X- -1898 Santiago) MD UCNY 1892. *Bost m & s jour* 139: 228, 1898. *Polk* 1893: 723.

BOWEN, ISRAEL MATHEWSON, Johnston, RI (b/I-27-1812 Coventry; d/V-27-1879) MD Castleton 1837. *Trans RI Med Soc* 2: 219, 1877-82.

BOWEN, JOHN BUCK, Bridgeton, NJ; CW-USA (b/XI 21-1839; d/XII-11-1888) MD UPa 1861. *Trans Med Soc NJ* 1889: 176-77. *U Pa med alum CW*: 1861. *Butler* 1878: 466.

BOWEN, JOHN G , San Antonio, Tex (d/VIII-17-1886 @ 31) MD NY Homeopathic 1882. *South jour hom* 7:60, 1886/87. *Minn med mo* 1: 164, 1886. *Polk* 1886:893. Homeopath.

BOWEN, JOSIAH S , Mt Washington, Md (b/III-1-1832; d/VIII-29-1900) MD UMd 1865. *Med annals Md*: 329. *Polk* 1886: 444.

BOWEN, PARDON, Providence, RI; RevWar-USA (b/III-22-1757; d/X-25-1826 Potowomuk, RI) Hon MD Brown 1812; ng UPa Med Sch 1798; AB Brown 1775. *Trans RI Med Soc* I: 12-14, 1859-1877.

BOWEN, SERANUS, Boston (d/IV-7-1889) MD Harvard 1876. *Bost m & s jour* 140: 368, 1899. *JAMA* 32: 1013, 1899. *Polk* 1896: 693.

BOWEN, WILLIAM, Providence, RI (b/III-8-1747; d/I-1832; ng UPa Med Sch nd; AB Yale 1766; Hon AM Brown 1770. *Trans RI Med Soc* 1:12, 1859-1877.

BOWEN, WILLIAM C , Providence, RI (b/VI-2-1785; d/IV-23-1815) MD Edinburgh 1807; AB Union 1803. *Trans RI Med Soc* I: 15-16, 1859-1877.

BOWEN, WILLIAM S , Bridgeport, Conn (d/III-23-1874) MD CPSNY 1835.*Med reg NY NJ Conn* 1874:270.

BOWER, CHARLES, New Hamilton & Harrisburg, Pa; CW-USA (b/XII-7-1816 Middleburg;d/X-11-1867) MD Jefferson 1838. *Med surg rep Phila* 17:370, 1867. *Tr AMA* 21:460-61 1870. *Trans Med Soc Pa* 1868:113-15.

BOWER [BOWERS], HENRY J , Myerstown, Pa (d/XII-31-1903 @ 62) MD Jefferson 1862. *Pa med jour* 7:278, 1903/04.

BOWER, WILLIAM, Myerstown, Pa (b/XI-6-1817; d/XI-27-1860) MD unknown. *Med surg rep Phila* ns5: 269, 1860/61.

BOWERMAN, MARTHA ALMINA (BRINK), Chicago (b/III-27-1841 Bergen, NY; d/VII-31-1897) MD Hahnemann Chic 1882. *Trans Am Inst Homeop* 1898: 48. *Polk* 1886: 260.

BOWERS, ANDREW J , Moore's Hill, Ind (b/VIII-17-1827; d/III-5-1902) MD Miami 1854. *Trans Ind St Med Soc* 1902: 409. *Polk* 1896: 382.

BOWERS, BENJAMIN FRANKLIN, NYC (b/IX-30-1796; d/II-7-1875) MD Yale 1819. *Trans Am Inst Homeop* 1875: 794. *NY homeop times* 3:21, 1875 (Apr). *Cleave*. Homeopath.

BOWERS, GEORGE WILLIAM, Oshkosh, Wis (d/III-8 1898 @ 29) MD Rush 1895; BS unknown. *JAMA* 30: 682, 1898.

BOWERS, JOSIAH, Huntington, Setauket, Smithtown, NY 1821- ; NYC 1854- (b/IX-1-1791 Billerica, Mass; d/XI-7-1868 Billerica) MD Yale 1816; MD Hahnemann Phila 1854. *Trans Am Inst Homeop* 1893: 130. *New Engl med gaz* 4:28, 1869. *Trans NY Homeop Soc* 9:625, 1871. *Phila med reg & dir* 1871: 299. *Cleave*. Homeopath.

BOWERS, P J , Coleman & Sanger, Tex (d/II-27-1906) MD U Louisville 1872. *Texas st jour med* 1: 352, 1905/06. *Polk* 1890: 1073.

BOWERS, SAMUEL SOWERS, Fond-du-Lac, Wis (b/XII-4-1836 Berlin, Ont; d/I-2-1900) MD UCNY 1856; MD Queens U Ont 1857. *JAMA* 34: 187, 1900. *Atkinson* I: 662. *Polk* 1886: 953.

BOWIE, HOWARD STRAFFORD, Baltimore (b/VIII-10-1846 Prince Geo Co, Md; d/II-26-1900) MD UMd 1870. *JAMA* 34: 639, 1900. *Med annals Md*: 329. *Polk* 1886: 435.

BOWKER, CYRUS KING, Auburn, Me (b/II-24-1824; d/IV-22-1865) MD Castleton 1853. *Trans Me Med Assn* 1866-68: 69-70.

BOWKER, WILLIAM T, Kansas City, Mo (d/I-9-1894) MD Kansas City Hosp Med Coll 1894. *JAMA* 22: 97, 1894. *Polk* 1890: 657.

BOWLBY, LUTHER CALVIN, Hackettstown, NJ; CW-USA (d/X-15-1874) MD Pa Med Coll 1851; MD CPSNY 1856. *Tr AMA* 27:653, 1876. *Trans Med Soc NJ* 1875: [104].

BOWLES, A P , Scottsville, Va (b/VII-14-1871 Hanover Co, Va; d/XI-27-1903) MD Med Coll Va 1897. *Trans Med Soc Va* 1904: 316. *Polk* 1900: 1775.

BOWLES, STEPHEN WALLACE, Springfield Mass (d/II-12-1895 @59) MD CPSNY 1859; AB Williams 1856. *Bost m & s jour* 132: 196, 504, 1895. *JAMA* 24: 497, 1895.

BOWLING, JAMES BUTLER, Logan Co, Va (b/X-25-1795; d/IX-29-1878) MD [?] UPa 1857. *Nashville jour m & s* 22: 179-184, 1878.

BOWLING, JAMES M , Nashville (d/XI-30-1893 @77) MD [?] U Nashville 1870. *JAMA* 21: 936, 1893.

BOWLING, WILLIAM K , Nashville, Tenn (b/VI-5-1808 Westmoreland Co,Va; d/VIII-6-1885) MD Cincinnati Coll Med Dept 1836. *So pract* 19: 177, 1897. *New Orl m & s jour* ns13: 324, 1885. *Nashville jour m & s* 35: 420-30, 1885. *Atkinson* I:161-62. *K & B* III: 133-34.

 Spec. educ'l status abbrev. as: ***ng*** = college verified attendance without degree;

BOWMAN, ALBION PERRY, LeMars, Ia 1884?–92; Sioux City, Ia 1892–1906 (b/V–27–1856; d/II–19–1906) MD Homeop Med Coll Chic 1878. *Trans Am Inst Homeop* 1906: 777–78. *Polk* 1886: 361. Homeopath.

BOWMAN, BENJAMIN, Chambersburg, Pa (b/II–18–1837 Cumberland Co, Pa; d/IX–20–1905) MD NY Homeop 1865. *Trans Am Inst Homeop* 1905: 762. *Polk* 1886: 795. Homeopath.

BOWMAN, EDWARD H , CW–USA; Andalusia, Ill (d/XI–30–1893 @ 77) MD Transylvania 1841. *JAMA* 21: 936, 1893. *Butler* 1878: 143.

BOWMAN, H B , Neffsville, Pa (d/VII–28–1869 @ 64) MD Pa Med Coll 1855. *Phila med reg & dir* 1871: 301.

BOWMAN, JOHN RAYMOND, Cheyenne, Wyoming Terr (b/VI–21–1849 Colon, Mich; d/II–11–1879) MD NY Homeop 1874; stud Albion Col. *Trans Am Inst Homeop* 1879: 1251. Homeopath.

BOWNE, JOHN, Ringoes,NJ (b/IX–2–1767 Monmouth, NJ; d/XI–4–1857) Stud w/Moses Scott, New Brunswick & Wm Shippen,Phila. *Trans Med Soc NJ* 1872:113–15. *Wickes*:163–64. *Med surg rep Phila* ns3:96–98, 1859/60.

BOWSER, WILLARD PARKER, Brooklyn (b/Canada; d/V–4–1889 @ 49) MD UCNY 1877. *Bost m & s jour* 140: 459, 1899. *JAMA* 32: 1072, 1889.*Polk* 1896: 993.

BOWYER, THOMAS MICHIE, CW–CSA; Roanoke & Bedford City, Va; Santa Rosalia, Chihuahua, Mex (b/II–22–1830 Botetourt Co, Va; d/IX–8–1900 Battle Creek, Mich) MD UVa 1852; MD UPa 1853; AB UVa 1851. *Trans Med Soc Va* 1900: 321–22. *Polk* 1886: 920.

BOYCE, CAPTAIN [sic] **WILLIAM**, Auburn, NY (b/VI–28–1822 Topsham, Vt; d/VIII–17–1900) MD NY Homeop 1862; MD Hahnemann Phila 1865 (special degree) ng Geneva 1843–44. *Clin rep* 13 [?]: 1900 (Sept)*Amer homeop* 26 [?] 1900. *Polk* 1886: 641. *Cleave*. Homeopath.

BOYD, ALFRED, Troy, Ala (b/Prosperity, SC; d/IX–21–1882) MD Med Coll SC 1856. *Trans Med Assn St Ala* 1883: 243.

BOYD, ALFRED JAMES, Watertown, NY (d/XII–11–1899 @ 33) MD UCNY 1889. *JAMA* 34: 62, 1900. *Polk* 1896: 986.

BOYD, ANDREW, Scottsboro, Ala (b/VI–11–1866; d/VI–22–1901) MD CPS Balto 1888; ng U Ala 1883. *Trans Med Assn St Ala* 1902: 129. *Polk* 1893: 163.

BOYD, DAVID, Charlton, NY (d/XII–12–1865) MD Fairfield 1839; AB Union 1833. *Tr AMA* 18: 316, 1867. *Med surg rep Phila* Phila 14: 80, 1866.

BOYD, GEORGE B , Scranton, Pa (d/XI–27–1893 @ 64) MD Jefferson 1863. *JAMA* 21:908, 936, 1893.

BOYD, GEORGE SHANNON, Beaver Falls, Pa (b/V–6–1850 New Sheffield, Pa; d/V–10–1901) MD Cleveland Homeop Hosp Coll 1880. *Trans Pa Homeop Soc* 1901. *Polk* 1886: 792.

BOYD, JAMES GREEN, Milan, Tenn (d/1878) MD Transylvania 1847. *Tr AMA* 30: 855–56, 1879. *Butler* 1878: 780.

BOYD, JAMES HARVEY, Jackson Co, Ala (d/I–31–1899 Scottsboro) MD U Tenn 1869. *Trans Med Assn St Ala* 1899:232.

BOYD, JAMES NEELEY, Madison, Wis (b/1851 Geneseo, NY; d/IX–10–1892) MD Rush 1881. *Trans Wis St Med Soc* 1893: 366; 1894: 502. *Polk* 1890: 1167.

BOYD, JAMES PETER, Albany, NY (b/II–24–1804; d/V–10–1881) MD UPa 1825; att? U St NY. *Trans Med Soc St NY* 1882: 358–61. *Atkinson* I: 207. *Butler* 1874: 529.

BOYD, JAMES W , La Place, Ala (d/IX– –1884) MD Med Coll SC 1856. *Trans Med Assn St Ala* 1885: 319.

BOYD, MONTAGUE L , Savannah, Ga (d/II–9–1898 @ 48) <MD Med Coll Ga 1875> *JAMA* 30: 570, 1898. *Polk* 1886: 231.

BOYD, RICHARD, CW–CSA; Clarksville, Va (b/II–9–1835; d/1892) MD Jefferson 1857. *Trans Med Soc Va* 1892: 255; 1893: 219; 1894: 198. *Blanton*: 395. *Polk* 1886: 928.

BOYD, ROBERT HENRY AGNEW, Philadelphia 1885–86; St Paul, Minn 1888– (b/VII–21–1861 South Easton, Pa; d/VII–1–1895 San Antonio, Tex) MD UPa 1885; AB Lafayette 1882; AM Lafayette. *Lafayette, Men of*: 239. *Polk* 1886: 813.

BOYD, SAMUEL, Brooklyn (d/III–17–1860 @ 54) MD CPSNY 1828; AB Dickinson 1824. *Med surg rep Phila* ns3: , 1859/60.

BOYD, SAMUEL SCOTT, Dublin, Ind (b/III–31–1820; d/IV–16–1888) MD Med Coll O 1849. *Trans Ind St Med Soc* 1888: 213. *Butler* 1878: 195.

BOYD, THOMAS J , USN 1820– (d/III–26–1839 Brooklyn) MD UPa 1818. *Med annals Md*: 330. *Hamersly*: 89.

BOYD, WENDELL CHARLES, Linneus, Me (d/VIII–3 1904 @ 34) MD Harvard 1893. *Bost m & s jour* 151: 197, 1904. *Polk* 1896: 637.

BOYDEN, JEREMIAH WESLEY, CW–USN (d/VIII–17–1866 at sea) MD unknown; AB Harvard 1860; AM 1861.*Tr AMA* 18: 359, 1867. *Harvard in CW*: 159–60. *Nat med jour* 1: 291, 1870/71.

BOYER, ALONZO HENRY, Philadelphia (d/III–17–1906 @ 60) MD UPa 1868. *Pa med jour* 9:524, 1905/06. *Polk* 1886: 813.

BOYER, P C , New Orleans, La (b/Phila; d/III–12–1881 @ 56) MD ULa 1852. *New Orl m & s jour* ns9: 396, 1881. *Butler* 1878: 293.

BOYER, PHILIP ALLEN, Selins Grove, Pa (d/X–23–1899 @ 43) MD UPa 1881. *JAMA* 33: 1182, 1899. *Polk* 1896: 1336.

BOYERS, HENRY M , Grafton, WVa (d/X–14–1898 @ 27) MD Balto Med Coll 1893. *JAMA* 31: 1066, 1898. *Polk* 1896: 1527.

BOYLE, CORNELIUS, CW–CSA; Washington, DC (b/I–12–1817; d/III–11–1878) MD Columbian DC 1844. *Tr AMA* 29:618–21, 1878. *Hist Med Soc DC*: 235–36.

Atkinson I: 381.

BOYLE, WILLIAM H , Chambersburg, Pa (b/1813 Ireland; d/IV- -1880) MD Pa Med Coll 1857. *Trans Med Soc Pa* 13: 307, 1880. *Butler* 1878: 705.

BOYNTON, CHARLES H , Lisbon, NH (b/New Hampton, NH; d/VIII-16-1903) MD Berkshire 1853. *Tr NH Med Soc* 1904: 295. *Polk* 1893: 773.

BOYNTON, EDWIN DANA, Worcester, Mass (b/d/IV-26-1902 @ 29 Harrington, Me) MD Harvard 1894. *Bost m & s jour* 147: 58, 1902. *Polk* 1896: 727.

BOYNTON, JAMES C , Richmond, Me (b/IV-1-1808; d/VII-27-1875) MD Bowdoin 1832. *Trans Me Med Assn* 1874-76: 430.

BOYNTON, JOSEPH JACKSON, So Framingham, Mass (b/VI-9-1833 Stowe, Vt; d/VI-17-1891) MD U Vt 1878. *Bost m & s jour* 136: 640, 1897. *JAMA* 29: 45, 1897.

BOYNTON, SOLON ROBINSON, Sparta, Ill (d/V-14-1904 @52) MD Homeop Med Coll St Louis 1883. *Clin rep* 1904 (June). *Polk* 1886: 298. Homeopath.

BOYSEN, THEOPHILUS HENRY, Egg Harbor City, NJ (b/I-14-1854 Rigarsville, O; d/III-12-1903) MD Buffalo 1874. *Trans Med Soc NJ* 1903: 379. *Polk* 1896: 936.

BOZARTH, DAVID, Stone Ford, Ill (d/IX-10-1900) Certif Exam. Bd. *Ill Med Soc* ns2: 286, 1900. *Polk* 1896: 442.

BOZEMAN, NATHAN, Jr, CW-CSA; NYC (b/III-26-1825 Butler Co, Ala; d/XII-16-1905) MD U Louisville 1848. *Bost m & s jour* 153: 736-37, 1905. *Atkinson* I: 380-81. *K & B* III:135. *Polk* 1896: 1042.

BRABSON, ALEX W , Millbrook, Tenn (b/1804; d/IX-1888) <MD @ Lexington,Ky> *So pract* 10:530-31,1888.

BRACE, EDWARD, W Hartford, Conn (b/XII-16-1799; d/XI-27-1879) MD Castleton 1828. *Proc Conn Med Soc* 1880: 164. *Butler* 1878: 73.

BRACE, HARRY MARTIN, Perth Amboy, NJ (b/1859 Catskill, NY; d/II-20-1906) MD CPSNY 1881. *Bost m & s jour* 154: 256, 1906. *Polk* 1896: 947.

BRACHT, [FRANC ?] FELIX [FRIDER ?], San Antonio, Tex (d/XII-16-1882 @ 73) MD U Berlin 1833; AB & Ph 1830. *Texas m & s rec* 3:551, 1883. *Butler* 1878: 783.

BRACKETT, ADINO NYE, Negro, Va (b/VII-11-1822 Lancaster, NH; d/V-13-1901) MD Woodstock 1851; AB Dartmouth 1844. *Dartmouth cat* 1940: 151. *Polk* 1896: 1490.

BRACKETT, ARTHUR B , Goldfield, Ia (d/X-9-1899) MD Rush 1869. *JAMA* 33: 1116, 1899. *Polk* 1890: 416.

BRACKETT, CHARLES, CW-USA (d/II-20-1863 Helena, Ark) *Nat med jour* 1: 291, 1870/71.

BRACKETT, LYMAN STEBBINS, Rochester, Ind (b/X-3-1818 Cherry Valley, NY; d/IV-7-1847) MD Fairfield 1839; ng Castleton 1836. *Ill & Ind m & s jour* 2:93, 1847.

BRADBURY, ALBION KEITH PARRIS, Hollis, Me (b/XI-13-1822; d/VI-23-1875) MD Harvard 1854. *Trans Me Med Assn* 1874-76: 430-32.

BRADBURY, ALLISON BEARD, Muncie, Ind (b/IX-17-1842 Jacksonburg, Ind; d/I-28-1892) MD LICH 1869. *Trans Ind St Med Soc* 1892: 289. *Butler* 1878: 195.

BRADBURY, JAMES CORCKETT, Howland & Oldtown, Me (b/III-5-1806 Buxton, Me; d/X-3-1865) MD Bowdoin 1829. *Tr AMA* 18:299-301, 1867. *Trans Me Med Assn* 1866-67: 55. *K & B* III: 137.

BRADBURY, MELISSA A , WilkesBarre, Pa (b/III-27-1837 Middlebury,Conn; d/VI-27-1878) MD Woman's Med Coll Pa 1872. *Trans Med Soc Pa* 12:787-90, 1879.

BRADBURY, OSGOOD NATHAN, Norway, Me; CW-USA (b/X-29-1828; d/I-22-1897) MD Bowdoin 1864. *Bost m & s jour* 137: 297, 1897. *Trans Me Med Assn* 12:627-30, 1897. *Atkinson* I: 1423. *Polk* 1896: 638.

BRADFIELD, THOMAS NAYLOR, Newark, NJ (d/VI-28-1891 @ 49) MD CPSNY 1872; DDS "elsewhere." *Bost m & s jour* 125:96, 1891. *Polk* 1886: 607.

BRADFORD, CHARLES H , Bel Air, Md (b/1810; d/III 28-1890) MD UMd 1830. *Med annals Md*: 330.

BRADFORD, FRANK STANDISH, Morristown, NJ; Charleston SC to 1860; CW-USA (b/V-20-1830; d/II-9 1900) MD Jefferson 1858; AB Brown 1853, AM. *Tr Am Inst Homeop* 1900: 829-30. *Cleave*. Homeopath.

BRADFORD, GEORGE W , Cortland Co, NY (b/V-9-1796 Otsego,NY; d/X-31-1863 Syracuse,NY) Lic Cortland Co Med Soc 1820. *Med reg NY NJ Conn* 1884: 223. *Trans Med Soc St NY* 1884: 394-400. *Butler* 1874: 529.

BRADFORD, JAMES HAWLINGS, Philadelphia; Canton, China 1825-35 (b/XI-4-1802; d/IV-9-1859) MD UPa 1823. *Trans CPP* centennial vol: 213. *Trans Med Soc Pa* 1860: 81-83.

BRADFORD, JOSHUA TAYLOR, Augusta, Ky (b/XII-8-1818; d/XII-31-1871) MD Transylvania 1839. *Tr AMA* 23: 585, 1872. *Trans Ky St Med Soc* 1873-76: 161-63. *K & B* III: 139-40.

BRADFORD, MILTON, Woodstock, Conn (b/I-12-1808; d/X-1-1878) MD Harvard 1831; AB Brown 1828. *Proc Conn Med Soc* 1879-80: 168. *Butler* 1878: 73.

BRADFORD, RICHMOND, Turner, Me 1829-35; Auburn, Me 1835- (b/IV-30-1801; d/XII-21-1874) MD Bowdoin 1829; AB 1825. *Trans Am Inst Homeop* 1875: 797. *NY Homeop times* 5:21, 1875. *New Engl med gaz* 10:96, 1875. *Amer jour homeop mat med* 8: 244, 1875? Homeopath 1845- .

BRADFORD, THEODORE DWIGHT, NYC (b/IX-1-1838 Auburn, Me; d/V-11-1883) MD CPSNY 1865; AB Bowdoin 1861; AM 1871. *NY med times* 11:119, 1883. *Butler* 1878: 494. Homeopath.

BRADFORD, THOMAS CULLY HILL, Cincinnati (b/X-3-1835; d/III-13-1864) MD Bellevue 1864; ng Jefferson 1862-63. *Trans Am Inst Homeop* 1896: 1186. *JAMA* 26: 642, 1896. *Polk* 1896:1160. Homeopath.

BRADISH, JAMES S , CW-USA (b/c1825; d/1865,

 Spec. educ'l status abbrev. as: ***ng*** = college verified attendance without degree;

Hilton Head, SC) Lic Med Soc St NY 1855. *Nat med jour* 1: 291, 1870/71.

BRADLEY, CHARLES, Norristown, Pa (d/IV-25-1906 @ 58) MD Jefferson 1875. *Pa med jour* 9: 607, 1905/06. *Flint* 1897: 811.

BRADLEY, CHARLES DAVID, Chicago (b/1851 Quebec; d/IV-7-1900) MD Harvard 1872; stud Paris 1871. *Chic med rec* 18: 487-99, 1900. *JAMA* 34:1021, 1900. *Trans Ill St Med Soc* 1899-1900: 574. *Polk* 1896: 376.

BRADLEY, E W , E Oakland, Calif (d/XII-28-1902) MD Hahnemann Chic 1879. *Calif st jour med* 1:70, 1903. *Polk* 1890: 190. Homeopath.

BRADLEY, EDWARD, NYC (b/VIII-25-1835 Burlington, Vt; d/III-5-1901) MD U Vt 1859. *Bost m & s jour* 144:294, 1901. *Polk* 1896: 1042.

BRADLEY, ROBERT SEYMOUR, New Haven, Conn (b/VIII-5-1863; d/II-1-1890) MD Yale 1887; AB 1885. *Med reg NY NJ Conn* 1890: 261. *Proc Conn Med Soc* 1890: 283-84.

BRADLEY, WILLIAM, CW-USN (d/I-30-1861 in Levant) *Nat med jour* 1: 291, 1870/71.

BRADLEY, WILLIAM ALFRED, USA (b/VIII-3-1831; d/II-27-1869 Point San José, Calif) *Phila med reg & dir* 1871:300. *Nat med jour* 1:219, 1870/71. *Tr AMA* 21:494, 1870. *Hist Med Soc DC*: 259. G.V.Henry: *Milit. rec*: 58.

BRADLEY, WILLIAM LOCKWOOD, New Haven, Conn (b/X-11-1837 NYC; d/VI-12-1903) MD Yale 1864; AB 1860. *Proc Conn Med Soc* 1904:515-16. *Atkinson* I:488. *Flint* 1897: 176.

BRADNACK, FOWLER, Buffalo, NY (b/England; d/III-18-1891) MD Buffalo Med Coll 1871. *Buff m & s jour* 30:694, 1891. *Polk* 1886: 672 (NYC).

BRADNER, FREDERICK HOUSTON, Middletown, NY (d/I-8-1880 @ 31) MD NY Homeop Med Coll 1873. *Trans Am Inst Homeop* 1880: 142. *Homeop times* 7:264, 1880? Homeopath.

BRADNER, IRA SMITH, CW-USA; Middletown, NY (b/VI-2-1820 Goshen, NY; d/X-24-1894) MD UCNY 1843; AB Princeton 1840. *Trans Am Inst Homeop* 1895: 215. *Polk* 1886: 668. Homeopath.

BRADSHAW, BENJAMIN H , Orangeville, Ill; Salem, Ore (d/X-14-1901) MD Rush 1861. *Ill med jour* ns3: 346, 1901. *Polk* 1896: 1240.

BRADT, GERRITT JAMES, Lowell, Mass (d/VII-1-1894 @ 45 N Chelmsford) MD UCNY 1880. *Bost m & s jour* 131:24,1894. *Polk* 1890:550.

BRADY, C C , Lincolnville, Ind (b/II-21-1852 Wabash Co; d/IX-10-1895) <MD Hosp Coll Med Louisville 1881> *JAMA* 25: 554, 1895. *Trans Ind St Med Soc* 1896: 255. *Polk* 1886: 319.

BRADY, FREDERICK L , NYC (d/XII-24-1902 @ 30) MD CPSNY 1899. *Bost m & s jour* 148: 28, 1903.

BRADY, SAMUEL JAMES, Brooklyn (d/IX-8-1892 @ 51) MD Bellevue 1868. *Med reg NY NJ Conn* 1893: 297. *Bost m & s jour* 127: 276, 1892. *Polk* 1890: 768.

BRADY, THOMAS ANDREW, Brooklyn (d/III-8-1877 @38) MD Bellevue 1867. *Med reg NY NJ Conn* 1877: 196.

BRAGG, IRA WILSON, CW-USA (d/X-21-1864 @ 36 New Orleans) MD Harvard 1859. *Bost m & s jour* 71: 308, 368, 1864. *Nat med jour* 1: 291, 1870/71. *Harvard in CW*: 152.

BRAGG, RALPH STAPLES, New Whatcom, Wash (d/I-21-1895) MD St Louis Med Coll 1880. *JAMA* 24:177, 1895. *Polk* 1890: 1142.

BRAGG, THOMAS H , Austin, Tex (d/VI-19-1891 Mexico) MD Rush 1871. *Tex med jour* 13: 95, 1897-98. *Polk* 1886: 880. Homeopath.

BRAGG, THOMAS M , Greenville, Ala (b/1794? d/XI-28-1882 @ 88) Certif County Bd. *Trans Med Assoc St Ala* 1883:243. *Butler* 1874: 15.

BRAILLY, COSMO, NYC (d/X-5-1890 @75) MD Paris 1840. *Med reg NY NJ Conn* 1891:269. *Polk* 1886: 672.

BRAILSFORD, WILLIAM MOULTRIE, Summerville, SC (b/Charleston; d/XII- -1886) MD Med Coll SC 1829. *New Orl m & s jour* ns14: 639, 1887.

BRAINARD, DANIEL, Chicago (b/V-15-1812 Whitesborough, NY; d/X-10-1866) MD Jefferson 1834. *Med surg rep Phila* 15: 448, 1866. *Chic med jour* 23: 529-38, 1866. *Tr AMA* 18: 348-49, 1867. *Trans Ill St Med Soc* 1867:9. *K & B* III: 40-41.

BRAINARD, DUDLEY S , Stacyville, Ia (b/I-3-1851 Williamsburg, NY; d/IX-9-1893 Osage, Ia) MD U Buffalo 1875. *JAMA* 21: 498, 1893. *Polk* 1886: 368.

BRAINARD, JEHU, Washington, DC; Cleveland, O (b/VII-8-1807; d/III- -1878) MD unknown. *Trans Am Inst Homeop* 1879: 1239. *Cleave*. Homeopath.

BRAKELEY, PHILIP FINE, Belvidere, NJ (b/VII-10-1818 Lopatcong; d/VII-2-1889) MD UPa 1842; stud Lafayette. *Trans Med Soc NJ* 1890: 332-35. *Med reg NY NJ Conn* 1890:261. *Butler* 1878: 466.

BRALEY, NORMAN WING, Pomfret, Vt (b/VIII-14-1823; d/IX-11-1880 Barre) MD Woodstock 1844. *JAMA* 1:520, 1883. *Butler* 1878: 803.

BRAMAN, AARON NEWELL, Brockport, NY 1874- ; Rochester 1897- ; (d/VII-6-1901) MD U Buffalo 1851. *Bost m & s jour* 145: 52, 1901. *JAMA* 37: 214, 1901. *Polk* 1896: 1018.

BRAMAN, CHANDLER BALCH, Brighton, Mass; USA (d/VII-15-1868 @ 27) MD Harvard 1866; AB 1864; AM 1865. *Phila med reg & dir* 1871: 297. *Bost m & s jour* ns2: 48, 1868. *Med surg rep Phila* 19: 180, 220, 1868. *Harvard in CW*: 204.

BRAMAN, JASON J, Healdsburg Calif (d/XI-15-1899 @83 [?]) MD U Cal Toland 1876. *JAMA* 33:1441, 1899.

BRAMWELL, HENRY V , Kansas City, Mo (d/IV-27-1868 @ 64) MD UMd 1828. *Phila med reg & dir* 1871:296. *Med surg rep Phila* 18: 486, 1868.

BRANCH, JOHN, St Albans, Vt (b/VIII-2-1805 Swanton; d/VII-4-1881) MD Castleton 1837. *Trans Vt Med Soc* 1883: 103. *Butler* 1874: 773.

BRANCH, LEROY K , Lecompte, La (d/IV-3-1898 @ 81+) MD Louisville Med Inst 1840. *New Orl m & s jour* 50: 670, 1898. *Polk* 1896: 614.

BRANDEGEE, ELISHAMA, Berlin, Conn (b/I-14-1814; d/II-17-1884) MD Yale 1838; AB 1833. *Proc Conn St Med Soc* 1884: 166. *Butler* 1878: 73.

BRANDEGEE, FRANK DESHON, New London, Conn (b/1827; d/1854) MD UCNY 1849. *Proc Conn St Med Soc* 1854: 19.

BRANDEGEE, WILLIAM PARTRIDGE, NYC (b/IV--1864 Brooklyn; d/VI-30-1906) MD CPSNY 1889. *Bost m & s jour* 155:161-62, 1906. *Polk* 1896: 1043.

BRANDIS, HERMANN M , NYC (b/England; d/III-16-1889 @ c65) MD New York Med Coll 1855. *Med reg NY NJ Conn* 1889: 268.

BRANDON, JOSEPH FRANCIS, Anderson, Ind (b/X-12-1835 Switzerland Co, Ind; d/I-6-1888) ng U Mich 1861. *Trans Ind St Med Soc* 1888: 210.

BRANDT, ELI BAINBRIDGE, Mechanicsburgh, Pa (d/I-16-1889 @ 60) MD Jefferson 1855. *Trans Med Soc Pa* 21: 261, 1889-90. *Butler* 1878: 705.

BRANDT, JOHN R , Chicago (b/NYC; d/VIII-18-1895 @57) MD Med Coll O 1875; att? Oberlin. *JAMA* 25: 342, 1895. *Chic med rec* 9:188, 1893. *Polk* 1890: 309.

BRANDT, JULIUS R , Warrenton, Mo (d/I-15-1895) MD St Louis Med Coll 1865. *JAMA* 24: 221, 1895. *Polk* 1890: 680.

BRANHAM, JOHN WILLIAM, US Marine Hosp Service (b/X-27-1868 Walker Co Ga; d/VIII-20-1893 Brunswick, Ga) MD CPS Balto 1889. *Bost m&s j* 129: 232, 1893. *New Orl m&s j* ns21: 436-37, 1893. *JAMA* 21:357, 1893. *NC m j* 32: 154, 1893. *Polk* 1890: 272.

BRANIN, HENRY ELY, Blackwood, NJ (b/I-8-1836 Medford, NJ; d/X-6-1897) MD Jefferson 1856. *Tr Med Soc NJ* 1898: 363-65. *Atkinson* I:390. *JAMA* 29: 816, 1897.

BRANNIGAN, PATRICK R , CW-USA (d/X-5-1864 New Bern, NC) MD unknown. *Nat med jour* 1:291, 1870/71.

BRANSTRUP, WILLIAM THEODORE, Vincennes,Ind 1875-83; La Porte; Topeka, Kans 1887- (b/III-18-1836 Pittsburgh, Pa; d/VIII-15-1899 Indianapolis) MD Cincinnati Ecl 1858; MD Hahnemann Chic 1877. *Med vis* 15: 629, 1899. *Tr Am Inst Homeop* 1900:830. *Hahn mo* 35:39 (news & advt) 1900 (Mar). *Polk* 1886: 385. Homeopath.

BRANTIGAM, C N , Ward's Isl, NYC (d/VI-1-1881) MD NY Homeop Med Coll 1881. *Amer homeop obs* 18: 392, 1881. *Hahn mo* 16:448, 1881. Homeopath.

BRASHEAR, BELT, Newmarket, Md (b/1770? Frederick Co, Md; d/XI-20-1834 @ 64) <stud med Phila> *Med annals Md*: 331.

BRASSFIELD, MILTON TURNER, Forkland, Ala (b/VI-25-1848; d/II-10-1887) MD UCNY 1869; AB U Ala. *Tr Med Assoc St Ala* 1887: 305. *Polk* 1886: 133.

BRATENAHL, GUSTAV WEBER, NYC (b/IV-19-1867 Cleveland, O; d/III-18-1895) MD CPSNY 1889. *Med reg NY NJ Conn* 1895: 216.

BRATT, BENJAMIN RICHARD, Reading, Pa (b/IV-22 1836 Boonton, NJ; d/I-31-1872) MD Hahnemann Phila 1858. *Tr Am Inst Homeop* 1893: 131. *Tr Hom Med Soc Pa* 1873: 166. Homeopath.

BRATT, JAMES D , Waterproof, La (d/IX-22-1855) MD Hahnemann Phila 1852. *Phila jour homeop* 4: 568, 1856. Homeopath.

BRATTON, WILLIAM DuBOSE, US MarHosp Service 1885-88; USN 1888?-97 (b/VI-23-1860 Fairfield Co SC; d/X-2-1897 Sabine Pass Tx) MD M C SC 1884; AB Univ South, Sewanee 1880. *NC med jour* 40: 315-17, 1897. *St Louis m & s j* 74: 119, 1898. *JAMA* 29:925, 1897. *Bost m & s j* 127:432, 1897. *Tex m j* 13: 249-50, 1897-98.

BRAUN, LOUIS, Elizabeth, NJ (b/VI- -1824 Baden Gny; d/XII-30-1880) MD Freiburg 1858. *Tr Med Soc NJ* 1880-81: 162-65. *Atkinson* I: 513. *Butler* 1878: 466.

BRAY, MADISON JAMES, CW-USA; Evansville Ind (b/I-1-1811 Turner, Me; d/VIII-22-1900) MD Bowdoin 1835. *Tr Ind St Med Soc* 1871:243 [as dead]. *Ind med jour* 19:122, 1900? *Atkinson* I: 38-39. *Butler* 1878: 195.

BRAYMER, ORANGE WHITNEY, Camden, NJ (b/VI-14-1865 Meadville, Pa; d/I-8-1898) MD Jefferson 1888. *Tr Med Soc NJ* 1898:365-66. *JAMA* 30:178, 1898.

BRAYTON, EDMUND CULLEN, Geneseo, Ill; Whitestown, NY (b/III-25-1847 Westernville; d/IX-17-1875) MD Jefferson 1878; AB Amherst 1867. *Amherst, Men of,* 1867.

BRAYTON, FORREST W , Carey, O (b/IX-10-1856 McCutchenville; d/XII-4-1890 Cincinnati?) MD Miami Med Coll 1880. *JAMA* 16: 428, 1891. *Tr Ohio Med Soc* 1891: 5, 344-45. *Polk* 1890: 897.

BRAYTON, SAMUEL NELSON, CW-USN; NYC (b/I-11-1839 Queensbury, NY; d/V-17-1893) MD CPSNY 1861. *Tr Am Inst Homeop* 1893: 131. Homeopath.

BRECHIN, WILLIAM PITT, Boston (d/XII-10-1899) MD Harvard 1872. *Bost m & s jour* 141: 616, 1899. *JAMA* 33: 1632, 1899. *Polk* 1896: 693.

BRECK, THEODORE FRELINGHUYSEN, Springfield, Mass (d/VI-26-1904 @ 58) MD Harvard 1866. *Bost m & s jour* 150: 716, 1904; 151: 27, 1904. *Polk* 1896: 723.

BRECK, WILLIAM GILMAN, Springfield, Mass (b/XI-14-1818 Franklin Co, Vt; d/I-22-1889 Chicopee) MD Harvard 1854. *Bost m & s jour* 120: 128, 1889. *Butler* 1878: 347.

BRECKENRIDGE, STEPHEN LONG, Riverside, Ill (d/II-21-1906 @ 44) MD St Louis Med Coll 1879. *Ill med jour* 9:463, 1906.

BRECKINRIDGE, ROBERT J , Houston, Tex; CW-

CSA (b/XII-4-1828 Ky; d/VII-8-1867) MD U Louisvl 1848; AB Center Coll. *Tr AMA* 21:487-8, 1870. *New Orl m&s j* 20:283-4, 1867. *Bost m&s j* 77:160, 1867. *Nashvl j m&s* ns2:92-93, 1867. *Med surg rep Phila* 17:87, 1867.

BRECKINRIDGE, STANHOPE P , Chattanooga (d/III 1887 @ 47) MD U Louisville 1862. *New Orl m & s jour* ns14: , 1887. *Polk* 1886: 862.

BREED, BOWMAN BIGELOW, Lynn, Mass; CW-USA (b/II-29-1832; d/XI-16-1873) MD Harvard 1857; AB Amherst 1853. *Bost m & s jour* ns12: 656, 1873; ns13 [or 90]: 25-26, 1874.

BREED, WILLIAM M , Philadelphia; CW-USA (d/II-12-1865) MD Jefferson 1855. *Med surg rep Phila* 12: 314, 1864/65. *Nat med jour* 1: 291, 1870/71.

BREEN, MICHAEL, Brooklyn (d/VII-28-1882 @ c42) <MD Queen's Univ, Ireland 1861; AB 1857> *Med reg NY NJ Conn* 1883: 222. *Butler* 1874: 514.

BREINIG, DAVID E , Brooklyn (d/V-31-1882) MD UCNY 1845. *Med reg NY NJ Conn* 1883: 222.

BREINIG, PETER B , Hellertown, Pa 1856-71; W Bethlehem, Pa 1873- (b/III-29-1829 Breinigsville, Pa; d/VI-1-1896) MD UCNY 1856. *Lehigh Valley med mag* 7:205-07, 1896. *Atkinson* I: 80.

BREISCH, RICHARD R , Ringtown, Pa (d/IV-23-1903 @ 49) MD Jefferson 1881. *Pa med jour* 7:278, 1903/04. *Flint* 1897: 833.

BREITENBACH, SAMUEL CYRUS, Philadelphia (d/II 27-1906 @ 80) MD CPSNY 1848. *Pa med jour* 9:524, 1905/06. *Flint* 1897: 814.

de BREMONT, LOUIS, NYC (b/VI-5-1834?; d/V-19-1882) <MD Paris 1867> *Med reg NY NJ Conn* 1883: 222.

BRENDEL, EMIL C, Springfield, Ill (d/I-6-1906 @ 72) <MD U Erlangen, Gny> *Ill med jour* 9:131, 1906. *Polk* 1896: 514.

BRENDLE, GEORGE FISHER, Mahanoy City, Pa (d/VIII-23-1906) MD UPa 1862. *Pa med jour* 9:893, 1905/06. *Flint* 1897: 808.

BRENEMAN, EDWARD DeWELDEN, CW-USA; Washington, DC (b/VIII-14-1839 Lancaster, Pa; d/X-11 1870) MD UPa 1861. *Hist Med Soc DC*:283. *U Pa med alum CW*: 1861. Henry, *Milit rec*: 59. *Tr AMA* 23: 581, 1872.

BRENGLE, WILLIAM DOWNEY, CW-CSA; Ridgeway, Va (b/IX-2-1838; d/IV-9-1900) MD UPa 1861. *JAMA* 34: 1021, 1900. *U Pa med alum CW*: 1861. *Polk* 1890: 1131.

BRENNAN, DANIEL H , Albion, NY (d/VIII-11-1896 Buffalo) MD U Buffalo 1885. *JAMA* 27: 449, 1896. *Polk* 1896: 986.

BRENNAN, GEORGE MARSDEN, USA (d/VII-21-1881 NYC @ 47) MD CPSNY 1862. *Med reg NY NJ Conn* 1882: 223.

BRENNAN, PATRICK THOMAS, NYC (b/III-4-1834 Ireland; d/I-18-1868) MD UCNY 1856. *Phila med reg & dir* 1871: 295. *Tr AMA* 19: 422, 1868. *Med reg NY NJ Conn* 1868: 323.

BRENNAN [BRENNEN], THOMAS, Dayton, O (d/1858) MD Med Coll O 1854. *Tr Ohio St Med Soc* 1873:362.

BRENNEMAN, TIMOTHY HENRY, Norfolk Va (b/VII 14-1871 Allen Co, O; d/I-28-1905) MD UVa 1900. *Tr Med Soc Va* 1905: 443-44. *Polk* 1902: 1963.

BRENT, COLUMBUS P, Cincinnati,O (d/VIII-21-1901) MD Miami 1854. *JAMA* 37:654,1901. *Polk* 1886: 741.

BRERETON, JOHN A , USN 1808-?, USA 1821- (b/Md; d/IV-22-1839) *Med annals Md*: 331. *Hamersly. Barton's List of surgeons in USN, 1814.*

BRESLIN, THOMAS HENRY, Portland, Me; CW-USA (b/X-3-1828; d/VI-17-1864 New Orleans) MD Bowdoin 1855. *Nat med jour* I:291, 1870/71.

BRESSLER, CHARLES H , York, Pa (d/II-21-1894 @ 72?) MD Jefferson 1844. *JAMA* 22: 391, 1894. *Off'l reg Pa phys* 1881-88: 414.

BRETT, W L, Denver (d/I-1-1891) MD Hahnemann Chic 1880. *Med vis* 7:48,1891. *Polk* 1886:183. Homeopath.

BREWER, A V , Southport, Ind (d/X-20-1868 @ 42) MD U Louisville 1853. *Phila med reg & dir* 1871: 298. *Med surg rep Phila* Phila 19: 390, 1868.

BREWER, GEORGE GASTON, Baltimore (d/IV-8-1895 @ 59) MD UMd 1856. *JAMA* 24: 609, 1895. *Med annals Md*: 332. *Butler* 1878: 317.

BREWER, HAMILTON, Middletown, Conn (b/VIII-3-1813 E Hartford; d/V-21-1855) MD Yale 1841; AB Wesleyan 1838. *Bost m & s jour* 52:347,1855.

BREWER, JOHN MAITLAND, Philadelphia; Beverly, NJ (b/IV-10-1781 Framingham, Mass; d/XI-5-1859) MD UPa 1837; AM Harvard 1804; ng Brown. *Bost m & s jour* 61:328, 1859. *Med surg rep Phila* ns3: 195, 1859/60. Palmer's *Necrol alum Harvard*: 303-04.

BREWER, NATHANIEL, Boston (b/VII-23-1795; d/V-17-1853) MD Harvard 1818; AM 1814. Palmer's *Necrol alum Harvard*: 16.

BREWER, THOMAS O , Monroe, La (d/XII-14-1902) MD Louisville Med Coll 1881. *New Orl m & s jour* 1855: 449, 1903. *Polk* 1886: 415.

BREWSTER, ETHAN ALLEN PAUL, CW-USA; Janesville, Wis; Escanaba, Mich (b/XI-23-1837 Salem, Mass; d/IV-5-1877) MD Harvard 1865; AB Amherst 1858. *Harvard in CW*: 290.

BREWSTER, FRANCIS GILBERT, Bridgeton, NJ (b/1768? d/VII-26-1828 @ 60) Lic c1785. *Tr Med Soc NJ* 1871-73: 147-48.

BREWSTER, JOHN MILTON, Pittsfield, Mass (d/X-15 1902 @ 84) MD Berkshire 1841. *Bost m & s jour* 147: 476, 1902. *Polk* 1896: 721.

BREWSTER, PHILANDER S , Lawsville Center, Pa; Berwick Co; (b/Wyalusing; d/III-5-1904 @ 73) Lic by years of practice. *Pa med jour* 8:334, 1904/05. *Reg Pa* *phys* 1881–88: 951. *Flint* 1897: 796.

BREYFOGLE, CHARLES WESLEY, CW–USA; Jeffersonville, Ind 1868; Louisville, Ky 1869; San José, Calif 1870–95 (b/VI–7–1841 Columbus, O; d/II–26–1895) MD Hahnemann Phila 1868; AB Wesleyan 1862. *Tr Am Inst Homeop* 1895: 216. *Polk* 1886: 175. *Cleave*. Homeopath.

BRICK, FRANCIS, Winchester, NH 1861–64; Keene 1864–75; Worcester, Mass 1875– (b/III–16–1838 Gard-ner, Mass; d/III–14–1906) MD Cleveland Homeop 1861. *New Engl med gaz* 41: , 1906 (May). Homeopath.

BRICKELL, DANIEL WARREN, CW–CSA; New Orleans (b/X–9–1824 Columbia SC; d/X–12 or XI–13–1881) MD U Pa 1847. *Chic med rev* 5:10, 1882. *UPa med alum CW*: 1847. *Med rec* 20:755 1881. *K&B* III:142.

BRICKELL, FRANK HAMAR, New Orleans (b/1857 Vicksburg, Miss; d/VIII–8–1898 Asheville, NC) MD ULa 1880. *JAMA* 31:427, 1898. *New Orl m & s jour* 51: 171, 1898. *Polk* 1890: 620.

BRICKER, SAMUEL REILEY, Reading, Pa; Spooner, Wis (b/XII–10–1867 Reading; d/XII–4–1895) MD Jefferson 1889. *Tr Wis St Med Soc* 30:553, 1896. *Polk* 1890: 1011.

BRICKER, WILLIAM R , Shelby, O (b/X–6–1820 Shafferstown, Pa; d/IX–6–1896) MD Cleveland Med Coll 1857. *Tr O Med Soc* 1897: 421–22. *JAMA* 27: 722, 1896. *Polk* 1896: 1211.

BRIDGE, W N , Marion, O; CW–USA (d/VIII–6–1864) MD Med Coll O 1852. *Tr O Med Soc* 1875: 193. *Nat med jour* 1: 291, 1870/71.

BRIDGES, ELISHA HALL, Ogdensburg, NY (d/XII–9–1903 @62) MD Bellevue 1866. *Bost m & s jour* 149: 692, 1903. *Tr Med Soc St NY* 1904: 420 (d/X–9–1903). *Polk* 1886: 700.

BRIDGES, ROBERT, Philadelphia (b/III–5–1806; d/II–20–1882) MD UPa 1828; AB Dickinson 1824. *Tr CPP* cent vol: 214. *Chic med rev* 5: 159, 1882. *Bost m & s jour* 106: 261, 1882. *K&B* III:144–45.

BRIDGES, VERNON ROE, Mattoon,Ill (d/XII–20–1895) MD Rush 1877 *JAMA* 26:93,1896. *Polk* 1890:339.

BRIDGMAN, FREDERICK, Tuskegee, Ala (b/III–26–1804; Belchertown, Mass; d/VII–20–1850) MD Harvard 1830; AB Yale 1826; ng Amherst 1826. *Amherst, Men of*: 1826.

BRIDGMAN, JOHN BAPTISTE, Boston (d/I–7–1862 @58) MD Harvard 1828. *Bost m & s jour* 65: 510, 1862.

BRIDGMAN, MARCUS FAYETTE, NH & Vt 1847–62; Brighton, Mass (b/III–11–1824 Windsor, Vt; d/I–20–1899) MD Dartmouth 1847. *Bost m & s jour* 140: 128, 1899. *Polk* 1886: 463.

BRIERLY, FRANK WALTER, NYC; Philadelphia 1896– (b/IV–13–1870 Beaver Falls, Pa; d/VI–17–1899) MD Hahnemann Phila 1894; BS Geneva. *Hahn mo* 34: 110 (news & advt) 1899 (July). *Tr Homeop Med Soc Pa* 1899. Homeopath.

BRIEVOGELLE, EUGENE ZACHARIAH, NYC (d/II 12–1897 @ 46) MD UCNY 1883. *JAMA* 28: 380, 1897. *Polk* 1896: 1043.

BRIGGS, CHARLES A ,NYC (d/XII–3–1869 @ 69) MD CPSNY 1829. *Phila med reg & dir* 1871:303.

BRIGGS, CHARLES EDWARD, CW–USA; Boston; St Louis, Mo (d/VI–17–1894 @62) MD Harvard 1856; AB 1853; AM 1860. *Bost m & s jour* 130:660, 1894. *Harvard in CW*: 64. *Butler* 1878:337.

BRIGGS, CYRUS, Augusta, Me (b/III–9–1800 Little Compton, RI; d/VI–20 or 24–1871) MD Harvard 1826; AB 1821. *Bost m & s jour* 7:440, 1871. *Tr Me Med Assn* 1871–73: 352–53.

BRIGGS, GEORGE CAREY, Franklin, Vt 1854?–75; Burlington 1875– (b/X–11–1829; d/II–11–1898) MD U Mich 1853; ng Castleton & Woodstock. *Tr Vt St Med Soc* 1898: 204–205. *JAMA* 30: 448, 1898. *Polk* 1896: 1473.

BRIGGS, JAMES A , Bowling Green, Ky (d/I–26–1900 @ 68) MD U Nashville 1852. *JAMA* 34: 381, 1900.

BRIGGS, JAMES CALVIN, Marblehead, Mass (b/VI–2–1816; d/XII–18–1856) MD Woodstock 1839; AB Yale 1835; Amherst ng 1833. *Amherst, Men of*: 1833. *Bost m & s jour* 55: 435, 1857.

BRIGGS, JOHN ABNER, Newburyport, Mass (b/VIII–18–1816 Salem; d/XII–11–1845) MD Harvard 1838; AB 1835; ng Bowdoin 1832. *Bowdoin cat*: 1835.

BRIGGS, JOHN M , Bowling Green, Ky (b/1798? d/IV–24–1882 @ 84) MD Transylvania 1824. *Nashville jour m & s* ns29:239, 1882; ns30: 1–20, 1882.

BRIGGS, LEMUEL WILLIAMS, Bristol, RI (b/VIII–28–1786 Middleboro, Mass; d/III–8–1840) MD AB Brown 1804. *Tr RI Med Soc* 1:42, 1859–77.

BRIGGS, LEMUEL WILLIAMS, Bristol, RI (b/V–21–1811; d/X–16–1889) MD Castleton 1833; ng Harvard Med Sch. *Bost m & s jour* 121:424, 1889. *Tr RI Med Soc* 1889–93: 102. *Atkinson* I: 357–58.

BRIGGS, THOMAS HENRY, Battle Creek, Mich (d/IV–7–1899) MD U Nashville 1864; MD UMich 1894 "1862 nunc pro tunc." *JAMA* 32:899,1899. *Polk* 1886: 483.

BRIGGS, WILLIAM AUGUSTUS, Boston (b/VII–12–1819; d/V–19–1859 Baltimore) MD Harvard 1841; AM 1838. *Bost m & s jour* 60: 348, 1859. Palmer's *Necrol alum Harvard*: 277.

BRIGGS, WILLIAM H , Rochester, NY (b/1822; d/VI–14–1901 @ 79) MD Geneva 1846. *JAMA* 37: 43, 1901. *Polk* 1886: 704.

BRIGGS, WILLIAM THOMPSON, Nashville, Tenn (b/XII–4–1828 Bowling Green, Ky; d/VI–13–1894) MD Transylvania 1849. *So pract* 16: 298–301, 1894. *JAMA* 22: 966–67, 1894. *New Orl med & surg jour* ns22: 77–78, 1894. *Nashville m & s jour* 76:37–49, 89–97, 145, 193, 241, 286, 1894. *Atkinson* I: 62. *K & B* III:145.

BRIGHAM, AMARIAH, Utica NY (b/XII–26–1798 New Marlborough, Mass; d/IX–8–1849) MD "not earned; stud med privately; att[?] lectures NYC." *Bost m & s jour* 41:

Spec. educ'l status abbrev. as: ***ng*** = college verified attendance without degree;

250–55, 1849. *Buff med jour* 5: 375, 397, 1849. *Tr AMA* 3: 434–36, 1850. *K&B* III: 145–46.

BRIGHAM, BRAYTON A , Lake Forest, Ill (d/X-11-1901) MD CPS Chicago 1886. *Ill med jour* ns3: 294, 1901. *Polk* 1886:260.

BRIGHAM, CHARLES BROOKS, San Francisco (b/I-17-1845 Boston; d/VIII-24-1903) MD Harvard 1870; AB 1866. *Calif st jour med* 1: 311, 1903. *Atkinson* I: 194. *Polk* 1896: 231.

BRIGHAM, FRANK FONTELLE, Lynn, Mass (b/X-15 1859 Westboro; d/III-10-1903) MD Harvard 1885; AB Brown 1882. *Bost m & s jour* 148:300 1903. *Polk* 1896: 716.

BRIGHAM, FRANKLIN WHITING, Shrewsbury, Mass CW-USA (b/1841; d/II-28-1899) MD Harvard 1865. *JAMA* 32: 563, 1889. *Harvard in CW*: 290. *Bost m & s jour* 140: 248, 364–65, 1899. *Polk* 1896: 722.

BRIGHAM, GERSHOM NELSON, Grand Rapids, Mich (b/III-3-1820 Fayston, Vt; d/VI-21-1886) MD Woodstock 1845. *Amer homeop* 12: 266, 1886. *Hahn mo* 21: 560, 1886. *Cleave*. Homeopath.

BRIGHAM, NORMAN, Mansfield, Conn (b/1790 S Coventry; d/X-15-1871) Lic Conn St Med Soc 1813. *Proc Conn Med Soc* 4:151, 1872. *Butler* 1878: 74.

BRIGHT, E C , Mt Sterling, Ky (d/V-4-1897) MD U Louisville 1855. *JAMA* 28: 1045, 1897. *Butler* 1878:269.

BRIGHT, GEORGE ADAMS, USN (b/IV-9-1837 Bangor, Me; d/III-12-1905 Washington, DC) MD Harvard 1860; AB Amherst 1858; ng Bowdoin 1856. *Harvard in CW*: 256.

BRILEY, JOHN J , Pittsburgh, Pa (b/X-12-1874; d/VI-4-1902) MD U Western Pa 1896. *Pa med jour* 5: 567, 1901/02; 6: 269, 1902/03.

BRILLANTOWSKY, SAMUEL, CW-USA (d/I-23-1866) <MD U Berlin 1846> *Med reg NY NJ Conn* 1866:206.

BRINCKERHOFF, ISAAC, Brooklyn? USN (d/IX-28-1874) MD UPa 1825. *Med reg NY NJ Conn* 1875: 196. *U Pa med alum CW*: 1825.

BRINCKLÉ, SAMUEL CRAWFORD, Greenville, Del; CW-USA; (b/IX-16-1835 Phila; d/VIII-26-1897 Wilmington, Del) MD UPa 1859. *U Pa med alum CW*: 1859. *Polk* 1886: 206.

BRINCKLÉ, THOMAS RODNEY, Philadelphia (b/IX-20-1804; d/VII-8-1853) MD UPa 1826. *Tr CPP* ns2: 291–94, 1854. *Phila med reg & dir* 2:77–78, 1853.

BRINCKLÉ, WILLIAM DRAPER, Philadelphia (b/II-9 1798 Kent Co, Del; d/XII-16-1862) MD UPa 1819; AB Princeton 1816. *Tr CPP* cent vol: 214. *K&B* III: 147–48.

BRINKER, THOMAS HENRY, Pleasant Unity, Pa (d/IV 27-1906 @ 87) MD Jefferson 1846. *Pa med jour* 9: 746, 1905/06.

BRINKERHOFF, JOHN J, Auburn NY (d/V-27-1896) MD Bellevue 1867. *JAMA* 26:1191 1896. *Polk* 1896:987.

BRINKERHOFF, SAMUEL B , Santa Barbara, Calif (b/Auburn, NY; d/III-25-1880) MD U Buffalo 1850. *Med rec* 17: 612, 1880.

BRINLEY, WILLIAM HENRY, Minneapolis (d/IX-1-1897) MD Yale 1881. *JAMA* 29:555,1897. *Polk* 1896: 790.

BRINSMADE, THOMAS CLARK, Troy, NY (b/VI-16-1802 New Hartford, Conn; d/VI-22-1868 @ 65) Hon MD Yale 1839; lic Conn St Med Soc 1823. *Bost m & s jour* ns1: 340, 1868. *Tr AMA* 21: 453–54, 1870. *Tr Med Soc St NY* 1869: 238–46.

BRINTON, DANIEL GARRISON, CW-USA; Philadelphia (b/V-13-1837, West Chester, Pa; d/VII-31-1899) MD Jefferson 1860; AB Yale 1858. *JAMA* 33: 427, 1899. *Atkinson* I: 648.

BRINTON, JEREMIAH BERNARD, Philadelphia (b/VIII-16-1835 New Hope, Pa; d/XII-6-1894) MD Jefferson 1859. *Bost m & s jour* 131: 600, 1894. *JAMA* 23: 961, 1894. *K&B* III: 148.

BRINTON, JOHN BOWEN, West Chester Pa (d/X-13-1881 @77) MD Jefferson 1826; MD UPa 1851 ad eundem. *Chic med rev* 4:495 1881. *Med bull m & s* 3: 266 1881.

BRINTON, WILLIAM BOWEN, West Chester, Pa; CW USA; (b/XI-30-1842; d/III-7-1883) MD UPa 1863. *Med bull med & surg* 5:117, 1883. *Tr Pa St Med Soc* 15:341–42, 1883. *U Pa med alum CW*: 1863.

BRIRY, MILTON STORY, Bath, Me (b/V-7-1825 Bowdoin; d/VIII-2-1899) MD Bowdoin 1853. *Hahn mo* 34:138 (news & advt) 1899 (Sept.) *Tr Am Inst Homeop* 1900: 830. *Cleave*. Homeopath.

BRISCOE, JOHN HANSON, Baltimore (b/XII-10-1789 Chaptico; d/IX-1855) MD UPa 1811. *Med ann Md*: 332.

BRISCOE, WALTER CLARKE, Washington, DC (b/XII-6-1837; d/V-16-1896) MD Georgetown 1869. *Hist Med Soc DC*: 296. *Polk* 1893: 268.

BRISTOL, MOSES, Clinton & Manlius, NY; Buffalo 1822–49 (b/X-21-1790 Clinton; d/XI-6-1869 Buffalo) MD Yale 1816; AB 1813. *Buff m & s jour* 9: 150, 1869.

BRISTOW, BENJAMIN W , Flatonia, Tex (d/VII-13-1896 @ c55) MD Rush 1859; MD Northwestern 1869. *Tex med news* 5: , 1895–96. *Polk* 1886: 885.

BRISTOW, JAMES C , Wayne City, Ill (d/VII-16-1905 @ 81) MD U Louisville 1872. *Ill med jour* 8: 185, 1905. *Polk* 1886: 279.

BRITTAIN, STEPHEN H , Loogootee, Ind (b/IX-25-1836 Washington Co; d/X-21-1904) MD Cincinnati Coll Med & Surg 1859. *Tr Ind St Med Soc* 1905: 443. *Polk* 1896: 480.

BRITTINGHAM, LITTLETON T , Hannibal, Mo (d/II-24-1901) MD Mo Med Coll (Kemper) 1847. *Ill med jour* ns2: 533, 1901. *Polk* 1886: 549.

BROCK, HENRY P, Trenton (b/IX-21-1847 Burlington Co; d/VIII-29-1886) MD UPa 1872. *Tr Med Soc NJ* 1886–87: 295.

BROCK, HUGH WORKMAN, Morgantown, WVa (b/I-

5–1830 Blacksville, Va; d/IV–24–1882) MD Jefferson 1852. *Tr AMA* 33:530–34, 1882. *Tr Med Soc W Va* 1882: 831–34. *K&B* I.

BROCK, WILLIAM E , Trenton, Ga (d/X–11–1881) MD U Nashville 1858. *Nashville jour m & s* ns28: 231, 1881. *Butler* 1878: 108.

BROCKBANK, JOSEPH WILLIAM, Philadelphia (b/ VII–1–1862 Elk Co, Pa; d/XI–7–1895) MD UMd 1883*JAMA* 25:911, 1895. *Med bull med & surg* 17:475.

BROCKENBROUGH, AUSTIN, Tappahannock, Va; Richmond Co (b/VI–11–1809; d/XII–31–1858) MD UPa 1831. *Med surg rep Phila* ns1:302, 1858/59.

BROCKETT, LINUS PIERPONT, Brooklyn (d/I–13–1893 @ c72) MD Yale 1843; AM Amherst 1857. *Med reg NY NJ Conn* 1893: 298.

BROCKWAY, FREDERICK JOHN, NYC (b/II–24–1860 Sutton, NH; d/IV–21–1901) MD CPSNY 1887. *Bost m & s jour* 144: 438, 1901. *Polk* 1896: 1043.

BROCKWAY, WILLIAM JOSEPH, NYC (b/IV–15–1861; d/XI–28–1894) MD UCNY 1889. *Med reg NY NJ Conn* 1895: 216.

BRODHEAD, CICERO, Waynesboro, Ga (b/XI–13–1851 Delaware Water Gap, Pa; d/II–6–1886?) MD UPa 1875; att? Lafayette. *Med surg rep Phila* 50:288, 1884.

BRODIE, WILLIAM, CW–USA; Detroit (b/VII–26–1823 Fawley Ct, Engl; d/VII–30–1890) MD CPSNY 1850; ng Berkshire, Woodstock. *Med age* 8:379, 419–21, 1890. *K&B* III: 149–50.

BRODIE, WILLIAM BIDDLE, Forest Grove, Pa (b/ Phila; d/IX–3–1897 @ 42) MD UPa 1879. *JAMA* 29:606, 1897. *Polk* 1886: 828.

BRODNAX, BENJAMIN H , Brodnax, La (d/X–17–1905 @ 73) MD unknown. *New Orl m & s jour* 58: 430, 1905. *Polk* 1886: 413.

BRODNAX, ROBERT WALKER, CW–CSA; Manchester, Va (b/I–12–1827 Jerusalem or Courtland, Va; d/VI–10–1888) MD UPa 1847. *U Pa med alum CW*: 1847.

BRODSKY, FRANCIS ALBERT, Jr, Racine, Wis (b/ IX–17–1859; d/IV–29–1899) MD CPSNY 1884. *JAMA* 32: 1074, 1899. *Tr Wis St Med Soc* 33: 516–17, 1899. *Polk* 1886: 672 (NYC).

BROKAW, WILLIAM A, St Louis (d/V–9–1899) MD Mo Med Coll 1896. *JAMA* 32:1133,1899. *Polk* 1896:866.

BROMLEY, CALVIN BARSTOW, Scotland, Conn (b/ V–11–1810 Lisbon; d/VII–17–1870) MD Berkshire 1835. *Proc Conn St Med Soc* 3:495–96, 1871.

BROMWELL, ROBERT EVANS, Port Deposit, Md (b/ II–28–1827 Cecil Co; d/III–21–1906) MD UMd 1850. *Med annals Md*: 333. *Atkinson* I: 320.

BRONAUGH, GEORGE W , Stanford, Ky (d/I–16–1899 @ 79) MD Transylvania 1843. *JAMA* 32: 263, 1899. *Polk* 1886: 406.

BRONSON, BENJAMIN FRANK, Syracuse, NY 1873–76; Bridgeport, Conn 1876– (b/1851 Bucksport, NY; d/XII–1905) MD Hahnemann Phila 1873. *Hahn mo* 41:22, 1906. Homeopath.

BRONSON, HENRY, New Haven, Conn (b/I–30–1804 Waterbury; d/XI–26–1893) MD Yale 1827; AM 1840. *Proc Conn St Med Soc* 1894:229–30. *JAMA* 21: 907–08, 1893. *Bost m & s jour* 129: 552, 1893. *K&B* III: 150. *Butler* 1878: 74.

BRONSON, HORACE, Cortland Co, NY (b/IX–8–1796; d/I–30–1874) MD Fairfield 1819; att? Hamilton Coll. *Med reg NY NJ Conn* 1874: 270.

BRONSON, JOHN O, Rhinebeck NY (b/XI–9–1827 Glastonbury, Conn; d/III–28–1897) MD NY Med Coll 1855. *Bost m&s jour* 136:341 1897. *JAMA* 28:714 1897.

BRONSON, JOHN RICHARDSON, Attleboro, Mass (b/ VI–5–1829; d/V–9–1900) MD Berkshire 1850; ng Woodstock 1850. *Bost m & s jour* 142: 528, 1900. *Tr RI Med Soc* 6:261–62, 1899–1903. *Polk* 1886:453.

BRONSON, ROSWELL, Oxford, Conn (d/XII–14–1855) MD Berkshire 1850. *Proc Conn St Med Soc* 1859:95–97.

BRONSON, STEPHEN HENRY, New Haven, Conn (b/ II–1844, Waterbury; d/VIII–19–1880) MD Yale 1866. *Proc Conn St Med Soc* ns2: 163–65, 1882–83. *Butler* 1878: 74.

BROOKE, BENJAMIN, Washington, DC; USA 1891 (b/ X–17–1866 Radnor, Pa; d/X–12–1900) MD UPa 1889; ng Haverford 1885. *Haverford Coll biogr cat*: 172.

BROOKE, CHARLES, Marshall, Tex (d/VI–9–1887) MD Tulane 1869. *Tex cour–rec med* 4: 488, 1887. *Polk* 1886: 890.

BROOKE, ENOS LEWIS, W Pikeland, Pa (d/IV–9–1897 @ 79) MD Pa Med Coll 1848. *JAMA* 28: 860, 1897.

BROOKE, JOHN, USA (b/II–22–1830 Radnor; d/V–13–1902) MD UPa 1854. *U Pa med alum CW*: 1854.

BROOKE, JOHN B , Reading, Pa (d/III–19–1898 @ 65) MD Jefferson 1858. *Lehigh Valley med mag* 9: 79, 1898. *JAMA* 30: 807, 1898. *Polk* 1896: 1331.

BROOKE, JOHN FRANCIS, USN (d/X–17–1849 Macao) MD UPa 1820. *Trans AMA* 3: 438, 1850.

BROOKFIELD, JOSEPH, Philadelphia (b/1789? d/XII–17–1872 @ 84) MD Jefferson 1836. *Med surg rep Phila* 28: 78, 1873.

BROOKS, A J , Marilla, NY (b/VIII–5–1832; d/IV–16–1890 @ 57) MD Albany 1860. *Buff m & s jour* 29: 735, 1890. *Polk* 1896: 796.

BROOKS, CHARLES ALLAN, Americus, Ga (d/XII–17 1894) MD Bellevue 1883. *JAMA* 23: 990, 1894. *Polk* 1890: 259.

BROOKS, CHARLES GROSVENOR, E Boston (b/III–24–1848 Keene, NH; d/III–15–1885) MD Harvard 1871; AB Amherst 1868. Stud NY Homeop 1871–72. *Tr Am Inst Homeop* 1885: 16. *Mass Homeop Med Soc* 1886. Homeopath.

BROOKS, EDWARD, CW–USA (b/Mass; d/IV–19–1866 Rockdale, NY) MD Jefferson 1862. *Nat med jour* 1: 291, 1870/71. G.V. Henry *Milit rec*: 60.

BROOKS, EUGENE WENTWORTH, Portland, Me (b/

 Spec. educ'l status abbrev. as: ***ng*** = college verified attendance without degree;

XII-21-1847; d/III-5-1885) MD CPSNY 1870. *Tr Me Med Assoc* 1883-85: 561-62. *Butler* 1878: 304.

BROOKS, FRANCIS R , Chicago (d/IV-12-1898 @ 31 Lake Geneva, Wis) MD UVa 1892; MD U Ill 1893. *JAMA* 30: 999, 1898. *Polk* 1896: 376.

BROOKS, GEORGE W , Ellsworth, O (d/III-10-1899 @ 73) MD Cleveland Med Coll 1851. *JAMA* 32: 733, 1899. *Polk* 1886: 754.

BROOKS, GEORGE WASHINGTON, NYC (d/VII-4-1904 @ 87) MD UCNY 1850. *Bost m & s jour* 150:660, 1904. *Polk* 1896: 1043.

BROOKS, HOMER, Haverhill, Mass (b/VIII-1-1855 Franconia, NH; d/IV-4-1893) MD NY Homeop 1881; AB Dartmouth 1877. *No Amer jour med* 41: 380, 1893. *Polk* 1886: 467. Homeopath.

BROOKS, JOHN G , Belfast, Me; Radnor, Pa (b/II-15-1821 York, Me; d/V-12-1902) MD Jefferson 1851; att? Dartmouth. *Pa med jour* 6: 259, 1902/03. *Atkinson* I:99. *Polk* 1886: 423.

BROOKS, PASCHAL PAOLI, La Crosse, Wis 1855- (b/ 1805? d/VII-22-1865 @ 60) MD UVt 1825. *Western homeop obs* 2: 171, 1865. *King* I: 339.

BROOKS, PELATIAH, Binghamton, NY CW-USA (b/ Lisle; d/III-2-1864 Nashville (MD CPSNY 1850. *Tr Med Soc St NY* 1865: 302-03.

BROOKS, PETER H , Lima, O (d/X-28-1898) MD U Miami 1872. *JAMA* 31: 1190, 1898. *Polk* 1886: 759.

BROOKS, RALPH ABRAM, USA (d/I-4-1903 Canton, Pa @ 27) MD UPa 1901. *Pa med jour* 7:278, 1903/04.

BROOKS, ROBERT FORSYTHE, CW-USN; Carthage, Mo (b/V-8-1839 Oxford, O; d/IX-6-1899) MD Bellevue 1864; AB U Miami 1858; AM 1863. *U Miami cat*: 1858. *Polk* 1886: 543.

BROOKS, SAMUEL DOOLITTLE, Springfield, Mass (d/II-26-1906 @ 89) MD Berkshire 1841. *Bost m & s jour* 154: 256, 1906. *Polk* 1886: 473.

BROOKS, SAMUEL T , Sherbrooke, PQ 1851-62; St Johnsbury, Vt 1862- (b/Stanstead, PQ XII-28-1823; d/III-13-1895) MD McGill 1851; att? Bishop's Coll 1854. *Tr Vt St Med Soc* 1895: 240-42. *JAMA* 24: 497, 1895. *Polk* 1890: 1107.

BROOKS, SILAS SWIFT, Philadelphia (b/V-30-1817 So Scituate, Mass; d/VII-2-1871) MD Jefferson 1844. *Tr Am Inst Homeop* 1893: 132. *Tr Pa Homeop Med Soc* 1873. Homeopath c1854- .

BROOKS, WILLIAM B, Dallas (b/1843 Charleston W Va; d/X-4-1896) MD Mo Med Coll 1876. *So pract* 18: 575-76, 1896. *Tex med jour* 12: 278, 1896-97. *Tex med news* 5:563 1895-96. *New Orl m & s jour* 24:367, 1896.

BROOKS, WILLIAM D F , Bridgeton, NJ (b/II-10-1813; d/X-4-1841) MD UPa 1839. *Tr Med Soc NJ* 1871: 178.

BROOKS, WILLIAM H , Fort Wayne, Ind (b/1813; d/ X-13-1894) MD Worthington Med Coll betw 1833 & 1838; MD Ecl Med Inst Cinc 1849. *JAMA* 23: 624, 1894. *Tr Ind St Med Soc* 1895: 405. *Butler* 1878: 195.

BROOM [BROOME], JOHN MACKALL, St Mary's City, Md (b/1808; d/VII-28-1887) MD Washington Med Coll Balto 1828. *Med annals Md*: 333. *Polk* 1886: 445.

BROSNAN, JOHN THOMAS JOSEPH, Brooklyn (d/IX 9-1904 @35) MD Bellevue 1894. *Bost m & s jour* 151: 308, 1904.

BROUGHTON, HENRY B, Port Deposit Md (b/1800 Cecil Co; d/X-6-1852) MD UMd 1822. *Med ann Md*: 333.

BROUS, HENRY A , Manhattan, Kans (d/V-10-1906 @ 51) MD Jefferson 1878. *Pa med jour* 9:672, 1905/06. *Polk* 1886: 813 (Philadelphia, Pa).

BROWER, JEREMIAH H , Lawrenceburgh, Ind (b/ 1798? d/VIII-1-1866 @ 69) MD unknown. *Tr AMA* 33: 529-30, 1882. Kemper, *Med hist Ind*: 246. *Tr Ind St Med Soc* 1871: 243. *Cinc jour med* 1:493-95, 1866. *Nashville jour m & s* ns1: 399, 488, 1866.

BROWER, ROBERT FULTON, Danbury, Conn (d/IV-29-1863 @ 39) MD CPSNY 1844. *Med surg rep Phila* 10: 64, 1863.

BROWN, AARON MERCER, CW-USA; Cincinnati (b/ VIII-3-1838 Milford, O; d/X-3-1902) MD UPa 1861. *U Pa med alum CW*: 1861. *Polk* 1886: 741.

BROWN, ALFRED, Hellertown, Pa (d/IX-11-1899 @ 54) MD UPa 1871; AB Lafayette 1868. *JAMA* 33: 808, 1899. *Polk* 1886: 802.

BROWN, ALPHONSO BICKFORD, Newburyport, Mass (d/X-17-1906 @41) MD Harvard 1898; AB Yale 1894. *Bost m & s jour* 155: 490, 1906.

BROWN, AMOS H , Zanesville, O; Brooklyn (d/I-26-1880 @ 74) MD CPSNY 1826. *Med surg rep Phila* 42: 176, 1880.

BROWN, ANDREW ROTHWELL, Washington, DC (b/ V-31-1847; d/XII-16-1900) MD Georgetown 1868. *Hist Med Soc DC*: 289.

BROWN, ANTHONY LEOPOLD, Springfield, Mass (d/ IV-22-1905 @ 42) MD Howard U, DC 1894. *Bost m & s jour* 152:508,534,1905. *Flint* 1897:480. Black.

BROWN, BEDFORD, CW-CSA; Alexandria, Va (b/I-17 1825 Caswell Co, NC; d/IX-12/13-1897) MD Transylvania 1848; MD Jefferson 1855. *JAMA* 29: 660, 1897. *Nashville jour m&s* 82:240 1897. *Hist Med Soc DC*:279.

BROWN, BELNO ADDISON, Milwaukee (d/V-11-1900 Kalamazoo, Mich) BD Nashotah 1872; MD Trinity Med Coll 1892: MD U Mich 1886. *Tr Wis St Med Soc* 35: 503, 1901.

BROWN, BENJAMIN STANTON, Bellefontaine, O (b/ VII-13-1800 Brownsville, Pa; d/XII-19-1873; MD Med Coll O 1828. *Tr AMA* 29: 621-22, 1878. *Tr Ohio St Med Soc* 1876: 93-95. *Butler* 1878: 621.

BROWN, BRINTON JAMES, Hastings, Mich; Detroit (b/XII- -1874 Derchan, Ont; d/VIII-30-1871) MD Cleveland Homeop Coll 1869; ng U Mich Med Sch 1867-68. *Am homeop obs* 1871: Homeopath.

BROWN, BUCKMINSTER, Auburndale, Mass (b/VII–13–1819 Boston; d/XII–26–1891) MD Harvard 1844. *Bost m & s jour* 125: 720, 1891; 126: 23, 74, 1892. *Atkinson* I:177–78. *K & B* III: 152–53.

BROWN, CALEB, Sac City, Ia (b/I–27–1850 Knox Co, O; d/VI–4–1899) MD Keokuk CPS 1877. *JAMA* 32: 1460, 1899. *Tr Ia St Med Soc* 18: 395–97, 1900. *Polk* 1896: 538.

BROWN, CARLOS M , Sacramento, Calif (d/1881) MD Jefferson 1879. *Med bull med & surg* 3: 91, 1881.

BROWN, CHARLES HENRY, NYC (d/X–15–1901 @ 45) MD UCNY 1879. *Bost m & s jour* 145: 478, 1901. *Polk* 1896: 1043.

BROWN, CHARLOTTE AMANDA BLAKE, SanFrancisco (b/1846 Philadelphia; d/IV–19–1904) MD Woman's Med Coll Pa, 1874. *Calif st jour med* 2: 172, 1904. *Bost m & s jour* 150:522, 1904. *Polk* 1886: 171.

BROWN, CLAY, CW–USA (d/III–19–1862) *Nat med jour* 1: 291, 1870/71.

BROWN, DAVID TILTON, Batavia, Ill (b/VIII– –1822; d/IX–4–1889) MD CPSNY 1844. *Med surg rep Phila* 61, 307–08, 1889. *K & B* III: 153.

BROWN, FRANCIS FREDERIC, CW–USA; Reading, Mass (b/VIII–12–1834 Sudbury, Mass; d/I–13–1890) MD Berkshire 1862; AB Amherst 1855. *Bost m & s jour* 122: 72, 192, 1890. *Polk* 1886: 471.

BROWN, FRANCIS WAYLAND, Rochester, NY (b/V–13–1840; d/IX–1–1885) MD UCNY 1877; AB Amherst 1867. *Amherst, Men of*: 1867. *Polk* 1886: 704.

BROWN, FRANK W , Detroit (d/IX–9–1893) MD Detroit Med Coll 1877. *JAMA* 21:498, 1893. *Polk* 1886:487.

BROWN, FRANK WARREN [also as **BROWN, ZENO**] Greenville, NC (b/III–16–1861 Pitt Co; d/V–15–1898) MD Bellevue 1884; stud UNC 1879–80. *NC med jour* 41:462, 1898. *Tr NC Med Soc* 1899: 174. *Polk* 1886: 729, as Zeno.

BROWN, FREDERIC DAVIS, Webster, Mass (d/XI–8–1886 @ 62) MD Castleton 1849. *Bost m & s jour* 115: 488, 1886.

BROWN, GEORGE, Baltimore (b/1755 Ireland; d/VIII–24–1822) <MD U Edinburgh 1799> *Med annals Md*: 333–34.

BROWN, GEORGE, Barre, Mass (d/VI–6–1892 @ 68) MD UCNY 1850. *Bost m & s jour* 126: 484, 1892. *Polk* 1886: 454.

BROWN, GEORGE WASHINGTON, Long Branch, NJ (b/VII–28–1857; d/V–11–1894) MD CPSNY 1879. *Med reg NY NJ Conn* 1894: 234 (d/III–12–1894). *Tr Med Soc NJ* 1894: 265. *JAMA* 22: 855, 1894.

BROWN, GUSTAVUS, Sr, Rich Hills, Md (b/IV–26–1689 Scotland; d/1765) *JAMA* 1: 600–01, 1883. *K & B* III: 154–55.

BROWN, GUSTAVUS, St Mary's Co, Md (b/1744 Edinburgh, Scotland; d/VII–3–1801) MD U Edinburgh 1770. *Med annals Md*: 334. *K & B* III: 155.

BROWN, GUSTAVUS ALEXANDER, Alexandria, Md (b/c1790; d/1835 Smithland, Ky) MD UPa 1815; AB Princeton 1806. *JAMA* 1:602,1883. *Hist Med Soc DC*:220.

BROWN, GUSTAVUS RICHARD, Rose Hill, Md (b/X–17–1747 Port Tobacco, Md; d/IX–30–1804) MD Edinburgh 1768. *JAMA* 1: 601–02, 1883. *Med annals Md*: 334. *K & B* III: 155–56.

BROWN, HARVEY ELLICOTT, USA (d/VIII–22–1889) MD UCNY 1858; AB Princeton 1854. *Med surg rep Phila* 61: 252, 1889.

BROWN, HENRY ALBERT, Reading, Mass (d/IX–3–1889) MD Boston U 1877. *Tr Am Inst Homeop* 1891. *Polk* 1886: 471. Homeopath.

BROWN, HENRI RIENZI, Leominster, Mass (d/II–16–1905 @ 63) <MD NY Homeop Med Coll 1867> *Bost m & s jour* 152: 234, 1905. *Polk* 1890: 550.

BROWN, HENRY WEEKS, NYC (b/VI–18–1828; d/XII 17–1864) MD UCNY 1850. *Med reg NY NJ Conn* 1865: 232. *Med surg rep Phila* 12:219, 1864/65.

BROWN, IGNATIUS C , Columbus Junction, Ia (d/III–21–1900) MD Jefferson 1861. *JAMA* 34: 830, 1900. *Polk* 1896: 516.

BROWN, IRA DEWITTE, Weedsport, NY (d/VI–23–1899 @ 64) MD Albany 1865. *JAMA* 33: 52, 1899. *Polk* 1896: 1111.

BROWN, ISAAC H , Waverly, Ill (b/X–28–1805 Goshen, Conn; d/IV–13–1874) MD Fairfield 1828. *Tr Ill St Med Soc* 1874: 156.

BROWN, JACOB NEWTON, San José, Calif (b/IV–25–1837; d/IV–2–1898) MD Med Coll O 1860; AB U Miami 1857. *U Miami cat*: 1857. *Polk* 1886: 275.

BROWN, JAMES, Baltimore (b/XI–12–1854; d/VI–16–1895 Boston) MD U Md 1875. *Med annals Md*: 334. *K & B* II: 154. *Polk* 1886: 435.

BROWN, JAMES LIVINGSTON, NYC (b/IV–2–1831; d/II–4–1873) MD UCNY 1856; AB Columbia 1852. *Med reg NY NJ Conn* 1873: 335. *Med rec* 8: 95, 120, 144, 162, 263, 327, 1873.

BROWN, JAMES M , Philadelphia (d/IV–13–1903 @ 58) MD Jefferson 1875. *Pa med jour* 7:278, 1903/04. *Polk* 1896: 1299.

BROWN, JAMES M , Spruce Creek, Pa (d/XI–28–1904. MD U Louisville 1882. *Pa med jour* 8:334, 1904/05.

BROWN, JAMES RAYMOND, Springfield, Mass (d/I–10–1892) MD Harvard 1870. *Bost m & s jour* 127: 638, 1892. *Polk* 1890: 556.

BROWN, JAMES WATSON, Framingham Mass (d/VII 7–1892) MD UPa 1851; AB Williams 1840. *Wms grads*.

BROWN, JEREMIAH N , Utica, NY (d/IX–18–1874) MD Buffalo Med Coll 1855. *Buff m & s jour* 14: 75–76, 1874.

BROWN, JOEL HENRY, West Newton, Mass (b/X–22–1815 Bradford, NH; d/III–15–1865) MD unknown; AB Dartmouth 1841. *Bost m & s jour* 72: 168, 1865.

 Spec. educ'l status abbrev. as: ***ng*** = college verified attendance without degree;

BROWN, JOHN, Lancaster, NY (b/I-10-1792; d/II-27-1852) MD unknown. AM Harvard 1813. Palmer's *Necrol alum Harvard*: 6-7.

BROWN, JOHN BALL, Boston (b/X-10-1784 Wilmington; d/V-14-1862) MD Harvard 1813; AB Brown 1806. *Bost m & s jour* 66:324, 362-64, 1862. *K&B* III: 156-57.

BROWN, JOHN WERT, Reading, Pa (d/V-1-1904 @ 69) MD UPa 1870. *Pa med jour* 8: 334, 1904/05. *Flint* 1897: 832.

BROWN, JOSEPH B , USA (d/X-21-1891 Albion, NY) MD Albany 1844. *Buff m & s jour* 31:239, 1891. *Med bull med & surg* 13: 467.

BROWN, JOSEPH R , Phoenix, NY 1848- ; Galveston, Tex 1853- (d/1854 Galveston) MD Hahnemann Phila 1854. *Tr Am Inst Homeop* 1893: 133.

BROWN, L C , CW-USA (d/XI- -1862) *Nat med jour* 1: 291, 1870/71.

BROWN, MARCUS A , Circleville, O (b/VIII-13-1824; d/X-21-1848) MD Jefferson 1847; AB U Miami 1844. *U Miami cat*: 1844.

BROWN, MYRON S , Danville, Ill (d/VI-28-1901 @ 69) MD U Nashville 1863. *Ill med jour* ns3: 141, 1901. *Polk* 1886: 275.

BROWN, NATHAN, Freedom, Md (d/1873) MD U Md 1826. *Med annals Md*: 335.

BROWN, NATHANIEL WEEDE, Pittsburgh, Pa (b/VI-6-1842 New Florence, Pa; d/X-6-1899) MD Jefferson 1866. *Pa med jour* 3:384-85, 1899/1900. *Flint* 1897:828.

BROWN, ORLANDO, Washington,Conn (b/IV-13-1827 Groton, Conn; d/VIII-3-1904) MD Yale 1851. *Proc Conn Med Soc* 1905: 77-78, 484-86. *Flint* 1897: 178.

BROWN, R F , Memphis,Tenn (d/X-8-1878) MD 1853 [where?] *Tr AMA* 30: 856, 1879. *Med rec* 14: 300, 1878.

BROWN, RALEIGH T , Washington, DC (b/Va; d/1859) MD UPa 1836; att? Washington & Lee. *Hist Med Soc DC*: 249.

BROWN, ROBERT S , Newport, Pa (d/X-18-1859 @38) MD Jefferson 1850 [?] *Med surg rep Phila* ns3:131, 1859/60.

BROWN, SAMUEL, Bladensburg, Va; New Orleans, Natchez, Miss; Lexington, Ky (b/I-30-1769 Augusta, Va; d/I-2-1830 Huntsville, Ala) Stud med Edinburgh; stud Phila w/B.Rush. *Transylvania jour med & assoc sci* 3: 151-52, 1830. *K & B* III: 157-58.

BROWN, SAMUEL, Philadelphia (b/VIII-16-1817 Scotland; d/III-22-1892) MD Hahnemann Phila 1858. *Tr Pa Homeop Soc* 1892. *Polk* 886:813. Homeopath.

BROWN, SAMUEL HINMAN, NYC; CW-USA (d/VII-31-1863 @39 Baton Rouge) MD UCNY 1850. *Med surg rep Phila* 10: 252, 1863. *Nat med jour* 1: 291, 1870/71.

BROWN, SEPTIMUS, Baltimore (b/1827; d/I-31-1883) MD UMd 1849; AB Princeton 1846; AM 1850. *Med annals Md*: 335. *Butler* 1874: 310.

BROWN, SILVANUS, Derry, NH (b/III-22-1807 Hamilton, Mass; d/X-24-1870) MD Bowdoin 1827. *Med surg rep Phila* 24: 112, 1871.

BROWN, THOMAS, Tenn (b/c1784 Wilkesboro, NC; d/1834) <ng UPa Med Sch> *Tr Med Soc Tenn* 1876: 80.

BROWN, THOMAS HUNTINGTON, Paris,Me (b/VIII-27-1813; d/VIII-3-1880) MD Jefferson 1837. *Tr Me Med Assoc* 1881: 383-85. *Butler* 1878: 305.

BROWN, THOMAS MORFORD, Sharpsville, Pa (b/1837; d/IX-5-1879) MD U Buffalo 1864. *Tr Med Soc Pa* 13: 425-26, 1880. *Butler* 1878: 705.

BROWN, THOMAS RICHARDSON, Baltimore; USN (b/IV-6-1845; d/I-26-1879) MD UMd 1866. *Tr AMA* 30:808-10, 1879. *Med annals Md*: 335. *Atkinson* I: 167.

BROWN, TITUS LONSON, Binghamton, NY (b/X-16-1828 Hillsdale, NY; d/VIII-17-1887) MD Hahnemann Phila 1853; ng UCNY Med Sch 1848. *Tr Am Inst Homeop* 1888: 226. *Med adv* 19: 287, 1887. *Med inst (Hahn)* 3: 41, 1888. *Polk* 1886: 642. *Cleave*. Homeopath.

BROWN, ULYSSES HIGGINS, Syracuse, NY (d/XII-27 1900 @ 48) MD NY Homeop Med Coll 1873. *Bost m & s jour* 144: 28, 1900. *Tr Med Soc St NY* 1901: 426. *Polk* 1890: 852. Homeopath?

BROWN, WELCOME OWEN, Providence, RI; Barton, Vt (b/III-27-1822; d/V-9-1888) MD UPa 1852. *Tr RI Med Soc* 1883-88:574-76. *Atkinson* I:235. *Polk* 1886: 903.

BROWN, WESLEY EVERETT, Paxton & Gilbertsville, Mass (d/VII-30-1894 @ 42) MD UVt 1878. *Bost m & s jour* 131: 124, 1894.

BROWN, WILLARD CHANNING, Centralia, Mo (d/XI 10-1899 @ 62) MD UCNY 1881. *JAMA* 33: 1441, 1899. *Polk* 1896: 742.

BROWN, WILLIAM, Alexandria, Va (b/1748 Scotland; d/1792) MD Edinburgh 1770. *JAMA* 1:602, 2883. *K&B* III: 159.

BROWN, WILLIAM, Philadelphia (b/Ireland; d/XI-8-1887 Phila) MD Hahnemann Phila 1852. *Med vis* 4:15, 1888. Homeopath.

BROWN, WILLIAM BELL, Bath, NY (b/X-23-1858; d/XI-30-1889) MD U Buffalo 1881. *Med reg NY NJ Conn* 1890:261. *Polk* 1886: 641.

BROWN, WILLIAM H , Butler, Pa (d/V-4-1905 @ 42) MD U Ill 1893. *Ill med jour* 7:611, 1905. Homeopath?

BROWN, WILLIAM HAMMOND, Bangor, Me 1850-57, 1860-82; St Louis, Mo 1857-60 (b/VI-14-1822 Bangor; d/XI-23-1882) MD Harvard 1850; AB Bowdoin 1842. *Tr Me Med Assoc* 1883-85: 150-51. *Bost m & s jour* 107: 528, 1882. *Atkinson* I: 667.

BROWN, WILLIAM K , Philadelphia (b/VIII-19-1850 Phila; d/X-3-1900) MD Phila U Med & Surg 1872; AB Niagara. *Tr Pa Homeop Med Soc* 1901: . Homeopath.

BROWN, WILLIAM KELLOGG, Brooklyn; Philadelphia (b/VII-8-1807 or 1806 Boston; d/VII-4-1879 Narragansett Pier, RI) MD Dartmouth 1829. *Med reg NY NJ Conn* 1880:233. *Proc Med Soc Co Kings* Bkln 4: 287-89. 1879-80. *Butler* 1878: 529.

BROWN, WILLIAM MORTIMER, Newark, NJ (b/IX-8-1816; d/IV-14-1864) MD Jefferson 1838. *Tr Med Soc NJ* 1865:79-83, 136-37. *Tr AMA* 16: 632, 1865.

BROWN, WILLIAM MOULTRIE, Chicago (d/IX-14-1905 @ 48) MD Rush 1881. *Ill med jour* 8:341, 1905. *Polk* 1890: 309.

BROWN, WILLIAM P , Greenville, Ill (d/XI-16-1899) Lic by years of practice. *Trans Ill St Med Soc* 1899-1900: 352. *Polk* 1896: 422.

BROWN, WILLIAM T , CW-USA (d/VI-27-1864) *Nat med jour* 1:291, 1870/71.

BROWN, WILLIAM WHITTIER, Manchester, NH (b/VIII-28-1805 Vershire, Vt; d/I-6-1874) MD Dartmouth 1835. *Tr NH Med Soc* 1874: 120-29.

BROWN, ZALMON KENT, Virginia, Minn (d/II-2-1900 @ 39) MD Jefferson 1890. *JAMA* 39: 446, 1900. *Polk* 1896: 802.

BROWN-SEQUARD, CHARLES E, Paris; NYC (b/1818 Mauritius; d/IV-1-1894 Paris) MD Paris 1846: BS 1839; LB 1838. *JAMA* 22: 523, 1894. *Med surg rep Phila* 15:169-72, 1866. *Atkinson* I: 700-01. *K & B* III: 158-59.

BROWNE, ALFRED L , Cornwall-on-Hudson, NY (d/V-3-1898 @ 36) MD Albany 1886. *JAMA* 30: 1248, 1898. *Polk* 1896: 1017.

BROWNE, GARDNER SHEPARD, Chicago (b/IX-12-1810 Alstead, NH; d/XII-29-1879) MD UCNY 1849; AM Dartmouth 1834. *Ohio med & surg rep* 11: 202, 1877. Homeopath.

BROWNE, JOHN MILLS, USN (b/V-10-1831 Hinsdale, NH; d/XII-7-1894) MD Harvard 1852. *JAMA* 23: 918, 1894; 24:101, 1895. *Harvard in CW*: 238. *Atkinson* I:132. *K & B* II: 158.

BROWNE, ROBERT BETHELL, CW-USA; Jeanesville, Pa (b/VI-19-1824; d/XI-13-1900 Phillipsburg, NJ) MD UPa 1846; AB Lafayette 1843. *U Pa med alum CW*: 1846.

BROWNELL, CLARENCE MELVILLE, E Hartford, Conn;(b/V-2-1828; d/V-22-1862) MD Berkshire 1848; ng Woodstock. *Proc Conn Med Soc* 2:161-66, 1865.

BROWNELL, MOSES, Troy & Albany, NY (b/1790? d/III-12-1879 Brooklyn @ 89) Lic Albany Med Soc 1816? *Med reg NY NJ Conn* 1879: 189.

BROWNELL, NATHAN PIKE, So Scituate, Mass (d/XII-29-1885 @ 60) <MD Dartmouth> *Bost m & s jour* 114: 24, 96, 1886. *Butler* 1878: 347.

BROWNELL, RICHMOND/RICHARD, Providence, RI (b/1789? d/X-29-1864 @ 74) MD Rutgers 1816; AB Union 1812. *Bost m & s jour* 71: 308, 1864.

BROWNELL, RUSSELL B , NYC (b/1838; d/1867 Egypt) MD Bellevue 1864; att? Marietta Coll. *Tr AMA* 19:409-10, 1868. *Med reg NY NJ Conn* 1867: 209.

BROWNELL, SEELY, CW-USA (d/V-19-1864 Memphis) MD unknown. *Nat med jour* 1:291, 1870/71.

BROWNELL, WILLIAM, Utica, Mich; CW-USA (b/XI 12-1830, Farmington, Mich; d/V-22-1884) MD U Mich 1852. *Med age* 2:197-98, 1884. *Atkinson* I:142-43. *Butler* 1878: 369.

BROWNELL, WILLIAM RICHMOND, Hartford, Conn (b/III-30-1828; d/XII-1-1873) MD UCNY 1852; AB Brown 1849. *Proc Conn Med Soc* 4:291 ff, 1874. *Butler* 1874: 74.

BROWNING, ALBERT GORDON, Providence, RI (b/1838 Woodstock, Conn; d/IV-5-1888) MD Yale 1863. *Tr RI Med Soc* 1883-88: 580. *Polk* 1886: 845.

BROWNING, JOHN BAILEY, CW-CSA; Ramsey, Ala (b/XI-24-1832; d/VIII- -1869) MD UPa 1855; att? U Ala 1851. *U Pa med alum CW*: 1855.

BROWNING, JOHN STROTHER, Flint Hill, Va; CW-CSA; (b/IX- -1828 Washington, Va; d/VI-28-1887) MD UPa 1851. *U Pa med alum CW*: 1851.

BROWNING, JOSEPH BOARDMAN, Kansas City, Mo (b/NY; d/XII-10-1893 @ c45 St Joseph, Mo) MD Rush 1873. *JAMA* 21: 982, 1893. *Polk* 1886: 550.

BROWNING, WILLIAM WEBB, Brooklyn (b/1852 Metuchen, NJ; d/X-4-1900) MD Bellevue 1884. *Bost m & s jour* 143: 384, 1900.

BROWNLEE, JAMES CARSON, Kansas City, Mo (b/II-9-1854 W Finley, Pa; d/XII-19-1900) MD Bellevue 1880; AB Amherst 1877. *Amherst, Men of*: 1877. *Polk* 1886: 550.

BROWNLEE, JAMES JEFFRAY [sic], USN (b/1809; d/XI-8-1879) MD CPSNY 1831. *Med surg rep Phila* 41: 462, 1879.

BROWNLEE, R W , Fort Deposit, Ala (d/I-7-1885) Cert Co Board. *Tr Med Assoc St Ala* 1885: 319.

BROWNLOW, JOHN H , Ogdensburgh, NY (d/X- -1899) MD Georgetown 1865. *Tr Med Soc St NY* 1900: 431. *Polk* 1886: 700.

BROWNSON, ROBERT SMITH, CW-USA; Mercersburg, Pa (b/X-19-1827; d/VI-15-1885) MD UPa 1851; AB Frank & Marsh 1847. *U Pa med alum CW*: 1851.

BROWNSON [BROWNELL], WILLIAM GREENE, New Canaan, Conn (b/VIII-6-1830 Peterboro, NY; d/ I-3-1899) MD UCNY 1865. *Proc Conn Med Soc* 1899: 362-64. *JAMA*32:92, 1899. *Polk* 1886: 194.

BRUBAKER, HENRY, Somerset, Pa (d/XI-12-1889) MD Jefferson 1851. *Med bull med & surg* 13: 26, 1890. *Polk* 1886: 835.

BRUBAKER, ISAAC P , Des Moines, Ia (b/IX-30-1851 Stoyestown, Pa; d/X-23-1892) MD Jefferson 1881. *Tr Ia St Med Soc* 11: xii, 1893; 14:328. 1896.

BRUCE, ARCHIBALD, NYC (b/II- -1777?; d/II-22-1810) MD Edinburgh 1800; AB Columbia 1795. *Med Soc Co NY* 1806-78: 332. *K & B* II: 158.

BRUCE, GEORGE D , Pittsburgh (d/V-28-1891 @ 79) MD UPa 1833. *Bost m & s jour* 124: 570, 1891. *Polk* 1886: 828.

BRUCE, R J , Thomasville, Ga (b/1817; d/1880) MD Transylvania 1846. *Tr AMA* 31: 1021-22, 1880.

 Spec. educ'l status abbrev. as: ***ng*** = college verified attendance without degree;

BRUCH, WILSON JOHN HARTMAN, CW-USA; Easton, Pa (b/VII-21-1837 Williams Twp; d/V-18-1880 Easton) MD UPa 1862. *U Pa med men CW*: 1862.

BRUCKHAUSEN, CASPER, Norwich, NY 1848- (d/XII-28-1891 @ 85) Stud med w/homeop physicians, esp Geo W Cook. *No Amer jour homeop* 40:63, 1892. *Cleave*. *Polk* 1886: 699. Homeopath.

BRÜCKHEIMER, MOSES, Washington, DC (b/IV-2-1836 Baden, Gny; d/VIII-7-1903) MD Columbian 1868. *Hist Med Soc DC*: 296. *Polk* 1893: 268.

BRUEN, EDWARD TUNIS, Philadelphia (b/VIII-12-1851; d/III-31-1889) MD UPa 1873; PhD 1873. *Tr CPP* cent vol: 214-15. *Tr Med Soc Pa* 21:265-266, 1889-90. *Bost m & s jour* 120:376, 1889.

BRUENINGHAUSEN, CHARLES, NYC? (b/Gny; d/1877) MD Berlin 1846? *Med reg NY NJ Conn* 1887:210. *Med surg rep Phila* 35: 200, 1876?

BRUMBY, GEORGE McDUFFIE, Delhi, La (d/VIII-27-1898 Biloxi, Miss) MD Jefferson 1859. *New Orl m & s jour* 51: 214, 1898. *Polk* 1890: 486.

BRUMLEY, JOHN DUANE, Newark, NJ (b/V-3-1834 Montville, Conn; d/I-8-1897) MD NY Med Coll 1858. *Tr Med Soc NJ* 1898: 373-75. *JAMA* 28: 184, 1897. *Atkinson* I: 451.

BRUMME, CARL, Detroit, Mich (b/Göttingen, Gny; d/V-13-1900 @ 83) MD Göttingen 1844. *JAMA* 34: 1273, 1900. *Polk* 1886: 487.

BRUMOND, PETER B , Idaho Springs, Colo (b/VII-19 1846 Prussia; d/IX-13-1889 @ 43) MD Chicago Med Coll 1868. *Tr Colo St Med Soc* 1898-99: 508. *Rec AAS USA* 1891: 27-28.

BRUN, CHARLES A , Columbus (d/III-29-1898 @ 28) MD Starling 1893. *JAMA* 30:933, 1898. *Polk* 1896:1179.

BRUNDAGE, AMOS H , CW-USA; Brooklyn (b/1828 Benton, Pa; d/III-19-1905) MD UCNY 1855. *Bost m & s jour* 152: 386, 1905. *Polk* 1896: 993.

BRUNDAGE, GEORGE W , Geneva, NY (d/IX-23-1899 @ 77) MD Geneva 1846. *JAMA* 33: 1308, 1899. *Polk* 1896: 1018.

BRUNDIGE, HENRY, Baltimore (b/V-15-1791 Dumfries Va; d/X-10-1865) MD UPa 1813. *Med annals Md*:336.

BRUNE, THOMAS BARTON, Baltimore (b/VI-4-1856; d/XI-9-1891) MD UMd 1878. *Bost m & s jour* 125: 336-37, 1891. *Med annals Md*: 336-37.

BRUNER, WILLIAM H , San Francisco, Calif (b/V-17-1826 Chester Co, Pa; d/VIII-10-1886) MD Jefferson 1848. *Tr Calif St Med Soc* 1887: 392-93.

BRUNNER, WILLIAM JOHN, NYC (d/XI-8-1906 @ 52) MD UCNY 1879. *Bost m & s jour* 155: 594, 1906. *Polk* 1896: 1043.

BRUNS, JOHN DICKSON, CW-CSA; Charleston, SC; New Orleans 1866- (b/II-24-1836; d/V-20-1883) MD Med Coll St SC 1857. *Med news* 42: 610, 1883. *Atkinson* I: 103-04. *K&B* III: 160.

BRUNT, SAMUEL F , Summitsville, Ind (b/I-20-1849 Madison Co, Ind; d/V-10-1883) MD Med Coll Ind 1874. *Tr Ind St Med Soc* 1884: 207.

BRUSH, FRANCIS V , Brooklyn (d/VII-8-1882 @ 37) MD CPSNY 1867. *Med reg NY NJ Conn* 1883: 222.

BRUSH, GEORGE RAWSON, USN (b/XI-3-1836 Smithtown, NY; d/XI-29-1894) MD CPSNY 1858. *Med reg NY NJ Conn* 1895: 217.

BRUSH, PLATTE EDWARD, CW-USA; ?Springville, Pa (b/X-14-1833 Bridgewater; d/VII-23-1896) MD Yale 1860; MD UPa 1866. *UPa med alum CW*: 1866.

BRUUER, AJALON, Philadelphia (b/II-4-1819 Wilbraham, Mass; d/XI-18-1896) <MD Jefferson 1844> AB Amherst 1839. *Amherst, Men of*: 1839.

BRUUER, LYCARTAS LUTHER, Wilbraham, Mass (b/X-26-1816; d/I-23-1845) MD Tulane 1843; AB Amherst 1836. *Amherst, Men of*: 1836.

BRYAN, JAMES, Elizabeth, NJ; CW-USA (b/VIII-23-1810 Merthyr Tydril, Wales; d/XI-5-1881) MD UPa 1834. *U Pa med alum CW*: 1834.

BRYAN, JAMES PETTIGREW, CW-CSA; Kinston,NC (b/VIII-31-1829 New Bern, NC; d/IV-14-1887) MD UPa 1852; AB UNC 1849. *U Pa med alum CW*: 1852.

BRYAN, JAY M , Philadelphia (d/III-14-1894) MD UPa 1892; AB Central HS Phila. *JAMA* 22:482, 1894.

BRYAN, JOHN, Beaver Falls, Pa (b/Washington Co; d/X-7-1905 @ 77) MD Homeop Hosp Coll Cleveland 1866. *Cleveland m & s rep*: 1905 (Dec). *Polk* 1886:792. Homeopath.

BRYAN, JOHN W , Beverley, NJ (b/1826? d/1871) MD Pa Med Coll 1859. *Tr AMA* 24: 359, 1873.

BRYAN, RICHARD S , Troy, NY (b/1796 Putnam Co, NY; d/III-5-1860 @ 64) Hon MD Cleveland Homeop 1851. *Tr Am Homeop Inst* 1860: 171. *Am hom rev* 2: 428 ff, 1860. Homeopath 1841-

BRYAN, THOMAS N , Indianapolis, Ind (b/III-26-1833 Southport, Ind; d/IV-3-1902) MD Louisville Med Coll 1857. *Tr Ind St Med Soc* 1902:407. *Polk* 1896: 472.

BRYAN, WILLIAM J , CW-USA; Corning, NY (b/XII-5-1837 Sonora; d/VII-13-1877) MD Cleveland Homeop 1869. *Tr Am Inst Homeop* 1878: 1122. *Homeop times* 5: 120. Homeopath.

BRYANT, ALBERT HENRY, CW-USA; Natick, Mass (d/VI-26-1877 @ 40) MD Harvard 1860. *Harvard in CW*: 257.

BRYANT, CHARLES G , Albany & Little Falls, NY; Calif 1854- (b/III-13-1829 Otsego Co, NY; d/VII-12-1864 San Francisco) MD Albany 1852. *Tr Am Inst Homeop* 1870: 645. Homeopath.

BRYANT, GEORGE SYNG, Lexington, Ky (b/III-4-1824 Powhatan Co, Va; d/VI-24-1875) MD Jefferson 1845;?att Hampden-Sidney. *Tr Ky St Med Soc* 1877:191.

BRYANT, HENRY, Boston; CW-USA (d/II-1-1867 @ 47 Porto Rico) MD Harvard 1843. *Harv in CW*: 14-15.

BRYANT, HORATIO, Independence, Ia (d/XI-2-1899)

MD Yale 1839; AB Union 1836; att? Amherst. *Amherst, Men of*: 1835.

BRYANT, JAMES K , Nashville, Tenn (d/II–14–1889) MD U Tenn 1885; DDS 1887. *So pract* 11:135–36,1889.

BRYANT, JOEL, Brooklyn 1849– (b/XI–10–1813 Northport, NY; d/XI–20–1868) <MD Pa Med Coll> *Tr Am Inst Homeop* 1893: 133. *Hahn mo* 4:353, 1869. *New Engl med gaz* 4:28, 1869. Homeopath.

BRYANT, MELLVILLE, Brooklyn (b/XII–8–1841 Northport, NY; d/XII–24–1893) MD NY Homeop 1862. *Tr Am Inst Homeop* 1894: 259. *JAMA* 22: 97, 1894. *Polk* 1886: 644.

BRYANT, WILLIAM W , Sycamore, Ill (d/XII–18–1899 @ 67) MD Worcester 1855. *Tr Ill St Med Soc* 1899–1900: 352. *JAMA* 34:62, 1900. *Polk* 1886: 299.

BRYARLY, WAKEMAN, Harford Co, Md (d/1821) MD UPa 1805. *Med annals Md*: 337.

BRYCE, PETER, Tuscaloosa, Ala (b/III–5–1834 Columbia, SC; d/VIII–14–1892) MD UCNY 1859; SC Milit Acad 1855. *Bost m & s jour* 127:176, 1892. *Atkinson* I:178. *Polk* 1886: 140.

BRYNE, JOHN, Brooklyn (b/1825 Ireland; d/X–1–1902 Switzerland) MD NY Med Coll 1853; MD Edinburgh 1846. *Bost m & s jour* 147: 422, 1902.

BUCHANAN, ALEXANDER, NYC (b/Glasgow, Scotland; d/IX–2–1896 @75) MD NY Med Coll 1862; MD Glasgow 1860. *JAMA* 27:661,1896. *Polk*1896: 1044.

BUCHANAN, ARCHIBALD H , Stone Mt, Ga (b/1808; d/VI–20–1863) MD UPa 1834. *So pract* 19:180, 1897. *Tr Med Soc Tenn* 1876: 80. *Nashville jour m & s* ns1: 67–69, 1866.

BUCHANAN, GEORGE, Baltimore; Philadelphia 1806– (b/IX–19–1763; d/VII–9–1808) MB UPa 1785; MD 1789; stud Edinburgh. *Med annals Md*: 337–38. *Balto med & phys recorder* 1:176, 1809. *K & B* III: 162–63.

BUCHANAN, JAMES ANDERSON Jr, CW–USA; (d/ VIII or IX–6 1869 @ 31) MD UPa 1862. *U Pa med alum CW*: 1862. *Phila med reg & dir* 1871: 294.

BUCHANAN, JOSEPH, Louisville, Ky (d/IX– –1829) MD . *Transylvania jour med & assoc sci* 2:594, 1829.

BUCHANAN, SAMUEL A , Philadelphia (d/VIII–27–1906 @ 30) MD UPa 1893. *Pa med jour* 10:52, 1906/07. *Flint* 1897: 815.

BUCHANAN, THOMAS B , Hot Springs, Ark (d/by V–1889) MD U Nashville 1858. *So pract* 11:231, 1889.

BUCHANAN, WILLIAM FAIRLAMB, CW–USA; Philadelphia (b/II–4–1836; d/II–16–1904) MD UPa 1862; PhG Phila Coll Pharm 1859. *U Pa med alum CW*: 1862. *Pa med jour* 8: 334, 1904/05. *Polk* 1897: 1299.

BUCHER, FREDERICK CHRISTIAN, Columbia, Pa (d/X–30–1906) MD UPa 1895; AB Princeton 1895; AM 1895. *Pa med jour* 10: 118, 1906/07.

BUCHLER, CHARLES W , NYC (d/XI–17–1891) <MD Würzburg 1850> *Tr Med Soc St NY* 1892: 495. *Polk* 1886: 673.

BUCHMAN, FRANCIS, Philadelphia (b/XI–14–1847 Houcksville, Md; d/VII–14–1898) MD Hahnemann Phila 1879. *Tr Pa St Homeop Soc* 1898.

BUCK, ALONZO MORRIS, Hyattsville, Md (b/I–24–1826 Glens Falls, NY; d/IX–29–1905) MD Georgetown 1867. *Hist Med Soc DC*: 285. *Polk* 1886: 211.

BUCK, CHARLES EDWARD, CW–CSA (d/1878) MD ULa 1859; AB Princeton 1856; AM 1859; ng U Miss. *Princeton alum cat* 1906: 192. *U Miss alum cat.*

BUCK, EPHRAIM, Philadelphia & Bridgeton, NJ (b/II–23–1795 Millville, NJ; d/VII–14–1855) MD UPa 1817. *Tr Med Soc NJ* 1871–73: 162–63.

BUCK, EPHRAIM, Mass (b/1786? d/I–2–1859 @ 73) MD unknown. *Med surg rep Phila* ns1: 302, 1858/59. *Mass Med Soc cat*: 1894.

BUCK, EPHRAIM WHITING, Los Gatos, Calif (b/III–20–1827 Troy, NY; d/X–5–1895) MD CPSNY 1857. *JAMA* 25:726, 1895. *Atkinson* I: 448. *Polk* 1896:212.

BUCK, ERASTUS J, CW–USA; Platteville, Wis (b/IX–5 1828 Heath, Mass; d/VI–20–1901) MD Jefferson 1854. *Tr Wis St Med Soc* 35: 453–54, 1901. *Polk* 1890: 1171.

BUCK, GURDON, NYC (b/V–4–1807; d/III–6–1877) MD CPSNY 1830. *Buff m & s jour* 16:235, 1877. *Tr Med Soc St NY* 1877: 367–74. *Med surg rep Phila* 13:34–36, 1865. *K & B* III: 164.

BUCK, JOHN STANSBURY, Warren Factory, Md (b/ 1803 nr Balto; d/1847) MD UMd 1825 *Med ann Md*:338.

BUCK, JONATHAN, Macon, Miss (b/IV–2–1824; d/III–29–1881) MD Jefferson 1848; AB UAla 1845; AM 1848. *U Ala cat*: 75.

BUCK, LLEWELLYN ADELBERT, El Reno, Okla; CW–USA (b/VIII–17–1840 Buckfield, Me; d/XII–13–1906) MD Georgetown 1866. *Hist Med Soc DC*: 280. *Polk* 1886: 383 (Peabody, Kans).

BUCK, SAMUEL PREBLE, Woolwich, Me (b/XII–13–1826; d/IV–24–1903) MD Bowdoin 1853; AB 1850. *Bowdoin cat. Polk* 1886: 430.

BUCK, WILBUR PARSONS, CW–USA; Moweaqua, Ill (d/IX–15–1893 @ 56) MD Chicago Med Coll 1871. *Chic med rec* 5: 277, 1893. *JAMA* 21: 498, 1893. *Butler* 1878: 144.

BUCK, WILLIM DENISON, Manchester, NH (b/III–25–1812 Williamstown, Vt; d/I–9–1872) MD CPSNY 1842; Hon AM Dartmouth 1866. *Tr AMA* 23:593, 1872; 24: 349–52, 1873. *Tr NH Med Soc* 1872: 89–96.

BUCKBEE, FRANK G, Fonda NY (d/X–22–1888) MD Albany 1871. *Tr Med Soc St NY* 1889:364. *Polk* 1886: 660.

BUCKINGHAM, CHARLES EDWARD, Boston (b/VI–27–1821; d/II–19–1877) MD Harvard 1844; AB 1840. *Trans AMA* 31: 1022–23, 1880. *Bost m & s jour* 105: 520–21, 1881. *K & B* III: 166.

BUCKINGHAM, HENRY GAYLORD, Clayton, NJ (b/ III–22–1837 Northfield, Conn; d/IV–4–1898) MD CPS NY 1874. *Tr Med Soc NJ* 1898: . *JAMA* 30: 933, 1898.

 Spec. educ'l status abbrev. as: ***ng*** = college verified attendance without degree;

BUCKINGHAM, RICHARD G , Denver (b/IX-14 1816 Troy, NY; d/III-18-1889) MD Berkshire 1836. *Tr Colo St Med Soc* 1898-99: 508. *Atkinson* I: 79. *Polk* 1886:183.

BUCKLER, JOHN, Baltimore (b/VIII-31-1795; d/II-24 1866) MD UMd 1817. *Trans AMA* 18:335-37, 1867. *Med annals Md*: 338.

BUCKLER, RIGGIN, Baltimore (b/XI-4-1831; d/VIII-31-1884 Narragansett Pier, RI) MD UMd 1853; AB Harvard 1851; AM 1855. *Bost m & s jour* 111: 288, 1884. *Med annals Md*: 338. *Atkinson* I:255.

BUCKLER, THOMAS HEPBURN, Baltimore; Paris, Fr 1866-90 (b/I-4-1812 Evergreen, Md; d/IV-20-1901) MD U Md 1835; AB St Mary's Coll, Balto. *Med annals Md*: 338-39. *K & B* III: 166-67.

BUCKLEY, BENJAMIN T, Freeport, Ill (d/I-4-1899 @ 74) MD Rush 1852. *JAMA* 32: 92, 1899. *Polk* 1896: 420.

BUCKLEY, CHARLES, Alexandria Bay, NY (d/IX-1-1891) MD UPa 1870. *Tr NY St Med Soc* 11: 741 ff, 1894. *Polk* 1890: 845.

BUCKLEY, HORATIO N , Delhi, NY (d/I-24-1894 @ 74) MD UCNY 1845. *Med reg NY NJ Conn* 1894: 234. *JAMA* 22: 202, 1894. *Polk* 1886: 658.

BUCKLIN, DANIEL D , Lansingburgh, NY (b/Brunswick, NY; d/IV-19-1890) MD Albany 1846. *Trans Med Soc St NY* 1892:428; 1894:741 ff. *Polk* 1886:665.

BUCKMAN, EDWIN DAWSON, Philadelphia; CW-USA (b/Bristol, Pa; d/V-21-1891 London, Engl) MD UPa 1848. *U Pa med alum CW*: 1848. *Polk* 1886: 813.

BUCKNAM, JOHN WINGATE, Somersworth, NH (b/XII-4-1833; d/XII-18-1870) MD Dartmouth 1860. *Tr NH Med Soc* 1872: 71-73.

BUCKNER, CHARLES S , Baltimore (b/1821 Richmond, Va; d/III-2-1899 @ 78) MD UMd 1843. *JAMA* 32:628, 1899. *Med annals Md*: 339. *Polk* 1896: 656.

BUDD, ANDREW ECKARD, Mt Holly, NJ (b/VII-18-1816 Woodbury; d/VII-18-1882) MD UPa 1842. *Tr Med Soc NJ* 1883: 279. *Atkinson* I:471. *Butler* 1878: 466.

BUDD, BERNARD WHEELER, NYC (b/VII-30-1793; d/I-3-1863) MD Rutgers 1816. *Med reg NY NJ Conn* 1865: 215. *Bost m & s jour* 67:490, 1862. *Med surg rep Phila* ns9:326, 1862/63.

BUDD, CHARLES AMOS, NYC (b/I-6-1831; d/V-17-1877) MD UCNY 1852; AB 1850. *Med reg NY NJ Conn* 1877:199. *Med rec* 12:335, 1877. *Atkinson* I: 127.

BUDD, CHARLES HENRY, ?Philadelphia; CW-USA (b/XII-8-1822; d/X-22-1880) MD UPa 1849; AB Franklin & Marshall 1851. *U Pa med alum CW*: 1849.

BUDD, JAMES HENRY, Geneva, NY (b/IV-15-1845; d/II-25-1890) MD Buffalo 1875 [Jas H Brown] *Med reg NY NJ Conn* 1890:262. *Tr NY St Med Soc* 11:74 ff, 1890.

BUDD, SAMUEL W , Petersburg, Va (d/V-13-1899 @ 47) MD Bellevue 1875. *JAMA* 32: 1269, 1899. *Polk* 1896: 1497.

BUDDEKE, RICHARD MILES, Memphis, Tenn (d/IX-19-1886) MD Memphis Hosp Med Coll 1883. *Med curr* 3:296, 1886. *Polk* 1886: 868. Homeopath.

BUDLONG, CALEB, Fairfield or Frankfort, NY (b/1791; d/1865) MD Fairfield 1817. *Trans AMA* 32:498, 1881.

BUDLONG, THOMAS RUSSELL, Jacksonville, Fla (b/I 7-1822 Lowell, Mass; d/I-6-1855) MD Harvard 1851; AB Brown 1842. *Brown hist cat*: 1842.

BUDLONG, WILLIAM HAGUE, Philadelphia (d/XI-12 1867 @32) MD Jefferson 1865. *Med surg rep Phila* 17: 458, 1867.

BUECHLER, CHARLES W , NYC (d/XI-17-1891 @ 64) MD Würzburg 1850. *Med reg NY NJ Conn* 1892: 272. *Polk* 1886:673.

BUEHLER, HENRY B , CW-USA; Harrisburg, Pa (d/II 1-1904 @ 69) MD Jefferson 1858. *Pa med jour* 8:334, 1904/05.

BUEL, HENRY WADHAMS, Litchfield, Conn (b/IV-7-1820; d/I-30-1893) MD CPSNY 1847; AB Yale 1844; AM 1847. *Med reg NY NJ Conn* 1893: 298. *Proc Conn Med Soc* 1893:233-36. *Butler* 1878: 74.

BUEL, SAMUEL, Litchfield, Conn (b/1782? d/by IV-1-1855) Hon MD Yale 1826. *Proc Conn Med Soc* 1855:21.

BUEL, WILLIAM, Litchfield Co, Conn (b/1768? d/1851) Hon MD Yale 1819; AM Williams 1810. *Proc Conn Med Soc* 1852: 17.

BUELL, RICHARD MILES, Brooklyn (b/V-10-1822; d/VI-30-1883) MD Yale 1852. *Med reg NY NJ Conn* 1884: 226. *Med surg rep Phila* 49: 56, 84, 1883.

BUFFET, EDWARD PAYSON, Jersey City, NJ (b/XI-7-1833 Smithtown, NY; d/IX-9-1904) MD CPSNY 1857; AB Yale 1854; AM 1857. *Bost m & s jour* 151: 308, 1904. *Atkinson* I:461. *Polk* 1896: 938.

BUFFINGTON, COLBY [COLLY] D , Atwater, Ill (d/V 11-1899 @ 52) Lic by years of practice. *JAMA* 32: 1269, 1899. *Polk* 1896: 361.

BUFFINGTON, JOHN ABRAM, New Windsor, Md (b/V-7-1862; d/X-17-1902) MD Jefferson 1884. *Med annals Md*: 339.

BUFFINGTON, JOHN FUSS, New Windsor, Md (b/XI-11-1829 Taneytown; d/II-4-1896) MD Jefferson 1855; AB Amherst 1852. *Med annals Md*: 339. *Polk* 1886: 444.

BUFFINGTON, LEE WOODWARD, Philadelphia (d/III 21-1873 @ 62) MD UPa 1837. *Med surg rep Phila* 28: 292, 1873.

BUFFINGTON, THOMAS J , Baton Rouge, La (d/XI-26-1903) MD Jefferson 1844. *New Orl m & s jour* 56: 571, 1904. *Polk* 1886: 412.

BUFFUM, FRANK PUTNAM, Chicago (d/I-6-1896) MD Rush 1890. *JAMA* 26:93, 1896. *McDonough's Ill med dir* 1895: 96.

BUGBEE, SAMUEL, Wrentham, Mass (d/1841) Hon MD Brown 1816; AB 1802. *Mass Med Soc cat* 1894.

BUGBEE, WILLIAM BROWN, Quincy, Mass (d/IV-2-1856 @ 33) MD Harvard 1847. *Bost m & s jour* 54: 227, 1856.

BUIST, EDWIN [EDWARD] SOMMERS, Greenville &

Charleston, SC; CW–CSA (b/III–31–1837; d/XI–7–1861 near Head Island) MD UCNY 1860; stud. UVa. Johnson, J L: *U Va alum who fell in CW*: 71–73.

BUIST, JOHN ROBINSON, Nashville, Tenn; CW–CSA; (b/II–13–1834; d/X–24–1905) MD UCNY 1857; AB SC Coll. *So pract* 27:634–35, 1905. *Nashville jour m & s* 97:519–21, 1905. *Atkinson* I: 266–67. *Butler* 1878: 765.

BULIS, HENRY CLAY, Decorah, Ia (b/XI–14–1830; d/IX–7–1897) MD Jefferson 1887; ng Woodstock 1853. *Tr Ia St Med Soc* 16:388–399, 1898. *Polk* 1890:412.

BULKELEY, JONATHAN ELIPHALET, CW–USA; Plymouth, Pa 1849–62; Wilkes-Barre, Pa 1862–64, 1865– (b/XI–16–1823; d/XII–20–1885) MD Jefferson 1846; AB Dickinson 1844; AM 1845. *Tr Med Soc Pa* 18: 245–46, 1886. *Atkinson* I: 32. *Butler* 1878: 706.

BULKLEY, EDWARD Jr, CW–USA; New Haven, Conn (b/V–15–1833; d/XI–5–1880) MD Yale 1856. *Proc Conn Med Soc* ns2: 213, 1881. *Atkinson* I: 673. *Butler* 1878: 74.

BULKLEY, HENRY DAGGETT, NYC (b/IV–4–1824 New Haven; d/I–4–1872) MD Yale 1830; AB 1821. *Med times* Phila 2:254,1872. *Tr AMA* 23:594–95,1872. *Med rec* 6:524–26,563,570, 1871–72. *K&B* III: 168.

BULKLEY, STURGIS, Waterbury, Conn (b/X–12–1799; d/VII–9–1857) Lic 1821; Hon MD Yale 1839. *Proc Conn Med Soc* 1: 69–70, 1860.

BULKLEY, SYLVESTER, Rocky Hill, Conn (b/VI–1–1787; d/II–1–1857) MD Dartmouth 1813; AB Yale 1810. *Proc Conn Med Soc* 1857: 21, 61–63.

BULL, BENJAMIN H D, Baltimore Co, Md (b/I–18–1824; d/VIII–25–1873) <MD Washington U Balto> *Med annals Md*: 339.

BULL, LOUIS ALEXANDER, Buffalo, NY (b/London, Ont; d/XI–30–1894 @37) <MD U Buffalo> MD NY Homeop Coll 1881. *Buff m & s jour* 34: 369–70, 1895. *Hahn mo* 30:4–5 (news & advt) 1895 (Jan). *No Amer jour homeop* 43:64,1895. *Polk* 1886:651.

BULL, RICHARD WILLIAM [WINTHROP], Bridgeport, Conn (b/V–16–1846; d/VII–2–1874) MD CPSNY 1869.*Med reg NY NJ Conn* 1875: 196. *Med rec* 9: 608, 1874.

BULLARD, ALFRED RODOLPHUS, Dedham, Mass (d/V–5–1867 @ 34, on board ship) MD Harvard 1859. *Bost m & s jour* 76: 364, 1867.

BULLARD, DAVID HOBBIE, Glens Falls, NY (b/XI–26–1812, Schuylerville; d/VII–1–1903) <Stud Albany Med Coll> *No Amer jour homeop* 51: , 1903. *Polk* 1886: 662. Homeopath.

BULLARD, EDWIN CHARLES, Jr, CW–USA; Dorchester, Mass (d/VI–20–1887 or IV–12–1889) MD UPa 1864 [as d/1887] *Mass Med Soc cat* 1894 [d/1889] *Bost m & s jour* 120: 400, 1889 [d/1889] *U Pa med alum CW*: 1864 [d/1887] *Polk* 1886: 455.

BULLARD, GATES BEZALEEL, St Johnsbury,Vt (b/II 1–1829 Plainfield, NH; d/IX–4–1901) MD Dartmouth 1855. *JAMA* 37:710, 1901. *Atkinson* I:436. *Polk* 1886:906.

BULLARD, TALBOTT, Indianapolis, Ind; CW–USA (b/1815 Sutton, Mass; d/VI–18–1863) MD ?Med Coll O 1845? *Tr AMA* 14:211, 1864. *Tr Ind St Med Soc* 1870: 159. *Med surg rep Phila* 10:156, 1863. *Nashville jour m & s* ns1: 317, 1866. Kemper *Indiana*: 247.

BULLARD, WILLIAM DUFF, NYC (b/1872; d/VI–20–1906) MD CPSNY 1895; AB Amherst 1892. *Bost m & s jour* 154: 750, 1906. *Polk* 1896: 104.

BULLARD, WILLIAM REED, Helena, Mont (b/Cambridge,Mass; d/II–17–1890) MD Harvard 1860;AB 1857. *Bost m & s jour* 122: 192, 1890. *Polk* 1890: 686.

BULLIONS, HENRY L, Troy, NY (b/1832? d/X–19–1858 @26) MD Albany 1854. *Med surg rep Phila* ns1: 76, 1858/59.

BULLITT, HENRY MASSIE, Louisville, Ky (d/II–5–1880) MD UPa 1838. *Med surg rep Phila* 42:176, 1880.

BULLOCH, WILLIAM GASTON, Savannah, Ga; CW–CSA; (b/VIII–3–1815; d/VI–23–1885) MD UPa 1838; AB Yale 1835. *JAMA* 5:195–96, 1885. *Atkinson* I: 209. *U Pa med alum CW*: 1838. *K&B* III:171–72. *Butler* 1878: 108.

BULLOCK, OTIS, Warren, RI (b/II–20–1806 Sterling, Conn; d/III–6–1884) MD Harvard 1832. *Bost m & s jour* 110:304–350, 616, 1884. *Tr RI Med Soc* 1883–88: 164–65. *Atkinson* I: 281. *Butler* 1878: 746.

BUMSTEAD, FREEMAN JOSIAH, NYC (b/IV–21–1826 Boston; d/XI–28–1880) MD Harvard 1851; AB Williams 1847; LLD 1879. *Bost m & s jour* 101: 821, 1879. *Med surg rep Phila* 41: 528, 568, 1879. *Atkinson* I: 16. *K&B* III: 172.

BUNCE, HENRY CLINTON, Glastonbury, Conn (b/I–17–1825; d/IV–15–1903) MD Yale 1850. *Proc Conn Med Soc* 1904: 513–14. *Flint* 1897: 174.

BUNCE, WILLIAM H, Oberlin, O (b/VI–29–1830 Paterson, NJ; d/II–13–1892) MD Cleveland Med Coll 1863. *JAMA* 18:340, 1892. *Atkinson* I: 64. *Butler* 1878:622.

BUNDY, SAMUEL H, Marion, Ill (d/XI–20–1899 @ 77) MD U Nashville & Vanderbilt 1875. *Tr Ill St Med Soc* 1899–1900: 352. *JAMA* 33:1441, 1899. *Polk* 1896: 429.

BUNKER, EDWARD SEAMAN, Brooklyn (d/VI–8–1897 @ 56) MD Bellevue 1871. *JAMA* 28:1202, 1897. *Bost m & s jour* 136: 636, 1897. *Polk* 1896: 993.

BUNKER, WILLIAM H, Hartwell O (d/III–6–1898) MD Med Coll O 1864. *JAMA* 30:682, 1898. *Polk* 1896: 1193.

BUNTON [BUNTIN], EDWIN A, Greensfork, Ind (b/VII–9–1846 near Moscow, O; d/II–26–1899) MD Med Coll O 1878. *Tr Ind St Med Soc* 1899: 407. *JAMA* 32: 562, 1899. *Polk* 1896: 470.

BURBANK, AUGUSTUS HANNIBAL, Yarmouth, Me (b/I–4 or 24–1823 Poland, Me; d/VI–27–1895) MD Harvard 1847; AB Bowdoin 1843. *Tr Me Med Assoc* 12:425–28, 1897. *Atkinson* I: 510. *K&B* III:173–74.

BURBANK, CHARLES HENRY, Portsmouth, NH; USN

(b/Me; d/I-30-1885) MD Harvard 1859. *Harvard in CW*: 252.

BURCHAM, ROBERT, Columbus, O (b/England? d/IX-25-1878 Memphis, Tenn) <MD Edinburgh> *Med rec* 14: 279, 1878. *Trans AMA* 30: 856, 1879.

BURCHARD, JEFFERSON GREGG, Peekskill, NY (b/X-25-1838; d/III-6-1870) MD NY Homeop Med Coll 1865. *Tr Am Inst Homeop* 1870:645. Homeopath.

BURCHARD, LEONIDAS S, Oakland, Calif (d/IV-23-1905) MD U Cal (Toland) 1882; PhB 1875. *Calif st jour med* 3:198, 1905. *Polk* 1886: 168.

BURCHARD, THOMAS HERRING, NYC (b/III-19-1850; d/XI-14-1896) MD Bellevue 1872. *Bost m & s jour* 135: 533, 1896. *Buff m & s jour* 36: 380, 1896. *Butler* 1878: 508.

BURCHARD, WILLIAM METCALF, Uncasville, Conn (b/X-31-1844 Bozrah; d/VI-1-1899) MD Georgetown 1867. *Proc Conn Med Soc* 1900:345-46. *Bost m & s jour* 140: 564, 1899. *Flint* 1897: 178.

BURCHFIELD, JAMES PENROSE, CW-USA; Clearfield, Pa (d/XI-8-1904 @ 67) MD U Mich 1862; AB Jefferson 1857. *Pa med jour* 8:334, 1904/05. *Flint* 1897: 798.

BURCKHALTER, THOMAS DE L, NYC (b/Aiken, SC; d/VI-20-1906 @ 32) MD Med Coll SC 1895. *Bost m & s jour* 154: 750, 1906.

BURDEN, FREDERICK LYSANDER, N Attleboro, Mass (d/II-23-1890 @ 41) MD Harvard 1869. *Bost m & s jour* 122: 216, 1890.

BURDEN, LEVI, Lagrange, Ind (d/III-3-1895) MD unknown. *JAMA* 24: 422, 1895. *Butler* 1878: 196. *Polk* 1890: 373.

BURDETT, ABRAHAM SMITH, Hackensack, NJ (b/XI 1830; d/II-4-1890) MD CPSNY 1852. *Med reg NY NJ Conn* 1890: 262. *Tr Med Soc NJ* 1890: 345-46. *Atkinson* I:435.

BURDETT, GEORGE WASHINGTON, Clinton, Mass (b/1819; d/V-10-1897) MD Harvard 1846. *Bost m & s jour* 136: 476, 528. *JAMA* 28: 1045, 1897.

BURDETT, JAMES F, CW-USA (d/VIII-5-1866) MD unknown. *Nat med jour* 1: 291, 1870/71.

BURDETT, JOHN BOGERT, Jersey City, NJ (b/IX-21-1833; d/V-21-1903) MD CPSNY 1856. *Bost m & s jour* 148: 600, 1903. *Polk* 1896: 938.

BURDICK, BURROWS, Stoughton, Wis (d/VI-3-1899 @ 76) MD UCNY 1849. *JAMA* 33: 302, 1899. *Polk* 1890: 1164.

BURDICK, FRANCIS, Johnstown, NY (b/IV-16-1818; d/22-1877) MD Fairfield 1840. *Tr Med Soc St NY* 1877: 374-76. *Butler* 1874: 530.

BURDICK, JOHN E, Johnstown, NY (d/IV-30-1900) MD Albany 1863. *Tr Med Soc St NY* 1901: 426. *Polk* 1886: 665.

BURDICK, JOHN LAFAYETTE, Winooski, Vt (b/XII-16-1824 Ira; d/XII-11-1897) MD Castleton 1852. *JAMA* 30: 106, 1898. *Polk* 1893: 1247.

BURDICK, PHINEAS H, Preble, NY (b/VI-3-1800 Ruyter; d/III-28-1870) MD Regents NY 1851; ng Castleton. *Med reg NY NJ Conn* 1871: 349. *Tr Med Soc St NY* 1871: 355-61.

BURDICK, STEPHEN POWELL, Oakland, Calif (b/XI-1-1829 Alfred, NY; d/XII-19-1891) MD LICH 1860. *Tr Am Inst Homeop* 1895: 217. *Med vis* 8:58. *Polk* 1886: 168. Homeopath.

BURG, HORACE W, Northumberland, Pa (d/II 15-1904 @ 58) MD Jefferson 1877. *Pa med jour* 8:334, 1904/05. *Flint* 1897: 812.

BURGE, JOHN HENRY HOBART, NYC-1855; Brooklyn (b/VIII-12-1823 Wickford, RI; d/III-24-1901) MD UCNY 1848; ng Harvard Med Sch. *Bost m & s jour* 144:342, 1901. *Tr Med Soc St NY* 1902:[484]. *Atkinson* I:261. *Polk* 1886: 644.

BURGESS, EBENEZER GEORGE, Paris (b/VII-2-1826 Dedham, Mass; d/V-14-1877) MD Jefferson 1853; AB Amherst 1852. *Amherst, Men of*: 1852.

BURGESS, HORACE, Moosup, Conn (d/1855?) MD UCNY 1848. *Proc Conn St Med Soc* 1855:21 (May).

BURGESS, MOWRY, Windham Co, Conn (b/1789? d/1856 @ 67) Hon MD Yale 1831. *Proc Conn St Med Soc* 1857: 21 (May).

BURGESS, SAMUEL NELSON, CW-CSA (b/IV-15-1835 Statesburg, SC; d/VII-16-1862) MD UPa 1855. *U Pa med alum CW*: 1855.

BURGESS, THOMAS, Nashville, Ill (d/I-30-1896 @ 69) MD UCNY 1857. *JAMA* 26:287, 1896. *Polk* 1890: 341.

BURGHER, JOHN C, Pittsburgh, Pa (b/XI-1-1822 Windham, O; d/VIII-11-1901) MD Hahnemann Phila 1854; ng Geneva. *Tr Am Inst Homeop* 1902: 839. *Tr Pa Homeop Soc* 1901. Homeopath.

BURGIN, GEORGE HORATIO, Jr, Philadelphia (d/I-2 1873) MD UPa 1843. *Med surg rep Phila* 28: 52, 1873.

BURIAN, JOSEPH JULIAN [JULES], NYC (d/XII-30-1890 @ 62) MD UCNY 1874. *Med reg NY NJ Conn* 1891: 269. *Polk* 1886: 672.

BURK, GEORGE L, Jamestown, Ind (b/IV-28-1820 Ky; d/XII-20-1891) <ng U Louisville Med Sch 1843> *Tr Ind St Med Soc* 1892: 282. *Butler* 1878: 196.

BURKE, ABRAHAM C, Brooklyn (b/VI-18-1818 Albany, NY; d/IV-15-1880) MD Albany 1845; AB Union 1838. *Tr Am Inst Homeop* 1880: 142. *Homeop times* 8:69, 1880 (June). *Amer homeop obs* 17: 576, 1880. *Homeop jour obs* 1:476. *Cleave*. Homeopath.

BURKE, ERNEST OSBORNE, Quincy, Mass (d/II-19-1903 @ 30) MD Harvard 1897; AB 1893. *Bost m & s jour* 148: 246, 1903.

BURKE, GEORGE W, CW-USA; New Castle, Ind (b/II-22-1841 Franklin Co, Pa; d/X-18-1901) <MD Jefferson 1865> *Ind med jour* 20:226, 1901? *Tr Ind St Med Soc* 1902:410. *Butler* 1878: 196.

BURKE, GEORGE WHITNEY, Middletown, Conn (b/

VI–1821 New Haven; d/VI–4–1904) MD Yale 1843; AB Wesleyan 1839. *Proc Conn Med Soc* 1905: 76–77, 538–41. *Flint* 1897:175.

BURKE, JOHN, NYC (d/IX–8–1886 @ 59) MD UCNY 1849. *Med reg NY NJ Conn* 1887: 255. *Bost m & s jour* 115:265, 1886. *Butler* 1878: 508.

BURKE, JOHN, Boston (d/VI–21–1889 @ 42) MD Harvard 1871. *Bost m s jour* 121:645, 1889. *Polk* 1889: 455.

BURKE, THOMAS F , DeWitt, Ia (d/I–23–1900 @ 45) MD CPS Chicago 1883. *JAMA* 34:312, 1900.

BURKE, THOMAS SOMERVEL, Corpus Christi, Tex (d/IX–21–1891) MD U La 1861. *Daniels Tex med jour* 7:150, 1891–92. *Polk* 1886: 883.

BURKITT, WILLIAM, Keokuk, Ia (d/III–12–1899) MD U Louisville 1845. *JAMA* 32:628, 1899.

BURLEIGH, DANIEL COFFIN, CW–USN; Franklin, NH 1869–73; Europe 1880–84; USA 1870–79? (b/IV–8 –1834 Sanbornton, NH; d/I–10–1884 Dresden, Gny) MD Bowdoin 1869; ng Harvard Med Sch 1863–64; AB Bowdoin 1858. *Bowdoin cat*: 1858. *Butler* 1878: 441.

BURLEIGH, WILLIAM A , Mobile La (d/VII–30–1901 @ 25) MD Tulane 1900. *New Orl m & s jour* 54: 200, 1901. *Polk* 1900: 1913, appendix.

BURLINGAME, FRANK W , McKeesport, Pa 1884– (b/VII–27–1859 Mt Morris, NY; d/XI–21–1903) MD Cleveland Homeop 1882. *Tr Am Inst Homeop* 1904: 961. *Tr Pa Homeop Soc* 1906. Homeopath.

BURLINGHAM, HARVEY DUDLEY, Plainfield, NJ; CW–USN (b/VII–14–1832 Pike, NY; d/III–17–1886) MD CPSNY 1857; AB Madison 1854; AM 1857. *Tr Med Soc NJ* 1886–87: 170–71. *Butler* 1878:479. *Atkinson* I: 436.

BURNAP, SEWALL GOODRICH, Holliston, Mass (b/ 1802; d/X–16–1874) MD Dartmouth 1826. *Bost m & s jour* 91:434, 1874.

BURNAP, SIDNEY ROGERS, Windsor Locks Conn (b/I 11–1833; d/IX–3–1901) MD CPSNY 1862; AB Union 1858. *Proc Conn Med Soc* 1902:422–24. *Flint* 1897:179.

BURNER, D F, Woodstock Va (d/VIII–23–1897) MD CPS Balto 1884. *JAMA* 29:502, 1897. *Polk* 1896: 1505.

BURNESON, JOHN B , Luzerne, NY (d/VIII–12–1893) MD Castleton 1852. *Med reg NY NJ Conn* 1894: 234.

BURNETT, CHARLES HENRY, Philadelphia (b/V–28–1842; d/I–29/30–1902) MD UPa 1867; AB Yale 1864; AM 1867. *Tr CPP* cent vol: 215. *Atkinson* I:269. *K&B* III:174–75. *Pa med jour* 5:277 1901/02; 6:259 1902/03.

BURNETT, D WALTON, NYC (d/X–19–1883 @ 23) MD Homeop Med Coll NY 1883. *Med surg rep Phila* 49:504, 1883. Homeopath.

BURNETT, JOHN, Scranton, Pa (d/IX–30–1898) MD CPSNY 1876. *JAMA* 31: 942, 1898. *Polk* 1896: 1335.

BURNETT, SWAN MOSES, Knoxville, Tenn 1870–75; Washington, DC 1876– (b/III–16–1847 Newmarket, Tenn; d/I–18–1906) MD Bellevue 1870; ng Miami Med Coll 1866–67; PhD Georgetown 1890. *Hist Med Soc DC*: 309. *Atkinson* I:187. *K & B* III:176.

BURNETT, WALDO IRVING, Boston (b/VII–12–1827; d/VII–1–1854) MD Harvard 1849. *So m & s jour*, 1854: 509. *Nashville jour m & s*: 9: , 1855.

BURNETT, WILLIAM, Petaluma, Cal (d/IV–6–1870 @ 55) MD unknown. *Phila med reg & dir* 1871: 304. *Tr AMA* 21: 489–91, 1870.

BURNETTE, EDWARD WORTHINGTON, NYC (d/IX 20–1895 @ 52) MD CPSNY 1869. *JAMA* 25: 595, 1895. *Bost m & s jour* 133:354, 1895.

BURNHAM, ABEL CONANT, Hillsborough Bridge, NH (b/V–2–1812 Amherst, NH; d/V–21–1896) MD Dartmouth 1840; ng Woodstock 1838. *Tr NH Med Soc* 1896: 181–82. *Bost m & s jour* 134: 604, 1896. *Polk* 1890: 709.

BURNHAM, COELEB, Lynn, Mass (b/II–13–1836 Essex; d/II–17–1892) MD Dartmouth 1869;AB 1865. *Bost m & s jour* 126: 204, 1892. *Polk* 1886: 469.

BURNHAM, N CLARK, Brooklyn (b/IX–15–1855; d/VII–22–1890) MD Hahnemann Phila 1881. *Med vis* 8: 57, 1892. *Polk* 1886: 644. Homeopath.

BURNHAM, WALTER, Lowell,Mass; CW–USA (b/I–12 1808 Brookfield, Vt; d/I–16–1883) MD UVt 1829; ng Castleton. *Bost m & s jour* 108:96, 1883. *Tr Vt Med Soc* 1883: 103. *Butler* 1878: 347. *K&B* III:176–77.

BURNS, EDWARD, New Britain, Conn (b/XII–12–1860; d/XII–27–1892) MD UCNY 1882. *Proc Conn Med Soc* 1893: 262. *Polk* 1886: 226 (Atlanta, Ga).

BURNS, JAMES, Louisville, Ky (b/XI–15–1820 Dayton, O; d/II–11–1895) MD Tulane 1859. *JAMA* 24:294, 1895. *Polk* 1890: 489.

BURNS, JOHN C , Philadelphia (d/II–1887) MD Hahnemann Phila 1885. *Hahn mo* 22:256,1887. Homeopath.

BURNS, JOHN FRANCIS, Long Island City, NY (b/XII–5–1863 NYC; d/VIII–9–1900) MD UCNY 1889. *Bost m & s jour* 143:172,1900. *Polk* 1896: 1030.

BURNS, ROBERT, CW–USA; Philadelphia (b/XI–7–1809 Glasgow, Scotland; d/III–12–1883) MD UPa 1839. *Tr CPP* cent vol: 215. *Atkinson* I:521. *U Pa med alum CW*: 1839. *Tr Med Soc St Pa* 17:376–81.

BURNS, WILLIAM, Littleton, NH (b/IV–15–1783 Merrimack; d/IX–22–1868) MD Dartmouth 1826. *Bost m & s jour* ns2: 144, 1868.

BURNS, WILLIAM WALLACE, Polo, Ill (d/IV–18 1905 @ 83) MD U Louisville 1843. *Ill med jour* 7: 611, 1905. *Polk* 1886: 293.

BURPEE, DAVID, Sheffield, NB 1851–59; Philadelphia 1859– ; CW–USA (b/IV–4–1827 Sheffield, NB; d/IX–14–1882) MD Pa Coll 1853. *Tr CPP* cent vol: 215. *Atkinson* I: 29; 293.

BURPEE, JOHN A, Malden, Mass (d/XI–10–1887 @ 65) MD Hahnemann 1854. *Hahn mo* 22:768, 1887. *New Engl med gaz* 22: 592, 1887. *Polk* 1886: 469. Homeopath.

BURR, CHARLES, Carbondale, Pa (d/IX–19–1904 @ 89) MD Berkshire 1838. *Pa med jour* 8:334, 1904/05.

 Spec. educ'l status abbrev. as: ***ng*** = college verified attendance without degree;

Flint 1897: 797.

BURR, CHARLES HARTWELL, Worcester, Mass 1859–60; Portland, Me 1860–85 (b/VI–22–1824 Mercer, Me; d/II–26–1885) MD Hahnemann Phila 1859; DDS Pa Coll Dent Surg 1853. *Tr Am Inst Homeop* 1885:97. *New Engl med gaz*: 20: 191, 1885. Homeopath.

BURR, FRANKLIN E , Greeley, Colo (b/I–5–1864 NY; d/IX–6–1898) MD U Buffalo 1890. *Buff med & surg jour* 38: 225, 1898. *JAMA* 31:673, 1898.

BURR, FRANKLIN KIMBALL, Chicago (b/1869? d/II–20–1905 @ 36) MD Rush 1895; PhG unknown. *Ill med jour* 7:379, 1905. *Polk* 1896:513.

BURR, GEORGE, Binghamton, NY (b/IV–5–1813; d/X–20–1882) MD unknown. *Tr Med Soc St NY* 1884: [365]. *Butler* 1874: 531.

BURR, HORACE, Middlesex Co, Conn; Wilmington, Del 1868– (b/XII–13–1817 Haddam, Conn; d/I–10–1899) MD Yale 1842. *JAMA* 32: 195, 1899. *Atkinson* I: 652.

BURR, LEMUEL, Paterson, NJ (b/1796 Fairfield, Conn; d/IV–22–1878) Lic Med Soc NJ VIII–1–1820. *Tr Med Soc NJ* 1878–79: 202–203. *Butler* 1878: 466.

BURR, RICHARD, Philadelphia (b/V–1–1819 Moorestown, NJ; d/III–30–1885 or X–5–1888) MD UPa 1846. *Med surg rep Phila* 52:512, 1885. *U Pa med alum CW*: 1846. *Tr Pa Homeop Soc* 1892. Homeopath.

BURRELL, BENJAMIN HENRY, Roxbury, Mass (d/IV 23–1906 Denver,Col) MD Ecl Med Inst Cincinnati 1878. *Bost m & s jour* 154:480, 1906. *Polk* 1896: 694.

BURRELL, JAMES LUTHER ALBERT, Williamsport, Pa (d/X–24–1891) MD UPa 1877. *Med bull med & surg* 13: 467, 1891. *Polk* 1886: 840.

BURRIER, GEORGE WASHINGTON, Clare, Mich (d/VI–5/8–1899) MD U Mich 1892. *JAMA* 32: 1460, 1899.

BURRIS, WILLIAM A , Hope Villa, La (d/XII–4–1885 @ 35) MD Jefferson 1873. *New Orl m & s jour* ns13: 578, 1886.

BURRITT, HENRY LEWELLEN WAKEMAN Bridgeport, Conn (d/VII– –1888) MD Yale 1844. *Med reg NY NJ Conn* 1889: 269.

BURRITT, WILLIAM H , Toledo, O (d/VII–2–1901 @ 59) MD CPS Keokuk 1873. *JAMA* 31:213, 1901.

BURROUGHS, BENJAMIN, Brooklyn (b/VI–7–1847 Brinkerhoffville, NY; d/III–7–1895) MD LICH 1888. *Med reg NY NJ Conn* 1895:217. *JAMA* 24:421, 1895.

BURROUGHS, CHARLES RICHARD, Trenton, NJ (b/II–12–1853 Pennington, NJ; d/XI–10–1897) MD LICH 1885. *Tr Med Soc NJ* 1898: 378–79.

BURROUGHS, FRANCIS VOLNEY, CW–USA; Manston, Wis (b/XII–16–1840; d/VI–24–1878) MD Bellevue 1869; ng U Mich. *Tr Wis St Med Soc* 1879: 294. *Atkinson* I:649.

BURROUGHS, LESTER M , Batavia, Ill (d/III–3–1906) Lic by years of practice. *Ill med jour* 9: 463, 1906. *Polk* 1886: 254.

BURROUGHS, RICHARD BERRIEN, Norfolk,Va (b/I–19–1833 Savannah, Ga; d/IX–11–1901) MD Jefferson 1856; AB UGa 1853. *JAMA* 37:847,1901. *K&B* III:178.

BURROWES, FRANCIS S , Lancaster, Pa (d/1853?) <MD U Dublin> *Tr Med Soc Pa* 4:32, 1854. *Practitioner*, Lancaster 1:60–61, 1883.

BURT, JOHN OTIS, Syracuse, NY; CW–USN (d/1894) MD CPSNY 1864; AB Harvard 1858. *Harvard in CW*: 109. *Polk* 1886: 710.

BURT, WILLIAM H , Chicago; Lincoln, Ill (b/II–25–1836 New Brunswick, Canada; d/I–30–1897. MD Cleveland Homeop 1858. *Tr Am Inst Homeop* 1897: 63. *Hahn mo* 32:35(news & advt, Mar) 1897. *Polk* 1886:260.

BURT, WILLIAM JEFFERSON, Ark to 1874; Austin, Tex (b/VI–15–1838 Dawsonville, Ga; d/VII–10–1886) MD Atlanta Med Coll 1860; stud CPSNY & Bellevue 1879–80. *Atkinson* I:264. *Tex cour-rec med* 3: 526–27, 1886. *Daniels Tex m jour* 2:23–25,1886. *Polk* 1886: 880.

BURTCH, HARRY MERCEIN, Salisbury, Conn (b/V–26–1859 Providence, RI; d/II–12–1896) MD Albany 1882. *Proc Conn Med Soc* 1896: 334. *Polk* 1896:284.

BURTON, CASPAR VAN WIE, Lansingburgh, NY (b/VI–15–1810 Albany; d/IX–23–1860) MD Albany 1842. *Tr AMA* 14:192–93, 1864. *Med & surg rep Phila* ns5: 26, 1860/61. *Tr Med Soc St NY* 1861: 175–79.

BURTON, CASWELL R , CW–USA (d/IX–30–1862 Woodsonville, Ky) MD U Mich 1861; BS U Indiana 1858. *U Mich cat*: 1861.

BURTON, GEORGE W , Mitchell, Ind (b/VII–22–1836 Lawrence Co; d/VII–13–1898) MD Med Coll Ind 1875 ad eundem; MD Hosp Med Coll Louisville 1877. *Tr Ind St Med Soc* 1899: 388–89. *JAMA* 31: 198, 1898. *Polk* 1896: 482.

BURTON, HENRY LYNE, La Grange, Tenn; CW–CSA (b/IX–12–1835; d/I–10–1873) MD UPa 1860. *U Pa med alum CW*: 1860.

BURTON, LEVI, West Topsham, Vt (b/1804? d/VIII–27 1867) MD Berkshire 1829. *Bost m & s jour* 77:160, 1867. *Med surg rep Phila* 17:260, 1897.

BURTON, MATTHEW HENRY, Troy, NY (b/III–16–1833 Albany; d/IV–28–1895 Bay Shore) MD Albany 1853. *Med reg NY NJ Conn* 1895:217. *JAMA* 24:907, 1895. *Tr Med Soc St NY* 1895? *Atkinson* I:192.

BURTON, THOMPSON, Fultonville, NY (b/III–17–1812 Charleston, NY; d/V–5–1892) MD Castleton 1835. *Med reg NY NJ Conn* 1892: 272. *JAMA* 18: 684, 1892. *Polk* 1886: 661.

BURTS, WILLIAM PAXTON, Fort Worth, Texas (b/XII 7–1827; d/IX–5–1895) MD Geneva 1852. *JAMA* 25:510, 1895. *Texas cour-rec med* 13: 54, 1895. *Texas med jour* 11:205, 1895–96. *Butler* 1878:784. *G P Red*:306–07.

BURTSELL, THOMAS E, NYC? (d/VII–16–1885 @ 68) MD UCNY 1844. *Med reg NY NJ Conn* 1886: 243.

BURWELL, GEORGE N, Buffalo(d/V–5/15–1891 @72) MD UPa 1843. *Buff m & s jour* 30: 693–94, 1891. *Bost m & s jour* 124:522, 1891. *Tr Med Soc St NY* 11: 794 ff.

BURWELL, HENRY de B , Richmond, Va (d/V-15-1889) MD Med Coll Va 1888. *Med reg NY NJ Conn* 1889/90: 269.

BUSEY, SAMUEL CLAGETT, Washington, DC (b/VII-23-1828 Montgomery Co, Md; d/II-12-1901) MD UPa 1848. *Hist Med Soc DC*: 240-42. *Bost m & s jour* 144:197, 1901. *K&B* III: 178.

BUSH, JAMES MILES, Lexington, Ky (b/V- -1808; d/II-8-1875) MD Transylvania 1833. *Tr Ky St Med Soc* 1877: 181-89. *K&B* III: 179-80.

BUSH, LEWIS POTTER, Wilmington, Del (b/X-19-1812; d/III-5-1892) MD UPa 1835; AB Jefferson 1831. *Med bull m & s* 14: 207, 1892. *Atkinson* I:255. *Polk* 1886:281. *K&B* III: 180.

BUSH, LEWIS R , E Stroudsburg, Pa (d/X-4-1892 @ 45) MD Jefferson 1872. *Lehigh Valley med mag* 4:36, 1892-93. *Butler* 1878: 706.

BUSH, ROBERT H, Huntsville Tex (d/IV-13-1898) MD Jefferson 1854. *JAMA* 31: 808, 1898. *Polk* 1896: 1436.

BUSH, ROBERT W , Clark Co, Ky (b/1815; d/1867) MD Transylvania 1835. *Tr AMA* 18: 344, 1867.

BUSH, WILLIAM P , CW-USA (b/c1831; d/X-3-1863) MD Albany 1858. *Nat med jour* 1:291, 1870/71.

BUSHNELL, KENYON A , Little Falls, NY (d/XII-24-1896 @ 40) MD Albany 1879. *JAMA* 28:92, 1897. *Polk* 1886: 666.

BUSHNELL, LAFAYETTE, NYC (b/X-12-1824 Winchester, Va; d/VII-9-1879) MD unknown; att? Union Theol Sem 1858. *Tr Am Inst Homeop* 1880: 144. *Butler* 1878: 495.

BUSHNELL, WILLIAM, E Boston (d/IV-28-1879 @ 78) <MD UPa 1855> AB Yale 1828. *Tr Mass Homeop Soc* 1880-83: 1890 (Sept). *Butler* 1874. Homeopath.

BUSHNELL, WILLIAM, Mansfield, O (b/1800? d/XII-13-1893 @ 93) Hon MD Cleveland Med Coll 1846. *JAMA* 21: 1010, 1893. *Polk* 1886: 760.

BUSS, CHARLES DELEVAN, Bradford, Pa (d/XII-24-1897) MD UCNY 1876. *Pa med jour* 1: 264-65, 1898. *Polk* 1890: 966.

BUSTEED, JOHN, NYC (b/1814; d/IV-10-1876) MD UCNY 1842. *Med reg NY NJ Conn* 1876: 241.

BUSWELL, ALBERT, NH & Vt; Lowell, Mass 1869- (b/VIII-15-1821 Hartland, Vt; d/III-11-1873) MD Woodstock 1847; Castleton 1851; Hahnemann Phila 1869. *Tr Mass Homeop Soc* 1890. *Cleave*. Homeopath.

BUTCHER, JOSEPH Jr, NJ (b/III-10-1824; d/X-17-1849) MD Jefferson 1849. *Tr Med Soc NJ* 1871:159-60.

BUTCHER, THOMAS S , Philadelphia (d/III-28-1902 @ 55 Mexico) MD Jefferson 1868. *Pa med jour* 6: 259, 1902/03. *Butler* 1874: 660.

BUTE, GEORGE HENRY, Philadelphia & Nazareth, Pa (b/V-27-1792 Schaumburg, Gny; d/II-13-1876) Stud homeop w/C Hering. *Am homeop obs* 13:232, 1876? *Hahn mo* 11:383, 1876. Homeopath.

BUTLER, ALLAN MACY, NYC (d/V-21-1888) MD CPSNY 1887; AB Harvard 1884. *Med reg NY NJ Conn* 1888: 242. *Bost m & s jour* 118: 557, 560, 1888.

BUTLER, ALVIN SNOW, Chicago (b/1837 Kalamazoo, Mich; d/VIII-4-1894) MD Hahnemann Chic 1884. *Tr Am Inst Homeop* 1895: 218. *Polk* 1886: 260. Homeopath.

BUTLER, CHARLES WOOSTER, Jamaica, NY (d/III-25-1900) MD UCNY 1885. *JAMA* 34: 957, 1900. *Polk* 1896: 1018.

BUTLER, CLARENCE WILLARD, Montclair, NJ (b/V 1-1848 Bellevue, O; d/XII-21-1904) MD NY Homeop 1872. *Tr Am Inst Homeop* 1905:839. Homeopath.

BUTLER, GEORGE O , Cleveland (d/XI-4-1897 @ 64) MD Cleveland Med Coll 1854. *JAMA* 26: 1081, 1897. *Polk* 1896: 1171.

BUTLER, J RUSSELL, Louisville, Ky (d/VI-11-1884) MD Louisville Med Inst 1850. *Med surg rep Phila* 51: 56, 1884.

BUTLER, JOHN, NYC (b/I-20-1844 Kilkenny, Irel'd; d/IV-10-1885) <MD RCPS Edinburgh> att? Trinity Coll, Dublin. *Tr Am Inst Homeop* 1885: 100. *New Engl med gaz* 20:336 1885. *Med adv* 15: 1885 (June). Homeopath.

BUTLER, JOHN DABNEY, CW-CSA; Sparta, Va (b/V-14-1819 Hanover Co; d/II-9-1905 near Bowling Green, Ky) MD UPa 1841; stud U Va. *Tr Med Soc Va* 1905: 444-45. *Polk* 1900: 1776.

BUTLER, JOHN SIMPKINS, Hartford, Conn (b/X-12-1803 Northampton, Mass; d/V-21-1890) MD Jefferson 1828; AB Yale 1825. *Bost m & s jour* 122: 536, 1890. *Atkinson* I: 585. *K&B* III:183.

BUTLER, LAWRENCE L , Muscatine, Ia (b/III-2-1857 [or 1849?] d/XII-27-1877 @ 28) MD Iowa St U 1874. *Tr Ia St Med Soc* 1879-80: 191-92; 1903: .

BUTLER, LORENZO FOWLER, Quincy, Mass (b/VII-17-1849; d/V-5-1882) MD Boston U 1877. *New Engl med gaz* 17: 224, 1882. Homeopath.

BUTLER, MOREAU S , Cherokee, Ia (b/IX-4-1830 Elyria O; d/III-2-1895) MD CPS Keokuk 1864. *JAMA* 24:422, 1895. *Tr Ia St Med Soc* 13: 409, 1900. *Polk* 1886: 353.

BUTLER, NEWTON JACOB [JACOB NEWTON?] Lempster, NH (b/II-6-1821 Lyndeborough; d/II-16-1903) MD Berkshire 1843. *Tr NH Med Soc* 1903: 236-37. *Polk* 1890: 710.

BUTLER, OLIVER H , Davenport, Ia (b/NY; d/X-1-1859 @ 24) MD Jefferson 1859. *Bost m & s jour* 61: 228, 1859. *Med surg rep Phila* ns3: 72, 1859/60.

BUTLER, SAMUEL STONE, E Berkshire, Vt (b/III-15-1787 Whiting; d/V-15-1869) Hon MD Woodstock 1840. *Med surg rep Phila* 20: 436, 1869.

BUTLER, SAMUEL WISWELL, Newport, RI (b/II-22-1816 Farmington, Me; d/IV-7-1881) MD Harvard 1843. *Tr AMA* 33: 534-36, 1882. *Tr RI Med Soc* 2: 388-89, 1877-82. *Atkinson* I: 111.

BUTLER, SAMUEL WORCESTER, Philadelphia (b/V-1-1823 Brainerd, Ga [or E Tenn?] d/I-6-1874) MD UPa

 Spec. educ'l status abbrev. as: *ng* = college verified attendance without degree;

1850. *Bost m & s jour* 90:203, 1874. *Tr Med Soc Pa* 1874: 369–70. *Med surg rep Phila* 30: 59–61, 1874. *K&B* III: 184.

BUTLER, WILLIAM E , Jackson, Tenn (b/1790? d/II–9 1882 @ 92) MD unknown. *Chicago med rev* 5:128, 1882. *Butler* 1878: 765.

BUTLER, WILLIAM HENRY, Buffalo, CW–USA (d/II 5–1864) MD Buffalo 1858. *Buff m & s jour* 3: 277–78; 319–21, 1864.

BUTLER, WILLIAM W S , Harrisonburg, Va (d/VIII–18–1901) MD Med Coll Va 1852. *JAMA* 37: 654, 1901.

BUTT, HOLT FAIRFIELD, CW–CSA; Portsmouth, Va (b/III–16–1835; d/X–9–1900) MD UPa 1856. *U Pa med alum CW*: 1856. *Polk* 1886: 924.

BUTT, RICHARD LEMUEL, CW–CSA; Midway, Ala (b/1825; d/XII–18–1901) MD UCNY 1846. *Tr Med Assoc St Ala* 1902: 129. *Polk* 1893: 159.

BUTT, WILLIAM BEALE, Washington, DC (b/VII–19–1827; d/VI–28–1877) MD Columbian 1850. *Hist Med Soc DC*: 259–60. *Tr AMA* 31: 1023–24, 1880.

BUTTERFIELD, HENRY LOWELL, Waupun, Wis; CW–USA; (b/IX–25–1817 Nashua, NH; d/VI–17–1882) MD Willoughby 1845. *Tr Wis St Med Soc* 1883: 127. *Butler* 1878: 859.

BUTTERFIELD, JOHN STODDARD, NH; Lake Co, O (b/XII–2–1817 Stoddard,NH; d/IX–7–1849 Salisbury, NH) MD CPSNY 1841. *Tr O St Med Soc* 1873: 262. *Tr AMA* 3:438, 1850. *Buff med jour* 5:525–26, 1849. *K&B* III: 184.

BUTTERMORE, SMITH, Connellsville, Pa (d/XII–30–1897) Lic by years of practice. *Pa med jour* 2: 101, 1898. *JAMA* 30:335, 1898. *Butler* 1878: 706.

BUTTON, H P , Denver, Colo (d/XI–29–1891) MD Hahnemann Chicago 1872. *Med vis* 8: 58, 1891. *Polk* 1886: 183. Homeopath.

BUTTON, HENRY HARRISON, Milwaukee (b/ VIII–28 1818; d/II–14–1890) MD UCNY 1845; AB Brown 1842. *Hist cat Brown*: 1842. Frank, L F, *Med hist Milw*.

BUTTRICK, ABNER WHEELER, Lowell, Mass (d/III 27–1882 @ 39) MD Harvard 1869; AB Williams 1865. *Bost m & s jour* 106:427, 1882; 107:618, 1882.

BUTTRICK, JAMES TYLER, Jamestown, RI (b/III–6–1825) MD NY Med Coll 1853. *Tr RI Med Soc* 2:315, 1877–82.

BUTTS, HENRY HOYLE, NYC (d/III–25–1906) MD U CNY 1885. *Bost m & s jour* 154:390, 1906. *Polk* 1896: 1044.

BUXTON, BENJAMIN FLINT, Warren, Me; CW–USA (b/XI–5–1810; d/X–8–1876) MD Bowdoin 1830. *Tr Me Med Assoc* 1877: 234–38. *K&B* III: 185.

BUZZARD, JOHN, Bangor, Pa (b/IX–21–1851 Northampton Co, Pa; d/IV–6–1895) MD LICH 1875. *Tr Med Soc Pa* 1896: 416–17. *Polk* 1886: 792.

BUZZELL, ANDREW JAMES HALE, CW–USA (b/ III–31–1831 NYC; d/III–28–1865 Wilmington, NC) MD Dartmouth 1854. *Nat med jour* 1: 291, 1870/71.

BUZZELL, JOHN, Portland, Me (b/XI–18 or 25–1825 or 1826; d/IV–10–1890) MD Bowdoin 1850. *Bost m & s jour* 122:328–32, 1890. *Tr Me Med Assoc* 1889–91:328. *Butler* 1878: 305.

BYERS, ALEXANDER R , Petersburg, Ind (b/VI–15–1829 Washington Co, O; d/VIII–15–1897) <MD Med Coll Evansville, Ind 1854> *Tr Ind St Med Soc* 1898: 378–79. *Polk* 1896: 487.

BYERS, JOHN EGGLESTON, Butler, Pa (d/II–8–1904 @ 40) MD UCNY 1879. *Pa med jour* 8:334, 1904/05. *Flint* 1897: 797.

BYFIELD, FREDERICK W , Sorento, Ill (d/III–20–1906 @ 76) Lic by years of practice. *Ill med jour* 9:463, 1906. *Polk* 1896: 441. Eclectic.

BYFORD, WILLIAM HEATH, Chicago (b/III–20–1817 Eaton, O; d/V–20/21–1890. MD Med Coll O 1845; AM Ashbury U. *Bost m & s jour* 122:536, 1890. *Buff m & s jour* 29:767, 1890. *Med bull* 13:263, 1880. *Tr Ill St Med Soc* 1891:12 ff. *K&B* III: 185–86.

BYFORD, WILLIAM HEATH Jr, Chicago (b/I–21–1850; d/X– –1883) MD Chicago Med Coll 1878. *JAMA* 2: 587, 1884. *Chic med rec* 1:190, 1891. *Tr Minn St Med Soc* 1883: 296.

BYINGTON, CHARLES, New Haven, Conn (b/1795? d/1857) MD Yale 1821. *Proc Conn Med Soc* 1858: 19.

BYINGTON, RODERICK, Johnsonsburg, Pa; Belvidere, NJ (b/X–27–1799 Stockbridge, Mass; d/VIII–18–1872) <Stud Jefferson Med Coll> also stud w/David Green & Geo McClellan. *Trans Med Soc NJ* 1873: 110–112.

BYNUM, DREW WILLIAMSON, Horn Lake, Miss; CW–CSA (b/De Soto, Miss; d/X–31–1878) MD UPa 1855. *U Pa med alum CW*: 1855.

BYNUM, JOSEPH MEDICUS, Rienzi, Miss; CW–CSA (b/III–15–1835 Pittsboro, NC; d/IX–26–1899 Booneville, Miss) MD UPa 1857. *U Pa med alum CW*: 1857. *Polk* 1886: 531.

BYRD, CHARLES CARTER, Frederick Co, Md (d/XII–14–1829 Clarke Co, Va) MD U Pa 1821. *Med annals Md*: 340.

BYRD, DANIEL ELLIS, Marvell, Ark (d/I–24–1888) MD Med Coll Va 1863. *New Orl m & s jour* ns15: 759, 1888. *Polk* 1886: 153.

BYRD, HARVEY LEONIDAS, CW–USA; Salem SC; Savannah; Baltimore (b/VIII–8–1820; d/XI–29–1884) MD UPa 1867; MD Pa Med Coll 1840. *Bost m & s jour* 111: 552,1884. *Med annals Md*: 340. *Med bull med & surg* 7:25,29,1884. *K&B* III: 186–87.

BYRD, WILLIAM ANDREW, Quincy, Ill (b/X–3–1843 Bath Co, Va; d/VIII–14–1887 Slater, Mo) MD Mo Med Coll 1867. *So pract* 9:397, 1887. *JAMA* 9:511–12, 1887. *Tr Ill St Med Soc* 1888:146–49. *Butler* 1878: 145. *K&B* III: 187.

BYRN, SPENCER, CW–USA; Marengo, Ind (d/IV–28–1895) MD Rush 1864. *JAMA* 24:731, 1895. *Kemper's*

Indiana: 190. *Polk* 1886: 327.

BYRNE, BARNARD M , USA (b/1807 Ireland; d/IX-6-1860 Sullivan's Isl SC) MD UMd 1828. *Bost m & s jour* 63:168, 1861. *Med annals Md*: 341.

BYRNE, CHARLES, St Johns River, Fla (b/Ireland; d/1854) MD UMd 1825. *Med annals Md*: 341.

BYRNE, HENRY VAUGHAN, Brooklyn (d/II-12-1895 @ 24 or 25) MD UVt 1892. *Med reg NY NJ Conn* 1895: 218. *JAMA* 24:337, 1895.

BYRNE, J G , ? (d/IX-2-1878 New Orleans) MD unknown. *Tr AMA* 30:857, 1879. *Med rec* 14:220, 1878.

BYRNE, JOHN, Brooklyn; San Francisco (b/X-13-1825 Kilkeel, Ireland; d/XI-1-1902 Switzerland) MD U Edinburgh 1846; att? Royal Inst Belfast 1842. *Calif st jour med* 1:13, 1902. *Atkinson* I: 586. *K&B* III: 187-88.

BYRNE, JOHN, St Mary's, Mo (b/X-20-1816; d/1887) MD UMd 1837. *Med annals Md*: 341. *Polk* 1886: 559.

BYRNE, WALTER J , CW-CSA; Russellville, Ky (d/VIII-1-1904 @ 80) MD St Louis U 1848. *JAMA* 43:558, 1904. *Polk* 1886: 405.

BYRON, JOHN MANUEL, NYC (b/VII-24-1861; d/V-8-1895) <MD U Naples 1877> *Med reg NY NJ Conn* 1895: 218. *Bost m & s jour* 132: 501, 1895. *Med rec* 47:590, 1895.

CABANISS, ALFRED BARWELL, Jackson, Miss (b/XII-10-1808; d/XI-21-1881) MD Transylvania 1833; MD Jefferson 1836 ad eundem. *Tr Miss St Med Assoc* 1874: 118. *Tr AMA* 33:536-37, 1882.

CABELL, HENRY LEE, CW-CSA; Cedarville? Va (b/XII-25-1828 Lynchburg; d/V-17-1906 Cedarville) MD UPa 1851. *U Pa med alum CW*: 1851.

CABELL, JAMES GRATTAN, CW-CSA; Richmond (b/VI-17-1817 Buckingham; d/III-18-1896) MD UMd 1841. *NC med jour* 37:277,1896. *Atkinson* I:334.

CABELL, JAMES LAWRENCE, Charlottesville, Va; CW-CSA; (b/VIII-26-1813 Nelson Co; d/VIII-13-1889 Overton) MD UMd 1834; AM UVa 1833. *NC med jour* 24:140-42, 1889. *K&B* III: 1899-89. *JAMA* 13: 287, 1889. *Bost m & s jour* 121:196, 1889. *Med surg rep Phila* 61:224, 1889.

CABELL, JOHN ROY, Danville, Va (d/VIII-26-1897) MD UVa 1850. *JAMA* 29:555, 1897. *Polk* 1886: 915.

CABELL, WILLIAM C , Danville, Va (d/VI- -1890) MD CPS Balto 1875. *Tr Med Soc Va* 1891: 250. *Polk* 1886: 915.

CABLE, WILLIAM W , Pittsburgh (d/VIII-25-1895 @ 71) <Med Coll Ohio 1846> *JAMA* 25:427, 1895. *Polk* 1886: 828.

CABOCHE, LOUIS, New Orleans (b/1791? France; d/XI 1863 @ 72) MD unknown. *Western homeop obs* 2:16, 1865. *King* I:189-90. Homeopath.

CABOT, SAMUEL, Boston (b/IX-20-1815; d/IV-13-1885) MD Harvard 1839; AB 1836. *Bost m & s jour* 112:384, 1885. *K&B* III:191-92.

CADDEN, CHARLES WILLIAM, Baltimore (b/III-11-1830 Shepherdstown, Va; d/III-26-1879) MD Washington U Balto 1850. *Med annals Md*: 341.

CADMUS, JAMES M , Hammondsport; Waverly, NY (b/VII-3-1834 Lodi, NY; d/V-10-1879) MD Cleveland Homeop 1866. *Tr Am Inst Homeop* 1880: 145. *Cleave. Butler* 1878:531. Homeopath.

CADWALLADER, DAVID WILLIS, CW-USA; Lower Wakefield Twp, Pa (b/III-11-1837; d/IV-7-1875) MD UPa 1858. *U Pa med alum CW*: 1855.

CADWALLADER-CROWDER, EDITH, Philadelphia (d/1906 Chicago) MD Woman's Med Coll Pa 1900. *Pa med jour* 10: 328, 1906/07.

CADY, WILLIAM FINCH, Lafayette, Ind (b/VI-26 or 30-1826 Keesville, NY: d/XII-24-1883) MD Albany 1853. *Hist Med Soc DC:*194. *Tr Ind St Med Soc* 1884: 224. *Butler* 1896: 196.

CAEMMERER, WILLIAM H, Brooklyn (b/India; d/VIII 30-1899 @78) <MD U Jena, Gny 1847> *JAMA* 33:683, 1899. *Bost m & s jour* 141:252, 1899. *Polk* 1896: 993.

CAGE, ALBERT H , Canton, Miss (b/IX-22-1833 Yazoo Co, Miss; d/IX-17-1878) MD ULa 1846. *Med rec NY* 14:260, 1878. *Tr Miss St Med Assoc* 1878: 57-58, 69-70. *Tr AMA* 30:857, 1879.

CAHEN, SOLOMON P , NYC (b/Gny; d/XII-6-1898) MD U Leipzig 1875. *JAMA* 31:1542, 1898.

CAHILL, GEORGE, Lynn, Mass (d/I-27-1881) MD Harvard 1870. *Bost m & s jour* 105:623, 1881.

CAIN, JOSEPH PALMER, CW-CSA; Berkeley, SC (d/X-14-1903 @ 67) MD Med Coll State SC 1859; AB So Carolina Coll 1856. *So pract* 26:114, 1904. *Waring*: 211.

CAINE, WILLIAM C , Ravenna, O; St Paul, Minn 1857; Stillwater (b/VIII-1-1819 Isle of Man; d/VI-19-1867) MD Cleveland Homeop 1851; <Geneva Med Coll 1842> *Tr Am Inst Homeop* 1895:1093. Homeopath.

CAINE, WILLIAM HARRIS, Stillwater, Minn 1877-95? Minneapolis (b/V-10-1854 Ravenna, O; d/IX-16-1902) MD Hahnemann Chic 1877. *Minneapolis hom mag* 11: 1902 (Sept). *Polk* 1886: 518.

CAIRNS, ROBERT W , NYC (d/IX-6-1881 @ 57) MD CPSNY 1833; AM ? *Med reg NY NJ Conn* 1862: 155.

CAKE, JOHN ADAM, Sunbury, Pa (b/I-10-1869; d/IV-24-1905) MD UPa 1893; stud Lafayette 1893. *Lafayette, Men of*: 277.

CALBREATH, THOMAS FRANKLIN, Cleopatra, Mo (d/I-9-1899) MD CPS Keokuk 1874; MD Bellevue 1877. *JAMA* 32:195-96, 1899. *Polk* 1886:544.

CALDWELL, CHARLES, Philadelphia (b/V-4-1772 Caswell Co, NC; d/VII-9-1853; Louisville, Ky) MD UPa 1796. *Phila med & surg jour* 2:76-77, 1853. *Bost m & s jour* 49:23, 1853. *Tr Ky St Med Soc* 1876:38-66. *K & B* III: 193.

CALDWELL, GEORGE B , Newberry, SC (d/VII-5-1901) MD CPS Baltimore 1886. *JAMA* 37:527, 1901.

CALDWELL, GEORGE O , Scranton, Pa (d/XI-18-

1905 @ 45) MD UCNY 1886. *Pa med jour* 9:221, 1905/06. *Flint* 1897: 834.

CALDWELL, HENRY [or HANSON] CLAY, USN (d/XII-1-1859 Lewisburg Va @ 28) MD UPa 1853; stud UVa Med Sch 1850-52. *Med surg rep Phila* ns3: 279, 1859. *Hamersly*: 123.

CALDWELL, JOHN B , Baltimore (d/1820) MD UMd 1816. *Med annals Md*: 341.

CALDWELL, JOHN JABEZ, CW-USA; Brooklyn 1866-73; Baltimore 1873- (b/IV-28-1836 Oakhill, Del; d/III-14-1878 Brooklyn) MD NY Med Coll 1859. *Med ann Md*:342. *Atkinson* I:176. *Polk* 1893:558.

CALDWELL, JOSEPH RUSSELL, CW-USA; Upper Chichester Twp; New Hamburg, Pa (b/VIII-31-1838 Delaware Twp; d/VII-21-1901 Marcus Hook) MD UPa 1867. *JAMA* 37:342, 1901. *Tr Pa Med Soc* 5:296, 314-15, 1901/02. *Polk* 1886: 809.

CALDWELL, JULIUS ANDREW, Salisbury, NC; CW-CSA (b/II-9-1830; d/XII-21-1905) MD UPa 1854 [as Julius Alexander]; AB UNC 1850. *Pa med alum CW*: 1854. *Polk* 1886: 726.

CALDWELL, MERLIN, Ford City, Pa (d/XII-23-1904 @ 30) MD U Western Pa 1904. *Pa med jour* 8: 334, 1904/05.

CALDWELL, WILLIAM A , Rockville, Md (b/IX-29-1862 WVa; d/VI-6-1903) MD Columbian 1892. *Hist Med Soc DC*:361.

CALDWELL, WILLIAM C , Fremont, O (d/IX-29-1896 @ 59) MD Cleveland Charity Hosp 1869. *JAMA* 27:825, 1896. *Polk* 1886: 755.

CALDWELL, WILLIAM R , Nunan, Ga (b/Charleston, SC; d/XI-15-1886 @ 44) MD unknown. *New Orl m & s jour* ns14: 639, 1887.

CALDWELL, WILLIAM SPENCER, Freeport, Ill (d/VI-7-1901) MD Jefferson 1864. *Ill med jour* ns3:91, 1901. *Polk* 1896: 420.

CALHOUN, ALBERT J , Goshenville, Pa (d/IX-29-1881 @ 32) MD Jefferson 1875. *Tr Med Soc Pa* 14:302-303, 1882.

CALHOUN, C P , Altoona, Pa (d/V-18-1902 @ 66) MD Cincinnati Coll M & S 1873. *Pa med jour* 6: 259, 1902/03. *Polk* 1896: 1267.

CALHOUN, CHARLES WILLIAM, Syria (d/1883) MD Bellevue 1880; AM Williams 1873; att? Union Theol Sem. *Med bull med & surg* 9:212, 1883.

CALHOUN, JAMES THEODORE, CW-USA; Rahway, NJ; Harts Island, NY (b/IX-17-1838; d/VII-19-1866) MD UPa 1859. *Tr AMA* 18:356, 1867; 19:431-32, 1868. *Tr Med Soc NJ* 1867: 147ff. *Med surg rep Phila* ns15: 106-07, 1866. *U Pa med alum CW*: 189. *Nat med jour* 1:291, 1870/71.

CALKINS, ABRAM RENSSELAER, Allegan, Mich; CW-USA (b/V-19-1822 Malta, NY; d/III-17-1873) MD Geneva 1845. *Tr St Med Soc Mich* 1873:146-47.

CALKINS, ALONZO, NYC (b/XI-27-1804 Conn; d/III-3-1878) MD CPSNY 1831; AB Williams 1825. *Med reg NY NJ Conn* 1878: 180. *Atkinson* I: 422.

CALKINS, GEORGE H , Waupaca, Wis (b/IV-21-1830; d/VI-25-1896) MD Buffalo 1857. *JAMA* 27:53, 1896. *Atkinson* I: 551-52. *Polk* 1886: 961.

CALL, NATHAN, Suncook, NH (b/IX-25-1827 Boscawen, NH; d/VI-15-1875) MD Dartmouth 1854. *Tr NH Med Soc* 1876: 165-68.

CALLAHAN, FELIX P , Peoria, Ill (d/I-29-1896) MD U Oregon 1888. *JAMA* 26:287, 1896. *Polk* 1890:190 (Nicolaus, Calif).

CALLAHAN, HENRY B , Leavenworth, Kans (d/XI-23 1895 @ 74) MD Med Coll Ohio 1843. *JAMA* 25: 968, 1895. *Polk* 1886: 380.

CALLAWAY, JAMES M , Galveston, Tex (d/II-12-1876 @ 46) MD ULa 1855. *Tr AMA* 29: 622, 1878. *Tr Tex St Med Assoc* 1876: [207].

CALLAWAY, THOMAS, Blooming Grove, Tex (d/I-4-1886) MD unknown. *New Orl m & s jour* ns13: 664, 1886. *Daniels Tex med jour* 1:339, 1886. *Tex cour-rec med*: 3:219, 1886.

CALLENDER, EMMA HULDAH, Middlebury, Vt (b/X 18-1839; d/V-31-1878) MD New Engl Female Med Coll 1869. *Tr Vt Med Soc* 1883: 105.

CALLENDER, JOHN HILL, CW-CSA; Nashville (b/XI-28-1832; d/VIII-3-1896) MD UPa 1855. *So pract* 18:423-29, 1896. *JAMA* 27:503, 1896. *Nashville jour m & s* 80:95,135-46, 1896. *Atkinson* I:119. *K&B* III: 195.

CALVERT, WILLIAM J, Denver (d/IV-1-1893 @48) MD NY Homeop 1865; MD Hahnemann Chic 1868. *Med vis* 9:173, 1893. *Tr Am Inst Homeop* 1895: 1093. *Polk* 1886: 183.

CALVIN, ABNER C , Meadville, Pa (b/Crawford Co; d/II-24-1906 @ 51) MD Jefferson 1878. *Pa med jour* 9: 524, 1905/06.

CAMAC, WILLIAM, Philadelphia (d/IV-3-1900 @ 71) MD Jefferson 1852. *JAMA* 34:957, 1900.

CAMBLOS, HENRY FISHER, Philadelphia (d/III-26-1906 @ 48) MD Jefferson 1881. *Pa med jour* 9:523, 1905/06.

CAMERON, CLARENCE, NYC (d/VI-1-1865) MD UCNY 1858. *Med reg NY NJ Conn* 1867: 210.

CAMERON, EDWARD MILLER, NYC (d/IX-28-1902 @ 73) MD CPSNY 1853. *Bost m & s jour* 147:422, 1902. *Polk* 1896: 1044.

CAMERON, JOHN W , CW-USA (d/XI-13-1865) MD unknown. *Nat med jour* 1:291, 1870/71.

CAMERON, RICHARD HUGH, Johnstown, NY (b/VII-6-1847 Perth, NY; d/IV-26-1890) MD Albany 1870. *Med reg NY NJ Conn* 1890: 262. *Tr Med Soc St NY* 1891:462-63. *Polk* 1886: 665.

CAMERON, WILLIAM OSCAR, Johnstown, Pa (d/I-5 1904 @ 33 or 35) MD Western Res U 1895. *Pa med jour* 8:334, 392, 1904/05. *Polk* 1896: 1266.

CAMMANN, GEORGE PHILIP, NYC (b/II-7-1804;

d/II-14-1863 Fordham) MD Rutgers 1828; AB Columbia 1825. *Tr AMA* 14:205, 1864. *Med reg NY NJ Conn* 1865:216.

CAMP, ARTHUR A , Minneapolis (b/1855 Hoboken, NJ; d/IV-9-1888 @ 33) MD NY Homeop 1878. *Tr Am Inst Homeop* 1888: 232. *Polk* 1886: 513.

CAMP, MARTIN V , Hoxie, Ark (d/VIII-30-1898) MD Hosp Med Coll Louisville 1885 [?] *JAMA* 31:673, 1898. *Polk* 1896: 200.

CAMPBELL, ABEL, CW-USA (d/III-28-1864) MD unknown. *Nat med jour* 1:291, 1870/71.

CAMPBELL, ARCHIBALD BARRINGTON, Philadelphia; USA (b/IV-18-1821; d/IX-1-1878 Chicago) MD Jefferson 1844; stud Amherst. *Tr AMA* 30:810-11, 1879.

CAMPBELL, CHARLES FITZHENRY, Springhill, NS; CW-USA (b/II-2-1823 England; d/XII-28-1906) MD UPa 1847. *U Pa med alum CW*:1847.

CAMPBELL, CORNELIUS NARE, NY; USA (b/VII-1825; d/XII-21-1888 Poughkeepsie, NY) MD UCNY 1848. *Med reg NY NJ Conn* 1890: 262.

CAMPBELL, DANIEL, Saxtons River, Vt (b/III-8-1820 Westminster; d/II-3-1898) MD Berkshire 1843; ng Woodstock 1842. *Tr Vt St Med Soc* 1898: 206-11. *JAMA* 30:570, 1898. *Polk* 1896: 1477.

CAMPBELL, ELIZA ANN LADD, Boston (b/1842? (d/IV-8-1890 @48) MD Boston U 1876. *Tr Am Inst Hom-eop* 1895:1093. *Polk* 1886:1093. *Cleave*. Homeopath.

CAMPBELL, FREDERICK R , Buffalo (b/1860; d/IX-14-1888) MD Buffalo 1883. *Buff med jour* 28: 166-69, 1888. *Polk* 1886: 651.

CAMPBELL, GAWN, NYC (d/II-20-1887) MD LICH 1874. *Med reg NY NJ Conn* 1887: 255. *Polk* 1886: 673.

CAMPBELL, GEORGE, NJ (b/VIII-15-1758 Irel'd; d/VIII-1818) <MD Dublin> *Tr Med Soc NJ* 1872:170-71.

CAMPBELL, GEORGE W , Columbia, Tenn (d/V--1834 Paris, Fr) MD Transylvania 1828. *Transylvania jour med & assoc sci* 6:427-28, 1834.

CAMPBELL, H F , Alleghany City, Pa (d/VI-14-1869 @28 Belfast, Ireland) MD Jefferson 1867. *Phila med reg & dir* 1871: 301. *Med surg rep Phila* 21: 68, 1869.

CAMPBELL, HARVEY, Voluntown, Conn (b/IX-30-1792; d/IX- -1877 Groton) MD Yale 1816. *Proc Conn Med Soc* 1879: 169. *Butler* 1878: 74.

CAMPBELL, HENRY FRASER, Augusta, Ga (b/II-10-1824 Savannah; d/XII-15-1891) MD Med Coll Ga 1842. *So pract* 14:89, 1892. *Med bull m & s* 14:74-75, 1892. *NW med jour* 20:16, 1892. *K&B* III: 196-97.

CAMPBELL, HENRY HANCOCK, Fairfield Center, Me 1849-57; Waterville 1857-94 (b/VII- -1820 Farmington; d/I-8-1895) MD Jefferson 1849; Dartmouth 1849; ng Bowdoin 1846. *Bost m & s jour* 132:72, 1895. *Butler* 1878: 304.

CAMPBELL, JAMES, Hartford Conn (b/III-14-1848; d/X-17-1899) MD UVt 1871. *JAMA* 33: 1115 1899. *Proc Conn Med Soc* 1900:347-50. *Polk* 1896: 279.

CAMPBELL, JAMES WILLIAM, Ottumwa, Ia (d/VIII-26-1894) MD Rush 1880. *JAMA* 23:362, 1894. *Polk* 1890: 423.

CAMPBELL, MELANCHTHON WHEELER, Stillwater, NY; Troy (b/XI-9-1822 Ft Edward, NY; d/III-1-1894 @ 72) MD Cleveland Homeop 1853. *Tr Am Inst Homeop* 1894: 260. *Polk* 1886: 712. Homeopath.

CAMPBELL, PATRICK HENRY, Dorchester, Mass (d/V-3-1895 @ 30) MD Harvard 1890. *Bost m & s jour* 132:476, 1895.

CAMPBELL, SAMUEL D , Charleston, SC; Norfolk, Va; Suisun, Calif 1864- (b/IV-24-1823 Greensboro, NC; d/IV-10-1875) MD UCNY 1846. *Tr Med Soc St Calif* 1874-75: 163-64.

CAMPBELL, SIDNEY A , W Pittston, Pa (b/1820 Eaton, Pa; d/IX-12-1903 @ 83) MD Jefferson 1849. *Pa med jour* 7:278, 1903/04. *Polk* 1886: 831.

CAMPBELL, SYLVESTER, CW-USA (d/II-6-1863 Camp Mansfield) MD UCNY 1858. *Nat med jour* 1: 291, 1870/71.

CAMPBELL, WILLIAM, Harmarville, Pa (d/VII-1 1873 @38 Tryon Plantation, Polk Co, NC) MD Jefferson 1859. *Med surg rep Phila* 29:126, 1873.

CAMPBELL, WILLIAM, Port Huron Mich (d/II-21 1900 @ 86) <MD Edinburgh 1838> *JAMA* 34:639, 1900. *Polk* 1896: 768.

CAMPBELL, WILLIAM CUNNINGHAM, NYC (d/II 5-1899 @ 44) MD CPSNY 1880; AB Princeton 1877. *JAMA* 32:385, 1899. *Polk* 1896: 1044.

CAMPBELL, WILLIAM H , Vanceburg, Ky (d/VIII 19-1896 @ 58) MD Starling 1863. *JAMA* 27: 555, 1896. *Polk* 1890: 479.

CAMPBELL, WILLIAM HENRY, Roxbury, Mass; CW USN (d/IV-24-1884 @ 52) MD Harvard 1865. *Bost m & s jour* 110:432, 1884.

CAMPBELL, WILLIAM JOSEPH, Boston (d/VI-14 1901 @ 26) MD Harvard 1900; AB Boston Coll 1896. *JAMA* 37:43, 1901.

CAMPBELL, WILLIAM MERRITT, CW-USA? (d/1862 @ 62, Charleston, SC) MD CPSNY 1847; AB UVt 1843. *CPSNY cat*: 1847.

CANDEE, JOEL GILLETT, West Farms, NY (d/I-26-1870 @ 71) MD Yale 1825. *Phila med reg & dir* 1871:303.

CANFIELD, ABRAHAM, Newark (b/VIII-9-1797; d/VIII-24-1846) MD unknown. *Tr Med Soc NJ* 1867: 129.

CANFIELD, WILLIAM BUCKINGHAM, Baltimore (b/1857; d/XII-27-1899 @ 42) MD UMd 1880; AB Princeton 1877. *Med annals Md*: 342. *JAMA* 34:61, 1900.

CANNADY, ISAAC GREEN, CW-CSA (b/Granville Co, NC; d/1884 So Lowell) MD UPa 1859. *U Pa med alum CW*: 1859.

CANTRELL, JAMES HENRY, Philadelphia (d/VI-3 1899 @ 66) MD Jefferson 1856. *JAMA* 32: 1460, 1899. *Polk* 1896: 1300.

Spec. educ'l status abbrev. as: *ng* = college verified attendance without degree;

CANTRELL, WILLIAM A , Philadelphia (d/I-7-1900 @ 58) MD Jefferson 1862. *JAMA* 34:187, 1900. *Polk* 1896: 1300.

CANTWELL, ALONZO WILLIAM, Davenport, Ia (d/XI-22-1899 @ 58) MD U Mich 1869. *Trans Iowa St Med Soc* 18:399-401, 1900. *JAMA* 33:1440, 1899. *Tr Ill St Med Soc* 1899: 352. *Polk* 1896: 517.

CAPEHART, B ASHBOURNE, Bermuda; NYC (b/IV-2-1865 Edenton, NC; d/XII-20-1904 NYC) MD UMd 1886. *Hist Med Soc DC*: 337.

CAPELLE, JOSEPH PHILIPPE EUGENE, Wilmington, Del; RevWar w/Lafayette, &c. (b/1757 Laurie, Flanders; d/XI-5-1796) MD unknown. *Trans AMA* 29: 622-23, 1878. *K & B* III: 195.

CAPERS, LeGRAND G , Vicksburg, Miss; New Orleans (b/IV-16-1834 Charleston, SC; d/XII-2-1877) MD Jefferson 1858. *Trans Miss St Med Assoc* 1878:164-65. *Butler* 1874: 389.

CAPERTON, GEORGE HENRY, Caperton, WVa; CW-CSA (b/XII-13-1828 Union, Va; d/I-13-1895 Balto) MD UPa 1853. *U Pa med alum CW*:1853. *Polk* 1880:940

CAPRON, GEORGE, Providence, RI (b/V-16-1802; d/IX-21-1882) MD Brown 1824. *Bost m & s jour* 107:334, 1882. *JAMA* 1:603, 1883. *Atkinson* I: 679. *Butler* 1878: 476. *Trans RI Med Soc* 2:545-50, 1877-82.

CAPRON, W J B , NYC? (d/XII- -1890) MD NY Homeop 1880. *Med vis* 7:113, 1891. Homeopath.

CARBEE, SAMUEL POWERS, Haverhill, NH (b/VI-14-1836 Bath, NH; d/I-31-1900) MD Dartmouth 1866. *JAMA* 34:446, 1900. *Trans NH Med Soc* 1900: 314. *Polk* 1886: 592.

CARBERRY, JOHN M , Waukesha, Wis (b/V-7-1853 Lisbon, Wis; d/I-13-1891) MD Chicago Med Coll 1884. *Trans Wis St Med Soc* 1891:356; 1892:385-86. *Polk* 1890: 1174.

CARD, DAVID CLARK, Willimantic, Conn (b/1822? d/X-16-1899 @ 77) MD UCNY 1850. *JAMA* 33: 1183, 1899. *Polk* 1896: 286.

CARDEN, PETER S , CW-CSA; Richmond, Va (d/X-11 1896 @ 60) MD UPa 1860. *NC med jour* 38:348, 1896. *JAMA* 27:1021, 1896. *Trans Med Soc Va* 1897: 268. *Polk* 1890: 1118.

CARDEZA, JOHN THOMAS MARTINEZ, Claymont, Del; CW-USA (b/1820 Phila; d/VI-27-1900) MD UPa 1844. *U Pa med alum CW*: 1844. *Polk* 1886: 205.

CAREY, ABEL, Salem, O (b/IX- -1809, Smithfield, O; d/I-9-1872) MD Cincinnati Coll Med 1839 [?] *Tr Ohio St Med Soc* 1872: 265-268.

CAREY, ALFRED W , Wild Rose, Wis (b/I-9-1853 Euphemia, Ont; d/III-23-1899) MD Mich Coll Med 1881. *JAMA* 32: 787, 1899. *Polk* 1896: 1566.

CAREY, A [?ANIZI?] B , CW-USA (d/IX-14-1862) MD Rush 1856 [Anizi B]. *Nat med jour* 1:291, 1870/71.

CAREY, GEORGE FRANCIS, NYC (b/Ireland; d/VI 17-1902 @ 66) MD CPSNY 1874. *Bost m & s jour* 146:706, 1902. *Polk* 1896: 1045.

CAREY, HENRY, NYC (d/III-9-1899 Lakewood, NJ) MD Ecl Med Coll NYC 1891. *Bost m & s jour* 140: 296, 1899. *Polk* 1896: 1045. Eclectic.

CAREY, MILTON T , Cincinnati (d/VII-15- 1901 @ 70) MD Med Coll Ohio 1850. *JAMA* 37:275, 1901. *Polk* 1886: 741.

CAREY, NELSON HOWARD, Durham, Me (b/I-5-1807 Bridgewater, Mass; d/IV-10-1877) MD Bowdoin 1828. *Trans Me Med Assoc* 1877: 240-42.

CAREY, SAMUEL, Quakertown, Pa (b/V-6-1797; d/VII-19-1864) MD CPSNY 1824. *Trans Med Soc Pa* 1:74, 1865. *Med surg rep Phila* 12:100, 1864/65.

CAREY, W B , CW-USA (d/I-20-1885) MD unknown. *Nat med jour* 1:291, 1870/71.

CAREY, WILLIAM ANTHONY, Philadelphia (d/I-29 1897 @ 35) MD UPa 1886. *JAMA* 28:380, 1897. *Polk* 1896: 1300.

CARLETON, CHARLES AUGUSTUS, Salem, Mass (b/II-27-1841 Orford, NH; d/VI-13-1902) MD Dartmouth 1861. *Boston m & s jour* 146:678, 1902. *Polk* 1896: 721.

CARLETON, CHARLES MONRO, Norwich Conn; CW USA (b/IV-28-1838 Waterford Me; d/XII-30-1886) MD Harvard 1861. *Harvard in CW*: 262. *Atkinson* I:363. *Butler* 1878:74. *K & B* I(1): 161.

CARLEY, DAVID W , Boscobel, Wis (d/V-27-1896) MD Rush 1856. *JAMA* 26:1144, 1896. *Polk* 1886: 951.

CARLIN, WILLIAM D , CW-USA (d/XII-26-1862) MD unknown. *Nat med jour* 1:291, 1870/71.

CARLISLE, RICHARD COLEMAN, CW-CSA; Newberry, SC (d/VIII-21-1906) MD UCNY 1862. *So pract* 28:598, 1906. *Butler* 1878: 753.

CARLISLE, STUART BROWN, Mt Vernon, NY (d/XII 8-1899 @ 51) MD Bellevue 1881. *JAMA* 33:1566, 1899; 34:61, 1900. *Polk* 1896: 1033.

CARLL, GEORGE GRIER, So Dennis, NJ (b/IX-28-1838 Hancocks Bridge; d/X-24-1890) MD UPa 1862. *Trans Med Soc NJ* 1892: 194.

CARMALT, CHARLES CHURCHILL, NYC (d/I-8-1905 @ 38) MD CPSNY 1891; ng Haverford 1887. *Bost m & s jour* 152:92, 1905. *Polk* 1896:1045.

CARMER, LEWIS CHARLES, Williamsville, NY (b/VI 16-1858 Clarence; d/VII-11-1892 Lancaster, NY) MD U Mich 1883. *Buff m & s jour* 32:430, 1893.

CARMICHAEL, EDWARD HACKLEY, Washington, DC (b/Glasgow, Scotland; d/1855) MD UMd 1817. *Hist Med Soc DC*: 247.

CARMICHAEL, GEORGE FRENCH, Fredericksburg, Va (b/III-9-1806; d/VIII-27-1882) MD UMd 1828. *JAMA* 1:224, 1883.

CARMICHAEL, JAMES A , NYC (d/XII-25-1899) MD UCNY 1844. *No Amer jour homeop* 46:20, 1898. *Polk* 1886: 674. Homeopath.

CARMICHAEL, SPOTSWOOD WELLFORD, CW-CSA; Fredericksburg, Va (b/XI-23-1830; d/III-18-

1904) MD Jefferson 1852; ng UVa Med Dept 1850/51. *Trans Med Soc Va* 1904:317–18. *Polk* 1900: 1763.

CARNCROSS, J AUGUSTUS, Philadelphia (d/III–19–1903 @ 58) MD Jefferson 1876. *Pa med jour* 7:278, 1903/04. *Polk* 1896: 1300.

CARNOCHAN, JOHN MURRAY, NYC (b/VII–14–1817 Savannah, Ga; d/X–28–1887) MD CPSNY 1836. *Med reg NY NJ Conn* 1888: 242. *Bost m & s jour* 117:442, 1887. *New Orl med & surg jour* ns15:494, 1887. *K & B* III: 199.

CARO, SALVATORE, Palermo, Sicily; NYC (b/II–15–1823 Palermo; d/IV–30–1881) MD U Palermo 1848; MD UCNY 1855. *Med reg NY NJ Conn* 1881: 234. *Chic med rev* 3:226, 1881. *Bost m & s jour* 104: 476, 1881. *Atkinson* I:223. *Butler* 1878: 495.

CAROLIN, SAMUEL J, CW–USA (d/XI–4–1862 Bowling Green, Ky) MD *Nat med jour* 1:291, 1870/71.

CAROTHERS, EDWARD J, Saltillo; San Antonio, Tex (b/Carlisle, Pa; d/IV–9–1891) MD UPa 1885. *Daniels Tex med jour* 6:34–35, 72–76, 1890–91.

CAROTHERS, WILLIAM HARSHA, St Paul, Minn; Melrose, Mass (b/XI–2–1854; d/X–23–1906) MD Jefferson 1883. *Bost m & s jour* 155:530, 1906. *Polk* 1890: 618.

CARPENTER, ALVAH, Mobile Ala (b/II–24–1790; d/XI–30–1824) MD AB Brown 1818. *Hist cat Brown*: 1818.

CARPENTER, ARTHUR BENJAMIN, Cleveland (b/1852 W Andover, O; d/X–15–1890) MD Wooster 1881. *Trans O Med Soc* 1891:5, 336–39. *Buff med & surg jour* 30:303, 1890. *Polk* 1886: 746.

CARPENTER, BENONI, Pawtucket, RI (b/III–12–1805 Rehoboth, Mass; d/XI–22–1877) MD Jefferson 1832; AB Brown 1829. *Hist cat Brown*: 1829.

CARPENTER, CHARLES FRANCIS, Louisville, Ky; CW–USA (b/VII–9–1826 W Bradford, Pa; d/I–5–1902 West Chester, Pa) MD UPa 1849. *U Pa med alum CW*: 1849.

CARPENTER, CHARLES H, Pittstown, NY; Troy 1865– (b/II–22–1825; d/IX–23–1883) MD Albany Med Coll 1857. *Trans Am Inst Homeop* 1884:666. *New Engl med gaz* 18:351, 1883. Homeopath.

CARPENTER, DRAPER, Pawtucket, RI (b/XII–30–1791 Rehoboth, Mass; d/VI–16–1848) MD Brown 1824; AB 1821. *Hist cat Brown*: 1821.

CARPENTER, FREDERICK BENONI, E Providence, RI (b/VI–18–1845 Pawtucket; d/XI–14–1891) MD Harvard 1868; ng Brown 1867. *Trans RI Med Soc* 4: 342–43, 1889–93. *Polk* 1890: 1025.

CARPENTER, GEORGE EDWARD, E Providence, RI (b/VIII–23–1849; d/IX–22–1893) MD CPSNY 1875; AB Brown 1873. *Trans RI Med Soc* 4:624–25, 1889–93. *Polk* 1890: 1025.

CARPENTER, GEORGE WASHINGTON, San Francisco (b/Indiana; d/X–3–1903 @ 79) MD U Mich 1853. *Calif st jour med* 1:385, 1903.

CARPENTER, HARVEY SESSIONS, Worcester, Mass (b/IV–4–1830 Warren, Mass; d/II–2–1875) MD Berkshire 1855; AB Amherst 1853. *Amherst, Men of*: 1853.

CARPENTER, HENRY BABCOCK, Rochester, NY (d/III–23–1900 @ 36) MD CPSNY 1890; AB UCNY 1886. *JAMA* 34:890, 1900. *Polk* 1896: 1093.

CARPENTER, ISAAC B, Cincinnati (d/VI–28–1883) MD Jefferson 1827. *Med surg rep Phila* 49:56, 1883.

CARPENTER, JAMES B, Gouverneur, NY (b/VII–9–1819 Johnstown; d/X–28–1895) MD Castleton 1847. *Bost m & s jour* 133:477, 1895. *Polk* 1886:662.

CARPENTER, JAMES STRATTON, Pottsville, Pa (b/1807 Carpenter's Landing, NJ; d/I–31–1872) MD UPa 1829. *Trans Med Soc Pa* 9:231–35, 1873. *Med times* Phila 2:216, 1871/72.

CARPENTER, JOHN, New Utrecht, NY (b/1790? d/XI–13–1864 @ 74) MD unknown. *Med surg rep Phila* 12:116, 1864/65.

CARPENTER, JOHN B, Groveton, NH (b/I–31–1862; d/VI–17–1897) MD Buffalo 1893. *Trans NH Med Soc* 1901: 331.

CARPENTER, JOHN E, CW–USA; Memphis; Washington, DC (b/II–14–1842 Aberdeen, O; d/V–5–1899) MD Charity Hosp Coll Cleveland 1866; MD U Buffalo 1893. *JAMA* 32:1133, 1899. *Hist Med Soc DC* 353.

CARPENTER, JOHN THOMAS, CW–USA; Pottsville, Pa (b/I–27–1833; d/I–22–1899) MD UPa 1855; AB 1852. *Pa med jour* 3:106–07, 1899/1900. *Atkinson* I:655. *Flint* 1897:832.

CARPENTER, MOSES, Kankakee, Ill (b/IX–24–1827; d/IX–9–1872) <MD Hahnemann Med Coll (?Chic)> *Trans Am Inst Homeop* 1895: 1093. *New Engl med gaz* 8:48, 1873. *Cleave*. Homeopath.

CARPENTER, REUBEN SOCRATES, ?NYC (d/XII–15 1874 @ 62) MD UCNY 1874. *Med reg NY NJ Conn* 1875: 196.

CARPENTER, SEBA, Attleborough, Mass (b/1783 Rehoboth; d/1854 @ 71) Stud med w/Dr Blackington. *Bost m & s jour* 51: 480–81, 1854.

CARPENTER, SIMEON BURT, Dedham, Mass (b/VI–5–1801; d/IV–24–1843) MD Harvard 1830; AB Brown 1827. *Hist cat Brown*: 1827.

CARPENTER, SOLOMON G, Chester, NY (d/IX–13–1901 @ 76) MD UCNY 1845. *JAMA* 37:847, 1901. *Polk* 1886: 656.

CARPENTER, WALTER, Burlington, Vt (b/I–12–1808 Walpole, NH; d/XI–9–1892) MD Dartmouth 1830. *Bost m & s jour* 127:492, 1892. *K & B* III: 200–01.

CARPENTER, WESLEY MANNEN, NYC; CW–USA (b/VIII–2–1839 Ericville, NY; d/I–7–1888) MD CPSNY 1863. *Med reg NY NJ Conn* 1888: 243. *Buff m & s jour* 118:53, 1888; 119:639, 1888. *Trans Med Soc St NY* 1888: 568–72.

CARPENTER, WILLIAM BLANDING, Providence, RI

 Spec. educ'l status abbrev. as: ***ng*** = college verified attendance without degree;

(b/Seekonk, Mass 1810; d/I-30-1830) Stud med Brown [?] 1829-30; AB Brown 1829. *Hist cat Brown*: 1829.

CARPENTER, WILLIAM D [B?], Leavenworth, Kans (d/XII-16-1893) MD Cleveland Med Coll 1853. *JAMA* 21:1010, 1893. *Butler* 1878:251 (as Wm. B.).

CARPENTER, WILLIAM M , New Orleans (1810? d/1850) MD ULa 1836. *Tr AMA* 3:438, 1850. *New Orl m & s jour* 3:409, 1848.

CARR, ALLEN B , Rochester, NY (b/II-15-1852 Ithaca; d/I-8-1901) MD NY Homeop Med Coll 1872. *Jour homeop* 49: 1901 (Feb). *Polk* 1886: 704. Homeopath.

CARR, ALONZO FERDINAND, Goffstown, NH (b/X-26-1817; d/XII-16-1887) MD Dartmouth 1839. *Tr NH Med Soc* 1888: 163-166. *Polk* 1886: 591.

CARR, ARTEMAS HOLMES, New Hampton, NH (b/II-28-1833 Sanbornton, NH; d/V-17-1862) MD Dartmouth 1858. *Tr NH Med Soc* 1862: 68.

CARR, BENJAMIN A, Bristol Md (d/III-21-1900 @ 68) MD UMd 1853. *JAMA* 34:957, 1900. *Polk* 1886: 441.

CARR, EDGAR Le ROI, Pittsfield, NH (b/V-12-1841 Gilmanton; d/XII-22-1903) MD Bowdoin 1864. *Tr NH Med Soc* 1904: 291-93. *Polk* 1890: 711.

CARR, EDSON, Canandaigua, NY (b/X-29-1801 Vershire; d/XI-28-1861) Lic Med Soc Ontario Co, NY 1826; Hon MD Regents NYU 1855. *Tr Med Soc St NY* 1862: 441-43. *Tr AMA* 14: 200-01, 1864.

CARR, EZRA SLOCUM, Pasadena, Calif (b/III-19-1819 Stephentown, NY; d/XI-27-1894) MD Castleton 1842; BS & CE Rensselaer 1838; Hon AM Middlebury 1843; Hon MD Rush 1867; LLD Lawrence U 1865. *JAMA* 23:918, 1894. *Atkinson* I:353. *Butler* 1878: 57.

CARR, GEORGE H , Galesburgh, Ill (d/X-23-1887) MD Hahnemann Chic 1870. *Med couns* 12:575, 1886/87. *Med vis* 4:15, 1888. *Polk* 1886: 280. Homeopath.

CARR, GEORGE W , Ligonier, Ind (b/I-30-1830 Stark Co, O; d/III-1-1895) MD Cleveland Med Coll 1856. *Tr Ind St Med Soc* 1895: 416. *Butler* 1896: 196.

CARR, JOHN, Gilmanton, NH (b/X-22-1786; d/1861) Hon MD Dartmouth 1839. *Tr NH Med Soc* 1861: 6.

CARR, JOSIAH, , Mechanic Falls, Me; CW-USA; (b/II-6-1814 Hebron, Me; d/VIII-12-1873) MD Bowdoin 1836. *Tr Me Med Assoc* 1877: 232-33.

CARR, MARVIN SAMUEL, Peoria, Ill 1852-59; CW-USA; Galesburgh, Ill (b/X-6-1823 Wilton, NY; d/IV-30 1899) MD Castleton 1848. *JAMA* 32: 1013, 1899. *Cleave*. *Polk* 1886: 280. Homeopath.

CARR, MORTIMER A R F , Cumberland, Md (b/1831 Va; d/III-24-1898 @ 68) MD UMd 1851. *JAMA* 30: 874, 1898. *Med annals Md*: 343.

CARRADINE, JAMES S , NYC (b/Yazoo, Miss; d/IV-23-1901) MD Pa Med Coll 1858. *Bost m & s jour* 144:438, 1901. *Polk* 1886: 674.

CARREAU, JOSEPH A , Brooklyn (d/XII-30-1890 @ 40) MD École de Med et de Chir Montréal 1875. *Med reg NY NJ Conn* 1891: 270.

CARREAU, JOSEPH STANISLAS, NYC (d/I-7-1902 @ 53) MD UCNY 1874. *Bost m & s jour* 146:76, 1902. *Polk* 1896:1045.

CARRERE, EDWARD W , ?Baltimore (d/I-31-1855 @ 53) MD UMd 1825. *Med annals Md*: 343.

CARRÉRE, MAYNARD EDWARD, Charleston SC; CW-USA (b/V-13-1813; d/IX-10-1879) MD UPa 1837. *U Pa med alum CW*: 1837. *Atkinson* I: 620.

CARRINGTON, EDWIN WELLS, Hartford Co, Conn (b/1805? d/1851) MD Yale 1828. *Proc Conn Med Soc* 1852: 17.

CARRINGTON, GEORGE CABELL, ?Halifax CH, CW CSA (b/X-13-1819 Coles Ferry, Va; d/IX-23-1880) MD UPa 1840. *U Pa med alum CW*: 1840.

CARRINGTON, HENRY AUSTEN, Bristol, Conn (d/VI 9-1906 @ 80) MD Harvard 1848. *Bost m & s jour* 154: 722, 1906. *Polk* 1896: 276.

CARRINGTON, PAUL JONES, Mt Laurel, Va; CW-CSA (b/V-21-1821 Halifax Co, Va; d/IV-17-1900) MD UPa 1845; AB Hampden-Sidney 1842. *U Pa med alum CW*: 1845. *Polk* 1886: 922.

CARRINGTON, PAUL S , New Orleans (d/II-6-1896 @68) MD Jefferson 1851; AB Princeton 1848. *New Orl m & s jour* ns23:542,1896. *Butler* 1878:296.

CARRINGTON, REED C , Sandidge's Va (d/XII-19 1899 @34) MD Med Coll Va 1887. *JAMA* 34:61, 1900.

CARRINGTON, WILLIAM FONTAINE, USN 1848-51; CW-CSA & CSN (b/Halifax Co, Va I-30-1822; d/IX-13-1883 Hot Springs, Ark) MD UPa 1845; AB Hampden-Sidney 1841. *U Pa med alum CW*: 1845.

CARRINGTON, WILLIAM WASHINGTON, ?Mayo, Va; CW-CSA (b/III-31-1808 S Boston, Va; d/I-4-1873 Mayo) MD UPa 1828. *U Pa med alum CW*: 1828.

CARROLL, ALEXANDER FORMAN, Brooklyn (b/VI-14-1866; d/XI-17-1894) MD LICH 1888. *Med reg NY NJ Conn* 1895: 218. *JAMA* 23:878, 1894.

CARROLL, ALFRED LUDLOW, NYC (b/VIII-3-1833; d/X-30-1893) MD UCNY 1855. *Med reg NY NJ Conn* 1894: 234. *JAMA* 21:746, 1893. *Atkinson* I:211.

CARROLL, GEORGE ATWOOD, USA 1817-18; Md (b/Montgomery Co, Md; d/VII-22-1844) MD UPa 1810. *Med annals Md*: 344. Heitman: *USA*.

CARROLL, GEORGE GREGORY, Rochester NY (d/IX 25-1905) MD Buffalo 1870. *Ill med jour* 8:430, 1905.

CARROLL, JAMES JOSEPH, Washington, DC (b/IV-14-1858; d/XI-5-1899) MD Columbian 1877. *JAMA* 33:1308, 1899. *Hist Med Soc DC*: 340. *Polk* 1890: 244.

CARROLL, JOHN G, Cleveland (d/IX-12-1897 @37) MD W Res 1884. *JAMA* 29:660,1897. *Polk* 1886: 746.

CARROLL, THOMAS, Cincinnati (b/1796? Irel'd; d/III 12-1871 @ 75) MD Transylvania 1826. *Tr O St Med Soc* 1872:263-64. *Med surg rep Phila* 24:262, 1871.

CARROLL, THOMAS JOSEPH, NYC (d/III-10-1889 @ 28) MD UCNY 1885; BS. *Med reg NY NJ Conn* 1889: 269.

CARROLL, THOMAS KING, Jr, Cambridge, Md (d/I-9 1900 @ 78) MD UMd 1846. *JAMA* 34:186, 1900. *Polk* 1886: 441.

CARROLL, WILLIAM EDWARD, Newark, NJ (b/ 1857; d/XII-2-1904) MD CPSNY 1884. *Bost m & s jour* 151: 640, 1904. *Polk* 1896: 942.

CARRUTHERS, WILLIAM H , Northfield, Minn (d/V-1-1894) MD Med Coll Ohio 1878. *JAMA* 22:764, 1894. *Polk* 1890: 612.

CARSCADDEN, RICHARD, York, Neb (d/VII-21-1890) MD Rush 1866. *Med surg rep Phila* 62[?]:214, 1890.

CARSON, EDWARD F , CW-USN (d/VII-1864, Philadelphia) *Nat med jour* 1:291, 1870/71.

CARSON, EDWIN, San Diego, Calif (d/XI-24-1898) MD U Miami 1883. *JAMA* 31: 1490, 1898.

CARSON, JAMES SEYMOUR, Webster, Pa (d/X-17-1893) MD Jefferson 1887. *JAMA* 21:700, 1893.

CARSON, JOHN, Philadelphia (b/XI-12-1752; d/X-26-1794) <MD Edinburgh> *Tr CPP* cent'l vol:215-16.

CARSON, JOSEPH, Philadelphia (b/IV-19-1808; d/XII-30-1876) MD UPa 1830; AB 1826. *Tr CPP* 3s4:xlv, 1879. *Am jour med sci* 73:568-70, 1877. *Tr Med Soc St Pa* 11:712-16, 1877. *K&B* III: 202.

CARSON, WILLIAM, Cincinnati (b/XI-25-1827 Chillicothe; d/VII-9-1893) MD UPa 1850; AB Miami 1849; LLD 1892. *JAMA* 21:94, 1893. *Polk* 1886:741.

CARSON, WILLIAM F , Huntington, Ind (b/XII-7-1853 Springfield, O; d/XI-25-1900) MD Starling 1880. *Tr Ind St Med Soc* 1901: 481. *Polk* 1896: 471.

CARSWELL, W A , Heber, Ark (b/Charleston, SC; d/ IX-8-1886) <MD Med Coll Ga> *New Orl m & s jour* ns14:317-18, 1886. *Polk* 1886: 156.

CARTÉE, CORNELIUS SOULE, Charlestown, Mass (b/VII-28-1806 Providence, RI; d/XII-23-1885) MD Harvard 1849; AB Brown 1825. *Brown hist cat*: 1825.

CARTER, BRIGGS THOMAS, Jefferson, Me (b/III-6-1814; d/IV-6-1874) MD Bowdoin 1845. *Tr Me Med Assoc* 1874-76: 164.

CARTER, CHARLES, Blowing Rock, NC; CW-USN 1861-63; USA 1863-65 (d/IX-9-1898 @ 62 Concordia, Pa) MD CPSNY 1861. *NC med jour* 42:214, 1898. *JAMA* 31:742, 1898. *Polk* 1896: 1120.

CARTER, CYRUS FAULKNER, Boston (b/XII-18-1861 Millbury, Mass; d/VI-14-1893) MD Harvard 1887. *Bost m & s jour* 128: 63, 659, 1893.

CARTER, DANIEL DRAKE, Versailles, Ky (b/X-12-1837; d/XII-12-1886) MD U Louisville 1862. *Butler* 1878: 270. *JAMA* 1:473-74, 1887.

CARTER, DAVID McA , Modoc, Ind (b/1834 Anderson; d/X-14-1893) MD Cincinnati Coll M & S 1859. *JAMA* 21:700, 1893. *Kemper's Indiana*: 213. *Polk* 1890:381.

CARTER, EZRA, Concord, NH (b/XII-27-1798; d/I-28 1879) MD Bowdoin 1824. *Tr NH Med Soc* 1879:161-63.

CARTER, FRANCIS, Columbus, O (b/1814 Ireland; d/ 1881) <MD King's Coll Dublin> *Tr AMA* 33:537-38, 1882.

CARTER, FRANK, Portland, Me (d/VI-23-1875 White Plains NY) MD Bowdoin 1866; ng Brown 1863. *Med reg NY NJ Conn* 1875:196. *Tr Me Med Assn* 1874-76:423.

CARTER, GALEN, NYC (b/VI-19-1795; d/III-2-1870) MD CPSNY 1823; AB Middlebury 1819. *Med reg NY NJ Conn* 1870: 314. *Tr AMA* 21:452-53, 1870. *Phila med reg & dir* 1871: 304. *Med rec* 5:164, 1870/71; 6:94, 1871/72.

CARTER, HERBERT H , Jacksonville, Ill (d/V-24 1899 @28) MD Hahnemann 1895; AB (in Illinois?) *Hahn mo* 34:110 (news & advt), 1899. Homeopath.

CARTER, JOHN CALVIN, Baltimore, Md; CW-USA (d/XII-30-1871) MD UMd 1858. *Med surg rep Phila* 24: 68, 1871.

CARTER, JOHN D, Knoxville,Tenn (d/V-19-1895) MD Jefferson 1868. *Polk* 1890: 1054. *JAMA* 24:861, 1895.

CARTER, JOHN L , Dallas, Tex; CW-CSA (b/IX-3-1833 Scoober PO, Miss; d/ca V-1-1896) MD UPa 1857. *Tex med jour* 11:648, 1895/96. *U Pa med alum CW*:1857. *G P Red*: 171.

CARTER, JOSEPH COLEMAN, Versailles, Ky (b/XII-23-1808 Charlottesville, Va; d/?-26-1875) MD Ohio Med Coll 1832. *Tr Ky St Med Soc* 1877: 195-98.

CARTER, LEWIS WARRINGTON, Richmond Va; CW CSA (b/XII-26-1819 Shirley; d/VIII-6-1888) MD UPa 1844; AB Wm & Mary 1840. *U Pa med alum CW*: 1844.

CARTER, MARION BRYCE, Richmond, Va; CW-CSA; (b/I-6-1836; d/X-28-1902) MD UPa 1859. *U Pa med alum CW*: 1859.

CARTER, MOSES, Concord, NH; Amesbury, Mass (b/1782? d/XI-27-1863 @ 81) MD unknown. *Bost m & s jour* 69:388, 1863.

CARTER, NORRIS M , Brooklyn (b/Ireland; d/VIII-11 1893 @ 52) MD Albany 1859. *JAMA* 21:356, 1893. *Polk* 1886: 644.

CARTER, RALPH, Glastonbury, Conn (b/1790? d/1854 @ 64) Hon MD Yale 1838. *Proc Conn Med Soc* 1855:21.

CARTER, RESTORE C, Cincinnati (d/XI-10-1874 @ 72) MD Med Coll O 1839. *Med s rep Phila* 31:500,1874.

CARTER, ROLLIN BERT, N Bennington, Vt to 1887: Akron, O (b/V-17-1858 Wellington, O; d/XII-23-1905 Cleveland) MD Homeop Hosp Coll Cleveland 1884; AB Ohio Wesleyan 1882. *Tr Am Inst Homeop* 1906: 774-75. *Cleave*. Homeopath.

CARTER, SAMUEL, ?Killingworth, Conn (b/VII-10-1779; d/1853) MD Hon Yale 1822. *Proc Conn Med Soc* ns2:149, 1882-83.

CARTER, THEODORE P , Orangeville, Ind (d/IX-17-1899) MD U Louisville 1858. *JAMA* 33:872, 1899. *Polk* 1890:384.

CARTER, THEOPHILUS RANSOM, Mt Vernon, NY (d/I-23-1906 @ 40) MD CPSNY 1890; AB Yale 1886. *Bost m & s jour* 154:142, 1906. *Polk* 1896: 1033.

CARTER, THERON HARLOW, Boston, Mass (b/X–25 1858 Charlemont; d/X–13–1899) MD Harvard 1895; AB Brown 1895. *Bost m & s jour* 141:400, 1899.

CARTER, W W , ? (d/IX or X–15–1878 Tangipahoa, La) MD unknown. *Tr AMA* 30: 857, 1879. *Med rec* NY 14:360, 1878.

CARTER, WILLIAM FREDERICK, Cohoes, NY (b/III 24–1812 Newburyport, Mass; d/VIII–22–1866) MD Dartmouth 1834. *Tr Med Soc St NY* 1867:442–46.

CARTER, WILLIAM GARDNER, Concord, NH (b/ VIII–8–1838; d/III–7–1904) MD Harvard 1869. *Tr NH Med Soc* 1904: 293–94. *Polk* 1890: 708.

CARTER, WILLIAM T , Louisville (b/Oldham Co; d/IV–11–1896 @ 49) MD Ky Sch Med 1870. *JAMA* 26:794, 1896. *Polk* 1896: 590.

CARTMELL, SIMON MORGAN, Maysville, Ky (d/VIII 4–1896 @ 78) MD UPa 1853. *JAMA* 27:449, 1896. *Polk* 1890: 472.

CARTWRIGHT, SAMUEL ADOLPHUS, Natchez Miss (b/XI–30–1793; d/V–2–1863) Stud "under B Rush." *Tr AMA* 24:345–48, 1873. *Med surg rep Phila* 10:96, 1863. *New Orl m & s jour* 19:432–36, 1866.

CARUTHERS, ROBERT EWING, Allegheny, Pa (b/XII 11–1848; d/I–5–1885 @ 37) MD Hahnemann Phila 1873. *Tr Am Inst Homeop* 1885: 101. *Hahn mo* 20: 127, 1885 (Feb). *Med adv* 15:391, 1885. Homeopath.

CARUTHERS [?CAROTHERS], WILLIAM Mc-DADE, Braddock, Pa (d/IV–12–1903 @ 45) MD UPa 1890; AB Wooster 1887. *Pa med jour* 7:278, 1903/04. *Flint* 1897: 796.

CARVALLO, CARLOS N , Boston; USA (b/Santiago, Chile; d/VII–23–1882) MD Berlin 1862. *Hist Med Soc DC*:276. *Butler* 1878: iv.

CARY, GEORGE, Houlton, Me; CW–USA (b/VIII–29–1839; d/XI–29–1899) MD CPSNY 1866; AB Bowdoin 1860. *JAMA* 33:1509, 1632, 1899. *Polk* 1896:636.

CARY, ROBERT HOWARD, Chelsea, Masss (b/1794? d/X–26–1867) MD Harvard 1820; AB 1816. *Bost m & s jour* 77:280, 1867.

CARY, WALES LEWIS, Brooklyn (b/II–13–1861 Boston; d/V–16–1890) MD LICH 1884. *Med reg NY NJ Conn* 1890: 263; 1891: 270.

CARY, WALKER, Buffalo (b/c1812; d/1881 Marseilles, Fr) MD UPa 1843. *Chic med rev* 4:520, 1881. *Buff med & surg jour* 21:190–91, 1881. *Butler* 1878: 537.

CARY, ZENAS, Albany, NY; Troy 1822– (b/VII–1787 Putney,Vt; d/V–11–1863) Lic Albany Co Med Soc 1813; ng CPSNY 1811–12. *Tr Med Soc St NY* 1863:389–91.

CASE, AUGUSTUS ROCKWELL, Forestville, Conn (d/IX–20–1872 @ 66) MD Castleton 1832. *Med surg rep Phila* 27: 332, 1872.

CASE, BENJAMIN WAITE, Newport, RI (d/1834) Hon AM Brown 1798. *Tr RI Med Soc* 1: 55, 1859–77.

CASE, DON CARLOS, Ocean Springs, Miss (b/1819 Liverpool, Engl; d/I–7–1886) MD Med Coll St Louis 1849. *New Orl m & s jour* ns13:664 1886. *Polk* 1886: 530.

CASE, IDA RACHEL GRIDLEY, Collinsville, Conn (b/ XI–3–1862 Canton; d/III–9–1904 as IRG) MD CPS Boston 1889; AB Wesleyan 1885. *Proc Conn Med Soc* 1904: 525–27.

CASE, MARY W , Troy, NY (d/VIII–19–1889) MD Woman's Med Coll Pa 1881. *Med reg NY NJ Conn* 1890: 263. *Med surg rep Phila* 61:251, 1889. *Tr NY St Med Soc* 11: 741 ff.

CASE, NATHAN, Riegelsville, NJ (b/III–17–1845 Pattenburgh; d/IV–27–1890) MD UCNY 1869. *Lehigh Valley med mag* 2:7, 1890–91. *Butler* 1878: 467.

CASEY, SAMUEL HARD, Oneonta, NY (b/XII–14–1808; d/I–10–1892) MD Fairfield 1829. *Med reg NY NJ Conn* 1892: 273. *JAMA* 18: 374, 1892. *Polk* 1886: 700.

CASE, THEODORE S , Kansas City, Mo (b/1832 Ga; d/ II–16–1900) MD Starling 1856. *JAMA* 34:573, 1900. *Polk* 1886: 550.

CASE, WILLIAM ELLICOTT, Morrisville, Pa (d/III–16–1894) MD UPa 1854. *Lehigh Valley med mag* 5:169, 1893–94. *Butler* 1878: 706.

CASEY, JOSEPH DANIEL, Latrobe, Pa (b/IV–1–1869; d/VIII–22–1903) MD Jefferson 1902. *Pa med jour* 7:278, 1903/04. *Flint* 1897: 807.

CASEY, NEWTON R , Mound City, Ill (d/VI–6–1899 @ 73) MD St Louis Med Coll 1857. *JAMA* 32: 1460, 1899. *Polk* 1896:430.

CASEY, WILLIAM BRYAN, Middletown, Conn (b/XII–28–1815; d/III–26–1870) MD UPa 1837; AB Columbia 1834. *Phila med reg & dir* 1871:304. *Proc Conn Med Soc* 1870: 403/05.

CASH, MERIT H , Wawayanda, NY (b/VII–20–1802; d/ IV–26–1861) Lic Med Soc Co NY 1825; Hon MD Reg NYU 1859. *Tr Med Soc St NY* 1862:445–47. *Tr AMA* 14:197–98, 1864. *Buff m & s jour* 1: 237, 1862.

CASON, EDWARD ASHLEY, La Grange, Ga (b/IX–1–1870 Jewells, Ga; d/IX–16–1897) MD Bellevue 1891. *JAMA* 29:709, 1897. *Polk* 1896: 334.

CASPARI, EDWARD, West Grove, Pa 1835– ; Louisville, Ky 1846– ; Norfolk, Va (b/Prussia; d/III–5–1870 @ 61) <MD Allentown Acad> *Western homeop obs* 7:128, 1871. *Hahn mo* 5:372, 1869/70. *Am hom obs* 7:256, 1870. *King* I:150, 174, 286. Homeopath.

CASS, NATHAN, Cameron, Tex (d/VIII–21–1906) MD Tulane 1882. *Tex st m jour* 2:168, 1906/07. *Polk* 1886:882.

CASSADY, FELIX F , Philadelphia (d/VIII–3–1904 @ 63) MD Jefferson 1867. *Pa med jour* 8:334, 1904/05. *JAMA* 43:558, 1904.

CASSELBERRY, ISAAC, Evansville, Ind; CW–USA; (b/XI–26–1821 Posey Co; d/VII–9–1873) MD Med Coll Ohio 1845. *Tr Ind St Med Soc* 1874:179–81. *Tr AMA* 26:463–64, 1875. *Kemper's Indiana*: 249.

CASSELBERRY, JESSE ROBERTS, Hazelton, Pa (b/ 1832? d/X–4–1892) MD Jefferson 1856. *Lehigh Valley* *med mag* 4:36, 1892–93. *Butler* 1878: 707.

CASSIDY, HUGH THOMAS, ?NYC (b/NYC; d/X–8–1888 @ 34) MD CPSNY 1887; att Xavier Coll. *Med reg NY NJ Conn* 1889: 269.

CASSIDY, PATRICK, Lancaster, Pa; CW–USA (d/VII–12–1864) MD Jefferson 1837. *Med surg rep Phila* 12: 68, 1864. *Nat med jour* 1:291, 1870/71. *Practitioner*, Lancaster 1:60–61, 1883.

CASTLE, ANDREW, New Haven Co, Conn (d/VIII–26–1861 @58) MD Yale 1825 *Proc Conn Med Soc* 1:67 app.

CASTLE, FREDERICK A, NYC (b/IV–29–1842 Fabius, NY; d/IV–28–1902) MD Bellevue 1866. *Bost m & s jour* 146:503, 1902. *Atkinson* I:320. *Polk* 1896: 1045.

CASTNER, JOHN DAVIS, Newark, NJ; Brooklyn (d/XI 13–1896 @ 27) MD UCNY 1893. *JAMA* 28:41, 1897. *Polk* 1896: 942.

CASTON, WILLIAM, Corsicana, Tex; Spokane, Wash; Denver, Colo (b/Hinds Co, Miss; d/IV–27–1896) MD Ky Sch Med 1880; stud Bart's London, 1883; Manhattan Eye & Ear, 1885–86. *Tex med jour* 11:648, 1895–96. *Polk* 1896: 1423.

CASWELL, EDWARD THOMAS, Providence, RI (b/IX 11–1833; d/IV–17–1887) MD Jefferson 1859; AB Brown 1803. *Bost m & s jour* 116:392, 438, 462, 1887; 117:616, 1887. *Tr RI Med Soc* 3:477, 1883–88.

CASWELL, JESSE, (b/IV–17–1809 Middletown, Vt; d/IX–25–1848 Bangkok, Siam) Stud Woodstock 1835; AB Middlebury 1832; att? Andover & Lane Theol Sem's. *Waite's Woodstock*, app.

CASWELL, WILLIAM, Brooklyn (d/XII–8–1893 @ 62) MD unknown. *JAMA* 21:936, 1893.

CATES, CHARLES BUNKER, Fall River, Mass 1845–47; Vassalboro, Me 1847–86 (b/IX–19–1820 Vassalboro; d/I–10–1888 Santa Monica, Calif) MD Jefferson 1845; ng Bowdoin Med Sch 1844. *Bowdoin cat*: 1844 med. *Polk* 1886: 425.

CATHCART, THOMAS LATIMER, York, Pa; Shepherdstown, W Va (b/VII–18–1807; d/X–28–1881) MD Jefferson 1830; AB Dickinson 1826. *Tr Med Soc Pa* 14: 391, 1882.

CATHERWOOD, THOMAS L , Shelbyville, Ill (b/VII–5–1827 Abington, Va; d/III–18–1906) MD Miami 1870. *Ill med jour* 9:464, 1906. *Polk* 1886: 297.

CATLETT, GEORGE CALMES, St Louis; CW–CSA; (b/VI–20–1830 Christian Co, Ky; d/V–19–1886 St Joseph) MD UPa 1851. *Atkinson* I:294–95. *New Orl m & s jour* ns13:1008, 1886. *Med surg rep Phila* 54:800, 1886. *Butler* 1878: 425.

CATLETT, HENRY C , Hickman, Ky (b/1812; d/1878) <MD U Louisville> *Trans AMA* 30:857, 1879.

CATLIN, ARCHIBALD M , Rockford, Ill (d/IX– –1892 @ 91) MD Fairfield 1827; ng Castleton 1825. *JAMA* 19:324–25, 1892. *Polk* 1886: 295.

CATLIN, BENJAMIN HOPKINS, Meriden, Conn (b/VIII–10–1801 Harwinton; d/II–18–1880) Hon MD Yale 1840. *Med surg rep Phila* 42:220, 1880. *Tr AMA* 33:538–39, 1882. *Proc Conn Med Soc* 1880: 164.

CATLIN, GEORGE EDWIN, Lake Geneva, Wis (b/III–19–1840 Catlin Hollow, Pa; d/VII–29–1898) MD Detroit Med Coll 1870. *Tr Wis St Med Soc* 33:517–18, 1899. *JAMA* 31:484, 1898. *Polk* 1896: 1552.

CATLIN, SAMUEL, CW–USA (d/XI–27–1866 New Orleans) MD Yale 1851 [?] *Nat med jour* 1:292, 1870/71.

CATLIN, THOMAS GILES, Youngstown, NY (b/1808 Burlington, Vt; d/III–10–1874 Brooklyn) Lic St Lawrence Co Med Soc 1830. *Med reg NY NJ Conn* 1874:271.

CATOR, HARVEY HULL, Syracuse, NY 1842–; Camden, NJ (b/VII–13–1815 Roxbury, NY; d/II–21–1882) MD Geneva 1840. *Tr Am Inst Homeop* 1884: 652. Homeopath 1842– .

CATTANACH, ANDREW J , Denver, Colo (d/V–30–1896 @ 49) MD McGill 1871. *Tr Colo St Med Soc* 1898–99: 509. *Polk* 1893: 233.

CATTELL, SAMUEL GILMORE, Deerfield, NJ (d/II–12–1877 @ 45) MD UPa 1855. *Tr AMA* 28: 627, 1877. *Tr Med Soc NJ* 1877: [127].

CATTO, WILLIAM MASON, Decatur, Ill (b/1858 Bothwell, Ont; d/I–27–1899) MD Mich Coll Med 1882. *JAMA* 32: 263, 1899. *Tr Ill St Med Soc* 49:27, 1899. *Polk* 1886: 301.

CAUSTEN, JAMES HYMAN Jr, Washington, DC (b/VII– –1818 Baltimore; d/X–3/5–1856) MD Columbian DC 1842. *Hist Med Soc DC*: 234.

CAVANAUGH, JAMES, Easton, Pa (d/VI–27/28–1897 @ 67) MD UPa 1850. *JAMA* 29:92, 1897.

CAVANAUGH, JAMES JOSEPH Jr, Easton, Pa (d/VIII–8–1893 @ 31) MD Bellevue 1884. *Lehigh Valley med mag* 5:59, 1893–94.

CAWLEY, THOMAS FRANKLIN, Saylorsburg, Pa (d/I 28–1904 @ 43) MD Bellevue 1880. *Pa med jour* 8:334, 1904/05.

CAYWOOD, JAMES BENNETT, Brooklyn (b/X– –1864; d/IV–13–1887) MD Bellevue 1886. *Med reg NY NJ Conn* 1887:255.

CECCARINI, GIOVANNI, NYC (d/XII–3–1888 Riccione, Italy) <MD Rome 1846> *Med reg NY NJ Conn* 1890: 263. *Butler* 1878: 496.

CECIL, THOMAS WITTEN, CW–CSA (b/II–22–1826 Tazewell CH, Va; d/XII–16–1868 Springfield, Mo) MD UPa 1858. *U Pa med alum CW*: 1858.

CENAS, AUGUSTUS HENRY, New Orleans (b/VIII–27 1808; d/I–10–1878) MD UPa 1830. *New Orl m & s jour* ns5: 736–37, 1878. *Atkinson* I: 135.

CENTARO, VINCENT, Chicago (d/IV–15–1901) <MD Naples 1880> *Ill med jour* ns3:47, 1901. *Polk* 1896:378.

CERNEA, ARTHUR B de, Philadelphia (d/VI–30–1883 @ 78) MD UPa 1831. *Med surg rep Phila* 49: 56, 1883.

CHABERT, ROMEO FELIX, Hoboken, NJ (b/1828 London; d/VIII–1–1904 Asbury Park, NJ) MD UCNY 1856. *Bost m & s jour* 151:228, 1904. *Polk* 1896: 937.

Spec. educ'l status abbrev. as: ***ng*** = college verified attendance without degree;

CHACE, DAVID E, NYC (d/II-2-1887 @41) MD U Buffalo 1868. *Med reg NY NJ Conn* 1887: 255.

CHADBOURNE, FRANCIS WATTS, Lowell Mass (b/X 23-1843 Kennebunk, Me; d/VIII-21-1902 @ 58) MD Bowdoin 1869. *Bost m & s jour* 147:256, 1902.

CHADBOURNE, THOMAS, Concord, NH (b/1791 Conway; d/IV-29-1864) MD Dartmouth 1813. *Bost m & s jour* 70:328, 1864: 4; 1872: 81-85.

CHADSEY, ALONZO GIDLEY, NYC (d/VII-15-1881) MD CPSNY 1875. *Med reg NY NJ Conn* 1882: 223.

CHADSEY, ALONZO J, NYC (d/VIII-29-1888 @ 84) MD Fairfield 1831. *Med reg NY NJ Conn* 1889: 269.

CHADWICK, GEORGE H, Portland, Me (b/VII-13-1831; d/II-25-1888) MD Albany 1857; AB Dartmouth 1854. *Tr Me Med Assoc* 1889: 170-71. *Butler* 1874: 305.

CHADWICK, JAMES READ, Boston (b/XI-2-1844; d/IX-24-1905 Chocorua, NH) MD Harvard 1871; AB 1865. *Bost m & s jour* 153:376, 1905. *Med annals Md*: 345. *K&B* III: 206-07.

CHADWICK, PAYSON MARTIN, Omaha, Nebr (d/VI-11-1898) MD U Vt 1875; MD UCNY 1876. *JAMA* 30:1534, 1898.

CHAFFEE, CALVIN CLIFFORD, Utica, NY (b/VIII-28-1811 Saratoga; d/VIII-8-1836) MD Woodstock 1835; Hon AM Amherst 1856. *JAMA* 27:449, 1896. *Butler* 1878: 347 [Springfield, Mass].

CHAFFEE, CHARLES W, Chicago (d/XI-21-1884) MD U Mich 1865. *Chic med jour* 50:267, 1885. *Butler* 1878:130.

CHAFFEE, HEMAN C, Tolono, Ill (d/V-21-1900 @ 84) MD Albany 1854. *JAMA* 34:1505, 1900. *Ill med jour* ns2(2):93, 1900. *Polk* 1896: 443.

CHAISTY, EDWARD J, Baltimore (b/XII-22-1813; d/VIII-16-1882) MD UMd 1837. *Med annals Md*: 336. *Butler* 1874: 311,

CHALKLEY, CHARLES H, Richmond, Va (b/VIII--1860; d/IX-13-1896) MD Med Coll Va 1880. *Tr Med Soc Va* 1897:255-56, 268. *JAMA* 27:721, 1896. *Med bull med & surg* 18: 430.

CHALLEN, JOSEPH, Lexington; Cincinnati (b/Lexington; d/VI-11-1833 @30) MD Transylvania 1827. *Transylvania jour med & assoc sci* 6:305, 1833.

CHALMERS, HENRY C, Springfield, Va; CW-CSA (b/VII-20-1837; d/II-7-1865) MD UCNY 1859; stud U Va 1854-56. Blanton: *CSA surg*: 397. Johnson's *UVa mem'l alum d/CW*: 754.

CHALMERS, THOMAS C, NYC (b/VI-18-1810 W Galway, NY; d/VI-4-1884) MD CPSNY 1835; AB Union 1831. *Med reg NY NJ Conn* 1885: 231. *Bost m & s jour* 110:571,1884. *Med surg rep Phila* 51:28,1884.

CHAMBERLAIN, ABRAM, Brooklyn; Susquehanna Co, Pa (d/III-21-1905 @ 74) Lic Susq. Co Med Soc. *Pa med jour* 8:546, 1904/05. *Polk* 1896:270.

CHAMBERLAIN, CHARLES H, Barre, Vt, 1863-(d/II-22-1881) MD Hahnemann Phila 1863. *Tr Am Inst Homeop* 1895: 1093. Homeopath.

CHAMBERLAIN, CHARLES WALTER, Hartford, Conn (b/VII-22-1844; d/VIII-21-1884) MD CPSNY 1871; AB Brown 1867. *Med reg NY NJ Conn* 1885: 231. *Proc Conn Med Soc* 1885:204-10. *Bost m & s jour* III:264, 1884. *Butler* 1878: 75.

CHAMBERLAIN, CYRUS NATHANIEL, Greenwich, Mass (b/III-8-1829 W Barnstable; d/VII-18-1899 Jamaica Plain) MD Woodstock 1850. *Bost m & s jour* 141:99, 1899. *K&B* II:204.

CHAMBERLAIN, DAVID CLEVELAND, Sudbury, Vt; Leroy, NY (b/I-8-1815 Quebec; d/VI-4-1896 Detroit) MD Castleton 1837. *JAMA* 26:1244, 1896.

CHAMBERLAIN, DAVID TAYLOR PARKER, Dover, NH (b/XI-21-1846 Lebanon, Conn; d/VII-21-1892) MD Bowdoin 1872. *Bost m & s jour* 127:100, 1892. *Tr NH Med Soc* 1893: 159-60.

CHAMBERLAIN [CHAMBERLIN], DWIGHT S, Lyons, NY; CW-USA (d/V-11-1903 @ 65) MD UCNY 1862. *Bost m & s jour* 148:572, 1903.

CHAMBERLAIN, GEORGE J, Dunmore, Pa (b/Pa; d/VII-2-1906 @ 91) MD Pa Med Coll 1850. *Pa med jour* 9:745, 105/06. *Flint* 1897: 800.

CHAMBERLAIN, JAMES N, Waterloo, Ind (b/III-22-1822 Cayuga Co, NY; d/II-6-1896) MD Cleveland Med Coll 1849. *Tr Ind St Med Soc* 1896:265-66. *Polk* 1896:496.

CHAMBERLAIN, MYRON NEWTON, Cheshire, Conn (b/1836 New Haven; d/I-10-1899) MD Yale 1857. *Proc Conn Med Soc* 1899: 365-67. *JAMA* 32:198, 1899. *Atkinson* I:407. *Polk* 1896: 277.

CHAMBERLAIN, NATHAN SAVERY, Marlborough, Mass (d/X-31-1884 @ 39) MD Harvard 1866. *Bost m & s jour* 111:456, 1884.

CHAMBERLAIN, SAMUEL B, Lawrenceburg Ind 1864- (b/1825 Northamp'shire, Engl; d/VIII-23-1897) Lic yrs pract. *Tr Ind St Med Soc* 1898:389. *Polk* 1886:329.

CHAMBERLAIN, WILLIAM, Moorestown, NJ (b/XI-27-1851 Crosswicks, NJ; d/XII-15-1893) MD UPa 1877. *Tr Med Soc NJ* 1894: 266.

CHAMBERLAIN, WILLIAM BAKER, Worcester, Mass; Keene, NH (b/IX-15-1827 Loudon; d/IV-19-1889) MD Cleveland Homeop 1854; ng Dartmouth Med Sch. *Tr Am Inst Homeop* 1890: 144. *Cleave*. Homeopath.

CHAMBERLAIN, WILLIAM HENRY, Oneida, NY (d/V-21-1900) MD UCNY 1875. *JAMA* 34:1505, 1900.

CHAMBERLAIN, WILLIAM MELLEN, NYC; CW-Sanitary Comm (b/X- 10-1826 Hanover NH; d/X-31-1887) MD Dartmouth 1853; AB 1845. *Med reg NY NJ Conn* 1888: 243. *Bost m & s jour* 117:464, 1887. *Tr Med Soc St NY* 1888: 564-568. *Atkinson* I: 228.

CHAMBERLAINE, JOSEPH E M, Easton, Pa (b/II-18-1826 Clora's Pt, Md; d/I-30-1901) MD UMd 1849. *Pa med jour* 5:296, 1901/02. *Med annals Md*: 346.

CHAMBERLAYNE, C EUGENE, Middleburg, Va (d/III-12-1899 @ 52) MD UMd 1875. *JAMA* 32:733, 1899. *Polk* 1886: 921.

CHAMBERLAYNE, LEWIS WEBB, Richmond, Va (b/I 9-1798 King Wm Co, Va; d/I-28-1854 Henrico Co, Va) MD UPa 1817. *Nashville jour med & surg* 6:271, 1854.

CHAMBERLIN, DE WITT CLINTON, Richmond, Me (b/III-12-1829; d/X-30-1870) MD Bowdoin 1852. *Trans Me Med Assoc* 1871-73: 186.

CHAMBERLIN, JOSIAH ADAMS, Manchester, NH; Washington, DC (b/III- -1833 Acton, Mass; d/IX-27-1868) MD Georgetown 1863. *Hist Med Soc DC*: 266.

CHAMBERLIN, PHELPS, San Francisco, Calif (b/Vermont; d/X-19-1877) MD St Louis Med Coll 1852. *Trans Calif St Med Soc* 1877-78: 240.

CHAMBERS, E W, Bentonville, Ark (d/IX-7-1886 @ 54) MD unknown. *Med adv* 16: 1887 (May). *Polk* 1886: 155. Homeopath.

CHAMBERS, JACOB, Kingston, NY (b/1851; d/IX-15-1904 @ 52) MD Buffalo 1875. *Bost m & s jour* 151: 338, 1904. *Polk* 1896: 1028.

CHAMBERS, JOHN E, Chicago (d/XI-24-1895) MD Jefferson 1877. *JAMA* 25:968, 1895. *Polk* 1890: 310.

CHAMBERS, JOHN TUCKER, Meridian, Va (b/V-15-1856 Dinwiddie Co, Va; d/I-19-1897) MD UPa 1877. *Tr Med Soc Va* 1897: 268. *Flint* 1897: 940.

CHAMBERS, MARTIN LUTHER, Port Jefferson, NY (d/VI-12-1905 @ 62) MD UCNY 1871. *Bost m & s jour* 152: 740, 1905. *Polk* 1896: 1091.

CHAMBERS, PASCAL H, Lexington,Mo (b/II-6-1824 Louisville, Ky; d/XII-22-1896) MD Louisville 1850; AB Miami 1845. *U Miami cat*: 1845. *Polk* 1886: 553.

CHAMBERS, WILLIAM MORTIMER, Sr, Charleston, Ill (b/IV-11-1814 Cynthiana, Ky; d/XI-12-1892) MD Transylvania 1846. *Tr Ill St Med Soc* 1893: 47-8. *Polk* 1890: 304.

CHAMPION, CHARLES STRATTON, Woodstown, NJ (b/XII-17-1842 Haddonfield; d/V-16-1876) MD UPa 1865. *Tr AMA* 28:625, 1877. *Tr Med Soc NJ* 1876: [128].

CHANCE, PERRY, Delano, Minn (b/IX-8-1834 Alliance, O; d/XI-19-1871) MD Charity Hosp Cleveland 1869. *Tr Minn St Med Soc* 1872: 118. *Tr AMA* 23:592-93, 1872.

CHANCELLOR, JAMES EDGAR, Charlottesville, Va (b/I-26-1826; d/IX-11-1896) MD Jefferson 1848. *Tr Med Soc Va* 1897:268. *JAMA* 27:721, 1896. *K&B* III:208-09.

CHANDLER, CHARLES, Chandlersville, Ill (b/VII-2-1806 Woodstock, Conn; d/IV-7-1879) MD Castleton 1829. *Tr Ill St Med Soc* 1879: 293.

CHANDLER, CHARLES BUCKLEY, Montpelier, Vt (b/IV-24-1796 Chelsea, Vt; d/I-8-1867) ng Castleton 1821. *Tr Vt Med Soc* 1883:104.

CHANDLER, CHARLES MARCELLUS, Montpelier; CW-USA (b/VII-1-1827 Tunbridge; d/III-19-1889) MD Harvard 1854; ng Castleton 1850. *Harvard in CW*: 241. *Polk* 1886: 905.

CHANDLER, CHARLES P, Addison, Me (b/XII-3-1824 Columbia Falls; d/II-22-1889) <MD Harvard 1848> *Tr Me Med Assoc* 1890:339-40. *Butler* 1878: 305. *Polk* 1886:423.

CHANDLER, GEORGE, Worcester, Mass (d/V-17-1893 @ 87) MD Yale 1831; AB Union 1829. *Bost m & s jour* 128:532, 1893. *Polk* 1886: 476.

CHANDLER, JOHN LOCKE, St Albans, Vt; CW-USA (b/III-4-1793 Powlet; d/V-24-1883) MD Castleton 1826. *Tr Vt Med Soc* 1883: 104. *Atkinson* I:334. *Butler* 1874: 774.

CHANDLER, JOSEPH A, Warsaw, Ind; CW-USA (d/VII-18-1901 @ 73) MD unknown. *JAMA* 37:276, 1901. *Polk* 1886: 328.

CHANDLER, THOMAS HENDERSON, Boston (d/VIII 27-1895) Hon MD Harvard 1872. *Bost m & s jour* 133:280, 1895.

CHANDLER, THOMAS KNOWLTON, CW-USN (d/II 5-1867 St Thomas, WI) MD CPSNY 1862. *Tr AMA* 18: 360, 1867. *Nat med jour* 1:292, 1870/71.

CHANDLER, WILLIAM S, ?Hopkinton, Vt (d/VII-18 -1884 @ 74) MD unknown. *Med surg rep Phila* 51:280, 1885.

CHANNELL, JAMES CLARK, CW-USA; Wrightsville, Pa (b/XI-11-1843 Fawn Twp, Pa; d/V-19-1903) MD UPa 1871. *Pa med jour* 7:278, 1903/04. *U Pa med alum CW*: 1871. *Flint* 1897: 840.

CHANNING, WALTER, Brookline, Mass (b/IV-5-1786 Newport, RI; d/VII-21-1879) MD Harvard ad eundem 1812; stud Phila, Edinb, Lond; AB Harvard 1808. *Bost m & s jour* 105:519-20,1881. *K&B* III:209-10.

CHAPEL, SANFORD W, Patchogue,NY (d/III-15-1884 c60) MD Buffalo 1851. *Med reg NY NJ Conn* 1885: 231.

CHAPIN, ALONZO, Winchester, Mass (b/II-24-1805 W Springfield; d/XII-25-1876) MD UPa 1831; AB Amherst 1826. *Tr AMA* 32:498-99, 1881.

CHAPIN, CORNELIUS A, CW-USA (d/IX-14-1863 NYC) MD UVt 1863. *Nat med jour* 1:292, 1870/71.

CHAPIN, CYRENIUS, Buffalo (b/II-7-1729; d/II-20-1838) MD unknown. *Buff med & surg jour* 7: 120+ 1868.

CHAPIN, EDWARD ROCKWELL, Brattleboro, Vt (b/I 1-1827 Chapinville, Conn; d/XII-7-1886) MD CPSNY 1842; att Yale Coll. *Med reg NY NJ Conn* 1887: 256.

CHAPIN, HENRY CLARK, Lincoln, Mass (d/X-31-1896 @ 81) MD Berkshire 1840. *Bost m & s jour* 135:480, 1896. *JAMA* 27:1169, 1896 (as of Lincoln Nebr). *Polk* 1886: 468 (Lincoln, Mass).

CHAPIN, JOSHUA BICKNELL, ? (b/VIII-19-1814 Hillsboro, NH; d/VI-7-1881) MD Berkshire 1838; AB Brown 1835. *Brown hist cat*: 1835.

CHAPIN, REUBEN SPENCER, NYC (d/VIII-2-1879) Lic NY St Med Soc 1849; Hon MD ? 1864. *Med surg rep Phila* 42:198, 1879. *Med reg NY NJ Conn* 1880: 234.

Spec. educ'l status abbrev. as: ***ng*** = college verified attendance without degree;

Med rec NY 16:143,1879. *Butler* 1874: 496.

CHAPIN, SAMUEL L , Saybrook, Ill (d/VIII-18-1904 @ 83 [?]) MD Jefferson 1885. *JAMA* 43:686, 1904. *Polk* 1886: 297.

CHAPIN, SYDNEY HERBERT, NYC (d/VII-26-1890) MD Bellevue 1873. *Med reg NY NJ Conn* 1891:280.

CHAPLIN, CHARLES FOSTER, Cambridgeport, Mass (d/VIII-17-1857 @ 57) MD Harvard 1829. *Bost m & s jour* 57:67, 1857.

CHAPMAN, CLARENCE ROGERS, Medina NY (d/VII 8-1899 @ 84 [?]) MD UCNY 1890. *JAMA* 33: 302, 1899.*Polk* 1896: 1031.

CHAPMAN, EDWIN NESBIT, Brooklyn (b/II-26-1819; d/III-2-1888) MD Yale 1842; MD Jefferson 1845. *Med reg NY NJ Conn* 1888: 244. *Atkinson* I: 379.

CHAPMAN, FRANK BOWDITCH, Middleton, Mass (d/VI-11-1897 @ 29) MD Dartmouth 1894; AB 1892. *Bost m & s jour* 137:640. *Polk* 1894:718.

CHAPMAN, HENRY D , Spencer, W Va (b/1799? d/III-12-1870 @ 71) MD Berkshire 1823. *Phila med reg & dir* 1871: 304. *Tr AMA* 21:483-84, 1870.

CHAPMAN, JAMES, CW-USA; Medina, NY (d/I or II-27-1901 @ 77) MD UCNY 1852. *Tr Med Soc St NY* 1901: [426]. *Polk* 1886: 667.

CHAPMAN, JOHN S , Plainfield, NJ (b/1826 Md; d/VII-15-1871) MD UMd 1847. *Hist Med Soc DC*: 269. *Med annals Md*: 347.

CHAPMAN, NATHANIEL, Philadelphia (b/V-28-1780 Fairfax Co, Va; d/VII-1-1853) MD UPa 1801. *Med examiner* ns9: 571-73, 1853. *Bost m & s jour* 40: 216-19, 242-43, 1849. *Phila med reg & dir* 2: 60, 76, 1853. Gross, *Am med biogr*. *Tr CPP* cent vol:216. *K&B* III:213.

CHAPMAN, NATHANIEL, Washington, DC (b/VIII-26 1842 Charles Co, Md; d/VIII-16-1898) MD UMd 1872. *JAMA* 31:551, 1898. *Med annals Md*: 347-48. *Polk* 1896: 301.

CHAPMAN, SAMUEL EDWARD, New Bern, NC (b/1807; d/1862) <MD UCNY 1847>; AB UNC 1826. *UNC cat*: 1826.

CHAPMAN, SHERMAN HARTWELL, New Haven, Conn (b/II-22-1846; d/IV-16-1903) MD CPSNY 1869; AB Yale 1866. *Proc Conn Med Soc* 1903: 408-14. *Polk* 1896: 282.

CHAPMAN, THOMAS LUCE, Longmeadow, Mass (d/VIII-20-1889 @72) MD Berkshire 1841. *Bost m & s jour* 121: 220,645, 1889. *Butler* 1878:348.

CHAPPELL, JOHN R , Petersburg, Va (d/IX-26-1898 @ 70) MD UPa 1877. *JAMA* 31:872, 1898. *NC med jour* 42:284, 1898. *Polk* 1896:1497.

CHAPPELLIER, FRANCIS, Natchez, Miss (b/I-1-1805 France; d/XI-20-1851) MD Paris 1838. *New Orl m & s jour* 11:574, 1855.

CHARBONNET, J NUMA, New Orleans (d/VII-23-1899 @ 33) MD Tulane 1887. *New Orl m & s jour* 52: 165, 1899. *JAMA* 33:367, 1899. *Polk* 1896: 620.

CHARLES, JOSEPH, USPH & MarServ; Newport News, Va, 1881- (b/I-19-1853 Hagerstown, Md; d/XII-12-1902) MD CPS Balto 1882; U Mich Med Sch ng 1880. *Tr Med Soc Va* 1903:269-70. *Bost m & s jour* 147:724, 1902. *Polk* 1900: 1768.

CHARLTON, ROBERT, Indianapolis,Ind; CW-USA (d/IV-21-1865 @32, Pleasant, Ind) MD U Mich 1856. *Tr Ind St Med Soc* 1866:9. *Kemper's Indiana*: 190.

CHARLTON, SAMUEL H , Seymour, Ind (b/XI-1-1826 Jefferson Co; d/I-12-1897) MD U Louisville 1871. *Tr Ind St Med Soc* 1897: 353. *JAMA* 28:284, 379, 1897. *Bost m & s jour* 136:196, 1897. *Polk* 1896: 490.

CHARLTON, SAMUEL TEMPLETON, NYC to 1852; Water St, Pa; Harrisburg (b/VII-25-1825 New Berlin, Pa; d/XI-9-1886) MD UCNY 1850; AB Jefferson 1846. *Hahn mo* 21:832, 1886. *Med vis* 3:41, 1887. *Tr Homeop Med Soc St Pa* 1887:? *Polk* 1886: 801. Homeopath.

CHARLTON, WILLIAM S , Philadelphia (d/II-2-1904 @ 58) MD UPa 1883. *Pa med jour* 8:334, 1904/05. *Polk* 1896: 1300.

CHASE, ABNER F . Philadelphia (d/IV-2-1898 @60) MD Jefferson 1874. *JAMA* 30:933, 1898. *Polk* 1896: 1300.

CHASE, BYRON S , CW-USA; Akron, O (b/I-8-1834 Jamaica, Vt; d/II-23-1878) MD U Mich 1860. *Tr O St Med Soc* 1878: 195-96.

CHASE, CHARLES, USN (b/1793? d/III-8-1877 Brooklyn) MD unknown. *Med reg NY NJ Conn* 1877:200.

CHASE, CHARLES, Deerfield, NH; Fayette Co, Ky 1862- (b/XII-14-1822 Cornish, NH; d/II-16-1892) MD Dartmouth 1850. *Tr NH Med Soc* 1864: 62-63.

CHASE, CHARLES EDMUND, Woburn, Mass (b/VI-25 1849 Deerfield, NH; d/XII-26-1902) MD UVt 1873. *Bost m & s jour* 148:108, 1903. *Polk* 1896: 727.

CHASE, CHARLES T , Brooklyn, NY (d/XI-5-1894 @ 63) MD Jefferson 1850. *Med reg NY NJ Conn* 1895:218. *JAMA* 23:768,802, 1894. *Butler* 1878: 530.

CHASE, DURFEE, Palmyra, NY (b/I-24-1793 Swansea, Mass; d/I-10-1872) MD Hahnemann Phila 1852; <MD "in NY" 1818> *Tr Mass Inst Homeop* 1895: 1094. *Tr Homeop Soc NY* 9:630. Homeopath 1840- .

CHASE, EDWARD WEBB, Omaha, Nebr (b/III-18-1860 Windham, Me; d/X-6-1899) MD Bowdoin 1886; AB 1883. *JAMA* 33:1661: 1899. *Polk* 1896: 906.

CHASE, ELI AYER, Brockton, Mass (d/X-3-1905 @ 58) MD LICH 1872. *Bost m & s jour* 153: 405, 1905. *Polk* 1896: 708.

CHASE, ENOCH, Milwaukee, Wis (b/I-16-1809 Derby, Vt; d/VIII-23-1892) MD Dartmouth 1831. *Med bull med & surg* 14:494, 1892.

CHASE, FRANCIS H , Kalamazoo, Mich (d/III-31-1899 @80) MD Berkshire 1840. *JAMA* 32:845, 1899.*Polk* 1886: 496.

CHASE, FREEMAN HERSEY, Bangor Me; CW-USA (b/IX-2-1838 Lincoln; d/VI-11-1901) MD Bowdoin

1866;AB 1859. *JAMA* 37:275,1901. *Polk* 1886:423.

CHASE, HENRY MELVILLE, Lawrence, Mass (b/VI–13–1838 Bristol, NH; d/VI–15–1903) MD Dartmouth 1864. *Bost m & s jour* 149:56, 1903. *Polk* 1886: 468.

CHASE, JAMES WILLIAM, Philadelphia (d/X–7–1859 @ 21) MD Pa Med Coll 1859. *Med surg rep Phila* ns3:92, 1859/60.

CHASE, LYMAN, Me & NH 1848–65 (as minister); Kennebunkport, Me 1878–85; Wells 1885- (as physician] (b/III–27–1821 Bridgton; d/XI–25–1894 Wellsbranch [?] Me) MD Dartmouth 1846; AB Colby 1843. *New Engl med gaz* 30: 1895 (June). *Polk* 1886: 426. Homeopath.

CHASE, PRESTON MARSHALL, Danvers, Mass (d/I–4 1887) MD Harvard 1857. *Bost m & s jour* 117: 636, 1887. *Polk* 1886: 465.

CHASE, SAMUEL WEBSTER, Addison, Livermore, Mt Vernon, Me (b/VII–17–1811 Fayette; d/VII–8–1863) MD Bowdoin 1837. *Med surg rep Phila* 10:180, 1863.

CHASE, SETH LYMAN, Colchester, Conn (d/II–15–1891) MD CPSNY 1860. *Bost m & s jour* 124:224, 1891. *Polk* 1886: 191.

CHASE, SUMNER BURNHAM, Osage, Ia (b/X–4–1821 Limington; d/VI–19–1891) MD Bowdoin 1849. *Tr Ia St Med Soc* 10:228, 1882. *Atkinson* I:95. *Polk* 1886: 365.

CHASE, WILLARD DUNLAP, Peterboro, NH (b/XII–4 1836 Claremont; d/IX–2–1894 @ 57) MD Harvard 1866; ng Dartmouth Med 1864. *JAMA* 23: 440, 1894. *Tr NH Med Soc* 1895: 159–60. *Butler* 1878: 454.

CHASE, WILLIAM, Mayville, NY (b/St Catherine's, Canada; d/XII–27–1891) MD CPSNY 1858. *Buff m & s jour* 31:383, 1892. *Tr NY St Med Soc* 1894:741 ff. *Polk* 1886: 667.

CHASE, ZALMAN F , Elmira, NY (d/XII–7–1891 @81) Lic by exam bd. *NW med jour* 20:16, 1892. *Butler* 1878:547. *Polk* 1890: 788.

CHASTANT, ALCÉE, New Orleans (d/I–20–1899 @63) MD Tulane 1852. *JAMA* 32:199, 1899. *New Orl m & s jour* 51:453, 1899. *Polk* 1886: 416.

CHATARD, FERDINAND EDME, Baltimore (b/VIII–3 1805; d/X–18–1888) MD UMd 1826. *Med annals Md*: 348. *Butler* 1874: 311.

CHATARD, FERDINAND EDME Jr, Baltimore (b/X–7 1839; d/VIII–27–1900) MD UMd 1861. *Med annals Md*: 348. *Polk* 1886: 435.

CHATARD, PIERRE, Baltimore (b/VII–18–1767 Santo Domingo; d/I–5–1848) MD U Montpelier 1788. *Med annals Md*: 348–49. *K&B* II: 210.

CHATHAM, BENJAMIN, Philadelphia (d/XI–26–1879) MD Pa Med Coll 1846. *Med surg rep Phila* 51:550, 1879.

CHAUVEAU, JEAN FRESNE, Sr, NYC (d/X–17–1903) MD Geneva 1853. *Bost m & s jour* 149:472, 1903. *Polk* 1902: 1395.

CHAZAL, JOHN PHILIP, Charleston, SC; CW–CSA; (b/XI–16–1814; d/I–8–1893) MD UPa 1836; stud Paris. *U Pa med alum CW*:1836. *Waring*: 211–12.

CHEATHAM, THOMAS J , Chesterfield CH, Va (d/VII 13–1901 @ 74) MD Med Coll Va 1850; AB ?UVa 1848. *Tr Med Soc Va* 1901: 279. *Polk* 1886:915 (as F.J.)

CHEATWOOD, LEIGHTON NICHOLAS, Bedford Co, Va; CW–CSA (b/VII–12–1839; d/II–23–1882) MD UPa 1861. *U Pa med alum CW*: 1861.

CHEESEMAN, NATHANIEL S , Scotia, NY (d/IX–12 1901 @ 67) MD Albany 1860. *JAMA* 37:848, 1901. *Polk* 1886: 708.

CHEESMAN, HOBART, NYC (b/VIII–13–1844 NY; d/IV–11–1903) MD UCNY 1878; ng Amherst 1871 [as Chessman] *Bost m & s jour* 148: 460, 1903. *Polk* 1896: 1045.

CHEESMAN, JOHN C , NYC (b/1787; d/X–11–1862) MD Rutgers 1812. *Tr AMA* 14:204, 1864. *Bost m & s jour* 67:248, 1862. *Med reg NY NJ Conn* 1865:213.

CHEESMAN, TIMOTHY MATLACK, NYC; CW–USA (b/X–27–1824; d/VII–7–1888) MD CPSNY 1859. *Med reg NY NJ Conn* 1889: 269. *Bost m & s jour* 119:69, 1888. *Polk* 1886: 674.

CHEEVER, CHARLES AUGUSTUS, Portsmouth, NH (b/XII–1–1793; d/IX–22–1852 Saugus, Mass) MD Harvard 1816; AB 1813. Palmer's *Necrol alum Harvard*: 16. *K&B* III: 216–17.

CHEEVER, HENRY SYLVESTER, Ann Arbor, Mich (b/VIII–8–1837 Exeter, NH; d/III–31–1877) MD U Mich 1866; AB 1863; AM 1866. *Tr AMA* 29:623–24, 1878. *K&B* III: 219.

CHEEVER, WILLIAM ROCKWELL, Kenosha, Wis (b/1868; d/VIII–30–1906) MD CPS Ill 1896. *JAMA* 57:795, 1906.

CHENAULT, ROBERT C , Lexington, Ky (b/Richmond, Ky; d/II–8–1895 @ 60) MD Jefferson 1854. *JAMA* 24:250, 1895. *Polk* 1886: 398.

CHENERY, ELISHA, Boston (d/VIII–1–1900 @ 70) MD Harvard 1853. *Bost m & s jour* 143: 148, 1900. *Polk* 1896: 694.

CHENEY, JASPER EDWIN, Brainerd, Minn (b/XII–5–1847 Pa; d/II–10–1884) MD Georgetown 1868; <ng UPa Med Sch> *Tr Minn St Med Soc* 1884: 181, 182.

CHENEY, OSCAR DUSTIN, Haverhill, Mass (b/XII–29 1845 Plaistow, NH; d/X–29–1896 Haverhill) MD Dartmouth 1872. *Bost m & s jour* 135:480, 1886. *JAMA* 27:1169, 1896. *Polk* 1890: 549.

CHENEY, WILLIAM FITCH, Chico, Calif (b/XII–30–1832 Richmond, NY; d/1879) MD UCNY 1863. *Tr AMA* 31:1024, 1880. *Atkinson* I: 136.

CHENOWETH, CHARLIE B , Huntington, Ind (d/XI–21–1899) MD Rush 1884. *JAMA* 33:1441, 1899.*Polk* 1896:534.

CHENOWETH, JOHN T , Winchester, Ind (b/XI–19–1833 Greenville, O; d/IV–19–1903) MD Med Coll Ohio 1875. *Trans Ind St Med Soc* 1903:335. *Polk* 1896:496.

CHESBROUGH, HENRY FREYER, Chicago, CW–CSA? (b/IX–19–1840 Totness, SC; d/XII–8–1870) MD Rush 1865. *Chic med jour* 28: 63, 1871.

CHESEBROUGH, NICHOLAS HALLAM, NYC (b/ Stonington, Conn; d/IV–6–1899 Summit, NJ) MD CPSNY 1845. *Bost m & s jour* 140:364, 1899. *Polk* 1896: 937.

CHESLEY, CHARLES PALMER, San Francisco (d/VI–14–1901 @ 67) MD UVt 1870; MD U Pacific 1870. *JAMA* 37:43, 1901. *Polk* 1886: 171.

CHESLEY, JAMES A , Calvert Co, Md (b/VI–20–1802; d/IV–9–1863) MD UMd 1823. *Med annals Md*: 349.

CHESLEY, NATHANIEL DARE, W River, Md (b/XII–16–1815; d/I–23–1878) MD UMd 1836. *Med annals Md*: 349. *Butler* 1874: 318.

CHESMORE, ALWYN HARDING, Huntington Vt;CW USA (b/X–17–1837 Warren; d/I–27–1891) MD U Vt 1860. *Bost m & s jour* 124:128 1891. *Butler* 1878: 804.

CHESTER, SAMUEL H , Jackson, Tenn (d/VI–10–1898) MD Jefferson 1850; MD Washington U Balto 1871. *JAMA* 30:1534, 1898. *Polk* 1886:866; 1896:1392.

CHESTON, CASPAR MORRIS, W River, Md (d/XII–1 1898) MD UPa 1871. *JAMA* 31:1542, 1898. *Polk* 1896: 676.

CHESTON, ELIJAH, CW–USA (b/XI–15–1832 Croyden, Pa; d/VIII–14–1863 en route from Vicksburg) MD UPa 1863. *U Pa med alum CW*: 1863. *Med surg rep Phila* 10:278, 1863. *Nat med jour* 1:292, 1870/71.

CHESTON, JAMES, W River, Md (b/V–10–1804 Balto; d/X–16–1885) MD UMd 1825. *Med annals Md*: 349.

CHETWOOD, GEORGE ROSS, Elizabeth, NJ (b/V–21 1802; d/IV–24–1886) MD CPSNY 1824. *Med reg NY NJ Conn* 1887: 256. *Tr Med Soc NJ* 1886–87: ?

CHEVES [CHEVIS], LANGDON A, (b/Savannah; d/ 1878, Memphis) MD UMd 1878. *Tr AMA* 30:857–58, 1879.

CHEW, PHILEMON, Tensas Parish, La (b/VII–2–1816; d/XI–21–1880) MD UPa 1836. *New Orl m & s jour* ns8: 991–92, 1881. *Butler* 1878: 296.

CHEW, SAMUEL, Baltimore (b/IV–29–1806; d/XII–28–1863) MD UMd 1829; AB Princeton 1825; AM 1828. *Tr AMA* 16:643–44, 1865; 31:1024–25, 1880. *Med ann Md*: 349–50. *Nashville jour m & s* ns1:318 1866. *K&B* III:22 220.

CHEW, THOMAS JOHN, Washington, DC (b/II–25–1846 Md; d/V–1–1904) MD UMd 1868; AB Princeton 1865; AM 1868. *Hist Med Soc DC*: 378. *Polk* 1900: 369.

CHEW, WILLIAM LOCKE, Birmingham, Ala (d/XII–4 1889) MD ULa 1886. *Tr Med Soc Ala* 1890: 217.

CHICKERING, JESSE, Jamaica Plain, Mass (b/VIII–31 1798 Dover; d/V–29–1855 @ 57) MD Harvard 1833; AB 1818; AM 1821. *Bost m & s jour* 367,1855.

CHILD, A A , Bucksfield, Me (d/VIII–4–1867 @ 34) MD unknown. *Bost m & s jour* 77:112, 1867.

CHILD, HENRY F , Lithgow, NY (d/I–1–1867) MD Fairfield 1835. *Med surg rep Phila* 16:40, 1867.

CHILD, THOMAS, Bath, Me (b/VIII–18–1808 Sturbridge, Mass; d/X–2–1872) MD Bowdoin 1831. *Tr Me Med Assoc* 1871–73: 482–83: *Med surg rep Phila* 27:398, 1872.

CHILDS, HENRY HALSEY, Pittsfield, Mass (b/VI–7–1783; d/III–21–1868) Hon MD Berkshire; AB Williams 1802; AM 1803. *Phila med reg & dir* 1871: 296. *Bost m & s jour* ns3?:126, 239, 1868. *Med surg rep Phila* 18:314, 1868. *K&B* III: 221.

CHILDS, TIMOTHY, Pittsfield, Mass (d/IX–3–1865) MD Berkshire 1844. *Med surg rep Phila* 13: 166, 1865. *Tr AMA* 18:315, 1867. *Buff m & s jour* 5:117, 1865. *Bost m & s jour* 73:168, 1865; 74: 45, 1866.

CHILDS, WILLIAM RIDDLE, Pittsburgh (b/II–18–1838; d/XI–11–1888) MD Hahnemann Phila 1863; AB Washington 1860. *Tr Am Inst Homeop* 1889:180. *Hahn mo* 23: 1888 (Dec.) *Med vis* 5:11, 1889. *Polk* 1886: 828. Homeopath.

CHILTON, ROBERT H , CW–USA; Albany & Louisville, Ky; Dallas, Tex 1880– (b/1844? Albany, Ky; d/VI–5–1901 @ 57) MD Miami 1870. *Tr Tex St Med Assoc* 1902:73–75. *Polk* 1896: 1424.

CHINN, JOSEPH GRAVES, Lexington, Ky (d/?IX– –1891) MD Transylvania 1846. *NW med jour* 19:151, 1891. *Butler* 1878: 271.

CHINN, RICHARD H , Brazoria, Tex (d/1868 @ 54) MD Tulane 1845. *Tr AMA* 21:488–89, 1870. *Phila med reg & dir* 1871: 296.

CHIPLEY, WILLIAM B , St Louis, Mo (d/III–16–1884 @ 83) MD unknown. *Med surg rep Phila* 50: 512, 1884.

CHIPMAN, ERASTUS DENNISON, CW–USA; Saugerties, NY (b/I–23–1835 Hope Valley RI; d/V–24–1895) MD Albany 1863. *Tr Med Soc St NY* 1896: 442. *Polk* 1886: 707.

CHIPMAN, M M , San Francisco & San Jose, Cal (d/X–16–1899 San Diego) MD Cooper 1874. *Tr Med Soc St Calif* 1900: 549. *Polk* 1893: 221.

CHISHOLM [CHISOLM], JULIAN JOHN, CW–CSA; Petersburg, Va; Baltimore (b/IV–16–1830 Charleston, SC; d/XI–1–1903) MD Med Coll SC 1850. *Med annals Md*: 350–51. *So pract* 25:710–11, 1903. *Bost m & s jour* 149: 558, 1903. *Waring*: 212–14. *K&B* III: 222.

CHISMORE, GEORGE, San Francisco (b/I–30–1840; d/I–11–1906) MD Cooper 1873. *Cal st jour med* 4:64–65, 1906. *Polk* 1886: 171.

CHITWOOD, GEORGE R , Connersville, Ind (b/V–10–1805 Gallipolis, O; d/V–6–1893) MD Cleveland Med Coll 1846. *Tr Ind St Med Soc* 1893: 251. *Polk* 1890:366.

CHITWOOD, JOSHUA, Connersville, Ind (b/II–12–1838 Liberty; d/V–13–1903) MD Med Coll Ohio 1859. *Tr Ind St Med Soc* 1903: 336. *Polk* 1886:314.

CHOATE, GEORGE CHEYNE SHATTUCK, Pleasantville NY (d/VI–26–1896 @70) MD Harvard 1849;AB 1846. *JAMA* 27:108–09 1896. *Polk* 1896:1090; 1045.

CHOPPIN, SAMUEL, CW–CSA; New Orleans (b/X–20 1828 Baton Rouge; d/V–2–1880) MD Tulane 1850. *Bost m & s jour* 102:452, 1880. *New Orl m & s jour* ns7:1153–54, 1880. *Atkinson* I: 337. *K&B* III: 223.

CHOVET, ABRAHAM, Engl; Jamaica; Philadelphia (b/V 25–1704 Engl; d/III–24–1790) MD unknown. *Tr CPP* cent vol: 217, 1887. *K&B* III: 223–24.

CHRISMAN, S ZACHARY TAYLOR, Warwick, Pa (d/VIII–26–1903 @ 64) MD UPa 1873. *Pa med jour* 7:278, 1903/04. *Polk* 1886: 838.

CHRISTIAN, JOHN HUNT, Richmond, Va (b/VIII–18–1845; d/III–13–1902) MD Med Coll Va 1867. *Med annals Md*: 351. *Polk* 1886: 435.

CHRISTIAN, MARCELLUS P , USN 1859–61; CW–CSN 1861–65; Lynchburg, Va (b/1832; d/1879) MD UCNY 1856. *Tr AMA* 31:1025–26, 1880.

CHRISTIAN, SAMUEL BEDLOE, Amherst, Va; CW–CSA (b/VI–5–1815 Buckingham, Va; d/IV–29–1879) MD UPa 1838. *U Pa med alum CW*: 1838.

CHRISTMAN, JEFFERSON D , Allentown, Pa (d/III 30–1906 @ 50) MD UPa 1876. *Pa med jour* 9:523, 1905/06. *Flint* 1897: 794.

CHRISTOPHER, WALTER S , Chicago (b/III–14–1859 Newport, Ky; d/III–2–1905 @ 46) MD Med Coll Ohio 1883. *Chic med rec* 28:253, 392–95, 1905. *Ill med jour* 7:302, 1905.

CHRISTY, JAMES H , Pittsburgh (b/I–23–1851 [?] Freeport, Pa; d/I–22–1896) MD Jefferson 1866. *Tr Med Soc Pa* 27:367–69, 1897. *Polk* 1890: 961.

CHRISTY, ROBERT W , Hollidaysburg, Pa (b/VI–27–1816 Juanita Co; d/VI–14–1873) MD Jefferson 1841. *Tr Med Soc Pa* 10:252 ff, 1874.

CHUNN, JAMES THOMAS, Baltimore (b/I–31–1829; d/I–4–1867) MD UMd 1851; stud UVa. *Med annals Md*: 351. *Tr AMA* 18: 339, 1867.

CHURCH, A W, Jersey City (d/III–13–1903 @33) <MD Edinburgh>; att CPSNY. *Bost m & s jour* 148: 328, 1903.

CHURCH, ALLEN S , NYC (b/1822; d/X–24–1884) MD Castleton 1848. *Med reg NY NJ Conn* 1885: 231. *Med surg rep Phila* 51:496, 1884.

CHURCH, AUSTIN, ? Conn (b/1799; d/VIII–7–1879) MD Yale 1823. *Med reg NY NJ Conn* 1880: 234. *Med surg rep Phila* 41:198, 1879.

CHURCH, ISAAC W, Walkerton, Ind (d/VIII–25–1902) MD Wooster 1871. *Wooster cat*: 1871 med. *Polk* 1886: 339.

CHURCH, J A , CW–USA (d/I–8–1864) MD unknown. *Nat med jour* 1:292, 1870/71.

CHURCH, MOSES DAVID [DAVIS], Cambridgeport, Mass (d/VIII–25–1890) MD Harvard 1880. *Bost m & s jour* 123: 629, 1890. *Polk* 1886: 464.

CHURCH, NELSON HORATIO, Chicago (d/III–5–1906 @ 43) MD Rush 1869. *Ill med jour* 9:463, 1906. *Polk* 1896: 378.

CHURCH, WILLIAM HENRY, NYC; CW–USA (b/VI–6–1826; d/IX–27–1866 Paris, Fr) MD CPSNY 1849. *Tr AMA* 19:410, 1868. *Med reg NY NJ Conn* 1867: 210. *Nat med jour* 1:292, 1870/71.

CHURCH, WILLIAM IRWIN, Pittsburgh (b/1827; d/IX 29–1862) MD Hahnemann Phila 1859. *Tr Am Inst Homeop* 1865: 109. *Tr Hom Med Soc St Pa* 1870/71. Homeopath.

CHURCH, WILLIAM LEE, Madison, Fla; CW–CSA (b/IV–21–1843; d/III–31–1871) MD unknown; AB UNC 1911 as of 1862. *UNC cat*: 1862.

CHURCHILL, ALONZO, Utica, NY (d/XII–28–1896 @ 85) Cert Exam Bd 1832; Hon MD 1855 Regents, UNY. *Buff m & s jour* 36: 542, 1897. *Tr Med Soc St NY* 1897: 479. *Polk* 1886: 713.

CHURCHILL, ANN ERVILLA (SHERMAN), Monroe, Wis 1848– (b/VI–10–1830 Albion, Pa; d/VII–26–1896 Guernseyville, Cal) MD Hahnemann Chicago 1886. *Tr Am Inst Homeop* 1897: 63. Homeopath.

CHURCHILL, ASA HOPKINS, Meriden, Conn (b/IX–8 1831 Litchfield; d/X–17–1903) MD Yale 1857. *Proc Conn Med Soc* 1905: 78–79, 487–88. *Atkinson* I: 553. *Polk* 1896: 280.

CHURCHILL, SEYMOUR, Milford, NY; CW–USA (d/XI–15–1869) MD Woodstock 1838. *Nat med jour* 1:292, 1870/71.

CHURCHMAN, VINCENT T [TAPP?], Greenville, Va (d/I–24–1872 @ 47) MD Jefferson 1848. *Tr Med Soc Va* 1872:26, 157–58.

CHUTE, JONATHAN ANDREW, Westport, Mo (b/IV–23–1811 Naples, Me; d/X–1–1838) MD Dartmouth 1835; ng Bowdoin 1829. *Bowdoin cat*: 183.

CILLEY, JONATHAN LONGFELLOW, Brooklyn (b/II 25–1838 Cincinnati; d/III–18–1903) MD Miami 1857; AB Harvard 1858. *Bost m & s jour* 148: 356, 1903. *Polk* 1886: 741.

CISNEROS, JUAN, Havana, Cuba; NYC (b/XI–21–1832; d/IX–30–1892) MD U Havana 1864. *Med reg NY NJ Conn* 1893:298. *Polk* 1886: 674.

CLAGETT, HORATIO C , Md (b/VII–1–1793; d/III–5–1858) MD UMd 1814; ng UPa Med Sch. *Med annals Md*: 351. *Tr AMA* 13: 807, 1860.

CLAGETT, JAMES HAWKINS, Pleasant Valley, Md (b/XII–25–1804 Montgomery Co; d/III–14–1869) MD UMd 1826. *Med annals Md*: 351–52.

CLAGETT, RICHARD H , Davidsonville, Md (d/I–24–1851 @42) Licensed; no MD. *Med annals Md*: 352.

CLAGETT, ZACHARIAH, Washington Co, Md (b/XI–19–1760 Rockville; d/I–28–1825) <ng UPa Med> *Med annals Md*: 352.

CLAIBORNE, GREGORY WELDON, CW–CSA, CSN (b/1837; d/I–25–1866 Brunswick Co, Va) MD UCNY 1859; att UVa 1856–57. *Med s rep Phila* 14:120,1866.

CLAIBORNE, JAMES WILLIAM, CW–CSA (b/VI–5–1825; d/XI–22–1906 Petersburg, Va) MD UPa 1848. *U*

 Spec. educ'l status abbrev. as: ***ng*** = college verified attendance without degree;

Pa med alum CW: 1848. *Polk* 1886: 924 (Petersburg).

CLANCY, THOMAS J , Scales Mound, Ill (d/VII-29-1901) MD U Ark 1897. *JAMA* 37:398, 1901.

CLAPP, ASAHEL, New Albany, Ind (b/X-5-1792 Mass; d/X-29 or XII-17-1862) MD unknown. *Bost m & s jour* 68: 44-45, 1863. *Tr Ind St Med Soc* 1871: 244. *Kemper's Indiana*: 251.

CLAPP, FAYETTE, Lee Center, Ill; CW-USA, USN (b/VI-5-1824 Chesterfield, Mass; d/VIII-29-1864) MD Castleton 1854; ng Harvard Med 1850; AB Brown 1848. *Harvard in CW*: 236. *Brown hist cat*: 1848.

CLAPP, HARVEY ERASTUS, Wrentham, Mass (d/VIII 7-1863 @ 49) MD Harvard 1840; AB 1837. *Bost m & s jour* 69: 48, 1863.

CLAPP, LEVI WHEATON, Pawtucket, RI (b/I-3-1849; d/IX-18-1894) MD Harvard 1873; AB Brown 1870. *JAMA* 23:561, 1894. *Bost m & s jour* 131: 304, 1894. *Butler* 1878: 749.

CLAPP, SYLVANUS, Pawtucket, RI (b/XI-22-1815 or 1816 Westhampton, Mass; d/VI-15-1879) MD Dartmouth 1837. *Tr AMA* 31:1026-27, 1880. *Bost m & s jour* 102:12, 1880. *Tr RI Med Soc* 2:218-19, 1877-82. *Atkinson* I:39.

CLARDY, THOMAS FLEMING, ?Christian Co, Ky; CW-CSA (b/1838; d/II-26-1885) MD UPa 1859. *U Pa med alum CW*: 1859.

CLARK, ALONZO, NYC (b/III-1-1807 Chester Village, Vt; d/IX-13-1887) MD CPSNY 1835; AB Williams 1828; Hon MD Woodstock 1841. *Med reg NY NJ Conn* 1888: 244. *JAMA* 9:415-16, 1887. *Atkinson* I:664. *K&B* III: 227.

CLARK, ALONZO F, Goffstown NH (d/XII-16-1887 @ 70) MD Darmstadt 1839. *Bost m & s jour* 117:616, 1887.

CLARK, BIRDSEY P , DeRay, Tenn (d/V-30-1900 @ 73) MD U Nashville 1857. *JAMA* 34:1574, 1900. *Polk* 1886: 872.

CLARK, CHARLES, Roodstown NJ (b/X-19-1773; d/II 25-1828) Lic Med Soc NJ. *Tr Med Soc NJ* 1871: 148.

CLARK, CHARLES, Montpelier, Vt (b/I-3-1800; d/VI 27-1874) ng Castleton 1820. *Tr Vt Med Soc* 1883: 104.

CLARK, CHARLES B , Kosciuszko, Miss (d/II-7-1899) MD UMd 1882. *JAMA* 32:442, 1899. *Polk* 1886: 528.

CLARK, CHARLES COLESWORTH PINCKNEY, Oswego, NY (b/III-10-1822 Tinmouth, Vt; d/I-11-1899) MD CPSNY 1847; AB Middlebury 1843. *Bost m & s jour* 138:547, 1899. *JAMA* 32:145, 1899. *Atkinson* I: 653. *Polk* 1896: 1088.

CLARK, CHARLES EDWARD, Lynn, Mass (d/X-29-1897 @56) MD Harvard 1877; AB Amherst 1873. *Bost m & s jour* 137:640, 1897. *Polk* 1896: 716.

CLARK, CHARLES FREMONT, Brooklyn (b/1856 Wheeling, WVa; d/IV-21-1892) MD CPSNY 1883; AM Jefferson 1878. *JAMA* 18: 658. 1858.

CLARK, CHARLES FRENCH, Gloucester Co, NJ (b/1800? d/X-16-1875 Woodbury) MD UPa 1823. *Tr AMA* 27:654, 1876.

CLARK [CLARKE], COURTNEY J , Selma, Ala (b/X-27-1816 Laurens Dist, SC; d/VIII-18-1893 Jacksonville, Ala) MD Jefferson 1844. *Atkinson* I: 51. *JAMA* 21: 356-57, 1893. *Butler* 1878: 16.

CLARK, DARIUS, Canton, NY (b/IV- -1798 Weybridge, Vt; d/I-23-1870) Lic Franklin Co Med Soc. *Med reg NY NJ Conn* 1871:350. *Trans Med Soc St NY* 1873: 183-84. *Trans AMA* 24:367-68, 1873.

CLARK, DAVID DAVIS, Philadelphia (b/VII-4-1822 Fall River, Mass; d/I-4-1877) MD UCNY 1850. *Trans Pa St Med Soc* 11:720-21, 1877.

CLARK, DEXTER SELWYN, Rockford, Ill (d/II-12-1898 @ 59) MD CPSNY 1865. *JAMA* 30:507, 1898. *Polk* 1896: 439.

CLARK, DOUGAN, Richmond, Ind (b/V-17-1828 Randolph, NC; d/X-10-1896) MD UPa 1861; att Haverford. *Haverford cat*: 45.

CLARK, E A , San José, Calif (b/Tiffin, O; d/III-30-1894) MD Med Coll Pacific 1877. *JAMA* 22:561, 1894. *Polk* 1890: 201.

CLARK, EDWARD STEPHEN, San Francisco (b/Ky; d/VI-1-1900 @ 44) MD Louisville Hosp Coll Med 1880. *JAMA* 34: 1574, 1900.

CLARK, EDWARD WIGHT, Englewood, NJ (b/X-20-1862 Manchester, NH; d/IV-11-1892) MD CPSNY 1887; AB Columbia 1883. *Med reg NY NJ Conn* 1892: 273. *Trans Med Soc NJ* 1892: 209. *JAMA* 18: 530, 1892.

CLARK, ELIJAH A, ?St Louis; CW-USA? (d/IV-16-1871 @35) MD Rush 1861. *Chic med jour* 28: 310, 1871. *Boston m & s jour* ns7: 272, 1871. *Med rec* 6:215-16, 1871-72.

CLARK, ELIPHALET, Portland, Me 1830- (b/1801 Strong, Me; d/VI-8-1883 @ 82) MD Bowdoin 1824. *Trans Am Inst Homeop* 1884: 650. *Am homeop obs* 20:192, 1883. *Hahn mo* 18:448, 1883. *New Engl med gaz* 18:224, 1885. Homeopath 1840-

CLARK, EPHRAIM, New Dorp, NY (b/1796? d/XI-20-1885 @ 89) MD unknown. *Med reg NY NJ Conn* 1887: 256.

CLARK, EUGENE, San Antonio, Tex; New Orleans (d/III-7-1898 @ 37) MD ULa 1883. *New Orl med & surg jour* 50:610, 1898. *JAMA* 30:683, 1898. *Polk* 1896: 620.

CLARK, FRANK M , Salem, O (b/I-14-1854 Strongsville; d/X-8-1892 @ 38) MD Homeop Hosp Cleveland 1880. *Tr Am Inst Homeop* 1893: 134. *Polk* 1886: 767.

CLARK, HENRY CLAY, Woodbury, NJ; CW-USA (b/XI-24-1831 Paulsboro; d/XII-26-1904) MD UPa 1853. *U Pa med alum CW*: 1853. *Polk* 1886: 612.

CLARK, HENRY GRAFTON, Boston (d/IX-23-1892 @ 88) MD Bowdoin 1834. *Bost m & s jour* 127:324, 1892. *Butler* 1878: 337.

CLARK, JAMES, Fairfax Co, Va (b/1731? Scotland; d/II-16-1815 @ 84) MD unknown. *Phila med & surg jour* 5:30-31, 1856.

CLARK, JAMES A , Erie, Pa (d/V-16-1899 @ 36) MD Northwestern 1885. *JAMA* 32:1269, 1899. *Polk* 1896: 379 (Chicago).

CLARK, JAMES HENRY, ?Newark, NJ (b/VI-23-1814; d/III-6-1869) MD CPSNY 1841; AM Princeton 1867. *Phila med reg & dir* 1871:200. *Med reg NY NJ Conn* 1869: 229-30. *Med rec* 4:48, 1869-70.

CLARK, JOHN SPANGLER, Chicago (b/Ontario? d/ VIII-31-1895 @ 74) MD Geneva 1843. *Chic med rec* 9:185, 1895. *JAMA* 25:427, 1895. *Ill st med reg* 1878/79. *Polk* 1886: 261.

CLARK, JOHNSON, Bridgewater & New Bedford, Mass; CW-USA (b/I-4-1818 Wakefield, NH; d/XII-8-1861 Fortress Monroe) ng Bowdoin Med Sch 1841. *Nat med jour* 1:292, 1870/71.

CLARK, JONATHAN, Lower Merion, Pa (d/XI-12-1869) MD UPa 1830. *Phila med reg & dir* 1871: 302.

CLARK, JOSEPH MANLY, Metamora, Ill (b/V-31-1829 Somerville, Mass; d/II-20-1870) MD Jefferson 1855; AB Amherst 1852. *Amherst, Men of*: 1852.

CLARK, LEON A , Rockford,Ill (b/1849;d/VII-22-1899) MD Tulane 1893. *JAMA* 33:367 1899. *Polk* 1896: 614.

CLARK, LEMON WILLARD, Elkhart, Ind (b/VIII-1-1858; d/II-8-1896) MD Rush 1882. *JAMA* 26:391, 1896. *Tr Ind St Med Soc* 1896:267. *Polk* 1890:348.

CLARK, LUCIUS, Rockford,Ill; CW-USA (b/I-10-1813 Amherst,Mass; d/XI-5-1878) MD Geneva 1835. *Chic med jour* 37: 670, 1878. *Atkinson* I:301. *Butler* 1878:146. *Tr Ill St Med Soc* 1879: 292-93.

CLARK, LUTHER, Waltham, Mass (b/VII-30-1810; d/ IX-26-1884 Lincoln) MD Harvard 1836; AB 1833. *Tr Am Inst Hom* 1885:87. *Med surg rep Phila* 51:420, 1884. *Bost m & s jour*111:336 1884. *Cleave*. Homeopath 1840-

CLARK, MICAJAH, Richmond Va; USA-1814 (b/ 1788; d/VIII-19-1849) UPa 1811. *Tr AMA* 31:1031-37, 1880.

CLARK, NORRIS G , Batavia, NY 1859- (b/Bloomfield; d/VII-22-1876 @ 58) MD stud w/preceptor. *Med surg rep Phila* 35:180, 1876.

CLARK, PATRICK HENRY, Halifax Co, Va; CW-CSA (b/IV-21-1837; d/VII-25-1862) MD Med Coll Richmond 1859; att UVa. Johnson's *U Va alum dec'd CW*: 199-203.

CLARK, REUBEN D , Albany, NY (d/VIII-11-1894 @ 47) MD LICH 1875. *Bost m & s jour* 131: 176, 1894. *Polk* 1890: 759.

CLARK, RIPLEY, Windsor Vt (b/VII-23-1817 Strafford; d/IV-23-1900) MD Dartmouth 1847. *JAMA* 34: 1146 1900. *Bost m & s jour* 142:469 1900. *Polk* 1896: 1478.

CLARK, ROBERT JAMES, CW-USA; Chestnut Level, Pa (b/VII-3-1839; d/VIII-19-1905) MD UPa 1868. *U Pa med alum CW*: 1868. *Polk* 1886: 795.

CLARK, RUFUS KING, Georgia Vt (b/1816 Rochester, Mass; d/II-12-1883) MD UVt 1865. *Tr Vt Med Soc* 1883: 104.

CLARK, S WELLMAN, Jersey City, NJ (b/V-29-1857 Newark; d/XII- -1899) MD NY Homeop 1881. *No Amer jour homeop* 48:13, 1900 (Feb "Curr Events") *Polk* 1886: 604. Homeopath.

CLARK, S WILLIAMS, Wallingford, Conn (d/IX-1852) MD UCNY 1848. *Proc Conn Med Soc* 1853: 19.

CLARK, SAMUEL LEWIS, Bangor, Me (b/X-11-1807 Winthrop Me; d/X-27-1851 Northampton, Mass) <MD Jefferson> AB Bowdoin 1826. *Bowdoin cat*: 1826.

CLARK, SAMUEL SHERRERD, Belvidere, NJ (b/XI-8 1825 Flemington; d/XI-23-1885) MD UCNY 1845; AB Princeton 1845; AM 1848; stud Lafayette. *Tr Med Soc NJ* 1886-87: 163-65. *Butler* 1878: 467. *Atkinson* 1:685.

CLARK, SHELDON SEARLES, St Albans, Vt; b/XII-9 1827 Isle La Motte; d/IV-21-1892) MD Castleton 1849. *Bost m & s jour* 126:432, 1892. *Butler* 1878: 804.

CLARK, SIMEON TUCKER, Lockport, NY (b/Canton, Mass; d/XII-24-1891 @55) MD Berkshire 1860. *Med reg NY NJ Conn* 1892: 273. *Buff med & surg jour* 31:383, 1892. *Tr NY St Med Soc*: 11:741 ff, 1894. *Bost m & s jour* 125: 720, 1891. *Polk* 1886: 666.

CLARK, STEPHEN JOHN, NYC; CW-USN (d/II-24-1901 Ossining, NY) MD UCNY 1861. *UCNY cat*: 1861. *Polk* 1886: 674.

CLARK, SUMNER, Effingham Ill (d/III-5-1906 @ 74) MD St Louis Med Coll 1871. *Ill med jour* 9:332, 1906.

CLARK, WALLACE CLEVELAND, NYC (d/V-19 1906) MD UCNY 1882. *Bost m & s jour* 154:642, 1906.

CLARK, WILLIAM EDWIN, River Forest, Ill; Rochester, NY (b/II-22-1819 Lebanon, Conn; d/III-22-1898) MD Woodstock 1841. *JAMA* 30:807, 1898.

CLARK, WILLIAM NELSON, Stafford, Conn (b/c1807 Chaplin; d/V-26-1888 @c81) Hon MD Yale 1830 *Proc Conn Med Soc* ns4: 250-52, 1889. *Butler* 1878: 75.

CLARK, WILLIAM PATTERSON, Wilkes Barre, Pa; Clinton, NJ; Belvidere (d/IX-4-1857) MD Rutgers 1817; AB 1814; Hon AM Princeton 1819. *Tr Med Soc NJ* 1872: 113.

CLARK, WILLIAM RUFUS SEARLE, Blufftown, Ind (b/1820; d/VII-20-1882) MD Willoughby 1842. *Tr Ind St Med Soc* 1883: 267.

CLARKE, ALPHEUS BRYANT, Holyoke, Mass (b/V-11-1814; d/XII-15-1869 Brooklyn) MD Yale 1850. *Med reg NY NJ Conn* 1870: 315. *Bost m & s jour* ns5:56, 1870.

CLARKE, ANDREW P , Baltimore (b/1850; d/VII-16-1888) MD UMd 1873. *Med annals Md*:353. *Polk* 1886: 435.

CLARKE, EDWARD HAMMOND, Boston (b/II-2-1820; d/XI-30-1877) MD UPa 1846; AB Harvard 1841. *Tr AMA* 29:624-27, 1878. *Chic med jour* 37:14, 1877. *Buff m & s jour* 17:230,1878. *Tr RI Med Soc* 2:159, 1859-77. *K&B* III:230.

CLARKE, GARDNER CARPENTER, CW-USA; Ni-

 Spec. educ'l status abbrev. as: ***ng*** = college verified attendance without degree;

agara Falls, NY (b/III-15-1841; d/III-22-1897) MD Bowdoin 1864. *Buff m & s jour* 36:711-13, 1897. *Polk* 1886:699 [as Clark].

CLARKE, GEORGE, Washington, DC (b/Essex Co, Va; d/X-5-1822) MD UPa 1810. *Hist Med Soc DC*: 217.

CLARKE, HENRY, Worcester, Mass (d/IV-17-1880 @ 55) MD Harvard 1850. *Tr AMA* 31:1028-30, 1880. *Bost m & s jour* 102:400, 475, 1880.

CLARKE, HENRY BRADFORD, New Bedford, Mass 1853-87; Coronado, Calif 1887- (b/X-18-1827 Cranston, RI; d/III-6-1888) MD Hahnemann Phila 1852. *Tr Am Inst Homeop* 1888: 219. *New Engl med gaz* 23:192, 1888. *Polk* 1886: 470. Homeopath.

CLARKE, JOHN JAY, CW-USA; Harrisburg, Pa (b/IX-25-1832 Monroe Twp,Pa; d/II-18-1895 Tampa Fla) MD UPa 1860. *U Pa med alum CW*:1860. *Polk* 1886: 801.

CLARKE, JOHN LEWIS, Scituate, RI; Fall River, Mass (b/XI-30-1812; d/X-25-1880) MD Hahnemann Phila 1854. *Am homeop obs* 18:56, 1880. *New Engl med gaz* 16:31, 1881. *Tr Am Inst Homeop* 1881:128, *Cleave*. Homeopath.

CLARKE, MOSES, E Cambridge, Mass (b/I-18-1818 Atkinson, NH; d/III-29-1864) MD Dartmouth 1843. *Bost m & s jour* 70: 188,307-08, 1864.

CLARKE, PATRICK JAMES, NYC (b/IV-26-1826; d/XII-1-1881) MD CPSNY 1849. *Med reg NY NJ Conn* 1882: 223. *Med rec* 20: 699, 1881.

CLARKE, PELEG, RI (b/VIII-5-1784 Richmond, RI; d/I-1-1875 E Providence) MD Hahnemann Phila 1813; ng Brown Med Dept 1813. *Tr Am Inst Homeop* 1875: 792. *New Engl med gaz*: 10:93, 1885. *Am homeop jour mat med* 8:244. *Cleave*. Homeopath.

CLARKE, RICHARD, Selma, Ala (d/I-30-1887 @ 73) MD UPa 1835. *Tr Med Assoc St Ala* 1887: 305. *Polk* 1886: 139.

CLARKE, ROWSE REYNOLDS, Whitinsville, Mass (d/II-4-1888 @ 65) MD Harvard 1847. *Bost m & s jour* 118:160, 510, 1888. *Butler* 1878: 348.

CLARKSON, CHARLES C , Newark, NJ; CW-USN (b/XI-10-1843; d/I-10-1871) MD UCNY 1868. *Tr Med Soc NJ* 1871: 240-42. *Tr AMA* 23:594, 1872. *Med surg rep Phila* 24:68, 1871.

CLARKSON, CHARLES DE SAUSSURE, Allendale, SC (d/IX-3-1901 @ 35) MD Med Coll SC 1890. *JAMA* 37:790, 1901.

CLARKSON, CORNELIUS VERMEULE, NYC (d/VI-1-1877 @ 64) MD CPSNY 1839. *Med reg NY NJ Conn* 1877: 200.

CLARKSON, GERARDUS, Philadelphia (b/1737; d/IX-19-1790) MD unknown. *Tr CPP* cent vol: 217.

CLARKSON, ROBERT W , Mayview, Mo (d/III-12-1900 @ 70) MD UPa 1849. *JAMA* 34:766, 1900. *Polk* 1896: 853.

CLARKSON, WILLIAM, Philadelphia (b/XI-7-1793; d/IX-9-1812) MD UPa 1785. *Tr CPP* cent vol: 217.

CLARY, LYMAN, Syracuse, NY (b/1803 Deerfield, Mass; d/VI-1-1876 @ 73) MD Berkshire 1827. *Tr Am Inst Homeop* 1877: 977. *Hahn mo* 12:44, 1876 (Aug; news & advt). Homeopath.

CLASON, ABRAHAM TRAVIS, Danbury, Conn (d/VI-16-1896 @ 56) MD UCNY 1866. *Proc Conn Med Soc* 1897:341. *JAMA* 26:1278,1896. *Butler* 1878:75 (Eclect)

CLASON, THOMAS S , Bellefontaine, O (b/XII-9-1827 Madisonville; d/IV-27-1873) MD Med Coll Ohio 1855. *Tr O St Med Soc* 1876:95-96. *Butler* 1878: 623.

CLAUDE, ABRAHAM, Annapolis, Md (b/XII-4-1818; d/I-10-1901) MD UMd 1838. *Med annals Md:* 354. *Polk* 1893: 557.

CLAUDE, DENNIS, Annapolis, Md (b/1779; d/XII-9-1863) <MD UPa 1802> *Med annals Md:* 354.

CLAUDY, JOHN C, Newville Pa (d/II-20-1897 @55) MD Bellevue 1865. *JAMA* 28:523,1897. *Polk* 1896:1295.

CLAUSS, HENRY OTHON, Jr, NYC (b/VIII-22-1833 Prussia; d/IX-19-1898) MD LICH 1865. *JAMA* 31:808, 1898. *Polk* 1886: 674.

CLAWSON, ISAIAH DUNN, Woodstown, NJ (b/III-30-1822; d/X-8 or 19-1879) MD UPa 1843; AB Princeton 1840; att Lafayette. *Med surg rep Phila* 41 [?]: 396, 1879. *US Congr biogr dir.*

CLAY, DAVID M, Shreveport La (b/1838; d/IX-9-1889) MD UCNY 1857. *UCNY cat*: 1857. *Polk*1886: 419.

CLAY, GEORGE BOLTON L , Moorestown, NJ; Germantown, Pa (b/I-11-1832 Evansburg, Pa; d/I-20-1898) MD Hahnemann Phila 1853; ng Princeton. *Cleave*. Homeopath.

CLAYTON, ALLEN B , Marinette, Wis; Chicago (b/Canada? d/IX-16-1900) MD Hahnemann Chicago 1869. *Ill med jour* ns2:237, 1900. *Polk* 1886: 955. Homeopath.

CLAYTON, WILLIAM GOODENOUGH, Point Pleasant, NJ (d/X-27-1884) MD Bellevue 1882. *Med surg rep Phila* 1884: 572.

CLEARY, REUBEN, US Marine Hosp Service; CW-CSA (b/IV-27-1835 Alexandria, DC; d/II-12-1898) MD Georgetown 1859. *Hist Med Soc DC*: 263.

CLEARY, THOMAS FRANCIS, Brooklyn (d/XI-19-1886) MD Bellevue 1883. *Med reg NY NJ Conn* 1887: 256. *Bost m & s jour* 115:508, 1896.

CLEAVELAND, CHARLES HARLEY, Cincinnati; CW-USA (b/1820 Lebanon, NH; d/XII-2-1863 Memphis) MD Dartmouth 1843 [d/XI-1875 Boston!]; ng Woodstock 1842. *Nat med jour* 1:292, 1870/71. *Chic med jour* xl:90, 1864. *K&B* III:231-32.

CLEAVELAND, MOSES PARKER, Bucksport Me; Newmarket NH (b/VII-6-1807 Brunswick Md; d/X-7-1840 Natick Mass) MD Bowdoin 1830; AB 1827. *Bowdoin cat*: 1826.

CLEAVELAND, PARKER, Brunswick Me (b/I-15-1780 Rowley, Mass; d/X-15-1858) Hon MD Dartmouth 1823; AM Harvard 1779; LLD Bowdoin 1824. *Tr AMA* 13:789,1860. *Bost m & s jour* 59:248,1859. *K&B* II: 228.

CLEAVER, HIRAM THOMAS, Keokuk, Ia; CW–USA (b/II–17–1822 Centreville, Pa; d/I–11–1888) MD CPS Keokuk 1862. *Tr Ia St Med Soc* 1890: 286 ff. *Atkinson* I: 588. *Polk* 1886: 361.

CLEAVER, ISAAC, Philadelphia (b/1786? d/II–10–1822 @ 36) MD UPa 1805. *Tr CPP* cent vol: 217.

CLEMENS, HENRY SWEITZER, Allentown, Pa (d/IV–8–1901 @ 63) MD UPa 1861 (d/III–27–1901) *Pa med jour* 5:296, 1901/02. *Polk* 1886: 791.

CLEMENT, ABRAHAM D , ?NYC (d/II–24–1866 @ 64) ng Castleton 1827. *Med reg NY NJ Conn* 1867: 212.

CLEMENT, JACOB B , Philadelphia (d/IX–23–1858 West Point, NY) MD UPa 1850. *Med surg rep Phila* ns1: 28, 1858/59.

CLEMENT, JAMES MOYES, Philadelphia (d/VI–12–1904 @ 67) MD UPa 1862. *Pa med jour* 8:334, 1904/05. *Polk* 1896: 1301.

CLEMENT, JOHN PHILLIPS, ?Norwich, Vt (b/III–2–1825 Andover, Mass; d/VI–22–1873 Norwich) MD Woodstock 1854; AB Dartmouth 1848. *Med surg rep Phila* 29:36, 1873.

CLEMENT, R HERBERT, San Francisco (d/XII–23–1902 @ 32) MD Hahnemann San Francisco 1893. *Pacific Coast jour homeop* 1903 (Jan). *Calif st jour med* 1:70, 1903. *Polk* 1896: 231. Homeopath.

CLEMENT, THOMAS RUNNELLS, Osterville Mass (d/IX–24–1898 @ 75) MD UVt 1863. *Bost m & s jour* 139:536, 1898*JAMA* 31:872, 1898.

CLEMENTS, JAMES WILLIAM GIFFING, NYC (b/VIII–1–1815; d/IX–14–1882) MD CPSNY 1835. *Med reg NY NJ Conn* 1883: 222.

CLENDENIN, PAUL, USA (d/VII–4–1899 @37 Santiago) MD Nat Med Coll 1884. *Bost m & s jour* 141:51, 1899. *JAMA* 33:111, 1899. *Polk* 1896: 694.

CLENDENIN, WILLIAM, Cincinnati (b/X–1–1829 Cumberland Co, Pa; d/V–23–1885) MD Med Coll O 1850. *Med bull m & s* 7:226, 1885. *Atkinson* I:13–14.

CLENDINEN, ALEXANDER, Baltimore (b/1786 York Dist, SC; d/1861) MD UMd 1815. *Med annals Md:* 354.

CLENDINEN, ALEXANDER, Englewood, NJ (b/VIII–16–1841; d/IX–27–1891) MD UMd 1859. *Med reg NY NJ Conn* 1892: 274. *Atkinson* I:493. *Tr Med Soc NJ* 1892: 209–10.

CLENDINEN, WILLIAM ALEXANDER, ?Baltimore (b/Balto; d/c1849 New Orleans) MD UMd 1840. *Med annals Md:* 354. *K&B* I (1): 186.

CLENDINEN, WILLIAM HAZLETT, Baltimore (b/1772 Cecil Co, Md; d/XI–6–1839) Hon MD UMd 1838; ng UPa Med Sch 1802/03. *Med annals Md:* 354–55.

CLENDINEN, WILLIAM HAZLETT Jr, Baltimore; CW–USA; (b/1833; d/VIII–25–1893) MD UMd 1850. *JAMA* 21:829,1893. *Med ann Md:*355. *Butler* 1878:318.

CLEVELAND, CHARLES LUTHER, Cleveland, O (b/VII–5–1857; d/I–14–1890) MD Cleveland Homeop 1883; stud CPSNY; AB ? *Tr Am Inst Homeop* 1890: 153. *Med adv* 24:192, 1890. *No Am jour homeop* 38:200, 1890. Homeopath.

CLEVELAND, EMELINE H , Philadelphia (b/XI–22–1829 Conn; d/XII–8–1878) MD Woman's Med Coll Pa 1855. *Med rec NY* 14:499, 1878.

CLEVELAND, PERCY E , Nashville (d/VI–25–1899 @ 37) MD U Nashville 1890. *Nashville jour m & s* 86:47–48, 1889. *JAMA* 33:175, 1899. *Polk* 1896: 1400.

CLEVELAND, WARNER, NYC (b/VI–12–1816 Hebron, NY; d/XII–31–1887) MD Castleton 1847. *Med reg NY NJ Conn* 1888: 249, *Polk* 1886: 674.

CLEVELAND, WILLIAM LARNED, Atlanta (b/VI–16 1809 Harrisburg, Pa; d/V–20–1876 @ 67) MD Homeop Coll Cleveland 1861. *Tr Am Inst Homeop* 1877: 966. *US med invest* 3:587, 1876. *Amer homeop obs* 13:496, 1876. *Cleave*. Homeopath.

CLEW, HORATIO S , Middlesex, NJ (b/IX– –1825 Princeton, NJ; d/I–15–1882) Lic Med Soc NJ 1849. *Tr Med Soc NJ* 1882–83: 177.

CLIFFORD, ARTHUR, New Bedford, Mass (b/IV–7–1852; d/II–26 or III–11–1881) MD Dartmouth 1878; AB Harvard 1874. *Bost m & s jour* 105:623, 1881.

CLIFFORD, GEORGE GAY, San Antonio Tex (d/VI–20 1905) MD Pulte 1888. *Texas st jour med* 1:84, 1905/06.

CLIFFORD, LEWIS WADE, Hartford, Conn (b/VIII–17 1805; d/IV–5–1854) MD Harvard 1845; AB Brown 1825; AM. *Brown hist cat*: 1825.

CLIFTON, JAMES BEVERLEY, Louisburg, NC; CW–CSA (d/XI–2–1902) MD UCNY 1857; att UVa 1855–56. *UCNY cat*: 1857. *Polk* 1886: 724.

CLINTON, ALEXANDER, NYC (b/IV–7–1793 Little Britain, NY; d/II–18–1878) MD CPSNY 1819; att Columbia Coll. *Med reg NY NJ Conn* 1878: 180.

CLIPPINGER, GEORGE W , Indianapolis, Ind; CW–USA (d/II–20–1870) MD UCNY 1845 *Tr Ind St Med Soc* 1870: 160. *Kemper's Indiana*: 190.

CLOKEY, ALLISON W [ANDREW ALLISON?] Louisville (b/VII–23–1863 Xenia, O; d/XI–27–1899) MD Hahnemann Phila 1889; stud Berlin; att U Mich 1884–86. *Tr Amer Inst Homeop* 1900: 831. *No Amer jour homeop* 48:3, 1900 ("curr events"). Homeopath.

CLOPTON, JOHN, Williamsburg, Va; CW–CSA; (b/1834 Richmond; d/VII– –1891) MD Med Coll Va 1857. *Butler* 1878: 825. Blanton, *Va CW surg*. *Polk* 1886: 929.

CLOSE, CHARLES FREDERICK, ?Los Angeles (d/V–29–1901) MD Iowa St U 1896. *Ill med jour* ns3: 91, 1901.

CLOUD, CHARLES REEVES, Burlington & W Hill, NJ (b/I–26–1844 Woodbury; d/XII–7–1876) MD Hahnemann Phila 1867. *Tr Am Inst Homeop* 1895: 1094; 1896:1186. *Tr AMA* 28: 627, 1877. *Tr Med Soc NJ* 1877: [127]. Homeopath.

CLOUD, JESSE ALBERT, Easton, Pa; CW–USA (b/X–26–1841 West Chester; d/III–4–1900) MD UPa 1866. *U Pa med alum CW*: 1866. *Cleave*. Homeopath.

Spec. educ'l status abbrev. as: ***ng*** = college verified attendance without degree;

CLOUGH, BENJAMIN FRANKLIN, Worcester, Mass (d/V–8–1899 @ 61) MD Harvard 1869. *Bost m & s jour* 141: 28, 1899. *Polk* 1896: 727.

CLOUGH, GREENLEAF CLARK, Greenland, NH (b/IX–19–1821 Sandown; d/VI–7–1871) MD Bowdoin 1844. *Tr NH Med Soc* 1872: 86–89.

CLOUGH, JOHN, Boston; Woburn (b/I–23–1809 Gilmantown, NH; d/XI–25–1879) MD Dartmouth 1837. *Bost m & s jour* 102:120, 1880.

CLOW, J BRUCE, San José, Calif (d/XII–11–1885 Oakland @ 29) MD Hahnemann Phila 1882. *Hahn mo* 21: 143, 1886. Homeopath..

CLOW, RODERICK F , NYC (d/II–26–1878 @48) Lic NY St Med Soc 1847. *Med reg NY NJ Conn* 1878: 180. *Butler* 1874: 509.

CLUSSMAN, WILLIAM H , ?NYC (d/VI–8–1861 @33) MD UCNY 1850. *Med reg NY NJ Conn* 1862:154.

CLUTTERBUCK, AUSTIN SAMUEL, Morristown, NJ (b/IX–15–1864 Co Tipperary, Ireland; d/III–28–1895) <Lic RCS Dublin 1886> *Med reg NY NJ Conn* 1895:218. *JAMA* 24:650, 1895. *Trans Med Soc NJ* 1895: 209.

CLUXTON, FREDERICK C , Bradford, Pa (d/II–16–1904 @ 57) <MD U Victoria, Ont 1871> *Pa med jour* 8:334, 1904/05.

CLYMER, GEORGE Jr, USN 1829–1871 (b/VII–24–1804 Morrisville, Pa; d/IV–13–1881 Washington, DC) MD UPa 1828. *U Pa med alum CW*: 1828.

CLYMER, MEREDITH, NYC; CW–USA (b/VI–6–1817 London, Engl; d/IV–20–1902) MD UPa 1837; AB 1835. *Tr CPP* cent vol: 217. *Bost m & s jour* 146:449,1902. *U Pa med alum CW*: 1837. *K&B* III:236.

COAD, JOSEPH R , Philadelphia (b/XII–4–1829 Lebanon, Pa; d/III–11–1868) MD Jefferson 1856. *Phila med reg & dir* 1871: 293. *Tr Med Soc Pa* 1869: 481–82.

COALE, SKIPWITH H , Baltimore (b/1787; d/1848) MD UMd 1816. *Med annals Md:* 355.

COALE, WILLIAM, Frederick Co, Md (b/1805; d/1842) MD UMd 1827. *Med annals Md:* 355.

COALE, WILLIAM EDWARD, USN 1837–43; Boston; CW–San Comm (b/II–7–1816 Balto; d/IV–24–1865) MD UMd 1836. *Bost m & s jour* 72:265, 307, 1865; 105: 521, 1881. *Tr AMA* 16:612–13, 1865. *Med ann Md:* 355.

COAN, CHARLES, Brooklyn (d/I–20–1894 NYC) MD LICH 1891. *Med reg NY NJ Conn* 1894: 235.

COAN, ELISHA SKINNER, CW–USA; Auburn, Me (b/I 26–1843 Exeter; d/V–30–1896) MD Bowdoin 1870; ng Dartmouth Med. *Tr Me Med Assoc* 12: 430–33, 1896. *Atkinson* I: 452. *Polk* 1886: 425.

COATES, ALFRED WASHINGTON, Mystic River, Conn (b/VII–8–1813 No Stonington; d/X–27–1880) MD Yale 1843. *Proc Conn Med Soc* 1881:220–21. *Butler* 1878: 75.

COATES, BENJAMIN HORNOR, Philadelphia (b/XI 14–1797; d/X–16–1881) MD UPa 1818. *Tr CPP* cent vol: 218. *Bost m & s jour* 105:409, 1881. *Atkinson* I:628. *K & B* III: 237.

COATES, ELIAS FRANKLIN, Mystic Bridge, Conn (b/VIII–21–1820 Plainfield; d/XII–5–1886) MD Yale 1843. *Proc Conn Med Soc* 1887: 184–85. *Atkinson* I: 479. *Butler* 1878: 75.

COATES, ISAAC TAYLOR, CW–USN & USA (b/III–17–1834 Coatesville, Pa; d/VI–23–1883 Socarro, NM) MD UPa 1859. *U Pa med alum CW*: 1859.

COATES, JESSE, Coatesville, Pa (b/1796? d/VIII–3–1868 @ 72) MD UPa 1819. *Phila med reg & dir* 1871: 297. *Med surg rep Phila* 19:240, 1868.

COATES, REYNELL, Philadelphia (b/XII–10–1802; d/IV–28–1886) MD UPa 1823. *Tr CPP* cent vol: 218. *Med surg rep Phila* 54: 608, 1886. *K&B* III:238.

COATS, JOHN, Easton, Md (b/VII–11–1751; d/XI–30–1810) <ng UPa Med Sch> *Med annals Md:* 356.

COATSWORTH, GEORGE, CW–USA (d/I–9–1863 Murfreesboro, Tenn) MD unknown. *Nat med jour* 1:292, 1870/71.

COBB, BENJAMIN FRANKLIN, Richmond, Va; CW–CSA; (b/I–1–1826 Wayne Co, NC; d/VIII–24–1888) MD Jefferson 1847. *Tr Med Soc Va* 1888: 275. *Atkinson* I:480.

COBB, JABEZ VAUGHN, Rome, NY (b/IV–13–1811 Carter, Mass; d/VIII–28–1877 Lockport, NY) MD Fairfield 1838. *Tr Med Soc St NY* 1879: 574–78. *Butler* 1874: 533.

COBB, JEDEDIAH, Cincinnati 1824–36; Louisville, Ky 1837–52; Manchester, Mass 1854–60 (b/II–27–1800 Gray, Me; d/XI–11–1860) MD Bowdoin 1823. *Med surg rep Phila* ns5:213, 1860/61. *Nashville jour m & s* 20:189, 1861. *K&B* III: 239.

COBB, JOHN EDWARD, CW–USN; Taunton, Mass 1865–69, 1874; New Bedford 1875–77 (d/IX–23–1877) MD Harvard 1861; AB 1858. *Harvard in CW*: 110.

COBB, MOSES BENNETT, Biddeford, Me (b/VII–16–1852 Saccarappa; d/VII–24–1894 Saco) MD Bowdoin 1887. *Tr Me Med Assoc* 12:186–87, 1895. *Bost m & s jour* 133:195, 1895. *Polk* 1890: 498.

COBB, WILLIAM ALMY, Baltimore (b/V–25–1823; d/VII–30–1845) MD UMd 1845; ng Haverford. *Haverford biogr cat*: 22.

COBB, WILLIAM B , Standish, Me (b/V–19–1832 Limington; d/IV–6–1890) MD Dartmouth 1856. *Tr Me Med Assoc* 1890: 332–34. *Butler* 1896: 305.

COBLEIGH, EDWARD A, Chattanooga (d/XI–29–1905) MD Atlanta Med Coll 1874. *So pract* 28: 48–49, 1906. *New Orl m & s jour* 58:609, 1906. *Polk* 1896: 1384.

COBLENTZ, JACOB, Dayton, O (b/III–17–1795 Frederick Co, Md; d/II–15–1861) MD UMd 1819. *Med annals Md:* 356.

COBLENTZ, JOSEPH, Reading, Pa; Vaughn, Wash (b/I 24–1820 Middletown Valley Md; d/VIII–6–1899) MD U Pa 1850; AB Frank & Marsh 1848. *JAMA* 33:620, 1899.

COBURN, GEORGE ALBERT, E Cambridge, Mass (b/

X-28-1845; d/IX-2-1898) MD Harvard 1873; AB Amherst 1868. *Bost m & s jour* 139:256, 1898. *Polk* 1896: 711.

COBURN, HENRY WILLIAM, Maysville, Ky (d/III-10 1829) MD Transylvania 1828. *Transylvania jour med & assoc sci* 2:297, 1829.

COCHRAN, CHARLES ALBERT, Winthrop, Me 1858– (b/IV-29-1833 Monmouth; d/VIII-13-1906) MD Bowdoin 1856. *Homeop rec* 1906 (Oct.) *Cleave*. Homeopath.

COCHRAN, GEORGE, Brooklyn (b/1831 Londonderry, Ireland; d/XI-19-1872) MD CPSNY 1852; stud Foyle Coll, Ireland 1848. *Med reg NY NJ Conn* 1873: 338. *Med surg rep Phila* 27:488, 1872. *Med rec* 7:551, 1872.

COCHRAN, HENRY KING, Seven Mile Ford, Va; CW-CSA; (b/VIII-5-1832 Charlottesville, Va; d/XI-27-1903) MD Jefferson 1856; stud UVa. *Tr Med Soc Va* 1904: 318. *Polk* 1900: 1775.

COCHRAN, JAMES, Spiceland, Ind (d/II-27-1894) MD Med Coll Ind 1876. *Tr Ind St Med Soc* 1894: 229. *Polk* 1886: 337.

COCHRAN, JEROME, CW-CSA; Mobile Ala 1865– (b/XII-4-1831 Moscow, Tenn; d/VIII-16-1896) MD U Nashville 1861, *Buff m & s jour* 36:135, 1896. *JAMA* 27: 448–449, 1896. *New Orl m & s jour* 24: 179, 1896. *Tex med jour* 12:143, 1896–97. *Atkinson* I:228. *K&B* III: 239.

COCHRAN, JOHN H, Havre de Grace, Md (b/VI-25-1833; d/X-10-1889) MD UMd 1860. *JAMA* 33:1116, 1899. *Polk* 1886: 443.

COCHRAN, MILTON B, Iowa City, Ia (d/V-29-1898) MD Western Reserve 1851. *JAMA* 30: 1481, 1898. *Polk* 1896: 527.

COCHRAN, WILLIAM ALEXANDER, Cambridge Ala CW-CSA (b/IV-1-1832; d/II or III- -1873) MD ? stud U Ala 1850. *U Ala cat*: 97. *SHSP* 22:188, 1893.

COCHRAN, WILLIAM ALLEN, Tuscaloosa, Ala (d/VII 29-1891) MD UPa 1839; AB U Ala 1834; AM 1837. *Med annals Md:* 356. *Polk* 1886: 140.

COCHRAN, WILLIAM BAILEY, Middleburg, Va (b/ 1809; d/VII-12-1898 @ 89) MD UPa 1831. *JAMA* 31: 198, 1898. *Polk* 1896: 1494.

COCHRANE, ADAM H, San José, Calif (d/IV-4-1895 @ 64) MD Albany Med Coll 1857. *JAMA* 24: 609, 1895. *Polk* 1886: 175.

COCHRANE, JOHN, Lowell, Mass (d/IX-9-1888 @ 40) MD CPS Boston 1883. *Bost m & s jour* 119:264, 1888. *Polk* 1886: 468.

COCHRANE, WILLIAM WINSTON, Atchison, Kans (b/IV-3-1820 Owen City, Ky; d/I-14-1899) MD Louisville Med Coll 1848. *JAMA* 32:195, 1899. *Atkinson* I: 284. *Polk* 1886: 374.

COCK, THOMAS, NYC (b/I-12-1782 Matinecock, NY; d/VI-14-1869) MD CPSNY 1805. *Tr AMA* 21:445–46, 1870. *Phila med reg & dir* 1871: 301. *Tr Med Soc St NY* 1871: 352–54. *Med reg NY NJ Conn* 1869:326; 1871: 350 as b/1783).

COCK, THOMAS FERRIS, NYC (b/VII-1-1819; d/VI-11-1896) MD UPa 1839; AB Haverford 1836; stud CPSNY. *JAMA* 27: 52, 1896. *Bost m & s jour* 134: 628–29, 1896. *Atkinson* I: 438. *Polk* 1896: 1046.

COCKCROFT, JAMES, NYC (b/1793? d/VII-19-1856) MD CPSNY 1815. *Bost m & s jour* 55:47, 1856.

COCKCROFT, WILLIAM, NYC (b/VII-25-1817; d/XI 18-1889) MD CPSNY 1838;AB Columbia 1834. *Med reg NY NJ Conn* 1890:263. *Bost m & s jour* 121:545, 1889.

COCKE, CARY CHARLES, ?Bremo, Va; CW-CSA (b/I 1-1814 Recess; d/VIII-16-1888) MDUPa 1838. *U Pa med alum CW*: 1838.

COCKE, JAMES, Baltimore (b/c1780 Va; d/X-25-1813) Md UPa 1804; stud Guy's Hosp, London. *Med annals Md:* 356. *K&B* III: 240.

COCKE, WILLIAM HENRY, Portsmouth, Va; CW-CSA (b/III-5-1832; d/IV-25-1865 Washington DC)MD UPa 1854; stud UVa 1849–52. *U Pa med alum CW*:1854 Johnson,*U Va alum dec'd CW*:712. Blanton, *Va CW surg*.

COCKE, WILLIAM IRBY, Belleville, Tex 1855?– (d/ VIII-6-1873 @ 43) MD Jefferson 1853. *Med surg rep Phila* 29:216, 1873. *Tr Texas St Med Assoc* 1874: 84.

COCKE, WILLIAM THOMPSON, Greensboro Ala CW CSA? (b/VII-13-1844; d/1862 nr Dandridge Tn) Med stud U ALA, matric 1861; <AB U Va> *U Ala cat*:154.

COCKERILLE, AMERICUS, Alexandria, La (b/1825 Fairfax Co, Va; d/IV-12-1888) MD Jefferson 1850. *New Orl m & s jour* ns15:914, 1888.

COCKEY, CHARLES, Queenstown, Md (b/VII-22-1842;d/VII-31-1904) MD UMd 1866. *Med ann Md*:357.

COCKEY, CHARLES HENRY, Baltimore (b/VII-4-1844; d/XI-19-1904) MD UMd 1867. *Med annals Md:* 1867. *Polk* 1900: 806.

COCKEY, JOHN PAUL, Frederick, Md (b/VIII-24-1796 Bloomfield; d/XI-27-1859) MD UMd 1817. *Med annals Md:* 357.

COCKEY, JOSEPH CROMWELL, Frederick, Md (b/ 1808; d/X-18-1881) MD UMd 1835. *Med annals Md:* 357. *Butler* 1874: 311.

COCKRILL, JAMES JACKSON, Baltimore; CW-USA (b/III-18-1815; d/VII-13-1878) MD UMd 1837; att St Mary's Coll, Balto. *Med annals Md:* 357. *Tr AMA* 30: 811–12, 1879.

COCKRILL, JOSEPH M, Baltimore (b/1849; d/VII-23 1898) MD UMd 1871. *Med ann Md*:357. *Polk* 1886: 436.

COCKS, DAVID CLARK, Harlem, NY (d/I-14-1890 @ 39) MD Bellevue 1874. *Med reg NY NJ Conn* 1890: 264.

CODMAN, BENJAMIN STORER, Boston (d/II-22 1894 @78) MD Harvard 1845. *Bost m & s jour* 130:228, 1894. *Butler* 1878: 338.

CODMAN, WILLARD WILD [WILLIAM?], Boston (d/XII-22-1886) MD Harvard 1843. *Bost m & s jour* 115: 630, 632, 1886. *Polk* 1886: 455.

CODY, JAMES, Watertown, Wis (b/VIII-22-1820 New-

 Spec. educ'l status abbrev. as: ***ng*** = college verified attendance without degree;

foundland; d/X-8-1894) MD Harvard 1844. *Tr Wis St Med Soc* 30:553-59, 1896. *Polk* 1890: 1174.

COE, ALGERNON SIDNEY, CW-USA; Oswego, NY (d/X-18-1893) MD CPSNY 1854. *Med reg NY NJ Conn* 1894: 235. *JAMA* 21:667, 1893. *Bost m & s jour* 129: 432, 1893.

COE, FRANZ HUNT, Seattle (d/VII- -1904) MD U Mich 1888. *Cal st jour med* 2:321,1904. *Polk* 1896:1514.

COE, MILTON F , Chicago (d/VIII-13-1892 @ 30) MD U Ill 1888. *Chic med rec* 3:515, 1892. *Polk* 1890:310.

COE, SARAH J , Wilkes-Barre, Pa (d/XI-4-1905) MD U Mich Homeop Coll 1878. *Pa med jour* 9:220, 1905/06. *Flint* 1897:829.

COE, WILLIAM HENRY, CW-USA; ?Auburn, NY (b/I 17-1841 Pavilion, NY; d/V-21-1904) MD UPa 1866. *U Pa med alum CW*: 1866.

COFFEEN, JOHN Q A , Wyoming, O (d/VIII-9-1883 @ 57) MD Eclectic Cincinnati 1863. *Med surg rep Phila* 49:252, 1883. *Med adv* 14? 1883 (Sept). Homeopath.

COFFIN, B F , Westfield, Ind (b/1816; d/XII-28-1898 @ 82) Lic by years of practice. *JAMA* 32:92, 1899. *Polk* 1890: 392.

COFFIN, FREDERICK GUSTAVUS, Great Falls, NH; Brockwayville, Pa (d/V-23-1897 @ 43) MD Boston U Sch Med 1878. *JAMA* 28:1092, 1897. *Polk* 1886: 591.

COFFMAN, JOHN R , Grenada, Miss (b/VIII-15-1840 St Genevieve Co, Mo; d/I-16-1873) MD U Nashville 1861. *Tr Miss St Med Assoc* 1876.

COGGESHALL, WILLIAM HARVEY, Oneida, NY; Henrico Co, Va (b/XII-24-1850 Fitchburg, Mass; d/IX-7-1884 or 1885) MD LICH 1871. *Tr Med Soc Va* 1885: 280-81. *New Orl m & s jour* ns13:420, 1885.

COGSWELL, GEORGE, Haverhill, Mass (b/II-5-1808 Atkinson, NH; d/IV-21-1901) MD Dartmouth 1830; AM 1865. *Bost m & s jour* 144:414, 1901.

COGSWELL, GEORGE BADGER, No Easton, Mass (b/IX-15-1834 Bradford, Mass; d/III-6-1896) MD Dartmouth 1857; AM 1880. *JAMA* 26:642, 1896. *Bost m & s jour* 134:280, 1896.

COGSWELL, MASON FITCH, Albany, NY; CW-USA (d/I-21-1865) MD CPSNY 1833; AB Yale 1829. *Tr AMA* 16:652, 1865; 18:310-11, 1867. *Nat med jour* 1: 292, 1870/71. *Tr Med Soc St NY* 1865:286-93. *Bost m & s jour* 72:28, 1865. *Med surg rep Phila* 12:284, 1864/65.

COGSWELL, WILLIAM, Bradford, Mass; CW-USA (b/IV-1-1821 Atkinson, NH; d/VIII-15-1891) MD Dartmouth 1845; ng Harvard Med 1844. *Bost m & s jour* 125:208, 1891. *Northwest med jour* 19:151, 1891. *Med bull m & s* 14:31, 1892. *Polk* 1886: 463. *Butler* 1878:348.

COHEN, JOSHUA I, Baltimore (b/1800/1 Richmond Va; d/1870) MD UMd 1823. *Med ann Md*:358. *K&B* III: 424.

COHEN, SALMON P, NYC (b/1845 Gny;d/XII-6-1898) <MD Leipzig 1877> *Bost m & s jour* 139: 636-37, 1898.

COHOON, JOHN THOMAS PHILIP COUPER, CW-CSA (b/1838 Suffolk, Va; d/IV- -1869 Elizabeth City, NC) MD UPa 1856. *U Pa med alum CW*: 1856.

COIT, BENJAMIN BILLINGS, San Francisco (b/1801; d/1867) MD Jefferson 1826; AM Yale 1822. *Tr AMA* 19:446-48, 1868. *Bost m & s jour* 76:544, 1867. *Med & surg rep Phila* 16:367, 418, 1867.

COIT, DAVID GARDINER, CW-CSA (b/VI-6-1829 Hunt's Bluff, SC; d/VII-21-1865 Cheraw) MD UPa 1857. *U Pa med alum CW*: 1857.

COIT, WILLIAM NOBLE, Champlain, NY (b/Plattsburgh; d/VIII-4-1886) MD UPa 1856. *Tr NY St Med Soc* 11:741 ff, 1894. *Butler* 1878: 548.

COKENOWER, HARVEY L , Clarinda, Ia (d/IX-19-1901) MD CPS Keokuk 1877. *Ill med jour* ns3:295, 1901. *Polk* 1886: 353.

COKER, JOHN H , New Orleans, La (d/I-3-1900) MD unknown. Lic by years of practice. *JAMA* 34:187, 1900. *Polk* 1886:416. Black.

COKER, S R , Mount Calm, Tex (d/XI-30-1899) MD Louisville Med Coll 1891. *JAMA* 33:1632, 1899. *Polk* 1896: 1442.

COLBURN, ZACCHEUS, Manchester, NH (b/I-6-1801 W Nottingham; d/XI-21-1864) MD Bowdoin 1829; AB Brown 1827. *Bost m & s jour* 71:368, 1864.

COLBY, ENOCH LANE, Cincinnati 1836-39; Claremont, NH 1839-49 (b/VI-11-1797 Bradford; d/VIII-24 1849) MD Jefferson 1836; ng Bowdoin Med Sch 1834; AB Amherst 1826. *Amherst, Men of*: 1826.

COLBY, GEORGE WASHINGTON, Waldoborough, Me (b/V-7-1818; d/II-24-1881) MD Bowdoin 1845. *Tr Me Med Assoc* 1881: 385. *Butler* 1878: 305.

COLBY, ISAAC, Concord, NH 1846- ; Salem, Mass 1851- (b/VIII-6-1793 Hopkinton, NH; d/VI-29-1866) MD Dartmouth 1817. *Tr Am Inst Homeop* 1893:134. Homeopath.

COLBY, JOHN CALVIN, Franconia, NH (d/XII-7-1852) MD UVt 1826. *Bost m & s jour* 48:99-102,1853

COLBY, JOHN LADD, NYC (d/II-4-1885) MD UCNY 1846. *Med reg NY NJ Conn* 1885: 232.

COLE, EDGAR B , Easton & Waterford, NY (b/IV-2 1826 Columbia Co, NY; d/XI-10-1871) MD Berkshire 1847. *Tr Am Inst Homeop* 1874: 660. *Tr NY St Hom Med Soc* 9:545. Homeopath.

COLE, ELI K , Carmel, NY (d/X-5-1865 Donaldson, La) Lic NY St Med Soc 1863. *Med surg rep Phila* 13: 310, 1865. *Nat med jour* 1:292, 1870/71.

COLE, GEORGE EDWARD, Sheboygan, Wis (b/1860? d/IX-26-1892 @ 32) MD Harvard 1887. *Bost m & s jour* 127:396, 1892. *Polk* 1890: 1172.

COLE, HENRY CLAY, Kokomo, Ind (b/I-28-1838 Ripley Co; d/IX-19-1881) ng U Mich Med Sch 1860; AB UCNY 1858. *Tr Ind St Med Soc* 1882: 197. *Butler* 1878: 197.

COLE, ISAAC, Carroll Co, Md (b/1806 Baltimore Co; d/VII- -1885) MD UMd 1827. *Med annals Md:* 358.

COLE, ISAAC GRISWOLD, St Johnsbury, Vt; CW-

USA; d/I-3-1866) MD Harvard 1855. *Harv in CW*: 291.

COLE, JAMES BLACKMER, Wabasha, Minn (d/VI-19 1898) MD U Mich 1882. *JAMA* 30:1534, 1898. *Tr Minn St Med Soc* 1899: 191. *Polk* 1886: 515.

COLE, JAMES GILLESPIE ROWE, CW-CSA; (b/IV-4-1831 New Bern, NC; d/V-14-1881 Demopolis, Ala) MD UPa 1855; AB Princeton 1852. *U Pa med alum CW*: 1855.

COLE, JAMES W , Hazelton, Pa (b/1861? Allentown; d/XII-15-1896 @ 35) MD Jefferson 1881. *JAMA* 28: 140, 1897. *Reg Pa Phys* 1881-88: 246.

COLE, JOHN TREADWELL, Newburyport, Mass (d/I-3-1871 @ 39 Charleston, SC) MD Bellevue 1864; AB Harvard 1860. *Bost m & s jour* 7:32, 220, 1871.

COLE, LORENZO STARRETT, Hallowell Me 1866-79 (b/IX-1-1828; d/II-13-1881 Peoria, Ill) MD Jefferson 1856; ng Bowdoin med 1853. *Bowdoin cat*: 1853 med.

COLE, MERRYMAN, Baltimore (b/V-19-1799; d/I-6-1872) "Licensed to practice." *Med annals Md:* 359.

COLE, PALMER COOK, CW-USA; NYC (b/1835 Claverack-on-the Hudson; d/VII-3-1906) MD Harvard 1858; AB Rutgers 1855. *Bost m & s jour* 155: 50, 1906. *Harvard in CW*: 251. *Polk* 1896: 1046.

COLE, RICHARD BEVERLY, Philadelphia; San Francisco (b/VIII-12-1829 Manchester, Va; d/I-17-1901) MD Jefferson 1849; MRCS (L) 1864. *JAMA* 32: 1212, 1899. *Atkinson*I: 184. *K&B* III: 245-46. *Polk* 1896: 231.

COLE, WILLIAM C , Fountain Co Ind (b/VII-16-1828 Washington; d/III-11-1894) MD Med Coll Ohio 1868. *JAMA* 22:482, 1894. *Tr Ind St Med Soc* 1894: 228. *Atkinson* I:586. *Butler* 1878: 197. Kemper's *Indiana*: 253.

COLE, WILLIAM J , Baltimore (b/1853? d/V-6-1888 @ 35) MD UMd 1877. *New Orl m & s jour* ns15: 1003, 1888. *Butler* 1886: 436.

COLEMAN, BYRON S , Rochester, NY (b/1861? d/VII 15-1899 @ 38) MD Buffalo 1883. *JAMA* 33:302, 1899. *Polk* 1886: 643.

COLEMAN, CHARLES SPOFFORD, San Leandro, Cal (b/VIII-17-1826 Seneca Co, NY; d/XI-27-1881) MD Geneva 1850. *Tr Cal St Med Soc* 1882:244-45. *Butler* 1878: 58.

COLEMAN, CHARLES WASHINGTON, CW-USA; Williamsburg, Pa (b/VII-18-1826; d/IX-15-1894) MD UPa 1847. *U Pa med alum CW*: 1847. *JAMA* 23:561, 1894. Blanton: *Va CW surg*: 1847. *Butler* 1878: 825.

COLEMAN, FRANCIS B , Church Hill, Miss (b/VII-4-1811 Lexington, Ky; d/II-7-1876) MD Transylvania 1832. *New Orl m & s jour* ns3:914-15, 1876.

COLEMAN, FRANCIS W , Rodney, Miss (d/V-29-1901, New Orleans) MD Tulane 1866. *New Orl m & s jour* 54:58, 1901. *Polk* 1890: 634.

COLEMAN, HENRY WALDBURG, Trenton, NJ (d/III-30-1897) MD CPSNY 1868; AM Columbia. *JAMA* 28: 714, 1897. *Polk* 1896: 950.

COLEMAN, ISAAC NEWTON, Cadillac, Mich (b/1850? d/I-17-1888 @ 38) MD Hahnemann, Chic 1879; ng U Mich Homeop Med Coll 1878. *Med couns* 13: 185, 1888. *Med vis* 4:206, 1888. *Polk* 1886: 485. Homeopath.

COLEMAN, ISAAC PEARSON, Pemberton, NJ (b/II-2 1804; d/XI-4-1869) MD Yale 1832. *Phila med reg & dir* 1871: 305. *Tr Med Soc NJ* 1870: 93-96. *Tr AMA* 21:468, 1870.

COLEMAN, JAMES BEAKS, Trenton, NJ (b/1806; d/II 19-1877) MD Yale 1829. *Tr AMA* 29:627-29, 1878. *Tr Med Soc NJ* 1878-79: 201-04. *Med rec* 13:455, 1878.

COLEMAN, JAMES WALTER, Uniontown, Ala (d/V-24-1886) MD Jefferson 1847; <att Med Coll SC> *Tr Med Assoc St Ala* 1887: 306. *Polk* 1886: 140.

COLEMAN, JOHN CLARK, USN 1852-58; CW-CSA (b/III-29-1829 Halifax CH, Va; d/VI-12-1898) MD UPa 1849; <AB UNC 1847> *U Pa med alum CW*: 1849.

COLEMAN, JOHN S , Augusta, Ga; CW-CSA (b/X-10 1837 Richmond Co, Ga; d/VI-19-1892) MD Jefferson 1852. *Atkinson* I:303-04. *Polk* 1886: 226.

COLEMAN, ROBERT THOMAS, CW-CSA; Richmond, Va (b/IX 3-1830 Hanover Co; d/III-4-1884) MD Jefferson 1852; MD UVa 1851; AB 1851. *Tr Med Soc Va* 1884:708. *Atkinson* I:286. *K&B* III:246-47. *Butler* 1878: 825.

COLEMAN, WILLIAM CLARK, CW-USA; Greensburg, Pa (b/XI 29-1839 Clarksburg; d/V-4-1880) MD LICH 1868. *JAMA* 3:82, 1884. *Atkinson* I: 127-28. *Butler* 1878: 707.

COLES, ABRAHAM, Newark, NJ (b/XII-26-1813 Scotch Plains; d/V-5-1891 Cal) MD Jefferson 1835; AM Rutgers; PhD Lewisburg 1860; LLD Princeton 1871. *Med reg NY NJ Conn* 1891: 270. *Tr NJ Med Soc* 1891:235-42. *JAMA* 17:387, 1891. *K&B* III:247-48.

COLES, JOHN W , USN (b/VIII-14-1838 NJ; d/IV-6 1895 Phila) MD Jefferson 1863. *JAMA* 24:609, 1895.

COLESCOTT, THOMAS W , Brookville, Ind (d/II-19-1900 @86) MD U Louisville 1842; MD Cincinnati Med Coll 1838. *JAMA* 34:573, 1900. *Polk* 1896: 158.

COLGAN, JOSEPH FRANCIS, Brooklyn (b/1865; d/IV 8-1898) MD LICH 1890. *JAMA* 30:999, 1898. *Polk* 1896: 994.

COLGAN, JOSEPH PATRICK Jr, Brooklyn; CW-USA (d/IV-13-1884 @ 50) MD CPSNY 1857. *Med reg NY NJ Conn* 1885: 232.

COLGATE, GEORGE, USN 1805-09; Westminster, Md (b/1783? d/V-1-1822 @ 39) *Med annals Md:* 359.

COLHOUN [CALHOUN], SAMUEL, Philadelphia (b/1787; d/IV-7-1841) MD UPa 1808; AB Princeton 1804. *Tr CPP* cent vol: 218. *K & B* III:195 [as Calhoun].

COLLARD, PHILANDER, Ossining, NY (b/1845 Westchester Co; d/V-7-1906) MD CPSNY 1883. *Bost m & s jour* 154:568, 1906. *Polk* 1896: 1100.

COLLER, LYMAN TANNER, Hingham, Wis (d/X-22-1897 @ 52) MD Rush 1883. *JAMA* 29:976, 1897. *Polk* 1896: 1550.

COLLETT, JOHN, Peekskill, NY (b/1804? d/1866) MD CPSNY 1831. *Tr AMA* 18:323, 1867; 19:410, 1868. *Med reg NY NJ Conn* 1867: 213. *Med surg rep Phila* 15:188, 1866.

COLLETT, WAIGHTSTILL AVERY, Morganton, NC (b/1830; d/1880) MD Jefferson 1856. *Tr NC Med Soc* 1881: 24. *Butler* 1878: 592.

COLLIER, ABNER A , Trenton, Mo (d/III–14–1895 @ 65) MD Jefferson 1852. *JAMA* 24:458, 1895. *Butler* 1878: 425.

COLLIER, HENRY. Coxsackie, NY; CW–USA (b/1833? d/I–22–1863) MD UCNY 1853. *Bost m & s jour* 68:48, 1863. *Nat med jour* 1:292, 1870/71.

COLLIER, THOMAS E , Atlanta, Ga (d/IV–12–1899 @ 64) MD UCNY 1857. *JAMA* 32:899, 1899. *JAMA* 32:899, 1899. *Polk* 1896: 324.

COLLIFLOWER, JOEL WASHINGTON, CW–USA (d/IX–23–1862 Washington, DC) ng U Mich Med 1861–62. *U Mich cat*: 659.

COLLIN, ROSWELL PARK, NYC (b/I–7–1852; d/XII–21–1891) MD CPSNY 1879; AB Williams 1876. *Med reg NY NJ Conn* 1892: 274. *Bost m & s jour* 125: 692, 1891.

COLLINGS, ISAAC S , CW–USA (d/IX–10–1865) MD unknown. *Nat med jour* 1:292, 1870/71.

COLLINS, ALMER MERCENA, Shelbyville, Ill (d/III–10–1903 @ 58) MD Ecl Med Inst Ohio 1873. *Ill med jour* ns4:889, 1903. *Polk* 1896: 440.

COLLINS, CHARLES SMITH, NYC (d/V–20–1900) MD CPSNY 1884; AB Columbia 1881; AM 1884. *Bost med surg jour* 142:580, 1900. *JAMA* 34:1574, 1900. *Polk* 1896: 1046.

COLLINS, CLARKSON T , NYC (b/I–8–1821 Smyrna, NY; d/IV–10–1881) MD UCNY 1843. *Tr AMA* 33:539–40, 1882. *Atkinson* I:41–42.

COLLINS, DANIEL B , St Peter, Minn (d/II–14–1898) MD Rush 1871. *JAMA* 30: 570, 1898. *Tr Minn St Med Soc* 1899: 191. *Polk* 1896: 915.

COLLINS, DENNIS, Chicago (d/XI–10–1905 @ 49) MD UCNY 1880. *Ill med jour* 8:530, 1905. *Polk* 1896: 379.

COLLINS, GEORGE, CW–USA (d/VII–25–1867 @ 28) ng U Mich 1861–62. *U Mich cat*: 659.

COLLINS, GEORGE E , Bethel, Me (b/X–16–1839 New Gloucester; d/VIII–26–1867) MD Berkshire 1862. *Tr Me Med Assoc* 1869–70: 174–75.

COLLINS, GEORGE LEWIS, Providence, RI (b/XII–31 1820 Hopkinton; d/VIII–21–1877) MD UCNY 1846. *Tr AMA* 29:629–30 1878. *Tr RI M Soc* 2:153–56 1877–82.

COLLINS, GEORGE MALIN, Tipton, Ind (b/I–10–1838; d/VIII–27–1896) MD Cincinnati Coll Med & Surg 1863. *Tr Ind St Med Soc* 1897: 363. *Polk* 1896: 494.

COLLINS, HENRY AUGUSTUS, Conway, Mass; Springfield 1852– (b/VIII–27–1826 S Hadley; d/V–13–1884) MD Yale 1850. *Tr Am Inst Homeop* 1893: 134. *Mass Homeop Soc* 1890 (Sept). Homeopath.

COLLINS, ISAAC GRIFFIN, Sing Sing, NY (b/VI–17–1832 Greenville; d/X–17–1885) DM Albany 1858. *Med reg NY NJ Conn* 1886: 243. *Bost m & s jour* 114: 398, 1886. *Tr Med Soc St NY* 1886: 626–30.

COLLINS, JAMES, Philadelphia; CW–USA (b/X–20–1831 Pineville Pa; d/X–7–1895) MD UPa 1860; AB Amherst 1858. *JAMA* 25:640,726, 1895. *Med bull m & s* 17:431,1895. *Atkinson* I:77. *U Pa med alum CW*: 1860.

COLLINS, JOHN MAURICE, Barneveldt, Wis (b/VI–? 1889) MD Rush 1883. *Tr Wis St Med Soc* 1891:256.

COLLINS, NAOMI A (PIERCE), Mahomet, Ill (d/V–3 1906 @ 44) MD Woman's Med Coll Chicago 1885. *Ill med jour* 9: 662, 1906.

COLLINS, RANSOM MALONE, E Feliciana, La (b/ 1794? d/III–12–1836 @ 42) MD Transylvania 1827. *Transylvania jour med & assoc sci* 9:560, 1836.

COLLINS, STEPHEN, Baltimore (b/1797 Del; d/XII–16–1871) MD UPa 1823; AB Princeton 1818; AM 1871. *Med annals Md:* 359.

COLLINS, THOMAS B , Rochester, NY (b/1827 Mendon; d/II–17–1888) MD Jefferson 1851; ng Woodstock 1849. *Tr NY Med Soc* 1894: 741 ff. *Polk* 1886: 704.

COLLINS, THOMAS SCULL, Blackwood, NJ (d/XII–12–1883 @ 27) MD UPa 1883; PhG Phila Coll Pharm 1880. *Med surg rep Phila* 49: 700, 1883.

COLLINS, WILLARD CLARK, CW–USA; Buckport, Me (b/IV–24–1826 Isle au Haut; d/1894) MD Bowdoin 1855. *JAMA* 22:158, 1894. *Butler* 1878: 305.

COLLINS, WILLIAM ANDREW, CW–USA; Madison, Ind (b/III–16–18__? Carrollton, Ky; d/V–18–1883) MD unknown; AB Hanover 1860. *Tr Ind St Med Soc* 1884: 208. Kemper's *Indiana*.

COLMAN, HENRY, Lynn, Mass (d/XI–12–1893 @ 53) MD Yale 1874. *Bost m & s jour* 129:504, 1893. *Butler* 1878: 348.

COLONY, GEORGE DANFORTH, Fitchburg, Mass (b/ Keene, NH; d/X–1/2–1898) MD UPa 1846; AB Dartmouth 1843. *Bost m & s jour* 139:356, 399–400, 1898. *Polk* 1896: 712.

COLT, EDWIN N , Brooklyn, NY (b/VIII–7–1811; d/ IX–15–1893) MD Berkshire 1833. *Med reg NY NJ Conn* 1894: 235. *JAMA* 21:498, 1893. *Bost m & s jour* 129:312, 1893.

COLTON, CHARLES M , CW–USA (b/Ohio; d/II–29–1864 Catlett's Station, Va) MD Med Coll Ohio 1862. *Tr AMA* 16:651, 1865. *Nat med jour* 1:292, 1870/71.

COLTON, D ALPHONSO, Chicago (d/X–17–1891 @ 70) MD Rush 1853. *Med vis* 7:365, 1891. *Polk* 1886:261. Homeopath 1854– .

COLTON, ELLSWORTH EARL, New Britain, Conn (d/ I–26–1900 @ 42) MD CPSNY 1882. *JAMA* 34: 381, 1900. *Polk* 1896: 1113.

COLTON, FRANCIS PARMELEE, NYC (b/XII–25 1824 Longmeadow, Mass; d/II–23–1852) MD CPSNY 1849; AB Amherst 1845. *Amherst, Men of*: 1845.

COLVILLE, ROBERT K , NYC (b/1810; d/VIII-12-1886) MD UCNY 1843. *Med reg NY NJ Conn* 1887:257.

COMAN, ISAAC W , Elkhorn, Wis (d/I-13-1890 @ 70) MD Hom Hosp Clev'd 1851 (Hon?) *Med vis* 6:45, 1890. *Tr Am Inst Hom* 1895: 1094. *Polk* 1886: 953. Homeopath.

COMBS, JOHN SHAW, CW-USA; Owensville O (b/XI 24-1820 Clermont Co;d/VIII-21-1901) MD Med Coll O 1850 *JAMA* 37:710 1901. *Atkinson* I:576. *Polk* 1886:764.

COMBS, WILLARD F , Flemington, NJ (b/NY; d/VIII-16-1854 @ 26) Lic Bd Censors, NJ; att med lectures NY. *Tr Med Soc NJ* 1871-73: 139-40.

COMEGYS, CORNELIUS GEORGE, Cincinnati (b/VII 23-1816 Kent Co, Del; d/II-10-1896) MD UPa 1848. *Buff m & s jour* 35:678, 1896. *Tr Ohio St Med Soc* 1896: 369-70. *JAMA* 26:390-91, 1896. *Atkinson* I:688-89. *K & B* III: 248-49.

COMEGYS, HENRY C , Scranton, Pa (b/Winborough, Md; d/XI-29-1904 @ 76) MD UMd 1854. *Pa med jour* 8:334, 1904/05. *Flint* 1897: 834.

COMFORT, JOHN E , Bronx, NY (b/X-6-1837; d/V-29-1901) MD Albany 1864. *Bost m & s jour* 144: 570, 1901. *Polk* 1896: 1046.

COMFORT, JONATHAN JONES, Cleveland, O (b/I-9-1830 Fallsington Pa; d/1906) MD U Mich 1858; MD Jefferson 1859; AB Haverford 1856. *Hav biog cat*: 60.

COMINGS, BENJAMIN NEWTON, New Britain, Conn (b/XI-2-1816 Cornish, NH; d/XII-4-1899) MD Castleton 1845; AB Dartmouth 1842. *Proc Conn Med Soc* 1900: 343-44. *JAMA* 33:632, 1899. *Polk* 1897: 281.

COMINGS, DAVID LAWRENCE MORRILL, W Swanzey NH; CW-USA (b/X-14-1825;d/VIII-1-1863) MD Castleton 1850. *Nat med jour* 1:292, 1870/71.

COMLY, EZRA, Philadelphia (d/I-4-1890) MD UPa 1862. *Med bull med & surg* 13: 68,1890. *Polk* 1886:814.

COMMANDER, JOSEPH, Jr, ?Elizabeth City, NC; CW-CSA; (b/X-10-1833 Nixonton; d/IX-28-1880) MD UPa 1860. *U Pa med alum CW*: 1860.

COMMLOSSY, FRANZ, NYC (d/1873) MD UCNY 1870. *Med reg NY NJ Conn* 1874: 271.

COMPTON, BENJAMIN TALBOTT, Corydon, Ky (d/VIII-10-1899 @ 29) MD U Louisville 1896. *JAMA* 33:493, 1899.

COMPTON, ISAAC LEWIS, Bound Brook, NJ (b/IX 28-1855 Liberty Corner; d/IV-5-1897) MD CPSNY 1879. *Tr Med Soc NJ* 1897: 302-303.

COMPTON, JAMES Mc , Shreveport, La (b/Ala; d/XII-16-1876 @ 38) MD U La 1872. *New Orl m & s jour* ns5: 164, 1877.

COMPTON, JOHN WILLIAM, Evansville, Ind (b/VII-22-1825 Hardensburg, Ky; d/V-28-1905 Terre Haute) MD Med Coll Evansville 1873. *Tr Ind St Med Soc* 1905: 444. *Atkinson* I: 606.

COMPTON, JOSEPH B , Bentonville, Va (d/X-8-1894) MD U Md 1880. *Tr Med Soc Va* 1894: 198.

COMPTON, WILLIAM, Lancaster, Pa (b/XII-30-1825 Cambridge; d/XII-15-1895) MD Phila Med Coll 1853. *JAMA* 25:1140, 1895; 26:93, 1896. *Tr Med Soc Pa* 27: 373-74. 1897. *Butler* 1878: 708.

COMPTON, WILLIAM McCORKLE, Jackson, Miss; CW-CSA (b/VIII-4-1833 Madisonville, Ky; d/X-23-1878) MD Jefferson 1854. *Tr AMA* 30:812-13, 1879. *Tr Miss St Med Assoc* 1879:40,43-48. *Atkinson* I:180.

COMSTOCK, ALBERT LEA, Bath, NY 1827- ; NYC 1837; Buffalo 1857- ; Mt Kisco 1864- (b/XII-12-1802 Butternuts; d/V-13-1876) Lic Herkimer Co Med Soc; stud Fairfield. *Tr Am Inst Homeop* 1895: 1094. *Cleave*. Homeopath 1857-

COMSTOCK, DAVID CLOSE, NYC (b/XII-2-1840; d/III-24-1892) MD Bellevue 1869. *Med reg NY NJ Conn* 1892: 275. *JAMA* 18:470, 1892. *Bost m & s jour* 126:328, 1892. *Polk* 1886: 675.

COMSTOCK, JOHN LEE, Hartford, Conn; War 1812-USA (b/1789? d/XI-21-1858 @ 71) MD unknown. *Bost m & s jour* 59:408, 1859.

COMSTOCK, JOSEPH, Liberty Hill, Conn (b/1777? d/XII-3-1867 @ 90) Hon MD Yale 1831. *Bost m & s jour* 77:428, 1867.

COMSTOCK, LUCIUS SAMUEL, NYC (d/XI-30-1876) MD Jefferson 1860? *Med s rep Phila* 35:526 1876.

CONANT, ABEL BLOOD, CW-USA (b/I-5-1837; d/XII-22-1864 NYC) MD CPSNY 1862. *Med reg NY NJ Conn* 1865:234. *Tr Med Soc St NY* 1866:345-46. *Med surg rep Phila* 12:236, 1864/65. *Nat med jour* 1:292, 1870/71.

CONANT, DAVID SLOAN, NYC; Burlington, Vt; Lyme, NH; CW-USA (b/I-21-1825 or 1828; d/X-8-1865 NYC) MD Dartmouth 1851; ng Bowdoin Med. *Tr Med Soc St NY* 1866:336-40. *Med reg NY NJ Conn* 1866:199. *Tr AMA* 18:314, 1867. *Med surg rep Phila* 14:81-83, 1866. *K&B* III: 249-50.

CONANT, GEORGE SEYMOUR, NYC (b/1853? d/IX-23-1904 @ 51) MD Bellevue 1877. *Bost m & s jour* 151:366, 1904. *Polk* 1896: 1046.

CONAWAY, WILLIAM KEITH, Ridgeway, Del (d/IX-4-1896) MD Jefferson 1890. *JAMA* 27: 661, 1896.

CONDELL, WILBUR R , Springfield, Ill (d/VII-17-1901) MD Hahnemann Chicago 1871. *Ill med jour* ns3:142, 1901. *Polk* 1886: 298.

CONDICT, HENRY FORD, Montgomery Co, Md (b/1804 Littleton, NJ; d/X-31-1893) MD Columbian DC 1830; AB Princeton 1822. *Hist Med Soc DC:* 228.

CONDICT, LEWIS, Morristown, NJ (b/III-3-1773; d/V-26-1862) MD UPa 1794. *Tr AMA* 14:207-08, 1864. *Bost m & s jour* 66:404, 1862. *Med surg rep Phila* ns8:234,360-61, 1862. *K&B* III:250. *US Cong biogr dir*.

CONDIE, DAVID FRANCIS, Morton, Pa (b/V-12-1796 Phila; d/III-21-1875) MD UPa 1818. *Phila m times* 5: 448, 1875. *Med rec* 10:265 & 447, 1875. *Tr CPP* cent vol: 218. *K & B* III: 250.

CONE, JONAH, E Haddam, Conn (b/V–17–1763; d/IX–18–1830) MD unknown. *Proc Conn Med Soc* ns2:150, 1882–83.

CONE, ROBERT CEPHAS, Durham, NY; NYC 1865– (d/XII–21–1879 @ 69) MD Yale 1837. *Med rec NY* 17:52, 1880. *Med surg rep Phila* 42:22, 1880.

CONE, THOMAS E, NYC (d/X–20–1906 @59) MD UCNY 1873. *Bost m & s jour* 155:490, 1906.

CONE, WILLIAM C, ? (d/IX–10–1878 Franklin, Tenn) MD unknown. *Tr AMA* 30:858, 1879. *Med rec NY* 14:240, 1878.

CONE, WILLIAM DAVIDSON, Conesville, Ia (d/XII–1 1899 @ 62) MD Bellevue 1868. *JAMA* 33:1504, 1899. *Polk* 1896: 516.

CONFER, FRANCIS MARION, Monroe, Wis (b/XII–18 1854 Green Co, Wis; d/XI–7–1900) MD Rush 1882. *Tr Wis St Med Soc* 35:454–57,1901. *Polk* 1890: 1170.

CONGDON, ISRAEL, Collins, NY (d/VI–21–1846) <MD Fairfield 1828> *Buff med jour* 2:124, 1846.

CONGER, FREDERICK HALSEY, Prairie du Sac, Wis (d/IV–7–1896) MD CPSNY 1872. *JAMA* 26:843, 1896. *Polk* 1896:1561.

CONGER, JOHN S, NYC (b/1785? d/I–27–1860 @ 74) MD CPSNY 1838; AB 1834; AM 1837. *Med surg rep Phila* ns3:425, 1859/60.

CONGER, STEPHEN H, Summit, NJ (d/XII–24–1897 @ 76) MD CPSNY 1843; AB Princeton 1839. *JAMA* 30:48, 1898.

CONKLIN, BENJAMIN F, Fayette Co, Pa (b/IX–18–1844 Washington Co; d/I–18–1873) MD Cleveland Med Coll 1869. *Tr Pa St Med Soc* 1874: 266–67. *Med surg rep Phila* 28: 184.

CONKLING, JOHN T, Brooklyn (d/III–17–1898 @ 73) MD CPSNY 1855. *Bost m & s jour* 138: 286, 1898. *JAMA* 30:744–45, 1898. *Polk* 1896:994.

CONKWRIGHT, ALLEN H, Sedalia, Mo 1872– (b/V–15–1837 Clark Co, Ky; d/XI–3–1896) MD Cincinnati Med Coll 1858; MD Jefferson 1861. *Tr Med Assoc St Mo* 1897:693–94. *Polk* 1886: 568.

CONLEY, ARTHUR VICTOR, Buffalo (d/VIII–23–1895) MD Niagara 1895. *Buff m & s jour* 35:178, 1895.

CONLEY, PATRICK HENRY, Chicago (d/II–3–1903 @ 42) MD Rush 1887. *Ill med jour* ns4: 665, 1903. *Polk* 1896: 379.

CONNELL, ALVA, Houston, Tex (b/1846 Hancock Co, Ga; d/VIII– –1872) MD Bellevue 1869. *Tr Tex St Med Assoc* 1874: 62. *Med surg rep Phila* 28:410.

CONNELLY, JOSEPH P, Williamsport, Pa (d/VI–23–1894 @ c35) MD CPS Balto 1886. *JAMA* 23: 86, 1894.

CONNER, DENNIS NUMBERS, Philadelphia (d/I–20–1904 @ 54) MD UPa 1867. *Pa med jour* 8:334, 1904/05. *Polk* 1896: 1301.

CONNER, GEORGE Cincinnati(d/I–12–1897 @53) MD U Miami 1872. *JAMA* 28:283–84 1897. *Polk* 1896:1161.

CONNER, JOHN A, Baltimore (b/1834 Annapolis; d/IX 26–1881) MD UMd 1862. *Med annals Md:* 360. *Butler* 1874: 360.

CONNER, PHINEAS SANBORN, Cincinnati (b/VIII–22 1813 Newburyport, Mass; d/IX–27–1854) MD Jefferson 1837; AB Dartm'th 1835. *Tr Ohio St Med Soc* 1875: 193.

CONNOLLY, JAMES J, NYC (d/VI–18–1871) MD UCNY 1861. *Med reg NY NJ Conn* 1872: 344.

CONNOLLY, JOHN J, Boston (b/IV– –1854; d/IV–16 1876) MD Boston U 1875; ng Harvard Med; stud theology. *New Engl med gaz* 11:288, 1876.

CONNOLLY, MICHAEL EMMET, Dubuque, Ia (d/II–2 1898 @ 54) MD Harvard 1870. *JAMA* 30: 448, 1898. *Polk* 1890:414.

CONOVER, CHARLES A, CW–USA; Marlborough, NJ (b/II–13– 1842 Manalpan; d/XI–2–1882) MD CPS NY 1865. *Tr Med Soc NJ* 1883: 297. *Atkinson* I: 603. *Butler* 1878: 466.

CONOVER, JACOB C, NYC (d/V–27–1888) MD Georgetown 1870. *Med reg NY NJ Conn* 1888: 249. *Polk* 1886: 675.

CONOVER, JAMES SIMMONS, Red Bank, NJ (d/1893 @ 45) MD Bellevue 1867. *JAMA* 21: 982, 1893. *Polk* 1890: 730.

CONOVER, JOHN R, Freehold, NJ (b/1813; d/1871) MD UCNY 1853. *Tr AMA* 24:358, 1873.

CONRAD, DANIEL BURR, USN 1854–61; CW–CSN 1862–65 (b/II–24–1831 Winchester, Va; d/IX–20–1898) MD UPa 1853. *U Pa med alum CW*: 1853. Blanton, *Va surg in CW*: 398.

CONRAD, HARRY BELL, NYC (d/X–20–1895 @ 43) MD UCNY 1877. *Bost m & s jour* 133:453, 1895. *Texas med jour* 11:330, 1895–96.

CONRAD, JAMES REED, Philadelphia (d/VIII–12–1891 @ 34) MD UPa 1879. *Med bull m & s* 13:391–92, 1891. *Polk* 1886: 814.

CONRAD, JOHN, Philadelphia (d/X–15–1881 @ 71) MD Jefferson 1844. *Bost m & s jour* 105: 409, 1881.

CONRAD, JOHN SUMMERFIELD, St Dennis, Md; CW–CSA (b/II–17–1839 Fairfax CH, Va; d/XII–7–1896) MD Nat Med Coll 1862. *Med annals Md:* 360. *Atkinson* I:127. *Polk* 1886: 445.

CONRAD, LOUIS, Brooklyn (b/XI– –1857 NJ; d/I–25–1895) MD UCNY 1887. *Med reg NY NJ Conn* 1895: 218. *JAMA* 24:336, 1895. *Butler* 1878: 509.

CONRAD, RUFUS, Louisville, Ky (d/IV–12–1893) MD unknown. *Med cent* 1893 (June). *Polk* 1886: 399. Black. Homeopath.

CONROE, ABRAM ENGLE, Moorestown, NJ (b/VII–8 1858 Burlington Co; d/VI–5–1899) MD UPa 1892; DVM 1891. *Tr Med Soc NJ* 1899: 284–85. *JAMA* 32: 1460, 1899.

CONSTANT, JOHN H, Peru Ind (d/VI–9–1866 @44) MD Rush 1851. *Med surg rep Phila* 14: 512, 1866.

CONVERSE, GEORGE V, Hillsboro Ia (d/VII–1–1899 @41) MD CPS Keokuk 1882. *JAMA*33:175, 1899.

CONVERSE, JOSEPH HENRY 2d, Boston (d/I-20-1905) 4th yr stud Harvard Med Sch; BS Harvard 1902. *Bost m & s jour* 152:120, 1905.

CONVERSE, SHUBAEL, Norwich, Vt (b/IX-7-1805 Randolph; d/VIII-6-1867) MD Dartmouth 1828. *Tr Vt Med Soc* 1883: 104.

CONWAY, CHARLES C, CW-CSA; Rapidan, Va (b/III 6-1843 Greene Co; d/II-17-1903) MD Wash'n U Balto 1869. *Tr Med Soc Va* 1903:270-71. *Polk* 1900: 1771.

CONWAY, JAMES HENRY, Woburn, Mass (d/VII-2-1901 @ 47) MD UCNY 1881 (Jas Francis) *JAMA* 37: 213, 1901. *Bost m & s jour* 145:52 1901. *Polk* 1896: 727.

CONWAY, JOHN JAY, Brooklyn (b/IV-16-1859; d/II-13-1903) MD LICH 1880; AM Mt St Mary's Coll 1885; stud St Francis Coll. *Bost m & s jour* 148: 222, 1903. *Polk* 1886: 644.

CONWAY, JOHN RICHARD, NYC (d/V-24-1888) MD CPSNY 1848. *Med reg NY NJ Conn* 1888: 249. *Polk* 1886: 675.

CONWAY, JOHN| RICHARD Jr, NYC (d/IV-22-1899 @ 36) MD CPSNY 1883; AB Columbia 1880. *JAMA* 32: 955, 1899. *Bost m & s jour* 140:440, 1899. *Polk* 1896:1047.

CONWAY, WILLIAM AUGUSTINE, NYC (d/IV-17-1894 @ 54) MD CPSNY 1866; att? St Francis Xavier. *JAMA* 22:674, 1894. *Bost m & s jour* 130: 429, 1894. *Butler* 1878: 510.

CONZELMAN, JOHN, St Louis, Mo (b/VI-19-1823 Württemberg; d/1888) MD St Louis Homeop 1869; stud Tübingen, Engl, Fr & Holl. *Clin rep* 1:153, 1888. *Med vis* 4:206, 1888. *Polk* 1886: 561. *Cleave*. Homeopath.

COOK, ABIJAH PERKINS, Chatham NY 1835- ; Hudson 1840- (b/XII-2-1808 Hyde Park; d/IX-23-1884) <MD Fairfield 1835> *Tr Am Inst Homeop* 1885: 88. *Med surg rep Phila* 51:420, 1884. *Cleave*. Homeopath.

COOK, ALEXANDER H , Chicago (d/I-8-1906 @ 83) MD UCNY 1846. *Ill m jour* 9:227 1906. *Polk* 1896: 379.

COOK, ARCHIBALD BROWN, Louisville, Ky; CW-CSA (b/IX-23-1828 Nobletown, Pa; d/I-2-1895 @ 66) MD Ky Sch Med 1853; AB Jefferson 1845; AM 1851. *JAMA* 24:67,1892. *Atkinson* I:656. *Butler* 1878: 264.

COOK, CHARLES, Jersey City, NJ (b/NJ; d/I-17-1867) MD UPa 1845. *Tr Med Soc NJ* 1867: 212-13. *Tr AMA* 19:431, 1868. *Med surg rep Phila* 16:120, 1867.

COOK, DANIEL, War 1812-USA; Waterville, Me 1815-36; Maumee, O (b/VII-29-1785 Kingston, Mass; d/III-22-1863) stud med Boston; AB Brown 1807. *Brown hist cat*: 1807.

COOK, DENNIS, Tiverton, RI (b/II-27-1785; d/1841) MD unknown; AB Brown 1805. *Tr RI Med Soc* 1859-77: 40.

COOK, EDGAR PUMPHREY, Mendota, Ill (b/V-2-1833 Wellsburg, WVa; d/X-31-1902) MD Cleveland Med Coll 1854. *Chic med rec* 23:377, 1902. *Ill med jour* ns4:387-88, 1902. *Flint* 1897: 281.

COOK, EDMUND HOWELL, NYC (d/IX-14-1902 @ 38) MD Bellevue 1893. *Bost m & s jour* 147:366, 1902. *Polk* 1896: 1047.

COOK, ELIHU GEORGE, Buffalo; Chicago; NYC (b/IV 26-1817 Oneida Co, NY; d/II-8-1893) Hon MD Cleveland Homeop 1863. *Med vis* 9:76, 1893. *No Amer jour homeop* 41:241, 1893. *Polk* 1886:675. Homeopath.

COOK, GEORGE PERRY, Canandaigua, NY (b/XI-20-1824; d/VI-12-1876) MD Geneva 1848; AB Hamilton 1844. *Med reg NY NJ Conn* 1876:241. *Tr Med Soc St NY* 1877: ? *Med rec med & surg* 11:422, 1876.

COOK, GEORGE W , Stockport, NY to 1836; Hudson, NY to 1844; NYC (b/V-21-1806 Hyde Park; d/X-1-1849) <MD CPSNY 1828> *Tr Am Inst Homeop* 1870:646. Homeopath 1838- .

COOK, HENRY, Sag Harbor, NY (b/1814 Engl; d/X-9-1887) MD UCNY 1842. *Bost m & s jour* 117: 394, 1887. *Polk* 1886: 706.

COOK, HENRY WHITE, NYC (b/W Hampton, Mass; d/III-14-1863) MD CPSNY 1862. *Med reg NY NJ Conn* 1865:219 (as Wm Henry). *Bost m & s jour* 68:209, 1863.

COOK, JAMES M , Muskegon, Mich (d/XII-21-1894) MD Rush 1868. *JAMA* 24:33, 1895. *Butler* 1878: 370.

COOK, JOHN SHERRED, Hackettstown, NJ (b/VI-19-1827 Stewartsville; d/I-1-1900) MD UPa 1850; AB Union 1847; stud Lafayette 1847. *Lehigh Valley med mag* 11:22, 1900. *Bost m & s jour* 142:76, 1900. *JAMA* 34:186-87, 1900. *Atkinson* I:351.

COOK, JOSEPH, CW-USA; Daretown, NJ (b/VIII-25-1825 Mullica Hill; d/III-10-1895) MD UPa 1847. *U Pa med alum CW*: 1847. *Polk* 1886: 602.

COOK, JOSEPH SWIFT, Washington, NJ; CW-USA (b/III-26-1830 Hackettstown; d/VII-4-1903) MD UPa 1856. *U Pa med alum CW*: 1856. *Polk* 1886: 612.

COOK, LEWIS CONDICT, Chicago 1857-61; Hackettstown, NJ (b/XII- -1818; d/I-11-1874) MD UPa 1842; AB Princeton 1838; AM 1842. *Tr AMA* 25:527-28, 1874. *Med surg rep Phila* 30:132, 1874. *Tr Med Soc NJ* 1874: 100-01.

COOK, MILTON R , Ashtabula, O (d/1895) MD Cincinnati Coll Med & Surg 1859. *JAMA* 25:1010, 1895. *NC med jour* 36: 380, 1895. *Butler* 1878: 624.

COOK, OSCAR L , CW-USA (d/III-23-1865) MD unknown. *Nat med jour* 1:292, 1870/71.

COOK, PARDON, CW-USA (d/VIII-31-1863 Duvall's Bluff, Ark) MD unknown. *Nat med jour* 1:292, 1870/71.

COOK, PETER McCAULEY, CW-USA; Webster's Mills, Pa (b/V-30-1843 Little Cove; d/I-31-1897 Harrisburg) MD UPa 1867. Polk 1886: 839.

COOK, PURCELL, Brooklyn (d/XII-24-1860) MD Regents St U NY 1851. *Med reg NY NJ Conn* 1862:153.

COOK, SIMEON A, Schaghticoke, NY; Troy 1848- (b/II-22-1803 Stillwater; d/II-9-1873) MD Castleton 1823. *Tr Am Inst Homeop* 1874: 653. Homeopath 1850-

COOK, SUSAN S PUTNAM, Buffalo; Chicago; NYC

(d/X-31-1895 @ 76) MD Cleveland Homeop 1863. *Tr Am Inst Homeop* 1897: 64. Homeopath.

COOK, THOMAS CHAPPELE, Weimar, Tex; CW-CSA (b/IX-19-1836 Tuscaloosa, Ala; d/II-19-1906) MD UPa 1859; AB Princeton 1857; stud U Ala. *Texas st jour med* 1:352, 1905/06. *U Pa med alum CW*: 1859. *Polk* 1886: 896.

COOK, THOMAS M , Sandusky O (b/IX-3-1816 Mansfield; d/III- -1896) MD Western Reserve 1847. *Tr O Med Soc* 1896: 398.

COOK, WARD, Pendleton, Ind (b/X-9-1808 Monroe Co, WVa; d/XII-24-1894) <MD Cincinnati Med Coll 1839> *JAMA* 24:33, 1895. *Tr Ind St Med Soc* 1895: 408. *Butler* 1878: 198.

COOK, WILLIAM, CW-USA (b/c1833 Bordentown, NJ; d/I-15-1864) MD UPa 1855. *U Pa med alum CW*: 1855.

COOK, WILLIAM J , Freeport, Pa (b/VII- -1849; d/XII-24-1885, Asheville, NC) MD Miami 1873. *Tr Med Soc Pa* 18:230-31, 1886.

COOK, WILLIAM WALLACE, Woodstock, Ill (d/II-4-1895 @ 39) MD Chicago Med Coll 1878. *JAMA* 24:221, 1895.

COOKE, JABEZ MILLS, Adams, Ind (d/IV-19-1884 @ 49) MD CPSNY 1857. *Med surg rep Phila* 50:640, 1884.

COOKE, JAMES P , Liberty, Tex (d/I-28-1892) MD UMd 1858. *Daniels Tex med jour* 7:296, 1891-92. *Tex cour-rec med* 9:136, 1892. *Polk* 1890: 1085.

COOKE, JOHN ESTEN, Lexington, Ky (b/1783 Boston; d/X-19-1853) MD UPa 1805. *Phila med & surg jour* 2:276, 1854. *Northwest m & s jour* 3:143, 1854. *K&B* III: 254-55.

COOKE, JOHN LOY, Henderson, Ky (b/1838; d/1878) MD U Louisville 1867; MD Bellevue 1870. *Tr AMA* 30: 858-59, 1879.

COOKE, LUCIUS, Montague, Mass (b/Amherst; d/X-10 1858 @ 44) MD Harvard 1840. *Bost m & s jour* 59:248, 306, 1859.

COOKE, NATHANIEL BOWEN, Lonsdale, RI (b/II-26 1816 Cambridgeport, Mass; d/IV-14-1871) MD Yale 1847; AB Brown 1840. *Brown hist cat*: 1840.

COOKE, NICHOLAS FRANCIS, Ship surg 1849-52; Providence, RI 1854; Chicago 1855- (b/VIII-25-1829 Providence; d/II-1-1885) MD Hahnemann Phila 1854; ng UPa Med Sch; ng Jefferson Med Sch. *Tr Am Inst Homeop* 1885: 112. *Med vis* 1:80, 1885; 2:196, 283, 1886. Homeopath.

COOKE, OCTAVIUS R , Baltimore (d/V-14-1888 @ 48) MD UMd 1862. *New Orl m & s jour* ns15: 1003. *Polk* 1886: 436.

COOKE, WARREN, Lonsdale, RI (b/VIII-10-1809 Uxbridge, Mass; d/V-15-1873) MD Columbian, DC 1834. *Trans RI Med Soc* 1:401, 1859-77.

COOKE, WILLIAM HARVEY, Nebr; Carlisle, Pa (b/I-1-1829 York Sulphur Springs; d/III-21-1879) MD Jefferson 1862. *Tr Am Inst Homeop* 1879: 1247. *Hahn mo* 14:384, 1879. *Cleave*. Homeopath.

COOKE [COOK], WILLIAM HENRY, Georgiana, Ala (d/III-15-1884) <MD Transylvania 1834> *Tr Med Assoc St Ala* 1885: 319.

COOKMAN, ALFRED, Williamsport, Pa (d/IX-14-1898 @ 26? Phila) MD Hahnemann Phila 1895; AB Wesleyan 1892. *Hahn mo* 33:146, 1898 (news & advt, Oct). Homeopath.

COOLEY, ORRIN , Chicago (b/VII-27-1843 S Deerfield, Mass; d/I-7-1877) MD UPa 1869; Amherst ng 1865. *Chicago med jour* 34:161, 1877.

COOLEY, R N , Hannibal Centre, NY (d/VII- 17-1901 @ 70) ng Castleton 1859. *Bost m & s jour* 145: 108, 1901. *Polk* 1896: 1025.

COOLIDGE, CYRUS HAMLIN, Buckfield, Me 1830-52; Calif 1852-60; Austin, Nev 1860-66 (b/V-11-1799 Canton, Me; d/VI-20-1851) MD unknown; AB Bowdoin 1825. *Bowdoin cat*: 1825.

COOLIDGE, JAMES, Athol Depot, Mass (d/X-16-1869 @ 38) MD Berkshire 1854. *Bost m & s jour* 4:216, 1869.

COOLIDGE, RICHARD HOFFMAN, USA (b/III-10-1820; d/I-23-1866 Raleigh, NC) MD CPSNY 1841. *Tr AMA* 18: 352-54, 1867. *Nat med jour* 1:292, 1870/71. *Hist Med Soc DC:* 124-25. *K&B* III:255.

COOLIDGE, SUMNER CURTIS, Middleton, Wis (b/II-9-1828 Orange, Mass; d/VI-1-1900) MD Berkshire 1856; ng Amherst 1850. *Tr Wis St Med Soc* 35:503, 1901; 34:423-24, 1900. *Polk* 1890: 1168.

COOLING, ALBERT A , Wilton, Ia (d/I-11-1900) MD Miami 1872. *JAMA* 34:251, 1900. *Polk* 1886: 370.

COOMBE, JAMES GRIFFITH, Washington, DC (b/I-1 1812; d/II-4-1883) MD UMd 1835. *Hist Med Soc DC:*235.

COON, HENRY CLARKE, Alfred Centre, NY (b/I-28-1828 W Edmeston; d/V-9-1898) <MD NY Homeop 1872> ng Bowdoin 1861? *Tr Am Inst Homeop* 1899: 925. *Polk* 1886: 640. Homeopath.

COON, HENRY PERRIN, San Francisco (d/XII-4-1884) MD UPa 1849; AB Williams 1844; att? Princeton Theol Sem. *Williams grads*: 1844.

COON, HIRAM LORENZO, Northfield, Minn 1861- (b/VIII-25-1828 Grafton, NY; d/X-16-1887) MD Rush 1855. *Tr Minn St Med Soc* 1888:169-70. *Atkinson* I: 475. *Polk* 1886: 516.

COON, SARAH A , ?NYC (b/1826? d/VI-30-1881 @ 55) MD Woman's Med Coll Pa 1868. *Med reg NY NJ Conn* 1882: 224.

COONE, ABNER B , CW-USA (d/III-4-1862) MD unknown. *Nat med jour* 1:292, 1870/71.

COOPE, ADELBERT FRANKLIN, Oil City, Pa (d/XII-14-1902) MD UMich 1870. *Pa med jour* 6:259, 1902/03. *Flint* 1897: 812.

COOPER, ALFRED M , Point Pleasant, Pa (b/IX-15-1830; d/IX-15-1898) MD Jefferson 1856. *Tr Med Soc NJ* 1899: 289-90. *Lehigh Valley med mag* 9:216-17,

1898. *JAMA* 31:808? 1898. *Butler* 1878: 708.

COOPER, CHARLES EBEN, San Francisco (b/XI-22-1860 Sacramento; d/VII-21-1901) MD Cooper 1889. *Calif st jour med* 1:229, 1903. *Polk* 1896: 232.

COOPER, CHARLES WENDELL, Northampton, Mass (b/V-16-1851 Calais, Me; d/II-7-1897 at sea) MD Harvard 1877; AB Amherst 1873. *Bost m & s jour* 136: 148, 263, 1897. *JAMA* 28:380, 1897.

COOPER, DAVID M , Hemphill, Tex (d/VI-16-1906 @ 83 Brooklands) MD St Louis U 1847. *Tex st jour med* 2:122, 1906. *Polk* 1886: 887.

COOPER, EDWARD CAMPBELL, Brooklyn NYC (b/II 1802 Peekskill, NY; d/1867) MD CPSNY 1824. *Med reg NY NJ Conn* 1867:213. *Tr AMA* 19:410-11, 1868.

COOPER, EDWIN HENRY, CW-USA; Henderson, Ill (d/VIII-15-1901) MD Rush 1865; MD Bellevue 1872. *Ill med jour* ns3:237, 1901. *Polk* 1886:280 (Galesburgh).

COOPER, ELIAS SAMUEL, San Francisco (b/Somerville, O; d/X-13-1862) MD St Louis Med Coll 1851 ad eundem. *Tr Ill St Med Soc* 1895: 65. *Bost m & s jour* 67: 228, 1862. *Tr AMA* 19:443-46, 1868. *K&B* III: 255-56.

COOPER, ESAIAS S , CW-USA; Galesburgh Ill (d/ 1893) MD St Louis Med Coll 1850 ad eundem; Hon MD Rush 1850. *JAMA* 21:829, 1893. *Polk* 1890:331.

COOPER, GEORGE EDWARD, USA 1847-76 (b/1824 Phila; d/IV-13-1881 San Francisco) MD UPa 1847. *U Pa med alum CW*: 1847.

COOPER, GEORGE FRANKLIN, CW-CSA; Americus, Ga (b/VII-31-1825 Wilks Co, Ga; d/XII-3-1882) MD Jefferson 1845. *Atkinson* I:517. *JAMA* 1:224, 1883. *Butler* 1878: 109.

COOPER, HENRY COOPER, NYC (d/III-4-1894) MD UCNY 1881. *Med reg NY NJ Conn* 1894:236. *Polk* 1893: 883.

COOPER, HENRY CROPSEY, Woodbridge, NJ (b/ 1829; d/VIII- -1893) MD UCNY 1853. *JAMA* 21: 248, 1893. *Bost m & s jour* 129: 152, 1893.

COOPER, HUNTER POPE, Atlanta, Ga (b/V-16-1860; d/VIII-21-1906) MD CPSNY 1883. *So pract* 27:597-98, 1906. *Flint* 1897: 215.

COOPER, JOHN, Brooklyn (b/London; d/III-29-1900 @ 85) Lic RCSE 1837 (as of Singapore); MD Castleton 1846. *Bost m & s jour* 142:368, 1900. *JAMA* 34:890, 1900. *Polk* 994: 1896.

COOPER, JOHN, Buffalo; CW-USA (b/X-24-1833 Cooper's Plains, NY; d/VII-11-1904) MD UPa 1857; AB Amherst 1854. *U Pa med alum CW*: 1857.

COOPER, JOHN FAWCETT, Allegheny City, Pa (b/IX 25-1822 E Liverpool, O; d/VIII-19-1899) MD Hahnemann Phila 1853. *Tr Homeop Med Soc Pa* 1870/71; 1899. *Tr Am Inst Homeop* 1900:831-32. *Cleave*. *Polk* 1886:790. Homeopath.

COOPER, JOHN J , Barnett, Ga (d/I-24-1900) MD Med Coll Ga 1851. *JAMA* 34:381, 1900. *Polk* 1886: 223.

COOPER, JOHN W , Elkton Md (b/II-16-1850 Kent Co; d/III-10-1906) MD Hahnemann Med Coll Phila 1884. *Hahn mo* 41:51,1906 (news &c Apr). Homeopath.

COOPER, JOSEPH L , New Castle, Pa (d/1900 @ 39) MD Jefferson 1884. *JAMA* 34:574 1900. *Polk* 1896: 124.

COOPER, JOSIAH C , Philadelphia (d/V-30-1898 @ 77) MD Jefferson 1862; AB Washington Coll, Pa 1846? *JAMA* 30:1481, 1898. *Polk* 1896: 1301.

COOPER, LEHMAN ADAMS, Raton, NM (b/XI- -1839; d/V-28-1879) MD UPa 1865; ng Haverford. *Haverford biogr cat*: 70.

COOPER, LLEWELLYN H , Coopersburg, Pa (d/II-14 1880) MD UPa 1874. *Med surg rep Phila* 42:198, 1880.

COOPER, RALPH LEE, Ogontz, Pa (d/VIII-2-1904 @ 82) MD Phila Coll Med & Surg 1858. *Pa med jour* 8:334, 1904/05. *Flint* 1897: 812.

COOPER, RICHARD MATLACK, Camden, NJ (b/VIII 30-1816; d/V-24-1874) MD UPa 1839; AB 1836; AM 1839. *Tr AMA* 26:469-70, 1875. *Tr Med Soc NJ* 1874: 108-09.

COOPER, THEODORE H , Warwick NY (d/I-2-1888) MD CPSNY 1855. *Med reg NY NJ Conn* 1888: 249.

COOPER, THOMAS BUCHECKER, Coopersburg, Pa (b/XII-29-1823; d/IV-4-1862) MD UPa 1843; att? Gettysburg 1843? *Med surg rep Phila* ns8:51, 1862. *US Congr biogr direct*.

COOPER, THOMAS E , Allentown, Pa (d/VIII-18-1893) MD Louisville Med Coll 1881. *JAMA* 21:357, 1893. *Polk* 1890: 975.

COOPER, WILLIAM, New Albany, Ind (b/III-27-1809 Chambersburg, Pa; d/VII-10-1879) MD Jefferson 1835. *Med rec* 16:119, 1879.

COOPER, WILLIAM D , Morrisville, Va (d/X-29-1897 @ 77) MD UPa 1845. *JAMA* 29:1028, 1897.

COOPER, WILLIAM G, Toledo O (d/IV-20-1900 @ 34) MD Balto Med Coll 1894. *JAMA* 34: 1146,1900.

COOPER, WILLIAM S , Troy, NY (b/Scotland; d/V-26 -1890) MD Albany 1861. *Tr NY St Med Soc* 11:741 ff, 1894. *Polk* 1894: 854.

COOVER, ELI H , Harrisburg Pa (b/X-1-1827 Cumberland Co; d/I-13-1903) MD Jefferson 1850. *Pa med jour* 7:278, 1903/04. *Atkinson* I:346. *Flint* 1897: 803.

COOVER, JOHN B , CW-USA (d/IX-27-1864 near Halltown, Va) MD Jefferson 1857. *Nat med jour* 1:292, 1870/71.

COOVER, JOSEPH H , Harrisburg, Pa (b/I-15-1838 Mechanicsburg; d/IX-25-1890) MD Jefferson 1863. *Med bull m & s* 13: 28, 1891. *Atkinson* I: 602. *Polk* 1886: 801.

COPELAND, ADONIRAM JUDSON, Aroostook Co, Me; Como & Geneseo, Ill (b/III-10-1814 Holden, Me; d/VIII-3-1855) MD Jefferson 1846; AB Bowdoin 1840. *Bowdoin cat*: 1840.

COPELAND, GEORGE WALTER, Middleborough, Mass (b/III-6-1846 Merigomish, NS; d/IV-29-1896) MD Jefferson 1869. *Bost m & s jour* 134: 476, 1896.

 Spec. educ'l status abbrev. as: ***ng*** = college verified attendance without degree;

Atkinson I: 186.

COPP, BENJAMIN D , Menominee, Wis (d/I–11–1899) MD Rush 1871. *JAMA* 32:196, 1899. *Polk* 1896: 1554.

COPPEDGE, CHARLES P , Wadesborough NC (d/VIII–1–1880) MD UCNY 1851. *NC med jour* 6:305, 1880.

COPPEDGE, OLIVER DeWITT, CW–CSA; Concrete, Tex (b/Castalia, NC; d/II–19–1906 Cuero, Tex) MD UPa 1857; att Wake Forest Coll. *Texas st jour med* 1:352, 1905/06. *U Pa med alum CW*: 1857.

CORBETT, WILLIAM D , Hickman, Ky 1865– (b/X–14–1829 Sumner Co, Tenn; d/X–10–1878) Stud w/B W Lauderdale, Paris, Tenn. *Tr AMA* 30:859, 1879.

CORBIN, JOHN L, Waverly, Pa 1848?–52; Athens 1852– (b/VII–26–1819 Warren; d/XI–30–1899) <ng Geneva Med Coll 1846–47> Hon MD Hahnemann Chicago 1874. *Tr Am Inst Homeop* 1900: 832. *Polk* 1886: 791. Homeopath.

CORBITT, WILLIAM BRINTON, ?Washington, DC (d/VII–17–1882 @42 Washington) MD Jefferson 1863; AB Haverford 1860. *Haverford biogr cat*: 79.

CORCORAN, [CORKRAN], A M , CW–USN (d/VII––1863 NY) MD unknown. *Nat med jour* 1:292, 1870/71.

CORCORAN, GEORGE L , Brimfield, Ill (b/1826 Ireland; d/IV–14–1898) <MD Glasgow 1849> *Tr Ill St Med Soc* 1888: 152–53. *Polk* 1886: 256.

CORCORAN, JOHN P , Detroit, Mich (b/Ireland; d/V–29–1899 @ 48) MD Detroit Coll Med 1874. *JAMA* 32: 1399, 1899. *Polk* 1896: 747.

COREY, CHARLES, Brooklyn (b/VI–13–1830 Dublin, NH; d/IV–4–1894) MD Dartmouth 1856. *Med reg NY NJ Conn* 1894: 236. *JAMA* 22:674, 1894. *Butler* 1896: 530.

COREY, CHARLES, Manchester, NH (b/III–19–1837 Stanbridge, PQ; d/X–21–1899) MD UVt 1863. *Tr NH Med Soc* 1900: 315. *Polk* 1890: 710.

COREY, JACOB, Sturbridge, Mass (b/I–13–1788; d/X–31–1841) MD unknown; AB Brown 1808. *Brown hist cat*: 1808.

COREY, LAVANNER, Van Buren, Ind (b/III–14–1834 Rush Co; d/XII–13–1896) MD Med Coll Ohio 1870. *Tr Ind St Med Soc* 1897: 350. *Polk* 1896:495.

COREY, SIMEON R, E Craftsbury, Vt (b/VI–3–1824; d/VII–4–1883) MD Berkshire 1851. *Tr Vt Med Soc* 1883: 104.

COREY, WATERMAN FRANKLIN, Washington, DC; CW–USA (b/II– –1835 Bridgeport, Vt; d/VI–16–1904) MD Howard 1880. *Tr Am Inst Homeop* 1904: 961. *JAMA* 43: 62, 1904. *Polk* 1886: 211. Homeopath. Black.

CORGAN, LAFAYETTE, Woodburn, Ill (d/I–22–1900) Cert by Exam Bd *Tr Ill St Med Soc* 1900: 415, 509. *JAMA* 34:313, 1900. *Polk* 1886: 258.

CORKINS, PHILIP G, Harwood Mo (d/VII–16–1896 @ 70) MD Rush 1853. *JAMA* 27:337 1896. *Polk* 1886: 568.

CORLEW, RUFUS M , Evansville, Ind (b/VIII–22–1843 Montgomery Co, Tenn; d/III–23–1896) MD U Nashville 1868. *Tr Ind St Med Soc* 1896: 272. *Polk* 1896: 465.

CORLISS, ALLEN TIMOTHY, Loganville, Wis (b/XII–17–1867 Sutton, Vt; d/III–19–1902) MD Rush 1894. *Tr Wis St Med Soc* 36:418, 1902. *Polk* 1896: 1553.

CORLISS, CORYDON T , Indianapolis, Ind (b/St Lawrence Co, NY; d/VII–5–1886 @ 68) Stud w/Hiram Corliss. *Med curr* 3:262, 1886. *Med adv* 17:192, 1886. *Polk* 1886: 322. Homeopath.

CORNELISON, JOHN MESIER, Hudson Co, NJ (b/IV–29–1802 Bergen, NJ; d/V–24–1875) MD CPSNY 1825; AB Union. *Trans Med Soc NJ* 1876: 134–36. *Med reg NY NJ Conn* 1875: 196. *Trans AMA* 27: 653, 1876.

CORNELIUS, ROBERT WILLIAM B , Philadelphia (b/1853 NYC; d/VIII–30–1903) MD Hahnemann Phila 1874. *JAMA* 41:799, 1903. *Polk* 1886:814. Homeopath.

CORNELL, FRANCIS O , Montgomery Co, NY (b/Glenville, NY; d/XII–3–1884) MD Albany 1880. *Tr NY St Med Soc* 1894: 741 ff.

CORNELL, WILLIAM MASON, Boston (b/X–16–1802 Berkeley, Mass; d/IV–14–1895) Hon MD Berkshire 1844; AB Brown 1827. *Bost m & s jour* 132:424, 1895.

CORNETT, WILLIAM T S , Madison, Ind (b/VII–11–1805 Carrollton, Ky; d/V–26–1897) Hon MD U Louisville 1852; ng Transylvania before 1823. *Tr Ind St Med Soc* 1897: 360. *Atkinson* I:60. *K&B* I(1): 202.

CORNICK, WILLIAM F , CW–CSA; Genito, Va (b/1837 Norfolk; d/VII–26–1906 Princess Anne Co) MD U Pa 1860. *U Pa med alum CW*: 1860. *Polk* 1886: 918.

CORNISH, AARON, New Bedford, Mass (b/1790? d/IV–10–1864 @ 74) MD Harvard 1820. *Bost m & s jour* 70:246–47, 1864.

CORNISH, AARON, New Bedford, Mass (b/I–7–1850 [!?] Plymouth; d/IX–27–1901) MD Castleton 1855. *Bost m & s jour* 145:394, 1901. *Polk* 1896: 719.

CORNISH, THEODORE OSGOOD, So Boston (b/II–19 1824 Plymouth; d/V–23–1904) MD Woodstock 1851. *Bost m & s jour* 150:604, 1904. *Polk* 1898: 774.

CORNWALL, EDWARD THOMAS, Cheshire, Conn (b/IX–22–1858; d/VIII–8–1899) MD CPSNY 1881. *Proc Conn Med Soc* 1901: 311–12. *Polk* 1896: 276.

CORRELL, JOHN WILLIAM, Baltimore (b/VIII–14–1825 Winchester, Va; d/I–20–1900) ng Winchester Med Coll. *Med annals Md:* 362. *JAMA* 34:312, 1900. *Polk* 1890: 512.

CORRELL, THOMAS ABRAHAM, Hagerstown, Md (b/Winchester, Va; d/X–14–1896) MD UMd 1875.*Med annals Md:* 362.

CORSE, JAMES MORRIS, Philadelphia (d/VIII–10–1885 @ 73) MD UPa 1851. *Tr CPP* cent vol: 218.

CORSON, ADAM CLARKE, CW–USA; NYC (b/I–20–1839 or 1840 Dumfries, Can; d/X–6–1873) MD Victoria, Ont 1864; MD CPSNY 1866. *Med reg NY NJ Conn* 1874: 271. *Proc Conn Med Soc* 1874: 293. *Med surg rep Phila* 29: 306, 462, 1873.

CORSON, EDWARD FOULKE, USN (b/X–14–1834 Montgomery Co, Pa; d/VI–22–1864) MD UPa 1856. *Nat* *med jour* 1:292, 1870/71. *Tr Med Soc Pa* 1865: 99–101. *Bost m & s jour* 71:28, 1864. *U Pa med alum CW*: 1856.

CORSON, HIRAM, Plymouth Meeting, Pa (b/X–8–1804; d/III–4–1896) MD UPa 1828. *Tr CPP* cent vol: 280. *JAMA* 26:541, 1896. *Bost m & s jour* 134:304, 1896. *Buff m & s jour* 35:750–51, 1896. *K&B* III: 258–59.

CORSON, JOHN R , Middletown, O (b/VI–20–1825; d/VI–19–1885) MD Ohio Med Coll 1862. *Tr Ohio Med Soc* 1886:396–97. *JAMA* 5:110, 1885. *Butler* 1878: 624.

CORSON, JOHN W , NYC (b/VIII–2–1816 Canada; d/VI–2 or X–1–1882 Orange, NJ) MD Albany 1842. *Med reg NY NJ Conn* 1883:223. *Tr Med Soc NJ* 1883:288–90.

CORSON, JOSEPH, CW–USA (b/I–20–1820 Montg y Co, Pa; d/VII–7–1866 Portsmouth, Ohio) MD UPa 1841. *U Pa med alum CW*: 1841.

CORSON, THOMAS FRANCIS, Philadelphia (d/V–29–1902 @62) MD UPa 1866. *Pa med jour* 6:259, 1902/03.

CORSON, THOMAS JOHNSON, Trenton, NJ (d/V–10–1879) MD UPa 1851. *Tr AMA* 33:540–42, 1882. *Tr Med Soc NJ* 1879:209–11. *Med rec NY* 15:479, 1879.

CORTELYOU, LAWRENCE V , NYC (d/VIII–5–1896 @ 50 or 57) MD Bellevue 1864. *Bost m & s jour* 135: 174, 1896. *JAMA* 27: 391, 1896.

CORWIN, JOSEPH ALBERT, Newark, NJ (b/V–17–1810; d/IX–8–1893) MD Yale 1835. *Tr Med Soc NJ* 1894: 259. *Med reg NY NJ Conn* 1889–90: 194. *Butler* 1878: 463.

CORY, ALPHONSO L , Chicago (d/IX–25–1902 @ 51?) MD Rush 1892. *Chic med rec* 27:472, 1902. *Ill med jour* ns4:425, 1902. *Flint* 1897: 258.

CORY, ANDREW JACKSON, San José, Calif (d/III–3–1892) MD Ohio Med Coll 1860; AB Miami 1855; AM 1858. *U Miami cat*: 1855. *Polk* 1886: 175.

CORY, BENJAMIN, San José, Calif (b/XI–17–1823 Oxford O; d/I–16–1896) MD Ohio Med Coll 1845; AB Miami 1842;AM 1847. *JAMA* 26:243,1896. *Polk* 1896: 240.

CORY, DAVID MAGIE, NYC (d/VIII–19–1901 @ 58) MD CPSNY 1866. *JAMA* 37: 595, 1901.

CORY, JEROME BONAPARTE, Denver, Colo (d/I–24 1892 @ 54) MD U Mich 1862. *Tr Colo St Med Soc* 1898–99: 509. *Polk* 1886: 183.

CORYELL, GEORGE, Riverside, Ill (d/XI–28–1898 @ 89) Lic by years of practice. *JAMA* 31: 1490, 1898.

CORYELL, WILLIAM, NJ (d/1829) MD UPa 1826. *Tr Med Soc NJ* 1872: 188.

COSENS, RICHARD, Dodgeville, Wis (b/XII–24–1840 Ontario; d/XI–1–1895) MD U Mich 1876. *Tr Wis St Med Soc* 30:559–60, 1896.

COSKERY, FELIX S , Baltimore (b/1815; d/1873) MD UMd 1836. *Med annals Md:* 363.

COSKERY, OSCAR J , Baltimore (b/1843; d/VII–5–1889 @ 46) MD UMd 1865. *Buff m & s jour* 24:52, 1889. *Med ann Md:* 363. *Med s rep Phila* 61:140, 1889.

COSKERY, WILLIAM, Baltimore (d/X– –1830) MD UMd 1827. *Med annals Md:* 363.

COSSITT, FREDERICK SILAS, Greenville, Pa (d/VIII 11–1902 @ 34) MD Western Reserve 1893; AB Thiel Coll 1889; AM 1892. *Pa med jour* 5:663, 1901/02; 6:259, 1902/03.

COTÉ, MARCELLIN, NYC to 1847; Pittsburgh, Pa (b/VIII–13–1815 Cacouna, Lower Canada; d/V–29–1878 @ 63) MD Bowdoin 1844. *Tr Am Inst Homeop* 1878: 1112. *Cleave*. Homeopath.

COTES, JOHN B , Batavia, NY (b/XII–31–1794 Springfield, NY; d/II–26–1859) <ng Fairfield 1817> stud Engl & Fr 1830–31. *Med & phys rep* Phila ns1:418, 1858/59. *Bost m & s jour* 60:128, 1859.

COTES, JOHN RICHARD, CW–USA; Batavia NY (b/X 8–1829; d/III–20–1884) MD Buffalo 1852. *Tr Med Soc St NY* 1894: 741 ff; 1885:326–28. *Butler* 1878: 549.

COTES, LEVANT BALLARD, Batavia, NY (b/VII–15–1801 Springfield; d/IX–11–1880) MD Fairfield 1826. *Tr Med Soc St NY* 1882:354–55. *Atkinson* I:655. *Butler* 1874: 534.

COTNAM, THOMAS TAYLOR, Stevenson, Ala (d/XII–11–1884) MD U Nashville 1855. *Tr Med Assoc Ala* 1885: 319. *Butler* 1874: 16.

COTTEN, JOSEPH, CW–CSA; Woodville, NC (b/VIII–12–1843; d/V–19–1877. MD UMd 1867; att UNC. *UNC cat*: 131.

COTTEN, ROBERT, Birmingham, Ala (d/XII–13–1901) MD Tulane 1867. *Tr Med Assoc St Ala* 1902: 130. *Polk* 1893: 151.

COTTING, BENJAMIN EDDY, Roxbury, Mass (b/XI–2 1812 Arlington; d/V–22–1897) MD Harvard 1837; AB 1834. *Bost m & s jour* 136:528, 532, 554, 583, 637, 1897. *JAMA* 28: 1045, 1897. *Tr NH Med Soc* 1897: 304. *K&B* III:259.

COTTON, CHARLES, Newport, RI (b/X–7–1788 Plymouth, Mass; d/II–3–1870) MD Brown 1813; AB Harvard 1808; AM 1811. *Phila med reg & dir* 1871: 303. *Bost m & s jour* 5:132, 1870.

COTTON, JOHN, Marietta, O (d/IV or V–2–1847) MD unknown. *Buff med jour* 2:752, 1847. *Ill & Ind m & s jour* 2: 191, 1847.

COTTRELL, JOSEPH FREDERICK, ?Washington, DC; CW–USN (b/III–16–1840 Columbia, Pa; d/IX–9–1894) MD UPa 1863; AB Princeton 1861. *U Pa med alum CW*: 1863.

COUCH, GRAFFINS MILLER, Altoona, Pa (d/IV–25–1897 @ 47) MD UMd 1883. *JAMA* 28:955, 1897. *Polk* 1886: 806.

COUCH, JOHN FRANCIS, Somerville, Mass (b/St Johns, Newfoundland; d/I–4–1903 @ 50) MD Harvard 1872. *Bost m & s jour* 148: 50, 52, 1903. *Polk* 1896: 722.

COUCH, JOSEPH DANIEL, Cambridge, Mass (d/III–16 1898) MD Harvard 1883. *Bost m & s jour* 138:288, 1898. *JAMA* 30:807, 1898. *Polk* 1896: 709.

COUDEN, WILLIAM CHASE, Denver 1889– (b/VI–30 1832 Cincinnati; d/X–4–1900) MD St Louis Homeop

Spec. educ'l status abbrev. as: ***ng*** = college verified attendance without degree;

Coll ? *Critique* (Oct 15) 1900. Homeopath.

COUDRICK [COWDRIC], CHARLES, Frenchtown, NJ (b/V-18-1833; d/XII-31-1871) MD Jefferson 1858. *Tr AMA* 24:360, 1873. *Tr Med Soc NJ* 1872:197.

COUES, ELLIOTT, Baltimore (b/IX-9-1842 Portsmouth, NH; d/XII-25-1899) MD Columbian DC 1863. *Atkinson* I: 226. *JAMA* 34:61, 1900. *K&B* III: 260.

COULTER, JOHN, Baltimore; RevWar-USN (b/1751 County Down, Ireland; d/V-24-1823) MD unknown. *Med annals Md:* 363.

COULTER, MIFFLIN, Baltimore; USN (b/1799; d/X-12-1840) MD UMd 1823. *Med annals Md:* 363.

COUPER, JAMES, New Castle, Del (b/X-3-1803; d/VIII-12-1865) MD UPa 1824. *Tr AMA* 18:333-35, 1867. *Bost m & s jour* 73:128,1865. *Med Soc Del*:42.

COURTNEY, HENRY, Des Moines, Ia (b/1813 Mason Co, Ky; d/VI- -1861) MD Med Coll Ohio 1850. *Tr Ia St Med Soc* 1867-71: 245-46.

COURTWRIGHT, ALVA P, Circleville, O (d/VI-23-1897) MD Miami 1867. *JAMA* 29:201 1897. *Polk* 1886: 745.

COVELL, CHARLES HENRY, CW-USN (d/VIII-9-1861 at sea off Ft Pickens @ 26) MD CPSNY 1860. *Tr AMA* 14:216, 1864. *Bost m & s jour* 65:148, 1861. *Nat med jour* 1:292, 1870/71.

COVENTRY, ALEXANDER, Hudson, NY 1785- ; Utica (b/VIII-16-1766 Hamilton, Scotl'd; d/XII-9-1831) Stud Glasgow & Edinb, 1784-85. *Tr Med Soc St NY* 1859: 366-69. *Am jour med sci* 10:272-74, 1832.

COVENTRY, CHARLES BRODHEAD, Utica NY (b/IV 20-1801 Deerfield; d/II-24-1875) MD Fairfield 1825. *Bost m & s jour* 45:159, 1851. *Tr AMA* 27:663-64, 1876.*Med rec* 10:174, 1875; 1876:429. *Tr Med Soc St NY* 1876:326-33.

COVERT, JOHN JAY, CW-USA; Pittsburgh (d/VII-12 1902 @81) MD U Buffalo 1851; ng U Mich Med 1854-55. *Pa med jour* 8:334, 1904/05. *Flint* 1897:829.

COVERT, JOHN M , Portsmouth, Va; Galveston, Tex; Brooklyn 1870- ; CW-CSA (b/VII-25-1832 St Augustine, Fla; d/II-18-1872) MD Med Coll SC 1855. *Med reg NY NJ Conn* 1872: 344.

COVEY, CALVIN EDSON, Chicago; Grand Ledge, Mich (d/IX-1-1898 @ 73) MD Hahnemann Chicago 1880. *JAMA* 31:673, 1898. *Polk* 1886: 492. Homeopath.

COWAN, H L , Ingleside, WVa (d/X-14-1894 @42) MD Med Coll Va 1876. *JAMA* 23:655, 1894.

COWAN, HARRY JEFFERSON, Danville, Ky (d/XII-20-1899 @ 38) MD CPSNY 1886; MB Centre Coll, Ky 1881. *JAMA* 34: 62, 1900.

COWAN, JACOB P , Ashland, O (d/VII-8-1895 @ 72) MD Starling 1855. *JAMA* 25: 169, 1895. *Tr Ohio Med Soc* 1896: 12. *Butler* 1878: 625.

COWAN, JOHN ALLEN, Auburn, Ind; CW-USA (b/III 1-1843 Decatur; d/VI-18-1885) MD Detroit Med Coll 1869. *Tr Ind St Med Soc* 1886: 200. *Butler* 1878: 198.

COWAN, THOMAS, Wilmington, NC; CW-USA (b/1840; killed @ Ft. Fisher 1865) MD unknown; stud UNC 1857-58. *UNC cat*: 134.

COWDEN, WILLIAM REYNOLDS, Lancaster Co, Pa (b/Porterville, Pa; d/IV-16-1897 @ 77) MD unknown. *Pa med jour* 1:513-14, 1898. *Butler* 1878:709.

COWDERY, JONATHAN, USN 1800-52; (d/XI-21-1852) *NW m & s jour* 1:384, 1852.

COWDREY, STEVENS GEORGE, NYC; USA (b/VI-13-1838 Plymouth, NH; d/II-22-1891) <MD Berkshire 1867> AB Harvard 1861; AM 1861. *Med reg NY NJ Conn* 1891:271. *JAMA* 16:428, 1891. *Bost m & s jour* 124:248, 1891.

COWEN, JESSE MILLER, Hennepin, Ill (b/I-2-1834 Zanesville O; d/IX-7-1890) MD Med Coll Ohio 1858. *Tr Ill St Med Soc* 1891: 17-18. *Butler* 1870: 148.

COWGILL, CLAYTON A , Philadelphia (d/II-5-1901 @ 75) MD Pa Med Coll 1846. *Pa med jour* 5:296, 1901/02. *Polk* 1886:219 (Penn, Fla).

COWGILL, TARVIN W , Greencastle, Ind (d/1850) MD Med Coll Ohio 1849. *NW med & surg jour* 3:90, 1850. *Proc Ind St Med Soc* 1850: 7.

COWIN, JOHN HENRY, Greensboro, Ala; CW-CSA (b/(IV-28-1839; d/V-3-1863 Chancellorsville, Va) MD Jefferson 1860; ng UVa med 1858; ng U Ala 1856. Johnson's *U Va alum dec'd CW*: 381 ff. *U Ala cat*: 125.

COWLES, ANDRE L , Spartansburg, Pa (b/Chautauqua, NY; d/II-18-1904 @ 40) MD Buffalo 1892. *Pa med jour* 8:334, 1904/05. *Flint* 1897: 836.

COWLES, CHESTER WILLIAM, Bentonsport, Ia (b/III 10-1808 Amherst, Mass; d/VIII-8-1891) MD Berkshire 1835; AB Amherst 1831. *Amherst, Men of*: 1831. *Polk* 1886:351.

COWLES, HENRY, Saxonville, Mass (b/VIII-8-1815 Amherst, Mass; d/X-8-1892) MD Harvard 1843; ng Amherst 1840. *Bost m & s jour* 127:372, 1892.

COWLEY, DAVID, Philadelphia 1853-61; Pittsburgh (b/XI-30-1830 Co Down Irel'd; d/X-30-1886) MD Hahnemann Phila 1853. *Tr Am Inst Homeop* 1887: 211. *Med vis* 3:41, 1887. *Tr Pa Homeop Soc* 1887. *Polk* 1886: 828.

COWLING, RICHARD OSWALD, Louisville, Ky (b/IV 9-1839 Georgetown, SC; d/IV-2-1881) MD Jefferson 1867. *Tr AMA* 32:499-501, 1881. *NC med jour* 7:250-51, 1881. *Bost m & s jour* 104:378, 402, 1881. *Med bull m & s* 3:118, 1881. *Atkinson* I:645. *K&B* III:261-62.

COX, ABRAHAM LIDDEN, CW-USA (b/1800 NYC; d/VII-28-1864 Lookout Mtn, Tenn) MD UPa 1823; Hon AM Princeton 1824 & Williams 1824? *Tr AMA* 16:652, 1865. *Med surg rep Phila* 12:84, 1864. *Nat med jour* 1:292, 1870/71. *U Pa med alum CW*: 1823.

COX, ANDREW P , Coraopolis, Pa (d/IV-21-1904 @ 59) MD Cincinnati Coll Med & Surg 1877. *Pa med jour* 8:334, 1904/05. *Polk* 1886: 792.

COX, BENJAMIN, Salem (d/XI-30-1871 @65) MD Harv 1829; AB 1826. *Bost m & s jour* 8:376, 390, 1871.

COX, CADER GREGORY, Richlands, NC; CW–CSA (d/1877) MD UCNY 1860; AB UNC 1858. *Tr Med Soc St NC* 1878: 26.

COX, CHRISTOPHER CHRISTIAN, Baltimore; Washington, DC (b/VIII–16–1816; d/XI–25–1882) MD Yale 1835; MD Wash Med Coll Balto betw 1831 & 1838. *JAMA* 1:223–24 1883. *Med ann Md:* 364. *K&B* II:254.

COX, E GOVER, Carroll Co, Md (b/VIII–11–1820; d/VIII–19–1883) <MD Ohio U 1840> *Med ann Md:* 364.

COX, EDWARD, Battle Creek, Mich (d/IX–19–1882) MD Geneva 1839. *JAMA* 1:256, 1883.

COX, GEORGE, Williamsburg, NY (b/II–2–1796 London; d/XI–11–1853) Stud Lond & Edinb. *Tr Am Inst Homeop* 1893: 134. Homeopath.

COX, GEORGE N , Detroit Mich (d/II–11–1900 @ 52) MD Med Coll Ind 1880. *JAMA* 34:511, 1900.

COX, GEORGE WILLIAM, Philadelphia (d/IV–19–1901 @ 60) MD unknown. *Pa med jour* 5:296, 1901/02.

COX, HARRY O , Philadelphia (d/X–1–1884 @ 26 Camden, NJ) MD Jefferson 1883. *Med surg rep Phila* 51:448, 1884.

COX, HENRY GEORGE, NYC (b/X–28–1818; d/V/29–1866) MD CPSNY 1849; AB Devonshire Coll, Bermuda 1838. *Med surg rep Phila* 14:479–80, 1866. *Tr AMA* 18:322, 1867. *Med reg NY NJ Conn* 1866: 214.

COX, HENRY MAJOR, Washington, NJ (d/XI–7–1902 @ 65) MD U Mich 1868. *Bost m & s jour* 147: 556, 1902. *Polk* 1886: 610.

COX, HENRY MILLER, NYC (d/IV–24–1904) MD CPSNY 1871; AB Union. *Bost m & s jour* 150: 496, 1904. *Polk* 1896: 1047.

COX, HENRY S , Columbia, Tenn (d/III–8–1894) MD UPa 1860. *JAMA* 22:482, 1894. *Butler* 1878: 766.

COX, J BARTON, St Genevieve, Mo (d/XII–31–1898) MD UPa 1851. *JAMA* 32:145, 1899. *Polk* 1896: 860.

COX, JAMES WILLIAM, Albany NY (b/II–5–1828 Gilbertsville; d/VI–10–1896) MD Albany 1852. *Tr Am Inst Homeop* 1896:1186. *No Am jour hom* 46:464, 1896.

COX, JOSEPH BRADFORD, San José, Cal (b/III–26–1840 Ohio; d/III–14–1884) MD LICH 1869; AB Portland Acad, Ore 1865. *Tr Cal St Med Soc* 1884:242. *Atkinson* I: 187.

COX, JULIUS W , Mapleton, Ia (d/IX–8–1898 Idaho) MD Iowa St U 1886. *JAMA* 31:872, 1898. *Polk* 1896:531.

COX, NOAH S , Beecher City, Ill (d/IX–17–1899) MD Mo Med Coll 1895. *Tr Ill St Med Soc* 1899: 287.

COX, RICHARD E [or H], Centerville, Va (b/XI– –1824 Carolina; d/VI–20–1886) MD Med Coll Va 1844. *Tr Med Soc Va* 1886: 390. *Butler* 1878: 826.

COX, THOMAS B , Lancaster Pa (b/I–8–1859; d/XII–17 1882) MD Jefferson 1879. *Tr Med Soc Pa* 15:367, 1883.

COX, TIMOTHY B , Frankfort, Ind (d/X–16–1895 @ 79) MD Med Coll Ohio 1853. *JAMA* 25:726, 1895. *Polk* 1890: 371.

COXE, EDWARD JENNER, New Orleans (b/1801; d/IX 22–1862 @ 60) MD UPa 1823. *Bost m & s jour* 67:268, 1862. *Med surg rep Phila* ns9:22, 1862.

COXE, ERNEST CLEVELAND, Baltimore (b/VII–9–1850 Hartford, Conn; d/X–13–1882) MD CPSNY 1873; AB Hobart 1871. *Med annals Md:* 364.

COXE, JOHN REDMAN, Philadelphia (b/IX–16–1773 Trenton, NJ; d/III–22–1864) MD UPa 1794. *Chic med jour* 21:284–85, 1864. *Bost m & s jour* 70:208, 1864. *Tr AMA* 16:642–43, 1865. *K&B* III: 262–63.

COXE, JOHN REDMAN Jr, Williamsport, Pa 1845–50; Philadelphia 1850– (b/II–19–1799; d/V–11–1863) MD Hahnemann 1850. *Tr Am Inst Homeop* 1893:135. Homeopath.

COXE, LORENZO LEWIS Jr, Philadelphia (d/XI–28–1866 @ 29) MD Hahnemann Phila 1858. *Tr Am Inst Homeop* 1868: 285. Homeopath.

COXE, WILLIAM SMITH, Philadelphia (b/IV–16–1790; d/VII–20–1837) MD UPa 1811. *Tr CPP* cent vol: 218.

COY, ERASTUS CALHOUN, Turner's Falls, Mass (b/VII–25–1831 Colerain; d/XII–28–1897) MD UVt 1861; ng Castleton 1860. *Bost m & s jour* 138:24, 1898. *JAMA* 30: 106, 1898. *Polk* 1896: 724.

COYLE, WALTER EDWARD, Canton, Mass (b/I–25–1870 Nasonville, RI; d/II–22–1897) MD UCNY 1892. *Tr RI Med Soc* 5:500, 1894–98.

COZAD, JAMES, Reynolds, Ill (d/VIII–15–1897 @61) MD Rush 1866. *JAMA* 29:453, 1897. *Polk* 1886: 295.

CRADDOCK, JOHN W , Black Walnut, Va (b/II–22–1824; d/VIII–11–1884) MD Jefferson 1846. *Tr Med Soc Va* 1885:281–82. *Butler* 1878: 826.

CRAEMER [CREAMER], JOSEPH M , Brooklyn (d/II 23–1900) MD UCNY 1873. *Bost m & s jour* 142: 236, 1900. *Polk* 1886: 644.

CRAFT, MIJAMAN SIDNEY, Jackson, Miss (b/VIII–6–1827; d/IV–8–1888) MD U Louisville 1849. *Tr Miss St Med Assoc* 1888:55–58. *Polk* 1886: 528.

CRAFTS, EDWARD GRIFFIN, Binghamton, NY (b/VII 4–1821; d/I–26–1894) MD Geneva 1852. *Med reg NY NJ Conn* 1894:236. *JAMA* 22:202,1894. *Polk* 1886:644.

CRAGIN, CHARLES HARTWELL, Alexandria DC (b/IX–7 or 17–1817 Alsted, NH; d/IV–1–1887) MD Columbian DC 1844; AB Amherst 1837. *Hist Med Soc DC:* 236. *Polk* 1886:211.

CRAGIN, FRANCIS WHITTEMORE, Greenfield, NH; Paramaribo, Dutch Guiana (b/VII–20–1803 Temple; d/VII–26–1858) MD Dartmouth 1830. *Bost m & s jour* 59:48, 1859.

CRAGIN, JOHN, Mobile, Ala (b/IV–7–1812 Worcester, Mass; d/V–24–1877) MD unknown; att Wm & Mary. *Hahn mo* 13:106, 1877. *Cleave*. Homeopath.

CRAIG, ALBERT B , Philadelphia (b/II–12–1867 Mo; d/III–14–1905) MD Jefferson 1901. *Bost m & s jour* 152:355, 1905. *Jeffersonian* 7:154–55, 1905.

CRAIG, ALEXANDER, Columbia, Pa (b/XII–22–1838 Hillside Station; d/VIII–16–1899) MD Jefferson 1865. *Pa med jour* 3:141, 220–21, 1900. *JAMA* 33:620, 1899. *Atkinson* I:104–05. *Flint* 1897:799.

CRAIG, BENJAMIN FANEUIL, CW–USA; Washington, DC (b/I–28–1829 Watertown, Mass; d/IV–10–1877) MD UPa 1851; AB 1849. *Hist Med Soc DC:* 246. *K&B* III:264.

CRAIG, JAMES, Jersey City, NJ (b/I–22–1834 Glasgow, Scotl; d/II–10–1888) MD UCNY 1861. *Med reg NY NJ Conn* 1888: 249. *Atkinson* I: 359. *K&B* III:264–68.

CRAIG, JAMES W , Churchville, NY; b/XI–8–1825 York, NY; d/VI–26–1891) MD Jefferson 1851. *Bost m & s jour* 31:113–14, 1891. *Polk* 1886: 656.

CRAIG, JOHN A, Baltimore Co, Md (b/1807 Cambridge; d/XII–10–1893) MD UMd 1830. *Med ann Md:* 365.

CRAIG, PRESLEY H , USA 1820– (b/Pa; d/VIII–8–1848) MD unknown. *Tr AMA* 3:453, 1850. Brown, *Med Dept USA*: 287.

CRAIG, ROBERT C , Pittsburgh Pa (d/XI–14–1906 Atlantic City NJ) MD UVa 1896. *Pa med jour* 10:294, 1906/07.

CRAIG, SAMUEL JAMES, Brooklyn (d/IX–29 1897 @ 25) MD CPSNY 1894. *JAMA* 29: 761, 1897.

CRAIG, WILLIAM D , Aledo, Ill (d/I–23–1901) MD Rush 1852. *Ill med jour* ns2: 533, 1901. *Polk* 1896:360.

CRAIG, WILLIAM H , Albany NY (b/XI–2–1825; d/X–4–1889) MD Albany 1852. *Med reg NY NJ Conn* 1890: 264. *Bost m & s jour* 121:400, 1889. *Polk* 1886: 638.

CRAIN, HENRY FOSTER, Springfield, Vt (b/IX–22–1810; d/III–16–1888) ng Dartmouth Med 1830. *JAMA* 13:143, 1889. *Polk* 1886: 906.

CRAM, CHARLES WARREN, Haverhill, Mass; Davenport, Ia (d/VII–13–1899 @ 65) MD Starling 1871; MD Bellevue 1874. *JAMA* 33:302, 1899. *Polk* 1886: 354.

CRAMPTON, HENRY E , NYC (b/IV–10–1837; d/V–28–1899 Glen Ridge, NJ) MD NY Med Coll 1857. *Bost m & s jour* 140:564, 1899. *JAMA* 32:1399, 1899.

CRAMPTON, JOSIAH O'BEAR, Winooski, Vt (b/VII 7–1838 Berkshire; d/V–2 or VII–4–1883) MD Castleton 1861; MD Bellevue 1862. *Tr Vt Med Soc* 1883:104. *Butler* 1874: 774.

CRANDALL, CASPAR LE ROY, Burlington, Wis; Salt Lake City (b/Hartford, Conn; d/III–22–1893) MD Hahnemann Chicago 1879. *Tr Am Inst Homeop* 1893: 135. *Polk* 1886: 951.

CRANDALL, CHARLES MILFORD, Belfast, NY; CW USA; (b/IV–11–1826 Amity; d/X–4–1867) MD Castleton 1850. *Tr Med Soc St NY* 1868:314–17. *Med surg rep Phila* 17:370, 1867. *K&B* III: 266.

CRANDALL, HENRY NEWTON, Westerly, RI (b/VII–13–1848 De Ruyter, NY; d/V–3–1888) MD Jefferson 1871. *Tr RI Med Soc* 3:581, 1883–88. *Polk* 1886:847.

CRANDALL, HIRAM S , Leonardsville, NY (d/XI–29–1897 or I–10–1898 @ 80) ?Cert Exam Bd 1840? *Tr Med Soc St NY* 1898:403. *JAMA* 29:1234 1897. *Polk* 1890:795.

CRANDALL, WILLIAM W , Andover, NY; Wellsville, (b/III–23–1828; d/IV–2–1899) MD U City NY 1858; ng Brown. *Tr Med Soc St NY* 1900: 431. *Polk* 1886: 640.

CRANE, CHARLES HENRY, USA (b/VII–19–1825; d/X–10–1883) MD Harvard 1847; AB Yale 1844; AM 1847. *Med reg NY NJ Conn* 1884:226. *So pract* 5:528, 1883. *JAMA* 1:464, 1883. *Bost m & s jour* 109:384, 526–27, 1883. *K&B* II:258.

CRANE, DELOS A , Holland Patent, NY (b/VI–11–1821 Marcy, NY; d/VII–22–1897) MD Castleton 1844. *JAMA* 29:251, 1897. *Polk* 1896:1025.

CRANE, HENRY BEDELL, Newark, NJ (b/VII–28–1856 Deckertown, NJ; d/III–23–1898) MD UPa 1883. *JAMA* 30:807, 1898. *Tr Med Soc NJ* 1898: 373.*Polk* 1896: 942.

CRANE, HORACE O , Green Bay, Wis (b/1810 Canfield, O; d/VI–3–1872) MD Cleveland Med Coll 1848. *Tr Wis St Med Soc* 1873:121–22.

CRANE, ISAAC L , CW–USA (d/I–31–1870) MD unknown. *Nat med jour* 1:293, 1870/71.

CRANE, JAMES, Brooklyn (b/1818; d/X–31–1888) MD Jefferson 1839; AB Princeton 1835; AM 1838. *Med reg NY NJ Conn* 1889: 270.

CRANE, JOB SYMMES, Elizabeth, NJ (b/IV–23–1825; d/III–26–1896 St Augustine, Fla) MD CPSNY 1849; AB Princeton 1843; AM 1846. *Bost m & s jour* 134: 354, 1896. *Tr Med Soc NJ* 1896:370–72. *JAMA* 26: 732, 1896. *Atkinson* I:446–47. *Butler* 1878: 468.

CRANE, JOHN JACOB, NYC (d/III–4–1890 @ 70) MD CPSNY 1844; AB Princeton 1840; AM 1843. *Med reg NY NJ Conn* 1890: 264. *JAMA* 14:467, 1890.

CRANE, JOHN JOSEPH, NYC; Phoenix, Ore (b/1851 Elizabeth, NJ; d/IV–18–1900 Adirondacks) MD CPSNY 1876; AB Princeton 1873; AM 1876. *Bost m & s jour* 142:444, 1900. *Polk* 1896: 1047. *JAMA* 34: 1084, 1900.

CRANE [CRAIN], JOSEPH, Hoguestown, Pa (b/XII–25 1803 Lancaster; d/IV–18–1876) <MD Jefferson 1829> *Tr Pa St Med Soc* 11:195–96, 1876.

CRANE, JOSEPH SIDNEY, NYC (b/Mass; d/V–20–1906 @ 85) MD UPa 1844. *Bost m & s jour* 154: 642, 1906. *Polk* 1886: 675.

CRANE, JULIUS A , Santa Ana, Cal (d/VI–6–1903) MD Western Reserve 1870. *Cal st jour med* 1:223, 1903. *Polk* 1896: 241.

CRANE, LYMAN MARK, Orange, NJ (b/1810 Bloomfield; d/XI–25–1880) Lic Med Soc NJ 1836. *Tr NJ Med Soc* 1881:158–59. *Butler* 1878:468.

CRANE, PHINEAS MILLER, E Boston (d/VIII–13–1882 @ 77) MD Harvard 1828; AB 1824. *Bost m & s jour* 107:618, 1882.

CRANE, THEODORE, Hackettstown, NJ (b/XII–5–1829; d/IX–12–1890) MD CPSNY 1855; AB Princeton 1850; AM 1854. *Med reg NY NJ Conn* 1892: 275. *Tr*

Med Soc NJ 1891:229–30. *Polk* 1886: 604.

CRANE, THOMAS H , Kent Co, Md (d/II–8–1887 @ 63) MD UMd 1848. *New Orl m & s jour* ns14: 723, 1887. *Butler* 1874: 318.

CRANE, WILLIAM BOWERS, Baltimore (d/II–19–1865 St Joseph Mo) MD UMd 1848 *Med annals Md:*366.

CRAPO, JOHN EUBEN, Terre Haute, Ind (b/X–3–1850; d/XII–19–1905) MD Med Coll O 1877. *Tr Ind St Med Soc* 1906: 503. *Polk* 1896: 493.

CRARY, DAVID, Hartford, Conn (b/IV–18–1806 Wallingford, Vt; d/IV–16–1894) MD Castleton 1834. *Med reg NY NJ Conn* 1894: 236. *JAMA* 22:818, 1894. *Bost m & s jour* 130:432, 1894. *Proc Conn Med Soc* 1894:231–32. *Atkinson* I: 562.

CRATER, HENRY, Somerville, NJ (b/VIII–27–1836 Chester Twp; d/V–1–1886) MD Hahnemann Phila 1872. *Tr Am Inst Homeop* 1886: 143. *Polk* 1886: 611. Homeopath.

CRAVEN, ELIJAH RICHARDSON, Washington, DC (b/II–3–1796 Morrisville, NJ; d/XII–4–1823) MD UPa 1819; AB Princeton 1815. *Hist Med Soc DC:* 223.

CRAVEN, GERSHOM, Ringoes, NJ; RevWar USA (b/1744; d/V–3–1819) <ng UPa Med Sch> AB Princeton 1765. *Tr Med Soc NJ* 1872:174–75. *Wickes*: 223.

CRAVENS, SAMUEL C , Bloomfield, Ind (b/I–3–1839 Hanover; d/IX–5–1903) MD Rush 1866; post-gr LICH 1870. *Tr Ind St Med Soc* 1904:351. *Polk* 1896: 459.

CRAWCOUR, ISAAC L , New Orleans (b/VI–14–1825 Devonshire, Engl; d/VII–25–1886) <MD London 1851> *New Orl m & s jour* ns14:160–61, 1886. *Polk* 1886: 416.

CRAWE, JOHN MORTIMER Sr, Watertown, NY (d/X 29–1901 @ 71) MD Jefferson 1859. *Bost m & s jour* 145:532, 1901. *Tr Med Soc St NY* 1902: [484]. *Polk* 1886: 714.

CRAWFORD, ADONIRAM JUDSON, Des Moines, Ia (d/1888) MD Bellevue 1883. *Tr Ia St Med Soc* 1886–89:529; 1896:328. *Polk* 1886: 356.

CRAWFORD, ALBERT H , Buffalo (d/I–20–1898 @ 58) MD U Buffalo 1865. *Buff m & s jour* 38:544–45, 1899. *JAMA* 32:363, 1899. *Polk* 1886: 651.

CRAWFORD, DAVID McLEAN, Mifflintown, Pa (d/VIII–25–1904 @ 78) MD UCNY 1851. *Pa med jour* 8: 334, 1904/05. *Flint* 1897: 809.

CRAWFORD, GEORGE CHAPPELL, Brooklyn (b/VII 24–1871 Middle Island, NY; d/VII–13–1903 @ 35) MD LICH 1894. *Bost m & s jour* 149:114, 1903.

CRAWFORD, HENRY M , ?CW–USA; St Charles, Ill (d/VI–25–1900) MD RCP(I) 1848. *Ill med jour* ns2:93, 1900; 3:141, 1900.*Polk* 1886: 296.

CRAWFORD, JOHN, Baltimore (b/V–3–1746 N Ireland; d/V–9–1813) <MD U Leyden> *Med annals Md:* 366.

CRAWFORD, JOHN B , Wilkes-Barre, Pa (d/X–7–1894) Lic by years of practice. *Lehigh Valley med mag* 6:70, 1894–95. *Butler* 1878: 708.

CRAWFORD, JOHN C , CW–USA (d/VIII–25–1864) MD unknown. *Nat med jour* 1:293, 1870/71.

CRAWFORD, JOHN S , Cambria, Pa 1838– ; Williamsport 1849– (b/XI–17–1808 Orwigsburg; d/XII–15–1879) MD Jefferson 1838. *Med surg rep Phila* 42:132, 1880. *Tr Med Soc Pa* 13:329–30, 1880. *Atkinson* I: 277.

CRAWFORD, JOHN T , USA (b/Pittsburgh; d/VI–7–1862 Kittanny, Pa) MD UPa 1847. *Tr AMA* 14:216, 1864. *U Pa med alum CW*: 1847. *Nat med jour* 1:293, 1870/71.

CRAWFORD, JOSEPH H , Brooklyn (b/Kans? d/VII–17–1876 @ c25) MD UCNY 1872. *Med reg NY NJ Conn* 1877: 200.

CRAWFORD, KATHERINE MARKLEY, Reading & Chambersburg, Pa (b/VIII–28–1856 Fayetteville; d/XII–2–1903 York, Pa) MD Hahnemann Chicago 1885. *Tr Am Inst Homeop* 1904: 961. Homeopath.

CREADICK, SAMUEL, Phila (d/X–19–1898 @ 57) MD UPa 1867. *JAMA* 31:1066, 1898. *Polk* 1896: 1301.

CREAMER, ALEXANDER DANIEL, Brooklyn (d/V–12–1878 @ 23) MD UCNY 1878. *Med reg NY NJ Conn* 1879: 189.

CREAMER, HENRY ALOYSIUS, Brooklyn (d/II–20–1897 @ 25) MD Bellevue 1892. *Bost m & s jour* 136:216, 1897. *JAMA* 28:429, 1897. *Polk* 1896: 994.

CREAMER, JOSEPH, Brooklyn (d/I–6–1893) MD CPS NY 1850. *Med reg NY NJ Conn* 1893: 298. *Chic med rec* 4:148, 1893.

CREHORE, CHARLES FREDERIC, Newton Lower Falls, Mass; CW–USA (d/1893) MD Harvard 1859. *JAMA* 21:784, 1893. *Bost m & s jour* 129:504, 1893. *Harvard in CW*: 255. *Butler* 1878: 349.

CREIGH, JOHN [?JAMES] War 1812–USA? Carlisle, Pa (b/IX–13–1773; d/XI–7–1841) MD UPa 1794? AB Dickinson 1792. *Dickinson cat*: 1792.

CREMIN, MICHAEL ALOYSIUS, New Haven, Conn (b/VII–15–1851 Limerick Co, Ire; d/XII–28–1895) MD CPSNY 1875. *Proc Conn Med Soc* 1896:332–33. *JAMA* 26:142, 1896.

CRENSHAW, JAMES C , Dermott, Ark (d/VIII–16–1901) MD U Louisville 1887. *JAMA* 37:594, 1901.

CRENSHAW, OCTAVIUS ASBURY, Richmond Va; CW–USA (b/VIII–11–1822 Goochland Co; d/X–22–1906) MD UPa 1844. *U Pa med alum CW*: 1844. *Polk* 1886: 925.

CRESSLER, ALONZO LEITNER, Wilkesbarre, Pa (d/II–23–1903 @ 75) MD Jefferson 1849. *Pa med jour* 7: 278, 1903/04. *Butler* 1878: 708.

CRESSON, CHARLES M , Philadelphia (b/II–3–1828 Cheltenham, Pa; d/XII–27–1893) MD Jefferson 1849. *JAMA* 22:31–32, 1894. *Bost m & s jour* 130:28, 1894.

CRESSON, HILBORN THOMPSON, Philadelphia (d/IX 6–1894 NYC) MD Jefferson 1891. *JAMA* 23:440, 1894.

CRESSY, EVERETT LARCOM, Beverly, Mass (d/V–28–1905; MD Harvard 1900; AB 1896. *Bost m & s jour* 152: 652, 1905.

CREWS, OCTAVIUS LYCURGUS, Alamuchee, Ala (b/XI-7-1837; d/VII-5-1871) MD Jefferson 1859; att U Ala 1856- ? *U Ala cat*: 126.

CRIM, WILLIAM HENRY, Baltimore (b/I-8-1845 Lovettsville, Va; d/XI-15-1902) MD UMd 1870. *Med annals Md:* 366. *Polk* 1886: 436.

CRIPPEN, E H , Milroy, Ind (b/VII-29-1833 New York; d/I-8-1896) MD UCNY 1856. *Tr Ind St Med Soc* 1896: 262. Kemper's *Indiana*: 153, 256.

CRISP, DAVID HARDIE, Uvalde, Tex (b/NC? d/VI-25 1906) MD UPa 1846. *Texas st jour med* 2:122, 1906.

CRISPELL, GARRETT D , Kingston, NY (b/IX-8-1801 Hurley, NY; d/XII-15-1880) Lic Ulster Co Med Soc 1823; MD ("special") NY Homeop 1869. *Tr Am Inst Homeop* 1881:124. Homeopath.

CRIST, DANIEL O , Indianapolis, Ind (b/VIII-28-1824 near Columbus, O; d/I-31-1899) MD Starling 1853. *Tr Ind St Med Soc* 1899:402. *JAMA* 32:385, 1899. *Polk* 1896:472.

CRIST, DAVID LEVI, Bloomington Ill (b/V-1817 Perry Co, O; d/III-18-1875) MD Starling 1852. *Tr AMA* 29:630-31,1878. *Tr Ill St Med Soc* 1876:177-78.

CRIST, LOUIS ARTHUR, Scranton, Pa (d/IV-3-1904 @33) MD UPa 1896. *Pa med jour* 8:334, 1904/05.

CRITCHFIELD, S T , CW-USA (d/IV-11-1865) MD unknown. *Nat med jour* 1:293, 1870/71.

CROCKER, FRANK HERBERT, Boothbay, Me, 1882-91; Machias 1891-99; Gardiner 1899-1903 (b/VIII-8-1851 Machias; d/VI-12-1903) MD Bowdoin 1882; AB 1877. *Bowdoin cat*: 1877. *Polk* 1886: 423.

CROCKER, ISAAC SENTER, Providence, RI (b/Barnstable, Mass; d/X-26-1866) MD Hahnemann Phila 1851. *Tr Am Inst Homeop* 1867: 157.

CROGGON, RICHARD C , Washington, DC (b/VII-15 1839; d/IX-23-1872) MD Georgetown 1860. *Tr AMA* 24:340-41, 1873. *Hist Med Soc DC:* 165.

CROGHAN, PATRICK, CW-USA; Washington, DC (b/Ireland; d/III-28-1874) MD Queens Coll Cork 1859. *Hist Med Soc DC:* 272. *Tr AMA* 25:526, 1874.

CROMBIE, JOHN BATES, Pittsburgh (b/II-22-1858 W Elizabeth, Pa; d/XII-22-1902) MD UMd 1883. *Pa med jour* 6:223, 259. 387. *Flint* 1897: 793.

CROMWELL, JOHN, Baltimore (b/1764 near Curtis Bay, Md; d/IX-14-1832) MD unknown. *Med annals Md:* 367.

CRONMILLER, JOHN, Elk Ridge, Md (b/VII-24-1793; d/X-9-1875) MD UMd 1826. *Med annals Md:* 367. *Butler* 1874: 318.

CRONMILLER, WILLIAM, Baltimore (b/1802; d/V-4-1843) MD UMd 1826. *Med annals Md:* 367.

CRONYN [CROMYER], JOHN, Fort Erie, Can 1850-59; Buffalo 1859- (b/XII-15-1823 or 1825 or 1827 Ireland; d/II-11-1898) MD U Toronto 1860; MB 1859. *Buff m & s jour* 37:619-622, 1898. *JAMA* 30:448, 1898; 30:507, 1898). *Atkinson* I:299. *Polk* 1886: 651.

CROOK, JAMES M , Dayton, O (b/XI- -1826 Montg'y Co; d/1857) MD UMd 1852; att Miami 1846-48. *Tr Ohio Med Soc* 1875: 194.

CROOK, JOHN TAYLOR, San Francisco (b/VII-14-1834 NYC; d/III-22-1879) MD CPSNY 1857. *Med rec NY* 15: 551, 1878. *Atkinson* I: 509.

CROOK, LURAD HEATH, CW-USA; Brooklyn (b/I-13-1839; d/V-10-1869) MD Bellevue 1865; AB Williams 1861. *Med reg NY NJ Conn* 1872: 344. *Med surg rep Phila* 20:327, 1869. *Phila med reg & dir* 1871:300.

CROOK, WILLIAM EUGENE, Snow Hill, Ala (b/VI-10-1849; d/XII-22-1880 Mobile) MD Tulane 1868; U Ala 1864- . *U Ala cat*: 196.

CROOKER, BENJAMIN TOWER, Boston, Bridgewater, Mass; CW-USA (d/III-21-1882) MD Harvard 1961. *Harvard in CW*: 262-63.

CROOKS, JAMES PALMER, Pittsburgh (d/X-11-1870) MD Hahnemann 1869. *Hahn mo* 6:181, 1870/71.

CROOKS, JOHN W , Shermansdale, Pa; CW-USA (d/X 16-1863 Sterrett's Gap @ 38) MD Phila Coll Med 1851; ng Dickinson 1848. *Nat med jour* 1:293, 1870/71. *Med surg rep Phila* 10:454, 1863.

CROOKS, ROBERT L, Convoy (d/VIII-12-1901) MD Med Coll Ft Wayne 1878. *JAMA* 37:527, 1901. *Polk* 1886:751.

CROPP, WILLIAM WARNER, CW-CSA; Burke's Mills, Va (b/II-28-1829 Burketown; d/X-25-1898) MD UPa 1859. *U Pa med alum CW*: 1859. *Polk* 1886: 914.

CROSBY, ALBERT HARRISON, CW-USA; Concord, NH (b/IV-23-1828 Gilmanton; d/IX-5-1886) MD Dartmouth 1860; AB 1848. *Bost m & s jour* 115:244, 1886. *Tr NH Med Soc* 1887:165-70. *K&B* III: 270.

CROSBY, ALPHEUS BENNING, Hanover, NH (b/II-22 1832 Gilmanton; d/VIII-9-1877) MD Dartmouth 1853; AB 1853. *Med reg NY NJ Conn* 1878:181. *Buff m & s jour* 17:110, 1877. *Atkinson* I: 75. *Tr NH Med Soc* 1878:153-175. *K&B* III:267-68.

CROSBY, ATWOOD, CW-USN; Waterville, Me (b/XI-1-1838 Albion; d/I-25-1883 Las Vegas NM) MD Bowdoin 1864. *Tr Me Med Assoc* 1883: 155-57.

CROSBY, DIXI, Hanover, NH (b/II-7-1800 Sandwich; d/IX-26-1873) MD Dartmouth 1824. *Bost m & s jour* ns12:346, 1873. *Tr NH Med Soc* 1874:105-19. *Med surg rep Phila* 29: 270, 1873. *K&B* III:268-70.

CROSBY, DIXI, NYC (b/VII-29-1869 Hanover, NH; d/I 20-1900) MD Dartmouth 1891. *Tr NH Med Soc* 1900: 317-18. *JAMA* 34:313, 1900. *Polk* 1896:218, 1891.

CROSBY, GEORGE AVERY, Manchester, NH (b/1831 Lowell, Mass; d/I-29-1888) MD Dartmouth 1855; AB 1852. *Bost m & s jour* 118:134, 1888. *Tr NH Med Soc* 1888: 159-63. *Polk* 1886: 592.

CROSBY, J B, Union Village NY (d/X-1-1865 @ 52) MD unknown. *Med surg rep Phila* 13:262, 1865.

CROSBY, JOSIAH, Epsom & Manchester, NH; Lowell, Mass (b/II-1-1794 Sandwich, NH; d/I-7-1875) MD

Dartmouth 1816. *Tr NH Med Soc* 1875: 143–54.

CROSBY, OBED H , Atlantic City, NJ (b/Middletown, NY; d/I–6–1885 @ 35) MD NY Homeop 1874. *Tr Am Inst Homeop* 1885:103. Homeopath.

CROSBY, ORRIS, Fredonia, NY c1817–37; Belvidere, Ill 1837– ; Pt Bluffs, Wis (b/VI–2–1791 Danbury, Conn; d/IV–8–1862) Stud w/Eliakim Crosby, Canada & Dr Mc-Cracken, Batavia, NY; lic Genesee Co Med Soc 1817. *Tr Med Soc St NY* 1865: 282.

CROSBY, THOMAS RUSSELL, Manchester, NH; CW–USA (b/X–22–1816 Gilmanton; d/III–7–1872 Hanover) MD Dartmouth 1841. *Tr AMA* 24:352–55, 1873. *Bost m & s jour* ns9: 1872. *Tr NH Med Soc* 1872: 74 ff. *K&B* II:263.

CROSS, ANDERSON G , Waynesburg, Pa (d/VIII–23–1904 @83) ng Jefferson 1858. *Pa med jour* 8: 334, 1904/05. *JAMA* 43:749, 1904. *Flint* 1897: 839.

CROSS, ELISHA WILD, Bradford, Vt; Rochester, Minn (d/XI–21–1899 @79) MD Woodstock 1851. *JAMA* 33: 1441, 1899. *Polk* 1886: 516.

CROSS, ENOCH, Newburyport, Mass 1845–88 (b/VII–19–1801 Methuen; d/V–17–1888) MD Dartmouth 1824. *Bost m & s jour* 118:536,1888. *Polk* 1886:470.

CROSS, GEORGE D , Chester, Pa (d/VIII–9–1903 @ 55) MD UPa 1889. *Pa med jour* 7:278, 1903/04. *Flint* 1897: 798.

CROSS, JEREMIAH A , Newark, NJ (b/II–21–1827 Schoharie, NY; d/III–30–1881) MD Albany 1856. *Tr Med Soc NJ* 1881: 169–70. *Atkinson* I: 672.

CROSS, JOSEPH B , Bainbridge, Ind (b/II–12–1824 Wayne Co; d/III–6–1889) MD Med Coll Ohio 1853. *Tr Ind St Med Soc* 1889: 215. *Butler* 1878: 198.

CROSS, WILLIAM PLUMMER, So Boston (b/VII–4–1816 Sanbornton, NH; d/IX–11–1890) MD Homeop Med Coll Cleveland 1853. *Tr Am Inst Homeop* 1891: 98. *New Engl med gaz* 26:160, 1891. *Med vis* 6:346, 1890. *Cleave*. *Polk* 1886: 473. Homeopath.

CROSSON, HENRY JOHN, Washington, DC (b/I–19 1803 Baltimore Co, Md; d/XI–21–1880) MD UMd 1836. *Hist Med Soc DC:* DC: 242. *Butler* 1874: 91.

CROSSWHITE, JOHN R, St Louis (d/VII–24–1901 @ 48) MD Mo Med Coll 1877. *JAMA* 37:398, 1901. *Polk* 1886: 561.

CROSWELL, ANDREW, Mercer, Me (b/IV–9–1778 Plymouth, Mass; d/VI–4–1858) MD unknown; AB Harvard 1798. *Bost m & s jour* 58:407,428, 1851. Palmer's *Necrol Harvard alum*: 168.

CROTHERS, ROBERT W , Delavan, Ill (b/IV–25–1833 Mt Pleasant, O; d/I–10–1890) MD Jefferson 1855. *Tr Ill St Med Soc* 1890: 37. *Polk* 1886: 276.

CROUCH, HENRY COOPER, Denver, Colo (d/IV–20–1898 @ 40) MD Giessen 1890; AB Yale 1879. *Tr Colo St Med Soc* 1898–99: 37, 509. *JAMA* 30: 1125, 1898. *Polk* 1896: 258.

CROUSE, JOHN LEWIS, Washington, DC (b/1833 Md; d/VI–30–1889) MD UMd 1859. *Hist Med Soc DC:* 281. *Polk* 1886: 211.

CROWELL, BENJAMIN FRANKLIN, Centreville, Tex; CW–CSA (b/V–29–1837; d/VIII–7–1885) MD U La 1861; AB U Ala 1857. *U Ala cat*:1857. *Butler* 1878:756.

CROWELL, EDWIN MELVILLE, Seneca Falls, NY (d/III–10–1862) ng U Mich Med 1857–59. *U Mich cat*:668.

CROWELL, ELISHA, CW–USA; Philadelphia (b/XI–10 1828; d/IV–6–1904) MD UPa 1851. *Pa med jour* 8:334, 1904/05. *U Pa med alum CW*: 1851. *Atkinson* I:308. *Polk* 1896: 1301.

CROWELL, GEORGE EDGAR, Sullivan, O (d/XII––1883 @ 31) MD Jefferson 1875. *Med bull m & s* 6:42, 1884.

CROWELL, JOHN Jr, Haverhill, Mass (b/IX–28–1823; d/IV–28–1890) MD Phila Coll Med 1850. *Bost m & s jour* 122: 462, 1890. *Butler* 1878: 348.

CROWELL, NATHANIEL SAVAGE, Bluffton, SC; USA; CW–CSA (d/XII–2–1867 Augusta, Ga) MD CPSNY 1851. *Tr AMA* 19:419, 1868. *Med surg rep Phila* 17:546, 1867.

CROWLEY, FREDERICK, Philadelphia (d/XI–14–1851?) MD Jefferson 1842. *Tr Med Soc Pa* 1:185, 1856.

CRUICE, JOHN JOSEPH, CW–USA; Philadelphia (d/VI–21–1863) MD UPa 1861. *Med surg rep Phila* 10: 156, 1863.

CRUICE, ROBERT BLAKE, Philadelphia; CW–USA (b/IX–29–1838 Irel'd; d/IX–23–1899) MD UPa 1859. *Tr CPP* cent vol: 218. *U Pa med alum CW*: 1859. *JAMA* 33:807: 1899.

CRUICE, WILLIAM ROBERT, Philadelphia (b/XII–23 1842 Irel'd; d/VIII–15–1886 Spring Lake, NJ) MD U Pa 1865. *Med age* 4:372–73,188_? *Tr CPP* cent'l vol: 218.

CRUIKSHANK, JAMES A , Bayou Rapides, La (d/XII–5–1897) MD UMd 1864. *New Orl m & s jour* 50: 433, 1898. *Polk* 1896: 613.

CRUISE, WILLIAM, NYC (d/VI–25–1879 @ 53) MD Harvard 1867; <att U Toronto c1850> *Med reg NY NJ Conn* 1880: 234. *Butler* 1878: 510.

CRUM, ELLEN GERTRUDE, Binghamton, NY (d/VIII 5–1898 @31) MD Woman's Med Coll of NY Infirmary 1886. *JAMA* 31:427, 1898. *Polk* 1896:989.

CRUM, GEORGE WASHINGTON, Jefferson, Md (b/III–12–1811; d/III–15–1896) MD UMd 1832. *Med ann Md:* 368. *Polk* 1893: 570.

CRUME, P M , Eaton, O (d/1869) MD Cincinnati Coll Med & Surg 1861. *Tr O St Med Soc* 1873: 263.

CRUMRINE, CLYDE W , Charleroi, Pa (d/VIII–29–1901 @32) MD W Penna Med Coll 1895. *Pa med jour* 5:39, 296, 1901/02. *JAMA* 37:710, 1901. *Polk* 1896:1288.

CRUSIUS, LOUIS, St. Louis (d/I–2–1898 @36) <MD St Louis Coll Phys & Surg 1890> *JAMA* 30:166, 1898. *Polk* 1896: 868.

CRUTCHER, THEOPHILUS P , CW–CSA; Nashville,

 Spec. educ'l status abbrev. as: ***ng*** = college verified attendance without degree;

Tenn (d/II-13-1898 @ 68) MD U Nashville 1856. *JAMA* 30:570, 1898. *Polk* 1886: 870. *SHSP* 22:189, 1893.

CRUTCHLEY, WILBUR F , Brooklyn (b/1842 Harper's Ferry, WVa; d/IX-18-1894 Lord's Valley, Pa) MD Columbian DC 1870. *Med reg NY NJ Conn* 1895: 218. *JAMA* 23:561, 1894. *Polk* 1886: 644.

CRUTTENDEN, ALBERT GALLATIN, Clifton Spr, NY (b/Covington; d/VI-7-1890) MD Willoughby 1840. *Tr Med Soc St NY* 1894: 741 ff. *Polk* 1886: 656.

CUDDEBACK, THOMAS, Big Hat, NY (b/VIII-31-1825; d/XI-3-1893) MD Yale 1847. *Med reg NY NJ Conn* 1894:236, *JAMA* 21:784, 1893. *Polk* 1886: 702.

CUDLIPP, CASSIUS LEE, Richmond, Va (d/III-14-1898 @ 33) MD Med Coll Va 1886. *JAMA* 30: 807, 1898. *Polk* 1896: 1498.

CULBERT, WILLIAM ACHESON McLEOD, Newburgh, NY (b/XI-4-1822 NYC; d/XI-10-1890) MD UCNY 1846. *New York med times* 18:283, 1890. *No Amer jour homeop* 38:846, 1890. *Med vis* 7:38, 1891. *Polk* 1886: 699. Homeopath?

CULBERTSON, HOWARD, Zanesville, O (b/II-24-1828; d/VI-18-1890) MD Jefferson 1848. *Bost m & s jour* 123:24, 1890. *Tr Ohio Med Soc* 1891:5. *Atkinson* I:29. *K&B* III:270-71.

CULBERTSON, JAMES, Lewistown, Pa (b/III-12-1783 Cumberland Co, Pa; d/III-30-1854) MD UPa 1827; AB Dickinson 1824. *Dickinson cat*: 1824.

CULBERTSON, ROBERT H , Brazil, Ind (d/IX-12-1899 @ 69) MD Med Coll Ohio 1869. *JAMA* 33: 808, 1899. *Polk* 1886: 312.

CULLEN, CHARLES ROCHE, Richmond, Va (b/VIII-16-1825; d/IV-6-1899) MD Med Coll Va 1848; AB Brown 1846. *Butler* 1878: 796. *Brown hist cat*: 1846.

CULLEN, FRANK CONNOR, Chicago (d/VIII-29-1901) MD Rush 1887. *Ill med jour* ms3:295, 1901. *Polk* 1896: 380.

CULLEN, HENRY JAMES, Brooklyn (b/VII-2-1805; d/VII-17-1874) <MD Geneva 1828> *Med reg NY NJ Conn* 1875: 196.

CULLEN, JOHN, Richmond, Va (b/1797 Dublin; d/XII-25-1849) <MD Dublin> *Tr AMA* 3:438, 1850. *K&B* III: 265.

CULLEN, JOHN M , New Orleans (b/Yazoo City, Miss; d/IX-22-1880 @ 33) MD U La 1869. *New Orl m & s jour* ns8:399, 1880; ns9:396, 1881. *Butler* 1878: 294.

CULLEN, JOHN SYNG DORSEY, Richmond, Va (b/VII-29-1832; d/III-22-1893) MD Med Coll Va 1853; att UVa*JAMA* 20:545, 1893. *Tr Med Soc Va* 1893: 219, 220. *Atkinson* I:315. *K&B* III: 272-73.

CULLEN, THOMAS FRANKFORD, Camden, NJ (b/X-3-1822; d/XI-21-1877) MD UPa 1844. *Tr AMA* 33:543, 1882. *Med rec* NY 13:455, 1878. *Tr Med Soc NJ* 1878:198-99.

CULLER, JAMES J , Jefferson, Md (d/III-13-1900) MD UMd 1848. *JAMA* 34:766, 1900. *Polk* 1886: 443.

CULLIMORE, THOMAS McINTYRE, Beatrice, Neb (d/III-4-1899 Jacksonville, Ill) MD UCNY 1877. *JAMA* 32: 628, 1899. *Polk* 1896: 424.

CULLINANE, JOHN J , Buffalo (d/III-31-1898 @ 31) MD Buffalo 1893. *JAMA* 30:933, 1898. *Polk* 1896: 1007.

CULLIS, CHARLES, Boston (b/III-7-1833; d/VI-18-1892) MD UVt 1857. *Tr Am Inst Homeop* 1893: 136. *Polk* 1886: 456. Homeopath.

CULPEPER, VERNON GRANT, Portsmouth Va (b/IX-25-1856; d/X-15-1905) MD UCNY 1877; att UVa 1873-74. *Tr Med Soc Va* 1905:445. *Polk* 1900: 1771.

CULVER, FREDERICK BURR, Washington, DC (b/1809 Frederick, O; d/VI-12-1879) MD Louisville Med Coll 1857. *Hist Med Soc DC:* 259. *Butler* 1874: 91.

CULVER, JANE KENDRICK, Boston (b/1827 Enfield, Mass; d/V-23-1901) MD Bost U Sch Med 1878. *Tr Am Inst Homeop* 1901:913-14. *Polk* 1886: 456. Homeopath.

CULVER, JOSEPH EDWIN, Jersey City, NJ (b/II-9-1823; Groton, Conn; d/XI-1-1897) MD CPSNY 1849. *Bost m & s jour* 137:505, 1897. *JAMA* 29:1028, 1897. *Atkinson* I: 287. *Polk* 1896: 938.

CULVER, JOSIAH HOWELL, CW-USN (b/IX-10-1837; d/IX-25-1868) MD UCNY 1860. *Phila med reg & dir* 1871: 298. *Tr AMA* 21:497-98, 1870. *Med reg NY NJ Conn* 1869: 230.

CUMMER, RALPH [ROBERT] J , Cleveland (d/X-22 1905 @ 52) MD Cleveland Med Coll 1880. *Cleveland m & s rep* 1905 (Dec) *JAMA* 45: 1513, 1905. *Polk* 1886: 485 (Cadillac, Mich).

CUMMING, JAMES RUSSELL, Bridgeport Conn; CW-USA (b/IV-16-1830; d/II-4-1891) MD CPSNY 1862. *Med reg NY NJ Conn* 1892:275. *Proc Conn Med Soc* 1891: 309-12. *Bost m & s jour* 124:176, 1891.

CUMMINGS, ALVAH R , Claremont, NH (b/VIII-27-1826; d/II-26-1905) MD Dartmouth 1852. *Bost m & s jour* 152:294, 1905. *Tr NH Med Soc* 1905: 276, 281-82. *Polk* 1896: 918.

CUMMINGS, ARIEL IVERS, Roxbury, Mass; CW-USA (b/VI-4-1823; d/IX-9-1863 Camp Grace Prison, Hempstead, Tex) MD UCNY 1851. *Bost m & s jour* 69:468, 1863. *Nat med jour* 1:293, 1870/71.

CUMMINGS, D J , Farmington, Minn (d/XI-9 1893 @ 75) MD *JAMA* 21:829, 1893. *Butler* 1878: 392.

CUMMINGS, E P , Newburyport, Mass; CW-USN & USA (d/IV-8-1878 @ 52) MD unknown. *Tr Mass Hom Soc* 1890 (Sept) Homeopath.

CUMMINGS, GEORGE HENRY, Portland, Me (b/IV-6 1850; d/VIII-22-1903 Boothbay Harbor) MD CPSNY 1875; AB Bowd'n 1872. *Bowd cat*:1872. *Polk* 1886:428.

CUMMINGS, HENRY THORNTON, Portland, Me 1844-74? Tacoma, Wash 1892-1901 (b/XI-12-1822 Yarmouth; d/XII-15-1901) MD Harvard 1844; AB Bowdoin 1841. *Bowdoin cat*: 1841. *Polk* 1886: 428.

CUMMINGS, HERBERT CYRUS, Concord, NH (b/VI-11-1860 Sutton; d/IX-1-1890) MD UCNY 1884. *Tr NH*

Med Soc 1891:254–55. *Polk* 1886:591.

CUMMINGS, ISAAC, NYC (b/VIII-2-1832 Royalston, Mass; d/XII-16-1868) MD Dartmouth 1858. *Phila med reg & dir* 1871: 299. *Tr AMA* 21:442, 1870. *Med surg rep Phila* 19:522, 1868. *Med reg NY NJ Conn* 1869: 231.

CUMMINGS, JAMES MERRILL, Nashua, NH; Cairo, Ill; Groton, Mass 1842; Portland, Me 1860– (b/VII-27-1810 Boston; d/VII-20-1883) MD Bowdoin 1834; AB 1830; AM 1852. *Tr Am Inst Hom* 1885:90. Homeopath.

CUMMINGS, JAMES PRESTON CHAPLIN, Fitchburg, Mass (d/1858 @ 28) MD Harvard 1851. *Bost m & s jour* 59:148, 1859. *Mass Med Soc cat* 1894.

CUMMINGS, JESSE E, Uvalde, Tex (b/1855 Tex; d/IV-30-1897) MD Mo Med Coll 1870. *Tex med jour* 13:44, 1897–98. *Polk* 1896: 1454.

CUMMINGS, JOHN ALFRED, Boston (b/VI-16-1816 Dunstable; d/III-4-1870) MD Woodstock 1840. *Bost m & s jour* 5:196, 1870.

CUMMINGS, JOHN CAMPBELL, CW–CSA (b/1827 Abingdon, Va; d/XII-2-1898 St Louis) MD UPa 1851. *U Pa med alum CW*: 1851. *Polk* 1886: 561.

CUMMINGS, JOHN MORLAND, Portland, Me (b/III-31-1814; d/III-28-1878) MD Bowdoin 1836; AB 1833. *Bowdoin cat*: 1833.

CUMMINGS, JOSEPHUS, Austin, Tex (b/XI-30-1849; d/VII-13-1895) MD Jefferson 1871. *Tex med jour* 11:86–87, 1895–96. *Atkinson* I: 413. *Polk* 1890:1069.

CUMMINGS, RALPH WARDLAW, CW–USA; Bay City, Mich; Minneapolis; San Francisco (b/IX-4-1832 No Yarmouth, Md; d/VIII-17-1880) MD Bowdoin 1855; NY Med Coll 1866; ng Bowdoin Coll 1853. *Bowdoin cat:* 1853.

CUMMINGS, SILAS, Fitzwilliam, NH (b/X-7-1803; d/VI-30-1882) MD Dartmouth 1827. *JAMA* 1:576, 1883. *Tr NH Med Soc* 1883:171–73. *Butler* 1878:454.

CUMMINGS, W J, CW–USA (d/X-13-1864) MD unknown. *Nat med jour* 1:293, 1870/71.

CUMMINS, DAVID, Louisville, Ky (d/IV-14-1883) MD U Louisville 1849. *Med bull med & surg* 5:138, 1883. *Butler* 1878: 260.

CUMMINS, JAMES, Wheeling, WVa (b/1827 Washington, Pa; d/VIII-18-1877) MD UPa 1849. *Tr AMA* 29: 631–33, 1878. *Tr Med Soc WVa* 1878: 434–35.

CUMMINS, ROBERT HAZLETT, Wheeling, WVa (b/II 1817 Washington Pa; d/IV-12-1873) MD UPa 1841; AB Wash & Jeff 1836. *Tr AMA* 24:389–91 1873. *Tr Med Soc WVa* 1873:470–71. *Med s rep Phila* 28:398, 1873.

CUMMINS, ROBERT HAZLETT, Wheeling, WVa (d/XII-13-1894) MD UPa 1891; att Washington & Jefferson Coll. *JAMA* 24: 33, 1895.

CUNKLE, LEVI J, Madison, Kans (d/XI-17-1899) MD Bellevue 1868. *JAMA* 33:1441, 1899. *Polk* 1896: 559.

CUNNEELY, HENRY CHARLES, Hoboken, NJ (d/X-1 1899 @ 38) MD Bellevue 1886. *JAMA* 33: 927, 1899. *Bost m & s jour* 141:380, 1899. *Polk* 1896: 937.

CUNNINGHAM, EDWARD LINZEE, Newport, RI (b/I 2-1810 Boston; d/I-29-1905) MD Harvard 1832; AB 1829. *Bost m & s jour* 152:148–49, 1905.

CUNNINGHAM, FRANCIS DEANE, Richmond Va; CW–CSA (b/1836 Goochland Co; d/IX-9-1885) MD Med Coll Va 1857; MD UCNY 1859. *Tr Med Soc Va* 1885:282–83. *Atkinson* I:100. *K&B* III:273.

CUNNINGHAM, J L, Fort Worth, Tex (b/Indiantown, SC; d/X-9-1896) MD UVa 1853. *Texas med news* 50: 38, 1896–97. *Polk* 1886: 887.

CUNNINGHAM, JOHN, Wooster, Pa (b/II-10-1792 Washington Co, Pa; d/I-21-1892) MD Jefferson 1827; att Washington Coll. *JAMA* 18:150–51, 1892.

CUNNINGHAM, JOHN ATKINSON, Richmond, Va (b/X-3-1803; d/III-21-1881) MD UPa 1826; AB Harvard 1823; AM 1850. *Tr AMA* 33:543–44, 1882.

CUNNINGHAM, JOHN S, Youngstown, O (b/II-4-1833 Ellwood, Pa; d/IV-4-1893) MD Jefferson 1860. *Tr O St Med Soc* 1893:384–85. *Butler* 1878: 625.

CUNNINGHAM, JOSIAH GUY, CW–USA; Kittanning, Pa (b/II-2-1842 Jefferson Co, O; d/XII-12-1898) MD Jefferson 1867. *Pa med jour* 2:426, 1899. *JAMA* 31: 1542, 1898. *Atkinson* I:586. *Butler* 1878: 709.

CUNNINGHAM, SAMUEL B, Jonesboro, Tenn (b/X-9 1797 Washington Co; d/IX-4-1867) MD Transylvania 1838. *Nashville jour m & s* ns3:287–88, 1867. *New Orl m & s jour* 20:205, 1868.

CUNNINGHAM, SMITH, Petersburg, O; Beaver, Pa (b/1804 Lancaster Co; d/X-25-1863) MD unknown. *Tr AMA* 18:327, 1867. *Tr Med Soc Pa* 1864: 407.

CUNNINGHAM, THEO NATHANIEL, Princeton, Ill (d/VI-122-1898 @ 54) MD Rush 1872. *JAMA* 31: 39, 1898. *Polk* 1886: 297.

CUNNINGHAM, WILLIAM FROST, Charlestown, Mass (d/VI-5-1894 Leamington, Engl @ 35) MD Harvard 1881. *Bost m & s jour* 130:636, 1894.

CUNNINGHAM, WILLIAM H, Burnt Corn, Ala (b/XI-26-1839; d/IX-21-1866) MD Tulane 1860; ng U Ala 1854. *U Ala cat*: 120.

CUNNION, ROBERT FRANCIS, Brooklyn (d/IV-7 1900 @ 30) MD CPSNY 1892; AB Manhattan 1889; AM 1892. *JAMA* 34:1021, 1900. *Polk* 1896:268.

CUPPLES, GEORGE, San Antonio, Tex (b/X-13-1815 Scotl; d/IV-9-1895) <ng Edinburgh> *JAMA* 24:650, 1895. *Texas cour rec med* 12:260, 1895. *Texas m jour* 10:606? 1894–95. *Polk* 1886: 893.

CURE, HIRAM W, Martinsville, Ind (b/IX-14-1830 Dearborn Co; d/XII-30-1900) Lic by years of practice. *Tr Ind St Med Soc* 1901: 482. *Polk* 1886: 327.

CURLEY, PETER FRANCIS, Newport, RI (b/IX-18-1861; d/XII-13-1900) MD Albany 1883. *Bost m & s jour* 143:646, 1900. *Tr RI Med Soc* 6:262–63, 1899–1903. *Polk* 1886: 845.

CURRAN, JOHN JOSEPH, NYC (b/Newport RI; d/VII-24-1897) MD CPSNY 1888. *JAMA* 29:350, 1897.

 Spec. educ'l status abbrev. as: ***ng*** = college verified attendance without degree;

CURRAN, JOHN P , Philadelphia (d/III–27–1885) MD UPa 1841. *Med surg rep Phila* 52:512, 1885. *Butler* 1878: 661.

CURREY, GEORGE W, Nashville (b/IX–13–1823; d/I–25–1886) MD U Tenn 1878. *So pract* 8:96–97, 1886. *New Orl m & s jour* ns13: 751 1886. *SHSP* 22:189 1893.

CURREY, JAMES HAMILTON, Baltimore (b/1832 Uniontown, Md; d/IV–20–1887) MD UMd 1859. *Med annals Md:* 369. *Polk* 1886: 436.

CURREY, RICHARD OWEN, Nashville; CW–CSA (b/VIII–28–1816; d/II–17–1865 Salisbury, NC) MD UPa 1840; AB U Nashville. *Tr Med Soc Tenn* 1876: 80. *SHSP* 22: 189, 1893. *U Pa med alum CW*: 1840.

CURREY, WILBUR C , Baltimore (d/V–28–1896) MD UMd 1889. *JAMA* 26:119, 1896.

CURRIE, DAVID MITCHELL, ?Brownsville Tenn; CW CSA (b/IX–3–1823 Caswell Co, NC; d/V–26–1903 Brownsville) MD UPa 1850. *U Pa med alum CW*:1850.

CURRIE, THOMAS HAINES, Lebanon, NH (b/IX–5–1821 Concord; d/IV–3–1898) MD Dartmouth 1845. *Tr NH Med Soc* 1898: 257–58. *Polk* 1896: 920.

CURRIE, WILLIAM, Chester, Pa; RevWar–USA (b/1754 Chester Co; d/VI–13–1828) <ng UPa Med Sch> *Tr CPP* cent vol: 219. *Hazard's reg* 9: 1830 (Sept). *K&B* III:274–75.

CURRIER, WILLIAM JACKSON, Lexington, Mass (d/X–27–1884 @ 69) MD Berkshire 1839. *Bost m & s jour* 111:620, 1884.

CURRY, JAMES HART, Shrub Oak NY (d/IX–24 1900) MD Yale 1852. *Bost m & s jour* 143:356, 1900. *Tr Med Soc St NY* 1901: [426]. *Polk* 1886: 708.

CURRY, WALKER, NYC; CW–USA (b/X–24–1835 Lincoln Co Ga; d/IX–20–1902) MD UPa 1857;AB U Ga 1852. *Bost m & s jour* 147:366, 1902. *Polk* 1896: 107.

CURTIS, EDWARD M , CW–USA; NYC: Sacramento 1871– (b/II–16–1840 Warren, Vt; d/V–12–1874) MD UVt 1863; ng Harvard 1859. *Tr Med Soc St Cal* 1874–75: 161–62. *Tr AMA* 29:633–34, 1878. *Harvard in CW*: 124. *Tr Cal Med Soc* 1875:161–62. *K&B* I(1): 214.

CURTIS, GEORGE BOARDMAN, Hawley, Pa (d/VI–9 1884 @ 48) MD UPa 1858. *Med surg rep Phila* 50:788, 1884. *Polk* 1886: 802 (!)

CURTIS, GEORGE L , Bartholomew Co, Ind (b/XI–21–1835 Columbus, O; d/IV–1–1898 Naples, Italy) MD Ind Med Coll 1877. *Tr Ind St Med Soc* 1890: 390–91.

CURTIS, HALL, CW–USA; Boston (d/VI–1–1906 Beverly Farms Mass) MD Harvard 1857; AB 1854. *Bost m & s jour* 154:664 1906. *Harv in CW:* 71. *Polk* 1896: 695.

CURTIS, J MONTGOMERY, Moundsville, WVa (b/XI 16–1844 W Liberty; d/VI–17–1875) MD Miami 1867. *Tr Med Soc W Va* 1876:216–17; 1884: 154.

CURTIS, JOHN BENEDICT, Somerville, Mass (d/X–1–1898 @31) MD Harvard 1891; AB Boston Coll. *Bost m & s jour* 139:350,356, 1898. *JAMA* 31:942 1898. *Polk* 1896: 722.

CURTIS, JONATHAN STRONG, Lawrence, Mass; Hartford, Conn 1853– (b/VI–11–1821 Epsom, NH; d/III–31–1897) MD Dartmouth 1844. *JAMA* 28: 714, 1897. *Polk* 1886: 192.

CURTIS, JOSIAH, Boston; CW–USA (b/IV–30–1816 Wethersfield, Conn; d/VIII–1–1883) MD Jefferson 1843; AB Yale 1840; AM 1861. *JAMA* 1:223,1883. *Med bull m & s* 5:211, 1883. *Atkinson* I:270–21. *K&B* III: 277.

CURTIS, LEVI, Philadelphia; CW–USA (b/V–5–1823 Wethersfield, Conn; d/XII–12–1904) MD Jefferson 1847. *Pa med jour* 8:334, 1904/05. *Atkinson* I:162. *Polk* 1896: 1301.

CURTIS, ROLAND, Richmond, Me (b/I–26–1846 Bowdoinham; d/X–13–1882) MD Bowdoin 1874. *Tr Me Med Assoc* 1883: 148–49.

CURTIS, ROMAINE J , Joliet, Ill (d/XI/XII 1900 @ 58) MD Med Coll Ohio 1864. *Chic med rec* 19: 470 1900. *Flint* 1897: 278.

CURTIS, THOMAS BUCKMINSTER, Boston (b/VII–19–1842; d/XII–13–1881) MD École de méd, Paris 1873; AB Harvard 1862) *Bost m & s jour* 105:575, 599–600 1881. *Med rec* 20:755, 1881. *Chic m rev* 5:10, 1882.

CURWEN, JOHN, Harrisburg & Warren, Pa (b/IX–20–1821 Lower Merion; d/VII–2–1901) MD UPa 1844; AB Yale 1841; LLD Jefferson 1862. *Pa med jour* 4:828, 1900/01; 5:296, 1901/02. *Atkinson* I:37. *Butler* 1878: 709. *K&B* III: 277.

CUSACK, THOMAS GEORGE, Orange NJ (d/IX–20–1899 @ 44) MD UCNY 1880. *JAMA* 33:994, 1899.

CUSHING, BENJAMIN, Boston (d/X–16–1895 @ 72) MD Harvard 1846; AB 1842. *JAMA* 25:1010, 1895. *Bost m & s jour* 133:454, 1893. *Polk* 1890: 536.

CUSHING, CLINTON, San Francisco (b/XII–13–1840 Aurora, Ill; d/V–11–1904 Washington, DC) MD Rush 1865. *Cal st jour med* 2:197, 1904. *Atkinson* I:446. *Polk* 1886: 171.

CUSHING, GEORGE WILLIAM, Brooklyn (b/1849 Montreal; d/III–21–1902) MD LICH 1874. *Bost m & s jour* 146: 350, 1902. *Polk* 1886: 644.

CUSHING, HENRY JOSEPH, Merrimac, Mass (d/XI–18 1902 @ 65) MD Harvard 1868. *Bost m & s jour* 147: 658, 1902. *Polk* 1896: 718.

CUSHING, JOHN SAMUEL, Sidney, Me 1860–71; CW USA; Skowhegan 1871– (b/VII–26–1830; d/II–4–1889) MD Harvard 1858; ng Bowdoin 1851–54. *Tr Me Med Assoc* 1889: 166–67. *Atkinson* I:433. *Butler* 1878: 305.

CUSHING, JOSEPH WHITNEY, Boston; Brookline; CW–USA (b/I–26–1837 Ashford, Conn; d/V–9–1897) MD Harvard 1861; AB Wesleyan. *Bost m & s jour* 136:475–76. 1897; 137:263, 1897. *Harvard in CW*: 263. *JAMA* 28:1045, 1897.

CUSHING, RUFUS KING, Brewer, Me 1824–34, 1836–70; Bangor 1834–36, 1870–89 (b/VII–23–1802 Brunswick, Me; d/III–28–1889) MD Bowdoin 1834; AB 1821. *Tr Me Med Assoc* 1889: 168–69. *Butler* 1878: 305.

CUSHING, STEPHEN, Boston (b/V–20–1841 Princeton, Mass; d/II–1–1892) MD Harvard 1866; ng Amherst 1863. *Bost m & s jour* 126:252, 1892. *Polk* 1890:536.

CUSHMAN, BARTHOLOMEW, Sandwich, Mass (b/ VIII 14–1782; d/I–11–1837) MD unknown; AB Brown 1805. *Brown hist cat*: 1805.

CUSHMAN, EARL, Orwell, Vt 1821– (b/V–10–1897 Middleboro, Mass; d/XI–2–1874) Hon MD Castleton 1854; <ng Harvard Med 1821> *Tr AMA* 29:634–35, 1878. *Med surg rep Phila* 31:460, 1874.

CUSHMAN, ISAAC SOMES, Topsham, Me; Biddeford, Me; Conway, NH; Winchendon, Mass; CW–USA (b/II–12–1823 New Gloucester, Me; d/IX–6–1870) MD Bowdoin 1847; AB 1844; AM 1847. *Bowdoin cat*: 1844.

CUSHMAN, JOSEPH, NYC (d/II–16–1887) MD Bellevue 1867. *Med reg NY NJ Conn* 1887: 257.

CUSHMAN, NATHAN SIDNEY SMITH BEMAN, Wiscasso Me (b/VII–26–1810; d/I–24–1890) MD Bowdoin 1836. *Tr Me Med Assoc* 1890:334. *K&B* II:272.

CUSHMAN, THADDEUS THOMPSON, Randolph, Mass (b/VI–20–1821 Sumner, Me; d/II–6–1896) MD Bowdoin 1844. *Bost m & s jour* 134:180, 1896. *Butler* 1878: 348.

CUSHMAN, WILLIAM BAXTER, Oxford, Mass (b/ 1856 Roxbury; d/II–25–1897) MD Bowdoin 1881. *Bost m & s jour* 136:476,503,1897. *Polk* 1886:471.

CUSHMAN, WILLIAM FLOYD, Ridgefield, Conn (d/ XII–2–1904 @ 65) MD CPSNY 1862; AB Columbia 1859. *Bost m & s jour* 151:640, 1904. *Polk* 1896:1048.

CUSTER, EMIL, Manchester, NH (d/V–18–1896 @ 76) <MD Würzburg 1845> *JAMA* 26:1092, 1896. *Polk* 1886: 592.

CUTBUSH, EDWARD, Geneva, NY (b/I–5–1772 Phila; d/VI–23–1843) MD UPa 1794. *Hist Med Soc DC:* 221–22. *K&B* III: 81–82.

CUTLER, GEORGE, Charlestown, Mass (b/III–31–1814 Holliston; d/I–17/18–1863) MD Harvard 1845; AB Brown 1839. *Bost m & s jour* 67:510, 1862.

CUTLER, GEORGE A , San Francisco (b/1832 Nashville, Tenn; d/III–22–1903) MD UCNY 1854; postgr Bellevue. *Cal st jour med* 1:173, 1903. *Polk* 1896: 217.

CUTLER, JOSEPH LEONARD, CW–USA; Bolivar NY (b/1829 Moravia; d/X–14–1900) MD UCNY 1881. *Bost m & s jour* 143:438, 1900. *Polk* 1896: 990.

CUTLER, KING R , Corpus Christi & Houston, Tex (b/ New Orleans; d/V–31–1906) MD Ecl Med Inst Ohio 1892. *Texas st jour med* 2:100, 1906.

CUTLER, WILLIAM CLARK, Chelsea, Mass 1866– (b/V–17–1837 Holliston; d/V–1–1899) <MD Hygeio-Therap Coll NY 1859> *Tr Am Inst Homeop* 1899: 75. *New Engl med gaz* 34: 1899 (June) *Polk* 1886: 464. Homeopath.

CUTTER, BENJAMIN, Woburn, Mass (b/1803 W Cambridge; d/III–9–1864) MD Harvard 1827; MD UPa 1857; AB Harv 1824. *Bost m & s jour* 70:148, 207–08, 1864.

CUTTER, CHARLES BENJAMIN, Brooklyn (d/VIII–29–1876) MD CPSNY 1873. *Med reg NY NJ Conn* 1877: 200.

CUTTER, DANIEL BATEMAN, Peterboro NH (b/V–10 1808 Jaffrey; d/XII–7–1889) MD Yale 1835; AB Dtmth 1833. *Bost m & s j* 121:620, 1889. *Polk* 1886: 594.

CUTTER, EDWARD JONES, Waverly, Mass (b/VII–5–1855 Peterboro NH; d/X–22–1900) MD Harvard 1881; AB 1877. *Bost m & s j* 143:489, 1900. *Polk* 1886: 468.

CUTTER, GEORGE ROGERS, NYC; CW–USA (b/III–21–1840; d/II–12–1891 Brooklyn) MD CPSNY 1861. *Med reg NY NJ Conn* 1891: 271. *Bost m & s jour* 124:196, 1891. *Atkinson* I:327. *K&B* III: 285.

CUTTER, NEHEMIAH, Pepperell, Mass (b/1799? d/III–15–1859 @ 60) MD Yale 1817; AB Middlebury 1814. *Bost m & s jour* 60:168, 227–28, 1859.

CUYLER, JOHN M, USA; Morristown NJ (b/III–9–1810 Savannah Ga; d/IV–26–1884) MD Med Coll SC 1833. *Tr Med Soc NJ* 1884: 174–75. *Med reg NY NJ Conn* 1884:228. *Med surg rep Phila* 50:570, 1884. *K&B* II:276.

CYPERT, JOHN REED, NYC (b/1830; d/VI–14–1894) MD U Nashville 1858. *Med reg NY NJ Conn* 1894: 237. *Butler* 1878: 510.

DABNEY, WILLIAM CECIL, Charlottesville, Va (b/ VII–4–1849 Albemarle Co; d/VIII–20–1894) MD UVa 1868. *Tr Med Soc Va* 1894:195–97. *JAMA* 23: 362, 1894. *K&B* III: 285.

DA COSTA, JACOB MENDEZ, Philadelphia (b/II–7–1833 St Thomas, W Indies; d/IX–11–1900 Villanova, Pa) MD Jefferson 1852; LLD. *Tr CPP* s3, v24:lxxxi–xcii, 1902. *Am jour med sci* ns125: 318–29, 1903. *Jeffersonian* 8:33–40, 1906/07/ *K&B* III: 286–87.

DADE, FRANCIS TOWNSHEND, CW–USA (b/Orange CH, Va; d/VI–2–1864 St Paul, Minn) MD U Pa 1864 *U Pa med alum CW*: 1864. *Nat med jour* 1:293, 1870/71.

DAGENAIS, ALPHONSE, Buffalo, NY (d/III–4–1897 @ 50) MD École de méd Montreal 1869. *Buff m & s jour* 36:708, 1897. *Polk* 1896: 1007.

DAGGETT, DAVID LEWIS, New Haven, Conn (b/VI–24–1820; MD Yale 1843; AB 1839. *JAMA* 26: 542, 1896. *Bost m & s jour* 134:252,1896. *Med bull med & surg* 18:191,1896. *Atkinson* I: 533. *Butler* 1878: 75.

DAGGETT, GREENLEAF DEARBORN, Boonton, NJ (b/Me; d/VII–23–1854) MD CPSNY 1848. *Tr Med Soc NJ* 1872: 167.

DAGGY, SAMUEL, Philadelphia (d/XII–15–1902 @ 79) <MD Starling 1853> *Pa med jour* 6:259, 1902/03.

DAHLSTRÖM, MAX, Philadelphia (b/Gny; d/I–4–1892 @ 38) MD Jefferson 1885. *Med bull med & surg* 14:73, 1892. *Polk* 1886: 814.

DAILEY, EDWARD D, Smyrna Del (d/X–6–1865 @ 41) MD Phila Coll M & S 1848. *Tr AMA* 31:1037, 1880. *Med surg rep Phila* 13:294, 1865. *Med annals Md:* 369.

DAILEY, JAMES J , Milton, Ind (b/1833 Raysville;

d/XII-17-1879) MD Med Coll Ohio 1872. *Tr Ind St Med Soc* 1880:230-31.

DAILEY, ROBERT WOOD, Romney Va; CW-CSA; (b/ 11-1802; d/IV-12-1902) MD UPa 1842. *U Pa med alum CW*: 1842. Blanton's *Va surg CW*. *Polk* 1886:994.

DAILEY, OLIVER A , Kansas City, Mo (b/DC; d/I-5-1896) MD Georgetown 1855. *Hist Med Soc DC:* 279.

DAILY, JOHN CALHOUN, Ft Smith, Ark (b/VIII-26-1860 Charleston, Ind; d/VII-31-1898 Stamford, Conn) MD Pulte 1883. *Tr Am Inst Homeop* 1889: 75. *No Amer jour homeop* 46: 720, 1898. *Polk* 1886: 151. Homeopath.

DAKE, CHARLES ROMEYN, Belleville, Ill (d/IV-22-1899 @ 50) MD CPSNY 1873. *JAMA* 32:956, 1899. *Polk* 1896:363.

DAKE, CHAUNCEY M , Genesee, Nunda, Rushville, NY; Genesee & Pittsburgh 1863-67; St Albans & Rochester, NY (b/XII-1-1816 Saratoga Co, NY; d/VII-15-1872 Springwater, NY) MD Hahnemann Phila 1856; lic 1836, ng Geneva. *Hahn mo* 8:119, 1872. *New Engl med gaz* 8:48, 1873. *Cleave*. Homeopath.

DAKE, DAVID MERRITT, Nunda, NY to 1846; Pittsburgh 1846-63; Reading (b/IV-14-1814 Greenfield NY; d/III-28-1891 De Funiak Spr, Fla) MD Castleton 1837; ng Geneva. *Hahn mo* 26:325, 1891. *Med vis* 7:192, 1891. *Cleave*. Homeopath.

DAKE, JABEZ PERCY [Jr] Nashville (b/IX-15-1857 Pittsburgh; d/XI-14-1886) MD U Mich 1879; ng U Tenn Med Dept. *Tr Am Inst Homeop* 1887: 212. *Hahn mo* 21: 832, 1886. *Amer homeop* 20:362, 379. *Polk* 1886: 870. Homeopath.

DAKE, JABEZ PHILANDER, Pittsburgh 1851-63; Nashville 1869- (b/IV-22-1827 Johnstown NY; d/X-28 1894) MD Hahnemann Phila 1851; AB Union 1849. *Tr Am Inst Homeop* 1895:218. *No Amer jour homeop* 42:759,788,1894. *US med inv* 1:159,1875. *Hahn mo* 29:801, 1894. *Polk* 1886: 870. *Cleave*. Homeopath.

DAKE, JABEZ W , Rochester, NY (d/II- -1886) MD Homeop Hosp Cleveland 1860. *Med adv* 17:384, 1886. *Polk* 1886: 704. Homeopath.

DALBY-NORRED, ELIZABETH, Minneapolis, Minn (b/X-14-1843 Wells Co, Ind; d/III-21-1898) MD Woman's Med Coll Chic 1881. *JAMA* 30:807, 1898. *Polk* 1886: 515.

DALE, EDWARD T , Texarkana, Ark (d/IX-19-1881 @ 40) MD LICH 1873. *Med rec* 20:503, 1881. *Tr AMA* 33:544-45, 1882. *Tr St Med Soc Ark* 1882: "In Mem."

DALE, GEORGE, Chicago (d/IV-24-1901) MD Bennett 1873. *Ill med jour* ns3:47, 1901. *Polk* 1886: 954 (Iola, Wis) Eclectic.

DALE, JOHN, Princ Anne, Md (d/XI-6-1899 @ 48) MD Bellevue 1874. *JAMA* 33:1441, 1899. *Polk* 1896: 723.

DALE, WILLIAM JOHNSON, Andover Mass; CW-USA (b/IX-5-1815 Gloucester;d/X-7-1903) MD Harvard 1840; AB 1837. *Bost m & s jour* 149:441-42, 444 1903. *Atkinson* I: 36. *Harv in CW*: 9-10. *Polk* 1896: 720.

DALLAM, JOHN MORTIMER, Philadelphia (b/c1826 Balto; d/V-2-1887 @ 61 or 62) MD UPa 1853. *Med surg rep Phila* 56:608, 1887. *Polk* 1886: 814.

DALLAM, WILLIAM H , Crewell, Md (d/VIII-31-1899 @ 77) MD UMd 1845. *JAMA* 33: 683, 1899. *Polk* 1886:441.

DALRYMPLE, AARON PITNEY, USA; NYC (b/XI-21 1824; d/II-26-1894) MD CPSNY 1851; AB Princeton 1847; AM 1850. *Med reg NY NJ Conn* 1894: 237.

DALRYMPLE, AUGUSTIN J , Baltimore (b/1830; d/VII-24-1895) MD UMd 1854. *Med annals Md:* 369. *JAMA* 25:209, 1895. *Butler* 1878: 318.

DALTON, EDWARD BARRY, NYC; CW-USA (b/IX-21-1834; d/V-13-1872 Santa Barbara, Cal) MD CPS NY 1858; AB Harvard 1855. *Med rec* 7:285, 1872. *Harvard in CW*: 80. *Med reg NY NJ Conn* 1872: 344.

DALTON, GEORGE OSGOOD, Woburn, Mass (d/II 12-1870) MD Jefferson 1855; AB Harvard 1853. *Bost m & s jour* 5:132, 1870.

DALTON, JOHN CALL, Lowell Mass (b/V-31-1795 Boston; d/1864) MD Harvard 1818; AB 1814. *Med reg NY NJ Conn* 1889: 270. *Tr AMA* 16:610-11, 1865. *Bost m & s jour*70:24-27, 1864; 71:487, 504, 517, 1864.

DALTON, JOHN CALL, CW-USA; NYC (b/II-2-1825 Chelmsford, Mass; d/II-12-1889) MD Harvard 1847; AB 1844; LLD Princeton 1886; LLD Columbia 1887. *Harvard in CW*: 23. *Bost m & s jour* 120: 228, 1889. *Med reg NY NJ Conn* 1889: 270. *So pract* 11:135, 1889. *K&B* III: 287.

DALY, JAMES PATRICK JOSEPH, NYC (d/X-15 1897) MD Bellevue 1886. *Bost m & s jour* 137:430, 1897. *JAMA* 29:925, 1897. *Polk* 1896: 1048.

DALY, JOHN JOSEPH, Rahway, NJ (b/1852; d/IV-14-1896) MD UCNY 1874. *JAMA* 26:934, 1896. *Bost m & s jour* 134:435, 1896. *Tr Med Soc NJ* 1896:374-75, 934. *Polk* 1890: 729.

DALY, WILLIAM HUDSON, USA; Pittsburgh, Pa (b/ VII or IX-11-1842 Indiana Co, Pa; d/VI-9-1901) MD U Mich 1866. *Pa med jour* 4:705-06, 1900/01; 5: 296, 1901/02. *Atkinson* I: 217. *K&B* III: 288.

DAMAINVILLE, LUCIEN, Kingsbridge, NY; CW-USA (d/XII-15-1891 @ 52) MD LICH 1860. *Med reg NY NJ Conn* 1892: 276. *Buff m & s jour* 31:366, 1892. *Bost m & s jour* 125:692, 1891. *Butler* 1878: 510.

DAMERAN, P , ? (d/1878 Thibodeaux, La) MD unknown. *Tr AMA* 30:859, 1879.

DAMON, EDWARD THOMAS, Wayland, Mass (b/IV-19-1834; d/XI-30-1859 as student) ng Harvard Med; AM 1857. Palmer's *Necrol alum Harvard*: 335-36.

DAMON, HOWARD FRANKLIN, Boston (b/V-6-1833; d/IX-17-1884) MD Harvard 1861; AB 1858. *Bost m&s jour* 111:312, 1884. *Atkinson* I: 615. *K&B* III: 289.

DAMON, ORISON BENJAMIN, Chicago (d/XI-18-1904 @ 67, Normal, Ill) MD Harvard 1866. *Ill med jour* 7:126, 1905. *Polk* 1896: 380.

DANA, ALFRED SANFORD, Yonkers, NY (d/VIII-22 1901 @ 50) MD CPSNY 1874. *JAMA* 37:654, 1901.

DANA, ANDERSON GREEN, Brandon, Vt (b/IX-17-1791 Mass; d/VIII-20-1861) Hon MD Castleton 1830; LLD Middlebury 1860. *JAMA* 1:604, 1883. *Bost m & s jour* 65:88, 1861. *Tr Vt Med Soc* 1883: 105.

DANA, CHARLES H , Tunkhannock, Pa (d/IV-17-1901 @ 45) MD unknown. *Pa med jour* 5:296, 1901/02.

DANA, DAVID, CW-USA; Lawrence, Mass (d/XII-10-1887 @ 64) MD Harvard 1847. *Bost m & s jour* 117: 292, 1887. *Harvard in CW*: 233-34.

DANA, EDWARD BARZILLAI, Metuchen, NJ (b/1863 Brooklyn; d/I-23-1904) MD CPSNY 1889. *Bost m & s jour* 151?:108, 1904. *Polk* 1896: 941.

DANA, FRANCIS, Cambridge, Mass (d/VII-8-1872 @ 65) MD Harvard 1831; AB 1827. *Bost m & s jour* ns10:40, 1872.

DANA, ISRAEL THORNDYKE, CW-USA; Portland, Me (b/VI-6-1827 Marblehead, Mass; d/IV-13-1904) MD Harvard 1850. *Bost m & s jour* 151:83, 1904. *Atkinson* I:260. *K&B* III: 289.

DANA, JAMES FREEMAN, NYC (b/IX-23-1793 Amherst, NH; d/IV-15-1827) MD Harvard 1817; MD Dartmouth 1821; AB Harvard 1813. *NY med & phys jour* 6:314-18. 1827.

DANA, JOHN ALLD, New Hampton, NH (b/V-3-1813; d/II-14-1882 Ashland) MD Dartmouth 1835; <ng Jefferson> *Tr NH Med Soc* 1882:177-78. *Butler* 1878: 454.

DANA, SIMEON SESSIONS, NJ (d/1861) MD Jefferson 1844. *Tr Med Soc NJ* 1872: 142.

DANA, WILLIAM LAWRENCE, Portland, Me (b/VI-30-1862; d/V-27-1897) MD Bowdoin 1886; AB Harvard 1883. *Bost m & s jour* 137:297, 1897. *Tr Maine Med Assoc* 12:630-31, 1897. *Med bull med & surg* 19:282, 1897. *Polk* 1896: 638.

DANCER, JOHN, So Milford, Ind (b/X-6-1830 Ashland Co, O; d/X-20-1896) MD Rush 1860. *Tr Ind St Med Soc* 1897: 362. *Atkinson* I: 78. *Polk* 1896: 492.

DANFORTH, GALEN BANCROFT, foreign missionary (b/XII-3-1846 E Boston; d/VII-9-1873 Tripoli) MD UCNY 1872; AB Amherst 1867. *Amherst, Men of*: 1867.

DANFORTH, GRACE, Granger, Tex (d/II-21-1895) <MD Woman's Med Coll Pa 1886> *JAMA* 24:370, 1895. *Tex cour-rec med* 12:164, 1895. *Tex med jour* 10:489, 1894-95. *Polk* 1890: 1080.

DANFORTH, SAMUEL, Newport, RI; Boston (b/1740 Cambridge, Mass; d/XI-16-1827 @ 87) Hon MD Harvard 1790; AB 1758. *Tr RI Med Soc* 1:9, 1859-77. *K&B* III: 291. Royalist.

DANFORTH, SAMUEL PARKMAN, Claremont, NH; Ludlow & Royalton, Vt (b/XII-12-1809? Barnard, Vt; d/X-19-1865) MD Dartmouth 1832. *Tr Vt Med Soc* 1883: 105.

DANFORTH, WILLIS W , Oswego, Ill 1850-54; Joliet 1854-70; Milwaukee (b/IX-26-1826 Lake Village, NH; d/VI-3-1891) <MD Rock Island Med Coll 1849> *Tr Am Inst Homeop* 1893:156. *Med era* 9:223, 1891. *Med vis* 7:230, 1891. *Polk* 1886:956. *Cleave*. Homeopath.

DANIEL, GUS, Waco & Robinson, Tex (d/XII- -1905 @ 65 San Bernardino, Cal) MD unknown. *Texas st jour med* 1:256, 1905/06.

DANIEL, JOHN MONCURE, Stafford Co, Va (b/IX-14 1769; d/X-7-1813) MD Glasgow 1791. *Med annals Md:* 369-70.

DANIEL, JOHN MONCURE, Stafford Co, Va (b/c1800; d/c1845) MD UMd 1822. *Med annals Md:* 370.

DANIELS, JOHN S , Rochester, NH (b/Barrington; d/III-6-1896) MD LICH 1875. *JAMA* 26:642, 1896. *Polk* 1896: 711.

DANKER, HENRY A , CW-USN (d/VIII-5-1864 on US Tecumseh before Mobile Forts, Ala) MD CPSNY 1864. *Nat med jour* 1:293, 1870/71.

DARBY, JOHN THOMSON, NYC; CW-CSA (b/XII-16 1836 Orangeburg Co, SC; d/VI-9-1879) MD UPa 1858. *Med reg NY NJ Conn* 1880: 234. *SHSP* 22: 192, 1893. *K&B* III: 292.

DARCY, JOHN S , Hanover Twp, NJ (b/1788; d/X-22 1863) MD unknown. *Tr AMA* 16:631-32, 1865. *Med surg rep Phila* 10: 356, 1863.

DARDEN, PETER EDWARD, Newsoms, Va (b/X-7-1871; d/VII-11-1894) MD Med Coll Va 1892. *Tr Med Soc Va* 1895: 212-13.

DARE, CHARLES HERBERT, Bridgeton, NJ (b/XI-22 1847; d/VIII-25-1894) MD UPa 1870. *JAMA* 23:479, 1894. *Tr Med Soc NJ* 1895: 203-04. *Atkinson* I:395. *Butler* 1878: 468.

DARKEN, EDWARD J , Jr, NYC; CW-USA (b/I-29-1836; d/1887?) MD NY Med Coll 1858. *Med reg NY NJ Conn* 1887: 257.

DARLING, ABEL L , Kilbourne, Ill (d/II-23-1906 @ 55) MD Cincinnati Ecl Med Inst 1881. *Ill med jour* 9:332, 464, 1906. *Polk* 1896: 434.

DARLING, CHARLES B , Lyndon, Vt (b/Burke; d/VI-10-1860 @ 41 or 42) MD Woodstock 1844; MD Hahnemann Phila 1852. *Tr Am Inst Homeop* 1867: 137. *US jour homeop* 1:796: 1860. Homeopath.

DARLING, ELIJAH, Dover, NH (b/XI-28-1794 Keene; d/VI-26-1855) MD Dartmouth 1825; AB 1819. *Bost m & s jour* 52:467, 1855.

DARLING, HENRY HUBBARD, Keene, NH (b/III-22-1824 Cambridge, Vt; d/V-10-1896) MD NY Homeop Med Coll 1861. *Tr Am Inst Homeop* 1898: 49. *No Amer jour homeop* 44:528, 1896. *New Engl med gaz* 31:259, 1896. *Med vis* 12:312, 1896. *Polk* 1886: 592.

DARLING, IRA A, Bangor NY (d/X-4-1891) MD Berkshire 1849. *Tr Med Soc St NY* 1892:471. *Polk* 1886: 715.

DARLING, JOSHUA B ,Chicago (d/I-19-1901) MD Miami 1872. *Ill med jour* ns2:533, 1901. *Polk* 1886: 361 (Laporte City, Ia).

DARLING, WILLIAM, NYC (b/1815 Berwickshire,

 Spec. educ'l status abbrev. as: ***ng*** = college verified attendance without degree;

Engl; d/XII-24-1884) MD UCNY 1842. *Med reg NY NJ Conn* 1885: 232. *Bost m & s jour* 112:21, 1885. *Med bull m & s* 7:25, 1884. *Atkinson* I:702. *K&B* III: 293.

DARLINGTON, WILLIAM, Chester Co, Pa (b/1782; d/IV-23-1863 @ 81) MD UPa 1804. *Tr AMA* 14:210-11, 1864. *Tr Med Soc Pa* 1864: 212. *K&B* III:294-95. *Med surg rep Phila* 10:64, 1863.

DARNALL, MILTON D, CW-USA(d/IX-2-1862 Bainbridge Ind) MD Rush 1848. *Nat med jour* 1:293 1870/71.

DARR, HIRAM HENRY, Caldwell, Tex (d/XI-23-1890) MD Ky Sch Med 1875; MD Louisville Med Coll 1875. *Tex med news* 6:41, 1896-97. *Polk* 1886: 882.

DARRACH, BARTOW [BARTON], CW-USA (d/VII-18-1863 @33 Vicksburg) MD Pa Med Coll 1852. *Med s rep Phila*10:228, 1863. *Nat med jour* 1:293, 1870/71.

DARRACH, WILLIAM Sr, Philadelphia (b/VI-16-1796; d/V-6-1865) MD UPa 1819; AB Princeton 1815; AM 1818. *Bost m & s jour* 72:416, 1865. *Tr CPP* ns4: 163-68, 1865. *Tr Pa St Med Soc* 1867: 266-68. *K&B* III:295-96.

DARRAH, ALEXANDER TAYLOR, Bloomington, Ill (b/1837 Delaware, O; d/IX-4-1889) MD Rush 1865. *JAMA* 13:431, 1889. *Tr Ill St Med Soc* 1890:28. *Butler* 1878: 149.

DARST, HENRY H , Toledo, O (d/VIII-25-1893 @ 72) MD ?Starling 1863? *JAMA* 21:390 1893. *Polk* 1886: 770.

DART, ALBERT, Goshen, O (d/I-15-1896 @ 94) MD unknown. *JAMA* 26:243, 1896.

DASH, THOMAS BUTLER, ?Washington, DC (d/V-13 1887 @ 55) MD CPSNY 1854. *Med reg NY NJ Conn* 1887: 257.

DASHIELL, NICHOLAS LEEKE, Baltimore (b/VII-1-1814; d/II-28-1895) MD UMd 1837. *Med annals Md:* 370. *Polk* 1893: 560.

DASHIELL, RUFUS V, Pr Anne, Md (b/V-10-1850; d/III-28-1900) <MD Washington U, Balto 1872> *JAMA* 34:957, 1900. *Med annals Md:* 370-71. *Polk* 1896: 674.

DASTLER, FRANCIS, NYC (d/1883 @ 45) MD CPSNY 1876. *Med reg NY NJ Conn* 1883: 223.

DAUGHERTY, JAMES D , Dayton, O (b/IV-22-1847; d/VII-12-1888) MD Med Coll Ohio 1872. *Tr Ohio St Med Soc* 1889:7, 266. *Polk* 1886: 752.

DAUGHERTY, PHILANDER, Vigo Co, Ind to 1870; Junction City Kans (b/III-10-1835 Greencastle, Ind; d/V-23-1904 @ 70) <MD Rush 1857> *Jour Kans Med Soc* 4:459-60, 1904. *Polk* 1886:379. *K&B* III:266.

DAUGHERTY, THOMAS, Baltimore (b/1830; d/IX-15-1885) MD UMd 1848. *Med annals Md:* 371.

DAUGHTREY, WILLIAM HENRY, Sunbeam, Va; CW-CSA (b/I-27-1835 Gates Co, NC; d/XII-14-1900) MD UPa 1855; att UVa 1853. *Tr Med Soc Va* 1901: 274-75. *Polk* 1886: 922.

DAVEIS, JOHN TAYLOR GILMAN, Portland Me (b/III 21-1816; d/V-9-1873) MD 1830 Bowd;MD 1837 UPa. *Tr Me Med Assn* 1871-73: 488-90. *K&B* III: 296-97.

DAVENPORT, JAMES, CW-USA (d/III-29-1863) MD unknown. *Nat med jour* 1:293, 1870/71.

DAVENPORT, JAMES HENRY, Roxbury, Mass (d/XII 26-1878 @32) MD Harvard 1871. MD CPSNY 1871; AB Harvard 1868. *Bost m & s jour* 100:38, 1879.

DAVENPORT, LOUIS, Wayne Co, Mich (d/X-22-1879) ng U Mich Med Sch 1850-51. *Mich med news* 2:247-48, 1879.

DAVENPORT, MARY RACHEL MYERS, med missionary (d/VII-18-1887 @ 28 Bengola, Afr) MD Boston Sch Med 1884. *New Engl med gaz* 22: 1887 (Dec). *Med couns* 12:576, 1888. Homeopath.

DAVENPORT, THEODORE, Warsaw, Ind (b/X-4-1828 Sullivan Co, NY; d/VII-4-1884) MD Albany 1851. *Tr Ind St Med Soc* 1885: 221.

DAVIDGE, JAMES BEALE, Birmingham, Engl; Baltimore (b/1768 Annapolis; d/VIII-23-1829) MD U Glasg 1793 [?as John?] *Transylvania jour med & assoc sci* 2:594, 1829. *Med annals Md:* 371. *K&B* III:298.

DAVIDSON, A S , New Orleans (d/V-11-1904 @ 66 Alexandria) Certif by Exam Bd. *New Orl m & s jour* 56:950, 1904.

DAVIDSON, AUGUSTUS REGINALD, Buffalo (d/V-25-1888 @ 43) MD U Buffalo 1878. *Med reg NY NJ Conn* 1889: 272. *Buff m & s jour* 27:516-20, 1888.

DAVIDSON, GARLAND HAMNER, Baltimore (b/1841; d/III-16-1900) MD UMd 1864. *Med annals Md:* 374.

DAVIDSON, HERMAN ELVERS, Boston (b/VIII-10-1815 Pelham, NH; d/VIII-10-1890) MD Harvard 1840; AB 1836. *Bost m&s jour* 123:629, 1890. *Polk* 1886: 456.

DAVIDSON, JAMES, Queen Anne's Co, Md (b/1743 Aberdeen, Scotl; d/1811) <MD Univ Aberdeen 1769> *Med annals Md:* 372.

DAVIDSON, JAMES, Queenstown, Md (b/III-3-1805 Rockland; d/II-24-1888) MD UMd 1827. *Med annals Md:* 372. *Butler* 1874: 318.

DAVIDSON, JAMES KING, Greencastle, Pa (b/II-10-1810 Franklin Co; d/VII-27-1892) MD Jefferson 1833; AB Dickinson 1829. *D'cksn cat*:1829. *Polk* 1886:800.

DAVIDSON, JOHN, Hempstead, NY (b/XI-28-1793; d/XII-26-1884) Lic NY St Med Soc 1829. *Med reg NY NJ Conn* 1885: 233. *Tr NY St Med Soc* 11:741 ff, 1894. *Butler* 1878: 550.

DAVIDSON, JOHN PINTARD, CW-CSA; New Orleans (b/XII-8-1812 Pinckneyville, Miss; d/III-30-1890) MD UPa 1832. *Bost m & s jour* 123:629, 1896. *K&B* III: 298-99. *New Orl m & s jour* ns19:41-44, 1891.

DAVIDSON, WILLIAM M W , Chicago (b/VIII-23-1849 Kenosha, Wis; d/III-2-1901) MD Hahnemann Chic 1878. *Tr Am Inst Homeop* 1901:914. Homeopath.

DAVIES, GEORGE WASHINGTON, Waterloo, Wis (d/IX-22-1906) MD CPS Chicago 1895; att U Wis 1893. *U Ill Coll Med alum*: 1895. *JAMA* 57: 1124, 1906.

DAVIES, JOHN, Oshkosh, Wis; Chicago 1858- (b/VI-18-1829 Oswestry, Engl; d/III-28-1873) MD Homeop

Med Coll Cleveland 1859. *US med & surg jour* 8:369, 1873. *Med invest* ns10:359, 1873. *Cleave*. Homeopath.

DAVIES, JOHN M, Warren, Pa (d/IX-4-1905) <MD Wooster 1874> *Med century* 1905 (Oct). *Polk* 1886:838. Homeopath.

DAVIES, WILLIAM B, CW-CSA (d/II-27-1863 Drainesville, Va) MD Jefferson 1855; AB Washington & Lee 1852. *Wash'n & Lee cat*: 1852. Blanton *Va surg CW*.

DAVIGNON, F F, Leadville, Col (b/1846? d/XI-6-1895 @ 49) MD McGill 1871. *Tr Colo St Med Soc* 1898-99: 509. *Polk* 1893: 241.

DAVIS, ALEXANDER McDONALD, Washington, DC (b/1807; d/V-29-1872) MD Columbian DC 1828. *Hist Med Soc DC:* 227.

DAVIS, ANDREW J, Pittsburgh, Pa (b/1826? d/VII-19 1899 @ 73) MD Jefferson 1850. *JAMA* 33:302, 1899. *Polk* 1896: 1324.

DAVIS, ARTHUR HARRISON, Philadelphia (b/1843? d/III-21-1906 @ 63) MD UPa 1865; BS Union. *Pa med jour* 9:524, 1905/06. *Polk* 1896: 1302.

DAVIS, BATEMAN WILLARD, Montgomery, Vt (b/VII 26-1844; d/VIII-21-1897) MD UVt 1875; att UCNY. *Tr Vt St Med Soc* 1897:194-95. *Polk* 1886: 905.

DAVIS, BUSHROD W, Marion, O (b/II-6-1813 Loudoun Co, Va; d/IV-16-1891) Hon MD Wooster 1872. *Tr Ohio St Med Soc* 1891: 6, 334-35. *Butler* 1878: 626.

DAVIS, CHARLES AUGUSTINE, Derry NH; CW-USA (b/1823? d/IV-9-1863) MD Harvard 1848; AB Dartmouth 1845. *Bost m & s jour* 68:230, 1863. *Nat med jour* 1:293, 1870/71.

DAVIS, CHARLES GILMAN, NYC (b/VIII-6-1857; d/IX-18-1887) MD NY Homeop 1882; Chirurgus Oculi et Auri, NY Ophth Hosp 1883; ng UCNY. *Med vis* 4:15, 1888. *No Amer jour homeop* 36: 1888 (Mar). *Polk* 1886: 674. Homeopath.

DAVIS, CHARLES HENRY, Worcester, Mass (b/1846? d/IX-16-1897 @ 51) MD Harvard 1867. *Bost m & s jour* 137:328, 1897. *Polk* 1896: 727.

DAVIS, CHARLES W, Chautauqua, NY (d/IV-9-1894) MD Buffalo 1887. *JAMA* 22: 601, 1894.

DAVIS, CHARLES WESLEY, Indianola, Ia; CW-USA (b/I-4-1828 Troy, O; d/VII-20-1881) MD Rush 1854; AB Wabash 1848. *Tr AMA* 33:545, 1882. *Tr Ia St Med Soc* 1881-82: 159-60. Fairchild's *Iowa* 229. *Butler* 1878: 234.

DAVIS, EDWARD EVERETT, Philadelphia (b/II-7-1833 Westport, Mass; d/IV-11-1892) MD Hahnemann Phila 1881. *Tr Am Inst Homeop* 1896: 1186-87. *Cleave*. *Polk* 1886: 814.

DAVIS, EDWARD [?EDWIN?] HAMILTON, Harlem, NY (b/I-22-1811 Ross Co, Ohio; d/V-15-1888) MD Cincinnati Med Coll 1838; AB Kenyon 1833. *Med reg NY NJ Conn* 1888: 250.*Bost m & s jour* 118:534, 1888. *K&B* III:300.

DAVIS, ELIJAH, Bellevue, Md (b/VII-22-1760 Chester Co, Md; d/VI-29-1829 Harford Co, Md) <MD Paris> ng UPa 1784-85. *Med annals Md:* 372.

DAVIS, EMORY HAWKINS, Plainfield, Conn (b/II-11-1845 Winfield, NY; d/III-15-1901) MD UVt 1872. *Proc Conn Med Soc* 1901: 307-10. *Polk* 1896: 284.

DAVIS, FRANCIS FLANEGIN, CW-USA; Oil City, Pa (b/VI-2-1838; d/X-31-1902) MD U Mich 1867. *Pa med jour* 6:153, 164, 250, 1902/03. *Flint* 1897: 812.

DAVIS, FRANK HOWARD, Chicago (b/VI-5-1848 NYC; d/VIII-17-1880) MD Chic Med Coll 1871. *Chicago med rev* 2:362, 540, 1880. *Chicago med jour* 41:333-35, 1880. *Bost m & s jour* 103:260, 1880. *Tr Ill St Med Soc* 1881:345-47. *K&B* III:303-04.

DAVIS, FREDERICK AUGUSTUS WILLIAM, Natchez, Miss (b/VI-28-1801 Washington, Ky; d/I-12-1885) MD Transylvania 1824. *Hahn mo* 20:169, 1885. *Cleave*. Homeopath.

DAVIS, GEORGE WASHINGTON, Holyoke, Mass (b/1847? d/IX-18-1894 @ 47) MD UVt 1868. *Bost m & s jour* 131:356, 1894. *Polk* 1886: 467.

DAVIS, H C, ? (d/XI-1878 St Louis Quarantine Hosp) MD unknown. *Tr AMA* 30:859, 1879.

DAVIS, HENRY GASSETT, Everett, Mass; Worcester & Milbury to 1855 (b/XI-4-1807 Trenton, NJ; d/XI-18-1896) MD Yale 1839. *Bost m & s jour* 135: 581, 1896. *JAMA* 27:1313, 1896. *K&B* III: 301.

DAVIS, HUGH HAMILL, Sonoma, Cal (b/1842? Pa; d/V-8-1904 @ 62) MD UPa 1868. *Calif st jour med* 2:197, 1904. *Polk* 1896: 243.

DAVIS, HUGH JOHNSTON, Scotland Neck, NC; CW-CSA (b/1822 Warrenton, Va; d/1864 Alexandria, Va) MD UPa 1845. *U Pa med alum CW*: 1845.

DAVIS, IRA SAMUEL, CW-CSA; Seven Springs, NC (b/VII-24-1825 Albertson, NC; d/VI-30-1899 Strabane, NC) MD UPa 1847. *U Pa med alum CW*: 1847. *Polk* 1886: 726.

DAVIS, ISAAC, USA (b/VII-27-1787 Chester Co, Pa; d/VII-21-1814 Ft Jackson, Miss) MD UPa 1810. *Med surg rep Phila* 1:126-27, 1854. *Heitman*.

DAVIS, JAMES AUBREY, Philadelphia (b/1865; d/VII-30-1902 @ 37) MD UPa 1887. *Polk* 1896: 1302. *Pa med jour* 6:259, 1902/03.

DAVIS, JAMES CADELL, Fort Atkinson, Wis (b/XI-12 1821 Rich Hill, O; d/IV-30-1879) MD Rush 1866. *Tr Wis St Med Soc* 1879: 296. *Butler* 1878: 860.

DAVIS, JAMES SHELTON, Iuka, Miss; CW-CSA (b/III 24-1819 Madison Co Ala; d/XI-29-1879) MD Jefferson 1854; MD *ad eund* U Louisv'le 1872. *Tr Miss St Med Assoc* 1881:166-68. *Atkinson* I:426. *Butler* 1874: 390.

DAVIS, JAMES W, Smyrna, Tenn (b/1821? d/X-31-1898 @ 77) MD U Tenn 1888. *JAMA* 31: 1190, 1898. *Polk* 1896: 1389.

DAVIS, JOHN, NYC (b/XI-4-1801 Bound Brook NJ; d/IV-1883) MD unknown *Med reg NY NJ Conn* 1883:223.

DAVIS, JOHN, Dayton, O (b/VIII-30-1818 Leesburg, Va; d/VI-10-1883) ng Starling 1844-46. *Tr O St Med Soc* 1884: 227.

DAVIS, JOHN, Cincinnati (d/XII-25-1890 @ 66) MD Med Coll Ohio 1843. *JAMA* 16:178, 1891. *Bost m & s jour* 124:52, 1891. *Butler* 1878: 610.

DAVIS, JOHN GAYLE, USA (b/Mo? or Lexington, Ky? d/XI-1-1900 Philippines) MD Georgetown 1868; MD Bellevue 1870. *Chic med rec* 19:357, 1900. *Ill med jour* ns2: 533, 1901. *Heitman*.

DAVIS [DAVIES], JOHN H, Waterloo, Wis (d/X-28-1894) MD CPS Chicago 1888. *JAMA* 23:768, 1894. *Polk* 1890: 1173.

DAVIS, JOHN IGNATIUS, CW-CSA (b/X-3-1839 Frederick Co, Md; d/XI-9-1863 Marietta, Ga) MD UPa 1861. *U Pa med alum CW*: 1861.

DAVIS, JOHN STAIGE, Charlottesville, Va 1845- (b/X-1-1824 Albemarle Co; d/VII-18-1885) MD UVa 1841; AM 1840. *JAMA* 5:138-39, 1885. *New Orl m & s jour* ns13:169-70, 1885. *Med bull med & surg* 7:257, 1884. *Atkinson* I:57.

DAVIS, JOHN WINDAL, Goldsboro, NC (b/VIII-8-1825 Lenoir Co; d/I-23-1869) MD UPa 1847. *U Pa med alum CW*: 264.

DAVIS, JOSEPH AUSTIN, Bloomfield, NJ (d/VIII-4-1886 @ 73) MD UPa 1836; MD Jefferson 1838; AB Princeton 1834. *Med reg NY NJ Conn* 1887: 258.

DAVIS, JOSHUA CULVER, Denver, Colo (d/X-8-1892 @ 66 Zurich, Sw) MD Castleton 1847. *Tr Colo St Med Soc* 1898-99: 509. *Polk* 1886: 183.

DAVIS, MEREDITH, ? Md (d/VII-18-1867 Frederick Co, Md) MD UPa 1825. *Med annals Md:* 373.

DAVIS, NATHAN SMITH, Chicago (b/I-9-1817; d/VI-16-1904) MD Fairfield 1837; AM NWU 1871; LLD Ill Wesleyan 1878. *So pract* 26:436, 1904. *Chic med rec* 26:461-62, 1904. *Nashville jour m & s* 96:518-22, 1904. *Tr Ill St Med Soc* 1895: 70. *K&B* III: 303-305.

DAVIS, NATHANIEL REYNOLDS, USN (b/XI-12-1825; d/VIII-23-1878 NYC) MD CPSNY 1848. *Med reg NY NJ Conn* 1879: 189.

DAVIS, PASCHAL, Keokuk, Ia (d/VII-16-1897) MD CPS Keokuk 1863. *JAMA* 29:252, 1897. *Polk* 1886:361.

DAVIS, PHILIP CHAPMAN, USA (b/Va; d/X-2-1871 Ft Benton, Mont) MD Columbian DC 1856. *Hist Med Soc DC:* 264. *Army List* 1815-1900: 275.

DAVIS, R FRANK, Tolersville, Va; Hermitage (b/XII-3 1854; d/III-15-1899) MD UVa 1876. *Tr Med Soc Va* 1900: 321. *Polk* 1886: 919.

DAVIS, REESE, Wilkes Barre, Pa (b/VII-5-1837 Warren; d/VIII-10-1895) MD Bellevue 1867; ng U Mich M Sch; AB Hamilton 1863. *Tr Luzerne Co (Pa) Med Soc* 1895:148-161. *JAMA* 25:342 1895. *K&B* III:305-06.

DAVIS, REZIN POLLARD, Parkersburgh, WVa (b/I-4-1840; d/VII-20-1876) MD CPSNY 1863. *Tr Med Soc W Va* 1875-82: 315-16.

DAVIS, ROBERT CHALMERS, NYC (d/IV-13-1906 @ 47) MD UCNY 1880; AB ? *Bost m & s jour* 154:452, 1906. *Polk* 1896: 1048.

DAVIS, ROBERT P, Portland Ind (b/XI-12-1836 Lawrence Co, O; d/III-28-1902) MD Cincinnati Coll Med & Surg 1873; postgrad 1883; postgrad NY 1884. *Tr Ind St Med Soc* 1902: 412. *Polk* 1886: 333.

DAVIS, ROBERT THOMPSON, Fall River, Mass (b/Irel; d/X-29-1906 @83) MD Harvard 1847. *Bost m & s jour* 155:525,530, 1906. *Butler* 1878:349.

DAVIS, ROGER, Chester Co, Pa (b/X-2-1762; d/XI-20 1815) <ng U Pa Med Sch> *Med rep [W Chester, Pa]* 1:96, 1854.

DAVIS, SAMUEL, Indianapolis, Ind (b/II-15-1814 Phelps, NY; d/IV-15-1886) MD Med Coll Ohio 1847. *Tr Ind St Med Soc* 1886: 216. *Butler* 1878: 199.

DAVIS, SEPTIMUS, Harford Co, Md (b/X-12-1801; d/I 7-1857) MD U Md 1824. *Med annals Md:* 373.

DAVIS, THOMAS JOHN, Brookville, Md (b/VII-25-1805;d/VII-11-1828) MD UMd 1828 *Med ann Md:* 373.

DAVIS, URIAH Q, CW-USA; Northumberland Co, Pa (b/VIII-16-1821 Limestone Valley; d/X-5-1887 Milton) MD UPa 1848. *U Pa med alum CW*: 1848. *Polk* 1886: 808.

DAVIS, WALTER S, Minneapolis (b/X-27-1870; d/IX 27-1898) MD Johns Hopkins 1897; AB Amherst 1892. *Amherst, Men of*: 1892.

DAVIS, WESLEY, Worcester, Mass (d/II-16-1906 @ 65) MD Berkshire 1866. *Bost m & s jour* 154:230, 1906. *Polk* 1896: 727.

DAVIS, WILLIAM BEESLEY, Camden, NJ to 1864; Philadelphia (b/XII-2-1820 Salem; d/III-7-1886 @ 66) MD Pa Med Univ 1860. *Tr Am Inst Homeop* 1886: 141. *Polk* 1886: 814. Homeopath.

DAVIS, WILLIAM BRAMWELL, CW-USA; Cincinnati (b/VII-22-1832; d/II-16-1893) MD Miami 1855; AB Ohio Wesleyan 1852. *JAMA* 20:224, 1893. *Atkinson* I:627. *K&B* III: 306.

DAVIS, WILLIAM ELIAS BROWNLEE, Birmingham, Ala (b/XI-25-1863 Trussville; d/II-24-1903) MD Bellevue 1884; AB Ohio Wesleyan. *Bost m & s jour* 148: 272, 1903. *New Orl m & s jour* 55:592, 1903. *Tr Med Soc St NY* 1904:[420]. *K&B* III: 306. *Polk* 1896: 135.

DAVIS, WILLIAM EPHRAIM, Boonsboro, Md (b/XII-28-1828 Funkstown; d/XII-17-1857) MD UPa 1853; AB Franklin & Marshall 1849. *F & M obit rec* I:114.

DAVIS, WILLIAM H, Baltimore (b/IX-22-1810; d/I-21-1881) MD UMd 1833. *Med annals Md:* 374. *Butler* 1874: 311.

DAVIS, WILLIAM W, Wilmington, NC (d/X-22-1879 @ 65) MD UPa 1842; ng UNC 1834-35. *Tr NC Med Soc* 1880: 15. *NC med jour* 4: 365, 1879. *Butler* 1878: 592.

DAVISON, JOHN B, Moline, Ill (b/VI-11-1826 Westmoreland Co, Pa; d/II-5-1897) MD Jefferson 1868. *JAMA* 28: 665, 1897. *Polk* 1896: 430.

DAVISON, REXFORD, Lockport, NY (b/1829; d/I-15-1888) MD Castleton 1851. *Med reg NY NJ Conn* 1888: 250.

DAVISON, SOLOMON W , Rochester, NY (d/X-21-1894 @ 72) Lic Med Bd Upper Canada 1852. *JAMA* 23: 697, 1894.

DAVIZAC, AUGUSTUS, New Orleans (d/1858 or 1859) Hon MD UCNY 1844. *Tr AMA* 13:820, 1860.

DAVOL, WILLIAM HALE, Fall River, Mass; St Paul, Minn; Brooklyn (b/VII-3-1823 Warren, RI; d/VI-12-1863 Warren) MD Harvard 1850; AB Brown 1844. *Med surg rep Phila* 10:144, 1863.

DAWBER, THOMAS B , Paterson, NJ (b/Engl; d/VII-9 1867 @ 29) MD UCNY 1867. *Tr Med Soc NJ* 1868:117.

DAWES, EBENEZER, Taunton, Mass (b/1791? Scituate, Mass; d/IV-20-1861 @ 70) Lic Mass Med Soc 1811. *Bost m & s jour* 64:295-96, 1861.

DAWES, EDMUND, CW-USA (d/XII-7-1862 Prairie Grove, Mo) ng U Mich Med 1861-62. *U Mich cat*: 675.

DAWES, FREDERICK, Washington, DC (b/I-26-1778 Huntingdon, Engl; d/II-10-1852) <MD England> *Hist Med Soc DC:* 229.

DAWES, THOMAS SPENCER, Saugerties, NY (b/ Cummington, Mass; d/IV-11-1897 @ 76) MD Albany 1848. *JAMA* 28:810, 1897. *Polk* 1886: 707.

DAWSON, BENJAMIN FREDERICK, NYC (b/VI-28-1847; d/IV-3-1888) MD CPSNY 1866. *Med reg NY NJ Conn* 1888: 251. *Bost m & s jour* 118: 384, 1888. *Atkinson* I:174. *K&B* III: 308 (as Benj. Franklin).

DAWSON, G R , Memphis, Tenn (d/X-24-1878) MD unknown. *Tr AMA* 30:859, 1879.

DAWSON, HARRY EMIL, Scranton, Pa (d/V-13-1901 @ 36) MD CPS Balto 1892. *Pa med jour* 5:296, 1901/02. *Flint* 1897:

DAWSON, JAMES, St Michaels, Md (b/XI-8-1805 Talbot Co, Md; d/c1882) MD UMd 1828. *Med annals Md:* 374. *Butler* 1874: 318.

DAWSON, JAMES H , Milton, Ill (b/I-29-1903) MD CPS Keokuk 1878. *Ill med jour* ns4: 665, 1903. *Polk* 1886: 288.

DAWSON, JESSE W , Canon City, Colo (d/I-8-1899 @ 65) MD Rush 1871. *Tr Colo St Med Soc* 1898-99: 38, 509. *JAMA* 32: 145, 1899. *Polk* 1896: 254.

DAWSON, JOHN, Columbus, O (b/V-11 or 20-1810 Va; d/IX-1-1866) MD Starling 1854. *Tr AMA* 18: 348, 1867. *Tr Ohio St Med Soc* 1867: 78-80. *K&B* III: 308-09.

DAWSON, JOHN LAWRENCE, Charleston, SC (b/III 1815 Moncks Cor; d/IX-17-1896) MD Med Coll SC 1836. *NC med jour* 38:219, 1896. *JAMA* 27: 776, 1896. *K&B* III: 309. *Waring* II: 218.

DAWSON, WILLIAM WIRT, Cincinnati (b/XII-19-1828 Berkeley Co, Va; d/II-16-1893) MD Med Coll Ohio 1850. *JAMA* 20:223, 1893. *Atkinson* I: 705. *K&B* III: 309-10.

DAY, ALBERT, Melrose Highlands, Mass (d/IV-26-1894 @ 72 or 74) MD Harvard 1866. *Bost m & s jour* 130:456, 1894. *Polk* 1886: 456.

DAY, ALEXANDER R A , St Paul, Minn (d/IX-24 1897 @ 29) MD McGill 1892. *JAMA* 29: 761, 1897.

DAY, ASBURY M, Farmington, Del (d/IX-4 1896 @ 60) MD Albany 1860. *JAMA* 27:661, 1896. *Polk* 1886: 205.

DAY, CHARLES BUTLER, Glencoe, Minn (d/I-13-1898) MD CPSNY 1889. *JAMA* 30: 279, 1898.

DAY, DAVID, St Paul, Minn (d/III-8-1896) MD UPa 1854. *Tr Minn St Med Soc* 1896:149. *Polk* 1890:618.

DAY, DWIGHT WASHINGTON, Eau Claire, Wis (b/V-15-1841 NY; d/XI-19-1901) MD Buffalo 1861. *Tr Wis St Med Soc* 36:410-13, 1902. *Tr Minn St Med Soc* 1902:306. *Polk* 1896: 1548.

DAY, FANNY M , Newark, NJ (d/X-21-1891) MD NY Hosp & Med Coll for Women 1880. *Med vis* 8:14, 1892. *Polk* 1886: 607. Homeopath.

DAY, IRA, Mechanicsburg, Pa (b/1799, Royalton, Vt; d/XI-27-1868) MD UVt 1828. *Med surg rep Phila* 20: 59-60, 1869. *Phila med reg & dir* 1871: 299. *Tr Med Soc Pa* 1869: 424-26.

DAY, LOREN TRUE, Westport, Conn (b/VIII-11-1860 Bridgeport, Conn; d/IV-1-1905) MD Yale 1880. *Proc Conn Med Soc* 1905: 510-11. *Polk* 1896: 286.

DAY, RICHARD HANCE, Baton Rouge, La (b/VI-9-1813 Bladensburg Md; d/XII-4-1892) MD Washington Med Coll Balto 1832. *New Orl m & s jour* 20:482-92, 1893. *Daniels Tex m j* 8:290, 1892-93. *Polk* 1886: 412.

DAY, SETH RICHARDSON, St Albans, Vt (b/V-31-1823 Essex; d/IV-5-1869) MD Woodstock 1848; ng Castleton. *Phila med reg & dir* 1871:300. *Med surg rep Phila* 20:327, 1869. *Tr Vt Med Soc* 1884: 105.

DAY, WALTER DeFOREST, NYC (b/1835; d/XI-27-1889) MD CPSNY 1863; AB Williams 1859. *Med reg NY NJ Conn* 1890:265. *Bost m & s jour* 121:568, 1889. *Polk* 1886: 676.

DAY, WILLIAM H , Kewanee, Ill (d/V-4-1901) Cert Chenango Co, NY 1849. *Ill med jour* ns3:47, 1901. *Polk* 1893: 367.

DAY, WILLIAM WALKER, Dayton, Wash (d/III-31-1893 @ 76) MD Cleveland Med Coll 1847. *Med vis* 9:174, 1893. *Amer homeop* 19:168, 1893? *Polk* 1886: 932. Homeopath.

DAYFOOT, HERBERT M , Mt Vernon & Rochester, NY (b/II-21-1846 Georgetown, Canada; d/IV-22-1894) MD Homeop Hosp Coll Cleveland 1867. *Tr Am Inst Homeop* 1894: 299. *Amer homeop* 20:175, 1894. *No Amer jour hom* 42:324, 405. *Hahn mo* 29:298 (news & advt) 1894. *Polk* 1886: 704. Homeopath.

DAYHUFF, A F , Kokomo Ind (b/1827 Orange Co, Ind; d/VII- -1884) <ng Rush> *Tr Ind St Med Soc* 1886: 195. *Med surg rep Phila* 51:280, 1884. *Butler* 1878: 199.

DAYTON, ABNER GILSON, Colosse, NY 1842-50; Mexico, NY 1850- ; Oswego (d/VIII-5-1889 Brooklyn) MD Geneva 1841. *Tr Med Soc St NY* 1891: 465-66.

 Spec. educ'l status abbrev. as: ***ng*** = college verified attendance without degree;

Med reg NY NJ Conn 1890: 265. *Med surg rep Phila* 61:223, 1889.

DAYTON, ALFRED BAILEY, Mattawan, NJ (b/XII-25 1812; d/VII-19-1870) MD CPSNY 1835; Hon AM Princeton 1862. *Tr AMA* 23:594, 1872. *Tr Med Soc NJ* 1871:240.

DAYTON, CHARLES BOLIVAR, E Hampton, NY (d/ VIII-17-1886) MD CPSNY 1848. *Med reg NY NJ Conn* 1887: 258.

DAYTON, CHARLES LEMON, Buffalo (b/Eden, NY; d/ IX-7-1893) MD Buffalo 1853. *Buff m & s jour* 33:172, 1893. *JAMA* 21: 464, 1893.

DAYTON, FERDINAND VANDERVEER, CW-USA; Natchez, Miss (b/VII-29-1834 Freehold, NJ; d/XI-8-1866) MD UPa 1857; AB Princeton 1854. *Med surg rep Phila* 15:445, 1866. *Nashville jour m & s* ns1:488, 1866. *U Pa med alum CW*: 1857.

DAYTON, LEWIS P , Buffalo (b/1819; d/V-14-1900) MD Geneva 1845. *Buff m & s jour* 39: 859, 1900. *Polk* 1886: 651.

DAYTON, SAMUEL W , Great Bend, Pa (d/I-1-1883) MD Jefferson 1863. *Med bull med & surg* 5:89, 1883.

DEAKYNE, A CLARK, Philadelphia (b/1838 Newcastle, Del; d/1899) MD Dept Pa Coll 1859. *Tr CPP* cent vol: 220. *Polk* 1886: 815.

DEAN, BENJAMIN DOUGLAS, Norwich, Conn; San Francisco (b/IV-5-1820 Freetown, Mass; d/X-6-1883) MD Berkshire 1843. *Tr Calif St Med Soc* 1884: 242-45. *Atkinson* I: 39. *Butler* 1878: 54.

DEAN, EDGAR EVERETT, Brockton, Mass (b/XII-17-1837; d/XII-31-1893) MD Harvard 1861. *New Engl med gaz* 29: 1894 (July) *Polk* 1886:463. Homeopath.

DEAN, GEORGE A , McComb, Ohio (b/IV-16-1822 Württemberg, Gny; d/II-28-1875) MD Western Reserve 1857. *Tr Ohio St Med Soc* 1876: 95.

DEAN, HENRY CLAUDIUS, Algonquin, Ill; CW-USA (d/XII-26-1867) MD Harvard 1861. *Bost m & s jour* 1:96, 1868. *Harvard in CW*: 263.

DEAN, HENRY SPALDING, So Coventry, Conn (b/VII-20-1823 Holland, Mass; d/I-15-1898) MD Jefferson 1852. *Proc Conn Med Soc* 1898: 361-62. *JAMA* 30:278-79, 1898. *Polk* 1896: 285.

DEAN, HENRY WALTER, Rochester, NY (b/VIII-22-1818; d/I-13-1878) MD Geneva 1841. *Buff m & s jour* 17:275, 1878. *Mich med news* 1:16, 1878. *Tr Med Soc St NY* 1880: 452=53. *Med rec* 13:75, 1878. *Atkinson* I: 542. *Butler* 1878: 550.

DEAN, JOHN, Florence, Italy (b/XII-21-1831 Salem, Mass; d/I-13-1888) MD Harvard 1860. *Bost m & s jour* 118:134, 1888.

DEAN, S EUGENE, Watertown & Buffalo, NY to 1887; Minneapolis (b/XII- -1858 Bloomington Twp, Minn; d/II-8-1894) MD Hahnemann Med Coll 1880; att Carleton Coll. *Hahn mo* 29:82 (news & advt) 1894. *Med vis* 10:363, 1894. *Minn hom mag* 1894 (Mar). Homeopath.

DEAN, WILLIAM F [?FRANKLIN] CW-USA (d/IX-17-1862 Georgetown, DC) MD ?Castleton 1843. *Nat med jour* 1:293, 1870/71.

DEANE, ADAM CALHOUN, Greenfield, Mass (d/XI-7-1899 @ 78) MD UCNY 1849. *Bost m & s jour* 141:484, 1899. *Atkinson* I:653. *Polk* 1896:713.

DEANE, FRANCIS H , Richmond, Va (d/I-24-1870 @59) MD UPa 1832. *Phila med reg & dir* 1871:303. *Tr AMA* 21:478-80, 1870.

DEANE, HORACE C , NYC (d/II-28-1899 @ 35) MD UCNY 1886. *JAMA* 32:563, 1899. *Polk* 1886: 1026.

DEANE, JAMES, Greenfield, Mass (b/II-24-1801 Coleraine; d/VI-8-1858) MD CPSNY 1831; Hon AM Amherst 1838. *Bost m & s jour* 58:406-07, 1858; 59:74-78, 1858. *Tr AMA* 13:790-94, 1860. *K&B* III: 311-12.

DEANE, JAMES ROBINSON, Newton Highlands, Mass (b/X-1-1833 Palermo, Me; d/XII-6-1901) MD Bowdoin 1860. *Bost m & s j* 145:664, 1901. *Polk* 1896: 719.

DEARBORN, ABRAHAM DRAKE, Malden, Mass (b/II-15-1802 Hampton, NH; d/XII-2-1871) MD Harvard 1825; ng Bowdoin Med Sch 1823; att Bowdoin 1820-21. *Bost m & s jour* 8:376, 1871.

DEARBORN, ALFRED RANDALL, Concord, NH (b/X 10-1843 Epsom; d/XII-18-1879) MD Bowdoin 1866. *Tr NH Med Soc* 1880: 123-24.

DEARBORN, ALVAH BURTON, E Salisbury, Mass 1870-74; Newburyport 1874-84; Somerville 1884- (b/VIII-3-1842 Topsham, Me; d/VIII-19-1906) MD Bowdoin 1870; AB 1863; AM 1866. *Bost m & s jour* 155: 270, 1906. *Butler* 1878: 349.

DEARBORN, FREDERIC MERRIWEATHER, USN (d/IV-24-1887) MD Harvard 1865. *Harvard in CW*: 292. *Callahan*.

DEARBORN, GEORGE S , Rockaway, NYC (d/III-26 1906 @ 71) MD Albany 1857. *Bost m & s jour* 154:390, 1906. *Polk* 1886:609 (Oxford, NJ)

DEARBORN, HENRY MARTIN, NH 3 yrs; Boston 7 yrs; NYC (b/XI-19-1846 Epsom, NH; d/II-16-1904) MD Bowdoin 1869. *No Amer jour homeop* 52:180-81, 1904. *Tr Am Inst Homeop* 1904: 954-55. Homeopath.

DEARBORN, SAMUEL GERRISH, Nashua, Mt Vernon, Milford, NH (b/VIII-10-1827 Northfield; d/V-8-1903) MD Dartmouth 1850. *Tr NH Med Soc* 1903:237-38. *Polk* 1896: 921.

DEARBORN, THOMAS BENTON, CW-USA; Milford, NH (b/IX- 1838 Northfield; d/VI-10-1879) MD Dartmouth 1865. *Tr NH Med Soc* 1879: 175-77.

DEAVER, JOHN T , Zanesville, O (d/VIII-7-1810 @ 22) MD unknown. *Med annals Md:* 374.

DEBOW, WILLIAM L, Englishtown, NJ (d/X-31-1858 @ 43) MD Berkshire 1836. *Tr Med Soc NJ* 1871: 88-89.

DEBOWES, THOMAS N , Brooklyn (b/Ireland; d/II-7-1903 @ 71) MD UCNY 1858; att Trinity Coll Dublin. *Bost m & s jour* 148:222, 1903. *Polk* 1896:994.

DE BRULER, JAMES P , Rockport & Evansville, Ind

(b/IX-21-1817 Orange Co, NC; d/VIII-12-1874. MD U Louisville 1847. *Med surg rep Phila* 31:360, 1874. *Tr AMA* 26:465, 1875.

DE BRULER, OLIVER E , Ireland, Ind (b/1857 Ind; d/IV-20-1892) MD Cincinnati Coll Med & Surg 1879. *Tr Ind St Med Soc* 1893:248.

DE BUTTS, ELISHA, Baltimore (b/1773 near Dublin, Irel; d/IV-3-1831) MD U Pa 1805. *Med annals Md:* 374-75. *Amer jour med sci* 8:270, 1831. *K&B* 312-13.

DE CAMP, WILLIAM HENRY, Grand Rapids, Mich (b/XI-6-1825 Auburn NY; d/VII-4-1898) MD Geneva 1847. *JAMA* 31:142,1898. *Polk* 1896:757. *K&B* III:313.

DeCAUSSEY, MARIAN, Sealy, Tex (d/X-21-1898 @ 56) MD Galveston Med Coll 1870. *JAMA* 31: 1128, 1898. *Polk* 1886: 881.

DECKER, DAYTON E , Woodbridge, NJ (b/VIII-1-1856 Metuchen; d/VII-20-1896 Princeton) MD LICH 1874. *Tr Med Soc NJ* 1897: 303.

DECKER, ELBRIDGE GERRY, Ft Fairfield, Me (b/IX-13-1827 Jefferson; d/I-29-1900) MD Bowdoin 1851. *JAMA* 34:381, 1900. *Polk* 1886: 425.

DECKER, SAMUEL, Griffin Corners, NY (d/XII-6-1898 @ 59) MD CPSNY 1867. *JAMA* 31: 1542, 1898. *Polk* 1896: 1024.

DECLARY, JOHN P , Louisville (d/VIII-1834) MD Transylvania 1823. *Transylv j m & assoc sci* 7: 428, 1834.

DE CORTEZ, CYRIO A PALMA, Hartford, Conn; Brooklyn (b/Spain; d/V-15-1873 @ 34) <MD U Bahia, Brazil> *Med reg NY NJ Conn* 1873: 339.

DEDOLPH, FRED, St Paul, Minn (b/1844 Gny; d/X-1890) MD Marburg Gny 1869. *Tr Minn St Med Soc* 1891: 198; 1893: 121-22. *Polk* 1890: 618.

DEDRICK, ALBERT CLINTON, Centreville, RI (b/VIII 27-1831 Warwick; d/IV-16-1889) MD Albany 1856. *Tr RI Med Soc* 4:103-04, 1889-93. *Med surg rep Phila* 61:28, 1889. *Polk* 1886: 844.

DE ECKE, THEODORE, Utica, NY (b/Gny; d/XII-16 1905) MD U Berlin 1857. *Bost m&s jour* 153:710, 1905.

DEEMER, AMOS, Philadelphia (b/1837? d/I-21-1859 @ 22) No MD: d/as med stud. *Med surg rep Phila* ns1:319, 1858/59.

DEERING [DEARING] HENRY LIVINGSTON, Boston; CW-USN (d/X-1-1864 Pensacola, Fla) MD Harvard 1864 as Dearing. *Bost m & s jour* 71: 248, 1864. *Med surg rep Phila* 12:196, 1864/65. *Harvard in CW*: 286, as Dearing.*Nat med jour* 1:293, 1870/71.

DEERING, ROGER M , Brooklyn; CW-USA (d/VIII 28-1864 Carrollton, La) MD LICH 1861. *Med surg rep Phila* 12:196, 1864/65. *Nat med jour* 1:293, 1870/71.

DEEY, EDWARD MORTIMER, NYC (d/I-13-1889 Engl; MD NY Med Coll 1856. *Med reg NY NJ Conn* 1889: 272.

DE FONTAINE, Z A , CW-USA (d/III-23-1865) MD unknown. *Nat med jour* 1:293, 1870/71.

DE FORD, HARRY S , Ottawa, Kans (d/V-24-1900) MD Jefferson 1864. *JAMA* 34:1574, 1900. *Polk* 1886:383.

DE FOREST, HENRY ALFRED, missionary to Syria; Rochester, NY (d/XI-24-1858 @ 44) MD Yale 1835; AB 1832. *Bost m & s jour* 59:407, 1859. *Med surg rep Phila* ns1:172, 1858/59.

DE FOREST, WILLIAM BRINTNAL, New Haven, Conn (b/X-3-1811; d/IX-21-1887) MD Yale 1840; AB 1831; stud. theol. *Proc Conn Med Soc* ns4:213-14, 1888. *Atkinson* I:492. *Butler* 1878: 75.

DE GERSDORF, ERNST BRUNO, Bethlehem, Pa; Boston; Andover, Salem, Mass 1849- (b/VII-18-1820 Esmarch, Gny; d/VI-28-1883 Pleasantville, NY) <MD Leipsic 1846> *Tr Am Inst Homeop* 1884: 656. *Amer homeop obs* 20: 192, 1884. *New Engl med gaz* 18: 221, 236, 1883. *NY med times* 11:160, 1883. Homeopath.

DE GRAFFENRIED, EDWIN F, CW-USA; ?Wynnton, Ga (b/Columbus; d/X-5-1902 Wynnton @ 79) MD UPa 1846. *U Pa med alum CW*: 1846. *SHSP* 22:190, 1893.

DEINENGER, CHARLES A , Crimean War-Russian Army (b/1834 Reading, Pa; d/X-25-1855 Russia) MD UPa 1855. *Tr Med Soc Pa* 1:54, 1856.

DEISINGER, JONAS, York Co, Pa (b/IV-18-1833; d/VIII-13-1903) MD UPa 1867. *Pa med jour* 7: 279, 1903/04.

DE JARNETTE, JOSEPH SPENCER, Spotsylvania Co, Va; CW-CSA (b/IX-19-1825 Louisa; d/V-21-1905) MD UPa 1848 *U Pa med alum CW*:1848. *Polk* 1886:920.

DE LACEY, JOHN, Philadelphia (b/1823: d/X-7-1868 @ 45) MD Jefferson 1849. *Phila med reg & dir* 1871: 293. *Med surg rep Phila* 19:412, 1868.

DE LA COSSETT, H , Greeneville, Pa (b/V-3-1800 Granby, Conn; d/III-1-1877) <Hon MD Fairfield 1825> *Tr Med Soc Pa* 11:646-48, 1877. *Butler* 1878: 719.

DELAFIELD, EDWARD, NYC (b/V-17-1794; d/II-1875) MD CPSNY 1816; AB Yale 1813. *Med reg NY NJ Conn* 1875: 197. *Med surg rep Phila* 15:509-12, 1866. *K&B* III: 315-16.

DELAMATER, JOHN, Cleveland, O (b/1787 Dutchess Co, NY; d/1867) Hon MD Berkshire 1824; lic Oswego Co Med Soc. *Tr O St Med Soc* 1867:76-77. *Tr AMA* 19: 425-27, 1868. *Med surg rep Phila* 16:412-13, 1867. *K&B* III: 316-17.

DELAMATER, STEPHEN G , Duanesburgh, NY (b/Bethlehem; d/VI-23-1888) MD Albany 1842. *Tr NY St Med Soc* 11:741 ff, 1894. *Polk* 1886: 658.

DELANEY, M G , CW-USN (d/IV-5-1866 Geneva) MD unknown. *Nat med jour* 1:293, 1870/71.

DELANO, JESSE, Milburn, NJ (b/II-12-1812 NY; d/VIII-8-1851) MD CPSNY 1837. *Tr Med Soc NJ* 1865-67: 131.

DELANY, ALFRED, USA (b/1839; d/II-11-1876 McPherson Barracks, Atlanta, Ga) MD Jefferson 1860. *Tr AMA* 28:636-37, 1877. *Med rec m & s* 11:119, 1876.

 Spec. educ'l status abbrev. as: ***ng*** = college verified attendance without degree;

DELANY, JAMES JOSEPH, NYC (d/IV-2-1886) MD CPSNY 1874. *Med reg NY NJ Conn* 1886: 243.

DELAP, GEORGE WASHINGTON, Brooklyn (d/IX-13 1901) MD LICH 1885. *JAMA* 37:847 1901. *Polk* 1886: 644.

DELAVAN, JOHN SAVAGE, CW-USA; Albany, NY; Washington, DC 1870- (b/X-18-1840 Ballston; d/I-8 or VIII-7-1885 Saranac Lake) MD Albany 1861. *Tr Am Inst Homeop* 1893:147. *Am obs* 21:143, 1885. *Hahn mo* 20:575, 1885. *New Engl med gaz* 20:432, 1885. *Cleave*. Homeopath.

DE LA VERGNE, CHARLES E , Brooklyn (b/VII-25 1857; d/VI-4-1892) MD LICH 1878; att Bklyn Polytech Inst. *Med reg NY NJ Conn* 1892:276. *JAMA* 18: 788, 1892. *Bost m & s jour* 126:592, 1892.

DE LEON, ABRAHAM, War 1812-USA; Camden, SC 1813?- ; Charleston 1848?- (d/XI-1867) MD unknown. *Waring* II:219-20.

DE LEON, DAVID CAMDEN, USA; CW-CSA; Mexico (b/V-16-1816 Camden, SC; d/IX-3-1872 Santa Fe, NM) MD UPa 1836; AB USC 1833. *U Pa med alum CW*: 1833. *Waring* II:220-21.

DELERY, CHARLES FRANÇOIS, New Orleans (b/I-28-1815 St Charles Parish, La; d/VI-12-1880) MD Paris 1842. *New orl m & s jour* ns7:583-85, 1880.

DELLENBAUGH, CHRISTIAN W , Cleveland (d/II-3-1898 @ 68) MD Jefferson 1865. *JAMA* 30:448, 1898. *Polk* 1896: 1172.

DELOFFRE, AUGUSTE A , USA (d/IX-4-1899 Ft Sam Houston, Tx) MD Tulane 1869; att U Ala 1862. *U Ala cat*: 196. *Polk* 1886: 68.

DELOUGHERY, EDWARD, Baltimore (b/1806; d/XI-18-1885) MD UMd 1829. *Med annals Md:* 375.

DEMAREST, SAMUEL, Cresskill, NJ (b/IX-8-1838; d/II-10-1867) MD CPSNY 1863. *Med reg NY NJ Conn* 1867: 215-16.

DEMENT, JOHN JEFFERSON, Huntsville, Ala; CW-CSA (b/V-13-1830 Madison Co; d/VIII-10-1891 Lithia Springs, Ga) MD UPa 1853; ng U Louisville. *JAMA* 17: 387-88, 1891. *U Pa med alum CW*: 1853. *Atkinson* I: 123-24. *Butler* 1878: 17.

DE MERRILL, ? , ? (d/X-10-1878 Point-a-la Hache, La) MD unknown. *Tr AMA* 30:859, 1879.

DEMING, EBENEZER SUMNER, Calais, Vt (b/XI-18 1816 Cornish, NH; d/IX-6-1857 Cornish) MD Dartmouth 1842; ng Woodstock. *Tr Vt Med Soc* 1883: 103.

DEMING, ELIZUR H , Lafayette, Ind 1833- (b/III-4-1797 Great Barrington, Mass; d/II-23-1855) MD unknown; AB Albany 1827; AM 1828. *Bost m & s jour* 52:127, 1855. *Tr Ind St Med Soc* 1855:8; 1857:53-56. *St Louis m & s jour* 13: 184, 1855. Kemper's *Indiana*.

DEMING, FENN, Westfield, NY (b/Berlin, Conn; d/X-11 1834 Lewiston, Ill) Lic Conn Med Soc. *Tr Med Soc St NY* 1865: 280.

DEMING, WILLIAM, Litchfield, Conn (b/III-16-1833; d/IX-20-1891) MD Yale 1856. *Proc Conn Med Soc* 1892: 862-63. *Atkinson* I:574.

DEMMING, AUGUSTUS E , CW-USA (d/I-6-1864 Ft Leavenworth, Kans) MD unknown. *Nat med jour* 1:293, 1870/71.

DEMOSS, WILLIAM RAMSEY, CW-USA (d/III-13-1864 Washington, DC) MD Georgetown 1863; ng U Mich med 1853-56. *U Mich cat*: 676. *Nat med jour* 1:293, 1870/71.

DE MUND, FREDERICK CORNELL, Brooklyn (d/XI-20-1900 @70) MD CPSNY 1855; AB Rutgers 1851. *Bost m & s jour* 143:570, 1900. *Polk* 1886: 669.

DE MUTH, CLARK, Denver, Colo (d/II-22-1887 Los Angeles @ 33) MD U Mich Hom Med Coll 1878. *Med vis* 3:138, 1887. *Polk* 1886: 183. Homeopath.

DENBY, EDWIN ROBINSON, USN (b/II-28-1832 Richmond, Va; d/V-3-1875 at sea aboard USS Lancaster) MD UPa 1853. *U Pa med alum CW*: 1853.

DENHAM, SILAS N, Kansas City Mo (d/VI-9-1906 @66) <MD St Louis Med Coll 1860> *JAMA* 43: 61, 1906[?]

DENIG, ROBERT M , Columbus (d/I-17-1897) MD Jefferson 1831. *JAMA* 28:380, 1897. *Polk* 1896: 1179.

DENISE, JACOB CONOVER, Dayton, O; CW-USA; Omaha 1868- (b/XII-3-1828 Montg'y Co; d/I-20 1899) MD Jefferson 1855. *JAMA* 32:263, 1899. *Proc Nebr St Med Soc* 1899: 21-22. *Atkinson* I: 240. *Polk* 1886: 582.

DENISON, EDWARD L, Marion Ill (d/XII-25-1900) Lic by yrs pract. *Ill med jour* ns2:533, 1901. *Polk* 1890: 338.

DENISON, JEREMIAH TOWNSEND, Fairfield, Conn (b/1806 New Haven; d/IV-25-1879) MD Yale 1828; AB 1824. *Tr Am Inst Homeop* 1879: 1235. *Amer homeop obs* 16:294, 1879? *New England med gaz* 14:168, 1879. Homeopath.

DENNIS, STEPHEN P , Salisbury, Md (d/III-15-1900 @ 73) MD Pa Coll 1856. *JAMA* 34:766? 1900. *Polk* 1886: 445.

DENNIS, WELDING FELL, Wilkes Barre, Pa (b/X-1-1818; d/V-1-1876) MD Jefferson 1842. *Tr Med Soc Pa* 11: 227-32, 1876.

DENNISTON, EDWARD EVANS, Northampton, Mass (b/1803 Ireland; d/V-10-1890) <MD Ireland> *Bost m & s jour* 122:486, 514, 1890. *Butler* 1878: 349.

DENNISTON, WILLIAM SCOTT, CW-USA (d/VII-22 1862 @ 30 James River, Va) MD CPSNY 1856; AB Yale 1853. *Med surg rep Phila* ns8:428.

DENNLER, ZACHARIAH P , Long Island City, NY (d/V-27-1890 @ 52) MD Geneva 1861. *Med reg NY NJ Conn* 1890:265.

DENNY, ANDREW, Jackson, Ala (b/IV-30-1812 Leicester, Mass; d/VI-9-1869) MD Harvard 1834; AB Amherst 1831. *Amherst, Men of*: 1831.

DENNY, THEODORE, Easton, Pa (b/VII-30-1788; d/I-20-1856 Eastern Shore, Md) MD U Pa 1810. *Med annals Md:* 375.

DENSMORE, DAVID T , Jamaica, Ia (d/VIII-28-1888 @ 28) MD CPS Chicago 1886. *Tr Ia St Med Soc* 8:285, 1890; 14: 328, 1896. *Polk* 1886: 360.

DENT, ARTHUR M , Coshocton, O (d/IV-5-1900) MD Columbus Med Coll 1882. *JAMA* 34:1146, 1900. *Polk* 1896:1183.

DENT, EMMET COOPER, NYC (b/X-11-1859 Macon, Miss; d/I-12-1906) MD Bellevue 1879. *Bost m & s jour* 154:82, 1906. *Polk* 1896: 1049.

DENTON, ASHLEY NEWTON, Austin, Tex (b/III-12-1836 Ft McIntosh, Choctaw Na, Ind Terr; d/III-4-1901) MD Tex Med Coll Galveston 1866; postgr Edinb 1879-80. *Tr Texas St Med Assn* 1901:47-48. *Polk* 1896: 1415.

DENTON, SAMUEL, Ann Arbor, Mich (d/VIII-17-1860) ng Castleton 1825. *Med surg rep Phila* nsr:510, 1860. *Nashville jour m & s* 19:383, 1860.

DEPPEN, DARIUS C , Bernville, Pa (b/Berks Co, Pa; d/XII-8-1902 @ 60) MD Pa Med Coll 1853. *Pa med jour* 6:260, 1902/03. *Flint* 1897: 796.

DEPREFONTAINE, JOSEPH R , California (b/Phila; d/III-25-1863 @ 54) MD Jefferson 1831. *Med surg rep Phila* 10:64, 1863.

DE PUY, CORNELIUS E , NYC (b/c1791 Ulster Co, NY; d/1822) MD CPSNY 1814. *NY med & phys jour* 4:266-77, 1825.

DERAISMES, EDWARD JOSEPH, Union, NJ (d/VI-18 1898 @ 39) MD UCNY 1838. *JAMA* 31: 39, 1898. *Polk* 1896:951.

DERBY, GEORGE, Boston; CW-USA (b/II-13-1819 Salem, Mass; d/VI-20-1874 @ 55) MD Harvard 1843; AB 1838. *Bost m & s jour* 90:636, 1874. *Harv in CW*:10. *K&B* III: 319.

DERICKSON, WILLARD POTTER, Wilmington, Del (d/VII-13-1904) MD Jefferson 1891. *JAMA* 43:276, 1904.

DERING, NICOLL HAVENS, NYC (b/I-1-1794 Shelter Island, NY; d/XII-19-1867) MD CPSNY 1817; AB Yale 1813; AM 1817. *Tr AMA* 19:417, 1868. *Buff m & s jour* 17:268, 1867. *Tr Med Soc St NY* 1868: 307-10.

DE ROSSET, ARMAND JOHN, Wilmington, NC (b/1767; d/IV-1-1859) MD UPa 1790. *Med surg rep Phila* ns2:51, 1859. *Tr AMA* 13: 814-16,1860. *K&B* III:321.

DE ROSSETT, MOSES JOHN, Wilmington, NC; NYC; CW-CSA (b/VII-4-1838 Pittsboro; d/V-1-1881) MD UCNY 1860. *Med reg NY NJ Conn* 1881: 235. *NC med jour* 7:309-13, 399-400, 1881. *Tr NC Med Soc* 1881: 23-24. *K&B* III: 321.

DERRICK, LAFAYETTE, Woodville, Ala (d/VII-6-1898) Cert 1882. *Tr Med Assoc St Ala* 1899:232. *Polk* 1893: 166.

DERRICKSON, JOHN B , Warren, Conn (b/II-9-1826 Paulsboro, NJ; d/I-12-1892) MD Jefferson 1850. *Proc Conn Med Soc* 1892:855. *Atkinson* I:618. *Butler* 1878:75.

DE SAUSSURE, HENRY W, Charleston (b/1815; d/1887 Thomasville Ga) MD Med Coll St SC 1836. *New Orl m & s jour* ns14:793-94,1887. *Waring* II:221-22.

DE SAUSSURE, HENRY W, Charleston (b/II-27-1843; d/VII-10-1897) MD Med Coll SC 1867. *JAMA* 29:201, 1897. *Polk* 1886: 852. *Waring* II: 222.

DESCHERE, MARTIN, NYC (b/1848 Hamburg, Gny; d/VII-21-1902) MD NY Homeop 1875. *Tr Amer Inst Homeop* 1903: 731-32. Homeopath.

DESHLER, CHARLES FRANKLIN, Hightstown, NJ (b/X-21-1843 Northampton Co, Pa; d/III-24-1879) MD UPa 1865. *Tr AMA* 33:545-46, 1882. *Tr Med Soc NJ* 1878 (!): 208-09. *Med rec NY* 15:565, 1879.

DESTEIGNER, EDWARD, San Marcos, Tex (d/XII-10-1893) MD Starling 1870. *Texas med jour* 9:351, 1893-94. *Polk* 1893: 1226.

DE TARR, DAVID N , Boone, Ia (b/X-9-1852 Boonsboro; d/1900) MD UMich 1880; AB 1878. *Tr Ia St Med Soc* 19:441-42, 1901. *Polk* 1886: 351.

DETMOLD, WILLIAM LUDWIG, NYC (b/XII-27-1808 Hanover Gny; d/XII-26-1894) MD Göttingen 1830. *Bost m & s jour* 132:20, 1895. *JAMA* 24:101, 1895. *Med rec NY* 47:22, 1895. *Atkinson* I: 284. *K&B* III:322.

DETWEILER, MOSES H , Hopewell, Pa (b/1842; d/IV-15-1902 @ 60) MD Jefferson 1870. *Pa med jour* 5:455, 1901/02; 6:260, 1902/03. *Flint* 1897: 805.

DETWILLER, HENRY, Hellertown, Pa; Easton 1852- (b/XII-13-1795 Langenbruck, Switz; d/IV-21-1887) <MD U Freiburg, Baden, 1836> *Tr Am Inst Homeop* 1887: 193. *No Amer jour homeop* 35:383, 1887. *Hahn mo* 20:124, 1885; 22:299, 1887. *Med adv* 18: 596, 1887. *Cleave*. Homeopath.

DETWILLER, JOHN WILLIAM, Bethlehem, Pa (d/IX-27-1898 @ 47 Newport, RI) MD UPa 1873. *JAMA* 31:871, 1898. *Polk* 1896: 1268.

DEVAN, SPENCER COXE, USMHS (d/II-3-1893 Phila) MD UCNY 1880. *Bost m & s jour* 128:152, 1893. *Polk* 1890: 779.

DEVANE, JAMES STUART, Cape Fear River, NC (d/I-1892) MD Med Coll SC 1857. *NC med jour* 29:122, 1892. *Polk* 1886: 727.

DEVENING, DANIEL, Buffalo (d/III-5-1890 @ 79) MD UCNY 1846. *Buff m & s jour* 29: 736-37? 1890. *Polk* 1886: 652.

DEVENS, DAVID STEARNS, Charlestown, Mass; Lake Village, NH (b/II-20-1810; d/VIII-30-1858) ng Dartmouth Med 1844; ng Amherst 1833. *Bost m & s jour* 59:128, 1859.

DEVER, BURNS H , Hume, Ill (d/VIII-14-1901 @ 42) MD Ky Sch Med 1882. *Ill med jour* ns3:237, 1901. *Polk* 1886: 283.

DEVEREUX, JOHN PIERRE, Philadelphia (d/II-9-1906 @ 35) MD UPa 1896. *Pa med jour* 9:430, 1905/06.

DEVINE, GEORGE C , Philadelphia (d/XII-26-1901 @ 43) MD Jefferson 1882. *Pa med jour* 5:296, 1901/02. *Flint* 1897: 816.

DEVLIN, HENRY JOHN, NYC (b/X-4-1838; d/IV-5-1864) MD CPSNY 1864 *Med reg NY NJ Conn* 1865:226.

DEVLIN, JOHN, NYC (d/X-31-1892 @ 44) MD UCNY 1876. *Med reg NY NJ Conn* 1893:299. *Polk* 1886:676.

DE VOE, ISAAC W, Wausau Wis (d/III-24-1888) MD Miami 1871. *Tr Wis St M Soc* 1891:356. *Polk* 1886: 962.

DEVOL, CHARLES, Albany, NY (d/III-5-1894 @ 85) MD Fairfield 1832. *Med reg NY NJ Conn* 1894:238. *JAMA* 22:482, 1894. *Butler* 1878: 550.

DEVOE [DEVOE], HENRY V , Indianapolis, Ind (b/IV-23-1854 Owen Co; d/IV-1-1892) MD Jefferson 1880. *Tr Ind St Med Soc* 1892: 293. *Polk* 1886: 320.

DEVRON, ALEXANDER JOHN GUSTAVUS, New Orleans (d/III-24-1900 @ 64) MD New Orl Sch Med 1860; PhG unknown. *New Orl m & s jour* 52:611, 1900. *JAMA* 34:957, 1900. *Polk* 1896: 620.

DE WEES, HARDMAN PHILLIPS, NYC (b/1810 Phila; d/X-11-1879) MD unknown; AB UPa 1831. *Med reg NY NJ Conn* 1881: 235.

DEWEES, OSCAR LORRAINE, Livingston, Miss (b/X-8-1816 Phila; d/XII-6-1859) MD UPa 1838; ng UPa Coll 1830-32. *Med surg rep Phila* ns3: 297, 1859/60.

DEWEES, WILLIAM POTTS, Philadelphia (b/V-5-1769; d/V-18-1841) MD UPa 1789. *Am jou med sci* ns2: 256, 1841. *K&B* III:322-23.

DEWEY, CHARLES FRANCIS, Goldsboro, NC (d/X--1866) MD UPa 1847; AB UNC 1844. *Tr NC Med Soc* 1867: 39.

DEWEY, CHESTER, Rochester, NY 1836- (b/X-25-1784 Sheffield, Mass; d/XII-22-1867) Hon MD Yale 1809; AB Williams 1806, &c. *Med surg rep Phila* 18: 22, 1867. *K&B* III:323-24.

DEWEY, DAVID ROBERT, North Adams, Mass; Span-Am War (b/Whitehall, NY; d/XI-5-1898 @ 34) MD CPSNY 1888; att Williams. *Bost m & s jour* 139:479,484,1898. *JAMA* 31:1297, 1898. *Polk* 1896:720.

DEWEY, EDWARD HOOKER, CW-USA; Meadville, Pa (d/XII-21-1904 @ 67) MD U Mich 1863. *Pa med jour* 8:334, 1904/05. *Flint* 1897: 809.

DEWEY, GEORGE CLINTON, NYC (b/XII-6-1840 Northampton, Mass; d/IV-17-1864 Northampton) MD CPSNY 1863; AB Williams 1860. *Med reg NY NJ Conn* 1865: 227.

DEWEY, JULIUS YEOMANS, Montpelier, Vt (b/1801; d/1877) MD U Vt 1824. *Tr AMA* 29:636-37, 1878. *Tr Vt Med Soc* 1883:105.

DE WITT, MANNING FORCE, WhiteHall Ill (b/1835;d/1870) MD Jefferson 1857. *Tr AMA* 23:583-84,1872.

DE WOLF, JAMES HENRY, Baltimore (b/Phila; d/I-17 1906 @ 51) MD Jefferson 1879. *Med annals Md:* 376. *Homeop recorder* 1906 (Mar) *Polk* 1886: 436.

DE WOLF, THADDEUS KINGSLEY, Chester, Mass (d/XI-4-1890 @89) MD Castleton 1845; Hon MD Berkshire 1857. *Bost m & s jour* 123:480, 1890.

DE WOLFE, STEPHEN, NYC (d/X-25-1890) MD UPa 1845. *Med reg NY NJ Conn* 1891: 272. *Polk* 1886: 676.

DEXHEIMER, JOHN, Brooklyn (d/XI-11-1894 @ 36) MD UCNY 1882. *Med reg NY NJ Conn* 1895: 220. *Polk* 1886: 676 (NYC).

DEXTER, JAMES EWINGS, Washington, DC (b/1822 Groton, NY; d/VI-17-1902) MD UCNY 1861. *Hist Med Soc DC:* 267. *Polk* 1886: 212.

DEXTER, RANSOM, Chicago (d/IV-2-1891 @ 60) MD U Mich 1862; AM U Chic 1873; LLD 1881. *Chic med rec* 1:188, 1891. *Bost m & s jour* 124:396, 1891. *Butler* 1878: 131.

DEYO, ABRAHAM, Gardiner, NY (d/V-4-1901 @ 71) MD UCNY 1851. *Bost m & s jour* 144:462, 1901.

DE YOUNG, PHILIP, Philadelphia (b/I-6-1809 Montgomery Co, Pa; d/IX-5-1880) MD UPa 1838. *Tr Med Soc Pa* 1884: 504.

DE ZOUCHE, ISAAC, Gloversville, NY (d/II-22-1895 @ 72) MD Albany 1869; att Queen's Coll, Irel. *JAMA* 24:370, 1895. *Butler* 1878: 550.

DIAL, WILLIAM HARRISON, Marshall, Tex; CW-CSA (b/Laurens Co, SC; d/1881) MD UCNY 1848. *UCNY-Bellevue cat* 1833-1905: 20.

DIBBLE, FREDERICK LEVI, New Haven, Conn (b/1830 Newtown; d/V-12-1898) MD Yale 1859. *Proc Conn Med Soc* 1899:354-56. *JAMA* 30:1366, 1898. *Polk* 1896: 282.

DICE, REUBEN B , Charlottesville, Va (b/1823 Franklin [W] Va; d/II-17-1892) MD Jefferson 1848. *Tr Med Soc Va* 1892: 195-96. *Butler* 1878: 826.

DICK, ELISHA CULLEN [CULLEN DICK, ELISHA] Alexandria, DC (b/1750 or 1752 [1762?] Chester Co, Pa; d/IX-22-1825) MD UPa 1782. *Hist Med Soc DC:* 219-20. *Tr Med Soc Va* 16:267, 1885. *K&B* III: 326-27.

DICK, FREDERICK N , CW-CSA; North Platte, Nebr (b/X-4-1842 Greensboro, NC; d/XII-29-1896) MD UVa 1867; MD Washington U, Balto 1869. *Proc Nebr St Med Soc* 1897: 15.

DICK, GEORGE HANDY, CW-CSA (b/I-29-1838 Phila; d/VI-6-1864 Phila) MD UPa 1862. *U Pa med alum CW:* 1862. *Nat med jour* 1:293, 1870/71.

DICK, JOHN G A , Alfordsville, NC (d/IV-12-1888 @ 60) att med lect in Phila [i.e., Harris' Med Inst?] AB Davidson. *NC med jour* 21:256, 1888. *Polk* 1886: 721.

DICK, LEONARD WHITE, Sumter Dist, SC; CW-CSA (b/XI-16-1834; d/XII-28-1882) MD UPa 1859; AB USC 1855. *U Pa med alum CW:* 1859.

DICK, WILLIAM A , Lumberton, NC (d/III-27-1879) MD UCNY 1852. *NC med jour* 3:282, 1879.

DICKEN, JAMES LINDSEY, CW-USA; Wabash, Ind (b/IV-15-1821 Fayette Co; d/III-26-1900) MD Ohio Med Coll 1851. *JAMA* 34:957, 1900. *Atkinson* I:644. *Butler* 1878: 200.

DICKENSHIED, CHARLES HENRY, Spinnerstown, Pa (b/II-11-1820 Upper Milford Twp; d/XII-5-1850 Trappe) MD UPa 1841; att Lafayette. *Laf'tte, Men of:*147.

DICKENSHIED, JOHN HENRY, Spinnerstown, Pa (d/X 17–1905 @ 80) MD UPa 1847. *Pa med jour* 9:127, 1905/06. *Flint* 1897: 831.

DICKERMAN, EDWARD T , Chicago (b/VIII–1867 Jacksonville, Ill; d/I–23–1903 Springfield) MD Northwestern 1890. *Ill med jour* ns4:558–59, 589, 1903.

DICKERMAN, JOHN LOCKE, Brattleboro, Vt (b/III 12–1790; d/XII–15–1857) Hon MD Castleton 1826; Hon AM Dartmouth 1857. *Bost m & s jour* 57:455, 1857.

DICKERMAN, LEMUEL, Foxboro, Mass (b/I–4–1826 Brattleboro, Vt; d/VIII–14–1895) MD Castleton 1845. *Bost m & s jour* 133: 308, 1895.

DICKERSON, P [or T] M , (d/IX–7 or 14–1878 Memphis) MD unknown. *Med rec* 14:220, 1878. *Tr AMA* 30: 859, 1879.

DICKERSON, THOMAS P , Salem, NJ (b/1812 Woodstown; d/IV–10–1882) MD UPa 1837. *Tr Med Soc NJ* 1882–83: 190–91.

DICKEY, HANOVER Jr, Lowell, Mass (b/IX–14–1809 Epsom, NH; d/V–29–1873) MD Havard 1837. *Tr NH Med Soc* 1873: 110–11.

DICKIE, JAMES W , CW–USA (d/I– –1864 David's Island NY) MD UCNY 1862. *UCNY–Bellevue cat.*

DICKINSON, C M , CW–USA (d/VII–7–1867) MD unknown. *Nat med jour* 1:293, 1870/71.

DICKINSON, FRANCIS LEMUEL, Rockville, Conn (b/ 1817 Chatham or Portland, Conn; d/VI–2–1897) MD Yale 1840. *Proc Conn Med Soc* 1898: 339–42. *JAMA* 28: 1202, 1897. *Polk* 1896: 294.

DICKINSON, J S , Denver, Col (d/1879) <Lic RCS(L)> *Tr Colo St Med Soc* 1898–99:508. *Butler* 1878: 66.

DICKINSON, JAMES PHILIP, Trappe, Md (b/c1801; d/ 1841) MD UPa 1825. *Med annals Md:* 376.

DICKINSON, JOHN, Ohio; CW–USA (d/I–18–1886 Cincinnati) MD Western Reserve 1857. *Nat med jour* 1:293, 1870/71.

DICKINSON, JOSHUA PRENTISS, Bangor, Me (b/VIII 21–1792 Holliston, Mass; d/XI–17–1856) MD Harvard 1816; AB Brown 1811. *Bost m & s jour* 55:355, 1857.

DICKINSON, L L , Colchester, Conn (d/VIII–2–1868) MD unknown. *Phila med reg & dir* 1871: 297. *Med surg rep Phila* 19:140, 1868.

DICKINSON, ROGER QUARLES, Albany, Ga (b/ 1797? Spotsylvania, Va; d/V– –1858) MD UPa 1826. *So m & s jour* 14:434, 1858. *Tr AMA* 13: 818, 1860. *Nashville jour m & s* 15: 91, 1858.

DICKINSON, SAMUEL PHILEMON, Trappe, Md (b/ 1804; d/IV–1862) MD UMd 1826. *Med annals Md:* 376.

DICKSON, GEORGE, Mississippi (d/X–5–1878 Crystal Springs) MD Tulane 1874[?] *Tr AMA* 30:859, 1879.

DICKSON, ISAAC N, Reisterstown Md (b/1817; d/1896) MD UMd 1838. *Med annals Md:*377. *Polk* 1893: 572.

DICKSON, JAMES G , Canonsburg, Pa (d/XI–14–1903 @ 78) MD Jefferson 1851. *Pa med jour* 7:279, 1903/04. *Flint* 1897: 797.

DICKSON, JAMES HENDERSON, Wilmington, NC (b/XII–1807; d/IX–28–1862) MD CPSNY 1827; AB UNC 1823. *NC med jour* 28:138–51, 1891. *Tr NC Med Soc* 1866: 7–8.

DICKSON, JOHN, Allen's Grove, Wis (b/IX–26–1820 near Meadville, Pa; d/XII–15–1875) MD Cleveland Med Coll 1848. *Tr Wis St Med Soc* 1876: 145–46.

DICKSON, LOUIS L , Reisterstown, Md (b/1807; d/1853) MD UMd 1824. *Med annals Md:* 377.

DICKSON, ROBERT D , Laurinburg, NC (b/V–19–1819 Wilmington, NC; d/IV–4–1896) MD UCNY 1845; AB UNC 1841. *NC med jour* 37:245–46, 1896. *Polk* 1886: 724.

DICKSON, SAMUEL HENRY, Charleston, SC; NYC 1847–50; Philadelphia 1858– (b/IX–30–1798; d/III–31–1872) MD UPa 1819; AB Yale 1814. *Med times* 2:278, 292–93, 1871–72. *Nashville jour m & s* ns9:206, 1872. *Phila med reg & dir* 1873:303. *K&B* III:327–28. *Waring* II:222–26.

DIEDERICHS [DIETRICHS], ALBERT, Denver, Colo (d/III–8–1895) <MD U Göttingen 1866 or 1868> *JAMA* 24:422, 1895. *Polk* 1890: 210.

DIEFFENBACHER, PHILIP L , CW–USA; Havana, Ill (b/II–6–1830 Northumberland Co, Pa; d/I–29–1905) MD Jefferson 1855. *Ill med jour* 7:242, 1905.

DIEFFENDERFER, EPHRAIM LUTZ, Ashley, Pa; Milwaukee (b/1839 White Deer; d/X–27–1901) MD UPa 1862. *Tr Wis St Med Soc* 36: 410, 1902. *Polk* 1886: 791.

DIESE, ERNEST, Willow Grove, Pa (d/X–31–1899 @ 78) <MD U Jena 1847> *JAMA* 33:1307, 1899. *Polk* 1896: 1302.

DIETRICH, C McD , Galesburg, Mo (d/XII–8–1898) MD Miami 1880. *JAMA* 31:542, 1898. *Polk* 1886: 547.

DIETRICH, HENRY J , Chicago (b/Switz; d/VII–22–1898 @ 48) MD U Bern 1873. *JAMA* 31?:314, 1898. *Polk* 1896: 381.

DIFFENDERFER, HENRY, Baltimore (b/1804; d/III–22 1832) MD UMd 1827. *Med annals Md:* 377.

DIFFENDERFER, MICHAEL, Baltimore (b/1789 Md? d/IV–17–1870) MD UPa 1814. *Med annals Md:* 377.

DIFFENDERFER, WILLIAM H , Baltimore (b/1822; d/ VII–7–1897) MD UMd 1843. *JAMA* 29:200–01, 1897. *Med annals Md:* 377.

DILDINE, DAVID DEMOTT, Hope, NJ (d/IX–1872 @ c26) MD UCNY 1870. *Tr Med Soc NJ* 1873: 112.

DILL, NATHANIEL C , DeSoto, Ind (b/IX–8–1860 Darke Co, O; d/II–14–1897) MD Med Coll Ohio 1881. *Tr Ind St Med Soc* 1897: 355. *Polk* 1896: 464.

DILLARD, JOHN L , Richmond, Tex (d/II–10–1899) MD Hosp Med Coll Louisville 1887. *JAMA* 32:442, 1899. *Texas med news* 8:252, 1899. *Polk* 1896: 1447.

DILLARD, RICHARD Sr, Edenton, NC; CW–CSA (b/ XII–1–1822? Sussex Co, Va; d/XI–29–1887 Chowan, NC) MD UPa 1844. *U Pa med alum CW*: 1844. *Tr NC Med Soc* 1889: 148–53.

 Spec. educ'l status abbrev. as: ***ng*** = college verified attendance without degree;

DILLARD, THOMAS, USN (b/I-24-1801 Va; d/III-2-1870) MD UPa 1825. *Phila med reg & dir* 1871:294. *Bost m&s jour* ns5:176, 1870. *U Pa med alum CW*: 1825.

DILLER, JOHN, Emmaus Pa (d/IX-29-1902 @ 65) MD Jefferson 1868 *Pa m jour* 6:260 1902/03. *Flint* 1897:801.

DILLON, ALEXANDER W , Bourbon Co, Ky (d/VI-30-1833) stud med Transylvania. *Transylvania jour med & assoc sci* 6:306, 1833.

DILLON, ANNIE BISSELL, Minneapolis, Minn (b/XII 3-1864; d/VI-7-1895 San Diego Cal) MD U Mich Homeop 1892. *Tr Amer Inst Homeop* 1896:1187.

DILLON, JOHN DALE, Philadelphia (b/1856; d/VII-28 1896 @ 40) MD Jefferson 1878. *JAMA* 27:337, 1896.

DILLS, THOMAS JOHNSON, Ft Wayne, Ind (b/VIII-10 1847 Spencerville; d/VI-3-1899 Pomona, Cal) MD U Mich 1871. *Tr Ind St Med Soc* 1899: 410-12. *Butler* 1878: 200.

DILWORTH, JOSEPH BANKSON, Philadelphia? (d/I 5-1871 @ 44) MD UPa 1860. *Med surg rep Phila* 24:46, 1871.

DILWORTH, RICHARD B , Juniata Co, Pa (b/I-24-1810 Philadelphia; d/XI-15-1851) MD Jefferson 1835. *Tr Med Soc Pa* 1858: 72-73. *Med reporter* (West Chester, Pa) 2:16-17, 1854.

DIMOCK, SUSAN J, Boston (b/IV-24-1847 Washington, NC; d/V-27-1875 at sea) MD Zurich 1871. *Bost m & s jour* ns15:695-96, 1875. *Med rec NY* 10:357, 1875. *Tr NC Med Soc* 1875:42; 1876:8. *K&B* III:329.

DIMOCK, THOMAS D B , NYC (b/VII-28-1855; d/V 12-1893) MD CPSNY 1883. *Med reg NY NJ Conn* 1893: 299. *Polk* 1886: 676.

DIMOCK, TIMOTHY, So Coventry, Conn (b/IV-7-1800; d/IV-29-1874) MD Yale 1823. *Proc Conn Med Soc* 4:435-36, 1875.

DIMON, THEODORE, Auburn, NY; CW-USA; (b/IX-19-1816 Fairfield, Conn; d/VII-22-1889) MD UPa 1838; AB Yale 1835. *Med reg NY NJ Conn* 1890: 266. *Med surg rep Phila* 61:140, 1889. *U Pa med alum CW*: 1838. *Buff m & s jour* 24: 125, 1889.

DINGEE, RICHARD, Newportville, Pa (d/X-6-1898 @ 70) MD Jefferson 1851. *JAMA* 31:1066, 1898. *Butler* 1878: 710.

DINGEE, WILLIAM H , Philadelphia (d/XII-30-1906 @ 32) MD UPa 1896. *Pa med jour* 10:294, 407, 1906/07.

DINSMOOR, CHARLES M , Omaha, Nebr (d/XII-8 1890) <MD Homeop Med Coll Mo 1881> *Med vis* 7:48, 1891. *Northwest jour homeop* 2:320, 1890? *Polk* 1886: 582. Homeopath.

DIOSSY, ADDISON SOPER Jr, NYC (d/X-14-1889) MD CPSNY 1878. *Med reg NY NJ Conn* 1890: 266. *Polk* 1886: 676.

DIRMEYER, GEORGE W , New Orleans (d/II-27-1881 @ 52) MD U La 1851. *New Orl m & s jour* ns9:396, 1881.

DISBROW, STEPHEN MORGAN, Farmingdale, NJ (b/X-12-1812 Brooklyn; d/VI-2-1894) MD CPSNY 1834. *Tr Med Soc NJ* 1894: 266-68.

DISBROW, STEPHEN MORGAN, Old Bridge, NJ (d/V-28-1895 @ 48) MD Bellevue 1877. *Med reg NY NJ Conn* 1895: 220. *Polk* 1886: 609.

DISBROW, WILLIAM GRAY, Dalhousie, NB (b/1830 St Johns; d/XII-12-1894) MD Harvard 1857. *Bost m & s jour* 132:48, 1895.

DISMOND, SAMUEL H , Richmond, Va (d/III-1-1898 @ 44) MD Howard 1883; Pharm D Howard. *JAMA* 30:682, 1898. *NC med jour* 41:307, 1898. *Polk* 1896: 1498. Black.

DISMUKES, THOMAS TERRELL, CW-CSA; Nashville (b/1832; d/1874) MD U Nashville 1855; AB UNC 1858. *UNC cat*: 164.

DISSE, CONRAD HENRY, Nauvoo, Ill (d/X-21-1905 @ 78) <MD Berlin 1853> *Ill med jour* 8:530, 1905. *Polk* 1896: 431.

DISSLER, HARRY S , Shoenecks, Pa (d/III-20-1904 @ 22) MD Medico-Chi Coll Phila 1903. *Pa med jour* 8: 334, 1904/05.

DITSON, ASA MOORES, New Carthage, La (b/II-10-1802 Wilton, Me; d/IX-8-1835) MD Bowdoin 1833; AB 1829. *Bowdoin cat*: 1829.

DIVAN, C P , Cincinnati (d/VI-28-1873 @28) MD Miami 1867. *Med surg rep Phila* 29:36, 1873.

DIX, JOHN HOMER, Boston (b/1813; d/VIII-25-1884) MD Jefferson 1836; AB Harvard 1833. *JAMA* 10:379, 1888. *Bost m & s jour* 111:240, 619, 1884. *Atkinson* I:618. *Butler* 1878: 338.

DIXON, HARRISON, Baltimore (b/1786? Caroline Co; d/X-12-1822 @ 36) MD unknown. *Med annals Md:* 378.

DIXON, JOHN, Fayetteville, Ala; CW-CSA (b/VI-21-1832 Tenn; d/IV-13-1902) MD Jefferson 1860. *Tr Med Assoc Ala* 1902: 149-50.

DIXON, JOSEPH EDWARD, ?Ashwood, Tenn; CW-CSA (b/VIII-14-1831 Maury Co; d/IV-7-1902) MD U Pa 1856. *U Pa med alum CW*: 1857. *SHSP* 22:195, 1893.

DIXON, LEWIS E , Moosup, Conn; CW-USA (b/1816; d/II-5-1863 Moosup) MD UCNY 1846. *Med surg rep Phila* ns9:398, 1862/63. *Nat med jour* 1:293, 1870/71.

DIXON, MAHLON COTTRILL, Hinsdale, NH (b/I-12-1844 Albany, Vt; d/VI-27-1900/1901?) MD UVt 1875. *Tr NH Med Soc* 1902: 317-18. *Polk* 1890: 709.

DIXON, ROBERT, Damariscotta, Me (b/I-28-1818 Plainfield, Conn; d/X-18-1888) MD Harvard 1846. *Tr Me Med Assoc* 1890: 334-36. *Butler* 1878: 305.

DIXON, ROBERT E LEE, ?NC (b/II-14-1861 Carteret Co, NC; d/1888?) MD Jefferson 1884. *NC med jour* 22: 317-19, 1888.

DIXON, W A , Ripley, O (d/VI-24-1899) MD Med Coll Ohio 1865. *JAMA* 33:174, 1899. *Polk* 1890: 932.

DIXON, WILLIAM CRESSON, CW-USA; Philadelphia (b/IV-13-1840; d/I-11-1902) MD UPa 1860. *Pa med jour* 5:277, 1901/02. *Polk* 1896: 1302.

DOAN, NATHAN W , Curtisville, Ind (b/V-4-1829 Knox Co, O; d/VII-2-1905) Lic by yrs pract. *Tr Ind St Med Soc* 1906: 501. *Polk* 1890: 383. Kemper's *Indiana*.

DOANE, AUGUSTUS SIDNEY, Staten Island, NYC (b/ IV-2-1808 Boston; d/I-27-1852. MD Harvard 1828. *Bost m & s jour* 46:466, 1852. Palmer's *Necrol Harvard alum*: 8.

DOANE, CHARLES RUSSELL, Brooklyn (b/VIII-30-1840; d/VI-9-1884) MD CPSNY 1872. *Med reg NY NJ Conn* 1885: 234.

DOANE, GEORGE MERRITT, Wilmington, Del (b/ 1851 Barnstable, Mass; d/III-19-1896) MD Hahnemann Phila 1890. *Hahn mo* 31:52-53, 103 (news & advt) 1896.

DOANE, GEORGE WASHINGTON, Hyannis, Mass (d/ XII-28-1905 @ 81) MD Harvard 1844. *Bost m & s jour* 154: 28, 1906. *Polk* 1896: 714. *Butler* 1878: 349.

DOBBINS, THOMAS, Marysville, Cal (b/1831 Ala; d/V-5-1900) MD Missouri Med Coll 1859; AB Brunswick 1855. *JAMA* 34:1273, 1900. *Polk* 1886:167.

DOCK, GEORGE, Philadelphia; CW-USA (b/V-23-1823 Harrisburg, Pa; d/VIII-17-1875 Clearfield, Pa) MD UPa 1844; AM Penna Coll 1854. *Tr Med Soc Pa* 1876: 197-201. *U Pa med alum CW*: 1844.

DOCKING, THOMAS, San Diego, Cal (d/VIII-20-1902) MRCS(L) 1866. *Tr Am Inst Homeop* 1903:732. *Polk* 1886: 168 (as Regular, i.e., non-homeopathic).

DODD, ISAAC DAVIS, Bloomfield, NJ (b/IV-23-1799 Steuben, NY; d/X-26-1869) Stud w/Dr Joseph S Dodd; lic Med Soc NJ 1827. *Med reg NY NJ Conn* 1870:317. *Phila med reg & dir* 1871: 302. *Tr Med Soc NJ* 1870:93.

DODD, ROBERT JOHN, Sulphur Springs, Md (d/VII-5 1816 Phila) MD UPa 1809. *Med annals Md:* 378.

DODGE, ASA, missionary to Syria, 1832- (b/XI-15-1802 Newcastle, Me; d/I-29-1835 Jeusalem) MD Bowdoin 1831; AB 1827. *Bowdoin cat*: 1827.

DODGE, AUGUSTUS W, S Baltimore (b/1837 NY; d/ III-3-1887) MD UMd 1864; ng U Mich M Sch 1862. *New Orl m&s jour* ns14:793, 1887. *Med annals Md:* 378.

DODGE, DANIEL ALBERT, Brooklyn (b/III-12-1829 SC; d/XII-12-1882) MD CPSNY 1852; AB UCNY 1848. *Med reg NY NJ Conn* 1883:224. *Atkinson* I:452.

DODGE, DAVID STUART NYC (d/V-23-1869 @ 65) MD Yale 1826. *Phila med reg & dir* 1871:301.

DODGE, EDGAR SIMON, Natick, Mass (b/X-21-1853 Enfield, NH; d/IV-5-1898) MD Dartmouth 1876. *Bost m & s jour* 138: 364, 1898. *Polk* 1886: 470.

DODGE, EDWARD FOSTER, Fond du Lac, Wis (b/ 1835 Augusta, NY; d/I-27-1891) MD Chicago Med Coll 1862. *Tr Wis St Med Soc* 1891:326-28. *Polk* 1890: 1165.

DODGE, EDWARD LEWIS, Brooklyn (d/I-3-1898 @ 39) MD UCNY 1889 *JAMA* 30: 166, 1898. *Polk* 1896:995.

DODGE, FRANKLIN, Harwich, Mass (b/XI-9-1809 Groton; d/VII-8-1872) MD Dartmouth 1838; AB Amherst 1834. *Bost m & s jour* ns10:76, 1872.

DODGE, ISRAEL S , Avondale, O (b/X-6-1807 Waterford; d/III-1-1872) MD Ohio Med Coll 1834. *Tr Ohio St Med Soc* 1872: 260-61.

DODGE, JOHN L , Groton, Conn; CW-USA; Peru (d/ VIII-14-1901) MD UCNY 1846. *JAMA* 37:595, 1901. *Polk* 1886: 192.

DODGE, JOSIAH H , Pana, Ill (d/VI-24-1897 @ 76) Lic yrs pract. *JAMA* 29:45, 1897. *Polk* 1890: 343.

DODGE, LEONARD, CW-USA (d/III-11-1864) MD unknown. *Nat med jour* 1:293, 1870/71.

DODGE, LEVI PARKER, Farmington, Minn (b/V-25-1839 Sunapee, NH; d/IX-29-1893) MD Dartmouth 1864. *JAMA* 21: 630, 1893. *Tr Minn St Med Soc* 1893: 131. *Butler* 1878: 392.

DODGE, LEWIS, Adrian, Mich; Cleveland, O; Chicago, 1873- (b/VI-27-1815 Utica, NY; d/VI-25-1890 Chicago) MD Hahnemann Phila 1850; ng Geneva Med Coll 1843-45; Ohio St & Union Law Sch 1840-43. *Med vis* 6:247, 1890. *Polk* 1886:262. *Cleave*. Homeopath.

DODGE, LORENZO, Wakefield, Mass (d/XI-4-1868 @ 32) MD Bowdoin 1865. *Bost m & s jour* 2:272, 1868.

DODGE, MOSES, Portland, Me 1846- (b/III-9-1812 Sedgwick, Me; d/X-18-1879) MD Bowdoin 1838. *Tr Am Inst Homeop* 1881: 122.

DODGE, WILLIAM CAMPBELL Jr, Chicago (d/I-12-1901) MD Jefferson 1864. *Ill med jour* ns2: 533, 1901. *Polk* 1896:316 (Florida).

DODSON, CAROLINE M , Philadelphia (b/1845 Keosauqua, Ia; d/I-9-1898) MD Woman's Med Coll Phila 1874. *JAMA* 30:278, 1898. *Polk* 1886: 815.

DODSON, WILLIAM B , New Orleans (d/V-11-1894 @93 Phila) MD Jefferson 1834. *Polk* 1886: 416.

DOE, ORLANDO WITHERSPOON, Boston (b/IX-1843 So Newbury, Vt; d/XII-10-1890) MD Harvard 1869; AB 1865. *Bost m & s jour* 123:580, 601, 630 1890; 124:190, 1891. *Polk* 1886: 456.

DOHERTY, ALEXANDER S , NYC (d/I-19-1875 @ 27) MD Bellevue 1869. *Med rec* 10:71, 1875.

DOHERTY, HUGH, So Boston (d/VII-31-1892 @ 49) MD Harvard 1867; AB Williams 1863. *Bost m & s jour* 127: 128, 1892. *Polk* 1890: 536.

DOLAN, ALBERT STANLEY, Athens, Mich; Fergus Falls, Minn (d/III-22-1904) MD U Mich Homeop Med Coll 1882. *Tr Am Inst Homeop* 1904:955. *Polk* 1886: 483. Homeopath.

DOLE, JOHN, Amherst, Mass; CW-USA (b/IX-14-1838 Augusta, Me; d/V-20-1872 at sea) MD Harvard 1864; AB Amherst 1861. *Bost m & s jour* ns9:396, 1872. *Harvard in CW*: 1864.

DOLLARHIDE, BENJAMIN E , Clinton, Ala (b/1813; d/1842) MD UPa 1837; AB U Ala 1836. *U Ala cat*: 50.

DOLLIVER, GEORGE CARROLL, Abington, Mass (b/ IX-29-1869 Gloucester; d/XII-30-1897) MD Harvard 1895; PhB Tufts 1891. *Bost m & s jour* 138: 24, 1898.

DONAGHE, WILLIAM RICE, ?NYC (b/IV-16-1830

 Spec. educ'l status abbrev. as: ***ng*** = college verified attendance without degree;

New Haven, Conn; d/VII-18-1866) MD UCNY 1852; MD & AB Yale 1859. *Tr AMA* 19:411-12, 1868. *Bost m & s jour* 75:28, 1866. *Med reg NY NJ Conn* 1867: 216-17. *Med surg rep Phila* 15:112, 1866.

DONALDSON, EBENEZER E , Wabash, Ind (b/XI-12-1830 Wilmington Pa [sic]; d/V-19-1898) MD Chic Med Coll 1873. *Tr Ind St Med Soc* 1899:383. *Polk* 1896: 495.

DONALDSON, FRANCIS, Baltimore (b/VII-23-1823; d/XII-8-1891) MD UMd 1846. *JAMA* 18:50, 1892. *Tr CPP* cent vol:280-81. *Bost m & s jour* 125:664. *Med bull med & surg* 14:35, 1892. *K&B* III:332 [d/1881!]

DONALDSON, HENRY CHAPMAN, Sterling, Ill (d/II-13-1896 @ 71) MD Rush 1851. *JAMA* 26:442, 1896. *Polk* 1896: 442.

DONALDSON, MILES LITTLEJOHN, Baltimore (b/1817; d/V-13-1845) MD UMd 1840. *Med ann Md:* 379.

DONALDSON, WILLIAM, Baltimore (b/1778 Calvert Co, Md; d/I-14-1835) Hon MD UMd 1818. *Med annals Md:* 379-380.

DONE, J BAYLY, NYC (d/XI-2-1873 @ 28 Yokohama, Japan) MD Bellevue 1864. *Med reg NY NJ Conn* 1874:272. *Med surg rep Phila* 30:66, 1874.

DONELSON, BENJAMIN RISLEY, CW-CSA; Pine Bluff, Ark (b/V-1-1834 Tenn; d/IX-4-1903) MD New Orl Med Coll 1861. *So pract* 25: 589, 1903. *SHSP* 22: 195, 1893.

DONLAN, JOHN MALACHI, Fitchburg, Mass (d/I-26-1905 @30) MD Harv 1897. *Bost m&s j* 152:178 1905.

DONLIN, PHILIP EUGENE, NYC (d/VI-12-1892 @ 43) MD UCNY 1870. *Med reg NY NJ Conn* 1893: 299. *Bost m & s jour* 126:620, 1892. *Polk* 1890: 811.

DONNAN, INGHAM WOOD, Pittsburgh (d/I-13-1903 @ 58) MD Bellevue 1874. *Pa med jour* 7:279, 1903/04. *Flint* 1897: 829.

DONNELL, JOTHAM, Houlton, Me; CW-USA (b/XI-18-1814 Alna; d/XI-10-1889) MD Bowdoin 1839; AB 1836. *Bowdoin cat*: 1836. *Polk* 1886: 426.

DONNELLY, MICHAEL, NYC (d/IV-10-1890 @ 52) MD Rush 1869. *Med reg NY NJ Conn* 1890:267.

DONOHO, CHARLES R , Triune, Tenn (d/VIII-14 1883 @ 46) MD Med Coll Va 1865. *Med surg rep Phila* 49:420, 1883.

DONOHUE, JAMES FRANCIS, New Britain, Conn (b/VII-12-1865 Waterbury; d/I-22-1898) MD UVt 1892. *Proc Conn Med Soc* 1898: 377.

DONOVAN, DONALD DAMIAN, Troy, NY (d/X-27 1899 @ 28) MD Albany 1895. *JAMA* 33:1308, 1899. *Flint* 1897: 638.

DONOVAN, SAMUEL MAGNER, Quincy, Mass (d/II-19-1894 @ 42) MD Harvard 1879. *Bost m & s jour* 130:200, 226-27, 251, 1894. *Polk* 1886: 771.

DONOVAN, THOMAS WASHINGTON, Staten Island, NYC 1848- (b/I-28-1809 Baltimore; d/IX-1-1890) Stud w/John W Francis, NY. *Tr Amer Inst Homeop* 1891: 85. Homeopath.

DOOLEY, JOHN JOSEPH, NYC (d/XII-10-1902 @ 35) MD CPSNY 1890. *Bost m & s jour* 147: 688, 1902. *Polk* 1896: 1049.

DOOLEY, JOHN THOMAS, Manchester, Conn (b/1865 Cohoes, NY; d/II-15-1902) MD UCNY 1887. *Proc Conn Med Soc* 1902:427-28. *Polk* 1896: 280.

DOOLITTLE, ANDREW F , Herkimer Co, NY (b/1811; d/V-22-1872) MD Fairfield 1833. *Med reg NY NJ Conn* 1873:339. *Tr Med Soc St NY* 1876:320-23.

DOREMUS, ROBERT OGDEN, NYC (b/1824; d/III-22 1906) MD UCNY 1851. *Bost m & s jour* 154:358-59, 1906. *Atkinson* I:709. *Polk* 1886: 676.

DORLAND, EDWARD [EDWIN] H , Chicago; Burlington, Ia (d/V-14-1898 @ 56) MD Miami 1880. *JAMA* 30:1305, 1898. *Polk* 1886:352.

DORLAND, ELIAS THOMAS, Buffalo, NY (b/IV-12-1832; d/II-20-1900) MD U Mich 1854. *Buff m & s jour* 39:617-18, 1900. *JAMA* 34:639, 1900. *Polk* 1886: 652.

DORLAND, PHILIP S , Hamburg NY (d/IV-29-1866) MD UCNY 1859. *Buff m & s jour* 6: 399-400, 1867.

DORN, JOHN A , NYC (b/1842 Johnstown, NY; d/VI-17-1904 London) MD Albany 1864. *Bost m & s jour* 150:716, 1904. *Polk* 1896: 1049.

DORR, CLIFFORD, Somerville, Mass (b/XI-2-1805 Boston; d/VIII-19-1858) MD Harvard 1829; AB 1825. *Bost m & s jour* 59:88, 1859. Palmer's *Necrol Harvard alum*: 269-70.

DORR, JAMES COLBY, Medford, Mass (d/IX-19-1880 Milton, NH) MD Dartmouth 1851. *Bost m & s jour* 103:329, 1890. *Tr AMA* 32:501, 1881.

DORR, JOSEPH HAWLEY, Philadelphia (b/XII-7-1807 Boston; d/IV-13-1855) MD Harvard 1837; AB Bowdoin 1827. *Bost m & s jour* 52:247, 1855.

DORR, SAMUEL G , Buffalo (b/1840 Dansville; d/IV-28-1901) MD Buffalo 1875. *Bost m & s jour* 144:462, 1901. *Polk* 1896: 1008.

DORRANCE, HENRY BOWEN, Philadelphia (d/XII-19 1872 @ 44) MD UPa 1847. *Med s rep Phila* 28:26, 1873.

DORSET, THOMAS B Jr, Manchester, Va (d/V-19-1898 @ 62) MD Jefferson 1859. *JAMA* 30:1366, 1898. *Polk* 1896: 1494.

DORSETTE [DORSAT], CORNELIUS N , Montgomery, Ala (d/XII-7-1897 @ 44) MD U Buffalo 1882. *Tr Med Assoc St Ala* 1898:240 [as "colored"] *JAMA* 30: 106, 1898. *NC med jour* 41:63, 1898. *Polk* 1890: 144. Black.

DORSEY, FREDERICK, Washington Co, Md (b/1774; d/X-26-1858) Hon MD UMd 1824. *Med annals Md:* 380. *Tr AMA* 13: 807-10, 1860. *K&B* III:334-36.

DORSEY, HARRY WOODWARD, CW-USA; Newmarket, Md (b/VII-15-1831; d/III-21-1903 Hyattsville) MD UPa 1857. *U Pa med alum CW*:187. *Polk* 1886: 444.

DORSEY, JOHN SYNG, Philadelphia (b/XII-23-1783; d/XI- -1818) MD UPa 1802. *K&B* III:336-37.

DORSEY, JOSIAH BURNAP, NYC (d/III-14-1875) MD UCNY 1853. *Med reg NY NJ Conn* 187: 198.

DORSEY, LLOYD, Frederick, Md (d/1857) MD UMd 1821. *Med annals Md:* 380.

DORSEY, NATHAN, Philadelphia (d/VII-2-1806) MD unknown. *Tr CPP* cent vol: 220.

DORSEY, NICHOLAS J, Joliet, Ill (b/1822; d/III-11-1906 @ 84) MD UMd 1847. *Ill med jour* 9:463, 1906. *Polk* 1886: 262.

DORSEY, RICHARD, Frederick, Md (d/IX-9-1827 @ 23 New Orleans) MD UMd 1824. *Med annals Md:* 381.

DORSEY, ROBERT RALSTON, Philadelphia (b/V-5-1869) MD UPa 1829; AB Princeton 1824; AM 1827. *Phila med reg & dir* 1871: 294. *Med surg rep Phila* 20:400, 1869.

DORSEY, ROBERT W, Baltimore (b/1835 near Catonsville, Md; d/II-24-1900) MD UMd 1856. *JAMA* 34: 446, 1900. *Polk* 1886: 917 [Fairfax CH, Va; MD UCNY 1868 (?)]

DORSEY, SEPTIMUS, Mt Vernon, Md (b/I-7-1819 Howard Co; d/III-6-1850) <MD Washington U Balto 1839> *Med annals Md:* 381.

DORSEY, WILLIAM TAGART, Baltimore (b/VI-4-1848; d/IV-15-1870) MD UMd 1870; AB Haverford 1867. *Haverford biogr cat*: 107.

DOTY, EDWARD WILBUR, Paterson, NJ (b/1856 Newark; d/VIII-21-1905) MD LICH 1886. *Bost m & s jour* 153: 262, 1905. *Polk* 1896: 946.

DOTY, HYLON, Vernon, NY; San Francisco 1849-52; Roxbury, NH; Canandaigua, NY (b/VII-19-1817 Northeast, NY; d/V-5-1876) MD Ecl Med Inst Cinc 1853; ng Hamilton. *US med inv* 4:203, 1876. *Cleave*. Homeopath.

DOTY, J M, CW-USA (d/IV-12-1865) MD unknown. *Nat med jour* 1:293, 1870/71.

DOTY, MARTIN, CW-USA (d/XII-10-1864 Nashville, Tenn) MD unknown. *Nat med jour* 1:293, 1870/71.

DOUBLEDAY, EDWIN THOMPSON, NYC; Boston (d/IV-23-1893 @ 33) MD Bellevue 1882. *Med reg NY NJ Conn* 1893: 299. *Bost m & s jour* 128:428, 1893. *Polk* 1886:676.

DOUGAL, CHARLES HAMMOND, CW-USA; Milton, Pa (b/IX-20-1838; d/IV-26-1902) MD UPa 1864; AB Princeton 1859. *Pa med jour* 6:260, 1902/03. *U Pa med alum CW*: 1864. *Flint* 1897: 810.

DOUGHERTY, ALEXANDER N, CW-USA; Newark, NJ (b/I-1- 1822; d/XI-29-1883) MD CPSNY 1845; AB Oberlin 1841; Hon AM Princeton 1866. *Med reg NY NJ Conn* 1883: 224. *Tr Med Soc NJ* 1883:299-302. *JAMA* 1:256, 1883. *Atkinson* I: 240.

DOUGHERTY, BERNARD A, Cumberland & Baltimore, Md (b/IX- -1825 York, Pa; d/IV-1-1875 NYC) MD UMd 1847. *Tr AMA* 26:468, 1875. *Med annals Md:* 381.

DOUGHERTY, MATTHEW C, Grafton, WVa; CW-USA (d/1880) MD Jefferson 1863. *Tr Med Soc WVa* 1884: 154. *Butler* 1878: 850.

DOUGHERTY, THOMAS DENNIS, Waterbury, Conn (b/1829 Ireland; d/XI-22-1878) MD NY Med Coll 1853. *Proc Conn Med Soc* 1879: 165. *Butler* 1878: 77.

DOUGHTY, JOHN HENRY, Matteawan, NY (d/I-28-1905 @ 74) MD U Mich 1873; AB Williams 1858; AM 1861. *Tr Med Soc St NY* 1905:[362] *Polk* 1886:667.

DOUGHTY, THOMAS JOHN, Matteawan, NY (d/VIII-20-1898 @ c31) MD U Mich 1896; ng 1890; stud pharmacy? 1891. *JAMA* 31: 427, 1898.

DOUGHTY, WILLIAM EVANS, CW-USA; Hartsville, Pa (b/VI-26-1836 Carversville; d/X-15-1902) MD UPa 1868. *Pa med jour* 6:260, 1902/03. *U Pa med alum CW*: 1868. *Flint* 1897: 804.

DOUGLAS, GEORGE HERBERT, Morgan City, La (d/II-7-1903 Pensacola, Fla) MD Tulane 1886. *New Orl m & s jour* 55:590, 1902. *Polk* 1896: 488.

DOUGLAS, JOHN [JONATHAN] HANCOCK, CW-US San Comm; NYC (b/VI-5-1824 Waterford, NY; d/X 2-1892 Washington, DC) MD UPa 1847; AB Williams 1843. *JAMA* 19:476, 1892. *Med reg NY NJ Conn* 1893: 299. *Bost m & s jour* 127:348, 1892. *U Pa med alum CW*: 1847.

DOUGLAS, SILAS HAMILTON, Ann Arbor, Mich (b/X 16-1816 Fredonia, NY; d/VIII-26-1890) Lic Mich St Med Soc 1842; ng U Mich. *JAMA* 15:483-84, 1890. *K&B* III: 339.

DOUGLAS, STUART, NYC (b/I- -1861 Alexandria, Va; d/X-14-1894) MD UVa ; MD CPSNY 1883; AB UVa. *Med reg NY NJ Conn* 1895:220. *JAMA* 23: 654, 1894. *Bost m & s jour* 131: 423, 428, 1894.

DOUGLASS, ELMORE, Sumner Co, Tenn (b/c1800; d/c1865) MD Transylv 1820. *Tr Med Soc Tenn* 1876: 81.

DOUGLASS, JAMES ALBERT, Center Star, Ala (d/IX-22-1898) MD U Nashville 1868. *Tr Med Assoc Ala* 1899: 233. *JAMA* 31:872, 1898.

DOUGLASS, JAMES S, Oswego, Vernon, Hamilton, NY; Milwaukee, Wis 1848- (b/VII-4-1801 Westmoreland, NY; d/VIII-6-1878 Macomb City, Miss) <MD Fairfield 1825> MA, Hon PhD Madison 1870. *Tr Am Inst Homeop* 1879: 1236. *Cleave*. Homeopath.

DOUGLASS, THOMAS J, Ottumwa, Ia (d/IX-2-1899 @ 72) MD Cleveland Med Coll 1854. *JAMA* 33: 745, 1899. *Polk* 1896: 535.

DOUGLASS, WILLIAM A, San Francisco (b/VI-23-1825 Va; d/III-26-1889) MD Columbian DC 1850. *Tr Med Soc Calif* 1889: 211. *Butler* 1878: 54.

DOUMEING, EMILE, New Orleans (d/I-18-1895) MD Tulane 1857. *New Orl m&s jour* ns22:636. *Polk* 1890:489.

DOUSMAN, JOHN B, Milwaukee, Wis (b/1807; d/II-4 1868) MD UVt 1827. *Tr AMA* 29:637, 1878. *Tr Wis St Med Soc* 1891: 356.

DOUTTEIL, HENRY, New Britain, Conn (b/IX-3-1848 Hesse, Gny; d/V-3-1898) MD Yale 1880. *Proc Conn Med Soc* 1899: 368-70. *JAMA* 30:1248, 1898. *Polk* 1896: 281.

DOVE, GEORGE McCAULEY, Washington, DC (b/X-5-1817; d/I-30-1874) MD UPa 1839. *Med annals Md:* 381. *Tr AMA* 25:525, 1874. *Hist Med Soc DC:* 239.

DOVE, JOHN, Richmond, Va (b/1782? d/XI-16-1876 @ 84) MD UPa 1814. *Med surg rep Phila* 35:459, 1876.

DOVILLIERS, LEOPOLD VICTOR, Annapolis Md; USA (b/II-15-1818 Paris; d/VIII-25-1892) MD Columbian DC 1850. *Hist Med Soc DC:*248. *Polk* 1886:212.

DOW, HORATIO, Elkington, Conn (b/I-30-1793 Ashford; d/IX-28-1859) Lic Conn Med Soc 1818; Hon MD Yale 1832. *Proc Conn Med Soc* 1860: 19, 59-63.

DOW, JOHN OSBORN, Reading, Mass (b/IV-5-1822 Lyndon, Vt; d/II-22-1897) MD Castleton 1846. *Bost m & s jour* 136: 220, 395, 1897. *Polk* 1886: 471.

DOW, THOMAS CHALMERS, Nashville, Tenn (b/XI-10-1845 Augusta, Ga; d/1879) MD U Nashville 1868. *So pract* 1:74-80, 1879. *Nashville jour m & s* ns23:43, 1879. *Atkinson* I:338.

DOW, VIRGIL MARO, New Haven Co, Conn (d/VII-4-1851) MD Castleton 1832; Hon MD Yale 1842. *Proc Conn Med Soc* 1852: 17.

DOW, WILLIAM WELLMAN, Somerville, Mass (d/V-8-1891 @ 57) MD Harvard 1867. *Bost m & s jour* 124:498, 1891. *Polk* 1890: 556.

DOWD, JOHN FRANCIS, Manchester, NH (b/II-19-1865; d/IV-12-1902) MD Dartmouth 1896. *Tr NH Med Soc* 1902: 316-17.

DOWDNEY, SAMUEL MOORE, Roadstown, NJ (b/III-11-1834; d/XI-17-1861) MD UPa 1855. *Tr Med Soc NJ* 1871:182.

DOWELL, GREENSVILLE, CW-CSA; Galveston, Tex (b/IX-1-1822 Albemarle Co, Va; d/VI-9-1881) MD Jefferson 1847; ng Louisville 1845/46. *Bost m & s jour* 105:622, 1881. *Tr AMA* 33:546-49, 1882. *Tex med & surg rec* 2:80, 1882. *Atkinson* I: 199. *K&B* III: 341-42.

DOWLING, JOHN WILLIAM, Hagerstown, Md; NYC (b/VIII-11-1837 NYC; d/I-4-1892 Goshen, NY) MD Hahnemann Phila 1857. *Tr Amer Inst Homeop* 1892:210. *Med adv* 15:219, 1884. *Med vis* 8:81, 1892. *Polk* 1886:676. *Cleave*. Homeopath.

DOWNES, AVERY, Preston, Conn (b/1761? d/1854 @ 93) Hon MD Yale 1818. *Proc Conn Med Soc* 1855: 21.

DOWNES, JESSE, Caroline Co, Md (d/V-24-1807 Hillsborough) *Med annals Md:* 382.

DOWNES, JOHN KENNEY, New Haven Co, Conn (d/1858) MD Yale 1854. *Proc Conn Med Soc* 1858: 19.

DOWNES, NATHANIEL, Boston (d/I-8-1903 @ 84) MD Harvard 1846. *Bost m & s jour* 148:80, 1903.

DOWNES, WILLIAM H Jr, CW-USA; Denton, Md (b/VIII-26- 1841; d/I-1-1891) MD UMd 1864. *Med annals Md:* 382. *Butler* 1874: 318.

DOWNEY, FINDLEY EDGAR, Clinton, Ill (d/I-5-1902) MD Pulte 1879. *Tr Am Inst Homeop* 1902:845-46. *Polk* 1886: 274.

DOWNEY, JAMES A , CW-USA (d/X-29-1864) MD unknown. *Nat med jour* 1:294, 1870/71.

DOWNEY, ROGER CHARLES, Middletown, Conn (b/1866 Ireland; d/II-15-1904) MD UVt 1892. *Proc Conn Med Soc* 1906:317-18. *Polk* 1896: 284.

DOWNING, ALFRED CLARK, Roxbury, Mass (b/1849? d/V-11-1885 @ 36) MD UVt 1875. *Bost m & s jour* 112:516, 1885.

DOWNING, CLARENCE WARE, Manchester, NH (b/VIII-12-1859 Marlow; d/IV-29-1897) MD UVt 1885. *Tr NH Med Soc* 1897:305.

DOWNING, ELEAZAR BUTLER, Preston City, Conn (b/XII-15-1786 Canterbury; d/I-20-1870) Hon MD Yale 1832. *Proc Conn Med Soc* 3:414 ff; 500-51, 1871.

DOWNS, CHARLES MANVILLE, Chicago (d/XI-24-1904) MD Yale 1883; PhB 1881. *Ill med jour* 7:126, 1904. *Polk* 1896: 381.

DOWNS, DIONYSIUS, Baltimore (d/VIII-2-1857 @ 54) MD unknown. *Med annals Md:* 382.

DOWNS, HENRY MITCHELL, Kansas City, Kans (d/VIII-13-1901 @ 41) MD U Mich 1880. *JAMA* 37:527, 1901.

DOWNS, HENRY S , NYC (b/1812; d/V-2-1879) MD CPSNY 1834. *Med reg NY NJ Conn* 1879: 189.

DOWNS, ISAAC M , Cape May CH, NJ (b/XII-5-1841 Berlin, NJ; d/III-1-1903) MD Jefferson 1882. *Tr Med Soc NJ* 1903:384. *Polk* 1890: 720.

DOWNS, MYRON, Roxbury, Conn (b/1805; d/IV-7-1887) MD Yale 1830. *Proc Conn Med Soc* ns4:217-18, 1888-91. *Butler* 1878: 76.

DOYLE, JOHN THOMAS JOSEPH, Wilkes-Barre, Pa (d/II-10-1894 @ 57) MRCS Ireland 1857. *JAMA* 22:234, 1894. *Reg Pa phys* 1881-88: 246.

DOYLE, OLIVER MILLER, CW-CSA; Calhoun, SC (b/I-31-1831 Richland; d/X-6-1897) MD UPa 1856. *JAMA* 29:867, 1897. *U Pa med alum CW*: 1856.

DOZIER, JOHN C , Birmingham, Ala (d/X-8-1897) MD U Nashville 1858. *Tr Med Assoc St Ala* 1898: 240. *Polk* 1886: 131.

DRAGGETT, DAVID LEWIS, New Haven, Conn (b/VI 24-1820; d/1896) MD Yale 1843. *Proc Conn Med Soc* 1896: 327 ff.

DRAKE, BENJAMIN, NYC (b/II-14-1805; d/I-11-1871) MD CPSNY 1828; AB Columbia 1824. *Med reg NY NJ Conn* 1871: 351. *Med rec* 6:94, 1871-72.

DRAKE, DANIEL, Cincinnati (b/X-20-1785 Essex Co, NJ; d/XI-5-1852) MD UPa 1816. *Phila med & surg jour* 1:215-17, 1852. *Bost m & s jour* 48:142-45, 1853. *Buffalo med jour* 8:457-58, 1852. *K&B* III:343-44.

DRAKE, EBENEZER WADE, Middleboro, Mass (d/VI-28-1887) MD Harvard 1847. *Bost m & s jour* 117:24, 1887. *Butler* 1878: 349.

DRAKE, ELIJAH HAMBLIN, Detroit, Mich 1853- (b/XI-16-1821 Wayne Co, NY; d/XI-16-1874 Ypsilanti) MD Rush 1855. *Tr Am Inst Homeop* 1875: 804. *Am obs* 11: 655, 1874. *Am j hom mat med* 8:121, 1875.

DRAKE, FREDERICK RICHARD SEWARD, NYC (d/III-1 or 9-1888 @ 43) MD UCNY 1871. *Med reg NY NJ Conn* 1888: 252. *Buff m & s jour* 27:403, 1888. *Bost m & s jour* 118:281, 1884. *Polk* 1886: 676.

DRAKE, ISRAEL L , Lebanon, O (b/1823; d/1891) MD Miami 1855. *JAMA* 16:827-28, 1891. *Tr O St Med Soc* 1891:6, 340-41. *Polk* 1886: 758.

DRAKE, JASON W , Dover, NH (b/I-29-1838 Easton, Mass; d/XI-20-1885 @ 47) MD NY Homeop 1870. *Tr Am Inst Homeop* 1888: 235.

DRAKE, LEWIS, Rahway, NJ (b/VIII-26-1802; d/VIII-17-1888) MD UPa 1829. *Med reg NY NJ Conn* 1889: 272. *Tr Med Soc NJ* 1889: 173-74. *Butler* 1878: 468.

DRAKE, MOSES CLAYTON, Ladoga, Ind; CW-USA (d/XII-17-1893 San Francisco) MD Bellevue 1873. *JAMA* 21:1010, 1893.

DRAKE, NELSON SAMUEL, USA (b/1831; d/V-31-1880) MD Woodstock 1852; MD CPSNY 1853. *Med reg NY NJ Conn* 1881:235.

DRAKE, WILLIAM F, NYC (d/III-1-1906 @39) MD U CNY 1889. *Bost m&s j* 154:282 1906. *Polk* 1896:1050.

DRAKE, WILLIAM M , Hillsborough Tex (d/IX-12-1896) MD Columbus Med Coll 1881. *Tex m news* 5:520, 1895-96. *Tex med jour* 12:208,1896. *Polk* 1893: 1215.

DRANE, HENRY AUGUSTUS, Philadelphia; CW-USA (b/1842; d/III-7-1866) MD UPa 1862. *Med surg rep Phila* 14:180, 1866. *U Pa med alum CW*: 1862.

DRANE, WALTER HAIGH, Batesville Miss (d/III-28-1905 @ 73) MD UCNY 1855. *So pract* 27: 335, 1905.

DRAPER, ABIJAH, Roxbury Mass (b/IX-22-1775 Dedham; d/III-25-1836) MD Brown 1819; AB 1797; AM. *Brown hist cat*: 1797. *Mass Med Soc cat* 1894.

DRAPER, EDGAR LEROY, Holyoke, Mass (b/XI-28-1842 Pelham; d/1906) MD Harvard 1867; AM Amherst 1863. *Amherst, Men of*: 1863. *Butler* 1878: 341.

DRAPER, HENRY, NYC (b/III-7-1837 Prince Edward Co, Va; d/XI-2-1882) MD UCNY 1858. *Med reg NY NJ Conn* 1883: 225. *So pract* 4: 391, 1882. *Bost m & s jour* 107:522, 1882. *K&B* II:330-32.

DRAPER, ISAAC, Jr, S Attleboro, Mass (b/I-4-1824; d/III-20-1855 Russia) Stud med Paris; AB Brown 1845. *Bost m&s j* 52:347, 1855. *Nashville m&s j* 9:161, 1855.

DRAPER, JOHN CHRISTOPHER, NYC (b/III-31-1835 Mecklenburg Co Va; d/XII-20-1885) MD UCNY 1857. *Med reg NY NJ Conn* 1886: 243. *Bost m & s jour* 113:658, 1885. *Atkinson* I:257. *K&B* III:345-46.

DRAPER, JOHN WILLIAM, NYC (b/V-5-1811 St Helen's nr Liverpool, Engl; d/I-4-1882 Hastings, NY) MD UPa 1836. *Med reg NY NJ Conn* 1882:224. *Chicago med rev* 5:6, 1882. *Med surg rep Phila* ns15:96-98, 1866. *Atkinson* I:504-06. *K&B* III:346-47.

DRAPER, JOSEPH, CW-USA; Brattleboro, Vt (b/II-16 1834 Warwick, Mass; d/III-17-1892 @ 58) MD Jefferson 1858. *Bost m & s jour* 126:304, 510, 1892. *Med bull med & surg* 14:328, 1892. *Atkinson* I:130-31.

DRAPER, JOSEPH RUTTER, Westford, Mass (d/X-30 1904) MD Harvard 1888; AB Williams 1885. *Bost m & s jour* 151:504, 1904. *Polk* 1896: 696.

DRAPER, JOSEPH RUTTER, So Boston; CW-USA (d/VIII-5-1885 @ 55) MD Berkshire 1863; AB Williams 1851. *Bost m & s jour* 113:168,504,1885.

DRAPER, LEMUEL JAMES, USN (b/V-14-1834 Milford, Del; d/VIII-30-1879 St Louis) MD UPa 1854. *Tr AMA* 31:1037-38, 1880. *Bost m & s jour* 101:459, 1879. *Hist Med Soc DC:* 281.

DRAPER, WILLIAM HENRY, NYC (b/X-14-1830 Brattleboro, Vt; d/IV-25-1901)MD CPSNY 1855; AB Columbia 1851; AM 1854 *Bost m & s jour* 144: 436-37, 1901. *Chic med rec* 20:525, 1901. *K&B* III: 347.

DRAVO, LEWIS H , Pittsburgh (b/1853? d/XI-18-1903 @ 50) MD Jefferson 1881. *Pa med jour* 7:279, 1903/04.

DRAWBAUGH, JOHN AMBROSE, Asheville, NC (b/XI-10-1863 Cumberland Co Pa; d/V-27-1898) MD Nat M Coll DC 1888. *Hist Med Soc DC*:355. *Polk* 1890: 244.

DRAYER, PETER, Hartford City, Ind (b/XII-5-1840 Montgomery Co, O; d/XII-20-1901) MD Starling 1865. *Tr Ind St Med Soc* 1903: 338. *Polk* 1896: 470.

DRAYTON, EDWARD F , Brooklyn (d/V-5-1894 @ 66) MD Jefferson 1848; AB Princeton 1845; AM 1848. *Med reg NY NJ Conn* 1894:238. *JAMA* 22: 818, 1894. *Butler* 1878: 530.

DRAYTON, HENRY EDWARD, Philadelphia (b/II-25-1823 Charleston, SC; d/IV-19-1862) MD UPa 1845. *Med surg rep Phila* ns8:156, 1862. *Tr AMA* 14:209, 1864. *Tr Med Soc St Pa* 1863:313-17.

DREIBELBIS [DREIBELLIS, DREIBILBIS] DAVID L , Reading, Pa (b/I-20-1842 Virginville; d/III-24-1872) MD Hahnemann Phila 1866. *Tr Pa Homeop Med Soc* 1882. Homeopath.

DRESSER, SIMEON PARKER, Hinsdale, Mass 1873-(b/I-16-1845 Londonderry, Vt; d/XI-15-1883) MD Dartmouth 1870. *Bost m&s j* 109:617 1883; 110:72 1884.

DREW, DAVID FOGG, Lynn, Mass (d/II-13-1886 @ 66) MD Albany 1855. *Bost m & s jour* 115:630, 1886.

DREW, FREDERICK PERKINS, CW-USA (d/III-20-1864 Junction City, Kans) MD CPSNY 1856. *Nat med jour* 1:294, 1870/71.

DREWRY, EMMET A , CW-CSA; Southampton Va (b/1838;d/1891) MD Med Coll Va 1860. *Tr Med Soc Va* 1892:201. Blanton, *Va surgs CW*: 399. *Polk* 1890: 119.

DREWRY, JAMES H , Drewrysville, Va; CW-CSA (b/VI-10-1839; d/VI-1-1864 nr Ashland, Va) UVa cand. for MD 1860. Johnson, J L: *U Va memorial...alum dec'd CW*: 611-13.

DREWRY, SAMUEL DAVIES, Richmond Va; CW-CSN (b/IX-12-1832; d/IV-2-1905) <Med Coll Va 1854> MD UPa 1855. *Tr Med Soc Va* 1905:445-46. *U Pa med alum CW*: 1855 (suppl.) *Polk* 1900: 1759.

DRINKARD, WILLIAM BEVERLEY, Washington, DC (b/XII-7-1842 Williamsburg, Va; d/II-13-1877) MD

Columbian DC 1866; lic RCS(E) 1865. *Tr AMA* 29:638–40, 1878. *Hist Med Soc DC:* 280. *Atkinson* I:669. *K&B* III: 347.

DRINKER, JOHN HENRY, New Bedford, Mass (b/III–28–1821 Phila; d/V–16–1859 Magnolia, Fla) MD Harvard 1844. *Bost m & s jour* 60:368, 1859. *Tr Med Soc Pa* 1860: 134–35.

DRINKWATER, SIDNEY, Haverhill, Mass (d/XI–20–1891 @ 79) MD Berkshire 1843. *Bost m & s jour* 125:718, 1891.

DROESCH, JOSEPH LOUIS, Brooklyn (d/II–19–1897 @ 40) MD CPSNY 1883. *JAMA* 28:569, 1897. *Polk* 1896:995.

DROUGHT, ALBERT M , Baltimore (b/V–17–1866; d/VII–17–1890) MD UMd 1888. *Med annals Md:* 382.

DROWN, EDWARD PAYSON, Malden, Mass (b/IV–30 1865 Keene, NH; d/V–25–1905) MD Harvard 1893; AB Amherst 1889) *Bost m & s jour* 152:652, 1905. *Polk* 1896:717.

DROWN, THOMAS MESSINGER, CW–USA; S Bethlehem, Pa (b/III–19–1842 Phila; d/XI–16–1904) MD UPa 1862; AB Central HS Phila 1859. *Pa med jour* 8: 334, 1904/05. *U Pa med alum CW*: 1862.

DROWNE, SOLOMON, RevWar–USA; Providence, RI (b/III–11–1753; d/II–5–1834 Foster) MD UPa 1781; Hon MD Brown 1804; AB Brown 1773; AM Dartmouth 1786. *Tr RI Med Soc* 1859–77: 25–35. *K&B* III:347–48.

DRUMELER, CORNELIUS MURREL, Pancora, Ia (b/VIII––18–1850; d/VIII–16–1899) MD St Louis Med Coll 1876. *Tr Ia St Med Soc* 18:391–392, 1900. *Polk* 1890: 425.

DRUMMOND, CHARLES ELMER, Bedford, NY (b/X–14–1839 N Sidney, Me; d/V–27–1894) MD Bowdoin 1867. *Med reg NY NJ Conn* 1894: 328.

DRURY, ALFRED C , S Canton, NY (d/IV–22–1899) MD UVt 1874. *JAMA* 32:1013, 1899. *Polk* 1896: 1014.

DRURY, ALFRED THOMAS, Brooklyn (b/I–8–1830 Hull, Engl; d/XI–1–1899) MD Castleton 1857. *JAMA* 33: 1308, 1899. *Bost m&s j* 141: 180, 1899. *Polk* 1896: 995.

DRURY, SAMUEL SMITH, Bristol, RI (d/X–9–1879) MD Harvard 1847. *Bost m & s jour* 101:600, 1879. *Butler* 1878: 746.

DRURY, WILLIAM HENRY, Columbus, O (d/V–30–1898 @ 65) MD CPSNY 1857. *JAMA* 30: 1481, 1898. *Polk* 1886: 750.

DRYDEN, THOMAS F , Clayton, Ind (b/X–20–1835 Aberdeen, O; d/III– –1896) MD Med Coll Ohio 1859. *Tr Ind St Med Soc* 1896:275. *Polk* 1896: 462.

DRYSDALE, THOMAS MURRAY, Philadelphia (b/VIII 14 or 31–1831; d/V–26–1904) MD Pa Med Coll 1852; Hon AM Lafayette 1879. *Pa med jour* 8:334–35, 1904/05. *Tr CPP* cent vol:221. *Atkinson* I:540–41.

DU BARRY, EDMUND LEWIS, Md; USN (d/VII–12–1853) MD UPa 1822. *Med annals Md:* 382.

DUBOIS, ABRAM, NYC (b/IV–5–1810; d/VIII–29–1891) MD CPSNY 1835; AB Trinity 1830. *Med reg NY NJ Conn* 1892:276. *JAMA* 17:423, 1891. *Bost m & s jour* 125:260, 1891. *K&B* III:350.

DUBOIS, COERT, NYC (b/I–6–1847 Johnstown, NY; d/I–1–1891) MD CPSNY 1872; AB Rutgers 1868; AM 1871. *Med reg NY NJ Conn* 1891:272. *Bost m & s jour* 124:76, 1891. *Polk* 1886: 676.

DUBOIS, FRANCIS LATTA, USN 1862–88; Portsmouth, NH (b/X–21–1837 New London, Conn; d/II–24–1895) MD UPa 1862. *Bost m & s jour* 132:244, 1895. *JAMA* 24:337, 1895. *Polk* 1890: 711.

DUBOIS, HENRY AUGUSTUS, New Haven, Conn (b/VIII–9–1808 NYC; d/I–13–1884) MD CPSNY 1830; AB Columbia 1827. *Bost m & s jour* 110:92, 1884. *Med bull med & surg* 6:66, 1884. *K&B* III:350–51.

DUBOIS, HENRY AUGUSTUS, Philadelphia; San Rafael, Cal (d/1897) <MD Yale 1861> PhB Yale 1859. *JAMA* 28:1156, 1897. *Polk* 1886: 176.

DUBOIS, ROBERT OGDEN, NYC (d/III–9–1895 @ 35) MD Yale 1886; PhB 1883. *Med reg NY NJ Conn* 1895: 220. *JAMA* 24:422, 1895. *Bost m&s j* 132:266, 1895.

DUBS, SAMUEL RICHARD, Doylestown, Pa (b/XI–8–1811; d/XII–26–1889) MD UPa 1836. *Tr Am Inst Homeop* 1890:133. *Med vis* 6:45, 1890. *Polk* 1886:797. *Cleave*. Homeopath.

DUCACHET, HENRY WILLIAM, Salem, Mass; Norfolk Va; Phila 1834– (b/1797 Charleston SC; d/XII–15 1865) MD CPSNY 1817; Hon AM Princeton 1822; DD UPa 1837. *Med surg rep Phila* 13:422 1865. *Med ann Md:* 382.

DUCACHET, HENRY WILLIAM Jr, CW–USA (b/VI–27–1821 NYC; d/X–11–1865 Georgetown, DC) MD Jefferson 1843; AM UPa 1840. *Med surg rep Phila* 13:278, 1865. *Tr AMA* 18:355, 1867. *Nat med jour* 1:294, 1870/71.

DUCATEL, JULES TIMOLEON, Baltimore (b/VI–6–1796; d/IV–23–1849) MD *Med annals Md:* 383.

DUCHEM, J B , Baton Rouge, La (d/XII–11–1903 @ 75) <MD Montpelier 1855> *New Orl m & s jour* 56:572, 1904. *Polk* 1896: 613.

DUCKETT, THOMAS BUCHANAN, Wash'n Co Md (b/1800; d/XII–27–1875) MD UMd 1824 *Med ann Md:*383.

DUDLEY, AUGUSTUS PALMER, Portland, Me to 1881; NYC (b/VII–4–1853 Phippsburg, Me; d/VII–15–1905 Liverpool Engl) MD Dartmouth 1878. *Tr Med Soc St NY* 1905:[362]. *K&B* III: 351. *Polk* 1886: 428.

DUDLEY, BENJAMIN WILLIAM, Lexington, Ky (d/VII–3–1884 @ 46) MD Keokuk 1861. *Med surg rep Phila* 51:84, 1884.

DUDLEY, BENJAMIN WINSLOW, Lexington, Ky (b/IV–12–1785; d/I–20–1870) MD UPa 1806. *Tr AMA* 21:482–83, 1870. *Bost m & s jour* ns5:112, 1870. *Med rec* 5:22, 1870/71. *K&B* III:352–53.

DUDLEY, WILLIAM EDMUNDS, Chicago (d/VIII–15–1891) MD Rush 1889. *Chicago med rec* 2:75, 1891.

DUDLEY, WILLIAM HENRY, Brooklyn (b/1811 Ireland; d/X-9-1886) MD CPSNY 1842; MRCS Ireland 1833. *Med reg NY NJ Conn* 1887:259. *Bost m & s jour* 115:361, 1886. *Atkinson* I:691-92.

DUER, ROBERT, Md (d/1840 Baton Rouge, La) MD UPa 1814. *Med annals Md:* 383.

DUFF, JAMES H , Pittsburgh (d/XII-22-1884 @ 61) <ng Jefferson Med Coll> *Med bull med & surg* 1885:60. *Reg Pa phys* 1881-87: 584.

DUFF, JAMES HENDERSON KIRK, Pittsburgh (b/ 1880? d/IV-16-1905 @ 25) MD Western Pa Med Coll 1904. *Pa med jour* 9:28, 1905/06.

DUFF, JOHN HENRY, Brooklyn (d/XII-29-1864 @ 32) MD CPSNY 1855. *Med surg rep Phila* 12:236, 1864/65.

DUFF, JOHN MILTON, Pittsburgh (b/X-16-1849 Newlinsburg, Pa; d/V-14-1904) MD Jefferson 1874. *Pa med jour* 7:335, 503, 1903/04.

DUFF, JOSIAS STEVENSON, Allegheny, Pa (b/1855 St Clarisville, O; d/III-23-1904) MD Columbus Med Coll 1881. *Pa med jour* 7:335, 391, 1903/04. *Polk* 1886: 739 (Cadiz, O).

DUFF, SAMUEL WATSON, Salem, Ind (b/1841? d/I-13 1894 @ 53) MD Miami 1878. *JAMA* 22:158, 1894. *Polk* 1886: 335.

DUFFAU, JUSTUS, Houston, Tex (d/X-9-1893 Austin) MD Jefferson 1887. *JAMA* 21:667, 1893. *Texas cour-rec med* 11:46, 1893. *Polk* 1890: 1082.

DUFFIELD, BENJAMIN, Philadelphia (b/XI-3-1753; d/XII-13-1799) <MD UPa 1774> AB 1771. *Tr CPP* ns4:449-50, 1863-74; cent vol: 221.

DUFFIELD, HENRY, Carlisle, Pa 1852-54; New London 8 yrs; Oxford (b/1801 Lancaster; d/XII-5-1865 Elkview, Pa) MD Hahnemann Phila 1852. *Tr Am Inst Homeop* 1866: 155. *Amer homeop obs* 3:103, 1866. *Med surg rep Phila* 13:430, 1865.

DUFFIELD, SAMUEL, Philadelphia (b/1732; d/XII-27-1814) MB UPa 1768. *Tr CPP* cent vol: 221.

DUFFIELD, SAMUEL, Kinzers Pa (b/VII-3-1795 Strasburg; d/II-24-1853 Salisbury) MD UPa 1817; AB 1811. *Matrics, Coll U Pa*: 47.

DUFFIELD, SAMUEL ELLIOT, McConnellsburg Pa (d/ X-21-1884 @ 63) MD UPa 1843. *Med surg rep Phila* 51: 604, 1884.

DUFFY, CHARLES Sr, Catherine Lake, NC (b/IX-2-1808 Ireland; d/VIII-24-1892 Newbern, NC) <MD Ireland> *Tr NC Med Soc* 1897: 181. *Butler* 1878:592.

DUFFY, CHARLES, Jr, Newbern, NC (b/VII-18-1838 Richland; d/1893?) MD UCNY 1859. *Tr NC Med Soc* 1893:23 *Atkinson* I:484. *Butler* 1878:592. *Polk* 1886:725.

DUGAS, LOUIS ALEXANDER, Augusta, Ga; CW-CSA (b/I-3-1806 Washington, Ga; d/X-19-1884) MD UMd 1827. *JAMA* 4:111-12, 1885. *So pract* 7:50, 1885. *New Orl m & s jour* ns12:415, 1884. *Butler* 1878:110. *Atkinson* I:10. *K&B* III-354.

DUGGAN, EDWARD H , Brooklyn (d/VI-24-1887 @ c48) MD LICH 1861. *Med reg NY NJ Conn* 1888:252. *Polk* 1886: 645.

DUGGER, HOBART COBBS, Van Dorn, Ala (d/VI-30-1887) MD U Ala 1879. *Tr Med Assoc St Ala* 1888:316. *Polk* 1886: 141.

DU HADWAY, CALEB, Jerseyville, Ill (d/XII-21-1901) MD Missouri Med Coll 1867. *Ill med jour* ns3:399, 1902. *Polk* 1897: 193.

DUHAMEL, WILLIAM HAMES CHAMBERLIN, Washington, DC (b/I or VI-18-1827; d/VIII-15-1883) MD UMd 1849. *JAMA* 1:288, 1883. *Hist Med Soc DC:* 247. *Med ann Md:* 383. *Med bull m & s* 5:258, 1883.

DU KATE, JOHN B , Vincennes, Ind (b/V-2-1849 Louisville, Ky (d/IX-12-1902) MD Louisville Med Coll 1871. *Tr Ind St Med Soc* 1903: 339. *Polk* 1896: 495.

DULIN, ALEXANDER FRANKLIN, Baltimore (b/V-7-1806; d/XI or XII-25-1874) MD UPa 1830. *Tr AMA* 26:467, 1875. *Med annals Md:* 384.

DULIN, ALEXANDER FRANKLIN, Baltimore (b/X-5-1856; d/XII-19-1891) MD UMd 1878. *Med annals Md:* 384. *Med surg rep Phila* 31:460, 1874. *Polk* 1886:436.

DULIN, CHARLES WILLIAM, Nevada, Mo; Kansas City, Mo (b/1873; d/III-23-1903) MD CPS Chicago 1895. *JAMA* 40:929, 1903.

DUMMER, JEREMIAH, Jacksonville, Ill 1833-35; Boonville, Mo 1835-36; Westport, Kans 1836-56 (b/III-6-1805 Hallowell, Me; d/XI-29-1856) MD Bowdoin 1828; AB 1825. *Bowdoin cat*: 1825.

DUN, WALTER ANGUS, Cincinnati (b/III-1-1857 London, O; d/XI-7-1887) MD Miami 1878. *Tr O Med Soc* 1888:708. *Polk* 1886: 741.

DUNAN, ADOLPHUS, Baltimore (b/1795? d/V-25-1838 @ 43) MD UMd 1827. *Med annals Md:* 384.

DUNBAR, ADOLPH WILLIAM, Brooklyn (d/VII-20-1901 @ 28) MD Bellevue 1897. *JAMA* 37:342, 1901.

DUNBAR, EDWARD MORRIS, Hartford, Conn (b/I-24 1843 Springfield, Mass; d/I-21-1876 New Haven) MD Harvard 1868; att Chandler Sci Sch, Dartmouth 1864. *Med reg NY NJ Conn* 1876: 242.

DUNBAR, EUGENE FILLMORE, Roxbury, Mass (d/II-20-1896 @44) MD Harvard 1880; PhG Mass C Pharm 1876. *Bost m&s jour* 134:228 355, 1896. *Polk* 1896: 696.

DUNBAR, HERVEY OWEN [HORACE O; HENRY ORIN], Athol, Mass (b/1849; d/XII-27-1894 @ 45) MD UCNY 1876 (as Hervey Owen). *Bost m & s jour* 132:24, 1895 (as Horace O?) *Mass Med Soc cat* 1894 (as Henry Orin). *Polk* 1886: 453 (as H O).

DUNBAR, JOHN RICHARD WOODCOCK, Baltimore (b/1804 Winchester, Va; d/VII-3-1871) MD UPa 1828; AB Dickinson 1824; AM. *Tr AMA* 23:588-89, 1872. *Med annals Md:* 384.

DUNBAR, ROBERT MACKEY, Winchester, Va (b/IX-25-1808; d/XI-27-1831) MD UPa 1830. *Med annals Md:* 381.

DUNCAN, CHARLES KANE, Montgomery, Ala (d/1892

Mobile) MD UCNY 1859. *UCNY cat*: 1859. *Polk* 1886: 137.

DUNCAN, CHARLES MORRIS, Shelburn, Mass (b/VII 1-1808 Dummerston, Vt; d/X-4-1884) MD Bowdoin 1833. *JAMA* 10, 284, 1888. *Bost m & s jour* 111:384, 1884. *Butler* 1878: 349.

DUNCAN, CHARLES T , Harrodsburg, Ky (d/I-13-1900 @ 35) MD Louisville Hosp Med Coll 1889. *JAMA* 34: 251, 1900.

DUNCAN, L DANIEL [DANIEL LEE], Warren & Sussex Co, NJ (b/1825 Weston, NY; d/XII-25-1883 NYC) MD Castleton 1848 (as Daniel Lee). *Med reg NY NJ Conn* 1884: 229.

DUNCAN, HENDERSON S [?HENRY STALLWORTH] Birmingham Ala (d/IX- -1889) MD U Nashville 1882. *Tr Med Soc Ala* 1890:217. *Polk* 1886: 131.

DUNCAN, WILLIAM FREESE, NYC (d/V-30-1892 @ 40) MD Bellevue 1875; BS Cornell 1873. *Med reg NY NJ Conn* 1893: 301. *Polk* 1886: 677.

DUNCAN, WILLIAM S , Greenup, Ill (d/VIII-2-1905 @80) Cert Exam Bd 1864. *Ill med jour* 8:341,1905.

DUNCAN, WILLIAM STEVENS, Brownsville Pa; CW-USA (b/V-24-1834; d/V-16-1892) MD UPa 1858. *Tr Med Soc Pa* 1892:178-79. *U Pa med alum CW*: 1858. *Atkinson* I:247. *Butler* 1878: 711.

DUNCAN, WILLIAM W , Louisville, Ill (d/II-1-1900 @ 71) MD Hosp Coll Louisville 1885. *Tr Ill St Med Soc* 1899-1900: 463, 509. *JAMA* 34:381, 1900.

DUNCANSON, HENRY A, Washington, DC; USA (b/III-4-1847 DC; d/I-28-1878 Las Cruces, NM) MD Columbian DC 1870. *Hist Med Soc DC:* 304.

DUNGAN, JACOB SHEARER, USN 1851-87 (b/I-29-1825 Bustleton, Pa; d/V- -1903 San Francisco) MD UPa 1848. *U Pa med alum CW*: 1848. Hamersly, *Rec liv off USN & MC*: 198.

DUNGAN, DAVID HAMILTON, Little Rock, Ark; CW-CSA (b/III-11-1839 or III-20-1840 Murray Co, Tenn; d/IV-16-1882 or 1883) MD UPa 1861. *JAMA* 2:725-26, 1884. *U Pa med alum CW*: 1861.

DUNGLISON, RICHARD JAMES, CW-USA Philadelphia (b/XI-13-1834; d/III-4-1901) MD Jefferson 1856; AB UPa 1852; AM 1855. *Pa med jour* 5:296, 1901/02. *Bost m & s jour* 144:269, 1901. *Atkinson* I:68.

DUNGLISON, ROBLEY, London; Charlottesville, Va 1825-35; Phila 1836- (b/I-4-1798 Keswick, Engl; d/X 1-1869) MD U Erlangen 1824; MRCS(E) 1819. *Tr CPP* ns4:294-313, 1869; cent vol: 222. *Tr AMA* 21:461-65, 1870. *Am jour med sci* ns58: 295-97, 1869. *Med annals Md:* 384-85. *K&B* III: 357.

DUNHAM, CARROLL, NYC & Newburgh, NY (b/X-29 1828 NYC; d/II-18-1877 Irvington-on-Hudson) <MD NY Med Coll 1850> Hon MD Hahn Phila 1870. *Tr Am Inst Homeop* 1877:961. *Hahn mo* 12:347, 1877. *Homeop times* 4:285, 1877. *New Engl med gaz* 12:226, 1877. Homeopath.

DUNHAM, CHARLES, Bordentown, NJ (b/II-7-1830 New Brunswick, NJ; d/XII-9-1875) MD UPa 1850. *Med reg NY NJ Conn* 1876: 242. *Tr AMA* 27:655-56, 1876. *Tr Med Soc NJ* 1876:136-37.

DUNHAM, CHARLES HENRY, Trenton, NJ (b/III-24-1839 Middlesex Co; d/X-16-1895) MD UPa 1864. *Tr Med Soc NJ* 1896: 364-65.

DUNHAM, GEORGE DANIEL, Plattsburgh, NY (d/XII 1-1891) MD Dartmouth 1862. *Northwest m jour* 20:16 1892. *Bost m & s jour* 125:612, 1891. *Tr Med Soc St NY* 1892: 464. *Butler* 1878: 551.

DUNHAM, VALENTINE, Madison Co, Ind (b/V-12-1812; d/II-22-1882) MD unknown. *Tr Ind St Med Soc* 1882: 201.

DUNKEL, GEORGE AUGUSTUS, Baltimore (b/1763? d/V-19 or VI-4-1838 @ 74) MD unknown. *Med annals Md:* 385.

DUNKEL [DUNKLE] THOMAS A , Reading, Pa (d/I-14-1894 @ 50) MD Jefferson 1865. *JAMA* 22:122, 1894. *Polk* 1886: 832.

DUNKLIN, W W [W A], Galveston, Tex (d/V- -1881) MD ?Galveston 1869. *Tex m & s rec* 2:80, 1882.

DUNLAP, ALEXANDER, Greenfield, O 1839-46; Ripley 1846-56; Springfield 1856- (b/I-12-1815 Brown Co; d/II-16-1894) <MD Cincinnati Med Coll 1839> AB Miami 1836. *Tr O Med Soc* 1894:36-38. *Buff m & s jour* 33:555-56, 1894. *JAMA* 22:276 1894. *Atkinson* I:626. *K&B* III:357-58.

DUNLAP, CHARLES ROBERT PINCKNEY, NYC; St Paul Minn; Brunswick, Md; Austin, Ill (b/II-26-1827 Brunswick, Me; d/II-23-1906) MD Bowdoin 1849; AB 1846; AM 1849. *Bowdoin cat*: 1846.

DUNLAP, JAMES, Northampton, Mass (b/II-13-1823 Pelham; d/VIII-3-1896) MD CPSNY 1850; ng Amherst 1847. *Bost m & s jour* 136:555, 1897. *JAMA* 27:449, 1896. *Polk* 1896: 720.

DUNLAP, JOHN McDOUGALL, Indianapolis, Ind (b/V 11-1829; d/III-13-1899) MD Med Coll Ohio 1859. *Tr Ind St Med Soc* 1899:408-09. *JAMA* 32:733, 1899. *Polk* 1886: 322.

DUNLAP, JOHN MILLER, Manheim, Pa (b/Lancaster Co; d/IV-4-1898 @ 76) MD Jefferson 1845. *JAMA* 30: 933, 1898. *Polk* 1886: 806.

DUNLAP, JOSEPH BISPHAM, CW-USA (b/V-1-1817 Phila; d/VIII-21-1871 Norristown, Pa) MD UPa 1840. *U Pa med alum CW*: 1840.

DUNLAP, JOSEPH PATTERSON, Syracuse, NY (d/III-29-1896 @ 82) MD Geneva 1842. *Tr Med Soc St NY* 1897:479. *Polk* 1886: 710.

DUNLAP, RICHARD W , Danville, Ky (b/VII-4-1817 Fayette Co; d/VII-27-1885) MD Transylvania 1839. *New Orl m & s jour* ns13: 256, 1885.

DUNLAP, WILLIAM HERBERT, Syracuse, NY (b/1853; d/XI-11-1895) MD Syracuse 1878. *JAMA* 25:968, 1895. *Polk* 1886: 710.

DUNN, D C , O'Fallon, Ill (d/VII-23-1905 @ 61) MD Louisville Med Coll 1872. *Ill med jour* 8:185, 1905. *Polk* 1886: 291.

DUNN, JAMES, CW-CSA; (b/V-7-1831 Petersburg, Va; d/I-19-1885) MD UPa 1852. *U Pa med alum CW*: 1852.

DUNN, JAMES B , Raleigh NC (b/Wake Forest, NC; d/XII-22-1895 @ 74) MD UPa 1849. *NC med jour* 37: 189-90, 1896. *Polk* 1886: 725.

DUNN, JOHN ALFRED, Cotile, La (b/IX-5-1860 Montgomery; d/X-31-1885) MD ULa 1881. *New Orl m & s jour* ns13: 914-15, 1886.

DUNN, JOHN SIMPSON, Pittsburgh (d/III-22-1905 @ 30) MD Western Pa Med Coll 1900. *Pa med jour* 9:523, 1905/06.

DUNN, JOHN WESLEY, Washington, DC (b/XII-30-1858 Phila; d/XII-30-1890) MD Columbian DC 1880. *Hist Med Soc DC:* 327. *Polk* 1886: 212.

DUNN, McCANN [?McLEAN], Bloomington, Ill (d/II-27-1882) MD Hahnemann 1862. *U S med inv* 15:312, 1882. Homeopath.

DUNN, RICHARD L , Yazoo City, Miss (d/VII-10-1896 @ 60) MD Tulane 1859. *JAMA* 27:226, 1896. *Polk* 1896: 816.

DUNN, ROSS, Nashville (d/VI-29/30-1899 @ 33) MD U Tenn 1889. *So pract* 21:408, 1899. *JAMA* 33:427, 1899.

DUNN, STEPHEN JOSEPH, Springfield, Mass (d/VI-27 1903 Hartford, Conn) MD Balto Med Coll 1896. *Bost m & s jour* 149: 114, 1903. *Polk* 1900: 891.

DUNN, THEOPHILUS CALHOUN, Newport, RI (d/II-26-1871) MD UPa 1871. *Tr AMA* 32:502 1881. *Med surg rep Phila* 24:344, 1871.

DUNN, THOMAS DEWITT, West Chester Pa (b/I-30-1854 Meadville; d/V-6-1898) MD UPa 1881. *Pa med jour* 2:436-38,1899. *JAMA* 30:1248,1898. *K&B* III:359.

DUNN, WESLEY A , Chicago (d/III-29-1897 Naples, Italy) MD Hahnemann Chic 1881. *JAMA* 28: ? ,1897. *No Amer jour homeop* 45:336, 1897. *Tr Am Inst Homeop* 1897: 63. *Polk* 1896: 382. Homeopath.

DUNN, WILLIAM ALLEN, CW-CSA; (b/1835 Raleigh, NC; d/1864, Ft Delaware Prison) MD UPa 1860. *U Pa med alum CW*: 1860. *UNC cat*: 174.

DUNNE, ALEXANDER J , Springfield, Mass (d/IV-22-1898 @ 36) MD CPS Balto 1884. *JAMA* 30: 1125, 1897. *Polk* 1886:197 (Thompsonville, Conn).

DUNNE, HENRY RUSSELL, Westerly, RI (b/II-18-1853 Bathurst, NB; d/X-15-1899) MD UCNY 1879. *Tr RI Med Soc* 6:132-33, 1899-1903. *Polk* 1896: 1354.

DUNNELL, HENRY GALE, NYC (b/1804 Albany; d/IX 24-1868) MD CPSNY 1826. *Tr Am Inst Homeop* 1893:139. *New Engl med gaz* 6:191, 1871. Homeopath.

DUNNELLS, JOHN EMERY, Harrison, Me (b/XI-24-1818 Newfield; d/I-3-1867) MD Bowdoin 1842. *Tr Me Med Assoc* 1866-68: 230-33.

DUNNIGAN, JOSEPH H, Buffalo (b/1864; d/I-4 1895) <MD Niagara U> *Buff m & s jour* 34: 429-30, 1895.

DUNNING, CHARLES HENRY, NYC (d/VI-29-1886 @ 25) MD NY Homeop Med Coll 1882. *No Amer jour homeop* 34:696, 1886. *Polk* 1886:677. Homeopath.

DUNNING, EDWIN B , PawPaw, Mich (d/VIII-3-1894) MD UCNY 1854. *JAMA* 23:248, 1894. *Butler* 1878: 372.

DUNNING, FREDERICK, Easton, Md (d/V-9-1896) MD Jefferson 1892. *JAMA* 26:1038, 1896. *Polk* 1896:670.

DUNOTT, THOMAS JUSTUS, Harrisburg, Pa (b/III or V-29-1831 Phila; d/V-28-1893) MD Jefferson 1852. *Tr Med Soc Pa* 24:384-85,1894. *Med annals Md:*386.

DUNPHY, JAMES WALTER, NYC (d/X-1-1901 @ 27) MD CPSNY 1895. *Bost m & s jour* 145: 419, 1901.

DUNPHY, JOHN F, NYC (d/VIII-12-1888 @38) MD Georgetown 1873. *Med reg NY NJ Conn* 1889:273. *Polk* 1886: 677.

DUNSTER, EDWARD SWIFT, NYC (b/IX-2-1834 Springvale, Me;d/V-3-1888 Ann Arbor, Mich) MD Med Coll NY 1859; AB Harv 1856; AM 1859? Hon MD Dartmouth 1881. *Med reg NY NJ Conn* 1888: 252. *JAMA* 10:762-63, 1888. *Bost m & s j* 118:536, 611, 1888. *K&B* III:359.

DUPEE, HORACE, Dorchester, Mass (d/VIII-7-1891 @81) MD Harvard 1837; AB 1832. *Bost m & s jour* 125:180,1891. *Atkinson* I:621. *Polk* 1890: 537.

DUPERRIER, ALFRED, New Iberia, La (d/III-22-1904 @ 73) MD Tulane 1847. *New Orl m & s jour* 56:795, 1904. *Polk* 1896: 619.

DUPRE [DUPREE], DANIEL, Dallas, Tex (d/XI-25-1898 @ 77) MD UPa 1847; att Wake Forest. *JAMA* 1542, 1898. *Polk* 1896: 1443.

DUPREE, JAMES W , Baton Rouge, La (d/V-26-1906 Cincinnati) <MD New Orl Sch Med 1861> *So pract* 28: 596, 1906. *New Orl m&s j* 59:86, 1906. *Polk* 1896: 613.

DURANT, JAMES STARRETT, Danville, Vt (b/X-22-1824 Walden, Vt; d/I-9-1892) MD Dartmouth 1855; AB Amherst 1852. *Amherst, Men of*: 1852. *Polk* 1886: 904.

DURFEE, NATHAN, Fall River, Mass (b/VI-18-1799; d/IV-6-1876) MD Harvard 1831; AB Brown 1824; AM. *Brown hist cat*: 1824.

DURGIN, FRANK ALBERT, Salem, Mass (d/XI-4-1886 @31) MD CPSNY 1881. *Bost m&s j* 115:464 1886.

DURGIN, OBADIAH ELKINS, Deering, Me (b/1795 Boscawen, NH; d/III-28-1879) MD Brown 1821. *Tr Me Med Assoc* 1879:685-56.

DURKEE, ROBERT ALOYSIUS, Baltimore (b/ca 1800; d/1848) MD UPa 1822; Hon MD Washington U, Balto 1840. *Med annals Md:* 386.

DURYEA, WILLIAM RICHMOND SMITH, Flemington, NJ; Jerseyville, Ill (d/VIII-30-1858) MD UPa 1833. *Tr Med Soc NJ* 1872:133.

DUSENBERY, EDWIN LAFAYETTE, Lexington, NC; CW-CSA (b/1824; d/1862 in battle) MD unknown; AB UNC 1845. *UNC cat*: 175.

DUSTMAN, WILLIAM HENRY, NYC (d/I-4-1899 @

42) MD Bellevue 1886. *Bost m & s jour* 140:50, 1899. *Polk* 1886: 1050.

DUTCHER, BENJAMIN C , Newark, NJ (d/X-20-1889 @ 85?) Cert Exam Bd 1832. *Med vis* 5:408, 1889. Homeopath; dentist 1869-

DUTCHER, GEORGE THOMAS, Pasadena, Cal (d/VI-23-1899 @ 30) MD CPSNY 1894. *JAMA* 33:174, 1899. *Polk* 1896: 1021 (Far Rockaway, NY).

DUTTON, THOMAS ALBERT, West Haven, Conn (b/I 29-1802 Oxford; d/IX-14-1881) Lic Conn Med Soc 1824. *Proc Conn Med Soc* ns2: 162, 1882.

DUVAL, CLAIBORNE ALEXANDER Sr, CW-CSA; Houma, La (d/I-23-1906 @ 73) MD Jefferson 1857. *New Orl m & s jour* 58:779, 1906. *Polk* 1890: 487.

DUVAL, EDMUND PARRY, Annapolis, Md (b/VI-28-1826 Montgomery Co; d/IX-5-1901) MD UPa 1847. *Med annals Md:* 386-87. *Polk* 1893: 557.

DUVAL, ELIAS R , USA 1858-59; CW-CSA Ft Smith, Ark (b/VIII-13-1836 Ft Smith; d/X-8-1885) MD UPa 1858. *New Orl m & s jour* ns13:420, 1885. *Atkinson* I:327. *Butler* 1878: 36.

DUVAL, JOHN S , Houston, Tex (b/Sumner Co, Tenn; d/XII-14-1858) MD U Louisville 1851. *Nashville jour m & s* 16:92-93, 1859.

DUVAL, WASHINGTON, Montgomery Co, Md (b/VI-23-1776; d/II-26-1874) MD UMd 1820. *Med annals Md:* 387. *Butler* 1874: 319.

DUVALL, GRAFTON, Frederick Co, Md (b/1780; d/VIII-22-1841) MD UPa 1802. *Med annals Md:* 387.

DUVALL, MARIUS, USN 1842-80; Baltimore (d/II-21-1891 @ 73) MD UPa 1848; MD Washington Med Coll Balto betw 1831 & 1838. *Bost m & s jour* 124: 224, 1891. *Hist Med Soc DC:* 275. *JAMA* 16, 428, 1891. Hamersly, *Rec living off USN & MC*: 195.

DUVALL, P M , Campbell, Ill (d/III-17-1899) MD Ky Sch Med 1877. *JAMA* 32: 787, 1899. *Polk* 1893: 324.

DUZAN, GEORGE NELSON, Indianapolis (d/XI-6-1893) MD U Nashville 1865; MD U Louisville 1872. *JAMA* 21:784, 1893. *Butler* 1878: 200.

DWIGGINS, MOSES FRAZIER, Richmond, Ind (b/IV-25-1852 Clinton, O; d/I-20-1890) MD Cincinnati Coll Med & Surg 1877. *Tr Ind St Med Soc* 1890:161.

DWIGHT, FRANCIS EDWIN, ? NYC (b/Clinton, NY; d/II-2-1885 NYC) MD CPSNY 1882. *Med reg NY NJ Conn* 1885:234.

DWIGHT, JOHN, Roxbury, Mass (b/XII-22-1773 Shirley; d/VIII-5-1853) Stud med w/Dr John Jeffries, Bost; AM Harvard 1800. Palmer's *Necrol Harv alum*: 28.

DWIGHT, WILLIAM, N Amherst, Mass (d/XI-13-1892 @ 71) MD Berkshire 1843. *Bost m & s jour* 127: 492, 1892. *Polk* 1886: 470.

DWIGHT, WILLIAM WHITE, ?NYC (d/VII-11-1861) MD Harvard 1830; AB Yale 1826; AM 1830. *Med reg NY NJ Conn* 1862: 154.

DWINELLE, JAMES ELLIOTT, Baltimore (b/I-30-1830 Cazenovia, NY; d/VII-18-1902) MD Jefferson 1854. *Med annals Md:* 387. *Polk* 1886: 436.

DWYER, JOHN, Hartford, Conn (b/Ireland; d/III-20-1898) MD UCNY 1871. *Proc Conn Med Soc* 1898: 366-68. *JAMA* 30: 807, 1898. *Polk* 1896: 279.

DWYER, PETER J , St Paul, Minn (d/III-30-1895 @ 55) <MD Queen's Coll Dublin 1869; MD Glasgow 1863> *JAMA* 24: 609, 1895. *Polk* 1886: 517.

DYAS, GEORGE KEATING, Chicago (b/Rathangan Ire; d/VIII-24-1895) MD Chic Med Coll 1869. *JAMA* 25: 383, 1895. *Chic med rec* 9:187,1895. *Polk* 1886: 262.

DYAS, WILLIAM GODFREY, Chicago (b/XI-4-1807 Dublin Ire; d/II-17-1895) <MRCS(I) 1830; FRCS(I) 1845> *JAMA* 24:294, 1895. *Chic med rec* 8:248, 259, 1895; 9:339, 1895. *Atkinson* I: 612.

DYCHE, DAVID R , Evanston, Ill (b/III-11-1827 Lebanon, O; d/VIII-4-1893) MD Med Coll O 1852. *JAMA* 21: 247, 1893. *Chic med rec* 5:141, 1893.

DYER, ANDERSON DANA, Brandon, Vt (d/IV-12-1886 @ 27) MD Bellevue 1883. *Bost m & s jour* 114: 360, 1886; 115:630, 1886.

DYER, AUGUSTUS EBENEZER, Natick Mass (d/IX 29-1865) MD Harv 1864. *Med s rep Phila* 13:262, 1865.

DYER, EDWARD C , Spencer, Mass (d/VII-1 1865 @ 50) MD unknown. *Bost m & s jour* 72:516, 1865.

DYER, ELIJAH, Norwich, Conn (b/III-22-1805 Canterbury; d/III-10-1882) MD Berkshire 1828; ng Bowdoin Med Sch. *Proc Conn Med Soc* 82:168. *Atkinson* I: 463. *Butler* 1878: 76.

DYER, EZRA, CW-USA; Cambridge, Mass; Newport, RI; Pittsburgh; Philadelphia (b/X-17-1836; d/II-9-1887) MD Harvard 1859; AB 1857. *Bost m & s jour* 116:172, 1887. *Harvard in CW*: 101. *K&B* III:362.

DYER, GEORGE, Trumbull, Conn (b/VIII-1-1802 Windham; d/V-28-1878) MD Yale 1827; AB Brown 1824. *Brown hist cat*: 1824. *Butler* 1878: 75.

DYER, HENRY, Boston (d/IX-21-1891 @ 87) MD Harvard 1829; AB 1826. *Bost m & s jour* 125: 336, 1891. *Polk* 1886: 677 (NYC).

DYER, JOHN F , Chicota, Tex (b/Knoxville Tenn; d/XI-23-1905 @39 Mineral Wells) MD West Reserve 1902. *Tex st jour med* 1:256, 1905/06.

DYER, JOHN IGNATIUS, St Mary's Co, Md; Washington, DC (b/V-17-1827 DC; d/V-9-1903) MD Columbian, DC 1847. *Hist Med Soc DC:* 240. *Polk* 1886:212.

DYER, JONAH FRANKLIN, Gloucester, Mass (b/IV-15 1826 Eastport, Me; d/II-9-1879) MD Bowdoin 1849. *Bost m & s jour* 100: 1879.

DYER, REUBEN F , CW-USA; Ottawa, Ill (b/I-29-1833 Strong, Me; d/I-25-1896) <MD Amer Med Coll (Ecl) Cincinnati 1856> *JAMA* 26:391, 1896. *Tr Ill St Med Soc* 1896: 56-58. *Polk* 1886: 291.

DYER, WILLIAM SNOW, ?Chicago; CW-USA (d/VIII 14-1882) MD unknown; att Harvard Med Sch 1857-58. *Harvard in CW*: 251.

DYSART, BENJAMIN G [or B] Paris, Mo (d/I-17-1904 @ 70) MD Jefferson 1859. *So pract* 26: 114, 1904. *Butler* 1878: 427.

EADIE, WILLIAM G , Staten Isl, NYC (d/VII-6-1870) MD CPSNY 1837. *Med reg NY NJ Conn* 1871: 354.

EADS, BENJAMIN FRANKLIN, CW-CSA; Marshall, Tex 1865- (b/III-9-1833 Caroline Co, Va; d/II-1-1903) MD UPa 1856; att UVa 1854; stud École de Paris. *Tr Tex St Med Assoc* 1903: 50-51. *Atkinson* I:442. *U Pa med alum CW*: 1856. *Polk* 1896: 1441.

EAGAN, EPHRAIM PRENTISS, CW-CSA (d/V-23-1864 @ 25) ng UMich M Dept 1858-59. *UMich cat*:687.

EAGER, WILLIAM BLAKE, Jr, Middletown, NY; CW-USA (b/XII-11-1824; d/I-18-1890) MD CPSNY 1848. *Med reg NY NJ Conn* 1890: 267. *Bost m & s jour* 122:170, 1890. *Polk* 1886: 668.

EAGLES, COLUMBUS W, Old Sparta NC (d/betw VII-15 & VIII-2-1886 @34) MD UPa 1875. *NC med jour* 18:196, 1886. *Polk* 1886: 725.

EAGLETON, JAMES MANDEVILLE, CW-USA; Philadelphia (b/XII-11-1838; d/I-1-1905) MD UPa 1859; AB Union (Tenn) 1855. *U Pa med alum CW*: 1859. *Polk* 1886: 815.

EALY, JACOB HUBERT, CW-USA; Palmyra, Mo (b/IV-17-1828 Schellsburg, Pa; d/X-11-1901) MD UPa 1850. *U Pa med alum CW*: 1850. *Polk* 1886: 557.

EARECKSON, RODERICK WINCHESTER, Elkridge, Md (b/II-12-1825 Kent Isl; d/III-1-1891) MD UMd 1848. *Med annals Md:* 388. *Polk* 1886: 442.

EARGLE, JAMES T , Lamkin, Tex (d/V-28-1895 @ 33) MD UTenn 1889. *Tex cour-rec med* 12:288, 1895.

EARHART, JACOB R , Philadelphia (b/II-2-1826 Lancaster, Pa; d/VI-22-1891) MD Hahnemann Phila 1855. *Med vis* 7:270, 1891. *Tr Pa St Hom Med Soc* 1891. *Polk* 815. Homeopath.

EARL, DAVID GARDNER, Lake Mills, Wis (b/I-14-1854 Aztalan; d/VIII-27-1892) MD Rush 1882: MS. *Tr Wis St Med Soc* 1894: 502. *Polk* 1890: 1167.

EARLE, CHARLES WARRINGTON, Chicago (b/IV-2 1845 Westford, Vt; d/XI-19-1893) MD Chic Med Coll 1870. *Buff m & s jour* 33:301, 1893. *Chic m rec* 5:445-47 1893. *JAMA* 21:829-30 1893. *K&B* III:363-34 34.

EARLE, FRANK MARSLAND, Philadelphia (d/XII-11-1893) MD Hahnemann Phila 1876. *Hahn mo* 29:82 (news & advt) 1894. *Polk* 1886: 815. Homeopath.

EARLE, FRANK O , Rye, NY (d/VII-19-1869) MD CPSNY 1865. *Phila med reg & dir* 1871:301.

EARLE, PLINY, Northampton, Mass (b/XII-31-1809; d/V-17-1892) MD UPa 1837. *Proc Conn Med Soc* 1893:231. *Bost m & s jour* 126:512, 1892. *Atkinson* I:336. *Butler* 1878: 349. *K&B* III:364-65.

EARLE, WESLEY CLARK, CW-USA; Buffalo (b/I-13 1835 Vt; d/VI-19-1899) MD Bellevue 1864. *Buff m & s jour* 38:939-40, 1899. *JAMA* 33:52, 1899.

EARLEY, CHARLES RICHARD, Ridgway Pa (d/V-16 1898 @74) <ng Cincinnati Coll Med & Surg; ng Jefferson> *JAMA* 30:1366,1898. *Polk* 1896: 1333.

EARLL, GEORGE W , Onondaga Co, NY (b/Mottville; d/VII-8-1890) MD Buffalo 1856. *Tr NY St Med Soc* 11:741 ff, 1894. *Polk* 1886:712 (Tully, NY) & 855 (Pickens CH, SC).

EARLY, MAURICE B , NYC (b/Richmond, Va; d/VI-21-1902 @ 53) MD UCNY 1869. *Bost m & s jour* 146:706, 1902. *Polk* 1896: 1050.

EASLEY, EDWARD TANDY, Little Rock, Ark (b/X-29 1842; d/IX-30-1878) MD Louisville Med Coll 1873; AM Madison. *Tr AMA* 30:813-16, 1879. *New Orl m & s jour* ns6:506-08, 1878-79. *Atkinson* I:347.

EASLEY, JOHN T , Stanton, Ill (d/V-11-1905 @ 51) MD Missouri Med Coll (Kemper) 1879. *Ill med jour* 7:611, 1905. *Polk* 1886: 252.

EASLEY, WILLIAM DANIEL, ?Montgomery, WVa; CW-CSA (b/XII-1-1831 Pearsburg, Va; d/IX-21-1877) MD UPa 1855. *U Pa med alum CW*: 1855.

EAST, HARRY H , Xenia, Ill (d/VI-2-1905 @ 45 St Louis) <MD Barnes Med Coll St Louis 1890> *Ill med jour* 8:80, 1905.

EAST, W A , Hallettsville & Austin, Tex (d/XII-9-1885) MD unknown. *Tex cour rec med* 3:219, 1886. *Daniel's Tex med jour* 1:339, 1886. *New Orl m & s jour* ns13:664, 1886. *Butler* 1878: 787.

EASTMAN, ALBERT FAXON, Abington, Mass (b/1843 Westford, Vt; d/II-13-1884) MD UVt 1873. *Bost m & s jour* 111:619, 1884.

EASTMAN, B D , CW-USA (d/II-19-1865) MD unknown. *Nat med jour* 1:294, 1870/71.

EASTMAN, CHARLES CARROLL, Binghamton, NY (d/IV-12-1900) <MD Geneva 1870> AB Hobart 1866; AM 1869. *JAMA* 34: 1021, 1900. *Polk* 1896: 989.

EASTMAN, EDMUND TUCKER, Boston (d/XI-7-1892 @73) MD Harvard 1850; AB 1846. *Bost m & s jour* 127:492. *Polk* 1890:537.

EASTMAN, HIRAM NEWTON, Candor & Owego, NY to 1859; Geneva 1861-73; Waverly, Ia 1 yr; Owego 1874- (b/VIII-10-1810 Fairfield; d/X-14-1879 Owego) MD Castleton 1844. *Tr Med Soc St NY* 1880:460-63. *Butler* 1874: 536.

EASTMAN, JOSEPH A , Indianapolis (b/I-29-1842 Fulton Co, NY; d/VI-5-1902) MD Georgetown 1865; MD Bellevue 1870. *Tr Med Soc St NY* 1903: [412]. *Tr Ind St Med Soc* 1903:340-41. *K&B* III:365-66.

EASTMAN, JOSEPH STEELE, Berkeley, Cal (b/VII-7-1854 Hanover, Ind; d/IV-19-1903) MD Missouri Med Coll (Kemper) 1878. *Calif st jour med* 1:173, 1903. *Polk* 1886:163.

EASTMAN, JOSIAH CALEF, Hampstead, NH (b/1811; d/XI-27-1897) MD Dartmouth 1837. *JAMA* 29: 1234, 1897. *Tr NH Med Soc* 1898: 255-256. *Polk* 1886: 592.

EASTMAN, LEONARD O , Union, NY (d/IX-15-1897)

 Spec. educ'l status abbrev. as: ***ng*** = college verified attendance without degree;

MD Buffalo 1889. *JAMA* 29:709, 1897. *Polk* 1896: 1108.

EASTMAN, LEWIS M , Baltimore (b/VII-17-1836; d/VI-27-1901) MD UMd 1859. *Med annals Md:* 388-89. *Polk* 1893: 560.

EASTMAN, SANFORD, Buffalo (b/IX-29-1821 Lodi, NY; d/I-8-1874 Riverside Cal) MD Buffalo 1851; AB Amherst 1841. *Buff m & s jour* 13:232-34, 1874.

EASTMAN, TIMOTHY, Eastmanville, Mich (b/1798? d/II-21-1868 @ 70) MD unknown. *Phila med reg & dir* 1871:295. *Med surg rep Phila* 18:226, 1868.

EASTWOOD, JOHN, Pittsfield, Mass (d/II-12-1861) MD Berkshire 1860. *Bost m & s jour* 64:60, 1861.

EATON, DARWIN GROVES, Brooklyn (b/III-6-1822; d/III-17-1895) Hon MD LICH 1864; att Albany Normal Coll 1864. *Med reg NY NJ Conn* 1895: 220. *JAMA* 24: 497, 1895.

EATON, GEORGE C, North Bend O (d/V-1-1866 @45) MD Med Coll Ohio 1842. *Med s rep Phila* 14: 400, 1866.

EATON, HARRISON, Merrimack, NH (b/XII-13-1813 Hopkinton; d/XI-19-1881 @ 68) MD Berkshire 1836. *Bost m & s jour* 105:628, 1881. *Tr NH Med Soc* 1882: 173-75. *Butler* 1878: 455.

EATON, HEZEKIAH HULBERT, Lexington, Ky (b/ VII-21-1809 Katskill, NY; d/VIII-16-1832) ?Stud Transylvania; AB Rensselaer 1826. *Transylvania jour med & assoc sci* 5:469-81, 1832.

EATON, HOSEA BALLOU, Camden, Me (b/III-24-1822 Plymouth; d/IV-19-1887) MD Bowdoin 1845. *New Engl med gaz* 22:256, 1887. *Tr Am Inst Homeop* 1887: 200. *Polk* 1886: 425. *Cleave*. Homeopath.

EATON, JOHN R , Wilton, Me (b/VII-14-1830; d/IV-1 1885) MD Bowdoin 1856. *Tr Me Med Assoc* 1885: 563-64. *Butler* 1878: 306.

EATON, JOSEPH, Newark, NJ (b/1750 Hopewell; d/V 10-1775) MD unknown; AB Brown 1769. *Brown hist cat* 1769.

EATON, JOSEPH, USA (b/VII-24-1784 Reading, Mass; d/III-17-1860) MD Harvard 1814; AB 1810; AM 1814. *Bost m & s jour* 62:292, 1860. Palmer's *Necrol Harvard alum*: 300. *Tr AMA* 13:822, 1860.

EATON, MORTON MONROE, CW-US San Comm; Cincinnati (b/IV-21-1839 Pelham, Mass; d/X-21-1889 @ 50) MD Rush 1861. *Med adv* 15:114, 1884. *Med vis* 5: 408, 1889. *Med couns* 14:528, 1889. *Polk* 1886: 741. Homeopath.

EATON, ROLLIN, Philadelphia; Enosburg, Vt (b/X-26-1810 Enosburg; d/X-13-1858) MD Woodstock 1840. *Med surg rep Phila* ns1:60, 1858/59.

EATON, SAMUEL WASHINGTON, Rowan Co, NC; CW-CSA (b/Davie Co, NC; d/1896) MD UPa 1868. *U Pa med alum CW*: 1868.

EATON, WILLIAM, Lloydsville, O (d/X-6-1896) MD Rush 1867. *JAMA* 27: 878, 1896.

EAVENSON, SARAH T ROGERS, Buck Hill Falls, Pa (d/VII-29-1906) <MD Amer Med Coll Phila 1860> *Pa med jour* 9:805, 1905/06. *Polk* 1896: 1303.

EBERLE, AUGUSTUS, CW-USA (d/XI-16-1864 Duvall's Bluff, Ark) MD unknown. *Nat med jour* 1:294, 1870/71.

EBERLE, JOHN, Lexington, Ky; Cincinnati (b/XII-10-1787 Lancaster Co, Pa; d/II-2-1838) <MD UPa 1809> *Transylvania jour med & assoc sci* 11:199-200, 1838. *Nashville jour m & s* ns1:319, 1866.

EBERT, CHARLES M , Mauch Chunk, Pa (b/Prussia; d/ 1906 @ 84) <MD Jefferson 1860> *Pa med jour* 9:805, 1905/06. *Off'l reg Pa phys* 1881-88: 102.

EBRIGHT, THOMAS McG , Akron, O (d/IV-11-1894) MD Starling 1851. *JAMA* 22:674, 1894.

ECCLES, JOHN, Philadelphia (d/I-18-1902 Boscas del Toro, Colombia) MD UPa 1896. *Penn med jour* 6:260, 1902/03.

ECKARD, FREDERICK SIMEON, Montgomery Co, Pa (d/VI-20-1856) MD UPa 1835. *Tr CPP* cent vol:281.

ECKEL, JOHN NICKOLEIUS, San Francisco (d/III-5-1901) <MD St Louis Homeop 1879> *Tr Am Inst Homeop* 1901: 914. *Polk* 1886: 171.

ECKELS, WILLIAM, Mechanicsburg, Pa (d/III-8-1906 @ 73) <ng UPa 1855; PhG Phila 1879> *Pa med jour* 9:524, 1905/06.

ECKERT, GEORGE NICHOLAS, Philadelphia (d/VI-28-1865 @ 63) MD UPa 1824. *Med surg rep Phila* 13:32, 1865.

ECKERT [ECHART] ROBERT PICKHAM, Chicago (d/VIII-28-1895) MD Rush 1892. *JAMA* 25: 427, 1895. *Polk* 1896: 382.

ECKFELDT, FREDERICK, Washington, DC (d/IV-10-1884 @ 44) MD Georgetown 1882. *Med surg rep Phila* 50:544, 1884.

EDDINS, SIMEON JACKSON, Tuscaloosa (b/1816; d/V 1859) MD UPa 1843; ng U Ala 1837. *U Ala cat*:55.

EDDY, HIRAM McC , Jersey City, NJ (b/VII-14-1848 Springville; d/XII-2-1895) MD UCNY 1872. *Bost m & s jour* 133:605, 1895. *Atkinson* I: 356. *Polk* 1886: 604.

EDDY, JOHN MATHEWSON, Providence, RI (d/1817 Havana, Cuba) Hon MD Brown 1815. *Tr RI Med Soc* I:44, 1859-77.

EDDY, LOREN L , Olean, NY (d/III-15-1900 @ 29) MD Buffalo 1897. *Buff m & s jour* 39:696, 1899. *JAMA* 34: 767, 1900.

EDDY, NORMAN, ?Indianapolis; CW-USA (b/XII-10-1810 Scipio, NY; d/I-28-1872 Indianapolis) MD UPa 1835. *U Pa med alum CW*: 1835.

EDEL, CARL, NYC (d/VIII-11-1894 @ 45) <MD U Würzburg 1872> *Med reg NY NJ Conn* 1895:221. *Polk* 1886: 677.

EDES, RICHARD EDWARD, Roxbury, Mass (d/XI-25-1901 @ 32) MD Harvard 1895; AB Johns Hopkins 1889. *Bost m & s jour* 145:610, 637, 1901.

EDGAR, ASBURY P, Collins Ia (d/III-15-1894 @ 40) MD St U Ia 1875. *JAMA* 22:523, 1894. *Polk* 1886: 354.

EDGAR, WILLIAM S, Jacksonville Ill; CW–USA (b/XII 22–1816 Phila; d/1878) <MD Kemper 1841> att Marion Coll, Mo. *Tr AMA* 30:816–17, 1879. *Atkinson* I: 381.

EDGE, BENJAMIN, Jersey City, NJ (b/V–17–1851; d/VII–26–1905) MD Bellevue 1879. *Bost m & s jour* 153:154, 1905. *Polk* 1896: 938.

EDGE, JOHN PENNELL, Downingtown, Pa (b/VI–22–1822 E Caln Twp; d/III–7–1904) MD Jefferson 1846. *Pa med jour* 8:335, 1904/05. *Atkinson* I: 181–82.

EDGERLEE, GEORGE W , Muncie, Ind; CW–USA (d/XI–11–1861) MD Cleveland Med Coll 1854. *Nat med jour* 1:294, 1870/71. *Tr Ind St Med Soc* 1873: 139. Kemper's *Indiana*: 153, 192.

EDGERLY, DAVID MARK, Cambridge, Mass (b/VII–11–1839 New Durham, NH; d/XII–20–1892) MD UCNY 1867; AB Dartmouth 1864. *Bost m & s jour* 127:640, 1892. *Polk* 1896: 545.

EDGERLY, EDWARD F , Moriah, NY (b/1839; d/VI–22–1889) MD Albany 1864. *Med reg NY NJ Conn* 1890:268. *Polk* 1886: 668.

EDGERTON, FRANCIS DANIELS, Middletown, Conn (b/VIII–26–1838 Chatham or E Hampton; d/I–19–1905) MD U Vt 1863; MD CPSNY 1864; AB Wesleyan 1861. *Proc Conn M S* 1905:79–81, 493–97. *Polk* 1900: 344.

EDGERTON, FRANCIS GRISWOLD, E Hampton, Conn (b/III–23–1797 Norwich; d/XI–2–1870) Stud w/Dr Wm P Eaton, Norwich; lic 1825. *Proc Conn Med Soc* 1871:488–91.

EDMISTON, THOMAS BLAND, Weston, WVa (b/XII–1–1844; d/IX–13–1875) MD Bellevue 1868. *Tr Med Soc WVa* 1876: 215; 1884: 154.

EDMONDS, SAMUEL C , Linwood, NJ (d/IX–18–1901 @ 72) MD Jefferson 1851. *JAMA* 37: 847, 1901. *Polk* 1886: 606.

EDMONSTON, RAPHAEL AUGUSTINE, USA (d/VI–5–1900 @ 27 Manila, PI) MD Georgetown 1897. *JAMA* 34: 1645, 1900.

EDMUNDS, JAMES J , Erie Co, NY (d/VIII–25–1869 @ 50) MD Buffalo 1851. *Buff m & s jour* 9:70, 1869.

EDSON, CYRUS, NYC (b/XII–8–1857 Albany; d/XII–3–1903) MD CPSNY 1881; AB Columbia. *Bost m & s jour* 149:662, 1903. *New Orl m & s jour* 56: 571, 1904. *Polk* 1896: 1050.

EDSON, EZRA, Manchester, Vt (d/IV–14–1884 @ 75) MD unknown. *Med surg rep Phila* 50:544, 1884.

EDSON, ISAAC C , Windsor, NY (d/II–23–1905 @ 82) MD Albany 1867. *Tr Med Soc St NY* 1905:[362]. *Polk* 1886: 716.

EDSON, SUSAN ANN, Washington, DC (b/I–4–1823 Aurelius, NY; d/XI–12–1897) MD Cleveland Homeop Med Coll 1854. CW–USA "as nurse & surgeon." *Tr Am Inst Homeop* 1898: 48; 1906: 883. *Polk* 1886: 212.

EDWARDS, CHARLES C , Binghamton, NY (b/Gibson, Pa; d/XI–16–1898 @ 73) MD Jefferson 1875. *JAMA* 31: 1319, 1898. *Polk* 1896:989.

EDWARDS, EMMA WOOD, Newark, NJ (b/VI–5–1845; d/III–29–1896) MD Woman's Med Coll NY Infirmary 1870. *Tr Med Soc NJ* 1896: 359–360.

EDWARDS, ENOCH, Philadelphia (b/1750; d/IV–1802) MD unknown. *JAMA* 3:418–19, 1884.

EDWARDS, FRANCIS SMITH, NYC (b/VI–2–1826; d/VI–1–1865) MD CPSNY 1854. *Med reg NY NJ Conn* 1866: 186.

EDWARDS, GEORGE KERR, Newcastle, Del; Princeton, NJ (d/VI–14–1897) MD UPa 1892; AB Princeton 1889. *JAMA* 28: 1252, 1897.

EDWARDS, GEORGE WILKINSON, Granby, Conn (b/X–12–1836 NYC; d/X–6–1884) MD UCNY 1862. *Proc Conn Med Soc* ns3: 212, 1885. *Med surg rep Phila* 51:496, 1884. *Butler* 1878: 76.

EDWARDS, JOSEPH F, Philadelphia (b/XII–8–1853; d/XII–6–1897) MD UPa 1874; AM Georg'n 1880. *JAMA* 29:1286, 1897. *Tr CPP* cent vol: 222. *Polk* 1886: 215.

EDWARDS, LAWRENCE STEWART, Patchogue, NY (d/VII–25–1903 @ 48) MD Bellevue 1876. *Bost m & s jour* 149: 166, 1903. *Polk* 1886: 701.

EDWARDS, LEWIS ALLISON, USA 1846–66 (b/IX–29–1823 Washington, DC: d/XI–8–1877) MD UPa 1845; AB Princeton 1842. *U Pa med alum CW*: 1845. *Tr AMA* 30: 817–18, 1879. *Hist Med Soc DC:* 257–58. *Med rec* 12:735, 1877.

EDWARDS, NATHAN BROWN, N Chelmsford, Mass (d/VI–12–1893 @ 73) MD Berkshire 1847. *Bost m & s jour* 128:612, 1893. *Butler* 1878: 349.

EDWARDS, THOMAS, Attalla, Ala (d/X–7–1886) MD Cincinnati Coll Med 1838? *Tr Med Assoc St Ala* 1887:305. *Polk* 1886: 130.

EDWARDS, THOMAS PAGE, Newark (b/Marcy, NY; d/VII–4–1900 @ 39) MD UCNY 1885. *Bost m & s jour* 143: 48, 1900. *Polk* 1896: 942.

EDWARDS, WILLIAM J [or H], Warrior Run, Pa (d/X–19–1894 @ 25) MD Jefferson 1893. *JAMA* 23:697, 1894. *Lehigh Valley med mag* 6: 70, 1894–95.

EDWARDS, WILLIAM MILAN, Kalamazoo, Mich (b/IX–17–1855 Peru, Ind; d/IV–26–1905 Ann Arbor) MD U Mich 1884. *Bost m & s jour* 152:536, 1905. *K&B* III:369–70.

EELLS, GEORGE E , Lithopolis, O (d/X–28–1866 @ 54) MD Berkshire 1838. *Tr Ohio St Med Soc* 1873: 265. *Med surg rep Phila* 17:480, 1867.

EELLS, SAMUEL HENRY, Detroit, Mich; CW–USA (d/I–31–1864) ng U Mich Med Dept 1860–61; AB Harvard 1858. *Harvard in CW*: 112. *Nat med jour* 1:294, 1870/71.

EGBERT, AUGUSTUS RILEY, USA 1861–89 (b/I–9–1831 Monmouth Battle Ground, NJ; d/IX–25–1890 Ft Omaha, Neb) MD UPa 1853; AB Princeton 1850. *U Pa med alum CW*: 1853.

EGBERT, DANIEL, USN 1829–71 (b/1799 Freehold, NJ; d/X–24–1875 Phila) MD UPa 1834. *U Pa med alum CW*: 1834.

EGBERT, DAVID NORMAN Jr Lower Merion Twp, Pa (d/II-11-1874 @ Winfield, Kans) MD UPa 1867. *Med surg rep Phila* 30: 204, 1874.

EGBERT, GEORGE, Marion, Ind (b/II-23-1823 Preble Co, O; d/VII-4-1886) MD Rush 1861; MD Bellevue 1871. *Tr Ind St Med Soc* 1887: 189. *Butler* 1878: 200.

EGBERT, JACOB, Pemberton, NJ (b/XII-25-1771; d/ 1831) Lic 1805. *Tr Med Soc NJ* 1871: 176.

EGELSTON, J Q [or D] Olathe, Kans (b/1828: d/I-11-1895) MD Keokuk Med Coll 1858. *JAMA* 24: 101, 1895. *Polk* 1886: 382.

EGGERS, JOHN THADDEUS, Kansas City, Mo (b/ Fairfield, Ia; d/II-21-1892 @ 35) MD Rush 1881. *Tr Med Ass St Mo* 35:266-67, 1892. *Polk* 1886: 551.

EGGMAN, JEREMIAH PATRICK, ?Ill (d/VIII-25-1900) MD St Louis Med Coll 1892) *Ill med jour* ns2: 237, 1900.

EGLE, WILLIAM HENRY, CW-USA; Harrisburg, Pa (b/IX-17-1830; d/II-10 or 19-1901) MD UPa 1859; Hon AM Lafayette. *Pa med jour* 5:296, 1901/02. *Milit surg* 10:93-96, 1901/02. *U Pa med alum CW*: 1859.

EHLE, A S , Greenbush, Wis ; CW-USA (d/IX-22-1867) MD Rush 1865. *Med surg rep Phila* 17:325, 1867.

EHLER, JOHN AUGUSTUS, Lancaster, Pa (b/X-30-1820; d/VI-29-1901) MD Pa Med Coll 1841. *Pa med jour* 4:782, 1900/01; 5:296, 1901/02. *Flint* 1897: 806.

EHRENZELLER, JACOB, West Chester, Pa; RevWar-USA (b/IX-1-1757 Phila; d/VII-18-1838) Stud w/Kuhn & Shippen. *Med reporter* (West Chester) 1:30-31, 1853.

EHRMAN, BENJAMIN, Harrisburg, Pa; Chillicothe, O 1848; Cincinnati 1849- (b/III-3-1812 Jagsthausen, Würtb'g; d/III-15-1886 @ 74) <MD Allentown Acad> *Tr Am Inst Homeop* 1886: 121. *Hahn mo* 21: 269, 1886. *Med adv* 16:763, 1886. *King* I:173, 181. Homeopath.

EHRMAN, ERNEST J , Evansville, Ind (b/X-29-1819 Württemberg; d/XI-24-1879) Stud w/father. *Cincinnati med adv* 8:64, 1880. *Cleave*. Homeopath.

EHRMAN, FREDERICK G , York Co Pa; Cincinnati (b/ Württemberg; d/VI-7-1890 @ 84) <MD Allentown Acad> *Med vis* 9:283 1892. *King*I:151. Homeopath.

EICHELBERGER, WILLIAM CHAMBERS, Terre Haute, Ind (b/VII-19-1840 Pa; d/V-18-1903 Jackson, Tenn) MD Rush 1870. *Tr Ind St Med Soc* 1903:342. *Polk* 1893: 493.

EICHLER, CARL A , NYC (b/Gny; d/I-4-1903 @ 76) "MD Germany" *Bost m & s jour* 148:80, 1893. *Polk* 1896: 1051.

EIDENBENZ, ANTON, NYC (b/Gny; d/XII-31-1903 @ 86) MD UCNY 1881; <MD Giessen 1846> *Bost m & s jour* 150:28, 1904. *Polk* 1896: 1051.

EIGENBRODT, DAVID L , NYC (b/1811; d/I-3 or X-3-1880) MD CPSNY 1836; att? Trinity Coll. *Med reg NY NJ Conn* 1880:235. *Med rec* 17:79, 1880. *Med surg rep Phila* 42:66, 1880.

EIGNUS, WILLIAM T , Kankakee, Ill (d/IX-19-1901) MD Rush 1901. *JAMA* 37:847, 1901. *Ill med jour* ns3: 237, 1901.

EISLER, MORRIS, NYC (b/VIII-17-1818 Hungary; d/ IV-11-1890) Lic NY St Med Soc 1853. *Med reg NY NJ Conn* 1890:268. *Polk* 1886: 677.

ELBERT, JOHN DOWNS, Keosauqua, Ia (b/V-16-1806 Fleming Co, Ky; d/III-28-1865) Lic Cincinnati 1829. *Tr Ia Med Soc* 1867-71: 243-45.

ELDER, ALEXANDER, NYC (b/VI-27-1804; d/II-3-1875) <MD Glasgow c1830> *Med reg NY NJ Conn* 1875: 198.

ELDER, B F , Knightstown, Ind; CW-USA (d/before 1870) MD Med Coll Ohio 1858. *Nat med jour* 1:294, 1870/71. *Tr Ind St Med Soc* 1870: 160.

ELDER, ELIJAH S , Indianapolis (b/1841 Hillsborough, Ind; d/V-9 or 19-1894) MD Med Coll Ohio 1867. *Buff m & s jour* 33:746-47, 1894. *JAMA* 22:854, 1894. *Tr Ind St Med Soc* 1895: 400.

ELDER, JENNIE S , Onondaga Co, NY (b/Syracuse; d/ II-2-1889) MD Syracuse 1878. *Tr NY St Med Soc* 11: 741ff, 1894. *Polk* 1886: 655.

ELDER, LORENZO WELTON, Hoboken, NJ (b/IV-15 1820 Guilford, NY; d/V-11-1892) MD CPSNY 1847. *Med reg NY NJ Conn* 1892:277. *Tr Med Soc NJ* 1893:177-79. *Bost m & s jour* 126:512, 1892. *Atkinson* I:356.

ELDER, SAMUEL M , Jacksonville, Pa (b/V-17-1831; d/VI-17-1868 Armagh) MD Jefferson 1861. *Phila med reg & dir* 1871:297. *Tr Med Soc Pa* 1869:442. *Med surg rep Phila* 19:140, 1868.

ELDER, WILLIAM A , Bloomington, Ill (d/I-3-1895 @ 69) MD Missouri Med Coll (Kemper) 1847. *JAMA* 24: 67, 1895. *Polk* 1890: 301.

ELDREDGE, CHARLES, E Greenwich, RI (b/1784 Brooklyn, Conn; d/IX-15-1838) <ng UPa Med Dept> *Tr RI Med Soc* 1:37-40, 1859.

ELDREDGE, JAMES HENRY, E Greenwich, RI (b/V-27-1816; d/II-20-1891) MD Jefferson 1837. *Bost m & s jour* 124:224, 1891. *Tr RI Med Soc* 1889-93:329-331. *Atkinson* I:543. *Butler* 1878: 746.

ELDRIDGE, CORNELIUS R , CW-USA (d/XII-19-1870 New Albany, Ind) MD UPa 1865. *U Pa med alum CW*: 1865.

ELDRIDGE, ISAAC N , Flint, Mich (b/VIII-5-1818 Richmond, NY; d/I-28-1893) <MD Homeop Hosp Cleveland 1864> *Med vis* 9:1893. *Polk* 1886:492. *Cleave*. Homeopath.

ELDRIDGE, JOHN STUART, US Marine Hosp Serv (d/ XI-19-1901 @ 60 Japan) <"MD in Phila"> *Bost m & s jour* 145:638, 723, 1901.

ELIASON, JOHN, Chestertown, Md (d/IV-4-1874) MD Jefferson 1873. *Med surg rep Phila* 28:452, 1873.

ELIOT, GEORGE, Boston (d/V-22-1891 Venice, Italy) MD Harvard 1890. *Bost m & s jour* 124:570, 1891.

ELIOT, JOHNSON, Washington, DC (b/VIII-24-1815;

d/XII-30-1883) MD Columbian DC 1843; Hon AM Georgetown 1869; DPharm Georgetown 1872. *JAMA* 2: 79-81, 1884. *Hist Med Soc DC:* 233-34. *Med surg rep Phila* 50:64, 1884.

ELKINTON, JOHN ABRAHAM, Philadelphia (b/1801; d/XII-15-1853) MD UPa 1822. *Med surg jour* Phila 2:230, 1854.

ELLEGOOD, ROBERT GRIFFITH, Laurel, Del (b/III-16-1829 Concord; d/III-22-1902) MD Pa Med Coll 1852. *Bost m & s jour* 146:350, 1902. *K&B* III: 358.

ELLEGOOD, WILLIAM THOMAS, CW-USA (b/III-17-1837 Concord, Del; d/XII-4-1867 Hannibal, Mo) MD UPa 1860. *U Pa med alum CW*: 1860.

ELLET, WILLIAM H , NYC (d/1859 @ 55) MD unknown. AB Columbia 1824. *Tr AMA* 13:800, 1860. *Buff m & s jour* 14:703, 1859. *Med surg rep Phila* ns1: 358, 1858/59.

ELLETT, ROBERT T , Christiansburg, Va; CW-CSA (d/V-27-1904) MD Med Coll Va 1858. *JAMA* 43: 61, 1904. Blanton, *Va surg in CW*: 400.

ELLICOTT, LINDLEY, Baltimore (b/I-26-1836; d/VIII-30-1876) MD UMd 1870. *Med annals Md:* 390. *Tr AMA* 28: 617, 1877. *Butler* 1874: 312.

ELLIGER, ARTHUR I, Phila (d/III-21 1871 @25) MD Jefferson 1871. *Med surg rep Phila* 24: 284, 1871.

ELLIOT, DANIEL MITCHELL, Peabody, Mass (d/VII-26-1882 @ 39) MD Harvard 1869; AB Dartmouth 1864. *Bost m & s jour* 107:216, 618, 1882.

ELLIOT, DAVID SANDERS, Fairmount, Ind (d/IV-4-1869 Richmond) MD U Mich 1859. *Tr Ind St Med Soc* 1871: 244.

ELLIOT, EDWARD PEARSON, Asylum Station, Mass (d/I-10-1897 @40) MD Harvard 1882; AB 1875. *Bost m & s jour* 136:48, 75, 121, 690, 1897. *JAMA* 28:236 1897.

ELLIOT, FREDERICK, NYC; CW-USA b/XI-15-1828 Chichester, Engl; d/XII-17-1884) MD CPSNY 1851. *Med reg NY NJ Conn* 1885: 235.

ELLIOT, FREDERICK WILLIAM, Roxbury, Mass (b/IV-1-1855 Contocook, NH; d/VI-28-1899) MD Boston U 1888; AB Brown 1886 [listed w/class 1879] *New Engl med gaz* 34: 1889 (Nov). *Polk* 1893: 589. Homeopath.

ELLIOT, GEORGE H , NYC (d/XII-17-1900 @ 55 Manchester, NH) MD U Denver 1882. *Bost m & s jour* 143:674, 1900. *Polk* 1896: 1051.

ELLIOT, GEORGE THOMPSON, NYC (b/V-11-1827; d/I-28-1871) MD UCNY 1849; AB Columbia 1845. *Med reg NY NJ Conn* 1871:354. *Phila med times* 1:226, 1870/71. *Bost m & s jour* ns7:88, 1871. *K&B* III: 373.

ELLIOT, JAMES WOODWARD, NYC (b/Engl; d/II-28 1896 @72) MD CPSNY 1850. *JAMA* 26:541, 1896. *Bost m & s jour* 134:249,1896. *Polk* 1886: 677.

ELLIOT, JOHN G , Poughkeepsie, NY (b/Engl; d/V-12 1902) MD Buffalo 1897. *Bost m & s jour* 146:560, 1902.

ELLIOTT, ALBERT SPENCE, Cleveland (d/VIII-2-1901 @ 30) MD West Res 1892. *JAMA* 37: 461, 1901.

ELLIOTT, JOHN B , USN 1834- (d/VI-4-1869) MD unknown. *Tr AMA* 21:498, 1870. *Phila med reg & dir* 1871: 301. *Med annals Md:* 390.

ELLIOTT, JOHN LEE, Duluth, Minn (d/XI-29-1897) MD UPa 1882; ng U Mich Med Dept 1879-81. *Tr Minn St Med Soc* 1899:191. *Polk* 1896: 785.

ELLIOTT, RALPH EMMS, SC (b/VII-15-1797 Beaufort, SC; d/VI-5-1853 NYC) MD CPSNY 1821; AM Harvard 1818. Palmer's *Necrol Harvard alum*: 17.

ELLIOTT, SCHUYLER C , Kansas City Ks (d/I-14-1904 @39) MD Cleveland Homeop 1886. *Cleveland m s rep* v?:940 (Feb). *JAMA* 42:324, 1903. Homeopath.

ELLIOTT, STEPHEN FULLER, Bowdoinham, Me; CW-USA (d/1864 San Francisco) MD Harvard 1848; ng Bowdoin Med Sch 1847. *Harvard in CW*: 235.

ELLIOTT, THOMAS ARTERS, Orangeburg, SC (b/XI-30-1802 Charleston; d/I-30-1884) MD Med Coll SC 1826. *NC med jour* 13:105-07, 1884.

ELLIOTT, THOMAS HOLLIDAY, Allegheny City, Pa; CW-USA (b/V-8-1818 Mercersburg; d/XI-25-1875) MD UPa 1841. AB Wash'n & Jeff'n 1836. *Tr Med Soc Pa* 11:160-61, 1876. *U Pa med alum CW*:1841.

ELLIOTT, WILLIAM N, White Pigeon Mich (b/1807; d/1881) MD CPSNY 1832. *Tr AMA* 33:549-51, 1882.

ELLIS, CALVIN, Boston; CW-USA (b/VIII-15-1826; d/XII-14-1883) MD Harvard 1849; AB 1846. *JAMA* 10: 505-06,1888. *Bost m & s jour* 109:598-99, 1883; 110:151,166,1884. *Med bull med & surg* 7:43, 1884. *Harvard in CW*: 30. *Atkinson* I:682. *K&B* III: 375-76.

ELLIS, CALVIN DORR, Hopkinton, Mass (b/XI-6-1802 W Brookfield; d/V-10-1844) MD Bowdoin 1829; AB Amherst 1826. *Amherst, Men of*: 1826.

ELLIS, CHARLES CURTIS, Somerville, Mass (b/1847 Berlin, Vt; d/I-28-1905) MD UVt 1867. *No Amer jour homeop* ?: 1905 (Apr). *JAMA* 44:487, 1905. Homeopath.

ELLIS, CHARLES S , Wabash, Ind; CW-USA (b/1824; d/1894) MD unknown. *JAMA* 23:878, 1894. *Indiana med jour* 13:337, 1894? Kemper's *Indiana*: 267.

ELLIS, DANIEL FULTON, Brunswick, Me (b/XII-14-1840 Dexter; d/IX-19-1882) MD Bowdoin 1866. *Tr Me Med Assoc* 1883: 152-53. *Butler* 1878: 306.

ELLIS, DAVID ELIJAH, Belvidere & Elgin, Ill; (d/III-18-1905 @ 85) MD Geneva 1843. *Ill med jour* 7:379, 1905. *Polk* 1890:298.

ELLIS, GEORGE W , ? (d/VI-5-1905 Paris, Fr) MD UPa 1861. *Pa med jour* 9:27, 1905/06.

ELLIS, HAMILTON ELMORE, Greencastle Ind (b/X-16-1826 Bledsoe Co, Tn; d/XI-17-1880) MD Med Coll O 1854. *Tr Ind St Med Soc* 1881:241. *Butler* 1878: 201.

ELLIS, JOHN, NYC; Grand Rapids, Mich (b/XI-26-1815; d/XII-3-1896) MD Berkshire 1841. *Homeop times* 1: ? 1897. *Cleave*. Homeopath.

ELLIS, JONATHAN W , Marion, Ind (d/IV-15-1889) MD Eclectic Med Inst Cincinnati 1854. *Med vis* 5:152, 1889. *Polk* 1886: 332. Homeopath.

 Spec. educ'l status abbrev. as: ***ng*** = college verified attendance without degree;

ELLIS, JOSEPH WILLARD, Augusta, Me (b/I-30-1825; d/III-7-1862) MD Jefferson 1849; AB Bowdoin 1847; AM 1849. *Bowdoin cat*: 1847.

ELLIS, JOSHUA JAMES, Newport, RI; CW-USA (b/IX 13-1826 Boston; d/III-17-1863) MD Harvard 1852; AB Brown 1847. *Bost m & s jour* 68:170, 1863. *Tr RI Med Soc* 1863-64: 209-10. *Harvard in CW*: 238.

ELLIS, ROBERT A , nr Cape Nome, Alaska (d/VI-15-1899) MD Kentucky Sch Med 1882. *JAMA* 34:1273, 1900. *Polk* 1886: 754 (Findlay, Ohio).

ELLIS, SAMUEL B , Dayton O (d/X-21-1899) MD Med Coll Ohio 1866. *JAMA* 33: 1183, 1899. *Polk* 1896: 851.

ELLIS, SAMUEL L, Chandler Okla (d/XI-29-1899) MD CPS Keokuk 1880. *JAMA* 33:1504,1899. *Polk* 1886: 542 (Brashear, Mo).

ELLIS, THOMAS H , Butte City, Mont (d/II-1-1896) MD Med Coll Va 1884. *JAMA* 26: 391, 1896. *Polk* 1886:913 (Amherst CH, Va).

ELLIS, WILLIAM BALDWIN, Brooklyn; CW-USA (d/XII-29-1866 Washington, DC @33) MD Dartmouth 1858. *Med surg rep Phila* 16:60, 1867.

ELLSBERRY, ANDREW M , Georgetown, O (b/III-25 1824 Bethel; d/VII-18-1896) MD Starling 1848. *Tr O Med Soc* 1897: 422-23. *Butler* 1878: 627.

ELLSBERRY, WILLIAM W , Georgetown, O (b/XII-18-1832 New Hope; d/IX-7-1894) MD Cincinnati Coll Med & Surg 1865; Med Coll Ohio 1876. *Tr O Med Soc* 1895: 52-53. *Butler* 1878: 627.

ELLSWORTH, C F , Elkhorn, Wis (b/1810 Hartwick, NY; d/X-19-1877) <MD Fairfield 1836> *Tr Wis St Med Soc* 1878:183; 1891:356. *Butler* 1878: 860.

ELLSWORTH, PINCKNEY WEBSTER, CW-USA; Hartford, Conn (b/XII-5-1814; d/XI-29-1896) MD CPSNY 1839. *Proc Conn Med Soc* 1897: 330-35. *JAMA* 27: 1260, 1896. *Bost m & s jour* 135:584, 1896. *Polk* 1896: 279.

ELLWOOD, LIVINGSTON, Schenectady, NY (d/VIII-29-1890 @ 65) MD U Buffalo 1848. *Tr Med Soc St NY* 1891: 457. *Polk* 1886: 707.

ELLZEY, SAMUEL S , Yarrellton, Tex (d/IV-25-1886) MD Tulane 1883. *Tex cour-rec med* 3:331, 1886.

ELMENDORF, JAMES LUDLUM HASBROUCK, ?NYC (b/1843 Hyde Park; d/XII-25-1880) MD LICH 1866; AB Rutgers 1863; AM. *Med reg NY NJ Conn* 1881: 235.

ELMER, EBENEZER, Bridgeton, NJ; RevWar-USA (b/VIII-23-1752; d/X-18-1843) Stud med privately. *Tr Med Soc NJ* 1871:155. *Biogr direct US Congress.*

ELMER, JOHN C , Springfield, NJ (b/IV-7-1817; d/X-17-1863) MD CPSNY 1840. *Med surg rep Phila* 10:356, 370, 1863. *Tr AMA* 16:631, 1865. *Tr M S NJ* 1867: 136.

ELMER, ROBERT WILLIAM, CW-USA; Bridgeton, NJ (b/III-4-1836; d/X-13-1885) MD UPa 1860; stud Princeton. *Tr Med Soc NJ* 1886-87: 160-61. *Atkinson* I:347. *Butler* 1878: 469. *U Pa med alum CW*: 1860.

ELMER, WILLIAM, ?NJ (b/III-23-1788; d/V-6-1836) MD UPa 1811. *Tr Med Soc NJ* 1871: 153-55.

ELMER, WILLIAM, Bridgeton, NJ (b/X-5-1814; d/VI or VII-27-1889) MD UPa 1836; AB Princeton 1832; AM 1835. *Tr Med Soc NJ* 1890: 340-41. *Med reg NY NJ Conn* 1890: 268. *Atkinson* I: 612.

ELMORE, TAYLOR, CW-USA (d/V-25-1864 Chattanooga) MD unknown. *Nat med jour* 1:294, 1870/71.

ELMORE, WILLIAM TREZEVAUNT, NYC (b/IV 10-1854 Montgomery, Ala; d/II-12-1898 @ 44) MD Dartmouth 1889. *JAMA* 30: 507, 570, 1898.

ELROD, EDWARD BELFORD, Flora, Mo (d/XI-8-1894) MD Miami 1876. *JAMA* 23:768, 802, 1894. *Polk* 1890: 331.

ELROD, LAWRENCE E , Colorado (d/VIII-18-1900) <MD Miami 1888> *Ill med jour* ns2: 189, 1900.

ELSBERG, LOUIS, NYC (b/IV-2-1836 Iserlohn, Prussia; d/II-19-1885) MD Jefferson Med Coll 1857. *Med reg NY NJ Conn* 1885:235. *JAMA* 4:252, 1885. *Tr Med Soc St NY* 1886:601-08. *Bost m & s jour* 112:212, 1885; 113:655, 1885. *Atkinson* I:405. *K&B* III:377-78.

ELSNER, CARL EUNOMOS, NYC (d/VIII-8-1898) <MD Halle Gny> *JAMA* 31:427, 1898. *Polk* 1886:677.

ELWELL, ALEXANDER, Vincentown, NJ (b/VIII-22-1824 Upper Pittsgrove; d/I-19-1889) MD UPa 1847. *Tr M S NJ* 1889:177-78. *Atkinson* I:457. *Butler* 1878:468.

ELY, ADRIEL GILBERT, Girard, Pa (d/III-27-1887 @ 67) MD Geneva 1840. *Med surg rep Phila* 56:512, 1887. *Polk* 1886: 800.

ELY, EDWARD TALBOT, NYC (d/IV-12-1885 @ 35 Rochester) MD CPSNY 1874; AB U Rochester 1871. *Med reg NY NJ Conn* 1885: 236.

ELY, HENRY POWELL, Medford, NJ (d/I-9-1873 @ 60) MD UPa 1834. *Med surg rep Phila* 28:78, 1873.

ELY, JAMES WINCHELL COLEMAN, Providence RI (b/X-2-1820 Windsor, Vt; d/V-7-1906) MD Harvard 1846; AB Brown 1842. *Bost m & s jour* 154:534, 1906. *Tr RI Med Soc* 7:427-30, 1904-09. *Polk* 1896: 1351.

ELY, JOHN SLADE, New Haven, Conn (b/XII-4-1860 NY; d/II-7-1906) MD CPSNY 1886; AB Yale 1881. *Proc Conn Med Soc* 1906:301-05. *Bost m & s jour* 154:198-99, 1906. *Polk* 1896: 1051.

ELY, SMITH, Newburgh & Kingston, NY (b/IV-28-1828 New Windsor; d/II-28-1896) MD Woodstock 1850. *Tr Med Soc St NY* 1897:479. *Bost m & s jour* 134:249, 1896. *JAMA* 26:541, 1896. *Polk* 1886:669.

ELY, SUMNER, Clarksville, NY (b/V-22-1787 Lyme, Conn; d/II-3-1857) Hon MD Geneva 1837; AB Yale 1804. *Tr Med Soc St NY* 1858:21-34.

ELY, WILLIAM ELWOOD, CW-USA (b/IX-13-1842 Horsham Twp, Pa; d/VII-6-1892 N Wales) MD UPa 1864. *U Pa med alum CW*: 1864.

ELY, WILLIAM WATSON, Manlius NY to 1839; Rochester 1839- (b/IV-30-1812 Fairfield, Conn; d/III-27-1879) MD Yale 1834; LLD U Rochester 1869. *Tr*

Med Soc St NY 1880:454–55.

ELZEY, ARNOLD, Washington DC; War 1812–USA (b/1756/58? Somerset Co, Md; d/VI–6–1818) MD unknown; AM Princeton 1775. *Hist Med Soc DC:* 219. *Med annals Md:* 391.

EMANUEL, A D, Antwerp, NJ (d/1876) MD Cincinnati Coll Med & Surg 1870. *Tr AMA* 28:629, 1877.

EMANUEL, LOUIS M, Linwood, Pa (b/London Engl; d/XII–27–1868) MD Med Dept Pa Coll 1859. *Phila med reg & dir* 1871:299. *Tr Med Soc Pa* 1869: 430. *Med surg rep Phila* 20:20, 1869.

EMBREE, GEORGE W, NYC (d/IX–22–1873) MD UPa 1839. *Med surg rep Phila* 29:270, 1873.

EMBREE, JAMES ROBERT, Colorado Spr; Flushing, NY (d/III–21–1892 @ 33) MD CPSNY 1883. *Bost m & s jour* 126:328, 1892. *Med reg NY NJ Conn* 1892:277. *Polk* 1886:660.

EMERSON, ARTHUR LLEWELLYN, Chester, NH (b/IV–2–1849 Hermon Me; d/VIII–16–1901) MD Bowdoin 1878. *Tr NH Med Soc* 1901:331. *Polk* 1890: 708.

EMERSON, EDWIN B, Stokes, Ill (d/III–18–1900) Lic by yrs of practice. *Tr Ill St Med Soc* 1899–1900: 509. *Polk* 1896: 442.

EMERSON, GOUVERNEUR, Philadelphia 1822– (b/VIII–4–1795 Dover, Del; d/VII–2–1874) MD UPa 1816. *Med surg rep Phila* 31:80, 1874. *Tr CPP* cent vol: 223. *K&B* III: 379.

EMERSON, JAMES, Ashby, NH; Gardner, Mass (b/VI–30–1827 Barnstead; d/I–21–1890) MD Dartmouth 1858; ng Amherst 1857. *Bost m & s jour* 122:96, 144, 1890. *Polk* 1886:466.

EMERSON, JOHN SHERMAN, Lynn, Mass (d/IX–23–1886 @ 54) MD Harvard 1855. *Bost m & s jour* 115:316, 1886. *Butler* 1878:349.

EMERSON, SAMUEL, RevWar–USA; Kennebunk, Me (b/IX–6–1765; d/VIII–7–1851) Hon MD Harvard 1824; AM 1785. Palmer's *Necrol alum Harvard*: 1.

EMERSON, WILLIAM CARROLL, Boston (d/X–8–1891 @ 37) MD Harvard 1880; AB 1875. *Bost m & s jour* 125:424, 1891.

EMERY, ALFRED EASTMAN, Concord NH; CW–USN (b/IV–21–1841; d/V–29–1900) MD UVt 1865; ng Harvard Med Sch 1864. *JAMA* 34:1574, 1900. *Tr NH Med Soc* 1900:315–16. *Harv in CW*:287. *Polk* 1896:922.

EMERY, F W, Chelsea, Vt (d/I–4–1880 @ 36) MD unknown. *Med surg rep Phila* 42:132, 1880.

EMERY, GEORGE W, Minneapolis to 1891; Chicago (d/VII–13–1895) MD Berkshire 1864. *Chic med rec* 9:122, 1895. *Polk* 1890: 614.

EMERY, JOHN P, Loveland O (d/IX–2–1883 @ 72) MD Med Coll Ohio 1840. *Med surg rep Phila* 49: 336, 1883.

EMERY, SAMUEL SANDS, Fla 1860–61; CW–USA (b/VII–3–1832 Buxton, Me; d/XII–13–1866 Buxton) MD Dartmouth 1860; ng Bowdoin 1857. *Bowdoin cat*: 1857.

EMLEN, JAMES VALENTINE, Philadelphia (b/IX–21–1820; d/II–29–1880) MD UPa 1849; att Haverford. *Tr CPP* cent vol:223.

EMLEN, SAMUEL, Philadelphia (b/III–6–1789 Chester Co; d/IV–17–1828) MD UPa 1812. *No Amer med & surg jour* 6:139, 1828. *Tr CPP* cent vol: 223.

EMMERTON, JAMES ARTHUR, Salem, Mass (b/VIII–28–1834; d/XII–31–1888) MD Harvard 1858; AB 1855. *Bost m & s jour* 120: 52, 1889.

EMMONS, EBENEZER, Albany, NY; Brunswick Co, NC (b/V–16–1799 Middlefield, Mass; d/XI–1–1863 NC) MD Berkshire 1830; ng Castleton 1820; AB Williams 1818. *Med surg rep Phila* 10:398, 1863.

EMMONS, LEWIS, Hartland, Vt (b/V–22–1804 Woodstock, Vt; d/VIII–13–1878) MD Dartmouth 1830. *Tr Vt Med Soc* 1883:105.

EMMONS, NATHANIEL, Delaware, O (d/VI–30–1889 Valparaiso, Chile) MD unknown. *Med surg rep Phila* 61:308, 1889.

EMORY, AUGUSTINE W, CW–USA (d/IV–9–1865 Park Hosp, Md) MD UMd 1852. *Nat med jour* 1:294, 1870/71.

EMORY, JOHN DAVIDGE, Centerville, Md (b/1779 Md; d/I–1–1834) MD unknown. *Med annals Md:* 391.

EMORY, JOHN KING BECK, Centerville, Md (b/1799? d/I–2–1873 @ 74) MD UMd 1822. *Med annals Md:* 391. *Butler* 1874: 312.

EMORY, RICHARD, Phoenix, Md (b/III–9–1839 Baltimore Co; d/VI–11–1895) MD UMd 1861. *Med annals Md:* 391. *Polk* 1893: 572.

ENDERLIN, CHARLES, US 1850– (b/IV–6–1813 Steinbach, Baden, Gny; d/IX–16–1854) MD Würzburg 1842. *Phila med & surg jour* 3:143–44, 1854.

ENDERS, EMANUEL ALLEMAN, CW–USA; Bismarck, Pa (b/III–10–1846 Enders, Pa; d/V–10–1889 Harrisburg) MD UPa 1868. *U Pa med alum CW*: 1868.

ENDERS, LEVI J, Williamstown, Pa (d/IX–11–1906 @ 52) MD US Med Coll (Ecl) NYC 1881. *Pa med jour* 10:53, 1906/07. *Polk* 1896: 1345. *Flint* 1897: 840.

ENGELMANN, GEORGE, St Louis, Mo (b/II–2–1809 Frankfort am Main; d/II–4–1884) <MD Würzburg> *Bost m & s jour* 110:240, 1884. *Med bull med & surg* 6:67, 1884. *K&B* III:384–85.

ENGELMANN, GEORGE JULIUS, St Louis; Boston (b/VII–2–1847 St Louis; d/XI–16–1903 Nashua, NH) MD Berlin; stud Tübingen; AB Washington U, St Louis. *Bost m & s jour* ?:582, 635, 718, 1903. *K&B* III:385–86.

ENGLE, SANFORD J, Susquehanna, Pa (b/VI–13–1855 Newark NJ;d/II–1–1899) MD Albany 1879 *Pa m j* 3:37–38, 1899/1900. *JAMA* 32:385, 1899. *Flint* 1897:837.

ENGLE, SARAH PARKER, Detroit, Mich (d/II–8–1889) MD UMich Homeop Med Coll 1878. *Med vis* 5:116, 1889. *Polk* 1886: 488. Homeopath.

ENGLEHARD, CARL, Chicago (d/XI–6–1898 @64) ng U Mich Med Sch 1866–67. *JAMA* 31:1257, 1898. *Polk* 1886: 262.

ENGLER, ROBERT SAYLOR, Philadelphia (d/II-8-1906 @ 31) MD Medico-Chirurg Coll Phila 1901. *Pa med jour* 9:360, 1905/06.

ENGLES, SOLOMON ALLEN, USN (b/I-9-1827 Phila; d/II-28-1865 Chelsea, Mass) MD UPa 1849; ng UPa Coll 1840. *Med surg rep Phila* 12:344, 1864/65. *Nat med jour* 1:294, 1870/71.

ENGLISH, DAVID COMBS, Springfield, NJ (b/I-24-1799; d/VIII-7-1865) MD CPSNY 1822. *Tr Med Soc NJ* 1866: 129-30; 1871: 82.

ENGLISH, JAMES Jr, NJ (b/1792? Englishtown, NJ; d/V-7-1834 @ 42) <ng UPa Med Dept; ng CPSNY>; lic Med Soc NJ. *Tr Med Soc NJ* 1871:81.

ENGLISH, JEREMIAH SMITH, Manalapan, NJ (b/XI-21-1798 Englishtown, NJ; d/X-9-1879) MD UPa 1820. *Tr Med Soc NJ* 1880-81:117-18.

ENGLISH, WILLIAM TIMOTHY, Arcadia, Wis; Winona, Minn (b/1864 Wis; d/II-8-1898) MD CPS Chicago 1886. *Tr Minn St Med Soc* 1899:191.

ENLOW, GEORGE W , Liberty, Ill (d/IV-1-1899 @ 48) <MD St Louis Med Coll 1877> *JAMA* 32: 845, 1899. *Polk* 1898: 484.

ENNETT, WILLIAM THOMAS, Rocky Pt, Burgaw, & Wilmington, NC (b/XI-19-1839; d/VI-15-1888 or 9) MD UMd 1867; att UNC 1859-61; AB UNC 1911 as of 1862. *NC med jour* 23:445-47,1889. *Atkinson* I:546.

ENOS, DEWITT CLINTON, Brooklyn (b/III-17-1820 De Ruyter, NY; d/XII-14-1868) MD CPSNY 1845. *Tr M S St NY* 1868:262-63. *Med reg NY NJ Conn* 1869:232. *Med rec* 3:496-97, 1868-69. *Tr AMA* 21:440-41, 1870.

ENSIGN, HERBERT DWIGHT, Boone, Ia (b/V-4-1844 Lake Co, O; d/X-2-1898) MD Chicago Med Coll 1875. *Tr Ia St Med Soc* 17:384-85, 1899. *JAMA* 31: 942, 1898. *Polk* 1886: 351.

ENSIGN, WILLIAM H, USA 1862-72; NYC (b/Middletown, Conn; d/X-26-1884) MD UCNY 1862; AB Norwich U, Vt 1854. *Med reg NY NJ Conn* 1886: 244. *Med surg rep Phila* 51:496, 1884.

ENSMINGER, WILLIAM H , Chicago (d/I-17-1905 @ 62) MD Jefferson 1871. *Ill med jour* 7:242, 1905. *Polk* 1896: 382.

ENTLER, GEORGE F , Oneonta, NY (d/IV-3-1899 @ 49) MD Jefferson 1879. *JAMA* 32:845, 1899. *Bost m & s jour* 140:364, 1899. *Polk* 1896:1088.

ENTRIKIN, FRANKLIN WAYNE, Findlay, O (b/VII-27-1830 West Chester, Pa; d/V-13-1897) MD Med Coll Ohio 1873. *JAMA* 28:1045, 1897. *K&B* III:387-88.

EPES, JAMES POAGUE, Blackstone, Va (b/IV-10-1869 Rockbridge Co; d/I-10-1899) MD Univ Coll Med Richmond 1900 [?]; <MD Hampden-Sidney 1891> *Tr Med Soc Va* 1902: 215-18.

EPLER, JOHN V , Reading, Pa (d/I-20-1903 @ 65) MD Pa Med Coll 1858. *Pa med jour* 7:279, 1903/04.

EPPERSON, JACOB POLLARD, Pulaski, Tenn (b/III-16-1812 Nashville; d/VIII-2-1866) MD U Louisville 1854. *Tr Med Soc Tenn* 1876: 81. *Nashville j m & s* ns1: 239, 1866.

EPPES, RICHARD, City Point, Va; CW-CSA (b/V-2-1824; d/II-17-1896) MD UPa 1847. *U Pa med alum CW*: 1847.

ERDMAN, MILTON S , Quakertown, Pa (b/XII-22-1858 Steinsburg; d/XI-9-1899) MD Bellevue 1883. *Pa med jour* 3:526, 1899/1900. *Lehigh Valley med mag* 10:93, 1899; 11:22, 1900. *JAMA* 28: 1156, 1897.

ERICH, AUGUSTUS FREDERICK, Baltimore (b/V-4-1837 Eisleben, Prussia; d/XII-7-1886) MD UMd 1861. *New Orl m & s jour* ns14:559, 1887. *Med annals Md:* 392. *Atkinson* I: 105.

ERICKSON, G B , USA (d/1865) MD unknown. *Tr AMA* 18:355-56, 1867.

ERICKSON, JAMES P, CW-USA (d/IX-21-1865 Ft Connor, Dakota Terr) MD unknown. *Nat med jour* 1:294, 1870/71.

ERNST, ALEXANDER B , Covington, Ky (b/VII-18-1863; d/IV-21-1896) MD Med Coll Ohio 1888. *JAMA* 26:934, 1896.

ERNST, CHARLES GUSTAF, Punxsutawney, Pa (d/VI-22-1902) MD Bellevue 1884. *Pa med jour* 5:260, 547, 1901/02. *Flint* 1897:832.

ERSKINE, ALBERT RUSSEL, Huntsville Ala; CW-CSA (b/I-17-1827; d/III-24-1903) MD UPa 1851. *UPa med alum CW*:1851. *SHSP* 22:197,1893. *Polk* 1886: 134.

ERSKINE, JOHN HENRY, CW-CSA; Memphis (b/XII-23-1834 Huntsville, Ala; d/IX-17-1878) MD UCNY 1858. *Tr M S Tenn* 1879:169-74. *Tr AMA* 30:860, 1879.

ESCH, KARL, Peoria, Ill (d/VI-10-1897 @ 37) <MD Northwestern Ohio Med Coll Toledo> *JAMA* 28:1203, 1897. *Polk* 1896: 435.

ESHLEMAN, JOHN K , Lancaster, Pa (d/X-7-1897 @ 87) MD Jefferson 1835. *JAMA* 29: 816, 1897.

ESKENS, FRANCIS X , Brooklyn (d/VI-29-1888) MD U Bonn 1866. *Med reg NY NJ Conn* 1888: 252. *Polk* 1886: 645.

ESKRIDGE, JEREMIAH THOMAS, Philadelphia; Denver, Col (b/VI-1-1848 Sussex Co, Del; d/I-15-1902 Denver) MD Jefferson 1875. *Tr CPP* cent vol: 223. *Pa med jour* 6:260, 1902/03. *K&B* III:389-90.

ESPY, JAMES OLIVER, New Palatine, Ind (b/II-23-1845 Rural Valley, Pa; d/XII-18-1881) MD Med Coll Ind 1880. *Tr Ind St Med Soc* 1885: 213.

ESRAY, S W , Monroe, NY (d/VIII-4-1873 @ 63) MD unknown. *Med surg rep Phila* 29:360, 1873.

ESREY, WILLIAM P , Norristown, Pa; Philadelphia (b/1818 Maple Twp; d/IX-28-1854) MD Jefferson 1844. *Tr Am Inst Hom* 1893:140. *Phila jour hom* 4:602, 1856. Homeopath.

ESSELSTYN, RICHARD, Red Hook, NY (b/1795? d/II-12-1868 @ 73) MD CPSNY 1819. *Phila med reg & dir* 1871: 295. *Med surg rep Phila* 18:182, 1868.

ESSROGER, PHILIP, NYC (d/IV-29-1875 @ 39) <MD

U Prague 1861> *Med reg NY NJ Conn* 1875: 198.

ESTABROOK, JOSEPH HUBBARD, Rockland, Me (b/X–15–1797 Athol, Mass; d/VII–5–1885) MD Harvard 1821; AB Williams 1818. *Tr Me Med Assoc* 1886: 145–148. *Butler* 1878: 306.

ESTERBROOK, FREDERICK R , ?Maine; CW–USA; (d/II–24–1863 New Orleans) MD unknown. *Nat med jour* 1:294, 1870/71.

ESTES, EDWARD M , McKinney, Ky (d/VI–19–1901 @ 45) MD U Louisville 1878. *JAMA* 37:126, 1901. *Polk* 1886: 401.

ESTILL, HENRY M , Lexington, Va (b/1811; d/VII–23–1867) MD UPa 1833; att UVa 1831. *Med surg rep Phila* 17:133, 1867.

ESTILL, JOHN MOFFET, CW–CSA; Tazewell, Va (b/IV–17–1821 Augusta Co; d/I–23–1899) MD UVa 1846; stud Wash & Lee. *Tr Med Soc Va* 1904: 318–19. *JAMA* 32: 385, 1899.

ESTILL, WALLACE, Winchester, Tenn; CW–CSA (b/II 12–1793 Greenbrier Co, Va; d/XI–23–1863) MD UPa 1816. *Tr Med Soc Tenn* 1876: 81–82.

ETHERIDGE, FRANCIS B , Hastings, Minn (d/1874) MD unknown. *Tr Minn St Med Soc* 1874:85. *Northwestern m & s jour* 4:345, 1874.

ETHERIDGE, JAMES HENRY, Chicago (b/III–20–1844 St Johnsville, NY; d/II–9–1899) MD Rush 1869. *Buff m & s jour* 38:626–27, 1899. *Tr Ill St Med Soc* 1899:24–26. *JAMA* 32:378–79, 1899. *K&B* III:390.

ETHRIDGE [ETHERIDGE] JAMES A , Macon, Ga (d/III–14–1897 @ c40) MD CPS Balto 1883. *Bost m & s jour* 136:362, 1897. *JAMA* 28:860, 1897. *Chic med rec* 12:357, 1897. *Polk* 1890: 269.

EVANS, ALEXANDER MASON, Middleway, WVa (b/1842; d/X–6–1899) MD UPa 1876. *JAMA* 33:1116, 1899. *Polk* 1896: 1529.

EVANS, AMOS ALEXANDER, Elkton, Md; USN 1808–24 (b/XI–26–1785; d/I–15–1848) MD Harvard 1814; <ng UPa 1806–07> *Med annals Md:* 392. *Callahan.*

EVANS, ASBURY, Cincinnati; Covington, Ky (d/IX–12–1858) MD U Louisville 1842. *Med surg rep Phila* ns1: 60, 1858/59.

EVANS, ASHTON, Templeville, Md (d/V–6–1865 @ c30) MD unknown. *Med surg rep Phila* 13:66, 1865.

EVANS, CHARLES, Philadelphia (b/XII–25–1802; d/IV 21–1879) MD UPa 1828. *Tr CPP* cent vol:223. *Atkinson* I:301.

EVANS, CHARLES HENRY, Canton, O (b/V–12–1898) MD Jefferson 1884. *JAMA* 30:1248, 1898. *Polk* 1896:1156.

EVANS, CHARLES POELLNITZ, Canton, Ala (b/1818; d/X– –1857) MD Louisville Med Inst 1848; ng U Ala 1836. *U Ala cat*: 50.

EVANS, CHARLES R, Lewisburg, Pa (d/IX–23–1867 @ 28) MD Jefferson 1867. *Med s rep Phila* 17:303, 1867.

EVANS, DANIEL, Cornville Me (b/X–5–1802 Hallowell; d/II–9–1867) MD Bowdoin 1824; AB 1821. *Bowdoin cat*: 1821.

EVANS, DAVID, Garland, Me (b/1821 Sweden, Me; d/V–25–1875) MD Bowdoin 1850. *Tr Me Med Assoc* 1879: 688–689. *Butler* 1878: 306.

EVANS, DAVID J , Richmond, Ind; CW–USA (d/XI–26 1868 @ 56) MD UPa 1851. *Med surg rep Phila* 19:488, 1868. *Phila med reg & dir* 1871:298. *U Pa med alum CW*: 1851.

EVANS, EARL, Winchester, NH (b/Brookline, Vt; d/VIII 27–1903 @ 69) MD Berkshire 1856. *Tr NH Med Soc* 1904: 295–97. *Polk* 1890:712.

EVANS, EDMUND HAUN, Philadelphia (b/I–26–1906 @ 45) MD Jefferson 1889. *Pa med jour* 9:360, 1906/07?

EVANS, EDWIN, Rome NY (d/VIII–16–1900 @ 56) MD CPSNY 1870. *Tr M S St NY* 1901: [426]. *Polk* 1886: 706.

EVANS, FRANCIS JOSEPH, USA 1880–82; NYC (d/III–11–1889 @ 35) MD Bellevue 1880; AB 1875; AM 1876. *Med reg NY NJ Conn* 1889: 273.

EVANS, GEORGE ADDISON, St Paul, Minn (d/XI–4–1875) MD Hahnemann Phila 1875. *Amer jour homeop mat med* 9:116, 1875? Homeopath.

EVANS, ISAAC NEWTON, Hatboro Pa (b/VII–29–1827 Nantmeal; d/XII–3–1901) MD Jefferson 1853; MD Bowdoin 1851. *Pa med jour* 5:296, 1901/02. *Butler* 1878: 711.

EVANS, JOHN, Port Deposit, Md (b/IV–25–1810; d/VI–13–1878) MD UMd 1832. *Med annals Md:* 393. *Atkinson* I:261–62.

EVANS, JOHN, Richmond, Ind (d/1894 @ 84) MD unknown. *JAMA* 23:918, 1894.

EVANS, JOHN, Chicago; Denver (b/III–9–1824 Waynesville O; d/VII–3–1897) MD Cincinnati Med Coll 1838. *Tr Ill St Med Soc* 1895:70. *Med bull m & s* 19:353, 1897. *JAMA* 29:200,1897. *K&B* III:370–1.

EVANS, JOSHUA R , Philadelphia (b/X– –1826 Doylestown, Pa; d/II–9–1884) MD Jefferson 1851. *Tr Pa St Med Soc* 16:507–08, 1884. *Med bull m & s* 6:67, 1884. *Med surg rep Phila* 50:288,1884. *Butler* 1878:687.

EVANS, JOSIAH THOMAS, Myrtlewood, Ala (b/XII–19–1812; d/I–3–1867) MD Jefferson 1837; ng U Ala 1831. *U Ala cat*: 41.

EVANS, ROBERT T , Philadelphia (d/II–26–1870) MD Pa Med Coll 1851. *Phila med reg & dir* 1871: 294.

EVANS, SIMEON ADAMS, CW–USA; Hopkinton, NH 1865–68; Conway 1869– (b/IV–14–1837 Fryeburg, Me; d/VI–24–1895) MD Bowdoin 1865; AB 1860. *Bowdoin cat*: 1860. *Polk* 1886: 591.

EVANS, THOMAS BENJAMIN, CW–USA; Baltimore (b/XI–5–1832; d/X–30–1891) MD Washington U Balto. *Med annals Md:* 393. *Atkinson* I:51–52. *Polk* 1886: 436.

EVANS, WILLIAM AUGUSTUS, Aberdeen, Miss (d/X–8–1903) MD UCNY 1859; AB U Miss 1857. *UCNY cat*: 1859. *Polk* 1886: 523.

EVARTS [EVERTS], FRANKLIN, Oswego, NY; CW–

USA; (b/1828; d/II-12-1864 Mexico, NY) MD CPSNY 1853; MD UCNY 1853? stud Paris 1 yr. *Tr AMA* 16: 627,1865. *Bost m & s jour* 70:148, 1864. *Tr Med Soc St NY* 1864: 441-42.

EVE, JOSEPH ADAMS, Augusta, Ga (b/VIII-1-1805 Charleston Co, SC; d/1886) MD Med Coll SC 1828. *Atkinson* I:51. *New Orl m & s jour* ns13: 751-52, 1886. *K&B* III: 391-392.

EVE, PAUL FITZSIMMONS, Nashville (b/VI-26-1806; d/XI-3-1877) MD UPa 1828; AB UGa 1826. *Nashville m & s jour* ns20:252-59, 1877. *So pract* 19:181, 1897. *Tr AMA* 29:641-46, 1878. *Tr Med Soc Tenn* 1878:83-88. *K&B* III:392-93.

EVELETH, FRANCIS MARION, Waldsboro, Me (b/V-22-1832 Phillips; d/IV-9-1895) MD Eclectic Med Inst Cincinnati 1856. *Tr Me Med Assoc* 1895:192-93. *Bost m & s jour* 133:195, 1895. *Polk* 1890:504.

EVELETH, JOHN MARSHALL, Poland, Me 1855-59; Mechanic's Falls 1861-80; Hallowell 1880- (b/II-24-1828 Windham; d/X-26-1894 Augusta) MD Bowdoin 1854; AB 1849. *Bost m & s jour* 131:452, 1894.

EVELETH, PHILEMON, Marblehead, Mass (b/IX-27-1845 Essex; d/V-14-1900) MD Dartmouth 1870. *Bost m & s jour* 143: 24, 1900. *Polk* 1896: 717.

EVERETT, CLAUD WARREN, Promise City, Ia (d/X-20-1898 @ 27) <MD St Louis Coll Phys & Surg 1892> *JAMA* 31:1128, 1898.

EVERETT, EDWARD BROOKS, Boston (b/V-6-1830 Medford, Mass; d/XI-5-1861) MD Harvard 1853; AB 1850. *Bost m & s jour* 65:320, 1861. Palmer's *Necrol alum Harvard*: 436-37.

EVERETT, FRANCIS M , Corydon, Ia (b/X-10-1840 Mason Co, Va; d/IX-28-1895) MD CPS Keokuk 1864. *JAMA* 25:640, 1895. *Tr Iowa St Med Soc* 14:319-20, 1896. *Polk* 1890:411.

EVERETT, JOSEPH H , CW-USA (d/V-4-1863 @ Pittsburg Landing) MD unknown. *Nat med jour* 1:294, 1870/71.

EVERETT, OLIVER, Sherburne, Mass (b/XI-11-1798 Dedham; d/XII-12-1851) MD Dartmouth 1824; AB Brown 1821. *Brown hist cat*: 1821. *Mass M S cat* 1894.

EVERETT, OLIVER, Dixon, Ill (b/IX-12-1811 Worthington, Mass; d/V-1-1888) MD Berkshire 1836. *Tr Ill St M S* 1889:xxv-xxx. *Atkinson* I:610. *Butler* 1878: 151.

EVERETT, ROBERT AUGUSTUS, Hillsdale, Mich; CW-USA (d/X-20-1897 @ 58) MD U Mich 1859. *JAMA* 29:926, 1897. *Polk* 1886: 494.

EVERETT, SAMUEL W , CW-USA; Quincy, Ill (b/VIII-25-1820 London, Engl; d/IV-6-1862 @ Pittsburg Landing) MD UCNY 1850. *Hist Med Soc DC:* 243-44. *Tr AMA* 14:212, 1863. *Nat med jour* 1:294, 1870/71.

EVERETT, WILLIAM, Memphis (d/X-19-1867 @ 51) MD unknown. *Med surg rep Phila* 17:458, 1867.

EVERHART, JOHN ROSKELL, CW-USA; West Chester, Pa (b/1827; d/X-8-1901) MD UPa 1853; AB Princeton 1850. *Pa med jour* 5:296, 1901/02. *U Pa med alum CW*: 1853.

EVERITT, DANIEL LAWRENCE, Brooklyn (b/XII-2-1823 Plattekill, NY; d/I-25-1889) MD CPSNY 1849. *Hahn mo* 24:178, 1889. *No Am jour hom* 37:208, 1896. *Med vis* 5: 152, 1889. *Polk* 1886:645. Homeopath.

EVERITT, EDWARD, Newark (d/II-27-1896) MD NY Homeop 1879. *NC med jour* 37: 189, 1896. *Med vis* 12:180, 1896. *Polk* 1886: 607. Homeopath.

EVERITT, EDWARD A , Burlington, Pa (d/XI-22-1903 @ 72) MD Albany 1856. *Pa med jour* 7:280, 297, 1903/04. *Flint* 1897:797.

EVERSFIELD, CHARLES, USN 1843- (b/Md; d/X-5-1873 No Conway, NH) MD unknown. *Med & surg rep Phila* 29:306, 1873. *Callahan.*

EVERSOLE, FRANK R , St Louis, Mo (d/VIII-4-1901 @ 46) MD Missouri Med Coll (Kemper) 1876. *JAMA* 37:461, 1901. *Polk* 1886: 562.

EVERTS, ORPHEUS, Cincinnati (b/XII-18-1826 Salem Settlem't, Ind; d/VI-19-1903) Hon MD Rush 1867. *So pract* 25:483, 1903. *Chic med rep* 25:86, 1903. *K&B* III:393.

EWELL, DOUGLASS, NYC (d/III-22-1897 @ 30) MD CPSNY 1891; AB Columbia 1888. *JAMA* 28:665, 1897.

EWELL, JESSE Sr, Hickory Grove, Va (b/III-22-1802 Dumfries; d/I-19-1897) MD Columbian DC 1826. *Tr Med Soc Va* 1897: 253-55, 268. *Butler* 1878: 827. *Polk* 1886: 1491.

EWEN, JOHN H , Alloway, NJ (d/VI-19-1883) MD unknown. *Med surg rep Phila* 49:56, 1883.

EWERS, HENRY FRANCIS, Troy, NY; Burlington, Ia (b/II- -1830; d/III-31-1899) MD Castleton 1853; AB Hamilton 1850; AM 1853. *Tr Ia St Med Soc* 17:385-86, 1899. *JAMA* 32:899, 1899. *Polk* 1896: 513.

EWING, AMOS W , Beaver Co, Pa (d/III-26-1873 @ 55) MD unknown. *Med surg rep Phila* 28:328, 1873.

EWING, GEORGE C, Dunlap's Cr'k Pa (d/I-26-1866 @ 31) MD Jefferson 1858. *Med s rep Phila* 14:180, 1866.

EWING, GEORGE V, Ogden, Col; Sacramento (d/1894) MD Cleveland Med Coll 1852. *JAMA* 22:391 1894.

EWING, JAMES, Hebron, O (b/I-15-1800 Huntington Co, Pa; d/XII-13-1884 Pataskala, O) MD Bd of Censors' diploma, Zanesville, O; stud Acad Med Zanesville [?] *Tr Ohio Med Soc* 1885: 213. *Butler* 1878: 628.

EWING, JAMES WILLIAM, CW-CSA; Pekin, NC (b/1833; d/VIII-9-1890) <MD Med Coll Charleston> att UNC. *UNC cat*: 190. *Polk* 1886: 725.

EWING, ROBERT BLACK, West Grove, Pa (b/IX-6-1841 Mechanics Grove; d/VII-3-1903) MD UPa 1865. *Pa m j* 7:279, 1903/04. *Atkinson* I:644. *Flint* 1897: 839.

EWING, WILLIAM BELFORD, Surg Brit Navy 1797; Greenwich, NJ (b/XII-12-1776; d/IV-23-1866) <ng UPa Med Dept> AB Princeton 1794. *Tr Med Soc NJ* 1867:207, 1871:170-72. *Med surg rep Phila* 14:400, 1866; 15: 428, 1866.

EYRICH, CHRISTOPHER GOTTFRIED, Newark, NJ (b/VI–20–1902 Nuremberg, Bavaria; d/XI–12–1876) <MD Erlangen> Lic Med Soc NJ. *Tr Med Soc NJ* 1877: 132–33. *Butler* 1874: 463.

EYSSEN, GERARD, St Louis; b/1829 Frankfurt a M; d/I–24–1859 @ 30) MD unknown. *St Louis m & s jour* 17:184–85, 1859.

EZELL, FRANCISCO, Fayette, Mo (d/VII–10–1901 @ 54) MD Washington U St Louis 1881. *JAMA* 37:276, 1901. *Polk* 1886: 554.

FABRICUS, FREDERICK WILLIAM, USA (d/VI–25 1899 @ 26 Santiago) MD Bellevue 1893. *Bost m s jour* 141:26, 73, 1899. *JAMA* 33:175, 1899.

FABYAN, CHARLES WESLEY, Providence, RI (b/III–11–1813 Scarborough, Me; d/VII–23–1886) MD Bowdoin 1837. *Tr RI Med Soc* 1883–88: 377–78. *Butler* 1878: 747.

FABYAN, GEORGE, Boston (b/VI–9–1810 Scarborough Me; d/V–25–1874) MD Bowdoin 1833. *Bost m & s jour* 90:564, 1874. *Med surg rep Phila* 31:140, 1874.

FACKLER, JOHN EHRSTINE, Versailles, O (b/IX–30–1836 Miami Co; d/I–7–1898) MD Med Coll Ohio 1863. *Tr Ohio Med Soc* 1898:444–46. *Butler* 1878: 628.

FAGET, JEAN CHARLES Sr, New Orleans 1845– (b/VI 26–1818; d/XII–8–1884) MD Paris 1844. *New Orl m & s jour* ns12:577, 1885. *Atkinson* I:44. *K&B* III: 394–95.

FAHNESTOCK, CAMILLUS S , La Port, Ind (d/1903 @ 55) MD NY Homeop Med Coll 1872. *Med vis* 19:377, 1903. *Polk* 1886: 325.

FAHNESTOCK, S , CW–USA (d/IV–13–1865) *Nat med jour* 1:294, 1870/71.

FAHNESTOCK, WILLIAM BAKER, Lancaster, Pa (d/IV–29–1886) MD UPa 1825. *Practitioner* (Lancaster) 1:60–61, 1883.

FAHS, CHARLES FREDERICK, USN 1851–61; CSN 1861–65; Georgia 1865?– (b/W Manch'r Twp Pa; d/XI 17–1873 Griffin Ga) MD UPa 1850. *Med s rep Phil* 1850 *Med s rep Phila* 30:22 1874. *U Pa med alum CW*:1850.

FAILOR, BENJAMIN M, Newton Ia (b/II–21–1831 Bucyrus, O; d/IX–12–1901) MD Jefferson 1855. *Tr Ia St Med Soc* 20:46–48, 1902. *Polk* 1896: 422.

FAIRCHILD, NELSON W , Milton, Vt (b/XII–16–1831; d/IV–10–1865) MD UVt 1858. *Bost m & s jour* 72:268, 1865. *Tr Vt Med Soc* 1883: 105.

FAIRCHILD, RICHARD VAN WYCK, Parcipany, NJ (d/1874 @53) MD UCNY 1843; AB Princeton 1839. *Med s rep Phila* 30:228,276, 1874. *Tr AMA* 26:469 1875.

FAIRCHILD, STEPHEN A , CW–USA (d/IV–5–1864) MD unknown. *Nat med jour* 1:294, 1870/71.

FAIRCLOTH, SILEY E , Chicago (d/II–23–1868) MD UPa 1854. *Phila med reg & dir* 1871:295. *Med surg rep Phila* 18:226, 1868.

FAIRFAX, ORLANDO, Richmond, Va; CW–CSA (b/II–24–1806 Alexandria; d/I–11–1882) MD UPa 1829. *U Pa med alum CW*: 1829. *Tr Med Soc Va* 1882: 516. *Chic med rev* 5:86, 1882. *Hist Med Soc DC*: 225. *Butler* 1878: 827. Blanton *Va surg CW*: 400.

FAIRLEIGH, ROBERT McLURE, Hopkinsville, Ky (b/I–17–1840; d/X–19–1888) MD Jefferson 1860. *JAMA* 12:141, 1889. *Butler* 1878: 273.

FAISON, HENRY WILLIAM, Faison, NC (d/XII–23–1885 @ 62) MD UPa 1844; AB UNC 1842. *NC med jour* 17:38, 63, 1885. *New Orl m & s jour* ns 13:751, 1886. *Butler* 1878: 593.

FAJANS, JULIAN, Philadelphia (d/VIII–26–1904 @48) MD Jefferson 1886. *Pa med jour* 8:335, 1904/05. *Polk* 1896: 1303.

FALCONER, CYRUS, Hamilton, O (b/I–21–1810 Washington Co, Pa; d/I–28–1895 @ 85) MD Cincinnati Med Coll 1837; att Miami. *JAMA* 24:250, 1895. *Atkinson* I:38. *Polk* 1890:918.

FALES, HORACE, Waterbury, Vt (b/II–16–1823 Sharon; d/IX–13–1882 or IX–15–1883) MD Woodstock 1848. *Tr Vt Med Soc* 1883: 105. *Butler* 1874: 774.

FALES, JOSEPH JAIRUS, E Boston (b/I– –1797 Wrentham, Mass; d/XII–15–1866) MD Brown 1825; AM 1820. *Bost m & s jour* 75:432, 1866. *Med surg rep Phila* 16:20, 1867.

FALING, PETER, Gasport, NY (d/XI–23–1901 @ 62) MD Albany 1854. *Tr Med Soc St NY* 1902: [484]. *Polk* 1886: 661.

FALK, JACOB MAYER, New Haven, Conn (b/IX–22–1856 Albany, NY; d/X–24–1893 Poughkeepsie) MD Albany 1884. *Proc Conn Med Soc* 1894: 248.

FALLIGANT, LOUIS ALEXANDER, Savannah Ga CW CSA (b/X–25–1836 Augusta; d/VII–5–1903) MD Hahnemann Phila 1888; AB Brown 1857. *Med adv* 41: 1903 (Sept). *Butler* 1878: 108. Homeopath.

FALLS, SAMUEL KEMP, Chicago (d/III–22–1906 @ 55) MD McGill 1875. *Ill med jour* 9:464, 1906. *Polk* 1896: 383.

FANNING, NELSON, Catskill, NY (d/II–28–1896 @ 88) MD Berkshire 1830. *JAMA* 26:642, 1896. *Bost m & s jour* 134:249, 1896.

FAQUINETTO [FAGUINETTI] RAMON, Brooklyn (d/VIII–26–1894 @ 41) Bensonhurst-by-Sea) MD UCNY 1886; DDS unknown. *JAMA* 23:440, 1894 [as Taguimetto]. *Med reg NY NJ Conn* 1895:221. *Polk* 1890:812.

FARIS, JAMES WHITE, Hickman, Ky (b/III–8–1844; d/IX–27–1878) MD U Nashville 1874. *Tr AMA* 30:860–61, 1879.

FARLEY, CHARLES K , San Josè, Cal (d/XI–6–1899 @ 77) MD Berkshire 1842. *JAMA* 33:141, 1899. *Polk* 1886:165.

FARLEY, WALTER B , Berwyn, Pa (d/V–25–1899 @ 31) MD Hahnemann Phila 1891. *Homeop phys* 1899 (July) *Hahn mo* 34:109 (news & advt) 1899. Homeopath.

FARNAM, GEORGE BRONSON, New Haven, Conn (b/VIII–21–1841; d/XII–21–1886) MD Yale 1869. *Med*

 Spec. educ'l status abbrev. as: ***ng*** = college verified attendance without degree;

reg NY NJ Conn 1887: 259. *Proc Conn Med Soc* 1887: 176. *Butler* 1878: 76.

FARNHAM, A E , Pittsfield, Me (d/VII-2-1898 @ 42) <MD UCNY 1886> *JAMA* 31:142, 1898. *Polk* 1896:635.

FARNHAM, BELA, E Haven Conn (b/III-15-1770 Killingworth, Conn; d/I-15-1857) Stud w/Dr Jonathan Todd, E Guilford, Conn; Hon MD Yale 1829. *Proc Conn Med Soc* 1859: 21, 91-94.

FARNHAM, HORACE PUTNAM, NYC (b/V-7-1822 Salem, Mass; d/VI-9-1886) MD Jefferson 1860; AB Harvard 1843; LLB 1846. *Med reg NY NJ Conn* 1887: 259. *Bost m & s jour* 114:577, 1886. *Tr Med Soc St NY* 1887: 567-74. *Atkinson* I: 425.

FARNISH, ROBERT D , Mayersville, Miss (d/II-3-1900 @ 54) MD Tulane 1869. *JAMA* 34:446, 1900. *Polk* 1896: 812.

FARNSWORTH, AMOS, Roxbury, Mass (b/1789? d/VII 31-1861 @ 72) MD Harvard 1813. *Bost m & s jour* 65: 28, 1862.

FARNSWORTH, CHARLES HENRY, E Cambridge, Mass (b/VI-14-1823 Portland, Me; d/VII-4-1894 @ 69) MD UCNY 1847. *Tr Am Inst Homeop* 1895: 220. *Polk* 1886:465. *Cleave*. Homeopath.

FARNUM, JOSEPH, Salem, Mass (b/XII-14-1814; d/XI 22-1874) MD Harvard 1835; AB Brown 1832. *Brown hist cat* 1832. *Mass Med Soc cat*: 1894.

FARNUM, JOSEPH WHITNEY, Philadelphia (b/1803 Providence, RI; d/II-2-1889) MD UPa 1830; AB Brown 1822. *Brown hist cat*: 1822.

FARQUAR, ALLEN HOWELL, Ridgeville, Ind (b/VIII 28-1835 Clinton Co, O; d/IV-18-1904) MD Eclectic Med Inst Cincinnati 1868. *Tr Ind St Med Soc* 1904:352. *Polk* 1896: 489.

FARQUHAR, CHARLES F N , Bentleysville, Pa (b/XII 11-1859; d/X-6-1889) MD UPa 1884. *Tr Med Soc Pa* 21:297, 1889/90.

FARQUHAR, QUINTIUS CURTIS, California, Pa (d/ III-28-1900) MD UPa 1877. *JAMA* 34:957, 1900. *Polk* 1896: 1275.

FARQUHARSON, ROBERT JAMES, USN 1847-55; CW-USA 1863-65; Davenport, Ia (b/VII-15-1824 Nashville, Tenn; d/IX-6-1884 Des Moines) MD UPa 1844. *Tr Ia St Med Soc* 6:466-67, 1883-85. *U Pa med alum CW*: 1844.

FARR, LEVI, Greene, NY (b/VII-22-1787 Pittsfield, Mass; d/VII-18-1859) Stud w/Dr Jonas Farr, Minden, NY; lic 1806 (med) 1807 (surg). Hon MD Regents St U NY 1842. *Tr Med Soc St NY* 1860:174-75.

FARRAND, DAVID OSBURN, Detroit; CW-USA (b/IV 23-1837 Ann Arbor; d/III-18-1883) MD CPSNY 1863. *Chic med jour* 46:433, 1883. *JAMA* 1:254-55, 1883. *Butler* 1878:372. *K&B* III:397-98.

FARRAR, CALEB FRANKLIN, Kingston, Miss; CW-CSA (b/IX-1-1824; d/IX-3-1904) MD UPa 1846. *U Pa med alum CW*: 1846. *Polk* 1886:528.

FARRAR, DANIEL, Leominster, Mass; CW-USA (d/VI 1875 @ 39) MD Harvard 1862. *Harvard in CW*: 272.

FARRAR, GEORGE, Derry, NH (b/X-6-1778; d/IX-15 1858) MB Dartmouth 1803; MD 1816; AB 1800; AM 1803. *Bost m & s jour* 59:188, 1859.

FARRAR, SAMUEL M , NYC (d/IV-18-1847) MD UCNY 1847. *Buff med & surg jour* 2?: 752, 1847.

FARRELL, THOMAS J , Columbus, O (b/1826 Ireland; d/IV-23-1880) MD Med Coll Ohio 1870. *Tr Ohio St Med Soc* 1880: 123.

FARRINGTON, EDWARD SHERMAN, NYC (d/IX-7-1896 @ 31) MD CPSNY 1892; AB Yale 1888. *JAMA* 27:722, 1896. *Polk* 1896: 1052.

FARRINGTON, ERNEST ALBERT, Philadelphia (b/I-1-1847 Williamsburg, NY; d/XII-17-1885) MD Hahnemann Phila 1868. *Tr Amer Inst Homeop* 1886: 134. *Hahn mo* 21:1, 1886. *Med adv* 16:468, 1887. *New Engl med gaz* 21:96, 1886. *No Amer jour homeop* 34:[203]-206, 1885/86. Homeopath.

FARRINGTON, JAMES BONAPARTE, Jefferson, Wis, 1862-63; CW-USA 1864-65; Salinas City, Cal 1868- (b/I-3-1831 Rochester, NH; d/III-22-1883) MD Rush 1862; AB Bowdoin 1854. *Bowdoin cat*: 1854.

FARRINGTON, STEPHEN H , Ashtabula, O (b/I-10 1800 Winchester, NH; d/III-8-1875) MD Castleton 1823. *Tr Ohio St Med Soc* 1877: 64-65.

FARROW, JOSEPH RUSLING SMITH, German Valley, NJ (b/X-2-1870 Middle Valley; d/VI-23-1898) MD LICH 1892. *Tr Med Soc NJ* 1898: 379-80.

FARWELL, DARIUS G , Brooklyn (d/V-5-1880 @ 48) MD UCNY 1860. *Med reg NY NJ Conn* 1880: 235.

FASSETT, OSCAR FITZALAN, Berkshire, Vt 1851-65; St Albans (b/II-28-1827 Enosburgh Falls; d/VII-22-1887) MD Woodstock 1851. *Tr NH Med Soc* 1888:169-170. *Bost m & s jour* 117:120, 1887. *Atkinson* I: 53-54. *Polk* 1886: 906.

FASSITT, LOUIS, Philadelphia (d/XII-9-1883 @ 57 Englewood, NJ) MD UPa 1848. *Tr CPP* 1887: 223. *Med surg rep Phila* 49:700, 1883.

FAUCETT [FAWCETT] RICHARD W , CW-USA (b/ c1832? d/VI-22-1864) <MD Dublin 1854> *Nat med jour* 1:294, 1870/71.

FAULKNER, ROBERT, Erie, Pa (b/1826 Erie Co; d/IV-1-1887) MD Starling 1848; MD NY Homeop 1867. *Hahn mo* 22:320, 1887. *Med vis* 3: 1887 (May). *Polk* 1886: 798. Homeopath.

FAUNTLEROY, ARCHIBALD MAGILL, USA 1860-61; CW-CSA 1861-65; Staunton, Va (b/VII-8-1837 Warrenton; d/VI-19-1886) MD UPa 1860. *U Pa med alum CW*: 1860. *Med annals Md*: 394. *New Orl m & s jour* ns14:162, 1886. *Tr Med Soc Va* 1886:388-89. *Atkinson* I:294. *K&B* III:399.

FAUST, JONATHAN L , Zieglersville, Pa (d/IV-14-1902 @ 60) MD Jefferson 1867. *Pa med jour* 6:260, 1902/03. *Flint* 1897: 841.

FAWCETT, CHARLES LITTLE, Monticello, Ia; Salem, O (d/VII-27-1902 @ 70) MD Jefferson 1863; ng U Mich 1861-62. *Polk* 1886: 767. *U Mich cat*: 1862.

FAWCETT, JOSEPH CARPENTER, Greensboro, Ind; CW-USA (d/XI- -1863 @ 29) ng U Mich Med Dep 1862-63. *U Mich cat*: 1863.

FAY, ALLEN CLARKE, Milford, Mass (b/IX-28-1803 Walpole, NH; d/VI-18-1880) MD Woodstock 1834. *Tr AMA* 32:502-03, 1881.

FAY, GEORGE WHITEFIELD, CW-USA; Baltimore (b/1832? Westboro, Mass; d/V?- -1872 Savannah, Ga) MD UMd 1860; AB Williams 1857. *Bost m & s jour* ns9:344, 1872.

FAY, GEORGE WYMAN, E Weymouth, Mass (b/Grafton, Mass; d/II-5-1889 @ 55?) MD Harvard 1863. *Bost m & s jour* 120:180, 276, 1889; 121:644, 1889. *Butler* 1878: 350.

FAY, WILLIAM M , Denver, Col (d/I-13-1889 @ 33) MD Kansas City Med Coll 1881. *Tr Col St Med Soc* 1898-99: 508. *Polk* 1886: 183.

FEARING, BENJAMIN, Wareham, Mass (d/XII-26-1889 @ 65) MD Jefferson 1851; AB Yale 1848. *Bost m & s jour* 123:629, 1890.

FEARING, ELISHA POPE, Nantucket, Mass (b/X-11-1785 Wareham; d/VI-25-1876) MD unknown; AB Brown 1807. *Brown hist cat*: 1807.

FEARING, JOSEPH WARREN, Providence, RI (b/IX-6 1800 Wareham, Mass; d/XI-24-1862) MD Brown 1827; AB 1823; AM. *Tr RI Med Soc* 1:207, 1859-77.

FEARING, SARAH J , Denver (d/I-11-1896 @ 38) MD Woman's Med Penna 1890. *Tr Col St M S* 1898-99: 509.

FEARN, HERBERT, Brooklyn (b/England; d/VI-25-1892 @ 58) MD N Y Med Coll 1857. *Med reg NY NJ Conn* 1893: 301. *JAMA* 19:57, 1892.

FEARN, RICHARD LEE, Mobile, Ala (b/1804; d/V-24-1868) MD UPa 1827; AB UNC 1824; AM 1828. *Phila med reg & dir* 1871:297. *Tr AMA* 21:486, 1870. *Proc Ala Med Soc* 1870:233.

FEATHERSTON, JOHN R , Bridgeport, Ind to 1871; Indianapolis (b/X-6-1840 or 1841 Lexington, Ky; d/IV-13-1886) MD Med Coll Ohio 1865. *Tr Ind St Med Soc* 1886: 215. *Atkinson* I:670. *Butler* 1878:201.

FECHTIG, SAMUEL CHRISTIAN, Wellersburg, Pa (d/XI-2-1902 @ 80) MD UPa 1846. *Pa med jour* 6:260, 1902/03. *Flint* 1897:838.

FEELY, JAMES FITZGERALD, Brooklyn (b/1841 London, Engl; d/VIII-30-1899) MD UCNY 1866. *JAMA* 33:683, 1899. *Bost m & s jour* 141:252, 1899. *Polk* 1896:995.

FEENEY, JOHN L , Stapleton, NY (b/1845; d/V-31-1901) MD UCNY 1866. *Bost m & s jour* 144:570, 1901. *Polk* 1896: 1101.

FEENY, JOSEPH, NYC; Jersey City, NJ (d/I-9-1866 @ 53) MD CPSNY 1850. *Med surg rep Phila* 14:60, 1866.

FEGLEY, ORLANDO L , Allentown, Pa; CW-USA (b/VI-8-1841 Boyertown; d/III-10 or 15-1900) MD UPa 1867; AB Gettysburg 1863. *U Pa med alum CW*: 1867. *JAMA* 34:766, 1900. *Polk* 1890: 963.

FEILD, ANDREW MEADE, CW-CSA (b/XI-20-1827 Sussex Co, Va; d/IX- -1865 Poplar Mount) MD UPa 1849. *U Pa med alum CW*: 1849.

FEILD, HUME, Dinwiddie Co, Va; CW-CSA (b/XI-10-1829 Ellenton; d/VIII-15-1891) MD UPa 1850. *Tr Med Soc Va* 1891:257-58. *U Pa med alum CW*: 1850. *Butler* 1878: 827.

FEILD, JULIAN C , CW-CSA; Denison, Tex (b/1841 Tenn; d/I-31-1906) MD Tulane 1861; MD U Louisville 1869. *So pract* 28:166, 1906. *Butler* 1878: 786.

FELKER, JOHN BOGGS, Amboy, Ill (b/XI-19-1839 Washington Co, Md; d/V-10-1888) MD Rush 1860. *Tr Ill St Med Soc* 1889:xxxi-xxxxii. *Butler* 1878:152.

FELL, JONATHAN W , Brandywine Springs, Del (b/V 5-1816 Phila; d/V-30-1868 Faulkland) MD UPa 1839; ng Haverford 1837. *Med surg rep Phila* 18:504, 1868.

FELL, SAMUEL W , New Hampton, NJ (b/1788? d/VII 11-1824 @ 36) MD unknown. *Tr Med Soc NJ* 1872:184.

FELLA, FRANCIS J , Toledo, O (d/VI-17-1899) <MD Northwestern Ohio Med Coll 1891> *JAMA* 33:53, 1899.

FELLGER, ADOLPHUS, Philadelphia (b/VI-14-1821 Gmund, Württemberg Gny; d/VII-19-1888) MD Hahnemann Phila 1869; stud Tübingen, Zurich, Strassburg. *Tr Am Inst Homeop* 1893: 140. *Med adv* 21:191, 1888. *Med vis* 4:276, 1888. *Polk* 1886: 815. *Cleave*. Homeopath.

FELLOWS, GEORGE B , Waukesha, Wis (d/I-31-1888 @ 57) MD Hahnemann Chic 1885. *Med couns* 13:100, 1888. *Med vis* 4:84, 1888. Homeopath.

FELLOWS, HENRY BARTON, Chicago (d/I-12-1901) MD Cleveland Homeop 1861. *Tr Am Inst Homeop* 1901: 915. *Ill med jour* ns2:533, 1901. *Polk* 1896: 383. Homeopath.

FELLOWS, ISAAC, Los Angeles (d/I- -1893) MD Hahnemann Chic 1876. *Med vis* 9:76, 1893. *Polk* 1886: 166. Homeopath.

FELLOWS, JOHN, Concord, NH (b/X-7-1815 Boscawen; d/IV-18-1873) MD unknown; AB Dartmouth 1838. *Dartmouth cat*: 1838.

FELLOWS, MILTON ALEXANDER, CW-USA (d/I-12-1863 Elmira, NY) MD U Mich 1860. *U Mich cat*: 1860.

FELT [PHELPS!] MARCELLUS HAZEN, Hillsboro Bridge, NH (b/VII-1-1845 Sullivan; d/VIII-21-1905) MD Dartmouth 1877. *Bost m & s jour* 153: 234, 1905. *Tr NH Med Soc* 1905:282. *Polk* 1896:919.

FELTER, MAHLON, Troy, NY (d/VII-19-1905 @ 74) MD Albany 1859; AB Union 1857. *Tr Med Soc St NY* 1905:[362]. *Butler* 1878: 537.

FELTON, HORACE WILCOX, Salinas, Cal (d/V-3-1899) MD Rush 1883. *JAMA* 32:1133, 1899.

FENGER, CHRISTIAN, Chicago (b/XI-3-1840 Copenhagen; d/III-7-1902) MD Copenhagen 1876. *Chic med*

 Spec. educ'l status abbrev. as: ***ng*** = college verified attendance without degree;

rec 22:267, 1902. *Bost m & s jour* 146:297, 1902. *K&B* III:402–03.

FENNEL, FRANK M , Miss (d/IX–17 or X–1–1878 nr Holly Springs, Miss) MD unknown. *Tr AMA* 30:861, 1879. *Med rec NY* 14:279, 1878. *New Orl m & s jour* ns6:506–08, 1878–79.

FENNEL, WILLIAM, Miss (d/X–5–1878 nr Holly Springs, Miss) MD unknown. *Tr AMA* 30:861, 1879. *New Orl m & s jour* ns6: 506–08, 1878–79.

FENNER, ALBERT GALLATIN, Dover, NH (b/XII–1–1813 Taunton, Mass; d/III–3–1891) MD Dartmouth 1850. *Bost m & s jour* 124:275, 1891. *Tr NH Med Soc* 1891:262–63. *Polk* 1890: 708.

FENNER, ERASMUS DARWIN, New Orleans (b/1807 Franklin, NC; d/1886) MD Transylvania 1829. *So med & surg jour* 21:363, 1866. *Tr AMA* 29:646–54, 1878. *Bost m & s jour* 74:388, 1866. *New Orl m & s jour* 19:138–39, 1866. *Nashville jour m & s* ns1:320, 1866.

FENNER, JUNIUS P , Jackson, Tenn (d/XII–17–1833) ng Transylvania 1833. *Transylvania jour med & assoc sci* 6:601, 1833.

FENWICK, GEORGE PHILIP, Washington, DC; USA (b/IV–26–1838 DC; d/VI–14–1905) MD Columbian 1859. *Hist Med Soc DC:* 266. *Polk* 1886: 212.

FERBER, AMANDUS, NYC (d/X–21–1890 @ 58) <MD Göttingen 1858> *Med reg NY NJ Conn* 1891:272.

FERGUSON, DAVID, CW–USA; Union City, Ind (b/VI–27–1818; d/III–18–1884) <ng Jefferson 1848> *Tr Ind St M S* 1884: 221. *Butler* 1878: 201. Kemper's *Indiana*: 269.

FERGUSON, H H , Jeffersonville, Ind (d/VI–15–1896 @51) MD U Lousville 1867. *JAMA*26:1278, 1896. *Polk* 1886:321.

FERGUSON, JAMES, Warren Co, NY (b/Kortright; d/X 27–1892) MD Castleton 1841. *Trans NY St Med Soc* 11:741 ff, 1894. *Polk* 1890:791.

FERGUSON, JAMES FRANCIS, NYC (b/X–10–1839; d/I–6–1904) MD U City NY 1861. *Boston m & s jour* 150:56, 1904. *Polk*1896: 1052.

FERGUSON, JOHN, Davenport, NY to 1866; Albany (b/IX–16–1812 Kortright; d/X–13–1874) MD Castleton 1836. *Tr M S St NY* 1876:311–12. *Med rec* 11:428, 1876.

FERGUSON, JOHN T , Brooklyn (d/X–11–1859 @ 55) MD Rutgers 1827; AB Columbia 1823. *Med surg rep Phila* ns3: 111, 1859/60.

FERGUSON, JOSEPH, Philadelphia; CW–USA (b/X–17 1839 Cookstown, Ireland; d/VII–26–1903) MD UPa 1867. *Pa med jour* 7:279, 1903/04.

FERGUSON, R MAUPIN, Louisville, Ky (d/VIII–1 1886 Basle, Sw) MD *New Orl m&s jour* ns14:317 1886.

FERGUSON, RICHARD Jr, Richmond. Va; Columbia SC 1900– (b/IV–4–1874 Chester; d/III–6–1902) MD U Coll Med Va 1897. *Trans Med Soc Va* 1902:218–220.

FERGUSON, WILLIAM C , CW–CSA; (d/I–23–1865 Richmond, Va) MD U City NY 1859. Blanton*: Va surg CW*:401. *U City NY cat.*

FERGUSSON, JAMES, Glens Falls, NY (d/V–22–1866 @39 NYC) MD Castleton 1848; MD CPSNY 1849. *Med reg NY NJ Conn* 1867:218. *Med surg rep Phila* 14:440, 1866.

FERNALD, ALBERTO FRANCIS, Shirley, Mass (d/II–17–1902 @ 33) MD Balto Med Coll 1894. *Bost m & s jour* 146:588, 1902. *Polk* 1896:722.

FERNALD, FRANK CLINTON, Washington DC (b/Portsmouth NH; d/VI–17–1889) MD Harvard 1884. *Hist Med Soc DC*: 322.

FERNSLER, EDWIN KURTZ, Terre Hill, Pa (b/Lebanon Co; d/V–22–1903 @ 61) MD Jefferson 1867. *Pa med jour* 7:279, 1903/04.

FERRE, HENRY, Dalton, Mass (d/VII–31–1881 @ 79) MD Berkshire 1833. *Bost m & s jour* 105:623, 1881.

FERREE, FRANK A , Indianapolis (b/1856; d/IX–8–1889) MD Med Coll Ind 1881. *Tr Ind St Med Soc* 1890: 155. *Polk* 1886: 322.

FERREE, SHADRACH LEONIDAS, Indianapolis (b/VII–14–1830 Clermont Co, O; d/I–30–1901) MD Med Coll Ind. *Tr Ind St Med Soc* 1901:483. *Polk* 1896: 473.

FERRELL, LEONIDAS C , La Grange, Ga; CW–CSA (d/VIII–19–1867) <MD U Ga>; MD U City NY 1851; AB UNC 1840. *UNC cat*: 196.

FERRER, HENRY, San Francisco; Santa Barbara, Cal (b/II–17–1850 Santiago de Cuba; d/X–22–1890) <MD Heidelberg 1872> *Tr Med Soc Calif* 21:318–319, 1891. *Polk* 1886:172.

FERRIN, SAMUEL A , Mineral Point, Wis (b/I–19–1831 St Thomas, Canada West; d/III–29–1875) MD Rush 1865. *Tr Wis St Med Soc* 1877: 149–150.

FERRIS, F W , Cincinnati (d/VII–19–1883 @ 60) MD *Med surg rep Phila* 49:196, 1883.

FERRIS, ISAAC WARD, Mt Vernon, NY (d/XII–25–1900 @ 60) MD Yale 1867; AB U City NY. *Bost m & s jour* 144: 28, 1901. *Polk* 1896: 1033.

FERRIS, SAMUEL, New Castle, Ind (b/III–13–1822 Franklin Co; d/XI?–4–1902) Certified by yrs pract. *Tr Ind St Med Soc* 1902: 413. *Polk* 1900: 606.

FERSON, JOHN LINDSAY, Kansas City Mo 1879; Pittsburgh, Pa 1880– (b/XI–8–1854; d/VII–9–1896) MD Hahnemann Phila 1879. *Med vis* 12:272, 312, 1896. *Hahn mo* 31:112 (news & advt) 1896. *Tr Am Inst Hom* 1898: 48. *Polk* 1886: 829.

FERSON, SHERMAN C , CW–USA (d/X–7–1864 @ Varnell's Station Ga) MD *Nat med jour* 1:294 1870/71.

FERTIG, HUGO FRANZ, Brooklyn, NY (d/I–20–1892 @ 67) <MD U Würzburg 1864> *Med reg NY NJ Conn* 1892:277. *JAMA* 24:135,1895. *Polk* 1886: 645.

FESSENDEN, BENJAMIN FREEMAN, Brooklyn, NY (b/IX–16–1818 Plymouth, NC; d/VII–27–1894) MD U Pa 1843. *Med reg NY NJ Conn* 1895: 221 *JAMA* 24; 135, 1895. *Polk* 1886: 645.

FESSENDEN, CHARLES STEWART DAVEIS, US MHS Portland, Me 1861–79; NYC 1879–82; St Louis

Mo 1882–85; Norfolk, Va 1885–88; Louisville, Ky 1888–93; Mobile, Ala 1893–95 (b/II–23–1828 Portland, Me; d/VII–23–1896 Salem Mass) MD Bowdoin 1851; AB 1848. *Bost m & s jour* 135:124, 1896. *JAMA* 27:337, 1896. *Atkinson* I:632. *Polk* 1890: 79.

FESSENDEN, ENOCH PERLEY, Bucksport, Me 1853–70 (b/VI–26–1822 Fryeburg; d/II–23–1882 Augusta) MD CPSNY 1853; AB Bowdoin 1844. *Bowd'n cat*:1844.

FESSLER, HENRY H , Williamsport, Pa (d/IV–9–1899 @ 64) MD Jefferson 1883. *JAMA* 32:1074, 1899. *Polk* 1886: 809.

FETTER, DAVID FOULKE, NYC (b/1823; d/X–2–1884) MD Med Coll Phila 1853. *Med reg NY NJ Conn* 1885: 236. *Med surg rep Phila* 51:448, 1884.

FEUSS, JOHN H USA (b/Gny; d/IX–26–1899 @ 35 at sea) MD *Bost m & s jour* 141:352, 1899.

FICKARDT, FREDERICK AUGUSTUS, Bethlehem, Pa (d/III–13–1890 @ 84) MD UPa 1827. *Bost m & s jour* 122:283, 1890. *Butler* 1878: 712.

FICKLIN [FICKLEN], JOSEPH BURRELL, Washington, Ga (b/IV–30–1830 Fairplay; d/III–3–1886) MD UPa 1853. *New Orl m & s j* ns13:915, 1886. *Polk* 1886: 236.

FICKLIN, WILLIAM AUGUSTUS, Thebodauxville, La (d/XI–16–1829 @ 24) MD Transylvania 1828. *Transylvania jour med & assoc sci* 3:152, 1830.

FIEGENBAUM, GEORGE A , St Joseph, Mo (d/IV–30 1896 @ 41) <MD St Joseph Med Coll 1880> *JAMA* 26: 995, 1896. *Polk* 1890: 698.

FIELD, CALEB CLESSON, Leominster, Mass (b/V–27–1810 Northfield Arms; d/V–6–1881) MD Dartmouth 1838; AB Amherst 1833. *Bost m & s jour* 104:504, 1881; 105: 623, 1881. *Atkinson* I:71. *Butler* 1878: 350.

FIELD, CHARLES, Boston (b/I–14–1803 Yarmouth, Me; d/VIII–22–1838 Plymouth) MD Bowdoin 1836; AB 1827. *Bowdoin cat*: 1827.

FIELD, CHARLES HAMPDEN, Rock Springs, Wyo; Alameda, Calif (d/VIII–6–1901) MD Med Coll Ala 1878. *Ill med jour* ns3: 237, 1901.

FIELD, CHAUNCEY MITCHELL, Plainfield, NJ (b/ Bound Brook; d/VII–17–1895 @ 45) MD CPSNY 1875; AB Princeton 1871; AM 1874. *JAMA* 25: 298, 1895.

FIELD, CONSTANT, Charlemont, Mass (b/X–31–1804; d/IX–30–1833) MD Berkshire 1829; AB Williams 1825; ng Amherst 1825. *Amherst, Men of*: 1825.

FIELD, CRIDLAND CROCKER, Easton, Pa (d/XI–26 or XII–2/3–1886 @ c70) MD UPa 1837. *New Orl m & s jour* ns14:559, 1887. *Bost m & s jour* 116:148, 1887. *Med bull m & s* 9:28, 1887. *Polk* 1886:798.

FIELD, EDWARD, Waterbury, Conn (b/Enfield, Conn; d/1840) Lic Hartford Co Med Soc. *Proc Conn Med Soc* 1859: 99–101.

FIELD, EDWARD GUSTAVUS, NYC (b/XII–7–1822 Waterbury, Conn; d/I–8–1899) MD Castleton 1847. *JAMA* 32:145, 1899. *Polk* 1896: 1052.

FIELD, EDWARD MANN, Bangor, Me (b/VII–27–1822 Belfast; d/VII–29–1887 @ 65) MD Jefferson 1849; AB Bowdoin 1845; AM 1850. *Tr Me Med Assoc* 1888:510–512. *K&B* II: 382–383.

FIELD, HENRY, Clinton, NJ (b/II–25–1805 Lamington [?] NJ; d/III–15–1878) Lic Med Soc NJ 1830. *Tr NJ Med Soc* 1878–79: 207–208. *Butler* 1878: 469.

FIELD, JACOB T , Bayonne, NJ; CW–USN (b/VIII–3–1839 North Branch; d/XI–25–1896) MD CPSNY 1863; ng Rutgers 1856–60. *Bost m & s jour* 135: 579, 1896. *Polk* 1896: 933.

FIELD, MATTHEW DICKINSON, NYC (b/VII–19–1853; d/III–8–1895) MD Bellevue 1879; AB Williams 1875. *Med reg NY NJ Conn* 1885: 236. *JAMA* 24: 457, 1895. *Bost m & s jour* 132:265, 1895. *Polk* 1886: 678.

FIELDS, EDWARD, Burlington, Conn; NYC 1846– (b/VII–4–1806 Chester; d/II–18–1867) MD Yale 1829; ng Yale Coll. *Med reg NY NJ Conn* 1867: 218.

FIFIELD, JOSEPH, Philadelphia (b/1794? d/XII–27–1868 @ 74) MD U City NY 1846 [?] *Phila med reg & dir* 1871:293. *Med surg rep Phila* 20: 40, 1869.

FIFIELD, MOSES, Centreville, RI (b/XII–23–1823 Warehouse Pt, Conn; d/IV–9–1900) MD UCNY 1844. *Tr RI Med Soc* 6:260–261, 1899–1903. *Polk* 1886: 844.

FIFIELD, WILLIAM CRANCH BOND, Boston (b/VIII 27–1828 Weymouth, Mass; d/IX–10–1896) MD Harvard 1851; MRCS (Eng) 1854. *Bost m & s jour* 135: 303–304, 1896. *JAMA* 27: 722, 1896. *Polk* 1896: 697.

FIGGAT, WILLIAM F , Christianburg, Va; CW–CSA (b/IV–25–1834 Fincastle; d/X–14–1878) MD Jefferson 1858; att Wash & Lee 1855. *Tr Med Soc Va* 1878: 510.

FILBERT, LUDWIG S , Philadelphia (b/III–12–1825 Berks Co, Pa; d/X–19–1903) MD Pa Med Coll 1847. *Pa med jour* 7:279,1903/04. *Atkinson* I:139. *Polk* 1886:815.

FILKINS, FRANK S , Barrington & Arlington Heights, Ill (d/II–20–1905 @ 65) Lic yrs pract. *Ill med jour* 7:524, 1905. *Polk* 1896: 446.

FILLER, CHARLES WRIGHT, Washington, DC; Baltimore (b/X–6–1852 Lovettsville, Va; d/III–22–1905) MD U Md 1876. *Hist Med Soc DC*: 358. *Polk* 1893: 560.

FILLMORE, CHARLES WESLEY, Providence, RI; CW–USA; (b/IX–22–1828 Lynn, Mass; d/VI–4–1893) MD Harvard 1856. *Harvard in CW*: 246. *Tr RI Med Soc* 4:618–622, 1889–93. *Polk* 1896: 1026.

FINCH, RODNEY GOVE DENNIS, Statesville, NC (b/ II–24–1858; d/IV–25–1885) MD UCNY 1881. *Med reg NY NJ Conn* 1885: 236.

FINCKE, CHARLES LOUIS, Brooklyn (b/III–29–1873; d/III–19–1906) MD LICH 1899; AB Yale 1896. *Bost m & s jour* 154: 360, 1906.

FINCKE, FREDERICK H , Baltimore (d/VIII–13–1899 Chicago) MD U Md 1891. *JAMA* 33:558, 1899.

FINDLEY, THOMAS FLEMING, Altoona, Pa (b/IX–25 1851 Frankstown; d/1879) MD UPa 1875. *Tr Med Soc Pa* 13: 252, 1879.

FINDLEY, WILLIAM MARTIN, Altoona, Pa; CW–

 Spec. educ'l status abbrev. as: ***ng*** = college verified attendance without degree;

USA (b/VII-6-1842 Manor Hill, Pa; d/VI-2-1906) MD UPa 1867. *Pa med jour* 9:760-61, 1905/06. *U Pa med alum CW*: 1867. *Atkinson* I:311. *Flint* 1897: 794.

FINFROCK, J H , Laramie, Wyo; Boise City, Idaho (d/II- -1894) MD Med Coll Ohio 1863. *Tr Colo St Med Soc* 1898-99: 509. *Polk* 1893: 1323.

FINK, ISAAC W , Hillsboro, Ill (d/IV-16-1903 @ 76) MD St Louis Med Coll 1854. *Tr Ill St Med Soc* ns4:889, 1903.

FINK, JACOB ASHER, Commerce, Mich (d/II-12-1894 Pontiac) MD U Mich 1886. *JAMA* 22: 313, 1894.

FINLAY, EDWARD S , NYC (b/VI-19-1820 St Croix, d/XII-2-1876) MD UCNY 1843; att Trinity Coll, Dublin. *Med reg NY NJ Conn* 1877: 200.

FINLAYSON, JOHN A , Armstrong, Ia (b/1860 Mt Carroll, Ill; d/V-9-1905) MD Ky Sch Med 1892. *Tr Ia St Med Soc* 23:367, 1905. *Polk* 1896: 511.

FINLEY, CLEMENT ALEXANDER, USA (b/V-11-1797 Newville, Pa; d/IX-8-1879 Phila) MD UPa 1834; AB Dickinson 1815. *Tr AMA* 31:1039-40, 1880. *Med surg rep Phila* 41:264, 286, 1879. *Atkinson* I: 365. *K&B* II: 383.

FINLEY, EBENEZER L , Streator, Ill (d/IX-1-1897) MD CPS Chic 1887. *JAMA* 29:555 1897. *Polk* 1896:442.

FINLEY, JAMES BROWN, Cincinnati (b/Cumberland Co, Pa) d/V-14-1851 So Bend, Ind) Stud law & med Cincinnati; AB Dickinson 1813. *Dickinson cat* 1813.

FINLEY, JOHN KNOX, Niles, Mich; CW-San Comm (b/VI-13-1800 Chillicothe, O; d/II-3-1885) MD UPa 1827. *U Pa med alum CW*: 1827.

FINLEY, JOHN W , Dubuque, Ia (b/VI-15-1807 Lincoln Co, NC; d/VIII-3-1877) MD Cincinnati Med Coll 1836. *Tr Ia St Med Soc* 1877-78: 67-70. *Iowa dir phys & surg* 1876:182.

FINLEY, MICHAEL ALLISON, Williamsport, Md (b/1786; d/III-25-1848) MD UPa 1808; AM Princeton 1804. *Med annals Md:* 395-396.

FINLEY, SAMUEL MOORE, USA 1862-65; 1878- (b/XII-22-1841 Phila; d/VIII-4-1885 Ft Concho, Tex) MD UPa 1864. *U Pa med alum CW*: 1864.

FINLEY, SYLVESTER J , Castle Fin, Pa (d/XI-12-1903 @ 73) <MD Washington U Balto 1853> *Pa med jour* 7:279, 1903/04. *Flint* 1897:798.

FINLEY, WILLIAM P , Fannin, Miss (b/XII-25-1836 Madison Co, Miss; d/V-15-1861) MD U La 1859. *Tr Miss St Med Assoc* 1882: 159.

FINN, JAMES ANTHONY, Roxbury, Mass (d/IX-?-1906) MD Harvard 1875. *Bost m & s jour* 155: 270, 1906. *Butler* 1878:339.

FINNELL, THOMAS CONSTANTINE, NYC; CW-USA; (b/VII-12-1826/27; d/IV-9-1890) MD UCNY 1849. *Med reg NY NJ Conn* 1890:268. *Proc Conn Med Soc* 1890:276. *Bost m & s jour* 122: 386, 1890. *Atkinson* I:268. *Butler* 1878: 512. *Polk* 1886: 678.

FINNEY, ADAM B , Washington, DC (d/VIII-9-1897 @ 61) MD Pa Med Coll 1860. *JAMA* 29:453, 1897. *Polk* 1896: 302.

FINNEY, JAMES BYERS, CW-USA (b/IX-5-1835 Halifax, Pa; d/X-8-1862 Schnee) MD UPa 1860. *U Pa med alum CW*:: 1860.

FINNEY, JAMES FRANCIS, New Orleans (b/1848; d/V 2-1902) MD Tulane 1871. *New Orl m & s jour* 54: 836, 1902. *Polk* 1886: 416.

FINNEY, JOHN JAMES OSWALD BOWMAN, Onancock, Va; CW-CSA (b/VII-2-1819 Accomac Co; d/VII 22-1900) MD UPa 1843; AB Washington & Jefferson 1840. *U Pa med alum CW*: 1843. *Polk* 1886: 923.

FINNEY, JOSEPH RUSSELL, Elbowoods, ND (d/XII-27-1899) MD UCNY 1879. *JAMA* 34:187, 1900. *Polk* 1886:706 (Rodman, NY).

FINNEY, LUDGER M , New Orleans (d/XI-28-1899 or 1900) MD Tulane 1890. *New Orl m & s jour* 53: 437, 1901. *Polk* 1896: 622.

FIRESTONE, JOHN LOWER, Medina, O (b/X-2-1829 Columbiana; d/II-6-1885) MD Castleton 1854; MD NY Med Coll 1856. *Tr Ohio St Med Soc* 1885: 207- 208. *Butler* 1878: 628.

FIRESTONE, LEANDER, Congress, O, 1845- ; Wooster 1856- (b/IV-11-1819 Wayne Co; d/XI-9-1888) MD Med Coll Cleveland 1846. *Tr Ohio Med Soc* 1889: 7. *Atkinson* I: 454. *Butler* 1878: 628. *K&B* III:406.

FIREY, WILLIAM, Topeka, Kans; CW-USA (b/XII-16 1823 Clear Spring, Md; d/IV-6-1896) MD UPa 1847; AB Franklin & Marshall 1843. *U Pa med alum CW*:1847.

FISCHER, FREDERICK J T , Elmhurst, Ill (d/IV-27-1906 @ 63) MD Med Coll Ohio 1878. *Ill med jour* 9:662, 1906. *Polk* 1896: 418.

FISCHER, FREDERICK L , NYC (b/VI-1-1817; d/VII 24-1887) <MD Tübingen Gny 1842> *Med reg NY NJ Conn* 1888: 253. *Polk* 1886: 678.

FISCHER, GEORGE A, Rochester NY (b/I-27-1848 Hanover Gny; d/VI-26-1893) MD CPS Balto 1879. *Chic med jour* 5:143, 1893. *JAMA* 21:250, 1893. *Polk* 1886: 704.

FISCHER, OTTO, Brooklyn (d/IX-9-1891) <MD U Würzburg 1874> *Med reg NY NJ Conn* 1892: 277. *Polk* 1886: 645.

FISCHER, W EMIL, Philadelphia (b/VI-22-1832 Bernstadt, Prussia; d/1899) MD Jefferson 1855. *JAMA* 33: 1632, 1899. *Tr CPP* cent vol: 24. *Atkinson* I: 138.

FISH, AUGUSTINE HALLETT, Philadelphia; Trenton, NJ; CW-USA (b/1828; d/VIII-3-1872) MD UPa 1851; AB Princeton 1847; AM 1850. *Phila med reg & dir* 1873: 303. *Tr AMA* 24: 363, 1873. *Med surg rep Phila* 27:142,1872. *Tr Med Soc St Pa* 9:219-20,1873.

FISH, CHARLES HERBERT, Chester, NH (b/XII-5-1865 Manchester; d/VIII-20-1892) MD Bowdoin 1891. *Tr NH Med Soc* 1893: 161-62.

FISH, DYER BALL NELSON, CW-USA; Amherst, Mass 1865- (d/VIII-10-1838; d/X-28-1895) MD

<Berkshire 1862> ng Amherst 1862. *JAMA* 25: 818, 1895. *Bost m & s jour* 133: 480, 1895. *Polk* 1890: 533.

FISH [FISK], HEZEKIAH, CW–USA (d/VIII–19–1864 Marietta, Ga) MD *Tr Iowa St Med Soc* 1867–71:247–48. *Nat med jour* 1:294, 1870/71.

FISH, JAMES S , Alexandria, La (d/III– –1887 @ 58) MD Jefferson 1849. *New Orl m & s jour* ns14:794, 1887. *Polk* 1886: 412.

FISH, TIMOTHY S , Wolcott, NY (d/VIII–10–1901 @ 55) MD Detroit Med Coll 1873. *JAMA* 37:527, 1901. *Polk* 1886: 716.

FISHER, ALEXANDER, Akron, O; Chicago (b/VIII–12–1804 Lancaster Mass; d/II–15–1882) MD Fairfield 1834. *Tr AMA* 33:553–54, 1882. *Chic med jour* 54:446–47, 1882. *Tr Ill St M S* 1882:? *Bost m&s jour* 106: 379, 1882.

FISHER, ALEXANDER MING, NYC (b/1857; d/II–13 1885 Cologne, Gny) MD CPSNY 1878. *Med reg NY NJ Conn* 1883: 228.

FISHER, CALVIN PETER WILLIAM, CW–USA; Boalsburg, Pa (b/V–20–1832 Linglestown; d/VII–31–1889) MD UPa 1857. *UPa med alum CW*: 1857. *Polk* 1886: 793.

FISHER, CHARLES HARRIS, Providence, RI (b/VI–30 1822 Killingly, Conn; d/X–21–1893 @ 71 Buffalo) MD Dartm'th 1848. *Bost m&s jour* 129: 432, 1893. *Tr RI Med Soc* 4:617 1889–93. *Atkinson* I:326–27. *Polk* 1890: 1026.

FISHER, CHARLES MORRISON, Oakland, Cal (b/Pa; d/VII–29–1898 @32) MD Cooper 1890. *JAMA* 31:366, 1898. *Polk* 1896: 223.

FISHER, CYRUS ARNDT, Bloomsburg, NJ (b/1848; d/1877) MD UPa 1876. *Tr AMA* 28:627–28, 1877.

FISHER, DANIEL, Edgartown, Mass (b/VI–14–1799 Sharon; d/XII–18–1876) MD Harvard 1825; AB Brown 1821. *Brown hist cat*: 1821.

FISHER, EDWARD ALBERT, Buffalo (d/III–1–1902 @ 42) MD U Mich Homeop Dept 1881. *Tr Amer Inst Homeop* 1902: 846–47. *Polk* 1886:653. Homeopath.

FISHER, EUSTACE WHIPPLE, NYC (d/III–5–1894 @ 51) MD CPSNY 1871; AB CCNY. *Med reg NY NJ Conn* 1894:238. *JAMA* 22: 482, 1894.

FISHER, GEORGE HADLEY, Sing Sing, NY (d/VII–23 1883 Baltimore, Ind) MD CPSNY 1878. *Med bull m & s* 5:212, 1883.

FISHER, GEORGE JACKSON, Sing Sing, NY 1851– (b/XI–27–1825; d/II–3–1893) MD UCNY 1849; Hon MA Madison 1859. *Med reg NY NJ Conn* 1893: 301. *Buff m & s jour* 23:502, 1893. *Bost m & s jour* 128:152, 1893? *Atkinson* I:340. *K&B* III: 408–409.

FISHER, HENRY M , Akron, O (d/I–21–1899 @ 57) MD Jefferson 1872. *JAMA* 32:263, 1899. *Polk* 1886:735.

FISHER, HENRY NEWTON, NYC; CW–USA (d/XI–25–1862 Fortress Monroe or III–16–1863 NYC) MD UCNY 1858. *Tr AMA* 14:205–06, 1864. *Med reg NY NJ Conn* 1865: 218. *Nat med jour* 1:294, 1870/71.

FISHER, JACOB, MD (b/XII–2–1796; d/II–18–1859) MD U Md 1821. *Tr AMA* 13:810–811, 1860. *Med annals Md:* 396.

FISHER, JAMES A, Reading Pa (d/III–6–1897 @56) MD Pa Med Coll 1853. *JAMA* 28:665, 1897. *Polk* 1896: 1331.

FISHER, JOHN, Pikesville, Md (b/VII– –1803 Balto Co, d/XII–22–1877) MD U Md 1824. *Med annals Md:* 396.

FISHER, JOHN, Baltimore (b/Gny; d/VIII–15–1899) MD CPS Balto 1892. *JAMA* 33: 620, 1899.

FISHER, JOHN DIX, Boston (b/III–27–1797 Needham, Mass; d/III–3–1850) MD Harvard 1825; AB Brown 1820. *Tr AMA* 3:439–40, 1850. *Buff med jour* 5:670, 1850. *Bost m&s j* 42: 106, 117–121, 1850. *K&B* III: 409.

FISHER, JOHN F Philadelphia (d/XII–9–1904 @60) MD Jefferson 1872. *Pa m j* 8:335, 1904/05. *Polk* 1886: 815.

FISHER, LEVI H , Shreveport, La (b/V– –1827 E Liverpool, O; d/I–10–1904) MD U La 1853. *New Orl m & s jour* 56:633, 1904. *Polk* 1896: 626.

FISHER, LEWIS, CW–USA; NYC (b/1839 Mobile, Ala; d/II–28–1887 Jacksonville, Fla) MD UCNY 1861. *Med reg NY NJ Conn* 1887: 260. *Bost m & s jour* 116:248, 1887. *Polk* 1886: 678.

FISHER, N H , CW–USA (d/I–25–1862) MD Med Coll Ohio 1862. *Nat med jour* 1:294, 1870/71.

FISHER, NATHANIEL AUGUSTUS, Providence, RI; CW–USA (b/VIII–3–1811 Attleboro, Mass; d/III or V–19–1883) MD Harvard 1834; AB Amherst 1831. *Harvard in CW*: 227–28. *Tr RI Med Soc* 3:67–68, 1883–88. *Butler* 1878: 747.

FISHER, PRESTON, Patten, Me 1855; CW–USA; Old Town 1865–68; Orono 1869–77; Boston 1891– (b/XI–9 1829 Corinna; d/IX–23–1901 Jamaica Plain, Mass) MD Jefferson 1851; Bowdoin [?] *Bowdoin cat*? *Polk* 1886:425.

FISHER, SAMUEL, Greencastle, Ind (b/VII–29–1823 New Columbia Pa; d/XI–13–1887) MD Med Coll O 1857. *Tr Ind St Med Soc* 1888: 207. *Butler* 1878: 202.

FISHER, WALTER W R , USA (b/1854 Va; d/VI–8–1896 Ft Meade, SD?) MD UVa 1878. *JAMA* 27: 52, 1896. *Army List* 1815–1900: 309. *Polk* 1896: 1371.

FISHER, WILLIAM, Pikesville, Md (b/1794 Balto Co; d/VIII–7–1879) MD U Md 1816. *Med annals Md:* 396.

FISK, CHARLES E , Peoria, Ill (d/V–2–1866 @ 39) MD *Med surg rep Phila* 14: 400, 1866.

FISK, CHARLES LEE Jr [?] Greenfield, Mass (d/IV–21–1906 @ 75) MD NY Med Coll 1858. *Bost m & s jour* 154: 480, 1906. *Polk* 1896: 713.

FISK, CYRUS MENTOR, Lowell, Mass; Bradford, NH (b/I–9–1825 Chichester; d/I–21–1895) MD Hon Dartmouth 1870; ng Dartm'th 1845. *Bost m & s jour* 132: 120, 1895.

FISK, MARCUS LYON, Warehouse Pt, Conn (b/XII–16 1817 Willington; d/IV–2–1883) MD Pa Med Coll 1842. *Proc Conn Med Soc* ns2:171–72, 1883. *Butler* 1878: 76.

FISK, S NEWELL, Chazy, NY (d/VI–11–1856 @ 47)

MD U Vt 1833. *Bost m & s jour* 54:407, 1856.

FISK, SAMUEL AUGUSTUS, Northampton, Mass (b/III 26–1821 Cambridge; d/XI–16–1884) MD UPa 1846; AB Yale 1844. *Bost m&s jour* 111:504, 1884; 112:264, 1885. *Med s rep Phila* 51: 604, 1884. *Atkinson* I: 323. *Butler* 1878: 350.

FISKE, CALEB, Scituate, RI; RevWar–USA (b/1753; d/ IX– –1835) Hon MD Brown 1821. *Tr RI Med Soc* 1:41–42, 1859–77.

FISKE, CALVIN PARK, Fiskdale, Mass (b/VII–27–1806 Sturbridge; d/VII–6–1874 Hillsdale/Hinsdale Ill) MD Harvard 1829;AB Brown 1826. *Bost m&s j* 91:124 1874.

FISKE, CYRUS K , Providence, RI (d/VIII?–29–1874 St Johns, NB) MD *Med surg rep Phila* 31: 180, 1874.

FISKE, DANIEL SHAW, Brookfield, Mass (b/XI–13–1820; d/IV–29–1878) MD Castleton 1846. *Tr AMA* 33: 554–55, 1882.

FISKE, EUGENE RUFUS, Salem, Ore (b/VI–4–1817 Cambridgeport, Mass; d/VIII–27–1877) MD Harvard 1863; AB Brown 1844. *Brown hist cat*: 1844.

FISKE, HENRY MORTIMER, Athens, Ill; San Francisco 1851– (b/XII–10–1823; d/IV–3–1896) <MD U St Charles 1843> MD Cooper 1870 ad eundem. *JAMA* 26: 794, 1896. *Atkinson* I:410. *Polk* 1896: 233.

FISKE, ROBERT TREAT PAINE, Hingham, Mass (d/V 8–1866 @ 66) MD Harvard 1821; AB 1818. *Bost m&s jour* 74: 308, 1866. *Med surg rep Phila* 14: 400, 1866.

FISKE, SAMUEL NELSON, CW–USA; Brooklyn (d/XI 10–1886) MD UCNY 1861. *Med reg NY NJ Conn* 1887: 260. *Bost m & s jour* 115:484, 1886.

FISKE, WILLIAM BOYD, Cambridge, Mass (d/V–9–1892 @ 30) MD Harvard 1887; AB 1882. *Bost m & s jour* 126: 484, 1892; 127: 27, 51, 1892.

FISKE, WILLIAM MEADE LINDSLEY, CW–USA; Brooklyn (b/V–10–1841; d/XII–21–1904) MD Bellevue 1863; MD NY Hom Med Coll 1864. *Tr Am Inst Homeop* 1905: 840. *Polk* 1886: 645.

FISLER, BENJAMIN, Port Elizabeth, NJ (b/1769; d/1854? @85) MD *Tr Med Soc NJ* 1871: 180–81.

FISLER, LORENZO FELIX, Camden, NJ (b/III–29–1797; d/III–30–1871) MD UPa 1818. *Tr AMA* 24:358, 1873. *Tr Med Soc NJ* 1871: 246–47.

FISLER, SAMUEL F , Clayton, NJ (b/X–16–1813; d/VI–20–1893) MD Jefferson 1844. *Tr Med Soc NJ* 1894:268–269. *Butler* 1878: 468.

FITCH, ANDREW TITCOMB, Naples & Bridgeton, Me; USA; NYC 1855–62; CW–USA (b/VIII–9–1826 Portland; d/II–14–1889) MD Bowdoin 1851; ng Bowdoin Coll 1844–47. *Bowdoin cat*: 1848. *Polk* 1886:427.

FITCH, CLARENCE LOVELL, New Haven, Conn (b/II 15–1858 Walton, NY; d/IV–13–1896) MD Dartmouth 1883. *JAMA* 26: 934, 1896. *Polk* 1890: 224.

FITCH, FREDERICK JAMES, Meriden, Conn (b/IX–17 1842 Chester, Vt; d/IV–25–1881) MD Bellevue 1865. *Proc Conn Med Soc* 1881: 213–14. *Butler* 1878: 76.

FITCH, GEORGE ARTHUR, Washington, DC (b/VII–30–1846 Morgantown, Va; d/XI–30–1875) MD Georgetown 1868; AM 1869. *Tr AMA* 29:654–55, 1878. *Hist Med Soc DC*: 290.

FITCH, GEORGE W , CW–USA (d/VI–1–1864 Pulaski, Tenn) MD *Nat med jour* 1:294, 1870/71.

FITCH, GRAHAM NEWELL, Logansport, Ind (b/XII–5 –1809 LeRoy NY; d/XI–29–1892) <MD Fairfield> *JAMA* 19:733,1892. *Chic med rec* 4:79,1893. Kemper, *Ind*: 270. *Biogr dir Congress* 1774–1961: 891.

FITCH, HENRY LEWIS, New Haven Co, Conn (d/1858 @ 24) MD Yale 1856. *Proc Conn Med Soc* 1859: 19.

FITCH, JAMES CLARK, Hope, NJ (b/XI–7–1792 Greensburgh, NY; d/III–22–1884) <MD Fairfield 1826> *Tr Med Soc NJ* 1884: 169–70. *Butler* 1878: 469.

FITCH, JAMES D , NYC (d/VII–20–1881 @ 80) MD CPSNY 1829; AB Union 1823. *Chic med rev* 4:346, 1881. *Med rec* 20: 195, 1881.

FITCH, LUTHER, Portland, Me 1846–50; Sacramento 1853–65 (b/IX–27–1821 Westbrook Md; d/I–3–1891) MD Bowdoin 1846; AB 1843. *Bowd'n cat*: 1843. *Polk* 1886: 427.

FITCH, LUTHER P , Charles City, Ia (b/III–26–1836 Groton Mass; d/II–26–1889) MD CPSNY 1864; AB Beloit. *Tr Ia St Med Soc* 7: 527–28 1889. *Atkinson* I: 545. *Polk* 1886: 353.

FITCH, WILLIAM, Dryden, NY (d/IX–14–1893 Franklin) MD Albany 1849. *JAMA* 21: 630, 1893. *Tr NY St Med Soc* 11: 741 ff.

FITCH, WILLIAM MOSELEY, CW–CSA; Charleston, SC (b/1823; d/1879) MD Med Coll SC 1845. *Tr AMA* 30: 818–19, 1879.

FITCH, WORHAM LEE, Nantucket, Mass (b/1803 Colebrook; d/VII–20–1872) MD *Bost m & s jour* ns10: 156, 1872.

FITHIAN, ENOCH, Bridgeton & Greenwich. NJ (b/V 10–1792 Roadstown; d/XI–15–1892) MD UPa 1815. *Tr NJ Med Soc* 1893: 179–80. *JAMA* 19: 733, 1892. *Bost m & s jour* 127: 516, 1892.

FITHIAN, HENRY CLINTON, Scotch Plains, NJ (b/ Bridgeton; d/VIII–22–1889 Port Norris) MD UPa 1877. *Med surg rep Phila* 61:252, 1889. *Polk* 1886: 610.

FITHIAN, JOSEPH, Woodbury, NJ (b/VI–25–1795 Fairton; d/I–8–1881) Lic by Supreme Court 1816. *Tr Med Soc NJ* 1881: 160–61.

FITHIAN, WASHINGTON, Paris, Ky (b/I–8–1825 NJ; d/VI–15–1904) MD Med Coll Ohio 1848; AB Miami 1845. *Miami cat*: 1845. *Polk* 1886: 404.

FITHIAN, WILLIAM, Danville, Ill (b/IV–7–1799 Cincinnati; d/IV–5–1890) Lic by Exam Bd. *Tr Ill St Med Soc* 1890:33–36. *Polk* 1886: 275.

FITTS, JOHN FRANKLIN, Francestown, NH (b/VIII–4 1839 Candia; d/X–19–1873) MD Dartmouth 1867. *Tr NH Med Soc* 1874: 10; 1875: 158–62.

FITTS, JOHN HENRY, Shongalo, Miss (b/II–20–1827;

d/VI–21–1851) MD Jefferson 1849; AB U Ala 1847. *Univ Ala cat*: 82.

FITZ, EDWARD SOUTHWORTH, Chicago; Neligh, Nebr (b/IX–6–1842 Pembroke, NH; d/III–14–1902) MD Rush 1881; AB Amherst 1871. *Amherst, Men of*: 1871. *Polk* 1886: 263.

FITZ, SAMUEL EATON, Roxbury, Mass (b/I–26–1836 Boston; d/X–20–1883) MD Harvard 1878; AB 1862. *Bost m & s jour* 109:430, 1883.

FITZGERALD, ALPHONSUS JOSEPH, NYC (d/III–29–1900) MD Bellevue 1889. *JAMA* 34: 957, 1900. *Polk* 1890: 813.

FITZGERALD, DAVID J , Glens Falls NY (b/Ireland; d/VII–17–1904 @ 46) MD Albany 1884. *Bost m & s jour* 151:212, 1904. *Polk* 1896: 1023.

FITZGERALD, JAMES HENRY, Chicago (d/III–29–1899) MD Bellevue 1878. *JAMA* 32:787, 1899. *Polk* 1896: 363.

FITZGERALD, JENKINS AUGUSTUS, Columbia, Pa (b/Ind; d/VIII–11–1879) MD Jefferson 1866. *Med rec NY* 16:192, 1879.

FITZGERALD, JOSEPH S , NYC (b/II–25–1843; d/I 7–1895) MD Georgetown 1870. *Med reg NY NJ Conn* 1895:222. *Bost m & s jour* 132:70, 1895. *JAMA* 24: 101, 1895. *Polk* 1890: 813.

FITZGERALD, PETER FLETCHER, CW–CSA; Grenada, Miss (b/XI–2–1836 Smithville, NC; d/X–13–1878) MD U La 1858. *Tr AMA* 30:861–63, 1879. *Tr Miss St Med Assoc* 1878–81: 41–42.

FITZHUGH, JOHN Jr, USN 1818–1826 (d/VII–6–1826) MD U Md 1817. *Med annals Md:* 397. *Hamersly*: 253.

FITZHUGH, P C , CW–USA (d/V–3–1866) MD *Nat med jour* 1:294, 1870/71.

FITZMAURICE, THOMAS J Paterson, NJ (d/V–20–1904 @35) MD Bellevue 1893. *Bost m & s jour* 150: 578, 1904.

FITZPATRICK, JAMES W , CW–USA (d/V–6–1864 Harwood Hosp DC) MD? CPSNY 1841. *Nat med jour* 1:294, 1870/71.

FITZPATRICK, PHILLIPS, CW–CSA; Wetumpka, Ala (b/III–15–1830; d/IV–29–1901) MD Tulane 1853; AB U Ala 1849. *Tr Med Assn St Ala* 1902: 129. *Polk* 1893: 165.

FITZSIMMONS, THOMAS DANA, Brooklyn (b/IV–13 1874; d/II–5–1900) MD LICH 1897. *Bost m & s jour* 142: 179, 1900. *JAMA* 34: 446, 1900.

FIX, IRA NIBLOCK, Turtle Creek, Pa (d/XI–22–1906) MD Jefferson 1893. *Pa med jour* 10: 214, 1906/07.

FLAGG, CHANDLER, Marblehead, Mass (b/I–1–1782 Grafton, Mass; d/IX–10–1878) MD ? AB Brown 1803. *Bost m & s jour* 59: 148, 1859.

FLAGG, JOSIAH FOSTER, Boston (b/I–11–1789; d/XII–30–1853) MD Harvard 1815. *Bost m & s j* 49: 492, 1853. *Phila jour homeop* 3: 564, 1854/55. Homeopath.

FLAGG, LEVI WELLS, Yonkers, NY (d/V–15–1884 @ 67) MD CPSNY 1847; AB Yale 1839; AM 1842. *Med surg rep Phila* 50: 704, 1884. *Tr Amer Inst Homeop* 1893:140. *Butler* 1878: 538. Homeopath.

FLAGG, ROBERT NEWTON, Yonkers, NY (d/X–1–1897 @38) MD NY Homeop 1880. *Tr Am Inst Homeop* 1898: 49. *Med vis* 13:349, 1897. *Polk* 1886: 716. Homeopath.

FLAGG, SAMUEL BENJAMIN, Grafton, Mass (b/VIII–6–1828; d/XI–16–1900) MD Berkshire 1854; AB Brown 1850. *Brown hist cat*: 1850.

FLAGG, URBANE HALLECK, Mittineague, Mass (d/XI 28–1894) MD Jefferson 1878. *Bost m & s jour* 131: 655, 1894. *Polk* 1886: 470.

FLANDERS, MARTHA [MARY?] JANE, Lynn, Mass (b/I–15–1823 Concord, NH; d/XI–3–1898) MD New Engl Female Med Coll 1861. *Tr Am Inst Homeop* 1899: 926. *Polk* 1886: 468.

FLANDRAU, THOMAS MACOMB, Rome, NY (b/VII–8–1826 NYC; d/VIII–8–1898) MD Natl Med Coll 1848. *Buff m & s jour* 38:139–40, 1898. *Atkinson* I: 202. *Butler* 1878: 553.

FLANNER, THOMAS WISTER, Philadelphia (b/NC; d/IV–18–1899) MD UPa 1851. *JAMA* 32: 955, 1899.

FLATLEY, THOMAS WILLIAM, Canton, Mass (d/IX–6–1873 @ 30) MD Harvard 1866. *Bost m & s jour* ns12: 276, 1873. *Med surg rep Phila* 29: 234, 1873.

FLEECE, E B , Campbellsville, Ky; Wildwood, Fla (d/XI–30–1898) MD Louisville Med Coll 1876. *JAMA* 31:1542, 1898. *Polk* 1886: 393.

FLEET, FRANCIS, NYC (d/V–8–1876 @ 69) MD UCNY 1849. *Med reg NY NJ Conn* 1876: 242.

FLEETWOOD, JOHN H , Thibodeaux, La (b/Tenn; d/III–7–1905 @75) MD Tulane 1872. *New Orl m & s jour* 57: 786, 1905. *Polk* 1896: 627.

FLEISCHAUER, FRANK WILLIAM, Brooklyn (d/XI–22–1891) MD LICH 1889. *Med reg NY NJ Conn* 1892: 278.

FLEISCHMAN, DAVID, Albany, NY (d/I–30–1892) MD Albany Med Coll 1881. *Tr Med Soc St NY* 1892: 457. *Polk* 1886: 638.

FLEISCHMAN, WILLIAM, ? (d/XI–23–1868 @ 70) MD ? *New Engl med gaz* 4:68, 1869. Homeopath.

FLEISHER, REBECCA, Philadelphia (d/1906) MD Woman's Med Coll Pa 1886. *Pa med jour* 10:118, 1906/07. *Flint* 1897: 817.

FLEMING, DAVID PETER, NYC (d/VII–9–1902 @ 36) MD Bellevue 1896. *Bost m & s jour* 147: 88, 1902.

FLEMING, JAMES ALOYSIUS, Boston; USA (d/IX–30 1883 @ 30) MD Harvard 1875. *Bost m & s jour* 109: 336, 358, 617, 1883. *Med bull m & s* 5:259, 1883.

FLEMING, JOHN McLEAN, Chicago (d/VI–10–1896 @50) MD Rush 1872. *JAMA* 26:1245 1896. *Polk* 1886: 263.

FLEMING, JOHN PERKINS, Baltimore (b/I–31–1829 Chester Co, Pa; d/VIII–13–1868) MD U Md 1851. *Med annals Md:* 397–98.

 Spec. educ'l status abbrev. as: ***ng*** = college verified attendance without degree;

FLEMING, JOHN ROBERT, Forkland, Ala (b/II-19-1830; d/1852) MD Med Coll St SC 1852; AB U Ala 1848; AM 1849. *U Ala cat*: 85.

FLEMING, WILLIAM JAMES, Philadelphia; CW-USA; (b/III-19-1828; d/III-1/3-1889) MD UPa 1851; AB 1848. *Med bull m & s* 11: 126, 1889. *Polk* 1886: 815.

FLEMMING, THORNTON H , Canton, Ill (d/IV-11-1894 @ 85) MD *JAMA* 22: 601, 1894. *Butler* 1878: 152. *Polk* 1890: 303.

FLESHER, FREDERICK CHARLES GREGORY, Faribault, Minn (d/VIII-14-1901) MD U Cal 1893. *JAMA* 37: 595, 1901.

FLETCHER, EZRA WOOD, Providence, RI (d/VI-25-1847) MD Harvard 1843; AB Brown 1839. *Brown hist cat:* 1839.

FLETCHER, GEORGE, Brooklyn (b/IV-23-1816 Lancaster, Engl; d/V-20-1882) MD LICH 1875; AB St John's, Cambr., Engl. *Med reg NY NJ Conn* 1883: 228.

FLETCHER, JOHN MURRAY, Belfast, Me (b/III-23-1846 Lincolnville; d/VIII-7-1899 @ 73) MD Bowdoin 1868. *JAMA* 33: 493, 1899. *Polk* 1896: 633.

FLETCHER, JOHN ROBINSON, Wartrace, Tenn; CW-CSA (b/Brunswick Co, Va; d/II-9-1890) MD UPa 1854. *U Pa med alum CW*: 1854. *Polk* 1886: 874.

FLETCHER, JOHN SWEPSON, Smithville, Tenn; CW-CSA (b/XI-21-1836 Murfreesboro; d/VI-1-1877) MD UPa 1860; MD U Nashville 1858. *U Pa med alum CW*: 1860 (suppl).

FLETCHER, SAMUEL MARK, Englewood, Ill (b/V-1-1822 Dunstable, Mass; d/X-3-1875) MD Hahnemann Phila 1856; AB Amherst 1846. *Amherst, Men of*: 1846. Homeopath.

FLIESBURG, OSCAR ALFRED, Stillwater & Minneapolis, Minn (b/1851; d/IX-12-1906) MD CPS Chicago 1885. *U Ill Coll Med alum*: 6. *JAMA* 57: 1124, 1906. *Polk* 1886: 518.

FLINT, AUSTIN Sr, Chicago; Buffalo 1847-52; Louisville, Ky 1852-56; New Orleans 1858-61; NYC 1861- (b/X-20-1812 Petersham, Mass; d/III-13-1886) MD Harvard 1833. *JAMA* 6:361-64 1886. *So pract* 8:187-93, 1886. *Bost m&s jour* 114: 264; 286-87, 1886. *Tr M S St NY* 1887:556-66. *Atkinson* I: 6-7. *K&B* III: 417-18.

FLINT, JOHN J , Albany, NY; Troy, NY 1886- (d/VII 19-1891 @ 72) MD Albany 1846. *Tr Med Soc St NY* 1892. *Polk* 1886: 712.

FLINT, JOHN SYDENHAM, Roxbury, Mass (d/IV-16-1887 @ 63) MD Harvard 1846; AB 1843. *Bost m & s jour* 116: 392, 1887. *Butler* 1878: 339.

FLINT, JOSHUA BARKER, Louisville, Ky (b/X-13-1801 Cohasset, Mass; d/III-19-1864) MD Harvard 1825; AB 1820. *Bost m&s jour* 70: 168, 1864. *Tr Ky St Med Soc* 1869. *K&B* III: 418-419.

FLINT, KENDALL, Haverhill, Mass (b/II-4-1807 Danvers; d/IX-28-1892) MD Harvard 1839; AB Amherst 1831. *Bost m&s j* 127: 348, 1892. *Polk* 1890: 549.

FLINT, THOMAS, San Benito Co, Cal (b/V-13-1824 Me; d/VI-19-1904) MD Jefferson 1849. *Cal st jour med* 2:232, 1904. *JAMA* 43:60, 1904.

FLOOD, PATRICK HENRY, Elmira, NY (b/Pa; d/III-12 1886) MD Geneva 1850. *Tr NY St Med Soc* 11:741 ff, 1894. *Butler* 1874: 538. *Polk* 1886: 660.

FLORES y HERNANDEZ, MAURICIO, Harrisburg, Pa (d/II-2-1906 @ 40) MD Howard 1903. *Pa med jour* 9: 608, 1905/06. Black?

FLOWER, BYRON L , CW-USA (d/X-24-1864? Ft Simonds, Georgetown, Va!) MD Castleton 1860. *Nat med jour* 1:295, 1870/71.

FLOWERS, JOAB R , Columbus, O (b/VII-25-1835 New Lisbon; d/V-27-1895) MD Cleveland Homeop 1861. *JAMA* 24: 861, 1895. *Tr Amer Inst Homeop* 1896: 1187. *Polk* 1890: 910.

FLOWERS, SAMUEL BRYCE, Mt Olive, NC?; CW-CSA (b/X-31-1835 Wayne Co, NC; d/VI-6-1886) MD UPa 1859; att Wake Forest Coll. *NC med jour* 18:66, 1886. *Tr NC Med Soc* 1887: 159. *Atkinson* 1878: 470. *U Pa med alum CW*: 1859. *Butler* 1878: 593.

FLOWERS, WILLIAM CALDWELL, USA 1863-73? Cambridge, Mass (d/X-10-1904 @ 72) MD Harvard 1861. *Bost m & s jour* 151: 478, 1904. *Harvard in CW*: 263-64. *Polk* 1896: 709.

FLOYD, CHARLES SLOCUM, Austin, Pa (d/XI-27-1896) MD Jefferson 1887. *JAMA* 27: 1360, 1896.

FLUD, DANIEL, Summerville, SC (d/III-24-1896 @ 77) <MD Med Coll SC> *NC med jour* 37:246, 1896. *Polk* 1886: 856.

FLYNN, JOHN, Philadelphia (d/VIII-24-1866) MD ? U Pa 1856. *Med surg rep Phila* 15: 208, 1866.

FLYNN, PERCIVAL HERBERT JOHN, NYC (d/XI-18-1888 @ c30) MD UCNY 1882. *Med reg NY NJ Conn* 1889:274.

FLYNN, WILLIAM D, Redwood Falls Minn (d/XI-23 1897 @ 56) MD Louisville Med Coll 1876. *JAMA* 29: 1181, 1897. *Polk* 1886:516 [as Wm D Flinn, Rush 1868].

FOARD, ANDREW JACKSON, Charleston, SC; CW-CSA; (b/Baldwin Co [?] d/I-18-1868 @ 42) MD Jefferson 1848. *New Orl m & s jour* 21:637, 1868. *Med surg rep Phila* 18:420, 1868. *SHSP* 22:203, 1893.

FOBES, JOSEPH BASSETT [BARTLETT?] E Bridgewater, Mass (d/VIII-30 or 31-1898) MD Harvard 1839. *Bost m & s jour* 139:256, 1898. *Polk* 1896: 708.

FOERTSCH, JACOB, NYC (b/VII-24-1812;d/I-1876) MD UCNY 1875. *Med reg NY NJ Conn* 1876: 242.

FOGG, DAVID SYLVESTER, Norwood, Mass (b/III-30 1821 Meredith, NH; d/VIII-30-1893) MD Dartmouth 1846. *Bost m&s jour* 129:260,358, 1893. *Polk* 1890: 554.

FOGG, EDMUND EASTMAN, Buxton Centre, Me (b/VI 7-1839 Limerick; d/IV-13-1887) MD Harvard 1869; AB Bowdoin 1861. *Bowdoin cat*: 1861.

FOGG, ELBRIDGE GERRY, Fairfield, Me 1873-82; Wakefield, Neb 1882- (b/XII-5-1842 Paris, Me; d/III-

21-1887) MD UCNY 1868; MD Bowdoin 1866. *Bowdoin med cat*: 1866.

FOGG, JOHN SAMUEL HILL, So Boston (b/V-21-1826 Eliot, Me; d/X-16-1893) MD Harvard 1850; AB Bowdoin 1846. *JAMA* 21:667, 1893. *Butler* 1878: 339.

FOGG, WILLIAM JOHN GORDON, So Boston (d/II-27-1894 @ 43) MD Harvard 1876; AB 1873. *Bost m&s jour* 130: 251-52, 1894. *Polk* 1886: 473.

FOGLE, JAMES O A, Columbus & Allapaha, Ga; CW-CSA (b/IX-12-1838; d/1888) MD Med Coll Va 1864; AB UNC 1860. *UNC cat*: 201. *Polk* 1886: 224.

FOLEY, JOHN BERNARD, Roxbury, Mass (d/VII-26-1882 @ 32) MD Harvard 1877. *Bost m & s jour* 107: 618, 1882.

FOLEY, WALTER LEMON, San Francisco; NYC (d/X-20-1883 @ 27) MD Bellevue 1877. *Med reg NY NJ Conn* 1884: 229.

FOLSOM, DAVID, Augusta, Me (b/III-24-1800 Tamworth, NH; d/VIII-11-1865) MD Bowdoin 1825. *Tr Me Med Assoc* 1866-68: 71.

FOLSOM, LEVI, New Bedford, Mass; NYC (b/XII-13-1802 Limerick, Me; d/X-25-1867) Hon MD Berkshire 1848; ng Bowdoin. *Tr AMA* 19: 414-15, 1868. *Med reg NY NJ Conn* 1868: 325.

FOLSOM, NORTON, CW-USA; Cambridge Mass (b/IV 15-1842; d/IX-12-1903) MD Harvard 1864. *Bost m & s jour* 149:332,359,1903. *Polk* 1896:709.

FOLSOM, ROBERT, CW-CSA (d/1864 "in battle") MD UCNY 1859. *UCNY* cat: 1859.

FOLTS, DANIEL VON, E Boston (b/VIII-31-1815 Frankfort, NY; d/V-27-1889) MD Albany 1840. *Bost m &s j* 120: 652, 1889; 121: 644, 1889. *Butler* 1896: 339.

FOLTZ, JONATHAN MESSERSMITH, USN (b/IV-25 1810; d/IV-12-1877 Phila) MD Jefferson 1830. *Tr AMA* 33:555-58, 1882. *Butler* 1878: xii. *K&B* III:420.

FOLWELL, JOSEPH N, New Orleans (d/III-31-1900 @ 71) MD Jefferson 1848. *JAMA* 34:957, 1900. *New Orl m & s jour* 52:694, 1900. *Polk* 1896: 622.

FOLWELL, MAHLON BAINBRIDGE, Buffalo (b/ 1841; d/XII-10-1895) MD Buff Med Coll 1867. *Buff m & s jour* 35:512 ff, 1895. *JAMA* 25:1108, 1895; 26: 93, 1896. *Butler* 1878: 537.

FONDA, DAVID BARTHOLOMEW, Chicago (d/ VI?- -1903) MD Bennett Ecl Med Coll 1878. *Chicago med rec* 25:88, 1903. *Flint* 1897: 260. Eclectic.

FONERDEN, JOHN, Baltimore (b/I-22-1804; d/V-6-1869) MD U Md 1823. *Tr AMA* 21:473-75, 1870. *Med annals Md:* 398. *K&B* III: 420-21.

FONTAINE, ABRAHAM WALTON, New Canton, Va (b/1832 Buckingham, Va; d/1883?) <MD U Va> *Tr Med Soc Va* 1883:188-89. *Butler* 1878: 828.

FONTAINE, JOHN B, CW-CSA (d/1864?) MD Med Coll Va 1860. *Med surg rep Phila* 12:164, 1864/65. Blanton, *Va surg in CW*: 401.

FOOTE, CHARLES CHENEY, New Haven, Conn (b/IX-5-1825 Jamestown, NY; d/XI-9-1871) MD Jefferson 1851; AB Union 1849. *New Engl med gaz* 6:568, 1871. *Tr Am Inst Hom* 1873: 509. Homeopath.

FOOTE, ELIAL TODD, Jamestown, NY (b/V-1-1796 Greenfield, Mass; d/XI-17-1877 New Haven, Conn) MD Hon Castleton 1828; lic Chenango Co, NY Med Soc 1815. *Tr Med Soc St NY* 1865: 277-79. *Tr Am Inst Hom* 1893:141. *New Engl med gaz* 12:567, 1877. *King* 1: 203. *K&B* III:421. Homeopath.

FOOTE, GEORGE ANDERSON, CW-CSA; Warrenton, NC (b/XII 16-1835 Warren Co; d/1899) MD Jefferson 1856; MD Med Coll Va 1884. *Atkinson* I:346-47. *Polk* 1886: 727.

FOOTE, GEORGE FRANKLIN, Stamford, Conn (b/III-13-1817 Albany, NY; d/V-8-1889) MD UCNY 1848. *Med vis* 5:262, 1889. *Tr Amer Inst Homeop* 1889: 173. *Polk* 1886: 196. Homeopath.

FOOTE, GEORGE W, Galesburgh, Ill (b/VII-4-1829 Hamilton, NY; d/IV-4-1892) MD Cleveland Homeop 1854. *Med vis* 8:341, 1892. *Polk* 1886: 280. Homeopath.

FOOTE, HENRY E, Cincinnati (d/VII-12-1871 @ 46) MD Med Coll Ohio 1847. *Tr Ohio St M S* 1872: 261-62.

FOOTE, HERSCHEL, Fayette Co, Pa; Philadelphia (b/1834 Westmoreland Co; d/II-6-1874) MD Jefferson 1863. *Med surg rep Phila* 30:180, 204, 1874.

FORBES, J G [or A], Round Rock, Ark (d/IX-24-1878 Memphis) MD *Tr AMA* 30:863, 1879.

FORBES, JAMES HARRISON, Brooklyn (d/II-6-1896 @ 76) MD UCNY 1857. *JAMA* 26: 490, 1896. *Polk* 1890: 770.

FORBES, SAMUEL FRANKLIN, Toledo, O; CW-USA; (d/1897 Socorro, NM) MD UCNY 1850. *JAMA* 29:1081, 1897. *Atkinson* I: 333. *Polk* 1896: 1216.

FORBES, WILLIAM SMITH, CW-USA; Philadelphia (b/II-10-1831 Falmouth, Va; d/II-17-1905) MD Jefferson 1852; MD UPa 1866. *Tr CPP* cent vol: 224; s3 29: liii-lxiv, 1907. *Bost m & s jour* 153: 708, 1905. *Atkinson* I:708. *K&B* III: 421-22.

FORCE, CHARLES FAIRCHILD, Cababa & Selma, Ala; CW-CSA (b/II-9-1827 DC; d/VIII-4-1884) MD Columbian DC 1852. *Hist Med Soc DC*: 251.

FORCE, H F [or J R] Hot Springs, Ark (d/X-13 1878 Memphis) MD ? *Tr AMA* 30: 863, 1879. *New Orl m&s j* ns6:506-08, 1878-79. *Med rec NY* 14:320, 1878.

FORD, ALONZO W, Newton, Ala (d/IX-15-1887) <MD Louisville 1874> *Tr Med Assoc St Ala* 1888: 316.

FORD, CHARLES MASON, Washington, DC; CW-USA (b/V-15-1840 near Troy, NY; d/II-15-1884) MD UPa 1861. *JAMA* 2:249-50, 1884. *U Pa med alum CW*: 1861. *Hist Med Soc DC*: 267. *Butler* 1878: 93.

FORD, CORYDON LA, Ann Arbor Mich (b/VIII-29-1813 Lexington NY; d/IV-14-1894) <MD Geneva 1842> *Med reg NY NJ Conn* 1895: 223. *Buff m&s j* 33: 625, 1894. *JAMA* 22:601, 1894. *Atkinson* I:545. *K&B* III: 423.

 Spec. educ'l status abbrev. as: ***ng*** = college verified attendance without degree;

FORD, DESAUSSURE, Augusta, Ga (d/II–5–1905) MD Med Coll Ga 1856. *So pract* 28: 166, 1906. *Butler* 1878: 111. *Polk* 1886: 226.

FORD, E C , ? (d/1878 Summerville, Tenn) MD *Tr AMA* 30:863, 1879.

FORD, GEORGE, Ward's Island, NY (b/1812; d/I–7–1881) Hon MD NY Med Coll 1863; MRCS (Engl) 1837. *Med reg NY NJ Conn* 1882:227. *Bost m&s j* 104:91 1881.

FORD, HENRY A , Gaboon Mission, Africa (d/II–2–1858 @ 38) MD UCNY 1850; AB Williams 1842. *Bost m & s jour* 58: 378–79, 1858.

FORD, JAMES BRADLEY, Norwalk, O (b/X–22–1826 Engl; d/VI–27–1896) MD U Mich 1857; AB Amherst 1854. *Amherst, Men of*: 1854. *Polk* 1886: 764.

FORD, JAMES H , Wabash, Ind (d/XII–30–1898) MD Med Coll Ind 1872. *JAMA* 32: 41, 1898.

FORD, JOHN FRANKLIN, CW–CSA; Lewisville Tx to 1874; Decatur Tx (b/IX–22–1844 Cleveland, Tn; d/VI–26–1904) MD UCNY 1874; att Emory & Henry. *Tex st j med* (Tr Tex St Med Assn) 1:242, 1906. *Polk* 1896:1425.

FORD, JOHN PRYOR, Nashville (b/I–7–1810 Cumberland Co, Va; d/VIII–17–1865) MD UPa 1831. *Tr Med Soc Tenn* 1876: 81. *Nashville j m & s* 4:320, 1866.

FORD, JOSEPH HALL, Auburn, Ind (b/IX–3–1823 Harrison Co, O; d/V–3–1905) MD Med Coll Ind 1872. *Tr Ind St Med Soc* 1905: 445. *Polk* 1896: 458.

FORD, LEWIS DE SAUSSURE, Augusta, Ga (b/XII–30 1801; d/VIII–21–1883) MD CPSNY 1822. *JAMA* 1: 320, 1883.

FORD, NATHANIEL, Alna, Me to 1854; Brooklyn 1854– (b/I–11–1814 Jefferson, Me; d/III–9–1885) MD Bowdoin 1836; att Bowdoin Coll 1831. *Bost m & s jour* 112: 308, 1885. *Med reg NY NJ Conn* 1885: 237. *Med surg rep Phila* 53:384, 1885.

FORD, SAMPLE, Wheeling, WVa (b/1827 W Alexander, Pa; d/IX–20–1887) <ng UPa Med Dept> *Tr Med Soc WVa* 1888: 590–91. *Butler* 1878: 850. *Polk* 1886: 945.

FORD, THOMAS JOHN INGOLDSBY, NYC (d/XI–11 1887) MD CPSNY 1874; AB CCNY 1871. *Med reg NY NJ Conn* 1888: 253. *Polk* 1886: 678.

FORD, WILLIAM HENRY, CW–USA; Philadelphia (b/X–7–1839; d/Bellmawr, NJ X–19–1897) MD Jefferson 1863; AB Princeton 1860. *Tr CPP* cent vol:224; s3, 20: liv, 1898. *Med bull med & surg* 19:434–35, 1897. *Atkinson* I: 192. *Polk* 1886: 816. *K&B* III: 423.

FORDYCE, BENJAMIN A , Union Springs NY (d/VI–3 1893 @70) Lic Cayuga Co Med Soc 1846. *Bost m & s jour* 129: 52, 1893. *Polk* 1896: 855.

FORE, JAMES H , Baltimore (d/V–16–1895) MD CPS Balto 1886. *JAMA* 24: 861, 1895. *Med annals Md:* 398.

FOREE, ERASMUS DARWIN, Louisville Ky (b/VII–25 1817 New Castle, Ky; d/1882) MD Louisville Med Inst 1839; AB Hanover Coll. *Tr AMA* 33:551–53, 1882. *Atkinson* I: 657.

FOREMAN, EDWARD, Washington, DC (b/1808 Balto; d/IV–14–1885) <MD Washington Coll, Balto 1830> *Med annals Md:* 399.

FOREMAN, EDWIN [EDISON?] KNOX, Littlestown, Pa (b/Frederick Co, Md; d/XII–12–1906) MD U Md 1862. *Pa med jour* 10: 295, 1906/07. *Butler* 1878: 712. *Flint* 1897: 807.

FORMAD, HENRY F, Philadelphia (b/1847 Russia; d/1892) MD UPa 1877. *JAMA* 19: 20, 1892. *Bost m & s jour* 126: 648, 1892. *Tr CPP* cent vol: 225. *Polk* 1886: 816.

FORMAN, AARON, Quakertown, NJ 1766–1794; Pittstown, NJ (b/II–4–1745; d/I–11–1805) MD ? *Tr Med Soc NJ* 1872: 172–73. *Wickes*: 260–61.

FORMAN, DAVID Sr, (b/1791? d/XII–26–1825 @ 34) Lic NJ Med Soc. *Tr Med Soc NJ* 1871: 79.

FORMAN, DAVID, Freehold, NJ (b/IX–23–1796; d/1826) <MD UPa 1820> *Tr Med Soc NJ* 1871: 79.

FORMAN, EUGENE S , Auburn, NY (d/IX–13–1898 @ 51) MD Buffalo Med Coll 1870. *Buff m&s jour* 38: 225, 1898. *JAMA* 31: 742, 1898. *Butler* 1878: 553.

FORMAN, SAMUEL, Freehold, NJ (b/VIII–3–1764; d/XII–11–1845) ng UPa Med Dept; lic V–1788. *Tr Med Soc NJ* 1871: 84–85.

FORMAN, SAMUEL RANDOLPH, Jersey City (d/II–19 1900 @64) MD CPSNY 1857; AB Princeton 1854. *Bost m & s jour* 142: 236, 1900. *JAMA* 34: 573–74, 1900. *Polk* 1896: 938.

FORMAN, WILLIAM, Princeton, NJ (b/VIII–17–1796; d/II–22–1848) MD CPSNY 1819. *Tr M S NJ* 1871: 86.

FORNEY, DANIEL SMICER, Burlington, Ia (d/IV–1898 @ 90) MD Washington U Balto 1828. *JAMA* 30: 1125, 1898. *Med annals Md:* 399. *Polk* 1896: 513.

FORREST, JOHN MURRAY, Kansas City, Mo; Alturas, Cal (d/II–12–1893) MD Bellevue 1868. *Tr Med Soc St Cal* 1894: 294. *Polk* 1886: 163.

FORREST, ROBERT FRANCIS, Cambridge, Mass (d/IX–18–1900 Watertown) MD Harvard 1898. *Bost m & s jour* 143: 332, 1900.

FORRESTER, JAMES Jr, NYC (b/1836; d/XII–14 1871)MD CPSNY 1858. *Med reg NY NJ Conn* 1872:346.

FORRESTER, JAMES CALVIN, NYC (d/VIII–20–1881) MD CPSNY 1835; AB Rutgers 1829. *Med reg NY NJ Conn* 1882: 227.

FORRY, SAMUEL, NYC; Gettysburg, Pa; Washington, DC (b/VI–23–1811 Berlin; d/XI–9–1844) MD Jefferson 1832. *Am j med sci* ns9:264, 1845. *Med annals Md:* 399. *Hist Med Soc DC*:230. *Tr AMA* 3: 440–41, 1850.

FORSAITH, FRANCIS FLINT, Weymouth, Mass (b/V–8–1824 Deering, NH; d/III–10–1894) MD Woodstock 1852. *Bost m & s jour* 130: 276, 1894. *Polk* 1886: 475.

FORSEE, EDGAR B , St Joseph, Mo (d/1894 "@ 50"!) MD U Louisville 1848. *JAMA* 23:768, 1894. *Butler* 1878: 428. *Polk* 1890: 669.

FORSHEE, JOHN M , CW–USA (d/X–25–1862 @26 Monroe, NY) MD UCNY 1858. *Nat med jour* 1:295, 1870/71.

FORST, DAVID, Kingwood, NJ (b/1786? d/VIII-6-1821 @ 35) Stud med w/Dr John Wilson. *Tr Med Soc NJ* 1872: 189–90.

FORSTER, EDWARD JACOB, Boston (b/VII-9-1846 Charlestown, Mass; d/V-15-1896) MD Harvard 1868. *Bost m & s jour* 134: 521, 550, 573, 1896. *JAMA* 26, 1191, 1896. *Med bull med & surg* 18: 272, 1896. *Polk* 1896: 697. *K&B* III:424–25.

FORSTER, WILLIAM CONDIE, Birmingham, Ala (d/X 22–1898 @ 37) MD U Louisville 1882. *Tr Med Assoc St Ala* 1899:233. *JAMA* 31:1128, 1898. *Polk* 1886: 137.

FORSYTH, FRANK LYMAN, Providence, RI (b/II-13-1854 Hampton, NH; d/V-11-1895) MD Harvard 1877. *JAMA* 24: 988, 1895. *Bost m & s jour* 133: 659, 1895. *Tr RI Med Soc* 5:253–54, 1894–98.

FORSYTH, JAMES BRANDER, Chelsea, Mass (d/III-8 1872 @62) MD Harvard 1834. *Bost m&s j* ns9:180 1872.

FORT, ALFRED J, Balto & Limestone Valley Md (d/XII 16–1842 @35) MD UMd 1827. *Med annals Md:* 399.

FORT, GEORGE FRANKLIN, Burlington & Monmouth Co, NJ (b/1809; d/IV-22-1872 New Egypt, NJ) MD UPa 1830. *Tr Med Soc NJ* 1873: 230–31. *Tr AMA* 24:361–62, 1873. *K&B* III:425.

FORT, WILLIAM SAXTON, CW–USN (b/XI-20-1839 Pemberton, NJ; d/III-24-1873 Rio de Janeiro) MD UPa 1860. *U Pa med alum CW*: 1860.

FORTINER, GEORGE ROSEMAN, Philadelphia; Camden, NJ (b/XI-28-1842; d/XI-29-1894 or 1895) MD Pa Med Univ 1879; MD Hahnemann 1887. *Hahn mo* 30:28 (news & advt) 1895. *Tr Amer Inst Homeop* 1895: 254. *Polk* 1886:601. Homeopath.

FORWOOD, WILLIAM STUMP, Darlington, Md except 1869–73 @ Phila & Clarke Co, Ala (b/I-27-1830 Harford Co, Md; d/I-2-1892) MD UPa 1854. *Med annals Md:* 399–400. *Atkinson* I: 121. *Butler* 1874: 319.

FOSS, SIDNEY ALDRIDGE, Pleasant Ridge Park, Ky (b/VI-12-1823 Madison, O; d/II-15-1898) MD Buffalo 1847. *New Orl m & s jour* ns15:836, 1888. *Atkinson* I: 535. *Polk* 1886: 404.

FOSS, STEPHEN, CW–USA; Brooklyn (b/VI-20-1825 New Portland, Me?; d/VII-31-1901) MD Harvard 1859; AB Bowdoin 1853. *Bost m & s jour* 145: 170, 1901. *Polk* 1896: 995.

FOSTER, ADDISON HOWARD, Oak Park & Chicago (d/III-3-1906) MD CPSNY 1866; AB Dartmouth 1863; AM 1883. *Ill med jour* 9:463, 1906. *Polk* 1896: 384.

FOSTER, ALSON JAMES, St Paul, Minn (d/VI-23-1901) MD U Minn 1901. *JAMA* 37: 126, 1901.

FOSTER, AVERY BELCHER, Providence, RI 1856–83; Auburn, Me (b/XII-26-1830 Livermore, Me; d/XII-17-1887) MD NY Med Coll 1856; stud Dartmouth & Bowdoin. *New Engl med gaz* 21:142, 1886. *Polk* 1886: 845. Homeopath.

FOSTER, CHARLES FRANCIS, Cambridge, Mass; CW–USA (d/IX-24-1865 @ 47) MD Harvard 1841; AB 1838. *Bost m&s jour* 72:188, 1865. *Harvard in CW*: 12.

FOSTER, DAVID LAWRENCE, Tuscaloosa, Ala (b/X-27-1831; d/IX-9-1891) MD Jefferson 1857; <ng UC NY> AB U Ala 1856. *U Ala cat*: 104. *Polk* 1886: 140.

FOSTER, EDWARD HORATIO, Concord, NH (b/X-13 1839 Canterbury; d/IV-5-1897) MD Bowdoin 1866. *JAMA* 28: 955, 1897. *Polk* 1896: 918.

FOSTER, GEORGE BARTLETT, Roxbury, Mass; Chicago (d/XI-6-1858 @ 30 or 33) MD Jefferson 1854. *Chic m j* 1:608, 1858. *Bost m&s j* 59:328, 448, 1859.

FOSTER, GEORGE WINSLOW, Washington, DC; Bangor, Me; LeMars Ia 188_; Salt Lake City (b/IX-28-1845 Bangor; d/there I-4-1904) MD Bowdoin 1871; AB 1868. *Bost m&s jour* 150: 56, 1904. *Hist M S DC*: 365. *Polk* 1886: 361.

FOSTER, HALSEY W, Pittsburgh (d/1895 @ 23) MD W Pa Med Coll 1895. *Med bull med & surg* 17:190, 1895.

FOSTER, HARRY STEWART, McKeesport, Pa (d/I-13 1906) MD Jefferson 1892. *Pa med jour* 9:361, 1905/06. *Flint* 1897: 808.

FOSTER, HENRY L , Keene, NH 1859; Joliet, Ill 1859– (d/IX-10-1867 @42) MD Hahnemann Phila 1857. *Med invest* 5:128, 1868. Homeopath.

FOSTER, J H , Iowa Falls, Ia (d/XII-14-1894) Rush 1865. *JAMA* 23: 990, 1894. *Polk* 1886: 360.

FOSTER, JAMES WOLCOTT, N Attleboro, Mass (d/IX 17–1885 @72) MD Berkshire 1854; ng Woodstock 1835. *Bost m & s jour* 113:312, 1885.

FOSTER, JOEL, Schoharie CH, NY 1826–35; NYC 1835– (b/III-10-1802 Barnard, Vt; d/VI-29-1884) MD Jefferson 1826. *Med reg NY NJ Conn* 1885: 237. *College & clin rec* (Jefferson) 5:183: 1884. *Bost m & s jour* 45: 1884. *Tr Med Soc St NY* 1885: 341–43.

FOSTER, JOHN DICKINSON, New Orleans; CW–CSA (b/1826 Nashville; d/XI-13-1867) MD UPa 1847. *New Orl m&s j* 21:203–04, 1868. *U Pa med alum CW*: 1847.

FOSTER, JOHN TOMPKINS, Meridian Miss (b/IV-7-1818; d/IX- -1884) MD ?; AB UAla 1838. *U Ala cat*:59.

FOSTER, ROBERT COLEMAN, Nashville (b/1825; d/I-11-1879) MD UPa 1847. *So pract* I: 80– , 1879.

FOSTER, ROBERT SAVIDGE, Foster's, Ala (b/II-9-1828; d/1855) MD Jefferson 1853; AB U Ala 1848; AM 1851. *U Ala cat*: 85.

FOSTER, SAMUEL CONANT, Boston (d/IV-18-1873) MD Jefferson 1837. *Med reg NY NJ Conn* 1873:339. *Med rec* 8:296,383 1873. *Med s rep Phila* 28:398, 1873.

FOSTER, SIMEON A, NYC (b/1843 Hillsdale, NY; d/III- 8-1885 Jacksonville Fl) MD UCNY 1867. *Med reg NY NJ Conn* 1885:238. *Med s rep Phila* 52:384, 1885.

FOSTER, THOMAS ALBERT, Portland, Me (b/II-20 1827; d/XI-27-1896) MD Pa Med Coll 1856. *Tr Me Med Assn* 12:633–36, 1897. *Bost m&s jour* 137: 297, 1897. *JAMA* 27: 1360, 1896. *Atkinson* I: 107–08. *K&B* III: 429–30.

FOSTER, W C , CW–USA (d/XII-6-1865 Matamoras,

Spec. educ'l status abbrev. as: ***ng*** = college verified attendance without degree;

Mexico) MD *Nat med jour* 1:295, 1870/71.

FOSTER, W P, Warsaw, Ind (d/VIII–17–1894 @ 50) MD Cinc Coll Med & Surg 1864. *JAMA* 23: 324, 1894.

FOSTER, WATT, Los Angeles (d/II–6–1900 @ 31) MD Medico–Chir Coll Phila 1891. *JAMA* 34: 573, 1900.

FOULKE, ANTRIM, Richland, Pa (b/1793; d/IX–6–1861) MD 1853. *Tr AMA* 14:208–09, 1864. *Tr Med Soc Pa* 1: 128–29, 1862.

FOULKE, CHARLES, New Hope, Pa (b/XII–14–1815 Penllyn; d/XII–27–1871) MD UPa 1838. *Tr Med Soc Pa* 87: 1872.

FOULKE, JOHN, Philadelphia (d/1796) MB UPa 1780. *Tr CPP* cent vol: 225.

FOULKE, JOHN LANCASTER, Philadelphia; CW–USA (b/II–14–1822 Gwynedd, Pa; d/X–30–1870) MD UPa 1841. *U Pa med alum CW*: 1841.

FOULKE, JOSEPH, Buckingham, Pa (b/I–27–1827 Gwynedd; d/II–10–1906 Milwaukee) MD UPa 1854. *Pa Med Soc* 9:430, 1905/06. *Atkinson* I:532. *Flint* 1897: 797.

FOULKE, LEWIS WILLIAM, Chillicothe O; Carlisle Pa (b/VIII–6–1809 Carlisle; d/1887) <MD UMd 1832> AB Dickinson 1829. *Dick'n cat*:1829. *Polk* 1886: 740.

FOULKE, SAMUEL L, Stroudsburg, Pa (d/IV–17–1903 @60) MD Jefferson 1874. *Pa med jour* 7:279, 1903/04.

FOULKES, JAMES FRANKLIN, CW–CSA; Oakland, Cal 1875– (b/I– –1829 Guilford CH, NC; d/V–22–1889) MD Jefferson 1852; AB Princeton 1849. *NC med jour* 23:472, 1889. *Polk* 1886: 168.

FOUNTAIN, EZRA JAMES, Davenport, Ia (b/1828; d/III–29–1861) MD CPSNY 1851; AB Princeton 1847; AM 1850. *Tr AMA* 14: 196–97, 1864. *Bost m & s jour* 64: 236, 1861. *Tr Iowa St Med Soc* 1867–71:251. *Nashville jour m & s* 20: 189, 1861.

FOURGRAND, VICTOR J, San Francisco (b/1816 SC; d/1875) MD Med Coll SC 1838; stud Paris. *Tr AMA* 31: 1040–41, 1880.

FOUTS, F F, Floresville [Tx] (d/VII–17–1889) MD ? *Med surg rep Phila* 61: 140, 1889.

FOWKES, WILLIAM E, Owensboro, Ky (d/IX–25 1898 @ 50) MD U Louisville 1873; <att Bellevue> *JAMA* 31: 872, 1898. *Polk* 1886: 392.

FOWLER, AMOS, Albany (d/X–23–1895 @ 76) MD UCNY 1846. *JAMA* 25: 818, 1895. *Polk* 1886: 638.

FOWLER, ARCHIBALD CAMPBELL, Allston, Mass (d/IX–16–1871 @ 33) MD Harvard 1867. *Bost m & s jour* 8: 192, 1871.

FOWLER, BENJAMIN F, Galena, Ill (d/VI–16–1899 @ 74) MD Geneva 1850. *JAMA* 32:1460 1899. *Polk* 1886: 280.

FOWLER, EDGAR OMERA, Danvers, Mass (b/V–7–1853 Alexandria, NH; d/V–1–1884) MD Dartmouth 1873. *Tr NH Med Soc* 1894: 199–203.

FOWLER, EDMUND B, USA (b/1811; d/IV– –1879) MD Berkshire 1834. *Med reg NY NJ Conn* 1879: 190.

FOWLER, EDWIN STANTON, Springfield, Ill (d/VII–11–1905 @ 77) MD UCNY 1852. *Ill med jour* 8:185, 1905. *Polk* 1896: 441.

FOWLER, EZEKIEL, Globe Village, RI (b/V–8–1787 Worcester, Mass; d/VII–21–1863) Lic Mass Med Soc 1812. *Tr RI Med Soc* 1: 212–15, 1859–77.

FOWLER, GEORGE HUGGINS, Mobile, Ala; CW–CSA (b/VII–24–1833; d/X–20–1897) MD UPa 1861. *Tr Med Assoc St Ala* 1898: 240. *U Pa med alum CW*: 1861. *Polk* 1886: 134.

FOWLER, GEORGE RYERSON, Albany, NY (b/XII–25–1848 NYC; d/II–6–1906) MD Bellevue 1871. *Chic med rec* 28:116, 1905, *Bost m & s jour* 154: 198, 1906. *Butler* 1878: 530. *K&B* III: 430–32.

FOWLER, JOSEPH, Columbia, Tenn (d/I–2–1894) MD Buffalo 1873. *JAMA* 22: 58, 1894. *Polk* 1890: 779.

FOWLER, JOSEPH CURTIS, Stockbridge, Mass (d/1855 @ 35) MD Woodstock 1849; AM U Vt 1840. *Bost m & s jour* 52:327, 1855.

FOWLER, REMUS MARCUS, Washington Conn (b/1793 Torrington; d/III–1–1879) MD ? ; Hon AM Yale 1834. *Proc Conn Med Soc* 1879:170. *Butler* 1878:76.

FOWNES, F C, NYC (d/X–3–1891) MD ? *Med vis* 7: 365, 1891. Homeopath.

FOX, CHARLES ANSON, Hartford, Conn (b/X–4–1865[?] Windsor Locks; d/V–10–1897) MD CPSNY 1881. *Proc Conn Med Soc* 1898: 373–74. *JAMA* 29:1028, 1897. *Polk* 1886: 444 (Muirkirk, Md).

FOX, CHARLES LEONARD, Lowell, Mass (d/X–5–1898 @ 28) MD Harvard 1892. *Bost m & s jour* 139:380, 1898. *JAMA* 31: 997, 1898. *Polk* 1896: 715.

FOX, DAVID RAYMOND, Plaquemines, La (b/X–14–1822 Woodville, Miss; d/XII–29–1893) MD U La 1845. *JAMA* 22: 97, 1894. *New Orl m & s jour* ns21: 711–12, 1894. *Polk* 1886: 414.

FOX, ELI, Mohawk, NY (b/Columbia, NY; d/X–13–1890) MD UCNY 1855. *Tr NY St Med Soc* 11: 741 ff, 1894. *Polk* 1886: 668.

FOX, GEORGE, Philadelphia (b/V–8–1806; d/XII–27–1882) MD UPa 1828; AB 1825. *Tr CPP* 3s 7:xlix–lxix, 1884. *Bost m & s jour* 108: 21–22, 1883. *Atkinson* I: 172. *K&B* III: 432.

FOX, ISAAC NEWTON, Woodstock & Rumney, NH; b/III–1–1862; d/III–2–1895) MD U Vt 1889. *Tr NH Med Soc* 1895: 161–62. *JAMA* 24:422, 1895. *Polk* 1893:775.

FOX, JOHN F, NYC (d/XII–17–1867) MD UCNY 1865. *Med reg NY NJ Conn* 1868: 325.

FOX, JOHN LAWRENCE, USN (b/I–8–1811 Salem, Mass; d/XII–17–1864 Roxbury) MD Harvard 1835; AB Amherst 1831. *Bost m&s jour* 71:428 464 505–06 1864. *Med s rep Phila* 12:236, 1864/65. *Harv in CW*: 228.

FOX, JULIUS C, Keyesport, Ill (bGny; d/III–12 1903 @ 65) Lic yrs pract. *Ill m j* ns4:889, 1903. *Polk* 1886:293. 293.

FOX, LORENZO SMITH, CW–USA; Lowell, Mass (d/VI–23–1891) MD Harvard 1863. *Bost m & s jour* 124:

646, 1891; 127: 638, 1892. *Harvard in CW*: 278. *Polk* 1886: 468.

FOX, ROSWELL, Wethersfield, Conn (b/XI-14-1825 Lebanon; d/X-25-1898) MD UCNY 1847. *Proc Conn M S* 1899: 350-51. *JAMA* 31: 1190, 1898. *Polk* 1886: 197.

FOX, SIDNEY ALLAN, Brooklyn (b/Mt Sterling Ky; d/XII-10-1890 or I-10-1891 @ 34) MD Bellevue 1880. *Med reg NY NJ Conn* 1891: 272. *Buff m & s jour* 30:372, 1891. *JAMA* 16: 754, 1891. *Tr Med Soc St NY* 1891: 457.

FOX, THOMAS SHELTON, Batesburg, SC; CW-CSA (d/III-5-1900) MD UCNY 1858. *JAMA* 34: 702, 1900. *Polk* 1896: 1358.

FOX, WILLIAM, Milwaukee (b/VI-22-1844 Dane Co, Wis; d/IV-12-1897) MD Rush 1870. *Tr Wis St Med Soc* 31:640-42, 1897. *Polk* 1890: 1168.

FOY, MICHAEL EYRE, NYC; CW-USA (d/VI-9-1861 East New-York) LRCS (Edinb) 1846. *Med reg NY NJ Conn* 1862: 154. *Nat med jour* 1:295, 1870/71.

FOY, JOHN WILSON, San Francisco; CW-USA (d/IV-1-1885) MD Harvard 1860. *Harvard in CW*: 258.

FRAER, JOSHUA M , Chattanooga, Tenn (d/XI-25-1891) MD Detroit Homeop MC 1872. *Med vis* 8: 122, 1892. *Polk* 1886: 862. Homeopath.

FRALEY, JAMES F , Fairbury, Ill (d/VII-31-1894 @83) Lic yrs pract. *JAMA* 23: 248, 1894. *Polk* 1896: 330. Eclectic.

FRANCE, JOHN M DUNCAN, St Joseph, Mo (b/1842 DC; d/V-9-1906) MD Georgetown 1865. *Hist Med Soc DC*: 275. *Butler* 1874: 415. *Polk* 1886: 560.

FRANCE, JOHN WILLIAM, Dunkirk, Ind (b/VI-22-1858; d/VII-10-1889) MD Miami 1882. *Tr Ind St Med Soc* 1892: 279. *Polk* 1886: 316.

FRANCIS, CHRISTOPHER C C , Clebourne, Tx (d/XI-16-1892) MD U Nashville 1859. *Daniels Tex med jour* 8:239-40, 1892-93. *Tex cour-rec med* 10:152, 1893. *Polk* 1886: 882.

FRANCIS, JOHN TAYLOR, Norfolk, Va (b/XI-27-1859; d/I-7-1893) MD UCNY 1883. *Tr Med Soc Va* 1893: 219.

FRANCIS, JOHN WAKEFIELD, NYC (b/XI-17-1789; d/II-8-1861) MD CPSNY 1811; AM Columbia 1809. *Tr AMA* 14: 194-96, 1864. *Med reg NY NJ Conn* 1862: 154. *Nashville jour m & s* 20:288-90, 1861. *Med surg rep Phila* ns5:547-48, 1860/61. *K&B* III:432-33.

FRANCIS, SAMUEL WARD, Newport, RI (b/XII-26-1835 NYC; d/III-25-1886) MD UCNY 1860; AB Columbia 1857. *Atkinson* I:197. *Tr RI Med Soc* 3:380-81, 1883-88.

FRANK, SAMUEL LEON, Baltimore (b/X-17-1841; d/VIII-3-1906) MD U Md 1862. *Med annals Md:* 400. *Polk* 1893: 560.

FRANKEL, EDWARD JULIUS, NYC (b/VII-25-1808 Breslau, Prussia; d/I-28-1881) <MD ?Pest 1836> *Med reg NY NJ Conn* 1881: 235. *Butler* 1878: 499.

FRANKISH, JOSEPH, Philadelphia (d/XII-3-1884 @ 58) MD ? *Med surg rep Phila* 51:732, 1884.

FRANKL, J WILHELM, ?NYC (d/I-8-1884 @ 42) <MD U Prague 1867> *Med reg NY NJ Conn* 1884: 229.

FRANKLIN, BENJAMIN, Newark, NJ (d/II-6-1901 @54) MD UCNY 1868. *Bost m & s jour* 144: 198, 1901. *Ill med jour* ns3:142, 1901.

FRANKLIN, DAVID, NYC (d/X-7-1903 @ 48) MD UCNY 1878. *Bost m&s j* 149: 494, 1903. *Polk* 1896: 1053.

FRANKLIN, EDWARD CARROLL, CW-USA; St Louis (b/Providence, RI; d/XII-17-1880) MD UPa 1860. *U Pa med alum CW*: 1860.

FRANKLIN, EDWARD CARROLL, CW-USA; San Francisco; Panama; Chicago; Ann Arbor, Mich; St Louis (b/1822 Flushing, NY; d/XII-10-1885 St Louis) MD UCNY 1846. *New Engl med gaz* 21:96, 1886. *Tr Am Inst Hom* 1886: 130. *Med adv* 16:467, 1886. *King* 3:99. Homeopath.

FRANKLIN, FREDERICK B, Portland Me (d/VIII-27 1855 @23) MD UCNY 1854. *Bost m&s j* 53: 155, 1855.

FRANKLIN, JOHN J , Columbia, Cal (d/V-9-1874 or 1875) MD Transylvania 1828. *Tr Cal Med Soc* 1875: 162. *Tr AMA* 31:1041-42, 1880.

FRANKLIN, JOHN R , Hornbeck, La (d/III-31-1905) MD Med Coll Ala 1880. *New Orl m & s jour* 57: 861, 1905. *Polk* 1896: 616.

FRANKLIN, THOMAS HARE, CW-USA; Atlantic City (b/IV-4-1840 Phila; d/I-9-1900) MD UPa 1868; PhG Phil Coll Pharm 1860. *U Pa med alum CW*: 1868.

FRANKLIN, THOMAS M, NYC (d/III-22-1896 Greenwich, Conn) MD UCNY 1847. *JAMA* 26:732, 1896.

FRANTZ, ELIAS H , Reading, Pa (d/XII-26-1903 @ 56) MD Jefferson 1873. *Pa med jour* 7: 209, 279, 1903/04. *Polk* 1886: 832.

FRARY, ROBERT G, Hudson NY (b/XI-15-1793; d/XII 29-1862) Hon MD Berkshire 1836; lic Columbia Co, NY Med Soc 1815. *Tr M S St NY* 1864: 435-40. *Tr AMA* 16:625-26, 1865. *Med s rep Phila* ns9: 326, 1862/63.

FRASER, EDWARD CLARENCE, Philadelphia (d/1901 @ 61) MD Jefferson 1884. *Pa med jour* 5:296, 1901/02.

FRASER, EDWIN IRVIN, CW-CSA (b/I-25-1834 Harper's Home, Va; d/1861) MD UPa 1857. *U Pa med alum CW*: 1857.

FRASER, JAMES W, Philadelphia (d/XI-27-1902) MD Jefferson 1876. *Pa m j* 6: 260, 1902/03. *Flint* 1897: 817.

FRAUENSTEIN, KARL HEINRICH GUSTAV, NYC (d/II-27-1895) MD CPSNY 1868. *JAMA* 24: 650, 1895. *Butler* 1878: 513.

FRAZER, JOHN GORDON, Asbury Park, NJ (d/X-4-1900) MD Bellevue 1865; AB Williams 1862. *Williams grads*: 1862. *Polk* 1886: 678 (NYC).

FRAZIER, D M , Bethel, O (d/III-17-1869) MD Med Coll Ohio 1844. *Phila med reg & dir* 1871: 300. *Med surg rep Phila* 20: 292, 1869.

FRAZIER, ROBERT Jr, Camden, NY (b/II-7-1817 Bethlehem, NY; d/V-10-1891) MD Castleton 1837.

Tr Med Soc St NY 1892: 428. *Polk* 1886: 656.

FRAZIER, WILLIAM A , St Louis, Mo; Staunton, Va (d/VIII–29–1894 @ 42) MD U Va 1873. *Tr Med Soc Va* 1894:194–95. *Polk* 1886: 562.

FREDENBURGH, BENJAMIN, Coeymans, NY (b/IX– –1797 Ghent, NY; d/VIII– –1888 Palatine Bridge) MD Castleton 1834. *Bost m & s jour* 119: 260, 1888. *Butler* 1878: 553.

FREE, JARED, CW–USA (d/X–10–1863 Rappahannock Station, Va) MD Jefferson 1863. *Nat med jour* 1:295, 1870/71.

FREE, JOHN LOWE, Stewartstown, Pa (d/IX–27–1904 @ 83) MD U Md 1848. *Pa med jour* 8:335, 1904/05. *Flint* 1897: 836.

FREEDLEY, SAMUEL, Philadelphia (b/II–2–1799; d/I–3–1886 Plymouth Meeting, Pa) MD UPa 1821. *Hahn mo* 21:143, 1886. *Polk* 1886: 816. Homeopath.

FREEL, FRANK JOHN, Brooklyn (d/III–9–1906 @ 48) MD LICH 1891. *Bost m & s jour* 154: 308, 1906.

FREELAND, EDWARD H , Md (d/VI–3–1834) MD U Md 1826. *Med annals Md:* 401.

FREELAND, JAMES BUYERS, CW–USA; Lancaster, Pa (b/III–31–1827 Salsbury Twp; d/VII–5–1895) MD UPa 1850. *U Pa med alum CW*:1850. *Polk* 1886: 804.

FREELAND, JAMES CHESTER, Fitchburg, Mass 1855– (b/VI–21–1831 Becket; d/IV–15–1870 or IV–23–1871) MD Cleveland Homeop 1862. *New Engl med gaz* 6: 328, 1871. *Tr Am Inst Hom* 1893: 141. Homeopath.

FREEMAN, ALFRED, NYC (b/XI–6–1793 Salem, NY; d/III–8–1861) <MD "NY 1817"> stud w/Dr Asa Fitch. *Med reg NY NJ Conn* 1862: 154. *No Am j hom* 9: 713, 1861. *US jour homeop* 2:460, 1861. *Tr Am Inst Hom* 1893: 141. *King* I:86–87. Homeopath.

FREEMAN, ELLIS BARRON, Woodbridge, NJ; CW–USA (b/1807; d/II–4–1877) MD CPSNY 1831; AB Yale 1826. *Tr ANA* 28:627, 1877. *Tr Med Soc NJ* 1877: 127. *Med reg NY NJ Conn* 1877: 200.

FREEMAN, GEORGE EDWARD, Brockton, Mass (d/VI–12–1898 @ 46) MD Bellevue 1867. *Bost m & s jour* 138: 580, 1898. *Polk* 1896: 709.

FREEMAN, GEORGE LLOYD, Glen Head, NY (d/XII–27–1904 @ 75) MD Cleveland Homeop Hosp Coll 1852; AB Columbus 1849. *Bost m & s jour* 152: 28, 1905.

FREEMAN, GEORGE W , Freemansburg, Pa (d/V–16–1898) MD UPa 1852; AM Lafayette 1866. *JAMA* 30: 1366, 1898. *Polk* 1896: 1279.

FREEMAN, JAMES R , Minneapolis (b/Biddeford, Me; d/I–4–1894 @ 38) MD Columbian DC 1879. *JAMA* 22: 97, 1894. *Polk* 1890: 614.

FREEMAN,JOHN N, CW–USA; NYC (b/1836; d/VIII–18–1888) MD UCNY 1862. *Med reg NY NJ Conn* 1889: 73.

FREEMAN, JOSEPH ADDISON, ?Paterson, NJ; CW–USA (b/VI–25–1833; d/XII–29–1864 Nashville) MD CPSNY 1856; AB Princeton 1852; AM 1855. *Nat med jour* 1:295, 1870/71. *Tr AMA* 16:633–34, 652,1865. *Tr NJ Med Soc* 1865: 78–9; 1867: 138–39.

FREEMAN, NATHANIEL MARSTON, NYC (d/IV–18 1902 @ 81) MD Yale 1852. *Bost m & s jour* 146: 450, 1902. *Polk* 1896: 1053.

FREEMAN, NELSON S , Charleston, Ill (d/VIII–7–1899 @ 70) MD ? *JAMA* 33:493, 1899. *Polk* 1896: 369.

FREEMAN, OTIS RUSSELL, Freehold, NJ (b/XII–30–1809 NH; d/VI–9–1902) MD Dartmouth 1843. *Bost m & s jour* 146: 678, 1902. *Polk* 1896: 936.

FREEMAN, ROBERT J , USN 1859–61; CW–CSN (b/IV–17–1837 Norfolk, Va; d/1874, Memphis) MD UPa 1859; MD UVa 1858. *U Pa med alum CW*: 1859.

FREEMAN, SAMUEL HUNTINGTON, Albany, NY (d/III–15–1906) MD Albany 1846. *Bost m & s jour* 154:332, 1906. *Polk* 1896: 984.

FREEMAN, WARREN, NYC (b/V–23–1815 Salem, NY; d/IV–5–1880) MD Hahnemann Phila 1854. *Am obs* 17:272, 1880. *Hom times* 8:24, 1880. *Tr Am Inst Hom* 1880: 146. *Cleave*. Homeopath.

FREEMAN, WILLIAM, Camden, Ind (b/IV–26–1809; d/IV–17–1883) MD Geneva 1835. *JAMA* 3: 196, 1884. *Tr Ind St Med Soc* 1883: 280.

FREEMAN, WILLIAM E , Wilmington, NC (b/1816 Hertford Co; d/II–23–1879) MD Med Coll SC: 1846. *Tr Am Inst Hom* 1881: 130. *Hahn mo* 14:320, 1879. *King* 1:405. Homeopath.

FREER, JACOB SANTA ANNA, NYC (d/I–27–1892) MD Geneva 1846. *Med reg NY NJ Conn* 1893: 302.

FREER, JAMES A, Washington, DC (d/II–4–1905) MD NY Hom Med Coll 1885. *Tr Am Inst Hom* 1905:839–40.

FREER, JOSEPH WARREN, Chicago (b/VIII–10–1816 Ft Ann NY; d/IV–12–1877) MD Rush 1849. *Tr AMA* 29:655–57, 1878. *Chic med jour* 34: 461–62, 1877. *Tr Ill St Med Soc* 1877:31–2,207–8. *K&B* III:435.

FRELIGH, MARTIN, Saugerties, NY 1834–40; Rhinebeck 1840–57; Kingston 1858?– (b/I–23–1813; d/VIII–31–1889) <MD Fairfield 1834> MD Hahn Phila 1858 (spec.degree) *Med vis* 5:346, 1889. *Tr Am Inst Hom* 1890: 138. *Cleave*. Homeopath.

FRENCH, ALVIN S , CW–USA (d/VI–10–1864 Guntown, Miss) MD ? *Nat med jour* 1:295, 1870/71.

FRENCH, AMELIA J , East Lynn, Ill (d/X–9–1899) MD Hahnemann 1880. *Tr Ill St Med Soc* 1899: 287. *Polk* 1886: 281 (Grand Crossing, Ill).

FRENCH, ANDREW, New Haven, Conn (d/1852 @68) Hon MD Yale 1831. *Proc Conn Med Soc* 1852:17.

FRENCH, ANNA DINSMORE, NYC (d/X–19–1871 San Francisco) MD Wooster 1873. *Med reg NY NJ Conn* 1892: 276. *Polk* 1886: 678.

FRENCH, GEORGE FRANKLIN, CW–USA; Minneapolis (b/X–30–1837 Dover, NH; d/VII–5–1897) MD Harvard 1862; AB 1859. *Harvard in CW*: 126. *JAMA* 29: 200, 1897. *Atkinson* I: 128. *Tr Minn St Med Soc* 1897: 152; 1899: 191. *Polk* 1896: 791. *K&B* III:436–37.

FRENCH, GEORGE MORRILL, Malden, Mass (b/Sandown, NH; d/II-23-1900 @ 45 Sancook, NY) MD Harvard 1884; AB Boston U 1880. *Bost m & s jour* 142:236, 1900. *Polk* 1896: 717.

FRENCH, HARRIET SCHNEIDER, Philadelphia (d/IX 5-1906 @ 82) MD Penn Med Univ 1864. *Pa med jour* 10:53, 1906/07. *Flint* 1897: 817. Homeopath.

FRENCH, HENRY MINOT, Concord, NH (b/IV-1-1853 Ashby, Mass; d/VI-13-1893 Manchester, NH) MD Dartmouth 1878; AB 1876. *Tr NH Med Soc* 1894: 187-89. *Polk* 1890: 708.

FRENCH, ISAAC SMITH, Loudon Ridge, NH (b/I-18-1834; d/IV-29-1878) MD Dartmouth 1855. *Tr NH Med Soc* 1878: 203-04. *Atkinson* I: 97.

FRENCH, JOHN ORDWAY, Chesterfield, NH 1845-55; Hanover, Mass 1855-87 (b/XI- -1821 Gilmanton, NH; d/III-26 or IX-29-1887) MD Dartmouth 1844. *Bost m & s jour* 117: 348, 1887. *Polk* 1886: 467.

FRENCH, JONATHAN JOHN, Kansas City, Mo (b/I-31 1845 Covington, O; d/VIII-24-1879) MD UPa 1866; ng Amherst 1866. *Amherst, Men of:* 1866.

FRENCH, LEONARD, Manchester, NH (b/XI-11-1817 Bedford, NH?; d/II-14-1892) MD Dartmouth 1846; AB 1843. *Tr NH Med Soc* 1892: 197-99. *Polk* 1890:710.

FRENCH, LEWIS, Noroton, Conn (d/I-27-1898) MD <W Med Coll [?] 1883> *JAMA* 30: 570, 1898.

FRENCH, LUTHER C , Hudson, Mich (d/IV-12-1895) MD Cleveland Med Coll 1848. *JAMA* 24: 609, 1895. *Polk* 1886: 495.

FRENCH, NATHAN, Malden, Mass (b/XI-13-1810 Sandown, NH; d/IV-27-1895) MD Dartmouth 1839. *Bost m & s jour* 132: 448, 1895. *Polk* 1890: 551.

FRENCH, NATHANIEL W, CW-USA (d/IV-14-1863 Baton Rouge) MD Yale 1862. *Nat m j* 1:295, 1870/71.

FRENCH, OTIS EVERETT, CW-USA; Garnett, Kans; Denver (b/III-1-1818 Boston; d/III-14-1884 Garnett or Calif) MD Harvard 1841. *Harv in CW*: 229.

FRENCH, ROBERT, Georgetown, Md; USA, USN (b/1787 DC; d/VIII-13-1835) MD UPa 1809. *Hist Med Soc DC*: 216.

FRENCH, WILLIAM FREEMAN, Noroton, Conn (b/VIII-18-1856 Sharon; d/I-27-1898) MD UCNY 1883. *Proc Conn M S* 1898: 375-76. *Polk* 1896: 283.

FRENCH, WILLIS WALTON, Greeley Col 1884-85; NYC 1886-88; USA (b/IV-27-1857 Portsmouth, NH; d/III-11-1888) MD CPSNY 1883; BSc Bowdoin 1878; MD 1881. *Med reg NY NJ Conn* 1888:253. *Polk* 1886:678.

FREY, LEVI, York, Pa (b/Frystown, Pa; d/XII-6-1894) MD UCNY 1850. *Tr Med Soc Pa* 26: 417, 1896. *Reg Pa phys* 1881-88: 416.

FREY [FRY], WILLIAM H , Keyser, WVa (b/Preston Co, WVa; d/VI-16-1900 @ 44) MD U Md 1852. *JAMA* 34: 1676, 1900. *Polk* 1886: 914.

FREYTAG, EBERHARD, Bethlehem, Pa (b/1764? d/III-14-1846 @ 82) MD Allentown Acad 1841. *Tr Am Inst Homeop* 1867: 157. *King* 1: 134. Homeopath.

FRICK, GEORGE, Baltimore (b/1793; d/III-26-1870 Dresden, Gny) MD UPa 1815. *Med annals Md:* 402. *K&B* III: 437-38.

FRICK, J CHARLES, Baltimore (b/VIII-8-1823; d/III 25-1860) MD U Md 1842. *Tr AMA* 13:813-14, 1860. *Bost m & s jour* 62:232, 1860. *Med annals Md:* 401-02. *JAMA* 26: 91, 1897. *K&B* III: 437.

FRICK, WILLIAM S , Philadelphia (b/XI-19-1826 Chester Co, Pa; d/I-7-1899) MD Jefferson 1849. *JAMA* 32: 195, 1899. *Polk* 1896: 1304.

FRICKÉ, ALBERT, Philadelphia (b/IX-13-1815; d/1899) <MD U Berlin 1839> *Pa med jour* 3: 441, 1899/1900. *Tr CPP* 3s22: xli ff, 1900. *JAMA* 33: 1441, 1899. *Polk* 1886: 816.

FRICKS, ASA T , Rising Fawn, Ga (d/VIII-10-1901) MD Washington U Balto 1869. *JAMA* 37: 527, 1901. *Polk* 1886: 234.

FRIDENBURG, EDWARD, NYC (b/1855; d/XII-9-1903) MD CPSNY 1878. *Bost m & s jour* 149: 692, 1903. *Polk* 1896: 1053.

FRIEDENWALD, AARON, Baltimore (b/XII-20-1836; d/VI-26-1902) MD U Md 1860. *Med annals Md:* 402. *Atkinson* 524. *Polk* 1893: 560. *K&B* III: 438-39.

FRIEND, NATHANIEL, CW-CSA; Lampasas, Tx (b/VIII-6-1834 Boligee Ala; d/XI-27-1877) MD UPa 1857; AB U Ala 1855. *U Pa med alum CW*:1857.

FRIEND, WILLIAM, Lancaster, Ill (d/XII-4-1905 Sumner) Lic 1877 yrs pract. *Ill med jour* 9:131, 1905. *Polk* 1896: 426.

FRIERSON, JAMES HERVEY, Columbia, Tenn (b/XI-? 1812; d/I-26-1846) MD Transylvania 1837; AB U Ala 1834. *U Ala cat*: 42.

FRIERSON, JAMES WHITE STEVENSON, Columbia, Tenn (b/III-5-1801 Sumter Dist, SC; d/I-29-1872) MD Transylvania 1824. *Tr Med Soc Tenn* 1876: 82.

FRIERSON, SAM W , Columbia, Tenn. (d/X-19-1878) MD ? *So pract* 1: 384, 1879. *Butler* 1874: 768.

FRIES, GEORGE, Cincinnati, O (d/XI-13-1866) MD *Tr AMA* 18: 349, 1867. *Tr Ohio St Med Soc* 1867: 77-78. *Nashville j m & s* ns4: 357, 1867.

FRIESE, MICHAEL, Carlisle & Mechanicsburg, Pa to 1866; Harrisburg, 1866- (b/II-7-1832; d/II-4-1880 Phila) MD Hahn Phila 1860. *Tr Am Inst Hom* 1881: 147. *Tr Hom Med Soc St Pa* 1880: 45-46. *Hahn mo* 15:256, 1880. *Cleave*. Homeopath.

FRINGER, GEORGE W , Pana Ill (b/III-24-1834 Taneytown Md; d/XII-17-1902) MD Missouri Med Coll 1869. *Ill med jour* ns4: 558, 1903. *Polk* 1886: 300.

FRINK, CHARLES SAFFORD, CW-USA; Elkhart, Ind (b/IV-3-1835 Jefferson Co, NY; d/VII-8-1893) MD U Mich 1859; MD Jefferson 1870. *JAMA* 21:94, 1893. *Tr Ind St Med Soc* 1893: 261. *Butler* 1878: 202.

FRINK, EDWARD AMES, CW-USA; Deer Isle, Me (b/

V-9-1831 Deerfield, Mass; d/XI-16-1894) MD UPa 1862. *U Pa med alum CW*: 1862. *Polk* 1886: 429.

FRIOU, GEORGE W , Brooklyn (b/ca 1834; d/IV-26 1889) MD Tulane 1856. *Med reg NY NJ Conn* 1889: 274. *Polk* 1886: 645.

FRISBIE, LEVI C, Vallejo, Cal (b/III-1-1821 Albany, NY; d/IX-24-1892) MD Albany 1841. *Tr Med Soc Cal* 23: 282, 1893. *Butler* 1878: 59.

FRISSELL, JOHN, Wheeling, WVa; CW-USA (b/III-8 1810 Peru, Mass; d/XI-16-1893) MD Berkshire 1834; AB Williams 1831; AM 1834. *JAMA* 21: 829, 1893. *Bost m & s jour* 129:528, 1893. *Atkinson* I: 410-11. *Butler* 1878: 850. *K&B* III: 439.

FRITZ, CRAWFORD ELLSWORTH, Hudson, NY (d/ IV-5-1904 @54) MD CPSNY 1875. *Tr Med Soc St NY* 1904:[420]. *Polk* 1886: 664.

FRITZ, P L , Alexandria, Ind (d/X-28-1899 @35) MD Mich Coll Med & Surg 1892. *JAMA* 33:1308, 1899.

FROMBERGER, JOHN HENRY, CW-USA (b/c1815 Del; d/IV-10-1885 Hampton, Va) MD UPa 1835; AB Wash'n & Jeff'n 1832. *U Pa med alum CW*: 1835.

FRONEFIELD, CHARLES, Philadelphia (d/VIII-6-1865 @56) MD UPa 1829. *Med s rep Phila* 13:133 1865.

FROST, CARLTON PENNINGTON, Brattleboro, Vt 6 yrs; Hanover, NH ca 25 yrs (b/V-29-1830 Sullivan, NH; d/V-24-1896) MD NY Med Coll 1857; MD Dartmouth 1856; AB 1852; att Woodstock, Bowdoin. *JAMA* 26: 1092, 1896. *Tr Vt St Med Soc* 1896: 408-14. *Bost m & s jour* 134: 552, 1896. *Atkinson* I: 197. *Polk* 1896: 919.

FROST, ELIAS, Meriden, NH (b/I-10-1782 Milford, Mass; d/III-31-1863) Hon MD Brown 1824; AB 1804; AM. *Brown hist cat*: 1804.

FROST, GEORGE MELVILLE, Peabody, Mass (b/IV-27-1843 Eliot, Me; d/VI-20-1898) MD Bowdoin 1869. *Bost m & s jour* 138: 628, 1898. *Polk* 1896: 720.

FROST, GEORGE W , Brooklyn (d/V-16-1887 @81) MD CPSNY 1830. *Med reg NY NJ Conn* 1887: 260.

FROST, GEORGE WASHINGTON, Iowa 1871-79; Emporia, Kans 1879- (b/VI-6-1836 Monmouth, Me; d/XII-3-1895) MD Rush 1871; ng Bowdoin Coll 1858-59. *Bowdoin cat*: 1862.

FROST, HENRY RUTLEDGE, Charleston, SC (b/X-6-1795; d/IV or V-7-1866) MD UPa 1816. *Bost m & s jour* 74:452,1866. *Med surg rep Phila* 14:420, 1866. *Waring* II:230-31. *K&B* III: 439-40.

FROST, JAMES HENRY PAINE, Bethlehem, Pa (b/V-24-1825 Bethel, Me; d/I-21-1875) MD Hahnemann Phila 1850; AB Amherst 1846; att Bowdoin 1842. *Tr Am Inst Hom* 1875: 801. *Am hom obs* 12: 240, 1875. *Cleave*. Homeopath.

FROST, JOHN, CW-CSA (d/III-30-1864) MD *SHSP* 22: 201, 1893.

FROTHINGHAM, EDWARD, USN (b/1841; d/I-24-1870 Yokohama Bay, Japan) MD CPSNY 1866. *Tr AMA* 21: 495-96, 1870. *Med rec* 6: 94, 1871-72. *Nat med jour* 1:295, 1870/71. *Phila med reg & dir* 1871:303.

FROTHINGHAM, GEORGE EDWARD, Detroit (b/IV-21-1836 Boston; d/IV-24-1900) MD U Mich 1864. *JAMA* 34:1145, 1900. *Atkinson* I: 100. *K&B* III: 440.

FROTHINGHAM, WILLIAM, NYC; CW-USA (b/ 1830; d/XI-19-1885) MD CPSNY 1854; att Union Coll 1851. *Med reg NY NJ Conn* 1886:248. *Bost m & s jour* 113: 549, 1885.

FROW, JOHN G , CW-USA (b/VII-31-1834 Mifflintown, Pa; d/III-24-1864 Blaine) MD UPa 1856; AB Jefferson 1853. *U Pa med alum CW*: 1856. *Nat med jour* 1:295, 1870/71.

FROWERT, CHARLES GILPEN, Philadelphia (d/I-9 1904 @ 53) MD UPa 1874. *Pa med jour* 8: 335, 1904/05. *Polk* 1886: 816.

FRÜH, ERNEST, Philadelphia (b/Gny; d/IX-7-1905) MD Jefferson 1886. *Pa med jour* 9:27, 1905/06.

FRUIT, JOHN, Hazleton, Pa (b/Jerseytown, Pa; d/IV-16-1906 @ 46) MD Jefferson 1881. *Pa med jour* 9: 608, 1905/06. *Flint* 1897: 804.

FRUIT, RICHARD B , Hazleton, Pa (b/VIII-12-1827 Jerseytown, Pa; d/XI-10-1895) MD Jefferson 1854. *JAMA* 25: 911, 1895. *Polk* 1886: 802.

FRUITNIGHT, JOHN HENRY, NYC (b/XI-9-1851; d/ XII-18-1900) MD Bellevue 1875; AB Coll City NY 1872; AM 1875. *Bost m & s jour* 143:674, 1900. *Polk* 1886: 679.

FRUITNIGHT, WILLIAM, NYC (b/IV-20-1858; d/VII 20-1884) MD Bellevue 1880; AB Coll City NY 1878. *Med reg NY NJ Conn* 1885: 238. *JAMA* 3: 106, 1884. *Med surg rep Phila* 51: 168, 1884.

FRY, THOMAS W , Lafayette, Ind (b/VIII-4-1814; d/II 24-1873) MD Transylvania 1837. *Tr Ind St Med Soc* 1874: 183-85. *Tr AMA* 26: 464-65, 1875. Kemper's *Indiana*: 273.

FRYE, DANIEL FISKE, Francestown NH (b/Deerfield, NH; d/X-11-1867 @ 53) MD Dartmouth 1840. *Bost m & s jour* 77:240, 1867.

FRYE, JOSEPH C , Peoria, Ill (b/IX-28-1809 or 1811 Winchester, Va; d/VIII-22-1887) MD Med Coll Ohio 1839. *Tr Ill St Med Soc* 1888:150-51. *Atkinson* I: 535. *Butler* 1878: 153.

FRYE, PETER Y , Oyster Bay, NY 1855- (b/X-1-1817 Deerfield, NH; d/X-9-1897) MD Dartmouth 1846. *JAMA* 29: 816, 1897. *Bost m & s jour* 137: 403, 1897. *Polk* 1886: 700.

FRYE, THOMAS, Rockland, Me (b/IX-13-1813 Vinal Haven; d/XI-20-1874) MD UCNY 1848. *Tr Me Med Assoc* 1874-76: 422; 1877-79: 483-84.

FRYE, THOMAS BAKER JOHNSON, Washington, DC (b/1820; d/V-31-1889) MD Columbian DC 1840. *Hist Med Soc DC*:235.

FRYER, JOHN P , Ypsilanti, Mich (d/VIII-26-1898) <MD Mich Coll Med & Surg 1893> *JAMA* 31: 618, 1898. *Polk* 1896: 776.

FÜLLGRAFF, OTTO, NYC (b/VIII-15-1819 Berlin; d/XI-14-1893) MD UCNY 1854. *No Am jour hom* 42: 1894 (Jan). *Tr Am Inst Hom* 1894: 261.

FÜRGANG, ALBERT J , East NY, NY (d/II-2-1886) MD UCNY 1861. *Med reg NY NJ Conn* 1886: 248.

FULDA, JOHN ALBIN, CW-USA; NYC (d/XII-9-1898) <MD Halle 1853> *JAMA* 31;1542, 1898. *Polk* 1886: 679.

FULKS, JAMES S , Baltimore (d/III-13-1898 @ 69) MD UMd 1864. *JAMA* 30:745,1898. *Polk* 1886:436.

FULLENWIDER, J A , Chicago (d/X-23-1901) MD ? *Ill med jour* ns3: 346, 1901.

FULLER, ANDREW JACOB, CW-USA; Bath, Me (b/IX-15-1817 or 1822; d/I-10-1897) MD Bowdoin 1841; <att Jefferson 1842> *Proc Conn Med Soc* 1904: 509-10. *Bost m & s jour* 136:48, 1897; 137: 297, 1897. *Tr Me Med Assoc* 1897: 632-33. *JAMA* 28:236, 1897.

FULLER, DANIEL, Conn (b/1775? d/XII-16-1843 @ 68) Hon MD Yale 1831. *Proc Conn Med Soc* 1903: 399.

FULLER, DANIEL, Pa (d/III-2-1870) MD Jefferson 1857. *Phila med reg & dir* 1871: 294.

FULLER, E E , Keokuk, Ia (d/XI-18-1897 @65) MD CPS Keokuk 1864. *JAMA* 29:1181, 1897. *Polk* 1886:361.

FULLER, EDWIN MARTIN, Sussex, Wis (b/III-27-1867 Merion, Wis; d/V-22-1892) MD Rush 1890; MD Hahnemann Chicago 1890. *Tr Wis St Med Soc* 1893:369; 1894:503. *Polk* 1890:312.

FULLER, FRAZER CHISOLM, NYC (b/1860; d/VII-18-1892) MD CPSNY 1882. *Med reg NY NJ Conn* 1893: 302. *JAMA* 19: 170, 1892.

FULLER, FREDERICUS, Manitou, Colo (d/1891) MD Harvard 1879; AB Colby 1873. *Northwestern med jour* 20:16, 1892. *Polk* 1890: 214.

FULLER, HENRY HOLTON, Charlestown, Mass (b/Lowell; d/XII-12-1888 @ 52) MD Harvard 1860. *Bost m & s jour* 119:641, 1888; 120:28, 1889. *Polk* 1886: 464.

FULLER, JACOB, Providence, RI (d/1839) MD Brown 1822. *Tr RI Med Soc* 1:44, 1859-77.

FULLER, JARED, E Corinth, Me (b/I-19-1806 Hampton, Conn; d/X-6-1878) MD Bowdoin 1836. *Tr Me Med Assoc* 1879:686-87. *Butler* 1878: 306.

FULLER, JOHN L , CW-CSA (b/III-12-1836 Lewisburg, NC; d/1862 Leesburgh, Va) MD UPa 1857. *U Pa med alum CW*: 1857.

FULLER, JOHN N, Calhoun, La (d/XII-23-1893) MD Tulane 1869. *New Orl m & s jour* 22: 551, 1894. *Polk* 1896: 486.

FULLER, JOSEPH BENJAMIN FRANKLIN, Norwich, Conn (b/XII-3-1811 Providence, RI; d/VII-31-1898) MD Castleton 1835. *JAMA* 31:366, 1898. *Polk* 1896:284.

FULLER, JUNIUS TAYLOR, CW-CSA; Roxboro, NC (b/I-29-1837 Lynnbank; d/XI-30-1889) MD UPa 1861. *NC med jour* 25:255, 1890. *Polk* 1886: 726.

FULLER, PHILIP HASTINGS, Brooklyn (b/1861 Painesville, O; d/II-12-1897) MD U Vt 1885. *JAMA* 28:380, 1897. *Polk* 1886: 996.

FULLER, ROBERT, Schenectady, NY (d/V-9-1894 @ 72) MD Albany 1875; AB Union 1840. *Med reg NY NJ Conn* 1894: 239. *JAMA* 22: 855, 1894.

FULLER, SAMUEL, Mass 1620- (b/I-20-1580 Redenhall, Norfolk, Engl; d/1633) MD? att Leyden? *Bost m & s jour* 105:494, 1881. *K&B* III: 441-42.

FULLER, SMITH, Uniontown, Pa (b/II-3-1818 Connellsville; d/III-12-1892) MD Jefferson 1847. *Tr Med Soc Pa* 177-78, 1892. *Polk* 1886: 838.

FULLER, SMITH Jr, Fayette Co, Pa (b/1856: d/XI-30-1890 @ 34 Phila) MD Jefferson 1878. *Tr Med Soc Pa* 22:213, 1891. *Polk* 1886: 838.

FULLER, STEPHEN EDWARD, Brooklyn, CW-USA (d/V 2-1895 @ 58) MD CPSNY 1858. *Med reg NY NJ Conn* 1895: 223. *JAMA* 24: 775, 1895.

FULLER, WINFIELD SCOTT, CW-USA; Fairport, NY (b/Walworth; d/I-13-1888) MD CPSNY 1861. *Tr NY St Med Soc* 11:741 ff, 1894. *Polk* 1886:660.

FULLERTON, JAMES, Bath, Ill (d/XII-6-1905 @77) Lic yrs pract 1878. *Ill m j* 9:130, 1906. *Polk* 1896: 362.

FULLILOVE, THOMAS WEIR, Vaiden, Miss 1886; Boerne, Tx (b/VII-31-1851 Carroll Co; d/IV-4-1905) MD Bellevue 1875; att Emory & Henry; att U Miss 1869-70. *Tex st jour med* 1:32, 1905/06. *Polk* 1886: 533.

FULMER, D A , Philadelphia (d/II-10-1902) MD ? *Pa med jour* 6:260, 1902/03.

FULMER, GEORGE, Mechanicsburg, Pa (d/V-1-1900) MD Jefferson 1853. *JAMA* 34:1211, 1900. *Polk* 1896: 1291.

FULMER, PHILIP FINE, Dingmans Ferry, Pa (b/VI-19 1830 Stewartsville, NJ; d/IV-29-1902 Port Jervis, Pa) MD UPa 1853; att Lafayette. *Pa med jour* 6:260, 1902/03. *Flint* 1897: 800.

FULTON, ALEXANDER, Philadelphia (d/III-1-1898 @43) MD UPa 1875; att Muhlenberg. *JAMA* 30: 625, 1898. *Polk* 1896: 1304.

FULTON, AMBROSE L , Astoria, Ore (b/1851 Ohio; d/XI-1-1899) <MD Northwestern Med Coll St Joseph, Mo 1881> *JAMA* 33:1375, 1899. *Polk* 1886: 777.

FULTON, FREDERICK SAMUEL, ?NYC (b/1858 Norwich, NY; d/V-26-1889) MD NY Homeop Coll 1885. *Tr Am Inst Hom* 1889: 187. *No Am jour hom* 37: 242, 1889. *Med couns* 14: 192, 1889. *Med vis* 5:222, 1889. Homeopath.

FULTON, JOHN BEVERIDGE, E Boston, Mass (d/II 19-1887 @ 52) MD Harvard 1868. *Bost m & s jour* 116:296, 1887; 117: 636, 1887. *Polk* 1886:465.

FULTON, JONATHAN [JOHN] BORDEN, Irvington-on-Hudson, NY (d/V-20-1899) MD Harvard 1869. *JAMA* 32:1269, 1899. *Bost m & s jour* 140:536, 1899. *Polk* 1896: 1027.

FULTON, ROBERT, Baltimore (b/IV- -1803 Frederick Co; d/V-30-1880) MD U Md 1827. *Med annals Md:* 403. *Butler* 1874: 312.

Spec. educ'l status abbrev. as: ***ng*** = college verified attendance without degree;

FUNDENBERG, GEORGE BEAR, Pittsburgh (b/XI-17 1815; d/VIII-15-1885) MD Pa Med Coll 1849. *JAMA* 5: 307-08, 1885.

FUNSTON, OLIVER RIDGWAY, CW-CSA; Richmond, Va (b/1817 Washington, Va; d/VII-14-1871) MD UPa 1837. *U Pa med alum CW*: 1837.

FUQUA, WILLIAM A , Charlotte Co, Va (d/VII-7-1867 @ c70) MD ? *Med surg rep Phila* 17:111, 1867.

FURBECK, PETER R , Gloversville, NY (b/VIII-9-1835 Guilderland, NY; d/I-17-1902 @67) MD LICH 1865. *Tr Med Soc St NY* 1902: 484. *Polk* 1886: 662.

FURMAN [FUHRMANN], GUIDO J F W , NYC (b/I 17-1831 Gny; d/XII-2-1896) MD UCNY 1856. *JAMA* 27: 1360, 1896: 1053. *Butler* 1878: 513.

FURNESS, JOHN R, Ogdensburg NY (b/1836; d/III-9 1873) MD UCNY 1861. *Med reg NY NJ Conn* 1874:272.

FURNISS, JOSEPH, Lancaster, Pa (d/XII-8-1905) MD UPa 1872. *Pa med jour* 9:281, 1905/06. *Flint* 1897: 805.

FURST, ROBERT GARDNER, Lockhaven, Pa (d/V-12 1900 @ 28) MD UPa 1894. *JAMA* 34:1356, 1900. *Polk* 1896: 1288.

FUSSELL, BARTHOLOMEW, Kennett Sq Pa (b/I-9 1794; d/II-15-1871) MD U Md 1824. *Med surg rep Ph* 24:178,262,1871. *Med annals Md*:403. *K&B* III:443.

FUSSELL, EDWIN, Pendleton, Ind; Philadelphia; Media Pa (b/VI-14-1813; d/1882) MD UPa 1835. *JAMA* 1: 255-56, 1883. *Tr Med Soc Pa*14: 318-19, 1882. *K&B* III: 443.

FUSSELL, MORRIS, Chester Springs, Pa (d/VI-29-1901) MD Jefferson 1851. *Pa med jour* 5:296, 1901/02. *JAMA* 37: 276. *Polk* 1886: 795.

FUSSELL, WILEY, Whitley, Ga (d/IX-12-1901) MD Atlanta Med Coll 1893. *JAMA* 37: 527, 1901.

FYFFE, EDWARD P , Urbana, O (b/IV- -1810; d/1867) MD Med Coll Ohio 1833. *Tr Ohio St Med Soc* 1868: 199-200; 1873: 265.

GABBY [GABBEY], R S , Rossville, Kans (d/I-25-1900 @ 69) MD Jefferson 1855. *JAMA* 34: 313, 1900. *Polk* 1896: 563.

GADBERRY, L L , Yazoo City, Miss (b/II-15-1852; d/XII-12-1877) MD Louisville Med Coll 1873. *Tr Miss St Med Asoc* 1878: 166.

GADBERRY [GADBURY] WILLIAM YOUNG, Yazoo City, Miss (b/VII-4-1822 Greenville, SC; d/V-12-1895) MD U Louisville 1845. *Tex med jour* 10:670, 1894-95. *Atkinson* I: 153-54. *Polk* 1890: 636.

GADDIS, ?J , Washington Co, Miss (d/1878) MD ? *Tr AMA* 30: 863, 1879. *Butler* 1874: .

GAETJENS, HEINRICH OTTO, Chicago (b/I-13-1838 Hamburg, Gny; d/II-26-1877 Denver, Colo) MD ? *Chic med jour* 34:362, 1877. *Butler* 1874: 133.

GAFFNEY, MATTHEW T , Newark, NJ (d/IV- -1906 @ 36) MD CPS Balto 1897. *Bost m & s jour* 154: 480, 1906. *Polk* 1900: 1144.

GAGE, CHARLES PINCKNEY, Concord, NH (b/IV-5-1811 Hopkinton; d/1894) MD Cinc Med Coll 1837; ng Dartmouth M S 1834. *JAMA* 23:918, 1894. *Bost m & s jour* 131:628, 1894. *Tr NH Med Soc* 1895:163-65. *Polk* 1886: 591.

GAGE, DANIEL PARKER, CW-USA; Lowell, Mass (d/I-31-1877 @ 48) MD Harvard 1855. *Harvard in CW*: 245. *Mass Med Soc cat*: 1894.

GAGE, FRANKLIN, Augusta, Me 1830-34; Bangor 1834-46? (b/XI-30-1806; d/IV-4-1851 Brooklyn) MD Bowdoin 1830; AB 1827. *Bowdoin cat:* 1827.

GAGE, FREDERICK FANNING, Huntsville, Ala (d/V--1889) MD UCNY 1876. *Tr Med Soc St Ala* 1891: 261. *Polk* 1886: 131.

GAGE, GEORGE CLARENCE, NYC (d/II-22-1903 @ 52) MD CPSNY 1872. *Bost m & s jour* 148:274, 1903. *Polk* 1896: 1053.

GAGE, WILLIAM HATHORNE, Taunton, Mass (d/IV 21-1885 @ 54) MD Harvard 1869. *Bost m & s jour* 112:432, 1885. *Butler* 1878: 350.

GAILLARD, EDWIN SAMUEL, NYC (b/I-16-1827 Charleston Dist, SC; d/II-1-1885 Ocean Beach, NJ) MD Med Coll SC 1854; AB SC Coll 1845. *Buff m & s jour* 24:380, 1886. *Bost m & s jour* 112: 163, 324, 1885. *Atkinson* I: 271-72. *New Orl m & s jour* ns12: 727, 1885. *Butler* 1878: 265.

GAILLARD, PETER CORDES, Charleston, SC (b/1815; d/I-14-1859) MD Med Coll SC 1837. *Tr AMA* 13: 816-18, 1860. *Buff m jour* 14:61, 703, 1859. *Bost m&s jour* 59:528, 1859. *Nashville jour m & s* 16: 375, 1859. *Waring* II: 232-33.

GAINES, EDMUND PENDLETON Mobile Ala (b/X-31 1824 St Stephens; d/XII-7-1884) MD UPa 1846. *New Orl m & s jour* ns12:577-78, 1885. *Tr Med Assoc St Ala* 1885:15-18, 319. *Butler* 1878:18.

GAITHER, NATHAN, War 1812-USA; Columbia, Ky (b/XII- -1785 or IX-15-1788 Rowan Co, NC; d/VIII-12-1862) <MD UPa> *Med surg rep Phila* ns8:516, 1862. *Biogr direct US Congress*.

GALBRAITH, THOMAS S , Seymour, Ind (b/III-9-1843 Bartholomew Co; d/II-23-1904) MD Med Coll Ohio 1866. *Tr Ind St Med Soc* 1904: 353.

GALE, ALEXANDER FRYER HERRICK, NYC (b/ Elizabeth, NJ; d/III-17-1905) MD CPSNY 1887. *Bost m & s jour* 152:386, 1905. *Polk* 1896:1053.

GALE, AMORY, Woonsocket, RI 1850- (b/X-15-1800 Warwick, Mass; d/II-20-1873) MD Brown 1824; ng Dartmouth 1843. *New Engl med gaz* 8:200, 1873. *Am j hom mat med* 6: 324, 1873? *King* 1:281 ff. *Cleave.* Homeopath.

GALE, C BERNARD, Newport, O (d/VI-1893) MD CPS Balto 1882. *JAMA* 21: 94, 1893. *Polk* 1890: 928.

GALE, ISRAEL NEWTON, Deerfield, NH (b/1799? d/IX-18-1869 @70) MD Dartmouth 1830. *Bost m & s jour* 4: 144, 1869.

GALE, JOHN H , Chicago (d/II–18–1905 @ 68) MD Chicago Homeop Coll 1893. *Ill med jour* 7:302, 1905. *Polk* 1896: 384.

GALE, LEROY, NYC (d/X–5–1883 New Haven, Conn) MD Bellevue 1877; PhB Yale 1874. *Med surg rep Phila* 49:448, 1883.

GALE, LEVI B , Boston (d/VIII–27–1859 @ 59 E. Kingston, NH) ng Brown Med 1822–24. *Bost m & s jour* 61: 108, 1859.

GALE, ROBERT, McKinney, Tex (b/Va; d/III–20 1899 @ 88) <MD Balto Med Coll 1835> *JAMA* 32: 787, 1899. *Polk* 1896: 1440.

GALE, STEPHEN MADISON, Derry, NH; Methuen, Mass 1839–50; Newburyport, Mass 1850– (b/X–20–1809 Kingston Plains, NH; d/I–26–1882) MD Harvard 1837. *New Engl med gaz* 17:96, 1882. *Tr Am Inst Hom* 1882: 140. Homeopath.

GALEN, GUSTAVUS E, Philadelphia (d/X–18–1865 @ 34) MD Pa Med Coll 1857.*Med s rep Phila* 13:294 1865.

GALER, JOSEPH B, Hampton Ia (b/Pa;d/IX–11–1895 @ 74) MD Rush 1869. *JAMA* 25:554, 1895. *Polk* 1890:416.

GALLAER, JOHN, Panama (d/VII–23–1862 Aspinwall, Colombia) MD CPSNY 1847. *Med reg NY NJ Conn* 1862: 153. *Med surg rep Phila* ns4:427, 1860 [sic].

GALLAGHER, CHARLES, La (d/1878) MD U La 1872. *Med rec* 14:240, 1878. *Tr AMA* 30: 863, 1879.

GALLAGHER, JOSEPH FRANCIS, Freeland, Pa (d/III–3–1891) MD Jefferson 1891. *JAMA* 28: 569, 1897.

GALLAGHER, JOSEPH H , Philadelphia (d/VIII–13–1866) MD ?Hahnemann Phila 1855. *Med surg rep Phila* 15: 188, 1866. Homeopath?

GALLAGHER, JOSEPH HENRY, Brooklyn (b/III–16–1876; d/IV–9–1902) MD LICH 1898; AB Villanova 1895. *Bost m & s jour* 146:426, 1902.

GALLAGHER, WILLIAM, Luzerne Co, Pa (b/1804; d/XII–15–1860) MD Jefferson 1829. *Tr Med Soc Pa* 1: 126–27, 1862. *Tr AMA* 14: 208, 1864.

GALLAHER, THOMAS JONES, CW–USA; Pittsburgh, Pa (b/X–4–1822; d/VIII–20–1888) MD UPa 1849. *U Pa med alum CW*: 1849. *Polk* 1886: 829.

GALLATIN, ALBERT HORATIO, NYC (d/III–25–1902 @63) MD UCNY 1862. *Bost m&s j* 146:374, 1902.

GALLERY, FRANK B , Rochester, NY (d/VIII–29–1885 @ 38) MD U Buffalo 1869. *Med reg NY NJ Conn* 1886: 248.

GALLIGAN, EDWARD FRANCIS, Taunton, Mass (d/IX–26–1905 @ 48) MD Harvard 1881. *Bost m & s jour* 153: 402, 1905. *Polk* 1896:724.

GALLION, ERNEST M , Harriman, Tenn (d/I–15–1900 @ 38) MD U Louisville 1889. *JAMA* 34: 312, 1900.

GALLISON, JEFFERSON CUSHING, Franklin, Mass (d/II–22–1904 @ 63) MD Boston U 1875. *Bost m&s j* 150:226, 1904. *Polk* 1890:466. *King* 3:199. Homeopath.

GALLOUPE, J ABBOTT, Beverly, Mass (d/VI–25–1901 @ 29) <att Harvard Med Sch> *JAMA* 37: 126, 1901.

GALLOWAY, GEORGE T , Findlay, O (b/IX–6–1846; d/I–30–1893) MD Western Reserve 1869. *Tr Ohio St Med Soc* 1893:387–88. *Butler* 1878: 629.

GALLOWAY, WILLIAM T , Eau Claire, Wis (d/V–5–1890) MD Castleton 1846. *Tr Wis St Med Soc* 1891: 357. *Polk* 1886: 953.

GALLUP, JOHN STARK, Plainfield, Conn (b/XI–24–1801 Hartland, Vt; d/XII–23–1869 Central Village, Conn) MD U Vt 1824; ng Castleton 1821. *Phila med reg & dir* 1871: 303.

GALLUP, JOSEPH ADAMS, Woodstock, Vt (b/III–30–1769 Stonington, Conn; d/X–12–1849) MD Dartmouth 1798. *Tr AMA* 3:442, 1850. *Bost m & s jour* 41:244, 1849. *K&B* III: 445–46.

GALLUP, LEWIS FREDERICK, Woodstock, Vt (b/V–22–1793 Hartland; d/VI–8–1866) MD Woodstock 1833. *Tr Vt Med Soc* 1883: 106.

GALLUP, WILLIAM, Plainfield, ? 1831–33; New Ipswich, Mass 1833–37; Concord, Mass 1837–44; Bangor, Me 1844– (b/VIII–30–1805 Plainfield, NH or Conn; d/II–13–1883) MD Dartmouth 1834. *Tr Am Inst Hom* 1883: 148. *New Engl med gaz* 18:319, 1883. *King* 1:233. Homeopath.

GALT, JAMES DICKIE, Norfolk, Va; CW–CSA (b/VI 4–1831; d/IX–11–1888) MD U Va 1852; MD UPa 1854. *Tr Med Soc Va* 1888: 275. *U Pa med alum CW*:1854.

GALT, JOHN MINSON, USA 1842–61; CSA 1861–65 (b/1810 Norfolk, Va; d/III–4–1868 Lynchburg) MD UPa 1831. *U Pa med alum CW*:1831 (suppl.)

GALT, ROBERT, CW–CSA (b/VI–8–1836 Richmond, Va; d/III–16–1877 Columbia) MD UPa 1860: AB Princeton 1858. *U Pa med alum CW*: 1860.

GALT, THOMAS, Rock Island, Ill (b/VII–13–1831 Lancaster Co, Pa; d/IV–26–1891) MD Berkshire 1855. *Tr Ill Med Soc* 1891: 19. *Butler* 1878: 153.

GALT, WILLIAM H , Louisville, Ky (d/IX–14–1893 @ 66) MD Kentucky Sch Med 1853. *JAMA* 21: 498, 1893. *Butler* 1878: 265.

GALVAN, JOHN JAMES, NYC (d/III–28–1867) MD CPSNY 1867. *Med reg NY NJ Conn* 1867: 219.

GALVIN, ANNIE STAMBACH, ? (d/IV–16–1872 @32) MD ? *Am jour hom mat med*: 5:412, 1872? Homeopath.

GAMBEL, FRANK W , Leadville Col (d/1882) MD Detroit Med Coll 1873. *Tr Colo St Med Soc* 1898–9:508.

GAMBELL, WILLARD PARKHAM [PARKMAN], Boston (b/IX–25–1820 Barnard, Vt; d/XII–1–1887 @ 67) MD Berkshire 1845. *Tr Am Inst Hom* 1888:219. *Polk* 1886: 456.

GAMBLE, GEORGE, Cincinnati, O; CW–USA (b/VIII–20–1838; d/V–26–1868 Folkestone, Engl) MD Bellevue 1864. *Med surg rep Phila* 19:80, 1868. *Phila med reg & dir* 1871:297 [as d/VI–26–1868 @ 29 Cincinnati].

GAMBLE, JAMES E , Altoona, Pa (b/Newton Hamilton, Pa; d/I–14–1891) MD Jefferson 1878. *Med bull med & surg* 13:110, 1891. *Polk* 1886: 791.

GAMBRILL, STEVENS, Annapolis, Md (b/VI-4-1799 Anne Arundel Co; d/XI-17-1851 Fountain Dale) ng U Md. *Med annals Md:* 405.

GAMMAGE, EMMETT THOMAS, Brooklyn (b/1840 Northampton, Engl; d/V-9-1886) <MRCP(L)> *JAMA* 26: 1092, 1896.

GAMWELL, HARLOW, Westfield, Mass (d/VIII-11-1898 @ 63) MD Berkshire 1858. *Bost m & s jour* 139:188, 1898. *JAMA* 31: 484, 1898. *Polk* 1896: 725.

GAMWELL, JOHN W , Princeton, Ill; Pittsfield, Mass (d/III-26-1905 Dayton, Fla) MD Berkshire 1852. *Ill med jour* 7: 378-79, 1905.

GANGLOFF, CHARLES, Pittsburgh (d/I-22-1898 @ 51) MD Cleveland Homeop Med Coll 1883. *JAMA* 30: 335, 1898. *Polk* 1896: 1325. Homeopath.

GANNAWAY, COLUMBUS E , Warren, Ark (d/III-12-1900) MD U Ark 1896. *JAMA* 34: 766, 1900.

GANNETT, JAMES CHURCH, Waterville, Yarmouth, Me 1878- (b/I-29-1849 Bath, Me; d/IV-4-1897) MD NY Homeop Med Coll 1872. *Tr Amer Inst Homeop* 1897: 63. *Polk* 1886: 430. Homeopath.

GANNON, JOHN, Mt Vernon, NY; NYC (d/V-22-1894) MD Bellevue 1881. *Med reg NY NJ Conn* 1894: 239.

GANNT, EDWARD, Georgetown, Md (b/1741? Pr Geo Co, Md; d/1837? Ky) att U Edinb.*Med annals Md:* 405.

GANTT, WILLIAM H , Galveston (b/St Louis; d/IX-8 1867) MD Mo Med Coll 1850. *Galveston m j* 2:111, 973, 1888 *New Orl m&s j* 21:205 1868. *Tr AMA* 19:429 1868.

GARBER, ABRAM PASCHAL, CW-USA; Renovo & Columbia, Pa (b/II-23-1838 Columbia; d/VIII-25-1881) MD UPa 1872; AB Lafayette 1868. *U Pa med alum CW*:1838. *K&B* III: 447-48.

GARBER, ALEXANDER MENZIES, Livingston, Ala (d/I-20-1891) MD Transylvania 1835. *Tr Med Assoc St Ala* 1891: 261. *Polk* 1886: 135.

GARBER, JAMES RHODES, Uniontown, Ala (b/II-14-1847; d/III-6-1896) MD Tulane 1867; att U Ala 1862. *U Ala cat*: 165. *Polk* 1886: 186 (Pueblo, Colo).

GARCEAU, TREFFLÉ, Roxbury, Mass (b/Montreal; d/XII-19-1897 @60) MD École mèd & chir Montr 1863. *Bost m & s jour* 137:663-64, 668, 1897. *Polk* 1896: 698.

GARCELON, ALONZO, Lewiston, Me (b/V-6-1813; d/XII-8-1906 Medford, Mass) MD Med Coll Ohio 1839; att Bowdoin 1836. *Bost m & s jour* 153: 728, 1906. *K&B* III: 448-49.

GARD, B F , Columbus, O (d/1849) MD Med Coll Ohio 1833. *Tr Ohio St Med Soc* 1873: 266.

GARDEN, WILLIAM ALSTON, CW-USA; Brownsville, Tx (d/II-21-1866 @ 41) MD UPa 1850. *Med surg rep Phila* 14:240, 1866. *Nat med jour* 1:295, 1870/71.

GARDENER, WILLIAM, Philadelphia (b/IX- -1814 Bristol, Engl; d/VI-1-1887) MD Pa Med Coll 1842. *Med surg rep Phila* 56:768, 1887. *Polk* 1886: 816.

GARDETTE, CHARLES DEMARAIS, Washington (b/1830? d/X-27-1884 @54) MD UPa 1851 *Med surg rep Phil* 51:572 1884.

GARDETTE, EMILE BLAISE, Philadelphia (b/VIII-12 1803; d/1887) MD Jefferson 1838. *Med bull med & surg* 10:264, 188. *Tr CPP* cent vol:225. *Butler* 1874, 662.

GARDINER, CHARLES, CW-USA; Hampton, Conn 1879-84; Emporia Kans 1884- (b/1847 Poughkeepsie, NY; d/IX-24-1903) MD Jefferson 1879. *Jour Kans Med Soc* 4:452-53, 1904. *Polk* 1886: 377.

GARDINER, DANIEL R , Woodbury, NJ 1863-71, 1886; Pottsville, Pa 1871-75 (b/X-21-1828 Newtown or Pottsville; d/VI-30-1889 Woodbury or White Sulphur Spr Va) MD Hahnemann Phila 1849; stud Hamilton U NY. *Med vis* 5:262, 1889. *Tr Amer Inst Hom* 1890:135. *King* 1:246. *Polk* 1886: 612.*Cleave.* Homeopath.

GARDINER, DAVID E , Manayunk Pa; Bordentown NJ 1858-70 (d/VI-10-1890 @ 56) MD Hahnemann Phila 1857. *Hahn mo* 25:556, 1890. *Med vis* 6: 283, 1890. *Polk* 1886: 816. Homeopath.

GARDINER, RICHARD, Philadelphia to 1870; Baltimore; Phila (b/II-21-1793 Darby Pa; d/III-22-1877) MD Hahnemann Phila 1850; <att UPa 1814> *Tr Am Inst Hom* 1877: 969. *Hahn mo* 12:540, 1877. *Tr Homeop Med Soc St Pa* 2:89-90, 1874-78. *Cleave.* Homeopath.

GARDINER, WILLIAM H , Brooklyn (b/XII-28-1822 NYC; d/I-7-1879) MD UCNY 1847. *Med reg NY NJ Conn* 1879: 191.

GARDNER, ALFRED WILD, NYC (b/Sharon Springs, NY; d/XII-10-1906) MD CPSNY 1890. *Bost m & s jour* 155: 762, 1906. *Polk* 1896:1054.

GARDNER, ARTHUR HENRY, NYC (b/Springfield, Mass; d/VI-12-1905) MD CPSNY 1898. *Bost m & s jour* 152: 740, 1905.

GARDNER, ASA BENNETT, Bellville, Tx (b/XI-7-1852 Warren Co, Ky; d/X-22-1902) MD U Louisville 1874. *Tex med jour* 14:655-57, 1898-99. *Tr Tex St Med Assoc* 1903: 44-46. *Polk* 1896: 1417.

GARDNER, AUGUSTUS KINSLEY, NYC (b/VII-31-1821 Roxbury, Mass; d/IV-7-1876) MD Harvard 1844. *Med surg rep Phila* 15:313-16, 1866. *K&B* III: 452.

GARDNER, BENJAMIN FRANKLIN, Atlanta, Ill (d/VII-21-1905 @87) MD Bennett 1887. *Ill med jour* 8: 185, 1905. *Polk* 1886: 253.

GARDNER, FRANK B, Baltimore (b/1848;d/IX-7-1895) MD U Md 1867. *Med ann Md:*405. *Polk* 1893:560.

GARDNER, FRANKLIN A , Washington, DC (d/II-13-1903) MD NY Homeop 1882. *Tr Am Inst Hom* 1903:731. *Polk* 1886: 212. Homeopath.

GARDNER, HARRISON SETH, Cedar Springs, Mich (d/VIII-22-1893 @ 53) MD Cleveland U Med & Surg 1881. *JAMA* 21: 357, 1893. *Polk* 1886: 486. Homeopath.

GARDNER, HENRY, Charlestown, Mass (b/IX-13-1772; d/VIII-22-1854) MD ? AM Harvard 1797. Palmer's *Necrol alum Harv*: 39. *Mass Med Soc cat*: 1894.

GARDNER, HENRY, Boston (b/VIII-2-1779; d/VI-19-1858) MB Harvard 1801; MD 1811; AB 1798; AM 1801.

Bost m&s j 58:427 1858. Palmer's *Necrol alum Harv*: 167.

GARDNER, HUGH WALLACE, Wilmington, NC; CW–CSA (b/VII–25–1835; d/1862 in battle) MD U Md 1861; AB UNC 1857. *UNC cat*: 213.

GARDNER, JOHN SEWALL, ? (b/V–16–1818 Hallowell, Me; d/XI– –1846 "in the South") MD CPSNY 1844; Amherst 1840. *Amherst, Men of*: 1840.

GARDNER, JOHNSON, Providence, RI (b/XI–22–1799; d/XII–12–1869 Pawtucket, RI) MD Brown 1824. *Tr RI Med Soc* 1:331–32, 1859–77.

GARDNER, LUCY M, ?LaPorte, Tx (d/II–6–1901) <MD Keokuk Coll Phys Surg 1896> *Ill m j* ns2: 533, 1901.

GARDNER, MATTHEW, San Francisco (b/1845 Ontario; d/IV–18–1903) MD McGill 1871. *Cal st j m* 1: 174, 1903. *Polk* 1896: 233.

GARDNER, SYLVESTER, Newport, RI (b/1717 So Kingston, Engl? d/1786) Stud in France & Engl. *Tr RI Med Soc* 1:8–9, 1859–77.

GARDNER, WILLIAM HENRY HARRISON, Rockwood, Pa (d/X–29–1904 @ 56) MD Bellevue 1873. *Pa m j* 8:335, 1904/05. *Polk* 1886: 800 (Glade, Pa).

GARDNER, WILLIAM WALLACE, Springfield, Mass (d/XII–11–1905 @79) MD UCNY 1865. *Bost m&s j* 153: 710, 1905. *Mass M S cat*: 1894. *Polk* 1896:72 723.

GAREY, DUMONT, New Albany, Ind (b/V–12–1855 Mauckport; d/VII–7–1907) MD U Louisville 1889. *Tr Ind St Med Soc* 1906: 492.

GARFIELD, LEONARD K , Algona, Ia (d/IX–2–1898 @ 78) MD CPS Keokuk 1878. *JAMA* 31: 673, 1898. *Polk* 1896: 510.

GARITEE, CLARENCE JOHN, Philadelphia (d/VIII–10 1903 @ 31) MD UPa 1894; AB 1890. *Pa med jour* 7: 279, 1903/04. *Flint* 1897: 817.

GARLAND, GEORGE WATERHOUSE, Lawrence, Mass (b/I–3–1813 Ranstead, NH; d/V–5–1881) MD Bowdoin 1837 [as Geo. Washington] *Bost m & s jour* 104:480, 1881; 105:449, 623, 1881. *Tr NH Med Soc* 1881:148–51. *Mass Med Soc cat*: 1894.

GARLAND, JOSEPH, Gloucester, Mass (b/I–22–1822 Hampton, NH; d/IX–4–1902) MD Jefferson 1849; AB Bowdoin 1844. *Bost m & s jour* 147: 312, 340, 1902.

GARNER, EDWARD SAMUEL, St Joseph, Mo (d/VII 7–1899) MD CPSNY 1883. *JAMA* 33: 175, 1889. *Polk* 1886: 212.

GARNER, HENRY C , Kansas City, Mo (d/XII–10–1895) MD Transylvania 1850. *JAMA* 25: 1108, 1895. *Polk* 1890: 658.

GARNER, JOHN E , Milwaukee (b/1823 St Mary's Co, Md; d/1887) MD U Md 1842. *Tr AMA* 27:668–69, 1876.

GARNER, LEVI S , CW–USA (d/V–7–1862) MD ? *Nat med jour* 1:295, 1870/71.

GARNETT, ALEXANDER YELVERTON PEYTON, Washington, DC; USN 1841–50; CW–CSA (b/IX–19–1820 Essex Co, Va; d/VII–11–1888 Rehoboth Beach, Del) MD UPa 1841. *U Pa med alum CW*: 1841. *Buffalo m & s jour* 28: 43, 1888. *South pract* 10:362, 1888. *JAMA* 11:105–107, 1888. *K&B* III: 454.

GARNETT, ALEXANDER YELVERTON PEYTON Jr, Washington DC (b/IX–18–1855; d/III–12–1886) MD UCNY 1882; att Wm & Mary. *Med reg NY NJ Conn* 1886: 248. *JAMA* 6:390–91, 1886. *New Orl m & s jour* 13:822,1886. *Med bull med & surg* 8:158, 1886.

GARNETT, JENIFER [male], Richmond, Va (b/I–25–1842 Kalamazoo, Va; d/XII–2–1885) MD Med Coll Va 1867. *New Orl m & s jour* ns13:664, 1886. *Tr Med Soc Va* 1885: 390–91. *Butler* 1878: 828.

GARNETT, JOHN MUSCOE, King & Queen Co, Va; CW–CSA (b/VIII–16–1819 Newtown; d/IV–4–1885) MD U Pa 1841. *U Pa med alum CW*: 1841.

GARNETT, JOHN N , Kansas City, Mo (b/Va; d/X–14–1893 @ 73) MD UPa 1844. *JAMA* 21: 667, 1893. *Polk* 1890: 658, as homeopath.

GARNETT, JUDSON WADE, Hunt Co, Tx 1870– ; Greenville, Tx 1880– (b/VIII–3–1848 Culpeper Co, Va; d/1906?) MD Washington U Balto 1871; att UVa. *Tex st jour med* 1:243, 1906. *Polk* 1896: 1432.

GARRAT [GARRETT], GRACE E , Peoria, Ill (d/X–29 1894) MD Hahnemann Chicago 1885. *JAMA* 23:735, 1894. *Polk* 1890: 344. Homeopath.

GARRATT, ALFRED CHARLES, Boston (d/VI–30–1891 @78) MD Berkshire 1842. *Bost m & s jour* 125: 48, 1891. *Polk* 1890: 537.

GARRETSON, JAMES EDMUND, Philadelphia (b/X–4 1828 Wilmington, Del; d/X–26–1895) MD UPa 1859. *Atkinson* I:75. *Med bull m & s* 17:472, 1895. *K&B* III:454–55.

GARRETSON, PETER H , Peoria, Ill (d/I–8–1900) MD St Louis Med Coll 1869. *Tr Ill St Med Soc* 1899–1900: 415. *JAMA* 34:187, 1900. *Polk* 1886: 287.

GARRETSON, VAN BIBBER [also used forename **FREDERICK**] Bound Brook, NJ (b/1837 Gloucester Co, Va; d/VIII–30–1887) MD U Md 1857. *Med annals Md:* 406. *Polk* 1886: 679.

GARRETT, EDMUND FRANKLIN, Philadelphia (d/XII 16–1891) MD Jefferson 1876. *Med bull med & surg* 14: 36, 1892. *Polk* 1886: 816.

GARRETTSON, JESSE, Cincinnati 1849– (d/VII–30–1876 @ 66) MD ? *Med surg rep Phila* 35: 180, 1876. *Am homeop obs* 13:496, 1876. Homeopath.

GARRETTSON, JOSEPH, Cincinnati (d/I– –1889 @82) MD ? *Med vis* 5:95,1889. *Polk* 1886: 742. *King* 1: 174. Homeopath.

GARRIES, GEORGE A , Erie, Pa (b/Bavaria; d/XII–25–1906 @ 60) MD Cleveland Med Coll 1881. *Pa med jour* 10:406–07, 1906/07. *Flint* 1897: 801.

GARRIGAN, THOMAS JAMES, N Brookfield, Mass (d/IV–20–1906 @ 51) MD UCNY 1879. *Bost m & s jour* 154: 538, 1906. *Polk* 1896:720.

GARRISH, JOHN POOL, NYC (d/IV–1–1891 @ 76) MD Jefferson 1846. *Med reg NY NJ Conn* 1891: 273.

 Spec. educ'l status abbrev. as: ***ng*** = college verified attendance without degree;

Bost m & s jour 124: 372, 1891. *Tr NY Med Soc* 11: 741ff, 1894. *Butler* 1878:513.

GARRISH, JOHN POOL Jr (b/I-23-1847; d/IV-25-1882) MD CPSNY 1866; AB "elsewhere." *Med reg NY NJ Conn* 1882: 228.

GARRISON, CHARLES, Swedesborough, NJ (b/III-17-1800 Deerfield; d/IV-11-1875) MD UPa 1822. *Tr Med Soc NJ* 1875: 107-08. *Tr AMA* 27:653, 1876.

GARRISON, JOSEPH FITHIAN, Camden, NJ (b/I-20-1823 Fairton; d/I-30-1892) MD UPa 1845; AB Princeton 1842; DD 1879. *Tr Med Soc NJ* 1892:195-96. *Butler* 1878: 469.

GARRISON, NELSON A , Brooklyn (b/1798? d/I-26-1872 @ 74) MD UCNY 1858. *Med reg NY NJ Conn* 1872: 346.

GARROTT, ERASMUS R , Chicago (d/IV-19-1898 @ 62) MD U Md 1856. *Chic med rec* 14:478, 1898. *JAMA* 30:1061, 1898. *Flint* 1897: 260.

GARSIDE, WILLIAM BRIGGS, Brooklyn 1868-87; Atlantic City, NJ 1889- (b/II-11-1835; d/XII-1-1899) MD NY Homeop 1868. *Tr Am Inst Hom* 1900: 832-33. *Polk* 1886: 645. Homeopath.

GARTON, WALTER A , Philadelphia (d/V-8 1906 @ 29) MD Temple 1899. *Pa med jour* 9:672, 1905/06.

GARVER, CHARLES, ? (b/X-13-1843 Scotland, Pa; d/1880) MD Jefferson 1868. *Tr M S Pa* 13:303-04, 1880.

GARVER, JANE KIMMELL, Harrisburg, Pa (b/VIII-31 1845; d/X-9-1902) MD Woman's Med Coll Phila 1872. *Pa med jour* 6:168, 259, 1902/03. *Flint* 1897: 804.

GARVER, JOHN JAMES, Indianapolis, Ind (b/II-14-1845 Silver Lake, O; d/XII-12-1900) MD Med Coll O 1877. *Tr Ind St Med Soc* 1901: 484. *Polk* 1896: 473.

GARVEY, PHILIP L , Atlanta Ga; Oakland Ill (d/VII-11 1897 @ 39?) MD Ky Sch Med 1883. *Tr Ind St Med Soc* 1898: 376. *JAMA* 29:252, 1897. *Polk* 1890: 342.

GARVIN, JOHN BROWN, Halifax NS; CW-USA (d/I-6-1870 Halifax) MD Harvard 1863. *Harv in CW*: 278.

GARVIN, J G , ? (d/1878 Williston, Tenn) MD ?UCNY 1847 [as Justin P, Tenn]. *Tr AMA* 30:863, 1879.

GARVIN, JOHN J , Philadelphia; CW-USA (b/VI-28-1819; d/1893) MD Hahnemann Phila 1864. *Hahn mo* 1893 (Mar). *Polk* 1886: 816. *Cleave.* Homeopath.

GARWOOD, WILLIAM T , San Francisco (b/Phila; d/XI-21-1902 @ 65) MD U Pacific (Cooper) 1864. *Cal st jour med* 1:43, 1902. *Polk* 1896: 233.

GARY, FRANKLIN F , Abbeville CH, SC; CW-CSA (b/1829 Cokesbury, SC; d/1887) MD Jefferson 1851. *Tr SC Med Assn* 1883: 27-36. *Waring* II:233-34. *Polk* 1886: 851.

GARY, GEORGE, Chepachet, RI (b/1794 Pomfret Conn? d/VIII-9-1828) MD ? ; AB Brown 1828. *Brown hist cat*: 1820.

GARY, JAMES F , Delhi, Ill (d/VI-19-1905 @ 55) MD Am Med Coll St Louis 1878. *Ill med jour* 8: 185, 1905. *Polk* 1886: 202.

GARY, THOMAS PORTER, Ocala, Fla (b/IV-10-1835 Abbeville, SC; d/VI-10-1891) MD Med Coll SC 1857. *Proc Fla Med Assn* 1892: 55-56. *Bost m & s jour* 124: 618, 1891. *Butler* 1878: 101.

GASTON, ALEXANDER K , Brandywine Twp, Pa (b/I-14-1814 Somerset Twp, NJ; d/XII-22-1882) MD Jefferson 1835. *Tr Med Soc Pa* 15:341, 1883; 16:440-41, 1884. *Butler* 1878: 713.

GASTON, EPHRAIM, Morristown, O (b/1799? d/V-30-1868 @ 69) MD ? *Tr Ohio St Med Soc* 1868-69: 175-76. *Med surg rep Phila* 19: 368, 1868. *Phila med reg & dir* 1871: 297.

GASTON, JAMES McFADDEN, Atlanta, Ga; Brazil (b/XII-27-1824 Chester, SC; d/XI-15-1903) MD Med Coll Ga 1846; AB So Carolina Coll 1843. *So pract* 25: 711, 1903. *K&B* III: 456.

GASTON, JOHN M , Indianapolis, Ind (b/IX-25-1818, Newbury, Pa; d/I-11-1901) MD UCNY 1848. *Tr Ind St Med Soc* 1901: 485. *Polk* 1896: 473.

GASTON, JOSEPH W , CW-USA (d/IX-13-1864) MD ? *Nat med jour* 1:295, 1870/71.

GATCHELL, ELISHA, Kennett Square, Pa (b/IV-18 1828 Chester Co; d/X-5-1857 Phila) MD UPa 1855. *Tr Med Soc Pa* 3:74-75, 1858.

GATCHELL [GETCHELL] HORATIO PAGE, Cincinnati, O; Kenosha, Wis; Asheville, NC (b/II-17-1814; d/III-27-1885) <MD Eclectic Med Coll Cinc 1842>; ng Bowdoin Coll 1831-33. *US med invest* 21:328, 1885. *Am hom obs* 21:47, 1885. *King* 1: 406; 3: 16. Homeopath.

GATES, CARLETON, Yonkers, NY (d/VIII-21-1869) MD CPSNY 1852; AB UCNY 1849. *Phila med reg & dir* 1871: 302. *Med surg rep Phila* 21:208, 1869.

GATEWOOD, D B , Cleburne, Tx (d/IX-19-1882) MD ? *Tex med & surg rec* 3:551, 1883.

GATEWOOD, J M , Keith, O (d/I-19-1894) MD Starling 1890. *JAMA* 22:122, 1894.

GATLING, RICHARD JORDAN, Hartford, Conn (b/IX 12-1818 Hertford Co, NC; d/II-26-1903) <MD Med Coll Ohio 1850> *Chic med rec* 24: 247, 1903.

GAUBERT, ALONZO LEWIS, Tryon, SC (b/VIII-28-1847 Richmond, Me; d/II-6-1896) MD Bowdoin 1874. *Tr Me Med Assn* 12:425 636-37, 1895-97. *Polk* 1886: 853.

GAUNTT, CHARLES STOCKTON, CW-USA; Philadelphia (b/VIII-23-1823; d/VIII-16-1906) MD UPa 1844. *Pa med jour* 9:894, 1905/06. *U Pa med alum CW*: 1844. *Flint* 1897: 817.

GAUNTT, FRANKLIN, CW-USA; Burlington, NJ (b/VII-19-1822; d/VII-7-1900) MD UPa 1847. *U Pa med alum CW*: 1847. *Polk* 1886: 601.

GAUS, GEORGE C , CW-USA (d/X-4-1864 Harrisonburg, Va) MD ? *Nat med jour* 1:295, 1870/71.

GAUSE, OWEN BEVERLY, Philadelphia (b/VI-22-1825 Wilmington, Del; d/I-11-1895) MD Hahnemann Phila 1857. *Hahn mo* 30:43 (news & advt), 1895 (Mar).

Tr Amer Inst Homeop 1895:221. *Polk* 1886: 816. Homeopath.

GAUSE, PERCIVAL OWEN BEVERLY, Aiken, SC 1885- (b/XI- -1860 Trenton, NJ; d/XI-10-1887) MD Hahn Phila 1881; postgr study @ London, Paris, Vienna. *Med vis* 4:15, 1889. *Hahn mo* 22:768, 1887. *Polk* 1886: 816. Homeopath.

GAUSE, THOMAS, Greenfork, Ind (b/II-2-1846 Dublin, Ind; d/VIII-29-1882) ng Med Coll Ohio. *Tr Med St Med Soc* 1883: 268.

GAWLEY, ECCLES W , Anamosa, Ia (d/III-20-1898 @ 50) MD Detroit Med Coll 1875. *JAMA* 30: 807, 1898. *Polk* 1890: 407.

GAY, CHARLES CURTIS FENN, Buffalo (b/I-27-1821 Pittsfield, Mass; d/III-27-1886) MD Berkshire 1845. *Buff m & s jour* 25:439, 482 ff, 1886. *Tr NY St Med Soc* 11: 741 ff, 1894. *Butler* 1878: 537.

GAY, GEORGE CLIFTON, Waterbury, Conn (b/X-29-1869 Washington Co, NY; d/III-22-1895) <MD U Mich 1890> *Proc Conn Med Soc* 1895: 361-62.

GAY, GEORGE HENRY, Boston (d/VIII-12-1878 @ 55) MD Harvard 1845; AB 1842. *Bost m & s jour* 99:225, 676, 1878.

GAY, GRENVILLE WARE, Boston (d/I-2-1865 @ 54 Bath, Me) MD Bowdoin 1841. *Bost m & s jour* 71:488, 1864. *Mass Med Soc cat* 1894.

GAY, HARVEY STAFFORD, NYC (d/III-25-1891 @ 65) MD UCNY 1849. *Bost m & s jour* 124: 372, 1891. *Butler* 1878: 513.

GAY, MARTIN, Boston (d/I-12-1850 @ 46) MD Harvard 1826; AB 1823; AM 1841. *Tr AMA* 3:441, 1850.

GAY, NORMAN, Columbus, O (d/V-6-1898 @78) MD Willoughby 1847. *JAMA* 30:1248, 1898. *Polk* 1890: 910.

GAYLORD, EDWARD PAYSON, Syracuse NY; Toledo O; Oshkosh & Ripon, Wis; Alameda, Cal 1892?- (d/IX-27-1895 @ 61) MD Hahnemann Phila 1854. *JAMA* 25: 640, 1895. *Polk* 1896: 223. Homeopath.

GAYLORD, HORACE, Pontiac, Ill (d/I-30-1895) MD Rush 1864. *JAMA* 24:221, 1895. *Polk* 1890: 345.

GEARY, JAMES STEPHEN, NYC (d/VII-18-1899 @ 30) MD Bellevue 1892. *JAMA* 33:302, 1899. *Bost m & s jour* 141:99, 1899. *Polk* 1896:1054.

GEARY, JOHN FITZGIBBON, Philadelphia; San Francisco 1862-83 (b/1814 Ireland; d/X-3-1883 Oakland, Cal) MD Hahnemann Phila 1855. *Am hom obs* 20:383, 1884. *Hahn mo* 18:704, 1883. Homeopath.

GEBHARD, LEWIS P , Philadelphia (b/VI-14-1791 Columbia Co, NY; d/XII-30-1873) MD UPa 1813. *Med surg rep Phila* 29:468, 1873. *Tr CPP* cent vol 1887: 225. *Tr Med Soc Pa* 10:361-68, 1874.

GEDDES, ANNIE LOWE, Glen Ridge & Montclair, NJ (b/VI-4-1855 Halifax, NS; d/VII- -1903) MD NY Coll & Hosp for Women 1890. *Tr Am Inst Hom* 1904: 956. Homeopath.

GEDDINGS, ELI, Charleston, SC (b/1799 Newberry; d/X-9-1878) MD Med Coll SC 1825; att U Pa Med Dept. *Med ann Md:* 406-07. *Tr AMA* 30:819-23, 1879. *Bost m & s jour* 99:742-43, 1878. *K&B* III:458-59. *Atkinson* I: 694.

GEDDINGS, JOHN FREDERICK MECKEL, Charleston, SC; CW-CSA (b/IX-14-1829; d/II-3-1887) MD Coll Med SC 1849. *Atkinson* I: 360. *New Orl m & s jour* ns14:723-24, 1887. *Polk* 1886: 852.

GEDDINGS, WILLIAM H , Aiken, SC (b/IV-23-1838 Charleston; d/VIII-27-1892 Bethlehem, NH) <g Med Coll SC> stud abroad. *Bost m&s j* 127: 586, 1892. *JAMA* 19:732-33, 1892. *Waring* II:238-39. *Atkinson* I:237.

GEDICKE, HERMAN W , Newark, NJ (d/III-5 1891 @ 42) MD Med Coll Evansville 1882. *Bost m&s j* 124: 275, 1891. *Polk* 1890: 726.

GEDNEY [GIDNEY] WILLIAM H , Milton, NY (d/I-18-1896 @ 73) MD Albany 1845. *Tr Med Soc St NY* 1896: 437. *Polk* 1886: 668.

GEE, EDWARD C , Lunenburg Co, Va (b/IV-15-1837; d/X-1-1893) MD Jefferson 1859. *Tr Med Soc Va* 1894: 189-90. *Butler* 1878: 828.

GEE, WILLIAM STANLEY, Hyde Park, Ill (b/VIII-6-1856 Clinton, Mo; d/XI-11-1890) MD Hahn Chic 1881. *Med vis* 6:376, 1890; 7:197, 1889. *Hahn mo* 25:843, 1890. *Tr Am Inst Hom* 1893: 142. *Polk* 1886: 283. Homeopath.

GEER, OLIVER P , Alloway, NY (d/XII-7-1894 @ 84) MD Geneva 1836. *JAMA* 23: 961, 1894.

GEER, SETH Jr, NYC (d/X-15-1866 Chatham, NJ) Lic Med Soc Co NY 1839. *Med reg NY NJ Conn* 1867: 219.

GEGAN, JOHN Jr, ? (d/II-15-1869) MD Jefferson 1851. *Phila med reg & dir* 1871: 293.

GEHRING, HENRY F , Malone, NY (d/1899?) MD Columbus Med Coll 1884. *Bost m & s jour* 142: 76, 1900. *JAMA* 34: 61, 1900. *Polk* 1896: 1015.

GEIGER, HENRY, Chicago (d/X-15-1898) <MD U Heidelberg 1861> *JAMA* 31: 1066, 1898. *Polk* 1896:384.

GEIGLEY, JESSE S , Canton, Ill (d/XI-2-1894 @ 36) MD Missouri Med Coll (Kemper) 1882. *JAMA* 23: 768, 1894. *Polk* 1890: 303.

GEIS, JOHN FRANK, Indianapolis, Ind (b/VIII-26-1868; d/III-7-1904) <MD Med Coll 1890> *Tr Ind St Med Soc* 1904: 354.

GEISSE, EMMA CORA, Chicago (b/IV-5-1846 Wellsville, O; d/XI-25-1895) MD Boston U 1885. *No Am j hom* 44:61, 1896. Homeopath.

GELCHICH, PETER G , Hermasillo, Mex (d/X-7-1883) MD ? *Med surg rep Phila* 49:532, 1883.

GELWIX, JAMES MONTGOMERY, Upper Strasbourg, Pa (b/1844; d/VII-10-1906) MD Jefferson 1866. *Pa med jour* 10: 167-68, 1906/07. *Flint* 1897: 838.

GEMMILL, JACOB M , Tyrone, Pa (b/Alexandria, Pa; d/VII-3-1906 @ 57) MD Jefferson 1870. *Pa med jour* 9:804, 1905/06. *Flint* 1897: 838.

GENTRY, R K , CW-CSA (d/XI-25-1863 Missionary

Ridge) MD ? *SHSP* 22:207, 1893.

GEORGE, JAMES HOSEA, Linden, Ala (d/XI-10-1901) MD Med Coll St SC 1876. *Tr Med Assoc St Ala* 1902: 130. *Polk* 1893: 159.

GEORGE, SILAS, Harrisburg, Pa (d/VIII-15-1823 @ 28?) MD UPa 1823. *Amer med recorder* 6: 772, 1823.

GEORGE, WILLIAM ALBERT, Keosauqua, Ia (b/1853; d/VI-3-1899) MD Bellevue 1876. *JAMA* 33: 175, 1899. *Polk* 1896: 741.

GERBERICH, MORRIS BASHORE, Lebanon Pa (b/VII 5-1861 E Hanover, Pa; d/XI-1-1905) MD Hahnemann Phila 1877. *Pa med jour* 9:221, 1905/06. *Flint* 1897: 806.

GERCKE, RUDOLPH O , Augusta, Ga (d/VI-4-1895 @ 52) <MD Med Coll Ga 1869> *JAMA* 24: 989, 1895. *Polk* 1890: 262.

GERDINE, A[LBINUS?] S , Miss (d/1878) MD U La 1869. *Tr AMA* 30:863-64, 1879.

GERDINE, JOHN, Athens, Ga (d/II-18-1903 @ 63) MD U La 1861. *So pract* 25:222-23, 1903. *Flint* 1897: 215.

GERET, BENJAMIN, St Charles, Mo (b/Bavaria; d/V-3 1900 @ 58) <MD U Erlangen 1868> *JAMA* 34: 1210, 1900. *Polk* 1896: 860.

GERHARD, ABRAHAM SCHULTZ, Philadelphia (b/VI 10-1840 Upper Hanover Twp, Pa; d/XII-15-1891) MD UPa 1866; AB Franklin & Marshall 1863. *Med bull med & surg* 14:36, 1892. *Polk* 1886: 816.

GERHARD, JEROME ZWINGLI, CW-USA; Harrisburg, Pa (b/XI-6-1842 Cherryville; d/XI-20-1906) MD UPa 1868; AB Fr & Marsh 1864. *Pa med jour* 10: 405-06, 1906/07. *UPa med alum CW*:1868. *Flint* 1897: 804.

GERHARD, MATTHIAS, Delaware, O (d/IV-20-1868) MD Pa Med Coll 1842. *Phila med reg & dir* 1871: 296. *Med surg rep Phila* 18: 398, 1868.

GERHARD, WILLIAM WOOD, Philadelphia (b/VII-23 1809; d/IV-28-1872) MD UPa 1830; AB Dickinson 1826. *Phila med reg & dir* 1873: 303. *Med times* (Phila) 2:319, 353, 1872. *Tr CPP* cent vol: 226. *K&B* III: 460.

GERLACH, RUDOLPH E , Mercer Co, NJ (b/X-24-1863 Gny; d/III-13-1891 Trenton) MD UPa 1889. *Tr Med Soc NJ* 1891:

GERRISH, JAMES W F , Seymour, Ind (b/II-12-1831 Monmouth, Me; d/VIII-4-1883) <MD Med Coll Ohio 1855> *JAMA* 3:335, 1884. *Tr Ind St Med Soc* 1884: 212. *Butler* 1878: 203.

GERRON, THOMAS J , Argo, Tx (d/IV-30-1906) MD Vanderbilt 1893. *Tex st jour med* 2:76, 1906.

GERRY, JAMES Jr, Shrewsbury, Pa (b/II-4-1839; d/VII-2-1903 @ 63) MD Jefferson 1863; ng Dickinson 1862. *Pa med jour* 7:279, 1903/04. *Flint* 1897: 836.

GERRY, SAMUEL RUSSELL, San Francisco (b/IV-18-1816 Marblehead, Mass; d/III-10-1893) MD Harvard 1838; AB Amherst 1835. *Amherst, Men of*: 1835. *Polk* 1886: 172.

GESCHEIDT, LOUIS ANTHONY, Hastings, NY (b/IV-8-1808; d/VIII-20-1877) MD Leipsig 1831. *Med reg NY NJ Conn* 1877: 201.

GETCHELL, ELLEN SOUTHARD, Boston (d/IX-26-1888 @ 49) MD Boston U 1884. *Med vis* 4:370, 1888. *Polk* 1886:457. Homeopath.

GETTY, THOMAS MURRAY, CW-USA (b/1823 Md; d/X-30-1867 Fort McHenry) MD UPa 1848. *U Pa med alum CW*: 1848. *Tr AMA* 19:453-54, 1868. *Nat med jour* 1:295, 1870/71.

GHISELIN, REVERDY, Nottingham, Md (b/c1765 Annapolis; d/1823) MD UPa 1788. *Med annals Md*:407-08.

GIBBES, ROBERT REEVE, Savannah, Ga; CW-CSA (b/XI-13-1836 Beaufort, SC; d/IV-29-1877) MD UPa 1858; ng Coll Charleston 1856-57. *U Pa med alum CW*: 1858. *Med reg NY NJ Conn* 1877: 202.

GIBBES, ROBERT WILSON, Columbia, SC (b/VII-8-1809 Charleston; d/X-15-1866) MD Med Coll SC 1834; AB So Carolina Coll 1827. *Amer jour med sci* 53:286, 1867. *Bost m & s jour* 75:312, 1866. *Med surg rep Phila* 15: 368, 1866. *K&B* III: 463.

GIBBON, J W , Charlotte, NC (b/1794? d/XII-16-1868 @ 74) MD ? *Phila med reg & dir* 1871: 299. *Med surg rep Phila* 19:522, 1868.

GIBBON, QUINTON V , Salem, NJ (b/VII-4-1813 Hopewell, NJ; d/VI-6-1894) MD UPa 1833. *Tr Med Soc NJ* 1894: 269-71. *Polk* 1886: 611.

GIBBON, ROBERT, CW-CSA; Charlotte, NC (b/1822 Phila; d/V-14-1898) MD Jefferson 1847; <att Yale> *NC med jour* 41: 371-72, 1898. *Polk* 1886: 721.

GIBBON, WILLIAM H , Chariton Ia (b/I-31-1832 Ellicott's Mills, Md; d/X-2-1895) MD Jefferson 1857. *Tr Ia St Med Soc* 1896: 320-21. *JAMA* 25:640, 1895. *Polk* 1890: 409.

GIBBONEY, SAMUEL RUSH, Belleville, Pa 1860; CW USA; Rock Grove, Ill; Osborne, Kans (b/V-17-1834; d/VI-18-1881) MD Jefferson 1860. *Tr St Med Soc Kans* 2:384, 1882.

GIBBONS, HENRY, Wilmington, Del to 1844; San Francisco (b/IX-20-1808 Wilmington; d/XI-5-1884) MD UPa 1829. *Tr CPP* cent vol: 226. *Atkinson* I: 641-42. *Med surg rep Phila* 51: 604, 1884. *Pacific m & s jour & Western lancet* 28:49-60, 1885. *K&B* III: 463-64.

GIBBONS, JAMES, Chester Co, Pa (b/c1776 E Bradford Twp, Pa; d/I-13-1808) Stud w/Dr Jacob Ehrenzeller; <ng UPa Med Dept c1799> *Med rep West Chester, Pa* 1: 128, 1854.

GIBBONS, JAMES EDWARD, Baltimore (b/VII-8-1844 Montg'y Co, Md; d/XII-2-1901) MD Washington U Balto 1868. *Med annals Md*: 408. *Polk* 1893:560.

GIBBONS, JOHN, Seaford, Del (b/1788 Ireland; d/1848) MD UPa 1809. *Med annals Md*: 408.

GIBBONS, JOHN H , Philadelphia (b/1759? d/X-5-1795 @ 36) MD Edinburgh 1786. *Tr CPP* cent vol: 226.

GIBBONS, JOSEPH, Philadelphia (d/XII-9-1883 @ 65 Bird-in-Hand, Pa) MD Jefferson 1845. *Med surg rep Phila* 49:700, 1883.

GIBBONS, THOMAS PYM, New Haven, Conn (b/IV-27-1824 Lancaster Co, Pa; d/IV-3-1886) MD Jefferson 1851. *Proc Conn Med Soc* ns3: 179-181, 1887.

GIBBONS, WILLIAM, Wilmington Del (b/1781; d/VII 24-1845) MD UPa 1805. *Tr AMA* 29:657-59, 1878.

GIBBS, BENJAMIN FRANKLIN, USN 1858- (b/VIII-18-1836 Pemberton, NJ; d/IX-9-1882 Trieste, Austria) MD UPa 1858. *U Pa med alum CW*: 1858.

GIBBS, EDWIN, Washington DC (d/VIII-15-1898 Lynnwood Va) <MD CPS Balto 1881> *JAMA* 31:484, 1898.

GIBBS, JOHN BLAIR, USN (b/IX-25-1858 Richmond, Va; d/VI-12-1898 Guantanamo Bay) MD UPa 1881; MD CPSNY 1882; AB Rutgers 1878; AM 1881. *Buff m &s j* 37:934-35, 1898. *Bost m&s j* 138:602-03, 1898. *JAMA* 30:1481, 1534, 1898. *Polk* 1886: 679 (NYC).

GIBBS, ORESTUS [?] C , Frewsburgh, NY (d/VII-28-1871 @ 47) MD Cleveland Med Coll 1849. *Buff m & s jour* 11: 40, 1871.

GIBBS, THERON ZADOC, Fort Ann, NY (b/XII-18-1826; d/VII-14-1896) MD Castleton 1853. *JAMA* 27: 279 1896. *Tr NY St Med Soc* 1897: 479. *Polk* 1896: 1022.

GIBBY, THOMAS HILL, Nashua, NH (d/X-16-1893 Manchester) MD Harvard 1858. *JAMA* 21:630, 1893. *Butler* 1878: 455.

GIBERSON, CHARLES HENRY, USN, Brooklyn (b/IX 5-1838 Bath, NB; d/IV-19-1879) MD U Vt 1861. *Med reg NY NJ Conn* 1879: 191. *Med rec NY* 15:528, 1879.

GIBERT, JAMES T , NYC (b/V-27-1804 Newport, RI; d/III-11-1867 Paris, Fr) MD ? ; AB Columbia 1824. *Tr AMA* 19:423, 1868. *Phila med reg & dir* 1871:295. *Med reg NY NJ Conn* 1868: 325.

GIBIER, PAUL, NYC (b/X-9-1851 France; d/VI-9-1900) <MD Paris 1884> *Bost m & s jour* 142: 645, 1900. *Med news NY* 76:967, 1900. *JAMA* 34:1574, 1900. *Buff m & s jour* 39:933-34, 1900.

GIBSON, BUSHROD RICE, Pomfret, Vt; (b/VIII-20-1823; d/III-25-1858) MD Woodstock 1847. *Tr Vt Med Soc* 1883: 105.

GIBSON, CHARLES BELL, Richmond, Va; CW-CSA (b/X-12-1815 Balto; d/IV-23-1865) MD UPa 1836; AB 1833. *Med annals Md:* 409. *U Pa Matriculates of the College*: 1833. *K&B* III:464-65.

GIBSON, GEORGE S , Baltimore (b/XII-11-1800; d/I 30-1872) MD U Md 1823. *Tr AMA* 23:590-91, 1872. *Med annals Md:* 409.

GIBSON, JAMES A , Foster & Richmond, Tx (d/VI-12-1893) MD U La 1852. *Tex cour-rec med* 10:344, 1893. *Polk* 1886: 892.

GIBSON, JAMES B , NYC (d/IV-10-1899 Colorado Spr) MD McGill 1886. *JAMA* 32: 899, 1899. *Bost m & s jour* 140:392, 1899. *Polk* 1896: 254.

GIBSON, JOHN GERARD, Chicago (d/V-24-1900) MD U Md 1883. *Ill med jour* ns2: 48, 1900.

GIBSON, JOHN J , USN (d/II-19-1870) MD Jefferson 1856. *Tr AMA* 21:498, 1870. *Phila med reg & dir* 1871: 304. *Nat med jour* 1:295, 1870/71.

GIBSON, JOHN St PIERRE, Staunton, Va (d/X-31-1898 @ 66) MD U Md 1858. *JAMA* 31: 1257, 1898. *Polk* 1886: 927.

GIBSON, JOSHUA GREGG, Shepherdstown [WVa?] (d/1894) MD UPa 1846; AB Jefferson Coll 1843. *Med annals Md:* 409.

GIBSON, ROBERT McQUEEN, Portsmouth, O (b/VII-4-1854 Troy, NY; d/VII-3-1885) MD Med Coll O 1876. *Tr Ohio Med Soc* 1886: 404-06. *Butler* 1878: 630. *JAMA* 5:390, 1885.

GIBSON, ROBERT PHILLIPS, NYC (b/1819; d/XII-27 1890) MD NY Med Coll 1855; AB Princeton 1840; AM 1854. *Med reg NY NJ Conn* 1891: 273. *Bost m&s jour* 124: 24, 1891.

GIBSON, SAMUEL, Williamsport, Pa (b/X-5-1819 Susquehanna; d/V-11-1875) MD Pa Coll Med 1850. *Tr Med Soc Pa* 10:654-55, 1875.

GIBSON, WILLIAM, Baltimore; Philadelphia (b/III-14-1788; d/III-2-1868) MD Edinburgh 1809; AB Princeton 1806. *New Orl m & s jour* 21:638, 1868. *Nashville jour m & s* ns3:478, 1868. *Med annals Md:* 409. *Med surg rep Phila* 18:271-74, 1868. *K&B* III: 465-66.

GIBSON, WILLIAM, Philadelphia 1853-55; Morris, Ill 1855-1860; Alexandria, Va 1860- (b/IV-2-1831 Armagh, Ireland; d/I-28-1903) MD Pa Med Coll 1853. *Tr Med Soc Va* 1903: 271. *Polk* 1900: 1755.

GIBSON, WILLIAM BORROWE, CW-USN (d/XI-8-1862 near Key West, Fla) MD Harvard 1862. *Tr AMA* 14:217, 1864. *Bost m & s jour* 67: 324-25, 1862. *Med surg rep Phila* ns9: 206, 1862/63. *Harvard in CW*: 272. *Nat med jour* 1:295, 1870/71.

GIBSON, WILLIAM C , Macon, Ga (d/IV-25-1896 @ 39 Vineville) MD Jefferson 1881. *JAMA* 26: 995, 1896. *Polk* 1886: 230.

GIBSON, WILLIAM R , Braddock, Pa (d/XI-7-1904 @ 49) <MD Edinburgh> *Pa med jour* 8:335, 1904/05. *Polk* 1896: 1269.

GIDDINGS, THEODORE, Housatonic, Mass (d/XII-28-1900 @ 64) MD CPSNY 1868. *Bost m & s jour* 144: 246, 1901. *Polk* 1896: 714.

GIDNEY, J CHAUNCEY, Shelby, NC (d/X-2-1889) MD Jefferson 1861. *NC med jour* 24: 383, 1889. *Polk* 1886: 726.

GIFFORD, DAVID S , Bedford, Mich (d/VII-16-1889 @ 51) MD ? *Med vis* 5: 300, 1889. *Polk* 1886: 484. Homeopath.

GIFFORD, GILBERT L , Hamilton, NY 1865- (b/XII-25-1842 Brookfield; d/VI-11-1906) MD Hahnemann Phila 1863. *Bost m&s j* 154:722, 1906. *Tr Am Inst Hom* 1906: 762-63. *Polk* 1896: 1025. *Cleave.* Homeopath.

GIFFORD, LA DETTE G, Watertown, NY (d/IV-8-1895 @38) MD UCNY 1884. *JAMA* 24:609 1895. *Polk* 1890: 856.

Spec. educ'l status abbrev. as: ***ng*** = college verified attendance without degree;

GIFFORD, SILAS SWIFT, Avon, Mass (b/XI-9-1823; d/IX-18-1902) MD Castleton 1852. *Bost m & s jour* 147:422, 1902. *Polk* 1886:645 (E Stoughton, Mass).

GIFFORD, THOMAS, Laurel, Ind (b/XII-16-1816 Penn Yan, NY; d/VI-14-1885) MD Med Coll Ohio 1846. *Tr Ind St Med Soc* 1886: 199. *Butler* 1878: 203.

GIGER, FREDERICK S , Baltimore; Philadelphia (b/V-14-1820; d/IV-20-1859) MD U Md 1844; AB Princeton 1841. *Med surg rep Phila* ns2:105, 144-45, 1859.

GIHON, ALBERT LEARY, USN 1855-95 (b/IX-28-1833 Phila; d/XI-17-1901 NYC) MD Phila Coll Med & Surg 1851; AB Central HS Phila; Hon AB Princeton 1854. *Bost m & s jour* 145:581, 1901. *Atkinson* I: 697. *Polk* 1890: 770. *K&B* II:438.

GILBERT, CHARLES HENRY, Morris, Conn (b/IV-15 1846 Portland; d/V-21-1883) MD ? *Proc Conn M S* ns2: 179, 1883. *Med bull m & s* 5:185, 1883. *Butler* 1878: 77.

GILBERT, DAVID, Gettysburg, Pa; Philadelphia (b/VII-27-1803 Adams Co; d/VII-28-1868) MD Jefferson 1828; AB Jefferson (Canonsburg Pa) 1825. *Tr CPP* cent vol: 226. *Phila med reg & dir* 1871: 293. *Bost m & s jour* 2:48, 1868. *Med s rep Phila* 19:120, 1868. *K&B* III: 467.

GILBERT [GUILBERT], EDWARD A , Galena, Ill (d/III-4-1900 Dubuque, Ia) MD Rush 1847. *Tr Ill St Med Soc* 1899-1900: 509. *Polk* 1886: 280.

GILBERT, GERSHOM CLARK HYDE, Westbrook, Conn (b/VII-17-1817 Mansfield; d/X-30-1889) MD Yale 1844. *Proc Conn M S* ns4:281 1890. *Polk* 1886:197.

GILBERT, J C , Commerce & Chisolm Tx (d/V-20-1905) <MD Barnes U St L> *Tex st j m* 1:154, 1905/06.

GILBERT, JAMES B , NYC (b/1852 Gilbertsville, NY; d/XII-9-1896) MD UCNY 1874. *JAMA* 28: 91, 1897. *Polk* 1896: 1054.

GILBERT, JOHN EDWIN, Gettysburg, Pa (b/VI-24-1852; d/IV-20-1882) MD UPa 1877; AB Penna Coll 1872; AM 1875. *Tr Med Soc Pa* 14:295-96, 1882.

GILBERT, JOHN HENRY, Quincy, Mass (b/Atkinson, NH; d/VIII-3-1899 @66) MD Harvard 1853; ng Dartmouth Med Coll 1849. *Bost m & s jour* 141:148,175, 1899. *JAMA* 33:427, 1899. *Polk* 1886:471.

GILBERT, JOSEPHUS C , Philadelphia; CW-USA (b/1832 Chestnut Hill, Pa; d/X-26-1895) MD Pa Med Coll 1853, 1854, 1855. *JAMA* 25:873, 1895. *Atkinson* I:248.

GILBERT, PORTEOUS C , Saratoga Springs, NY (d/VI-11-1898 @ 57) MD Albany 1863. *Bost m & s jour* 138:601, 1898. *Polk* 1896: 1098.

GILBERT, VAN BUREN, Gilbertsboro, Ala; CW-CSA (b/II-6-1837; d/XII-19-1870) MD U Nashville 1857. *Nashville j m & s* ns7:239-40, 1870. *SHSP* 22:207, 1893.

GILBERT, WILLIAM KENT, Philadelphia (b/XII-28-1829 Northumberland Co, Pa; d/VI-28-1880) MD Pa Med Coll 1852; AB Penna Coll 1848. *Tr CPP* cent vol: 226. *Tr AMA* 32:503-04 1881. *Chic med rev* 2:349 1880.

GILCHRIST, EDWARD, Chelsea, Mass; USN (b/Charlestown, NH; d/XI-6-1869 @ 52) MD ? ; Hon AM Harvard 1852. *Phila med reg & dir* 1871: 302. *Bost m & s jour* ns4:265, 268, 1869. *Nat med jour* 1:295, 1870/71.

GILCHRIST, JAMES GRANT, Ann Arbor, Mich; Iowa City Ia 1883- (b/IV-28-1842; d/III- -1906) MD Hahnemann Phila 1863. *Tr Am Inst Hom* 1906: 772-73. *Polk* 1886: 360. Homeopath.

GILCHRIST, WILLIAM N , NYC (Kortright, NY; d/XII-3-1897 @ 74) MD Castleton 1846. *Bost m & s jour* 137: 609, 1897.

GILES, ALBERT, Racine & Madison, Wis (b/V-10-1809 Kingston, NY; d/VI-7-1862 @ 53) MD Berkshire 1831. *Am hom rev* 3:240, 1862? *Tr Am Inst hom* 1893: 143. *King* 1:339. Homeopath.

GILFILLAN, GEORGE, Brooklyn (b/1799? d/II-5-1879 MD CPSNY 1834. *Med reg NY NJ Conn* 1879: 192.

GILFILLAN, THOMAS, Northampton, Mass (d/IX-9-1905 @ 75) MD Berkshire 1854. *Bost m & s j* 153: 318, 1905. *Polk* 1896: 720.

GILFILLAN, WILLIAM, Brooklyn (b/Ireland; d/XII-18 1904 @ 71) MD Edinburgh 1855. *Bost m & s jour* 151: 726, 1904. *Polk* 1896: 996.

GILFORD [GIFFORD], JACOB TOWNSEND, NYC(b/VIII-2-1805; d/XII-27-1868) <MD Geneva> AB Columbia 1824. *Med reg NY NJ Conn* 1869:326; 1870:318.

GILKEY, WALTER R , CW-USA (d/VI-6-1863 Winchester, Va) MD Cleveland Med Coll 1857. *Nat med jour* 1:295, 1870/71.

GILL, CHARLES, Mays Landing, NJ (b/X-18-1814; d/I 14-1886) Lic yrs pract; <att U Pa Med Dept> *Tr NJ Med Soc* 1886: 165-67. *Polk* 1886: 606.

GILL, CHARLES ROBERT, NYC (d/VII-12-1891 @ 70) MD CPSNY 1844. *Bost m & s jour* 125: 124, 1891.

GILL, GEORGE FULLER, St Louis, Mo (d/VI-4-1892 @ 49) <MD St Louis Med Coll 1864> *Bost m & s jour* 127: 28, 1892. *Polk* 1890: 672.

GILL, HENRY SALVIN, NYC (d/I-16-1891) MD CPS NY 1880; <att Edinburgh> *JAMA* 16:179, 1891. *Bost m & s jour* 124: 15, 1891. *Polk* 1886: 679.

GILL, JOSEPH W , Louisville (d/IV-2-1895 Danville, Ky) MD UPa 1847. *JAMA* 24: 609, 1895.

GILL, WILLIAM B , Dallas, Tx (b/Tipperary Co, Ireland; d/II-12-1887 @37) MD U La 1884. *New Orl m & s jour* ns14: 722, 1887. *Tex cour-rec med* 4: 286-87, 333, 1887. *Polk* 1886:416 (New Orleans).

GILLAND, S W , ? (d/X-23 or XI-2-1878 Vicksburg, Miss) MD ? *Tr AMA* 30:864, 1879. *Med rec NY* 14:360, 1878.

GILLANE, PATRICK T, Cincinnati (d/X-2-1873 @ 37) MD M Coll O 1864. *Med surg rep Phila* 29: 306, 1873.

GILLEN, RICHARD H , Wabash, Ind (d/I-22-1899 DeLand, Fla) MD Jefferson 1871. *JAMA* 32:324, 1899.

GILLESPIE, ?, ?(d/IX-5 or 14-1878 Grenada Miss) MD *Tr AMA* 30: 864, 1879. *Med rec NY* 14:220, 1878.

GILLESPIE, JAMES HENRY, Louisa Co, Va (d/IV-27 1868 @36) MD UPa 1854. *Bost m&s jour* ns1:240,1868.

GILLESPIE, JOHN, Boston (d/VI-5-1896 @ 36) MD Harvard 1885; AB 1882. *JAMA* 26: 1245, 1896. *Polk* 1896: 698.

GILLESPIE, JOHN E , Philadelphia; USN (d/VI-29-1872) MD UPa 1866. *Med surg rep Phila* 27: 22, 1872. *Tr AMA* 24:394-96, 1873.

GILLESPIE, JOSEPH S, Chickamauga, Tenn (d/III-27 1896 @75) MD ? *NC med jour* 37:246, 1896. *Polk* 1886: 863.

GILLESPIE, RICHARD, Cairo, Tenn (b/VI-2-1785 Sumner Co; d/III-4-1826) <att UPA Med Sch> *Tr Med Soc Tenn* 1876: 83-84.

GILLESPIE, W H , CW-USA; Sistersville, WVa (b/X-8-1840 Fredericksburg, Va; d/XI-8-1897 NYC) MD CPS Balto 1881; Va Milit Inst 1862. *Tr St Med Soc W Va* 1898: 215-16.

GILLESPIE, WILLIAM A , Louisa Co, Va (d/I-10-1875 @70) <MD U Md 1831> *Tr Med Soc Va* 1875:65-66. *Tr AMA* 26:477-78, 1875.

GILLESPIE, WILLIAM JOSEPH, Philadelphia (d/III-14-1904 @ 35) MD Jefferson 1890. *Pa med jour* 8:335, 1904/05. *Flint* 1897: 816.

GILLETT, BUCKLAND, Franklin, Pa 1834- (b/I-18-1807 there or Broome, NY; d/X-19-1881) Hon MD Wooster 1873. *Tr AMA* 33:558-59 1882. *Atkinson* I:319.

GILLETT, LESLIE B , Beatrice, Neb (d/IV-24-1899 @ 63) MD CPS Chicago 1885. *JAMA* 32: 1013, 1899. *Polk* 1886: 381 (Medicine Lodge, Kans).

GILLETT, OMER TOUSEY, Evansville, Ind; Colorado Springs (d/X-5-1894) MD CPSNY 1869; ng U Mich Med Dept; AB Indiana St U 1866. *JAMA* 23: 624, 1894. *Polk* 1886: 360 (Iowa City, Ia).

GILLETT, WILLIAM J , Parsons, Kans (d/X-30-1901) MD CPS Keokuk 1868. *Ill med jour* ns3: 346, 1901. *Polk* 1886: 283 (Ipava, Ill).

GILLETTE, AUGUSTUS FREDERICK, Wayne Co NY (b/X-8-1839 Sweden, NY; d/XII-3-1880) MD Bellevue 1868. *Med reg NY NJ Conn* 1881: 237.

GILLETTE, FIDELIO BUCKINGHAM, Brooklyn; USA 1862-69 (b/X-31-1833 Nile, NY; d/VII-1-1895 De Ruyter, NY) MD UPa 1856. *JAMA* 25: 123, 1895. *Atkinson* I: 468, 1878.

GILLETTE, HORACE CORNELIUS, S Windsor, Conn (b/1806; d/1878) MD Yale 1829. *Tr AMA* 33:559-60 1882.

GILLIAM [GILLAM], JAMES SOTHORON [SKELTON], USN (b/Petersburg Va; d/VI- -1861 at sea abd US Levant) MD UPa 1847;AB Princeton 1844;AM 1847. *Tr AMA* 14:216, 1864. *Nat med jour* 1:295, 1870/71.

GILLIAM, THEOPHILUS FEILD, ? CW-CSA (n/1829 Petersburg, Va; d/XI-29-1904) MD UPa 1851. MD UPa 1851. *U Pa med alum CW*: 1851.

GILLIAM, WILLIAM CLEMENT, ? (d/XI-13-1894) MD UCNY 1877; att U Va 1876. *Med reg NY NJ Conn* 1895: 223.

GILLIAMS, JACOB, Philadelphia (b/1783? d/II-4-1868 @ 85) MD ? *Phila med reg & dir* 1871: 293. *Med surg rep Phila* 18: 159-60, 1868.

GILLINGHAM, EZRA, Baltimore (d/1825) MD U Md 1816. *Med annals Md:* 410-11.

GILLINGHAM, WILLIAM HEYWARD, Philadelphia (b/1798; d/1863) MD UPa 1817. *Tr AMA* 16:634-35, 1865. *Tr Med Soc Pa* 3:526-30, 1864. *Med surg rep Phila* ns9:326, 1862/63.

GILLIS, JOHN P R , Whaleysville, Md (b/1806; d/VIII 7-1881) MD U Md 1829. *Med annals Md:* 411. *Butler* 1874: 319.

GILLUM, IRA HAMILTON, Milford, Ill (d/III-7-1906) MD Rush 1874. *Ill med jour* 9:464,1906. *Polk* 1896:529.

GILMAN, ALBERT OTIS, St Cloud, Minn (b/II-11-1847 Gilmanton, NH; d/VII-16-1897) MD Dartmouth 1868. *JAMA* 29: 201, 1897. *Tr Minn St Med Soc* 1899: 191. *Polk* 1886: 516.

GILMAN, CHANDLER ROBBINS, NYC (b/IX-13-1802 Marietta, O; d/IX-26-1865) MD UPa 1824; att Harvard. *Tr AMA* 18:313-314, 1867. *Med reg NY NJ Conn* 1866: 191. *Amer jour med sci* ns51:566, 1866. *Tr Med Soc St NY* 1866:341-44. *K&B* III: 468-69.

GILMAN, HENRY ARTEMAS, Mt Pleasant, Ia (b/I-15-1845 Gilmanton, NH; d/X-9-1898) MD Dartmouth 1867. *Tr Ia St Med Soc* 17: 389, 1899. *JAMA* 31: 997, 1898. *Polk* 1890: 421.

GILMAN, JOHN HENRY, Lowell, Mass; CW-USA; (b/II-24-1836 Sangerville, Me; d/VI-11-1890 E Barrington, NH) MD Harvard 1863. *Bost m & s jour* 122: 622, 1890. *Harvard in CW*: 278. *Atkinson* 1878:276-77.

GILMAN, JOHN TAYLOR, Portland, Me 1832- (b/V-9-1806 Exeter, NH; d/I-16-1884) MD Bowdoin 1829; AB 1826. *Bost m & s jour* 110:92, 1884. *Tr Me Med Assoc* 1884: 368-70, 373-80. *K&B* III: 469.

GILMAN, JUDSON, Baltimore (b/XII-22-1818 Meredith, NH; d/VIII-1-1883) MD U Md 1845; att Colby, Me. *JAMA* 1:288, 1883. *Med annals Md:* 411. *Med bull med & surg* 5:258, 1883. *Atkinson* I:133.

GILMARTIN, PETER PAUL, Detroit, Mich; CW-USN (b/VI-29-1839 Boston; d/IV-1-1893) MD Harvard 1865. *Harv in CW*: 292. *Bost m & s jour* 128: 380, 1893. *Atkinson* 1878: 69. *Butler* 1878: 374.

GILMER, MAURICIO W , Philadelphia (d/III-17-1902 @ 40) MD Jefferson 1881. *Pa med jour* 6: 260, 1902/03. *Flint* 1897.

GILMER, PEACHY HARMER, Lynchburg, Va (b/1813 Henry Co; d/III-10-1872) MD U Md 1835. *Tr Med Soc Va* 1872: 26, 155.

GILMORE, ALEXANDER W, CW-USA (d/V-13-1865 Nashville, Tenn) MD *Nat med jour* 1:295,1870/71.

GILMORE, ARNOLD PLUMER, Chicago (d/X-10-1906 @ 55) MD Jefferson 1874. *Chic med rec* 28: 591, 1906. *Polk* 1896: 385. *Flint* 1897: 260.

GILMORE, CHARLES MARSH, Markesan, Wis (b/XI-

 Spec. educ'l status abbrev. as: ***ng*** = college verified attendance without degree;

14–1858 Mackford; d/IV–9–1897) MD CPS Chic 1889. *Tr Wis St Med Soc* 31: 638 ff, 1897. *Polk* 1896: 1553.

GILMORE, JOHN TAYLOR, CW–CSA; Noxubee, Miss (b/1835; d/1875) MD Jefferson 1858; AB UNC 1856. *UNC cat*: 221.

GILMOUR [GILMORE], SAMUEL BAYARD, Philadelphia (d/VIII–13–1899 @ 23) MD UPa 1899. *JAMA* 33: 620, 1899.

GILPATRICK, BENJAMIN, Boston (d/V–28–1868 @28 Anoka, Minn) MD ? *Phila med reg & dir* 1871: 297. *Med surg rep Phila* 18: 542, 1868.

GILSON, WILLIS O , Erie, Pa (d/I–25–1894 @ 35) MD Western Reserve 1883. *JAMA* 22:202, 1894.

GILTENAN, JAMES J, Chicago (d/IV–20 1905 @62) MD Cinc Coll Med & Surg 1869. *Ill m j* 7:611, 1901.

GINDRAT, ABRAM, Montgomery, Ala; CW–CSA (d/ 1884?) MD UCNY 1846. *Tr Med Assoc St Ala* 1885: 320. *Butler* 1874: 18.

GINKINGER, WILLIAM HENRY HARRISON, Philadelphia; CW–USA (b/III–20–1837 Allentown, Pa; d/I–2 1878) MD UPa 1861. *U Pa med alum CW*: 1861.

GIRARD, CHARLES, Washington, DC (b/III–9–1822 Mülhausen, Fr; d/I–29–1895 Fr) MD Georgetown 1856. *Hist Med Soc DC*: 258. *K&B* III: 471.

GIRVIN, ROBERT M , Philadelphia (b/II–3–1836 Strasburg Pa; d/1900) MD Jefferson 1862. *JAMA* 34:830 1900. *Atkinson* I: 101. *Tr CPP* cent vol: 226.

GISSEY, CHARLES E V , Breese, Ill (d/II–21–1901) <MD St Louis Med Coll 1875> *Ill med jour* ns2:532, 1901. *Polk* 1886: 256.

GITTINGS, ALLEN, Weston, WVa (b/Clarksburg; d/II 7–1884) MD CPSNY Balto 1874. *Tr Med Soc W Va* 1884: 150.

GITTINGS, DAVID STERRET, Baltimore (b/VIII–17–1797; d/III–12–1887) MD U Md 1818. *Med annals Md:* 411. *Polk* 1886: 446.

GIVAN, SANFORD E , Burney, Ind (d/X–25–1898) Cert by Exam Bd. *JAMA* 31:1190, 1898. *Polk* 1890:380.

GIVEN, ADAM, Louisville, Ky (b/X–15–1829 Warm Springs, Va; d/IX–18–1896) MD Chicago Homeop 1864; MD Northwestern 1864. *Tr Amer Inst Homeop* 1897: 63. *Polk* 1886: 399. Homeopath.

GIVEN, JAMES G , Austin, Tex (b/1852 Paducah, Ky; d/VIII– –1886) MD U La 1872; <stud Edinburgh> *New Orl m & s jour* ns14: 318, 1886. *Polk* 1886: 880.

GIVEN, ROBERT AIKEN, Philadelphia (b/III–15–1816; d/I–10–1888) MD UPa 1839. *Tr CPP* 3s10:lxxiii, 1888. *Med bull med & surg* 10:61, 1888. *Tr Med Soc Pa* 20:304–05, 1888. *Butler* 1878: 713.

GIVEN, SINGLETON ALEXANDER MERCER, Clifton Heights, Pa (b/1861 Carlisle; d/II–23–1901) MD UPa 1887. *Pa med jour* 5:165, 296, 1901/02.

GIVHAN, JOSEPH P , Calera, Ala (d/XI–8–1899) MD Med Coll Ala 1873 *JAMA* 33:1441 1899. *Polk* 1886:136.

GLADDEN, GEORGE, Homestead Pa (d/I–18–1900)MD Jefferson 1875. *JAMA* 34:251,1900. *Polk* 1896:1283.

GLANTY, JULIUS, CW–CSA (d/II–10–1863) MD *SHSP* 22: 203, 1893.

GLASS, ROBERT GEORGE, NYC (d/V–7–1877) MD Bellevue 1873. *Med reg NY NJ Conn* 1877: 202.

GLATZMAYER, WILLIAM, Newark, NJ (d/1900 @42) MD UCNY 1885. *JAMA* 34: 702, 1900. *Polk* 1896: 942.

GLEASON, AARON R , Keene, NH (b/VI–1–1835 Warren, Vt; d/III–4–1904) MD Georgetown 1864. *Tr NH Med Soc* 1904: 297–98. *Polk* 1896: 920.

GLEASON, CLOYES WILLIAM, Philadelphia (d/V–30 1902 @ 80) MD UPa 1844. *Pa med jour* 6:260, 1902/03. *Flint* 1897: 818.

GLEASON, JUBAL CONVERSE, Rockland Mass (b/XI 9–1837 Hubbardston; d/XI–1–1890) MD Harvard 1867; AB Amherst 1863. *Bost m & s j* 123:456 1890. *Polk* 1886: 472.

GLEASON, SILAS ORSEMUS, Elmira, NY (b/XI–3–1818 Colerain, Mass; d/IV–4–1899 Buffalo) MD Castleton 1844. *JAMA* 32: 845, 1899. *Buff m & s jour* 38: 790, 1899. *Butler* 1878: 555.

GLEAVES, SAMUEL CROCKETT, CW–CSA; Wytheville, Va (b/X–12–1823; d/I–14–1890) MD UPa 1848. *U Pa med alum CW*: 1848. *Polk* 1886: 929.

GLEAVY, JOHN JOSEPH, Brooklyn (b/VI– –1851; d/ VII–9–1891) MD Bellevue 1872. *Med reg NY NJ Conn* 1892: 278.

GLENN, ATCHISON L , Springfield, Ill (b/Newville, Pa; d/X–16–1854) MD ? AB Lafayette 1849. *Lafayette, Men of*: 164.

GLENNAN, MICHAEL AUGUSTINE, Ludlow, Ill (d/ IV–11–1906) MD Rush 1878. *Ill med jour* 9:661, 1906. *Polk* 1896: 428.

GLENTWORTH, GEORGE, Philadelphia; RevWar–USA (b/VII–22–1735; d/XI–4–1792) MD U Edinburgh 1785. *Tr CPP* cent vol: 53–54. *Columbian mag* 2:367–68, 1792.

GLENTWORTH, PLUNKET FLEESON, Philadelphia (b/VII–27–1760; d/I–16–1833) MD UPa 1790. *Tr CPP* cent vol: 227.

GLOCKER, THEODORE W , Baltimore; CW–CSA (b/VI–11–1841; d/XI–15–1894) MD U Md 1861. *Med annals Md:* 412. *Polk* 1893.

GLONINGER, CYRUS DORSEY, Lebanon, Pa CW–USA; (b/III–13–1824; d/VII–23–1872) MD UPa 1846; st abroad; att Franklin & Marshall. *F&M obit rec*:41–42.

GLONINGER, DAVID STANLEY, Philadelphia (b/IV–27–1827 Lebanon, Pa; d/IX–13–1889) MD UPa 1849; AB Franklin & Marshall 1846. *Bost m & s jour* 121: 320, 1889. *Med surg rep Phila* 61:364, 1889.*U Pa med alum CW*: 1849. *Polk* 1886: 816.

GLOVER, LEWIS JOSEPH, Quincy, Mass (b/II–26–1807 Dorchester; d/VI–24–1856 Pepperell, Mass (MD Harvard 1835; AB 1832) *Bost m & s jour* 54: 447, 1856. Palmer's *Necrol Harvard alum*: 95.

GLOVER, RALPH, NYC (b/1798? d/VII-5-1869 @ 71) MD Jefferson 1826. *Phila med reg & dir* 1871: 301. *Med surg rep Phila* 21: 68, 1869.

GLOVER, WILLIAM AUGUSTUS, Woodbury, NJ; Atlanta Ga; Seabreeze Fla (b/VI-19-1847; d/XI-13-1903 Woodbury) MD Hahnemann, Phila 1876. *Hahnemann biogr index*: 124. *Polk* 1886: 612. Homeopath.

GMELIN, CHARLES H , ?Philadelphia (b/1798? d/IV 8-1874 @ 76) MD ? *Med surg rep Phila* 30: 396, 1874.

GOBLE, JABEZ GWINNEP, NJ (b/XI-13-1799; d/II-7 1859) MD CPSNY 1823; AB Hamilton 1819. *Tr AMA* 13:800-01, 1860. *Tr NJ Med Soc* 1867:132-33. *Med surg rep Phila* ns1:378, 1858/59.

GOBRECHT, WILLIAM H , Washington, DC (b/III-7 1828; d/VII-19-1901) MD Pa Med Coll 1849. *Pa med jour* 4:876-77, 1901. *Tr CPP* cent vol: 227.

GODDARD, CHARLES E , USA (d/I-4-1886 Fort Yates, Dakota Terr) MD CPSNY 1859. *Bost m & s jour* 114: 48, 1880.

GODDARD, KINGSTON Jr, Philadelphia; CW-USN (b/XI-27-1839 Brooklyn; d/I-17-1902) MD UPa 1860. *Pa med jour* 6:260, 1902/03. *U Pa med alum CW*:1860. *Butler* 1878: 686.

GODDARD, PAUL BECK, CW-USA; Philadelphia (b/I-26-1811 Balto; d/VII-3 or 5-1866) MD UPa 1832; AB Washington Coll 1828. *U Pa med alum CW*: 1832. *Tr CPP* cent vol: 227. *Nat med jour* 1:295, 1870/71. *Bost m & s jour* 75: 28, 1866. *K&B* III: 474.

GODDARD, THOMAS FARRIE, Boston (d/II-12-1872 @ 27) MD Harvard 1870. *Bost m&s jour* ns9:116, 1872.

GODDARD, WHARTON H , CW-USA (d/VIII-18-1863 NY) MD ? *Nat med jour* 1:295, 1870/71.

GODDARD, WILLIAM, Boston (b/IV-22-1796 Portsmouth, NH; d/V-27-1888) MD Harvard 1820; AB 1815. *Bost m & s jour* 118: 558, 1888.

GODDING, ALVAH, Winchendon, Mass (b/XI-5-1796; d/I-11-1875) MD Bowdoin 1825. *Tr AMA* 31:1042-44; 1880. *Mass Med Soc cat* 1894.

GODDING, WILLIAM WHITNEY, Washington DC (b/V-5-1831 Winchendon Mass; d/V-6-1899) MD Castleton 1857; AB Dartmouth 1854; LLD 1896. *JAMA* 32: 1073-74, 1899. *Bost m & s jour* 140: 488, 1899. *Hist Med Soc DC*: 304. *K&B* III: 474.

GODFREY, JAMES YOUNG, Georgia, Vt (b/VII-26-1832; d/III-20-1873) MD U Vt 1866. *Med reg NY NJ Conn* 1874: 273. *Med surg rep Phila* 28:310, 346, 1873.

GODFREY, JONES, Taunton, Mass (b/XII-26-1770; d/XII-11-1831) MD ? AB Brown 1793; AM *Brown hist cat*: 1793.

GODMAN, JOHN DAVIDSON, Philadelphia (b/XII-20-1794 Annapolis, Md; d/IV-17-1830) MD U Md 1818. *Am j med sci* 6:274-75, 1830. *Med annals Md:* 412. *K&B* III: 474-75.

GODON, FREDERICK WILLIAM, NYC; San Francisco (b/VI-2-1845 Phila; d/IX-23-1876 San Rafael, Cal) MD Bellevue 1873; grad Penna Polytechnic Coll 1870; AM Harvard 1870. *Med reg NY NJ Conn* 1877: 202. *Med rec NY* 11: 726, 1876.

GODON, VICTOR L , USN 1835-44; Philadelphia (d/1849) MD UPa 1834. *Tr CPP* cent vol: 227.

GODRICH, THOMAS, London, Engl; Gravesend, NY 1885- (b/London; d/VII-27-1892 @ 53) LRCP (L) 1862; MRCS (Engl) 1858. *Med reg NY NJ Conn* 1893: 302. *JAMA* 19:238, 1892.

GOELL, A C , Philadelphia (d/IX-27-1884 @ 79) MD *Med surg rep Phila* 51:448, 1884.

GOERSEN, GEORGE F , Philadelphia (d/III-3-1880 @62) MD ? *Med surg rep Phila* 42:286, 1880.

GOERTZ, ADOLPH, NYC (b/Russia; d/XI-6-1881 @ 40) <MD St Petersburg 1870> *Med reg NY NJ Conn* 1882: 228. *Med rec NY* 20:586, 1881.

GOFF, ISAAC NEWTON, Cazenovia, NY (d/X-13-1902 @ 69) MD CPSNY 1858. *Tr Med Soc St NY* 1903: [412]. *Polk* 1886: 656.

GOFF, SARAH (ALLEN), Kansas; Leadville, Col 1892- (b/VII-10-1846 Chambersburg, Pa; d/VI-4-1900 Canyon City, Colo) MD Hahnemann Chicago 1886. *Tr Am Inst Homeop* 1901: 915. Homeopath.

GOLD, A N , CW-USN (d/IX-1-1862 abd ship Huntsville) MD ? *Nat med jour* 1:295, 1870/71.

GOLD, SAMUEL WADSWORTH, Cornwall, Conn (b/IX-27-1794; d/1869 @ 75) Hon MD Yale 1836; AB Williams 1814. *Bost m & s jour* 4: 180, 1869. *Proc Conn Med Soc* 1870:410-11, 414 ff.

GOLDBERG, PHILIP, NYC (d/IV-12-1883 @ 54) MD *Med surg rep Phila* 1883: 229.

GOLDING, JOHN FREDERICK, Brooklyn (b/1854; d/VI-7-1903) MD CPSNY 1875. *Bost m & s jour* 148: 684, 1903. *Polk* 1896: 996.

GOLDSBOROUGH, CHARLES BLOOMFIELD, New Orleans; US Marine Hosp Serv (b/1850 Md; d/I-5-1890) MD UPa 1876. *New Orl m & s jour*ns17: 616-17, 1890. *Polk* 1890: 490.

GOLDSBOROUGH, CHARLES HENRY, Walkersville, Md (b/II-4-1800; d/VIII- -1862) MD U Md 1823. *Med annals Md:* 413.

GOLDSBOROUGH, EDWARD YERBURY, Frederick Co, Md (b/XII-5-1797; d/XI-14-1850) MD U Md 1825. *Med annals Md:* 413.

GOLDSBOROUGH, HOWES, Dorchester Co, Md (b/XI 20-1771; d/X-20-1804) MD ? *Med annals Md:* 413.

GOLDSBOROUGH, HOWES, Howard Co, Md (b/III-11-1789 Talbot Co; d/1862) MD UPa 1812. *Med annals Md:* 413-14.

GOLDSBOROUGH, LEANDER WORTHINGTON, Philadelphia (b/V-21-1804 Frederick, Md; d/VI-28-1891) MD U Md 1828. *Med annals Md:* 414. *Butler* 1874: 663.

GOLDSBOROUGH, ROBERT, Centerville Md (b/XII-4 1772 Talbot Co; d/IX-30-1849) MD ? *Med ann Md:*414.

 Spec. educ'l status abbrev. as: ***ng*** = college verified attendance without degree;

GOLDSMITH, [orig SMITH], **ALBAN,** Danville, Ky; Cincinnati; NYC (b/1788? d/186–?) MD ? *Med reg NY NJ Conn* 1862: 154. *K&B* III:476–77.

GOLDSMITH, MARCUS KAUFMANN, NYC (d/I–16–1903 @55) MD UCNY ? . *Bost m&s j* 148: 108, 1903.

GOLDSMITH, MIDDLETON, Rutland, Vt; CW–USA (b/VIII–5–1818 Fort Tobacco, Md; d/XI–26–1887) MD CPSNY 1840; AB Hanover 1835; AM 1840. *Med reg NY NJ Conn* 1888: 253. *Bost m & s jour* 117: 636, 1887. *K&B* III: 477–78.

GOLDSMITH, ROBERT H , Baltimore (b/1832; d/I–13 1903) MD U Md 1852. *Med annals Md:* 414. *JAMA* 40: 324, 1903. *Butler* 1874: 312.

GOLDSMITH, WILLIAM BENJAMIN, Providence, RI (b/I–11–1854 Bellona, NY; d/III/21 or 23–1888) MD CPSNY 1877; AB Amherst 1874. *Bost m & s jour* 118:332, 388, 510, 1888. *Tr RI Med Soc* 1889: 576–79. *Polk* 1886: 465. *K&B* II:448.

GOLDTHORPE, ELMER E, Chicago (b/1866; d/V–18 1901) MD U Ill Coll Med 1893; DDS U Mich 1892. *JAMA* 36: 1723, 1901.

GOLDTHWAITE, HENRY, CW–CSA; NYC (b/IV–13–1842 Mobile, Ala; d/I–4–1895) MD Bellevue 1876; AB Princeton 1860. *Med reg NY NJ Conn* 1895: 223. *Buff m & s jour* 34:430–31, 1895. *JAMA* 24: 101, 1895. *Bost m & s jour* 132: 445, 1895.

GOLL, GUSTAV G , ?Chicago (b/IV–30–1845 Saxony; d/III–29–1877) MD Rush 1871. *Chic med jour* 34: 362, 1877. *Tr Ill St Med Soc* 1877: 32.

GONTNER, AARON MARTIN, York, Pa (b/Lancaster Co; d/V–17–1903 @ 47) MD Jefferson 1878. *Pa med jour* 7:279, 1903/04.

GOOCH, PHILIP CLAIBORNE, Richmond, Va (b/1825 Henrico Co; d/1853 Norfolk) MD UVa 1844. *New Hampshire jour med* 6:214–15, 1856.

GOOD, HENRY W , NYC (b/XI–17–1827 Lehigh Co, Pa; d/II–17–1878 Brooklyn) MD LICH 1863. *Med reg NY NJ Conn* 1878: 181. *Butler* 1878: 514.

GOOD, JAMES MARKOE [or **MARTYN**], West Chester, Pa (b/VI–11–1840; d/1867) MD UPa 1862. *Med surg rep Phila* 16: 512, 1867. *Tr Med Soc Pa* 1870:94.

GOODALE, LINCOLN, Columbus, O (b/1781? Mass; d/IV–30–1868 @ 87) MD ? *Med surg rep Phila* 18:420, 1868. *Phila med reg & dir* 1871: 296.

GOODBRAKE, CHRISTOPHER, Clinton, Ill (b/VI–14–1816 Gny; d/III–15–1891) MD Rush 1855. *Bost m & s jour* 124: 324, 1891. *Tr Ill St Med Soc* 1891: 20. *Atkinson* I: 340. *Butler* 1878: 154.

GOODE, SAMUEL GEORGE, Jersey City (b/1871; d/II –24–1903) MD UCNY 1887. *Bost m&s j* 148:274, 1903.

GOODELL, JONATHAN WOODWARD, Lynn, Mass (d/III–12–1902 @72) MD Berkshire 1856. *Bost m&s j* 146: 322, 1902. *Polk* 1896: 716.

GOODELL, WILLIAM, Philadelphia (b/X–27–1829 Malta; d/X–27–1894) MD UPa 1871; MD Jefferson 1854; AB Williams 1851; AM. *JAMA* 23: 697, 1894. *Med ann Md:* 414–15. *Med bull med & surg* 1895: 269. *Tr CPP* cent vol:227. *K&B* III:479. *Atkinson* I: 448–49.

GOODENOUGH, JOSEPH BORDEN, Long Branch, NJ (b/IX–21–1825 Farmingdale; d/II–1–1899) MD CPSNY 1852. *Tr Med Soc NJ* 1899: 290–91. *JAMA* 32:385, 1899. *Butler* 1878: 469.

GOODENOUGH, LEVI, Sudbury, Mass (d/IV–3–1886 @ 82) MD U Vt 1830. *Bost m&s jour* 114: 360, 1886; 115: 630, 1886.

GOODHUE, JOSIAH, Pittsfield, Mass (b/I–17–1759; d/IX–9–1829 Keene, NH) Hon MD Dartmouth 1800; att Harvard. *Am j m sci* 6:275–76, 1830. *K&B* III: 479–480.

GOODHUE, PERLEY EBEN, Haverhill, Mass (d/V–19–1890 @ 31) MD U Vt 1882. *Bost m & s jour* 122: 514, 536, 1890. *Polk* 1886: 467.

GOODLETT, ADAM BIGG, War 1812–USA; Nashville (b/X–1782 Orange Co Va; d/IV–19–1848 Rutherford Co, Tn) Stud Ky & Phila. *Tr Med Soc Tenn* 1876:82.

GOODLETT, JAMES E , Lake Charles, La (d/XI– –1887 @53) MD U Nashville 1861. *New Orl m & s jour* ns15:493, 1887. *Polk* 1887: 414.

GOODLETT, WILLIAM CAMPBELL, CW–CSA; St Louis (b/VII–16–1824 Nashville; d/III–1–1903) MD UPa 1849. *U Pa med alum CW*:1849.

GOODMAN, HENRY EARNEST, CW–USA; Philadelphia (b/IV–12–1836 Speedwell, Pa; d/I–3–1896) MD UPa 1859. *JAMA* 26:340, 1896. *Tr CPP* cent vol: 227–28; 3s19:xxxix ff, 1897. *U Pa med alum CW*: 1859. *Atkinson* I: 137.

GOODMAN, JULIA (MERGENTHALER), Hamilton, O (b/VII–20–1848; d/VI–6–1902) MD NY Woman's Coll 1888. *Tr Am Inst Hom* 1902: 847. Homeopath.

GOODMAN, R J, Sparks Ga (d/VI–16–1897) MD Atlanta Med Coll 1890. *JAMA* 28:1252,1897. *Polk* 1890: 339.

GOODRICH, CALVIN GIBSON, Oxford, O 1849–68; Minneapolis, Minn (b/V–11–1820 Petersburg, Va; d/1880) <MD Med Coll Cinc 1845> *Tr AMA* 32:504–05, 1881. *Chic med jour* 41:667, 1880. *Atkinson* I:524.

GOODRICH, CHARLES S, Brooklyn (b/1803; d/III–28–1883) MD Berks 1826. *Med reg NY NJ Conn* 1883: 229.

GOODRICH, HARRIET RAWSON, Salem, Mass (d/VIII–23–1904 @ 35) MD ? *Bost m&s j* 151: 256, 1904.

GOODRICH, OSMAN D , Allegan, Mich 1836–45? 1855– ; Conn 1845–55 (b/V–10–1808 New Hartford, NY; d/XI–3–1887) MD Berkshire 1834. *Med adv* 20:160, 1888? *Med couns* ns3:100, 1888. Homeopath.

GOODSELL, THOMAS, New Haven Co & Whitesboro NY (b/VI– –1775 Washington, Conn; d/I–12–1865) Hon MD Yale 1822; <att UP 1809> *Tr Med Soc St NY* 1865: 294–297.

GOODSON, BENJAMIN F , Hopkins, Mo (d/I–28–1899 @ 47) MD CPS Keokuk 1878. *JAMA* 32: 324, 1899. *Polk* 1886: 549.

GOODWIN, AZRO E , Rockford Ill (b/VIII–11–1826

Chelsea, Vt; d/V-14-1889) MD Berkshire 1850. *Tr Ill St Med Soc* 1889:34. *Butler* 1878:154. *Polk* 1886:295.

GOODWIN, FRANCIS, Brooklyn (b/X-22-1829 Ireland; d/X-15-1882) MRCS (Engl) 1851. *Med reg NY NJ Conn* 1883: 229. *Butler* 1878: 531.

GOODWIN, JAMES SCAMMON, Portland, Me (b/XI-11-1793 So Berwick, Me; d/III or V-14-1884) MD Dartmouth 1814. *Tr Me Med Assoc* 1884: 370-71. *Atkinson* I: 472. *K&B* III: 481-82.

GOODWIN, RALPH SCHUYLER, Thomaston, Conn (b/VI-24-1839 Litchfield; d/1904) MD CPSNY 1866. *Proc Conn Med Soc* 1904:519-22. *Atkinson* I: 525. *Polk* 1896: 285.

GOODYEAR, GEORGE H, Toledo, O (d/XI-26-1897) MD Detroit Coll Med 1897. *JAMA* 29:1234, 1897.

GOODYEAR, MILES, NYC & Conn (b/XI-14-1793; d/III-1?-1870) MD Yale 1816. *Med reg NY NJ Conn* 1871: 356.

GORDON, CHARLES, Boston (b/XI-17-1809 Hingham Mass;d/III-2-1872) MD Harvard 1832;AB Brown 1829; stud med Paris 1835-36. *Bost m&s j* ns9: 164, 208, 1872.

GORDON, CHARLES OSCAR, Lakewood, NJ (b/IV-1 1841 Solon, Me; d/III-18-1881 Bricksburg, NJ) MD Dartmouth 1868. *Tr NJ Med Soc* 1880-81: 167-169. *Atkinson* I:533. *Butler* 1878: 469.

GORDON, DAVID HUME, NYC (b/Schenectady, NY; d/IV-8-1891) MD Med Coll Ohio 1879. *Bost m & s jour* 124: 396, 1891. *Polk* 1890: 814.

GORDON, GEORGE ALEXANDER, CW-USA; Charlestown, WVa; Sandusky, O 1886-92; Chillicothe (b/1841 Washington, Pa; d/I-31-1905) MD Cleveland Hom 1870. *Tr Am Inst Hom* 1906: 764. *Polk* 1886:767.

GORDON, JAMES, Carlyle, Ill (Huntsville, Ala; d/VIII-11-1895 @77) <MD Memphis Med Coll 1857> *JAMA* 25:342 1895. *Tr Ill St M S* 1896:58-59. *Polk* 1886: 281.

GORDON, JAMES WILLIAM, Sandy Hook, Conn (b/XII-22-1862 St Louis; d/I-26-1904) MD UCNY 1889; AB St Johns 1885. *Proc Conn Med Soc* 1904: 523-24. *Polk* 1896: 283.

GORDON, JENNIE MAY (TAYLOR), foreign missionary (b/XII-13-1867 Concord, Pa; d/XII-29-1897 W Africa) MD Woman's Med Coll Pa 1892; AB Dickinson 1889. *JAMA* 30: 624, 1898.

GORDON, JOHN N, Harrisonburg, Va (b/Va; d/VII-27-1882) MD Jefferson 1852; att U Va 1850. *Med annals Md:* 415. *Butler* 1874: 798.

GORDON, JOSEPH C, Mt Vernon O(d/X-2-1895 @54) MD Jefferson 1868. *JAMA* 25:640 1895. *Polk* 1886: 762.

GORDON, JOSEPH NICHOLSON, Chestertown Md (b/X-9-1775 Kent; d/IV-28-1849) MD ?*Med ann Md*:415.

GORDON, L CHARLES, Baltimore (b/1851; d/X-30-1880) MD U Md 1877. *Med annals Md:* 415.

GORDON, LEONARD JAMES, Jersey City, NJ (b/1844 NYC; d/I-17-1905) MD Bellevue 1875. *Bost m & s jour* 152: 122, 1905.

GORDON, M D, Huey, Ill (d/II-23-1895) MD Missouri Med Coll 1882. *JAMA* 24:337, 1895.

GORDON, PETER ALBERT, Jersey Ridge, Ky to 1871; Flemingsburg (b/XI-20-1844 Mason Co; d/II-2-1891) MD NY Homeop 1868; att Hahnemann Phila 1867-68. *Med vis* 7:125, 1891. *Polk* 1886: 395.

GORDON, RICHARD P, Hebron, Ky (d/VI-20-1893) MD Med Coll Ohio 1887. *JAMA* 21: 58, 1893.

GORDON, THOMAS, Philadelphia (d/V-4-1874 @ 52) MD Jefferson 1845. *Med surg rep Phila* 30: 468, 1874.

GORDON, THOMAS B, Jacksonville, Ill (d/IV-10-1905 @ 42) <MD Missouri Med Coll 1889> *Ill med jour* 7:611, 1905. *Polk* 1890: 339.

GORDON, THOMAS W, Georgetown, O (b/IX-23-1819 Warren; d/IV-21-1900 @ 81) MD Cleveland Med Coll 1846. *JAMA* 34: 1273, 1900. *Atkinson* I: 260. *Polk* 1896: 1191.

GORDON, W C, CW-USA (d/1862) MD ? *Nat med jour* 1:295, 1870/71.

GORDON, WILLIAM ALEXANDER, New Bedford, Mass (d/I-14-1887 @77) MD Harvard 1829; AB 1826. *Bost m & s jour* 116: 100, 1887. *Butler* 1878: 351.

GORE, JOEL R, Chicago (b/Wilkes-Barre, Pa; d/II-25 1900 @ 89) MD UCNY 1850. *Tr Ill St Med Soc* 1899-1900: 509. *JAMA* 34:573, 1900. *Polk* 1896: 385.

GORE, JOSHUA, Bloomfield, Ky (d/I-6-1869) MD Louisville Med Inst 1846. *New Orl m & s jour* 22:192, 1869. *SHSP* 22: 207, 1893.

GORE, WILLIAM M, Philadelphia (d/XI-24-1864 High Bridge, Pa) MD ? *Med surg rep Phila* 12:219, 1864/65.

GORGAS, ALBERT C, USN (d/VI-29-1895 Germantown, Phila) MD Jefferson 1856. *JAMA* 25: 76, 1895. *Bost m & s jour* 133: 52, 1895.

GORGAS, SOLOMON R, Philadelphia; Harrisburg, Pa (d/VI-30-1894) MD Jefferson 1874. *JAMA* 23:86, 1894. *Butler* 1878: 687.

GORHAM, BENEDICT FENWICK, Providence, RI (b/II-12-1850; d/I-13-1886) MD Harvard 1877. *Tr RI Med Soc* 3:381-82, 1883-88.

GORHAM, HENRY CLAY, Canandaigua, NY (d/III-6-1871 @ 27) MD Bellevue 1870. *Med reg NY NJ Conn* 1872: 347.

GORHAM, JOHN, Cambridge, Mass (b/1783; d/III-27-1829) MD Harvard 1811; MB 1804; AB 1801. *New York med & phys jour* ns1:229-30, 1829. *Amer jour med sci* 4: 538-39, 1829. *K&B* III: 482-83.

GORRELL, J G O, Fort Wayne, Ind (d/1878 Memphis) MD ? *Tr AMA* 30:864, 1879.

GORTON, WILLIAM ARTHUR, Providence, RI (b/VI-21-1854 No Brookfield, NY; d/V-1-1899 Boston) MD UCNY 1876. *Bost m & s jour* 140: 440, 459-60, 1899. *JAMA* 32:1074, 1899. *Tr RI Med Soc* 6:128-31, 1899-1903. *Polk* 1896: 1352.

GOSEWISCH, JOHN CHARLES, Wilmington, Del 1839- (b/V-14-1808 Peine, Hanover, Gny; d/V-11-

 Spec. educ'l status abbrev. as: ***ng*** = college verified attendance without degree;

1854) <MD N Amer Acad Homeop, Allentown> *Tr Am Inst Hom* 1854: 74; 1867: 157. *King* 1:271. Homeopath.

GOSH, JOHN DEITRICK, ?Northumberland Co, Pa; CW-USA (b/VI-7-1836 Dewart; d/VII-27-1877) MD UPa 1865. *U Pa med alum CW*: 1865.

GOSLEE, LEVIN E, Carrollton & Lakeland Ky (b/ Versaille, Ky; d/I-19-1900 @ 66) MD Ky Sch Med 1854. *JAMA* 34:251, 1900. *Polk* 1893: 501.

GOSLING, WILLIAM EUGENE, Shelbyville, Tenn (b/XI-20-1840; d/IV-11-1876) MD Jefferson 1865; ng Amherst 1861. *Amherst, Men of*: 1861.

GOSS, JAMES M, CW-USA; Freedom, Ind (b/XII-10 1840 Owen Co; d/I-22-1892) MD U Louisville 1872. *Tr Ind St Med Soc* 1892: 288. Kemper's *Indiana*: 193.

GOSS, OLIVER, Lakeport, NH (b/X-26-1819 Northfield; d/IV-2-1896) MD Dartmouth 1846. *Bost m & s jour* 134:404, 1896. *Tr NH Med Soc* 1896:182-83. *Polk* 1890: 710.

GOSS, OSSIAN WILBUR, Lakeport, NH (b/III-21-1856 Laconia; d/X-8-1903) MD Harvard 1882. *Bost m & s jour* 149: 444, 1903. *Polk* 1886: 592.

GOTT, LEMUEL, Berlin, Mass (b/XII-23-1808 Gloucester; d/VI-16-1888) MD Harvard 1836; ng Bowdoin 1831-33. *Bowdoin cat*: 1835. *Polk* 1886: 454.

GOTTHELF, B H , ? (d/1878 Warren Co, Miss) MD ? *Tr AMA* 30:864, 1879.

GOTTSCHALK, WILLIAM VON, Providence, RI (d/IX 15-1888 @ 68) MD ? *Tr Am Inst Hom* 1889: 177. *N Am jour hom* 36: 679, 1888. *New Engl med gaz* 25: 480, 1890. *Med vis* 4:335, 1888. *Polk* 1886: 845. Homeopath.

GOTTSCHALK, WILLIAM VON Jr, Central Falls, RI (d/IV-3-1902) MD Boston U 1877. *Tr Am Inst Hom* 1902: 849-850. *Polk* 1886:844. Homeopath.

GOTWOLD, JACOB HENRY, CW-USN (b/Phila; d/II-2-1863 at sea off Charleston, SC) MD UPa 1861. *Med surg rep Phila* ns9:374, 1862/63. *Tr AMA* 14:217, 1864. *U Pa med alum CW*: 1861. *Nat med jour* 1:295, 1870/71.

GOULD, AUGUSTUS ADDISON, Boston (b/IV-23-1805 New Ipswich, NH; d/IX-15-1866) MD Harvard 1830; AB 1825; AM 1830. *Tr AMA* 18:308-09, 1867. *Nashville jour m & s* ns1: 488, 1866. *Med surg rep Phila* 15: 268, 1866. *K&B* III: 483-84.

GOULD, FREDERICK B , Kent, NY (d/II-13 1898 @38) MD Buffalo 1895. *JAMA* 30: 570, 1898.

GOULD, HUGH H, Box Station Tn (d/VIII-6-1886) MD U Nashville 1881. *Nashville j m & s* ns37: 414-15, 1886.

GOULD, JAMES BREWSTER, USN 1839-54; Rome, It (b/1810 Sharon, Conn; d/XII-15-1879 NY) MD CPSNY 1838. *Med reg NY NJ Conn* 1880: 235. *Med surg rep Phila* 42: 22, 1880.

GOULD, JOSEPH FERDINAND, So Boston; CW-USA (d/VI-5-1885) MD Harvard 1859. *Bost m & s jour* 112:590, 1885. *Harvard in CW*: 253. *Butler* 1878: 329.

GOULD, JOSHUA BAYLEY, W Somerville, Mass (d/ XII- -1904 @85 Phila) MD Woodstock 1850. *Bost m & s jour* 151: 726, 1904. *Polk* 1896:722.

GOULD, LAWRENCE MERVIN, Hyde Park, NY (d/X-7-1900 Portland, Me) MD Harvard 1877. *Bost m & s jour* 143: 384, 1900. *Polk* 1896: 714.

GOULD, PUTNAM F , Nashville (b/VIII-2-1824; d/VI-19-1889 Kirkwood, Del) MD UPa 1848. *Nashville jour med & surg* 82:43-44, 1897.

GOULD, SAMUEL HERRICK, Brewster, Mass (b/XII-19-1814; d/VIII-25-1882) MD Bowdoin 1840. *Bost m & s jour* 107: 618, 1882. *Butler* 1878: 351.

GOULD, SAMUEL LAMPSON, CW-USN (b/VII-6-1839 Dixmont Me; d/VIII-21-1862 at sea off Fla) MD Harvard 1862; ng Bowdoin med 1862. *Bowd'n cat*: 1862.

GOULEY, LOUIS PETER GABRIEL, NYC (b/1845; d/ X-17-1879) MD UCNY 1868; att Georgetown. *Med reg NY NJ Conn* 1880: 235.

GOURDIN, SAMUEL, CW-CSA (b/II-5-1829 Charleston, SC; d/IV-2-1865 Isl of Great Inaqua, Bahamas) MD UPa 1852. *U Pa med alum CW*: 1852.

GOURRIER, ALFRED R , CW-CSA; St Gabriel, Iberville Par, La (d/XI-5-1885 @ 47) MD New Orl Sch Med 1860. *New Orl m & s jour* ns13: 505, 1885. *Butler* 1878: 298. *SHSP* 22: 209, 1893.

GOVAN, WILLIAM, CW-USA; Rockland Co, NY (b/ VIII-12-1818 Barnet, Vt; d/XII-22-1894) MD NY Med Coll 1854; AB Dartmouth 1839; AM 1842. *Med reg NY NJ Conn* 1894: 239. *Tr NY St Med Soc* 1895:380-81.

GOWAN, JAMES E, Metropolis, Ill (d/X-27-1899) MD Rush 1866. *Tr Ill St Med Soc* 1899: 287. *Polk* 1896: 429.

GOWER, JAMES, CW-USA (d/X-15-1863) MD ? *Nat med jour* 1:296, 1870/71.

GRACE, JOHN THOMAS, Allenton, Ala (b/V-22-1832; d/V-7-1859) MD ? att U Ala 1850. *U Ala cat*:101.

GRADY, MARY ELIZABETH, Brooklyn (d/VII-29-1896) MD NY Med Coll & Hosp for Women 1884; MD NY Ophth Hosp Coll 1886. *Tr Am Inst Hom* 1897: 64. *Med vis* 12:312, 1896. *No Am jour hom* 44:663, 1896. *Polk* 1886: 645. Homeopath.

GRAFF, HAROLD, St Paul, Minn (d/VII-29-1894) <MD U Christiana, Norway 1881> *JAMA* 23:207, 1894. *Tr Minn St Med Soc* 1894: 125. *Polk* 1890: 1164.

GRAFF, MILTON BRAYTON, Cincinnati, O; CW-USA (b/Cincinnati; d/I-7-1877) MD UPa 1864; MD Cinc Coll Med & Surg 1862. *U Pa med alum CW*: 1864.

GRAFIUS, WILLIAM, Alexandria, Pa (b/IV-20-1826; d/IX-14-1857 at sea) MD UPa 1854; att Pa Med Coll 1854; att Hahnemann Phila 1 yr; AB Franklin & Marshall 1846. *F & M obit rec*: 67 ff.

GRAHAM, ANDREW E , Richland, Ind (b/V-29-1824 Ky; d/XII-23-1897) ng Med Coll Ohio 1848-49. *Tr Ind St Med Soc* 1898: 384. *Polk* 1890: 386.

GRAHAM, CHAUNCY WILLIAMS, Kenansville, NC (b/1810 or 1819; d/IX-14-1866) MD UPa 1844; att UNC. *Tr NC Med Soc* 1868: 38.

GRAHAM, DANIEL McLEAN, CW-CSA; Wallace, NC

(b/III-30-1835; d/V-4 or 5-1898) MD Jefferson 1860; AB UNC 1857. *JAMA* 30:1248, 1898. *Polk* 1896: 1130.

GRAHAM, FREDERICK RIDGELY, Chester, Pa (b/VII 31-1826 Chillicothe, O; d/I-27-1895) MD Jefferson 1850; AB Amherst 1847. *JAMA* 24: 250, 1895. *Butler* 1878: 713.

GRAHAM, GEORGE S , Burgettstown, Pa (d/IX-10-1902 @62) MD Jefferson 1866. *Pa med jour* 6:260, 1902/03. *Polk* 1886: 799.

GRAHAM, JAMES, Cincinnati, O (b/V-28-1819 New Lisbon, O; d/XI-6-1879) Stud w/Dr McCosh; AB Wash & Jeff. *Tr AMA* 31:1044-45, 1880. *K&B* III: 486.

GRAHAM, JOHN, Plainville, Ill (d/I or II-23-1903 @65) MD Eclectic Med Inst Cleveland 1877. *Ill med jour* ns4: 665, 760, 1903. *Polk* 1896: 436. Eclectic.

GRAHAM, JOHN ALEXANDER, Lexington, Va; CW-CSA (b/XII-25-1833; d/1894) MD Jefferson 1858; MD UCNY 1859. *Tr Med Soc Va* 1894: 256; 1895: 227. Blanton's *Va surg CW*: 403. *Butler* 1878: 828.

GRAHAM, JOSEPH DRAPER, CW-CSA; Draper's Valley, Va (b/I-22-1835 Wythe Co; d/V-1-1898) MD UPa 1860. *U Pa med alum CW*:1860. *Polk* 1886:916.

GRAHAM, LEONIDAS J , Henderson, Tx (d/IV-15-1891) MD Jefferson 1855. *Daniel's Tex med jour* 6:477, 1890-91. *Polk* 1890: 1081.

GRAHAM, MERRITT EUGENE, Brockport, NY (b/ 1855; d/VIII-3-1905) MD U Mich Sch Homeop 1878. *Tr Am Inst Hom* 1906: 777. *Polk* 1886: 643.

GRAHAM, PERCY MALCOLM, Philadelphia (d/IV-23 1901 @ 40) MD Jefferson 1888. *Pa m j* 5:296, 1901/02.

GRAHAM, ROBERT HENDERSON, Washington, DC (b/I-20-1849 Yellow Springs, O; d/VIII-24-1903) MD Columbus Med Coll 1879. *Hist Med Soc DC*: 374. *Polk* 1893: 270.

GRAHAM, SAMUEL, Butler, Pa (d/VI-21-1898 @62) MD Jefferson 1862. *JAMA* 31: 38, 1898. *Polk* 1896: 579 (in Briensburgh, Ky) & 1270 (Butler, Pa).

GRAHAM, THOMAS A , Jeffersonville, Ind (d/IX-14 1901) MD Med Coll Ohio 1871; MD U Louisville 1873 ad eundem. *JAMA* 37:847, 1901. *Polk* 1886: 324.

GRAHAM, THOMAS P, Pittsburgh (d/IV-14-1901) MD Albany 1865. *Ill m j* ns3: 142, 1901. *Polk* 1886: 829.

GRAM, HANS BURCH, Copenhagen; NYC (b/1786 Boston; d/II-26-1840 @54) MD Copenhagen 1814. *New Engl med gaz* 4:375, 386, 1869. *Homeop examiner* 1:101, 1840. *King* 1:60-67. *Cleave*. Homeopath.

GRAMM, GUSTAVUS EDWARD, Phila (b/XI-18-1823 Halle; d/XI-2-1901) MD Hahnemann 1867. *Pa med jour* 5:296, 1901/02. *Tr am inst hom* 1902: 840-42. Homeopath.

GRANBERY, WILLIAM BISHOP, CW-CSA; Somerville, Tenn (b/XI-20-1834 Hertford Co, NC; d/V-30-1906) MD UPa 1858. *U Pa med alum CW*: 1858.

GRANDIN, JOHN FORMAN, Camden, NJ (b/VI-6-1827; d/VIII-26-1889) MD UPa 1852; AB Union 1850. *Med reg NY NJ Conn* 1890:269. *Med surg rep Phila* 61:332, 1889. *Polk* 1886: 602.

GRANGER, LYMAN COUCH, Pittsford, Vt; CW-USN (b/II-12-1832; d/IX-26-1864) MD UCNY 1855; ng Castleton. *Med surg rep Phila* 12: 164, 1864/65. *Nat med jour* 1:296, 1870/71.

GRANNISS, JOHN HENRY, Old Saybrook, Conn (b/IV 16-1844 Ridgebury; d/II-17-1905) MD Yale 1868. *Proc Conn M S* 1905:81-82, 498-500. *Polk* 1896:284.

GRANT, CHARLES S, Saratoga NY (d/II-5-1899 @ 54) MD Albany 1866. *JAMA* 32:385, 1899. *Polk* 1886: 707.

GRANT, EDWARD INGLETON, Trenton, NJ (b/XI-11 1812; d/III-13-1871) MD UPa 1837; AB Princeton 1833; AM 1836. *Tr AMA* 24:358-59, 1873. *Tr Med Soc NJ* 1871: 240, 245-46.

GRANT, HARRY ALLEN, Enfield, Conn (b/1813 St Simons Island, Ga; d/XI-30-1884) MD U Md 1834. *Med surg rep Phila* 51: 732, 1884.

GRANT, JAMES FRANKLIN, CW-CSA; Nashville (b/ IX-25-1837 Lincoln Co; d/VII-22-1905 Hermitage) MD U Pa 1856. *U Pa med alum CW*: 1856 (suppl) *Polk* 1886: 870.

GRANT, JASPER SPURZHEIM, CW-USA (b/II-6-1838 Wakefield, NH; d/VIII-4-1865 Washington, DC) MD Bowdoin 1863; AB Dartmouth 1861. *Nat med jour* 1:296, 1870/71.

GRANT, JOSEPH PERKINS, Saco, Me (b/III-11-1813; d/VII-20 or 26-1881 Portland) MD Bowdoin 1837. *Tr Me Med Assn* 1882:414; 1883:144-46. *Butler* 1878: 307.

GRANT, WILLIAM ROBERTSON, Philadelphia (b/XII 22-1811; d/III-28-1852) MD Jefferson 1839. *Tr CPP* ns1:498-517, 1850-53. *Tr Med Soc Pa* 1: 84, 1856.

GRAVATT, JOHN JAMES, CW-CSA; Port Royal, Va (b/XI-27-1817; d/IX-23-1886) MD U Pa 1842; att Wm & Mary. *U Pa med alum CW*: 1842. Blanton, *Va surg CW*: 403.

GRAVES, EZRA J , Amsterdam, NY (d/VII-1-1895 @ 56) MD Buffalo 1865; att NY Polyclinic 1885. *JAMA* 25: 169-70, 253, 1895. *Polk* 1886: 640.

GRAVES, FRANK WALKER, Woburn, Mass (b/VI-26 1842 Rumney, NH; d/III-13-1900) MD U Vt 1866. *Bost m & s jour* 142: 288, 1900; 143: 331-32, 1900. *Tr NH Med Soc* 1900: 316-17. *Polk* 1886: 727.

GRAVES, HENRY STEDMAN, Somerville, Mass (b/V-16-1861 Boston; d/VI-8-1898) MD NY Homeop Med Coll 1885; AB Brown 1883. *No Am jour hom* 46: 462, 1898. *Polk* 1893: 890.

GRAVES, IRVING FRED, Nashua, NH (d/XII-15-1898 @ 32) MD CPSNY 1889. *JAMA* 32: 41, 1899. *Polk* 1896: 921.

GRAVES, JOHN JAMES, Baltimore (b/1800 NY; d/I-19 1890) MD CPSNY 1825 [?] *Med annals Md:* 416. *Polk* 1886: 436.

GRAVES, JOHN WHEELOCK, Lowell, Mass (b/1810 Deerfield, NH; d/XI-28-1873) MD Berkshire 1851. *Med*

 Spec. educ'l status abbrev. as: ***ng*** = college verified attendance without degree;

surg rep Phila 29:462, 1873. *Bost m&s j* ns12:572, 1873.

GRAVES, LELAND JOSHUA, Langdon & Claremont, NH (b/V–24–1812 Berkshire, Vt; d/II–22–1891) MD Dartmouth 1842. *Bost m&s j* 124: 224, 1891. *Tr NH Med Soc* 1891: 246–48.

GRAVES, MILAN, Bath, Me (b/VII–17–1830 E Andover, NH; d/IX–5–1873) MD Dartmouth 1856. *Tr Me Med Assoc* 1874–76; 163–64.

GRAY, ASA, Cambridge, Mass (b/XI–18–1810 Paris, NY; d/I–30–1888) MD Fairfield 1831. *Buff m&s jour* 27: 365, 1888. *Bost m&s j* 118: 134, 1888. *K&B* III: 488–89.

GRAY, CHARLES CARROLL, Geneva, NY (b/III–28–1838 Chester; d/XI–22–1884) MD Geneva 1861. *Bost m & s jour* 111:549,1884. *Butler* 1874:540.

GRAY, CLIFTON SYDNEY, Little Rock, Ark (d/II–14 1899 @ c49) MD St Louis Med Coll 1872; <att Bellevue 1881> *JAMA* 32:563, 1899. *Polk* 1886: 151.

GRAY, ELDRED P , Buffalo; USA (b/1824; d/VIII–9–1872 St Joseph, Mo) MD Buffalo 1849. *Buff m & s jour* 12: 39, 1872.

GRAY, GEORGE, Denison, Tx (d/II–15–1879) MD ? *Michigan med news* 2:44, 1879.

GRAY, HENRY MARTYN, San Francisco (b/NYC; d/VIII–24–1863 @ 42) MD Geneva 1844; att Lafayette. *Med surg rep Phila* 10:370, 1863. *Bost m & s jour* 69: 188, 1863. *Nashville jour m & s* ns1: 317, 1866.

GRAY, HENRY VINCENT, CW–CSA; Washington, DC; Roanoke, Va (b/VII–28–1839 Bedford Co; d/VII–15–1894) MD Med Coll Va 1860. Blanton's *Va surg CW*: 403. *Tr Med Soc Va* 1894:192–92. *Polk* 1886: 926.

GRAY, JAMES A, Atlanta (d/IX–27–1887 @37) MD Atlanta Med Coll 1879. *New Orl m&s j* ns15: 413, 1887. *Daniels Tex med j* 3: 151–52, 1887. *So pract* 9:486, 1887. *Bost m&s j* 117: 635, 1897. *Polk* 1886: 224.

GRAY, JOHN, Buffalo, NY (d/V–21–1883) MD Buffalo 1883. *Med bull med & surg* 5:166, 1883.

GRAY, JOHN ALFRED, Princeton & Rocky Hill, NJ; (b/VII–6–1812; d/1872) MD Jefferson 1836; AB Princeton 1832; AM 1835. *Tr Med Soc NJ* 1873:112–13. *Tr AMA* 24:363–64, 1873.

GRAY, JOHN FRANKLIN, NYC (b/IX–28–1804 Sherbourne, NY; d/VI–6–1882) MD CPSNY 1826. *Tr Am Inst Hom* 1882: 126 ff. *New Engl med gaz* 17: 224, 231, 1882. *Amer hom obs* 19:08, 1882. *King* 1:65–70. *Cleave*. Homeopath.

GRAY, JOHN M , Noblesville, Ind (d/VIII–28–1899 @ 63) MD Med Coll Ohio 1858. *JAMA* 33:683, 745, 1899. *Polk* 1886: 331.

GRAY, JOHN PURDUE, Utica, NY (b/VIII–6–1825 Half Moon, Pa; d/XI–29–1886) MD UPa 1849; Hon AM Dickinson 1852. *Med reg NY NJ Conn* 1887: 260. *Buff m & s jour* 26:283–84, 1887. *Tr Med Soc St NY* 1888:541–44. *JAMA* 7:671–72, 1886. *K&B* III: 488–89.

GRAY, JOHN W, Avon NY (d/IV–17–1886) MD UCNY 1856. *Tr NY St M S* 11: 741 ff, 1894. *Butler* 1878: 555.

GRAY, JOSEPH G , Loudoun Co, Va (b/II–21–1807; d/II–3–1864) MD UPa 1828; AB Dickinson 1825. *Dickinson cat*: 1825.

GRAY, LANDON CARTER, NYC (b/IV–3–1850; d/V–8–1900) MD Bellevue 1873. *Buff m & s jour* 39: 861–62, 1900. *Chic med rec* 19:49, 1900. *Proc Conn Med Soc* 1900: 342. *JAMA* 34:1273, 1900. *Flint* 1897: 673.

GRAY, PHILANDER, Litttle Compton, RI (b/I–6–1804; d/III–12–1834) ng Castleton 1823; ng Amherst, 1824. *Amherst, Men of*: 1824.

GRAY, ROBAH F , Danville, Va; Winston, NC (b/XII–24–1852; d/III–5–1900) MD Louisville Med Coll 1877. *Tr M S St NC* 47: 175, 1900. *JAMA* 34: 703, 1900. *Polk* 1886: 727.

GRAY, ROGER M , Stratford, Conn (b/X–1–1833 Huntington; d/XII–19–1873) MD UCNY 1856. *Proc Conn Med Soc* 1874: 291 ff.

GRAY, ROTHEUS AUGUSTUS, US Marine Hosp Serv; Colusa Cal 1876– (b/VIII–5–1851 Dublin Irel; d/XI–19 1903 Belmont, Cal) MD Bowdoin 1872; AB 1874; AM 1877. *Bowdoin cat*:1874. *Atkinson* I:191. *Polk* 1886:165.

GRAY, SAMUEL C, Warsaw, Ind (b/II–20–1821 Warren Co, O; d/IV–25–1883) MD Ft Wayne Med Coll 1881. *Tr Ind St Med Soc* 1883: 276. Kemper's *Indiana*: 130, 277.

GRAY, WILLIAM BURKE, Richmond, Va; CW–CSA (b/II–20–1833 Bowlesville; d/V–11–1878) MD UPa 1851. *U Pa med alum CW*: 1851.

GRAY, WILLIAM DeCLIFFORD, Philadelphia; CW–USA (b/Moundsville, WVa; d/VI–16–1870 @ 28) MD UPa 1865. *U Pa med alum CW*: 1865.

GRAY, WILLIAM HARKNESS, Philadelphia (d/III–10 1868) MD UPa 1860. *Phila med reg & dir* 1871: 293. *Med surg rep Phila* 18: 314, 1868.

GRAY, WILLIAM KELLY, Madison, NJ (b/1821 Patchogue, NY; d/VII–7–1896) MD UCNY 1868. *Tr M S NJ* 1897:303. *Bost m&s j* 135:73 1896. *Butler* 1878:469.

GRAY, WILLIAM N, Allegheny, Pa (d/X–10–1901) MD UCNY 1846. *Pa m j* 5:296, 1901/02. *Polk* 1896: 1262.

GRAYBILL, PETER KUNE, Amsterdam, Va (b/VII–7–1849 Botetourt Co; d/XII–26–1884) MD Jefferson 1874. *Tr Med Soc Va* 1885: 283–84.

GRAYDON, ANDREW W , Philadelphia; Cincinnati, O (d/II–28–1900) MD Jefferson 1877. *JAMA* 34: 639, 1900. *Polk* 1890: 993.

GRAYDON, ROBERT GEDDES, Southport, Ind (b/VIII 17–1819 Lancaster, Pa; d/VII–23–1898) MD UPa 1845; AB Dartmouth 1842. *JAMA* 31:314,1898. *Polk* 1886:336.

GRAYSON, WRAY, Washington, Pa (b/1826; d/II–2–1899 Orlando, Fla) MD Jefferson 1853. *Pa med jour* 2: 497–98, 1899. *JAMA* 32: 385, 1899. *Butler* 1878: 713.

GRAYSTON, FREDERICK SAMUEL COOPER, Huntington, Ind (b/IV–6–1823 Woodbridge, Engl; d/XI–5–1898) MD Chicago Med Coll 1861. *Tr Ind St Med Soc* 1899: 398. *JAMA* 31: 1257, 1898.

GREATHOUSE, JAMES A , Morganville, Ky (d/IX–

1897) MD Tulane 1897. *New Orl m&s jour* 50: 269, 1897.

GREELEY, ADONIRAM JUDSON, Providence, RI (b/IX-10-1818 Hudson NH; d/IX-1-1893 @75) MD Harvard 1845; AB Brown 1841. *Bost m&s j* 129:260,1893. *Tr RI Med Soc* 4:622, 1888-1893. *Butler* 1878: 747.

GREELEY, MOSES REUBEN, So Weymouth, Mass; CW-USA (d/IV-23-1895 @67) MD Harvard 1850. *Bost m&s jour* 132:448, 1895. *Harvard in CW*: 236-37.

GREEN, ALFRED WISE, CW-USA; Meadville, Pa (b/X-26-1822 Germantown, Pa; d/III-19-1901 Greeley, Colo; MD UPa 1844. *U Pa med alum CW*: 1855.

GREEN, BENJAMIN THORP, CW-CSA (b/XII-25-1834 Oak Hill, NC; d/1885 Franklinton) MD UPa 1855; AB UNC 185_? *U Pa med alum CW*: 1855.

GREEN, CALEB, Homer, NY (b/XI-14-1819 Lafayette, NY; d/V-10-1893) MD Geneva 1844; Hon AM Madison. *Med reg NY NJ Conn* 1893: 302. *Atkinson* I: 538.

GREEN, CHARLES DANIEL Jr, CW-USA; ?Smyrna, Del (b/III-10-1827 Smyrna; d/VI-19-1889) MD UPa 1848. *U Pa med alum CW*: 1845.

GREEN, CLINTON ROGERS, Wonewoc Wis (b/XII-29 1850 Marshall; d/II-26-1894 Milton Jnct) MD U Mich 1875. *Tr Wis St M S* 1894:472-73. *Polk* 1890: 1175.

GREEN, CUTHBERT SEWELL, Cecil Co, Md (d/XI-2 1843) MD UPa 1824. *Med annals Md:* 416.

GREEN, DANIEL SMITH, USN 1833-61; CSN 186_? (b/II-29-1812 Greenwood, Va; d/III-5-1864 Lynchburg) MD UPa 1832. *U Pa med alum CW*: 1832.

GREEN, DeWITT C , Woodstock, Ill; Florence, Tenn (d/II-14-1900) MD Jefferson 1882. *Tr Ill St Med Soc* 1899-1900: 509. *Polk* 1886: 302; 1896: 1008.

GREEN, ELIJAH DIX, Charleston, SC (b/VII-4-1769 Worcester, Mass; d/IX-21-1795) MD ? AB Brown 1792. *Brown hist cat*: 1792.

GREEN, FRANK BERTANGUE, NYC (d/IX-30-1887 @38 Nyack, NY) MD CPSNY 1875. *Med reg NY NJ Conn* 1888: 254.

GREEN, HARVEY [HENRY] M , Grand Rapids, Mich (b/Steuben Co, NY; d/XII-17-1872 NYC @ 33) MD UCNY 1867. *Tr St Med Soc Mich* 1873: 147.

GREEN, HORACE, NYC (b/XII-24-1802 Chittenden, Vt; d/XI-29-1866 Sing Sing, NY) MD Castleton 1824; Hon AM U Vt 1834; LLD 1853; Hon AM Middlebury 1834. *Tr AMA* 18: 323, 1867; 19:412-14, 1868. *Med surg rep Phila* 16:64-66, 1867. *Med reg NY NJ Conn* 1867: 220. *K&B* III: 490.

GREEN, JAMES COLQUHOUN, Danville, Va; CW-CSA (b/II-26-1838; d/III- -1884) MD U Va 1860; att UNC. *Tr Med Soc Va* 1884: 7. *Butler* 1878: 828.

GREEN, JAMES H, Seymour Ind (d/III-19-1900) MD Med Coll Ohio 1884 *JAMA* 34:830 1900. *Polk* 1886:331.

GREEN, JAMES SPROAT, Elizabeth, NJ (b/VII-2-1829 Princeton; d/VII-2 or 20-1892) MD UPa 1851; AB Princeton 1848; AM 1851. *Med reg NY NJ Conn* 1893: 303. *JAMA* 19: 83-84, 1892. *Tr Med Soc NJ* 1893: 173. *Atkinson* I: 391. *Butler* 1878: 464.

GREEN, JAMES W, Shelbyville, Ind (b/II-5-1825 Rush Co; d/VII-27-1896) MD Rush 1856. *Tr Ind St Med Soc* 1897: 346. *Polk* 1896: 490.

GREEN, JOHN, Worcester, Mass (b/IV-19-1784; d/X-17-1865) MD Brown 1826; AB 1804; Hon MD Harvard 1826; AM 1815. *Tr AMA* 18: 306-07, 1867. *Bost m & s jour* 73: 265-66, 1865.

GREEN, JOHN ORNE, Lowell Mass (b/V-14-1799 Malden; d/XII-23-1885) MD Harvard 1822; AB 1817. *Bost m & s jour* 113: 657, 1885; 114:24, 1886. *Atkinson* I: 636-37. *Butler* 1878: 351. *K&B* III: 492-93.

GREEN, JONAS, Philadelphia; Washington, DC (b/1798? d/XII-25-1868 New Orleans) MD UPa 1822. *Phila med reg & dir* 1871: 299. *Med surg rep Phila* 20: 20, 1869. *Tr Am Inst Hom* 1870:631. *King* 1:145-47 319. Homeopath.

GREEN, LOT, Rushville, Ind (b/VII-29-1847 Arlington; d/II-23-1905) MD Med Coll Ind 1881. *Tr Ind St M S* 1905: 446. *Polk* 1896: 489.

GREEN, RALPH EMERSON, Lebanon, Conn (b/IX-22 1815 Auburn Mass; d/V-20-1874) MD Berkshire 1839; AB Amherst 1835. *Pr Conn M S* 4: 287-88 291 ff, 1874.

GREEN, SAMUEL FISK, Worcester Mass (d/V-28-1884) MD CPSNY 1845. *Med s rep Phila* 51:28, 1884.

GREEN, SIMON THOMAS, CW-CSA; Warrenton, NC (b/X- 1827 Franklin Co; d/VIII-11-1900) MD UPa 1849. *U Pa med alum CW*: 1849. *Polk* 1886: 727.

GREEN, TRAILL, Easton, Pa (b/V-25-1813; d/IV-29-1897) MD UPa 1835; AM Rutgers 1841; LLD Wash & Jeff 1866. *Tr CPP* cent vol: 281-82. *JAMA* 28: 1045, 1897. *Pa med jour* 2: 40-41, 1898. *Atkinson* I: 378-79. *K&B* III: 495-96.

GREEN, WILLIAM, Trenton, NJ (b/I-30-1839 Nottingham, Engl; d/X-27-1891) MD UPa 1860. *Tr Med Soc NJ* 1892: 196-97. *Atkinson* I:393. *Butler* 1878: 469.

GREENE, GEORGE HERBERT, No Andover, Mass (b/VII-1-1837 Chicopee; d/I-3-1875) MD Bowdoin 1866; AB Brown 1863. *Brown hist cat*: 1863.

GREENE, HENRY BOWEN CLARKE, Saco, Me (d/VIII-7-1862) MD Harvard 1851 *Bost m&s j* 67:68 1862.

GREENE, JAMES M, Aberdeen Miss (d/I-20-1896) MD Jefferson 1858. *NC med jour* 37: , 1896. *Polk* 1886: 523.

GREENE, JAMES MONTGOMERY, USN 1824-71 (b/IX-24-1795 Ireland; d/VI-9-1871) MD UPa 1823. *Tr AMA* 23:603-06, 1872. *Phila med reg & dir* 1873: 303. *U Pa med alum CW*: 1823.

GREENE, JOSEPH C , Buffalo, NY (b/VII-31-1829 Vt; d/I-3-1899) MD Albany 1855. *Buff m&s jour* 38: 543-44, 1898. *JAMA* 32:92, 1898. *Tr Med Soc St NY* 1899: 435. *Butler* 1878: 537.

GREENE, MARSHALL L [or S], Pontiac, Mich (d/I-11-1870 @35) MD Jefferson 1859. *Phila med reg & dir* 1871: 303.

GREENE, MOSES COLLINS, Manchester, NH; Somerville, Mass (b/VI-9-1810 Deerfield; d/XI-20-1889) MD

 Spec. educ'l status abbrev. as: ***ng*** = college verified attendance without degree;

Dartmouth 1836. *Bost m & s jour* 121: , 1889. *Polk* 1886: 472.

GREENE, ROBERT WARREN, NYC (b/IV-20-1860 Augusta, Ga; d/X-28-1892) MD Bellevue 1887; AB Brown 1884: AM 1888. *Med reg NY NJ Conn* 1893: 303.

GREENE, WILLIAM WARD BOWEN, Providence, RI & US MarServ (b/IV-14-1840; d/VII-25-1880 NY) MD Berkshire 1864. *Tr RI Med Soc* 2:316, 1877-82.

GREENE, WILLIAM WARREN, Portland, Me (b/III-1 1831 Waterford;d/IX-10-1881 at sea) MD U Mich 1855. *Atkinson* I: 572. *Tr Me Med Assn* 1882: 414; 1883: 146. *Bost m&s j* 105:282,309-10,603, 1881. *K&B* III:497-98.

GREENE, WILLIS NEWLAND, Webster City, Ia (d/V-9-1895 @ 39) MD Rush 1881. *JAMA* 24: 776, 80, 1895. *Polk* 1886: 368.

GREENE, WILSON, New Geneva, Pa (b/XII-1-1829; d/VII-2-1894) <MD Western Reserve; Winchester Med Coll 1853> *Tr Med Soc Pa* 25:414-15, 1895. *Reg Pa phys* 1811-88; 180. *Butler* 1878: 713.

GREENFIELD, WILLARD TYLER, McKean, Pa (b/Crawford Co; d/I-5-1906 @ 46) MD Miami 1883. *Pa med jour* 9: 361, 1905/06. *Polk* 1886: 798.

GREENLEAF, FRANK EDGAR, ?NYC (b/1851; d/VII-16-1888 @ 37) MD CPSNY 1882. *Med reg NY NJ Conn* 1889: 275

GREENLEAF, MOSES P, So Weymouth, Mass (d/IV-23-1895 @ 68) MD UCNY 1846. *JAMA* 24: 690, 1895. *Butler* 1878: 351.

GREENLEAF, ROBERT WILLARD, Boston (b/Charlestown; d/IV-28-1901 @45) MD Harvard 1885; AB 1877 *Bost m&s j* 144:438 459-60, 1901. *Polk* 1896:698.

GREENLEE, ELISHA GRIGSBY, Christiansburg, Va; Australia, Miss; CW-CSA (b/I-8-1828 Natural Bridge; d/VII-10-1885) MD UPa 1854; MD UCNY 1857; att Washington & Lee. *U Pa med alum CW*: 1854.

GREENOUGH, FRANCIS BOOTT, CW-USA; Brookline, Mass (b/XII-24-1837 Boston; d/X-16-1904) MD Harvard 1866; AB 1859. *Bost m&s j* 151:452 476, 1904. *Harv in CW*: 126. *Atkinson* I: 624-25. *K&B* III:498-99.

GREER, ROBERT, Boston Harbor, Mass (d/I-28-1873 @67) MD Harvard 1849. *Bost m&s jour* ns11:152, 1873.

GREER, THOMAS B , Rocky Mount, Va (b/1827; d/XII-26-1891) MD Pa Med Coll 1859 ad eundem. *Tr Med Soc Va* 1892: 191. *Polk* 1886: 926.

GREGG, HENRY, Roanoke, Ind (b/VII-15-1815 Washington Co, Pa; d/II-21-1887) MD Starling 1850. *Tr Ind St Med Soc* 1887: 195. *Butler* 1878: 203.

GREGG, JAMES POTTER, CW-USA (b/X-7-1834 Penns Valley, Pa; d/IX-30-1864 Poplar Spring Church, Va) MD UPa 1858. *U Pa med alum CW*: 1858.

GREGG, JAMES SANSOM, Indianapolis, Ind (b/XII-16 1830 Belleville, Pa; d/I-18-1890) MD Jefferson 1866. *Tr Ind St Med Soc* 1890: 160. *Butler* 1878: 204.

GREGG, RICHARD S , Manor, Tx (d/I-22-1897) MD Tulane 1873. *Tex cour-rec med* 14:200, 1897. *Tex med news* 6: 180, 1896-97. *Tex med jour* 12: 465-66, 1896-97. *Polk* 1890: 1086.

GREGG, ROLLIN ROBINSON, Canandaigua & Buffalo, NY (b/VIII-12-1828 Palmyra; d/VIII-1-1886) MD Hahnemann, Phila 1853; att Cleveland Homeopathic. *Minn med mo* 1886: 164. *Tr Am Inst Hom* 1887: 202. *Med adv* 17:191, 1887. *Med vis* 2:348, 1886. Homeopath.

GREGG, SAMUEL, Medford, Mass 1825-1838; Boston 1840-72 (b/VII-1-1799 New Boston NH; d/X-25-1872 Pelham) MD Dartmouth 1825. *Bost m&s jour* ns10: 332, 1872. *New Engl med gaz* 8:47, 1873. *Amer obs* 10:176, 1873. Homeopath.

GREGG, VINCENT H , CW-CSA; Connersville, Ind (b/I 25-1825 Brecken Co, Ky; d/IX-12-1895) Lic yrs pract. *Tr Ind St Med Soc* 1896:256. *Polk* 1890: 366.

GREGOR, ALEXANDER R , Hammond, NY (d/VI-3-1890 @ 75) MD Geneva 1846. *Med reg NY NJ Conn* 1891: 273.

GREGORY, ELISHA HALL, St Louis (b/IX-10-1824 Russellville Ky; d/II-11-1906 Ormond Fla) MD St Louis Med Coll 1849. *JAMA* 32:1211,1899. *K&B* III:499.

GREGORY, FRANCIS ROGER, CW-CSA; Sassafras Fork, NC (b/I-20-1838 Oxford, NC; d/III-23-1899 Stovall, NC) MD UPa 1861. *U Pa med alum CW*: 1861.

GREGORY, H N , CW-CSA (d/VI-9-1862) MD ? *Nat med jour* 1:296, 1870/71.

GREGORY, HARVEY HOLMES, Harlem, NYC (b/X-2 1829; d/V-1-1877) MD CPSNY 1853; Hon AM Wesleyan 1867. *Med reg NY NJ Conn* 1877: 202. *Med rec* 12: 288, 318, 1877.

GREGORY, IRA, Norwalk, Conn (d/IX-2-1872 @ c68) MD Yale 1829. *Med surg rep Phila* 27:260, 356, 1872.

GREGORY, JOSEPH SHERWOOD, Mt Vernon, NY (d/III-3-1881 @ 56) MD CPSNY 1848; AB Princeton 1845 [?] *Med reg NY NJ Conn* 1881: 237.

GREGORY, JUSTUS E , Brooklyn (b/1841; d/X-26-1890) MD Albany 1863. *Med reg NY NJ Conn* 1891: 274. *Polk* 1886: 645.

GREGORY, LEVI MONTGOMERY, Stevens Point Wis (b/VIII-27-1827 Harpersfield O; d/VII-21-1902) MD Cleveland Med Coll 1869. *Tr Wis St M S* 36: 419, 1902.

GREGORY, OSCAR, CW-CSA; Oxford, NC (b/1835 Va; d/1896?) MD Jefferson 1854; att U Va 1852. *NC med jour* 35: 43-44, 1896.

GREGORY, THOMAS LITTLEPAGE, Blenheim, Va; CW-CSA (b/II-27-1827 King William Co; d/IV-8 1884) MD UPa 1850. *Med surg rep Phila* 50:544, 1884. *U Pa med alum CW*: 1850 [suppl].

GREIS, WILLIAM, Reading, Pa (b/1796 Womelsdorf, Pa; d/IV-12-1857) MD UPa 1823. *Tr Med Soc Pa* 3: 45-46, 1858.

GRETHER, EDWARD, Brooklyn (b/Gny; d/IX-22-1897) <MD Würzburg 1869> *JAMA* 29: 817, 1897. *Polk* 1896: 996.

GREY, JOSEPH EDWARD, Brooklyn (d/III-26-1886

@ 36) MD Bellevue 1866. *Med s rep Phila* 14: 280, 1866.

GRIDLEY, HORATIO, Hartford, Conn (b/IX-10-1792 Berlin; d/XI-9-1864) MD Yale 1833; AB 1815; AM 1820. *Med surg rep Phila* 12:252, 1864/65. *Proc Conn Med Soc* 2:160-61, 1865.

GRIER, MATTHEW JAMES, CW-USA; Philadelphia (b/III-8-1838; d/X-27-1900) MD UPa 1863. *Tr CPP* cent vol: 228. *U Pa med alum CW*: 1863. *Atkinson* I: 231-32.

GRIER, SAMUEL L, Natchez Miss (d/VII-30-1864 @ 41) MD Tulane 1848; att Lafayette. *Laf'te, Men of*:145.

GRIER, WILLIAM POTTER, USA (b/XII- -1834 Pittsburgh; d/I-22-1866 Arkansas River) MD UPa 1858; ng Coll UPa 1850-51; ng Brown 1855. *Tr AMA* 18: 355, 1867. *Nat med jour* 1:296, 1870/71. *Med surg rep Phila* 14: 140, 1866.

GRIERSON, GEORGE TONEY [TORREY], Lowell, Mass (d/I-28-1894 @25) MD LICH 1893. *Bost m & s jour* 130:128, 1894.

GRIESEMER, CALVIN H , ?Berks Co, Pa (b/III-9-1828 Oley; d/XII-5-1855) MD Jefferson 1854. *Tr Med Soc Pa* 1: 54, 1856.

GRIFFEE, HOWARD MALCOLM, Taylorsville, Pa (d/X-28-1906) MD UPa 1875. *Pa med jour* 10: 118, 404, 1906/07. *Flint* 1897: 837.

GRIFFIN, BRADNEY, CW-USA; NYC (b/V-16-1843; d/VII-7-1872) MD Bellevue 1863. *Med reg NY NJ Conn* 1873: 339. *Med surg rep Phila* 27: 94, 1872.

GRIFFIN, CHARLES BEALE, CW-CSA; Salem, Va (b/VIII-29-1833; d/1885) MD UPa 1855. *Tr Med Soc Va* 1888: 275. *U Pa med alum CW*: 1855. *Butler* 1878:828.

GRIFFIN, EDWARD DORR, Lyme Conn (d/V-8-1887) MD CPSNY 1865. *Med reg NY NJ Conn* 1887: 262, *Polk* 1886: 193.

GRIFFIN, EZRA LEONARD, Nashua & Derry, NH; Fond du Lac, Wis 1855- (b/IX-21-1821 Hillsboro, NH; d/I-25-1892) MD Berkshire 1849; stud Dartmouth. *Atkinson* I:77. *Chic med rec* 1:570, 1892. *Tr Wis St Med Soc* 1892: 386-391; 1894: 503. *Butler* 1878: 861. *Polk* 1890: 1165. *K&B* III: 499-500.

GRIFFIN, FREDERICK HINTZE, Philadelphia (d/XII- -1904 or I-1-1905 @ 47) MD UPa 1880. *Pa med jour* 8:335, 1904/05. *Flint* 1897: 818.

GRIFFIN, JAMES M , W Hurley, NY (b/VI-13-1842; d/VI- -1892) MD Albany 1869. *Med reg NY NJ Conn* 1893: 304. *Polk* 1886: 715.

GRIFFIN, JOHN F , Stamford Conn 1873-77; Williamsport, Pa 1877-84; Plainfield, NJ 1884- (b/III-2-1824 N Castile NY; d/IV-10-1892) MD NY Homeop 1873. *Tr Am Inst Hom* 1892:220. *Polk* 1886:840. Homeopath.

GRIFFIN, JOHN STROTHER, USA; Los Angeles (d/VIII-24-1898 @82) MD UPa 1837. *JAMA* 31: 551, 1898. *Polk* 1896: 218.

GRIFFIN, LANSING, Great Bend, Pa; CW-USA; Binghamton, NY 1865- (b/II-5-1827 Albany Co; d/XI-12-1894) MD Albany 1857. *Tr Med Soc St NY* 1895:381-82. *Polk* 1886: 642.

GRIFFIN, PETER EVANS, CW-CSA; Columbia, SC (b/1831 Society Hill SC; d/V-18-1904) MD UPa 1855; AB USC 185-. *U Pa med alum CW*:1855. *Polk* 1886:853.

GRIFFIN, SAMUEL OSGOOD, Pascoag, RI (b/VI-23-1827 Epsom, NH; d/VI-12-1874) MD Dartmouth 1853. *Tr RI Med Soc* 1: 464-65, 1859-77.

GRIFFIN, SAMUEL STUART, Williamsburg, Va (b/1781? d/XII-19-1864 @83) MD Edinburgh 1805; <grad Wm & Mary> *Med surg rep Phila* 13:358, 1865.

GRIFFIN, THOMAS BRADNEY, NYC (b/II-22-1813; d/VI-21-1871) MD UCNY 1843. *Med reg NY NJ Conn* 1872: 347.

GRIFFIN, WILLIAM ALBERT, Carver, Minn (b/IX-25 1824 Lee, NH; d/XII-24-1899 Superior, Wis) MD Dartmouth 1854. *JAMA* 34: 61, 1900. *Polk* 1890: 611.

GRIFFITH, ALEXANDER L , Md (b/1791? d/IV-1 1815 @24) MD UPa 1813. *Med annals Md:* 418.

GRIFFITH, BENJAMIN M , Springfield, Ill (b/IV-14 1831 Shelby Co, Ky; d/IX-24-1898) MD St Louis Med Coll 1859. *Buff m & s jour* 38: 304, 1898. *JAMA* 31: 871, 1898. *Tr Ill St M S* 49: 26-27, 1899. *Butler* 1878: 155.

GRIFFITH, DAVID S , Durango, Colo (b/III-13-1840 Indiana, Pa; d/1886) MD Jefferson 1863. *Atkinson* I:499. *Tr Colo St Med Soc* 1898-99: 508.

GRIFFITH, JETHRO JOHNSON, Lacon, Ill 1857; CW-USA; Philadelphia (b/I-13-1826 Canandaigua, NY; d/VII-25-1893) MD Hahnemann Phila 1856. *Tr Homeop Med Soc Pa* 1893. Homeopath.

GRIFFITH, JOSEPH, Kimberton, Pa (b/VIII-29-1790 Bucks Co, Pa; d/VIII-10-1849) MD UPa 1821. *Med reporter* (W Chester) 3:121-22, 1856.

GRIFFITH, LEWIS, Western Run Valley, Md (b/Havre de Grace, Md; d/XI- -1854) MD U Md 1818. *Med annals Md:* 418.

GRIFFITH, ROBERT EGLESFIELD, Philadelphia (b/II-13-1798; d/VI-26-1850) MD UPa 1820. *Med annals Md:* 418. *K&B* III: 500.

GRIFFITH, WILLIAM BREWER, Baltimore (b/I-23-1843 West River, Md; d/XI-2-1885 Dakota Terr) MD U Md 1870; AB Princeton 1865; AM 1868. *Butler* 1874: 312. *Med annals Md:* 419.

GRIFFITHS, AMOS, Bucks Co, Pa (b/1771 Chester Co, Pa; d/XI-17-1863 @ 93) Stud med w/B.Rush. *Med surg rep Phila* 10:426, 1865.

GRIFFITHS, CHARLES G M , CW-USA (b/1833? d/X -1865 Chester, Pa?) MD Pa Med Coll 1857. *Med surg rep Phila* 13:246, 1864/65. *Nat med jour* 1:296, 1870/71.

GRIFFITHS, JESSE W , Providence Twp, Pa (b/1798? d/XII-23-1864 @ 66) MD Jefferson 1826. *Med surg rep Phila* 12:236, 1864/65.

GRIFFITHS, WATKINS WYNNE [or WILLIAM], Concord, NH (b/VII-29-1870 Wales; d/XI-26-1903) MD U Vt 1895. *Tr NH Med Soc* 1904: 300-01.

 Spec. educ'l status abbrev. as: ***ng*** = college verified attendance without degree;

GRIFFITHS, WILLIAM EDWARD, Brooklyn (b/1842 NYC; d/II-21-1905) MD CPSNY 1868. *Bost m & s jour* 152: 262, 1905. *Polk* 1896: 996.

GRIFFITHS, WILLIAM MANDEVILLE, Louisville, Ky (b/II-16-1855; d/XII-24-1893) MD U Louisville 1876. *JAMA* 22: 31, 1894. *Tr Ky St Med Soc* ns3: 274, 1894. *Polk* 1860: 469.

GRIFFITHS, WILLIAM PATTON, Towanda, Pa (b/VIII-14-185-? Germantown, Pa; d/IX-21-1898) MD UPa 1881. *JAMA* 31: 872, 1898. *Polk* 1896: 1340.

GRIFFITTS, ELIJAH, Philadelphia (d/VII-4-1847) MD UPa 1804. *Tr CPP* cent'l vol: 228.

GRIFFITTS, SAMUEL POWEL, Philadelphia (b/VII-21-1759; d/V-12-1826) MB 1781 "U St Pa" [i.e., UPa] *Tr CPP* cent'l vol: 124-26; 229. *No Amer m & s jour* 3:151-63, 1827. *K&B* III: 500.

GRIGG, ELIJAH HENDRICK, CW-CSA; Pamplin City, Va (b/XII-19-1834 Buckingham Co, Va; d/XII-19 1900) MD Med Coll Va 1860; <att Jefferson>; stud U Va. *Tr Med Soc Va* 1902:221. *Polk* 1886:923.

GRIGGS, EDWARD LUTHER, Waterbury, Conn (b/VII 18-1838 S Windsor; d/I-6-1904) MD LICH 1864. *Proc Conn Med Soc* 1904: 517-18. *Polk* 1896:286.

GRIGGS, JOHN G , CW-CSA; Tuskegee, Ala (b/Le Grange, Ga; d/X-21-1900 Birmingham) MD UPa 1853. *U Pa med alum CW*: 1853.

GRIGGS, OLIVER BURNHAM, Willimantic, Conn; Providence, RI (b/VIII-31-1823 Homer, NY; d/XII-22-1899 @ 77) MD UCNY 1847. *JAMA* 34:61, 1900. *Atkinson* I: 558. *Polk* 1896: 1352.

GRIGGS, STEPHEN CHANDLER, Brooklyn (b/1820? d/II-1-1901 @ 81) MD UCNY 1849; AB Brown 1845. *Bost m & s jour* 144: 150, 1901. *Polk* 1896: 996.

GRIGGS, THOMAS THURSTON, Grafton, Mass (d/VIII-12-1890 @ 72) MD Harvard 1849. *Bost m & s jour* 123: 216, 1890. *Polk* 1886: 466.

GRIGSBY, ALEXANDER S , CW-CSA; Marion, Ark (d/III-16-1895) MD UPa 1859; MD UVa 1858. *JAMA* 24: 497, 1895. Blanton's *Va surg CW*: 403.

GRIM, WILLIAM L , W Washington, Pa (d/IV-24-1902 @ 63) MD Western Reserve 1875. *Pa med jour* 6:260, 1902/03. *Flint* 1897: 839.

GRIMES, JOHN, Boonton, NJ (b/1802 Parsippany, NJ; d/IX-12-1875) Lic Med Soc NJ 1827. *Tr Med Soc NJ* 1876: 140-41. *Tr AMA* 28:623, 1877.

GRIMES, JOHN HARRIS, Mishawaka, Ind (d/V-25-1895 @ 42) MD Bennett 1878. *JAMA* 24:908, 1895. *Polk* 1890: 381. Eclectic.

GRIMES, W S , Denver, Colo (d/XII-21-1889 @53) MD Miami Med Coll 1857. *Tr Colo St Med Soc* 1898-99: 508. *Polk* 1886: 183.

GRIMES, WILLIAM HENRY, Bakersville, Md (b/1807; d/V-19-1892) MD UMd 1828. *Med annals Md:* 419. *Polk* 1886: 435.

GRIMSHAW, ARTHUR HARPER, CW-USA; Wilmington, Del (d/V-17-1891 @66) MD UPa 1845. *Bost m & s jour* 124:522,1891. *Polk* 1886: 206.

GRINDER, E D , USA (d/XI-25-1867 New Orleans) MD ? *Med surg rep Phila* 17:502, 1867. *Nat med jour* 1:296, 1870/71.

GRINDER, GEORGE WASHINGTON, Washington, DC (b/XII-1-1862; d/XII-31-1901) MD Nat'l U Wash 1885. *Hist Med Soc DC* : 378. *Polk* 1893: 270.

GRINNAN, ANDREW GLASSELL, Madison CH, Va to 1859; Brampton (b/VIII-14-1827 Fredericksburg; d/V 9-1902) MD UPa 1848. *Tr Med Soc Va* 1902: 222.

GRISCOM, JOHN DENN, Philadelphia (b/III-25-1809; d/1890) MD UPa 1838. *Tr CPP* cent vol: 229. *Bost m & s jour* 123:144, 1890.

GRISCOM, JOHN HOSKINS, NYC (b/VIII-13-1809; d/IV-28-1874) MD UPa 1832. *Med reg NY NJ Conn* 1874: 273. *Med surg rep Phila* 15:118-22, 1866. *K&B* III: 501-02.

GRISSOM, EUGENE, CW-CSA; Granville Co, NC (b/V-8-1831 Wilton; d/VII-27-1902 Washington, DC) MD UPa 1858. *U Pa med alum CW*: 1858. *K&B* III: 502-03. *Polk* 1886: 725.

GRISWOLD, ELISHA, Pittsburgh, Pa (b/III-14-1828 Chester Co, Pa; d/X-7-1896) MD Jefferson 1853. *JAMA* 27: 878, 1896. *Butler* 1878: 714.

GRISWOLD, GASPAR, NYC (b/IV-24-1856; d/III-4-1886) MD & AB Bellevue 1879; MRCS (Engl?) 1883. *Med reg NY NJ Conn* 1886:248. *Bost m & s jour* 114:236,1886. *Med bull med & surg* 8:132, 1886.

GRISWOLD, H DWIGHT, Sherman, Mich (d/I-30-1899) ng U Mich Med Sch 1863-64. *JAMA* 32: 324, 1899. *Polk* 1886: 503.

GRISWOLD, NELSON L , Utica, NY (d/VII-8-1901 @ 79) MD ? *JAMA* 3:376, 1901.

GRISWOLD, RUFUS WHITE, Rocky Hill, Conn (b/II-1825 Manchester; d/VIII-17-1902) MD CPSNY 1854. *Proc Conn Med Soc* 1903: 397-405. *Flint* 1897: 178.

GRISWOLD, SAMUEL H , Hoosick, NY; Clarendon Spr, Vt; W Rutland 30 yrs (b/IX-14-1818 Chester, NY; d/VII-13-1896) MD Castleton 1844. *Tr Vt St Med Soc* 1896:419-21. *JAMA* 27:226,1896. *Polk* 1886:906.

GRISWOLD, SAMUEL L , ? (d/I-24-1882 @ 73) <MD Geneva Med Coll> *Med reg NY NJ Conn* 1882: 228.

GRISWOLD, STEPHEN, NYC; CW-USA (d/XI-30-1861 @ 37 Castle Pinckney, Charleston, SC) MD UCNY 1850. *Tr AMA* 14:201, 1864. *Med reg NY NJ Conn* 1862: 155. *Bost m&s j* 65: 460, 1861. *Nat m j* 1:296, 1870/71.

GROENEVELT, JOHN F , New Orleans (d/VI-29-1891) MD Tulane 1889. *JAMA* 17: 161, 1891. *Bost m & s jour* 125: 96, 124, 1891.

GROESBECK, ABRAM, Chicago (d/XI-25-1884) MD ? *Med surg rep Phila* 51:732, 1884.

GROESS, EDWARD L , Black Rock, ?(d/VI-19-1901 @ 38) MD Buffalo 1893. *JAMA* 37: 43, 1901.

GROFF, JOHN HUMPRHEYS, Penns Grove, NJ (d/VI-

19–1901) MD U Md 1866. *JAMA* 37:126 1901. *Polk* 1886: 610.

GROOT, CORNELIUS A , Auburn, NY (d/VIII–12–1897) MD Albany 1864. *JAMA* 29: 453, 1897. *Polk* 1886: 655.

GROSH, BENJAMIN FRANKLIN, Andersonburg, Pa (b/I–4–1818 Marietta; d/XI–9–1857) MD Woodstock 1840; <MD Geneva 1839> *Tr Med Soc Pa* 1858: 85–88.

GROSS, CHESTER L , Penn Argyll, Pa (d/X–9–1901 @ 65) MD Jefferson 1861. *Pa m j* 5: 296. *Flint* 1897: 812.

GROSS, FERDINAND HERMAN, CW–USA; Philadelphia (b/VIII–18–1831 Gudensburg, Gny; d/II– –1891 Boston) MD Jefferson 1855. *Tr CPP* cent vol: 229. *Atkinson* I: 234–35.

GROSS, HENRY SAMUEL, CW–USA; Philadelphia (b/II–3–1840 Skippack, Pa; d/II–21–1897) MD UPa 1862. *JAMA* 28:523, 1897. *U Pa med alum CW*: 1862. *Butler* 1878: 687.

GROSS, MARIA MAXWELL (TOOKER). Chicago (b/III–28–1833 Elmira, NY; d/VIII–11–1899) MD Cleveland Homeop 1859. *Tr Ill St Med Soc* 1899: 287. *Polk* 1896: 386. *Cleave.* Homeopath.

GROSS, SAMUEL DAVID, Easton, Pa; Cincinnati, O 1833–40; Louisville, Ky 1840–55; Philadelphia 1855– (b/VII–8–1805 Easton; d/V–6–1884) MD Jefferson 1828; LLD 1861; LLD 1884 Cambridge (Engl); Edinburgh, UPa; DCL Oxford 1872. *Tr CPP* cent vol 229–30; 3s7: xcv–cxxi, 1884. *JAMA* 4:527–30, 1885. *Med surg rep Phila* 50:607–08, 1884. *So pract* 6:304–05, 1884. *Bost m&s j* 110:465, 522–23, 1884; 111: 618, 1884. *K & B* III: 503–06.

GROSS, SAMUEL WEISSEL, Philadelphia; CW–USA (b/II–4–1837 Cincinnati; d/IV–16–1889) MD Jefferson 1857. *Tr CPP* cent vol: 230. *Bost m&s j* 120:396 424, 1889. *Buff m&s j* 28: 620, 1889. *JAMA* 12:611, 1889. *K&B* III: 506.

GROSVENOR, DAVID AUGUSTUS Jr, Danvers, Mass (b/I–1–1811 Manchester; d/IX–27–1889) MD Dartmouth 1835. *Bost m&s j* 121: 348, 1889. *Polk* 1886: 465.

GROSVENOR, EDWIN PRESCOTT, Newburyport, Mass (b/by VIII–17–1823 Reading; d/XII–13–1856 @35) MD Woodstock 1842. *Bost m&s j* 55:415, 1857.

GROUARD, JOHN HANSON, Allegheny Co, Pa (b/VIII 9–1828 Rochester, NH; d/I–7–1876) MD Dartmouth 1855. *Tr Med Soc Pa* 1877: 584–85.

GROUX, EUGENE A , Williamsburgh, Brooklyn, NY (b/1833 Hamburg; d/X–15–1878) <MD Göttingen> *Med reg NY NJ Conn* 1879: 192. *Butler* 1878: 541.

GROVE, DAVIS BRAINARD, Hanover, Pa (b/V–29–1860; d/VI–30–1893) MD NY Homeop 1883) *Med vis*: 9:358, 1893. *No am jour hom* 41: 167, 1893. Homeopath.

GROVE, FRANK PAUL, Alexandria, Pa (d/VIII–20–1906 @36) MD UPa 1901. *Pa m j* 10: 404–05, 1906/07.

GROVE, GEORGE, Big Springs, Pa (b/VIII–7–1811 Chambersburg; d/IX–14–1892) MD Jefferson 1836. *Tr Med Soc Pa* 23:243–44, 1893. *Butler* 1878: 714.

GROVE, JOHN BRIGHT, CW–USA; Columbus, Ind (b/VIII–2–1829 Augusta Co, Va; d/I–27–1882) MD UPa 1849. *U Pa med alum CW*: 1849.

GROVE, JOHN HEISTAND, CW–USA; Philadelphia (b/I–13–1825 E Donegal Twp Pa; d/I–1–1896) MD UPa 1849. *U Pa med alum CW*: 1849. *Tr CPP* cent'l vol: 230.

GROVE, WILLIAM ROBERTS, Columbia, Pa; Lancaster, Pa (Columbia Co; d/I–3–1903 @ 65) MD U Md 1865. *Pa med jour* 7:279, 1903/04. *Flint* 1897: 799.

GROVER, WILLIAM B , E Orange, NJ (b/VIII–23–1818 Caldwell; d/VIII–20–1885) Lic Med Soc NJ 1845; <att CPSNY> *Tr Med Soc NJ*: 1886–87: 158.

GROVES, ARTHUR ISAAC, Creston, Ia (d/XI–15–1899 @ 33) MD Iowa St U 1889. *JAMA* 33:1441, 1889. *Tr Iowa St Med Soc* 1900:398; 1903:448. *Polk* 1890: 404.

GROVES, MICHAEL FREYTAG, Philadelphia (b/1809: d/XI–20–1876 @67) MD UPa 1830. *Med surg rep Phila* 35: 504, 526, 1876.

GROW, AMBROSE G , Oakley, La (d/I–19–1849) MD Buffalo Med Coll 1848. *Buff m j* 4:714, 1849.

GRUBE, FRANKLIN, CW–USA (b/II–10–1831 E Coventry, Pa; d/VI–11–1869 Jacksonville, Ore) MD UPa 1854; AB Yale 1852. *U Pa med alum CW*: 1854.

GRUEL, LOUIS T, Philadelphia (d/IX–19 1898 @28) MD Jefferson 1890. *JAMA* 31:808, 1898. *Polk* 1896:1305.

GRUEL, THEODORE H E , Philadelphia (d/VII–31–1898 @ 52) MD Jefferson 1867. *JAMA* 31: 366, 1898. *Polk* 1895: 1305.

GRUENHUT, BERNARD W, NYC (d/VIII–22–1894 at sea) MD CPSNY 1870; AB Coll City NY 1867; AM. *Med reg NY NJ Conn* 1895:224. *JAMA* 24:609, 1895.

GRUWELL, JOHN PENNOCK, Alliance, O (b/V–19–1810 Marlboro; d/I–20–1896) MD UPa 1849. *JAMA* 26: 287, 1896. *Atkinson* I: 484. *Polk* 1890: 926.

GRYMES, JAMES M , Washington, DC (b/Norfolk, Va; d/1862) MD Georgetown 1853. *Hist Med Soc DC*: 253.

GUARD, CHARLES C , CW–USA (d/IV–4–1862) MD ? *Nat med jour* 1:296, 1870/71.

GUDEN, WILLIAM T, NYC (b/1846 Gny;d/IV–1–1890) MD CPSNY 1872. *Med reg NY NJ Conn* 1890: 269.

GUELICH, EMIL, Alton Ill (d/X–15–1893) <MD St Louis Med Coll 1859> *JAMA* 21:630 1893. *Butler* 1878:155.

GUENTHER, JULIUS, Quincy, Ill (b/1827 Berwalde, Saxony; d/VIII–17–1891) MD New Orl Sch Med 1857. *JAMA* 17: 980, 1891. *Butler* 1878: 155.

GUERNSEY, DESAULT, CW–USA; Amenia, NY (b/VI 13–1830; d/XII–9–1885) MD CPSNY 1850. *Med reg NY NJ Conn* 1886: 249. *Bost m&s j* 114: 398, 1886. *Butler* 1878: 556.

GUERNSEY, EGBERT, NYC (b/VII–8–1823 Litchfield, Conn; d/VIII–19–1903 Fishkill, NY) MD UCNY 1846. *Tr Am Inst Hom* 1904: 958–59. *No am jour hom* 44:398,

Spec. educ'l status abbrev. as: ***ng*** = college verified attendance without degree;

1904. *Cleave.* Homeopath.

GUERNSEY, HENRY NEWELL, Philadelphia (b/II-10 1817 Rochester, Vt; d/VI-27-1885 @68) MD UCNY 1844. *Tr Am Inst Hom* 1886:115. *Tr Hom Med Soc St Pa* 1885: 23-24.

GUERNSEY, PETER BENNETT, Dutchess Co, NY (b/ II-22-1804; d/XI-26-1873 Amenia) MD ? *Med reg NY NJ Conn* 1874: 276. *Med s rep Phila* 29: 440, 1873.

GUERNSEY, WILLIAM FULLER, Frankford Pa (b/XII 12-1814 Rochester, Vt; d/II-16-1877 Phila) MD Hahnemann Phila 1852. *Tr Am Inst Hom* 1877: 984. *Tr Hom Med Soc St Pa* 2:86-87 1874-78. *Cleave.* Homeopath.

GUICE, NAPOLEON L , Natchez & Meridian, Miss (d/VII-7-1899) MD Tulane 1858. *New Orl m & s jour* 52:111, 1899. *Polk* 1890: 532.

GUILBEAU, FELIX, Lafayette Parish, La (d/III-3-1885 @34) MD Tulane 1872. *New Orl m&s j* ns13: 86, 1885.

GUILBERT, EUGENE A , McGregor, Ia; Jackson, Miss (d/IX-14-1891) MD Homeo Med Coll Mo 1883. *No am jour hom* 39: 698, 1891. *Med vis* 7: 298, 1891. *Polk* 1886: 362. Homeopath.

GUILD, JAMES Jr, CW-CSA; Tuscaloosa, Ala (b/I-18-1831; d/VI 18-1890) MD Jefferson 1855; att U Ala 1851. *Tr Med Assoc St Ala* 1891: 261. *Polk* 1886: 140.

GUILD, LAFAYETTE, San Francisco (b/XI-23-1826; d/VII-4-1870) MD Jefferson 1848; AB U Ala 1845; AM 1848. *U Ala cat*: 75.

GUILD, PHINEAS K , Boston; Los Angeles (b/III-9-1827 W Halifax Vt;d/VI-13-1891 Santa Barbara) MD U City NY 1853. *No am jour hom* 39:698,1891. *Med vis* 7: 298,1891. *Polk* 1886:166. Homeopath; Eclectic.

GUILLAUDEU, EMILE, NYC (d/I-7-1860 @ 48) MD CPSNY 1833. *Med reg NY NJ Conn* 1862: 153.

GUILLOU, CHARLES FLEURIS BIENAIMÉ, USN 1838-54; Hawaii 1854-66; Petersburg, Va 1869-82; NYC (b/Philadelphia VII-26-1813; d/I-1-1899 NYC) MD UPa 1836. *Bost m & s jour* 140:50, 1899. *Med rec NY* 55:23, 1899. *Polk* 1896: 1056.

GUINAN, JAMES, Carson City, Nev (b/Manchester, Mich; d/III-24-1900 Chicago) MD U Mich 1867. *JAMA* 34: 1084, 1900. *Polk* 1886: 587.

GUINN, HOUSTON THOMAS, Rogers Prairie, Tx (d/II 27-1906) MD U Tex 1892. *Texas st jour med* 1:532, 1905/06. *Polk* 1898: 1568.

GUION, EDWARD M , NYC (d/IV-14-1871 @ 62) MD ? *Med surg rep Phila* 24:344, 1871.

GULEKE, HERMAN F , NYC (b/1836 Russia; d/VIII 18-1896) MD NY Med Coll 1858. *Bost m & s jour* 135:225, 1896. *Polk* 1896: 1056.

GULICK, JOHN WILEY, Corsicana, Tex (d/VII-23-1898 @ 69) MD UPa 1855. *JAMA* 31:314, 1898. *Polk* 1896: 1423.

GULICK, LUTHER HALSEY, missionary to Pacific isl, Spain (d/IV-8-1891 Springfield, Mass) MD UCNY 1850. *JAMA* 16: 612, 1891.

GULICK, SELAH, S Brunswick, NJ (b/1808; d/VI-25-1879) MD UPa 1830. *Butler* 1878: 470.

GULICK, WILLIAM JAMES, Stroudsburg, Pa (d/IX-20 1891) MD UPa 1865. *Lehigh Valley med mag* 4:18, 1892-93. *Polk* 1886: 836.

GULLETT, THOMAS FRANKLIN, CW-CSA; Amite City, La (b/ XII-7-1825 Union Co, Ga; d/II-14-1878) MD UPa 1851. *U Pa med alum CW*: 1851.

GULLIVER, DANIEL F , Norwichton, Conn (d/V-22-1895 @ 69) MD Jefferson 1852. *JAMA* 24: 908, 1895. *Butler* 1874: 76.

GUMBES, CHARLES W , CW-USA; Oaks, Pa (b/XI-2 1891 Phila; d/I-31-1903) MD Jefferson 1864. *Pa med jour* 7: 279, 1903/04. *Records Assn AAS USA* 1891: 45-46. *Off'l reg Pa phys* 1881-88: 274.

GUMMERT, C L , Brownsville, Pa (d/VIII- -1891) MD CPS Balto 1882. *Tr Med Soc Pa* 23:179, 1892.

GUMPERT, BENJAMIN BARTON, Philadelphia (b/III 1-1815; d/VI-23-1904) MD Hahnemann Phila 1853. *Tr Am Inst Hom* 1905: 843-44. *Polk* 1886: 817. Homeopath.

GUMPERT, EDWARD, Wilkes-Barre, Pa (b/Offenbach, Gny; d/VI-3-1904 @ 78) MD U Würzburg 1856. *Pa med jour* 8:335, 1904/05. *Polk* 1886: 840.

GUNDRY, RICHARD, Athens, O; Baltimore (b/X-14-1830 London, Engl; d/IV-23-1891 Spring Grove, Md) MD Harvard 1851. *JAMA* 16: 754, 1891. *Bost m & s jour* 124: 474, 1891. *Med bull med & surg* 13:313, 1891. *Butler* 1878:631. *K&B* III: 509. *Med annals Md:* 420-21.

GUNKLE, WILLIAM H , Glenloch, Pa (d/X-3-1874) MD Pa Med Coll 1851. *Tr Med Soc Pa* 10:619-20, 1875. *Med & surg rep Phila* 31: 340, 1874.

GUNN, ALEXANDER N , NYC (b/I-8-1811; d/XII-21 1871) MD CPSNY 1833; AB Columbia 1828; AM Rutgers 1832. *Med reg NY NJ Conn* 1872: 347. *Med rec* 6:526, 551, 1871-1872; 7:33, 1872.

GUNN, MOSES, Chicago (b/IV-20-22 Ontario Co, NY; d/XI-4-1887) MD Geneva 1846. *Buff m & s jour* 27: 365, 1888. *So pract* 9:425-26, 1887. *Tr Ill St Med Soc* 1888: 141-44. *Atkinson* I: 455. *K&B* III: 510.

GUNN, NEIL K , CW-USA (b/Nova Scotia; d/VI-2 or 3-1863 nr Potomac, Va) MD Harvard 1863. *Harvard in CW*: 279. *Med surg rep Phila* 10: 216, 1863. *Bost m & s jour* 68: 390, 1863. *Nat med jour* 1:296, 1870/71.

GUNNELL, JAMES SAMUEL, Washington, DC (b/III--1788; d/1852. MD UPa 1820. *Hist Med Soc DC:* 40.

GUNTER, ADOLPHUS BIRUM, Charlestown, Mass (d/ VII-15-1901 @ 50) MD Harvard 1877. *Bost m & s jour* 145: 108, 1901. *Polk* 1896:698.

GUNTER, LEVERETT DUNCAN, Chelsea, Mass (d/XI 7-1888 @49) MD Harvard 1868. *Bost m & s jour* 119: 544, 1888. *Polk* 1886: 464.

GUNTERMANN, PETER, Louisville (b/Gny; d/V-1-1898 @55) MD U L'ville 1869. *JAMA* 30:1191-92 1898.

GUSHEE, ALMOND, Warren, RI (d/VI-30-1859) MD

Harvard 1834. *Bost m & s jour* 60: 468, 1859.

GUTHRIE, GUION S , CW–USA (d/II–20–1864 Huntsville, Ala) MD Jefferson 1853. *Nat med jour* 1:296, 1870/71.

GUTHRIE, SAMUEL, Sackett's Harbor, NY (b/1782 Brimfield, Mass; d/X–19–1848) Stud U Pa Med Dept 1815; King's Coll, NY 1810–11. *Bost m & s jour* 119: 21, 1888. *K&B* II: 477–79.

GUY, ALEXANDER, Oxford, O (d/XI–30–1893 @93) MD Med Coll Ohio 1831. *JAMA* 21: 936, 1893.

GUY, SAMUEL SMITH, Brooklyn; Visalia, Cal (b/I–18 1818 Kingsbury, NY; d/1900) MD Albany Med Coll 1846. *Tr Am Inst Hom* 1901: 916. *Polk* 1886: 645. *Cleave.* Homeopath.

GUYER, OSCAR K , Lewisville, Ind (b/III–9–1853 NC; d/III–29–1902) MD Med Coll Ohio 1882. *Tr Ind St Med Soc* 1902: 414. *Polk* 1886: 326.

GUYOL, LEONCE P , Pilot Town La (d/V–5–1878) MD Tulane 1874. *New Orl m & s jour* ns5:986, 1878.

GUYTON, BENJAMIN AUGUSTUS, Sioux City, Ia (b/X–15–1844 Hartford Co, Md; d/IX–1–1886 Lebanon, O) MD U Md 1869. *Tr Iowa St Med Soc* 7:518–19, 1886–89. *Polk* 1886: 367.

GWALTNEY, JAMES A , Baltimore (d/XII–18–1886) MD CPS Balto 1878. *No am jour hom* 35: 127, 1887. *Med vis* 3:74, 1881. *Polk* 1886: 436. Homeopath.

GWATHMEY, WILLIAM HENRY, Richmond, Va; CW CSA as civilian (b/IX–22–1819 Burlington; d/V–2–1886 Richmond) MD UPa 1842; AB Wm & Mary 1839. *U Pa med alum CW*: 1842.

GWINN [GWYNN], WILLIAM B , Littlestown, Pa (d/VII–4–1873 Phila) MD U Md 1827. *Med annals Md:* 421. *Med surg rep Phila* 29: 36, 1873.

GWYNN, HENRY B , Baltimore (b/1855; d/X–11–1900) MD Balto U 1887. *Med annals Md:* 421. *Polk* 1896:660.

GWYNN, ROBERT S C , Madrid, Ia (b/X–29–1848 Sarahsville, O; d/VII–24–1884) MD Ky Sch Med 1875. *Tr Ia St Med Soc* 6: 462–63, 1883–85.

GYGAX, PAUL, Milwaukee, Wis (b/VIII– –1861, Switzerland; d/XII–17–1899) MD Bern 1890. *Tr Wis St Med Soc* 34:426–27, 1900.

HAAS, HAROLD, Wabash, Ind (d/II–4–1894 Deland, Fl) MD Northwestern 1893. *JAMA* 22: 202, 1894.

HAASE, CHARLES F W , NYC (d/X–15–1901 @74) MD UCNY. *Bost m&s j* 145: 78, 1901. *Polk* 1886: 680.

HABEL, A , NYC (d/I–1–1879 @60?) <MD Vienna 1846> *Med reg NY NJ Conn* 1879: 192.

HACKEDORN, GEORGE GEDDES, Lima, O (b/IX–19 1828 Huntington Co, Pa; d/IX–1–1874) MD Starling Med Coll 1850. *Med surg rep Phila* 31: 380, 1874.

HACKETT, CHARLES WARREN, Malden, Mass 1874–77; Belmont, NH 1881–87 (b/IX–8–1852 Belmont; d/VI–30–1887) MD Dartmouth 1874. *Bost m & s jour* 117: 24, 1887. *Polk* 1886: 590.

HACKETT, COLIN J , LeMars, Ia (d/XI–26–1896 @ 56) MD Med Coll Va 1860; MD UCNY 1861. *JAMA* 27: 1360, 1896. *Polk* 1896: 529.

HADDOCK, CHARLES W , Beverly Mass (d/X–10–1889 @67) MD Dartmouth 1847; AB 1844. *JAMA* 13: 614, 1889. *Bost m & s jour* 121:400, 1889.

HADLEY, EVAN, Mooresville, Ind (b/I–4–1845; d/V–12 1903) MD Indiana Med Coll 1870. *Tr Ind St Med Soc* 1903: 343. *Polk* 1896: 473.

HADLEY, GEORGE, Buffalo (b/VI–20–1813; d/X–16–1877 @64) MD Fairfield 1840. *Buffalo m & s jour* 17: 146–50, 1887.

HADLEY, JACOB MILTON, LaGrange NC; CW–CSA (b/XI–30–1835 Hadley's Mills; d/XII–13–1901) MD U Pa 1860. *U Pa med alum CW*: 1860. *Polk* 1886: 723.

HADLEY, JAMES, Fairfield, NY 1812–40; Geneva 1840–53; Buffalo 1856– (b/VII–5–1785 Weare, NH; d/X–18–1869) MD ? *Buff m&s jour* 9:112–113, 1869; 12:153, 1872. *Tr Med Soc St NY* 1871: 345–49.

HADLEY, OWEN, Montgomery Co, NC (b/Chatham Co; d/VI–25–1869) MD UCNY 1846. *Tr Med Soc St NC* 1870: 11–12.

HADRA, BERTHOLD ERNEST, Texas 1872– {Dallas, Austin, Galveston, San Antonio} (b/1842 nr Breslau, Gny; d/VII–12–1903) MD U Berlin 1866. *Tex st jour med* 1:243, 1906. *New Orl m & s jour* 56: 240, 1903. *Polk* 1896: 1448. *G P Red*: 320–21.

HAESSLER, CHARLES HERMANN, Pottsville, Pa (d/I 23–1903 @73) MD CPSNY 1853. *Pa med jour* 7:279, 1903/04. *Flint* 1897: 832.

HAGAN, HUGH, Atlanta, Ga (d/III–22–1898 @ 35) MD CPSNY 1888. *JAMA* 30: 874, 1898.

HAGAR, JOSEPH, Marshfield, Mass (d/IV–9–1895 @ 75) MD UCNY 1846. *Bost m & s jour* 132: 396, 1895. *Polk* 1890: 547.

HAGARD, MARTIN L , Midlothian, Tex (d/VI– –1897) MD U La 1871. *Tex cour–rec med* 14:354, 1897. *Polk* 1890: 1087.

HAGEN, HERMANN AUGUST, Cambridge, Mass (b/Prussia; d/XI–10–1893 @76) <MD Königsberg 1840> *Bost m & s jour* 129: 504, 1893.

HAGGARD, WILLIAM D Sr, Gallatin, Tenn (b/X–17 1826 Ky; d/I–25–1901 Columbia, Tenn) MD Jefferson 1851. *So pract* 23:125–28, 1901. *Butler* 1878: 769. *Nashville j m & s* 89:92–93, 1901.

HAGGART, DAVID, Indianapolis (d/XI–19–1888) MD Hahnemann Med Coll Chic 1872. *Med couns* 13: 484, 1888. *Med vis* 5:11, 1889. *Polk* 1886:322. Homeopath.

HAGGERTY, ROBERT J , Elkhart Co, Ind (b/1822 NJ; d/I–16–1880) MD Cleveland Med Coll 1865. *Tr Ind St Med Soc* 1880: 229–30. *Tr AMA* 33: 560, 1882.

HAGGOTT, JOHN P , Eaton, O; CW–USA (d/IV–30–1862 @ 58) MD Med Coll Ohio 1831. *Bost m & s jour* 66: 404, 1862. *Tr Ohio St Med Soc* 1873: 267. *Med surg rep Phila* ns8:257, 1862. *Nat med jour* 1:296, 1870/71.

 Spec. educ'l status abbrev. as: ***ng*** = college verified attendance without degree;

HAGNER, DANIEL RANDALL, Washington, DC (b/VII-19-1830; d/III-4-1851; AB St John's Coll, Md; AM. *Hist Med Soc DC*: 250. *Nat med rev* 2:21, 1893-94. *Atkinson* I:233.

HAGY, JOSEPH ALBERT, CW-USA; Dobbs Ferry, NY (b/Phila; d/1894 Phila) MD UPa 1863; AB Bucknell 1855. *U Pa med alum CW*: 1863. *Polk* 1886: 658.

HAHN, HEINRICH N , St Paul, Minn (d/II-22-1898) MD Marburg, Gny 1874. *JAMA* 30:570, 1898. *Polk* 1896: 799.

HAHN, SAMUEL, NYC (b/1840 Neutra, Hungary; d/III-6-1880) MD U Md 1875; stud med Vienna 1862. *Med reg NY NJ Conn* 1880: 236.

HAIGH, THOMAS, CW-USA; NYC (b/III-14-1840; d/VI-8-1871) MD CPSNY 1865; BS Mich St Agr Coll 1862. *Med reg NY NJ Conn* 1872: 348.

HAIGHT, CALEB W, Pleasantville NY (d/III-5-1874 @ 54) MD UCNY 1846. *Med s rep Phila* 30:252 300, 1874.

HAIGHT, NATHANIEL DRAKE, Stamford, Conn (b/1803 Peekskill NY; d/IX-12-1879/80) MD in NY 1825? Hon Yale 1870. *Proc Conn Med Soc* 1882-83: 169-70. *Med surg rep Phila* 41:308, 1879. *Butler* 1878:77.

HAILE, ASHBEL BRADFORD, Norwich, Conn (b/V-29-1806 Putney, Vt; d/III-8-1880) MD Yale 1842. *Proc Conn Med Soc* 1879-80:168-70. *Med surg rep Phila* 42: 286, 1880. *Butler* 1878: 77.

HAINES, ABRAM B , Aurora, Ind; CW-USA (b/XI-20 1823 Rising Sun; d/VII-20-1887) MD ? *Tr Ind St Med Soc* 1888: 216. *Polk* 1886: 311.

HAINES, GEORGE, Medford, NJ (b/1798? d/IV-12-1877 @78) MD UPa 1821. *Tr AMA* 28: 628, 1877.

HAINES, ISAAC SNOWDEN, Burlington, NJ (b/1808; d/VI-1848) MD UPa 1833. *Tr AMA* 3:442-43, 1850.

HAINES, JOB, Dayton, O (b/X-28-1791 NJ; d/VII-17-1860) MD ? ; stud UPa Med Dept; AB Princeton 1812. *Bost m & s jour* 63:68, 1861; 67:188, 188, 1862. *Tr Ohio St Med Soc* 1873: 267. *K&B* II: 479.

HAINES, WILLIAM ELLIS, Springfield, Pa (b/X-30-1816; d/IV-18-1846) MD UPa 1837. *Med reporter* (W Chester, Pa) 3:90-94, 1856.

HAINES, WILLIAM SHIPLEY, ? (d/I-3-1855) MD UPa 1839. *Tr Med Soc Pa* 1856: 185.

HAKES, HARRY, Wilkes-Barre, Pa (b/VI-10-1825 Harpersfield, NY; d/IV-21-1904) MD Castleton 1846. *Pa med jour* 8:335, 1904/05. *Tr Luzerne Co* (Pa) *Med Soc*: 1904: 11-12. *Flint* 1897: 840.

HALBAUER, THOMAS KIRKBRIDE, St Clair, Pa (b/I 17-1851 Phila; d/I-12-1885) MD UPa 1871. *Tr Med Soc Pa* 18:255-66, 1886.

HALBERSTADT, GEORGE, Pottsville, Pa (b/III-12-1805 Phila; d/XI-9-1860) MD UPa 1829; ng Coll U Pa 1821. *Med surg rep Phila* ns5: 185, 1860/61.

HALDEMAN, GEORGE WASHINGTON, Newville, Pa to 1870; Paola, Kans (b/VII-11-1830 Perry Co, Pa; d/III-14-1884) MD Jefferson 1854. *Tr Kans St Med Soc* 2:401, 1884. *Atkinson* I: 318-19.

HALE, BENJAMIN, Augusta & Newburyport Mass 1859- (b/XI-23-1797 Newbury; d/VII-15-1863) Hon MD Dartmouth 1827; AB Bowdoin 1818; AM 1821; DD Columbia 1836. *Bowdoin cat*: 1818.

HALE, DANIEL MASON, W Bloomfield, NY (b/IV-17 1808 Swansea, Mass; d/X-4-1882) MD Harvard 1833; AB Brown 1828; AM. *Brown hist cat*: 1828.

HALE, EDWIN MOSES, Jonesville, Mich; Chicago 1864- (b/II-2-1829 Newport, NH; d/I-15-1899) <stud Western Coll Homeop 1850, 1858> *Tr Am Inst Hom* 1899: 927-28. *Med vis* 15: 115-17, 1899. *King* 1:331-32. *Polk* 1886: 264. *Cleave*. Homeopath.

HALE, ELIAS WHITE, Lewistown, Pa (b/VI-6-1824; d/II-20-1892) MD UPa 1848. *U Pa med alum CW*: 1848.

HALE, ENOCH, Boston (b/I-19-1790 W Hampton; d/XI 12-1848) MD Harvard 1813. *Buffalo med jour* 5:551, 1849. *Tr AMA* 3:443-44, 1850. *K&B* III:512-13.

HALE, JOSIAH LITTLE, Brookline, Mass (b/IV-1-1841 Geneva, NY; d/XII-21-1903) MD Harvard 1868; AB Hobart 1860. *Bost m & s jour* 149:748, 1903; 150:54, 1904. *Polk* 1896: 698.

HALE, MOSES, Troy, NY 1804- (b/VI-12-1780 Alstead, NH; d/I-3-1837) Hon MD U Vt 1825. *Tr Med Soc St NY* 1857: 73-78.

HALEY, GEORGE WILLIAM, CW-USA; Peabody Mass (b/IX-21-1819 Bath, Me; d/VIII-23-1884) MD Bowdoin 1847. *Bowdoin cat*: 1841. *Butler* 1878: 343. Homeopath.

HALEY, JAMES H , Moffett, Tex (b/XI-5-1831 Carroll Co, Miss; d/II-20-1887) MD Jefferson 1856. *College & clin rec* (Jefferson) 8:86, 1887. *Daniel's Tex med jour* 2: 380-82, 1887. *New Orl m & s jour* ns14: 794, 1887. *Tex cour-rec med* 4:331-32, 1887.

HALL, ABBIE GALE, Champaign, Ill (d/IX-11-1898) MD Hahnemann Chic 1890. *JAMA* 31: 742, 1898. *Polk* 1896: 366. Homeopath.

HALL, ADINO BRACKETT, Boston (b/X-17-1819 Northfield, NH; d/IV-21-1880) MD Dartmouth 1846. *Bost m & s jour* 102:451, 1880; 103:207, 1880. *Tr AMA* 31:1045-46, 1880.*Butler* 1878: 340.

HALL, ALEXANDER POWE, Mobile, Ala (d/X-22-1905 @ 69) MD U La 1859. *So pract* 28: 704, 1905. *Butler* 1878: 18.

HALL, ANDREW DOUGLASS, CW-USA; Philadelphia (b/VII-2-1833; d/IV-25-1905) MD Jefferson 1854; AB UPa 1851; AM. *Tr CPP* cent vol:230. *Atkinson* I:90.

HALL, C B , Millersport, O (b/III-24-1829 Chester Co, NH; d/II-17-1876) MD Starling 1852. *Tr Ohio St Med Soc* 1878:196. *Butler* 1878: 640.

HALL, CHARLES, Swanton, St Albans, Burlington, Vt (b/II-2-1786 Cornish, NH; d/XII-3-1847) MD Dartmouth 1821. *Tr AMA* 29: 659-660, 1878.

HALL, CHARLES J , Glen Cove, NY (d/III-29-1900 @53) MD U Mich 1870; MD Bellevue 1882. *JAMA* 34:

891, 1900. *Polk* 1886: 662.

HALL, CHARLES WESLEY, Amherst, NH (b/III-29-1825 Sudbury, Vt; d/IX-18-1894) MD Castleton 1846. *JAMA* 23:561, 1894. *Polk* 1886: 453.

HALL, CHAUNCEY AUSTIN, Madison, Wis (b/III-14-1811 Blandford, Mass; d/V-8-1856) MD UPa 1837; AB Amherst 1833. *Amherst, Men of*: 1833.

HALL, DANIEL D , Connersville, Ind (b/1803 Va? d/1871) MD UMd 1828. *Tr AMA* 23:584-85, 1872. *Med annals Md:* 422.

HALL, EDWARD, Hoosick, NY 1848-58; Auburn, NY 1858- (b/II-28-1821 Keene, NH; d/IV-28-1871 Messina, Italy) MD Harvard 1843; AB Dartmouth. *Tr Med Soc St NY* 1872: 333-35.

HALL, EDWARDS, NYC (b/X-16-1818 Washington Co, NY; d/XII-10-1898) MD Albany 1844. *Bost m&s j* 139: 636, 1898. *JAMA* 31: 1542, 1898. *Polk* 1896: 1056.

HALL, EDWIN, Newcastle, Me 1841-44; Saco 1844-52 (b/X-16-1816 Alfred; d/XI-19-1852) MD Dartmouth 1841; AB Bowdoin 1836. *Bowdoin cat*: 1836.

HALL, FRANK STEVENS, Cumberland Center, Me (b/XII-30-1839 Windham; d/VII-26-1872) MD Bowdoin 1867; ng Haverford 1861-63. *Tr Me Med Assoc* 1872:481. *Med surg rep Phila* 27:398, 1872.

HALL, FRIEND MABEL, Berkshire Vt 1819?- (b/1785? d/IX-6-1868) MD ? ; AB Middlebury 1812. *Phila med reg & dir* 1871: 298. *Med surg rep Phila* 19:260, 1868.

HALL, GEORGE DOUGLAS, Courtney, Tex; CW-CSA (b/III-24-1824 New Berne, Tex; d/XII-22-1899) MD UPa 1848. *U Pa med alum CW*: 1848. *Polk* 1886: 873.

HALL, GEORGE MARTIN, Swanton Falls, Vt (b/1825; d/1874) MD Berkshire 1848. *Tr AMA* 29:660-61, 1878. *Tr Vt Med Soc* 1883: 106. *Med s rep Phila* 31: 220, 1874.

HALL, GEORGE MIFFLIN DALLAS, Huntingdon, Pa; CW-USA; (b/I-19-1845 Milesburg; d/V-18-1872) MD UPa 1866. *U Pa med alum CW*: 1866.

HALL, GEORGE ROGERS, Brush Hill Road, Mass (d/XII-24-1899 @ 78) MD Harvard 1846; AB Trinity, Conn, 1842. *JAMA* 34: 187, 1900.

HALL, HARRISON B , Riverton, NJ (b/Bridgeton; d/III-8-1901) MD Hahnemann Phila 1869. *Pa med jour* 5:296, 1901/02. *Polk* 1890: 730. Homeopath.

HALL, HENRY CLAY, Leslie NY (d/I-6-1887) MD UC NY 1870. *Tr NY St M S* 11:741 ff, 1894. *Polk* 1886: 666.

HALL, HENRY NEWBERY, Chicago (d/II-23-1896 @ 32) MD UPa 1888. *Chic med rec* 10:219, 1896. *JAMA* 26: 442, 1896.

HALL, HENRY P , Jamestown, NY (d/V-26-1895 @59) MD Buffalo 1868. *Med reg NY NJ Conn* 1895:224. *JAMA* 24: 908, 1895. *Polk* 1886: 664.

HALL, JACOB, RevWar-USA; Harford Co Md (b/1747; d/V-7-1812) MD Edinburgh 1771. *Med annals Md*:422.

HALL, JAMES, Philadelphia (d/IX-16-1801) MD ? *Tr CPP* cent'l vol: 230.

HALL, JAMES CROWDHILL, Washington, DC (b/I-10-1805 ?Alexandria; d/VI-7-1888) MD UPa 1827; AB Jefferson 1823. *Hist Med Soc DC: 228*. *Bost m & s jour* 102: 621, 1880. *Tr AMA* 32: 506, 1881. *Atkinson* I: 395.

HALL, JAMES KING, CW-CSA; Greensboro NC (b/I-13-1816 Iredell Co; d/XI-13-1885) <ng UPa 1848> *Tr NC Med Soc* 1887: 158-59. *Butler* 1878: 593.

HALL, JEREMIAH FORREST, Portsmouth, NH; CW-USA (b/XII-2-1816; d/III-1-1888) Hon MD Dartmouth 1860; ng 1835. *Tr NH Med Soc* 1888: 166-68. *Atkinson* I: 133. Conn's *NH surg, WarRebel*:183. *Polk* 1886: 594.

HALL, JOHN CALVIN, Millerstown, Pa (d/II-11-1903 @ 48) MD CPS Balto 1879. *Pa med jour* 7:279. 1903/04. *Off'l reg Pa phys* 1881-88: 873.

HALL, JOHN CAMBRIDGE, Medical Lake, Wash; Monroe Wis; CW-USA (b/Vt; d/XI-29-1896 @75) MD Harvard 1852. *JAMA* 28:92, 139, 1897. *Polk* 1886: 958.

HALL, JOHN COFFEE, Frankford, Pa (b/III-12-1842 Mt Pleasant, O; d/VI-8 or VII-4-1893) MD UPa 1868. *JAMA* 21:94, 1893. *Chic med rec* 5:206, 1893. *Atkinson* I: 688.

HALL, JOHN E , Green Island, NY (b/New Marlboro, Mass; d/XI-3-1886) MD Albany 1877. *Tr NY St Med Soc* 11:741 ff, 1894. *Polk* 1886: 662.

HALL, JOHN L , Crockett, Tex (b/I-29-1853; d/III-20 1904) MD U Louisville 1883. *Tex st jour med* 1:243, 1906. *Polk* 1896: 1424.

HALL, JOHN STORRS, Ripon Wis (b/X-11-1871 Sheboygan; d/III-5-1902) MD Milwaukee Med Coll 1897. *Tr Wis St Med Soc* 36: 415-16, 1902.

HALL, JOSEPH UNDERWOOD, San Jose, Cal (d/XI-14-1898 @ 85) MD Jefferson 1859. *JAMA* 31: 1319, 1898. *Polk* 1886: 187.

HALL, JOSIAS CARVIL, Md; RevWar-USA (b/VII-7-1746 Harford Co; d/1814) MB UPa 1769. *Med annals Md:* 422-3.

HALL, JULIUS Upper Marlboro, Md (d/IX-4-1899 @ 80) MD U Md 1841. *JAMA* 33:745 1899. *Polk* 1886:436.

HALL, LAURENS, Alleghany Co, NY (b/1779? d/1865) MD ? *Tr AMA* 18: 315, 1867.

HALL, LEWIS A , Newark 1834- ; Trenton 1854- (b/X 2-1794 Salem Co; d/V-23-1872) <MD UPa 1820> *Tr Med Soc NJ* 1872: 231. *Tr AMA* 24: 362-63, 1873.

HALL, MATTHEW R , CW-CSA; Warrenton, Ga (b/1843; d/I-28 1905) MD UCNY 1857. *UCNY cat*: 1857. *Polk* 1886: 236.

HALL, MILTON WILDER, Roxbury, Mass (b/X-24-1848 Me; d/I-9-1900) MD Bowdoin 1872. *Bost m&s j* 142: 76, 1900. *JAMA* 34: 251, 1900.

HALL, NELSON FRANKLIN, Fulton, NY (d/IV-24-1899 @43) MD CPS Balto 1886. *JAMA* 32: 1013, 1899.

HALL, NEWTON BUSHNELL, Branford, Conn (b/III-14-1828 Canaan, Pa; d/VII-21-1878) MD Yale 1863. *Proc Conn Med Soc* 1879-80: 166 ff. *Butler* 1878: 77.

HALL, ORRAN RENSSELAER, Buckfield, Me 1867-72; Weston Mass 1872-83 (b/IV-23-1838 Naples, Me;

Spec. educ'l status abbrev. as: ***ng*** = college verified attendance without degree;

d/XI-24-1903 Buckfield) MD Bowdoin 1867; ng Bowdoin Coll 1860-63. *Bowdoin cat*: 1863. *Polk* 1886:429.

HALL, RANDOLPH NATHANIEL, Chicago (b/IV-2-1844 Eaglesville, O; d/XII-30-1901) MD Rush 1882. *Chic med rec* 20: 202-03, 1901. *Ill med jour* ns2:533, 1901. *Flint* 1897: 261.

HALL, RICHARD JOHN, NYC (b/Ireland; d/I-24-1897 @41 Santa Barbara, Cal) MD CPSNY 1878; AB Princeton 1875. *Bost m & s jour* 136: 120, 1897. *JAMA* 28:327, 1897. *Polk* 1896: 241.

HALL, RICHARD WILMOT, War 1812-USA; Baltimore (b/1785 Harford Co Md; d/IX-14-1847) MD UPa 1806. *Med annals Md:* 423. *K&B* III: 515.

HALL, STANTON L , Bennington, Vt 1875-80; Port Chester, NY 1880- (b/IX-7-1842 Pittsfield, Mass; d/I 12-1895 @53) MD NY Hom Med Coll & Hosp 1875. *No am j hom* 43:128, 1895. *Polk* 1886: 702. Homeopath.

HALL, THEODORE FRANCIS, CW-USA; Rochester, NY (b/1827; d/III-5-1869) MD CPSNY 1855; AB Union 1850. *Tr AMA* 21:442, 1870. *Phila med reg & dir* 1871: 300. *Med rec* 4:236, 1869-70.

HALL, THOMAS PARRY, Baltimore (d/IX-21-1825) MD U Md 1816. *Med annals Md:* 423.

HALL, WALTER LANGDON, Medford, Mass (d/X-25 1906 @60) MD Bellevue 1868. *Bost m & s jour* 155: 530, 1906. *Polk* 1886: 469.

HALL, WESLEY C , CW-USA; Franklin, Ind (b/1830; d/XII-24 or 25-1899) MD ? *JAMA* 34:187, 1900. Kemper's *Indiana*: 278. *Ind med jour* 18:361, 1899?

HALL, WILLIAM BONNELL, CW-CSA; Lowndesborough, Ala (b/IX-9-1834; d/I-14-1906) MD UPa 1856. *U Pa med alum CW*: 1856.

HALL, WILLIAM C , Fayetteville, O (b/IX-2-1834; d/V-5-1872) MD Starling 1857. *Tr Ohio St Med Soc* 1872: 264-65.

HALL, WILLIAM EDWARD, Tarrytown, NY (d/V-25-1878 @33) MD CPSNY 1870. *Med rec* 13: 516, 1878.

HALL, WILLIAM JAMES, Korea (d/XII- -1894 @35) MD Bellevue 1889. *JAMA* 24: 33, 1895.

HALL, WILLIAM WOOD, USA; CW-CSA (b/VIII-17 1839 Grenada, Miss; d/VIII-29-1878) MD U Nashville 1860. *Tr AMA* 30:864-70, 1879. *Tr Miss St Med Assoc* 1879: 54-56. *Med rec* 14: 220, 1878.

HALL, WILLIS WOODBURY, USA 1880-81; Springfield, O (b/XII-18 1855 Washington Co; d/IV-8-1898 @ 42) MD Miami Med Coll 1880. *JAMA* 30:999, 1898. *Records AAS USA* 1891: 46.

HALLAM, ALBERT COBERG, Brooklyn (b/1845 Watertown, Conn; d/I-9-1895) MD Yale 1866. *Med reg NY NJ Conn* 1895:224. *JAMA* 24:101, 421-22, 1895. *Bost m & s jour* 132: 70, 1895.

HALLAM, WILLIAM L , Bloomington, Ill (d/I-24-1898 @45) MD Med Coll Ohio 1874. *JAMA* 30: 335, 1898. *Polk* 1896: 364.

HALLER, FRANCIS B , Vandalia, Ill (b/X-13-1826 Lewistown, Pa; d/IX-14-1895) MD Mo Med Coll 1851. *JAMA* 25:510, 1895. *Tr Ill St Med Soc* 1896: 50-52. *Polk* 1896:444. *Polk* 1886: 300 (MD Jefferson 1865).

HALLER, JACOB, Wytheville, Va (b/XI-29-1796 York Co; d/I-28-1877) MD ? *Tr Med Soc Va* 1877: 307. *Butler* 1878: 829.

HALLETT, ARNOLD, Brooklyn (b/XII-11-1825 St John, NB; d/III-10-1895 Norwalk, Conn) MD UCNY 1848. *Med reg NY NJ Conn* 1895: 225. *JAMA* 24: 422, 1895. *Butler* 1874: 531.

HALLMAN, NATHANIEL FRANKLIN, Slatington, Pa (d/III-18-1906 @66) MD UPa 1862. *Pa med jour* 9:524, 1905/06. *Flint* 1897: 836.

HALLOCK, LEWIS, NYC (b/VI-30-1803; d/III-3-1897) MD CPSNY 1826. *Tr Am Inst Hom* 1897: 63. *No Amer jour hoeop* 45: 204, 1897. *King* 1: 91-92. *Polk* 1886: 680. Homeopath.

HALLOCK, WINTHROP BAILEY, Cromwell, Conn (b/II-2-1838 Utica, NY; d/IX-24-1898) MD LICH 1864. *Proc Conn Med Soc* 1899: 359-61. *JAMA* 31: 871, 1898. *Atkinson* I: 481.

HALLOWELL, EDWARD Jr, Philadelphia (b/IX-14-1808; d/II-20-1860) MD UPa 1830; AB 1827; stud med in Paris. *Tr CPP* cent vol: 230. *K&B* III:515-16.

HALLUM, RICHARD ANDREW RAPLEY Jr, CW-CSA (b/IX-18-1843 Winnsboro, NC; d/I-17-1901 Canadian Okla) MD UPa 1871. *U Pa med alum CW*: 1871.

HALSEY, CHARLES EDWARD, NYC; CW-USA (d/VIII-30-1862 @28 Balto) MD CPSNY 1858; AB Williams 1856. *Med surg rep Phila* ns8:444, 1862. *Nat med jour* 1:296, 1870/71.

HALSEY, GAIUS LEONARD, Unadilla, NY (d/II-17-1891) MD Fairfield 1840. *Bost m & s jour* 124: 221, 1891. *Tr Med Soc St NY* 1892: 428.

HALSEY, JOHN CONDIT, Brooklyn (d/V-7-1885 @83) MD CPSNY 1834; AB Union 1830. *Med reg NY NJ Conn* 1895: 224. *JAMA* 24: 810, 1895.

HALSEY, LUTHER F , Swedesboro, NJ (b/X-25-1843 Churchville, Pa; d/VII-7-1895) MD Jefferson 1854. *Tr Med Soc NJ* 1896: 362-64. *Butler* 1878: 470.

HALSEY, ROBERT SEYMOUR, Plymouth, NC; CW-CSA (b/III-5-1828 Halifax; d/VIII-29-1880) MD UPa 1848. *U Pa med alum CW*: 1848.

HALSTEAD, JOHN COOLEY, NYC (d/VI-17-1903 @45) MD UCNY 1883. *Bost m & s jour* 148: 712, 1903. *Polk* 1896: 1056.

HALSTEAD, MILTON A , CW-USA; Jacksonville, Ill 1877- (b/IX-17-1838 Mich; d/I-6-1904) MD Cleveland Homeop 1861; ng U Mich 2 yrs. *Tr Am Inst Hom* 1904:962. *Polk* 1886: 283. Homeopath.

HALSTED, THADDEUS MILLS, NYC (d/X-8-1870) MD CPSNY 1838; AB Princeton 1835; AM 1838. *Med rec* 5:407, 1870/71; 6:94, 1871/72 (d/VII-26-1870).

HAM, ABNER, Rochester & Dover, NH 1847-57 (b/II-12-1820 Farmington; d/VIII-14-1866 Charleston, SC)

MD UCNY 1847; AB Bowdoin 1844. *Bowd'n cat*: 1844.

HAM, SYLVESTER CLAY, Auburn Ill (d/II-22-1898 @40) MD Rush 1877 *JAMA* 30:570 1898. *Polk* 1886:253

HAMER, ELLIS P, Lincoln, Nebr (d/VII-18-1901 @ 78) MD Jefferson 1851. *JAMA* 37:275 1901. *Polk* 1886: 581.

HAMER, JAMES, Collegeville, Pa (d/III-24-1900 @81) MD UCNY 1844. *JAMA* 34:957, 1900. *Polk* 1886: 796.

HAMILL, GEORGE A , Martinsburg, WVa; CW-CSA (b/X-9-1819 Shippensburg, Pa; d/XII- -1865) MD Pa Med Coll 1855. *Tr AMA* 23:597, 1872. *Tr Med Soc WVa* 1884: 154; 1872: 354.

HAMILL, GEORGE SAGER, Philadelphia (d/VI-15-1863 @39) MD UPa 1849. *Med s rep Phila* 10:144 1863.

HAMILL, JOHN RANSOM, Davis, Ill (b/III-1-1828 Baldwinsville, NY; d/X-7-1869) MD Geneva 1849. *Chicago med jour* 22: 64, 1870.

HAMILL, ROBERT C, Chicago (b/XI-26-1808 Xenia O; d/VII-21-1886) Hon MD Rush 1861. *Chic m j* 53: 298-99 1866. *Tr Ill St M S* 1887:169-71. *Butler* 1878:132.

HAMILTON, ALBINUS OTIS, Dorchester, Mass (d/X-4 1894 @62) MD Harvard 1877. *Bost m & s jour* 131: 380, 1894. *Polk* 1886: 465.

HAMILTON, ALEXANDER, Corpus Christi, Tex (d/VII 16-1882) MD Tulane 1849. *Tex m & s rec* 3:550, 1883.

HAMILTON, BENJAMIN FRANKLIN, Emlenton, Pa (b/VI-21-1838; d/VIII-2-1906) MD Charity Hosp Med Coll Cleveland 1867. *Pa med jour* 9:893, 1905/06; 10: 168-69, 1906/07. *Flint* 1897: 801. *Atkinson* I: 608.

HAMILTON, CHARLES BEALE, USN; Washington DC (b/1792;d/IV-24-1851) MD ? *Hist Med Soc DC*:223.

HAMILTON, EDWARD L , Richmond, Ark (d/VII-5-1899 @63) MD Tulane 1858. *JAMA* 33:175, 1899. *Polk* 1886: 155.

HAMILTON, ERSKINE ERASMUS, Springfield, Ill (b/XII-25-1866 Somers, Conn; d/I-24-1901) MD CPS NY 1892; ng Amherst 189_. *Bost m & s jour* 144:126, 1901. *Polk* 1896: 723.

HAMILTON, EVERETT V , Austin, Tex (b/Wilson Co, Tn; d/II-11-1906 @40) MD U Louisville 1889. *Tex st jour med* 1:352, 1905/06. *Polk* 1900:1680.

HAMILTON, FREDERICK A , Chico, Cal (d/IV-20-1899) MD Eclect Med Inst Cincinnati 1873. *JAMA* 32: 1013, 1899. *Polk* 1886: 163.

HAMILTON, FRANK HASTINGS, Buffalo, Brooklyn; CW-USA; NYC (b/IX-10-1813 Wilmington, Vt; d/VIII 11-1886) MD UPa 1835; AB Union 1830. *Med reg NY NJ Conn* 1887: 262. *Buff m&s j* 26: 90-91, 1886. *Bost m & s j* 115: 170-71, 196, 338, 429, 629, 1886. *K&B* III: 519 *Atkinson* I: 156.

HAMILTON, FRANK HASTINGS Jr, NYC; CW-USA (b/VI-24-1841 Rochester, NY; d/XI-5-1869) MD Bellevue 1863. *Phila med reg & dir* 1871: 302.

HAMILTON, GEORGE, Centreville, Del 1833-44; Philadelphia 1844- (b/XI-15-1808; d/X-30-1885) MD UPa 1831. *Tr CPP* cent'l vol: 230, 3s8: xlv-liii, 1886. *Med bull med & surg* 8:23, 1886. *Atkinson* I: 160.

HAMILTON, HORATIO A , Perrysburg, O (d/IX-9-1897 @68) MD UCNY 1852. *JAMA* 29:660, 709, 1897. *Polk* 1886: 765.

HAMILTON, HOSEA ALEXANDER, Oneonta, NY (d/XII-6-1898 @76) MD Castleton 1837. *JAMA* 31: 1542, 1898. *Polk* 1886: 700.

HAMILTON, INCREASE S , Tecumseh, Mich (d/VII-25-1891 @82) MD Fairfield 1835. *JAMA* 17: 236, 1891. *Butler* 1878: 374.

HAMILTON, JAMES, Baltimore (b/Scotland; d/1854 at sea) MD UMd 1838. *Med annals Md:* 424.

HAMILTON, JAMES, Del (b/III- -1826 Newcastle Co; d/X-29-1874) MD Jefferson 1848. *Med annals Md:* 424.

HAMILTON, JAMES FRANCIS, Philadelphia (d/IX-1-1902 @32) MD UPa 1893. *Pa med jour* 6:260, 1902/03. *Flint* 1897: 818.

HAMILTON, JOHN BROWN, Chicago (b/XII-1-1847 Jersey Co, Ill; d/XII-24-1898 Elgin) MD Rush 1869. *Chic med rec* 16:88-89, 1899. *So pract* 21:88-91, 1899. *Tr Ill St M S* 49:22-24, 1899. *St Louis m & s j* 76:82-83, 1879. *K&B* III: 250.

HAMILTON, JOHN V , USA (d/VII-26-1899 Matanzas, Cuba) MD ? *JAMA* 33: 367, 1899.

HAMILTON, JOHN W , USN; Brooklyn (b/XI-12-1819; d/IV-4-1880) MD Jefferson 1855. *Med reg NY NJ Conn* 1881: 237.

HAMILTON, JOHN W , Allegheny, Pa (b/1827 Ohio; d/II-12-1897 Lake Worth, Fla) MD Jefferson 1881. *JAMA* 28: 476, 1897. *Polk* 1896: 1295.

HAMILTON, JOHN W , Lampasas, Tex (d/III-29-1905 @45) MD Tulane 1887. *Tex st jour med* 1:32, 1905/06.

HAMILTON, JOHN WATERMAN, Columbus, O (d/I 1-1898 @ 72) MD Willoughby 1847. *JAMA* 30: 106, 1898. *Polk* 1896: 1180.

HAMILTON, JOSEPH COURTIN, Mobile, Ala (d/IV-27-1887) MD UPa 1846. *Tr Med Assoc St Ala* 1887: 306. *Polk* 1886: 136.

HAMILTON, JOSEPH ORMOND, Jerseyville, Ill (b/IV 2-1824 New Design; d/VIII-21-1882) MD Mo Med Coll 1850. *Tr Ill St M S* 1884: 267-69. *Atkinson* I: 627.

HAMILTON, RAYBURN B , Longview, Tex (d/VI-23 1897) MD U Nashville 1883. *Tex cour-rec med*: 14: 354, 1897. *Polk* 1890: 1085.

HAMILTON, THOMAS B , CW-USA (d/III-17-1865 Nashville) MD ? *Nat med jour* 1:296, 1870/71.

HAMILTON, WILLIAM AUGUSTUS, Camden, NJ; Baltimore (b/IV-15-1848; d/V-10/14-1888) MD U Md 1869. *Med ann Md*:425. *New Orl m&s j* 15:1003, 1888.

HAMILTON, WILLIS D , Kennett Square, Pa (d/VII-3 1903 @36) MD Jefferson 1889. *Pa med jour* 7: 279, 1902/03. *Flint* 1897: 806.

HAMLIN, AUGUSTUS CHOATE, Bangor, Me; CW-

 Spec. educ'l status abbrev. as: ***ng*** = college verified attendance without degree;

USA (b/VIII-29-1829 Columbia; d/XI-18-1905 @76) MD Harvard 1855; AB Bowdoin 1851. *Bost m & s jour* 153: 597, 1905. *Harvard in CW*: 245. *Atkinson* I: 318. *K&B* III: 520-21.

HAMLIN, CHARLES FRANKLIN, Medway, Mass 1895-1903 (b/VII-14-1869 Otisfield, Me; d/V-16-1903) MD Bowdoin 1892. *Bost m&s j* 148: 656, 1903.

HAMLIN, CHARLES WILLARD, CW-USA Middleville, NY (b/XII-21-1839 Holland Patent; d/X-7-1897) MD Bellevue 1866. *Tr Med Soc St NY* 1898: 403, 411-12. *Polk* 1886: 668.

HAMLIN, CHESTER, E Granby, Conn (b/III-14-1795 Farmington; d/X-5-1872) Hon MD Yale 1856; lic Conn St M S 1823. *Proc Conn Med Soc* 4:219-21, 225, 1873.

HAMLIN, NORMAN SCOTT, Yuba City & Marysville, Cal (d/IV-12-1891) MD Keokuk Med Coll 1860. *Tr Med Soc Cal* 22: 263-64, 1892. *Butler* 1878: 59.

HAMMER, ADAM, St Louis, Mo (b/XII-27-1818 Baden, Gny; d/VIII-4-1878 Baden) <MD Tübingen> *Tr AMA* 30:832-24, 1879. *St Louis m & s jour* 35: 1878. *K&B* III:485-486.

HAMMER, CHARLES, Schenectady, NY (b/I-25-1832 Gny; d/1897) <MD Göttingen 1854> *Bost m & s jour* 136: 366, 1897. *JAMA* 28: 760, 1897.

HAMMER, ROBERT BROWN, Greensburg, Pa (d/IX-17-1905 @46) MD UPa 1881. *Pa med jour* 9:28, 1905/06. *Flint* 1897: 803.

HAMMETT, CHARLES MASSEY, Washington, DC (b/VIII-4-1835 St Mary's Co, Md; d/XI-22-1898) MD Geo't'n 1856. *JAMA* 31: 1377, 1898. *Hist M S DC:* 320.

HAMMOND, ALBERT, Hagerstown, Md (b/XII-14-1847; d/XI-8-1879) MD Hahnemann Phila 1871; att Frank & Marsh. *Tr Am Inst Hom* 1893: 144. Homeopath.

HAMMOND, CORNELIUS ELIJAH, Portland, Conn (b/1824 Ellington; d/IX-17-1888) MD UCNY 1848. *Proc Conn M S* ns4:253-58, 1888-91. *Butler* 1878: 77.

HAMMOND, DAVIS M, Evansville, Ind (d/XI-18-1895 @42) MD Kentucky Sch Med 1875. *JAMA* 25:968 1895. *Polk* 1890: 372.

HAMMOND, FRANCIS JAMES, Indianapolis (b/1837 Yorkshire, Engl; d/II-1-1895) <MRCS(E) 1860> *JAMA* 24: 221, 1895. *Tr Ind St Med Soc* 1895: 409. Kemper's *Indiana*: 279. *Polk* 1890: 375.

HAMMOND, GEORGE, USA (d/1863) MD U Md 1854. *Tr AMA* 16: 651, 1865.

HAMMOND, GEORGE H , Freeport, NY (d/V-29-1904 @58) MD UCNY 1872. *Bost m & s jour* 150: 390, 1904. *Polk* 1896: 1022.

HAMMOND, GEORGE W , CW-CSA (b/VII-24-1828; d/VIII-14-1863 Cloyd's Farm, Va) MD UPa 1851. *U Pa med alum CW*: 1851.

HAMMOND, JOHN FOX, USA 1847-84 (b/XII-7-1820 Columbia, SC; d/IX-29-1886 Poughkeepsie, NY) MD UPa 1841. *Med reg NY NJ Conn* 1887: 266.

HAMMOND, JOSIAH STURTEVANT, Plympton, Mass (b/V-14-1810 Carver; d/XI-28-1886) MD Berkshire 1834; ng Amherst 1832. *Bost m&s jour* 115: 536, 1886.

HAMMOND, JUSTIN, Killingly, Conn (b/III-2-1804 Hampton; d/VII-5-1873) MD Harvard 1830; AB Brown 1827. *Proc Conn Med Soc* 4:273, 1874. *Butler* 1878: 77.

HAMMOND, NICHOLAS, Easton, Md (b/1795; d/1831) MD U Md 1823. *Med annals Md:* 425.

HAMMOND, SAMUEL FERDINAND, Fairfield, Ia (d/1887) MD Rush 1880. *Tr Ia St Med Soc* 18:410, 1900. *Polk* 1886: 358.

HAMMOND, THOMAS H , Dover Plains, NY (d/XII-27-1895 @73) MD UCNY 1859. *Tr Med Soc St NY* 1896: 437. *Polk* 1886: 658.

HAMMOND, WILLIAM ALEXANDER, USA 1849-64, 1878- ; NYC (b/VIII-28-1828 Annapolis, Md; d/I-5-1900) MD UCNY 1848. *Tr CPP* cent vol: 230-31. *JAMA* 34: 122, 1900. *Med surg rep Phila* 16: 165-66, 1867. *Atkinson* I: 364-65. *K&B* III:521-22.

HAMMOND, WILLIAM M , San Francisco (b/XI--1824 Hagerstown, Md; d/IV-29-1905) MD U Md 1845. *Cal st jour med* 3: 195, 1905.

HAMPTON, ISAAC HARRIS, Bridgeton, NJ (d/IX-4-1860) MD UPa 1808. *Med surg rep Phila* ns4:510, 1860; ns5:409, 1860/61.

HANAFORD, JAMES BOARDMAN, Apponang, RI (b/II-22-1849 New Hampton, NH; d/XII-6-1898) MD UCNY 1872. *JAMA* 31: 1542, 1898. *Tr RI Med Soc* 5: 645, 1894-98.

HANCE, EDMUND, Trenton, NJ (b/I-15-1816; d/XI-29 1872 Glassboro, NJ; <MD ? 1853> *Med surg rep Phila* 27: 524, 1872. *Tr AMA* 24: 365, 1873.

HANCE, EDMUND Jr, Mt Holly, NJ (d/II-25-1874 @ 22) MD UPa 1871. *Med surg rep Phila* 30:276. 1874.

HANCE, FRANCIS WATERMAN, CW-USA; Freeport, Ill (b/VII-23-1825 Barnesville, O; d/IX-16-1896) MD UPa 1849. *JAMA* 27: 721, 1896. *Butler* 1896: 156. *U Pa med alum CW*: 1849.

HANCHETT, MARY E , Chittenango, NY (d/1889) <MD Albany 1848> *Bost m&s j* 121: 144, 1889. *Polk* 1886: 656.

HANCK, FRANCIS M , CW-USA (d/II-11-1862) MD ? *Nat med jour* 1:296, 1870/71.

HANCOCK, ALEXANDER STANLEY, NYC (b/Engl; d/II-28-1903 @65) <MD Buffalo> att Trinity Coll Toronto. *Bost m & s jour* 148:274, 1903.

HAND, DANIEL WHILLDIN, CW-USA; St Paul, Minn (b/VIII-18-1834 Cape May CH, NJ; d/VI-1-1889) MD UPa 1856. *JAMA* 12:898, 1889. *Tr Minn St Med Soc* 1889:234-39. *U Pa med alum CW*: 1856. *K&B* II:487.

HAND, FRANCIS C , ?Philadelphia (d/IX-9-1881) MD UPa 1874. *Tr CPP* cent vol: 231.

HAND, GEORGE F, CW-CSA (d/XI- -1862 or 63) MD U Mich 1857. *SPHS* 33:212, 1893.

HAND, HENRY CLAY, St Paul, Minn (b/III-17-1848 Cape May, NJ; d/III-2-1876) MD UPa 1870. *Tr Minn St*

Med Soc 1876: 147–49.

HANDY, CHARLES W , Md (d/IX–29–1859 Washington, DC @48) MD Columbian 1832. *Med surg rep Phila* ns3:72, 1859/60.

HANDY, ISAAC HENRY, Wilmington, Del (d/XII–7–1853) MD UPa 1833. *Phila m & s jour* 2:216, 1853. *Tr Pa St Med Soc* 1:185, 186 (as John Henderson Handy)

HANDY, LITTLETON DENNIS [DENNIS MIDDLETON] Princess Anne, Md (b/1808 Snow Hill; d/1856) MD UMd 1828. *Med annals Md:* 426.

HANDY, SAMUEL KERR, Md (b/X–23–1800; d/XII–15–1859) MD U Md 1821. *Tr AMA* 13:811, 1860. *Med annals Md:* 426.

HANDY, WASHINGTON R , Baltimore (b/1811 Somerset Co, Md; d/1857) MD Wash Med Coll Balto 1834. *Bost m & s jour* 57:495,1857. *Med annals Md:*427.

HANDY, WILLIAM, NYC (b/IX–21–1766 Newport, RI; d/IX–22–1828) MD Edinburgh 1788. *New York med & phys jour* 7:440–41, 1828.

HANDY, WILLIAM NASSAU, CW–USA (b/XI–15–1835 Phila; d/VI–28–1861) MD UPa 1856. *U Pa med alum CW*: 1856. *Nat med jour* 1:296, 1870/71.

HANDY, WILLIAM W , Baltimore (b/1785 Somerset Co, Md; d/1865) MD U Md 1819. *Med annals Md:* 427.

HANEY, JOHN RIEGEL, CW–USA; Camden NJ (b/XI–4–1833 Riegelsville Pa; d/VIII–27–1887) MD UPa 1861. *Tr Med Soc St NJ* 1888–89:154–55. *Butler* 1878:470.

HANFORD, SAMUEL CULLEN, Hempstead, NY (d/II 24–1903 @80) MD UCNY 1846. *Bost m & s jour* 148: 274, 1903. *Polk* 1896: 996.

HANGER, JOHN M , Staunton, Va (b/Augusta Co; d/II–25–1900 @60) MD Jefferson 1857. *JAMA* 34: 639, 1900. *Polk* 1896: 1503.

HANK, JOHN WILLIAM FLETCHER, Baltimore (b/1826 Ohio; d/XI–3–1881) MD UPa 1850. *Med annals Md:* 427.

HANKINS, JOHN W , Carlinville, Ill (d/III–19–1901) Lic yrs pract. *Ill med jour* ns2:533, 1901.

HANKS, HORACE TRACY, NYC (b/VI–27–1837 E Randolph, Vt; d/XI–18–1900) MD Albany 1861. *Bost m &s jour* 143:570, 1900. *Tr Med Soc St NY* 1901: [426]. *K&B* III:524–25. *Polk* 1886: 680.

HANKS, JOHN ARMSTRONG, Pittsboro, NC (d/IV–26 1889 @75) MD UPa 1837. *NC med jour* 23: 471, 1889.

HANKS, LUCIEN ALBERT, CW–CSA; Pittsboro, NC (b/X–23–1841; d/I–15–1896) MD UPa 1872. *U Pa med alum CW*: 1872. *Polk* 1886: 725.

HANLON, NICHOLAS JOHN, Waterbury, Conn (b/V–8 1864; d/I–25–1895) MD Dartmouth 1891. *Proc Conn Med Soc* 1895: 364.

HANLY, MICHAEL ABBOTT, Philadelphia (d/VII–18 1885 @50) MD Jefferson 1855. *Med bull m & s* 7:255, 1895.

HANNA, GEORGE S, Hedgesville Md (d/IX–8–1898 @ 70) MD UMd 1858. *JAMA* 31:742, 1898. *Polk* 1886:942.

HANNA, JOHN, Hunterdon Co, NJ (b/1731? d/XI–4–1801) <MD UPa> AB Princeton 1755; AM 1758. *Tr Med Soc NJ* 1872:169–170. Blane, *Hunterdon Co*:81–82.

HANNA, ROBERT H , Galveston, Tex (b/La; d/IX–5–1867 @27) MD Galv Med Coll 1866. *Galv med jour* 2:1014,1867; 3:117,1868. *Tr AMA* 19:428,1868.

HANNAN, JOHN C , NYC (b/Ireland; d/V–30–1885) MD UCNY 1866. *Med reg NY NJ Conn* 1886: 249.

HANSON, JACOB CLEMENTS, Great Falls, NH (b/IX–29–1812 Rochester; d/VII–18–1875) MD Dartmouth 1839. *Tr NH Med Soc* 1876:169–70.

HANSON, SWAN, Moline, Ill (d/X–30–1905 @84) Lic yrs pract. *Ill med jour* 8:530, 1905. *Polk* 1886:288.

HAPPERSETT, EFFINGER, W Nantmeal, Pa (b/1778? d/I–20–1862 @84) MD ? *Med surg rep Phila* ns7:456, 1861/62.

HAPPERSETT, JOHN C G , USA (d/IV–9 1893 @56 Plainfield NJ) MD Jefferson 1859. *Bost m&s j* 128:380, 1893.

HAPPOLDT, CHRISTOPHER, Morganton, NC; CW–CSA (b/1823; d/X–11–1878 Vicksburg, Miss) MD Med Coll SC 1851. *NC med jour* 2: 299–300, 1878. *Tr AMA* 30:873, 1879.

HARCOURT, H DeWITT, Tompkinsville, Staten Isl, NY (d/VII–26–1866 @52) MD CPSNY 1839. *Med surg rep Phila* 15: 132, 1866.

HARCOURT, JAMES, Staten Isl, NY (d/VII–31–1870) MD CPSNY 1831. *Med surg rep Phila* 1871: 357. *Med rec* 6: 94,1871–72.

HARD, ABNER, Aurora, Ill (d/III–20–1885) MD CPS Keokuk 1854; Hon MD Rush 1868. *Chic med jour* 50: 378, 1885. *Ill st med reg* 1878/79. *Butler* 1878: 156.

HARD, CHESTER A , Ottawa, Ill; Los Angeles (b/II–8 1827 Mt Morris, NY; d/IV–18–1896) MD Mo Med Coll (Kemper) 1854. *JAMA* 26: 843, 1896. *Tr Ill St Med Soc* 1896: . *Atkinson* I: 625.

HARD, NICHOLAS, Aurora, Ill (b/VII–4–1818 Geneva, NY; d/1851) MD Med Coll Ohio 1841. *Tr AMA* 29: 661–62, 1878. *NW m & s jour* 4:306, 1851. *Buff m j* 7:448, 1851. *K&B* III: 525–26.

HARDACKER, HENRY D , Hortonville, Wis (d/III–26–1900 @ 53) MD Chicago Med Coll 1875. *JAMA* 34:890, 1900. *Polk* 1896: 1550.

HARDAWAY, DANIEL HORACE, CW–CSA; Blacks & Whites, Va (b/VI–24–1839 Somerset; d/VI–7–1906 nr Blackstone, Va) MD UPa 1861. *U Pa med alum CW*: 1861. *Polk* 1886: 914.

HARDAWAY, GEORGE STANFIELD, Columbus, Ga (d/X–16–1859 @25) MD UCNY 1857. *Med surg rep Phila* ns3: 151, 1859/60.

HARDAWAY, JAMES JARRATT, Macon, Ga (b/VI–30 1848; d/XII–20–1877) MD UCNY 1870; AB U Ala 1865. *U Ala cat*: 199.

HARDEN [HARDER], CHARLES STEWART, Bloomsburg, Pa (b/II–14–1841 Catawissa; d/IV–5–

 Spec. educ'l status abbrev. as: ***ng*** = college verified attendance without degree;

1883) MD U Vt 1866. *Tr Med Soc Pa* 15: 357, 1883.

HARDESTY, CHARLES, CW-USA (d/VII-7-1863) MD *Nat med jour* 1:296, 1870/71.

HARDEY, WILLIAM H, Clarksville, Md (b/1820? d/X 9-1899 @ 79) MD U Md 1852. *JAMA* 33: 1116, 1899.

HARDIE, CHARLES JOHN, Chicago; Ariz (d/VI-? 1898 Ariz) MD U Ill Coll Med 1893. *U Ill Coll Med alum.*

HARDING, ABRAHAM, So Hero, Vt (b/IV-15-1801 Hartland, Vt; d/XI-21-1880) MD Woodstock 1830. *Tr Vt Med Soc* 1883: 106.

HARDING, ERASTUS G, Wyoming, NY (d/VII-9-1892) MD Buffalo 1892. *Buffalo m & s jour* 32: 60, 1892. *Polk* 1886: 716.

HARDING, FRANK H, Mansfield, O (b/1862? d/II-25-1895 @33 Norwalk, O) MD UPa 1888. *JAMA* 24:422, 1895. *Polk* 1890: 994.

HARDING, GEORGE AUSTIN, Sault Ste Marie, Mich (d/X-20 or XI-22-1884) MD U Mich 1879. *Med age* 3:15, 1885.

HARDING, JOHN, Hartland, Vt (d/VIII-1-1863 @ 62) MD "never graduated" *Tr Vt Med Soc* 1883: 106.

HARDING, MYRON HAWLEY Sr, Lawrenceburg, Ind (b/VIII-10-1810 Williamson, NY; d/IX-18-1883) MD Med Coll Ohio 1837. *Tr Ind St Med Soc* 1886: 205. *Atkinson* I: 103. *Butler* 1878: 204.

HARDING, MYRON HAWLEY Jr, Lawrenceburg, Ind (b/I-3-1855; d/I-12-1879) MD Ohio Med Coll 1878. *Tr Ind St Med Soc* 1880: 241.

HARDING, PHILANDER HARRISON, Ellsworth, Me (b/XII-22-1829 Hampden, Me; d/III-1-1875) MD Jefferson 1855. *Tr Me Med Assoc* 1874-76: 427-28.

HARDING, THOMAS JEFFERSON, Nashville Tenn (b/I-18-1827; d/VI-23-1901 Vicksburg Miss) MD UPa 1849. *Nashville jour med & surg* 90:43-44,1901. *Polk* 1886: 870.

HARDING, WILLIAM G, Terrill, Tex (d/II-8-1888) MD U Louisville 1881. *Daniels Tex med jour* 3:407, 1888. *Polk* 1886: 895.

HARDMAN, WILLIAM B J, Commerce, Ga (b/1822? d/VIII-21-1904 @82) MD Jefferson 1850. *JAMA* 43: 749, 1904. *Polk* 1886: 232.

HARDRICK, HERMAN, Brooklyn (b/NYC; d/X-4-1896 @42) MD UCNY 1876. *JAMA* 27:1020,1896.

HARDY, BENJAMIN FRANKLIN, San Francisco (b/1809; d/XI-22-1886) MD UPa 1840; AB Haverford 1842. *JAMA* 1:252, 1887. *Butler* 1878: 54.

HARDY, DANIEL WARREN, Chicago 1867-69 (b/VII-24-1834 Wilton, Me; d/VII-28-1901 Bellerica, Mass) MD Bowdoin 1863; ng 1858-60. *Bowdoin cat*: 1861.

HARDY, SAMUEL, Cornish Flat, NH (b/1805? d/VIII-8 1879 @ 74) MD *Med surg rep Phila* 41:242, 1879.

HARDY, THOMAS J, Norfolk, Va (d/X-31-1886) MD Hahnemann Phila 1853. *Med vis* 3:138, 1887. *Polk* 1886: 922. Homeopath.

HARDY, WILLIAM LEWIS, NYC (b/V-18-1849; d/IV 24-1886) MD Bellevue 1871. *Med reg NY NJ Conn* 1886: 249. *Bost m & s jour* 114: 428, 1886.

HARE, ALBERT, McKeesport, Pa (b/1856? d/IV-26-1901 @45) MD CPS Balto 1883. *Pa med jour* 5:296, 1901/02. *Polk* 1886: 837.

HARE, ANDREW JACKSON, Milwaukee, Wis (b/1838? d/VII-6-1898 @60) MD Boston U 1877. *JAMA* 31: 198, 1898. *Polk* 1886: 957. Homeopath.

HARE, HORACE BINNEY, Philadelphia; CW-USA (b/VIII-30-Burlington, NJ; d/III-25-1879) MD UPa 1866; ng Harvard 1861. *U Pa med alum CW*: 1866. *Harvard in CW*: 209. *Phila med times* 9:320, 1879.

HARE, ROBERT, Philadelphia (b/I-17-1781; d/V-15-1858) Hon MD Harvard 1816; Hon AM Yale 1806. *Tr AMA* 13:802-03, 1860. *Buffalo med jour* 14: 318, 1858. *Phila m & s jour* 6:455-58, 1858. *Nashville jour med & surg* 15: 88-90, 1858? *K&B* III: 526.

HARGIS, ROBERT BELL STURGIS, Pensacola, Fla; CW-CSA; US Marine Hosp Serv (b/VI-7-1818 Hillsboro, NC; d/XI-30-1893) MD Tulane 1844. *New Orl med & surg jour* ns21:539-43. *Polk* 1890: 255. *K & B* III: 527.

HARGROVE, WILLIAM SMITH, New Salem, Ind (b/VIII-27-1843 Shelby Co, Ind; d/VIII-25-1894) MD Western Res 1886; ng U Mich 1865. *Tr Ind St Med Soc* 1895: 403. *Butler* 1878: 204.

HARING, ISAAC C, W Nyack, NY (d/IV-15-1900) MD UCNY 1850. *Bost m & s jour* 142:444, 1900. *JAMA* 34: 1085, 1900. *Polk* 1896: 1112.

HARKER, FRANK SCOTT, Richmond, Va (b/III-9-1858 Gisbro, Yorks, Engl; d/XII-7-1900) MD Med Coll Va 1882. *Tr Med Soc Va* 1901: 275-77.

HARKNESS, HARVEY W, San Francisco (d VII-10-1901 @80) MD Berkshire 1847. *JAMA* 37: 275, 1901.

HARLAN, DAVID, USN (b/XI-30-1809; d/VII-12-1893 @84) MD Wash'ton Med Coll Balto betw 1831 & 1838. *Bost m & s jour* 129: 104, 1893. *Med annals Md:* 428.

HARLAN, L B, Hot Springs, Ark (d/IX-16-1878 Memphis) MD *Med rec NY* 14:240, 1878. *Tr AMA* 30: 870, 1879.

HARLEY, EDWARD T, Cincinnati (d/V-16-1884) MD Med Coll Ohio 1879. *Med surg rep Phila* 50: 704, 1884.

HARLOW, EDWIN AUGUSTUS WARREN, Wollaston, Mass (b/1813? X-12-1902 @89) MD Harvard 1846; AB 1841. *Bost m & s jour* 147: 448, 1902.

HARLOW, HENRY MILLS, Augusta, Me (b/IV-19-1821 Westminster, Vt; d/IV-5-1893) MD Berkshire 1844. *Tr Me Med Assoc* 1893: 363-66. *Bost m & s jour* 128: 380, 1893. *Atkinson* I:35. *K&B* III:529.

HARLOW, JAMES FREDERICK, Quincy Point, Mass (b/1820? d/III-8-1889 @69) MD Harvard 1847. *Bost m & s jour* 120: 276, 1888.

HARLOW, LEWIS DAVIS, CW-USA; Philadelphia (b/

VI-16-1818 Windsor, Vt; d/VI-23-1895) MD UPa 1845; AB Dartmouth 1843; AM 1857. *U Pa med alum CW*: 1845. *Tr CPP* cent'l vol: 231-32. *JAMA* 25:39, 1895. *Polk* 1886: 817.

HARLOW, ROSCOE LINCOLN, Auburn, Me (b/V-22-1827 Minot, Me; d/VI-3-1885) MD Dartmouth 1852. *Tr Me Med Assoc* 1886: 140-44. *Butler* 1896: 307.

HARMAN, OLIVER S , Pawlet Mass (b/I-19-1769 Suffield, Conn; d/V-25-1852) MD *Bost m & s jour* 47: 185-86, 1852.

HARMON, ELIJAH DEWEY, Chicago; Bennington, Vt; War 1812-USN (b/VIII-20-1782 Bennington; d/II-3-1869) Stud med w/Dr Swift, Manchester, Vt. *Phila med reg & dir* 1871: 299. *K&B* III: 529-30.

HARMON, JOSEPH W , Chicago (b/1815? d/III-29-1900 @85) MD Albany 1845. *Tr Ill St Med Soc* 1900: 574. *JAMA* 34:891, 1900. *Polk* 1896: 364.

HARMON, ROBERDEAU, Oakland, Cal (d/V-18-1904) MD U Cal 1879; PhB 1876. *Calif st jour med* 2:197, 1904. *Polk* 1886: 168.

HARMON, SAMUEL TAPPAN, W Roxbury, Mass (b/1859? d/II-7-1891 @37) MD Harvard 1881. *Bost m & s jour* 134: 180, 1896. *Polk* 1896: 699.

HARNAN, WILLIAM R , New Orleans (b/1861? d/XII 27-1899 @38) MD Tulane 1887. *JAMA* 34:186, 1900. *Polk* 1896: 622.

HARNE, FRANKLIN H , Santee's Mill, Pa (b/1852? d/1906 @54) <MD CPS Balto 1880> *Pa med jour* 10: 118, 1906/07. *Reg Pa phys* 1881-1888: 286. *Flint* 1897:834.

HARNED, SAMUEL P , Woodbridge NJ (d/I-18-1898) MD UCNY 1868. *JAMA* 30:279, 1898. *Polk* 1896: 951.

HARNEY, BENJAMIN FRANKLIN, USA (b/1785? Del; d/VIII-29-1858 Baton Rouge, La) <stud UPa Med Dept> *Tr AMA* 13:821-22, 1860. *Med surg rep Phila* ns1:28, 1858/59. *New Orl m & s jour* 16: 754,1859.

HARNISH, CHARLES ALEXANDER, Alexandria, Pa (b/III-13-1866; d/I-2-1902 Phila) MD UPa 1891. *Pa med jour* 5:211, 260, 295, 1901/02. *Flint* 1897: 793.

HARNISH, TOBIAS, Alexandria, Pa (b/III-6-1826 Waterstreet, Pa; d/III-21-1897) MD Jefferson 1856; AB Franklin & Marshall 1849. *Franklin & Marshall obit rec* 1:114-16. *Polk* 1886: 789.

HARPER, JAMES KENT, Centerville, Md (d/1856) MD UPa 1810. *Med annals Md:* 429.

HARPER, JOSEPH T , CW-USA (d/VII-26-1865) MD *Nat med jour* 1:296, 1870/71.

HARPER, W D , Minden, La (b/1851? d/IX-22-1901 @50) MD Tulane 1880. *New Orl m & s jour* 54: 342, 1901. *Polk* 1886: 415.

HARPKE, HENRY, Milwaukee, Wis (b/1827? d/I-12-1895 @68) MD Würzburg 1879. *JAMA* 24:221, 1895. *Polk* 1890: 1168.

HARRELL, WILLIAM JAMES, Bainbridge, Ga (b/1848; d/1881) MD Jefferson 1869 [?] *Tr AMA* 32: 513-15, 1881.

HARRIMAN, BENJAMIN EVANS, Manchester, NH (b/X-20-1854 Concord, NH; d/V-23-1880) MD Dartmouth 1878. *Tr NH Med Soc* 1880: 125-28.

HARRIMAN, HERBERT JAMES, E Peacham, Vt; Revere, Mass (b/IV-9-1858; d/IV-14-1889) MD Dartmouth 1882; AB 1879.*Bost m & s jour* 120:424, 1889; 121:644, 1889. *Polk* 1886: 472.

HARRIMAN, JAMES LANG, Hudson, Mass (b/V-11-1833 Peacham, Vt; d/XII-28-1905) MD Bowdoin 1857. *Bost m & s j* 154: 28, 1906. *Polk* 1896: 714.

HARRIMAN JOHN W , Iowa City, Ia (d/I-25-1904) MD Iowa St U 1891. *Tr Iowa St Med Soc* 22:341, 1904.

HARRINGTON, DELOS W , Lockport NY (d/X-11-1889 @55) MD U Buffalo 1862. *Med reg NY NJ Conn* 1890:270. *Med s rep Phila* 61:476,1889. *Polk* 1886: 660.

HARRINGTON, HENRY LEONARD, Chicago (d/VIII-31-1896 @50) MD Rush 1875. *JAMA* 27: 613, 1896. *Polk* 1886: 289.

HARRINGTON, I F , Richland & Jackson, Miss (b/I-23-1824; d/III-23-1874) MD Med Coll SC 1848. *Tr AMA* 33:560-61, 1882.

HARRINGTON, JOSIAH V , CW-USA (d/XII-1-1864 Sterling, Conn) MD UCNY 1857. *Nat med jour* 1:296, 1870/71.

HARRIOT, HAMPTON, NYC (b/III-16-1825; d/IV-2-1868) MD CPSNY 1848; AB UCNY 1844. *Tr AMA* 19:421-22, 1868. *Med reg NY NJ Conn* 1868: 325. *Phila med reg & dir* 1871:296. *Med rec* 3:120, 1868-69.

HARRIS, AUGUSTUS, Colebrook, NH (b/IX-29-1811 Paris Me; d/IV-20-1874) MD Bowdoin 1838; ng Dartmouth Med 1837. *Bost m & s j* 90:466, 1874.

HARRIS, BENJAMIN H , Groveland, Ill (d/IV-6-1895) MD St Louis Med Coll 1855. *JAMA* 24: 609, 1895. *Polk* 1890: 333.

HARRIS, CHAPIN AARON, Baltimore (b/V-6-1806 Onondaga Co, NY; d/IX-29-1860) Lic Bd Med Censors 1829. *Med surg rep Phila* ns5:[26] 1860/61. *Nashville jour med & surg* 19:480, 1860. *Bost m & s j* 63:208,1861. *Med annals Md*:429. *K&B* III:531-32.

HARRIS, CHARLES MORRIS BAINBRIDGE, Washington, DC; CW-USN (b/X-2-1827 Phila; d/I-8-1901) MD UPa 1848; AB 1845. *Matrics Coll UP*: 1845.

HARRIS, CHARLES TAYLOR, Ypsilanti Mich (b/II-10 1818 Cato, NY; d/VI-4-1890) <MD "NY 1856"> *Med vis* 6:247, 1890. *Polk* 1886:710. *Cleave.* Homeopath.

HARRIS, CLEMENT R, Staunton Va(d/XI-1-1872) MD Jefferson 1842. *Tr Med Soc Va* 1872:26; 1875:102.

HARRIS, DOUGLASS, Whitney, Tex (d/V-15-1899) MD Pa Med Coll 1857. *JAMA* 32:1269, 1899. *Tex med jour* 14:715, 1898-99. *Polk* 1896: 1457.

HARRIS, EDWARD W , ? (d/1878 Sumnerville, Tenn) MD *Tr AMA* 30:870, 189.

HARRIS, ELISHA, NYC; CW-US San Comm; (b/III-5 1824 Westminster, Vt; d/I-31-1884 Albany) MD CPSNY 1849. *JAMA* 2:194-95, 1884. *Bost m & s j* 110:

141, 1884. *Atkinson* I:676. *K&B* III:532.

HARRIS, FRANCIS LEE, Buffalo (b/Pa; d/II-22-1876 NYC) MD UPa 1832. *Med reg NY NJ Conn* 1876: 242.

HARRIS, GEORGE ROBERT, Rayne, La (d/VII-31-1904) MD CPSNY 1885. *New Orl m & s j* 57: 284, 1904.

HARRIS, HENRY S , Warren NJ (b/XII-6-1795 Weston; d/VI-21-1881) Lic 1818-19 Med Soc NJ. *Tr Med Soc NJ* 1882:184-86. *Butler* 1878: 470.

HARRIS, JAMES A, ?Tenn (d/1901) MD Jefferson 1884. *JAMA* 37:276, 1901. ?*Polk* 1886:916 (Cornsville, Va)

HARRIS, JAMES BURR, Sag Harbor, NY (d/IV-17-1896 @36) MD CPSNY 1882. *JAMA* 26:1038, 1896. *Polk* 1890: 787.

HARRIS, JAMES OTEY, Washington, DC; CW-CSA (b/1840 Alexandria, Va; d/XII-9-1882) MD UPa 1861. *U Pa med alum CW*: 1861. *Hist Med Soc DC* :275. *Butler* 1874: 92.

HARRIS, JOANIS ORLANDO, Ottawa, Ill (d/I-10-1905 @76) MD Geneva 1851. *Ill med jour* 7:242, 1905.

HARRIS, JOHN STUART, Fountain City, Ind (b/II-22-1836 Westminster, NC; d/VII-23-1890) MD U Mich 1864; ng Haverford. *Hav'd biog cat*:82. *Polk* 1886:319.

HARRIS, JONAS COWDREY, Arlington Mass (b/1820? d/II-10-1895 @75) MD Berkshire 1840. *Bost m & s j* 132:172, 1895.

HARRIS, JOSEPH V [or H], Canton, Ill (d/V-7-1900 @61) MD Rush 1871. *Ill med jour* ns2: 48, 1900. *JAMA* 34: 1356, 1900. *Polk* 1896:365.

HARRIS, LUTHER METCALF, War 1812-USA; Jamaica Plain, Mass (b/V-7-1789 Brookline, Mass; d/I-28 1865) MD Brown 1811; AB 1811. *Bost m & s j* 72:46, 1865. *Brown hist cat*: 107.

HARRIS, MARY BRIGGS, Andover, Mass (b/III-25-1847 E Machias, Me; d/I-6-1886) MD Boston U 1875; att New Engl Female Med Coll 1872. *New Engl med gaz* 21:143, 1886. *Polk* 1886: 453. Homeopath.

HARRIS, MAYNARD W , Bivins & Queen City, Tex (d/VII-20-1906 @29 San Angelo) MD Georgia Coll Ecl Surg 1899; stud U Ga. *Tex st jour med* 2: 144,1906.

HARRIS, NATHAN COY, Auburn, Me (b/I-25-1817 Minot; d/V-15-1875) MD Bowdoin 1842. *Tr Me Med Assoc* 1874-76: 428-29.

HARRIS, NATHAN OVERTON, Atlanta, Ga (d/III-6-1896) <MD Southern Med Coll Atl 1881> MD Bellevue 1883. *NC med jour* 37: 189, 1896. *Polk* 1886: 225.

HARRIS, RALPH, Macomb, Ill (d/III-19-1895 @82) MD Hahnemann Chic 1869. *JAMA* 24: 497, 1895. *Polk* 1890: 338.

HARRIS, RICE C , Elletsville Ind (b/XI-15-1834 Owen Co, Ind; d/X-15-1894) ng U Mich Med Dept 1856-57. *Tr Ind St Med Soc* 1895: 406. *Butler* 1878: 205.

HARRIS, ROBERT, Washington, DC (d/XII-26-1880) MD UPa 1860. *Hist Med Soc DC:* 300.

HARRIS, ROBERT LOCKE, Fulshear, Tex (b/1838; d/X-11-1905 NYC) MD Tulane 1861. *Tex st jour med* 1: 184, 1905/06.

HARRIS, ROBERT PATTERSON, CW-USA; Philadelphia (b/XI-15-1822; d/II-20-1899) MD UPa 1844; AB 1841. *JAMA* 32: 506, 1899. *Tr CPP* cent vol: 232. *K&B* III: 533. *Matrics Coll UPa*: 124.

HARRIS, STEPHEN, Pa (d/XI-18-1851) MD UPa 1819. *Tr Med Soc Pa* 1:185, 1856. *Med reporter* (W Chester) 2:16-17, 1854.

HARRIS, STEPHEN R , San Francisco (b/1801; d/1879) MD CPSNY 1826. *Tr AMA* 31:1046-47, 1880.

HARRIS, THADDEUS WILLIAM, Cambridge, Mass (b/XI-12-1795; d/I-16-1856) MD Harvard 1820; AB 1815. Palmer's *Necrol Harv alum*: 86. *K&B* III:523-24.

HARRIS, THOMAS, USN (b/1784; d/III-4-1861) MD UPa 1809. *Med surg rep Phila* ns5:635, 1860/61. *Nashville j m & s* 20:492, 1861. *Tr AMA* 14:216, 1864.

HARRIS, THOMAS WEST, Chapel Hill, NC; CW-CSA (b/XII-15-1839; d/1888) MD UCNY 1868; <MD Paris> AB UNC 1859. *Tr NC M S* 1894:[203] *Polk* 1886: 721.

HARRIS, WILLIAM, Chester Co, Pa (b/VIII-18-1792; d/III-3-1861) MD UPa 1812. *Tr AMA* 14:209, 1863. *Tr M S Pa* 1:128-30, 1862. *Med s rep Phila* ns5: 606, 1860/61.

HARRIS, WILLIAM AUGUSTUS, USN 1844-61 (b/III 4-1822 Phila; d/X-25-1881 Baltimore) MD UPa 1843; AB Princeton 1840. *U Pa med alum CW*: 1843.

HARRIS, WILLIAM C , Roachdale, Ind (b/IX-5-1827 Knox Co, Tenn; d/V-1-1901) MD Rush 1848. *Tr Ind St Med Soc* 1901: 486. *Butler* 1878: 205.

HARRIS, WILLIAM F , Ferris, Ill (d/XI-3-1901) MD CPS Keokuk 1885. *Ill med jour* ns3:346, 1901.

HARRIS, WILLIAM HUME, Louisville (d/III-20-1894 @ 60) MD U Nashville 1856. *JAMA* 22:523, 1894. *Polk* 1890: 470.

HARRIS, ZINA H , Brooklyn to 1840 (b/c1792 Vt; d/IV 30-1859) MD ? *Tr Am Inst Hom* 1870:647. *King* 1:89. Homeopath.

HARRISON, BENJAMIN, Richmond & Mill Wood, Va (d/IX-10-1900) MD UVa 1883. *Tr Med Soc Va* 1900: 334-35. *Polk* 1886: 921.

HARRISON, BENJAMIN FRANKLIN, Wallingford, Conn; CW-USA (b/IV-19-1811 N Branford; d/IV-23-1886) MD Yale 1836. *Proc Conn Med Soc* ns3:165-68, 1887. *Atkinson* I: 306-07. *Butler* 1878: 77.

HARRISON, DAVID, Middlesex Co, Conn (d/1856) MD Yale 1825. *Proc Conn Med Soc* 1857: 21. *Bost m & s j* 56: 287, 1857.

HARRISON, ELISHA, Washington, DC (b/1762 Cecil Co, MD; d/VIII-24-1819) MD ? *Med annals Md:* 430. *Hist Med Soc DC:* 218.

HARRISON, GEORGE BYRD, CW-CSA; Washington, DC (b/VIII-30-1844 Ampthill, Va; d/VII-19-1898 Cape May, NJ) MD UVa 1879; stud CPSNY & UCNY. *JAMA* 31: 314, 1898. *Hist M S DC:* 316. *Polk* 1896: 303.

HARRISON, GEORGE E , Springfield, NY (b/1858? d/

IV–24–1902) MD Bennett 1880. *Bost m & s j* 146:480, 1902. *Polk* 1886:736 (Ashland, O).

HARRISON, ISHAM, White Rock , Tex (d/XI–21–1892) MD U Louisville 1885. *Tex cour–rec med* 10:92, 1892. *Polk* 1890: 628.

HARRISON, JOHN, Washington, DC (b/Prince Georges Co, Md; d/III–4–1825) MD *Hist Med Soc DC:*217.

HARRISON, JOHN BATES, Union City, Tenn (d/VIII–27–1899 @70) MD St Louis Med Coll 1872. *JAMA* 33:683, 1899. *Tex m news* 8:587, 1898. *Polk* 1886: 874.

HARRISON, JOHN HOFFMAN, New Orleans (b/VIII–30–1808; d/III–19–1849) <MD U Md 1831> *New Orl m &s j* 6:306–20, 1849. *Buff m&s j* 5:528–38, 555, 1849. *Tr AMA* 29:662–71.

HARRISON, JOHN POLLARD, Louisville; Cincinnati (b/VI–5–1796 Louisville; d/IX–1–1849) MD UPa 1819. *Bost m & s j* 2:296, 1849. *Southern m & s j* 5:640, 1849. *Tr AMA* 3:444–45, 1850. *K&B* III: 534–35.

HARRISON, OSCAR GEORGE, NYC (d/I–14 or III–4–1894) MD CPSNY 1891; PhG NY Coll Pharm 1890. *Med reg NY NJ Conn* 1895: 225.

HARRISON, RANDOLPH, ?Williamsburg, Va; CW–CSA (b/II–12–1831 Richmond; d/VI–14–1894) MD UPa 1853. *U Pa med alum CW*: 1853.

HARRISON, RANDOLPH, USN 1851–56; CSA 1861– (b/I–16–1828 nr Richmond; d/IX–23–1863) MD UPa 1851; AB Princeton 1848; AM 1851. *U Pa med alum CW*: 1851.

HARRISON, ROBERT HENRY, W Tenn; Miss; Columbus, Tex 1869– ; CW–CSA (b/XI–13–1826 Gainesville Ga; d/X–17–1905) <MD Botanico–Med Coll Cinc 1846> MD Med Coll Ala 1873. *Tex st jour med* 1:220, 1905/06.

HARRISON, VIRGINIUS WILLIAMS, Mt Pleasant, Va; CW–CSA (b/X–7–1829; d/IV–29–1873) MD UPa 1851; att Randolph–Macon. *U Pa med alum CW*:1851.

HARRISON, WILLIAM DAVID, Philadelphia; CW–USA (b/1838 London, Engl; d/IV–21–1876) MD UPa 1866. *U Pa med alum CW*: 1866.

HARRISON, WILLIAM GILPIN Jr, Baltimore (b/1842 Howard Co, Md; d/VIII–30–1895) MD Bellevue 1864. *Med annals Md:* 430. *Polk* 1893: 560.

HARRISS, WILLIAM WHITE, CW–CSA; Wilmington, NC (b/I–13–1824; d/XII–7–1901) MD UCNY 1846; AB UNC 1842; AM 1847. *UNC cat*: 262.

HARROD, SANFORD HICKMAN, Canton, Ind (b/VIII 20–1827 Austin, Ind; d/II–11–1888) MD Med Coll Ohio 1857. *Tr Ind St Med Soc* 1888: 199. *Butler* 1878:205.

HARRY, SAMUEL McCLAINE, Rising Sun, Md (d/V–25–1868 @35) MD UPa 1856. *Phila med reg & dir* 1871: 297.

HARSEN, JACOB Jr, NYC (b/II–16–1808; d/XII–31–1862) MD CPSNY 1829; AB Columbia 1825. *Tr AMA* 14:204–05, 1864. *Bost m&s j* 67: 490, 1862. *Med surg rep Phila* ns9: 325–26, 1862/63.

HARSH, ISAIAH MORSE, Cumberland, Griswold, Marne, Ia (d/1891 @41) MD CPS Chicago 1883. *Tr Ia St Med Soc* 18: 410, 1900.

HARSHBERGER, ABRAM Jr, CW–USA; Philadelphia (b/XI–23 1839 Zion, Pa; d/IV–10–1902) MD UPa 1868. *Pa med jour* 6:260, 1902/03. *U Pa med alum CW*: 1868. *Flint* 1897: 818.

HART, ALEXANDER, New Orleans (b/V–30–1813 Charleston, SC; d/V–14–1877) MD U La 1836. *New Orl m & s j* 5:249–50, 1877.

HART, ALEXANDER CHAMBERS, Philadelphia (d/X 30–1884 @73) MD UPa 1836. *Med surg rep Phila* 51:572, 1884. *Butler* 1878: 664.

HART, ANDREW J , Pacific Grove, Cal (d/V–7–1899 @67) MD Castleton 1860. *JAMA* 32: 1269, 1899. *Polk* 1886: 167.

HART, ARCH COOMBS, San Francisco (b/I–14–1869 China, Me; d/V–28–1901) MD CPS San Francisco 1897; PhG; DDS. *Cal st jour med* 1:229–30. 1903.

HART, BYRON, CW–USA (d/X–8–1864) MD Jefferson 1854. *Nat med jour* 1:296, 1870/71.

HART, CHARLES A , USA; Plainfield NJ (b/XII–27–1842; d/VII–24–1885) <MD NY Med Coll 1860> *Med reg NY NJ Conn* 1887: 267. *Tr M S NJ* 1886–87: 155 ff.

HART, CHARLES S, NYC (b/V–25–1868) MD ? *Med s rep Phila* 18: 504, 1868. *Phila med reg & dir* 1871:297.

HART, HENRY W , Council Bluffs, Ia (d/1886) MD Geneva 1846. *Tr Ia St Med Soc* 13: 410, 1900. *Polk* 1886: 354.

HART, JOHN, NYC; CW–USA (b/II–9–1810 Danville, Vt; d/VIII–9–1867 Pittsfield, Mass) MD CPSNY 1835. *Med reg NY NJ Conn* 1868: 326. *Tr AMA* 19: 407–08, 1868.

HART, JOHN, Boston Highlands, Mass (d/VII–29–1873 @ 49) MD Harvard 1863. *Bost m&s j* ns12:148, 1873. *Mass Med Soc cat* 1894.

HART, JOHN BEAUREGARD, Towson, Md (b/VI–20–1862 Baltimore; d/VI–29–1901) MD U Md 1883. *Med annals Md:* 431. *Polk* 1893: 561.

HART, MARTIN G , Chicago (d/XI–26–1904) MD Bennett 1883. *Ill med jour* 7:126,1905. *Polk* 1886:264. Ecl.

HART, SAMUEL, Beverly, Mass 1821–28; Oswego & Brooklyn NY 1829–55 (b/XI–27–1796 Reading, Mass; d/IX–13–1878) MD Harvard 1821; AB 1817. *Med reg NY NJ Conn* 1879: 193. *Bost m & s j* 99: 742, 1878. *Tr Med Soc St NY* 1879:579–80. *Atkinson* I:297.

HART, SAMUEL WALDO, New Britain, Conn (b/V–22 1825; d/XII–31–1891) Hon MD Yale 1855; att Berkshire & Woodstock. *JAMA* 18: 82, 1892. *Proc Conn Med Soc* 1882: 860–61. *Atkinson* I: 329. *Butler* 1878: 77.

HART, WILLIAM H , Pittsburgh (d/1894) <MD Hahnemann Chic 1883> *JAMA* 23:918, 1894. *Polk* 1886: 829. *Off'l reg Pa phys* 1881–88: 32.

HART, WILLIAM WESLEY, Lodi, Miss (b/IV–26–1828 Robertson Co, Tenn; d/V–27–1887) MD U Louis–

ville 1849. *Tr Miss St Med Assoc* 1888: 63. *Atkinson* I: 665. *Polk* 1886: 529.

HARTIGAN, JAMES FRENCH, Washington (b/XII-20 1843 Limerick Ire; d/I-31-1894 Trieste Aus) MD Georgetown 1868. *Hist M S DC:*295. *Polk* 1886: 212.

HARTLOFF, RICHARD, Evansville, Ind (b/VIII-16-1845 Prussia; d/VI-18-1900) MD U Louisville 1870. *Tr Ind St Med Soc* 1901: 487. *JAMA* 34:1676, 1900. *Polk* 1886: 317.

HARTMAN, ANDREW, Towson, Md (b/V-4-1818 Greencastle, Pa; d/XII-15-1884) MD Wash U Balto 1839; att Pa Coll, Gettysburg. *Med ann Md:* 431. *Med bull m & s* 7:32, 1884. *Atkinson* I: 350. *Butler* 1874: 312.

HARTMAN, CHARLES A , Cleveland, O; CW-USA (d/V-3-1863 Chancellorsville, Va) MD ? *Nat med jour* 1:296, 1870/71. *Med surg rep Phila* 10: 112, 1863. *Buffalo m&s j* 2:354, 1863. *Bost m&s j* 68: 430, 1863.

HARTMAN, ROBERT L , Independence, Pa (b/France; d/IV-24-1897 @66) MD ? *JAMA* 28: 1045, 1897. *Off'l reg Pa phys* 1881-88: 394. *Polk* 1896: 1284.

HARTMAN, WILLIAM BENJAMIN, CW-USA; St Marys, Pa (b/IX-14-1833 Williamsport; d/XI-11-1899) MD UPa 1864. *Pa med jour* 3:384, 1899/1900. *JAMA* 33: 1441, 1899. *U Pa med alum CW*: 1864. *Butler* 1878: 715.

HARTMAN, WILLIAM DELL, West Chester, Pa (b/XII 25-1817 Chester Co Pa; d/VIII-17-1899) MD UPa 1839. *Pa med jour* 4:158-61, 1900/01. *JAMA* 33:558, 1899. *Flint* 1897: 839.

HARTMANN, ALEXIS CARL, St Louis, Mo (d/I-10-1899 @60) MD St Louis Med Coll 1878. *JAMA* 32:145, 1899. *Polk* 1886: 562.

HARTMANN, JACOB, NYC (d/VIII-18-1901 @63) MD St Louis Med Coll 1875; MD U Toronto 1878; MD CPS Ontario 1878; MD Trinity Med Coll 1878; RCPS (Edinb) 1875. *JAMA* 37:595, 1901. *Polk* 1886: 680.

HARTNETT, MAURICE KING, Boston (d/V-14-1894 @70) MD Harvard 1859. *Bost m & s j* 130: 528, 1894. *Butler* 1878: 340.

HARTSHORNE, EDWARD, Philadelphia; CW-US San Comm (b/V-14-1818; d/VI-22-1885) MD UPa 1840; AB Princeton 1837; AM. *Tr CPP* cent vol: 232. *U Pa med alum CW*: 1840. *Atkinson* I:46. *K&B* III:536.

HARTSHORNE, HENRY, Philadelphia; Tokyo (b/III 16-1823; d/II-10-1897) MD UPa 1845; AM Haverford 1860; LLD 1884. *Tr CPP* cent vol: 232-33; 3s19: lxv-lxxvi, 1897. *Bost m & s j* 136:196, 1897. *JAMA* 28: 380, 1897. *Atkinson* I: 458.

HARTSHORNE, JOSEPH, Philadelphia (b/XII-12-1779 Alexandria, Va; d/VIII-20-1850 Brandywine Spr, Pa) MD UPa 1805. *Tr CPP* cent vol: 233; ns1:201-19, 1850/53. *K&B* III: 537.

HARTSWICK, JOHN GEORGE, Clearfield, Pa (b/IV-17-1830 Boalsburg; d/III-14-1896) MD UPa 1854. *Pa med jour* 2:163-64, 1898. *Butler* 1878: 715.

HARTT, HENRY LE BARON, NYC (b/1841; d/II-20-1880) MD NY Med Coll 1863. *Med reg NY NJ Conn* 1880: 236. *Med rec NY* 17:274, 1880. *Med surg rep Phila* 42:220, 1880. *Butler* 1878: 514.

HARTT, JOHN CHARLES, Brooklyn (b/X-21-1861; d/XI-24-1901) MD LICH 1892. *Bost m&s j* 145: 638, 1901.

HARTWELL, BENJAMIN HALL, Ayer, Mass (d/I-6-1904 @59) MD Jefferson 1868. *Bost m&s j* 150:56, 576-77, 1904. *Polk* 1896: 691.

HARTWELL, FRANCIS WAYLAND, Manitou Spr, Colo 1884- (b/1857 New Marlborough, Mass; d/VIII-20-1890 @33) MD Boston U 1878. *New Engl med gaz* 25:440, 1890. *Polk* 1886: 186. Homeopath.

HARTZELL, FRANKLIN KERR, Churchtown, Pa (d/XI 4-1894 @50) MD UPa 1868. *JAMA* 23:768, 1894.

HARVEY, CHARLES W, Buffalo (b/III-17-1810 Albany; d/X-15-1886) MD Buffalo 1848; att Lafayette 1836; Union 2 yrs. *Lafay'te, Men of*:139. *Polk* 1886:652.

HARVEY, EDWARD J , Brooklyn (d/X-27-1895 Red Bank, NJ) MD LICH 1874. *JAMA* 25:911, 1895.

HARVEY, ELLWOOD, Chester, Pa (b/XI-30-1820 Chadd's Ford; d/III-23-1889) MD UPa 1843. *Med bull med & surg* 11:124,1889. *Atkinson* I:572. *Polk* 1886:795.

HARVEY, EZRA WILSON, Bancroft, Mich (d/VIII-1893) MD Detroit Med Coll 1877; ng U Mich Med Dept 1874-75. *Chic med rec* 5:206, 1893. *Polk* 1886: 483.

HARVEY, HENRY PRENTISS, Crawford, Miss; USN 1872- (d/XII-25/26-1892) MD ? *Bost m&s j* 128:28, 1893.

HARVEY, JAMES [JOSEPH] ALBERT, Philadelphia (d/II-12-1902 @30) MD Hahnemann Phila 1900. *Pa med jour* 6:260, 1902/03. Homeopath.

HARVEY, JOHN GORIN, Blue Mound & Decatur, Ill (b/c1839; d/VIII-17-1905) MD U Louisville 1862. *Ill med jour* 8:256, 1905. *Polk* 1886: 255.

HARVEY, JOHN MURDOCK, NYC (b/IX-28-1842 Newport,NS; d/XII-4-1875) MD Bellevue 1871. *Med reg NY NJ Conn* 1876: 242. *Med rec NY* 11: 16, 1876.

HARVEY, JOSEPH R PAUL, Allegheny City, Pa (b/XI 25-1836 Northampton; d/VII-7-1866 @29) MD Hahnemann Phila 1865. *Med surg rep Phila* 15:84, 1866. *Tr Am Inst Hom* 1893: 144. *Hahn mo* 2:48. 1866/67. Homeopath.

HARVEY, OBED, Galt, Cal (b/IX-7-1825 Wayne Co, NY; d/I-17-1894) Hon MD UCNY 1858; <MD U Iowa 1858> *JAMA* 22:314, 1894. *Tr Med Soc Cal* 24:294, 1894. *Polk* 1890: 186.

HARVEY, ROBERT S , Spokane Falls, Wash (d/I-9-1894) MD Wash U Balto 1872. *JAMA* 22:97, 1894. *Polk* 1890: 1141.

HARVEY, THOMAS B , Indianapolis, Ind (b/XI-29-1827 Clinton, O; d/XII-5-1889) MD Med Coll Ohio 1857. *Tr Ind St Med Soc* 1889:158. *Buffalo m&s j* 29: 384, 1890. *JAMA* 13:865, 1889. *Bost m&s j* 121:596, 1889. *Butler* 1878: 205.

HARVEY, ZACHARY T, Council Grove, Kans (d/XI-15 1901) MD CPS Chic 1883. *Ill med jour* ns3:399, 1902.

HARWOOD, DANIEL, Dorchester, Mass (b/III-21-1801; d/X-2-1881) MD Bowdoin 1828. *Bost m&s j* 105: 556, 623, 1881.

HARWOOD, EDWARD COKE, NYC (b/XI-28-1838 or XI-26-1839 Barrington, Vt; d/I-13-1891) MD Bellevue 1868. *Bost m&s j* 124:104,1891. *Med reg NY NJ Conn* 1892:278. *Med rec* 13:72,1891. *Atkinson* I: 530.

HARWOOD, JOHN MARTIN, Shelbyville, Ky (b/XII-24-1840 Hartford; d/1897) MD U Louisville 1865. *Tr Ky St Med Soc* 6:297-98, 1897. *Polk* 1886:405.

HASBROUCK, CHARLES, Hackensack, NJ (b/XI-11-1818, NYC; d/XI-25-1877) MD Fairfield 1839. *Tr AMA* 29:671-72, 1878. *Med rec* 13:455, 1877. *Atkinson* I:607.

HASBROUCK, DU BOIS, Paramus, NJ (b/IX-16-1825 NY; d/III-30-1865) MD UCNY 1848. *Tr AMA* 18: 332, 1867.

HASBROUCK, EVERETT, Brooklyn (d/III-16-1906) MD NY Homeop 1865. *Tr Am Inst Hom* 1906: 767-68. *Polk* 1886: 646. Homeopath.

HASBROUCK, JACOB L , Monticello, NY (b?I-25-1807; d/VII-15-1891) MD CPSNY 1833. *Med reg NY NJ Conn* 1892: 278. *Northwest med jour* 19:118, 1891.

HASBROUCK, JOSIAH, Port Ewen, NY (b/I-1-1830 Marbletown; d/III-25-1889) MD Albany 1855. *Tr Med Soc St NY* 1892: 439. *Butler* 1874: 542.

HASBROUCK, MOSES CANTINE, Nyack, NY (b/XI-23-1808 Marbletown; d/X-28-1870) MD Fairfield 1835. *Tr Med Soc St NY* 1872: 354 ff.

HASBROUCK, STEPHEN, NYC (b/IV-24-1794; d/XII 28-1881) MD CPSNY 1817; AB Union Coll 1815. *Med reg NY NJ Conn* 1882: 228.

HASKELL, BENJAMIN CUMMINS, Rockport, Mass (b/X-22-1810 Gloucester; d/I-21-1878) MD Bowdoin 1837; AB Amherst 1832. *Amherst, Men of*: 1832.

HASKELL, CHARLES HENRY, So Abington, Mass (d/XI-10-1863 @31) MD ? *Bost m&s j* 69:348 368, 1863.

HASKELL, JOSEPH HENRY, Philadelphia (b/Mass; d/IV-13-1863) MD Jefferson 1844. *Tr Med Soc Pa* 3:533, 1864. *Bost m & s j* 68:290, 1863. *Tr AMA* 16:640, 1865. *Med surg rep Phila* 10: 48, 1863.

HASKELL, PELEG SPRAGUE, Parkman, Me 1856-57; Hartland 1857-59; Stockton 1859-79; St Paul, Minn 1879- (b/V-11-1832 St Albans, Vt; d/IX-26-1890) MD Bowdoin 1856. *Tr Minn St Med Soc*1891: 198; 1893: 121. *Polk* 1890: 619.

HASKINS, ALFRED LEONARD, Boston (b/III-10-1838 Hardwick, Mass; d/IV-2-1876) MD Harvard 1865; AB Amherst 1861. *Bost m&s j* ns17: 431, 1876. *Med rec med & surg* 11:277, 1876.

HASKINS, E B , Clarksville, Tenn (d/IV-11-1868) MD U Louisville 1851. *Bost m&s j* 1:386, 1868. *Nashville j m & s* ns3:567-68; ns5:531, 1870.

HASLETT, J D S , CW-USA (d/X-8-1862 Perry, Ky) MD ? *Nat med jour* 1:296, 1870/71.

HASLETT, JOHN, USN (b/XII- -1799; d/IX-28-1878) MD UPa 1822; AB Harvard 1819. *Med reg NY NJ Conn* 1879: 193.

HASSE, EDWARD, St Louis (d/IV-30-1887) MD St Louis Med Coll 1852. *New Orl m&s j* ns14: 985-86, 1887. *Polk* 1886: 563.

HASSELL, EBENEZER, NYC (d/I-12-1862 Bridgetown, Barbadoes @30) MD CPSNY 1853. *Med surg rep Phila* ns7:504, 1861/62.

HASSENPLUG, JACOB H , Philadelphia (d/XI-25 1899) MD Jefferson 1851. *JAMA* 33:1504, 1899. *Polk* 1896: 1306.

HASSLER, JAMES POWER, Cochranton, Pa (d/IX 1899 Meadville) MD U Mich 1864; AM Allegheny Coll 1858. *Pa med jour* 3:386,1899/1900. *Polk* 1886:795.

HASSON, ALEXANDER BRECKINRIDGE, USA 1849-77 (b/1825 Baltimore; d/III-19-1877 Ft Trumbull, Conn) MD ? *Med rec* 12:208, 1877. *Tr AMA* 28:641-42, 1877. *Butler* 1878: iii. *Heitman*.

HASTINGS, ADELAIDE CURTIS, NYC (d/II-7-1882) MD Woman's Med Coll NY 1880. *Med reg NY NJ Conn* 1882: 229.

HASTINGS, BENJAMIN FRANKLIN, Whitman, Mass (b/VIII-23-1836 Richmond; d/VI-28-1901) MD UCNY 1863. *Bost m&s j* 145:28, 52, 1901. *Polk* 1896: 726.

HASTINGS, DAN HYDE, NYC (d/IV-15-1884 @72) MD NY Med Coll 1859. *Med s rep Phila* 50: 544, 1884.

HASTINGS, JOHN, USN 1841-50 (d/XII-12-1891 San Francisco) MD UPa 1840. *Tr CPP* cent vol: 233.

HASTINGS, JOSEPH WILCOX, Warren, Mass; CW-USA (b/II-19-1834 Lenox; d/IX-23-1895) MD Harvard 1856. *Bost m&s j* 133:356, 1895. *Harvard in CW*: 246. *Polk* 1886: 475.

HASTINGS, PANET MARSHALL, Hartford Conn (b/VIII-17-1816 Clinton, NY; d/VI-4-1898) MD CPSNY 1842; AB Hamilton 1838. *Proc Conn Med Soc* 1899: 375-78. *Polk* 1896: 279.

HASTINGS, WILLIAM HENRY ROWE, Boston (d/II-16-1900 @ c60) MD Harvard 1868. *Bost m&s j* 142:208, 234, 314, 1900. *JAMA* 34:60, 1900. *Polk* 1896: 699.

HATCH, ELISHA, Hillsboro, NH (b/VII-17-1796 Alstead; d/XI-12-1863) MD Dartmouth 1824. *Med surg rep Phila* 10:426, 1863.

HATCH, HENRY, Quincy, Ill (b/II-22-1848 Phila; d/VII-24-1905) MD Louisville Med Coll 1873; MD LICH 1880. *Ill med jour* 8:185, 1905. *Polk* 1886: 294.

HATCH, HENRY LEE, Jacksonville, Ill (d/XI-24-1899 @55) MD Missouri Med Coll 1873. *Tr Ill St Med Soc* 1899-1900: 352. *Polk* 1886: 283.

HATCH, HORACE, Burlington, Vt to 1854 (b/V-13-1788 Tunbridge, Vt; d/X-17-1872 NYC) MD Dartmouth 1817; AB 1814: "d/X-18-1873." *Med surg rep Phila* 29:360, 1873. *Tr Vt Med Soc* 1883: 106.

HATCH, HORACE, New Haven, Conn (d/VIII-28-

Spec. educ'l status abbrev. as: ***ng*** = college verified attendance without degree;

1891) MD Harvard 1846; AB U Vt 1842. *Bost m&s j* 125: 284, 1891.

HATCH, IRA, Warrensville, Ill (b/XI-7-1800 Alstead, NH; d/X-1-1879) MD Castleton 1829; AB Union 1826. *Chic med jour* 39: 557, 1879.

HATCH, JOHNSON C , Kent, Conn (b/IX-20-1792; d/VIII-24-1854) MD Yale 1823. *Proc Conn Med Soc* 1855: 51-53.

HATCH, PHILO LEWIS, Dubuque, Ia 1852-58; Minneapolis 1858-92; Santa Barbara, Cal 1892- (b/V-21 1823 Sherburne, NY; d/V-24-1904) MD Cleveland Homeop 1857. *Tr Am Inst Hom* 1905:843. *Minn med monthly* 2:113, 1887. *Polk* 1886: 514. Homeopath.

HATCH, THURSTON B , San Francisco (b/1845; d/1875) MD LICH 1865. *Tr AMA* 31:1047-49, 1880.

HATCH, WILLIAM, Sidney, Me 1827-31; Georgetown, Ky 1831-40 (b/VII-27-1806 Exeter, NH; d/VII-23-1876 Hannibal, Mo) MD Bowdoin 1827; AB 1824. *Bowdoin cat*: 1824.

HATCHARD, THOMAS, Huron, SD (d/II-15-1900 Milwaukee, Wis) <MRCPS (Lond) 1840> *JAMA* 34:574, 1900. *Polk* 1886: 957.

HATCHER, J E , Bowling Green, Ky (d/III-10-1900 @34 Okla) MD ? *JAMA* 34:766, 1900.

HATFIELD, GEORGE L , Uniontown, Pa (d/IX-26-1906 @31) MD Jefferson 1900. *Jeffersonian* 8:9, 1906. *Pa med jour* 10: 53, 1906.

HATFIELD, NATHAN LEWIS, Philadelphia (b/VIII-2-1804; d/VIII-29-1887) MD Jefferson 1826. *Tr CPP* 1887: 233.

HATHAWAY, CHARLES E, NYC (d/IX-25 1863 @29 St Johns NB) MD CPSNY 1855. *Bost m&s j* 69:248, 1863.

HATHAWAY, EDMUND VALENTINE, Berkeley, Cal (b/I-18-1818 Freetown, Mass; d/XII-10-1899) MD UPa 1844; AB Brown 1840; AM. *Brown hist cat*: 1840.

HATHAWAY, FRANK ALTON, Taunton, Mass (b/X-29-1861; d/VI-14-1891) MD UCNY 1883; ng Amherst 1882. *Amherst, Men of*: 1882.

HATHAWAY, JOHN EATON, Shrewsbury, Mass (d/I-12-1862 @ 34) MD Harvard 1852. *Bost m&s j* 65: 510, 1861.

HATHAWAY, JOSEPH CUSHMAN, Ottawa, Ill (d/I-21 1901) MD Jefferson 1856. *Ill med jour* ns2:533, 1901.

HATHAWAY, MARY TUFTS, E Wareham, Mass (d/V-13-1887 Lapeer, Mich) MD U Mich Homeop Med Coll 1886. *Med vis* 3:207, 1887. *Polk* 1886:465. Homeopath.

HATHEWAY, CHARLES EDWIN, St John, NB (b/V-14-1834; d/IX-29-1863) MD CPSNY 1855; ng Bowdoin Coll 1851. *Bowdoin cat*: 1854.

HATTON, JOHN B , Des Moines, Ia (b/VII-7-1839; d/VIII-7-1898) MD CPS Keokuk 1870. *JAMA* 31: 427, 1898. *Polk* 1886: 366.

HAUGHEY, JAMES, Scooba, Miss (d/VII-26-1896 @ 78) MD U Louisville 1846. *JAMA* 27: 503, 1896.

HAUPTMANN, JOHN HENRY, Erie, Pa (d/III 6-1898 @34) MD U Mich 1892. *JAMA* 30:683, 1898.

HAUSMANN, WILLIAM, Kewaskum, Wis (b/XII-6-1855 Buffalo; d/I-14-1902) MD Chicago Med Coll 1874. *Tr Wis St M S* 36:417-18, 1902. *Polk* 1896: 1551.

HAUXHURST, D CLAUDE, Battle Creek, Mich (d/II-16-1882 @39 Paris, Fr) MD U Mich 1877; DDS 1876. *JAMA* 1:254, 1883.

HAVA, JEAN G , New Orleans, La (b/VII-12-1833 Cuba; d/I-15-1894) MD Paris 1859. *New Orl m&s j* 21:712-15, 1894. *Polk* 1890: 490.

HAVEN, ALFRED HOUSTON, CW-USA (d/1895) MD Harvard 1861; AB 1867 [listed w/class of 1858] AM 1870. *Harvard in CW*: 113.

HAVEN, ALLISON M , Pennellville, NY (d/I-7 1899 @42) MD Balto U 1890. *JAMA* 32: 196, 1899.

HAVEN, CYRUS, Hannibal, NY (d/I-25-1895) MD Bellevue 1872. *JAMA* 24: 221, 1895. *Polk* 1886: 663.

HAVEN, GEORGE, Boston (b/VII-13-1861; d/IX-27-1903) MD Harvard 1883. *Bost m&s j* 149: 388, 414, 608, 1903. *Polk* 1896: 699.

HAVEN, SAMUEL FOSTER, CW-USA (b/V-20-1831 Dedham, Mass; d/XII-13-1862 Fredericksburg, Va) MD Harvard 1855; AM 1852. *Nat med jour* 1:296, 1870/71. *Harvard in CW*: 56. Palmer's *Necrol Harv alum*: 492-94.

HAVEN, WILLIAM CHADBOURNE, Coventry Conn (b/IX-15-1851 Charlton Mass; d/XII-26-1904) MD UC NY 1877. *Proc Conn M S* 1905: 506-09. *Polk* 1896: 277.

HAVENS, JONATHAN, Newton, NJ (b/VIII-16-1840 Deckertown; d/XI-27-1882) MD CPSNY 1862. *Tr Med Soc NJ* 1882-83: 186-87. *Butler* 1878: 470.

HAVILAND, ABRAHAM A , NYC; CW-USA (d/VI-14-1864 Washington, DC) MD ? *Med surg rep Phila* 12: 52, 1864/65. *Nat med jour* 1:296, 1870/71.

HAWES, CARY NICHOLAS, Paris, Ky; CW-CSA (b/VIII- -1834 Winchester; d/VII- -1874) MD UPa 1858. *U Pa med alum CW*: 1858. *SHSP* 22:219, 1893.

HAWES, ELIAS, New Berne, SC [NC?] (b/I-15-1768 Wrentham, Mass; d/1829) MD ? AB Brown 1790. *Brown hist cat* 1790.

HAWES, GEORGE E, Palatka, Fla (d/X-27-1896) MD UCNY 1846. *Proc Fla Med Assoc* 1897: "In memoriam" 26 ff. *Flint* 1897: 207.

HAWES, JESSE, Greeley, Colo (b/VIII-21-1843 Corinna, Mo; d/VIII-4-1901) MD U Mich 1868; MD LICH 1871. *JAMA* 37: 460, 1901. *Polk* 1886: 185.

HAWES, JOHN Q A , Hallowell, Me (b/I-28-1830 Paris; d/III-17-1889) MD NY Med Coll 1857. *Tr Me Med Assoc* 1889: 169-70. *Butler* 1878: 307.

HAWES, OLIVER, Society Hill, SC (b/VI-24-1766 Wrentham, Mass; d/X- -1821) MD ? AB Brown 1878; AM. *Brown hist cat*: 1787. *Waring* I:382.

HAWES, WILLIAM, Boston (b/IV-2-1817; d/II-4-1854) MD Harvard 1840; AB Bowdoin 1837. *Bowdoin cat*: 1837.

HAWKES, EDWIN GREEN, Philadelphia (b/IV-15 1866; d/IV-5-1906) MD Jefferson 1892. *Pa m j* 9: 523, 1905/06. *Flint* 1897: 818.

HAWKES, ESTHER (HILL), Lynn, Mass (b/VIII-4 1833 or V-6-1834 Hookset, NH; d/V-7-1906) MD New Engl Female Med Coll 1857. *Bost m & s j* 154: 594-95, 1906. *Polk* 1896: 716.

HAWKES, JOHN MARSHALL, NYC (b/Windsor, Me; d/V-25-1895 @ 47) MD CPSNY 1890. *Med reg NY NJ Conn* 1895: 225. *JAMA* 24:1023, 1895. *Bost m & s j* 132: 606, 1895.

HAWKES, WILLIAM HINES, CW-USA; Washington, DC (b/X-25-1845 Meriden Conn; d/III-13-1904 DC) MD UPa 1874; AB Brown 1867. *Hist Med Soc DC:* 331. *Records AAS USA* 1891:47-48. *Polk* 1886: 212.

HAWKINS, ABSALOM WILLIAM HENRY HARRISON, CW-USN (b/I-22-1839 E Bethlehem Twp, Pa; d/XI-10-1876 Mansfield, O) MD UPa 1861; AB 1858. *U Pa med alum CW*: 1861.

HAWKINS, E R, CW-CSA; Daingerfield, Tex; Greenville 1883- (b/II-211-1831 NC; d/I-8-1904) <MD Med Coll Ga 1854> *Tex st m j* 1:243, 1906. *Polk* 1886: 887.

HAWKINS, HAMILTON S, USA 1824- (b/Md; d/VIII 7-1847) MD UMd 1822. *Med annals Md:* 432. *Heitman.*

HAWKINS, LEROY, Pittsfield Ill (d/IX-7-1901) Lic yrs pract. *Ill med jour* ns3:237, 1901. *Polk* 1896: 437. Ecl.

HAWKINS, NATHAN, Greene Co Tn (d/VIII-15 1859 @34) MD U Nashville 1856. *Nashvl j m&s* 17:286 1859.

HAWKINS, WILLIAM HARRISON, CW-CSA; Texarkana, Ark (b/XI-25-1832 Franklin Co, NC; d/IX-7-1887 Rocky Comfort) MD UPa 1857. *U Pa med alum CW*: 1857. *New Orl m & s j* ns15:413, 1887. *Atkinson* I:589. *SHSP* 22: 212,1893. *Polk* 1886:156.

HAWLEY, ALMON, Jefferson, O (d/1873 @74) MD ? *Med surg rep Phila* 28: 345, 1873.

HAWLEY, AUGUSTINE BOYER, Red Wing, Minn (b/ Tompkins Co, NY; d/IX-27-1878 @44) MD Geneva 1854. *Tr Minn St Med Soc* 1879: 155-56.

HAWLEY, GEORGE BENJAMIN, Hartford, Conn (b/II 13-1812 Bridgeport, Conn; d/IV-17-1883) MD Yale 1835; AB 1833. *JAMA* 1: 687, 1883. *Proc Conn Med Soc* 1883: 164. *Butler* 1878: 77.

HAWLEY, GEORGE T, Clinton, NY (d/1898) MD NY Hom 1886. *No Am j hom* 46: 200, 1898. *Polk* 1886: 657.

HAWLEY, JOEL EDWIN, Ithaca NY (b/IX-14-1802 Bethany, Conn; d/VIII-1-1859) MD Yale 1829. *Tr Med Soc St NY* 1860:173. *Buff m j* 15:633, 1860.

HAWLEY, LIVERUS B, MexWar-USA; Phoenixville, Pa 1855-63, 1872-90; Waverly NY 1863-72 (b/VIII-22 1828 Delaware Co, NY; d/III-20-1890) MD Hahnemann Phila 1853. *Tr Am Inst Hom* 1891:93. *Med vis* 6: 173, 1890. *Polk* 1886: 828. *Cleave.* Homeopath.

HAWLEY, ROSWELL, Bristol, Conn (d/XII-1867 @55) MD Yale 1842. *Proc Conn Med Soc* 3:19, 1868.

HAWLEY, WILLIAM AGUR, Syracuse, NY (b/VIII-28 1820 Hinsdale, Mass; d/V-15-1891) MD Albany 1851; AB Williams 1842. *Med adv* 26: 399, 1891. *Med vis* 7:230, 1891. *Polk* 1886: 710. Homeopath.

HAWTHORN, FRANK, New Orleans; CW-CSA (b/IX-20-1835 Conecuh Co, Ala; d/II-24-1876) MD UCNY 1859. *New Orl m&s j* ns3:760-62, 1876. *Med rec m& s* 11: 229, 1876.

HAWTHORNE, RICHARD FRANKLIN, New Orleans; CW-CSA (b/IX-20-1835; d/II-24-1876) MD Bellevue 1859; att U Ala 1854. *U Ala cat*: 116.

HAXALL, ROBERT WILLIAM, Richmond, Va (b/1802 Petersburg; d/III- -1871) MD U Md 1826; AB Yale 1823; att UPa Med Dept. *Tr Med Soc Va* 1872:26, 1855. *Tr AMA* 23:599-601, 1872.

HAY, EDWARD P, Buffalo (d/VIII-10-1901) MD Buffalo 1899) *JAMA* 37:527, 1901.

HAY, GEORGE, Pittsburgh (d/VII-4-1901 @64) MD UPa 1876. *JAMA* 37: 213, 1901.

HAY, JACOB, York, Pa (d/X-18-1897 @54) MD U Md 1855. *JAMA* 29: 976, 1897. *Polk* 1886: 841.

HAY, JOHN, York, Pa (d/VIII-26-1868 @42) MD U Md 1848. *Phila med reg & dir* 1871: 298. *Med surg rep Phila* 19:200, 1868.

HAY, WALTER, Chicago 1857- ; Dubuque, Ia 1877- ; Annapolis Md (b/VI-13-1830 Georgetown DC; d/III [?] 1893 or 1889 [?] Annapolis) MD Columbian DC 1853. *Chic med rec* 4:229, 1893. *Tr Ill St Med Soc* 1893: 58. *Atkinson* I: 416. *Polk* 1886: 264. *K&B* III: 543-44.

HAY, WILLIAM, CW-CSA (b/I-19-1833 Clarke Co, Va; d/I-1-1864 Staunton, Va) MD UPa 1858. *U Pa med alum CW*:1858. Blanton, *Va surg CW*: 404.

HAYDEN, HORACE H, Baltimore (b/X-13-1769 Windsor, Conn; d/I-26-1844) Hon MD Jefferson 1837. *Med annals Md:* 433. *K&B* III: 544.

HAYDEN, JOHN COLE, Cambridge, Mass (d/VII-30-1869) MD Harvard 1823; AB 1820; AM 1823. *Phila med reg & dir* 1871: 301. *Bost m&s j* ns4:48, 1869.

HAYES, AUGUSTUS ALLEN, Boston (b/II-28-1805 Windsor, Vt; d/VI-21-1882) MD Dartmouth 1846. *Bost m&s j* 107: , 1882 (Dec 28).

HAYES, CHARLES, CW-USA; Wisconsin; Illinois; Providence, RI (b/III-7-1840 N Berwick, Me; d/VI-8-1894) MD Dartmouth 1865; ng Bowdoin 1862. *Tr Am Inst Hom* 1894: 262. *Med vis* 10:364, 1894.

HAYES, ISAAC ISRAEL, CW-USA; NYC (b/III-5-1832; d/XII-17-1881) MD UPa 1853. *Tr CPP* cent vol: 233. *Chic med rev* 5:10, 1892. *Med surg rep Phila* 45: 740, 1881. *K&B* III: 545.

HAYES, JACOB, Charlestown, Mass (Berwick, Me; d/IX 28-1861 N Conway, NH) MD Bowdoin 1836. *Bost m&s j* 65: 188, 1861.

HAYES, JOHN J, Sharpsburg, Md (d/VII- -1823) MD U Md 1819. *Med annals Md:* 433.

HAYES, JOSEPH BYRON, Canandaigua, NY (d/1890) MD UPa 1860; AB Williams 1854. *Williams grads*:

1854. *Polk* 1886: 655.

HAYES, NATHAN, Unionville, Pa (b/II-5-1787; d/VII--1819) MD UPa 1808. *Med rep* (West Chester, Pa) 3:60-61, 1855.

HAYES, PLINY HAROLD, Buffalo & Binghamton, NY (b/1823 Bristol; d/IV-9-1894) MD Jefferson 1848. *JAMA* 22:601, 1894. *Polk* 1886: 652.

HAYES, PLYMMON SANFORD, Chicago (b/XII-1-1850 Shalesville O; d/V-14-1894) MD Rush 1872. *Tr Ill St Med Soc* 1894: 50. *Atkinson* I: 587. *Polk* 1886: 264.

HAYES, R T D, ? (d/IX-28-1878 Memphis) MD ? *Tr AMA* 30:870, 1879.

HAYES, THOMAS JOSEPHUS, Beverly, Mass (b/I-24-1862; d/VIII-25/26-1897) MD Harvard 1887; AB Boston Coll. *Bost m&s j* 137:248, 1897. *JAMA* 29: 555, 1897.

HAYMAKER, GEORGE W, Charleston, Ind (b/VI-6-1831 Oregon; d/VII-12-1900) MD Kentucky Sch Med 1857. *Tr Ind St M S* 1901: 488-89. *JAMA* 34:1676, 1900. *Polk* 1896: 462.

HAYMAN, WILLIAM HENRY, Chicago (d/XII-2-1896) MD Rush 1886. *JAMA* 28: 92, 1897.

HAYMOND, WILLIAM SUMMERVILLE, Indianapolis (b/II-23-1823 Harrison Co, WVa; d/XII-24-1885) MD Med Coll Ohio 1859; MD Bellevue 1872. *Tr Ind St Med Soc* 1886: 211. *Butler* 1878: 205.

HAYNEL, ADOLPH FERDINAND, Baltimore (b/1796? Gny? d/VIII-28-1877 @81 Dresden, Gny) Stud w/CF Hahnemann. *Hom times* 5:216, 1877. *Med annals Md:* 433. *King* 1:198-99. Homeopath.

HAYNES, ARETUS C, Kansas City, Mo (d/VI-29-1898 @55) <MD St Louis Med Coll 1864> *JAMA* 31:142, 1898. *Polk* 1896: 846.

HAYNES, FRANCIS LEADER, Los Angeles (b/VII-11 1850; d/X-18-1898) MD UPa 1871. *Buff m&s j* 38: 386, 1898. *JAMA* 31:1128, 1898. *K&B* III:545.

HAYNES, JOHN RUSS, Indianapolis, Ind (d/III-10-1902) MD Cincinnati Eclectic 1860. *Tr Am Inst Hom* 1902: 842. Homeopath.

HAYNES, THOMAS BAXTER, Hurricane, Ill (d/I-28-1905 @78) MD St Louis CPS 1880. *Ill med jour* 7:242, 1905. *Polk* 1896: 424.

HAYNES, TIMOTHY, Concord, NH; CW-USA (b/IX-5 1808 Alexandria; d/VI-28-1883) MD Jefferson 1836. *JAMA* 1:224, 1883. *Butler* 1878: 456. Conn *NH surg in CW*: 268.

HAYNES, WILLIAM HENRY, Brooklyn (d/XI-15-1902 @46) MD UCNY 1878. *Bost m&s j* 147:606, 1902. *Polk* 1886: 680.

HAYNIE, EZEKIEL, Princess Anne, Md; RevWar-USA (b/IX-29-1750 Northumberland Co, Va; d/1803) MD ? *Med annals Md:* 433-34.

HAYNIE, SAMUEL G, Austin, Tex (b/1806; d/1877) MD Galveston 1871. *Tr AMA* 29:672, 1878. Nixon, *Med ... early Texas*: 478.

HAYS, ADAM, War1812-USA, USN; Carlisle & Pittsburgh, Pa 1829- (b/1792 Cumberland Co; d/VIII-18 1857) MD UPa 1811; ng Dickinson 1808. *Dick'n cat*: 1808.

HAYS, DAVID S, CW-USA; Hollidaysburg, Pa (b/XII 11-1833 Huntingdon Co; d/VII-10-1898 @65) MD U Pa 1856. *U Pa med alum CW*: 1856. *JAMA* 31: 198, 1898. *Atkinson* I:349-350. *Polk* 1896: 1283.

HAYS, EDGAR C, Hannibal, Mo (d/VII-8-1901 @60) MD Washington U St Louis 1868. *JAMA* 37: 213, 1901. *Polk* 1886: 548.

HAYS, GEORGE C, Hillsboro, Ind (b/I-22-1836; d/X-26-1903) MD Med Coll Ind 1878. *Tr Ind St Med Soc* 1904: 355. *Butler* 1878: 205.

HAYS, H, CW-USA (d/IX-4-1864) MD ? *Nat med jour* 1:297, 1870/71.

HAYS, ISAAC, Philadelphia (b/VII-5-1796; d/IV-12-1879) MD UPa 1820: AB 1816. *Tr CPP* cent vol: 233-34; 3s5: lxxvii-cxv, 1880. *Am j m sci* ns78: 281-92, 1879. *Phila med times* 9:391 ff, 1879. *Med rec* NY 15:382-83, 1879. *K&B* III: 545-46.

HAYS, JACOB, Chicago (d/I-2-1903 @62) MD U Vienna 1863. *Ill med jour* ns4:589, 1903. *Polk* 1896:388.

HAYS, JAMES MACKINTOSH, Greensboro, NC (b/III 9-1863 Oxford; d/V-15-1897) MD Med Coll SC 1883. *Buff m&s j* 36:872-73, 1897. *Tr NC Med Soc* 1897: 180-81. *Polk* 1896: 1123.

HAYS, JOHN BROWN, Columbia, Tenn (b/1794 Rockbridge Co, Va; d/1868) MD UPa 1809. *Tr Med Soc Tenn* 1876: 82-83.

HAYS, W W, San Luis Obispo Ca (d/VII-3-1901) MD Georgetown 1861. *JAMA* 37:213, 1901. *Polk* 1886: 176.

HAYS, WILLIAM, Covington, Ky (b/I-21-1835 Butler Co; d/II-8-1869) MD Cincinnati Coll Med 1857; AB Miami 1858; AM. *Phila med reg & dir* 1871:300.

HAYS, WILLIAM L, Philadelphia (d/V-4-1867 @25) MD Jefferson 1863. *Med surg rep Phila* 16: 418, 1867.

HAYT, CHARLES WALKER, Corning NY (d/VII-23/24 1901 on Lake Erie) MD CPSNY 1889. *JAMA* 37: 398, 1901.

HAYWARD, ELISHA, Raynham, Mass (b/VI-26-1791 Easton; d/III-16-1868) MD Yale 1820; AB Brown 1817. *Brown hist cat*: 1817.

HAYWARD, GEORGE, Boston (b/III-9-1791; d/X-7-1863) MD UPa 1812; AB Harvard 1809; AB Yale 1809; AM Yale. *Tr AMA* 16:610, 1865. *Bost m&s j* 69:208, 225, 268, 1863. *Buff m&s j* 3: 120, 1863. *K&B* III:547.

HAYWARD, GEORGE, Boston (d/III-30-1901 @81) MD Harvard 1843; AB 1839. *Bost m&s j* 144: 342, 1901.

HAYWARD, HARRY, Mississippi City [La?] (b/New Orleans; d/VII-23-1895 @35) MD Tulane 1886. *New Orl m&s j* ns23: 127, 1895. *Polk* 1890: 490.

HAYWARD, JOHN McLEAN, CW-USA; Wayland, Mass (d/III-9-1886 @48) MD Harvard 1858. *Bost m&s j* 114:264, 1886. *Harvard in CW*: 252. *Butler* 1878: 340.

HAYWARD, JOSEPH WARREN, Taunton, Mass 1866-

CW–USA (b/VII–11–1841 Easton; d/XI–21–1905) MD Bowdoin 1864; ng Harvard Med Sch 1862–63. *Tr Am Inst Hom* 1906: 763–64. *King* 1:321. *Polk* 1886: 474.

HAYWARD, JOSHUA HENSHAW, Boston (b/II–6–1897; d/XII–2–1856) MD Harvard 1821: AB 1818. *Bost m&s j* 55:395, 1857. Palmer's *Necrol Harvard alum*: 130.

HAYWARD, NATHAN, St Louis; CW–USA (d/VIII–17 or 24–1866) MD Harvard 1855; AB 1850. *Nashville j m&s* ns2:358, 1867. *Harvard in CW*: 47.

HAYWOOD, EDMUND BURKE, CW–CSA; Raleigh NC (b/I–13–1825; d/I–18–1894) MD UPa 1849; att UNC 1847. *JAMA* 22:202, 1894. *Tr NC Med Soc* 1894: 201. *NC m j* 35: 71–79, 1895. *U Pa med alum CW*: 1849. *Atkinson* I: 264. *K&B* III: 547–48.

HAYWOOD, FRANCIS PHILEMON, Smithville, NC; CW–CSA (b/1810; d/X–23–1900) MD ? *UNC cat*: 269.

HAYWOOD, RICHARD BENNEHAN, Raleigh, NC (b/XI–5–1819; d/I–2–1889) MD Jefferson 1844; AB UNC 1841. *Tr NC Med Soc* 1889: 157–59. *Atkinson* I:472. *Butler* 1878: 594.

HAZEL, FRANKLIN BUTLER, CW–USA; Philadelphia (b/II–24–1846 Dover, Del; d/III–28–1900) MD UPa 1869. *JAMA* 34: 890, 1900. *Polk* 1896: 1306.

HAZELTINE, LABAN, Jamestown, NY (b/VIII–7–1789 Wardsborough, Vt; d/V–1–1852) Lic Vt Med Soc 1815; att Dartmouth Med Coll. *Tr M S St NY* 1865: 279–80.

HAZELTINE, WILLIAM VINCENT, Warren, Pa (b/VIII–26–1840 Busti, NY; d/IV–23–1902) MD LICH 1883; att U Mich Med Sch 1862–63; att Harvard Med Sch 1864–65. *Pa med jour* 5: 452, 520, 1901/02; 6:260, 1902/03. *Flint* 1897: 838.

HAZEN, ALLEN, NYC (d/XI–17–1903 @36 Jericho Centre, NH) MD CPSNY 1895. *Bost m&s j* 149: 610, 1903.

HAZEN, DAVID HENRY, Washington, DC (b/VIII–10–1846 Mt Bethel, Pa; d/XI–6–1906) MD Georgetown 1873. *Hist Med Soc DC:* 304–05. *Polk* 1893: 270.

HAZLET, HARRY FOSTER, Pueblo, Colo (d/III–4–1900 @34) MD Jefferson 1892. *JAMA* 34: 703, 1900. *Polk* 1896: 267.

HAZLET, SAMUEL WINTERTON, NYC (d/I–30–1860 @39) MD UCNY 1844. *Med surg rep Phila* ns3:425, 1859/60.

HAZLETT, JOHN, NYC (b/V–17–1817 Ireland; d/III–4 1870) MD Willoughby 1846. *Med reg NY NJ Conn* 1870: 320. *Phila med reg & dir* 1871: 304.

HAZLETT, ROBERT W , CW–USA; Wheeling, WVa (b/IV–16–1828 Washington, Pa; d/IX–2–1899) MD Jefferson 1851. *JAMA* 33: 683, 1899. *Atkinson* I: 475. *Polk* 1890: 1153. *K&B* III: 548.

HAZZARD, WILLIAM H , Philadelphia (d/I–2–1867 @51) MD Phila Coll Med & Surg 1856. *Med surg rep Phila* 16: 40, 1867.

HEACOCK, STACY L , Rohrsburg, Pa (d/VI–6–1881) MD Jefferson 1881. *Med bull m & s* 3: 164, 1881.

HEACOCK, WILLARD AVERY, NYC (b/1866 Gloversville; d/II–24–1899) MD CPSNY 1892; AB Rutgers 1888. MD CPSNY 1892; AB Rutgers 1888. *JAMA* 32: 506, 1899. *Bost m&s j* 140: 222, 1899. *Polk* 1896: 1057.

HEAD, JAMES H , Centralia, Mo (d/X–29–1898) MD St Louis Med Coll 1867. *JAMA* 31:1190 1898. *Polk* 1886: 544.

HEADLEY, WILLIAM SALISBURY, Syracuse, NY; NYC (b/Walton, NY; d/III–31–1883) MD ? <AB Union> *Med reg NY NJ Conn* 1883: 230.

HEADY, WILLIAM SHIELDS, Jamestown, Ind (b/XII–24–1849 Putnam Co; d/V–3–1903) MD Cinc Coll Med & Surg 1875. *Tr Ind St M S* 1903:344. *Polk* 1886: 324.

HEALEY, THOMAS A, Cumberland Md (d/VIII–9–1892) MD U Md 1835. *Med annals Md:* 434. *Butler* 1874: 320.

HEALEY, THOMAS MICHAEL, Cumberland, Md (b/VI–16–1840; d/VIII–13–1892) MD LICH 1866. *Hist Med Soc DC:* 299. *Polk* 1886: 441.

HEALY, JAMES JOSEPH, Newburyport, Mass (d/XI–11–1904 @55) MD CPSNY 1872. *Bost m&s j* 151: 556, 1904. *Polk* 1896: 719.

HEALY, JOHN JOSEPH, Philadelphia (d/V–8–1903 @54) MD UPa 1872. *Pa med jour* 7:279, 1903/04. *Flint* 1897: 819.

HEALY, ROBERT HAMES, Raleigh, NC; CW–CSA (b/IX–13–1837; d/XII–31–1863) MD Med Coll Ga 1858; att U Ala 1853. *U Ala cat*: 105.

HEAP, DAVID PORTER, Philadelphia; CW–USA (d/VIII–11–1866 @ c40) MD UPa 1850; MD Franklin Med Coll 1847. *Med surg rep Phila* 15:188, 1866.

HEARD, GEORGE WASHINGTON, Ipswich, Mass (b/II–5–17993; d/IV–21–1863) MD Harvard 1815; AB 1812. Palmer's *Necrol Harvard alum*: 458–59.

HEARD, JOHN S , Newburgh, NY (d/XII–18–1885 @70) MD CPSNY 1837; AB Columbia 1834; AM 1837. *Med reg NY NJ Conn* 1886: 250.

HEARD, JOHN THEODORE, CW–USA; Boston (d/IX 2–1906 @70) MD Harvard 1859.*Bost m&s j* 155: 298, 1906. *Harvard in CW*: 253–54. *Butler* 1848: 340.

HEARD, THOMAS JEFFERSON, Galveston, Tex (b/V 14–1814 Morgan Co, Ga; d/III–8–1899) MD Tulane 1845; att Transylvania Med Coll 1836–37. *JAMA* 32: 628, 1899. *New Orl m&s j* 51:592, 1899. *Atkinson* I: 500. *Polk* 1896: 1431. *K&B* III: 548–49.

HEARIN, HEZEKIAH B , Pine Bluff, Ark (d/XII–23–1873 @35) MD New Orl Sch Med 1860. *Med surg rep Phila* 30: 156, 1873.

HEATH, ASAHEL HAWLEY, NYC (d/III–10–1899 @ 78) MD Castleton 1859. *JAMA* 32:628 1899. *Polk* 1890: 816.

HEATH, JOHN FRANCIS, ?Smithville, NC; CW–CSA (b/XI–15–1819 Petersburg, Va; d/X–7–1862 Smithville) MD UPa 1853. *Med surg rep Phila* ns9: 138, 1862/63. *U Pa med alum CW*: 1853.

Spec. educ'l status abbrev. as: ***ng*** = college verified attendance without degree;

HEATH, MOTT C , Cadillac, Mich (d/V-2-1886 @38) MD Fort Wayne Coll Med 1883. *JAMA* 26: 1038, 1896. *Polk* 1896: 743.

HEATH, NICHOLAS JOHN, NYC (d/XII-15-1867) <LRCS Ireland> *Med reg NY NJ Conn* 1868: 328.

HEATH, WILLIAM HENRY, Stoneham, Mass; CW-USA (d/VIII-23-1864 Chattanooga, Tenn) MD Harvard 1853. *Bost m&s j* 71:128, 1864. *Nat med jour* 1:297, 1870/71. *Harvard in CW*: 240.

HEATON, CARLTON R, Owego NY (d/VII-19-1900 @ 58) MD Geneva 1864. *Tr Med Soc St NY* 1901: [426]. *Polk* 1886: 700.

HEATON, CHARLES WILLIAM, Dedham Mass (d/ 1869) MD Harvard 1867;AM 1863. *Bost m & s j* 4:128, 1869.

HEATON, GEORGE, Boston (b/IV-19-1808 Alton, Ill; d/VIII-I-1879) <MD UPa 1840> *Med rec NY* 16: 95-96, 1879.

HEAVENRIDGE, ALLEN, Stilesville, Ind (b/III-22-1829 Union Co, Ind; d/II-10-1902) MD Rush 1858. *Tr Ind St Med Soc* 1902: 415. *Polk* 1896: 492.

HEBB, THOMAS WILLIAM, Poplar Hill, Md (d/VIII-15-1858) MD Columbian 1853. *Med annals Md:* 434.

HEBELER, KARL G , Pittsburgh (b/Gny; d/XII-23-1906 @ 72) <MD U Marburg 1852> *Pa med jour* 10: 295, 1906/07.

HEBERSMITH, ERNEST [orig. Smith, Heber] USN (b/I-20-1840; d/III-11-1888) MD CPSNY 1861. *Med reg NY NJ Conn* 1889: 275.

HECKEL, CHARLES A , Robeson Twp, Pa (d/XII-10-1876 @45) MD Pa Med Coll 1853. *Med surg rep Phila* 35: 548, 1876.

HECKEL, FREDERICK WILLIAM, CW-USA; Spring City, Pa (b/II-24-1829 E Vincent Twp; d/III-4-1900) MD UPa 1849. *JAMA* 34: 703, 1900. *U Pa med alum CW*: 1849.

HECKERMAN, JOHN H , Tiffin, O (d/III-11-1900) MD Columbian DC 1846. *JAMA* 34: 766, 1900. *Polk* 1896: 1214.

HECKERT, CALVIN J , Harrisburg, Pa (b/III-23-1853 Linglestown; d/XI-13-1898) MD LICH 1875. *JAMA* 31: 1319, 1898.

HEDENBURG, JAMES, Medford, Mass (d/VII-25/26-1905 @74) MD Castleton 1852. *Bost m&s j* 153: 154, 1905. *Polk* 1896: 717.

HEDGES, JACOB E , NJ (d/VII-22-1841 @29) MD *Tr NJ Med Soc* 1872: 133.

HEDGES, JOSEPH, Newton, NJ (d/IV-14-1906 @78) MD CPSNY 1859; AB Princeton 1858; AM 1862. *Bost m&s j* 154:480, 1906. *Polk* 1886: 601 (Branchville, NJ).

HEDGES, JOSEPH, Newark (d/II-14-1890) MD CPS NY 1853. *Med reg NY NJ Conn* 1890:270. *Polk* 1886: 607.

HEDGES, SMITH E , Chester, NJ (b/XI-20-1830; d/IV 1-1892) MD UCNY 1852. *Tr NJ Med Soc* 1892: 197-98. *Polk* 1890: 720.

HEDGES, URBAN D, Wilmington, Del (d/XI 4-1865 @ 58) MD Jefferson 1835. *Med s rep Phila* 13: 326, 1865.

HEDLER, FRANCIS LUDWIG, NYC 1854- ; CW-USA (b/XII-22-1807 Rastadt, Gny; d/VII-21-1873) <MD Freiburg 1834> *Med reg NY NJ Conn* 1874: 277.

HEED, HARMON, Warehouse Pt, Conn (b/IV-6-1840 Yardleyville, Pa; d/V-18-1888) MD UPa 1865. *U Pa med alum CW*: 1865. *Polk* 1886: 197.

HEFLIN, CHARLES S , Falmouth, Va (d/XII-13-1886) MD CPS Balto 1882. *New Orl m & s j* ns14: 639, 1887.

HEFLIN, EDGAR H , Minneapolis (d/VII-26 1901 Stillwater) <MD U Iowa 1883> *JAMA* 37: 398, 1901. *Polk* 1886: 514.

HEILMAN, AMOS E , Rural Valley, Pa (d/IX 10-1903 @47) MD CPS Balto 1884. *Pa med jour* 7:279, 1903/04.

HEILNER, HENRY C , Lykens, Pa; CW-USA (d/XII-1 1868) MD LICH 1861. *Phila med reg & dir* 1871: 299. *Med surg rep Phila* 19: 508, 1868.

HEINMULLER, ROBERT JOHN, NYC (b/II-13-1855; d/VIII-30-1884) MD UCNY 1875. *Med reg NY NJ Conn* 1885: 239.

HEISKELL, HENRY LEE, USA (b/III-16-1803; d/VIII 12-1855) MD UPa 1828. *Amer jour med sci* 30:551, 1855. *Bost m & s j* 53: 87, 175, 1856.

HEITZ, P A , Hastings, Minn (b/II-12-1820 Gny; d/IV-9-1888) <MD Heidelberg 1846> *Tr Minn St Med Soc* 1888: 170. *Polk* 1886: 512.

HELDMANN, JOEL A , Baltimore (b/XI-20-1820 Gny; d/III-23-1898) MD U Marburg 1845. *JAMA* 30:807, 1898. *Med annals Md:* 435. *Polk* 1886: 437.

HELFFENSTEIN, ABRAHAM, Kensington, Phila (b/ 1804; d/1864) MD UPa 1826. *Tr AMA* 18: 328-29, 1867. *Tr Med Soc St Pa* 1865: 139-40. *Med surg rep Phila* 12: 180, 1864/65.

HELFRICH, JACOB S, Philadelphia (d/II-22-1874) MD Pa Med Coll 1853. *Med s rep Phila* 30:228, 300, 1874.

HELFRICH [HELFFRICH], JOHN HENRY, Allentown, Pa (d/VII-29-1903 @83) MD Pa Med Coll 1846. *Pa med jour* 7: 279, 1903/04. *Flint* 1897: 794.

HELLEN, BENJAMIN JOHNSON, Washington, DC (b/III-20-1830; d/VII-2-1864) MD Columbian DC 1854; AB 1850; AM 1854. *Tr AMA* 23:575-76, 1872. *Hist Med Soc DC:* 259.

HELLER, JACOB A , Factoryville, Pa (d/I-12-1906 @ 52) MD Jefferson 1881. *Pa med jour* 9:359, 1905/06. *Flint* 1897: 802.

HELLER, JACOB LOUIS, Philadelphia (d/I-12 1903 @ 36) MD Jefferson 1892. *Pa med jour* 7:279, 1903/04. *Flint* 1897: 819.

HELLER, RAYMOND L , Napoleon, O (d/XII-14-1897 @26) MD Starling 1896. *JAMA* 30:48, 1898. *Polk* 1896: 1202.

HELM, JOHN, New Brunswick, NJ (b/XII-27-1838; d/ XI-7-1898) MD UCNY 1861. *Tr NJ Med Soc* 1899:

290. *JAMA* 31: 1257, 1898. *Butler* 1878: 470.

HELM, JOHN HAMPTON, Peru Ind (b/IV–23–1826 Elizabethton Tn; d/V–1–1889) MD Med Coll Ohio 1847. *JAMA* 32:1074,1889. *Atkinson* I:52. *Butler* 1878: 205.

HELM, JOHN NEWTON, CW–CSA (b/V–20–1833 Natchez, Miss; d/VII–15–1862 Richmond, Va) MD UPa 1855. *U Pa med alum CW*: 1855.

HELM, MEREDITH, Springfield, Ill (b/III–8–1802 Williamsport, Md; d/III–2–1866) MD U Md 1825. *Tr Ill St Med Soc* 1895: 68. *Med surg rep Phila* 14:260, 1866.

HELM, SCOTT, Phoenix, Ariz (d/X–8–1897 @ 35) MD Rush 1883. *JAMA* 29: 816, 1897. *Chic med rec* 13: 296, 1897. *Polk* 1886: 264.

HELM, WILLIAM HENRY, CW–USA; Sing Sing, NY (b/I–19–1840 Nashville; d/II–5–1898) MD UPa 1864; AB Princeton 1860. *U Pa med alum CW*: 1864. *JAMA* 30:448, 1898. *Tr M S St NY* 1899: 435. *Polk* 1896: 1100.

HELME, THOMAS, McKownville, NY (d/III–17–1889) MD Albany 1854. *Tr Med Soc St NY* 1889: 364. *Polk* 1886: 667.

HELMUTH, WILLIAM SHAEFF, Philadelphia (b/II–19 1801; d/IV–8–1880) MD UPa 1824; AB 1819; Hon MD Hahnemann Phila 1857. *Tr Am Inst Hom* 1880: .*Hahn mo* 16: 127, 1881. *Hom times* 8:48, 1880. Homeopath.

HELMUTH, WILLIAM TOD, Philadelphia 1853–58; St Louis Mo 1858–70; NYC (b/X–30–1833; d/V–15–1902) MD Hahnemann Phila 1853. *Tr Am Inst Hom* 1901: 829–31. *No Am jour hom* 43: 319. *Polk* 1886: 680. *Cleave.*

HELPER [HEPLER?], HARRY A , Reading, Pa (d/VIII 18–1906) MD U Pa 1888. *Pa med jour* 10: 53, 1906/07. *Reg Pa phys* 1881–88: 64.

HELWIG, ANDREW F, Praworenville, NY (d/1891) <MD Mich Coll Med 1883> *Buff m&s j* 30:695,1891. *Polk* 1886: 710.

HELWIG, THEODORE AUGUSTUS, CW–USA; Minersville, Pa (b/VII–5–1835 Zweibrücken, Bavaria; d/XII 22–1898) MD UPa 1856; <MD Heidelberg 1844!> *U Pa med alum CW*: 1856. *Polk* 1886: 808.

HEMMING, F W BOYD, CW–USA? (d/II–3–1865 Alacrunes, Cuba) MD ? *Med surg rep Phila* 12: 344, 1864/65.

HEMPEL, CHARLES JULIUS, Philadelphia to 1860; Grand Rapids, Mich 1860– (b/IX–5–1811 Solingen, Prussia; d/IX–24–1879) MD UCNY 1845. *Amer obs* 16: 524, 1879. *New Engl med gaz* 14: 275, 1879. *King* 1: 333. *Cleave.* Homeopath.

HEMPSTEAD, G S B, Portsmouth O (d/VII–9–1883) MD Med Coll Ohio 1822. *Med s rep Phila* 49: 196, 1883.

HENDEE, HORATIO S , Lowville, NY (b/XI–11–1829 Greig, NY; d/I–5–1892) MD Castleton 1851. *Bost m & s j* 126: 48, 1892. *Polk* 1886: 666.

HENDERSON, ALVIN CHARLES, Brooklyn (b/VII–4 1845 Cadiz, O; d/II–6–1899) MD U Mich 1872; MD LICH 1872. *Bost m & s j* 140: 172, 1899. *JAMA* 32: 384, 1899. *Polk* 1896: 997.

HENDERSON, ANDREW AUGUSTUS, USN 1841– (b/II–14–1816; d/IV–4–1875) MD Jefferson 1838. *Tr AMA* 33: 561–64, 1882. *Med reg NY NJ Conn* 1875:198. *Tr CPP* cent vol: 234. *K&B* II: 514.

HENDERSON, FRANCES IDA, Titusville, Pa (b/II–2 1856; d/II–13–1895) MD Cleveland Homeop Coll 1888. *Tr Am Inst Hom* 1896: . *Hahn mo* 30:152 (news & advt) 1895. Homeopath.

HENDERSON, GEORGE ROBINSON, Brooklyn (d/VII 28–1896 @45) MD Yale 1876; AB Lincoln 1872. *JAMA* 27: 503, 1896. *Polk* 1890: 771. Black.

HENDERSON, HARVEY DINWIDDIE, Salem, Ind (b/IX–6–1819; d/III–11–1896) MD Transylvania 1842. *Tr Ind St Med Soc* 1896: 270. *Polk* 1886: 335.

HENDERSON, HENRY GLOVER, Ala (d/III–11–1883) MD Jefferson 1870. *Tr Med Assoc St Ala* 1883: 243.

HENDERSON, JAMES MILTON, CW–USA (b/Newark, O; d/XII–27–1864 Nashville, Tn) MD UPa 1864. *U Pa med alum CW*: 1864

HENDERSON, JAMES PATTERSON, Newville, O (b/I 17–1803 Elizabethtown, Pa; d/VII–1–1889) Hon MD Willoughby 1842; AB Wash'n Coll, Pa 1825; AM 1828. *Tr Ohio M S* 1890:7. *Atkinson* I:559. *Butler* 1878: 632.

HENDERSON, JAMES T , Covington, Ind (b/VIII–10–1846 Parke Co; d/III–2–1905) MD Med Coll Ind 1875. *Tr Ind St Med Soc* 1905: 447. *Polk* 1896: 463.

HENDERSON, JOPHANUS, E Somerville, Mass (d/VIII 7–1869 @60) MD Jeff'n 1854. *Bost m&s j* 4:48, 1869.

HENDERSON, NATHANIEL POTTER, Johnsontown, Va; CW–CSA (b/II–21–1839 Franklin, Va; d/I–5–1895 Bridgetown, Va) MD UPa 1861. *U Pa med alum CW*: 1861. *Polk* 1886: 919.

HENDERSON, NELSON H , Chicago, Ill (d/VI–23–1903 @45) MD CPS Chicago 1885. *JAMA* 41:47, 1903.

HENDERSON, PLEASANT P , Zanesville, O (d/IX–12 1899 @42) MD Jefferson 1890. *JAMA* 33:872, 1899. *Polk* 1898: 1342.

HENDERSON, THOMAS, Warrenton, Va; Washington, DC (b/I–6–1789 Dumfries; d/VIII–11–1854 Lexington) MD UPa 1809. *Hist Med Soc DC:* 214–15.

HENDERSON, WILLIAM B , Steelton, Pa (b/Hummelstown, Pa; d/II–22–1897) MD Pa Med Coll 1853. *JAMA* 28: 523, 1897. *Reg Pa phys* 1881–88: 148.

HENDERSON, WILLIAM CHURCH, ?Mexico (d/IX–23–1883 Hermosillo, Mex) MD ? *Med surg rep Phila* 49:448, 1883.

HENDREE, JOHN, Dixie, Ala (d/V–6–1883) MD UPa 1821? *Tr Med Assoc St Ala* 1883:243. *Butler* 1874:19.

HENDRICK, GUSTAVUS, Brundidge, Ala (d/1898) MD Pa Med Coll 1853. *Tr Med Assoc St Ala* 1899: 233. *Polk* 1893: 152.

HENDRICKS, GEORGE A , Minneapolis, Minn (b/VII–16–1852 Shippensburg, Pa; d/IX–25–1899) MD U Mich 1877. *Tr Minn St Med Soc* 1899: 191. *JAMA* 33: 872, 1899. *Polk* 1890: 615. *K&B* II: 515.

 Spec. educ'l status abbrev. as: ***ng*** = college verified attendance without degree;

HENDRIE, JAMES DUNLAP, CW–USA; Chicago (b/IX–25–1833 Bucks Co, Pa; d/XII–27–1900) MD UPa 1855. *U Pa med alum CW*: 1855.

HENDRIE, WILLIAM SCOTT, CW–USA; Doylestown, Pa (b/XII–17–1798 Sussex Co, NJ; d/IV–20–1875) MD UPa 1824. *U Pa med alum CW*: 1824.

HENDRIE, WILLIAM SCOTT, CW–USA; Philadelphia (b/X–25–1835 Hilltown, Pa; d/XII–10–1881) MD UPa 1860; AB 1856. *Matrics Coll UP*: 195.

HENDRY, BOWMAN, Haddonfield, NJ; CW–USA (b/1820? d/V–8 1868 @48) MD Jefferson 1846. *Phila med reg & dir* 1871: 296. *Med surg rep Phila* 18:5421, 1868.

HENDRY, CHARLES DUFFIELD, Haddonfield, NJ (b/1811; d/IV–25–1869 Camden) MD UPa 1833. *Tr NJ Med Soc* 1869: 108. *Tr AMA* 21:467–68, 1870. *Phila med reg & dir* 1871: 300.

HENDRY, JOHN A , ?Morristown, NJ (b/1786; d/VI–23 1834) Lic by exam 1808. *Tr NJ Med Soc* 1872: 117–19.

HENGST, DAVID ALFRED, Denver, Colo; Pittsburgh, Pa (d/IV–24–1899) MD Jefferson 1870. *JAMA* 32: 1013, 1899. *Polk* 1896: 1326.

HENION, EGBERT B , Sweden, NY (d/VI–11–1896) MD CPS Balto 1882. *JAMA* 26: 1278, 1896.

HENKEL, ABRAM MILLER, Staunton, Va (b/X–13–1843 New Market; d/IV–19–1904) MD UCNY 1868. *Tr Med Soc Va* 1904: 320–22. *Polk* 1900:1776.

HENKEL, FREDERICK LEWIS, Staunton, Va (b/V–1854 New Market; d/V–27–1904 Lebanon Church) MD UPa 1879. *Tr Med Soc Va* 1905:446. *Polk* 1900:1776.

HENKLE, ELI J , Baltimore (b/1829; d/XI–1–1893) MD U Md 1850. *JAMA* 21: 746, 1893. *Med annals Md:* 437.

HENLEY, LEONARD, CW–CSA; Williamsburg, Va (b/IV–11–1821; d/VIII–5–1904) MD UPa 1847; att Wm & Mary. *Tr Med Soc Va* 1904: 322–23. *U Pa med alum CW*: 1847 (suppl) Blanton *Va surg CW*: 405.

HENNA, WILLIAM ARTHUR, NYC (d/XI–27 1886 @ 26) MD CPSNY 1885. *Med reg NY NJ Conn* 1887: 267.

HENNESSY, THOMAS CHARLES, ?Montreal Que (b/X–9–1849 Providence, RI; d/XII–25–1899 [?] Montreal) MD Bellevue 1874; AB Brown 1871. *Brown hist cat* 1871.

HENNIG, EMIL E , Wheeling, WVa (b/X–9–1831 Leipzig; d/VIII–27–1899) MD U Vienna 1851. *Med vis* 15:601–02, 1899. *Polk* 1886: 945. Homeopath.

HENNING, ROBERT, Jeffersonville, Ind (b/XII–28–1847 Wooster; d/IV–17–1897) MD U Louisville 1879. *Tr Ind St Med Soc* 1897: 358.

HENOT, JOHN LOUIS, Winsted Conn; Poultney Vt (d/VII–26–1896 @38) MD UVt 1888. *JAMA* 27: 449, 1896. *Polk* 1896: 285.

HENROTIN, FERNAND, Chicago (d/XII–9–1906 @59) MD Rush 1868. *Chic med rec* 27: 698, 712, 1906. *Flint* 1897: 262.

HENRY, ABIJAH F , Alamo, Ind (d/III–29–1898) MD Rush 1866. *JAMA* 30:874, 1898. *Polk* 1886: 315.

HENRY, B BROWN, W Newton, Pa (d/XI–17 1903 @ 26) <MD Univ Coll Med Va 1900> *Pa med jour* 7: 279, 1903/04.

HENRY, BERNARD, USN 1844–50; Philadelphia (d/IV 15–1860) MD UPa 1844. *Tr CPP* cent vol: 234.

HENRY, CHARLES FRANCIS, Mobile, Ala (b/VIII–29 1828; d/VIII–22–1862 Warm Springs, Ga) MD UPa 1849; AB U Ala 1847. *U Ala cat*: 83.

HENRY, FRANCIS G , Kansas City, Mo (b/1828 Paris, Ky; d/II–26–1898) MD Med Coll Ohio 1851. *JAMA* 30: 624, 1898. *Polk* 1896: 846.

HENRY, GREENBURY RIDGELY, Burlington Ia (b/IX 28–1828 Hopkinsville Ky; d/V–14–1885) MD Louisville Med Inst 1849. *JAMA* 6:616, 1886. *Tr Ia St Med Soc* 6:469–70, 1883–85. *Atkinson* I: 543. *Butler* 1878: 237.

HENRY, JAMES HERVEY, Brooklyn (b/II–22–1806; d/XI–1–1875) MD Berkshire 1827. *Med reg NY NJ Conn* 1876: 242.

HENRY, JOHN POWELL, Jersey City, NJ (d/III–15 1906) MD CPSNY 1881. *Bost m & s j* 154: 360, 1906. *Polk* 1896: 939.

HENRY, JOSEPH NICHOLSON, USA; Devon, Pa (d/X 3–1904 @75) MD ? *Pa med jour* 8: 335, 1904/05.

HENRY, MORRIS HENRY, CW–USA; NYC (b/VII–26 1835 London, Engl; d/V–15–1895) MD U Vt 1860; AM 1876; LLD UNC 1885. *Med reg NY NJ Conn* 1895: 225. *JAMA* 24: 810, 1895. *Bost m & s j* 132: 552, 1895. *K&B* III: 554–55.

HENRY, SAMUEL H, Baltimore (b/1819; d/VII–12–1887) MD UPa 1839. *Med ann Md:*436. *Butler* 1874: 320.

HENRY, THOMAS CHARLTON, USA 1853–59, 1864–65 (d/I–5–1877) MD Jefferson 1850; AB Williams 1846. *Williams grads*: 1846.

HENRY, WILLIAM, Philadelphia (b/1808; d/I–5–1860) MD UPa 1834. *Tr Med Soc Pa* 1862: 125–26. *Med surg rep Phila* ns3: 340, 1860.

HENRY, WILLIAM F , Tuscaloosa, Ala (b/Rutland, Mass; d/XII–13–1855 @53) MD ? *Bost m & s j* 53:555, 1856.

HENSCHEL, CHARLES, NYC 1832– (b/II–25–1809 Minden, Prussia; d/IX–18–1872 Zürich, Switz) <MD U Würzburg> *Med reg NY NJ Conn* 1873: 339–41. *Med rec* 7: 448, 174, 1872; 8:21, 22, 24, 1872.

HENSCHEL, EDWARD KARSCH, NYC (d/II–28–1890 @38) MD CPSNY 1872 *Med reg NY NJ Conn* 1890:270.

HENSHAW, GEORGE BRIDGES, Cambridge, Mass (d/XII– –1901 @34 New Rochelle, NY) MD Harvard 1894; AB 1890. *Bost m & s j* 145: 726, 1901.

HENSLEE, JOHN THOMAS, Dickson, Tenn (b/V–5–1838 Calloway Co, Ky; d/VII–27–1895) MD U Nashville 1874. *Nashville j m & s* 79: 47–48, 1896.

HENSLEY, JOHN H , Vincennes, Ind (b/III–24–1857 Owen Co; d/IV–22–1897) MD U Louisville 1881. *Tr Ind St Med Soc* 1897; 361. *Polk* 1896: 495.

HENTHORN, LEWIS S , Indianapolis, Ind (b/1846; d/II 25–1895) MD Med Coll Ind 1877. *JAMA* 24: 370, 1895. Kemper's *Indiana*: 284.

HENTZ, CHARLES ARNOLD, Quincy, Fla (b/V–28–1827; d/VI–30–1894) MD Med Coll Louisville 1848; MD (?) U Ala 1844. *U Ala cat*: 77.

HEPBURN, JAMES, Harford Co, Md (d/I–21–1878 Williamsport, Pa) MD UPa 1823. *Med annals Md:* 436.

HEPLER [HELPER], BENJAMIN F , Ft Scott, Kans (d/IX–22–1894) MD Phila Med Coll 1858. *Bost m & s j* 131:328,1894. *Butler* 1878:253 *Polk* 1886:378.

HEPWORTH, FREDERICK J , Paterson, NJ (d/V–12 1893) MD LICH 1881. *Tr NJ Med Soc* 1893: 174. *Polk* 1890: 728.

HERBEIN, ISAAC S , Strausstown, Pa (b/Berks Co; d/XI–14–1905 @69) MD Jefferson 1865. *Pa med jour* 9: 220, 1905/06. *Flint* 1897: 837.

HERBERT, CHARLES DICKINSON, Rutland, Mass 1866–76; Hebron, NY 1886–93 (b/IX–28–1818 Ellsworth, Me; d/X–13–1893) MD Hahnemann Phila 1866; AB Bowdoin 1841. *Bowdoin cat*: 1841. Homeopath.

HERBERT, JOSEPH WELLS, Washington, DC (b/X–3 1837 St Marys Co, Md; d/X–21–1903) MD Georgetown 1859. *Hist Med Soc DC:*269. *Butler* 1874: 92.

HERBERT, RICHARD, Rowley, Mass (b/1798? d/VII–28–1859 @ 61) MD Dartmouth 1822. *Bost m & s j* 61: 28, 1860.

HERBERT, THOMAS, New Iberia La (d/VI–8–1895) MD U La 1880.*New Orl m & s j*ns23:127 1895.

HERBERT, THOMAS SNOWDEN, Anne Arundel Co, Md (b/III–13–1806; d/IV–1–1852) MD UPa 1828. *Med annals Md:* 436.

HERBERT, WILLIAM PAUL, Churchville, Md (b/1797 Harford Co; d/1821) MD U Md 1818. *Med ann Md:* 436.

HERBST, JOHN EDWARD, Hagerstown, Md 1865–79; Abilene Kans 1879–87; Kansas City Mo 1887–99 (b/II–24–1828 Gettysburg Pa; d/VI–19–1899) MD Pa Med Coll 1853; AB Gettysburg Coll 1846. *Gett'bg cat*:1846.

HERBST, JOHN S , Pike, Pa (d/I–27–1859 Phila) stud @ Jefferson 1859. *Med surg rep Phila* ns1: 337, 1858/59.

HERBST, WILLIAM S , Trexlertown, Pa (b/IX–24–1833; d/XII–22–1906 @73) MD Jefferson 1855. *Med bull med & surg* 3:45,1881. *Pa med jour* 10:295,1906/07. *K&B* III: 555–56. *Flint* 1897: 837.

HERDMAN, THOMAS JEFFERSON, Eastern Shore, Md (b/Del; d/XII–22–1842 Newark, Del) MD UPa 1823. *Med annals Md:* 436.

HEREFORD, FRANCIS MARION, Montgomery Ala (b/VII–26–1814 Mason Co, WVa; d/I–22–1881) MD Jefferson 1836. *Tr M S St Ala* 1881: 271. *Butler* 1874: 19.

HERING, CONSTANTINE, Paramaribo, Surinam 6 yrs; Philadelphia 1833– (b/I–1–1800 Oschatz, Sax'y; d/VII 23–1880) MD U Würzburg 1826. *Tr am inst hom* 1881: 45 ff, 115 ff. *Med counselor* 3:193 ff, 1880. *New Engl med gaz* 15:307 ff, 1880. *K&B* III: 556–58. Homeopath.

HERING, EDWIN A , Sabillisville, Md 1855–57; Waynesboro, Pa 1857–59; Cross Keys, Va 1879–92; Harrisonburg 1892– (b/XI–24–1826 Big Pike Creek; d/II–25–1905) MD U Md 1855. *Tr Med Soc Va* 1905: 446–47. *Polk* 1900: 1764.

HERITAGE, JOSEPH, Philadelphia (b/W Jersey c1830; d/1878) MD Phila Coll Med & Surg 1851. *Tr Med Soc Pa* 12:408, 1878. *Butler* 1878: 688.

HERNDON, CHARLES L CUVIER, CW–USA; New Orleans (b/1833; d/1878) MD Jefferson 1858. *Tr AMA* 30: 870–72, 1879. *Med rec* 14: 240, 1878.

HERNDON, JAMES CARMICHAEL, CW–CSA; Fredericksburg, Va (b/IX–22–1831; d/X–18–1877 Fernandina, Fla) MD Jefferson 1852; att U Va. *Bost m & s j* 112:514, 1885. *Med rec* 13: 119, 1878. *Atkinson* I: 563.

HEROLD, THEODORE, Elgin, Ill (d/I–31–1900) MD Bern & Zürich, Switz 1887. *Tr Ill St Med Soc* 1899–1900: 509. *Polk* 1896: 418.

HERR, ELIAS BEANE, Lancaster, Pa (d/IV–27–1904 @ 70) MD UCNY 1854. *Pa med jour* 8:335, 1904/05. *Flint* 1897: 806.

HERR, MARTIN L, Lancaster Pa (d/II–8–1902 @63) <MD St Louis Med Coll 1863> *Pa m j* 5:314 464 1901/02.

HERRICK, ALBERT SHAW, Lowell, Mass 1873– (b/XII–28–1844 Greenwood, Me; d/VI–5–1882 @38 Bethel) MD Dartmouth 1873. *Bost m & s j* 107: 618, 1882.

HERRICK, HENRY JUSTUS, CW–USA; Cleveland (b/I 20–1833 Aurora, O; d/I–28–1901) MD Rush 1861; AB Williams 1858. *Bost m & s j* 144:126, 1901. *Atkinson* I:106. *K&B* III: 558.

HERRICK, JOHN CLAUDIUS, Denver, Colo (b/1844 Southampton; d/IX–30–1898) MD Yale 1865; <MD LICH 1865> *Tr Colo St Med Soc* 1898–99: 37, 509. *JAMA* 31: 942, 1898. *Polk* 1893: 234.

HERRICK, ORSON QUINCY, Kansas, Ill; CW–USA (b/1831; d/VIII–19–1873) MD U Mich 1854. *Tr AMA* 25: 530–31, 1874. *Tr Ill St Med Soc* 1877: 218.

HERRICK, WILLIAM BENTLEY, Louisville; Chicago; Auburn, Me; MexWar–USA (b/IX–20–1813 Durham, Me; d/XII–31–1865) MD Dartmouth 1837; att Bowdoin Med Coll. *Chicago med jour* 23: 913, 1866. *Med surg rep Phila* 14: 80, 1866. *Tr Ill St Med Soc* 1869: 151–55. *K&B* III: 559.

HERRICK, WILLIAM SLADE, Stewart, Ill (d/V–10–1885 @47) MD Rush 1866. *New Orl m&s j* ns13:86, 1885.

HERRING, BENJAMIN A , Clarksville, Tenn; Decatur, Ga (d/IX–19–1898 @76) MD U Louisville 1846. *JAMA* 31: 872, 1898. *Polk* 1886: 863.

HERRMAN, CHRISTIAN A , Chicago (d/I–22–1905 @59) MD Hahnemann Chic 1894. *Ill med jour* 7:292, 1905. *Polk* 1896: 388. Homeopath.

HERRON, JAMES A , Pittsburgh 1856– CW–USA (b/II–14–1834; d/XI–15–1868) MD Hahnemann Phila

 Spec. educ'l status abbrev. as: ***ng*** = college verified attendance without degree;

1856. *Tr Homeop Med Soc Pa* 1869:125, 158, 173.

HERRON, JAMES BLAKELY, Allegheny, Pa (d/III-17 1899 @76) MD UCNY 1848. *JAMA* 32: 787, 1899.

HERSEY, GEORGE EVERETT, Manchester, NH (b/IX 1-1847 Sanbornton: d/I-8-1878) MD UCNY 1871. *Tr AMA* 29:672-73, 1878. *Tr NH Med Soc* 1878: 199-201.

HERSEY, HERBERT SEWALL, Philadelphia; Bismarck, DakTrerr (b/IV-7-1855 Paris, Me; d/VI-2-1901) MD Detroit Med Coll 1878; ng Amherst. *Amherst, Men of*: 1876. *Polk* 1886: 200.

HERSHEY, ANDREW H, CW-USN (d/II-6-1863 abd "Amando") MD CPSNY 1862. *Nat m jour* 1:297, 1870/71.

HERSOM, NAHUM ALVAH, Portland, Me (b/VIII- -1835 Lebanon; d/V-1-1881 Dublin, Ire) MD UPa 1861. *U Pa med alum CW*:1861. *JAMA* 1:687-88, 1883. *Tr Me Med Assoc* 1881: 385-86. *Butler* 1878:307.

HERVEY, FRANK F , Fortville, Ind (b/I-19-1856; d/V-20-1893) MD Med Coll Ind 1879. *Tr Ind St Med Soc* 1894: 215. *Polk* 1886: 328.

HERWISCH, CHARLES, Philadelphia? (b/IV-2-1852 Austria; d/XII-14-1899) <MD Vienna> *Pa med jour* 3: 615-16, 1899/1900. *JAMA* 33: 1632, 1899.

HERZBERG, EMANUEL, NYC (b/XII-13-1812; d/III-5-1880) MD Berlin 1839. *Med reg NY NJ Conn* 1880: 236. *Butler* 1878: 501.

HERZOG, CARL, NYC (d/III- -1886) MD UCNY 1879. *Med reg NY NJ Conn* 1886: 250.

HERZOG, MAX, NYC (b/VI-4-1830; d/IV-12-1881) MD U Würzburg 1854. *Med reg NY NJ Conn* 1881: 237. *Bost m & s j* 105: 622, 1881.

HESS, ELIZABETH, Iowa City (b/III-23-1845 Ohio; d/IV-21-1898) MD Iowa St U 1874. *JAMA* 30:1125,1898. *Tr Ia St Med Soc* 16:366-68,1898. *Polk* 1896: 527.

HESS, LOUIS, Brooklyn (b/NY; d/IX-11-1898 @38) MD CPSNY 1886. *JAMA* 31: 742, 1898. *Polk* 1896: 997.

HESS, THOMAS M , Berwick Ill (d/IV-9-1896 @77) MD Rush 1871 hon. *JAMA* 26:843 1891. *Polk* 1896:363.

HESSE, HENRY JOSEPH, Brooklyn (b/1853; d/V-19-1895) MD LICH 1876. *Med reg NY NJ Conn* 1895:226. *JAMA* 24: 861, 1895.

HESTER, ABNER, New Orleans (d/XII-1-1853) MD UPa 1837. *New Orl m & s j* 10:555- 62, 1854. *Northwest m & s j* 3:143, 1854.

HESTER, B O , Haskell, Tex (d/VI-23-1906 @34) MD Univ Med Coll Va 1896. *Tex st jour med* 2:122, 1906. *Polk* 1902: 1916.

HESTER, MANLY LEE, Jasper, Tex (b/III-16-1828; d/XII-24-1854) MD U La 1853; AB U Ala 1849; AM 1852. *U Ala cat*: 89.

HESTER, WILLIAM, Tuscaloosa, Ala (b/VI-9-1841; d/II-11-1899) MD UCNY 1867; att U Ala. *Tr Med Assoc St Ala* 1899: 233. *Polk* 1893: 164.

HESTER, WILLIAM WEIR, Chicago (b/IV-18-1835 Charlestown, Ind; d/VII-18-1902) MD Jefferson 1863. *Ill med jour* ns4:480-81, 1903. *Polk* 1896: 388.

HESTON, GEORGE THOMAS, Newtown, Pa (b/II-17-1826; d/VIII-15-1904) MD UPa 1852; att Haverford Coll. *Haverford biogr cat*: 30. *Flint* 1897: 811.

HETRICK, JEREMIAH SMITH, New Freedom, Pa (b/XII-28-1849 York Co; d/III-27-1904) MD Washington U Balto 1873. *Pa med jour* 7: 335, 390, 1903/04. *Flint* 1897: 811.

HETZELL, DAVID GEORGE, Philadelphia (d/X-25-1904 @68) MD Jefferson 1861. *Pa med jour* 8: 335, 1904/05. *Flint* 1897: 819.

HEUEL, FRANZ, NYC (b/Westphalia; d/I-4-1898) MD NY Med Coll 1857. *Bost m & s j* 138: 45, 1898. *JAMA* 30:166, 1898. *Polk* 1896: 1058.

HEUSER, PAUL E , Brooklyn (b/Gny; d/VII-10-1905 @81) MD ? *Bost m & s j* 153: 94, 1905.

HEUSER, WILLIAM FERDINAND, Brooklyn 1853- (b/IV-30-1815 Hersfeld, Gny; d/VIII-9-1870 Gny) <MD U Marburg 1843> *Med reg NY NJ Conn* 1871: 357.

HEWELL, JOHN ALFRED RAGLAND, Brewersville, Ala; CW-CSA (b/I-1-1832; d/X-7-1863) MD ? att U Ala 1848. *U Ala cat*: 91.

HEWINS, LEVI TOMLINSON, Lodi, Ill (b/IX- -1821 Munson, O; d/VII-26-1873) MD Starling 1854; <stud CPSNY and Jefferson> *Tr AMA* 29:673-74, 1878. *Tr Ill St Med Soc* 1874: 157-58.

HEWIT, HENRY STUART, CW-USA; NYC (b/XII-26 1825 Fairfield, Conn; d/VIII-19-1873) MD UCNY 1847. *Med reg NY NJ Conn* 1874: 277. *Med rec* 8:440, 462, 576, 1871.

HEWITT [HERWITT], ELI M , CW-USA (d/VII-24-1864) MD ? *Nat med jour* 1:297, 1870/71.

HEWITT, ROBERT CARSON, Louisville (d/XII-22-1891) MD Transylvania 1844. *JAMA* 18: 172, 1892.

HEWLETT, PETER V P , Newark, NJ (b/XII-3-1846; d/III-13-1906) MD UCNY 1868. *Bost m & s j* 154: 332,1906. *Atkinson* I: 553. *Polk* 1896:943.

HEWSON, ADDINELL, Philadelphia (b/XI-22-1828; d/IX-11-1889) MD Jefferson 1850; AB UPA 1847. *Tr CPP* cent vol:234; 3s12:xxxiii-xliv,1890. *JAMA* 13:505 1889. *Med surg rep Phila* 61:336,1889.*K&B* III:562.

HEWSON, DAVID CALDWELL, CW-CSA (b/New Orleans; d/X-30-1869 Orange, Tex) MD UPa 1848. *U Pa med alum CW*: 1848.

HEWSON, THOMAS TICKELL, Philadelphia 1800- (b/IV-9-1773 London; d/II-17-1848) Hon MD UPa 1822; stud Lond, Edinb; AB UPa 1789. *Tr AMA* 3: 445-47, 1850. *Tr CPP* ns3:2-10, 1849/50. *NJ med rep* 1:216-19, 1848. *K&B* III: 563-64.

HEWSON, WILLIAM, Detroit (d/XI-11-1899) <MD Montreal Med Inst 1843> *JAMA* 33:1441, 1899. *Polk* 1890: 585 (as homeopath).

HEYDOCK, MILLS OLCOTT, Chicago (d/IV-17-1881) MD Dartmouth 1851. *Chic med jour* 42:549, 1881. *Butler* 1878: 133.

HEYL, HENRY F , Philadelphia (b/1781? d/II-15-1866 @ 75) MD ? *Med surg rep Phila* 14:180, 1866.

HEYWOOD, BENJAMIN, Worcester, Mass (b/VII-16-1821; d/VII-21-1860) MD UPa 1844; AB Harvard 1840. *Bost m & s j* 62: 526, 1860. *Med surg rep Phila* ns4:466, 1860. Palmer's *Necrol Harvard alum*: 376-77.

HEYWOOD, BENJAMIN FRANKLIN, Worcester, Mass (b/IV-24-1792; d/XII- -1869) MD Yale 1815; AB Dartmouth 1812. *Phila med reg & dir* 1871:303. *Bost m & s j* ns4: 344, 1869.

HEYWOOD, CHARLES FREDERICK, NYC (b/1823 Boston; d/II-14-1893) MD Harvard 1846; AB 1843. *Bost m & s j* 128:204,1893. *Butler* 1878:515.

HEYWOOD, FREDERICK, Worcester, Mass (d/VIII-20 1855 San Salvador) MD UPa 1848; att Dartmouth. *Boston m & s j* 53: 515, 1856.

HEYWOOD, JOHN WICKS, Buffalo (d/V-19-1854) MD Buffalo 1854; AB ? . *Buff med jour* 10: 64, 1854.

HIATT, ALFRED H , Chicago (d/IV-27-1901) MD Med Coll Ohio 1846. *Ill med jour* ns3:47, 1901.

HIATT, JOHN MILTON, CW-CSA; Peoria, Ill (b/1840? d/III-20-1869 @29) MD Rush 1864. *Phila med reg & dir* 1871:300. *Med surg rep Phila* 20:346, 1869.

HIBBARD, CHARLES C , No Branch, Mich (b/Detroit; d/IV-5-1878 @25) MD Detroit Med Coll 1876; AB U Mich 1874. *Mich med news* 1:67, 1878.

HIBBARD, CLEON MELVILLE, St Louis; Boston (d/VIII-22-1898) MD Harvard 1895. *Bost m & s j* 139:254, 1898. *JAMA* 31:551, 1898. *Polk* 1896: 699.

HIBBARD, RUFUS, Elizabeth, NJ (d/V-17-1884 @79) MD ? *Med surg rep Phila* 50:704, 1884.

HIBBARD, TIMOTHY RUSS, Yonkers, NY (d/XI-2-1866 @ 61) MD CPSNY 1831. *Med surg rep Phila* 15: 407, 1866.

HIBBEN, JAMES, Brooklyn (b/IX-1-1824 Charleston, SC; d/IV-14-1856) MD NY Med Coll 1852; AB Amherst 1846. *Amherst, Men of*: 1846.

HIBBEN, JOHN BASCOME, Kansas City, Kans (d/X-27-1899 @46) MD UCNY 1878. *JAMA* 33:1183, 1899. *Polk* 1896: 564.

HIBBERD, JAMES FARQUHAR, Calif 1849-55; Richmond, Ind; CW-USA (b/XI-4-1816 New Market, Md; d/IX-8-1903) MD CPSNY 1849; att Yale Med Sch. *Tr Ind St Med Soc* 1904: 356. *Atkinson* I: 59-60. *K&B* III: 564.

HIBLER, AUGUSTUS, Bellefonte, Pa (d/I-16-1902) <MD Freiburg, Gny> *Pa med jour* 5:260, 276, 1901/02. *Polk* 1886: 792.

HICHBORN, ALEXANDER, CW-USA (d/V-5-1865 Chancellorsville, Va) MD Dartmouth 1856; ng Woodstock. *Nat med jour* 1:297, 1870/71.

HICKEY, AMANDA (SANFORD), Auburn, NY (b/VIII 28-1838 New Bedford [Mass?] d/X-17-1894) MD U Mich 1871; <att Woman's Med Coll Pa> *Med reg NY NJ Conn* 1895: 226. *JAMA* 23: 655, 1894. *K&B* II: 525.

HICKEY, THOMAS BERNARD, Shamokin Pa (d/VIII-6-1902) MD Jefferson 1894. *Pa med jour* 6:260, 1902/03.

HICKLIN, O B , New London, Mo (b/IX-24-1833; d/VI 28-1905) MD CPS Keokuk 1876. *So pract* 27:637,1905.

HICKMAN, JOSEPH, Chester Co, Pa (b/IV-12-1804; d/V-14 or 15-1856) MD Jefferson 1829. *Tr Med Soc Pa* 1857: 137-38.

HICKMAN, THOMAS G , Vandalia, Ill (d/IX-21-1899) MD U Louisville 1859. *Tr Ill St Med Soc* 1899: 287. *JAMA* 33:927, 1899. *Polk* 1886: 300.

HICKMAN, WILFORD, Spencer, Ind (b/XII-25-1856 Owen Co; d/XI-22-1904) MD Med Coll Ind 1883. *Tr Ind St Med Soc* 1905: 450. *Polk* 1896: 492.

HICKOK, OLIVER STARR, Ridgefield, Conn (b/XII-9 1834 Bethel; d/IV-9-1885) MD Berkshire 1855. *Proc Conn Med Soc* 1885: 217-18. *Butler* 1878: 78.

HICKS, BENJAMIN BLOUNT, Oxford, NC; CW-CSA (b/1835; d/1874) MD UPa 1857. *U Pa med alum CW*:1857.

HICKS, HERBERT DEXTER, Amherst, NH (b/II-14-1852 Boston; d/IV-8-1891) MD Harvard 1879. *Tr NH Med Soc* 1891: 256-57. *Polk* 1890: 707.

HICKS, J W , Ala; Miss; Moulton, Tex (b/Elyton, Ala; d/VIII-23-1905 @74) MD Tulane 1855 [?] *Polk* 1886: 890. *Texas st jour med* 1:154, 1905/06.

HICKS, JAMES WOOD, CW-CSA; Orlando, Fl (b/1826/27 Granville Co, NC; d/I-14-1895) MD UPa 1851; AB UNC 1847. *JAMA* 24: 177, 1895. *U Pa med alum CW*: 1851. *Polk* 1890: 254.

HICKS, JOHN B , Rutherford Co, Tenn (b/II-5-1857 Murfreesboro; d/IX-16-1878 Memphis) MD Vanderbilt 1877. *Tr Med Soc Tenn* 1879: 174-75.

HICKS, JOHN HENRY [HENBY], CW-CSA; Sampson Co, NC (b/1832; d/1883) MD UPa 1861; att UNC 1856-58. *U Pa med alum CW*: 1861.

HICKS, JOHN R , CW-CSA; Vicksburg, Miss; Murfreesboro, Tn (b/1839; d/X-7-1878 Ala) MD U La 1861. *Tr AMA* 30:872, 1879. *Tr Miss St M Assn* 1879: 37-38.

HICKS, JOHN TATUM, CW-CSA (b/VIII-26-1826; d/V-25-1863 White Co, Ark) MD UPa 1851. *U Pa med alum CW*: 1851.

HIESTER, FRANK MUHLENBERG, Reading, Pa; CW-USA (b/III-11-1829; d/IV-9-1864) MD UPa 1853; AB Princeton 1849; AM 1852. *Tr AMA* 16:652, 1865. *Nat med jour* 1:297, 1870/71.

HIESTER, ISAAC, Reading, Pa (b/1785? d/IX-12-1855) MD UPa 1808. *Bost m & s j* 53:175, 1856.

HIGDAY, TOMPKINS, Laporte, Ind (b/VIII- -1826 Tompkins Co, NY; d/X-5-1876) MD Ind Med Coll 1847; MD Jefferson 1852. *Tr Ind St M S* 1880: 236-37.

HIGGINBOTHAM, EDWARD GARRIGUES, CW-CSA; Richmond, Va (b/VII-20-1824; d/V-4-1901) MD UPa 1845. *U Pa med alum CW*:1845. Blanton *Va surg CW*: 405. *Polk* 1886: 925.

 Spec. educ'l status abbrev. as: ***ng*** = college verified attendance without degree;

HIGGINS, ARCHIBALD ALEXANDER, Manasquan, NJ (b/IX-29-1827 Princeton; d/X-9-1897) MD Pa Med Coll 1854; AB Princeton 1846. *Bost m & s j* 137: 403, 1897. *Atkinson* I: 538-39. *Polk* 1896:940.

HIGGINS, CARTER B, Peru, Ind (b/XII-15-1843 Preble Co, O; d/XI-14-1894) MD Rush 1866. *JAMA* 23: 802, 1894. *Tr Ind St Med Soc* 1895: 407. *Butler* 1878: 206.

HIGGINS, EDWARD M , Hot Springs, Ark (d/VII-18-1897 @43) MD Queens U, Ont 1877. *JAMA* 29: 251, 1897. *Polk* 1890: 166.

HIGGINS, FRANCIS WESLEY, Cortland, NY (d/XII-18-1903 @46) MD UCNY 1881. *Bost m & s j* 149: 720, 1903. *Tr Med Soc St NY* 1904: [420].

HIGGINS, GEORGE ZOETH, Strong, Me (b/XII-29-1832 Exeter;d/XII-11-1898) MD Bowdoin 1858. *Bost m &s j* 139:609 1898. *JAMA* 31:1542 1898. *Polk* 1896:640.

HIGGINS, JOHN FRANCIS, Port Jervis, NY (d/VIII-20 1893) MD Bellevue 1879. *JAMA* 21:390, 1893.

HIGGINS, JOHN JACOB, NYC (d/VIII-28-1906 @78) MD CPSNY 1850; AB Madison 1846. *Boston m & s j* 155: 298, 1906. *Polk* 1896: 1058.

HIGGINS, JONATHAN MITCHELL, Philadelphia (d/XII-15-1899 @58) MD UPa 1861. *JAMA* 34: 61, 1900.

HIGGINS, SEABURY M , Memphis, NY (b/Brewster, Mass; d/XII-9-1889) MD UCNY 1848. *Tr NY St Med Soc* 11:741 ff, 1894. *Polk* 1886: 667.

HIGGINSON, FRANCIS JOHN, Brookline, Mass (d/III-9-1872 @65) MD Harvard 1828; AB 1825. *Bost m & s j* ns9:180, 1872. *Mass Med Soc cat* 1894 (as of Grand Rapids, Mich).

HIGH, LOUIS FIELDING, Woodburn, NC; Danville, Va; Southern Pines, NC 1901- (b/III-4-1867; d/V-3-1905) MD CPS Balto 1891. *Tr Med Soc Va* 1905: 448-49. *Polk* 1900: 1761.

HIGHMAN, LOUIS W , New Harmony, Ind (b/XII-9-1845 Posey Co; d/I-22-1879) MD Cincinnati Coll Med & Surg 1874. *Tr Ind St Med Soc* 1880: 227-28.

HIGINBOTHAM, SAMUEL, CW-USA (d/V-29-1863 Triune, Tenn) MD Rush 1857. *Nat m j* 1:297, 1870/71.

HILBURN, EBER WHITFIELD, Washington, Ind (b/XII-31-1837; d/X-24-1897) MD Miami Med Coll 1871. *Tr Ind St Med Soc* 1898: 382. *Butler* 1878:206.

HILDRETH, CHARLES C , Zanesville, O (b/IV-28-1811 Marietta; d/VIII-11-1889) MD Med Coll Ohio 1833. *Med surg rep Phila* 61: 307, 1889. *Atkinson* I: 568. *Polk* 1886: 774.

HILDRETH, CHARLES FLOYER POND, CW-USA; Manchester, NH (d/VIII-18-1903 @71) MD Harvard 1861. *Bost m&s j* 149: 276, 1903. *Harv in CW*: 264.

HILDRETH, CHARLES HOSEA, Gloucester, Mass (d/V-18-1884 @58) MD Harvard 1851. *Bost m & s j* 110: 504, 1884.

HILDRETH, CHARLES LEWIS, Southampton, NY (d/VIII-12-1896 @40) MD LICH 1889. *JAMA* 27: 661, 1896. *Polk* 1890: 850.

HILDRETH, EUGENIUS AUGUSTUS, Wheeling, WVa (b/IX-13-1821; d/VIII-31-1885) MD Med Coll Ohio 1844; AB Kenyon 1840. *New Orl m&s j* ns13: 324, 1885. *Tr Med Soc W Va* 1886: 335-37. *K&B* III: 565.

HILDRETH, JOSEPH S , CW-USA; Chicago (b/Somerville, Mass; d/VII-22-1870) *Chic med jour* 27:512, 1870. *Tr Ill St M S* 1870: 108. *Med rec* 5:336, 1870/71.

HILDRETH, SAMUEL PRESCOT, Marietta, O (b/IX-30-1783 Methuen, Mass; d/VII-24-1863) Lic Med Soc Mass 1805. *Bost m&s j* 41:229-32. *Nashville j m & s* ns4: 319, 1886. *K&B* III:565.

HILDRETH, THADDEUS, CW-USA; Gardiner, Me (b/V-1-1826 or 1827; d/VIII-25-1880) MD Dartmouth 1856. *Tr Me Med Assoc* 1881: 387-88. *Atkinson* I: 583. *Butler* 1878: 307.

HILDRETH, WILLIAM HARTWELL, Newton, Mass (b/IV-19-1843 New Ipswich, NH; d/I-13-1903 Newton Upper Falls, Mass) MD Dartmouth 1868. *Bost m&s j* 148: 108, 1903. *Polk* 1896: 719.

HILEMAN, JOHN SAX, W Pittston, Pa (b/XII-12-1863; d/VIII-6-1904) MD UPa 1889. *Pa m j* 8: 335, 1904/05. *Tr Luzerne Co Med Soc* 1904: 189-91. *Polk* 1896: 1330.

HILL, ALBERT D , Chicago (d/III-4-1906 @57) MD Albany 1879. *Ill med jour* 9:463, 1906.

HILL, CHARLES HOWARD, Philadelphia (d/VII-18-1889 @85) MD Jefferson 1835. *JAMA* 33: 302, 1899. *Polk* 1896: 1307.

HILL, CHARLES JUDSON, Utica NY (b/II-13-1830 Burford, Can W; d/II-15-1891) MD Hahnemann Phila 1859. *No Am j hom* 39:211, 1891. *New Engl med gaz* 26:158, 1877/78. *Polk* 1886:713. Homeopath.

HILL, EDWIN ALLEN, E Killingly, Conn (b/IX-27-1825 Griswold; d/V-30-1896) MD Harvard 1850. *Proc Conn Med Soc* 1897:339-40. *JAMA* 26:1245, 1896. *Atkinson* I: 378.

HILL, FRANCIS HAMILTON, Washington, DC (b/1826 or 27; d/I-30-1906) MD Columbian 1849. *Hist Med Soc DC:* 246. *Polk* 1900: 371.

HILL, HAMPTON EUGENE, Saco, Me (b/IV-21-1850; d/I-9-1894) MD U Mich 1871. *Buff m&s j* 33:555, 1894. *Tr Me Med Assoc* 1894: 573-78. *JAMA* 22:122, 1894. *Bost m&s j* 130:52, 1894. *K&B* III: 567.

HILL, HENRY CLAY, CW-USA; Lockport, NY (b/1832 Vt; d/II-8-1901) MD U Mich 1859. *Bost m&s j* 144:174, 1901. *Polk* 1886: 666.

HILL, HENRY HOWARD, Everett, Pa (d/V-22-1902 @57) MD Jefferson 1867. *Pa med jour* 6: 260, 1902/03. *Flint* 1897: 802.

HILL, HIRAM HOVEY, Augusta, Me (b/IV-30-1810 Turner; d/XII-2-1889) MD Bowdoin 1836. *Tr Me Med Assoc* 1890:336-39. *K&B* III: 567-68.

HILL, J W , Knoxville, Tenn (d/XII-4-1898) MD Strassburg, Gny 1878. *JAMA* 31: 1542, 1898. *Polk* 1886:867.

HILL, JAMES HYSER, Springfield, Ill (d/III-6-1906

@81) MD U Louisville 1850. *Ill med jour* 9:463, 1906. *Polk* 1886: 279.

HILL, JAMES SENECA, Tewksbury Mass; Sacramento, Cal (b/III–3–1825 Pawtucket; d/IV–21–1857) MD Harvard 1855; AB 1852; ng Amherst 1852. *Bost m&s j* 56: 407, 1857. Palmer's *Necrol Harv alum*: 155.

HILL, JOHN, S Norwalk, Conn (b/I–19–1820 or 1821 Sterling, Conn; d/IX–18–1880) MD UCNY 1845. *Proc Conn Med Soc* 1881: 221–22. *Butler* 1878: 78.

HILL, JOHN DAVIDSON, Buffalo (d/II 27–1892 @70) MD Buff 1849 *Buff m&s j* 31:556 1892. *Butler* 1878:537.

HILL, JOHN EDWARD, CW–USA (b/III–24–1835 Eliot, Me; d/IX–11–1862 Georgetown, DC) MD Harvard 1860; ng Bowdoin Med Coll 1858. *Nat med jour* 1:297, 1870/71. *Harvard in CW*: 258.

HILL, JOHN LAWRENCE, Gettysburg, Pa (d/1903) MD Pa Med Coll 1846. *Pa med jour* 7:279, 1903/04.

HILL, JOHN SHELTON, Baltimore (b/1849 Va; d/XI–26–1883) MD U Md 1871. *Med annals Md:* 438. *Butler* 1874: 312.

HILL, JOSEPH SPENCER, Tenn (d/1878 Moscow, Tn) MD Washington U Balto 1874. *Tr AMA* 30: 872, 1879.

HILL, LESTER SENECA, Providence, RI (b/XII–19–1843; d/IX–9–1907) MD UCNY 1872. *Tr RI Med Soc* 7:720, 1904–09. *Polk* 1896:1352.

HILL, LEVI GERRISH, Dover, NH (b/VII–7–1812 Strafford; d/III–3–1898 @85) MD Dartmouth 1838. *Bost m&s j* 138: 364, 1898. *Tr NH Med Soc* 1898: 258–65. *Atkinson* I:125. *Polk* 1896: 918.

HILL, LUKE, Biddeford, Me; CW–USA (b/VI–20–1812; d/XII–24–1863) MD Bowdoin 1841; AB 1835. *Bowdoin cat*: 1835.

HILL, NATHAN BRANSON, Minneapolis (b/V–13–1817 NC; d/1875) MD Med Coll Ohio 1848; ng Haverford 1839. *Tr AMA* 29: 674–75, 1878. *Tr Minn St Med Soc* 1876: 121–23.

HILL, NATHAN S , CW–USA; Neville, O (b/VII–20–1828 Cynthiana, Ky; d/IV–13–1896) MD Med Coll Ohio 1862. *JAMA* 26:890 1896. *Atk'n* I:517. *Butler* 1878:633.

HILL, THOMAS, CW–CSA; Goldsboro, NC (b/X–26–1832; d/II–20–1906) MD UCNY 1854; att UNC 1849–51. *UNC cat*: 282. *Polk* 1886: 722.

HILL, THOMAS PRENTISS, Sanbornton, NH 1816–44; Hanover 1844–66 (b/VIII–1781 Conway; d/VIII–3–1866) MD Dart'th 1816. *Med s rep Phila* 15:188 1866.

HILL, THOMAS RUFUS, MexWar–USA; Montgomery, Ala (b/1818 Trenton, Tenn; d/XI–27–1872) MD ? *Tr AMA* 23: 573–74, 1872.

HILL, WILLIAM, Bloomington, Ill (d/III–1–1906 @77) MD Jefferson 1856. *Ill med jour* 9:463, 1906.

HILL, WILLIAM GEDDY, Raleigh, NC (b/IX–11–1806; d/III–4–1877) MD UPa 1828; att UNC. *Tr NC Med Soc* 1877:9; 1878:105. *Tr AMA* 29:657–76, 1878.

HILL, WILLIAM OTHO, CW–CSA; Harrisonburg, Va (b/XI–1–1839 Woodstock; d/XI–23–1883) MD Va Med Coll 1861. *Tr Med Soc Va* 1883: 1867. Blanton *Va surg CW*: 405.

HILLBISH, FREDERICK SOBIESKI, Fremont, O (d/VIII–25–1898 @56) MD Bellevue 1869. *JAMA* 31: 618, 1898. *Polk* 1886: 755.

HILLEGAS, JOHN PETER, Philadelphia (d/II–12–1898) MD UPa 1886. *JAMA* 30:570, 1898. *Polk* 1896: 1307.

HILLIARD, CHARLES EUGENE, Asheville, NC (b/VIII 24–1864; d/XII–19–1898) MD Jefferson 1888. *Tr NC Med Soc* 1899: 174. *Polk* 1896: 1119.

HILLIARD, PHINEAS KIRKBRIDE, CW–USA; Manahawkin, NJ (b/I–22–1842 Vincentown; d/XII–22–1890) MD UPa 1864. *U Pa med alum CW*: 1864.

HILLIS, DAVID BURK, Keokuk, Ia (b/VII–24–1825 Madison, Ind; d/IX–9–1900) MD St Louis Med Coll 1847; MD St Louis Med Coll 1872 hon; att So Hanover Coll, Ind. *Tr Ia St Med Soc* 19: 442–43, 1901. *Ill med jour* ns2:286, 1900. *Polk* 1890: 418.

HILLMANTEL, JOSEPH L, Milwaukee (d/XI–7–1899 @36) MD Northwestern 1887. *JAMA* 33: 1441, 1899.

HILLS, ERASMUS DARWIN, Montour Falls, NY (d/IV 19–1900 @61) MD Buffalo 1867. *JAMA* 34: 1146, 1900.

HILLS, RALPH, Delaware, O (b/XII–13–1810 Worthington, O; d/X–9–1879) Stud med w/Eli Todd, Hartford, Coll. *Tr O St Med Soc* 1880: 118–19.

HILLS, SAMUEL AUGDEN, NYC (d/II–26–1898 @76) MD Yale 1846. *JAMA* 30: 624, 1898.

HILS, JOSEPH, Woonsocket, RI (b/IX–21–1849 Quebec; d/II–23–1906) MD McGill 1873. *Tr RI Med Soc* 7:430–31, 1904–09.*Polk* 1896: 1355.

HILTON, ABRAHAM TEN EYCK, E Orange, NJ (d/XII–21–1883 @70) MD CPSNY 1835. *Med surg rep Phila* 50:64, 1884.

HILTON, CHARLES W , Monroe, La (d/V– –1906 @45) MD Tulane 1887. *New Orl m&s j* 58: 979, 1906. *Polk* 1896: 618.

HILTON, , JOHN R , CW–USA (d/III–17–1863) *Tr Med Soc NJ* 1866: 18.

HILTON, JOSEPH, NYC (d/I–7–1892 @77) Lic M S St NY 1837. *Bost m&s j* 126:48 1882. *Polk* 1890:817.

HIMES, ISAAC NEWTON, CW–USA; Cleveland, O (b/XII–4–1834 Shippensburg, Pa; d/IV–1–1895) MD CPS NY 1856. *Tr Ohio Med Soc* 1895: 49–51. *Med bull med & surg* 17:235, 1895. *Butler* 1878: 616. *K&B* III: 569.

HIMOE, H CLARENCE, Albuquerque, NM (d/VII–3–1898) MD Kansas City Med Coll 1890. *JAMA* 31: 142, 1898. *Polk* 1896: 846.

HINCKLEY, DONALD ROSE, New Haven, Conn (b/IX 18–1869 Northampton, Mass; d/X–14–1901) MD Harvard 1896; AB Yale 1892. *Proc Conn Med Soc* 1902: 429–30. *Bost m & s j* 145: 504, 1901.

HINCKLEY, JOHN WESLEY, Boston; Onogra Ill (d/III 28–1865 @44) MD Harv 1847. *Bost m&s j* 72:208 1865.

HINDE, THOMAS, Newport, Ky (b/1736? d/IX– 1828

 Spec. educ'l status abbrev. as: ***ng*** = college verified attendance without degree;

@92) MD ? *Transylvania j m & assoc sci* 2: 298, 1829.

HINDS, FREDERIC JONAS, Salem, NY (b/E Greenwich; d/IV-26-1887) MD Bellevue 1876. *Tr NY St Med Soc* 11: 741 ff. 1894. Polk 1886: 706.

HINDS, WILLIAM HENRY WEED, CW-USA; Milford, NH (d/VII-29-1897 @64) MD Harvard 1861. *Tr Am Inst Hom* 1898: 49. *Polk* 1886: 593. Homeopath.

HINES, ANDREW J , Doylestown, Pa (d/I-21-1902 @ 75) MD Jefferson 1853. *Pa med jour* 6: 260, 1902/03. *Polk* 1886: 797.

HINES, FRANCIS EDWARD, Salem, Mass (d/IX-30-1901 @49) MD Harvard 1879. *Bost m & s j* 145:394, 1901. *Polk* 1896:722.

HINES, THOMAS F , Middle Creek, O (d/V-13-1896) MD CPS Keokuk 1892. *JAMA* 26: 1092, 1896.

HINISH, WILLIAM WATSON, Chicago (d/II-10-1903 @60) MD Miami 1875. *Ill med jour* ns4: 665, 1903. *Polk* 1886: 265.

HINKLE, HENRY CONRAD, Oakland, Cal (d/VII-13-1897) MD UCNY 1886. *JAMA* 29: 252, 1897. *Polk* 1896: 234.

HINKLEY, ALONZO SQUIRE, Buffalo (d/II-25-1898 @75) MD Cleveland U Med & Surg 1856. *Buffalo m & s j* 37: 698-99. 1898. *Butler* 1878: 537.

HINKS, EZEKIEL FRANKLIN, Hyde Park, Mass; Thomaston Me; Marlboro Mass (b/VIII-10-1820 Bucksport Me; d/II-12-1886) MD NY Hom 1867. *Tr Am Inst Hom* 1886: 142. *Polk* 1886: 466. Homeopath.

HINKSON, ADDISON CYRUS, San Francisco (d/-IV 21-1903) MD CPS San Francisco 1901. *Calif st jour med* 1:174, 1903.

HINMAN, GEORGE ADAM, Holland, Vt (b/XI-29-1817; d/II-11-1880) MD Woodstock 1841. *Tr Vt Med Soc* 1883: 106.

HINMAN, RICHARD H , CW-USA (d/V-22-1862 Brooklyn) MD CPSNY 1858. *Nat m j* 1:297, 1870/71.

HINSEY, JOSEPH CRAWFORD, Ottumwa, Ia (b/VI-9 1829 Butler Co, O; d/IV-10-1892) MD Rush 1851; MD Pa Med Coll 1855. *Tr Ia St Med Soc* 10:229-230, 1892. *Atkinson* I: 558-59. *Polk* 1886: 365.

HINTON, JOHN HENRY, NYC (b/1827; d/IV-26-1905) MD CPSNY 1852. *Bost m & s j* 152: 536, 1905. *Polk* 1896: 1058.

HINTON, JOHN ROBERT, Petersburg, Va; CW-CSA (b/VII-13-1833 Clarksville; d/X-11-1890) MD UPa 1860. *U Pa med alum CW*: 1860. Blanton *Va s CW*: 405.

HINTON, RUFUS KING, Philadelphia; CW-CSA (b/I-7 1830 Brookesville, Miss; d/IV-24-1904) MD Jefferson 1852; att U Ala. *Pa med jour* 8: 335, 1904/05.

HINTZE, FREDERICK E B , Baltimore (b/1803; d/X-12-1865 Wilmington, Del) MD UMd 1823. *Tr AMA* 18: 337-38, 1867. *Med annals Md:* 439.

HIRIART, PAUL J , Plaquemine, La (d/XII-15-1876 @ 62) MD Tulane 1869. *New Orl m & s j* ns4: 599, 1877.

HIRSCH. SIMON, NYC 1848- (b/V-13-1816 Stebbach, Bavaria; d/IV-23-1878) <MD Munich 1840>. *Med reg NY NJ Conn* 1878: 181. *Butler* 1878: 515.

HIRSCHMANN, LEOPOLD, NYC (d/III-15-1906 @35) MD Cornell 1899; AB. *Bost m&s j* 154:332, 1906.

HIRST, CYRUS J , Altoona, Pa; Galesburg, Ill (d/IX-1-1859 @40) MD Jefferson 1850. *Med surg rep Phila* ns3: 72, 1859/60.

HISEROTE, A J , Union, Ia (d/XI-1-1893) MD ? *JAMA* 21:869, 1893. *Butler* 1878: 238.

HISLOP, JOHN G , NYC (d/X-19-1867 @ 46) MD UCNY 1858. *Tr AMA* 19:423, 1868. *Med reg NY NJ Conn* 1868: 328.

HITCHCOCK, ALFRED, Fitchburg Mass (b/1813 Westminster, Vt; d/III-31-1874) MD Dartmouth 1837; MD Jefferson 1845. *Bost m&s j* 90:372, 394, 1874. *K&B* III:570-71.

HITCHCOCK, CHARLES H , Aurora, Ill (d/VI-28-1905 @74) MD Amer Med Coll Cincinnati 1857. *Ill med jour* 8:185, 1905. *Polk* 1896: 362.

HITCHCOCK, DANIEL DWIGHT, CW-USA; Ft Gibson, Cherokee Nation (b/1823; d/VII-17-1867) MD Bowdoin 1851. *Med surg rep Phila* 17: 155, 1867.

HITCHCOCK, ELIZUR, Akron, O (b/1832 Talmadge, O; d/V-21-1899) MD Cleveland Med Coll 1860. *JAMA* 32:1399, 1899. *Polk* 1896: 1149.

HITCHCOCK, FRANK EASTMAN, Rockland, Me (b/III-3-1847 Damariscotta; d/X-25-1896) MD Bowdoin 1871; AB 1868. *Bost m&s j* 137: 297, 1897. *Tr Me Med Assoc* 12: 637-39, 1897. *Polk* 1886:428.

HITCHCOCK, JOSEPH GREEN STEVENS, Clarendon Hills, Mass (d/VIII-24-1891 @68) MD Harvard 1850; AB Middlebury 1844. *Bost m & s j* 125: 232, 1891. *Polk* 1890: 548.

HITCHCOCK, THOMAS BARNES, Newton, Mass; CW-USA (d/VI-24-1874 @35) MD Harvard 1860. *Bost m & s j* 41: 24, 1874. *Harvard in CW*: 258.

HITCHCOCK, WILLIAM AARON, Shoreham, Vt (b/I-13-1805 Great Barrington, Mass; d/II-25-1868) MD Castleton 1829. *Tr AMA* 19:437-38, 1868.

HITT, WILLIS WASHINGTON, Vincennes, Ind (b/II-11-1801 Bourbon, Ky; d/VIII-18-1876) MD U Md 1825. *Med annals Md:* 440. *Tr AMA* 28: 613-14, 1877. *K&B* II: 533.

HITZROT, HENRY W , McKeesport, Pa (d/VI-23-1906 @58) MD CPS Balto 1880. *Pa med jour* 9: 804, 1905/06. *Polk* 1886: 806.

HOADLEY, ALBERT EDWARD, Chicago (b/1847 Chenango Forks, NY; d/I-16-1900) MD Chic Med Coll 1872. *JAMA* 34:186, 1900. *Tr Ill St Med Soc* 1899-1900: 415, 463. *Polk* 1886: 265.

HOADLEY, FREDERICK HODGES, ?W Palm Beach, Fla (b/1850 New Haven, Conn; d/II-2-1895) MD Yale 1876; AB 1870. *Med reg NY NJ Conn* 1895: 227. *JAMA* 24: 422, 1895.

HOAG, CLITUS SPURZHEIM, Bridgeport, Conn (b/I-

31–1855 Gaysville, Vt; d/VII–18–1900) MD Hahnemann Phila 1877. *No Am j hom* 48: 1900. *Tr Am Inst Hom* 1901:916–17. *Polk* 1886: 190.

HOAG, GUY DUDLEY, New Castle, Pa (d/X–6–1906 @31) MD Bellevue 1899. *Pa med jour* 10:118, 1906/07.

HOAGLAND, CHRISTOPHER COLUMBUS, Des Moines (b/V–10–1810;d/IV–11–1869) MD Yale 1832; AB Rutgers 1828; AM. *Phila m reg & dir* 1871:30 300. *Tr M S NJ* 1872:178–79. *Med s rep Phila* 20: 310, 1869.

HOAGLAND, CORNELIUS MEIGS, Brooklyn (b/XI–23–1828 Neshanic, NJ; d/IV–24–1898) MD Western Reserve 1852. *Bost m&s j* 138: 433, 1898. *JAMA* 30: 1125, 1898. *K&B* III: 572–73.

HOAR, WILLIAM MICHAEL, Lowell, Mass (d/I–12–1890 @40) MD Bellevue 1873. *Bost m&s j* 122: , 1890.

HOBART, ANDREW JACKSON, CW–USA; Clinton, Ia (b/VII–15–1828 Penn Yan, NY; d/XII–6–1895) MD U Mich 1859. *JAMA* 25:1058, 1108, 1895. *Tr Iowa St Med Soc* 14:329, 1896. *Atkinson* I: 483. *Polk* 1890: 410.

HOBART, ANSON LOOMIS, Worcester, Mass (b/VII–14–1814 Columbia, NH; d/XII–31–1890) MD Castleton 1844; AB Williams 1836. *Williams grads*: 1836. *Polk* 1886: 476.

HOBART, ISAAC EASTMAN, Milford, Mass (b/VII–8–1863 Edmunds, Me; d/V–15–1894) MD Bellevue 1888. *Tr Me Med Assoc* 1894: 580–81.

HOBBINS, JOSEPH, Brookline, Mass; Madison, Wis 1854– (b/XII–28–1816 Wednesbury, Engl; d/I–24–1894) LRCS (Lond) 1840; <MD Columbian, DC> *Tr Wis St Med Soc* 1894: 473–76. *JAMA* 22: 158, 1894. *Polk* 1890: 1167. *K&B* II: 533–34.

HOBBS, BENJAMIN, CW–USA (b/Wakefield, NH; d/VIII–28–1866 White's Ranch, Tex @25) MD Dartmouth 1863. *Med surg rep Phila* 15: 287, 1866. *Bost m&s j* 75: 232, 1866. *Nat med jour* 1:297, 1870/71.

HOBBS, EBENEZER, Waltham Mass (b/1794? d/1863 @ 69) MD Harvard 1817; AB 1814. *Bost m&s j* 69:408, 1863.

HOBBS, MARMADUKE W , Richmond, Ind (d/VI–16–1899 @65) MD Bellevue 1865. *JAMA* 32: 1460, 1899. *Polk* 1896: 488.

HOBBS, PHILIP M , Wymore, Nebr (d/IX–4–1899) MD Cincinnati Coll Med & Surg 1875. *JAMA* 33: 745, 1899. *Polk* 1896: 912.

HOBBS, WILLIAM T, Mound, Ill (d/VII–18 1897 @ 58) MD CPS Keokuk 1869. *JAMA* 29:297, 1897 *Polk* 1886: 289.

HOBSON, JOSEPH VIRGINIUS, Richmond, Va 1865–? Lynchburg (d/X–10–1894/1895 @85) MD UPa 1832; att Hampden Sidney; att U Paris. *JAMA* 25:726, 1895. *Tr Am Inst Hom* 1896: 1189. Homeopath 1856– .

HOBSON, THOMAS, Philadelphia (d/XI–12–1853) MD UPa 1841. *Tr Med Soc Pa* 1856: 185.

HOBSON, WILLIAM HEVERIN, Philadelphia (d/I–30–1906 @36) MD Jefferson 1895. *Pa med jour* 9: 361, 1905/06. *Flint* 1897: 819.

HOCHETT [HOCKETT], ZIMRI, Morrow, O 1855–58; Anderson, Ind 1867– (b/I–17–1830 Clinton Co, O; d/X–10–1890) <MD Physio-Med Inst, Cinc 1864> *Med vis* 6:376, 1890. *Med adv* 25:399, 1890. *Polk* 1886: 310. Homeopath.

HOCKETT, OLIVER O, Newman, Ill (d/II–8–1901) MD Hahn Chic 1889. *Ill med jour* ns2:533, 1901. Homeopath.

HOCKING, JOHN W , Govanstown, Md (b/1857 Frostburg; d/VII–26–1897) MD U Md 1884. *JAMA* 29:350, 1897. *Med annals Md:* 440.

HODGDON, RICHARD LORD, Arlington, Mass (b/IV–11–1825 S Berwick, Me; d/I–30–1893) MD Jefferson 1852; AB Bowdoin 1845. *Bost m&s j* 128: 128, 1893. Atkinson I:109. *Butler* 1878: 532.

HODGDON, WALTER H A , San Francisco (b/1851 Medford, Me; d/II–23–1891) MD U Calif 1876. *Tr Med Soc Calif* 1891: 320. *Polk* 1886: 172.

HODGE, CHARLES, Jr CW–USA; Trenton, NJ (b/III–22–1832 Princeton; d/VII–31–1876 Clifton Springs, NY) MD UPa 1855; AB Princeton 1852, AM 1855. *Tr AMA* 28: 626, 1877. *Tr Med Soc NJ* 1877:[126]. *Med surg rep Phila* 35: 180, 1876.

HODGE, HENRY, Roby, Tex 1880– (b/Crittendon Co, Ky; d/V–10–1904) MD Nashville Med Coll 1889. *Tex st med jour* 1:243, 1906. *Polk* 1896: 1452.

HODGE, HUGH, RevWar–USA;NJ (d/VII– –1798 @ 43) MD ? ; ?AB Princeton 1773. *Tr CPP* cent vol: 235. *K&B* III: 574.

HODGE, HUGH LENOX, Philadelphia (b/VI–27–1796; d/II–26–1873) MD UPa 1818; AM Princeton 1814; LLD 1872. *Tr Med Soc Pa* 10:349–61, 1874. *Am j m sci* 63: 576–78, 1873. *Tr CPP* cent vol: 235. *Med times* (Phila) 3:414–15, 1873. *K&B* III: 574–75.

HODGE, HUGH LENOX, CW–USA; Philadelphia (b/VII–30–1836; d/VI–10 or 16–1881) MD UPa 1858; AB 1851. *Tr CPP* cent vol 1887: 235. *Tr M S St Pa* 1882: 357–65. *Atkinson* I:148–49. *U Pa med alum CW*: 1855.

HODGEN, HARRY, St Louis (b/VIII–21–1855 Pittsfield, Ill; d/VIII–29–1896 Alma, Mich) MD St Louis Med Coll 1883. *Tr Med Ass St Mo* 1897:691–92. *Polk* 1886: 563.

HODGEN, HARRY A , St Louis (d/IX– –1896) MD St Louis Med Coll 1833. *JAMA* 27: 1169, 1896. *Med bull med & surg* 18:395, 1896. *Polk* 1886: 563.

HODGEN, JOHN THOMPSON, St Louis (b/I–17–1826, Hodgenville, Ky; d/IV–28–1882) MD Missouri Med Coll 1848; att Bethany Coll WVa. *Tr Med Assoc St Mo* 1883: 252–56. *Tr AMA* 33:565–72, 1882. *Tr CPP* cent vol: 282. *K&B* III: 575–76.

HODGES, BENJAMIN F , CW–USA (d/XII–31–1863 @27) MD ? *Nat med jour* 1:297, 1870/71.

HODGES, FRED JENNER, Ashland, Wis (b/XI–11–1865; d/II–18–1901 Chicago) MD Northwestern 1888. *Tr Ill St M S* ns2:533, 1901. *Tr Wis St M S* 1901:457–59.

HODGES, RICHARD MANNING, Boston (b/XI–6 1827

 Spec. educ'l status abbrev. as: ***ng*** = college verified attendance without degree;

Bridgewater, Mass; d/II-9-1896 @68) MD Harvard 1850; AB 1847. *Bost m & s j* 134: 180, 202–03, 1896. *Med bull med & surg* 18: 151, 1896. *Atkinson* I: 686. *Polk* 1890: 538.

HODGES, ROLAND CARROLL, Houston, Tex (d/III-13-1906 Del Rio) MD Detroit Med Coll 1878. *Tex st jour med* 1:352, 1905–06. *Polk* 1886: 883.

HODGES, TISDALE, Bristol, RI (b/IV-21-1783 Norton, Mass; d/1808 off Afr coast) MD ? AB Brown 1804. *Brown hist cat*: 1804.

HODGES, W R, Memphis (d/1878) MD U Md 1860 [?] *Tr AMA* 30: 872, 1879. *Med rec* 14:220, 1878.

HODGES, WILLIAM DONNISON, Nahant, Mass (b/1854 Boston; d/III-6-1893 @39) MD Harvard 1881; AB 1877. *Bost m & s j* 128: 274, 276, 1893.

HODGES, WILLIAM HAMMATT, Boston? (d/IV-11 1872 @25 Italy) MD Harvard 1871. *Bost m&s j* ns9:308, 1872.

HODGKINS, DAVID WEBB, E Brookfield, Mass (d/IV 19-1898 @63) MD CPSNY 1863. *Bost m&s j* 138: 412, 1898. *Polk* 1896: 711.

HODGMAN, ABBOTT, NYC (b/XI-15-1832 W Townsend, Mass; d/II-26-1901 @68) MD UCNY 1858. *Bost m & s j* 144:246, 1901. *Polk* 1896:1058.

HODGMAN, WILLIAM HENRY, Saratoga, NY (d/VII-15-1898 @46) MD CPSNY 1873. *JAMA* 31:198, 1898. *Polk* 1896: 1098.

HODGSON, GEORGE W, White Plains, NY (b/IX-10-1811 NYC; d/V-12-1886) Lic NY St Med Soc 1831; att CPSNY. *Med reg NY NJ Conn* 1887:267. *Bost m & s j* 114: 523, 1886. *Butler* 1878: 558.

HOEGEL, FRANK C, Allegheny, Pa (d/II-2 1903 @27) MD W Pa U 1897. *Pa med jour* 7:279, 1902/03.

HOFF, ALEXANDER HENRY, USA (b/XII-18-1822 Phila; d/VIII-19-1876) MD Jefferson 1845. *Med rec* 11: 582, 1876. *Tr AMA* 28: 638–39, 1877.

HOFFA, JACOB P, Washingtonville, Pa (d/X-27-1902 @50) MD Jefferson 1876. *Pa med jour* 6:153, 260, 1902/03. *Flint* 1897: 839.

HOFFENDAHL, HERMANN LOUIS HENRY, Boston (b/IV-10-1830 Waldeck, Mecklenburg-Strelitz; d/III-16-1881) MD Harvard 1852; AB 1849. *Tr Am Inst Hom* 1881: 125. Homeopath.

HOFFMAN, ADAMS CLAY, Jersey City, NJ (d/XI-14 1887) MD CPSNY 1876 *Med reg NY NJ Conn* 1888:254.

HOFFMAN, CARL, Baltimore (d/IV-8-1895) <MD Giessen 1870> *JAMA* 24:609, 1895. *Polk* 1886: 437.

HOFFMAN, CARL OTTO, Oaklin, Cresco PO, Pa (d/I-10-1903 @95) <MD Giessen 1843> *Pa med jour* 7:279, 1903/04. *Polk* 1886: 808.

HOFFMAN, CHARLES I, Lebanon, Pa (d/XI 27-1906 @59) MD Jefferson 1870. *Pa med jour* 10:213, 1906/07.

HOFFMAN, EDWARD SETON, CW-USA; Morristown NJ(d/II-28-1876) MD CPSNY 1855; AB Colum 1851. *Tr AMA* 27:656, 1876. *Med reg NY NJ Conn* 1876: 243.

HOFFMAN, G F THEODORE, Niles, Ill (d/XI-1-1905 @85) Hon MD Rush 1861. *Ill med jour* 8: 530, 1905. *Polk* 1896: 432.

HOFFMAN, HERMAN H, Pittsburgh (b/XII-21-1821 nr Leipzig; d/IV-4-1891) MD Leipzig 1848. *Med vis* 7: 191, 1891. *Hahn mo* 27: 324, 1892. *Tr Am Inst Hom* 1891: 93. *Polk* 1886: 829. Homeopath.

HOFFMAN, JOSEPH REED, Morristown, NY (d/XII 11-1893) MD NY Homeop 1883. *JAMA* 21: 1010, 1893. *Butler* 1878: 558. *No Am j hom* 42: 1894. Homeopath.

HOFFMAN, LOUIS A, Texarkana, Tex; Newark, NJ (b/XII-30-1855 Berks Co, Pa; d/VI-1-1895 @39) MD Hahnemann Phila 1880; att Lafayette. *JAMA* 25: 39, 1895. *Polk* 1893: 791. Homeopath.

HOFFMAN, RICHARD KISSAM, NYC; War 1812-USN (b/1790? d/XII-25-1860) MD CPSNY 1820. *Tr AMA* 14: 194, 1864. *Med reg NY NJ Conn* 1862: 153.

HOFFMAN, WALTER JAMES, Reading, Pa (b/V-30-1846 Weidasville; d/XI-8-1899) MD Jefferson 1866. *JAMA* 33:1308, 1899. *Bost m & s j* 141:508, 1899. *Rec act'g asst surg USA* 1891: 48–52. *K&B* III: 577–78.

HOFFMAN, WASHINGTON ATLEE, CW-USA; Philadelphia (b/IX-17-1844; d/IX-20-1874 Bryn Mawr) MD UPa 1868; AB Amherst 1864. *Tr Med Soc Pa* 10:761–63, 1875. *Phila med times* 5:18 & 32, 1874–75. *Med surg rep Phila* 31: 240, 280, 300, 1874.

HOFFMAN, WILLIAM S, Port Byron, NY (b/V-23-1816 Shawangunk; d/I-8-1882) Lic NY St Bd Med Censors. *Tr Med Soc St NY* 1882: 357–58.

HOFMANN, ERNST F, NYC (b/IV-25-1832 Coburg, Gny; d/III-11-1897) MD UCNY 1858. *Tr Am Inst Hom* 1897: 64. *No Am j hom* 45: 263, 1897. *Polk* 1886: 681. *Cleave*. Homeopath.

HOFSTETTER, J J, Sabula, Ia (d/IX-20-1894 @74) <MD Giessen 1844> *JAMA* 23:561 1894. *Polk* 1890:419.

HOGAN, EDWARD KELLY, CW-USA (d/VII- 26-1867) MD CPSNY 1863. *Tr AMA* 19:419, 1868. *Med reg NY NJ Conn* 1868: 329.

HOGAN, JAMES KLEIN, NYC (b/I-15-1858 Ireland; d/IX-3-1898) MD LICH 1888. *JAMA* 31: 618, 1898. *Polk* 1896: 1058.

HOGAN, MICHAEL, NYC (b/1820; d/XII-17-1882) MD Kings & Queens Coll Dublin 1858; LRCS (Dublin?) 1858. *Med reg NY NJ Conn* 1883: 230. *Butler* 1878: 502.

HOGAN, MICHAEL KELLY, CW-USA; NYC (b/1830; d/II-25-1894) MD CPSNY 1858. *Med reg NY NJ Conn* 1894: 239. *Polk* 1886: 680.

HOGAN, ROBERT, ?NYC (d/XII-5-1861 @61) MD ? *Med reg NY NJ Conn* 1862: 155.

HOGEBOOM, CHARLES LAWRENCE, Brooklyn & Lawrence, NY (b/1827? d/III-13-1895 @68) MD CPSNY 1851. *Med reg NY NJ Conn* 1895: 227. *JAMA* 24:497, 1895.

HOGG, SAMUEL, Tenn; War 1812-USA (b/IV-18-1783 Caswell Co, NC; d/V-28-1842) Hon MD U Md

1818. *Tr Med Soc Tenn* 1876: 83. *Proc Med Soc Tenn* 1843: 13–22; 1876: 83. *US Congr biogr direct.*

HOGUE, JAMES HERBERT, Altoona, Pa (b/XI–5–1860 Watsontown; d/VIII–30–1904) MD CPSNY Balto 1885. *Pa med jour* 8: 66, 1904/05. *Flint* 1897: 794.

HOGUE [HOGG], WILLIAM PATRICK, Charlestown, Jefferson Co, WVa (b/I–24–1820; d/XII–7–1897) ng Ohio Med Coll 1863. *Tr St Med Soc WVa* 1898: 219–24. *JAMA* 30:106, 1898. *Polk* 1890: 1148.

HOITT, GEORGE COTTON, Manchester, NH (b/VII–20–1835 Thorntons Ferry; d/XII–9–1897) MD Dartmouth 1882. *Bost m&s j* 137: 640, 1897. *JAMA* 30: 106, 1898. *Tr NH Med Soc* 1898: 255. *Polk* 1896: 921.

HOKE, AMOS F, Detroit, Mich (d/X– –1886) MD Detroit Med Coll 1875. *Med age* 4: , 1886.

HOLAHAN, JOHN FREDERICK, York, Pa; CW–USA (b/XI–3–1840 Milesburg; d/1880) MD UPa 1867. *U Pa med alum CW*: 1867. *Atkinson* I: 163.

HOLBROOK, CLARENDON GORHAM, Boston; S Abington, Mass (d/IX–21–1863 @57) MD Harvard 1837; AB 1832. *Bost m & s j* 69: 188, 1863.

HOLBROOK, JOHN EDWARDS, Charleston SC (b/XII 30–1794 Beaufort; d/IX–8–1871 Norfolk, Mass) MD UPa 1818; AB Brown 1815. *Bost m&s j* ns8:192, 1871. *Tr AMA* 23:595–97, 1872. *K&B* III: 578. *Waring* II: 243.

HOLBROOK, LOWELL, Brooklyn, 1850–53; Thompson Conn (b/X–6–1818; d/X–16–1905) MD UCNY 1849; att Brown. *Proc Conn Med Soc* 1906: 315–16. *Bost m&s j* 153:484 1905. *Atkinson* I:460 *Polk* 1896:285.

HOLBROOK, THOMAS JEFFERSON, Morrisville, Vt (b/1835; d/XII–17–1899) MD U Vt 1864. *JAMA* 34:62, 1900. *Polk* 1886: 906.

HOLBROOK, URIAH HOPKINS, Providence, RI (b/X–10–1850; d/V–8–1884) MD Harvard 1877; AB Brown 1874. *Tr RI Med Soc* 3:166–67, 1883–88.

HOLBROOK, WILLIAM, Palmer, Mass (d/IV–27–1903 @79) MD UCNY 1848. *Bost m & s j* 149: 486, 1903. *Polk* 1896: 720.

HOLCOMBE, HENRY, Alexandria, NJ (b/VIII–5–1797; d/IV–7–1859) MD UPa 1821; AB Princeton 1818. *Tr Med Soc NJ* 1872: 129–30.

HOLCOMBE, HUBERT VINCENT CLAIBORNE, Branford, Conn (b/I–5–1828 W Granville, Mass; d/VIII–4–1874) MD Castleton 1850. *Proc Conn Med Soc* 4: 441–42, 1875. *Butler* 1878: 78.

HOLCOMBE, JOHN RANDOLPH, Philadelphia (b/I–13–1849 Lancaster Co; d/XII–18–1896) MD UPa 1871. *Tr Am Inst Hom* 1897:63. *Polk* 1886: 818.

HOLCOMBE, VINCENT, W Granville, Mass (b/1795? d/IX–11–1863 @68) MD ? *Bost m & s j* 69: 288, 1863.

HOLCOMBE, WILLIAM FREDERIC, NYC (b/IV–2 1827 Sterling Mass; d/III–17–1904) MD Albany 1858. *Bost m&s j* 150:310,904. *K&B* III:579–80.

HOLCOMBE, WILLIAM HENRY, Madison, Ind 1847–50; Cincinnati 1850–52; Natchez 1852–55; Waterproof, La to 1864; New Orleans (b/V–29–1825 Lynchburg, Va; d/XI–28–1893) MD UPa 1847; att Washington & Lee. *No Am j hom* 42: , 1894. *Tr Am Inst Hom* 1894: 264. *King* 1:192. *Cleave.* Homeopath.

HOLDEN, LEVI HALL, USA 1840–68 (b/V–6–1817 Providence, RI; d/V–12–1874 Vineland, NJ) MD UPa 1839; AB Brown 1835. *U Pa med alum CW*: 1839. *Tr AMA* 25: 539, 1874. *Med rec* 9:304, 1874.

HOLDERNESS, ROBERT CHARLES, Black Jack Grove, Tex (b/X–11–1827 Yanceyville, NC; d/VI–2–1905 Cumby, Tex) MD UPa 1850. *U Pa med alum CW*:1850. *Polk* 1886: 881.

HOLLADAY, ROBERT C, Hot Springs, Ark (d/VIII 23–1899) MD CPS Keokuk 1878. *JAMA* 33: 621, 1899. *Polk* 1886: 500 (Joplin, Mo).

HOLLAND, DANIEL J, Atchison, Kans (d/by IX–16 1890) MD Jefferson 1876. *Kans med jour* 2: 695–96, 1890. *Polk* 1886: 374.

HOLLAND, G H, Mt Perry O (d/III–11–1900 @65) MD Starling 1869. *JAMA* 34: 766, 1900. *Polk* 1896: 1202.

HOLLAND, JAMES WILLIAM, Westfield, Mass (d/XII 29–1905) MD UPa 1894. *Bost m & s j* 154: 28, 1906. *Polk* 1896: 725.

HOLLAND, JOHN T, Baltimore (Queen Anne's Co, Md; d/II–5–1900 @65) MD UMd 1862. *JAMA* 34:446, 1900. *Polk* 1886: 445.

HOLLAND, JOSEPH BASSETT, Boston (b/VII–10–1833 Fayetteville, Vt; d/II–14–1902) MD Dartmouth 1866; ng Amherst 1855. *Amherst, Men of*: 1855.

HOLLAND, JOSIAH GILBERT, Richmond, Va; Vicksburg, Miss; Springfield, Mass; NYC 1869– (b/VII–24 1819 Belchertown; d/X–12–1881) MD Berkshire 1845. *Chic med rev* 4:470, 1881. *K&B* III:580–81.

HOLLAND, PHILO L, Chicago (d/III–2–1899) MD Northwestern 1890. *JAMA* 32:563, 1899. *Chic med rec* 16:366, 456, 1899. *Polk* 1896: 389.

HOLLAND, WILLIAM TURPIN, Jarretts, Va (b/I–30–1869; d/XI–1–1894) MD Med Coll Va 1891. *Tr Med Coll Va* 1895:215. *Polk* 1893: 1260.

HOLLENBACK, CHARLES EDGAR, Halsey Valley, NY (d/IX–13–1901 @51) MD Bellevue 1874. *JAMA* 37:848, 1901. *Polk* 1886: 663.

HOLLENBUSH, C G, USA (d/VIII–6–1861 McKey's Half Falls, Pa) MD Pa Med Coll 1856. *Tr AMA* 14: 216, 1864. *Nat med jour* 1:297, 1870/71.

HOLLIDAY, CHARLES H, Carlinsville, Ill (b/VI–12 1822 Scottsville, Ky; d/VI–14–1891) MD Mo Med Coll (Kemper) 1849. *Tr Ill St Med Soc* 1892:33–34. *Polk* 1890: 303.

HOLLIDAY, SAMUEL TAYLOR, CW–CSA; Winchester, Va (b/I–3–1836; d/VIII–8–1893) MD UPa 1860. *Tr Med Soc Va* 1894: 197–98. *Butler* 1878: 830.

HOLLIFIELD, HORATIO N, Sandersville, Ga (d/IX–23–1895 @63) MD Jefferson 1854. *JAMA* 25: 595, 1895. *Polk* 1890: 272.

 Spec. educ'l status abbrev. as: ***ng*** = college verified attendance without degree;

HOLLINGSWORTH, CHARLES MILTON, Harrisonburg, Va (b/Winchester; d/XI-9-1902) MD U Md 1882. *Tr Med Soc Va* 1903: 271-72. *Polk* 1900: 1764.

HOLLINGSWORTH, JOSEPH, Mt Airy, NC (d/I-20-1887 @66) MD Jefferson 1847. *Tr NC M S* 1887: 159.

HOLLINGSWORTH, SAMUEL LOVERING, Philadelphia (b/V-22-1816; d/XII-14-1872) MD UPa 1842. *Med times* (Phila) 3:267-68, 1872/73. *Tr CPP* cent vol:235. *Phila med reg & dir* 1873: 303. *Med surg rep Phila* 28:26, 1873.

HOLLIS, THOMAS H , CW-CSA; Nacogdoches, Tex (b/VII-22 1829 Tenn; d/II-3-1888) <MD UPa 1854> *Daniels Tex med jour* 3:407-08, 1888. *Butler* 1878:788.

HOLLISTER, EDWIN ORLANDO, E Bloomfield, NY (b/Batavia; d/X-8-1887) MD Bellevue 1874. *Tr NY St Med Soc* 11:741 ff, 1894. *Polk* 1886: 659.

HOLLISTER, HORACE, Scranton, Pa (d/XII-29-1893 @71) MD UCNY 1846. *JAMA* 22: 31, 1894. *Butler* 1878: 716.

HOLLOWAY, JAMES MONTGOMERY, CW-CSA; Louisville (b/VII-14-1834; d/XI-13-1905) MD U La 1857. *So pract* 27: 700-02, 1905. *Nashville j m & s* 97: 562-63, 1905. *Butler* 1878: 265. *K&B* III: 581.

HOLLOWAY, JOSEPH KUNKLE, Nittany Hall, Pa 1861-70; Akron, O 1870- (b/1834 Aaronsburg; d/IV-16-1874) MD LICH 1861; ng Jefferson Med Coll. *Med surg rep Phila* 30:444, 1874.

HOLLOWAY, THOMAS A J , Bishopville, Md (d/c1898 @70) MD CPS Keokuk, Ia. *Med annals Md:* 441. *Polk* 1893: 566.

HOLMAN, JAMES A , Pittsburgh (d/II-18 1896 @38) MD Jefferson 1879. *JAMA* 26:442,1896. *Polk* 1890:961.

HOLMAN, JAMES WILSON, CW-CSA; Winona, Miss (b/X-5-1829 Marion, Ala; d/IV-21-1881) MD U Louisv'l 1851. *Tr Miss St M Assn* 1833:141. *Atkinson* I:665.

HOLMAN, SILAS ATHERTON, CW-USA; York Harbor, Me (d/ XII-24-1894) MD Harvard 1855. *Bost m & s j* 132: 24, 1895. *Harvard in CW*: 245.

HOLMEAD, ANTHONY Jr Washington, DC (b/1822; d/X-26-1855) MD Columbian 1841. *Hist M S DC:* 234.

HOLMES, ALEXANDER REED, CW-USA; Canton, Mass (b/New Bedford; d/XI-11-1894 @68) MD UPa 1849; att Harvard. *Bost m & s j* 131: 500, 1894. *Harvard in CW*: 235. *Butler* 1878: 352.

HOLMES, ALMAN, CW-CSA; Clinton, NC (b/II-17-1831; d/II 24-1899) MD UPa 1852. *Tr Med Soc St NC* 47:178-79. *Butler* 1878: 574.

HOLMES, CHARLES MOSES, Northampton, Mass (b/I-8-1862 Sunapee, NH; d/X-7-1898) MD Dartmouth 1889. *Bost m & s j* 139:380, 1898. *JAMA* 31: 997, 1898.

HOLMES, CHRISTOPHER COLUMBUS, Milton, Mass; CW-USA; (b/IX-14-1817 Kingston; d/VII-16-1882) MD Harvard 1840; AB 1837; AM 1840. *JAMA* 1: 254 1883. *Bost m&s j* 107:120 618 1882. *Harv in CW*:10.

HOLMES, DANIEL, Leraysville, Pa; CW-USA; Elmira, NY 1866- (b/IV-28-1818 Chenango Co, NY; d/II-15-1869) MD UPa 1850. *Tr Med Soc St Pa* 2:406-08, 1869. *Med surg rep Phila* 20:200, 1869. *Tr AMA* 31: 1049-50, 1880. *U Pa med alum CW*: 1850.

HOLMES, EDGAR A , N St Paul, Minn (d/VIII 8-1897 @45) MD Northwestern 1880. *Tr Minn St Med Soc* 1899: 191. *JAMA* 29: 400, 1897.

HOLMES, EDWARD LORENZO, Chicago (b/I-28-1828 Dedham, Mass; d/II-11-1900) MD Harvard 1854; AB 1849. *Bost m & s j* 142:208,1900. *Chic med rec* 18:322, 1900. *JAMA* 34: 445, 1900. *Tr Ill St Med Soc* 1899-1900:463, 509. *K&B* III:582.

HOLMES, ESTHER B , Colorado Springs; Olathe, Kans (d/IV-10-1897) MD Eclectic Med Inst Cinc 1848. *Tr Am Inst Hom* 1897: 64. *Polk* 1886: 182, 382. Homeopath.

HOLMES, EZEKIEL, Portland & Augusta, Me (b/VIII-24-1801 Kingston, Mass; d/II-6-1865) MD Bowdoin 1824; AB Brown 1821. *Med surg rep Phila* 12:340, 1864/65. *Bost m & s j* 72:268, 1865.

HOLMES, FREELAND SALMON, Foxcroft, Me 1856-62; CW-USA (b/IX-8-1827; d/VI-23-1863 nr Germantown, Va) MD G Wash'n U 1854; AB Bowdoin 1850. *Med surg rep Phila* 10:180, 216, 1863. *Nat med jour* 1:297, 1870/71.

HOLMES, HENRY Hartford Conn (b/II-14-1795 Litchfield; d/VII-31-1870) MD Yale 1825; MD CPSNY 1831. *Proc Conn Med Soc* 3:484 ff, 503, 1871.

HOLMES, HOWLAND, Lexington, Mass (b/I-16-1815 Halifax; d/1893) MD Harvard 1848; AB 1843; AM 1846. *Bost m & s j:* 129: 528, 1893; 130: 148, 1894. *Butler* 1878: 352.

HOLMES, JAMES, Allentown NJ (d/VI-26 1878) MD Jefferson 1869. *Tr Med Soc NJ* 1878-79: 203-04.

HOLMES, OLIVER WENDELL, Boston (b/VIII-29-1809; d/X-7-1894) MD Harvard 1836; AB 1829. *Chic med rec* 7:287, 1894. *Buffalo m&s j* 34: 249, 1894. *Bost m & s j* 131: 375-80, 1894. *K&B* III: 583-86.

HOLMES, WALTER HAMLIN, Waterbury, Conn (b/VI 23-1854 Calais, Me; d/XI-27-1898) MD Harvard 1879; AB Bowdoin 1875. *Proc Conn Med Soc* 1900: 357. *Polk* 1886: 197.

HOLMES, WILLIAM COE, Waterbury, Conn (d/II-24 or VIII-25-1898) MD CPSNY 1880. *JAMA* 30:625, 1898 (III-15).

HOLMES, WILLIAM H, Orange, NJ (d/1903 @69) MD NYMC 1859. *Bost m&s j* 149:692, 1903. *Polk* 1886: 609.

HOLMS, LEWIS WARFIELD, Baltimore (b/III-12-1831; d/X-17-1883) MD U Md 1855; AB Amherst 1852. *Amherst, Men of*: 1852. *Butler* 1878: 313.

HOLROYD, EUGENE E , Chicago (d/VII-10-1905 Orchard, Ala) MD CPS Keokuk 1878. *Ill med jour* 8:256, 1905. *Polk* 1886: 265.

HOLSTEN, GEORGE D, NYC (b/1857;d/VIII-21-1896) MD UCNY 1882. *JAMA* 27:555, 1896. *Polk* 1896: 997.

HOLSTON, JOHN GEORGE FREDERICK Sr, CW-

USA; Cleveland, O; Washington, DC (b/1809 Hamburg, Gny; d/V–1 1874) MD Jefferson 1867; MD Cleveland Med Coll 1846; ng U Mich Med Dept. *Phila m times* 4: 544, 1873/74. *Tr AMA* 26: 454–55, 1875. *Buff m&s j* 13: 396, 1874. *Tr Ohio St M S* 1874: 382. *K&B* II: 545–46.

HOLT, ALFRED CHARLES, Summit, Miss (b/VII–11–1820 Augusta, Ga; d/X–5–1891) MD Jefferson 1842. *New Orl m & s j* ns9:393–97, 1891.

HOLT, ALFRED FAIRBANKS, CW–USA; Boston (b/XII–15–1838 Lyndeborough, NH; d/XII–28–1890 Fla) MD U Vt 1860; att Harvard. *JAMA* 16: 143, 1891. *Bost m & s j* 124:22, 189, 248, 1891. *Harvard in CW*: 254. *Polk* 1886: 464.

HOLT, DANIEL, Lowell, Mass 1845– (b/VII–2–1810 Hampton, Conn; d/IV–11–1883) MD Yale 1835. *Amer hom observ* 20: 144, 1883/84. *New Engl med gaz* 18: 191, 1883. *Tr Am Inst Hom* 1883: 150. *King* 1: 202–203, 227–28. *Cleave.* Homeopath.

HOLT, DAVID, Woodville, Miss (b/V–12–1792 Bedford Co, Va; d/XI–25–1881) MD UPa 1819. *New Orl m & s j* ns9:712–14, 1882.

HOLT, EDWARD BROWN, Lowell, Mass (b/Glastonbury, Conn; d/VII–18–1904) MD Harvard 1868; MD Hahnemann, Phila 1870. *Tr Am Inst Hom* 1905: 842. Homeopath.

HOLT, HIRAM, Pomfret, Conn (b/I–31–1798 Chaplin; d/XI–30–1870) Hon MD Yale 1834. *Proc Conn Med Soc* 3: 495–99, 503 ff, 1871.

HOLT, JOSEPH WILLIAM, Montgomery, Ala (d/IV–27–1881) MD Med Coll Ga [?] *Chic med rev* 4:301, 1881. *Butler* 1878: 19.

HOLT, PLEASANT ALLEN, Jacksonville, Fla; CW–CSA (b/IV–24–1826 Orange Co, NC; d/XII–31–1881) MD UCNY 1861; AB UNC 1845. *UNC cat*: 293.

HOLT, SAMUEL DOAK, Montgomery, Ala (b/X–14–1803 Elberton, Ga; d/IV–23–1863) MD Med Coll SC 1827. *Proc Med Assoc Ala* 1870: 233.

HOLT, SUMNER GREENLEAF, CW–USA (b/V–16–1839 Albany, Me; d/III–23–1863 Pensacola, Fla) MD Bowdoin 1862. *Nat med jour* 1:297, 1870/71.

HOLT, WILLIAM ALEXANDER, CW–CSA; ?Davidson, NC (b/VIII–17–1828 Orange Co; d/IX–16–1886) MD UPa 1861. *U Pa med alum CW*: 1861.

HOLT, WILLIAM FLEWELLEN, CW–CSA; Macon, Ga (b/VIII–23–1835 Bibb Co; d/IX–10–1901) MD Jefferson 1857. *JAMA* 37: 847, 1901. *Atkinson* I: 488. *Polk* 1886: 23.

HOLT, WILLIAM MORRIS, Anchorage, Ky (b/Henderson; d/VIII–4–1896 @56) MD Louisville Med Coll 1874. *JAMA* 27:390–91, 1896. *Polk* 1886: 391.

HOLTON, DAVID PARSONS, NYC (d/VI–7–1883 @ 71) MD CPSNY 1839. *Med bull m & s* 5:166, 1883.

HOLYOKE, EDWARD AUGUSTUS, Essex, Mass (b/VIII–1–1728 Marblehead; d/III–31–1829 @100) Hon MD Harvard 1783. *NY m & phys j* ns1:229–30, 1829. *K&B* III: 588–89.

HOLYOKE, EDWARD AUGUSTUS, Jr [orig Turner, Edward Augustus Holyoke] Salem, Mass; Syracuse, NY (b/VII–12–1796 or 97; d/XII–17–1855) MD Harvard 1821; AB 1817. *Bost m & s j* 53: 455, 1856. Palmer's *Necrol Harvard alum*: 90–91.

HOLYOKE, WILLIAM COOKE, Boston (d/XI–26–1896 @54) MD Harvard 1872. *Bost m & s j* 135: 508, 1896. *Polk* 1896: 699.

HOLZHAUSEN, CHARLES HENRY, NYC (d/XI–4–1899 @29) MD Bellevue 1898; att CCNY. *Bost m & s j* 141: 508, 1899.

HOMANS, CHARLES DUDLEY, Boston (b/XII–5–1826 Brookfield, Mass; d/IX–2–1886 Bar Harbor, Me) MD Harvard 1849; AB 1846. *Bost m&s j* 115:268, 1886. *Atkinson* I: 686. *Butler* 1878: 340. *K&B* III:589–90.

HOMANS, JOHN, Boston (d/IV–30–1868 @74) MD Harvard 1815; AB 1812. *Bost m & s j* ns1: 192, 204, 1868; 105: 521, 1881. *Med rec* 3:287, 1868–69. *K&B* III: 590 (mention only).

HOMANS, JOHN, CW–USN & USA; Boston (b/XI–26–1836; d/II–7–1903) MD Harvard 1862; AB 1858. *Bost m & s j* 148: 191, 194, 1903. *Harvard in CW*: 114. *Atkinson* I:536. *Polk* 1896:699. *K&B* III:590–91.

HOMANS, JOHN 2d, Boston (d/V–4–1902 @45) MD Harvard 1882; AB 1878. *Bost m & s j* 146: 503, 1902.

HOMER, HORACE, CW–San Comm US; Hagerstown, Md; Plainfield, NJ; Brooklyn; Philadelphia (b/III–16–1841 NYC; d/VIII–23–1883) MD Hahnemann Phila 1863. *Med surg rep Phila* 49: 364, 1883.

HOMET, VOLNEY, Wyalusing, Pa (b/III–20–1833 Homet's Ferry, Pa; d/XII–26–1906) MD Jefferson 1856. *Pa med jour* 10:912–13, 1906/07. *Flint* 1897: 840.

HOMEYARD, JOHN COOPER, Staten Isl, NYC (d/XI–20–1879) MD CPSNY 1834. *Med reg NY NJ Conn* 1880: 236. *Med surg rep Phila* 41: 506, 1878.

HOMISTON, JOSEPH MANSFIELD, Brooklyn (d/IV–8–1879 @50) MD Yale 1872. *Med reg NY NJ Conn* 1880: 237.

HOMMELL, PHILEMON, Jersey City, NJ (b/Alsace; d/IX–14–1893 @57) MD CPSNY 1883. *JAMA* 21:498, 1893. *Polk* 1886: 605.

HONEYMAN, JOHN, New Germantown, NJ (b/1798; d/I–2–1874) Lic 1825; <ng UPa Med Dept 1822–24> ng Middlebury. *Med surg rep Phila* 30: 66, 1874. *Tr Med Soc NJ* 1874: 101–02. *Tr AMA* 25: 527, 1874.

HONNOLD, ALBERT M , CW–USA (d/XI–27–1863 Memphis) MD ? *Nat med jour* 1:297, 1870/71.

HONSINGER [HOUSINGER], WILLIAM S , Chazy, NY (d/VII–15–1895 @74) MD Castleton 1846. *JAMA* 25:170, 1895. *Polk* 1886:715.

HOOD, HUMPHREY H , Litchfield, Ill (b/IX–23–1823; d/II–20–1903) MD Jefferson 1851. *Ill med jour* ns4:655, 1903. *Polk* 1896: 427.

HOOD, THOMAS BEAL, CW–USA; Columbus, O;

 Spec. educ'l status abbrev. as: ***ng*** = college verified attendance without degree;

Washington, DC (b/III-19-1829 Fairview, O; d/III-15-1900) MD Western Reserve 1861; ng U Md Med Sch. *Hist Med Soc DC:*335. *JAMA* 34:766,1900. *K&B*II: 551.

HOOK, JOSIAH STACY, Adrian, Mich (b/III-4-1803 Castine, Me; d/1844) MD Harvard 1827; AB Bowdoin 1823; AM 1826. *Bowdoin cat*: 1823.

HOOKE, BENJAMIN PENNOCK, Loysville, Pa (d/III-11-1903 @74) MD UPa 1855. *Pa med jour* 7: 279, 1903/04. *Flint* 1897: 808.

HOOKER, ALFRED EDWARDS, NYC (d/IV-23-1887) MD CPSNY 1885; AB Yale 1880; PhB 1882. *Med reg NY NJ Conn* 1887: 267.

HOOKER, ANSON, E Cambridge, Mass (b/VII-17-1799 Westhampton; d/XI-1869) MD Harvard 1822; AB Williams 1819. *Bost m&s j* ns4:265, 1869; 105:520, 1881.

HOOKER, ANSON PARKER, CW-USA; E Cambridge, Mass (d/XII-31-1873 @41) MD Harvard 1855; AB 1851. *Bost m&s j* 90: 51, 52, 1874. *Med surg rep Phila* 30:66, 68, 1874. *Harvard in CW*: 53.

HOOKER, CHARLES, New Haven, Conn (b/1799; d/III 19-1863) MD Yale 1823; AB 1820. *Proc Conn Med Soc* 1865:137. *Tr AMA* 14:187-90, 1864. *Am jour med sci* ns45: 536, 1863.

HOOKER, EDWARD, ?S Hadley, Mass (b/1835; d/IV-26-1858) MD ? ; <att Williams> *Bost m & s j* 58:297-99, 1858.

HOOKER, GEORGE, Longmeadow, Mass (b/1794? d/III-14-1884 @90) MD Yale 1817; AB 1814. *Bost m & s j* 111:619, 1884.

HOOKER, JOHN, Springfield, Mass (d/VII-11-1892) <MD Worcester 1848> *Bost m&s j* 127:52, 1892. *Polk* 1890: 557.

HOOKER, JOHN W , New Haven, Conn (d/I 26-1863 @29) MD Yale 1857; AB 1854. *Bost m&s j* 68:68, 1863.

HOOKER, WILLIAM, Westhampton, Mass (b/1767? d/II-27-1861 @94) Hon MD Harvard 1825. *Bost m & s j* 64: 148, 1861.

HOOKER, WORTHINGTON, New Haven, Conn (b/III-2-1806 Springfield, Mass; d/XI-6-1867) MD Harvard 1829; AB Yale 1825; AM 1829. *Proc Conn Med Soc* 1870: 397-402. *Tr AMA* 19: 442, 1868. *Bost m & s j* 77:319, 1867. *K&B* III: 592.

HOOKS, JOHN FRANKLIN, CW-USA; Paris, Tex (b/IV-14-1837 Tuskegee, Ala; d/X-19-1895) MD UPa 1861. *Tex med jour* 11:262, 1895-96. *Tex med news* 5: 39,1895-96. *U Pa med alum CW*:1861. *Polk* 1890: 1088.

HOOKS, JOHN JAMES, Memphis (d/V-13-1868) MD UPa 1845. *Phila med reg & dir* 1871: 297. *Med surg rep Phila* 18: 542, 1868.

HOON, ANTHONY WILBUR, Pittsburgh (d/XII-16-1902 @25) MD Jefferson 1902. *Pa m j* 6:260, 1902/03.

HOOPER, ELIHU MORGAN, CW-CSA; Wilson, La (b/VII-14-1837 E Baton Rouge; d/X-12-1896 Iberville) MD U La 1862. *Tr La St Med Soc* 19:19-20, 1898. *Polk* 1886: 413.

HOOPER, FRANKLIN HENRY, Boston (b/IX-19-1850 Dorchester; d/XI-22-1892) MD Harvard 1877. *Bost m&s j* 127:539-40, 1892; 128:71, 1893. *K&B* III: 592.

HOOPER, HENRY MARTYN, Rutherford, NJ (b/XI-16 1850 Griggstown; d/XII-19-1894) MD CPSNY 1889; AB Trinity. *Tr M S NJ* 1894:201-02. *JAMA* 24:33, 1895.

HOOPER, LEMUEL WASHINGTON, Newport, Tenn (d/X-6-1899) MD Bellevue 1872. *JAMA* 33:1116, 1899. *Polk* 1896: 1403.

HOOPER, PETER, Philadelphia (d/VII-1-1898) MD U Pa 1880; AB Trinity. *JAMA* 31:142,1898. *Polk* 1896:1307.

HOOPER, ROBERT WILLIAM, Cambridge, Mass (b/X-25-1810 Marbletown; d/IV-13-1885) MD Harvard 1836; AB 1830. *JAMA* 9: 767, 1887. *Bost m & s j* 112: 384, 1885. *Butler* 1878: 340.

HOOPER, WILLIAM DAVIS, Bedford City, Va (b/VIII 28-1843 Beaver Dam; d/VII-3-1893) MD Med Coll Richmond 1865. *Tr Med Soc Va* 1893: 221-23. *Polk* 1890: 1123. *K&B* III: 593.

HOOPER, WILLIAM HENRY, Philadelphia (b/VIII-7-1824 Worcester Co, Va; d/XII-18-1883) MD UPa 1849; AB 1849. *Tr Pa St M S* 1884:505-07. *Tr CPP* cent vol:235. *Med surg rep Phila* 49:708, 1883.

HOOPES, PASCAL JOSEPH, Philadelphia (b/XII-5-1827; d/IV-25-1879) MD UPa 1852; att Lafayette. *Lafayette, Men of*: 164. *Butler* 1878: 664.

HOOPLE, HEBER NELSON, Brooklyn (b/1856 Wales, Ont; d/V-9-1905) MD Toronto 1885; MD Bellevue 1885. *Bost m & s j* 152: 592, 1905. *Polk* 1896: 997.

HOORNBECK, STEPHEN E DeWITT, Ellenville, NY (b/1844 Wawarsing; d/X-3-1900) MD CPSNY 1865. *Bost m & s j* 143:384, 1900. *Polk* 1886:715.

HOOVER, EMERY C, Dayton O (d/VI-13-1896) MD Med Coll O 1878. *JAMA* 26:1278 1896. *Polk* 1896:1184.

HOPE, GEORGE HERBERT, Brooklyn (d/VIII-17-1886 @25) MD LICH 1886. *Med reg NY NJ Conn* 1887: 267.

HOPE, JAMES S , NYC; USA (d/VII-1-1896) MD UVa 1888. *JAMA* 27: 165, 1896.

HOPE, JESSE PENDERGAST, Hampton, Va (b/XI-17-1828; d/VI-30-1883) MD Jefferson 1851. *Tr Med Soc Va* 1892:188-89.

HOPE, THOMAS P , Hampton, Va (d/I-20-1899) MD Med Coll Va 1893. *JAMA* 32: 195, 1899.

HOPKINS, DICKINSON STEWART, CW-USA (d/VII 18-1864 Petersburg, Va) MD Geneva 1861. *Nat med jour* 1:297, 1870/71.

HOPKINS, MARK, Williamstown, Mass; NYC (bII-4-1802 Stockbridge; d/VI-17-1887) MD Berkshire 1829; AB Williams 1824; DD Dartmouth 1837; DD Harvard 1841; LLD U St NY 1857. *Williams grads*:1824.

HOPKINS, SAMUEL C , Philadelphia (d/IV-28-1818; MD UPa 1816. *Tr CPP* cent vol: 235.

HOPKINS, STEPHEN WORCESTER, Lynn, Mass

(b/I-24-1829 Irasburg, Vt; d/VI-23-1895) MD Boston U 1880. *Tr Am Inst Hom* 1896: 1189. *Polk* 1886: 469. Homeopath.

HOPKINS, WAKEMAN B, Darlington Md (d/XII? 1860) MD U Md 1828. *Med surg rep Phila* ns5: 353, 1860/61.

HOPKINS, WILLIAM BARTON, Philadelphia (d/V-5-1904) MD UPa 1874. *Pa med jour* 8: 335, 1904/05. *Tr CPP* cent vol: 235. *Flint* 1897: 819.

HOPKINS, WILLIAM SMITH, Vergennes, Vt (b/II-28-1825 Panton; d/V-8-1892) MD Castleton 1849; AB Middlebury 1846. *Bost m&s j* 126: 484, 1892. *Butler* 1878: 806.

HOPKINS, WOOLSEY, NYC; Stamford, Conn (d/II-14 1900 @35) MD CPSNY 1890. *Polk* 1896: 1059. *Bost m & s j* 142: 208, 1900.

HOPKINSON, JOSEPH Jr, USN 1840-52; USA 1862- (b/III-30-1816; d/VII-11-1865) MD UPa 1838. *Tr AMA* 18:335, 1867. *Tr CPP*cent vol: 236. *Nat med jour* 1:297, 1870/71. *Med surg rep Phila* 13:66, 1865. *U Pa med alum CW*: 1838.

HOPPER, ABRAHAM, Hackensack, NJ (b/IV-26-1797 Hohokus; d/XII-14-1872) MD CPSNY 1818. *Tr AMA* 24:365, 1873. *Tr Med Soc NJ* 1873: 114-16.

HOPPER, HENRY ABRAHAM, Hackensack, NJ (b/VIII-8-1824 Bergen; d/VII-8-1882) MD CPSNY 1847. *Med reg NY NJ Conn* 1883: 231. *Tr Med Soc NJ* 1883: 290-91. *JAMA* 1: 352, 1883.

HOPPIN, CARRINGTON, ? (b/VII-4-1812 Providence, RI; d/II-17-1879 Zurich) <Stud med Phila> AB Brown 1834. *Brown hist cat*: 1834.

HOPPIN, COURTLAND, Providence, RI (b/IX-5-1834; d/X-19-1876) MD CPSNY 1860; AB Brown 1855. *New Engl med gaz* 12:78. *Hahn mo* 12: 303, 1877. *Tr Am Inst Hom* 1877: 985. Homeopath.

HOPPIN, WASHINGTON, Providence, RI (b/I-1-1827; d/IV-1-1867) MD Hahnemann Phila 1850; ng Brown 1847. *Bost m & s j* 76: 228, 1867. *Tr Am Inst Hom* 1893: 145. *King* 1: 277, 280.

HOPSON, H R, ? (d/VIII-25-1878 Memphis) MD ? *Tr AMA* 30:873, 1879. *Med rec* 14:220, 1878.

HOPSON, JAMES A, Piermont, NY (d/II- -1887) MD Fairfield 1830. *Med reg NY NJ Conn* 1887: 267. *Polk* 1886: 701.

HORD, WILLIAM TALIAFERRO, USN 1851-93; Washington, DC (b/III-3-1832 Mason Co, Ky; d/IV-1-1901) MD UPa 1853. *U Pa med alum CW*: 1853. *Polk* 1886: 212.

HORLBECK, HENRY B, CW-CSA; Charleston, SC (b/1839; d/VII-31 or VIII-2-1901) MD Med Coll SC 1859. *Bost m&s j* 145: 170, 1901. *JAMA* 37:397, 1901. *Waring* II: 247.

HORLBECK, WILLIAM CHISOLM, CW-CSA; Charleston, SC (d/1871) MD Med Coll St SC 1850. *Tr AMA* 24:381-82, 1873.

HORN, GEORGE HENRY, CW-USA; Philadelphia (b/IV-7-1840; d/XI-24-1897) MD UPa 1861. *Tr CPP* cent vol: 236. *JAMA* 29: 1181, 1897. *U Pa med alum CW*: 1861. *K&B* III: 594-95.

HORN, LOUIS C, Baltimore (b/VI-2-1840 Gny; d/X-23-1898 in SC) MD U Md 1869. *JAMA* 31:1128, 1898. *Med annals Md:* 443.

HORNADAY, EZEKIEL, CW-CSA; Willow Green, ND (b/IV-4-1838 Chatham Co, NC; d/III-20-1900) MD Washington U Balto 1868. *Tr Med Soc St NC* 47: 173-75, 1900. *Polk* 1886: 727.

HORNBECK, EDWARD MOLTON [or MOLTON EDWARD] CW-USA (b/I-23-1842 Allentown, Pa; d/X-9 1905 Catasauqua) MD UPa 1865. *U Pa med alum CW*: 1865. *Atkinson* I: 350. *Polk* 1886: 794.

HORNBROOK, WILLIAM P, Union, Ind (b/I-1-1828; d/VII-3-1883) <att Med Coll Evansville 1849-50> *Tr Ind St Med Soc* 1884: 211. *Butler* 1878: 206.

HORNE, JOHN, Yorktown, Ind (b/II-14-1814 Scotland; d/X-16-1880) MD Med Coll Ohio 1840. *Tr Ind St Med Soc* 1881:240. *Butler* 1878: 206.

HORNE, SAMUEL S, Jonesboro, Ind 1847- (b/Scotland; d/IV-19-1874) <MD Edinburgh> *Tr Ind St Med Soc* 1875: 176. *Butler* 1878: 206-07. Kemper's *Indiana*: 128.

HORNER, CHARLES, CW-USA; Gettysburg, Pa (b/V-5-1824; d/I-25-1893) MD UPa 1846; AB Pa Coll Gtbg 1843. *U Pa med alum CW*: 1846. *Polk* 1886: 800.

HORNER, EDWARD STANTON, Turbotville Pa (d/XII 21-1906 @40) MD Medico-Chi Phila 1899. *Pa med jour* 10:373, 1906/07.

HORNER, FREDERICK, USN 1851-61; Marshall, Va (b/VI-26-1828 Berry's Ferry; d/VI-14-1902) MD UPa 1851; AB UVa 1848. *Tr Med Soc Va* 1902:222-24.

HORNER, GUSTAVUS RICHARD BROWN, USN 1826-71? Philadelphia (b/VI-17-1804 Warrenton, Va; d/VIII-8-1892) MD UPa 1826. *U Pa med alum CW*: 1826. *Polk* 1886: 818.

HORNER, WILLIAM EDMONDS, Philadelphia (b/VI-3-1793 Warrenton, Va; d/III-13-1853) MD UPa 1814. *Northwest m&s j* 1:568, 1853. *Phila m&s j* 1:319, 359, 1853. *Tr Med Soc Va* 1853: 14. *Bost m&s j* 41:114-18, 1849. *K&B* III: 595-97.

HORNOR [HORNER], CALEB W, CW-USA; Philadelphia (d/II-27-1903 @74) MD Jefferson 1849. *Pa med jour* 7: 279, 1903/04. *Flint* 1897: 819.

HORR, ASA, CW-USA; Dubuque, Ia (b/IX-2-1817 Worthington O; d/VI-2-1896) MD Cleveland M C 1846. *JAMA* 26:1244, 1896. *Atkinson* I:237. *K&B* III: 597-98.

HORR, OREN ALONZO [ALPHONSE], Lewiston, Me (b/X-8-1834 or 35 Waterford; d/V-28-1893) MD Bowdoin 1861; AB Bates 1858. *Tr Me Med Assoc* 1893: 366-67. *Bost m & s j* 128:560, 1893; 129:44, 1894. *Atkinson* I: 112.

HORSAY, JOHN A E, Somerset Co, Md (b/Va; d/IX-27-1841) MD U Md 1831. *Med annals Md:* 443.

HORSFIELD, THOMAS W, NYC (d/II-19-1868 @64,

 Spec. educ'l status abbrev. as: ***ng*** = college verified attendance without degree;

Manhasset) MD CPSNY 1840. *Tr AMA* 19:419, 1868; 21:436, 1870.

HORTON, FREEMAN, Lynn, Mass (d/III-3-1861) MD Hahnemann Phila 1853 ad eundem? *Bost m&s j* 64:120, 1861. *Tr Am Inst Hom* 1893: 145. Homeopath.

HORTON, HENRY L , Morrisania, NY (b/XII-6-1826; d/III-24-1885) MD Albany 1859. *Med reg NY NJ Conn* 1885: 239.

HORWITZ, EUGENE, Baltimore (b/XII-7-1863 Phila; d/XI-10-1893) MD U Md 1889. *JAMA* 21: 829, 1893.

HORWITZ, PHINEAS JONATHAN, USN 1847-73? Philadelphia (b/III-3-1822 Baltimore; d/XI-28-1904) MD U Md 1845. *Pa m jour* 8: 335, 1904/05. *Bost m&s j* 151:394, 1904. *Atkinson* I:203-04. *Tr CPP* cent vol: 236.

HOSACK, ALEXANDER EDDY, NYC; Newport, RI (b/IV-6-1805; d/III-2-1871) MD UPa 1824; stud Paris, etc. *Med surg rep Phila* 13:358-63, 1865; 24:240, 262, 1871. *K&B* III: 599-600.

HOSACK, DAVID, NYC (b/VIII-31-1769; d/XII-22-1835) MD UPa 1791; AB Princeton 1789; LLD. *Amer jour med sci* 17:548, 1836. *K&B* III: 600-01.

HOSFELD, GEORGE, Cape May Point, NJ (d/XI-9-1884) MD ? *Med surg rep Phila* 51: 604, 1884.

HOSKINSON, WILLIAM HARVEY, Trimble, Ill (d/II-20-1905 @50) MD Miami 1882. *Ill med jour* 7:524, 1905. *Polk* 1886: 300.

HOSMER, ALFRED, Watertown, Mass (b/IX-11-1832 Newton Upper Falls; d/V-14-1891) MD Harvard 1856; AB 1853. *JAMA* 16: 828, 1891. *Bost m&s j* 124: 522, 545, 1891. *Med bull med & surg* 13: 267-68, 1891. *Atkinson* I: 112.

HOSMER, ARTHUR BURLEY, Chicago (d/V-5-1906 @62) MD Chic Med Coll 1876. *Chic med rec* 28: 301, 1906. *Ill med jour* 9:662, 1906. *Flint* 1897: 262.

HOSMER, HIRAM, Watertown, Mass (b/1799? d/IV-15 1862 @63) MD Harvard 1824. *Bost m&s j* 66:264, 1862.

HOSSIE, THOMAS R , Gouverneur, NY (d/IV-14-1900 @41) MD Queens U, Ont 1878. *JAMA* 34: 1084, 1900. *Polk* 1896: 1024.

HOTTENSTEIN, CYRUS D , CW-USA; Philadelphia (d/V-1-1902 @73) MD Jefferson 1848. *Pa med jour* 6:260, 1902/03. *Polk* 1886: 818.

HOTTERMAN [HALTERMAN], N S , Glenwood, Minn (d/VII-18-1895) Cert by Exam Bd. *JAMA* 25: 170, 1895. *Polk* 1896: 612.

HOUARD, JOHN EMILIO, Cienfuegos, Cuba (b/IX-15 1815 Phila; d/II-11-1882) MD Jefferson 1843. *College & clin record* (Jefferson) 3:67-68, 1882. *Hahn mo* 17:192, 1862. Homeopath.

HOUARD, JOHN GUSTAVUS, Philadelphia (b/II-11-1812; d/IV-24-1878) MD Hahnemann 1851. *Tr Hom Med Soc St Pa* 2:92-93, 1874-78. Homeopath.

HOUCK, JACOB W , New Orleans (b/1823 Balto; d/V 22-188 Balto) MD U Md 1842. *New Orl m & s j* ns 16: 79, 1888. *Med annals Md*:444. *Polk* 1886:437.

HOUGH, ALANSON HODGES, Essex, Conn (b/X-26-1803; d/VIII-18-1886) MD Yale 1832. *Proc Conn Med Soc* ns3:185-87, 1887. *Butler* 1878: 78.

HOUGH, DEWITT CLINTON, CW-USA; Rahway, NJ (b/XII-31-1826 Pt Pleasant, Pa; d/VIII-25-1897) MD Jefferson 1847. *Tr Med Soc NJ* 1898: 380-381. *JAMA* 29:502, 1897. *Atkinson* I:670. *Butler* 1878: 470.

HOUGH, ERASTUS C , Naperville, Ill (d/VII-27-1849) MD Rush 1848. *Northwest m & s j* 2:297, 1849.

HOUGH, GEORGE THOMAS New Bedford Mass (d/III 24-1898) MD NY Med Coll 1857. *JAMA* 30:874, 1898. *Bost m & s j* 138:312, 1898. *Polk* 1886: 470.

HOUGH, HENRY WRIGHTMAN, Putnam, Conn (b/II 6-1810 Bozrah; d/1897) MD Yale 1836. *Proc Conn Med Soc* 1897: 327-29. *Butler* 1878: 78.

HOUGH, JOHN STOCKTON, Trenton, NJ (b/XII-5-1845 Yardley, Pa; d/V-6-1900 @54) MD UPa 1868; BChem Polytechnic Coll, Pa 1867. *JAMA* 34:1210, 1900. *K&B* III: 603.

HOUGH, THOMAS L , Elizabeth, NJ (b/1832 Doylestown, Pa; d/VI-12-1896) MD Jefferson 1856. *Bost m & s j* 134: 629, 1896. *Tr Med Soc NJ* 1896: 373-74. *JAMA* 27:108, 1896. *Butler* 1878: 470.

HOUGHTON, ASAHEL, NYC (d/X-27-1869 @61) MD Castleton 1829. *Phila med reg & dir* 1871: 302.

HOUGHTON, DOUGLAS, Ann Arbor, Mich (b/IX-21-1809; d/X-13-1845 Lake Superior) Lic Chautauqua Med Soc NY 1831; AB Rensselaer Polytech. *Tr AMA* 3: 447-449, 1850. *K&B* III: 603-04.

HOUGHTON, ELIHU RUSSELL, NYC (b/III-26-1864 Jersey City, NJ; d/II-19-1905) MD Bellevue 1888; AB Amherst 1885. *Bost m & s j* 152:262, 1905.

HOUGHTON, HENRY ARVIN, Lyndon, Vt 4 yrs; Keeseville NY 21 yrs; Charlestown, Mass (b/XII-25-1826 Lyndon; d/I-15-1899) MD Hahnemann Phila 1852; ng Woodstock 1850. *Tr Am Inst Hom* 1899: 928. Homeopath.

HOUGHTON, HENRY CLARKE, NYC (b/I-22-1837 Roxbury, Mass; d/XII-1-1901) MD UCNY 1867; att Bowdoin Med Sch. *Tr Am Inst Hom* 1902: 842-43. Homeopath.

HOUGHTON, JONATHAN SPAULDING, Solon, Me 1859-61; CW-USA; Skowhegan 1863-69; San Francisco 1869-70; Port Gamble, Wash 1870-78; Goldendale, Wash 1878-83; Seattle 1883-94 (b/II-1-1828 Anson, Me; d/VII-2-1894) MD Bowdoin 1859. *Bowdoin cat*: 1859. *Polk* 1886: 932.

HOUSE, HENRY H , Rockland Lake, NY (b/Ulster Co, NY; d/II-21-1896) MD UCNY 1863. *JAMA* 26: 542, 1896. *Polk* 1896: 1096.

HOUSE, JOHN G , Independence, Ia (b/IV-26-1816 Cazenovia, NY; d/I-1-1880) MD Columbian, DC 1841; ng Jefferson. *Tr Ia St Med Soc* 1879-80:185-86. *Atkinson* I: 547. *Butler* 1878: 238.

HOUSE, WILLIAM SANDERS, Haverstraw, NY (d/I-

27–1900 @62) MD UCNY 1859. *Bost m & s j* 142:124, 1900. *JAMA* 34:312, 1900. *Polk* 1896: 1025.

HOUSEKEEPER, BENJAMIN, Philadelphia (d/III–30–1870 @62) MD UPa 1843. *Phila m reg & dir* 1871: 294.

HOUSEMAN, WILLIAM W , Philadelphia (d/IX–7–1875 @22) MD Jefferson 1875. *Phila med times* 5: 816, 1874–75.

HOUSTON, JAMES ALEXANDER, Co Antrim, Ireland; NYC; Washington, DC (d/IX–17–1849 NYC) MD ? *Bost m & s j* 41:162, 314–19, 1849.

HOUSTON, PUGH, Iuka, Miss (d/VI–8–1884 @81) MD UPa 1827. *Med surg rep Phila* 51: 56, 1884.

HOUTZ, ABRAHAM, Canal Fulton, O (d/VII–27–1879 @56) MD Jefferson 1848. *Med surg rep Phila* 41: 176, 1879. *Butler* 1878: 634.

HOVEY, ARIEL B , Tiffin, O (d/X–2–1884 @56) MD Western Reserve 1852. *Tr Ohio St Med Soc* 1885: 212. *Butler* 1878: 634.

HOVEY, DANIEL ALFRED, Killingly, Conn (b/II–24–1809 Hampton; d/X–11–1878) Hon MD Yale 1847. *Proc Conn Med Soc* 1879: 168–69. *Butler* 1878: 78.

HOVEY, FREDERICK FREEMAN, Jericho, Vt (b/I–24 1826 Thetford; d/III–7–1872. MD Woodstock 1853. *Tr Vt Med Soc* 1883: 106.

HOW, LYMAN BARTLETT, Manchester, NH (b/II–25 1838 New Bedford, Mass; d/IX–15–1893) MD Dartmouth 1863; AB 1860. *JAMA* 21: 498, 1893. *Bost m & s j* 129:312, 1893. *Tr NH Med Soc* 1894: 185 ff. *Atkinson* I: 207. *Polk* 1890: 710.

HOWARD, BENJAMIN, Elberon, NJ (b/Engl; d/VI–21 1900) MD CPSNY 1858; Hon AM Williams 1860. *JAMA* 34:1675–76, 1900. *Atkinson* I: 675.

HOWARD, E W , Akron, O (b/IV–14–1816 Andover, Vt; d/VIII–9–1890) MD Berkshire 1838. *Tr Ohio Med Soc* 1891: 6, 342. *Butler* 1878: 634.

HOWARD, EDWARD LLOYD, CW–CSA; Balto (b/I–14–1837; d/IX–5–1881) MD U Md 1861. *Tr AMA* 33, 572–76, 1882. *Med rec* 20:641, 1881. *Med annals Md:* 444. *Atkinson* I: 705. *K&B* III: 604.

HOWARD, ELIJAH J , Hazelton, Ind (b/III–6–1831 Bledsoe Co, Tenn; d/X–4–1882) ng Nashville Med Coll 1857. *Tr Ind St Med Soc* 1883: 269. *Butler* 1878:207.

HOWARD, FLODOARDO, Washington, DC (b/III–11–1811 Stafford, Va; d/I– –1888) MD Columbian 1841; PharmD Georgetown 1872. *Hist Med Soc DC:* 232. *Atkinson* I: 34. *Polk* 1886: 445.

HOWARD, FREDERICK, Randolph, Mass (d/IX–24–1870 @50) MD Harvard 1843; AB 1839. *Bost m & s j* 6: 212, 260, 1870.

HOWARD, GEORGE W , Vicksburg, Miss (d/I–12–1903) MD Med Coll Va 1863. *So pract* 25: 223, 1903. *Polk* 1896: 816.

HOWARD, HAMILTON PLEASANTS, DC to 1848 (b/1820 Brookville, Md; d/XII–29–1863) MD UVa 1891. *Hist Med Soc DC:* 238.

HOWARD, HENRY, Brookville, Md (b/V–28–1792; d/III–2–1874 Charlottesville, Va) MD UPa 1837. *Tr AMA* 25:533–34, 1874. *Med annals Md:* 444.

HOWARD, HENRY CHITTENDEN, Akron, O (d/IV–23–1887 @45) MD Bellevue 1871. *JAMA* 10: 379, 1888. *Polk* 1886: 736.

HOWARD, HENRY SLATTER, Montgomery, Ala (d/VIII–26–1868 Chattanooga, Tenn) MD U Md 1867; att U Ala 1864. *U Ala cat*: 201.

HOWARD, JOHN C , Washington, DC (b/1847; d/VIII–8–1889) MD Columbian DC 1871. *Med reg NY NJ Conn* 1890: 270.

HOWARD, JOSEPH, Hartford, Conn (d/IV–14–1879 @72) MD CPSNY 1831; AB Amherst 1827. *Med reg NY NJ Conn* 1880: 237.

HOWARD, LEVI, Lowell, Mass; Chelmsford 1848– (b/V–26–1820 Bolton; d/I–23–1885) MD Dartmouth 1846. *JAMA* 10:378, 1888. *Bost m & s j* 112:120, 1885; 113:657, 1885. *Butler* 1878: 352.

HOWARD, NOBLE P Sr, Greenfield, Ind (b/IX–11–1822 Wayne Co, O; d/VIII–25–1895 @73) MD Med Coll Ind 1878. *JAMA* 25: 427, 1895. *Tr Ind St Med Soc* 1896: 254. *Polk* 1890: 372.

HOWARD, ORLANDO, Elgin, Ill (d/II–25–1899 @83) Lic by yrs of practice. *JAMA* 32:563, 1899.

HOWARD, ROBERTSON, St Paul, Minn (b/XII–12–1847 DC; d/XII–1–1899) MD Georgetown 1867; AM 1870; LLB 1874. *Hist Med Soc DC:* 291.

HOWARD, WILLIAM, Baltimore (b/XII–16–1793; d/VIII–25–1834) MD U Md 1817; stud Paris & Edinburgh. *Med ann Md:* 444–45. *K&B* III:606–07.

HOWE, APPLETON, S Weymouth, Mass (b/XI–26–1792 Hopkinton; d/X–10–1870) MD Harvard 1819; AB 1815. *Bost m & s j* 6: 260, 317, 318, 1870.

HOWE, CHARLES, Taunton, Mass (d/II–12–1903 @82) MD Harvard 1848. *Bost m&s j* 148: 460, 1900. *Polk* 1896: 724.

HOWE, DANIEL, Sanbornton, NH 1825–31; Lowell, Mass 1831– (b/Pembroke, NH 1790; d/XI–3–1860) MD Dartmouth 1819. *Bost m & s j* 63:426, 1861.

HOWE, ESTES, RevWar–USA; Belchertown, Mass (b/VI 24–1747; d/III–3–1826) MD ? *Bost m&s j* ns16:117, 1875.

HOWE, ESTES, Cambridge, Mass (b/Northampton; d/I 1887 @72) MD Harvard 1835; AB 1832. *Bost m & s j* 116: 72, 100, 1887.

HOWE, GEORGE MARSHALL, Framingham, Mass (d/IX–16–1882) MD Harv 1854. *Bost m&s j* 107:618, 1882.

HOWE, JAMES SETH MASON, ? (b/IX–25–1824 Pepperell, Mass; d/XI–9–1888) MD ? ng Amherst 1846. *Amherst, Men of*: 1846.

HOWE, JOHN, NYC (b/1838; d/VIII–11–1876) MD NY Med Coll 1859; <AB UCNY 1856> *Med reg NY NJ Conn* 1877:203. *Med surg rep Phila* 35: 180, 1876.

HOWE, JOHN TWEEDIE, Chatham, NB (d/XII–1–1890

 Spec. educ'l status abbrev. as: ***ng*** = college verified attendance without degree;

NYC?) MD UCNY 1889 *Med reg NY NJ Conn* 1891:274.

HOWE, JOSEPH WILLIAM, NYC (b/IX-30-1843 Chatham, NB; d/VI-7-1890) MD UCNY 1865. *Buff m & s j* 29:767, 1890. *JAMA* 14:941-42, 1890. *Bost m&s j* 122: 617-18, 1890. *Atkinson* I: 573. *Butler* 1878: 516.

HOWE, SAMUEL, Boston (d/IV-30-1879) MD Harvard 1875; AB 1871. *Bost m & s j* 100: 662, 1879.

HOWE, SAMUEL GRIDLEY, S Boston (b/XI-10-1801; d/I-9-1876) MD Harvard 1824; AB Brown 1821. *Bost m & s j* ns17: 78-79, 1876. *K&B* III:608-09.

HOWE, WILLIAM FRANKLIN, Brooklyn Wis (d/ 1889) MD Rush 1880. *Tr Wis St Med Soc* 1891: 357. *Polk* 1886: 951.

HOWE, WILLIAM RUDY, Blain, Pa (b/XI-10-1826 Newport; d/V-24-1859) MD Jefferson 1836. *Tr Med Soc St Pa* 4:90-91, 1859.

HOWELL, ARCHIBALD ALEXANDER, Milford, NJ; Carversville, Pa; Allentown, NJ (b/V-10-1818 Trenton; d/XI-23-1881) MD Jefferson 1841; att Lafayette & Princeton. *Lafayette, Men of*: 147, 185. *Atkinson* I: 584. *Polk* 1886: 600.

HOWELL, EDWARD YERKES, Philadelphia (d/III-13 1850) MD UPa 1822; AB Princeton 1813. *Tr CPP* cent vol: 236.

HOWELL, GEORGE HOCKER, USN (d/X-7-1859 @ 34) MD Jefferson 1848. *Med surg rep Phila* ns3:92, 1859/60.

HOWELL, GEORGE W , Philadelphia (d/IV-24-1869 @55) <MD Eclectic Med Coll Pa 1853> *Phila med reg & dir* 1871: 294. *Med surg rep Phila* 20:363, 1869.

HOWELL, HENRY S , Kansas City, Mo (d/XI-13-1898 @40) MD Meharry 1893. *JAMA* 31: 1319, 1898. *Polk* 1896: 846. Black.

HOWELL, SAMUEL BEDELL, Philadelphia (b/IX-20-1834; d/XII-12-1903) MD UPa 1858. *Tr CPP* cent vol:236. *Atkinson* I: 66.

HOWELL, WILLIAM, CW-USN (d/VII-26-1862 NY) ?MD UCNY 1860 [as Wm A] *Nat m j* 1:297, 1870/71.

HOWELL, WILLIAM S , NYC (d/I-6-1874) Hon MD NY Med Coll 1856. *Med surg rep Phila* 30:132, 1874.

HOWERTER, EMANUEL L , Kempston, Pa (d/III-26-1904 @41 Allentown) MD UPa 1889. *Pa med jour* 8: 335, 1904/05.

HOWES, JOSIAH, Burlington, Ia (b/IX-24-1819 New Sharon, Me; d/XII- -1881 Clarinda, Ia) MD U Cincinnati 1851; AB Bowdoin 1844. *Bowdoin cat*: 1844.

HOWES, WOODBRIDGE RUGGLES, CW-USA Hanover, Mass (d/II-5-1898 @80) MD Harvard 1854. *Bost m&s j* 138:144, 1898. *Harv in CW*:242. *Polk* 1896:713.

HOWETH, V A , Gainesville, Tex; Pomona, Cal (d/IX 18-1899) MD Jefferson 1873. *Tex med news* 8:586, 1898-99. *Polk* 1890: 1079.

HOWLETT, BENJAMIN H , Broguesville, Pa (b/Harford Co, Md; d/VIII-17-1903 @56) MD CPS Balto 1878) *Pa med jour* 7: 279, 1903/04. *Flint* 1897: 797.

HOWZE, J T , Hunstville Tex (d/VIII-30-1888) MD Louisville Med Coll 1887. *Daniels Tex m j* 4:134, 1888.

HOXTON, WILLIAM WILMER, Washington, DC; USA (b/DC; d/VIII-23-1855) MD UPa 1834. *Hist Med Soc DC:* 232.

HOY, FRANCIS, Bavaria 38 yrs; to US 1836 @63; Columbus, O 1861- (b/XII-8-1770 Bavaria; d/II-6?-1874 @103) MD ? *Med surg rep Phila* 30:204,1874.

HOY, PHILO ROMAYNE, Racine, Wis (b/1816; d/XII-8-1892 @76) MD Med Coll Ohio 1842. *Bost m&s j* 127: 588, 1892. *K&B* III: 611-12.

HOYNE, TEMPLE STOUGHTON, Chicago (b/X-16-1841; d/II-4-1899) MD Bellevue 1865. *Med vis* 15: 129-32, 1899. *Tr Am Inst Hom* 1899: 76. *Polk* 1886: 76. *Cleave*. Homeopath.

HOYT, AHIRA B , CW-USN; Grafton, NH (b/IV-6-1826; d/VII-1-1881) MD Berkshire 1850. *Tr NH Med Soc* 1882: 171-72. *Conn & NH surg in CW*: 349.

HOYT, CHARLES, CW-USA (d/VII-24-1863 Memphis) MD ? *Nat med jour* 1:297, 1870/71.

HOYT, CHARLES S , Canandaigua, NY (b/1822; d/XII 13-1898) MD Geneva 1842. *JAMA* 31: 1584, 1898.

HOYT, DIXI CROSBY, Milford, Mass; CW-USA (b/VIII-24-1833 Northfield, NH; d/XI-1-1864 New Bern NC or Mower Hosp, Phila) MD Harvard 1860; AB Amherst 1855. *Bost m & s j* 71:328, 1864; 72:248, 1865. *Nat med jour* 1:297, 1870/71. *Harvard in CW*: 259.

HOYT, ENOS, Farmington, NH (b/VIII-14-1875 Henniker, NH; d/III-25-1875) MD Dartmouth 1821. *Tr NH Med Soc* 1875: 7.

HOYT, FRANKLIN MARCELLUS, Brooklyn (d/VII-18-1887 @28) MD Bellevue 1877. *Med reg NY NJ Conn* 1888: 254.

HOYT, GEORGE ASA, Framingham, Mass (d/X-15-1857 @32) MD Harvard 1851; AB Dartmouth 1847. *Bost m & s j* 57:247, 1857.

HOYT, GEORGE M , Athol, Mass (d/VI-24 1866 @65) MD Berkshire 1825. *Med surg rep Phila* 15: 28, 1866.

HOYT, HORACE, E Aurora, NY (d/VI-17-1896 @73) MD Buffalo Med Coll 1848. *Buffalo m & s j* 35: 975, 1896. *JAMA* 26: 1278, 1896. *Polk* 1886: 659.

HOYT, JAMES M , Walled Lake, Mich (d/IV-10-1894) MD Geneva 1839. *JAMA* 22: 601, 1894. *Polk* 1890: 604.

HOYT, LESTER [LESLIE] MASON, Chicago (d/VII-3 1901 @42) MD Rush 1883. *Ill med jour* ns3: 189, 1901. *JAMA* 37:213, 1901. *Polk* 1896, 443.

HOYT, OSCAR F , CW-USA; (d/VII-27-1865) MD ?UCNY 1865. *Nat med jour* 1:297, 1870/71.

HUARD, LOUIS OCTAVE, New Orleans (d/VI-17-1896 @67) MD Tulane 1857. *JAMA* 27: 52, 1896. *Polk* 1896:622.

HUBBARD, DENISON HALE, Clinton, Conn (b/IX-1-1805 Bolton; d/VIII-12-1874) MD Yale 1829. *Proc Conn Med Soc* 1875: 291 ff; 437-40.

HUBBARD, CALVIN, Springfield, Vt (b/1795? d/VII-12 1872 @77) MD ? *Med surg rep Phila* 27: 118, 1872.

HUBBARD, EDWARD D , Clinton, Conn; CW-USA as med cadet (d/VII-25-1864 @22 Cumberland Hosp Tenn) *Bost m & s j* 71:108, 1864.

HUBBARD, GEORGE, Boston (b/VIII-18-1808 Brimfield, Mass; d/III-19-1889) MD Yale 1835; AB Amherst 1829. *Bost m & s j* 120: 324, 1889.

HUBBARD, GEORGE C , Staten Isl, NYC (b/Ohio; d/ VIII-3-1898 @67) MD UCNY 1859. *Bost m & s j* 139: 150, 1898. *JAMA* 31: 366, 1898. *Polk* 1896: 1106.

HUBBARD, GEORGE ELIJAH, NYC (d/III-24-1893 @36) MD UCNY 1883. *Med reg NY NJ Conn* 1893: 304.

HUBBARD, GEORGE FRANCIS, Des Moines (b/V-12 1841 Ipswich, Mass; d/XII-29-1876 Ashtabula, O) MD Dartmouth 1865. *Tr Ia St Med Soc* 1877-78: 62-64.

HUBBARD, GEORGE HARRIS, Manchester, NY 1855-; CW-USA; Lansingburgh, NY 1865- (b/VI-8-1823 Hopkinton, NH; d/I-19-1876) MD U Vt 1845; Hon AM Dartmouth 1869. *Tr Med Soc St NY* 1876: 323-25. *Tr AMA* 30:824-25, 1879. *Med rec med & surg* 11:428, 1876.

HUBBARD, HENRY BABCOCK, Taunton, Mass (d/VII 5-1870 @61) MD Harvard 1834. *Bost m&s j* 6:16, 1870.

HUBBARD, HENRY C , Bloomington, Ill (d/IX-24-1899 @53) MD Louisville Med Coll 1879. *JAMA* 33: 872, 1899. *Polk* 1898: 416.

HUBBARD, JOHN COLEMAN, Ashtabula, O; CW-USA (b/VII-22-1820 Trenton, NJ [?]; d/VI-5-1883) MD CPSNY 1844. *Tr Ohio St Med Soc* 1884:226-27. *Med bull med & surg* 5: 162, 1883. *Atkinson* I: 30-31.

HUBBARD, OLIVER PAYSON, Hanover, NH (b/III-31 1809 Pomfret, Conn; d/III-9-1900 NYC) <Hon MD Med Coll St SC 1837> *Tr Med Soc St NY* 1901: [426]. *JAMA* 34:702,1900. *Polk* 1886:681. *K&B* III:613.

HUBBARD, ROBERT, Bridgeport, Conn (b/IV-27-1826 Cromwell; d/VII-18-1897) MD Yale 1851. *Pr Conn M Soc* 1898:350-60. *JAMA* 29:252 1897. *Polk* 1896: 276.

HUBBARD, SAMUEL THOMAS, NYC (b/II-19-1808 Haddam, Conn; d/VI-1-1894) MD CPSNY 1835. *Med reg NY NJ Conn* 1894: 240. *Polk* 1886: 681.

HUBBARD, SIMEON P , Taunton, Mass (d/VII-20-1897 @70) MD Worcester 1852. *JAMA* 29: 297, 1897. *Polk* 1886: 474.

HUBBARD, STEPHEN GROSVENOR, New Haven, Conn (b/X-16-1816 Rome, NY; d/VI-30-1905) MD Dartmouth 1843. *Proc Conn Med Soc* 1906:287-91. *Atkinson* I: 547.

HUBBARD, VAN BUREN, USA 1862-95 (b/V-1-1833 La Grange, O; d/IX-6-1895 Fort McPherson, Ga) MD Bellevue 1862; AB Yale 1855. *JAMA* 25: 510, 1895. *Polk* 1890: 68.

HUBBARD, WILLIAM HUSTACE, NYC (b/III-24-1859; d/V-29-1884) MD CPSNY 1883; AB Columbia 1880. *Med reg NY NJ Conn* 1885: 240.

HUBBELL, CHARLES LYMAN, CW-USA; Williamstown, Mass (b/IX-16-1827; d/X-7-1890) MD Berkshire 1848; AB Williams 1846. *Bost m & s j* 123: 360, 1890. *Atkinson* I: 155.

HUBBS, WILLIAM N , Brooklyn (d/III-31-1874 @47) MD Albany 1850. *Med surg rep Phila* 30: 372, 1874.

HUBER, HENRY STATE, Gettysburg, Pa (b/IX-17-1814 Phila; d/X-21-1873) MD Pa Med Coll 1846. *Tr Med Soc St Pa* 10:229-30, 1874.

HUBER, JOHN F , Lancaster, Pa; CW-USA (d/II-15-1868 @31) MD Pa Med Coll 1859. *Phila med reg & dir* 1871: 295. *Med surg rep Phila* 18: 203, 1868.

HUCKEL, JACOB, Philadelphia (b/XI-1800 Frankford; d/I-1877) MD Phila Coll Med & Surg 1848. *Tr Med Soc St Pa* 11:721-22, 1877.

HUCKINS, DAVID THOMPSON, Watertown Mass (b/II 19-1819 New Hampton NH; d/VII-21-1894) MD Dartmouth 1843. *Bost m & s j* 131: 96, 1894. *Polk* 1890: 558.

HUDELSON, LUCIUS ROLLIN, Milroy, Ind (b/IV-8-1861 Princeton; d/XII-6-1905) MD Jefferson 1896. *Tr Ind St Med Soc* 1906: 500.

HUDSON, ADRIAN, USN 1861-aft 1888 (b/XII-25-1837 Montreal; d/II-7-1890) MD ? *JAMA* 14:322, 1890. *Callahan*.

HUDSON, E J , Richmond, Va (d/VIII-30-1860 Balto) MD ? *Med surg rep Phila* 21: 224, 1869.

HUDSON, EDWARD, USN (b/1819; d/I-23-1859 Brooklyn) MD UPa 1839. *Tr AMA* 13: 825-26, 1860. *Buffalo med jour* 14:703, 1859.

HUDSON, ERASMUS DARWIN, Greenwich, Conn (b/ XII-15-1805 Torrington; d/XII-31-1880) MD Berkshire 1827. *Med reg NY NJ Conn* 1881: 237. *K&B* III:614.

HUDSON, ERASMUS DARWIN, NYC (b/XI-10-1843 Northampton, Mass; d/NYC V-9-1887) MD CPSNY 1867; AB Coll City NY 1864. *Med reg NY NJ Conn* 1887: 267. *Bost m & s j* 116:490, 1887. *K&B* III: 614.

HUDSON, FREDERICK R , Hoosick Falls, NY (d/X-25 1906 @50) MD Cleveland Homeop Hosp 1882. *Bost m & s j* 155: 530, 1906. *Polk* 1890: 793. Homeopath.

HUDSON, HERBERT S, Selma Ala (d/III- 1895) MD U Md 1868. *New Orl m&s j* ns22:765 1895. *Polk* 1890:148.

HUDSON, JOHN M , Tupelo, Ala (d/VIII-15-1890) MD - "non-grad" *Tr Med Assoc St Ala* 1891: 260.

HUDSON, ROBERT B , Roanoke, Va (d/III-15-1900 @72) MD Jefferson 1850. *JAMA* 34:766, 1900. *Polk* 1896: 1492.

HUDSON, WILLIAM MILLER, CW-USA; Hartford, Conn (b/III-14-1833; d/X-31-1901) MD Jefferson 1855. *Proc Conn Med Soc* 1902: 416-21. *Bost m & s j* 145:532, 1901. *Atkinson* I:415. *Polk* 1896:279.

HUEBNER, GEORGE WILLIAM, Johnstown, Pa (d/XII 21-1906 @40) MD Jefferson 1893. *Pa med jour* 10: 373, 1906/07. *Flint* 1897: 805.

HUFF, JOSEPH A , Pittsburgh (d/XII-30-1902) Student

 Spec. educ'l status abbrev. as: ***ng*** = college verified attendance without degree;

@ W Pa Univ Sch Med. *Pa med jour* 6: 260, 1902/03.

HUFF, SANFORD W , Sigourney, Ia (b/1826; d/1879) MD Buffalo 1851. *Tr AMA* 31: 1050, 1880. *Tr Ia St Med Soc* 1881–82: 163; 1896: 329.

HUFTY, NEWTON L , Delavan, Ill (d/II-28 1900 @77) Lic by yrs of practice. *JAMA* 34:703, 1900. *Tr Ill St Med Soc* 1900: 509. *Polk* 1896: 416.

HUGART, ALEXANDER, NYC (b/Gny; d/1887?) MD UCNY 1872. *Med reg NY NJ Conn* 1888: 254.

HUGGINS, JACOB, CW–CSA; New Berne, Ala (b/VII-13–1836; d/XI-21–1906) MD UPa 1860. *U Pa med alum CW*: 1860. *Polk* 1886: 137.

HUGHES, A H , Auburn, Wash (b/Warren Co, Mo; d/III-2–1897 @78) <MD Mo Med Coll 1850> *JAMA* 28: 569, 1897. *Polk* 1886: 932 [?].

HUGHES, BERNARD, NYC (d/IV-11–1898 @52) MD UCNY 1868. *JAMA* 30: 999, 1898. *Polk* 1896: 1054.

HUGHES, BRYCE MARTIN, Birmingham, Ala (b/III-19–1857 Franklin, Tenn; d/VII-3–1888) MD U La 1882. *New Orl m & s j* ns16:157–58, 1888. *Tr Med Assoc St Ala* 1889: 229. *Polk* 1886:131.

HUGHES, DANIEL E , Easton, Pa; Philadelphia (b/VIII 5–1850 or 51; d/X-28–1902) MD Jefferson 1878. *Pa med jour* 6:260, 1902/03. *Bost m & s j* 147: 504, 1902. *Flint* 1897: 819.

HUGHES, DYER Jr, Hampton, Conn (b/XI-12–1797; d/III-10–1882) Stud w/John & W A Brewster, Hampton. *Proc Conn Med Soc* ns2:181–82, 1883. *Butler* 1878: 78.

HUGHES, EDWARD W , Grenada, Miss (b/III-15–1819 Charleston, Va; d/VIII-31–1878) MD U Louisville 1847. *Med rec* 14: 220, 1878. *Tr AMA* 30: 826, 1879. *Tr Miss St Med Assoc* 1879: 38, 51–56. *Atkinson* I: 510.

HUGHES, ELLIS, Baltimore (b/VIII-9–1813; d/X-5 1866) MD U Md 1834. *New Orl m & s j* 19:714–18, 1867. *Med annals Md:* 446.

HUGHES, HUGH, Washington, NJ (b/III-17–1794; d/IV-22–1856) Stud med in Phila. *Tr Med Soc NJ* 1872:187. Blane, *Hunterdon Co*: 99.

HUGHES, I L , Stamford, Tex (d/V-27–1906 Fort Worth) MD ? *Tex st jour med* 2:100, 1906.

HUGHES, ISAAC SIMPSON, Springfield, Ill (d/XI-2–1893 @49) MD St Louis Med Coll 1873. *JAMA* 21: 746, 1893. *Polk* 1886: 298.

HUGHES, ISAAC WAYNE, New Bern, NC 1825– (b/II 14–1804 Montg'y Co, Pa; d/II-21–1881) MD UPa 1825. *NC med jour* 7: 187, 1881.

HUGHES, ISAAC WAYNE, CW–USA; Philadelphia (b/X-14–1832 Norristown, Pa; d/IV-26–1895) MD UPa 1853. *JAMA* 24:689–90, 1895. *U Pa med alum CW*: 1853. *Atkinson* I: 91.

HUGHES, JAMES BETTNER, CW–CSA; New Bern, NC (b/VI-9–1830; d/V-30–1900) MD UPa 1856; AB UNC 1853 [as Hunter, James Bettner) *U Pa med alum CW*: 1856. *Polk* 1886: 725.

HUGHES, JAMES HENRY, CW–USN; Honeybrook, Pa (b/VII-31–1840; d/XI-12–1870) MD UPa 1866. *U Pa med alum CW*: 1866.

HUGHES, JAMES W , Berlin, O (b/Clarksburg, Md; d/I-2–1869 @61) <Lic Med & Chir Fac Md> *Tr Ohio St Med Soc* 1869: 176–77.

HUGHES, JOHN, Valley Junction, O (b/IX-21–1816 Hamilton Co; d/II-23–1880) MD Med Coll Ohio 1839. *Med s rep Phil* 42:264 1880. *Tr Ind St M S* 1880:245–46.

HUGHES, JOHN S , Hughesville, NJ (b/1770; d/VII-7 1825 @55) MD ? *Tr Med Soc NJ* 1872: 205–06.

HUGHES, JOHN W , Latrobe, Pa (Jefferson Co, Pa; d/IX 11–1902 @64) MD Cincinnati Coll Med & Surg 1863. *Pa med jour* 6: 27, 260, 1902/03. *Flint* 1897: 807.

HUGHES, JOSEPH CLOKEY, Keokuk, Ia 1850– (b/IV 1–1821 Washington Co, Pa; d/VIII-10–1881) MD U Md 1845; <att Jefferson Coll, Pa> *Tr AMA* 33:576–77, 1882. *Tr Ia St Med Soc* 1881–82: 161–63. *Atkinson* I: 336–37. *Butler* 1878: 238.

HUGHES, LEANDER, Franklin, Tenn (d/VIII-20–1828) MD Transylvania 1828. *Transylvania jour med & assoc sci* 1:596, 1828.

HUGHES, MICHAEL J , Wilmington, Del (d/VI-19–1904 Bedford Springs, Pa) MD Jefferson 1883. *JAMA* 43:60, 1904. *Polk* 1886: 207.

HUGHES, THOMAS, , Baltimore (d/I-29–1884 @27) <MD CPS Balto 1879> *JAMA* 2:250, 1884.

HUGHES, WILLIAM LAFAYETTE TODD, Bedford, Pa (d/XII-21–1902) MD UPa 1873. *Pa med jour* 6: 260, 1902/03. *Flint* 1897: 795.

HUHN, GEORGE, CW–USA (d/X-24–1864 @55) MD ? *Med surg rep Phila* 12: 148, 1864/65. *Nat med jour* 1: 297, 1870/71.

HUHNE, AUGUSTUS, Kingston, NY (b/Hanover, Gny; d/XII-2–1897 @ c77) MD NY Med Coll 1858. *JAMA* 29: 1234, 1897. *Polk* 1886: 706.

HUIDEKOPER, RUSH SHIPPEN, Philadelphia; Span-Amer War–USA (b/V-3 1854–Meadville, Pa; d/XII-17–1901) MD UPa 1877. *Pa med jour* 5:296,1901/02. *Boston m & s j* 145:692,1901. *Milit surg* 11:101– 02, 1902. *Tr CPP* cent vol: 236. *Polk* 1896: 1059.

HUKILL, WILLIAM, W Liberty, WVa (b/IV-13–1840 Brooke Co; d/IX-4–1877) MD Miami 1867; AB Bethany Coll. *Tr Med Soc WVa* 1878:439–40; 1884:154. *Bost m & s j* 1878: 850.

HULBERT, CHAUNCEY MUNSELL, So Dennis, Mass (b/1818 E Sheldon, Vt or Weymouth, Mass; d/XI-6–1893) MD Woodstock 1844. *JAMA* 21: 784, 1893. *Bost m & s j* 129: 659, 1893.

HULBERT, JOEL C , Rochester, NY (d/XII-6 1891 @76) MD ? *Northwestern med jour* 20:16, 1892. *Butler* 1878: 559. *Polk* 1890: 846. Eclectic.

HULL, AMOS GERALD, Newburgh, NY; NYC (b/1810 New Hartford, NY; d/IV-25–1859) <MD Rutgers 1832> Lic NY Co Med Soc; AB Union 1828. *Amer homeop rev* 1:384, 427, 1858/59. *Tr Am Inst Hom* 1859: 163,

1870:649. *King* I:72–73. *Cleave.* Homeopath.

HULL, GEORGE SHRINER, Chambersburg, Pa (b/XII–26–1853; d/VIII–28–1902 Calif) MD UPa 1876. *Pa med jour* 6:33, 260, 1902/03. *Flint* 1897: 798.

HULL, HENRY V , Schenectady, NY (d/IV–7 1890 @38) MD Albany 1874. *Med reg NY NJ Conn* 1890: 270. *Polk* 1886: 707.

HULL, LAURENS, Bridgewater, NY (b/VI–6–1779 Woodbury, Conn; d/VI–27–1865) MD ? 1802; MD Regents NYU 1827; stud w/David Hull, Fairfield, Conn. *Tr Med Soc St NY* 1867: 439–41.

HULL, TYLER, Dimondale, Mich (d/VII–17–1897) <MD Detroit Med Coll 1871> *JAMA* 29: 252, 1897. *Polk* 1886:490.

HULL, WILLIAM H , Poestenkill, NY (b/Petersburgh, NY; d/XII–1–1894) MD Albany 1866. *Tr NY St Med Soc* 11: 741 ff, 1894. *Polk* 1886: 702.

HULL, WILLIAM R , CW–USA; Williamsport, Pa (b/Milton; d/VII–17–1903 @66) MD Pa Med Coll 1858. *Pa med jour* 7:279,1903/04. *Atkinson* I:708. *Flint* 1897: 840.

HULLIHEN, MANFRED F , Wheeling, WVa (b/XII–28 1835; d/V–11–1884) MD Jefferson 1870. *Tr Med Soc WVa* 1884: 154; 1886: 334. *Butler* 1878: 851.

HULSHIZER, ALLEN H , Philadelphia (b/III–28–1851 Springtown, NJ; d/V–19–1902) MD Jefferson 1878. *Pa med jour* 5:508, 1901/02; 6:298, 1902/03. *Polk* 1886:818.

HULSHIZER, HENRY, Port Oram, NJ (b/III–28–1827 Stewartsville; d/III–8–1885) MD Phila Coll Med & Surg 1856. *Tr Med Soc NJ* 1885:164–67. *Butler* 1878: 471.

HULSHIZER, PHILIP FINE, Stewartsville, NJ (b/II–11 1828 Greenwich Twp; d/X–23–1893) MD Pa Med Coll 1851. *Tr M S NJ* 1894: 291,340. *JAMA* 21:700, 1893. *Lehi Val'y m mag* 5:84–87 1893–94. *Butler* 1878:470.

HUMESTON, LUTHER F , Highland Springs, Va (d/II 2–1899 @74) MD Berkshire 1852. *JAMA* 32: 324, 1899.

HUMMEL, ARTHUR L , NYC? Denver, Col (b/Hummelstown, Pa; d/X–13 or 24–1887 @39) MD U Md 1884. *St Louis m & s j* 74: 30, 1898. *Buffalo m & s j* 37:378–79,1897. *JAMA* 29:1028, 1897.

HUMMEL, CHARLES CARROLL, Mechanicsburg Pa (b/Dauphin Co; d/1906 @51) MD Jefferson 1877. *Pa med jour* 9:804,1905/06;10:169,1906/07. *Flint* 1897:809.

HUMPHREY, CHARLES HAYS, CW–USA; Cherryville, Pa (b/III–4–1805 Weaversville; d/VI–3–1892) MD UPa 1831. *U Pa med alum CW*:1831 suppl.

HUMPHREY, GIDEON, Beverly, NJ (b/1776 or 78 Simsbury, Conn; d/VIII–3–1872) MD ? ; <ng Columbia Coll> *Am jour hom mat med* 6:37, 1872? *Tr AMA* 24:363, 1873. *Med surg rep Phila* 27:188, 1872. *King* 2:144–45. Homeopath 1835– .

HUMPHREY, JOHN RUFUS, Washington, DC; Ac-Worth, Ga (d/II–7–1900) MD U Md 1874. *JAMA* 34: 446, 1900. *Polk* 1886: 212, 224.

HUMPHREYS, GEORGE HOPPIN, NYC (b/1835 Phila; d/IV–15–1898) MD Jefferson 1856; AB UPa 1854. *Bost m & s j* 138: 386, 1898. *JAMA* 30: 999, 1898. *Polk* 1896: 1059.

HUMPHREYS, GEORGE L , Monroe, Nebr (d/III–30–1900) MD Jefferson 1874. *JAMA* 34: 957, 1900. *Polk* 1896: 905.

HUN, EDWARD REYNOLDS, Albany, NY (b/IV–17–1842; d/III–14–1880 Stamford, Conn) MD CPSNY 1866; AB 1863. *Med surg rep Phila* 42: 308, 1880. *Tr AMA* 31: 1050–52, 1880. *Bost m&s j* 102:308, 1880. *Tr M S St NY* 1881: 368–69. *Atkinson* I: 318. *K&B* III: 616.

HUN, THOMAS, Albany, NY (b/IX–14–1808; d/VI–23–1896) MD UPa 1830; AB Union 1826. *Buffalo m & s j* 36:65, 1896. *JAMA* 27: 52, 1896. *Atkinson* I: 188. *Butler* 1878: 559. *K&B* III: 617.

HUNDLEY, LARKIN, Centre Cross, Va (b/IV–8–1875 Rose Hill; d/II–19–1904) MD U Md 1896. *Tr Med Soc Va* 1904: 322–23. *Polk* 1900: 1759.

HUNGERFORD, HENRY, Stamford, Conn (b/II–8–1857 Brooklyn; d/II–5–1893) MD CPSNY 1880. *Proc Conn Med Soc* 1893: 258–59. *Med reg NY NJ Conn* 1893:304. *Bost m & s j* 128: 152, 1893.

HUNGERFORD, ROBERT, Seymour, Conn (b/II–22–1862 Chester, Conn; d/IX–22–1888) MD CPSNY 1885. *Proc Conn Med Soc* 1889: 267–68.

HUNICKE, GEORGE WILLIAM [WILLIAM G] St Louis (d/XI–30–1894) MD Washington U St L 1879. *JAMA* 23: 918, 1894. *Polk* 1890: 673.

HUNKINS [HUNKING] BENJAMIN, War 1812–USN; Lancaster, NH (b/I– –1782 Newbury, Vt; d/XII–21–1868) MD Dartmouth 1808. *Phila med reg & dir* 1871: 299. *Med surg rep Phila* 20: 20, 1869.

HUNKINS, SETH CHELLIS, Windham & Portland Me (b/XII–10–1821 Sanbornton NH; d/IV–19 or V–15–1867) MD Dartmouth 1846. *Tr Me Med Assn* 1866–68: 227–29.

HUNNEWELL, WALTER, Watertown, Mass (b/VIII–10 1769 Cambridge; d/X–19–1855) Hon MD Harvard 1825; AB 1787. *Bost m & s j* 53:294–95, 1856. Palmer's *Necrol Harvard alum*: 70.

HUNT, AZARIAH P , Somerset Co, NJ (b/II–22–1821 Hunterdon Co; d/II–26–1895) <MD UPa> Lic 1848. *Tr Med Soc NJ* 1895: 210–11. *Butler* 1878: 470.

HUNT, CHARLES A , CW–USA (d/VIII–2–1863 Mound City, Ill) MD ? *Nat med jour* 1:297, 1870/71.

HUNT, CHARLES WILLIAM, CW–USA; NH (b/XII–8 1832 Gilford; d/VIII–20 or 24–1863 Hammond Hosp) MD Dartmouth 1857. *Nat med jour* 1:297, 1870/71.

HUNT, CHESTER, Windham, Conn (b/II–24–1789; d/VIII–20–1869) Hon MD Yale 1833. *Phila med reg & dir* 1871: 302. *Proc Conn Med Soc* 3:414, 1871. *Med surg rep Phila* 21: 208, 1869.

HUNT, CICERO, Ringoes, NJ (d/XII–1–1876 @76?) MD CPSNY 1825. *Tr AMA* 28:626–27, 1877. *Tr M S NJ* 1872: 175–76; 1877: 134–35. Blane, *Hunterdon Co*: 87.

HUNT, DAVID BRAINERD, NYC (b/I–29–1846; d/IX–

25–1876) MD CPSNY 1870; AB Princeton 1866; AM 1869. *Med reg NY NJ Conn* 1877: 203. *Med rec* 11:646, 649, 1876. *Med surg rep Phila* 35: 326, 1876.

HUNT, DAVID PAGE, Marksborough, NJ (d/1835) Lic Bd Censors 1824; AB Princeton 1818; AM 1823. *Tr M S NJ* 1872: 132.

HUNT, EBEN, NYC (b/1845 NH; d/IX–3–1880) MD UCNY 1879; AB Dartmouth 1870. *Med reg NY NJ Conn* 1881: 238.

HUNT, EBENEZER KINGSBURY, Hartford Conn (b/VIII–26–1810 Coventry; d/V–2–1889) MD Jefferson 1838. *Pr Conn Med Soc* 1889:235–44. *K&B* III:617–18.

HUNT, ELEAZAR, Coventry, Conn (b/XII–28–1786; d/III–14–1867) Hon MD Yale 1826. *Proc Conn Med Soc* 1867:321–22; 1870:446.

HUNT, ELLSWORTH ELIOT, Metuchen, NJ (b/V–15–1855; d/VIII–17–1886 Pensacola, Fla) MD CPSNY 1878; AB Princeton 1875; AM 1878. *Med reg NY NJ Conn* 1887:268. *Tr Med Soc NJ* 1886: 293–94. *New Orl m & s j* ns14:318, 1886. *K&B* III: 618 (mention only).

HUNT, EZRA MUNDY, CW–USA; Metuchen, NJ (b/I–4 1830; d/VII–1–1894) MD CPSNY 1852; AB Princeton 1849; AM 1852; LLD Lafayette. *Med reg NY NJ Conn* 1895: 228. *JAMA* 23: 86, 1894. *Tr Med Soc NJ* 1895: 206–09. *Atkinson* I: 249. *K&B* III: 618.

HUNT, FLORENCE W , Milwaukee (d/V–27–1903 @45) MD Chicago Woman's Med Coll 1885. *Chic med rec* 24: 449–50, 1903.

HUNT, FRANKLIN L, CW–USA (d/XI–7–1862) MD Dartmouth 1861. *Bost m&s j* 67: 388, 1862. *Nat med jour* 1:297, 1870/71.

HUNT, HENRY, Washington, DC (b/1782 Calvert Co, Md; d/1838) <MD U Md 1824> *Med annals Md:* 447.

HUNT, HENRY FRANCIS, Camden, NJ (b/III–29–1838 Evanston, RI; d/X–3–1895 Providence, RI) MD Hahnemann Phila 1864. *Hahn mo* 30:144 (news & advt), 1895 (Nov) *Tr Am Inst Hom* 1896: 1189–90. *Cleave.* Homeopath.

HUNT, HENRY HASTINGS, Gorham, Me 1868–82; Portland 1882– (b/VII–7–1842; d/XI–30–1894) MD Bowdoin 1867; AB 1862; <MD Jefferson 1867> *Bost m & s j* 133: 195, 1895. *Tr Me Med Assoc* 1895: 188–90. *Atkinson* I: 568. *Butler* 1878: 308.

HUNT, HIRAM H , Independence, Ia (d/IX–25 1896 @72) No MD. *JAMA* 27: 776, 1896. *Polk* 1886:360.

HUNT, ISRAEL THORNDIKE, Charlestown, Mass (d/II 16–1905 @65) MD Harvard 1870. *Bost m&s j* 152:234, 1905. *Polk* 1896: 700.

HUNT, J SPAFFORD, Chicago (b/1834: d/XII–10–1897 @63) MD Miami 1855; MD Jefferson 1856. *JAMA* 29: 1286, 1897. *Polk* 1886: 265.

HUNT, JACOB, Utica, NY (b/I–25–1811; d/IV–21–1888) MD Fairfield 1836. *Med reg NY NJ Conn* 1889: 275. *Butler* 1878:559.

HUNT, JAMES HALSEY, Port Jervis, NY (b/Centreville, NY; d/XII–20–1892. MD Bellevue 1872. *Tr Med Soc St NY* 11: 741 ff, 1894. *Polk* 1890: 843.

HUNT, JAMES L, Brooklyn (d/VIII–2–1886 @71) MD Med Coll Cinc 1851. *Med reg NY NJ Conn* 1887: 268.

HUNT, JOHN GIBBONS, Philadelphia (b/VII–26–1826 Darby, Pa; d/IV–29–1893 Lansdowne) MD UPa 1850. *Tr CPP* cent vol: 236. *K&B* III: 619.

HUNT, LEWIS STOUT, Montrose, NJ (b/IX–12–1846 Wertsville; d/II–28–1875 or III– –1876 Hopewell) MD UPa 1868. *Tr AMA* 28:628, 1877. *Tr M S NJ* 1877:133.

HUNT, MOSES NOWELL, Danversport, Mass (b/XII–11–1839 Danvers; d/XI–17–1873 St Louis) MD Harvard 1867; ng Amherst 1862. *Bost m & s j* ns12: 572, 1873.

HUNT, MYRON WINSLOW, Falls City, Nebr (b/XII–5–1846 Madras, India; d/VIII–10–1881) MD Mo Med Coll 1890; ng Amherst 1870. *Amherst, Men of*: 1870.

HUNT, OTIS EUGENE, Newtonville, Mass (b/VII–7–1822 Sudbury; d/I–20–1905) MD Berkshire 1847. *Bost m & s j* 152: 120, 1905. *Polk* 1886:470.

HUNT, OWEN T , LaCrosse, Ark (b/1833 Tenn; d/IX–22 1886) MD UPa 1855. *New Orl m&s j* ns14: 559, 1887. *Polk* 1886: 153.

HUNT, SAMUEL P , Cincinnati (b/1802 Connellsville, Pa; d/XI–2–1884) Stud w/Dr Hoover, Barnesville, O. *Tr O M S* 1886: 398–99. *Med surg rep Phila* 51: 604, 1884.

HUNT, SYLVESTER HENRY, CW–USA; Long Branch, NJ (b/VI–21–1837; d/V–5–1891) MD Jefferson 1865. *Tr Med Soc NJ* 1891: 255–61. *Med reg NY NJ Conn* 1891:275. *Atkinson* I: 384–85. *Butler* 1874: 471.

HUNT, THOMAS, New Orleans (b/V–18–1808 Charleston, SC; d/III–20–1867) MD UPa 1829. *New Orl m&s j* 20:141–52 1867; ?ns22:41–42 1894. *Tr AMA* 18:349–50 1867. *Nashville j m&s* ns3:428 1868. *K&B* III:619–20.

HUNT, THOMAS BENJAMIN, Warsaw, Ill (d/XI–17–1905 @74 or 75) MD U Louisville 1864. *Ill med jour* 9:131, 332, 1906. *Polk* 1886: 301.

HUNT, TILGHMAN, Plainfield, Ind (b/IV–8–1838 Friendship, NC; d/VI–12–1906) MD Ind Med Coll 1872. *Tr Ind St Med Soc* 1906: 496. *Polk* 1886: 314.

HUNT, WILLIAM, CW–USA; Philadelphia (b/IX–26–1825; d/IV–17–1896) MD UPa 1849. *Bost m&s j* 134: , 1896. *U Pa med alum CW*: 1849. *JAMA* 26:890,1896. *Tr CPP* 3s19:xlvff,1897. *K&B* III:620.

HUNT, WILLIAM ALLEN, Anderson, Ind (b/X–26–1822 Wayne Co; d/II–20–1889) <MD Starling 1849> *Tr Ind St Med Soc* 1889:214. Kemper's *Indiana*: 218–19. *Polk* 1886: 310.

HUNT, WILLIAM C, Chicago (d/II–28–1891 @68) MD Rush 1852. *Chic med rec* 1:91, 1891. *Butler* 1878: 132.

HUNT, WILLIAM G , Brooklyn (d/XI–16–1887 @77) Lic NY St Med Soc 1832. *Med reg NY NJ Conn* 1889: 276. *Butler* 1878: 531. *Polk* 1886: 646.

HUNT, WILLIS HENRY, Camden, NJ (d/IV–11–1900 @45) MD Harvard 1877. *JAMA* 34:1021, 1900. *Polk* 1886: 602.

HUNTER, ALEXANDER STUART, NYC (b/1839 Conesville; d/II-13-1896 Spuyten Duyvil) MD UCNY 1863; gr NY St Normal Sch 1859. *Buffalo m&s j* 35: 678, 1896. *Bost m&s j* 134: 201, 1896. *JAMA* 26: 442, 1896. *Polk* 1890: 818.

HUNTER, ANDREW, CW-CSA (b/VI-22-1838 Charlestown, WVa; d/1864? nr Winchester, Va) MD UPa 1860. *U Pa med alum CW*: 1860.

HUNTER, CHARLES, Colorado Spr, Col (d/I-14-1899) MD CPSNY 1882. AB ? *JAMA* 32: 196, 1899. *Polk* 1896: 255.

HUNTER, CHARLES THOMAS, Philadelphia (b/I-13-1843 N Bloomfield, O; d/IV-27-1884) MD UPa 1868. *Med s rep Phila* 50: 608, 1884. *Tr M S St Pa* 17:381-84, 1885. *Chic med jour* 48: 657, 1884. *Tr CPP* cent vol:237, *Atkinson* I: 170.

HUNTER, GALEN, NYC (b/I-2-1800 Vt; d/VIII-6-1872) MD Dartmouth 1824. *Med reg NY NJ Conn* 1873: 341. *Med rec* 7:448, 1872; 8:161, 1873.

HUNTER, HORATIO MILTON, Lowell, Mass (b/IX-29-1830 Lyndon, Vt; d/I-11-1899) MD Hahnemann Phila 1857; att Dartmouth Med Sch & UVt Med Sch. *Tr Am Inst Hom* 1899: 928. Homeopath.

HUNTER, JAMES BRADBRIDGE, NYC; CW-USA (b/IV-30-1837 Geneva, NY; d/VI-10-1889) MD CPSNY 1866. *Med reg NY NJ Conn* 1890: 270. *Buff m&s j* 24: 52, 1889. *Nashville j m&s* 43:264, 1889. *Bost m&s j* 121: 644, 1889. *Atkinson* I: 260. *Butler* 1878: 516.

HUNTER, JOHN, ? (d/1878 Bell's Depot, Tenn) MD ? *Tr AMA* 30:873, 1879.

HUNTER, JOHN, Washington, DC (d/VII-10-1883 @ 79) MD UPa 1826. *JAMA* 1: 64, 1883.

HUNTER, JOHN A , CW-CSA (b/Louisburg, Va; d/IV 1870) MD UPa 1842; att Washington & Lee. *U Pa med alum CW*: 1842. Blanton, *Va surgs CW*: 406.

HUNTER, JOHN POWELL, West Chester, Pa (b/1865 Williamstown; d/III-27-1901) MD UPa 1893; AB Brown 1888. *Pa med jour* 296, 1901/02.

HUNTER, LEWIS BOUDINOT, USN 1828-1866 (b/X-9-1804 Princeton, NJ; d/VI-24-1887 Philadelphia) MD UPa 1828. *U Pa med alum CW*: 1828.

HUNTER, REUBEN, CW-USA (d/IX-19-1864 Annapolis, Md) MD ? *Nat med jour* 1:297, 1870/71.

HUNTER, ROBERT, NYC (b/Ayrshire, Scot; d/VII-29-1899 @76) MD UCNY 1846. *JAMA* 33: 367, 427, 1899. *Polk* 1896: 1059.

HUNTER, WARREN, Hampton, Ill (b/X-18-1833 Strong, Me; d/I-6-1905) MD Bowdoin 1860. *Ill med jour* 7:242, 1905. *Polk* 1896: 422.

HUNTER, WILLIAM CHARLES, NYC (b/IX-25-1829; d/IX-20-1885) MD CPSNY 1857. *Med reg NY NJ Conn* 1886: 250.

HUNTER, WILLIAM RUSSELL, Pembroke, Me 1848-56; St Cloud, Miss 1856-73 (b/X-14-1814 Strong, Me; d/IV-25-1874 Brownsdale, Minn) MD Jefferson 1848; AB Bowdoin 1842. *Bowdoin cat*: 1842.

HUNTINGTON, ALFRED THOMAS, Boston (b/1868; d/II-13-1899) MD Harvard 1898. *Bost m&s j* 140:198-99, 200, 1899.

HUNTINGTON, DAVID LOW, USA 1862-98 (b/IV-10 1834 Charlestown, Mass; d/XII-20-1899 Rome, Italy) MD UPa 1857; AB Yale 1855. *JAMA* 34:61, 1900. *U Pa med alum CW*: 1857. *K&B* III: 621.

HUNTINGTON, ELIPHALET, Windham, Conn (b/III-3 -1816; d/XII-30-1882) MD Dartmouth 1848. *Pr Conn M S* 1883:180-81. *Atkinson* I: 564-65. *Butler* 1878: 78.

HUNTINGTON, ELISHA, Topsfield & Lowell, Mass (b/IV-9-1876; d/XII-13-1865) MD Yale 1823; AB Dartmouth 1823. *Tr AMA* 18: 305-06, 1867. *Bost m&s j* 73: 428, 1865; 74:45, 1866. *Med surg rep Phila* 13:422, 1865. *K&B* III: 621.

HUNTINGTON, HENRY KENT, City Island, NY (b/III-27-1845 Hartford, Conn; d/II-28-1897) MD UCNY 1871; AB Trinity 1866. *Bost m & s j* 136: 240, 1897. *JAMA* 28: 523, 1897.

HUNTINGTON, JOSHUA, Washington, DC (b/II-11-1812 Boston; d/III-23-1900) MD Yale 1838; AB 1832; ng Amherst 1831. *Amherst, Men of*:1831. *Polk* 1893:270.

HUNTLEY, OSMAN LORENZO, Fitchburg, Mass (b/IX 20-1819 Marlow, NH; d/II-25-1856) MD Woodstock 1841. *Bost m & s j* 54: 87, 1856.

HUNTON, ARIEL, Hyde Park, Vt (b/1789 Unity, NH; d/XI-25-1857) Hon MD Dartmouth 1847; <MD Cincinnati Eclectic Med Inst 1855> *NH jour med* 8:29, 1858.

HUNTSMAN, HENRY CLAY, Oskaloosa, Ia; CW-USA (b/IX-16-1825 Dayton, O; d/I-14-1887) MD U Mich 1851; att Laporte Med Coll. *Tr Ia St Med Soc* 7:521-24, 1886. *Atkinson* I: 521. *Polk* 1886: 365.

HUNTT, HENRY, Washington, DC (b/1782 Md; d/IX 21-1838) Hom MD U Md 1824; lic Med & Chir Fac Md. *Hist Med Soc DC:* 214. *Med exam* Phila : 363, 1838.

HURD, CAROLINE AMANDA, Taunton, Mass (d/I-22 -1878 @55) MD Boston U 1875. *New Engl med gaz* 13: 132, 1878. Homeopath.

HURD, EDWARD PAYSON, Newburyport, Mass (b/VIII-29-1838 Newport, Can; d/II-24-1899) MD McGill 1865. *Bost m & s j* 140:223-24, 416, 1899. *JAMA* 32: 563, 1899. *Polk* 1886: 719. *K&B* III: 622-23.

HURD, EDWIN HENRY, Rochester, NY (b/V-8-1825 North East, NY; d/V-15-1891) MD Geneva 1847. *Med vis* 7:230, 1891. *Tr Am Inst Hom* 1891: 99. *Polk* 1886: 704. Homeopath.

HURD, FREDERIC W , Brooklyn (d/III-1-1869 @56) Lic Med Soc St NY 1834. *Phila med reg & dir* 1871:300. *Tr AMA* 21:442 1870 *Med reg NY NJ Conn* 1869:234.

HURD, JOHN SIDNEY, Wright Co, Ia 1855-59; Hampton 1859-62; CW-USA; Chapin 1868- (b/XII-28 1831 Fryeburg, Me; d/VII-23-1901) <att UPa Med Dept to 1855> AB Bowdoin 1851; AM 1852. *JAMA* 37: 397, 1901. *Polk* 1886: 353.

 Spec. educ'l status abbrev. as: ***ng*** = college verified attendance without degree;

HURD, JOSIAH STEARNS, Charlestown, Mass (d/III 25–1855 @59) MD Harvard 1818. *Bost m & s j* 52: 167, 186, 1855. *Mass Med Soc cat* 1894.

HURD, SAMUEL HUTCHINS, CW–USA; Charlestown, Mass (b/IV–27–1830; d/II–5–1897 Atlantic City, NJ) MD UPa 1858; AB Harvard 1852. *Bost m&s j* 136:148, 1897. *Harv in CW*: 57. *U Pa med alum CW*: 1858 suppl.

HURD, WILLIAM S, Paterson, NJ (b/1847 Fishkill Landing, NY; d/VIII–18–1893) MD UCNY 1877. *JAMA* 21: 357, 1893.

HURD, YORICK GORDON, Ipswich, Mass (b/1827; d/IX–24–1888) Hon MD Bowdoin 1876; AB Dartmouth 1854. *Bost m & s j* 119: 320, 1888.

HURDSFIELD, JOHN, NYC (b/XII–6–1843; d/III–3–1884) MD CPSNY 1869. *Med reg NY NJ Conn* 1884: 230. *Med surg rep Phila* 50: 448, 1884.

HURLBUT, GEORGE ALMARIN, Glastonbury, Conn (b/IX–28–1833; d/X–10–1882) MD CPSNY 1857. *Proc Conn Med Soc* 1883: 170–71.

HURLBUT, HORATIO NELSON, Chicago (d/XI–5–1891 @85) MD Starling 1840. *Chic med rec* 2:288, 1891. *Polk* 1886: 265.

HURLBUT, VINCENT LOMBARD, Chicago (b/VI–28 1829 W Mendon, NY; d/VII–24–1896) MD Rush 1852. *JAMA* 27:279, 1896. *Polk* 1890: 315.

HURLBUTT, LEWIS RAYMOND, Stamford, Conn (d/ II–14–1898 @78) MD Yale 1850; AB 1843; AM. *JAMA* 30:570, 1898. *Polk* 1890: 226.

HURLEY, JOHN, NYC; CW–USA (d/IV–14–1863 nr Falmouth, Va) MD CPSNY 1859. *Nat med jour* 1:297, 1870/71. *Med surg rep Phila* 10: 64, 1863.

HURST, HARRY HERBERT, Wilkinsburg, Pa (d/I–31 1903 @28) MD UPa 1897. *Pa med jour* 7: 279, 1903/04.

HURT, RICHARD THWEATT CW–CSA; Petersburg Va (b/VIII–6–1840; d/V–27–1871) MD U Md 1861. *Tr Med Soc Va* 1872:26, 155. Blanton *Va surgs CW*:406.

HURTER, P C, CW–USA (d/I– –1866) MD *Nat med jour* 1:297, 1870/71.

HUSE, EDWARD CARROLL, Rockford, Ill (b/ Mass; d/ V–14–1900 @65) MD CPSNY 1866; AB Harvard 1856. *Ill med jour* ns2:48, 1900. *JAMA* 34:1356, 1900. *Polk* 1886: 295.

HUSE, FRED J, San Francisco (d/VIII–7–1893 @50) MD Chic M C 1873; att NW U 1868. *JAMA* 21:247–48 1893.

HUSE, RALPH CROSS, CW–USA; Georgetown, Mass (d/VI–1–1892 @49) MD Harvard 1866. *Rec Assoc Act'g Asst Surg USA* 1891:52–53. *Bost m & s j* 126: 592, 1892. *Polk* 1890: 548.

HUSE, STEPHEN, Methuen, Mass (b/1799? Edgartown, Mass; d/VIII–3–1864 @65) MD Harvard 1823. *Bost m & s j* 71: 68, 1864.

HUSSON, FRANÇOIS CHARLES, NYC (b/X–7–1863; d/II–27–1893) MD CPSNY 1885. *Med reg NY NJ Conn* 1893: 304.

HUSTED, JARVIS NICHOLS, NYC (b/VI–27–1823; d/ IV–13–1893) MD UCNY 1850; AB Wesleyan 1845;AM 1848. *Med reg NY NJ Conn* 1893: 305. *Polk* 1886: 682.

HUSTED, NATHANIEL C, CW–USA; NYC (b/X–22–1825 Greenwich, Conn; d/XI–19–1891 Tarrytown, NY) MD UCNY 1850. *Med reg NY NJ Conn* 1892: 279. *Proc Conn Med Soc* 1893: 230. *Bost m & s j* 125: 584, 1891. *Atkinson* I:114.

HUSTON, ANTHONY S, Anderson, Ind (b/1848; d/XII 28–1894) <MD Physio–Med Coll Ind 1876> *JAMA* 24: 67, 1895. Kemper's *Indiana*:219. *Polk* 1886: 332.

HUSTON, FREDERICK NICKELS, CW–USA; Damariscotta, Me 1873–91 (b/X–1–1839; d/V–7–1891) MD Bowdoin 1873; AB 1863. *Bowdoin cat*: 1863.

HUSTON, JOHN, Salisbury, Md (b/II–20–1768; d/I–23–1828) MD ? *Med annals Md:* 448.

HUSTON, ROBERT MENDENHALL, Philadelphia (b/ V–19–1795 Abingdon, Va; d/VIII–3–1864) MD UPa 1825. *Med surg rep Phila* 12: 68, 1864/65. *Bost m & s j* 71: 148, 1864. *K&B* III: 624.

HUSTON, WILLIAM A, CW–USA (d/VI–25–1864) MD *Nat med jour* 1:297, 1870/71.

HUSTON, WILLIAM AUGUSTUS, Damariscotta Mills & Rockland, Me; Boston (b/II–5–1843 Bristol, Me; d/V–26–1904) MD CPSNY 1879; att Bowdoin 1862–64. *Bowdoin cat*: 1866.

HUTCHINGS, JOHN W, Murfreesboro, NC (d/II–17–1870 @49) MD UPa 1845; Hon AM Princeton 1846. *Tr NC Med Soc* 1870: 10–11.

HUTCHINS, ALEXANDER, Brooklyn (d/VII–30–1906 @71) MD NY Med Coll 1860. *Bost m & s j* 155: 162, 1906. *Polk* 1896: 1060.

HUTCHINS, CORYDON CHADWICK, CW–USA (b/ VI–13–1836 New Portland, Md; d/VII–10–1863 Washington, DC) MD Bowdoin 1861. *Bowdoin cat*: 1861.

HUTCHINS, EDWARD RIDGWAY, CW–USA & USN; Clyde, O (b/X–21–1841 Concord, NH; d/II–28–1894 @48) MD Jefferson 1866; AB Williams 1862. *JAMA* 22:391, 1894.

HUTCHINS, SAMUEL, Danielsonville, Conn (b/VI–3–1818 Seekonk, Mass; d/I–16–1886) MD Harvard 1841. *Proc Conn Med Soc* ns3: 181–82, 1886. *Bost m & s j* 114: 120, 1886. *Butler* 1878: 78.

HUTCHINSON, EDWIN, CW–USA; Utica, NY (b/II–1–1840; d/X–19–1887) MD CPSNY 1866; PhB Yale 1860. *Med reg NY NJ Conn* 1888: 254. *Tr Med Soc St NY* 1888: 554–60. *Atkinson* I: 257. *K&B* III: 624.

HUTCHINSON, IRA, Cromwell, Conn (b/III–1–1800; d/ VIII–8–1881) MD Yale 1825. *Proc Conn Med Soc* ns2: 177–79, 1882. *Atkinson* I: 623. *Butler* 1878: 78.

HUTCHINSON, JAMES, RevWar–USA USN; Philadelphia (b/I–29–1752 Wakefield; d/IX–7–1793) MB U Pa 1774;AB. *Tr CPP* cent vol:237. *K&B* III:624–25.

HUTCHINSON, JAMES HOWELL, CW–USA; Philadelphia (b/VIII–3–1834 Cintra, Port; d/XII–27–1889) MD UPa 1858; AB 1854; AM 1857. *Tr CPP* cent v: 237;

3s12:xlv–lviii, 1890. *Bost m & s j* 122: 22,1890. *U Pa med alum CW*:1858. *K&B* III: 625–26.

HUTCHINSON, JAMES M , Chicago (d/V–6–1905 @ 62) MD Chicago Med Coll 1867. *Ill med jour* 6: 611, 1905. *Polk* 1896: 389.

HUTCHINSON, MAHLON PALMER, Philadelphia (d/IX–16–1895) MD UPa 1842. *Tr CPP* cent vol:237.

HUTCHINSON, MORISON THOMAS, Englewood, NJ (d/IX–11–1897 @33) MD CPSNY 1889; PhB Yale 1886. *JAMA* 29:660,1897. *Polk* 1896:936,1060 [NYC].

HUTCHINSON, [HUTCHISON], NATHANIEL GERHARD, Brooklyn (b/1854? d/IV–10–1877 @23) MD CPSNY 1875. *Med reg NY NJ Conn* 1877: 203. *Med rec* 12: 303, 1877.

HUTCHINSON, PROSPER KIMBALL, Rice City, RI (b/VIII–29–1817 Plainfield, Conn; d/XI–1–1872) <MD Yale 1847> AB Amherst 1841. *Amherst, Men of*: 1841.

HUTCHINSON, ROBERT C , Yardville, NM (d/II–27–1906 @49 at sea) MD UPa 1878. *Bost m & s j* 154: 308, 1906. *Polk* 1896: 951.

HUTCHINSON, WILLIAM FRANCIS, Providence, RI (b/X–28–1838 Oswego, NY; d/X–2–1893) MD Heidelberg 1858; MD Buffalo 1873; AM Central HS Phila 1856. *JAMA* 21:667, 1893. *Chic med rec* 5:361, 1893. *Tr RI Med Soc* 4:623–24, 1889–93. *Bost m & s j* 130:198, 1894. *Polk* 1890: 1027.

HUTCHISON, JOSEPH CHRISMAN, Brooklyn (b/II–23–1827 Old Franklin, Mo; d/VII–17–1887) MD UPa 1848. *Proc Conn M S* 1891: 295. *Med reg NY NJ Conn* 1888: 255. *Bost m&s j* 117: 93, 348, 1887. *K&B* III: 626.

HUTCHISON, WILLIAM NOBLE, Oxford, Pa; CW–USA (b/IV–8–1845; d/X–4–1877) MD UPa 1866. *U Pa med alum CW*: 1866.

HUTTON, ERNST LEROY, Kansas City, Mo (d/VI–1–1898) MD Rush 1884. *JAMA* 30: 1481, 1898.

HUTTON, WILLIAM HENRY HARRISON, Edinburgh, Ind; US Marine HospServ (d/VI–14–1897 @59) MD LICH 1875. *Bost m & s j* 137:45,1897. *JAMA* 28:1203, 1897. *Polk* 1886: 400 (Louisville, Ky)

HUXLEY, ASAHEL M , Goshen, Conn (b/IX– –1805 New Marlborough, Mass; d/I–10–1864 Alexandria, Va) MD Berkshire 1832. *Bost m & s j* 69: 528, 1863. *Proc Conn Med Soc* 2:61–63, 1864.

HUYETT, HERMAN JOSEPH, Rock Island, Ill (d/XII–10–1905 @43) MD Jefferson 1885. *Ill med jour* 9:130, 1906. *Polk* 1896: 429.

HUYETT, JOSEPH, Milan, Ill (d/X–6–1905 @85) MD Jefferson 1843. *Ill med jour* 8:430, 1905. *Polk* 1896: 429.

HUZZA, THOMAS HARRY, Atlanta, Ga (b/IX–12–1863 St Louis; d/XII–9–1898 NY) MD Jefferson 1887. *JAMA* 31: 1584, 1898. *Bost m & s j* 139: 637, 1898. *Polk* 1896: 325.

HYATT, AARON SANFORD, Lansing, Mich (d/I–12–1899 @38) MD UCNY 1879. *JAMA* 32:196, 1899. *Polk* 1896: 762.

HYATT, ELIJAH [ELISHA] H , Delaware, O (b/II–19 1827 Wooster, O; d/XII–24–1898) MD Starling 1857; AB Ohio Wesleyan 1849. *JAMA* 32: 41, 1898. *Atkinson* I:581. *K&B* III: 587.

HYATT, PULASKI F , Jersey Shore, Pa (d/I–17–1904 @67) MD Georgetown 1865. *Pa m j* 8: 335, 1904/05.

HYDE, EPHRAIM AUGUSTUS, Freeport, Me 1841–(b/VIII–10–1814; d/IV–15–1871) MD Berkshire 1840; ng Bowdoin 1831–33. *Bowdoin cat*: 1835.

HYDE, FREDERICK, Cortland, NY (b/I–27–1807; d/X–15–1887) MD Fairfield 1835. *Med reg NY NJ Conn* 1888: 256. *Bost m & s j* 117: 544, 1887. *Tr Med Soc St NY* 1889: 365–73. *Atkinson* I: 208. *K&B* III: 626–27.

HYDE, GEORGE SMITH, Boston (d/XII–11–1905 @74) MD Harvard 1856; AB 1853. *Bost m & s j* 153: 710, 1905. *Polk* 1896:700.

HYDE, JOHN ANGIER, Freeport, Me (b/VII–10–1771 Rehoboth, Mass; d/II–19–1857) Hon MD Bowdoin 1831. *Bost m & s j* 56: 107, 1857.

HYDE, SENECA TOBIAS, Dorchester, Mass (d/II–17–1901 @60) MD U Vt 1866. *Bost m & s j* 144:222, 1901. *Polk* 1886: 469.

HYDE, WILLIAM, Stonington, Conn (b/X–27–1808; d/IX–25–1873) MD Harvard 1830. *Pr Conn M S* 4: 267–72, 293, 1874. *Med s rep Phila* 29:263, 305–06, 1873.

HYER, WILBUR F , Meridian, Miss (d/XI–18 1897 @59) <MD Shelby Med Coll, Tenn> *New Orl m&s j* 50: 380, 1897. *Polk* 1896: 812.

HYLAND, HENRY, Princess, Md (b/1788; d/VI–17–1852) MD UPa 1812. *Med annals Md:* 448.

HYSLOP, JAMES, NYC (b/IV–8–1816; d/V–17–1870) MD CPSNY 1842; AB Union 1836. *Med reg NY NJ Conn* 1871:359. *Med rec* 5:498, 1870/71; 6:94, 1871/72.

IBACH, FREDERICK GUSTAVUS, Mauch Chunk, Pa (b/Lebanon Co, Pa; d/IX–12–1902 @44) MD Jefferson 1879. *Pa med jour* 6:260, 1902/03. *Flint* 1897: 809.

IHRIE, ROSS R , CW–USA; Pittsboro, NC (b/III–24–1828 Easton, Pa; d/VI–28–1889) MD UPa 1850. *U Pa med alum CW*: 1850.

IKE, EDGAR MILTON, Altoona, Pa (b/III–21–1867; d/VII–29–1897) MD Jefferson 1888. *JAMA* 29:350, 1897. *Polk* 1896: 1266.

IKIRT, J J , E Liverpool, O (d/V–18–1897 @70) MD Starling 1865. *JAMA* 28: 1045, 1897. *Butler* 1878: 634.

ILGEN, ERNST, Brooklyn (b/Munich, Gny; d/III–5–1897) MD U Munich 1836. *Bost m & s j* 136: 240, 1897. *JAMA* 28:523, 1897. *Polk* 1896: 997.

ILIFF, JOSEPH N , Melrose, Kans; Welch, Indian Terr (d/VIII–23–1904) MD CPS Kansas City 1895. *Jour Kans Med Soc* 4: 460, 1904.

ILLINSKI, ALPHONSO XAVIER, E St Louis, Ill (b/Poland; d/V–29–1897 @90) MD Mo Med Coll 1842. *JAMA* 28: 1156, 1897. *Polk* 1886: 277.

IMPERATORE DI RINALDO, CARLO, NYC (b/1832

 Spec. educ'l status abbrev. as: ***ng*** = college verified attendance without degree;

Italy; d/VII-26-1902) MD Bellevue 1874. *Bost m & s j* 147:144, 1902. *Polk* 1896: 1060.

INCHES, HERMAN BRIMMER, Boston (d/VIII-19-1889 @77) MD Harvard 1834; AB 1831. *Med surg rep Phila* 61: 307, 1889. *Bost m&s j* 121:196, 1889. *Polk* 1886: 458.

INGALLS, LUCIEN, Andover, Me 1861- ; Falmouth, Me 1872- (b/IV-29-1833 Merrimac, NH; d/V-3-1881) MD Dartmouth 1870. *Tr Me Med Assoc* 1881: 388-89. *Atkinson* I: 667. *Butler* 1878: 308.

INGALLS, PASCHAL PIERCE, CW-USA; S Boston (b/X-8-1836 Harrison, Me; d/XI-20-1874) MD Jefferson 1860; ng Bowdoin Med Sch 1858-59. *Bost m&s j* 91:532, 1874.

INGALLS, WILLIAM, Wrentham, Mass (b/V-3-1769 Newburyport; d/IX-9-1851) Hon MD Harvard 1801; Hon MD Brown 1813; MB Harvard 1794; AB 1790. *Bost m & s j* 45:106, 1851. Palmer's *Necrol Harvard alum*: 2. *Tr Am Inst Hom* 1852: 44. *K&B* III: 631. Homeopath [?]

INGALLS, WILLIAM, CW-USA; Boston (b/I-12-1813; d/XII-1-1903) MD Harvard 1836; AB 1835. *Bost m & s j* 149: 661-62, 1903; 150:106, 1904. *Atkinson* I: 329. *Polk* 1896: 700. *K&B* III: 631. *Harvard in CW*: 8.

INGALS, EPHRAIM, Chicago (b/V-20-1823 Pomfret, Conn; d/XII-18-1900) MD Rush 1847. *Chic med rec* 20: 246-47, 1901; 21:100, 1901. *Ill med jour* ns2:356-57, 1901. *K&B* III:629-30.

INGELS, JOHN B , Meriden, Ia (b/III-29-1852 Wabash Co, Ind; d/1895) MD Bellevue 1878. *Tr Ia St Med Soc* 1896: 323-24. *Polk* 1890: 421.

INGERSOLL, DENMAN BEVIS, CW-USA Med cadet; May's Landing, NJ (b/I-26-1831; d/VIII-29-1890) MD UPa 1865. *U Pa med alum CW*: 1865. *Med reg NY NJ Conn* 1892: 279. *Tr Med Soc NJ* 1891: 228-29. *Butler* 1874: 471.

INGERSOLL, ELLEN A, Canton, Ill (b/IV-24-1844; d/XI-29-1888) MD Woman's M C Pa 1874. *JAMA* 12: 898-99, 1889. *Tr Ill St M S* 1889:xxxiii ff. *Polk* 1886: 257.

INGHAM, JOHN HOWARD, Philadelphia (d/II-16-1866 @62) MD UPa 1832. *Med s rep Phil* 14: 180, 1866.

INGHAM, JONATHAN, NJ (b/1744? d/X-1-1793 Solebury, Pa) MD ? *Tr Med Soc NJ* 1872: [202-03].

INGLIS, ROY, Jersey City, NJ (d/IV-23-1901 Denver, Col) MD CPSNY 1891. *Bost m & s j* 144:438, 1901.

INGRAHAM, CHARLES WILSON, Binghamton NY (d/I-3-1900 @29) MD UCNY 1892. *JAMA* 34: 187, 1900. *Polk* 1896: 990.

INGRAHAM, TIMOTHY MURPHY, Brooklyn (b/I-12 1821 Amenia, NY; d/XI-5-1894) MD Woodstock 1845. *Med reg NY NJ Conn* 1895: 228. *JAMA* 23: 768, 802, 1894. *Butler* 1878: 559.

INGRAM, ALEXANDER, CW-USA (b/XII-12-1837 Scotl; d/VII-30-1865 at sea) MD Med Coll Ohio 1861; att Dartmouth 1854. *Amer jour med sci* ns52: 287-88, 1866. *Tr AMA* 18: 354-55, 1867. *Nat med jour* 1:297, 1870/71. G V Henry: 83-84.

INGRAM, E W , Mt Erie, Ill (d/IV-5-1900) Lic yrs of pract. *Tr Ill St Med Soc* 1899-1900: 574. *Polk* 1896: 431.

INGRAM, FRANK HAROLD, Logansport, Ind (b/VII-19-1861; d/III-17-1893 NYC) MD Bellevue 1883. *Med reg NY NJ Conn* 1893: 305. *Bost m & s j* 128: 304, 1893.

INLOES, HENRY AUGUSTUS, Baltimore (b/I-4-1811; d/V-28-1874) MD U Md 1833. *Tr AMA* 26:466, 1875. *Med annals Md:* 449.

INLOW, JOHN J , Manilla, Ind (b/II-13-1826 Fleming Co Ky; d/I-24-1896) ng Med Coll Ohio 1840-50. *Tr Ind St Med Soc* 1896: 263. *Butler* 1878: 207.

INMAN, BENJAMIN W , Leota Landing, Miss (d/XII-11-1905) MD Tulane 1885. *New Orl m & s j* 58: 683, 1906. *Polk* 1896: 816.

INSLEY, WILLIAM QUINN, Terre Haute, Ind (b/VIII-27-1827 Attica; d/VI-21-1880) MD Med Coll Ohio 1863. *Tr Ind St Med Soc* 1881:233. *Butler* 1878:207.

IRELAND, DAVID CALDWELL, Baltimore (b/V-4-1844 Annapolis, Md; d/I-14-1901) MD UPa 1867. *Med annals Md:* 449. *Polk* 1893: 561.

IRELAND, JAMES W, Lewisport Ky (b/Eminence; d/III 15-1896 @58) MD ? *JAMA* 26:642 1896 *Polk* 1896:588.

IRELAND, JOHN F , Lower Marlboro, Md (d/VIII-4-1899 @60) MD U Md 1856. *JAMA* 33:493, 1899. *Polk* 1893: 570.

IRELAND, JOSIAS ALEXANDER, Louisville (d/IX-20 1901 @77) MD Kentucky Sch Med 1851. *JAMA* 37: 847, 1901. *Polk* 1886: 400.

IREMONGER, FRANCIS WILLIAM, Rossville, NY (b/II-3-1825; d/XI-24-1869) MD UCNY 1850. *Med reg NY NJ Conn* 1871: 360.

IRISH, DELILA [DELLA] SUSAN, Davenport, Ia (b/VII-24-1842 Franklin Co NY; d/V-7-1878) MD Woman's Med Coll Pa 1868; <MD Milwaukee Female Med Coll 1863> *Tr Ia St M S* 1877-78: 187. *Butler* 1878: 238.

IRISH, FRANKLIN, Pittsburgh; CW-USA (b/I-12-1820; d/VIII-7-1869 Newcastle, Pa) MD UPa 1841. *Tr Med Soc Pa* 8:81-82, 1870. *U Pa med alum CW*: 1841.

IRLAND, WILLIAM PENN, Philadelphia; Bedford, Pa; Fairfield, Ia (b/Milton, Pa; d/IX-9-1859 Oreapolis, Nebr Terr) MD Jefferson 1840. *Med surg rep Phila* ns3: 92, 1859/60.

IRONS, WILLIAM R , Allegheny, Pa (d/V-24-1903 @ 42) MD Jefferson 1890. *Pa med jour* 7:279, 1902/03. *Flint* 1897: 793.

IRVIN, SPENCER POTTER Jr, Philadelphia (d/V-30-1906 @27) MD UPa 1900. *Pa med jour* 9: 672, 1905/06.

IRVIN, WILLIAM, CW-San Comm US (b/XI-15-1805 Linden Hall, Pa; d/IX-9-1865 Amoy, China) MD UPa 1829. *U Pa med alum CW*: 1829.

IRVINE, JOSEPH S KANAGA, CW-USA; Lock Haven

Pa (b/IX-8-1842 Silver Spring Twp; d/IV- 1871) MD UPa 1866. *U Pa med alum CW*: 1866.

IRVINE [IRVIN], WILLIAM, Evans City, Pa (d/IV-6-1898 @70) MD Jefferson 1855. *JAMA* 30:999, 1898. *Off'l reg Pa phys* 1881-88: 666.

IRWIN, AARON J , CW-USA (d/V-8-1864) MD U Nashville 1864. *Nat med jour* 1:297, 1870/71.

IRWIN, E HOWARD, Lodi, Wis (b/VII-1-1833; d/IV-2-1892) MD Rush 1866. *Tr Wis St Med Soc* 1892: 391-93; 1894: 503. *Polk* 1890: 1167.

IRWIN, JAMES HERVEY, NYC (d/X-16-1872 @46) MD UCNY 1852. *Med s rep Phila* 27:398, 416, 1872.

IRWIN, LUTHER MARTIN, Lafayette, Ind (b/VII-2-1855 Dayton, O; d/IX-17-1903) MD Rush 1882. *Tr Ind St Med Soc* 1904: 357. *Polk* 1896: 478.

IRWIN, OLIVER H , Sheldon, Ill (d/III-23-1905 Elk City, Okla) MD Med Coll Indiana 1871. *Ill med jour* 7:379, 1905. *Polk* 1896: 440.

IRWIN, ROBERT ALEXANDER, Sistersville, WVa (b/I 4-1879 Danville Ky; d/I-14-1899) MD UPa 1895. *Tr St Med Soc WVa* 1899:337-38. *JAMA* 32:196, 1899. *Polk* 1896: 1326.

IRWIN, W S , Louisville, Ky (d/III-8-1894) MD U Louisville 1867. *JAMA* 22: 482, 1894. *Polk* 1890: 465. *Butler* 1878: 277.

IRWIN, WILLIAM FULLERTON, Monroe, Ia (b/IV-22 1816 Pa; d/XII-31-1872) MD UPa 1839; att Washington & Jefferson. *Med surg rep Phila* 28: , 1873.

ISAACS, CHARLES EDWARD, NYC (b/VI-24-1811 Bedford, NY; d/VI-16-1860 Brooklyn) MD U Md 1833; att CPSNY. *Med s rep Phila* ns4:268, 1860. *Tr AMA* 14: 190-92, 1864. *Nashvl j m&s* 19:191 1860. *K&B* III:631.

ISH, MILTON A , Edgewood, Va (b/Aldis; d/XII-15-1890 @52) MD Med Coll Va 1861. *Tr Med Soc Va* 1891: 256-57. *Polk* 1886: 922.

ISHAM, JOHN H , Louisville (d/VI-22-1899 @40) <MD Louisville Med Coll 1886> *JAMA* 33:53, 1899.

ISHAM, JOHN SIDNEY, Cleveland (d/II-10-1898 @50) MD Bellevue 1874. *JAMA* 30:570,1898. *Polk* 1896:1174.

ISHAM, NELSON, Little Falls NY (d/IX-18-1898 @ 90) MD Yale 1828. *Bost m & s j* 133: 330, 1895.

ISHAM, OLIVER KINGSLEY, Tolland, Conn (b/III-27 1797; d/III-10-1872) MD Yale 1822. *Proc Conn Med Soc* 1872: 153.

ISHAM, RALPH NELSON, Chicago (b/III-16-1831 Manheim, NY; d/V-28-1904) MD UCNY 1854. *Chic med rec* 26:399, 1904. *Tr Med Soc St NY* 1904: [420]. *K&B* III: 633.

ISHAM, RICHARD H, Louisville (d/VI-30-1894 @62) MD U Louisvl 1868 *JAMA* 23:87 1894. *Butler* 1878:265.

ISOM, JOHN F , Cleveland (d/IX-26-1898 @67) MD Cleveland Med Coll 1877. *JAMA* 31:871, 1898. *Polk* 1896: 1174.

ISOM, THOMAS DUDLEY, Oxford, Miss (B/IV-5-1816 Maury Co, Tenn; d/V-4-1902) MD Jefferson 1839. *New Orl m&s j* 54:836, 1902. *Atkinson* I: 526-27. *Polk* 1896: 633.

ISZARD, JACOB, Glassboro, NJ (b/V-23-1829; d/X-20 1900) MD Hahnemann Phila 1870. *Hahn mo* 1886:603, 1900 (Dec). *Polk* 1886: 603.

IUTZI, JOSEPH, Richmond, Ind (b/1846 Butler Co, O; d/VIII-19-1902) MD Med Coll Ohio 1871. *Tr Ind St Med Soc* 1903: 345. *Polk* 1896: 488.

IVES, AMBROSE, Waterbury, Conn (b/Wallingford; d/ 1852 @66) Lic 1808. *Proc Conn Med Soc* 1860: 67-68.

IVES, ANSEL W , Fishkill, NY (b/VIII-31-1787; d/II-5-1838) MD CPSNY 1814; AB Yale 1821. *Amer jour med sci* 22:257-58, 1838. *K&B* III: 633-34.

IVES, CHARLES E , Savannah, Ga (d/IX-19 1894 @63) MD ? *JAMA* 23: 561, 1894.

IVES, CHARLES LINNAEUS, New Haven, Conn (b/VI 22-1831; d/III-20-1879) MD Jefferson 1854. *Proc Conn Med Soc* 1879: 162. *Atkinson* I: 499-500.

IVES, ELI, New Haven, Conn (b/II-7-1779; d/X-8-1861) MD Conn St Med Soc 1811; AB Yale 1799; AB 1811. *Buffalo m & s j* 2:382, 1863. *Proc Conn Med Soc* 1: 67 (appendix); 2:311-20. *K&B* III:634-35.

IVES, GEORGE WHITFIELD, NYC (b/VIII-22-1819; d/XII-6-1874) MD Yale 1846; AB 1841. *Med reg NY NJ Conn* 1875: 199.

IVES, LEVI, New Haven, Conn (b/VII-13-1816; d/XI 30-1891) MD Yale 1838. *Med reg NY NJ Conn* 1892: 280. *JAMA* 17: 980, 1891. *Proc Conn Med Soc* 1892: 845-46. *Bost m & s j* 125: 612, 1891.

IVES, NATHAN BEERS, New Haven, Conn (b/VI-4-1806; d/VI-18-1869) MD Yale 1828. *Proc Conn Med Soc* 3: 414, 1871.

IVINS, HORACE FREMONT, Philadelphia (b/X-30-1856 Penn's Manor, Pa; d/I-1-1899 Easton) MD Hahnemann Phila 1879. *Tr Am Inst Hom* 1899: 928. Homeopath.

IZARD, HENRY, Meridian, Miss (d/IV-28-1899 @65) MD Med Coll SC 1856. *JAMA* 32: 1074, 1899. *Polk* 1886: 529.

IZARD, JOHN, Roanoke, Va (d/XI-22-1899 @45) MD Louisville Hosp Med Coll 1881. *JAMA* 33: 1504, 1899.

JACK, JOHN ANDREW, Oley, Pa; CW-USA (b/X-10-1837 Pottsgrove Twp; d/IV-8-1887 Friedensburg) MD UPa 1862. *U Pa med alum CW*: 1862. *Polk* 1886: 811.

JACKMAN, FRANK, Indianapolis, Ind (b/VI-26-1855 Milroy; d/XI-15-1884 Orlando, Fla) MD Bellevue 1880. *Tr Ind St Med Soc* 1885: 217.

JACKSON, ABRAHAM REEVES, CW-USA; Chicago (b/VI-17-1827 Phila; d/XI-12-1892) MD Pa Med Coll 1851; Hon MD Rush 1873. *Buff m&s j* 32:374, 1893. *Chic med rec* 3:861, 1892. *Tr Ill St M S* 1893: 44-47. *So pract* 14: 543, 1892. *Butler* 1878: 133. *K&B* III: 635.

JACKSON, ALBERT LAFAYETTE, Washington DC (d/X-17-1899 @42) MD Howard 1889. MD George-

 Spec. educ'l status abbrev. as: ***ng*** = college verified attendance without degree;

town 1886. *JAMA* 33:1116. *Polk* 1896: 298. Black.

JACKSON, ALEXANDER, Plymouth, Mass (b/V-18-1819 Winthrop; d/XII-12-1901) MD Harvard 1843; AB Amherst 1840. *Bost m&s j* 145:692 1901. *Polk* 1896:700.

JACKSON, ARTHUR HARPER, Middletown, Conn (b/XI-7-1826 Phila; d/III-9-1869) MD CPSNY 1850; AB Amherst 1846. *Amherst, Men of*: 1846.

JACKSON, CHARLES THOMAS, Somerville, Mass (b/VI-21-1805 Plymouth; d/VIII-29-1880) MD Harvard 1829. *Bost m & s j* 103:233, 1880. *Mich med news* 3:294-95, 1880. *K&B* III: 635.

JACKSON, DONALD, Tex; USA 1865- (b/1838 Canada; d/IX-22-1876) <MD Victoria College Can> *Tr AMA* 28:639-40, 1877. *Army List*, 1815-1900.

JACKSON, EBEN, Somerville, Mass (d/VI-22-1898 @ 73) MD Castleton 1856. *Bost m&s j* 138: 628, 1898. *JAMA* 31: 38-39, 1898. *Polk* 1896:722.

JACKSON, EVAN OWEN, Philadelphia; CW-USA (d/VIII-4-1863 @26 Washington, DC) MD Pa Med Coll 1855. *Med surg rep Phila* 10: 216, 1863. *Nat med jour* 1:297, 1870/71.

JACKSON, FRANCES MARIA WHITE, Emporia, Kans (d/VIII-7-1900) MD Boston U 1882. *Ill med jour* ns2: 237, 1900. *Polk* 1890: 438.

JACKSON, GEORGE FOLLANSBEE, NYC (b/X-7-1827 Pittston, Me; d/XI-10-1895) MD Jefferson 1853; AB Bowdoin 1850. *JAMA* 25:911,1895. *Butler* 1878:516.

JACKSON, JAMES, Boston (b/X-3-1877 Neburyport, Mass; d/VIII-17-1867) MB Harvard 1802; MD 1809; AB 1796; AM 1802; LLD 1854. *Tr AMA* 19:438-40, 1868. *Buff m&s j* 7:79, 1867. *Bost m&s j* 77:86, 106-09, 1867. *K&B* II:638-40.

JACKSON, JAMES CALEB, LeRoy, NY (d/VII-10-1895 @84) MD ? *JAMA* 25:170, 1895.

JACKSON, JAMES CORBIN, Hartford Conn (b/VIII-22 1818 Cornish NH; d/II-7-1882) MD Jefferson 1847. *Pr Conn Med Soc* ns2:151-55,1882-83. *Atkinson* I: 409-10.

JACKSON, JOHN BARNARD SWETT, Boston (b/V I5-1806; d/I-6-1879) MD Harvard 1829; AB 1825 *Bost m&s j* 100:63 188 437 1879. *Atkinson* I:489. *K&B* III: 640-41.

JACKSON, JOHN DAVIS, CW-CSA; Danville, Ky (b/1834; d/XII-8-1875) MD UPa 1857; AB Centre Coll 1854. *Tr AMA* 29: 676-82, 1878. *U Pa med alum CW*:1857. *New Orl m & s j* 3: 607, 1876. *Nashvl j m&s* ns17:43-44, 1876. *K&B* III: 641-42.

JACKSON, JOHN F, Richmond, Va (b/1825; d/III-16 1900) MD UPa 1847 *JAMA* 34:930, 1900. *Polk* 1896:1499.

JACKSON, JOHN M B, Ickesburg Pa (b/IX-6-1827 Savannah, Ga; d/X-11-1866) MD Pa Med Coll 1859. *Tr Pa St Med Soc* 1868: 161-62. *Tr AMA* 21:457-58, 1870.

JACKSON, JOHN WESLEY, Kansas City, Mo (b/1834 Va; d/III-13-1890) MD CPSNY 1873. *Bost m&s j* 122: 312, 1890.

JACKSON, JOSEPH AVERY, Pittston & Readfield, Me; Green Bay & Depere, Wis; Amboy, Ill; CW-USA (b/II 25-1824; d/III-20-1865) MD Bowdoin 1846. *Bowdoin cat*: 1846.

JACKSON, M C, CW-USA (d/III-5-1865) MD ? *Nat med jour* 1:297, 1870/71.

JACKSON, M S, Mineral Wells, Tex (d/V-19 1906 @ 80) MD ? *Tex st jour med* 16: 100, 1906.

JACKSON, MERCY [MARY] (RUGGLES) BISBE, Boston (b/IX-17-1802 Hardwick, Mass; d/XII-13-1877) MD New Engl Female Med Coll 1860. *Tr Am Inst Hom* 1878: 1117. *New Engl med gaz* 13:27, 1878. *King* 3:169. *Cleave*. Homeopath.

JACKSON, ROBERT MONTGOMERY SMITH, Cresson, Pa; CW-USA (b/1820; d/I-17-1865 Chattanooga) MD Jefferson 1838. *Nat med jour* 1:297, 1870/71. *Med s rep Phila* 12:314, 1864/65. *Bost m&s j* 71:528, 1864. *Tr AMA* 16:652, 1865.

JACKSON, SAMUEL, Philadelphia (b/III-22-1787; d/IV 4-1872) MD UPa 1808. *Tr CPP* cent vol: 238. *Tr AMA* 24:377-79, 1873. *Med times* Phila 2:308, 319, 1872. *Bost m&s j* 41:319-22, 1849; ns9: 308, 1872. *K&B* III: 642.

JACKSON, SAMUEL, Northumberland, Pa; USN (d/XII 17-1869) MD UPa 1812. *Tr CPP* cent vol:238. *Tr AMA* 13: 825, 1860.

JACKSON, SAMUEL Jr, USN 1838-79 (b/IV-1-1817 Phila; d/VII-22-1905 Washington, DC) MD UPa 1838. *U Pa med alum CW*: 1838.

JACKSON, THOMAS JEFFERSON, Baltimore (d/X-26 1899 @50) <MD CPS Balto 1879> *JAMA* 33: 1183, 1899. *Polk* 1886: 444.

JACKSON, WILLIAM FRANCIS, Gardiner, Me 1849-53; Roxbury, Mass 1853- (b/XI-15-1824 Brunswick, Me; d/IV-3-1879) MD Jefferson 1849; AB Bowdoin 1847; AM 1849. *New Engl med gaz* 14: 144, 1879. *Butler* 1878: 333. Homeopath.

JACKSON, WILLIAM H H, Oil City, Pa (b/Aurora, O; d/X-30-1903 @63) MD Cleveland Med Coll 1868. *Pa med jour* 7:279, 1903/04. *Flint* 1897: 812.

JACKSON, WILLIAM HENRY, NYC (b/1810; d/XI-25 1893) MD CPSNY 1835. *Med reg NY NJ Conn* 1894: 241. *JAMA* 21: 908, 1893.

JACKSON, WILLIAM LEAVITT, Boston (b/I-23-1853 Gardiner, Me; d/VI-21-1905 Bad Neuheim, Gny) MD Harvard 1876. *Tr Am Inst Hom* 1906: 768-69. *Polk* 1886: 458. Homeopath.

JACKSON, WILLIAM S, Bucyrus, O (b/1863 Wabash, Ind; d/V-1895 in south) <MD Hahnemann Chicago> *Tr Am Inst Hom* 1896: 1190. Homeopath.

JACKSON, WILLIAM WILEY, NYC (d/IX-14-1886 @56) MD UCNY 1874. *Med reg NY NJ Conn* 1887: 269. *Bost m & s j* 115: 289, 1886.

JACOB, NATHANIEL, Canandaigua, NY (b/VII-16 1782 Hanover, Mass; d/II-3-1861) MB Dartmouth 1809; AM Harvard 1806. Palmer's *Necrol Harv alum*: 352-53.

JACOBI, MARY PUTNAM, NYC (b/VIII-31-1842 London, Engl; d/VI-11-1906 @63) MD Woman's Med Coll Pa 1864; MD École de Méd Paris 1871. *Bost m&s j* 154: 690, 1906. *Nashvl j m&s* 98: 328-29, 1906. *K&B* III: 643-45.

JACOBS, BENJAMIN FRANKLIN, CW-USA (d/IX-23-1864 Chicago) MD U Mich 1864. *Nat med jour* 1:297, 1870/71.

JACOBS, CHARLES H , Youngsville, Pa (d/XI-14-1905 @49) MD Western Reserve 1883. *Pa med jour* 9:434, 1905/06. *Polk* 1896: 1347.

JACOBS, FERRIS, Delhi, NY (b/I-10-1802; d/IX-9-1887) MD Columbian, DC 1830. *Tr Med Soc St NY* 1888:545-46. *Butler* 1874: 544.

JACOBS, JAMES KENT HARPER, Centerville, Md (b/II-11-1856; d/XII-18-1901) MD U Md 1877. *Med annals Md:* 451. *Polk* 1893: 370.

JACOBS, JOHN CALVIN, CW-CSA (b/IV-1-1836 Northampton Co, NC; d/IX- -1881 Henderson) MD UPa 1859; AB UNC. *U Pa med alum CW*: 1859.

JACOBS, LUTHER DAVID, CW-USA; Emporia, Kans (b/V-20-1842 Franklin Co, Pa; d/IV-28-1904 Chicago) MD UPa 1866. *Jour Kans Med Soc* 4:453-54, 1904. *U Pa med alum CW*: 1866. *Polk* 1886: 377.

JACOBS, WILLIAM ARMSTRONG, CW-USA; Centre Hall, Pa (b/V-5-1846 Shingletown; d/VIII-16-1899) MD UPa 1875. *JAMA* 33: 620, 1899. *U Pa med alum CW*: 1875. *Polk* 1896: 1271.

JACOBSON, C H , Preston, Minn (d/X-11-1882 @26 Danneborg, Nebr) MD Bennett 1879. *Minn med mirror* 1882 (Nov): 163.

JACOBSON, DAVID, Brooklyn (d/XII-31-1902 @38) MD UCNY 1887. *Bost m&s j* 148: 52, 1903. *Polk* 1896: 997, 1060.

JACOBSON, EDWARD H , Hope, Ind 1864-67; Bethlehem, Pa (b/III-31-1831 Salem, NC; d/VII-6-1896) MD Jefferson 1854. *Hahn mo* 31: 111 (news & advt) 1896. *Tr Am Inst Hom* 1898: 49. *Cleave.* Homeopath 1855-77? *Polk* 1886: 792 [as "regular" pract.]

JAEGER, C HERMANN, Galveston, Tex (b/VIII-9-1806 Leipzig, Gny; d/X-15-1863) <MD U Leipzig 1830> *Tr Tex St Med Assoc* 1878: 20.

JAGGARD, WILLIAM WRIGHT, Chicago (d/VI-30-1896 Phila @40) MD UPa 1880. *Buff m&s j* 35: 677, 1896. *Chic med rec* 10: 160, 1896.

JAMES, ALFRED SCOTT, CW-CSA; Montgomery, Ala (b/VI-7-1832; d/II-28-1874) MD Med Coll SC 1855; att U Ala 1851. *U Ala cat*: 101.

JAMES, BUSHROD WASHINGTON, Philadelphia (b/VIII-25-1836 Somerton, Pa; d/I-6-1903) MD Hahnemann 1857; AB Central HS Phila. *Med vis* 19:30, 1903. *Tr Am Inst Hom* 1903: 727-28. Homeopath.

JAMES, CHARLES PIERSON, Brooklyn (b/1867; d/V-22-1894) MD LICH 1891. *Med reg NY NJ Conn* 1894: 241. *Bost m & s j* 130:649, 1894. *JAMA* 22: 967, 1897.

JAMES, DAVID, Philadelphia (d/VI-6-1873 @68) MD Jefferson 1828. *Med surg rep Phila* 38: 488, 1873. *New Engl med gaz* 9:48, 1874. *Tr Homeop Med Soc St Pa* 1873: 320. Homeopath.

JAMES, DERASTUS HANKS, NYC (d/II-6-1883) MD UCNY 1876. *Med reg NY NJ Conn* 1883: 231.

JAMES, EDWARD CONWAY, CW-CSA (b/XII-27-1834 Courtland, Ala; d/I-27-1881) MD UPa 1861. *U Pa med alum CW*: 1861.

JAMES, H C , Ouray, Colo (d/I-4-1890 @50) MD Jefferson 1870. *Tr Colo St Med Soc* 1898-99: 508. *Polk* 1886: 183.

JAMES, HIRAM HOWARD, Rahway, NJ; CW-USN (b/VII-11-1836 Deerfield; d/IX-11-1885 Saratoga Springs, NY) MD UPa 1863. *Tr Med Soc NJ* 1886-87: 158-60. *Butler* 1878: 471.

JAMES, ISAAC, Trenton, NJ; Bustleton, Pa 1852- (b/1777 Radnor; d/I-22-1874) MD CPSNY 1825. *Tr Am Inst Hom* 1874: . *Med surg rep Phila* 30: 110, 1874. *Hahn mo* 9:332, 1874. *Amer homeop obs* 11: 192, 1874. Homeopath.

JAMES, JOHN SEXTON, foreign missionary (b/1818 Phila; d/IV-15-1848 Hong Kong) MD Jefferson 1846; AB Brown 1842; AM. *Brown hist cat*: 1842.

JAMES, JOHN WARREN, Pittsburgh (d/X-6-1902 @65) MD Jefferson 1895. *Pa med jour* 6: 260, 1902/03. *Flint* 1897: 829.

JAMES, OLIVER P , Doylestown, Pa (d/II-19 1894) MD Jefferson 1840. *JAMA* 22: 314, 1894. *Lehigh Valley med mag* 5:169, 1893-94. *Butler* 1878:718.

JAMES, S T , Park Springs, Tex (d/X-4-1905 @36) MD Atlanta Coll Phys & Surg 1898. *Tex st jour med* 1: 184, 1905/06. *Polk* 1900: 1712.

JAMES, SILAS, Warwick, RI (d/1850) MD Brown 1820; MD Yale 1821. *Tr RI Med Soc* 1:40, 1859-77.

JAMES, THOMAS CHALKLEY, Philadelphia (b/VIII-31-1766; d/VII-5-1835) MD UPa 1787; MD 1811. *Amer jour med sci* ns6:91-106, 1843. *K&B* III: 646-47.

JAMES, THOMAS CHARLES, Bradford, Pa (d/II-25-1894 @42) MD Bellevue 1874. *JAMA* 22:391, 1894.

JAMES, THOMAS E , Greenville, SC (d/XI-15-1899) MD Med Coll Va 1853. *JAMA* 33: 1441, 1899. *Polk* 1886: 219 (Midway, Fla).

JAMES, THOMAS H , Cheraw, SC (d/III-16-1900) MD Med Coll SC 1895. *JAMA* 34: 830, 1900.

JAMES, THOMAS L , Waterloo, Ill (d/X-12-1900) <MD Marion-Sims 1895> *Tr Ill Med Soc* ns2: 286, 1900. *Polk* 1898: 486.

JAMES, WILLIAM MALCOLM, Utica, NY (d/VIII-26 1901 @62) MD CPSNY 1862. *JAMA* 37: 710, 1901. *Polk* 1886: 713.

JAMESON, HORATIO GATES, Baltimore; Washington, DC; Philadelphia (b/1778 York, Pa; d/VIII-24-1853 NYC)MD UMd 1813 *Med ann Md:*452 *K&B* III:648-49.

JAMESON, RUSH, Columbia Tx (b/II-20-1803 Adamstown; d/XII-3-1836) MD U Md 1827. *Med ann Md:* 453.

JAMESON, T F F, Ala to 1859; Rusk Tx (b/IX-27 1827 Wilcox, Ala; d/X-3-1888) MD Transylvania 1853 (as Thomas Y. T.) MD Med Coll Ga 1854 (as F. Y. T.) *Daniel's Tex med jour* 4:177, 1888.

JAMIESON, EGBERT, CW-CSA (d/VI-17-1863) MD Castleton 1837. *Nat med jour* 1:297, 1870/71.

JANES, EDWARD HOUGHTON, NYC (b/X-3-1820; d/III-12-1893) MD Berkshire 1847. *Med reg NY NJ Conn* 1893: 306. *JAMA* 20: 488, 1893. *Bost m&s j* 128: 276, 1893.

JANEWAY, THOMAS L, New Brunswick, NJ (b/1843; d/XI-27-1887 Eureka Spr. Kans) MD CPSNY 1867; AB Rutgers 1863; AM 1866. *Med reg NY NJ Conn* 1888: 262. *Tr Med Soc NJ* 1888-89:161-62. *Polk* 1886:608.

JANEWAY, THOMAS THEODORE, NYC (b/1860 Princeton, NJ; d/I-15-1897 Bermuda) MD CPSNY 1883. *Bost m&s j* 136: 74, 1897. *Polk* 1896: 1060.

JANIN, JULES V, New Orleans (d/VII-6-1902 @45) MD Tulane 1878. *New Orl m & s j* 55:132, 1902. *Polk* 1896: 488.

JANNEY, BENJAMIN SAY, Philadelphia (b/II-21-1790 or 1799? d/I or VI-8-1859) MD UPa 1813. *Tr Med Soc St Pa* 1860: 145-48. *Med surg rep Phila* ns2: 237, 1859. *Tr CPP* cent vol: 238.

JANNEY, DANIEL, Purcel's Store, Loudoun Co, Va (b/1792? d/X-13-1859) MD Hahnemann Phila 1850, ad eundem. *Tr Am Inst Hom* 1867:157; 1868: 285.

JANNEY, EDGAR, Washington, DC (b/I-18-1853 Loudoun Co, Va; d/I-3-1898) MD Howard U 1882; MD Hahnemann Phila 1883. *Tr Am Inst Hom* 1898: 49. *Polk* 1886: 212. Black.

JANUARY, DERICK P, Crowley La (d/III-17-1904) MD Tulane 1860. *New Orl m&s j* 56:794, 1904. *Polk* 1886: 416.

JANVIER, EDGAR, Philadelphia (d/XII-26-1877)MD U Pa 1847; AB Lafayette 1843; AM. *Lafayette, Men of*:152.

JAQUETT, GEORGE PETERSON, CW-USA (b/ Woodstown, NJ; d/X-6-1882) Philadelphia 1860. *U Pa med alum CW*: 1860.

JARRETT, MERCHANT MAUDSLEY, CW-USA (b/II 29-1842 Horsham, Pa; d/VIII-22-1864 Phila) MD UPa 1864. *Nat med jour* 1:298, 1870/71. *U Pa med alum CW*: 1864. *Med surg rep Phila* 12: 100, 1864/65.

JARVIS, EBENEZER [EBENETUS] P, Centre Moriches NY (b/IV-5-1829; d/II-24-1892) MD UCNY 1852. *Med reg NY NJ Conn* 1892:280. *JAMA* 18:340, 1892.

JARVIS, EDWARD, Boston (b/I-9-1803 Concord, Mass; d/X-31-1884) MD Harvard 1830; AB 1826. *Bost m & s j* 111:456, 598-99, 1884. *Atkinson* I: 134-135. *K&B* III:655.

JARVIS, GEORGE CYPRIAN, CW-USA; Hartford, Conn (b/IV-21-1834 Colebrook; d/1901) MD UCNY 1860. *Proc Conn Med Soc* 1901: 294-300. *Atkinson* I: 547-48.

JARVIS, GEORGE OGLEVIA. Portland, Conn (b/VII-14-1795 New Canaan; d/II-3-1875) Lic 1817; Hon MD Yale 1846. *Proc Conn Med Soc* 1875: 430-32, 442.

JARVIS, JOHN FURNESS, Boston (d/II-10-1893 @66) MD Harvard 1853; AB Dartmouth 1848. *Bost m&s j* 129: 659, 1893. *Butler* 1878:340.

JARVIS, NATHAN S, USA 1833-62 (b/New York; d/V 12-1862 Baltimore, Md) MD CPSNY 1822. *Med surg rep Phila* ns8:182, 1862. Henry, Guy V. *Milit rec*: 85. *Nat med jour* 1:298, 1870/71.

JARVIS, SAMUEL GARDINER, W Claremont, NH (b/ VIII-30-1816; d/III-5-1892) MD Jefferson 1838. *Bost m & s j* 126: 252, 1892. *Tr NH Med Soc* 1892: 203-04. *Butler* 1878: 476.

JARVIS, WILLIAM CHAPMAN, Willets Point, NY (b/ V-13-1855 Fort Monroe, Va; d/VII-30-1895) MD U Md 1876. *Bost m & s j* 133:145, 1895. *JAMA* 25:253, 1895. *K&B* III: 655-57.

JAUNCEY, JOSEPH, Westport, Conn (d/IV-7-1858 @50) MD CPSNY 1829. *Bost m & s j* 58: 227, 1858.

JAY, JOHN CLARKSON, Westchester Co, NY (b/IX-11 1808 NYC; d/XI-15-1891) MD CPSNY 1830; AB Columbia 1827. *Med reg NY NJ Conn* 1892: 280. *Bost m&s j* 125: 560, 1891. *K&B* III: 657.

JAY, MILTON, Chicago (d/IV-1-1905 @71) MD Ecl Med Inst Cincinnati 1859; <MD Rush 1895 ad eundem> *Ill med jour* 7: 378, 1905. *Polk* 1896: 390.

JAY, WILLIAM CHARLES, Richmond, Ind (b/XII-2-1860 Farmers' Inst; d/I-10-1898) MD Bennett 1883; ng Haverford 1882. *Hav'fd biogr cat*: 157. *Polk* 1886: 334.

JAYNE, DeWITT CLINTON, Florida, NY (d/XI 9-1897 @80) MD Yale 1839. *Tr Am Inst Hom* 1898: 49. *Polk* 1886: 660.

JEANES, JACOB, Philadelphia (b/X-4-1800; d/XII-18 1877) MD UPa 1823; Hon MD Hahnemann Phila 1856. *Tr Am Inst Hom* 1878: 1064, 1123. *Tr Hom Med Soc St Pa* 2:90-91, 1874-78. Homeopath.

JEBB, FRED, CW-USA (d/VI-20-1863 abd USS Red Rover) MD ? *Nat med jour* 1:298, 1870/71.

JEFFERDS, GEORGE PAYSON, Kennebunkport, Me 1845-60; Bangor 1860- (b/V-7-1816 Kennebunkport; d/V-9 1904) MD Bowdoin 1844; AB 1844; AB 1838. *Bowdoin cat*: 1838. *Polk* 423. Homeopath.

JEFFRIES, JOHN, Boston (b/II-5-1745; d/1819) Hon MD Harvard 1819; AB 1763. *Bost m&s j* 105: 496, 1881. *K&B* III: 658-59.

JEFFRIES, JOHN AMORY, Boston (d/III-25 1892 @32) MD Harvard 1884; AB 1881. *Bost m&s j* 126: 326, 328, 538, 1892. *Polk* 1890: 539.

JEFFRIES, WILLIAM GEORGE, Tapahannock, Va (d/ III-3-1899 @68) MD UPa 1850. *JAMA* 32: 628, 1899. *Polk* 1896: 1503.

JELKS, JAMES THOMAS, Hot Springs, Ark (d/VI-24-1902 @53) MD U Nashville 1870. *Chic med rec* 23:77, 149, 1902. *Polk* 1886: 153.

JELLECKER, FRANK AUGUSTINE, NYC (d/ VII-3-1901 @32) MD Bellevue 1892. *Bost m&s j* 145: 52, 1901. *Polk* 1896: 1060.

JENCKES, HUGH L , Galena, Ill (d/XI-20-1899) MD Northwestern 1879. *JAMA* 33: 1441, 1899. *Tr Ill St Med Soc* 1899:352. *Polk* 1898: 476.

JENKINS, ALVIN, Great Falls, NH (b/V-25-1812 Eliot, Me; d/V-3-1892 @79) MD Dartmouth 1862. *Bost m & s j* 126: 540, 1892.

JENKINS, JOHN CARMICHAEL, Natchez, Miss (b/XII-22-1809 Lancaster Co, Pa; d/X-14-1855) MD UPa 1833; AB Dickinson 1828. *Dickinson cat*: 1828.

JENKINS, JOHN E , Charleston, Ill (d/IX-25-1897) MD Northwestern 1885. *JAMA* 29: 761, 1897.

JENKINS, JOHN FOSTER, NYC 1849-56; Yonkers, NY 1856- ; CW-US San Comm (b/IV-15-1826 Falmouth, Mass; d/X-9-1882) MD UPa 1848; AB Union 1845. *Med reg NY NJ Conn* 1883: 231. *Bost m&s j* 107: 401, 1882. *Tr M S St NY* 1884: 367-387. *K&B* III: 659.

JENKINS, JOHN PURVIS, New Orleans (d/XII-22-1872 @32) MD Tulane 1862. *Med s rep Phil* 28:78 1873.

JENKINS, SOLOMON MARTIN, Easton Md (b/1803; d/V-15-1848) MD UPa 1831. *Med annals Md:* 454.

JENKINS, THOMAS JARRETT, Oroville, Cal (b/XI-4 1824 Marshall Co, Ky; d/X-16-1890) MD U Nashville 1877. *Tr Med Soc Cal* 21:319-20,1891. *Polk* 1886: 169.

JENKS, DANIEL S, Plano Ill (d/V-12-1900) MD Northwestern 1866. *Ill med jour* ns2: 48, 1900. *Polk* 1886: 293.

JENKS, ERNEST POTTER, NYC b/V-18-1866 Boston; d/V-18-1902) MD CPSNY 1898. *Bost m&s j* 147: 30, 1902.

JENKS, OLIVER BOWEN, CW-CSA; Madison CH, Va (b/II-5-1820 Newport, NH; d/III-27-1876) MD UPa 1850. *Tr Med Soc Va* 1877: 116-17. *Butler* 1878:830.

JENKS, PHILIP FREDERICK, Newtown, Pa; CW-USA (b/II-27-1832; d/I-9-1863 St Louis) MD UPa 1854. *Med surg rep Phila* ns9:350, 1862/63. *U Pa med alum CW*: 1854. *Nat med jour* 1:298, 1870/71.

JENKS, THOMAS LEIGHTON, Boston (b/1830 Conway, NH; d/X-31-1899) MD Harvard 1854. *Bost m &s j* 141:456, 460, 1899. *JAMA* 33: 1308, 1899. *Polk* 1896: 700.

JENKS, WILLIAM FURNESS, Philadelphia (b/V-15-1842; d/X-31-1881) MD UPa 1866; AB Harvard 1863. *Bost m&s j* 105: 503-04, 1881. *Chic med rev* 4:566, 1881. *Med bull m & s* 3:288, 1881. *Butler* 1878: 689.

JENNER, CHARLES W , Denver, Colo (d/VIII-11-1895 @55) MD Western Reserve 1882. *Tr Colo St Med Soc* 1898-99: 509. *Polk* 1893: 235.

JENNESS, RICHARD PEARSON, Saccarappa, Me (b/V 9-1826 Deerfield, NH; d/XII-5-1878) MD Bowdoin 1850; ng Dartmouth 1847. *Tr Me M Assn* 1879: 684-85.

JENNINGS, CHARLES B, Dubuque (d/III-11-1898 @ 64) MD UPa 1857. *JAMA* 30: 683, 1898. *Polk* 1896: 522.

JENNINGS, JACOB, Hunterdon Co, NJ (b/1744 Somerset Co; d/II-17-1803 Pa) MD ? *Wickes*: 296-97. *K&B* III: 661, mention only.

JENNINGS, JOHN HENRY, New Bedford, Mass (d/VII 31-1882) MD Harvard 1847. *Bost m&s j* 107: 618, 1882.

JENNINGS, NAPOLEON B , Haddonfield, NJ (b/IV 22-1831 Manahawken; d/IV-17-1885) MD Jefferson 1856. *Tr M S NJ*: 167. *Atkinson* I: 494. *Butler* 1878: 471.

JENNINGS, ROBERT PRATT, Delavan, Ill (b/XI-9-1839 Delaware, O; d/X-5-1889) MD Starling 1863. *Tr Ill St Med Soc* 1890: 39. *Polk* 1886: 276.

JENNINGS, ROSCOE GREEN, CW-CSA; Little Rock, Ark (b/VI-11-1833 Leeds, Me; d/IV-5-1899) MD Bowdoin 1856. *JAMA* 32: 899, 1899. *Polk* 1896: 194.

JENNINGS, SAMUEL KENNEDY, Baltimore; Tuscaloosa, Ala 1845-53 (b/VI-6-1771 Essex Co, NJ; d/X-10 1854) Hon MD U Md 1818; att Rutgers. *Med ann Md:* 454. *K&B* III: 661.

JENNINGS, SAMUEL KENNEDY Jr, Baltimore; Erie, Ala; Austin, Tx (b/VIII-13-1796; d/VII-13-1877 Jackson, Tenn) MD U Md 1820. *Med ann Md:* 454-55. *K&B* III: 661.

JENNINGS, SELDEN, Richmond, Mass (d/IV-15-1864 @50) MD ? *Bost m & s j* 70:248, 1864.

JENNINGS, THOMAS REID, Nashville (b/1805 Steubenville, O; d/VI-7-1874 Narragansett, RI) MD U Md 1826; att Washington Coll, Pa. *Tr Med Soc Tenn* 1876: 83. *Med surg rep Phila* 31: 120, 140, 1874. *Nashvl j m & s* ns14: 120-24, 1874.

JENNINGS, WILLIAM MORGAN, Titusville, Pa (b/XI 19-1832 Venango Co; d/II-10-1869) MD UPa 1860. *Tr Med Soc St Pa* 2: 417-18, 1869.

JERMAN, JEFFERSON S , Spring Lake, Mich (d/VII-25-1874 @63) MD Transylvania 1840. *Med surg rep Phila* 31: 160, 1874.

JERMANE, PERCY LEE, Holton Ks (b/III-3-1868 Jeffersonville, Ind; d/III-22-1904) MD Jefferson 1892. *Jour Kans Med Soc* 4: 455, 1904.

JEROME, JAMES HENRY, Saginaw City, Mich (b/IX-28-1812; d/VIII-8-1883) Hon MD Geneva 1855; ng 1837. *Med age* 1:250, 1883. *Med s rep Phila* 49: 252, 1883. *JAMA* 1:223, 1883; 2:814-15, 1884. *Butler* 1878: 376. *K&B* I:43-44.

JESSOP, ABRAHAM, Ashland, Md (b/X-5-1801 Ridgley's Forges; d/XI-17-1827) MD U Md 1821. *Med ann Md:* 455.

JESSUP, ROBERT B Sr, Vincennes, Ind (b/1828; d/XI-9-1893) MD Jefferson 1853. *JAMA* 21: 784, 1893. Kemper's *Indiana*: 291. *Polk* 1890: 391.

JETER, VIRGIL SHAKESPEARE, Atlanta, Tex (d/IV-19-1905) MD Bellevue 1879. *Tex st jour med* 1:83, 1905/06. *Polk* 1886: 880.

JEWELL, JAMES GRAY, San Francisco (b/1830 Allegheny Co, Pa; d/IX-17-1894) MD Georgetown 1855. *JAMA* 23: 561, 1894.

JEWELL, JAMES STEWART, Chicago (b/IX-8-1837

 Spec. educ'l status abbrev. as: ***ng*** = college verified attendance without degree;

Galena, Ill; d/IV-18-1887) MD Chic Med Coll 1860. *Chic m jour* 54:533-34, 1887. *Tr Ill St Med Soc* 1887:172. *JAMA* 1:502-03, 1887. *K&B* III: 661-62.

JEWELL, JOSEPH HAYDEN, Manchester, NH (b/VIII 18-1847 Brentwood; d/III-29-1872) Stud med Harvard 1871-72; AB Brown 1871. *Brown hist cat*: 1871.

JEWELL, WILSON, Philadelphia (b/XI-12-1800; d/XI-4-1867) MD UPa 1824. *Tr CPP* cent vol: 238. *Tr AMA* 31: 1052-53, 1880. *Tr Pa St Med Soc* 1880:368-74. *K&B* III: 662-63.

JEWESSON, GEORGE WALTER, Staten Isl, NYC (b/III-4-1805; d/I-12-1867) <MD Med Coll Ga 1833> *Med reg NY NJ Conn* 1867:221; 1868:329.

JEWETT, CHARLES COGSWELL, Brooklyn (b/I-31-1831 Me; d/VI-12-1884) MD NY Med Coll 1854; att Dartmouth 1851. *Med reg NY NJ Conn* 1885: 240.

JEWETT, GEORGE, CW-USA; Fitchburg, Mass (d/XII 16-1894 @69) MD Berkshire 1846; stud med Harvard. *Bost m&s j* 131:628 1894. *JAMA* 24:33 1895. *Butler* 1878: 352.

JEWETT, HARVEY, Canandaigua, NY (b/XI-19-1809 Langdon, NH; d/IX-4-1888) <MD Fairfield 1832; MD Buffalo 1851> *Tr M S St NY* 1889: 374-79. *Buff m&s j* 38:223, 1888. *Polk* 1886:655.

JEWETT, HENRY ALFRED, Northborough, Mass (d/VIII-23-1895 @75) MD Pa Med Coll 1847. *Bost m&s j* 133: 659, 1895.

JEWETT, HOMER OCTAVIUS, Cortland, NY (b/III-31-1819 Lebanon; d/I-30-1901) MD UCNY 1843. *Bost m & s j* 144: 150, 1901. *Polk* 1886:657.

JEWETT, JEREMIAH PEABODY, Lowell Mass (d/VI 3-1870 @62) MD Dartm 1832. *Bost m&s j* 5:448 1870.

JEWETT, JOSEPH FRANKLIN, Granby & New Haven, Conn (b/VIII-22-1788; d/I-5-1860) Lic Hartford Co M S 1812; Hon MD Yale 1841. *Proc Conn M S* 1860: 57-58.

JEWETT, PLINY ADAMS, CW-USA; New Haven, Conn; Aiken SC (b/VI-4-1816 Hampton, NY; d/IV-10-1884 Providence, RI) MD Yale 1840. *Proc Conn M S* 1884-87: 169-72. *Med s rep Phila* 50: 544, 1884. *Bost m&s j* 3:384, 618, 1884.

JEWETT, RENSSELAER, NYC (b/XII-26-1818; d/III-7-1890) MD Albany 1844. *Med reg NY NJ Conn* 1890: 271.

JEWETT, THEODORE HERMAN, South Berwick, Me; CW-USA (b/III-24-1815; d/IX-20-1878) MD Jefferson 1840; AB Bowdoin 1834. *Bost m & s j* 99:420,1878. *Tr NH Med Soc* 1879:180-81. *Tr Me Med Assoc* 1879: 680-84. *Atkinson* I:208. *K&B* II: 625-26.

JEWETT, THOMAS BACKUS, Birmingham, Conn (b/I 9-1850 New Haven, Conn; d/VIII-6-1885) MD Yale 1879. *Proc Conn Med Soc* 1887: 173-74.

JILLSON, BENJAMIN CUTLER, Pittsburgh (b/VII-15 1830 Willimantic, Conn; d/VII-19-1899) MD U Nashville 1857; ng Amherst 1854. *Amherst, Men of*: 1854. *Atkinson* I: 686.

JIMENEZ, SATURNINO M , NYC (b/1851 Cuba; d/II 17-1897) MD Jefferson 1878. *Bost m & s j* 136: 194, 1897. *JAMA* 28:429, 1897. *Polk* 1896: 1060.

JIRKA, FRANK JOSEPH, Chicago (d/VII-9-1895) MD Rush 1880. *Chic med rec* 9:64, 1895.

JOBS, EUGENE, Springfield, NJ (b/II-23-1821 Liberty Corner; d/V-22-1875) MD UPa 1844. *Tr AMA* 27: 653, 1876. *Tr Med Soc NJ* 1875:[105]; 1876: 129-30.

JOBS, NICHOLAS CONOVER, Springfield, NJ (d/XI-1889 @38) MD CPSNY 1874; AB Cornell 1873. *Med reg NY NJ Conn* 1890: 271.

JOCELYN, CORNELIUS B , Brooklyn; Springfield, Mass (d/X-18-1864) MD NY Homeop 1864. *Med surg rep Phila* 12:196, 1864/65. *No Am j hom* 13: 543, 1865. *Amer hom obs* 2: 88, 1865.

JOHNES, HARVEY C , Decatur, Ill (b/1819; d/IV-22 1900) MD Jefferson 1844. *JAMA* 34: 1146, 1900.

JOHNES, JOHN BLANCHARD, Morristown, NJ (b/1785; d/1863) MD UPa 1809; AB Princeton 1804; AM 1807. *Tr AMA* 16: 631, 1855.

JOHNS, CYRUS, NYC (b/IX-24-1811 Huntington, Vt; d/II-9-1865) MD CPSNY 1855. *Med reg NY NJ Conn* 1865: 235. *Med surg rep Phila* 12: 314, 1864/65.

JOHNS, MONTGOMERY, Baltimore (b/1830? d/1871) MD U Md 1853; AB 1847. *Med annals Md:* 455.

JOHNS, THOMAS M, Taylorsville, Ill (d/I-12-1905 @ 50) Certif Exam Bd. *Ill m j* 7:242, 1905. *Polk* 1896: 443.

JOHNSON, AARON TERRELL, CW-USA; New Vienna, O (b/VI-1-1829 Leesburg; d/IX-19-1887) MD M C Ohio 1859; MD UPa 1868. *U Pa med alum CW*: 1868.

JOHNSON, AMOS HOWE, Salem, Mass (b/VIII-4-1831 Boston; d/V-12-1896) MD Harvard 1865; AB 1853; gr Amherst Th Sem. *Bost m&s j* 134:500, 522, 1896. *JAMA* 26:1092 1896. *Atkinson* I:601. *Polk* 1896:722.

JOHNSON, ARTEMAS, Rehoboth, Mass (b/XI-18-1780 Sherborn; d/XII- -1827) MD Brown 1816; AB 1808. *Brown hist cat*: 1808.

JOHNSON, BENJAMIN, Dover, Me (b/VI-14-1802 Limerick; d/XI-20-1869) MD Bowdoin 1824. *Bost m & s j* 4:364, 1869.

JOHNSON, BENJAMIN FRANKLIN, Notasulga, Ala (d/I-5-1890) MD Med Coll SC 1843. *Tr Med Soc Ala* 1890: 217. *Polk* 1886: 138.

JOHNSON, BENJAMIN K , Norristown, Pa (d/IV-23-1898) MD Pa Coll Med Dept 1861. *JAMA* 30: 1125, 1898. *Polk* 1886: 810.

JOHNSON, BEVERLY, Colbert Co, Ala (d/III- -1899) <MD Nashville 1898> *Tr Med Assoc St Ala* 1899:232.

JOHNSON, BURWELL R , Gowanda, NY (d/I-21-1899) MD Buffalo 1893. *Buff m & s j* 38: 546-47, 1899. *JAMA* 32: 263, 1899. *Polk* 1896: 1024.

JOHNSON, C C , Gowanda, NY (d/I-7-1898) <MD Ecl Med Coll Phila 1864> *Buff m&s j* 37: 935, 1898.

Butler 1878: 560.

JOHNSON, CALEB CLARK, Hillsdale, Mich (d/VIII-28-1898 @84) MD Geneva 1843. *JAMA* 31: 551, 1898. *Polk* 1886: 494.

JOHNSON, CHARLES, CW-USA (d/IV-5-1863) MD ? *Nat med jour* 1:298, 1870/71.

JOHNSON, CHARLES EARL, Raleigh, NC (b/III-15-1812 Edenton; d/IV-1-1876) MD UPa 1835. *Tr NC Med Soc* 1876: 9-10, 11-18. *Tr AMA* 29:682-85, 1878. *U Pa med alum CW*: 1835. *K&B* III: 663-64.

JOHNSON, CHARLES HATCH, Otsego, Mich (d/II-2-1867 Binghamton, NY @31) MD ? *Med surg rep Phila* 16: 224, 1867.

JOHNSON, CHARLES HENRY, Brooklyn (d/IX-1902 @48) MD UCNY 1880. *Bost m&s j* 147: 366, 1902. *Polk* 1896: 998.

JOHNSON, CHARLES S , Harveysburgh, Ind (b/IX-14 1824 Ohio; d/XI-21-1885) Stud med Kansas City, Mo. *Tr Ind St Med Soc* 1886: 209. *Polk* 1886: 321.

JOHNSON, CHARLES WORTHINGTON, Frederick Co, Md (b/IX-28-1805; d/1833) MD UPa 1828; AB Princeton 1825. *Med annals Md:* 455.

JOHNSON, DAVID POWELL, Muscatine, Ia (d/II-14-1900 @87) MD Med Coll Ohio 1840. *JAMA* 34: 574, 1900. *Polk* 1896: 533.

JOHNSON, E M , CW-USA (d/III-15-1865) MD ? *Nat med jour* 1:298, 1870/71.

JOHNSON, EDWARD C , Hammond, Ind (d/II-5-1898) MD Syracuse 1885. *JAMA* 30: 391, 1898.

JOHNSON, ELBRIDGE MONROE, Williamsburg, Mass (d/V-16-1874 @35) MD CPSNY 1862. *Bost m & s j* 90:516, 539, 1874.

JOHNSON, FRANCIS EMERSON, Pawtucket, RI (d/XI 27-1898 @65) MD Dartmouth 1881. *JAMA* 31: 1542, 1898. *Polk* 1886: 468 (Lawrence, Mass).

JOHNSON, FRANCIS MARION, CW-CSA; Platte City, Mo 1855-78; Kansas City, Mo, 1878- (b/VIII-27 1828 Georgetown, Ky; d/IV- -1893) MD U Louisville 1854. *Tr Med Assn St Mo* 36:361-62, 1893. *Daniel's Tex m j* 8:522, 1892-93. *Atkinson* I:667. *K&B* III: 664-65.

JOHNSON, FRANCIS UPTON, New Brighton, NY (d/XI-20-1892 @66) MD CPSNY 1852. *Bost m & s j* 127: 516, 1892. [Probably identical w/Johnston, Francis Upton, q.v.]

JOHNSON, FREDERICK LEIGHTON, NYC (d/XII-10-1899 @30) MD UPa 1860; PhG 1880. *JAMA* 33: 1632, 1899.

JOHNSON, GEORGE, Frederick, Md (b/1832; d/X-26-1905) MD UPa 1854; AB Princeton 1851; AM 1854. *Med annals Md:* 456. *Polk* 1893: 568.

JOHNSON, GEORGE L , Denver, Colo (d/1876) MD U Iowa 1872. *Tr Colo St Med Soc* 1898-99: 508.

JOHNSON, GEORGE W , Chicago (b/1861; d/VI-4-1906) MD CPS Chicago 1895. *JAMA* 46: 1782, 1906.

JOHNSON, HENRY, CW-USN; New Bedford, Mass (d/IV-19-1880) MD Harvard 1865. *Bost m & s j* 102:456, 1880. *Harvard in CW*: 293.

JOHNSON, HORATIO HUNTINGTON, Belfast, Me (d/VIII-4-1896 @51) MD Harvard 1869; AB Tufts 1864. *JAMA* 27: 449, 1896. *Butler* 1878: 308.

JOHNSON, HOSMER ALLEN, Chicago (b/X-6-1822 Wales, NY; d/II-26-1891) MD Rush 1852; AB U Mich 1849; AM 1852? *Chic med rec* 1:69-71, 1891. *JAMA* 16: 365-68, 1891. *Tr Ill St M S* 1891:22-25. *Atkinson* I: 88. *K&B* III: 665.

JOHNSON, HOWARD A , Milltown, Ala (d/VI-20-1891) Cert County Bd Tuscaloosa 1881. *Tr Med Assoc St Ala* 1891: 260. *Polk* 1886: 136.

JOHNSON, J B , Montgomery, O (d/VI-30-1870) MD Med Coll Ohio 1861. *Phila med reg & dir* 1871:305.

JOHNSON, JAMES, Milwaukee (d/II-2-1882) MD Berkshire 1839. *Chic m rev* 5:86, 1882. *Butler* 1878: 862.

JOHNSON, JAMES MADISON, Baltimore; Scotland Neck, NC (d/VI-9-1896 @70) MD UPa 1852. *NC med jour* 37: 372, 1896. *Polk* 1886: 437.

JOHNSON, JAMES T , Frederick, Md (b/XI-18-1794; d/IX-4-1867) MD UPa 1816. *Med annals Md:* 456.

JOHNSON, JAMES THOMAS, Huntsville, Ala; New-market, Va to 1861; CW-CSA; Va, Md, Ala (b/VII-26-1828 Charles Co, Md; d/VIII-9-1899) MD U Md 1848. *JAMA* 33:493,1899. *Polk* 1896:162. *Med annals Md*:456.

JOHNSON, JOHN BRIDGES, New Orleans (b/Charleston, SC; d/XII-15-1880 @34) MD U La 1868. *New Orl m & s j* ns9:396, 1881. *Butler* 1878: 294.

JOHNSON, JOHN GIDEON, Lowndesville, SC (d/V-25 1896) MD Bellevue 1875. *NC med jour* 37:1896, 373. *Polk* 1886: 855.

JOHNSON, JOHN MILTON, Atlanta; CW-CSA (b/I-15 1812 Centreville, Ky; d/V-18-1886) MD Atlanta Med Coll 1875. *New Orl m&s j* ns14:77, 1886. *Atkinson* I: 589-90. *Polk* 1886: 120.

JOHNSON, JONATHAN GREENLEAF, Newburyport, Mass (b/1790? d/IX-6-1868 @78) MD Harvard 1813; AB 1810. *Bost m & s j* ns2:112, 1868.

JOHNSON, JOSHUA JEWETT, Northborough, Mass (d/I-29-1884 @74) MD ? *Bost m & s j* 110: 144, 1884.

JOHNSON, LAURENCE, CW-USA; NYC (b/VI-7-1845; d/III-18 1893) MD Bellevue 1868; Hon AM Wesleyan 1880. *Med reg NY NJ Conn* 1893: 307. *Buff m&s j* 32: 564, 1893. *Bost m&s j* 128: 304, 1893. *K&B* III: 666.

JOHNSON, LEVI H , Detroit (b/IX-16-1842 Uniontown, Pa; d/I-30-1896) MD Nortwestern 1880. *JAMA* 26: 442, 1896. *Polk* 1886: 489. Black.

JOHNSON, LINUS, CW-USA (d/IV-30-1865) MD ? *Nat med jour* 1:298, 1870/71.

JOHNSON, MARTIN V B , Sioux City, Ia (b/1842; d/XII-9-1897 @55) MD Med Coll Ohio 1865. *JAMA* 30: 106, 1898. *Polk* 1896: 539.

JOHNSON, MAYHEW, Penns Grove, NJ (b/V-28-1828 Pittsgrove; d/XII-30-1894) MD UPa 1850; stud Lafay-

 Spec. educ'l status abbrev. as: ***ng*** = college verified attendance without degree;

ette. *Lafayette, Men of*: 161. *Polk* 1886: 610.

JOHNSON, NATHAN, Cambridge City, Ind (b/Loudoun Co, Va; d/I-4-1872 @77) <Hon MD Starling 1850> att UPa Med Dept 1834-35. *Tr AMA* 23:584, 1872. *Bost m&s j* ns9:64, 116, 1872. *Tr Ind St M S* 1873:141, 141.

JOHNSON, OLIVER C , St Charles, Mo (d/VII-30-1866 @42) MD St Louis Med Coll 1853. *Med surg rep Phila* 15: 248, 1866.

JOHNSON, ORVILLE, Worthington, O (b/XII-4-1822 Henderson, NY; d/1896) MD Starling 1852. *Tr Ohio Med Soc* 1897: 421-24. *Polk* 1886: 774.

JOHNSON, OTHELLO OTIS, Framingham Mass (d/I-3 1882 @64) MD Harvard 1843. *Bost m&s j* 107:618 1882.

JOHNSON, OTIS HENRY, Haverhill, Mass (d/VII-16-1904 @63) MD Harvard 1866. *Bost m & s j* 151: 84, 1904. *Polk* 1896: 713.

JOHNSON, PETER ROOSEVELT, Sag Harbor, NY (d/II-12-1905 @77) MD CPSNY 1851. *Bost m & s j* 152: 234, 1905.

JOHNSON, RASSELAS B , Morrison, Ill (d/XI-29-1888) MD Hahnemann Chic 1876. *Med vis* 5:11, 1889. *Polk* 1886: 289.

JOHNSON, REASON P , Chicago (d/X-9-1901) MD Cinc Coll Med & Surg 1861. *Ill med jour* ns3:295, 1901. *Polk* 1886: 739 (Canton, O).

JOHNSON, RICHARD H , Baltimore; Vandalia, Mo (d/XI-21-1899 @57) MD Howard 1894. *JAMA* 33: 1441, 1899. *Polk* 1896: 661. Black.

JOHNSON, RICHMOND, Washington, DC (b/1791 Annapolis, Md; d/III-12-1874. Not MD: accoucheur. *Hist Med Soc DC:* 225. *Tr AMA* 25:526, 1874.

JOHNSON, ROBERT PORTER, CW-USA; Wilmington, Del (b/X-11-1825; d/I-16-1890) MD UPa 1850; AB Yale 1847. *U Pa med alum CW*: 1850. *Atkinson* I: 556. *Polk* 1886: 207.

JOHNSON, SAMUEL, Bozrah Conn (b/VII-1-1805; d/II 12-1879) *Proc Conn Med Soc* 1879:167. *Atkinson* I:655.

JOHNSON, SHELDON CRITTENDEN, Seymour, Conn (b/XI-6-1797 Bethany; d/XI-13-1887) Lic Med Soc Conn 1825. *Proc Conn Med Soc* 1888: 215-16. *Butler* 1878: 79.

JOHNSON, STEPHEN THEODORE, Easton, Md (d/VII-16-1813) MD UPa 1789. *Med annals Md:* 457.

JOHNSON, THOMAS, Baltimore (b/II- -1766; d/XI-1-1831) MD UPa 1793) *Med annals Md:* 457-58.

JOHNSON, THOMAS R , Baltimore; USA (b/Washington Co, Md; d/VII-11-1837) *Med annals Md:* 458.

JOHNSON, UZAL, NJ; RevWar-Loyalist (b/IV-17-1751; d/V-22-1827) MD CPSNY 1772. *Tr NJ Med Soc* 1865-67: 124-25. *Wickes*: 304.

JOHNSON, WEBSTER B , Savannah, Ia (d/VIII-31-1899 @25) MD Northwestern 1894. *JAMA* 33:745, 1889.

JOHNSON, WILLIAM, Whitehouse, NJ (b/II-18-1789 Princeton; d/I-13-1867) Lic Med Soc NJ 1811; att UPa Med Dept. *Tr Med Soc NJ* 1867: 213-17; 1872: 110-11. *Med surg rep Phila* 16: 199, 1867.

JOHNSON, WILLIAM, USN 1831-71 (b/I-4-1804 Shrewsbury, Del; d/IV-7-1876 Washington, DC) MD UPa 1826. *U Pa med alum CW*: 1826.

JOHNSON, WILLIAM Jr, USN 1855-70 (b/V-10-1833 Wilmington, Del; d/VIII-20-1872 Smyrna) MD UPa 1855. *U Pa med alum CW*: 1855.

JOHNSON, WILLIAM C , Springfield, Ill (d/VI-13 1905 @66) MD Rush 1869. *Ill med jour* 8:80, 1905. *Polk* 1896: 434.

JOHNSON, WILLIAM NORTON Sr, Germantown, Pa (b/1807; d/VI-22-1870) MD UPa 1829; stud med Paris 1829-31; AB Dickinson 1826. *Phila med reg & dir* 1871: 294.

JOHNSON, WILLIAM OTIS, Boston; CW-USA (d/VIII-17-1873 @48) MD Harvard 1848; AB 1845. *Bost m & s j* ns12:247, 1873. *Harvard in CW*: 29.

JOHNSON, WOOLSEY, NYC (b/Stratford, Conn; d/VI-21-1887 @45) MD CPSNY 1863; AB Princeton 1860; AM 1863. *Med reg NY NJ Conn* 1888: 262; 1889: 265. *Bost m & s j* 116: 645-646, 1887.

JOHNSTON, ABNER NASH, Natural Bridge, Va (b/III-25-1851; d/V-10-1904) MD Med Coll Va 1873. *Tr Med Soc Va* 1904: 323-24. *Polk* 1900: 1768.

JOHNSTON, CHARLES GARRETT, Barryville, NY (b/VIII-14-1845; d/III-20-1889) MD CPSNY 1875. *Med reg NY NJ Conn* 1889: 276.

JOHNSTON, CHRISTOPHER, Baltimore (b/IX-27-1822; d/X-11-1891) MD U Md 1843. *Tr CPP* cent vol: 282-83. *Med annals Md:* 458. *JAMA* 17:740, 1891. *Atkinson* I: 280. *K&B* III: 667.

JOHNSTON, FRANCIS UPTON Jr, Staten Isl, NYC (d/XI-20-1892) MD CPSNY 1852. *Med reg NY NJ Conn* 1893: 307. *Polk* 1886: 669. [Probably identical w/ Johnson, Francis Upton, q.v.]

JOHNSTON, GEORGE WINSTON, Fairmont, Nebr; Lynchburg, Va; Los Angeles; Joplin, Mo; Chicago (b/VII-30-1851 Pearisburgh, Va; d/IV-21-1897 Geneva, Nebr) MD Bellevue 1872; att Emory & Henry Coll. *Proc Nebr St M S* 1897: 15-16. *Polk* 1893:758.

JOHNSTON, JAMES, Hudson, Ill (b/1845; d/III-26-1905) MD Med Coll Ohio 1872. *Ill med jour* 7:379, 1905. *Butler* 1878: 160.

JOHNSTON, JOHN KEYS, Philadelphia (d/1903 @75) MD U Mich 1866. *Pa med jour* 7:279, 1903/04. *Polk* 1886: 818.

JOHNSTON, JULIUS A , Alexandria, La (d/X 19-1898 @45) MD Med Coll Ala 1880. *JAMA* 31: 1128, 1898. *Polk* 1890: 485.

JOHNSTON, LINDSEY M , Storm Lake, Ia (d/XI-20-1899) MD Iowa St U 1878. *JAMA* 33: 1441, 1899.

JOHNSTON, ROBERT, Yorkshire, Engl; NYC 1852- (b/VIII-27-1828 Roscommon, Ire; d/V-31-1867) <MD Dublin & London> *Med reg NY NJ Conn* 1867: 222.

JOHNSTON, ROBERT L , Craig, Mo (d/I-24-1899)

<MD Emsworth Med Coll Mo 1892> *JAMA* 32:263, 1899. *Polk* 1896: 837.

JOHNSTON, STEPHEN BURR, Carrollton, Miss (b/V-13-1818; d/X-8-1863) <MD Med Coll Augusta 1851> AB U Ala 1840. *U Ala cat*: 61.

JOHNSTON, WILLIAM EDWIN, Paris, Fr (b/II-16-1822; d/II-14-1886) MD UCNY 1847. *JAMA* 7: 111-12, 1886.

JOHNSTON, WILLIAM HENRY, CW-CSA; Birmingham, Ala (b/III-28-1839 Lincoln Co, NC; d/IV-3-1898) MD UCNY 1867; att UNC. *NC med jour* 41:279, 1898. *Tr Med Assoc St Ala* 1898: 43-45, 240, 1898. *JAMA* 30:933, 1898. *Atkinson* I:107. *Polk* 1896: 156.

JOHNSTON, WILLIAM MONCRIEFF, Hernando Ms; Sewickley Pa (b/X-22-1807 Newburgh, NH; d/XII-20-1887) MD Berkshire 1833; att Jefferson Med Coll; AB Amherst 1827. *Amherst, Men of*: 1827. *Polk* 1886:834.

JOHNSTON, WILLIAM PATRICK, Washington, DC (b/VI-11-1811 Savannah; d/X-24-1876) MD UPa 1836; AB Yale 1833. *Tr AMA* 29:686-88, 1878. *Hist Med Soc DC*: 231-32. *K&B* III: 668-69.

JOHNSTON, WILLIAM POYNTELL, Philadelphia (b/IX-23-1811; d/II-26-1856) MD UPa 1836; AB 1830. Matrics Coll UPa: 81.

JOHNSTON, WILLIAM POYNTELL Jr, CW-USA; Philadelphia (b/1844; d/X-4-1872) MD UPa 1871. *U Pa med alum CW*: 1871.

JOHNSTON, WILLIAM SEMPLE, Hamburg, Ala (d/IV 31-1886) MD Med Coll SC 1858. *Tr Med Assoc St Ala* 1887: 306. *Polk* 1886: 134.

JOHNSTON, WILLIAM WARING, Washington, DC (b/XII-28-1843; d/III-21-1902 Atlantic City, NJ) MD UPa 1865; AB St James Coll Md; stud Edinburgh. *Bost m & s j* 146:349, 1902. *Hist Med Soc DC*: 291-92. *Atkinson* I: 319. *K&B* III:669-70.

JOHNSTON, WIRT, Jackson Miss (b/VIII-31-1846; d/I-25-1900) MD Jefferson 1868. *New Orl m&s j* 52: 547, 1900. *JAMA* 34:381 1900. *Atkinson* I:52. *Polk* 1896:811.

JOHNSTONE, HOWISON J , Brooklyn (d/VII-10-1882 @40) <MD Dublin & Edinburgh> *Med reg NY NJ Conn* 1883: 232. *Butler* 1878: 532.

JOINER, GEORGE BERTRAM, Chicago (b/Watseka, Ill; d/VII-7-1896) MD Rush 1893; AB Amherst 1890. *Amherst, Men of*: 1890.

JOLLY, MATTHEW ARNOLD, CW-CSA; Mt Hebron, Ala (b/VIII-4-1835; d/IX-19-1880) MD Jefferson 1869; stud med Nashville; AM Mt Hebron; AM Franklin Coll, Tn 1856. *Tr M S St Ala* 1881: 271. *Butler* 1874: 20.

JONAS, METHA (HELFRITZ), Omaha (b/I-23-1857 Arlington, Wis; d/X-28-1895 Balto) MD Woman's Med Coll Chicago 1889; AB U Iowa. *Proc Nebr St Med Soc* 1896: 21-22. *Polk* 1893: 762.

JONES, A H , Sheridan, Wyo (d/V-20-1899 @32) MD *JAMA* 32: 1399, 1899.

JONES, ADOLPHUS E, Cincinnati (d/VII-27-1889) MD ?UPa 1841. *Med surg rep Phila* 61:168, 1889. *Polk* 1886: 743.

JONES, ALANSON SYLVESTER, NYC (b/I-10-1819; d/V-20-1881) MD CPSNY 1839. *Med reg NY NJ Conn* 1881: 238; 1882: 229. *Chicago med rev* 4:301, 1881. *Butler* 1878: 516.

JONES, ALBERTUS C , Cambridge, Md (d/VIII-3-1893) <MD Balto Med Coll 1890> *Med annals Md*: 459.

JONES, AMBROSE W , Line, La (b/V-31-1856 Morehouse Parish; d/III-16-1906 Plantersville) MD Tulane 1883. *New Orl m&s j* 58:862, 918, 1906. *Polk* 1890: 488.

JONES, ANDREW BARRY, Portsmouth, O (b/IV-30-1829 Hillsborough; d/X-15-1876) MD Cleveland 1850. *Med s rep Phila* 35:370, 1876. *Tr O St M S* 1877: 61-62.

JONES, BENJAMIN RUSH, Montgomery, Ala (d/VI-26 1887) MD Jefferson 1836. *Tr Med Assoc St Ala* 1888: 316. *Polk* 1886: 137.

JONES, CALEB MORDECAI, St Mary's Co, Md (b/1788; d/1869) MD UPa 1813. *Med annals Md*: 459.

JONES, CALEB V , MexWar-USA; CW-USA; Covington, Ind (b/III-22-1812 Peekskill, NY; d/X-5-1883) Lic Herkimer Co Med Soc NY 1834; att Fairfield. *Tr St Med Soc Ind* 1884: 213. *JAMA* 1:602-03, 1883. Kemper's *Indiana*: 292.

JONES, CHARLES DeHAVEN, Staten Isl, NYC (d/II 24-1877) MD Chicago Med Coll 1860. *Med reg NY NJ Conn* 1877: 204.

JONES, CHARLES EDMUND, Albany, NY (b/II-15-1849; d/XII-1-1899) MD NY Homeop 1873 or 1882; MD Albany 1872. *Tr Am Inst Hom* 1900:833. *No Amer jour homeop* 48:3 (curr events), 1900. Homeopath.

JONES, CHARLES HYLAND, CW-USA; Baltimore (b/X-1-1828; d/XII-17-1897) *JAMA* 30:48, 1898. *Atkinson* I: 674. *Med annals Md*: 460.

JONES, CHARLES WESLEY, USA (b/II-11-1829 Milford Del; d/XII-19-1878 Wilmington) MD UPa 1857 *Tr AMA* 32:515-16, 1881. *U Pa med alum CW*: 1857.

JONES, CLAUDIUS MARCELLUS, Boston (b/II-22-1845 Worcester; d/I-24-1892) MD Harvard 1875; AB 1866. *Bost m&s j* 126:104 130 155 1892. *Polk* 1886: 458.

JONES, CYRUS V , Kniman, Ind (d/XI-7-1895 @40 San Jose, Calif) MD Med Coll Ind 1888. *JAMA* 25:467, 1895. *Polk* 1896: 477.

JONES, DANIEL T , Baldwinsville, NY (b/VIII-17-1801 Coventry, Conn; d/III-29-1861) Lic Med Soc Conn 1826; att Yale Med Sch 1826; Hon MD Geneva 1844. *Tr M S St NY* 1861: 267-273. *Tr AMA* 196, 1864.

JONES, DAVID T , Plymouth, Pa (b/1856 So Wales, Pa; d/I-16-1894) MD Jefferson 1881. *Lehigh Valley med mag* 5: 152, 1893-94.

JONES, EDWIN TEGID, Queens, NY (d/VI-10-1906 Utica, NY) MD UCNY 1883. *Bost m&s j* 154: 722, 1906. *Polk* 1896: 998, 1092.

JONES, ELIJAH UTLEY, Taunton, Mass (b/V-2-1826; d/XI-26-1893) MD Hahnemann Phila 1854; ng Bow-

 Spec. educ'l status abbrev. as: ***ng*** = college verified attendance without degree;

doin Med 1851–52. *Hahn mo* 29:82 (news & advt) 1894. *Tr Am Inst Hom* 1894: 265. *New Engl med gaz* 29: 1894 (Jan) Homeopath.

JONES, EMERY C , Virden, Ill (d/III–21–1900) MD U Louisville 1880. *Tr Ill St Med Soc* 1899–1900: 509, 574.

JONES, ERASMUS DARWIN, Albany, NY (b/IX–10–1818 Upper Jay; d/VIII–17–1895) MD Albany 1841. *Hahn mo* 30: 134 (news & advt) 1895 (Oct). *Tr Am Inst Hom* 1896:1190. *King* 1:98. Homeopath 1844– .

JONES, EUSEBIUS LEE, NYC (b/XII–20–1829; d/I–30 1876 Calif) MD Columbian 1850; AB Princeton 1847. *Med reg NY NJ Conn* 1876: 243. *Med rec med & surg* 11: 134, 1876.

JONES, FRANCIS DUVAL, CW–CSA; Lancaster Co Va (b/X–18–1802 Petersburg; d/XII–18–1881) MD UPa 1825. *U Pa med alum CW*: 1825.

JONES, FREDERICK, New Ipswich, NH (b/VII–20–1813 Dublin, NH; d/VII–6–1892) MD Dartmouth 1859 (ng 1835); AB Harvard 1835; AM 1859. *Bost m&s j* 127: 52, 1892. *Med bull m & s* 14: 496, 1892. *Polk* 1890: 711.

JONES, GEORGE HENRY W , Prince Frederick Md (b/VIII–19–1845 Calvert Co; d/X–16–1899 @54) MD U Md 1867. *JAMA* 33:116, 1899. *Med annals Md:* 460. *Polk* 1886: 445.

JONES, GEORGE NELSON, Burlington, Ia (b/V–18–1852; d/X–17–1900) MD McGill 1874. *Tr Ia St Med Soc* 19:442–43, 1901. *Polk* 1890: 409.

JONES, GEORGE P , E New Market, Md (d/IV–2–1901 @55) MD U Md 1865. *Pa med jour* 5:296, 1901/02. *Flint* 1897: 449. *Polk* 1896: 670.

JONES, GEORGE SPROSON, Covington, Ind (d/VIII–25–1897 @56) MD U Mich 1867; AM DePauw 1880. *JAMA* 29:555, 1897. *Polk* 1886: 315.

JONES, GEORGE STEVENS, Boston (d/II–2–1888 @70) MD Harvard 1846. *Bost m&s j* 118: 160, 1888.

JONES, GEORGE WASHINGTON, Cleveland (b/II–22 1871 Liverpool, O; d/VIII–6–1906) MD Cleveland Homeop 1901; LLB Harvard Law 1894. *Tr Am Inst Hom* 1906: 776–77. Homeopath.

JONES, GEORGE WHEELER, Danville Ill (d/I–7 1895) MD Chic Med Coll 1862. *Tr Ill St M S* 1895: 74.

JONES, HENRY NEWELL, Canaan, NH 1841–49; Kingston, Mass 1849–1902 (b/X–15–1815 Epping, NH; d/XII–18–1902) MD Dartmouth 1841. *Bost m&s j* 148: 28, 1903. *Polk* 1896: 715.

JONES, HENRY WYCKOFF, NYC (d/VII–27–1862 at sea) MD CPSNY 1847; AB 1843 Rutgers. *Med surg rep Phila* ns9: 22, 1862/63.

JONES, HIRAM G , Evansville, Ind (b/VII–15–1824 Staunton, Va; d/IV–30–1884) MD Starling 1850. *Tr Ind St M S* 1885: 215. *Med surg rep Phila* 50:640, 760, 1884.

JONES, JAMES, New Orleans, La (b/XI–18–1807 Georgetown, DC; d/X–10–1873) MD UPa 1828. *Med surg rep Phila* 29:306, 1873. *Tr AMA* 29: 689–96, 1878. *New Orl m&s j* ns1:460–61, 1873. *K&B* III: 674–75.

JONES, JAMES A , CW–USA (d/VII–9–1864) MD ? *Nat med jour* 1:298, 1870/71.

JONES, JAMES R, Paris, Tx (d/VII–7–1905 @91 Dalby Spr) MD UPa 1837. *Tex st jour med* 1:84, 1905/06. *Polk* 1886: 891.

JONES, JOE S, Baton Rouge La (b/IX–28–1852 Jackson; d/X–23–1896) MD Tulane 1875. *Tr La St Med Soc* 19:17–19,1898. *New Orl m & s j* ns24:368, 1896.

JONES, JOHN, Philadelphia; RevWar–USA (b/1729;d/VI 23–1791) MD Rheims 1751. *Tr CPP* cent vol: 239. *Amer med & philos reg* 3:325–37,1814. *K&B* III:675–6.

JONES, JOHN, Middle Granville, NY (d/X–23–1897 @ 35) MD Albany 1893. *Bost m&s j* 137: 427–28, 1897.

JONES, JOHN CLARK, Wymore, Neb (d/X–10–1894) MD Rush 1881. *JAMA* 23: 735, 1894. *Polk* 1886: 582.

JONES, JOHN CURTIS, CW–CSA; Gonzales, Tx (b/1837 Lawrence Co, Tx; d/I–25–1904) MD Edinburgh 1860. *Tex st med jour* :1: 243, 1906. *Polk* 1896: 1432.

JONES, JOHN DAVIS, Providence, RI (b/X–15–1839; d/VII–13–1867) MD Harvard 1861. *Tr RI Med Soc* 1859–77: 320–22.

JONES, JOHN LEVI, New Middleton, Tenn (d/XII–4–1898) MD U Nashville 1872. *JAMA* 31:1542, 1898. *Polk* 1886: 871.

JONES, JOHN RANDOLPH, CW–CSA; Hicksford Va (b/XI–3–1835 Greensvl Co;d/III–25–1904 Emporia) MD UPa 1858. *U Pa med alum CW*: 1858. *Polk* 1886: 919.

JONES, JOHN WESLEY, CW–CSA; Tarboro, NC (b/IX 26–1831 Edgecombe Co, NC; d/I–28–1904) MD UPa 1857; att UNC 1853–54. *U Pa med alum CW*: 1857. *Atkinson* I: 141.

JONES, JOHNSTON BLAKELY, Charlotte, NC (b/IX–13–1814 Rock Rest; d/III–1–1889) MD Med Coll SC 1841; att UNC 1831–36. *Tr NC Med Soc* 1889: 153–57. *Bost m&s j* 120:276, 1889. *Atkinson* I:674. *K&B* III: 676.

JONES, JONATHAN C , Mankato, Minn (b/IX–16–1841 Canada; d/XII–4–1872) MD McGill 1865. *Tr Minn St Med Soc* 1873: 115–117.

JONES, JOSEPH, CW–CSA; New Orleans (b/IX–6–1833 Liberty Co, Ga; d/II–17–1896) MD UPa 1855; AB Princeton 1853; AM 1856. *JAMA* 26: 441–42, 1896. *Buff m&s j* 35: 676, 1896. *New Orl m&s j* 23:540–42, 1896. *Atkinson* I: 253. *K&B* III: 676–77.

JONES, JOSEPH B , Brooklyn (b/1828 NYC; d/X–12–1905) MD CPSNY 1855. *Bost m&s j* 153: 460, 1905. *Polk* 1896: 998.

JONES, JOSEPH E, West Chester, Pa (d/V–6–1899) MD UPa 1856. *Tr Am Inst Hom* 1899: 929–30. Homeopath.

JONES, LAFAYETTE J, CW–CSA; Franklin Ky (b/IV–22–1839; d/VI–11–1904 @66) MD Jefferson 1861. *JAMA* 43: 60, 1904. *Polk* 1886: 395.

JONES, LEONIDAS M , Brooklyn, Mich (b/VIII–24 1822; d/I–30–1905) MD Cleveland Homeop 1858. *Tr Am Inst Hom* 1905: 844. *Polk* 1886: 485. Homeopath.

JONES, LEWIS J , Wichita, Kans (b/1830 Ky; d/V–20–

1900 Galena) MD Ky Sch Med 1868. *JAMA* 34: 1504–05, 1900. *Polk* 1886: 386.

JONES, LUKE M , Lick Creek, Ill (d/III–5–1901) Lic by yrs of pract. *Ill med jour* ns3: 91, 1901.

JONES, NATHANIEL M , Cleveland (d/VIII–1–1901 @61) MD Charity Hosp Med Coll 1866. *JAMA* 27: 461, 1901. *Polk* 1866: 747.

JONES, PHILIP LIVINGSTON, NYC (b/IX–24–1812; d/X–1–1883) MD CPSNY 1835; AB Columbia 1832. *Med reg NY NJ Conn* 1884: 231. *Med surg rep Phila* 49: 448, 1883.

JONES, PRIDE, CW–CSA; Hillsboro, NC (b/XI–21–1815 Halifax Co; d/IV–6–1889) MD UPa 1837; AB UNC 1834. *U Pa med alum CW*: 1837.

JONES, RALPH KNEELAND, Vineyard Haven, Mass 8 yrs; Bangor, Me (b/VII–13–1823; d/1888) MD Harvard 1847; ng Berkshire. *Bost m & s j* 119: 561–62, 1888. *Atkinson* I: 462. *K&B* I:2, 57.

JONES, ROBERT E , Indianapolis, Ind (b/IV–7–1847 Fayette Co, WVa; d/XII–23–1891) MD Ind Med Coll 1878. *Tr Ind St Med Soc* 1892: 284.

JONES, SAMUEL JEREMIAH [?], CW–USN; Chicago (b/III–22–1836 Bainbridge, Pa; d/X–4–1901) MD UPa 1860; AB Dickinson 1857; AB 1860. *U Pa med alum CW*: 1860. *Ill med jour* ns2:295, 1901; ns4:479, 1903. *Atkinson* I: 319. *K&B* III: 679.

JONES, SAMUEL OLIVER, Allenton, Ala (b/IX–16–1859; d/XI–26–1886) MD Med Coll Ala 1883; att U Ala 1877– . *Tr Med Assoc St Ala* 1887: 306. *Polk* 1886: 130.

JONES, SAMUEL PRESTON, Merchantville, NJ (d/III 13–1891 @59) MD UPa 1855. *Bost m&s j* 124: 324, 1891. *Polk* 1886: 606.

JONES, SAMUEL SEABURY, NYC (b/Oyster Bay, NY; d/I–21–1902 @55) MD UCNY 1869. *Bost m & s j* 146: 128, 1902. *Polk* 1886: 683.

JONES, SELDON WILEY, Leavenworth, Kans (b/XII–26–1826 Boston; d/XII–16–1896) MD Bowdoin 1853. *JAMA* 28: 92, 139, 1897. *Polk* 1896: 558.

JONES, STACEY, Darby, Pa (b/XI–3–1828 Moorestown, NJ; d/XII–12–1905 Darby? or Seattle, Wash?) MD Hahnemann Phila 1853. *Pa med jour* 9:360, 1905/06. *Butler* 1878: 718. Homeopath.

JONES, STARLING W , Pine Bluff, Ark (d/1879) MD UCNY 1859. *Tr St Med Soc Ark* 1882: In Mem.

JONES, THOMAS, CW–USA (d/V–15–1864 in Wilderness) MD UPa 1856. *U Pa med alum CW*: 1856.

JONES, THOMAS B , Lynnville, Ind (b/XI–28–1841 Spencer Co, Ind; d/VII–21–1902) MD Med Coll Ohio 1870. *Tr Ind St Med Soc* 1903: 346. *Butler* 1878:208.

JONES, THOMAS F [or S], Cartersville, Ga (d/XI–14–1899 @60) MD Louisville Med Coll 1887. *JAMA* 33: 1441, 1899.

JONES, TOLAND, CW–USA; London, O (b/I–10–1820; d/II–18–1894) <Hon MD Cleveland Med Coll> *Tr Ohio St M S* 1894: 39. *Butler* 1878: 635. *K&B* I(2): 57–58.

JONES, WALTER FREDERICK, CW–CSA; Sassafras, Va (b/XII–25–1821 Petersburg; d/III–17–1901 Gloucester Co; MD UPa 1848. *U Pa med alum CW*: 1846. *Polk* 1886: 918, 926.

JONES, WILLIAM, Washington, DC; War 1812–USA (b/IV–12–1790; d/VI–25–1867) MD UPa 1812. *Hist Med Soc DC:* 215. *Med annals Md:* 461. *Tr AMA* 19: 433–34, 1868.

JONES, WILLIAM B, USN (d/II–26–1869) MD UCNY 1849. *Tr AMA* 21:498 1870. *Phila m reg & dir* 1871:300.

JONES, WILLIAM CLINTON, Grass Valley, Cal; Walnut Spr, Tx (b/VIII–25–1833 Athens, Tn; d/XII–26–1906) MD Bellevue 1886; att Hiawassee Coll. *Tex st med jour* 2:286,1906/07. *Atkinson* I:208. *Polk* 1896:1456.

JONES, WILLIAM HENRY, USN (b/XII–15–1840 Christian Spr, Pa; d/XII–13–1900 Bethlehem) MD UPa 1863. *U Pa med alum CW*: 1863.

JONES, WILLIAM J , Baltimore (b/1858; d/I–10–1894) MD U Md 1883. *Med annals Md:* 462. *Polk* 1893: 562.

JONES, WILLIAM KENNON, CW–CSA; Union Spr, Ala (b/II–17 1835 Petersburg, Va; d/V–9–1901 Montgomery) MD UPa 1856. *U Pa med alum CW*: 1856.

JONES, WILLIAM PALMER, Nashville, Tenn 1849– (b/X–17–1819 Adair Co, Ky; d/IV–25–1897) MD Med Coll Ohio 1842; <MD Memphis> *So pract* 19:475, 1897. *JAMA* 29:709, 1897. *Nashvl j m & s* 82:190, 1897. *Atkinson* I: 684. *K&B* III: 680.

JONES, WILLIAM W , NYC (b/1813; d/VII–11–1891) MD CPSNY 1842; AB Rutgers 1832. *Med reg NY NJ Conn* 1892: 281. *Bost m & s j* 125:72, 1891.

JONES, ZEBEDEE RING, Philadelphia; CW–USA; (d/III–28–1867 @38) MD UPa 1851; MD Phila Coll Med & Surg 1850. *Med surg rep Phila* 16:296, 1867. *U Pa med alum CW*: 1851.

JORDAN, ALEXANDER STAHR, CW–USA; Riegelsville, Pa (b/IV 10–1839 Lehigh Co; d/XI–23–1900) MD UPa 1863. *U Pa med alum CW*: 1863. *Polk* 1886: 833.

JORDAN, DEWITT, Coxville, Ind (b/VII–27–1871 Rosedale, Ind; d/XII–13–1901) MD Ky Sch Med 1892. *Tr Ind St Med Soc* 1902: 416. *Polk* 1896: 474.

JORDAN, GEORGE W , CW–CSA; Smith's PO, SC (d/I–20–1906) MD UCNY 1859; att SC Coll 1854–56. *JAMA* 46: 450, 1906.

JORDAN, HERBERT STANTON, Waltham, Mass (d/I–10–1889 @30) MD Harvard 1882. *Bost m & s j* 120:78, 1889; 121:644, 1889. *Polk* 1886: 475.

JORDAN, JAMES CAREY, Richmond, Va (d/V–21–1897 @61) MD Med Coll Va 1864. *JAMA* 28:1091, 1897. *Polk* 1886: 925.

JORDAN, JAMES P , Green Bay, Wis (b/VII–26–1858 Martins Ferry, O; d/VII–3–1899 Rockland, Mich) MD U Cinc 1886. *Tr Wis St M S* 34:424–25, 1900; 35:504 1901.

JORDAN, JAMES REID, Montgomery, Ala (b/III–4–1860 Lexington, Va; d/III–27–1898) MD U Md 1884. *Tr Med Assoc Ala* 1898: 45–46, 240. *Tex med jour* 13:531,

 Spec. educ'l status abbrev. as: ***ng*** = college verified attendance without degree;

1897–98. *Polk* 1890: 144.

JORDAN, MORTIMER HARVEY, CW–CSA; Birmingham, Ala 1872– (b/VI–10–1844 Jefferson Co; d/II–6–1889) MD Miami Med Coll 1867; att U Ala 1860– *Tr Med Assn St Ala* 1889:29–31, 229. *Atkinson* I: 285. *Polk* 1886: 131.

JORDAN, NAHUM, Eastham, Mass (b/XI–29–1807 Ellsworth, Me; d/III–22–1831) MD Bowdoin 1830; AB 1827. *Bowdoin cat*: 1827.

JORDAN, NESBIT F , Bloomington, Ill (d/XII–28–1902 @38) MD Med Coll Ohio 1882. *Ill m j* ns4: 589, 1902.

JORGENSEN, JOSEPH, USA; Portland, Or (b/II–11–1844 Phila; d/I–21–1888 Portland) MD UPa 1865. *U Pa med alum CW*: 1865.

JOSLIN, BENJAMIN FRANKLIN, Albany, NY; NYC (b/XI–25–1796 Exeter, RI; d/XII–31–1861) MD CPSNY 1826; MD UCNY 1849; AB Union 1821. *New Engl med gaz* 20:336, 1885. *Med reg NY NJ Conn* 1862: 155. *Tr Am Inst Hom* 1867: 157. Homeopath.

JOSLIN, BENJAMIN FRANKLIN Jr, ?NYC (d/IV–18–1885 @55) MD UCNY 1852. *Tr Am Inst Hom* 1885: 92.

JOSLYN, HENRY, Buffalo (b/1862 Engl;d/X–27–1898) MD Buffalo 1898.*Buff m & s j* 38:627–28 1899.

JOSLYN, ZARA W , Dansville, NY (b/XI–6–1815 Cayuga; d/IV–25–1889) MD Castleton 1842. *Med surg rep Phila* 61:112, 1889.

JOSSE, JOHN MICHAEL, Fort Wayne, Ind (b/VII–17–1818 Bavaria; d/IV–13–1880) <MD Heidelberg 1843> *Tr Ind St Med Soc* 1880:231–34. *Butler* 1878:203.

JOSSELYN, ELI EDWARDS, Philadelphia (d/IX–19–1903) MD UCNY 1873. *Pa med jour* 7:279, 1903/04.

JOUSSET, ALBERT DEMAY, Paterson, NJ (d/XII–9–1899) MD Bellevue 1883. *JAMA* 33:1632, 1899. *Polk* 1890: 728.

JOWERS, EMMETT, Channing, Tex; New Orleans (b/Preston, Ga; d/V–22–1905 @46) MD Tulane 1890. *Tex st m j* 1:32, 1905/06. *New Orl m&s j* 58:82, 1905. *Polk* 1896: 622.

JOYCE, AUGUSTUS THADDEUS, NYC (d/II–16–1891) MD UCNY 1886. *Med reg NY NJ Conn* 1891:275.

JOYCE, ROBERT DWYER, Boston 1866–83 (b/1828 Limerick Co, Ire; d/X–23–1883 Dublin) <MD Ireland> *Bost m&s j* 109:479 1883. *Butler* 1878:333. *K&B* III:681.

JOYNES, HENRY, CW–CSA (b/IV–2–1820 Poplar Grove, NC; d/VI–12–1868 Raleigh) MD UPa 1844. *U Pa med alum CW*: 1844.

JOYNES, LEVIN SMITH, CW–CSA; Baltimore 1844–46; Phila 1846–48; Accomac, Va 1849–55; Richmond 1855– (b/ V–13–1819; d/I–18–1881) MD U Va 1839; AB Wash & Jeff 1835. *So pract* 3:99–100, 1881. *Tr AMA* 32: 516–18, 1881. *Med annals Md:* 462. *Atkinson* I: 280. *K&B* III: 681–82.

JUDD, HERBERT, Galesburg, Ill (b/Franklin, NY; d/I–10–1894 @50) MD Albany Med Coll 1867. *Buff m&s j* 33:437, 1894. *JAMA* 33: 158, 1894. *Chic med rec* 6:217, 1894. *Tr Ill St Med Soc* 1894: 50.

JUDD, JAMES FREDERICK, Philadelphia (b/Engl; d/VIII–5–1899 @38) MD Jefferson 1897. *JAMA* 33: 493, 1899. *Polk* 1896: 1308.

JUDKINS, DAVID, Cincinnati (d/XI–12–1893 @75) MD Med Coll Ohio 1842. *JAMA* 21: 784, 1893. *Chic med rec* 5:452, 1893. *Butler* 1878: 611.

JUDKINS, ELAM IRWIN, Greenfield, Ind (b/I–5–1830 Wayne Co; d/IV–15–1890) MD Med Coll Ind 1878. *Tr Ind St M S* 1890: 167. *Atkinson* I: 667. *Butler* 1878: 208.

JUDKINS, EMERY GLIDDEN, Claremont, NH; CW–USN (b/VII–27–1830 Unity; d/VI–29–1863 Waitsfield, Vt) MD Dartmouth 1853. *Tr NH Med Soc* 1864: 63–64. *Bost m&s j* 68:530, 1863. Conn's *NH surg CW*: 350–51.

JUDKINS, GEORGE B , Wetumpka, Ala (d/III–8–1900) MD Jefferson 1860. *JAMA* 34:766,1900. *Polk* 1896:171.

JUDKINS, JESSE P , Cincinnati (d/XII–6–1867 @52) MD Med Coll Ohio 1838. *Tr Ohio St M S* 1868: 198–99. *Chic m j* 24:622, 1867. *Med surg rep Phila* 18:36, 1868.

JUDKINS, WILLIAM, Cincinnati (b/1861) MD Miami 1855. *Bost m&s j* 65:28, 1862. *Tr Ohio St M S* 1873: 268.

JUDSON, AZARIAH, Athens, Pa (d/III–3–1904 @82) MD Berkshire 1845. *Pa med jour* 8:335, 1904/05.

JUDSON, ELIZA E, Staten Isl NYC (d/II–2–1880) MD Wom Med Coll Pa 1872 *Med reg NY NJ Conn* 1880:237.

JUDSON, FREDERICK JOSEPH, Fairfield Co Conn (d/II–6–1862 @58) MD Yale 1820. *Proc Conn Med Soc* 1: 67, 1862?

JUDSON, OLIVER ALBERT, CW–USA; Philadelphia (b/IX–28–1830 Cornwall, Conn; d/III–30–1898) MD Jefferson 1851. *JAMA* 30: 874, 1898. *Tr CPP* cent vol: 239. *Atkinson* I: 394. *K&B* III: 683.

JUDSON, WALTER RICE BARTLETT, New Orleans (b/I–30–1800 Uxbridge Mass; d/XI–1–1825) MD Harvard 1821; AB Brown 1818; AM. *Brown hist cat*: 1818.

JULE, IVER A , Eau Claire, Wis (d/XI–22–1897 Norway) <MD U Christiania 1887> *JAMA* 29:1181, 1897.

JUMP, JULIA (CHAPIN), Oberlin (b/I–20–1832 Vernon, NY; d/III–18–1897) MD Cleveland Homeop 1884. *Tr Am Inst Hom* 1897: 63. *Polk* 1886: 764. Homeopath.

JUMP, SAMUEL VAUGHN, New Burlington Ind (b/VI 27–1822 Kent Co Del; d/VIII–13–1887) MD MedColl O 1860. *Tr Ind St Med Soc* 1888:204. *Butler* 1878:208.

JUNG, G O , Vicksburg, Miss (d/IX–14–1888) MD ? *Med vis* 5:44, 1889. *Polk* 1886: 533.

JUNKIN, JOHN MILLER, CW–USA; Philadelphia; Easton, Pa (b/VII–21–1821 Milton; d/I–18–1889) MD Jefferson 1845; att Lafayette 1841. *Atkinson* I:38. *Polk* 1886: 819.

JUSTICE, JAMES M , Logansport, Ind (d/XI–2–1894 @77) MD Ohio Med Coll 1848. *JAMA* 23: 735, 1894. *Butler* 1878: 208.

JUSTICE, JOHN H , Greenfield, Ind (b/IX–9–1854 Madison Co; d/XI–16–1902) MD Med Coll Ind 1882. *Tr Ind St Med Soc* 1903: 347. *Polk* 1896: 481.

KAEMMERER, JULIUS, Atlantic City, NJ; Philadelphia (b/XI-29-1830 Bavaria; d/V-13-1895) <MD Paris 1856> *JAMA* 24:810, 1895. *Med reg NY NJ Conn* 1895: 228. *Tr Med Soc NJ* 1895:199-200. *Butler* 1878: 689. *Polk* 1890: 718.

KAHLE, WILLIAM G , Franklin, NY; Span-Am War-USA (d/III-7-1899 Pinar del Rio) MD UCNY 1890. *Bost m & s j* 140:269, 1899. *Polk* 1890:1216.

KAHLER, HENRY DAVID, Shelby, O (b/Bolivar; d/II-20-1898 @32) MD West Res 1895. *JAMA* 30:682 1898.

KAHN, SOLOMON LEE, Leadville, Colo (b/1867 Morrison, Ill; d/II-26-1899) MD Rush 1889. *JAMA* 32: 563, 1899. *Tr Colo St M S* 1898-99:38, 509. *Polk* 1896: 266.

KAMERER, JOSEPH W B , Greensburg, Pa (b/IX-29 1845; d/I-14-1902) MD Jefferson 1871. *Pa med jour* 5: 277, 520, 1901/02; 6:260, 1902/03. *Flint* 1897: 803.

KAMMERER, JOSEPH, NYC (b/III-4-1822; d/VI-10-1875) <MD Göttingen 1850> *Med reg NY NJ Conn* 1875: 199.

KANE, EDWARD, Detroit ((b/1801; d/1875) MD U Vt 1824. *Trans AMA* 29:696, 1878.

KANE, ELISHA KENT, Philadelphia; USN (b/II-20-1820; d/II-16-1857 Havana, Cuba) MD UPa 1842. *Northwestern m&s j* 6:186-88, 1857. *Bost m&s j* 56: 67:129-31, 1857. *New Hampshire j m* 4:125-26, 1857. *K&B* III: 684.

KANE, FRANCIS BAILEY, San Francisco (b/I-25-1845 Irel'd; d/XII-29-1888) <MD Queens, Dublin 1872> *Trans Med Soc Cal* 1889: 208-210. *Butler* 1878: 55.

KANTZ, ANDREW JACKSON, Berrysburg, Pa (d/II-12 1899 @61) MD CPS Keokuk 1865. *JAMA* 32:506, 1899. *Polk* 1886: 792.

KAPP, HIRAM, Orwell, Pa (b/II-19-1805 Springfield, NY; d/X-18-1865) MD ? *Tr Med Soc Pa* 1865:69-70.

KAPPEL, JOHN H [or A] Fort Wayne, Ind (b/V-26 1870; d/X-31-1898) <MD Ft Wayne Coll Med 1893> *JAMA* 31:1257, 1898. *Trans Ind St Med Soc* 1899: 397. Kemper's *Indiana*: 293.

KAPPES, DAVID A, Philadelphia (d/II-14-1903 @44) MD Jefferson 1889. *Pa m j* 7:279 1903/04. *Flint* 1897: 820.

KARSNER, CHARLES, Philadelphia (b/V-26-1814; d/VI-6-1883 Ocean Grove, NJ) MD Jefferson 1859; stud theol Dickinson. *Cleave*: 214. Homeopath.

KAST, THOMAS, Boston (d/1820) MD ? AM Harvard 1774. *Bost m&s j* 105:497, 1881.

KATZENMEYER, GUIDO, NYC (b/1832 Gny; d/X-13 1906) <MD Gny> MD Bellevue 1883. *Bost m&s j* 155:490, 1906. *Polk* 1896: 1061.

KAUFFMAN, GEORGE ROYER, Chambersburg, Pa (d/VIII-13-1897 @56) MD Bellevue 1867. *JAMA* 29: 502, 1897. *Polk* 1896: 1285.

KAUWERTZ, FRED H , Milwaukee (d/XI-25-1897 @ 28) MD Louisville Med Coll 1893. *JAMA* 29:1234,1897.

KEALHOFER, RICHARD H, Hagerstown, Md (b/V-26 1844; d/V-1-1900 Phila) MD U Md 1866; AB Franklin & Marshall 1863. *JAMA* 34:1210, 1900. *Polk* 1886: 564.

KEANE, THADDEUS J , NYC (d/XII-17-1894 @36) MD UCNY 1883. *Med reg NY NJ Conn* 1895: 229.

KEARBY, E P , Emory, Tx (d/II-16-1897 @79) MD ? *Tex med news* 6:177, 1896-97.

KEARNEY, EDWARD C , McKeesport, Pa (d/VIII-31 1903 @50) MD Cleveland Med Coll 1876. *Pa m j* 7:279, 1903/04. *Polk* 1896:2327 (appendix).

KEARNEY, THOMAS JOHN, NYC (d/IX-24-1902 @ 51) MD Bellevue 1875. *Bost m&s j* 147:394 1902. *Polk* 1896: 1061.

KEARNS, DENNIS JAMES, Alpena, Mich (d/V-13 1899 @42) MD U Mich 1883. *JAMA* 32: 1269, 1899.

KEARNS, WILLIAM DICKEY, Pittsburgh (d/II-24 1902 @71) MD UCNY 1857. *Pa m j* 6:260, 1902/03. *Flint* 1897: 829.

KEASBEY, JOHN BRICK, Washington, DC; Woodbury, NJ; CW-USA (b/VIII-5-1833 Salem; d/VIII-25 1886) MD UPa 1854. *Hist Med Soc DC*: 259. *Polk* 1886: 612.

KEATING, JOHN MARIE, Philadelphia (d/XI-18-1893 Colorado Spr) MD UPa 1873. *JAMA* 21: 829, 1893. *Trans CPP* cent'l vol: 239; 3s16: xxxv-xxxviii, 1894. *Daniel's Tex m j* 9:415, 1893-94.

KEATING, JOHN R , CW-CSA; Cleburne, Tx 1873- (d/ IV-30-1906) MD UCNY 1857. *Tex st m j* 2: 276, 1906.

KEATING, MICHAEL TONNEL, CW-USA; New Orleans (b/ Irel'd; d/X-18-1878 Memphis) MD ? *Tr AMA* 30:873, 1879.

KEATING, WILLIAM VALENTINE, CW-USA; Philadelphia (b/IV-4-1823; d/IV-18-1894) MD UPa 1844; AB St Mary's 1842. *Tr CPP* cent vol:239; 3s17: xxxix f, 1895. *U Pa med alum CW*: 1844. *JAMA* 22: 764-65, 1894. *K&B* III: 686.

KEEDY, SAMUEL H , Washington Co, Md (d/V-14-1900 Balto) MD U Md 1864. *JAMA* 34: 1505: 1900.

KEEFE, JOHN FRANCIS, NYC (d/VII/VIII-26-1891 @ 46?) MD UCNY 1881. *Med reg NY NJ Conn* 1892: 281. *Bost m&s j* 125:284, 1891. *Tr M S St NY* 1882: 495.

KEELER, EDGAR A, Little Falls NJ (d/VI-7-1897) MD CPS Balto 1880. *JAMA* 28:1202, 1897. *Polk* 1886:606.

KEELER, WILLIAM THADDEUS, NYC (d/VII-30-1891 @42) MD CPSNY 1875. *Med reg NY NJ Conn* 1892: 281. *Polk* 1886: 683.

KEELEY, LESLIE E, Dwight Ill (d/II-21-1900 Los Angeles @68) MD Rush 1864. *Tr Ill St Med Soc* 1899-1900: 463, 509. *Chicago med rec* 17:251, 1900. *Flint* 1897: 274.

KEELING, SOLOMON S, Norfolk, Va (b/VIII-21-1840 Princess Anne Co; d/V-16-1885) MD Med Coll Va 1865. *Tr Med Soc Va* 1885: 284. *Butler* 1878: 831.

KEEN, ALFRED W , Quarryville, Pa (d/IX-8-1904 @43) MD Jefferson 1884. *Pa m j* 8:735, 1904/05.

KEENAN, THOMAS, S Lynnfield, Mass (d/I-17-1865

@61) MD ? *Bost m&s j* 71:528, 1864.

KEENE, GEORGE FREDERICK, Howard, RI (b/X-22 1853 Whitman, Mass; d/III-13-1905) MD Harvard 1879; AB Brown 1878. *Bost m&s j* 152:414, 1905. *Tr RI Med Soc* 7:282-84, 1904-09. *Polk* 1896: 1350.

KEENE, JOSEPH WADSWORTH, Boston 1871-73, 1876-78; Buffalo, NY 1878-87; National City, Cal 1888- (b/I-23-1847 Bremen, Me; d/I-30-1902 Fallbrook, Cal) MD Harvard 1878; MD Bowdoin 1875; AB 1870; AM 1873. *Bowdoin cat*: 1870. *Polk* 1886: 653.

KEENE, MARCELLUS, Hillsborough, Md (b/V-12-1782 Dorchester; d/X-8-1845) <MD UPa 1805> *Med ann Md:* 463.

KEENE, STEPHEN STONE, Providence, RI (d/VI-16-1888 Roseville, NJ) MD UPa 1835; stud Paris. *Tr RI Med Soc* 111:513-74, 1883-88. *Polk* 1886:846.

KEENER, WILLIAM H , Baltimore (b/XI-31-1822; d/V-21-1880) MD U Md 1845. *Med ann Md:* 464. *Butler* 1878: 320.

KEENEY, JOHN HARVEY, Oswego, NY (d/III 26-1898 @38) MD NY Homeop 1883. *Tr Am Inst Hom* 1898: 49. *Polk* 1886: 700. Homeopath.

KEENEY, JOSEPH, CW-USA (d/1863) MD Albany 1851; AB Williams 1847. *Williams grads*: 1847.

KEENON, JOHN G , CW-USA (d/1864?) MD Jefferson 1851. *Trans AMA* 16: 652, 1865.

KEEP, LESTER, FairHaven NY to 1860; Brooklyn 1860- (b/IX-6-1797 Lee, Mass; d/VIII-20-1882) MD Fairfield 1828. *Hahn mo* 17: 460, 1882. *Tr Am Inst Hom* 1883: 142. *King* 1:205-06. Homeopath 1839- .

KEEP, S HOPKINS, Brooklyn (b/V-12-1846; d/X-26 1887) MD NY Homeop 1866. *Tr Am Inst Hom* 1888: 229. *Med vis* 4:107, 1888. *Polk* 1886: 646. Homeopath.

KEEP, SAMUEL HAMILTON, Boston (d/IX-30-1863 @30) MD Harvard 1855. *Bost m&s j* 69:208, 1863.

KEESE, HOBART, NYC (b/IX-18-1831; d/XI-7-1871) MD Yale 1855. *Med reg NY NJ Conn* 1872: 349.

KEEVER, JAMES H , Dalton, Tex (d/XII-8 1906 @36) MD Balto Med Coll 1894. *Tex st m j* 2: 286, 1906/07.

KEEVER, MOSES H , Ridgeville, O (b/IV-28-1810 Warren Co; d/IV-7-1878) MD Med Coll Ohio 1834. *Tr Ohio St Med Soc* 1878: 193-94. *Butler* 1878: 636.

KEFFER, FREDERICK AUGUSTUS, New Orleans; CW-USA (b/VI-27-1839 Phila; d/IX-27-1873) MD UPa 1863. *Med surg rep Phila* 29:288, 342, 1873. *U Pa med alum CW*: 1863.

KEIDEL, GEORGE, Baltimore (b/1799 Hildesheim, Hanover; d/XI-13-1874 Catonsville, Md) <MD Bonn 1828> *Tr AMA* 26: 467, 1875. *Med annals Md:* 464.

KEIR, WILLIAM GEORGE, Philadelphia (b/V-12-1830 Irel'd; d/IX-11-1884) MD Pa Coll Med 1856. *Tr Med Soc Pa* 1886: 261-62.

KEIRN, WALTER LEAKE, CW-CSA; Itta Bena, Miss (d/1901) MD UPa 1852; AB Princeton 1848; stud law U Miss 1883. *Princeton cat*: 174.

KEISER, JAMES W , Reading, Pa (d/VI-20-1904 @43) MD UPa 1882. *Pa m j* 8: 335, 610-11, 1904/05. *Flint* 1897: 833.

KEITH, ERNEST WARDWELL, Chicago (d/VII-26 or VIII-1-1901) MD Boston U 1885. *Ill m j* ns3:189, 1901. *Polk* 1896: 390.

KELLAM, FREDERICK C A , Pungoteague, Va (d/VIII-6-1896 @83) MD Jefferson 1837. *NC m j* 38: 155, 1896. *JAMA* 27: 449, 1896.

KELLEAM, JAMES M , Fort Smith, Ark (d/III-23-1906 @47) MD U Louisville 1882. *Tex st m j* 2: 36, 1906. *Polk* 1886: 151.

KELLER, FRANKLIN B , Pottstown, Pa (d/III-24-1900 @51) MD Jefferson 1874. *JAMA* 34: 957, 1900. *Polk* 1896: 1330.

KELLER, JAMES IRWIN, Hot Springs, Ark (b/1855; d/IX-29-1886 @31) MD Louisville Med Coll 1876. *JAMA* 7: 475-76, 1886. *Polk* 1886: 152.

KELLER, JOSIAH GOODE, Baltimore (b/II-16-1839; d/IV-8-1897) MD U Md 1863. *Med annals Md:* 465. *Polk* 1886: 437.

KELLER, SILAS WILLIAM, New Kensington, Pa (d/1903 @45) MD Western Reserve 1885. *Pa m j* 7: 209, 279, 1903/04. *Polk* 1896: 1343.

KELLER, WILLIAM HENRY, Harrisburg, Pa (d/II-2-1906 @48) MD UCNY 1890. *Pa m j* 9: 360, 1905/06. *Polk* 1896: 1102 (Stony Pt, NY).

KELLEY, CYRUS KINGSBURY, Plymouth, NH (b/VI-23-1820 Gilmartin, NH; d/VI-21-1898 @77) Hon MD Dartmouth 1867; MD Woodstock 1844. *JAMA* 30:1534, 1898. *Polk* 1886: 594.

KELLEY, EDWARD B P , Perth Amboy, NJ (b/VII-4-1835 Lebanon, Pa; d/XI-25-1891) MD U Vt 1857; MD Jefferson 1858. *Tr M S NJ* 1892: 198-99. *Polk* 1890:729.

KELLEY, ELBRIDGE GERRY, Newburyport, Mass (d/IX-13-1881) MD Jefferson 1838. *Chicago med rev* 4: 469, 1881. *Butler* 1878: 353.

KELLEY, GEORGE WALLACE, Barnstable, Mass (d/V-20-1896 @39 Pasadena, Cal) MD Harvard 1878. *Bost m&s j* 134: 552, 1896. *Polk* 1896:691.

KELLEY, HIRAM R , Galion, O (b/II-7-1835 Northumberland Co, Pa; d/I-4-1897) MD Starling 1865. *Tr Ohio Med Soc* 1897: 426-27. *JAMA* 28: 283, 1897. *Butler* 1878: 636.

KELLEY, JAMES STEPHEN, Archibald, Pa (d/XI-16-1898 @27) MD UPa 1893. *JAMA* 31:1377, 1898. *Polk* 1896: 1296.

KELLEY, JOHN CLAWSON, NYC (b/1793? d/V-19-1863 @70) MD ? *Med surg rep Phila* 10:80, 1863.

KELLEY, SAMUEL BOWDOIN, Franklin, NH (d/I-9 1871 @51) MD Dartmouth 1844. *Bost m&s j* 7:68, 1871.

KELLEY, THOMAS, San Jose Cal (d/II-4-1906 @ c70) MD Rush 1871. *Cal st j m* 4:137, 1906. *Polk* 1886: 175.

KELLEY, WILLIAM DENNIS, Galveston, Tex; CW-CSA (b/XI-20-1825 Cainsville, Tenn; d/VII-9-1888)

MD UPa 1848. *U Pa med alum CW*: 1848. *Tr Tex St Med Assoc* 1889: In Memoriam. *Polk* 1886: 886.

KELLEY, WILLIAM M , Knox, Ind (d/VIII–28–1896) MD Med Coll Ind 1870. *JAMA* 27: 722, 1896.

KELLEY, WILLIAM PHILIP, Boston (d/IV–26 1882 @26) MD Harvard 1878; AB Boston Coll 1878. *Bost m&s j* 107: 618, 1882.

KELLIHER [KELLEHER], MICHAEL WILLIAM , Pawtucket, RI (b/II–20–1864 Palmer, Mass; d/X–31–1900) MD UCNY 1886. *Tr RI Med Soc* 6:263–64, 1899–1903. *Polk* 1896: 1350.

KELLNER, MAX G [?KELLMER, GEORGE MAX], Chicago (d/VIII–2 or 10–1901) MD Rush 1882; <PhG> *Ill m j* ns3: 237, 1901. *JAMA* 37: 398, 1901.

KELLO, SAMUEL BLYTHE, Ivor, Va (d/VII–1–1888 Southampton Co, Va) MD UPa 1841. *Tr Med Soc Va* 1888: 275. *Butler* 1878: 831.

KELLOG, PHINEAS, Plainfield, Vt (b/VIII–14–1822 Brookfield; d/X–10–1862) MD Woodstock 1851. *Tr Vt Med Soc* 1883: 106.

KELLOGG, JOHN LEONARD, Washington Heights, Ill (b/IV–8–1811 Manlius NY; d/IV–27–1893) MD Woodstock 1837. *Med vis* 9:173, 1893. *Polk* 1886: 278. Homeopath.

KELLOGG, S WILSON, USN 1837–67 (d/I–7–1867) MD ? *Tr AMA* 18:360, 1867; 19:455, 1868. *Nat m j* 1:298,1870/71. *Med surg rep Phila* 16:179, 1867.

KELLS, ROBERT, Jackson Miss (b/VI–19–1820 Claverack, NY; d/IV– –1888) MD Albany 1840. *Tr Miss St Med Assoc* 1888: 59–60. *Atkinson* I: 429. *Polk* 1886:528.

KELLY, FRANK B [or P], Philadelphia; Phoenixville, Pa (d/IX–19–1881 @29) MD Jefferson 1881. *Med bull med & surg* 3:266, 1881.

KELLY, HENRY JUDSON, NYC (d/X–15–1899 @42) MD CPSNY 1880. *JAMA* 33:1183,1899. *Polk* 1896: 1061.

KELLY, HUGH, Statesville, NC (b/VII–15–1815 Moore Co; d/IX–I–1883) Hon MD UCNY 1859; att 1844–45. *Tr NC M S* 1887: 157. *NC m j* 12: 245, 1883. *Butler* 1878: 595.

KELLY, JAMES, NYC (d/VIII–2–1866) MD ? *Med reg NY NJ Conn* 1867: 222.

KELLY, JOHN J , Brooklyn (d/III–9–1877 @65) MD ? *Med reg NY NJ Conn* 1877: 204. *Butler* 1874: 517.

KELLY, JOHN W , Washington, Pa (d/X–30–1899 @76) MD ? *JAMA* 33: 1308, 1899. *Polk* 1886: 838.

KELLY, MARTIN CROCKER, Mt Clemens, Mich (d/XII–23–1898) MD U Mich 1875; PhG 1871. *JAMA* 32: 41, 1899. *Polk* 1886: 499.

KELLY, MATTHEW, CW–USA (d/VIII–23–1864) MD ? *Nat m j* 1:298, 1870/71.

KELLY, WILLIAM, Madison Parish, La (d/1897) MD Bellevue 1876. *Tr La St M S* 19:27, 1898. *Polk* 1896:627.

KELSEY, BENJAMIN, NYC (b/1846; d/IV–27–1888) MD Bellevue 1884. *Med reg NY NJ Conn* 1888: 262.

KELSEY, JEREMIAH S , Converse, Ind (b/XI–29–1842 Dayton, O; d/IX–2–1893) MD Med Coll Ohio 1869. *Tr Ind St Med Soc* 1894:220.

KELSEY, LEVERETT SILLIMAN, Mt Vernon, O (b/IX 4–1854; d/IV–9–1897) MD Med Coll Ohio. *JAMA* 28: 760, 1897. *Polk* 1896: 488.

KELSEY, W J , Cassopolis, Mich (d/1893) MD Rush 1865. *JAMA* 21: 936, 1893. *Butler* 1878:376.

KELSO, REESE DAVIS, Waveland, Ind (b/1866; d/X–30–1896) MD Rush 1892. *Trans Ind St Med Soc* 1897:349. *Polk* 1896: 496.

KEMBLE, ARTHUR, CW–USN; Salem, Mass (b/V–8–1839 Wenham; d/X–27–1898) MD Harvard 1863; ng Amherst 1861; stud Paris, Vienna, Edinburgh. *Bost m&s j* 139: 460, 1898. *Harv in CW*: 279. *Polk* 1896: 722.

KEMBLE, GEORGE SHOWERS Jr, CW–USA; Mifflinburg, Pa (b/1827 Harrisburg; d/IX–2–1884) MD UPa 1850. *U Pa med alum CW*: 1850.

KEMBLE, LAURENCE GRAFTON, Salem, Mass (d/VIII–7–1899 @37) MD Harvard 1883. *Bost m&s j* 141: 176, 1899. *Polk* 1896: 722.

KEMBLE, WARREN, CW–USA; Saugerties, NY (d/VIII 10–1898 @57) MD CPSNY 1868. *JAMA* 31: 427, 1898. *Polk* 1896: 1099.

KEMP, ALBA ENOCH, E Douglas, Mass (b/VII–21–1822 Sullivan, NH; d/X–29–1883) MD Dartmouth 1852; ng Woodstock 1851. *Bost m&s j* 109: 617, 1883. *Butler* 1878: 353.

KEMP, CHARLES PARKE, Rugby, Tenn (d/II–12–1892 @51) MD Harvard 1866; AB 1862. *Bost m&s j* 126: 204, 1892. *Polk* 1886: 872.

KEMP, FRANKLIN MIDDLETON, NY; USA (d/II–3–1903) MD LICH 1893. *Bost m&s j* 148: 274, 1903.

KEMP, JOHN D , Ohio (b/X–19–1830; d/IV–17–1884) MD U Md 1856. *JAMA* 2: 727, 1884. *Tr O St Med Soc* 1885: 206.

KEMP, SAMUEL T , Trappe, Md (d/1856) MD UPa 1817. *Med annals Md:* 466.

KEMP, WILLIAM MILLER, Baltimore (b/II–21–1814 Frederick Co, Md; d/IX–6–1886) MD UPa 1834. *New Orl m&s j* ns14: 318, 1886. *Med annals Md:* 466. *Atkinson* I:295–96. *Butler* 1878: 320.

KEMP, WILLIAM MITCHELL, NYC (d/IV–20–1899 @53) MD Bellevue 1870. *Bost m&s j* 140: 416, 1899. *JAMA* 32:956, 1899. *Polk* 1896: 1061.

KEMP, WILLIAM T , CW–USN (d/III–31–1864 St Michael, NH) <MD U Md 1863> *Nat m j* 1:298, 1870/71.

KEMPER, EDWARD Y , Cincinnati (b/1782? d/VI–10–1863 @81) MD ? *Med surg rep Phila* 10:144, 1863.

KEMPER, MEADE C , Norfolk, Va (b/V–2–1857 Madison Co; d/II–22–1886) MD Med Coll Va 1877. *Tr Med Soc Va* 1886: 386–88. *New Orl m&s j* ns13: 821, 1886.

KEMPF [KEMP], MATHEW, Louisville (b/IX–25–1827 Gny; d/III–29–1880) MD U Louisville 1850. *Tr Ind St M*

 Spec. educ'l status abbrev. as: ***ng*** = college verified attendance without degree;

S 1881: 231. *Med rec* 17: 499, 1880. *Butler* 1878: 208.

KEMPF, PAUL H , Ferdinand, Ind (b/III-12-1861 Dubois Co; d/IV-16-1896) MD U Louisville 1880. *Tr Ind St Med Soc* 1897: 344. *Polk* 1896: 466.

KENDALL, ALBERT, CW-USA (d/IX-17-1862 Antietam @34) MD UCNY 1852; ng Woodstock 1851. *Bost m&s j* 67: 188, 1862. *Nat m j* 1:298, 1870/71.

KENDALL, JAMES E , CW-USA; Elizabeth, WVa to 1882; Parkersburg (b/III-9-1840 Monongalia Co; d/VIII -6-1897) MD Cleveland Med Coll 1869. *Tr St M S WVa* 1898: 217-18. *JAMA* 29: 400, 1897. *Polk* 1886: 943.

KENDALL, JAMES VARANNAS, Baldwinsville, NY (b/III- -1878 Oswego Co; d/VIII-5-1901) MD Geneva 1844. *Bost m&s j* 145: 200, 1901. *Tr M S St NY* 1902: [484]. *Atkinson* I: 19.

KENDALL, JOSHUA, Seymour Conn (d/I-19-1891 @ 84) MD Castl'n 1832 *JAMA* 16:179 1891 *Butler* 1878:79.

KENDALL, LUCIAN HOWARD, CW-USN; Reading, Pa (b/XI-10-1838; d/X-27-1871) MD UPa 1862. *U Pa med alum CW*: 1862.

KENDALL, PIERSON THURSTON, Clinton, Mass (b/ 1792? d/I-11-1865 @73) MD Harvard 1816. *Bost m&s j* 71: 508, 1864. *Med surg rep Phila* 12: 268, 1864/65.

KENDALL, RICHARD L, Aurora Ill (b/I-31-1872;d/I-1 1906 San Diego Cal) MD Hahnemann Chic 1897. *Tr Am Inst Hom* 1906: 778. *Ill m j* 9:228, 1906.

KENDERDINE, ROBERT STOCKTON, CW-USA; Philadelphia (b/1831; d/III-27-1882) MD UPa 1853. *U Pa med alum CW*: 1853.

KENDRICK, TIMOTHY F , Utica, NY (b/VII-8-1849 Franklin, NH; d/I-29-1879 Naples, Italy) <MD LICH 1874> *Tr NH Med Soc* 1879: 169-70.

KENEGY, CHARLES H, Scales Mound Ill (d/IV-21 1901) MD CPS Keokuk 1877. *Ill m j* ns3:47, 1901. *Polk* 1886: 279.

KENGLA, LOUIS A, San Francisco (b/Washington, DC; d/III-26-1904) MD Georgetown 1886; BS 1882; AB 1883. *Cal st j m* 4: 134, 1904. *Polk* 1896: 234.

KENNARD, THOMAS, Elmwood, Md; St Louis 1858- (b/VI-1-1834; d/XI-9-1879) MD UCNY 1856; AB U Va 1855. *Tr Mo St Med Assn* 1880: 128-30. *New Orl m&s j* ns7: 739-40, 1880. *Med rec NY* 16: 576, 1879. *Butler* 1874: 405.

KENNARD, WILLIAM RUFUS, CW-CSA; Rockdale, Tx (b/IX-29-1834 Livingston Ala; d/IX-16-1902) MD UPa 1860. *U Pa med alum CW*: 1860. *Polk* 1886: 893.

KENNEDY, ALFRED L , CW-USA; Philadelphia (b/X 25-1818; d/I-31-1896) MD UPa 1848. *Tr CPP* cent vol: 240. *U Pa med alum CW*: 1848. *Atkinson* I: 118. *K&B* III: 691-92.

KENNEDY, ALONZO LEWIS, Boston (b/X-22-1844 Newcastle Me; d/IV-13-1905) MD Boston U 1875; stud Bowdoin. *Tr Am Inst Hom* 1905: 844. *Polk* 1886: 458.

KENNEDY, CHARLES VAN BUREN, Altoona, Pa (d/II 11-1900) MD Bellevue 1875. *JAMA* 34:511, 1900. *Polk* 1896: 1284.

KENNEDY, DAVID, Kingston, NY (d/VIII-5-1901) MD CPSNY 1860. *JAMA* 37: 460, 1901. *Polk* 1886: 706.

KENNEDY, DAVID DICKEY, CW-USA; Oxford, Pa (b/XII-27-1829; d/IX-5-1881) MD UPa 1853. *U Pa med alum CW*: 1853.

KENNEDY, HENRY A , Cape May, NJ (b/VIII-31-1845; d/VII-17-1891) MD UPa 1868. *Tr Med Soc NJ* 1891:233-34. *Polk* 1886: 602.

KENNEDY, HOWARD, Hagerstown, Md (b/1809; d/VI-12-1855) MD U Md 1828. *Med annals Md:* 466.

KENNEDY, JAMES, NYC (d/III-29-1884 @84) MD ? *Med reg NY NJ Conn* 1884: 231. *Med surg rep Phila* 50:512, 1884. *Butler* 1878: 517.

KENNEDY, JAMES, San Antonio, Tx (d/III-30 1895) MD ? *JAMA* 24: 609, 1895. *Tex cour rec med* 12: 230, 1895. *Tex m j* 10:543-44, 1894-95.

KENNEDY, JAMES CHARLES, MexWar-USA; Batavia, O (b/II-11-1809 Butler Co; d/1890) MD Med Coll O 1839. *Tr O Med Soc* 1892:377-78. *Atkinson* I: 674.

KENNEDY, JAMES CHARLES, Chicago (d/XI-3-1899) MD Bellevue 1882.*Tr Ill St Med Soc* 1899:287.

KENNEDY, LUTHER PRESSLY, Atlanta (d/VI- -1892 Due East, SC) MD UCNY 1887; att Erskine Coll. *JAMA* 19:170, 1892.

KENNEDY, PHILIP, Deavertown, O (b/Dublin, Irel'd; d/IV-26-1882) MD Med Coll Ohio 1864. *Tr AMA* 33: 578-79, 1882.

KENNEDY, ROBERT AMMERMAN, Shamokin, Pa (d/ II-6-1900 @44) MD UPa 1881. *JAMA* 34: 511, 1900. *Polk* 1896: 1336.

KENNEDY, ROBERT S, New Sheffield Pa (d/II-8-1906 @64) MD Jefferson 1866. *Pa m j* 9: 524, 1905/06.

KENNEDY, SAMUEL, NYC (d/II-25-1900) MD UCNY 1870. *JAMA* 34: 574, 1900. *Polk* 1896: 1061.

KENNEDY, SAMUEL SHERRERD, Stewartsville, NJ (d/VI-22-1888) MD CPSNY 1857; AB Lafayette 1853; AM. *Lafayette, Men of*: 168.

KENNEDY, STEWART, CW-USN (d/III-8-1864 Harrisburg, Pa) MD Jefferson 1854. *Nat m j* 1:298, 1870/71.

KENNEDY, STIRLING DeVERE, New Orleans (d/VII-6-1892 @33) MD U La 1880. *New Orl m&s j* ns20: 136-38, 1892. *Polk* 1890: 490.

KENNEDY, WILLIAM, Warren Co, NJ to 1857; Dade Co, Mo; CW-CSA (b/II-6-1829; d/X-23-1864 Westport, Mo) MD U Pa 1851; AB Lafayette 1847; AM. *U Pa med alum CW*: 1851.

KENNEY [KENNY], ARTHUR G , W Troy & Watervliet, NY (d/VI-25-1896 @52) MD Albany 1877. *JAMA* 27: 109. *Polk* 1886: 715.

KENNING, RICHARD H , Chicago (d/III-6-1906 @58) <MD Manitoba Med Coll 1883> *Ill m j* 9:463, 1906. *Polk* 1896: 390.

KENNON, C[HARLES?] E , La (d/1878 Tangipahoa, La) MD? Tulane 1866. *Tr AMA* 30:873, 1879.

KENNON, JOHN G , CW–USA (d/VIII–12–1862 Memphis) MD ? *Nat m j* 1:298, 1870/71.

KENT, BARKER BROOKS, Boston (b/1844; d/II–2–1873) MD Harvard 1869. *Bost m&s j* ns11: 1873 (Feb 6).

KENT, ERASMUS MARBLE, Bristol Vt (d/I–26–1894 @57) MD U Vt 1866 *JAMA* 22:202, 1894. *Polk* 1890:1104.

KENT, J EMERSON, Philadelphia (b/1811 Engl; d/XI–20–1889) MD King's Coll Lond 1839. *Med surg rep Phila* 61: 620, 1889. *Polk* 1886: 619. Homeopath.

KENT, JAMES, CW–CSA; Birmingham, Ala (b/I–8–1830 Petersburg, Va; d/V–22–1881) MD UPa 1850. *U Pa med alum CW*: 1850.

KENT, JAMES McGAVROCK, CW–CSA (b/IV–15–1825 Shawsville, Va; d/IV–5–1881 Roanoke) MD UPa 1845. *U Pa med alum CW*: 1845.

KENT, JOSEPH, Pr George Co, Md (b/I–14–1779 Calvert Co; d/XI–24–1837 Bladensburg) <MD UPa c1800> admitted to pract Lower Marlborough 1799. *Med annals Md:* 467. *Biogr direct US Congress.*

KENT, RIDLEY, Paterson, NJ (b/1810 Trowbridge, Engl; d/IX–30–1878) Lic Med Soc NJ; MD CPSNY 1853. *Tr Med Soc NJ*: 204–05. *Butler* 1878: 471.

KENYON, JOB, CW–USA; Warwick, RI (b/VII–8–1821 Exeter; d/VIII–5–1889) MD Yale 1846. *Tr RI Med Soc* 4:96–101, 1889–93. *Atkinson* I: 627. *Polk* 1886: 846.

KENYON, LORENZO MARCELLUS, Buffalo; Youngs town, Pa; Westfield, NY 1856– (b/III–18–1821 Sheridan, NY; d/XI–25–1887) MD Homeop Med Coll St Louis 1875. *Med adv* 20: 160, 1888. *Tr Am Inst Hom* 1888: 216. *Polk* 1886: 653. Homeopath.

KENYON, NAPOLEON BONAPARTE, Riverpoint RI (b/II–17–1840 Richmond; d/XII–3–1899) MD Yale 1864. *Tr RI M S* 6:132–33, 1899–1903. *Polk* 1896: 1354.

KERLIN, ISAAC NEWTON, CW–USA; Elwyn, Pa (b/V–27–1834 Burlington, NJ; d/X–25–1893) MD UPa 1856. *JAMA* 21:746 1893. *Tr M S Pa* 24:386–7 1894. *Atknsn* I:111. *K&B* III:692–93. *U Pa m alum CW*: 1856.

KERLIN, J M , CW–USA (d/VIII–12–1864) MD ? *Nat m j* 1:298, 187071.

KERN, THEODORE, Kokomo, Ind (d/IX–21–1894 @ 39) MD Med Coll Ind 1876. *JAMA* 23: 561, 1894. *Polk* 1886:325.

KERNAHAN, GEORGE, Chicago (d/IV–17–1901) MD Rush 1880. *Ill m j* ns3:47, 1901. *Polk* 186: 390.

KERNAN, THOMAS D , Marion, Va (d/VI–18–1896) MD UPa 1853. *JAMA* 27: 53, 1896. *Butler* 1878: 831. *Polk* 1896: 1494.

KERNAN, WILLIAM JAMES, Albany, NY (d/XI–26–1897) MD Albany 1891. *JAMA* 29: 1234, 1897. *Polk* 1896: 984.

KERR, GEORGE W , Waelder, Tx (d/IV– –1891) MD U La 1873. *Tex cour–rec med* 8:234, 1891. *Daniel's Tex m j* 6:478, 1890–91. *Polk* 1890: 1095.

KERR, JAMES WILSON, York, Pa (b/IX–19–1813 Maytown; d/VI–10–1889) MD UPa 1839; AB Jefferson 1833. *Tr M S Pa* 1889–90: 299. *JAMA* 13:757, 1889. *Butler* 1878: 719. *U Pa med alum CW*: 1839.

KERR, JOHN W, Allegheny, Pa (d/II–9–1896 @41) MD Jefferson 1854. *JAMA* 26:391,1896. *Polk* 1896:1262.

KERRIGAN, JOSEPH AMBROSE, NYC (b/XII–7–1833; d/I–17–1879 Hoboken, NJ) MD CPSNY 1858; AB St Johns 1852; AM 1855. *Med reg NY NJ Conn* 1879: 194.

KERSEY, JONATHAN HODSON, Stuart, Ia (b/IX–11–1840 Hendricks Co, Ind; d/XI–28–1899) MD Bellevue 1866. *Tr Iowa St Med Soc* 18:393–94, 1900. *JAMA* 33: 1504, 1899. *Polk* 1896: 540.

KERSEY, VIERLING, Richmond, Ind (b/IX–8–1809; d/VI–3–1875) MD Med Coll Ohio 1851; ng Jefferson 1837–38. *Tr Ind St Med Soc* 1876: 146–48. *Tr AMA* 614–17, 1877. Kemper's *Indiana*: 294.

KERWIN, MICHAEL HAMILTON, Seymour & Milwaukee, Wis (b/V–14–1855 Menasha; d/III–7–1891) MD U Mich 1876; MD CPSNY 1882. *Tr Wis St M S* 1891: 329–30. *Polk* 1890: 1172.

KESSINGER, ELLIS M , Sanborn, Ind (b/VIII–19–1857; Bruceville; d/V–21–1905) MD Hosp Coll Med Louisville 1891. *Tr Ind St Med Soc* 1905: 451. *Polk* 1896: 490.

KETCH, SAMUEL, NYC (d/XII–14–1899 @44) MD Bellevue 1875; att Coll City NY. *JAMA* 33: 1632, 1899. *JAMA* 33: 1632, 1899. *Bost m&s j* 141: 644, 1899. *Polk* 1896: 1062.

KETCHAM, JOHN DYE, Tunnelton, Ind (b/VIII–23 1865 Monroe Co; d/VI–4–1900) <MD CPS Indianapolis 1891> *Tr Ind St M S* 1901: 490. *JAMA* 34: 1574, 1900.

KETCHAM, ORLANDO CRISMAN, Washington, DC (b/I–30–1839 Northumberland Co, Pa; d/VII–30–1892) MD Georgetown 1871. *Hist Med Soc DC:* 313. *Polk* 1886: 212.

KETCHUM, BENJAMIN F , Brattleborough, Vt (b/XII 25–1837 Troy, NY; d/I–9–1897) MD UCNY 1860. *JAMA* 28: 184–85, 1897. *Polk* 1896: 1473.

KETCHUM, GEORGE AUGUSTUS, CW–CSA; Mobile, Ala (b/IV 6–1825 Augusta, Ga; d/V–29–1906) MD UPa 1846. *New Orl m&s j* 59: 86, 1906. *U Pa med alum CW*: 1846. *Polk* 1896: 164.

KEY, JOHN P , Brenham, Tx (d/1867) MD ? *New Orl m&s j* 21:204, 1868. *Tr AMA* 19: 428, 1868.

KEY, LUCINDA DAVIS, Chattanooga, Tenn (d/VIII–27 1896) MD Meharry 1894. *JAMA* 27: 555, 1896. *Polk* 1896: 1385. Black.

KEYS, ROBERT S H , Monongahela, Pa (b/Fayette Co, Pa; d/VI–24–1899 @67) MD ? *JAMA* : 53, 1899. *Butler* 1878: 719. *Polk* 1890: 983.

KEYSER, PETER DIRCK, Philadelphia (b/II–8–1835; d/III–9–1897) <MD Jena 1864> AB Delaware Coll 1852; AM 1854. *Bull Acad Med Easton Pa* 3:258–60 1897–98. *JAMA* 28:569 1897. *Atkinson* I:189. *K&B* III:694.

KEYT, ALONZO THRASHER, Cincinnati (b/I-10-1827 Higginsport, O; d/XI-9-1885) MD Med Coll Ohio 1848. *JAMA* 5: 615, 1885. *Bost m&s j* 113: 526, 1885. *Butler* 1878: 611. *K&B* III: 694.

KIBBEE, GEORGE W , NYC (d/IX-25-1878 New Orleans) MD ? *Tr AMA* 30:873,-74, 1879. *Med rec NY* 14: 279, 1878.

KIBBEE, GIDEON, Wilbraham, Mass (b/1779; d/III-7-1859 @80) MD ? *Bost m&s j* 60: 148, 1859.

KIDD, H B , Yazoo City, Miss (b/XI-18-1820 Fayette Co, Ky; d/VIII-11-1877) MD Louisville Med Inst 1845. *Tr Miss St Med Assoc* 1878: 156.

KIDD, JOHN QUINCY, CW-CSA; Grand Lake, Tx (b/1828 Chester Dist, SC; d/1890) MD ? att U Ala 1836. *U Ala cat*: 51.

KIDD, W W , Jackson CH & Ripley, WVa (b/I-26-1854 Liberty Twp; O (d/VIII-20-1897) MD CPS Balto 1878. *Tr St M S WVa* 1899: 336. *Polk* 1886: 942.

KIDD, WILLIAM ANDREW, Independence, Pa (d/XII-11-1902 @35) MD West Res 1897. *Pa m j* 6: 260, 1902/03.

KIDDER, EDWARD HAMILTON, Fall River, Mass (b/Lincoln; d/VII-16-1898 @33) MD Harvard 1893; AB 1888. *Bost m&s j* 139: 76, 1898. *JAMA* 31:257, 1898. *Polk* 1896: 712.

KIDDER, FREDERICK T , NYC (d/II-19-1880 @72) MD ? *Med surg rep Phila* 42: 220, 1880.

KIDDER, JEROME HENRY , CW-USN; Washington, DC (b/X-26 1842 Baltimore; d/IV-8-1889) MD U Md 1866; MD NY Homeop 1869 {?]; AB Harvard 1862. *Med reg NY NJ Conn* 1889: 276. *So pract* 11:230, 1889. *Bost m&s j* 120:400, 1889; 121: 641, 1889. *K&B* III: 695.

KIDDER, MOSES WARREN, Lowell & Lincoln, Mass (b/IX-11-1828; d/VIII-15-1900) MD Berkshire 1852. *Bost m&s j* 143: 196, 1900. *Polk* 1886:468.

KIEFER, LOUIS FRANCIS NYC (d/VII-23-1897 @45) MD CPSNY 1886. *JAMA* 29:267 1897. *Polk* 1896: 1062.

KIEFFER, STEPHEN BARNETT, Rockdale, Pa (b/IX-6-1824; d/X-27-1887) MD UPa 1851; AB Franklin & Marshall 1848. *Atkinson* I: 528. *Polk* 1886: 794.

KIEHL, HARRY LUTHER, Fayette City & Bentleyville, Pa (d/XI-29-1902) MD Western Pa Univ 1896. *Pa m j* 6: 260. *Polk* 1896: 1268, 1278.

KIELTY, JOHN DANIEL, Fitchburg, Mass (d/VIII-27 1901 @43) MD Bellevue 1884. *Bost m&s j* 145: 290, 1901. *Polk* 1896, 712.

KIERLAND, PETER E , Rushford, Minn? (d/1871) MD Rush 1869. *Tr AMA* 23: 593, 1872.

KIERNAN, JAMES LAWLOR, CW-USA; NYC (b/1835 Ireland; d/XI-26-1869) MD UCNY 1857; AB Trinity, Dublin. *Med reg NY NJ Conn* 1870:321. *Tr AMA* 21:449-50,1870. *Phila med reg & dir* 1871: 302.

KILBOURNE, ALBERT WELLS, Albany, NY (b/1851 Liberty; d/I-14-1897) MD UCNY 1874. *JAMA* 28: 380, 1897. *Polk* 1886: 638.

KILBOURNE, EDWIN ARTHUR [or ARIUS], NYC Aurora, Ill (b/III-12-1837 Chelsea, Vt; d/II-27-1890) MD CPSNY 1868. *JAMA* 14: 431-32, 1890. *Tr Ill St Med Soc* 1890: 29-32. *Butler* 1878: 161.

KILBOURNE, JEDEDIAH SAGE, NYC (d/VII-12-1877) MD CPSNY 1837 *Med reg NY NJ Conn* 1877:210.

KILBY, JOHN DENNYS, Bangor, Me (b/VIII-26-1826 Dennysville; d/IX-19-1849) Stud med Bowdoin 1849. *Bowdoin cat*: 1847.

KILLOUGH, THOMAS, Hanover, Ill (d/VIII-25-1896) MD Northwestern 1873. *JAMA* 27: 555, 1896. *Polk* 1896: 422.

KILPATRICK, ANDREW ROBERT, Navasota, Tx (b/III-20-1817 Cheneyville, La; d/IX-19-1887) MD Med Coll Ga 1837; att Jefferson 1 yr. *Daniel's Tex m j* 3: 159-62, 1888. *New Orl m&s j* ns15: 413, 493, 1887. *Atkinson* I: 152-53. *K&B* III: 695-96.

KIMBALL, ARTHUR HERBERT, Battle Creek, Mich (d/VIII-6-1894 @44) MD Dartmouth 1876; AB 1873. *JAMA* 23: 248, 1894. *Polk* 1886: 483.

KIMBALL, BOWEN NYE, Augusta, Me; CW-USA Med cadet (b/III-15-1841 Milo, Me; d/IX-2-1864 Augusta) Stud med Bowdoin 1864. *Bowdoin cat*: 1864.

KIMBALL, DANIEL STARKWEATHER, Sackett's Harbor, NY (b/I-7-1806 Charlestown; d/XII-12-1882) <MD Fairfield 1828> *Tr Am Inst Hom* 1884: 618. *King* 1:97. *Cleave*. Homeopath.

KIMBALL, FRANK DUANE, Blackwell's Isl, NY (d/IV 12-1900 @24) MD UCNY 1898;<AB Dartmouth> *Bost m&s j* 142:120 1900. *JAMA* 34:102 1900. *Polk* 1900: 1274.

KIMBALL, GILMAN, Lowell, Mass (b/XII-8-1804 New Chester, NH; d/VII-27-1892. MD Dartmouth 1827; Hon MD Berkshire 1837; Hon MD Woodstock 1840; Hon MD Yale 1856. *Proc Conn Med Soc* 1893: 231-32. *Nwest m j* 20:160, 1892. *Bost m&s j* 127:12 128, 1892. *Atkinson* I:571. *Butler* 1878:353. *K&B* III: 696-97.

KIMBALL, JARVIS, CW-USN (d/II-6-1864 abd USS Pequot) MD U Vt 1863. *Nat m j* 1:298, 1870/71.

KIMBALL, JOHN ELI LELAND, Saco, Me (b/VI--1819 Pembroke, NH; d/VI-2-1892) MD Woodstock 1847. *Tr Me Med Assoc* 1892: 198. *Bost m&s j* 126:592, 1892. *Butler* 1878: 308.

KIMBALL, JOHN ROBINSON, Suncook, NH (b/XII-28-1844 Pembroke; d/I-8-1893) MD Bowdoin 1869. *Tr NH Med Soc* 1893: 161. *Polk* 1890:712.

KIMBALL, JOSEPH EDWIN, Nashua, NH (b/1859; d/VI-8-1900 Chelsea, Mass) MD U Vt 1886. *JAMA* 34: 1645, 1900.

KIMBALL, WALTER HENRY, Andover, Mass (b/VI-20-1820 Boxford; d/IX-30-1881 @61) MD Dartmouth 1844; AB 1841. *Bost m&s j* 105: 449, 623, 1881.

KIMBARK, EVERETT HOFFMAN, NYC (b/VIII-30-1818; d/VIII-29-1872) MD CPSNY 1850. *Med reg NY NJ Conn* 1873: 341.

KIMBERLIN, JOHN J , Medora, Ind (d/1863) MD Ky Sch Med 1859. *Tr Ind St Med Soc* 1866: 9.

KIMBLEY, JOHN F, Owensburgh Ky (d/V-24-1897) MD Jefferson 1849. *JAMA* 28:1091,1897. *Polk*1896:600.

KIMERER, JOHN R, Danville Pa (d/VII-1 1903 @43) MD CPS Balto 1885. *Pa m j* 7:279, 1903/04. *Polk* 1896: 1274.

KIMLIN, THOMAS, Quincy, Ill (d/II-24-1900 @62) MD UCNY 1865. *JAMA* 34:639, 1900. *Polk* 1886: 570 (Trenton, Mo).

KINARD, G ALLEN, Pine Grove, SC (d/III-29-1897) MD ? *NC m j* 39:324, 1897.

KINCH, FREDERICK ADRIAN, Westfield, NJ (d/IV-27-1890) Cert Exam Bd 1851. *Polk* 1886: 612. *Med reg NY NJ Conn* 1890: 271.

KINCHLOE, DAVID ANDERSON, MexWar-USA; CW CSA; Sardis, Miss (b/X-18-1823 Barren Co, Ky; d/IX-9-1878) MD Med Coll Ohio 1846. *Tr AMA* 31:1054-55, 1880. *Tr Miss St M Assn* 1878-81:39. *Atkinson* I:445-46.

KINDERMANN, ALEXANDER, Eugene, Ind (b/XII-5-1858; d/IV-2-1905) MD Rush 1883. *Tr Ind St Med Soc* 1905: 452. *Polk* 1896: 465.

KINDRICK, CYRUS MAXCY, Gardiner, Me 1850-52; Litchfield 1852- (b/IX-6-1825; d/IV-4-1904) MD Jefferson 1850; ng Bowdoin Med 1849. *Bowdoin cat*: 1849. *Polk* 1886: 426.

KING, ABSALOM PRIDE, Providence, RI (b/V-1-1820; d/X-16-1868) Lic 1845; att Berkshire. *Tr RI Med Soc* 4:349-50, 1889-93.

KING, ASA HOWE, Old Saybrook, Conn (b/1798 New Haven; d/XI-20-1870) Hon MD Yale 1821; MD Bowdoin 1824. *Proc Conn Med Soc* 1871: 502 ff.

KING, BENJAMIN, Weston, Md (b/VIII-24-1798 Calvert Co; d/VI-24-1888) MD U Md 1818. *Hist Med Soc DC:* 227.

KING, BENJAMIN W , NYC (b/XI-2-1829; d/XII-18-1889) MD Castleton 1856. *Med reg NY NJ Conn* 1890:272.

KING, CHARLES GOODRICH, Providence, RI (b/I-3-1840; d/VIII-27-1881) <Stud med Phila 1 yr> AB Amherst 1861. *Amherst, Men of*: 1861.

KING, CHARLES HENRY, Staten Isl, NYC (d/III--1883) MD ?LICH 1864. *Bost m&s j* 108: 307, 1883.

KING, CHARLES RAY, Philadelphia (b/III-16-1813; d/IV-15-1901) MD UPa 1834; AB Columbia 1831. *Pa m j* 5: 296, 1901/02. *Tr CPP* cent vol: 240.

KING, COURTENAY S , Charleston, SC (d/III or IV--1855 Crimea) MD ? ; stud abroad. *Bost m&s j* 52: 407, 1855. *Waring* II: 252.

KING, DAN, Taunton, Mass (b/I-27-1791 Mansfield, Conn; d/XI-13-1864 Smithfield, RI) Lic 1815; stud Yale. *Bost m&s j* 71: 368, 1864. *Tr RI Med Soc* 1889-93: 344 ff. *K&B* III: 700.

KING, DAVID, Newport, RI (b/IV-2-1774 Raynham, Mass; d/XI-14-1836) Hon MD Brown 1821; AB 1796. *Tr RI Med Soc* 1:10, 50-55, 1859-77. *K&B* III:700.

KING, DAVID Jr, Newport, RI (b/V-10-1812; d/III-7-1887) MD Jefferson 1834; AB Brown 1831. *Tr AMA* 33: 579-82,1882. *Bost m&s j* 106:373, 1882. *Tr RI Med Soc* 2:540-44,1877-82. *Atkinson* I:652-53.

KING, ENOCH WOOD, New Albany, Ind (b/VI-24-1846 Rollingham, Ky; d/XI-14-1882) MD U Louisville 1869. *Tr Ind St Med Soc* 1883: 270. *Butler* 1878:209.

KING, FREDERICK GORE, NYC (b/1801 Engl; d/IV-24-1829) MD ? *Amer j m sci* ns4:539, 1829.

KING, GEORGE Jr, Franklin, Mass (d/IV-24-1902 @79) MD CPSNY 1847. *Bost m&s j* 146: 678, 1902. *Polk* 1896: 712.

KING, GEORGE ANDREW, Lancaster, Pa (d/V-16 1891 @48) MD Jefferson 1866. *Bost m&s j* 124: 522, 1891. *Polk* 1886: 804.

KING, GEORGE W , Pendleton, Or (d/VIII-23-1899 @55) MD Med Coll Ohio 1883. *JAMA* 33:745, 1899. *Polk* 1890: 946.

KING, HENRY [C ?], Phenix, RI (b/VII-24-1828; d/II-21-1891 @63) MD UCNY 1855. *Bost m&s j* 124:224, 1891. *Tr RI M S* 4:350-51, 1889-93. *Polk* 1890: 1026.

KING, HOWARD WILLIAMS, Providence, RI (b/V-1 1824 Charlestown; d/III-12 or 15-1875) MD Bowdoin 1853. *Tr RI Med Soc* 1:466-67, 1859-77.

KING, J FRANCIS, CW-CSA; Wilmington, NC (d/XII 7/11 1879 @48) MD NY Med Coll 1853. *Tr NC Med Soc* 1880: 15. *NC m j* 4:430, 1879. *Med surg rep Phila* 41: 554, 1879. *Butler* 1878: 595.

KING, JAMES, Pittsburgh; CW-USA (b/I-18-1816; d/III-10-1880) MD Transylvania 1838; <MD UPa 1838> *Tr CPP* cent vol: 283. *Tr AMA* 31:1055-58, 1880. *Tr Pa St Med Soc* 1880: 247-48. *Atkinson* I:548.

KING, JAMES C J , CW-CSA; Waco, Tx (b/Tenn; d/III-21-1906) MD Tulane 1871. *Tex st j m* 2:36, 1906. *Polk* 1886: 896.

KING, JAMES E , Buffalo (d/II-1-1888) MD Buffalo 1848. *Buff m&s j* 27:381, 1888. *Tr Med Soc St NY* 11:741 ff, 1894? *Butler* 1878: 537.

KING, JOHN BOWNE, Nantucket, Mass (b/NYC; d/VII 27-1889 @81) MD CPSNY 1832. *Bost m&s j* 121: 266, 1889. *Butler* 1878: 353.

KING, JOHN F , Washington, DC (d/III-25-1873) MD Jefferson 1855; ?AB Georgetown 1852. *Hist Med Soc DC:* 255.

KING, JOHN SKILES, Mercersburg, Pa; CW-USA (b/XII-20-1826; d/VI-2-1869) MD UPa 1848; AB Franklin & Marshall 1844. *U Pa med alum CW*: 1848.

KING, JOSEPH H THOMAS, Laredo, Tex (d/IX-30 1890 Victoria, Mex) MRCP London 1858. *Daniel's Tex m j* 6:225-26, 1890-91. *Polk* 1886: 889.

KING, KENNETH KIRK, Rutherford, NJ (b/X-3-1850 Beaufort, NC; d/XI-9-1882) MD Bellevue 1877. *Tr Med Soc NJ*: 278, 1882-83.

KING, LORESTON J , Santa Rosa, Calif (b/NY; d/VII-

 Spec. educ'l status abbrev. as: ***ng*** = college verified attendance without degree;

22–1901 @52) MD Columbus Med Coll 1880. *JAMA* 37: 398, 1901. *Polk* 1886: 177.

KING, M F , Philadelphia? (d/IV–14–1862 @57) MD ? *Med surg rep Phila* ns8: 104, 1862.

KING, M W , Decatur, Tx (d/VII–7–1882) MD ? *Tex med & surg rec* 3:550, 1883.

KING, NATHAN SHERWOOD, Yonkers, NY (b/1824 Fishkill; d/XII–11–1898) MD CPSNY 1852; AB Wms 1849. *Bost m&s j* 139:636 1898. *JAMA* 31:1542, 1898.

KING, O , Honesdale, Pa (b/1798? d/III–6–1867 @69) MD ? *Med surg rep Phila* 16:224, 1867.

KING, RICHARD DAVIS, Bells, Tx (d/VIII–19–1901) MD U Nashville 1854. *JAMA* 37: 710, 1901.

KING, SHUBAL [SAMUEL] S , McKinley, Ala (d/XI–8 1899 @75) MD U Louisville 1847. *Tr Med Assoc St Ala* 1899: 233. *Polk* 1893: 159.

KING, STEPHEN HENRY, Providence, RI; Baltimore (b/IV–10–1844 Boyle, Irel'd; d/VI–5–1902 London) MD Harvard 1872. *Tr RI Med Soc* 6:546–47, 1899–1903. *Med annals Md:* 468. *Polk* 1896: 1352.

KING, THEODORE F , Brooklyn (b/c1805; d/IX–2 1868) MD CPSNY 1827; AB Columbia 1822. *Tr AMA* 21:436, 1870. *Med reg NY NJ Conn* 1869: 234. *Med surg rep Phila* 19: 239, 1868.

KING, THOMAS JEFFERSON, Machias, NY (b/VI–4–1825; d/XI–5–1889) MD Albany 1855; AB Williams 1848; AM 1852. *Med reg NY NJ Conn* 1890: 272. *Buffalo m&s j* 24: 318, 1889. *Med surg rep Phila* 61: 680, 1889. *Butler* 1878: 560.

KING, W NORREL, Abilene Kans (d/III–19–1895 @69) MD Jefferson 1858. *JAMA* 24:497, 1895. *Polk* 1886:374.

KING, WILLIAM F , Centerville, Ind (b/IV–19–1824 Georgetown DC;d/II–4–1892) MD Ind Central Med Coll 1851. *Tr Ind St Med Soc* 1892: 290. *Polk* 1886: 313.

KING, WILLIAM H H , Jacksonville Ill (d/XI–15 1897) MD Rush 1866. *JAMA* 29:1129, 1897. *Polk* 1886: 283.

KING, WILLIAM HEBRON, CW–USA (b/S Egremont, Mass; d/III–21–1863 Newark, NJ) MD Bellevue 1862. *Nat m j* 1:298, 1870/71. *Med reg NY NJ Conn* 1865: 223 [as Wm Henry]. *Bost m&s j* 68: 209, 1863. *Med surg rep Phila* Phila ns9:441, 1862/63.

KING, WILLIAM HOWARD, USA 1863–68? Philadelphia (b/X–7–1840; d/VIII–23–1883) MD UPa 1863; AB Princeton 1862. *U Pa med alum CW*: 1863.

KING, WILLIAM HOWARD, Yreka, Calif (b/XII–15–1848 RI; d/XI–16–1884) MD Bellevue 1874. *Tr RI Med Soc* 4: 350, 1889–93.

KING, WILLIAM M , USN 1858–75? (b/VI– –1836 Phila; d/III–14–1880) MD Jefferson 1858. *Med surg rep Phila* 42: 264, 1880. *Tr CPP* cent vol: 240.

KING, WILLIAM RUFUS, Boston (d/II–17–1905 @37) MD Harvard 1890. *Bost m&s j* 152:294, 1905.

KING, WILLIAM SHAKESPEARE, USA 1837– (b/Pa; d/VIII–2–1895) MD UPa 1833. *U Pa med alum CW*: 1833. G V Henry, *Milit rec*: 87–88.

KINGMAN, ABEL WASHBURN, Brockton, Mass (b/IV 22–1806 N Bridgewater; d/V–4–1883) MD Columbian 1831; ng Amherst 1829. *Amherst, Men of*: 1829.

KINGSBURY, CHARLES WOOD, Framingham, Mass (b/V–27–1831; d/XII–9–1853) <ng UCNY 1852–54> AB Amherst 1842. *Amherst, Men of*: 1852.

KINGSBURY, JOSEPH BYRON, Holbrook, Mass (b/ VII–29–1836 Braintree, Vt; d/III–24–1906) MD Dartmouth 1871. *Bost m&s j* 154:360, 1906. *Polk* 1896: 714.

KINGSBURY, NATHANIEL, Temple, NH (b/VI–28–1798 Rindge; d/III–3–1870 Shirley, Mass) MD Bowdoin 1829. *Phila med reg & dir* 1871: 304.

KINGSLEY, CHARLES, Marlboro, Mass (d/XII–29–1899 @30) MD Jefferson 1891. *Bost m&s j* 142:48, 1900. *JAMA* 34: 187, 1900. *Polk* 1896: 712.

KINGSLEY, GEORGE LYLE, Boston (b/1864 Rome, NY; d/IX–25–1890) MD Harvard 1890; AB Yale 1886. *Bost m&s j* 123: 336, 1890.

KINGSLEY, JEDEDIAH H [or S] Rome, NY (d/IV–26 1899 @77) MD U Vt 1866. *JAMA* 32: 1074, 1899. *Polk* 1893: 928.

KINGSLEY, LESTER, Moretown, Vt (b/III–16–1805 Ira; d/I–4–1881) MD Castleton 1826. *Tr Vt Med Soc* 1883: 107.

KINGSTON, THOMAS A , Jerseyville, Ill (d/1900 @68) MD Washington U, St Louis 1864. *Tr Ill St Med Soc* 1899–1900: 415, 463, 509. *Polk* 1886: 284.

KINLOCH, GEORGE C , Charleston, SC (b/1859; d/ VI–7–1886) MD Med Coll St SC 1881; stud Austria & Gny. *New Orl m&s j* ns14: 77, 1886. *K&B* III: 702 (mention). *Waring* II: 252.

KINLOCH, ROBERT ALEXANDER, CW–CSA; Charleston, SC (b/II–20–1826; d/XII–23–1891) MD UPa 1848, AB 1845. *JAMA* 18: 29–30, 1892. *Bost m&s j* 125: 720, 1891. *Tr CPP* cent vol: 283. *Waring* II: 253–54. *K&B* III: 791–92.

KINNAMAN [KINSMAN], JACOB W , Lancaster, O (b/X–18–1815 Ellsworth, O; d/VII–18–1874) MD Med Coll Cleveland 1847. *Tr Ohio St M S* 1876: 90–91. *Butler* 1878: 638.

KINNE, AMASA FARRINGTON, Ypsilanti Mich (b/IV 13–1813 Waterford, Vt; d/II–14–1894) MD Dartmouth 1841; AB 1837. *JAMA* 22:314,1894. *Polk* 1890: 605.

KINNE, THEODORE YOUNG, CW–USA; Paterson, NJ (b/VIII–27 1838 Syracuse, NY; d/III–4–1904) MD Albany 1862. *Tr Am Inst Hom* 1904: 954. *No Am jour hom* 52:249–50, 1904. *Polk* 1886: 609. Homeopath.

KINNE, WILLIAM B [W], CW–USA (d/IV–25–1864) MD Berkshire M C 1835. *Nat m j* 1:298, 1870/71.

KINNEMON, GEORGE S , Baltimore (b/1848; d/XII–12–1884) MD U Md 1874. *Med annals Md:* 468. *Med bull* 7:32, 1884. *Butler* 1878: 320.

KINNEMON, PERRY SPENCER, Baltimore; CW–USA (b/XII–7–1809; d/I–1–1877) MD U Md 1833. *Tr AMA* 28:617–18, 1877. *Med annals Md:* 468–69.

KINNEY, CHARLES, CW–USA (d/II–15–1865 Ft Gibson, Ind Terr) MD Dartmouth 1850; AB U Vt 1846. *Nat m j* 1:298, 1870/71.

KINNEY, ELIJAH C , Norwich, Conn (b/VII–25–1829; d/X–19–1892) MD NYMC 1858. *Proc Conn M S* 1893: 237–39. *Bost m&s j* 127: 420, 1892. *Polk* 1890: 225.

KINSEY, THOMAS JEFFERSON, CW–CSA; ?Washington, Va (b/VII–11–1833 Madison Co; d/VII–11–1895) MD UPa 1860. *U Pa med alum CW*: 1860.

KINSLEY, HUDSON, Yonkers, NY (b/1795? d/III–26–1868 @73) MD CPSNY 1823. *Phila med reg & dir* 1871: 296. *Med surg rep Phila* 18:314, 1868.

KINSMAN, BENJAMIN WILLIS, Toledo, O (b/I–8–1833; d/XI–26–1855 Paris, Fr) MD Harvard 1855; AB Brown 1852. *Bost m&s j* 53:476, 1856.

KIRBY, HIRAM, Canton, O (d/I–20–1899 @56) MD Bellevue 1871. *JAMA* 32: 263, 1899.

KIRBY, JOHN, Trenton, NJ (b/IX–13–1826 Swedesboro, NJ; d/II–27–1897) MD UPa 1852. *Tr Med Soc NJ* 1897:300. *JAMA* 28: 523, 1897.

KIRBY, STEPHEN REYNOLDS, NYC (b/V–21–1801 Middle River, Bedford, NY; d/III–6–1876) MD *Tr Am Inst Hom* 1893:147. *King* 1:79. Homeopath.

KIRBY, THEODORE, NYC (d/VIII–10–1863 @38) MD *Med surg rep Phila* 10: 228, 1863.

KIRK, JOSEPH PATTON, E Waterford, Pa; USN (d/II–13–1867 @54) MD ? *Med s rep Phila* 16: 199, 1867.

KIRK, WILLIAM T , Atlanta, Ill (b/X–27–1833 Simpsonville, Ky; d/III–25–1887) MD U Louisville 1854. *Tr Ill St Med Soc* 1887:166–69. *JAMA* 1: 380, 1887.

KIRKBRIDE, JOSEPH JOHN, Philadelphia (b/VIII–4 1842;d/V–4–1899) MD UPa 1872; PhG Phila Coll Phar 1870. *JAMA* 32:1074, 1899. *Tr CPP* cent vol: 240.

KIRKBRIDE, THOMAS STORY, Philadelphia (b/VII–31–1809; d/IV–16–1885) MD UPa 1832; LLD Lafayette 1880. *Med surg rep Phila* 49: 708, 1883; 50:31–32, 1884. *Tr Pa St Med Soc* 17:384–85, 1885. *Tr CPP* cent vol: 240. *K&B* III: 703–04.

KIRKBRIDE, THOMAS STORY Jr, Philadelphia (b/VII–25–1869; d/VII–19–1900) MD UPa 1893; att Haverford. *Haverford biogr cat*: 202.

KIRKER, JOHN, Allegheny City, Pa (d/I–23–1897) MD Bellevue 1864; MD Cleveland Med Coll 1857. *JAMA* 28: 380, 1897. *Polk* 1896: 1262.

KIRKLAND, JOHN RANDOLPH, CW–CSA; Meridian, Miss (b/XII–20–1835 Warsaw, Ala; d/IV–7–1901) MD UPa 1859. *New Orl m&s j* 53:708, 1901. *U Pa med alum CW*: 1859. *Polk* 1896: 812.

KIRKPATRICK, HENRY AUGUSTUS, Stanton, NY (d/IX–29–1851 @35) <ng Jefferson> stud w/Dr Cicero Hunt. *Tr Med Soc NJ* 1872: 193–94.

KIRKPATRICK, JOHN WEST, Wyoming, Ia (b/X–9–1862 Phila; d/V–13–1903) MD Rush 1888. *Tr Iowa St Med Soc* 22: 341, 1904. *Polk* 1896: 543.

KIRKPATRICK, ROSS C , Los Angeles (b/1842 New Bethlehem, Pa; d/1903) MD Starling 1870. *Cal st j m* 1:173, 1903. *Polk* 1896: 219.

KIRKSCEY, E JEHU, USA; CW–CSA; Columbus, Ga (b/1837; d/1877) MD Jefferson 1858. *Tr AMA* 31: 1058–59, 1880. *SHSP* 22: 227, 1893.

KIRSCHSTEIN, HERMAN, Chicago (d/IV–29–1906 @ 77) <MD Breslau 1862> *Ill m j* 9: 662, 1906. *Polk* 1886: 266.

KIRSTEN, ADOLPH, Jersey City, NJ (b/1824 Gny; d/I 23–1896) MD UCNY 1869. *JAMA* 26: 340, 1896. *Polk* 1896: 939.

KIRTLAND, JARED POTTER, E Rockport, O; CW–USA (b/XI–10–1793 Wallingford, Conn; d/XII–10–1877) MD Yale 1815; LLD Williams 1861. *Tr Ohio St M S* 1879: 186. *Atkinson* I:704–05. *K&B* III: 704–05.

KIRWAN, GEORGE HENRY, Wilkes Barre, Pa (b/VII–21–1856 Hawley; d/XII–28–1895) MD CPSNY 1882. *Lehigh Valley med mag* 7:13–14, 1896. *JAMA* 26: 142, 1896. *Tr Luzerne Co (Pa) Med Soc* 1–4:162–66, 1895; 5–6: 201, 1897. *Polk* 1886: 840.

KISSAM, DANIEL EMBURY, Huntington, NY (b/X–3–1817; d/XII–23–1903) MD CPSNY 1848. *Bost m&s j* 149: 748, 1903. *Polk* 1886: 646.

KISSAM, DANIEL WHITEHEAD, Brooklyn (d/IX–9–1890) MD CPSNY 1865. *Med reg NY NJ Conn* 1891: 275. *JAMA* 15: 555, 1890.

KISSAM, GEORGE HOFFMAN, Jamaica, NY (b/1810; d/XI–19–1865) MD CPSNY 1838; AB Trinity 1830; AM 1833.*Med surg rep Phila* 13: 326, 1865.

KISSAM, GEORGE PURDY, Brooklyn (d/VII–8–1877 or 1878 @28) MD UCNY 1874. *Med reg NY NJ Conn* 1878: 182.

KISSAM, JAMES B, NYC (d/IV–26–1886 @74) MD ? *Med reg NY NJ Conn* 1886: 250. *K&B* III: 1043 (mention)

KISSAM, RICHARD SHARPE, Hartford, Conn; NYC (b/X–2–1808; d/XI–28–1861) MD CPSNY 1830. *Tr AMA* 14: 199–200, 1864. *Med reg NY NJ Conn* 1862: 155. *K&B* III: 705.

KISSAM, WILLIAM AYMAR, NYC (d/IV–12–1877 @ 32) MD CPSNY 1867. *Med reg NY NJ Conn* 1877: 204.

KISSANE, WILLIAM ELWOOD, Brooklyn (d/IV–26–1899) MD UCNY 1885. *JAMA* 32:1013, 1899. *Polk* 1896: 998.

KISTLER, JACOB K, Lehighton Pa (d/XII–9–1899 @ 51) MD Jefferson 1875. *JAMA* 33:1632 1899. *Polk* 1896: 1287.

KITCHEL, EDWIN MATHEWS, NYC (d/VIII–26–1897) MD CPSNY 1893. *Buff m&s j* 33: 140–41, 1897. *JAMA* 29: 554, 1897. *Med bull m & s* 19:398–99, 1897.

KITCHELL, WILLIAM, Madison, NJ (d/XII–29–1861 @34) MD UCNY 1850. *Med surg rep Phila* ns7: 360, 1861/62.

KITCHEN, FRANCIS ANDREW, CW–USA; Toledo, O (b/VI–6–1829 Easton, Pa; d/XII–18–1903) MD UPa 1856. *U Pa med alum CW*: 1856. *Polk* 1886: 770.

Spec. educ'l status abbrev. as: ***ng*** = college verified attendance without degree;

KITCHEN, JAMES Jr, Philadelphia (b/III-8-1800; d/VIII-19-1894) MD UPa 1822; AB 1819. *Hahn mo* 29: (news & advt) 1894 (Oct); 30: (news & advt) 1895 (June). *Tr Am Inst Hom* 1895: 223. *Bost m&s j* 131: 228, 1894. *Polk* 1886: 819. *Cleave.* Homeopath 1839- .

KITCHEN, JOHN SMYTHE, USN 1855- ? (b/XI-29-1831 Phila; d/V-8-1872) MD UPa 1855. *Phila med reg & dir* 1873: 303. *Tr AMA* 24: 392-94, 1873. *Bost m&s j* ns9: 344, 1872. *U Pa med alum CW*:1855.

KITE, JOHN ALBAN, Nantucket, Mass (d/V-14-1891) MD UPa 1880. *Bost m&s j* 125: 718, 1891.

KITLOE, EDWARD R , Galena, Ill (d/II-18-1903 @57) MD NWU 1869. *Ill m j* ns4:760, 1903. *Polk* 1886: 280.

KITRELL, BENJAMIN H, Winona, Miss (d/VIII-17-1901 Fourth Lake NY) MD Tulane 1897. *JAMA* 37:595 1901.

KITTINGER, LEONARD, Bordentown & Flemington, NJ; Wilmington, Del 1866- (b/IV-27-1834 Phila; d/IV 16-1903) MD Hahnemann Phila 1863. *Tr Am Inst Hom* 1905:846-47. *Polk* 1886: 206. *Cleave.* Homeopath.

KITTINGER, MARTIN S, Lockport, NY (d/IX-11-1904 @77) MD CPSNY 1853. *Tr M S St NY* 1905: 362. *Polk* 1886: 666.

KITTREDGE, BENJAMIN F , Hinsdale, Mass (d/IV-18 1862) MD Berkshire 1824. *Bost m&s j* 66: 264, 1862. *Med surg rep Phila* ns8: 130, 1862.

KITTREDGE, CHARLES MARSH, Mt Vernon, NY [sic] (b/IV-30-1838 Mt Vernon, NH [sic]; d/VIII-19-1896) MD Harvard 1867; AB Amherst 1862. *Bost m&s j* 135: 249, 1896. *JAMA* 27:1119, 1896.

KITTREDGE, EDMUND FOSTER, S Danvers Mass (d/III-14-1865) MD Harv'd 1862. *Bost m&s j* 72:188 1865.

KITTREDGE, EDWARD AUGUSTUS, Auburndale, Mass (b/1811 Salem; d/II-25-1869) MD Bowdoin 1831. *Bost m&s j* 3: 88, 1869.

KITTREDGE, FLOYER GALEN, Peabody, Mass; CW-USA; (d/VI-1-1878) MD Harv'd 1845. *Harv in CW*:231.

KITTREDGE, GEORGE WASHINGTON, New Market, NH 1835- (b/I-31-1805 Epping, NH; d/II-6-1880 or III-6-1881) ng Harvard Med Dept. *Med surg rep Phila* 42: 264, 1880. *Biogr direct US Congress*.

KITTREDGE, INGALLS, Beverly, Mass (b/1770? d/VI-17-1856 @86) <att Harvard> *Bost m&s j* 54: 427, 1856.

KITTREDGE, INGALLS, Beverly Mass (b/1779? d/II-14-1867) MD Harvard 1823; AB 1820. *Bost m&s j* 76:68, 1867.

KITTREDGE, JOHN THEODORE, Framingham, Mass (b/I-24-1811; d/IX-25-1837) MD Harvard 1833; AB Amherst 1828. *Amherst, Men of*: 1828.

KITTREDGE, JOSIAH, Nashua NH; Montclair NJ (b/X-15-1793; d/X-29-1872) Hon MD Dartmouth 1832. *Bost m&s j* ns10: 332, 1872. *Med surg rep Phila* 27: 416, 1872. *Tr AMA* 24:365, 1873.

KITTREDGE, KENDALL, Billerica, Mass (b/1773? d/XII-5-1857 @84 Mt Deseret, Me) MD ? *Bost m&s j* 57: 475, 1857.

KITTREDGE, RUFUS, Portsmouth, NH (b/VI-28-1789 Tewksbury, Mass; d/II-21-1854) MD ? AM Harvard 1810. Palmer's *Necrol Harv alum*: 30-31.

KITTREDGE, RUFUS JAY, Cincinnati, O (b/1828 Chester, NH; d/IX-3-1850) ng Dartmouth Med 1848; AB 1847. *New Hamp j m* 1:198, 1851.

KITTRELL, BENJAMIN FRANKLIN, CW-CSA; Black Hawk, Miss (b/XII-24-1836 Greensboro, Ala; d/IV-22-1897) <MD New Orl Sch Med 1861> *JAMA* 28: 955, 1897. *Atkinson* I: 460. *Polk* 1886: 524.

KLAMER, HUGO, NYC (d/XI-16-1899 @40) MD UCNY 1894. *JAMA* 33: 1375, 1899. *Polk* 1896: 1062.

KLAPP, HENRY MILNOR, Philadelphia (d/VI-4-1873) MD UPa 1859. *Med surg rep Phila* 28:470, 1873.

KLAPP, JOSEPH Jr, CW-USA; Philadelphia (b/I-17-1817; d/II-26 1885) MD UPa 1839; AB 1837. *Med surg rep Phila* 52:384, 1885. *Atkinson* I: 186. *Tr Pa St Med Soc* 17: 385-87, 1885.

KLAPP, WILLIAM HENRY, Philadelphia (b/X-14-1808; d/IV-28-1855 or 86. *Tr CPP* cent vol: 241. *Tr Pa St Med Soc* 1857: 166-71.

KLAPPER, FREDERICK, NYC (d/III-4-1873 at sea) <MD Berlin 1868> *Med reg NY NJ Conn* 1873: 342.

KLAWITTER, DAVID RICHARD, Brooklyn (b/VII-15 1839 Danzig; d/X-30-1871) MD Greifswald 1863. *Med reg NY NJ Conn* 1872: 349.

KLEEFUS, JOSEPH MICHAEL, Detroit (d/VII-30-1898 @40) MD U Mich 1883. *JAMA* 31: 366, 1898. *Polk* 1896: 749.

KLEIN, ALEXANDER, Corryville O (b/XII-8-1862 Hungary; d/I-22-1900) MD LICH 1889. *JAMA* 34: 313, 1900.

KLEINSCHMIDT, CARL HERMANN ANTON, Washington, DC; CW-CSA (b/X-12-1839 Petershagen, Westphalia; d/V-20-1905) MD Georgetown 1862; PhD 1889. *Atkinson* I:531. *Hist M S DC:* 286. *K&B* III: 706.

KLEMMER, WILLIAM NICHOLAS, Germania, Pa (d/I 23-1906 @46) MD Jefferson 1893. *Pa m j* 9:359, 1905/06. *Flint* 1897: 802.

KLINE, E P , Thomasville, Miss (d/IV-2-1895) MD ? *New Orl m&s j* ns23: 254, 1895. *Polk* 1886: 524.

KLING, FRANKLIN B , Williamstown, Pa (d/X-4-1905) <MD Balto 1876> *Pa m j* 9:127, 1905/06. *Flint* 1897: 840.

KLINGENSMITH, ISRAEL PUTNAM, Blairsville, Pa (d/IX-27-1904 @54) MD Jefferson 1875. *Pa m j* 8: 335, 1904/05. *Flint* 1897: 796.

KLINGHAMMER, WILLIAM JEROME, Roxbury, Mass (d/X-1-1888 @31) MD Harvard 1884; AB Tufts 1879. *Bost m&s j* 119: 348, 1888.

KLOPSCH, OSMAR EGINHARD HUGO [or Eginhard Hugo Osmar] NYC (d/VI-21-1891) MD Berlin 1842. *Med reg NY NJ Conn* 1892:281. *Polk* 1886: 683.

KLUEBER, CHARLES JULIUS, Baltimore (b/IV-10-

1839 Gny; d/VI–21–1878) MD U Md 1872. *Med annals Md:* 469. *Butler* 1878: 320.

KNAFFLE, RUDOLPH, Knoxville, Tenn (b/II–20–1809 Austria; d/III– –1881) <MD Vienna 1835> *Tr M S Tenn* 1883: 65–66. *Butler* 1878: 742.

KNAPEN, ASA PALMER, Jamesburgh, NY (b/IX– –1837 Herkimer Co; d/I–7–1879) MD U Vt 1865; AB Williams 1864. *Tr Med Soc NJ* 1879: 206–07. *Butler* 1878: 471.

KNAPP, EDWIN ABBOTT, Onondaga Co, NY (d/XII–7 1890) MD Geneva 1851. *Tr Med Soc St NY* 11: 741 ff, 1894. *Polk* 1886:665.

KNAPP, EPHRAIM, Attleboro, Mass (b/1780? d/XII–17 1860 @80) MD *Bost m&s j* 63: 468, 1861.

KNAPP, GIDEON LEE, NYC (d/XII–7–1895 @39) MD CPSNY 1878. *Bost m&s j* 133:605–06, 1895.

KNAPP, JAMES B, Bardolph Ill (d/VII–1–1906) MD Buffalo 1870. *Ill m j* ns2:141,1900. *Polk* 1886: 254.

KNAPP, JOHN HALL, Cortland Co, NY (b/New Fairfield, Conn; d/IV–30–1886) Lic Chenango Co M S 1843; Hon MD Geneva 1861. *Tr M S St NY* 11: 741 ff, 1894.

KNAPP, MOSES LONG, Balto 1829–30; Keokuk Ia; Indiana 1847; Mexico (b/1799 NY; d/1879 Cadereyta, Mex) MD Jeff'n 1826. *Med ann Md:*469. *K&B* III:708.

KNAPP, WARREN A BICKEL, Pottstown, Pa (d/XII 8–1894 @30) MD Jefferson 1893. *JAMA* 23: 961, 1894.

KNEASS, NICHOLAS WILLIAMSON, Baltimore; CW USA (b/IX–21–1840 Phila; d/XI–25–1896) MD Hahnemann 1868. *Tr Am Inst Hom* 1897: 63. *Polk* 1886: 437.

KNEELAND, JONATHAN, S Onondaga, NY (d/V–21–1898 @66 Syracuse) Cert 1848. *JAMA* 30:1366, 1898. *Tr Med Soc St NY* 1899:435(In Mem). *Polk* 1890:851.

KNEELAND, SAMUEL, Boston; CW–USA (b/VIII–1–1821; d/IX–27–1888) MD Harvard 1843; AB 1840. *Bost m&s j* 119:372, 1888. *Atkinson* I:60. *Harv in CW*: 15. *K&B* III: 709.

KNEPFLER, NATHAN, Shelbyville, Ky (b/X– –1803 Hungary; d/I–10–1859) <MD Pesth & Göttingen, Gny> *Tr Ind St Med Soc* 1859: 46–48.

KNICKERBOCKER, SIMEON C , Watertown, NY (d/II–10–1890) MD Homeop Hosp Cleveland 1861. *Med vis* 6:103, 1890. *Polk* 1886: 714. Homeopath.

KNIEF, JOHN DIEDRICK, NYC (d/IX–8–1898) MD Bellevue 1887. *JAMA* 31:808, 1898.

KNIGHT, ALBION WILLIAMSON, White Springs, Fla 1849–72; Jacksonville 1872– (b/I–5–1822 Falmouth, Me; d/IX–7–1889) MD Bowdoin 1848; AB 1841. *Bowdoin cat*: 1841. *Polk* 1886: 218.

KNIGHT, AQUILLA LEIGHTON, W Columbia, WVa (b/XII–25–1823; d/V–27–1897 @74) MD Cleveland Med Coll 1850. *JAMA* 28: 1156, 1897. *Atkinson* I: 330. *Polk* 1896: 1153.

KNIGHT, BENJAMIN, Santa Cruz Calif (d/1905) MD Harvard 1869. *Cal st j m* 3: 234, 1905. *Polk* 1896: 242.

KNIGHT, CARLOS WALSH, USN 1864– (b/V–26–1843 Matamoras, Mex; d/X–27–1876 or XI–18–1875 San Antonio, Tx) MD UPa 1864. *U Pa med alum CW*: 1864. *Phila med times* 6:168, 1875–76.

KNIGHT, CYRUS W , Covington, La (d/I–24–1901) MD St Louis Med Coll 1863. *New Orl m&s j* 53:515, 1901. *Polk* 1890: 493.

KNIGHT, EBENEZER, Brimfield, Mass (b/1789? d/VII–4–1857 @68) MD ? *Bost m&s j* 56: 467, 1857.

KNIGHT, EBENEZER ADAMS, Springfield, Vt (b/X–19–1819 Hancock, NH; d/V–6–1872) MD Berkshire 1843; ng Woodstock 1841. *Tr Vt Med Soc* 1883: 106.

KNIGHT, ELAM CLARK, Slatersville, RI; Quincy, Ill; New Haven Conn, 1860?– (d/III–21–1888 Woodbury) MD Berkshire 1845. *Tr Am Inst Hom* 1888:233. *New Engl med gaz* 23:240, 1888. *Med vis* 4: 174, 1888.

KNIGHT, GRANVILLE, Malden, Mass (b/1836 Limerick, Me; d/1900) <MD U Vt> *JAMA* 34:1432, 1900. *Polk* 1890: 708.

KNIGHT, HARVEY, Bellview, Fla (b/II–14–1846 Haverhill, NH; d/III–21/26–1891) MD U Vt. *Bost m&s j* 124:348, 1891. *Polk* 1886:468 (Lowell, Mass).

KNIGHT, HENRY MARTIN, Salisbury, Conn (b/VIII–11–1827 Stafford; d/I–22–1880 Fla) MD Berkshire 1849. *Proc Conn M S* 1880:180–185. *Tr AMA* 33:586–87, 1882. *Atkinson* I: 374–75.

KNIGHT, ISAAC DONALDSON, CW–USA (b/Md; d/I 13–1867 Phila) MD UPa 1837. *U Pa m alum CW*: 1837.

KNIGHT, JAMES, NYC (b/II–14–1810; d/X–24–1887) MD Washington Med Coll, Balto 1832. *Med reg NY NJ Conn* 1888: 262. *Bost m&s j* 117: 442, 1887. *Atkinson* I:27. *Med ann Md:* 469. *K&B* III:712.

KNIGHT, JAMES SCOTTEN, USN 1861–84 (b/X–4–1834 Dover, Del; d/III–21–1886 Hyannis, Mass) MD UPa 1861. *U Pa med alum CW*: 1861.

KNIGHT, JONATHAN, New Haven Conn (b/IX–4 1789; d/VIII–25–1864) <MD Yale 1818> AB 1808. *Tr AMA* 16: 619–23,1865. *Bost m&s j* 71:108, 1864. *Proc Conn Med Soc* 1865: 147–51. *K&B* III: 712–13.

KNIGHT, LUTHER MARTIN, Franklin Falls, NH (b/IV 11–1810 Franconia; d/II–4–1887) MD Dartmouth 1834. *Tr NH Med Soc* 1888: . *Bost m&s j* 116: 148, 1887. *Butler* 1896: 456.

KNIGHT, MOSES DAVIS, Clinton, NJ (d/III–6–1904 @ 70) MD UPa 1861. *Bost m&s j* 150:282, 1904. *Polk* 1896: 935.

KNIGHT, SAMUEL ROBINSON, Philadelphia (b/II–28 1825 Engl; d/XI–14–1891) MD UPa 1869. *Med bull m & s* 14:32, 1892. *Atkinson* I: 101. *Polk* 1886: 819.

KNIGHT, SAMUEL THOMAS, Baltimore (b/XII–20–1817;d/I–20–1881) MD UMd 1835.*Med annals Md:*470.

KNIGHT, WILLIAM, Metuchen, NJ (d/VIII–6–1872) MD UCNY 1851; MD Med Dept Pa Coll 1852. *Tr AMA* 24:363, 1873. *Med surg rep Phila* 27: 188, 1872.

KNIGHT, WILLIAM LAMBDIN, Philadelphia (b/1811; d/1877) MD Jefferson 1837. *Tr AMA* 30:826–29, 1879.

Tr Pa St Med Soc 1878: 391–403.

KNIPE, FRANCIS M , Pottstown, Pa (d/VIII–4–1894 @60) MD Jefferson 1857. *JAMA* 23:248, 1894. *Butler* 1878: 719.

KNOB, JACOB, Philadelphia (d/X–29–1902 @70) MD ? *Pa m j* 6: 260, 1902/03. *Polk* 1896: 1309.

KNODE, GEORGE E , Markleburg, Pa (b/X–19–1864 Alexandria, Pa (d/VII–8–1901) MD UPa 1893. *Pa m j* 4:817, 829–30, 1900/01; 5:296, 1901/02.

KNOLL, WALTER F , Chicago (b/VIII–24–1851 Stephenson Co; Ill; d/XI–23–1893) MD Chicago Homeop 1879. *Minn med mag* 2:312, 1893. *Polk* 1886: 266. *Cleave.* Homeopath.

KNOTT, THOMAS M , CW–USA (d/IV–5–1862) MD ? *Nat m j* 1:298, 1870/71.

KNOWLTON, CHARLES, Winchendon, Mass (b/V–10–1800 Templeton; d/II–20–1850) MD Dartmouth 1824; MD Berkshire 1827. *Bost m&s j* 45: 109–20, 1851; 46:28, 1852. *Nashville j m & surg* 1: 362–75, 1851.

KNOWLTON, CHARLES LORENZO, Northampton, Mass (d/IV–5–1898 @74) MD Jefferson 1845. *JAMA* 31:198, 1898. *Bost m&s j* 139: 52, 1898. *Polk* 1896: 720.

KNOX, JAMES SUYDAM, Chicago (b/VII–28–1840 Nassau, NY; d/VI–28–1892) MD CPSNY 1866; AB Princeton 1860. *Tr Ill St M S* 1893: 48–52. *Bost m&s j* 127: 28, 1892. *Polk* 1890: 316.

KNOX, M D , Hillsboro, Tx (d/VIII–27–1899) <MD St Louis U 1875> *Tex med news* 8:579, 1899.

KNOX, ORTHO S , Waterloo, Ia (b/V–23–1845 Bedford, Pa; d/IV–9–1885) MD Albany 1866. *Tr Iowa St Med Soc* 6:467–69, 1883–85. *Butler* 1878: 239.

KNOX, ROBERT TAGGART, Gonzalez, Tx (b/Danville, Ky; d/VII–22–1898) MD Louisville Med Inst 1854. *Tex m j* 14:275–76, 1898–99. *Polk* 1886:887.

KNOX, WILLIAM MORROW, Louisville (d/IV–28 1862 @32) MD CPSNY 1854; AB Columbia 1849. *Bost m&s j* 66:304, 1862. *Nat m j* 1:298, 1870/71.

KOCH, JOHN WILLIAM, Quincy, Ill; Minn 14 yrs (b/IV–6–1828 Fr Rhineland; d/XI–10–1887) MD Hahnemann Chic 1869. *Med vis* 4:14, 1888. *Polk* 1886: 294. *Cleave.* Homeopath.

KOCH, WILLIAM H , CW–USA (d/VIII–6–1862) MD ? *Nat m j* 1:298, 1870/71.

KOEBERLIN, FREDERICK, Freeburg, Ill (d/IV–8–1901) Lic yrs pract. *Ill m j* ns3:91, 1901. *Polk* 1896: 420.

KOEBIG, ALBERT, Houston, Tx 17 yrs (d/VIII–30–1905 ca 65) MD Würzburg 1873. *Tx st j m* 1:154, 1905/06. *Polk* 1900: 1702.

KOEHLER, H F , Arcadia, Nebr (d/I–21–1900) MD CPSNY 1893. *JAMA* 34: 313, 1900. *Polk* 1896: 901.

KOEHLER, JOHN G , Schuylkill Haven, Pa (b/1816 Lebanon; d/IX–29–1875) MD Pa Med Coll 1841. *Tr Med Soc Pa* 1876: 312–13.

KOEHNE, HENRY FRANCIS, Ohio (b/1833; d/1858) MD Med Coll Ohio 1854. *Tr AMA* 13:820–21, 1860.

Bost m&s j 58: 207, 1858.

KOEPSEL, R L , Kansas City, Kans (d/X–16–1895 @ 31) MD Kans City M C 1888. *JAMA* 25: 781, 1895. *Polk* 1890: 440.

KOHLER, JOHN PETER KERN, Egypt, Pa (b/VIII–4–1841; d/V–27–1866) MD UPa 1861; AB Franklin & Marshall 1859. *U Pa med alum CW*: 1861.

KOHNSTAMM, LORENZO JUDAH, NYC (d/IV–18 1904 @42) MD UCNY 1889. *Bost m&s j* 150: 470, 1904. *Polk* 1896: 1062.

KOINER, ARTHUR ZIRKLE, Roanoke, Va (b/1855 Augusta Co, Va; d/III–22–1893) MD UVa 1875. *Tr M S Va* 1893:219, 220–221. *Polk* 1886: 926.

KOLB, MATTHEW G , Cleveland (d/III–6–1900) MD W Reserve 1884. *JAMA* 34:703, 1900. *Polk* 1886: 747.

KOLLOCK, CORNELIUS, Cheraw, SC; CW–CSA; (b/XII–7–1824; d/VIII–17–1897) MD UPa 1848; AB Brown 1845; AM. *U Pa med alum CW*: 1848. *Buff m&s j* 37:303, 1897. *JAMA* 29:453. *Atkinson* I: 588,–89. *Waring* II: 255. *K&B* III: 713.

KOLLOCK, JOHN McDOWELL, CW–USA (b/VI–26–1836 Elizabethtown, NJ; d/1881 Seattle, Wash) MD UPa 1857. *U Pa med alum CW*: 1857.

KOLLOCK, LEMUEL, Savannah (b/1766; d/IV– –1823) MD Harvard 1822; AB Brown 1786; AM. *Brown hist cat*: 1786.

KORDENAT, CARL F W , Reedsburg Wis (b/1854; d/IX 21–1904) MD CPS Chicago 1887. *JAMA* 43:1074 1904.

KORTRIGHT, JAMES LITTLE, Middletown, NY (b/1859 Brooklyn; d/VIII–14–1899) MD CPSNY 1881; BS UCNY 1878. *JAMA* 33: 620, 1899.

KRACKOWIZER, ERNST, NYC (b/XII–3–1821 Austria; d/IX–23–1875 Sing Sing, NY) <MD Vienna> *Med reg NY NJ Conn* 1876:244. *Tr AMA* 27:664–67, 1876. *Med rec NY* 10:671 686 752 832 1875. *K&B* III: 713–14.

KRAMER, ERNST, Milwaukee (d/IV–18–1897 @64) MD Berlin 1856. *JAMA* 28:955, 1897. *Polk* 1886: 956.

KRAUSE, JOEL H , Plumsteadville, Pa (b/III–23–1836 Norristown; d/IX–12–1892) MD Starling 1863. *Lehigh Valley med mag* 4:18–19,36, 1892–93. *Butler* 1878: 719.

KRAUSE, LOUIS, London, Engl; NYC 1855– (b/1823 Koenigsberg, Gny; d/X–14–1872) MD Berlin 1853. *Med reg NY NJ Conn* 1873: 342.

KREBS, JOHN J , Clearspring, Md (d/XI–24–1893) MD UPa 1885. *JAMA* 21: 907, 1893.

KREBS, RUDOLPH FRANCIS, Reading, Pa (b/V–28–1832 Gny; d/IV–5–1890) <MD Prague 1853> MD NY Homeop 1874. *Hahn mo* 25:316, 1890. *Med vis* 6: 173, 1890. *Polk* 1886: 833. Homeopath.

KREHBIEL, AUGUST, NYC (d/II–11–1904 @67) MD U Würzburg 1864. *Bost m&s j* 150: 198, 1904. *Polk* 1886: 684.

KREHBIEL, VALENTINE, NYC (b/Bavaria; d/II–26 1869) MD Erlangen 1833? *Med reg NY NJ Conn* 1870: 322.

KREIDER, HENRY WAGNER, Galesburg, Ill (d/V-25-1905 @86) MD Rush 1856. *Ill m j* 8:80, 1905. *Butler* 1878: 162.

KREIDER, JACOB BOWMAN, CW-USA; Bucyrus, O (b/II-3-1840 Millheim, Pa; d/XII-14-1899) MD UPa 1866. *JAMA* 34: 187, 1900. *U Pa med alum CW*: 1866.

KREIDER, MICHAEL ZIMMERMAN, Lancaster O (b/1803 Huntingdon, Pa; d/VII-20-1855) Lic Columbus O 1825. *Tr Ohio St Med Soc* 1875:194. *K&B* III:715.

KREITZER, MICHAEL C , Philadelphia (d/IX-25-1903 @77) MD Jefferson 1850. *Pa m j* 7:77, 1903/04. *Polk* 1886: 819.

KREMIEN, JOHN D , Baltimore (b/ca 1846 Gny; d/I 23-1901) <MD Greifswald 1894> *Med annals Md:* 471.

KREPPS, JAMES TAYLOR, Pittsburgh (d/III-31-1901 @55) MD Jefferson 1875. *Pa m j* 5:296, 1901/02. *Flint* 1897: 830.

KRESS, EDWARD HENRY, Cambria Co, Pa (d/I-8 1901 @27) MD Jefferson 1897. *Pa m j* 4:491-92, 1900/01; 5:296, 1901/02.

KRETCHMAR, GODFREY AUGUSTUS, CW-USA; NYC (d/II- -1888) MD Bellevue 1864; <MD Jena 1867> *Med reg NY NJ Conn* 188:263. *Polk* 1886: 684.

KRETZ, HENRY F , NYC (d/IV-23-1899 @55) MD Munich 1869. *JAMA* 32: 956, 1899. *Bost m&s j* 140: 440, 1899. *Polk* 1896: 1063.

KRETZSCHMAR, PAUL H, NYC (b/VI-7-1847 Dresden; d/IV-27-1891) MD LICH 1877; att Holy Cross, Dresden. *Med reg NY NJ Conn* 1891:275. *Bost m&s j* 124:474, 1891. *Med bull med & surg* 13:266, 1891.

KRISE, COLUMBUS W , Carlisle, Pa (b/Gettysburg; d/I-23-1900) MD U Md 1871. *Pa m j* 4:157, 1900/01. *JAMA* 34: 312, 1900. *Flint* 1897: 797.

KRISSINGER, WILLIAM R , Berlin, Pa (d/VII-4-1901) MD CPS Balto 1878. *JAMA* 37:213, 1901. *Polk* 1886: 792.

KROESER, RICHARD, Lambertville NY (d/III-19 1807 @40) Stud med w/Jacob Jennings. *Tr M S NJ* 1872: 188.

KROG, ALBERT FRANZ EMIL [Albert E W] NYC (b/Gny; d/VIII-10-1897 @50) MD UCNY 1881. *Bost m&s j* 137:189, 1897. *JAMA* 29:400,1897.

KROG, CHARLES ALBERT THEODOR, NYC (b/IV-23-1826; d/X-2-1882) MD UCNY 1866. *Med reg NY NJ Conn* 1883: 232.

KROUSE, FREDERICK W , Saladasburg, Pa (d/X-7 1860 @45) MD ? *Med s rep Phila* ns5:213, 1860/61.

KUECHLER, MAX, NYC (b/VII-30-1829 Gny; d/VII-30-1886) MD ? *Med reg NY NJ Conn* 1887:269.

KUEHN, ADELBERT FRANZ, NYC (b/1852 Pittsburgh; d/X-22-1895) MD CPSNY 1893; PhG NY Coll Pharm 1873. *JAMA* 25: 819, 1895.

KUENSTLER, HUGO, NYC (d/XI-26-1882 @37) MD CPSNY 1871. *Med reg NY NJ Conn* 1883: 232.

KUFNER, JOSEPH, NYC (b/Gny; d/IX-14-1898 @60) MD Bellevue 1883. *JAMA* 31:808,1898. *Polk* 1896:1063.

KUGLER, BENJAMIN, Philadelphia (d/VI-8-1859) MD UPa 1810. *Med surg rep Phila* ns2:304-05, 1859.

KUHN, ADAM, Philadelphia; RevWar-USA (b/XI-17-1741 Germantown, Pa; d/VII-5-1817) MD Edinburgh 1767. *Eclectic repertory* 8: 1818. *K&B* III:715-17.

KUHN, JOSEPH FRANCIS, Brooklyn (b/1864 Ft Townsend, Wash; d/IX-12-1898 @34) MD LICH 1887. *JAMA* 31:742, 1898. *Polk* 1896: 998.

KUMPÉ, GEORGE ERNEST, Leighton, Ala; Montana (b/1819 Kassell, Gny; d/I-29-1887) MD UPa 1847. *Tr Med Assoc St Ala* 1888: 31, 315. *Atkinson* I:112-13. *Polk* 1886: 135.

KUMPE, JOSEPH MARTIN, White Sulphur Springs, Mont (d/VIII-4-1905 @58) MD Med Coll Ala 1873. *Ill m j* 8:256, 1905.

KURTZ, ALFRED J , Philadelphia (b/1866 Allentown, Pa; d/XII-25-1903) MD Hahnemann 1893. *Tr Am Inst Hom* 1904: 962. Homeopath.

KUYPERS, SAMUEL SCHUYLER, NYC (b/III-8-1795; d/I-10-1870) <MD Rutgers> *Med reg NY NJ Conn* 1870: 323. *Tr AMA* 21:452, 1870. *Phila med reg & dir* 1871: 303.

KYLE, C W , Sherwood, O (d/II-16-1900) MD ? *JAMA* 34: 574, 1900. *Polk* 1886: 768.

KYLE, FRANCES ELIZABETH, Sioux Falls, SD (d/VII 24-1895 Chicago) MD U Mich 1889. *JAMA* 25:209, 1895. *Polk* 1890: 352.

KYLE, JOHN G, Xenia O (b/IX-22-1819; d/III-4-1870) MD M C Ohio 1848. *Tr Ohio St M S* 1870: 249-52.

KYLE, THOMAS M , Aurora, Ind (d/1899? @57) MD Miami 1871. *JAMA* 32: 506, 1899. *Polk* 1886: 325.

LA BARTE, J N , Erie, Pa (b/Ireland; d/I-9-1876) <MD Ireland> *Bost m&s j* ns17:105, 1876.

LACHENOUR, HENRY D , Easton, Pa (d/XI-6-1893 @55) MD Jefferson 1859; AB Lafayette 1859. *JAMA* 21:784, 1893. *Lehigh Valley med mag* 5:108, 1893-94. *Butler* 1878: 719.

LACKERSTEEN, MARK H , Chicago (d/1897?) <MD U St Andrews 1858> MRCP London 1869; MRCS London 1858. *Chicago med rec* 13:490, 1897. *JAMA* 29: 1286, 1897. *Polk* 1896: 392.

LACKEY, HARPER BEECHER, Scranton, Pa (d/IX-30 1902 @58) MD Bellevue 1868. *Pa m j* 6: 260, 1902/03. *Flint* 1897: 835.

LACKEY, ROBERT M, CW-USA; Oak Park, Ill (d/IV-29-1895 @59) MD Rush 1861. *JAMA* 24:690, 1895. *Records AAS USA* 1891:57-58. *Polk* 1890: 342.

LADD, ABIJAH, Tolland, Conn (b/1788? d/VI-18-1855 @67) Hon MD Yale 1834. *Bost m&s j* 53:27, 1856. *Proc Conn Med Soc* 1870: 429.

LADD, HENRY, Melmore, O (d/I-30-1896 @83) MD ? *JAMA* 26:287, 1896. *Polk* 1890: 925.

LADD, JOHN GARDINER, Brooklyn (b/VII-4-1820 Alexandria, DC; d/VIII-19-1853 Saratoga Spr) MD

UVa 1845; AM Harvard 1843. Palmer's *Necrol Harv*: 34.

LAFON, THOMAS, Sandwich Isl; Paterson, NJ; Newark 1847– (b/1802 Chesterfield Co, Va; d/III–20–1876 @74) MD Transylvania 1827; <att Phila Med Coll> *Homeop times* 4:45, 1877? *King* 1:244. Homeopath.

LAGLE, LUTHER A , Tuscola, Ill (d/XII–9–1896) MD U Louisville 1886. *JAMA* 28:92, 1897. *Polk* 1896: 1456.

LAGRANGE, ORIAN DEMAND, Iowa Falls, Ia (d/XI–24–1899) MD Rush 1883. *JAMA* 33: 1504, 1899. *Polk* 1886: 369.

LAIDLAW, HORACE, San Francisco (d/VIII–2–1905 @ 45) MD U Calif 1880. *Ill m j* 8:256, 1905. *Calif st j m* 3:410, 1905. *Polk* 1886: 168.

LAIDLEY, LEONIDAS H , Carmichaels, Pa; St Louis (b/IX–20–1844; d/VII–28–1881) MD Jefferson 1868. *Chicago med rev* 4:401, 1881. *Butler* 1878: 719.

LIDLEY, THOMAS MORTIMER, Oakland, Tx (d/XII 12–1889 @64) MD Jefferson 1849. *Daniel's Tex m j* 5:271, 1889–90. *Polk* 1890: 1088.

LAIGHTON, WILLIAM, Portsmouth, NH (b/VIII–7–1809; d/IX–6–1870) MD Harvard 1850. *Tr NH M S* 1871: 109–110.

LAINE, JOSEPH R , San Francisco (b/1846 Canada; d/XII–15–1902) MD Buffalo 1876. *Cal st j m* 1:70, 172–73, 1903. *Polk* 1896: 227.

LAIRD, FRANK FOSTER, Utica, NY 1881–1900; Los Angeles 1900–04 (b/IV–15–1856 Stittsville, NY; d/VIII–20–1906 Atlantic City, NJ) MD Hahnemann Phila 1880; AB Hamilton. *Tr Am Inst Hom* 1906: 770–71. *Polk* 1886: 713. Homeopath.

LAIRD, JOHN BOAL, CW–USA; ?Bellwood, Pa (b/VIII 25–1825 Milton; d/XI–12–1898) MD UPa 1847; AB Wash & Jeff 1849. *U Pa med alum CW*: 1847.

LAIRD, WILLIAM TOWNSEND, Augusta, Me; Watertown, NY (d/X–7–1899) MD NY Homeop 1872. *Tr Am Inst Hom* 1900: 834. *Polk* 1886: 423.

LAJUS, DANIEL PAUL, Philadelphia (b/XII–4/5–1815; d/XI–25–1860) MD UPa 1837. *Tr CPP* cent vol:241. *Med surg rep Phila* ns5:241, 1860/61.

LAMB, FREDERICK DeFOREST, Great Bend Village, NY (b/XI–21–1849 Barker's, NY; d/V–27–1897) MD Buffalo 1875. *Pa m j* 1: 379, 1897.

LAMB, GEORGE ALLEN, Benton Harbor, Mich (b/VII 1–1837 Ashtabula, O; d/III–1–1883) MD Rush 1863. *Tr Minn St Med Soc* 1884: 181, 183.

LAMB, HENRY A, Portland, Me (d/IX–16–1901 @24) MD Vanderbilt 1901. *JAMA* 37:848, 1901.

LAMB, JAMES, Aurora, Ind (b/1818 Pa; d/III–1–1894) MD U Mich 1853. *Tr Ind St Med Soc* 1894: 227. *Butler* 1878: 209.

LAMB, JOHN FERGUSON, Philadelphia (b/XII–28–1791 Pittsylvania Co, Va; d/IV–26–1869) MD UPa 1820. *Tr Pa St Med Soc* 1871:419–22. *Phila med reg & dir* 1871: 294.

LAMB, MILTON M , Lansingburgh, NY (b/Veronica; d/IV–10–1892) MD Castleton 1856. *Tr NY St Med Soc* 11: 741 ff, 1894. *Polk* 1890: 794.

LAMB, THEODORE, Augusta, Ga (d/IV–14–1896) <MD Med Coll Ga> *NC m j* 37:277, 1896. *Med bull med & surg* 18:232, 1896. *Polk* 1886: 226.

LAMB, THOMAS WHITE, Vermillion Grove, Ill (b/II–1 1840 Belvidere, NC; d/VII–13–1878) MD UPa 1871; AB Haverford 1861. *Haverford biogr cat*: 85.

LAMB, WILLIAM WALLACE, Philadelphia (b/II–7–1841 Blackwood, NJ; d/1900) MD LICH 1862. *JAMA* 34: 574, 1900. *Polk* 1886: 819.

LAMBERT, EDWARD WILBERFORCE, NYC (b/ 1831; d/VII–17–1904) MD CPSNY 1857; AB Yale 1854; AM 1857. *Bost m&s j* 151:110, 1904. *Polk* 1896: 1063.

LAMBERT, JOHN, Pa (b/III–17–1807 Washington Co, Md; d/IX–27–1872. *Tr Pa St Med Soc* 1873: 156–57.

LAMBERT, THOMAS SCOTT, NYC (b/1819 Mass; d/ III–31–1897) MD Castleton 1845. *JAMA* 28:665, 1897. *Polk* 1896: 1063.

LAMONT, JOHN CAMPBELL, Sodus, NY (b/Edinburgh, Scotl'd; d/XII–13–1887) MD UCNY 1862. *Tr Med Soc St NY* 11: 741 ff, 1894. *Polk* 1886: 708.

LAMONT, WILLIAM, Charlotteville, NY (b/IX–4–1810; d/VIII–16–1877) ng Berkshire. *Tr Med Soc St NY* 1878:232–33. *Butler* 1874: 546.

LAMPHEAR, ELISHA FREDERICK, Providence, RI (b/XI–14–1851 Warwick, RI; d/XII–8–1880 Phoenix, Ariz) MD CPSNY 1879; AB Brown 1875; AM. *Tr RI Med Soc* 2:317 ff, 1877–82.

LAMPLEY, CALEB BLISS, Greenville, Ala (b/VII–22–1830 Rockingham, NC; d/I–16–1885) MD UCNY 1851. *Tr Med Assoc St Ala* 1885: 319. *Atkinson* I: 673. *Butler* 1874:21.

LAMPORT, LEWIS R , NYC (d/XI–12–1867 @20) MD UCNY 1868 [sic] *Med surg rep Phila* 17:458, 1867.

LAMSON, DANIEL LOWELL, Fryeburg, Me (b/VI–18 1834 Hopkinton, NH; d/II–13–1894) MD UCNY 1857. *Tr Me Med Assoc* 1894: 578–80. *Atkinson* I: 427–28. *K&B* II:677–78.

LANBECK, ALFRED, CW–USN (d/IV–21–1865 US Govt Hosp for Insane) MD ? *Nat m j* 1:298, 1870/71.

LANCASTER, CHARLES C , Knoxville, Tenn (d/II–3–1891) MD Med Coll Va 1884. *JAMA* 16:321, 1891.

LANCASTER, F M , Wayside, Md (d/I–30–1899 @70) MD Georgetown 1857; AB 1851; AM 1857. *JAMA* 32:385, 1899. *Polk* 1890: 524.

LANDIS, EDMUND MATTHEW, Chicago (d/V–6–1881) MD Rush 1875. *Butler* 1878: 134. *Chic med rev* 3: 226, 1881.

LANDIS, HENRY Jr, Reading, Pa (b/XI–27–1836 Lancaster Co; d/X–18–1898) MD UPa 1861. *Lehigh Valley med mag* 9:217, 1898. *Pa m j* 2: 325 387 1898. *Flint* 1897: 833.

LANDIS, HENRY GARDNER, Columbus & Niles, O (b/

VI-4-1848 Phila; d/V-22-1886 Phila) MD Jefferson 1870; AB Yale 1867. *Med bull m & s* 8:230, 1886. *Atkinson* I: 413. *Butler* 1874: 615.

LANDON, DILLON STEVENS, Brooklyn (d/IV-20-1873) MD UCNY 1849; AB 1843. *Med reg NY NJ Conn* 1873: 342. *Med surg rep Phila* 28:364, 1873.

LANDON, JOHN PARSON, Telluride, Colo (d/1900?) MD Bellevue 1875. *JAMA* 34:1210, 1900 (May 12). *Polk* 1896: 268.

LANDON, NEWELL EGBERT, Newark, NY (d/II-9-1906 @54) MD CPSNY 1876. *Bost m&s j* 154: 200, 1906. *Polk* 1896: 1033.

LANE, EDWARD G , CW-USA (d/XI-5-1862 @26, Washington, DC) MD Jefferson 1862. *Med surg rep Phila* ns9:190, 1862/63. *Nat m j* 1:298, 1870/71.

LANE, GEORGE ERASTUS, Williamstown, Vt 14 yrs; Ludlow (b/VII-13-1834 Westminster; d/XI-7-1895) MD U Vt 1864; AB Middlebury 1859. *Tr Vt Med Soc* 1897: 192-93. *Polk* 1886: 905.

LANE, GEORGE WASHINGTON, Boston (b/VII-7-1804 Readfield, Me; d/V-19-1833) MD Bowdoin 1831; AB 1828. *Bowdoin cat*: 1828.

LANE, JOHN FOSTER WILLIAMS, Boston (b/VI-14-1817; d/VIII-25-1861) MD Harvard 1840; AB 1837. *Bost m&s j* 65:88 1861. Palmer's *Necrol alum Harv*: 429.

LANE, JONAS HENRY, Boston (b/I-28-1800 Lancaster; d/IX-5-1861) MD Harv'd 1826; AB 1821. *Bost m&s j* 65:128 1861. Palmer's *Necrol alum Harv*: 419-20.

LANE, LEVI COOPER, San Francisco (b/V-9-1830 Cincinnati; d/1902) MD Jefferson 1851; AM Union; MRCS London 1875. *Bost m&s j* 146: 242, 1902. *Cal st j m* 1:227-28, 1903. *Polk* 1890: 198. *K&B* III: 719.

LANE, LEWIS, Toms River, NJ (d/1873) MD CPSNY 1831. *Med surg rep Phila* 28:238 1873. *Tr AMA* 24:366, 1873.

LANE, MARY JANE, Webberville, Mich (d/III-10-1895) ng U Mich 1870-73. *JAMA* 24:458, 1895. *Polk* 1886: 505.

LANE, MILTON, Lincoln, Nebr (b/VIII-14-1837 Boone Co, Ind; d/IX-1-1889) MD Jefferson 1869. *Bost m&s j* 121: 348, 1889.

LANE, NICHOLAS BITTINGER, Fred'k Co Md (d/IV 18-1853 Chamb'g Pa) MD UPa 1822. *Med ann Md:* 471.

LANE, ROBERT, Sutton NH (b/IV-2-1786 Newport; d/V-3-1872) MD Dartm 1815. *Bost m&s j* ns9:344 1872.

LANE, SAMUEL GETTYS, CW-USA; Chambersburg, Pa (b/VIII-26-1826; d/VI-2-1889) MD UPa 1849. *U Pa med alum CW*: 1849. *Polk* 1886: 795.

LANE, WILLIAM CULBERTSON, CW-USA; Mercersburg, Pa (b/III-22-1825 Chambersburg; d/III-4-1890) MD UPa 1851. *U Pa med alum CW*: 1851.

LANE, WILLIAM NOURSE, Charlestown, Mass; USN (d/III-23-1862 @42) MD Harvard 1853. *Bost m&s j* 66: 184, 1862.

LANG, EDMUND, Philadelphia (d/1856) MD UPa 1840; AB Princeton 1837; AM 1840. *Tr CPP* cent vol: 241.

LANG, IRA M, Deerfield Centre NH (b/Canton; d/V-2 1886 @50) MD LICH 1869. *Med reg NY NJ Conn* 1886: 250.

LANGAN, JOHN THOMAS, Oswego, NY; Lowell, Mass (b/Lowell; d/XI-5-1896 @40) MD U Vt 1888; MD Bellevue 1891. *Bost m&s j* 135: 506, 1896. *JAMA* 27: 1169, 1896. *Polk* 1896: 1088.

LANGDON, OLIVER MONROE, MexWar-USA; Cincinnati (b/II-2-1817 Columbia; d/1878) MD Med Coll Ohio 1838. *Tr AMA* 33:584-86, 1882. *Atkinson* I:599.

LANGE, CHARLES CASSIMIR, Pittsburgh; CW-USA (b/VI-10-1843; d/I-3-1899) MD UPa 1867. *U Pa med alum CW*: 1867. *JAMA* 32: 92, 1899. *Polk* 1896:1326.

LANGE, CONRAD, NYC (d/VI-28-1894 Berlin) <MD Königsb'g 1872> *Chic m rec* 7:150 1894. *Polk* 1890:821.

LANGER, PHILIP JOSEPH, Philadelphia; USN (d/V-9-1887 @45) MD Hahnemann Phila 1883. *Med vis* 3: 229, 1887. *Hahn mo* 22:384, 1887. *Polk* 1886: 819. Homeopath.

LANGFORD, GEORGE WASHINGTON, Williamston, Mich (d/X-28-1897 @57) MD U Mich 1869. *JAMA* 29: 1028, 1897. *Polk* 1896: 775.

LANGWORTHY, FRANK ABNER, Lakewood, NJ (d/VIII-31-1884 @34 Havilah, Cal) MD Columbian 1877; AB Yale 1872. *Bost m&s j* 111:264, 1884.

LANGWORTHY, HENRY HOBART, Rochester, NY (d/II-5-1889) MD Geneva 1848. *Buff m&s j* 28:561-62, 1889. *Butler* 1878: 561.

LANIER, EMMETT SYKES, Columbus, Miss (b/III-24 1844; d/V-5-1896) MD U La 1871; U Ala 1863- . *U Ala cat*: 183. *Polk* 1886: 525.

LANIER, ISAAC DICKENS, Calera, Ala (d/IV-3-1887) MD Jefferson 1856. *Tr Med Assn St Ala* 1887: 306. *Polk* 1886: 132.

LANIER, JAMES AUGUSTUS, CW-CSA (d/VIII-6-1862 or XII- -1862 Louisville) MD UCNY 1858. *SHSP* 22: 227, 1893.

LANING, SYLVESTER, Kingman, Kans (d/III-4-1898 @ c56) MD U Mich 1853. *JAMA* 30: 683, 1898.

LANKFORD, GEORGE ADREON, Harrisburg, Tx (d/XI-30-1899 @30) MD CPS Balto 1892. *JAMA* 33: 1632, 1899.

LANKREIT, BRUNO, CW-USA (d/X-25-1862 St Louis) MD ? *Nat m j* 1:298, 1870/71.

LANOIX, WILLIAM H , Quincy, Ill (d/III-18-1895 @51) <MD Chaddock 1883> *JAMA* 24: 497, 1895. *Polk* 1890: 346.

LANSDALE, PHILIP, USN 1847-79; Philadelphia (b/1817 Leonardtown, Md; d/VIII-21-1894 Coscob, Conn) MD UPa 1838. *Med reg NY NJ Conn* 1895: 229. *JAMA* 23:362 1894. *Bost m&s j* 131:228 1894. *Butler* 1878: viii.

LANSDALE, WILLIAM, Leonardtown, Md (b/c1765; d/III- -1801) <Dipl RCP(L)> *Med annals Md:* 472.

LANSING, EDWARD SANDERS, Burlington, NJ (b/

 Spec. educ'l status abbrev. as: ***ng*** = college verified attendance without degree;

VII- -1827 Albany; d/V-29-1895) MD CPSNY 1849. *Med reg NY NJ Conn* 1895:229. *JAMA* 24:907-08, 1895.

LANSING, JOHN V, Albany NY (b/II-16-1824 Lansingburgh; d/V-9-1880) MD NYMC 1854; AB Rutgers 1843; AM 1846. *Tr M S St NY* 1881: 376-78. *Butler* 1874: 546.

LANSINGH, KILLIAN V R , Denver, Colo (d/1879) MD Albany 1870. *Tr Colo St Med Soc* 1898-99: 508.

LARABEE, GEORGE HERMAN, CW-USA; Suncook, NH (b/IX-15-1840 Bradford, Vt; d/X-31-1896) MD Harvard 1864. *Tr NH Med Soc* 1897: 307. *Harv in CW*: 288. *Polk* 1896: 712.

LARCADE, J A, Opelousas La (d/X-12-1886) MD ULa 1876. *New Orl m&s j* ns14:402, 1886. *Polk* 1886: 418.

LARCOMBE, GEORGE GARMANY, Savannah (d/VI-28-1895 @34) MD Bellevue 1885; AB Princeton 1882; AM 1885. *JAMA* 25: 1895.

LARENDON, JOSHUA, CW-CSA; Houston, Tx (b/VIII 21-1838 Charleston, SC; d/III-7-1907. MD Med Coll SC 1861. *Tex st m j* 1:243. 1906. *Atkinson* I: 701-02. *Polk* 1896: 1435.

LARGE, JONATHAN L , Galveston, Tx (d/IV-4-1891 De Leon, Tx) MD U Md 1851. *Tex cour-rec med* 8: 234, 1881. *Polk* 1886: 886.

LARGE, THEODORE M , Dolington, Pa (b/X-3-1830; d/XII-12-1864) MD ? *Tr Med Soc NJ* 1872: 193.

LARISON [LARRISON], GEORGE HOLCOMBER, Lambertville, NJ (b/I-4-1831 Delaware Twp; d/III-7-1892) MD UPa 1858. *Tr Med Soc NJ* 1892:? *Atkinson* I:147. *Butler* 1878: 472.

LARKIN, JAMES J , Chicago (d/III-12-1903 @49) MD NWU 1880. *Ill m j* ns4:760, 1903. *Polk* 1886: 298.

LARKIN, JAMES J , Brooklyn (b/VIII-24-1839 NYC; d/III-10-1880) MD UCNY 1859. *Med reg NY NJ Conn* 1880: 237.

LARKIN, JOHN, San Francisco (b/1835; d/X-19-1890) MD Tulane 1886. *Tr M S Cal* 21:317-18, 1891. *Polk* 1890: 198.

LARKIN, JOHN BRADFORD, Mitchell, Ind (b/VI-24-1833 Vt; d/XI-5-1901) MD Hosp Med Coll Louisville. *Tr Ind St Med Coll* 1902: 417. *Polk* 1896: 482.

LARKIN, LYMAN BEECHER, Ballston Spa, NY (b/XI-8-1804 Marlboro, Mass; d/VI-9-1883) MD Berkshire 1838; AB Amherst 1835. *Amherst, Men of*: 1835. *Butler* 1878: 546. Homeopath.

LARKIN, WILLIAM RICHARD, NYC (d/X-15-1900 @42) MD Bellevue 1883. *Bost m&s j* 143:438, 1900. *Polk* 1886: 684.

LARNED, EDWARD STUART, Westchester Co, NY (b/IX-13-183- Detroit; d/VIII-23-1889) <att UCNY M S> stud Paris; AB Amherst 1852. *Amherst, Men of*: 1852.

LA ROCHE, RENÉ, War 1812-USA; Philadelphia (b/1795; d/XII-9-1872) MD UPa 1820. *Tr CPP* cent vol: 241. *Tr AMA* 24:380-81, 1873. *Med times Phila* 3:445-46, 1873. *K&B* III: 720-21.

LAROE, JAMES GILLIAM, Greenpoint, NYC (d/V-30 1906 @59) MD Bellevue 1873. *Bost m&s j* 154: 692, 1906. *Polk* 1886: 647.

LAROQUE, ALFRED, Baltimore (d/1876) MD U Md 1847. *Med annals Md:* 472.

LAROS, JOHN ANDREW, Coopersburg, Pa (d/XI-15 1906 @68) MD UPa 1862. *Pa m j* 10:214, 1906/07. *Flint* 1897: 799.

LARRABEE, JOHN ALBERT, CW-USA; Louisville (b/V-17-1840 Gorham, Me; d/VI-12-1898) MD Bowdoin 1864. *Buff m&s j* 37:934, 1898. *JAMA* 30: 1533-34, 1898. *Atkinson* I: 109. *Butler* 1878: 266.

LARRABEE, WALTER WILLIS, Saco, Me (d/I-15-1881 @25) MD Harv'd 1879. *Bost m&s j* 104:117, 1881.

LARUE, BENJAMIN, Portland Mills, Ind (b/VIII-22-1848 Park Co; d/IV-7-1891) MD Miami 1879. *Tr Ind St Med Soc* 1891: 285. *Polk* 1886: 333.

LASH, HUGH MORRISON, Indianapolis, Ind (b/VI-11 1844 Athens Co, O; d/IX-19-1903) MD Cinc Coll M & S 1870. *Tr Ind St Med Soc* 1904: 358. *Polk* 1896: 474.

LASHELLS, THEODORE B , Meadville, Pa (b/III-20-1839 New Berlin; d/V-9-1906) MD Columbian 1863. *Pa m j* 9:672, 1905/06. *Atkinson* I:189. *Flint* 1897: 809.

LASHER, JAMES H , Fulton, NY (d/XII-12-1873 @ 25) MD Albany 1871. *Med surg rep Phila* 30: 44, 1874.

LATANÉ, WILLIAM, Essex Co, Va; CW-CSA (d/VI-13/14/15?-1862) MD Med Coll Va 1853; att UVa Med 1851. *U Va Mem'l...alum d/CW*: 141.

LATE, WILLIAM M , Bridgeport, WVa; CW-USA (b/X-4-1833 Flint Hill, Va; d/IX-4-1905) MD UPa 1855. *U Pa med alum CW*: 1855. *Polk* 1886: 940.

LATHAM, HENRY, Lynchburg, Va (d/IV-13-1884 @76) MD Med Coll Va 1841. *Tr Med Soc Va* 1841. *Tr Med Soc Va* 1884:6. *K&B* III: 721 (mention).

LATHAM, HENRY GREY, Lynchburg, Va; CW-CSA (b/III-4-1831; d/V-5-1903) MD U Va 1851. *Tr Med Soc Va* 1903:272-73. *Polk* 1900:1766. *K&B* III:721-22.

LATHAM, SAMUEL C, Enfield, Ill (d/I-28-1906 @72) MD CPS Keokuk 1870. *Ill m j* 9:332 1906. *Polk* 1886:278.

LATHAM, WILLIAM HARRIS, Indianapolis (b/III-6-1814 Lyme, NH; d/IV-5-1904) MD Ohio M C 1843; AB Dartm 1836; gr Lane Th Sem 1839. *Dartm cat*: 1836.

LATHROP, CHARLES CORNING, Denver, Colo (b/IV 9-1853 New Orleans; d/V-28-1889) MD Bellevue 1875; AB Princeton 1873; AM 1875. *Tr Colo St Med Soc* 1898-99: 508. *Med surg rep Phila* 61:140, 1889. *Atkinson* I: 580. *Polk* 1886: 183.

LATHROP, DeWITT CLINTON, Norwich, Conn; CW-USA; (b/VI-20-1819 Franklin; d/IV-13-1862 New Bern, NC) MD Yale 1846. *Bost m&s j* 66:284, 1862. *Proc Conn M S* 1864:64-65. *Nat m j* 1:298, 1870/71.

LATHROP, GEORGE DERBY, Ann Arbor, Mich (d/XII 31-1895 Los Angeles) MD Northwestern 1883; att U Mich Med Sch 1881-82. *JAMA* 26:142, 1896. *Cal offl* *reg* 1889: 69 (Oakland).

LATHROP, HORACE, Cooperstown, NY (d/VII–15–1905 @52) MD Jefferson 1852. *Tr Med Soc St NY* 1905:[362]. *Polk* 1866: 657.

LATHROP, J M, Dover, O (d/II–9–1894) MD Cleveland Med Coll 1862. *JAMA* 22:313 1894. *Polk* 1890:915.

LATHROP, JAMES CAMPBELL, N Grosvenordale, Conn (b/III–19–1852 Sterling; d/VII–16–1879 Griswold) MD Bellevue 1875. *Proc Conn M S* 1880:178–79.

LATHROP, SAMUEL SALISBURY, Norwich, Conn (b/VI–5–1864 Griswold; d/XI–8–1903) MD CPSNY 1900. *Proc Conn Med Soc* 1904: 528–29.

LATIMER, EDWIN WALTER, Pr Wm Co, Va; CW–CSA (b/VI–6–1826; d/IV–20–1880 DC) MD Columbian 1860. *Hist Med Soc DC:* 289. *Butler* 1874: 801.

LATIMER, HENRY, Wilmington, Del; RevWar & War 1812–USA (b/IV–24–1752 Newport; d/XII–19–1819 Phila) ng Edinburgh Med Sch; AB UPa 1770; AM 1773. *Tr AMA* 29:697, 1878. *K&B* III: 722.

LATIMER, JAMES ABERCROMBIE, Cambridge, Mass (d/VIII–10/11–1893 @46) MD Harvard 1873. *Bost m&s j* 129:180, 1893. *Butler* 1878:341.

LATOUR, ISIDOR PERRIN, Fort Lee, NJ (d/IV–20 1886 @44) MD CPSNY 1869. *Med reg NY NJ Conn* 1886: 251. *Polk* 1886: 603.

LATTA, ELMER FREEMONT, Unadilla, Nebr (d/I–29 1894) MD Rush 1876. *JAMA* 22:234,1894. *Polk* 1886:584.

LATTA, MILTON MILLER, Goshen, Ind (b/VII–9–1822 Champaign Co, O; d/XI–30–1899) Hon MD Rush 1856. *JAMA* 33: 1504, 1899. *Atkinson* I:548. *Butler* 1878: 209.

LATTIN, GEORGE, Cattaraugus NY (d/IV–11–1900) MD Bellevue 1875. *Buff m&s j* 39:782 1900. *Polk* 1886: 655.

LAUB, CHARLES H, USA (b/1804 Georgetown; d/XII –2–1876) MD Columbian DC 1833. *Med ann Md:* 474. *Tr AMA* 28:640–41, 1877.

LAUBACH, AMANDAS JOSIAH, Ft Wayne, Ind; CW–USA (b/XII–9–1843 Allen Twp, Pa; d/III–7–1892) MD UPa 1867. *U Pa med alum CW*: 1867. *Polk* 1886: 318.

LAUBER, MARTIN, W Earl, Pa (d/XII–24–1905 @69) MD ? *Pa m j* 9:280, 1905/06.

LAUCK, ISAAC STREIGHT, Georgetown, DC (b/III–11–1820 Martinsburg, Va; d/V–17–1864) MD Pa Med Coll 1842. *Hist Med Soc DC:* 240.

LAUER, EUGENE, NYC (b/Gny; d/X–31–1866 @40) MD Marburg 1868. *Med reg NY NJ Conn* 1887: 269. *Tr Med Soc St NY* 11: 741 ff, 1894. *Polk* 1886: 684.

LAUGHTON, SUMNER, Orono & Bangor, Me (b/IV–5–1812 Norredgewock; d/II–8–1898) MD Bowdoin 1834. *JAMA* 30: 507, 1898. *Atkinson* I: 330. *Polk* 1896: 633.

LAURENT, HENRY ADOLPH, NYC (b/Gny; d/X–12–1906 @43) <MD Gny> MD UCNY 1896. *Bost m&s j* 155: 490, 1906.

LAUTERMAN, GEORGE SALADAY, Bellevue, O (d/I–29–1900 @55) MD U Mich 1868. *JAMA* 34:380, 1900. *Polk* 1890: 894.

LAVISON, ANDREW B, Hunterdon Co, NJ (d/1873) MD ? *Tr AMA* 24:363, 1873.

LAW, CHARLES KNAPP, Jersey City, NJ (d/XII–13 1904 @36) MD UCNY 1893. *Bost m&s j* 151: 700, 1904. *Polk* 1896: 939.

LAW, GEORGE E, Brooklyn (d/V–25–1895 @35) MD Jefferson 1883. MD Jefferson 1883. *Med reg NY NJ Conn* 1895: 229. *JAMA* 24: 908, 1895.

LAW, JOHN SANDERSON, Ga; Columbia, Tenn (b/1802 Liberty Co, Ga; d/III–2–1844) <MD UPa> *Tr Med Soc Tenn* 1876: 84.

LAWALL, LEVI HENRY,Bethlehem Pa(d/I–24–1900 @ 70) MD UPa 1864 *JAMA* 34:313,1900. *Polk* 1896:1268.

LAWDER, WILLIAM G, Brooksburg, Ind (b/X–19–1841 Cincinnati; d/XI–18–1890) MD Med Coll O 1868. *Tr Ind St Med Soc* 1891: 281. *Butler* 1896: 209.

LAWING, JOHN MEANS, CW–CSA; Lincolnton NC (b/VIII–21–1836; d/III– –1894) MD UPa 1860; AB UNC 1857. *UNC cat*: 355. *Polk* 1886: 724.

LAWRENCE, AMOS, Oshkosh, Wis (d/I–17–1881) MD ? *Tr Wis St Med Soc* 1881: 172.

LAWRENCE, AMOS ORLANDO, Indianapolis (b/IV–10–1849 Fitchburg, Mass; d/IV–22–1879) MD Med Coll Ind 1877. *Tr Ind St Med Soc* 1880: 239–40.

LAWRENCE, DANIEL HOWLAND, Baltimore Co, Md (b/II–29–1812; d/X–27–1879) MD U Md 1869. *Med annals Md:* 474.

LAWRENCE, EBENEZER, Hampton, NH (b/I–9–1770 Pepperell, Mass; d/VI–14–1856) MD ? AM Harvard 1795. *Bost m&s j* 54:427, 1856. Palmer's *Necrol alum Harvard*: 74–75.

LAWRENCE, EDWARD STUART, Philadelphia (d/I 22–1894 Atlantic City, NJ) MD Jefferson 1879. *JAMA* 22:202, 1894. *Polk* 1886: 819.

LAWRENCE, GEORGE CARLISLE, N Adam, Mass (d/I–6–1884 @63) MD Berkshire 1847. *Bost m&s j* 110:70, 168, 1884; 111:619, 1884.

LAWRENCE, GEORGE W, Colorado Spr (b/1849; d/VII–30–1902) MD NY Homeop 1873. *Tr Am Inst Hom* 1904: 962–63. *Polk* 1886: 182.

LAWRENCE, GEORGE WASHINGTON, Baltimore; Cal; Hot Springs, Ark; USN 1843–45; CW–CSA (b/VII 4–1823 Plymouth, Pa; d/XII–30–1889 or I– –1890) MD UPa 1846. *Med ann Md:* 474. *U Pa med alum CW*: 1846. *Med bull m & s* 13:70, 1890. *Atkinson* I:56–57.

LAWRENCE, JASON VALENTINE O'BRIEN, Philadelphia (b/1791 New Orleans; d/VIII–19–1823) MD UPa 1815. *Phila j m & phys sci* 7:171–75, 1823.

LAWRENCE, JOHN CROWDER, Murfreesboro, NC; CW–CSA (b/X–16–1847; d/VI–21–1886) MD UPa 1868. *U Pa med alum CW*: 1868.

LAWRENCE, JOHN MYERS, Allegany Co, Md; War

 Spec. educ'l status abbrev. as: ***ng*** = college verified attendance without degree;

1812–USA (b/IX-26-1787; d/VI-20-1850) MD UPa 1810. *Med annals Md:* 474.

LAWRENCE, JONATHAN S , CW-USA; NYC (b/I-1-1808; d/ VII-10-1884) MD Geneva 1847. *Med reg NY NJ Conn* 1885:241. *Atkinson* I: 78.

LAWRENCE, MORDECAI Jr, Philadelphia (d/II-21 1880 @77) MD UPa 1827. *Med s rep Phil* 42:220, 1880.

LAWRENCE, SAMUEL STERRY, Brooklyn (b/1804 NYC; d/VI-29-1876) MD CPSNY 1828. *Med reg NY NJ Conn* 1878:182. *Med s rep Phila* 35:120, 1876.

LAWSON, FRANK, CW-USA; Osseo & St Paul, Minn (b/I-1838 Pr Edw Isl; d/XII-28-1877) MD Harv'd 1865. *Tr Minn St M S* 1878:183; 1902:306. *Harv in CW*: 294.

LAWSON, LEONIDAS MOREAU [or Merion], Cincinnati (b/IX-10-1812 Nicholas Co, Ky; d/I-21-1864) MD Transylvania 1838. *Tr Ohio St Med Soc* 1865: 76-77. *Bost m&s j* 70: 68, 1864. *K&B* III:723-24.

LAWSON, THOMAS, USN 1809; USA 1813-65 (b/ 1781? Va; d/V-15-1865 Norfolk) MD ? *Nat m j* 1:298, 1870/71. *K&B* III: 724.

LAWTON, CHARLES HENRY, Wilmington, Del (b/II-15-1832 Newport, RI; d/VII-6-1894) MD Hahnemann Phila 1871. *Tr Am Inst Hom* 1895:224. *King* 1:275. *Polk* 1886: 206. Homeopath.

LAWTON, ELON J , Rome, NY (d/IV-18-1895 @59) MD Albany 1858. *Med reg NY NJ Conn* 1895: 229. *JAMA* 24: 650, 689, 1895.

LAWTON, JOHN WILLIAM, Syracuse, NY (d/1874) MD Yale 1859. *Bost m&s j* 91: 116, 1874.

LAWTON, R H , Memphis (d/IX-21-1878 Louisville, Ky) MD ? *Tr AMA* 30:874, 1879.

LAWTON, THOMAS CLARK, Cranston, RI (b/II-8-1834 Hartland, Conn; d/XI-9-1895) MD Berkshire 1859. *Tr RI Med Soc* 5:253, 1894-98. *Polk* 1890: 1027.

LAWVER, WINFIELD PETER, Washington, DC (b/XI 28-1848 Stevenson Co, Ill; d/VIII-29-1891) MD Columbian 1874. *Hist Med Soc DC:* 307. *Polk* 1886:213.

LAWYER, THOMAS, CW-USA (d/VIII-23-1862) MD Albany 1852. *Tr Med Soc St NY* 1863: 421.

LAY, WILLOUGHBY LYNDE, Bradford Conn (d/1859) MD Yale 1816. *Bost m&s j* 60:568, 1859.

LAYMAN, JOHN MARION, Maysville, Ala (d/III-23 1900 @74) MD U Nashville 1870. *JAMA* 34:957, 1900.

LAYMAN, WILLIAM S , Schoharie Co, NY (d/IX-5-1895 @65) MD Albany 1857. *JAMA* 25:554, 1895.

LAYTON, LEWIS PENFIELD, Buffalo (d/1819 Erie Co; d/V-14-1900) MD Geneva 1845. *JAMA* 34:1356, 1900.

LAZEAR, JESSE WILLIAM, USA (b/V-20-1866 Balto; d/IX-26-1900 Cuba) MD CPSNY 1892; AB Johns Hopkins 1889. *Bost m&s j* 144: 596-97, 1901. *Med annals Md:* 474-75. *K&B* III: 724.

LAZEAR, LYTTLETON LYON, Denver, Colo (b/XII-21-1867 Pittsburgh; d/II-6/8-1898 Tucson, Ariz) MD Hahnemann Phila 1890; stud Berlin, Paris, Innsbruck 1892-94. *Tr Am Inst Hom* 1898: 49.

LAZIER [LAZEAR], HENRY BAIRD, Monongalia, WVa (d/V-11-1899 @69) MD Jefferson 1853. *JAMA* 32: 1269, 1899.

LAZZELL, JAMES M'LEAN, Fairmount, WVa; CW-USA (b/XI-28-1824 Morgantown; d/VIII-15-1885) MD Jefferson 1856; MD Pa Med Coll 1859. *Tr Med Soc WVa* 1885: 335. *Butler* 1878: 851.

LEA, CALVIN D , CW-CSA (b/XI-19-1836 Yanceyville, NC; d/IV-29-1864) MD UPa 1858. *U Pa med alum CW*: 1858 [suppl].

LEA, CALVIN GRAVES, CW-CSA (b/I-21-1834 Milton, NC; d/I-12-1906 Milton) MD UPa 1858. *U Pa med alum CW*: 1858.

LEA, GEORGE GALLATIN Jr, CW-CSA (b/II-24-1847 Leasburg, NC; d/VII-4-1876 Princeton, Ark) MD UPa 1871. *U Pa med alum CW*: 1871.

LEA, WILLIS MONROE, Marshall Co, Miss (b/XI-5 1802 Leasburg, NC; d/XII-8-1878 Holly Springs, Miss) MD UPa 1826; AB UNC 1821. *Tr Miss St Med Assoc* 1879: 37. *Atkinson* I: 575-76.

LEACH, EZEKIEL WALTER, Boston (b/VII-1-1809 Manchester, Mass; d/III-2-1842 at sea) MD Harvard 1835; ng Amherst 1828. *Amherst, Men of*: 1828. *Mass Med Soc cat* 1894.

LEACH, HAMILTON E , Washington, DC (b/III-10-1850; d/V-9-1893) MD Georgetown 1872. *Hist Med Soc DC:*308. *Polk* 1886: 213.

LEACH, THOMAS WALTER, Newmarket, NH; USN 1858-75? (d/XII-30-1894 @58) MD Harvard 1857. *Bost m&s j* 123:48,1895. *Polk* 1890:76,711.

LEACH, WILLIAM, Vineyard Haven, Mass (d/IV-1-1903) MD Harvard 1856. *Bost m&s j* 148: 408, 1903. *Polk* 1896: 724.

LEAKE, EPHRAIM FITHIAN, CW-USA; Philadelphia (b/VIII-15-1821 Millville, NJ; d/XII-13-1901) MD UPa 1845; Hon ? Lafayette 1865. *Pa m j* 5:296, 1901/02. *Butler* 1878: 690.

LEAKE, JAMES, Bayou Sara, La 1884-85 (b/1862; d/ XI-28-1896 New Orleans) MD Tulane 1884. *Tr La St Med Soc* 19:20, 1898. *New Orl m&s j*ns24:418, 1897. *Tex cour-rec med* 14:123-24, 1896. *Polk* 1890: 485.

LEAL, JOHN ROSE, Paterson, NJ (b/X-20-1823 or 1825 Meredith, NY; d/VIII-28-1882) MD Berkshire 1848. *JAMA* 1:406-07, 1883. *Tr Med Soc NJ* 1883:292-94. *Atkinson* I: 388. *Butler* 1878: 472.

LEAMAN, BRAINERD, Leaman Place, Pa (b/1842; d/I-28-1904) MD Jefferson 1864; att Lafayette. *Pa m j* 7:447-48, 1903/04; 8:335, 1904/05. *Flint* 1897: 807.

LEAMING, JAMES ROSEBRUGH, NYC (b/II-25-1820 Groveland NY; d/XII-5-1902) MD UCNY 1849. *Med reg NY NJ Conn* 1893:308. *JAMA* 19:733-34, 1892. *Bost m&s j* 127:564,1892. *K&B* III: 725.

LEAMING, WALTER S , Cape May, NJ (b/III-4-1854; d/ III-29-1903) MD Jefferson 1882. *Tr Med Soc NJ* 1903: 382-83.

LEANING, JOHN K , Cooperstown, NY (d/IV-4-1902 @79) MD Castleton 1849. *Tr Med Soc St NY* 1903: [412] *Polk* 1886: 660.

LEARNED, EBENEZER TURELL, Weymouth, Mass; Fall River 1847- (b/VII-19-1812 Gardner; d/II-12-1885) MD Dartmouth 1838. *Bost m&s j* 112: 192, 1885.

LEARY, JAMES BONAVENTURA, Brooklyn (d/III-6-1886) MD Bellevue 1873; AB 1869. *Med reg NY NJ Conn* 1886: 251.

LEARY, WILLIAM BARRY, Quantico, Va (b/X-28-1836 Va; d/XI-26-1890) MD Jefferson 1859. *Tr Med Soc Va* 1891: 260. *Butler* 1878: 831.

LEAS, THOMAS B , Freeling, Pa (d/1878) MD Jefferson 1878. *Tr Med Soc Pa* 13: 780, 1881.

LEASON, JAMES A , Dillon, Md (d/IV-21-1898 @43) MD U Md 1881. *JAMA* 30:1123, 1898. *Polk* 1886: 360 (Kalo, Iowa)

LEASURE, DANIEL, CW-USA; New Castle, Pa 21 yrs; Allegheny; St Paul, Minn (b/Westmoreland Co, Pa; d/X-9-1886 @67) MD Jefferson 1846. *Tr Minn St Med Soc* 1887: 184-85. *Atkinson* I: 122. *Polk* 1886: 517.

LEAVENWORTH, DANIEL CARROLL, New Haven, Conn (b/IV-29-1828 Woodbury; d/XII-19-1896) MD Yale 1865. *Proc Conn Med Soc* 1899:374. *Polk* 1886:194.

LEAVENWORTH, FRANCIS P, St Louis (d/V-17 1857 @32) MD UCNY 1849. *Bost m&s j* 57:87, 1857. *St Louis m&s j* 15:376-379, 1857.

LEAVENWORTH, MELINES CONKLIN, CW-USA (b/I-5-1796 Waterbury, Conn; d/XI-18-1862 New Orleans) MD Yale 1817. *Proc Conn Med Soc* 1866: 269. *Nat m j* 1:298, 1870/71. *K&B* III: 725-26.

LEAVITT, DANIEL FRYE, NYC; CW-USA (d/VI-23-1883) MD Harvard 1862. *Harvard in CW*: 273.

LEAVITT, J EDWARDS, NYC (d/I-20-1863 @36 St Croix, WI) MD UCNY 1852. *Bost m&s j* 68: 90, 1863. *Med surg rep Phila* ns9:398, 1862/63.

LEAVITT, JOHN, Baptist Town NJ (b/NH; d/IV-4-1876 @57) MD UCNY 1847. *Tr AMA* 27: 657, 1876. *Tr Med Soc NJ* 1876: 133.

LEAVITT, THADDEUS LAURISTON, Philadelphia; CW-USA (b/IX-20-1840 Allegheny City, Pa; d/II-23-1880) MD UPa 1865. *U Pa med alum CW*:1865. *Med surg rep Phila* 42:220,242,1880. *Tr CPP* 3s5: cxxxv-cxl, 1881.

LEAVITT, WILLIAM BRADBURY, Athens, Me (b/1840; d/X-6-1879) MD Bowdoin 1863. *Tr Me Med Assoc* 1881: 389-90. *Butler* 1878: 308.

LeBARON, LEMUEL, Jamaica Plain, Mass (b/I-10-1780 Mattapoisett; d/XII-5-1843 Bergen, NY) Stud w/Dr Thos Kittredge, Andover; AB Brown 1799; AM. *Brown hist cat*: 1799.

LEBBY, ROBERT, Charleston, SC (b/1805; d/III-18 1887) MD Med Coll SC 1826. *New Orl m&s j* ns14:794, 1887. *Polk* 1886: 852.

LEBERKNIGHT, ADAM K , Orrstown, Pa (b/Franklin Co; d/III-5-1906 @55) MD Jefferson 1878. *Pa m j* 9:524, 1905/06. *Flint* 1897: 812.

LeBLANC, L PIERRE, Bayou Tigre, La; Abbeville 1895- (b/II-16-1861 Vermilion Parish; d/VII-17-1897) MD Tulane 1885. *Tr La St Med Soc* 19:26, 1898.

LeBLOND [LEBBOND], JOHN BYERS, Sioux Falls, SD (b/II-27-1825 Belleville, O; d/VII-24-1895) <MD Cleveland Med Coll 1850> *JAMA* 25: 209, 1895. *Tr Minn St M S* 1899:191. *Polk* 1886:202. *Atkinson* I:664.

LeBOUTILLIER, C W , CW-USA (d/IV-3-1863 St Peter, Minn) MD ? *Nat m j* 1:298, 1870/71.

LeCARPENTIER, JULES, Fairplay, Colo (d/1876) <MD Paris 1865> *Tr Colo St Med Soc* 1898-99: 508. *Butler* 1874: 68 (suppl).

LeCATO, GEORGE W , Northampton Co, Va; NYC 1869- ; Wachapreagus (b/VIII-1-1842 Accomac Co; d/I- -1903 Richmond) MD U Md 1864. *Tr Med Soc Va* 1904:274. *Polk* 1900: 1777.

LeCONTE, JOHN, CW-CSA; Savannah; Columbia, SC; Berkeley, Cal (b/XII-4-1818 Woodmaston, Ga; d/IV-29 1891) MD CPSNY 1841; AB U Ga 1838. *Tr M S Cal* 22:260, 1892. *Atkinson* I:17-18. *K&B* III:726-27.

LeCONTE, JOHN LAWRENCE, CW-USA; Philadelphia (b/V-13-1825; d/XI-15-1883) MD CPSNY 1846; AB St Mary's Coll Md 1842. *Tr CPP* cent vol: 242. *Atkinson* I: 37. *K&B* III: 727.

LeCONTE, JOSEPH, Oakland, Calif (b/II-26-1823 Woodmanston, Ga; d/VII-5-1901 Yosemite Valley, Cal) MD CPSNY 1845; AB U Ga 1841. *JAMA* 37: 125, 1901. *Atkinson* I:150. *K&B* III: 727-28.

Le CRONE, JOHN, Effingham, Ill (d/1897 @81) Lic by yrs pract. *JAMA* 29:297, 1897. *Polk* 1896: 417.

LEDBETTER, WILLIAM LEAK, CW-CSA; Anson Co, NC (b/1831; d/1870) MD Med Coll SC 1858; AB UNC 1854. *UNC cat*: 358.

LEDLIE, JOSEPH H , Pittsfield, Ill (d/V-25-1896) <MD Dublin 1854; MRCPS (Irel'd) 1854> *JAMA* 26: 114, 1896. *Polk* 1896: 436.

LEE, ALEXANDER F , Jacksonville, Ill (b/V-31-1861 Shelbina, Mo; d/VIII-19-1892) MD Mo Med Coll 1883. *Tr Ill St M S* 1893: 58. *Polk* 1890: 346.

LEE, ALFRED B , CW-USA (d/IV-25-1864 Iowa City, Ia) MD ? *Nat m j* 1:298, 1870/71.

LEE, ALFRED HOWLAND, Washington, DC (b/IV-19 1819 Ridgefield, Conn; d/X-24-1903) MD Jefferson 1839. *Hist Med Soc DC:* 238. *Butler* 1874: 93.

LEE, BENJAMIN, Pr George's Co, Md (d/X- -1863) MD U Md 1818. *Med surg rep Phila* 10:370, 1863.

LEE, CHARLES ALFRED, CW-US San Comm; NYC (b/III-3-1801 Salisbury, Conn; d/II-14-1872 Peekskill, NY) MD Berkshire 1826; AM Williams 1822. *Med reg NY NJ Conn* 1872: 349. *Tr AMA* 32:518-23, 1881. *Bost m&s j* 42:467-70, 1850. *K&B* III:729.

LEE, CHARLES CARROLL, CW-USA; NYC (b/III-24

1839 Phila; d/V-10-1893) MD UPa 1859; AB St Mary's Coll Md 1856. *Med reg NY NJ Conn* 1893: 309. *Buff m &s j* 32:693-94 1893. *JAMA* 20:696 1893. *K&B* III: 730.

LEE, CHARLES J , CW-USA (d/VIII-24-1864 Ft Smith, Ark) MD ? *Nat m j* 1:298, 1870/71.

LEE, CHARLES MILTON, Ringoes, NJ (b/XII-9-1842 Baptisttown; d/VI-11-1875) <MD Geneva> att Bellevue *Tr AMA* 27:653-54, 1876. *Tr Med Soc NJ* 1876: 131-32.

LEE, DUNCAN C , NYC (d/IV-25-1874) MD UCNY 1869. *Med reg NY NJ Conn* 1874: 278.

LEE, DWIGHT MORGAN, CW-USA; Oxford, NY (b/I 25-1843 Georgetown; d/X-5-1895) MD Albany 1864; AB Hamilton 1863. *JAMA* 25: 911, 1895. *Tr Med Soc St NY* 1896: 438-440. *Butler* 1878: 562.

LEE, EDWARD H , Chicago (d/IV-24-1904) MD Würzburg 1892. *Chic med rec* 26: 26:339, 1904. *Flint* 1897: 263.

LEE, GEORGE P , Merced, Cal (b/Mass; d/VII-26-1891 @52) MD Cooper 1876. *Tr Med Soc Cal* 22: 262-63, 1892. *Polk* 1886: 167.

LEE, JAMES, Mechanicsville, NY (b/XI-15-1818 Fishkill; d/IV-13-1866) ng Castleton 1843. *Tr Med Soc St NY* 1867:466-67. *Med surg rep Phila* 14:340, 1866.

LEE, JAMES MASON, Clarksburg, WVa (b/IV-12-1895; d/VII-8-1875) MD Jefferson 1867. *Tr Med Soc WVa* 1876: 215-16; 1884:154. *Butler* 1878: 851.

LEE, JOHN K , Philadelphia (b/V-2-1824 Allegheny; d/XI-10-1887) MD Hahnemann 1851. *No Amer jour homeop* 35:776, 1887. *Hahn mo* 22:767, 1887. *Med vis* 4:15, 1888. *Polk* 1886: 819. Homeopath.

LEE, JOHN KIDD, Johnstown, Pa (b/VIII-14-1841 Freeport; d/V-31-1889 in flood) MD Hahnemann 1869. *Med vis* 5:222, 1889. *Hahn mo* 24:587, 1889. *Polk* 1886:803.

LEE, JOHN LAWRENCE, NYC (d/II-25-1892 @ c45) MD CPSNY 1865. *Med reg NY NJ Conn* 1892: 281.

LEE, JONATHAN EDWARDS, Philadelphia (d/X-8-1868 @46) MD CPSNY 1845; AB Williams 1841. *Phila med reg & dir* 1871: 293. *Tr AMA* 21:455-57, 1870.

LEE, JONATHAN HAMILTON, Killingworth, Conn (b/IV-10-1837 Madison; d/X-8-1881) MD Yale 1859. *Proc Conn Med Soc* ns2:179, 1882.

LEE, JOSEPH, Roesville, Ill (d/XII-23-1893) Lic by yrs pract. *JAMA* 22:97, 1894. *Polk* 1886: 296.

LEE, LUCIUS J W , Brooklyn (d/I-7-1901 @64) <MD U Med & Surg 1865> *Bost m&s j* 144:78, 1901. *Polk* 1890: 219 (Bridgeport, Conn)

LEE, PAUL CORNELIUS, Montgomery, Ala (b/I-10-1835; d/III-13-1875) MD Jefferson 1858; AB U Ala 1853. *U Ala cat*: 119.

LEE, RICHARD HENRY, Philadelphia (b/V-13-1827 Pineville, Pa; d/III-21-1881) MD UPa 1848. *U Pa med alum CW*: 1848 [did not serve].

LEE, THOMAS Jr, Pr Geo Co, Md (d/IX-6-1888 Elizabeth, NJ) MD UPa 1830. *Med annals Md:* 475. *Polk* 1886: 603.

LEE, THOMAS FISHBOURNE, Tuscaloosa, Ala (b/IV-8-1837; d/VI-22-1865) MD UPa 1860; att U Ala 1855. *U Ala cat*: 121.

LEE, WILLIAM, Washington, DC (b/III-12-1841; d/III-2-1893) MD CPSNY 1863. *JAMA* 20: 649-50, 1893. *Hist Med Soc DC:* 274. *Atkinson* I: 111. *Butler* 1878:95.

LEE, WILLIAM, Stevenson, Md (b/1844 Balto Co, Md; d/IV-16-1898) MD U Md 1865. *Med annals Md:* 475. *Polk* 1886: 437.

LEECH, JOHN STUART, Downingtown, Pa (b/Harrisburg; d/I-23-1901) MD Jefferson 1841; AB 1834; AM 1839. *Pa m j* 5:296, 1901/02. *Flint* 1897: 800.

LEEDOM, JOHN MOORE, CW-USA; Philadelphia (b/VII-15-1837;d/I-8-1885) MD UPa 1859;AB Haverford *Tr CPP* cent vol:242. *Haverford Coll biogr cat*:66.

LEEMAN, S W , Honey Grove Tx; Dallas (d/VIII-5-1905) <MD CPS St Louis 1895> *Tex st m j* 1:83 1905/06.

LEET, FREDERICK H , Greenville, Pa (d/VI-23-1906 @84) MD Western Reserve 1858. *Pa m j* 9:805, 1905/06

LEET, NATHAN YOUNG, CW-USA; Scranton, Pa (b/III-2-1830 Friendsville; d/XII-6-1902) MD UPa 1855. *Pa m j* 6:260, 1902/03. *U Pa med alum CW*:1855. *Flint* 1897: 835.

LEETE, JAMES MADISON, CW-USA; St Louis (b/II-10-1833 De Ruyter, NY; d/IV-7-1897 Mineral Pt, Wis) MD UPa 1861. *UPa med alum CW*. *Polk* 1886: 564.

LEFEVRE, ALFRED, Kansas City, Mo (b/1822 Troy, O; d/VII-4-1897) MD Cincinnati Med Coll 1845. *JAMA* 29: 200, 1897. *Polk* 1886: 752.

LEFFINGWELL, FREDERICK O , New Haven, Conn (d/VI-15-1857 @32) MD Yale 1847. *Bost m&s j* 56: 487, 1857.

LEFFINGWELL, JAMES GIBSON, Pittsburgh (d/I-29 1903 @57) MD U Mich 1873. *Pa m j* 7:279, 1903/04.

LeFORGEE, WALKER LITSTER, Ill (d/VII-11-1883 @23) MD Rush 1881. *JAMA* 1: 96, 1883.

LEFTWICH, THOMAS W , CW-CSA; Bedford City, Va (d/VII-14-1901 @70) MD UVa 1849. *JAMA* 37:342 1901. *Polk* 1886: 914.

LEGRANDE, JOHN C , Birmingham, Ala (d/III-21 1906) MD Atlanta Med Coll 1886. *New Orl m&s j* 58:863, 1906. *Polk* 1890: 133.

LEHLBACH, CHARLES FREDERICK JACOB, Newark, NJ (b/III-16-1835 Baden, Gny; d/VIII-14-1895) MD CPSNY 1856. *JAMA* 25:426-27, 1895. *Tr Med Soc NJ* 1896:360-62. *Butler* 1878: 463.

LEHMAN, GEORGE F , Mt Holly, NJ (b/1806! d/IX-22 1859 @53) MD UPa 1813! *Bost m&s j* 61:208, 1859. *Med surg rep Phila* ns3:36, 1859/60.

LEHMAN, ISIDORE, ? (d/IX-12-1878 New Orleans) MD ? *Tr AMA* 30:874, 1879. *Med rec NY* 14:240.

LEHR, GEORGE Y , Philadelphia (b/1847 Gratz, Pa; d/VIII-18-1897) MD Jefferson 1863. *JAMA* 29:502, 1897.

Polk 1896: 1310.

LEHWESS, RUDOLPH, NYC (b/VI-24-1810; d/V-30-1875) <MD Gny> *Med reg NY NJ Conn* 1876: 251. *Butler* 1878 [!] 504.

LEIB, HENRY FRANKLIN, Philadelphia (b/III-4-1811; d/V-16-1856) MD UPa 1833. *Tr M S Pa* 1857: 171-72.

LEIDY, JOSEPH, Philadelphia (b/IX-9-1823; d/IV-30-1891) MD UPa 1844; LLD Harvard 1886. *Tr CPP* cent vol:243-44. *Chic med rec* 1:374, 1891. *Bost m&s j* 125: 717, 1891. *K&B* III:732-36.

LEIDY, PHILIP, CW-USA; Philadelphia (b/XII-29-1838; d/V-1 1891) MD UPa 1859. *Tr CPP* cent vol:244. *Bost m&s j* 124:474, 1891. *Med bull m & s* 13:274, 1891.

LEIGH, EDWIN, Somerville, Mass 1849-51; Townsend, 1851-54; St Louis; Brooklyn (b/IX-10-1815 S Berwick, Me; d/IV-9-1890 Kerr Co, Tex) MD Harvard 1850; AB Bowdoin 1835. *Bowdoin cat*: 1835.

LEIGH, HEZEKIAH GILBERT, Petersburg, Va (b/III-12-1833 Mecklenburg, Va; d/X-17-188) MD NY Med Coll 1856; att UVa Med Sch 1855. *JAMA* 31:1066, 1898. *Atkinson* I: 406.

LEIGH, JAMES W , Norfolk, Va (b/1829 Greenville; d/VIII-28-1859) MD Med Coll Va 1859. *Tr Med Soc Va* 1875: 66-67.

LEIGHTON, NATHANIEL WILSON, Brooklyn (b/VI-11-1833 Falmouth, Me; d/VIII-12-1899) MD Bowdoin 1857; MD NYMC 1858. *JAMA* 33:493, 1899. *Bost m&s j* 141: 204, 1899. *Polk* 1896: 998.

LEIGHTON, WALTER H , Togus, Me (d/XI-30-1896 Togue Lake) MD Jefferson 1864. *JAMA* 28: 92, 1897. *Polk* 1896: 640.

LEINBACH, AUGUSTINE NATHANIEL, Bethlehem, Pa (b/VIII-28-1832 Salem, NC; d/VIII-23-1877) MD UPa 1859. *Tr Med Soc Pa* 12:372-73, 1878.

LEININGER, AUGUSTUS, Canton O (d/XII-30-1898 @39) MD Wooster 1880. *JAMA* 32:92,1899. *Polk* 1886: 739.

LEIPER, JAMES WASSON, Philadelphia (d/XII-3-1851) MD UPa 1845. *Tr Med Soc Pa* 1856: 185.

LELAND, AARON LARKIN, Detroit (b/VIII-21-1813 Sherburne, Mass; d/1858) MD ? ; AB Harvard 1835. *Tr AMA* 13:821, 1860. *Bost m&s j* 59: 467-68, 1859. Palmer's *Necrol alum Harvard*: 275.

LELAND, ALBERT J , Trumbull, O (b/1843 Hartsburgh; d/XII-1-1883) MD Cleveland Med Coll 1869. *Tr Ohio St Med Soc* 1884: 229. *Butler* 1878: 637.

LELAND, ANTON GRANGER, Whitewater, Wis (d/XII 24-1904) MD Hahnemann Chic 1865. *Tr Am Inst Hom* 1905: 845. *Polk* 1886: 962.

LELAND, FRANCIS, Milford, Mass; CW-USA (b/XII-24-1817 Sherburne; d/X-5-1867 Boston) MD Harvard 1842; AB Brown 1838. *Tr AMA* 19:441, 1868. *Bost m&s j* 77: 220, 1867. *Harvard in CW*: 229.

LEMKE, AUGUST F , Chicago, Ill (d/I-6-1906 Pasadena, Ill @32) MD U Ill 1895. *Ill m j* 9:131, 1906.

LEMOINE, EDWIN SPOTSWOOD, St Louis (d/VII-17 1901 @74) MD UPa 1848; AB Princeton 1843; AM 1848. *Ill m j* ns3: 189, 1901. *JAMA* 37:75, 1901. *Polk* 1896: 873.

LEMOYNE, FRANCIS JULIUS, Washington Pa (b/IX 4-1798; d/X-14-1879) MD UPa 1823; AB Wash'n Coll. *Mich med news* 2:268,1879. *Med rec NY* 16:408, 1878. *Med surg rep Phila* 41:374, 1879. *K&B* III:737-38.

LENCE, WILLIAM C , Jonesboro, Ill (d/VIII-1-1900) MD Mo Med Coll (Kemper) 1893. *Ill m j* ns2:189, 1900.

L'ENGLE, WILLIAM JOHNSON, CW-CSA (b/VII--1831 Pensacola, Fla; d/V-11-1861) MD UPa 1852. *U Pa med alum CW*: 1852.

LENNOX, RICHMOND, Brooklyn (d/XI-14-1895 @34) MD CPSNY 1883. *JAMA* 25:968, 1895.

LENOX, EDWIN SEWALL, Boston & Worcester, Mass (b/II-19-1830 Newcastle, Me; d/I-7-1895) MD Bowdoin 1859; AB 1854; AM 1859.

LENTE, FREDERIC DIVOUX, Cold Spring, NC (b/XII 23-1823 New Bern; d/IX-17-1883) MD UCNY 1849; AB UNC 1845; AM 1848. *Med reg NY NJ Conn* 1884: 232. *Bost m&s j* 109:380, 467, 1883. *Med bull m & s* 5:278, 1883. *Atkinson* I: 131. *NC m j* 12:245-46, 1883.

LENTZ, LEVI R , Fleetwood Pa (b/XII-23-1836 Whitehall; d/V-27-1902) MD Hahnemann Phila 1865. *Tr Am Inst Hom* 1904:963. *Polk* 1886:899. Homeopath.

LEON, ALEXIS, Philadelphia; New Orleans; NYC (b/IV- -1815; d/IX-2-1866 Long Branch, NJ) <MD Jefferson> *No Am j hom* 15:303, 1867. *Amer homeop obs* 3:487, 1866. *Tr Am Inst Hom* 1893: 748. *Med surg rep Phila* 15:228, 1866. *King* I:190. Homeopath.

LEONARD, ALFRED MARCY, Clarkson, NY (b/1802; d/XII-13-1856) MD Bowdoin 1828. *Buff m j* 12:640, 1857.

LEONARD, BENJAMIN F , Baltimore (b/IV-14-1847; d/IV-10-1900) MD U Md 1876. *Med annals Md:* 476. *JAMA* 34:1021, 1900. *Polk* 1886: 437.

LEONARD, CHARLES P , Philadelphia (d/XI-23-1902 @24) MD Medico-Chir Coll Phila 1902. *Pa m j* 6:260, 1902/03.

LEONARD, ELBRIDGE KNOWLTON, Rockville, Conn (b/XI- -1833 Stafford; d/VI-13-1900) Lic Conn St Med Soc 1866; stud med Phila; <att Yale> *Proc Conn Med Soc* 1901:301-03. *Bost m&s j* 142:674, 1900. *JAMA* 34:1645, 1900. *Polk* 1896: 284.

LEONARD, EZRA, Gloucester, Mass (b/1775 Raynham; d/IV-22-1832) MD Brown 1826; AB 1801. *Brown hist cat*: 1801.

LEONARD, GEORGE H , CW-USA (d/II- -1863) MD Buffalo Med Coll 1859. *Nat m j* 1:298, 1870/71.

LEONARD, GEORGE WILLIAM, NYC (b/1847 Newburg, NY; d/IV-16-1898) MD UCNY 1879. *JAMA* 30: 1061, 1898.

LEONARD, HENRY, Mass 60 yrs (d/I- -1849) MD ? *Tr AMA* 3:449, 1850.

LEONARD, HENRY BAXTER, No Haverhill, NH (d/II 17–1869 @51) ng Dartmouth Med Sch 1840. *Bost m&s j* 3:88, 1869.

LEONARD, J HENRY, Chicago, Ill (d/V–19–1895 @ 28) MD U Ill 1895. *JAMA* 24: 810, 1895. *Chic med rec* 8: 458, 1895.

LEONARD, JONATHAN Sandwich, Mass (b/I–7–1805; d/I–29–1882) MD Harvard 1828. *JAMA* 9:512, 1887. *Butler* 1878: 363.

LEONARD, MARCUS BLOOMFIELD, E Boston, Mass (b/Sugar Grove, Pa; d/V–6–1887 @66) MD Harvard 1848. *Bost m&s j* 116:464, 568, 1887.

LEONARD, O L, ?Chicago (d/IV–1–1864) MD ? *Chicago m j* 21:190, 1864.

LEONARD, RENSSELAER, Mauch Chunk, Pa (b/IV–12 1821 Hancock, NY; d/X–25–1888) MD Castleton 1845. *Lehigh Val'y m mag* 1:45–46 1889–90. *Butler* 1878:720.

LEONARD, SOMERVILLE E, New Albany Ind (b/X–28–1804 Balto; d/VIII–8–1854) MD ? *Med ann Md:*476. *Tr Ind St M S* 1855:8; 1857:72. Kemper's *Indiana*: 299.

LEONARD, THEOBALD M, Pensacola, Fla (d/1885? @34) MD Med Coll Ala 1875. *New Orl m&s j* ns13: 167–68, 1885.

LEONARD, WILLIAM L, Winterset, Ia (b/X–6–1823; d/XII–19–1893) MD Jefferson 1874; MD Ohio Med Coll 1852. *JAMA* 22:97, 1894. *Tr Iowa St Med Soc* 14:329, 1896. *Atkinson* I:434, 1878. *Polk* 1886: 370.

LEONARD, WILLIAM SMITH, Hinsdale, NH (b/X–13 1832 Dublin, NH; d/VI–14–1902) MD Dartmouth 1860; AB 1856. *Tr NH Med Soc* 1902: 319. *Polk* 1896:920.

LEONARD, ZEPHANIAH, Lumberton, NC 20 yrs (b/ IV–18–1773 Raynham, Mass; d/IX–11–1823 Raynham) MD ? AB Brown 1793. *Brown hist cat:* 1793.

LERAN, WALLACE ADAM, Slatington, Pa (d/IX–16–1902 @35) MD Jefferson 1890. *Pa m j* 6:261, 1902/03. *Flint* 1897: 836.

LEROY, DAVID, Streator, Ill (d/II–27–1905 @83) MD Med Coll Ohio 1848. *Ill m j* 7:379, 1905. *Polk* 1896: 442.

LESLIE, ALEXANDER, Petersburg, Ind (b/I–15–1815 Camden Co, NC; d/IV–30–1887) MD U Md 1833? *Tr Ind St Med Soc* 1887?:201. Kemper's *Indiana*:299. *Polk* 1890:385.

LESLIE, DANIEL HEISEY, CW–USA; Spring City, Pa (b/III–12–1847 N Annville; d/II–2–1888) MD UPa 1874. *U Pa med alum CW*: 1874. *Pa off'l reg phys* 1881–87: 689 [as Lester].

LESTER, JAMES R, Lebanon, Tenn (d/II–14–1895) MD Jefferson 1860. *JAMA* 24: 337, 1895.

LESTER, SULLIVAN WARD, Troy, NY (b/Niantic, Conn; d/I–5–1890) MD UCNY 1881. *Tr Med Soc St NY* 11: 741 ff, 1894. *Polk* 1886: 712.

LESTER, WILLIAM, S Hadley, Mass (d/XII–24–1892 @72) MD Berkshire 1844. *Bost m&s j* 127: 640, 1892. *Polk* 1886: 473.

LETCHER, JOSEPH PERKINS, Lexington, Ky (b/VI–8 1807 Lancaster, Ky; d/I–6–1894) MD Transylvania 1840. *Tr Ky St Med Soc* ns3:280–88. *Butler* 1878: 278.

LETCHER, JOSEPH STEPHENS, Dallas, Tex (b/Ala; d/XI–30–1896 @46) MD Med Coll Ala 1872. *New Orl m&s j* ns24:481, 1897. *Tex cour–rec med* 14: 92, 1896. *Tex med news* 6:94, 1896–97. *Tex m j* 12:341, 1896–97.

LETCHER, SAMUEL McKEE, Richmond, Ky (b/IX–10 1841 Lexington; d/X–4–1891) MD U Louisville 1875. *Tr Ky St Med Soc* ns1:337–40, 1892. *Polk* 1886:404.

LETHERMAN, JOSEPH H, Valparaiso, Ind (b/III–4–1819 Wash'n Co, Pa; d/III–29–1886) MD CPS Keokuk 1871. *Tr Ind St Med Soc* 1886: 214. *Polk* 1886: 339.

LETTERMAN, JONATHAN, USA (b/XII–11–1824 Canonsburg, Pa; d/III–15–1872) MD Jefferson 1849. *Bost m&s j* ns9: 196, 1872. *K&B* III:739.

LEUBKEMANN [LUEBKEMANN], THEODORE, Eau Claire, Wis (d/XI–28–1893) MD ? *JAMA* 21: 907, 1893. *Polk* 1890: 1165.

LEVAN, JEREMIAH REBER, Philadelphia (d/XII–16/17–1906 @73) MD UPa 1861. *Pa m j* 10: 295, 1906/07. *Flint* 1897: 821.

LEVENGOOD, JAMES A, Honeybrook, Pa (d/VII–15–1903 @74) MD M C Pa 1851. *Pa m j* 7:279, 1903/04.

LEVEQUE, JOSEPH A, Bermuda; Natchitoches Parish, La 25 yrs (d/XII–15–1893) MD Med Coll Pa 1855. *New Orl m&s j* ns21:551, 1894. *Polk* 1890:485.

LEVERETT, FREDERICK PERCEVAL, CW–CSA (b/ VIII–10–1831 Prince Wm, SC; d/VII–23–1864 Richmond, Va) MD UPa 1856; AB Harvard 1852. *U Pa med alum CW*: 1856 suppl.

LEVERIDGE, BENJAMIN CHASE, NYC (b/1799? d/ IV–16–1862 @63) MD CPSNY 1826; AB Columbia 1840; AM 1844. *Med reg NY NJ Conn* 1865: 212. *Med surg rep Phila* 8:104, 1862. *Tr AMA* 14:204, 1864.

LEVERIDGE, JOHN H, NYC (d/XII–20–1888 @ 61) MD UCNY 1852. *Med reg NY NJ Conn* 1889: 276. *Polk* 1886: 684.

LEVERING, JOSEPH H, Philadelphia (d/II–13–1866 @ 47) MD Jefferson 1839. *Med surg rep Phila* 14:180 1866

LEVICK, JAMES JONES, CW–USA; Philadelphia (b/VII–28–1824; d/VI–25–1893) MD UPa 1847; AB Haverford 1842. *U Pa med alum CW*: 1847. *JAMA* 21: 94, 1893. *Atkinson* I: 279. *K&B* III:354 [Mention].

LEVINGS, NOAH C, NYC (b/III–4–1824; d/VI–10–1883) MD UCNY 1844. *Med reg NY NJ Conn* 1884: 232. *Med bull med & surg* 5:166, 1883. *Butler* 1878: 518.

LEVIS, MAHLON M, Philadelphia (d/XII–27 1872 @77) MD Jefferson 1833. *Med surg rep Phila* 28: 52, 1873.

LEVIS, RICHARD J, Philadelphia (b/VI–28–1827; d/XI 12–1890 Cedarcroft, Pa) MD Jefferson 1848. *JAMA* 15: 880, 1890. *Bost m&s j* 123:504, 1890. *Nashville j m&s* 46:530–31 1890. *K&B* III:739. *Butler*1878:690.

LEVISON, HUGO ADOLPH, NYC (d/III–17–1901) MD CPSNY 1896. *Bost m&s j* 144: 318, 1901.

LEWI, JOSEPH, Albany, NY (b/VIII–17–1820 Radnitz,

Austria; d/XII-19-1897) MD U Vienna 1847. *Buffalo m&s j* 37: 542, 1898. *Tr Med Soc St NY 1878*: 409-10. *Polk* 1890: 760.

LEWIS, AARON, Waukegan, Ill (d/VI-24-1901 @83 Louisa, Va) MD Ind Med Coll 1845. *JAMA* 37:43, 1901. *Polk* 1886: 301.

LEWIS, AMOS C , Fordham Heights, NYC (d/XII-28-1901 @59) MD Cincinnati Coll Med & Surg 1871. *Bost m&s j* 146: 28, 1902. *Polk* 1896:1064.

LEWIS, CHARLES GRIGSBY, Ottumwa, Ia (b/X-25-1832 Urbana, O; d/V-8-1900) MD CPS Keokuk 1859. *Tr Ia St Med Soc* 19:444-46, 1901. *Polk* 1886:535.

LEWIS, CHARLES STUART, Charlie Hope, Va (d/VIII 13-1873) MD UPa 1838. *Tr Med Soc Va* 1874:54.

LEWIS, D[AVID?] T[HACKER?], CW-USN (d/IX-3-1862 abd Ethan Allen) <ng Castleton 1835> *Nat m j* 1:298, 1870/71.

LEWIS, DAVID WILLIAM, Pittsburgh (d/XI-9-1873 @50) MD Jefferson 1846? *Med s rep Phil* 29:418, 1873.

LEWIS, EDWARD Jr, Rutland Co, Vt to 1835; Jackson, Mich (b/VII-6-1796 Hampton, NY; d/I-1-1867) MD Castleton 1824. *Bost m&s j* 76:28, 1867. *Med surg rep Phila* 16:80, 1867.

LEWIS, EDWIN, Jersey City, NJ (d/VII-5-1876) MD Berkshire 1835. *Tr AMA* 28:625, 1877. *Tr Med Soc NJ* 1877:[126]. *Med surg rep Phila* 35:120, 1876.

LEWIS, FRANCIS WEST, CW-USA; Philadelphia (b/VI-17-1825; d/II- -1902) MD Jefferson 1846; AB UPa 1843. *Tr CPP* cent vol:244; 3s25:li-lvi, 1903. *Pa m j* 6:260-61, 1902/03. *K&B* III: 740-41.

LEWIS, FREDERICK W , Philadelphia (d/XII-8-1873) MD UPa 1867. *Tr CPP* cent vol: 244.

LEWIS, GEORGE, NYC (b/IX-1-1823; d/IV-24-1863 St Paul, Minn) MD CPSNY 1851; att Dartmouth Med Sch 1 yr. *Med reg NY NJ Conn* 1865:220. *Tr AMA* 14:206, 1864. *K&B* III: 741.

LEWIS, GEORGE F , Brooklyn (d/1867) MD LICH 1866. *Med reg NY NJ Conn* 1868: 330.

LEWIS, HENRY G , Plymouth, NC (b/V-31-1842 Tyrrell Co; d/I-19-1880) MD CPS Balto 1873. *NC m j* 5:136, 1880.

LEWIS, J K , CW-USA (d/X-12-1862) MD ? *Nat m j* 1:298, 1870/71.

LEWIS, JOHN, Denison, Tex (d/IX-26-1878 Holly Springs, Miss) MD ? *Tr AMA* 30:874, 1879.

LEWIS, JOHN, Charlottesville, Va (d/IX-5-1884) MD ? *Tr Med Soc Va* 1884: 8. *Butler* 1878:832.

LEWIS, JOHN C , Panama, NY (d/II-6-1897 @48) MD Buffalo 1874. *Buffalo m&s j* 36:618-19, 1897. *JAMA* 28: 523, 1897.

LEWIS, JOHN P , Eatontown, NJ (b/X-1-1788; d/II-27 1861) <att CPSNY 1810> *Med surg rep Phila* ns5:635, 1860/61. *Tr Med Soc NJ* 1871: 89.

LEWIS, JOHN ROWLAND, King William CH, Va (d/XII-9-1899) MD ?UVa 1842. *JAMA* 33: 1632, 1899. *Polk* 1896: 1492.

LEWIS, LOUIS, Philadelphia (b/Engl; d/II-19-1902 @63) MRCPS(L) 1862; <MD U London 1862 MD Rostock 1865> *Bost m&s j* 146:242, 1902. *Pa m j* 6:260, 1902/03. *Polk* 1893: 1108.

LEWIS, MAGNUS MEWES, Alexandria, Va; CW-CSA (b/II-8-1824 Jefferson Co; d/I-19-1884) MD Jefferson 1846; att UVa Med Dept. *Tr Med Soc Va* 1884:7. *Atkinson* I:453-4. *JAMA* 2:222-23,1884. *Butler* 1878:832.

LEWIS, RICHARD F , Lumberton NC; CW-CSA (d/VII 14-1901 @64) <MD UCNY> att UNC 1855-58. *JAMA* 37:398, 1901. *Polk* 1886: 724.

LEWIS, RICHMOND A , Richmond, Va (b/1824; d/III-18-1900) MD Transylvania 1847. *JAMA* 34:830, 1900. *Polk* 1886: 925.

LEWIS, ROBERT S, Culpeper Va (d/XI-28-1897 @ 68) MD Jeff'n 1856. *JAMA* 29:123, 1897. *Polk* 1896: 1488.

LEWIS, ROLAND SEARS, Dubuque (b/1810; d/1869) MD Geneva 1840. *Tr AMA* 31:1060, 1880. *Tr Ia St Med Soc* 1867-71: 265.

LEWIS, SAMUEL, Philadelphia (b/XI-16-1813 Barbadoes; d/XI-15-1890) MD Edinburgh 1840; MRCS(L) 1839. *Tr CPP* cent vol: 244; 3s12:xci-ciii, 1890. *K&B* III: 741.

LEWIS, SMITH HAINES, Mercer Co NJ (b/V-15-1858; d/III-12-1891) MD UPa 1881. *Tr M S NJ* 1891: 231-32.

LEWIS, THOMAS Jr, Mahanoy City Pa (d/X-9-1906 @ 45) MD CPS Balto 1881. *Pa m j* 10: 295, 1906/07.

LEWIS, WILLIAM ALBERT, Moosup, Conn (b/VIII-25-1829 W Greenwich, RI; d/IV-20/28-1895) MD Harvard 1851. *JAMA* 24: 690, 1895. *Proc Conn Med Soc* 1896:335-36. *Butler* 1878: 79.

LEWIS, WINSLOW, Boston (b/VII-8-1799; d/VIII-3-1875 Granville) MD Harvard 1822; AB 1819. *Bost m&s j* 16:199-200, 1875. *K&B* III: 742.

LEWITT, WILLIAM, San Francisco (b/1828 Leicester, Engl; d/VIII-3-1883) MD Jefferson 1855. *Tr Cal St Med Soc* 1884: 245-46.

LEYDA, JAMES HARVEY, CW-USA; Allegheny, Pa (b/IV-4-1843 Bentleysville; d/IV-22-1899) MD UPa 1870. *U Pa med alum CW*: 1870. *Polk* 1886: 790.

LIBBY, ALVAN, Wells, Me (b/I-10-1818 Newfield; d/VI-21-1874) MD Dartmouth 1843. *Tr Me Med Assoc* 1874-76: 424-26 [?]

LIBBY, ANSEL JOSEPH, CW-USA (b/VIII-24-1834 Dexter, Me; d/XII-25-1862 E New York) MD Bowdoin 1860. *Nat m j* 1:298, 1870/71.

LICHTENTHALER, HENRY ALBERT, CW-USA; Lock Haven, Pa (b/1829 Limestoneville; d/V-3-1872) MD UPa 1851. *U Pa med alum CW*: 1851.

LICHTENTHALER, HERNY C , Lock Haven, Pa; Larned, Kans (b/1860; d/III-19-1895 Lock Haven) MD UPa 1882. *JAMA* 24: 497, 1895.

LICKLE, JOHN D , Baltimore (d/III-20-1900 @ c56) MD Balto U 1887. *JAMA* 34:830, 1900. *Polk* 1896: 662.

 Spec. educ'l status abbrev. as: ***ng*** = college verified attendance without degree;

LIDDLE, HERBERT JAMES, NYC (b/Bkln; d/VI-25-1906 @32) MD LICH 1896. *Bost m&s j* 155: 26, 1906.

LIDELL, JOHN A , NYC (b/XI-10-1823; d/VII-10-1883) MD Albany 1848. *Med reg NY NJ Conn* 1884: 232. *Med s rep Phila* 49:84, 1883.

LIEBER, FRANCIS, USA (b/1869 St Paul, Minn; d/X-10-1898 Fernandia, Fla) MD UPa 1891. *JAMA* 31:997, 1898. *Hist Med Soc DC:* 363. *Polk* 1896: 304.

LIEBERMANN, CHARLES H , Washington, DC (b/IX 15-1813 Riga, Russia; d/III-27-1886) <MD U Berlin 1838; AM Dorpat 1836> *Hist Med Soc DC:* 235. *JAMA* 7: 222-23. *K&B* III: 742.

LIEBMANN, GUSTAV, Boston (b/I-27-1833 Gny; d/II-20-1904) MD Tübingen 1856. *Bost m&s j* 150:226, 1904. *Polk* 1896: 701.

LIEBOLD, CARL THEODORE, NYC (d/XI-29-1886 @55) MD ? *No Am j hom* 35:1, 1887. *Med vis* 3: 12, 1887. *Polk* 1886: 685. Homeopath.

LIGGETT, GEORGE, Wooster O (d/XII-24-1893 @60) Med Coll Ohio 1857. *JAMA* 22:31,1894. *Polk* 1890: 941.

LIGGETT, JOSHUA WILLARD, Philadelphia (d/I-26-1902) MD UPa 1898. *Pa m j* 5:277, 1901/02; 6:261, 1902/03.

LIGHT, ABIAH HUTCHINSON, CW-USA; Lebanon, Pa (b/1839 Avon; d/VII-21-1901) MD UPa 1862. *Pa m j* 5:296. 1901/02. *U Pa med alum CW*: 1862. *Butler* 1878: 720.

LIGHT, AMOS BURKHOLDER, N Vernon, Ind (b/X-15-1843 Lebanon Co, Pa; d/VII-4-1901) MD UPa 1866. *Tr Ind St Med Soc* 1902: 418. *Polk* 1896: 485.

LIGHT, SAMUEL BAHL, CW-USA; Lebanon, Pa (b/III-15-1839; d/VII-7-1886) MD UPa 1863; AB Franklin & Marshall 1858. *U Pa med alum CW*: 1863.

LIGHTFOOT, PHILIP F , Murrayville, Ill (d/I-14-1906 @82) Lic yrs pract *Ill m j* 9:228, 1906. *Polk* 1896: 431.

LIGON, EDWIN T C , Black Jack Grove, Tex (d/IV-5-1883) MD Tulane 1873. *Tex med & surg rec* 3:717, 1883. *Polk* 1886: 881.

LILES, JASPER DAVID, Roanoke, Ala (d/II-13-1897) MD U Louisville 1870. *Tr Med Assoc St Ala* 1899: 233. *Polk* 1893: 163.

LILIENTHAL, JAMES EDWARD, NYC to 1887; San Francisco (b/X-3-1844 Hamburg SC; d/IX-27-1895) MD NY Homeop 1880. *Tr Am Inst Hom* 1896: 1191. *Polk* 1886: 685. Homeopath.

LILIENTHAL, SAMUEL, NYC (d/X-3-1891 @75) MD U Munich 1838. *No Amer jour homeop* 39:749, 1891. *Med vis* 7:352, 363, 1891. *Polk* 1886: 685. Homeopath.

LILLISTON, ALBERT HERBERT, Accomac CH, Va (d/XII-19-1904 @c30) MD UVa 1898; <pg Johns Hopkins> *Tr Med Soc Va* 1905:449-51. *Polk* 1900: 1755.

LILLY, HENRY MARTIN, CW-USA; Fond du Lac Wis (b/1831; d/XI-28-1870) MD U Mich 1857; AB Beloit 1853. *Tr AMA* 23:597-99, 1872. *Nw m&s j* 2:297-302, 1871. *Tr Wis St Med Soc* 1881: 357.

LILLY, JOHN, Lambertville, NJ (b/1783 Engl; d/1848) Stud w/Dr Samuel Stringer; lic 1807. *Tr Med Soc NJ* 1872: 125-26.

LILLY, SAMUEL, Lambertville, NJ (b/X-15-1815 Geneva, NY; d/IV-3-1880) MD UPa 1837. *Tr Med Soc NJ* 1880: 118-21. *Tr AMA* 31:1061-64, 1880. *Atkinson* I: 507. *Butler* 1878: 472.

LILLY, THOMAS W , La (d/1878 Delhi, La) MD Tulane 1857. *Tr AMA* 30:874, 1879.

LIMBERG, FERDINAND AUGUST, Rimersburg, Pa to 1879; La Java, Colo (b/I-31-1852 Manitowoc, Wis; d/V 12-1890) MD Jefferson 1875; AB Franklin & Marshall 1873. *F&M obit rec*: 227-28. *Polk* 1886: 182 (Conejos, Colo).

LIMPERT, LUDWIG G W , NYC (b/V-2-1831 Gny; d/VI-14-1887) <MD U Marburg 1854> *Med reg NY NJ Conn* 188: 263. *Polk* 1886: 685.

LINCECUM, GIDEON, War 1812-USA; Long Point Tx; Tuscaloosa, Ala; Mississippi (b/IV- -1793 Hancock Co, Ga; d/XI-28 1873) Stud med in Ga. Owen's *Dict Ala biog* 4:1048.

LINCOLN, ARTHUR TALBOT, Dennysville, Me (d/X-18-1899) MD Harvard 1889; att Amherst 1879. *JAMA* 33: 1183, 1899.

LINCOLN, BENJAMIN, Boston 1827-29; Burlington, Vt 1829-34 (b/X-11-1802 Dennysville, Me; d/II-26-1835) MD Bowdoin 1827; AB 1823. *Bowdoin cat*: 1823. *K&B* III: 743-44.

LINCOLN, FRANCIS MINOR, CW-USN & USA; Wareham, Mass (b/I-29 1830 Boston; d/V-3-1868) MD Harvard 1854. *Bost m&s j* ns1: 224, 273, 1868. *Harvard in CW*: 242.

LINCOLN, GEORGE COOK, Natick, Mass (d/I-9-1873 @51) MD Harvard 1859. *Bost m&s j* ns11: 124, 1873. *Med surg rep Phila* 28: 130, 1873.

LINCOLN, HENRY, Lancaster, Mass (b/VIII-11-1804 Leominster; d/II-29-1860) MD UPa 1834; AM Harvard 1830. Palmer's *Necrol alum Harvard*: 328.

LINCOLN, ISAAC, Brunswick, Me (b/1779? d/III-6-1868 @89) Hon MD Bowdoin 1831; AM 1806; AB Harvard 1800; AM 1806. *Phila med reg & dir* 1871: 295. *Bost m&s j* ns1: 96, 1868.

LINCOLN, JOHN CLIFFORD, Hyde Park, NY (d/VI-18-1902) MD Harvard 1884. *Bost m&s j* 146: 706, 1902. *Polk* 1896: 714.

LINCOLN, JOHN DUNLAP, Brunswick, Me (b/VI-1-1821; d/VI-3-1877) MD Bowdoin 1846; AB 1843. *Tr Me Med Assoc* 1877:246-48. *Butler* 1878:308.

LINCOLN, JOHN RANDOLPH, Boston (d/VIII-22-1857 @28) MD Harvard 1851. *Bost m&s j* 57:87, 1857.

LINCOLN, MARK H , Philadelphia (d/XI-26-1898) MD UPa 1885. *JAMA* 32:41, 1899. *Polk* 1896: 1310.

LINCOLN, NATHAN SMITH, Washington, DC (b/IV-3 1828 Gardner, Mass; d/X-14-1898) MD U Md 1851; AB Dartmouth; AM; LLD. *Bost m&s j* 139: 404, 666,

1898. *Hist Med Soc DC:* 155. *Polk* 1896:304, 1898. *Buffalo m&s j* 38:304–05, 1898. *JAMA* 31: 997,

LINCOLN, RUFUS PRATT, CW–USA; NYC (b/IV–27 1840 Belchertown, Mass; d/XI–27–1900) MD Harvard 1868; AB Amherst 1862. *Bost m&s j* 143: 592–93, 1900. *Polk* 1896: 1064. *K&B* III: 744–45.

LINCOLN, SAMUEL W , Nelson, Pa; Moline, Ill (d/II–7–1900 @44) <MD CPS Balto 1879> *Tr Ill St Med Soc* 1899–1900; 413, 509. *Polk* 1886: 809.

LINCOLN, WILLIAM LEAVITT, Wabasha, Minn (b/ VIII–5–1824 W Townsend, Mass; d/XI–29–1889) MD Harvard 1882; AB 1850. *Tr Minn St Med Soc* 1891: 198; 1893: 121. *Atkinson* I:632. *Butler* 1878: 393.

LINDERMAN, HERBERT, Philadelphia (d/V–15–1904 @37) MD Medico–Chir Coll Phila 1891. *Pa m j* 8: 335, 1904/05.

LINDHEIM, GEORGE WASHINGTON, NYC (d/IX–16–1898) MD CPSNY 1897. *Bost m&s j* 139: 303, 1898. *JAMA* 31: 871, 1898.

LINDLEY, LUTELLUS W , Connellsville, Pa (b/II–1 1808 Athens, O; d/X–25–1881) MD Jefferson 1873. *Tr Med Soc Pa* 1882: 333–34.

LINDLEY, NEWTON ADAMS, ? (d/IX–28–1878 Grand Junction, Tenn) MD CPSNY 1869. *Tr AMA* 30:874, 1879.

LINDSAY, ANDREW, Bryn Mawr, Pa (d/1905 @76) MD Jeff'n 1855. *Pa m j* 9:221, 1905/06. *Flint* 1897: 797.

LINDSAY, EDWARD O , Greensboro & Chapel Hill, NC; St Louis (b/I–27–1849; d/IX–3–1887) MD Washington U Balto 1871; att UNC & UVa. *NC m j* 20:200, 1887. *New Orl m&s j* ns15:413, 1887. *Polk* 1886: 722.

LINDSAY, GEORGE, NYC (d/1880? @76) <MD Glasgow 1825> *Med reg NY NJ Conn* 1881:239. *Butler* 1878: 504.

LINDSEY, B ABBOTT, NYC (b/Lancaster, NH; d/XI–13–1898 @42) MD CPSNY 1881. *JAMA* 31: 1319, 1898. *Polk* 1896: 1064.

LINDSLEY, CHARLES AUGUSTUS, New Haven, Conn (b/VIII–19–1826 Orange, NJ; d/III–9–1906) MD Yale 1852; AB Trinity 1849. *Proc Conn M S* 1906: 292–97. *Bost m&s j* 154:307, 1906. *Atkinson* I: 687–88. *Butler* 1878: 79.

LINDSLEY, HARVEY, Washington, DC (b/I–11–1804 Morris Co, NJ; d/IV–28–1889) MD Columbian 1828; AB Princeton 1820; AM 1823. *Bost m&s j* 120:476, 1889. *JAMA* 32:1207, 1899. *Atkinson* I: 119. *K&B* II: 705. *Hist Med Soc DC:* 225.

LINDSLEY, JOHN BERRIEN, CW–CSA; Nashville, Tenn (b/X 24–1822 Princeton, NJ; d/XII–7–1897 @75) MD UPa 1843; AB U Nashville 1839; LLD Princeton 1856. *So pract* 19:176, 1897; 20:35, 1898. *Nashville j m & s* 83:47–52, 1898. *NC m j* 40:[426] 1897. *JAMA* 29: 1285, 1897. *Atkinson* I: 88.

LINDSLEY, VAN SINDEREN, Nashville, Tenn (b/X 13–1840 Greensboro, NC; d/XI–15–1885) MD U Nashville 1863. *So pract* 7:878–80, 1885. *New Orl m&s j* ns13:578, 1886. *Nashville j m & s* ns36: 562, 1885. *Atkinson* I: 613. *Butler* 1878: 772.

LINDSLEY, WEBSTER, USA (b/X–6–1835 DC; d/VIII 8–1866) MD Harvard 1857. *Nashville j m & s* ns4: 320, 1866. *Hist Med Soc DC:*? *Tr AMA* 18: 357, 1867. *Harvard in CW*: 249. *Nat m j* 1:298, 1870/71.

LINDSTRÖM, ALFRED HERMAN, Boston (b/III–21–1869 Sweden; d/V–17–1900) MD Harvard 1894. *Bost m&s j* 142:556, 1900. *Polk* 1896: 701.

LINEAWEAVER, JOHN KROUSE, Columbia, Pa (b/IV 30–1831 Lebanon, Pa; d/X–18–1903) MD Jefferson 1861. *Pa m j* 7:224, 279, 1903/04. *Flint* 1897:799.

LINEHAN, JOHN BERNARD, NYC (d/I–5–1890 @35) MD UCNY 1876. *Med reg NY NJ Conn* 1890: 273.

LINGENFELDER, J P , St Louis, Mo (d/1894 @50) <MD Humboldt 1861> *JAMA* 22: 276, 1894. *Butler* 1878: 418. *Polk* 1890: 674.

LINGLE, RICHARD W , Orleans, Ind (b/XI–26–1838; d/VI–10–1901) MD U Louisville 1861. *Tr Ind St Med Soc* 1902: 419. *Polk* 1896: 486.

LINN, ALEXANDER, Deckertown, NJ 30 yrs (b/VII–17 1811; d/V–12–1868) MD Jefferson 1836. *Phila med reg & dir* 1871:296. *Tr AMA* 21:465, 1870. *Tr Med Soc NJ* 1868:118–21. *Med surg rep Phila* 18:486, 1868.

LINN, HENRY C , Butler, Pa (b/Crawford Co; d/IV–3–1902 @90) MD St Louis Med Coll 1864. *Pa m j* 6:261, 1902/03. *Flint* 1897: 797.

LINN, TIMOTHY THOMPSON, Bourbon, Ind (b/X–31 1819 Washington Co, Ky; d/III–24–1896) MD Rush 1864; ng U Mich Med Dept. *Tr Ind St Med Soc* 1896: 273. *Butler* 181878: 210.

LINN, WILLIAM H , Newton, NJ (d/X–4–1877) MD Jefferson 1848. *Tr Med Soc NJ* 1878: 197–98. *Butler* 1878: 472.

LINNENBRINK, JOSEPH, Zelienople, Pa (b/IV–26–1808 Prussia; d/IX–5–1871) <MD Berlin> *Tr Pa St Med Soc* 9:76–77, 1872.

LINQUIST, CHARLES FREDERICK, New Haven, Conn (d/XII–20–1889 @28) MD Yale 1883. *Med reg NY NJ Conn* 1890: 273.

LINSLEY, JOSEPH HATCH, Burlington, Vt (b/V–29–1859 Windsor; d/II–17–1901) MD U Vt 1880. *Bost m&s j* 144:219, 1901. *Polk* 1896: 1473.

LINSLY, JARED, NYC (b/1803 N Branford, Conn; d/VII–12–1887) MD CPSNY 1829; AB Yale 1826. *Med reg NY NJ Conn* 1889: 276. *Bost m&s j* 117:68–69, 1887.

LINSLY, WILLIAM BALDWIN, CW–USA; Pawling, NY (d/VI–10–1890 @ c50) MD CPSNY 1864. *Med reg NY NJ Conn* 1891: 276.

LINSON, JOHN J , Tarrytown, NY (b/1837 NYC; d/VIII 27–1899) MD ? Coll 1856. *Bost m&s j* 141: 252, 1899. *JAMA* 33:620, 683, 1899. *Polk* 1886: 711.

LINTHICUM, D A , Helena, Ark (d/VIII–1–1899 @80)

Spec. educ'l status abbrev. as: ***ng*** = college verified attendance without degree;

MD St Louis Med Coll 1872 ad eundem. *JAMA* 33:427, 1899. *Polk* 1886: 152.

LINTHICUM, WILLIAM ANTHONY, Roseville, Ark (d/XII–4–1872 @39) MD ? *Med s rep Phil* 38:184, 1873.

LINTON, JOHN, Garnavillo, Ia (b/X–5–1811 Ky; d/VI–27–1878) MD St Louis M C 1850. *Chic m j* 28:220 1879.

LINTON, MOSES LEWIS, St Louis (b/IV–12–1808 Nelson Co, Ky; d/VI–1–1872) MD Transylvania 1835. *Tr AMA* 29:697–701, 1878. *K&B* III: 748.

LINTON, THOMAS J , CW–USA (d/IX–20–1862 Norfolk, Va) MD ? *Nat m j* 1:298, 1870/71.

LINVILL, LEWIS M , Columbia City, Ind (b/X–30–1860; d/III–31–1896) MD Mich Coll Med 1883. *Tr Ind St Med Soc* 1896: 274. *Polk* 1890: 701.

LIONBERGER, D B , Denver (d/1873) MD St Louis Med Coll 1873. *Tr Colo St Med Soc* 1898–99: 508.

LIPPE, ADOLPH, Gny to 1839; Carlisle, Pa; Pottstown 1842?–48? Philadelphia 1848? (b/V–11–1812 Gurletz, Prussia; d/I–23–1888) MD Allentown Homeop Acad 1841: stud Berlin. *Minn med mo* 1888:39. *Tr Am Inst Hom* 1888: 212. *Med adv* 20:156, 1888. *King* I: 153. *Cleave*. Homeopath.

LIPPINCOTT, ALLEN, Fallsington, Pa (d/III–5–1863 @24) MD UPa 1860; att Pa Med Coll 1856. *Med surg rep Phila* ns9:422, 1862/63.

LIPPINCOTT, DeWITT GOSMAN, Campbell Hall, NY (b/IV–15–1861 Ulster Co; d/VI–8–1905) MD Jefferson 1883; att Rutgers 1877–78. *Bost m&s j* 152:712, 1905. *Polk* 1886: 662.

LIPPINCOTT, SAMUEL WESLEY, Philadelphia (d/IX 22–1906 @36) MD UPa 1897. *Pa m j* 10: 54, 1906/07.

LIPPITT, WILLIAM FONTAINE, Charlestown, WVa (b/IX–27–1833 Leesburg, Va; d/III–11–1902) MD Jefferson 1873; MD U Va 1884. *Hist Med Soc DC:* 253. *Polk* 1886: 941.

LIPSCOMB, ELIAS D , New Market, Ala (d/III–29 1898 @34) Lic by Exam Bd. *JAMA* 30:874: 1898. *Polk* 1896: 166.

LIPSCOMB, THOMAS, Shelbyville, Tenn (b/VII–22–1808 Va; d/XII–22–1891) MD U Louisville 1850. *So pract* 14: 41–44, 1892. *Nashville j m & s* 71:45–46, 1892. *Atkinson* I: 303. *Butler* 1878: 772.

LISTER, GEORGE, Galveston, Tex (b/1817; d/1849) Stud med Dublin; att U Ala 1835. *U Ala gen'l cat*: 51.

LITTELL, NORVAL W , Baltimore (b/IX–28–1829 Newmarket, Va; d/II–11–1897) MD Jefferson 1853. *Med annals Md:* 477–78. *Atkinson* I: 282.

LITTELL, SQUIER, Philadelphia (b/XII–3–1803 Burlington NJ; d/VII–4–1886 Bay Head) MD UPa 1824. *Tr CPP* cent vol: 245. *Atkinson* I: 95–96. *K&B* III:748.

LITTIG, THOMAS, Baltimore (b/1801; d/III–30–1886) MD U Md 1830. *Med annals Md:* 478.

LITTLE, BENJAMIN RUSH, Mercersburg, Pa 1851–56; Keokuk, Ia 1856–57 (b/V–2–1829 Mercersburg; d/XII–7 1857) MD UPa 1851; AB Franklin & Marshall 1847. *F & M obit rec*: 86–87.

LITTLE, CHARLES, Acton, Mass (d/XI–17–1869 @33) MD ? *Bost m&s j* 4:324, 1869.

LITTLE, DANIEL, Goffstown Center, NH (b/III–4–1798; d/IX–4–1874) MD Dartmouth 1827. *Bost m&s j* 91: 292, 1874.

LITTLE, GEORGE STEBBINS, Brooklyn (b/I– –1826 Middletown, NY; d/III–31–1898) MD UCNY 1848. *Bost m&s j* 138:336 1898. *JAMA* 30:874 1898. *Polk* 1896:999.

LITTLE, HOSEA A , Linton, Ind (d/IX–9–1899 @30) <MD Barnes Med Coll St Louis> *JAMA* 33:808, 1899.

LITTLE, JAMES LAWRENCE, NYC (b/II–19–1836 Brooklyn; d/IV–4–1885) MD CPSNY 1860. *Med reg NY NJ Conn* 1885: 241. *Chicago m j* 50:378, 1885. *JAMA* 4:444–45, 1885. *Bost m&s j* 112: 382, 1885; 113:491, 655, 1885. *K&B* III: 749.

LITTLE, JOHN ANDREW, Delaware, O (b/XII–7–1825; d/I–13–1877) MD UPa 1848. *Tr Ohio St Med Soc* 1878: 194–95.

LITTLE, JOHN PEYTON, CW–CSA (b/I–15–1823 Wilmington, Del; d/VII–15–1869 Williamsburg, Va) MD UPa 1845. *U Pa med alum CW*: 1845.

LITTLE, JOSEPH HARRIS, Washington, Pa (d/V–16 1900 @65) MD Columbian DC 1861; AB Washington Coll 1855. *JAMA* 34: 1505, 1900. *Polk* 1896: 1342.

LITTLE, ROBERT PARKER, Mercersburg, Pa 1842–53; Columbus, O (b/I–19–1818; d/III–17–1856) MD UPa 1842; AB Franklin & Marshall 1839. *F & M obit rec*: 11.

LITTLE, WILLIAM, Raleigh, NC (b/I–31–1838; d/XII– –1879) MD UCNY 1861; AB UNC 1858. *Tr NC Med Soc* 1880: 15. *NC m j* 5: 67–68, 180. *Atkinson* I:524–35. *Butler* 1896: 595.

LITTLE, WILLIAM AVERY, Castine, Me (b/VII–20–1806; d/VIII–8–1828) MD Harvard 1827; AB Bowdoin 1824. *Bowdoin cat*: 1824.

LITTLE, WILLIAM RABY, Bloomsbury, NJ (b/X–27–1850 Chester Co, Pa; d/II–13–1897) MD UPa 1878; CE Lafayette 1873. *JAMA* 28:523, 1897. *Tr Med Soc NJ* 1897: 299–300.

LITTLE, WILLIAM SEELY, Philadelphia; NYC (d/II 11–1887 @38) MD Bellevue 1873; MD Jefferson 1877; AB Princeton 1869; AM 1872. *Med reg NY NJ Conn* 1887: 269. *Bost m&s j* 117:634, 1887. *Med bull med & surg* 9:85, 1887.

LITTLEFIELD, JOSEPH DANA, Jamestown, NY (d/III 11–1899) MD UPa 1876. *JAMA* 32:628, 1899. *Polk* 1896: 1027.

LITTLEWOOD, JAMES B , Washington, DC (b/VI–23 1843 Ashton, Engl; d/II–7–1906) MD Georgetown 1868. *Hist Med Soc DC:* 292. *Polk* 1896: 304.

LIVERMORE, ABEL CUTTING, Stow, Mass (d/III–15 1891) MD Harvard 1859. *Bost m&s j* 124:300, 1891.

LIVERMORE, FRANK, CW–USA; NYC; Paris 1865–70 (d/XI–18–1902 @61) MD Bellevue 1864; MD U

Paris 1868. *Bost m&s j* 147:606, 1902. *Polk* 1886: 685.

LIVERMORE, GEORGE EDWARD, Lowell, Mass (b/IV–4–1855 Fitchburg, Mass; d/IX–4–1891) MD Dartmouth 1884. *Bost m&s j* 125:284, 1891. *Polk* 1890: 550.

LIVEZEY, ABRAHAM, Yardley, Pa (b/1821 Solebury twp, Pa; d/VIII–31–1896) MD Jefferson 1845; AB Princeton 1842. *JAMA* 27: 661, 1896. *Polk* 1896:1345.

LIVEZEY, EDWARD, CW–USA; Philadelphia (b/VIII–28–1833 Plymouth Mtg, Pa; d/IV–15–1876) MD UPa 1858. *U Pa med alum CW*: 1858.

LIVINGOOD, LOUIS A, Womelsdorf Pa (d/I–4–1899 @ 68) MD Jefferson 1854. *JAMA* 32:92,1899. *Polk* 1896: 1345.

LIVINGOOD, LOUIS EUGENE, Baltimore (d/VII–4–1898 @32 at sea) MD UPa 1895; AB Princeton 1890. *JAMA* 31: 141–42, 1898.

LIVINGSTON, BEVERLY, NYC (b/1852; d/VII–2–1883 @31) MD CPSNY 1877; PhB Yale 1874. *Med reg NY NJ Conn* 1884: 233. *JAMA* 1:64, 1883. *Med surg rep Phila* 49: 56, 1883.

LIVINGSTON, JOSEPH ALEXANDER, W Cornwall, Conn (b/VIII–27–1869 Bklyn; d/XII–31–1896) MD LI CH 1890. *Proc Conn Med Soc* 1897:351–52. *JAMA* 28:236, 1897.

LIVINGSTON, WATTS CADY NYC (d/XII–19–1892 @73) MD CPSNY 1852. *Med reg NY NJ Conn* 1893: 309. *Bost m&s j* 127: 640,1892. *Polk* 1890: 822.

LLOYD, EDWARD MORRIS, Yardley, Pa (d/VI–21–1901) MD Jefferson 1886. *JAMA* 37: 125, 1901.

LLOYD, GRANDIN, Freehold NJ (b/X–13–1807; d/V–30–1852) <att UPa Med Dept> *Tr M S NJ* 1871: 86–87.

LLOYD, JAMES, Boston (b/IV– –1728; d/III–14–1810) Hon MD Harvard 1790. *Bost m&s j* 105:496, 1881. *K&B* III: 751.

LLOYD, SAMUEL, New Haven Co, Conn (d/VIII–3 1868 @55) *Proc Conn Med Soc* 1: 67 (app) 1861?

LOAR, JAMES, Bloomington, Ill (d/VI–14–1894 @64) <MD Physio–Med Inst Cincinnati 1867> *JAMA* 23:42, 1894. *Polk* 1890:301. Eclectic.

LOBAUGH, JOHN J, Farmington, Ill (b/Pa; d/V–18 1897 @68) MD Amer Coll 1857. *JAMA* 28:1091, 1897. *Polk* 1890: 330. Homeopath.

LOBDELL, HENRY, Danbury, Conn (b/I–25–1827; d/III–25–1855 Asia Minor) MD Yale 1850; AB Amherst 1849. *Bost m&s j* 52: 467, 1855.

LOCHMAN, LUTHER M, York, Pa (b/VIII–4–1829 Harrisburg; d/V–22–1897) MD Pa Med Coll 1852. *Pa m j* 1:184, 1897. *JAMA* 28:1092, 1897. *Polk* 1886: 841.

LOCKE, JOHN, Cincinnati (b/II–19–1792 Fryeburg, Me; d/VII–16–1856) MD Yale 1819. *Bost m&s j* 54:487, 1856. *K&B* III: 751–52.

LOCKWOOD, GEORGE BERTRAND, Sharon, Mass (b/VIII–14–1873 or 74; d/VII–12–1905 Albuquerque, NM) MD Jefferson 1897; ng Amherst 1897. *Bost m&s j* 153:94, 1905. *Polk* 1898: 796.

LOCKWOOD, JOHN ALEXANDER, USN 1832–65; San Francisco (b/XII–23–1811 Dover, Del; d/III–11 1900 Bournemouth, Engl) MD UPa 1832; AB Union 1830. *JAMA* 34:890, 1900. *U Pa med alum CW*: 1832. *Polk* 1890: 198.

LOCKWOOD, TIMOTHY T, Erie Co, NY (d/XII–27–1870) MD Jefferson 1835. *Buffalo m&s j* 10: 477, 1871.

LOCKWOOD, WILLIAM AUGUSTUS, Norwalk Conn; Brooklyn (d/XII–8–1899 @60) MD CPSNY 1864. *JAMA* 33:1566, 1632, 1899. *Bost m&s j* 141: 616, 1899. *Atkinson* I: 501. *Polk* 1896: 284.

LODER, N SHERMAN, Philadelphia (d/I–5–1892 @27) MD Jefferson 1884. *Med bull med & surg* 14:78, 1892. *Polk* 1886: 820.

LODGE, GILES HENRY, Boston (d/XII–17–1888) MD Harvard 1828; AB 1825. *Bost m&s j* 119: 644, 1888.

LOEBER, FREDERICK, New Orleans (b/I–2–1839 Giessen, Gny; d/X–18–1901) MD New Orl Sch Med 1866. *New Orl m&s j* 54:345–46, 407–08, 1901. *Polk* 1886: 417.

LOELING [LOEHRIG], GERHARD, Philadelphia (b/Gny; d/III–23–1902 @69) MD Jefferson 1874. *Pa m j* 5:386, 1901/02; 6:261, 1902/03. *Flint* 1897: 821.

LOEWENSTEIN, HENRY, Brooklyn (d/VI–10–1897 @ 59) MD Giessen 1857. *JAMA* 28:1252, 1897. *Polk* 1890: 772.

LOEWENTHAL, AUGUST ERNST, Hoboken, NJ (d/XII–7–1886) MD CPSNY 1879. *Med reg NY NJ Conn* 1887: 269.

LOEWENTHAL, HERMAN, NYC (b/Berlin; d/IV–21–1896 @60) <MD U Berlin 1860> *JAMA* 26: 1038, 1896.

LOFTUS, THOMAS VINCENT, Scranton, Pa (d/VII–2 1903 @26) MD UPa 1901. *Pa m j* 7: 279, 1903/04.

LOGAN, ABNER LOUIS, Whitesburg, Ala (d/XII–8–1886) MD U Nashville 1858. *Tr Med Assoc St Ala* 1887:306. *Polk* 1886: 141.

LOGAN, CHARLES MULDRUP, San Francisco (b/VII–31–1808 Charleston, SC: d/II–13–1876 Sacramento) MD SC Med Coll 1828; stud London & Paris. *Tr AMA* 29: 701–07, 1878. *K&B* III: 754–55.

LOGAN, CORNELIUS AMBROSE, Leavenworth Ks (b/VIII–24–1832 Deerfield Mass; d/I–30–1899 Los Angeles) MD Miami 1853 *JAMA* 32:506 1899. *K&B* III:753.

LOGAN, GEORGE, Charleston, SC; USN 1810–29 (b/I–4–1778; d/II–13–1861 New Orleans) MD UPa 1802. *Bost m&s j* 64:356, 1861. *Tr AMA* 19:442–43, 1868. *K&B* III: 754 [mention only]

LOGAN, JAMES M, Kansas City, Mo (d/VIII–12–1899 @54) MD Med Coll Ohio 1874. *JAMA* 33: 621, 1899.

LOGAN, JOHN ADDISON, Newport, Va (b/IV–6–1845 Roanoke; d/III–17–1877) MD Med Coll Va 1868. *Tr Med Soc Va* 1877:307–08. *Butler* 1878: 832.

LOGAN, JOHN DICKINSON, Philadelphia (b/VI–21–1819; d/IV–25–1881) MD UPa 1842. *Tr CPP* cent vol 1887: 245.

 Spec. educ'l status abbrev. as: ***ng*** = college verified attendance without degree;

LOGAN, JOHN R , Grand Forks, ND (b/Fenelon, Ont; d/III-18-1894) <MD Trinity Med Coll Toronto; MRCS (L)> *JAMA* 22:523, 1894.

LOGAN, JOSEPH PAYNE, Marietta, Ga; CW-CSA (b/ XI- -1820 Botetourt Co, Va; d/VI-2-1891 Atlanta; MD UPa 1841; att Wash'n & Lee. *JAMA* 17:161, 1891. *Bost m&s j* 124: 594, 1891. *Atkinson* I: 685.

LOGAN, SAMUEL, Pittsburgh (b/VIII-21-1830 New Salem, Pa; d/III-19-1872) MD Jefferson 1855. *Tr Pa St Med Soc* 9:241-44, 1873.

LOGAN, SAMUEL, New Orleans; CW-CSA (b/IV-16-1831 Charleston, SC; d/I-14-1893) MD SC M C 1853. *New Orl m&s j* ns20:598-604, 804-05, 1893. *Daniel's Tex m j* 8:333, 1892-93. *Atkinson* I:123. *K&B* III:753.

LOGAN, SAMUEL MOORE, E Boston (d/1893 @65 Riverside, Cal) MD Harvard 1861. *JAMA* 21: 936, 1893. *Bost m&s j* 129:580, 659, 1893. *Butler* 1878: 341.

LOGIER, WILLIAM, Black Hawk, Wis (d/V or VI- -1889) <MD St Louis 1866> *Tr Wis St Med Soc* 1891: 357. *Polk* 1886: 960.

LOINES, JONAS POWELL, Mt Vernon, NY; NYC (b/IV-30-1821 LI; d/XII-15-1873) MD UCNY 1849. *Med reg NY NJ Conn* 1874:278. *Med rec* 9:47, 71, 80, 1874. *Med surg rep Phila* 30:22, 110, 1874.

LOMAX, CONSTANTINE, Marion, Ind (b/XII-31-1814; d/III-6-1884) MD Med Coll Ohio 1851; <MD Indiana Med Coll 1848> *Tr IndSt Med Soc* 1885:214. *Butler* 1878: 210.

LOMAX, JOSEPH DODSON, Troy, NY (b/IV-4-1829 Engl; d/VII-22-1899) MD CPSNY 1862. *Tr Med Soc St NY* 1900: 431. *JAMA* 33: 367, 1899. *Atkinson* I: 78. *Polk* 1896:1107.

LOMAX, WILLIAM, Marion, Ind (b/III-15-1813 Guilford Co NC;d/IV-27-1893) MD UCNY 1850. *JAMA* 20: 614, 1893. *Tr Ind St Med Soc* 1893: 259. *Atkinson* I: 27. Kemper's *Indiana*: 300. *Butler* 1878: 210.

LOMBARD, FREDERICK HOWARD, Boston (d/XII-15-1885 @33) MD Harvard 1882; AB 1874. *Bost m&s j* 113:632, 1885.

LOMBARD, JOSIAH STICKNEY, London Eng 1876- (d/V-18-1903) MD Harvard 1864. *Bost m&s j* 148:684, 1903.

LONERGAN, WILLIAM D , Chicago (d/VIII-28-1898 @57) MD Mo Med Coll (Kemper) 1882. *JAMA* 31:551, 1898. *Polk* 1896: 395.

LONG, ALFRED JEROME, Whitehall, NY (d/VIII-10 1895 @71) MD UCNY 1853; AB Middlebury 1851. *Tr Med Soc St NY* 1896: 437. *Polk* 1886: 715.

LONG, CRAWFORD WILLIAMSON, Athens, Ga (b/ XI-1-1815 Danielsville; d/VI-16-1878) MD U Pa 1839. *Atkinson* I: 525-26. *New Orl m&s j* ns6: 387-88, 1878. *Med reg NY NJ Conn* 16:168, 236-37, 1879. *K&B* III: 755-56.

LONG, ED T, Bethlehem, Ky (d/VII-21-1898 @78) MD U Louisville 1848. *JAMA* 31:366, 1898. *Polk* 1896:578.

LONG, EDWIN R , USA (d/III-11-1845 Detroit) MD Rush 1845. *Buff m&s j* 1:263, 1845. *Ill & Ind m&s j* 1:54-55, 1846.

LONG, FREDERICK FARWELL, Chester, Pa (b/III-15 1865 Pittsfield, Ill; d/V-27-1906) MD UPa 1888. *Pa m j* 9: 671, 708, 1905/06. *Flint* 1897: 798.

LONG, GEORGE H , Barry, Ill (d/VII-29-1901 @71) MD Mo Med Coll 1855. *JAMA* 37: 527, 1901.

LONG, HIRAM, Sunbury, Pa (b/1831 Upper Mt Bethel; d/IV-27-1903) MD NY M C 1859; AB Lafayette 1858. *Pa m j* 7: 279, 1903/04. *Flint* 1897:827.

LONG, JAMES F , Washington, NC; New Bern 1870- (d/1888) MD Med Coll NY 1858. *NC m j* 21:62-63, 1888. *Polk* 1886: 725.

LONG, MANOAH SNYDER, CW-USA; Mertztown, Pa (b/XII-8-1837 Longswamp; d/III-16-1897) MD UPa 1862. *JAMA* 28:665, 1897. *U Pa med alum CW*: 1862. *Butler* 1878: 721.

LONG, R D , Greenville, SC (d/VIII-17-1886 @56) MD Med Coll SC 1855. *New Orl m&s j* ns14: 317, 1886. *Butler* 1878: 756.

LONG, SAMUEL, Springfield, Ill (b/1825; d/1863) MD ? *Tr AMA* 16: 647-48, 1865.

LONG, WILLIAM H , US Marine HospServ (b/Ky; d/I 5-1892 Cincinnati) MD Ky Sch Med 1866 [as Wm C] MD Bellevue 1870. *JAMA* 18:50, 1892. *Bost m&s j* 126: 48, 1892. *Med bull m & s* 14: 73, 1892. *Polk* 1886: 489 (Detroit, Mich).

LONGENECKER [LONGNECKER], JOHN HENRY, Islip, NY (b/Lancaster, Pa; d/VIII-19-1902 @80) MD Jefferson 1846. *Bost m&s j* 147: 256, 1902.

LONGFELLOW, A J, Fostoria O (d/V-15-1899 @68) MD M C O 1860. *JAMA* 32:1269 1899. *Butler* 1878:638.

LONGLEY, RUFUS, Haverhill Mass (b/VII- -1789 Shirley; d/III-12-1855) MD Dartmouth 1811; MD Harvard 1850. *Bost m&s j* 52:355-59, 1855.

LONGSHAW, WILLIAM, CW-USA (d/I-15-1865 abd Minnesota, at Fort Fisher, NC) MD U Mich 1859; att U Mich Sch Arts 1858-59. *Bost m&s j* 72: 28, 1865. *Nat m j* 1:298, 1870/71.

LONGSHORE, EVAN J, Scranton Pa (d/VI-7-1897 @ 53) Cert Exam Bd. *JAMA* 28:1203,1897. *Polk* 1886:832.

LONGSHORE, HANNAH ELIZABETH MYERS, Philadelphia (d/X-18-1901 @83) MD Wom Med Coll Pa 1852. *Pa m j* 5:296, 1901/02. *Butler* 1878: 690.

LONGSHORE, JOSEPH SKELTON, Philadelphia (d/ XII-5-1879 @70) MD UPa 1834. *Med surg rep Phila* 41: 550, 1879; 26:554, 1879. *Butler* 1878: 690.

LONGSTREET, DELAVAN W , Lackawaxon, Pa (d/ XII-12-1906 NY) MD Balto 1889. *Pa m j* 10:295, 1906/07. *Flint* 1897.

LONGSTREET, HENRY HENDRICKSON, Bordentown, NJ (b/I-11-1819; d/VII-6-1890) MD CPSNY 1842. *Med reg NY NJ Conn* 1891: 276. *Tr Med Soc NJ* 1891: 227-28. *JAMA* 15: 232, 1890. *Atkinson* I: 519.

LONGWELL, ALBERT, CW-USA (d/III-19-1865 Camp Chase, O) MD ? *Nat m j* 1:298, 1870/71.

LONGWORTH, LANDON RIVES, Cincinnati (b/XII-25-1846; d/I-14-1879) MD CPSNY 1873. *Tr Ohio St Med Soc* 1879: 189. *Bost m&s j* 100: 440, 1879. *Med rec NY* 15:96, 1879. *K&B* III: 757.

LOOMIS, ALFRED LEBBEUS, NYC (b/X-16-1831 Bennington, Vt; d/I-23-1895) MD CPSNY 1852; AB Union 1851. *Med reg NY NJ Conn* 1895: 230. *Buff m&s j* 34:431-32, 1895. *Chic med rec* 8:171, 1895. *Tr M S St NY* 1895: 370-74. *Atkinson* I: 279-80. *K&B* III:758-59.

LOOMIS, CHARLES LINCOLN, Washington, DC; Denver (b/IX-9-1859 DC; d/IV-6-1888) MD U Vt 1882. *Hist Med Soc DC:* 321. *Polk* 1886: 212.

LOOMIS, EDWARD, Dodgeville, NY (d/VII-14-1895 @89) MD Fairfield 1831. *JAMA* 25: 170, 1895. *Polk* 1886: 700. Homeopath.

LOOMIS, HORATIO N, Buffalo (b/III-25-1807 Franklin, Conn; d/III-22-1881) MD Fairfield 1828. *Nashville j m & surg* 20:424, 1881. *Butler* 1878: 537.

LOOMIS, SILAS LAWRENCE, CW-USA; DC; Fla (b/V-22-1822 N Coventry Conn; d/VI-22-1896) MD Georgetown 1857. *Hist Med Soc DC:* 287. *K&B* III:759.

LOOP, DENNIS D, North East Pa (d/IV-2-1904 @76) MD Buff 1865. *Pa m j* 8:335, 1904/05. *Flint* 1897:812.

LOOSE, CYRUS ALBRIGHT, CW-USA; Peabody, Kans (b/X-2-1843 Myerstown, Pa; d/XI-6-1893) MD UPa 1873; AB Dickinson 1870. *JAMA* 21: 784, 1893. *U Pa med alum CW*: 1873.

LOPER, WILLIAM FRANCIS, ?Millville, NJ (b/VII-18 1839 Millville; d/I-15-1864) MD Jefferson 1863; AB Princeton 1861. *Tr Med Soc NJ* 1871:185-86.

LORAINE, HENRY, Clearfield, Pa (b/1799? d/III-8-1859) MD UPa 1825. *Tr AMA* 13:804-05, 1860. *Med surg rep Phila* ns1:462-63, 1858/59.

LORD, FRIEND DRAKE, Newton Lower Falls, Mass (b/III-3-1822 Limington, Me; d/XII-8-1883) MD Bowdoin 1847. *Bost m&s j* 109:599, 1883.

LORD, GEORGE EDWIN, USA (b/II-17-1846; d/VI-25-1876 Little Big Horn, Mont) MD Chicago Med Coll 1871; AB Bowdoin 1866. *Tr AMA* 28:637-38, 1877. *Med rec med & surg* 11: 501, 1876.

LORD, ROBERT McCURDY, Kansas City, Mo 1857- (b/1833 Lyme, Conn; d/V-11-1894 San Diego, Cal) MD CPSNY 1857; AB Yale 1853. *Med reg NY NJ Conn* 1894: 242.

LORD, RUFUS S, Springfield Ill (b/VII-31-1818 St Lawrence Co, NY; d/X-27-1880) MD UCNY 1846. *Tr Ill St Med Soc* 1884:269-70, 1884. *Butler* 1878: 164.

LORD, SAMUEL AUGUSTUS, S Danvers, Mass (b/II-13-1822; d/X-29-1862) MD Dartmouth 1847; AB 1843. *Bost m&s j* 67: 288, 1862.

LORET [LORETTE], FRANCIS MORELAND, Brooklyn (b/London; d/I-29-1897 @84) MD CPSNY 1843. *JAMA* 28:328, 1897. *Polk* 1896: 999.

LORING, CHARLES PARKMAN, Providence, RI (b/VII-25-1834 Danville, Me; d/I-27-1877) MD Bellevue 1863; AB Bowdoin 1858. *Bowdoin cat*: 1858.

LORING, EDWARD GREELY, NYC (b/IX-28-1837 Boston; d/IV-23-1888) MD Harvard 1864. *Med reg NY NJ Conn* 1888:263. *Chic m j* 56:325, 1888. *Bost m&s j* 118: 440, 462, 586, 1888; 119: 640, 1888. *K&B* III: 760.

LORING, GEORGE BAILEY, Salem, Mass (b/XI-8-1817 No Andover; d/IX-14-1891) MD Harvard 1842; AB 1838. *Bost m&s j* 125:308, 1891. *K&B* III: 760.

LORING, JOSEPH, ? (b/VIII-11-1768 Boston; d/cIII-1 1857 Lisbon, Port.) Stud w/Dr Sam'l Danforth, Boston; AM Harvard 1786. Palmer's *Necrol Harvard alum*: 107.

LORING, PARK H, CW-USA (d/II-16-1865) MD ? *Nat m j* 1:298, 1870/71.

LORING, RICHMOND, Aux Cayes, Haiti (b/X-29-1801 N Yarmouth, Me; d/1854 France) MD Bowdoin 1825; AB 1822; AM 1827. *Bowdoin cat*: 1822.

LOSEY, E T, Honesdale, Pa (b/1797? d/III-9-1870 @ 73) MD ? *Phila med reg & dir* 1871: 304.

LOTHROP, CHARLES HENRY, CW-USA; Lyons, Ia (b/IX-3-1831 Taunton, Mass; d/II-6-1890) MD UCNY 1858. *JAMA* 14:915-16, 1890. *Tr Ia St M S* 1890: 285-86. *Atkinson* I:94-95. *Butler* 1878:240. *Polk* 1886: 362.

LOTHROP, JOSHUA RICH, ?Buffalo, NY (d/VII-22-1869) MD Harvard 1852; AB Dartmouth 1844. *Buffalo m&s j* 8: 479, 1869; 9:29, 1869.

LOTT, CHARLES F, Quakertown, Pa (b/1780? d/VII-8 1866 @86) MD ? *Med surg rep Phila* 15:112, 1866.

LOTZ, GEORGE, ?Boston (b/III-16-1836 New Berlin, Union Co, Pa; d/VII-23-1879) MD UPa 1858. *U Pa med alum CW*: 1858.

LOTZ, JOSEPH R, Philadelphia (b/VIII-26-1797; d/I 19-1875 @75) <MD UPa> *Phila med times* 5:304, 1875.

LOUGEE, ISAAC WILLIAM, Rochester, NH (b/VIII-1 1818 Gilmanton, NH; d/I-4-1893) MD Dartmouth 1845. *Tr NH Med Soc* 1893: 155-56. *Polk* 1890: 711.

LOUGEE, WILLIAM HATCH, Lawrence, Mass; Methuen 5 yrs (b/II-3-1832 Hanover; d/XI-18-1897) MD Hahnemann, Phila 1857; stud Dartmouth 1855-56. *Tr Am Inst Hom* 1898: 49. *Polk* 1886: 468.

LOUGHLIN, DENNIS J, Philadelphia (b/VIII-10-1847; d/XII- -1902) MD Jefferson 1881. *Pa m j* 6:261, 1902/03. *Flint* 1897: 821.

LOUGHLIN, THOMAS JOHN, NYC (d/V-9-1889 @ 33) MD CPSNY 1877. *Med reg NY NJ Conn* 1890: 273. *Polk* 1886: 685.

LOUGHRAN, ROBERT, Kingston NY (d/IV-11-1899 @67) MD Albany 1857. *Bost m&s j* 140: 392, 1899. *JAMA* 32: 899, 1899. *Polk* 1886:665.

LOUGHRAN, THOMAS HUGH AUGUSTINE, Brooklyn (d/VI-13-1891 @33) MD Bellevue 1882. *Med reg NY NJ Conn* 1892: 282. *Polk* 1886: 647.

LOUNDES, C T, CW-USA (d/II-2-1865) MD ? *Nat m j* 1:298, 1870/71.

LOUNSBERY, SETH STEPHENS, Westchester Co, NY; CW-USA (b/1838; d/IV-26-1872) MD CPSNY 1861; AB Lafayette 1860. *Med reg NY NJ Conn* 1872: 355.

LOVE, ALBERT CLARENCE, La (b/XII-2-1851; d/VII-29-1884) MD Louisville Med Coll 1875. *JAMA* 3: 419-20, 1884.

LOVE, ISAAC NEWTON, St Louis; NYC (b/1848 Barry, Ill; d/VI-18-1903) MD St Louis Med Coll 1872. *Bost m&s j* 148:712, 1903. *So pract* 25:484-85, 1903. *Chic med rec* 25:87-88, 1903. *Polk* 1896:874.

LOVE, JOHN H , Ventura, Calif (b/Ohio; d/VII-23-1906 @58) MD Cincinnati Coll Med & Surg 1870. *Cal st j m* 4:202, 1906. *Polk* 1896: 244.

LOVE, JOHN JAMES HERVEY, CW-USA; Montclair, NJ (b/IV-3-1833 Harmony; d/VII-30-1897) MD UC NY 1855; AB Lafayette 1851; AM 1854. *Tr Med Soc NJ* 1898:369-72. *Bost m&s j* 137: 142, 1897. *JAMA* 29:297, 1897. *Butler* 1878: 472.

LOVE, JOSEPH G , Savanna, Ill (d/III-24-1895 @52) MD LICH 1878. *JAMA* 24:497, 1895. *Polk* 1890: 348.

LOVE, MARTIN JAMES, Bennington, Vt (b/III-22-1821; d/XII-4-1869) MD Woodstock 1848; AB Williams 1845. *Tr Vt Med Soc* 1883: 107.

LOVE, THOMAS, Cockeysville, Md (b/III-25-1753 Cecil Co, Md; d/III-1-1821) MD ? *Med ann Md:* 479.

LOVE, WILLIAM ABRAHAM, Atlanta; CW-CSA (b/V 16-1824 Camden, SC; d/I-21-1898) MD UPa 1846. *JAMA* 30:334, 1898. *U Pa med alum CW*: 1846. *Atkinson* I:496. *Polk* 896: 326.

LOVE, WILLIAM SAMUEL, Baltimore (b/III-12-1803; d/VI-25-1872) MD Wash U Balto 1837. *Med annals Md:* 479.

LOVEJOY, CHARLES WARREN, Keene, NH (b/VI-2 1866 Orford; d/IV-23-1897 Greeley or New Windsor, Col) MD Dartmouth 1892. *Tr NH Med Soc* 1897:305.

LOVEJOY, DANIEL HEYWOOD, Boston (b/X-18-1838 Rindge, NH; d/II-27/28-1881) MD Bowdoin 1865. *Bost m&s j* 105: 623, 1881.

LOVEJOY, EZEKIEL, Bradford Co, Pa 1841- ; Owego, NY 1845- (b/VII-6-1803 Stratford, Conn; d/VIII-15-1872) MD Rutgers 1827; AB Union 1823. *Tr Hom M S Pa* 1873: 167. *Tr Am Inst Hom* 1873: 514. *King* I:100. Homeopath.

LOVEJOY, JAMES WILLIAM HAMILTON, Washington, DC (b/XII-15-1824; d/III-18-1901) MD Jefferson 1851. *Hist Med Soc DC:* 249. *Atkinson* I: 64. *Polk* 1886: 213.

LOVELACE, ARTHUR S , San Francisco (d/IX-23 1897 @42) MD Cooper 1878. *JAMA* 29: 761, 1897. *Polk* 1886: 178 (Willow, Calif).

LOVELACE, CURT H , Dukedom, Tenn (d/XI-7-1894 @40) MD Nashville Med Coll 1881. *JAMA* 23:768,1894.

LOVELACE, LEONARD M , Lemoore, Cal (b/XII-30 1837 McCracken Co, Ky; d/III-4-1890) MD Jefferson 1868. *Tr Med Soc Cal* 20:328, 1890. *Polk* 1886:166.

LOVELL, JOSEPH, Washington, DC; USA (b/XII-22-1788 Boston; d/X-17-1836) MD Harvard 1811. *Hist Med Soc DC:* 223. *K&B* III: 761.

LOVELL, JOSEPH M , New Orleans (d/IX-22-1897) MD Tulane 1894. *New Orl m&s j* 50:269, 1897. *JAMA* 29:816, 1897. *Polk* 1896: 623.

LOVERIDGE, A , Brooklyn (b/1788? d/XI-30-1865 @77) MD ? *Med surg rep Phila* 13:390, 1865.

LOVERING, JOHN DUDLEY, Newton Highlands, Mass (b/1827 Raymond, NH; d/III-18-1891) MD Albany 1860; att Dartmouth 1853. *Bost m&s j* 124: 324, 1891. *Butler* 1878: 353.

LOVETT, SAMUEL, Langhorne, Pa (d/XII-22-1893) MD UPa 1855. *Lehigh Valley med mag* 5: 108, 1893-94. *Butler* 1878: 721.

LOW, JAMES, Albany, NY (d/1822 @39) MD Edinburgh 1807. *New York med & phys jour* 1:128, 1822.

LOWBER, EDWARD, Philadelphia (b/X-6-1784; d/I-6-1870) MD UPa 1807; AB 1804; AM 1807. *Phila med reg & dir* 1871: 294.

LOWBER, WILLIAM, USN 1847-88 (b/X-9-1824 Phila; d/II-24-1888) MD UPa 1845; AB 1842; AM 1845. *U Pa Coll matriculants*: 130.

LOWE, JOHN NEWTON, Milford, NJ (b/VIII- -1824; d/I-5-1903) MD UCNY 1862. *Hahn mo* : 1903 (Mar). *Polk* 1886: 606. Homeopath.

LOWE, JOHN THOMAS, Aberdeen, Miss; CW-CSA (b/XI-6-1824; d/189_?) MD UPa 1846; AB U Ala 1842; AM 1851. *U Ala cat*: 66. *U Pa med alum CW*: 1846.

LOWE, LEE G , Algiers, Ala (d/I-9-1900 @31) MD Tulane 1890. *JAMA* 34:251, 1900.

LOWE, LEWIS GOULD, CW-USA med cadet; Brookline, Mass (b/VIII-17-1828 Boston; d/IX-30-1899) MD Harvard 186; MD Dartmouth 1864; CE Rensselaer Polytech 1848; BNS 1849. *Harvard in CW*:288. *Polk* 1886:463. Homeopath 1869-75.

LOWE, MORGAN M, Algiers La (d/VI- 1906) MD Tulane 1885. *New Orl m&s j* 59:86, 1906. *Polk* 1896: 623.

LOWELL, ABRAM LELAND, CW-USA & USN; Brooklyn (b/VI-3-1832 Chester, Vt; d/X-12-1882) MD UCNY 1861; att Hartford Coll? *Med reg NY NJ Conn* 1883:232. *Bost m&s j* 107: 482, 1882.

LOWMAN, WEBSTER BODINE, Johnstown, Pa (b/III-25-1841 Indiana, Pa; d/XII-5-1904) MD Jefferson 1867. *Pa m j* 8:186-87, 335, 1904/05. *Atkinson* I: 565. *Flint* 1897: 805.

LOWRY, JAMES, Shelbyville, Ky (b/II-4-1817 Irel'd; d/XII-4-1876) MD Transylvania 1844. *Tr Ky St Med Soc* 1877: 199-203.

LOWRY, J R , Parkersburg, WVa (b/XI-17-1844 Covington Va;d/X-17-1885) MD Louisville Med Coll 1871. *Tr Med Soc WVa* 1886: 337-38. *Butler* 1878: 851.

LOWRY, SYLVANUS TODD, San Antonio, Tex (b/Elkhorn, Ky; d/VI-30-1890 @44) MD Jefferson 1867; AB Bethel 1865. *Daniel's Tex m j* 6:40-41, 1890-91. *Polk*

1886: 893.

LOWRY, WILLIAM MARTIN, CW–CSA (b/IV– 1833 Bedford Co, Pa; d/1897 Bartow, Fla) MD UPa 1856. *U Pa med alum CW*: 1856.

LOWRY, WILLIAM R , Memphis (d/X–6–1878) MD ? *Tr AMA* 30:874, 1879. *Med rec* 14: 300, 1878.

LOZIER, ABRAHAM W , NYC (d/I–14–1896) MD NY Med Coll 1861. *JAMA* 26:192, 1896. *No Am j hom* 44: 126, 1896. *Polk* 1886:685. Homeopath.

LOZIER, CLEMENCE SOPHIE (HARNED), NYC (b/ XII–13–181? Plainfield, NJ; d/IV–26–1888 @65?) <MD NY Central M C (Ecl) 1853> *Med vis* 4:174 1888. *King* III: 125–36, 151–55. *Polk* 1886: 685. *K&B* III: 763. Homeopath.

LUBBOCK, CLINTON HENRY, Alameda, Cal (b/1861; d/V–21–1903) <MD Mo Coll 1880> MD UCNY 1881. *Cal st j m* 1:194, 1903. *Polk* 1896: 211.

LUCE, ABRAHAM B , Riverhead, NY (b/1818; d/I–21 1892) <MD Berkshire 1840> *Med reg NY NJ Conn* 1892: 282. *Polk* 1886: 703.

LUCE, HIRAM C , Bloomington, Ill (b/XII–26–1839 Harbor Creek, Pa; d/II–27–1888) MD Rush 1860. *Tr Ill St Med Soc* 1888: 145. *Butler* 1878: 164.

LUCE, JACOB B , E Newark, NJ (b/1841 Riverhead, NY; d/II–24–1865) MD Bellevue 1862. *Med surg rep Phila* 12: 344, 1864/65.

LUCE, LYMAN HORACE Falmouth & W Tisbury Mass (b/IV–10–1846;d/I–30–1892) MD Bowdoin 1869. *Bost m&s j* 126:132,1892. *Polk* 1890: 558.

LUCHSINGER, SAMUEL CHARLES, Milwaukee (b/ IV–19–1872 Green Co; d/VI–23–1900) MD Milwaukee Med Coll 1898; <stud pharm Phila> *Tr Wis St Med Soc* 35:459, 1901.

LUCK, S M , ?Collierville, Tenn (d/1878) MD ? *Tr AMA*, 30:874, 1879.

LUCK, WILLIAM J [or W] Middleburg, Va (d/II–20 1898) MD Med Coll Va 1857. *NC m j* 41:307, 1898. *Polk* 1886: 921.

LUCKETT, ROBERT L, Alexandria, La (d/IV–24–1895 @57) MD Tulane 1860. MD New Orl Sch Med 1860. *JAMA* 24:730, 1895. *New Orl m&s j* 22:892, 1895. *Polk* 1896: 613.

LUCKETT, ROBERT L Jr, Alexandria, La (d/VIII–29–1901 @37)MD Tulane 1891 *New Orl m&s j* 54:269, 1901.

LUCKETT, WILLIAM FLEET, Washington, DC (b/III–6–1838 Middleburg, Va; d/III–30–1901) MD U Louisville 1860. *Hist Med Soc DC:* 327. *Polk* 1886: 445.

LUCKEY, FRANKLIN NEELY, CW–CSA; Rowan Co, NC (d/VIII 8–1878 @55) <Stud 1845 (& 1846?) NY> *Tr NC m j* 2:232, 1878.

LUDEN, JOHN BERNHARD, Huntingdon Pa (d/IX– –1865) att Pa M C 1844. *Med s rep Phila* 14:40, 1866.

LUDLAM, JACOB W , Deerfield, NJ; Evanston, Ill 1855– (d/VII– –1858) MD UPa 1837. *Tr Med Soc NJ* 1871: 166.

LUDLAM, REUBEN Jr, Chicago (d/IV–19–1899) MD UPa 1852. *Tr Am Inst Hom* 1899: 930–31. *No Amer jour hom* 47: , 1899 (June). *King* I:353–54. Homeopath.

LUDLOW, BENJAMIN CHAMBERS, Los Angeles; CW–USA (b/1831 Ludlow Station, O; d/I–10–1898) MD UPa 1854. *U Pa med alum CW*: 1854. *JAMA* 30: 334, 1898.

LUDLOW, EDMUND, Los Angeles (d/IV–5–1903) MD NW U 1895. *Chicago med rec* 24:383, 1903.

LUDLOW, EDWARD GREENFIELD, NYC (b/1793; d/ VII–7–1877) <MD CPSNY 1823> *Med reg NY NJ Conn* 1878: 182.

LUDLOW, JACOB REPELYE, Easton, Pa (b/XI–22–1825 Somerset Co, NJ; d/II–10–1904) MD UPa 1845. CW–USA. *Pa m j* 8: 335, 1904/05. *Flint* 1897:801.

LUDLOW, JOHN LIVINGSTON, Philadelphia (b/V–14 1819; d/VI–21–1888) MD UPa ? *Tr CPP* cent vol:245.

LUDLOW, OGDEN CURTIS, NYC (d/III–2–1904) MD UCNY 1883. *Bost m&s j* 150:254 1904. *Polk* 1896:1065.

LUDLOW, RICHARD GABRIEL, CW–USA; Neshanic, NJ (b/V–29–1840; d/XII–5–1879 Belvidere) MD UPa 1863; ng Rutgers 1858–60. *U Pa med alum CW*: 1865. *Med s rep Phila* 42: 22, 1880. *Tr M S NJ* 1880–81: 212.

LUDLUM, WILLIAM SIMMONS, NYC (d/III–1–1890 @60) MD CPSNY 1862; AB 1847; AM 1850. *Atkinson* I: 675–76.

LUDWIG, GARDINER, Portland, Me (b/VI–20–1812 Waldoboro; d/II–17–1896) MD Bowdoin 1833. *Tr Me Med Assoc* 12:428–29, 1896. *Butler* 1878:309.

LUDWIG, GEORGE W , Chambersburg, Pa (d/VI–23–1902 @46) <MD U Md> *Pa m j* 6:261, 1902/03.

LUDWIG, MARTIN, West Earl, Pa (d/VI–3–1906 @74) MD Pa Med Coll 1850. *Pa m j* 9:894, 1905/06.

LUDWIG, MOSES ROBINSON, Thomaston, Me (b/I/II 2–1799 Waldoboro; d/IX–6–1872) MD Castleton 1824; AB Middlebury 1824. *Tr Me M Assn* 1871–73: 346–48.

LUECK, A W , Maysville, Wis (b/VI–2–1838 Prussia; d/XII–11–1878 or I–8–1879) MD Rush 1865. *Chic m j* 38:220–21, 1879. *Tr Wis St Med Soc* 1879: 1891: 357. *Butler* 1878: 863.

LUEDERWALD, RICHARD, NYC (d/XII–9–1876) MD Greifswald 1860. *Med reg NY NJ Conn* 1877: 204. *Butler* 1878: 519.

LUKE, ELIJAH J , Arthur, Ill (d/XI–3–1895) MD Wooster 1886. *Tr Ill St M S* 1899: 352. *Polk* 1886: 269.

LUKE, JOHN C , South Fork, Pa (d/VIII–2–1903 @70) MD Cleveland Med Coll 1871. *Pa m j* 7:279, 1903/04. *Flint* 1897: 836.

LUKENS, CASPAR PENNOCK, Philadelphia (d/VII–26 1862 @34) MD Phila Coll Med & Surg 1855. *Med surg rep Phila* ns8: 428, 1862.

LUKENS, CHARLES, Philadelphia (d/III–1–1855) MD UPa 1816. *Tr CPP* cent vol: 245.

LUKENS, ISAIAH, Wilmington, Del (d/VIII–19–1887 @70) MD UPa 1848. *Med vis* 3:292, 1887. *Hahn mo*

Spec. educ'l status abbrev. as: ***ng*** = college verified attendance without degree;

22:592, 1886? *Polk* 1886: 206. Homeopath.

LUKENS, ISRAEL, Rahway, NJ (d/II-10-1890 @79) MD ? *Med vis* 6:71, 1890. *Amer homeop* 16:112, 1890? Homeopath.

LULL, ALMON, Berkeley, Calif (d/III-16-1894 @89) MD ? att Waterville Coll, Me 1831. *JAMA* 22:523, 1894.

LUMBARD [LOMBARD], JOHN PATRICK, Dorchester, Mass (d/III-21-1905 @44) MD UCNY 1887. *Bost m&s j* 152: 386, 1905. *Polk* 1896:701.

LUMMIS, JOSEPH E , Maxwell, Ind (b/VI-1-1866 Eden, Ind; d/VI-26-188) MD Med Coll Ind 1894. *Tr Ind St Med Soc* 1899: 385.

LUND, OLIVER P , Philadelphia (d/X-13-1901 @39) MD Jefferson 1886. *Pa m j* 5:296, 1901/02. *Off'l reg Pa phys* 1881-87: 350.

LUNGREN, SAMUEL SMITH, Toledo, O (b/VIII-22-1827 York Co, Pa; d/III-7-1892) MD Jefferson 1850; MD Hahnemann 1852. *Tr Am Inst Hom* 1892: 217. *Med vis* 8:187, 1892. *Polk* 1886: 770. Homeopath.

LUNN, VASTINE CRITTENDEN, LaGrange, Tex (b/IX-10-1874 Warda, Tex; d/III-5-1904) <MD Rush 1895> att Tulane & Marion Sims Coll St Louis. *Tex st m j* 1:243-44. *Polk* 1900: 1705.

LUNNEY, GEORGE, Malden, Mass (d/VII-21-1892 @38) MD Columbian 1875. *Bost m&s j* 127: 100, 1892. *Polk* 1886: 469.

LUPFER, GEORGE W , Neff's Mills, Pa (d/XI-2-1905 @49) <MD CPS Balto 1881> *Tr Pa St Med Soc* 9:148, 1905/06. *Flint* 1897: 811.

LUSK, NATHAN LORENZO, Penn Yan, NY (d/XII-4-1893 @ c50) MD Buffalo 1865. *JAMA* 21: 936, 1010, 1893. *Butler* 1878: 563.

LUSK, OBED L , Long Island City, NY (d/VI-20-1902) MD Chicago Med Coll 1882. *Bost m&s j* 146: 706, 1902.

LUSK, WILLIAM THOMPSON, CW-USA; NYC (b/V 23-1838 Norwich, Conn; d/VI-12-1897) MD Bellevue 1864. *Bost m&s j* 136: 610-11, 1897; 137: 67, 689, 1897. *Proc Conn Med Soc* 1899: 343-49. *So pract* 19:310-11,1897. *Atkinson* I:149. *K&B* III:764-65.

LUSTIG, JULIUS, NYC (b/VIII-24-1835 Gleiwitz, Silesia; d/IX-24-1866) MD U Berlin 1858; att U Breslau 1854-56. *Med reg NY NJ Conn* 1867: 222.

LUTHER, MARTIN, Reading, Pa (b/II-16-1826 New Holland; d/II-22-1894) MD Jefferson 1848. *Tr M S Pa* 1894:381-82. *JAMA* 22: 314 818 1894. *Butler* 1878:721.

LUTKENS, OCTAVIO A , NYC (d/I-13-1882 @37) MD Würzburg 1869. *Med reg NY NJ Conn* 1882: 230.

LUTKINS, ALFRED AUGUSTINE, Jersey City (d/ V-9 1894 @68) MD UCNY 1878. *Med reg NY NJ Conn* 1894: 242. *JAMA* 22:855, 1894. *Butler* 1878:472.

LYMAN, DANIEL LEE,Royalton, Vt (b/II-2-1804; d/VI-19-1870) MD Woodstock 1837; Hon AM Royalton 1852. *Phila med reg & dir* 1871: 305.

LYMAN, E S , Sherburne, NY (b/Torrington, Conn; d/XI-20-1892) Cert 1834 Exam Bd Chenango Co, NY. *Tr Med Soc St NY* 11: 741 ff, 1894. *Polk* 1890: 850.

LYMAN, EDWARD PHELPS, New Preston, Conn (b/IV 1-1821 Glastonbury; d/IV-5-1882) MD Yale 1842. *Proc Conn Med Soc* 1882: 176. *Butler* 1878: 79.

LYMAN, ELIPHALET, Lancaster, NH (b/IX-11-1781 Woodstock, Conn; d/VII-19-1858) MD Dartmouth 1830. *Bost m&s j* 59:28, 1859.

LYMAN, FRANCIS ROMEYN, Sherburne, NY; USA (d/XI-14-1862 Wash'n, DC) MD UCNY 1861. *Med reg NY NJ Conn* 1865:213. *Bost m&s j* 67:368, 1862. *Med s rep Phila* ns9:206, 1862/63. *Nat m j* 1:298, 1870/71.

LYMAN, GEORGE HINCKLEY, CW-USA; Boston (b/VII-18-1819 Northampton Mass; d/VIII-19-1891 London, Engl) MD UPa 1843. *U Pa med alum CW*: 1843. *JAMA* 17:387,1891. *Bost m&s j* 125:232, 256,257,534, 1891; 126:313-18, 1892. *Atkinson* I:201.

LYMAN, HENRY MUNSON, Evanston, Ill (b/XI-26-1835 Sandwich Isl; d/XI-21-1904) MD CPSNY 1861; AB Williams 1858. *Bost m&s j* 151:637, 1904. *Chicago med rec* 24: 825, 1904. *Atkinson* I: 201. *K&B* III: 767.

LYMAN, JABEZ BALDWIN, Salem Mass (b/VI-18-1820 Easthampton; d/VI-29-1893) MD Jeff'n 1857; AB Amherst 1841. *Bost m&s j* 129:24 1893. *Polk* 1886: 472.

LYMAN, NORMAN, Warren, Conn (b/IX-6-1787 Torringford; d/IV-20-1850/1851) Lic c1809 Bd Censors Litchfield Co; Hon MD Yale 1831. *Proc Conn Med Soc* 1864:55-57.

LYMAN, WILLIAM CULLEN, Chicago (b/1838; d/I-27 1879 @41) <MD Harvard 1859> *Tr Ill St Med Soc* 1879: 293. *Butler* 1878: 134.

LYMAN, WILLIAM M , Rockford, Ill (b/Schenectady, NY; d/XII-19-1865) MD Woodstock 1832. *Chic m j* 22:572, 1865. *Med surg rep Phila* 14:60, 1866.

LYNCH, DAVID VALENTINE, NYC (b/III-10-1847; d/IX-11-1885) MD CPSNY 1868. *Med reg NY NJ Conn* 1886: 251.

LYNCH, JOHN, NYC (d/II-26-1877 @34) MD UCNY 1863. *Med reg NY NJ Conn* 1877: 204.

LYNCH, JOHN S , Clifton, Ala; Baltimore; CW-CSA (b/XI-24-1828 St Mary's Co, Md; d/IX-27-1888) MD U Md 1853. *Buff m&s j* 28:223, 1888. *Med annals Md:* 480. *Atkinson* I: 230. *Polk* 1886: 437.

LYNCH, PATRICK J, NYC (b/1828 Irel'd; d/IV-22-1905) MD UCNY 1857. *Bost m&s j* 152:508, 1905. *Polk* 1896: 1065.

LYNCH, SAMUEL BARTLETT, Boston (d/I-14-1899 @38) MD UCNY 1885. *JAMA* 32:263, 1899. *Polk* 1896: 701.

LYNCH, SAMUEL D, Anne Arundel Co, Md (b/1814 Pa; d/II- -1871) MD Washington Med Coll, Balto 1834. *Med annals Md:* 480.

LYNCH, THOMAS, S Boston (d/1857 @25) MD UCNY 1854. *Bost m&s j* 57:147, 1857. *Mass Med Soc cat*: 1894.

LYNCH, THOMAS A , Queen Anne's Co, Md (d/V-20

1893 @ c70) MD ?U Md 1877. *Med annals Md:* 480. *Polk* 1886: 446.

LYNDE, JAMES PORTER, Athol, Mass (b/III-21-1827 Gardiner; d/I-21-1890) MD Harvard 1852. *Bost m&s j* 122: , 1890.

LYNES, SAMUEL, Norwalk Conn (b/XII-1-1821 Ridgefield; d/VII-29-1878) MD CPSNY 1846; AB Yale 1842. *Proc Conn Med Soc* 1879-80: 173-74. *Atkinson* I: 578.

LYNN, EDWARD E , CW-USA; (d/IV-9-1863) MD ? *Nat m j* 1:298, 1870/71.

LYNN, GEORGE Jr, Cumberland, Md (b/VIII-8-1805; d/XII-8-1860) MD U Md 1829. *Med annals Md:* 481.

LYNN, ISAIAH P , Chicago (d/II-28-1866) MD Rush 1866. *Bost m&s j* 74:148, 1866. *Chic m j* 23:143-44, 1866. *Med surg rep Phila* 14:220, 1866.

LYNN, KLINE WILLIAM, Cortland, O (d/VIII-7-1899 @29) MD Western Reserve 1893. *JAMA* 33: 493, 1899. *Polk* 1896: 1183.

LYON, CALEB, Rossville, NY (d/IX-11-1897) MD Albany 1871. *JAMA* 29: 660, 1897. *Polk* 1886: 706.

LYON, CHARLES L , Farragut, Pa (b/VIII-24-1821 Hughsville; d/1897) MD Jefferson 1842. *Pa m j* 1: 277, 1897. *Atkinson* I: 650.

LYON, DAVID STUART, Peekskill, NY (b/1839 NY; d/IX-11-1895) MD UCNY 1878. *Bost m&s j* 133: 300.

LYON, EDWARD, Williamsport, Pa (b/XI-7-1846 or 1847; d/IV-14-1900) MD UPa 1867. *Pa m j* 3: 655, 1899/1900. *JAMA* 34:1211, 1900. *Flint* 1897:840.

LYON, EDWARD RANSOM, Bethel, Conn (b/VII-22-1861; d/X-10-1888) MD CPSNY 1885. *Proc Conn Med Soc* 1889: 266.

LYON, GEORGE GAINES, Chicago (d/I-17-1906 @45) MD Pulte 1888. *Ill m j* 9:228, 1906. *Tr Am Inst Hom* 1906:775. *Polk* 1896: 164.

LYON, IRVING WHITEHALL, Hartford, Conn (b/X-18-1840 Bedford, NY; d/III-4-1896) MD U Vt 1862; MD CPSNY 1863. *Proc Conn Med Soc* 1896:327-31. *Butler* 1878: 74.

LYON, J E , ? (d/1878 Handsboro, Miss) MD ? *Tr AMA* 30: 874, 1897.

LYON, JAMES L , NYC (d/XII-24-1858 @50) MD ? *Med surg rep Phila* ns1:236, 1858/59.

LYON, RANSOM PERRY, CW-USA (d/VIII-6-1863) MD Yale 1853. *Nat m j* 1:299, 1870/71.

LYON, SAMUEL HALL, Booneville, Mo (b/c1800 Baltimore Co, Md; d/X- -1840) MD U Md 1827; AB Harvard. *Med annals Md:* 481.

LYON, SAMUEL KUYPERS, NYC (d/V-4-1901 @63) MD CPSNY 1866; AB Columbia 1860. *Bost m&s j* 144: 462, 1901. *Polk* 1896: 1065.

LYONS, ANDREW WOLFF, Bridgeport, Conn (b/VIII-11-1852 McArthur, O; d/X-6-1904. *Proc Conn Med Soc* 1905: 503-04. *Flint* 1897: 173.

LYONS, IRA ELLIS, Huntington, Ind (b/1822 New Castle, Del; d/II-7-1898) MD Rush 1864. *JAMA* 30:448, 1898. Kemper's *Indiana*: 301. *Polk* 1886: 321.

LYONS, J A , San Antonio, Tex (d/I- -1881) MD ? *Tex med & surg rec* 2:80, 1882.

LYONS, JOHN C , Philadelphia; CW-USA (d/VII-5 1865 @51) MD Pa Med Coll 1854. *Med surg rep Phila* 13: 48, 1865.

LYONS, JOHN J , New Orleans (d/XI-6-1896 @63) MD Tulane 1859. *New Orl m&s j* ns24:367, 1896. *Polk* 1890: 491.

LYONS, WILLIAM A , St Francisville, Ill (d/IX-14-1899) MD U Tenn 1884. *Tr Ill St Med Soc* 1899: 287. *Polk* 1890: 348.

LYONS, WILLIAM B , Huntington, Ind (b/IX-2-1818 Newcastle Co, Del; d/V-22-1899) MD Rush 1865. *JAMA* 32: 1399, 1899. *Atkinson* I:464.

LYSTER, HENRY FRANCIS, Detroit (b/XI-6-1837 Sanderscourt, Irel'd; d/X-3-1894) MD U Mich 1860; AB 1858; AM 1861. *JAMA* 23: 593, 1894. *Butler* 1878: 378. *K&B* III: 768.

LYTLE, WILLIAM J, Princeton, NJ (d/I-22-1899 @75) MD UCNY 1848. *JAMA* 32: 263, 1899. *Polk* 1896: 948.

LYTTLE, HERBERT GEORGE, Long Island City, NY (d/XII-1-1892 @39) MD UCNY 1878. *Med reg NY NJ Conn* 1893: 310. *NW m j* 20:16, 1891. *Bost m&s j* 125: 640, 1891.

Note: Entries beginning Mc are alphabetized among those beginning Mac.

MABBETT, HARRY, Quitman, Ga; Calhoun Co, Ala (d/II-24-1891) <MD Savannah 1876> *Tr Med Assoc St Ala* 1891: 260. *Polk* 1886: 234.

MABRY, ALBERT GALLATIN, Selma, Ala (b/IX-7-1810 Jerusalem, Va; d/II-23-1874) MD UPa 1837. *Tr Ala St Med Assoc* 1878:288-311. *Proc Med Assoc Ala* 1874: 425-26.

McABEE, HENRY M , CW-USA (d/IX- -1864) MD Cleveland Med Coll 1851. *Nat m j* 1:299, 1870/71.

McADAM, ALEXANDER HUTCHINSON, Philadelphia (d/IX-9-1896 @57) MD UPa 1863. *JAMA* 27: 722, 1896. *Butler* 1878: 690.

McADAM, WILLIAM R , USMarineHospServ (d/X-12 1899 Key West, Fla) MD Jefferson 1897. *JAMA* 33:1116, 1899. *Polk* 1898: 1466.

McADEN, JOHN HENRY, CW-CSA; Charlotte, NC (b/III-13-1835; d/VIII-15-1904) MD Jefferson 1857; stud UNC 1853-54. *JAMA* 43:686, 1904.

McADORY, JAMES SADLER, Uniontown, Ala (b/IX-24-1839; d/I-19-1865. MD Jefferson 1860; att U Ala 1838. *U Ala cat*: 138.

McALISTER [McALLISTER], OLIVER HUSTON, McAlisterville, Pa; CW-USA (b/X-27-1832; d/II-15-1883) MD UPa 1871; att UMich. *UPa m alum CW*: 1871.

McALLISTER, GEORGE, NYC; CW-USA (d/VII-29-1864 @37) MD ? *Med surg rep Phila* 12: 68, 1864/65. *Nat m j* 1:299, 1870/71.

 Spec. educ'l status abbrev. as: ***ng*** = college verified attendance without degree;

McALLISTER [McCALLISTER], JAMES C, Genoa, Ill (d/IX-25-1905 @90) MD Castleton 1850. *Ill m j* 8:430, 1905. *Polk* 1886: 280.

McALLISTER, JOHN J, Cincinnati (d/IV- -1874) MD ? *Med surg rep Phila* 30: 420, 1874.

McALLISTER [McALISTER], JOHN W, Albany, Miss (d/IX-17-1895) MD U Nashville 1875. *JAMA* 25: 595, 1895. *Polk* 1886: 870 (Nashville).

McALLISTER, THOMAS, Brooklyn (d/III-19-1879 @ 50) MD CPSNY 1852. *Med reg NY NJ Conn* 1879: 194.

McALLISTER, WILLIAM L, Pasadena, Calif (d/IV-8 1899) MD Med Coll Ind 1873. *JAMA* 32: 899, 1899.

McALPINE, JAMES N, Sommerville, Md (b/1825 Clarksburg, Va; d/IV-9-1899) MD UPa 1847. *JAMA* 32: 899, 1899.

McALPINE, SAMUEL [or SUMNER] MANDEVILLE, Alpine, Ala (d/VII- -1889) MD UPa 1856. *Tr Med Assoc Ala* 1890:218.

McARTHUR, JOHN AMBROSE, Lynn, Mass (d/IX-28 1887 @56/57) MD Harvard 1872. *Bost m&s j* 117: 348, 1887. *Polk* 1886: 469.

McARTHUR, POLYDORE S, LaCrosse Wis (d/IX-19 1896 @74) MD Geneva 1847. *JAMA* 27: 776, 1896. *Polk* 1886: 655.

McARTHUR, ROBERT M, Ottawa, Ill (b/III-24-1825 Ayrshire, Scotl'd; d/VIII-12-1886) MD Rush 1854. *Tr Ill St Med Soc* 1887: 174-75. *Butler* 1878: 165.

McAULEY, EDWARD ALOYSIUS, Brooklyn (b/Irel'd; d/III-11-1884. *Med reg NY NJ Conn* 1885:243. *Butler* 1878: 532.

MACAULEY, PATRICK, Baltimore (b/1792 Yorktown, Va; d/IX- -1849) MD UPa 1815. *Med annals Md:* 481.

McBARRON, PATRICK AUGUSTUS, NYC (d/IX-30-1859 @36) MD CPSNY 1844. *Med surg rep Phila* ns3: 72, 1859/60.

McBLAIR, JOHN HOLLINS, Washington, DC (b/XI-12 1843; d/XII-3-1899) MD Georgetown 1869. *Hist Med Soc DC:* 294. *Polk* 1893: 271.

McBRAYER, JOHN ALLEN, USA (b/X-3-1817; d/III 24-1850) MD U Louisville 1842. *Tr Ky St Med Soc* 1860 [Spilman,CH: Rep't on med biogr Ky, 1860:10-14].

McBRAYER, VICTOR, Shelby NC(d/IX-19-1897 @46) MD UCNY 1878. *NC m j* 40:245 1897. *Polk* 1886:726.

McBRIDE, ALEXANDER, Berea, O (b/I-12-1822 Summit Co; d/VIII-5-1876) MD Cleveland Med Coll 1845. *Tr Ohio St Med Soc* 1877: 63-64.

McBRIDE, ALEXANDER, Decatur, Ill (d/VIII-14-1901 @71) MD Jefferson 1854. *Ill m j* ns3:237, 1901. *JAMA* 37: 1901. *Polk* 1886: 291.

McBRIDE, EDWARD H, Springfield, Mo (d/IX-5-1897) MD Louisville Med Coll 1873. *JAMA* 29:660, 1897. *Polk* 1886: 569.

MACBRIDE, ISAAC, CW-USA; Philadelphia (b/I-31-1831; d/X-2-1904) MD UPa 1854; AB Washington & Jefferson 1850. *Pa m j* 8:335, 1904/05. *U Pa med alum CW*: 1854. *Flint* 1897: 821.

MACBRIDE, LEWIS ARNOLD, Jersey City (b/XII-28-1844 Finchville, NY; d/XII-7-1891) MD Bellevue 1871. *Tr Med Soc NJ* 1892: 199. *Butler* 1878: 479.

McBRIDE, THOMAS ALEXANDER, NYC (d/VIII-31-1886 @40 @sea) MD CPSNY 1871; AB elsewhere. *Med reg NY NJ Conn* 1887: 269. *Bost m&s j* 115: 265, 1886.

McBRYAR, WILLIAM L, Pittsburgh (d/IV-10-1899 @37) MD Jefferson 1886 [as Bryar] *JAMA* 32:899, 1899. *Polk* 1896: 1266.

McCAA, DAVID, Baton Rouge (d/IX- -1887) MD Tulane 1881 *New Orl m&s j* ns15:329 1897. *Polk* 1886:412.

McCAA, JOHN Sr, Kirkwood SC (d/VIII-31-1859) MD UPa 1814;att SC Coll. *Med surg rep Phila* ns2:408 1859.

McCAFFRAY, CHARLES, NYC (b/1806; d/II-11-1870 @64) MD ? *Med reg NY NJ Conn* 1870: 323.

McCAIN, JOHN SIDNEY, CW-CSA; Lexington, Miss (d/IX-8-1898 @70) MD UPa 1851. *JAMA* 31:808. *Polk* 1896: 811.

McCALL, CHARLES ARCHIBALD, CW-USA; Philadelphia (b/XI-4-1837 Tampico Tx; d/III-12-1903) MD UPa 1858. *Pa m j* 7:279 1903/04. *UPa m alum CW*:1858

McCALL, JOHN, War 1812-USA; Deerfield Corners, NY; Utica 1823- (b/I-25-1787 Hebron; d/X-5-1867) Att CPSNY 1809/10 & 1811/12. *Buffalo m&s j* 7:268, 1868. *Tr Med Soc St NY* 1868: 318-23.

McCALL, WILLIAM, Omro, Wis (b/VI-13-1810 Franklin, NY; d/VIII-25-1879) MD Fairfield 1832. *Tr Wis St Med Soc* 1880: 206.

McCALLA, JOHN MOORE, Washington, DC (b/V-24-1835 Lexington, Ky; d/IV-30-1897) MD Columbian 1853. *Hist Med Soc DC:* 253.

McCALLA, WILLIAM HOLLINGSHEAD, Woodbury, NJ (b/VI- -1792; d/VIII-16-1824) MD UPa 1819. *Tr Med Soc NJ* 1871: 175-76.

McCALLMONT, GEORGE F, Philadelphia (d/VIII-5 1874 @73) MD UPa 1835. *Med s rep Phil* 31:160, 1874.

McCALLUM, G C, Lake Station, Miss (b/VIII-9 1845 Californe, Miss; d/IX-7-1878) MD Tulane 1868. *Tr AMA* 30:875, 1879. *Tr Miss St Assoc* 1879:38, 64-65.

McCANDLESS, ALEXANDER G, Pittsburgh (b/1816; d/II-24-1875) MD Cleveland Med Coll 1849. *Tr Med Soc Pa* 11:158-59, 1876.

McCANDLESS, MORRIS D, Youngstown, O (b/Great Bend, Pa; d/I-18-1892 @52) MD Jefferson 1875. *Tr Ohio Med Soc* 1892:383.

McCANE, THOMAS A, Toluka Ala (d/IV-3-1885)<MD Graffenburg Inst 1854> *Tr M Assn St Ala* 1885:319.

McCANN, JAMES, CW-USA; Pittsburgh (b/IV-12-1837 Verona, Pa; d/VII-13-1893) MD UPa 1864; LLB Heidelberg Coll, O. *Buff m&s j* 33: 50-52, 1893. *U Pa med alum CW*: 1864. *JAMA* 21: 58, 1893. *K&B* III: 770-71. *Butler* 1878: 700.

McCANN, THOMAS, Pittsburgh (d/V-9-1903 @40) MD Bellevue 1886. *Pa m j* 7: 279,1903/04. *Flint* 1897:830.

McCANN, WILLIAM G , Marshall, Ill (d/II-23-1900) MD Bennett 1872. *Tr Ill St Med Soc* 1899-1900: 509. *Polk* 1886: 287. Eclectic.

McCARTHY, HENRY C , Altoona, Pa (d/VI-6-1897 @56) MD Jefferson 1874. *JAMA* 28: 1203, 1897.

McCARTHY, JEREMIAH JOSEPH, Charlestown, Mass (b/Irel'd; d/II-25-1883 @35) MD Harvard 1870. *Bost m&s j* 108:502, 1883; 109:617, 1883.

McCARTHY, MARTIN CHARLES, Brooklyn (d/VIII-12-1896 @30) MD UCNY 1891. *JAMA* 27:503, 1896. *Polk* 1896: 999.

McCARTHY, MICHAEL, E Boston (d/X-30-1881? @ 38) MD LICH 1877. *Bost m&s j* 105: 623, 1881.

McCARTIN, HENRY EMMET, NYC (b/V-31-1838; d/III-12-1869) MD CPSNY 1863. *Med reg NY NJ Conn* 1869:236. *Tr AMA* 21:445, 1870. *Phila med reg & dir* 1871: 300.

McCARTY, CHARLES BARNEY, New Haven Co Conn (d/1859) MD Yale 1826. *Proc Conn Med Soc* 1860: 19.

McCARTY, JAMES HENRY, Birmingham, Ala (d/VI-11-1901) MD Atlanta 1880. *Tr Med Assoc St Ala* 1902: 130. *Polk* 1893: 151.

McCARTY, JAMES JOSEPH, Brooklyn (d/XII-23-1871 Jacksonville, Fla) MD CPSNY 1868. *Med reg NY NJ Conn* 1872: 355.

McCASKEY, HUGH, Hamersville, O (b/Beaver Co, Pa; d/XI-5-1885 @73) MD M C Ohio 1846. *Tr O St Med Soc* 1886: 407.

McCAULEY, B M , W Salem, O (d/V-3-1898 @50) MD ? *JAMA* 30: 1248, 1898.

McCAW, JAMES BROWN, CW-CSA; Richmond, Va (b/VII-12-1823; d/VIII-13-1906) MD UCNY 1843. *Atkinson* I: 267. *Tr Med Soc Va* 1893: 294. *K&B* III: 771.

McCHESNEY [MECHESNEY], ALEXANDER C, Chicago (d/IV-14-1894 @53, Nice, Fr) MD LICH 1867. *JAMA* 22:601, 1894. *Polk* 1890: 317. *Butler* 1878:165.

McCHESNEY, CHARLES G , Trenton, NJ (d/III-7-1861 @61) MD ? *Med surg rep Phila* ns5:665, 1860/61.

McCHESNEY, JACOB NEWTON, NYC (b/1852; d/VI-33-1885) MD Bellevue 1875. *Med reg NY NJ Conn* 1886: 251.

McCHESNEY, WILLIAM S , Staunton, Va (d/1884) MD Jefferson 1847. *Tr M S Va* 1884:7. *Butler* 1878: 832.

McCHORD, ALEXANDER, Lexington, Ky (b/Ala; d/VI-12-1833) Student @ Transylvania Med Dept. *Transylvania j m & assoc sci* 6:306, 1833.

McCLAIN, HENRY, NYC (d/II-23-1878) MD CPSNY 1855. *Med reg NY NJ Conn* 1876: 182.

McCLATCHEY, ROBERT JOHN, Philadelphia (b/IV-6 1836; d/I-15-1883) MD Hahnemann Phila 1856. *New Engl med gaz* 18:95, 1883. *Tr Homeop Med Soc St Pa* 1883: 40-43. Homeopath.

McCLEARY, THOMAS FRANCIS, Brooklyn (b/XII-25 1870; d/XII-15-1906) MD LICH 1893. *Bost m&s j* 155: 792, 1906. *Polk* 1896: 999.

McCLELLAN, CHRISTOPHER RABORG, Brooklyn (b/X-18-1813; d/I-13-1887) MD U Md 1835; AB Yale 1833. *Med reg NY NJ Conn* 1887: 270.

McCLELLAN, DAVID WENTWORTH BOISSEAU, Baltimore (b/1796 Gettysburg, Pa; d/V- -1854) MD U Md 1829. *Med annals Md:* 493.

McCLELLAN, ELY, USA (b/VIII-23-1834 Philadelphia; d/V-8-1893 Chicago) MD Jefferson 1856; att UPa Coll 1854. *Chic med rec* 4:377, 1893. *Bost m&s j* 128: 508, 1893. *K&B* III: 772.

McCLELLAN, GEORGE, Philadelphia (b/XII-23-1796 Woodstock Conn; d/V-18-1847) MD UPa 1819; AB Yale 1816. *Ill & Ind m&s j* 2:190-91, 1847. *Tr AMA* 3: 451-53 1850. *Buff m&s j* 5:473 ff 1850 *K&B* III:772-73.

McCLELLAN, HENRY M , York, Pa (d/VIII-14-1869) MD ? *Med surg rep Phila* 21:205, 1869.

McCLELLAN, JOHN, Greencastle, Pa (b/1761? d/VI-10 1845 @84) MD UPa 1788 "not publicly conferred"; <Cert by Benj Rush> *Med s rep Phila* ns9:127, 1862/63.

McCLELLAN, JOHN, Seneca Co, NY 1796-97; Livingston to 1842; Hudson 1842- (b/VI-22-1773 Colerain, Mass; d/X-18-1855) Stud w/Dr Hyde, Guilford, Conn. *Tr Med Soc St NY* 1857: 79-83.

McCLELLAN, JOHN HILL BRINTON, CW-USA (b/VIII-13-1823 Phila; d/VII-20-1874) MD UPa 1844. *Med surg rep Phila* 31:100, 160, 1874. *K&B* III:774.

McCLELLAN, ROBERT MILLER, Philadelphia (b/West Chester, Pa; d/II-16-1887 @53) MD Jefferson 1879; AB Yale 1854; stud Lafayette. *Lafayette, Men of*: 167. *Polk* 1886: 820.

McCLELLAN, SAMUEL, Schodack, NY (b/VII-13-1787 Colerain, Mass; d/IV-8-1855) Stud w/Dr John McClellan, NY. *Tr M S St NY* 1857: 51-72.

McCLELLAN, SAMUEL, Philadelphia (d/I-4-1854) MD ? *Phila m&s j* 2:244, 1854. *Nw m&s j* 3:142, 1854.

McCLELLAN, SAMUEL B , Hudson, NY (d/1890? @ 84, Kenosha, Wis) MD ? *JAMA* 15:232, 1890.

McCLELLAND, COCHRAN C , Philadelphia (d/II-16-1903 @59) MD Jefferson 1873. *Pa m j* 7: 279, 1903/04. *Flint* 1897: 820.

McCLELLAND, FREEMAN, Cedar Rapids, Ia (d/II-13-1896 @66) MD Jefferson 1855. *JAMA* 26:391, 1896. *Polk* 1890: 409.

McCLELLAND, JOHN, NYC (b/IV-23-1805; d/II-20-1875) MD CPSNY 1838; AB Union 1832. *Med reg NY NJ Conn* 1875: 201. *Med record* 10:174, 1875.

McCLELLAND, R H , Glenwood, Tex (d/III-28-1905) MD ? *Tex st m j* 2:36, 1906. *Polk* 1900: 1699.

McCLENACHAN, MORRIS, Philadelphia (d/III-21-1860 @62) MD UPa 1823. *Med s rep Phila* ns3: 570, 1879/60.

McCLENAHAN, JOHN SPENCE, Pittsboro, NC; CW-CSA (b/I-3-1833; d/X-10-1889) MD UPa 1867. *U Pa med alum CW*: 1867.

McCLENAHAN, WILLIAM, Oenaville, Tex; CW-CSA

(b/V-5-1836 Pittsboro, NC; d/IX-30-1904) MD UPa 1860. *U Pa med alum CW*: 1860.

McCLENDON, CAMILLUS FEW, Springville, Ala (d/VIII-8-1887) Cert County Bd 1875. *Tr Med Assoc St Ala* 1887:306. *Polk* 1886: 140.

McCLERY [McCLEARY] JAMES F [J OR T], CW-CSA; Washington, DC (b/I-24-1820; d/II-16-1871) MD Columbian 1842. *Hist Med Soc DC:* 236-37. *Tr AMA* 23: 581-82, 1872.

McCLINTOCK, G K , CW-USA (d/XI-5-1862 @26) MD ? *Nat m j* 1:299, 1870/71.

McCLINTOCK, JAMES, Philadelphia (b/1809 Lancaster Co; d/X-18-1881) MD Jefferson 1829. *Bost m&s j* 43: 493-96, 1851.

McCLINTOCK, JAMES L , Galva Ill (d/XI- -1899) MD Atlanta Med Coll 1858. *Tr Ill St Med Soc* 1899: 287.

McCLINTOCK, WILL H , Loudoun, Pa (d/X-12-1882) MD Jefferson 1882. *Med bull med & surg* 5:18, 1883.

McCLOSKEY, JAMES F X , Philadelphia (d/V-18-1859 @39) MD Pa Med Coll 1856. *Med surg rep Phila* ns2: 189, 1859.

McCLOSKEY, JOHN B , Mill Hall, Pa (b/IV-19-1849 Cook's Run; d/VI-13-1899) MD UPa 1874. *Pa m j* 32: 460, 1899. *Flint* 1897: 809.

McCLUER, BENJAMIN, CW-USA; Dubuque, Ia (b/V 8-1824 Franklinville, NY; d/XI-4-1894) MD Harvard 1852. *JAMA* 23:768, 1894. *Harvard in CW*: 238. *Atkinson* I: 457. *Butler* 1878: 240.

McCLURE, ANDREW WILSON, CW-USA; Mt Pleasant, Ia (b/VI-10-1828 Lebanon Co, O; d/V-20-1905) MD Med Coll Ohio 1853; MD UPa 1860. *Tr Iowa St Med Soc* 1905: 367-69. *U Pa med alum CW*: 1860.

McCLURE, DAVID, Jeffersonville, Ind (b/III-17-1815 Allegheny, NY; d/II-16-1896) <MD Albany 1838> *Tr Ind St Med Soc* 1896: 268. *Polk* 1890: 377.

McCLURE, JESSE D , Jeffersonville, Ind (b/XII-2-1855 Frankfort; d/IX-29-1885) MD Louisville M C 1884. *Tr Ind St Med Soc* 1886: 206.

McCLURE, JOSEPH FORBES, Beaver Dam, Wis (b/I-6 1824 Chelsea, Vt; d/VI-27-1892) MD Woodstock 1847. *Tr Wis St M S* 1892:393; 1894:503. *Polk* 1890: 1161.

McCLURE, V C , Chicago (d/IX-16-1895 @80) MD Geneva 1846. *JAMA* 25:510, 1895. *Butler* 1878: 134.

McCLURE, VIRGIL, Warsaw, Ky (d/VIII-1-1874 @67) MD ? *Med surg rep Phila* 31:180, 1874.

McCLURE, WILLIAM J , York, Pa (d/I-24-1891 @52) MD U Md 1866. *JAMA* 16:320, 1891. *Bost m&s j* 124: 152, 1891. *Butler* 1878: 721.

McCLURG, JOHN RUSSELL, West Chester, Pa (d/XI-3 1896 @76) MD Jefferson 1846. *JAMA* 27:1169, 1896.

McCOLLAM, SAMUEL, CW-USA; Columbus & Chillicothe, O (b/Phila; d/III-7-1895) MD UPa 1865. *U Pa med alum CW*: 1865. *Polk* 1886: 750.

McCOMB, ALONZO DEXTER, W Milville, Pa (b/XII-4-1853 Dayton, Pa; d/IX-5-1901 @47) MD Western Reserve 1880. *Pa m j* 5:296,3-5-16, 1901/02. *Flint* 1897: 804.

McCOMBS, JAMES P, CW-CSA; Charlotte NC (d/VII 23-1901 @65) MD UCNY 1860. *JAMA* 37:398 1901.

McCOMBS, ROBERT SHELMERDINE, Philadelphia (b/XI-23-1848; d/I-18-1899) MD UPa 1868. *JAMA* 32:263, 1899. *Polk* 1896: 1311.

McCONE, JAMES FRANCIS, San Francisco (b/1871 Silver City, Nev; d/XII-7-1902) MD U Cal 1892. *Cal st j m* 1:43, 1902.

McCONKEY, ALLEN G, Modesta, Ill (d/VI-13-1899 @ 28)<MD Marion Sims St Louis 1895> *JAMA* 33:53 1899.

McCONNELL, HIRAM SMITH, New Brighton, Pa (d/I 15-1906 @54) Md Bellevue 1875. *Pa m j* 9:359, 435, 1905/06. *Flint* 1897: 811.

McCONNELL, JOHN B , ?Nashville (b/VI-5-1822 NC; d/VII-1-1879) MD U Nashville 1852. *So pract* 1:351-52, 1879. *Nashville j m & s* ns24: 135-36, 1879.

McCOOK, GEORGE, Pittsburgh (b/1794? d/VI-23-1873 @79 New Lisbon, O) MD Jefferson 1836. *Med surg rep Phila* 29:36, 1873.

McCOOK, GEORGE M L , Morrison Ill (d/I-6-1874) MD ? *Med surg rep Phila* 30:132, 1874.

McCOOK, JOHN, Steubenville, O (d/X-11-1865 Washington, DC) MD ? *Med surg rep Phila* 13:293, 1865.

McCOOK, L A , Pekin, Ill (d/VIII-23-1869 @48) MD ? *Phila med reg & dir* 1871: 302.

McCORD, D H , Centralia, Ill 30 yrs (d/IV-2-1884 @63) MD St Louis M C 1855. *St Louis m&s j* 46:557, 1884.

McCORD, DAVID O , CW-USA?; York, Ill (b/1830; d/1874) MD M C Ohio 1854. *Tr AMA* 26:460-61, 1875.

MacCORD, GEORGE T , Pittsburgh (b/Venice, Pa; d/VI-7-1897) MD Jefferson 1879. *JAMA* 28: 1203, 1897. *Med bull m & s* 19:277,1897. *Polk* 1896: 1327.

McCORKLE, ALFRED LEYBURN, Carrollton Mo; CW CSA (b/VIII-17-1832; d/VII-11-1893) MD UPa 1857; MD UVa 1856. *UPa m alum CW*:1857. *Polk* 1886: 543.

McCORMACK, CHARLES, CW-USA; Washington DC (b/II-19-1841; d/VII-30-1868) MD Georgetown 1861. *Phila med reg & dir* 1871: 297. *Tr AMA* 21:481-82, 1870. *Hist Med Soc DC:* 273.

McCORMACK, JOHN, NYC (d/IV-1-1879 @31) MD UCNY 1874. *Med reg NY NJ Conn* 1879: 194. *Butler* 1878: 519.

McCORMICK, CHARLES, USA 1846- (b/1807 DC; d/IV-28-1877) MD U Md 1835. *Tr AMA* 28:642-46, 1877. *Med rec* 12:288, 1877.

McCORMICK, CYRUS, CW-CSA?; Berryville, Va (b/Clarke Co; d/I-12-1905) MD U Md 1868. *Tr Med Soc Va* 1905:452. *Polk* 1900: 1756.

McCORMICK, JOHN, Greensburg, Pa (b/IV-28-1860 New Florence; d/1905) MD Cleveland Med Coll 1882 [as Jas] *Pa m j* 8:545-46, 1904/05. *Polk* 1896: 1280. *Off'l reg Pa phys* 1881-88: 404.

McCORMICK, PETER J , CW-CSA; Yazoo City, Miss

(d/I-3-1905) MD UCNY 1858. *New Orl m&s j* 57:625, 1905. *Polk* 1896: 816.

McCOSKER, THOMAS, Brooklyn (b/1845; d/II-19-1886) MD CPSNY 1873 *Med reg NY NJ Conn* 1886:252.

McCOSKRY, CHARLES NISBET, USN (d/XI-16-1821) MD UPa 1819; AB Dickinson 1815. *Dickinson cat*: 1815.

McCOUGHLIN, JAMES, Albany, NY (d/II-12-1886) MD ? *Bost m&s j* 114:164, 1886.

MACCOUN, ROBERT TOLAND, USN 1844-79 (b/IV 19-1817 Phila; d/III-20-1890 Balto) MD UPa 1843. *U Pa med alum CW*: 1843.

McCOY, GEORGE, USA (b/1828 Dublin, Irel'd; d/X-8-1880) MD Georgetown 1857. *Hist Med Soc DC:* 261. *Butler* 1874: 93.

McCOY, GEORGE K , CW-USA (d/XII-18-1864) MD U Louisville 1858. *Nat m j* 1:299, 1870/71.

McCOY, GILBERT RODMAN, Doylestown, Pa (d/XI-7-1882 or 1883) MD UPa 1840; AB Princeton 1837; AM 1840. *Tr Med Soc Pa* 1883:339-40.

McCOY, JAMES A C , Tacoma, Wash (d/IV- -1898 @71) MD U Louisville 1859. *JAMA* 30: 1061, 1898; 31: 39, 1898. *Polk* 1886: 933.

McCOY, JOHN M , Centre Co, Pa (b/II-4-1817 Greenwood, Pa; d/I-19-1879) MD UPa 1838. *Tr Med Soc Pa* 12:753-54, 1879.

McCOY, WILLIAM A , Madison, Ind (b/X-27-1843 Wooster, O; d/V-8-1904) MD Med Coll Ind 1872. *Tr Ind St Med Soc* 1904: 359. *Polk* 1896: 480.

McCOY, WILLIAM A , Dallas, Tex (d/IV-25-1905 @60) MD Jefferson 1884. *Tex st m j* 1:32, 1905/06. *Polk* 1896: 1075.

McCOY, WILLIAM NEWTON, Jeffersonville, Ind (b/XII-13-1833 Harrison Co; d/II-19-1892) MD Bellevue 1871; MD U Louisville 1860. *Tr Ind St Med Soc* 1892: 291. *Butler* 1896: 210.

McCRACKAN, THOMAS, Puyallup, Wash (d/IV-11-1906) MD CPS Chicago 1886. *JAMA* 57: 220, 1906.

McCRACKEN, WILLIAM A , CW-USA; Springfield, O (d/XII-25-1868 @28) MD Med Coll Ohio 1863. *Phila med reg & dir* 1871:299. *Tr Ohio St Med Soc* 1869: 173-75. *Med surg rep Phila* 20:40, 1869.

McCRANOR [McCRANER], CHARLES D, St Joseph Mo (d/VI-9-1895) MD Jefferson 1895. *JAMA* 24:989, 1895.

McCREA, THOMAS PLEASANTS, CW-USA; Philadelphia; Logansport, Ind (b/IX-28-1816; d/III-10-1885) MD UPa 1850; ng UPa Coll 1833-34 *Matrics, Coll UPa*.

McCREADY, BENJAMIN WILLIAM, NYC (b/X-28-1813; d/VIII-9-1892) MD CPSNY 1835. *Med reg NY NJ Conn* 1893: 310. *JAMA* 19:262, 1892. *Bost m&s j* 127: 176, 1892.

McCREARY [McCREERY], JACOB, CW-USA (d/VIII 3-1863 Helena, Ark) MD ? *Nat m j* 1:299, 1870/71.

McCREERY, JOHN ALEXANDER, NYC (d/XI-10-1899) MD Bellevue 1871; AM St John's 1867. *JAMA* 33: 1308, 1899. *Bost m&s j* 141:536, 1899. *Polk* 1896: 1065.

McCROSSEN, THOMAS, City Isl, Westchester, NY (b/1851 NYC; d/IX-18-1896) MD UCNY 1879. *JAMA* 27: 1215, 1896. *Polk* 1896: 1016.

McCULLEY, WILLIAM A , Independence, Kans (d/I-22-1895) MD Med Coll Ohio 1862. *JAMA* 24:221, 1895. *Polk* 1890: 441.

McCULLOCH, CHARLES, Gloversville, NY (d/X-15-1898 @50) MD Albany 1877. *JAMA* 31: 1066, 1898.

McCULLOUGH, ALBERT MORRIS, Bellefont, Ala (d/XII-22-1887) Cert Exam Bd 1880. *Tr Med Assoc Ala* 1888:316. *Polk* 1886: 130.

McCULLOUGH, ALEXANDER JOHN, Meadville, Pa (d/IV-26-1902 @49) MD Western Reserve 1882; BS, PhG. *Pa m j* 6: 261, 1902/03.

McCULLOUGH, HOWARD, Ft Wayne, Ind (b/I-28-1858; d/I-8-1892) MD UPa 1882. *JAMA* 18: 212, 1892. *Tr Ind St Med Soc* 1892:285. *Polk* 1886: 318.

McCULLOUGH, J HAINES, Pt Deposit, Md (b/IX-15 1837 Rising Sun Md; d/VII-5-1889) MD U Md 1861. *Med annals Md:* 495. *Polk* 1886: 445.

McCULLOUGH, JAMES HAINES Jr, Baltimore (b/Md; d/1836?) MD UPa 1814. *Med annals Md:* 494-495.

McCULLOUGH, JOSEPH W , CW-USA; Blackwoodtown, NJ (b/ VIII-12-1837 Wilmington, Del; d/III-15-1881) MD Jefferson 1860. *Tr Med Soc NJ* 1881: 166-167. *Butler* 1878: 473.

McCULLOUGH, THOMAS P , Fort Wayne, Ind (d/II 18-1898 @75) MD Jefferson 1847. *JAMA* 30:570, 1898. *Polk* 1896: 467.

McCULLOUGH, WILLIAM H , Tarentum, Pa (d/VIII-28-1906 @55) MD Cincinnati Coll Med & Surg 1878. *Pa m j* 10:54, 1906/07. *Off'l reg Pa phys* 1881-88: 20. *Flint* 1897: 837.

McCUNE, JOHN N , McKeesport, Pa (d/V-17-1903 @52) MD Cleveland Med Coll 1878. *Pa m j* 7: 279, 1903/04. *Flint* 1897: 808.

McCUNE, JOSEPH ANDRE, Greenup Co, Ky (d/XI-27 1870) MD ? *Med surg rep Phila* 24:90, 134, 1871.

McCURDY, ROBERT L , Freeport, Pa (d/VIII-28-1906 @55) MD Cleveland Med Coll 1853. *Pa m j* 10: 54, 1906/07. *Flint* 1897: 802.

McDANIEL, CORNELIUS WINBURN, Washington, Ind (b/1823 Randolph Co, NC; d/VI-19-1880) MD Med Coll Ohio 1848 [not confirmed]. *Tr Ind St Med Soc* 1881: 232. *Butler* 1878: 210.

McDANIEL, EDWARD DAVIES, Coy, Ala (b/VII-7-1822 Chester Dist, SC; d/VI-27-1898 Denver Colo) MD Med Coll SC 1857. *JAMA* 31: 132, 1898. *New Orl m&s j* 51:453, 1899. *Atkinson* I:273.

McDANIEL, JAMES H , Centreville, Tex (b/V-27-1849 Leon Co; d/XI-26-1900) MD U Louisville 1870. *Tr Tex St Med Assoc* 1902:70-71. *Polk* 1886: 882.

McDAVITT, M , Alvin, Tex (b/I-21-1834 Franklin, Ky;

 Spec. educ'l status abbrev. as: ***ng*** = college verified attendance without degree;

d/V-13-1897?) MD ? *Tex med news* 7:349, 1898.

McDERMOTT, GEORGE C , Cincinnati (d/V-8-1901) MD Cleveland Homeop 1870; MD NY Ophth Hosp 1875. *Tr Am Inst Hom* 1901: 917-18. *Polk* 1886: 743. Homeopath.

McDERMOTT, JOHN ROGERS, Newark, NJ (d/II-2-1891) MD UCNY 1877. *Med reg NY NJ Conn* 1891: 276. *Polk* 1886: 608.

McDERMOTT, WILLIAM J , NYC (b/Portland, Me; d/III-1904 @73) MD UCNY 1854. *Bost m&s j* 150: 310, 1904. *Polk* 1896: 1065.

McDILL, DAVID, Burlington, Ia (b/V-12-1832 Hamilton, O; d/V-6-1891) MD St Louis Med Coll 1855. *Tr Ia St Med Soc* 1892: 227. *Polk* 1890: 408.

McDONALD, ALEXANDER, S Boston (b/1831; d/IV-20-1867 NY) MD Harvard 1861. *Bost m&s j* 76: 256, 1867.

MACDONALD, ALEXANDER EDWARD, NYC (b/1845 Toronto; d/XII-7-1906) MD UCNY 1870. *Bost m&s j* 155:727, 1906. *Polk* 1896: 1066.

McDONALD, C M, Leesburg, Ga (d/XI-12-1899) <MD CPS Balto 1880> *JAMA* 33:1441, 1899. *Polk* 1886:231.

McDONALD, CALVIN D , Kansas City, Mo (d/VI-19 1898 @63) MD Starling 1864. *JAMA* 31:39, 1898. *Polk* 1886: 551.

McDONALD, CLAUDE MEREDITH, USA; Princeton, Ind (d/I-23-1899 @28 Greenfield, NC) MD U Louisville 1893. *JAMA* 32: 263, 1899.

McDONALD, DAVID L , Shiremanstown & Concord, Pa (d/IV-11-1899) MD Columbus Med Coll O 1881. *JAMA* 32:899, 1899. *Polk* 1886: 796.

MACDONALD, DONALD W , Brookline, Mass (d/VII-21-1901 @42) MD U Vt 1898. *JAMA* 37:342, 1901.

McDONALD, FRANK HEWITT, Harlem, NY (d/VIII-2 1890 @46) MD UCNY 1880. *Med reg NY NJ Conn* 1891: 276.

McDONALD, J T , Celeste, Tex 7 yrs (b/1853 Tippah, Miss; d/VIII-29-1904) <MD Memphis 1889> *Tex st m j* 1:244, 1906. *Polk* 1900: 1685.

MACDONALD, JAMES, NYC (b/IV-19-1803 White Plains, NY; d/V-5-1849) MD CPSNY 1825. *Tr AMA* 3:450-51, 1850. *K&B* III:781-82.

MACDONALD, JOHN, NYC (d/V-21-1900 Phila) MD ? *Bost m&s j* 142: 580, 1900. *JAMA* 34:1432, 1900. *Polk* 1896: 1066.

McDONALD, JOHN BANN, Dickinson, ND to 1896; Spokane, Wash 1896- (b/XII-17-1838; d/III-1901) MD Harvard 1865; att Bowdoin 1862. *Bowdoin cat*: 1865. *Polk* 1886: 200.

McDONALD, JOHN [?JAMES] E, USA (b/NY; d/IX-10 1866 NY) MD NYMC 1853. *Tr AMA* 18:357, 1867. *Nat m j* 1:299, 1870/71. *US Army list* 1815-1900: 466.

McDONALD, JOHN ROBERT, Courtland, Ala (d/I-5-1902) MD U Nashville 1867. *Tr Med Assoc St Ala* 1902: 130. *Polk* 1893: 164.

McDONALD, T T, New Carlisle, Ind (d/II-7-1898 @66) Lic by yrs pract. *JAMA* 30:448, 1898. *Polk* 1890: 382.

McDONNELL, EDWARD, Texas & NYC (b/VII-9-1817 Irel'd; d/XII-29-1867) Lic RCS(E) 1842. *Med reg NY NJ Conn* 1869: 237.

McDONNELL, PATRICK WILLIAM, NYC (b/1816; d/III-8-1884) <MD Dublin 1836> MD UCNY 1845. *Med reg NY NJ Conn* 1888:263. *Med surg rep Phila* 50: 448, 1884.

McDONOUGH, ANTHONY A , Reading, Pa; Ill; CW-USA (d/IX-22-1863 Paducah, Ky) MD UCNY 1858. *Nat m j* 1:299, 1870/71. *Med s rep Phila* 10:328, 1863.

McDONOUGH, CHARLES, CW-USA; Reading, Pa (d/V-5-1902 @76) MD Pa Med Coll 1847. *Pa m j* 6: 261, 1902/03. *Flint* 1897: 833.

McDONOUGH, EDWARD JAMES, NYC (d/XI-30-1906 @44) MD UCNY 1887. *Bost m&s j* 155: 698, 1906. *Polk* 1896: 1065.

McDONOUGH, LAWRENCE JOHN, Lowell, Mass (d/III-2-1901 @42) MD U Vt 1886. *Bost m&s j* 144:438, 1901. *Polk* 1886: 716.

McDOW, JOHN RAMSAY, CW-CSA (b/IV-15-1829 Gainesville, Ala; d/II-15-1864 Harrisonburg, La) MD U Pa 1855; AB U Ala 1852. *U Pa med alum CW*:1855.

McDOWELL, AUGUSTUS WILLIAM, Morristown NJ; CW-USA (b/XI-11-1820; d/III-6-1878) MD UPa 1840; AB Princeton 1837; AM 1840. *U Pa med alum CW*: 1840.

McDOWELL, EPHRAIM, Danville, Ky (b/XI-11-1771 Rockbridge Co, Va; d/VI-20-1830) Hon MD U Md 1832? att Edinburgh 1793-94. *Tr AMA* 29:708-12, 1878. *K&B* III: 782-83.

McDOWELL, GEORGE MONTGOMERY, CW-CSA; Barnesville, Ga (b/VII-22-1834 Pike Co; d/VII-26-1883) MD Jefferson 1855. *JAMA* 1: 128, 1883. *Atkinson* I: 686-87. *Butler* 1878: 115.

McDOWELL, JAMES H , Jersey City, NJ (d/X-23-1889 @64) MD U Md 1857. *Med reg NY NJ Conn* 1890: 273. *Polk* 1886: 605.

McDOWELL, JAMES HENRY TRANIS, CW-CSA; Martin, Tex (b/X-14-1833 Hanover Co, Va; d/X-15 1901) MD UPa 1855. *U Pa med alum CW*: 1855.

McDOWELL, JOHN D , St Louis, Mo (d/VII-8-1868 @61) MD ? *Med rec* 3:312, 1868-69.

McDOWELL, JOHN JAMES, St Louis (d/III-27-1880 Hot Springs, Ark) MD Mo Med Coll 1855. *Tr AMA* 32:523-24, 1881. *Bost m&s j* 102:427, 1880. *Butler* 1878: 418.

McDOWELL, JOSEPH NASH, St Louis (b/1803 Lexington, Ky; d/IX-25-1868) MD Transylvania 1827. *Phila med reg & dir* 1871: 298. *Bost m&s j* ns2: 192, 1868. *Nashville j m & s* ns4:185-86, 1868. *Med s rep Phila* 19:312, 1868. *K&B* III: 783-84.

McDOWELL, LUCIEN, Flemingsburg Ky (d/1903) MD U Louisville 1849. *So pract* 25:222,1903. *Polk* 1896:584.

McDOWELL, MAXWELL, Baltimore; York, Pa 1804- (b/1771; d/1847) Hon MD U Md 1818; AM Dickinson 1792. *Med annals Md*: 496.

McDOWELL, WILLIAM JEFFERSON, Portsmouth, O (b/IX-14-1821; d/II-23-1878) MD UPa 1845. *Tr Ohio St Med Soc* 187_: . *Tr AMA* 29: 712-14, 1878. *Butler* 1878: 639.

McDUFFIE, WILLIAM CHARLES, CW-CSA; Fayetteville, NC (b/II-10-1829 Cumberland Co; d/X-31-1899) MD UCNY 1855. *Tr Med Soc St NC* 47:177-78, 1900. *JAMA* 33:1440, 1899.

MACE, SAMUEL VEIRS, Cecil Co, Md (b/1828 Rossville; d/1864) MD U Md 1849. *Med annals Md:* 482.

MACE, SAMUEL VEIRS, Rossville, Md (b/I- -1860; d/X-14-1899) MD U Md 1884. *JAMA* 33:1183, 1899. *Med annals Md:* 482.

McEACHIN, H G , Plano, Tex (b/NC; d/VII-13-1906 @73 Ft Worth, Tex) MD ? *Tex st m j*2: 122, 1906. *Polk* 1896: 1434.

McELDERRY, HENRY, Hot Springs, Ark (d/IV-17-1898) MD U Md 1865. *JAMA* 30:1061, 1898.

McELFRESH, JOHN HAMMOND, Frederick City, Md (b/V-27-1796 Frederick Co; d/VIII-4-1841) MD U Md 1817; AB elsewhere; stud law. *Med annals Md:* 496.

MACELLAN, KENNETH F , NYC (d/I-29-1899) <MD Glasgow 1867> *JAMA* 32: 324, 1899.

McELMURRAY, HENRY S , Charleston, Mo (d/VI-16 1899 @28) MD ? *JAMA* 33:53, 1899.

McELRATH, JAMES B , Jackson Center, Pa (d/VI-30-1904 @60) MD Jefferson 1871. *JAMA* 43:414, 1904. *Pa m j* 8:335, 1904/05. *Flint* 1897: 805.

McELROY, JAMES TYRONE, NYC (d/VI-25-1889 @ 30) MD Bellevue 1880. *Med reg NY NJ Conn* 1890: 273. *Polk* 1886: 685.

McENROE, WILLIAM MICHAEL HALEY, NYC (b/ VIII-15-1854 Charlotteville NY; d/V-17-1899) MD UCNY 1883. *Bost m&s j* 140:508 1899. *Polk* 1896:1065.

McEUEN, THOMAS, Philadelphia (b/X-18-1799; d/II-27-1873) MD UPa 1821; AB 1819; AM 1821. *Med surg rep Phila* 28:238, 256, 1873?

McEWEN, JOHN BETTS, NYC (d/X-7-1867 @59) MD CPSNY 1831. *Med reg NY NJ Conn* 1868: 330.

McEWEN, ROBERT CHARLES, CW-USA; Saratoga Springs, NY (d/XII-26-1893 @60) MD CPSNY 1856; AB Williams 1853. *Med reg NY NJ Conn* 1894: 243. *JAMA* 22:31,1894. *Tr Med Soc St NY* 11:741 ff,1894.

McFALL, HOWARD M , Mattoon, Ill (d/XI-10-1899 @39) MD Rush 1882. *JAMA* 33: 1375, 1899. *Tr Ill St Med Soc* 1899-1900: 352. *Polk* 1890: 339.

McFALLS, DAVID, St Lawrence Co, NY (b/I-10-1822; d/IV-6-1891) MD Castleton 1849. *Med reg NY NJ Conn* 1891: 276. *Polk* 1886: 662, 899 (Utah).

McFARLAN, EBENEZER, NYC (d/II-25-1900) MD UCNY 1845. *JAMA* 34: 573, 1900. *Polk* 1896: 1066.

McFARLAND, ANDREW, Jacksonville, Ill (b/VII-17-1817 Concord, NH; d/XI-22-1891) MD Dartmouth 1840; att Jefferson 1843; MD Rush 1870. *Chicago med rec* 2:371, 1891. *Polk* 1890: 335.

McFARLAND, ELIZABETH, Sharon, Pa (d/II-7-1903 @26) MD Woman's Med Coll Pa 1901. *Pa m j* 7:279, 1903/04.

McFARLAND, GEORGE C , Jacksonville, Ill (b/Concord, NH; d/I-15-1905 @65) MD Rush 1863. *Ill m j* 7:242, 1905. *Polk* 1896: 424.

McFARLAND, JOHN A , Tiffin, O (b/VI-10-1811 Waynesboro, Pa; d/VI-1-1883) MD Jefferson 1837. *Tr Ohio St Med Soc* 1884: 225-26.

McFARLAND, JOHN P , Lebanon, Tenn (d/II-16-1891) MD Jefferson 1868. *So pract* 13:136 ff, 1891. *Nashville j m & surg* 49: 140, 1891.

McFARLAND, LAFAYETTE, Springfield, Mass; Boston (d/X-30-1887 @63) MD Hahnemann Phila 1854. *Med vis* 4:14, 1888. *New Engl med gaz* 22:591, 1886. *Polk* 1886: 474. Homeopath.

McFARLAND, SOLOMON FENTON, Binghamton, NY (d/IV-26-1900 @71) MD U Mich 1857. *Tr Med Soc St NY* 1901: [426]. *Polk* 1886: 642.

McFARLAND, WILLIAM C , NYC (d/II-28-1891) MD CPSNY 1867. *Med reg NY NJ Conn* 1891: 276. *Butler* 1878: 519.

McFARLANE, ANDREW, Philadelphia (d/XI-7-1906) MD UPa 1874. *Pa m j* 10:118, 1906/07.

McFETRIDGE, WILLIAM CROMWELL, Philadelphia (b/X-2-1864; d/I-3-1900) MD UPa 1886; att Coll UPa 1881-83. *JAMA* 34:186, 1900. *Polk* 1896: 1311.

McGAHAN, GEORGE, NYC 1866- (b/Irel'd; d/VI-16-1873 @38) <MRCS (Ireland) 1858> *Med reg NY NJ Conn* 1874: 281.

McGALLIARD, BENJAMIN WALTON, Trenton, NJ (d/VI-14-1905 Phila) MD UPa 1889; att Lafayette. *JAMA* 45: 57, 1905.

McGAUGHY, ANDREW JACKSON, Linton, Ind (b/XI 1-1855 Daviess Co, Ind; d/XI-29-1904) MD U Louisville 1884. *Tr Ind St Med Soc* 1905: 453.

McGAY, JOHN YOUNG, Brooklyn (d/X-12-1894 @40) Lisbon Centre, NY) MD UCNY 1880. *Med reg NY NJ Conn* 1895: 232. *JAMA* 24: 176-77, 1895.

McGEE, JOHN A, Rice Tex (d/VII-1-1905) MD U Louisville 1875. *Tex st m j* 1:84, 1905/06. *Polk* 1886: 892.

McGEE, NATHAN J, ? (d/VIII-23-1878 Canton, Miss) MD ? *Tr AMA* 30:875, 1879. *Med rec NY* 14:220, 1878.

McGEE, WILLIAM HENRY [HARVEY?], Belvidere, NJ (d/V-11-1904 @56) MD Bellevue 1872; AB Princeton 1869; AM 1872. *Bost m&s j* 150: 552, 1904. *Polk* 1896: 933.

McGHEE, WILLIAM A , Dripping Spr, Tex (d/XII- -1890) MD Tulane 1880. *Daniel's Tex m j* 6:319-20, 1890-91. *Polk* 1890: 1095.

MacGILL [McGILL], CHARLES, Chesterfield Co, Va; CW-CSA (b/1806; d/V-5-1881) MD U Md 1823? *Med*

 Spec. educ'l status abbrev. as: ***ng*** = college verified attendance without degree;

*ann Md:*482. *Tr AMA* 32:524–25 1881. *Butler* 1878: 833.

McGILL, GEORGE McCULLOCH, CW–USA (b/IV–20–1838 Hannah Furnace, Pa; d/VII–21–1867 Fort Lynn, Colo Terr) MD UPa 1861; AB Princeton 1858; AM 1861. *Nat m j* 1:299, 1870/71. *Med surg rep Phila* 17: 177, 1867. *Tr AMA* 19:451–52, 1868. *Med reg NY NJ Conn* 1868: 330.

McGILL, WARDLAW, Asheville, NC (b/V–22–1846 Frederick Co, Md; d/X–26–1888) MD U Md 1867. *NC m j* 23: 395, 1889. *Med annals Md:* 497.

McGILL, WILLIAM, Frenchtown, NJ (b/1769? d/VI–23 1815 @47) MD ? *Tr Med Soc NJ* 1872: 181–82. *Wickes, NJ*: 325. *Blane, Hunterdon Co*: 93–94.

MacGILL, WILLIAM D , Hagerstown, Md (b/1802; d/III–13–1833) MD U Md 1823. *Med annals Md:* 483. *K&B* III: 785.

McGILLICUDDY, TIMOTHY JOSEPH, NYC (b/Lewiston, Me; d/I–16–1899 @41) MD UCNY 1882. *Bost m &s j* 140:103 1899. *JAMA* 32:195 1899. *Polk* 1896:1065.

McGINNIS, ALLEN B , Guyandotte, WVa (d/V–11–1898 @79) MD Med Coll Ohio 1854. *JAMA* 30:1305, 1898. *Polk* 1896: 1527.

McGINNIS, WILLIAM T , Eminence, Ky (d/II–13 1895) <MD Louisville Med Coll> AB Centre Coll. *JAMA* 24: 294, 1895.

McGIVERN, JOHN HENRY, NYC (d/VII–21–1896 Nova Scotia) MD UCNY 1883. *Bost m&s j* 135:122, 1896. *JAMA* 27:449,1896. *Polk* 1896: 1065.

McGLOUGHEN, JOHN, NJ 1787?– (b/Mourne, Irel'd; d/IX–17–1835) Appr to surg in Irel'd. *Tr Med Soc NJ* 1872: 190–92. *Blane, Hunterdon Co*: 102–03.

McGLYNN, EDWARD, Roxbury, Mass (d/VII–26–1895 @32) MD Harvard 1886. *Bost m&s j* 133: 659, 1895.

McGOUGH, PETER Jr, Pittsburgh (d/I–24–1906 @51) MD UPa 1878. *Pa m j* 9:360, 1905/06. *Flint* 1897: 830.

McGOVERN, MICHAEL H , Pen Yan, NY (d/VI–10–1896 @38) MD CPS Balto 1884. *JAMA* 26: 1278, 1896.

McGOWAN, CHARLES EDWARD, S Boston (d/XI–12 1887 @36) MD Harvard 1875. *Bost m&s j* 117: 492, 1887. *Butler* 1878: 341.

McGOWAN, JOHN JOSEPH, Providence, RI; NYC (b/X–12–1824; d/III–26–1871) MD Harvard 1847. *Med reg NY NJ Conn* 1871: 361.

McGRATH, EDWARD COMIO, NYC (d/II–21–1868 Brooklyn) MD CPSNY 1854. *Tr AMA* 19:423, 1868. *Phila med reg & dir* 1871: 295.

McGRATH, MICHAEL FRANCIS, Fishkill–on–Hudson, NY (d/VIII–11–1903 @35) MD CPSNY 1885. *Bost m&s j* 149:220, 1903.

McGRATH, ROBERT, Philadelphia (d/VI–24–1873 @ 66) MD Jefferson 1836. *Med surg rep Phila* 29:18, 1873.

McGRAW, JAMES F , Brooklyn (d/II–19–1891 @82) <MD U Md 1878> *Med reg NY NJ Conn* 1891: 277.

MacGREGOR, ANDREW, Providence, RI (b/VII–8–1868 New Glasgow, NS; d/X–15–1899) MD Jefferson 1893. *Tr RI Med Soc* 6:134, 1903. *Polk* 1896:1352.

McGREGOR, G K , Yellow Prairie, Tex (b/V–12 1839 Scotland; d/X–12–1884) <MD in New Orleans 1870> *Daniel's Tex m j* 1:481–82, 1886.

MacGREGOR, JAMES ROBINSON, NYC (d/II–5–1903 @71) MD CPSNY 1853. *Bost m&s j* 148: 194, 1903. *Polk* 1896: 1066.

McGREGOR, JOHN, Providence, RI (b/X–10–1819 Coventry, RI; d/XI–4–1867) MD UCNY 1845. *Med surg rep Phila* 17:436, 1867. *Tr RI Med Soc* 1:322–23, 1867.

McGREGOR, JOHN LOMA, Whitefield, NH (b/IX–5–1855; d/IV–17–1895) MD Dartmouth 1884; MD Hahnemann Phila 1883. *Tr NH Med Soc* 1895: 162–63. *Polk* 1890: 712.

McGREGOR, THOMAS H , Garland & Mt Zion, Tenn (d/IX–15–1878 Memphis) Stud med U La. *Med rec* NY 14:240, 1878. *Tr AMA* 30:875–76, 1879.

McGREGOR, WILLIAM, Sioux City, Ia (d/VIII–5–1898) MD UCNY 1861. *JAMA* 31:427, 1898. *Polk* 1886: 267 (Chicago).

McGRONEN, HARRY A , Brooklyn (d/I–21–1904 @35) MD Ill Med Coll 1898. *Bost m&s j* 154: 84, 1906.

McGUGAN, DAVID L , Keokuk, Ia (b/1807 W Middleton, Pa; d/1865) Hon MD U Md 1844. *Tr AMA* 18: 350–52, 1867. *Buff m&s j* 5: 498,1866. *Tr Ia St Med Soc* 1867–71: 240–43. *Med s rep Phila* 13:113, 118, 1865.

McGUIRE, CALVIN BRIDGES, Fayetteville, Tenn (d/III–25–1906 @75) MD U Nashville 1856. *So pract* 28:303, 1906. *Butler* 181878: 772.

McGUIRE, DAVID J, Detroit (d/VIII–18–1888 @43) MD Wooster 1869. *Med vis* 4:301, 1888. *Polk* 1886: 489. Homeopath.

McGUIRE, HUGH HOLMES, Winchester Va; CW–CSA; (b/XI–6–1801;d/VIII–9–1875) MD UPa 1822 *Tr M S Va* 1875:67. *Tr AMA* 31:1064–5 1880. *K&B* III:786.

McGUIRE, HUNTER HOLMES, Richmond, Va; CW–CSA (b/X–11–1835; d/IX–19–1900) MD Winchester M C 1855; MD Va Med Coll 1859; LLD UNC 1887. *So pract* 22:466, 1900. *Tr Med Soc Va* 1900: 325–32. *New Orl m&s j* 53:300, 1900. *Tr CPP* cent vol: 284. *Atkinson* I:107. *K&B* III: 782.

McGUIRE, JAMES MERCER GARNETT, CW–CSA; ?Berryville, Va (b/IV–20–1832 Theolog. Seminary, Va; d/I–24–1903) MD UPa 1855. *U Pa med alum CW*: 1843.

McGUIRE, JOHN S , Seattle; b/Engl; d/1898? @65) <MD Trinity Coll, Dublin 1854> *JAMA* 31: 38, 1898.

McGUIRE, ROBERT LEWIS, CW–CSA (b/1822 Fredericksburg, Va; d/IV–10–1876) MD UPa 1843. *U Pa med alum CW*: 1843.

McGUIRE, WILLIAM B , NYC (d/XI–26–1883 @33) MD UCNY 1871. *Med reg NY NJ Conn* 1884: 233.

MACHAN, GEORGE STOVER, Providence, RI (b/VII–21–1867 Argenta, Ill; d/IV–6–1901) MD Bowdoin 1896; AB 1893. *Tr RI St Med Soc* 6:548–49, 1899–1903.

McHENRY, JAMES, Baltimore (b/XI–16–1753 Bally–

mena, Irel'd; d/V-3-1816) Stud med w/B Rush. *Med ann Md:* 497.

McHENRY, THOMAS, CW-USN; (d/IX-18-1863 Key West, Fla) MD ? *Nat m j* 1:299, 1870/71.

MACHETT, J F, Brenham, Tex (d/IV- -1881) MD Tulane 1851. *Tex m&s j* 2:80, 1882.

McILROY, SAMUEL HENDERSON, NYC (b/VI-21-1839 Scotland, Pa; d/I-5-1898) MD LICH 1864. *JAMA* 30: 166, 1898. *Polk* 1886: 686.

McILROY, SAMUEL PAUL, Brooklyn (d/III-4-1886 @60) MD CPSNY 1858; att Queen's Univ, Irel'd. *Med reg NY NJ Conn* 1886: 252.

McILVAIN [McILVAINE], JAMES PATRICK, Media, Pa (b/II-21-1830; d/XI-10-1854 Springton Manor) MD UPa 1853. *Tr Med Soc Pa* 1855: 135-36.

McILVAINE, ROBERT R, Cincinnati (d/VII-28-1881 NYC) MD Cinc Med Coll 1840> *Med reg NY NJ Conn* 1882: 230; 1889: 265. *Med rec* NY 20:419, 1881.

McILWAINE, GEORGE D, Washington, DC (b/1866 Pittsburgh; d/XII-25-1901) MD Western Pa Coll 1895. *Pa m j* 5:222, 277, 296, 1901/02.

McINTIRE, ALEXANDER, Cummington Mass (b/1794? d/VII-15-1859) Palmyra, NY) MD ? *Bost m&s j* 61: 48, 1860.

McINTIRE, HARVEY GRAVES, Concord, NH (d/V-9-1892) MD Harvard 1848. *Bost m&s j* 126: 484, 1892. *Polk* 1886: 591.

McINTOSH, LYMAN D, Chicago (d/II-29-1892) Lic Sheboygan Co, Wis, Med Soc 1868. *Chicago med rec* 3: 76, 1892. *NW m j* 20:46, 1892. *Polk* 1886: 267.

McINTYRE, GEORGE D, London, Kans; CW-USA (b/II-14-1840 Phila; d/X-14-1871 Emporia, Kans) MD U Pa 1864, AB Lafayette 1862. *U Pa med alum CW*: 1864.

McINTYRE, JOHN BRADY, NYC (d/V-6-1888 @43) MD CPSNY 1877. *Med reg NY NJ Conn* 188: 264. *Polk* 1886: 686.

MacIVOR, ABBIE HAMLIN, ?NYC (d/II- -1900) MD NYMC & Hosp Women 1886. *No Am j hom* 46:32, 1900. Homeopath.

MACK, WILLIAM, Salem, Mass (d/VI-9-1895 @80) MD Harvard 1838; AB 1833. *Bost m&s j* 133:659, 1895. *Polk* 1893: 608.

MACKALL, LEONARD, Baltimore (b/1803 Georgetown, DC; d/I-1-1892) MD U Md 1826. *Med annals Md:* 483. *Polk* 1886: 438.

MACKALL, LOUIS, Georgetown, DC (b/I-7-1801; d/VII-3-1876) MD U Md 1824. *Med annals Md:* 483. *K&B* III: 788.

MACKALL, LOUIS Jr, Washington, DC (b/IV-10-1831 Pr Geor Co, Md; d/IV-18-1906) MD U Md 1851. *Hist Med Soc DC:* 252. *Polk* 1893: 271.

MACKALL, RICHARD, Baltimore (b/I-21-1805; d/III-2-1875) Hon MD U Md 1838. *Med annals Md:* 483-84. *Tr AMA* 26: 468, 1875.

MACKALL, RICHARD COVINGTON, Elkton, Md (b/1821; d/II-16-1906) MD U Md 1847. *Med ann Md:* 484.

MACKAY, BERNARD, NYC (b/Engl; d/V-12-1904) <MD Engl> *Bost m&s j* 150: 552, 1904.

MACKAY, EDWARD, Buffalo (b/II-17-1810 Irel'd; d/1867) MD ? *Buff m&s j* 6:478-80, 1867.

MCKAY, ISAIAH R, Northumberland, Pa (d/1858 Tucson, Ariz) MD Jefferson 1836; stud Lafayette 1837. *Lafayette, Men of*: 142.

MACKAY, JAMES C, Buffalo (d/X-13-1862) MD ? *Buff m&s j* 2:127-28, 1862.

MACKAY, OLIVER PERRY, Fayette City, Pa (d/XI-24 1900 @56) Lic by yrs pract. *Pa m j* 4: 368-69, 1900/01. *Offl reg Pa phys* 1881-88: 180.

MACKEAIG, SAMUEL M, CW-CSA (d/III-12-1863 Shelbyville, Tenn) MD ? *SHSP* 22:233, 1893.

MACKEAN, H C, Johnson, Ia (d/XI-4-1865 @36) MD ? *Med surg rep Phila* 13:406, 1865.

McKEE, ALBERT BLAKEMAN, Edwardsville, Ill (d/III-17-1903 @40) MD Rush 1893. *Ill m j* ns4: 760, 1903. *Polk* 1896: 417.

McKEE, JAMES COOPER, USA; Butler, Pa (b/V-18-1830; d/XII-11-1897) MD UPa 1852. *JAMA* 30:106, 1898. *NC m j* 41:63, 1898. *Polk* 1896: 1294.

McKEE, JOHN COOPER, New Castle, Pa (d/IX-25-1900) MD Miami 1874. *Pa m j* 4: 671, 1900/01. *Butler* 1878: 722.

McKEE, WILLIAM HENRY, Raleigh, NC (b/IX-7-1814; d/1877) MD UPa 1839. *Tr AMA* 29:714-16, 1878. *Tr NC Med Soc* 1875: 6-7.

McKEEHAN, SAMUEL, W Alexander, Pa; Wellsburg 1803- ; War 1812-USA (b/1775 Cumberland Co, Pa; d/IX- -1866 @92) MD ? <AB Dickinson> *Med surg rep Phila* 16: 454, 1867.

McKEEN, JAMES, Topsham, Me (b/XI-27-1797 Beverly, Mass; d/XI-28-1873) MD Harvard 1820; AB Bowdoin 1817; AM 1820. *Tr Me Med Assoc* 1874-76: 423-24. *Med surg rep Phila* 29: 462, 1873. *Bost m&s j* ns12:572, 1873. *K&B* III: 790.

McKEEN, JOSEPH, CW-USA; Topsham, Me (b/X-15-1832 Brunswick; d/I-15-1881) MD Bowdoin 1856; AB 1853; AM 1856. *Bowdoin cat*: 1853. *Butler* 1878: 302.

McKELVEY, JAMES BOYD, Bloomsburg, Pa (d/I-14/15-1901 @76) MD UPa 1848. *Pa m j* 5:296, 1901/02. *Bost m&s j* 1878: 722.

McKELWAY, ALEXANDER JEFFREY, Williamstown, NJ; CW-USA (b/XII-6-1813 Glasgow, Scotl'd; d/XI-7-1885) MD Jefferson 1835. *Tr Med Soc NJ* 1886-87: 161-62. *Butler* 1878: 473.

McKELWAY, JOHN, Trenton, NJ (b/1787? d/IV-23-1877 @90) MD ? *Tr M S NJ* 1872:109-10; 1877:[127].

McKENNAN, HARRY, Paris, Ill (d/III-30-1906) MD U Mich 1889. *Ill m j* 9:464, 564, 1906.

McKENNAN, HENRY S, Washington, Pa (b/X- -1849; d/I-9-1889) MD UPa 1874. *Tr Pa St M S* 21: 296, 1889.

McKENNAN, THOMAS, CW-USA; Washington, Pa (b/

V–21–1825; d/VIII–8–1895) MD UPa 1846; AB Wash'n Coll 1842; AM 1846. *Tr M S Pa* 27:377–78, 1897. *JAMA* 25:342, 1895. *Atkinson* I: 402. *Butler* 1878: 722.

MACKENZIE, AUGUSTUS C , Negaunee, Mich (d/VII 13–1896) MD LICH 1868. *JAMA* 27: 337, 1896. *Polk* 1890: 599.

MACKENZIE, COLIN, Baltimore (b/1775; d/IX–1–1827) MD UPa 1797. *Med ann Md:* 484.

MACKENZIE, COLIN, NYC (d/I–7–1892 @53) MD Cleveland MedColl 1860. *Med reg NY NJ Conn* 1892: 282. *Bost m&s j* 126:48, 1892. *Polk* 1886:686.

MACKENZIE, GEORGE BROWN, Baltimore (b/1807; d/1833) MD U Md 1828. *Med annals Md:* 484.

MACKENZIE, JOHN CARRERE, Baltimore (b/1824; d/IV–4–1866) MD U Md 1847. *Med annals Md:* 484. *Med surg rep Phila* 14: 300, 1866.

McKENZIE, JOHN F , Leroy, Ill (d/IV–14–1896) MD Louisvl M C 1874. *JAMA* 26:843, 1896. *Polk* 1886: 286.

MACKENZIE, JOHN MILNE, Fall River, Mass (b/V–7 1855; d/VII–11–1896) MD Harvard 1890; AB Brown 1876. *Bost m&s j* 135:76, 1896. *Polk* 1896: 712.

MACKENZIE, JOHN PINKERTON, Baltimore (b/IV–8 1800; d/I–14–1864) MD U Md 1821. *Med annals Md:* 485. *Tr AMA* 16:644, 1865.

McKENZIE, SULTAN WESTMORELAND, CW–CSA; Gadsden, SC (b/V–14–1837 Ft Motte; d/VI–18–1896 Eastover) MD UPa 1860. *U Pa med alum CW*: 1860. *Polk* 1886: 854.

McKENZIE, THOMAS GREER, Md; CW–USA (d/I–1 1867 Washington, DC) MD ? *Tr AMA* 18:357, 1867; 19:450, 1868. *Nat m j* 1:299, 1870/71.

McKENZIE, WILLIAM VALENTINE Jr, Metuchen, NJ (b/XI–14–1841 Irel'd; d/II–14–1906) MD CPSNY 1884; att Lafayette. *Bost m&s j* 154:230, 1906. *Polk* 1896: 941.

MACKEW, DENNIS I , Baltimore (b/XI–5–1829; d/II–10–1885) MD U Md 1850; AB St Mary's Coll 1848. *Med annals Md:* 498. *Med bull med & surg* 7:98, 1884. *Atkinson* I: 295. *Butler* 1874: 313.

MACKEY, ARGYLE, Baltimore (b/1868 NC; d/VIII–28 1896) MD U Md 1890. *Hist Med Soc DC:* 356. *JAMA* 27: 555, 1896. *Polk* 1893: 271.

MACKEY, CHARLES DAVID, Montrose, Pa (d/VII–31 1906) <MD Balto Med Coll 1882> *Pa m j* 9:894, 1905/06.

MACKEY, CHRISTOPHER, Hunterdon Co, NJ (d/IV 6–1862) MD CPSNY 1857. *Tr M S NJ* 1872: 185–86.

MACKEY, EDWARD, Buffalo, NY (d/VII–7–1867) <MD Dublin> *New Orl m&s j* 21:205, 1868.

MACKEY, HORATIO NELSON, Morgantown WVa (d/I–21–1896 @67) MD Rush 1872; MD Bellevue 1880. *JAMA* 26: 243, 1896. *Polk* 1886: 943.

McKIBBIN, DAVID JAMES, CW–USA; Ashland, Pa (b/X–15–1824 Phila; d/XII–19–1888) MD UPa 1846; att Coll UPa 1839. *Lehigh Valley med mag* 1:117–19, 1889–90. *Butler* 1878: 722.

MACKIE, ANDREW, New Bedford, Mass (b/I–24–1794 Wareham; d/V–2–1871) MD Brown 1817;AB 1814. *Bost m&s j* 7:324, 1871.

MACKIE, BENJAMIN S , USN (d/VII–25–1895 @50) MD Jefferson 1866. *Bost m&s j* 133: 176, 1895.

McKIE, JOHN, Providence, RI (b/VIII–1–1780 Wareham, Mass; d/II–22–1833) MD Dartmouth 1812; Hon MD Brown 1813; AB 1800. *Brown hist cat*: 1800.

MACKIE, JOHN HOWELL, CW–USN; New Bedford, Mass (b/VIII–24–1826 Plymouth; d/III–4/5–1891) MD Jefferson 1850; att Harvard 1849. *Harvard in CW*: 236. *Bost m&s j* 124: 276, 1891. *Butler* 1878:354.

McKIE, NATHAN W , Canton, Miss (b/VII–5–1849; d/VIII–19–1878) MD Wash U Balto 1870; att U La. *Tr AMA* 30:876–77, 1879. *Tr Miss St M S* 1878–81: 40–41.

de MACKIEWICZ, WILLIAM SEYDEL, NYC (d/III–24–1894 @70) <MD U Zurich 1854> *Med reg NY NJ Conn* 1894: 242. *Polk* 1886: 686.

McKIM, J W , St Louis (d/IX–9–1878 Memphis) MD ? *Tr AMA* 30: 877, 1879.

McKIM, JOHN DUNCAN, Washington, DC (b/I–4–1864 Staunton, Va; d/IV–23–1892) MD U Va 1886. *Hist Med Soc DC:* 336.

McKIM, SAMUEL AUCHMETY HARRISON, Washington, DC (b/IV–17–1826 Charlestown, Mass; d/VII 26–1900) MD Columbian 1852. *Hist Med Soc DC:* 248. *Polk* 1886: 213.

MACKIN, THOMAS HENRY, Reading, Pa (d/X–29 1906 @29) MD UPa 1900. *Pa m j* 10:328, 1906/07.

McKINLEY, JOHN, New Wilmington, Pa (d/XII–12 1902 @67) <MD Jefferson> *Pa m j* 6:261, 1902/03.

McKINLEY, JOHN AMBROSE, El Paso, Tex (b/V–26–1868 Postville, Ia; d/III–8–1901) MD NWU 1894. *Ill m j* ns3: 47, 1901. *Chic m rec* 20:605, 1901; 21:54–55, 1901.

McKINLEY, WILLIAM, Polk, Pa (d/IX–14–1901 @44) MD CPS Keokuk 1882. *Pa m j* 5:296, 1901/02.

McKINNEY, DAVID Jr, New Brighton, Pa (b/XII–12–1839 Centre Co; d/VIII–20–1901) MD Jefferson 1860. *Pa m j* 5:90 296 1901/02. *Atkinson* I:22. *Flint* 1897:811.

McKINNEY, GEORGE WEBSTER, Marion, Ind (b/XII 23–1849 Grant Co; d/V–2–1902) MD Bennett 1874; MD Ind M C 1884. *Tr Ind St M S* 1903: 348. *Polk* 1896: 477.

McKINNEY, W O , ? (d/X–1–1878 Holly Springs, Miss) MD ? *Tr AMA* 30:877, 1879.

McKINSTRY, JOHN F , Jonesboro, Ind (b/XI–22–1842 Preble Co, O; d/XII–6–1882) MD CPS Indianapolis 1875. *Tr Ind St Med Soc* 1883: 271.

McKISSACK, PETER DITMARS, Somerset Co, NJ (d/III–22–1872) MD UCNY 1842; AB Princeton 1837. *Tr AMA* 24:361, 1873. *Tr Med Soc NJ* 1872: 230.

McKISSACK, WILLIAM D , Millstone, NJ; War 1812–USA (d/III–6–1853) <att med lect NY> AB Princeton 1802. *Tr Med Soc NJ* 1872:163–65. *Med surg rep Phila* 6:414, 1861. *Blane, Hunterdon Co*: 75–77.

McKNAB, JOHN, Wells River, Vt (d/VII–20–1878) MD Dartmouth 1824 [as McNab] *Tr Vt Med Soc* 1883:107.

McKNEW, WILBERFORCE RICHMOND, CW–CSA; Baltimore (b/IX–28–1839 Pr Geor Co; d/V–31–1904) MD UMd 1862. *Med annals Md:*498. *JAMA* 43:61, 1904.

McKNIGHT, CHARLES G , Providence, RI (d/XI–4 1899 @83) MD UCNY 1848. *JAMA* 33:1441, 1899. *Polk* 1886: 846. Homeopath.

McKNIGHT, HATTON H, Nashville, Tn (d/XI–7–1898 Charlotte, NC) MD U Nashville 1892. *Polk* 1896: 1402.

McKNIGHT, JOSEPH GILLIES, Parkesburg, Chester Co, Pa (b/XI–13–1840 W Caln Twp; d/VIII–22–1866 @25) MD UPa 1866; AB Oberlin 1865. *U Pa med alum CW*: 1866. *Med s rep Phila* 15:228, 1866.

McKNIGHT, LEWIS, Milwaukee (b/NJ; d/VIII–21 1896 @71) MD UPa 1841; AB Princeton 1838; AM 1841. *JAMA* 27: 503, 1896. *Butler* 1878: 863.

McKUNE, ALBERT B , Council Bluffs, Ia (d/1883) MD Rush 1868. *Tr Ia St Med Soc* 13:410, 1900. *Butler* 1878:241.

McLACKLIN, D S , CW–USA (d/V–17–1864 Washington, DC) MD ? *Nat m j* 1:299, 1870/71.

McLAIN, DAVID HUBBARD, Gurley, Ala (b/IV–23–1851 Winston Co; d/V–31–1897) MD Med Coll Ala 1875. *Tr M Assn Ala* 1898: 35–36 (app). *Polk* 1893: 159.

McLANE, ALLEN, War 1812–USA; Wilmington, Del (b/1785 Smyrna; d/I–11–1845) MD UPa 1811; AB Princeton 1807; AM 1810. *Tr AMA* 29:716–18, 1878. *Med annals Md:* 498. *Hist Med Soc Del:* 40.

McLAREN, ADAM N , Boston; USA 1833– (b/Scotland; d/VIII–1–1874) MD M C SC 1829. *Bost m&s j* 91: 148, 1874. *Tr AMA* 28:629–33, 1877. *Med rec* 9:471, 1874.

McLAUGHLIN, ANDREW C , Tremont, O 1836– (b/VIII–1–1809 Concord Twp, O; d/X–12–1882) MD Starling 1876. *Tr Ohio St M S* 1884:223. *Atkinson* I: 110. *Butler* 1878: 640.

McLAUGHLIN, CORNELIUS W, NYC (d/X–23–1861 @ 31) MD NYMC 1852 *Med reg NY NJ Conn* 1862:155.

McLAUGHLIN, DANIEL CHARLES, Philadelphia (d/XII–6–1906) MD UPa 1905. *Pa m j* 10:295, 1906/07.

McLAUGHLIN, ISAAC THOMAS, NYC (b/IV–11–1844 Lewisburg, Pa; d/XI–27–1873) MD Bellevue 1869; att Lewisburg U. *Med reg NY NJ Conn* 1874: 281.

McLAUGHLIN, J M C , Kansas City, Mo (d/III–6–1895) MD ? *JAMA* 24:422, 1895.

McLAUGHLIN, MOSES A , San Francisco (b/Irel'd; d/XI–20–1899 @65) MD Toland 1878. *JAMA* 33: 1375, 1899. *Polk* 1886: 173.

McLAURIN, HUGH C , Brandon, Miss (b/IX–30–1813 Marlborough Dist, SC; d/VII–13–1880) MD UPa 1845. *Tr Miss St Med Assoc* 1881: 166. *Butler* 1874: 394.

McLAURY, WILLIAM MUIR, NYC(d/IX–8–1896) MD UCNY 1860. *JAMA* 27:722, 1896. *Polk* 1896: 1066.

McLAURY, WILLIAM PLATT, Catskill, NY (d/VIII–30–1904 @55) MD CPSNY 1875; AB Union 1869. *Tr Med Soc St NY* 1902: [484]. *Polk* 1886: 655.

MACLAY, ARCHIBALD, NYC (b/III–20–1812; d/XI–2 1892) MD CPSNY 1834.*Med reg NY NJ Conn* 1893:311

MACLAY, CHARLES BENJAMIN, Delavan, Ill; Petersburg, Pa; Gallipolis, O (b/IV–23–1824 Shippensburg, Pa; d/XI–3 1890) <MD Med Coll O 1852> AB Franklin & Marshall 1843. *F & M obit rec*: 45–46.

MACLAY, JOHN ANDREW, Greenvillage, Pa (d/X–15 1869) MD UPa 1867. *Phila med reg & dir* 1871: 302.

MACLAY, ROBERT H, NYC (b/X–20–1803; d/X–14 1868 @64) MD CPSNY 1824. *Med reg NY NJ Conn* 1869: 235. *Tr AMA* 21:437, 1870. *Phila m reg & dir* 1871: 298.

MACLAY, SAMUEL, Milroy Pa; CW–USA (b/X–5 1803 Mifflin Co; d/XII–17–1891 Washington, DC) MD UPa 1829; AB Dickinson 1825. *U Pa med alum CW*: 1829. *Polk* 1886: 808.

MACLEAN, ARCHIBALD M , Leadville, Colo (d/1886) MD U Mich 1874. *Tr Colo St Med Soc* 1898–99: 508. *Polk* 1886: 185.

McLEAN, CHARLES, Baltimore (b/1808 Washington, DC; d/VIII–17–1883) MD Columbian 1828. *Med annals Md*: 498. *Butler* 1874: 313.

McLEAN, DAVID, CW–USN; Nova Scotia (b/V–17–1836 Green Hill, NS; d/VIII–30–1876 Stellarton, NS) MD UPa 1864. *U Pa med alum CW*: 1864.

McLEAN, HENRY CORNELIUS, Brooklyn (b/New Hamburgh on Hudson, NY; d/XII–23–1904) MD UCNY 1873; att Manhattan Coll. *Bost m&s j* 151: 726, 1904. *Polk* 1896: 999.

McLEAN, J H , Cass City, Mich (d/X–21–1895) <MD Mich Coll Med 1833> *JAMA* 25: 781, 1895.

McLEAN, JOHN KNOX, Cheraw, SC; CW–CSA (b/I–18–1835; d/I–3–1883) MD UPa 1860; att UNC. *U Pa med alum CW*: 1860.

McLEAN, JOHN WILSON, Norwalk, Conn (d/IV–19 1897 @59) MD CPSNY 1859. *JAMA* 28:860, 1897. *Polk* 1896: 284.

McLEAN, JOSEPH R , Scranton, Pa (d/V–5–1897) MD UPa 1895. *JAMA* 28: 1045, 1897. *Polk* 1896:1335.

McLEAN, LEROY, CW–USA; Troy, NY (d/IV–23–1897 @66) MD Albany 1855. *Buff m&s j* 36: 783–84, 1897. *Bost m&s j* 136:418, 1897. *JAMA* 28: 860, 1897. *Tr Med Soc St NY* 1898: 403. *Atkinson* I: 236.

McLEAN, PETER, Laurinburg, NC (d/IX–20–1880) MD City NY 1879; att U Va. *Tr Med Soc NC* 1881: 32. *NC m j* 6: 242, 1880.

McLEAN, SAMUEL H , Hillsboro, Ill (d/III–18–1903 @53) MD Ecl Med Inst Cleveland 1874. *Tr Ill St Med Soc* ns4:760, 1903. *Polk* 1896: 423.

McLEAN, WILBUR FISK, Elyria, O (b/VII–26–1833 Northampton; d/X–5–1898 @65) MD LICH *Nat m j* 1: 299, 1870/71; ng U Mich 1855–65. *JAMA* 31: 942, 1898.

McLELLAN, ARCHIBALD C, Gloucester Mass (b/Pr Edw Isl; d/X–17–1896 @35) MD McGill 1890; LRCS

(Edinb) 1890. *JAMA* 27:1021, 1896. *Polk* 1896: 713.

McLELLAN, CHARLES HUGH PATTERSON, Gray, Me 1825–30; Portland 1830–36; Poughkeepsie NY 1837– (b/VI–5–1803 Gorham; d/IV–2–1862) MD Bowdoin 1825; AB 1822; AM 1839. *Bowdoin cat*: 1822.

McLELLAN, FRANCIS MILLER, Maspeth, NY; CW–USA (b/I–21–1817 Boston; d/XI–12–1863) MD Harvard 1843; AB Brown 1839. *Harvard in CW*: 230. *Med surg rep Phila* 10:426, 1863. *Nat m j* 1:299, 1870/71.

McLEMORE, ROBERT S , Greenwood, Miss (d/XI–23 1905 @63) MD Tulane 1872. *New Orl m&s j* 58: 609, 1906. *Polk* 1886: 530.

McLENAHAN, ROBERT MILLS, New Hampton, NJ (d/IV–28–1864) MD CPSNY 1839. *Tr Med Soc NJ* 1872: 185. *Blane, Hunterdon Co, NJ* : 97.

McLENDON, ERASTUS HOOD, Rock Mills, Ala (d/VII–20–1898) <MD Graffenburg 1860> *Tr Med Assoc St Ala* 1899: 233. *Polk* 1893: 162.

McLENNAN, KENNETH FAIRBAIRN, NYC (b/Scotl'd; d/I–30–1899 @54) MB U Glasgow 1867; MD 1877. *Bost m&s j* 140:172, 1899. *Polk* 1886:686.

McLEOD, GEORGE INGELS, Philadelphia (b/I–19–1832 Tioga Co; d/XII–20–1905 Bryn Mawr) MD UPa 1857; AB Bucknell 1852. *Pa m j* 9:281, 1905/06. *Polk* 1896: 1311.

McLEOD, SAMUEL BROWN WYLIE, NYC (b/II–1–1832; d/VIII–23–1899) MD CPSNY 1852; AB UPa 1849. *Bost m&s j* 141: 228, 1899. *JAMA* 33:620, 1899. *Polk* 1896: 1066.

MACLIN, WILLIAM T , DuQuoin, Ill (d/XII–6–1899) MD Ecl Med Inst Cinc 1868; MD Memphis Hosp Med Coll 1881. *Tr Ill St M S* 1899–1900:352. *Polk* 1896: 417.

MACLIN, WILLIAM W , Richmond, Va (b/Greenville Co; d/VIII–14–1878 @28) MD Med Coll Va 1877. *Tr Med Soc Va* 1878: 510.

MACLOCHLIN, JAMES ALPHONSUS, NYC (d/VII–16–1897 Saratoga) MD UCNY 1874. *JAMA* 29: 201, 1897. *Polk* 1896: 1066.

McMAHAN, SAMUEL W , Indianapolis, Ind (b/1847 Madison Co, Ky; d/IX–12–1901) MD Med Coll Ind 1879. *Tr Ind St Med Soc* 1902: 420. *Polk* 1886: 335.

McMAHON, J POINTE COULANT, USA 1817–34 (d/IV–1837 New Orleans) MD ? *Hist Med Soc DC*:216.

MACMAMUS, CHARLES, Mex War–USA; Matamoros, Mex (d/VIII–16 1906 @86) MD Tulane 1846. *Tex st m j* 2:144, 1906.

McMANIGAL, JOSEPH M, Hoboken Pa (d/VIII–29 1902 @39) MD U Md 1886. *Pa m j* 6:261, 1902/03.

McMANUS, CHARLES WILLIAM, NYC (d/I–5–1899 @ 22) MD LICH 1898. *Bost m&s j* 140:50, 1899.

McMANUS, FELIX R, Baltimore (b/V–30–1807; d/III–3 1885) MD U Md 1829; att Georgetown. *Tr Am Inst Hom* 1885:93. *New Engl med gaz* 20:192, 1885. *Amer hom obs* 21:47, 1885. *King* I: 196–96. Homeopath.

McMANUS, J J , Rutland, Vt (d/V–15–1895) MD ? *JAMA* 24:861, 1895.

McMANUS, THOMAS FRANCIS, Pittsburgh (b/X–3–1860 Youngstown, O; d/XI–5–1902) MD West Pa M C 1890. *Pa m j* 6:153, 223, 261, 1902/03. *Polk* 1896: 1327.

McMASTER, JOHN T B , Pocomoke City, Md (b/XII 18–1889 Worcester Co; d/VIII–28–1889) MD U Md 1850. *Med s rep Phila* 61: 308, 1889. *Med bull m & s* 11:334, 1889.

McMEEN, JAMES M , Danville, Ill (d/XII–28–1894 @65) MD U Louisville 1887. *JAMA* 24:33, 1895. *JAMA* 24:33, 1895. McDonough's *Ill dir* 1895: 252.

McMEENS, ROBERT RICHEY, Sandusky, O; CW–USA (b/1820 Long Reach, Pa; d/X–30–1862 Perryville, Ky) MD UPa 1841. *Tr Ohio St Med Soc* 1875: 195. *U Pa med alum CW*: 1841. *Nat m j* 1:299, 1870/71.

McMILLAN, CHARLES, NYC; CW–USA (b/Livingstone Co, NY; d/I–7–1890 Washington, DC) MD CPS NY 1849. *Med reg NY NJ Conn* 1890: 274. *Buff m&s j* 29: 445–46, 1890. *JAMA* 14:250, 1890. *Bost m&s j* 122: 712? 1890.

McMILLAN, F MARION, CW–CSA (d/I– –1868 SC) MD UCNY 1859. *UCNY cat*: 1859.

McMILLAN, WALLACE, Dorchester, Mass (d/III–31–1899 @31) MD McGill 1893. *Bost m&s j* 140:344, 1899. *Polk* 1896: 701.

McMILLAN, WILLIAM PENN, Biloxi, Miss (d/I–27 1899 @68) MD New Orl Sch Med 1857. *JAMA* 32: 506, 1899. *Polk* 1896: 807.

McMILLEN, JOHN W , Columbus, O (b/IX–13–1849 Sunbury, Del; d/1891) MD LICH 1873. *Tr Ohio Med Soc* 1891: 349–50.

McMILLIN, THOMAS, USA 1862– (d/IV–6–1873 Camp Von Bremer, Calif) MD ?U Louisville 1864. *Med surg rep Phila* 28:328, 1873. *Med rec* 8:214, 1873. *Tr AMA* 25: 536–37, 1874.

McMORRIS, NOBLE CALVIN, Duncannon, Pa (d/XII–27–1904 @75) MD Pa Med Coll 1859. *Pa m j* 8:335, 1904/05. *Flint* 1897: 800.

McMULLEN, THOMAS, Greenville, Pa (b/1826 Franklin Co; d/II–12–1884) MD Jefferson 1856. *Tr Pa St Med Soc* 1884:450–51. *Butler* 1878: 723.

M'MUNN, JOHN B , Port Jervis, NY (d/VIII–5–1869 @68) MD ? *Med surg rep Phila* 21:170, 1869. *Phila med reg & dir* 1871: 301.

McMURRAY, ANDREW STEWART, Philadelphia (b/XII–29–1810 Irel'd; d/IV–7–1884) MD Jefferson 1842. *Tr Pa St M S* 17:387 1885. *Med s rep Phila* 50:544 1884.

McMURRAY, GEORGE H , ? (d/VII–12–1901 @36) MD Albany 1887. *JAMA* 37: 276, 1901.

McMURRAY, GERALD J , Philadelphia (d/II–10–1900 @30) MD Jefferson 1894. *JAMA* 34: 511, 1900. *Polk* 1896: 1311.

McMURRAY, JOHN, Perry, Kans (b/1835 Canada; d/I–14–1891) MD Mo Med Coll 1869. *Tr Kans St Med Soc* 1881: 129. *Butler* 1878: 254.

McMURRAY, ROBERT, NYC 1844– (b/I–17–1817 Salem, NY; d/IV–15–1896) MD Fairfield 1840. *Tr Am Inst Hom* 1896:1191–92. *No Am j hom* 44:400, 1896.

McMURRAY, WILLIAM J , Nashville (b/IX–22 1842; d/XII–4–1905) MD U Nash 1869. *So pract* 28:47–48, 1906. *New Orl m&s j* 58:609, 1906. *Butler* 1878: 773. *Nashville j m & s* 97:564, 1905.

McMURTRIE, DANIEL, USN 1862–98 (b/Phila; d/XI–21–1899 Washington, DC) MD UPa 1863. *U Pa med alum CW*: 1863.

McMURTRIE, GEORGE SALTAR, Denver (b/I–3–1826 Phila; d/VIII– –1887) MD Pa M C 1860. *Tr Colo St Med Soc* 1898–99: 508. *Atkinson* I: 139. *Polk* 1886: 184.

MacNAIR, AUGUSTUS HARVEY, Tarboro, NC (b/XII–22–1819; d/III–29–1882) MD UPa 1842. *NC m j* 9:364–65, 1882.

McNAIR, SAMUEL, Kalamazoo, Mich (d/VI–30–1898 @75 Elburn, Ill) MD Rush 1859. *JAMA* 31: 142, 1898.

McNAIRY, BARTLETT YANCY, CW–CSA (b/1823 Guilford NC; d/X–28–1871 Aberdeen, Miss) MD UPa 1846; AB UNC 1843. *U Pa med alum CW*: 1846, suppl.

McNAIRY, BOYD, Nashville (d/XI–20–1856) MD UPa 1809. *Tr M S Tenn* 1876:84. *Nashvl j m&s* 11:545, 1856.

McNAIRY, CHARLES BINGLEY, Fillmore, Ind (b/III–11–1841 Putnam Co; d/VII–9–1880) MD Med Coll Ind 1875. *Tr Ind St Med Soc* 1881: 234. *Butler* 1896:211.

McNAIRY, JOHN SIMS, Nashville, Tenn (d/VI or VIII–18–1849) MD UPa 1835. *Tr AMA* 3:453, 1850. *NW m&s j* 2:370, 1849.

McNAIRY, WALTER SIMS, Washington, DC (d/IX–3 1898 @81) MD UPa 1842. *JAMA* 31:674, 1898.

McNAIRY, WILLIAM JAMES, CW–CSA (b/III–12–1836 Pulaski, Tenn; d/IX–20–1863 Chickamauga) MD UPa 1856. *U Pa med alum CW*: 1856, suppl.

McNAMARA, JAMES HUGHES, Hartford, Conn (b/II–22–1863; d/II–27–1892) MD UCNY 1887. *Proc Conn Med Soc* 1892: 871–72.

McNAMARA, LAWRENCE JOSEPH, NYC (d/I–28 1897 @37) MD Bellevue 1882. *Bost m&s j* 136:120, 1897. *JAMA* 28:328, 1897. *Polk* 1896: 1066.

McNARY, HUGH FLOURNOY, CW–USA; Princeton & Lakeland, Ky (b/I–15–1837; d/V–12–1897) MD Harvard 1863. *JAMA* 28: 1045, 1897; 29:297, 1897. *Rec AAS USA* 1891:61. *Polk* 1896: 2339, app.

McNARY, WILLIAM H , Martinsville, Ill (d/V–28–1898 @71) Lic by yrs pract. *JAMA* 30:1481, 1898. *Polk* 1896: 429.

McNAUGHTON, ALEXANDER W , San Francisco (d/1865) MD New Orl S M 1848. *Tr AMA* 19:449, 1868.

McNAUGHTON, HENRY G , Albany, NY (d/IV–18–1898) MD Albany 1856. *JAMA* 30:1125, 1898. *Polk* 1886: 639.

McNAUGHTON, JAMES, Albany, NY (b/XII–10–1796 Kenmore, Scotl'd; d/VII–11–1874 Paris, Fr) MD Edinburgh 1816. *Tr M S Co Albany* 3:363, 1883. *Med s rep Phila* 30:91–92, 1874. *Tr M S St NY* 1875:384–87. *K&B* III: 796.

McNAUGHTON, WILLIAM H , Watervliet, NY (d/VII 22–1897 @34) MD Albany 1886. *JAMA* 29:251, 1897.

McNEIL, BERNARD A , Philadelphia; CW–USA (d/I 27–1865 @31) MD Jefferson 1856. *Med surg rep Phila* 12:300, 1864/65. *Nat m j* 1:299, 1870/71.

McNEIL, C HOLMES, Jersey City, NJ (d/XII–18–1898) MD NY Homeop 1872. *JAMA* 32:41, 1899. *Polk* 1890: 723. Homeopath.

McNEIL, CURTIS, CW–USA (d/VIII–2–1864) MD ? *Nat m j* 1:299, 1870/71.

McNEIL, DANIEL, Jersey City (d/XI–9–1883 @69) MD ? *Med s rep Phila* 49: 616, 1883. *King* I:252. Homeopath.

McNEIL, JOHN, Demont, Pa (d/XI–3–1873 @62) MD Jefferson 1853. *Med s rep Phila* 28:345, 1873.

McNEILL, BERNARD, Philadelphia (b/1785? d/XI–7–1858 @73) MD CPSNY 1825. *Med s rep Phila* ns1: 124, 1858.

McNEILL, ERNEST, Morrisania, NY (b/1842 Brunswick, Me; d/I–5–1893) <MD Berkshire 1867> *Bost m&s j* 128: 52, 1893. *Polk* 1890: 824.

McNERNEY [McNANARY], STEWART A , Danbury Ia (d/1888) MD St U Iowa 1884. *Tr Iowa St Med Soc* 18:411, 1900; 21:449, 1903. *Polk* 1886: 355.

MacNIEL, DUGALD, Buffalo (b/1843 Scotl'd; d/III–21–1885) MD Buffalo 1871. *Buff m&s j* 24: 430–33, 1884. *Med bull med & surg* 7: 255, 1884. *Butler* 1878: 537.

McNULTY, CHARLES A , Harlem & Virginia City, Mont (d/X–6–1904) MD CPS Chicago 1887. *JAMA* 44: 232, 1905.

McNULTY, FREDERIC JOSEPH, Roxbury, Mass (b/1835 Richmond, Va; d/VI–13–1897) MD Georgetown 1860. *Bost m&s j* 136: 612, 1897. *JAMA* 28: 1252, 1897. *Polk* 1886: 472.

McNULTY, JOHN M , CW–USA; Fort Dodge, Ia (d/IX–14–1899 @75) MD UCNY 1853. *JAMA* 33:872, 1899. *Polk* 1890: 415.

McNUTT, JOHN S , Philadelphia (d/IX–28–1901) MD Cincinnati Coll Med & Surg 1867. *Pa m j* 5: 296, 1901/02. *Butler* 1878: 691.

MACOMB, EDWARD, USN 1866;USA 1871– (b/VIII–1 1843; d/I–14–1873 Ft Duncan Tx) MD CPSNY 1866; AB Hobart 1862; AM 1865. *Med reg NY NJ Conn* 1873: 343.

MACOMBER, (Mrs) FIDELE GRAY, Atlantic, Ia (d/V–29–1887) MD Hahnemann Chic 1879. *Med vis* 3:229, 1887. *Polk* 1886:351. Homeopath.

MACOMBER, GEORGE S , Melrose, Mass (d/I–1–1866 @46) MD Worcester 1849. *Bost m&s j* 73: 488, 1865. Homeopath?

MACOMBER, JAMES H , CW–USN (d/II–18–1865 Navy Hosp Land's End) MD ? *Nat m j* 1:299, 1870/71.

MACOMBER, JOSHUA MASON, Uxbridge, Mass (b/X 12–1811 New Salem; d/II–9–1887) <MD ?CPSNY

1834> MD NYMC 1854; AB Brown 1835; AM 1862. *Brown hist cat*: 1835.

MACON, GIDEON HUNT, CW-CSA; Littleton, NC? (b/IV-8-1832; d/X-23-1877) MD UPa 1854; att Randolph Macon. *Tr NC Med Soc* 1878: 26; 1879: 27. *Atkinson* I: 567.

MacOWEN, MICHAEL A , Utica, NY (d/I-19-1896 @76) MD ? *JAMA* 26: 243, 1896. *Polk* 1890: 855.

McPHAIL, DANIEL, Franklin, Tenn; Mex War-USA (b/ Scotl'd; d/1846) MD ? *Tr Med Soc Tenn* 1876: 84.

McPHAIL, LEONARD C , Brooklyn; CW-USA? (d/III-23-1867) "Stud med in Europe." *Tr AMA* 18:324-25, 1867. *Med reg NY NJ Conn* 1867: 222. *Med surg rep Phila* 16: 296, 1867.

McPHEETERS, JOHN [JOSEPH/] G , Bloomington, Ind (b/I-21-1811 Fayette Co, Ky; d/IV-2-1888) MD Transylvania 1840; AB U Ind 1834. *Tr Ind St Med Soc* 1888: 212. *Butler* 1878: 212

McPHEETERS, WILLIAM AUGUSTUS, CW-CSA; Natchez, Miss (b/III-11-1833 Jefferson Co, Miss; d/IX-27-1905 Springville, Mo) MD UPa 1855. *U Pa med alum CW*: 1855. *Polk* 1886: 530.

McPHEETERS, WILLIAM MARCELLUS, CW-CSA; St Louis (b/XII-3-1815 Raleigh, NC; d/III-15-1905) MD UPa 1840; <att UNC> *U Pa med alum CW*:1840. *Polk* 1886: 564.

McPHERSON, ANDREW GORDON, Quinton, NJ (b/XI 20-1841; d/I-29-1886 Stratford, Ont) MD UPa 1866. *Tr Med Soc NJ* 1886: 167-68. *Butler* 1878:473.

McPHERSON, E MELVIN, Janesville, Wis (d/VIII-12 1897 @35) MD Ecl Med Inst Cincinnati 1888 <MD Colo Sch Med 1894> *JAMA* 29:400, 453, 1897.

McPHERSON, J CHESTER, Brunswick, Me (d/I-4-1899 @42) MD U Md 1880. *JAMA* 32: 145, 1899. *Polk* 1893: 572.

McPHERSON, J T , Cambridge, O (d/XII-15-1894 @70) MD ?Med Coll Ohio 1849. *JAMA* 23:990, 1894. *Polk* 1890: 896.

McPHERSON, SAMUEL McCLUNG, CW-CSA (b/X-11-1837 Lewisburg, WVa; d/VI-14-1863 nr Richmond, Va) MD UPa 1861; AB Dickinson 1858; att UVa 1859. *U Pa med alum CW*: 1861.

McPHERSON, WILLIAM SMITH, Baltimore (b/III-4-1792 Adam Co, Pa; d/XI-20-1879) MD UPa 1817. *Med annals Md:* 499. *Butler* 1874: 313.

McPHETERS, JAMES A , Natchez, Miss (d/V?- -1848) MD ? *New Orl m&s j* 5:129, 1848.

McPHETERS, WILLIAM D , Hookstown, Pa (d/VII-20 1896 @45) MD Cleveland Med Coll 1870. *JAMA* 27: 337, 1896. *Polk* 1896: 1283.

McQUEEN, J K , Dallas, Tex (d/XII-14-1885 Montgomery, Ala) MD ? *Tex cour-rec med* 3:219,1886.

McQUEENEY, FRANCIS JOSEPH, Boston (b/II-29-1859; d/X-1-1906) MD Harvard 1890. *Bost m&s j* 155:389, 394, 1906. *Polk* 1896: 701.

McQUESTON, EUGENE FORREST, Nashua, NH (b/X 11-1842 or 1843 Litchfield; d/VII-18-1906 Squirrel Isl, Me) MD Jefferson 1866. *Tr NH Med Soc* 1906:239-40. *Polk* 1890: 711.

McQUILLAN, JOHN HUGH, Philadelphia (b/II-12 1826; d/III-3-1879) MD Jefferson 1852. *Med rec NY* 15: 240, 1879.

MacRAE, JAMES A , Fayetteville, NC; MexWar-USA; CW-CSA (d/III?- -1887) MD UCNY 1845. *NC m j* 19: 272, 1887. *Tr NC Med Soc* 1887: 159.

McRAE, P P , Ga (d/VIII- 1868 @45 Columbia Tx) MD ? *Phila med reg & dir* 1871: 298. *Tr AMA* 21:489, 1870.

McREA [McREE], JAMES FERGUS Sr, Wilmington, NC (b/XI-18-1794; d/VIII-9-1869) MD CPSNY 1814. *Phila med reg & dir* 1871: 301. *Tr AMA* 21:484-85, 1870. *Tr NC Med Soc* 1870:8-9. *NC m j* 29:10 ff, 1892. *K&B* III:798-99.

McREYNOLDS, HUGH WASHINGTON, Bloomsburg, Pa (b/VII-2-1822 Montour Co, Pa; d/IV-17-1906) MD UPa 1848. *Pa m j* 9:707, 1905/06. *Flint* 1897: 796.

McREYNOLDS, WILLIAM H , Cincinnati, O (d/XI-29 1890) MD Med Coll Ohio 1858. *Buffalo m&s j* 30:372, 1891. *Butler* 1878: 612.

McRUER, DANIEL, Bangor, Me; CW-USA (b/I-12 1802 Scotl'd; d/IV-5-1873) MD UPa 1834. *Tr Me Med Assoc* 1871-73: 484-86. *U Pa med alum CW*: 1834.

McSHEEHY, JOHN JAMES, CW-USA Boston (d/IX-13-1884) MD Harvard 1864. *Harvard in CW*: 288.

McSHERRY, HENRY F , USN 1860- (d/X-1-1867 abd Wyoming) MD U Md 1858. *Tr AMA* 19:455, 1868. *Med s rep Phila* 17: 524, 1867. *Nat m j* 1:299, 1870/71.

McSHERRY, RICHARD, USN & USA; Baltimore (b/XI 21-1817 Martinsburg, Va; d/X-7-1885) MD UPa 1841. *Chic m j* 51:486, 1885. *New Orl m&s j* ns13:420, 1885. *Med ann Md*:500. *Atkinson* I:22. *K&B* III:799-800.

McTAGGART, JAMES, Detroit (d/X-18-1899) <MD Detroit Med Coll 1893> *JAMA* 33: 1183, 1899.

McTAMMANY, GEORGE H , Cohoes, NY (b/Troy; d/IV-12-1891) MD Albany 1884. *Tr Med Soc St NY* 11:741 ff, 1894. *Polk* 1886: 657.

McTAMMANY, WILLIAM FRANCIS, Troy, NY (d/ VII- -1888) MD Bellevue 1880; AB St John's, NY 1877. *Med reg NY NJ Conn* 1889: 278.

McTAVISH, DUNCAN A , West Bay City, Mich (b/1855 Glencoe, Ont; d/XI-17-1898) MD Toronto 1881; LRCS Edinburgh. *JAMA* 31:1377, 1898. *Polk* 1880: 605.

McVAY, HARLAN E , USA (b/Ohio; d/I-4-1899 Manila) <MD Miami> *JAMA* 32: 195, 1899.

McVICKAR, JOHN AUGUSTUS, NYC (b/VI-16-1812 Schenectady, NY; d/I-29-1892) MD CPSNY 1833. *King* I:90. *Med vis* 8:122, 1892. *Cleave.* Homeopath 1843- .

McWAYNE, LEROY D, Hoosick Falls NY (d/V-10-1906) MD ? *Bost m&s j* 154:568 1906. *Polk* 1896: 1014.

McWHARTER, A A , ?Burkeville, Tex 1849- (b/Ala; d/VII-15-1906 @81) MD ? *Tex st m j* 2:122, 1906.

McWHINNEY, ARTHUR, Philadelphia (d/XII-25-1871 @52) MD Jefferson 1851. *Phila med reg & dir* 1873: 303. *Med times* Phila 2:192, 1871/72.

McWHORTER, ALEXANDER B, Mt Carmel, Ala (d/ 1859?) MD ? *So m&s j* 15:791–92, 1859.

McWHORTER, ALEXANDER B, Mt Carmel, Ala (d/ 1887?) MD UCNY 1846. *Tr Med Assoc St Ala* 1888:316. *Butler* 1874: 22. *Polk* 1886: 316.

McWILLIAMS, ALEXANDER, Washington, DC; USN (b/1775 St Mary's Co Md; d/III-31-1850) MD Columbian 1841; stud UPa> *Hist M S DC*:215–16. *K&B* III: 800.

McWILLIAMS, ALEXANDER BARTON, Washington, DC; b/1823 or 1827; d/V-17-1898) MD Columbian 1846. *JAMA* 30:1366, 1898. *Hist Med Soc DC*:283. *Rec AAS USA* 1891: 68. *Polk* 1886: 213.

MacWITHEY, EDWARD LEWIS CHICHESTER, NJ (b/II-11-1852; d/X-24-1879) MD CPSNY 1871. *Med reg NY NJ Conn* 1880: 237. *Med rec NY* 16:432, 1879.

MACY, BENJAMIN CLASBY, New Harmony Ind 183–; Elyria, O; Brooklyn (b/XI-26-1809 Hudson, NY; d/IX-16-1864) MD UCNY 1836. *Tr Amer Inst Hom* 1865: 109. *Med surg rep Phila* 12:132, 1864/65.

MADDEN, EDWARD GEORGE, New Haven, Conn (b/ VIII-5-1864 Irel'd; d/III-12-1896) MD Yale 1885. *Proc Conn Med Soc* 1897: 354.

MADDEN, PETER HENRY, Woonsocket, RI (b/VI-29-1828 Irel'd; d/IV-21-1895) <MD Louvain, Belg 1857> *Tr RI Med Soc* 5:252–53, 1894–98. *Polk* 1890:1029.

MADDEN, WILLIAM B, Johnstown, Pa (d/X-9-1889) MD UPa 1877. *Med s rep Phila* 61:447, 1889. *Polk* 1886: 803.

MADDOX, CHARLES J, Rockville, Md (d/VII-26-1899 @80) MD U Md 1843. *JAMA* 33: 367, 1899. *Polk* 1886: 445.

MADDOX, JAMES HAMILTON, Deason, Miss (d/III-4 1900) MD Memphis Hosp Med Coll 1882. *JAMA* 34: 703, 1900.

MADDOX, THOMAS H, Rapides, Miss (b/1793 Md; d/I 1888 @95) MD ? *New Orl m&s j*ns15: 669–70, 1888. *Polk* 1886: 527.

MADDOX, WILLIAM ROBEY, Washington DC (b/III-8-1855 Erie, Pa; d/X-25-1899) MD Jefferson 1877. *Hist M S DC*: 360. *JAMA* 33:1183, 1899. *Polk* 1896: 305.

MADDUX, THOMAS CLAY, CW-CSA (b/II-10-1836; d/XI-8-1881) <MD Winchester Med Coll 1859> Washington U Balto 1868. *Tr AMA* 33: 587–88, 1882. *Med annals Md*: 485.

MADDUX, WILLIAM D, Monticello, Ga (d/VII-22-1901 @87) MD UCNY 1842. *JAMA* 37: 398, 1901. *Polk* 1886: 232.

MADILL, THOMAS F, Wysox Pa (d/VI-27-1906 @ 78) MD Jeff'n 1855. *Pa m j* 9:745, 1905/06. *Flint* 1897: 840.

MADISON, ROBERT LEWIS, Lexington, Va (b/Orange Co, Va; d/V-26-1878 @50) MD Jefferson 1850. *Tr Med Soc Va* 1878: 509–510. *Butler* 1878: 832.

MADISON, THOMAS COOPER, Lynchburg, Va; CW-CSA (b/VI-10-1818 Madison Co; d/XI-7-1865 Tallahassee, Fla) MD UPa 1838. *Med surg rep Phila* 13: 390, 1865. *U Pa med alum CW*: 1838.

MAGEE, ANTHONY BERNARD, Lawrence, Mass (d/I-31-1887 @38) MD Dartmouth 1874. *Bost m&s j* 116: 124, 1887. *Polk* 1886: 469.

MAGEE, JAMES J, CW-USN (d/II-14-1864 Phila) MD ? *Nat m j* 1:299, 1870/71.

MAGER, HUGO, Colo (d/VII-18-1898 @48) MD NW Med Coll 1883. *Tr Colo St Med Soc* 1898–99: 38, 509. *Polk* 1893: 236.

MAGGINI, J C F, Port Perry, Pa (b/VI-17-1820 Balto; d/III-1-1877) MD Med Coll Ohio 1841. *Tr Med Soc Pa* 1877: 585–586.

MAGILL, ARTHUR H, Brooklyn (d/II-27-1869 @69) MD ? *Med reg NY NJ Conn* 1869: 235. *Phila med reg & dir* 1871: 300. *Med surg rep Phila* 20: 199, 1869.

MAGILL, CHARLES ARTHUR, Niles, Mich (d/XI-14 1884 @67) MD UCNY 1846. *Med surg rep Phila* 51: 732, 1884.

MAGILL, MARY J, Sacramento (b/III-23-1855 Dubuque, Ia; d/VIII-15-1891) MD Woman's Med Coll Chic 1864. *Tr M S Cal* 22: 263, 1892. *Polk* 1890: 193.

MAGNESS, GEORGE HOSMER, White Plains, NY (b/ 1851 NYC; d/VI-25-1901) MD Bellevue 1876. *Bost m&s j* 145:28, 1901. *Polk* 1896:1112.

MAGOFFIN, JOHN, St Louis (d/XI-3-1893 @74 Kirkwood) MD Transylvania 1847; AB Centre Coll, Danville, Ky 1842. *JAMA* 21:784,1893. *Butler* 1878:418.

MAGNIN, JULIUS A F, CW-USN; (d/II-10-1864 @21) MD Pa Med Coll 1861. *Nat m j* 1:299, 1870/71.

MAGRAW, JAMES MARTIN, Thomas Run, Harford Co, Md (b/1841 Cecil Co; d/VII-13-1889) MD UPa 1866. *Med annals Md*: 485–86. *Polk* 1886: 446.

MAGRUDER, HEZEKIAH, Washington, DC (b/V-24-1804 Montg'y Co, Md; d/VII-20-1874) MD U Md 1826. *Hist Med Soc DC*: 242. *Tr AMA* 31:1065–66, 1880.

MAGRUDER, J T, Canton, Miss (d/1878) MD U La 1872. *Tr AMA* 30:874–75, 1879.

MAGRUDER, WILLIAM BOWIE, Baltimore (b/II-11-1810; d/V-30-1869 Washington, DC) MD U Md 1831. *Med surg rep Phila* 20:436, 1869. *Tr AMA* 23:577–78, 1872. *Phila med reg & dir* 1871: 301.

MAGRUDER, ZADOK, ?Baltimore (b/V-10-1765 Montg'y Co; d/XII-2-1809) <MD UPa 1786> *Med ann Md*: 486.

MAGUIRE, CHARLES, Baltimore (b/Irel'd; d/1847) MD U Md 1829. *Med annals Md*: 486.

MAGUIRE, PHILIP JAMES, NYC (d/I-9-1899 @54) MD CPSNY 1871. *Bost m&s j* 140:76, 1899. *Polk* 1896: 1066.

MAGUIRE, ROBERT, Kent Co, Md (d/XII-23-1821 Turners Crk) MD ? AM St Johns 1804? *Med ann Md* 486

MAHON, ALFRED N, Pittsburgh (d/I-11-1902 @29)

MD Jefferson 1897. *Pa m j* 6:261, 1902/03.

MAHON, CHARLES L , Smyrna, Del (d/I–3–1873) MD ? *Med surg rep Phila* 28:202, 1873.

MAHON, DAVID NELSON, USN 1821–24; Carlisle, Pa (b/1797 or 1798 nr Pittsburgh; d/VIII–29–1876) MD UPa 1820; AB Dickinson 1815. *Dickinson cat*: 1815.

MAHON, JAMES ARTHUR, Boston (b/II–7–1865 Nova Scotia; d/IX–14–1905) MD Harvard 1896. *Bost m&s j* 153:348, 1905; 154:114, 1906.

MAHON, ORMSBY S , Baltimore (b/1826 Pa; d/IV–3–1894) MD Jefferson 1849. *Med annals Md:* 486.

MAILLY, HAMILTON, Bridgeton, NJ (b/1867 Del; d/VIII–30–1899 @32) MD UPa 1891. *JAMA* 33: 683, 1899. *Polk* 1896:934.

MAIN, JOHN H T , Ft Smith, Ark; Jackson, Mich (d/X 1–1891) MD Castleton 1857. *Med bull med & surg* 13:471, 1891. *Polk* 1886: 495.

MAINES, ELIJAH WOLSEY, Flatbrookville, NJ (b/V–29–1832 Stillwater, NJ; d/III–13–1876) MD Jefferson 1859; att Geneva. *Med reg NY NJ Conn* 1876: 251. *Tr AMA* 27:657, 1876. *Tr Med Soc NJ* 1876: 146–47.

MAJER, ADOLPH, CW–USA (d/1866 NYC) MD ? *Nat m j* 1:299, 1870/71.

MALECH, GUSTAVUS H, San Francisco (d/I–10–1900) MD Phila Coll Med & Surg 1850. *JAMA* 34: 251, 1900. *Polk* 1886: 173.

MALIN, GEORGE W , Penn Yan, NY; Germantown, Pa 1856– (b/VIII–3–1802/03?; d/I–18–1883) MD Homeop Coll St NY 1842. *Tr Hom Med Soc St Pa* 1883: 43 ff. *Hahn mo* 18:122, 1883. Homeopath.

MALIN, JOHN, Naples, NY; Germantown, Pa (b/II–2–1833 Penn Yan, NY; d/XI–29–1889) MD Hahnemann Phila 1860; stud dentistry. *Tr Am Inst Hom* 1890:143. *Tr Hom Med Soc St Pa* 1892: . *Polk* 1886: 821.

MALLESON, PHILIP ARTHUR OSMOND, NYC (b/XII–25–1859 Glens Falls, NY; d/IX–19–1898) MD CPSNY 1885. *JAMA* 31: 808, 1898. *Polk* 1886: 686.

MALLET-PREVOST, WASHINGTON, Wilkes-Barre, Pa; Mexico City 1890– (b/V–4–1864 Zacatecas, Mex; d/V–13–1895 Fresnillo, Mex) MD UPa 1888; ng Coll UPa 1887. *JAMA* 24:861, 1895.

MALLORY, MAITLAND LORENZO, Rochester NY (d/IV–28–1894 @46) MD CPSNY 1873. *Med reg NY NJ Conn* 1894: 242. *Buff m&s j* 33:693, 1894. *JAMA* 22:764, 1894.

MALONE, BENJAMIN, CW–USA (b/X–26–1807 Buckingham Twp, Pa; d/XII–28–1871 Phila) MD UPa 1831. *U Pa med alum CW*: 1831, suppl.

MALONE, DANIEL C , So Bethlehem, Pa (d/IX–24–1902 @58) MD UPa 1869. *Pa m j* 6:261, 1902/03.

MALONE, EDWARD, Brooklyn (d/VI–16–1890 @ c52) MD UCNY 1859. *Med reg NY NJ Conn* 1891: 277.

MALONE, H B , Gallatin, Tenn (d/X–29–1876 @46) MD ? *Med surg rep Phila* 35: 414, 1876.

MALONE, HENRY B , Cincinnati; Indian Bay, Ark (d/X–4–1868) MD ? *Phila med reg & dir* 1871: 298. *Med surg rep Phila* 20: 199, 1869.

MALONE, JOHN, CW–USA (d/V–31–1863 Phila) MD ? *Nat m j* 1:299, 1870/71.

MALONE, JOHN A , Princeton, Ind (b/XII–10–1837 Owensville; d/II–16–1893) att U Mich Med Dept 1864/65. *Tr Ind St Med Soc* 1893: 257.

MALONE, LOUIS A , Jacksonville, Ill (d/X–14–1905 @47 Indianapolis) MD NWU 1885. *Ill m j* 8:430, 1905.

MALONEY, JAMES ALOYSIUS, Washington, DC (b/II 24–1846 Balto; d/X–29–1897) MD Columbian 1891. *Hist Med Soc DC:* 345. *Polk* 1893: 271.

MALONY, JOHN M , Allegheny, Pa; Eddytown (d/II 12–1896 @52) MD Georgetown 1870. *JAMA* 26: 391, 1896. *Polk* 1886: 659.

MANCHESTER, CHARLES FENNER, Pawtucket, RI (b/II–7–1805 Johnston; d/IV–5–1878) MD Harvard 1828; AB Brown 1825. *Brown hist cat*: 1825.

MANCHESTER, CONSTANT WOOD, Lebanon NH (b/IV–20–1831 Plainfield; d/VIII–4–1892) MD U Vt 1858. *Tr NH Med Soc* 1893:157–58. *Polk* 1890:710.

MANCHESTER, DARWIN L , Waupaca, Wis (b/II–25 1833 Cornish, NH; d/VIII–11–1895) MD Dartmouth 1867; MD Chicago Med Coll 1870. *JAMA* 25: 342, 1895. *Tr Wis St M S* 29:539–46. *Butler* 1878: 863.

MANDELBAUM, GERSON, NYC (b/I–25–1835 Gny; d/X–17–1882) MD ? *Med reg NY NJ Conn* 1883: 232. *Butler* 1874: 505.

MANDEVILLE, AUSTIN, Rochester, NY (d/VIII–31–1888) MD Berkshire 1845. *Tr Med Soc St NY* 1889: 364. *Polk* 1886: 704.

MANDEVILLE, DORRANCE KIRTLAND, Brooklyn (b/1828 New Brunswick, NJ; d/III–12–1896) MD CPS NY 1853; att Hamilton Coll 1849. *JAMA* 26: 642, 1896. *Bost m&s j* 134:302, 1896. *NC m j* 37:214, 1896.

MANDEVILLE, HENRY ADDISON, Orange NJ (b/XII 16–1858 Newburgh; d/I–31–1903) MD CPSNY 1881; AB UCNY. *Bost m&s j* 148:166 1903. *Polk* 1896, 949.

MANEY, HARDY JAMES, CW–CSA (b/VI–14–1834 Franklin, Tenn; d/VIII–3–1881 Auburn) MD UPa 1857. *U Pa med alum CW*: 1857, suppl.

MANGUM, HOWELL Y , Metropolis, Ill (d/XII–26 1898) Certified by Exam Bd. *JAMA* 32:145, 1899. *Polk* 1886: 284.

MANLEY, GARRIT V , Long Isl City, NY (d/III–10–1862 @38) MD ? *Med s rep Phila* ns7:624, 1861/62.

MANLEY, IRA, Markesan, Wis (b/X–2–1822; d/XII–9–1892) MD CPSNY 1848. *Tr Wis St Med Soc* 1894: 503. *Polk* 1890: 1167.

MANLEY, JAMES R , NYC (b/1782? d/XI–21–1851 @69) MD ? ; AB Columbia 1799. *So m&s j* 8: 67, 1852. *NW m&s j* 4:380, 1852? *NH j m* 2:167, 1852.

MANLEY, THOMAS HENRY, NYC (b/Irel'd; d/I–14–1904) MD UCNY 1875. *Bost m&s j* 152: 90, 1905. *Polk* 1896: 1066.

MANLY, CHARLES S, Denver (d/XI-13-1895 @29) MD Denver 1891. *Tr Colo St Med Soc* 1898-99:509. *Polk* 1893: 236.

MANLY, LANGDON CHEVES, CW-CSA; Raleigh, NC (b/1822; d/1888) MD UPa 1848; AB UNC 1845; AM 1849. *U Pa med alum CW*: 1848.

MANN, BENJAMIN, Roxbury, Mass (b/III-31-1814 Randolph, Mass; d/IV-21-1874 Brooklyn) MD Harvard 1840; AB Amherst 1837. *Bost m&s j* 90:444, 466, 1874.

MANN, DELOS H, Brooklyn (b/Delhi, NY; d/V-2-1906 @70) MD Albany 1848 [!] *Bost m&s j* 154:538, 1906. *Polk* 1886:647.

MANN, GEORGE R, CW-USN (d/VIII-20-1864 abd US Pocahontas) MD ? *Nat med jour* 1:299, 1870/71.

MANN, JOHN PRESTON, NYC (d/I-13-1893 Syracuse @71) MD Geneva 1842. *Med reg NY NJ Conn* 1894:242.

MANN, JONATHAN, Boston (d/VI-15-1889 @73) MD Berkshire 1840. *Bost m&s j* 120:652, 1889.

MANN, THOMAS THEODORE, St Paul, Minn (b/Phila; d/1884?) MD ? *Tr Minn St Med Soc* 1893:121.

MANNERS, JOHN, Clinton, NJ (b/IV-8-1786; d/VI-24 1853) MD UPa 1812; Hon AM Princeton 1812. *Tr Med Soc NJ* 1872:135-36.

MANNEY, JAMES LEWIS, Beaufort, NC (d/III-18-1889 Wilmington) MD CPSNY 1848. *NC med jour* 23: 234, 1889. *Polk* 1886: 720.

MANNHEIMER, MICHAEL, Chicago (b/Batavia; d/VIII 31-1891) MD Tulane 1870; stud Europe. *Chic med rec* 2:79-80, 1891.

MANNING, ANDREW, Plainfield, NJ (b/I-6-1861; d/V-19-1898) MD CPSNY 1883; att Rutgers. *Bost m&s j* 138:529, 1898. *Tr Med Soc NJ* 1898:381-82. *JAMA* 30: 1366, 1898.

MANNING, CHARLES D, Chicago (b/1848 Dixon, Ill; d/IX-24-1898) MD Rush 1870. *JAMA* 31: 872, 1898. *Polk* 1886: 267.

MANNING, EDMUND ROACH, Albany & Stamford, Tex (b/VI-9-1854 Bellville; d/I-14-1904) MD Mo Med Coll 1897. *Tex st m j* 1:244, 1906. *Polk* 1902: 1912.

MANNING, FREDERICK ARNOLD, Denver (b/V-4-1859 Eddyville, Ind; d/XII-3-1896) MD CPSNY 1884; AB Yale 1881. *JAMA* 28:140, 1897. *Bost m&s j* 135: 610, 1896.

MANNING, JOHN, Rockport, Mass (b/X-12-1789 Gloucester; d/II-7-1852) MD Harvard 1813; AB 1810. Palmer's *Necrol Harvard alum*: 6.

MANNING, JOSEPH, Rockport, Mass (b/XI-7-1826 Waldoboro; d/XII-10-1894) MD Bowdoin 1852. *Bost m&s j* 131: 600, 1894. *Polk* 1886: 472.

MANNING, MASON, Mystic, Conn (b/VIII-27-1796 Lisbon; d/II-10-1883) Hon MD Yale 1840. *Proc Conn Med Soc* 1883: 173-77. *Butler* 1878: 80.

MANNING, PETER, Lowell, Mass (b/1791? d/VIII-4-1855 @64) ng Dartmouth M S 1814. *Bost m&s j* 53: 47, 1856.

MANNING, THOMAS D, Austin, Tex (d/IX-20-1878 Holly Springs, Miss) MD U La 1861. *Tr AMA* 30:875, 1879. *Tr Tex St Med Assoc* 1884: 61-65.

MANNING, WILLIAM PRICE, Washington, DC (b/XII 8-1844 Va; d/II-9-1901) MD U Md 1869. *Hist Med Soc DC:* 327. *Polk* 1893: 271.

MANNY, JAMES HARVEY Jr, Chicago (d/XII-6-1897 @38) MD CPS Chicago 1890; MD CPSNY 1892. *JAMA* 29: 1286, 1897. *Polk* 1896: 396.

MANOR [MANER], FRANKLIN B, Itasca, Tex (d/1905?) MD Vanderbilt 1880. *Tex st med jour*1:84, 1905/06. *Polk* 1886: 885.

MANSFIELD, JOHN ROBBINS, Wakefield, Mass (d/XI 11-1906 @74) MD Harvard 1859. *Bost m&s j* 155: 666, 1906. *Polk* 1896: 724.

MANSFIELD, RICHARD W, Baltimore (b/XII-14 1846 Chestertown; d/VI-2-1898) MD U Md 1865. *JAMA* 30: 1534, 1898. *Med annals Md:* 488.

MANSON, GEORGE W, Philadelphia (d/I-9-1863 @43) MD Phila Coll Med & Surg 1849. *Med surg rep Phila* ns9:326, 1862/63.

MANSON, HENRY WALKER, Rockwall, Tex (d/X-27 1905 @64) MD U Nashville 1867. *So pract* 27: 704, 1905. *Polk* 1886: 893.

MANSON, JOHN C, Pittsfield Me (b/X-2-1830 Meredith, NH; d/IV-8-1885) MD UCNY 1853. *Tr Me M Assn* 1885:564-66. *Atkinson* I:676-77. *Butler* 1878:309.

MANSON, OTIS FREDERICK, NC 1841- ; Richmond, Va 1862- ; CW-CSA (X-10-1822 Richmond; d/I-25 or II-1-1888) MD Hampden-Sydney 1841. *NC m j* 21: 125-28, 150, 1888. *Tr Med Soc Va* 1888: 275. *New Orl m&s j* ns15:836, 1888. *Atkinson* I: 344. *K & B* III: 807.

MANWARING, ROBERT ALEXANDER, New London, Conn (b/VIII-2-1811; d/IX-1-1890) Hon MD Yale 1845. *Med reg NY NJ Conn* 1892:282. *JAMA* 15: 555, 1890. *Proc Conn Med Soc* 1891:304-06. *Bost m&s j* 123: 264, 1890.

MAPES, JAMES JAY, NYC (d/1896 Saranac Lake, NY) MD CPSNY 1891;AB Columbia 1888. *Buff m&s j* 35: 828 1896. *JAMA* 26:890 1896. *Bost m&s j* 134:425 1896.

MARBLE, WALTER H, Chicago (b/Ashburnham, Mass;d/I-13-1899) MD Chicago Med Coll 1886. *JAMA* 32:195, 1899. *Polk* 1893: 346.

MARBURY, WILLIAM, Washington, DC (b/II-9-1824; d/XII-18-1879) MD UPa 1847. *Tr AMA* 31:1066-67, 1880. *Hist Med Soc DC:* 253.

MARCH, ALDEN, Albany, NY (b/IX-20-1795 Sutton, Mass; d/VI-17-1869) MD Brown 1820; LLD Williams 1868. *Phila med reg & dir* 1871: 301. *Chic m j* 26:428, 1869. *Buff m&s j* 8:552, 1859. *Tr AMA* 21:447-48, 1870. *Tr Med Soc St NY* 1870:287-308. *K & B* III: 808-809.

MARCH, DANIEL Jr, Winchester, Mass (b/V-25-1844 New Haven, Conn; d/I-1-1897) MD UPa 1871; AB Amherst 1865. *Bost m&s j* 136: 24, 121, 1896. *JAMA* 28:236, 1897.

 Spec. educ'l status abbrev. as: ***ng*** = college verified attendance without degree;

MARCH, DAVID, Sutton, Mass (b/I-29-1785; d/V-13-1829) MD Brown 1816; AB 1811. *Brown hist cat*: 1811.

MARCH, HENRY, Albany, NY; CW-USA (b/XII-13-1826 or 1827; d/V-7-1886 Santa Barbara, Cal) MD Albany 1853. *Tr Med Soc St NY* 1887: 565 ff. *Atkinson* I: 374. *K & B* III: 803 [mention only]. *Butler* 1874: 549.

MARCH, MARVIN M , NYC (d/1868) MD New Orl Med Sch 1841. *Tr AMA* 21: 447, 1870.

MARCY, ERASTUS EDGERTON, NYC (b/XII-9-1815 Greenwich, Mass; d/XII-27-1900) MD Jefferson 1837; AB Amherst 1834. *Tr Am Inst Hom* 1901: 917. *Med vis* 17:113, 1901. *Cleave*. Homeopath.

MARCY, LORENZO, Woodstock, Conn (b/1793; d/I-4-1875) Hon MD Yale 1839; att Harvard Med 1816. *Med reg NY NJ Conn* 1876: 252.

MARCY, SAMUEL SIMONSON [SUMNER?], Cape May, NJ (b/XII-7-1793 Willington, Conn; d/II-13-1882) Hon MD Yale 1817. *Tr Med Soc NJ* 1882: 188.

MARCY, SIMEON, Canajoharie NY (b/VIII-19-1770; d/XII-6-1853) MD ? AB Brown 1795. *Brown hist cat*.

MARION, OTIS HUMPHREY, Allston, Mass (b/I-12-1847 Burlington; d/XI-27-1906) MD Harvard 1878; AB Dartmouth 1873. *Bost m&s j* 155:666 1906. *K&B* III:810.

MARIS, EDWARD, Philadelphia (d/VI-13-1900 @68) MD Jeff'n 1855. *JAMA* 34:1645 1900. *Polk* 1896: 1311.

MARIS, EDWARD ALEXANDER, Baltimore (b/VIII-19-1820; d/IV-20-1902) MD U Md 1841. *Med annals Md:* 488. *Polk* 1886: 438.

MARIX, MARTIN MAYER, Buffalo 1857; Appleton, Wis; Denver 1870 (b/1832? d/1877) <MD U Leipzig> *US med inv* 5:318, 1877. *King* I: 407, 415. *Cleave*. Homeopath.

MARKHAM, GEORGE E , Burnside, Conn (b/III-9-1857; d/VII-4-1890) MD UCNY 1882. *Proc Conn Med Soc* 1893: 237-38.

MARKHAM, HOMER C , Independence, Ia (d/VIII-18 1901 @63) MD UCNY 1859. *JAMA* 37:654, 1901. *Polk* 1886: 360.

MARKHAM, T H , Huntsville, Tex (b/VI-20-1823 Chesterfield Co, Va; d/VIII-6-1897) MD Memphis Med Coll 1853. *Tex med news* 7:36, 1897. *So pract* 19:431-32, 1897. *Polk* 1890: 1083.

MARKLEY, ARTHUR DONALDSON, CW-USN (b/IV 19-1832 Columbia, Pa; d/IV-6-1896 Hatboro) MD UPa 1857. *U Pa med alum CW*: 1857.

MARKOE, THOMAS MASTERS, NYC (b/IX-13-1819 Phila; d/VIII-26-1901) MD CPSNY 1841; AB Princeton 1836. *Bost m&s j* 145: 289, 1901. *JAMA* 37: 654,1901. *Atkinson* I:676. *K & B* III:810. *Polk* 1886:686.

MARKS, ELIAS, Washington, DC (b/1790? d/VI-22-1886 @96) MD CPSDNY 1815. *Med reg NY NJ Conn* 1887: 269.

MARKS, JOHN IRWIN, Milroy, Pa; CW-USA (b/IV-9 1826 Lewistown; d/I-12-1883) MD UPa 1853; AB Wash & Jeff 1846. *Tr Med Soc Pa* 16:476-77, 1884.

MARKS, PIERRE A , Chicago; CW-USN (d/V-12-1905 @61) MD Miami 1867. *Ill med jour* 7:611, 1905. *Polk* 1886: 294 (as Peter A.)

MARLOWE, NICHOLAS PERKINS, Tuscaloosa, Ala (b/X-15-1833; d/IX-1-1898) MD Jefferson 1857; att U Ala 1853-54, 1856-57. *Tr Med Assn St Ala* 1899: 233. *Polk* 1893: 164.

MARQUIS, DAVID STEWART, Rochester, Pa (b/IV-6-1821 Beaver; d/I-31-1900) MD Med Coll Ohio 1845. *Pa med jour* 3:645-46, 1899/1900. *JAMA* 34:381, 1900. *Flint* 1897: 833.

MARR, CHARLES, CW-USA (d/1865 Scranton, Pa) MD Jefferson 1857. *Med surg rep Phila* 12:268, 1864/65. *Nat med jour* 1:299, 1870/71.

MARR, DANIEL PRICE PERKINS, Bolivar Co, Miss (b/1816; d/VIII-1-1853 Wyandotte, Va) MD ? att U Ala 1831. *U Ala cat*: 42.

MARR, DELOS DANFORTH, Chesterton, Ind (b/VII-28-1852 Laporte Co; d/IX-12-1889) MD Rush 1875. *Tr Ind St Med Soc* 1890: 156.

MARR, JOHN HARDIN, Panola Co, Miss (b/1818; d/X-23-1840 Yellowbushe Co, Miss) MD ? ; AB U Ala 1836. *U Ala cat*: 47.

MARSDEN, JOHN HATTON, York Springs, Pa 1840-(b/1803; d/VIII-27-1883) MD Jefferson 1848; AB 1825. *Tr Hom Soc Pa* 1884:32-34. *Amer obs* 20:287, 1883/84. *King* I: 153-54. Homeopath.

MARSEE, JOSEPH WILKINS, Indianapolis (b/X-28 1848; d/XII-3-1898) MD CPSNY 1871. *Tr Ind St Med Soc* 1899: 399-400. *JAMA* 31:1542, 1898.

MARSEILLES, FREDERICK W , CW-USA (d/IV-23 1864 Bowling Green, Ky) MD Cleveland Med Coll 1852. *Nat med jour* 1:299, 1870/71.

MARSELIUS, WILLARD C , Albany, NY (d/XII-24 1893 @36) MD Albany 1884. *Med reg NY NJ Conn* 1894: 243. *Buff m&s j* 33:436, 1893. *JAMA* 22: 31, 1894.

MARSH, ALF F , CW-USA (d/III-31-1865) MD ? *Nat med jour* 1:299, 1870/71.

MARSH, ANNA ELIZABETH PORTIA (EASTMAN), Greeley, Colo (b/IX-6-1837 Mich; d/II-20-1896) MD U Mich Homeop Dept 1879. *Tr Am Inst Hom* 1896: 1191. *King* I:408. *Polk* 1886:185. Homeopath.

MARSH, AUSTIN, Carlisle, Mass (b/IX-15-1811 Sharon, Vt; d/II-2-1900) MD Dartmouth 1835. *JAMA* 34: 446, 1900 [as Oscar]. *Bost m&s j* 142: 154, 1900. *Polk* 1896: 710.

MARSH, CHARLES PITT, Kalamazoo, Mich (d/XI-17-1863 @35) MD U Mich 1851. *Chic m j* 6:573, 1863. *Med s rep Phila* 10:440, 1863. *Bost m&s j* 69:448, 1863.

MARSH, EDWIN WASH, Darien, Pa (b/II-22-1831 Bethany, NY; d/XI-4-1877) MD Buffalo 1866; att Lafayette. *Lafayette, Men of*: 175.

MARSH, GRAFTON, War 1812-USA; Towson, Md (b/VI-17-1792; d/X-10-1825) MD U Md 1813; ng Dickinson 1810. *Med annals Md:* 488.

MARSH [MARRH], JAMES F, Rochelle, Ill (d/I-3 1880 @ c50) MD Rush 1857. *Med s rep Phila* 42:88, 1880.

MARSH, JOHN, Contra Costa, Calif (b/VI-5-1799 Danvers, Mass; d/IX-24-1856) Stud med privately; AM Harvard 1823. Palmer's *Necrol Harvard alum*: 137-40.

MARSH, JOHN McLELLAN, Delphos, O (d/XI-2-1898 @35) MD Miami 1890. *JAMA* 31:1257, 1898. *Polk* 1896: 1186.

MARSH, JOSIAH, Towson, Md (b/VI-15-1797; d/VII-17-1850) MD U Md 1819. *Med annals Md:* 489.

MARSH, LEONARD, Burlington, Vt 1855- (b/VI-29-1900 Harford; d/VIII-16-1870) MD U Vt 1832; AB Dartmouth 1827. *Bost m&s j* 6:128, 1870. *Med rec* 5:336, 1870/71.

MARSH, ROLPH DENMAN, NYC (b/VII-9-1858 Rahway, NJ; d/IV-29-1884) MD UCNY 1879. *Med reg NY NJ Conn* 1884: 233.

MARSH, STEPHEN W , Canton Bend, Ala (d/1868) MD ? ng U Ala 1831. *U Ala cat*: 38.

MARSHALL, ALBERT QUINCY, New Gloucester, Me (b/VIII-12-1836 Hebron; d/V-3-1880) MD Bowdoin 1867. *Tr Me Med Assoc* 1880: 203-04. *Butler* 1878:309.

MARSHALL, CALVIN PHILLIPS, CW-USA (b/IV-2-1834 Newcastle, Del; d/V-28-1891 Wichita, Kans) MD UPa 1856. *U Pa med alum CW*: 1856.

MARSHALL, CHARLES, Huntington, Quebec (d/XI-13 1903 NYC) MD UCNY 1872. *Bost m&s j* 149:582 1903.

MARSHALL, DANIEL Mc , Columbia City, Ind (b/III 5-1823 Winchester; d/X-13-1892) MD Rush 1856. *Tr Ind St Med Soc* 1893: 250. *Butler* 1878: 212. *Polk* 1886: 352 (Burlington, Ia).

MARSHALL, EDWARD JAMES, West Chester, Pa (d/ I-28-1901 @60) MD UPa 1867. *Pa med jour* 5:296, 1901. *Polk* 1886: 810.

MARSHALL, GEORGE W , Lima, Ill (d/IV-28-1905 @81) MD Keokuk CPS 1873. *Ill med jour* 7:611, 1905. *Polk* 1886: 286.

MARSHALL, GUY C, CW-USA (d/VII-25-1862) MD ? *Nat m j* 1:299, 1870/71. *Med reg NY NJ Conn* 1865: 212.

MARSHALL, HUGH, Monmouth, Ill (b/XII-15-1825 SC; d/IV-10-1903) MD Rush 1852. *Ill med jour* ns4: 851, 889, 1903. *Polk* 1896: 430.

MARSHALL, JOHN CARROLL, Lyme, NH (b/II-28-1845 Weare, NH; d/IX-3-1882 Post Mills, Vt) MD Dartmouth 1872. *Tr NH Med Soc* 1883: 179-80.

MARSHALL, JOHN ELLIS, Mayville, NY 1809-15; Buffalo 1815-38 (b/III-1785 Norwich, Conn; d/XII-27-1838) Stud w/Dr Philemon Tracy, Norwich; lic Conn Med Soc 1808. *Tr Med Soc St NY* 1865:275.

MARSHALL, JOSEPH D , USA (d/VIII-5-1864) MD ? *Nat med jour* 1:299, 1870/71. *Tr AMA* 18: 355, 1867.

MARSHALL, MOSES, Wilmington, Del (b/XI-20-1758 Chester Co, Pa; d/X-1-1813) Stud med w/Nicholas Way 1776-79. *Med rep* (W Chester, Pa) 1:31-32, 1853. *K&B* III: 811-12.

MARSHALL, ORSEMUS WARD, Jeffersonville O (b/ VII-9-1827 Boonville NY; d/VII-23-1886) MD Cincinnati Coll M & S 1865; att U Mich Med Dept 1852. *Tr Ohio Med Soc* 1887: 233-34. *Butler* 1878: 641.

MARSHALL, RANDOLPH, Tuckahoe, NJ (d/II-19-1879) MD UPa 1834. *Med rec NY* 15:239, 1879.

MARSHALL, THOMAS, CW-CSA (b/XI-19-1834 Fauquier Co, Va; d/IX-1-1861) MD UPa 1856. *U Pa med alum CW*: 1856.

MARSHALL, THOMAS HASTINGS, Mason Village, NH (b/XII-2-1805 Jaffrey; d/XII-16-1872; d/XII-16 1872) MD Dartmouth 1835. *Tr AMA* 24:355-58, 1873. *Bost m&s j* ns11:229-30 1873. *Tr NH M S* 1873:112-17.

MARSTON, DANIEL EDWARD, Monmouth, Me (b/V-13-1836 W Gardiner; d/IV-18-1894 @58) MD Bowdoin 1859. *Bost m&s j* 130:404, 1894. *Tr Me Med Assoc* 1892-94: 581-82. *Polk* 1890: 501.

MARSTON, DANIEL WILLIAM, NYC (d/1901 Schenectady NY) MD Bellevue 1898. *Bost m&s j* 144:628 1901.

MARSTON, ENOCH QUIMBY, Centre Sandwich, NH (b/V-20-1847; d/II-1-1904) MD Harvard 1876. *Tr NH Med Soc* 1904: 301-02. *Polk* 1890: 708.

MARSTON, JOHN J , Cheyenne, Wyo (d/IV-17-1897) MD McGill 1863. *JAMA* 28: 860, 1897. *Polk* 1896:1569.

MARTIN, ALEX DONALD WILLIAM, Boston (d/III-5 1896 @67) MD Harv'd 1851. *Bost m&s j* 134:304, 1896.

MARTIN, ALFRED JACOB, Allentown, Pa (b/III-24 1837; d/XII-8-1896) MD UPa 1857. *Lehigh Valley med mag* 8:48, 1897. *Butler* 1878: 723.

MARTIN, CHARLES, USN 1848- (b/VIII-21-1822; d/I 14-1892 NYC) Stud med Albany. *Med reg NY NJ Conn* 1892: 283. *Bost m&s j* 126: 76, 1892. *Butler* 1878: viii.

MARTIN, CHARLES DETWILLER, Allentown, Pa (d/ VII-15-1902 @55) MD Bellevue 1867. *Pa med jour* 6:261, 1902/03. *Flint* 1897: 794.

MARTIN, CHARLES HENRY, Allentown, Pa (d/IX-25 1860 @53) MD UPa 1830. *Med surg rep Phila* ns5:104, 1860-61.

MARTIN, DEWEES JACOB, Allentown, Pa (d/VI-20 1874 @39) MD UPa 1859. *Med s rep Phila* 31: 80, 1874.

MARTIN, EDGAR E, Belcher, La (d/X-6-1905 Rhome, Tx? <MD Memphis Hosp Med Coll 1902> *Tex st med jour* 1:220, 1905/06. *Polk* 1904: 885. [See entry below for George E.]

MARTIN, EDWARD F , Elmhurst, LI, NY (d/II-24-1900 @44) MD ? *Bost m&s j* 142: 236, 1900.

MARTIN, EDWARD JOHN, Gilmore City, Ia (d/III-28-1899 @42) MD Iowa St U 1892. *JAMA* 32:845, 1899.

MARTIN, EDWIN GOUNDIE, CW-USA; Allentown, Pa (b/X-3-1836; d/VIII-30-1893) MD UPa 1856. *U Pa med alum CW*: 1856. *Lehigh Valley med mag* 5:34-37, 1893-94. *Butler* 1878: 723.

MARTIN, ENNALLS, Easton, Md; RevWar-USA (b/ VIII-23-1758 Hampden;d/XII-16-1834) MB UPa 1782

 Spec. educ'l status abbrev. as: ***ng*** = college verified attendance without degree;

Hon MD UMd 1818. *Med ann Md:*489. *K&B* III:812–13.

MARTIN, ERNEST DUDLEY, USN (b/VII–1–1843 Phila; d/VII–17–1868 abd Powhatan in Pacific) MD UPa 1865. *Phila med reg & dir* 1871: 297. *Tr AMA* 21: 495, 1870. *Nat m j* 1:299, 1870/71. *U Pa med alum CW*: 1865.

MARTIN, FRANKLIN BENJAMIN, Catasauqua, Pa (d/X–19–1868 @46) MD UPa 1842. *Phila med reg & dir* 1871: 298. *Med surg rep Phila* 19:350, 1868.

MARTIN, FRED DELAMATER, Norwalk, O (d/VII–7–1893 @37) MD Clev'd M C 1878. *JAMA* 21:94, 1893.

MARTIN, GEORGE, NYC (b/V–17–1842; d/XI–26–1870) MD CPSNY 1870 *Med reg NY NJ Conn* 1871:361.

MARTIN, GEORGE E , Belcher, La (d/X–6–1905 Roane, Tex) MD Keokuk CPS 1882. *New Orl m&s j* 58:430, 1905. [See entry above for Edgar E.]

MARTIN, GEORGE T , Elkridge Landing, Md (b/IV–17 1793 Easton; d/XI–18–1860) MD U Md 1819. *Med ann Md:* 490.

MARTIN, HENRY AUSTIN, Roxbury, Mass; CW–USA (b/VII–23–1824 London; d/XII–7–1884) MD Harvard 1845; Hon AM Dartmouth 1883. *JAMA* 4:55–56, 1885. *Bost m&s j* 111:576, 1884; 112:33–34, 47, 1885. *Harvard in CW*: 232. *K & B* III: 813.

MARTIN, HENRY M , USN 1870–90 (d/I–16–1891 Phila) MD UPa 1869. *JAMA* 16:178,1891. *Bost m&s j* 124:152,1891. *Med bull med & surg* 13:70, 1891.

MARTIN, HENRY NEWELL, Baltimore 1876–93 (b/VII–1–1848 Newry, Ire; d/X–27–1896 Burly Eng) MB U London 1871; DS 1872; AB Cambr 1874; AM 1877. *JAMA* 28:41, 1897. *Med ann Md:*490. *K&B* III: 814–15.

MARTIN, HENRY NOAH, Philadelphia (b/X–20–1829 Albion, NY; d/VIII–31–1889) MD Hahnemann Phila 1865; stud law. *Med surg rep Phila* 61:336, 1889. *Med vis* 5:346, 1889. *Polk* 1886: 821.

MARTIN, HOWARD B , Philadelphia (b/XII–29–1863; d/II–3–1902) MD Jefferson 1885. *Pa med jour* 5:314, 1901/02; 6:261, 1902/03. *Polk* 1896: 1311.

MARTIN, HUGH McDONALD, Fredericksburg, Va; CW–CSA (b/1828 Scotl'd; d/VI–23–1904) MD U La 1855. *JAMA*43:61, 1904. *Polk* 1886: 917.

MARTIN, ISAAC J Jr, Elliot City, Md (d/XI–10–1899 @40) MD CPS Balto 1884. *JAMA* 33:1375, 1899.

MARTIN, ISAAC W, Des Moines (b/XI–11–1838 Tippecanoe Co Ind; d/VI–20–1889) MD Bennett 1877. *Med surg rep Phila* 61:112, 1889. *Polk* 1886:356. Eclectic.

MARTIN, JAMES STANSBURY, Baltimore (b/IV–2–1824; d/IV–14–1900) MD Wash'n U Balto 1845. *JAMA* 34:1084, 1900. *Med annals Md:* 490. *Polk* 1896: 668.

MARTIN, JOHN, Georgetown Pa (b/1822; d/X–8–1885) MD Jefferson 1845. *Tr M S Pa* 18:244, 1886. *Butler* 1878: 723.

MARTIN, JOHN D , Savannah (d/VIII–3–1898 @40) <MD Savannah Med Coll 1861> *JAMA* 31:427, 1898. *Polk* 1896: 339.

MARTIN, JOHN H L , Arcadia, Ind (b/V–1–1850 Hummelstown, Pa; d/XI–10–1885) MD Med Coll Ind 1880. *Tr Ind St Med Soc* 1886: 208.

MARTIN, JOHN RUSSELL, Havana, Cuba (b/V–27–1790 Providence, RI; d/V–24–1817) MB Dartmouth 1810, & MD?; AB Brown 1807. *Brown hist cat*: 1807.

MARTIN, JOSEPH, NYC (b/1797? d/1864) MD ? *Tr AMA* 16: 628, 1865.

MARTIN, JOSEPH BLAIR, Baltimore (b/1800; d/1847) MD U Md 1823. *Med ann Md:* 491.

MARTIN, JOSEPH LLOYD, Boston 1847– ; Baltimore 1861? (b/V–1–1820 Monmouth Co, NJ; d/VI–29–1889) MD UCNY 1846. *Med s rep Phila* 61:140,1889. *Tr Am Inst Hom* 1890:137. *Polk* 1886: 438. *Cleave.* Homeopath.

MARTIN, MATHEW C , Wauwatosa, Wis (d/II–21–1901 Milwaukee) MD Milwaukee Med Coll 1899. *Tr Ill St Med Soc* ns2:533, 1901. *Polk* 1900: 1844.

MARTIN, NOAH, Dover, NH (b/VII–26–1801 Epsom; d/V–28–1863. *Bost m&s j* 68: 370, 1863.

MARTIN, ORAMEL, New Braintree, Mass 1833–45? Worcester 1845– (b/VII–21–1810 Hoosick, NY; d/IV–15–1892 @81) MD Castleton 1832; <MD Berkshire 1833> stud Paris. *Bost m&s j* 126: 404, 1892. *Atkinson* I: 311. *Butler* 1878: 354.

MARTIN, RICHARD A, Philadelphia (d/IV–22–1906 @ 71)MD UPa 1860 *Pa m j* 9:672 1905/06 *Polk* 1896:1311.

MARTIN, ROBERT, Nashville (b/1799 Chatham Co NC; d/I–28–1873 Knoxville) MD U Nashville 1866; att lect Phila 1829. *Tr M S Tenn* 1876:85. *Nashvl j m & s* ns10: 375, 1872.

MARTIN, ROBERT J , Augusta, Me (d/VI–19–1901 @36) MD UCNY 1887. *JAMA* 37:43, 1901.

MARTIN, SABIN, New Orleans (d/VIII–21–1883 @75) <MD Paris> *New Orl m&s j* ns11:330–31, 1883. *Butler* 1878: 295.

MARTIN, SAMUEL, Xenia, O (b/1797? d/VI–21–1879 @82) MD ? *Med s rep Phila* 41: 44, 1879.

MARTIN, SAMUEL BLAIR, Baltimore (b/V– –1785; d/XII–21–1875) Hon MD U Md 1838; att lect UPa 1806/07? *Med ann Md:* 491. *Tr AMA* 27:649, 1876.

MARTIN, SAMUEL K , Martinsville, NJ (d/VII–24–1868 @60) Lic 1830; att CPSNY. *Med surg rep Phila* 19: 140, 1868. *Phila med reg & dir* 1871:297. *Tr AMA* 21:466, 1870. *Tr Med Soc NJ* 1869: 103–04.

MARTIN, SAMUEL M , Greenfield, Ind (d/VI–14–1897 @55) MD Bennett 1884. *JAMA* 28:1252, 1897. *Polk* 1886: 320.

MARTIN, SOLOMON CLAIBORNE, St Louis (b/X–26 1837 Claiborne Co, Miss; d/III–27–1906) MD Tulane 1866; att U Mich 1859; ng Med Dept 1859–61. *So pract* 28: 302–03, 1906. *New Orl m&s j*58:922, 1906. *Polk* 1886: 564.

MARTIN, STEPHEN CROSBY, Brookline, Mass (d/XI–5–1893 @33) MD Harvard 1874. *JAMA* 21:784. *Polk* 1886: 472.

MARTIN, THOMAS J , Dixon's Springs, Tenn (d/VIII–

18–1833) MD Transylvania 1832. *Transylv j m & assoc sci* 6:305–06, 1833.

MARTIN, THOMAS TILGHMAN, Allentown, Pa (b/IX 10–1851; d/IV–15–1896) MD UPa 1877. *Lehigh Valley med mag* 7:162–63, 1896.

MARTIN, URBAN FRANCIS, NYC (d/IX–6–1905 @ 28) MD ? *Bost m&s j* 153:318, 1905.

MARTIN, WALLACE D, CW–USA (b/Middletown, Pa; d/XII–7–1873 Baldwin) MD UPa 1863. *U Pa med alum CW*: 1863.

MARTIN, WALTER FRANKLIN, Weaversville, Pa (d/ II–21–1862 @30) MD UPa 1855. *Med surg rep Phila* ns7: 528, 1861/62.

MARTIN, WILLIAM H, Jefferson, Tenn (b/VI–3–1854; d/IV–4–1880) MD U Nashville 1880. *Nashvl j m & s* ns25: 234, 1880.

MARTIN, WILLIAM L, Rancocas, NJ (b/I–19–1827 Chester Co, Pa; d/I–22–1903) MD Jefferson 1852. *Tr Med Soc NJ* 1903: 380–81. *Polk* 1890: 729.

MARTINACHE, NARCISSE JOSEPH, San Francisco (b/XI–24–1834 France; d/XII–23–1892) <MD Paris 1861> *Tr M S Cal* 23:282–83, 1893. *Butler* 1878: 55.

MARTINDALE, FRANK E [or L], Port Richmond, NY (d/X–26–1902 @72) MD Albany 1853. *Bost m&s j* 147: 532, 1902. *Tr M S St NY* 1903: [412]. *Polk* 1886: 702.

MARTINEZ, JUSTO PASTOR, NYC(d/I–8–1886 @66) MD UCNY 1876. *Med reg NY NJ Conn* 1886: 252.

MARVIN, A TOLLS, Northampton, NY (d/XI–2–1864 @30) <MD Bellevue> *Med reg NY NJ Conn* 1865:231. *Med surg rep Phila* 12:252, 1864/65.

MARVIN, GEORGE, Brooklyn (b/II–23–1798 Norwalk, Conn; d/XII–23–1874) MD UPa 1821; AB Yale 1817; AM 1821. *Med reg NY NJ Conn* 1875: 200.

MARVIN, JONATHAN D, Morristown, NJ (b1789? d/ 1872) MD ? *Med surg rep Phila* 27: 212, 1872. *Tr AMA* 24: 363, 1873.

MARYOTT, ERASTUS EDGAR, Coxsackie, NY (b/IX–29–1845; d/II–29–1904) MD Albany 1882; AB Brown 1870; AM. *Brown hist cat* 1870. *Polk* 1886: 474.

MASON, ALFRED, ?NYC (b/III–24–1804 Portsmouth, NH; d/IV–12–1828) ng Bowdoin Med Dept 1825–26; AB Bowdoin 1825. *Bowdoin cat*: 1825.

MASON, AUGUSTUS, Brighton, Mass; CW–USA (b/X–2–1823 Waltham; d/V–24–1882) MD Harvard 1844; AB Brown 1841; AM. *JAMA* 1:191–92, 1883. *Bost m&s j* 106: 522, 1882. *Harvard in CW*: 231. *Butler* 1874: 354.

MASON, CHARLES, Peekskill, NY (d/IV–19–1899) MD Bellevue 1875. *Bost m&s j* 140:416, 1899. *Tr Med Soc St NY* 1900: 431. *Polk* 1886: 701.

MASON, CHARLES H, CW–USN (d/X–1864 abd USS Virginia) MD UCNY 1856. *Nat m j* 1:299, 1870/71.

MASON, CHARLES R, Hartford City, Ind (b/I–12–1846 Wells Co; d/III–8–1906) MD Cincinnati Coll M & S 1870. *Tr Ind St Med Soc* 1906:490. *Polk* 1896: 470.

MASON, DAVID H, Athens, Ala (d/summer 1834) MD Transylvania 1828. *Transylv j m & assoc sci* 7: 427, 1834.

MASON, EDMUNDS, Wetumpka, Ala (b/XI–29–1825 Brunswick Co, Va; d/XII–17–1877) MD Jefferson 1848. *Tr St Med Assoc Ala* 1878: 132, 153.

MASON, EDWARD BROMFIELD, CW–USA (d/IX–14 1863 Readville, Mass) MD Harvard 1861; AB 1858. *Harvard in CW*: 115. *Nat med jour* 1:299, 1870/71.

MASON, EDWIN GAILLARD, NYC (b/Hagerstown, Md; d/V–24–1904 @31) MD Bellevue 1887. *Bost m&s j* 150: 604, 1904. *Polk* 1896: 1067.

MASON, ELIPHALET HASTINGS, Towanda, Pa (b/IV 28–1815 Monroeton; d/II–3–1871) MD Jefferson 1838. *Tr Med Soc St Pa* 8:317–19, 1871.

MASON, ERSKINE, NYC (b/V–8–1837; d/IV–13–1882) MD CPSNY 1860; AB Columbia 1857; AM 1860. *Med reg NY NJ Conn* 1882: 230. *Chicago med rev* 5:197, 1882. *Atkinson* I:233–34.

MASON, FRANK, Taylorville, Ill (d/XII–7–1897) MD CPS Chicago 1896. *U Ill Coll Med alum*: 1896.

MASON, GEORGE EDWARD, CW–USA; Providence, RI (d/XI–28–1882 @42) MD Harvard 1865. *Bost m&s j* 107: 552, 1882. *Tr RI Med Soc* 3: 163–64, 1883–88. *Harvard in CW*: 294.

MASON, GEORGE LINDSLY, Moultonborough, NH (b/X–10–1854; d/V–14–1888) MD Bellevue 1876. *Tr NH Med Soc* 1888: 168–69. *Polk* 1886: 593.

MASON, GEORGE WILCOXSON, Bloomington, Ill (b/VIII–8–1850 Palo; d/X–8–1887) MD Chicago Med Coll 1880. *Tr Ill St Med Soc* 1888:136–40.

MASON, GERARD F, Charlestown, WVa (b/1815 Va; d/I–30–1900) MD Jefferson 1842. *JAMA* 34:380, 1900. *Polk* 1896: 1825.

MASON, JARVIS KING, Suffield, Conn (b/XI–8–1831 Enfield; d/IV–8–1905) MD Harvard 1861; AB Yale 1855; AM 1859. *Proc Conn Med Soc* 1906: 284–86, 1906. *Bost m&s j* 152: 444, 1905. *Atkinson* I: 368–69. *Butler* 1878: 80.

MASON, JOHN KEMBLE, Philadelphia (d/X–2–1872) MD UPa 1842. *Tr CPP* cent vol: 246. *Med surg rep Phila* 27:356, 1872. *Phila med reg & dir* 1873: 303.

MASON, JOSEPH, Providence, RI (b/X–8–1768; d/VII–20–1843) MD ? AB Brown 1786. *Tr RI M S* 1: 44, 1859–77.

MASON, JOSEPH, CW–USA as med cadet (d/IX–23–1862 Mill Creek, Ft Monroe, Va) stud med Harvard w/class of 1863. *Harvard in CW*: 281.

MASON, MOSES, Bethel, Me 1813– (b/VI–2–1789 Dublin, NH; d/VI–18–1866) MD ? *Med surg rep Phila* 15: 56, 1866. *US Congr biogr dir*.

MASON, RANDOLPH FITZHUGH, USN 1859–61; CSN 1861– (b/III–1–1822 Fairfax Co, Va; d/VIII– –1862 Jones' Springs, NC) MD UPa 1844. *U Pa med alum CW*: 1844.

MASON, RICHARD CHICHESTER, CW–CSA; Fau–

quier Co, Va (b/1793 Fairfax; d/1867) MD UPa 1816. *U Pa med alum CW*: 1816.

MASON, RUFUS OSGOOD, NYC (b/I-22-1830 Sullivan, NH; d/V-11-1903) MD CPSNY 1859; AB Dartmouth 1854. *Bost m&s j* 148:572, 1903. *Polk* 1896: 1067.

MASON, STEPHEN ROBEY, Duvall's Bluff, Ark; Sheffield, Ill 20 yrs (b/VI-18-1827 Chichester, NH; d/VIII 20-1903) MD Rush 1851. *Tr Am Inst Hom* 1905: 845-46. Homeopath.

MASON, SUMNER APPLETON, NYC (b/NJ; d/III-12 1897 @58) MD UPa 1868. *Bost m&s j* 136: 269-70, 1897. *JAMA* 28:620, 1897. *Polk* 1886: 687.

MASON, THEODORE LEWIS, Brooklyn (b/IX-30-1803 Cooperstown, NY; d/II-12-1882) MD CPSNY 1825. *Med reg NY NJ Conn* 1882: 231. *Chic med rev* 5: 126, 1882. *Bost m&s j* 107:618, 1892. *Atkinson* I: 691.

MASON, WILLIAM, Bucksport, Me 1832-52; Charlestown Mass 1852- (b/V-8-1805 Castine; d/III-18-1881) MD Harvard 1832; AB Bowdoin 1824. *Bost m&s j* 105: 623, 1881.

MASON, WILLIAM BOND, Dartmouth, Mass [!] (b/1782? d/1856 @74) ng Dartmouth Med 1807. *Bost m&s j* 55: 375, 1857.

MASON, WILLIAM HENRY HARRISON, Moultonborough, NH 1842-89 (b/XII-14-1817 Gilford; d/I-29-1892) MD Dartmouth 1843. *Bost m&s j* 126:132, 1892. *Tr NH Med Soc* 1892: 199-202.

MASSSER, GEORGE W , Scranton, Pa (d/III- -1870) MD UPa Med Coll 1842. *Phila med reg & dir* 1871:304.

MASSEY, ISAAC, CW-USA; West Chester, Pa (b/II-15 1838 W Goshen; d/I-31-1898) MD Jefferson 1864. *JAMA* 30:391, 1898. *Rec AAS USA* 1891:60. *Atkinson* I: 146. *Polk* 1896: 1343.

MASSIE, JAMES B , Fayetteville, Ark (d/VIII-24-1901 @45) <MD St Joseph Coll, Mo 1887> *Tr Tex St M Assoc* 1902: 75-76. *JAMA* 37:654, 1901. *New Orl m&s j* 54: 269, 1901.

MASSON, LUC H J , San Francisco (b/Canada; d/X-14 1901 Paris) MD CPS Quebec 1890; stud Belgium & Paris. *Cal st jour med* 1:31, 1902.

MASTA, JOHN BATISTE, Barton, Vt (b/IV-26-1819 St Francis, Que; d/X-21-1861) MD Dartmouth 1850. *Tr Vt Med Soc* 1883:107. Indian.

MASTEN [MASTER], CHARLES HERMAN, Nyack-on-Hudson, NY (d/V-1-1902 @62) MD Bellevue 1867. *Bost m&s j* 146:504, 1902. *Polk* 1886:709.

MASTERS, BEZIN REECE, NYC (d/IX-17-1860 Bermuda) MD CPSNY 1848. *Tr AMA* 14:192, 1864.

MASTIN, CHARLOTTE EVANGELINE, Wellsboro, Pa (b/II-10-1872 Cayuga Co, NY; d/V-20-1905) MD Buffalo 1897. *Pa med jour* 9:71-72, 1905/06.

MASTIN, CLAUDIUS HENRY, CW-CSA; Mobile, Ala (b/VI-4-1826 Huntsville, Ala; d/X-3-1898) MD UPa 1849; AB U Va 1874; LLD UPa 1875. *NC m j* 42: 284, 1898. *Buff m&s j* 38:305, 1898. *Tr Med Assoc St Ala* 1899: 233. *K&B* III: 816-17.

MATAS, N H , Brownsville, Tex; Tucson, Ariz (d/IV-13-1904 @67) <MD New Orl Sch Med 1859> *New Orl m&s j* 56:877, 1904. *Polk* 1893: 170.

MATHER, SAMUEL, CW-USA (d/V-21-1865) MD ? *Nat med jour* 1:299, 1870/71.

MATHER, WILLIAM HENRY, Suffield, Conn; CW-USA (b/III-15-1834 Windsor Locks; d/V-22-1888) MD UCNY 1862. *Proc Conn Med Soc* ns4: 261-65, 1889. *Atkinson* I: 429-30. *Polk* 1886: 196.

MATHES, JESSE MARION, Sullivan Ind (d/V-5-1899 @58) MD Rush 1877. *JAMA* 32:1074, 1899. *Polk* 1896:461.

MATHESON, JOHN, NYC (b/Pr Edw Isl Can; d/XII-8 1905 @35) MD UCNY 1896. *Bost m&s j* 153:682, 1905.

MATHEWS [MATTHEWS], CHARLES HENRY, Bucks Co, Pa (d/VII-25-1849) MD UPa 1827. *Tr Med Soc Pa* 1850: 13.

MATHEWS, CLUREN O , Dennison, Tex (d/XII-14-1899 @39) MD CPS Balto 1884. *JAMA* 34: 62, 1900.

MATHEWS, JOHN, Brooklyn (b/Bath, Me; d/VIII-30 1875 @53) MD Bowdoin 1845. *Med reg NY NJ Conn* 1876: 253.

MATHEWS [MATHENY], LORENZO D , Springfield, Ky (d/II-7-1837) MD Transylvania 1836. *Transylvania jour med & assoc sci* 10: [167], 1837.

MATHEWS, THOMAS P , Pamplin City, Va to 1875; Manchester, Va 1875- (b/VIII-27/29-1835 Appomattox Co; d/I-12-1905) MD Med Coll Va 1856; MD Jefferson 1856; att Va Mil Inst 1856 [!] *Tr Med Soc Va* 1905: 451.

MATHEWSON, HARLEY PHILLIPS, Omaha, Nebr; Los Angeles (b/XII-14-1828 Wheelock, Vt; d/VIII/3 or 19/1901) MD Dartmouth 1863. *JAMA* 37:654, 1901. *Polk* 1886: 581.

MATHEWSON, RUFUS WELLINGTON, Durham Conn (b/III-24-1814 Coventry RI; d/V-5-1893) MD CPSNY 1835. *Proc Conn M S* 1894:233-35. *Atkinson* I: 398. *Butler* 1878:80. *Med reg NY NJ Conn* 1893: 312.

MATHIEU, FERDINAND CHARLES, Baltimore (b/1849 Prussia; d/I-7-1890) <MD Bonn 1868> *Med annals Md*: 492. *Polk* 1886: 438.

MATHIEU, JULES A , New Orleans (b/1824; d/XII-7-1899) MD Tulane 1854. *New Orl m&s j* 52:426, 1900. *Polk* 1896: 623.

MATHIEU [MATTHEW], LEVI, St Anne, Ill (d/XII-11 1904 @54) MD CPS Chic 1883. *Ill m j* 11:242, 1905.

MATHIOT, HENRY B , Smithfield, Pa (d/II-24-1894 @78) MD Jefferson 1852. *JAMA* 22: 391, 1894. *Butler* 1878: 723.

MATLACK, CHARLES FRENCH, Germantown, Phila (b/1799? d/VIII-1-1874) MD UPa 1820. *Med s rep Phila* 31:120, 280, 1874. *Tr Am Inst Hom* 1874: 656. Homeopath.

MATLACK, JAMES M , Turtle Creek, Pa (b/III-23-

1833 Chester Co, Pa; d/IV-2-1877) MD UPa 1861. *Tr Pa St Med Soc* 1877:585. *Butler* 1878: 723.

MATLACK, WILLIAM HENRY, Downingtown, Pa (b/E Brandywine; d/VII-12-1896 @59) MD Jefferson 1859. *JAMA* 27:449, 1896. *Butler* 1878: 723.

MATSON, ALBERT F , Logansville, O (d/IV-9-1867 @43) MD Western Reserve 1852. *Tr Ohio St Med Soc* 1868-69: 200.

MATSON, EDWIN AMES, Sonora, Calif (d/1881 or 1882) MD U Va 1871. *Tr Cal St Med Soc* 1882:247.

MATSON, SYLVESTER G , Viola, Ia (b/III-5-1808; d/II-5-1898) MD U Vt 1832. *JAMA* 30: 507, 1898. *Polk* 1896: 541.

MATSON, WILLIAM BUCKINGHAM, Brooklyn (b/1853; d/III-10-1893) MD Bellevue 1876. *Med reg NY NJ Conn* 1893: 311. *Polk* 1886: 647.

MATTER, GEORGE F , Shenandoah, Pa (d/X-22-1897 @57) MD Jefferson 1866. *Lehigh Valley med mag* 8:341, 1897. *JAMA* 29:977, 1020, 1897. *Butler* 1878: 723.

MATTERN, WILLIAM K, Philadelphia (b/VIII-5-1847 Berks Co, Pa; d/IV-16-1896) MD Jefferson 1882; PhB Phila Coll Pharm 1874. *JAMA* 26:843, 1896. *Med bull med & surg* 18: 193, 1896.

MATTESON, JOHN C, Dunkirk NY (d/V-8-1867 @38) MD Jefferson 1851. *Buff m & s jour* 7:408, 1867.

MATTHES, GUSTAVUS FELIX, Berlin & Schweldt, Pr; New Bedford, Mass 1849- ; Boston (b/XII-31-1809 Pr; d/V-17-1889) <MD Halle 1836> *New Engl med gaz* 24: 193, 1889. *Med vis* 5:222, 1889. *King* I: 228-29. Homeopath 1845- .

MATTHEWS, ALEXANDER, Oxford, Md (b/V-27-1825 DC; d/X-5-1891) MD U Md 1847. *Hist Med Soc DC:* 276. *Polk* 1886: 444.

MATTHEWS, CALEB BENTLEY, Philadelphia (d/V-25-1851 @50) MD UPa 1824. *No Am j hom* 1: 412, 1851. *Nw j hom* 3:268, 185_? *King* III:56-57. Homeopath 1836- .

MATTHEWS, DAVID, CW-USA; NYC (d/VII-9-1891 @60) MD CPSNY 1860. *Med reg NY NJ Conn* 1892: 283. *Bost m&s j* 125: 96, 1891.

MATTHEWS, FREDERICK LAWSON, Springfield, Ill (b/Engl; d/XII-24-1891) MD U Mich 1867; MD Rush 1869 ad eundem. *Tr Ill St Med Soc* 1892: 31-32. *Polk* 1890: 350.

MATTHEWS, HENRY CLAY, Brooklyn, NY (b/IV-3-1844 Granby, Vt; d/X-23-1902) MD U Vt 1870. *Bost m&s j* 147: 504, 1902. *Polk* 1896:999.

MATTHEWS, HENRY WYLLY EDMUND, New Haven, Conn (b/XII-10-1827 St Simons Isl, Ga; d/I-29-1875) MD Yale 1850; AB Trinity Coll, Conn 1847. *Proc Conn Med Soc* 1875: 427, 442.

MATTHEWS, JAMES R , Bloomville, NY (d/VII-13-1890 @45) MD Albany 1871. *JAMA* 15: 232, 1890. *Polk* 1886: 642.

MATTHEWS, RICHARD ALEXANDER, ?NYC (d/X-14-1893 @28) MD UCNY 1892. *JAMA* 21:630, 1893.

MATTHEWS, YOUNG A , Atlanta, Tex (b/Fayetteville, NC; d/XI-20-1906 @69) MD Shelby Med Coll 1859. *Tex st med jour* 2:260, 1906/07.

MATTINGLY, THOMAS, Florence, Ala (d/VIII-11-1867 New Iberia, La) MD Columbian 1842. *Med surg rep Phila* 17:177, 1867. *New Orl m&s j* 21:205, 1868.

MATTOX, J F , Pine Ridge, Tex (d/VII-1-1905) MD ? *Tex st med jour* 1:83, 1905/06. *Polk* 1900: 1699.

MAUCHER, JOHN E, Carrolltown, Pa (d/V-21-1904 @ 78) <MD Munich 1851> *Pa med jour* 8:335, 1904/05. *Flint* 1897: 1271.

MAUGHS, G M B , St Louis (d/III-23-1901) MD Mo Med Coll (Kemper) 1848. *Ill med jour* ns2: 601, 1901. *Butler* 1878: 418.

MAULL, DAVID W , Delaware (b/Georgetown, Del; d/II-22-1896 Wilmington @65) MD Jefferson 1853. *JAMA* 26: 490, 1896.

MAULSBY, GEORGE, USN 1838-72 (b/XII-27-1810 Plymouth Mtg, Pa; d/X-27-1886 Washington, DC) MD UPa 1831. MD UPa 1831. *U Pa med alum CW*: 1831.

MAUPIN, GEORGE WASHINGTON OPIE, Portsmouth, Va (d/VI-28-1888) MD UPa 1844. *Tr Med Soc St Va* 1888: 270-75. *Butler* 1878: 833.

MAUPIN, SOCRATES, Richmond, Va (b/1808 Albemarle Co; d/1871) MD U Va 1830; AM. *Tr AMA* 24: 384-86, 1873. *Tr Med Soc Va* 1872: 26, 155-56.

MAURAN, ANTOINE JOSEPH, Creston, Ia (b/XII-10 1831 Providence, RI; d/XI-1-1899) MD CPSNY 1854; AB Brown 1851. *Tr Iowa St M S* 18: 398- 99, 1900. *Polk* 1896: 516.

MAURAN, JOSEPH, Providence, RI (b/XII-22-1796 Barrington; d/VI-8-1873 NY) MD CPSNY 1819; AB Brown 1816. *Med surg rep Phila* 28: 488, 1873. *Tr RI Med Soc* 1: 430-06, 1859-77.

MAURAN, PIERRE BOWEN, NYC (d/III-8-1887 @ 64) MD CPSNY 1853; AB Harvard; AM; LLB 1845. *Med reg NY NJ Conn* 1887: 269.

MAURER, JACOB S, Philadelphia; CW-USA (d/XII-18 1882 @45) MD Jefferson 1859 *Med bull m&s* 5:20 1883.

MAURER, JOHN, E New York, NY (d/VI-4-1890 @69) MD NY Med Coll 1855. *Med reg NY NJ Conn* 1891:277.

MAURER, O , CW-USA (d/VI-25-1862) MD ? *Nat med jour* 1:299, 1870/71.

MAURY, FRANK FONTAINE, Philadelphia ; CW-USA (b/VIII-9-1840 Danville, Ky; d/VI-4-1879) MD Jefferson 1862; AB Centre Coll, Ky 1859. *Tr Pa St Med Soc* 1880: 374-77. *Bost m&s j* 100:869-70, 1879. *Phila med times* 9:468. 1879. *Atkinson* I: 687. *K&B* III: 818.

MAURY, RUTSON, NYC (d/V-5-1892 @27, 32 or 37!) MD Bellevue 1887. *Med reg NY NJ Conn* 1892: 283. *JAMA* 18: 683, 1892. *Bost m&s j* 126:484, 1892. *Polk* 1890: 825.

MAURY, THOMAS FAYLES, CW-CSA; Washington, DC (b/VIII-16-1838; d/IX-19-1871 Mt Holly Springs,

 Spec. educ'l status abbrev. as: ***ng*** = college verified attendance without degree;

Pa) MD UPa 1856. *U Pa med alum CW*: 1856. *Hist Med Soc DC:* 260. *Tr AMA* 23:582–83, 1872.

MAUSS, RICHARD G , Washington, DC (b/VIII–24–1842 Gny; d/V–2–1891) MD Georgetown 1872. *Hist Med Soc DC:* 305. *Polk* 1886: 213.

MAUSTELLER, JAMES DALLAS, Danville, Pa (b/1844; d/VIII–26–1883 Denver, Colo) MD UPa 1871. *Tr Pa St Med Soc* 16:489–90, 1884.

MAUTNER, RUDOLPH FRIEDRICH, Turkey; Hungary; Stapleton, NY (b/VII–24–1840; d/VIII–5–1887) MD Vienna 1864. *Med reg NY NJ Conn* 1888:264. *Polk* 1886: 709.

MAVITY, WILLIAM K , Denver (d/1886) MD Jefferson 1865. *Tr Colo St Med Soc* 1898–99: 508.

MAXON, EDWARD H , Brooklyn (d/XII–14–1895) MD ? *Bost m&s j* 134: 25, 1896.

MAXON, ORRIN T , Evanston, Ill (d/V–9–1895) MD Rush 1849. *JAMA* 24:810 1895. *Butler* 1878:167. *Polk* 1890:330.

MAXSON, GEORGE W , Scott, NY (b/VIII–15–1800; d/III–27–1888) Lic Herkimer Co Med Soc 1828. *Med reg NY NJ Conn* 1888: 265.

MAXWELL, ARCHIBALD STEPHEN, Davenport, Ia (b/VI–22–1818 Tuscarawa Co, O; d/III–13–1884 Cal) MD Western Reserve 1848. *Atkinson* I: 147. *Tr Iowa St Med Soc* 6:465–66, 1883–85; 14:329, 1896.

MAXWELL, CHARLES DUVALL, USA 1836–37; USN 1837–73 (b/X–21–1806 Middletown, Del; d/IV 18–1890 Washington, DC) MD UPa 1836. *U Pa med alum CW*: 1836. *Polk* 1886: 213.

MAXWELL, ELIJAH ASHTON, NYC (d/IX–25–1893 @47) MD Bellevue 1869. *Med reg NY NJ Conn* 1894: 243. *Polk* 1886: 687.

MAXWELL, GEORGE TROUPE, CW–CSA; Jacksonville, Fla (b/VIII–6–1827 Bryan Co, Ga; d/IX–9–1897) MD UCNY 1848. *Proc Fla Med Assoc* 1897:26 ff. *Flint* 1897: 206. *Atkinson* I: 45. *K&B* III: 819.

MAXWELL, JAMES DARWIN Sr, Bloomington, Ind (b/V–19–1815 Hanover; d/IX–30–1892) MD Jefferson 1844; AM U Ind 1834. *Tr Ind St Med Soc* 1894: 214. *Atkinson* I: 142. *Butler* 1878: 212.

MAXWELL, JAMES DARWIN Jr, Bloomington, Ind (b/VII–14–1850; d/I–6–1891) MD Miami 1878. *Tr Ind St Med Soc* 1891: 282. *Polk* 1886: 311.

MAXWELL, JOHN CHAPPELL, CW–CSA; Greenwood, SC (b/XI–10–1837 Chappell's Depot; d/VIII–12–1899) MD UPa 1859. *JAMA* 33:621, 1899. *U Pa med alum CW*: 1859. *Polk* 1896: 1362.

MAXWELL, JOHN KELLY, CW–USA; Worthington, Pa (b/X–24–1825 Kellersburg; d/X–21–1903) MD UPa 1867. *U Pa med alum CW*: 1867. *Atkinson* I:607. *Polk* 1886: 840.

MAXWELL, SAMUEL, Johnstown NY (d/XII–9–1863 @80) MD CPSNY 1812. *Bost m&s j* 69:448, 1863.

MAXWELL, SAMUEL C , Duluth, Minn (b/1840 Crawfordsville, Ind; d/V–13–1900) MD Rush 1866. *JAMA* 34: 1505, 1900. *Polk* 1886: 333 (Remington, Ind).

MAXWELL, WILLIAM H , NYC (b/1813; d/VII–16–1889) MD CPSNY 1838. *Med reg NY NJ Conn* 1889: 278. *Butler* 1878: 519.

MAY, FRANCIS, Nashville 1802–04; Knoxville 1804–(d/1817 Nashville) MD ? *Tr Med Soc Tenn* 1876: 84.

MAY, FREDERICK, Washington, DC (b/XI–16–1773 Boston; d/I–23–1847) MB Harvard 1795; MD 1811; AB 1792. *Hist Med Soc DC:* 218. *K & B* III: 819–20.

MAY, FREDERICK JOHN [JOHN FREDERICK], Washington, DC (b/V–19–1812; d/V–2–1891) MD Columbian 1834; AB 1831. *JAMA* 17:121–23, 1891. *Hist Med Soc DC:*229–30. *Med annals Md:*492. *K&B* III:820.

MAY, GEORGE WASHINGTON, Washington, DC (b/1789 Boston; d/1845) MD Harvard 1813; AB 1810. *Hist Med Soc DC:* 218.

MAY, HENRY CLAY, Washington, DC; Corning, NY; CW–USA (b/XII–24–1830 Bath, NY; d/I–27 or II–?–1894) MD U Mich 1856; ng Amherst 1854. *Amherst, Men of*: 1854. *Polk* 1886: 657.

MAY, IRVING N, Danville, Va (b/IX–25–1875 Oakland; d/VII–27–1902 El Paso, Tex) MD U Med Coll Va 1896. *Tr Med Soc Va* 1902: 224–25. *Polk* 1900: 1761.

MAY, JAMES, Petersburg, Va (b/IV–11–1798 Dinwiddie Co; d/XI–15–1873) MD UPa 1820. *Tr M S Va* 1875:102; 1877:118. *Tr AMA* 25: 532–33, 1874. *K & B* II: 771.

MAY, OLIVER THEODORE, Monroeville, Ind (b/IV–29–1863 Adams Co; d/III–23–1903) MD Ft Wayne Med Coll 1888. *Tr Ind St Med Soc* 1903: 349.

MAY, VANCE W , Lawrence, Kans (d/II–4–1895) MD Jefferson 1867. *JAMA* 24: 221, 1895. *Butler* 1878:254.

MAY, W B , ? (d/XI–13–1878 Grenada, Miss) MD ? *Tr AMA* 30:875, 1879. *Med rec* NY 14:220, 1878.

MAY, WILLIS L, Crawfordsville, Ind (b/X–8–1828 Carrollton Co, Ky; d/X–24–1900) MD Rush 1858. *Tr Ind St Med Soc* 1901: 492. *Polk* 1896: 463.

MAYBERRY, EDWIN, E Weymouth, Mass (d/VII–18 1895 @68) MD Bowdoin 1849. *Bost m&s j* 133: 659, 1895. *Polk* 1886: 475.

MAYBIN, DAVID CRAWFORD, Morenci, Mich (b/IX–7–1814 Philadelphia; d/II–2–1881) MD Castleton 1855; ng Amherst 1835. *Amherst, Men of*: 1835.

MAYBURY, WILLIAM, Philadelphia (b/VI–13–1816 Montgomery Co, Pa; d/XI–20–1873) MD UPa 1843; AB Franklin & Marshall 1840. *Tr CPP* cent vol: 247. *Med s rep Phila* 29:462, 1873. *Tr Pa St Med Soc* 1875: 755–61.

MAYER, CARL F , Ft Wayne, Ind 23 yrs (b/I–12–1830 Gny; d/I–15–1885 Gny) <MD Tübingen> *Tr Ind St Med Soc* 1886:197. *Butler* 1878: 207.

MAYER, EDWARD RODMAN, Wilkes Barre Pa (b/VII 18–1823; d/VIII–16–1891) MD UPa 1844; AB 1841; AM. *Tr CPP* cent vol: 247. *Tr Luzerne Co (Pa) Med Soc* 1891: 104–06. *Atkinson* I: 705.

MAYER, GOTTFRIED, Brooklyn(d/I–4–1875 @43)

MD ? *Med reg NY NJ Conn* 1875:201. *M rec* 10:48 1875.

MAYES, SAMUEL, SC; Maury, Tenn (b/1759 Carlisle, Pa; d/1841) <MD UPa> *Tr Med Soc Tenn* 1876: 84.

MAYFIELD, GEORGE ANDREW, Nashville (b/III-13 1814 Williamson Co, Tenn; d/VII-20-1864) <MD U Nashville> *Tr Med Soc Tenn* 1876: 84.

MAYHEW, GEORGE ERNEST. Red Bluff, Calif (b/ 1872; d/VII-19-1904 Colyear Springs) MD CPS Chicago 1897; AB Wabash Coll 1894. *U Ill Coll Med alum.*

MAYHEW, JULIUS STEWART, New Bedford, Mass (b/1791? d/IX-20-1859 @68) MD Harvard 1826. *Med surg rep Phila* ns3:72, 1859/60.

MAYNADIER, HENRY, Annapolis, Md; RevWar-USA (b/1756; d/XI-11-1849) MD ? *Tr AMA* 3:449, 1850. *Med annals Md:* 492.

MAYNARD, ELIAS FRENCH, NYC (b/1800? d/1869) MD Yale 1829. *Med reg NY NJ Conn* 1869: 236.

MAYNARD, JOHN PARKER, Dedham, Mass (b/Boston; d/II-26-1898 @81) MD Harvard 1848. *Bost m&s j* 138:216 237-38 1898. *JAMA* 30:624 1898 *Polk* 1896:711.

MAYO, HENRY OBED, USN (b/IX-1-1819 Ogdensburgh, NY; d/I-1-1892) MD Albany 1842; ng Woodstock 1840; AB Amherst 1838. *JAMA* 18: 82, 1892.

MAYO, ROBERT, Richmond Va; Washington DC 1830- (b/IV-25-1787 Powhatan Co, Va; d/X-31-1864) MD U Pa 1808; att Wm & Mary. *Med annals Md:* 493. *K&B* III: 820-21.

MAYO, THEODORICK P, CW-CSA; Richmond Va (d/ VI-20-1889 @59) MD Med Coll Va 1853. *Med surg rep Phila* 61:28,1889. *Med bull m & s* 11:263, 1889.

MAYO, WILLIAM STARBUCK, NYC (b/IV-20-1812 Ogdensburgh, NY; d/XI-22-1895 NYC) MD CPSNY 1832. *JAMA* 25: 1010, 1895.

MEACHEM, EDWARD H G , Milwaukee, Wis (d/ VIII-10-1887) MD Geneva 1843. *Tr Wis St Med Soc* 1891:357. *Polk* 1886:957.

MEACHEM, JOHN GOLDSBOROUGH, Racine, Wis 1862- (b/V-27-1823 Axbridge, Engl; d/II-1-1896) MD Castleton 1843; MD Bellevue 1863. *JAMA* 26:287, 1896. *Tr Wis St Med Soc* 30:561-63, 1896. *Atkinson* I: 81. *K & B* III: 822-23. *Polk* 1890: 1172.

MEACHER, WILLIAM, Portage, Wis (b/V-27-1833 Suffolk, Engl; d/IV-22-1898) MD Rush 1862. *JAMA* 30:1125, 1898. *Tr Wis St Med Soc* 32:553-55, 1898. *Polk* 1886: 959.

MEACOM, JOHN FRANCIS, Beverly, Mass (d/IX-27-1871 @24) MD Harvard 1870. *Bost m&s j* 8: 1871.

MEAD, EDWARD, Ohio & Boston (b/1819 Engl; d/VI-28-1883 at sea) MD Med Coll Ohio 1841. *JAMA* 2: 726, 1884. *Bost m&s j* 109:139, 1883. *K&B* III:823.

MEAD, JOHN AMES, Pearlington, Miss (b/VII-16-1842 Portland, Me; d/I-30-1891 New Orleans) MD Harvard 1869; AB Amherst 1865. *JAMA* 16:428, 1891. *Bost m&s j* 124: 224, 1891. *Polk* 1890: 633.

MEAD, JOHN CALVIN, NYC (b/VI-11-1844; d/VIII-24-1868) MD CPSNY 1866. *Tr AMA* 21:435-36, 1870. *Med reg NY NJ Conn* 1869:240. *Med rec NY* 3: 334, 1868-69.

MEAD, SYLVESTER, Greenwich, Conn (b/1807; d/XII-21-1894) MD Yale 1829. *Med reg NY NJ Conn* 1895: 232. *JAMA* 24: 33, 1895.

MEAD [MEADE], W C , Hopefield, Ark (d/IX-28 1878 Memphis, Tenn) MD ? *Tr AMA* 30:877, 1879. *Med rec NY* 14:220, 1878.

MEADE [MEAD], EUTHANASIA SHERMAN, San Jose, Cal (b/1836 Genesee, NJ; d/1895) MD Wom M C Pa 1869. *Tr M S Cal* 26:320-22, 1896. *Polk* 1890: 1704.

MEADE, HODIJAH BAYLIES, CW-CSA (b/III-2-1838; d/1875 Danville, Va) MD UPa 1861. *U Pa med alum CW*: 1861. Blanton *Va surgs in CW*: 410.

MEAKER, CYRUS TRUMAN, Carbondale, Pa (b/I-3-1856 Hawleyton, NY; d/V-9-1904) MD Dartmouth 1887; DDS U Pa 1881. *Pa med jour* 8:335, 1904/05. *Flint* 1896: 1270.

MEALIA, EDWARD JOSEPH, Brooklyn (b/XII-24-1859; d/VI-6-1890) MD CPSNY 1883; AM St Francis Xavier Bkln. *Med reg NY NJ Conn* 1891: 278.

MEANS, ROBERT, Fairfield Dist, SC (d/IX-18-1858 @30) MD M C SC 1850. *Med surg rep Phila* ns1: 28, 1858/59.

MEANS, ROBERT MARKLE, Dehaven, Pa (d/II-14 1903 @35) MD Jefferson 1893. *Pa med jour* 7: 279, 1903/04. *Flint* 1897: 800.

MEANS, THEOPHILUS HOLTON, CW-CSA (b/c1835 Mecklenburg Co, NC; d/VII-9-1879 Charlotte) MD UPa 1859. *U Pa med alum CW*: 1859.

MEANS, THOMAS SUMTER, CW-USA; Spartanburgh, SC (b/IV-1-1833 Union Co; d/VI-18-1900) MD UPa 1859. *U Pa med alum CW*: 1859. *Polk* 1886: 856.

MEARES JOHN LOUDON, San Francisco (b/1822 or 1823 Wilmington, NC; d/I-13-1888) MD Jefferson 1846; AB UNC 1843. *NC m j* 21:62, 1888. *Tr Cal St Med Soc* 1888: 300. *Butler* 1878: 61.

MEARES, T W , ? (d/IX-29-1878 Memphis) MD ? *Tr AMA* 30:877, 1879.

MEARS, GEORGE WASHINGTON, Indianapolis, Ind (b/VI-27-1803 Harrisburg, Pa; d/V-20-1879) MD Jefferson 1827. *Tr AMA* 31:1067-69, 1880. *Tr Ind Med Soc* 1879:183, 185-86, 234-36.

MEARS, JAMES HOWELL, CW-USN; Philadelphia (b/ II-8-1837; d/IV-5-1887) MD UPa 1859. *U Pa med alum CW*: 1859.

MEARS, WESLEY NATHAN, Cohan, Ala (d/VII-1-1898?) MD ? *Tr M Assn St Ala* 1899:233. *Butler* 1874:22.

MEASE, JOHN N , Oswego, NY (d/III-11-1898 @71) Lic Oswego Co Med Soc. *Bost m&s j* 138: 262-63, 1898. *JAMA* 30:682, 1898. *Polk* 1896: 1088.

MEASE, LEVI A , Freeport, Ill (d/1881) MD Rush 1851;

 Spec. educ'l status abbrev. as: ***ng*** = college verified attendance without degree;

MD Jefferson 1856. *Chic med jour* 43: 541, 1881.

MEBANE, BENJAMIN FRANKLIN, Orange Co NC (b/V–28–1823; d/1884 Mebane NC) MD UPa 1850; AB U NC 1847. *UNC cat*: 422.

MEBANE, WILLIAM THOMAS, Mebanesville, Ark (b/1825; d/1891) MD UPa 1849; AB UNC 1845; AM 1850. *UNC cat:* 423. *Polk* 1886: 154.

MECHEM, ABEL F , USA 1860–67? (b/Md; d/VII–14 1871 Pleasantville) MD U Md 185. *Med rec* 6:263, 1871.

MECRAY, ALEXANDER McKENZIE, CW–USA med cadet; Cape May, NJ (b/X–5–1839; d/VI–26–1902 Maple Shade) MD UPa 1864; PhG Phila Coll Pharm 1860. *U Pa med alum CW*: 1864. *Polk* 1886: 602.

MECUEN, GEORGE EDWARD, Roxbury, Mass (d/X–21–1902 @59) MD Harvard 1875. *Bost m&s j* 147:504, 1902. *Polk* 1886: 472.

MEDILL, WALTER W , Indianapolis; Denver (d/III–14 1901) MD Med Coll Ind 1889; MD U Ill Coll Med 1891. *Ill med jour* ns2:601, 1901. *Polk* 1893: 236.

MEEK, EDWIN G , Nevada, Calif; Jacksonville, Ill (d/IX–1–1866) MD ? *Chic med jour* 23:527–28, 1866. *Tr Ill St Med Soc* 1895: 64–65.

MEEK, JAMES T , Ennis, Tex (b/1842 SC; d/XI–11 1886) MD Med Coll Va 1863. *JAMA* 7:697, 1886. *New Orl m&s j* ns14:559, 1887. *Tex cour–rec med* 4:242–43, 1887. *Polk* 1886: 885.

MEEK, JOHN WILLIAM, Carrollton, Ala (b/XI–6–1822; d/V–1–1851 Tuscaloosa) MD New Orl Sch Med 1859; AB U Ala 1840. *U Ala cat*: 61.

MEEKER, SAMUEL F , Lecompte, La (b/1836 W Feliciana Parish; d/II–12–1899) MD U La 1859. *New Orl m&s j* 51:528, 1899. *Polk* 1896: 617.

MEEKINS, THOMAS, Williamsburg, Mass (d/VIII–5–1881 @84) MD Berkshire 1827. *Tr AMA* 32: 525–26, 1881. *Bost m&s j* 105: 623, 1881.

MEEKS, EDWIN JOSEPH, Stamford, Conn (b/XII–16–1864 Lower Sancon, Pa; d/VI–9–1895) MD Bellevue 1890; AB Harvard 1887. *Med reg NY NJ Conn* 1895:233. *Proc Conn M S* 1897: 353. *Bost m&s j* 132: 654, 1895.

MEEM, ANDREW RUSSELL, Abingdon, Va; CW–CSA (b/VI–27–1821; d/II–26–1865) MD UPa 1844; <att Princeton> att U Va. *U Pa med alum CW*: 1844. Johnson, J.L. *U Va memorial ... alum d/CW*: 702.

MEERS [MEARS], HAMILTON H , NYC; CW–USA (d/I–8?–1863 @ c30) MD UCNY 1847. *Med surg rep Phila* ns9:325, 1862/63. *Nat med jour* 1:299, 1870/71.

MEETER, WILLIAM H , Chestertown, Md (b/XI––1824 Newark, Del; d/1882) MD Jefferson 1847. *Med annals Md:* 500. *Butler* 1874:321.

MEGEE, WILLIAM K , Rushville, Ind (d/III–17 1900 @40) MD Mo Med Coll 1884. *JAMA* 34: 380, 1900.

MEHARD, JAMES W, Painesville O (d/IX–25–1883 @ 35) MD Jefferson 1872. *Med bull m & s* 5:257, 1883.

MEIER, CARL T , NYC (b/1810 Prussia; d/II–2–1865) MD ? *Nashville jour med & surg* ns1:318, 1866.

MEIGNEN, LEOPOLD, Philadelphia (b/1793; d/VI–4–1874) <MD Jefferson> att Paris Conservatoire. *Med surg rep Phila* 28: 470, 1873?

MEIGS, CHARLES DELUCENA, Philadelphia (b/II–19 1792 St George, Bermuda; d/VI–22–1869) MD UPa 1817; AB U Ga 1809. *Tr CPP* ns4:417–48, 1874. *Tr AMA* 24:374–77, 1873. *K&B* III: 828.

MEIGS, JAMES AITKEN, Philadelphia (b/VII–31–1829; d/VII–8–1879) MD Jefferson 1851; AB Central HS Phila 1848. *Tr CPP* cent vol: 248; 3s5:cxvii–cxxxiv, 1881. *Tr Pa St Med Soc* 1880: 385–400. *Tr AMA* 31:1069–75, 1880. *K&B* III: 829.

MEIGS, JOHN FORSYTH, Philadelphia (b/X–3–1818; d/XII–16–1882) MD UPa 1838. *Tr CPP* cent vol: 248; 3s7:lxxi–xciii, 1884. *Atkinson* I: 694. *K&B* III:829.

MEIGS, WILLIAM, Kennebec Co, Me 1844–54; WVa 1854–57; Ohio 1857–65; Vineland, NJ 1874–80; NC & Va 1880–84; Quiet Dell, Harrison Co, WVa 1884–91 (b/III–9–1816 Easton, NY; d/II–15–1891) MD Bowdoin 1844. *Bowdoin cat*: 1844.

MEISEL, HARRY, Elmira, NY (b/1824; d/1872) MD Leipzig 1849. *Tr AMA* 31: 1075, 1880.

MELHORN, JOHN F , CW–USA (d/X– –1863) MD ? *Nat med jour* 1:299, 1870/71.

MELICK, DANIEL RAMSEY, Light St, Columbia Co, Pa (d/IV–17–1866 @26) MD Jefferson 1865. *Med surg rep Phila* 14: 458, 1866.

MELIUS, ROBERT A , Morrisania, NY (d/1877?) MD Albany 1864. *Med reg NY NJ Conn* 1877: 204.

MELLEN, GEORGE FROST, Sartartia, Miss 1851– ; CW–CSA (b/II–28–1826 Durham, NH; d/II or V–23–1877) MD Jefferson 1851; AB Bowdoin 1846; AM 1849. *New Orl m&s j* ns4:899–900, 1877.

MELLEN, WILLIAM MICHAEL EDWARD, Chicopee, Mass (d/V–14–1906 @58) MD U Mich 1876. *Bost m&s j* 154, 568, 1906. *Polk* 1896: 710.

MELLINGER, HENRY SCHOP, Cresswell, Pa (d/II–7 1901 @79) MD Jefferson 1845. *Pa m j* 5: 296, 1901/02. *Flint* 1897: 799.

MELLISH, ERNEST JOHNSON, Chicago(d/IV/V–1905 El Paso Tx) MD Rush 1886. *Chico med rec* 27: 404, 1905. *Tex st med jour* 1:32, 1905. *Flint* 1897:265.

MELOU, ETIENNE, Brownsville, Tx (b/XII–23–1833 Toulouse, Fr; d/XI–25–1888) MD New Orl Sch Med 1869? *Tex health jour* 1:141, 1888. *Daniel's Tex med jour* 4:267, 1888.

MELROSE, JAMES, Canton, Ill (d/VII–5–1860) MD ? *No Amer jour homeop* 9:348, 1861. *Amer homeop rev* 2:480, 1860. *King* III:158. Homeopath.

MELVIN, McCARTHY B , Washington, DC (b/1814 Va; d/V–21–1904) MD U Md 1849. *Hist Med Soc DC:* 248. *Polk* 1886: 213.

MELVIN, WALTER, CW–USA; Felton, Del (b/XII–18–1834 Caroline Co, Md; d/IX–16–1876) MD UPa 1859. *Med s rep Phila* 35: 526, 1876. *UPa m alum CW*: 1859.

MENDEL, JACOB, Milwaukee (d/XI-12-1895 @50) <MD Breslau 1870> *Tr Med Soc Wis* 30:563-64, 1896. *JAMA* 25: 968, 1895. *Polk* 1890: 1169.

MENDENHALL, ELIJAH R , Indianapolis, Ind (d/XI-3 1897 @82) MD Cinc Coll Med & Surg 1865. *JAMA* 29: 1028, 1897. *Polk* 1886: 323.

MENDENHALL, GEORGE, Cincinnati; CW-US San Comm (b/V-5-1814 Chester Co, Pa; d/VI-4-1874 Phila) MD UPa 1835. *Med surg rep Phila* 31: 20, 1874. *JAMA* 32:1209, 1899. *K&B* III: 832.

MENDENHALL, NATHAN, Thorntown, Ind (b/X-31-1831 Canton, Ind; d/VIII-18-1880) MD Med Coll Ohio 1858. *Tr AMA* 33:582, 1882. Kemper's *Indiana*:310.

MENDENHALL, NEREUS, Greensboro, NC (b/1819 Jamestown; MD Jefferson 1845; AB Haverford 1839. *Haverford biogr cat*: 12.

MENDENHALL, WILLIAM O'NEAL, Richmond, Ind (b/IV-18-1834 Montgomery Co, Ind; d/VII-16-1905) MD Rush 1870. *Tr Ind St Med Soc* 1906:504.

MENDENHALL, WINFIELD SCOTT, Springfield, Ill (d/I-25-1899 @51) MD Miami 1869. *JAMA* 32:324, 1899. *Polk* 1896: 168.

MENEES, GEORGE W , Springfield, Tenn (b/II-22-1824 Robertson Co; d/VIII-2-1904) MD Nashville 1855. *Nashvl j m & s* 96:708-09, 1904. *Polk* 1896: 1407.

MENEES, ORVILLE HARRISON, Nashville (b/IV-15 1859 Springfield; d/II-17-1895) MD Vanderbilt 1879; MD U Tenn 1880. *So pract* 17:126,1895. *JAMA* 24: 337, 1895. *Nashvl j m & s* 77:139-42, 1895.

MENEES, THOMAS, Nashville, Tenn (b/VI-26-1823 Davidson Co; d/IX-6-1905) MD Transylvania 1842. *Nashvl j m & s* 97:415-19, 465-67, 1905. *New Orl m&s j* 58:348, 1905. *Atkinson* I: 697. *Polk* 1896: 1402.

MENEES, THOMAS WILLIAMS, Nashville (b/Robertson Co; d/XI-15-1878 Memphis) MD U Nashville & Vanderbilt 1876. *Tr AMA* 30:877-78, 1879. *Med rec* 14:240, 1878.

MENEES, YOUNG HOOPER, Springfield, Tenn (d/XII-12-1883 @27) MD U Nashville & Vanderbilt 1879. *So pract* 6:40-41, 1884. *Nashvl j m&s* ns32: 374-75, 1883.

MENNINGER, HENRY J, Brooklyn; CW-USA (b/1838; d/IX-8-1889) MD UCNY 1863. *Med surg rep Phila* 61: 364, 1889.

MENNINGER, JOHN, NYC (b/Gny; d/X-27-1881 @ 75) <MD Giessen 1832> *Med reg NY NJ Conn* 1882: 232. *Butler* 1878: 519.

MENOCAL, OSCAR A , Washington, DC (d/II-9-1898 @28) MD Columbian 1890. *JAMA* 30:570, 1898.

MENSCH, PETER CALVIN, Collegeville, Pa (d/VII-29 1901 @38) MD Bellevue 1889. *Pa med jour* 5:296, 1901/02. *JAMA* 37:398, 1901. *Polk* 1890: 986.

MERCER, JOHN CYRUS, USN 1832-40; CW-CSA (d/III-26-1884 Va) MD UPa 1832. *UPa m alum CW*: 1832.

MERCER, THOMAS C, Jeffersonville Ind (b/1819 Louisville; d/II-28-1884) MD Louisville Med Inst 1841. *Med surg rep Phila* 50:448, 1864. *Tr Ind St M S* 1884: 222. Kemper's *Indiana*; 310.

MERCER, WILLIAM, Princeton, Ill (d/I-4-1895 @80) Lic by yrs pract. *JAMA* 24:101, 1895. *Polk* 1890: 345. Eclectic.

MERCHANT, HARRY ALVIN, Monson, Mass (d/VI-25-1901 @34) MD Albany 1897. *JAMA* 37: 125, 1901.

MERCIER, ARMAND, New Orleans (d/IV-7-1888 @ 73) MD Paris 1840. *New Orl m&s j* ns13:323, 1885. *Butler* 1878: 293.

MEREDITH, HENRY CLAY, CW-USN; Pughtown, Pa (b/X-13-1842; d/V-9-1891) MD UPa 1865. *U Pa med alum CW*: 1865. *Polk* 1886: 832.

MEREDITH, JOHN QUINCY ADAMS, CW-USA; ?Albuquerque, NM (b/VIII- -1840 Pughtown, Pa d/V-2 1900 Albuqu) MD UPa 1861. *UPa m alum CW*: 1861.

MEREDITH, MARION, Vinton, Ia (b/V- -1831 Greensburg, Ind; d/XII-28-1904) MD Med Coll Ohio 1866. *Tr Iowa St M S* 23:369, 1905. *Polk* 1896: 541.

MERENESS, DWIGHT, Milwaukee (b/VI-8-1859 Sharon; d/V-29-1901) MD LICH 1886; <att Chicago Homeop Coll 1886> ng U Mich 1883-85. *Tr Wis St Med Soc* 35:460-62, 1901. *Polk* 1896: 1556.

MERGLER, MARIE J , Chicago (b/1851 Main Stockheim, Bavaria; d/V-18-1901 Chic or LA) MD Woman's M C Chic 1879; grad St Normal Sch Oswego, Ill. *Chic m rec* 20:605, 1901; 21:53-54, 1901. *Bost m&s j* 144:537, 1901. *Ill med jour* ns3: 47, 1901. *K&B* III: 835-36.

MERILLAT, JOHN CHARLES MARTIN, CW-CSA (b/III-1811 Bordeaux, Fr; d/1875 WVa) MD UPa 1837. *UPa med alum CW*: 1837. Blanton *Va surgs CW*: 490.

MERIWETHER, GEORGE MATHEWS, Mathews Station, Ala b/1814; d/X-13-1873) MD UPa 1838; att U Ala 1833. *U Ala cat*: 44.

MERIWETHER, JOHN SAMUEL, Eutaw, Ala (b/I-28-1830; d/V-26-1879) MD Med Coll SC 1853; AB U Ala 1850, AM 1853. *U Ala cat*: 94.

MERIWETHER, ROBERT THOMAS, CW-CSA; Tuscaloosa, Ala (b/XI-24-1828; d/VIII-15-1862 Richmond) MD U Nashville 1858; AB U Ala 1848; AM 1851. *U Ala cat*: 86.

MERKLE, ISAAC H, NYC (b/Gny; d/III-25 1865 @70) Lic NY Co Med Soc. *Med reg NY NJ Conn* 1865: 236.

MERKLE, JOSEPH FRANKLIN, Perkasie, Pa (d/XI-17 1903 @43) MD UPa 1894. *Pa m j* 7:279, 1903/04.

MERRIAM, EPHRAIM CARLOS, Washington DC (b/XII-9-1838 Pittsburgh; d/XI-27-1895) MD Dartmouth 1864; ng Amherst 1862. *Hist M S DC*:279. *Polk* 1886:213.

MERRIAM, JOSEPH WAITE, CW-USA (d/1900 Iquique, Peru [or Chile?]) MD Harvard 1862; AB 1856. *Harv in CW*: 97. *Mass Med Soc cat* 1894.

MERRIAM, ROYAL AUGUSTUS, Topsfield, Mass (b/I 30-1786; d/XI-13-1864) MB Dartmouth 1811; MD 1820; AB 1808. *Bost m&s j* 71:328, 1864.

MERRICK, CHARLOTTE LAVINIA, Utica, NY (d/1899? @49) MD Woman's Med Coll Pa 1878. *JAMA* 32: 787, 1899. *Polk* 1886: 713.

MERRICK, FREDERICK T , Barclay, Md (d/XI-4-1898 @36) MD Jefferson 1888. *JAMA* 31: 1257, 1898. *Polk* 1896: 667.

MERRICK, MYRA K, Cleveland (d/XI-11-1899 @74) <MD Central Med Coll Rochester NY 1852; MD Homeop Hosp Cleveland 1890> *Buffalo m&s j* 39: 385,1899. *Polk* 1886:748. *Polk* 1896:1174. Homeopath.

MERRILL, FRANKLIN BENJAMIN, Garrettsburg, Ky 1847-49; Alfred, Me 1852- (b/II-16-1825 Buxton, Me; d/V-2-1899) MD Jefferson 1852; AB Bowdoin 1847. *Bowdoin cat*: 1847. *Polk* 1886: 423.

MERRILL, JAMES CUSHING, USA (b/III-26-1853 Cambridge, Mass; d/X-27-1902) MD UPa 1874; AB Harvard. *Bost m&s j* 148: 107, 1903. *K&B* III: 836-37.

MERRILL, JESSE, Franklin, NH 1820-45; Hopkinton, Mass 1845-60 (b/VIII-1-1794 Peacham, Vt; d/XI-18-1860) MD Dartmouth 1819; AB 1806. *Bost m&s j* 63: 348, 1861; 66:291-94, 1862.

MERRILL, JOHN, Portland, Me (b/III-2-1782 Conway NH; d/VI-7-1855) MD Harvard 1807; MD 1811; AM 1804. *Bost m&s j* 52:387, 1855. *Tr Am Inst Hom* 1893: 149. *King* I:312. Homeopath 1841- .

MERRILL, JOHN CUMMINGS, Lewiston, Me; St Paul, Minn; Natchez, Miss; CW-CSA; Portland, Me 1866-96 (b/XI-3-1831 Portland; d/VIII-8-1900) MD NY Med Coll 1854; AB Bowdoin 1851; ng Amherst 1851. *Hom rec*: 1900. *Bowdoin cat*: 1851. Homeopath.

MERRILL, JOHN WESLEY, Boston (b/XI-22-1849 Dorchester; d/I-14-1884) MD Dartmouth 1881. *Tr NH Med Soc* 1884:205. *Med surg rep Phila* 50:192 1884.

MERRILL, JOSEPH, Gardiner, Me (d/X-29-1863 @58) MD Bowdoin 1829. *Bost m&s j*69:388, 1863.

MERRILL, SIDNEY SMITH, Calif (b/V-25-1827 Greene, Me; d/I-6-1891) MD Berkshire 1851; ng Amherst 1851. *Amherst, Men of*: 1851.

MERRILL, SUAYZE B L , Chicago (d/IX-11-1894) MD U Ill Coll Med 1886. *JAMA* 23: 440, 1894.

MERRIMAN, ANDREWS, Madison, O (b/VII-14-1795 Dalton, Mass; d/1867 @72) Hon MD Willoughby 1839. *Tr Ohio St Med Soc* 1870: 252-55.

MERRIMAN, H R , CW-USA (d/IX-18-1864) MD ? *Nat med jour* 1:299, 1870/71.

MERRITT, CHARLES AUSTIN, Charlotte, Mich (d/XII-26-1898 @74) MD U Mich 1855. *JAMA* 32:92, 1899. *Polk* 1886: 486.

MERRITT, DANIEL SMITH, Philadelphia (b/II-11-1835 NYC; d/IV-11-1869) MD UPa 1857; AB 1853; AM 1856. *Med s rep Phila* 20: 327, 1869. *Phila med reg & dir* 1871: 294.

MERRITT, JESSE FROST, Pleasant Plains, NY (d/III-30-1868 @38) MD CPSNY 1852. *Phila med reg & dir* 1871: 296. *Med surg rep Phila* 18:420, 1868. *Amer hom obs* 5:299, 1868. Homeopath.

MERRITT, JOHN, New Castle, Del (b/III-21-1816 St Georges; d/I-5-1872) MD UPa 1843. *Tr AMA* 23:575, 1872. *Med Soc Del*: 46.

MERRIWEATHER, H C , CW-USA (d/IV-11-1865) MD ? *Nat med jour* 1:299, 1870/71.

MERROW [MERRON], JAMES MONROE, CW-USA; W Newfield, Me (b/XII- -1869) MD Dartmouth 1859. *Nat med jour* 1:299, 1870/71.

MERRYMAN, MOSES W , Baltimore; Atlantic City, NJ (b/II-15-1827; d/I-25-1904 Gettysburg) MD U Md 1850; AB Gettysburg 1847. *Med annals Md:* 501.

MERSEREAU, CHARLES HENRY, NYC (d/V-2-1900 @37) MD CPSNY 1884. *Bost m&s j* 142:528, 1900. *JAMA* 34:1210, 1900. *Polk* 1896: 1068.

MERSHOM, RICHARD BLACKWELL, Newark, NJ (b/I-12-1812 Lawrenceville, NJ; d/III-22-1895) MD Jefferson 1839; AB Princeton 1834. *Med reg NY NJ Conn* 1895: 233. *JAMA* 24: 497, 1895.

MERVY, ALPHONSE T , San Diego, Cal (d/XI-17-1903) MD Med Coll Pacific 1876. *Cal st j m* 1:489, 1903. *Polk* 1886: 173 (San Francisco).

MESSEMER, MICHAEL JEAN BAPTISTE, NYC (d/II 21-1894 Mentone, Fr) MD Bellevue 1875; att St Xavier's Coll. *Med reg NY NJ Conn* 1894:243. *JAMA* 22: 392, 1894. *Butler* 1878: 519.

MESSENGER, JOHN, NYC (b/VI-20-1819; d/V-19-1892) MD CPSNY 1852. *Med reg NY NJ Conn* 1892:283 *Bost m&s j* 126:540,1892. *Polk* 1890: 825.

MESSERSMITH, JOHN S , USN 1837-72 (d/II-16-1891 @81 Lancaster, Pa) MD Jefferson 1833. *JAMA* 16: 428,1891. *Bost m&s j* 124:200, 1891. *Med bull med & surg* 13:195, 1891.

METCALF, CHARLES NATHANm Indianapolis (b/IV-25-1846 Herkimer, NY; d/III-10-1896) MD U Mich 1872. *Tr Ind St M S* 1896:269. *Med bull m&s* 18: 192, 1896.

METCALF, EDWARD AUGUSTUS, Kinderhook, NY (d/I-11-1874 Huimanguillo, Mex) MD UCNY 1849. *Med surg rep Phila* 30:372, 1874.

METCALF, GEORGE REUBEN, St Paul, Minn (b/XII-17-1848 Brattleboro, Vt; d/II-28-1905) MD CPSNY 1874; ng Amherst 1872. *Amherst, Men of*: 1872. *Polk* 1886: 517.

METCALF, JOHN GEORGE, Mendon, Mass (b/IX-10-1801 Norfolk, Mass; d/I-13-1892) MD Harvard 1826; AB Brown 1820; AM. *Bost m&s j* 126: 76, 1892. *Polk* 1886: 469.

METCALF, SAMUEL C , Fort Wayne, Ind (d/VIII-10 1895 @51) MD Western Reserve 1870. *JAMA* 25: 342, 1895. *Polk* 1890: 371.

METCALF, VOLNEY, Natchez, Miss (b/IX-19-1804 Flemming Co, NY; d/X-19-1852) MD UPa 1831; AB Yale 1828. *New Orl m&s j* 9:484-87, 1853.

METCALFE, ERNEST GEORGE, Brooklyn (d/II-2

1900 @49) MD LICH 1872. *Bost m&s j* 142: 154, 1900. *JAMA* 34:380, 1900. *Polk* 1896:1000.

METCALFE, FRANCIS JOHNSTON, Florence, Italy (b/NY; d/II-9-1892 @42) MD CPSNY 1871. *Med bull med & surg* 14:203, 1892.

METCALFE, JAMES, Natchez, Miss (b/1789? d/VI-1-1867 @78) MD UPa 1816. *New Orl m&s j* 20: 282-83, 1867.

METCALFE, JOHN THOMAS, NYC (b/Natchez, Miss; d/I-30-1802 @83 Thomasville, Ga) MD UPa 1843. *Bost m&s j* 146: 154, 1902. *Atkinson* I:676.

METTAUER, JOHN PETER, Pr Edw Co, Va (b/1787; d/XI-22-1875) MD UPa 1809; AB Hampden-Sidney 1806. *Tr Med Soc Va* 1877:117-18. *Nashvl j m & s* ns17: 44, 1876. *K&B* III: 837-39.

METZ, ABRAM, Massillon, O (b/1828 Stark Co; d/1876) MD Cleveland Med Coll 1848. *Tr Ohio St Med Soc* 1875:195; 1876: 91-92. *K&B* II: 787.

METZ, JACOB K , Allensville, Pa (d/IX-11-1903 @78) MD Jefferson 1852. *Pa med jour* 7: 279, 1903/04. *Flint* 1897: 794.

METZGER, ISAAC, NYC (b/1849? Alsace; d/III-24-1873 @24) MD Bellevue 1872. *Med reg NY NJ Conn* 1873: 343.

METZGER, LEOPOLD LOWELL, Brooklyn (d/XII-4-1898 @35) MD LICH 1894. *JAMA* 31: 1542, 1898.

MEYER, CHARLES, Macungie, Pa (d/IX-2-1904 @77) MD U Berlin 1848. *Pa med jour* 8:335, 1904/05. *Flint* 1896: 1290.

MEYER, JOHN M , Danville, Ky (d/IX-5-1901 @84) MD Transylvania 1843. *JAMA* 37: 789, 1901.

MEYER, LOUIS, Cleveland (d/X-29-1897) MD Göttingen 1840. *JAMA* 29:1028, 1897. *Polk* 1886: 748.

MEYER, THEODORE, ?NYC (d/1864 @35) MD ? *Med reg NY NJ Conn* 1865: 235.

MEYER, WILLIAM C Cleveland (d/XII-21-1898 @78) MD Göttingen 1842. *JAMA* 32:41,1899. *Polk* 1886:748.

MEYERS [MYERS], CHARLES W , Clinton, Ia (d/IV-21-1898) MD Western Reserve 1862. *JAMA* 30:1125, 1898. *Polk* 1896: 515.

MEYLERT, ASA P , CW-USA; NYC (b/La Porte, Pa; d/XI-11-1893 Wilkes Barre) MD UCNY 1857. *JAMA* 21: 829, 1893.

MICHAEL, J EDWIN, Baltimore (b/V-15-1843 Hartford Co; d/XII-2-1895) MD U Md 1873; AB Princeton 1871; AM 1874. *Buff m&s j* 35:514-15, 1895. *Chic med rec* 10:83 1896. *JAMA* 25:1058, 1895. *Med ann Md:* 502.

MICHAELIS, MORITZ, NYC (b/X-18-1811; d/VI-22-1883) MD U Berlin 1835. *Med reg NY NJ Conn* 1884: 233. *Med surg rep Phila* 49: 28, 1883. *Butler* 1878: 505.

MICHAELS, A LOUIS, Kansas City, Mo (b/1854 Ill; d/VI-29-1898) <MD Louisville; MD Starling> *JAMA* 31:142, 1898. *Polk* 1896: 848.

MICHAL, GEORGE WASHINGTON, CW-CSA; Hickory, NC (b/X-19-1825 Rutherfordton; d/I-11-1892) MD UPa 1847; att Med Coll SC. *UPa m alum CW*: 1847.

MICHEL, WILLIAM MIDDLETON, Charleston, SC; CW-CSA (d/I-22-1822; d/VI-4-1894) MD M C SC 1846; Dipl École de Med Paris 1845. *So pract* 16: 301, 1894. *Atkinson* I: 701. *K&B* III: 840-41. *Waring* II: 266.

MICHELENA, GUILLERMO, Caracas, Venezuela 1848-65; Havana, Cuba 1865-68; NYC 1868- (b/IV-6-1817 Curaçao; d/I-15-1873 NYC) MD Paris 1847. *Med reg NY NJ Conn* 1873:344. *Med rec* 8: 185, 1873.

MICHENER, EZRA, New Garden Twp, Pa (b/XI-24-1794 London Grove Twp; d/VI-24-1887) MD UPa 1818. *Med bull* 9:213, 1887. *K&B* III: 841.

MICHIE, THEODORE ADOLPHUS, CW-CSA; Earlysville, Va (b/ IX-23-1821 Albemarle Co; d/VI-12-1890 Chancellorsville) MD UPa 1843. *U Pa med alum CW*: 1843. *Polk* 1886: 916.

MICKS, THOMAS RICHÉ SWIFT, CW-CSA (b/IX-16-1833 Gosport Navy Yd; d/VI-18-1869 Red River, La) MD UPa 1859. *U Pa med alum CW*: 1859.

MIDDLEBROOK, ELIJAH, Fairfield Conn (d/1860?) MD CPSNY 1813. *Proc Conn Med Soc* 1:19, 1860.

MIDDLETON, HORACE PECHIN, Washington, DC (b/XI-1-1839; d/X-27-1867) MD UPa 1863. *Tr AMA* 19:434-35, 1868. *Hist Med Soc DC:* 272.

MIDDLETON, JAMES, Baltimore (d/1818) MD UPa 1813. *Med annals Md:* 503.

MIDDLETON, JOHN D , Wheeling, WVa 1848-51; Baltimore (d/IV-26-1870) MD U Md 1847. *Tr Am Inst Hom* 1893: 150. *King* 1:404. Homeopath.

MIDDLETON, PASSMORE, USA 1862-91 (b/IV-2-1835 Phila; d/II-14-1895 Pewee Valley, Ky) MD UPa 1862. *U Pa med alum CW*: 1862.

MIDDLETON, ROZIER, Washington, DC (b/IX-18-1861 Herndon, Va; d/I-31-1901) MD Columbian DC 1889. *Hist Med Soc DC:* 352. *Polk* 1893: 272.

MIDDLETON, WILLIAM DRUMMOND, Davenport, Ia (b/IV-26-1844 Bervie, Scotl; d/IV-5-1902) MD Bellevue 1868. *Tr Iowa St Med Soc* 20:44-46, 1902. *Atkinson* I: 312. *Polk* 1896: 518.

MIFFLIN, CHARLES HENRY, Boston (b/VII-19-1805 Phila; d/XII-9-1875) MD UPa 1826; AB 1823. *Bost m & s j* ns16: 718-19, 1875.

MIGHILL, STEPHEN, S Boston (b/1821 Georgetown, Mass; d/IX-6-1872) MD Dartmouth 1851; ng Woodstock 1851. *Bost m&s j* ns10:192, 1875.

MIGNAULT, DEODAT, CW-USA; Lowell, Mass (d/XI 11-1862 @29 Camp Meigs) MD Harvard 1857. *Bost m & s j* 67:308, 1862. *Nat med jour* 1:299, 1870/71.

MILAN, E E , ? (d/1878 Paris, Tenn) MD ? *Tr AMA* 30:878, 1879.

MILBANK, ROBERT, NYC (d/VIII-4-1904 @56) MD UCNY 1878. *Bost m&s j* 151:228 1904. *Polk* 1896:1068.

MILBURY, FRANCIS STEPHEN, Brooklyn (b/1857 New Brunswick; d/VIII-29-1900) MD Cinc Coll Med & Surg 1888. *Bost m&s j* 143: 248, 1900. *Polk* 1896: 1000.

 Spec. educ'l status abbrev. as: ***ng*** = college verified attendance without degree;

MILES, ALBERT BALDWIN, New Orleans (b/V-18-1852 Prattville, Ala; d/VIII-5-1894) MD Tulane 1875. *Buff m&s j* 34:174-75, 1894. *JAMA* 23: 248, 1894. *New Orl m&s j* ns22:185-88, 321-25, 1894. *K&B* III:842.

MILES, ARCHIBALD, NYC (d/II-18-1869 @65) MD ? *Phila m reg & dir* 1871: 300. *Med s rep Phila* 20: 1869.

MILES, B J, Merit, Tex (d/XII-26-1905 @42) <MD Memphis Hosp M C 1892> *Tex st m j* 1:352, 1905/06. *Polk* 1900: 1708.

MILES, BENJAMIN BRISCOE, Baltimore (b/1840; d/II-8-1878) MD U Md 1861. *Med annals Md:* 503. *Butler* 1874: 314.

MILES, EDGAR, Sag Harbor, NY (d/XI-30-1899 @75) MD ? *Bost m&s j* 141:616, 1899. *JAMA* 33: 1504, 1899. *Polk* 1896: 1097.

MILES, FRANCIS TURQUAND, CW-CSA; Baltimore (b/1827 Charleston, SC; d/VII-30-1903) MD Med Coll St SC 1854. *So pract* 25:588, 1903. *Waring* II: 267-68. *K&B* III: 842.

MILES, JOHN M, Acton, Mass (d/III-22-1865) MD Dartmouth 1828. *Bost m&s j* 72: 1865.

MILHAU, JOHN JEFFERSON, USA 1851-76; NYC (b/XII-28-1828 France; d/V-8-1891) MD CPSNY 1850. *Med reg NY NJ Conn* 1891: 278-79. *Bost m&s j* 124:498, 1891. *Atkinson* I: 98.

MILLAR, JAMES, Fruit Hill, RI (b/1806 Glasgow, Scotl; d/V-15-1884) <MD Glasgow> *Tr RI Med Soc* 3:165-66, 1883-88.

MILLARD, HENRY BENTON, NYC (d/IX-14-1893) MD UCNY 1858; AB Hamilton 1855. *Med reg NY NJ Conn* 1894: 243. *Bost m&s j* 129:312, 1893.

MILLARD, PERRY HENRY, St Paul, Minn (b/V-14-1848; d/II-1-1897 Balto) MD Rush 1872 *Bost m&s j* 136:172, 1897. *Tr Minn St M S* 1897:152; 1899:191. *Chic m rec* 12:207, 1897. *JAMA* 28:327, 1897. *K&B* III: 843.

MILLEN, GEORGE RUFUS, CW-CSA (b/V-16-1829 & d/XII-19-1892 Savannah) MD UPa 1856. *U Pa med alum CW*: 1856 suppl.

MILLER, AARON WOOLLEY, CW-CSA; Washington, DC (b/VIII-26-1818 Pittsburgh; d/I-6-1881) MD Columbian 1846. *Tr AMA* 32:526, 1881. *Hist Med Soc DC:* 242-43.

MILLER, ABNER MYERS, Bird-in-Hand, Pa (b/XI-8-1833 Honeybrook Twp, Pa; d/VII-28-1902) MD Pa Med Coll 1858. *Atkinson* I: 508. *Pa med jour* 5: 663,676 1901/02; 6:261, 1902/03. *Flint* 1897: 796.

MILLER, ABRAHAM SCHULTZ, CW-CSA; New Market, Va (b/XI-27-1830 Winchester; d/IV-16-1896) MD UPa 1854. *NC med jour* 37: 310, 1896. *U Pa med alum CW*: 1854.

MILLER, ABRAM J, Paris, Ill (d/V-22-1901 @78) MD Rush 1858. *Ill med jour* ns3:91,140, 1901. *Polk* 1896: 434.

MILLER, ABRAM O, Lebanon Ind (b/X-2-1827 Madison Co; d/IV-25-1901) MD U Louisville 1856. *Tr Ind St Med Soc* 1901: 493.

MILLER, ADAM, CW-USA; Chicago (b/1810; d/VII-29 1901) MD UCNY 1847. *Ill med jour* ns3: 189, 1901. *Med vis* 17:502, 1901. Homeopath.

MILLER, ALBERTUS A, Greencastle, Pa (b/II-18-1843 Williamsport, Pa; d/VI-30-1880) MD Jefferson 1868; ng Dickinson 1868. *Dickinson cat*: 1868.

MILLER, ALFRED, Ashburnham, Mass (b/III-18-1815 Westminster, Vt; d/XI-15-1877 Fitchburg) MD Woodstock 1845; AB ?1840; AM 1843. *Tr AMA* 31:1075-76, 1880.

MILLER, ALFRED, New Ulm, Minn (d/III-3-1896 Switzerland) MD Jefferson 1878. *JAMA* 26: 843, 1896. *Polk* 1896: 853.

MILLER, AMBROSE M, Lincoln, Ill (d/IV-2-1898) MD Washington U Balto 1853. *JAMA* 30:933, 1898.

MILLER, AMOS S, Scotch Plains NJ (d/XII-8-1866 @ 65) MD CPSNY 1825. *Med surg rep Phila* 15:508, 1866.

MILLER, CALEB, Bristol, RI (b/1776 Rehoboth, Mass; d/XI-13-1826) MD Brown 1816. *Tr RI Med Soc* 1: 42, 1859-77.

MILLER, CHARLES A, CW-USA; Cincinnati (d/XI-21 1890) MD Med Coll Ohio 1862. *JAMA* 16:178-79, 1891.

MILLER, CLARKSON, CW-USA (d/XII-20-1864) MD ? *Nat med jour* 1:299, 1870/71.

MILLER, DAVID MAGIE, Elizabeth, NJ (b/V-21-1858 Newark; d/XII-3-1895) MD CPSNY 1883; AB Princeton 1878. *JAMA* 25:1058, 1895. *Tr M S NJ* 1896:372-73.

MILLER, DE LASKIE, Chicago (b/V-29-1818 Niagara Co, NY; d/VII-9-1903) MD Geneva 1842. *Chicago med rec* 25:186, 1903. *Atkinson* I: 600.

MILLER, EDWARD, NYC; War1812-USA (b/V-9 1760 Dover, Del; d/III-17-1812) MD UPa 1785. *NY med & philos jour & rev* 3:320, 1811 [sic]. *No Amer m&s j* 5:127-148. *K&B* III: 843.

MILLER, EDWARD C, Chicago (d/X-23-1898) MD NWU 1891. *JAMA* 31:1128, 1898.

MILLER, EDWARD P, Sullivan, Ill (d/X-7-1902 @37) MD Ky Sch Med 1891. *Ill med jour* ns4: 425, 1902.

MILLER, EDWIN JOHN, Intercourse, Pa (b/I-16-1869; d/VII-24-1903) MD Jefferson 1896. *Pa med jour* 7: 56, 279, 1903/04.

MILLER, EDWIN SYLVESTER, Altoona, Pa (d/II-10-1901) MD UPa 1878. *Pa med jour* 5:296, 1901/02.

MILLER, ERASMUS DARWIN, Dorchester, Mass (b/VIII-7-1813 Franklin; d/VII-5-1881) MD Berkshire 1835; AB Brown 1832. *Tr AMA* 33:582-84, 1882. *Bost m&s j* 105: 384-85, 623, 1881.

MILLER, ERNEST J, Sycamore, Ill (b/1854; d/XI-19 1906) MD CPS Chicago 1888. *JAMA* 57: 1846, 1906.

MILLER, FRANCIS, Brooklyn (d/I-5-1892 @74) <MD Giessen 1842> *Med reg NY NJ Conn* 1892: 284.

MILLER, G [or D] W, Brush Valley, Pa (d/VI-15-1906) MD Western Reserve 1881. *Pa med jour* 9: 746,

1905/06. *Flint* 1897: 797.

MILLER, GEORGE AUGUSTUS, CW-USA (b/1819 Middlebury, Vt; d/VII-2-1867 Humboldt, Kans) MD Castleton 1844; AB Middlebury 1839. *Nat med jour* 1:299, 1870/71.

MILLER, GEORGE McCLELLAN, USA 1863-77 (b/ NJ; d/X-18-1888 River View, Del) MD UPa 1854; AB Princeton 1849; AM 1852. *U Pa med alum CW*: 1854.

MILLER, GEORGE P , Middleburgh, Pa (d/1895? @27) MD Med-Chir Phila 1891. *Med bull m&s* 17: 434, 1895.

MILLER, GEORGE RICHARDS, Washington DC (b/I 10-1846; d/VI-5-1872) MD UPa 1868;att Columbian & Bellevue. *Tr AMA* 24:340, 1873; 31:1076-77, 1880.

MILLER, GEORGE W, Wickenburg, Az; d/X-29 1869) ?MD Jefferson 1854. *Phila med reg & dir* 1871: 302.

MILLER, GEORGE W, Lampeter Pa (d/VI-2-1898) MD UPa 1860. *JAMA* 30:1534,1898. *Polk* 1896: 1286.

MILLER, GOTTLIEB, Ottawa Ill (d/I-4-1901) Hon MD CPS Keokuk 1882. *Ill m j* ns2:533, 1901. *Polk* 1886:291.

MILLER, HENRY, Harrodsburg & Louisville, Ky (b/XI-1-1800; d/II-8-1874) MD Transylvania 1822. *Tr Ky St M S* 1874: 38-43. *Nashvl j m & s* ns 13: 188-90, 1874. *Tr AMA* 26: , 1875.

MILLER, HOMER VIRGIL MILTON, Rome, Ga (d/V 31-1896 @82) MD Med Coll SC: 1835. *NC med jour* 37:373, 1896. *Polk* 1886: 225.

MILLER, ISAAC J Jr, Cincinnati (d/X-23-1898 @30) MD Med Coll Ohio 1889. *JAMA* 31:1128, 1898.

MILLER, J EDWIN, Pittsburgh (d/X-6-1902) MD Jefferson 1870. *Pa med jour* 6:261,1902/03. *Flint* 1897:830.

MILLER, JACOB S , NYC 1837- (b/1793; d/I-5-1869) Lic Med Soc Albany. *Phila m reg & dir* 1871: 299. *Med s rep Phila* 20: 60, 1869. *Med reg NY NJ Conn* 1869:241.

MILLER, JAMES A, CW-CSA; Wilmington NC (d/1881 Rocky Pt) MD UCNY 1855. *NC med jour* 8:34 1881.

MILLER, JAMES C , Jeanette, Pa (d/IX-22-1906 @50) MD Jefferson 1885. *Pa med jour* 10:53, 118, 1906/07. *Flint* 1897: 805.

MILLER, JAMES HENRY, Baltimore (b/I-20-1788 Millerstown, Pa; d/V-25-1853) MD UPa 1810. *Med annals Md:* 504.

MILLER, JEDEDIAH NYC (b/IX-17-1811 Berlin Vt;d/ XII-27-1867) MD Dartmouth 1839;AM U Vt 1864. *Tr AMA* 19:423, 1868. *Med reg NY NJ Conn* 1868: 336.

MILLER, JESSE, CW-USA (b/V-4-1837 Damascoville, O; d/X-24-1884 Alliance) MD UPa 1861. *U Pa med alum CW*: 1861.

MILLER, JESSE C , Markleysburg, Pa (d/XII-21-1899) MD Jefferson 1886. *JAMA* 34:61, 1900. *Polk* 1896:1283.

MILLER, JOHN, USN; Truxton, NY (b/XI-10-1774 Amenia; d/III-30-1862) Stud med w/B Rush; lic Vt Med Soc 1800. *Tr AMA* 14:202-03, 1864. *Tr Med Soc St NY* 1862:449-60. *K&B* III: 845-46.

MILLER, JOHN, NYC (b/1807; d/I-13-1863) MD CPSNY 1829. *Med reg NY NJ Conn* 1865: 215. *Tr AMA* 14:205, 1864.

MILLER, JOHN, Sussex Co, NJ (d/VIII-1-1888 @72) MD ? *Tr Med Soc NJ* 1890: 331-32. *Med reg NY NJ Conn* 1889: 278.

MILLER, JOHN A , Ligonier, Pa (b/IX-14-1836; d/XII-12-1871) MD Jefferson 1865. *Tr Pa St Med Soc* 1873: 240-41.

MILLER, JOHN FULLENWIDER, Goldsboro, NC (b/ XII-25-1834; d/I-7-1906) MD Jefferson 1858; att UNC 1854-55. *UNC cat*: 429. *Polk* 1886: 722.

MILLER [MILLS], JOHN H , Pana, Ill (d/X-16-1900) MD Mo Med Coll 1880. *Tr Ill Med Soc* ns2:286: 1900. *McDonough* 1895: 277. *Polk* 1896: 434.

MILLER, JOHN LELAND, Sheffield, Mass (d/IV-16-1889 @76 or 77) MD Berkshire 1837. *Bost m&s j* 120:424, 1889; 121:645, 1889. *Polk* 1886:472.

MILLER, JONATHAN DICKINSON, USN 1836-72; Princeton, NJ (b/1810 NYC; d/I-29-1891 Phila) MD UPa 1835; AB Princeton 1829. *JAMA* 16:320-21, 1891. *Bost m&s j* 124: 152, 1891. *U Pa med alum CW*: 1835.

MILLER, JOSHUA, Flagstaff, Ariz; Kansas City, Mo (d/ VII- -1901 @55) MD U Mich 1872 *JAMA* 37:398 1901. *Polk* 1886: 551.

MILLER, KATHARINE, Lincoln, Ill (b/NH; d/VIII-1-1901 @45) MD NWU Women's Med Coll 1882. *Ill med jour* ns3:189, 1901; ns4:480, 1903. *Polk* 1886:286.

MILLER, LEVI DeWITT, Newton, NJ (b/II-15-1836 Harmony; d/VII-21-1895) MD CPSNY 1855. *JAMA* 25: 253, 1895. *Tr M S NJ* 1896:369-70. *Butler* 1878: 473.

MILLER, LEWIS LEPRILETE, Providence, RI (b/I-6-1798 Franklin, Mass; d/III-8-1870) MD Brown 1820; AB 1817. *Phila med reg & dir* 1871:304. *Bost m&s j* ns5:196, 1870. *Tr RI Med Soc* 1:332-33, 1865-72.

MILLER, LOUIS, Kinston, NC 1854-65; Stockbridge, Mass 1886 (b/1828? NC; d/I-3-1896) MD ? *NC m j* 37: 1896. *Polk* 1886: 474.

MILLER, MAURICE NORTON, NYC (b/1838; d/XII-8 1888) MD UCNY 1877. *Med reg NY NJ Conn* 1889:279.

MILLER, NATHANIEL, Fireplace, LI, NY (b/1784? d/V 7-1863 @79) MD ? *Med surg rep Phila* 10:96, 1863.

MILLER, SAMUEL JAMES FERGUS, CW-USA;Cincinnati & Dayton, O; Milwaukee (b/III-12-1837 Pleasant Ridge; d/VIII-9-1893 Togus, Me) MD UPa 1862. *Bost m&s j* 129:208, 1893. *U Pa med alum CW*: 1862. *Butler* 1878: 612.

MILLER, SAMUEL TYLER, CW-USA; Paulsboro, NJ (b/XI-21-1826 Greenwich Twp, NJ; d/IV-2-1905) MD UPa 1850. *U Pa med alum CW*: 1850.

MILLER, SELINA H , Lincoln, Ill (d/VI-22-1905 @73) MD Homeop Med Coll Mo 1886. *Ill med jour* 8:185, 1905. *Polk* 1896: 427.

MILLER, THEODORE De CLEMENT, NYC (d/I-28-1901 @59) MD Bellevue 1866. *Bost m&s j* 144:150, 1901. *Polk* 1866: 1068.

MILLER, THOMAS, Washington DC (b/II-18-1806 Pt

 Spec. educ'l status abbrev. as: ***ng*** = college verified attendance without degree;

Port Royal, Va; d/III or IX-20-1873) MD UPa 1829. *Bost m&s j* ns12:346, 1873. *NW m&s j* 4:197, 1873. *Tr AMA* 25:523-24, 1874. *Hist M S DC:* 226-27. *K&B* III:846. .

MILLER, THOMAS JEFFERSON, CW-CSA; ?Central Plains, Va (b/III- -1810 Woodstock; d/XII- -1894) MD UPa 1833. *U Pa med alum CW*: 1833.

MILLER, TRUMAN W , Chicago (b/III-2-1840; d/V-31-1900) MD Geneva 1864. *Chic m rec* 17:opp p 487, 1900. *JAMA* 34: 1425, 1645, 1900. *Ill med jour* ns2: 93, 1900. *Polk* 1893: 346.

MILLER, VIRGIL MARONIS, Townley, Ala (b/IV-26-1852; d/IX-9-1898 Jasper) MD U Nashville 1880; MD Vanderbilt 1879; AB U Ala 1873. *Tr M S St Ala* 1898: 241. *Polk* 1886: 135.

MILLER, W H H , Chadwick, Ill (b/1861; d/I-31 1906) MD CPS Chicago 1893. *Ill m j* 9: 228, 1906.

MILLER, WARWICK, Sadsbury, Pa (b/III-18-1785 Chester Co; d/IV-23-1825) <ng U Pa Med Dept> *Med rep* (W Chester, Pa) 2:127-28, 1855.

MILLER, WILLIAM F, Louisville (d/VI-17-1898 @74) MD U Louisvl 1843. *JAMA* 31:39, 1898. *Polk* 1886: 400.

MILLER, WILLIAM H,Pittsburgh (d/IV-16-1903 @34) MD Western Pa U 1897. *Pa med jour* 7:279, 1903/04.

MILLER, WINTHROP, Minneapolis (b/XII-22-1850 Dorchester, Mass; d/X-14-1884) MD Harvard 1877; AB 1873. *Tr Minn St M S* 1884:225. *Butler* 1878:394.

MILLET, ASA, E Bridgewater, Mass (b/VI-22-1813 Leeds, Me; d/III-21-1893) MD Bowdoin 1842. *Bost m & s j* 128:304, 671, 1893. *Polk* 1886: 465.

MILLIGAN, FRANCIS HENRY, Wabasha, Minn; CW-USA (b/XII-8-1830 Philadelphia; d/XII-5-1888) MD Jefferson 1851. *Tr Minn St M S* 1889: 242-44, 1889. *Atkinson* I:109. *Polk* 1886: 518.

MILLIGAN, HARVEY WILLIAM, Jacksonville, Ill (d/ VII-16-1902) MD UPa 1863; AB Williams 1853. *Williams grads*: 1853.

MILLIKEN, CHARLES JAMES, Cherry Field, Me (d/X 16-1898 @55) MD Harvard 1866. *JAMA* 31: 1128, 1898. *Polk* 1896: 634.

MILLIKEN, CHARLES WIDGERY, Oquawka, Ill 1865-71; Shullsburg, Wis 1871- (b/III-17-1836 Buxton, Me; d/VI-14-1880 Limerick, Me) MD U Mich 1865; AB Bowdoin 1862. *Bowdoin cat*: 1862.

MILLIKEN, JOHN M , Scarborough, Me (b/1808; d/XI 24-1867) Bowdoin 1831. *Bost m&s j* 77: 380, 1867.

MILLIKEN, MURRAY GAYLORD, Hamilton, O (b/VI 14-1849; d/VII-14-1874) MD Bellevue 1869; att U Miami Coll. *Med rec* NY 9:439, 1874.

MILLINGTON, STEPHEN ROBINS, Poland, NY (d/XI 28-1898 @72) MD Geneva 1848. *JAMA* 31: 1542, 1898. *Polk* 1886: 702.

MILLMAN, JOHN HENRY, Washington, Ind (b/VIII-17-1845 Cumberland, Me; d/X-12-1881) att Ind Med Coll 1874-75. *Tr Ind St M S* 1882: 149.

MILLS, ANDREW M, Newark (d/VIII-11-1891 @55) MD UVt 1859 *Bost m&s j* 125:208 1891 *Butler*1878:463.

MILLS, CHARLES DRAKE, Pittsfield, Mass (d/1878 @ 51) MD Berkshire 1851. *Bost m&s j* 100: 38, 1879. *Mass Med Soc cat* 1894.

MILLS, GEORGE W Jr, Sedalia, Mo (d/X-16-1898 @ 46) MD Louisville Med Coll 1875. *JAMA* 31:1066, 1898. *Polk* 1886: 554.

MILLS, JAMES N , CW-USA (d/II-8-1863 Helena, Ark) MD ? *Nat med jour* 1:299, 1870/71.

MILLS, MADISON, USA 1834 (b/1810 NY; d/IV-1-1834) MD Fairfield 1832. *Tr AMA* 25:537-38, 1874. *Med times* 3:508, 526, 1873. *Med rec* 8:240, 1873.

MILLS, MYRON HOLLY, Mt Morris, NY (d/VIII-14-1897) MD Geneva 1845. *Buffalo m&s j* 38: 141, 1897. *Polk* 1886:668.

MILNE, CHARLES, NYC (d/IX-28-1896 @56) MD UC NY 1873. *JAMA* 27:825 1896. *Bost m&s j* 135:373 1896.

MILNE, JAMES A , Fruit Valley, NY (d/XII-8-1885) MD U Mich 1865. *Med reg NY NJ Conn* 1887: 271.

MILNER, JAMES PALMER, CW-USN; Phila (b/I-8-1844; d/X-25-1892) MD UPa 1867; PhG Phila Coll Pharm 1868. *UPa med alum CW*: 1867. *Polk* 1886: 821.

MILNOR, WILLIAM HENRY, CW-USA (d/VII-25-1862 Savage's Station, Va) MD CPSNY 1832; AB Columbia 1826. *Nat med jour* 1:299, 1870/71. *Med surg rep Phila* ns8:428, 1862.

MILTENBERGER, GEORGE WARNER, Baltimore (b/ III-17-1819; d/XI-11-1905) MD U Md 1840. *Bost m&s j* 153:710, 1905. *Med ann Md:* 505-06. *Atkinson* I: 301. *K&B* III: 846-47.

MILTON, JOHN L, ? (d/VIII-19-1878 Grenada, Miss) MD ? *Tr AMA* 30:878, 1879. *Med rec* NY 14:220, 1878.

MIMS, ALEXANDER DOWSING, CW-CSA (b/III-5-1839 Vernon, Ala; d/IX-16-1878 Prattville) MD UPa 1860; MD Tulane 1859. *U Pa med alum CW*: 1860.

MINER [MINOR], DAVID WORTHINGTON, Ware, Mass (d/I-2-1895 @74) MD Berkshire 1844. *Buff m&s j* 34:431, 1895. *Bost m&s j* 132:48, 1895.*Butler* 1878:354.

MINER, EBENEZER BOWMAN, Wilkes Barre, Pa (d/ XII-29-1869) MD UPa 1852; AB Columbia 1849. *Phila med reg & dir* 1871: 303.

MINER, JOHN J , Brooklyn (d/II-7-1892 @60) MD CPS Keokuk 1879. *Med reg NY NJ Conn* 1892: 284.

MINER, JOHN OWEN, New London, Conn (b/1762? d/ 1851 @89) Hon MD Yale 1816 *Proc Conn M S* 1852:17.

MINER, JOSHUA LEWIS, Wilkes Barre, Pa (b/XI-11-1855 NYC; d/VII-27-1889) MD UPa 1881; AB Lafayette 1878; AM. *Polk* 1886: 840. *Lafayette, Men of*: 222.

MINER, JULIUS FRANCIS, CW-USA; Buffalo (b/II-16-1823 Peru, Mass; d/XI-5-1886) MD Albany 1847; <MD Berkshire 1846> *Med reg NY NJ Conn* 1887: 271. *Buff m&s j* 26:233-37,1886? *Bost m&s j* 115:460,1886. *Atkinson* I:45-46. *K&B* III:847.

MINER, WILLIAM, NYC (d/XI-16-1859 @44) MD

CPSNY 1836. *Med surg rep Phila* ns3:217, 1859/60.

MINER, WILLIAM SAMUEL, Morrisania, NY 1886– (b/XII–8–1863; d/I–21–1896 Harlem) MD NY Homeop 1884. *Tr Am Inst Hom* 1896:1192. *No Amer jour homeop* 44:128, 1896. *Polk* 1886: 830.

MINER, WILLIAM W , NYC (b/1780? d/III–20–1863 @83) MD ? *Med reg NY NJ Conn* 1865: 218. *Med surg rep Phila* ns9: 441, 1862/63.

MINICH, ANDREW K , Philadelphia (b/1846 Lancaster, Pa; d/III–11–1901) MD Jefferson 1870; AB Lafayette; PhD Wagner Free Inst Sci, Phila. *Pa med jour* 5: 296, 1901/02. *Butler* 1878: 691.

MINIS, DAVID, CW–USA (b/IX–7–1831 Beaver Co, Pa; d/II–4–1862 Roanoke Isl, NC) MD UPa 1854; AB Wash & Jeff. *U Pa m alum CW*:1854. *Nat m j* 1:299, 1870/71.

MINOR [MINER], GARRY HINMAN, Morris, Conn (b/ 1802 Woodbury; d/XII–9–1882) MD Yale 1824. *Proc Conn Med Soc* ns2:178–79, 1883.

MINOR, ISAAC N , CW–USA (d/XII–13–1862) MD ? *Nat med jour* 1:299, 1870/71.

MINOR, JAMES MONROE, Brooklyn (b/XI–7–1815; d/III–23–1879) MD UPa 1837; att Kenyon. *Med reg NY NJ Conn* 1879: 194. *Med rec* NY 15:360, 1879.

MINOR, LEWIS WILLIS, USN 1832–61; CSN 1861–65 (b/I–29–1808 & d/II–9–1872 Hazel Hill, Va) MD UPa 1831. *U Pa med alum CW*: 1831.

MINOR, PHILIP PENDLETON BARBOUR, CW–CSA Forkland Ala (b/I–22–1828 Huntsville; d/1884) MD UPa 1852; ng U Ala 1843. *U Pa med alum CW*: 1852.

MINOR, THOMAS, Middleton Conn (b/X–15–1777; d/ IV–23–1846 Worcester Mass?) Hon MD Yale 1819; AB 1796. *Pr Conn M S* ns2:145, 1882–83. *K&B* III:848–49.

MINOT, FRANCIS, Boston (b/IV–12–1821; d/V–11 1899 @78) MD Harvard 1844; AB 1841; AM Trin 1860. *Bost m&s j* 140:488, 511–12, 1899. *K&B* III: 1851.

MINTIE, ROBERT L , Chicago (d/V–21–1895 @45) MD Bennett 1881. *JAMA* 24:861, 1895. *Polk* 1890:319.

MINTON, HENRY BREWSTER, CW–US San Comm; Brooklyn (b/III–4–1831 Dover, NJ; d/VI–1–1895) MD Hahnemann Phila 1853; att CPSNY. *Hahn mo* 30:107–08 (news & advt) 1895. *Tr Am Inst Hom* 1895: 226. *No Amer j hom* 43:519, 1895. *Cleave.* Homeopath.

MIRRIELEES [MIRRIDIES], GEORGE JOHN, Brooklyn (b/1859; d/V–17–1896) MD LICH 1882. *No Am j hom* 44: 462, 1863. *Polk* 1886: 647. Homeopath?

MISH, PHYSICK BICKEL, Lebanon, Pa; CW–USA (b/ VI–11–1827; d/VII–16–1886) MD UPa 1849. *U Pa med alum CW*: 1849.

MITCHELL, A H , Warm Springs, Mont (b/Ky; d/XII 20–1898 @67) MD ? *JAMA* 32:195, 1899.

MITCHELL, ALBERT LESHMAN, CW–USA; Cape Breton (d/X– –1864) MD Harvard 1863; AB King's Coll 1859. *Harvard in CW*: 281.

MITCHELL, ARCHIBALD, Kingston, Mich (d/V–17–1900 Los Angeles) MD U Mich 1872. *JAMA* 34:1356, 1900. *Polk* 1886: 485.

MITCHELL, BENJAMIN RUSH, USN (d/III–8–1862 @ 41) MD Kentucky Sch Med 1853. *Med s rep Phil* ns7: 576, 1861/62. *Nat med jour* 1:299, 1870/71.

MITCHELL [MITCHEL], CHARLES, CW–USA (d/ VIII–28–1864 Key West, Fla) MD ? *Nat med jour* 1: 299, 1870/71.

MITCHELL, CHARLES, Nashville (d/X–3–1900) MD U Louisvl 1871 *Nashvl j m&s* 4:190 1900 *Polk* 1896: 1402.

MITCHELL, CHARLES ANDREWS, CW–CSA; Memphis, Ala [sic] (b/X–7–1838; d/1868) MD ? AB UNC 1857. *UNC cat*: 432.

MITCHELL, CHARLES H , Baltimore (b/VII–29–1857; d/VII–22–1898) <MD CPS Balto 1879> *Med ann Md:* 506. *JAMA* 31: 314, 1898. *Polk* 1896: 663.

MITCHELL, CHARLES J , Vicksburg, Miss (b/Ky; d/I or II–1886 @73) MD Transylvania 1834. *Tr Miss St Med Assoc* 1886: 14.

MITCHELL, CHAUNCEY LEEDS, Brooklyn (b/XI–20 1813 New Canaan, Conn; d/V–8–1888) MD CPSNY 1836; AB Union 1833; AM 1836. *Med reg NY NJ Conn* 1888: 265. *Atkinson* I: 576.

MITCHELL, EDWARD DANA, CW–CSA; Memphis, Tenn (b/X–6–1846 Hinds Co, Miss; d/IV–26–1896) MD UPa 1869. *U Pa med alum CW*: 1869. *Polk* 1886: 869.

MITCHELL, ELBRIDGE KENNEY, Portland, Me; W Newton, Mass (b/IX–12–1819 N Yarmouth; d/1850) MD Harvard 1846; ng Bowdoin 1840–42. *Bowdoin cat*: 1844.

MITCHELL, ELISHA V , CW–USA (d/III–31–1865) MD UCNY 1854. *Nat m j* 1:300, 1870/71.

MITCHELL, FRANK ALBERT, Bridgton, Me; Chicago (b/VIII–19–1847 Kennebunkport; d/I–23–1898) MD Bellevue 1874; ng Bowdoin 1868–71. *JAMA* 30: 335, 1898. *Polk* 1896: 634.

MITCHELL, FREDERICK A, Amherst Mass (d/VII–27 1869 @80) ng Dartmouth Med 1812. *Phila med reg & dir* 1871: 301. *Med surg rep Phila* 21:170, 1869.

MITCHELL, GEORGE EDWARD, Washington, DC (b/ III–3–1781 Cecil Co, Md; d/VI–28–1832) MD UPa 1805. *Med ann Md:* 506–07.

MITCHELL, GEORGE F , Mansfield, O (b/V–9–1808 Washington Co, Pa; d/III–31–1869) MD Med Coll Ohio 1844. *Tr Ohio St M S* 1868–69: 177–78.

MITCHELL, GEORGE V , Kishcoquillas Valley, Pa (d/ VII–21–1876 @65) MD Jefferson 1834. *Med s rep Phila* 35: 414, 1876.

MITCHELL, GILES BEDFORD Mooresville Ind (b/V–17–1822 Bartholomew Co; d/X–6–1880) <MD Med Coll O 1845> *Tr Ind St M S* 1881:239. *Butler* 1878: 213.

MITCHELL, GOODRICH, CW–CSA (b/1837 Fauquier Co, Va; d/VII–4–1864 [i.e., 1863] Gettysburg, Pa) MD UPa 1861. *U Pa med alum CW*: 1861.

MITCHELL, GOVE, Hatboro Pa (b/X–27–1781 Bristol; d/V–4–1856) <MD UPa 1802> *Tr M S Pa* 1860:133–34.

MITCHELL, HENRY, Coventry & Norwich, NY (b/1784 Woodbury, Conn; d/I-12-1856) Hon MD Yale 1824; lic Conn St Med Soc 1805. *Tr Med Soc St NY* 1857: 85-90. *US Congr biogr dir.*

MITCHELL, HENRY HOOPER, Elkton, Md (d/VIII or IX-27-1896 @76) MD UPa 1842. *JAMA* 27: 895, 1896. *Polk* 1896: 670.

MITCHELL, HOWARD E , Troy, NY (d/VIII-8-1894) MD U Md 1882. *Polk* 1886: 712. *Med reg NY NJ Conn* 1895: 233.

MITCHELL, JACOB, Kennebunkport, Me 1831-41; Wellfleet, Mass 1852-73 (b/IX-14-1802 N Yarmouth; d/VI-11-1873 Norwich) MD Bowdoin 1830; ng 1825. *Bost m&s j* ns11: 616, 1873.

MITCHELL, JAMES, ?NYC (b/1812; d/II-19-1894) <MD U Prague 1839> *Med reg NY NJ Conn* 1894:244. *Polk* 1886: 688.

MITCHELL, JAMES E , Baltimore (b/II-20-1843 West River, Md; d/XI-7-1873) MD U Md 1865. *Med annals Md:* 507. *Med surg rep Phila* 29:418, 1873.

MITCHELL, JAMES ROGERS, Milford, Del (b/VII-30 1806; d/V-26-1867) MD U Md 1827. *Med Soc Del*: 46. *Tr AMA* 19:432, 1868.

MITCHELL, JOHN KEARSLEY, Philadelphia (b/V-12 1793 Shepherdstown Va; d/IV-14-1858) MD UPa 1819; AB Edinburgh. *Tr AMA* 13:802-02, 1860. *Tr CPP* cent vol:249. *Tr Pa St M S* ns4:93-98, 1859. *K&B* III:853.

MITCHELL, JOSEPH DAVIS, St Stephens, NB; Jacksonville, Fla (d/VII-15-1893 @70) MD Harvard 1850. *Bost m&s j* 129:80, 1893. *Mass Med Soc cat* 1894.

MITCHELL, JOSEPH SIDNEY, Chicago (d/XI-4-1898) MD Bellevue 1867. *Tr Am Inst Hom* 1899: 931. *Polk* 1886: 268.

MITCHELL, MILTON, Mansfield, O (b/VI-5-1835; d/IV-7-1864) MD Miami 1857. *Tr Ohio St Med Soc* 1865:77-78. *Nashvl j m & s* ns1:318, 1866.

MITCHELL, NATHANIEL, Colon, Mich (b/XI-27-1808 Calais, Vt; d/I-26-1879) MD Woodstock 1834. *Med rec NY* 15:617, 1879.

MITCHELL, ORLANDO, Marshall, Ill (d/IV-3/5-1901 @45) MD Med Coll Ind 1878. *Ill med jour* ns3:47, 189, 1901. *Polk* 1886: 287.

MITCHELL, ROBERT WOOD, Memphis (b/VIII-26 1831; d/XI-2-1903) MD U La 1856. *So pract* ? 1903. *Polk* 1896: 1397.

MITCHELL, SAMUEL, Cameron Mills, NY (b/I-19-1821; d/VI-17-1889) <MD Berkshire 1847> *Med reg NY NJ Conn* 1890: 275. *Polk* 1886: 664.

MITCHELL, SAMUEL BROWN WYLIE, CW-USA; Philadelphia (b/VIII-16-1828; d/VIII-16-1879) MD UPa 1854; AB 1852. *Tr AMA* 32:527, 1881. *Med surg rep Phila* 41: 176, 1879. *Med rec* 16:238, 1879.

MITCHELL, SAMUEL ROBERT, CW-USA; Ottumwa, Ia (b/IV-14-1826 Springfield, Ill; d/VII-8-1895) MD St Louis Med Coll 1864. *JAMA* 25: 170, 1895. *Atkinson* I: 573. *Polk* 1890: 423.

MITCHELL, THOMAS DUCHÉ, Cincinnati; Philadelphia (b/1791; d/V-13-1865) MD UPa 1812; Hon AM Princeton 1830. *Bost m&s j* 45:390 ff 1851. *K&B* III:857.

MITCHELL, THOMAS J , Bement, Ill (d/VIII-3-1905 @82) <MD U Louisvillle 1848> *Ill med jour* 8:185, 256, 1905. *Polk* 1890: 301.

MITCHELL, WILLIAM, Monmouth, Ill (d/X-14-1894 @82) Lic 1878 as of 20 yrs' practice. *JAMA* 23:654-55, 1894. *Polk* 1890: 340.

MITCHELL, WILLIAM A , Mangohick, Va (b/V-2-1844 King & Queen Co; d/II-1-1905) MD Med Coll Va 1873. *Tr Med Soc Va* 1905: 452. *Polk* 1900: 1767.

MITCHELL, WILLIAM STANTON, New Orleans; CW-CSA (b/IX-25-1835 Natchez, Miss; d/IV-18-1887) MD New Orl S M 1860; AB & CE Ky Mil Inst 1855. *New Orl m&s j* ns14:887-88, 1887. *Atkinson* I: 81. *Polk* 1886: 417.

MITCHILL, SAMUEL LATHAM, NYC (b/VIII-29-1764 N Hempstead, NY; d/IX-7-1831) Stud med Edinburgh. *NY med jour* 2:487-89, 1831. *K&B* III:857-59.

MITMAN, ELSIE, Freeburg, Pa (b/II-12-1843 Winfield, Pa; d/III-15-1886) MD Woman's Med Coll Pa 1882. *Tr Pa St Med Soc* 18: 271-72, 1886.

MITTER, ROBERT G , Chicago (d/cXII-24-1891) MD Rush 1882. *Chic m rec* 3:73,1892. *Polk* 1886:268.

MIX, JUDD W , Byron, Ill (d/XII-28-1897 @42) MD Northwestern 1883. *JAMA* 30:106, 1888. *Polk* 1886:256.

MIX, WILLIAM BARNEY, Milwaukee (d/IX-17-1894 @52) MD LICH 1871. *JAMA* 23: 561, 1894.

MIXER, SYLVESTER FRINK [FREDERICK], Buffalo (b/XII-27-1815 Morrisville, NY; d/IX-17-1883) MD Yale 1841; MD CPSNY 1847. *Med reg NY NJ Conn* 1884:234. *JAMA* 1:406, 1883. *Buff m&s j* 23:142-43, 1883.

MIXSELL [MIXWELL], AARON JACKSON, Rye, NY (d/X-31-1896) MD Bellevue 1872. *Bost m&s j* 135: 477, 1896. *Polk* 1896: 1031.

MIXSELL, JOSEPH, Easton, Pa 1867-82; Philadelphia 1882- (b/V-24-1886; d/VII-3-1888) MD UPa 1868; PhD 1881; Hon AM Lafayette 1880. *Tr Med Soc Pa* 21:263-64, 1889-90. *Butler* 1878: 724.

MIZER, HENRY W , Lovilla, Fla (b/X-25-1830 Annapolis, O; d/XII-10-1898) MD Keokuk 1864. *Tr Ia St Med Soc* 17: 386, 1899. *Polk* 1890: 419.

MOBERLEY, ELDRED W , Newmarket, Md (b/I-3-1803; d/IX-24-1887) MD UPa 1824. *Med ann Md:* 508. *Polk* 1886: 444.

MOCK, JOHN WESLEY, Covington, Ind (b/XII-30-1835 Middletown, Md; d/IX-26-1905) MD Med Coll O 1863. *Tr Ind St M S* 1906: 493. *Polk* 1896: 493.

MOEHRING, GOTTHILF, Philadelphia (b/XII-14-1802; d/X-9-1881) MD U Berlin 1825. *Tr CPP* cent vol: 249.

MOELLER, EDWARD, CW-USA (d/XI-10-1863 Ft

Lyon, Va) MD ? *Nat med jour* 1:300, 1870/71.

MOEUR, JOHN B, CW–CSA; Tenn; Del Rio, Tex (b/I–31–1834 New Orleans; d/V–20–1904 Ariz; <MD St Charles Med Sch New Orl> stud Paris. *Tex st med jour* 1: 244, 1906. *Polk* 1896: 1425.

MOFFAT, JOSEPH, Washingtonville, NY (d/VIII–16 1901 @68) MD U Mich 1862; AB Antioch 1858; AM 1861. *JAMA* 37: 654, 1901. *Polk* 1886: 714.

MOFFATT, SAMUEL STEWARD, Washington, DC (d/IV–25–1896) MD U Mich Hom Med Coll 1878. *Tr Am Inst Hom* 1896: 1192.

MOFFATT, THOMAS CLARKSON, Stapleton, NY (d/XII–26–1869) MD UCNY 1851. *Phila med reg & dir* 1871:303. *Med reg NY NJ Conn* 1870: 324.

MOFFETT, FRANK TIFFT, Littleton, NH (b/VIII–6–1841; d/VII–12–1896) MD Harvard 1870. *Tr NH Med Soc* 1896:188. *Polk* 1890: 710.

MOFFETT, GEORGE BOONE, CW–CSA; Parkersburg, WVa (b/X–20–1820 Augusta Co, Va; d/VIII–21–1887) MD UPa 1844; ng Amherst 1843. *Tr M S WVa* 1888: 590. *U Pa med alum CW*: 1844. *Butler* 1878:852.

MOFFETT [MOFFATT], JOHN, Rushville, Ind (b/X–28–1823 Washington Co, Va; d/V–7–1903) MD M C O 1849. *Tr Ind St Med Soc* 1903: 350. *Butler* 1878: 213.

MOFFETT, RICHARD, Philadelphia (d/_–4–1876 @37) MD UPa 1868. *Med surg rep Phila* 35: 504, 1876.

MOFFITT, ROBERT H, Mt Pleasant, Ia (d/VI–10 1897 @30) MD NWU 1894. *Tr Iowa Med Soc* 16:391–92, 1898. *JAMA* 28:1203, 1897. *Polk* 1896: 533.

MOHR, CHARLES A, Asheville, NC; Mobile, Ala (d/VII–17–1901) MD U Ala 1884. *JAMA* 37:342, 1901. *Polk* 1886: 136.

MOHR, RICHARD J, Pasadena, Calif (d/III–9–1900 @60) MD CPS Keokuk 1861. *JAMA* 34:639, 703, 766, 1900. *Polk* 1886:358 (Fairfield, Ia).

MOLONY, ALVAH JOHNSON, CW–USA (b/XI–15–1827 Phila; d/IX–25–1867 Norristown, Pa) MD UPa 1851. *U Pa med alum CW*: 1851.

MONCURE, JAMES DUNLAP, Williamsburg Va (b/VIII–2–1842 Richmond; d/XI–9–1898) MD U Md 1868. *JAMA* 31:1319, 1898. *Atkinson* I:444. *Polk* 1886: 929.

MONCURE, JOHN EDRINGTON DANIELS, CW–CSA (b/1812 Stafford Co, Va; d/I– –1875 Dry Grove, Miss) MD UPa 1836. *U Pa med alum CW*: 1836.

MONELL, JOSEPH AUGUSTUS, NYC (b/IX–25–1826 Middletown, NY; d/VIII–12 or 17–1896) MD CPSNY 1850. *JAMA* 27:503, 1896. *Polk* 1896: 1068.

MONELL, JOSEPH SAYER, NYC (b/VI–10–1828; d/III–15–1881 Fla) MD UCNY 1861. *Med reg NY NJ Conn* 1881: 239.

MONETTE, WILLIAM E, CW–CSA (b/I–7–1834 Warren Co, Miss; d/1878 Monroe Co) MD UPa 1857. *Tr AMA* 30: 878, 1879. *Tr Miss St M Assn* 1878–81: 39.

MONGES, JOHN ARMENTAIRE, Philadelphia (b/1759; d/V–20–1827) MD ? *Phila med reg & dir* 14: 338–43, 1827?

MONKUR, JOHN CAVENDISH SMITH, Baltimore (b/1800; d/I–21–1867) MD U Md 1822. *Med ann Md:* 508. *Bost m&s j* 75: 492, 1866. *Tr AMA* 18:338–39, 1867.

MONLEY, THOMAS, ? (d/IX–28–1878 New Orleans) No MD. *Tr AMA* 30:880, 1879.

MONMONIER, JOHN FRANCIS, Baltimore (b/IV–4–1813; d/VI–8–1894) MD U Md 1834; att St Mary's Coll. *Atkinson* I:13. *Med annals Md:* 508. *Polk* 1886: 438.

MONMONIER, JOHN N K, Baltimore (d/VI–11–1896) MD U Md 1858. *Med annals Md:* 508. *Polk* 1886: 438.

MONROE. ALEXANDER Le BARON, Granby & Medway, Mass (b/1807; d/1879) MD Yale 1831. *Tr AMA* 31: 1077–79, 1880.

MONROE, FRANCIS Le BARON, CW–USA; Meriden, NH (d/VIII–14–1904 @69 Woburn, Mass) MD Harvard 1861; AB Williams 1857. *Harv in CW*: 266. *JAMA* 43: 784, 1904.

MONROE, HOLLIS, Belfast, Me (b/1789; d/VI–21–1861) MD Yale 1819. *Bost m&s j* 64:476, 1861. *K&B* I(2): 184–85.

MONROE, NAHUM PARKER, Belfast, Me (b/I–4–1808 Surry, NH; d/IV–22–1873 Baltimore) MD Albany 1839. *Tr Me Med Assoc* 1871–73: 486–88. *Med surg rep Phila* 28: 380, 1873.

MONROE, THOMAS J C, Ohio; USA 1811–39 (b/Va; d/X–23–1839) MD ? *Med annals Md:* 509.

MONROE, WILLIAM ROBERT, Baltimore (b/1821 Pr Geo Co; d/II–13–1894) MD Washington U Balto 1849. *Med annals Md:* 509. *Polk* 1886: 438.

MONSON, ALFRED SHEPARD, New Haven, Conn (b/IX–22–1795; d/V–22–1870) MD UPa 1819; AB Yale 1815. *Proc Conn Med Soc* 1871: 414.

MONTAGUE, ALEXANDER, Galt, Calif (b/IX–16–1845; d/V–21–1902) MD UCNY 1868; att UNC. *UNC cat*: 434. *Polk* 1886: 165.

MONTES, ANDREW, NYC 10 yrs (b/XI–30–1846 Matanzas Cuba; d/VIII–6–1882 Asbury Park NJ) MD Bellevue 1879; att coll Cuba. *Med reg NY NJ Conn* 1883: 233.

MONTFORD, ROBERT V K, Newburgh, NY (b/1835 Fishkill; d/XII–28–1900) MD Albany 1856. *Bost m&s j* 144: 54, 1901. *Polk* 1856: 1034.

MONTGOMERY, BENJAMIN RUSH Jr, Tenn (b/1848; d/X–9–1878) MD U Tenn 1877. *Tr AMA* 30: 878–80, 1879.

MONTGOMERY, DANIEL CAMERON, Greenville, Miss (d/III–26–1898) MD UPa 1855. *Tex med jour* 1897–98:531. *Polk* 1890: 630.

MONTGOMERY, DAVID B, Cynthiana, Ind (b/III–26 1834 Gibson Co; d/IX–1–1885) MD Rush 1858. *Tr Ind St Med Soc* 1886: 203. *Butler* 1878: 213.

MONTGOMERY, DAVID H, Mifflinville, Pa (d/XI–28 1902 @68) MD Phila Coll Med & Surg 1852. *Pa med jour* 6:261, 1902/03. *Flint* 1897: 808.

MONTGOMERY, EDWARD, St Louis (b/XII–20–1816

Ballymena, Irel'd; d/X-19-1883) <MD Edinburgh 1838> Hon MD Mo Med Coll 1862. *JAMA* 1:548, 1883. *Atkinson* I:108-109. *Butler* 1874: 405.

MONTGOMERY, GEORGE, CW-USA; Newburyport, Mass (b/VII 23-1834 Stratford, NH; d/III-18-1892 NYC) MD Bowdoin 1854. *JAMA* 18:408, 1892. *Bost m&s j* 126:304, 1892. *Butler* 1878: 354.

MONTGOMERY, HARVEY FITZ-HUGH, CW-USA; Rochester, NY (b/VII-21-1818; d/XI-8-1884) MD UPa 1842; AB Princeton 1839. *Med s rep Phila* 51:604, 1884. *U Pa med alum CW*: 1842. *Butler* 1878: 550.

MONTGOMERY, JAMES, Baltimore (b/1790 Harford Co; d/IV-11-1878) MD U Md 1819. *Med ann Md:* 509. *Butler* 1874: 314.

MONTGOMERY, JOSEPH FAUNTLEROY, Nelson Co, Va 1834-36, 1842-50; Jackson, Miss 1836-42; Sacramento 1850- (b/XI-15-1812; d/X-6-1883) MD U Va 1833; AB 1833?; MD UPa 1834. *JAMA* 1:716, 1883. *Atkinson* I: 258-59. *Butler* 1878: 61.

MONTGOMERY, THOMAS A , Wrightstown, Wis (b/ Lake Co, O; d/VI-16-1876 @25) MD Cleveland Med Coll 1872. *Tr Wis St Med Soc* 1876:144; 1891:357.

MONTGOMERY, THOMAS JOHNSON, CW-USA; Springfield, Ky 1838; Longwood, Mo 1857; Georgetown, Mo 1859; Sedalia 1865- (b/VIII-19-1812 Danville, Ky; d/V-17-1877) MD Louisvl Med Coll 1838. *Tr Mo St M Assn* 1878: 154-55. *Tr AMA* 29:718-19, 1878.

MONTGOMERY, W H , San Antonio, Tex (d/IV-28-1882) MD ? *Tex med & surg rec* 3:550, 1883.

MONTGOMERY, WILLIAM, ? (d/X-5-1878 Greenville, Miss) MD ? *Tr AMA* 30:880, 1879. *Med rec NY* 14:320, 1878.

MONTGOMERY, WILLIAM T , Shrewsbury, Pa (b/ Harford Co, Md; d/IX-1-1881) MD U Md 1851. *Med annals Md:* 509.

MOODY, ANSON, New Haven, Conn (b/II-25-1792 S Hadley, Mass; d/II-11-1855) Hon MD Yale 1840; AB 1814; lic 1817. *Proc Conn Med Soc* 1861: 125-28, 1861.

MOODY, BENJAMIN, Pernambuco, Brazil (d/V-16-1807 Falmouth, Me; d/1839 Maracaibo, Venez) MD Dartmouth 1835; AB Bowdoin 1826. *Bowdoin cat*:1826.

MOODY, C L , Moody, Tex (d/IX-22-1906) <MD Ky Sch Med 1876> *Tex st med jour* 2:194, 1906.

MOODY, DANIEL, Clinton, Me 1864-89 (b/IV-26-1831 Limington; d/IV-26-1889) MD Dartmouth 1877. *Tr Me M Assn* 12:627, 1897. *Bost m&s j* 137:297, 1897.

MOODY, GEORGE, Georgetown, Mass (d/III-4-1866 @66) MD Harvard 1830. *Med s rep Phila* 14:240, 1866.

MOODY, GEORGE OWEN, CW-USA; Titusville Pa (b/ VII-17-1833 Lebanon, Me; d/II-6-1887) MD Dartmouth 1863; AB Bowdoin 1859; AM 1862. *Med surg rep Phila* 56:256, 1887. *Polk* 1886: 837.

MOODY, GEORGE WASHINGTON, Huron, SD (d/X-13-1894) MD NWU 1878. *JAMA* 23:624, 1894. *Polk* 1886: 201.

MOODY, HORACE P , Susquehanna, Pa (b/X-16-1835 Asylum, Pa; d/VIII-3-1869) MD Geneva 1858. *Tr Pa St Med Soc* 1870: 92-93.

MOODY [MOODEY], JOHN W , Greensburg, Ind (b/VI-12-1816 Shippensburg, Pa; d/VIII-27-1867) MD ? *Tr Ind St Med Soc* 1870: . *Med surg rep Phila* 17:199, 1867. *Tr AMA* 19:455-56, 1868. Kemper's *Indiana*: 313.

MOODY, RICHARD E , Mansfield & Meridian, Tex; Sweetwater 1881- (b/II-23-1849 Tenn; d/XI-11 1904) MD U Tenn @ Nashvl 1872; stud NY Polyclinic 1884; Chicago 1901. *Tex st m j* 1:244, 1906. *Polk* 1896: 1452.

MOODY, THOMAS H , Cross Roads, Miss (d/II-26-1888) MD Jefferson 1851. *New Orl m&s j* ns 15: 836, 1888. *Polk* 1886: 526.

MOODY, WILLIAM BRADSTREET, Franconia, NH (b/XII-25-1827 Easton, NH; d/VI-1-1891) MD Dartmouth 1850. *Tr NH M S* 1891:248-52. *Polk* 1890: 709.

MOOERS, BENJAMIN J , ?Plattsburgh, NY (b/IX-11-1787 Haverhill, Mass; d/V-20-1869) Hon MD NYU Regents 1833; lic Clinton Co Med Soc 1812. *Tr Med Soc St NY* 1870:309. *Med surg rep Phila* 20:476, 1869.

MOON, ADDISON S , Beaver Falls, Pa (d/VII-17-1901 @42) MD Cleveland Med Coll 1884. *Pa med jour* 5: 296, 1901/02. *JAMA* : 342, 1901. *Flint* 1897.

MOONEY, FLETCHER D , St Louis Mo (d/XI-8-1897) MD Mo Med Coll 1880. *Buffalo m&s j* 37: 379, 1897. *Flint* 1897: 569.

MOONEY, HENRY CLAY, Laketon, Ind (b/VII-27-1850 Marshall Co; d/III-24-1905) MD NWU 1876. *Tr Ind St Med Soc* 1905: 454.

MOONEY, JOSEPH HENRY, Kansas City, Kans (d/IV 19-1899 @47) <MD U Med Coll KC 1888> *JAMA* 32:955, 1899. *Polk* 1896: 848.

MOOR, GEORGE WASHINGTON, Hampton, NH (b/I-2-1820 Princeton, Mass; d/IX-9-1866) MD UPa 1843; AB Dartmouth 1841. *Med surg rep Phila* 15:308, 1866.

MOORE, ALLEN T [Y], Cleveland, O (d/IV-16-1887 @26) MD Homeop Hosp Cleveland 1881. *Med vis* 3:170, 1887. *Clin rev* 2:121, 1887? *Polk* 1886: 748. Homeopath.

MOORE, ALVIN A , Parker's Landing, Pa (d/IV-14-1902 @41) MD Cincinnati U 1886. *Pa med jour* 5:452, 1901/02; 6:261, 1902/03. *Flint* 1891: 812.

MOORE, ANDREW BARRY, SC (b/II-11-1771 Spartanburg Dist, SC; d/I-3-1848) MD ? AB Dickinson 1795. *Dickinson cat*: 1795.

MOORE, CHARLES D , Des Moines (d/1889 @32) MD Miami 1885. *Tr Ia St M S* 18:411, 1900. *Polk* 1886:356.

MOORE, CHARLES TURNER BEALE, CW-USA; Pt Pleasant, WVa (b/V-29-1841 Mercer's Bottom, Va; d/ IV-17-1875) MD UPa 1865; AB Wash & Jeff 1862. *Tr Med Soc WVa* 1875: 121-22. *U Pa med alum CW*: 1865.

MOORE, CHARLES VAIL, Stillwater, NJ (b/XI-14-1822 Franklin, NY; d/III-5-1892) MD UCNY 1845. *Tr Med Soc NJ* 1892: 199-201. *Butler* 1878: 473.

MOORE, CHARLES VERLING, Fairmount, Ind (b/IV-

17–1849 Montg'y Co; d/IV–26–1897) MD Louisvl Med Coll 1878. *Tr Ind St Med Soc* 1897: 359. *Polk* 1886: 317.

MOORE, DAVID O , Bloomington, Ill (d/III–15–1901) Lic Exam Bd. *Ill med jour* ns2:533, 1901. *Polk* 1896:364.

MOORE, EBENEZER GILES, Concord, NH 1844– (b/1797 Dorchester; d/III–2–1870) MD Dartmouth 1829. *Phila med reg & dir* 1871: 304. *Bost m&s j* 5:196, 1870.

MOORE, EDWARD BUCKNAM, Epping, NH; Boston (b/VI–12–1801; d/IX–16–1874) MD Bowdoin 1828. *Tr AMA* 29:719–22, 1878? *Mass Med Soc cat* 1894.

MOORE, EDWARD G , Spring Valley, Ill (d/VIII–11 1898) MD NWU 1884. *Tr Ill St Med Soc* 1899–1900:509. *JAMA* 31:427, 551, 1898. *Polk* 1896:442.

MOORE, EDWARD MOTT, Rochester, NY (b/VII–15–1814 Rahway, NJ; d/III–3–1902) MD UPa 1838. *Tr CPP* cent vol: 283. *Proc Conn Med Soc* 1902:413. *Tr Med Soc St NY* 1903:415–18. *K&B* III:863–64.

MOORE, ELI HERDMAN, Wellsburg, WVa (b/IV–4–1814; d/I–17–1878) MD Jefferson 1840; AB Washington 1834. *Tr Med Soc WVa* 1884:154; 1878:438–39. *Tr AMA* 29:722–23, 1878. *Butler* 1878: 852.

MOORE, ENOCH W , Decatur, Ill (d/V–19–1899 @78, Cleburne, Tex) MD St Louis Med Coll 1853. *JAMA* 32: 1269, 1899. *Polk* 1886: 76.

MOORE, GEORGE EVERTSON, NYC (d/IV–15–1891) MD CPSNY 1879. *Med reg NY NJ Conn* 1891: 279. *Bost m&s j* 124:420, 1891.

MOORE, GEORGE W , Springfield, O (d/XII–1–1892 @59) MD Homeop Hosp Cleveland 1870. *Med vis* 9:8, 1893. *Polk* 1886: 769. Homeopath.

MOORE, GODWIN COTTEN, St Johns, NC (b/XI–6–1806; d/V–1–1880) MD UPa 1828; att UNC 1822. *UNC cat*: 437.

MOORE, H W , Salona, Tex (d/V–30–1897) MD Mo Med Coll 1884. *Tex med jour* 13:47, 1897–98. *Polk* 1896: 1439.

MOORE, HAYS WHITE, Ft Worth, Tex (b/III–5–1856 New Orl; d/IX–26–1886) MD Louisville Med Coll 1877. *Tex cour–rec med* 4:87–90,1886. *Daniel's Tex med jour* 2:170–73,1886. *New Orl m s j* ns14:483,1886.

MOORE, HENRY B , Colorado Springs (d/II–20–1900) MD Jefferson 1886. *JAMA* 34:573, 1900. *Polk* 1896:255.

MOORE, IRA LORISTON, Boston (b/XI–24–1824 Candia, NH; d/X–2–1897) MD Jefferson 1851; ng Amherst 1851. *Bost m&s j* 137:384, 1897. *JAMA* 29:816–17, 1897. *Polk* 1896: 702.

MOORE, J W, Midlothian Tx (d/V–29–1906 Dallas) <MD St Louis Coll Ph & S 1900> *Tex st m j* 2:100, 1906.

MOORE, JAMES ALBERT, New Haven, Conn (b/VII–9 1866 Oxford, NY; d/III–9–1905) MD Yale 1894; AB 1892. *Proc Conn Med Soc* 1905: 516–17.

MOORE, JAMES ALEXANDER, NYC; Helena, Mont (d/XI–29–1898 @53) MD Bellevue 1883; AB Yale 1867. *JAMA* 31:1490, 1898. *Bost m&s j* 139:586, 1898. *Polk* 1896: 893.

MOORE, JAMES FREDERICK, Brooklyn (d/II–19 1893 @54) MD UCNY 1861. *Med reg NY NJ Conn* 1893: 312. *Polk* 1886: 647.

MOORE, JAMES MOODY, Concord, NH (b/VI–20 1832; d/II–3–1870) MD Dartmouth 1860. *Phila med reg & dir* 1871: 303.

MOORE, JAMES OTIS, Haverhill, Mass (b/IV–12–1822 Parsonfield, Me; d/XI–16–1886) MD Castleton 1848. *New Engl med gaz* 21:608, 1886. *Med vis* 3:12, 1887. *Polk* 1886: 467. *Cleave.* Homeopath.

MOORE, JOE L , Shreveport, La (d/XI–12–1878 @41) MD Mo Med Coll 1857. *New Orl m&s j* ns6: 673, 1879.

MOORE, JOHN, Philadelphia (b/V–4–1778; d/V–23–1836) MD UPa 1800. *Tr CPP* cent vol: 250.

MOORE, JOHN CALVIN WEBSTER, Concord, NH (b/I–30–1837 Wells, Me; d/XI–28–1897) MD Bowdoin 1865. *JAMA* 29:1234, 1897. *Polk* 1886: 591.

MOORE, JOHN GEORGE, NYC (d/V–1–1891) MD CPSNY 1886; AB Coll City NY. *Med reg NY NJ Conn* 1892: 284. *Bost m&s j* 126:484, 1892.

MOORE, JOHN GORDON, Elba, Ala (d/XI–3–1887) <MD Med Coll St SC 1845; MD Atlanta 1871> *Tr Med Assoc St Ala* 1888: 315.

MOORE, JOHN JAY, Syracuse, NY (b/X–21–1861 Scottville; d/X–3–1897) MD UCNY 1882. *JAMA* 29: 816, 1897. *Polk* 1896: 1105.

MOORE, JOHN ROWLAND, Parnassus, Pa (d/X–12–1901 @76) MD Jefferson 1854. *Pa med jour* 5:296, 1901/02. *Polk* 1886: 794.

MOORE, JOHN WESLEY F , Butler, Pa (d/VI–24–1903 @35) MD Jefferson 1894. *Pa med jour* 7:279, 1903/04. *Flint* 1897: 797.

MOORE, JOHN WILSON, Philadelphia (b/1789? d/VI–25–1865) MD UPa 1812. *Med surg rep Phila* 13:16, 1865. *Tr CPP* cent vol: 250.

MOORE, JOSEPH, West Chester, Pa (b/ca 1758; d/VII 5–1799) stud med Phila. *Med reporter* [Chester Co, Pa] 1:61–62, 1853.

MOORE, JOSEPH B , CW–USA (d/IX–5–1864) MD ? *Nat med jour* 1:300, 1870/71.

MOORE, JOSEPH F Sr, CW–CSA; Meridian, Miss; Tyler, Tx 1894– (b/XII–16–1829 Fairfield Dist, SC; d/XI–18–1903) MD Tulane 1855. *Tex st med jour* 1:244, 1906. *Polk* 1896: 1454.

MOORE, JOSEPH F , Autaugaville, Ala (d/XI–8–1888) MD Med Coll Ala 1882. *Tr Med Assoc St Ala* 1889: 229. *Polk* 1886: 130.

MOORE, JOSEPH W , NYC (d/IX–9–1886) MD Castleton 1860. *Med reg NY NJ Conn* 1887: 271.

MOORE, LEVI, Albany, NY (b/I–28–1827 Duanesburgh; d/VI–30–1880) MD Albany 1851. *Tr Med Soc St NY* 1883: 279–81. *Butler* 1874: 550.

MOORE, MARCUS AURELIUS, Waltham, Mass (d/III–30–1864 @39) MD Harvard 1847. *Bost m&s j* 70:208, 1867. *Mass Med Soc cat* 1894.

MOORE, MATTHEW D , Sussex Co, Va (d/1859) Med stud at Jefferson. *Med surg rep Phila* ns3:195, 1859/60.

MOORE, MERIWETHER GAINES, Wetumpka, Ala (d/ III-27-1890) MD UPa 1846. *Tr Med Assn St Ala* 1890: 217. *Polk* 1886: 141.

MOORE, RICHARD HOFFMAN, NYC (d/VI-29-1875) MD CPSNY 1861 *Med reg NY NJ Conn* 1875:201.

MOORE, RICHARD S , Mt Vernon, Ind (b/III-19-1843 Peterboro, Ont; d/XII-3-1881) MD Miami 1872. *Tr Ind St Med Soc* 1882: 200.

MOORE, SAMUEL, Philadelphia (b/II-8-1774; d/II-18-1861) MD ? AB UPA 1792; AM 1795. *Tr Med Soc NJ* 1871: 183-84.

MOORE, SAMUEL LAWRENCE, Boston (d/III-13-1892 @56) MD Harvard 1868. *Bost m&s j* 126: , 1892. *Polk* 1890: 541.

MOORE, SAMUEL PRESTON, Richmond, Va; CW-CSA (b/1813 Charlestown; d/V-31-1889) MD Med Coll SC 1834. *So pract* 11:313-16, 1889; 23:381-86, 1901. *Bost m&s j* 120:572, 1889. *K&B* III:865.

MOORE, THOMAS, Germantown, Phila (b/VII-2-1827; d/III-25-1882) ?MD UPa 1848; MD Hahnemann 1868. *Tr Hom M S St Pa* 1882:51. *Hahn mo* 17:256, 1882. Homeopath.

MOORE, THOMAS JEFFERSON, Richmond, Va 1882- (b/IV-30-1840 NC; d/II-24-1898) MD UCNY 1868. *NC med jour* 41:307, 1898. *JAMA* 30:624, 1898. *Polk* 1896: 1500.

MOORE, W H , Runge, Tex (d/III-11-1903) MD ? *Tr Tex St Med Assoc* 1903:51-52.

MOORE, WILLIAM, Womelsdorf, Pa (b/VII-28-1810 Reading; d/V-23-1872) MD CPSNY 1836. *Tr Med Soc Pa* 10: 230-31.

MOORE, WILLIAM, ? (d/1878 Port Gibson, Miss) MD ? *Tr AMA* 30: 880, 1879.

MOORE, WILLIAM HARDING, Goldsborough, NC (b/1828; d/1881) MD ?Ky Sch Med 1870; att UNC 1845-46. *Tr NC Med Soc* 1882: 34.

MOORE, WILLIAM JAMES, USMarHospServ 1855-61; CSA 1861-65; Norfolk, Va (b/VI-21-1819; d/V-19 1888) MD UPa 1841. *Tr Med Soc Va* 1888:275. *Atkinson* I: . *Butler* 1878: 833.

MOORE, WILLIAM S , CW-USA (d/VII-2-1863) MD ? *Nat med jour* 1:300, 1870/71.

MOORE, WILLIAM WEBSTER, Oakfield, Wis (d/ 1890) MD UCNY 1886. *Tr Wis St Med Soc* 1891: 357.

MOOREHEAD, JAMES, NYC (d/I-19-1884 @39) MD Bellevue 1873. *Med reg NY NJ Conn* 1884:234. *Med surg rep Phila* 50:160, 1884.

MOOREHEAD, WASHINGTON, Zanesville, O (b/VI-27-1807; d/IV-25-1862) MD UPa 1829. *Tr Ohio St Med Soc* 1862: 121-22.

MOOREHOUSE, WILLIAM D , Wauwautosa, Wis (b/ X-7-1832 Ottawa, Can; d/I-17-1896 @64) MD Rush 1866. *JAMA* 26: 243, 1896. *Tr Wis St Med Soc* 30:564-66, 1896. *Polk* 1890: 1174.

MOORES, DANIEL, Baltimore (d/1802) MD Edinburgh 1787. *Med annals Md:* 509-10.

MOORHEAD, JOHN FRANCES Jr, Joplin, Mo (d/I-26 1899 @45) MD UCNY 1883. *JAMA* 32:324, 1899. *Polk* 1896: 843.

MOORMAN, JOHN J , Va (b/Bedford Co, Va; d/I-18-1885) <MD Phila> *Med annals Md:* 510.

MORAN, JAMES E , Braidwood, Ill (d/VI-1-1891 @ 23) MD Bellevue 1888. *JAMA* 30: 1481, 1898.

MORAN, JOHN J , Baltimore; Falls Church, Va (b/1820; d/XII-13-1888) MD U Md 1845. *Med annals Md:* 510. *Polk* 1886: 213, 917.

MORAN, JOHN JOSEPH, Dorchester, Mass (d/IX-22 1894 @29) MD Harvard 1892. *Bost m&s j* 131:328, 1894.

MORAWETZ, LEONARD FRANZ, Baltimore (b/XII-2 1818 Austria; d/X-26-1892) <MD U Vienna 1844> *Med annals Md:* 510-11.

MOREHOUSE, GEORGE READ, CW-USA; Philadelphia (b/III-25-1829 Mt Holly, NJ; d/XI-12-1905) MD Jefferson 1851; MD UPa 1875; AB Princeton 1848. *Tr CPP* cent vol:250; 3s28:lix ff, 1905. *Atkinson* I:149. *K&B* III: 865-67.

MORELAND, ANDREW O , Jamestown, Pa (d/V-18 1899 @42) MD Cleveland Med Coll 1882. *JAMA* 32: 1269, 1899. *Polk* 1886: 803.

MORENZY, DEMONT F , Decatur, Ill (d/IV-8-1905 @78) MD Phila Coll Med & Surg 1854. *Ill med jour* 7:378, 1905. *Polk* 1886: 256.

MORFIT, JOHN C , Chicago (d/I-8-1858) MD ? *Bost m&s j* 57: 535, 1857.

MORGAN, ALBERT W C, DeWitt Ia (d/1893 @58)MD CPS Keokuk 1870 *Tr Ia St M S* 1896:329 *Polk* 1890:414.

MORGAN, ALONZO CALVIN, Dugansville, Ky (d/X 3-1898) MD U Louisville 1882. *JAMA* 31: 997, 1898. *Polk* 1893: 503.

MORGAN, ANNA E , Denver (d/I-23-1896) MD New Engl Female Med Coll 1869; MD Denver 1892. *Tr Colo St Med Soc* 1898-99: 509. *Polk* 1893: 236.

MORGAN, ASA, Cedar Bayou, Tex (d/VIII-24-1895 @ 67) MD CPS Keokuk 1852. *JAMA* 25: 427, 1895. *Polk* 1886: 882.

MORGAN, BENJAMIN FRANKLIN, Bennington, Vt (b/1799; d/II-4-1887) MD Castleton 1825. *Med reg NY NJ Conn* 1887: 271.

MORGAN, CHARLES EDWARD, NYC (d/VIII-4-1867 @34) MD CPSNY 1857; AB Columbia 1854. *Tr AMA* 19: 416-17, 1868. *Bost m&s j* 77:112, 1867. *Med surg rep Phila* 17:155, 1867. *Med reg NY NJ Conn* 1868: 330.

MORGAN, EDWARD NOADIAH SWIFT, Bennington, Vt (b/I-25-1826 Pownal; d/VI or VII-20-1884) ng Woodstock 1846; Berkshire 1847; AB Williams 1844. *Med surg rep Phila* 51: 168, 1884.

MORGAN, EDWIN DENISON Jr, Suffield, Conn (b/IX 8–1834; d/VIII–10–1879) MD Bellevue 1871. *Med reg NY NJ Conn* 1880: 237. *Med s rep Phila* 41: 176, 1879. *Med rec* 17: 160–61, 1880.

MORGAN, ETHELBERT CARROLL, Washington, DC (b/II–10–1856 DC; d/V–5–1891) MD UPa 1877; AB Gonzaga 1874; PhD Georgetown 1888. *Hist Med Soc DC:* 311. *K&B* III: 867.

MORGAN, GERARD EDWIN, CW–USA; Baltimore (b/I–7–1828 Harrisonb'g Va; d/XII–1–1874) MD Wash U Balto 1852. *Tr AMA* 26:468, 1875. *Med ann Md:* 511.

MORGAN, J B, Joplin Mo (d/III–30–1895 @72) MD ? *JAMA* 24: 609, 1895.

MORGAN, JAMES, New London, Conn (b/III–20–1802 Engl; d/VII–3–1859) MD Jefferson 1828. *Proc Conn Med Soc* 1860: 65–66.

MORGAN, JAMES ETHELBERT, Washington, DC (b/IX–25–1822 St Mary's Co, Md; d/VI–2–1889) MD Columbian DC 1845; att St Mary's Coll. *Hist Med Soc DC:* 237–38. *NY med jour* 49:638, 1889. *Med rec NY* 35: 692, 1889. *Atkinson* I: 116–17. *K&B* III: 816 (mention).

MORGAN, JAMES H, Roanoke Va (d/IX–30–1892) MD Hosp C M Louisvl 1887. *Tr M S Va* 1892:286; 1893:219.

MORGAN, JOHN, Philadelphia; RevWar–USA (b/1735; d/X–15–1789) MD Edinburgh 1763; AB 1757. *Phila j m & phys sci* 1: 439–42, 1820. *No Amer m&s j* 4:362–86, 1827. *Amer museum* 6:353–55, 1789. *K&B* III: 868–70.

MORGAN, JOHN C, Sioux Falls, SD (d/V–19–1900) MD Rush 1869. *JAMA* 34:1146, 1900. *Polk* 1886: 202.

MORGAN, JOHN COLEMAN, Hamilton, Ill 1856; Alton, Ill 1858; Philadelphia 1865–75; Los Angeles (b/II–9–1831 Phila; d/VI–19–1899) MD Pa Med Coll 1852; Hahnemann Phila 1886. *Tr Am Inst Hom* 1900: 834–35. *King* I:358. Homeopath.

MORGAN, JOHN VINCENT, NYC (b/1841; d/VII–25–1879) MD CPSNY 1870. *Med reg NY NJ Conn* 1880: 238. *Med surg rep Phila* 41: 132, 1879.

MORGAN, RALPH GREGORY, Indianapolis (b/I–18–1873 Plainfield, Ind; d/I–1–1903) <MD Med Coll Ind 1898> *Tr Ind St Med Soc* 1903: 351.

MORGAN, SAMUEL B, Crawfordsville, Ind (b/I–30–1813 NJ; d/VI–22–1886) MD Med Coll Ohio 1869. *Tr Ind St M S* 1887: 188. *Butler* 1878: 213.

MORGAN, SIDNEY ELY, Hartford Conn (d/II–20–1900 @28) MD LICH 1897. *JAMA* 34:573, 1900.

MORIARTY, JOHN MOSELY, E Boston (b/X–14–1807 Salem, Mass; d/X–20–1865) MD Harvard 1831; AB Brown 1827. *Med surg rep Phila* 13:294, 1865. *Bost m&s j* 73:268, 1865.

MORIARTY, JOSEPH, Boston (d/XII–4–1847) MD Harvard 1834; AB Brown 1830. *Brown hist cat*: 1830.

MORISEY, SAMUEL BUNTING, CW–CSA (b/1830 Sampson Co, NC; d/1884 Clinton) MD UPa 1854. *U Pa med alum CW*: 1854.

MORISON, ALEXANDER, Newark, NJ (d/V–1–1892 @35) MB CM Glasgow 1883; MD 1887. *Med reg NY NJ Conn* 1892: 284.

MORISON, JAMES, Calif; Quincy, Mass (b/VI–20–1818; d/V–20–1882) MD U Md 1846; AB Harvard 1844; AM 1864. *JAMA* 1: 192, 1883. *Bost m&s j* 106: 504, 621–22, 1882. *Butler* 1878: 354.

MORISON, JAMES M, Baltimore (d/XI–13–1899 @ 62) MD U Md 1859. *JAMA* 33:1375, 1899. *Polk* 1886: 438.

MORISON [MORRISON], ROBERT BROWN, Baltimore (b/III–13–1853; d/IX–30–1897) Stud Harvard 1869; Göttingen; MD U Md 1874. *Bost m&s j* 137:408, 1897. *Med annals Md:* 511: 873.

MORLEY, FRANK W, Huron, O (d/1903) MD Cleveland Hom 1884. *Tr Am Inst Hom* 1904:963. Homeopath.

MORONG, JOSEPH F, Philadelphia (d/X–30–1874 Charleston, SC) MD ? *Med s rep Phila* 31:380, 1874.

MORRILL, ALPHEUS, Akron, O 1846; Columbus 1848; Concord, NH (d/V–9–1874 @62) MD ? *New Engl med gaz* 9:288,1874. *Tr Am Inst Hom* 1874:647. *King* I:175. Homeopath.

MORRILL, EDWIN C, Norwalk, O (d/I–3–1900) MD Cleveland Homeop 1886. *Tr Am Inst Hom* 1900: 835–36. *Polk* 1886:764. Homeopath.

MORRILL, HENRY EDWIN, Brooklyn (b/XII–29–1813 Boston; d/III–6–1874) MD U Pa 1840; ng Amherst 1837. *Med surg rep Phila* 30:300, 1874. *Tr Am Inst Hom* 1874:656. Homeopath.

MORRILL, ISAAC, Borodino & Chemung, NY (b/IX–1808 Cornish, Me; d/IX–8–1887) MD Bowdoin 1832. *Tr Med Soc St NY* 11: 741 ff, 1894. *Polk* 1886: 660.

MORRILL, SAMUEL, Boston (b/II–4–1800 Wells, Me; d/III–27–1872) MD Bowdoin 1823; AB 1820; AM 1823. *Bost m&s j* ns9:228, 1872.

MORRILL, SHADRACH CATE, Concord, NH (b/VII–20–1839 Loudon; d/X–8–1904) MD Homeop Hosp Coll Cleveland 1866; ng Brown 1863. *Bost m&s j* 151, 242, 1904. *Tr NH M S* 1905:284–85. *Polk* 1886: 591. Homeopath.

MORRIS, AUSTIN FLINT, NYC (d/VIII–22–1906 @ 38) MD Bellevue 1893. *Bost m&s j* 155: 242, 1906. *Polk* 1900: 1281.

MORRIS, CASPAR, Philadelphia (b/V–2–1805; d/III–17 1884) MD UPA 1826 *Tr CPP* cent vol:250; 3s10: xxxiii–lx, 1888. *Med surg rep Phila* 50:416, 1884. *Atkinson* I: 24. *K&B* II: 872.

MORRIS, FLORILLO BALDWIN, CW–USA; Philadelphia (b/II–14–1829 Buffalo; d/VIII–16–1894) MD UPa 1865. *U Pa med alum CW*: 1865. *Polk* 1886: 821.

MORRIS, FRANCIS D, CW–USA (d/IX–23–1864) MD ? *Nat med jour* 1:300, 1870/71.

MORRIS, JOHN, Philadelphia (b/X–27–1759; d/IX–7–1793) MD UPa 1783. *Tr CPP* cent vol: 251.

MORRIS, JONATHAN, Marple & Darby, Pa (b/V–1729; d/IV–7–1819) No MD. *Med reporter* (West Chester, Pa) 3:30–32, 61–64, 1855.

 Spec. educ'l status abbrev. as: ***ng*** = college verified attendance without degree;

MORRIS, JONATHAN, Ironton, O (b/XII-1-1823 Morgan Co; d/XII-26-1895) MD Cleveland M C 1847. *Tr O M S* 1896:399 *JAMA* 26:142 1896. *Butler* 1878:642.

MORRIS, MOREAU, NYC (b/VI-19-1825 Stillwater, NY; d/III-17-1904) MD CPSNY 1848. *Bost m & s jour* 150:310, 1904. *Atkinson* I:227-28. *Polk* 1896:1069.

MORRIS, RICHARD LEWIS, NYC (b/XI-4-1805; d/VI-14-1880) MD CPSNY 1830; AB Columbia 1826. *Med reg NY NJ Conn* 1881: 239.

MORRIS, SPENCER, Mt Morris, Pa (b/1903) MD M C Ohio 1847. *Pa med jour* 7:279, 1903/04.

MORRIS, WILLIAM BOWEN, Charlestown, Mass (b/III-4-1826 Washington, DC; d/III-16-1878) MD Harvard 1849; AB Brown 1846. *Brown hist cat*: 1846.

MORRIS, WILLIAM SMITH, Island Hts, NJ; Philadelphia (d/I-30-1895) MD Hahnemann Phila 1887. *Hahn mo* 30:80 (news & advt) 1895 (June). Homeopath.

MORRISON, ALBERT, Windsor, Conn (b/III-13-1820; d/V-13-1873) MD CPSNY 1847. *Pr Conn M S* 4:281, 293, 1874. *Med surg rep Phila* 29: 72, 1873.

MORRISON, AMBROSE, Nashville (b/V- -1847; d/VIII-3-1898) MD U Nashville 1876. *So pract* 20:392-93, 1898. *JAMA* 31:427, 1898. *Tex med jour* 14: 154, 1898-99. *Flint* 1897: 884.

MORRISON, EDWIN T, Baltimore (d/VIII-7-1896 @ 47) MD U Md 1887. *JAMA* 28:449,1896. *Polk* 1896:663.

MORRISON, HIEL, Philadelphia (d/XII-6-1883 @79) MD ? *Med surg rep Phila* 49:700, 1883.

MORRISON, JOHN, Greensburg, Pa (b/1797? d/VIII-11 1869) MD ? *Med surg rep Phila* 21:190, 1869.

MORRISON, JOHN A , Cochranville, Pa (d/VII-26-1904 @93) MD Jefferson 1837. *Pa med jour* 8:335, 1904/05. *Flint* 1897: 799.

MORRISON, JOHN M , USA (b/1836; d/1880 Robertson Co, Tex) <MD New Orl Sch Med> *Tr AMA* 31: 1079-80, 1880.

MORRISON, MAURICE, Havana, Cuba (b/1807 Md; d/IX-14-1842) MD U Md 1831. *Amer jour med sci* ns5: 252, 1843. *Med annals Md:* 512.

MORRISON, THOMAS SCOTT, CW-USA; Coatesville, Pa (b/II-17-1840 E Fallowfield; d/XI-9-1881) MD UPa 1861; att Princeton. *Tr Pa St Med Soc* 14:309-10, 1882. *U Pa med alum CW*: 1861.

MORRISON, WILLIAM CLINGAN, CW-USA (b/VII-2-1840 Cochranville, Pa; d/XI-18-1884) MD UPa 1861. *U Pa med alum CW*: 1861.

MORRISS, BEVERLY PRESTON, Amherst CH Va (b/X-29-1822 Big Island; d/III-7-1903) MD UPa 1849; att U Va 1847. *Tr M S Va* 1903: 274-75. *Polk* 1900: 1756.

MORRISSY, WILLIAM P, Brooklyn (d/III-13-1898 @ 51) MD UCNY 1869. *JAMA* 30:745, 1898. *Polk* 1896:1000.

MORROGH, CLIFFORD T, New Brunswick, NJ (b/VII 31-1821 Cork, Irel'd; d/III-13-1882) MD UCNY 1847. *Med reg NY NJ Conn* 1882:232 *Tr M S NJ* 1883:189-90.

MORROW, JAMES, CW-CSA (b/VIII-7-1821 Willington, SC; d/XII-11-1865) MD UPa 1846. *UPa med alum CW*: 1846.

MORROW, JOHN WILSON, Tionesta, Pa (b/VI-2-1837; d/VIII-5-1905) MD Jefferson 1873. *Pa med jour* 9:238, 1905/06. *Flint* 1897: 837.

MORROW, WILLIAM HENRY, Fayetteville, NC; CW-USA (b/1828; d/1868) MD ? AB UNC 1853 *UNC cat*:445.

MORSE, CHARLES WHITE, Dowagiac, Mich (d/I-24 1899 @71) MD U Buffalo 1866. *JAMA* 32: 385, 1899. *Polk* 1886: 490.

MORSE, EBENEZER, Walpole, NH (b/VIII-13-1785 Dublin; d/XII-30-1863) MD Dartmouth 1813; AB 1810. *Bost m&s j* 69: 468, 1863.

MORSE, GEORGE MASON, Clinton, Mass (d/IX-23 1901 @80) MD Harvard 1843. *Bost m&s j* 145:366, 1901. *Polk* 1896: 710.

MORSE, HORATIO GILEAD, Roxbury, Mass (b/IV-14 1817; d/V-12-1886 @69) MD Harvard 1843; AB Brown 1840; AM. *Bost m&s j* 114: 480, 524, 1886. *Butler* 1878: 354.

MORSE, HUMPHREY, Newburyport, Mass (b/IV-6-1808; d/IV-4-1836) MD Dartmouth 1834; AB Amherst 1834. *Amherst, Men of*: 1834.

MORSE, JAMES EPHRAIM, W Hartford, Conn 1850-65; Royalton, Vt 1865-82 (b/IV-12-1824 Craftsbury, Vt; d/V-14-1882) MD Dartmouth 1850. *Tr Vt Med Soc* 1883: 107.

MORSE, JOEL, CW-USA (d/V-27-1865 or 1866 Brownsville, Tex) MD U Mich 1853. *Tr AMA* 18:357, 1867. *Nat med jour* 1:300, 1870/71.

MORSE, JOHN FREDERICK, Brooklyn NY to 1849; Sacramento to 1863; San Francisco (b/XII-27-1815 Essex, Vt; d/XII-30-1874) MD UCNY 1844. *Tr Med Soc St Calif* 1874-75: 158-60.

MORSE, JOHN FREDERICK, San Francisco (b/Calif; d/VIII-4-1898) MD Cooper Med Coll 1878; MD Fr Wilh U Berlin 1881. *Chicago med rec* 15:281, 1898. *JAMA* 31: 551, 1898. *Polk* 1886: 173.

MORSE, LUTHER BLODGETT, Watertown, Mass (b/VIII-13-1820 Rochester; d/V-26-1900) MD Woodstock 1844; ng Castleton 1841. *Bost m&s j* 142:580, 1900. *Polk* 1896: 725.

MORSE, NATHAN RANSOM, Salem, Mass (b/II-20-1831 Stoddard, NH; d/VIII-5-1897) MD U Vt 1862; AB Amherst 1857. *Med vis* 13:324, 1897. *Tr Am Inst Hom* 1898:49. *Hahn mo* 32: 1897 (Sept). *Cleave.* Homeopath.

MORSE, VERRANUS, Brooklyn (b/1818 Springfield, NH; d/III-9-1904) MD UCNY 1849; AB Dartmouth 1845. *Bost m&s j* 150: 282, 1904. *Polk* 1896: 1000.

MORTLAND, JAMES CALDWELL, Edgerton, O (b/V-23-1834; d/IV-20-1897) MD Bellevue 1871. *JAMA* 28:860, 1897. *Polk* 1896: 1187.

MORTON, ARCHIBALD J , Williamstown & Elmwood, Ill (b/II-1-1855 Ayrshire, Scotl; d/VII-1-1898) MD CPS Chicago 1889. *Tr Ill St Med Soc* 1899: 29- 30. *Polk* 1890: 354.

MORTON, DAVID B , St Louis, Mo (d/III-5-1900 @ 85) MD ? *JAMA* 34:702, 1900.

MORTON, EDWARD WATTS, Kennebunk Me (b/VIII 30-1828 Portland; d/I-10-1894) MD Hahnemann Phila 1856; AB Bowdoin 1848. *Bowd cat*: 1848. Homeopath?

MORTON, JOHN HAMILTON, Dallas (d/VII-18-1887) MD UPa 1852. *Tex cour-rec med* 4:580, 1887. *Daniel's Tex m jour* 3:156-57, 1887.

MORTON, LLOYD, CW-USA; Halifax, Mass; Pawtucket, RI (b/ XII-3-1827; d/X-16-1888) MD Woodstock 1851; AB Brown 1849. *Tr RI Med Soc* 1888:569-73. *Atkinson* I:647. *Polk* 1886: 845.

MORTON, SAMUEL GEORGE, Philadelphia (b/I-26-1799; d/V-15-1851) MD UPa 1820; MD Edinb 1823. *Tr CPP* cent vol:251; ns1: 1850-53. *Bost m&s j* 41:56-58, 1849; 44:344-45, 398-401, 1851. *K&B* III: 874-77.

MORTON, THOMAS GEORGE, Philadelphia; CW-USA (b/VIII-8-1835; d/V-20-1903 Cape May, NJ) MD UPa 1856. *Tr CPP* cent vol: 251-52; 3s36: lxviii- lxxii, 1914. *Pa med jour* 7:280, 1903/04. *U Pa med alum CW*: 1856. *Atkinson* I:43. *K&B* III:877-78.

MORTON, WALTER ALFRED, Brooklyn (b/IX-1-1859 Westmoreland Co, Va; d/VII-22-1895) MD Dartmouth 1890; AB Bates 1886; AM 1893. *JAMA* 25: 208, 1895.

MORTON, WILLIAM A , Liberty, Mo (d/XII-10-1894 @82) MD ? *JAMA* 23:961, 990, 1894.

MORTON, WILLIAM JOSEPH, Racine, Wis (d/VIII-14-1896 @89) <MD Louisville Med Coll> *JAMA* 27: 449, 1896.

MORTON, WILLIAM THOMAS GREEN, Boston (b/ VIII-9-1819 Charlton, Mass; d/VII-15-1868 NYC) Stud Coll Dental Surg Balto 1840. *Phila med reg & dir* 1871: 297. *Bost m&s j* ns2: 32, 1868. *Med surg rep Phila* 19:100, 1868. *K&B* III: 878-79.

MOSELEY, CHARLES FLOYD, CW-CSA; Gold Hill, Va (b/VII-23-1822; d/X-27-1901) MD UPa 1849. *U Pa med alum CW*: 1849. *Polk* 1886: 918.

MOSELEY, DANIEL W , Richmond, Va (d/VI-15-1904 @76) MD Jefferson 1850. *JAMA* 43:61, 1904.

MOSELEY, NATHANIEL RICHARDS, CW-USA; NYC (b/1825 Mass; d/II-9-1889) MD UPa 1855. *Med reg NY NJ Conn* 1889:279. *U Pa med alum CW*: 1855.

MOSELEY, SAMUEL, Philadelphia (d/VI-9-1873 @ 72) MD U Pa 1826. *Med surg rep Phila* 28:488, 1873.

MOSELEY, WILLIAM OXNARD Jr (d/1879 Switz) MD Harvard 1878; AB 1869. *Bost m&s j* 101: 316, 1879.

MOSELY, LUTHER, Arlington, Vt (d/XI- -1876) MD Berkshire 1833. *Tr Vt Med Soc* 1883: 107.

MOSER, IRA D, Philadelphia (d/X-21-1905) MD Jefferson 1880. *Pa med jour* 9:127, 1905/06. *Polk* 1896: 1313.

MOSER, PHILIP S , Muscatine, Ia 1852; Boone 1854-(b/VII-17-1829 Charleston, SC; d/IX-26-1894) MD Pa Med Coll 1852. *JAMA* 23:561, 1894. *Atkinson* I:465-66.

MOSES, ISRAEL, NYC (d/X-4-1870) MD CPSNY 1845; AB Columbia 1841. *Med rec NY* 6:94, 1871-72.

MOSES, MONTEFIORE J , CW-CSA; NYC (b/1841 Charleston, SC; d/IV-11-1878) MD UCNY 1863. *Med reg NY NJ Conn* 1878:182. *Med rec NY* 13:358, 1878.

MOSES, SAMUEL DODGE, CW-CSA; Knoxville (b/X 17-1826; d/VI-16-1873 @46) MD U Va 1852; AB Williams 1848. *Med surg rep Phila* 29:36, 90, 1873.

MOSES, SIMON GRATZ, St Louis (b/X-6-1813 Phila; d/II-22-1897) MD UPa 1835; AB 1832. *JAMA* 28:429, 1897. *Polk* 1896: 875.

MOSGROVE, ADAM, Urbana, O (b/VIII-12-1790 Tyrone, Irel'd; d/III-3-1875) <MD RCS Dublin> *Tr Ohio St Med Soc* 1876: 96-97. *Butler* 1878: 642.

MOSHER, CORNELIUS D , Albany NY (b/1829 Bethlehem; d/1890) MD Albany 1859. *Bost m&s j* 123:336, 1890. *Polk* 1886: 639.

MOSHER, DANIEL J, Norwich, NY (d/IX-8-1896) MD Detroit M C 1869. *JAMA* 27:721, 1896. *Polk* 1886: 699.

MOSHER, JACOB SIMMONS, CW-USA; Albany, NY; NYC 1870-76 (b/III-19-1834, Coeymans; d/VIII-13-1883) MD Albany 1863; Rutgers 1853. *JAMA* 1:407, 1883. *Tr Med Soc St NY* 1885: 319-325. *Med bull med & surg* 5:212, 1883. *K&B* III: 879-80.

MOSHER, MARK ANTHONY, CW-USA; Austin Ill (d/ IX-12 1899 @80) MD ? ; AB U Mich 1846; AM 1866. *JAMA* 33: 745, 1899. *Polk* 1896: 1556.

MOSHER, WILLIAM B , Baltimore (b/1797? d/VII-15 1869) MD U Md 1823. *Bost m&s j* 3:480, 1869. *Med annals Md:* 512.

MOSS, BENJAMIN HART, New Orleans, La (b/1817 Orangeburg, SC; d/IV-7-1873) MD Med Coll SC 1839. *New Orl m&s j* ns1:131-32, 1873. *Med surg rep Phila* 28: 346, 1873.

MOSS, JOHN WILLIAM, Parkersburg WVa; CW-USA (d/I-2-1864 Petersburg Va) MD UPa 1838. *Tr AMA* 16:644-45 1865 *Nat med jour* 1:300, 1870/71. *U Pa med alum CW*:1838.

MOSS, MARY DENISON, Providence, RI (b/VIII-3-1840 Stonington, Conn; d/III-25-1904) MD Boston U 1875. *Tr Am Inst Hom* 1904: 963. Homeopath.

MOSS, MICHAEL, Paterson, NJ (b/Irel'd; d/XII-26-1886 @59) MD NY Med Coll 1851; MD Hahnemann Phila 1852. *Tr Med Soc NJ* 1886-87: 297-300. *Med reg NY NJ Conn* 1887: 272. *Polk* 1886: 609.

MOSS, NATHANIEL B , CW-CSA (d/III-9-1863 Murfreesboro, Tenn) MD ? *SHSP* 22: 236, 1893.

MOSS, OSCAR BURNHAM, Topeka, Kans; Kansas City (b/1845; d/VI-27-1901 Grand Rapids, Mich) MD Cleveland Homeop 1870; AB Allegheny Coll 1879. *King* II: 77. Homeopath.

MOSS, THOMAS H , Hartford, Mo (b/1832; d/XII-25 1895 @64) MD ? *JAMA* 26: 142, 1896.

MOSS, THOMAS R, Dyersburg, Tenn (d/I-7-1899) MD Vanderbilt 1881. *JAMA* 32:145, 1899. *Polk* 1886: 864.

MOSSER, DAVID O , Breinigsville, Pa (b/Lynn Twp, Pa; d/II-22-1861) MD UCNY 1845. *Med surg rep Phila* ns5: 606, 1860/61.

MOSSER, MARTIN BRENNEMAN, USA (b/1836; d/ 1881 Mechanicsburg, Pa) MD Jefferson 1862. *Tr AMA* 32: 527, 1881.

MOSSOP, STEPHEN E , Seymour, Ind (d/X-16-1894 @79) <MRCS(Engl) 1844> *JAMA* 23:655, 1894. *Polk* 1890: 388.

MOTER [MOTTER], HERMAN, Reading, Pa (d/II-22-1904 @83) <MD Giessen 1847> *Pa med jour* 8:335, 1904/05. *Flint* 1897: 1332.

MOTHERSHEAD, JOHN L , Indianapolis, Ind (d/XI- -1854 @c46) MD Transylvania 1830. *Tr Ind St M S* 1855: 8; 1857: 73.

MOTT, ALEXANDER BROWN, CW-USA; NYC (b/ III-31-1826; d/VIII-12-1889 Yonkers, NY) MD Castleton 1850; MD NY Med Coll NY 1851; MD UPa 1857. *Med reg NY NJ Conn* 1890: 275. *Buff m&s j* 24: 125, 1889. *Atkinson* I: 697-98. *K&B* III:880-82.

MOTT, ARMISTEAD RANDOLPH Sr, Leesburg Va (b/ VIII-2-1822; d/1894) MD Jefferson 1845. *Tr M S Va* 1894:191. *Polk* 1886: 920.

MOTT, ARMISTEAD RANDOLPH Jr, Leesburg Va (b/ 1857; d/V-6-1884 @26) MD U Va 1878. *Med reg NY NJ Conn* 1884:234. *Tr M S Va* 1884:8. *Butler* 1878: 833.

MOTT, EUGENE K, Chester Pa (b/1842 Scranton; d/II 22-1897) MD Jefferson 1868. *JAMA* 28:476, 1897. *Polk* 1886: 795.

MOTT, JOSEPH VARNUM, NYC (b/1851; d/I-23-1904 @53) MD CPSNY 1872. *Bost m&s j* 150:108 1904.

MOTT, VALENTINE, NYC (b/VIII-20-1785 Glen Cove, NY; d/IV-26-1865) MD CPSNY 1806. *Med reg NY NJ Conn* 1865:236-46. *Bost m&s j* 43:370-74, 1851. *Tr AMA* 16:628-30, 1865. *K&B* III: 880-82.

MOTTE, JACOB RHETT, USA; Oakly Sta, SC (b/IX-22-1811 Charleston; d/XII-6-1868 @56) MD Med Coll SC 1835; AB Harvard 1832. *Bost m&s j* __:320, 1868. *Waring* II: 271-72.

MOTTER, GEORGE TROXELL, CW-USA Med cadet; Taneytown Md (b/IV-5-1842 Emmittsb'g; d/I-16 1903) MD U Nashville 1865; att Bellevue; AB Dickinson 1862. *Med annals Md:* 513. *Polk* 1886: 446.

MOULTON, BENJAMIN FRANCIS, Lawrence, Mass (d/V-3-1904 @58) MD Harvard 1867. *Bost m&s j* 150: 552, 1904. *Polk* 1896: 715.

MOULTON, CHARLES A , CW-USA (d/IV-24-1864 New Orleans) MD ? *Nat med jour* 1:300, 1870/71.

MOULTON, CHARLES FRED, W Roxbury Mass 1891-96; Boston 1897- (b/VI-23-1865 Canton, Me; d/IV-24-1906) MD Dartmouth 1890; stud Paris, London; AB Bowdoin 1887. *Bost m&s j* 154: 508, 1906. *Polk* 1896: 702.

MOULTON, CHARLES THOMPSON, Cumberland Center, Me (b/III-4-1836 Lisbon;d/VI-1-1894) MD Bowd'n 1879. *Tr Me M Assn* 1896:582-83. *Polk* 1886:424.

MOULTON, PETER, Westchester Co, NY (b/X-7-1794; d/XII-7-1873) Hon MD UCNY 1860; att Dartmouth. *Med reg NY NJ Conn* 1874: 281-83.

MOULTRIE, JAMES Jr, Charleston SC (b/III-27-1793; d/V-29-1869) <MD UPa >; AB Coll Charleston 181_?; stud England. *Tr AMA* 29:724-25, 1878. *Waring* II:272. *K&B* III:882.

MOUNT, JOHN EZEKIEL, CW-CSA; Mountville, Va (b/IX-10-1817; d/X-5-1897) MD UPa 1845. *U Pa med alum CW*: 1845. *Polk* 1886: 922.

MOUNT, WILLIAM, Cumminsville, O (b/1799 Armstrong, Pa; d/II-17-1866 Phila) MD Med Coll Ohio 1826. *Tr Ohio St M S* 1867:74-75. *Bost m&s j* 74:188, 1866. *Nashvl j m & s* ns1:319, 1866.

MOWBRAY, JARVIS B, Bay Shore NY (d/VII-27-1886) MD UCNY 1844. *Med reg NY NJ Conn* 1887:272.

MOWER, THOMAS GARDNER, USA 1812- ; NYC (b/II-19-1790; d/XII-7-1853) MD CPSNY 1818; AB Harvard 1810. *Phila m&s j* ns2: 216, 1853. *Amer jour med sci* ns27:555-56, 1854. *NW m&s j* 3:143, 1854. *K&B* II: 830.

MOWRY, ROBERT B , Allegheny City, Pa (b/XII-23 1813 Pittsburgh; d/III-4-1895) MD Jefferson 1836; AB U W Pa 1834. *Tr CPP* cent vol: 283. *Tr Med Soc Pa* 25:414, 1895. *Polk* 1886: 790.

MOYER, ALFRED C , Bethlehem, Pa (b/IV-19-1863 Rittersville, Pa; d/VIII-7-1890) MD UPa 1884. *Tr Pa St Med Soc* 22:221, 1891.

MOYER, DANIEL PRICE, Dublin, Pa (b/III-4-1847 Towamencing Twp, Pa; d/V-11-1890) MD UPa 1872. *Lehigh Valley med mag* 2: 8, 1890-91.

MOYER, JOSEPH, Hilltown, Pa (b/1821 Leidytown; d/ IV-12-1862 @40) MD Jefferson 1844. *Med surg rep Phila* ns8: 104, 1862.

MOYERS, LESLIE E , Fairdale, Ill (b/1864; d/IX-2 1902 @38 Colorado Spr) MD CPS Chicago 1889. *Ill med jour* ns4:425, 1902. *Polk* 1896: 419.

MUDD, GEORGE DYER, Baltimore (b/XI-20-1826; d/ XII-1-1899) MD U Md 1848. *JAMA* 33:1504, 1899. *Polk* 1886: 441.

MUDD, HENRY HODGEN, St Louis, Mo (b/IV-27-1844 Pittsfield, Ill; d/XI-20-1899) MD St Louis Med Coll 1866. *Buff m&s j* 39: 460, 1900. *Atkinson* I: 579. *K&B* III: 883. *JAMA* 33:1375, 1899.

MUDD, SAMUEL ALEXANDER (b/1833; d/I-3-1883 Bryanstown, SC) MD ? *Chic med jour* 46: 330, 1883.

MUDGE, SELDEN JOHNSON, Olean, NY (d/IV-19-1899 @48) MD Buffalo 1877. *JAMA* 32:956, 1899. *Polk* 1886: 700.

MUDIE, ARCHIBALD FINN, CW-USA(d/II-18-1879 @37) MD CPSNY 1860 *Med reg NY NJ Conn* 1879:195

MUELLER, AUGUSTE FREDERICK, Philadelphia; CW–USA; (b/XII–3–1840 Colmar, Alsace–Lorraine; d/X–19 1904) MD UPa 1868. *Pa m j* 8:335, 1904/05. *U Pa med alum CW*: 1868. *Flint* 1897: 822.

MUELLER, CHARLES, CW–USA (d/IX–11–1862 Covington, Ky) MD ? *Nat med jour* 1:300, 1870/71.

MUELLER, FREDERICK A , ?NYC (d/V–1–1891) MD UCNY [?as Franz Adam, 1887?] *Med reg NY NJ Conn* 1891: 279.

MUELLER, FREDERICK WILLIAM HERMANN [or Henry] Henderson, Minn (b/1850 Yonkers; d/VIII–30–1879) MD UCNY 1876. *Tr Minn St M S* 1882:260–62.

MUELLER, GUSTAVUS ADOLPHUS, Allegheny, Pa; Menasha Wis (d/X–5–1894 @40) MD Ecl Med Inst Cinc 1878. *JAMA* 23:624,1894. *Polk* 1890:1167. Eclectic.

MÜTTER, THOMAS DENT, Philadelphia (b/III–9–1811 Richmond, Va; d/III–16–1859 Charleston, SC) MD UPa 1831; AB Hampden–Sidney. *Tr AMA* 13:805–06, 1860. *Med s rep Phila* ns2:24–25, 113–18, 1859. *Tr Pa St Med Soc* 1860: 148–54. *K&B* III:896–97.

MUFFAT, MAXIMILIAN, Palatine, Ill (b/1852; d/IX–30 1902) MD CPS Chicago 1880. *Chicago med rec* 23:299, 1902. *Ill med jour* ns4:425, 1902. *Polk* 1890: 354.

MUFFE, FREDERICK PETER, San Francisco (d/III–10 1899 @50) MD UCNY 1887. *JAMA* 32:733, 1899. *Polk* 1896: 236.

MUHLENBERG, FRANCIS, ?Lancaster, Pa; CW–USA (b/IV–4–1844; d/IX–8–1844) MD UPa 1867; AB Gettysburg 1864. *U Pa med alum CW*: 1867.

MUHLENBERG, FREDERICK AUGUSTUS HALL, Lancaster, Pa (b/III–14–1795; d/VII–5–1867) MD UPa 1814. *Med surg rep Phila* 17:62, 1867.

MUHLENBERG, HIESTER HENRY, Reading, Pa CW–USA; (b/I–15–1812; d/V–5–1886) MD UPa 1833; AB Dickinson 1829. *Med surg rep Phila* 54:608, 1886.

MUHLFELD, HENRY, NYC (d/I–15–1890 @35) MD Bellevue 1876. *Med reg NY NJ Conn* 1890: 277. *Polk* 1886: 688.

MUIR, JAMES L , Bardstown, Ky (d/II–23–1900) MD U Louisville 1850. *JAMA* 34:639, 1900. *Polk* 1886:391.

MULFINGER, JOHN LEONARD, Chicago (d/VII–20–1900 @46) MD Rush 1880; PhG. *Ill m j* ns2: 141, 1900. *Polk* 1896: 398.

MULFORD, ISAAC BUSBY, Camden NJ (b/1843 Millville;d/XI–21–1882) MD UPa 1871; AB Princeton 1865; AM 1868 *Tr M S NJ* 1883:297–99 *Butler* 1878:473. 473.

MULFORD, ISAAC SKILLMAN, Camden, NJ (b/XII–31–1799 Alloways Creek; d/II–16–1873) MD UPa 1822. *Tr M S NJ* 1873: 121. *Tr AMA* 24:366, 1873. *Med bull m & s* 5: 21, 1883.

MULFORD, SYLVANUS SANFORD, NYC (d/IX–9 1896 @66) MD CPSNY 1855; AB Yale 1850. *Bost m&s j* 135: 300, 1896. *Polk* 1896: 1069.

MULHALL, JOSEPH ALOYSIUS C , St Louis (d/I–11 1900) MD St Louis Med Coll 1873 <LRCS Dublin 1874> *JAMA* 34:186, 251, 1900. *Polk* 1886: 565.

MULHALLON, WILLIAM E , Brooklyn (b/V–24–1819; d/V–8–1872) MD Jefferson 1841. *Med reg NY NJ Conn* 1872: 355.

MULHERON, EDWARD, Binghamton, NY (d/IV–6 1900 @53) MD Buffalo 1872. *Buff m&s j* 39:782, 1900. *JAMA* 34: 957, 1900. *Polk* 1896: 990.

MULL, THOMAS MILLER, CW–USA (b/V–16–1840 New Hanover Twp, Pa; d/VI–22–1864 Washington, DC) MD UPa 1864. *U Pa med alum CW*: 1864.

MULLANE, JOSEPH, Lyons, Ind (b/III–18–1856 NYC; d/X–16–1898) MD Central CPS Indianapolis 1881. *Tr Ind St M S* 1899: 394.

MULLEN, ALEXANDER J Sr? St Louis (b/1813 Irel'd; d/IX–22–1897) <MD Louisville 1838> *JAMA* 29:761, 1897. *Polk* 1886: 565.

MULLEN, ALEXANDER J Jr? Michigan City, Ind (d/V 4–1897 @40) MD St Louis Coll Phys & Surg 1881. *JAMA* 28: 1045, 1897. *Polk* 1886: 328.

MULLEN, FRANCIS HENRY, Dorchester, Mass (d/III–15–1888 @31) MD Harvard 1879. *Bost m&s j* 118:308, 1888. *Polk* 1886:459.

MULLEN, HENRY, Philadelphia (d/VII–31–1898 @64) MD Jefferson 1864. *JAMA* 31:366,1898. *Polk* 1886: 821.

MULLEN, JOHN, Portsmouth, NH (b/X–19–1861 Gorham; d/XII–17–1905 @42) MD Dartmouth 1888. *Bost m&s j* 153:710, 1905. *Polk* 1896: 922.

MULLENS, JAMES H , Waco, Tex (d/X–30–1898) MD U Louisville 1850. *JAMA* 31: 1257, 1898.

MULLIKEN, EDWARD, Montpelier, Vt (b/I–21–1827 Stowe, Mass; d/VII–24–1857) <MD U St NY 1850> AB Harvard 1846. *Bost m&s j* 57: 27, 1857.

MULLINIX, MASTON G, CW–USA; Spencer, Ind (b/X 18–1827 Putnam Co; d/X–22–1886) Stud med Chicago 1853–54. *Tr Ind St Med Soc* 1887: 193.

MUMFORD, DAVID E, Rehoboth Md (d/IV–21–1859 @ c28) MD U Md 1852. *Med surg rep Phila* ns2:105, 1859.

MUNCASTER, MAGRUDER, Washington, DC (b/II–13 1859; d/XI–28–1901) MD U Md 1883. *Hist Med Soc DC:* 324–25. *Polk* 1893: 272.

MUND, CONRAD, NYC (d/III–2–1902 @28) MD CPSNY 1900. *Bost m&s j* 146:298, 1902.

MUNDAY, BENJAMIN, USA; Richmond, Va (d/V–4–1899) MD Med Coll Va 1880. *JAMA* 32:1074, 1899.

MUNDAY, JOHN C , Lake Charles, La (d/XII–7–1901 @ San Antonio, Tex) MD Tulane 1872. *New Orl m&s j* 54:508, 1902. *Polk* 1896: 488.

MUNDÉ, PAUL FORTUNATUS, NYC 1849– , 1872– ; Franco–Prus War (b/IX–7–1846 Dresden; d/II–7–1902) MD Harvard 1866. *Chicago med rec* 22: 266, 1902. *Bost m&s j* 146:185, 1902. *Nashvl j m & s* 91:144–45, 1902. *Atkinson* I:140–41. *K&B* III: 886–87.

MUNDELL, JOHN HODGES, Washington, DC (b/VIII–29–1827 Upper Marlboro, Md; d/V–12–1900) MD U Md 1849. *Hist Med Soc DC:* 319. *Polk* 1893: 272.

MUNFORD, SAMUEL E , Princeton, Ind (b/VI-17-1837 Gibson Co; d/VII-31-1893) MD Jefferson 1861. *Tr Ind St Med Soc* 1894: 219. *Bost m&s j* 129:180, 1893. *Butler* 1878: 214. Kemper's *Indiana*: 177, 197, 317.

MUNGER, ELISHA, New London, Conn (b/IV-17-1848 Northfield; d/V-14-1897) MD Yale 1875. *Pr Conn Med Soc* 1897: 347-50.

MUNGER, ERASTUS A, Waterville, NY (b/II-12-1813 Copenhagen NY; d/XI-4-1879) <MD Jefferson 1835> *Tr NY St Hom Soc* 10:631, 1879? *Tr Am Inst Hom* 1880: 152. *Hom j obstet* 1:362, 18__? *Hom times* 7:213, 1879. *King* I:100. Homeopath.

MUNN, JEPHTHA BALDWIN, Chatham, NJ (b/XII-29 1780; d/VI-22-1863) MD ? *Tr Med Soc NJ* 1867:107-08. *Tr AMA* 16:630-31, 1865. *Med surg rep Phila* 10:156, 1863.

MUNN, WILLIAM H , Bronx, NYC (d/IX-24-1900 @53) MD UCNY 1868. *Bost m&s j* 143: 384, 1900.

MUNRO, GEORGE ALBERT, Providence, RI (d/XII-3 1897 @60) MD Harvard 1866. *JAMA* 29:1286, 1897. *Polk* 1896: 1353.

MUNRO, JOHN ROSS, Highland Falls, NY (b/VI-28-1838 Glasgow, Scotl'd; d/V-27-1899) MD LICH 1868. *Bost m&s j* 140:564, 1899. *Polk* 1896:1025.

MUNRO, THEODORE, Union, SC (d/X-10-1897) MD UCNY. *JAMA* 29: 867, 1897. *Polk* 1896: 1366.

MUNSELL, GEORGE NELSON, CW-USA; Harwich, Mass (d/XI-2-1905 @70) MD Harvard 1860. *Bost m&s j* 153:540, 1905. *Harv in CW*: 260. *Polk* 1896: 713.

MUNSEY, BARTON, CW-USA; Curaçao; Wilmington, NC (b/NH; d/1888) MD Hahnemann Phila 1850. *King* I: 405. Homeopath.

MUNSON, BYRON WOOSTER, Sharon, Conn (b/XII-3 1845 Oxford, Conn; d/I-3-1897) MD Yale 1869. *Proc Conn Med Soc* 1897: 342-46. *Bost m&s j* 136:24, 1897. *JAMA* 28: 236, 1897. *Butler* 1878: 80.

MUNSON, OWEN, CW-USA; (d/1868 Washington, DC) MD ? *Nat med jour* 1:300, 1870/71.

MUNZ, CARL, CW-USA (d/I-13-1862 Ironton, Mo) MD ? *Nat med jour* 1:300, 1870/71.

MURBACH, ANDREW J , Archbold O (d/III-26-1900 @ 62) MD Starling 1864. *JAMA* 34:957, 1900. *Polk* 1886:736.

MURDOCH, HENRY MARTYN, New Richmond, Wis (b/X-19-1825 Antwerp, NY; d/X-7-1899) MD Woodstock 1846. *JAMA* 33:1116, 1899. *Polk* 1890: 1170.

MURDOCH, JAMES BISSETT, CW-USA; Oswego, NY 1855-72; Pittsburgh 1872- (b/X-16-1830 Scotl'd; d/X-29-1896) MD CPSNY 1854. *Buff m&s j* 36:381, 1896. *JAMA* 27:1073-74, 1896. *Atkinson* I: 188. *K&B* III: 890.

MURDOCH, THOMAS FRIDGE, Baltimore (b/V-9-1829; d/II-18-1901) MD U Md 1850; AB Princeton 1847; AM 1850. *Med annals Md:* 514. *Polk* 1886: 438.

MURPHY, CORNELIUS H , CW-USA; Brooklyn (d/VII-21-1869 @31) MD UCNY 1857. *Med reg NY NJ Conn* 1870: 325.

MURPHY, CORNELIUS TATE, Clinton, NC (b/VI-20-1827 New Hanover Co; d/I-9-1882) MD Jefferson 1848. *NC m j* 9:57-58, 1882. *Tr NC M S* 1882:33. *Atkinson* I: 74. *Butler* 1878: 597.

MURPHY, DANIEL, Brooklyn (d/III-24-1891 @45) MD UCNY 1869. *Med reg NY NJ Conn* 1891: 279.

MURPHY, DANIEL FRANCIS, Woburn, Mass(d/I-31-1904 @44) MD Harvard 1887. *Bost m&s j* 150: 138, 1904. *Polk* 1896: 727.

MURPHY, DAVID C , Edwardsville, Kans 30 yrs (d/VIII-22-1904) MD Keokuk 1874. *Jour Kans Med Soc* 4:454, 1904. *Polk* 1886: 377.

MURPHY, EDMUND ANDREW, New Orleans (b/1836 Dublin,Ire; d/I-25-1898) <MD Hom Med Coll St Louis 1866> *New Orl m&s j* 50:548, 1898. *Polk* 1890: 491.

MURPHY, J S , Burlington, NC (d/XII-20-1897) MD ? *NC med jour* 41:100, 1898. *Polk* 1896: 728.

MURPHY, JAMES, CW-USA; San Francisco (b/Tyrone Co, Irel'd; d/ VII-7-1890) MD Cooper Med Coll 1862; MD Rush 1867 ad eundem. *Tr Med Soc Calif* 21:315-16, 1891. *Polk* 1886: 173.

MURPHY, JOHN, CW-USA; Menominee Mich (d/III 11-1870) MD Rush 1861. *Chic m j* 27:241-49, 1870.

MURPHY, JOHN, Peoria, Ill (d/I-21-1903 @86) MD Edinburgh 1840. *Ill m j* ns4:589,1903. *Polk* 1896: 435.

MURPHY, JOHN ALEXANDER, CW-USA; Cincinnati (b/I-23-1824 Hawkins Co, Tenn; d/II-28-1900) MD Med Coll Ohio 1846. *JAMA* 34:639, 1900. *Atkinson* I: 605. *K&B* III: 891-92.

MURPHY, JOHN D , USN (d/X-26-1867 Pensacola Fla) MD ? *Nat m j* 1:300, 1870/71. *Tr AMA* 19: 455, 1868.

MURPHY, JOHN GAMBLE, CW-USA; Philadelphia (b/XI-19-1824; d/XI-10-1878) MD UPa 1850; AB 1842. *Matrics cat Coll UPa*: 131.

MURPHY, JOHN HENRY, CW-USA; St Paul, Minn (b/I-22-1826 New Brunswick, NJ; d/I-31-1894) MD Rush 1851. *Chic m rec* 6: 151, 1894. *Tr Minn St M S* 1894: 125. *Atkinson* I: 565. *Butler* 1878:394.

MURPHY, JOHN HOMAN, Brooklyn (b/1834; d/XI-5-1872) MD UCNY 1858. *Med reg NY NJ Conn* 1873:433.

MURPHY, JOSEPH, Taunton, Mass (d/IX-15-1890 @ 72) <MRCS (Engl)> *Bost m&s j* 123:288, 1890. *Polk* 1886: 474.

MURPHY, JOSEPH A, CW-USA; Wilkes Barre, Pa (b/II-17-1842 Chanceford; d/IV-4-1896) MD UPa 1868. *Tr Pa St M S* 1897:374-77. *Tr Luzerne Co* [Pa] *M S* 1896: 167-72. *Lehigh Valley med mag* 7: 135-37, 1896. *JAMA* 26: 794, 1896.

MURPHY, PATRICK JOSEPH, Washington, DC (b/X-10-1844 Dublin, Irel'd; d/X-3-1891) MD Georgetown 1873; AM 1873; stud Maynooth Coll, Irel'd. *Bost m&s j* 125:392, 1891. *Hist M S DC:* 300.

MURPHY, RICHARD, Milford, Mich (d/I-20-1894

Detroit) MD U Mich 1875. *JAMA* 22:122, 1894. *Polk* 1886: 499.

MURPHY, ROBERT MAURICE, Kingston, NY (d/VIII 22–1901 @52) MD Bellevue 1880. *JAMA* 37:654, 1901. *Polk* 1886: 706.

MURPHY, SAMUEL M, CW–USA (d/XI–16–1864 Bald Eagle Pa) MD Jefferson 1863. *Nat m j* 1:300, 1870/71.

MURRAY, CHARLES PEMBERTON, Lamanda Park, Cal (d/V–3–1891 @32) MD CPSNY 1879; AB Princeton 1875; AM 1878. *Med reg NY NJ Conn* 1891: 279.

MURRAY, GEORGE W, Alvaton, Ky (d/I–20–1899) MD Starling 1892. *JAMA* 32:263, 1899. *Polk* 1896: 577.

MURRAY, JABEZ WOODMAN, Machias, Me 1848–72; Lewiston 1872–74; Minneapolis 1874– (b/XII–22–1823; d/IV–20–1892) MD Bowdoin 1848. *NW med jour* 20:108, 1892. *Tr Minn St Med Soc* 1893:122.

MURRAY, JAMES, Annapolis, Md (b/1739; d/XII–17–1819) Stud med Edinburgh. *Med annals Md:* 515.

MURRAY, JAMES F, Gloversville, NY (d/XII–5–1897 @52) MD Albany 1866. *JAMA* 29:1286, 1897. *Polk* 1886: 662.

MURRAY, JOHN L, Louisville, Ky (b/1874? d/XII–19 1859 @75) MD ? *Bost m&s j* 61: 488, 1859.

MURRAY, ROBERT DRAKE [DRAY or DREW], US MarHosp Serv 1872– ; Key West, Fla (b/IV–21–1845 Ohlton O; d/XI–22–1903 Laredo Tx) MD Cleveland M C 1868; MD Jefferson 1871. *Chic m rec* 25:423, 1903. *Atknsn* I:690 *New Orl m&s j* 56:489 1903. *K&B* III:893.

MURRAY, SANFORD JAMES, NYC (b/XI–6–1847 Luzerne NY; d/III–27–1902 Hot Spr SD) MD UVt 1878. *Bost m&s j* 146:426, 1902. *Polk* 1896:1069.

MURRAY, THOMAS, Stone Fort, Ill (d/1873? @50) MD ? *Med surg rep Phila* 29: 234, 1873.

MURRAY, THOMAS WALKER, Philadelphia (d/II–25 1906 @45) MD Jefferson 1885. *Pa med jour* 9:524, 1905/06. *Polk* 1896: 1313.

MURRAY, WILLIAM, NYC (d/1862) <MD Edinburgh> *Tr AMA* 14:202, 1864. *Med reg NY NJ Conn* 1865:212.

MURRELL, THOMAS EDGAR, St Louis (b/XI–1–1850 Bolivar, Tenn; d/VI–26–1898 Denver) MD U Md 1875. *JAMA* 31: 141, 1898. *Atkinson* I: 369.

MURRELL, WILLIAM J, Mobile, Ala; Atlanta & Columbia, Ga (b/1832 Penscaola, Fla; d/V–17–1890) MD UCNY 1861; AB Princeton 1854; MD NY Homeop 1861. *Tr Med Assoc St Ala* 1891:261. *Med vis* 6:247, 1890. *Tr Am Inst Hom* 1890:149. *Polk* 1886: 136. Homeopath.

MURREY, NICHOLAS H, Nashville (d/1902) MD U Nashville 1858. *So pract* 24:141–42, 1902.

MURSICK, GEORGE ANDREW, CW–USA; Nyack, NY (b/1834; d/X–17–1895) MD CPSNY 1860. *JAMA* 25:819, 1895. *Bost m&s j* 133: 428, 1895.

MURTHA, EUGENE BERNARD, NYC (d/VIII–25–1886 @41) MD CPSNY 1869. *Med reg NY NJ Conn* 1887: 272.

MUSCROFT, CHARLES SIDNEY, Cincinnati (b/II–14 1820 Engl; d/1888?) MD Med Coll Ohio 1843. *Tr Ohio Med Soc* 1888: 7. *Atkinson* I:102. *Butler* 1878:612.

MUSGRAVE, JOHN FREEDLY, CW–USA; Swedesboro, NJ (b/Phila; d/VI–11–1891) MD UPa 1864. *U Pa med alum CW*: 1864.

MUSGRAVE, JOSEPH P, Philadelphia (d/I–3–1865) MD UPa 1831. *Med surg rep Phila* 12:236, 1864/65.

MUSGROVE, CHARLES W, McEwensville, Pa (d/VII 29–1906 @68) MD Jefferson 1879. *Pa med jour* 10:52, 1906/07.

MUSICK, J T, Pittsburg, Tex (b/Ala; d/VIII–22–1905 @61) MD Tulane 1869. *Tex st med jour* 1:154, 1905/06. *Polk* 1886: 889.

MUSSER, BENJAMIN, Strasburg, Pa (d/VII–14–1883 @63) MD Jefferson 1846. *Med surg rep Phila* 49:84, 1883. *Butler* 1878: 701.

MUSSER, FRANCIS MARTIN, Witmer, Pa (b/I–1–1850; d/IX–12–1885) MD Jefferson 1870. *Tr Pa St Med Soc* 18:243, 1886. *Butler* 1878: 725.

MUSSER, HENRY ELMER, Witmer, Pa (b/II–17–1852 Lancaster Co, Pa; d/IX–22–1906) MD Jefferson 1875. *Pa med jour* 10:169–70, 1906/07. *Flint* 1897:840.

MUSSER, MILTON B, Philadelphia (b/X–20–1846 Strasburg, Pa; d/1888) MD Jefferson 1868. *Bost m&s j* 118:282, 1888. *Atkinson* I:193. *Tr CPP* cent vol:252. *Butler* 1878: 692.

MUSSEY, FRANCIS B, Cincinnati (b/Hanover, NH; d/V 12–1900 @71) MD Med Coll Ohio 1844; AB Dartmouth 1840. *JAMA* 34: 1432, 1900. *Polk* 1896: 1166.

MUSSEY, REUBEN DIMOND, Cincinnati (b/VI–23–1780 Pelham, NH; d/VI–21–1866 Boston) MD Dartmouth 1805; AB; LLD 1854; MD UPa 1809. *Tr Ohio St Med Soc* 1867: 80–81. *Bost m&s j* 74: 451,452, 491–92, 1866. *Tr NH Med Soc* 1869:61–81. *Tr AMA* 18:347–48, 1867. *K&B* III:895–96.

MUSSEY, WILLIAM HEBERDEN, CW–USA; Cincinnati (b/IX–30–1818 Hanover, NH; d/VIII–1–1883) MD Med Coll Ohio 1848. *JAMA* 1:405, 1883. *Atkinson* I: 690–91. *K&B* III: 896.

MUSSEY, WILLIAM LINDSLEY, Cincinnati (d/IX–8–1898 France) MD Miami 1887. *JAMA* 31: 742, 1898.

MUSTARD, DAVID L, Lewes, Del (d/IV–2–1900 @64) MD Pa Med Coll 1858. *JAMA* 34: 1084, 1900. *Polk* 1886: 206.

MUSTIN, JOHN BURTON, Philadelphia (b/1844; d/V–31–1871) MD UPa 1868; AB Brown 1866. *Phila med reg & dir* 1873:303.

MUTCHLER, JOHN PACE, Stroudsburg, Pa (d/IX–29–1902) MD Jefferson 1875. *Pa med jour* 6:261, 1902/03. *Flint* 1897: 836.

MUZZY, ARTHUR THOMAS, NYC (b/X–20–1851 India;d/III–4–1902) MD CPSNY 1879; AB Amherst 1874. *Bost m&s j* 146:298, 1902. *Polk* 1896: 1069.

MYERS, FRANK F, Allegheny Pa (d/III–29–1900 @ 33)

 Spec. educ'l status abbrev. as: ***ng*** = college verified attendance without degree;

MD UPa 1890. *JAMA* 34:1146, 1900. *Polk* 1896:1262.

MYERS, HENRY K , Edinburgh, Ind (d/II–16–1900) MD U Md 1867. *JAMA* 34:574, 1900. *Polk* 1886: 806 (Lykens, Pa).

MYERS, ISAAC N , CW–USA (d/VIII–25–1862 Evansville, Ind) MD Jefferson 1862. *Med surg rep Phila* ns8: 492, 1862. *Nat med jour* 1:300, 1870/71.

MYERS, JOHN J , Winchester, Va (b/I–23–1807 Balto; d/VIII–4–1854) MD Washington Med Coll Balto 1828. *Med annals Md:* 516.

MYERS, JOHN T , CW–USA (b/Newburg, Pa; d/X–28 1867 Key West, Fla) MD UPa 1864. *U Pa med alum CW:* 1864.

MYERS, JOSEPH, NYC (b/1849; d/VI or VII–6–1871) MD UCNY 1871. *Med reg NY NJ Conn* 1872: 355.

MYERS, MILES G , Wautoma, Wis (b/1831 Lakeville, Mich; d/I–18–1880) MD Buffalo 1868. *Tr Wis St Med Soc* 1880:206; 1881:158. *Butler* 1878: 864.

MYERS, REUBEN SHERMAN, Clarence Centre, NY (b/II–24–1839 Mountville, Pa; d/IX–30–1904) MD U Vt 1875. *Tr Med Soc St NY* 1905: [362]. *Polk* 1886: 656.

MYERS, WILBUR FISKE, Franklin, Pa (d/X–4–1905 @ 44) MD UPa 1875. *Pa med jour* 9:127, 1905/06. *Flint* 1897: 802.

MYNDERSE, BARENT A , Schenectady, NY (b/VI–15 1829; d/X–2–1887) MD Albany 1853; AB Union 1849. *Tr Med Soc St NY* 1888: 546–48. *Butler* 1874: 551.

MYNTER, HERMAN, Buffalo (d/II–9–1903 @53) <MD Copenhagen 1871> lic Med Soc St NY 1875. *Bost m&s j* 148:222, 1903. *Tr Med Soc St NY* 1904: [420]. *Polk* 1896: 1011.

MYRICK, LOT, Augusta, Me (d/V–8–1863 @72) MD Dartmouth 1815. *Med s rep Phila* 10:96, 1863.

NAGLE, FRANK O , Philadelphia (b/X–3–1857; d/II–1 1884) MD UPa 1879. *Tr Pa St M S* 17:387–90, 1885. *Med bull m & s* 6:66, 1884. *Med s rep Phila* 50:255–56 1884.

NAGLE, GEORGE L , Philadelphia (d/VIII–15–1879 @74) MD Phila Coll Med & Surg 1848? *Med surg rep Phila* 41: 220, 1879.

NAGLE, HIESTER MUHLENBERG, Reading, Pa (b/ XII?–23–1824 Williamsport; d/I–30–1893) MD Jefferson 1857. *Tr Pa St Med Soc* 24:382–83, 1894. *Butler* 1878: 725.

NAGLE, ISRAEL EMAUS [sic], New Orleans; St Augustine, Fla; Winstead, Conn (d/V–16–1887 @54) MD Woodstock 1852. *New Orl m&s j* ns15: 73, 1887. *Polk* 1886: 219, 600 (Asbury Park, NJ)

NAGLE, MAURICE CORNELIUS, NYC (d/VII–31 1882 @26) MD Bellevue 1877. *Med reg NY NJ Conn* 1883: 233.

NAGLE, RICHARD JOSEPH, Dixon, Ill (b/1866; d/II–12–1905) MD CPS Chicago 1895; BS No Ill St Normal Sch. *Ill med jour* 7:302, 1905. *Polk* 1896: 416.

NALL, BURR F , Ky (d/1870 or early 1871) MD Jefferson 1861. *Med surg rep Phila* 24: 90, 1871.

NANCE, WILLIAM HARRISON, Nashville; Gunnison, Miss (d/I–26–1899) MD Bellevue 1888. *JAMA* 32: 324, 1899.

NANCREDE, JOSEPH GUERARD, Philadelphia (b/VI– –1793 Boston; d/II–2–1857) MD UPa 1813. *Phila m&s j* 5:252–53, 1857. *K&B* III: 898.

NANCREDE, SAMUEL JOSEPH GUERARD, Philadelphia (b/XII–31–1831 Washington, DC; d/II–6–1871) MD UPa 1850; AB 1848. *Med reg NY NJ Conn* 1871: 361. *K&B* III: 898 (mention).

NAPHEYS, GEORGE HENRY, Philadelphia (b/III–5–1842; d/VII–1–1876) MD Jefferson 1866. *Tr Pa St Med Soc* 1877: 719–20.

NASH, CHARLES E , Little Rock, Ark (d/1903 @70) MD Mo Med Coll 1849. *So pract* 25:475, 1903. *Polk* 1897: 194.

NASH, CRANSTON W , Nashville (d/IV–3–1895) MD U Nashvl & Vandblt 1878. *Nashvl j m & s* 77: 188, 1895.

NASH, FREDERICK, ? (d/VI–16–1861 Bonchurch Isle of Wight @34) MD CPSNY 1850; AB Columbia 1846. *Med reg NY NJ Conn* 1862: 154.

NASH, GEORGE WASHINGTON, Indianapolis (b/X–15–1835 Hendricks Co; d/VII–26–1903) MD Central Coll Phys & Surg 1888. *Tr Ind St Med Soc* 1904:360.

NASH, JOHN W , Williamsburg, Va (d/IX–21–1899 @ 73) Lic yrs pract. *JAMA* 33:927, 1899. *Polk* 1896: 1395.

NASH, JOSEPH D, Philadelphia (d/XII–9–1906 @70) MD Jeff'n 1865. *Pa m j* 10:294 1906/07. *Flint* 1897: 822.

NASH, SAMUEL ANDRIS, N Berwick, Me (b/VI–26 1840 E Raymond; d/I–5–1893) MD Bowdoin 1869. *Tr Me Med Assoc* 1893: 369–70. *Bost m&s j* 129: 44, 1893. *Butler* 1878: 309.

NASH, WILLIAM BURR, Bridgeport, Conn (b/1785? d/XII–9–1872 @87) Hon MD Yale 1852. *Med surg rep Phila* 27: 542, 1872.

NASSAU, WILLIAM W , CW–USA; Burlington, Ia (b/IV–11–1832 Montgomery Co, Pa; d/V–23–1891) MD UPa 1855; AB Lafayette 1832. *Bost m&s j* 124: 546, 1891. *Tr Ia St Med Soc* 1892: 228. *Polk* 1890: 401.

NAU, J H , Carroll, O (d/XII–5–1875) MD Miami 1872. *Tr Ohio St Med Soc* 1876:92–93.

NAUDAIN, ARNOLD [S ?], Dover, Del (b/I–6–1790 Snowland; d/I–4–1872 Odessa) MD UPa 1810; AB Princeton 1807. *Tr AMA* 30:829–31 1879. *Med S Del*:39.

NAUDAIN, ARNOLD, NYC (d/IV–16–1899 @68) MD U Pa 1852. *JAMA* 32: 956, 1899. *Polk* 1896: 1070.

NAVITY [MAVITY], JAMES S , Fowler, Ind (b/II–19 1845 Ripley Co; d/IV–21–1901) MD Hospital Med Coll Louisville 1884; att Ind Med Coll 1870–71. *Tr Ind St Med Soc* 1901: 491. *Polk* 1886: 319.

NAYLOR, WALTER WILLIAMS, Philadelphia (d/XII–17–1905) MD UPa 1889. *Pa med jour* 9:280, 1905/06. *Flint* 1897: 822.

NAYLOR, WILLIAM HAMILTON, NYC (d/IX–20–

1887 @34) MD UCNY 1879. *Med reg NY NJ Conn* 1888: 265. *Polk* 1886: 688.

NAYLOR, WILLIAM LOVEJOY, Washington, DC (b/V–20–1844; d/VI–3–1890) MD U Md 1869. *Hist Med Soc DC:* 305. *Polk* 1886: 213.

NEAL, JOHN GEORGE, Santa Rosa, Cal (b/Ky; d/X–11 1903) MD Kentucky Sch Med 1890. *Cal st jour med* 1: 385, 1903.

NEAL, THOMAS L , CW–USA; Dayton, O (b/IX–9–1830 Mechanicsburg; d/II–12–1885) MD Miami 1854. *Tr Ohio St Med Soc* 1885: 209–10.

NEAL, VANDY M , Forest Co, Miss (d/XII–20–1905 @ c70) MD Tulane 1860. *New Orl m&s j* 58:683, 1906. *Polk* 1896: 810.

NEALE, BENNETT ALOYSIUS, Baltimore (b/III–6–1815 Port Tobacco, Md; d/II–13–1878) MD U Md 1838. *Med annals Md:* 517. *Butler* 1874: 314.

NEALE, FRANCIS C , NYC (d/I–17–1895 @60) MD U Md 1852. *JAMA* 24:177, 1895. *Polk* 1886: 438 (Balto).

NEALIS, WILLIAM THOMAS, NYC (b/II–12–1841; d/I–15–1879) MD CPSNY 1862; AB St Joseph's Coll, O 1858; AM 1860. *Med reg NY NJ Conn* 1879: 195.

NEALL, SAMUEL W , Philadelphia (d/III–29–1884 @ 76) MD ? *Med surg rep Phila* 50: 512, 1884.

NEALS, J J , Mill Creek, Pa (d/VII–2? –1874) MD ? *Med surg rep Phila* 31:100, 1874.

NEBINGER, ANDREW Jr, Philadelphia; CW–USA (b/XII–12–1819; d/IV–12–1886) MD UPa 1850. *Tr CPP* cent vol: 252. *Atkinson* I: 34–35. *Med surg rep Phila* 54: 544, 1886. *Butler* 1878: 693.

NEBINGER, GEORGE WASHINGTON, CW–USA (b/VII–23–1824 Phila; d/III–8–1868 Phila) MD UPa 1862. *Phila m reg & dir* 1871: 293. *U Pa med alum CW*: 1862.

NEEDHAM, JOHN GREGORY, Pawtucket, RI (b/IV–7 1801 Walpole, Mass; d/VIII–29–1867) MD Brown 1824; AB 1821. *Brown hist cat*: 1821.

NEEDHAM, WILLIAM C H , Gallipolis, O (b/1845 Gorton, Mass; d/1882) MD Jefferson 1868. *Bost m&s j* 106:72, 1882. *Butler* 1878: 642.

NEELY, SHAW FREW, CW–USA; Leavenworth, Kans (b/IV–18–1842 Lancaster Co, Pa; d/VII–20–1906) MD UPa 1865; MD Pa M C 1861. *U Pa med alum CW*: 1865.

NEFF, CHARLES, Philadelphia (d/IX–20–1871 @47) MD Jefferson 1852; ng Amherst 1843. *Phila med reg & dir* 1873: 303.

NEFF, CHARLES WESLEY, Baltimore (b/I–22–1838 Frostburg, Md; d/I–17–1900) MD UCNY 1864; AB Dickinson 1861. *JAMA* 34: 251, 1900. *Polk* 1886: 438.

NEFF, HENRY K , Huntingdon, Pa (d/II–21–1868) MD Jefferson 1851. *Phila med reg & dir* 1871: 295. *Med surg rep Phila* 18: 203, 1868.

NEFF, HENRY SAGENDORPH, Bethayres, Pa (b/Phila; d/VI–22–1895) MD Hahnemann Phila 1894. *Hahn mo* 30:145, 1895; 31:104 (news & advt) 1896.

NEFF, PETER D , Centre Hall, Pa (b/XI–23–1816 Cedar Spring; d/IV–7–1886) MD Jefferson 1848. *Tr Pa St Med Soc* 13: 259–60, 1880.

NEFTEL, WILLIAM BASIL, NYC (b/IX–22–1830 Russia; d/I–20–1906) <MD Petersburg 1852> *Bost m&s j* 154: 142, 1906. *Atkinson* I: 309.

NEGLEY, W H , Dayton, O (d/I–5–1898) <MD Miami 1886> *JAMA* 30:166, 1898.

NEIDECKER, GEORGE WILLIAM, Brooklyn (d/VII–17–1899 @38) MD LICH 1889 *Bost m&s j* 141:99 1899.

NEIDHARD, CHARLES, Philadelphia (b/1809 Bremen, Gny; d/IV–17–1895) MD Allentown Acad 1837. *Hahn mo* 30:66–67, 80–81, (news & advt) 1895. *Tr Am Inst Hom* 1895: 229. *Cleave*. Homeopath.

NEILL, BENJAMIN DUFFIELD, Philadelphia (b/1811; d/1872) MD UPa 1833. *Tr CPP* cent vol:252. *K&B* III:898.

NEILL, HENRY, Philadelphia (b/III–12–1783; d/X–7–1845) MD UPa 1807. *Tr CPP* cent vol: 253, 2:320–23, 1846/49. *Tr AMA* 3:453–54, 1850. *K&B* II:898.

NEILL, JOHN, Philadelphia; CW–USA (b/VII–9–1819; d/II–11–1880) MD UPa 1840; AB 1837. *Tr CPP* cent vol:253; 3s5: clxi–clvi, 1881. *Med s rep Phila* 42:176, 1880. *Bost m&s j* 102: 208–09, 1880. *K&B* III: 899.

NEILSON, JOHN L , Boston; USN (d/IX–1–1898 @53) MD Med Coll Ohio 1866. *JAMA* 31: 672–73, 1898.

NEILSON, ROBERT, Pleasant Unity, Pa (b/III–26–1817 Irel'd; d/XII–30–1860) MD Jefferson 1850. *Tr Pa St Med Soc* 1862: 136–37.

NEILSON, WILLIAM, Salem, Mass (d/V–2/3–1889 @ 80) MD Harvard 1855. *Bost m&s j* 120: 476, 1889; 121: 645, 1889. *Butler* 1878: 354.

NEILSON, WILLIAM HOWARD, New Rochelle, NY (b/1858 New Brunswick, NJ; d/VII–6–1899) MD Bellevue 1891. *JAMA* 33:174, 1899. *Bost m&s j* 141: 52, 1899. *Polk* 1896: 1034.

NELAN, JAMES ROLAN, Pittsburgh (d/III–28–1901 @50) MD UPa 1877. *Pa med jour* 5:296, 314, 1901/02; 6:261, 1902/03. *Polk* 1886: 794.

NELDEN, CHARLES R Stanhope, NJ (d/V–2–1897 @55) MD Bellevue 1864. *JAMA* 28:1045,1897. *Polk* 1896: 949.

NELLIS, ALEXANDER Jr, Willard, NY (b/II–11–1847; d/XII–27–1893) MD Albany 1872. *Med reg NY NJ Conn* 1894: 244. *Polk* 1886: 716.

NELSON, ALDEN E , ?NYC (d/III–22–1864) MD UCNY 1862. *Med reg NY NJ Conn* 1865: 225.

NELSON, BENJAMIN DAY, Wyoming, Va (b/V–15–1810 Bleak Hill; d/VI–21–1846) MD UPa 1836; AB Amherst 1831. *Amherst, Men of*: 1831.

NELSON, DANIEL E, Chattanooga (b/1859; d/1905 @47) MD Vanderbilt 1882; MD U Nashville 1883. *So pract* 28:702–03, 1905. *Nashvl j m&s* 97: 563–64, 1905.

NELSON, DAVID BATCHELDER, Laconia, NH (b/VI–7–1823 Roxbury; d/VII–5 or IX–9–1898) MD Harvard 1849. *JAMA* 31:141, 1898. *Tr NH Med Soc* 1899:292–

 Spec. educ'l status abbrev. as: ***ng*** = college verified attendance without degree;

93. *Polk* 1896: 920.

NELSON, G W H, CW-USA (d/IX-17-1865) MD ? *Nat med jour* 1:300, 1870/71.

NELSON, HUGH THOMAS, Charlottesville, Va (d/III-26-1906) MD U Va 1875. *So pract* 28:355-56, 1906. *Flint* 1897: 935.

NELSON, JAMES BARNES, NYC (b/IX-14-1813; d/IX 28-1874) MD CPSNY 1837. *Med reg NY NJ Conn* 1875: 201.

NELSON, JAMES W, Winnetka, Ill (d/XII-5-1893) MD NWU 1886. *Chic med rec* 5:452, 1893. *Polk* 1890: 354.

NELSON, JOHN A, CW-CSA (b/I-3-1836; d/X-12-1863) MD Jefferson 1857; stud UVa. Johnson, *U [Va] memorials...alum CW*:492. Blanton, *Va surgs CW*:411.

NELSON, JUDSON CALEB, CW-USA; Truxton NY (b/VI-3-1824 Danby; d/VII-11-1895) MD Geneva 1848. *Tr Med Soc St NY* 1896: 440-41. *Polk* 1886: 712.

NELSON, ROBERT, NYC (b/I or VIII-1794 Montreal; d/III-1-1873 Staten Isl, NYC) MD ? *Med reg NY NJ Conn* 1873:344. *Med rec* 8:144, 1873. *Med surg rep Phila* 28: 256, 1873. *K&B* III: 900.

NELSON, ROBERT WESLEY, Walkersville Md (d/IV-28-1863) MD UPa 1846. *Med s rep Phila* 10:96, 1863.

NELSON, SAMUEL NEWELL, Revere, Mass (d/II-25 1893 @36) MD Harvard 1882; AB 1878. *Bost m&s j* 128:228, 1893.

NELSON, THOMAS C, Clinton Miss (d/1834) MD Transylvania 1830. *Transylv j m & ass sci* 7:427-28, 1834.

NELSON, WILLIAM, Danville, Va (b/1852 Hanover Co; d/IV-5-1899) MD U Va 1881. *JAMA* 32:845, 1899. *Polk* 1893: 1257.

NELSON, WILLIAM ARMISTEAD, USN 1839-54; CSA; NYC (b/IV-18-1818 Petersburg, Va; d/VI-5-1902 Arnold Station, Mo) MD UPa 1839. *Bost m&s j* 146:678, 1902. *U Pa med alum CW*: 1839.

NELSON, WILLIAM WHEELOCK, Taberg, NY (d/VII 22-1899 @36) MD UCNY 1888. *JAMA* 33:367, 1899. *Polk* 1886: 711.

NELSON, WILLIAM Y, CW-USA (d/VI-26-1864 Kingston, Ga) MD ? *Nat med jour* 1:300, 1870/71.

NES, CHARLES M, York, Pa 36 yrs (d/VI-12-1896 @69) <MD Columbian DC 1845> *JAMA* 26:1278, 1896. *Polk* 1890: 1022.

NESBIT, LOUIS ROBERT, CW-CSA (b/VIII-16-1836 Athens, Ala; d/V-1-1862 Shiloh, Tenn) MD UPa 1860. *U Pa med alum CW*: 1860.

NESBITT, GEORGE WASHINGTON, Sycamore, Ill (d/IV-24-1894 @46) MD Buffalo 1866. *Buffalo m&s j* 33:693, 1894. *Tr Ill St M S* 1894: . *Butler* 1878: 170.

NESMITH, ROBERT DILLON, CW-USA; NYC (d/XII 23-1880 @ 40) MD UCNY 1863; AB Columbia 1860. *Med reg NY NJ Conn* 1881: 239.

NESMITH, W J, ? (d/1878 Warren Co, Miss) MD U La 1870. *Tr AMA* 30: 880, 1879.

NETHERTON, ROBERT T, Taylorsville, Ky (d/III-7-1866 @35) MD ? *Med surg rep Phila* 14: 479, 1866.

NETTLES, RICHARDSON CLARKE, Marlin, Tex (b/IV-4-1842 SC; d/V-6-1897) MD SC Med Coll 1867. *Tex st med jour* 13:246-48, 1897-98. *Polk* 1886: 890.

NEUHAUS [NEWHAUS], CHARLES F, Brooklyn; CW USA (d/VII-26-1866 @48) MD Berlin 1846. *Med surg rep Phila* 15:132, 1866. *Nat med jour* 1:300, 1870/71.

NEUMER, EMIL, NYC (d/XI-4-1890) MD Bellevue 1879. *Med reg NY NJ Conn* 1891: 279.

NEVIN, HENRY WILLIAM, Brooklyn (d/IX-1-1891 @ 35) MD Bellevue 1878; AB St Francis Xavier 1872; AM 1875. *Med reg NY NJ Conn* 1892:284. *Polk* 1886:648.

NEVIN, JOSEPH PIERCE, Easton, Pa (b/X-24-1851 Shippensburg; d/III-17-1878) MD UPa 1875; AB Lafayette 1874. *Tr Pa St Med Soc* 12:309, 1878.

NEVINS, JOHN C, Summit Hill, Pa (d/X-28-1903 @ 64) MD Jefferson 1874. *Pa med jour* 7: 280, 1903/04. *Flint* 1897: 837.

NEW, GEORGE WASHINGTON, Indianapolis (b/II-27 1819 Madison; d/IV-10-1891) MD Med Coll Ohio 1840. *Tr Ind St Med Soc* 1891: 286.

NEWBERRY, JOHN STRONG, New Haven, Conn (b/XII-22-1822 Windham; d/XII-7-1892) MD Cleveland Med Coll 1848; AM, LLD Western Reserve. *Bost m&s j* 127: 585, 588, 1892. *K&B* III: 901-02.

NEWBERRY, JOSEPH ALLEN, Clio, Ala (d/XII-10-1890) MD U Ala 1887. *Tr Med Assoc St Ala* 1891: 260.

NEWBOLD, THOMAS, Philadelphia (b/III-14-1829; d/XII-28-1873) MD UPa 1852; AB 1848; AM 1852. *Med surg rep Phila* 30: 66, 1874.

NEWBY, GEORGE RAYSON, NYC (d/III-2-1892 @ 31) MD CPSNY 1888. *Med reg NY NJ Conn* 1892: 284.

NEWCOMB, DARWIN ERASMUS, Carleton, Mich (d/IX-10 or 16-1901) MD Detroit Med Coll 1885; att U Mich Med Dept 1867-68. *JAMA* 37:848, 1901. *Polk* 1886: 485.

NEWCOMB, GEORGE, Quincy, Ill (b/I-21-1811 Braintree, Mass; d/X-18-1859) MD Harvard 1835; AB Amherst 1832. *Amherst, Men of*: 1832.

NEWCOMB, ROLAND B C, Blissfield, Mich (d/VI-2 1881 @58) MD Starling 1848. *Mich m news* 4:168, 1881.

NEWCOMER, DAVID, Mt Morris, Ill (d/X-19-1900) MD Jefferson 1859 *Ill m j* ns2:286 1900. *Polk* 1896:431.

NEWCOMER, FRISBY SNIVELY, Indianapolis; CW-USA (b/XII-10-1828 Hagerstown, Md; d/IX-13-1889 Lake Bluff, Ill) MD UPa 1851; AB Franklin & Marshall 1848. *Tr Ind St Med Soc* 1890: 157. *Butler* 1878:214.

NEWCOMET, HENRY WALBORN, Philadelphia (b/VI 20-1838 Crosskill Mills, Pa; d/VI-3-1885 St Louis) MD UPa 1865; att Franklin & Marshall. *Med surg rep Phila* 52:768, 1885. *Butler* 1878: 668.

NEWELL, AZARIAH D, New Brunswick, NJ (d/III-9 1895) MD UPa 1838. *Bost m&s j* 132:266, 1895.

NEWELL, HENRY EDWARD, Derry, NH (b/III-12-

1851 Nashua; d/II-24-1903) MD LICH 1873. *Tr NH Med Soc* 1903: 241. *Polk* 1896: 918.

NEWELL, ROBERT WINGATE, Boston (d/IV-9-1896 @81) MD Harvard 1845. *Bost m&s j* 134: 404, 1896. *Polk* 1890: 541.

NEWELL, SELIM, Lyndon, Vt (d/I-28-1881) <MD Dartmouth 1835> *Tr Vt Med Soc* 1883: 107.

NEWELL, TIMOTHY, Providence, RI (b/III-29-1820 Sturbridge, Mass; d/VI-20-1901) MD Woodstock 1850; att Brown. *Tr RI Med Soc* 1899-1901: 402-05. *Atkinson* I: 71. *Polk* 1896: 1352.

NEWELL, WILLIAM AUGUSTUS, Allentown, NJ (b/ 1817 Ohio; d/VIII-8-1901) MD UPa 1839; AB Rutgers 1836. *JAMA* 37: 460, 1901. *Atkinson* I: 677. *Polk* 1886: 932 (Olympia, Wash).

NEWELL, WILLIAM DUNHAM, Imlaystown, NJ (b/II 20-1823; d/XI-22-1869) MD Columbian DC 1844. *Phila m reg & dir* 1871: 302. *Tr M S NJ* 1870: 83; 1871: 98-100.

NEWHALL, EDWARD L , Lynn, Mass (d/VI-15-1905 @83) MD Harvard 1848. *Bost m&s j* 152: 712, 1905. *Polk* 1896: 717.

NEWHALL, HORATIO, Galena, Ill (b/1797? d/1870 @ 73) MD Harvard 1821; AM 1817; Hon AM Beloit. *Bost m&s j* 6:212, 227, 1870.

NEWHALL, THOMAS KENDALL, Providence, RI (b/ XII-23-1817 Turner, Me; d/VI-21-1900 Edgewood) MD Harvard 1846. *Tr RI Med Soc* 6:259-60, 1899-1903. *Polk* 1896: 1350.

NEWING, WILLIAM EDWARD, Long Branch, NJ (d/ VII-11-1895 @29) MD CPSNY 1888. *JAMA* 25:298, 1895.

NEWKIRK, ABRAM F , Wilmington, NC (d/I-25-1891 @69) MD UCNY 1844. *NC med jour* 27:113, 1891. *Polk* 1886: 727.

NEWKIRK, JACOB, Roxbury & Binghamton, NY (d/ VIII-13-1894 @89) MD Fairfield 1830. *Med reg NY NJ Conn* 1895: 233. *JAMA* 23: 479, 1894.

NEWKIRK, NATHANIEL REEVES, Greenwich, NJ 1852-59; Bridgeton 1859- (b/VII-22-1817; d/XI-10-1866) MD UPa 1843; AB Lafayette 1840. *Tr M S NJ* 1867:208-09; 1871:172-73. *Med s rep Phil* 16:15 1867.

NEWLAND, BENJAMIN, Bedford, Ind (b/VII-19-1821 Jackson Co; d/IV-5-1889) MD U Louisville 1847. *Tr Ind St M S* 1889: 216. *Butler* 1878: 214.

NEWLAND, JAMES HARVEY, Valparaiso, Ind (b/XII-9-1820 Lawrence Co; d/VI-21-1889) MD Chicago Med Coll 1869. *Tr Ind St M S* 1890:152. *Butler* 1878: 214.

NEWLAND, T J, Ellensburg, Wash (d/XI-20-1899 @40) MD Willamette 1884. *JAMA* 33:1441, 1899. *Polk* 1896: 1512.

NEWMAN, JAMES BARBOUR, Great Falls, Mont; Ashland, Ore (d/VIII-13-1893) MD U Md 1868. *JAMA* 21: 357, 1893. *Polk* 1890: 944.

NEWMAN, JAMES C , Miss (d/X-6-1878 Vicksburg, Miss) MD ? *Tr AMA* 30:80, 1879.

NEWMAN, JAMES FREELAND, Gorham, Me (b/IV-30-1845 Canton; d/V-10-1890) MD Bowdoin 1873. *Tr Me Med Assoc* 1890:340-41. *Butler* 1878: 309.

NEWMAN, JOSEPH CHAMBERS, ?Nashville (b/1818; d/X- -1870) MD Louisville Med Coll 1840 [!] *Nashvl j m & s* ns6: 238-40, 1870.

NEWMAN, S T , St Louis (b/XI-30-1816; d/VII-15-1883) MD Transylvania 1839. *JAMA* 1:128, 1883. *Butler* 1878: 41.

NEWMAN, WILLIAM,Brooklyn (b/Eng; d/XII-31-1896 @76) Hon MD NY St Univ 1847? *Bost m&s j* 136:22, 1897. *JAMA* 28:139,1897. *Polk* 1897, 1001.

NEWMAN, WILLIAM GEORGE HENRY, Washington, DC (b/III-17-1827 Pr Anne Md; d/XI-6-1883) MD U Md 1849. *JAMA* 1:603-04, 1883. *Hist M S DC:* 259. *Med surg rep Phila* 49:560,1883. *Butler* 1878: 95.

NEWMARK, VALENTINE, Benicia Cal (b/Prussia;d/ XI -21-1889 @50) MD Toland 1868. *Tr M S Cal* 20:329, 1880.

NEWNAN, JOHN, Nashville (b/c1770 Salisbury, NC; d/c 1825-1827 Nashville) MD UPa 1793? *Tr Med Soc Tenn* 1876: 85.

NEWS, ANNE, NYC; Newport, RI (b/X-13-1846 Croton, NJ; d/II-7-1896) MD U Mich 1872. *JAMA* 26: 340, 1896. *Tr RI Med Soc* 5: 365, 1894-98.

NEWTON, ADIN HUBBARD, Everett, Mass (d/VII-7-1904 @87) Lic Mass Med Soc? *Bost m&s j* 151:56, 1904. *Polk* 1886: 471.

NEWTON, FRANK BROWNLIE, Stafford Springs, Conn (b/XII-23-1874; d/II-19-1903) MD U Vt 1899. *Proc Conn Med Soc* 1903: 415-16.

NEWTON, GEORGE M , Augusta, Ga (b/I-6-1859) MD UPa 1833. *Tr AMA* 13:819, 1860. *So m&s j* 20:142-44, 1859. *Buff m&s j* 14:703, 1859. *Med s rep Phila* ns1: 302, 1858/59.

NEWTON, LEWIS E , Washington, DC (b/IX-3-1840 DC; d/II-3-1889) MD Georgetown 1868. *Hist Med Soc DC:* 302. *Polk* 1886: 213.

NEWTON, ROBERT, MexWar-USA; Philadelphia (d/ VIII-9-1848 New Orleans) MD UPa 1845; AM Lafayette 1842. *Lafayette, Men of*: 150. *Heitman*.

NEWTON, ROBERT SAFFORD, NYC (b/1858 Cincinnati; d/III-26-1903) MD Ecl Med Coll NY 1876. *Bost m&s j* 148: 382, 1903. Eclectic.

NEWTON, THOMAS, Va; CW-CSA (b/II-2-1816 Norfolk; d/III-3-1862 or 1864) MD UPa 1838; att U Va 1834-35. *U Pa med alum CW*: 1838. Johnson, *U \[Va] Mem'l..alum d/CW*: 279. Blanton, *Va surg CW*: 1838.

NEWTON, WILLIAM T , Indianapolis, Ind (b/IV-12-1854 Sugarbranch; d/X-21-1900) MD Med Coll Ohio 1876. *Tr Ind St Med Soc* 1901: 495. Kemper's *Indiana*: 321. *Polk* 1886: 321.

NICHOL, WILLIAM LYTLE, USN 1852-55; CSA 1861-65; Nashville (b)X-8-1828; d/VI-23-1901) MD

 Spec. educ'l status abbrev. as: ***ng*** = college verified attendance without degree;

UPa 1849; AB U Nashville 1845. *JAMA* 37?:43, 1901. *So pract* 23: 369–70, 1901. *U Pa m alum CW*:1849. *Butler* 1878: 775.

NICHOLAS, CHARLES EARL, Clayville, RI (b/1825 Coventry; d/II–24–1863) MD UCNY 1851. *Tr RI Med Soc* 1:210–12, 1859–77.

NICHOLAS, HENRY, North Bay, NY (d/II–10–1900) Cert by Exam Bd. *JAMA* 34: 574, 1900. *Polk* 1896:1087.

NICHOLAS, JAMES, NJ (b/I–30–1815; d/I–17–1849) MD CPSNY 1839. *Tr Med Soc NJ* 1867: 129–30.

NICHOLLS, BENJAMIN FRANKLIN, CW–CSA; Childersburg, Ala (b/IV–25–1821 Spartanburg, SC; d/V–19–1884) MD U Pa 1842. *U Pa med alum CW*: 1842.

NICHOLLS, WILLIAM CHARLES, Newberne, Ala CW–CSA (b/I 13–1833; d/I–31–1871) <MD U La 1858; AB UNC 1854> att U Ala 1849. *U Ala cat*: 102. *SHSP* 22:242, 1893.

NICHOLS, CHARLES HENRY, NYC; Washington DC; CW–USA (b/X–19–1820 Vassalboro Me; d/XII–16 1889 NYC) MD UPa 1843; Hon AM Union; LLD Columbia. *Med reg NY NJ Conn* 1890:277. *JAMA* 14: 35, 1890. *Bost m&s j* 121:646,1889. *K&B* III: 902–03.

NICHOLS, ELIAS S , LI, NY (b/IV–23–1801; d/XI–5–1880) MD Castl'n 1846. *Med reg NY NJ Conn* 1881: 239.

NICHOLS, GEORGE BURRITT, San Luis Obispo, Cal (b/XI–28–1841 Augusta, Ga; d/1905) MD LICH 1871. *Cal st jour med* 3:410, 1905.

NICHOLS, GEORGE HENRY, Boston (b/VIII–26–1815 Portland, Me; d/II–5–1890) MD UPa 1836; AB Harvard 1833. *Bost m&s j* 122:168, 1890.

NICHOLS, HAYDN, Brooklyn (b/XI–28–1832 Wilton, Conn; d/III–4–1899 @62) MD LICH 1883. *Bost m&s j* 140:246, 1899. *JAMA* 32:563, 1899.

NICHOLS, HORACE, Osage, Ia (d/VI–23–1898 @ c/66) MD Rush 1866. *JAMA* 31:142,1898. *Polk* 1886: 365.

NICHOLS, ISAAC A , Newark, NJ (b/II–24–1828; d/XI 22–1880) MD CPSNY 1850. *Tr Med Soc NJ* 1881:137–38. *Bost m&s j* 103:576, 1880.

NICHOLS, JAMES, Bradford, Pa (d/II–16–1895 @70) MD Buffalo 1864. *Buffalo m&s j* 34: 501, 1895. *JAMA* 24: 337, 1895.

NICHOLS, JAMES EPHRAIM H , NYC (d/IX–10–1898 @41 Sapphire, NC) MD CPSNY 1885; AB Rochester 1878. *Bost m&s j* 139: 354, 1898. *JAMA* 31:742, 1898. *Tr Med Soc St NY*: 1899. *Polk* 1896: 1070.

NICHOLS, JAMES ROBINSON, Haverhill, Mass (b/VII–19–1819 W Amesbury; d/I–2–1888) MD Dartmouth 1867; AM 1867. *Bost m&s j* 118:26, 27, 28, 1888; 119: 232, 1888. *K&B* III: 903–04.

NICHOLS, JOHN H , Wapakoneta, O (d/I–9–1899 @55) MD Med Coll Ohio 1872. *JAMA* 32:196, 1899. *Polk* 1886: 772.

NICHOLS, JOHN S , ? (d/I–15–1862 @36) MD ? *Tr Am Inst Hom* 1867:158. *Mass Homeop Soc* 1890: (Sept). Homeopath.

NICHOLS, JOSEPH, Springfield, NH (b/XII–24–1796; d/V–18–1853) ng Dartmouth 1819. *Bost m&s j* 49: 98–100, 1854.

NICHOLS, JOSEPH DEAN, Taunton, Mass (d/V–26 1879 @77) MD Harvard 1841. *Bost m&s j* 101:496 1879

NICHOLS, LEMUEL BLISS, Worcester, Mass (b/X–6–1816 Bradford, NH; d/IX–28–1883) MD Phila Coll Med & Surg 1850; AB Brown 1842. *Tr Am Inst Hom* 1884: 655. *King* I: 234. Homeopath.

NICHOLS, PAUL LEWIS, Kingston, Mass (b/V–24–1823; d/IV–28–1852) MD Harvard 1849; AM 1845. Palmer's *Necrol Harv alum*: 9.

NICHOLS, S H , Bloomingdale, NY (d/XII–17–1889) MD ? *Med surg rep Phila* 61: 726, 1889.

NICHOLS, STELLA BLANCHE H , Corning, NY (d/IX–30–1898 @63) MD Chicago Woman's Med Coll 1882. *JAMA* 31: 942, 1898. *Polk* 1890: 319.

NICHOLS, THOMAS BRAINERD, Plattsburgh, NY (b/III–21–1817 Enosburg, Vt; d/X–3–1899) MD Castleton 1850; AB U Vt 1853; AM 1856. *Tr Med Soc St NY* 1900: 431. *Polk* 1886: 701.

NICHOLS, WHITFIELD, NJ (b/II–6–1807; d/XII–9–1851) <MD Rutgers 1829; MD Geneva> AB Princeton 1825. *Tr Med Soc NJ* 1867: 130–31.

NICHOLS [NICOLS], WILLIAM HENRY, Rockford, Ia (b/XII–28–1845 Harpers Ferry, Va; d/XI–18–1886) MD Iowa St U 1872. *Tr Ia St Med Soc* 7:524–25, 1888–89. *Polk* 1886: 367.

NICHOLSON, E G , Del Rio, Tex (d/II–3–1893) MD Tulane 1870. *Tex cour–rec med* 10:209, 1893. *Polk* 1886: 884. *Daniel's Tex jour med* 8:335, 1892–93.

NICHOLSON, JOHN, CW–USA (d/VIII–1–1862 Washington, DC) MD Jefferson 1861. *Nat m j* 1:300, 1870/71.

NICHOLSON, JOHN COGBURN, CW–CSA; Mt Meigs, Ala (b/VIII–1830 Haywood, Tenn; d/1902?) MD Jefferson 1855. *Tr M Assn St Ala* 1902:130. *Polk* 1893: 160.

NICHOLSON, WILLIAM, Washington, DC; Mass 1896– (b/V–16–1853 Camden, Ark; d/X–5–1896) MD Columbian 1879. *Hist Med Soc DC:* 314.

NICHTERN, PONCE MARIE, Brooklyn (d/I–26–1887 @75) MD CPSNY 1846 *Med reg NY NJ Conn* 1887:272.

NICKELSON [NICHOLSON], CLARK A , Beekman, NY (d/1888) MD UCNY 1847. *Tr Med Soc St NY* 1889: 364. *Polk* 1886: 641.

NICKERSON, ASA HARDEN, Central Falls, RI (b/VII–1–1854 So Dennis, Mass; d/IV–28–1897) MD Harvard 1882. *Bost m&s j* 137: 263, 1897. *Tr RI Med Soc* 5:498–99, 1894–98. *Polk* 1896: 1350.

NICOLL, LEONARD FRANCIS, NYC (d/XI–25–1906 @30) MD Columbia 1903; AB Harvard 1899. *Bost m&s j* 155: 698, 1906.

NICOLL, SAMUEL BENJAMIN, Shelter Isl, NY (d/I–4 1899 @73) MD CPSNY 1852; AB UCNY 1848. *JAMA* 32: 92, 1899. *Polk* 1896: 1100.

NICOLSEN, WILLIAM L , Fort Dodge, Ia (d/1892) MD Ia CPS Des Moines 1883. *Tr Ia St M S* 18: 411, 1900. *Polk* 1890: 415.

NIELSEN, NIELS JULIUS, Chicago (d/IV-17-1895) MD Chic Med Coll 1878. *Chic med rec* 8:393, 1895. *Polk* 1886: 268.

NIGHTINGALE, HENRY B , Rosemont, NJ (d/IX-10 1873 @ c50) MD Jefferson 1850. *Tr AMA* 25: 527, 1874. *Med surg rep Phila* 29: 270, 1873. *Tr M S NJ* 1874: 109.

NIGHTINGALE [NIGHTENGALE], JOHN, San Francisco (d/VI-3-1900 @45) MD Cooper 1875. *JAMA* 34: 1574, 1900.

NIGHTINGALE, LIONEL BRYDGES, Engl; NYC (d/ III-14-1889) <MD King's Coll Hosp London 1865> *Med reg NY NJ Conn* 1889: 279. *Polk* 1886: 648.

NIGLAS, JOHN N , Peoria, Ill (b/1819 Austria; d/III-3 1890) MD Rush 1854. *Tr Ill St M S* 1890:38. *Butler* 1878: 171.

NILES, AUGUSTUS, Wellsboro, Pa (d/VII-23-1906 @ 52) MD Bennett 1875. *Pa med jour* 9: 805, 1905/06. *Polk* 1896: 1343. Eclectic.

NILES, DANIEL WATERHOUSE, Worcester, Mass (b/I-28-1826 Portland, Me; d/VII-17-1890) MD Dartmouth 1880. *Bost m&s j* 123:96, 1890. *Polk* 1886:476.

NILES, HARRY HALE, Post Mills, Vt (b/X-1-1807 W Fairlee; d/I-28-1881) <MD Dartmouth> *Tr Vt M S*: 1883, 107.

NILES, WILLIAM GORDON, Philadelphia (d/III-16-1906) MD Jefferson 1904. *Pa med jour* 9:524, 1905/06.

NIMAN, CHARLES HENRY, Elkhart, Ind (b/IV-1-1855 Lagrange; d/I-14-1904) MD Bellevue 1880. *Tr Ind St Med Soc* 1905: 455. *Polk* 1896: 465.

NIMAN, JONAS POLLARD, Lagrange, Ind (b/XII-7-1828 Mansfield, O; d/VII-19-1888) MD Ft Wayne 1882; att Starling 1850. *Tr Ind St Med Soc* 1889: 209. *Polk* 1886: 325.

NIMS, DWIGHT BOYDEN, Jackson, Mich (b/IX-12-1808 Conway, Mass; d/IV-15-1879) MD Berkshire 1833. *Tr AMA* 31:1080, 1880. *Mich med news* 2:142, 1879. *Atkinson* I: 392.

NISBET, JOHN N, Waxhaw NC (b/1823;d/VIII/IX 1899) MD Med Coll SC 1847. *NC med jour* 44: 153, 1899.

NISBET, JOHN YOUNG, Jacksonville, Ala (d/I- -1888) MD U Louisville 1854. *Tr Med Assoc St Ala* 1888: 315. *Polk* 1886: 135.

NIVER, C , Ancram, NY (d/I-31-1867 @52) MD ? *Bost m&s j* 76:48, 1867.

NIVISON, MARK, NYC (d/V-19-1899 @61) <MD Eclectic Med Coll NY 1874> *JAMA* 32:1399, 1899. *Polk* 1886: 689. Eclectic.

NIXON, ALEXANDER B , CW-USA; Sacramento (b/III 1-1820 Butler Co, O; d/XI-1-1889) MD Ohio Med Coll 1846; att Miami. *Tr Med Soc Calif* 20:327-28, 1890. *Atkinson* I: 113. *Butler* 1878: 61.

NIXON, FRANCIS MARION, Guntersville, Ala (d/IX-24-1889) MD ? *Tr Med Assoc St Ala* 1890: 217. *Polk* 1886: 133.

NIXON, J L , Troy, Ala (d/I-21-1859) MD ? *Bost m&s j* 60:48, 1859.

NIXON, U H , Monterey Mex; Killeen Tex 189_- (b/XI 21-1864 Campbellton, Ga; d/XI-11-1903) <MD Barnes 1893> att Galveston Med Coll. *Tex st m j* 1:244, 1906.

NIXON, WILLIAM CADDIS, Shannon, Ga (d/I-13-1898 @55) MD U Va 1870. *JAMA* 30: 279, 1898. *Polk* 1886: 233.

NIXON, WILLIAM GOODWYN, CW-CSA; Uniontown, Ala (b/ XII-20-1834 Pichula, Miss; d/X-23-1902) MD UPa 1855. *U Pa med alum CW*: 1855. *Polk* 1886: 140.

NOBLE, FRANCIS E, Jersey City (b/1824 NY; d/VI-29 1899) MD Western Reserve 1851. *Bost m&s j* 141: 28, 1899. *JAMA* 33:175, 1899. *Polk* 1886: 605.

NOBLE, HARRISON, Heyworth, Ill (b/1812 Hamilton Co, O; d/1870) MD Med Coll Ohio 1847. *Tr AMA* 29: 725-26, 1878. *Chicago med jour* 28: 311-12, 1871.

NOBLE, STEPHEN WARD [WOOD], Bloomington, Ill (b/1826 Hamilton Co, O; d/1871) MD Med Coll Ohio 1848. *Tr AMA* 29:726-27, 1878.

NOBLE, WILLIAM D, Federalsburg Md (d/I-18 1880 @ 50) MD U Md 1851. *Med surg rep Phila* 42:154, 1880.

NOCK, WILLIAM J , Ft Adams, Miss (d/III-8-1896) MD ? *NC med jour* 37: 214, 1896.

NOE, ALLEN T , Paducah, Ky (d/IV- -1856) MD Transylvania 1843. *Nashvl j m & s* 11:170, 1856.

NOEL, HENRY REGINALD, CW-CSA; Baltimore (b/ 1836 Essex Co, Va; d/I-23-1878) MD U Va 1859. *Med annals Md*:519. *Tr AMA* 32:528,1881. *Atkinson* I:516.

NOEL, JOHN A , Des Moines, Ia (b/XII- -1852 Redfield, Ia; d/IV-23-1897) MD Mo Med Coll 1886. *Tr Ia St Med Soc* 15:368-69, 1897. *Polk* 1890: 424.

NOEL, PERRY ECCLESTON, Centerville, Md (b/1768; d/X-4-1813) MD Edinburgh 1794. *Med annals Md*:519.

NOLAN, JOHN, NYC (d/III-11-1900) MD CPSNY 1868. *JAMA* 34: 766, 1900. *Polk* 1886: 689.

NOLAN, PATRICK HOPKINS, CW-USA; NYC (b/V-11-1833; d/X-22-1874) MD CPSNY 1858.

NOLAN, ROBERT GRAFTON [or GEORGE], Bayonne NJ (b/1856 Norwich Conn; d/I-23-1895) MD UVt 1877. *Med reg NY NJ Conn* 1895: 233. *JAMA* 24:337, 1895.

NOLAND, BUD A , Pittsburg, Tex (d/VIII-10-1897) MD Atlanta Med Coll 1886. *Tex cour-rec med* 14:427, 1897. *Tex med news* 6:434, 1896-97. *Polk* 1896: 1424.

NOLAND, STACY T , Delphi, Ind (b/IV-17-1845 Loudon Co, Va; d/VIII-7-1887) MD Washington U Balto 1873. *Tr Ind St Med Soc* 1888: 217.

NOONEY, EDWIN DeWITT, Stratford, Conn (d/VII-18 1889) MD CPSNY 1871. *Med reg NY NJ Conn* 1890: 278. *Polk* 1886: 196.

NORBURY, JOHN F , NYC (d/I-13-1895) MD Albany 1844. *Med reg NY NJ Conn* 1895: 234.

NORCOM [NORCUM], WILLIAM AUGUSTUS BLOUNT, Edenton, NC; CW–CSA (b/V–24–1836; d/II 28–1881 Balto) MD UPa 1857. *Tr AMA* 33:588–89, 1882. *U Pa med alum CW*:1857. *K&B* II:852. *Atkinson* I:204.

NORDMAN [NORDMANN], FREDERICK RUDOLPH, Baltimore (b/I–29–1859; d/X–22–1902) MD CPS Balto 1884. *Med annals Md:* 520. *Polk* 1866: 438.

NORDMANN, LOUIS E, Philadelphia (d/III–25–1872 @ 57) MD Jefferson 1858. *Phila med reg & dir* 1873: 303.

NORDQUIST, CHARLES J , Tuckahoe, NY (b/Sweden; d/III–6–1890) <MD Sweden> MD UCNY 1856. *Bost m &s j* 122: , 1890.

NORFOLK, WILLIAM H , Baltimore (d/XI–28–1899 @64) MD U Md 1856. *JAMA* 33:1504, 1899.

NORRED, CHARLES H , Lincoln, Ill; Minneapolis (d/I 11–1905 @62) MD Jefferson 1886. *Ill med jour* 7:242, 1905. *Polk* 1896: 793.

NORRIS, BASIL, USA 1852– (b/III–9–1828 Montgomery Co, Md; d/XI–10–1895 San Francisco) MD U Md 1849. *JAMA* 25:873, 1895; 26:287, 1896. *Buffalo m&s j* 35:423–24, 1895. *Tr M S Cal* 1896: 322. *Polk* 1886: 213.

NORRIS, BENJAMIN, Pittsfield, Ill (b/X–13–1803 Bris tol, RI; d/XII–19–1870) MD Brown 1826; AB 1823. *Brown hist cat*: 1823.

NORRIS, GEORGE CALVIN, Mountain Creek, Ala (d/III–3–1889) MD Med Coll Ala 1883. *Tr Med Assoc St Ala* 1889: 229. *Polk* 1886: 137.

NORRIS, GEORGE DASHIELS, Newmarket, Ala (b/ 1812? d/II–12–1890) MD U Md 1831. *JAMA* 14:323, 1890. *Tr Med Assoc St Ala* 1890:217; 1891:261. *Med annals Md:* 520. *Butler* 1878: 23.

NORRIS, GEORGE WASHINGTON, Philadelphia (b/ XI–6–1808; d/III–4–1875) MD UPa 1830; AB 1827. *Tr CPP* cent vol: 253; 3s2: xxvii–xliii, 1876. *K&B* III: 906.

NORRIS, H EUGENE, Marietta Pa (b/Wakefield Md; d/ X–12–1885) MD UMd 1874. *Tr Pa St M S* 18:244 1886.

NORRIS, HENRY LEE, W Hoboken NJ (d/II–23–1900 @49) <MD Edinburgh> *JAMA* 34:574, 1900. *Polk* 1896: 951.

NORRIS, JAMES BARBY, Chattanooga (b/V– –1849 Delaware, O; d/IX–10–1878 Vicksburg) MD Detroit M C 1872; AB Kenyon 1866. *Tr AMA* 30:880–81, 1879. *Tr M S Tenn* 1879:175–76. *Med rec* NY 14:240, 1878.

NORRIS, JOHN CLEMENTS, Philadelphia; CW–USA (b/X–2–1834; d/III–13–1885) MD Jefferson 1862. *Tr CPP* cent vol: 253. *Atkinson* I: 241.

NORRIS, JOHN H , Metropolis, Ill (d/VIII–13–1896 @ 66) MD CPS Keokuk 1870. *JAMA* 27:449, 1896. *Polk* 1890: 339.

NORRIS, THOMAS PETER, USA 1856–60; CW–USA; Brooklyn (d/XII–21–1894) MD UCNY 1854. *Med reg NY NJ Conn* 1895: 234. *JAMA* 24:33, 1895.

NORRIS, WILLIAM FISHER, CW–USA; Philadelphia (b/I–6–1839;d/XI–18–1901) MD UPa 1861;AB 1858. *Tr CPP* cent vol: 254; 3s24: lxxii–lxxx, 1902. *Pa m j* 5: 143–44,296, 1901/02. *Atkinson* I:143. *K&B* III: 907.

NORRIS, WILLIAM H , Baltimore (b/1829 Carroll Co, Md; d/II–2–1892) MD U Md 1853. *Med ann Md:* 520–21. *Polk* 1886: 438.

NORTH, ALFRED, Waterbury, Conn (b/X–5–1836; b/ XI–5–1836; d/XI–17–1893) MD CPSNY 1861; AB Brown 1858; PhB . *Med reg NY NJ Conn* 1894:244. *JAMA* 21:869, 1893. *Pr Conn M S* 1894:242–44.

NORTH, EDWARD, Hammonton, NJ (b/VII–29–1841 W Waterville Me; d/II–11–1899) MD Jefferson 1868. *Tr Med Soc NJ* 1899:283–84. *JAMA* 32: 385, 1899. *Butler* 1878: 473.

NORTH, EUGENE BENTON, Peru, Ind (b/III–10–1854 Franklin Co, Me; d/VII–8–1887) MD St Louis Med Coll 1876. *Tr Ind St Med Soc* 1888: 203.

NORTH, MILO LINUS, Saratoga Springs, NY (b/1790? d/II–22–1856 @66) MD Yale 1834; AB 1813. *Boston m & s jour* 54:107, 1856. *Proc Conn Med Soc* 1857: 21.

NORTH, NELSON LUTHER, Brooklyn (b/IV–20–1830; d/XI–23–1904) MD CPSNY 1854. *Bost m&s j* 151:610, 1904. *Polk* 1896: 1000.

NORTH, WILLIAM BURRITT, Cornwall, Conn (d/III or IV–1866 @31) MD Yale 1863. *Med surg rep Phila* 14:280, 1866.

NORTHROP, JAMES, Woodstock, Ill (d/VIII–9–1896 @ 71) MD Geneva 1857. *JAMA* 27: 449, 1896. *Polk* 1890: 354.

NORTHROP, JOSEPH NORMAN, Mississippi 1840? Albany & Decatur, NY 1840–59 (b/XI–20–1817 Decatur; d/IX–17–1878) MD Castleton 1841; ng Transylvania. *Tr Med Soc St NY* 1879: 581–83.

NORTHROP, KATHERINE, Warren, Pa (d/VII–13–1899) MD Woman's Med Coll Pa 1889. *Pa m j* 33: 272, 1899/1900. *JAMA* 33:302, 1899. *Polk* 1896:1342.

NORTHWAY, ZENAS ARTHUR, CW–USA (d/IX–27–1864) MD Buffalo 1861. *Nat med jour* 1:300, 1870/71.

NORTON, ALBERT B , Washington, DC (b/Mass; d/VII –5–1873) MD Berkshire 1849. *Hist Med Soc DC:* 293.

NORTON, BENJAMIN, Hornellsville, NY (d/X–3–1893) Lic Allegany Co Med Soc 1875. *JAMA* 21:630, 1893. *Butler* 1878: 567.

NORTON, CLAUDE R , Philadelphia (d/V–31–1906) MD NY Homeop Med Coll 1872. *Pa med jour* 9: 672, 1905/06. *Polk* 1896: 1313. Homeopath.

NORTON, EMMA VIRGINIA (BAKER), Lancaster, Pa (d/VIII–6–1903 @50) MD Woman's Med Coll 1878. *Pa med jour* 7:280, 1903/04.

NORTON, GEORGE SALMON, NYC (b/XII–8–1851 Great Barrington, Mass; d/I–31–1898 @39) MD NY Homeop Med Coll 1872. *Tr Am Inst Hom* 1891:96. *No Am j hom* 39:119, 1891. *Med vis* 7: 125, 1891. *Polk* 1886:689. Homeopath.

NORTON, GREENLEAF C , CW–USA (d/VIII–10–1862) MD ? *Nat med jour* 1:300, 1870/71.

NORTON, JOHN BLAKELY, Boston (b/II-4-1868 Tinmouth Vt; d/XII-8-1901) MD Dartmouth 1900; BS 1897. *Bost m&s j* 145: 663, 1901.

NORTON, THOMAS MARSHALL, Washington, DC (b/XI-21-1863 Fauquier Co, Va; d/I-9-1892 Alexandria) MD U Va 1885. *Tr M S Va* 1892: 288; 1893: 219; 1894: 198. *Hist M S DC:* 327.

NORTON, WILLIAM ABNER, Eclectic, Ala (d/1889?) MD Med Coll Ala 1888. *Tr Med Assoc St Ala* 1899: 232. *Polk* 1893: 154.

NORTON, WILLIAM S, Ft Edward, NY (b/1796 Easton; d/II-20-1863) Hon MD Regents St Univ NY 1857; ng Castleton 1824. *Tr Med Soc St NY* 1863: 392.

NORWOOD, JOHN, CW-CSA; Columbus, Ga (b/VIII-5 1836; d/VI-28-1897) MD Jefferson 1859; stud UNC 1853-55. *JAMA* 29:92, 1897. *Polk* 1890: 264.

NORWOOD, WILLIAM D , Shreveport, La (b/Marshall, Tex; d/I-13-1906) MD Hering 1895. *New Orl m&s j* 58:779, 1906. Homeopath.

NOTHHELFER, JULIUS, St Louis (d/VIII-14-1899 @43) MD St Louis Med Coll 1881. *JAMA* 33:621, 1899. *Polk* 1896: 876.

NOTSON, WILLIAM, Philadelphia (d/XII-9-1893 @ 69) MD Jefferson 1846. *JAMA* 21: 982, 1893.

NOTT, ALBERT, W Newton, Mass (b/X-15-1846 Claremont, NH; d/X-10-1903 @56) MD U Vt 1869. *Bost m&s j* 149:444, 1903. *Polk* 1896:726.

NOTT, GUSTAVUS ADOLPHUS, New Orleans (b/VI-29-1816 Columbia SC; d/VI-6-1867 Montgomery, Ala) MD M C SC 1837. *New Orl m&s j* 20: 280-82, 1867. *Bost m&s j* 77:160, 1867.

NOTT, JAMES DEAS, CW-USA (b/1836 Mobile, Ala; d/IX-20-1863 Chickamauga, Tenn) MD UPa 1858. *U Pa med alum CW*: 1858.

NOTT, JOSIAH CLARKE, Mobile, Ala; Columbia, SC; CW-CSA (b/III-31-1804; d/III-31-1873) MD UPa 1827. *U Pa m alum CW*: 1827. *Tr AMA* 29:727-33, 1878. *Tr M Assn St Ala* 1877: 118. *Waring* II: 278-79. *K&B* III: 910-11.

NOTTINGHAM, CURTIS BELL, Macon Ga (b/1818; d/1876) <MD Jefferson 1840> *Tr AMA* 29: 733-34, 1878.

NOTTINGHAM, JOHN, Syracuse, NY (d/III-3-1897) MD Hahnemann, Phila 1870. *Tr Am Inst Hom* 1898: 49. *Med vis* 13:1897. *Polk* 1886:711. Homeopath.

NOUEL, AUGUSTE ADOLPHE, Brooklyn (d/IV-9-1902 @56) MD Bellevue 1876. *Bost m&s j* 146: 426, 1902.

NOURSE, AMOS, Hallowell & Bath, Me (b/XII-17-1794 Boston; d/IV-7-1877) Stud med w/Dr Randall, Boston; AB Harvard 1812. *Tr Me M Assn* 1877: 238-39.

NOURSE, CHARLES JOSEPH, Washington, DC; USN 1876- (b/XII-15-1854 Annapolis, Md; d/VII-23-1880 Hartmansville, WVa) MD Columbian DC 1876; AB Lafayette. *Lafayette, Men of*: 204.

NOXON, MARY WOOLSEY, NYC (d/I-16-1895 @40) MD NY Med Coll & Hosp for Women 1873. *JAMA* 24:177, 1895. *No Am j hom* 43:128, 1895. *Polk* 1890: 827. Homeopath.

NOYES, FRANCIS ASBURY, Somerville, Mass (b/IV-11-1823 Landalf, NH; d/III-27-1859 @36) MD Woodstock 1849. *Bost m&s j* 60: 188, 1859.

NOYES, HELON F , Pulaski, NY; Stillwater, Minn 1855- ; Milwaukee, Wis (d/I-15-1872 @70) MD UCNY 1843. *Tr Minn St Med Soc* 1873: 117.

NOYES, HENRY ALLEN, NH (b/1865; d/1903) MD Hahnemann, Chicago 1891. *Tr Am Inst Hom* 1905: 846.

NOYES, HENRY DRURY [DEWEY], NYC (d/XI-12 1900 @68) MD CPSNY 1855; AB UCNY 1851; AM 1854. *Tr Med Soc St NY* 1901:[426]. *Chicago med rec* 19, 466, 1900. *Bost m&s j* 143:541, 1900. *K&B* III: 912.

NOYES, JAMES FANNING, Detroit 1863- ; Providence, RI (b/VIII-2-1817 S Kingstown, RI; d/II-16-1896) MD Jefferson 1846; stud Berlin, Vienna, Paris. *JAMA* 26: 442, 1896. *Tr RI Med Soc* 5:359-62, 1894-98. *Polk* 1890:587. *K&B* III: 912-13.

NOYES, JOHN, Lyme, Conn (d/1854 @46) MD Yale 1836; AB 1834. *Proc Conn Med Soc* 1855: 21.

NOYES, JOHN WESLEY, Racine, Wis (d/VII-24-1897 @76) MD Woodstock 1846. *JAMA* 29: 297, 1897. *Polk* 1886: 960.

NOYES, JOSEPH F , Providence, RI (d/II-3-1896 @78) MD ? *NC med jour* 37: 189, 1896.

NOYES, JOSIAH, Needham, Mass (b/X-8-1801 Acton; d/I-7-1871) MD Dartmouth 1825. *Bost m&s j* 7:32, 404, 1871.

NOYES, SELDON WALKLEY, Higganum & Haddam, Conn (b/IX-1-1855; d/VII-12-1897) MD UPa 1868. *Proc Conn Med Soc* 1898: 364-65. *JAMA* 29: 252, 1897.

NOYES, WALTER, Butte City, Mont (d/II-29-1894) MD ? *JAMA* 22:234, 1894. *Polk* 1893: 748.

NUGENT, P C , St Louis (d/IX-14-1878 Memphis) MD Mo Med Coll 1877. *Tr AMA* 30:881, 1879. *Med rec NY* 14:240, 1878.

NUGENT, WASHINGTON GEORGE, Pittston Pa; CW USA (b/XII-29-1822 Phila; d/III-9-1877) MD U Pa 1842. *Tr M S Pa* 1877:624-26. *U Pa m alum CW*: 1842.

NURCROSS, G J , CW-USA (d/XII-6-1865) MD ? *Nat med jour* 1:300, 1870/71.

NUTT, FREDERICK L , Marengo, Ill (d/V-23-1901) MD NWU 1878. *Ill med jour* ns3: 91, 1901.

NUTT, RUSH, Gillen's Landing, Ark (d/IV-24-1874 @ 35) MD ? *Med surg rep Phila* 28:410, 1873.

NUTTALL, JOSEPH H , Natchez, Tenn [? Miss] St Louis Mo (d/IV-20-1886) MD UPa 1861. *New Orl m&s j* ns13:1008, 1886. *Polk* 1886: 869.

NUTTING, THOMAS, Georgiaville, RI (b/III-6-1814 Coventry, RI; d/III-21-1886) MD Berkshire 1837. *Tr RI Med Soc* 3:378 ff, 1883-8. *Butler* 1878: 748.

NUZUM, DAVID P , Elwood, Ind (b/1842; d/VIII-23 1895) MD Eclectic Med Inst Cinc 1883. *JAMA* 25:427,

1895. Kemper's *Indiana*: 220. *Polk* 1886: 334.

NYCE, NATHAN JOHN, CW–USA (b/Knauertown, Pa; d/1868) MD UPa 1865. *U Pa med alum CW*: 1865.

NYE, ELISHA BOURNE, Middletown, Conn (b/XI–7–1812 Sandwich Mass; d/III–7–1889) MD Yale 1837; AB Wesleyan 1835. *Pr Conn Med Soc* ns4:245–49, 1889.

NYE, JAMES MONROE, Lynn, Mass (b/IX–26–1818 Salisbury, Mass; d/IV–21–1872) ND Woodstock 1841. *Bost m&s j* ns9: 276, 1872.

OAKES, SILVESTER, Auburn, Me (b/I–31–1820 Temple; d/III–30–1887) MD Dartmouth 1844. *Tr Me Med Assoc* 1887: 318–20. *Polk* 1886: 423.

OAKES, THOMAS FLETCHER, Titusville, Pa; CW–USA d/1876) MD Harvard 1852. *Harvard in CW*: 239.

OAKLEY, LEWIS WILLIAM, CW–USA; Elizabeth, NJ (b/XI–22–1828; d/III–3–1888) MD CPSNY 1852; AB Princeton 1849. *Med reg NY NJ Conn* 1888: 265. *Tr Med Soc NJ* 1888:163–65.

OAKLEY, THOMAS ABNER, Leasburg, NC; CW–CSA (b/II–27–1835; d/XII–4–1885) MD UPa 1861. *U Pa med alum CW*: 1861.

OATLEY, EUGENE LYMAN, Philadelphia; Utica, NY (b/X–13–1859; d/XI–1–1891) MD Hahnemann Phila 1886; AB Cornell 1881. *Tr Am Inst Hom* 1894: 268.

OATMAN, EDWARD DAVIS, O'Fallon, Ill (d/VII–30 1898 @51) MD St Louis Med Coll 1876. *JAMA* 31: 366, 1898. *Polk* 1896: 433.

OATMAN, IRA E, Sacramento; CW–USA (b/X–18 1819 New Albany, Ind; d/XII–19–1888) MD Rush 1845. *Tr M S Cal* 1889: 208. *Atkinson* I:298–99. *Butler* 1878: 61.

OATMAN, JAMES J , Altoona, Pa (d/I–30–1900 @62) MD Jefferson 1897. *JAMA* 34: 381, 1900.

OATMAN, JOEL S , NYC (b/II–6–1807 Middletown, Vt; d/X–2–1876) ng Castleton 1831. *Med reg NY NJ Conn* 1877: 204. *Med surg rep Phila* 35:326, 1876.

OBER, BENJAMIN, Wilkes Barre, Pa; San Francisco 1849– (d/V–13–1867 @61) <ng Bowdoin 1837> *Bost m &s j* 76:544 1867. *Tr Am Inst Hom* 1867:158. Homeopath.

OBER, LEVI ELIHU, Moline, Ill 1850– ; LaCrosse, Wis 1857– (d/III–26–1881 @63) MD Eclectic Med Inst Cinc 1850. *Clinique* 2: 144, 1881? Homeopath.

OBETZ, FRANCIS, Grove City, O (d/II–20–1895) MD Starling Med Coll 1851. *JAMA* 24: 370, 1895.

O'BRIEN, CABEL S , Bloomsburgh, Pa (d/XI–16–1893) MD Jefferson 1890. *JAMA* 21: 829, 1893.

O'BRIEN, CHARLES D , Ackley, Ia (d/IV–4–1895) <MD Rush> *JAMA* 24: 609, 1895. *Tr Ia St M S* 14:329, 1896; 18:411, 1900; 21:449, 1903.

O'BRIEN, J T , Waco, Tex; Ft Worth 1903– (d/VII–22–1906) <MD New Orleans> *Tex st med jour* 2:144, 1906.

O'BRIEN, JOHN, CW–CSA (b/IX–28–1832 Norfolk, Va; d/VII–26–1902 Aurelian Spr, NC) MD UPa 1854. *U Pa med alum CW*: 1854. *Polk* 1886: 723.

O'BRIEN [O'BYRNE], JOHN M, Ocean View, Cal (d/VII–10–1899 @39) MD Buff 1889. *JAMA* 33:302, 1899.

O'BRIEN, JOHN N, Milwaukee (b/Pa; d/IV–22–1900 @62) MD Rush 1864 *JAMA* 34:1146,1900. *Polk* 1886:957.

O'BRIEN, JUNIUS D , Hopkinsville, Ky (d/VIII–23 1901 @70) MD UCNY 1858. *JAMA* 37:710, 1901.

O'BRIEN, LUCIUS, Baltimore; USA 1832–35, 1837–38 (b/Md; d/I–7–1841 Tampa, Fla) <MD Washington U Balto 1828> *Med annals Md:* 521.

O'BRIEN, STEPHEN D , Kalamazoo ((d/III–2–1899 @38) MD Detroit Med Coll 1886. *JAMA* 32:563, 1899.

O'BRIEN, THOMAS FRANCIS, NYC (d/XI–19–1885) MD Bellevue 1876. *Med reg NY NJ Conn* 1886: 252.

O'BRIEN [BRYAN], WALTER, NYC (d/VI–26–1905 @38) MD UCNY 1889. *Bost m&s j* 153: 36, 1905. *Polk* 1896: 1000.

O'CALLAGHAN, THOMAS ALBERT, Worcester, Mass (d/IV–13–1901 @46) MD McGill 1880; AB. *Bost m&s j* 144:540, 1901. *Polk* 1896: 728.

O'CALLAGHAN, THOMAS C , Jersey City, NJ (b/1831 Irel'd; d/XII–27–1899) MD UCNY 1862. *Bost m&s j* 142:24, 1900. *JAMA* 34: 61, 1900. *Polk* 1886: 605.

O'CALLAHAN, F L , CW–USA (d/X–8–1864) MD ? *Nat med jour* 1:300, 1870/71.

O'CONNELL, JEFFERSON J, Honesdale Pa (b/1859; d/IV–1–1897) MD CPS Chicago 1887*JAMA* 28:955,1897.

O'CONNELL, PATRICK ALOYSIUS, Boston (b/1835 Irel'd; d/I–6–1874/Santa Barbara Cal) MD Harvard 1860; AB 1857. *Bost m&s j* 90: 76,202, 1874.

O'CONNOR, DAVID P , Charleston, Ill (d/X– –1899) MD Mo Med Coll 1895. *Tr Ill St Med Soc* 1899:287.

O'CONNOR, HARRY [HENRY] R , Pittsburgh (d/VIII 30–1897 @44) MD Jefferson 1875. *JAMA* 29:555, 1897.

O'CONNOR, JAMES JOHN, Holyoke, Mass (d/XII–14 1888 @46) MD Harvard 1865. *Bost m & s j* 120: 102, 1889; 121:644, 1889. *Butler* 181878: 355.

O'CONNOR, JOHN, Baltimore (b/1791? d/IX–30–1819) MD U Md 1812. *Med annals Md:* 521.

O'CONNOR, JOHN ZENUS, Elwood, Ind (b/VII–4–1868 Phila; d/IV–7–1898) MD Louisville Med Coll 1897. *Tr Ind St Med Soc* 1898: 387.

O'CONNOR, THOMAS HENRY, Clinton, Mass (d/I–1 1899 @41 Nice, Fr) MD Bellevue 1883. *Bost m&s j* 140:28, 1899. *JAMA* 32: 145, 1899.

O'CONOR [OCONNOR], J FITZGERALD, NYC (d/VI–25–1878 @37) MD UCNY 1869; AB Trinity Coll, Dublin. *Med reg NY NJ Conn* 1879: 196.

OCTERLONY [OUCHTERLONY], JOHN ARVID, CW–USA; Louisville (b/VI–24–1838 Sweden; d/X–9–1905) MD UCNY 1861. *So pract* 27:636, 1905. *Atkinson* I: 640. *Butler* 1878: 266. *K&B* III: 926.

O'DELL, BENJAMIN F , Belcherville, Tex (d/IX–27 1882) MD Eclectic Med Inst Cinc 1885. *Tex cour–rec med* 10: 27, 1892–93. *Polk* 1890: 1070.

ODELL, T R, Armington Ill; Spokane Wash (d/VII-1-1898 @82) MD ? *JAMA* 31:366,1898. *Polk* 1886: 253.

ODEN, , ? (d/1878 Stoneville, Miss) MD ? *Tr AMA* 30: 881, 1879.

ODENEAL, JAMES PATRICK, CW-USA; Shuqualak, Miss (b/ VIII-21-1831; d/XII-8-1861) MD New Orl Med Sch 1856; att U Ala 1852. *U Ala cat*: 106.

ODIN, JOHN, Somerville, Mass (d/IX-4-1864) MD Harvard 1833; AB 1830. *Bost m&s j* 71:128, 1864. *Mass Med Soc cat* 1894.

ODIORNE, WALTER BURLINGAME, Cambridge, Mass (d/VII-15-1906 @33) MD Harvard 1899; AB 1895. *Bost m&s j* 155: 77, 419, 1906.

ODLIN, CHARLES CUSHING, Melrose, Mass (b/X-31 1847 Exeter, NH; d/XII-18-1906 @59) MD Dartmouth 1869. *Bost m & s jour* 155:792, 1906. *Polk* 1896: 718.

O'DONNELL, DOMINICK A , Baltimore (b/1809 Co Donegal, Irel'd; d/VIII-26-1874) MD Jefferson 1833. *Tr AMA* 26:466, 1875. *Med annals Md:* 521.

O'DONNELL, WILLIAM, NYC (b/I-25-1795 Clareen Co, Irel'd; d/IV-21-1875. Lic Med Soc St NY. *Med reg NY NJ Conn* 1875: 202.

O'DONOGHUE, EUGENE, Bergen NY (d/XII-3-1867 @75) MD ? *Med reg NY NJ Conn* 17:560, 1867.

O'DONOGHUE, FLORENCE [male] Washington DC (b/1832; d/VI-29-1882) MD U Md 1855; att Jesuits' Coll DC. *Med reg NY NJ Conn* 1883:233. *Hist M S DC:* 274.

O'DONOVAN, CHARLES, Baltimore (b/IX-20-1829; d/XII-23-1889) MD U Md 1853. *Bost m&s j* 122:48, 1890. *Med ann Md:* 421. *Med bull m & s* 13:69, 1890.

O'DONOVAN, JOHN H , Baltimore (b/1802 Irel'd; d/VI 18-1869) MD U Md 1824. *Phila med reg & dir* 1871: 301. *Tr AMA* 21:477, 1870. *Med annals Md:* 521-22.

O'DWYER, JOSEPH, NYC (b/X-12-1841 Cleveland, O; d/I-7-1898) MD CPSNY 1866; AB St Johns; LLD Fordham 1891. *JAMA* 30:166, 1898. *Nashvl j m & s* 83:93-94, 1898. *Bost m&s j* 138:46, 1898. *K&B* III: 915.

OERTEL, GEORGE FREDERICK, NYC (b/VI-19-1825? d/VII-8-1898 @73) MD NY Homeop 1876. *No Amer jour homeop* 46:1898. *Polk* 1886: 689. Homeopath.

OESTERLIN, CHARLES, Findlay, O (d/I-18-1889) MD Homeop Hosp Cleveland 1861. *Med vis* 5:116, 1889. *Polk* 1886: 754. Homeopath.

O'FARRELL, GERALD DUNNE, CW-USA; Philadelphia (b/X-18 1832 Co Galway, Irel'd; d/III-27-1902) MD UPa 1862. *Pa med jour* 5:386, 1901/02; 6:261, 1902/03. *U Pa med alum CW*: 1862.

O'FARRELL, JOHN, CW-CSA (b/XI-1-1845 Harper's Ferry, WVa; d/XI-11-1871) MD UPa 1869. *U Pa med alum CW*: 1869.

O'FARRELL, THOMAS, New Britain, Conn; Monterey, Mex (b/IX-1-1832; d/IV-8-1874) MD UPa 1852 [as Farrell]. *Med reg NY NJ Conn* 1874: 284. *Proc Conn Med Soc* 1874: 291.

O'FERRALL, ROBERT M , Lafayette, Ind (b/I-17-1826 Piqua, O; d/XII-13-1896) MD UCNY 1847. *Tr Ind St Med Soc* 1897: 351. *Butler* 1878: 214.

OFFUTT, BARRACK, Rockville, Md (b/1835? d/1893?) MD UMd 1859. *JAMA* 21:784, 1893. *Butler* 1878:329.

OFFUTT, GEORGE W, Washington, DC (b/1851; d/IX-13-1878) MD Georgetown 1874. *Hist Med Soc DC:* 305.

O'FLAHERTY, JOHN, Hartford (b/Irel'd; d/VII-31-1904 @62) MD Albany 1864. *Proc Conn Med Soc* 1904: 79, 490-92. *Butler* 1878: 80.

OGDEN, BENJAMIN, NYC (b/X-14-1797; d/VI-18-1867 College Pt, LI NY) MD CPSNY 1820. *Med surg rep Phila* 17:22, 1867. *Tr AMA* 19:406-07, 1868. *Med reg NY NJ Conn* 1868: 331-34.

OGDEN, E RUSSELL, Chicago (d/II-4-1892) MD NWU 1844. *Chic med rec* 1:566, 1892. *Polk* 1886: 269.

OGDEN, EDWIN ROSS, Orange, NJ (d/IX-21-1905) MD ? *Bost m&s j* 153: 376, 1905.

OGDEN, ISAAC, New Germantown, NJ (d/1829) MD ? AB Princeton 1784. *Tr Med Soc NJ* 1872:128-29.

OGDEN, OLIVER WAYNE, NJ (b/c1778; d/c1840 @62) <Stud med Phila> *Tr Med Soc NJ*__: 126-27.

OGIER, SEPTIMUS A , Chester Valley, Pa (b/IX-17-1821 Charleston, SC; d/XI-26-1857) MD Med Coll SC 1844. *Tr Pa St Med Soc* 1858: 70-72.

OGIER, THOMAS LOUIS Jr, Charleston, SC; CW-CSA (d/VIII-26-1863 Morton, Miss) MD Med Coll SC 1859. *SHSP* 22:244, 1893.

OGIER, WILLIAM HUFFE, Columbus, O (d/II-24-1900 @29) MD Bellevue 1897. *JAMA* 34: 639, 1900.

OGLE, GEORGE COOKE, Baltimore (b/1816; d/XI-27 1890) MD UMd 1838 *Med ann Md:*522. *Polk* 1886: 438.

OGLE, S A , Duffau's Mills, Tex (d/I-26-1888) MD ? *Daniel's Tex med jour* 3:407, 1888.

OGLESBY, BENJAMIN A, Louisville (d/VIII-14-1901) <MD Hosp C M Louisvl 1890> *JAMA* 37: 461, 1901.

O'GORMAN, WILLIAM, Newark, NJ (b/VII-12-1824; d/XI-10-1887) <MRCP [Irel'd?] 1848> *Med reg NY NJ Conn* 1888:266 *Tr M S NJ* 1889:171-2. *Butler* 1878:463.

O'GORMAN, WILLIAM, Newark, NJ (d/IV-15-1893 @32) MD CPSNY 1887; att Seton Hall. *Med reg NY NJ Conn* 1893: 313.

O'HANLON, PHILIP Sr, NYC (b/1786? d/V-18-1866 @80) MD ? *Med reg NY NJ Conn* 1867: 222.

O'HARA, MICHAEL, USN 1854-58; USA 1862-63; Philadelphia (b/I-2-1832; d/I-31-1905) MD UPa 1852; AB Central HS Phila 1848. *U Pa med alum CW*: 1852. *Atkinson* I: 121.

O'HEAR, JOHN SANDERS, ?Wando, SC (b/IX-6-1806 Charleston; d/IX-21-1895) MD UPa 1827. *U Pa med alum CW*: 1827.

O'HEARN, WILLIAM HENRY, Lawrence, Mass (d/VI-4-1900 @30) MD UCNY 1891. *Bost m&s j* 142:614, 1900. *Polk* 1896: 715.

OHL, JOSIAH G , Summit Hill, Pa (b/Buckthorn; d/V-

20–1863) MD Jefferson 1855. *Med surg rep Phila* 10: 128, 1863.

OHLENSCHLAGER, EMIL , CW–USA (d/X–13–1864) MD ? *Nat med jour* 1:300, 1870/71.

OHLINGER, CONRAD R , Cleveland, O; USA (d/VIII–20–1901 Philippine Isl) MD Ohio Wesleyan 1898. *JAMA* 37: 790, 1901.

O'KEEF, PATRICK, Menominee, Mich (b/XII–31–1846 Chatham, Ont; d/VI–27–1899) MD Victoria, Toronto 1869. *Tr Wis St Med Soc* 34:425–26, 1900; 35:505, 1901.

O'KEEFE, DAVID, Baltimore (d/III–2–1870 @41) MD Wash'n U Balto 1848. *Phila med reg & dir* 1871: 304.

OKIE, ABRAHAM HOWARD, Providence RI 1842– (d/IX–21–1882) <MD Allentown Acad Homeop> MD Pa Med Coll 1840. *Hahn mo* 17:640, 1882. *King* 1:275. Homeopath.

OKIE, RICHARDSON BROGNARD, Berwyn, Pa (d/VII–30–2904 @54) MD UPa 1870. *Pa med jour* 8:335, 1904/05. *Flint* 1897: 796.

OLCOTT, AUSTIN, Conn (b/1775? d/1843 @68) Hon MD Yale 1823. *Proc Conn Med Soc* 1882–83: 144.

OLCOTT, CHARLES AUGUSTUS, Brooklyn (d/III–30 1905 @50) MD Bellevue 1876. *Bost m&s j* 152: 416, 1905. *Polk* 1896: 1001.

OLCOTT, CORNELIUS, Brooklyn (b/I–24–1828 Jersey City; d/V–2–1897) MD UCNY 1849. *JAMA* 28: 1045, 1897. *Bost m&s j* 136:474, 1897. *Polk* 1896: 1001.

OLCOTT, EDGAR, Jersey City, NJ (b/II–24–1807; d/V–27–1868) MD ? *Med surg rep Phila* 18: 542, 1868. *Phila med reg & dir* 1871: 297. *Tr AMA* 21:468–69, 1870. *Med reg NY NJ Conn* 1869/70:241–42.

OLCOTT, EUGENE SANDS, Brooklyn; CW–USN? (d/IX–2–1864 @23) MD UCNY 1862. *Med surg rep Phila* 12:100, 1864/65.

OLCOTT, GEORGE, Wethersfield, Conn (d/1864) MD ? AM Yale 1805. *Proc Conn Med Soc* 1882: 144.

OLDROYD, WILBUR FISK, Big Prairie, O (d/I–24–1891) MD Wooster 1871. *Polk* 1886: 738. *Wooster cat.*

O'LEARY, CHARLES, Providence, RI (b/1830 Irel'd; d/VI–1–1897) MD LICH 1860. *Tr RI Med Soc* 5: 493–95, 1894–98. *JAMA* 28:1202, 1897.

O'LEARY, CORNELIUS M , NYC (b/Irel'd; d/XII–12–1903 @64) MD UCNY 1864; AB Coll Montreal. *Bost m&s j* 149:720, 1903. *Polk* 1896: 1071.

OLIPHANT, DAVID, RI (b/1720? d/1802 @82) MD ? *Tr RI Med Soc* 1:7, 1859–77.

OLIPHANT, DAVID SEWALL, New Orleans 1850–53; Toronto (b/VI–18–1816 Keene NH; d/XI–13–1903) MD Homeop Med Coll St Louis 1861; AB Amherst 1836. *Amherst, Men of*: 1836.

OLIPHANT, ROBERT WOODRUFF, St Louis (b/XII–28–1824 Beverly, Mass; d/X–9–1883) MD Harvard 1848; AB Amherst 1845. *Bost m&s j* 109:408, 1883. *Butler* 1878: 419.

OLIVER, ALLEN H , NYC (b/New Orleans; d/III–27–1906 @58) MD UPa 1882. *Bost m&s j* 154: 390, 1906. *Polk* 1886: 689.

OLIVER, ANDREW S , Kingston, Ont (d/II–15–1900 @60) MD Hahnemann Phila 1881. *JAMA* 34: 511, 1900.

OLIVER, DANDRIDGE H , Indianapolis (b/1826; d/II–3–1895) MD U Louisville 1856; <att Kans Med Coll; att Jefferson> *JAMA* 24:250, 1895. *Tr Ind St M S* 1895: 410–11. Kemper's *Indiana* :332. *Polk* 1886: 323.

OLIVER, DAVID, Oxford, O (b/1792? d/VI–15–1869 @77) MD ? *Med surg rep Phila* 21:46, 1869. *Phila med reg & dir* 1871: 301.

OLIVER, E W , Mulberry Grove, Ill (d/VIII–9–1900) MD Keokuk 1874. *Ill m j* ns2:237, 1900. *Polk* 1886: 289.

OLIVER, FITCH EDWARD, Boston (b/XI–25–1819; d/XII–8–1892) MD Harvard 1843; AB Dartmouth 1839; AM; Hon AM Trinity Coll. *Bost m&s j* 127:588,611, 1892. *K&B* III: 917–18.

OLIVER, GEORGE HENRY, CW–USA; ?New Mexico (d/III–17–1881 Mesina, NM) MD Harvard 1854. *Harvard in CW*: 243.

OLIVER, GEORGE POWELL, CW–USA; Philadelphia (b/1824; d/II–10–1884) MD Phila Coll Med & Surg 1851; MD UPa 1859. *Med bull med & surg* 6:68, 1884. *Med surg rep Phila* 50:288, 1884.

OLIVER, JAMES M , CW–USA (d/X–10–1863) MD ? *Nat med jour* 1:300, 1870/71.

OLIVER, JOSEPH L , Coatesville, Pa (b/X–9–1837; d/I–2–1865) MD U Md 1859. *Tr M S Pa* 1:76–77, 1865. *Tr AMA* 18:329–30, 1867. *Nat med jour* 1:300, 1870/71.

OLIVER, JOSEPH P , Boston (b/III–28–1845; d/IX–11 1903 Paris) *Bost m&s j* 149: 332, 498, 1903. *Atkinson* I: 699. *Polk* 1896: 703.

OLIVER, MATTHEW H , Ennis, Tex (b/IX–1–1833 Columbia, SC; d/IX–8–1893) MD U Nashville 1855. *Tex cour–rec med* 11:73, 1893. *Daniel's Tex med jour* 9:139–40, 1893–94. *Atkinson* I:428. *Polk* 1886: 885.

OLIVER, NATHAN WARREN, Portsmouth, NH (b/V–31–1819 Waltham, Mass; d/IX–23–1868) MD Harvard 1840. *Bost m&s j* 2:144, 160, 1868. *Tr NH M S* 1869: 82–84.

OLIVER, O M , CW–USA (d/IV–29–1864) MD ? *Nat med jour* 1:300, 1870/71.

OLIVER, RICHARD E , Half–Way, Ky (d/IX–27–1899) MD U Nashville 1890. *JAMA* 33:927, 1899. *Polk* 1893: 522.

OLLIFFE, WILLIAM JOHN, NYC (b/VII–8–1807; d/X 7–1865) MD CPSNY 1833. *Med reg NY NJ Conn* 1866: 196. *Med surg rep Phila* 13:278, 1865.

OLLIPHANT, SAMUEL R , Mobile, Ala (d/III–3–1899 @71) MD Tulane 1855. *Tr M Assn St Ala* 1899:233. *JAMA* 32: 628, 1899. *Polk* 1896: 165.

OLMSTEAD, JAMES, Middletown, Conn (b/New Haven; d/XII–4–1897) MD Yale 1874; AB 1872. *Proc Conn Med Soc* 1898: 370–72. *Bost m&s j* 137:609, 1897. *JAMA* 29:1234, 1897. *Butler* 1878: 85.

OLMSTEAD, JOSEPH, Warehouse Pt, Conn (b/XII-31-1826 Enfield; d/VIII-9-1864) MD UCNY 1843. *Proc Conn Med Soc* 1865: 156-57.

OLMSTEAD, LOUIS JUBA, Kansas City, Mo (d/II-11-1889 @27) MD *Med vis* 5:116, 1889. *Tr Am Inst Hom* 1889: 188. *Polk* 1886:551. Homeopath.

OLMSTEAD, SAMUEL HAWLEY, Brooklyn (b/VIII-9 1838; d/XII-22-1893) MD Yale 1861. *Med reg NY NJ Conn* 1894:245. *JAMA* 22: 31, 1894. *Butler* 1878: 533.

OLSTAD, G , Galveston, Tex (d/XII-12-1890) MD ? *Tex cour-rec med* 8:137, 1891.

O'MALLEY, EDWARD GEORGE, Wilkes Barre, Pa; New Haven, Conn (d/VII-19-1890 @33) MD UCNY 1881. *JAMA* 15: 232, 1890.

O'MALLEY, JAMES AUSTIN, Pittston, Pa (d/1906? @43) MD UCNY 1887. *Pa med jour* 9:524, 1905/06. *JAMA* 46: 904, 1906. *Flint* 1897: 831.

O'MALLEY, MICHAEL, Philadelphia; CW?-USA; (b/Irel'd; d/XII-26-1903 @77) MD ? *Pa med jour* 7: 280, 1903/04.

O'MALLEY, WILLIAM HENRY INGRAM, Span-Am War-USA; San Francisco (b/1862? d/V-24-1900 @38) MD U Cal 1896. *JAMA* 34: 1504, 1900.

O'MEAGHER, WILLIAM, NYC (b/1829 Irel'd; d/II-24 1896) MD UCNY 1857; grad Queen's Coll, Galway, Irel'd. *Bost m&s j* 134:250, 1896. *JAMA* 26:542, 1896. *Polk* 1886: 689.

OMO, JOSEPH HARVEY, Harlan, Ind (b/XII-8-1832 New Berlin, Pa; d/X-21-1898) MD U Nashville & Vanderbilt 1865. *JAMA* 31:1128, 1898. *Tr Ind St M S* 1899: 396. *Polk* 1886: 320.

O'NEAL, WILLIAM S , Lancaster, Ky (b/X-3-1836 Verona; d/III-15-1898) MD Med Coll Med Ohio 1861. *JAMA* 30:744, 1898.

O'NEILL, ALEXANDER A, San Francisco(b/1847 NYC; d/X- -1880) MD U Cal 1867. *Tr Cal St M S* 1880: 330.

O'NEILL, TIMOTHY HAYES, Providence, RI (d/VIII-29-1899) MD UCNY 1876. *JAMA* 33:745, 1899. *Polk* 1886: 846.

ONSTOTT, JEREMIAH WILLIAM, McKees Rocks, Pa (d/IV-4-1902 @43) MD Wooster 1885. *Pa med jour* 6: 261, 1902/03. *Flint* 1897: 808.

OPDYCKE, W , Philadelphia (d/III-14-1880) MD ? *Med surg rep Phila* 42: 308, 1880.

ORCUTT, ALMON MITCHELL, Hardwick, Mass (b/Cummington; d/II-11-1889 @64) MD CPSNY 1849. *Bost m&s j* 120:204, 1889. *Butler* 1878:355.

ORD, JAMES LYCURGUS, USA 1846-91? (d/X-3 1898 @75 Washington DC) MD Jefferson 1846. *JAMA* 31: 942, 1898. *Records AAS USA* 1891:68-70. *Polk* 1896: 225 (Monterey, Calif)

ORDWAY, JOHN POND, CW-USA; Boston (b/1824; d/IV-27-1880) MD Harvard 1861. *Tr AMA* 31:1080-81, 1880. *Bost m&s j* 102:451, 1880. *Harvard in CW*: 266.

O'REAR, CHARLES D , Montgomery Co, Ky (b/XI-12 1839; d/I-23-1884) MD Med Coll Ind 1876. *Tr Ind St Med Soc* 1884: 216.

O'REILLEY, J J , Louisville?; Galveston, Tex (d/II--1880) MD ? *Med surg rep Phila* 42:198, 1880.

O'REILLEY [O'RILEY], PATRICK, NYC; Greenville, Pa (d/V-21-1897 @58) MD UVt 1884. *JAMA* 28: 1092, 1897.

O'REILLY, JAMES, NYC (b/1828 Irel'd; d/VI-26-1899) MD U Vt 1875; <MRCP Dublin?> *Bost m&s j* 141:28, 1899. *JAMA* 33: 175, 1899. *Polk* 1886: 689.

O'REILLY, JAMES C, Maury Co, Tenn (b/1776 Dublin; d/1850) <MD Dublin> *Tr Med Soc Tenn* 1876: 85.

O'REILLY, JOHN, NYC (b/1813 Scotl'd; d/XII-6-1868) MD Glasgow 1839; FRCS (Dubl) 1845. *Phila med reg & dir* 1871: 299. *Tr AMA* 21:437-40, 1870. *Med reg NY NJ Conn* 1869/70:242-44. *Med rec* 3: 475-76, 1868-69.

O'REILLY, LUKE, ?NYC (b/1804; d/IV-1-1864) <MD Glasgow 1826> *Med reg NY NJ Conn* 1865: 225.

O'REILLY, PHILIP ROBERT, ?NYC (b/1818; d/VII-22-1867) MD CPSNY 1847. *Med reg NY NJ Conn* 1868: 334. *Tr AMA* 19:420, 1868.

O'REILLY, THOMAS, St Louis (d/II-24-1901) <MRCS (E) 1849> MD St Louis Med Coll 1856 ad eundem. *Ill med jour* ns2: 533, 1901.

OREN, JESSE, Laporte City, Ia (d/VIII-25-1897 @73) MD Penn Med U Phila 1854 ad eundem. *JAMA* 29:606, 1897. *Polk* 1896: 529.

ORME, LEWIS H , Atlanta (d/II-3-1873 NYC?) MD UCNY 1857. *Med surg rep Phila* 28:256, 1873.

ORMES, CORNELIUS, Jamestown, NY (b/VIII-4-1807; d/IV-20-1886 @79) MD Castleton 1832. *Med adv* 17:383, 1886. *Polk* 1886: 665. *Cleave*. Homeopath.

ORMISTEAD, O W , Lynchburg & Mecklenburg Co, Va (d/IX-13-1873) MD ? *Med s rep Phila* 29:270, 1873.

ORMISTON, ROBERT Jr, CW-USA; Brooklyn (b/1834 Ox Bow, NY; d/IX-19-1905 Stamford, NY) MD UPa 1858. *Bost m&s j* 153: 376, 1905. *U Pa med alum CW*: 1858. *Polk* 1896: 1001.

ORMOND, JOHN JAMES, Faunsdale, Ala (b/I-27-1831; d/I-2-1896) MD U La 1853; att U Ala 1847. *U Ala cat*: 94.

ORMOND, AUGUSTUS P , Kansas City, Mo (d/V-18-1898) MD Med Coll Ohio 1882. *JAMA* 30:1366, 1898. *Polk* 1896: 848.

ORMSBY, ORANGE B Sr, Murphysboro, Ill (d/VI-13 1899 @63) MD Rush 1858. *JAMA* 32:1460, 1899. *Butler* 1878: 171. *Polk* 1896: 431.

O'RORKE, JAMES, NYC (d/VII-30-1893) MD Jefferson 1847. *JAMA* 21: 357, 1893. *Polk* 1886: 689.

ORR, ADAM, Allegheny, Pa (d/IX-25-1906 @66) <MD Queens Coll Cork 1862> *Pa med jour* 19:53, 1906/07.

ORR, [DANIEL?] JAMES, Hill Co & Kaufman Co, Tex; Terrell 1879- (b/X-1850 Jefferson Co, Miss; d/XII-25-1904) MD Tulane 1871; AB U Miss 1868. *Tex st med jour* 1:244-45, 1906. *Polk* 1886: 1453.

ORR, HECTOR, E Bridgewater, Mass (b/III-24-1770; d/IV-26 or 29-1855) Hon MD Harvard 1818; AB 1792. *Bost m&s j* 52: 267, 1855.

ORR, HENRY B , Pittsburgh (d/III-29-1906 @46) MD Jefferson 1883. *Pa med jour* 9: 608, 1905/06. *New Orl m&s j* 58:82, 1906. *Flint* 1897: 830.

ORR, JOHN CRAWFORD, USA; Chambersburg Pa (b/VI-4-1870; d/IX-12-1901 Philippine Isl) MD UPa 1895. *Pa med jour* 5:144, 296, 1901/02.

ORR, THOMAS S , Alexandria, Ky (d/XII-7-1896 @56) MD Med Coll Ohio 1869. *JAMA* 27: 1313, 1896. *Polk* 1896: 577.

ORRICK, JOHN CROMWELL, Baltimore (b/VI-16-1805; d/XII-29-1863) MD UMd 1831 *Med ann Md*:523.

ORRICK, JOHN HENRY, Stevens' Pt, Wis (b/1835 Orricktown, Md; d/1876) MD U Md 1857. *Tr AMA* 27: 669, 1876. *Tr Wis St Med Soc* 1880: 305.

ORRIS, GEORGE Q , Seymour, Ind (d/XII-13-1897 @47) MD Louisville Med Coll 1876 (as Orvis). *JAMA* 29:1286, 1897. *Polk* 1886: 335.

ORTH, ADOLPH, NYC (b/1837; d/IV-26-1878) MD Munich 1866. *Med reg NY NJ Conn* 1878: 183.

ORTON, AZARIAH G , Lisle, NY (b/1789? d/I-28-1865 @76) MD ? *Med s rep Phila* 12: 300, 1864/65.

ORTON, JAMES, Caldwell, NJ (b/1787? d/IX-17-1869 @82) MD ? *Phila med reg & dir* 1871: 302.

ORTON, MILSON T , CW-USA (d/II-2-1864 Hatteras, NC) MD ? *Nat med jour* 1:300, 1870/71.

ORWIG, ALBERT D , Toledo, O (d/I-15-1900 @ 42) MD Western Reserve 1884; AB. *JAMA* 34:251, 1900.

ORWIG, GEORGE R, Cleveland (d/III-14-1899 @44) MD Jefferson 1876 *JAMA* 32:733 1899. *Polk* 1896:1175.

OSBORN, CHARLES, Dubuque, Ia (d/II-2-1901) MD Rush 1890. *Ill med jour* ns2: 533, 1901.

OSBORN, CORRA, Westfield, NJ (b/1793? d/VI-8-1868 @75) MD ? *Phila med reg & dir* 1871: 297. *Tr AMA* 21:466, 1870. *Med surg rep Phila* 19:22, 1868.

OSBORN, FRANCIS M , Port Chester, NY (d/VIII-30-1894 @53) MD ? *Med reg NY NJ Conn* 1895:234.

OSBORN, FREDERICK SAMUEL, NYC (b/IX-26-1852; d/VII-18-1876) MD CPSNY 1874. *Med reg NY NJ Conn* 1877:205. *Med s rep Phila* 35:120, 1876.

OSBORN, JOHN, NYC (b/1818; d/III-4-1882) MD CPSNY 1839; AB Columbia 1836. *Med reg NY NJ Conn* 1882: 232.

OSBORN, MARY E , Cincinnati & Canton, O (d/IV-5-1896 @40) MD Woman's Med Coll Pa 1883. *JAMA* 26: 843, 1896: 1157, 1166.

OSBORN, MOSES C , Delmar, Ia (d/IV-23-1894) MD St U Iowa 1882. *JAMA* 22:764, 1894. *Polk* 1890: 412.

OSBORN, THOMAS CRUTCHER, Greenville, Ala; La; Cleburne, Tex 1882- (b/V-4 or 9-1818 Nashville; d/VIII-19-1902) <Hon MD Memphis Med Coll 1861> *Tr Tex St Med Assoc* 1903: 47-50. *So pract* 23:9-17, 1901; 24: 516, 1902. *Atkinson* I: 41. *Polk* 1900: 1686.

OSBORNE, ARUNDEL CAULFIELD, ?Pa (d/VI-21-1874 @25) MD Med Coll Va 1869. *Med surg rep Phila* 31: 60, 1874.

OSBORNE, CHARLES HORACE, CW-USA; NYC (b/IV-4-1837; d/I-29-1878) MD CPSNY 1858. *Med reg NY NJ Conn* 1878: 183.

OSBORNE, EDWARD, E Hampton, NY (d/XII-4-1905 @70) MD Bennett 1878. *Bost m&s j* 153: 682, 1905. *Polk* 1886:363 (Mason City, Ia). Eclectic.

OSBORNE, EDWARD A , Newark, NJ (b/1823 Longwood, NJ; d/X-24-1891) MD Jefferson 1848. *Med reg NY NJ Conn* 1892: 284. *Tr Med Soc NJ* 1892: 295. *Bost m&s j* 125:480, 1891. *Butler* 1878:436.

OSBORNE, F M , CW-USA (d/IX-22-1864) MD ? *Nat med jour* 1:300, 1870/71.

OSBORNE, GEORGE, Peabody, Mass (b/1799? d/IX-21 1882 @83) MD Harvard 1829; AB 1818. *Bost m&s j* 107: 619, 1882.

OSBORNE, GEORGE STERNE, CW-USA; Salem, Mass (d/V-25-1901 @62) MD Harvard 1863; AB 1860. *Bost m&s j* 144: 540, 568, 1901. *Harvard in CW*: 145. *Polk* 1896: 720.

OSBORNE, HENRY, Council Bluffs, Ia (b/1830; d/1880) MD CPS Keokuk 1858. *Tr AMA* 32:528-29, 1881. *Tr Ia St Med Soc* 1879-80: 192-94. *Butler* 1878: 242.

OSBORNE, JOSEPH DAVIS, CW-USA; Newark, NJ (d/VI-2-1900 @67) MD CPSNY 1859. *JAMA* 34: 1574, 1900. *Polk* 1896: 943.

OSBORNE, WILLIAM, Chicago (d/IV-19-1906) MD Bennett 1882. *Ill med jour* 9: 661, 1906.

OSGOOD, BENJAMIN, Westford, Mass (b/1781? d/II-1 1863 @82) MD ? *Bost m&s j* 68:28, 1863.

OSGOOD, ERASTUS, Lebanon, Conn 1803-50? Norwich 1850- (b/III-7-1780 Pomfret; d/XII-22-1867) Stud med w/Thos Hubbard, Pomfret. *Med s rep Phila* 18: 21 1868. *Pr Conn M S* 1868:19. *Bost m&s j* 77:468 1867.

OSGOOD, GEORGE, Danvers, Mass (d/V-26-1863) MD ? *Bost m&s j* 68:370, 1863.

OSGOOD, JONATHAN WALTER DANDOLO, Greenfield, Mass (b/VII-29-1802; d/V-15-1885) MD Dartmouth 1826; AB 1823. *JAMA* 9:479-80, 1887. *Bost m&s j* 112:540, 1885; 113:657, 1885. *Butler* 1878:355.

OSGOOD, WILLIAM, Boston (d/IV-10-1885 @62) MD Jefferson 1855; AB Harvard 1850. *Bost m&s j* 112: 384, 1885.

OSGOOD, WILLIAM, N Yarmouth, Me (b/XI-12-1825; d/XII-25-1894) MD Bowdoin 1850; AB 1846. *JAMA* 24: 67, 1895. *Bost m&s j* 133:195, 1895. *Tr Me Med Assoc* 1895: 187-88.

OSMUN, LEWIS MACKEY, Warren Co, NJ (b/XI-2-1835; d/III-20-1884 Phillipsburg, NJ) MD Columbian DC 1860. *Tr Med Soc NJ* 1884: 166-67.

OSTERSTOCK, JOSEPH HINKLE, Easton, Pa (b/1836; d/VII-30/31-1901) MD U Pa 1872. *Pa med jour* 5:296, 1901/02. *U Pa med alum CW*: 1872. CW-USA.

OSTRANDER, CHAUNCY B , Fairbury, Ill (d/V–30–1905 @87) <MD Fairfield 1836> *Ill med jour* 8:80,1905.

OSTRANDER, EZEKIEL, Brooklyn (b/1778? d/V–23–1860 @82) MD CPSNY 1804. *Bost m&s j* 62:372, 1860.

OSTRANDER, FERDINAND WILLIAM, Brooklyn (b/VI–4–1804 NYC; d/I–30–1895) Lic 1828 NY Med Soc. *Bost m&s j* 132:141, 1895. *JAMA* 24: 337, 1895. *Med reg NY NJ Conn* 1895:234. *Med bull m & s* 17:148, 1895.

OSTRANDER, JASPER ANNIS, Suisum, Calif (b/1855 Snelling; d/I–22–1899) MD Hahnemann San Francisco 1888. *Tr Am Inst Hom* 1900: 836. Homeopath.

OSTRANDER, WALTER D McJ, Philadelphia; Danville & Pittston, Pa (b/VIII–4–1839 New Brunswick, NJ; d/VIII–23–1881) MD Hahnemann Phila 1864. *Chic m rev* 4:401,1851. *Butler* 1878:726. *Cleave*. Homeopath.

OSTROM HENRY H , Alton NY (d/XII–8–1898 @73) MD UCNY 1850. *JAMA* 31:1542,1898. *Polk* 1896: 986.

O'SULLIVAN, GEORGE BRENDON, Brooklyn (b/II–11–1866; d/X–11–1896) MD LICH 1887; att St Francis Coll 1883. *JAMA* 27: 1020–21, 1896. *Polk* 1896: 1001.

O'SULLIVAN, THOMAS JEFFERSON, Derby, Conn (b/III–1852 Preston; d/II–9–1900) MD Bellevue 1876. *Pr Conn M S* 1900: 254–56. *JAMA* 34:446, 1900. *Flint* 1897: 174.

OTEY, PAUL H , CW–CSA; Tenn (d/IX–29–1878 Memphis) MD Jefferson 1846. *Tr AMA* 30:881, 1879. *SHSP* 22: 243, 1893.

OTIS, DANIEL GREEN, RI (d/1858) MD Harvard 1850. *Tr AMA* 13:796, 1860.

OTIS, FESSENDEN NOTT, NYC (v/V–6–1825 Ballston Spa, NY; d/V–24–1900 New Orleans) MD NY Med Coll 1852; AB Union. *Buff m&s j* 39:861, 1900. *JAMA* 34: 1431, 1900. *New Orl m&s j*52:754, 1900. *K&B* III: 923–24. *Atkinson* I: 338.

OTIS, GEORGE ALEXANDER, USA 1861– (b/XI–12 1830 Boston; d/II–23–1881 Washington, DC) MD UPa 1852: AB Princeton 1849; AM 1852. *U Pa m alum CW*: 1851. *Tr AMA* 32: 520–34, 1881. *Bost m&s j* 104: 211 261 383 1881; 105:621–22 623 1881. *K&B* III: 924–25.

OTIS, GEORGE WASHINGTON Jr, Chelsea, Mass (d/VIII–5–1872 @72) MD Harvard 1821; AB 1818. *Bost m&s j* ns10:124, 1872.

OTIS, HENRY SHARWOOD, Hartford, Conn (d/VIII–4 1889) MD Harvard 1883. *Bost m&s j* 121: 148, 1889.

OTIS, JENKS HARRIS, Boston; USN 1851– (d/VIII 27–1864 @34) MD Harvard 1851; ng Harvard Coll 1847. *Bost m&s j* 71:108, 1864. *Med s rep Phila* 12:100, 1864/65. *Nat med jour* 1:300, 1870/71.

OTIS, ROBERT MENDUM, Roslindale, Mass (d/III–19 1886 @42) MD Bellevue 1869; AB Harvard 1866. *Bost m&s j* 114: 288, 1886.

OTIS, WILLIAM KELLY, NYC (b/NY; d/IX–22–1906) MD CPSNY 1885; AB Columbia 1882. *Bost m&s j* 155: 389, 661, 1906. *Polk* 1896: 1071.

O'TOOLE, MICHAEL C , San Francisco (b/Wexford, Irel'd; d/XI–23–1897 @65) MD U Mich 1862; MD UCNY 1865. *JAMA* 29:1181, 1897. *Polk* 1886: 174.

OTTERSON, ANDREW, Brooklyn (b/II–22–1822 Amsterdam, NY; d/IV–14–1897) MD UCNY 1844. *JAMA* 28:860, 1897. *Polk* 1896: 1001.

OTTERSON, WILLIAM CARTER, CW–USA; Brooklyn (b/IX–17–1828 LI, NY; d/VIII–17–1898) MD CPSNY 1853. *Bost m&s j* 139: 202, 1898. *JAMA* 31:484, 1898. *Polk* 1896: 1001.

OTTILIE, CHARLES, La Crosse, Wis (b/IV–3–1831 Gny; d/IV–30–1895) <MD Berlin 1856> *JAMA* 24:731, 1895. *Tr Wis St M S* 29:540–43, 1895. *Polk* 1890: 1310.

OTTO, JOHN CONRAD, Philadelphia (b/III–14–1774 Woodbury NJ; d/VI–26–1844) MD UPa 1796; AB Princeton 1772. *Tr CPP* cent vol: 254; 1:303–18, 1841–46. *Tr AMA* 3:454–56,1850. *K&B* III:925–26.

OTTO, JOHN HENRY, Milwaukee (d/I–15–1898 @36) MD UCNY 1885. *JAMA* 30:279, 1898. *Polk* 1896:1556.

OTTO, JOHN MARTIN, NYC (d/XII–29–1903) MD UCNY 1889. *Bost m&s j* 150:28, 1904. *Polk* 1896: 1071.

OVERFIELD, FERDINAND S , Brookville, Ill (d/VIII–16–1905 @76) Lic yrs pract. *Ill med jour* 8:341, 1905. *Polk* 1896: 365.

OVERHOLT, FRANK, Harlan & Des Moines, Ia (b/I–22 1866 Jackson Co; d/XII–10–1896) MD Bellevue 1889. *JAMA* 28:92, 1897. *Tr Iowa St M S* 15:370–71, 1897. *Polk* 1890: 417.

OVERSTREET, WALTER C Jr, Monmouth Ill (d/VII–26–1895) MD Mo M C 1878. *JAMA* 25:209, 253, 1895.

OVERTON, JAMES, Nashville & Rock Castle, Tenn (b/VIII–1785 Louisa Co Va;d/IX–23–1865) MD UPa 1809. *Tr Med Soc Tenn* 1876:85–86. *Nashvl j m & s* ns1:42–52, 1886. *Tr AMA* 18:342–44, 1867.

OVERTON, JOHN B , Brooklyn (d/V–5–1879 @51) <Stud med Phila & CPSNY> *Med reg NY NJ Conn* 1880:238. *Butler* 1878: 533.

OVERTON, MARTIN LUTHER, Lorraine, NY (d/I–13–1900) MD CPSNY 1865. *JAMA* 34:313, 1900. *Polk* 1896: 1030.

OVERTON, WILLIAM P , Cold Spring Harbor, NY (d/X–24–1894 @74) MD ? *Med reg NY NJ Conn* 1895: 234. *JAMA* 23:735, 840, 1894. *Polk* 1886: 657.

OWEN, ABRAHAM MICONIUS, Evansville, Ind (b/III–14–1849 Hopkinsville, Ky; d/IX–18–1898) MD Bellevue 1871. *Buff m&s j* 38:224, 1898. *JAMA* 31: 1898. *Atkinson* I: 539.

OWEN, ALFRED M, USN (d/VIII–1883 Pensacola, Fla) MD Jefferson 1869. *Med bull med & surg* 5:239, 1883.

OWEN, CHARLES SYLVESTER, Wheaton, Ill 1885– (b/VII–29–1858 Marion Co, O; d/XII–27–1903 Chic) MD Chicago Homeop 1883. *Tr Am Inst Hom* 1904:963–64. *Polk* 1886:301. Homeopath.

OWEN, DAVID DALE, New Harmony, Ind (b/Scotl'd? d/XI or XII–13–1860) MD Med Coll Ohio 1836. *Med surg rep Phila* ns5: 241, 1860/61. *K&B*

Spec. educ'l status abbrev. as: ***ng*** = college verified attendance without degree;

OWEN, EDWARD W , CW–USA; Brooklyn (d/III–30–1889 @76) MD Castleton 1846. *Med reg NY NJ Conn* 1890:279. *Butler* 1878: 533.

OWEN, GORONWY, Mobile, Ala; CW–USA (b/II–11–1835; d/III–30–1903) MD UPa 1857; AB U Ala 1854. *U Pa m alum CW*: 1857. *Polk* 1886: 137.

OWEN, JESSE, Cincinnati (d/V–1–1884 @68) MD ? *Med surg rep Phila* 50:640, 1884.

OWEN, JOHN, Baltimore (b/IX–17–1775 Annapolis; d/X– –1824) Hon MD U Md 1818. *Med annals Md:* 524.

OWEN, JOSEPH RICHARDSON NIMMO, Indian & Mex Wars–USA; Eureka, Nev (b/1818; d/V–3–1900) MD Transylvania 1838; att U Ala 1831. *U Ala cat*: 43. *Polk* 1886: 185.

OWEN, JOSHUA T , Chester, Pa (d/II– –1880) MD ? Jefferson 1840. *Med surg rep Phila* 42:176, 1880.

OWEN, SCOTT, Syracuse, NY (d/I–3–1899) MD Syracuse 1883. *JAMA* 32:92, 1899. *Polk* 1886: 711.

OWEN, THOMAS LUCIAN MORELAND, Jonesboro, Ala; CW–CSA? (b/XII–23–1834; d/II–6–1862) <MD Mobile> AB U Ala 1859. *U Ala cat*: 136.

OWEN, WILLIAM OTWAY Jr, CW–CSA; Lynchburg, Va (b/X–20–1820;d/II–15–1892) MD UCNY 1845. *Tr M S Va* 1892:193–5. *NW m j* 20:112, 1892. *K&B* III:872.

OWEN, WILLIAM R , Sublette, Ill (b/1840; d/VIII–27 1905 Minneapolis) MD CPS Chicago 1889. *Ill med jour* 8:341, 1905. *Polk* 1896: 443.

OWENS, ISAAC B , Baltimore (b/1812; d/1854) MD U Md 1833. *Med annals Md:* 524.

OWENS, R C , Ben Franklin Tx (d/VII–10–1894) MD ? *Tex cour–rec med* 11 [ie 12?]:286, 1894. *Polk* 1890: 1086.

OWENS, SAMUEL A, USA; Waco, Tex 1859–89? (d/XI 19–1905 @81 Center City, Tex) MD Mo Med Coll 1849. *Tex st med jour* 1:256, 1905/06. *Polk* 1886: 896.

OWENS, SAMUEL R , Somerset, Ky (d/VIII–29–1901 @76) MD U Tenn 1886. *JAMA* 37:790, 1901.

OWENS, THOMAS ROBERT, Boston (d/IX–3–1861 @ 36) MD Harvard 1850. *Bost m&s j* 65: 108, 1861.

OWENS [OWEN], WILLIAM, Lynchburg, Va (b/I–12–1788 Staunton, Va; d/I–22–1875) MD UPa 1815. *Tr M S Va* 1875: 67. *Tr AMA* 26:476–77, 1875. *K&B* III: 928.

OWENS, WILLIAM, CW–USA; Cincinnati (b/IV–24–1823 Warren; d/XII–15–1897 @74) MD Eclectic Med Inst Cinc 1849. *Tr Am Inst Hom* 1898: 49. *Polk* 1886: 744. Homeopath.

OWINGS, HARRY W , Baltimore (b/IX–15–1837; d/XI–15–1890) MD U Md 1860. *Med annals Md:* 524. *Polk* 1886: 438.

OWINGS, THOMAS, Anne Arundel Co, Md (b/XII–11–1802; d/XII–18–1866) MD U Md 1825. *Tr AMA* 18: 338, 1867.

OXNER, J HARRIS, Rome, NY (d/VI–8–1900 @58) MD U Mich 1880. *JAMA* 34: 1645, 1900. *Polk* 1896: 1097.

PACETTI, JOSEPH A , Jacksonville, Fla (b/1838 St Augustine; d/I–12–1894) MD U Md 1858. *JAMA* 22: 122, 1894. *Polk* 1890: 253.

PACKARD, ALPHEUS SPRING, Providence, RI (b/II–19–1839 Brunswick, Me; d/II–14–1905) MD Bowdoin 1864; AB 1861. *Tr RI Med Soc* 7:280–282, 1904–09.

PACKARD, FREDERICK ADOLPHUS, Philadelphia (b/XI–17–1862; d/XI–1–1902) MD UPa 1885; AB 1882. *Pa m j* 6: 153, 1902/03. *Bost m&s j* 147:578, 1902. *Flint* 1897: 823. *K&B* III:928–29.

PACKARD, GEORGE, Saco, Me 1825–42; Andover, Mass 1843–45; Lawrence 1846–76 (b/V–23–1803 Wiscasset; d/XI–30–1876) MD Bowdoin 1825; AB 1823; stud Theol Sem Fairfax Co, Va. *Bowdoin cat:*1823.

PACKARD, LIBERTY DODGE S Boston (b/IX–13–1831 N Bridgewater; d/I–15–1895) MD NY Homeop 1862; att Harvard 1860–61. *Tr Am Inst Hom* 1895: 231. *Polk* 1886: 473. Homeopath.

PADDOCK, FRANKLIN KITTREDGE, Pittsfield, Mass (b/XII–19–1841 Hamilton, NY; d/VII–26–1901) MD Berkshire 1864. *Bost m&s j* 145: 139, 140, 1901. *Polk* 1896: 721.

PADGETT, DAVID ANDERSON, Fackler, Ala (d/V–31 1887) MD Vanderbilt 1882. *Tr M Assn St Ala* 1887: 306.

PADULA, THOMAS FRANCIS, Quincy, Mass (d/II–9–1905 @45) MD Harvard 1887; AB Holy Cross. *Bost m &s j* 152: 206, 1905. *Polk* 1896: 703.

PAGANI, JOSEPH, Boston (b/Italy; d/VII–15–1894 @ 58) <MD Parma> *Bost m & s j* 131:72, 1894. *Polk* 1890:541.

PAGE, ALPHEUS FELCH, Orland, Me 1849–51; Bucksport 1851– (b/XII–7–1824 Limington; d/XII–28–1880) MD Bowdoin 1849; att Bowdoin Coll 1844–46. *Tr Me Med Assoc* 1880–82: 517–18. *Butler* 1878:309.

PAGE, BEZIN ARNOLD, Washington, DC (d/III–14 1879 @30) MD Georgetown 1871. *Med reg NY NJ Conn* 1880:238. *Butler* 1878: 96.

PAGE, CALVIN GATES, Boston; CW–USA (d/V–29–1869 @39) MD Harvard 1855; AB 1852. *Bost m&s j* ns3:328, 1869; 105:521, 1881. *Harvard in CW*: 58–59.

PAGE, CHARLES GRAFTON, Washington, DC (d/V 5–1868 @57) MD ? *Med surg rep Phila* 18: 442, 1868. *Phila med reg & dir* 1871: 296.

PAGE, CHARLES H , USN (b/NH; d/XII–24–1867 or 68 Japan) MD ? *Nat med jour* 1:300, 1870/71. *Tr AMA* 19:455, 1868; 21:495, 1870. *Med surg rep Phila* 18: 204, 1868. *Phila med reg & dir* 1871: 299.

PAGE, EDWARD AUGUSTUS, Philadelphia; CW–USA (b/X–23–1830 Moorestown, NJ; d/II–19–1881) MD UPa 1852. *U Pa med alum CW*: 1852. *Tr CPP* cent vol: 255.

PAGE, FREDERIC BENJAMIN, Donaldsville, La (b/VII–5–1798 Hallowell, Me; d/VII–26–1857 Edwards, Miss) MD Harvard 1821; AB Bowdoin 1818; AM 1821. *Bowdoin cat*: 1818.

PAGE, HORATIO NELSON, Chelsea, Mass; Bangor, Me (b/VI–20–1806 Fryeburg, Me; d/IX–16–1893

Milwaukee) MD Bowdoin 1831. *JAMA* 21: 498, 1893. *Chic med rec* 5:277, 1893. *Bost m&s j* 129: 336, 1893.

PAGE, JAMES, USN 1807–24, 1827–32; Baltimore (b/Kent Co, Md; d/III–15–1832) MD UPa 1808. *Med annals Md:* 525–26.

PAGE, JESSE WILLIAM, Merry Hill, NC 1848–58; NYC 1858–61; Baltimore 1886 (b/X–14–1820 and d/III–21–1888 Bath, Me) MD UMd 1848; AB Bowdoin 1842. *Bowdoin cat*: 1842. *Polk* 1886: 438.

PAGE, JOHN RANDOLPH, Charlottesville, Va (b/VI–3 1834; d/III–11–1901) MD UCNY 1859. *Med ann Md:* 526. *Butler* 1874: 314.

PAGE, JOHN TAYLOR, Somersworth, NH; Winchendon Mass (b/V–29–1822 Dover NH;d/XII–25–1866)MD Jefferson 1849; AB Bowdoin 1844. *Bowdoin cat*: 1844.

PAGE, MELVIN EARNEST, Oswego, NY (b/Broome Co; d/IX–10–1906 @40) MD Bellevue 1889. *Bost m&s j* 155: 324, 1906.

PAGE, PRINCE WOODMAN, Boston (d/IX–29–1891 @50 Calif) MD Harvard 1871. *Bost m&s j* 125: 392, 1891. *Butler* 1878: 342.

PAGE, R ARNOLD, NYC (b/DC; d/1878) MD Georgetown 1871. *Hist Med Soc DC:* 303.

PAGE, RICHARD CHANNING MOORE, NYC; Philadelphia (b/I–2–1841 Keswick, Va; d/VI–19–1898) MD UCNY 1868. *JAMA* 31:38, 1898. *Polk* 1896:1071.

PAGE, RICHARD HENRY, Columbus, NJ (b/IX–22–1828 Medford, NJ; d/I–2–1890) MD UPa 1850. *Tr Med Soc NJ* 1890: 341–43.

PAGE, THOMAS, Tuckerton, MJ (b/VI–8–1798 Cross Roads; d/II–18–1876) MD UPa 1821. *Tr AMA* 27:656, 1876. *Tr Med Soc NJ* 1876: 137–38.

PAGE, WILLIAM BYRD, Philadelphia (d/II–18–1877 @59) MD UPa 1839; att Kenyon. *Tr CPP* cent vol: 255.

PAGE, WILLIAM MEADE, USN 1855–61; CSA 1861–65; Fauquier Co, Va (b/VI–13–1831 Millwood; d/V–8–1906) MD UPa 1855; MD U Va 1853. *Hist Med Soc DC:* 307. *U Pa med alum CW*: 1855.

PAIGE [PAGE], HOMER R , Des Moines, Ia (d/1892) MD Ia St U 1871. *Tr Ia St Med Soc* 18:411, 1900; 21:449, 1903. *Polk* 1890: 413.

PAIGE, WILLIAM F , Johnstown, O (b/IV–19–1820 Licking Co; d/XII–2–1878) ng Med Coll NY 1844–45 [!] *Tr O St Med Soc* 1880: 111–12. *Butler* 1878: 644.

PAINE, CHARLES F , Comanche, Tex (b/VII–29–1849 De Soto Co, Miss; d/IX–13–1893) MD Tulane 1875. *Tex cour–rec med* 11:51, 1893. *Daniel's Tex m j* 9:350–52, 1893–94. *Polk* 1886: 883.

PAINE, CHARLES FORREST, Troy, Pa (d/XI–14–1901) MD UPa 1866; AB Kenyon 1862. *Pa med jour* 5: 296, 1901/02.

PAINE, D L , Oregon City (d/IX–30–1898 @55) MD Columbus Med Coll 1878. *JAMA* 31:942, 1898. *Polk* 1890: 966.

PAINE, FREDERICK T , Comanche, Tex (d/IV–16–1891) MD Transylvania 1836. *Tex cour–rec med* 8:234, 1891. *Daniel's Tex med jour* 6:479, 1890.

PAINE, HORACE MARSHFIELD, Albany & Clinton, NY to 1895; Atlanta (b/XI–19–1827 Paris, NY; d/XII–5 1903 Atlanta) MD UCNY 1849. *Tr Am Inst Hom* 1904: 953–54. *Polk* 1886: 63. Homeopath.

PAINE, HORATIO, CW–USA; NYC (d/V–1–1882 @40 London, Engl) MD UPa 1864; AB Harvard 1859. *Med reg NY NJ Conn* 1882:233. *U Pa med alum CW*: 1864.

PAINE, MARTYN, NYC (b/VII–8–1794 Vt; d/XI–10–1877) MD Harvard 1816; AB 1813. *Med reg NY NJ Conn* 1878: 183. *Med surg rep Phila* ns15:63–67, 1866. *Med rec* 12:735, 1877. *Atkinson* I:12–13. *K&B* III:931.

PAINE, OAKMAN SPRAGUE, NYC (d/XI–8–1891 @53) MD Buffalo 1864. *Bost m&s j* 125:560, 1891. *Butler* 1878: 521.

PAINE, RICHARD KENDALL, CW–USA; Manitowoc, Wis (b/X–5 1841 Orange Vt; d/XI–7–1904) MD Hahnemann Chicago 1873. *Tr Am Inst Hom* 1905: 842. *Polk* 1886: 955. Homeopath.

PAINE, ROTHEUS EMERY, Camden, Me (b/X–18–1834 Exeter; d/V–31–1882) MD Bowdoin 1857. *Tr Me Med Assoc* 1882:414: 1883:154. *Butler* 1878: 309.

PAINE, STEPHEN ATKINS, Provincetown, Mass (b/IX –26–1807; d/IX–3–1869) MD Harvard 1835; AB Amherst 1832. *Amherst, Men of*: 1832.

PAINE, STERLING LEWIS, Aberdeen & Corinth, Miss; CW–CSA (b/XII–14–1824 Giles Co, Tenn; d/IV–28–1890 Muldon, Miss) MD UPa 1847. *U Pa med alum CW*: 1847. *Atkinson* I: 512. *Polk* 1886: 531.

PAINTER, EDWIN THOMAS, Redlands, Calif (d/I–22–1900 @44) MD CPSNY 1885; BS Worcester Polytechnic Inst. *JAMA* 34: 380, 1900. *Polk* 1896: 227.

PALEN, GILBERT EZEKIEL, Philadelphia (b/1832; d/VII–28–1901 Ocean City, NJ) MD Albany 1855. *JAMA* 37:398, 1901. *Polk* 1886: 822.

PALLEN, MONTROSE ANDERSON, CW–CSA; St Louis; NYC (b/I–2–1836 Vicksburg, Miss; d/X–1–1892) MD St Louis M C 1856; AB St Louis U 1853; AM 1856. *Med reg NY NJ Conn* 1891: 280. *Bost m&s j* 123:360, 1890. *JAMA* 15:734, 1890. *Atkinson* I:162–63. *K&B* III: 931–32.

PALLEN, MOSES MONTROSE, St Louis (b/IV–29–1810 K & Q Co Va; d/IX–25–1876) MD U Md 1832; ng U Va 1832. *Tr AMA* 28:620–21,1877. *K&B* III: 932.

PALMEDO, ULRIC, Brooklyn (b/VII–4–1810; d/IX–25 1876) MD Berlin 1831. *Med reg NY NJ Conn* 1877:205.

PALMER, ALDEN DWINAL, CW–USA (b/1837 Orono Me; d/III–20–1865 Wilmington NC) MD Bowdoin 1862. *Nat med jour* 1:300, 1870/71.

PALMER, ALONZO BENJAMIN, Ann Arbor, Mich; CW–USA (b/X–6–1815 Richfield, NY; d/XII–23–1887) MD Fairfield 1839. *Bost m&s j* 119:56, 1888. *Tr Me Med Assoc* 1888: 512–13. *Med age* 5:558, 1887. *Atkinson* I: 13. *K&B* III: 932.

 Spec. educ'l status abbrev. as: ***ng*** = college verified attendance without degree;

PALMER, BENJAMIN RUSH, Woodstock, Vt; Louisville (b/V-8-1813 Clarendon; d/VII-4-1865) Hon MD Berkshire 1843; AB Woodstock 1831; AM Dartmouth 1834. *Bost m&s j* 72:496, 1865. *Tr AMA* 29:735-36, 1878. *Tr Vt Med Soc* 1883: 108.

PALMER, BENJAMIN R [B ?], Sauk Centre, Minn (b/III-5-1815 Berwick Me; d/V-6-1882) MD U Md 1844. *Tr Minn St M S* 1882:267-68. *Butler* 1878: 394.

PALMER, BENJAMIN WOOD, Detroit (d/I-4-1895) MD CPSNY 1880. *Med reg NY NJ Conn* 1895: 235. *New Orl m&s j* ns24:637, 1895. *Chic med rec* 8:253, 1895. *Polk* 1886: 489.

PALMER, CHARLES, CW-USN; Strafford, NH 1852-65; Ipswich, Mass 1868-1903 (b/XI-11-1825 Dover, NH; d/I-11-1906) MD Jefferson 1848; AM Dartmouth 1877; ng Bowdoin Med Coll 1845. *Bowdoin cat*: 1845. *Polk* 1886: 467.

PALMER, CHARLES THOMAS, CW-USA; Pottsville, Pa (b/IX-8-1843; d/XII-11-1893) MD UPa 1865. *Lehigh Valley m mag* 5:108, 1893-94. *JAMA* 22: 31, 1894. *U Pa m alum CW*: 1865. *Butler* 1878: 727.

PALMER, CHARLES W, New Hope, Pa (d/III-9-1903 @36) MD Jefferson 1902. *Pa med jour* 7:280, 1903.

PALMER, DAVID, Brooklyn (b/1790; d/XI-14-1873 @83) MD ? *Med s rep Phila* 29:418 1873; 30:228 1874.

PALMER, EDWARD DORR GRIFFIN, Boston (b/IV-17-1818; d/VI-28-1869) MD Harvard 1842; AB Brown 1839. *Bost m&s j* ns3:408, 1869; 105:521, 1881.

PALMER, EDWARD RUSH, CW-USA; Louisville (b/XI-18-1842 Woodstock, Vt; d/VII-6-1895) MD U Louisville 1864. *Tr Ky St M S* 6:290-96 1897. *JAMA* 25: 76, 123, 1895. *Buff m&s j* 35:122, 1895. *Atkinson* I: 692.

PALMER, FREDERIC NILES, Boston (b/III-19-1814; d/V-10-1886) MD Hahnemann Phila 1853. *New Engl m gaz* 21:336, 1886. *Med vis* 2:243, 1886. *Polk* 1886:460.

PALMER, GEORGE E, Stonington, Conn (b/IV-15-1803; d/V-8-1868) MD CPSNY 1826. *Phila med reg & dir* 1871: 296. *Proc Conn Med Soc* 1869:299-304.

PALMER, GEORGE S, Buffalo (d/IV-14-1900 @38) MD U Buff 1886. *Buffalo m&s j* 39:782,1900.

PALMER, GIDEON STINSON, CW-USA; Washington, DC (b/VI-14-1813 Gardiner, Me; d/XII-8-1891) MD Bowdoin 1841; AB 1838. *JAMA* 18:29, 1892. *Hist Med Soc DC:* 299. *Med bull med & surg* 14:79, 1892.

PALMER, HARRIS ORLANDO, Hubbardston, Mass (b/VIII-19-1841 Orford, NH; d/II-17-1901) MD Dartmouth 1867. *Bost m&s j* 144:540, 1901. *Polk* 1886: 467.

PALMER, HENRY, Janesville, Wis (b/VII-30-1827 New Hartford, NY; d/VI-15-1895) MD Albany Med Coll 1854. *JAMA* 24:989, 1895. *Tr Wis St Med Soc* 29: 543-46, 1895. *Polk* 1890: 1166.

PALMER, HENRY H, Ludlow, Vt (b/VIII-1-1819; d/VIII-9-1872 @53) MD Woodstock 1843. *Tr Vt Med Soc* 1883: 108. *Med surg rep Phila* 27:260, 1872.

PALMER, ISAAC, Augusta, Me 1838-39; N Anson 1839- (b/IX-26-1807 Fayette; d/II-28-1880) MD Berkshire 1837; AB Bowdoin 1833. *Bowdoin cat*: 1833.

PALMER, JOSEPH, Boston (b/1797? d/III-3-1871 @74) MD Harvard 1826; AB 1820. *Bost m&s j* 7:172, 1871.

PALMER, LUCIUS N, Brooklyn (d/VI-17-1885 @63) MD UCNY 1849. *Med reg NY NJ Conn* 1886: 252.

PALMER, R H, CW-USA (d/XI-7-1862 Buffalo) MD ? *Nat med jour* 1:300, 1870/71.

PALMER, RICHARD H, CW-USA (d/XII-4-1864 @ c44) <Cert Med Soc NY 1863> *Med surg rep Phila* 12: 268, 1864/65. *Nat med jour* 1:300, 1870/71.

PALMER, THOMAS M, Monticello, Fla (d/VI-3-1895) MD U Md 1844. *JAMA* 24:989, 1895. *Polk* 1890: 254.

PALMER, WILLIAM GRAY, Pr Geo Co, Md; Washington, DC 1852- (b/II-22-1824 Montgomery Co, Md; d/XI-23-1893) MD UPa 1844. *JAMA* 21:908, 1893. *Hist Med Soc DC:* 247. *Atkinson* I: 511.

PALMER, WILLIAM H, Jackson, Mich (d/IX--1897 @60) MD ? *JAMA* 29:606, 1897. *Polk* 1886:495.

PALMER, WILLIAM HENRY, Leroy, Ill (b/XII-24-1849 Morgan Co; d/III-5-1873) MD Rush 1870. *Chicago med jour* 30: 256, 1873.

PALMER, WILLIAM PENNELL, Sandy Spring, Md (b/XI-19-1792 Concord, Pa; d/XII-27-1869) MD UPa 1815. *Med annals Md:* 527.

PALMER, WILLIAM PRICE, ?Richmond, Va; CW-CSA (b/VIII-17-1821; d/III-3-1896) MD UPa 1842; MD U Va 1840. *U Pa med alum CW*: 1842. Blanton *Va surgs CW*: 412.

PANCAKE, D A [PANKAKE, A D] ?Columbus, O (d/VIII-28-1890) MD ?Starling 1865. *JAMA* 21:390, 1893.

PANCOAST, DILWYN PARRISH, CW-USA; Camden, NJ (b/III-11-1836 Mullica Hill; d/IV-11-1899 @63) MD UPa 1859. *JAMA* 33: 1375, 1899. *Polk* 1886: 602.

PANCOAST, GEORGE LAURIE, Washington, DC; CW-USA (b/XII-9-1838 Burlington Co, NJ; d/XII-15-1868) MD Jefferson 1859. *Tr AMA* 23:578-81, 1872. *Hist Med Soc DC:* 278. *Phila med reg & dir* 1871: 299.

PANCOAST, JOSEPH, Philadelphia (b/XI-23-1805 Burlington, NJ; d/III or V-7-1828. *Bost m&s j* 106:260, 261, 1882. *Tr CPP* cent vol: 255. *Coll & clin rec* (Jefferson) 3:89, 1882. *K&B* III:934-35.

PANCOAST, SETH, Philadelphia (b/VII-28-1823 Darby, Pa; d/XII-16-1889) MD UPa 1852. *Med surg rep Phila* 61:726, 1889. *Polk* 1886: 822.

PANCOAST, WILLIAM HENRY, Philadelphia (b/X-16 1834; d/I-5-1897) MD Jefferson 1856; AB Haverford 1853; AM. *Tr CPP* cent vol: 255. *Bost m&s j* 136:48, 1897. *JAMA* 28: 91, 1897. *Med bull med & surg* 19:70, 74-75, 1897. *K&B* III: 935-36.

PANGBURN, DAVID, Judson, Ark (b/VIII-7-1813 Schenectady Co, NY; d/1880) MD Albany 1847. *Tr AMA* 32:534-35, 1881. *Tr St Med Soc Ark* 1882: "In memoriam." *Atkinson* I: 385.

PANNILL, WILLIAM, Chatfield, Tex 1894- ; Corsicana (b/IV-20-1851 Petersburg, Va; d/X-21-1904) MD Tex Med Coll Galveston 1878; att VMI. *Tex st med jour* 1:245, 1906. *Polk* 1896: 1423.

PAOLI, GERHARDT CHRISTIAN, Springfield, O; Chicago (b/III-23-1815 Drontheim, Norway; d/I-29-1898) Hon MD Rush 1866. *Chicago med rec* 14: 173-74, 1898. *JAMA* 30: 391, 1898. *Flint* 1897: 266.

PAPE, GEORGE EDWARD, Baltimore (b/Hanover, Gny; d/1900) MD Göttingen 1833 <att U Md 1856> *Med annals Md:* 527.

PAPE, GEORGE W , Baltimore (b/1848 Hanover, Gny; 2/1882) MD U Md 1871. *Med annals Md:* 527. *Butler* 1874: 314.

PAPE, WILLIAM BARNEMORE, Mobile, Ala (d/VIII-29-1901 @51) MD Med Coll Ala 1882. *Tr Med Assn St Ala* 1902:130. *JAMA* 37:710,1910. *Polk* 1893:159.

PARCEL, JAMES H, Anna Ill (d/III-16-1905 @76) Cert 1878 yrs pract. *Ill med jour* 7:379,1905. *Polk* 1886: 301.

PARCHER, GEORGE, Ellsworth, Me (b/XI-19-1803 Hallowell; d/XII-29-1884) MD Bowdoin 1830. *Tr Me Med Assoc* 1885:559-61. *Butler* 1878: 309.

PARDEE, CHARLES INSLEE, NYC (b/IV-13-1838 Seneca Co; d/XI-4-1899) MD UCNY 1860. *Bost m&s j* 141:480, 1899. *Buffalo m&s j* 39:385, 1899. *JAMA* 33: 1307, 1899. *Atkinson* I: 234. *Polk* 1896: 1072.

PARDEE, DANIEL, Fulton, NY (d/VIII-25-1891 @57) MD Albany 1855; AB Union 1852; AM 1855. *NW med jour* 19:151, 1891. *Bost m&s j* 125:284, 1891. *Tr Med Soc St NY* 1892:428. *Butler* 1878: 568.

PARISH, ASBURY, Flemington, NJ (b/V-17-1846 Franklin, NJ; d/XII-17-1891) MD Jefferson 1874. *Lehigh Valley med mag* 4:17, 1892-93. *Tr Med Soc NJ* 1892: . *Polk* 1890: 721.

PARISH, CHARLES W , Marshallton, Pa (b/II-5-1793 London, Engl; d/XII-17-1856) ng UPa Med Dept 1821. *Tr Pa St Med Soc* 1857: 135-37.

PARISH, WILLIAM HENRY, Philadelphia (b/X-23-1845; d/VII-20-1903) MD Jefferson 1870. *Pa m j* 7:280 1903/04. *Butler* 1878 693. *Tr CPP* cent vol:255-56.

PARK, AUGUSTUS VITELIUS, Chicago (d/VIII-14-1901 @50) MD Rush 1883. *Ill med jour* ns3:237, 1901. *JAMA* 37:527, 1901. *Polk* 1896: 400.

PARK, CEPHAS, Oquawaka, Ill (d/IX-23-1901) MD Cleveland Med Coll 1854. *Ill med jour* ns3:295, 1901. *Polk* 1886: 291.

PARK, CREDNER S , Mt Pleasant, Mich (d/VII-25-1897) MD Detroit Med Coll 1884. *JAMA* 29:297, 1897.

PARK, EDWIN AVERY, New Haven, Conn (b/I-27-1817 Preston; d/I-17-1879) MD Yale 1846. *Proc Conn Med Soc* 1879: 163. *Butler* 1878: 81.

PARK, H EUGENE, Whitehouse Station, NJ (d/I-8-1906 @56) MD ? *Bost m&s j* 154:84,1906.

PARK, JOHN GRAY, CW-USN; Worcester & Groton, Mass (b/1838; d/VIII-29-1905 @67) MD Harvard 1866; AB 1858. *Bost m&s j* 153:290, 1905. *Harvard in CW*: 117-18. *K&B* III: 936.

PARK, WILLIAM HENRY, Tyler, Tex (b/VI-15-1835/36 Lowndesboro Ala; d/XI-4-1883 or 1885) MD UCNY 1857; stud Bellevue 1872. *New Orl m&s j* ns13: 578, 1886. *Tex cour-rec med* 3:128, 1885. *Daniel's Tex m j* 1:290-91, 1885.

PARK, WILLIAM W, Woodbury, Ill (d/X-19-1905) Lic yrs pract. *Ill m j* 8:530, 1905. *Polk* 1890: 352. Eclectic.

PARKE, ALEXANDER GASTON BOWEN, CW-USA; Gap, Pa (b/I-28-1842 Downingtown; d/VII-1-1905) MD UPa 1866. *U Pa med alum CW*: 1866.

PARKE, CLIFFORD DANIEL, CW-CSA; Selma, Ala (b/IX-27-1826 Wadesboro, NC; d/V-8-1886) MD Jefferson 1850. *Tr Med Assoc St Ala* 1887: 305. *Atkinson* I: 511. *Polk* 1886: 139.

PARKE, JOHN SITER, Radnor, Pa (b/1828; d/X-29-1865) MD UPa 1851. *Med surg rep Phila* 13:326, 1865.

PARKE, THOMAS, Philadelphia (b/VIII-6-1749; d/I-9-1835) MB UPa 1770. *Tr CPP* cent vol: 132-34, 256.

PARKE, WILLIAM WING, NYC; CW-USA (d/VIII-3 1863 Cincinnati) MD UCNY 1858. *Nat med jour* 1:300, 1870/71. *Med surg rep Phila* 10:228, 1863.

PARKER, BENNETT W , Conn; NJ (b/V-12-1808; d/V-18-1859) Lic 1836 Med Soc St Conn; Lic 1838 Med Soc NJ. *Tr Med Soc NJ* 1871: 167-68.

PARKER, BRADLEY, Brooklyn (d/I-16-1869 @69) MD ? *Bost m&s j* 2:400, 1869.

PARKER, CARY K, Bonita La (d/IV-10-1906) MD Tulane 1896. *New Orl m&s j* 58:922, 1906. *Polk* 1900: 770.

PARKER, CHARLES EDMUND, Beardstown, Ill (b/X-14-1813 Amherst; d/VIII-23-1882) MD Yale 1837; AB Dartmouth 1834; AM. *Tr Ill St Med Soc* 1884: 269.

PARKER, CHARLES EDWIN, Princeton, Mass (d/VII-10-1905 @41) MD U Vt 1889. *Bost m&s j* 153:94 [?], 1905. *Polk* 1896: 721.

PARKER, CHARLES FREDERICK, Boston (b/XII-23 1859 Halifax, NS; d/III-24-1903 @43) MD U Vt 1883. *Bost m&s j* 148:382, 1903. *Polk* 1886:703.

PARKER, CINCINNATUS M , Denver (d/VIII-12-1892 @54) <MD U La 1859> MD Med Coll Va 1863. *Tr Colo St Med Soc* 1898-99: 509. *Polk* 1886: 184.

PARKER, CLIFFORD J, Philadelphia (d/II-12-1880 @ 43) MD Pa M C 1859. *Med surg rep Phila* 42:198, 1880.

PARKER, D HERBERT, Cairo Ill (d/XII-8-1891 @42) MD Med Coll Ohio 1873. *Chic med rec* 1:477, 1892. *Med bull m & s* 14:77, 1892. *Butler* 1878: 171.

PARKER, DAVID, Gardiner, Mass (b/1802; d/V-1802; d/V-8-1886) MD Castleton 1827. *Bost m&s j* 114:456, 1886.

PARKER, DAVID McCAIRE, Boston (d/X-8-1887 @ 71) MD Woodstock 1846. *Bost m&s j* 117: 372, 616, 1887.

PARKER, DAVID TAYLOR, Farmington, NH (b/IV-10 1813 Brandon, Vt; d/XII-1-1888) MD Bowdoin 1836.

 Spec. educ'l status abbrev. as: ***ng*** = college verified attendance without degree;

Tr NH Med Soc 1889: 155. *Polk* 1886: 591.

PARKER, EDGAR, CW–USA; Bridgewater Mass (d/IV 9–1892 @51) MD Harvard 1863. *Bost m & s j* 126: 380,1892. *Harvard in CW*:1863. *Polk* 1890: 541.

PARKER, EDWARD HAZEN, Poughkeepsie NY (b/III 7–1823 Boston; d/XI–10–1896) MD Jefferson 1848; AB Dartmouth 1846; ng Bowdoin Med 1848. *Tr Med Soc St NY* 1897:479, 481–82. *Polk* 1886:702. *K&B* III:938.

PARKER, GEORGE A , CW–USN (d/VI–18–1864 abd USS DeSoto) MD ? *Nat med jour* 1:300, 1870/71.

PARKER, HENRY CLINTON, Bedford, NH 1838–54; Manchester 1855– (b/IV–11–1813; d/XII–8–1861) MD Jefferson 1838; stud Bowdoin Med 1836. *US med invest* 2:382, 1875. Homeopath.

PARKER, ISAAC, Chester Hill, O (d/1893 @78) MD ? *JAMA* 21:357, 1893.

PARKER, JAMES MONROE, Buffalo, Ia (b/XI–13–1859 Florence, Nebr; d/IX–17–1893) MD Ia St Univ 1885; <att Bellevue> *Tr Ia St M S* 11:133, 1893. *Polk* 1890: 412.

PARKER, JAMES PLEASANT, St Louis (b/1854 Marshall, Ala; d/II–6–1896) MD Jefferson 1886. *JAMA* 26:843, 1896. *K&B* I(2): 244. *Polk* 1896: 876.

PARKER, JOHN GIDEON, Dublin, NH 1852–65; Warner (b/VII–2–1818 Peterborough; d/IX–12–1869) MD Dartmouth 1852; AB Norwich 1847. *Tr NH Med Soc* 1871: 103–05.

PARKER, JOSEPH, Colfax, Ind (b/XII–10–1849; d/IV–17–1897) MD Miami 1881. *Tr Ind St Med Soc* 1897: 364–65. *Butler* 1878: 215.

PARKER, JULIAN NEWELL, Mansfield, Conn to 1872; S Manchester; CW–USA (b/VII–3–1839 Mansfield; d/II 7–1901) MD Yale 1867. *Proc Conn Med Soc* 1901: 304–06. *Atkinson* I: 423. *Butler* 1878: 81.

PARKER, KATE, Newark, NJ (b/1848; d/II–13–1895) MD NY Infirmary for Women Med Coll 1876. *Med reg NY NJ Conn* 1895: 235.

PARKER, LYMAN, New Haven Co, Conn (b/1791? d/IV–25–1862 @71) Hon MD Yale 1832. *Proc Conn Med Soc* 1: 67.

PARKER, LYMAN P L , Akron, NY (d/I–1–1899 @ 70) MD Buffalo 1854. *Buff m&s j* 38:546, 1899. *JAMA* 32: 92, 1899.

PARKER, NATHANIEL CHAMBERLAIN, Farmington, NH; CW–USA (b/III–30–1835 Lebanon, Me; d/XII 31–1866) MD Bowdoin 1856. *Tr NH Med Soc* 1867:4. Conn, *NH surg in CW*: 370.

PARKER, ORLANDO KELLOGG, Clarence, NY (b/ VIII–16–1826 Wyoming, NY; d/XI–16–1872) MD Geneva 1848. *Buff m&s j* 12:153, 194–95, 1872. *Butler* 1878: 568.

PARKER, P M , Barry, Ill (d/XII–26–1893) MD ? *JAMA* 22: 31, 1894.

PARKER, PETER, Washington, DC (b/VI–18–1804; d/1888) MD Yale 1834; AB 1831; AM 1858; stud Yale Theol Sem 1831–33. *Tr CPP* cent vol: 284. *Bost m&s j* 118: 84, 1888. *Butler* 1878: 96.

PARKER, SAMUEL JUNIUS, Ithaca, NY (b/V–19–1819 Danby; d/I–30–1898) Hon MD NY Med Coll 1860; AB Amherst 1841. *Amherst, Men of*: 1841. *Polk* 1886: 664. Homeopath.

PARKER, THOMAS IVERS, Boston (b/III–29–1784; d/XII–10–1856) MB Harvard 1806; MD 1811; AM 1806. *Bost m&s j* 55: 415, 1857. Palmer's *Necrol Harv alum*: 116.

PARKER, W W , Davenport, Ia 1854– (b/1818 Onondaga, NY; d/VIII–8–1868) Lic 1839 Cumberland Co, NC. *Med surg rep Phila* 19: 160, 1868. *Tr Iowa St Med Soc* 1867–71: 266. *Phila med reg & dir* 1871: 297.

PARKER, WILLARD, NYC (b/IX–2–1800 Lyndeboro, NH?; d/IV–25–1884) MD Harvard 1830; AB 1826; LLD Princeton. *Med reg NY NJ Conn* 1884: 235. *Bost m & s j* 110:427–28, 1884. *Med s rep Phila* 13:17–19, 1865; 50: 576, 1884. *Trans M S St NJ* 1885:328–29. *K&B* III: 939.

PARKER, WILLIAM C, Santa Cruz Cal (b/NY; d/VIII–11–1896) MD Starling 1869. *JAMA* 27:503, 1896.

PARKER, WILLIAM MARSHALL, Milford, Mass (d/ III–1–1883 @54) MD Berkshire 1853. *Boston med & surg jour* 109:617, 1883.

PARKER, WILLIAM S, Piqua O (d/VI–9–1895 @54) MD Jefferson 1864. *JAMA* 24:989 1895 *Butler* 1878:644.

PARKER, WILLIAM THORNTON, Jamaica, Mass (b/I 8–1818 Bradford; d/III–12–1855) MD Harvard 1841; AB Dartmouth 1838. *Boston med & surg jour* 52:127, 144–45, 1855.

PARKER, WILLIAM W , Richmond, Va (d/VIII–3–1899 @75) MD Med Coll Va 1848. *JAMA* 33: 427, 1899. *Polk* 1896: 1500.

PARKES, CHARLES THEODORE, Chicago (b/VIII–19 1842 Troy, NY; d/III–28–1891) MD Rush 1868. *Buffalo m&s j* 30:631 1891. *Chic m rec* 1:153–5 1891. *JAMA* 16: 500, 1891. *Trans Ill M S* 1891: 26–27. *K&B* III:940–41.

PARKES, EDWARD, Brooklyn (d/III–14–1893) MD Bellevue 1885. *Med reg NY NJ Conn* 1893:313. *Polk* 1886: 648.

PARKES, THOMAS FRANCIS, Brooklyn (d/XII–21 1894) MD LICH 1890. *Med reg NY NJ Conn* 1895: 237. *JAMA* 24: 33, 1895.

PARKHILL, CLAYTON, Denver (b/IV–18–1860 Vanderbilt, Pa; d/I–16–1902) MD Jefferson 1883. *Chic m rec* 22:186, 1902. *Bost m & s j* 146:128, 1902. *Flint* 1897: 160. *K&B* III: 941.

PARKHILL, MYRON H , Howard, NY (d/III–26–1901 @35) MD Buffalo 1886. *Bost m & s j* 144: 342, 1901. *Polk* 1896: 1026.

PARKHURST, CHARLES B , Irasburg, NY to 1870; Owego to 1872; Chicago 1872–74; Colorado Spr (b/XI–10–1842 Troy, Vt; d/I–16–1877) MD NY Homeop 1866. *US med invest* 5:222, 1877. Homeopath.

PARKHURST, LUMEN BOYDEN, Northampton, Mass

1879– (b/X–26–1874 [!] Milford; d/XI–7–1896) MD Boston U 1879. *Tr Am Inst Hom* 1897: 64. *Polk* 1886: 471. Homeopath.

PARKHURST, W H, Dunbar, Nebr (d/II–25–1898) <MD Ensworth, St Joseph, Mo 1885> *JAMA* 30:625, 1898.

PARKHURST, WILLIAM H H , Frankfort, NY (b/XI–5–1813 Winfield; d/I–22–1901) MD Fairfield 1840. *Tr M S St NY* 1901: 428–29. *Polk* 1893: 861.

PARKIN, JOHN STILL WINTHROP, St Stephens, Ala 1818–25; NYC (b/III–9–1792; d/XI–2–1866) Lic NY St Med Soc 1825; AB Yale 1809. *Med reg NY NJ Conn* 1867: 223. *Med surg rep Phila* 15: 407, 1866.

PARKIN, RALPH, Minnesota Lake, Minn (b/II–9–1848 Durhamshire, Engl; d/IV–16–1882) MD Rush Med Coll 1874. *Tr Minn St M S* 1883: 292.

PARKINS, WILLIAM EDWARD, Mt Sidney, Va; Bramwell, WVa 1903– (b/IV–1–1875 Ft. Defiance, Va; d/VI–19–1904) MD Maryland Med Coll 1901. *Tr M S Va* 1904: 325–26.

PARKINSON, EDWARD ALVIN, Hart, Mich (d/VII–12 1898) MD Detroit Med Coll 1879. *JAMA* 31:198, 1898. *Polk* 1886: 269 (Chicago).

PARKMAN, SAMUEL, Boston (b/VI–21–1816 Boston; d/XII–15–1854) MD Harvard 1838. *Bost m & s j* 52:425, 1854. Palmer's *Necrol Harv alum*: 58.

PARKS, JAMES F , Bourbon, Ind (d/II–28–1895) MD Med Coll Ind 1872. *JAMA* 24:370, 1895. *Polk* 1890:367.

PARKS, LUTHER, Boston (b/1789? d/X–25–1869 @80) MD ? *Bost m & s j* 4: 236, 1869.

PARKS, LUTHER, (b/XI–4–1823; d/XI–9–1886 Paris, Fr) MD Harvard 1847; AB 1843. *JAMA* 9:448, 1887. *Bost m & s j* 115:512, 533, 1886. *Butler* 1878: 342.

PARKS, RAVEL BERTRAM, Jamestown, NY (d/XI–17 1897 @48) MD Buffalo 1886. *JAMA* 29: 1181, 1897. *Buff m & s j* 27: 37, 1897.

PARKS, SENECA ELIAS, Swanton, Vt (b/1811 Orwell, Vt? d/XII–22–1863) MD Castleton 1835. *Bost m & s j* 69:468, 1863.

PARKS, WILLIAM HENRY, Great Barrington, Mass (b/X–11–1823 Wells, Vt; d/VI–21–1898 @75) MD Castleton 1847. *JAMA* 31:141, 1898. *Polk* 1886:466.

PARMLY, ELEAZAR, NYC (b/1797? d/XII–13–1874 @77) MD ? *Med rec* 10: 8, 1875.

PARR, JOHN, Buel, NY (b/1817? d/XII–7–1898) MD UCNY 1850. *Tr M S St NY* 1899? *JAMA* 31: 1542, 1898. *Polk* 1896: 1005.

PARRAGA, JOSE MIGUEL, NYC (d/IX–2–1892) <MD U Madrid 1879> *Med reg NY NJ Conn* 1893:313. *Polk* 1886: 690.

PARRAN, RICHARD, Shepherdstown, Va (b/I– –1811 Calvert Co, Md; d/II–1–1851) MD U Md 1830. *Med annals Md:* 528.

PARRAN, THOMAS, St Leonards, Md (d/ca 1877) MD U Md 1817. *Med annals Md:* 528.

PARRIS, SAMUEL BARTLETT, Attleboro Falls, Mass (b/I–30–1806 Marshfield; d/IX–21–1827) MD Harvard 1825; AB Brown 1821; AM. *Brown hist cat*: 1821.

PARRISH, EDWARD, Philadelphia; Swarthmore, Pa (b/1822; d/IX–9–1872 Ft Sill, Indian Terr) MD Jefferson 1844. *Nashvl j m & s* ns10: 1872. *Med s rep Phila* 260: 307, 308, 1872.

PARRISH, ISAAC, Philadelphia (b/III–19–1811; d/VII–31–1852) MD UPa 1832. *Trans CPP* cent vol:256; ns1: 427–51, 1850–53. *New Jersey med rep* 6:343–45, 1853. *K&B* III: 941.

PARRISH, JAMES , Portsmouth, Va; CW–CSA (b/1838; d/I–21–1894) MD U Va 1858; MD UCNY 1861. *Tr M S Va* 1894; 193–94. *Bost m & s j* 130: 252, 1894. Blanton *Va surgs CW*: 412. *Butler* 1878: 834.

PARRISH, JAMES M , Elkton & Lexington, Ky (d/III–19–1831) Student at Transylvania. *Transylv j m & assoc sci* 4:148, 1831.

PARRISH, JOSEPH, CW–US San. Comm; Burlington, NJ (b/XI–11–1818 Phila; d/I–15–1891) MD UPa 1844; ng Coll 1844. *Tr M S NJ* 1891:243–54. *Med annals Md:* 528–29. *Med reg NY NJ Conn* 1891: 280. *K&B* III: 942. *Atkinson* I: 440.

PARRISH, JOSEPH, Philadelphia (b/IX–2–1779; d/III–18–1840) MD UPa 1805. *Tr CPP* cent vol: 256. *Western j m & s* 1:387, 1840. *Am j m sci* 26:258–60, 1840. *K&B* III: 941–42.

PARRISH, ROBERT G, Goochland Co Va (d/IX–4–1884 @75) MD UPa 1836. *Med s rep Phil* 52: 280 1884.

PARRY, CHARLES, Ind'pls (d/VIII–11–1861 @47) MD UPa 1835 *Bost m&s j* 65:260 1861 *Tr Ind St MS* 1870: .

PARRY, GEORGE RANDOLPH, New Hope, Pa (b/IX–23–1889 Phila; d/VI–12–1893) MD UPa 1867; PhG Phila Coll Pharm 1862. *Tr Med Soc NJ* 1894:273–74.

PARRY, HENRY CHESTER, CW–USA; Philadelphia & Orwigsburg, Pa (b/VI–17–1839 Pottsville; d/XI–7–1893) MD UPa 1861. *JAMA* 21: 829, 1893. *UPa m alum CW*: 1861. *Polk* 1886: 822 (Germantown) & 831 (Pottsville).

PARRY, JOHN STUBBS, Philadelphia (b/I–4–1843 Drumore Pa; d/III–11–1876 Jacksonvl Fl) MD UPa 1865 *Med s rep Phil* 35:40 1876. *Tr CPP* cent vol:256; 3s2: xlv–lviii, 1876. *Phila m times*6:336 1876. *K&B* III: 944.

PARSHALL, J B , Cincinnati (d/VIII–2–1873 @59) MD ? *Med surg rep Phila* 29:126, 1873.

PARSONS, ALFRED, ?Pa (b/1797 Enfield, Conn; d/X––1865) <MD Fairfield> *Tr Pa St Med Soc* 1865: 70.

PARSONS, ANDREW BUCK, Atlanta (b/X–10–1822 Fairfax, Vt; d/XI–10–1885?) MD Berkshire 1846. *Buff med & surg jour* 25: 280, 1886.

PARSONS, ANSON, CW–USA; Springboro, Pa (b/VI–19 1830 Sunderland, Vt; d/II–25–1903) MD U Md 1865. *Tr Am Inst Hom* 1904:964. Homeopath.

PARSONS, CHARLES WILLIAM, Providence, RI (b/IX–6–1823; d/IX–2–1893) MD Harvard 1840; hon MD Brown 1848; stud Charité, Paris, 1844. *Bost m & s j* 129: 284, 1893. *Tr RI M S* 5:245–48 1894–98. *Atkinson* I:666.

 Spec. educ'l status abbrev. as: ***ng*** = college verified attendance without degree;

PARSONS, EZEKIEL W , Colchester, Vt (b/1785? d/XI 9-1868 @83 NYC) MD ? *Bost m & s j* 2:272, 1868.

PARSONS, FRANK, Manasquan, NJ (b/VI-30-1852; d/XI-23-1878 Morristown) MD CPSNY 1876. *Med reg NY NJ Conn* 1879:196. *Tr M S NJ* 1879?: 206.

PARSONS, GEORGE L , Philadelphia (d/XII-14-1903 @75) MD Berkshire 1854. *Pa med jour* 7:280, 1903/04.

PARSONS, HENRY L , ?NYC (d/VII-28-1860 @29) MD UCNY 1849. *Med reg NY NJ Conn* 1862: 153.

PARSONS, HOMER LEE, Terrell, Tex (d/I-22-1893) MD Yale 1857. *Tex cour-rec med* 10:183, 1893. *Polk* 1886: 889, 895.

PARSONS, ISRAEL, Marcellus, NY (d/III-24-1904 @82) MD CPSNY 1848. *Trans Med Soc St NY* 1904: [420]. *Polk* 1886: 667.

PARSONS, RALPH ALFRED, W Roxbury, Mass (d/IV-3/4-1891 @29) MD ? *Bost m & s j* 124:396, 474, 1891.

PARSONS, USHER, War 1812-USN. Providence, RI (b/VIII-18-1788; d/XII-19-1868) MD Harvard 1818. *Bost m&s j* ns2:336, 1868. *Phila m reg & dir* 1871:299. *Tr AMA* 21:430-31, 1870. *Med reg NY NJ Conn* Phila 20: 96-97, 1869. *Tr RI M S* 1865-72: 329-30. *K&B* III: 945.

PARSONS, WILLIAM, Sheffield, Conn (b/X-30-1802; d/IV-18-1830) MD Yale 1829; ng Amherst 1825. *Amherst, Men of:* 1825.

PARTRIDGE, OLIVER, Stockbridge, Mass (b/IV-15-1751 [os] Hatfield; d/VII-24-1848) Stud med w/Dr Erastus Sargent. *Tr AMA* 3:456-57, 1850. *K&B* I(2): 256.

PARTRIDGE, ORLANDO HOLBROOK, Truro, Mass 1829-36; Philadelphia 1838- (b/IX-19-1805 Augusta, Me; d/V-11-1859) MD Bowdoin 1829. *Med surg rep Phila* ns2:171, 1859.

PARVIN, CHARLES ROCHESTER, Philadelphia (b/III-23-1850 Rochester NY; d/VI-3-1871) MD UPa 1871;att Coll UPa 1866-68. *Phila m reg & dir* 1873:303.

PARVIN, HOLMES, Deerfield, NJ; Cincinnati (b/XII-7 1794; d/II-6-1842) <MD UPa 1815> *Tr M S NJ* 1871: 178-79.

PARVIN, JAMES B , Cedarville, NJ (b/VI-3-1779; d/X-28-1834) Lic Supr Ct NJ. *Tr M S NJ* 1871: 152-53.

PARVIN, THEOPHILUS, Indianapolis; Philadelphia (b/I 9-1829 Buenos Aires; d/I-29-1898) MD UPa 1852; AB St U Ind 1847; AM 1850; LLD Hanover Coll. *Buff m & s j* 38:622-23, 1898. *JAMA* 30:333-34, 1898. *Chic m rec* 14:173, 1898. *K&B* III:947-48.

PARVIS, GEORGE W , Centerville, Md (d/I-26-1894 @67) MD Jefferson 1853. *JAMA* 22:202, 1894. *Butler* 1878: 329.

PASCHALL, BENJAMIN H , Arrington, Tenn (d/XI-1-1898 @73) MD U Louisville 1849. *JAMA* 31:1190, 1898. *Nashvl j m & s* 84:238, 1898. *Polk* 1886: 860.

PASK, WILLIAM, Erie Co, NY (b/Engl; d/VIII-24-1884) MD Buffalo 1884. *Tr M S St NY* 11:741 ff, 1894.

PASSMORE, EDWARD C , NYC (b/1817; d/VI-21-1890) <Lic Med Soc St 1844> Stud Apothecaries' Hall, Dublin 1835. *Bost m & s j* 123: 165, 1890. *Med reg NY NJ Conn* 1892: 285. *Polk* 1886:690.

PATCH, FRANKLIN FLETCHER, Boston (d/XI-12 1891 @76) MD Harvard 1850. *Bost m & s j* 125: 560, 1891. *Polk* 1890: 541.

PATILLO, R H , ? (d/IX-11-1878 Memphis) MD ? *Trans AMA* 30:881, 1879.

PATON, WILLIAM, Mobile (d/III-17-1898) MD U Ala 1876. *Tr M Assn St Ala* 1898:240. *Polk* 1886: 136.

PATRICK, WILLIAM S , Woodstown, NJ (b/IX-14-1864 Quinton; d/XI-17-1898) MD UPa 1889. *Tr M S NJ*: 380, 1898.

PATTEE, ASA FLANDERS, CW-USA; Boston (b/III-5 1835 Warner, NH; d/V-31-1897) MD Dartmouth 1857. *Bost m & s j* 136:556, 1897. *JAMA* 28: 1202, 1897. *Rec AA Surgs USA* 1891: 71-72. *Polk* 1896: 703.

PATTEE, LUTHER, Canada; Boston; Warner & Manchester, NH (b/XII-1-1831 Warner; d/XI-27-1895 Manchester) MD Woodstock 1853. *JAMA* 25: 1058, 1895. *Tr NH M S* 1896:184-85. *Butler* 1878:457.

PATTEE, WILLIAM SEWELL [SAMUEL?], Quincy, Mass (d/IX-18-1881 @57) MD Harvard 1851. *Bost m & s j* 105:623, 1881.

PATTEN, JAMES COMFORT, Francisco, Ind (b/III-8 1826 Maury Co, Tenn; d/II-19-1903) MD Med Coll Evansvl 1850. *Tr Ind St M S* 1903: 352. *Polk* 1886: 468.

PATTEN, JULIA MARIA, Holyoke Mass (d/IX-8-1902 @43) MD Woman's Med Coll Chic 1880. *Bost m & s j* 147:366, 1902. *Polk* 1896: 714.

PATTEN, SUMNER AUGUSTUS, CW-USA; Searsport, Monson & Skowhegan, Me (b/XII-6-1820 Skowhegan; d/XII-19-1898) MD Harvard 1848; ng Bowdoin Med 1846. *Harvard in CW*: 235. *JAMA* 32:41, 1899. *Atkinson* I: 649, *Polk* 1886: 429.

PATTERSON, B [P?] M , CW-USA (d/XII-15-1862 Georgetown, DC) MD ? *Nat med jour* 1:300, 1870/71.

PATTERSON, CHARLES GORDON, NJ (b/IX-4-1796;d/II-18-1835) <MD CPSNY> *Tr M S NJ* 1871:82.

PATTERSON, CHARLES WEBB, Nashville (d/V-3 1890) MD Louisville Med Coll 1879. *Nashvl j m & s* 45:217-21, 1890. *Polk* 1886: 870.

PATTERSON, DeWITT CLINTON, Washington, DC (b/VIII-3-1826 Mt Washington Twp, Mass; d/XII-20-1893) MD Cleveland Med Coll 1851. *JAMA* 22:57-58, 1894. *Hist M S DC:* 289. *Butler* 1878: 96.

PATTERSON, E E , Waco, Tex (d/IV-4-1906 Winnsboro) MD ? *Tex st med jour*2:36, 1906.

PATTERSON, G M D , Franklin, Tex (d/VII-8-1895) MD ? *Tex m j* 11:87, 1895-96. *Polk* 1890:1079.

PATTERSON, GEORGE W , Philadelphia (d/cVIII-5 1852) MD UPa 1839. *Tr Pa St Med Soc* 1856:185.

PATTERSON, HENRY M, Staunton, Va (b/1831; d/XI-10-1896) MD UVa 1851. *Tr M S Va* 1897:268. *NC med jour* 38:347-48, 1896. *Polk* 1890: 1133.

PATTERSON, HENRY STUART, Philadelphia (b/VIII-

15–1815; d/IV–27–1854) MD UPa 1836. *Tr Pa St M S* 1854:32; 1856:185. *New Orl m & s j* 11:134–38, 1854. *Med reporter* (W Chester, Pa) 2:32, 1854. *K&B* III: 949.

PATTERSON, JAMES E, Harvey's Pa (d/V–8–1901)MD Jefferson 1869. *Pa m j* 5:296,1901/02. *Polk* 1886:801.

PATTERSON, JAMES H , Shrewsbury, NJ (d/VII–4–1890) MD UCNY 1857. *Med reg NY NJ Conn* 1891:280. *Polk* 1886: 611.

PATTERSON, JOHN H, Baltimore (b/1817; d/V–25–1893) MD UMd 1837 *Med ann Md*:529 *Butler* 1874:314.

PATTERSON, JOHN HENRY, Harwich, Mass (b/III–2 1863 S Merrimack, NH; d/IV–29–1894) MD Dartmouth 1889; AB 1886. *Bost m & s j* 130:456, 1894.

PATTERSON, JOHN KENNIER, Philadelphia (d/I–14–1904 @61) MD Jefferson 1868. *Pa med jour* 8:335, 1904/05. *Polk* 1886: 822.

PATTERSON, MARIE B , NYC (d/V–13–1892) MD NY Infirmary Woman's Med Coll 1883. *Med reg NY NJ Conn* 1892: 285. *Polk* 1886: 690.

PATTERSON, RICHARD JOHN, Chicago (b/IX–14–1817 Mt Washington, Mass; d/IV–27–1893 Batavia, Ill) MD Berkshire 1842. *Chic m rec* 4:435, 1893. *Atkinson* I: 62. *K&B* III: 949.

PATTERSON, THEOPHILUS, Salem, NJ (b/X–18–1827; d/IX–7–1894) MD Jefferson 1848. *Med reg NY NJ Conn* 1895: 235. *Polk* 1886: 611.

PATTERSON, WILLIAM, Frederick Co, Md (b/1802; d/1876)MD UMd 1826 *Med ann Md*:529. *Butler* 1874:322.

PATTERSON, WILLIAM HALSTEAD, Buenos Aires (b/XII–6–1813 Newark, NJ; d/VII–5–1836) MD UPa 1835; AB 1831; ng Amherst 1832. U Pa Coll, *Matrics cat*: 85. *Amherst, Men of*: 1832.

PATTERSON, W M , Campbell, Tex (d/IV–8–1899 @68) MD ? *JAMA* 32: 956, 1899. *Polk* 1886: 892.

PATTILLO, T M , Mt Vernon, Tex (d/I–24–1888) MD ? *Daniel's Tex med jour* 3:407, 1888. *Polk* 1886: 891.

PATTISON, GRANVILLE SHARP, Philadelphia 1818–20, 1831–41; Baltimore 1820–26; NYC 1841– (b/Glasgow 1791; d/IX–12–1851) MD Glasgow 1813? *So med & s j* 8:67, 1852. *NW m & s j* 4:350, 1852. *NH j m* 6:167, 1852. *Med annals Md*: 529. *K&B* III: 950–51.

PATTISON, MATTHEW MONCRIEFF, Brooklyn (d/IV–13–1884 @38) MD UCNY 1876. *Med s rep Phila* 50: 544, 1884.

PATTON, ELLA MARTHA, Quincy, Ill (b/X–18–1860 Shelbina, Mo; d/II–16–1899 St Louis) MD U Mich 1882. *Tr Ill M S* 1899: 29. *JAMA* 32:506, 1899. *Polk* 1886: 295.

PATTON, GEORGE W, Pana Ill (d/VII–24–1898 @65) MD Mo M C 1882. *JAMA* 31:314, 1898. *Polk* 1896:434.

PATTON, JAMES HUGH, Trenton, Mo (d/I–12–1900 @ 56) MD U Mich 1879 *JAMA* 34:251,1901 *Polk* 1886:570

PATTON, NATHANIEL NEWTON, Monongahela City, Pa (d/VII–14–1896 @50) MD Jefferson 1873. *JAMA* 27: 337, 1896. *Off'l reg Pa phys* 1881–88: 8.

PATTON, WALTER STEELE, Knoxville (b/IX–6–1827; d/1859) MD U La 1853; AB U Ala 1850; AM 1854. *U Ala cat*: 94.

PATZE, ADOLPHUS, Hampton, Va (b/IV–4–1804 Stettin, Prussia; d/X–24–1886) <MD U Berlin 1838> *Hist Med Soc DC*: 268. *Polk* 1886: 213.

PAUL, COMEGYS, Philadelphia (d/VI–29–1906 @59) MD UPa 1869. *Pa med jour* 9: 805, 1905/06.

PAUL, JOHN HODGDON, Dover, NH 1846– (b/VI–23 1818 Rollinsford; d/XI–12–1858) MD Jefferson 1846; ng Bowdoin Med 1845. *Bowdoin cat*: 1845.

PAUL, JOHN MARSHALL, Belvidere, NJ (b/I–2–1800; d/XII–18–1879) MD UPa 1822. *Tr CPP* 3s5: , 1881. *Med surg rep Phila* 42:22, 44, 1880.

PAUL, JOHN MARSHALL Jr, CW–US San Comm; Belvidere, NJ (b/XII–1 1842 Phila; d/III–17–1887) MD UPa 1868; AB Williams 1864. *Med reg NY NJ Conn* 1887: 272. *U Pa med alum CW*: 1868. *Butler* 1878: 474.

PAUL, JOHN RODMAN, Philadelphia (b/I–24–1802; d/X–13–1877) MD UPa 1823; AB 1820. *Tr CPP* cent vol: 257; 3s4: xxv–xliii, 1879.

PAUL, JOSEPH BLODGETT, Havana, Ill (d/XII–2–1893) MD Rush 1857. *JAMA* 21: 936, 1893. *Butler* 1878: 172.

PAULDING, MOSES JOHNSON, CW–USA; Daretown, NJ (b/III 16–1843 Phila; d/XII–26–1893 Woodstown) MD UPa 1865. *Med reg NY NJ Conn* 1894:246. *Tr M S NJ* 1894:274. *JAMA* 22:31 1894. *U Pa m alum CW*:1865.

PAULUS, AUGUSTUS DAVID, Flatonia, Tex (b/VII–18 1817 Copenhagen; d/IX–4–1893 @78) <MD Kiel 1839> *Tex med jour* 11:197–99, 1895–96. *Polk* 1886: 894.

PAWLING, JOHN A , Boyle Co, Ky (d/V?– –1868) MD U Louisville 1865. *Med surg rep Phila* 18:542, 1868. *Trans Ky St Med Soc* 1872: 79.

PAWLING, WILLIAM, Danville, Ky (b/1797; d/1872) MD Transylvania 1838. *Trans AMA* 23:587–88, 1872.

PAXSON, FRANKLIN VAN CLEVE, Trenton, NJ; CW–USA (b/II–28–1844 Princeton; d/XI– –1868 nr Omaha) MD UPa 1864. *U Pa med alum CW*: 1864.

PAYN, FREDERICK GEORGE, Jersey City & Bergen Pt, NJ (b/1825 Engl; d/III–5–1894) MD Jefferson 1856. *Med reg NY NJ Conn* 1894:246. *Tr M S NJ* 1894:275–76. *JAMA* 22:482, 1894. *Butler* 1878: 474.

PAYNE, ALBAN SMITH, Markham, Va (b/VI–1–1821 Granville, Va; d/IX–20–1891) MD Castleton 1845; MD CPSNY 1846; MD Southern Med Coll 1880. *Tr M S Va* 1891:258–59. *Butler* 1878: 834.

PAYNE, FLEMING RICE, Marshall, Ill (b/1821; d/1873) MD ? *Tr AMA* 25:531, 1874.

PAYNE, FRANK HOWARD, Berkeley, Calif (b/1850? d/1904) MD Rush 1874. *Calif st jour med* 2:286, 1904. *Polk* 1886: 163.

PAYNE, FREDERICK W , Boston (b/I–1–1845 Bath, Me; d/VII–17–1903) MD Hahnemann Phila 1868. *Tr Am Inst Hom* 1904: 956. *Polk* 1886: 460. *Cleave*.

PAYNE, HENRY R , Kansas City, Mo (d/XII–29–1895

 Spec. educ'l status abbrev. as: ***ng*** = college verified attendance without degree;

@68) MD U Louisville 1853. *JAMA* 26:142, 1896. *Polk* 1890: 660.

PAYNE, J SCOTT, Rahway, NJ (b/1839 Barbadoes, WI; d/V-10-1882) MD UCNY 1863. *Tr M S NJ* 1882: .

PAYNE, JANSEN TASMAN, CW-USA; New Orleans (d/1891) MD Harvard 1862. *Harvard in CW*: 274.

PAYNE, JOHN, Hillman, Ala (d/V-31-1901) MD Jefferson 1880. *Tr M Assn St Ala* 1902:130. *Polk* 1893: 149.

PAYNE, LYCURGUS VIRGINIUS, Belfast, Me (b/X-28-1824 Gorham; d/VII-8-1853) MD Bowdoin 1846. *Tr Am Inst Hom* 1854: 72. Homeopath.

PAYNE, MARTIN, Portland, Ore (d/XII-2-1898 @62) MD ? *JAMA* 31:1542, 1898.

PAYNE, ROBERT LEE Sr, CW-CSA; Lexington, NC (b/XII-29 1834; d/II-25-1895) MD Jefferson 1857. Stud UNC 1852-53. *NC med jour* 36:257-59, 1895. *Tr NC M S* 1895: 207-14. *Atkinson* I: 93. *Butler* 1878:597.

PAYNE, ROBERT SPOTSWOOD, CW-CSA; Lynchburg, Va (b/VIII-21-1840 Goochland Co; d/V-16-1885 or IX-28-1884) MD UPa 1861; <MD Med Coll Va 1863> *Tr M S Va* 1885:284-85. *Atkinson* I:380. *U Pa med alum CW*:1861.

PAYNE, WILLIAM ELISHA, Bath, Me (b/XI-25-1815 Unity; d/III-9-1877) MD Bowdoin 1838. *New Engl med gaz* 12:364, 1877. *US med invest* 5:409, 1877. *Cleave*. *King* I:305. Homeopath.

PAYNE, WILLIAM W, CW-USA (d/VIII-6-1863 abd steamer Westmoreland Mississippi River) MD ?Ecl Med Inst Cincinnati 1854. *Nat med jour* 1:300, 1870/71.

PAYNTER, CHRISTIAN S [or L], Salem, Ind (b/II-19-1824 Washington Co; d/XII-10-1893) MD U Louisville 1853. *Tr Ind St Med Soc* 1895: 399. *Polk* 1886: 335.

PEABODY, JOSEPH, Buffalo (d/1853 @59) MD Yale 1821. *Buff m & s jour* 9:126-27, 1853.

PEABODY, LEONARD WOOD, Henniker, NH 1844-45; 1871- ; Epsom 1845-71 (b/IX-13-1817 Newport; d/I-13-1899) MD Woodstock 1844. *Tr NH M S* 1899: 294. *JAMA* 32:263, 1899. *Atkinson* I:214. *Polk* 1886:592.

PEACE, EDWARD, Philadelphia (d/IX-9-1879 @68) MD UPa 1833. *Trans CPP* cent vol: 257. *Med s rep Phila* 41:214, 1879.

PEACE, JOSEPH Jr, Philadelphia (b/I-14-1807 Charleston, SC; d/VII-25-1845 Bristol, Pa) MD UPa 1829; AB 1825. *Tr CPP* cent vol: 257; 1:417-19, 1841-46.

PEACE, PLEASANT P, Wake Co, NC (b/Granville Co; d/VI-25-1886) MD UPa 1845; att Wm & Mary 1842. *NC m j* 18:65, 1886. *Tr NC M S* 1887:159.

PEACO, JOHN W, USN 1814-27? (b/Annapolis, Md; d/V-23 or VI- -1827 Savannah) MD ? *Med annals Md:* 530. Callahan: *USN*.

PEACOCK, RUFUS WILIE, Jersey City (b/VI-18-1827 Goldsborough, NC; d/II-7-1899) MD UCNY 1876. *Bost m&s j* 140:172 1899. *JAMA* 32:385 1899. *Polk* 1896:939.

PEACOCK, WILLIAM CARSON, Prairieville, Tex (b/IX-14-1846; d/IX-14-1885) MD Bellevue 1868. *Tex cour-rec med* 3:77, 1885. *New Orl m & s j* ns13:505, 1885. *Polk* 1886: 892.

PEAK, ORIN, CW-USA; Oak Park, Ill (d/X-8-1905 @ 79) MD U Mich 1854 *Ill m j* 8:530, 1905. *Polk* 1886:291.

PEALE, JAMES BURD, CW-USA; Holmesburg, Phila (b/VII-10 1833 NYC; d/III-2-1882) MD UPa 1856 as d/III-2-1881. *U Pa med alum CW*:1856. *Trans Pa St Med Soc* 1882: 365-68.

PEARCE, FRANK SAVARY, Philadelphia (d/V-27 1904 @37 Steubenville, O) MD UPa 1891. *Pa m j* 8:335, 1904/05. *Chic m rec* 26:398, 1904. *Bost m & s j* 150:660, 1904. *Flint* 1897: 823.

PEARCE, HIRAM M, Cincinnati (d/IX-16-1878 Memphis) MD Med Coll Ohio 1865. *Tr AMA* 30:881 1879.

PEARCE, J R, CW-USA (d/VIII-27-1863) MD ? *Nat med jour* 1:300, 1870/71.

PEARCE, JEREMIAH BURRITT, Lyons, NY (b/1790; d/1862) MD ? *Tr AMA* 14:203-04, 1864.

PEARMAN, FRANCIS M, Warsaw, Ind (d/IX-3-1897 @61) MD Ft Wayne Med Coll 1884. *JAMA* 29:555, 1897. *Polk* 1886: 332. Kemper's *Indiana*: 168, 327.

PEARMAN, JOHN T, CW-USA; Champaign, Ill (b/1829 Hardin Co, Ky; d/V-25-1896) MD Rush 1858. *JAMA* 26:1144, 1896. *Atkinson* I:635. *Butler* 1878:172.

PEARSALL, JERE R, Manchester, NC (d/1894) MD U Md 1888. *Tr NC M S* 1894:[203]. *Polk* 1890:871.

PEARSALL, JOSEPH DICKSON, CW-CSA; Sampson Co, NC (b/XII-8-1829 Duplin Co; d/IV-28-1876) MD UPa 1853. *U Pa med alum CW*: 1853 suppl.

PEARSE [PEARCE], SIMEON H, Mt Vernon, Ind (d/VII-16-1896 @66 Friendship, NY) MD Castleton 1854. *JAMA* 27:337, 1896. *Polk* 1890: 382.

PEARSON, C H, ?CW-USN (d/XII-2-1863 at sea) MD ? *Bost m & s j* 70:68, 1864.

PEARSON, CHARLES DEWEY, Indianapolis (b/IV-20 1820 Paoli, Ind; d/II-4-1890) MD UCNY 1878; MD Cinc Coll M & S 1859; att Asbury U Indianapolis 1851. *Tr Ind St M S* 1890:165. *Polk* 1886:323. Kemper's *Indiana*:327.

PEARSON, CHARLES L, Trenton NJ (b/Phila; d/IV-12 1883 @ c75) Lic M S NJ 1844. *Tr M S NJ* 1883: 302.

PEARSON, CLEMENT, Wellsville, O 1850-57; Iowa 1857-74? Washington, DC 1874-86 (b/XII-19-1819 Mercer Co, Pa; d/I-29-1886 @67) MD Western M C Homeop Cleveland 1857. *Hahn mo* 21:143, 1886. *Med adv* 16: 665, 776, 1886. *King* I:386. *Cleave*. Homeopath.

PEARSON, EDWIN OSGOOD, Manchester, NH (d/X-29-1886 @33) MD Dartmouth 1879; BS 1874. *Tr NH Med Soc* 1887: 172-73.

PEARSON, JOHN SAPPINGTON, Louisiana, Mo (d/VI-2-1899 @67) MD UPa 1849. *JAMA* 32:1460, 1899. *Polk* 1896: 852.

PEARSON, JOSIAH WILSON, Camden, Me; Providence, RI (b/IV-7-1856 Morrill; d/XII-2-1901) MD U Vt 1883. *Tr RI M S* 6:249, 1899-1903. *Polk* 1896: 634.

PEARSON, NILS P, Chicago (d/IV 1897 @72) <MD Copenhagen 1853>*Chic m rec* 12:360 1897. *Polk* 1896:400.

PEARSON, ROBERT CALDWELL, CW–CSA; Morganton NC (b/III–27–1837; d/I–28–1906) MD UCNY 1860; stud UNC 1855–57. *UNC cat*:482. *Polk* 1886:724.

PEARSON, ROBERT P Sr, Starkville, Miss (d/III–6–1895) MD Med Coll SC 1845. *New Orl m & s j* ns23: 767, 1895. *Polk* 1886: 532.

PEASE, CHARLES E, Middletown Pa (b/LI NY; d/IX–12/13–1904 @ 47) MD UPa 1882. *Pa med jour* 8: 335, 1904/05. *Flint* 1897: 809.

PEASE, CLARKE E , CW–USA (d/VI–27–1864 Janesville, Wis) MD ? *Nat med jour* 1:300, 1870/71.

PEASE, DANIEL PEARSON, NYC (d/XII–7–1902 @45 Paris) MD Bellevue 1882. *Bost m & s j* 147:685 1902. *Tr M S St NY* 1903: [412] *Polk* 1896: 1072.

PEASE, GEORGE CHANCY, Kalamazoo, Mich (d/I–25 1895 @50) MD U Mich 1875. *JAMA* 24:177, 1895. *Polk* 1886: 492.

PEASE, GEORGE MANLIUS, CW–USA; Bridgton, Me (b/XII–15 1841; d/XII–18–1873) MD Bowdoin 1867; AB 1863. *Bowdoin cat*: 1863.

PEASE, GILES MOSELEY, CW–USN; USA; San Francisco (d/XII–14 1891 @53) MD Harvard 1863. *Tr Am Inst Hom* 1892:214. *Harvard in CW*: 282. *Med vis* 8:58, 1892. *Polk* 1886: 174.

PEASE, L T , Williamsburg, O (d/1874) MD Med Coll Ohio 1841. *Tr Ohio St M S* 1874:388–89.

PEASE, PHILO C, CW–USA; Westchester Co NY (d/II–6–1868 @32) MD LICH 1860 *Phila med reg & dir* 1871: 295.

PEASE, ROBERT H , Detroit (d/VI–26–1885) <MD Detroit Med Coll 1883> *Med age* 3:252, 1885.

PEASE, ROGER WILLIAM, CW–USA; Syracuse, NY (b/V–31–1828; d/V–28–1886) MD Geneva 1848. *Med reg NY NJ Conn* 1887: 272. *K&B* III: 645.

PEASLEE, EDMUND RANDOLPH, Hanover NH; NYC (b/I–22–1814; d/I–21–1878) MD Yale 1840; AB Dartm 1836; AM 1839. *Med reg NY NJ Conn* 1878: 185. *Chic m j* 36:443–44, 1878. *Buff m & s j* 17:317–18, 1878. *Tr M S St NY* 1879:578–79. *Atkinson* I:358. *K&B* III:952.

PEAT, EDWARD, Delphos, O (d/IV–19–1883) MD Jefferson 1881. *Med bull med & surg* 5:166, 1883.

PECK, AARON EDGERTON, Brooklyn (d/III–8–1900 @65) MD CPSNY 1855. *Bost m & s j* 142: 288, 1900. *JAMA* 34: 702, 1900. *Polk* 1896: 1001.

PECK, AUGUSTUS T , CW–USN (d/VIII–29–1867 Pensacola, Fla) MD ? *Nat med jour* 1:300, 1870/71.

PECK, CHARLES A , NYC (d/VI–4–1860 @38) MD ? *Med reg NY NJ Conn* 1862: 153. *Med surg rep Phila* ns4:215, 1860.

PECK, CHARLES W, CW–USN (d/IX–4–1863 abd ship Relief, Pensacola, Fla) MD ? *Nat m j* 1:300, 1870/71.

PECK, CLARENDON, Sicily Isl, La (d/VIII–1–1837 @ 25) MD Transylv 1835. *Transylv j m &c* 10:594–5 1837.

PECK, EDGAR FENN, Brooklyn (d/I–20–1888 @81) MD CPSNY 1833; Hon MD Rutgers 1832. *Med reg NY NJ Conn* 1888:266; 1889:279.

PECK, GEORGE, USN; Lake Mohonk, NY (b/Orange, NY; d/VII–26–1906) MD CPSNY 1847. *Bost m & s j* 155:133, 1906. *Polk* 1896: 1017.

PECK, GEORGE BACHELOR, CW–USA; Providence, RI (b/1834; d/I–22–1906 Dorchester, Mass) MD Yale 1871; MD Harvard 1863; AB Miami 1857; AB Brown 1864; grad Auburn Theol Sem 1868. *Harvard in CW*: 282. *Polk* 1886: 846. Homeopath.

PECK, LOUIS E , Hartford, Wis (b/V–30–1819 Barra, Vt; d/III–26–1877 Milwaukee) MD Cleveland Med Coll 1844. *Tr Wis St M S* 1878: 185–86.

PECK, MARVIN R , Glens Falls, NY (b/Sand Lake, NY; d/IV–4–1884) MD Albany 1851. *Tr M S St NY* 11: 741ff, 1894. *Butler* 1878: 568.

PECK, SAMUEL W, Washington Ind (b/II– –1817 Eaton, NY; d/V–16–1895) MD Fairfield 1838. *JAMA* 24: 861:1895. *Tr Ind St M S* 1895:413. *Polk* 1886:340.

PECK, THOMAS W , Shiloh, NJ (b/XI–4–1779 Stoe Cr; d/VIII–30–1852) MD ? *Tr M S NJ* 1871:160.

PECK, WASHINGTON F , Davenport, Ia (b/I–22–1841 Galen, NY; d/XII–12–1891) MD Bellevue 1863. *JAMA* 17:995, 1891. *NW m j* 20:10, 16, 1892. *Bost m & s j* 125: 664, 1891. *Tr Ia St M S* 10: 229, 1892. *Atkinson* I: 222.

PECK, WILLIAM DANDRIDGE, Sterling, Mass (b/XI–10–1812 Cambridge; d/VI–2–1890) MD Harvard 1836; AB 1833. *Bost m & s j* 123:48, 1890. *Polk* 1886: 474.

PECKHAM, CYRUS BENEDICT, Hallowell, Me (b/III–20–1833 MIddleton, RI; d/X–14–1904) MD Bowdoin 1884; AB Brown 1866; AM. *Brown hist cat*: 1866.

PECKHAM, FENNER HARRIS, Killingly, Conn to 1852; Providence, RI 1852– ; USA 1861–72? (b/I–27 1820 Killingly; d/II–7–1887) MD Yale 1842. *Bost m & s j* 116:200, 1887. *Tr RI M S* 3: 471–75, 1883–88. *Atkinson* I:299–300. *Butler* 1878: 748.

PECKHAM, WALTON H, NYC (b/Palmyra; d/XII–6/7 1879) MD ? *Med surg rep Phila* 41: 550, 1879. *Med reg NY NJ Conn* 1880: 238. *Med rec NY* 16: 576, 1879.

PEDIGO, WILLIAM EMORY, Edmonton, Ky (d/VIII–11–1899 @55) MD U Louisville 1876. *JAMA* 33:621, 1899. *Polk* 1890: 463.

PEEBLES, BERLIN, Memphis (d/1878) MD U Nashville 1878. *Trans AMA* 30:881–82, 1879.

PEEBLES, G HIAL, Lincoln Nebr (d/III–15–1894 @ 53) MD Rush 1864. *JAMA* 22: 482, 1894.

PEEBLES, JOHN F , Petersburg, Va (d/XII–6–1853) MD U Va 1834. *Nashvl j m & s* 10:167,1856.

PEEBLES, ROBERT STOCKTON JOHNSON, CW–CSA; Petersburg & Richmond, Va (b/IX–24–1839; d/III–13–1873) MD Med Coll Va 1862; AB UPa 1859; AM 1862; att UPa Med Dept 1859–61. *Tr AMA* 24:386–88, 1873. *Tr M S Va* 1873:37, 112.

PEEK, JESSE HOPE, Hampton, Va (b/VII–3–1854; d/

IX-20-1902) MD U Va 1874. *Trs M S Va* 1902:225-26. *Polk* 1886: 918.

PEEK, WILLIAM HOPE, CW-CSA (b/II-18-1838; d/VII-14-1863 Williamsport, Md) MD UVa 1860. Johnson, *U Va Mem'l...alum d/CW*: 754. Blanton, *Va surgs in CW*: 412.

PEELER, JAMES P , Kissimee, Fla (d/XII-13-1891) MD Ky Sch Med 1876. *Proc Fla Med Assoc* 1892: 57. *Polk* 1890: 253.

PEEN, WILLIAM H , Brooklyn (d/XI-13-1887 @66) MD UCNY 1851. *Med reg NY NJ Conn* 1888:267. *Polk* 1886: 648 [as Peer].

PEERY, THOMAS RITCHIE, Tazewell Co, Va; (b/XI-16-1859; d/VIII-17-1895) MD CPS Balto 1882. *Tr M S Va* 1902: 225.

PEET, DUDLEY, NYC (d/IV-18-1862 @31) MD CPS NY 1856; AB Yale 1852. *Bost m & s j* 66: 284, 1862. *Med s rep Phila* ns8: 104, 1862.

PEETE, GEORGE WASHINGTON, Galveston, Tex (b/ 1809 Va; d/IX-16-1875) MD UPa 1834. *Tr Tex St M Assn* 1876: 23. G.P.Red: 205-06.

PEETE, J S , ? (d/1878 Mason, Tenn) MD ? *Tr AMA* 30:882, 1879.

PEGAN, EMANUEL, CW-USA (d/V-16-1865 Dover, Del) MD Cincinnati Coll Med & Surg 1863. *Nat med jour* 1:300, 1870/71.

PEGG, AUSTIN J , Ossian, Ia (d/I-29-1894) MD McGill 1872. *JAMA* 22:313, 1894. *Polk* 1890: 423.

PEGG, WILLIAM H , Atlanta (d/VIII-10-1873) MD ? *Med surg rep Phila* 29: 144, 1873.

PEGRAM, JOHN COMBE Jr, Providence, RI (b/VII-25 1870 Bristol; d/IV-26-1906) MD Harvard 1897; AB Brown 1892. *Bost m & s j* 154:506-07, 508, 1906. *Tr RI M S* 7:431-32, 1904-09.

PEGUES, CHARLES AUGUSTUS, Abbeville, Miss (b/ VI-26-1827; d/XII-25-1895) MD Charleston 1852; att U Ala 1846. *U Ala cat*: 88.

PEIRCE, AUGUSTUS FREDERIC, Tyngsborough, Mass (b/VIII-11-1827 Nashua, NH; d/X-18-1855) MD Bowdoin 1849. *Bost m & s j* 53:275, 1856.

PEIRCE, BENJAMIN FRANKLIN, CW-USN (b/II-23 1837; d/III-9-1864 Mississippi River) MD Harvard 1860; ng Bowdoin Med 1857, 1859. *Harvard in CW*: 260. *Nat med jour* 1:301, 1870/71.

PEIRCE, CHARLES HENRY, Cambridge, Mass (b/I-8-1814 Salem, Mass; d/VI-16-1855) MD Harvard 1836; AB 1833. *Bost m & s j* 52:427, 1857. Palmer's *Necrol Harv alum*: 58.

PEIRCE, GEORGE WASHINGTON, Leominster, Mass (d/V-1-1886 @66) MD Harvard 1846. *Bost m & s j* 114:480, 1886; 115:630, 1886. *Polk* 1886:468.

PEIRCE, JAMES, Methuen, Mass (d/VIII-25-1902 @ 54) MD UCNY 1871. *Bost m & s j* 147: 340, 1902. *Polk* 1886: 469.

PEIRCE, JAMES L , Philadelphia (d/XI-26-1883 @77) MD ? *Med s rep Phila* 49:644, 700, 1883.

PEIRCE, WARREN, Plymouth, Mass (d/VII-10-1898 @ 50?) MD Harvard 1869. *JAMA* 31:198, 1898. *Polk* 1896:721.

PEIRSON, ABEL LAWRENCE, Salem, Mass (b/XI-25 1794 Biddeford, Me; d/V-6-1853) MD Harvard 1816; AM 1812. Palmer's *Necrol Harv alum*: 16. *K&B* III:956.

PEIRSON, EDWARD BROOKS, Salem, Mass (d/XI-18 1874 @57) MD Harvard 1844; AB 1840. *Bost m & s j* 91:532, 554-55, 1874.

PELL, RICHARD VARICK, Blackwell's Isl, NY (b/VII-28-1843; d/VIII-22-1866) MD Bellevue 1865; AB Columbia 1862. *Tr AMA* 19:414, 1868. *Med reg NY NJ Conn* 1867:223.

PELTON, CLARENCE WHITFIELD, Dedham, Mass (d/VI-14-1892 @26) MD Harvard 1890. *Bost m & s j* 126:648, 1892.

PELTON, D R , Wahoo, Nebr; Topeka, Kans (d/XI-4 1896) MD CPS Keokuk 1875. *JAMA* 27: 1169, 1896. *Polk* 1890: 701.

PELTON, LOUIS FREDERICK, Mt Kisco, NY (b/II-13 1828 Westfield, Mass; d/IX-17-1883) MD UCNY 1851; AB Wesleyan Conn 1846. *Med reg NY NJ Conn* 1884: 237. *JAMA* 1:406, 1883. *Med surg rep Phila* 49: 392, 1883. *Polk* 1886:748 (Cleveland, O).

PELTZ, SAMUEL HENRY, CW-USN (d/VII-5-1865 abd ironclad, Charleston Harbor) MD UPa 1862. *Med s rep Phila* 12: 284, 1864/65. *Nat m j* 1:301, 1870/71.

PELZER, ANTHONY P , Charleston, SC (d/II- -1886 @67) MD Med Coll SC 1841. *New Orl m & s j* ns13: 751, 1886. *Butler* 1878: 757.

PEMBERTON, CHARLES, Asbury Park, NJ (d/VII-13-1894) MD Jefferson 1882. *JAMA* 23:164, 1894. *Polk* 1886: 600.

PEMBERTON, JOHN PRICE, Long Beach, NJ (d/XI-9 1895 @63) MD CPSNY 1864; AB Columbia 1849. *Bost m & s j* 133: 500, 1895. *Polk* 1886: 606.

PENCE, JOHN C , Carlinsville, Ill (d/IV-29-1899 @31) MD Ft Wayne Coll Med 1882. *JAMA* 32: 1074, 1899.

PENDER, W D , Tarboro, NC (d/IX-24-1884) MD U Md 1883 @ 19. *NC med jour* 14:262, 1884.

PENDERGAST, PATRICK, CW-USA; Brooklyn (b/XII 24-1836; d/II-5-1875) MD CPSNY 1863. *Med reg NY NJ Conn* 1875: 203.

PENDLETON, JAMES F , Marion, Va (b/X-24-1844; d/II-1-1883) MD Med Coll Va 1868. *Trs M S Va* 1883: 189-190.

PENDLETON, LEWIS WARRINGTON, Portland, Me (b/III-18-1844 Camden; d/I-12-1898) MD Albany 1864. *JAMA* 30:278, 1898. *K&B* III: 956-57.

PENDLETON, PLEAS H , Pine Bluff, Ark (d/III-26-1899 @45) MD Louisville Med Coll 1875. *JAMA* 32:787, 1899. *Polk* 1890: 163.

PENGRA, CHARLES PHILIP, Boston (d/I-31-1892 @31) MD U Mich 1881; PhC 1883. *Bost m & s j* 126:

132, 1892. *Polk* 1890: 541.

PENISTON, THOMAS, New Orleans (d/XII-2-1863) MD Jefferson 1835; LLB Harvard 1845. *Bost m & s j* 74: 452, 1866. *Nashvl j m & s* 1:320, 1866.

PENN, J E, ? (d/IX-16-1878 Memphis) MD ? *Tr AMA* 30:882, 1879.

PENN, JAMES, CW-CSA; Sulphur Spr, Tex (b/XII-19-1818 Tenn; d/IX-23-1886) MD Med Coll Ga 1853. *Tex cour-rec med* 4:285-86, 1887. *Polk* 1886: 866.

PENNEBAKER, AMOS, Philadelphia (d/XII-29-1869 or 1870) MD UPa 1829. *Med surg rep Phila* 24:22, 1871.

PENNELL, RICHARD, NYC (b/Engl; d/IV-16-1861 @ 62) MD CPSNY 1821. *Med reg NY NJ Conn* 1864: 154.

PENNEPACKER, HENRY, CW-USA; Scranton Pa (b/V 25-1839 Chester Spr; d/II-7-1893) MD UPa 1866. *U Pa med alum CW*: 1866. *Polk* 1886: 834.

PENNEY, EDWARD WINTHROP, Providence, RI (b/ XII-23-1853 Cold Lake, Miss; d/I-13-1890) MD UCNY 1884. *Tr RI Med Soc* 4:341-42, 1889-93. *Bost m & s j* 122:283, 1890. *Polk* 1886:946.

PENNIMAN, JESSE ALLEN, Great Barrington, Mass (b/XII-3-1817 New Braintree; d/II-11-1878) MD UPa 1843; ng Amherst 1837. *Amherst, Men of*: 1837.

PENNINGTON, ISAAC, Compassville & Jersey Shore, Pa; Hampshire Co, Va; St Clairsville, O; Oakland Co, Mich (b/IX- -1789 Chester Co, Pa; d/V- -1849) MD Washington Coll Balto 184_ [hon?] *Med reporter* (West Chester, Pa) 3:94-96, 1856.

PENNINGTON, JOEL, Milton, Ind (b/II-11-1799 Huntington Co, Pa; d/I-9-1887) MD Ohio Med Coll 1847. *JAMA* 1:252, 1887. Kemper's *Indiana*: 327. *Atkinson* I: 259. *Butler* 1878: 215.

PENNINGTON, JOHN CONDICT, NYC; Colorado Spr (d/VII-27-1897) MD CPSNY 1875; AB Princeton 1871; AM 1874. *JAMA* 29:297, 1897. *Polk* 1896: 1072.

PENNINGTON, SAMUEL HAYES, Newark, NJ (b/ 1806; d/III-14-1900) Cert by Exam Bd 1880; AB Princeton 1825; AM 1828; LLD 1891. *JAMA* 34:766, 1900. *Bost m & s j* 142:316, 1900. *Pr Conn M S* 1900: 338-41. *Atkinson* I: 259.

PENNISSE, J G, Indianapolis (d/1878 Memphis) MD ? *Tr AMA* 30:882, 1879.

PENNOCK, CASPAR WISTAR, Philadelphia (b/VII-2-1799; d/IV-16-1867) MD UPa 1828. *Tr CPP* cent vol:257; ns4:245-46, 1863. *Tr AMA* 21:457, 1870. *Med s rep Phila* 16:344, 1867. *K&B* III: 957.

PENNY, JESSE S, Elizabeth, Pa (d/I-26-1867 @52) MD ? *Med surg rep Phila* 16: 139, 1867.

PENNYPACKER, ISAAC ANDERSON, Philadelphia (b/VII-9-1812 Chester Co, Pa; d/II-13-1856) MD UPa 1835. *Tr Pa St M S* 1857:138-141. *Phila m & s j*4: 287, 1856. *Med reporter* (West Chester, Pa) 3:114-15, 1856.

PENNYPACKER, JOSEPH JUDSON, CW-USA; West Chester, Pa (b/III-2-1838; d/X-4-1905) MD UPa 1865. *Pa med jour* 9:127, 1905/06. *U Pa med alum CW*:1865.

PENNYPACKER, MATTHIAS JACKSON, Philadelphia (d/VIII-29-1899 @48) MD UPa 1876. *JAMA* 33: 745, 1899.

PENROSE, THOMAS NEALL, CW-USN; Philadelphia (b/VI-6-1835; d/II-13-1902 @67) MD UPa 1858. *Pa m j* 6:261, 1902/03. *U Pa m alum CW*: 1858. *Nat m j* 1:301, 1870/71 [as d/Galveston @23 nd abd "Harriet Lane"].

PENTZ, EDWARD H, York, Pa (d/XI-30-1873) MD UCNY 1848. *Med surg rep Phila* 30:44, 86, 1874.

PENWELL, ENOS S, Shelbyville, Ill (d/XII-24-1904 @83) MD Ind Med Coll 1847. *Ill med jour* 7:242, 1905. *Polk* 1896: 440.

PEPINO, W C, Mexico, Mo; Des Moines (d/1896?) <MD U Md 1873> *Med bull med & surg* 18:307, 1896. *Polk* 1886: 555.

PEPPER, GEORGE, CW-USA; Philadelphia (b/VI-1-1841; d/IX-14-1872) MD UPa 1865; AB 1862; AM 1865. *Phila med reg & dir* 1873: 303. *Med surg rep Phila* 27: 332, 1872. *K&B* III: 957-58.

PEPPER, WILLIAM, Philadelphia (b/I-21-1810; d/X 15-1864) MD UPa 1832; AB Princeton 1829. *Tr CPP* cent vol:257; ns4:168-74, 354, 1863-74. *Med s rep Phila* 12:180, 196, 1864/65. *Tr Pa St M S* 1865: 141-43. *K&B* III:958-59.

PEPPER, WILLIAM, Philadelphia (b/VIII-21-1843; d/ VII-28-1898 Pleasanton Cal) MD UPa 1864; AB 1862; AM 1865; LLD Lafayette 1881. *Tr CPP* cent vol: 258; 3s23:xlvii-lxvii, 1901. *JAMA* 31: 313-14, 1898. *Bost m & s j* 139:119-20, 1898. *So pract* 20:391-92, 1898. *Atkinson* I: 474-75.

PEPPER, WILLIAM J, Connersville, Ind (b/IX-26 1830 Mason Co, Ky; d/VIII-31-1892) MD Cleveland Med Coll 1856. *Tr Ind St Med Soc* 1893:249. *Polk* 1890: 367.

PERCHMENT, ALBERT H, Allegheny City, Pa (d/XII-13-1867 @32) MD Jefferson 1860. *Med surg rep Phila* 18: 66, 1867.

PERCIVAL, WARREN, Fairfield Co, Conn (d/1852? @65) MD ? *Proc Conn Med Soc* 1852: 17.

PERCY, EDWARD ROTTON, Brooklyn (d/I-4-1875 @ 56) MD CPSNY 1850. *Med reg NY NJ Conn* 1875: 203. *Med rec* 10:48, 1875.

PERCY, ROBERT, Newellton, La (d/II-2-1900 @ 67) MD UPa 1856. *JAMA* 34: 446, 1900. *Polk* 1886: 415.

PERCY, SAMUEL ROTTON, NYC (b/IV-24-1816 Somerset, Engl; d/IV-10-1890) MD CPSNY 1846; AB Charterhouse Coll 1833. *Med reg NY NJ Conn* 1890:279. *Bost m & s jour* 122:435, 1890. *Atkinson* I: 257-58.

PERHAM, DANIEL WEBSTER, NYC (b/VIII-23-1852; d/IV-27-1882) MD Bellevue 1877. *Med reg NY NJ Conn* 1882: 233.

PERIN, GLOVER, USA 1847-87 (b/Ohio; d/XII-15-1890 St Paul Minn) MD M C Ohio 1846. *JAMA* 16:143. 1891.

PERINE, FRANCIS M, Dansville, NY (d/VII-13-1903 @72) MD Buffalo 1855. *Trans Med Soc St NY* 1904:

 Spec. educ'l status abbrev. as: ***ng*** = college verified attendance without degree;

[420]. *Polk* 1886: 658.

PERKINS, CHARLES JAMES, Upperville, Va 1840– (b/X–19–1818 Farmington, Me; d/II–12–1843) Stud Jefferson; AB Bowdoin 1839. *Bowdoin cat*: 1839.

PERKINS, CHAUNCEY F , Erie Co, Pa (d/IX–24–1872 @90) MD CPSNY 1818. *Trans Pa St Med Soc* 9:149, 1873. *Med surg rep Phila* 27:359–61, 1872.

PERKINS, CONSTANTINE HUME Sr, Tenn (b/IV–24 1824; d/1868) MD ? att U Ala 1840. *U Ala cat*:70.

PERKINS, DANIEL CHUTE, S Danvers, Mass (b/XI–11 1824 Royalston; d/XI–3–1863) MD Harvard 1850; ng Amherst 1849. *Bost m & s j* 69:308, 1863.

PERKINS, EDWARD AUGUSTUS, Boston (d/II–20 1900 @72) MD Harvard 1854. *Bost m & s j* 142: 236, 1900. *Polk* 1896: 703.

PERKINS, EDWIN STANLEY, USN 1864–68; Philadelphia (b/XI–23–1845; d/V–6–1901) MD UPa 1869. *Pa med jour* 5:296, 1901/02. *Butler* 1878: 693.

PERKINS, GEORGE AUGUSTUS, Salem, Mass; missionary to Africa 1836?–50 (b/X–15–1813; d/V–18–1895) MD Harvard 1844. *JAMA* 24:861, 1895. *Bost m & s j* 132:532, 1895.

PERKINS, GEORGE THOMAS, USA 1861–76? Boston 1865– ; Newton Lower Falls, Mass (d/XII–7–1880 @42) Stud med Harvard 1857. *Harvard in CW*: 249–50.

PERKINS, HENRY COIT, Newburyport, Mass (d/II–1 1873 @69) MD Harvard 1827; AB 1824. *Bost m & s j* ns11:152, 175, 1873. *Med surg rep Phila* 28: 202, 1873.

PERKINS, JOHN DAY, Smyrna, Del (b/VIII–27–1790 Baltimore; d/VIII–13–1860) MD UPa 1811. *Tr AMA* 14: 211,1864. *Med annals Md:* 532. *Hist M S Del*:44.

PERKINS, JOSEPH Jr, Castleton, Vt (b/IV–1–1798 Bridgewater; d/I–6–1872) MD Castleton 1821; Hon AM Middlebury 1837. *Tr AMA* 29:736–37, 1878. *Bost m & s j* ns9:84, 1872. *Tr Vt M S* 1883: 107. *K&B* I(2): 267.

PERKINS, JOSEPH FLEMING, Baltimore (b/I–28–1806 Pa; d/1854) MD U Md 1833. *Med annals Md:* 532.

PERKINS, LEWIS G , Jackson & Norwood, La (d/VIII–7–1906 @79) MD Tulane 1850. *New Orl m & s j* 59:86, 1906. *Polk* 1896: 625.

PERKINS, NATHANIEL SHAW, New London, Conn (b/II–11–1792; d/V–25–1870) MD Yale 1829. *Proc Conn Med Soc* 3:414, 478–81, 1871.

PERKINS, P A , ? (d/IX–17–1878 Collierville, Tenn) MD ? *Tr AMA* 30:882, 1879.

PERKINS, S J, Norwood, La (d/VI–11–1899 @39) MD Tulane 1887. *JAMA* 32:1460–61, 1899. *Flint* 1897: 421.

PERKINS, SELAH GRIDLEY, Castleton, Vt; CW–USA (b/XI–26–1826; d/IX–24–1862 Ashby Gap, Va) MD Castleton 1851. *Bost m & s j* 67:268, 1862. *Med surg rep Phila* ns9:22, 1862/63. *Nat med jour* 1:301, 1870/71.

PERKINS, THOMAS P , Trevillian Depot, Va; CW–CSA (d/VII–13–1873 @40) MD Med Coll Va 1860; att U Va 1853. *Tr Med Soc Va* 1873: 37, 112.

PERKINS, WILLIAM HENRY, Hancock, Md (b/XI–18 1841 Lewiston; d/IX–11–1896) MD LICH 1868. *JAMA* 27:776, 1896. *Med annals Md:* 532. *Polk* 1886: 443.

PERKINS, WINSLOW LEWIS, New London, Conn (b/XII–8–1834) MD Yale 1863; ng Amherst 1857. *Bost m & s j* 71:448, 1864.

PERL, MICHAEL, Houston, Tex (b/XI–1–1835 Vienna, Aus; d/I–2–1895) <MD Pesth, Hung 1861> *Tex cour-rec med* 12:106, 1894. *Tex med jour* 10:361, 1894–95. *Polk* 1890: 1082. G.P.Red, *251–52.*

PERLEY, DANIEL, Lynn, Mass (b/III–24–1804 Boxford; d/I–31–1881) MD Dartmouth 1831; AB 1828. *Bost m & s j* 104:139,1881. *Butler* 1878: 355.

PERLEY, THOMAS FITCH, Portland, Me (b/II–23–1816; d/III–22–1889) MD Bowdoin 1841; AB 1837. *Bost m & s j* 120:324, 1889. *Butler* 1878:310.

PERO, JOSEPH THOMAS, Indian Orchard, Mass (d/VII–10 or 19–1901 @34) <MD CPS Balto 1891> *Bost m & s j* 145:108, 1901. *JAMA* 37:342, 1901. *Polk* 1896: 714.

PERRIN, NELSON, Smithfield, RI (b/IV–13–1809 Seekonk, Mass; d/III–31–1843) MD Harvard 1836; ng Amherst 1832. *Amherst, Men of*: 1832.

PERRINE, EDMUND K , Philadelphia (b/XII–6–1862; d/IX–18–1902) MD Jefferson 1886; <MRCS (Lond)> *Pa med jour* 6:27, 264, 1902/03. *Flint* 1897: 823.

PERRINE, GEORGE W , Lyons & Syracuse, NY 1839?–55; Milwaukee 1855– (b/XII–16–1816; d/IV–10 1872) MD Geneva 1839. *Med invest* 9:334, 1872? *Tr Am Inst Hom* 1874: 650. *King* I:339. *Cleave.* Homeopath.

PERRINE, WILLIAM La RUE, Stockbridge, Mass 1845–51; Hudson, NY 1851–55; Brooklyn 1855– (b/XI –8–1813 Bloomfield, NJ; d/XII–16–1889) MD CPSNY 1845. *Tr Am Inst Hom* 1890:140. *Polk* 1886: 648. Homeopath.

PERRY, BENJAMIN F , Hillsville, Va (b/Md; d/III–21 1898 Carroll Co Va) MD U Md 1829. *Hist Med Soc DC:* 232. *Med annals Md:* 532. *Polk* 1886: 919.

PERRY, CHRISTOPHER GRANT, Philadelphia (b/IV–2–1812 Newport, RI; d/IV–7–1854) MD UPa 1837; AB Brown 1830; AM. *Brown hist cat*: 1830.

PERRY, DANA DUANE, NYC (d/IV–24–1893) MD Bellevue 1882. *Med reg NY NJ Conn* 1893: 313.

PERRY, EDGAR, Boston (b/X–19–1855 Rehoboth, Mass; d/IV–7–1903) MD Harvard 1898; AB Brown 1880; AM. *Bost m & s j* 148:408, 1903.

PERRY, EDGERTON, CW–USA (d/IV–17–1863 Camp Collins, Colo) MD UCNY 1849. *Nat med jour* 1:301, 1870/71.

PERRY, EUGENE BEAUHARNAIS, Melvin, Ill (b/1844? d/VI–22–1905 @61) MD Rush 1880. *Ill med jour* 8:185, 1905. *Polk* 1896: 429.

PERRY, FRANK PARKER, Bucksport Me (d/I–13 1906 @55) MD LICH 1873. *Bost m & s j* 154:84, 1906.

PERRY, GEORGE THOMPSON, Warwick, RI (b/II–18 1839; d/VIII–29–1892) MD Bellevue 1864. *Trans RI*

Med Soc 4:488–89, 1889–93. *Polk* 1890: 1025.

PERRY, GEORGE W , Yonkers, NY (d/XI–15–1883 Orange, NJ) MD ? *Med surg rep Phila* 49: 616, 1883.

PERRY, GIDEON B Sr, Hopkinson Ky (d/IX–30–1879 @78) MD ? *Nashvl j m & s* ns24:233, 1879. *Med surg rep Phila* 41: 352, 1879. *Bost m & s j* 101:570, 1879.

PERRY, GIDEON B Jr, Brooklyn (b/c1826 Hopkinsville, RI; d/XII–30–1890) MD UCNY 1851. *Med reg NY NJ Conn* 1891:280. *Bost m & s j* 124:76, 1891. *Butler* 1878: 533.

PERRY, JOSEPH SMITH, NYC (b/1785? d/I–3–1874) Lic Med Soc Ulster Co, NY 1826; att lect CPSNY 1818–19. *Med reg NY NJ Conn* 1874:284.

PERRY, MARSHALL SEARS, Boston (d/XI–18–1859 @ 54) MD Harvard 1830. *Bost m & s j* 61:347, 1859. *Nashvl j m & s* 18:92, 1860.

PERRY, NATHANIEL MALLORY, Troupsburg NY (d/IV–3–1894) MD Geneva 1845. *JAMA* 22:601, 1894.

PERRY, NEHEMIAH, Ridgefield, Conn (d/II–12–1866) Hon MD Yale 1832. *Bost m & s j* 74:128, 1866.

PERRY, SAMUEL, No Kingston, RI (b/c1778 Perryville; d/1831) MD ? AB Brown 1802. *Brown hist cat*:1802.

PERRY, THOMAS WELLS, Providence RI (b/Hopkinton; d/I–5–1884 @60 Boston) MD UCNY 1846. *Bost m & s jour* 110:70, 304–05, 616–17, 1884. *Tr RI Med Soc* 3:166, 1883–88. *Med bull med & surg* 6:43, 1884.

PERRY, VAN LEAR, CW–CSA; Navassa, WI [?] (b/IV–20–1837 Cumberland, Md; d/X–26–1869 Navassa) MD Jefferson 1859; AB Franklin & Marshall 1856. *F & M obit rec*: 159–160.

PERRY, WILLIAM, Exeter, NH (b/XII–20–1788 Norton, Mass; d/I–11–1887) MD Harvard 1814; AB 1811. *Bost m & s j* 116:72, 100, 1887.

PERRY, WILLIAM FENWICK, Mansfield, Mass (b/XII–9–1809 Easton; d/X–17–1873) MD Bowdoin 1833. *Bost m & s j* ns12:654, 1873.

PERSONETTE, STEPHEN, Verona, NJ (b/1813; d/II–3–1880 @67) Lic Med Soc NJ 1834. *Tr M S NJ* 1880–81: 121–23. *Med s rep Phila* 42:154, 1886. *Butler* 1878: 474.

PETER, ARMISTEAD, CW–USA; Georgetown, Md (b/II–22–1840 Montgomery Co, Md; d/I–28–1902) MD Columbian, DC 1861. *Hist M S DC:* 266. *Rec AAS USA* 1891: 74. *Atkinson* I: 430. *Polk* 1886:213.

PETER, ROBERT, Lexington, Ky (b/I–21–1805 Cornwall Engl; d/IV–26–1894 Minton) MD Transylvania 1834. *Tr Ky St M S* ns3:276–79, 1894. *K&B* III: 961–62.

PETERS, ALFRED C , Iowa City, Ia (d/XII–18–1895 @34) MD Iowa St U 1887. *JAMA* 26: 93, 1896. *Polk* 1890: 418.

PETERS, CHARLES AUGUSTUS, NYC (b/VI–20–1861; d/1887 @26) MD CPSNY 1882. *Med reg NY NJ Conn* 1887: 273.

PETERS, DeWITT C , USA 1854–56, 1860–66 (d/IV–22–1876 @47) MD ? *Tr AMA* 28:637, 1877. *Med rec med & surg* 11:294, 1876.

PETERS, GEORGE ABSALOM, NYC (d/XII–6–1894) MD CPSNY 1846; Hon AM Williams 1851; Hon AM Yale 1881. *Med reg NY NJ Conn* 1895:235. *JAMA* 23: 990, 1894. *Bost m & s j* 131:600, 1894.

PETERS, GEORGE JOHNSON, Butler, Pa (d/IX–20–1902) MD Western Pa Med Coll 1887. *Pa med jour* 6: 261, 1902/03. *Flint* 1897: 797.

PETERS, GOODWIN EDEN, Storm Lake, Ia; Dallas, Tex (b/IX–18–1852 Wabash, Ind; d/II–28–1892) MD Wooster 1876. *Tex cour–rec med* 9:219, 1892. *Polk* 1886: 884. Plunkett, *Med man in Tex*: 175–76.

PETERS, JOHN CHARLES, NYC(b/VII–6–1819 NYC; d/II–21–1893 LI, NY) <Stud med Vienna, Berlin, CPSNY> *Med reg NY NJ Conn* 1894:247. *JAMA* 21:667, 1893. *Atkinson* I: 31. *K&B* III: 963. Homeopath?

PETERS, JOHN SAMUEL, Hebron, Conn (b/IX–21–1772; d/III–30–1858) Hon MD Yale 1818; stud med Phila 1797? *Proc Conn Med Soc* 1858:115–20.

PETERSON, FRANCIS MARION, Greensboro, Ala (b/VIII–29–1821; d/1897 {Oct} to 1898 {Feb}) MD UCMY 1869; stud med UPa 1845. *Tr M Assn St Ala* 1898:39–41, 240. *Atkinson* I:690. *Polk* 1886: 134.

PETERSON, WILSON, NYC; CW–USA (b/X–17–1831 Fayette, NY; d/II–19–1898) MD Hahnemann, Phila 1858. *No Amer jour hom* 46:270, 1898. *Polk* 1886:60.

PETHERBRIDGE, JOHN BUDD, USA (b/Pennington, NJ; d/II–23–1867 NY or Carlisle Barracks, Md) MD UPa 1847. *U Pa m alum CW*:1847. *Tr AMA* 18:357, 1867. *Med s rep Phila* 16:199, 1867.

PETHERBRIDGE, JOHN F , Annapolis, Md (b/1811; d/X–28–1897) MD U Md 1832. *Med ann Md:* 533. *Polk* 1886: 442.

PETIT [PETTIT], FREDERICK HASEN, Moriah, NY; CW–USA (b/V–15–1817 No Hero, Vt; d/XII–25–1863 Washington, DC) MD Dartmouth 1840. *Nat med jour* 1:301, 1870/71.

PETRIE, HERBERT L, Jackson Miss (b/I–29–1851; d/X 26–1875) MD Jefferson 1873. *Tr Miss St M Assn* 1876.

PETRIE, JAMES S , Elkton, Ky (d/II–2–1887) <MD Vanderbilt 1886> *Nashvl j m & s* ns39:94–95, 1887.

PETRIE, ROBERT MAITLAND, Jersey City (b/1845 Liberty, NY; d/VIII–3–1905) MD UPa 1869; AB Lafayette 1869. *Bost m&s j* 153:178 1905. *Polk* 1896:939.

PETTEE, JOHN HARRIS, Roxbury, Mass (d/III–6–1906 @34) MD Harvard 1897. *Bost m&s j* 154:282 1906.

PETTICOLAS, A E , Richmond, Va (b/1824; d/XI–28 1868 Williamsburg) MD ? *Phila med reg & dir* 1871: 299. *Trans AMA* 21:480–81, 1870.

PETTINGILL, EDWARD HENRY, Saxton's River, Vt (b/1837 Grafton; d/II–8–1900) MD Harvard 1866. *Bost m & s j* 142:179, 1900. *JAMA* 34:446, 1900.

PETTINGILL, SARAH BROOKS (FELT), Philadelphia (b/V–16–1810 Charlestown, Mass; d/III–29–1877) MD Pa Med U 1860. *Tr Am Inst Hom* 1893:152. *Cleave*. Homeopath.

 Spec. educ'l status abbrev. as: *ng* = college verified attendance without degree;

PETTUS, JAMES THOMAS Jr, NYC (d/VII-13-1896 Reading, Pa) MD CPSNY 1884. *JAMA* 27: 279, 1896. *Polk* 1896: 1073.

PETTUS, JOHN R [or A], Galveston, Tex 1853- ; CW-CSA (b/1818? Lunenburg Co, Va; d/IX-26-1870) MD UPa 1840. *Galveston med jour* 5:341, 1870.

PETZOLD, EDWARD, NYC (d/VII-8-1887) <MD Leipzig 1839> *Med reg NY NJ Conn* 1888: 267. *Polk* 1886:690.

PEUGNET, EUGENE EMILE RAMSAY, Fordham, NY (b/III-17-1837; d/X-10-1879) MD CPSNY 1858. *Med reg NY NJ Conn* 1880:239. *Bost m&s j* 101:600, 1879. *Med s rep Phil* 41:374 376 1879. *Med rec* 16:383, 1879.

PEYTON, CRAVEN, CW-CSA; Little Rock, Ark (d/ 1872) MD U Louisville 1846. *Tr AMA* 24:337-38, 1873.

PFAFF, CHARLES, NYC (d/V-30-1860 @29) MD Harvard 1856. *Bost m & s j* 62:392, 1860.

PFAFF, JESSE C , Philadelphia (d/IX-6-1903 @22) MD Med-Chi Coll Phila 1902. *Pa m j* 7:280, 1903/04.

PFARRE, PHILIP HERMAN, Brooklyn (b/1869; d/VI-8 1894) MD LICH 1893. *Med reg NY NJ Conn* 1894: 247.

PFEIFFER, CHARLES WILLIAM, NYC (b/1854 Phila; d/V-22-1899) MD Bellevue 1878. *Bost m & s j* 140:63,1899. *JAMA* 32:1399,1899. *Polk* 1886:1074.

PFEIFFER, P C , Lebanon Co, Pa; CW-USA (d/IX-10 1863) MD ? *Med s rep Phila* 10:292, 1863. *Nat med jour* 1:301, 1870/71.

PFEIFFER, PHILIP PETER, Drums, Pa (d/VII-18-1904 @74) <MD UPa 1859> MD Amer U Phila 1856 [fraudulent?] *Pa med jour* 8:336, 1904/05. *Off'l reg Pa phys* 1881-87: 244. *Polk* 1896:1275. *Flint* 1897:800.

PHARES, JOHN H, Clinton La(d/XII-12-1899) MD Atlanta Med Coll 1866. *JAMA* 34:62, 1900. *Polk* 1886:413.

PHELAN, ARTHUR QUIN, Lowell Mass (d/I-7-1890 @42) MD UCNY 1876. *Bost m & s j* 123: 629, 1890.

PHELAN, GREGORY J , Sacramento (b/XII-23-1822 NY; d/XI-5-1902) MD UCNY 1847. *Cal st jour med* 1:13, 172, 1902/03. *Polk* 1896: 237.

PHELPS, ABEL MIX, Burlington, Vt; Chateaugay, NY (b/I-27-1851 Alburgh Spr Vt; d/X-6-1902 NYC) MD U Mich 1873. *Bost m&s j* 147:447 474 1902. *Tr M S St NY* 1903: 418-22. *Nashvl j m&s* 92:182, 1902. *Polk* 1886: 656.

PHELPS, ABNER, Dorchester, Mass (b/1780? d/II-24-1873 @93) Hon MD Yale 1814; AB Williams 1806. *Bost m & s j* ns11:332, 1873.

PHELPS, ALONZO J , Nittayuma, Miss (d/IX-28-1897) MD Starling 1853. *JAMA* 29:761, 1897. *Polk* 1886: 530.

PHELPS, CHARLES ABNER, Boston (b/X-20-1820; d/ 1902) MD Harvard 1844; AB Union 1841. *Bost m & s j* 146:504, 1902.

PHELPS, EBENEZER SMITH, Middleton, Mass (b/ 1792? d/V-28-1882 @90) Lic Mass Med Soc 1816. *Bost m & s j* 107: 61, 1882.

PHELPS, EDWARD ELISHA, Windsor, Vt; CW-USA; (b/IV-24-1803 Peacham; d/XI-26-1880) MD Yale 1825; AM U Vt 1837; LLD 1857. *Trans AMA* 32:535-38, 1881. *Tr Vt M S* 1883:108. *Tr NH M S* 1881:153. *Atkinson* I:527. *K&B* III: 964-65.

PHELPS, FRANCIS P , Cambridge, Md (b/I-31-1799 Del; d/XI-18-1886) MD U Md 1853. *Med annals Md:* 533. *Biogr Encycl Md & DC* 1879: 410-11.

PHELPS, HENRY, Gloucester, Mass (d/1852 at sea) Stud med w/Joshua Plummer, Salem; AB Harvard 1789. Palmer's *Necrol Harvard alum*: 1-2.

PHELPS, JAMES LUDOWICK, NYC (b/IV-16-1785; d/X-17-1869) MD ? *Med reg NY NJ Conn* 1870: 325. *Phila med reg & dir* 1871: 302. *Med rec* 4:449, 1869-70.

PHELPS, ROLLIN HORACE, Pepperell, Mass (b/II-22 1833; d/I-28-1905 Littleton; MD Dartmouth 1862. *Bost m & s j* 152:620, 1905. *Polk* 1896:715.

PHELPS, THADDEUS, No Attleboro, Mass (b/VII-21 1809 Windsor, Conn; d/V-31-1879) MD Woodstock 1832. *Bost m & s j* 101: 496, 1879.

PHILIPS [PHILLIPS], ALBERT J , Baltimore (d/XI-24 1898 @44) MD Balto U 1895. *JAMA* 31:1490, 1542, 1898. *Polk* 1896: 664.

PHILLIPS, BUTLER HUBBARD, Suncook, NH (b/VIII 17-1815 Loudon, NH; d/V-25-1893 @78) MD Bowdoin 1841. *Bost m & s j* 128:560, 1893. *Tr NH M S* 1893:155. *Butler* 1878: 457.

PHILLIPS, CHARLES W , Rocky Ford, Colo (b/VI-4 1859 Jennings Co, Ind; d/IX-25-1901) MD Med Coll Ohio 1887. *Tr Ind St Med Soc* 1902: 421.

PHILLIPS, DAVID, NYC (d/V-28-1891 @39) MD CPS NY 1873. *Bost m & s j* 124:570, 1891. *Butler* 1878: 522.

PHILLIPS, HENRY JOHN, CW-USA; NYC (b/X-2-1830 Engl; d/X-16-1879) MRCS(E) 1849[!] <att St Andrews, Sc 1857> *Med reg NY NJ Conn* 1880:239. *Med s rep Phila* 41:396, 1879. *Med rec NY* 16:383, 1879.

PHILLIPS, HENRY PADDLEFORD, No Adams, Mass (d/XI-24-1881 @74) MD Berkshire 1826. *Bost m & s j* 106:24, 1882. *Med rec* 20:558, 1881.

PHILLIPS, JAMES J , Edgecombe, NC (b/III-12-1798; d/IV-10-1874) Stud med NC w/Dr Cullen Battle; stud med Phila. *Tr NC M S* 1892:205-09; 1875: 20-21. *NC m j* 30:350-54, 1892.

PHILLIPS, JAMES RICHARDS, Millport, Ala (b/XI-13 1848; d/VI-4-1893) MD Louisville Med Coll 1873; att U Ala 1871. *U Ala cat*: 220.

PHILLIPS, JAMES WILLOUGHBY, Burn Brae, Pa (b/ V- 1847 Montreal; d/IX-19-1900) MRCS(E) 1873. *Pa med jour* 5:164, 296, 1901/02.

PHILLIPS, JERRIE KNOWLTON, Bangor, Me (b/II-25-1858; d/XI-5-1899) MD Harvard 1885. *Bost m & s j* 141:484, 1899. *Polk* 1896: 633.

PHILLIPS, JOHN, Mellonville, NY (d/XII-17-1859) MD ?Brown 1817. *Med surg rep Phila* ns3:297, 1859/60.

PHILLIPS, JOHN, Bristol, Pa (b/VIII-28-1790 NJ; d/I-

1-1861) MD UPa 1812; AB Princeton 1808; AM 1811. *Med surg rep Phila* ns5:438, 1860/61.

PHILLIPS, JOHN, Lickdale, Pa (d/I-23-1906 @28) MD Med-Chir Coll 1905. *Pa med jour* 9:524, 1905/06.

PHILLIPS, JOHN BARNARD, St Paul, Minn (b/III-23-1821 Kennett Square Pa; d/IV-27-1877) MD UPa 1855. *Tr Minn St M S* 1877:149-51; 1902:307 *Butler* 1874:385.

PHILLIPS, JOHN HOWELL, Pennington, Pa; CW-USA (b/III-31-1814 Titusville, NJ; d/III-1-1878 Beverly) MD UPa 1837. *U Pa m alum CW*: 1837. *Tr AMA* 33: 589-90, 1882. *Tr M S NJ* 1878-79; 204-05. *Med rec* 13:455, 1878.

PHILLIPS, JOSEPH AUGUSTUS, CW-USA; Pittsburgh (b/XII-23 1832 Louisville; d/X-25-1895) MD UPa 1855. *JAMA* 25: 818, 1895.

PHILLIPS, JOSIAH LOCKE, Sioux Falls, SD (b/VI-8-1835 Farmington, Me; d/VI-12-1882) MD Rush 1857; ng Bowdoin 1852-53. *Bowdoin cat*: 1854.

PHILLIPS, LESLIE ALMON, Boston (b/VIII-19-1847 Fitzwilliam, NH; d/V-9-1896) MD Boston U 1877. *Tr Am Inst Hom* 1896:87. *No Am j hom* 44:528, 1896. *Med couns* ns1: 1896 (May). *Polk* 1886:460. Homeopath.

PHILLIPS, MATTHEW B , Brooklyn (d/IX-22-1866 @26) MD ? *Med reg NY NJ Conn* 1867: 224.

PHILLIPS, NEWTON F , St Clair, Tenn (d/XI-26-1883 @38) MD U Nashville 1872. *So pract* 6:95, 1884.

PHILLIPS, SAMUEL B , NYC (d/1857? @54) MD UCNY 1842. *Bost m & s j* 56:127, 1857.

PHILLIPS, WILLIAM WILSON LATTA, Trenton, NJ; CW-USA (b/II-19 or 29-1829 Lawrence Twp; d/IV-27 1896) MD Jefferson 1851; AB Princeton 1848. *Tr M S NJ* 1896: 365-68. *Atkinson* I: 510.

PHILLIPSON, ABRAHAM, ?NYC (d/II-10-1866) <MD Göttingen 1840> *Med reg NY NJ Conn* 1866: 206.

PHINNEY, CHARLES FREMONT, Bound Brook, NJ (d/XI-29-1892) MD U Vt 1886. *Tr M S NJ* 1893: 174. *Polk* 1890: 719.

PHINNEY, ELIHU [or **ELISHA**], Yantic, Conn (b/III 1809 Canterbury; d/X-15-1892) <MD Yale 1835> *Proc Conn Med Soc* 1892: 873-74. *Polk* 1890: 225.

PHINNEY, ERASTUS OTIS, Melrose, Mass (b/II-26-1810 Sandwich; d/VII-8-1883) MD Harvard 1841; AB Wesleyan 1838. *Bost m & s j* 109:617, 1883.

PHIPPS, JAMES MONROE, Boston (b/V-1-1818 Hopkinton; d/II-15-1865 @47) MD Harvard 1845; AB Brown 1842. *Bost m & s j* 72: 88, 1865.

PHIPPS, JOHN M, Evansville Ind (d/VI-8-1896 @79) MD Rush 1850. *JAMA* 26:1244-5,1896. *Polk* 1886:317.

PHISTER, BENJAMIN Jr, Philadelphia (d/V-17-1883 @48) MD Jefferson 1856. *Tr Pa St M S* 1884: 504-05. *Butler* 1878: 693.

PHOENIX, LEWIS, Morristown, NJ (d/XI-30-1865) MD ? *Med surg rep Phila* 13:490, 1865.

PHYSICK, PHILIP SYNG, Philadelphia (b/VII-7-1768; d/XII-15-1837) MD Edinburgh 1792; stud w/John Hunter London; AB UPa 1785. *Amer j m sci* 21: 542, 1838; 24:93-128, 1839. *So m & s jour* 2:321-22, 1837. *K&B* III: 965-966.

PHYTHIAN, CHARLES TAYLOR, Newport, Ky (b/1861; d/III-14-1897) MD Med Coll Ohio 1885. *JAMA* 28: 620, 1897.

PHYTHIAN, JOHN L , Newport, Ky (b/1833 Johns town, Pa; d/II-12-1896) MD U Louisville 1856. *JAMA* 26:391, 1896. *NC m j* 37:150, 1896. *Polk* 1886:403.

PIATT, WILLIAM A, Cherrytree Pa (d/VIII-21-1860 @ 35) MD Jefferson 1851. *Phila m & s j*ns4:486, 1860.

PICK, ALBERT EDWARD, Brockton, Mass (d/II-12-1899 @34) MD Boston U 1890. *Bost m & s jour* 140:176, 1899. Homeopath?

PICK, AUGUSTUS T, USN 1867 (d/VIII-29-1867) MD U Md 1853. *Tr AMA* 19:455, 1868. *Hamersly*: 567.

PICKARD, ADONIRAM JUDSON, CW-USA; Pensacola, Fla 1872-79 (b/XII-24-1838 Hampden, Me; d/XII-26-1882 Carmel, Me) MD Homeop Hosp Coll Cleveland 1872; AB Bowdoin 1863. *Bowdoin cat*: 1863. Homeopath?

PICKARD, ISAIAH LOVELL, CW-USA (b/III-6-1831 Canterbury, NH; d/VII-20-1865 Indianola, Tex) MD Bowdoin 1863; ng Dartmouth Med 1861. *Nat med jour* 1:301, 1870/71.

PICKETT, COLUMBUS M , Kinsley, Kans (d/X-3-1890 @62) MD Pulte 1881. *Med vis* 6:346, 1890. *Polk* 1886: 380. Homeopath.

PICKETT, JOHN HENRY, Elizabeth, NJ (d/VIII-9-1898 @68) MD Buffalo 1865. *Buff m&s j* 38:141, 1898. *JAMA* 31:427, 1898.

PICKETT, JOHN SCOTT, Danville, Ala (d/IX- -1886) MD U Louisville 1851. *Tr M Assn St Ala* 1887: 306. *Polk* 1886: 133.

PICKETT, NOBLE BENNETT, Great Barrington, Mass (d/II-5-1884 @83) MD Yale 1834. *Bost m & s jour* 110:168, 1884.

PICKING, CHRISTIAN S , York Co, Pa (d/V-25-1877 @54) MD Pa Med Coll 1846. *Tr Pa St M S* 11:751, 1877. *Butler* 1878: 727.

PICOT, MITCHELL HENRY d'ESPINVILLE, Geneva, NY (b/VI-5-1896) MD Jefferson 1861. *JAMA* 26: 1245, 1896. *Polk* 1896: 1023.

PICTON, JOHN MOORE WHITE, New Orleans (b/1804 Woodbury, NJ; d/X-28-1858) MD U Pa 1832; grad 1824 US Mil Acad. *Tr AMA* 13:819-20, 1860. *Bost m&s j* 59:468, 1859. *K&B* I(2): 273.

PIERCE, ALEXANDER B , Weldon, NC (d/II-21 1896 @72) MD UPa 1845; att Randolph Macon. *Tr NC M S* 1896:148-50. *Butler* 1878: 597.

PIERCE, ANDREW MARTIN, New Bedford, Mass (d/XI-6-1905 @53) MD CPSNY 1873. *Bost m & s jour* 153:540, 1905. *Polk* 1886: 470.

PIERCE, CALEB, Madrid, NY (b/1799? d/VI-14-1887 @88)Lic Exam Bd 1831. *Med reg NY NJ Conn* 1888:267.

 Spec. educ'l status abbrev. as: ***ng*** = college verified attendance without degree;

PIERCE, CHARLES R , CW-USA (d/VII-29-1863) MD Cleveland Med Coll 1848. *Nat m j* 1:301, 1870/71.

PIERCE, DELANO, Grafton, Mass (b/1787? d/I-9-1871 @84) MD ? *Bost m & s jour* 7:120, 1871.

PIERCE, ELBRIDGE GERRY, Holyoke, Mass; USA (d/1862 @46) MD Berkshire 1838. *Bost m & s jour* 67:105, 1862.

PIERCE, FRANKLIN WILLIAMS, Marstons Mills, Mass (d/X-19-1896 Edgartown) MD UCNY 1879; AB Yale 1876. *Bost m&s j* 135:456, 1896. *Polk* 1890:551.

PIERCE, GARDNER CARPENTER, Ashland, Mass (b/II-22-1838 Foxboro, Mass; d/V-18-1900) MD Harvard 1866; AB Dartmouth 1863. *Bost m & s jour* 142:580,1900. *JAMA* 34:1505,1900. *Polk* 1896:691.

PIERCE, GEORGE AUGUSTUS, Providence, RI (b/VIII-12-1828; d/VIII-20-1885) MD UPa 1854. *Tr RI M S* 3:253, 1883-88. *Butler* 1878:748.

PIERCE, H LINDSLEY, CW-USA (d/XI-5-1863 Libby Prison) MD U Md 1862. *Nat m j* 1:301, 1870/71.

PIERCE, JOHN, Edgartown, Mass (b/XI-25-1805 Lebanon, Conn; d/III-22-1885) MD Bowdoin 1833. *Bost m & s jour* 112:360, 516, 1885; 113:657, 1885. *JAMA* 9:735, 1887. *Butler* 1878: 355.

PIERCE, JOHN GREELEY, Yarmouth, Me (b/X-28-1842; d/X-28-1897) MD Bowdoin 1867; ng Harvard. *Bost m & s jour* 138:364, 1898. *Polk* 1896: 641.

PIERCE, MOSES, West Chester, Pa (b/VI-18-1782; d/VI-18-1808) <Stud U Pa before 1805> *Med reporter* (West Chester, Pa) 2:64, 1854.

PIERCE, SAMUEL NEWELL, Cedar Falls, Ia (b/V-6-1832 Barnard, Vt; d/1900) MD Woodstock 1856. *Tr Iowa St M S* 19:446, 1901. *Polk* 1896: 513.

PIERCE, THOMAS WILLIAM, CW-CSA; Knoxville, Ala (b/XII-25-1836; d/VI-1-1898) MD U Va 1856; att U Ala 1853. *U Ala cat*: 111.

PIERPONT, HENRY, New Haven, Conn (b/IV-20-1831 Morris; d/VIII-26-1892) MD Yale 1853. *Proc Conn M S* 1893:244-46. *Butler* 1878: 81.

PIERREPONT, WILLIAM AUGUSTUS, Brooklyn (d/I 6-1902 @46) MD UCNY 1882; LLB Columbia 1876. *Bost m & s jour* 146: 76, 1902.

PIERSON, C M , Newark, NJ (d/VIII-13-1873) MD ? *Med surg rep Phila* 29: 144, 1873.

PIERSON, CHARLES EDWIN, So Bergen, NJ; NYC (b/1787? d/VIII-6-1865 @78) MD UPa 1813; AB Princeton 1807; AM 1810. *Med s rep Phila* 13:133, 1865.

PIERSON, CHARLES H, Avon, Ill (d/I-25-1906 @80) MD ? *Ill med jour* 9:227, 1906.

PIERSON, DANIEL C , Cedarville, NJ to 1817; Augusta (b/X-9-1782; d/I-29-1857) MD UPa 1814. *Tr M S NJ* 1871: 164-65.

PIERSON, E M , Somonauk, Ill (d/II-4-1866 @42 Ukia City, Cal) MD ? *Med s rep Phila* 14:240, 1866.

PIERSON, EDWARD AUGUSTUS, CW-USA & USN (b/III-22-1836; d/V-22-1863 abd "Penobscot" off Wilmington, NC) MD CPSNY 1858. *Tr AMA* 14:217, 1864. *Nat m j* 1:301 1870/71 *Med s rep Phil* 10:96, 1863.

PIERSON, MOSES, Metuchen, NJ (d/VI-13-1874) MD CPSNY 1850. *Tr M S NJ* 1875:[104]. *Tr AMA* 27: 652, 1876.

PIERSON, WILLIAM, Orange, NJ (b/1832; d/VI-12-1900) MD UCNY 1852. *Bost m & s jour* 142: 676, 1900. *JAMA* 34:1645, 1900. *Polk* 1896: 945.

PIERSON, WILLIAM J , Orange, NJ (b/XII-4-1796; d/X-1-1882) Lic M S NJ 1820; AB Princeton 1816; AM 1821. *Med reg NY NJ Conn* 1883: 233. *Tr M S NJ* 1883: 294-96. *JAMA* 1:407. 1883. *Bost m&s j* 107: 356, 1882.

PIERSON, WILLIAM SEWARD, Windsor, Conn (b/1787? d/VII-16-1860 @73) MD Dartmouth 1813; AB Yale 1808. *Bost m&s j* 62:536, 1858. *Proc Conn M S* 1: 133-41, 1861.

PIGGOT, AARON SNOWDEN, Baltimore (b/1822 Phila; d/II-13-1869) MD U Md 1845; AB Yale 1841. *Med annals Md:* 533-34.

PIKE, CHARLES COLBY, Peabody, Mass (b/V-5-1844 New London, NH; d/I-27-1894) MD Dartmouth 1869. *Bost m&s j* 130:128, 1894. *Tr NH M S* 1894:191-92. *Polk* 1890: 554.

PIKE, GEORGE ALBERT, Bristol, RI (b/VIII-21-1848; d/XI-8-1892) MD Harvard 1873. *Tr RI M S* 4:624, 1889-93. *Polk* 1890: 1025.

PIKE, NATHAN S , Windham Co, Conn (d/1857 @40) MD UCNY 1842. *Proc Conn M S* 1857: 21.

PILE, CHARLES HENRY, CW-USN (b/VII-28-1839 Phila; d/XII-23-1862 abd "Paul Jones" off Ga) MD UPa 1860. *Nat med jour* 1:301, 1870/71. *Med surg rep Phila* ns9:326, 1862/63. *U Pa med alum CW*: 1860.

PILGRIM, MAURICE FISCHER, NYC (d/X-18-1903 @46) MD Howard 1884; AB; Pharm D. *Bost m & s jour* 149:500, 527, 1903. *Polk* 1896:639. Black.

PILLOW, ANTHONY LECHLEY, Columbia, Tenn (d/VII-14-1904 @85) MD Jefferson 1845. *JAMA* 43:621, 1904. *Polk* 1886: 863.

PILLSBURY, BURKE, Middletown, NY (d/VI-18-1900 @52) MD Harvard 1872. *JAMA* 34:1676, 1900. *Tr M S St NY* 1901:[426] *Polk* 1896, 1032.

PILLSBURY, ENOCH HILTON, Hubbardstown, Mass (d/XII-23-1857 @33) MD Harvard 1854. *Bost m & s jour* 57:455, 1857.

PILLSBURY, LEVI, Fitchburg, Mass (b/IV-2-1817 Winchendon; d/II-4-1895) MD Dartmouth 1842. *Bost m & s jour* 132:144, 1895. *Polk* 1890: 548.

PINCHEN, THOMAS F , NYC 1878- (b/Irel'd; d/XI-8 1880 @33) MD ? *Med reg NY NJ Conn* 1880: 239.

PINCKNEY, CHARLES, Atlanta (d/VIII-13-1889) MD Med Coll St SC 1855. *Med surg rep Phila* 61:336, 1889. *Polk* 1886: 225.

PINCKNEY, SAMUEL GREY COURTNEY, Atlanta (b/VII-14-1869 Nyack, NY; d/IX-20-1906) MD CPS NY 1893. *Bost m&s j* 155:364, 1906. *Polk* 1896: 1073.

PINCKNEY, WILLIAM EDWARD, Annapolis, Md (d/II-25-1822) MD UPa 1808. *Med annals Md:* 524. *Biogr dir Congr.*

PINDAR, JOHN, Hoboken, NJ (d/IV-11-1893 @63) MD UPa 1853. *Tr M S NJ* 1893:180-81. *Polk* 1886: 604.

PINDELL, RICHARD, Lexington, Ky; RevWar-USA (b/1755 Hagerstown, Md; d/III-20-1833) MD ? *Med annals Md:* 534. *Transylvania jour med & assoc sci* 6:149, 1833. Heitman's *Officers Continental Army*.

PINDELL, WILLIAM NICK, Newark (b/XII-25-1828 Anne Arundel Co, Md; d/VIII-4-1892) MD U Md 1848. *Atkinson* I:415. *Tr M S NJ* 1893:181. *Bost m&s j* 127: 152, 1892. *Butler* 1878:463.

PINEO, PETER, Boston; W Somerville, Mass; Hyannis; CW-USA (b/III-6-1825 Cornwallis, NS; d/IX-10-1891) MD Bowdoin 1847; att Harvard Med Sch. *Bost m & s j* 125:368, 1891. *Atkinson* I:73. *Harvard in CW*: 232. *Butler* 1878: 355.

PINKHAM, CHARLES ELLIOTT, Sacramento (b/1839; d/VI-30-1901) <MD Ecl Med Coll Pa 1868> *Tr Am Inst Hom* 1902: 850. *Polk* 1886: 170. Homeopath.

PINKHAM, JOHN WARREN, Montclair, NJ (b/V-14-1834 Gardiner, Me; d/XII-7-1894) MD Bellevue 1866; AB Haverford 1860. *Med reg NY NJ Conn* 1895:237. *Tr M S NJ* 1895:197. *JAMA* 23:961, 1894.

PINKNEY, HOWARD, CW-USA; NYC (b/I-9-1838; d/V-5 or 14-1888 London, Engl) MD CPSNY 1860; AB UCNY 1856; AM 1859. *Med reg NY NJ Conn* 1888:267. *Bost m & s jour* 118:534, 1888. *Butler* 1878:522.

PINKNEY, NINIAN, USN 1834-77? (b/1811; d/1877) MD Jefferson 1833. *Tr AMA* 29:737-41, 1878. *K&B* III:970. Hamersly, *Rec...Off USN & MC*: 191.

PINKNEY, WILLIAM HENRY, Pittsburgh; NYC (d/V-2-1889) MD CPSNY 1885. *Med reg NY NJ Conn* 1889: 280.

PINNEO, JOSEPH OTIS, Elizabeth, NJ (b/III-29-1842; d/V-19-1891) MD CPSNY 1865. *Tr M S NJ* 1891: *Polk* 1886:603. *Butler* 1878: 474.

PINNEO, TIMOTHY STONE, Norwalk, Conn (d/VIII 9-1893 @89) MD ?Med Coll Ohio 1834; AB Yale 1824. *JAMA* 21:247, 1893. *Boston m & s jour* 129:208, 1893.

PINNER, FRANCIS, NYC (d/VII-3-1891 @51) <MD U Berlin 1866> *Med reg NY NJ Conn* 1892: 285. *Tr M S St NY* 1892:495. *Polk* 1886: 690.

PINNEY, CHARLES HITCHCOCK, Derby, Conn (b/IV 25-1831 New Windsor; d/V-16-1893 Evanston, Ill) MD CPSNY 1853. *JAMA* 20:649, 1893. *Pr Conn M S* 1894: 239-41. *Chic m rec* 5:63, 1893. *Bost m&s j* 128: 532, 1893. *Atkinson* I:395.

PINNEY, CHARLES HURLBURT, CW-USA; Council Bluffs, Ia (b/VIII-30-1842 Elyria, O; d/VIII-9-1894 Lincoln, Nebr) MD U Mich 1864; MD UPa 1866. *U Pa med alum CW*: 1866. *Tr Ia St M S* 12:201-03, 1895.

PIPER, WATSON JOHN, CW-USA; Allegany Co, Md (b/VIII-17-1842; d/1884) MD U Md 1867. *Med annals Md:* 535. *Butler* 1874: 322.

PIPER, WILLIAM A , Philadelphia (d/VII-6-1896 @77) MD Jefferson 1844. *JAMA* 27:279: 1896. *Polk* 1896: 1315.

PIPER, WILLIAM EVANS, Ellicott City, Md (b/I-17 1807 Balto; d/1858) MD U Md 1830; AB Kenyon 1826. *Med annals Md:* 535.

PIPES, JOHN H , Cameron, WVa; Wheeling 1873-98) b/V-22-1839 Greene Co, Pa; d/III-16-1899 Albuquerque, NM) MD Charity Hosp Med Coll Cleveland 1866; MD Bellevue 1873. *Polk* 1886: 945.

PIPINO, WILLIAM C , Des Moines (b/Balto; d/VI-3-1896 @46) MD U Md 1873. *Tr Ia St M S* 14:329, 1896: 15:369, 1897. *JAMA* 28:907, 1897. *Polk* 1890: 413.

PIRIE, W T , Waco, Tex (d/II-2-1899) <MD Aberdeen Scotl 1884> *JAMA* 32:385, 1899. *Polk* 1896: 1455.

PIROSH, BERTHOLD B, Chicago (d/I-25-1906 @52) <MD St Petersburg 1879> *Ill med jour* 9:228, 1906.

PITCHER, ZINA, USA 1832-39; Detroit (b/IV-12-1797; d/IV-5-1872) MD Castleton 1822. *Buff m&s j* 11: 362, 1872. *Tr AMA* 23:591-92, 1872. *Bost m&s j* ns9: 308, 1872. *K&B* III:970-71.

PITCHFORD, THOMAS JEFFERSON, Warren, NC (b/VI-13-1810;d/XI-1883) MD UPa 1834; AB UNC 1831. *UNC cat*: 495.

PITKIN, LEONARD FOX, NYC (b/1858 Hartford, Conn; d/XII-1-1904) MD UCNY 1879. *Bost m&s j* 151: 640, 1904. *Polk* 1896: 1073.

PITMAN, JOHN, Memphis (d/X-18-1885) MD ? *New Orl m & s j*ns13:663, 1886.

PITMAN, JOSEPH HENRI, N Conway, NH (b/VII-30-1857 Bartlett; d/I-11-1891) MD Dartmouth 1884. *Tr NH M S* 1891: 255-56. *Polk* 1890: 711.

PITMAN, SAMUEL S , Chipley, Ga (d/IV-21-1900 @41) MD U Md 1882. *JAMA* 34: 1146, 1900.

PITNEY, AARON, War1812-USA; Auburn, NY; Chicago 1836- (b/1793? Mendham, NJ; d/II-7-1865 @72) Stud w/V Mott. *Amer homeop obs* 2:63, 1865. *Tr Am Inst Hom* 1893. *King* I:345-46. Homeopath.

PITNEY, JONATHAN, Absecon, NJ (b/X-29-1797; d/VIII-7-1869) MD ? *Med surg rep Phila* 21:170, 1869. *Phila med reg & dir* 1871: 301.

PITT, WILLIAM, Boston (d/III-11-1868 @ c50 Valparaiso, Chile) MD Harvard 1848. *Bost m & s jour* ns2:32, 1868. *Mass M S cat* 1894.

PITTINOS, JAMES W , CW-USA; Philadelphia (d/II-2 1894) MD Phila Coll Med & Surg 1857; MD Pa Med Coll 1859. *JAMA* 22:235, 1894. *Butler* 1878:693.

PITTMAN, BENJAMIN HERBERT, Hillsdale, Pa (d/X 19-1904 @69) MD U Mich 1864. *Pa med jour* 8:336, 1904/05. *Flint* 1897: 804.

PITTMAN, NEWSOM JONES, Tarboro, NC; CW-CSA (b/VIII-9-1818 Halifax Co; d/V-14-1893) MD UPa 1839. *Tr M S NC* 1894: 193-94. *NC m j* 32:58-59, 1893. *U Pa m alum CW*:1839. *Atkinson* I:265. *Polk* 1886: 726.

 Spec. educ'l status abbrev. as: ***ng*** = college verified attendance without degree;

PITTWOOD, LOUIS N , Watseka, Ill (d/IX-29-1897 @67) Lic yrs pract. *JAMA* 29:761, 1897. *Polk* 1886:301.

PITZER, ANDREW BAKER, Tipton, Ind (b/1845; d/III-22-1895) MD Med Coll Ind 1875; AB. *JAMA* 24:497, 1895. *Tr Ind St M S* 1895: 412. Kemper's *Indiana*: 328.

PLACE, NELSON Jr, NYC (b/III-11-1839; d/VII-7-1881) MD NY Med Coll 1864; AB UCNY 1862; AM 1865. *Med reg NY NJ Conn* 1882: 233. *Atkinson* I: 552.

PLAGEMAN, HENRY, Woodland & Hustisford, Wis (b/III-12-1852; d/V-19-1894) MD Würzburg 1879. *Tr Wis St M S* 29:546-47, 1895. *Polk* 1886:962.

PLAISTED, SAMUEL, Waterville, Me (b/XI-24-1801 Gardiner; d/IV-14-1860) MD Bowdoin 1828; AB Brown 1825; AM. *Brown hist cat*: 1825.

PLANK, DAVID A , CW-USA; St Clairsville, Pa (b/1838; d/IV-12 1902 @64) <MD Jefferson 1870> *Pa med jour* 5:455, 1901/02; 6:261, 1902/03. *Flint* 1897: 834.

PLANK, EDWARD HAMLIN, Christina, Pa (d/II-5-1902 @52) MD Jefferson 1870. *Pa med jour* 6:261, 1902/03. *Flint* 1897: 798.

PLANK, JACOB R , York Springs, Pa (d/V-24-1903 @76) MD Washington U, Balto 1874. *Pa m j* 7: 280, 1903/04. *Flint* 1897: 841.

PLANK, W H , Deer Creek Ind (d/X-11-1898 @45) MD Ky Sch Med 1881. *JAMA* 31:1066, 1898. *Polk* 1886:315.

PLANT, WILLIAM TOMLINSON, Syracuse CW-USN (b/VII-27-1836 Marcellus;d/X-27-1898) MD U Mich 1860. *JAMA* 31:1128 1898. *Atknsn* I:385. *K&B* III:971.

PLATT, ELIPHALET, Rhinebeck, NY (b/1797? d/V-16 1868) MD ? *Phila med reg & dir* 1871: 297. *Med surg rep Phila* 18:522, 1868.

PLATT, GIDEON LUCIAN, Waterbury, Conn (b/VII-20 1813 Middlebury; d/XI-11-1889) MD Yale 1838. *Proc Conn M S* 1890:277-78. *Atkinson* I:686. *Butler* 1878:81.

PLATT, THOMAS, Dayton, O (b/1797? d/III-29-1870 @73) MD ? *Phila med reg & dir* 1871: 304.

PLIMPTON, DANIEL BACON, Putnam, Conn (b/III-4 1821 Southbridge, Mass; d/IV-1-1875) MD ? ng Amherst 1846. *Mass M S cat* 1894.

PLUMB, EDWARD B , Ames, Ia (b/1858; d/1893) MD NWU 1882. *Tr Ia St M S* 14:329, 1896. *Polk* 1890: 407.

PLUMB, OVID, Litchfield Co, Conn (b/1786? d/1857? @ 71) Hon MD Geneva 1849. *Proc Conn M S* 1857:21.

PLUMER, ALEXANDER, Smithfield, Ill; CW-USA (d/V-18-1862 @28) MD ? *Med surg rep Phila* 12:164, 1864/65. *Nat med jour* 1:301, 1870/71.

PLUMER, WILLIAM D , CW-USA (d/VII-10-1864 Chattanooga) MD NWU 1864. *Med surg rep Phila* 12: 164, 1864/65. *Nat med jour* 1:301, 1870/71.

PLUMMER, C , Wooster, O (d/VII-27-1895 @74) MD ? *JAMA* 25:253, 1895.

PLUMMER, HENRY LYNE, Warrenton, NC (b/I-1-1798; d/I-21-1864) MD UPa 1819; AB UNC 1815. *UNC cat*: 497.

PLUMMER, JOHN THOMAS, Richmond, Ind (b/1807; d/1865) MD Yale 1828. *Tr AMA* 18:345, 1867.

PLUMMER, RICHARD HENRY, San Francisco (b/1840 Cambridge, O; d/IV-23-1899) MD Toland 1866; MD Rush 1870 ad eundem. *Tr M S St Calif* 1900: 546-47. *JAMA* 32:955, 1899. *Polk* 1896: 237.

PLUMMER, SAMUEL C Sr, Rock Isl, Ill (b/Pa; d/IV-29-1900 @79) MD Cleveland Med Coll 1856. *JAMA* 34:1210, 1900. *Tr Ill St M S* 1899/1900:574, 1900/1901: 48. *Polk* 1886: 296.

PLUNKETT, EDWARD LEICESTER, NYC (d/I-10 1890 @33) MD CPSNY 1885; att Lafayette. *Med reg NY NJ Conn* 1890: 279. *Bost m & s jour* 122: 1890.

PLUNKETT, FRANCIS CHARLES, Lowell, Mass (b/1842 Irel'd; d/XI-29-1899) <MRCS [?Dublin] 1863> *Bost m & s jour* 142:153, 1900. *JAMA* 33:1566, 1899. *Polk* 1893: 604.

PLYMPTON, HENRY SYLVANUS, Cambridge, Mass; CW-USA & USN (d/IX-25-1863 @25) MD Harvard 1860; MD CPSNY 1861. *Bost m & s jour* 69: 188, 1863. *Harvard in CW*: 260-61.

POCOCK, ELI DUDLEY, Shreve O (d/XII-16-1893) MD Bellevue 1870 *Butler* 1878:645. *JAMA* 21:1010, 1893.

POHLE, J C, NYC (b/1829 Gny; d/X-7-1895) MD NY M C 1864. *Bost m&s j* 133: 406, 1895. *Polk* 1890: 199.

POLHEMUS, DANIEL, Englishtown, NJ (b/IX-28-1806; d/III-1-1858) Lic Monmouth Co M S NJ 1828; <MD CPSNY 1828> *Tr M S NJ* 1871:88.

POLIN, JOHN H , Springfield, Ky (b/1799? d/VII-6 1867) MD Transylv 1837. *New Orl m&s j* 21:205, 1868.

POLIS, GEORGE S , Philadelphia (d/VIII-30-1899 @ 49) MD UPa 1878. *JAMA* 33:683, 1899. *Polk* 1890:1000.

POLK, JOHN METCALFE, NYC (d/III-29-1904 @28) MD Cornell 1899; BP Yale 1896. *Bost m & s j* 150:390, 1904.

POLLARD, ABIATHAR, Westport, NY (d/IV-15-1892 or 1893 @91) MD Castleton 1831. *Tr M S St NY* 1892: 470; 1894:741 ff. *Polk* 1890: 857.

POLLARD, GEORGE WILLIAM, Edgehill, Va (b/XII-28-1847; d/XII-5-1885) MD U Va 1868. *Tr M S Va* 1885:286-87.

POLLARD, JAMES RIVES, SC; Richmond, Va; CW-CSA (b/1825 Lovingston, Va; d/II-20-1862) MD UPa 1848. *U Pa m alum CW*: 1848 [d/1868] *Med s rep Phila* ns7: 552, 1861/62. Blanton's *Va surgs CW*: 413.

POLLARD, WADE H , Fort Worth, Tex (d/XI-23-1893 @82) MD Mo Med Coll 1858. *JAMA* 21:907, 1893. *Butler* 1886: 886.

POLLOCK, ALEX McC , Pittsburgh (b/I-7-1820; d/1892) MD Med Coll O 1841. *Tr CPP* cent vol: 285. *JAMA* 19:20, 1892. *Atknsn* I: 708. *Butler* 1878: 700.

POLLOCK, J D , Aurora, Ill (d/XII-14-1896 @86) MD ? *JAMA* 28:92, 1897.

POLLOCK, SAMUEL, Williamsport, Pa (b/X-23-1808 Milton, Pa; d/IV-28-1887) MD UPa 1832; AB Dicknsn

1828. *Atkinson* I: 510. *Polk* 1886: 840.

POLLOCK, THOMAS C , Williamsport, Pa (d/III–28–1870 @36) MD ? *Phila med reg & dir* 1871: 304.

POMEREN [POMERON], JOEL, Millersburg, Pa; CW–USA (d/IX–15–1881 @56) MD Jefferson 1858. *Bost m & s jour* 105:622, 1881. *Med rec* 20:390, 1881.

POMEROY, CHARLES G , NYC (b/II–22–1817 Madison Co, NY; d/XII–14–1887 Newark, NJ) MD Jefferson 1851. *JAMA* 10:64, 1888. *Tr M S St NY* 11: 741 ff, 1894. *K&B* III: 973.

POMEROY, OREN DAY, NYC (b/X–11–1834 Somers, Conn; d/III–18–1902 @68) MD CPSNY 1860; stud Berkshire. *Bost m & s jour* 146:350, 1902. *Atkinson* I: 494. *K&B* III: 973.

POMEROY, THOMAS FULLER, Detroit 1857– ; Providence, RI (b/V–11–1816 Cooperstown, NY; d/IV–2–1892) MD Hom Hosp M C Cleveland 1853; AB Union 1836. *Tr Am Inst Hom* 1892:205. *Polk* 1886: 489. *Cleave*. Homeopath.

POMROY, HERBERT JASON, Providence, RI (b/IV–7 1856 Lincoln, Me; d/XI–27–1893) MD Harvard 1881. *Tr RI M S* 4:625–26, 1889–93. *JAMA* 21:907, 1893.

POND, BENJAMIN, Westboro, Mass (d/VI–7–1857 @68?) MD Dartmouth 1813. *Bost m&s j* 56:447, 1857.

POND, EDWARD PAYSON, NYC (d/IV–3–1889) MD CPSNY 1887; BS. *Med reg NY NJ Conn* 1889: 280.

POND, ERASMUS ALLINGTON, Rutland, Vt (d/V–29 1889 @67) MD Harvard 1853. *Bost m & s jour* 120:572, 1889. *Butler* 1878: 808.

POND, JAMES OTIS, NYC (b/VIII–21–1790 Grafton, Mass; d/II–1–1879) Hon MD Yale 1827. *Med reg NY NJ Conn* 1881:240. *Bost m&s j* 106: 470, 1882. *Atkinson* I: 634. *Butler* 1878: 622.

POOL, JOHN HERSEY, South Mills, NC (b/II–6–1835 Pooltown; d/VII–29–1903) MD UPa 1859; att UNC 1854–57. *UNC cat*: 499. *Polk* 1886: 726.

POOL, WILLIAM GASKINS, Elizabeth City, NC (d/III 15–1887) MD UPa 1851; AB UNC 1849. *UNC cat*: 499. *Polk* 1886: 722.

POOLE, AUGUSTUS, ? (b/III–30–1819 Easton, Mass; d/VIII–9–1883) Stud w/Dr E A Potter. *Tr Am Inst Hom* 1884:663. *Cleave*. Homeopath.

POOLE, HENRY BULEY, New Brunswick, NJ (b/IV–24 1791 Engl; d/XII–2–1861) Lic Distr M S Somerset Co NJ 1820? AB Rutgers 1813; AM Queens 1816. *Tr M S NJ* 1872:112–13.

POOLE, JOHN, Bradford, Vt (b/1792? d/IV–14–1869 @77) MD Dartmouth 1817. *Phila med reg & dir* 1871: 300. *Med surg rep Phila* 20: 346, 1869.

POOLEY, JAMES HENRY Sr, Dobbs Ferry, NY (b/1810 Engl; d/VI–3–1890 Engl) <MD Engl> *Bost m & s jour* 122:591–92, 1890.

POOLEY, JAMES HENRY Jr, CW–USA; Yonkers, NY 1863–75; Columbus & Toledo (b/XI–17–1839 Engl; d/XII–10–1897) MD CPSNY 1860. *JAMA* 29:1286, 1897. *Atkinson* I: 224. *Polk* 1896: 1217.

POPE, ALEXANDER BARNETT, NYC (b/Washington, Ga; d/VI–12–1895 @35) MD CPSNY 1884; att U Va. *Med reg NY NJ Conn* 1895:237. *JAMA* 25:39, 1895.

POPE, ALEXIS DARWIN, Washington, Ark (d/XII–11–1880 Columbus) MD UPa 1835; AB U Ala 1833. *U Ala cat*: 35.

POPE, ASA WILLIE, Marshall, Tex (b/II–17–1858 Washington, Ga; d/XI–3–1892) MD Tulane 1882. *Daniel's Tex med jour* 8:194–95, 1892–93. *Polk* 1890: 1086.

POPE, BOLLING A , New Orleans; Galveston (d/VII–3 1894 @69) MD UCNY 1856. *JAMA* 23:164, 1894. *New Orl m&s j* ns22:308–09, 1894. *Tex cour–rec med* 11 [ie12?]:287, 1894. *Tex m j* 10: 31–32, 1894–95.

POPE, CHARLES ALEXANDER, St Louis (b/III–15–1818 Huntsville, Ala; d/VII–6–1870 Paris, Mo) MD UPa 1839. *Med rec* 5:238, 1870–71. *Bost m&s j* ns6: 30, 1870. *Tr AMA* 29:741–47, 1878. *K&B* III:974.

PORCHER, FRANCIS PEYRE, CW–CSA; Charleston, SC (b/XII–14–1825; d/XI–19–1895) MD Med Coll St SC 1847; AB SC Coll 1844. *Tr CPP* cent vol: 285. *JAMA* 25:1108, 1895. *Bost m&s j* 133:580, 1895. *Atkinson* I: 58. *K&B* III: 975–76.

PORTEOUS, JAMES GEORGE, Poughkeepsie & Luzerne, NY; CW–USA (b/I–3–1839 Moriah; d/V–12–1895) MD Harvard 1866. *Med reg NY NJ Conn* 1895: 237. *JAMA* 24:907, 1895. *Butler* 1878: 569.

PORTER, ALBERT AUGUSTUS, Wrentham, Mass (d/III–26–1871 @30) MD Harvard 1865. *Bost m & s jour* 7: 240, 1871.

PORTER, ALEXANDER SHAW, Lonaconing, Md 1893; USA 1893–99; Redlands, Calif 1899– (b/II–15–1868; d/I–6–1901) MD U Md 1889; PhB Dickinson 1887; AM 1890. *Med annals Md:* 536. Heitman.

PORTER, AMELIA ABIGAIL, Waterbury, Conn (d/I–2 1891) MD Boston U 1885. *New Engl med gaz* 26:160, 1891. *Med vis* 7:125, 1891. Homeopath.

PORTER, ANDREW, Harrisburg, Pa (b/1822 Huntingdon; d/VIII– –1859 Cape May, NJ) MD UPa 1846; att Lafayette 1843? *Lafayette, Men of*: 152.

PORTER, BENJAMIN, Northfield, Vt (b/1788 Conn; d/II–20–1876) ng Dartmouth Med Sch 1814. *Tr Vt M S* 1883: 107.

PORTER, BYRON, Waterville & Dixmont Me 1833–51 (b/V–11–1802 Vienna; d/II–24–1871 Worcester, Mass) MD Bowdoin 1827. *Tr Me M Assn* 1871–73: 187–88.

PORTER, CHARLES HOGEBOOM, Albany, NY (b/XI 11–1834 Ghent; d/XI–21–1903 Canandaigua) MD Albany 1861; Hon AM Yale 1857. *Tr M S St NY* 1904: 421–22. *Atknsn* I:513. *K&B* III:976–77. *Polk* 1886:639.

PORTER, CHARLES JULIUS, Calais, Me 1836–53; 1855–75; Terr Hawaii 1853–55 (b/III–20–1813 Peterboro, NH; d/XII–14–1875) MD Bowdoin 1836; MD UPa 1851; AB Bowdoin 1832. *Bowdoin cat*: 1832.

PORTER, DANIEL REA, Queens Co, NY (d/VIII–17–

 Spec. educ'l status abbrev. as: ***ng*** = college verified attendance without degree;

1888) MD Bel'vue 1866. *Med reg NY NJ Conn* 1889:280.

PORTER, DENNIS WILSON, Decatur, Ill (b/IV-25-1844 Barnesville, O; d/X-23-1901) MD Rush 1878. *Ill med jour* ns3: 348, 1901. *Polk* 1886: 364.

PORTER, EBENEZER, Poultney, Vt (b/V-11-1801; d/XII-12-1869) MD Dartmouth 1824; ng Castleton 1822. *Phila med reg & dir* 1871: 303.

PORTER, EDMUND, Frenchtown, NJ (b/VI-18-1791; d/VII-18-1791; d/VIII-12-1826) MD ? *Tr M S NJ* 1872: 120-24.

PORTER, EDWARD EVELYN, NYC (b/IX-25-1842; d/X-26-1892) MD U Nashville 1864. *Med reg NY NJ Conn* 1873: 346.

PORTER, EDWARD MULFORD, Greenwich & Bridgeton, NJ (b/VIII-20-1825 Camden; d/I-10-1853) MD UPa 1849. *Tr M S NJ* 1871:161-62.

PORTER, EVELYN HART, Onondaga Co, NY (d/X-22 1875)MD Fairfield 1831 *Med reg NY NJ Conn* 1876:253.

PORTER, FRANK MERITHEW, Louisville, Ga (b/III 13-1860 Searsport, Me; d/IX-28-1888) MD Vanderbilt 1882; att Bowdoin Coll 1878-79; ng Bowdoin Med Sch 1880. *Bowdoin cat*: 1882. *Polk* 1886: 231.

PORTER, GABRIEL ELLIS, Lonaconing, Md (b/VII-9 -1830 Frostburg; d/XII-30-1889) MD Jefferson 1853. *Med annals Md:* 536.

PORTER, GEORGE WASHINGTON, Harrisburg, Pa (d/V-7-1906 Spring Lake NJ @81) MD UPa 1851. *Pa m j* 9:612 1905/06. *JAMA* 96:1546 1906. *Flint* 1897: 804.

PORTER, HENRY NORTON, Washington, DC (d/IX-12-1899) MD Geneva 1841. *JAMA* 33:872, 1899.

PORTER, HENRY WILLIAM [WITHEN?], NYC (d/ 1847) MD CPSNY 1846; AB Williams 1842. *Williams grads*: 1842.

PORTER, HERBERT KENT, Duluth (d/III-2-1894 @ 30) MD Miami 1888; MD CPSNY 1889. *JAMA* 22:391, 1894.

PORTER, HORACE THORNBULL, Georgetown, DC; Philadelphia (b/III-11-1849; d/VIII-14-1879) MD Geo'town 1870. *Tr AMA* 32:538-39, 1881. *Hist M S DC:* 303. *Phila med times* 9:612, 1878-79. *Med surg rep Phila* 41:176, 1879.

PORTER, ISAAC, Lebanon, NH (b/X-11-1783 Voluntown, Conn; d/IX-2-1854 Porter, Wis) MD Dartmouth 1814; AB Brown 1808. *Brown hist cat*: 1808.

PORTER, ISAAC GLEASON, New London, Conn; CW-USA (b/VI-29-1806 Waterbury, Conn; d/IV-30-1892) MD UPa 1833; AB Yale 1826. *Med reg NY NJ Conn* 1892: 285. *JAMA* 18: 818, 1892. *Proc Conn M S* 1892: 837-42. *Atkinson* I: 62.

PORTER, JAMES JEFFERSON, Georgetown, DC; CW-USA (b/1803 Phila; d/XII-19-1884) MD UPa 1824. *U Pa med alum CW*: 1824 suppl.

PORTER, JOHN, Duxbury, Mass (b/1793? d/III-23-1865) MD Dartmouth 1820. *Bost m&s j* 72: 188, 1865.

PORTER, JOHN BLISS, USA 1833- (b/VII-3-1804 Coventry, Conn; d/VI-15-1869) MD Berkshire 1829. *Phila med reg & dir* 1871: 301. *Proc Conn M S* 1871: 414; 1875: 433. *Tr AMA* 21:493-94, 1870.

PORTER, JOHN GUERNSEY, Chicago (b/VII-1-1868 Clinton, Ill; d/IV-24-1906) MD Chic Hom 1899. *Tr Am Inst Hom* 1906:775-76. *Ill m j* 9:662 1906. Homeopath.

PORTER, JOHN P , CW-USA (d/XI-1-1864) MD ? *Nat med jour* 1:301, 1870/71.

PORTER, JOSHUA, N Bloomfield, Mass (b/X-20-1808; d/I-6-1874) MD Bowdoin 1834; ng Amherst 1833. *Bost m & s jour* 90:76, 1874.

PORTER, MARIA W , Davenport, Ia 1860- (b/IV-23 1823 Nottingham, Engl; d/IX-8-1888) MD Woman's Med Coll Phila 1859. *Med adv* 21:567, 1888. *Med vis* 4:335, 1888. *King* I:387. *Polk* 1886: 355. Homeopath.

PORTER, MORTIMER G , NYC (b/X-26-1826; d/XI-24-1863) MD Buff 1848. *Med s rep Phila* 10:440, 1863. *Tr AMA* 16: 627, 1865. *Med s rep Phila* 1865: 222-23.

PORTER, PACIFICUS B , Chicago (d/II-8-1903 @58) MD NWU 1869 *Tr Ill M S* ns4:665 1903. *Polk* 1886:279.

PORTER, PHILIP CHESTER, Berkley, Mass (b/IV-17 1833; d/I-11-1895) MD Berkshire 1866; AB Amherst 1855. *Amherst, Men of*: 1855.

PORTER, ROBERT MASSINGILL, Nashville (b/IV-12 1818; d/VII-1-1856) MD UPa 1845; AB U Nashville 1836; LLD Harvard 1838. *So pract* 19:188, 1897. *Tr M S Tenn* 1876:86. *Bost m&s jour* 55:151, 1857. *Nashvl j m & s* 11:163-66, 1856; 12:335-39, 1857.

PORTER, ROBERT ROBINSON, Wilmington, Del (b/ 1811; d/IV-14-1876) MD UPa 1833. *Tr AMA* 27: 647-48, 1876. *K&B* II: 925.

PORTER, SAMUEL, Tenn (b/II-3-1795 Chesterville, SC; d/I-25-1873) MD Transylvania 1825. *Tr M S Tenn* 1876: 86.

PORTER, SIDNEY, Providence RI (d/VI-30-1880) ng U Mich 1876-7; AB Brown 1876; AM. *Brown hist cat*: 1876.

PORTER, WILFRED WICKLIFF, Geddes, NY (b/VII-24-1826 Fayston Vt; d/VI-2-1885) MD Castleton 1851. *Atknsn* I:309 *Tr M S St NY* 1886:630-2. *Butler* 1874:554.

PORTER, WILLIAM, Skaneateles, NY (d/XI-9-1884 @54) MD Buffalo 1851. *Med s rep Phila* 51:604, 1884.

PORTER, WILLIAM B , Richhill Twp, Pa (d/IV-18 1868 @56) MD ? *Med surg rep Phila* 18:542, 1868. *Phila med reg & dir* 1871: 296.

PORTER, WILLIAM B , Chicago (d/XII-12-1895) <MD Mich Coll Med 1890> *JAMA* 25:1108, 1895.

PORTER, WILLIAM D, Higginsville Ill (b/1826 Lewis Co, Ky; d/VIII-20-1890) Lic 1881 by yrs. pract; att Rock Isl Med Coll. *Tr Ind St M S* 1891: 279.

PORTER, WILLIAM GIBBS Jr, Philadelphia (b/IV-25 1846; d/I-30-1906) MD UPa 1868, *Tr CPP* cent vol: 258. *Pa m j* 9:359, 1906. *Atkinson* I:237. *Flint* 1897:823.

PORTER, WINSLOW BURROUGHS, Walpole, NH (b/ XI-21-1823 Morristown, Vt; d/XI-3-1891) MD Dartmouth 1853. *Tr NH M S* 1892: 202–03. *Polk* 1890: 712.

PORTZER, FRANK L , Greensburg, Pa (d/III–27–1902 @35) MD U Western Pa 1888. *Pa m j* 5:386, 1901/02; 6:261, 1902/03. *Flint* 1897: 803.

POSEY, DAVID R , Philadelphia (d/II–3–1896 @66 Jersey City, NJ) <Stud homeop Phila> *Med vis* 12:124, 1896. *Hahn mo* 31:34 (news & advt) 1896. Homeopath.

POSEY, JOHN F , MexWar–USA; Savannah (b/1792 NC; d/1860) MD ? *Med surg rep Phila* ns3:396, 1859/60. *Bost m & s jour* 62:88, 1860.

POSEY, JOHN L , New Orleans (d/XI–6–1895 @42) MD Tulane 1877. *New Orl m & s j* ns23:378, 1895. *Polk* 1890: 491.

POSEY, JOHN WESLEY, Petersburg, Ind (b/IV–10–1801 SC; d/VIII–10–1884) Lic 1825 Wabash Valley M S. *Tr Ind St M S* 1886: 196.

POSEY, MORDECAI AIKEN, Chanceford, Pa (b/York Co; d/X–28–1904 @58) MD Jefferson 1882. *Pa m j* 8: 336, 1904/05. *Flint* 1897: 798.

POST, ALFRED CHARLES, NYC (b/I–13–1806; d/I or II–7–1886) MD CPSNY 1827; AB Columbia 1822. *Med reg NY NJ Conn* 1886: 252. *Bost m & s jour* 114: 165, 1886. *Tr M S St NY* 1886:541–551. *Med surg rep Phila* 12:53–55, 1864/65. *K&B* III: 978.

POST, MINTURN, NYC (b/VI–28–1808; d/IV–26–1869) MD UPa 1832; AB Columbia 1828. *Tr AMA* 21: 448–49, 1870. *Med reg NY NJ Conn* 1869:245. *Tr M S St NY* 1871:350–51. *K&B* III: 979.

POST, PHILIP WRIGHT, NYC (b/II–19–1766 Hempstead, NY; d/VI–14–1828) Hon MD CPSNY 1814; stud w/Richard Bayley, NY & John Sheldon, London. *NY med & phys jour* 9:324, 428–39, 1828. *Amer jour med sci* 2:495–96, 1828. *K&B* III: 980–81.

POST, WILLIAM ELISHA HOWELL, Quogue, NY (b/II–27–1848; d/VII–23–1877) MD Bellevue 1873; AB Williams 1870. *Med rec* 12:511, 1877. *Med reg NY NJ Conn* 1878: 187.

POST, WILLIAM H B , NYC (d/XI–4–1886 @43) MD UCNY 1865; AB. *Med reg NY NJ Conn* 1887: 273.

POSTELL, PHILIP S , Plaquemine, La (d/VIII–3–1900) MD Med Coll SC 1858. *New Orl m & s j* 53:179, 1900. *Polk* 1896: 625.

POTT, J C C , Philadelphia (d/XII–9–1884 @80) MD ? *Med surg rep Phila* 51: 732, 1884.

POTTER, ALBERT, Chepachet, RI (b/II–28–1831 Sturbridge, Mass; d/X–2–1902) MD Harvard 1855. *Tr RI M S* 6:543–45, 1899–1903. *Polk* 1896: 1350.

POTTER, AUGUSTUS OWEN, CW–USA (d/IX–13–1864 Helena, Ark) MD U Mich 1856. *Nat med jour* 1:301, 1870/71.

POTTER [PORTER] CHARLES HENRY, Brooklyn (d/VIII–6–1881) MD Bellevue 1868; AB Princeton 1863; AM. *Med reg NY NJ Conn* 1882: 233. *Butler* 1878: 533.

POTTER, DAVID T , CW–USA (d/IX–28–1862 Ballston, NY) MD CPSNY 1859; AB ? . *Med surg rep Phila* ns9:22, 1862/63.

POTTER, FRANK HAMILTON, Buffalo (b/I–8–1860 Cowlesville; d/VI–6–1891) MD Buffalo 1882. *Med reg NY NJ Conn* 1892:285. *Buff m&s j* 31:37 ff, 1891? *JAMA* 17:161, 1891. *Bost m&s j* 125:96, 1891. *K&B* III: 982.

POTTER, FREDERICK EUGENE, MexWar–USA? USN 1861–76; Portsmouth, NH (b/VII–3–1839 Rumney; d/XI–18–1902 or 1903) MD U Vt 1860. *Tr NH M S* 1903:240–41. Conn, *NH surgs CW*: 373–75.

POTTER, GEORGE L , CW–USA (d/VIII–2–1879 @ 56) MD UPa 1847. *U Pa med alum CW*: 1847.

POTTER, HANDLEY B , LaFargeville, NY (b/1840? d/II–17–1901 @61) MD ? *Bost m & s jour* 144:222, 1901. *Polk* 1886: 665. Eclectic.

POTTER, HAZARD ARNOLD, Potter Twp, NY; CW–USA (b/XII–22–1810; d/XII–3–1869) MD Bowdoin 1835. *Buffalo m & s j* 9:196, 1870. *Bost m&s j* ns4:384, 1869. *Tr AMA* 21:450–52, 1870. *K&B* III: 982.

POTTER, HENRY, New London, Conn (b/1825; d/III 10–1880) MD Yale 1867. *Proc Conn M S* 1880: 167–68. *Butler* 1878: 81.

POTTER, HORACE S , CW–USA (d/VI–2–1864 Acworth, Ga) MD ? *Nat med jour* 1:301, 1870/71.

POTTER, JAMES BARRON, Bridgeton, NJ (b/VII–18–1823; d/VI–11–1892 on ship) MD UPa 1847; AB Princeton 1844; AM 1849. *Tr M S NJ* 1893:181–82. *JAMA* 19:84, 1892.

POTTER, JOHN DONALDSON, Pittsburgh (d/VII–22 1906 @60) MD Cleveland Med Coll 1871. *Pa med jour* 9: 805, 1905/06. *Polk* 1896: 1327.

POTTER, JOSEPH FITCH, Cincinnati (b/XI–28–1808 Sebago, Me; d/IV–5–1868) MD Bowdoin 1835. *Tr Ohio St M S* 1868:200. *Bost m&s j* ns1:187, 1868. *Phila med reg & dir* 1871:296.

POTTER, M E , Attica, NY (d/XI–1–1875 @60) MD ? *Buff m&s j* 15:156, 1875.

POTTER, MERRITT FRANKLIN, Hinckley, Ill; Claremont Mass (d/1886) MD Harv'd 1846; AB Will'ms 1839. *Wms grads*:1839. *Mass M S cat* 1894. *Polk* 1886:282.

POTTER, MILTON GROSVENOR, Buffalo (b/VIII–29 1843 Bennington, Vt; d/I–28–1878) MD Buffalo 1867. *Tr AMA* 30:831–33, 1879. *Buff m&s j* 17:316, 1878. *Atkinson* I: 513.

POTTER, NATHANIEL, Baltimore (b/1770 Easton, Md; d/I–2–1843) MD UPa 1796; att Princeton. *Med annals Md:* 537. *K&B* III: 983–84.

POTTER, SAMUEL, Lancaster, NY (b/III–22–1816 Wells, Vt; d/VI–12–1897) MD Castleton 1836. *Buffalo m & s j* 36:938, 1897. *Flint* 1897: 661.

POTTER, SILAS ALLEN, Roxbury, Mass (d/VII–10 1892 @38) MD Harvard 1884; AB 1876. *Bost m & s jour* 127:52, 1892. *Polk* 1886: 460.

POTTER, THOMAS BURNSIDE, CW–USA; Phillipsburg, Pa (b/XI–21–1829 Potters Mills, Pa; d/I–12–1906) MD UPa 1851. *Pa med jour* 9:360, 1905/06. *Atkinson*

 Spec. educ'l status abbrev. as: ***ng*** = college verified attendance without degree;

I:645, 1878. *Flint* 1897: 828. *U Pa m alum CW*:1851.

POTTER, THOMAS CLIFFORD, CW-USA; Philadelphia (b/1846; d/I-7-1906 @59) MD UPa 1871. *Pa med jour* 360:1906. *Tr CPP* cent vol:258. *Flint* 1897:823.

POTTER, THOMAS GULLIVER, Providence, RI (b/VIII-3-1821 Gloucester, RI; d/X-22-1894) MD Berkshire 1843. *Tr RI M S* 5:135, 1894-98. *Polk* 1890: 1028.

POTTER, THOMAS MAWNEY, USN 1839-76; Kingston, RI (b/VIII-12-1814; d/IV-13-1890) MD UPa 1838; AB Brown 1834. *U Pa med alum CW*: 1838.

POTTER, URIAH, Ft Plain, NY (b/I-11-1809 Salisbury, NY; d/XII-16-1869) MD Fairfield 1834. *Tr M S St NY* 1870: 317 ff.

POTTS, [?EDGAR N], La (d/IX-13-1878 Vicksburg, Miss) MD ?Tulane 1870. *Tr AMA* 30:882, 1879. *Med rec* 14:240, 1878.

POTTS, JAMES F , Detroit (d/VI-8-1896 @59) MD Jefferson 1865. *JAMA* 26: 1278, 1896. *Polk* 1896: 366.

POTTS, RICHARD, USA 1853-61; CSA 1861-65 (b/VII- -1826 Frederick, Md; d/1867 Memphis) MD UPa 1852. *U Pa med alum CW*: 1852.

POTTS, THOMAS READ, Natchez; Galena, Ill 10 yrs; St Paul 1849- (b/II-10-1810 Phila; d/X-6-1874) MD UPa 1831. *Med s rep Phila* 31: 400, 1874. *Tr AMA* 31:1081, 1880. *Tr Minn St M S* 1882: 272.

POTTS, WILLIAM Jr, Western Shore Md (b/1786; d/IV 13-1818 Frederick) MD UPa 1810. *Med ann Md:* 537.

POUCHER, CHARLES H C , Indianapolis (b/1868 Loogootee; d/II-6-1901 Swanton, Nebr) <MD Med Coll Ind 1893> *Tr Ind St M S* 1901: 496.

POULSON, PETER WILLIAM, San Francisco (b/XII-14-1831 Copenhagen; d/III or IV- -1894) MD NY Homeop 1866. *Tr Am Inst Hom* 1896: 87. *Polk* 1886: 354. Homeopath.

POWELL, ALBERT EUGENE, Marion, Ind (d/IX-21-1905 @36) MD U Mich 1892. *Ill med jour* 8:430, 1905.

POWELL, ALFRED, NYC; CW-USA (d/VIII-23-1876/1877) MD CPSNY 1853 *Med reg NY NJ Conn* 1877:205.

POWELL, BELITHA, CW-CSA; Houston, Tex (b/V-3 1832 Md; d/VI-16-1893) MD Jefferson 1853. *Tex cour-rec med* 10:316, 1893. *Daniel's Tex med jour* 9:40, 1893-94. G.P. Red, *Med man in Texas*: 247-48.

POWELL, EDWAIN [or ERMINE], Chicago (b/X-12 1837 Jefferson Co, NY; d/III-10-1899) MD Rush 1858; Hon AB Williams 1870. *JAMA* 32:733, 1899. *Atkinson* I: 597-98. *Polk* 1886: 269.

POWELL, ISRAEL A , Homer, Ill (d/V-1-1905 @79) Lic by yrs pract. *Ill med jour* 7:611, 1905.

POWELL, J W , Hernando, Miss (d/X- -1878) MD ? *Tr AMA* 30:882, 1879.

POWELL, JOHN, Pa (d/I-28-1895 Zacatecas, Mex) MD ? *JAMA* 24: 177, 1895.

POWELL, JOHN W , Peoria, Ill (d/VIII-8-1897 @59) MD Rush 1865. *JAMA* 29:350, 400, 1897.

POWELL, MacDONALD MONROE, Collinsville Ill (d/VI-19-1897) MD St Louis M C 1885 *JAMA* 28:1252 1897.

POWELL, SAMUEL, CW-USA (d/VIII-8-1864 in prison) MD ? *Nat med jour* 1:301, 1870/71.

POWELL, SAMUEL F , Baltimore (b/XI-3-1838; d/IV-21-1894) MD U Md 1861. *Med annals Md:* 538. *Polk* 1886: 438.

POWELL, THOMAS E , Hearne, Tex (d/XI-12-1885) MD Tulane 1875. *Tex cour-rec med* 3:171, 1885. *New Orl m & s j* ns13:578, 1886. *Polk* 1886:887.

POWELL, THOMAS SPENCER, Atlanta (b/1826 Brunswick Co, Va; d/XII-30-1895) MD UPa 1846. *JAMA* 26:93, 1896. *Med bull med & surg* 18:113, 1896. *Atkinson* I: 542. *Polk* 1890: 261.

POWELL, WILLIAM D [or O], Mackinaw, Ill (d/I-23 1906 @43) MD ? *Ill med jour* 9: 130, 1906.

POWER, HENRY JAMES, McKeesport, Pa (d/VI-15-1904 @49) MD UPa 1881; AB Princeton 1877. *Pa med jour* 8:336, 1904/05. *Flint* 1897: 808.

POWER, WILLIAM, Baltimore (b/1813; d/VIII-15-1852) MD U Md 1835; AB Yale 1832. *Buff m j* ?: 760 ff, 1854. *Med ann Md:* 538. *K&B* III: 987.

POWER, WILLIAM, NYC (b/1797? Ireland; d/IX-15-1858 @61) MD CPSNY 1826; <MD & AB Dublin> *Med surg rep Phila* ns1: 28, 1858/59.

POWERS, EDWIN D, Lafayette Ind (b/1827; d/II-15-1899) MD Geneva 1851. *JAMA* 32:563, 1899. *Polk* 1886: 325.

POWERS, GEORGE HENRY, Acworth, NH (b/IX-26-1852 Groton; d/IV-12-1893) MD Dartmouth 1881. *Tr NH M S* 1893:158-59. *Polk* 1890: 707.

POWERS, HARRY A , Buffalo (d/X-24-1898 @28) MD Buffalo 1895. *Buff m&s j* 38:385-86, 1898.

POWERS, HORACE, Morrisville, Vt (b/X-27-1807 Croydon, NH; d/XII-4-1867) MD Woodstock 1832. *Med surg rep Phila* 17: 546, 1867.

POWERS, JOSEPH W , Salt Lake City (d/III-25-1895 @37) MD Rush 1885. *Tr Col St M S* 1898-99: 509. *Polk* 1893: 240.

POWERS, THOMAS ELEAZAR, Woodstock, Vt (b/XI-14-1808; d/XII-28-1876 or II- -1877) MD Dartmouth 1827. *Tr Vt M S* 1883:108.

POWERS, TITUS WILLIAM, NYC(d/III-1-1863 @55) MD Yale 1831. *Med & surg rep* Phila ns9:441, 1862/63.

P'POOL, E J , S Nashville (b/Va; d/V-17-1880) MD U Nashvl 1875. *Nashvl j m&s* ns25: 279, 1880. *Butler* 1878: 775.

PRAEGER, EMIL ARNOLD, Los Angeles (b/1855; d/III-6-1898 @43) Lic Fac Phys & Surg Glasgow 1883; Lic Soc Apoth Engl 1883. *Tr Obst Soc London* 41:91, 1900. *Buff m&s j* 37: 698, 1898. *JAMA* 30: 745, 1898. *Flint* 1897: 113.

PRAEGER, HUBERT F , Brooklyn (b/Sweden; d/VI-23 1905 @52) MD Jefferson 1878. *Bost m & s jour* 147:30, 1902. *Polk* 1896: 1001.

PRALL, WILLIAM, Reaville, NJ (b/1771? Amwell, NJ; d/II-9?-1825 @54) Stud w/Dr Moses Scott. *Tr M S NJ* 1872:182-83. *Wickes*: 366. Blane, *Hunterdon Co*: 94-95.

PRALL, ZACHARIAH, Willow Grove, Pa (b/1790? d/X-11-1850 @60) MD UPa 1816. *Tr M S NJ* 1872: 183. Blane, *Hunterdon Co*: 95. Homeopath?

PRATHER, HUGH L, Mo; Hickman Ky (b/1854; d/1878) MD U Louisville 1877. *Tr AMA* 30:882, 1879.

PRATHER, RICHARD CATLETT, Hickman Ky (b/1852; d/1878) MD Jeff'n 1875. *Tr AMA* 30:883, 1879.

PRATT, AMBROSE, CW-USA; Chester, Conn (d/VI-18 1891) MD Columbian 1843; AB Yale 1837. *Bost m & s jour* 124: 646, 1891. *Polk* 1886: 91.

PRATT, CALVIN BARTON, Bridgewater, Mass (b/IV-15-1806 Middleboro; d/VIII-23-1862) MD Dartmouth 1833; AB Amherst 1828. *Amherst, Men of*: 1828.

PRATT, CHARLES SUMNER, Shrewsbury, Mass (b/IV 18-1852; d/IX-20-1904) MD Boston U 1879; ng Amherst 1879. *Amherst, Men of*: 1879. *Polk* 1886: 472. Homeopath.

PRATT, EDWIN J , NYC (b/1843; d/1896) MD NY Homeop 1881. *No Amer jour homeop* 44:319, 1896. *Polk* 1886: 690. Homeopath.

PRATT, EUGENE BEAUHARNAIS, Mt Sterling, O (b/II-12-1835 Pickaway Co; d/XI-5-1884) MD Starling 1862. *Tr O St M S* 1885: 205-06.

PRATT, FOSTER, CW-USA; Kalamazoo, Mich (b/I-9 1823 Mt Morris NY; d/VIII-12-1898) MD UPa 1849. *U Pa m alum CW*:1849 *JAMA* 31:484 1898 *K&B* III:987-88.

PRATT, GUSTAVUS PERCIVAL, Cohasset, Mass; CW-USA (b/II-14-1840; d/IV-29-1887) MD Harvard 1863. *Bost m & s jour* 116:438, 1887. *Harvard in CW*: 282. *Butler* 1878: 356.

PRATT, HARDEN DeVALSON, Elmira, NY (b/IX [?]-12-1856 Waverly; d/I-12-1899) MD CPSNY 1881; stud Heidelberg & Vienna; ng Amherst 1877. *JAMA* 32: 145, 196, 1899. *Buff m&s j* 38:546, 1890. *Tr M S St NY* 1899:436-37. *Polk* 1896: 1020.

PRATT, J HOWELL, Philadelphia (d/XII-21-1866 @ 43) MD ? *Med surg rep Phila* 16:20, 1867.

PRATT, J M , Hillsboro, Tex (d/X-14-1893) MD Louisville Med Coll 1879. *Tex med jour* 9:237, 1893-94. *Polk* 1890: 1069.

PRATT, JEFFERSON, Hopkinton, Mass (b/VI-6-1803 Belchertown; d/VI-26-1883) MD Berkshire 1827. *JAMA* 9:639 1887. *Bost m&s j* 109:617 1883. *Butler* 1878:356.

PRATT, LEONARD, Rock Creek, Ill 12 yrs; Wheaton & Chicago 21 yrs; San Jose, Cal 1890- (b/XII-26-1819 Rome, Pa; d/IV-29-1900) MD Hahnemann Phila 1852; att Jefferson 1841-42; att Lafayette. *Tr Am Inst Hom* 1900:836. *Cleave.*

PRATT, MARCUS LESTER, Albany, NY 1854-93; Homer 1893- (b/IV-25-1818 Pratt's Hollow; d/VII-6-1901) MD Hahnemann Phila 1854. *Tr Am Inst Hom* 1903: 733. *Polk* 1886: 639. Homeopath.

PRATT, NATHAN, CW-USA; Milford, Del (b/IX-19-1834 Camden; d/VI-18-1899) MD UPa 1860. *U Pa med alum CW*: 1860. *JAMA* 33:52, 1899. *Polk* 1896: 292.

PRATT, THOMAS T , London, Engl; CW-CSA (d/VIII 29-1891 Paris, Fr?) MD UCNY 1861. *JAMA* 17:740, 1891. *Bost m & s jour* 125:260, 1891.

PRATT, WHITCOMB ELIPHALET, Buckingham CH, Va (b/II-27-1849 Clay Bank; d/V-16-1901 Richmond) MD CPS Balto 1875; stud Med Coll Va & Jefferson. *Tr M S Va* 1901:277-78. *Polk* 1886: 914.

PRATT, WILLIAM MADISON, NYC (b/VII-4-1831 Fabius, NY; d/I-1-1889) MD NY Homeop 1861. *Med vis* 5:95, 152, 1889. *No Amer j hom* 37:135, 1889. *Polk* 1886: 690. *Cleave.* Homeopath.

PRAY, ISAIAH FRANKLIN, NYC (b/1846 Me; d/IV-23 1896) MD UCNY 1874; AB Dartmouth 1870. *JAMA* 26: 1038, 1896. *Bost m&s j* 134:449, 1896. *Polk* 1886: 690.

PRAY, ORESTES M , Brooklyn (d/IV-23-1869) MD Bellevue 1863. *Med reg NY NJ Conn* 1869: 245. *Tr AMA* 21:444-45, 1870. *Med surg rep Phila* 20:346 1869. *Med rec* 4:148, 192, 1869-70.

PRAY, THOMAS JEFFERSON WORCESTER, Dover, NH (b/IX-2-1819 Lebanon, Me; d/XII-9-1888) MD Harvard 1848; AB Bowdoin 1844. *Tr NH M S* 1889: 156. *Polk* 1886: 591.

PREFONTAINE, LOUIS AURELE, Springfield, Mass (d/VI-19-1905 @39) MD UPa 1892. *Bost m & s jour* 153: 36, 1905.

PREGIZER, WILLIAM, Stapleton, NY (b/Gny; d/VIII 14-1876 @47) MD NY Med Coll 1863. *Med reg NY NJ Conn* 1877: 206.

PRENDERGAST, JEDIAH [JEDEDIAH?], Thorold Canada to War 1812; Mayville, NY 1812- (b/V-8-1776 Pawling; d/III-2-1842) Lic by judge Rensselaer Co; stud w/Dr Wm Chase. *Tr M S St NY* 1865:275-76.

PRENDERGAST, PAUL PETER, Brooklyn (d/VII-10-1896 @23) MD CPSNY 1894. *JAMA* 27:279, 1896.

PRENDERGAST, WILLIAM, Mayville, NY (b/II-28-1791 Pawling; d/III-11-1857) Stud w/Dr Jediah Prendergast Thorold, Can. *Tr M S St NY*: 1865, 276.

PRENTICE, PIERPONT ISHAM, Duluth (b/X-16-1860 Albany, NY; d/I-4-1890) MD NWU 1888; ng Amherst 1888. *Amherst, Men of*: 1888.

PRENTICE, WALTER MEAD, CW-USA (d/V-28-1864) MD ?Willoughby 1847. *Nat m j* 1:301, 1870/71.

PRENTISS, DANIEL WEBSTER, Washington, DC; CW-USA (b/V-21-1843; d/XI-20-1899) MD UPa 1864; PhB Columbian 1861; AM 1864. *Hist M S DC:* 271. *JAMA* 33: 1375, 1899. *U Pa med alum CW*: 1864. *Atkinson* I: 305. *K&B* III: 988.

PRENTISS, JOHN H , Govanstown, Md (b/1827; d/I-26-1888) MD U Md 1848. *Med annals Md:* 539. *Polk* 1882: 442.

PRENTISS, JOHN HART, Augusta, Me (b/XI-26-1837 Bangor; d/VII-3-1859) MD Jefferson 1859; AB Union

 Spec. educ'l status abbrev. as: ***ng*** = college verified attendance without degree;

1857; stud med Bowdoin 1858. *Bowdoin cat*: 1858.

PRENTISS, NATHANIEL SHEPHERD, W Cambridge, Marlborough, Roxbury, Mass (b/VIII-7-1766; d/XI-5 1853) Stud med w/Israel Atherton, Lancaster, Mass; AM Harvard 1878. Palmer's *Necrol Harv alum*: 25.

PRENTISS [PRENTICE], OBADIAH, Monroeville, O (b/1821 Lowville, NY; d/XII-29-1893 Norwalk) MD Worthington 1848. *JAMA* 22:58, 1894. *Butler* 1878:645.

PRESCOTT, JOSIAH, Belfast & Farmington, Me (b/IX-2-1785 Winthrop, Me; d/X-5-1864 @79) MD Dartmouth 1810. *Med surg rep Phila* 12:192, 1864/65.

PRESCOTT, OLIVER, Newburyport, Mass (b/IV-27-1831 Groton; d/IV-17-1804) Hon MD Harvard 1791; AB 1750; stud med w/Dr Eben Robie, Sudbury. *Bost m & s jour* 105:497, 1881. *K&B* III: 989.

PRESCOTT, ROYAL BLOOD, CW-USA; NYC; Nashua, NH (b/1839; d/I-2-1902 @63) MD LICH 1867. *Bost m&s j* 146: 52, 1902. Conn, *NH surgs in CW*: 156.

PRESTON, ABRAM WILLIAM, Rumney, NH; CW-USA (b/II- -1822; d/XI-13-1864) MD Dartmouth 1847. *Nat med jour* 1:301, 1870/71.

PRESTON, ALBERT GALLATIN, Greencastle, Ind (b/IV-17-1813 Lynchburg, Va; d/VII-4-1889) MD M C Ohio 1840. *Tr Ind St M S* 1890:153. *Butler* 1878: 216.

PRESTON, ALEXANDER B , Abingdon, Va (b/XII-5-1805; d/III-5-1874) MD Jefferson 1848. *Tr AMA* 25: 534-35, 1874. *Tr M S Va* 1874: 54-55.

PRESTON, ANN, Philadelphia (b/XII-1-1813 West Grove, Pa; d/IV-18-1872) MD Woman's Med Coll Pa 1852. *Med rec* 7:237, 1872. *K&B* III: 930.

PRESTON, COATES, Chester, Pa (b/I-20-1820 West Grove; d/VIII-9-1881 Wilmington, Del) MD Hahnemann Phila 1853. *Tr Am Inst Hom* 1882: 138. *Tr Homeop M S St Pa* 1881: 43-44.

PRESTON, DANIEL, Hopkinsville, Ky (b/c 1769? d/III-16-1829 @60?) MD ? *Transylvania jour med & assoc sci* 2:297-98, 1829.

PRESTON, GEORGE HENRY, Kane, Pa (d/VI-11-1901 @45) <MD UCNY 1879> *Pa med jour* 5:296, 1901/02. *JAMA* ?36:43, 1901. *Flint* 1897: 806.

PRESTON, GILBERT HOWARD, Tolland, Conn (b/XI 14-1820; d/V-8-1883) MD Castleton 1844. *Proc Conn M S* ns2:182-84, 1883.

PRESTON, JOHN C , Cleveland (b/XII-8-1819 Tallmadge, O; d/I-4-1890) MD Cleveland Med Coll 1863. *Tr Ohio M S* 1890:7, 303-04. *Butler* 1870:645.

PRESTON, MAHLON, Norristown, Pa (b/I-22-1839 E Caln; d/X-2-1895) MD Hahnemann Phila 1861. *Hahn mo* 30:144-45 (news & advt) 1895. *Nat med jour* 1:301, 1870/71.95. *Med vis* 11:381, 1895. *Tr Am Inst Hom* 1896: 87. *Polk* 1886: 810. Homeopath.

PRESTON, SAMUEL C , Greencastle, Ind (b/X-15-1846; d/I-6-1893) MD Miami 1870. *Tr Ind St M S* 1893: 253. *Polk* 1890: 390.

PRESTON, WILLIAM S , Patchogue, NY (b/I-15-1810 Ashford, Conn; d/II-16-1897) Lic Mass M S 1835. *JAMA* 28:523, 1897. *Polk* 1893: 922.

PRETERRE, PIERRE A , NYC (d/III-20-1886 Paris, Fr) MD CPSNY 1849. *Med reg NY NJ Conn* 1862: 154.

PRETLOW, THOMAS JEFFERSON Jr, CW-CSA; Jerusalem, Va (b/VI-18-1845 Southampton Co; d/IX-3-1898) MD UPa 1867. *Polk* 1886: 919.

PREWITT, J[AMES ?] H[ILL?], Grand Junction, Tenn (d/1878) MD ? *Tr AMA* 30:883, 1879.

PREWITT, NATHAN HILL, Fayetteville, Tenn (b/1829; d/1878) MD UCNY 1851. *Tr AMA* 30:883-84, 1879.

PRICE, ANDREW BAILLIE, Frostburg Md (b/1841 Nanjemoy; d/IV-15-1900) MD U Md 1867; AB. *JAMA* 34: 1084, 1900. *Med ann Md:* 539. *Polk* 1886: 442.

PRICE, BURROUGHS, Philadelphia (b/VII-6-1830 Landisville, Pa; d/XII-8-1874) MD UPa 1853. *Tr M S Pa* 10:763-64, 1875.

PRICE, EDWARD B , Alexandria, La (b/1822 Balto; d/I-30-1895 @72) MD U Md 1849. *New Orl m & s j* ns22:639, 1895. *Med ann Md:* 540. *Polk* 1890:485.

PRICE, ELIAS C, Baltimore 1865- (b/IV-16-1826;d/VI 16-1902) MD UMd 1848 *Tr Am Inst Hom* 1902:843-44. *King* II:166. *Polk* 1886:438. *Cleave.* Homeopath.

PRICE, JACOB, W Chester, Pa (b/VIII-4-1826; d/VI-9 1905) MD Jefferson 1850. *Pa med jour* 9:257-58, 1905/06. *Atkinson* I: 220.

PRICE, JOHN FRANCIS, Washington, DC (b/XI-23-1850 Charles Co, Md; d/XI-7-1903) MD Washington U, Balto 1875. *Hist M S DC:* 337.

PRICE, JOSEPH, Randolph, O (b/X-15-1823 Stark Co; d/X-22-1895) MD Starling 1851. *Tr Ohio M S* 1896: 399-400. *Butler* 1878: 645.

PRICE, LEWIS, NYC (b/Austria; d/II-18-1893 @33) MD UCNY 1882; BS. *Med reg NY NJ Conn* 1893:313. *Polk* 1886: 691.

PRICE, MICHAEL, Harrisburg, Pa (d/X-11-1895) MD ? *JAMA* 25: 726, 1895. *Polk* 1890: 1016.

PRICE, MORDECAI, Philadelphia (b/1844 Rockingham Co, Va; d/X-29-1904) MD UPa 1869. *Pa m j* 8:336, 1904/05. *Bost m&s j* 151:528, 1904. *Flint* 1897: 823.

PRICE, RICHARD N , Graham, Tex (b/Va; d/1903) MD Jefferson 1853. *Tex cour-rec med* 20:21-22, 1903.

PRICE [PRYCE], RICHARD W , Iowa City, Ia (d/1880) MD Jefferson 1868. *Tr Ia St M S* 1880: 184; 1896: 329; 1903: 449.

PRICE, THOMAS H [or F], Philadelphia (d/XI-22-1902 @54) MD Jefferson 1876; <att U Va 1873> *Pa med jour* 6:261, 1902/03.

PRICE, WILLIAM, Philadelphia; Cincinnati (b/1788; d/II-27-1860 @72) MD UPa 1813. *Med surg rep Phila* ns3: 425, 1859/60.

PRICE, WILLIAM B , New Berlin, Ill (d/I-6-1900 @75) MD Jefferson 1857. *JAMA* 34:251, 1900. *Polk* 1896: 431.

PRICHARD, JOHN ELIAS, Baltimore (b/II-3-1830

Wales; d/III-1-1899 @64) MD Albany 1857. *JAMA* 32: 563, 1899. *Med annals Md:* 540. *Polk* 1886: 439.

PRICKETT, SANFORD H, Mineral Wells, WVa (b/XII 27-1839 Marion Co; d/VI-8-1885) MD Miami 1873. *Tr M S WVa* 1887:500; 1888:589. *Butler* 1878: 852.

PRIDE, JOHN M , Algona, Ia (d/1895) MD St U Ia 1878. *JAMA* 25: 818, 1895. *Polk* 1886: 370.

PRIESON, GUSTAV ADOLPH, CW-USA; Lock Haven, Pa (d/XII 2-1905 @73) <MD U Würzburg 1852> *Pa m j* 9:281, 1905/06. *Polk* 1893: 1088.

PRIEST, GEORGE ARTHUR, Manchester, Mass (d/IV-25-1888 @59) MD Woodstock 1853. *Bost m&s j* 118: 488, 1888; 119:641, 1888. *Butler* 1878: 356.

PRIESTLEY, CRAYKE SIMPSON, Des Moines (b/I-21 1875 Northumberland Pa; d/V-12-1904) MD UPa 1896. *Tr Iowa St M S* 23:369-70, 1905. *Polk* 1896: 520.

PRIESTLEY, JOHN, NYC (d/IV-24-1871) <MD Glasgow> *Med reg NY NJ Conn* 1871: 361.

PRIESTLEY, JOSEPH, Northumberland, Pa (b/IX-22 1819; d/III-10-1883) MD UPa 1844. *Med bull med & surg* 5:86-87, 1883. *Atkinson* I: 207.

PRIMM [PRIMER?], THOMAS J , Athens, Ill (d/I-15-1899 @77) MD Mo Med Coll 1850. *JAMA* 32:263, 1899. *Flint* 1897: 251.

PRIMM, THOMAS WILSON, Lincoln, Ill (d/II-20-1900 @62) Lic by yrs. pract. *JAMA* 34:574, 1900. *Tr Ill St M S* 1900: 509. *Polk* 1896: 427.

PRIMROSE, HENRY C , Philadelphia; CW-USA (d/X 24-1864 @23) MD Jefferson 1854. *Med surg rep Phila* 12:219, 1864/65. *Nat med jour* 1:301, 1870/71.

PRINCE, CHRISTOPHER, NYC (b/1823 Brooklyn; d/III-5-1900 Irvington-on-Hudson) MD CPSNY 1846. *Bost m&s j* 142:288, 1900. *Polk* 1886:691.

PRINCE, DAVID, CW-USA; Jacksonville, Ill (b/VI-21-1816 Brooklyn, Conn; d/XII-19-1889) MD Med Coll O 1840; stud Fairfield. *Tr Ill St M S* 1890: 26-27. *Bost m&s j* 122: 72, 1890. *Atkinson* I: 638. *K&B* III: 989.

PRINCE, JOSIAH EDMUND, Corpus Christi, Tex (b/IV 12-1832; d/VI- -1896) MD Jefferson 1852; AB U Ala 1850; AM 1854. *U Ala cat*: 94. *Polk* 1886: 888.

PRINCE, WILLIAM HENRY, Newton, Mass (d/V-15 1883 @67) MD Harvard 1841; AB 1838. *Bost m & s jour* 109:617, 1883.

PRINGLE, G W , New Concord, O (d/X-12-1876 @63) MD ? *Med surg rep Phila* 35: 414, 1876.

PRIOLEAU, WILLIAM H , Summerville, SC (d/VIII-7 1896) MD Med Coll SC 1860. *NC med jour* 38: 1896.

PRIOR, ISRAEL, N Stamford, Conn (d/III-6-1900 @58) MD Bellevue 1864. *JAMA* 34:702, 1900. *Polk* 1890: 226.

PRIOR, PHILEMON F , Oyster Bay, NY (d/XII-17-1867 @46) MD ? *Med surg rep Phila* 17:560, 1867.

PRIZER, GRANVILLE W , Lionville, Pa (d/IV-5-1899 @58) MD ? *JAMA* 32: 899, 1899. *Polk* 1896:1288.

PROCTOR, ALPHEUS, Chelsea, Mass (d/VIII-21-1862 @57) MD ? *Bost m & s jour* 67:148, 1862.

PROCTOR, G W , Louisville (d/XI-16-1860 @34 Sacramento) MD U Louisvl 1848. *Bost m&s j* 63: 448, 1861.

PROCTOR, LEONARD, Fultonville, NY; Michigan City, Ind (b/1798? d/III-8-1856) MD Harvard 1824. *Bost m & s jour* 54:117, 1856.

PROCTOR, RICHARD, NY (d/IX-22-1888) MD ? *So pract* 10: 441-42, 1888.

PROEBSTING, LOUIS, CW-USA (d/X-31-1864 Cairo, Ill) MD ? *Nat med jour* 1:301, 1870/71.

PROEHL, LEWIS J , Akron, O (b/VII-18-1850; d/IV-29-1887) MD Ohio M C 1879. *Tr Ohio M S* 1887: 235.

PROFILET, LOUIS EMILE, Natchez; CW-CSA (b/X 13-1834; d/1898) MD New Orl Sch Med 1861; AB Yale 1857. *Yale, Class 1857 record. Polk* 1886: 530.

PROUDFIT, JAMES O , ? (d/VI-1-1861) MD ? *Med reg NY NJ Conn* 1862: 154.

PROVINS, CLARK BREADING, Ottawa, Ill (d/VI-4-1906) MD Rush 1882. *Chic m rec* 28:413 1906. *Polk* 1886: 286.

PRUYN, JOHN M , Kinderhook, NY (b/X-24-1806; d/II 1806) MD CPSNY 1828. *Tr M S St NY* 1867: 464-65.

PRUYN, PETER VAN SCHAACK, Kinderhook, NY (b/XI-19-1841; d/V-4-1891) MD CPSNY 1863; AB Union 1860. *Med reg NY NJ Conn* 1891: 280. *Tr M S St NY* 1895:382-87. *Polk* 1886: 665.

PRYER, WILLIAM CHARDAVOYNE, New Rochelle, NY; CW-USA (b/1834; d/IX-24-1888) MD CPSNY 1862. *Med reg NY NJ Conn* 1889:280. *Polk* 1886: 669.

PRYNE, PETER, Herkimer NY (d/IV-13-1899 @79) MD Geneva 1846. *Bost m&s j* 140:392, 1899. *JAMA* 32: 899, 1899.

PRYOR, THOMAS HENRY, CW-USA Boston (d/1888) MD Harvard 1862; AB 1859. *Harvard in CW*: 130.

PRYOR, WILLIAM RICE, NYC (b/1859; d/VIII-25-1904 @45) MD CPSNY 1881. *Bost m&s j* 151:255, 1904. *K&B* III: 996.

PUE, ARTHUR Jr, Ellicott City, Md (b/1804 Balto; d/IX-20-1881) MD U Md 1826. *Med ann Md:* 541. *Butler* 1874: 322.

PUGH, JOHN HOWARD, CW-USA; Burlington, NJ (b/VI-23-1827 Unionville, Pa; d/IV-30-1905) MD UPa 1852. *Bost m&s j* 152: 563, 1905. *U Pa m alum CW*: 1852. *Polk* 1896: 934.

PUGH, JOHN McGINNESS, Philadelphia (b/X-11-1809 Chester Co, Pa; d/IX-24-1863) MD Jefferson 1831. *Tr AMA* 16: 640-42, 1865. *Tr Pa St M S* 1864:533-34. *Med surg rep Phila* 10: 316, 1863.

PUGH, JOHN W , Upland, Ind (b/I-27-1827 Guernsey Co; d/IX-24-1896) MD Ohio Med Coll 1867. *Tr Ind St M S* 1897: 347-48. *Butler* 1878: 216.

PUGH, MAHLON, Upland, Ind (b/X-14-1835 Grant Co, Ind; d/XI-10-1883) Att Med Coll Ohio 1865-66. *Tr Ind St M S* 1884: 214. *Butler* 1878: 216.

PUGH, WILLIAM A [or M], Rushville, Ind (b/III-7 1829; d/XI-5-1893) MD Med Coll Ohio 1857. *JAMA*

21:829, 1893. *Tr Ind St M S* 1895: 398. Kemper's *Indiana*: 330. *Butler* 1878: 216.

PULLEN, WILLIAM B , Chireno & Jacksonville, Tex (b/IX–28–1871 Bedford City, Va; d/IV–17–1904) MD Louisville Hosp Coll Med 1889. *Tex st med jour* 1:245, 1906. *Polk* 1896: 1421.

PULLIAM, ALFRED BARNETT, CW–CSA; Somerville, Tenn (b/1838 Granville Co NC; d/II–11–1885) MD UPa 1861; att UNC 1855–59. *U Pa med alum CW*: 1861.

PULLIAM, ROBERT M , Richmond, Va (d/IX–5–1897 @66) MD Med Coll Va 1855. *NC med jour* 40:209, 1897. *JAMA* 29: 606, 1897. *Polk* 1886: 925.

PULLING, EZRA REED, NYC (b/II– –1828 Saratoga Co, NY; d/VI–5–1899) MD CPSNY 1853. *Bost m&s j* 140:596, 1899. *JAMA* 32:1460, 1899. *Polk* 1896: 1073.

PULSIFER, MOSES RUST, Eden, Sullivan, Minot & Ellsworth, Me 1851– (b/X–9–1799 Poland, Me; d/I–27 1877) MD Bowdoin 1822. *New Engl med gaz* 12:126, 1877. *King* I:310. *Cleave*. Homeopath.

PULSIFER, NATHAN GOLDSMITH HOWARD, Waterville, Me 1851– (b/I–24–1824 Eden; d/XII–2–1893) MD Dartmouth 1849. *JAMA* 21:982, 1893. *Butler* 1878: 310. *Polk* 1886: 429.

PULTE, JOSEPH HIPPOLYTE, NYC; Allentown, Pa; Cincinnati (b/X–6–1811 Gny; d/II–24–1884) <MD Marburg 1833> *Med s rep Phila* 50:448, 1884. *Tr Am Inst Hom* 1884:643. *Am hom obs* 20:430, 1883/84. *Tr Hom M S St Pa* 1884:33–37. *King* I:152, 171; 2:221 ff. Homeopath.

PULTZ, MONROE TAVER, Stanfordville, NY (d/IX–9 1902) MD CPSNY 1868. *Bost m&s j* 147: 340, 1902. *Polk* 1886: 709.

PUNDERSON, SAMUEL, New Haven, Conn (b/I–22–1791; d/III–13–1870) MD Yale 1834. *Proc Conn M S* 3:414, 1871.

PURCELL, JOHN, NYC (b/Irel'd; d/IX–30–1904 @86) <Grad Apothecaries' Hall, Dublin 1841> *Bost m&s j* 151: 394, 1904. *Butler* 1878: 508.

PURCELL, THOMAS AQUINAS, Holyoke, Mass (d/V 31–1897 @36) MD UCNY 1884 or 1885; AB. *JAMA* 28: 1203, 1897. *Polk* 1896: 714.

PURCELL, WILLIAM JOSEPH, NYC (d/II–17–1896) MD Bellevue 1867. *JAMA* 26:542,1896. *Polk* 1896:1073.

PURDY, ALBERT GALLATIN, Eaton, NY to 1859; Oneida (b/I–31–1809 Sherburne Four Corners; d/IV–5 1875) <MD Fairfield> *Tr M S St NY* 1879: 573. *Med rec NY* 15:158, 1879. *Butler* 1874: 555.

PURDY, ALFRED SEAMAN, NYC (b/XII–14–1808; d/VII–22–1886) MD CPSNY 1831; AB Wesleyan 1859. *Med reg NY NJ Conn* 1887:273. *Bost m&s j* 115:93–94 1886.

PURDY, CHARLES WESLEY, Chicago (b/1846 Kingston, Ont; d/VI–20–1901) MD Queen's Kingston 1869; LLD. *Chic m rec* 20:212, 247–48, 1901. *Nashvl j m & s* 89:93–94, 1901.

PURDY, GEORGIE B , Manhasset, NY (b/1792? d/I–16 1865 @73) MD CPSNY 1816; AB Columbia 1811. *Med s rep Phila* 12:268, 1864/65.

PURDY, ISAAC, Mongaup Valley, NY (b/Walkill; d/XII–6–1885) MD Castleton 1850. *Tr NY St M S* 11: 741 ff, 1894. *Butler* 1878: 570.

PURDY, JOTHAM, Elmira NY (b/V–4–1799 Spencer; d/VIII–11–1858) <MD CPSNY 1822> *Tr AMA* 31:1082, 1880. *Tr M S St NY* 1860: 172. *Buff m j* 15:633, 1860.

PURDY, SAMUEL AUGUSTUS, NYC (b/I–28–1812; d/I–12–1888) MD CPSNY 1834. *Med reg NY NJ Conn* 1888: 268. *Polk* 1886: 691.

PURMAN, WILLIS H , Bloomsburg, Pa (d/X–2–1905 @49) MD Howard 1887. *Pa med jour* 9:127, 1905/06. *Polk* 1890:246. Black.

PURNELL, CHESED, Snow Hill, Md (d/1862) MD UPa 1819. *Med annals Md:* 541.

PURNELL, GEORGE WASHINGTON, Hazlehurst, Miss (d/IV–4–1905 @70) MD UPa 1858. *New Orl m & s j* 57:861, 1905. *Polk* 1886: 527.

PURNELL, HORTENSIUS W , Holly Springs, Miss (d/VII–3–1888 @49) MD U La 1862. *Daniel's Tex med jour* 4:33, 1888. *Polk* 1886: 869.

PURNELL, JAMES ROBINS SPENCE, Worcester Co, Md (d/VIII–22–1848) MD UPa 1830. *Med ann Md:* 542.

PURNELL, JOHN ROBINS, Selma, Ala 1839– (b/Worcester, Md; MD UPa 1819. *Med ann Md:* 542.

PURNELL, ROBERT JENKINS HENRY, Worcester Co, Md (b/XII–14–1786; d/VIII–13–1825) MD UPa 1811. *Med ann Md:* 542.

PURNELL, WILLIAM, Berlin, Md (d/1835) MD UPa 1811. *Med ann Md:* 542.

PURNELL, WILLIAM ISAAC FRANKLIN, CW–CSA (b/X–18–1839 Berlin, Md; d/XI–5–1896 Haddonfield, NJ) MD UPa 1860. *U Pa med alum CW*: 1860.

PURPLE, JOHN G , Painesville, O (d/V–15–1862 @36) MD Cleveland M C 1851. *Tr Ohio St M S* 1862: 124.

PURPLE, SAMUEL SMITH, NYC (b/VI–24–1822 Lebanon, NY; d/IX–29–1900) MD UCNY 1844. *Bost m&s j* 143:354, 1900. *Tr M S St NY* 1901:[426]. *Atkinson* I:653. *Polk* 1896: 1073. *K&B* III: 997–98.

PURPLE, WILLIAM D , Greene, NY (b/IV–2–1802; d/V–19–1886) Hon MD Regents St U NY 1846. *Med reg NY NJ Conn* 1887: 274. *Butler* 1878: 570.

PURRINGTON, TOBIAS, Washington, DC (b/III–19–1801 Windham, Me; d/V–3–1880) MD Bowdoin 1826. *Hist M S DC:* 257.

PURROY, FRANCIS MICHAEL, NYC (b/1846; d/XI–25–1886) MD Bellevue 1870. *Med reg NY NJ Conn* 1887: 275. *Polk* 1886: 691.

PURSEL [PURSELL], WILLIAM WILSON, White House Station, NJ (b/IX–9–1849 Wilkes-Barre, Pa; d/XII–9–1906) MD Jefferson 1874; stud Lafayette. *Bost m & s jour* 155: 762, 1906. *Polk* 1896: 951.

PURSELL, ISAAC, Danville, Pa (b/Northampton Co, Pa;

d/III-27-1888) Stud UPa Med Dept 1845/46. *Tr Pa St M S* 21:262, 1889-90. *Butler* 1878: 728.

PURSELL, JOHN L , CW-USA (d/V-26-1862) MD ? *Nat med jour* 1:301, 1870/71.

PURVIANCE, GEORGE, USN; Philadelphia (d/X-20 1904 @ 74) MD Jefferson 1867. *Pa m j* 8:336, 1904/05. *Polk* 1886: 744 (Cincinnati).

PURVIANCE, SAMUEL M , Crawfordsville, Ind (b/VII 29-1823 New Paris, O; d/XI-10-1891) MD Starling 1848. *Tr Ind St M S* 1892: 283. *Polk* 1890: 367.

PUSEY, HENRY K , Lakeland, Ky (d/IX-2-1896 Garnetsville; MD U Louisville 1849. *JAMA* 27:613, 1896. *Polk* 1886: 400.

PUTNAM, ARCHELAUS FULLER, Beverly, Mass (b/VII-3-1792 Danvers; d/VIII-11-1859) MD Dartmouth 1829; AB 1819. *Bost m&s j* 61:88, 1859.

PUTNAM, CHARLES GIDEON, Boston (b/1805 Salem; d/II-5-1875) MD Harvard 1827; AB 1824. *Bost m&s j* ns15:163-64, 1875; 105:520, 1881. *Mass M S cat* 1894.

PUTNAM, DANA BOARDMAN, Ipswich, Mass; Fredonia, Ala 1852-54; LaGrange, Ga 1855-68; Boston 1868- (b/IX-19-1825 Rumford; d/II-11-1881) <MD Ga M C 1854> MD Jefferson 1855; AB Bowdoin 1852. *Bost m & s jour* 105: 623, 1891.

PUTNAM, E C , Alma, Nebr (d/VIII-9-1897 @44) MD Louisville Med Coll 1875. *JAMA* 29: 502, 1897.

PUTNAM, ISRAEL, Bath, Me (b/XII-25-1805 Sutton, Mass; d/VI-30-1876) MD Bowdoin 1830; AB Brown 1827. *Tr Me M Assn* 1877:249-50. *K&B* III:999.

PUTNAM, SUMNER, Montpelier, Vt (b/II-21-1818; d/VIII-20-1887) MD Woodstock 1842. *Bost m & s jour* 117:192,1887. *Atkinson* I:21. *K&B* II:949-50.

PUTNEY, JAMES, CW-CSA; Kanawha Salines WVa (b/VII-5-1816; d/IX-6-1876) MD Cincinnati M C 1846. *Tr M S WVa* 1878: 435-38; 1884:154. *Butler* 1878: 853.

PUTNEY, WILLIAM ROBERT, CW-CSA; New Canton, Va (b/III 26-1834; d/XI-21-1901) MD UPa 1858. *U Pa m alum CW*: 1858. *Polk* 1886: 922.

PYATT, JAMES, Amwell, NJ (b/1784: d/X-26-1864 @ 80) <Att med lectures NY> *Tr M S NJ* 1872:138.

PYE, EDWARD A , Calvert, Tex (d/XI-9-1873 @54) MD U Md 1842; AB Georgetown. *Med surg rep Phila* 30: 44, 1874.

PYLAND, W J, Wimberly Tx (d/III-4-1906) MD Vanderbilt 1867[!] *Tex st m j* 1:352 1905/06 *Polk* 1900:1711.

PYLE, EDWIN WOLLASTON, Jersey City (b/1849 Unionville, Pa; d/II-8-1902) MD UPa 1873. *Bost m & s jour* 146: 214, 1902.

PYLE, J SAPPINGTON, Delta, Pa (d/XI-12-1901 @ 81) MD ? *Pa m j* 5:296, 1901/02.

PYLES, MADISON, Louisville (d/IV-26-1866) MD U Louisvl 1846. *Tr Ky St M S* 1869: 111. *Med s rep Phila* 14:360, 1866.

PYLES, NEWTON CYRUS, Clinton, Ala (d/IX-18-1888) MD Jefferson 1860. *Tr Med Assn St Ala* 1889: 229. *Butler* 1874: 24.

PYNCHON, JOSEPH CHARLES, Springfield, Mass (b/III-3-1815; d/IV-9-1889) MD U City NY 1843; ng Amherst 1836. *Amherst, Men of*: 1836.

QUACKENBOS, HENRY FELTUS, NYC (b/IX-29-1819; d/VIII-21-1888) MD CPSNY 1841; <AB Columbia> *Med reg NY NJ Conn* 1889:281. *Med s rep Phil* 41: 506, 1875. *Bost m&s j* 119:216, 1888. *Butler* 1878: 522.

QUACKENBUSH, JOHN VAN PELT, Albany, NY (b/VI-3-1819; d/VI-8-1876) MD Albany 1842; AB Williams 1838. *Med reg NY NJ Conn* 1876:253. *Tr M S St NY* 1876:333-342. *Med rec m & s* 11:404, 1876.

QUATTLEBAUM, JOSEPH, CW-CSA; Ridge Spr, SC (d/I-6-1892) MD UCNY 1845. *NYU Bellevue alumni* 1833-1905: 10.

QUETIL, CHARLES EDOUARDES, Philadelphia (b/1860? d/IX-26-1903 @43 Kingston, Jamaica) MD UPa 1895. *Pa med jour* 7:280, 1903/04.

QUICK, EMMETT W, Cincinnati (d/VII-19-1873 @23) MD M C Ohio 1873. *Med s rep Phila* 29: 108, 1873.

QUICK, THEODORE, Milton & Harlem, NY (b/X-29-1826 Platterill, NY; d/IV-4-1877) MD Hahnemann, Phila 1855; ng Castleton. *Tr Am Inst Hom* 1877: 989. *NY homeop times* 5:68, 1877. Homeopath.

QUIGLEY, WENTWORTH HENRY, Boston (d/X-7-1873 @31) MD Harv'd 1869. *Bost m&s j* ns12: 396, 1873.

QUIMBY, ISAAC NEWTON, Jersey City (b/VIII-5 1831 Bernardsville; d/V-6-1898) MD UCNY 1859 *Tr M S NJ* 1898:376-78. *Bost m&s j* 138:456, 1898. *JAMA* 30: 1191,1898; 31:1199-1200 1898. *Tex m j* 13:636 1897-8.

QUIMBY, SAMUEL FOSTER, Salem, Mass (d/XII-21 1903 @63) MD Harvard 1864. *Bost m & s jour* 149:720, 1903. *Polk* 1896: 722.

QUIN, JAMES M, Morrisania NY (b/1806 NYC; d/III-27 1868) MD Rutgers 1833; AB Columbia 1827; AM 1833. *Phila m reg & dir* 1871:296. *Med s rep Phil* 18:314, 1868. *Tr Am Inst Hom* 1868:286; 1870: 654. *Am hom obs* 5:301, 1868. *New Engl m gaz* 3:180, 1870. Homeopath.

QUINAN, JOHN RUSSELL, Baltimore (b/VIII-7-1822 Lancaster, Pa; d/XI-11-1890) MD Jefferson 1844. *NC m j* 27:249-55, 1891. *Med ann Md*:543.*Polk* 1886:439. *K&B* III: 1003.

QUINBY, JOSIAH, Readington, NJ (b/II-2-1783; d/II-14-1854. <Att lect NY 1815> read w/Dr John S Darcy. *Tr M S NJ* 1872: 137.

QUINCY, HENRY PARKER, Boston (b/X-28-1838; d/III-11-1899) MD Harvard 1867; AB 1866. *Bost m&s j* 140:270 272 1899. *JAMA* 32:628 1899. *Polk* 1896:704.

QUINLAN, CHARLES HARVEY, Evanston, Ill (b/II-19 1821 Albany, NY; d/XII-6-1897 @76) MD Rush 1865; stud dentistry. *JAMA* 29: 1286, 1897.

QUINN, JOHN CAMPBELL, NYC (d/V- -1884 @30) MD U Vt 1875. *Med reg NY NJ Conn* 1884:237.

QUINN, JOHN HEMPHILL, West Chester, Pa (b/IX-3

1793; d/XII-1-1823) MD UPa 1814. *Med reporter* (West Chester) 2:128, 1855.

QUINN, JOHN PAUL, USN (d/VI-6-1869 Havana) MD ? *Med s rep Phila* 20:476, 1869. *Tr AMA* 21:48, 1870. *Nat med jour* 1:301, 1870/71.

QUIRK, WILLIAM F , Alta, Ia (b/Isle of Man; d/III-31-1889 @36) MD Rush 1877. *Tr Iowa St M S* 7:526-27, 1886-89. *Polk* 1886: 351.

QUISENBERRY [QUESENBERRY], WILLIAM DeJARNETTE, CW-USA; Milford Co, Va (d/XII-8-1901) MD UPa 1849. *U Pa m alum CW*: 1849 suppl.

RABINEAU, JOHNSON, Va (d/X-13-1862 @48) MD ? *Med surg rep Phila* ns9: 86, 1862/63.

RABORG, SAMUEL A , NYC (d/I-4-1888) MD U Md 1860. *Med reg NY NJ Conn* 1888:269. *Polk* 1886: 691.

RACE, GORTON HERBERT, Great Barrington, Mass (d/VII-22-1903 @50) MD Albany 1880. *Bost m&s j* 149: 166, 1903. *Polk* 1896: 713.

RACE, HENRY, Pittstown, NJ (b/II-23-1814 Kingwood; d/IV-20-1901) MD UPa 1843; att Lafayette 1842; AM 1871. *Lafayette, Men of*: 150.

RADCLIFFE, SAMUEL JACOBS, Washington, DC; CW-USA (b/II-2-1829; d/VII-9-1903) MD Georgetown 1852. *Hist M S DC:* 251-52. *Rec AAS USA* 1891: 80. *Polk* 1886: 213.

RADEKE, GUSTAV, Providence, RI (b/X-30-1842 Hamm,Gny; d/1892) MD Friedr Wilh U Berlin 1868. *Tr RI M S* 4:483-87, 1889-93. *Polk* 1886:846.

RADFORD, WILLIAM JAMES, S Boston (d/VII 29-1864 @43) MD Harvard 1863. *Bost m&s j* 71:428, 1864.

RADMORE, C C , CW-USA; Winona, Ill (d/VIII-19-1893 Lincoln, Nebr) MD ? *JAMA* 21:357, 1893. *Butler* 1878: 448.

RAE, JOHN, Clifton [?Pa] (b/1795? Aberdeenshire, Scotl; d/VII-12-1872 Clifton) MD ? *Med surg rep Phila* 27: 118, 1872.

RAE, WALTER, NJ (b/IX-29-1849 Annan, Scotl; d/XII 10-1891) MD UCNY 1876. *Med reg NY NJ Conn* 1892: 286. *Tr M S NJ* 1892:201. *Butler* 1878:479.

RAFFERTY, THOMAS HENRY, Stafford Spr, Conn (b/III-24-1867 Stonington; d/IV-10-1898) MD CPSNY 1890; AB Holy Cross 1886. *Proc Conn M S* 1898: 363. *JAMA* 30:999, 1898. *Polk* 1896:285.

RAHAUSER, GEORGE GILLESPIE, Pittsburgh (d/X--1901 @58) MD Jefferson 1866. *Pa med jour* 5:90, 294, 1901/02. *Flint* 1897: 830.

RAIFORD, MARSHAL D , Waller, Tex (d/IX-30?-1899) MD U Nashville 1870. *JAMA* 33:808, 1899. *Polk* 1893: 1216.

RAINES, CHARLES B, Rusk Tex (b/I-17-1808 Va;d/VI 28-1894) MD Transylvania 1830. *Tex cour-rec med* 11 [i.e.12?]: 280 1894. *Polk* 1890: 1086. *JAMA* 23:86, 1894.

RAINEY, HARVEY WARD, Indianapolis (b/X-8-1854 Lafayette, Ind; d/X-15-1902) MD LICH 1882. *Tr Ind St M S* 1903:353. *Polk* 1896: 475.

RAINEY, JAMES M , Nashville (d/XII-10-1896) MD Vanderbilt 1853. *JAMA* 28:92, 1896. *Polk* 1886: 870.

RAINEY, JOHN B , Gilmer, Tex (b/Ky; d/XII-11-1890) MD Ky Sch Med 1881. *Daniel's Tex med jour* 6:413-14, 1890-91. *Polk* 1886: 887.

RAINIER, FRANK C, Fort Scott, Kans (d/XII-15-1899) MD Starling 1896. *JAMA* 34:61, 1900. *Polk* 1896: 2342.

RALSTON, G W , Pine Bluff, Ark (d/X-8-1867 @36) MD ? *Med surg rep Phila* 17:392, 1867.

RALSTON, WILLIAM WILSON, Horton, Kans (d/XII-6-1899 @41) MD Rush 1886. *JAMA* 34:61, 1900.

RAMSAY, ANDREW M , Philadelphia (d/I-26-1881 @ 82? or 86?) MD Jeff'n 1868. *Med bull m&s* 3: 65, 1881.

RAMSAY, CYRUS, MexWar-USA; Ohio; NYC 1853- (b/VI-3-1820 Martinsburg, WVa; d/IV-13-1871) MD UCNY 1853; MD Cleveland Med Coll 1850. *Med reg NY NJ Conn* 1871: 362.

RAMSAY, GEORGE McILVAIN, CW-USA; Washington, Pa (d/ IV-13-1902 @82) MD Jefferson 1852. *Pa med jour* 6:261, 1902/03.

RAMSDELL, EDWIN D , NYC (d/VI-12-1896 @66) MD UCNY 1855. *JAMA* 26:1278, 1896. *Polk* 1896:1074.

RAMSEY [RAMSAY], A K , Belton, Tex (b/III-11 1833 Marengo Co Ala;d/I-23-1881) MD ULa 1855; AB UVa *New Orl m&s j* ns8:989, 1881. *Tex m&s rec* 2:80, 1882.

RAMSEY, ALEXANDER, Parsonfield, Me (b/1754 London; d/XI- -1824 Scotland?) <MD Dublin & Edinburgh> *Tr Me M Assn* 1883:161 ff. *K&B* III:1004-06.

RAMSEY, GEORGE P , Xenia, Ill (d/VII-18-1901) Lic by 25 yrs' pract. *Tr Ill M S* ns3: 189, 1901.

RAMSEY, J G M , Knoxville (b/1797? d/IV-11-1884 @87) MD ? *Med surg rep Phila* 50:544, 1884.

RAMSEY, JAMES BARTLETT, Washington Ala; Kemper Co Miss; Vermilion Par La 1872- (b/VIII-27-1820 Chatham Co, NC; d/VI-7-1897 Abbeville) <MD Transylv 1843> att U Ala 1840. *Tr La St M S* 19:26-27, 1898.

RAMSEY [RAMSAY], JUNIUS NAPOLEON, CW-CSA; Seaboard, NC (b/III-31-1836; d/II-26-1900 or 1904) MD UPa 1859; AB UNC 1857. *U Pa med alum CW*: 1859. *Polk* 1886: 726.

RAMSEY, WILLIAM RICHARDSON, CW-USA; Norristown, Pa (b/I-28-1833; d/V-3-1900) MD UPa 1855. *U Pa med alum CW*: 1855. *JAMA* 34: 1356, 1900.

RAND, BENJAMIN HOWARD, Philadelphia (b/X-1-1827; d/II-14-1883) MD Jefferson 1848. *Tr CPP* cent vol: 259. *Med bull m & s* 5:68, 1883. *K&B* III: 1008.

RAND, HENRY WALTER, Brooklyn (b/1851 Nova Scotia; d/1895) MD Bellevue 1877; AB Acadia U, NS 1873; AM 1878. *JAMA* 25:467, 1895. *Med bull m&s* 17: 447, 1895. *Polk* 1886: 648.

RAND, ISAAC, Boston (b/IV-27-1743; d/IX-11-1822) Hon MD Harvard 1799; AB 1761. *Bost m & s j* 105: 1881. *K&B* III: 1008-09.

RAND, JOHN MILTON, Newark, NJ (b/XII–1–1834 Lyndeboro, NH; d/XII–18–1905) MD Dartmouth 1859; <AB Harvard> *Bost m&s j* 153:738 1905. *Polk* 1896:943.

RAND, NEHEMIAH WHEELER, Monson, Mass (b/IX–14–1853 Francestown, NH; d/XI–5–1898) MD NY Hom 1878; stud Dartmouth & Boston U. *Tr Am Inst Hom* 1899: 932. *No Am j hom* 46:770, 1898. *Polk* 1886: 470.

RANDALL, BENJAMIN PRINCE F, Boston (d/1855 @ 36) MD Harvard 1844. *Bost m & s jour* 53: 155, 1856. *Mass M S cat*: 1894.

RANDALL, BURTON, Williamsport, Md; CW–USA (b/IV–7–1805 & d/II–8–1886 Annapolis) MD UPa 1828; AB St Johns; AM. *Med ann Md:* 543–44. *U Pa m alum CW*: 1828.

RANDALL, DAVID, Morrisville Vt (b/VI–14–1832 Wilton Me or XI–28–1823 Fayston Vt; d/X–25–1898) MD Castleton 1848. *JAMA* 31:1190, 1898. *Polk* 1886: 905.

RANDALL, EDWARD, Galveston, Tex (b/IV–26–1826 Montevallo, Ala; d/XI–13–1889) MD U La 1849. *Tr Tex St M Assn* 1889: In Mem. G P Red, *Med man in Tex*: 216.

RANDALL, FREDERICK JOHN, NYC (b/III–31–1838; d/XII–25–1869) MD UCNY 1867. *Med reg NY NJ Conn* 1870: 326.

RANDALL, GEORGE HENRY, N Rehoboth, Mass (d/I 18–1896 @70) MD ? *Bost m & s jour* 134:100, 1896. *Polk* 1893: 607.

RANDALL, HENRY RAYMOND, Winona, Minn (b/XI 20–1864 St Peter; d/XII–7–1890) MD Rush 1890. *Tr Minn St M S* 1893: 123.

RANDALL, ROBERT ALEXANDER, Lewistown, Ill (d/VIII–19–1900) MD Rush 1881. *Ill med jour* ns2:237, 1900. *Polk* 1886: 286.

RANDALL, JOHN WITT, Boston (d/I–25–1892 @78) MD Harvard 1839; AB 1834. *Bost m&s j* 126: 104, 1892.

RANDALL, MENZIES RAYNER, N Rehoboth, Mass (b/1794? Easton; d/VII–23–1882) MD Brown 1824. *Bost m&s j* 107:619, 1882. *Mass M S cat* 1894.

RANDALL, RICHARD, USA 1818–21; Washington, DC (b/V–13–1796 Annapolis; d/IV–19–1829 Liberia) MD UPa 1818; att St Johns Coll. *Hist M S DC:*220–21.

RANDALL, SAMUEL, Galveston, Tex (b/XI–11–1824 Ala; d/XII–8–1866) MD UCNY. *Galveston m j* 2: 504, 534, 1886.

RANDALL, WILLIAM H , Hillisburgh, Ind; Augusta, Ia (b/VI–12–1832 Wilton, Me; d/XII–23–1899) MD Castleton 1857. *JAMA* 34:123, 1900. *Polk* 1896: 511.

RANDEL, JOHN MASSEY, Philadelphia (b/VII–14–1831 New Castle, Del; d/VII–13–1858) MD Hahnemann Phila 1852. *Tr Am Inst Hom* 1859: 166.

RANDEL, OGDEN MOSES, Oneida, NY (d/IX–15–1895 @68) MD U Mich 1854. *JAMA* 25:554, 1895. *Butler* 1878: 570.

RANDLE, GEORGE H , Waco, Tex (d/I–5–1906 @66) <MD U Nashville 1856> *Tex st jour med* 2:76, 1900.

RANDLETT, HOWARD MALCOLM, CW–USA; USN 1864–68 (b/II–20–1837 Stratham, NH; d/V–26–1873 Annapolis, Md) MD Harvard 1864; AB Bowdoin 1859. *Harvard in CW*: 289. *Bowdoin cat*: 1859.

RANDOLPH, ARCHIBALD CARY, Mill Wood Va; CW–CSA (b/IV–13–1833 Clarke Co; d/III–30–1887) MD UPa 1860. *U Pa m alum CW*: 1860. *Polk* 1886: 921.

RANDOLPH, ISRAEL, NYC (d/VI–2–1877 @74) MD CPSNY 1828. *Med reg NY NJ Conn* 1877: 206.

RANDOLPH, JACOB, Philadelphia (b/XI–25–1796;d/II 29–1848) MD UPa 1817 *Tr CPP* cent vol:259; 2: 283–89, 1846–49. *Tr AMA* 3:457–59 1850. *K&B* III:1009–10.

RANDOLPH, JAMES HENRY, ?Tallahassee; CW–CSA (b/VII–3–1809 Va; d/1892) MD UPa 1831. *U Pa m alum CW*: 1831.

RANDOLPH, JOHN FIELD, Philadelphia; USA 1855–65? (b/1828 Va; d/V–14–1880) MD UPa 1850. *Med rec NY* 17:611, 1880. Heitman.

RANDOLPH, NATHANIEL ARCHER, Philadelphia (b/XI–7–1858; d/VIII–21–1887) MD UPa 1882. *Tr CPP* cent vol:259; 3s10:lxi–lxvi, 1888. *New Orl m & s j* ns15:329, 1897. *K&B* III: 1010.

RANDOLPH, RICHARD Jr, Philadelphia (b/IV–27 1822; d/I–10–1906) MD UPa 1847; AB Haverford 1835. *Pa med jour* 9:360, 1905/06.

RANDOLPH, RICHARD H , Fla; CW–CSA; NYC 1877?– (b/Fla; d/VII–4–1878) MD Med Coll SC 1855. *Med reg NY NJ Conn* 1879: 196.

RANDOLPH, WILLIAM, CW–USA (d/VI–5–1865) MD U Louisville 1855. *Tr AMA* 18:356, 1867. *Nat med jour* 1:301, 1870/71.

RANDOLPH, WILLIAM HENRY, Brooklyn (b/IX––1840; d/III–17–1893) MD U Mich 1862. *Med reg NY NJ Conn* 1893: 313.

RANEY, GEORGE MONROE, Smoky Ordinary, Va (d/I 24–1899) MD UPa 1851. *JAMA* 32:324, 1899. *Polk* 1896: 1502.

RANKIN, FRANCIS HUNTINGTON, Newport, RI (b/IX–25–1845 Fishkill–on–Hudson; d/XI–9–1896) MD UCNY 1869. *Boston m&s j* 135:535, 536, 1896. *Tr RI M S* 5:363–64, 1894–98. *Polk* 1896: 1350.

RANKIN, JAMES COFFIELD MITCHELL, Ashland, Tenn; Bellemina Ala (d/II–18–1906)MD U Nashvl 1858. *So pract* 28:301 1906. *Butler* 1878:776. *Polk* 1886:130.

RANKIN, JOHN STEPHEN, Pittsburgh (b/IV–7–1831 Carroll Co, O; d/IV–21–1899) MD Hahnemann Phila 1858. *Tr Am Inst Hom* 1899: 932. *Polk* 1886: 830. Homeopath.

RANKIN, ROBERT G , Baltimore (d/IX–26–1897 @71) MD U Md 1850. *JAMA* 29: 761, 1897.

RANKIN, ROBERT McKEEVER, Hopewell, NJ (b/II–17–1845; d/X–14–1884) MD UCNY 1877. *Tr M S NJ* 1885: 163.

RANKIN, WILLIAM Jr, Newark, NJ (b/III–13 or 18–1848; d/II–26–1904 @56) MD CPSNY 1871; AB Rutgers 1868; AM 1871. *Bost m&s j* 150:226, 1904. *Atkin*–

 Spec. educ'l status abbrev. as: ***ng*** = college verified attendance without degree;

son I: 361. *Polk* 1896: 943.

RANNEY, AMBROSE LOOMIS, NYC (b/1848 Hardwick Mass; d/XII-2-1905) MD UCNY 1871; AB Dartm'th 1868. *Bost m&s j* 153:656, 1905. *K&B* III:1010-11.

RANNEY, EVANDER W , NYC (d/VI-22-1888 @78) MD Berkshire 1834. *Med reg NY NJ Conn* 1889: 282.

RANNEY, HENRY D , NYC (b/Vt; d/1878 @61?) MD Albany 1840. *Med reg NY NJ Conn* 1879: 196.

RANNEY, JAMES W , NYC (b/IX-28-1824 Townsend, Vt; d/II-28-1889) MD UCNY 1849. *Med reg NY NJ Conn* 1889: 282. *Bost m & s j* 120:252, 1889.

RANNEY, LAFAYETTE, Wardsboro, Vt (b/VIII-16-1819; d/II-15-1883 NYC) MD Dartm'th 1846; AB 1842. *Med reg NY NJ Conn*1883:234 *Med bull m&s* 5:89 1883.

RANNEY, MARK, Mt Pleasant, Ia (b/VII-7-1827 Westminster, Vt; d/II-1-1882) MD Woodstock 1849. *JAMA* 2: 726, 1884. *Atkinson* I: 82. *Tr Ia St M S* 6:457-58, 1883-85; 18:411, 1900. *Butler* 1878: 243.

RANNEY, MOSES HARRIS, Vt; NYC (b/VIII-16-1814; d/XII-7-1864 Blackwell's Isl, NYC) MD Berkshire 1833; ng Castleton 1837. *Bost m&s j* 71:508, 1864. *Tr AMA* 18:310, 1867. *Med surg rep Phila* 12:219, 1864. *Med reg NY NJ Conn* 1865: 232.

RANNEY, STEPHEN ELEAZAR, N Bennington, Vt (d/III-3-1899 @76) MD CPSNY 1845. *JAMA* 32:628, 1899. *Polk* 1896: 1476.

RANNEY, WALTER LAFAYETTE, NYC (d/VIII-17 1888) MD UCNY 1880. *Med reg NY NJ Conn* 1889:283. *Polk* 1886: 691.

RANSOM, ANSON AMESBURY, S Orange, NJ (b/II-18 1824; d/III-11-1894) MD UCNY 1867. *Med reg NY NJ Conn* 1894:247. *Tr M S NJ* 1894:262. *JAMA* 22:482, 1894. *Butler* 1878: 474.

RANSOM, WALTER JAMES, Lockport, NY (d/VIII-1897) MD UCNY 1876. *Buff m & s j* 37: 303-04, 1897. *Flint* 1897: 662.

RANSONE, ALEX L , Hyattstown, Md (b/XII-24-1847 Norfolk Va; d/IX-30-1899) MD CPS Balto 1875. *JAMA* 33:994, 1899. *Polk* 1886: 443.

RAPHAEL, BENJAMIN I , NYC (b/XI-8-1818; d/III-17-1880) MD CPSNY 1839. *Med reg NY NJ Conn* 1880: 241. *Med surg rep Phila* 42:308, 1880. *Atkinson* I: 329. *Butler* 1878: 523.

RAPHAEL, HENRY, NYC (b/Russia; d/VIII-4-1888 @47) MD Bellevue 1862. *Med reg NY NJ Conn* 1889: 283. *Bost m & s jour* 119:164, 1888. *Butler* 1878: 523.

RATCLIFFE, CHARLES S , Alexandria, La (d/XI--1887 @61) MD Jefferson 1853. *New Orl m & s j* ns15: 494, 1887. *Polk* 1886: 412.

RATHBONE, JOSHUA HENRY, Jamestown, NY (b/1832; d/1877) MD Pa M C 1857. *Tr AMA* 29:747, 1878.

RATHGEBER, EUGENE ALBERT, NYC (d/VI-5-1895) MD UCNY 1891. *Med reg NY NJ Conn* 1895: 237. *Polk* 1893: 908.

RATRIE, GEORGE T , Lexington, Ky (b/c1798? Md; d/XII-18-1828 @30?) MD Transylvania 1824. *Transylvania jour med & assoc sci* 2: 147, 1829.

RAU, FREDERICK [FRANK] CHRISTOPHER, W Hoboken NJ (d/IX-30-1876)MD Bellevue 1869. *Tr Med Soc NJ* 1877: [127]. *Med rec med & surg* 11:694, 1876.

RAU, JACOB, Newark, NJ (b/1824 Württemberg, Gny; d/V-7-1896) Lic Exam Bd. *JAMA* 26:1038, 1896. *Polk* 1890: 728.

RAUB, HENRY E, Quarryville Pa (d/VII-20-1901 @ 71) MD Pa M C 1857. *JAMA* 37:342, 1901. *Polk* 1886:832.

RAUB, JACOB FRANKLIN, CW-USA (b/V-13-1840; d/V-21-1906) MD LICH 1864. *Pa m j* 9:671, 1905/06; 10:913, 1906/07. *Flint* 1897:197 (Washington, DC).

RAUB, JOHN ANGLE, Philadelphia (b/III-15-1835 Blairstown, NJ; d/IX-29-1897) MD UPa 1862; AB Lafayette 1858; AM 1864. *JAMA* 29:925, 1897. *Polk* 1896: 1315.

RAUCH, JOHN HENRY, CW-USA; Iowa; Lebanon, Pa; Ill (b/IX-4 1828 Lebanon; d/III-24-1894 Lebanon or Chicago) MD UPa 1849. *Chic med rec* 6:294, 1894. *Tr Ill St M S* 1894: 57-59. *JAMA* 22:481-82, 1894. *U Pa med alum CW*: 1849. *K&B* III: 1011-12.

RAUE, CHARLES GOTTLIEB [GODLOVE], Philadelphia (b/V-11-1820 Nieder Cunnersdorf, Saxony; d/VIII-21-1896) MD Phila C M 1850; Hon MD NY Homeop 1871; Hon MD Hahnemann Phila 1896. *Hahn mo* 31:130-32 (news & advt) 1896. *Tr Am Inst Hom* 1897:64. *No Am j hom* 44:664, 1896. *Hom rec* 11:529-35, 1896.

RAVENSCROFT, FRANK H, Friendsvl Md (d/VIII-19 1901 @31) MD KySchMed 1893 *JAMA* 37:710. 1901.

RAWLINS, SAMUEL W , New Orleans (d/III-31-1880 @22) MD Tulane 1879. *New Orl m & s j* ns7:984, 1880.

RAWSON, ALLEN A , Corning, Ia (b/III-14-1831 O; d/II-26-1900) MD Rush 1855. *Tr Iowa St M S* 18:399, 1900. *JAMA* 34:639, 1900.

RAWSON, CHARLES HAMILTON, Des Moines (b/VII 6-1828 Orleans Co, Vt; d/VI-27-1884) MD CPSNY 1851; ng Woodstock 1847. *Tr Iowa St M S* 6: 463-64, 1883-85.

RAWSON, EDMUND GRINDAL, NYC (b/XI-30-1803; d/1882) MD CPSNY 1830; AB Union 1826; AM 1830. *Med reg NY NJ Conn* 1883: 234. *Butler* 1878: 523.

RAY, BENJAMIN LINCOLN, Philadelphia (b/XII-31-1836 Eastport, Me; d/XII-9-1879) MD Harvard 1859; AB Brown 1856. *Med surg rep Phila* 41:550, 1879. *Butler* 1878: 670.

RAY, DUNCAN WILLIAM, CW-CSA (b/III-11-1812 Columbia,SC; d/X-18-1868 Richland, SC) MD UPa 1842; AB Coll SC 1837. *U Pa med alum CW*: 1842.

RAY, ISAAC, Portland, Me 1827-29; Eastport 1829-41; Augusta, 1841-45; Providence, RI 1845-67; Philadelphia 1867-81 (b/I-16-1807 Beverly, Mass; d/III-31-1881) MD Bowdoin 1827; AB 1826; LLD Brown 1879. *Tr CPP* cent vol: 259; 3s5: , 1881. *Tr RI M S* 2:391-404,

1877–82. *Bost m&s j* 104:332 353 1881. *K&B* III: 1014.

RAY, JESSE HYDE, USN 1809–35 (d/IX–7–1835) MD ? AM St Johns 1802. *Med ann Md:* 544. *Callahan.*

RAY, JOHN AUGUSTUS, Brooklyn (b/1851; d/VI–22–1892 @40) MD CPSNY 1874. *Med reg NY NJ Conn* 1893:313. *Bost m&s j* 127:28,1892. *Polk* 1886:648.

RAY, JOHN TODDINGTON, Greenville & Meadville, Pa (b/1817 Frankford; d/1874) MD UPa 1838. *Tr AMA* 26:471–72, 1875.

RAY, JOSEPH H , Huntington, NY (b/1805; d/III–23–1875) MD ? *Med reg NY NJ Conn* 1875: 203.

RAY, PETER WILLIAM, Brooklyn (d/XI–26–1906 @82) MD Castleton 1850. *Bost m&s j* 155: 692, 1906. *Polk* 1896: 1001.

RAY, ROBERT Jr, NYC (d/1860 @28) MD CPSNY 1856; AB Columbia 1852. *Tr AMA* 14:192, 1864. *Med reg NY NJ Conn* 1862: 153.

RAYMOND, JONAS C, Utica NY 1848–77; Oakland Cal 1878–98 (b/IV–23–1823 Troy; d/III–3–1901) MD Hahnemann, Phila 1851; att UCNY Med Sch 1 yr. *Tr Am Inst Hom* 1901: 918. *Tr NY St Homeop Soc* 10:637, Homeopath.

RAYMOND, MAHLON HARRISON, Grass Lake, Mich (d/X–21–1896 @60) MD U Mich 1859; MD Bellevue 1869. *JAMA* 27:1021, 1896. *Polk* 1886: 494.

RAYNES, JOHN BENSON, Lebanon, NH (b/VI–2–1857 Detroit; d/V–22–1896 Holeb, Me) MD Dartmouth 1883. *Tr NH M S* 1896: 186.

RAYNOR, GEORGE C, Joliet Ill (d/IV–23–1905 @79) MD UCNY 1852. *Ill m j* 7:611, 1905. *Polk* 1896: 425.

REA, ADELINE V MARTIN, York, Pa (b/1871 Chester; d/XI–23–1899) MD Woman's Med Coll Phila 1893. *Pa med jour* 3:440–41, 1889/1900. *JAMA* 33: 1566, 1899. *Flint* 1897: 840.

REA, ALBUS [ALBERT], Portland, Me (b/II– –1795 Windham; d/X–14–1848) MD Bowdoin 1822. *Tr Am Inst Hom* 1893:153. *King* I:312. Homeopath.

REA, FRANK L , Chicago (d/VIII–10–1883 @24) MD Chic Med Coll 1882. *Chic med jour* 47:663–66, 1883. *Med bull med & surg* 5:213, 1883.

REA, GEORGE NATHANIEL, New Castle, Ind (b/VII–28–1852 Lewisville; d/II–19–1885) MD Med Coll Ohio 1878. *Tr Ind St M S* 1885: 219.

REA, JOHN, New Castle, Ind (b/II–10–1819 Rockbridge, Va; d/II–24–1899) MD Med Coll Ohio 1855. *JAMA* 32: 506, 1889. *Tr Ind St M S* 1899: 405. *Polk* 1886:330.

REA, ROBERT LAUGHLIN, Chicago (b/VII–1–1827 Rockbridge Co, Va; d/VII–10–1899) MD Med Coll Ohio 1855.*Chic med rec* 17:33–34, 1899. *Tr Ill St M S* 1899: 90. *Butler* 1878:136. *Flint* 1897: 267.

READ, ALEXANDER, New Bedford, Mass (b/VI–10–1786 Milford; d/XI–20–1849) MD Yale 1816; AB Dartmouth 1808; MB 1811. *Bost m & s jour* 41:336 [i.e. 346], 377–79, 1849. *Tr AMA* 3:459–60, 1850.

READ, GEORGE MUMFORD, Dorchester, Mass (b/IV–16–1856 Providence RI; d/III–16–1890 @33) MD Harvard 1877. *Bost m & s jour* 122:288, 388, 1890.

READ, IRA BEMAN, CW–USA; NYC (d/VII–4–1897) MD U Mich 1867; MD Bellevue 1868; AB Western Reserve 1862; AM 1865. *Bost m & s jour* 137:69, 1897. *JAMA* 29: 200, 1897. *Polk* 1896: 1074.

READ, JOHN BRAHAN, Tuscaloosa (b/VI– –1816; d/I–20–1899) MD Tulane 1846; AB U Ala 1834; AM 1850. *Tr Med Assoc St Ala* 1899:233. *JAMA* 32:263, 1899.

READ, LOUIS WERNWAG, Crimean War–Russian Army 1856; CW–USA 1861–66; Norristown, Pa (b/VII–5–1828 Plymouth; d/X–31–1900) MD UPa 1849. *U Pa med alum CW*: 1849.

READ [REED], NATHANIEL [NEWTON] SEDGWICK, Chandlersville, Ill (b/VII–25–1820 Williamsfield, O; d/VIII–11–1901) MD Cleveland Med Coll 1844. *Ill m j* ns3:347–48, 1901. *JAMA* 37: , 1901.

READ, ROBERT McLELLAN, Boston (d/IV–21–1907 @55) MD Harvard 1877. *Bost m & s jour* 150: 470, 1904. *Polk* 1896: 704.

READ, WILLIAM, Boston (b/Amherst, NH; d/V–6–1889 @69) MD Harvard 1842; AB Amherst 1839. *Bost m & s jour* 120:476, 500, 1889. *Atkinson* I: 699.

READ, WILLIAM CONNER, Brownsville, Tenn (d/IV–7–1887) MD Memphis Hosp Coll Med 1886. *New Orl m & s j* ns14: 985, 1887.

READ, WILLIAM PRATT, Philadelphia (d/X–8–1898 @51) MD UPa 1871. *JAMA* 31:997 1898. *Polk* 1896:1315.

READ, ZACHARIAH, Mt Holly, NJ (b/1808; d/VII–28–1879) MD UPa 1830. *Tr AMA* 33:590–91, 1882. *Tr M S NJ* 1880:124. *Med surg rep Phil* 41:176 1879. *Butler* 1878:475.

READELL, JOHN DIDIER, Baltimore (b/1790 Phila; d/V–31–1854) MD UPa 1811. *Med annals Md:* 544–45.

READING, EDWARD, Hatboro, Pa (b/I–3–1829 Somerton, Pa; d/III–3–1889) MD Hahnemann Phila 1853. *Tr Am Inst Hom* 1889: 175. *Med vis* 5:116, 1889. *Polk* 1886: 801. Homeopath.

REAGAN, ROBERT S , Broad Ford, Pa (d/XII–13–1903 @52) MD Jefferson 1880. *Pa m j* 7:280, 1903/04. *Polk* 1886: 793.

REAGAN, T J , Beckville, Tex (d/V–9–1887) <MD Med C Ga> *Tex cour–rec med* 4:535, 1887. *Polk* 1886: 880.

REAMER, FRANCIS C , CW–USA (b/Bedford, Pa; d/IV–28–1870) MD UPa 1845. *U Pa med alum CW*:1845.

REAMY, LEONIDAS M , Zanesville, O (d/IX–7–1897 @61) MD Med Coll Ohio 1872. *JAMA* 29:660, 1897. *Polk* 1886: 774.

REARDON, JEREMIAH JOHN, Natick, Mass (dI–22–1882 @32) MD Harvard 1876 *Bost m&s j* 107:619, 1882.

REASONER, WILLIAM MARTIN, Sulphur Sprs Ind (b/III–24–1828; d/VII–6–1887) MD Cinc C M & S 1872. *Tr Ind St M S* 1888:202. *Butler* 1878:217. *Polk* 1886:337.

REBER, WILLIAM McCLELLAN, Bloomsburg, Pa (b/

 Spec. educ'l status abbrev. as: ***ng*** = college verified attendance without degree;

III-4-1842 Lewisburg, Pa; d/XI-17-1904 @61) MD Jefferson 1863. *Pa med jour* 8: 187, 336, 1904/05. *Atkinson* I: 168. *Flint* 1897: 796.

REBMAN, GEORGE A , Wrightsville, Pa (b/W Manchester; d/III-9-1903 @50) MD U Md 1876. *Pa med jour* 7:280, 1903/04. *Flint* 1897: 840.

RECTOR, PIERSON, Jersey City (b/I-11-1840 Duanesburg, NY; d/I-21-1899) MD Albany 1863. *JAMA* 16: 320, 1891. *Med reg NY NJ Conn* 1891: 280. *Tr M S NJ* 1892: 203. *Bost m & s jour* 124:128, 1891.

RED, GEORGE CLARK, Washington, Tex (b/VIII- -1820 Newberry, SC; d/VIII- -1880 or 1881) MD Charleston M C 1842. *Tex m & s rec* 2:80, 1882. G P Red, *Med man in Texas*.

REDDEN, JOSEPH W, CW-USA; Topeka, Kans (b/VIII 30-1834 Bridgeville, Del; d/VIII-5-1893) MD Jefferson 1857; AB Dickinson 1856. *JAMA* 21: 357, 1893.

REDFIELD, JOHN S , Ft Scott, Kans (d/VI-15-1876 @ 56) MD Jefferson 1850. *Tr Kans M S* 1:470, 1877. *Butler* 1878: 255.

REDMAN, JOHN, Philadelphia (b/II-27-1722; d/III-19-1808) MD Leyden 1748. *Tr CPP* cent vol: 259. *Med museum* 5 (1): 49-56. 1808. *K&B* III: 1018.

REDWINE, COLUMBUS L , CW-CSA; ?Atlanta (b/ 1832; d/VI-8 1903) MD UCNY 1855. *UCNY cat*: 1855.

REECE, MADISON, ?Abingdon, Ill; CW-USA (b/VII-18-1836 Lima, O; d/V-20-1884) MD UPa 1866; MD Rush 1861. *U Pa med alum CW*: 1866.

REED, ALFRED GRAHAM, Philadelphia; CW-USA (b/ IX-23-1837 Lowville, NY; d/XII-4-1898) MD UPa 1868; <MD Pa Med Coll> *U Pa med alum CW*: 1868. *Polk* 1886: 823.

REED, CALEB RICHMOND, Middleport, O (d/X-31 1899 @73) MD Jefferson 1853. *JAMA* 33:1307, 1899. *Polk* 1896: 1201.

REED, CHARLES L, LaCrosse, Wis (d/XI-5-1893) MD Castleton 1846. *JAMA* 21:734, 1893. *Polk* 1890:1166.

REED, CHARLES M , Dotsero, Colo (d/IX-29-1894 @24) MD U Louisville 1892. *Tr Colo St M S* 1895: 43; 1898-99: 509.

REED, JACOB Jr, Colorado Springs (d/XII-15-1896 @57) MD Jefferson 1866. *Tr Colo St M S* 1898-99: 509. *Polk* 1893: 231.

REED, JOHN BURNS, Wheeling, WVa (b/XII-14-1846 Washington Co, Pa; d/X-17-1887) MD Western Reserve 1872. *Tr M S WVa* 1888:591-92. *Polk* 1886:945.

REED, JOSEPH ALLISON, Dixmont, Pa (b/XII-31-1823 Washington, Pa; d/XI-6-1884) MD Jefferson 1847. *Tr Pa St M S* 1885:298-300. *JAMA* 4: 110-11, 1885. *Atkinson* I: 76-77. *Butler* 1878: 729.

REED, JOSEPH O , Middletown, NY (b/IX-14-1865 Niles, NY; d/IV-22-1889 Rio de Janeiro) MD NY Homeop 1887. *Tr Am Inst Hom* 1889:190. Homeopath.

REED, LEWIS, Ocean Grove, NJ (b/1806 Bridgeton, NJ; d/III-22-1898) MD ? *JAMA* 30: 807, 1898.

REED, LOUIS WILLIAM, Woodstown, NJ (b/V-10-1851; d/IV-15-1889) MD UPa 1877. *Tr M S NJ* 1889: 178. *Polk* 1886: 612.

REED, MARO McLEAN, Jacksonville, Ill 1830- (b/X 18-1801 E Windsor, Conn; d/VI-28-1877) MD Castleton 1826; AB Yale 1822. *Amer homeop* 1: 40, 1877. *Tr Am Inst Hom* 1878:1115. *King* I:358. Homeopath.

REED, ORANGE BENTON, Lenox, Mich (d/XI-8-1894 @90) ng U Mich Med Dept 1851-53. *JAMA* 23:802, 1894. *Polk* 1886: 502. *Butler* 1878: 381.

REED, SAMUEL P , Cane Isl, SC (d/IV-14-1855 @39) MD Med Coll SC 1838. *Bost m & s jour* 52:247, 1855.

REED, STUART HANCKEL, Madison, NJ (b/X-10-1854 SC; d/I-6-1904) MD CPSNY 1881; AB Williams 1878. *Bost m & s jour* 150: 56, 1904.

REED, THOMAS BAIRD, Philadelphia (d/1891 @ 56) MD Jeff'n 1859; MD UPa 1882. *Tr CPP* cent vol: 259. *Bost m&s j* 124:372, 1891. *Med bull m&s* 13:196, 1891.

REED, THOMAS GRANT, Bridgeton, NJ (b/XI-12-1837; d/IX-12-1866) MD UPa 1858. *Tr M S NJ* 1867: 208. *Med surg rep Phila* 16: 80, 1867.

REED, THOMAS SYDENHAM, Philadelphia (b/1822; d/IX-11-1889 Cape May, NJ) MD Jefferson 1846. *Bost m&s j* 121:292, 1889. *Med surg rep Phila* 61:336, 1889. *Med bull med & surg* 11:333, 1889. *Polk* 1886: 823.

REED, WALTER, USA 1874- (b/IX-13-1851 Glouc'tr Co, Va; d/XI-22-1902 Washington, DC) MD U Va 1869; MD Bellevue 1872. *Bost m&s j* 147: 630, 1902. *Cal st jour med* 1:69-70,1903. *K&B* III:1018-20.

REED, WILLIAM ASHTON, Philadelphia (b/VI-25-1827; d/I-15-1895) MD Hahnemann Phila 1852; AB Madison & Lewisburg. *Hahn mo* 30(1): 80; (3):43, 1895 (news & advt). *Polk* 1886: 823. Homeopath.

REED, WILLIAM BARRETT, Waterville, NY (b/I-3 1813; d/XII-6-1846) MD Med Coll Va 1842; AB Amherst 1837. *Amherst, Men of*: 1837.

REES, WILLIAM T , Owenton, Ky (d/XII-9-1888 @ 65) MD ? *Med adv* 22:64, 1889. *Med vis* 5:44, 1889. *Polk* 1886:403. Homeopath 1879?- .

REES, JOHN THOMAS, Philadelphia (b/1780? Del; d/1833 @53) MD UPa 1805. *Med annals Md:* 545.

REESE, AUGUSTUS JORDAN, CW-CSA; Mobile Ala (b/IV-22-1826 Autauga; d/IX-14-1889) MD ULa 1849. *Tr M S Ala* 1890: 218. *Atkinson* I: 550. *Polk* 1886: 162.

REESE, DAVID MEREDITH, Baltimore (b/1800 Phila; d/V-13-1861 NYC) MD U Md 1819. *Med reg NY NJ Conn* 1862:154. *Tr AMA* 14:198-99 1864. *Bost m&s j*64: 356 374-75, 1861. *Med ann Md:*545. *K&B* III:1021-22.

REESE, JOHN JAMES, CW-USA; Philadelphia (b/VI-16-1818; d/IX-4-1892 Atlantic City) MD UPa 1839; AB 1836. *JAMA* 19:535, 1892. *Bost m&s j* 127:25, 1892. *Tr CPP* cent vol:260. *Atkinson* I: 23. *K&B* III: 1022.

REESE, WILLIAM WOODWARD, Brooklyn (d/X-20-1894 @82) MD UPa 1845. *Med reg NY NJ Conn* 1895: 237. *JAMA* 23:697, 1894. *Bost m&s j* 131: 470, 1894.

Butler 1878: 534.

REEVE, DANIEL L , Jersey City, NJ (b/1822 NYC; d/II-25-1899) MD UCNY 1845. *JAMA* 32: 506, 1899. *Polk* 1896: 939.

REEVES, ABNER, Newark, NJ (d/1871) MD ? *Tr AMA* 24:360, 1873.

REEVES, EDWARD LAFFERTY, Paulsboro, NJ (d/IX-21-1899 @68) MD UPa Coll 1859. *JAMA* 33:872, 1899. *Polk* 1886: 610.

REEVES, JAMES EDMUND, Chattanooga (b/IV-5-1829 Annisville Va; d/I-4-1896) MD UPa 1860 *New Orl m&s j* ns23:438-39 501-02 1896. *JAMA* 26:93, 141, 1896. *Nashvl j m&s* 79:48-49, 1896. *K&B* III: 1024-25.

REEVES, URIAH G , Clifty, Ind (b/X-3-1820 Warren Co, O; d/V-27-1882) MD ? *Tr Ind St M S* 1883: 266. *Butler* 1878: 217.

REEVES, W W , Cedar Pt, Will's Pt, Austin, Tex (b/VI-23-1847 Va; d/XII-29-1891) <MD CPS Balto 1879> *Daniel's Tex m j* 7:260-64, 1891-92. *Med bull m&s* 14: 74, 1892. *Tex cour-rec m* 9:136, 1892. *Polk* 1886: 897.

REGAN, MATTHEW FRANCIS, Brooklyn; CW-USA (d/VII-19-1878 @42) MD CPSNY 1856. *Med reg NY NJ Conn* 1879: 196. *Butler* 1878: 534.

REGENSBERGER, JOSEPH, NYC (b/1816; d/XI-26-1870) MD ? *Med reg NY NJ Conn* 1871:362.

REGESTER, WILSON GRAY, CW-CSA; Baltimore (b/II-16-1845 Bath Co, Va; d/IV-22-1882) MD Washington U, Balto 1869; att Roanoke Coll, Salem, Va. *Tr AMA* 33:591, 1882. *Med annals Md:* 546.

REID, HENRY C , Mariposa, Calif (d/IX-7-1895) MD Ky Sch Med 1881. *JAMA* 25:467, 1895. *Polk* 1890: 189.

REID, J T , Fairfield, O (d/1864) MD ? *Tr Ohio St M S* 1873: 223.

REID, JAMES ANDERSON, Davenport, Ia (d/II-4-1901) MD Ecl Med Inst Cincinnati 1856. *Ill m j* ns2:533, 1901. *Polk* 1886: 355. Eclectic.

REID, JAMES RANSOM M, Thomasville Ga (d/VI-13 1898) MD UPa 1844 *JAMA* 30:1534 1898 *Polk*1896:340.

REID, JOHN K , Philadelphia (d/II-2-1906 @87) MD Pa M C 1850. *Pa m j* 9:360, 1905/06. *Polk* 1886: 796.

REID, KENNETH, Tompkinsville, NY (b/I-22-1840; d/I-22-1882) MD McGill 1864. *Med reg NY NJ Conn* 1882: 234. *Butler* 1878?: 570.

REID, NEVILLE C , ?Philadelphia (d/III-23-1870 @ 61) MD Jefferson 1840. *Phila med reg & dir* 1871:294.

REID, ROBERT KING, SC 1yr; Stockton, Calif 1849-CW-USA (b/I-21-1820 Erie, Pa; d/II-4-1891) MD UPa 1849; AB Wash & Jeff 1842. *Tr M S Cal* 21:320-21, 1891. *Atkinson* I: 26. *Butler* 1878: 62.

REILEY, ASHER, Frenchtown NJ (b/I-8-1821; d/IV-10 1891. MD UCNY 1849. *Tr M S NJ* 1892: ? *Butler* 1878: 474. *Polk* 1890: 721.

REILEY [REILAY], JAMES, CW-USA; Succasunna, NJ (b/1829 Durham, Pa; d/III-23-1872) MD CPSNY 1852; AB Union 1849. *Tr M S NJ* 1872:141; 1873:110. *Tr AMA* 24:361, 1873. *K&B* III:1271, mention only.

REILLY, BERNARD SYLVESTER, CW-USA (d/IX-28-1867 Rio Grande, Tex) MD U Mich 1866. *Nat med jour* 1:301, 1870/71.

REILLY, JOHN REDMUND, Appleton, Wis (b/VII-13 1844 Chelsea, Mich; d/V-10-1897) <MD Rush 1868> ng U Mich Med Dept 1865-66. *Tr Wis St M S* 31:639-40, 1897. *Polk* 1890: 1161.

REILLY, THOMAS AUGUSTUS, Philadelphia; CW-USA (b/VI-20-1819 Irel'd; d/XII-6-1873) MD UPa 1840. *U Pa med alum CW*: 1840 suppl.

REILY, JAMES ROSS, CW-USA; College Park Md (b/III-23-1835 York, Pa; d/X-12-1904) MD UPa 1859. *Hist M S DC:*276 *U Pa m alum CW*:1859 *Butler* 1874:94.

REIMANN, LOUIS, Louisville, Ky (d/VII-30-1883 Lacrosse, Wis) MD ? *Med surg rep Phila* 49:252, 1883.

REIMAR, AUGUST F W , NYC (d/IV-29-1904 @66) MD Göttingen 1850. *Bost m&s j* 150: 524, 1904. *Polk* 1896: 1017.

REIMER, J R [or S], Indianapolis (b/IX-16-1878 Memphis) MD ? *Med rec* NY 14:240, 1878. *Tr AMA* 30: 884, 1879.

REINFELDER, MAXIMILIAN JOSEPH, Yonkers, NYC (b/III-4-1821; d/XI-30-1888) MD UCNY 1869; <MD U Munich 1846> *Med reg NY NJ Conn* 1889:283. *Bost m&s j* 119:561,1888. *Butler* 1878: 570.

REINHARD, WILSON J , Hellertown, Pa (d/III-13-1899) MD Jefferson 1885. *JAMA* 32:733, 1899. *Polk* 1896: 1282.

REINHARDT, ERNEST GOTTHOLT, Roberts, Ill (d/V 5-1899 @38) MD Rush 1891. *JAMA* 32:1133, 1899. *Polk* 1896: 438.

REINHARDT, LOUIS, Milwaukee (d/XI-20-1893) MD U Marburg 185. *JAMA* 21:829, 1893. *Butler* 1878: 865. *Polk* 1890: 1169.

REINHOLD, C G , Philadelphia 1830-34; Pa (b/XI-8 1802 Muhlhausen, Gny; d/VI-28-1865) Stud med Leipzig. *King* I:150. Homeopath.

REINHOLD, HAHNEMANN ETZLER, Williamsport, Pa (b/IV-9-1844 Lewistown; d/III-6-1876 Phila) MD Hahnemann Phila 1869. *Tr Am Inst Hom* 1880: 44-45. Homeopath.

REINOEHL, JOHN KRAUSE, Lebanon, Pa (d/VII-10 1902 @43) MD UPa 1882. *Pa med jour* 6:261, 1902/03. *Flint* 1897: 807.

REISINGER, JOHN S , Galion, O (b/X-11-1811 Heidelberg, Pa; d/X-14-1866) MD ? *Tr Ohio St M S* 1867: 75-76.

REISMAN, ADOLPH, Pittsburgh (d/XI-13-1906 @75) MD ? *Pa med jour* 10:295, 1906/07.

REISSNER, KARL LUDWIG EUGENE, ? (b/XI-6-1867; d/VII-29-1894) MD ? *Med reg NY NJ Conn* 1895: 238.

REMICK, AUGUSTUS, Providence, RI (b/VIII-28-1830 N Bridgewater, Mass; d/X-5-1903) MD Harvard 1868.

 Spec. educ'l status abbrev. as: ***ng*** = college verified attendance without degree;

Tr RI M S 6:678–79, 1899–1903. *Polk* 1896:1353.

REMINGTON, EDGAR WILSON, Providence, RI (b/VIII-27-1861 Riverport; d/I-15-1905) MD Bellevue 1888; AB Brown 1885. *Tr RI M S* 7:284–85, 1904–09. *Polk* 1896: 1353.

REMINGTON, FREDERICK ADELBERT, Woonsocket, Dakota Terr (b/VIII-12-1852 nr Omro, Wis; d/VI-1-1903) MD St U Iowa Hom Dept 1884. *Tr Am Inst Hom* 1903: 732. *Polk* 1886:203.

REMINGTON, ISAAC, Philadelphia (b/I-5-1804; d/XI-10-1862) MD UPa 1824. *Tr CPP* cent vol: 260, ns3: 475–83, 1856–62. *Tr Pa St M S* 1863: 319–20. *Tr AMA* 14: 210, 1864.

REMINGTON, WASHINGTON B , Rochester, NY (d/VII-19-1901 @57) <MD Phila U Med & Surg 1871> *JAMA* 37: 342, 1901. *Polk* 1886: 701.

RENDELL, JOHN, Brooklyn (b/III-6-1840; d/IX-16-1897) MD LICH 1885. *Bost m&s j* 137:327 1897. *JAMA* 29: 660, 1897. *Polk* 1896: 1002.

RENFRO, JAMES C B , LaGrange & Houston, Tex (b/X-26-1835 Dade Co, Mo; d/VII- -1898) MD Tulane 1872. *Tex m news* 12:252, 1898. *Tex m j* 14: 38, 1898–99. *Atkinson* I:432. *Polk* 1886: 889.

RENNER, JOHN GEORGE EMIL, Indianapolis (b/I-2-1850 Gny; d/IX-16-1878 Memphis) <MD U Louisville 1877> *Tr Ind St M S* 1880: 238–39. *Tr AMA* 30:884, 1879. Kemper's *Indiana*: 332–33.

RENNOLDS, HENRY STHRESHLEY, USN 1841–61 (b/VI-22-1806 Tappahannock, Va; d/IX-28-1869 Pikesville, Md) MD UPa 1831. *Tr AMA* 21:498, 1870. *Nat m j* 1:301, 1870/71. *Phila med reg & dir* 1871: 302.

RENTON, JOHN, Boston (d/XII-15-1893 @74) MD Woodstock 1842. *Bost m&s j* 129:632, 1893. *Butler* 1878: 343.

RENTON, PETER, Boston (b/V-5-1801 Trawbourne, Scotland; d/II-10-1865) Hon MD Woodstock 1832. *Bost m & s jour* 72:68, 1895.

RENZ, GUSTAV H, Morrisania NY(d/IV-11-1883 @46) MD ? *Med reg NY NJ Conn* 1884:237. *Butler* 1878:570.

REPLOGLE, HENRY M , Udell, Iowa (b/IV-3-1865; d/V-27-1904) MD Rush 1895; DVM ? *Tr Ia St M S* 22: 341–42, 1904.

RETEL, MICHAEL, Buffalo (d/V-20-1896 @38) MD Buffalo 1886. *Buff m&s j* 35:917, 1896. *Polk* 1896: 1011.

REVELL, HENRY M , Asbury, Md (b/IX-12-1854 Anne Arundel Co; d/VII-2-1901) MD U Md 1876. *Med ann Md:* 548. *Polk* 1886: 435.

REVERE, EDWARD HUTCHINSON ROBBINS, Canton, Mass; CW-USA (b/1827? d/IX-17-1862 Sharpsburg, Md) MD Harvard 1849; att Harvard Coll 1846. *Harv in CW*: 35. *Nat m j* 1:301, 1870/71.

REVERE, FREDERICK B , ?NYC (d/X-6-1873 Tours, Fr) MD UCNY 1846. *Med s rep Phila* 29: 306, 1873.

REVERE, JOHN, Philadelphia; NYC (b/III-17-1787; d/V-1-1847) MD Edinburgh 1811; AB Harvard 1807 *Tr AMA* 3:460–61, 1850. *Med annals Md:* 548. *Ill & Ind m & s j* 2:191, 1847. *K&B* III: 1028.

REWKOWSKI, CASIMIR V , Chicago (d/I-23-1894) <MD Charkow, Russia 1873> *JAMA* 22:202, 1894. *Polk* 1886: 270.

REX, GEORGE ABRAHAM, Philadelphia (d/II-4-1895 @50) MD UPa 1868. *JAMA* 24:250, 1895. *Butler* 1878:694.

REYBURN, ROBERT, Washington, DC; CW-USA (b/VIII-1-1833 Glasgow, Scotl'd; d/III-25-1899) MD Phila Coll M & S 1856; Hon AM Howard 1871. *Hist M S DC:* 281–282. *Atkinson* I:83–84. *Polk* 1886: 214.

REYBURN, THOMAS, St Louis (d/IV-8-1857 @38) MD Transylvania 1839. *Bost m&s j* 56:428, 1857. *St Louis m & s j* 15:280, 285, 1857.

REYNOLDS, ALBERT, CW-USA; Clinton, Ia (b/VIII-18-1837 Grand Isl, Vt; d/II-23-1899) MD U Vt 1864. *Tr Iowa St M S* 1899:387–88. *Atkinson* I:200. *JAMA* 32:506, 1899. *Polk* 1896: 515.

REYNOLDS, BENJAMIN FRANKLIN, Hulton Pa (b/NY; d/VI-12-1901 @67) <MD Jefferson 1858> *JAMA* 37:43, 1901. *Polk* 1886: 802.

REYNOLDS, BENJAMIN H , Manchester, Ia (b/VII-22 1839;d/XI-13-1883) MD Iowa St U 1872 *JAMA* 2: 473–74, 1884. *Tr Iowa St M S* 6:461–62, 1883–85. *Butler* 1878: 244.

REYNOLDS, BENN P, Chicago (d/XII-8-1897) <MD Eclectic Med Coll Pa 1857 or 1863> *Chic med rec* 13:486, 1897. *Flint* 1897: 267. *Polk* 1896: 402.

REYNOLDS, CHARLES HENRY, Bay City, Mich 1861–65; Gorham, Me 1866– (b/VII-5-1835 Portland; d/XI-5-1877 Turner) MD CPSNY 1861; AB Bowdoin 1857. *Tr Me M Assn* 1879; 680. *Butler* 1878:310.

REYNOLDS, DAVID C, Philadelphia (d/XI-12-1901 @ 71) MD UPa 1852 *Pa m j* 5:296 1901/02. *Polk* 1886:823.

REYNOLDS, DAVID ELLIOT, New Orleans 1851- (b/XI-21-1826 Chambersburg, Pa; d/IX-9-1853) MD UPa 1850; AB Frankl & Marsh 1848. *F & M obit rec*:109.

REYNOLDS, DUDLEY SHARPE Jr, Louisville; Collinsville, Ill (b/II-70-1873; d/X-22-1894) MD Hosp Coll Med Louisville 1893. *JAMA* 23:697, 1894.

REYNOLDS, EDWARD, Boston (b/II-28-1793; d/XII-25-1881) Hon MD Brown 1825; Hon MD Bowdoin 1825; AB Harvard 1811. *Bost m&s j* 105:623, 624, 1881; 106:20, 1882; 107:618, 1882. *Tr AMA* 33:592–93, 1882. *K&B* III: 1029.

REYNOLDS, EDWIN, Brooklyn (b/Warwick, NY; d/XII-15-1905 @60) MD CPSNY 1877. *Bost m&s j* 153: 710, 1905. *Polk* 1896: 1002.

REYNOLDS, GIDEON PERRY, Guilford, Conn (d/XII-9-1897 @68) MD UCNY 1852. *JAMA* 29: 1286, 1897. *Polk* 1896: 279.

REYNOLDS, HENRY, Wilton NY (b/1788 Columbia Co; d/XII-20-1857) <MD Fairfield> *Tr M S St NY* 1858: 47–48.

REYNOLDS, JAMES BANKS, NYC (b/IV-8-1833; d/VIII-18-1882) MD CPSNY 1856. *Med reg NY NJ Conn* 1883:234. *Butler* 1878: 523.

REYNOLDS, JAMES D, Creston Ia (b/1838 Irel'd; d/III-2-1899) MD CPS Keokuk 1873; MD Rush 1877 ad eundem. *Tr Iowa St M S* 17:387, 1899. *Polk* 1896:517.

REYNOLDS, JOHN HENRY, CW-USA; Saratoga, NY (b/VIII-17-1828 Wilton; d/IV-3-1870) MD Albany 1851. *Tr M S St NY* 1872: 349-53; 1873: 182.

REYNOLDS, JOSEPH BROWN, CW-USA; Concord, Mass (b/I-28-1834 Rockport; d/VIII-8-1871 Griggsville or New Salem, Ill) MD Harvard 1862; AB Amherst 1855. *Harv in CW*: 274-75. *Bost m&s j* 8: 1871.

REYNOLDS, MARY J , Milwaukee (d/V-31-1888) MD Woman's Med Coll Pa 1861. *Tr Wis St M S* 1891: 357. *Polk* 1886: 955.

REYNOLDS, R BRUCE, Brooklyn (d/IV-7-1863 @28) MD ? *Med surg rep Phila* 10:32, 1863.

REYNOLDS, ROBERT C , CW-USA (d/IX-11-1862 Mound City, Ill) MD ? *Nat med jour* 1:301, 1870/71.

REYNOLDS, ROBERT TODD, Chicago (d/II-28-1897 @85) MD McGill 1836. *JAMA* 28: 523, 1897.

REYNOLDS, RUFUS C , Pittsford, NY (b/Columbia, NY; d/XII-22-1886) MD Fairfield 1830. *Tr NY St M S* 11:741 ff, 1894. *Butler* 1878: 570.

REYNOLDS, TABOR B , Saratoga Springs, NY (d/VII-3-1901 @81) MD Albany 1842. *Bost m & s jour* 145:52, 1901. *Tr M S St NY* 1902: [484]. *Polk* 1896: 1098.

REYNOLDS, THOMAS NOBLE, San Antonio (b/II-4-1843 Picton, Ont; d/II-14-1885) MD U Toronto 1870. *Med age* 3:91-92 1865 [?] *Med bull m&s* 7: 122, 1884.

REYNOLDS, WASHINGTON, Kittanning, Pa (d/XII-14 1872 @50) MD ? *Med surg rep Phila* 28:26, 104, 1873.

REYNOLDS, WILLIAM HENRY TOBEY, Albany, NY (b/IV-26-1846; d/XII-9-1894) MD CPSNY 1870; AB Union 1866; AM 1869. *Med reg NY NJ Conn* 1895: 238. *Polk* 1886: 629.

REYNOLDS, WILLIAM SNEAD, NYC (b/VII-3-1850 Charleston, SC; d/XII-1-1872) MD Bellevue 1872; MD U SC 1871; AB 1869. *Med reg NY NJ Conn* 1873: 347. *Med rec* 8:72, 1873.

RHEES, MORGAN JOHN, Mt Holly, NJ; Calif 1849-55? Hollidaysburg Pa 1869-; Newtonville, Mass 1873- ; Wheeling, WVa 1878- (b/VII-15-1824 Philadelphia; d/III-26-1899) MD Jefferson 1846. *Tr Am Inst Hom* 1899: 932-33. *King* I:245. Homeopath.

RHEINHART, HENRY H , Hope, NJ (d/XI- -1878) MD ? *Med rec* NY 15:565, 1879.

RHETT, BENJAMIN, Summerville, NC (b/III-23-1826 Charleston, SC; d/VI-9-1884) MD Med Coll SC 1848. *Hist M S DC:* 261. *Butler* 1874: 730.

RHETT, ROBERT BARNWELL Jr, Charleston, SC (b/1854 Huntsville, Ala; d/VIII-7-1901 @47) MD Med Coll SC 1879. *JAMA* 27:527, 1901. *Tr SC Med Assoc* 1901: 23. *Waring* II:289-90.

RHOADS, EDWARD, Philadelphia (b/IX-29-1841; d/I-15-1871) MD UPa 1863; AB Haverford 1859. *Med surg rep Phila* 24:90, 1871. *Tr CPP* cent vol:260; ns4: 403-411, 1863-74. *Phila med times* 1:164-65, 1871. *Proc Amer Philos Soc* 12:171-73, 1871-72.

RHOADS, EDWARD E , Reading, Pa (d/IX-13-1905 @ 31) MD ? *Pa med jour* 9: 27, 1905/06.

RHOADS, ELAM, ? Pa; CW-USA (d/X-18-1872 @31) MD UPa 1867; PhG Phila Coll Pharm. *U Pa med alum CW*: 1867.

RHOADS, JAMES E , Bryn Mawr, Pa (b/1828; d/I-2-1895) MD UPa 1851. *JAMA* 24: 67, 1895.

RHOADS, MICHAEL ALBERT, Reading, Pa (b/IV-18 1847 Colebrookdale, Pa; d/V-4-1901) MD Jefferson 1868. *Pa m j* 4:672, 1900/01. *Flint* 1897:833.

RHODES, D S , Rocky Point, NC (d/XI-6-1893) MD ? *NC med jour* 32:251, 1893.

RHODES, DUDLEY WOODBRIDGE, Zanesville, O (b/ Stonington, Conn; d/X-10-1815) MD ? *Western j m&s* 2:481-83, 1840.

RHODES, ROBERT H , Brooklyn (d/V-31-1890 @64) MD UCNY 1850. *Med reg NY NJ Conn* 1891:281. *Butler* 1878: 534.

RIBBLE, JAMES IRVINE BROWN, Trenton, NJ (b/XII 28-1830 Belvedere, NJ; d/I-9-1890) MD CPSNY 1853. *Tr M S NJ* 1890: 434 ff. *Butler* 1878: 475.

RIBBLE, WILLIAM R [or B] E Millstone, NJ (d/VI-10-1900 @75?) MD Berkshire 1849; att Lafayette 1851. *JAMA* 34:1645, 1900. *Polk* 1886: 603.

RICE [RICH], ALVIN BUTTON, Jamestown, NY (b/X-24-1841 Panama, NY; d/V-7-1903) MD Bellevue 1867; ng Amherst 1866. *Tr Am Inst Hom* 1904: 964-65. *Polk* 1886: 701. Homeopath.

RICE, CHARLES DARWIN, Woodstock, NB 1836-50; Eastport, Me 1850- (b/II-12-1810 New Salem, Mass; d/II-27-1853) MD Bowdoin 1836; AB 1831. *Bowdoin cat*: 1831.

RICE, CYRUS STRICKLER, Disco, Ill (d/XII-29-1899) MD U Mich 1876. *Tr Ill St M S* 1899-1900: 415, 463. *JAMA* 34: 187, 1900.

RICE, DAVID, Leverett, Mass (b/VII-25-1819 Rowe; d/VIII-29-1878) MD Berkshire 1842. *JAMA* 9:639, 1887. *Butler* 1878: 356.

RICE, DE WITT CLINTON, Marysville, Calif (b/1823; d/1870) MD New Orl Sch Med 1848; MD Albany 1848. *Tr AMA* 23: 574, 1872.

RICE, FRANK HORTON, Passaic, NJ (b/I-6-1831 Rowe, Mass; d/III-27-1905) MD Woodstock 1854. *Bost m&s j* 152:416, 1905. *Polk* 1886:609.

RICE, GEORGE, Troy, NY (b/Mechanicsville; d/I-12-1894) MD Albany 1872. *Tr NY St M S* 11:741 ff, 1894. *Polk* 1886: 712.

RICE, HYLAND WASHINGTON, Elgin, Ill 1870-71; Aurora, Ill (b/II-19-1847 Wilmington, Del; d/VII-23-1884) MD Hahnemann Phila 1870. *Calif homeopath*

 Spec. educ'l status abbrev. as: ***ng*** = college verified attendance without degree;

2:192, 1884? *Cleave.* Homeopath.

RICE, JAMES NELSON, Scranton, Pa (d/XII-9-1902 @ 58) MD Bellevue 1868. *Pa m j* 6:261, 1902/03. *Flint* 1897: 835.

RICE, JESSE WILSON, Wilbraham, Mass (b/1794? d/ III-2-1860 @66) MD ? *Bost m&s j* 62:152, 1860.

RICE, JOEL, Madison, Wis; Bridport, Vt; (b/VIII-15 1792; d/VIII-28-1860 Blooming Grove, Wis) MD Castleton 1822; AB Middlebury 1819; AM 1822. *Bost m&s j* 63:548, 1861. *Tr Wis St M S* 1891: 357.

RICE, JOHN McDOWELL, CW-USN (b/IX-19-1841 Phila; d/VI-15-1868 abd US Ossipee, Acapulco) MD UPa 1862; AB 1859. *Tr AMA* 21:495, 1870. *Phila med reg & dir* 1871: 293. *Bost m&s j* 2:48, 1868. *Med surg rep Phila* 19: 120, 1868.

RICE, JOSEPH MARCUS, Worcester, Mass (d/XI-11-1901 @74) MD Castleton 1853. *Bost m&s j* 145: 554, 724, 1901. *Polk* 1896: 728.

RICE, LEVI J , Hillsdale, Mich (d/VIII-31-1898 @ 94) MD ? *JAMA* 31:673, 1898. *Polk* 1886: 494.

RICE, OLIVER WASHINGTON, Patchogue NY (d/XI-12-1869) MD UMich 1854 *Phila m reg & dir* 1871: 302.

RICE, RICHARD C , Smithland, Ia (d/I-25-1898 @60) MD Buffalo 1865. *JAMA* 30:335, 1898. *Polk* 1886: 368.

RICE, THOMAS HARPER, Pottstown, Pa (d/III-14-1903 @25) MD UPa 1895. *Pa med jour* 7:280, 1903/04. *Flint* 1897: 832.

RICE, WILLIAM, CW-USA; Trenton, NJ (b/III-16-1836 Solebury Twp, Pa; d/II-13-1901) MD UPa 1860. *U Pa med alum CW*: 1860. *Polk* 1886: 612.

RICE, WILLIAM EDMUND, S Boston (d/VII-19-1865 St Augustine, Fla) MD Harvard 1861. *Bost m & s jour* 73: 68, 1865. *Med surg rep Phila* 13:150, 1865.

RICH, ARTHUR Jr, Baltimore (b/1815 Cambridge, Md; d/IV-25-1880) MD U Md 1836. *Med annals Md:* 548. *Butler* 1874: 315.

RICH, HOSEA, Bangor, Me; War 1812-USA (b/X-1-1780 Charlestown, Mass; d/I-30-1866) Hon MD Bowdoin 1851; stud w/preceptors. *Tr Me Med Assoc* 1866-68: 59-63. *K&B* II: 974.

RICH, JOSHUA BARTLETT, Worcester, Mass (d/II-25 1896 @51) MD Jefferson 1874; AB Yale 1870. *Bost m & s jour* 134: 252, 1896. *Polk* 1896: 728.

RICH, KENDALL EBEN, Wenona, Ill (b/VIII-24-1824 Warwick, Mass; d/IX-28-1890) MD Missouri Med Coll 1850. *Tr Ill St M S* 1891:28-30. *Butler* 1878:175.

RICH, THOMAS C , CW-USA; Williamsport, Pa (d/V-27-1903 @59) MD Jefferson 1878; MD Georgtn 1869 [as Rice]. *Pa m j* 7:280, 1903/04. *Polk* 1886: 283 (Phila).

RICHARD, VICTOR PETER, NYC (b/V-16-1825; d/X 3-1868) MD UMd 1850. *Phila m reg & dir* 1871:298. *Tr AMA* 21:436-7 1870. *Med reg NY NJ Conn* 1869: 246.

RICHARDS, CHARLES HENRY, Georgetown, Del (b/ XI-22-1827; d/I-10-1899) MD UPa 1851. *JAMA* 32: 263, 1899. *Polk* 1896: 291.

RICHARDS, DANIEL W , CW-USA; Pa (b/IV-20-1838 Williamstown; d/III-23 or 24-1902) MD Jefferson 1863. *Pa med jour* 5:407-08; 486, 1901/02; 6:110-11, 261, 1902/03. *Flint* 1897: 801.

RICHARDS, GEORGE WASHINGTON, NYC; Newark & Orange, NJ (b/XI-28-1829 Columbia, NJ; d/V-2-1893 @64) MD CPSNY 1853. *Med vis* 9:174, 1893. *King* I:244. *Cleave.* Homeopath.

RICHARDS, J WESLEY, NYC (d/VI-3-1906 @37) MD ? *Bost m & s jour* 154:692, 1906.

RICHARDS, JACOB, Hanover Mass (b/VI-24-1795; d/I 2-1864) MD ? ; AB Brown 1824. *Brown hist cat:* 1824.

RICHARDS, JAMES AUSTIN, New Haven, Conn (b/X-24-1827 Maui, Sandwich Isl; d/VI-4-1859) MD Yale 1858; ng Amherst 1851. *Amherst, Men of*: 1851.

RICHARDS, JAMES FORSYTH, Andover, Mass (d/V-13-1903 @70) MD CPSNY 1859. *Bost m&s j* 148:600, 1903. *Polk* 1896: 691.

RICHARDS, JOHN ALMOND, Farmington, Me (b/IX-26-1829 Strong; d/VIII-28-1897) MD Bowdoin 1854. *JAMA* 29: 555, 1897. *Polk* 1886: 425.

RICHARDS, JOHN C , Washington, DC (b/X-15-1815 Co Antrim, Irel'd; d/I-19-1862) MD U Md 1834. *Hist M S DC:* 248.

RICHARDS, JOHN CUSTIS, Chambersburg, Pa (b/VI-1 1812 Balto; d/VI-11-1874) MD U Md 1834. *Tr Pa St M S* 10: 638-41, 1875.

RICHARDS, JOSEPH B, NYC (b/Oneida Co; d/VI-4 1860) MD CPSNY 1859 *Med reg NY NJ Conn* 1862:153.

RICHARDS, LEWIS, New Canaan, Conn (b/VII-28-1797; d/III-29-1880) Hon MD Yale 1855; att lect NYC *Proc Conn M S* 1880:174-76. *Butler* 1878: 81.

RICHARDS, THOMAS LINCOLN, NYC (b/Ft Atkinson, Wis? d/X-1-1893 @29 NYC) MD CPSNY 1891. *JAMA* 21: 590, 1893.

RICHARDS, WALTER OSCAR, Waterloo & Black Hawk, Ia (b/XI-21-1820 Riga, NY; d/III-2-1898) ng U Mich Med Sch 50-51, 54-55. *JAMA* 30:682, 1898. *Tr Iowa St M S* 1898: 390-91. *Polk* 1890:428.

RICHARDSON, ABEL PARKER, Walpole, NH (b/II-19-1834 Lempster, NH; d/II-3-1900) MD Dartmouth 1865. *JAMA* 34:445-46, 1900. *Bost m&s j* 142:154 1900. *Tr NH M S* 1900:311-13. *Polk* 1896: 283 (Newtown, Conn) & 293.

RICHARDSON, BENJAMIN FRANKLIN, Cincinnati, O (d/XII-24-1890 @73) MD Starling 1848. *Bost m & s jour* 124:52, 1891. *Polk* 1886: 744.

RICHARDSON, BRATON, Brooklyn, Pa (b/X-9-1803 Attleborough, Mass; d/III-20-1864) MD Fairfield 1834. *Tr Pa St M S* 1865: 149-50.

RICHARDSON, DAVID DORRINGTON, Norristown, Pa (b/V-11-1832 Richmond, Va; d/III-6-1906) MD UPa 1871; MD Transylvania 1858. *Pa med jour* 9:523, 1905/06. *Atkinson* I:124.

RICHARDSON, EBENEZER COOLIDGE, Ware, Mass

(d/I-10-1886 @65) MD Harvard 1842. *Bost m & s jour* 114:48, 1886. *Butler* 1878: 356.

RICHARDSON, EDWARD TRASK, Brooklyn (d/VIII 14-1881 @67) MD CPSNY 1839; AB Brown 1835. *Tr Am Inst Hom* 1882: 133. *New Engl med gaz* 16:320, 1881. Homeopath.

RICHARDSON, ELLIOT, Philadelphia (b/XII-3-1842; d/V-9-1887) MD UPa 1867. *Tr CPP* cent vol: 260. *Med s rep Phila* 56:640 1887? *Tex cour-rec med* 4:436 1887.

RICHARDSON, GEORGE N , Richmond, Va (b/1828; d/XII-7-1873 Staten Isl, NYC) MD U Va 1850. *Med surg rep Phila* 30:22, 1874.

RICHARDSON, GEORGE T, CW-USA; Delphi, Ind (b/ IX-26 1834 Tippecanoe Co; d/X-6-1880) MD UCNY 1855. *Tr Ind St M S* 1881: 238. Kemper's *Indiana*: 333.

RICHARDSON, HAYNES L, NYC(d/IV-11-1893 @64) <MD Castleton 1861> *Med reg NY NJ Conn* 1893: 314.

RICHARDSON, HENRY AUGUSTUS, Cambridge, Mass; CW-USN (b/XI-25-1836; d/VII-1-1863) MD Harvard 1861; AM 1858. Palmer's *Necrol Harvard alum*: 507. *Harvard in CW*: 119.

RICHARDSON, HORACE, Boston (d/VI-18-1891 @ 61) MD Harvard 1855; AB 1852. *Bost m & s jour* 124: 646, 1891.

RICHARDSON, IDA E , Philadelphia (d/V-9-1902 @57) MD Woman's Med Coll Pa 1879. *Pa med jour* 5: 508, 1901/02; 6:261, 1902/03. *Flint* 1897: 824.

RICHARDSON, JOHN A , Ben Franklin, Tex (d/X-25 1905 Paris, Tex @45) MD Tulane 1884. *Tex st med jour* 1:220, 1905/06. *Polk* 1902: 1864.

RICHARDSON, JOHN EDWARD, Brooklyn (b/Albany; d/III-23-1902 @51) MD CPSNY 1877. *Bost m&s j* 146: 350, 1902. *Polk* 1896: 1002.

RICHARDSON, JOHN HENRY, Medfield, Mass (d/VII 22-1902 @74) MD UCNY 1854. *Bost m&s j* 147: 116, 1902.

RICHARDSON, JOSEPH GIBBONS, Philadelphia (b/I 10-1836; d/XI-13-1886) MD UPa 1862. *Tr CPP* cent vol: 260. *Med bull m&s* 8:397, 1886. *Atkinson* I: 594. *K&B* III: 1032. *Polk* 1886: 823.

RICHARDSON, NEHEMIAH, Vernon, Ind (d/XI-13 1899 @72) MD West Res 1853. *JAMA* 33: 1441, 1899.

RICHARDSON, NICHOLAS D, Nashville (b/XI-30-1832 Athens, Ala; d/I-3-1895) MD Jeff'n 1853. *Nashvl j m&s* 1:47-48 1895. *Atknsn* I:520. *Polk* 1890: 1059.

RICHARDSON, ROSS B , ? (d/VIII-6-1862 @45) MD Jefferson 1837. *Med surg rep Phila* ns8: 444, 1862.

RICHARDSON, SAMUEL, Watertown, Mass (b/1795; d/ 1879) ng Dartmouth Med Sch 1819. *Tr AMA* 33:593- 94, 1882. *Butler* 1878: 368.

RICHARDSON, THOMAS FARRAR, New Orleans; US PHS (b/New Orleans; d/III-19-1906) MD Tulane 1897. *New Orl m & s j* 58:779, 1900.

RICHARDSON, TOBIAS GIBSON, CW-CSA; New Orleans (b/I-3-1827; d/V-26-1892) MD U Louisville 1848. *Daniel's Tex med jour* 7:452-53, 1891/92. *JAMA* 18: 754, 1892. *New Orl m & s j* ns19:952 ff, 1892; ns20: 805, 1893. *K&B* III: 1034-35.

RICHARDSON, WENTWORTH RICKER, CW-USN (b/1829 Poland, Me; d/VII-20-1864 Key West, Fla) MD Dartmouth 1852. *Nat med jour* 1:301, 1870/71.

RICHARDSON, WILLIAM, Slatersville, RI 1813-17; Portsmouth 1817-38; Johnston 1838- (b/III-13-1788 Boston; d/IX-30-1864) MD Harvard 1813; AB Bowdoin 1809. *Bowdoin cat*: 1809.

RICHARDSON, WILLIAM HENRY, Mansfield, Conn (b/XII-5-1808; d/XII-14-1878) MD Yale 1834. *Proc Conn M S* 1879-80: 171-72. *Butler* 1878: 81.

RICHARDSON, WILLIAM HILLER H , Montpelier, Vt to 1867; Winona, Minn 1867- (b/1824 Orange, Vt or naturalized Vt 1856? d/VI-3-1874) MD Berkshire 1849. *Tr Minn St M S* 1902:307. *NW m & s j* 4:467, 1874. *Tr AMA* 27:650-51, 1876. *Tr Vt M S* 1883: 108.

RICHARDSON, WILLIAM PUTNAM, Salem, Mass to 1846; Kendall, Ill 1846- (b/VIII-15-1815 Salem; d/III-27-1857) MD Harvard 1837; AB 1834. Palmer's *Necrol Harv alum*: 148.

RICHEY, ROBERT THEODORE, Asbury, NJ (d/IX-14 1841 @24) MD UPa 1841; AB Princeton 1838; att Lafayette 1837. *Lafayette, Men of*: 142.

RICHMOND, JOHN M, CW-CSA; St Joseph, Mo (b/IX 17-1837 Fairfield Dist SC; d/VII-16-1900) MD UCNY 1860; AB UNC 1858. *UNC cat*: 523. *Polk* 1886: 560.

RICHMOND, JOHN WILKES, Providence, RI (b/IX-25 1775 Little Compton; d/III-4-1857 Phila) MD ? AB Brown 1794. *Bost m & s jour* 56:127, 1857.

RICHMOND, LEMUEL, Derby Line, Vt (b/VII-26-1804 Barnard; d/VIII-5-1874) MD Woodstock 1834. *Tr Vt M S* 1883: 108. *Med surg rep Phila* 31:180, 1874.

RICKARD, TRUMAN, Woburn, Mass (b/II-12-1814 Cornish, NH; d/1861) MD Dartmouth 1847; AB 1842. *Bost m & s jour* 65:47, 1862.

RICKER, CHARLES HENRY, Lowell, Mass (d/III-16 1898 @42) MD Dartmouth 1881. *Bost m & s jour* 138: 288, 1898. *Polk* 1886: 468.

RICKER, CLINTON JOSIAH, Chatham, Mass (d/III-15 1886 @39) MD CPSNY 1874. *Bost m&s j* 115:630 1886.

RICKER, RICHARD RUSSELL, Lewiston, Me (b/III-12-1825; d/IV?- -1902) MD Bowdoin 1847 *Bost m & s jour* 146: 450, 1902. *Polk* 1896: 637.

RICKERT, WILLIAM, Baltimore (b/1855; d/IX-22-1897) MD CPS Balto 1879. *JAMA* 29: 761, 1897. *Med annals Md:* 549. *Polk* 1886: 439.

RICKETTS, DAVID F , CW-USN (d/I-8-1866 @33 Balto) MD U Md 1859. *Med surg rep Phila* 14:60, 1866. *Nat med jour* 1:301, 1870/71.

RICKETTS, GIRARD R , Proctorville, O (b/1829 Va; d/ IX-20-1897) ng West Res 1853-54. *JAMA* 29:721, 926, 1897. *Polk* 1886: 766.

RICKEY, ROBERT N, Gray's Lake, Ill (d/IV-30-1906

 Spec. educ'l status abbrev. as: ***ng*** = college verified attendance without degree;

@55) MD Rush 1869 *Ill m j* 9:662 1906. *Polk* 1896 422.

RICORD, PHILIPPE, Paris, Fr (b/XII-23-1800 Balto; d/X-22-1889) MD Paris 1826; stud med Phila. *Med surg rep Phila* 61:504, 1889. *New Orl m&s j* ns17: 383, 1889. *Bost m&s j* 121: 424, 447, 1889. *K&B* III: 1037.

RIDDELL, JOHN LEONARD, New Orleans (b/II-20-1807 Leyden, Mass; d/X-7-1896) Hon MD Cincinnati M C 1836. *Med s rep Phila* 13:292, 1865. *New Orl m&s j* 19:284-7, 1866. *Tr AMA* 29:748-52, 1878. *K&B* III: 1037-38.

RIDDELL, WILLIAM PITT, CW-CSA; Houston (d/1872) MD U La 1856; AB Yale 1851. *Tr Tex St Med Assoc* 1874: 62-63.

RIDDICK, JOSEPH HENRY, Baltimore; CW-CSA (b/183_; d/1865 Balto) MD UPa 1859; att Haverford. *U Pa med alum CW*: 1859.

RIDDICK, REUBEN BRIGGS, ? (b/XII-24-1831 Gates Co, NC; d/VI-22-1867) MD UPa 1857; ng Haverford. *Haverford biogr cat*: 59.

RIDENOUR, ALBERTUS WARD, CW-USA; Massillon, O (b/IX-2 1843 Washington Co, Md; d/VI-26-1891) MD Med Coll Ohio 1868. *Med bull med & surg* 14:38, 1892. *Atkinson* I: 207-08. *Polk* 1886: 761.

RIDENOUR, W T, Toledo, O (d/VI-6-1894) MD Med Coll Ohio 1858. *JAMA* 23:86, 1894. *Polk* 1890: 937. *Butler* 1878: 647.

RIDER, WILLIAM C, Baltimore (d/V-31-1886) MD UPa 1842. *New Orl m&s j* ns14:77 1886. *Polk* 1886: 445.

RIDGE, JAMES MARSHALL, Camden, NJ (b/1826 Bucks Co, Pa; d/I-30-1903) MD UPa 1852. *Tr M S NJ* 1903:381-82. *Polk* 1890: 720.

RIDGWAY, CHARLES, Burlington & Jacksonville, NJ (b/VIII-21-1824 Sharpstown; d/ca 1873? Shamong) MD Jefferson 1845; att Lafayette. *Tr AMA* 24:360, 1873.

RIDINGS, E W, Dickson, Tenn (d/VII-8-1905) <MD Vanderbilt 1889> *Nashvl j m&s* 97:327, 1905.

RIDOUT, JOHN, Hagerstown, Md (d/I-28-1882 @89) MD UPa 1816; AB St Johns 1810. *Med annals Md:* 549.

RIEFFEL, AUGUST JOSEPH, NYC (b/XI-24-1802; d/III-10-1879) MD Leipzig 1828. *Med reg NY NJ Conn* 1879: 196. *Butler* 1878: 508.

RIEGEL, GEORGE, NYC (b/XII-19-1831; d/VI-23-1881) <MD Giessen 1856> *Med reg NY NJ Conn* 1882: 234. *Butler* 1878: 508.

RIEGEL, THOMAS F, Philadelphia (d/V-7-1902 @22) MD Jefferson 1901. *Pa m j* 6:261, 1902/03.

RIEHLE, CHARLES B, CW-USA (d/IX-14-1862 Washington, DC) MD ? *Nat med jour* 1:301, 1870/71.

RIEKER, GEORGE A, New Brunswick, NJ; CW-CSA; Panama (d/I-14-1879 Panama) MD Jefferson 1865. *Med rec* 15: 48, 1879.

RIFFE. JOHN M, Covington Ky (d/I-21-1899 @75) MD U Louisville 1847. *JAMA* 32:263, 1899. *Polk* 1886:394.

RIGBY, WILLIAM WASHINGTON, Spartanburg, SC (d/IX-4-1901 @30) MD Balto Med Coll 1892. *JAMA* 37:790, 1901.

RIGGS, BENJAMIN HOGAN, Selma, Ala; CW-CSA (b/VIII-19-1838; d/I-11-1888) MD UPa 1859. *Tr M Assn St Ala* 1888:32-33, 316. *U Pa med alum CW*: 1859. *Atkinson* I:122-123. *Polk* 1886: 139.

RIGGS, CLARENCE E, New Orleans (d/III-14-1894 @27) MD Tulane 1891. *JAMA* 22:482, 1894.

RIGGS, EDWARD ELDER, Pittsburgh (d/XI-2-1901 @37) MD Jefferson 1886. *Pa med jour* 5:296, 1901/02. *Flint* 1897: 830.

RIGGS, JETUR R, MexWar-USA; Drakeville, NJ (b/IV-20-1809; d/XI-5-1869) MD CPSNY 1836. *Tr M S NJ* 1870:96-97. *Tr AMA* 21: 468, 1870. *Phila med reg & dir* 1871:302.

RIGGS, LEANDER, Elizabeth, Pa (b/1846 Allegheny Co; d/V-3-1904 @58) MD Cleveland Med Coll 1870. *Pa med jour* 8:336, 1904/05. *Flint* 1897: 801.

RIGGS, LEWIS, Homer, NY (b/I-16-1789; d/XI-7-1870) Hon MD Reg St U NY 1849. *Med reg NY NJ Conn* 1871: 363.

RIGHTER, WASHINGTON, Philadelphia (d/VII-16 1902 @57) MD Jefferson 1866. *Pa m j* 6:261, 1902/03.

RIGHTMIRE [RIGHTMORE], WILLIAM VANDERVEER, Brooklyn (d/II-4-1900 @36) MD UCNY 1892. *Bost m&s j* 142:179, 1900. *JAMA* 34: 446, 1900. *Polk* 1896: 1074.

RIHL, JACOB L, Philadelphia (d/XI-13-1891 @70) MD Jefferson 1856 *Med bull m&s* 14:31 1892 *Polk* 1886:823.

RILEY, EDWARD W, Kansas City, Mo (d/I-27-1898 @47) MD Jefferson 1880. *JAMA* 30:391, 1898. *Polk* 1896: 849.

RILEY, HENRY AUGUSTUS, NYC (d/VI-9-1892) MD ? *Chic med rec* 3:512, 1892. Homeopath.

RILEY, JOHN CAMPBELL, CW-USA; Washington, DC (b/XII-15 1828 Georgetown; d/II-22-1879) MD Columbian 1851. *Hist M S DC:* 247. *Tr AMA* 30:833-34, 1879. *K&B* III: 1039-40.

RILEY, JOSHUA, Washington, DC (b/I-19-1800 Balto; d/II-11-1875) MD U Md 1824. *Chic med jour* 32:317, 1875. *Tr AMA* 26:453-54, 1875. *Hist M S DC:* 225. *Med rec* ?: 212- , 1875.

RILEY, THOMAS, Adams Mass (d/III-4-1901 @57)MD U Mich 1874 *Bost m&s j* 144:246 1901. *Polk* 1874:688.

RILEY, WILLIAM, Baltimore (b/II-17-1807; d/VIII-15 1887) MD UPa 1832. *Med ann Md:*550. *Polk* 1886:439.

RILEY [REILEY], WILLIAM F, Decatur, Ind (b/IV-21-1828; d/XI-21-1895) MD Med Coll Ohio 1858. *Tr Ind St M S* 1896:259-60. *Butler* 1878: 217.

RING, CHARLES AUGUSTUS, Portland, Me 1873- (b/II-6-1845; d/VII-8-1903) MD Bowdoin 1872; MD CPSNY 1873; AB Bowdoin 1868. *Tr Me Med Assoc* 15: 1904. *Polk* 1886:428. *K&B* I(2):324.

RING, FRANK WHITMAN, NYC (b/VIII-28-1848 Portland, Me; d/VII-17-1896 New Haven, Conn) MD Bowdoin 1878; AB 1869. *JAMA* 27:337, 1896. *Bost m &*

s jour 135:96, 1896. *Polk* 1896: 1074.

RING, HAMILTON, Urbana, O 1851–57, 1865–84; Port Gibson, Miss 1857–65 (b/1821 Balto; d/XI–12–1884) MD Hahnemann Phila 1851. *Med couns* 9:576, 1884/85. *King* I:180–181. Homeopath.

RING, WILLIAM, Buffalo (b/XI–17–1824 DeRuyter; d/IV–21–1887) MD Buffalo 1847. *Buff m&s j* 26: 480, 523–25, 1887. *Butler* 1878:538.

RINGER, ERNEST, NYC (b/Gny; d/I–29–1898) Lic NY Co M S 1874. *JAMA* 30:278, 1898. *Polk* 1886:691.

RINGGOLD, RICHARD SMITH, CW–CSA; Mayfield & Hickman, Ky; Grenada, Miss (b/I–26–1829 Md; d/IX–8–1878) MD ? *Tr AMA* 30:884: 1879. *Med rec NY* 14: 240, 1878.

RINGO, JAMES L , Elwood, Ind (b/XI–22–1866 Henry Co, Ind; d/V–28–1901) MD Louisville Med Coll 1891. *Tr Ind St M S* 1902: 422.

RIPLEY, JOHN HOWARD, NYC (b/V–16–1837 Conn; d/II–14–1896 Fla) MD UCNY 1866. *Bost m & s jour* 134:225, 1896. *Buffalo m & s j* 35:676–77 1896. *JAMA* 26:442, 462, 1896. *Polk* 1886: 691.

RIPPETOE, A H , Brenham, Tex (d/IV– –1881) MD ? *Tex med & surg rec* 2:80, 1882.

RISCH, ERNEST J , Brooklyn (b/Goslau, Gny; d/VI–17 1900 @77) <MD Braunschweig 1843> *JAMA* 34:1676, 1900. *Polk* 1896: 1002.

RISING, ARETUS, Suffield, Conn (b/XII–15–1801; d/III–27–1884) MD Berkshire 1826 *Pr Conn M S* ns3: 163–66, 1884. *Med surg rep Phil* 50:512, 1884. *Butler* 1878:81.

RISK, CLARENCE HENDERSON, Philadelphia (b/I–21–1849 Lewisburg; d/VII–3–1894) MD UPa 1877; att Lafayette. *Lafayette, Men of*: 193.

RISK, WILLIAM HENRY, CW–USA; Summit, NJ (b/II 25–1842 Muncy, Pa; d/II–7–1905) MD UPa 1866; att Lafayette 1864. *Bost m&s j* 152:206, 1905. *U Pa m alum CW*: 1886. *Polk* 1886: 611.

RISLEY, JAMES C , Camden, NJ 1844; Columbia, Pa 1849–56; Muscatine, Ia 1856–61; New Brighton, Pa 1861–64; Woodstown, NJ 1864– (b/VI–1817; d/XI–21–1866) MD Jefferson 1844; Lic M S NJ west distr 1838. *Tr M S NJ* 1867: 209–211. *Med s rep Phila* 16: 20, 1867.

RISLEY, STEPHEN GOODALE, Rockville, Conn (b/V 11–1820 E Windsor, Conn; d/VIII–2–1894) MD UCNY 1846. *Proc Conn M S* 1895:353–55.

RISTINE, HENRY, Cedar Rapids, Ia (b/IX–21 or 28 1818; d/V– –1893) MD Med Coll Ohio 1852. *JAMA* 21: 1010, 1893. *Tr Ia St M S* 14:330, 1896. *Butler* 1878: 244.

RITCHEY, JOHN A , Oil City, Pa (b/XI–28–1838 Wayne Twp; d/V–2–1906) MD Jefferson 1871. *Pa m j* 9: 759–60, 1905/06. *Flint* 1897: 812.

RITCHEY, P , CW–USA (d/III–13–1864) MD ? *Nat med jour* 1:301, 1870/71.

RITCHIE, ALBERT, Frederick, Md (d/1858) MD UPa 1826. *Med annals Md:* 550.

RITCHIE, JAMES, New Orleans (d/VII–31–1873) MD UPa 1841. *Med surg rep Phila* 29:108, 1873.

RITCHIE, JOSHUA A , Washington, DC (b/VII–1–1815 DC; d/XI–2–1887) MD Jefferson 1839. *Hist M S DC:* 230–31. *Polk* 1886: 214.

RITCHIE, LOUIS WARFIELD, USA 1869–87 (b/III–4 1843 or III–8–1845; d/IX–9–1901 Washington, DC) MD Georgetown 1863. *Hist M S DC:* 268. *Rec AAS USA* 1891: 82–83. *Polk* 1886: 214.

RITCHIE, ROBERT R , USA 1847–48; CW–CSA (b/IV–13–1816 Richmond, Va; d/1866, Lower Brandon, Va) MD UPa 1837. *U Pa med alum CW*: 1837.

RITCHIE, THOMAS HENDRY [HENRY], Philadelphia (b/III–20–1801; d/IX–16–1836) MD UPa 1822. *Tr CPP* cent vol: 261.

RITTENHOUSE, SAMUEL REINER, Reading, Pa 1868– (b/I–16–1832 Montg'y Co; d/VI–26–1895) MD UPa 1853. *Tr Am Inst Hom* 1896: 87. *Cleave.* Homeopath. *Polk* 1886: 832.

RITTER, CHARLES F E , NYC (d/VI–20–1889) <MD US Med Coll NY 1882> *Med s rep Phila* 61: 84, 1889. *Polk* 1886: 648.

RITTER, NEWTON H , Philadelphia (d/XII–16–1899 @50 Wernersville, Pa) MD Jefferson 1884. *JAMA* 34: 61, 1900. *Polk* 1886: 1316.

RITTER, WASHINGTON, Morrisania, NY (b/1803? d/VIII–30–1875 @72) MD ? *Med reg NY NJ Conn* 1876: 254. *Butler* 1874: 556.

RITZ, AMBROSE HENRY, Lewistown, Pa (d/XI–2–1861 @29) MD UPa 1856. *Med surg rep Phila* ns7:143, 1861/62.

RITZMANN, OTTO, Albany, NY (b/1857 Albany; d/VIII–19–1889 Lake Champlain, NY) MD Albany 1879. *Med surg rep Phila* 61:392, 1889. *Polk* 1886: 639.

RIVARD, PETER E , Rochester, NY (d/X–19–1898 @46) MD Buffalo 1883. *JAMA* 31:1066, 1898. *Polk* 1896: 1095.

RIVELY, MARTIN P , Philadelphia (d/III or IV–1 1891 Denver) MD Jefferson 1885. *Med bull m & s* 13:229, 1891. *Polk* 1886: 823.

RIVERS, HENRY WHEATON, RI; CW–USA (b/IX–21 1814 Providence; d/XII–3–1868) MD UPa 1839; att Harvard Med Sch 1838. *Phila m reg & dir* 1871: 299. *Bost m&s j* ns2: 320, 1868. *Tr RI M S* 1865–72: 327–29. *U Pa med alum CW*: 1839.

RIVERS, WILLIAM E, New Hope Ala (d/XII–18–1890) Lic Co Bd 1878. *Tr Med Assoc St Ala* 1891: 261.

RIVES, ALEXANDER Jr, Floreyville, Miss; CW–CSA (b/1838 Albemarle Co, Va; d/1875) MS UCNY 1861; att U Va 1857–58. *UCNY cat*: 1861.

RIVES, EDWARD, Cincinnati (d/IX–26–1883 @50) MD CPSNY 1857. *Med surg rep Phila* 49:448, 1883. *Butler* 1878: 592.

RIVES, GEORGE, CW–CSA; Snowden, Ala (b/VIII–26 1827 Coosada; d/II–15–1896) MD UPa 1852. *U Pa m*

 Spec. educ'l status abbrev. as: ***ng*** = college verified attendance without degree;

alum CW: 1852. *Polk* 1886: 139.

RIVES, GEORGE EDWARD, Rives Va (b/Pr Geo Co; d/ 1885?) MD Jefferson 1849.*Tr M S Va* 1885:285–86.

RIVES, JOHN G , Edgecombe Co, NC (b/VII–10–1818 Pitt Co; d/XII–16–1882) MD UCNY 1845. *NC m j* 11: 111, 1883.

RIVES, LANDON CABELL, Cincinnati, O (b/X–24–1790 Nelson Co, Va; d/VI–3–1870) MD UPa 1821; AB Wm & Mary. *Phila med reg & dir* 1871: 305. *Tr Ohio St M S* 1870:255; 1873:273. *Bost m & s jour* ns5: 504, 1870. *K&B* II: 984.

RIVES, SAMUEL HENRY, Liberty, Tex (b/VIII–18–1818; d/X–21–1872 Collirene, Ala) MD ? AB U Ala 1838; AM 1843. *U Ala cat*: 59.

RIVES, WILLIAM HENRY, CW–CSA (b/X–27–1816 Petersburg, Va; d/II–2–1864 Montgomery, Ala) MD UPa 1839. *U Pa med alum CW*: 1839.

RIVES, WRIGHT, Washington, DC (d/IV–2–1899 @ 24) <MD Columbian 189_> *JAMA* 32: 845, 1899.

RIVINUS, EDWARD FLORENS, Washington, DC (b/I–1–1802 Dueben, Saxony; d/II–14–1873 Hyeres, Fr) MD UPa 1830. *Hist M S DC:* 232.

RIX, LEVI, Royalton, Vt (d/IX–5–1876 @76) ng Dartmouth Med Sch 1826. *Med surg rep Phila* 27:332, 1872.

RIXEY, SAMUEL ROBERT, Culpeper Co, Va; CW–CSA (b/III– –1833; d/I– –1883) MD UPa 1854. *U Pa med alum CW*: 1854. Blanton's *Va surgs CW*: 414.

RIZER, MARTIN, CW–USA; Philadelphia (d/1876) MD Phila Coll M & S 1850. *Med s rep Phila* 35:120, 1876.

ROACH, BENJAMIN TYLER, Norwich, Conn (b/VI–11 1810; d/I–8–1881) ng Castleton 1833. *Proc Conn M S* 1881: 219.

ROACH, J E , Atlanta; Sipe Springs, Tex (d/IV–10–1893) <MD Med Coll Ga 1882> *Daniel's Tex med jour* 8:425, 1892–93. *Tex cour–rec med* 10:240–41, 1893. *Polk* 1890: 1093.

ROACH, J W , ? (d/IX–26–1878 Vicksburg, Miss) MD ? *Tr AMA* 30:884, 1879. *Med rec NY*:279, 1878.

ROACHE, JAMES ALOYSIUS, Brooklyn (b/V–15–1869 NYC; d/V–2–1903) MD LICH 1890; att St Francis Coll. *Bost m & s jour* 148: 544, 1903.

ROANE, JAMES, Nashville (b/V– –1790 Jefferson Co, Tenn; d/II–27–1833) MD CPSNY 1817. *Transylvania j m & assoc sci* 6:144–48, 1833. *Tr M S Tenn* 1876: 86.

ROANE, THOMAS WALTER, Covington, Tenn; CW–CSA (b/V–17–1830 Gloucester CH, Va; d/I–19–1896) MD UPa 1854; MD U Va 1853. *U Pa m alum CW*: 1854.

ROBB, ANDREW JAMES, Owosso, Mich (d/II–26–1895) MD Ecl Med Inst Cinc 1878. *JAMA* 24:370, 1895. *Polk* 1886: 501.

ROBB, WILLIAM H , Montgomery Co, NY (d/I–12–1898 @54 Selma, Ala) MD Albany 1865. *Bost m&s j* 138: 70, 1898. *Buff m&s j* 138: 543, 1898. *JAMA* 30:278, 1898. *Butler* 1878: 571.

ROBB, AUGUSTUS, Brooklyn (d/IX–13–1855) MD Harvard 1832. *Bost m & s jour* 53:215, 1856.

ROBBINS, CHANDLER, Boston (b/VIII–21–1796 Hallowell, Me; d/V–24–1836 Cheraw, SC) MD Harvard 1818; AB Bowdoin 1815. *Bowdoin cat*: 1815.

ROBBINS, EDWARD HUTCHINSON, Boston (d/I–1850 @58) MD Harvard 1815; AB 1812. *Tr AMA* 3: 462, 1851.

ROBBINS, EMILY RIDGEWAY, Philadelphia (d/VIII 31–1903 @71) MD Pa Med Univ 1859. *Pa m j* 7: 279, 1903/04. *Bost m&s j* 149:304, 1903. *Polk* 1896: 1316.

ROBBINS, EUGENE PATTERSON, Boston; CW–USN (d/VI–27–1863) MD Harvard 1863. *Harv in CW*: 282.

ROBBINS, GEORGE R , Hamilton Square, NJ (b/IX–24 1808 Monmouth Co, NJ; d/II–22–1875) MD Jefferson 1837. *Tr AMA* 28:622, 1877. *Tr M S NJ* 1876: 134. *US Congr biogr direct.*

ROBBINS, JAMES HENRY, Hingham, Mass (b/VII–22 1839 Corliss, Me; d/VIII–22–1900) MD Harvard 1867; AB Amherst 1862. *Bost m&s j* 143:224, 248, 1900. *Polk* 1890: 549.

ROBBINS, JAMES WATSON, Uxbridge, Mass (b/XI–18–1901 Colebrook, Conn; d/I–10–1879) MD Yale 1828; AB 1822. *Bost m&s j* 100:169–70, 1879. *K&B* III: 1040–41.

ROBBINS, WILLIAM EATON, Hamburg, NY (b/XII–7 1860 Iowa; d/XII–5–1899) MD Buffalo 1885. *Buff m & s j* 39: 458–59, 1900. *JAMA* 33: 1632, 1899.

ROBE, WILLIAM E, Maxwell, Cal (b/VI–30–1849 Chicago; d/IX–6–1888) MD M C Pacific 1878. *Tr Cal St M S* 1889:207. *Nat m j* 1:301, 1870/71. *Polk* 1886: 167.

ROBERSON, W C , Hardy, Tex (d/IX–16–1893) MD ? *Tex cour–rec med* 11:46, 1893.

ROBERT, JOHN COWENHOVEN, ?NYC (d/XI–12–1893) MD UCNY 1877. *Med reg NY NJ Conn* 1894:248.

ROBERT, JOSEPH THOMAS, Atlanta (b/XI–28–1807 Robertville, SC; d/III–5–1884) MD Med Coll SC 1831; AB Brown 1828; AM. *Brown hist cat*: 1828.

ROBERTS, ABEL COMMINS, CW–USA; Ft Madison, Iowa (d/VII–28–1901 @71) MD U Mich 1853. *JAMA* 37: 397, 1901. *Polk* 1886: 358.

ROBERTS, ALGERNON SYDNEY Jr. Philadelphia (b/ XII–19–1855; d/VIII–17–1896) MD UPa 1877. *Tr CPP* cent vol: 261. *JAMA* 27, 503, 1896. *Med bull m & s* 18: 352, 1896. *K&B* III: 1041–42.

ROBERTS, C S , Sulphur Springs, Ky (d/IX–29–1878) MD ? *Tr AMA* 30:884, 1879. *Med rec NY* 14: 279, 1878.

ROBERTS, D W , New Salem, Pa (b/1792? d/IV–3–1870 @78) MD ? *Phila med reg & dir* 1871: 304.

ROBERTS, DAVID, Boston (b/XI– –1826; d/VIII–15–1863 @36) MD Bowdoin 1854. *Bost m&s j* 69:68, 1863.

ROBERTS, E W , Harrisburg, Pa 1830?- (d/XI–10 1865) MD ? *Med s rep Phila* 13:358, 1865.

ROBERTS, FREDERICK ALBERT, Wilmington, Mass? (d/VIII–11–1906 @33) MD CPS Balto 1897. *Bost m & s j* 155: 298, 1906. *Polk* 1902:992.

ROBERTS, GEORGE, Baltimore (b/Easton, Md; d/VIII-2 1827) Hon MD U Md 1818. *Med annals Md:* 551.

ROBERTS, GEORGE C M , Baltimore (b/VI-29-1806; d/I-15-1870) MD U Md 1826; DD Newton U Balto. *Tr AMA* 21:475-76, 1870. *Med rec* 5:47, 1870-71. *Med ann Md:* 551.

ROBERTS, GEORGE M , Union Centre, Ill (d/VII-25 1896) MD Hosp Coll Med Louisville 1880. *JAMA* 27: 337, 1896. *Polk* 1886: 300.

ROBERTS, GRACE, Washington, DC (d/XI-1-1899) MD U Mich Homeop Med Dept 1878; MD Howard 1877. *Tr Am Inst Hom* 1900: 837. *Polk* 1886: 214. Homeopath. Black.

ROBERTS, HENRY CLINTON, Nashville (b/XII-31 1832; d/II-14-1894) MD U Tenn 1888. *So pract* 16: 128-29, 1894. *Nashvl j m & s* 75: 145-46, 1894. *JAMA* 22: 313, 1894.

ROBERTS, J E , Lone Star, Tex (d/V-23-1893) MD ? *Daniel's Tex m j* 8:322, 1892-93. *Polk* 1890: 1085.

ROBERTS, JACOB, CW-USA; Philadelphia (b/III-21-1839; d/VII-20-1890) MD UPa 1862. *Tr CPP* cent vol: 261. *Bost m&s j* 123:120, 1890. *U Pa m alum CW*: 1862.

ROBERTS, JEROME ELMER, CW-USA (d/II-19-1865) MD Harvard 1864. *Harvard in CW*: 289.

ROBERTS, JOHN LOUTHAIN, NYC (b/1831; d/I-3-1866) MD UCNY 1857. *Med surg rep Phila* 14:40 1866.

ROBERTS, JOHN MACKALL, Washington, DC (b/VI-11-1815; d/IX-11-1865) MD Jefferson 1836. *Tr AMA* 23: , 1872. *Hist M S DC:* 231.

ROBERTS, JOHN W , Clarksdale, Mo (d/IX-19-1897 @30) <MD St Joseph Med Coll 1889> *JAMA* 29: 709, 1897. *Polk* 1886: ? .

ROBERTS, MICHAEL, Lawrence, Mass (d/II-10-1884 @56) MD Harvard 1862. *Bost m&s j* 110: 240, 1884; 111:619, 1884.

ROBERTS, MILTON JOSIAH, NYC (b/1850 Ohio; d/IV-26-1893) MD UCNY 1878; att Cornell. *Med reg NY NJ Conn* 1893:14. *JAMA* 20:545, 1893. *Chic m rec* 5:61, 1893. *K&B* III: 1042.

ROBERTS, THOMAS A , Cecilton, Md (b/V-4-1804; d/VIII-8-1871) MD U Md 1825. *Med annals Md:* 551.

ROBERTS, THOMAS P , Johnstown, Pa (d/XI-6-1859 @27) MD ? *Med s rep Phila* ns3:195, 1859/60.

ROBERTS, WALTER CLARENCE, Maywood, Ill (d/VI-4-1898 @45) MD Rush 1881. *JAMA* 30:1481, 1898. *Polk* 1886: 950 (Albany, Wis).

ROBERTS, WILLIAM CURRIE, NYC (b/IX-9-1810 London, Engl; d/XII-9-1873) MD CPSNY 1832. *Med reg NY NJ Conn* 1874:284. *Med rec* 9:24, 46, 71, 1874. *Med s rep Phila* 30:22, 1874. *K&B* III: 1042.

ROBERTS, WILLIAM ELDER, Washington, DC (b/VIII-9-1839; d/IV-13-1892) MD Bellevue 1863. *Hist M S DC:* 270. *Polk* 1886: 214.

ROBERTSON, CHARLES, Bainsville, O 1824- ; Mc-Connellsville 1876- (b/VII-13-1799 Leesburg, Va; d/III-24-1884) MD Jefferson 1849. *JAMA* 2:474, 1884. *Atkinson* I: 412.

ROBERTSON, CHARLES ARCHIBALD, CW-USA; Albany, NY (b/X-15-1825 or 1829 Mobile, Ala; d/IV-1 1880) MD Jefferson 1853; AB Harvard 1850. *Harv in CW*: 47. *Tr M S St NY* 1881:372-76. *Med rec NY* 17:413, 1880. *Atkinson* I:268. *K&B* III:1043-44.

ROBERTSON, CHARLES GRAY, Clarkston, Mich (d/VII-18-1901 @70) MD Buffalo 1862; att U Mich Med Dept 1850-51. *JAMA* 37:342, 1901. *Polk* 1886:486.

ROBERTSON, ELISHA BRYANT, Copperopolis & Jackson, Cal (b/X-22-1826 Sumner Co, Tenn; d/X--1899 San Francisco) MD U Pacific 1864. *Tr M S St Cal* 1900:551. *Atkinson* I: 628.

ROBERTSON, FELIX RANDOLPH, Nashville (b/I-11 1781; d/VII-8 or 10 or 15-1865) MD UPa 1805. *Tr M S Tenn* 1876: 87. *Bost m&s j* 73: 27- 28, 1865. *Nashvl j m & s* ns1:210-14, 1866. *Buff m&s j* 5:232, 1866.

ROBERTSON, FLAVIUS JOSEPHUS, US 1847-48; CW-CSA (b/VI-28-1825 Nashville; d/II-13-1862) MD UPa 1846. *U Pa med alum CW*: 1846.

ROBERTSON, FRANCIS MARION, CW-CSA; Charleston, SC (b/1807 Abbeville Dist; d/VII-15-1892) MD Med Coll SC 1830. *Tr M S Va* 1891: 271; 1892:196-200. *Tr SC Med Assoc* 1893: 18-20, 62. *Waring* II:290-91.

ROBERTSON, HENRY DAVID, San Francisco (d/X-19 1899) MD U Pacific 1876. *JAMA* 33: 1183, 1899.

ROBERTSON, JAMES, Hanoverton, O (d/X-14-1868 @ 68) MD ? *Med surg rep Phila* 19:412, 1868.

ROBERTSON, JAMES B, Calvert Co Md (b/White Haven; d/1856 @53) MD U Md 1826. *Med annals Md:* 552.

ROBERTSON, JAMES CARSON, Council Bluffs, Ia (b/VI-6-1845 Dutch Creek; d/IX-16-1899) MD Iowa St U 1873; MD Bellevue 1883. *Tr Iowa St M S* 18:397 ff, 1900. *JAMA* 33:872, 1899. *Polk* 1896:516.

ROBERTSON, JAMES E , Sulphur Springs, Tex (d/II 12-1893) MD UPa 1845; att Washington & Lee. *Tex cour-rec med* 10:183, 1893. *Polk* 1886: 895.

ROBERTSON, JAMES M, Muscatine, Ia (d/1888) MD Jeff'n 1875 [?] *Tr Ia St M S* 18:411, 1900; 21:449, 1903.

ROBERTSON, THOMAS SETON [SEXTON], NYC (b/Glasgow; d/IX-7-1898 @45) MD UVt 1879 *Bost m &s j* 139:354, 1898. *JAMA* 31:672, 1898. *Polk* 1876: 1075.

ROBERTSON, WILLIAM HENRY, Farmville, Va; CW CSA (b/XI-11-1829 Amelia Co; d/VI-8-1873) MD U Pa 1851. *U Pa med alum CW*: 1851.

ROBERTSON, WILLIAM STEVENSON, Columbus City & Muscatine, Ia; CW-USA (b/VI-5-1831 Lancaster Co, Pa; d/I-20-1887) MD Jefferson 1856. *Tr Iowa St M S* 7:516-18, 1886-89. *Med s rep Phila* 56:224, 1887. *Atkinson* I: 94. *Polk* 1886: 364.

ROBESON, ROBERT R , Kyle's Landing, NC (d/IV-1886) MD UCNY 1858. *New Orl m&s j* ns13: 1007, 1886. *Polk* 1886: 723.

ROBEY, DANIEL L , Stewardson, Ill (d/I-20-1906 @

77) Lic by yrs pract. *Ill m j* 9:130, 227, 1906. *Polk* 1896: 441. Eclectic.

ROBINETT, GEORGE HERMAN, Philadelphia (d/IV-9-1872) MD UPa 1851. *Phila med reg & dir* 1873:304.

ROBINSON, ABRAHAM HAZEN, Concord, NH (b/1813; d/X-31 or XI-10-1898) MD Yale 1867; AB 1835. *Bost m&s j* 139:479, 1898. *JAMA* 31:1257, 1898. *Polk* 1896: 918.

ROBINSON, ALEXANDER CHARLES, Baltimore (b/1810; d/XI-9-1871) <MD U Md 1831> AB Yale 1829. *Tr AMA* 23:589-90, 1872. *Med annals Md:* 552.

ROBINSON, BENJAMIN WEST, Fayetteville, NC (b/III-31-1811; d/II- -1885) MD Jefferson 1835. *NC m j* 14:179-80, 1885. *Atkinson* I: 408. *Polk* 1886: 722.

ROBINSON, BENJAMIN WOOLDRIDGE, Marblehead, Mass (d/I-10-1863 S Danvers) MD Harvard 1862. *Bost m&s j* 67:510, 1862.

ROBINSON, CHARLES McLEAN, CW-USA; Elmer, NJ (b/XI-10-1836 Fairfield, Pa; d/VIII-29-1889 Millville) MD U Pa 1862. *U Pa med alum CW*: 1862.

ROBINSON, CHARLES THOMSON, NYC (d/IX-11-1899 @26) MD CPSNY 1895; AB. *JAMA* 33:807, 1899. *Bost m&s j* 141: 304, 1899.

ROBINSON, CHAUNCEY CLARK, Milwaukee (d/1897 @76) MD Geneva 1849. *JAMA* 29: 45, 1897. *Polk* 1886:957.

ROBINSON, CLEOPAS V , Petersburg, Va (b/VII-16 1850; d/XI-22-1899) MD Med Coll Va 1873. *Tr M S Va* 1900: 325. *JAMA* 33: 1441, 1899. *Polk* 1886: 924.

ROBINSON, ELIJAH, Charleston, Vt (d/1866 @56) ng Bowdoin Med 1833. *Bost m&s j* 74:248, 1866.

ROBINSON, GEORGE LAW, Baltimore (b/II-7-1844; d/IX-11-1873) MD U Md 1865. *Med annals Md:* 552. *Med surg rep Phila* 29:252, 1873.

ROBINSON, GEORGE TAYLOR, Camden, NJ (b/1861; d/VI- -1895) MD UPa 1882. *Med reg NY NJ Conn* 1895: 238. *Tr M S NJ* 1896:397-99. *JAMA* 25: 76, 1895.

ROBINSON, HORATIO, Stonington, Conn 12 yrs; Auburn, NY 1841- (b/II-4-1803 Lebanon; d/VII-28-1889) MD Berkshire 1825. *Tr Am Inst Hom* 1890: 132. *King* I:95-96. Homeopath.

ROBINSON, HORATIO Jr, Auburn, NY (b/VI-24-1830 Westerly, RI; d/IV-27-1891) MD Hom Hosp Coll Cleveland 1851; ng Castleton 1849-1850. *Tr Am Inst Hom* 1892: 220. *Med vis* 7: 192, 1891. *Polk* 1886: 641. Homeopath.

ROBINSON, J KING, CW-USA; Salt Lake City (d/by III-1886) MD Bellevue 1864. *Med s rep Phila* 18: 218, 1868.

ROBINSON, JAMES S , CW-CSA; Elizabethtown, NC (d/XI-9-1883 @45) MD Charleston 1861. *NC m j* 12: 310, 1883.

ROBINSON, JAMES W , Philadelphia (b/Irel'd; d/XII-13-1896 @51) MD Jefferson 1889. *JAMA* 28:140, 1897. *Polk* 1896: 1316.

ROBINSON, JESSE Jr, Hartwick NY; Vacaville Cal (d/V-4-1899) MD Woodstock 1847. *JAMA* 32:1133, 1899. *Polk* 1886: 168.

ROBINSON, JOHN, NYC 1839- (b/I-4-1809; d/XI-27 1879) <MD Dublin 1838> att Trinity Coll. *Med reg NY NJ Conn* 1880: 241. *Med rec NY* 16:503, 1879. *Butler* 1878: 509.

ROBINSON, JOHN A , CW-USA; Brooklyn (b/1837 Dublin; d/VI 12-1885) MD CPSNY 1862. *Med reg NY NJ Conn* 1886: 253.

ROBINSON, JOHN F , CW-USA (d/II-8-1864 Washington, DC) MD ? *Nat med jour* 1:301, 1870/71.

ROBINSON, JOHN LOMBARD, CW-USA; Manchester, NH (b/1835 Pembroke; d/VI-13-1890) MD Harvard 1859. *Bost m&s j* 134:632, 1896; 135:313, 1896. *Harvard in CW*: 255. *JAMA* 26: 1278, 1896. *Polk* 1890: 710.

ROBINSON, JOHN Q , W Newton, Pa (b/VII-22-1817; d/V-28-1900) MD UCNY 1849. *Pa med jour* 7:266, 1900/01. *JAMA* 34:891, 1900. *Flint* 1897: 839.

ROBINSON, JOHN WINTER, CW-USA; Richmond & Rockland, Me (b/XII-23-1824 Litchfield, Me; d/XII-10 1863) MD Bowdoin 1849. *Nat med jour* 1:301, 1870/71.

ROBINSON, JONATHAN HENRY, Southboro, Mass (b/1831 Surrey, NH; d/III-11-1904) MD Albany 1856. *Bost m&s j* 150:254, 1904. *Polk* 1886: 722.

ROBINSON, JOSEPH, Bethel, Md (d/VIII- -1873 @38) MD ? *Med surg rep Phila* 29: 306, 1873.

ROBINSON, JOSEPH W , CW-USA; Hornellsville, NY (b/Angelica; d/I-4-1887) MD Buffalo 1860. *Tr M S St NY* 11: 741 ff, 1894. *Polk* 1886: 664.

ROBINSON, JOSIAH WARREN, Providence, RI (b/XII 12-1807 Plainfield, Conn; d/II-7-1886) MD Yale 1829. *Tr RI M S* 3: 376, 1883-88. *Butler* 1878: 748.

ROBINSON, LUCIUS GAIN, Detroit (d/V-7 1858) MD Albany 1852. *Tr AMA* 13: 821, 1860. *Bost m&s j* 58:407, 1858. *Chic m j* 1:477, 1858. *Nashvl j m&s* 15:91 1858.

ROBINSON, LUKE, Colusa & San Francisco, Cal (b/VI-15-1842 St Joseph, Mo; d/X-10-1897) MD U Cal 1867; <MRCP(L) 1884> *JAMA* 29:816, 1897. *Polk* 1886:174.

ROBINSON, MARCUS TULLIUS, Jamaica Plain, Mass (d/III-13-1864 @50) MD Harvard 1860. *Bost m&s j* 70: 148, 1864.

ROBINSON, MATTHEW FULLERTON, Newville, Pa (b/IV-26-1820 Greencastle; d/I-7-1874) <MD Washington U Balto 1847> *Tr Pa St M S* 10:263- 64, 1874. *Tr AMA* 29:752, 1878.

ROBINSON, MORTON, Newark, NJ (d/1893 @69) <MD Metrop Med Coll NY 1854> *JAMA* 21:784, 1893. *Polk* 1890: 727.

ROBINSON, ORLANDO CHESTER, Huntingdon Valley, Pa (d/VIII-4-1904 @44) MD UPa 1881. *Pa med jour* 8:336, 1904/05. *Flint* 1897: 804.

ROBINSON, R C , Pittsburgh (d/V-15-1904 @67) <MD Jefferson 1860> *Pa med jour* 8:336, 1904/05.

ROBINSON, ROBERT EMMET, CW-CSA (b/XI-12-

1810 Farmville, Va; d/XII-10-1865 NY) MD UPa 1836. *U Pa med alum CW*: 1836.

ROBINSON, SAMUEL CURTIS, Brooklyn (b/IX-1830 Guilford, Conn; d/XII-20-1891) MD Yale 1855; AB 1852. *JAMA* 18:309-10 1892. *Bost m&s j* 125:692 1891.

ROBINSON, SAMUEL QUINCY, USA 1877-99 (b/I-29-1853 Boston; d/XI-6-1899 Hot Springs, Ark) MD Harvard 1876; AB Dartmouth 1872. *JAMA* 33:1308, 1899. *Polk* 1890: 789.

ROBINSON, THADDEUS PULASKI, Newton Mass (d/I 6-1874 @48) MD Harv'd 1860. *Bost m&s j* 90:76, 1874.

ROBINSON, WALTER R, Macomb, Ill (d/V-24-1896) MD NWU 1891. *JAMA* 26: 1144, 1896. *Polk* 1896: 428.

ROBINSON, WALTER SCOTT, Taunton, Mass (d/VI-3 1896 @57) MD Dartm 1864. *Bost m&s j* 134: 604, 1896.

ROBINSON, WILLIAM, CW-USA (d/V-22-1864) MD ? *Nat med jour* 1:301, 1870/71.

ROBINSON, WILLIAM, Chicago (d/X-10-1905) MD Buff 1862. *Ill m j* 8:530, 1905.

ROBINSON, WILLIAM CHAFFEE, Portland, Me (b/XI-27-1822 Chaplin, Conn; d/VI-30-1872) MD UCNY 1849. *Tr Me M Assn* 1871-73: 479-80. *NW m & s j* 3: 81, 1872. *K&B* III: 1046-47.

ROBINSON, WILLIAM FRANCIS, Chicago (b/Wis; d/V-12-1899 @36) MD Rush 1893. *JAMA* 32:1133, 1899. *Polk* 1896: 403.

ROBINSON, WILLIAM H, ? Tex (b/V-20-1820 SC; d/1886) MD Transylvania 1847. *Tex cour-rec med* 4:286, 1887.

ROBINSON, WILLIAM THOMPSON, Philadelphia CW-USA (b/1838 Boston; d/IV-15-1900) MD UPa 1859. *U Pa m alum CW*: 1859. *JAMA* 34:1145-46, 1900.

ROBINSON-MESSNER, AGNES B, Philadelphia (d/VI-5 or 6-1902) MD Woman's Med Coll Pa 1896. *Pa med jour* 5:547, 568, 1901/02; 6:261, 1902/03.

ROBISON, JAMES DICKEY, CW-USA; Wooster O (d/V-9-1895 @75) MD Jefferson 1843. *JAMA* 24:776, 1895. *Tr Ohio M S* 1897: 427-28. *Bost m&s j* 132:556, 1895. *Polk* 1890: 941.

ROBITAILLE, OLIVER, Quebec (b/XII- -1811; d/XI- -1896) MD Harvard 1838; MD Bowdoin 1838. *Bost m & s jour* 137:263, 1897.

ROBSON, BENJAMIN R, NYC (b/1783 or 1785? d/VIII-18-1878) MD ? *Med reg NY NJ Conn* 1879: 197. *Bost m&s j* 99:320, 1878. *Med rec NY* 14: 160, 1878.

ROBY, JAMES WILLIAM EDWARD, Brooklyn (d/VI 25-1901 @38) MD UCNY 1887. *Bost m&s j* 145: 28, 1901. *Polk* 1896: 1002.

ROBY, JOSEPH, Boston; Brunswick, Me; Hanover, NH; Baltimore (b/VIII-25-1807 Boston; d/VI-3-1860) MD Harvard 1831; AB Brown 1828. *Bost m & s jour* 62:392, 1860. *Med annals Md:* 553. *K&B* III: 1047.

ROCHE, MANNING B, New Bedford, Mass 1841- (b/1790 Wilmington, Del; d/VII-3-1862 Riverside, NJ) <MD Homeop Acad Allentown 1835> att Princeton. *Tr Am Inst Hom* 1870: 656. *King* I:228-29.

ROCHESTER, THOMAS FORTESCUE, CW-USA; Buffalo (b/X-8-1823; d/V-24-1887) MD UPa 1848; AB Hobart 1845. *Med reg NY NJ Conn* 1888:269. *Buff m & s j* 26:517-23, 1887. *Tr M S St NY* 1888: 572-76. *K&B* III: 1047.

ROCKWELL, ALMON FERDINAND, ? (d/1903) MD Hahnemann Phila 1858; AB Williams 1856. *Williams grads*: 1856. Homeopath?

ROCKWELL, FRANCIS WARREN, Brooklyn (b/XII-22-1843; d/IV-30-1889) MD CPSNY 1868; AB Amherst 1865; AM 1868. *Med reg NY NJ Conn* 1889: 283. *Bost m & s jour* 120:476,1889. *Butler* 1878: 534.

ROCKWELL, SIDNEY WILLIAMS, S Windsor, Conn (b/VI-4-1818; d/V-17-1890) Hon MD Yale 1855. *Med reg NY NJ Conn* 1892:286. *Proc Conn M S* 1891: 307-08. *Butler* 1878: 81.

ROCKWELL, WILLIAM, NYC (b/VII- -1800; d/XII-30-1868 Long Branch, NJ) MD Reg NY St U 1858; lic c1822; att Yale. *Tr M S St NY* 1869:256-59. *Tr AMA* 19:432, 1868. *Med surg rep Phila* 18:44, 1868.

ROCKWELL, WILLIAM HAYDEN, Brattleboro, Vt (b/II-15-1800 Conn; d/XI-30-1873) MD Yale 1831; AB 1824; AM Trinity 1829. *Bost m&s j* ns12: 653, 1873. *Tr Vt M S* 1883:108. *Med s rep Phila* 29:468, 1873; 30:22, 1874. *K&B* I(2): 328.

RODENSTEIN, CHARLES FREDERICK, CW-CSA; Fordham & Tremont, NY (b/XI-16-1826 Frankfort-am-Main; d/III-18-1876) MD CPSNY 1867; AB Somerville Coll, Ala; AM. *Med reg NY NJ Conn* 1876: 254. *Med rec med & surg* 11:229, 1876.

RODES, JOSEPH, Philadelphia 1887-89; San Diego 1891- (b/X-15-1863 Phila; d/XII-20-1896 La Jolla) MD Hahnemann, Phila 1887.*Tr Am Inst Hom* 1897: 64.

RODGERS, JOHN KEARNY, NYC (b/1793; d/XI-9-1851) MD CPSNY 1816; AB Princeton 1811. *So m&s j* 8: 67, 1852. *NW m & s j* 4:380, 1852. *NH jour med* 2:167, 1852. *K&B* III: 1047-48.

RODGERS, JOHN RICHARDSON BAYARD, RevWar USA; NYC (b/1757; d/I-29-1833) MB UPa 1784; MD Edinburgh; AB Princeton 1775. *Tr CPP* cent vol: 261.

RODGERS, ROBERT, Springfield, O (b/IX-26-1807 Cumberland Co, Pa; d/II-4-1880) MD UPa 1828. *Tr O St M S* 1880: 121-122. *Atkinson* I: 605.

RODGERS, SAMUEL SAFFIELD, CW-USA; Millsboro Pa (b/VI-23-1822 Brownsville; d/II-28-1902) MD UPa 1849. *U Pa med alum CW*: 1849. *Polk* 1886: 808.

RODGERS, WILLIAM OLIVER, Omaha, Nebr (d/III-10-1898) MD Buffalo 1883. *Buff m&s j* 37:699, 1898. *JAMA* 30:682, 1898. *Tex m j* 13: 530, 1897-98. *Polk* 1896: 908.

RODMAN, HUGH, Frankfort, Ky (b/VI-4-1818 Newcastle; d/II-5-1871) MD U Louisville 1842. *Tr AMA* 23: 586-87, 1872. *Tr Ky St M S* 1873:163-65.

RODMAN, LEWIS, Bustleton & Philadelphia (b/VI-12

Spec. educ'l status abbrev. as: ***ng*** = college verified attendance without degree;

1806 Bucks Co; d/VI-20-1890) MD UPa 1827. *Tr CPP* cent vol:261-62; 3s14:143 ff, 1892. *Polk* 1886:824.

RODMAN, THOMAS, Newport, RI 1680- (b/1647? d/ 1727 @80) MD ? *Tr RI M S* 1:5, 1859-77.

RODMAN, WILLIAM WOODBRIDGE, New Haven, Conn (b/IV-1-1817 Stonington; d/III-30-1900) MD Jefferson 1844; AB Yale 1838; AM 1841. *JAMA* 34: 891, 1900. *Tr Am Inst Hom* 1900:837-38. *King* I:206. *Polk* 1896: 282. Homeopath.

RODOLPH, SAMUEL F , San Francisco (d/X-9-1895) <MD U Würzburg> *JAMA* 25:726,1895. *Polk* 1896: 224.

ROE, JOSEPH BISPHAM, CW-USA; Woodbury NJ (b/ II-26-1836 Haddonfield; d/II-5-1904) MD UPa 1861; AB Princeton 1858. *Bost m&s j* 150:168, 1904. *UPa m alum CW*: 1861.

ROE, URIAH C , Franklin Grove, Ill (d/VII-3-1900) <MD Physio-Med Inst Cinc 1866> *Ill m j* ns2: 141 1900.

ROE, WILLIAM J , Vienna, NJ (b/XII-28-1821 Morris Co, NJ; d/II-11-1899) MD Pa Coll Med 1847. *Tr M S NJ* 1899: 291. *Polk* 1886: 602.

ROEDER, AUGUSTUS, Omaha (b/1824 Schweinfurt, Bavaria; d/1869) <MD Humboldt Med Inst St Louis> *Tr AMA* 24: 348-49, 1873.

ROESSLER, ANATOL, Newark, NJ (b/NYC 1862; d/ XII-30-1886) MD Bellevue 1885. *Med reg NY NJ Conn* 1887: 275.

ROETH, ADOLPHE GASTON, Boston (b/X- -1850; d/ XII-10-1896) <MD Univ Coll London 1878> *Bost m & s jour* 135:636, 1896. *Polk* 1890: 542.

ROGERS, ALBERT S , Pavilion, NY (d/VI-30 or VII-10-1897 @55) MD CPSNY 1867. *JAMA* 29: 92, 200, 1897. *Polk* 1896: 1089.

ROGERS, ALEXANDER, Hopkinton, NH (b/II-13-1814 Exeter; d/X-4-1886) MD Dartmouth 1861. *Tr NH M S* 1887: 173-74. *Butler* 1878: 457.

ROGERS, ALEXANDER W , Paterson, NJ (b/1814 Ireland; d/V-14-1905) MD CPSNY 1836. *Bost m&s j* 152: 620, 1905. *Polk* 1886: 947.

ROGERS, BENJAMIN, Hartford, Conn (b/IV-5-1779 Norwich; d/X-17-1859) Hon MD Yale 1845. *Pr Conn M S* 1860: 53-55.

ROGERS, CHARLES HENRY, Plainfield, Conn (b/II-6 1818 Pomfret; d/V-23-1897) MD Yale 1847. *Proc Conn M S* 1898: 343-45. *Polk* 1896: 277.

ROGERS, DAVID L , NYC; CW-USA (b/VI-7-1799 Mamaroneck, NJ; d/XI-10-1877) MD CPSNY 1822. *Med reg NY NJ Conn* 1878: 187-89. *K&B* III: 27 (mention only).

ROGERS, GUSTAVUS A, Chicago; Bath NY (d/XII-26 1872 @75) MD ? *Med surg rep Phila* 27: 524, 1872.

ROGERS, HENRY RAYMOND, Dunkirk, NY (b/V-15-1822 Winslow Me; d/X-19-1901) MD Jefferson 1851; ng Bowdoin Med 1851. *Bowdoin cat*: 1851. *Polk* 1886:659.

ROGERS, JACOB DRAKE, NYC (b/IX-30-1842; d/IV-8-1875) MD UCNY 1870. *Med reg NY NJ Conn* 1875: 203.

ROGERS, JAMES BLYTHE, Philadelphia (b/II-11-1802; d/VI-15-1852) MD U Md 1822; att Wm & Mary. *Med annals Md:* 533. *K&B* III: 1050.

ROGERS, JAMES HENRY, CW-USA; Sag Harbor, NY (d/1901) MD Jefferson 1855; AB Williams 1852. *Williams grads*: 1852. *Polk* 1886: 706.

ROGERS [RODGERS], JOEL J , Huntsville, Pa (b/Wilkes Barre; d/III-23-1902 @84) Stud U City NY Med Dept 1842-43; lic yrs pract. *Pa m j* 6:261, 1902/03. *Tr Luzerne Co* [Pa] *M S* 1902: 151 ff. *Flint* 1897: 805.

ROGERS, JOHN ALEXANDER, Paterson, NJ (b/I-7-1852; d/XII-30-1883) MD CPSNY 1875; BS UCNY 1872. *Med s rep Phila* 50:64, 1884. *Tr M S NJ* 1884: 165-66. *Butler* 1878: 479.

ROGERS, JOHN CAVE, Memphis (d/VIII-25-1878) MD UPa 1843; att Wake Forest. *Tr AMA* 30:884, 1879. *Med rec NY* 14:220, 1878.

ROGERS, LEMUEL H, Bloomington Ill (d/VI-3-1901) MD Rush 1863 *Ill med jour* ns3:91,1901. *Polk* 1890:338.

ROGERS, LEWIS, Louisville (b/X-22-1812 Lexington; d/VI-13/17-1875) MD UPa 1836; AB Transylv 1831; AB Georgtn 1831. *Tr Ky St M S* 1876:34. *K&B* III: 1052.

ROGERS, LYMAN, Bennington Vt (b/XI-10-1832 Tinsmouth; d/I-22-1900) MD U Vt 1858. *JAMA* 34: 312, 1900. *Polk* 1896: 1472.

ROGERS, MOSES, Falmouth, Mass (b/IX-26-1817; d/1862) MD Jefferson 1846; att Bowdoin 1839-42. *Bowdoin cat*: 1843.

ROGERS, PATRICK KERR, Philadelphia; Baltimore; Williamsburg, Va 1819- (b/1776 Irel'd; d/VIII-1-1828) MD UPa 1802. *Med annals Md:* 554. *K&B* III:1052-53.

ROGERS, PENNOCK BROWNING, NYC (II-11-1906) Student @ Manhattan Eye, Ear, Nose & Throat Hosp, NYC at death. *Boston m & s jour* 154:230, 1906.

ROGERS, ROBERT EMPIE, CW-USA; Philadelphia (b/III-29-1813 Balto; d/IX-6-1884) MD UPa 1836; LLD Dickinson 1883. *Tr CPP* cent vol: 262. *Coll & clin rec* (Jefferson) 6:203-10, 1885. *Proc Amer Philos Soc* 23: , 1885. *Atkinson* I: 705. *K&B* III:1053-54.

ROGERS, S H , Abilene, Tex (d/I-6-1892) MD ? *Tex cour-rec med* 9:136, 1892.

ROGERS, SETH, Pomfret, Conn (b/II-13-1823 Danby, Vt; d/VIII-6-1893) MD Castleton 1849. *JAMA* 21:498, 1893. *Bost m & s jour* 129: 206-07, 1893.

ROGERS, SHEPHERD ASHE, Memphis (d/I?- -1898) MD Memphis Hosp Coll 1884. *JAMA* 30:335, 1898. *Polk* 1886: 869.

ROGERS, STEPHEN, Chile (b/I- -1826 Tyre, NY; d/V 23-1878 Valparaiso) Hon MD NY Med Coll 1857; Hon MD Starling 1859. *Med reg NY NJ Conn* 1879: 198. *K&B* III: 1054-55.

ROGERS, THOMAS COOPER, Willow Grove, Del (b/1827; d/X-16-1878 Harrington) MD UPa 1855. *Tr AMA* 33: 594-96, 1882.

ROGERS, WILBUR J , Sparta, Ga (d/V-14-1884) MD ? *Med surg rep Phila* 50:704, 1884.

ROGERS, WILLIAM, NYC (d/1883?) MD UCNY 1876. *Med reg NY NJ Conn* 1883: 235.

ROGERS, WILLIAM E , Memphis (d/V-21-1885 @58) MD Jefferson 1848. *Med bull med & surg* 7:256, 1885. *Med surg rep Phila* 52:736, 1888. *Polk* 1886: 869.

ROGERS, WILLIAM N , Waco, Tex (d/V-1-1900) MD Louisville Med Coll 1877. *JAMA* 34:1211, 1900.

ROGERS, WILLIAM S , Galveston (d/1887?) MD New Orl Med Sch 1858. *Tex cour-rec med* 4:488, 1887. *Daniel's Tex jour med* 2:508-09, 1887. *Polk* 1886: 886.

ROHÉ, GEORGE HENRY, Baltimore (b/I-26-1851; d/II-6-1899 New Orleans) MD U Md 1873. *New Orl m&s j* 51:527, 1899. *Buffalo m&s j* 38: 624 ff, 1899. *Med annals Md:* 554. *JAMA* 32: 385, 1899. *K&B* III: 1055.

ROHRER, JOHN S , Philadelphia (d/VIII-29-1863) MD Jefferson 1831. *Med surg rep Phila* 10:264, 1863.

ROJAS, MARCO AURELIO, San Fernando de Apure, Venez to 1856; Cuba 1859-65; NYC 1865- (b/1833 Caracas; d/VI-17-1866) <MD U Caracas> stud Europe 1856-59. *Med reg NY NJ Conn* 1867: 224.

ROLAND, WILLIAM SEEGER, CW-USA; York, Pa (b/XI-16-1814 New Holland; d/I-23-1897) MD UPa 1835. *JAMA* 28:328, 1897. *Polk* 1896: 1346.

ROLANDO, HENRY, Baltimore (b/1861; d/X-4-1888) MD U Md 1883.*Med annals Md:*544-55. *Polk* 1886:439.

ROLERFORT, GEORGE W , Newark, NJ (b/Va; d/ 1903 @43) MD Shaw U 1889. *Bost m & s jour* 149: 194, 1903. *Polk* 1896: 943. Black.

ROLLER, WILLIAM CALVIN, CW-USA; Hollidaysburg, Pa (b/III-6-1838 Williamsburg; d/III-11-1897 @59) MD Jefferson 1861; AB Lafayette 1857. *JAMA* 28: 620, 1897. *Polk* 1896: 1283.

ROMIG, JOHN, Allentown, Pa (b/I-3-1804; d/II- -1885) MD UPa 1825. *Hahn mo* 20:192, 1884/85. Homeopath.

ROMIG, WILLIAM HENRY, Allentown, Pa (b/VIII-22 1846; d/XII-10-1884) MD UPa 1867; MD Hahnemann, Phila 1871. *Hahn mo* 20: 126, 1884/85. Homeopath.

RONAYNE, DAVID PATRICK, Boston (d/IV-1-1899 @33) MD Harvard 1895; AB Holy Cross 1889. *Bost m & s jour* 140:344, 1899. *Polk* 1896: 704.

ROOF, CHARLES BULKLEY, NYC? (d/XII-19-1881 @34 Brewsters, NY) MD CPSNY 1875. *Med reg NY NJ Conn* 1882: 234. *Butler* 1878: 523.

ROOF, STEPHEN WHITE, CW-USA; NYC (b/Somerstown, NY; d/I-10-1895) MD CPSNY 1864. *Med reg NY NJ Conn* 1895: 238. *JAMA* 24: 101, 136, 1895. *Bost m & s jour* 132: 70, 1895. *Butler* 1878: 523.

ROOKE, THOMAS CHARLES BYOE, Kailua, Hawaii (d/XI-28-1858 @52) <FRCS (?)> *Bost m & s jour* 60: 68, 1859.

ROOME, EDWARD, Washington, DC (d/XI-27-1891) MD Columbian 1888; MD Hahnemann Phila 1889. *Med vis* 8:15, 1892. Homeopath.

ROONEY, JOSEPH GEORGE, Hoboken, NJ (d/II-4-1904) MD UCNY 1891. *Bost m & s jour* 150:168, 1904.

ROONEY, MICHAEL, Quincy, Ill (b/I-31-1837 NYC; d/IX-10-1897) MD Miami 1866; MD LICH 1874. *Tr Ill St M S* 1899:27-29. *JAMA* 29:660, 1028, 1897. *Polk* 1890: 437.

ROOSEVELT, JAMES WEST, NYC (b/VII- -1858; d/IV-10-1896) MD CPSNY 1880. *Bost m & s jour* 134:402, 1896. *Buffalo m & s j* 35:827-28, 1896. *Polk* 1886: 692.

ROOT, A M , ?Mobile, Ala (d/VI-26-1860 Phila) Med stud UPa @ death. *Med surg rep Phila* ns4: 288, 1860.

ROOT, DAN S , Chicago (d/IV?- -1882) MD Rush 1867. *Chic med jour* 44:447, 1882. *Bost m & s jour* 106:378, 1882. *Butler* 1878: 136.

ROOT, FRANKLIN WILLOUGHBY, Kent, O (d/II-26 1898 Cleveland) MD U Mich 1871. *JAMA* 30: 625, 1898. *Polk* 1886: 763.

ROOT, LOUIS FELLOWS, Tarrytown, NY (b/II-19-1859 Chatham; d/IX-3-1897) MD CPSNY 1882. *JAMA* 29: 555, 1897.

ROOT, MARTIN Jr, Byfield, Mass (b/VII-8-1802 Montague; d/X-28-1880) MD Castleton 1825. *JAMA* 9: 830-31, 1887. *Bost m&s j* 105: 449-50, 1881. *Butler* 1878: 356.

ROOT, MARTIN NELSON, Charleston, NH (b/XII-14-1829 S Byfield, Mass; d/VII-28-1895) MD Harvard 1853; AB Amherst 1849. *Amherst, Men of*: 1849.

ROOT, OLIVER DEAN, CW-USN (d/X-30-1863 New Orleans) MD Harvard 1854. *Med surg rep Phila* 10:426, 1863. *Bost m&s j* 114: 212, 1886. *Harvard in CW*: 243. *Nat med jour* 1:301, 1870/71.

ROOT, RUFUS W, Fond du Lac Wis (d/I-31-1856 @28) MD U Buffalo 1848. *Buff m & s j* 11:703, 1856.

ROOT, FRANCIS CODMAN, CW-USA; Boston (d/IX-15-1869 @31) MD Harvard 1860; AB 1857. LRCP (E); LRCS(E); FRCS(E). *Bost m&s j* 4:140, 144, 321-22, 1869. *Harvard in CW*: 105.

ROS, LEONCIO, NYC (b/Cuba; d/IV-30-1897) MD CPSNY 1895. *JAMA* 28: 907, 1897.

ROSA, ARTHUR J , CW-USA (d/II-20-1864) MD Med Coll Ohio 1862. *Nat med jour* 1:301, 1870/71.

ROSA, LEMUEL KEMBLE, Painesville, O (d/II-9-1853) MD Eclectic Med Inst Cinc 1849. *Tr Am Inst Hom* 1854: 73. Homeopath.

ROSA, STORM, Painesville, O (b/1794? Coxsackie, NY; d/V-3-1864 @73) MD ? 1816. *Am hom rev* 5:142, 1865? *Med invest* 3:88, 1867? *Tr Am Inst Hom* 1870: 656. Homeopath.

ROSE, DANIEL, Thomaston, Me (b/IV- 1813 Boothbay, Me; d/III-21-1871) MD Bowdoin 1837. *Tr Me Med Assoc* 1871-73: 349-51.

ROSE, EDWARD P , Salt Lake City; Aspen, Colo; (d/XI 6-1895 @40) MD Med Coll St SC 1878. *Tr Colo St M S*

1898–99: 509. *Polk* 1893: 230.

ROSE, GEORGE S , CW–USA (b/1838 Kingston, Ont; d/1876) MD Queen's Coll, Kingston 1860; AB. *Tr AMA* 28:640, 1877.

ROSE, JOSEPH GREEN, CW–CSA; Smithfield, NC (b/VIII–30–1860 Bentonville, NC; d/XI–18–1887) MD UPa 1859. MD UPa 1859. *U Pa med alum CW*: 1859.

ROSE, MADISON H , Thorntown, Ind (b/XII–2–183; d/XII–16–1904) MD Buffalo 1861. *Tr Ind St M S* 1905: 456. *Polk* 1896: 494.

ROSE, WILLIAM M , Columbia, Ill (b/Gny; d/VII–26 1896) MD CPS Keokuk 1878. *JAMA* 27:337, 1896. *Polk* 1886: 274.

ROSEBERRY, CHARLES IHRIE, CW–USA; Easton, Pa (b/VIII–31–1831 Phillipsburg, NJ; d/IX–11–1905) MD UPa 1860; MD NY Homeop 1861. *Pa m j* 9: 27, 1905/06. *Ill m j* 8:430, 1905. *U Pa m alum CW*: 1860. *Flint* 1897: 801.

ROSEBERRY, JAMES A , Forrest, Ill (d/III–24–1901) MD Med Coll Ohio 1882. *Ill med jour* ns3:47, 1901. *Polk* 1886: 751 [Columbus, O] & 753 [Dayton, O].

ROSECRANCE, JAMES E , New Milford, Ill (d/IV–6 1901) Lic by yrs pract. *Ill med jour* ns2:601, 1901. *Polk* 1896: 432. Eclectic.

ROSENBERG, EMIL, NYC (b/Gny; d/XI–4–1903 @74) <MD Berlin 1855> *Bost m&s j* 149:558, 1903. *Polk* 1896: 1075.

ROSENBERGER, PRESLEY A , Petersburg, Ill (d/IV–8 1905 @80 El Remo, Okla) MD St Louis Med Coll 1859. *Ill med jour* 7:524, 1905. *Polk* 1896: 435.

ROSENBERGER, SIMON, Pasadena, Calif (d/XII–4–1899 @68) MD Pa Med Coll 1861. *JAMA* 33: 1632, 1899. *Polk* 1886: 824 (Phila). Eclectic.

ROSENFELD, ALBERT, Cincinnati (d/I–8–1897) <MD U Vienna 1848> *Tr Ohio M S* 1897:429. *Polk* 1896: 1167.

ROSENMILLER, LEWIS ADOLPHUS, NYC (d/V 1875) MD CPSNY 1847 *Med reg NY NJ Conn* 1875:203.

ROSENSTOCK, HENRY, Philadelphia (d/II–23–1904 @34) MD Jefferson 1896. *Pa m j* 8:336, 1904/05. *Flint* 1897: 824.

ROSENTHAL, DAVID, Chicago (d/VII–18–1899 @70) <MD U Pesth Austr> *JAMA* 33:302 1899 *Polk* 1896:404.

ROSENTHAL, JACOB, Chicago (b/XII–7–1862 Phila; d/VIII–24–1896) MD Jefferson 1888. *JAMA* 27:556, 1896. *Polk* 1896: 404.

ROSKOTEN, ROBERT, Peoria, Ill 1850– ; CW–USA (b/II–5–1816 Prussia; d/V–8–1897) <MD Jena 1848> *JAMA* 28:1045, 1897. *Atkinson* I: 642. *Polk* 1886: 293.

ROSMAN, JOHN GAUL, Brooklyn (d/I–27–1892 @56) MD Hahnemann Phila 1856. *No Am j hom* 40:135, 1892. Homeopath.

ROSMAN, ROBERT, Brooklyn (b/X–18–1807 Clavo-rack, Columbia; d/XII–25–1859) MD CPSNY 1832. *Bost m&s j* 61: 488, 1859. *Med surg rep Phila* ns3: 340, 1859/60. *Tr Am Inst Hom* 1860: 174. Homeopath.

ROSS, BENJAMIN F , Cobden, Ill (b/1832 Franklin Co, Pa; d/XII–15–1886) MD Rush 1858. *Med surg rep Phila* 56: 32, 1887. *Polk* 1886: 274.

ROSS, CHARLES AUSTIN, Leopold, Ind; SpanAmer War–USN? (d/II–2–1901 Philippines) MD Ky Sch Med 1897. *Tr Ind St M S* 1901:497–98.

ROSS, FRANCIS ARMSTRONG, MexWar–USA; CW–CSA; Mobile (b/II–24 1821 St Stephens; d/X–17–1884) MD UPa 1841; att U Va. *Tr M Assn St Ala* 1885: 14–15, 319. *UPa m alum CW*: 1841. *Atkinson* I: 615. *Butler* 1874: 25.

ROSS, GEORGE, Lebanon, Pa; b/Elizabethtown; d/XI–30–1880 @59) MD Jefferson 1849. *Med bull med & surg* 3: 65, 1881.

ROSS, GEORGE A, Mobile (b/1821; d/X–17–1884) MD UVa 1861. *New Orl m & s j* ns12:493, 1884.

ROSS, HIRAM W , St Helen, Ore (d/1899? @77) MD Rush 1853. *JAMA* 32:628, 1899. *Polk* 1886: 778.

ROSS, ISAAC EDGAR, Dorranceton, Pa (b/II–22–1832 Pike, Pa; d/VII–21–1901) <MD Geneva 1869> *Tr Luzerne Co* [Pa] *M S* 1901: 197–99.

ROSS, J M , Brenham, Tex (d/II–10–1889) MD ? *Daniel's Tex med jour* 4:350, 1889.

ROSS, JAMES, NYC (d/X–22–1897 @72 Lincoln, Neb) MD NY Med Coll 1851. *Med reg NY NJ Conn* 1893: 314. *Bost m&s j* 127:444, 1892. *Butler* 1878: 523.

ROSS, JAMES PRICE, Henderson, Ky (d/X–31–1867) MD ? *Med surg rep Phila* 17: 436, 1867.

ROSS, JOHN DEAN, Williamsburg, Pa (b/IX–2–1806 Indiana, Pa; d/III–5–1901) MD UPa 1832. *Pa med jour* 4:614, 1900/01. *Atkinson* I: 225, 1878. *Butler* 1878:730.

ROSS, JONATHAN, Blountsville, Ind (b/II– –1828 Wayne Co, Ind; d/II–5–1888) ng Med Coll Ohio 1867. *Tr Ind St M S* 1888: 211. *Butler* 1878: 218.

ROSS, JONATHAN SMITH, CW–USA; Great Falls, NH (b/IV–12–1822 Lisbon, NH; d/XI–22–1877) MD UPa 1846; AB Dartmouth 1843. *U Pa med alum CW*:1846.

ROSS, JOSEPH PRESLEY, Chicago 1853– (b/I–7–1828 Ohio; d/VI–15–1890) MD Med Coll Ohio 1852. *JAMA* 14: 941, 1890. *Bost m&s j* 122:650, 1890. *Tr Ill St M S* 1891: 31. *K&B* III: 1059.

ROSS, JUSTIN P , Marion, Ind (b/1840 Ohio; d/I–1–1896) MD Rush 1868. *Tr Ind St M S* 1896: 261. *Butler* 1878: 218.

ROSS, LUCRETIUS DEWEY, Poultney, Vt (d/VIII–25–1902 @75) MD Castleton 1857; AB Middlebury 1852. *Bost m&s j* 147: 284, 1902. *Polk* 1896:1476.

ROSS, OLIVER E , Rockport, Me (b/XI–16–1840 Cornwall, Vt; d/V–16–1890 Charleston, SC) MD Berk-shire 1862 *Tr Me M Assn* 1891:500–01. *Butler* 1878:310.

ROSS, SAMUEL McNUTT, Altoona, Pa (d/IX–13–1897 @73 or 76) MD Jefferson 1850. *JAMA* 29:817, 1897. *Polk* 1896: 1266.

ROSS, THOMAS, Lancaster, Ont to 1870; Woodland &

Sacramento (b/XI–26–1839 or V–30–1840 Lancaster; d/II–11–1906) MD McGill 1863. *Cal st j m* 4:105, 1900. *Atkinson* I: 200. *Polk* 1896: 227.

ROSS, W FRANK, Champaign, Ill (d/I–23–1901) <MD CPS Balto 1881> *Ill m j* ns2:533, 1901. *Polk* 1886: 439.

ROSS, WILLIAM, Brooklyn (b/1849 Tullanee, Irel'd; d/XI–2–1880) <MD Queen's Dublin 1873> AB 1871. *Med reg NY NJ Conn* 1881: 241.

ROSS, WILLIAM HENRY, NYC (b/VII–17–1844; d/XI 20–1900) MD Georgetown 1869. *Hist M S DC:* 298. *Atkinson* I:709. *Polk* 1893: 909.

ROSS, WILLIAM HENRY Jr, Mobile; Pensacola(b/I–16 1847; d/VIII–8–1896) MD CPSNY 1868; AB UAla 1865 *JAMA* 27:449,1896. *Atkinson* I:604. *Polk* 1896:317.

ROSSE, IRVING COLLINS, Washington, DC (b/X–20–1843 E Newmarket, Md; d/V–3–1901) MD U Md 1866. *Bost m&s j* 144:486, 1901. *Hist M S DC:* 317–18. *K&B* III: 1059–1060.

ROSSE, ZADOK HENRY, Cambridge Md (b/1799 Snow Hill; d/IV–19–1860) MD U Md 1822. *Med ann Md:* 555.

ROSSEAU [ROUSSEAU] LOUIS MAJORIQUE, Pittsburgh (b/II–3–1820 Quebec City; d/IX–25–1882) MD Bowdoin 1845; att Coll Nicolet 1837. *Tr Am Inst Hom* 1883: 152. *Tr Hom M S St Pa* 1883:38– 40. *NY m times* 10:255, 1882. *Cleave.* Homeopath.

ROSSEAU, WILLIAM H , Washington, Ia (b/1816 Ky; d/1883 @66) MD CPS Keokuk 1854. *Tr Iowa St M S* 18:411, 1900. *Fairchild*: 46.

ROSSITOR, JOSEPH PENNYPACKER, Norristown, Pa; CW–USA (b/IV–22–1832; d/IV–22–1864 Washington, DC) MD UPa 1860. *Tr AMA* 18:328, 1867. *Tr M S Pa* 3:468, 1864. *U Pa med alum CW*: 1860. *Nat med jour* 1:301, 1870/71.

ROTH, AMOS ASHENFELTER, Frederick, Md (b/X–19–1846 Harrisburg, Pa; d/VI–24–1890) MD Hahnemann, Phila 1870; att Gettysburg. *Med vis* 6:247, 1890. *Hahn mo* 25:618, 1890/91. Homeopath.

ROTH, CHARLES [CARL] M[AXIMILIAN], NYC (b/Giessen Gny; d/X–27–1897 @72) MD CPSNY 1866; PhD Giessen 1853 *JAMA* 29:1028 1897. *Polk* 1896:1875.

ROTH, JOHN C , Baltimore (d/II–7–1900 @35) MD Balto U 1890. *JAMA* 34:511, 1900.

ROTH, JULIUS AUGUSTUS, NYC (b/1858; d/I–5–1899) MD Bellevue 1882. *Bost m&s j* 140: 103, 1899. *JAMA* 32:195, 1899. *Polk* 1896: 1075.

ROTH, THEODORE, Philadelphia (d/XII–1–1876 @42) MD Jefferson 1865. *Med s rep Phila* 35:526, 1876.

ROTHACKER, WILLIAM ADAM, Cincinnati (b/IX–3 1853; d/1896) MD Cinc Coll Med & Surg 1877. *JAMA* 27:449, 1896. *Atkinson* I: 329. *Polk* 1886: 744.

ROTHROCK, ABRAHAM, CW–USA; McVeytown, Pa (b/IV–19–1806 Derrytownship; d/IX–9–1894) MD UPa 1835. *U Pa m alum CW*: 1835. *Atkinson* I: 549. *Polk* 1886: 806.

ROTZELL, JOSEPH M , Gloucester City, NJ (d/II–27 1874) MD ? *Med surg rep Phila* 30:276, 1874.

ROUNDTREE, J T , Troupe, Tex (d/VI–30–1897) MD ? *Tex med news* 6:392, 1896–97.

ROUP, DAVID, Muncie, Ind (b/X–20–1831 Portsmouth, O; d/VIII–23–1891) <MD Med Coll Ohio 1865> *Tr Ind St M S* 1892: 281.

ROUS, HANNAH CULLOMBINE, Vevay, Ind (b/I–12–1854 Switzerland Co; d/V–12–1905) MD U Mich 1886. *Tr Ind St M S* 1905: 457. *Polk* 1896: 495.

ROUSE, JOSEPH W , Philadelphia (d/I–11–1866 @35) MD ? *Med surg rep Phila* 14:60, 1866.

ROW, ELHANON WINCHESTER, CW–CSA; Orange CH, Va (b/XI–8–1833; d/V–23–1900) MD UPa 1858. *Tr M S Va* 1900:322–23. *U Pa m alum CW*: 1858. *Polk* 1886: 923. *K&B* III: 1064.

ROWAN, BENJAMIN C , Ft Wayne, Ind; CW–USA (b/IX–17–1817 Westmoreland Co Pa; d/IV–15–1863) MD UCNY 1848 *Tr Ind St M S* 1866:9. Kemper's *Indiana*:27.

ROWAND, JOHN RANDOLPH, Philadelphia; CW–USA (b/III–20–1811 Haddonfield, NJ; d/V–24–1880) MD UPa 1836. *U Pa med alum CW*: 1836 (suppl).

ROWAND, JOSEPH T , Camden, NJ (d/1876) MD Phila Coll Med & Surg 1849. *Tr AMA* 28:626, 1877. *Med surg rep Phila* 35: 180, 1876.

ROWAND, THOMAS GARWOOD, Camden, NJ (b/VIII 27–1829 Carpenter's Landing, NJ; d/I–25–1897) MD Phila Coll Med & Surg 1847. *JAMA* 28:379, 1897. *Tr M S NJ* 1897: 295–97. *Butler* 1878: 479.

ROWE, CHARLES HENRY, USA (d/IX–4–1867 Galveston, Tex) MD Yale 1864; AB 1862. *Tr AMA* 19: 452, 1868. *Nat med jour* 1:301, 1870/71.

ROWE, EUGENE ORVILLE, NYC (b/IX–5–1841; d/I–12–1864) MD Bellevue 1864. *Med reg NY NJ Conn* 1865: 224.

ROWE, ISAIAH JOSIAH WILLIS, Gorham, NH (b/X–19–1814 Bethel; d/1893) MD ? *JAMA* 21: 907, 1893.

ROWE, JOHN, ?Horsham Twp, Pa (b/1799? d/II–26–1862 @63) MD ? *Med s rep Phila* ns7:552, 1861/62.

ROWELL, ISAAC, San Francisco (b/IX–23–1818 Stark, NH; d/I–4–1871) MD Dartmouth 1850. *Tr AMA* 23: 574–75, 1872. *Med surg rep Phila* 24: 46, 1871.

ROWELL, SAMUEL NEWELL, Jersey City, NJ (b/1821; d/XI–3/4–1893) MD Yale 1852; AB 1849. *Med reg NY NJ Conn* 1894:248. *Tr M S NJ* 1894: 276–77. *JAMA* 21:784, 1893.

ROWLAND, CHARLES, Brooklyn (d/VIII–9–1879 @79) MD Yale 1824. *Med reg NY NJ Conn* 1880: 241. *Med surg rep Phila* 41:176, 198, 1879.

ROWLAND, EDWARD, Sunbury, O (b/XI–18–1809 Windsor, Conn; d/VIII–1–1845) AB Amherst 1832. *Amherst, Men of*: 1832.

ROWLAND, JOSEPH, CW–USA; Media, Pa (b/IV–18–1814 Radnor; d/IV–29–1895) MD UPa 1840. *JAMA* 24: 689, 1895. *Polk* 1886: 807.

ROWLAND, JOSEPH S C , Hartford, Conn (d/III–21–

1893 @62) <MD Cleveland Med Coll 1867> *Med reg NY NJ Conn* 1893: 314.

ROWLAND, MARVIN [MARION] C , Genesee, NY (d/I-15-1895 @67) MD UCNY 1862. *Med reg NY NJ Conn* 1895:239 *Buff m&s j* 34:429 1895 *Butler* 1878:571.

ROWLAND, MELSON LAWS, ? CW-USA (b/III-1-1838; d/I-25-1901) MD UPa 1859; ng Coll U Pa 1853-55. *Matrics cat Coll UPa*: 203.

ROWLAND, WILLIAM B , Rowlandsville & Port Deposit, Md (b/1811; d/IX-6-1885 Phila) MD U Md 1834; AM Columbia. *New Orl m & s j* ns13: 324-25, 1885. *Med annals Md:* 556. *Butler* 1878: 330.

ROYAL, WOODMAN WATSON, E Portland, Ore (d/VII-22-1896 @61) MD Bowdoin 1863. *JAMA* 27: 503, 1896. *Polk* 1896: 1239.

ROYER, LEWIS, Pottstown & Trappe, Pa (d/X-27-1904 @82) MD UPa 1844. *Pa m j* 8: 336. 1904/05. *Flint* 1897:837.

ROYER, SAMUEL S , Allentown, Pa (d/1906 @59) MD ? *Pa med jour* 10:119, 1906/07.

ROYSTER, THOMAS SALTERWHITE, Townesville, NC (b/IX-14-1856; d/XI-7-1898) MD Bellevue 1882. *NC med jour* 43:74, 1899. *Polk* 1886: 727.

RUAN, JOHN, Philadelphia (b/VI-9-1771 St Croix, WI; d/VII-2-1845 Bucks Co) <MD Edinburgh> AB Princeton 1790; AM. *Tr AMA* 3:462-63, 1850. *Tr CPP* 1:326-29, 1841-46.

RUBLEE, CHAUNCEY MOORE, Montpelier, Vt (b/XI 25-1821; d/I-26-1870) MD Woodstock 1846. *Phila med reg & dir* 1871: 303. *Tr Vt M S* 1883: 108.

RUBUSH, DAVID PAUL, CW-USA; Sharpsville, Ind (b/II-25-1847 Rockingham Co, Va; d/II-20-1904) <MD Med Coll Ind 1875> *Ind m j* 22:473. *Tr Ind St M S* 1906: 502. *Polk* 1886: 336.

RUCKER, THOMAS H , New Albany & Evansville, Ind (d/III-31-1894 @79) MD Transylvania 1835. *JAMA* 22: 561, 1894. *Butler* 1878: 218.

RUCKER, WILLIAM R , Murfreesboro, Tenn (b/Va; d/VIII- -1861) MD UPa 1819. *Tr M S Tenn* 1876: 87.

RUDDACH, WILLIAM HENRY, Philadelphia (d/X-16 1884 @56) MD UPa 1852 *Med s rep Phila* 51:668, 1884.

RUDDEROW, FRANCIS, Philadelphia (b/VI-8-1862 Phila; d/I-22-1904 @42) MD UPa 1887: AB 1884. *Pa med jour* 8:336, 1904/05. *Flint* 1897: 824.

RUDEN [RUDDEN], CARL F , Joliet, Ill (d/IV-9-1894 @62) <MD U Berlin 1854> *JAMA* 22:601, 1894. *Polk* 1890: 335.

RUDENSTEIN, JOHN, USN (d/XII-9-1869 Pensacola, Fla) MD U Md 1842. *Phila med reg & dir* 1871: 303.

RUFFIN, GEORGE WASHINGTON, CW-CSA (b/III-19-1822 Louisburg, NC; d/VI-5-1862 Wilson Co, NC) MD UPa 1846. *U Pa med alum CW*: 1846 (suppl).

RUFFIN, JAMES SHERLING, Demopolis, Ala (b/1826; d/XII-13-1896 Birmingham, Ala) MD UPa 1850; AB UNC 1840. *UNC cat*: 540. *Polk* 1886:133.

RUFFIN, JOHN KIRKLAND, CW-CSA; Wilson NC (b/III-6-1834 Alamance; d/V-21-1903) MD UPa 1857; AB UNC 1854.*UPa med alum CW*:1857. *Polk* 1886:727.

RUFFIN, WILLIAM HEYWOOD, CW-CSA; Choctaw Co, Ala (b/ II-22-1817 Louisburg, NC; d/IV-26-1879) MD UPa 1838; stud UNC 1833-36. *U Pa m alum CW*: 1838 (suppl).

RUGGLES, AUGUSTUS DENNETT, CW-USA; NYC (d/XII-27-1903 @63) MD UPa 1865. *Bost m&s j* 150: 28, 1904. *U Pa med alum CW*: 1865.

RUGGLES, DWIGHT, NYC & WVa (b/III-31-1816; d/VII-18-1884) MD Phila Coll Med & Surg 1849. *Med reg NY NJ Conn* 1885: 243. *Med surg rep Phila* 51: 168, 1884. *Butler* 1878: 523.

RUGGLES, EDWARD, Brooklyn (d/III-10-1867) MD ? *Med surg rep Phila* 16: 224, 1867.

RUGGLES, PAUL, Carmel, Me (b/VI-20-1801; d/V-13 1857) MD Bowdoin 1832. *Bost m&s j* 56: 287, 1857.

RULISON, WILLIAM H , CW-USA (d/VIII-20-1864 Shenandoah Valley, Va) MD Albany 1855. *Med surg rep Phila* 12:100, 1864/65. *Nat med jour* 1:301, 1870/71.

RUMSEY, JAMES S , Fishkill-on-Hudson, NY (b/1799? d/XI-1-1872 @73) MD CPSNY 1824; AB Columbia 1819. *Med surg rep Phila* 27: 452, 1872.

RUNDELL, ALPHARIS E , Center Point, Ind (b/III-10-1850 Greene Co, O; d/XII-28-1900) MD Evansville 1874. *Tr Ind St M S* 1901: 499. *Polk* 1896: 461.

RUNDLETT, HENRY ALBERT, Brooklyn (d/III-8-1904 @47) MD Harvard 1887; AB Bates 1878. *Bost m&s j* 150: 282, 1904.

RUPERT, DELOS WHITE, Lexington, Ind; CW-USA (d/X-2-1862 Nashville, Tenn) MD Geneva 1849. *Nat med jour* 1:301, 1870/71.

RUPPANER, ANTHONY [ANTOINE], NYC (b/1825 Switzerland; d/VIII-2-1892 Pittsburgh) MD Harvard 1857; AB 1855. *JAMA* 19:238, 1892. *Bost m&s j* 127:152, 1892. *K&B* III: 1065. *Butler* 1878:523.

RUPPRECHT, LOUIS LUDWIG, NYC (b/XII-31-1830; d/II-21-1874) <MD Giessen 1850> ?MD Munich 1862. *Med reg NY NJ Conn* 1874: 288-89.

RUSCHENBERGER, WILLIAM SAMUEL WAITHMAN, USN 1826-71; Philadelphia (b/Bridgeton, NJ IX-4-1807; d/III-24-1895) MD UPa 1830. *Tr CPP* cent vol:262; 3s18:xxxv-xli, 1896. *JAMA* 24: 527, 1895. *Bost m&s j* 132:344, 1895. *Atkinson* I: 74. *K&B* III: 1066.

RUSH, BENJAMIN, RevWar-USA; Philadelphia (b/XII-24-1745; d/IV-19-1813) MD Edinburgh 1768; AB Princeton 1760. *Phila jour med & phys sci*7: 162-71, 1823. *Eclectic repertory* 3: 1813 (July). *Transylvania jour med & assoc sci* 12:92-116, 1839. [*Note*: The bulk of contemporary notices of BR appeared in pamphlet form and are accessible through monographic indexes.] *K&B* III: 1066-1069.

RUSH, JAMES, Philadelphia (b/III-1-1786; d/V-26-1869) MD UPa 1809; AB Princeton 1805; AM 1808.

Phila m reg & dir 1871: 294. *Med s rep Phila* 20: 436, 1869. *K&B* III: 106–70.

RUSH [RUYCH], ROBERT BRYSON, Salem, O 1858– (b/X–3–1825 Milton, Pa; d/III–28–1899) MD Cleveland Homeop 1860. *Tr Am Inst Hom* 1899:76, 933–34. *No Am hom* 47:73, 1899. *Polk* 1886: 767. Homeopath.

RUSHING, STEPHEN HARRIS, CW–CSA; Alexandria, La (b/X–26–1830 Wadesboro, NC; d/IV–20–1905) MD UPa 1853. *So pract* 27:335, 1905. *U Pa med alum CW*: 1853. *SHSP* 22:254, 1893. *New Orl m & s j* 57: 864, 1905. *Butler* 1878: 300.

RUSHMORE, EDWIN CLOWES, Hempstead, NY (b/ VIII–7–1824; d/II–4–1885) MD UCNY 1854; AB Wesleyan Conn 1846. *Med reg NY NJ Conn* 1885: 243. *Butler* 1878: 571.

RUSHTON, WILLIAM, New Orleans (b/1808 Bolton, Engl; d/XI–21–1862) <MD Edinburgh 1827> *New Orl m & s j* 19:137–38, 1866. *South jour med sci* 1: 394, 1866. *Nashvl j m&s* ns1:320, 1866.

RUSS, JOHN DENNISON, Pompton, NJ (b/IX–1–1801 Essex, Mass; d/III–1–1881) MD Yale 1825; AB 1823. *Bost m&s j* 104:283, 1881. *K&B* III:1070.

RUSS, KIMBALL, Pomfret, Vt (b/VI–21–1800 Woodstock; d/XII–28–1875) MD Woodstock 1827. *Tr Vt M S* 1883: 108.

RUSSSEL, CHARLES PORTER, CW–USA; NYC (d/ VI–11/12–1886) MD CPSNY 1858. *Med reg NY NJ Conn* 1887: 275. *Butler* 1878: 523.

RUSSELL, CHARLES, Conway, NH 1848–50; W Paris, Me 1850–65; Fayette, Me 1865–68 (b/VII–19–1820 Bethel, d/VII–4–1858) MD U Md 1848; att Bowdoin 1844. *Bowdoin cat*: 1848.

RUSSELL, CHARLES PATTERSON, Utica, NY (d/X–26–1906) MD Bellevue 1874. *Bost m&s j* 155:530, 1906. *Polk* 1890: 855.

RUSSELL, EDMUND, Lewiston, Me (b/XI–23–1824 Temple, Me; d/XII–20–1880) MD Bowdoin 1847. *Tr Me Med Assoc*1881: 391. *Butler* 1878: 310.

RUSSELL, EDWARD, CW–USA; Wollaston, Mass (d/X 22–1891 @50) MD Harvard 1862. *Bost m&s j* 125: 480, 1891. *Harvard in CW*: 275.

RUSSELL, GEORGE, Boston (b/IX–23–1795 Lincoln, Mass; d/II–18–1883) MD Harvard 1820. *New Engl med gaz* 18:96, 1883. *Cleave.* Homeopath.

RUSSELL, HOWARD C , Stapleton, NY (b/IX–25–1868 Washington, DC; d/III–1/2–1904) MD UPa 1891. *Bost m&s j* 150: 254, 1904. *Hist M S DC:* 347.

RUSSELL, IRA, Winchendon, Mass (b/XI–9–1815 Rindge, NH; d/XII–19–1888) MD UCNY 1844; AB Dartmouth. *Bost m&s j* 119:641, 1888; 120:28, 1889. *Atkinson* I: 310–11.

RUSSELL, ISAAC S , CW–USA (d/VIII–3–1864 Atlanta) MD ? *Nat med jour* 1:301, 1870/71.

RUSSELL, ISAAC WADHAMS, Mt Vernon, O (d/IV–12–1876) MD U Mich 1869. *Tr Ohio St M S* 1876: 90.

RUSSELL, JOHN T , Troy, Ala (d/1890) MD UCNY 1851. *Tr Med Assn St Ala* 1891: 261. *Polk* 1886:140.

RUSSELL, JOHN WADHAMS, Mt Vernon, O (b/I–28–1904 Canaan, Conn; d/III–22–1887) MD Jefferson 1827; ng SC, Yale, Berkshire. *Tr Ohio M S* 1887: 238–42. *JAMA* 8:380, 1887; 9:285–86, 1887. *Atkinson* I: 242. *K&B* III:1070–71.

RUSSELL, JOSEPH PYNCHON, USA 1814–49 (b/ 1790? Bennington, Vt; d/IX–19–1849 NY) MD ? *Tr AMA* 3:464, 1850. *Heitman.*

RUSSELL, LE BARON, Boston (b/VII–29–1814; d/ VIII–19–1889 Plymouth) MD Harvard 1836; AB 1832. *Bost m&s j* 121:196,645, 1889. *Polk* 1886: 461.

RUSSELL, LEONIDAS, CW–CSA; Washington, DC (b/ Ind; d/VI 26–1901 @66) MD Jefferson 1855. *JAMA* 37: 397, 1901.

RUSSELL, MOSES WADLEIGH, Concord, NH (b/XI–4 1835 Sutton; d/IV–18–1896) MD Dartmouth 1864. *Tr NH M S* 1896:187–8. *JAMA* 26:890 1896 *Polk* 1886:591.

RUSSELL, PETER H , St Louis; CW–USN (b/VII–17 1838 Warren Co, NJ; d/V–28–1904) MD UPa 1864. *U Pa med alum CW*: 1864.

RUSSELL, PRESTON W, Philadelphia (d/VII–9–1865 @37) MD Jefferson 1851. *Med s rep Phila* 13:48, 1865.

RUSSELL, SELWYN A , Poughkeepsie, NY (d/I–12–1906 @55) MD Albany 1877. *Bost m&s j* 154:84, 389, 1906. *Polk* 1886: 639.

RUSSELL, STEPHEN C , New Orleans (d/VI– –1902 @82) MD Tulane 1848. *New Orl m&s j* 55: 68, 1902. *Polk* 1886: 417.

RUSSELL, WALTER A , Pittsfield, Mass (d/VII–19–1897) MD Tulane 1891. *JAMA* 29: 297, 1897.

RUSSELL, WILLIAM, Utica, NY (b/VI–5–1821 Glasgow, Scotl; d/VI–27–1890) MD Berkshire 1848; att CPSNY 1849. *Tr M S St NY* 1891: 458–61.

RUSSELL, WILLIAM L , Baltimore (d/XII–21–1899 @ 65) MD U Md 1869. *JAMA* 34:61, 1900. *Polk* 1886:439.

RUSSELL, WILLIAM LAMBERT, Barre, Mass (d/V–6 1899 @99) MD Harvard 1831; AB 1826. *Nashvl j m& s* 86:131, 1899. *JAMA* 32:1074, 1899. *Bost m&s j* 140:458–59, 1899.

RUSSELL, WILLIAM P , Middlebury, Vt (b/III– –1804 Charlotte; d/VI–4–1872) MD Berkshire 1831; att Castleton 1832. *Tr Vt M S* 1883: 108.

RUSSELL, WILLIAM R, CW–USA; Beloit Wis; Washington, DC (b/VII–21–1836 Somersetshire, Engl; d/IV–21–1883) MD Rush 1862. *Hist M S DC:* 282.

RUSSELL, WILLIAM THOMAS, Spartanburg, SC (d/II–23–1899 @72) MD UPa 1850. *JAMA* 32: 506, 1899. *Polk* 1896: 1365.

RUST, GEORGE W , Luray, Va (d/V–12–1888 @65) MD Jefferson 1846. *New Orl m&s j*ns15:1003, 1888. *Polk* 1886: 920.

RUST, JOHN McAFEE, CW–CSA (b/VI–6–1836 Jackson Co, Ind; d/1862 Winchester, Tenn) MD UPa 1858. *U*

 Spec. educ'l status abbrev. as: ***ng*** = college verified attendance without degree;

Pa med alum CW: 1858.

RUST, MELVIN N , CW-USA (d/VIII-13-1865 Nashville) MD Northwestern 1865. *Nat med jour* 1:301, 1870/71.

RUTH, MELANCHTHON LUTHER LORE, USN (b/VII-9-1845 Lebanon, Pa; d/XII-14-1891 Brooklyn) MD UPa 1866. *Med reg NY NJ Conn* 1892: 287. *JAMA* 17:995, 1891. *Bost m&s j* 125:664, 1891.

RUTHERFORD, ALFRED JOSEPH, Milwaukee (b/I-11-1860 Peterboro, Ont; d/VII-11-1896) MD Buffalo 1889. *JAMA* 27:226, 1896. *Tr Wis St M S*: 30, 566-67, 1896. *Polk* 1896: 1557.

RUTHERFORD, HIRAM, Oakland, Ill (d/IV-30-1900) MD Jefferson 1838. *Ill m j* ns2:48, 1900. *Polk* 1896:432.

RUTHERFORD, J W , Stony, Tex (d/I-26-1892) MD ? *Tex cour-rec med* 9:136, 1892.

RUTHERFORD, ROBERT MITCHELL, Houston, Tex (b/Columbus, Ga; d/III-31-1899) MD UCNY 1881. *JAMA* 32:845, 1899. *New Orl m&s j* 51:647, 1899. *Daniel's Tex m j* 2:379-80, 1887. *Tex m j* 14:587, 1898-99. *Polk* 1886: 888.

RUTHERFORD, WILLIAM W , Harrisburg, Pa (d/III-12-1872 @67) MD Jefferson 1832. *Med s rep Phila* 28: 292, 1873.

RUTTER, CHARLES LINDLEY, Chicago (b/VIII-14-1842 Phila; d/X- -1898) MD Chic M C 1867. *Chic m rec* 15:365, 1898. *Atkinson* I: 613.

RUTTER, DAVID, Philadelphia (d/IV-16-1865 Chicago) MD UPa 1823. *Chic med jour* 22:238, 1865.

RUTTER, EDWARD JOHN, USN (b/Balto; d/IV-30-1852 at sea) MD U Md 1837. *Med annals Md:* 557.

RUTZ, GALLUS, Highland, Ill; Port Townsend, Wash (d/XI-1-1898 @68) MD Humboldt 1861. *JAMA* 31: 1257, 1898. *Polk* 1886: 282.

RYAN, CHARLES THOMAS, NYC (d/X-1-1897) MD Bellevue 1869. *JAMA* 29:761, 1897.

RYAN, GEORGE W, Niantic Ill (d/VII-30-1899 @51) MD St Louis CPS 1890. *JAMA* 33:427, 1899. *Polk* 1896:432.

RYAN, GEORGE W , Cincinnati (b/Louisville; d/VII-11 1896 @36) MD Louisville U 1878. *JAMA* 27: 165, 1896. *Med bull med & surg* 18:356, 1896.

RYAN, JOHN, CW-USA; Boston (d/II-2-1878 @43) MD Harvard 1860. *Harvard in CW*: 261.

RYAN, JOHN FRANCIS, Roxbury, Mass (d/IX-1-1900 @29) <MD Mo M C 1891> *Bost m&s j* 143:248, 1900.

RYAN, THOMAS JOSEPH ALOYSIUS, Providence, RI 1869- (b/VI-13-1840 Ireland; d/III-5-1873) MRCP Edin; MRCS Edin 1868. *Tr RI M S* 1:399-400, 1859-77.

RYAN, TOWNSEND, CW-USA; Anderson, Ind 1843- (b/1813 Lancaster, Pa; d/XII-30-1880) <MD Jefferson> *Med s rep Phila* 42:88, 1880. Kemper's *Indiana*: 145, 158, 178, 183, 199, 221.

RYBURN, JOHN STEWART, Ottawa, Ill (b/V-5-1852; d/IX-21-1892) MD Rush 1876. *Tr Ill St M S* 1893: 57-58. *Polk* 1896: 1388.

RYERSON, THOMAS, Newton, NJ (b/II-18-1821 Myrtle Grove, NJ; d/V-27-1887) MD CPSNY 1844; AB Princeton 1840; AM 1843; att Lafayette. *Tr M S NJ* 1887: 300-03. *Tex cour-rec med* 4:487, 1887.

RYLAND, KIRTLEY, USA 1859- (b/Mo; d/IX-22-1861) MD St Louis U 1853. *Tr AMA* 14:216, 1864. *Heitman*.

RYND, CHARLES, Adrian, Mich (b/1835 Ireland; d/VIII-20-1884) MD U Mich 1861. *Med age* 2:259-66, 1884. *Butler* 1878: 382.

RYND, JOHN, CW-USA (d/I-23-1866) MD ? *Nat med jour* 1:301, 1870/71.

SABIN, HENRY LYMAN, Williamstown, Mass (b/V-29 1801; d/II-24-1884) Hon MD Berkshire 1839; AB Williams 1821. *JAMA* 10:506-07, 1888. *Bost m&s j* 110:216, 288, 1884. *Med s rep Phila* 50: 320, 1884. *Atkinson* I: 89. *Butler* 1878: 356.

SABIN, ROBERT HALL, W Troy, NY (d/XII-4-1888) MD Albany 1856. *Bost m&s j* 119:590, 1888. *Tr M S St NY* 11:741 ff. *Butler* 1878:571.

SABINE, GUSTAVUS A , NYC (b/VI-27-1809 Engl; d/XI-17-1896) <MRCS (L) 1832> *JAMA* 27: 1214-1215. *Butler* 1878: 523.

SABINE, THOMAS TAUNTON, NYC (b/1841? d/VIII-23-1888 @47) MD CPSNY 1864; AB Columbia 1861; AM 1864. *Med reg NY NJ Conn* 1889:284. *Bost m&s j* 119:216,1888. *Atkinson* I:681-82. *Butler* 1878:523.

SACHSE, GEORGE J , Columbus, O (b/III- -1800 Westphalia; d/VII-2-1860) MD Heidelberg 1830. *Tr Ohio St M S* 1862:122-24.

SACKETT, SOLON PHILO, Ithaca, NY (b/1818; d/XII-18-1893) MD Geneva 1843. *JAMA* 22:31, 58, 1894. *Med reg NY NJ Conn* 1894: 248. *Butler* 1878: 571.

SACKETT, WALLACE A , Dallas, Tex (b/1869? New Albany, Ind; d/VI-28-1894 @25) MD U Louisville 1893. *JAMA* 23:86, 1894.

SACKRIDER, CHARLES H , Mason, Mich (b/1832; d/XI-8-1881) MD U Mich 1856; MD Jefferson 1863. *Tr AMA* 33:596-98, 1882.

SACKVILLE, JOHN C , Washington, Pa (b/1814? d/IX-23-1896 @82) <MRCS (L) 1838> *JAMA* 27:776, 1896. *Polk* 1896: 1342.

SADLER, LEWIS H , ?Tenn (d/1881) MD U Tenn 1880. *So pract* 3:68, 1881.

SADLER, RICHARD B , Bastrop, La (d/VII-27-1894) MD U Nashville 1861. *New Orl m & s j* ns22: 313, 1894. *Polk* 1890: 485.

SADLER, WILLIAM KING, CW-USA (b/IX-20-1833 Hatfield, Mass; d/XII-2-1864) MD UPa 1859. *U Pa med alum CW*: 1859. *Nat med jour* 1:302, 1870/71.

SAFFOLD, REUBEN WASHINGTON, Summerfield, Ala (b/II-14-1820; d/VII- -1892) MD ? att U Ala 1837. *U Ala cat*: 58. *Polk* 1886: 138.

SAFFORD, MARY JANE, Boston (b/Hyde Pk, Vt; d/XII 8–[1891?] Tarpon Spr, Fla) MD NY Med Coll & Hosp for Women 1869. *Med vis* 8:1892. *Cleave. Polk* 1886: 461. Served CW.

SAGER, ABRAM, Ann Arbor, Mich (b/XII–22–1810 Bethlehem, NY; d/VIII–6–1877) MD Castleton 1834; att Yale; AB Rensselaer Polytech 1831; Hon AM U Mich 1852. *Tr AMA* 29:752–57, 1878. *Atkinson* I: 58–59. *K&B* III: 1073.

ST CLAIR, T C , Vaiden, Miss (d/1878 Memphis) MD ? *Tr AMA* 30:885, 1879.

ST JOHN, CHARLES, USA (d/V–22–1901 Philippine Isl) MD ? *JAMA* 37: 397, 1901.

ST JOHN, J T , Vernon, Tex (d/VIII–23–1892) MD ? *Tex cour–rec med* 10:27, 1892.

ST JOHN, ORSON S , Buffalo (b/1810; d/VII–9–1897 @ 87) MD Fairfield 1831. *Buff m&s j* 27: 58, 1897. *JAMA* 29: 200, 1897.

ST JOHN, SAMUEL, New Canaan, Conn (b/III–29–1813; d/IX–9–1876) <MD Castleton 1840> Hon MD West Res 1851; Hon MD CPSNY 1857; AB Yale 1834. *Med reg NY NJ Conn* 1877:206. *Med surg rep Phila* 35: 348, 1876. *K&B* III: 1073–74.

SALE, LE ROY P , Pembroke, Ky (d/V– –1883 @76) MD ? *So pract* 5:288, 1883. *Butler* 1878:284.

SALISBURY, AUGUSTUS HARRISON, Minneapolis (b/VII–22–1840 Canandaigua, NY; d/VIII–26–1893) MD Bellevue 1867. *JAMA* 21:390, 1893. *Tr Minn St M S* 1893: 131. *Atkinson* I: 529. *Butler* 1878: 395.

SALISBURY, SAMUEL THURBER, Plymouth, Conn (b/III–14–1814 Providence, RI; d/III–1–1874) MD Yale 1836. *Proc Conn M S* 1874:284–86, 291.

SALLADE [SALLADA], FRANKLIN L , Womelsdorf, Pa (d/X–24–1897) MD Jefferson 1866. *Lehigh Valley m mag* 8:341, 1897. *JAMA* 29:1028, 1897.

SALMON, GEORGE P , Hudson, NY (d/IV–11–1891 @60) MD ? *Tr M S St NY* 1892: 428. *Polk* 1890: 793.

SALMON, ROBERT G , Brazoria, Tex (d/1867) MD ? *Tr AMA* 19:429, 1868.

SALTER, FRANCIS, Washington, DC (b/1831 Engl; d/V–3–1879) <LRCP & S Edinb 1850> *Hist M S DC:* 294. *Butler* 1878: 94.

SALTER, JOSEPH ELY, Saltersville, NJ (d/II–25–1896 @36 Bayonne) MD Bellevue 1881. *NC m j* 37: 189, 1896. *Polk* 1886: 611.

SALTER, RICHARD HENRY, Boston (d/VIII–4–1893 @86) MD Yale 1831. *Bost m&s j* 129:152, 1893. *Butler* 1878: 343.

SALTER, SOLOMON CARR, Lena, Ill (d/VIII–1–1895 @64) MD U Mich 1863. *JAMA* 25:253, 1895. *Butler* 1878: 711.

SALTONSTALL, GILBERT DUDLEY, Hoboken, NJ (d/VI–17–1895 @66) MD UCNY 1852. *Med reg NY NJ Conn* 1895:239. *JAMA* 24: 1023, 1895. *Bost m&s j* 132:654, *Butler* 1878: 475. *Polk* 1886: 604.

SALTONSTALL, GURDON, NYC (b/1827; d/VI–20–1857 @30) MD UCNY 1850. *Bost m&s j* 56:527, 1857.

SALZER, HENRY, Baltimore (b/1841 Gny; d/VI–19 1896) <MD Giessen 1866> *Tr AMA* 27:52, 1896. *Med annals Md:* 557. *Polk* 1896: 664.

SAMO, JAMES B , Buffalo (d/III–12–1897) MD CPSNY 1832. *Buff m&s j* 36:710, 1897. *JAMA* 28:665, 1897. *Flint* 1897: 652.

SAMPLE, G F , Austin, Tex (d/X–7–1878 Memphis) MD ? *Tr AMA* 30:885, 1879.

SAMPLE, SAMUEL RAMSEY, Intercourse, Pa (d/IX–30 or X–1–1906 @72) MD Jefferson 1857. *Pa med jour* 10: 53, 1906/07. *Flint* 1897: 805.

SAMPSEL, D S Sr, Ashland O (d/XII–10–1893 @71) MD ? *JAMA* 21: 936, 1893. *Polk* 1890:893. *Butler* 1878:648.

SAMPSON, GEORGE W Sr, Tiffin, O (d/1895 @93) MD Med Coll O 1835. *JAMA* 24:457, 1895.

SAMPSON, IRA, Taunton, Mass (b/III–23–1815 Middleboro; d/III–2–1870) MD Harvard 1841; AB Brown 1838. *Brown hist cat*: 1838. *Mass M S cat* 1894.

SANBORN, ALBERT HOYT, Leipsic, Md (b/II–12–1822 Sandwich Vt; d/I–6 or 12–1867) MD Franklin M C 1846; MD Bowdoin 1848. *Med s rep Phil* 16:179, 1867.

SANBORN, BENJAMIN, Belgrade, Me 1830–36; Falmouth 1836 (b/VIII–24–1799; d/II–27–1846) MD Dartmouth 1827; AB Bowdoin 1822; AM 1825. *Bowdoin cat*: 1822.

SANBORN, EASTMAN, Andover, Mass (d/XII–8–1859 @59) MD ? *Bost m&s j* 61: 408, 1859.

SANBORN, EBENEZER KIMBALL, CW–USA; Rutland, Vt (b/I–24–1828 New Chester, NH; d/IV–3–1862 Ship Isl, Miss) MD Berkshire 1847. *Bost m&s j* 66: 304, 1862; 67:27–28, 1862. *Buff m&s j* 1:341–42, 1862. *Nat m j* 1:302, 1870/71.

SANBORN, JESSE APPLETON, Plymouth, NH (b/XII–5–1820 Meredith; d/VI–15–1888) MD Dartmouth 1842. *Tr NH M S* 1888:170–71. *Polk* 1886: 594.

SANBORN, JOHN EASTMAN, CW–USA; Melrose, Mass (b/VIII–17–1824 Gilmanton, NH; d/IV–1–1903) MD Harvard 1850; AB Wesleyan 1845. *Bost m&s j* 148: 408, 1903. *Harvard in CW*: 237. *Polk* 1896: 718.

SANBORN, JOHN H , Franklin, NH (b/IX–23–1830 Meredith; d/XII–19–1905) MD Berkshire 1852. *Tr NH M S* 1906:235–36. *Polk* 1896: 919.

SANBORN, NATHAN, Henniker, NH (b/III–7–1791 Sanbornton; d/XII–15–1858) Hon MD Dartmouth 1834; lic 1816. *Tr NH M S* 1859:76–79.

SANBORN, NOAH, Bayonne, NJ (b/V–14–1837 Tamworth, NH; d/IX–6–1894) MD Dartmouth 1862. *Med reg NY NJ Conn* 1895: 239. *Tr M S NJ* 1895:204–05. *Bost m&s j* 131:304, 1894. *Polk* 1890: 718.

SANBORN, THOMAS, Newport, NH (b/IX–26–1811 Sanbornton; d/VII–1875) MD Dartmouth 1841. *Tr NH M S* 1876:161–4. Conn, G P, *NH s in CW*: 192–3, 195, 197.

 Spec. educ'l status abbrev. as: ***ng*** = college verified attendance without degree;

SANBORN, THOMAS BARTON, Newport, NH (b/VII-9-1852; d/VI-30-1894) MD Bellevue 1876. *Tr NH M S* 1895:160. *Polk* 1890: 711.

SANBORN, THOMAS MOOR, Lake Village, Vt (d/ 1869) att Dartmouth 1838-39. *Phila med reg & dir* 1871: 299. *Med s rep Phila* 20: 199, 1869.

SANBORN, WILBUR [WILLIAM] FISKE, N Sandwich, NH (d/III-19-1884 @34) MD Harvard 1875. *Bost m&s j* 111:619, 1884.

SANDERS, ABRAHAM B , Charlestown, Mass (d/IX-4 1854) MD Hahnemann Phila 1854. *Tr Mass Hom M S* 1890: (Sept). Homeopath.

SANDERS, CHARLES PEAKE, Pleasant Ridge Ala (b/ IX-1-1812 Charleston, SC; d/VI-25-1889) MD Transylv 1844. *Tr M Assn St Ala* 1889: 229. *Polk* 1886: 138.

SANDERS, JOHN H , Indianapolis (d/1849 or 1850) MD Transylv 1823. *NW m&s j* 3:90 1850. *Pr Ind St M S* 1850: 7.

SANDERS, JOSEPH, NYC (b/VII-6-1867; d/X-20-1901 Oil City, Pa) MD Bellevue 1892. *Bost m&s j* 145: 503, 1901. *Polk* 1896: 1076.

SANDERS, LABAN MILES, Barnstead, NH (d/I? -1867) MD Dartmouth 1864. *Med surg rep Phila* 16:100, 1867.

SANDERS, ORREN STRONG, Boston (b/IX-24-1820 Epsom NH; d/X-23-1898) MD Castleton 1843; att Dartmouth 1841. *Tr Am Inst Hom* 1899: 934. *No Am jour hom* 47: 1899 (Feb). Homeopath.

SANDERS, RICHARD WALTON, Max Meadows, Va (b/XI-17-1826 Wythe Co; d/II-13-1906) MD UPa 1851; att U Va 1849; att Emory & Henry. *Tr M S Va* 1905:452-53. *Polk* 1900: 1767.

SANDERSON, IRA LEAVITT, USA 1872- (b/III-13-1840 Littleton, Mass; d/I-17-1899 Sturgis, SD) MD CPSNY 1869. *JAMA* 32: 263, 1899. *Records AAS USA* 1891:88-89. *Polk* 1896: 1373.

SANDERSON, WILLIAM RAYMOND, Frederick, Md (b/1810 Md; d/XI-17-1887) MD U Md 1834. *Med ann Md:* 557.

SANDS, AUSTIN LEDYARD, Cold Spring, NY; NYC; Newport, RI (b/XII-14-1825 Phila; d/XII-20-1877 Cairo Egpt) MD CPSNY 1848 *Med s rep Phil* 1878:189.

SANDS, D JEROME, Port Chester, NY (d/IV-31-1888 @73) MD CPSNY 1840. *Med surg rep Phila* 1888: 270.

SANDS, DAVID, NYC (d/VII-31-1859 @47) MD CPSNY 139. *Med surg rep Phila* ns2: 408, 1859.

SANDS, HENRY BERTON, NYC (b/IX-27-1830; d/XI 17-1888) MD CPSNY 1854 *Med reg NY NJ Conn* 1889: 284. *Chic m j* 57:362, 1888. *Bost m&s j* 119: 515, 542-43, 1888? *JAMA* 11:755, 1888. *K&B* III: 1075.

SANDS, SAMUEL, Darien, Conn (b/XI-10-1819 S Salem, NY; d/VII-15-1891) Lic M S Westchester Co, NY 1848. *Proc Conn M S* 1892: 852-854. *Bost m&s j* 125: 96, 1891.

SANDS, WILLIAM, Baltimore (b/1803; d/VI-24-1879) MD U Md 1823. *Med annals Md:* 558. *Butler* 1874: 315.

SANDT, JOHN, Easton, Pa (b/VI-9-1822 Mt Bethel Twp, Pa; d/V-1-1889) MD UPa 1850; AB Lafayette 1846. *Lehigh Valley med mag* 1:110-120, 1899-90. *Atkinson* I:549-550. *Butler* 1878: 730.

SANDT, SAMUEL, CW-USA; Easton, Pa (b/XI-15-1815 Northampton Co; d/IX-29-1892 or IX-1-1902!) MD UPa 1844; AM Lafayette 1871. *Lehigh Valley m mag* 4: 35, 1892-93. *U Pa m alum CW*:1844. *Butler* 1878: 730.

SANFORD, ABBOTT, Everett, Mass (b/IX-6-1854 E Bridgewater, Mass; d/VII-12-1893) MD Harvard 1885; AB Amherst 1877. *Amherst, Men of*: 1877.

SANFORD, GEORGE WILLIS, Tariffville, Conn (b/ XII-20-1807 Litchfield; d/IX-23-1892) MD Berkshire 1836. *Proc Conn M S* 1893:240-41. *Atkinson* I: 366. *Butler* 1878: 82.

SANFORD, JAMES HENRY, Shelbyville, Ind (b/VI-22 1838 Albany, NY; d/IX-7-1903) ng Centr CPS Indianapolis 1885. *Tr Ind St M S* 1904: 361.

SANFORD, JOHN WILLIAM, CW-CSA; Fayetteville, NC (b/1834; d/1881) MD Jefferson 1857; AB UNC 1854. *UNC cat*: 544.

SANFORD, LEONARD JACOB, New Haven, Conn (b/ XI-8-1833; d/XII-12-1896) MD Jefferson 1854. *Bost m&s j* 135:636, 1896. *JAMA* 27:1360, 1896. *Polk* 1896: 283. *Butler* 1878: 82.

SANFORD, WILBUR FISK, Greenpoint, NY (b/V-21-1845; d/XII-12-1880) MD UCNY 1867; AB Wesleyan 1865; LLB Columbia 1887. *Med reg NY NJ Conn* 1881:241.

SANGER, EUGENE FRANCIS, CW-USA; Bangor, Me 1865- (b/X-18-1829 Waterville; d/VII-24-1897) MD Jefferson 1853; ng Bowdoin Med Dept 1852; AB Dartmouth 1849. *Bost m&s j* 137:166, 1897. *JAMA* 29:297, 1897. *Atkinson* I: 37. *Polk* 1897: 633.

SANGER, WILLIAM WALLACE, NYC (b/VIII-10-1819 Conn; d/V-8-1872) MD CPSNY 1846. MD CPS NY 1846. *Med reg NY NJ Conn* 1872: 356.

SANGREE, ERNEST B , Harrisburg, Pa (b/V-28-1862 McConnellstown; d/II-23-1900) MD Medico-Chir Coll, Phila 1889; att Franklin & Marshall. *JAMA* 34: 573, 1900. *Tr Ill St M S* 1900:463, 509. *Polk* 1896: 1316.

SANNS [SARMS], JOHN, Gallipolis, O (d/I-29-1898 @ 73) MD UPa 1850; att Wash & Jeff. *JAMA* 30:391, 1898. *Polk* 1890: 917.

SANTEE, WILBUR R , ?Philadelphia (d/VIII-31-1862 @23) MD ? *Med surg rep Phila* ns8:516, 1862.

SAPPINGTON, , ? (d/IX-13-1878 Vicksburg, Miss) MD ? *Tr AMA* 30:885, 1879. *Med rec NY* 14:240, 1878.

SAPPINGTON, JOHN, Darlington, Md; York Co, Pa (b/ 1801 Harford Co; d/IX-18-1869 @67) MD UPa 1825. *Phila m reg & dir* 1871: 302. *Med annals Md:* 558.

SAPPINGTON, THOMAS, Baltimore (b/X-16-1816 Libertytown; d/VIII-11-1901) MD UPa 1839. *Med annals Md:* 559.

SARGEANT, JAMES HOVEY, Medway, Mass (b/1781? d/VIII-31-1869 @88) MD ? *Bost m&s j* 4: 112, 1869.

SARGENT, F D, Cincinnati (d/XI-13-1883) MD ? *Med surg rep Phila* 49:616, 1889.

SARGENT, FITZWILLIAM, Philadelphia; Europe (b/V 17-1820, Gloucester, Mass; d/IV-27-1889 Bournemouth, Engl) MD UPa 1843; AB Jefferson. *K&B* III: 1076-77.

SARGENT, GEORGE WOODBURY, Lawrence, Mass (d/I-1-1893 @58) MD Albany 1857. *Bost m&s j* 128: 28, 1893. *Butler* 1878: 356.

SARGENT, GORHAM P, Bryn Mawr, Pa (d/I-11-1891 @56) MD LICH 1863. *Med bull m & s* 13:70, 1891. *Polk* 1886: 794.

SARGENT, HENRY, Worcester, Mass (b/Leicester; d/IV-27-1858 @36) MD Harvard 1847; AB Yale 1841. *Bost m&s j* 58:285-86, 1858.

SARGENT, HOWARD, Boston (d/IX-14-1872 @61) MD Harvard 1832; AB 1829. *Bost m&s j* ns10:208 1872.

SARGENT, JOSEPH, Worcester, Mass (b/XII-15-1815 Leicester; d/1888) MD Harvard 1837; AB 1834. *Proc Conn M S* 1893:229. *Bost m&s j* 119: 396, 512, 1888. *K&B* III: 1077.

SARGENT, LUCIUS MANLIUS, CW-USA (b/IX-15-1826 Boston; d/XII-9-1864 Belfield, Va) MD Harvard 1857; AM 1848; AB 1859! *Bost m&s j* 71: 428, 486, 1864; 105:521, 1881. *Harvard in CW*: 38. *Nat med jour* 1:302, 1870/71.

SARGENT, ORIN SHAW, Boston (d/III-28-1902 Phila) MD CPS Boston 1889. *Pa med jour* 6:261, 1902/03. *Polk* 1896: 704.

SARGENT, RUFUS, Philadelphia 1857-62; 1865- (b/IV-16-1824 Essex Co, Mass; d/IV-10-1886 or 1887 Wernersville, Pa) MD Phila Coll M & S 1851; MD Hahnemann 1852. *Hahn mo* 21: 336, 1886. *Tr Am Inst Hom* 1887: 215. Homeopath.

SARGENT, SENECA, Lawrence, Mass (d/1873 @70) MD Dartmouth 1839. *Bost m&s j* ns12: 198, 1873.

SARGENT, WINTHROP Jr, CW-USA; Philadelphia; Newton, Mass (b/VII-8-1822 Gloucester; d/III-17-1896 Roxbury) MD UPa 1847; AB Dartmouth 1842. *JAMA* 26: 732, 1896. *Tr CPP* cent vol: 263. *Butler* 1878: 694. *Polk* 1886: 470.

SARNER, F, ? (d/VIII-15-1878 Memphis) MD ? *Tr AMA* 30: 885, 1879. *Med rec NY* 14:220, 1878.

SARTWELL, HENRY PARKER, War 1812-USA; Penn Yan, NY (b/IV-18-1792 Berkshire Co, Mass; d/XI-15-1867) MD U Md 1841; PhD Hamilton 1864. *Tr AMA* 19: 419, 1868. *Tr M S St NY* 1865: 277. *K&B* III:1078.

SASS, LOUIS J, NYC (b/Havana; d/XI-19-1896 @76) Hon Med NY Med Coll 1859. *Bost m&s j* 135: 579, 1896. *JAMA* 28: 236, 1897.

SASSER, LEWIS L, Smithfield, NC (b/I-16-1860; d/II 24-1896 Richmond, Va) MD U Va 1883. *JAMA* 26: 794, 1896. *NC m j* 37: 150, 1896. *Tr NC M S* 1896: 150. *Polk* 1896: 1128.

SATCHWELL, SOLOMON SAMPSON, Burgaw, NC (b/X-26-1821 Beaufort Co; d/X-9-1892) MD UCNY 1845; att Wake Forest. *NC med jour* 30:319, 1892. *Tr NC M S* 1893: 20; 1899: 172-74. *Butler* 1878: 598.

SATTERFIELD, JAMES L, MexWar-USA; Iberia Parish, La (d/V-15 1885 @71) MD UPa 1837. *New Orl m & s j* ns14: 86, 1885. *Butler* 1878: 300.

SATTERLEE, RICHARD SHERWOOD [SMITH], USA 1822-69; NYC (b/XII-6-1798; d/XI-10-1880) MD ? *Bost m&s j* 103:527, 1880. *Tr RI M S* 2:318, 1877-82. *Med reg NY NJ Conn* 1881: 241. *Atkinson* I: 354. *K&B* II: 1019-1020.

SAULISBURY, STEPHEN, Boston (b/1812; d/1875) MD Harvard 1835; AB 1832. *Tr AMA* 31:1082-83, 1880.

SAULSBURY, GOVE DENTON, Dover, Del (b/V-29 1815; d/VII-31-1881) MD UPa 1842. *JAMA* 2:24, 1884. *Chic med rev* 4:401, 1881. *Butler* 1878: 79.

SAUNDERS, ALBERT AINSWORTH, Carolina, RI (b/X-6-1833 Hopkinton; d/X-2-1897) MD Buffalo 1861. *Tr RI M S* 5:495-96, 1894-98. *Polk* 1896: 1025.

SAUNDERS, FREDERICK WARD, USN 1859-61; USA 1864-65; Philadelphia (b/VI-29-1829 Webster, Mass; d/I-20-1897 Phila) MD UPa 1864. *U Pa med alum CW*: 1864.

SAUNDERS, HENRY G, Grand Rapids, Mich (d/XII-22 1899 @80) MD UCNY 1847.*JAMA* 34:61.*Polk* 1896:758

SAUNDERS, JOHN S, Bonham Tex (b/II or IX-22-1826 Barren Co, Ky; d/VIII-22-1892) MD U Louisville 1854. *Tex cour-rec med* 10:119-20, 1892. *Atkinson* I:516.

SAUNDERS, RICHARD WESTROP, Cincinnati (d/III-16-1884) MD ? *Med surg rep Phila* 50:480, 1884.

SAUNDERS, THOMAS JEFFERSON, CW-USA; Davenport, Ia (b/II-6-1819 Woodbury, NJ; d/X-18-1897) MD UPa 1843. *U Pa med alum CW*: 1843.

SAUNDERS, WILLIAM EDWARD, CW-CSA; Sherman, Tex (b/IV-5-1828 Wilson Co, Tenn; d/I-14-1885) MD UPa 1868; att Nashville Med Coll 1853. *Tex cour-rec med* 2:665-67, 1885. *New Orl m&s j* ns13: 1008, 1886. *JAMA* 6:530-31, 1886. *Butler* 1876: 793.

SAUNDERS, WILLIAM H, ? (b/1820; d/II-11-1857 San Juan, Nicaragua) MD UPa 1848. *Bost m&s j* 56:187, 1857. *Hist M S DC:* 240.

SAUNDERS, WILLIAM STURGIS, Sturbridge, Mass (b/c1815; d/XI-5-1862) MD Dartmouth 1837. *Bost m&s j* 67:308, 1862.

SAUTER, EMILE, Covington, La (d/XII-22-1901 @35) <MD U Md 1894> *New Orl m&s j* 54:564, 1902. *Polk* 1896: 624.

SAUVÉ, HENRY P, New Orleans (d/V- -1895 @62) MD Tulane 1856. *New Orl m&s j* ns22: 892, 1895. *Polk* 1890: 491.

SAVAGE, CHARLES MAURY, Louisville 1870-71; Columbus, O 1871- (b/XI-16-1846 Columbus; d/VIII-16-1904) MD Hahnemann, Phila 1870. *Med vis* 1904: ?

 Spec. educ'l status abbrev. as: ***ng*** = college verified attendance without degree;

(Oct). Homeopath.

SAVAGE, JOHN JAMES, Lowell, Mass (d/I-12-1897 @24) MD Harvard 1895. *Bost m&s j* 136: 76, 1897.

SAVAGE, W E, CW-USA (d/XI-21-1867 Ringgold Barracks, Tex) MD ? *Nat med jour* 1:302, 1870/71.

SAVERY, L P, Denmark, Me c40 yrs (d/X-10-1864) MD ? *Med surg rep Phila* 12: 196, 1864/65.

SAVERY, PHINEAS, Attleborough, Mass (b/1800 Wareham, Mass; d/V-19-1853) MD Harvard 1827; AB Brown 1824. *Bost m&s j* 48: 362, 1853.

SAVERY, WILLIAM, CW-USA; Philadelphia (b/X-20-1832; d/III 13-1896) MD UPa 1861; PhB Coll Pharmacy 1854. *U Pa m alum CW*: 1861. *JAMA* 26: 732, 1896.

SAVILLE, HENRY MARTYN, CW-USA; Boston; NYC (b/VII-29-1833 Quincy, Mass; d/I-11-1881) MD UPa 1857; AB Amherst 1855; ng Harvard Med 1856. *Bost m&s j* 105:624, 1881. *Harvard in CW*: 247. *U Pa med alum CW*: 1857. *Butler* 1878: 343.

SAVORY, CHARLES AUGUSTUS, Lowell, Mass (b/XII-25-1813 Beverly; d/II-2-1892) MD Dartmouth 1836. *Bost m&s j* 126:132, 1892. *Med bull m & s* 14:160, 1892. *Polk* 1890: 550.

SAWTELLE, MARY P, San Francisco (b/NY; d/IV-22 1894 @59 NYC) MD NY Med Coll for Women 1872. *JAMA* 22:674, 1894. *Polk* 1886: 616 (Albuquerque NM).

SAWYER, ALFRED ISAAC, Monroe, Mich 1857- (b/X 31-1827 Lyme, O; d/V-7-1890) MD Homeop Med Coll Cleveland 1854. *Hahn mo* 26:573, 1890? *NW j hom* 1: 208, 1891. *Med vis* 7:230, 1891. Homeopath.

SAWYER, CONANT, Auburn, NY (d/II-21-1898) MD Albany 1865. *Bost m&s j* 138:212, 1898. *JAMA* 30:570, 1898. *Polk* 186: 988.

SAWYER, EDWARD, Bridgewater, Mass (d/XII-21 1891 @53) MD Harvard 1865. *Bost m&s j* 125:692, 1891. *Polk* 1890: 545.

SAWYER, EDWARD JULIUS, Gardner, Mass (b/VIII-3 1829 W Haven, Conn; d/V-10-1883) MD Castleton 1853. *JAMA* 2:726-27, 1884. *Bost m&s j* 109:617, 1883. *Butler* 1878: 356.

SAWYER, FREDERIC AUGUSTUS, CW-USA; Wareham, Mass (d/II-10-1895 @62) MD Harvard 1856. *Bost m&s j* 132:172, 1895. *Harvard in CW*: 247.

SAWYER, JOHN WOODBURY, Providence, RI (b/XI-5-1834 Danvers, Mass; d/XII-14-1885) MD Harv'd 1859; Hon AM Brown 1881;ng Amherst 1858 *Bost m&s j* 113:623 632 656 1885 *Tr RI M S* 111:254-5 1883-88.

SAWYER, LANGDON, Springfield, Vt (d/XI-1-1879 @61) MD Castleton 1843; Hon MD Dartmouth 1867. *Med surg rep Phila* 41:528, 1879.

SAWYER, PLATT ROGERS HALSTED, Bedford NY (b/VIII-14-1834 Westport; d/III-31-1885) Lic St Bd Censors 1870; ng U Vt Med Sch. *Tr M S St NY* 1886: 635-36. *Med s rep Phila* 52:512 1885. *Butler* 1874: 557.

SAWYER, SAMUEL, Cambridge, Mass (b/III-20-1803; d/I-4/5-1859) MD Harvard 1831; AB 1826. *Bost m&s j* 59:468, 1859. Palmer's *Necrol Harv alum*: 270-71.

SAWYER, SYLVESTER J, CW-USA; NYC (b/V-21-1828; d/V-21-1828; d/XI-25-1870) MD CPSNY 1854. *Med reg NY NJ Conn* 1871: 363. *Med rec* 6:94, 1871-72.

SAWYER, THOMAS H, CW-USA (d/VIII-23-1862 Phila) MD ? *Med surg rep Phila* ns8:492, 1862. *Nat m j* 1:302, 1870/71.

SAWYER, WILLIAM, Boston (b/II-1-1771 Newburyport; d/IV-18-1859) MD ? AB Harvard 1800. *Bost m&s j* 60:268 1859. Palmer's *Necrol Harv alum* 212-14.

SAXE, ARTHUR WELLESLEY, Vt; Santa Clara, Cal (b/X-20-1820 Plattsburgh, NY; d/V-26-1891) MD Castleton 1842. *Tr M S Cal* 22:260-62, 1892. *K&B* III: 1078-79.

SAY, BENJAMIN, Philadelphia (b/1756; d/IV-23-1813) <MD U St Pa 1780> *Tr CPP* cent vol:263. *Congr biogr direct*. *K&B* III: 1079.

SAYERS, GEORGE W, CW-USA (d/XII-26-1862 Bowling Green, Ky) MD ? *Nat m j* 1:302, 1870/71.

SAYLER, WILLIAM, Winchester, O (b/XI-8-1837; d/IX-18-1885) MD Med Coll Ohio 1871. *Tr Ohio M S* 1886: 400-401.

SAYLOR, ANDREW JACKSON, Frankfort, Ind (d/XII 1-1895 @45) MD Eclectic Med Inst Ohio 1877. *JAMA* 25: 1058, 1895. *Polk* 1890: 371.

SAYLOR, GEORGE WALLACE, Philadelphia; CW-USA (b/IX-26-1842 Schuylkill Haven, Pa; d/XI-26-1883) MD UPa 1864; MD Hahnemann, Phila 1876. *Med surg rep Phila* 49: 644, 700, 1883. Homeopath.

SAYLOR, HENRY A, Weisenburg, Pa (d/XI-29-1898 @68) <MD UPa> *Lehigh Valley med mag* 9:246, 1898. *Butler* 1878: 731. *Polk* 1886: 803.

SAYLOR, OBADIAH L, Bethlehem, Pa (b/Pa; d/IV-4 1906 @72) MD Jefferson 1853. *Pa m j* 9:608, 1905/06. *Flint* 1897: 796.

SAYRE, CHARLES HENRY BALL, NYC (b/V-14-1850; d/III-11-1880) MD Bellevue 1878. *Med reg NY NJ Conn* 1880:241. *Med rec NY* 17:444, 1880. *K&B* III: 1080 [mention only].

SAYRE, DAVID MARTIN, Newton, NJ (b/III-26-1807 Hanover; d/VIII-3-1876) MD CPSNY 1836. *Tr AMA* 29: 757-58, 1878. *Tr M S NJ* 1877: [129]-131.

SAYRE, JOHN STANFORD, Monticello, Mo (b/VIII-7-1857; d/XI-29-1899) MD U Mich 1881; MD Bellevue 1884; AB Princeton 1878. *JAMA* 33:1504, 1899.

SAYRE, LEWIS ALBERT, NYC (b/Bottle Hill, NJ; d/IX 21-1900) MD CPSNY 1842. *Med s rep Phila* 12: 133-34, 1864/65. *So pract* 22:457, 1900. *Bost m&s j* 143:331, 1900. *K&B* III: 1079-80.

SAYRE, LEWIS HALL, NYC (d/I-3-1890 @39) MD Bellevue 1876. *Med reg NY NJ Conn* 1890: 279. *Buff m & s j* 29: 446, 1889. *Med bull m & s* 13: 71: 1890. *K&B* III: 1080 [mention only].

SAYRES, DAVID, Bastrup, Tex (d/VII-2-1886 @75) MD ? *Tex cour-rec med* 3:527, 1886.

SCALES, THOMAS SIDNEY, Mobile, Ala (d/VI-5-1901) MD CPSNY 1867; AB UNC 1862; AM 1868. *Tr Med Assn St Ala* 1902: 130. *New Orl m&s j* 54:59, 1901. *Polk* 1893: 159.

SCALES, WILLIAM B , Sedalia, Mo (d/VIII-27-1898 @57) MD Med Coll Ohio 1878. *JAMA* 31:618, 1898. *Polk* 1896: 889.

SCAMMEL, ALEXANDER, Milford, Mass (d/I-28-1858 @49) MD ? *Bost m&s j* 58: 47, 1858.

SCAMMELL, LUCIUS LESLIE, CW-USA; St Louis (b/XII-17-1819 Bellingham, Mass; d/II-13-1892) MD Harvard 1842; AB Dartmouth 1837. *Bost m&s j* 127:638, 1892. *Harvard in CW*: 229.

SCANLAND, J E , ?Chicago (d/1871) MD Rush 1867. *Chic m j* 28:310-11, 1871.

SCANLON, MICHAEL D , Washington, Ind (d/V-30-1904 @75) MD Jefferson 1869. *JAMA* 43: 61, 1904. *Polk* 1886: 340.

SCANNELL, MICHAEL EDWARD, Worcester, Mass (d/XI-16-1905 @41) MD Harvard 1891. *Bost m&s j* 153:656, 1905.

SCARBORO, H , Ellaville, Ga (d/IX-8-1898 @86) MD ? *JAMA* 31: 742, 1898.

SCARBOROUGH, J H , Trenton, NC (d/III-20-1886) MD CPS Balto 1882. *New Orl m&s j* ns13: 1007, 1896. *Polk* 1886: 727.

SCHAADT, CLINTON JOSEPH, Egypt, Pa (d/IV-4-1904 @40) MD UPa 1890. *Pa med jour* 8:336, 1904/05.

SCHAAKE, FREDERICK HENRY, Lawrence, Mass (d/III-27-1899 @34) MD Harvard 1888. *Bost m&s j* 140: 320, 1899.

SCHAEFER, FREDERICK C , Chicago (d/VI-3-1904) MD Chic Med Coll 1876. *Chic med rec* 26:399, 1904. *Flint* 1897: 268.

SCHAEFFER, CHARLES, CW-USA; Philadelphia (b/II 4-1838; d/ XI-23-1903) MD UPa 1859. *Tr CPP* cent vol:263. *Atkinson* I:199. *K&B* III:1081. *Flint* 1897: 824.

SCHAEFFER, EDWARD MORTON, Baltimore (b/1856; d/IV-23-1901) MD U Md 1880. *Med annals Md:* 560. *Polk* 1886: 439.

SCHAEFFER, LEON A, Kansas City Mo (d/V-1-1899 @57) MD KC Med Coll 1894. *JAMA* 32:1074, 1899.

SCHAFER, ALBERT FRANKLIN, So Bend, Ind (b/XII 16-1863 Decatur; d/IX-17 or X-16-1898 Cleveland, O) MD U Mich 1887. *Tr Ind St M S* 1899: 391. *JAMA* 3:808, 1898. *Polk* 1896: 492.

SCHAFER [SHAEFFER], CHARLES MARTIN, Pittsburgh (d/VII-25-1904 @27) MD W Pa Med Coll 1900. *Pa med jour* 8: 336, 1904/05.

SCHAFORTH, ERNEST, S Bethlehem, Pa (d/II-10-1869) MD ? *Phila med reg & dir* 1871: 300. *Med surg rep Phila* 20:160, 1869.

SCHANK, JOHN STILLWELL, Princeton, NJ (b/II-24 1817 Freehold; d/XII-16-1898) MD UPa 1843; AB Princeton 1840; LLD Lafayette. *JAMA* 32:41, 1899. *Polk* 1896: 948.

SCHAPER, ALFRED, Boston (b/V-25-1863 Europe; d/1905 Europe) MD ? *Bost m&s j* 154: 55, 1906.

SCHAPER, CHARLES, Sheboygan, Wis (b/XI-24-1857 Lippe Detmold, Gny; d/XII-29-1901) MD Rush 1885. *Tr Wis St M S* 36: 414-15, 1902. *Polk* 1896: 1549.

SCHAPPS, CORNELIUS HANFORD, NYC (d/IX-1-1899 @82) Lic NY St M S 1840. *JAMA* 33:683, 1899. *Polk* 1896: 1002.

SCHELL, HENRY AUGUSTUS, CW-CSA; Gallatin, Tenn (b/XI-26-1831 Phila; d/IX-25-1885) MD UPa 1858. *So pract* 7:489-90, 1885. *U Pa med alum CW*: 1858. *SHSP* 22:257, 1893.

SCHELL, HENRY SAYLER, USA 1860-69; Philadelphia (b/VI-1-1835; d/III-15-1890 San Diego) MD UPa 1857; AB 1853 Central HS, Phila; AM 1858. *Tr CPP* cent vol: 263. *U Pa med alum CW*: 1853. *Atkinson* I: 323. *Med bull med & surg* 13: 147, 1890.

SCHELL, JOSEPH GRABILL, CW-CSA; Frederick, Md (b/VII-18-1837; d/X-19-1897) MD UPa 1866. *U Pa med alum CW*: 1866.

SCHELLING, AUGUST, Brooklyn (d/III-8-1884 @57) MD ? *Med reg NY NJ Conn* 1885: 243.

SCHENCK, AUGUST H , Kenney, Tex (b/1866 Bellville; d/VIII-21-1900) MD U Louisville 1888; att Bellevue. *Tr Tex St M Assn* 1901:48-49. *Polk* 1896: 1437.

SCHENCK, FERDINAND SCHUREMAN, Six Mile Run, NJ (b/1790; d/V-13-1860) MD CPSNY 1814. *Tr AMA* 29:758-60, 1878.

SCHENCK, HENRY H , RevWar-USA; Neshanic, NJ (b/VIII- -1760 Millstone, NJ; d/1838) MD ? *Tr M S NJ* 1872:210-11.

SCHENCK, HENRY H Jr, USA (b/II-1782 NY; d/XII 20-1823 @41) MD ? *Tr M S NJ* 1872: 119-120.

SCHENCK, JOHN FRELINGHUYSEN, Flemington, NJ (b/VI-6-1799 Neshanic; d/II-6-1881) <Lic NJ 1821> *Tr M S NJ* 1880-81: 165-66. *Butler* 1878: 475.

SCHENCK, JOHN P , Matteawan, NY (b/1797? d/IX-7 1872 @75) MD CPSNY 1819. *Med surg rep Phila* 27: 332, 1872.

SCHENCK, JOHN VOORHEES, Camden, NJ (b/XI-17 1824; d/VII-25-1882) MD UPa 1847; AB Rutgers 1844; AM 1847. *JAMA* 1:408, 1883. *Tr M S NJ* 1883:291-92. *Atkinson* I: 213. *Butler* 1878: 475.

SCHENCK, PETER VOORHIS, CW-USA; ?St Louis (b/V-23-1838 Six Mile Run, NJ; d/III-11-1885 St Louis) MD UPa 1860. *U Pa med alum CW*: 1860.

SCHENCK, TEUNIS L , Brooklyn (d/VIII-15-1899 @58) MD CPSNY 1865; AB Union 1859. *JAMA* 33:558, 1899. *Bost m&s j* 141:204,1899. *Polk* 1896:1110.

SCHENKEL, NICHOLAS, Allegheny, Pa (d/VI-19-1897 @40) MD Jefferson 1878. *JAMA* 28:1252, 1897. *Polk* 1886: 790.

SCHERZER, WILLIAM, Savannah 1866-68, 1880-82; NYC 1868-80 (b/VIII-7-1825 Bavaria; d/II-21-1882)

<MD Leipsig> MD Hahnemann Phila 1859. *NY m times* 10:24, 1882? *Tr Am Inst Hom* 1882: 144. Homeopath.

SCHEU [SCHEER], PHILIP, NYC (d/X-21-1899 @41) MD CPSNY 1884; PhG NY Coll Pharm. *JAMA* 33:1183, 1899. *Bost m&s j* 141: 460, 1899. *Polk* 1890: 832.

SCHEURMANN, CASPER, Milwaukee (b/1834 Gny; d/XII-21-1899) <MD Würzburg 1855> *JAMA* 34:61, 1900. *Polk* 1890: 116.

SCHIFF, GUSTAV, San Francisco; Dallas, Tex (d/IX-2 1901 @68) <MD U Würzburg 1856> *JAMA* 37: 789, 1901. *Polk* 1886: 884.

SCHIFF, HERMAN JAMES, NYC (d/VII-24-1905 Alexandria Bay) MD CPSNY 1884. *Bost m&s j* 153: 154, 1905. *Polk* 1896: 1077.

SCHILLING, ERNST, NYC (b/XII-25-1809 Salzburg, Austria; d/IV-25-1872) <MD U Vienna> *Med reg NY NJ Conn* 1872: 356.

SCHILTNECK, VANDYKE G , Hagerstown, Ind (b/Frederick, Md; d/I-3-1900 @55) MD U Md 1882. *JAMA* 34: 380, 1900. *Polk* 1886: 316.

SCHIRMER, WILLIAM, NYC (b/1808; d/VII-8-1878) <MD U Marburg 1832> att U Würzburg. *Med s rep Phila* 1879: 199. *Butler* 1878: 509.

SCHIVELY, GEORGE P , Philadelphia; Chambersburg, Pa (d/I-7-1873 @59) MD Jefferson 1856. *Med surg rep Phila* 28: 202, 1873.

SCHIVELY, GEORGE SINGE, Philadelphia (d/IX-28-1901 @78) MD Jefferson 1851. *Pa med jour* 5:296, 1901/02. *Polk* 1886: 824.

SCHLAGENHAUF, GEORGE, Altamont, Ill (b/I-10-1901) <MD St Louis Med Coll 1875> *Ill m j* ns2:533, 1901. *Polk* 1896: 360.

SCHLAWIG, JOHN JACOB, Sioux City, Ia (b/1867; d/IX-8-1902) MD CPS Chic 1891. *JAMA* 39: 714, 1902.

SCHLEMM, WILLIAM E , Reading, Pa (d/II-25 or 29-1904 @79) MD UPa 1854. *Pa med jour* 8: 336, 1904/05. *Flint* 1897.

SCHLENKER, T W , Ridgetown, Ont (d/VIII-25-1892 Austin, Tex) MD ? *Daniel's Tex m j* 8:118, 1892-93.

SCHLOETZER, GEORGE, Chicago; Highland, Ill (d/XII-5-1893 Carlsruhe, Gny) MD U Munich 1843. *JAMA* 22:97, 1894. *Chic med rec* 67: 1894. *Polk* 1886: 282.

SCHMELTZER, ROBERT P , Brooklyn (b/Gny; d/X-11-1906 @54) <MD Würzburg 1879> *Bost m&s j* 155: 458, 1906. *Polk* 1900: 1212.

SCHMIDT, ERNST, Chicago (d/VIII-26-1900 @70) MD Würzburg 1852. *Chic med rec* 19: 203, 1900. *Ill med jour* ns2:237, 1900. *Polk* 1896: 405.

SCHMIDT, HENRY D , CW-CSA; New Orleans (b/1823 Marburg, Prussia; d/XI-23-1888) MD UPa 1858. *Chic med jour* 57:361-62, 1888? *U Pa med alum CW*:1858. *K&B* III: 1082-83. *Polk* 1886: 418.

SCHMIDT, JACOB, Philadelphia; Baltimore 1844-80 (b/VI-29-1813 Kreutznach, Prussia; d/III-20-1880) MD Allentown Acad 1843; MD Hahnemann Phila 1867. *Tr Am Inst Hom* 1881:120. *King* I: 198. Homeopath.

SCHMIDT, RUDOLPH HENRY, Seymour, Wis (b/1846? d/VII-29-1899 @53) MD Rush 1886. *JAMA* 33:427, 1899. *Polk* 1890: 328.

SCHMINKEY [SCHWINKEY], I [J] S [F], Gratz, Pa (d/II-19-1900 @67) MD ? *JAMA* 34:574, 1900. *Polk* 1886: 800.

SCHMITTLE, JULIUS FREDERICK, New Orleans (b/VI-20-1864; d/IX-19-1897) MD Tulane 1888; MD Charity Hosp NO 1888. *Tr La St M S* 19: 23, 1898. *New Orl m&s j* 50:269, 1897. *JAMA* 29: 706, 1897. *Tex med pract* 10-11: 83, 1897-98. *Polk* 1886: 162.

SCHMITZ, CHARLES, Ft Wayne, Ind (b/XI-24-1809 Hanover, Gny; d/III-10-1887) <MD U Bonn 1833> *Tr Ind St M S* 1887: 196. *Butler* 1878: 218.

SCHNECK, BENJAMIN FRANCIS, CW-USA (b/VII-7-1824 Lebanon, Pa; d/X-2-1865) MD UPa 1846; att Franklin & Marshall. *U Pa med alum CW*: 1846. *Tr AMA* 18: 331, 1867.

SCHNEIDER, LOUIS, Williamsport, Pa (b/VI-22-1844 Huntingdon; d/XII-29-1900) MD Ky Sch Med 1865. *Pa m j* 4:496, 1900/01. *Off'l reg Pa phys* 1881-88:260.

SCHNEIDER, NATHANIEL, Cleveland (d/II-4-1895) MD Cleveland Homeop 1864. *No Am j hom* 43: 318, 1895. *Hahn mo* 30:37, 1895. *Polk* 1886:748. Homeopath.

SCHNETTER, JOSEPH, NYC (b/1822; d/1903) <MD Würzburg 1848> *Chic med rec* 25:288, 1903. *Med rec NY* 64:422, 1903. *Bost m&s j* 149:304, 1903.

SCHOALES, JOSEPH DAFFRON, CW-USA; Philadelphia (b/XI-27-1837 Irel'd; d/X-24-1895) MD UPa 1857. *U Pa med alum CW*: 1857. *JAMA* 25:818, 873, 1895. *Med bull m & s* 17:467,1895. *Polk* 1886:824.

SCHOFIELD, EDWARD LANE, Chambersburg, Pa (d/XI-19-1893) MD UPa 1867. *JAMA* 21:869, 1893. *Butler* 1878: 731.

SCHOLFIELD, EDWIN, Philadelphia (d/1871? @56) MD UPa 1855. *Phila med reg & dir* 1873:304. *Tr CPP* cent vol: 263.

SCHOLL, JOSEPH, Washington, DC; Newark, NJ (b/III-12-1823 Carlsruhe, Gny; d/VI-6-1902) <MD Tübingen 1850> *Hist M S DC:* 277. *Butler* 1878:94.

SCHOONMAKER, EPHRAIM JOACHIM, Magee's Corners NY (b/Ulster Co; d/VIII-19-1889) MD Geneva 1848. *Tr M S St NY* 11:741, 1894. *Polk* 1886: 667.

SCHOONOVER, WARREN Jr, NYC (d/VI-12-1905) MD Bellevue 1898. *Bost m&s j* 152: 740, 1905.

SCHOPEN, EMIL, Yonkers, NY (d/XI-17-1898) MD Bern 1884. *JAMA* 31:1319, 1898. *Polk* 1896: 1114.

SCHORSE, WILLIAM, Milwaukee (b/V-2-1846 Braunschweig, Gny; d/XII-11-1898) MD Göttingen 1877. *JAMA* 32:41, 1899. *Tr Wis St M S* 33:518-19, 1899. *Polk* 1886: 857.

SCHOTT, ARNOLD HEINRICH ARTHUR, Philadelphia (b/1827 Gny; d/III-18-1897) MD Jefferson 1868. *JAMA* 28: 655, 1897. *Polk* 1896: 1316.

SCHOTT, CHARLES, Troy, Ill (d/V–21–1901) MD Homeop Med Coll St Louis 1878. *Ill m j* ns3: 91, 1901. *Polk* 1886: 300.

SCHRACK, DAVID Jr, Jeffersonville, Pa (d/IV– –1883) MD Jefferson 1865. *Tr Pa St M S* 15:40–41, 1883.

SCHRACK, FREDERICK AUGUSTUS SETZLER, CW–USA (b/VIII–26–1843 Norristown, Pa; d/1891) MD UPa 1868. *U Pa med alum CW*: 1868.

SCHRENCK, ANDREW, NYC (d/VIII–20–1899) MD Bellevue–UCNY 1889 *JAMA* 33:621 1899. *Polk* 1890:832.

SCHRIVER, ALBERT, USN (b/1829; d/1873) MD Jefferson 1850; AB Princeton 1848. *Tr AMA* 24:397–98, 1873. *Med s rep Phila* 28: 130, 1873.

SCHROEDER, HERMAN, Bloomington, Ill (d/IV–7 1905 @84) <MD West Res 1849> *Ill m j* 7:611, 1905. *Polk* 1896: 364.

SCHROEDER, J ERNST, So Brooklyn, NY (b/III–26–1852; d/I–13–1900) MD LICH 1882 [as Ernest]. *JAMA* 34: 251, 1900.

SCHRUBERT [SCHUBERT?], JOHN, Joliet, Ill (d/III 20–1899 @57) MD Med Dept Ill Coll 1888. *JAMA* 32: 787, 1899.

SCHUHL, CHARLES A G, W Hoboken, NJ (b/VIII–31–1842 Offenbach, Gny; d/I–15–1890) <MD Giessen; AM 1861> *Tr M S NJ* 1890:344–45. *Polk* 1890:723.

SCHULTZ, EDWARD FRANK, Milwaukee (b/VI–9–1872 Reedsburg, Wis; d/IX–30–1899) MD Rush 1897. *Tr Wis St M S* 34:426, 1900; 35:505, 1901.

SCHULTZ, OSCAR T, Mt Vernon, Ind (b/XI–9–1848 Prussia; d/II–12–1890) MD Hosp Med Coll Louisville 1875. *Tr Ind St M S* 1890: 164.

SCHULTZ, SOLOMON SCHULTZ, CW–USA; Danville, Pa (b/ VII–5–1831 Berks Co; d/IX–21–1891) MD UPa 1856; AB Princeton 1852; AM 1855. *Lehigh Valley med mag* 4:16–17, 1892–93. *Bost m&s j* 125:392, 1891. *Med bull med & surg* 13:431, 1891. *Atkinson* I: 47. *Butler* 181878: 731.

SCHULTZE, ALBERT FERDINAND LOUIS, CW–USA; NYC (b/XI–6–1822 Berlin; d/II–8–1887) MD NY Med Coll 1861; stud med Berlin & Heidelberg. *Med reg NY NJ Conn* 1887: 275. *Polk* 1886: 693 [as Louis F).

SCHULTZE, WILLIAM S, Louisville (d/IV–24–1897 @35) MD Ky Sch Med 1893. *JAMA* 28:1092 1897.

SCHULZE [SCHULTZ], RUDOLPH B, Reading Pa (d/XI–3–1894 @34) MD Jefferson 1883. *JAMA* 23:768, 1894. *Lehigh Val m mag* 6:70 1894–95. *Polk* 1890:1012.

SCHUPPERT, MORITZ, New Orleans (b/1817 Marburg, Gny; d/V–2–1887) ng Marburg. *New Orl med & surg jour* ns14:986–88, 1887. *Tr La St M S* 10:51–53, 1888. *Med surg rep Phila* 56:608, 1887. *K&B* III:1084.

SCHUPPERT, WILLIAM E, New Orleans (d/VII–9–1895) <MD Charity Hosp NO 1875> *New Orl med & surg jour* ns23:127, 1895. *Polk* 1890: 491.

SCHUREMAN, ALBERT JEREMIAH, Newark, NJ (d/VII–29–1903 @74) MD UCNY 1872. *Bost m&s j* 149:166, 1903. *Polk* 1896: 944.

SCHUREMAN, IRVING C, Toms River, NJ (d/VIII–6–1899 @59) MD Albany 1869. *Bost m&s j* 141: 174, 1899. *JAMA* 33:493, 1899. *Polk* 1886: 611.

SCHUYLER, CLARKSON C, Troy, NY (d/VIII–16 1905 @55) MD Albany 1875. *Bost m&s j* 153:234, 1905. *Polk* 1886: 712.

SCHUYLER, PHILIP ALEXANDER, Greenville, Miss (d/II–25–1859) MD UPa 1835; AB Rutgers 1835; AM 1838. *Med surg rep Phila* ns1: 378, 1858/59.

SCHUYLER, WILLIAM DAVID, NYC (b/1834; d/XII–31–1887) MD CPSNY 1869. *Med reg NY NJ Conn* 1888:270. *Butler* 187: 527.

SCHWAB, JOSEPH, Brooklyn (b/1806; d/IX–4–1876) MD Munich 1832. *Med reg NY NJ Conn* 1877: 206. *Butler* 1878: 519.

SCHWARTZE, EDWARD, Baltimore (b/XII–1–1805; d/III–1–1805; d/III–12–1886) MD Washington Med Coll Balto 1828. *Med annals Md:* 561. *Butler* 1874: 315.

SCHWEIG, J HENRY, NYC (b/III–8–1810; d/I–2–1866) <MD U Berlin 1835> *Med reg NY NJ Conn* 1866: 205.

SCHWENK, SAMUEL G, Schwenksville, Pa (d/V–24–1863 @ 24) MD Jefferson 1853. *Med surg rep Phila* 10: 96, 1863.

SCOBEY, WILLIAM H, Hamilton, O (d/II–27–1895) MD Cleveland Med Coll 1851. *JAMA* 24:370, 1895. *Butler* 1878: 649.

SCOFIELD, DARIUS, Corinth, NY 1859–63; CW–USA; Washington, Ia 1869– (b/VII–31–1834 Hadley, NY; d/1893) MD Albany 1858; att Bellevue 1877–78. *Tr Ia St M S* 14:330, 1896. *Atkinson* I: 413. *Polk* 1890: 428.

SCOGGINS, CHARLES M, Graham, Tex (d/XII–22–1896 @ c35) <MD So Med Coll Atlanta 1886> *Tex med jour* 12:400, 1896/97. *Tex med news* 6:130, 1896–97. *Polk* 1896: 1432.

SCOLLAY, SAMUEL, Smithfield, Va (b/I–21–1782 Ashburnham, Mass; d/I–11–1857) MD UPa 1816; AM Harvard 1808. Palmer's *Necrol Harv alum*: 119.

SCOTT, ABRAHAM O, CW–USA; Fairfield, Pa (b/II–21–1828 Gettysburg, Pa; d/VII–7–1903) MD UPa 1853. *Pa med jour* 7:280, 1903/04. *U Pa med alum CW*: 1853. *Flint* 1897: 802.

SCOTT, AMOS, Seward, Ill (d/IX–17–1901) Lic 1877 by 16 yrs' pract. *Ill med jour* ns3:295, 1901. *Polk* 1890: 344.

SCOTT, CHESTER WALTER, Lyndon, Vt 1859–70; Lawrence, Mass 1870–1900 (b/XI–10–1832 Barre; d/VI–10–1903) MD Hahnemann Phila 1854. *Tr Am Inst Hom* 1903: 732–33. Homeopath.

SCOTT, DANIEL ARNOLD, Akron, O (b/1822 Cadiz, O; d/I–23–1890) MD Wooster 1880. *Tr Ohio St M S* 1890: 7, 301. *Polk* 1886: 736.

SCOTT, DANIEL VOORHEES, Jeffersonville, Ind (b/IV 14–1872 Floyd Co; d/I–6–1904) MD U Louisville 1894.

 Spec. educ'l status abbrev. as: ***ng*** = college verified attendance without degree;

Tr Ind St M S 1904: 363. *Polk* 1900: 597.

SCOTT, GEORGE WOODSON, Madison Run, Va (b/II–8–1871; d/V–14–1901) MD Med Coll Va 1894. *Tr M S Va* 1901: 278. *Polk* 1900: 1766.

SCOTT, GIDEON B , Greentown, Ind (b/VII–17–1838 Roseburgh; d/I–20–1898) MD Med Coll Ind 1870. *Tr Ind St M S* 1898: 388. *Polk* 1896: 470.

SCOTT, HORACE B , Wallingford, Conn; USN (b/ 1857; d/V–29–1900 @43) MD Jefferson 1882; AB Trinity 1878. *JAMA* 34: 1505, 1900.

SCOTT, J T H , Barren Plains, Tenn (d/VIII–17–1906) MD NY Med Coll 1861. *Nashville jour med & surg* 98: 428, 1906. *Polk* 1900: 1641.

SCOTT, JAMES L , Coatesville, Pa 1867– (b/X–1–1838 E Fallowfield; d/VIII–15–1876) MD Hahnemann Phila 1860. *Med surg rep Phila* 35:282, 1876. *Tr Am Inst Hom* 1877: 992. *Hahn mo* 12: 351, 1877.

SCOTT, JAMES W, Chillicothe O (d/IX–7–1833 @21) MD Transylvania 1833. *Trnslv j m & ass sci* 6:457 1833.

SCOTT, JAMES WARD Jr, Belair, Md (b/St Louis; d/VI–15–1899 @54) MD U Md 1866. *JAMA* 32: 1460, 1899. *Polk* 1886: 441.

SCOTT, JOHN, San Francisco (b/1821 Tyrone Co, Irel'd; d/XII–24–1886) MRCS (Ireland) 1841. *Tr Calif St M S* 1887: 293–94.

SCOTT, JOSEPH BION, Gettysburg, Pa (b/VIII–29–1859; d/IX–23/24–1904 Phila) MD UPa 1881: AB Gettysburg 1877. *Pa med jour* 8: 336, 1904/05. *Flint* 1897: 802.

SCOTT, JOSEPH T , New Orleans (b/Ky; d/VI–25–1896) MD Mo Med Coll 1856. *New Orl med & surg jour* ns24: 112, 1896. *JAMA* 27: 108, 1896. *Polk* 1890: 491.

SCOTT, MARTIN PICKETT, ?Va; CW–CSA (b/VI–12 1823 Warrenton, Va; d/XII–30–1904 Va) MD UPa 1846. *U Pa med alum CW*: 1846.

SCOTT, MATTHEW THOMPSON Jr, Lexington, Ky (b/III–14–1855 NYC; d/I–26–1894 San Antonio, Tex) MD UCNY 1877. *JAMA* 22:202, 1894. *Tr Ky St M S* 1894: 288–89. *Polk* 1890: 468.

SCOTT, NORMAN B , Hagerstown, Md (b/V–8–1819 Bruceville, Md; d/IX–21–1905) MD UCNY 1844. *Med annals Md:* 562. *Polk* 1886: 443.

SCOTT, PRESTON B , Louisville, Ky (b/IX–12–1832; d/IX–24–1900) MD U Louisville 1856. *So pract* 22: 463–66, 515, 1900. *Nashville jour med & surg* 88: 191–92, 1900. *Butler* 1878: 266.

SCOTT, ROBERT W , Milan, Tenn (d/VIII–24–1879) MD Jefferson 1859. *Med surg rep Phila* 41:286, 1879. *Butler* 1878: 777.

SCOTT, THOMAS F [or A], Petersburg, Va (d/VII–11 1883 @80) MD UPa 1839. *JAMA* 1:64, 1883. *Med surg rep Phila* 49: 84, 1883.

SCOTT, THOMAS J , Velasco & Alvin, Tex (b/Decatur, Ala; d/X–1–1906 @68) MD New Orl Sch Med 1860. *Tex st jour med* 2:194, 1906/07. *Polk* 1900: 1722.

SCOTT, UPTON, Annapolis, Md (b/1722 Ireland; d/II–23 1814) <MD U Glasgow 1753> *Med annals Md:* 563. *K&B* III: 1084–85.

SCOTT, WILLIAM JAMES, Philadelphia (d/VI–18–1899 @32) MD UPa 1892. *JAMA* 33:53, 1899. *Polk* 1896: 1317.

SCOTT, WILLIAM JOHN, White Plains, NY (b/XII–15 1847; d/I–25–1895 Jersey City, NJ) MD CPSNY 1871. *Med reg NY NJ Conn* 1895: 240.

SCOTT, WILLIAM JOHNSON, Cleveland (b/I–25–1822 Culpeper Co, Va; d/V–5–1896) MD Starling 1855. *Tr Ohio M S* 1896: 400–02. *JAMA* 26:995, 1896. *Med bull med surg* 18:272, 1896.

SCOTT, WILLIAM MAXWELL, CW–USA; Kulpsville, Pa (b/III–10–1832 Phila; d/XI–24–1872) MD UPa 1856; AB Brown 1852. *Tr Pa M S* 9:179–80, 1873.

SCOVILLE, SHELDON SMITH, CW–USA; Lebanon O (d/IX–22 1899 @76) MD Cincinnati Coll Med & Surg 1859. *JAMA* 33: 994, 1899. *Polk* 1886: 758–59.

SCRAMBLING, WILLIAM HOLMES, Slash, Ind (b/VI 16–1842 Lawrence, NY; d/VII–15–1881) MD Med Coll Ind 1872. *Tr Ind St M S* 1882: 196.

SCRATCHLEY, EDWARD, New Orleans (b/Ceylon; d/VIII–29–1881 @65) <MD France 1839> *New Orl med & surg jour* ns9:397, 1881.

SCREVEN, JAMES PROCTOR, Hot Springs, Va (d/VII 15–1859) MD UPa 1820; att SC Coll. *Bost m&s j* 61:168, 1859.

SCRIBNER, JAMES WILLIAM, Tarrytown, NY (b/ 1820; d/I–31–1879 or 1880) MD CPSNY 1847. *Tr AMA* 31: 1083–84, 1880. *Med reg NY NJ Conn* 1880: 241. *Med surg rep Phila* 42:154,176, 1880. *Butler* 1878: 572.

SCRIBNER, JOHN K , Finleyville Pa (d/III– 1902 @ 32) MD Jefferson 1894. MD Jefferson 1894. *Pa med jour* 6: 261, 1902/03.

SCRIBNER, WILLIAM AUGUSTUS, New Albany, Ind (b/II–19–1800 Mass; d/IV–16–1868) MD *Phila med reg & dir* 1871:296. Kemper's *Indiana*: 340.

SCRIVEN [SCRIVENS], ZEBULON W , Long Branch, NJ (b/IX–1–1826Petersburg, NY; d/II–11–1876) MD Albany 1852; MD New Orleans Sch Med 1852; AB Madison 1849. *Tr AMA* 27:656, 1876. *Tr M S NJ* 1876: 130–31. *Med reg NY NJ Conn* 1876: 255.

SCRUGGS, S OGLESBY, Natchitoches, La (b/1788? d/ III– –1886 @98) MD Med Inst Louisville 1840. *New Orl med & surg jour* ns13: 822, 1886.

SCUDDER, CHARLES DAVIES, Northport, NY (b/IX–24–1856; d/VII–19–1892) MD CPSNY 1878; AB Trinity 1875. *Med reg NY NJ Conn* 1893: 315. *Bost m&s j* 127:100, 1892. *Polk* 1886: 693.

SCUDDER, JOEL N [or JOE WILLSON?], Chesterfield, NH; Jacksonville, Vt 1889– (b/VIII–15–1851 So Granville, NY; d/VII–13–1899) MD Dartmouth 1887 [JW]. *Tr Vt St M S* 1899: 209–10.

SCUDDER, JOHN, Kadal Kamal, India (missionary) (b/X

29–1835 India; d/V–23–1900 India) MD LICH 1860; AB Rutgers 1857. *JAMA* 34:1431, 1900.

SCUDDER, SAMUEL OSBORNE, Rome, NY (b/III–19 1818 Roxbury; d/III–2–1895) MD Hahnemann, Phila 1849. *JAMA* 24:422, 1895. *No Amer jour homeop* 43:518, 1895. Homeopath.

SCUDDER, SILAS DOREMUS, India (missionary) b/XI 6–1836 Ceylon; d/XII–24–1877 Brooklyn) MD NY Med Coll 1858; AB Rutgers 1856. *Med reg NY NJ Conn* 1878: 190. *K&B* III: 1087.

SCULL, DAVID CLARENCE, Lebanon, Ind (b/II–4–1839 Moscow, Ind; d/VII–23–1897) Lic yrs pract. *Tr Ind St M S* 1898: 377. *JAMA* 29:297, 1897. *Polk* 1886: 326.

SCULL, WILLIAM JASPER, CW–USA (b/1838 Prince Wm Co, Va; d/V–9–1879 Chattahoochee, Fla) MD UPa 1861. *U Pa med alum CW*: 1861.

SCULLY, DANIEL J , Lindsay, Ont; Aspen, Colo (d/IV 21–1895 @33) MD McGill 1887. *Tr Colo St M S* 1898–99: 509. *Polk* 1893: 230.

SCULLY, FRANCIS PATRICK, Portland, Me (d/XI–12 1886 @34) MD Harvard 1879. *Bost m&s j* 115:488 1886.

SEABROOK, E M , Richmond, Va (b/SC; d/I–2–1887) <MD Med Coll St SC> *New Orl med & surg jour* ns14: 639, 1887. *Polk* 1886: 926.

SEABROOK, JOHN GABRIEL, CW–CSA; Columbia, SC (b/IX–13–1820 Edisto Isl; d/I–20–1903) MD UPa 1844; AB SC Coll 1841. *U Pa med alum CW*: 1844. *Polk* 1886: 853.

SEABURY, BENJAMIN FRANKLIN, Orleans, Mass (d/ II–26–1890 @82) MD Harvard 1830. *Bost m&s j* 123: 629, 1890. *Polk* 1886: 471.

SEABURY, JOHN HENRY, Yonkers, NY (d/III–16–1899 @51) MD CPSNY 1872. *JAMA* 32: 733, 1899. *Polk* 1896: 1114.

SEAMAN, FRANK G , Seneca Falls, NY (d/VII–12–1898 @35) MD Albany 1881. *JAMA* 31:198, 1898. *Polk* 1886: 708.

SEAMAN, MARINUS W , Shipman, Ill (d/IX–16–1897 @67 Denver, Colo) MD Albany 1853. *JAMA* 29:709, 1897. *Polk* 1886: 297.

SEAMAN, STEPHEN M , Lenhartsville, Pa (d/VIII–7 1903 @28) MD Medico–Chir Coll 1899. *Pa med jour* 7: 280, 1903/04.

SEAMAN, WILLIAM FERRIS, NYC (b/1797? d/IV–19 1855 @58) MD UPa 1818. *Bost m&s j* 32: 247, 1855.

SEARCEY [CEARSEY], O O , Temple Tx (d/X–19 1895) MD ? *Tex m j* 11:261 1895–6. *JAMA* 25:781 1895.

SEARCY, REUBEN, Tuscaloosa, Ala 1830– (b/Chapel Hill, NC; d/1887?) MD Transylvania 1832. *Tr Med Assoc St Ala* 1887: 306. *Polk* 1886: 140 [?].

SEARCY, ROBERT THOMAS, Fayetteville, Tenn to 1861; Cullman, Ala (b/I–11–1824 Bedford Co, Tenn; d/I–27–1889) MD U Nashville 1853. *Tr Med Assoc St Ala* 1890: 217. *Atkinson* I: 593. *Polk* 1886: 132.

SEARING, BYRON HUDSON, Auburn, NY (b/IV–9–1860; d/VI–4–1892) MD CPSNY 1885; BS Cornell 1882. *Med reg NY NJ Conn* 1893: 315.

SEARING, O W , E Oakland, Calif (d/VIII–22–1895 @65) MD ? *JAMA* 25: 427, 1895.

SEARLE, DAYTON WYCOFF, NYC (d/XI–15–1899 @ 62) MD CPSNY 1866; AB UCNY 1855; AM 1859. *JAMA* 33:1375: 1899. *Polk* 1896: 1077.

SEARS, GEORGE H , Blooming Grove, NY (d/III–4 1871) MD ? *Med surg rep Phila* 24:262, 1871.

SEARS, JOHN HENRY, Waco, Tex 1854– ; Port Sullivan (b/X–9–1826 Appomattox CH, Va; d/XII–4–1901) MD SC Coll Med 1852. *Tr Tex St M Assn* 1902: 70. *Atkinson* I: 323. *Polk* 1896: 1455.

SEARS, JOHN WILLIAM, CW–CSA; Birmingham, Ala (b/I–21–1830 Sandy Hook, Va; d/XII–13–1896) MD UPa 1850. *U Pa med alum CW*: 1850.

SEARY, CHARLES WESLEY, Philadelphia; CW–USA (b/1842 Media, Pa; d/V–8–1882 Phila) MD UPa 1865. *U Pa med alum CW*: 1865.

SEASTRUNK, T R , Burkeville, Tex (b/SC; d/VIII–20 1906 @8_?) MD Charleston Med Coll 1844. *Tex st med jour* 2:168, 1906/07. *Polk* 1886: 881.

SEATON, BERNARD COLE, Bolivar Pa (b/Westmoreland Co, Pa; d/X–9–1903 @55) MD Jefferson 1873. *Pa med jour* 7:280, 1903/04. *Flint* 1897: 796.

SEATON, JOHN, Ft Wayne, Ind (d/VIII–17–1894) MD *JAMA* 23:324, 1894. *Polk* 1890: 371.

SEATON, LEANDER, Stauffer, Pa (d/XII–11–1898 @ 40) MD CPS Balto 1886. *JAMA* 31: 1542, 1898.

SEATON, THOMAS, Bolivar, Pa (d/IV–29–1895 @82) MD ? *JAMA* 24: 731, 1895.

SEATON, W H , Indianapolis, Ind (d/VIII–6–1899) MD Med Coll Ind 1895. *JAMA* 33:493, 1899. *Polk* 1896: 475.

SEAVERNS, JOEL, CW–USA; Roxbury, Mass (b/V–25 1828 W Roxbury or Jamaica Plains, NY; d/II–1–1894) MD Harvard 1854; AB 1850. *JAMA* 22:392, 1894. *Bost m&s j* 130:252, 327, 1894. *Harvard in CW*: 47–48. *Butler* 1878: 343.

SEAVEY, CALVIN, Bangor, Me (b/VI–15–1809; d/VIII 1–1886 @77) MD Bowdoin 1837; AM 1863. *Bost m&s j* 155: 148, 186. *Butler* 1878: 310.

SEAVEY, HENRY HILL, Bangor, Me (b/IX–22–1841 Stetson; d/XI–26–1872) MD Bowdoin 1862. *Tr Me Med Assoc* 1871–73: 483–84. *Butler* 1878: 310.

SEAWELL, FABIUS HAWOOD, CW–CSA; Emit, NC (d/V–30–1904 @63) MD ? *JAMA* 43: 62, 1904.

SEAY, GEORGE W , Nashville (d/IX–26–1900 @35) <MD Vanderbilt 1887> *Nashvl j m&s* 88: 193–94, 1900.

SEAY, JOHN Jr, Nashville (d/V–9–1898 @73) MD UPa 1846. *JAMA* 30: 1248, 1898. *Polk* 1896: 1402.

SEBRELL, WILLIAM P , Southampton Co, Va (b/XII–30–1850 Jerusalem; d/IV–13–1885) MD Med Coll Va 1872. *Tr M S Va* 1885: 287.

SECOR, ISAAC R , Sing Sing, NY (d/VI–24–1889) MD

 Spec. educ'l status abbrev. as: ***ng*** = college verified attendance without degree;

Pulte 1877. *No Am j hom* 37:503, 1889. *Polk* 1886: 708. Homeopath.

SECREST, CONRAD, Watseka, Ill (d/IV-28-1896 @67) MD Rush 1870. *JAMA* 26:996, 1896. *Polk* 1886: 301.

SEDGWICK, HARRY HOWARD, Martin's Ferry, O (d/VIII-19-1893) MD West Res 1887. *JAMA* 21:357, 1893. *Polk* 1890: 924.

SEDGWICK, LOUISE, Wheaton, Ill (b/1864? d/VI-5-1891) <MD Woman's Med Coll Chic> *Chic med rec* 1:485, 1891.

SEDGWICK, W H, Granville, O (d/X-25-1895) MD ? *JAMA* 25: 818, 1895.

SEEBOLD, JOHN P, Pearl City, Ill (d/III-21-1901) MD Jefferson 1846. *Ill m j* ns2:533, 1901. *Polk* 1890: 354.

SEELEY, E K, Louisville (d/IX-25-1865) MD ? *Med surg rep Phila* 13:278, 1865.

SEELEY, THADDEUS POMEROY, CW-USA; Chicago (d/V-16-1898) MD U Mich 1856; AB Union 1852; AM 1855. *Chic m rec* 14:543, 1898. *JAMA* 30:1305, 1898. *Flint* 1897: 268.

SEELYE, SAMUEL DIBBLE, NYC; Montgomery, Ala (b/III-14-1829 Bethel, Conn; d/II-23-1898) MD UCNY 1855. *Tr Med Assoc St Ala* 1898: 42, 240. *JAMA* 30:625, 1898. *Atkinson* I: 54. *Polk* 1896: 165.

SEEM, ASA K, Martin's Creek, Pa (b/VII-14-1830 Kreidersville; d/VI-9-1896) MD Jefferson 1853. *Lehigh Valley med mag* 7:229-30, 1896. *Polk* 1886: 807.

SEEMAN, CHARLES L, New Orleans (d/VIII-15-1893 @30) MD Tulane 1885. *JAMA* 21:357, 1893. *New Orl m&s j* ns21:234-35, 1893. *Polk* 1886:418.

SEGER, CHARLES E, New Hackensack, NY (d/XII-10 1896 @54) MD Albany 1863. *JAMA* 28:91, 1897. *Butler* 1878: 572.

SEGNITZ, BERNARD, NYC (b/1811; d/II-23-1894) MD Marburg 1834. *JAMA* 22: 392, 1894. *Butler* 1878: 524. *Polk* 1890: 833.

SEGUIN, EDOUARD [O EDOUARD], NYC (b/I-20-1812 Clamecy, France; d/X-28-1880) MD UCNY 1861. *Med reg NY NJ Conn* 1881: 241. *Bost m&s j* 103: 453-54, 1880. *Chic m rev* : 498, 1880 (Oct). *K&B* III: 1089.

SEGUIN, EDWARD CONSTANT, NYC (b/1843 Paris; d/II-19-1898) MD CPSNY 1864. *Buff m & s j* 37:624, 1898. *Bost m&s j* 138: 191, 1898. *K&B* III: 1088-89.

SEIBERT, JOHN, Chicago (d/X-9-1896 @78) MD UPa 1845. *JAMA* 27: 878, 1896. *Polk* 1896: 405.

SEIFFERT, RUDOLPH, Chicago (b/Vienna; d/X-4-1894 @69) <MD Heidelberg 1882> *JAMA* 23:593, 1894. *Butler* 1878: 137.

SEILER, CARL, Reading, Pa (b/IV-14-1849 Switzerland; d/X-10-1905) MD UPa 1871. *Pa m j* 9:434-35, 1905/06. *Atkinson* I: 292, 1878.

SEILER, JOHN PERRY, CW-USA; Harrisburg, Pa (b/W Hanover; d/I-5-1888) MD UPa 1865. *U Pa med alum CW*: 1865.

SEILER, ROBERT H, Harrisburg, Pa (d/XI-21-1873) MD Jefferson 1863. *Med surg rep Phila* 28: 345, 1873.

SEIP, AARON KREIDER, CW-USA; Milford, Nebr; Holland, Mich (b/II-12-1842 Easton, Pa; d/IV-27-1902 Holland) MD UPa 1869. *U Pa m alum CW*: 1869.

SEIP, AMOS, CW-USA; Easton, Pa (b/X-11-1821 or 1822; d/III-21 1904) MD UPa 1848. *Pa med jour* 7: 504, 1903/04; 8:336, 1904/05. *U Pa med alum CW*: 1848. *Flint* 1897: 800.

SEIP, GEORGE W, Erie Pa (d/II-21-1902) MD Jefferson 1862. *Pa m j* 6:261, 1902/03. *Polk* 1886: 832.

SEIPLE, WILLIAM GEORGE MARX, Lehighton, Pa (d/III-1-1901 ca 55) MD UPa 1867. *Pa m j* 4:671-72, 1900/01; 5:296, 1901/02. *Butler* 1878: 731.

SEITZ, JOHN LANDIS, Harrisburg, Pa (d/XI-28-1902 @46) MD Jefferson 1882. *Pa m j* 6:261, 1902/03. *Flint* 1897: 804.

SEITZINGER, FRANKLIN S, Reading, Pa (d/X-9 1868) MD Pa Med Coll 1860. *Phila med reg & dir* 1871: 298. *Med surg rep Phila* 19: 350, 1868.

SELBY, JEREMIAH B, Milwaukee (d/V-31-1897 @75) MD UCNY 1845. *JAMA* 28:1156,1897. *Polk* 1896: 1557.

SELDEN, HENRY, Norfolk, Va (d/X-2-1855 @38) MD UPa 1841. *Nashvl j m&s* 10:147-49, 1856.

SELDEN, WILLIAM, CW-CSA; Norfolk, Va (b/VIII-15 1808; d/ XI-7-1887) MD UPa 1830. *U Pa m alum CW*: 1830. *Tr M S Va* 1888: 275. *NC m j* 20:328, 1887. *K&B* III: 1091.

SELER, CHARLES A, Allentown, Pa (d/III-18-1902 @ 32 Hay Fork, Cal) MD UPa 1892. *Pa m j* 6:261, 1902/03.

SELFRIDGE, JAMES MARS, Oakland Cal (d/1906) MD Buffalo 1852; MD Jefferson 1856. *Cal st j m* 4:150, 1906. *Polk* 1896:224. *Butler* 1878:62. Homeopath.

SELL, JACOB, Greensburg, Pa (d/IX-10-1901 @39) MD W Pa Med Coll 1889. *JAMA* 37: 847, 1901.

SELLARDS, ANDREW WATSON, Scranton, Kans (d/XI-30-1899 @55) MD Miami 1877. *JAMA* 33:1441, 1899. *Polk* 1886: 396 (Greenup, Ky).

SELLERS, JESSE SHENTON, Philadelphia; Chicago (b/IV-1828; d/VII-1-1873) MD UPa 1852; att Coll UPa. *Med surg rep Phila* 29:36, 1873.

SELLERS, TOBIAS, Pottstown, Pa (b/1781? d/XI-2-1862 @81) MD ? *Med s rep Phila* ns9:190, 1862/63.

SELMAN, JOEL L, Chattanooga (d/VI-23-1896 @39) MD U Louisville 1882. *JAMA* 27:108, 1896.

SEMMES, ALEXANDER JENKINS, DC to 1860; CW-CSA; Savannah & Macon, Ga (b/XII-17-1828; d/IX- -1898 New Orleans) MD Georgetown 1852; MD Columbian 1851. *Hist M S DC:* 249-50. *Atkinson* I: 271. *K&B* III: 1092.

SEMMES, ALPHONSUS T, Canton, Miss (d/I-9-1895) MD Tulane 1853. *New Orl m&s j* ns22:638, 1895. *Polk* 1890: 627.

SEMMES, THOMAS, Alexandria DC (b/VIII-13-1778/9 Pr Geo Co Md; d/VII-31-1833) MD UPa 1801. *Hist M S DC:* 220. *Am j m sci* 17:272, 1835. *K&B* II:1033.

SEMPLE, EDWARD ARMISTAD, Montgomery, Ala (b/XI-9-1818 Williamsburg, Va; d/XI-22-1877) MD Tulane 1852. *Tr Med Assn St Ala* 1878: 132, 153.

SEMPLE, GEORGE WILLIAM McKENZIE, Hampton, Va (b/III-10-1812 Williamsburg; d/XI-17-1883) MD U Pa 1834; AB Wm & Mary 1831. *Tr M S Va* 1884:6-7. *Atkinson* I:467. *Butler* 1878: 835.

SEMPLE, JOHN, Wilkinsburg, Pa (b/IX-16-1822 Hoboken, Pa; d/X-9-1901) <MD Jefferson 1848> *Pa med jour* 5:38, 294, 1901/02. *Flint* 1897: 840.

SEN, W , ? (d/1878 Memphis) MD ? *Tr AMA* 30:885, 1879.

SENDERLING, PHILIP MEYER, Jersey City, NJ 1857-62; 1877- ; CW-USA (b/III-19-1831 Brunswick, NY; d/1895) MD UPa 1856; AB Williams 1852. *U Pa med alum CW*: 1856. *Atkinson* I: 630. *Polk* 1886:605.

SENKLER, ALBERT EDWARD, St Cloud, Minn; St Paul 1880- (b/III-8-1842 Docking, Engl; d/XII-10-1899) MD McGill 1863. *Tr Minn St M S* 1899:191. *JAMA* 33:1632, 1899. *Polk* 1890:620. *K&B* III: 1092-93.

SENSEMAN, HIRAM, Tremont City, O (b/V-10-1826 Lancaster Co, Pa; d/V-25-1883) MD Jefferson 1849. *Tr Ohio St M S* 1884: 224-25.

SENSENEY, EDGAR [EDWARD] N , Chambersburg, Pa (d/X-2-1884) MD Jefferson 1870. *Med bull med & surg* 6:280, 1884.

SENSENY, ABRAHAM H , Chambersburg, Pa (b/VIII-5-1811; d/VII-17-1879) MD Jefferson 1835. *Tr Pa St M S* 13:305-06, 1880. *Med surg rep Phila* 41:88, 1879. *Butler* 1878: 731.

SENSENY, B RUSH, Chambersburg, Pa (b/1841; d/III-28-1880 @39) MD St Louis Med Coll 1863. *Tr Pa St M S* 13:306, 1880. *Med s rep Phila* 42:308, 1880.

SENTER, HORACE, Savannah (b/1776? Newport, RI; d/I-12-1804) MD ? AB Brown 1796; AM. *Brown hist cat*: 1796.

SENTER, ISAAC, RevWar-USA; Newport, RI (b/1753/1754 Londonderry, NH; d/XII-10 or 20-1799) Hon MD Brown 1787; ? Hon AM 1799; AM Harvard 1793. *Tr CPP* cent vol: 286. *Tr RI M S* 1:708, 1859-77.

SERFASS, JOHN JAY, Easton, Pa (b/I-10-1854; d/VI-22-1892) MD UPa 1879; AB Lafayette. *Lehigh Valley med mag* 4:17-18, 1892-93.

SERRIN, JAMES S , Detroit, Mich; Indianapolis (d/XII-13-1896 @65) MD Med Coll Ind 1881. *JAMA* 28:92, 139, 1897. *Polk* 1890: 587.

SESSIONS, EDWARD L , Hillsboro Tx (d/X-14-1905) MD Louisvl M C 1879. *Tex st med jour* 1: 184, 1905/06.

SESSOMS, JOHN WILLIAM, CW-CSA; Powellsville, NC (b/Bertie Co; d/VI-1-1906) MD UPa 1852; att Wake Forest. *U Pa med alum CW*: 1852.

SESSUMS, JOHN L H , CW-USA?; Lonoke, Ark (d/I-19-1884) MD UCNY 1866; <MD Memphis M C 1860> att Trenton Coll, Tenn. *Med surg rep Phila* 50:288, 1884.

SEVERANCE, LA GRANGE, Huntingdon, Ind (b/XII-28-1839 Newport, Me; d/I-26-1893) MD Ecl Med Inst Cinc 1868. *Tr Ind St M S* 1893:256. *Polk* 1886: 321.

SEVERIN, CHARLES AUGUSTUS, CW-USA; NYC (b/1830; d/1866?) <MD Hamburg> *Tr AMA* 19:414, 1868. *Med reg NY NJ Conn* 1867: 225. *Nat med jour* 1:302, 1870/71.

SEVERSON, FRANK M , Seneca Falls, NY (d/III-1-1904 @40) MD CPSNY 1889; AB Union 1885. *Tr M S St NY* 1904: [420].

SEVIER, CHARLES H , Brownsville, Tenn (d/IX-30-1898 @59) MD U Nashville 1870; MD Vanderbilt 1877. *JAMA* 31:942, 1898. *Polk* 1886: 861.

SEVIER, W R , Jonesboro, Tenn (d/VIII-22-1882) MD ? *So pract* 4:294, 1882.

SEWALL, JOHN GALLISON, NYC (b/XI-2-1822; d/I 18-1874) MD Harvard 1847; AB 1843. *Med reg NY NJ Conn* 1874: 289.

SEWALL, LUCY ELLEN, Boston (b/IV-26-1837; d/II-13-1890) MD New Engl Female Med Coll 1862. *Bost m&s j* 122:240, 1890. *Am hom* 16:147, 1890. *Med vis* 6:103, 1890. *K&B* III: 1095. Homeopath.

SEWALL, STEPHEN BAYLEY, Somerville, Mass; Weaverville, Cal (b/XI-22-1815 Chesterville, Me; d/XII 23-1864) MD Harvard 1843; att Bowdoin 1836-38. *Bowdoin cat*: 1840.

SEWALL, THOMAS, Washington, DC (b/IV-16-1786 Augusta, Me; d/IV-10-1845) MD Harvard 1812. *Hist M S DC*: 222. *Tr CPP* cent vol: 286. *Med exam* 1:291, 1845. *South m & s j* 1:352, 1845. *K&B* III: 1096.

SEWARD, JONES J , Erie, Pa (d/X-22-1899 @43) MD Med Coll O 1883. *JAMA* 33:1183, 1899. *Polk* 1886: 799.

SEXTON, HORATIO G , Rushville, Ind (b/I-21-1796 Andover, NH; d/VI- -1865) MD ? *Tr Ind St M S* 1866:9. Kemper's *Indiana*: 340.

SEXTON, MARSHALL, Rushville, Ind (b/1823; d/I-9-1892) MD Med Coll Ohio 1844. *Tr Ind St M S* 1892: 286. *Polk* 1890: 387.

SEXTON, SAMUEL, NYC (b/1833 Ohio; d/VII-11-1896) MD U Louisville 1856; ng U Mich Med Dept 1853-54. *Bost m&s j* 135:73, 1896. *JAMA* 27:225, 1896. *Med bull m & s* 17:312-13, 1896. *Polk* 1896:1077.

SEYBERT, ADAM, Philadelphia (b/V-16-1773; d/V-2-1825 Paris, Fr) MD UPa 1793. *Tr CPP* cent vol:264. *K&B* III: 1096.

SEYDELL, ARTHUR, Chinendega, Nicaragua (d/IV-11 1862 @28) MD Jefferson 1860. *Med surg rep Phila* ns8: 412, 1862.

SEYFERT [SEIFERT], SIMON JOHN, Pine Grove, Pa (d/II-13/14-1904 @61) MD UPa 1871. *Pa m j* 8: 336, 1904/05. *Flint* 1897: 828.

SEYFFARTH, EDMUND, Lawrence, Mass (d/VII-21-1874 @47) MD ? *Bost m&s j* 91:124, 1874.

SEYMOUR, ABBIE JANET, Buffalo (d/X-17-1895 @42 or 48) MD Hahnemann Chic 1873. *JAMA* 25:781, 1895. *Buff m & s j* 35:356, 1895. *Tr Am Inst Hom* 1896:

87. *Polk* 1886: 654. Homeopath.

SEYMOUR, EDWARD WILLIAM, Junction City, Kans (d/II–24–1880) MD Jefferson 1858. *Tr Kans St M S* 1881: 129. *Butler* 1878: 255.

SEYMOUR, GEORGE, Litchfield, Conn (b/XII–27–1816; d/I–29–1861) MD Fairfield 1838. *Proc Conn M S* 1861: 117–21.

SEYMOUR, JAMES DWIGHT, Whately, Mass (d/IX–11–1906 @46) MD Harvard 1872. *Bost m&s j* 155:324, 1906. *Polk* 1896: 726.

SEYMOUR, JOSEPH EGGLESTON, CW–CSA; Pine Bluff, Ark (d/VII–14–1884) MD UPa 1855. *Med surg rep Phila* 51:196, 1884. *Butler* 1878: 41.

SEYMOUR, WILLIAM PIERCE, Troy, NY (b/X–17–1825; d/IV–7–1893) MD UPa 1848; AB Williams 1845; AM 1848. *JAMA* 20:488, 1893. *Bost m&s j* 128:380, 1893. *Tr M S St NY* 1895:376–80. *Atkinson* I: 669. *K&B* III: 1097.

SEYMOUR, WILLIAM WOTKYNS, Troy, NY (d/X–18 1904 @51) MD Harvard 1878; AB Yale 1875. *Bost m&s j* 151:478, 503, 1904. *Tr M S St NY* 1905: [362]. *Polk* 1896: 1108.

SHAAF [SHAAFF], JOHN THOMAS, Annapolis, Md; Georgetown, DC (b/1763 Frederick Co; d/IV–28 or V–3 1819) <MD Edinburgh> *Hist M S DC:* 218. *Med annals Md:* 564.

SHACKLEFORD, J F, CW–CSA; Trenton, Tenn (d/IX–1–1904 @77) <MD Med Coll Ga 1850> *JAMA* 43: 749, 1904. *Polk* 1886: 873. Blanton's *Va surg CW*:415.

SHACKLEFORD, LEE, Meridian, Miss (b/XII–15–1833 Perry Co, Ala; d/V–19–1878) MD U La 1858. *Tr Miss St Med Assoc* 1879: 68–69.

SHADE, J A, Shade Gap, Pa (d/XII–2–1876) MD ? *Med surg rep Phila* 35:526, 548, 1876.

SHAFFER, CHARLES H, Elizabeth, Pa (b/Allegheny Co; d/XI–21–1902 @44) MD West Res 1882. *Pa med jour* 6: 261, 1902/03. *Flint* 1897: 801.

SHAFFER, EDWARD LIVINGSTON, NYC (b/1849; d/III–12–1888) MD UCNY 1874. *Med reg NY NJ Conn* 1888: 270. *Butler* 1878: 524.

SHAFFER, JOHN ECKERT, Elizabeth, Pa 1845–81 (b/II–22–1821 Washington, Pa; d/V–31–1889) MD UPa 1845; AB Washington Coll 1840. *Med surg rep Phila* 61: 28, 1889. *Polk* 1886: 798.

SHAIN, FRANCIS, Jersey City, NJ (d/I–16–1896) MD Jefferson 1882. *Bost m&s j* 134:125, 1896.

SHAKESPEARE, EDWARD ORAM, Philadelphia (b/V 19–1846 New Castle, Del; d/VI–1–1900) MD UPa 1869; AB Dickinson 1867. *Tr CPP* cent vol: 264. *Bost m&s j* 142:614, 1900. *Atkinson* I:190–91. *JAMA* 34: 1504, 1900. *K&B* III: 1097.

SHALLCROSS, JOSEPH, Darby, Pa (b/XII–12–1759 Wilmington, Del; d/V–22–1811) MD ? *Med reporter* (W Chester, Pa) 2:63–64, 1854.

SHALLCROSS, MORRIS CADWALADER, Philadelphia (b/1791; d/XI–28–1871) MD UPa 1813. *Tr CPP* cent vol: 264. *Phila med reg & dir* 1873: 304.

SHALLENBERGER, HORACE MANN, Rochester, Pa (b/X–2–1853; d/V–12–1906) MD Jefferson 1876. *Pa med jour* 9:761–62, 1905/06. *Flint* 1897: 833.

SHANELY, CHARLES MILLER, Mt Blanchard, O; Barataria, La (d/X–9–1905) MD Balto Med Coll 1894. *New Orl m&s jour* 58:430, 1905. *Polk* 1896: 1202.

SHANKS, JOHN, NYC (b/III–28–1800 Glasgow; d/VIII–10–1870) MD UCNY 1842. *Med reg NY NJ Conn* 1871: 364. *Med rec* 5:353. *K&B* III:360 (mention only).

SHANNON, BENJAMIN FRANKLIN, Shannonville, Pa (b/II–9–1827; d/VIII– –1878) MD UPa 1849. *Tr M S Pa* 12:880–81, 1879.

SHANNON, JAMES GRISWOLD, Rutland, Mass (d/XII–29–1889 @46) MD Harvard 1870. *Bost m&s j* 123:629, 1890. *Polk* 1886: 472.

SHANNON, JESSE CLEMENT, CW–CSA (b/VIII–13 1835 Portsmouth, Va; d/XII–10–1868 Great Bridge) MD UPa 1859. *U Pa med alum CW*: 1859.

SHANNON, NATHANIEL, Loudon, NH; Knightsville, Me (b/VIII–22 or 28–1822 Pittsfield, NH; d/V–19–1890 Charlestown, Me) MD Dartmouth 1849. *Tr Me M Assn* 1890:327–28. *Atkinson* I: 706. *Polk* 1886: 428.

SHANNON, SAMUEL H, Schuylkill Haven, Pa (b/1814 Shannonville; d/I–17–1879) MD Jefferson 1836. *Med rec NY* 15:95, 1878.

SHANNON, THOMAS JEFFERSON, CW–USA (d/X–19–1864 Silver Creek, Va) MD Jefferson 1857. *Nat med jour* 1:302, 1870/71.

SHANNON, WILLIAM CUMMINGS, USA 1875–95? Elkhorn, Nebr (b/V–8–1851 Loudon, NH; d/IV–21–1905 Oakland, Cal) MD Bellevue 1874; AB Bowdoin 1872. *Bowdoin cat*: 1872. *Polk* 1886: 582.

SHANTZ, SAMUEL ERB, CW–USA; Utica, NY; St Peter, Minn 1866– (b/Waterloo Twp, Canada; d/VIII–22 1868) MD Harvard 1863; stud U Toronto. *Phila med reg & dir* 1871: 297. *Med surg rep Phila* 19:240, 1868.

SHAPARD, J CAMPBELL, Winchester, Tenn (b/VIII 30–1823; d/I–4–1892) MD U Nashville 1858. *Nashvl j m&s* 71:233–36, 1892. *So pract* 14:44, 1892. *NW m j* 20: 10, 1892. *Polk* 1890: 1063.

SHAPLEIGH, ALFRED LINDSAY, Shanghai, China (d/1905 @35) MD Harvard 1894; AB 1892. *Bost m&s j* 152:262, 1905.

SHAPLEIGH, ELISHA BACON, Philadelphia (b/XI–6 1823 or 1824 York Co, Me; d/1892) MD UPa 1849; AB Yale 1846. *Tr CPP* cent vol: 264. *Bost m&s j* 127:588, 1892. *Atkinson* I:215. *K&B* III: 1097.

SHARER, JOHN PETER, Little Falls NY (d/I–7–1899 @75) MD CPSNY 1848; AM Albany 1846. *JAMA* 32: 144–5, 1899. *Bost m&s j* 140:102 1899. *Polk* 1896:1029.

SHARETTS, UPTON ABRAHAM, Frederick, Md (b/XII–27–1857; d/X–8–1905 Colorado Springs) MD Hahnemann Phila 1883; stud Gny & Switz. *Tr Am Inst*

Hom 1906: 771–72. *Polk* 1886: 442.

SHARP, JOHN CAULDWELL, Boston (d/IX–22–1890) MD Harvard 1890. *Boston m & s jour* 123:360, 1890.

SHARP, JOHN W , Dayton, Pa (d/IV–2–1904 @80) MD UPa 1850. *Pa m j* 8:336, 1904/05. *Flint* 1897: 800.

SHARP, ROBERT CAULFIELD, Atglen, Pa (b/Weymouth, Engl; d/I–2–1904 @52) MD Jefferson 1881. *Pa med jour* 8:336, 1904/05. *Flint* 1897: 795.

SHARP, SAMUEL C Jr, ?Pa (b/X–30–1834 Camden Co, NJ; d/I–28–1866) MD Jefferson 1857. *Tr Pa St M S* 1867: 288.

SHARP, SOLOMON Jr, USN 1829–65 (b/VIII–1806 Pa; d/I–7–1870 Wilmington Del) MD UPa 1826. *Tr AMA* 21: 498, 1870. *Bost m&s j* ns5:76, 1870. *Phila m reg & dir* 1871:303. *U Pa med alum CW*: 1826.

SHARP, WILLIAM, Jackson, Cal (b/III–5–1826 Canada; d/III–18–1881) MD Phila Coll Med & Surg 1857. *Tr Cal St M S* 1882:247. *Butler* 1878: 63.

SHARP, WILLIAM McDOWELL, Newville, Pa (b/VII–23–1798 Cumberland Co; d/VIII–20–1835) MD UPa 1819; AB Dickinson 1815. *Dickinson cat*: 1815.

SHARPE, WILLIAM, ?Pa (d/XII–18–1869 @63) MD Jefferson 1829. *Phila med reg & dir* 1871: 294.

SHARPE, WILLIAM REECE, Fulton, NC (b/XI–30–1822 Iredell Co, NC; d/XI–21–1877) MD Jefferson 1851; MD Bellevue 1877 ad eundem. *Tr NC M S* 1878: 26. *NC m j* 1:64, 1878. *Butler* 1878: 598.

SHARPLESS, FRANCES (LINTON), W Chester, Pa (b/I 6–1856 Abington, Pa; d/V or IX–15–1906) MD Woman's Med Coll Pa 1886. *Pa m j* 9:672, 1905/06.

SHARPLESS, JACOB, Downingtown, Pa (b/1792? d/II–18–1863 @71) MD UPa 1817. *Med s rep Phila* ns9: 398, 1862/63.

SHARPLESS, JOHN TOWNSEND, Philadelphia (d/IV–22–1883 @82) MD UPa 1822. *Tr CPP* cent vol: 264.

SHARPNACK, THOMAS H , Jefferson, Pa (b/Greene Co; d/II–22–1902) MD Jefferson 1872. *Pa m j* 5: 452, 1901/02; 6:261, 1902/03. *Flint* 1897: 805.

SHATTUCK, GEORGE, Nugent's Grove, Ia (b/XII–21–1843 Ticonderoga, NY; d/X–6–1873) MD U Vt 1871; AB Amherst 1867. *Amherst, Men of*: 1867.

SHATTUCK, GEORGE CHEYNE, Boston (b/VII–17–1784 Templeton, Mass; d/III–18–1854) MD UPa 1807: Hon MD Dartmouth 1812; MB 1806; AB 1803; LLD 1853. *Bost m&s j* 49:184–86, 1854. *So m&s j* 10:388, 1854. *K&B* III: 1098–99.

SHATTUCK, GEORGE CHEYNE, Boston (b/VII–22–1813; d/III–22–1893) MD Harvard 1835; AB 1831; AM 1834. *Bost m&s j* 128:328, 354–55, 1893. *JAMA* 20: 512, 1893. *Tr CPP* cent vol: 286. *Atkinson* I:699–700. *K&B* III: 1099–1100.

SHATTUCK, GEORGE FRANCIS, Wilcox, Fla; CW–USA (d/XI–7–1884) MD Harvard 1862 *Harv in CW*:275.

SHATTUCK, RAYMOND WILBUR, NYC (d/IV–20–1903 @31) MD CPSNY 1897. *Bost m&s j* 148:486 1903.

SHAW, ALEXANDER B , St Louis (d/1896 @49) MD St Louis Med Coll 1867; AB. *JAMA* 27:923, 1896. *Med bull m & s* 18:430, 1896. *Polk* 1886: 566.

SHAW, BENJAMIN F , Kansas City, Mo (d/IV–1–1900) MD Univ Kansas 1892. *JAMA* 34: 957, 1900.

SHAW, BENJAMIN SHURTLEFF, Boston (b/IX–12–1827; d/V–2/3–1893 @65) MD Harvard 1850; AB 1847. *Bost m&s j* 128: 452, 478, 1893. *Atkinson* I: 440. *Butler* 1878: 343.

SHAW, CHARLES STONER, Pittsburgh (b/1856; d/XII 28–1899) Albuquerque, NM) MD UPa 1879. *Pa m j* 3: 420, 439, 455, 525, 1899/1900. *JAMA* 34:123, 1900. *K&B* III: 1100.

SHAW, GEORGE R , Antigo, Wis (d/X–12–1893) MD CPSNY 1853. *JAMA* 21:667, 1893. *Polk* 1890: 1161.

SHAW, HENRY CHARLES, CW–USA (b/c1833 Waitsfield, Vt; d/IX–7–1862 Alexandria, Va) ng Dartmouth 1858. *Nat med jour* 1:302, 1870/71.

SHAW, HENRY MARCHMORE, CW–CSA (b/XI–20–1817 Newport, RI; d/II–1–1864 New Bern, NC) MD UPa 1838. *U Pa med alum CW*: 1838.

SHAW, JOHN, Canada 1803–05; Annapolis, Baltimore 1807– (b/V–4–1778 Annapolis; d/I–10–1809 at sea) <ng UPa Med Dept> ng Edinburgh. *Med annals Md*: 565. *Balto m & phys rec* 1:366, 1809. *K&B* III:1100–01.

SHAW, JOHN CARGILL, Brooklyn (b/IX–25–1845 Jamaica, WI; d/I–23–1900) MD CPSNY 1874. *Bost m&s j* 142:124, 1900. *JAMA* 34:312, 1900. *K&B* III: 1101.

SHAW, JOSEPH BACON, CW–USA; Delaware Water Gap Pa (b/IX–17–1845 Cape May NJ; d/VII–18–1904) MD UPa 1877. *Pa m j* 8:336 1904/05. *Flint* 1897: 800.

SHAW, JOSEPH G , NYC (d/V–25–1870 @35) MD UCNY 1856. *Phila med reg & dir* 1871: 305.

SHAW, MERRILL EUGENE, Buffalo (d/X–17–1867 @ 26) MD Buff 1864. *Buff m&s j* 7:158, 1867.

SHAW, MORTIMER WRIGHT, NYC (d/II–22–1905 @37 Middletown, NY) MD LICH 1892. *Bost m&s j* 152:262, 1905. *Polk* 1896: 1003.

SHAW, P M, Rome Ia (d/XI–3–1899 @62) <MD EclMed Coll Pa 1871> *JAMA* 33:1441, 1899. *Polk* 1896:1293.

SHAW, SAMUEL FRANCIS, CW?–USN; Philadelphia (d/XII–7–1884) MD ? *Med s rep Phila* 51:732, 1884.

SHAW, THOMAS WILSON Jr, CW–USA; Pittsburgh (b/I–25–1826 Allegheny Co; d/I–18–1899) MD UPa 1849. *JAMA* 32: 263, 1899. *Pa m j* 2:425–26, 497, 1899. *Polk* 1896: 1328.

SHAW, WILLIAM ALLEN, Wickford RI (b/VI–4–1805 d/V–5–1878) MD Harvard 1827. *Tr RI M S* 2: 156–58, 1871–72.

SHAW, WILLIAM CHESLEY, Belleville, Ala (d/XI–12 1898) MD U Ala 1885. *Tr M Assn St Ala* 1899: 232. *Polk* 1893: 150.

SHEA, ANDREW FRANCIS, Lawrence, Mass (d/VII–25 1893 @35) MD Harvard 1882 *Bost m&s j* 129:104, 1893.

SHEA, DANIEL FRANCIS, Franklin, Mass (d/XII–22

 Spec. educ'l status abbrev. as: ***ng*** = college verified attendance without degree;

1898 @31) MD LICH 1890. *JAMA* 32:41, 1899.

SHEAD, EDWARD WADSWORTH, Seattle (d/VIII–26 1905 @32) MD Harvard 1901. *Bost m&s j* 153:262, 290, 1905.

SHEAHAN, JOSEPH MAURICE, Quincy, Mass; Quincy, Ill (b/1853 Braintree; d/IX–21–1905) <MD Paris, Fr 1879> AB Harvard 1873. *Bost m&s j* 153: 376, 482–83, 1905. *Ill med jour* 8:430, 1905. *Polk* 1896: 721.

SHEARDOWN, SAMUEL BARNARD, Stockton, Minn; CW–USA (b/X–7–1826 Catlin NY; d/VIII–1–1889) MD Geneva 1850. *Tr Minn St M S* 1890:75–76; 1891:198. *Polk* 1896: 620.

SHEARER, JAMES M, Dillsburg, Pa (b/1833; d/XII–14 1881 @48) MD Pa M C 1858. *Tr Pa St M S* 14:390–91, 1882.

SHEASBY, SAM, Elgin, Tex (d/I–19–1883) MD ? *Texas med surg rec* 3:600, 1883.

SHEETS [SHUTZ], JOHN, Philadelphia (d/XII–28–1898 @40) MD UPa 1880. *JAMA* 32:? 1899 (Jan) *Polk* 1896: 1317.

SHEETS, JOHN WILLIAM, CW–USA; Northumberland, Pa (b/X–7–1844 W Fairview; d/VIII–4–1904) MD UPa 1871. *U Pa med alum CW*: 1871.

SHEFFER, DANIEL, York Sulphur Springs, Pa (b/V–24 1783 York; d/II–16–1880) Stud med UPa. *Med surg rep Phila* 42:220, 1880. *Biog dir Congr*.

SHEFFIELD, HULDAH H, ? (d/XI–19–1887 @66) MD ? *Med couns* 12:576, 1887/88. *Med vis* 4:15, 1888. Homeopath.

SHEFFIELD, JAMES, Earlville, NY (d/III–23–1849) MD ? *Trans AMA* 3:464, 1850.

SHEFFREY, CHARLES WOOLEY, Bridgeport, Conn (b/IX–17–1832 Engl; d/II–12–1892) MD Yale 1862. *Proc Conn Med Soc* 1892:864–65. *Butler* 1878: 82.

SHEIBLEY, JAMES POLK, CW–USA; Landisburg, Pa (b/IV–11–1842; d/X–25–1906) MD UPa 1868. *U Pa med alum CW*: 1868. *Polk* 1886: 804.

SHEILD, WILLIAM HENRY, CW–CSA; Yorktown, Va (b/VII–15–1834; d/X–1894) MD UPa 1856. *Polk* 1886: 929. *UPa med alum CW*:1856. Blanton, *Va surgs CW*:1856.

SHELBY, JOHN, Nashville (b/V–24–1786 Sumner Co; d/V–15–1859) MD UPa 1809 *Tr Med Soc Tenn* 1876:87.

SHELDON, BENJAMIN A, San Francisco (b/1825; d/1864) <MD Tulane 1847> *Trans AMA* 19:446, 1868.

SHELDON, DANIEL, Washington, Conn (b/X–19–1750 Hartford; d/IV–10–1840) MD ? *Pr Conn M S* 3:408–09, 1870.

SHELDON, HORACE PRESTON, Wakefield, Mass (b/1853 NYC; d/IV–17–1891) MD CPSNY 1877; AB Middlebury 1874; AM. *Bost m&s j* 124: 420, 1891.

SHELDON, JAY W, Syracuse, NY (d/IX–16–1906) MD Cleveland Homeop 1864. *Tr Am Inst Hom* 1906: 764–66. *Polk* 1886: 711.

SHELDON, LEONARD RAWSON, Boston (d/VIII–2–1873 @45) MD Castleton 1851. *Bost m&s j* ns12:148, 1873.

SHELDON, SILAS E, Topeka, Kans (b/1837 Carlisle, O; d/IV–19–1900) MD Cleveland Med Coll 1860. *JAMA* 34:1084, 1900. *Polk* 1890: 449.

SHELLER, ADAM, Mt Joy, Pa (b/I–12–1808 Big Cliques; d/XI–29–1882) MD NY Reformed MC 1830 [!] *Tr Pa St M S* 1883: 366. *Butler* 1878: ?

SHELLY, AARON F, Philadelphia (d/X–13–1883 @60) MD Jefferson 1850. *Med s rep Phila* 49:448, 1883. *Butler* 1878: 671.

SHELLY, JESSE, CW–USA (d/V–8–1864) MD ? *Nat med jour* 1:302, 1870/71.

SHELMERDINE, ROBERT C, Philadelphia (b/1799? d/IX–23–1876 @77) MD U Md 1820. *Med surg rep Phila* 35: 326, 1876.

SHELMERDINE, ROBERT Q, Philadelphia (d/IV–13 1870) MD Jefferson 1847 *Phila med reg & dir* 1871:294.

SHELTON, CHARLES OSCAR, St Louis; CW–CSA (b/XII–27–1835; d/IV–22–1862 New Orleans) MD UCNY 1859; stud med U Va. Johnson, J L, *Univ [Va] Mem... alum d/CW*: 108.

SHELTON, JAMES HOVEY, Huntington, Conn (d/V–10–1868 @63) MD *Pr Conn M S* 1868: 19.

SHELTON, JOHN D, Jamaica, NY (d/XII–10–1862 @ 47) MD UPa 1840; AB Princeton 1836. *Med s rep Phila* ns9: 278, 1862/63.

SHELTON, NATHAN, Jamaica, NY (b/1784? d/VII–25 1864 @80) MD Yale 1835; AB 1902. *Med surg rep Phila* 12:84, 1864/65.

SHELTON, WILLIAM TOMLINSON, Stratford, Conn (d/III–6–1868) Hon MD Yale 1832. *Bost m&s j* 1:128, 1868. *Pr Conn M S* 3:19, 1868.*Phila m reg & dir* 1871: 295. *Med s rep Phila* 18:270, 1868.

SHENK, OTTO, CW–USA (d/VIII–21–1864) MD ? *Nat med jour* 1:302, 1870/71.

SHEPARD [SHEPHARD], CHARLES UPHAM, Charleston, SC (b/VI–29–1804 Little Compton, RI; d/V–1 1886) Hon MD Dartmouth 1836; AB Amherst 1824; LLD? *New Orl m&s j* ns13:1008, 1886. *Waring* II: 291. *K&B* III: 1102.

SHEPARD, EDWARD TAYLOR, New Orleans (b/Cincinnati; d/VIII–15–1899 @56) MD Tulane 1867. *New Orl m&s j* 52:166–67, 1899. *JAMA* 33:621, 1899. *Polk* 1896: 624.

SHEPARD, FREDERIC WILLIAM, Essex, Conn (b/III 18–1812 Plainfield; d/V–2–1860) MD Yale 1834. *Pr Conn M S* 1861: 123–24.

SHEPARD, JESSIE, Buffalo (d/VIII–24–1901) MD Boston U 1888. *Tr Am Inst Hom* 1902:817–18. Homeopath.

SHEPARD, JOEL, Montague, Mass (b/1764? d/XII–9–1859 @95) MD ? *Bost m&s j* 61:448, 1859.

SHEPARD, JOSEPH CHRISTOPHER, Wilmington, NC (b/I–7–1840; d/III–5–1903) MD UCNY 1860; att

UNC. *UNC cat*: 558. *Polk* 1886: 726.

SHEPARD, ORLANDO WATERS, Edwardsville, Ala (d/II–17–1899) <MD Graffenburg 1854> *Tr M Assn St Ala* 1899: 232. *Polk* 1894: 154.

SHEPARD, THOMAS PERKINS, Providence, RI (b/III–16–1817 Salem, Mass; d/V–5–1877) MD Harvard 1840; AB Brown 1836; AM. *Brown hist cat:* 1836.

SHEPARD, WILLIAM HENRY HASTON, Westminster, Mass (d/II–7–1886 @44) MD ? *Bost m&s j* 114: 480, 1886.

SHEPHERD, CORNELIUS, Trenton, NJ (b/I–21–1837 Bucks Co, Pa; d/X–7–1903) MD UPa 1861. *Bost m&s j* 149:444,1903. *Atkinson* I:375. *Polk* 1896: 950.

SHEPHERD, FRANCIS COKE, Bruceton, WVa (b/I–18 1829 Newville, Pa; d/V–19–1872) MD Jefferson 1853. *Tr M S WVa* 1873: 472–74.

SHEPHERD, LUCIAN H , Oswego, NY (d/I–24–1903 @37) <MD Syracuse 1895> *Bost m&s j* 148: 166, 1903. *Polk* 1900: 1304.

SHEPPARD, FREDERICK C , Philadelphia (b/1857 Bridgeton, NJ; d/IV–14–1884 Colo) MD UPa 1879. *Tr Pa St M S* 1885: 390–91. *Tr CPP* cent vol: 264. *Med surg rep Phila* 50: 544, 1884.

SHEPPARD [SHEPPERD], FREDERICK P, Asbury NJ (b/XI–1–1844; d/V–12–1869) MD UCNY 1866. *Phila m reg & dir* 1871:301. *Tr M S NJ* 1870:82; 1872: 208.

SHEPPARD, JOHN HANNIBAL, Cal 1849–65; Boston 1865– (b/III–7–1822 Wiscasset, Me; d/XII–23–1870) MD Harvard 1849; AB Bowdoin 1845. *Bowd cat*: 1845.

SHEPPARD [SHEPHERD], JOHN W , NYC (d/X–5–1868) MD UCNY 1852. *Med reg NY NJ Conn* 1869:246. *Tr AMA* 21:431, 1870. *Med s rep Phila* 19:328, 1868.

SHEPPARD, JOSEPH H , CW–USA; Bridgeton, NJ (b/VI–23–1828; d/X–23–1902) MD UPa 1849. *Tr M S NJ* 1903: 384–85. *Rec AAS USA* 1891: 91. *Atkinson* I: 359. *Polk* 1890: 719.

SHEPPARD, MARK J , Westfield, Mass (d/XI–7–1899 @45) MD UCNY 1878. *JAMA* 33:1441, 1899. *Polk* 1896: 986.

SHEPPARD, W A , New Vienna, O (d/1872) MD Miami 1856; MD Cinc Med & Surg 1856. *Tr Ohio St M S* 1875: 195.

SHERARD, CHRISTOPHER COLUMBUS, Mobile, Ala; CW–CSA (b/X–8–1829 Edgecombe Co, NC; d/I–30–1885) MD UPa 1860; AB UNC 1852. *Tr M Assn St Ala* 1885:320. *U Pa med alum CW*: 1860.

SHERIDAN, CAMPBELL, Johnstown Pa (d/X–18–1904 @85) MD Jefferson 1849. *Pa m j* 8:336, 1904/05. *Flint* 1897:805.

SHERIDAN, PETER HERBERT, Brooklyn (d/X–11 1879 @34) MD UCNY 1876. *Med reg NY NJ Conn* 1879: 199.

SHERK, JOHN HENRY, Philadelphia (b/II–24–1841 Lebanon Co, Pa; d/V–25–1870) MD UPa 1860. *Phila m reg & dir* 1871: 294. *Tr Pa St M S* 9:189–90, 1872.

SHERK, JOHN LIGHT, CW–USA (b/I–14–1837 Lebanon, Pa; d/XII–29–1864 Bardstown, Ky; MD UPa 1857. *Med s rep Phila* 12:252, 1864/65. *U Pa med alum CW*: 1857. *Nat m j* 1:302, 1870/71.

SHERMAN, AUSTIN B , Mahanoy City, Pa (d/XII–11 1906 @62) MD Jefferson 1865. *Pa m j* 10:295, 1906/07. *Flint* 1897: 808.

SHERMAN, BENJAMIN FRANKLIN, Ogdensburg, NY (b/V–24–1817 Barre, Vt; d/V–30–1897 @80) MD Albany 1841. *Buff m&s j* 37:59, 1897. *JAMA* 29:502, 1897. *Tr M S St NY* 1898:407–09. *Atkinson* I: 67–68. *K & B* III: 1102–03.

SHERMAN, FRANKLIN ADAMS, Ballston Spa, NY (b/XI–9–1828 Barre, Vt; d/IV–22–1903) MD Castleton 1850. *Bost m&s j* 148:486, 1903. *Polk* 1896: 988.

SHERMAN, GEORGE EDWIN, Oakland, Cal (b/V–27 1842 Galena, Ill; d/IX–19–1881) MD UCNY 1867. *Med bull m&s* 3:188, 1881. *Tr Cal St MS* 1882: 246–47. *Butler* 1878: 62.

SHERMAN, JAMES AUGUSTUS, Cherokee, Ia (b/X–1 1846 Erie, Pa; d/X–10–1899) MD Keokuk CPS 1873. *Trans Ia St Med Soc* 18: 392–93, 1900. *JAMA* 33:1116, 1183, 1899. *Polk* 1890: 515.

SHERMAN, JULIAN S , ?Chicago (b/Quincy, Ill; d/VIII–16–1876) MD Chic Med Coll 1864. *Chic med jour* 33:1032, 1876.

SHERMAN, SARAH EVA, Salem, Mass (d/XII–6–1900) MD Boston U 1876. *Trans Amer Inst Homeop* 1901:918. Homeopath.

SHERMAN, SOCRATES NORTON, Ogdensburg, NY (b/VII–22–1801 Barre, Vt; d/II–1–1873) MD Castleton 1824. *Med reg NY NJ Conn* 1873:347–49. *US Congr Biog dir*.

SHERMAN, THOMAS, Dresden, Me 1829–39 (b/VI–29 1803 Edgecombe; d/VIII–20–1842) MD Bowdoin 1828; ng Bowdoin Coll 1825. *Bowdoin cat*: 1829.

SHERMAN, THOMAS FOSTER, Boston (d/IX–26–1893) MD Harvard 1881; AB 1877. *Bost m&s j* 129:359, 1893.

SHERMAN, WASHINGTON, CW–USN (d/V–4–1864 Phila) MD ? *Nat med jour* 1:302, 1870/71.

SHEROW, ELTON JOHN, NYC (b/Sing Sing, NY; d/I–1–1898) MD CPSNY 1890. *Bost m&s j* 138:45, 1898. *JAMA* 30:106, 1898. *Polk* 1896: 1100.

SHERRERD, JOHN BROWN, Scranton, Pa (b/XI–19–1820 Warren Co, NJ; d/V–3–1852) MD UPa 1845; AB Princeton 1839; AM 1842; att Lafayette 1836. *Lafayette, Men of*: 139.

SHERRILL, HUNTING, Hyde Park, NY 23 yrs; NYC 1840– (b/IV–3–1773 Easthampton; d/I–16–1866) MD Geneva 1809. *Med surg rep Phila* 14: 80, 1866. *Amer homeop rev* 6:359, 1866. *Trans Amer Inst Homeop* 1870: 657. *Trans NY Homeop Med Soc* 1866: . Homeopath.

SHERROD, J H , Paoli, Ind (d/II–26–1895 @52) MD ? *JAMA* 24:370, 1895. *Polk* 1890: 269 (Lothair, Ga).

SHERWOOD, EBENEZER, Readington & German Valley, NJ (b/VI-16-1782; d/II-25-1854) MD ? *Tr M S NJ* 1872: 179-80.

SHERWOOD, JUSTUS, Southport Conn (b/1805;d/1878) MD Yale 1827;AB 1824. *Proc Conn M S* 1880:176.

SHERWOOD, THOMAS HUMPHRIES, Washington, DC; CW-USA (b/IX-24-1834 Milford, Del; d/II-9-1905) MD UPa 1858. *Bost m&s j* 152:206, 1905. *Polk* 1886: 824.

SHEW, ABRAM MARVIN, CW-USA; Middletown, Conn (b/IX-18-1841 Leroy, NY; d/IV-12-1886) MD Jefferson 1864. *Proc Conn Med Soc* ns3:182-87, 1886. *Atkinson* I:541. *K & B* III:1103.

SHIDLER, ARTHUR L , Ellisville, Ill (d/IX-1-1899) MD CPS Chic 1886. *Trans Ill St Med Soc* 1899: 287. *Polk* 1896: 418.

SHIDLER, SCHUYLER F , Sheridan, Mo (d/I-3-1903) MD CPS Chic 1888. *JAMA* 40:185, 1903.

SHIELD, MALLORY A , Hampton, Va (b/XII-7-1845 Elizabeth City; d/XI-10-1874 or 1875) MD U Va 1867. *Tr M S Va* 1875: 65, 102. *Med s rep Phila* 31: 420, 1874.

SHIELD, RICHARD H , Winton, NC (d/I-1-1870 @45 Murfreesboro) MD Med Coll Va 1845. *Trans NC Med Soc* 1870: 9.

SHIELDS, CHARLES M , Richmond, Va (b/I-1-1856; d/IV-16-1897) MD Med Coll Va 1879. *Trans Med Soc Va* 1897: 256-58. *JAMA* 28: 955, 1897. *Polk* 1896:1500.

SHIELDS, GEORGE WASHINGTON, Philadelphia; CW-USN (b/1840 Germantown; d/VIII-10-1867 New Orleans) MD UPa 1866. *Med surg rep Phila* 17:155, 1867. *U Pa m alum CW*: 1866. *Nat m j* 1:302, 1870/71.

SHIELDS, ISAAC HAYES, CW-USA; Philadelphia (b/XII-2-1838 Coatesville; d/I-13-1903) MD UPa 1858. *Pa med jour* 7:280, 1903/04. *U Pa med alum CW*: 1858.

SHILLING, GEORGE WILLIAM, Sharon, Pa (d/IV-21 1901 Cambridge Spr @58) MD UPa 1875. *Pa med jour* 5:296, 1901/02.

SHIMER, HENRY, Mt Carroll, Ill (d/VII-30-1895 @65) MD Northwestern Univ 1866. *JAMA* 25:253, 1895. *Butler* 1878: 178.

SHIMER, JACOB SCHANTZ, Philadelphia (d/VII-27/28-1898 @62) MD UPa 1857. *JAMA* 31:366, 1898.

SHIMER, REUBEN LUTZ, CW-USA; Redington, Pa (b/1834; d/II-13-1905) MD UPa 1858. *U Pa med alum CW*: 1858.

SHIMWELL, BENJAMIN T , Philadelphia (d/II-5-1903 @51) MD Jefferson 1875. *Pa med jour* 7:280, 1903/04. *Polk* 1886: 824.

SHIPLEY, GEORGE THOMPSON, CW-USN; Honolulu (d/XII-7-1880) MD Harvard 1861. *Harv in CW*: 267.

SHIPMAN, AZARIAH BOOTH, ortland, NY 1833-49; Syracuse, NY (b/III-22-1803 Roxbury, Conn; d/IX-15-1868 Paris, Fr) MD Jefferson 1844; MD Castleton 1835. *Bost m & s jour* 2:208, 1868. *Tr M S St NY* 1869: 247-55. *Med rec* 3:557, 1868-69. *K & B* I(1): 366-67.

SHIPMAN, GEORGE ELIAS, Chicago (d/I-20-1893 @73) MD CPSNY 1843; AB UCNY 1839. *Med vis* 8:77, 1892. *Med curr* 9:92, 1893. *US med invest* 1: ?, 1875. Homeopath.

SHIPMAN, NORBOURN N, Seymour Ind (b/IX-21-1829 New Orleans; d/I-7-1902) MD Med Coll Ohio 1874. *Tr Ind St M S* 1902: 423. *Polk* 1896: 490.

SHIPMAN, WILLIAM, Still Valley, NJ (b/V-16-1817 Stewartsville; d/II-5-1893) MD Jefferson 1836. *Tr Med Soc NJ* 1893:184. *Butler* 181878: 475.

SHIPPEN, CHARLES CARROLL, Baltimore (b/X-29-1856 Phila; d/1905) MD U Md 1879; AB Harvard 1877. *Med annals Md:* 566. *Polk* 1900: 816.

SHIPPEN, EDWARD, CW-USA; Baltimore (b/VI-23-1827 Bristol, Pa; d/IV-22-1895) MD Pa Med Coll 1853; MD UPa 1857; AB 1846. *JAMA* 24:690, 1895. *U Pa med alum CW*: 1857.

SHIPPEN, WILLIAM, Philadelphia; RevWar-USA (b/X-21-1736; d/VII-11-1808) MD Edinburgh 1761; AB Princeton 1754. *Tr CPP* cent vol: 265. *Phila jour med & phys sci* 5: 1822. *K & B* III: 1104-06.

SHIPPEN, WILLIAM, Philadelphia (b/I-29-1792; d/VI-6-1867) MD UPa 1814; AB 1810; AM. *Med surg rep Phila* 16: 511, 1867.

SHIREMAN, HENRY L , Nazareth, Pa (d/XI-5-1904 @ 63) MD Toledo M C 1885; MD Hahnemann Phila 1886. *Pa m j* 8:336, 1904/05. *Polk* 1886: 809. Homeopath?

SHIRLEY, ELIJAH STEVENS, Xenia, Ill (d/II-21-1900 @73) MD St Louis M C 1878. *Tr Ill St M S* 1899-1900: 463, 509. *JAMA* 34:381, 1900. *Polk* 1886: 302.

SHIRMER, CHARLES DAVID, NYC (d/IX-15-1898) MD CPSNY 1890. *JAMA* 31: 808 1898. *Polk* 1896:1078.

SHIVE, PETER C , Plainsville, Pa (b/VIII-18-1830 Bucks Co, Pa; d/V-12-1893) MD Pa Med Coll 1861. *Lehigh Valley med mag* 5:37, 1893-94. *Butler* 1878:732.

SHIVELY, GEORGE C , Waynesboro, Va (d/IX-20-1893) MD Jefferson 1878. *JAMA* 21: 546, 1893.

SHIVELY, JAMES SCOTT, Marion, Ind (b/IV-8-1813 Morgantown [W] Va; d/IV-11-1893) MD M C O 1873; stud w/Wm Kerr, New Castle, Ind. *Tr Ind St M S* 1893: 260. Kemper's *Indiana*:? *Ind m j* 11:376, 1893?

SHIVERICK, ARTHUR A , NYC (d/X-3-1863 @38) MD LICH 1862. *Med surg rep Phila* 10:342, 1863. *Bost m&s j* 69:228, 1863.

SHIVERS, JAMES KNIGHTON, CW-USA (b/XI-14-1821 Phila; d/XII-24-1864 nr Savannah or Atlanta) MD UPa 1843; ng Coll UPa 1840. *Nat med jour* 1:302, 1870/71. *U Pa med alum CW*: 1843.

SHIVERS, OFFA LUNSFORD, Marion, Ala (b/1815; d/III-14-1881) <MD Transylvania> att U Ala 1836. *Tr M Assn St Ala* 1881:271. *Butler* 1874: 25.

SHOAFF, PARIS, Newcastle, Pa (d/VI-6-1906 @37) MD West Pa Med Coll 1892. *Pa m j* 9:745-46, 1905/06.

SHOEMAKER, AUSTIN DENISON, Kingston, Pa? (d/1857) MD Yale 1849; AB Lafayette 1845; AM 1857.

Lafayette, Men of: 154.

SHOEMAKER, BENJAMIN FRANKLIN, Brownsville, Pa (d/VII–23–1902 @73) MD UPa 1870. *Pa m j* 5: 607, 1902/03; 6:261, 1902/03. *Flint* 1897: 797.

SHOEMAKER, CHARLES E , Reading, Pa (d/VII–18 1891) MD Pa Med Coll 1860; <att Bellevue 1876> *NW m j* 19:118, 1891. *Polk* 1886: 832.

SHOEMAKER, CLINTON L, Philadelphia (d/V–29–1904 @33) MD Med–Chi Phil 1903. *Pa m j* 8:336, 1904/05.

SHOEMAKER, JESSE GROOM, Phoenixville, Pa (d/XII–14–1901 @35) MD UPa 1886; AB 1883. *Pa m j* 5: 296, 1901/02.

SHOEMAKER, JOSEPH TURNER, Philadelphia; CW–USA (b/IV–5–1835 Chester; d/XII–6–1900) MD UPa 1860. *U Pa m alum CW*: 1860. *Polk* 1886: 824.

SHOEMAKER, NATHAN, Philadelphia (b/1789? d/V–11–1868 @79) MD UPa 1810. *Phila med reg & dir* 1871: 293. *Buff m&s j* 7:458, 1867. *Med s rep Phila* 19:80, 1868; 18:542, 1868. *Med rec* 3:312, 1868–69.

SHOEMAKER, SAMUEL BINES, Philadelphia (b/1861; d/IV–2–1893) MD UPa 1886; AB Haverford 1883. *Haverford Coll biogr cat*: 160.

SHOOK, JAMES W , Chillicothe, O (d/II–18–1894) MD Columbus Med Coll 1855. *JAMA* 22:391, 1894. *Polk* 1890: 896.

SHOPTAUGH, SHELTON H , Princeton, Ind (b/X–30–1840; d/VII–13–1898) MD Keokuk CPS 1864. *Tr Ind St Med Soc* 1899:387. *Polk* 1896:488.

SHORB, EDMUND F , Laurel, Md (d/I–15–1895 @69) MD U Md 1846. *JAMA* 24:177, 1895.

SHORB, JOSEPH CAMPBELL, San Francisco (b/IV–20 1837 Emmitsburg, Md; d/X–1–1889) MD UPa 1860. *U Pa med alum CW*: 1860. *Polk* 1886: 174.

SHORT, CHARLES WILKINS, Louisville (b/X–6–1794; d/III–7–1863) MD UPa 1815; AB Transylvania 1810. *Am j m sci* ns45:535–36,1863. *K&B* III:1107–08.

SHORT, JAMES C , Indiana, Pa (b/X–5–1840 Huntington Co, Pa; d/X–9–1894) MD Jefferson 1882. *Tr Med Soc Pa* 26:465 [?], 1896. *Polk* 1886: 793.

SHORT, ROBERT N , Centerville, Pa (b/IX–6–1831 Pulaski Co, Ky; d/XII–1–1897) <MD Georgia 1853> MD Miami 1871 ad eundem. *Pa med jour* 2:164–65, 1898. *JAMA* 29:1286, 1897. *Polk* 1890: 982.

SHORT, URIAH MERWIN, Grand Rapids, Mich (d/XII 13–1899 @54) MD U Mich 1868. *JAMA* 33:1632, 1899. *Polk* 1886: 493.

SHORTER, ELI SEMMES, CW–CSA; NYC (b/XI–23–1840 Columbus, Ga (d/V–12–1887) MD UPa 1870. *Med reg NY NJ Conn* 1887: 276. *New Orl m&s j* ns15:73, 1887. *Butler* 1878: 524.

SHOTWELL, JOHN T , Cincinnati (b/I–10–1807 Mason Co, Ky; d/VII–23–1850) MD Med Coll O 1832. *NW m & s jour* 3:266, 1850. *Tr Ohio St M S* 1873: 274. *Buff m&s j* 6:192, 1850. *K & B* III: 1108.

SHOVE, HARMON WILLIAM, Woodbury, Conn (b/VII 30–1832 Warren, Conn; d/I–24–1892) MD Yale 1853. *Proc Conn Med Soc* 1892:856–57. *Bost m&s j* 126:132, 1892. *Butler* 1878: 82.

SHOVE, SETH, Katonah, NY (b/VIII–8–1805 Warren, Conn; d/II–24–1878) MD Yale 1829. *Med rec* 13:220, 1878.

SHOWALTER, D T, Montpelier Ind (b/XII–20–1845; d/I–23–1883) MD M C Ind 1880. *Tr Ind St M S* 1883: 272.

SHOWER, JACOB, Manchester, ? (b/II–22–1803; d/V–25–1879) MD U Md 1825. *Med annals Md:* 566. *Butler* 1874: 323.

SHOWERMAN, JAMES M , Rome, NY (d/V–25–1899 @59) <MD Buffalo CPS Homeop 1881> *JAMA* 32:1399, 1899. *Buff m&s j* 38:941, 1899. *Flint* 1897: 694.

SHOYER, CHARLES C , Leavenworth, Kans (d/XII–7–1883/1884) MD Jefferson 1860 *Med bull m&s* 7:26 1885.

SHRINER, SAMUEL, New Texas, Pa (d/IV–12–1868 @ 46) MD ? *Phila m reg & dir* 1871:296. *Med s rep Phila* 18:376, 1868.

SHRIVER, JACOB L , Jollytown, Pa (d/V–7–1906) MD ? *Off'l reg Pa phys* 1881–87: 192. *Pa med jour* 9:607, 1905/06. *Flint* 1897: 805.

SHRYOCK, LOUISA MAY, Butler, Pa (d/1903 @36) MD Wooster 1893. *Pa med jour* 7:280, 1903/04.

SHUEY, JAMES W , Amsterdam, Va 1859–78; Sherman, Tex 1879–82 (b/VIII–25–1829 Augusta Co; d/1882) MD UCNY 1858; att U Va Med Dept 1857; AB Gettysburg 1856. *Gettysburg cat*: 1856.

SHUMARD, BENJAMIN FRANKLIN, Philadelphia; St Louis (b/1820; d/IV–14–1869) MD Louisville Med Inst 1843. *Phila m reg & dir* 1871:300. *Med s rep Phila* 20: 346, 1869. *K&B* III: 1109–10.

SHUMARD, GEORGE GETZ, Cincinnati (b/1825; d/X–6–1867) MD Louisville Med Inst 1845. *Tr AMA* 19:425, 1868. *Med s rep Phila* 17:347, 1867.

SHURE, CHARLES A, Port Deposit Md (d/V–14–1898 @57) MD U Md 1862. *JAMA* 30:1366, 1898. *Polk* 1886: 445.

SHURLOCK, WILLIAM CHARLES, Beaver Falls, Pa; CW–USA; Fargo ND (b/I– 6 or 10–1835 Enon Valley; d/I–17–1892) MD Jefferson 1858. *JAMA* 18:172, 1892. *Atkinson* I:189. *Butler* 1878: 732.

SHURTLEFF, AUGUSTINE, Brookline, Mass (b/VIII–24–1826 Boston; d/I–27–1901) MD Harvard 1849; AB Brown 1846. *Bost m&s j* 144:126, 1901.

SHURTLEFF, BENJAMIN, Boston (b/XI–7–1774 Plympton, Mass; d/IV–12–1847) MD Harvard 1802; AB Brown 1796; AM. *Brown hist cat*: 1796.

SHURTLEFF, CARLETON ATWOOD, CW–USA (d/VI–26–1864 Brookline, Mass) Med cadet at death; AB Harvard 1861. *Harvard in CW*: 174.

SHURTLEFF, GEORGE AUGUSTUS, Stockton, Cal (b/VIII–5–1819 Carver, Mass; d/II–11–1902) MD Woodstock 1845. *Cal st j m* 1:228, 1903. *Polk* 1896:243.

SHURTLEFF, HERBERT STERLING, Campello, Mass (d/III–31–1882 @32?) MD Albany 1869. *Bost m&s j* 106: 408, 1882.

SHURTLEFF, NATHANIEL BRADSTREET, Boston (b/VI–29–1810; d/X–17–1874) MD Harvard 1834; AB 1831. *Bost m&s j* 91:411, 1874. *Med s rep Phila* 31:360, 1874. *K&B* III: 1110–11.

SHURTLEFF, SIMEON, Simsbury, Conn (b/VII–9–1808 Montgomery, Mass; d/XII–23–1865) MD Berkshire 1835; AB Amherst 1832. *Amherst cat*: 1832.

SHUTE, CHARLES BAILEY, Malden, Mass (d/XI–25–1888 @45) MD Harvard 1870; AB 1865. *Bost m&s j* 119:544, 1888. *Butler* 1878: 357.

SHUTT, JOHN T , Greenville, Pa (d/III or V–4–1902) <MD CPS Balto 1880> *Pa med jour* 5:508, 1901/02; 6:261, 1902/03.

SHUTT, MARGARET TAYLOR, Springfield, Ill (d/I–24–1903 @35) MD Cornell 1899. *Ill med jour* ns4:557–58, 590, 1903. *Polk* 1902:613.

SHUTTLEWORTH, JOHN GEORGE, Brooklyn (b/VIII–15–1844; d/I–8–1876) MD UCNY 1867. *Med reg NY NJ Conn* 1876: 255.

SIBERT, WILLIAM HENRY, Kansas City, Mo (d/I–13–1898 @48) MD NWU 1873. *JAMA* 30:279, 1898. *Polk* 1886: 552.

SIBLEY, CHARLES WILBUR, Fairfield, Ill (d/I–13–1903 @64) MD Bellevue 1877. *Ill med jour* ns4:590, 1903. *Polk* 1886: 279.

SIBLEY, WALLACE A , Rochester, NY (d/X–28–1900) MD Buffalo 1875. *Bost m&s j* 143: 490, 1900. *Polk* 1886: 705.

SICKLER, JASPER BRITTON, Rockville, Pa (d/XII 11–1901) MD Bellevue 1890. *Pa med jour* 5:296, 1901/02. *Flint* 1897: 813.

SICKLER, JOHN ROWAN, Mantua, NJ (b/IX–20–1800 Chews Landing, NJ; d/IV–11–1886) MD Jefferson 1829. *Tr Med Soc NJ* 1886:171–72. *Butler* 1878: 475.

SIDDALL, HUGH WAGSTAFF, CW–USA; Philadelphia (b/VIII–16–1824 Lower Providence; d/II–28–1889) MD UPa 1847. *UPa med alum CW*:1847. *Polk* 1886:824.

SIDES, BENJAMIN FRANKLIN, Furniss, Pa (d/XI–14–1904 @84) MD Jefferson 1846. *Pa med jour* 8:336, 1904/05. *Flint* 1897: 802.

SIDWELL, NATHAN H , Wilmington, O (b/X–18–1840 Georgetown, O; d/VI–13–1883) MD Miami Med Coll 1871. *Tr Ohio St Med Soc* 1884: 227–29.

SIEBER, JOHN A , Owensboro, Ky (b/IX–14–1853 Evansville, Ind; d/III–19–1883) MD Evansville Med Coll 1879. *Tr Ind St Med Soc* 1883: 279.

SIEGFRIED, CHARLES A , Newport, RI (d/I–15–1900) MD Jefferson 1872. *JAMA* 34: 186, 1900.

SIEWERS, NATHANIEL SHOBER, CW–USA; Salem, NC (b/XI–15–1845; d/I–12–1901) MD UPa 1867. *U Pa med alum CW*: 1867. *Polk* 1886: 726.

SIGLINGER, CHARLES J, Philadelphia (d/VII–12–1899) MD Jefferson 1890. *JAMA* 33: 302, 1899. *Polk* 1896: 1317.

SIGWORTH, FRANKLIN P , Cranesville, Pa (d/I–8–1906 @50) <MD CPS Balto 1883> *Pa m j* 9: 361, 1905/06.

SILL, HARVEY NEWELL, Strawberry Point Ia (b/X–29 1832 Hinsdale NY; d/IV–13–1892) MD Iowa St U 1873. *Tr Iowa St M S* 10:230–31, 1892. *Polk* 1890: 436.

SILLIMAN, BENJAMIN, New Haven, Conn (b/VIII–8–1879 No Stratford; d/XI–24–1864) MD Bowdoin 1818; AB Yale 1796; AM 1818. *Bost m&s j* 71: 368, 1864. *K & B* III: 1111–1112.

SILLIMAN, BENJAMIN, New Haven, Conn (b/XII–4–1816; d/I–14–1885) Hon MD SC Med Coll 1849; AB Yale 1837; LLD Jefferson M C 1884. *Med bull m & s* 7: 91, 1885. *Atkinson* I:477–78. *K & B* III: 1112.

SILLIMAN, HENRY RIDGWAY, USA 1861–67; Philadelphia (b/X–29–1832 Pottsville; d/I–1–1883) MD U Pa 1855. *UPa med alum CW*: 1855. *Tr CPP* cent vol:265.

SILLS, DAVID NICHOLSON, CW–CSA; Castalia, NC (b/IV–20–1836 Belford; d/X–19–1897) MD UPa 1858. *U Pa med alum CW*: 1858.

SILVA, CHRISTOPHER C P , Chicago (d/XII– –1896) <MD Lisbon 1861> *Chic med rec* 12:84, 1897.

SILVER, DAVID H , CW–USA (d/VI–26–1864 Chattanooga) MD ? *Nat med jour* 1:302, 1870/71.

SIM, FRANK L, Memphis (b/IV–29–1834 Golconda, Ill; d/XI–23–1894) MD U Louisville 1855; MD Pa Med Coll 1857. *So pract* 16: 519–20, 1894. *Buff m&s j* 34: 370, 1895. *JAMA* 23:840, 1894. *Nashvl j m&s* 76:285, 1894.

SIM, THOMAS, Washington, DC (b/1770 Fred'k Co Md; d/IX–13–1832) <MD UPa 1823> *Hist Med Soc DC:* 215.

SIMABAUGH, M N , CW–CSA (d/VII– –1863 Shelbyville, Tenn) MD ? *SHSP* 22:256, 1893.

SIMCOX, WILLIAM N , Pittsburgh (d/VI–30–1902 @ 76) <MD Jefferson> *Pa med jour* 6: 261, 1902/03. *Flint* 1897: 831.

SIMINGTON, ROBERT SIMINGTON, Danville, Pa CW–USA (b/V–10–1831 White Deer; d/XI–23–1889) MD UPa 1854. *U Pa med alum CW*: 1854. *Atkinson* I: 654. *Polk* 1886: 797.

SIMMONDS, THOMAS W , Martinsville, Va (d/XI–21 1898 @38) MD Med Coll Va 1884. *JAMA* 31: 1490, 1898. *Polk* 928.

SIMMONS, ARTHUR RAYMOND, Utica, NY (d/III–27 1904 @56) MD CPSNY 1875; AB Amherst 1871. *Tr M S St NY* 1904: [420]. *Polk* 1886: 669.

SIMMONS, DUANE BUCKBEE, Tokyo 1859– (b/1826? d/II–19–1889) MD CPSNY 1855. *Med reg NY NJ Conn* 1889:285. *Bost m&s j* 120:348, 1889.

SIMMONS, ELECTA G U , Erie, Ill (d/II–28–1901) MD NWU 1879. *Ill m j* ns2:533 1901. *Polk* 1886:278.

SIMMONS, FRANCIS A, St Joseph Mo (d/VI–5–1899 @70?) MD NW M C St Jos 1880. *JAMA* 32: 1460, 1899.

SIMMONS, JOHN, NYC (d/VI–24–1867) MD UCNY

1853. *Tr AMA* 19: 421, 1868. *Med reg NY NJ Conn* 1868: 334.

SIMMONS, JOHN F , Houston, Tex (d/1895) MD Jefferson 1865. *JAMA* 24:861, 1895. *Polk* 1886: 155 (Pine Bluff, Ark).

SIMMONS, JOHN HOLMES, CW–USA; Ashford, Conn (b/XI–21–1811; d/XI–12–1891) MD Yale 1833. *Pr Conn M S* 1892:866. *Atkinson* I:438. *Butler* 1878:82.

SIMMONS, JOSEPH M R , USN (b/1846; d/1872) MD U Va 1870. *Tr AMA* 24:396–97, 1873.

SIMMONS, MARSHALL EDWIN, CW–USA; Wareham, Mass (d/V– –1874 @42) MD Harvard 1860. *Harvard in CW*: 261.

SIMMONS, SAMUEL SMITH, Natchitoches, La (b/Ga; d/VII–22–1877 @62) MD Tulane 1838. *New Orl m&s j* ns5:250, 1877.

SIMMONS, THOMAS WARFIELD, Hagerstown Md (b/VI–16–1836; d/XII–30–1905) MD Jefferson 1861. *Med annals Md:* 567. *Polk* 1886: 443.

SIMMS, HENRY C , Brooklyn (b/1828 DC; d/II–18 1883) MD Jefferson 1855. *Med reg NY NJ Conn* 1883: 235. *Hist Med Soc DC:* 248.

SIMONS, BENJAMIN BONNEAU, Charleston, SC (b/XII–5–1776; d/IX–27–1844) MD Glasgow 1800; AB Brown 1796. *Brown hist cat*: 1796. *Waring* II: 212, 223. *K&B* III: 1112–13.

SIMONS, LEWIS EDWARD, Saxton's River, Vt (b/1825; d/1865) MD Harvard 1853. *Tr AMA* 29:760, 1878.

SIMONS, O H , Magnetic Spr, Cal (b/1846 Ohio; d/VIII–22–1903) <MD UPa> *Cal st j m* 1:323, 1903.

SIMONS, THOMAS YOUNG, Charleston, SC (b/1797; d/VI–8–1857) MD Edinburgh 1820. *Bost m&s j* 56: 447, 1857. *Waring* II: 295–96.

SIMONTON, A C , Vernon, La (d/III–6–1899 @ 67) MD New Orl Sch Med 1857; att U Va Med Sch. *JAMA* 32: 628, 1899.

SIMONTON, PUTNAM, Searsport, Me (b/IX–10–1812; d/II–13–1870) MD Bowdoin 1835. *Tr Me Med Assoc* 1870: 329–30.

SIMONTON, WILLIAM B , Oakland, Cal (b/V–26–1827 Bloomfield, Pa; d/VII–19–1890) MD Pa Med Coll 1850. *Tr Med Soc Cal* 21: 316–17, 1891. *Polk* 1886:168.

SIMPSON, CHARLES T , Temple & Austin, Tex (d/II–25–1906 Cananea, Mex) MD Med Coll Ala 1877. *Texas st jour med* 1: 352, 1905/06. *Polk* 1886: 895.

SIMPSON, EDWARD BASIL, Harney, Md (d/X 7–1899 @60) MD UMd 1862. *JAMA* 33:994 1899. *Polk* 1886: 443.

SIMPSON, J B , Mountain Home, Ark (d/XII 31–1898 @47) MD U Louisville 1882. *JAMA* 32:92 1899. *Polk* 1890: 169.

SIMPSON, J L , Houston Heights, Tex (d/V–19–1906 @50) MD ? *Tex st jour med* 2:100, 1906.

SIMPSON, JAMES, San Francisco (b/VIII–12–1829 Calais, Me; d/X–22–1897) MD UCNY 1855; stud Albany Med Coll. *Bost m&s j* 137:456, 1897. *Atkinson* I: 681. *Butler* 1878: 55.

SIMPSON, JAMES, Philadelphia (d/VI–20–1904 @66) MD Jefferson 1865 *Pa med jour* 8:336, 1904/05. *Flint* 1897:825.

SIMPSON, JAMES F, Point Caswell, NC (d/IX–28–1897 @78) MD Jefferson 1846. *NC med jour* 40: 245, 1897.

SIMPSON, JAMES THOMAS, Glen Springs, SC (d/XII–3–1899 @50) MD Memphis Hosp Med Coll 1882. *JAMA* 33: 1632, 1899.

SIMPSON, JOSIAH, USA 1837– (b/II–27–1815 New Brunswick, NJ; d/III–3–1874 Balto) MD UPa 1836; AB Princeton 1833; AM 1836. *Tr AMA* 25:538–39, 1874. *Med rec* 9:157, 1874. *Med surg rep Phila* 30:276, 1874.

SIMPSON, JULIUS MANNING, Schraalenburgh NJ (b/II–22–1838 Franklin Que; d/VI–11–1896) MD Bellevue 1866 *Tr M S NJ* 1897:295. *Atksn* I:372. *Butler* 1878: 475.

SIMPSON, RICHARD FRENCH, USA 1840–61 (b/Loudoun Co Va; d/VII–4–1861 Key West Fla) MD UPa 1840. *Tr AMA* 14:216, 1864. *Nat m j* 1:302, 1870/71.

SIMPSON, ROBERT BOYD, Pittsburgh (d/II–5–1866 @57) MD UPa 1833. *Med s rep Phila* 14: 140, 1866. *Nat m j* 1:302, 1870/71.

SIMPSON, ROBERT M , Moulton, Ala (d/V–1–1897) MD Vanderbilt 1885. *Tr M Assn St Ala* 1898:240.

SIMPSON, S LAFAYETTE, NH (b/VIII–20–1825 Concord, NH; d/III–10–1877) MD Berkshire 1847. *Tr NH Med Soc* 1877: 116–19.

SIMPSON, WILLIAM L , Ill (d/I–26–1901 NYC) MD Bennett 1882. *Ill m jour* ns3:142, 1901. *Polk* 1890: 330.

SIMS, JAMES HENRY, Harwood, Tex (b/VII–2–1846; d/VI–24–1893) MD Nashville U 1868; att U Ala. *U Ala cat*: 188.

SIMS, JAMES MARION, NYC (b/I–15–1813 Lancaster Distr, SC; d/XI–13–1883) MD Jefferson 1835; AB SC Coll 1825. *Chic m j* 48:111–12, 1884. *JAMA* 1:659, 1883. *Tr M S Va* 1884:9. *So pract* 5:561–65. 1883. *K&B* III: 1114.

SIMS, WALTER HIGHTOWER, Wartrace, Tenn (b/X–16–1815 Brentwood; d/VII–2–1882) MD U Louisville 1844. *Tr M S Tenn* 1883: 63–64. *Butler* 1878: 777.

SINCLAIR, WILLIAM BEVERLY, USN 1838–61; CW–CSN (b/I–22–1818 Norfolk, Va; d/IX–27–1895 Balto) MD UPa 1838. *U Pa med alum CW*: 1838.

SINGER, JAMES JONES, Connellsville, Pa (d/III–29–1903 @53) MD Jefferson 1871. *Pa med jour* 7:280, 1903/04. *Flint* 1897: 799.

SINGLETON, JAMES WILLIAM, Paducah, Ky; CW–CSA (b/VIII 23–1829 Grant Co; d/IX–25–1881) MD U Louisville 1854. *So pract* 3:359–66, 1881. *Tr AMA* 33: 603–05, 1882. *Atkinson* I: 84–85.

SINGLETON, WILLIAM, Covington, Ky (d/VII–23 1901 @73) MD Ky Sch Med 1851. *JAMA* 37: 398, 1901. *Polk* 1886: 134.

SINKLER, SEAMAN DEAS, Charleston, SC (d/I–19–

 Spec. educ'l status abbrev. as: ***ng*** = college verified attendance without degree;

1847 @30) MD UPa 1837. *Tr AMA* 3:464–65, 1850.

SINNETT, JOHN HARRIS, NYC (d/III–22–1894 @28) MD Bellevue 1889; AB U Iowa 1886. *Med reg NY NJ Conn* 1894: 249.

SISSON, WILLIAM H H , CW–USA; Omaha 1868–73 (b/II–8–1842 New Bedford, Mass; d/I–25–1873) MD Hahnemann Phila 1863. *Tr Am Inst Hom* 1873: 513. *New Engl m gaz* 8:200, 1873. *Am j hom mat med* 6:324, 1873?

SKEER, JOHN DUGAN, Chicago (b/1825? d/III–7–1898 @73) MD U Nashville 1876. *Chic m rec* 14:248, 1898. *JAMA* 30:682, 1898. *Polk* 1896: 405.

SKELTON, CHARLES, Trenton, NJ (b/IV–19–1806 Bucks Co, Pa; d/V–20–1879) MD Jefferson 1837. *Tr AMA* 33:598–603, 1882. *Tr Med Soc NJ* 1879: 211–15. *Butler* 1878: 476.

SKELTON, JOHN GIFFORD, CW–CSA; Richmond, Va (b/IV–19–1815 Powhatan; d/X–31–1899) MD UPa 1838. *U Pa med alum CW*:1838. *Atkinson* I: 286.

SKELTON, LEONARD LAWSHEE, Chicago (d/III–14 1906 @42) MD NWU 1889. *Ill med jour* 9:464, 1906.

SKENE, ALEXANDER JOHNSTON CHALMERS, CW–USA; Brooklyn (b/VI–17–1837 Fyvie, Scotl; d/VII–4–1900) MD LICH 1863; att U Mich Med Dept. *So pract* 22:457, 1900. *Pr Conn M S* 1901: 276–79. *K&B* III: 1117–18. *Butler* 1878: 534.

SKERRETT, DAVID CHRISTIE, Philadelphia (b/1797? d/I–27–1873) MD UPa 1820. *Med surg rep Phila* 28: 148, 1873.

SKIFF, CLARK, Selma, Ind (b/I–16–1826 Clinton, O; d/X–12–1888) ng Miami Med Coll 1854–55. *Tr Ind St M S* 1889: 212. *Butler* 1878: 219.

SKIFF, GEORGE VARNUM, CW–USA; NYC (d/I–28–1890 @52) MD UCNY 1860. *Med reg NY NJ Conn* 1890: 279. *Butler* 1878: 525.

SKIFF, PERRIN A , Utica, NY (d/III–13–1895 @68) MD Albany 1851. *JAMA* 24:497, 1895. *Polk* 1890: 790.

SKILLMAN, ABRAHAM, Bound Brook, NJ (b/1796; d/XII–10–1862) MD ? ; AB Princeton 1819; AM 1822. *Tr AMA* 14:208, 1864. *Med s rep Phila* ns9:278, 1862/63.

SKILLMAN, JACOB T B , New Brunswick, NJ (b/III 10–1794; d/VI–24–1864) Lic XI–8–1825. *Med s rep Phil* 12:18, 1864/65. *Tr AMA* 16:632–33, 1865. *Tr M S NJ* 1865: 72–75.

SKILTON, JULIUS A , Brooklyn (b/VI–29–1833 Troy, NY; d/XI–20–1897) MD Albany 1855; AB Wesleyan 1853. *JAMA* 29: 1180, 1897.

SKINNER, ALDEN B , CW–USA (d/III–30–1862 Baton Rouge, La) MD ? . *Nat m j* 1:302, 1870/71.

SKINNER, ALBERT GALLATIN, Youngstown, NY (d/VII–18–1891 @84) MD Dartmouth 1835. *Med reg NY NJ Conn* 1892: 287. *NW m j* 19:118, 1891. *Bost m&s j* 125: 124, 1891. *Butler* 1878: 573.

SKINNER, BENJAMIN FRANKLIN, Enfield, NH (d/III–13–1868 @38) MD Woodstock 1856; ng Dartmouth Med Dept 1855. *Phila med reg & dir* 1871:295. *Bost m&s j* 1:160, 1868. *Tr NH M S* 1868:60.

SKINNER, CALVIN, Malone, NY (b/V–29–1818 Royalton, Vt; d/IX–24–1903) MD Dartmouth 1841. AB U Vt 1836. *Bost m&s jour* 149:388, 1903. *Polk* 1896: 1031.

SKINNER, DANIEL MOORE, CW–USA; Belleville, NJ (b/V–1–1835 Orange; d/IX–26–1906) MD UCNY 1858. *Bost m&s j* 155:394 1906. *Atkinson* I:359 *Polk* 1896:933.

SKINNER, DAVIS NEVENS, Auburn, Me (b/XI–17–1841 Lewiston; d/VI–18–1892) MD Bowdoin 1867. *Bost m&s j* 126:648, 1892; 129:44, 1893. *Tr Me Med Assoc* 1893:370–71. *Polk* 1886: 423.

SKINNER, EUGENE CARROLL, Detroit (d/I–24–1899 @57) <MD Detroit Med Coll 1887> *JAMA* 32:324, 1899. *Polk* 1896: 752.

SKINNER, RICHARD BAXTER, Barton, Vt (b/1834; d/1900) MD Harvard 1858. *JAMA* 34:380, 1900. *Polk* 1896: 1472.

SKINNER, THOMAS H , Philadelphia (d/V–10–1884 Hartford, Conn) MD ? *Med reg NY NJ Conn* 1884: 239. *Med surg rep Phila* 50:640, 1884.

SKINNER, WILLIAM MORRELL, Anamosa, Ia (d/1893) MD Woodstock 1850. *Tr Ia St M S* 18:411, 1900. *Polk* 1890: 407.

SKINNER, WILLIAM WESLEY, Forrest, Ill (d/VII–25 1897 @27) MD Rush 1891. *JAMA* 29:297, 1897.

SKINNER, WINSLOW WARNER, NYC (b/1856; d/III–29–1900 Viareggio, Italy) MD Paris 1885. *JAMA* 34:891, 1900. *NY m j* 71:520, 1900. *Polk* 1890: 833.

SKIVINGTON, JOHN, Morganza, Pa (d/I–18–1906 @ 76) MD Med Coll Ohio 1857. *Pa m jour* 9:607, 1905/06.

SLACK, HENRY, Fishkill–on–Hudson, NY (b/1831; d/XII–10–1886) MD Albany 1852. *Med reg NY NJ Conn* 1887:276. *Bost m&s j* 115:582, 1886.

SLACK, JOHN HAMILTON, Bloomsburg, NJ (b/IX–23 1834 Bordentown; d/VIII–27–1874) MD UPa 1860; AB 1856. *Tr CPP* cent vol: 266. *Med surg rep Phila* 31: 220, 240, 1874. *Tr AMA* 26: 471, 1875.

SLACK, WILLIAM HENRY, ?Nashville (b/II–21–1854; d/IV–21–1876 @23) MD Vanderbilt 1876. *Nashvl j m & s* ns17:236–37, 1876.

SLADE, DANIEL DENISON, Boston (b/V–1–1823; d/II–11–1896) MD Harvard 1848; AB 1844. *JAMA* 25:391 1896. *Bost m&s j* 134:204 474, 1896. *K&B* III:1119–20.

SLADE, JAMES BOG, New Orleans; MexWar–USA (b/1803 NC; d/XI–30–1847 Mex City) MD UPa 1826; stud UNC 1822. *New Orl m & s j* 4:548, 1848.

SLADE, THOMAS TURNER, Lincolnton, NC; CW–CSA (b/1822; d/1863 in battle) MD ? AB UNC 1845. *UNC cat*: 568.

SLAUGHTER, ALFRED E , Gordonsville, Va (b/VIII 24–1839; d/I–11–1883)MD UVa 1860. *JAMA* 1:436, 1883. *Med bull m & s* 5:279, 1883.

SLAUGHTER, CHARLES, Duluth, Minn (d/I–23–1898) MD UVa 1876. *JAMA* 30:335, 1898. *Tr Minn St M S* 1899: 191. *Polk* 1886:921 (Lynchburg, Va).

SLAUGHTER, JAMES, Philadelphia (b/1794? d/II-25 1863) MD Jefferson 1828. *Med s rep Phila* ns9: 422, 1862/63.

SLAUGHTER, THOMAS TOWLES, Madison Co, Va; CW-CSA (b/VI- -1804 Culpeper Co; d/II-21-1890) MD UPa 1825. *U Pa med alum CW*: 1825. *Tr M S Va* 1892: 189-90. *Butler* 1878: 836.

SLEVIN, WILLIAM H , Toledo (d/VIII-18-1897 @30) <MD Detroit Coll Med 1891> *JAMA* 29: 502, 1897.

SLICER, JOHN EDWIN, St Joseph, La (d/II-8-1899 @ 69) MD Jeff'n 1854. *JAMA* 32:442, 1899. *Polk* 1886:419.

SLOAN, A C , Corsicana, Tex (d/XI-30-1906 @63) MD U Louisville 1870. *Tex st m j* 2:260, 1906/07. *Polk* 1886: 883.

SLOAN, GEORGE WHITE, Indianapolis (b/VI-28-1835 Harrisburg, Pa; d/II-15-1903) Hon MD Ind Med Coll; PhD 1880. *Tr Ind St M S* 1903:354.

SLOAN, JAMES GORDON, Monongahela City, Pa (b/I 18-1841 Frankford; d/XI-2-1897) MD Georgetown 1869. *Pa m j* 1:565-66, 1898. *JAMA* 29: 1081, 1897. *Butler* 1878: 732.

SLOAN, JOHN, CW-USA; New Albany, Ind (b/IX-15-1815 Westbrook, Me; d/IV-13-1898) MD Bowdoin 1838. *Tr Ind St M S* 1898: 392-93. *JAMA* 30:1305, 1898.

SLOAN, WILBERT K, Moline Ill (d/I-1-1901) MD CPS Keokuk 1875. *Ill m j* ns2:533, 1901. *Polk* 1886: 288.

SLOAN, WILLIAM JAMES, USA 1837- (b/Pa; d/III-17 1880 St Paul Minn) MD Jefferson 1836. *Med rec NY* 17: 359, 1880. *Tr Minn St M S* 1880:186-87. *Heitman*.

SLOCUM, ALFRED MARSHALL, Philadelphia (b/XII-2-1822; d/VI-21-1882) MD UPa 1847. *Tr CPP* cent vol: 266.

SLOCUM, JOHN OSTRANDER, Camillus, NY (b/IV-4 1820 Delphi or Pompey; d/III-3-1885) MD Castleton 1846. *Tr NY St M S* 11:794 ff, 1894. *Butler* 1878: 573.

SLOCUM, M W , Buchanan, Mich (d/II-7-1887) MD Hahnemann Chic 1884. *Med vis* 3:74, 1887. *Polk* 1886: 485. Homeopath.

SLOUGH, GRANVILLE BROBST, CW-USN; Easton Pa (d/XI-27 1899 @61) MD Jefferson 1861; att Lafayette. *JAMA* 33:1504, 1899. *Polk* 1896: 1276.

SLOVER, GEORGE, New Bern, NC (b/X-8-1843; d/VI 30-1904) MD Johns Hopkins 1869!! AB UNC 1866;AM 1868. *UNC cat*: 570.

SMALL, ALVAN EDMOND, Philadelphia 1845-56; Chicago 1856- (b/III-4-1811 Wales, Me; d/XII-31-1886) MD Pa Med Coll 1841. *Med vis* 3:39-41, 1887. *US m invest* 22:576, 1886. *Hahn mo* 22:112, 1887. *Tr Am Inst Hom* 1887:198. *Polk* 1886:271. *Cleave*. Homeopath.

SMALL, ANDREW V , Sedalia, Mo (d/III-10-1896 @75) MD Paris 1839. *Tex m news* 5:232, 1895-96. *Polk* 1886: 568.

SMALL, HORATIO NELSON, CW-USA; Portland, Me (b/XI-10-1839/1840 Buxton; d/XII-26\28, 1886) MD Dartmouth 1863. *Tr Me M Assn* 1887:315-17. *Bost m&s j* 116:24, 1887. *K&B* 1120-21.

SMALL, JOHN MEGQUIER, Exeter & Lewiston, Me (b/III-14-1818 New Gloucester; d/XII-4-1897 @80) MD Bowdoin 1847. *JAMA* 29:1286, 1897. *Atkinson* I: 421. *Polk* 1886: 426.

SMALL, P M , Eaton, O (d/XI-3-1899 @65) MD Miami 1872. *JAMA* 33:1441, 1899. *Butler* 1878: 650.

SMALLEY, ADONIRAM, Lebanon, NH (b/IX-14-1803 Randolph, Vt; d/V-14-1876) MD Dartmouth 1831. *Tr NH M S* 1876: 157-60.

SMALLEY, GEORGE LYMAN, CW-USA (d/XI-23-1862) MD Harvard 1862. *Bost m&s j* 67:368, 1862. *Nat med jour* 1:302, 1870/71 [as d/XI-23-1864].

SMALLWOOD, EDWARD FLEET, CW-CSA; New Bern, NC (b/IX-25-1822; d/VII-11-1881) MD UCNY 1846; att UNC 1839-40. *NC m j* 8:111- , 1881.

SMART, ANSON R, Toledo O (b/VII-4-1841 Adrian; d/ 1891) MD LICH 1872. *Tr Ohio M S* 1891:6, 346-48.

SMART, CHARLES, USA (b/1841 Scotl; d/IV-23-1905 St Augusine, Fla) <MD Aberdeen 1882> *Bost m&s j* 152:534, 1905. *K&B* III:1121-22.

SMART, DANIEL STEVENSON, Fredricksburg Tx; USA (b/VI-28-1844 Baltimore; d/V-15-1877) MD Jefferson 1870; AB Amherst 1867. *Amherst, Men of*:1867.

SMEAD, ROBERT B , Altona, Ill (d/II-18-1900 @61) MD CPS Keokuk 1874. *Tr Ill St M S* 1899-1900: 463, 509. *JAMA* 34:574, 1900. *Polk* 1886: 300.

SMEDLEY, ISAAC GARRETT, Philadelphia (b/II-10-1855 W Chester, Pa; d/XII-1-1899 Bryn Mawr) MD Hahnemann Phila 1885. *Tr Am Inst Hom* 1900:838. *Med vis* 16:56, 1901. *No Am jour hom* 48:7 (curr events) 1900. *Polk* 1886: 825. Homeopath.

SMEDLEY, JAMES, North-East, Pa (b/1790? d/I-26-1868 @78) MD ? *Phila med reg & dir* 1871: 295. *Med surg rep Phila* 18: 314, 1868.

SMEDLEY, ROBERT CLEMENS, W Chester Pa 1863-(b/IV-5-1832 Willistown; d/I-2-1883) MD Hahnemann Phila 1860; att UPa. *Tr Am Inst Hom* 1891: *Cleave*. Homeopath.

SMILEY, ANDREW JACKSON, Philadelphia (d/1867) MD UPa 1854. *Med surg rep Phila* 17: 436, 1867.

SMILEY, JAMES C , Kewanee, Ill (d/II-27-1901) Cert by yrs pract. *Ill m j* ns2:533, 1901. *Polk* 1896:426.

SMILEY, JAMES FRANCIS, Marshall, Mich (d/IX-29 1899 @64) MD U Mich 1862. *JAMA* 33: 994, 1899. *Polk* 1896: 764.

SMILEY, THOMAS TUCKER, Philadelphia; CW-USA (b/XI-15-1795 Luzerne Co, Pa; d/XII-17-1879) MD UPa 1831; AM Geo Wash U 1833. *Med surg rep Phila* 42:22, 1880. *U Pa med alum CW*: 1831.

SMITH, A T , Marshall, Tex (d/VI-12-1883 @ c75) MD ? *Tex med & surg rec* 3:804, 1883.

SMITH, AARON, Hardwick, Vt 1811-65; Montpelier (b/ 1786 Hanover, NH; d/IX-28-1868) ng Dartmouth 1811. *Phila med reg & dir* 1871:299. *Bost m&s j* ns2:272, 336,

1868. *Med surg rep Phila* 19:412, 1868.

SMITH, ABNER MARSHALL, Pittsfield, Mass (d/V-23 1889 @68) MD Berkshire 1846. *Bost m&s j* 121: 645, 1889.

SMITH, ABRAHAM CARPENTER, Bloomsburg, NJ (b/XII-11-1828; d/III-23-1895) MD UPa 1850; AB Lafayette 1850. *Tr M S NJ* 1895: 205-06.

SMITH, ABRAM CLARKSON, Columbia, Pa (d/1856) MD UPa 1852; stud Lafayette. *Lafayette, Men of*: 166.

SMITH, ALAN PENNIMAN, Baltimore (b/II-3-1840; d/VII-18-1898) MD UMd 1861; <AB Princeton> *JAMA* 31:257, 1898. *Med ann Md:* 569. *Polk* 1886: 439.

SMITH, ALANSON T , Brooklyn (d/VI-17-1901) MD UCNY 1885. *JAMA* 37:43, 1901. *Polk* 1886: 649.

SMITH, ALBERT, Peterborough, NH (b/VI-18-1801; d/II-22-1878) MD Dartmouth 1833; AB 1825. *Tr NH M S* 1878:189-95. *Tr Vt M S* 1883:109. *Tr AMA* 29:760-62. *K&B* III: 1122.

SMITH, ALBERT, New Rochelle, NY (b/1798? d/II-19-1884 @86) MD CPSNY 1820. *Med reg NY NJ Conn* 1884: 239. *Butler* 1878: 573.

SMITH, ALBERT, Queechee, Vt (b/X-16-1842 Randolph; d/VIII-31-1880) MD Dartmouth 1869. *Tr Vt M S* 1883: 109.

SMITH, ALBERT DOUGLASS, Holden, Mass (d/X-26 1858 @36) MD ? *Bost m&s j* 59:288, 1859.

SMITH, ALBERT HENRY, Meridian, Miss (b/VI-3-1815 Charlotte Co, Va; d/III-13-1895) MD Transylvania 1837. *New Orl m&s j* ns22:766, 1895. *Atkinson* I: 453. *Polk* 1890: 632.

SMITH, ALBERT HOLMES, Philadelphia (b/VII-19-1835; d/XII-14-1885) MD UPa 1856; AB 1853. *Tr CPP* cent vol: 266; 3s9: cdxxxiii-cdxlvii, 1887. *Buff m&s j* 25:329, 1886. *New Orl m&s j* ns13:664, 1886. *Atkinson* I: 63-64. *K&B* III:1122-23.

SMITH, ALVAN, Monson, Mass (b/V-23-1808 Palmer; d/VIII-2-1882) MD Harvard 1837; ng Amherst 1833. *Bost m&s j* 107:312, 1882.

SMITH, AMOS BIRD, Geneva, NY (d/XII-18-1894 @ 75) MD Geneva 1845; <MD CPSNY 1846> *JAMA* 23: 990, 1894. *Polk* 1886: 661.

SMITH, ANDREW KINGSBURY, USA 1852- (b/II-9 1826; d/VIII-14-1889 West Point, NY) MD Jefferson 1849; MD NYMC 1852; AB Williams 1847; AM 1868. *Tr CPP* cent vol: 266. *Bost m&s j* 141:204, 1899.

SMITH, ANDREW MURRAY, Williamstown, Mass (b/1826; d/X-25-1896) MD Berkshire 1847. *Bost m&s j* 135:535, 1896. *Polk* 1896: 726.

SMITH, ASHBEL, Cedar Bayou, Tex (b/VIII-13-1805/1806 Hartford, Conn; d/I-21-1886) MD Yale 1828; AB 1824. *Daniel's Tex med j* 1:376-78, 441-55, 1886. *Tex m & s rec* : 193-99, 1881. *K&B* III:1123-24.

SMITH, BENJAMIN F , Mt Upton, NY (d/II-23-1895) MD Albany 1857. *JAMA* 24:370, 1895. *Polk* 1886:668.

SMITH, BERWICK BRUCE, Baltimore (b/VII-4-1826; d/III-20-1860) MD UMd 1849; AB Princeton 1846; AM 1853. *Med ann Md:* 569. *Tr AMA* 13:812-13, 1860.

SMITH, C L , Orange, Tex (d/X-23-1882) MD ? *Tex m&s rec* 3:551, 1883.

SMITH, CHARLES, New Brunswick, NJ (b/XII-4-1767; d/V-7-1848) Hon MD Rutgers 1792; AB Princeton 1786. *Tr AMA* 3:465-66, 1850.

SMITH, CHARLES, Middle Haddam, Conn (d/1848 @ 47) MD Yale 1825. *Proc Conn M S* ns2:146, 1882-83.

SMITH, CHARLES DICKINSON, NYC (b/XI-14-1824 [i.e.1814?] d/XII-4-1891 @77) MD UPa 1837. *Med reg NY NJ Conn* 1892:287. *Bost m&s j* 125:640, 1891. *Polk* 1886: 693.

SMITH, CHARLES GILMAN, CW-USA; Chicago (b/I 4-1828 Exeter, NH; d/I-10-1894) MD UPa 1851; AB Harvard 1847; AM 1851. *JAMA* 22:97, 1894. *Bost m&s j* 130: 80, 1894. *Harvard in CW*: 35. *U Pa med alum CW*: 1851. *Atkinson* I: 344.

SMITH, CHARLES H , Nyack, NY (d/II-16-1895) MD Albany 1859. *JAMA* 24: 337, 1895.

SMITH, CHARLES MAGILL, CW-CSA; St Mary's Co, Md; Franklin, La (b/I-26-1826 Winchester, Va; d/XI-7-1901) MD UPa 1847. *Med annals Md:* 570. *U Pa med alum CW*: 1847.

SMITH, CHARLES McKNIGHT, Perth Amboy, NJ (b/IX-29-1803 Haverstraw, NY; d/II-3-1873/1874) MD CPSNY 1827. *Tr M S NJ* 1874: 104-06. *Med surg rep Phila* 30:180, 204, 1874.

SMITH, CHARLES P , Chester, NY (d/X-12-1894 @ 66) MD Castleton 1851. *Med reg NY NJ Conn* 1895: 240. *JAMA* 23: 654, 1894. *Butler* 1878: 574.

SMITH, CHESTER, Portland, Mich (d/I-2-1904) MD Cleveland Homeop 1859. *Polk* 1886: 502. *Tr Am Inst Hom* 1904: 957. Homeopath.

SMITH, CLIFTON G , Akron, O (d/X-2-1899 @35) MD Buffalo 1887. *Buff m&s j* 39:299, 1899. *JAMA* 33: 994, 1899.

SMITH, COURTNEY L, Aurora Ill (d/IV-15-1905 @ 47) MD Rush 1879. *Ill m j* 7:611 1905. *Polk* 1896:362.

SMITH, CURRAN C , Richmond, Ky (d/VIII-13-1896) MD U Louisville 1850. *JAMA* 27:449, 1896.

SMITH, CYRUS, CW-USA; Jackson, Mich (d/II-10-1899) MD U Mich 1857. *JAMA* 32:442, 1899. *Polk* 1886: 495.

SMITH, CYRUS BURNETT, Granby, Mass (d/IX-7-1879) MD Berkshire 1859. *Bost m&s jour* 101:570, 1879. *Med surg rep Phila* 41:308, 1879.

SMITH, DAVID, NYC (b/VII-31-1802 Ridgefield Conn; d/I-17-1867) Stud med w/Dr Chas Smith. *Med reg NY NJ Conn* 1867:226. *Tr AMA* 18:324, 1867.

SMITH, DAVID AUGUSTINE, NYC (b/VI-24-1843; d/IV-8-1872) MD CPSNY 1866. *Med reg NY NJ Conn* 1872: 357.

SMITH, DAVID MILLIGAN, Pen Yan, NY (b/NYC; d/III-19-1891) MD Bellevue 1877. *Tr NY St Med Soc* II:

741 ff, 1894. *Polk* 1886: 701.

SMITH, DAVID PAIGE, Springfield, Mass (b/X-1-1830 Westfield; d/XII-27-1880) MD Jeferson 1853. *Bost m&s j* 103:646,1880; 104:24, 1881; 105:17, 1881. *Tr AMA* 32:539-40, 1881. *Atkinson* :706. *K&B* III:1124-25.

SMITH, DAVID SHEPARD, Chicago 1843- (b/IV-28-1816 Camden, NJ; d/IV-29-1891) MD Jefferson 1836. *Tr Am Inst Hom* 1891:83. *Med vis* 7:19, 1891. *NW j hom* 3:91, 1891. *Polk* 1886: 271. *Cleave.* Homeopath.

SMITH, DAVID SOLON CHASE HALL, RI (b/1796; d/1859) MD Yale 1816. *Tr AMA* 13: 796, 1860.

SMITH, DAVIDSON HEERMANCE, NYC (d/X-23-1903 @28) MD CPSNY 1902; AB Columbia 1899. *Bost m&s j* 149:500, 1903.

SMITH, DRIESBACH, San Francisco (b/X-9-1861 Ohio; d/XI-15-1904) MD Cooper Med Coll 1885. *Cal st jour med* 2:379, 1904; 3:26, 1905.

SMITH, DUDLEY, Keene, NH 1839-56; DeKalb, Ill 1856- (b/IX-15-1799 Gilsum, NH; d/III-28-1874) MD Dartmouth 1825. *Med surg rep Phila* 30:468, 1874.

SMITH, EDMOND, Dayton O (b/VII-1-1816 LI; d/VIII-15-1851) MD CPSNY 1838; AB Miami 1850. *Tr Ohio St M S* 1873: 274.

SMITH, EDWARD ALEXANDER, CW-USA; NYC (b/IX-14-1830 Stonington, Conn; d/XII-10-1900) MD U Pa 1851. *Bost m&s j* 144:28, 1901. *U Pa med alum CW.*

SMITH, EDWARD DORR GRIFFIN, USN; Newark, NJ (b/XI-7-1826; d/VI-15-1878) MD CPSNY 1851; Hon AM Rutgers 1856. *Tr M S NJ* 1878-79: 199-201. *Med rec NY* 15:565, 1879.

SMITH, EDWARD H , Fullerton, Nebr (b/III- -1858 Montreal; d/XII-29-1896 Omaha) MD McGill 1881. *Pr Nebr St M S* 1897: 15. *Polk* 1893: 757.

SMITH, EDWARD [EDWIN] M , Philadelphia (d/III-29 1900 @77) MD Jefferson 1846. *JAMA* 34: 957, 1900. *Polk* 1896: 1318. Homeopath?

SMITH, EDWARD SUTTON, NYC (d/VII-20-1891 @ 61) MD Harvard 1856; AB 1853; AM. *Med reg NY NJ Conn* 1892:287. *Bost m & s j* 125:124, 1891. *Polk* 1886:693.

SMITH, ELIAS ELY, Newtown, Pa (d/I-20-1884) MD Jefferson 1847. *Med surg rep Phila* 50:160, 1884. *Butler* 1878: 708.

SMITH, ELIJAH HERMAN, St Paul, Minn (d/II-19-1871 St Paul or New Canaan, Conn @29) MD CPSNY 1865. *Tr AMA* 23:592, 1872. *Tr Minn St M S* 1872: 117-18; 1899:191. *NW m&s j*1: 309-10, 1870. *Med s rep Phil* 24:198, 1871.

SMITH, ELLERY P , CW-USA (d/VII-7-1864 Pine Bluffs, Ark) MD Jefferson 1853. *Nat m j* 1:302, 1870/71.

SMITH, ELLSWORTH F , St Louis (d/VIII-19-1896 Ft Missoula, Mont) MD St Louis Med Coll 1848. *JAMA* 27: 555-56, 1896. *Polk* 1886: 566.

SMITH, ENOS, Ashfield, Mass (b/I-16-1770 S Hadley; d/X-11-1856) MD ? AB Dartmouth 1793. *Bost m&s j* 55:275, 1857.

SMITH, FISHER COLEMAN, Columbus, Nev (b/X-1825 Phila; d/VIII-14-1873 Cal) MD UPa 1847; ng Coll UPa 1845. *Med surg rep Phila* 29:216, 1873.

SMITH, FRANCIS ASBURY, NYC (b/VIII-29-1852; d/XI-4-1881) MD Bellevue 1874. *Med reg NY NJ Conn* 1882: 234. *Butler* 1878: 525.

SMITH, FRANCIS B , Stowe, Vt (d/IX-23-1899 @76) MD UCNY 1850. *JAMA* 33:994, 1899.

SMITH, FRANCIS GURNEY Jr, CW-USA; Philadelphia (b/III-8-1818; d/IV-6-1878) MD UPa 1840; AB 1837. *Tr AMA* 29:762-63, 1878. *Tr Pa St M S* 1878: 404-08. *Tr CPP* cent vol: 266. *Atkinson* I:25-26. *K&B* III: 1125-26.

SMITH, FRANK BUCHANAN, Springfield, Ill (d/VIII-24-1901 @42) MD Rush 1880. *Ill m j* ns3:237, 1901. *JAMA* 37: 654, 1901. *Polk* 1896: 442.

SMITH, FRANKLIN, NYC (b/NY; d/X-9-1900 @76) MD UCNY 1895. *Bost m&s j* 143: 414, 1900.

SMITH, FRANKLIN RUSHTON, St Paul Minn (b/II-19 1809 Burlington, NJ; d/VIII-5-1892 Ft Adams, RI) MD UPa 1838. *Tr Minn St M S* 1893:121. *Butler* 1878: 395.

SMITH, FREDERICK AUGUSTUS, Leominster, Mass (b/VI-18-1830 Peterborough, NH; d/XII-20-1856) MD Dartmouth 1855; AB 1852. *NH jour med* 7:61-68, 1857.

SMITH, GEORGE ALLEN, Henton, Ill (d/III-30-1900 @50) MD St Louis M C 1879. *Tr Ill St Med Soc* 1899-1900: 574.

SMITH, GEORGE CLARK, CW-USA; Kingston, NY (d/IV-14-1893 @59) MD UCNY 1862. *Med reg NY NJ Conn* 1893: 315. *Tr M S St NY* 1895: 369. *Butler* 1878: 574.

SMITH, GEORGE F , Atlanta (d/XI-5-1899 @77) MD Med Coll Ga 1856. *JAMA* 33: 1441, 1899.

SMITH, GEORGE H , NYC (d/VII-15-1895 @67) MD Bellevue 1865. *Bost m&s j* 133:97, 1895.

SMITH, GEORGE RICHARD, NYC (d/X-17-1897) MD ? *JAMA* 29:925, 1897.

SMITH, GOUVERNEUR MATHER, CW-USA; NYC (b/NY; d/XII 8-1898) MD CPSNY 1855; AB UCNY 1852. *Bost m&s j* 139:610, 1898. *JAMA* 31: 1542, 1898. *Atkinson* I: 249. *Polk* 1896: 1078.

SMITH, HARRIS K , Towanda, Pa (d/IV-7-1881 Middletown, NJ [NY?] MD Jefferson 1879. *Med bull med & surg* 3:142, 1881.

SMITH, HARVEY W , Mt Vernon, O (d/XII-15-1874 @48) MD UCNY 1848. *Med rec NY* 10: 8, 1875.

SMITH, HENRY A M , Gloucester City, NJ (b/VII-30 1839 Doylestown, Pa; d/III-29-1899 @59) MD Jefferson 1864. *Tr Med Soc NJ* 1899: 285-86. *JAMA* 32:845, 1899. *Polk* 1886: 603.

SMITH, HENRY HOLLINGSWORTH, Philadelphia (b/XII-10-1815; d/IV-11-1890) MD UPa 1837; AB 1834; AM; LLD Lafayette 1885. *Tr CPP* cent vol: 266-67. *Tr Phila Co M S* 11:xix-xxvii, 1890. *JAMA* 14:698-9 1890.

 Spec. educ'l status abbrev. as: *ng* = college verified attendance without degree;

Med bull m & s 13:184, 188–89, 1890. *Atkinson* I: 11–12. *K&B* III: 1127.

SMITH, HENRY LYLE, Hudson, NY (d/II–11–1904 @ 59) MD CPSNY 1864. *Bost m&s j* 150: 198, 1904. *Tr Med Soc St NY* 1904: [420].

SMITH, HENRY MELVILLE, S Orange, NJ (b/II–3–1847 Meredith, NY; d/XI–28–1902) MD CPSNY 1871. *Tr Med Soc NJ* 1903: 387. *Polk* 1896: 939.

SMITH, HENRY MITCHELL, NYC (d/1901) MD NYMC 1860. *Tr Am Inst Hom* 1900: 918–20. *Med vis* 17:233, 1901. *Polk* 1886: 694. Homeopath.

SMITH, HENRY SUTTON BURGESS, Bowdoinham, Me 1865–78; Middleboro, Mass 1878– (b/VII–12–1864 [!]; d/X–30–1894) MD Berkshire 1865; AB Bowdoin 1861. *Bost m&s j* 131: 476, 1894. *Polk* 1890:552.

SMITH, HERMAN BANGS, Westville, Conn (d/VII–16 1891) MD Yale 1876. *Bost m&s j* 125: 124, 1891. *Polk* 1886: 197.

SMITH, HIRAM, Guilford, Vt (d/I–30–1883 @28) MD ?Jefferson 1878. *Med surg rep Phila* 50:160, 1884.

SMITH, HIRAM STROWBRIDGE, Wappinger's Falls, NY (b/III– –1828 Crown Pt; d/VI–9–1876) MD Castleton 1851; MD NYMC 1854. *Med rec NY* 11:453, 1876.

SMITH, HIRAM T , Preston, La (d/VIII–10–1895 @66) <MD Memphis Med Coll 1857> *New Orl m&s j* ns23: 256, 1895. *Polk* 1890: 493.

SMITH, HORATIO SOUTHGATE, Augusta, Me 1844–46; Eastport, 1846–47; Brooklyn 1847– (b/VII–28–1820 Portland; d/IV–27–1875. MD Bowdoin 1843; AB Dartmouth 1840; ng Bowdoin 1836–38. *Med reg NY NJ Conn* 1876: 255.

SMITH, HOWARD, CW–CSA; New Orleans (b/1823; d/I–30–1892) MD UPa 1847; AB Yale 1844. *Bost m&s j* 126:132, 1892. *U Pa med alum CW*: 1847.

SMITH, HUGH MONTGOMERY, Brooklyn (d/VIII–30 1897) MD NY Hom 1876. *Med vis* 13:349, 1897. *Tr Am Inst Hom* 1898: 49. *No Am jour hom* 45:650, 651, 1897. *Hahn mo* 32: 1897? *Polk* 1886:649. Homeopath.

SMITH, IRA P, Bath NY (d/V–26–1905 @69) MD Albany 1859. *Bost m&s jr* 152:652, 1905. *Polk* 1896:989.

SMITH, IRVIN WHEAT, Charles City, Ia (b/III–1–1851 E Franklin, NY; d/X–29–1895 Cal) MD Jefferson 1875. *Tr Iowa St M S* 1896:321–22. *Polk* 1890: 410.

SMITH, ISAAC, Portland, Conn (b/1772? d/1839 @67) Hon MD Yale 1828. *Pr Conn M S* ns2:145–46, 1882–83.

SMITH, ISAAC Jr, Fall River, Mass (b/XII–9–1841 E Stoughton; d/I–20–1882 @40) MD Dartmouth 1863; AM 1876. *Bost m&s j* 107:619, 1882. *Butler* 1878: 357.

SMITH, J A , Piqua, O (d/1858) MD Med Coll O 1843. *Tr Ohio St M S* 1873:274; 1880: [list dec'd members].

SMITH, J AUGUSTINE, NYC (b/1781? d/II–9–1865) MD ? *Tr AMA* 16: 630, 1865.

SMITH, J B , CW–USA (d/V–12–1865) MD ? *Nat med jour* 1:302, 1870/71.

SMITH, JAMES, Chestnut Hill, Pa (b/XI–26–1786 Hightstown, NJ; d/I–30–1854) MD UPa 1809. *Tr Pa St Med Soc* 1856:185; 1862:80–81.

SMITH, JAMES, Pikesville, Md (b/1771 Elkton; d/VII–12–1841) <MD UPa 1794> AM Dickinson 1792. *Med annals Md:* 571.

SMITH, JAMES, Clarington, O (d/VII–29–1877) MD Cinc Coll Med & Surg 1864. *Tr Ohio St M S* 1878: 191.

SMITH, JAMES McCUNE, NYC (b/IV–18–1813; d/XI–17–1865) MD Glasgow 1837; att Glasgow 1835 & 1836. *Med reg NY NJ Conn* 1866: 201–04. *Med s rep Phila* 13: 358, 1865.

SMITH, JAMES OWENS, NYC (b/1802 Coxsackie, NY; d/I–30–1885) MD CPSNY 1825. *Med reg NY NJ Conn* 1885: 244. *Bost m&s j* 112: 189, 1885. *Med bull m & s* 7:90, 1884. *Butler* 1878: 525.

SMITH, JAMES PASCAL, Chicago (b/XI–21–1833 Albany, NY; d/X–11–1872) MD UCNY 1858; AB Princeton 1855; AM 1858. *Med reg NY NJ Conn* 1873: 350. *Med surg rep Phila* 27:398, 1872. *Tr AMA* 24: 364, 1873. *Tr M S NJ* 1873: 113–14.

SMITH, JAMES R , Cincinnati (d/1869 @48) MD ?CPS NY 1845 [James Rawson]. *Phila m reg & dir* 1871:299.

SMITH, JAMES WILLIAM, Paterson, NJ (d/III–29–1906 @49) MD Bellevue 1882. *Bost m&s j* 154:422, 1906. *Polk* 1896: 947.

SMITH, JARED KNAPP, Sandwich Isl (d/IX–24–1897) MD CPSNY 1876. *JAMA* 29: 925, 1897.

SMITH, JEFFERSON, Dover NH (b/1803 Berwick Me; d/V–17–1864) MD Bowdoin 1832 *Tr NH Med Soc* 1864:61–62.

SMITH, JEREMIAH P , Linglestown, Pa (d/XI–1–1906 @38) MD Jefferson 1887. *Pa med jour* 10: 214, 1906–07. *Flint* 1897: 807.

SMITH, JEREMIAH RANLETT, Gloucester, Mass (b/IV–2–1822 Gilmanton, NH; d/I–25–1902) MD Woodstock 1845. *Tr NH M S* 1902: 318–19. *Polk* 1893: 601.

SMITH, JEROME CANDEE, Boston; NYC (b/XI–2–1831; d/VI–19–1888 Germantown) MD Berkshire 1854. *Med reg NY NJ Conn* 1889: 286.

SMITH, JEROME VAN CROWNINSHIELD, Richmond, Mass (b/VII–20–1800 Conway, NH; d/VIII–20 1879) MD Brown 1818; AM Dartmouth 1855 *Bost m&s j* 101:318–19 1879. *Mass M S cat* 1894 *K&B* III:1128–29.

SMITH, JERVIS JOHNSON, Gloucester, RI (b/1801; d/1863 or 1864) MD Yale 1827. *Tr AMA* 16:614–16, 1865. *Tr RI Med Soc* 1863–64: 216–17.

SMITH, JOB LEWIS, NYC (b/X–15–1827 Spafford, NY; d/VI–6–1897) MD CPSNY 1853; AB Yale 1849; AM 1853. *Buff m&s j* 36:936–37, 1897. *JAMA* 28: 1202, 1897. *Bost m&s j* 136:611, 1897. *Med bull m & s* 19:277, 282, 1897. *K&B* III: 1129.

SMITH, JOB LEWIS Jr, NYC (d/VII–8–1889 @28) MD Bellevue 1884; AB Columbia 1881. *Med reg NY NJ Conn* 1890: 280. *Med s rep Phila* 61:140, 1889. *Butler* 1878: 525. *K&B* III:1129 (mention only).

SMITH, JOEL WASHINGTON, Charles City, Ia (b/VII 23–1824 Franklin, NY; d/VI-6–1897 @72) MD Yale 1850. *Bost m&s j* 136: 640, 1897. *JAMA* 28:1252, 1897. *Atkinson* I: 56. *Polk* 1896: 514.

SMITH, JOHN, Wilkesbarre, Pa (b/XI-4–1789 Kingston; d/VIII-24–1869) MD ? *Tr Luzerne Co (Pa) M S* 1889: .

SMITH, JOHN ABSALOM PERSON, Greensville Co, Va; CW–CSA (b/Northampton Co, NC; d/XII- –1897) MD UPa 1848. *U Pa med alum CW*:1848 (suppl).

SMITH, JOHN DERBY, CW–USN; Bridgewater, Mass (b/IV-9–1812 Hanover, NH; d/IV-26–1884) MD UMd 1846; AB Yale 1832. *Med annals Md:* 572.

SMITH, JOHN E , NYC (b/III-25–1840 DC; d/I-22 1884) MD Georgetown 1867. *Hist Med Soc DC:* 283.

SMITH, JOHN GREER, Philadelphia (d/XI-30–1906 @ 32) MD Med–Chi Phila 1898. *Pa m j* 10:294, 1906/07.

SMITH, JOHN ISAAC, Shannon, Ill (d/X- –1899) MD Rush 1872. *Tr Ill St Med Soc* 1899:287. *Polk* 1896: 440.

SMITH, JOHN MANCHESTER, Vineyard Haven, Mass (d/XII- –1887 @61) MD Harvard 1852. *Bost m&s j* 117:616, 1887. *Butler* 1878: 357.

SMITH, JOHN T S , Spuyten Duyvil, NY d/X-3–1876 @71) MD ? *Med surg rep Phila* 35:326, 1876. *Tr Am Inst Hom* 1877:987. Homeopath.

SMITH, JOHN W , Ames, Ia (b/1851; d/1895 @44) MD Jefferson 1877. *Tr Ia St M S* 1896:330; 1903:450. *Polk* 1886:326 (Lebanon, Ind).

SMITH, JOHN WILLIAM, Gosport, Ind (b/V-11–1830 Clark Co; d/I-9–1904. MD Ky Sch Med 1853. *Tr Ind St M S* 1903: 355. *Polk* 1896: 469.

SMITH, JOSEPH, Lexington, Ky (b/I-18–1815 Danville; d/1875) MD Transylvania 1836; <att UPa Med Dept 1838> *Tr Ky St M S* 1877:211–16.

SMITH, JOSEPH ELY, Yardley, Pa (d/XI-18–1898) MD UPa 1857. *Lehigh Valley m mag* 9:246–47, 1898. *Butler* 1878: 733.

SMITH, JOSEPH F , CW–USA (d/VIII-22–1862) MD ? *Nat med jour* 1:302, 1870/71.

SMITH, JOSEPH H , Plattsburgh, NY (b/1821? d/X-4 1899 @78) MD Albany 1846. *Bost m&s j* 141:380, 1899. *JAMA* 33:994, 1899.

SMITH, JOSEPH HAVEN, Lowell, Mass (b/XI-17–1805 Rochester, NH; d/II-25–1886) MD Bowdoin 1829. *Bost m&s j* 114:216, 1886. *Tr NH M S* 1885: 143–44. *Butler* 1878: 357.

SMITH, JOSEPH HEBER, Boston (b/XII-5–1842 Bucksport, Me; d/X-23–1898) MD Hahnemann Phila 1866. *Tr Am Inst Hom* 1899: 935. *Polk* 1886: 461. *Cleave.* Homeopath.

SMITH, JOSEPH MATHER, NYC (b/III-14–1789 New Rochelle, NY; d/IV-22–1866) MD CPSNY 1815. *Tr AMA* 18:318–22, 1867. *Bost m&s j* 74:268, 1866. *Med reg NY NJ Conn* 1866: 206. *Tr M S St NY* 1867: 447–63. *K&B* III: 1131–32.

SMITH, JOSEPH SIM, USA 1861–67 (b/Va; d/IX-8–1867) MD Georgetown 1857. *Tr AMA* 19:452–53, 1868. *Nat med jour* 1:302, 1870/71. *Heitman.*

SMITH, JOSEPH T , Canandaigua, NY (b/Farmington; d/XII-9–1890) MD Jefferson 1854. *Tr M S St NY* 11:741 ff, 1894. *Polk* 1886: 655.

SMITH, JOSHUA VINCENT, CW–USA; Richmond Me 1869–72; Boston 1873–75; Melrose Mass 1875– (b/IX-9–1845 Bridgeton; d/IV-18–1887) MD Bowdoin 1869; AB 1867 *Bost m&s j* 116:392 1887. *Polk* 1886:469.

SMITH, JUDSON CLARK, NYC (d/I-28–1899) MD U Vt 1889. *JAMA* 32:263, 1889. *Polk* 1896:1078.

SMITH, JUSTIN EDWARDS, Cleveland (d/V-17–1894 @68) MD Cleveland Hom 1877. *Tr Am Inst Hom* 1896: 87. *Polk* 1878: 264. Homeopath.

SMITH, L BYRON, Canton, Pa (d/VI-21–1906 @70) Lic by yrs pract. *Pa med jour* 9:745, 1905/06.

SMITH, LATHAM AVERY, New Milford Pa (b/VIII-14 1816 Brooklyn, Pa; d/VI-12–1890) ng Fairfield. *Tr Pa St M S* 22:222–23, 1891. *Off'l reg Pa phys* 1881–89: 374.

SMITH, LAWRENCE SAVERY, Philadelphia (d/VIII 17–1898 @32 at sea) MD UPa 1891 *JAMA* 31:551 1898. *Bost m&s j* 139:203, 1898. *Polk* 1896:1318.

SMITH, LAWRENCE SUMNER, Haverhill, Mass (d/ VII-2–1901 @49) MD UCNY 1873. *Bost m&s j* 145:140, 1901. *Polk* 1896: 713.

SMITH, LEANDER B , Lexington, Ky (d/XI-18–1893) MD CPS Keokuk 1878. *JAMA* 21:907, 1893. *Polk* 1890: 694 (Fremont, Nebr).

SMITH, LEANDER CHAPMAN, Brooklyn (d/XII-9–1898) MD UCNY 1878. *JAMA* 31:1542, 1898. *Polk* 1896: 1003.

SMITH, LLOYD H, Easton Md (d/IV-3–1898 @45) MD West Res 1877. *JAMA* 30:933, 1898. *Polk* 1896: 670.

SMITH, LOUIS PERCY, Manila, Philippines (b/XII-10 1871 DC; d/I-8–1901) MD CPSNY 1893. *Hist Med Soc DC:* 357. *Polk* 1900: 99.

SMITH, LOUIS TURNER, CW–CSA; Henderson, NC (b/V-7–1833 Granville Co; d/II-6–1895 Durham) MD UPa 1860. *U Pa m alum CW*:1860. *Polk* 1886: 723.

SMITH, LUCIUS, CW–USA (d/X-21–1867 Hempstead, Tx) MD ? *Nat m j* 1:302, 1870/71.

SMITH, LUCIUS ANTHONY, Conn; Brooklyn (b/VII-11–1831; d/I-5–1894) MD Yale 1853. *Med reg NY NJ Conn* 1894: 249. *JAMA* 22:97, 1894.

SMITH, LUCIUS B , CW–USA (d/VII-13–1864 Tupelo, Miss) MD ? *Nat med jour* 1:302, 1870/71.

SMITH, LYNDON ARNOLD, Newark (b/XI-11–1795 NH; d/XII-15–1865) MD Dartmouth 1823; MD Berkshire 1824; AB Dartmouth 1817; AM 1820. *Tr AMA* 18: 332–33, 1867. *Tr M S NJ* 1866:139–42; 167:141. *Med s rep Phila* 13:430, 1865.

SMITH, MARCELLUS R , Cincinnatus, NY (b/Taylor; d/XII-11–1890) MD Geneva 1847. *Tr M S St NY*: 11: 741 ff, 1894. *Polk* 1886: 656.

SMITH, MASON G , Perry, NY (b/1797? d/IV-10–1857

 Spec. educ'l status abbrev. as: ***ng*** = college verified attendance without degree;

@60) MD ? *Bost m&s j* 56:267, 1857.

SMITH, MATTHEW JOSEPH, Jersey City (d/XI-16 1899) MD CPSNY 1890. *JAMA* 33:1375, 1899. *Polk* 1896: 939.

SMITH, MONTROSS LESLIE, NYC (b/VII-1-1840; d/ VII-18-1871) MD CPSNY 1864. *Med reg NY NJ Conn* 1872: 357.

SMITH, MOSES BLACKFAN, Philadelphia (b/IX-29 1787 Solebury, Pa; d/VII-15-1855) MD UPa 1814. *Tr Pa St Med Soc* 1856:185-95. *Bost m&s j* 53:215, 1856. *K&B* III:1122 (mention only).

SMITH, NATHAN, New Haven, Conn (b/IX-30-1762 Rehoboth, Mass; d/VII-26-1828) MD Harvard 1790. *Transylv j m & ass sci* 5:276-81 1832 *K&B* III:1132-35.

SMITH, NATHAN RYNO, Baltimore (b/V-21-1797 Cornish, NH; d/VII-3-1877) MD Yale 1820; AB 1817. *Med ann Md:* 573. *Med rec NY* 12:464, 1877. *Tr AMA* 29:763-68, 1878. *Atkinson* I:448-49. *K&B* III:1135-37.

SMITH, NATHANIEL, Bennington, Vt (b/1797? d/XII-22-1867 @70, Columbia Cross Roads, Pa) Hon MD Berkshire 1837; ng Castleton. *Bost m&s j* 77:468, 1867.

SMITH, NORMAN, Groton, Mass (d/V-24-1888 @76) MD Berkshire 1853. *Bost m&s j* 118:560, 1888; 119:641 1888.

SMITH, NORMAND, Yonkers, NY (d/VII-30-1896 Keene Valley, NY) MD CPSNY 1861; AB Yale 1858. *JAMA* 27:503, 1896. *Butler* 181878: 525.

SMITH, ORRIN, Montpelier, Vt (b/VII-27-1806 Marlow, NH; d/VIII-13-1867 Chicago) MD UVt 1831; AM 1859 *Tr Vt M S* 1883:109. *Med s rep Phila* 17:199, 1867.

SMITH, ORSAMUS, CW-USA; Mobile, Ala (b/II-26-183 Butternuts, NY; d/IX-19-1876 Patterson, NY) MD Bellevue 1867. *Med surg rep Phila* 35:348, 1876. *Med rec NY* 11:694, 1876.

SMITH, RALPH C , Philadelphia (b/1839; d/II-20-1896) MD Hahnemann Phila 1869. *Hahn mo* 31:42, 103 (news & advt) 1896. *Polk* 1886: 824. Homeopath.

SMITH, REUBEN, Ithaca, NY (d/IV-4-1889 @56) MD Pa Med Coll 1847! MD LICH 1866. *Med reg NY NJ Conn* 1889: 286. **BEGIN**

SMITH, REUBEN C , Greenville, Ind (d/III-24-1884 @ 81) MD ? *Med surg rep Phila* 50:512, 1884.

SMITH, RICHARD ALEXANDER, Raleigh NC(b/1828; d/X-12-1904) MD ? att UNC 1847-48 *UNC cat*: 576.

SMITH, ROBERT MARK, Athens, Ga (b/1826; d/1879) MD Jefferson 1847. *Tr AMA* 31:1084-85, 1880.

SMITH, ROBERT P , Santa Rosa, Cal (d/X-19-1899 @ 50) MD Med Coll SC 1861. *JAMA* 33:1183, 1899. *Polk* 1886: 176.

SMITH, ROBERT S , Bound Brook, NJ (b/II-19-1800 Flaggtown; d/VIII-20-1874) Cert Med Soc NJ 1820. *Tr M S NJ* 1875:[104,106] *Med s rep Phila* 31:200, 1874.

SMITH, S RICHARD, Philadelphia (d/XII-27-1862 @53) MD ? *Med surg rep Phila* ns9:326, 1862/83.

SMITH, SAMUEL DeHAVEN, USN; Piqua, O (b/X-13-1839 McClellansville, Del; d/II-6-1898) MD UPa 1863. *JAMA* 30:682, 1896. *Polk* 1896: 1207.

SMITH, SAMUEL HANBURY, Brooklyn (b/II-15-1810 Staffordshire, Engl; d/IX-13-1894) <MD U Coll London 1831; MChir Stockholm 1840> att Starling? *Med reg NY NJ Conn* 1895:240. *JAMA* 23:510, 561, 1894. *Bost m&s j* 131:380, 1894. *Atkinson* I:382. *Polk* 1886:694.

SMITH, SAMUEL MITCHELL, CW-USA; Greenfield & Columbus, O (b/XI-28-1816; d/XI-30-1874) MD U Pa 1840; AB Miami. *Med surg rep Phila* 31:500, 1874. *Tr Ohio St Med Soc* 1875:195. *K&B* III: 1138.

SMITH, SAMUEL PARISH, Prattville, Ala 1843- (b/IX 8-1814 Clinton, Ga; d/III-28-1891) MD ULa 1838. *Tr M Assn St Ala* 1891:260. *Atkinson* I:680. *Polk* 1886:138.

SMITH, SAMUEL PRICE, CW-USA; Cumberland, Md (b/XII-21 1795 Frederick; d/III-1-1882) MD U Md 1817. *Tr AMA* 33:605-06, 1882. *Med annals Md:* 574. *Atkinson* I: 141.

SMITH, SAMUEL R S , Ardmore, Pa (d/VI-1-1902 @80) MD ? *Pa m j* 6:262, 1902/03. *Polk* 1890: 963.

SMITH, SAMUEL ST JOHN, Perth Amboy, NJ (d/I-4-1872 @c35 Providence, RI) MD CPSNY 1866. *Bost m&s j* ns9:32, 1872. *Tr AMA* 24:360, 1873. *Med reg NY NJ Conn* 1872:357.

SMITH, SARAH, Council Bluffs, Ia (d/XII-22-1901) MD Hahnemann Chic 1887. *Tr Am Inst Hom* 1902:849. Homeopath.

SMITH, THEODORE V , Westfield NY (d/IX-13-1901 @50) MD NY Hom 1873. *Bost m&s jour* 145:366, 1901. *Polk* 1900:1153. Homeopath.

SMITH, THEOPHILUS EMORY, Columbus, Ind (b/IX 7-1846 Sussex, Del; d/III-7-1890) ng Med Coll Ind 1882-83. *Tr Ind St Med Soc* 1890: 166. *Polk* 1886:314.

SMITH, THMOAS, Society Hill, SC (b/Engl; d/1875) MD UPa 1821. *Tr AMA* 31:1085-86, 1880.

SMITH, THOMAS BLANCH, Rockland Co, NY (b/XI-27-1835; d/IV-14-1875 Nyack) MD CPSNY 1857. *Med reg NY NJ Conn* 1875:204. *Med rec* 10:302, 1875.

SMITH, THOMAS LUDINGTON, USN; Brooklyn (b/ VIII- -1800 Orange, NJ; d/VIII-13/14-1891) MD CPSNY 1822. *Med reg NY NJ Conn* 1892:287. *NW med & surg jour* 19:150, 1891. *JAMA* 17:387, 1891. *Bost m&s j* 125:208, 1891. *Butler* 1878: xii.

SMITH, THOMAS STANLEY, Reading, Pa (b/I-25-1845 Robeson Twp; d/XI-25-1887) MD Jefferson 1868; ng Amherst 1865. *Butler* 1878:709. *Amherst, Men of.*

SMITH, VESPASIAN, Duluth, Minn (d/X-11-1897 @ 79) MD Cleveland Med Coll 1852. *JAMA* 29:867, 1897. *Polk* 1886: 511.

SMITH, VINE, Lisbon, Conn (b/1790? d/1852) MD Yale 1843 hon. *Proc Conn Med Soc* 1853: 19.

SMITH, WALTER, Baltimore (d/VII-10-1863 Danville, Va) MD U Md 1863? *Med surg rep Phila* 10:204, 1863.

SMITH, WALTER PRESCOTT, Baltimore (b/VI-16-1868; d/VII-18-1902) MD U Md 1890. *Med annals Md:*

575. *Polk* 1896: 665.

SMITH, WICKLIFFE C , Delphi, Ind (d/XII-29-1899 @48) MD Med Coll Ohio 1874. *JAMA* 34:187, 1900. *Polk* 1886: 315.

SMITH, WILL C J, St Clair, Pa (d/VI-1-1906 @68) MD CPSNY 1866. *Pa m j* 9:671, 1905/06. *Flint* 1897: 834.

SMITH, WILLARD EVERETT, Boston (d/VII-14-1890 @33) MD Harvard 1882; AB 1879. *Bost m&s j* 123: 72, 1890.

SMITH, WILLIAM ANTHONY, CW-USA; Philadelphia (b/XI-13-1809 Huntington; d/X-20-1887) MD U Pa 1832. *Rec AAS USA* 1891:92-93. *UPa m alum CW*:1832.

SMITH, WILLIAM AUGUSTUS, CW-USA; Sidney & Norwich, NY; Newark, NJ (b/III-30-1820 Guilford, NY; d/VIII-4 1892) MD Geneva 1847. *Med reg NY NJ Conn* 1893: 315. *Tr M S NJ* 1893:184-85. *Butler* 1878: 464.

SMITH, WILLIAM CONRAD, Linglestown, Pa (d/VI-16-1901 @73) MD UPa 1850. *Pa m j* 5:296, 1901/02. *Butler* 1878: 733.

SMITH, WILLIAM DANGERFIELD, La (d/IX-25-1878 Smithfield Plantation) MD ? *Tr AMA* 30:885 1879.

SMITH, WILLIAM F, Chicago (b/1845 Urbana, O; d/IV-7-1891) MD Miami 1868. *Chic m rec* 1:274, 1891.

SMITH, WILLIAM FARES, CW-USA; McCall's Ferry, Pa (b/I-13 1836 Chanceford; d/III-4-1900) MD UPa 1861. *U Pa med alum CW*:1861. *Polk* 1886: 806.

SMITH, WILLIAM GEORGE, Chicopee, Mass (b/XII-31-1812 Engl; d/I-16-1892) MD Bowdoin 1841. *Bost m&s j* 127:638, 1892.

SMITH, WILLIAM GRAY, Winchester, Ind (b/IV-18-1837 New Carlisle, O; d/VIII-7-1892) MD Med Coll Ohio 1869. *Tr Ind St M S* 1893:247. *Butler* 1878: 220.

SMITH, WILLIAM H , Akron, O (d/II-6-1900 @59) MD Cincinnati Coll M & S 1872. *JAMA* 34:446, 1900.

SMITH, WILLIAM HARMANY, Intercourse, Pa (b/I-15-1854; d/III-16-1898) MD Jefferson 1877. *Pa med jour* 2:39-40, 1898. *JAMA* 30:807, 1898.

SMITH, WILLIAM HENRY, Philadelphia (b/I-11-1811 Warwickshire, Engl; d/II-12-1880) MD Hahnemann Phil 1864; att Med Coll Pa 1848-49; att Jefferson 1831-32. *Med surg rep Phila* 42:198, 1880. *Tr Am Inst Hom* 1891:__. *Cleave.* Homeopath.

SMITH, WILLIAM HENRY, Glenwood, Ia (b/VIII-21-1844 Licking Co, O; d/1882) MD Chic Med Coll 1873. *Tr Ia St Med Soc* 1881-82:181; 1883-85:460-61; 1903: 450. *Butler* 1878: 246.

SMITH, WILLIAM HENRY CLAY, CW-USA; Millville, NJ (b/ VIII-2-1848 Phila; d/II-12-1902) MD UPa 1866. *U Pa med alum CW*: 1866. *Polk* 1886: 606.

SMITH, WILLIAM MANLIUS, Syracuse, NY (d/V-5-1900 @76) MD UPa 1849; AB Yale 1844. *Tr Med Soc St NY* 1901:[426]. *Atkinson* I:669. *Polk* 1886:711.

SMITH, WILLIAM PETER, Salina, Kans (d/IV-23-1900) MD Rush 1879. *JAMA* 34:1146, 1900. *Polk* 1886: 350 (Alta, Ia).

SMITH, WILLIAM R , Lexington, Ky (b/Henry Co, Ky; d/II-21-1829) Student @ Transylvania. *Transylv jour med & assoc sci* 2:297, 1829.

SMOLT, CHARLES FREDERICK, Newton, Kans (d/III-14-1899) MD Rush 1878. *JAMA* 32:787, 1899. *Polk* 1896: 561.

SMOOT, SAMUEL CLEMENT, Washington, DC (b/II-3-1818; d/IX-29-1866) MD Jefferson 1838. *Tr AMA* 18:340, 1867. *Hist Med Soc DC*:234.

SMYSER, HENRY LANIUS, Crimean War-Russ Army; CW-USA (b/XII-8-1825 York, Pa; d/IX-16-1900 York) MD UPa 1847. *U Pa med alum CW*: 1847.

SMYTH, FRANCIS GARDEN, Philadelphia (b/XII-29 1843; d/VII-24-1879) MD UPa 1866; AB 1863. *Tr CPP* cent vol: 267. *Phila med times* 9:540, 1878-79. *Tr Pa St M S* 1880: 377-81. *Med surg rep Phila* 41:198, 1879.

SMYTHE, GONZALVA CORDOVA, Greencastle, Ind (b/X-31-1836 Putnam Co; d/II-9-1897) MD Rush 1864; MD LICH 1870. *Tr Ind St Med Soc* 1897:354. *Med bull med & surg* 19:157, 1897. *Polk* 1896: 469.

SMYTHE, JOHN J , Scranton, Pa (d/XII-1-1905 @73) <MD Trinity Coll Dublin> *Pa med jour* 9:280, 1905/06.

SNARE, EDMUND, CW-USA; Huntingdon, Pa (b/XII-14-1828; d/II-27-1867) MD UPa 1860; AB Washington & Jefferson 1847. *U Pa med alum CW*: 1860.

SNAVELY, CYRUS J , Manheim, Pa (d/II-26-1894 @ 75) MD Pa Med Coll 1849. *JAMA* 22:391, 1894. *Butler* 1878: 733.

SNEAD, ALBERT, Richmond, Va; CW-CSA (b/VII-3-1807 Hanover Co; d/XI-22-1873) MD UPa 1830. *Tr AMA* 25:531-32, 1874. *Tr Med Soc Va* 1873:37, 112. *Med s rep Phila* 29:418, 1873. *U Pa m alum CW*: 1830.

SNEAD, EDWARD FRANKLIN, Lynchburg, Va (b/II-19-1852 Bedford Co; d/III-6-1897) MD Washington U Balto 1871. *Tr Med Soc Va* 1897: 258-59, 268. *Polk* 1896: 1393.

SNELL, ARIE B , Bayou Goula, La (b/Amsterdam NY; d/V-28-1885 @49) MD Albany 1855. *New Orl m & s jour* ns13:169, 1885. *Butler* 1878: 300.

SNELL, CHARLES, Augusta, Me 1828-33; Bangor 1833- (b/VI-17-1805 Winthrop, Me; d/X-20-1868) MD Bowdoin 1828; AB 1825. *Bowdoin cat*: 1825.

SNELL, HIRAM W , CW-USA (d/VIII-16-1863) MD ? *Nat med jour* 1:302, 1870/71.

SNELL, ISSACHAR, Augusta, Me (b/IV-16-1775 Bridgewater, Mass; d/X-7-1847) Stud med w/Dr Ephr Wales & surg w/Dr Nath'l Miller; AB Harvard 1797. *Bost m&s j* 41: 251-55, 1850.

SNELL, JACOB G , Stone Arabia, NY 1832-42? Port Jackson 1842?-55; Amsterdam 1855- (b/VI-16-1808 Palatine; d/IX-15-1882) MD Castleton 1847; MD UC NY 1854; att Fairfield. *Tr Med Soc St NY* 1884: 367-69. *Butler* 1874:559.

SNELLING, FREDERICK GREENWOOD, NYC; CW

USA; (b/ VII–26–1831; d/XI–26–1878) MD UCNY 1859. *Med reg NY NJ Conn* 1879: 199. *Med rec NY* 14: 499, 1878. *Butler* 1878: 525.

SNIDER, THORNTON A , Sacramento (d/I–12–1900 @ 74)MD Tulane 1848. *JAMA* 34:251 1900. *Polk* 1886:170.

SNITCHER, ELIJAH JEFFRIES, Camden, NJ (b/VIII–1–1849 Salem; d/II–5–1888) MD Chicago Med Coll 1874. *Tr Med Soc NJ* 1888:162–63. *Polk* 1886: 602.

SNIVELY, JOSEPH CULBERTSON, CW–CSA; Brooklyn (b/I–17 1836 Greencastle, Pa; d/I–29–1875 or III 22–1885 @49) MD LICH 1865; AB Dickinson 1857. *Med reg NY NJ Conn* 1885: 244. *Med surg rep Phila* 52:512, 1885. *Butler* 1878: 534.

SNODDY, PATRICK CRAWFORD, Spartanburgh dist, SC (d/I–31–1830 @22) Stud @ Transylvania. *Transylv jour med & assoc sci* 3:152, 1830.

SNODGRASS, JAMES H, Pittsburgh (d/VII–1885 @52) MD Jefferson 1866. *JAMA* 5:391, 1885. *Butler* 1878:701.

SNODGRASS, THOMAS, Cassville & Crossville, Tenn (d/IX–22–1898 @76) Lic yrs pract. *Polk* 1890:1047, 1049. *JAMA* 31:872, 1898.

SNOW, ALBION PARRIS, Winthrop, Me (b/III–14–1826 Brunswick; d/X–25–1898) MD Bowdoin 1854; ng Dartmouth Med Sch. *Bost m&s j* 139:432, 1898. *JAMA* 31:1190, 1898. *Atkinson* I:124. *K&B* III: 1141.

SNOW, ASA B , NYC; CW–USA (d/X–9 or 11–1864) MD Fairfield 1832. *Nat m j* 1:302, 1870/71. *Bost m&s j* 71:508, 528, 1865. *Med surg rep Phila* 12:219, 1864/65.

SNOW, CALEB HOPKINS, Boston (b/IV–1–1796; d/ VII–6–1835) MD Brown 1821; AB 1813; AM. *Brown hist cat*: 1813. *Mass Med Soc cat* 1894.

SNOW, EDWIN MILLER, Providence, RI (b/V–8–1820 Pomfret, Vt; d/XII–22–1888) MD CPSNY 1849; AB Brown 1845; AM 1848. *Bost m&s j* 119:641, 1888; 120:28, 1889. *Tr RI Med Soc* 4:92–96, 1889–93. *Atkinson* I:375. *Butler* 181878: 749.

SNOW, GEORGE WALTER, Middleboro, Mass (d/V–7 1867 @58) MD ? *Bost m&s j* 76:344, 1867.

SNOW, GEORGE WILLIAMS, Newburyport, Mass (b/ X–31–1837 Chelsea, Mass; d/V–21–1893 @58) MD Jefferson 1859. *Bost m&s j* 128:532, 1893. *Atkinson* I: 126. *Polk* 1886: 470.

SNOW, JESSE WALKER, Somerville, Mass (d/VI–12 1890 @69) MD ? *Bost m&s j* 122:622, 1890. *Polk* 1886: 461.

SNOW, NORMAN LESLIE, CW–USA; Albany, NY (b/ IV–7–1839 Root; d/XII–19–1885) MD CPSNY 1861; AB Union 1859. *Tr Med Soc St NY* 1886:633–35. *Butler* 1874:558 (Canajoharie).

SNOW, SAMUEL, Boonville, NY; Canadaway 1816–(b/ V–28–1770 Hardwick, Mass; d/VI–28–1830) Lic VII–8 1807 Oneida Co Med Soc. *Tr Med Soc St NY* 1865: 280.

SNOW, SIMEON, Root, NY (b/II–18–1803 Mansfield, Mass; d/IX–20–1865) MD Berkshire 1828. *Bost m&s j* 73:228, 1865. *Tr Med Soc St NY* 1866:347–49.

SNOWDEN, CHARLES F, ?New Orleans (d/II–25–1847 @40) MD ? *New Orl m & s jour* :822, 1847.

SNOWDEN, JOHN WIEGAND, Waterford, NJ 1846– (b/IV–22–1823 Phila; d/V–28–1888 Hammonton, NJ) MD UPa 1844. *Tr Med Soc NJ* 1888:167–69. *Med reg NY NJ Conn* 1889: 297. *Atkinson* I:355. *Butler* 1878:476.

SNOWDEN, THOMAS, Peekskill, NY (b/1825; d/X–11–1889 @64) MD CPSNY 1849. *Med reg NY NJ Conn* 1890:280. *JAMA* 13:686, 1889. *Butler* 1878: 574.

SNOWDEN, THOMAS JEFFERSON, S River, Md (d/ VII–3–1835 Magnolia Fl) MD UPa 1832. *Med annals Md:* 576.

SNYDER, ELMER REIFF, Hilltown, Pa (d/III–16–1898 @31) MD UPa 1889. *Lehigh Valley m mag* 9:79, 1898.

SNYDER, HARVEY LEON, N Wales, Pa (b/II–1–1868; d/X–21–1898) MD UPa 1890. *Lehigh Valley med mag* 9: 215–16, 1898.

SNYDER, HENRY D , N Wales, Pa (d/X–22–1898 @33) MD U Md 1890. *JAMA* 31:1128, 1898.

SNYDER, HENRY W , Reisterstown, Md (d/X–22 1840) Clark Co, Va) MD UMd 1825. *Med annals Md:* 576.

SNYDER, JOHN MARSHALL, Washington, DC (b/XII 21–1828 Charleston, Va; d/VIII–2–1863) MD UCNY 1850. *Tr AMA* 31:1086–87, 1880. *Hist Med Soc DC:*253.

SNYDER, MORGAN, Fort Plain, NY (b/X–3–1809 Marbletown; d/IX–15–1883) MD Jefferson 1833. *Tr Med Soc St NY* 1884:392–94. *Butler* 1874: 559.

SOCKETT, RICHARD GALEN, Howard Co, Md (b/II–7–1776 Anne Arundel Co, Md; d/II–27–1861) Hon MD UMd 1826. *Med annals Md:* 584.

SOHN, EDWIN CHRISTIAN, Tiffin, O 1854–56; Galesburg, Ill 1856– (b/VIII–15–1824 Greencastle, Pa; d/XI–23–1887) MD U Md 1854; AB Franklin & Marshall 1847. *F & M obit rec*: 92.

SOLES, J MARION, Bryan, Tex (b/XII–18–1834 Lowndes Co, Ala; d/IX–8–1898) MD Med Coll SC 1856. *Tex med jour* 14:343, 1898–99. *Polk* 1886: 881.

SOLIDAY, JOHN A , CW–USA (d/III–27–1865 Galesboro, NC) MD ? *Nat med jour* 1:302, 1870/71.

SOLIS, WILLIAM HENRY, Calumet, Mich (b/1850 Pontiac, Mich; d/X–21–1885) MD U Mich 1873. *Med age* 3:517, 1885. *Butler* 1878: 383.

SOMERS, JOB BRADDOCK, Lindenwood, NJ (b/1841 Somers' Pt, NJ; d/IV–8–1895) MD Jefferson 1859. *Tr Med Soc NJ* 1895:200–01. *Med bull med & surg* 17:195, 1895. *Butler* 1878: 476.

SOMERS, LEWIS SUMMEL [SUMMERL], ?Pa (d/IV–30–1869 @58) MD UPa 1831. *Phila med reg & dir* 1871: 294. *Med surg rep Phila* 29:364, 1869.

SOMERS, ROBERT H , LeMars, Ia (b/VIII–23–1872 Toronto; d/I–3–1905) <MD Toronto 1869> *Tr Ia St Med Soc* 23:369, 1905. *Polk* 1902: 742.

SOMERVILLE, HENRY, Culpeper Co Va (b/II–6–1853; d/I–3–1892) MD UVa 1876;AB *Tr MS Va* 1894:184–85.

SOMERVILLE, JOHN ALEXANDER, Union Hill, NJ

(b/I-11-1860 NYC; d/IV-3-1884) MD UCNY 1882. *Tr Med Soc NJ* 1884: 170-71.

SOMERVILLE, WALTER, CW-CSA; Mitchell's Station, Va (d/XI-25-1890 @86) MD UPa 1826. *Tr Med Soc Va* 1891: 260. *Butler* 1878: 836.

SORSBY, NICHOLAS T , CW-CSA (b/VI-20-1818 Havana, Ala; d/1867 Eutaw) MD UPa 1841. *U Pa med alum CW*: 1841.

SOTHORON, JAMES THOMAS, Washington, DC (b/VII-9-1892 Charlotte Hall, Md; d/IX-27-1897) MD Georgetown 1865. *JAMA* 29:761, 1897. *Hist Med Soc DC:* 304. *Polk* 1896: 307.

SOTHORON, WILLIAM H , Washington, DC (d/IX 27-1897) MD ? *Med annals Md:* 577.

SOTO, JOSEPH BONIFACE, Brunswick, Me (b/1842 Callao, Peru; d/XI-19-1874) MD Bowdoin 1870. *Tr Me Med Assoc* 1874-76: 426-27.

SOULE, HORATIO SPRAGUE, Winthrop, Mass (b/III-4-1823 Duxbury; d/X-7-1895 @72) MD Bowdoin 1854; ng Harvard Med 1854. *Bost m&s j* 133:384, 1895.

SOULE, WILLIAM, Jewett City, Conn (b/VIII-24-1827 Chaplin; d/V-15-1900) MD Yale 1851. *JAMA* 34:1356, 1900. *Polk* 1896: 280.

SOUTH, EPHRAIM W , Plainfield, NJ 1870-86; Philadelphia 1887- (b/IX-8-1835 Bristol, Pa; d/IV-8-1888) MD Hahnemann 1869. *Tr Am Inst Hom* 1888: 231. *Polk* 1886: 610.

SOUTHACK, JOHN W Jr, NYC (b/XII-21-1839; d/XII-14-1869) MD Bellevue 1865; AB Columbia 1860; AM 1865. *Med reg NY NJ Conn* 1870: 330. *Tr AMA* 21:453, 1870. *Phila med reg & dir* 1871:302. *Med rec* 4: 575-76, 1869-70.

SOUTHALL, JAMES BARRETT, CW-CSA (b/Smithfield, Va; d/XII-10-1862 Richmond) MD UPa 1833. *U Pa med alum CW*: 1833.

SOUTHALL, JAMES H , Little Rock, Ark (d/VII-22 1901) MD UPa 1861 *JAMA* 37:342 1901. *Polk* 1886:153.

SOUTHARD, JAMES M , Marysville O (b/XII-16-1825 Adams Co; d/III-16-1891) MD Starling 1854. *Tr Ohio Med Soc* 1892:379-82. *Butler* 1878: 651.

SOUTHARD, LOTT, Newark (b/VIII-12-1826 Basking Ridge, NJ; d/V-14-1898) MD Geneva 1851. *Tr Med Soc NJ* 1899:288-89. *JAMA* 30:1366, 1898.

SOUTHERLAND [SUTHERLAND], JOHN H , Southerland's Spr, Tx (b/1794? d/1867? @73) MD ? *Med surg rep Phila* 16:472, 1867.

SOUTHGATE, FREDERIC, Texas; Burlington, Ia 1841 (b/X-23-1814 Portland, Me; d/II-29-1844 Quincy, Ill) MD Cinc 1840; AB Bowdoin 1835. *Bowdoin cat*:1835.

SOUTHGATE, ROBERT, USA 1836-56; CSA 1861- (b/Va; d/III-23-164 Richmond) MD UPa 1835. *U Pa med alum CW*: 1835.

SOUTHWICK, EDWARD M , Philadelphia (d/III-25 1906 @39) <MD Balto Med Coll 1898> *Pa med jour* 9: 523, 1905/06. *Polk* 1900: 1562.

SOUTHWORTH, CHARLES TRACEY, Havana, Cuba 1849-51; MexWar-Mexico 1856-59; Monroe, Mich 1859- ; CW-USA (b/V-19-1827 Coventry, NY; d/VIII-14-1884) <MD Madrid 1849> ng U Mich; ng CPSNY 1845-46. *JAMA* 3:560, 1884. *Med age* 2:246-47, 1884. *Atkinson* 1:421-22.

SOUTHWORTH, EDWARD, NYC (b/Mass; d/VIII-15-1882) MD CPSNY 1882; AB Yale 1879. *Med reg NY NJ Conn* 1883: 235.

SOUTHWORTH, JOHN WILLARD, Rochester, NY (d/1889) MD U Mich 1867. *Buff m & s jour* 28:54, 1889.

SOUTHWORTH, MOSES DANIELS, Millville, Mass (b/VII-9-1805 Mendon, Mass; d/VI-9-1875) MD Bowdoin 1831; AB Brown 1828. *Brown hist cat*: 1828. *Mass Med Soc cat*: 1894.

SOUTHWORTH, RICHMOND JOSEPH, Washington DC; Yonkers NY (b/1841 Wis; d/VII-27 or VIII-2-1900) MD CPSNY 1866. *Hist M S DC:*285. *Polk* 1886: 716.

SOUTHWORTH, SLOCUM, Kampsville Ill (d/XI-1899) Lic yrs pract. *Tr Ill St M S* 1899: 287. *Polk* 1896: 425.

SOWDEN, CHRISTOPHER, Larwill, Ind (d/XII-14 1899 @57) MD Cinc Coll Med & Surg 1870. *JAMA* 34: 61, 1900 [as Souder].

SOWERBY, JOSEPH JOHN, USN 1862-68, 1873-79 (b/VII-13-1838 Olney, Phila; d/I-1895 Holmesburg, Phila) MD UPa 1861. *U Pa med alum CW*: 1861.

SOZINSKEY, THOMAS S , Philadelphia (d/IV-19 1889) <MD UPa 1874> *Med bull med & surg* 11:157, 1889. *Polk* 1886: 825.

SPACKMAN, MARY D , Washington, DC (d/V-26-1904) MD Howard 1872. *JAMA* 43:211, 1904. *Polk* 1886:214. Black.

SPACKMAN, REUBEN V , Dubois, Pa (b/Bellefonte, Pa; d/III-20-1906) MD Jefferson 1870. *Pa med jour* 9:523, 1905/06. *Flint* 1897: 800.

SPAIN, ARCHIBALD W , Terre Haute, Ind (b/XI-22-1837 Patoka; d/I-4-1898) MD Cinc Coll Med & Surg 1863. *Tr Ind St Med Soc* 1898: 385. *Polk* 1896: 494.

SPALDING, ANDREW J , Leonardtown, Md (d/X-5-1897) MD Jefferson 1849. *JAMA* 29:867, 1897. *Med annals Md:* 577. *Polk* 1886: 443.

SPALDING, ASA LEFFINGWELL [LUTHER?], Enfield, Conn (b/IX-18-1806 Killingly; d/I-7-1864) MD Yale 1832; Hon MD Berkshire 1833. *Bost m&s j* 69:508, 1863. *Proc Conn Med Soc* 2:66, 1864.

SPALDING, CHARLES PARKER, Lowell, Mass (d/III-25-1895 @46) MD Harvard 1877; AB 1870. *Bost m&s j* 132:448, 1895.

SPALDING, EDWARD, Nashua, NH (d/VI-24-1895 @ 80) MD Harvard 1837; AB Dartmouth 1833; LLD 1886. *JAMA* 25:76, 1895. *Polk* 1886: 593.

SPALDING, GEORGE ATHERTON, NYC (d/X-2-1906 @57) MD CPSNY 1875. *Bost m&s j* 155:426, 1906. *Polk* 1896: 1079.

SPALDING, JAMES, Montpelier, Vt (b/1792; d/III-15-1858) MD Dartmouth 1814; Hon MD Castleton 1823. *Tr AMA* 29:768-69, 1878. *Bost m&s j* 58:294-97, 1858. *Tr Vt Med Soc* 1883: 109.

SPALDING, JOEL, Lowell, Mass (d/I-30-1888 @68) MD Berkshire 1843. *Bost m&s j* 118:160, 1888.

SPALDING, MATTHIAS, Amherst, Mass (b/VI-25-1769 Chelmsford; d/V-22-1865) Hon MD Dartmouth 1817; AB Harvard 1798. *Tr NH Med Soc* 1865: 4. *Tr AMA* 18:301-05, 1867.

SPANG [SPRANG], FREDERICK K , Reading, Pa (b/Oley; d/II-17-1894 @57) MD Jefferson 1860. *JAMA* 22: 313, 1894.

SPANN, BENJAMIN F , Anderson, Ind (b/V-14-1830 Jefferson Co; d/II-2-1894) MD Med Coll Ohio 1880. *JAMA* 22:235, 1894. *Tr Ind St Med Soc* 1894: 225. *Butler* 1878:220. Kemper's *Indiana*: 223.

SPANNHAKE, LOUIS HENRY, NYC (d/XII-29-1898 @58) MD UCNY 1867. *JAMA* 32:92, 1899. *Polk* 1896: 1079.

SPARE, JOHN, CW-USN; New Bedford, Mass (b/XI-13 1816 Canton; d/V-22-1901) MD Harvard 1842; AB Amherst 1838. *Harvard in CW*: 230. *Polk* 1886: 470.

SPARHAWK, GEORGE E, Gaysville Vt 1857-80; Burlington 1880- (b/II-15-1829 or II-30-1830 Rochester; d/III-22-1906) MD Woodstock 1852; MD Hahnemann Phila 1853. *Tr Am Inst Hom* 1905: 758-59. *Polk* 1886: 904. Homeopath.

SPARHAWK, THOMAS, Newburyport, Mass (b/1807; d/V-17-1874 @67) MD Harvard 1833; AB Dartmouth 1828. *Bost m&s j* 90:516, 563, 1874.

SPARKMAN, JAMES RITCHIE, Plantersville, SC (b/1815 Georgetown Co; d/1897) MD Med Coll SC 1836. *JAMA* 29:1234, 1897. *Waring* II: 303. *Butler* 1878:758.

SPARKS, GEORGE W , Philadelphia (d/1902) MD Jefferson 1865. *Pa m j* 5:314, 1901/02; 6:262, 1902/03.

SPARKS, JAMES B , Carthage, Ind (b/VI-15-1833 Nicholasville, Ky; d/VIII-22-1895) MD Transylvania 1857. *Tr Ind St Med Soc* 1896: 253. *Polk* 1886: 313.

SPARKS, PETER B , Griggsville, Ill 1867- (b/VII-1834 Rushville; d/1890 @57) <MD St Louis Homeop 1873> *Polk* 1886: 276. *Cleave.* Homeopath.

SPARKS, R B , Lone Oak, Tx (d/X-20-1885) MD ? *New Orl m & s jour* ns13:578, 1886. *Polk* 1886: 889.

SPARROW, ORSON COWLES, CW-USA; Tenn; Brooklyn; Valdosta, Ga 1875- (b/IX-3-1832 Killingly, Conn; d/IX-13-1877) MD LICH 1864; AB Yale 1854; PhB Sheffield 1858. *Med reg NY NJ Conn* 1878: 191.

SPARROW, WILLIAM EDWARD, Mattapoisett, Mass (d/V-15-1899 @75) MD Yale 1847. *Bost m&s j* 140:512, 1899. *Polk* 1896: 717.

SPATZ, JOHN H , Leesport, Pa 1864-74; Centreport 1874- (d/I-1890) MD Pa M C 1848. *Med bull m&s* 13: 68, 1890. *Polk* 1886:795. *Off'l reg Pa phys* 1881-87:646.

SPAULDING, JOSEPH PAYSON, Richmond, Me (b/IX 19-1839 Bingham; d/VI-30-1877) MD Bowdoin 1866. *Tr Me M Ass* 1880:202-3; 1881:391-2. *Butler* 1878:311.

SPAULDING [SPALDING], STEPHEN HODGEMAN, S Natick, Mass (b/1789? d/VII-15-1865 @76) MD ? *Bost m&s j* 72:516, 1865. *Mass Med Soc cat* 1894.

SPAULDING, STILLMAN, Lexington, Mass (b/1788? d/V-26-1860 @72) MD ? *Bost m&s j* 62:372, 1860.

SPAULDING, W R , Louisville; Austin, Tx (d/XII-9-1888) MD Louisville 1887. *Daniel's Tex m j* 4:278, 1888.

SPAULDING, ZACHARIAH, Bingham, Me (b/XI-13-1790; d/XI-16-1865 @66) MD Bowdoin 1827. *Bost m&s j* 75:152, 1866.

SPEAKE, RUFUS HOLMEAD, Washington, DC (b/IV-17-1807; d/IV-20-1867) <AB Georgetown> MD Wash Med Coll Balto 1829. *Tr AMA* 19:435, 1868. *Hist Med Soc DC:* 242. *Med annals Md:* 577.

SPEARS, HUGH C , Hillsboro, Tx; Longwood, Mo (d/V 18-1906) MD Transylvania 1850. *Polk* 1886: 554. *Tex st jour med* 2:100, 1906.

SPEARS [SPIRES], JOAB B , Texarkana, Tx (d/IX-12 1905) MD Tulane 1859. *Tex st jour med* 1:154, 1905/06. *Polk* 1893: 537.

SPEED, EDWARD B , CW-USA (d/IX-14-1864) MD ? *Nat med jour* 1:302, 1870/71.

SPEER, JAMES RAMSEY, Pittsburgh (b/1796; d/IX-6 1891) MD UPa 1821. *NW med jour* 19:150, 1891. *Bost m&s j* 125:284, 1891.

SPEES, F T , Tuscola, Ill (d/IV-8-1900 @76) Lic yrs pract. *Tr Ill St Med Soc* 1899-1900: 574. *Polk* 1896: 444.

SPEES, GEORGE, Milwaukee (d/IX-13-1895 @62) MD Med Coll Ind 1871. *JAMA* 25:510, 1895. *Polk* 1890: 372.

SPEES, SAMUEL T , Tuscola, Ill (d/I-29-1898) MD M C Ohio 1880. *JAMA* 30:391, 1898. *Polk* 1896: 444.

SPEIR, SAMUEL FLEET, Brooklyn (b/1838; d/XII-19-1895 @56) MD UCNY 1860. *JAMA* 25:1140, 1895. *Atkinson* I: 578. *Polk* 1886: 649.

SPELLMAN, HENRY, CW-USA (d/V-21-1862 Mt Vernon, Ind) MD Willoughby 1839. *Med surg rep Phila* ns8:258, 1862. *Nat med jour* 1:302, 1870/71.

SPENCE, GIDEON O, Salem O (b/II-25-1830 Seneca Co NY; d/X-23-1886) MD Albany 1854; MD Cleveland Hom 1869. *Med vis* 3:12, 1887. *Cleave.* *Polk* 1886: 749.

SPENCE, JOHN, Dumfries, Va (b/1766? d/V-18-1829 @63) Hon MD UPa 1828. *Am j m sci* 5: 262-64, 1829.

SPENCE, JOHN Jr, Boston (d/II-7-1851) MD Harvard 1839; AB Brown 1839; AM. *Bost m&s jour* 44:46 1851.

SPENCER, A J , San Antonio, Tx (d/X-14-1893) MD ? *Tex med jour* 9:235, 1893-94.

SPENCER, ALEXANDER JOSEPHUS, San José, Cal (d/I-10-1885 @74) MD Castleton 1831. *Med reg NY NJ Conn* 1885: 244. *Butler* 1878: 62.

SPENCER, CALVIN, Clarendon, Vt (g/1799; d/X-28-1870) MD Castleton 1833. *Bost m&s j* 6:304, 1870.

SPENCER, EDWARD CURRAN, St Paul, Minn (b/XII-8-1858; d/XII-26-1891 Coronado Beach, Cal) att St

Paul Med Sch 1882. *Tr Minn St Med Soc* 1893:123. *Med bull med & surg* 14:76, 1892.

SPENCER, ETHAN, Evansville, Ind (b/1812 NYC; d/X-17-1895 NYC) MD ? *JAMA* 25:726, 1895. *Polk* 1890: 369. Eclectic.

SPENCER, GAIUS L, Triangle, NY (b/III-9-1794 Anadilla; d/VI-17-1852) Lic Del Co Med Soc NY 1817. *Nashvl jour m & s* 3:271-73, 1852. *Bost m&s j* 47: 194-95, 1852.

SPENCER, H D, S Bainbridge, NY (b/Lisle; d/1857 @ 34) MD Berkshire 1848. *Bost m&s jour* 57:136-37 1857.

SPENCER, HENRY GORDON P, Watertown, NY (d/VI-27-1899 @78 Minneapolis) MD Jefferson 1846. *Buff m & s jour* 39:141-42, 1899. *Tr Med Soc St NY* 1900: 431. *JAMA* 33:175, 1899. *Polk* 1896: 1111.

SPENCER, HENRY WORTHINGTON, Paris, Fr (d/XI--1893 @86) MD UPa 1853. *Bost m&s j* 129:630, 1893.

SPENCER, JAMES T, Farmville, Va (b/I-22-1820 Halifax Co; d/IV-27-1886) MD UVa 1841. *Tr Med Soc Va* 1886: 389-90.

SPENCER, JOHN E, Moorestown NJ (d/1874 Santa Barbara, Cal) MD Jefferson 1870. *Med s rep Phila* 31: 120, 1874. *Med rec NY* 10:733, 1875. *Tr AMA* 26: 470, 1875.

SPENCER, THOMAS, Philadelphia; Geneva, NY (b/X-22-1793 Great Barrington, Mass; d/V-30-1857) MD Fairfield 1820; att UPa Med Dept 1832-33. *NW med & surg jour* 6:340, 1857. *Phila med & surg jour* 6:377-78, 1858. *Tr M S St NY* 1858: [35]-46. *K&B* III: 1146-47.

SPENCER, THOMAS RUSH, Geneva, NY; USA 1861-70 (b/1818; d/VI- -1872 Santa Fe, NM) MD UPa 1840; AB Hobart 1838. *Med reg NY NJ Conn* 1873: 349. *U Pa med alum CW*: 1840.

SPENCER, WILLIAM DAVID, Saybrook, Conn (b/VII-15-1852 New Haven; d/VI-3-1904) MD CPSNY 1873. *Proc Conn Med Soc* 1905: 505.

SPENCER, WILLIAM OCTAVIUS, Red River Co, Tx (b/XI-12-1840; d/1898) <MD Med Coll Ala 1862> ng U Ala 1856. *U Ala cat*: 142.

SPENS, CONRAD, Joliet, Ill (b/Stockholm, Sw; d/IV-27 1900) MD Upsala 1869. *JAMA* 34:1146, 1900. *Ill med jour* ns2:48, 1900.

SPENZER, PETER IGNATIUS, Cleveland (d/IV-27 1896 @59) MD Wooster 1873. *JAMA* 26:995, 1896. *Polk* 1886: 749.

SPERRY, JOHNSON, Delafield, Wis (b/IX-22-1822 Manchester, Vt; d/I-14-1879) Stud med w/Dr Goodwin, Burton, O. *Tr Wis St M S* 1879:288. *Butler* 1878: 866.

SPICER, HIRAM L, Baltimore (b/III-24-1840; d/II-12 1898) MD U Md 1860. *JAMA* 30:570, 1898. *Med annals Md:* 578. *Polk* 1886: 439.

SPICER, JAMES, Goldsboro NC (d/IV-5-1897 @35) MD Bellevue 1884. *NC m j* 39:324 1897. *Polk* 1886:722.

SPICKLER, DAVID HEWITT, Ashton, Ill (b/III-18-1830 Middleburgh, Pa; d/X-28-1879) MD Rush 1857. *Chic m j* 39:670, 1879. *Med s rep Phila* 41:462, 1879.

SPIER, ROBERT FLEET, Brooklyn (d/VIII-13-1896) MD U Vt 1866. *JAMA* 27:503, 1896. *Polk* 1896:1003. [*See also Speir, Samuel Fleet, above.*]

SPILLMAN, CHARLES HARVEY, Yazoo City, Miss; Nicholsville, Harrodsburg & Hopkinsville, Ky (b/V-20 1805 Garrard Co, Ky; d/XII-15-1892) MD Transylvania 1835; AB Centre Coll. *Tr Ky St Med Soc* ns2:16, 1893. *Atkinson* I: 407-08.

SPINNER, WILLIAM, Montvale, Va (d/III-3-1900 @38) <MD CPS Balto 1879> *JAMA* 34: 703, 1900.

SPINNING, JOHN NEWTON, Covington, Ind (b/VIII-29-1822 Ohio; d/II-11-1890) MD ? *Tr Ind St Med Soc* 1890:162. *Polk* 1886: 315.

SPITLER, DANIEL, Iroquois, Ill (b/1843 Page Co, Va; d/VII-23-1884) MD Rush 1867. *Med surg rep Phila* 51: 392, 1884.

SPOFFORD, JEREMIAH, Hampstead, NH to 1817; E Bradford, Mass (b/XII-8-1787 Georgetown; d/IX-16 1880) ng Dartmouth Med Coll; lic Worcester Distr Med Soc 1813. *Tr AMA* 32:540-41, 1881. *Bost m&s j* 103: 332, 1880; 104:116, 1881. *K&B* III: 1149.

SPOFFORD, MORRIS, Groveland Mass (d/III-7-1884 @55) MD ? *Bost m&sj* 111:61 1884 *Mass M S cat* 1894.

SPOFFORD, RICHARD SMITH, Newburyport, Mass (b/1788? d/1872 @83) MD Harvard 1816. *Bost m&s j* ns9:64, 1872. *Med rec* 7:120, 1872.

SPOONER, EDWARD AMASA,b Philadelphia (b/I-7-1830; d/XI-6-1887) MD Jefferson 1854; MD UPa 1866; ng Harvard Med Sch.*Tr CPP* cent vol:267. *Atknsn* I: 120.

SPOONER, PAUL, New Bedford, Mass (b/1786? d/VII-13-1862 @76) MD ? *Bost m&s j* 66:524, 1862.

SPOTSWOOD, WILLIAM AUGUSTINE WASHINGTON, USN 1828-61; CSN 1861-65; Mobile, Ala (b/X-2-1806 Orange Co, Va; d/IX-7-1891) <MD U Va> stud med Phila. *Bost m&s j* 125:284, 1891. *Hamersly*.

SPRAGUE, ALDEN SPOONER, Springville, NY 1826-28; Buffalo 1828-53 (b/I-19-1801 Haverhill, NH; d/I-8 1863) MD Dartmouth 1826; ng Pa Med Coll 1843. *Tr Med Soc St NY* 1868: 311-13.

SPRAGUE, CHARLES AZRO L, Milton, Vt (b/I-26 1809 New Haven, Conn; d/V-31-1872 Williston, Vt) MD Castleton 1841. *Tr Vt Med Soc* 1883:109.

SPRAGUE, EDWARD, Coraopolis, Pa (d/VIII-12-1899 @65) MD ? *JAMA* 33:621, 1899.

SPRAGUE, HAVILAH MOWRY, Fordham & Fremont, NY (b/VII-4-1835 Windham, Conn; d/V-30-1874) MD UCNY 1861; AB Amherst 1858. *Med reg NY NJ Conn* 1874: 291. *Med rec NY* 9:383, 1874.

SPRAGUE, JENKS S, Carlisle, NY 1825-28? Exeter 1828-60; Cooperstown to 1869; Hastings Minn 1870 (b/X-14-1800 Otsego;d/I-22-1879) MD Fairfield 1825. *Tr M S St NY* 1879: 589-91. *Tr Minn St M S* 1879: 151-53.

SPRAGUE, JOSEPH, Dubuque, Ia (d/1878) ?MD Med Coll Ohio 1851. *Tr AMA* 31: 1088, 1880.

SPRAGUE, LESTER S, Williamson, NY (d/1897 @78)

MD Geneva 1841. *JAMA* 30:106, 1898. *Polk* 1886:716.

SPRAGUE, PHOEBE A, Springfield, Mass; Holley, NY (b/1845; d/XII- -1904) MD Womans Med Chic 1873. *Bost m&s j* 152:89, 1905. *Polk* 1896: 723.

SPRAGUE, RICHARD, Boston (b/1859; d/VI-28-1892) MD Harvard 1887; AB 1881. *Bost m&s j* 126:672, 1892; 127:27, 1892.

SPRAGUE, SETH BILLINGTON, Jersey City (b/I-12 1840 Dexter, Md; d/VI-5-1901) MD Bowdoin 1867. *Bost m&s j* 14_?:600, 1901. *Polk* 1896: 939.

SPRAGUE, THOMAS JEFFERSON Jr, Joliet Ill (d/X-3 1893) MD Rush 1879. *JAMA* 21:590, 1893. *Polk* 1886:289.

SPRAGUE, WELCOME WHIPPLE, NYC (b/II-16-1828; d/III-26-1884) MD Bellevue 1875. *Med reg NY NJ Conn* 1884: 240. *Butler* 1878: 525.

SPRAGUE, WILLIAM BISHOP, Pavilion, NY (b/1836; d/III-16-1891) MD Buffalo M C 1857. *Bost m&s j* 124: 324, 1891. *Buff m&s j* 30:570, 1891. *Butler* 1878: 575.

SPRAGUE, WILLIAM LAWRENCE, Boston (d/VI-22 1884 @34) MD Harvard 1881; AB 1871. *Bost m&s j* 111:619, 1884.

SPRATT, W D, ? (d/X-1-1878 Port Gibson, Miss) MD ? *Tr AMA* 30:885, 1879. *Med rec NY* 14:300, 1878.

SPRAY, JOHN CAMPBELL, Chicago (d/II-20-1906 @ 60) MD Chic Med Coll 1873. *Ill med jour* 9:332, 1906. *Polk* 1896:406.

SPRENKLE, JOSIAH EDWIN, Hanover, Pa (b/IV-18-1858; d/VIII-4-1897) MD Jefferson 1884; AB Franklin & Marshall 1881. *Fr & Marsh obit rec*: 266-67.

SPRING, CHARLES EDWARD, Holliston, Mass (b/III-19-1842 Grafton, Vt; d/X-25-1890) MD Albany 1864. *Bost m&s j* 123:432, 1890; 124:190, 1891. *Polk* 1886: 467.

SPRING, CHARLES HARRISON, Boston (b/VIII-22-1831 Hillsboro, NH; d/XII-9-1887) MD Albany 1857; ng Amherst 1856. *Bost m&s j* 117:292, 1887.

SPRING, CLARENCE WALTER, Fitchburg, Mass (d/XI-9-1906 @47) MD Harvard 1884; AB Dartmouth 1880. *Bost m&s j* 155:594, 1906. *Polk* 1896: 712.

SPRING, MARSHALL, Watertown, Mass (b/1732? d/1818 @76) Hon MD Harvard 1807; AB 1762. *Bost m&s j* 105:497, 1881.

SPRING, SAMUEL, NYC (b/1807? d/IV-8-1869 @62) MD CPSNY 1830. *Phila med reg & dir* 1871: 300.

SPROAT, HENRY HAMILTON, Freetown, Mass (d/III-15-1892 @50) MD Harvard 1865. *Bost m&s j* 126: 304, 1892. *Polk* 1890: 548.

SPROAT, LOUIS D, NYC (b/Chillicothe, O; d/X-28-1833) MD CPSNY 1869 *Med reg NY NJ Conn* 1884:240. *Med surg rep Phila* 49:588, 1883.

SPROSTON, GEORGE SAXON, USN (d/I-27-1842 Baltimore) MD Harvard 1817. *Med annals Md:* 578.

SPROULL, CHARLES GEORGE, NYC (b/Phila; d/I 25-1902 @34) MD UCNY 1893; AB Princeton 1890. *Bost m&s j* 146:128, 1902. *Polk* 1896: 1079.

SPURRIER, JOHN H, Rushville, Ind (b/II-15-1829 Blue Lick, Ky; d/I-9-1902) MD Med Coll Ind 1879; ng Rush. *Tr Ind St Med Soc* 1902:424. *Polk* 1886: 335.

SPURZHEIM, GASPAR, Prussia (b/XII-31-1775 Longvich, Prussia; d/XI-11-1833 Boston) MD Vienna. *Transylvania jour med & assoc sci* 6:115-31, 1833.

SQUIBB, EDWARD ROBINSON, Brooklyn (b/1819; d/X-26-1900) MD Jefferson 1845. *Chic med rec* 19:354, 1900. *Proc Conn Med Soc* 1901:273-75. *Atkinson* I:684.

SQUIRE, LUCIUS MELANDER, Paynette, Wis (b/VI-11-1866; d/III-7-1898) MD Rush 1891. *JAMA* 30:745, 1898. *Tr Wis St Med Soc* 1898:556-57.

SQUIRE, TRUMAN HOFFMAN, Elmira, NY (b/III-31-1823 Quasia, NY; d/XI-27-1889) MD CPSNY 1848. *Med reg NY NJ Conn* 1890: 280. *Buff m & s jour* 29:445, 1889. *K&B* III: 1150.

SQUIRE, WILLIAM H, Germantown, Pa (d/XII-8-1865 @40) MD Jefferson 1851. *Med s rep Phila* 13:406 1865.

STAATS, BARENT P, Albany, NY 1821- (b/IX-25-1796 Schodack; d/VII-9-1871) Hon MD Geneva 1849; lic 1818. *Tr AMA* 24:367, 1873. *Buff m&s j* 10:474, 1871. *Bost m&s j* ns8:32, 1871. *Tr Med Soc St NY* 1873: 180-81.

STACHELBERG, ISIDORE, NYC(d/VI-12-1877)<MD St Petersburg 1860> *Med reg NY NJ Conn* 1877: 210. *Butler* 1878: 525.

STACKHOUSE, HENRY C, Miss (b/VI-4-1843 Crystal Spr; d/1877) MD New Orl Sch Med 1868. *Tr Miss St Med Assoc* 1878: 166.

STACKPOLE, PAUL AUGUSTINE, Dover, NH (b/II-12-1814 Rocheser; d/III-28-1900) MD Dartmouth 1842; AM 1880. *Bost m&s j* 142:368, 1900. *Pr Conn M S* 1900:337. *Tr NH M S* 1900:309-10. *Polk* 1890: 708.

STACY, CLINTON, Gorman, Me (b/XI-30-1868 Porter; d/I-15-1899) MD Bowdoin 1896; AB 1892. *Bowdoin cat*: 1892.

STACY, HORACE, Boston 1844- (b/VI-30-1814 Acton, Me; d/V-5-1882) MD Dartmouth 1838. *Bost m&s j* 107:619, 1882.

STACY, ROBERT Q, NYC (b/Ga? d/XI-6-1882) MD Jefferson 1858. *Med reg NY NJ Conn* 1883: 235.

STAFFORD, JAMES ROMEYN, NYC (d/XI-5-1867 @ 60) MD ? *Med surg rep Phila* 17:458, 1867.

STAFFORD, JOHN, Baltimore (b/1801; d/XII-24-1829) MD UMd 1823. *Med annals Md:* 578.

STAFFORD, JOSEPH B, Allentown, NJ (d/VIII-15-1872 @62) MD Phila Coll Med & Surg 1848. *Med surg rep Phila* 27:260, 1872.

STAFFORD, M L, Luray, Mo (d/I-26-1896 @45) MD Missouri Med Coll 1877. *JAMA* 26:287, 1896. *Polk* 1890: 554.

STAHL, ALBERT THOMAS, Boston (b/VI-4-1846 Attleboro, Mass; d/III-16-1892 @45) MD Bowdoin 1875. *Bost m&s j* 126:304, 1892. *Polk* 1890: 543.

STAHL, DANIEL, Quincy, Ill; USA (d/X-26-1874 @70) MD ? *Med surg rep Phila* 31:460, 500, 1874. Kemper's *Indiana*: 19.

STALEY, GEORGE LEWIS Jr, Baltimore (b/1857 Washington, Md; d/IX-9-1901) MD CPS Balto 1878. *Med annals Md:* 579. *Polk* 1886: 439.

STALL, JOHN F, Clermont Co, O (d/X-2-1867 @65) MD ? *Med surg rep Phila* 17:347, 1867.

STALLARD, H H, Menlo Park, Cal (d/XI-15-1899 @ 77) <MRCP(L) 1857> *JAMA* 33:1441, 1899.

STALNAKER, JOHN WILLIAM, CW-CSA; Austin, Tx (b/1831 Lewisburg, WVa; d/XI-11-1883) MD UPa 1855. *U Pa m alum CW*: 1855. Blanton *Va surgs CW*:416.

STAMPS, WILLIAM LIPSCOMBE, Milton, NC (b/II-17-1816; d/I-19-1896) MD UPa 1839; AB UNC 1836. *UNC cat*: 587.

STANARD, ALBERT CUSHMAN, NYC (d/III-19-1894 @29) MD Harvard 1889; BLitt U Mich 1884. *Med reg NY NJ Conn* 1894:249. *Bost m&s j* 130:503, 1894.

STANBRO, EDWARD EVERETT, ?Buffalo (b/1869; d/XI-5-1899) MD U Buffalo 1892. *Buff m & s jour* 39: 384, 1899.

STANCELL, ROBERT HENRY Jr, Margarettsville, NC (b/V-26-1872; d/I-23-1896) MD UMd 1892; att UNC 1888. *Tr Med Soc NC* 1896:150. *Polk* 1886:724.

STANDIFORD, ABRAHAM G, Westville, Ind (d/II-10 1894) MD ? *JAMA* 22:276, 1894. *Polk* 1890: 392.

STANFORD, FRANCIS A, Columbus, Ga (d/IX-15 1885 Marietta) MD UCNY 1848. *New Orl m & s jour* ns13:420, 1885. *Butler* 1878:119.

STANLEY, CHARLES WESLEY, Chicago (b/V-28-1828 Conway, NH; d/X-26-1893) MD UCNY 1867. *Med reg NY NJ Conn* 1894:249. *JAMA* 21:784, 1893. *Butler* 1878: 137.

STANLEY, CLAUDE GRAHAM, NYC (b/1847; d/V-24-1877) MD Bellevue 1870. *Med reg NY NJ Conn* 1877: 206. *Butler* 1878: 525.

STANLEY, FRANK [FRANCIS] ALBERT, Chicago (d/I-16-1900) MD CPSNY 1870. *Tr Ill St Med Soc* 1899-1900: 509. *Polk* 1896: 406.

STANLEY, GEORGE WASHINGTON, Slatersville, RI (b/VII-18-1817 Readfield, Me; d/V-28-1892) MD Dartmouth 1844. *Tr RI Med Soc* 5:132-33, 1894-98. *Polk* 1890: 1028.

STANLEY, J C, Lancaster, Pa (d/XI-18-1858 @53) MD ? *Med surg rep Phila* ns1:156, 1858/59.

STANLEY, JAMES PHILIP, CW-CSA (b/VIII-29-1833 Haywood Co, Tenn; d/IX-8-1899 Pine Bluff, Ark) MD UPa 1858. *U Pa med alum CW*: 1858.

STANLEY, JOSIAH, New Calif, Wis (d/I-26-1854) MD Rush 1853. *NW med & surg jour* 3:96, 1854.

STANLEY, WILLIAM STILLMAN, Wrentham, Mass (b/I-17-1803 Attleboro; d/VII-11-1884) MD Brown 1828; AB 1825. *Brown hist cat*: 1825.

STANNARD, FRANK DRAKE, Chicago (d/IX-1-1895 @33) MD Rush 1890. *JAMA* 25:427, 1895.

STANSBURY, EMORY, Appleton, Wis (d/IV-3-1899 @60) MD Bellevue 1867. *JAMA* 32:845, 1899. *Polk* 1896: 1544.

STANTON, BENJAMIN, Salem, O (d/1861) MD Cleveland Med Coll 1845. *Tr O St Med Soc* 1873: 274.

STANTON, DAVID, CW-USA; New Brighton, Pa (b/VI 9-1829 Salem, O; d/XI-5-1871) MD Cleveland Med Coll 1850; MD UPa 1857; att Jefferson 1856? *Tr Pa St Med Soc* 9:77-79, 1872. *U Pa med alum CW*:1857.

STANTON, JAMES, San Francisco (d/XII-28-1897) MD U Calif 1882 *JAMA* 30:166 1898. *Polk* 1886: 174.

STANTON, JOSHUA OTIS, CW-USA; Washington, DC (b/X-22-1837 Strafford, NH; d/IV-9-1891) MD Bowdoin 1862. *JAMA* 16:828, 1891. *Bost m&s j* 124:396, 1891. *Hist Med Soc DC:* 295. *Atkinson* I:355. *Butler* 1878: 97.

STAPLES, GEORGE DENNETT, N Berwick, Me (b/VIII-17-1808 Limerick; d/II-11-1879) MD Bowdoin 1838. *Tr Me Med Assoc* 1879: 680. *Butler* 1878: 311.

STAPLES, GEORGE McLELLAN, Dubuque, Ia; CW-USA (b/IV-26-1827 Buxton, Me; d/1895) MD Harvard 1856; AB Colby 1849. *Tr Ia St Med Soc* 18:411, 1900. *Atkinson* I:188-89. *Polk* 1890:414.

STAPP, JAMES T, Vicksburg, Miss (d/VII- 1882) MD ?Jefferson 1879. *Med bull med & surg* 5:18, 1883.

STARK, CHARLES ALVAN, Marshfield, Mass (d/I-22-1897 @35) MD Dartmouth 1883. *JAMA* 28:328, 380, 1897. *Bost m&s j* 136: 100, 1897.

STARK, JOHN, ?Brooklyn (d/V-25-1875 @49) MD CPSNY 1853; AB Union 1849. *Med reg NY NJ Conn* 1875: 204. *Med rec* 10:39, 1875.

STARK, JOHN K, CW-USA; St Louis (d/I-26-1895 @66) MD Royal Coll Glasgow 1863. *JAMA* 24:250, 1895. *Polk* 1890: 660.

STARK, WILLIAM GEDDES, Philadelphia (d/XII-12-1905) <MD CPS Toronto> *Pa med jour* 5:281, 1905/06.

STARKEY, HERBERT A, Sloatsburgh, NY (d/XI-21-1903) MD Med-Chir Coll Phila 1889. *Bost m&s j* 149:610, 1903. *Polk* 1896: 1097.

STARKWEATHER, EDWARD PAYSON, Bridgeport, Conn (d/IX-17-1871) MD Berkshire 1847. *Bost m&s j* 8:392, 1871.

STARKWEATHER, ROBERT, Chesterfield, Mass (d/V 8-1858 @92) MD ? *Bost m&s j* 58:327, 1858.

STARLEY, SILAS F, Tyler, Tx (b/IX-5-1823/1824 Autauga Co Ala; d/XII-19-1887) MD U Louisville 1854. *Daniel's Tex med jour* 3:293, 1887. *Atkinson* I:406. *Polk* 1886: 895.

STARNES, E CLINGMAN, Asheville, NC (d/I-6-1900 @39) MD Jefferson 1888. *JAMA* 34: 251, 1900. *Polk* 1896: 1119.

STARR, DAVID L, Pittsburgh (d/IV-13-1895 @83) <MD "Mass Med Coll" 1833> *JAMA* 24:650, 1895. *Hahn mo* 30:76 (news & advt) 1895. *Med vis* 11:221,

 Spec. educ'l status abbrev. as: ***ng*** = college verified attendance without degree;

1895. *Polk* 1886: 833. Homeopath.

STARR, HEZEKIAH, Baltimore (d/X-23-1898 @82) MD UMd 1836. *JAMA* 31:1128, 1898. *Med annals Md:* 579. *Polk* 1886: 439.

STARR, JOHN, War 1812-USA; Northwood.,NH 38 yrs (b/XII-3-1783; d/IX-8-1851) Stud med w/Dr Matthias Spalding; AB Harvard 1805. Palmer *Necrol Harv alum*:5.

STATHEM, THOMAS EWING, CW-USA; Greenwich, NJ (b/V-10 1837; d/VI-10-1891) MD UPa 1860. *Tr M S NJ* 1892:203-04. *U Pa m alum CW*: 1860. *Atkinson* I:250.

STATLER, EMANUEL J B , Marshalltown, Ia (b/St Thomas, Pa; d/I-1-1892 @65) MD Jefferson 1868. *JAMA* 18:82, 1892. *Polk* 1886: 363.

STATON, JAMES RODERICK, Tarboro, NC (b/VIII-14-1856; d/XII-23-1883 @26) MD Bellevue 1881; ng UNC 1875-77. *Tr Med Soc St NC* 1887: 157.

STAUFFER, WALTER O, Indianapolis (d/IX-11-1895) MD M C Ind 1881. *JAMA* 25:554, 1895. *Polk* 1890: 388.

STAUGHTON, JAMES MARTIN, Cincinnati; Washington, DC (b/1800 Bordentown, NJ; d/VIII-7-1833) MD UPa 1821; AM Princeton 1821. *Hist Med Soc DC:* 224. *K&B* II: 1090.

STAYMAN, ABRAHAM FLETCHER, CW-USA (b/II-23-1831 Carlisle, Pa; d/IV-20-1871 Tyrone) MD UPa 1865; ng Dickinson 1850 (?) *U Pa med alum CW*: 1865.

STAYMAN, JACOB ASBURY, CW-USA; Baltimore (b/V-4-1826 Carlisle, Pa; d/I-31-1897) MD UPa 1865; <att Dickinson> *U Pa med alum CW*: 1865.

STEADMAN, AUGUSTA ALICE, Amsterdam, NY (d/II 1-1901 @50) MD Woman's Med Coll Inf NY 1881. *Bost m&s j* 145:80, 1901. *Polk* 1896: 987.

STEARNS, CHARLES WOODWARD, USA 1841-42; 1861-63 (b/IX-24-1817 Springfield, Mass; d/IX-8-1887 Longmeadow, Mass) MD UPa 1840; AB Yale 1837. *U Pa med alum CW*: 1840.

STEARNS, DANIEL WALDO, Newton, Mass (d/I-9-1902 @38) MD Harvard 1888. *Bost m&s j* 146:76, 1902. *Polk* 1896: 719.

STEARNS, GEORGE, Groton, Mass (d/III-7-1882 @ 79) MD Harvard 1827. *Bost m&s j* 106:427, 1882; 107:619, 1882.

STEARNS, HAROLD, Idaho Spr, Col (b/V-31-1863 Bombay, India; d/VII-4-1890) MD Denver Med Coll 1886? ng Kansas City Med Coll 1884; ng Amherst 1885. *Amherst, Men of*: 1885.

STEARNS, HENRY PUTNAM, CW-USA; Hartford, Conn (b/IV-18-1828 Sutton, Mass; d/III-27-1905) MD Yale 1855; AB 1853; ng Harvard 1854; stud med Edinburgh. *Proc Conn M S* 1906:273-80. *Bost m&s j* 152: 650-55, 1905. *Harvard in CW*: 244. *Atkinson* I: 337-38. *K&B* III:1152-53.

STEARNS, ISAAC HOLDEN, Cliftondale, Mass (d/IX-6 1897 @72) MD Columbian DC 1860. *Bost m&s j* 137: 304, 1897. *Polk* 1890: 551.

STEARNS, J M , CW-USA (d/I-22-1864 St Louis) MD ? *Nat med jour* 1:302, 1870/71.

STEARNS, JEHIEL, War 1812-USA; Pompey, NH (b/II 6-1790 Rockingham, Vt; d/X-6-1878) <MD Dartm'th> Hon MD Geneva 1839. *Tr M S St NY* 1879: 583-87.

STEARNS, JOHN, Waterford, NY 1793-1810; Albany, NY 1810- (b/V-16-1770 Wilbraham, Mass; d/III-17-1848 NYC) Hon MD U St NY 1812; AB Yale 1788; AM 1812. *Tr AMA* 3:366-67, 1850. *K&B* III: 1153.

STEARNS, JOHN, CW-USA; Mass; Washington, DC (b/Mass; d/ VIII-26-1898) MD Harvard 1860; AB 1846. *Hist Med Soc DC:* 297. *JAMA* 31:618, 1898. *Harvard in CW*: 32. *Polk* 1886: 214.

STEARNS, OWEN E , Freeport, Ill (d/XII-13-1893) Lic yrs pract. *Chic med rec* 6:66, 1894. *Polk* 1886: 279.

STEBBINS, ALBERT M , Fertile, Minn (d/VII-21-1897) MD U Minn 1894. *JAMA* 29: 297, 1897.

STEBBINS, DANIEL, Northampton, Mass (b/1760? d/X-7-1856 @96) MD ? AB Yale 1788. *Bost m & s j* 55: 255, 1857.

STEBBINS, DWIGHT DELAVAN, CW-USA; Detroit, Mich (b/1835; d/VII-18-1862 @27 Cairo, Ill) MD CPSNY 1860. *Med surg rep Phila* ns8: 444, 1862. *Nat med jour* 1:302, 1870/71.

STEBBINS, SUMNER, Unionville, Pa (b/IV-12-1809 Peterboro, NY; d/VII-12-1884 Chester Co, Pa) <MD UPa 1834> *Tr Pa St M S* 1885:337-38. *Butler* 1878: 733.

STEBBINS, WALTER GAY, Boston (d/X-8-1893) MD Harvard 1892; AM 1892; AB Yale 1886. *JAMA* 21:630, 1893. *Bost m&s j* 129:382-83, 404, 1893.

STEDMAN, CHARLES GRISWOLD, CW-USA; Ravenna, O (b/X-13-1845 Shakopee, Minn; d/VIII-30-1869 Shakopee) MD Bellevue 1868. *Phila med reg & dir* 1871: 302.

STEDMAN, CHARLES HARRISON, Boston (d/VI-8-1866 @61) MD Harvard 1828; Hon AM Yale 1855. *Bost m&s j* 74:412, 1866.

STEDMAN [STEEDMAN], HARRY COOKE, CW-USA (b/VII-12-1832 Lewisburg, Pa; d/V-23-1876 Mifflinburg) MD UPa 1861. *U Pa med alum CW*: 1861.

STEDMAN, JOSEPH, Jamaica Plain, Mass (b/X-13-1835 Medfield; d/V-16-1898 Watkins Glen, NY) MD UCNY 1864. *Bost m&s j* 138: 506, 526, 584, 1898. *JAMA* 30:1366, 1898. *Polk* 1896: 706.

STEEL, DAVID, CW-CSA; Petersburg, Va (b/XII-27-1826 Ayrshire, Scotl; d/III-6-1886) MD Med Coll Va 1852. *Tr Med Soc Va* 1886:391. Blanton *Va surgs CW*:416. *Atkinson* I: 285.

STEELE, ARMSTRONG THOMAS, Waveland, Ind (b/IX-13-1834 Owen Co; d/IV-12-1884) MD U Louisville 1857. *Tr Ind St Med Soc* 1887:187. *Butler* 1878:221.

STEELE, CHARLES G , Buffalo (d/II-11-1888) MD Buffalo 1886. *Buff m & s jour* 27:381, 1888.

STEELE, EBENEZER W , CW-USA (d/IX-2-1862) MD Med Coll Ohio 1847. *Nat med jour* 1:302, 1870/71.

STEELE, HARRISON, Peoria, Ill (d/XI-14-1902 @66) MD Rush 1867. *Ill m j* ns4:425, 1902. *Polk* 1896: 434.

STEELE, HENRY K , CW-USA; Denver (b/IV-1-1825 Dayton, O; d/I-20-1892) MD UCNY 1848. *Tr Colo St Med Soc* 1898-99:509. *Atkinson* I:322-23. *K&B* III: 887. *Polk* 1893: 238.

STEELE, HENRY SHERWOOD, Dixon, Ill (b/IX-5-1828 Hartford Conn; d/III-18-1857 Roxbury Mass) MD Rush 1853; AB Yale 1847. *Bost m&s j* 56:167 237 1857.

STEELE, JAMES ELNATHAN, CW-USA; NYC (b/1828 Kidderminster Engl; d/V-28-1878) MD NYMC 1861. *Med reg NY NJ Conn* 1879:200. *Med rec* 13:500, 1878.

STEELE, JOHN, Lexington, Ky (d/VI-11-1833) MD Transylvania 1833. *Transylv j m & assoc sci* 6:305 1833.

STEELE, ROBERT JOHNSON, CW-CSA; Rockingham, NC (b/Richmond Co; d/VII-24-1887) MD UPa 1842. *U Pa med alum CW*: 1842.

STEELING, WILLIAM, Philadelphia (b/1785; d/1856) <MD Jefferson 1826> *Tr Med Soc NJ* 1871: 163-64.

STEGER, ROBERT W , Chicago (d/I-10-1906 @48 NYC) MD Vanderbilt 1877. *Ill med jour* 9:131, 1906. *Nashville jour m & s* 98:39, 1906. *Polk* 1886: 271.

STEIGERS, ALONZO F , USA (d/IV-12-1899 @55) MD ? *JAMA* 32: 955-56, 1899.

STEIN, ALEXANDER W , NYC (b/III-3-1841 Hungary; d/XII-5-1897) MD UCNY 1867. *JAMA* 29:1286, 1897. *Atkinson* I: 114, 1878. *K&B* III: 1155.

STEIN, EDWARD M , USN (d/VII-14-1877 @38) MD UPa 1860. *Med reg NY NJ Conn* 1878: 192.

STEINACH, ADELRICH, NYC (b/IV-26-1826 Switz; d/VIII-25-1892) <MD U Strasbourg 1854> *Med reg NY NJ Conn* 1893:315. *Polk* 1886: 694.

STEINER, HENRY HEGNER, USA 1839-52; CSA 1861-65; Augusta, Ga (b/I-8-1816 Frederick, Md; d/II-13-1892) MD UPa 1838. *U Pa med alum CW*: 1838. *Polk* 1886: 226.

STEINER, LEWIS HENRY, CW-US San Comm; Baltimore (b/V-4-1827 Frederick; d/II-18-1892) MD UPa 1849; AB Marshall 1846; AM 1849; AM St James 1854; AM Yale 1869. *JAMA* 18:438, 1892. *Bost m&s j* 126:204, 1892. *Med annals Md:* 579-80. *U Pa med alum CW*: 1849. *K&B* III: 1155.

STEINFUEHRER, GUSTAVUS ADOLPHUS FRIEDRICH, Schenectady NY (b/Gny; d/VII-2-1890) MD CPSNY 1874 *Tr M S St NY* 11:741 1894. *Polk* 1886:707.

STEINMETZ, CHARLES RAMSEY, CW-USA (b/IX-21-1843 Norristown, Pa; d/VIII-10-1869) MD UPa 1865. *U Pa med alum CW*: 1865.

STEINMEYER, OTTO Jr, Carlinville, Ill (d/II-9-1899) MD ? *JAMA* 32: 442, 1899.

STEINSIECK, CHARLES HY[?] GUSTAVUS, NYC (d/XII-3-1901 @43) MD UCNY 1882. *Bost m&s j* 145: 664, 1901.

STELLE, EPHRAIM M , Bernardsville, NJ (b/XI-28-1856 Millington, NJ; d/XI-18-1894) MD CPSNY 1884. *Tr Med Soc NJ* 1894:277.

STELLE, GEORGE W , ?Philadelphia (d/X-18-1868) MD ? *Med surg rep Phila* 19:368, 1868.

STELLE, NELSON, Metuchen to 1839; NYC (b/IV-29-1812 Piscataway, NJ; d/III-3-1864) MD Fairfield 1835. *Med reg NY NJ Conn* 1865: 224.

STEPHENS, FREDERICK PHILIP, NYC (b/Ithaca; d/XII-4-1884) MD Bellevue 1877; BS Cornell 1875. *Med reg NY NJ Conn* 1885:245. *Tr Med Soc St NY* 11:741 ff, 1894. *Med surg rep Phila* 51: 732, 1884.

STEPHENS, HENRY WILLIAM, Brooklyn (b/Saratoga Spr; d/II-22-1891 @33) MD CPSNY 1882; AB Williams 1879. *JAMA* 16:576, 1891.

STEPHENS, JAMES J , Tappan, NY (b/NYC; d/III-3-1898 @75) MD CPSNY 1846. *Bost m & s jour* 138:237, 1898. *JAMA* 30:624, 1898. *Polk* 1896: 1106.

STEPHENS, WILLIAM C , Waelder, Tx (d/IX- 1886) Lic by 25 yrs pract. *So pract* 9:37, 1887. *Polk* 1886:896.

STEPHENS, WILLIAM GREEN, CW-CSA (b/VIII-18 1839 Leasburg, NC; d/II-10-1896 Caswell Co) MD UPa 1861. *U Pa med alum CW*: 1861.

STEPHENSON, BENJAMIN FRANKLIN, Springfield, Ill (b/X-3-1823 Wayne Co, Ill; d/VIII-30-1871 Rock Creek, Ill) MD Rush 1850. *Tr Ill St Med Soc* 1895:68-69. *K&B* III:1156-57.

STEPHENSON, EZRA, Hingham, Mass (d/V-20-1874 @68) MD Harvard 1832. *Bost m & s jour* 90:540, 1874.

STEPHENSON, JOSEPH, Pendleton, Ind (b/IV-19-1819 Warren Co, O; d/III-16-1886) MD Med Coll Ohio 1850. *Tr Ind St Med Soc* 1886: 213.

STEPHENSON, MARCUS P , NYC (d/X-23-1885 @ 52) MD Jefferson 1857. *Med reg NY NJ Conn* 1886: 254. *Butler* 1878: 525.

STEPHENSON, MARK, Brooklyn (b/VII-7-1803 Hudson, NY; d/VIII-28-1865) MD CPSNY 1826. *Tr AMA* 18:313, 1867. *Med surg rep Phila* 13:166, 198, 1865. *Med reg NY NJ Conn* 1866: 189.

STEPHENSON [STEVENSON], WILLIAM GEORGE, Nyack, NY (d/II-3-1888) MD CPSNY 1865. *Med reg NY NJ Conn* 1888: 271. *Butler* 1878: 575.

STEPTOE, HENRY C , Lynchburg, Va (d/VII-30-1874 @52) MD Jefferson 1847. *Tr Med Soc Va* 1874: 54.

STERLING, JOHN, CW-USA (b/1831 Ireland; d/IV-6-1869) MD UPa 1856.*U Pa med alum CW*: 1856.

STERLING, JOHN WILLIAMS, NYC (b/VI-12-1795; d/VII-7-1881) Hon MD Yale 1819; stud med Dublin, London, Paris. *Med reg NY NJ Conn* 1888:235. *Atkinson* I: 704. *Butler* 1878: 575.

STETSON, ALBERT EVERETT, Dorchester, Mass (d/VII-5-1857 @32) MD Harvard 1849; AB Yale 1846. *Bost m & s jour* 56:467, 1857.

STETSON, EZRA, Princeton, Ill (d/IV-28-1895 @78) MD Fairfield 1837. *JAMA* 24:690, 1895.

STETSON, JOHN, W Harwich, Mass (b/1814 Abington;

d/II-19-1896 @81) MD Dartmouth 1851. *Bost m & s jour* 134:228, 1896. *Polk* 1886: 475.

STETTINIUS, JOHN W D, Washington, DC (b/1826; d/VII-20-1863) MD Columbian 1848 *Hist M S DC:*265.

STETTLER, CORNELIA SOMARINDYCKS, Chicago (d/X-20-1899 or VIII-7-1898 @39) MD Hahnemann Chic 1891. *Tr Ill St Med Soc* 1899:287. *Tr Am Inst Hom* 1898: 935. Homeopath.

STEUART, JAMES, Baltimore (b/1755 Annapolis; d/1845) MD Edinburgh 1779. *Med annals Md:* 580.

STEUART, JAMES A, Baltimore (b/IV-3-1828; d/III 27-1903) MD UMd 1850; AB St Mary's Coll Balto. *Med ann Md:* 581. *Bost m&s j* 148:408, 1903. *Polk* 1890: 516.

STEUART, JAMES HENRY, Baltimore (d/X-8-1892 @57) MD UMd 1857; AB Princeton 1855; AM 1858. *JAMA* 19: 535, 1892.

STEUART, RICHARD SPRIGG, Baltimore (b/XI-1-1797; d/VII-13-1876) MD UMd 1822. *Tr AMA* 28:618-20, 1877. *Med annals Md:* 581. *K&B* III:1160-61.

STEVENS, ALEXANDER HODGDON, NYC (b/VII or IX-4-1789 NYC; d/III-30-1869) MD UPa 1811; AB Yale 1807. *Tr M S St NY* 1874:288-300. *Med reg NY NJ Conn* 1869:247. *Buff m&s j* 7:386 1869. *Med s rep Phila* 13:5-7, 1865. *Tr AMA* 21:442-44, 1870. *K&B* III:1161.

STEVENS, ALLEN AUGUSTUS, Sinclairville, NY (d/X-13-1893) MD Buffalo 1873. *Med reg NY NJ Conn* 1894:249. *Buff m&s j* 33:237, 1893. *JAMA* 21:667, 1893.

STEVENS, BELA NETTLETON, Washington, DC; CW-USA (b/XII-29-1833 Newport NH; d/VII-5-1865) MD Dartmouth 1859; AB 1854; AM 1854. *Bost m & s jour* 72:536, 1865. *Med surg rep Phila* 13:48, 1865.

STEVENS, CALVIN, Boston (d/III-1-1898 @81 Auburndale) MD Harvard 1845. *Bost m & s jour* 138:216, 1898. *Polk* 1896: 706.

STEVENS, CHARLES AUGUSTUS, Palmyra, NY 1842; Buffalo 1844; Cortland, Coxsackie & Hudson, NY 1855- ; Scranton, Pa 1860- (b/Harpersfield, NY; d/I-17-1881 @63) MD Geneva 1841. *Tr Hom Med Soc St Pa* 1881:43. *Tr Am Inst Hom* 1881:119. *Cleave.* Homeopath.

STEVENS, CHARLES WISTAR, Charlestown, Mass (d/I-25-1901 @64) MD Harvard 1870; AB 1860. *Bost m & s jour* 144:126, 1901. *Polk* 1896: 706.

STEVENS, DODDRIDGE A, Dallas (b/V-14-1857 Bedford Co, Va; d/I-18-1886) MD Vanderbilt 1883. *Tex cour-rec m* 3:219, 1886. *New Orl m&s j* ns13:751, 1886.

STEVENS, EDWARD BRUCE, Lebanon, O (b/1823; d/VII-11-1896) MD Med Coll Ohio 1846. *Tr Ohio St Med Soc* 1897:430. *K&B* III: 1162.

STEVENS, ELBRIDGE GERRY, Kennebunk & Biddeford, Me (b/III-30-1811 Pittston; d/III-26-1898) MD Bowdoin 1834. *JAMA* 30:933, 1898. *Polk* 1886:423.

STEVENS, FRANK DANA SWITZER, Lynn, Mass (b/V-30-1860 Auburn; d/II-10-1896) MD Bowdoin 1881. *Bost m & s jour* 134:180, 1896. *Polk* 1896: 717.

STEVENS, HENRY WILLIAM, Brooklyn (d/II-22-1891 @33) MD CPSNY 1882; AB Williams 1879; AM. *Med reg NY NJ Conn* 1891: 281. *Bost m & s jour* 124: 246, 1891.

STEVENS, HIRAM FAIRCHILD, St Albans, Vt (b/VIII 3-1825; d/I-15-1866) MD CPSNY 1850; ng Woodstock. *Bost m&s j* 74:46, 1866. *Tr Vt Med Soc* 1883:109.

STEVENS, HORACE, Cambridge, Mass (b/IV-19-1816 Piedmont, NH; d/1889) MD Woodstock 1842. *Bost m & s jour* 120:228, 1889.

STEVENS, JOHN, Boston (b/1789? d/VII-10-1863 @ 74) MD ? *Bost m & s jour* 68:490, 1863.

STEVENS, JOHN ALEXANDER, Boston (d/X-7-1870 @58) MD ? *Bost m & s jour* 6:244, 1870.

STEVENS, JOHN HORACE, CW-CSA; Jackson Parish, La; Dallas (b/1828 Harrisonburg, Va; d/II-24-1882) MD UVa 1846; ng Dickinson 1845. *Med rec* 20:700, 1881.

STEVENS, JONATHAN HUMPHREY PETTIBONE, Norfolk, Conn (b/XII-9-1830; d/XII-18-1885) MD CPSNY 1852. *Proc Conn Med Soc* ns4:216-? 1888.

STEVENS, JOSEPH, ? ; La (b/IX-7-1832 Bangor, Me; d/VIII-7-1872) MD Tulane 1859; ng Amherst 1852. *Amherst, Men of*: 1852.

STEVENS, JOSEPH LOWE, Castine, Me (b/1790 Gloucester, Mass; d/II-19-1879) MD Harvard 1814; AB 1810. *Bost m & s jour* 100:411-12, 1879.

STEVENS, OLIVER P, CW-USA; Maxinkuckee Ind (b/XI-11-1820 Stark Co O; d/IV-19-1880) MD ? *Tr Ind St M S* 1888:214. *Polk* 1886:328. Kemper's *Indiana*: 344.

STEVENS, SELTON W, Scranton, Pa (d/IV-25-1901 @39) MD Jefferson 1894. *Pa med jour* 5:296, 1901/02. *Flint* 1897: 835.

STEVENS, THADDEUS MORRELL, Indianapolis (b/VIII-29-1829 or 1830; d/XI-8-1885) <MD Ind Med Coll 1853> ng Jefferson. *Tr Ind St Med Soc* 1886: 207. *Atkinson* I: 341. *Butler* 1878: 221. *K&B* III:1162-63.

STEVENS, WILLIAM B, Nelson, Pa (d/XII-11-1902 @37) MD Jefferson 1891. *Pa med jour* 6:262, 1902/03. *Flint* 1897: 811.

STEVENS, WILLIAM BRADFORD, Bedford, NH (b/I-27-1820; d/II-18-1861) ng Dartmouth Med Coll 1853. *Tr NH Med Soc* 1861: 6.

STEVENS, WILLIAM FLINT, Stoneham, Mass (d/1879 @72) MD ? *Bost m & s jour* 100:555, 1879.

STEVENS, WILLIAM LeROY, ?NYC (d/VI-24-1877 @22) MD UVa 1876. *Med reg NY NJ Conn* 1878: 192.

STEVENS, WILLIAM STANFORD, Augusta, Ga (d/XI 29-1898) MD Harvard 1883; AB Amherst 1876. *JAMA* 31: 1542, 1898. *Polk* 1896: 706.

STEVENS, WINTHROP FLINT, Stoneham, Mass (d/IX-5-1890 @42) MD Harvard 1872; AB Dartmouth 1869. *Bost m & s jour* 123: 264, 336, 1890.

STEVENSON, JAMES S, Baltimore (b/1815 Ky; d/VII 2-1882) MD UMd 1841. *JAMA* 1:576, 1833. *Butler* 1878: 323. *Med annals Md:* 582.

STEVENSON, JOHN B , NYC (b/1795? d/VIII–25–1863 @68) MD CPSNY 1815; AB Columbia 1811. *Med surg rep Phila* 10:252, 1863.

STEVENSON, JOHN FLETCHER, CW–USA (d/XI–8–1865 NYC?) MD Harvard 1861. *Harvard in CW*: 267.

STEVENSON, JOHN M , CW–USA; Baltimore (b/1842; d/III–6 1879) MD UMd 1862. *Med annals Md:* 582. *Butler* 1874: 316.

STEVENSON, JOSEPH H, Centerville, NJ (d/II–7–1861 Somerville @35) MD ? *Tr Med Soc NJ* 1872:196–97.

STEVENSON, JOSEPH M , Pittsburgh (b/1829 Murraysville, Pa; d/II–3–1896) MD Jefferson 1859. *Tr Pa St Med Soc* 27:367, 1897. *Butler* 1878: 701.

STEVENSON [STEPHENSON], ROBERT, Adrian, Mich (b/VIII– –1823 Ireland; d/VIII–9–1890 Vienna) <MD U Glasgow 1845> *JAMA* 15: 626, 1890. *Polk* 1886: 482.

STEVENSON, THOMAS Jr, NYC (d/X–27–1906 @41) <MD Bellevue 1888> *Bost m & s jour* 155, 562, 1906.

STEVENSON, THOMAS COLLINS, Carlisle, Pa (b/Pittsburgh; d/XII–19–1879) MD Hahnemann Phila 1851; stud West Point; att Wash'n Med Coll, Balto. *Tr Am Inst Hom* 1881:123. *Cleave*. Homeopath.

STEVENSON, WILLIAM GEORGE, Poughkeepsie, NY (d/VII–31–1890 @47) MD CPSNY 1865. *Tr Med Soc St NY* 1891:457. *Polk* 1886: 702.

STEWARDSON, THOMAS Jr, Savannah; Philadelphia (b/VII–10–1807; d/VI–30–1878) MD UPa 1830. *Tr CPP* cent vol:286; 3s7:xxix–xlviii, 1884.

STEWART, ALEXANDER, Shippensburg, Pa (d/XII–6 1893 @84) MD Wash'n Med Coll Balto 1831? *JAMA* 22: 97, 1894. *Butler* 1878: 734.

STEWART, ALLEN W , Philadelphia (d/II–14–1896 @ 24) MD Hahnemann, Phila 1893. *Hahn mo* 31:104 (news & advt) 1896. Homeopath.

STEWART, D M , Denton, Tx (d/IV–19–1906 @81) MD U Louisville 1869. *Tex st jour med* 2:100, 1906. *Polk* 1886: 879.

STEWART, DAVID, Port Penn, Del (b/II–14–1813; d/IX 2–1899) MD UMd 1844. *Med annals Md:* 582–83. *K&B* III: 1164.

STEWART, FERDINAND CAMPBELL [orig CAMPBELL, FERDINAND STEWART], NYC to 1855? (b/VIII–10–1815 Williamsburg, Va; d/II–11–1899 Pisa, It) MD UPa 1837; stud Wm & Mary. *Med surg rep Phila* 15:249–53, 1866. *K&B* III: 1165.

STEWART, GEORGE WASHINGTON, Danville, Ia (b/V–30–1847 Chester, Vt; d/IV– –1882) MD Rush 1869; att Med Coll Ohio. *Tr Ia St Med Soc* 6:458–59, 1883–85. *Atkinson* I:539. *Butler* 1878: 246.

STEWART, J R , Bryan, Tx (d/III–10–1883) MD Tulane 1858. *Tex med & surg rec* 3:642, 1883.

STEWART, JACOB HENRY, St Paul, Minn (b/I–15–1829 Peekskill, NY; d/VIII–25–1884) MD UCNY 1851; ng Yale Coll. *Bost m & s jour* 111:619, 1884. *Tr Minn St Med Soc* 1884:181. *K&B* III: 1165–66.

STEWART, JAMES, NYC (b/IV–7–1799; d/IX–12–1864) MD CPSNY 1823; hon AM Amherst 1840. *Tr AMA* 18:309–10, 1867. *Bost m&s j* 69:28, 1863! *Med reg NY NJ Conn* 1865:229–31. *Tr M S St NY* 1865: 304–13. *K&B* III: 1166.

STEWART, JAMES H , Pittsburgh (d/X–31–1872) MD ? *Med surg rep Phila* 28:78, 1873.

STEWART, JAMES LOGAN, CW–USA?; Erie, Pa (b/VIII–1–1825 Pittsburgh; d/XII–6–1890) MD UPa 1848. *Buff m & s jour* 30:372, 1891. *JAMA* 15:915–16, 1890; 16:179, 1891. *U Pa med alum CW*: 1848. *Bost m & s jour* 123: 604, 1890. *Atkinson* I: 102.

STEWART, JAMES MARTIN, CW–USA; Indiana, Pa (b/1791 Huntingdon; d/III–27–1869) MD UPa 1829. *Phila med reg & dir* 1871:300. *Med surg rep Phila* 20: 310, 1869. *U Pa med alum CW*: 1829.

STEWART, JAMES TORRANCE, CW–USA; Peoria, Ill (b/VI–20 1824 Greenville; d/IV–12–1901) MD UPa 1850. *Ill med jour* ns2:601, 1901. *U Pa med alum CW*: 1850. *Polk* 1896: 435.

STEWART, JAMES W , Brooklyn (d/XII–27–1867) MD ?UPa 1833. *Med surg rep Phila* 18:22, 1867.

STEWART, JOHN L , New Albany, Ind (b/XI–28–1835 Switzerland Co, Ind; d/VII–12–1898) MD Ky Sch Med 1865. *Tr Ind St Med Soc* 1899:386. *Polk* 1896: 484.

STEWART, JOHN Q A , Farmdale, Ky (b/II–13–1829 Louisville; d/I–25–1898) MD Ky Sch Med 1859. *JAMA* 30:334, 1898. *Polk* 1886: 395.

STEWART, JOHN S , Philadelphia (d/1892) MD Medico–Chir Coll 1885. *Med bull med & surg* 14:206, 1892. *Polk* 1886: 825.

STEWART, JOSEPH DePUY, ? Pa (b/Pa; d/IV–12–1854 Phila) MD UPa 1837. *Med rep* 2:32, 1854. *Tr Pa St Med Soc* 1856: 185.

STEWART, JOSEPH F , Jacksonville, Pa (b/1832; d/IX–29–1865) MD Jefferson 1864. *Tr Pa St M S* 1865: 83.

STEWART, JOSIAH, Philadelphia (b/1792? d/VI–3–1867 @75) MD UPa 1812. *Med s rep Phila* 16:511 1867.

STEWART, LAWRENCE, CW–CSA (b/VIII–13–1836 Laurinburg, NC; d/IX–1–1862 Chantilly, Va) MD UPa 1860. *U Pa med alum CW*: 1860.

STEWART, PHILANDER, Roxbury, Conn to 1836? Peekskill, NY (b/VI–20–1810 Danbury; d/II–11–1874) MD Jefferson 1834. *Tr Med Soc St NY* 1875: 379–84. *Med surg rep Phila* 30:276, 1874. *Butler* 1874: 561.

STEWART, ROBERT, No Chatham, NY (b/II–11–1829 Natchez, Miss; d/II–11–1905) ng UPa Med Dept 1853; AB Amherst 1851. *Amherst, Men of*. *Polk* 1886: 694.

STEWART, ROBERT COCHRAN, Shippensburg, Pa (d/II–9–1899) MD UPa 1872. *JAMA* 32:385, 1899. *Polk* 1896: 1337.

STEWART, W R , York Spr, Pa (d/III–9–1867 @65) <MD UMd> *Med surg rep Phila* 16:531, 1867.

STEWART, WALLACE B , Armagh, Pa (d/V–27–1874

 Spec. educ'l status abbrev. as: ***ng*** = college verified attendance without degree;

@55) MD ? *Med surg rep Phila* 31:120, 1874.

STEWART, WALTER MONTEITH, CW–USA; Philadelphia (b/Johnstown NY; d/XI–4–1866) MD UPa 1865. *Med s rep Phila* 16:199, 1867. *U Pa m alum CW*: 1865.

STEWART, WILLIAM G , Newville, Pa (b/Allegheny Co, Pa; d/IV–14–1899 @59) MD Western Reserve 1874. *JAMA* 32: 956, 1899. *Polk* 1894: 1094.

STEWART, WILLIAM S , Philadelphia (b/XI–13–1838 Stewart's Station Pa; d/XI–25–1903) MD Jefferson 1863. *Pa med jour* 7:155, 280, 1904/04. *Atkinson* I: 203.

STICKEL, HENRY L , Harrisburg, Pa (d/I–24–1901 @48) MD Jefferson 1873. *Pa med jour* 5:296, 1901/02. *Butler* 1878: 743.

STICKLER, JOSEPH WILLIAM, Orange, NJ (b/I–25–1854 Hoboken; d/V–19–1899) MD CPSNY 1879; BS U CNY 1876. *Bost m & s j* 140:636, 1899; 142: 200, 1900. *JAMA* 32:1269, 1899. *Tr Med Soc NJ* 1899: 286–87.

STICKNEY, CHARLES WILSON, CW–USA; Newark (b/I–4–1833 Milford, Pa; d/IV–23–1889) MD UPa 1858. *Med reg NY NJ Conn* 1889:287. *U Pa med alum CW*: 1858. *Butler* 1878: 464.

STICKNEY, HORATIO GATES, Springfield, Mass (d/1878 @43) MD ? *Bost m & s jour* 100:39, 1879.

STICKNEY, JAMES MILTON, Pepperell, Mass (b/XI–24–1813 Antrim, NH; d/XI–28–1889) MD Woodstock 1842. *Bost m & s jour* 121: 645, 1889.

STICKNEY, PIERRE LE BRETON, Springfield, Mass (d/XI–5–1887 @73) MD Jefferson 1842. *Bost m & s jour* 117:468, 1887. *Polk* 1886: 474.

STIDHAM, JOSEPH PENROSE, Philadelphia (b/XII–9 1824 Wilmington Del;d/VIII–7–1893) MD UPa 1851; AM Lafayette 1848. *Laf'tte Men of*:160. *Polk* 1886: 825.

STIEREN, EDWARD, Natrona, Pa (d/III–27–1868 @65) MD ? *Med surg rep Phila* 18:356, 1868.

STIGER, JOHN D , Stanton, NJ (b/X–8–1857 White House, NJ; d/X–19–1890) MD CPS Balto 1884. *Tr Med Soc NJ* 1892:204.

STIGLEMAN, CALOHILL MINIS, CW–CSA; Floyd, Va (b/III–24–1833; d/1904?) MD Med Coll Va 1857. *Tr Med Soc Va* 1905: 453. *Polk* 1900: 1762.

STILES, GEORGE MITCHELL, CW–USA; Conshohocken Pa (b/II–14–1844 Burlington NJ; d/VI–8–1904) MD UPa 1866; att Princeton. *U Pa m alum CW*: 1866. *Pa m j* 8:336, 1904/05. *Atkinson* I:647. *Flint* 1897: 799.

STILES, JOSEPH NATHAN, Windsor, Vt (b/VIII–13–1818; d/VIII–31–1875) MD Dartmouth 1839. *Tr AMA* 29:769–70, 1878.

STILES, RICHARD CRESSON, CW–USA;Brooklyn (b/X–3–1840 Phila; d/IV–16–1873 W Chester Pa) MD UPa 1854; AB Yale 1851. *Med reg NY NJ Conn* 1873: 350; 1874:295. *Med s rep Phil* 35:460 1876. *UPa m alum CW*: 1854. *Med times* (Phila) 3:508, 1872/73. *K&B* III: 1168.

STILES, SAMUEL EDWARD, Brooklyn (b/VIII–26–1844; d/X–9–1901 @57) MD LICH 1870. *Bost m & s jour* 145: 450, 1901. *Polk* 1896: 1003.

STILES, WALTER, Philadelphia (d/IV– –1892) Student @ Med–Chir Coll Phil. *Med bull m & s* 14: 205, 1892.

STILLÉ, ALBERT OWEN, Philadelphia; CW–USA (b/VI–29–1827; d/VI–23–1862) MD UPa 1851; AB 1848; AM 1851. *Nat m j* 1:302 1870/71. *Tr AMA* 14:210 1864. *Tr Pa St M S* 2:318–19, 1863. *Tr CPP* cent vol: 268.

STILLÉ, ALFRED, CW–USA; Philadelphia (b/X–13–1813; d/IX–24 1900) MD UPa 1836; LLD 1859 Pa Coll; Hon AM Yale; AB UPa 1832. *Tr CPP* cent vol:268; 3s 24:lviii–lxxi 1902. *UPa m bull* 15:126–32 1902/03. *Atknsn* I:151. *Chic m rec* 19:275 1900. *K&B* III:1169–70.

STILLÉ, BENJAMIN Jr, New Orleans (b/III–17–1814 Philadelphia; d/III–28–1882) MD UPa 1837; AB 1834. *New Orl m & s jour* ns9:797, 1882. *Atkinson* I:275. *Butler* 1878: 295.

STILLÉ, LOUIS SYDENHAM, Philadelphia (d/V–7–1872 @23) MD UPa 1871; PhD 1871. *Phila med reg & dir* 1873: 304. *Med times* 2:308, 1872.

STILLÉ, MORETON, Philadelphia (b/X–22–1822; d/VIII–20–1855) MD UPa 1844; AB 1841. *Tr CPP* cent vol:268; ns3:5–35, 1856–62. *Tr Pa St M S* 1856:185, 195–98. *Nashville jour m & s* 9:352, 1855; 12: 238–41, 1857. *K&B* III:1170–71.

STILLEY, EDWARD J , Hope Church, Pa (d/I–3–1904 @40) MD Western Pa U 1889. *Pa m j* 8:336, 1904/05. *Flint* 1897: 805.

STILLMAN, A G , Troy, NY (d/III–21–1884) MD ? *Med surg rep Phila* 50:448, 1884.

STILLMAN, CHARLES FREDERICK, Plainfield, NJ (b/1853; d/IV–30 or V–1–1892) MD CPSNY 1876; BS Rutgers 1873. *JAMA* 18:684, 1892. *Chic med rec* 3:263, 1892. *Bost m & s jour* 126:484, 1892. *Butler* 1878:476.

STILLMAN, CHARLES HENRY, Plainfield, NJ (b/I–25 1817 Schenectady, NY; d/XII–11–1881) MD CPSNY 1840; AB Union 1835. *Tr Med Soc NJ* 1883: 286–87. *Med rec* 20:697, 1881. *Butler* 1878:476.

STILLMAN, EDWIN M , Andover, NY (d/XII–5–1898 @57?) MD Buffalo Med Coll 1865. *Buff m & s jour* 38: 461, 1899. *JAMA* 31:1542, 1898.

STILLMAN, HENRY W , Woonsocket, RI (b/V–4–1825 Potter Hill, RI; d/II–5–1892) MD Berkshire 1845. *Bost m & s jour* 126:156, 1892. *Tr RI Med Soc* 4:487–88, 1889–93. *Butler* 1878: 748.

STILLMAN, ROSWELL FOX, No Haven, Conn (b/XII–6–1815 Cooperstown, NY; d/XII–21–1879) MD UCNY 1843. *Tr AMA* 33:606, 1882. *Pr Conn M S* 1880:166–67.

STILLSON [STILSON], EDWARD HENRY,Knoxville; Keokuk, Ia (d/V–30–1897) MD Hahnemann Phila 1871. *Tr Am Inst Hom* 1898: 49. *Polk* 1866: 285.

STILLSON, JOSEPH, Bedford Ind(b/VIII–8–1815 Newtown, Conn; d/IX–15–1885) ng U Louisville. *Tr Ind St Med Soc* 1886:204. *Butler* 1874: 216.

STILLWELL, JOHN EDWIN, NYC (b/VII–25–1813 NYC; d/XI–26–1873) MD CPSNY 1836; AB Columbia 1832. *Med reg NY NJ Conn* 1874:291. *Med surg rep*

Phila 29:440, 1873. *Med rec NY* 9:71, 1874.

STILLWELL, JOSEPH A, CW–USA; Brownstown, Ind (b/IV–11–1831 Pleasant Grove; d/V–30–1894) MD Med Coll Ohio 1866; stud Louisvl 1853. *Tr Ind St M S* 1895: 401–02. *Polk* 1886: 312. Kemper's *Indiana*:300, 345.

STILLWELL, THOMAS, Fremont, O (d/XI–30–1897 @ 82) MD Jefferson 1839; att Lafayette. *JAMA* 29:1234, 1897. *Polk* 1886: 755.

STILLWELL, WILLIAM EDGAR, NYC (b/III–14–1807; d/II–6–1867) MD CPSNY 1830. *Med reg NY NJ Conn* 1867: 227. *Med surg rep Phila* 16: 139, 1867.

STILWELL, WILLIAM R, CW–USA (d/IX–19–1864 @ 24 Washington, DC) MD ? *Med surg rep Phila* 12: 1864/65. *Nat med jour* 1:302, 1870/71.

STIMPSON, ALFRED O, Thompson, Pa (d/V–20–1899) MD McGill 1868. *JAMA* 32:1399 1899. *Polk* 1896:1340.

STIMSON, HOIT S, Athens, O (d/II–25–1894) MD ? *JAMA* 22:391, 1894. *Butler* 1878: 652. Eclectic.

STIMSON, JEREMY, Dedham, Mass (b/1783? d/VIII–12–1869 @86) Hon MD Harvard 1852; AB 1804. *Bost m & s jour* 4:48, 1869. *Mass Med Soc cat* 1894.

STINSON, MARY HENDERSON, Norristown, Pa (d/1889 @70) MD Woman's Med Coll Pa 1869. *Bost m & s jour* 120:204, 1889.

STIRLING, THOMAS BRUCE, NYC (d/VI–10–1877) MD CPSNY 1857. *Med reg NY NJ Conn* 1877: 206. *Med rec* 12:370, 1877.

STITES, HARRY, Harrisburg, Pa (d/I–25–1906 Havana Cuba) MD UPa 1876. *Pa m j* 9:524, 1905/06. *Flint* 1897: 804.

STITSON, AUSTIN B, Windsor, NY (b/IX–17–1849; d/IV–27–1887) MD UCNY 1876. *Med reg NY NJ Conn* 1888: 271.

STITZEL, GEORGE, Nevada, Ia (b/Pa; d/1894 @65) MD Pa Med Coll 1858. *Tr Ia St Med Soc* 14:330, 1896. *Polk* 1890: 422.

STOCKBRIDGE, THOMAS, N Bridgewater Mass (b/1793; d/I–13–1863 @70) MD ? *Bost m&s j*67:610 1862.

STOCKBRIDGE, TRISTRAM GILMAN, Bath, Me (b/VIII–18–1806; d/I–20–1871) MD Bowdoin 1828. *Bost m&s j* 7:88, 1871. *Tr Me M Assn* 1871–73: 184– 85. *K&B* I(2): 417–18.

STOCKDELL, HUGH, CW–CSA; Petersburg, Va (b/VIII–28–1835; d/V–23–1901) MD Jefferson 1859; ng UVa. *Tr Med Soc Va* 1901:278–79. Blanton *Va surgs CW*: 416. *Polk* 1886: 924.

STOCKER, ANTHONY EUGENE, CW–USA; Philadelphia (b/III–5–1819;d/V–23–1897) MD UPa 1840;AB 1837. *Tr CPP* cent vol: 268. *JAMA* 28:1092, 1156, 1897.

STOCKMAN, CHARLES OSWALD, New Haven, Conn (b/1809 Gny; d/IX–8–1873) MD Rostov 1836. *Pr Conn Med Soc* 1874: 293.

STOCKTON, ELIAS ALANSON, Stockton, Cal (b/IX–19–1830 Phila; d/VI–30–1886) MD Med Coll Ohio 1853. *Tr Cal St Med Soc* 1887:396. *Butler* 1878: 63.

STOCKTON, RICHARD W, North East, Pa; NY; War 1812–USA (b/IX–13–1785; d/IX–29–1868) Lic Del Co NY 1804; ng Columbia Coll, NY. *Phila med reg & dir* 1871: 298. *Med surg rep Phila* 19:330, 1868.

STOCKWELL, CYRUS M, CW–USA; Port Huron, Mich (b/VI–20–1823 Colesville, NY; d/XII–9–1899) MD Berkshire 1850. *JAMA* 33:1632, 1899. *Polk* 1896: 768. *K&B* II: 1109.

STOCKWELL, SARAH FOWLER, South Bend, Ind (b/XI–11–1841 Lagrange Co, Ind; d/IV–9–1904) MD U Mich 1876. *Tr Ind St M S* 1904:362. *Polk* 1896: 492.

STODDARD, GEORGE W, Ramsey, Ill (d/X–11–1895 @33) MD Mo Med Coll 1891. *JAMA* 25:682, 1895. *Tr Ill St Med Soc* 1896: 59.

STODDARD, J C, CW–USA; (d/VII–26–1864 Wallace's Ferry, Ark) MD ? *Nat med jour* 1:302, 1870/71. *Med surg rep Phila* 12: 68, 1864/65.

STODDARD, SAMSON, Jackson, Mich (b/II–7–1806 Vienna, NY; d/VIII–24–1876) MD Fairfield 1829. *JAMA* 2:110–11, 1884.

STODDARD, SAMUEL FELLOWS, Lake Crystal, Minn (b/III–22–1844 Farmington, Me; d/XII–16–1875) MD Dartmouth 1868. *Tr Minn St Med Soc* 1877:152.

STODDARD, THOMAS, Seymour, Conn (b/III–11–1813 Oxford, Conn; d/IX–29–1887) MD Yale 1836. *Proc Conn Med Soc* ns4:212–13, 1888. *Butler* 1878: 82.

STOECKEL, GUSTAVE MOZART, Norfolk, Conn (d/II–15–1900 @51) MD CPSNY 1874; AB Yale 1871; AM 1874. *JAMA* 34:511, 1900. *Polk* 1896: 1080.

STOKES, J SPENCER, Moorestown NJ (b/X–4–1842;d/IX–18–1868) MD Jefferson 1864; AB Haverford. *Phila m reg & dir* 1871:298. *Med s rep Phila* 19: 260, 1868.

STOKES, J WILLIAM, Corinth, Miss; Orangeburg, SC (d/VII–6–1901) MD Vanderbilt 1881; MD U Nashville 1882. *JAMA* 37:213, 1901. *Polk* 1886: 525.

STOKES, JAMES, W Chester, Pa; CW–USA (b/I–19 1832 Germantown, Pa; d/VI–23–1895 Gtn) MD UPa 1855. *U Pa med alum CW*: 1855. *Polk* 1886:839.

STOKES, JOHN HINCHMAN, Moorestown, NJ (b/1808;d/I–20–1873) MD UPa 1828 *Tr AMA* 24:366 1873. *Tr M S NJ* 1873: 118. *Med s rep Phila* 28: 120, 1873.

STOKES, JOHN M, Sumner, Ill (d/II–10–1900 @38) MD Hosp Med Coll Louisville 1882. *Tr Ill St Med Soc* 1899–1900: 509. *JAMA* 34: 574, 1900. *Polk* 1886: 299.

STOKES, N NEWLIN, Moorestown, NJ (d/IV–19–1905 @72) MD Jefferson 1854. *Bost m & s jour* 152:508, 1905. *Polk* 1896: 941.

STOKES, THOMAS D, Danville, Va (b/II– –1817 Caswell Co, NC; d/VII–30–1886) MD UPa 1839. *Tr Med Soc Va* 1886:391–92. *Butler* 1878: 836.

STOKES, WILLIAM HUGHES, Mobile, Ala 1835–40; Baltimore 1842– (b/I–21–1812 Havre de Grace, Md; d/V–7–1893) MD UMd 1834; AB Yale 1831; stud Dublin, London, Paris. *Bost m & s jour* 128:480, 1893. *Med annals Md:* 584. *Butler* 1878: 323.

 Spec. educ'l status abbrev. as: ***ng*** = college verified attendance without degree;

STOLTZE [STOLZE], JOHN, Reading, Pa (d/IX-11-1906 @73 Geneva, Wis) MD Eclectic Coll Pa 1865. *Pa med jour* 10:53, 1906/07. *Flint* 1897: 833.

STONE, ALPHEUS FLETCHER, Greenfield, Mass (b/V-7-1778 Rutland, Mass; d/IX-5-1851) Hon MD Berkshire 1825. *Bost m & s jour* 45:217 ff, 1851.

STONE, DEWEY H , Homer, NY (d/III-14-1892 @36) MD UCNY 1879. *Med reg NY NJ Conn* 1892: 288. *NW med jour* 20:112, 1892.

STONE, EBENEZER, Walpole, Mass (b/X-10-1797 Sharon; d/VIII-13 or 15-1869) MD Harvard 1824; AB Brown 1820. *Bost m & s jour* 4:48, 1869.

STONE, EBENEZER, Stevens Plains, Me (b/1818 Gorham or Unity; d/1880) MD Bowdoin 1842. *Tr Me Med Assoc* 1880: 205-06. *Butler* 1878: 311.

STONE, ELIZE PFEIFER, Oakland, Cal (b/1819 Mainz, Gny; d/V-30-1880) MD Woman's Med Coll Phila 1867; stud Giessen, Gny. *Tr Cal St M S* 1880:327-28.

STONE, EPHRAIM, Boston (d/VI-26-1860 @89) MD ? *Bost m&s j* 62:476, 1860. *Mass M S cat* 1894.

STONE, GEORGE H , Savannah (d/II-19-1899) MD Georgetown 1868. *JAMA* 32:506, 1899. *Polk* 1890:273.

STONE, GEORGE WILLIAM, Rome, Pa (d/III-14-1894 @80) MD ? *JAMA* 22:523, 1894. *Off'l reg Pa phys* 1881-88: 82.

STONE, HENRY E , Fairhaven, Conn; Otego, NY 1856- (b/VII-20-1820; d/I-27-1886) MD Castleton 1847. *New Engl med gaz* 21:143, 1886. *Cleave.* Homeopath.

STONE, HENRY MORRILL, Perth Amboy, NJ (b/III-25-1825; d/III-3-1866) MD CPSNY 1850. *Tr Med Soc NJ* 1867:203. *Bost m & s jour* 74:128, 1866.

STONE, HENRY OSGOOD, Salem, Mass (d/VIII-23 1888 @67) MD UPa 1844; AB Harvard 1841. *Bost m & s jour* 119:216, 1888. *Butler* 1878: 358.

STONE, JAMES, Phillipston, Mass (b/1783? d/XII-18-1857 @74) MD ? *Bost m & s jour* 57: 455, 1857.

STONE, JAMES H , Tappan, O (d/VI-7-1898 @67) MD Columbian 1889. *JAMA* 30: 1534, 1898. *Polk* 1886:769; 1896: 1214.

STONE, JAMES L , Roanoke, Va (d/VIII-17-1899) MD ? *JAMA* 33: 621, 1899. *Polk* 1890: 1131.

STONE, JAMES WINCHELL, Dorchester, Mass (d/VIII-22-1863 @40) MD Harvard 1847; AB 1843. *Bost m & s jour* 69: 88, 1863.

STONE, JOHN OSGOOD, NYC (b/II- -1813; d/VII-7-1876) MD Harvard 1836; AB 1833. *Med reg NY NJ Conn* 1876-77: 256-57. *Med rec med & surg* 11:404, 438, 470. *Med surg rep Phila* 35:40, 120, 1876.

STONE, JONATHAN COOLIDGE, West Farms NY (b/X-23-1826 Newburyport Mass; d/IV-8-1868) MD Bellevue 1863; AB Harvard 1848. *Phila med reg & dir* 1871:296. *Med reg NY NJ Conn* 1868: 335. *Bost m & s jour* ns1:265, 1868. *Med surg rep Phila* 18:376, 1868.

STONE, JOSEPH, Hardwick, Mass (b/XI-12-1789 Shrewsbury; d/VI-27-1849) Stud med w/Dr Flint of Shrewsbury. *Bost m&s j* 41:149-52, 289-95, 1849. *Tr AMA* 3:467, 1850.

STONE, OSCAR WHITNEY, Camden Me (b/I-10-1852 Milford; d/IV-30-1896 Boulder, Mont) MD Bowdoin 1878. *JAMA* 26: 995, 1896. *Tr Me M Assn* 12:425, 1896. *Polk* 1886: 424.

STONE, RALPH LANE, Norristown, Pa (d/XI-5-1886 @22) MD UPa 1885. *Med reg NY NJ Conn* 1887: 276.

STONE, ROBERT, NYC (d/III-7-1901 @64) MD CPSNY 1858. *Bost m & s jour* 144: 270, 1901. *Polk* 1886: 716 (Yonkers).

STONE, ROBERT KING, Washington, DC (b/1822; d/IV-23-1872) MD UPa 1845; AB Princeton 1842: AM 1846. *Tr AMA* 24:338-40, 1873. *Hist M S DC*:238-39. *K&B* III: 1173-74.

STONE, SELDON AUGUSTUS, Parkersburg & Monongah, WVa (b/II-25-1860 Vienna, WVa; d/III-30-1899) MD CPS Balto 1886; PhB Marietta. *Tr St Med Soc WVa* 1899:336-37. *JAMA* 32:845, 1899. *Polk* 1890: 1151.

STONE, SILAS EMLYN, CW-USA; Walpole, Mass (d/I 29-1887 @48) MD Harvard 1860. *Bost m & s jour* 116: 122, 124, 1887. *Harv in CW*: 261. *Butler* 1878: 358.

STONE, THOMAS M , Jasper, Tex (d/I-18-1892) <MD New Orl Sch Med 1869> *Tex cour-rec med* 9:191, 1892. *Daniel's Tex med jour* 7:295, 1891-92. *Polk* 1886: 888.

STONE, THOMAS NEWCOMB, Wellfleet, Mass 1844-75; Provincetown 1875- (b/V-30-1818; d/V-15-1876) MD Dartm'th 1844; AB Bowd'n 1840. *Bowd'n cat:* 1840.

STONE, THOMAS RITCHIE, Washington, DC (b/VII-18-1856/1857?; d/V-31/VI-1? 1902) MD UVt 1884. *Hist Med Soc DC:* 331: *Polk* 1886: 214.

STONE, WARREN, New Orleans (b/II-3-1808 St Albans, Vt; d/XII-6-1872) MD Berkshire 1830. *Tr AMA* 24: 341-44, 1873. *New Orl m&s j* ns22:769-88 1895. *Med rec* 8:46, 1873. *Tr Miss St Med Assn* 1873:150. *K&B* III:1174.

STONE, WARREN Jr, CW-CSA; New Orleans (b/1843; d/I-3-1883) MD Tulane 1867. *New Orl m & s jour* ns10: 639, 1883. *Butler* 1878: 295. *K&B* III: 1174.

STONE, WILLIAM CORLIDGE, Lakewood, NJ (b/II-21-1857 Brooklyn; d/II-5-1893) MD Bellevue 1880. *Med reg NY NJ Conn* 1893: 185-86.

STONE, WILLIAM NEWCOMB, Wellfleet, Mass (d/X 17-1898 @53) MD Harvard 1869. *Bost m & s jour* 139: 536, 1898. *Polk* 1896: 725.

STONE, WILLIAM PARKER, Sydnorsville, Va (b/1870 Franklin Co, Va; d/VII-29-1898) MD CPS Balto 1893. *Tr Med Soc Va* 1900: 324.

STONE, WILLIAM PAYSON, Burke, NY; USA (b/VII-29-1809 Reading, Vt; d/X-23-1872 @67) MD Dartmouth 1835. *Bost m & s jour* ns10:312, 1872.

STONER, ANDREW J , Jacksonville, Ill (d/XI-13 1901) MD Jefferson 1853; <MD St Louis Med Coll 1860> *Ill med jour* ns3:399, 1902. *Polk* 1896:416.

STONER, CHARLES E , Des Moines (d/X- -1901) MD

CPS Keokuk 1882. *Ill med jour* 3:346, 1901. *Tr Ia St Med Soc* 20:48–49, 1902; 21:450, 1903. *Polk* 1896: 521.

STONER, WILLIAM BRUCE, Sunbury, Pa (b/X–25–1845 Westminster, Md; d/I–9–1906 Clifton Spr, NY) <MD Edinburgh; MD Phila Coll M & S 1866> MD Ky Sch Med 1892. *Pa m j* 9:359, 637–38, 1905/06. *Flint* 1897: 837.

STONG, PHILIP, CW–USA (b/VIII–19–1843 Plymouth Mtg, Pa; d/XII–29–1881 Williston Twp) MD UPa 1864. *U Pa med alum CW*: 1864.

STOOKEY, LYMAN P , Belleville, Ill (d/VIII–2–1901 @37) MD Mo Med Coll 1872. *Ill med jour* ns3: 189, 1901. *JAMA* 37:461, 1901. *Polk* 1886: 255.

STORCK, CHARLES, Chicago (b/VI–9–1826 Baden, Gny; d/V–6–1898) MD Albany 1855. *JAMA* 30:1192, 1898. *Polk* 1890: 323.

STORCK, EDWARD, Buffalo (d/VII–26–1897 @66) MD U Mich 1854. *Buff m & s jour* 37:138 ff, 1897. *JAMA* 29: , 1897. *Butler* 1878: 538.

STORER, DAVID HUMPHREYS, Boston (b/III–26–1804 Portland, Me; d/IX–10–1891) MD Harvard 1825; AB Bowdoin 1822; LLD 1876. *JAMA* 17:533–34, 1891. *NW m j* 19:151, 1891. *Bost m&s j* 125:303, 308, 1891; 126:291, 313, 1892. *Atkinson* I:16. *K&B* III: 1174.

STORER, EBENEZER, NYC (b/VIII–20–1803 Portland, Me; d/V–20–1879) MD CPSNY 1825. *Med reg NY NJ Conn* 1880: 242. *Butler* 1878: 525.

STORER, JOHN W , Triadelphia, WVa to 1883; Elm Grove (b/IV–22–1830 Allegheny Co, Pa; d/by X–1–1897 Clearfield, Pa) MD Jefferson 1854; AB Wash'n & Jeff'n 1847. *Tr St M S WVa* 1898:216. *Butler* 1874: 821.

STORER, THOMAS RICHARD, Scenery Hill, Pa (d/XI 25–1903 @61) <MD Jefferson 1866> *Pa med jour* 7: 280, 1903/04. *Flint* 1897: 834.

STORMONT, DAVID WASSON, Grand View, Ill 1845–62; Topeka, Kans (b/IX–26–1820 Princeton, Ind; d/VIII–18–1887) MD UPa 1860; AB U Ind; AM. *Tr St Med Soc Kans* 2:519–22, 1888. *Atkinson* I:58.

STORROW, SAMUEL APPLETON, Washington, DC; USA 1861–? (b/Va; d/VII–12–1879 San Francisco; MD Jefferson 1852. *G. V. Henry*: 116. *Hist Med Soc DC*:259. *Med rec NY* 16: 118, 1879.

STORRS, MELANCHTHON, Hartford, Conn (b/1823? Mansfield; d/VI–9–1900) MD Yale 1853; AB 1852. *Bost m&s j* 142:674, 1900. *Proc Conn Med Soc* 1901:282–90. *Buff m&s j* 39:934, 1900. *JAMA* 34: 1574, 1900.

STORY, DYER, W Windsor Vt (b/178–?; d/1868? @80+) ng Dartmouth 1813. *Med surg rep Phila* 19:487, 1868.

STORY, GEORGE W , Cooper, Tex; Santa, Ala (d/IX–4 1905 @84) MD U Nashville 1855. *Tex st jour med* 1: 154, 1905/06. *Polk* 1886: 139.

STOUT, GEORGE W , Easton, Pa (b/III–6–1859; d/IV 12–1881) MD Jefferson 1881; att Lafayette. *Med bull med & surg* 3:115, 1881.

STOUT, SAMUEL HOLLINGSWORTH, Clarendon, Tex; CW–CSA (b/III–3–1822 Nashville; d/IX–18–1903) MD UPa 1848; AB U Nashville 1839. *So pract* 25:586–87, 1903. *U Pa med alum CW*: 1848. *Atkinson* I: 305. *Polk* 1896: 1425.

STOUT, THOMAS JEFFERSON, NYC (b/XI–24–1822 Phila; d/X–10–1878) MD UPa 1849. *Med reg NY NJ Conn* 1879: 200.

STOUT, WESSEL TEN BROECK, Princeton, NJ (d/II–26–1862) MD UPa 1846. *Med surg rep Phila* ns7:624, 1861/62.

STOVALL, JOHN THOMAS, Columbia, Ala (d/I–8–1889) MD ? *Tr M Assn St Ala* 1889: 229. *Polk* 1886:132.

STOVALL, JOSEPH BARNETT, CW–CSA (b/X–3–1838 Tally Ho, NC; d/XII–18–1863 Stovall) MD UPa 1861. *U Pa med alum CW*: 1861.

STOVALL, STEPHEN BENJAMIN, CW–CSA; Vienna, Ga (b/XII–6–1826 Lincolnton, Ga; d/X–10–1904) MD UPa 1848. *U Pa med alum CW*:1848. *Polk* 1886: 236.

STOVEL, DAVID, Detroit (d/V–1–1900 @61) <MD Toronto Med Coll & Detroit Med Coll> *JAMA* 34:1211, 1900. *Polk* 1886: 490.

STOVERING, WILLIAM LAWRENCE, Cleveland (d/III–3–1895) MD Wooster 1895. *JAMA* 24: 422, 1895. *Polk* 1890: 909.

STOWE, WILLIAM HARVEY, Wellfleet, Mass (d/X–17–1898 @53) MD Yale 1888. *JAMA* 31:1128, 1898.

STOWELL, ASHLEY LIVINGSTONE, Peru, Mass [?] (d/X–3–1891 @25) MD UVt 1889. *Med reg NY NJ Conn* 1892: 288.

STOWELL, DAVID PATHER, ?Waterville, Me (b/IX–22–1838; d/II–12–1903 or VIII–31–1904) MD UCNY 1862; ng Amherst 1861. *Polk* 1886: 429. *Amherst, Men of*: 1861.

STOWELL, LUTHER E , Peoria, Ill (d/VIII–26–1905 @30) MD ? *Ill med jour* 8:341, 1905.

STRACHAN, A RUSSELL, NYC (b/Scotl; d/III–1–1898) <MD Victoria U 1861> *JAMA* 30:624, 1898. *Polk* 1886: 694.

STRACHAN, W T , Lancaster, Pa (d/VII–23–1895 @ 65) MD ? *JAMA* 25:209, 1895.

STRAIT, JAMES LAWRENCE, CW–CSA (b/III–13–1831 Chester, SC; d/XI–16–1895 Cooksville, Miss) MD UPa 1858. *U Pa med alum CW*: 1858 suppl.

STRALEY [STRAHLEY], SIDNEY B , Newton, NJ (b/IX–28–1861 Huntsville; d/IV–15–1903) MD CPS Balto 1887. *Tr M S NJ* 1903:390–91.

STRANAHAN, DANIEL V , Warren, Pa (d/1892 @45) MD Buffalo 1872. *Buff m & s jour* 32: 60, 1892. *Butler* 1878: 734. *Off'l reg Pa phys* 1881–88: 388.

STRANG, ALBERT, Yorktown, NY (d/II– –1888) MD Bellevue 1867. *Med reg NY NJ Conn* 1888: 271. *Butler* 1878: 576.

STRANGEWALD, H , Nunana Valley, Hawaii (b/1829 Dresden, Gny; d/VIII–1–1899) <MD Vienna> *JAMA* 33: 493, 1899.

Spec. educ'l status abbrev. as: ***ng*** = college verified attendance without degree;

STRATTON, ALBERT GALLATIN, CW–USA; Philadelphia (b/IV–17–1845; d/XI–15–1904) MD UPa 1875. *UPa med alum CW*: 1875.

STRATTON, BENJAMIN HARRIS, Mt Holly, NJ (b/II 6–1804; d/XII–31–1875) MD UPa 1827; AB Princeton 1823; AM 1827. *Tr AMA* 27:655, 1876. *Tr Med Soc NJ* 1876:143–46.

STRAUSSER, SIMON, Philadelphia; Chicago (b/1833 Bavaria; d/IV–22–1886) MD Rush 1879. *JAMA* 7: 84, 1886.

STRAW, JACOB, Henniker, NH (b/1781? d/IX–13–1856 @75) ng Dartmouth 1816. *Bost m & s jour* 55:171, 1857.

STRAW, WILLIAM R , Vinita, Ind Terr (d/XI–21–1898) MD CPS Balto 1892. *JAMA* 31:1377, 1898. *Polk* 1896: 1545.

STRAWBRIDGE, JAMES DALE, CW–USA; Danville, Pa (b/IV–7 1824 Montour Co; d/VII–19–1890) MD UPa 1847; AB Princeton 1844; AM 1847; MD Jefferson 1875. *Tr Pa St M S* 1891: 218–19. *JAMA* 15: 232, 1890. *Jeff Coll & clin rec* 11:194, 1890. *Biogr dir Congr*.

STRAWN, BENJAMIN F , Philadelphia (d/IV–25–1868 @30) MD Jefferson 1862. *Med surg rep Phila* 18:398, 1868. *Phila med reg & dir* 1871: 293.

STRECKER, C F , E St Louis (d/XI–26–1894 @43) MD Am M C 1878. *JAMA* 23:878, 1894. *Polk* 1890: 328.

STREET, CHARLES CARROLL, Boston (d/V–17–1900 @64) MD Harvard 1861. *Bost m & s jour* 142:500, 1900. *Polk* 1896: 706.

STREET, SHERMAN S , Arkville, NY (d/IV–2–1897 @94) <MD Vt> *JAMA* 28:860, 1897. *Polk* 1886: 640.

STREETER, GEORGE DALLAS, Waco, Tex (b/1844 Tioga, Pa; d/XI–18–1904) MD Hahnemann Phila 1872. *Tr Am Inst Hom* 1905:838. *Polk* 1886: 896. Homeopath.

STREETER, JOHN WILLIAMS, Lake Forest, Ill (d/VI–4–1905 @64) MD Hahnemann Chic 1868. *Ill med jour* 7: 611, 1905. *Polk* 1886:272. Homeopath.

STREETER, JOSEPH HERMAN, Roxbury, Mass (b/VII–11–1820 Springfield; d/V–30–1891) MD Woodstock 1841; AB Norwich. *Bost m & s jour* 124:570, 1891. *Butler* 1878: 358.

STREETS, DAVID REESE, Bridgeton, NJ (d/VII–15 1906 @48) MD UPa 1880. *Pa med jour* 9:805, 1905/06.

STREW, WILLIAM WALLACE, CW–USA; NYC (d/II 7–1894) MD UCNY 1844. *Med reg NY NJ Conn* 1894: 249. *Butler* 1878: 525.

STRIBLING, FRANCIS TALIAFERRO, Staunton, Va (b/II–20–1810; d/IV–23–1874) MD UPa 1831. *Tr M S Va* 1874:55–56; 1875:102. *K&B* III:1177–1178.

STRICKER, JULIUS J , Portage, Pa (b/Prussia; d/VI–20 1904 @50) MD Jefferson 1878. *Pa m j* 8:336, 1904/05. *Polk* 1886: 831.

STRICKLAND, FRANKLIN BRAINARD, NYC (b/IV–11–1847 Vt; d/IX–22–1885) MD UCNY 1876. *Med reg NY NJ Conn* 1886: 254. *Butler* 1878: 525.

STRICKLAND, RIAL, Enfield, Conn (b/1814 Stafford Spr; d/1903) MD Albany 1839. *Pr Conn M S* 1905:75, 477–80. *Polk* 1896: 285.

STRINGFELLOW, JOHN HENRY, CW–USA; St Joseph, Mo (b/XI–4–1819 Raccoon Ford, Va; d/VII–24 1905) MD UPa 1845. *UPa med alum CW*:1845 suppl. *Polk* 1886:560.

STROBRIDGE, J G , ? (d/X–1–1878 Port Gibson, Miss) MD ? *Tr AMA* 30:885, 1879. *Med rec NY* 14:300, 1878.

STRONACH, JAMES WATSON, NYC (b/Scotl; d/I–23 1901) MD UCNY 1872. *Bost m & s jour* 144:126, 1901. *Polk* 1896: 1080.

STRONG, ADONIJAH, Honesdale, Pa (b/1800; d/XII–5 1879) MD "Med Coll Conn" [not confirmed Yale] *Med surg rep Phila* 41: 554, 1879.

STRONG, ALBERT BLISS, Chicago; Kankakee, Ill (b/V 22–1845 Galesburg; d/III–16–1900) MD Rush 1872; AB Kenyon 1868. *Chic med rec* 8:488–89, 1900. *Tr Ill St M S* 1899–1900: 589. *JAMA* 34:766, 1900. *Atkinson* I: 592. *Polk* 1896: 407.

STRONG, CHARLES G , Eau Claire Wis (d/III–3–1887) MD Buffalo 1882. *Tr Wis St Med Soc* 1891:357. *Polk* 1886: 953.

STRONG, CHARLES PRATT, Boston (b/XII–19–1855 Springfield, Mo; d/III–14–1893) MD Harvard 1881; AB 1876. *JAMA* 20:677–78, 1893. *Chic med rec* 5:62, 1893. *Bost m & s jour* 128:276, 303, 379, 402, 558, 1893.

STRONG, ELISHA HALL, CW–CSA; West Point, Miss (b/VII–28–1824 Lexington, Ga; d/X–6–1896) MD UPa 1846. *U Pa med alum CW*: 1846. *Polk* 1886: 534.

STRONG, FREDERICK EMERSON, Lancaster, Wis (d/XII–13–1898 @40) MD Harvard 1884. *JAMA* 31: 1542, 1898. *Polk* 1896: 1552.

STRONG, HENRY PARTRIDGE, CW–USA; Beloit, Wis (b/II–8–1832 Brownington, Vt; d/VI–30–1883) MD Castleton 1853. *Tr Wis St M S* 1883:123–25. *Atkinson* I: 107. *Butler* 1878: 867.

STRONG, HENRY TUNSTALL, NYC (d/XII–12–1876 @31) MD CPSNY 1868; stud med Paris; AB Williams 1865. *Med reg NY NJ Conn* 1877:207.

STRONG, JAMIN, Cleveland (d/I–28–1895 @69) MD Cleveland Med Coll 1849. *JAMA* 24:221, 1895. *Chic med rec* 8:255, 1895. *Med bull med & surg* 17:148, 1895.

STRONG, JOHN MASON, Charlotte, NC (d/III–16–1898) MD Jefferson 1847. *NC med jour* 41:307, 1898. *JAMA* 30:807, 1898. *Polk* 1896: 1121.

STRONG, JOHN THOMAS, Plainfield, Ind (d/IX–10 1895 @55) MD U Mich 1864; LLB NW Christ U 1864. *JAMA* 25: 510, 1895.

STRONG, MALTBY, Rochester, NY 1831–68 (b/XI–24 1796 Heath, Mass; d/VIII–5–1878) MD Bowdoin 1822; AB Yale 1819; ng Harvard. *Tr M S St NY* 1880: 453.

STRONG, PHINEAS HARMAN, Buffalo (b/VIII–6–1817 Pawlet, Vt; d/II–10–1890) MD Albany 1839; ng Castleton. *Buff m&s j* 29:497, 1890. *Tr M S St NY*: 457.

STRONG, SYLVESTER S , Saratoga, NY (d/II–1–1891

@78) MD UCNY 1855. *Bost m & s jour* 124: 176, 1891. *Butler* 1878: 576.

STRONG, WOODBRIDGE, Boston (b/1795? d/1861 @ 66) MD Yale 1818; AB 1814. *Bost m & s jour* 64:231–32, 1861. *Mass Med Soc cat* 1894.

STROTHER, TOBIAS CLARENCE, Canton Bend, Ala (d/V–8–1874) MD Tulane 1869; att U Ala 1864. *U Ala cat*: 210.

STROTHER, WILLIAM AUGUSTINE, CW–CSA; Albany, Ga (b/1839 Edgefield, SC; d/V–2–1896) MD UCNY 1861. *JAMA* 26: 995, 1896. *Polk* 1886: 224.

STROUD, WILLIAM DANIEL, Philadelphia (b/X–5–1825 Stroudsburg; d/IX–25–1883) MD UPa 1846; AB Haverford. *Tr CPP* cent vol: 268. *Med s rep Phila* 49: 420, 1883.

STROUP, WILSON W , Harrisburg, Pa (d/IX–30–1903 @55) MD UPa 1874. *Pa med jour* 7:280, 1903/04. *Flint* 1897: 804.

STROZER, LYCURGUS L , CW–CSA; Albany, Ga (d/1871) MD UCNY 1859. *UCNY cat*: 1859.

STRUBLE, HUGH McDONALD, Middletown, NJ (b/1852 Newton, NY; d/IV–30–1897) MD UPa 1875. *Bost m&s jour* 136:474, 1897. *JAMA* 28:955, 1897.

STRUBLE, WILLIAM McDANOLDS [sic], Trenton, NJ (b/1860 Branchville; d/VIII–28–1902) MD UPa 1885. *Tr M S NJ* 1903:388–89. *Polk* 1896: 950.

STRUDWICK, EDMUND CHARLES FOX, Hillsboro, NC (b/III–25–1802 Long Meadows; d/XI– –1879) MD UPa 1824. *NC m j* 5:129–36, 1880. *Med surg rep Phila* 41:550, 1879. *Tr M S St NC* 1880: 15. *K&B* III:1178–79.

STRUNK, EDWARD P , Brewster, NY (d/III–12–1897) MD NY Homeop 1874. *Tr Am Inst Hom* 1897:63. *No Am jour hom* 45:407, 1897. *Polk* 1886:642. Homeopath.

STRYKER, JACOB R [or K], Califon, NJ (d/IX–8–1862 @41) MD UCNY 1849. *Tr M S NJ* 1872: 195–96.

STUART, ABSALOM BAYLIS, CW–USA; W Hampton Mass; Macomb Ill; Winona Minn; Santa Barbara Cal (b/VIII–27 1830 Williamsburgh Pa; d/VII–30–1887) MD Berkshire 1856; MD Bellevue 1866. *JAMA* 10:410–11, 1888. *Tr Minn St M S* 1887:182–84; 1896:149. *Atkinson* I:232–33. *Butler* 1878: 395.

STUART, EDWARD PAYSON, Penn Yan NY (b/1851; d/VI–23–1901) MD UCNY 1883. *JAMA* 37:126, 1901.

STUART, JAMES CLARK, Syracuse (b/V–1–1812 Andover, Mass; d/III–24 or 31–1870) MD Berkshire 1837; AB Yale 1831, ng Amherst 1830. *Phila med reg & dir* 1871: 304.

STUART, JOHN R , Sussex Co, NJ (b/III–11–1809 Newton; d/I–15–1873) Lic M S NJ 1831; att CPSNY; <att Rutgers Coll> *Tr AMA* 24: 365–66, 1873. *Tr M S NJ* 1873:116–18. *Med surg rep Phila* 28:104, 1873.

STUCKSLAGER, CYRUS R , CW–USA; McKeesport, Pa (d/1904 @75) MD Jefferson 1856. *Pa med jour* 8:336, 1904/05. *Flint* 1897: 808.

STUDDIFORD, JAMES HERVEY, Lambertville NJ (b/IX–12–1832; d/III–23–1870) MD UCNY 1854; AB Princeton 1852; AM 1855. *Tr AMA* 21:469, 1870; 23: 593–94, 1872. *Tr M S NJ* 1870:97–99; 1872:144–46. *Phila med reg & dir* 1871: 304.

STUDDIFORD, THEODORE HENRY, CW–USA; Hunterdon, NJ (b/I–17–1842; d/IV–15–1882 Lambertville) MD UCNY 1864; Hon AM Princeton 1864. *Tr M S NJ* 1882–83:191–92. *Butler* 1878: 477.

STUDLEY, WILLIAM HARRISON, CW–USA; NYC (d/VII–14–1882) MD CPSNY 1860; AB Trinity Conn 1850; AM 1853. *Med reg NY NJ Conn* 1883: 235.

STUDY, JAMES MADISON, CW–USA; Richmond, Ind (d/1866 @31) MD CPSNY 1866; MD Med Coll Ohio 1859. *Tr AMA* 18:348, 1867.

STULL, THEODORE W , Marengo, Ill (b/1833 Smithford, Pa; d/V–8–1879) MD Rush 1861. *Chic med jour* 39:219–20, 1879. *Med surg rep Phila* 41:154, 1879.

STURDIVANT, MARSHALL K , Avinger, Tex (d/IV–26–1906) MD Tulane 1870. *Tex st jour med* 2:100, 1906.

STURGEON, WILLIAM H , Uniontown, Pa (b/I–24 1826; d/X–15–1900) Lic 20 yrs pract; <MD Jefferson 1849> *Pa med jour* 4:329, 1900/01. *Atkinson* I:550. *Off'l Reg Pa phys* 1881–88: 180.

STURGIS, RUSSELL Jr, Boston (b/XII–16–1856; d/VII–17–1899) MD Harvard 1881; AB 1878. *Bost m&s j* 141:76, 99, 1899. *JAMA* 33:302, 1899. *Polk* 1896:706.

STURTEVANT, EDWARD LEWIS, Framington, Mass 1887– (b/I–23–1842 Boston; d/VII–20–1898) MD Harvard 1866; AB Bowdoin 1864. *JAMA* 31:366, 1898.

STUTSMAN, SAMUEL H , Burlington, Ia (b/X–25–1836 Morgan Co, Ind; d/IV–3–1891) MD CPS Keokuk 1863. *Tr Iowa St Med Soc* 1892: 227. *Polk* 1886: 352.

STYER, ALBANUS, Ambler, Pa (d/VII–1–1902) MD Jefferson 1849. *Pa m j* 6:262, 1902/03. *Flint* 1897: 795.

STYER, CHARLES, CW–USA; Philadelphia (b/V–3–1840 Norristown; d/VII–6–1896) MD UPa 1862. *JAMA* 27:165, 1896. *U Pa m alum CW*:1862. *Polk* 1896: 1319.

STYLES, THOMAS WRIGHT, Stephensville, Tex (b/Laurens Dist SC; d/VII–16–1893 @35) MD Tulane 1883. *Tex med jour* 9:143, 1893–94. *Polk* 1890: 1088.

SUCKLEY, GEORGE, NYC; USA 1853–56; 1861–65 (b/IX–30–1830; d/VII–30–1869) MD CPSNY 1851. *Tr AMA* 21:445, 1870. *Nat med jour* 1:302, 1870/71. *Med reg NY NJ Conn* 1870:331. *K&B* III:1180.

SUDDARDS, JAMES, USN 1849–75 (b/II–27–1827 Hull Engl; d/VIII–31–1888 Atlantic City) MD UPa 1847; AB 1844; AM 1847. *Med reg NY NJ Conn* 1889: 287. *Butler* 1878: ix.

SUDDUTH, JAMES McCREARY, Bloomington, Ill (d/IX–20–1895 @68 Colton, Cal) MD Rush 1854. *JAMA* 25: 554, 1895.

von SUESSMILCH, FREDERICK L , Delavan, Wis (b/Hanover, Gny; d/II–10–1898 @77) <MD Dresden 1848> *JAMA* 30:448, 1898. *Polk* 1896: 1547.

SUGGETT, JAMES M , Flora, Ill (d/X–9–1900) MD

 Spec. educ'l status abbrev. as: ***ng*** = college verified attendance without degree;

Transylv 1847. *Tr Ill M S* 1900: 286. *Polk* 1890: 331.

SULLARD, A E, Franklin, NY (d/XI-19-1898 @79) MD Albany 1844. *JAMA* 31:1377, 1898. *Polk* 1890:790.

SULLIVAN, DANIEL HENRY, Pawtucket, RI (b/1870 Providence; d/I- -1897) MD CPS Balto 1893. *Tr RI M S* 5:499, 1894-98. *Polk* 1896: 1349.

SULLIVAN, GEORGE ROBERT, Flemington, NJ (b/1836 Md; d/VIII-29-1893) MD UMd 1859. *Tr Med Soc NJ* 1894:277-78. *Med reg NY NJ Conn* 1894: 250. *JAMA* 21:434, 1893. *Butler* 1878: 476.

SULLIVAN, JAMES FRANCIS, CW-USA; San Francisco (b/V-18 1838 Roxbury, Mass; d/I-24-1899) MD Harvard 1861. *JAMA* 32:324, 1899. *Harvard in CW*: 268. *Polk* 1896: 239.

SULLIVAN, JAMES JOSEPH, Lowell, Mass (d/VIII-11 1885 @28) MD UCNY 1879. *Bost m&s j* 113:192, 1885.

SULLIVAN, JOHN JOSEPH, NYC (d/III-26-1899 @ 42) MD UCNY 1886. *JAMA* 32: 787, 1899. *Polk* 1896: 1080.

SULLIVAN, JOHN LANGDON, Malden, Mass (b/III-8 1827 Keene, NH; d/IX-5-1900) MD Harvard 1849. *Bost m&s j* 143:276, 1900. *Atkinson* I: 94. *Polk* 1896: 717.

SULLIVAN, JOHN McKEW, Baltimore (b/1828 Irel'd; d/IV-27-1881) MD UMd 1861. *Med annals Md:* 586-87. *Butler* 1874: 316.

SULLIVAN, RICHARD HENRY, Brooklyn (d/III-27 1905 @50) MD UCNY 1883. *Bost m & s jour* 152: 416, 1905. *Polk* 1896: 1004.

SULLIVAN, TIMOTHY, Lawrence, Mass (d/III-2-1891 @58) MD UCNY 1868. *Bost m & s jour* 124:275, 1891. *Polk* 1886: 468.

SULOFF, SAMUEL ANGHEY, Patterson, Pa (d/XI-23 1902 @45) MD Rush 1882. *Pa med jour* 6:262, 1902/03. *Flint* 1897: 812.

SUMAN, WILLIAM, Madison Co, Ind 38 yrs; Anderson Co 22 yrs (b/VIII-27-1829; d/IX-19-1898) Att med lect Cincinnati; ng Bellevue 1867-68. *Tr Ind St M S* 1899: 393. Kemper's *Indiana*: 223.

SUMMERELL [SUMMERILL], JOSEPH JOHN, Salisbury, NC (b/XI-1 or 13-1819 Halifax Co; d/XII-17-1893) MD UPa 1844; AB UNC 1842. *Tr M S St NC* 1894: 194-95. *Atkinson* I: 573. *Butler* 1878: 599.

SUMMERS, OSA RAY, Middletown, Ind (b/IX-12-1874; d/VI-8-1904) <MD Ind Med Coll 1897> *Tr Ind St Med Soc* 1905: 458. Kemper's *Indiana*: 347.

SUMMERS, REUBEN, Martinsburg WVa (b/1801 Montgomery Co, Md; d/XII-29-1866) MD UMd 1824. *Tr AMA* 340-41, 1867. *Med annals Md:* 587.

SUMMERS, THOMAS OSMOND, St Louis, Mo (d/VI-13-1899 @ c47) MD U Nashvl 1871; MD U London 1875; AB U Ala 1864; AB Southern U Greensboro. *JAMA* 32:1460, 1899. *Nashvl j m&s* 86:45, 1899. *Polk* 1896: 879.

SUMNER, ALLEN MELANCHTHON, Boston (b/I-31-1844; d/V-25-1901) MD Harvard 1868; BS 1865. *Bost m&s j* 144: 540, 568, 1901. *Polk* 1896: 706.

SUMNER, CHARLES FLETCHER, Bolton, Conn (b/III 28-1817 Gilead or Hebron; d/VII-12-1904) MD Fairfield 1840. *Proc Conn Med Soc* 1905:75-76, 481-83. *Atkinson* I:373. *Polk* 1893: 246.

SUMNER, FREDERICK AUGUSTUS, Charlestown, NH (d/X-10-1873 @71 Boston) MD Harvard 1827; AB 1823. *Med surg rep Phila* 29:324, 1873.

SUMNER, GEORGE, Hartford, Conn (b/XII-13-1794 Pomfret; d/II-20-1855) MD UPa 1817. *Proc Conn Med Soc* 1855: 53.

SUMNER, JEANETTE JUDSON, Washington, DC (b/XI-15-1846 Constantine, Mich; d/XII-12-1906) MD Wom M C Pa 1883. *Hist M S DC:*340. *Polk* 1896:214.

SUPLEE, WILLIAM A, Philadelphia (d/IV-19-1869) MD UPa 1867. *Phila med reg & dir* 1871: 294. *Med surg rep Phila* 20:346, 1869.

SUTER, ALLEN [ALEXANDER] F, USA 1835- (b/DC; d/XII-17-1847) MD Columbian 1832. *Med annals Md:* 587. *Heitman.*

SUTHERLAND, CHARLES, USA 1852-93; Washington, DC (b/V-29-1830 Philadelphia ; d/V-10-1895) MD Jefferson 1849. *Bost m & s jour* 132:504, 1895. *K&B* II: 1117. *JAMA* 24:776, 1895. *Heitman.*

SUTHERLAND, DONALD EGBERT, Span-Amer War-USA; Bay City, Mich (d/I-25-1904 Detroit) MD CPS Chic. *JAMA* 42: 387, 1904.

SUTHERLAND, JOSEPH H, Niagara Falls, NY (b/X 18-1840; d/VI-18-1900) MD ?NY Eclectic 1867. *Flint* 1897: 688. *Buff m & s jour* 39:932-33, 1900.

SUTHERLAND, LEWIS W, Pittsburgh (d/XI-12-1904 @73) MD Albany 1855. *Pa med jour* 8:336, 1904/05. *Flint* 1897: 831.

SUTPHEN [SUTPHIN], JOHN C, Plainfield, NJ (b/1836 Somerset Co; d/IV-13-1878) MD UPa 1859; AB Princeton 1856. *Tr M S NJ* 1878: 208-09. *Med rec* 13: 455, 1878.

SUTPHEN, REUBEN MORRIS, Newark (b/Princeton; d/IX-3-1902 @83) MD UCNY 1847. *Bost m & s j* 147: 312, 1902. *Tr M S NJ* 1903:387-88. *Polk* 1896:644.

SUTTON, EMMA FRANCES, Providence, RI (b/VI-30 1850 Seekonk, Mass; d/VI-29-1892) MD Woman's M C Pa 1886. *Tr RI M S* 4:489, 1889-93. *Polk* 1890: 1028.

SUTTON, GEORGE, Aurora, Ind (b/VI-16-1812 London, Engl; d/VI-13-1886) MD M C Ohio 1836. *JAMA* 6:56, 1886. *K&B* III:1180-81. *Butler* 1878: 221.

SUTTON, GEORGE LEMUEL [SAMUEL], Massena, NY (b/Louisville, NY; d/IX-6-1888) MD CPSNY 1859. *Tr M S St NY* 11:741 ff, 1894. *Polk* 1886: 667.

SUTTON, JAMES A, Argos, Ind (b/V-1-1840 Starke Co, O; d/VI-12-1893) ng Med Coll Ohio. *Tr Ind St M S* 1894: 216. *Butler* 1878: 221.

SUTTON, RHODES STANSBURY, USA 1863-65, 1898; Pittsburgh (b/VII-8-1841; d/IV-21-1906) MD UPa 1865; AB Wash & Jeff 1862. *U Pa med alum CW*:

1865. *Polk* 1886: 830.

SUTTON, RICHARD E , Rome, NY (d/XI-10-1897) MD UMd 1851. *JAMA* 29:1129, 1897. *Polk* 1886: 706.

SUTTON, WILLIAM, NYC (b/Kent, Engl; d/VI-20-1884 @70) MD ? *Med reg NY NJ Conn* 1886: 254. *Med surg rep Phila* 51:28, 1884.

SUTTON, WILLIAM H , Dallas (b/Louisville; d/XI-23-1895) MD U Louisville 1862. *Tex med jour* 11:332-33, 1895-96. *Tex med news* 5:88, 1895-96. *Polk* 1890:1075.

SUTTON, WILLIAM THOMAS Jr, CW-CSA; Norfolk, Va (b/III-5-1839 Elmwood, NC; d/II-7-1899) MD UPa 1860; AB UNC 1850. *U Pa med alum CW*: 1860. *Polk* 1886: 923.

SUTTON, WILLIS E , Aurora, Ind (b/VI-2-1848; d/II-24-1879) MD Med Coll Ohio 1872; <MD Jefferson 1873> *Tr AMA* 30:834-35, 1879. *Tr Ind St M S* 1880: 242-43. Kemper's *Indiana*: 347.

SWALLOW, EDWARD EMERSON, Waltham, Mass (d/XII-31-1887 @34 Wilmington, NC) MD Jefferson 1880; AB Yale 1874. *Bost m & s jour* 118:28, 1888.

SWALLOW, FRANK LEWIS, Pittsburgh (d/XI-17-1903 @27 Manor, Pa) MD UPa 1900. *Pa med jour* 7: 280, 1903/04.

SWALLOW, GEORGE CLINTON, Kansas City Mo; Evanston, Ill (b/XI-17-1817 Buckfield, Me; d/IV-21-1899) MD M C Mo 1869; AB Bowdoin 1843. *Bowdoin cat*: 1843.

SWALM, SAMUEL J , Brooklyn (b/XII-30-1808 Montgomery, NY; d/VIII-29-1872) Hon MD Regents St U NY 1856. *Med reg NY NJ Conn* 1873: 352.

SWAN, CALEB, Easton, Mass (d/III-19-1870 @75) MD ? AB Harvard 1814. *Phila med reg & dir* 1871: 304.

SWAN, DANIEL, Medford, Mass (d/XII-5-1864 @83) MD ? AB Harvard 1803. *Bost m & s jour* 71:408, 1864.

SWAN, GEORGE FRANCIS, NYC (d/XI-5-1901) MD Bellevue 1899; AB. *Bost m & s jour* 145: 556, 1901. *Polk* 1896: 1080.

SWAN, LYMAN L, RI (b/XII-16-1838 Smithfield; d/IX 21-1872) MD LICH 1864 *Tr RI M S* 1:402-03 1859-77.

SWAN, SAMUEL, NYC; Montgomery, Ala (b/VII-4-1815 Medford, Mass; d/X-18-1893) MD Hahnemann Phila 1867. *Hahn mo* 29:82, 1894. *No Am j hom* 41: , 1893. Homeopath.

SWAN, SAMUEL M, Johnstown Pa (d/VII-23-1898 @ 68) MD Jeff'n 1854. *JAMA* 31:314, 1898. *Polk* 1886:803.

SWAN, WILLIAM EDWARD, NYC; Saratoga Spr (d/II 4-1906) MD CPSNY 1890. *Bost m & s jour* 154:200, 1906. *Polk* 1896: 1098.

SWANN, JOHN, Wilmington, NC (d/III-11-1870 @52) ng Castleton 1846. *Phila med reg & dir* 1871: 304. *Tr AMA* 21: 485, 1870.

SWANSTON, WILLIAM EDWARD, Devil's Lake Mo (d/X-14-1898) MD Wooster 1883 *JAMA* 31:1066, 1898.

SWARTS, DAVID J , Beaver Co, Okla (b/VI-30-1832 Ashland Co, O; d/III-3-1905) MD M C Ohio 1860. *Tr Ind St M S* 1905:459. *Polk* 1896: 458.

SWARTWOUT, LEANDER, Prospect, NY (d/III-10-1904 @61) MD Albany 1880. *Tr M S St NY* 1904:[420]. *Polk* 1886: 703.

SWARTZ, GEORGE NEUCHOMER, Pen Argyl, Pa (b/Lehigh Gap; d/V-23-1906 @55) MD Bellevue 1875; MD Jeff'n 1876. *Pa m j* 10:170, 1906/07. *Flint* 1897: 12.

SWARTZWELDER, ADAM CLARKE, USA 1861-67; Waco, Tex (b/Lancaster, Pa; d/III-5-1881) MD UPa 1845. *U Pa med alum CW*: 1845.

SWASEY, CHARLES LAMSON, New Bedford, Mass (b/1815 Limerick; d/XI-24-1888 @73) MD Bowdoin 1838. *Bost m & s jour* 119:640, 1888; 121:644, 1889. *Butler* 1878: 358.

SWASEY, H A , ? (d/IX-18-1878 Tangipahoa, La) MD ? *Tr AMA* 30: 885, 1879.

SWASEY, WILLIAM, Limerick, Me (b/VIII-25-1805; d/XII-26-1883) MD Bowdoin 1828. *Tr Me Med Assoc* 1884:368. *Atkinson* I:521-22. *Butler* 1878: 311.

SWAVING, JOHN CHRISTIAN G , Pottsville, Pa (d/XI 26-1901 @80) <MD Giessen 1849> *Pa med jour* 5:144, 296, 1901/02. *Butler* 1878: 735.

SWAYNE, CALEB, West Chester, Pa (b/VII-10-1827; d/X-20-1859) MD UPa 1852. *Tr Pa St M S* 1862: 58-59.

SWEARINGEN, RICHARD MONTGOMERY, Austin, Tex (b/IX-26-1838 Noxubee Co, Miss; d/VIII-7-1898) MD New Orl Sch Med 1867; Hon MD Louisville 1887. *Tex med jour* 14:144-48, 1898-99. *New Orl m & s jour* 51:170, 1898. *JAMA* 3:427, 1898. *Polk* 1890: 1069.

SWEAT, JOHN B , Parsonfield, Me (d/XI-21-1856 @30) MD UCNY 1847. *Bost m & s jour* 55:435, 1857.

SWEAT, MOSES, Parsonfield, Me 66 yrs (b/III-18-1788 Portland; d/VIII-25-1865) MD Bowdoin 1823. *Med s rep Phila* 13:166, 1865. *Bost m & s jour* 73:108, 1865. *K&B* III: 1180-81.

SWEAT, WILLIAM, Hollis, Me (b/X-16-1794 Portland; d/III-17-1880) ng Dartmouth 1826. *Tr Me Med Assoc* 1883: 158-60.

SWEAT, WILLIAM WEDGWOOD, New Bedford, Mass 1845-50; Portland, Me 1850-60; Mattapoisett Mass 1860 (b/1820 Parsonfield; d/VII-12-1872) MD Jefferson 1842; ng Bowdoin 1840. *Bowdoin cat*: 1840.

SWEENEY, GEORGE ALPHONSO, Chester Pa (d/VIII 7-1901) MD UPa 1898. *Pa med jour* 5:296, 1901/02.

SWEENEY, JAMES, Brooklyn (b/Irel'd; d/II-18-1892 @ 56) MD Albany 1859. *Med reg NY NJ Conn* 1892:288. *JAMA* 18:310, 1892. *Bost m & s jour* 126:204, 1892. *Butler* 1878: 535.

SWEET, RICHARD FOSTER, Norton, Mass (b/III-11-1801; d/III-21-1841) <MD "Boston Med Coll" 1827> AB Brown 1824. *Brown hist cat*: 1824.

SWEETSER, WILLIAM, NYC (b/IX-8-1797 Boston; d/X-13-1875) MD Harvard 1818: AB 1815. *Med reg NY NJ Conn* 1876: 257. *K&B* III: 1182.

SWENEY [SWEENEY], WILLIAM WILSON, Red

 Spec. educ'l status abbrev. as: ***ng*** = college verified attendance without degree;

Wing, Minn (b/XII-18-1818 Wilson, Pa; d/VIII-12 1882) MD Rush 1857. *JAMA* 2:26, 1884. *Tr Minn St Med Soc* 1882:288-89; 1883:288-89. *Atkinson* I: 178. *Butler* 1878: 395.

SWETT [SWEET], GEORGE JAY, CW-USN; Buffalo (b/1832; d/ VIII-12-1868) MD UCNY 1854. *Buff m & s jour* 7:79, 1868.

SWETT, GEORGE WOODBURY, Jamaica Plain, NY (d/1869 @23 Bonn, Gny or Jamaica Plain) MD Harvard 1868; AB 1865; AM 1869. *Phila m reg & dir* 1871: 301. *Med s rep Phila* 21:170, 1869. *Bost m&s j* ns4: 15, 1869.

SWETT, JOHN APPLETON, NYC (b/XII-3-1808 Boston; d/IX-18-1854) MD Harvard 1831; AB 1828. *Buff m&s j* 10:383, 1854. *Bost m&s j* 51:486, 1854. *Nashvl j m&s* 7:436, 1854. *Phila m reg & dir* 3(6):111-12, 1854. *K&B* III: 1182.

SWETT [SWEET], JOHN LANGDON, Newport NH (b/ II-17-1810 Claremont; d/IV-30-1900) MD Jeff'n 1836. *Tr NH M S* 1900:303-09. *Atkinson* I:55. *Polk* 1890: 711.

SWETT, JOSEPH BENJAMIN Jr, Albany, NY (d/X-3-1897 @29) MD Albany 1893. *JAMA* 29:817, 1897.

SWETT, RICHARD LEWIS, Brunswick, Me (b/IX-5-1858; d/XII-26-1884) ng CPSNY 1884; AB Bowdoin 1880; AM 1884. *Bowdoin cat*: 1880.

SWETT, SAMUEL BOURNE, Jamaica Plain, Mass (b/ 1810; d/XII-6-1890) MD Jefferson 1834. *JAMA* 15: 915, 1890. *Bost m&s j* 123:580, 1890. *Polk* 1886: 467.

SWETTING, GEORGE RODNEY, Clinton, NY; Berlin, Wis 1855- (b/XII-1-1819 Westmoreland, NY; d/V-30 1866) ng Buffalo & Harvard. *Med invest* 3:132, 1866? *Cleave*. Homeopath.

SWIFT, EARL, Mansfield, Conn (b/IV-8-1784; d/VI-14 1869) Hon MD Yale 1830?; AB 1805; lic 1808. *Proc Conn Med Soc* 3:413-14, 1870.

SWIFT, EDWARD, Easton, Pa (b/I-15-1805 Bustleton; d/XI-6-1869) MD UPa 1826. *Tr Pa St M S* 1870: 144.

SWIFT, EDWARD CLEMENT, CW-USA; Easton, Pa (b/I-30-1842; d/IX-23-1903) MD UPa 1868. MD UPa 1868. *Pa med jour* 7:280, 1903/04. *U Pa med alum CW*: 1868. *Flint* 1897: 801.

SWIFT, EDWIN DWIGHT, Hamden, Conn (b/V-8-1828 Cornwall, Conn; d/IV-19-1901) MD UCNY 1849. *Proc Conn Med Soc* 1902:431-32. *Polk* 1896: 279.

SWIFT, FOSTER, CW-USA; NYC; Geneva, NY (b/X-31-1833; d/ V-10-1875 Santa Cruz, WI) MD CPSNY 1857; AB Harvard 1854; AM 1857; AB Geneva 1852; AM 1855. *Med reg NY NJ Conn* 1875:204. *Med rec* 10:384, 704, 1875. *Harvard in CW*: 76.

SWIFT, GEORGE BAKER, Manchester, NH; Lawrence, Mass (b/VII-30-1806 Andover; d/II-15-1872 Nyack, NY) MD Harvard 1830; ng Bowdoin 1825-26. *Bowdoin cat*: 1829.

SWIFT [SWEET], GRIFFIN, Fairfield, NY (b/III-13 1813 Norway, NY; d/IV-22-1879) MD Fairfield 1839; att Jefferson 1 course 1841? *Tr M S St NY* 1880: 456-57.

SWIFT, JOHN MARCUS, Northville, Mich (d/VIII-30 1897 @65) MD Rush 1864; MD Ecl Med Inst Cinc 1854. *JAMA* 29:55, 606, 1897. *Polk* 1886: 500.

SWIFT, LAWRENCE CHEW, Pittsfield, Mass (b/Geneva, NY; d/VI-1-1905) MD CPSNY 1878. *Bost m & s jour* 152:679, 680, 1905. *Polk* 1896: 721.

SWIFT, SAMUEL, Yonkers, NY (b/Brooklyn; d/VII-29-1896) MD CPSNY 1872; AB Yale 1868 *Bost m&s j* 135: 149-50, 1896. *Tr M S St NY* 1897:479. *Polk* 1886: 716.

SWIFT, THOMAS DELANO, NYC (b/Geneva NY; d/III 3-1888 @34) MD CPSNY 1879; AB Rutgers 1875; AM 1878. *Med reg NY NJ Conn* 1888: 271. *Polk* 1886: 694.

SWIFT, WILLIAM, Brooklyn; USN 1813-61 (b/1779? d/XII-27-1864 @85) MD Harvard 1812; AB 1809. *Med surg rep Phila* 12:236, 1864/65. *Nat med jour* 1:302, 1870/71. *Callahan*.

SWIFT, WILLIAM, Brooklyn (b/V-6-1819 St Albans, Vt; d/IV-5-1885) MD CPSNY 1843. *Med reg NY NJ Conn* 1885: 245. *Med surg rep Phila* 52:512, 1885. *Butler* 1878: 535.

SWILER, WILLIAM E , Mechanicsburg, Pa (d/III-8-1906 @73) MD Jefferson 1857. *Pa med jour* 9:523, 1905/06. *Flint* 1897: 809.

SWINBURNE, JOHN, CW-USA; Albany, NY (b/V-30-1820 Deer River; d/III-28-1889) MD Albany 1846. *Med reg NY NJ Conn* 1889: 287. *Bost m & s jour* 120:345, 1889. *Atkinson* I: 668. *K&B* III: 1184.

SWINBURNE, RALPH ERSKINE, NYC (b/XII-27-1853 Rouse's Point, NY; d/II-14-1897) MD Bellevue 1877. *JAMA* 28:429, 1897. *Polk* 1896: 1080.

SWING, CHARLES, Sharpstown, NJ (d/I-4-1860) MD UPa 1815. *Med surg rep Phila* ns3:490, 1859/60.

SWINGLEY, FREDERICK, Bucyrus, O (d/VI-14-1900 @92) MD Med Coll Ohio 1841. *JAMA* 34:1676, 1900.

SWINNEY, JOHN GILLETTE, CW-USA; Smyrna, Del (d/XII-27-1894 @50 Shiloh or Bridgeton, NJ) MD Hahnemann Phila 1872. *King* I:273. Homeopath.

SWISHER, WILLIAM FESTUS, Woodburn, Ia (d/VI-23-1898) MD U Md 1892. *JAMA* 31:39, 1898. *Polk* 1896:543.

SWOPE, JOHN, Taneytown, Md (b/VIII-16-1797; d/IV--1870) MD UMd 1821. *Med annals Md:* 587.

SWOPE, SAMUEL, Taneytown Md (b/XI-21-1806; d/ 1897) MD UMd 1830. *Med ann Md*:587. *Polk* 1886:446.

SYDNOR, CHARLES W , CW-CSA; Strasburg, Va (d/ V-11-1900) <MD CPS Baltimore 1881> *Tr MS Va* 1900:335. *JAMA* 34:1356, 1900. *Polk* 1886: 927.

SYKES, ANDREW JACKSON, Courtland, Ala (d/IV-8-1887) MD U Louisville 1851. *Tr M Assn St Ala* 1887: 306. *Polk* 1886: 132.

SYKES, FRANCIS WINFIELD, Courtland & Decatur, Ala (b/IV-19-1816 Chatham Co, NC; d/I-26-1883) MD Transylvania 1840. *Tr M Assn St Ala* 1883:243.

SYKES, LUCIAN MELVILLE, Muldon, Miss (b/V-4-1838 Decatur Ala; d/VII-16-1879) MD UCNY 1866. *Tr*

Miss St M Assn 1880:174–5 *Med s rep Phil*41:132 1879.

SYKES, WILLIAM EDMUNDS, CW–CSA (b/I–28–1835 Decatur, Ala; d/X–27–1864 Decatur) MD UPa 1855. *U Pa med alum CW*: 1855.

SYKES, WILLIAM H, Plymouth O (d/IX–20–1898) MD Clevel'd M C 1866. *JAMA* 31:872, 1898. *Polk* 1886:765.

SYLVESTER, A A, Columbia, SC (d/IX–11–1898 @64) MD U Nashvl 1861 *JAMA* 31:742 1898. *Polk* 1896:1360.

SYLVESTER, GEORGE, Washington DC (d/1879?) MD Georget'n 1864. *Hist Med Soc DC:* 270. *Butler* 1874: 95.

TABB, ROBERT BRUCE, CW–CSA; Indian Crk, Va (b/VIII–10–? Elizabeth City;d/XI–12–1906 E Falls Church) MD UPa 1855. *U Pa m alum CW*: 1855. *Polk* 1886: 919.

TABB, SHERRARD RUTHERFORD, US Marine Hosp Serv (d/IV–30–1900 @30?) MD UVa 1892. *Tr M S Va* 1900: 335.

TABER, CHARLES R, CW–CSA; Fort Motte SC (b/1837 Charleston; d/I–27–1898) MD M C SC 1860; stud Bellevue. *JAMA* 30:891, 1898. *Waring* II: 307. *Polk* 1896: 1361.

TABER, HIRAM, Marilla, NY (b/1827? d/V–8–1873 @ 46) MD Buffalo 1852. *Buff m & s jour* 12:396–97, 1873.

TADLOCK, ROBERT E LEE, La Crosse, Wis (d/III–15 1906 @38) MD CPS Keokuk 1896. *Ill m j* 9:464, 1906.

TAFT, MARCUS L, NYC (b/1821; d/II–8–1850 @29) MD UCNY 1845. *Tr AMA* 3: 467, 1850.

TAGERT [TAGGART], ADELBERT HUGH, Chicago (b/X–2–1845 Hinesburgh, Vt; d/V–27–1903) MD UVt 1866. *Chic med rec* 24:448, 1903. *Flint* 1897: 269.

TAGERT, ALONZO D, Chicago (d/VI–16–1897) MD U Vt 1866. *Chic m rec* 13:54, 1897. *JAMA* 28: 1252, 1897. *Flint* 1897: 269.

TAGGART, C T, Sullivan, Ill (b/1847? d/X–28–1904 @57) MD CPS Indianapolis 1886. *Ill m j* 7:126, 1905. *Polk* 1896:413.

TAGGART, CHARLES, Jersey City (b/V–14–1820 Ireland; d/IX–15–1867) MD Jefferson 1854; <MD Edinburgh 1841> *Med surg rep Phila* 17:281, 1867. *Tr AMA* 19:422–23, 1868. *Med reg NY NJ Conn* 1868: 336–37.

TAGGART, CHARLES JAMES, Beloit, Wis (b/1824; d/1873 or 1875) MD CPSNY 1860. *Tr AMA* 25:528–30, 1874; 29:770–71, 1878.

TAGGART, GRAY, Galesburgh, Ill (d/IV–2–1899 @33) MD NWU 1894. *Tr Ill St M S* 1899: 21. *JAMA* 32: 787, 1899. *Polk* 1896: 421.

TAGGART, SAMUEL CHILDS, Charlestown, Ind (b/1828 Lexington, Ky; d/III–1901) MD U Louisville 1851. *Tr Ind St Med Soc* 1901: 500. *Polk* 1896: 462.

TAGGART, WILLIAM HEMBEL, Philadelphia; CW–USA 1861–63; USN 1864–65 (b/VII–15–1830 Winchester, Va; d/IX–20–1899) MD UPa 1852; AB 1849; AM 1852. *Tr CPP* cent vol:269. *JAMA* 33: , 1899. *Atkinson* I:706.

TAIT, CHARLES WILLIAM, USN 1838–43; MexWar–Tex vols; CW–CSA; Columbus, Tex (b/VI–4–1815 Elbert Co, Ga; d/XI–2–1878) MD UPa 1837; AB U Ala 1834;AM 1843. U Ala cat:40. *U Pa med alum CW*: 1837.

TAIT, WILLIAM T, Galesburg, Ill (d/1905? @66 St Louis) <MD Physio–Med Coll Cincinnati 1866> *Ill m j* 8:530, 1905. *Polk* 1896: 421.

TALBOT, GEORGE W, Denver (d/V–15–1895) MD Louisvl M C 1878. *JAMA* 24:810, 1895. *Polk* 1890: 212.

TALBOT, MICHAEL, Niagara Falls (b/V–12–1846 Ireland; d/I–26–1898) MD Buff 1871. *Buff m & s jour* 37: 623–24, 1898. *JAMA* 30:391, 1898.

TALCOTT, ALVAN, Guilford, Conn (b/VIII–17–1804 N Bolton or Vernon, Conn; d/I–17–1891) MD Yale 1831; AB 1824; AM 1827. *Med reg NY NJ Conn* 1892: 289. *JAMA* 16:321, 1891. *Proc Conn Med Soc* 1891:300–01. *Bost m & s jour* 124:104, 1891. *Atkinson* I: 56.

TALCOTT, FREDERICK COOLIDGE, Brooklyn (b/VII–31–1850 Oswego, NY; d/V–31–1878) MD CPSNY 1875. *Med reg NY NJ Conn* 1879: 200.

TALCOTT, SELDEN HAINES, Middletown, NY (d/VI–15–1902) MD NY Hom 1872. *Tr Am Inst Hom* 1902: 832–33. *Polk* 1886:668. Homeopath.

TALIAFERRO, CHARLES THOMAS, Stephens City, Va; Hicksville, NY 1894– (b/VII–4–1859 Rockingham Co; d/II–15–1901) MD CPS Balto 1888; att UVa 1886–89. *Tr M S Va* 1902:226–28.

TALIAFERRO, FOUNTAIN NEWTON, Hicksville, NY (b/1861? Va; d/I–16–1895 Aiken, SC) MD UCNY 1889. *Med reg NY NJ Conn* 1895:241. *JAMA* 24:177, 1895.

TALIAFERRO, GARLAND, Brownsville, Tenn (b/IV–25–1822 Amherst Co, Va; d/IX–4–1859) <MD in Louisville> *Nashville jour m & s* 17:478, 1859.

TALIAFERRO, HORACE DADE, USN 1838–44; CW–CSA (b/VI–6–1815 Rose Hill, Va; d/I–21–1891 Farmville) MD UPa 1836; att UVa. *U Pa m alum CW*: 1836.

TALIAFERRO, VALENTINE HAM, CW–CSA; Atlanta (b/IX–24–1831 Oglethorpe Co Ga; d/IX–2–1887 Tate Spr, Tex) MD UCNY 1852. *Med bull med & surg* 9:346, 1887. *NC med jour* 20:254, 1887. *Atkinson* I:379–81. *Polk* 1886: 225. *K&B* III: 1185.

TALIAFERRO, WILLIAM T, Cincinnati; War 1812 USN? (b/1795 Newington, d/III–1–1871) MD UPa 1827. *Tr Ohio St M S* 1872:262–63. *Med surg rep Phila* 24: 284, 322, 1871. *K&B* III: 1185.

TALL, REUBEN JAMES HOOPER, Baltimore (b/VII–9 1844 Dorchester Co; d/V–12–1902) MD UMd 1865. *Med annals Md:* 588. *Polk* 1886: 439.

TALLEY, ALEXANDER NICHOLAS, CW–CSA; Columbia, SC (b/X–27–1827 Washington, Ga; d/VII–6–1897) MD Med Coll SC 1851. *JAMA* 29:201, 1897. *Atkinson* I: 30, 1878. *Waring* II: 308.

TALMAGE, JOHN FRELINGHUYSEN, Brooklyn (b/III–11–1833 Somerville, NJ; d/VI–30–1897 Rye, NY) MD UCNY 1859; AB Rutgers 1852; AM 1855. *JAMA* 29: 92, 1897. *Tr Am Inst Hom* 1898: 49. *Polk* 1896:1004.

Homeopath.

TALMAGE, SAMUEL, Brooklyn (b/1831? d/XI-20-1903 @72) MD UCNY 1870. *Bost m & s jour* 149:610, 1903. *Polk* 1896: 1004. Homeopath.

TAMAYO, RAFAEL y BOU, NYC (b/1851 Santiago de Cuba; d/VI-30-1881) MD Bellevue 1875. *Med reg NY NJ Conn* 1882: 235. *Butler* 1878: 526.

TANDY, DAVID CASTLEMAN, St Louis (b/1824? d/1875) MD St Louis Med Coll 1850; stud med Florence, Paris. *Tr AMA* 27:651-52, 1876.

TANEY, AUGUSTINE, Baltimore Co, Md (b/1797; d/1853) MD UMd 1821. *Med annals Md:* 588.

TANNER, ELY JUDSON, Chicago (d/II-18-1900 @ 36?) MD Rush 1880. *Tr Ill St M S* 1899-1900: 463, 509. *JAMA* 34:574, 1900. *Polk* 1896: 408.

TANNER, JAMES, Wheeling [W] Va (b/Balto; d/XII-26 1858) MD UMd 1823. *Med s rep Phila* ns1:302 1858/59.

TANNER, JOHN ALEXANDER, Dorchester, Mass (d/VI-21-1906 @53) MD UVa 1875. *Bost m & s jour* 154: 750, 1906. *Polk* 1896: 706.

TANNER, JOSEPH H , New Haven, Ill (d/VII-26-1897) MD Louisville Med Coll 1893. *Chic med rec* 13: 52, 1897. *JAMA* 29:44, 1897. *Polk* 1896: 432.

TANNER, NELSON BRIGGS, N Abington, Mass (d/XI 25-1887 @70) MD Harvard 1862. *Bost m & s jour* 117: 514, 1887. *Polk* 1886: 472.

TANSLEY, JOHN OSCROFT, NYC (d/III-25-1905 @60) MD CPSNY 1877. *Bost m & s jour* 152:416, 1905. *Polk* 1896: 1080.

TAPLIN, NEHEMIAH Jr, Corinth, Me (b/VII-8-1814; d/IV-25 or V-8-1856 Mokelumne Hill, Cal) MD Berkshire 1837; ng Woodstock. *Bost m&s j* 54:407, 1856.

TAPLIN, WILLIAM T, Cadillac Mich (d/VI-18-1899 @ 77) MD Geneva 1859 *JAMA* 33:53 1899. *Polk* 1890:590.

TAPPAN, BENJAMIN, CW-USA (b/Jefferson Co, O; d/III-22-1866 Cottonwood Spr, Ariz) MD UPa 1836. *U Pa med alum CW*: 1836. *Nat med jour* 1:303, 1870/71.

TAPPAN, BENJAMIN, Steubenville, O (b/IV-1-1812; d/I-17-1884) MD ? *Tr Ohio St M S* 1884: 230.

TAPPAN, W C , Baltimore (d/IV-10-1896 @78) MD ? *JAMA* 26:843, 1896. *Polk* 1886: 439.

TARBELL, GEORGE GROSVENOR, CW-USA;Boston (b/IX-9-1841 Lincoln, Mass; d/XII-31-1900) MD Harvard 1865; AB 1862. *Bost m&s j* 144:28, 52, 1901. *Atkinson* I:184. *Harvard in CW*: 189. *Polk* 1896: 706.

TARKINGTON, A K [or R], Hot Spr, Ark (d/II-4-1905) <MD Memphis Hosp M C 1891> *New Orl m&s j* 57: 705, 1905.

TARKINGTON, JOSEPH ASBURY, Washington, DC (b/XI-25-1837 Indiana; d/V-1-1902 Greensburg, Ind) MD Georgtn 1870. *Hist M S DC:* 300. *Polk* 1893: 273.

TATE, CHARLES N , Alexis, Ala (d/VIII-4-1897) Cert by Exam Bd. *JAMA* 29:400, 1897. *Polk* 1890: 133.

TATE, R H , Cincinnati (d/IX-29-1878 Memphis) MD ? *Tr AMA* 30:885, 1879. Black [?]

TATE, ROBERT HUNTER, New Hanover, NC (b/1826; d/1864) MD Jefferson 1849; AB UNC 1847. *Tr M S St NC* 1870: 24.

TATE, WILLIAM C , Morganton, NC (d/III-11-1869) MD M C SC 1831. *Tr M S St NC* 1869: 12.

TATEM, WILLIAM ALEXANDER, Denton, Md (d/III-1877) MD UPa 1823. *Med annals Md:* 589.

TAUSZKY, RUDOLPH, NYC (d/XI-21-1889) MD Pesth 1861; MD Vienna 1874. *Bost m&s j* 121:572 1889.

TAXIL, L V M , New Orleans (b/1796? France; d/VIII-6-1864) MD Hahnemann Phila 1858; MD Western Hom 1858. *Med invest* 2:43, 1864? *King* I:189.

TAYLOE, DAVID THOMAS, Washington, NC; CW-CSA (b/II-21-1826; d/III-25-1884) MD UCNY 1849. *NC m j* 13:217, 1884. *Tr M S St NC* 1887: 157-58.

TAYLOR, ALFRED, CW-USA (d/V-23-1863 Ohio River) MD ? *Nat med jour* 1:303, 1870/71.

TAYLOR, ARCHIBALD, USA 1852-56; CSA 1861-65; ?Richmond, Va (b/VIII-10-1829 Gloucester CH; d/III-3 1893) MD UPa 1849. *U Pa med alum CW*:1849.

TAYLOR, ARTHUR KENNON, Hot Spr, Ark (b/IV-5 1818; d/VI-19-1886) MD UPa 1840. *Tex cour-rec med* 3:482, 1886. *Atkinson* 1878: 557.

TAYLOR, ASHMUN [ASHMAN] HINCKLEY, Shelbourne Falls, Mass (d/IV-13-1887 @64) MD Berkshire 1842. *Bost m&s j* 117:636 1887. *Mass Med Soc cat* 1894.

TAYLOR, AUGUSTUS FITZ-RANDOLPH, New Brunswick, NJ (b/X-6-1809; d/III-6-1889) Lic M S NJ 1832; AB Rutgers 1829. *Med reg NY NJ Conn* 1889:288; 1890:281. *Butler* 1878: 479.

TAYLOR, CEPHAS RODNEY, Hardwick, Vt (d/1865 Irasburgh) MD Dartmouth 1842. *Tr Vt M S* 1883: 109.

TAYLOR, CEPHUS BLAIR, Rock Mills, Ala (d/II-7-1890) MD Graffenburg 1849. *Tr M Assn St Ala* 1890: 218. *Polk* 1886: 139.

TAYLOR, CHARLES FAYETTE, Los Angeles (b/IV-25-1827 Williston, Vt; d/I-25-1899) MD UVt 1856. *Bost m&s j* 140:127, 1899. *Buff m&s j* 38: 789-90, 1899. *K&B* III: 1186.

TAYLOR, CHARLES HIRAM, Philadelphia (d/XII-15-1862 @42) MD UPa 1843 *Med s rep Phil* ns9:278, 1862.

TAYLOR, CLARENCE ORSEN, NYC (d/VIII-18-1892 @46) MD Bellevue 1879. *Med reg NY NJ Conn* 1893: 316.

TAYLOR, DANIEL THOMAS, Hot Spr, Ark (d/VIII-29 1901) MD New Orl Sch Med 1859. *JAMA* 37:710, 1901. *Polk* 1886: 152.

TAYLOR, DAVID [DANIEL] NELSON, Amsterdam, NY (b/II-1-1850 Albany; d/III-29-1900) MD LICH 1884. *JAMA* 34:891, 1900. *Polk* 1886: 640.

TAYLOR, DeWITT CLINTON, Philadelphia (d/V-10 1886 @36) MD UPa 1856. *Med s rep Phil* 14:420 1866.

TAYLOR, EDWARD, ?Philadelphia (b/V-27-1762 Upper Freehold, NJ; d/V-2-1835) <MD UPa 1786> AB Princeton 1783. *Tr M S NJ* 1871: 83. *Wickes*: 49.

TAYLOR, EDWARD, Cleveland (d/II–27–1868 @57?) MD CPSNY 1826. *Phila med reg & dir* 1871: 295. *Med surg rep Phila* 18: 270, 1868.

TAYLOR, EDWARD B, Chicago (d/IX–7–1901) MD Bennett 1877. *Ill m j* ns3:295 1901. *Polk* 1886:272. Ecl.

TAYLOR, ESTHER W , Boston (d/VIII–5–1905) MD Hahnemann Chic 1872. *Tr Am Inst Hom* 1905:846. *Polk* 1886: 462.

TAYLOR, GEORGE, USA (d/VIII–5–1867 Galveston, Tx) MD UMd 1851. *Med annals Md:* 589. *Tr AMA* 19: 452, 1868. *Nat med jour* 1:303, 1870/71.

TAYLOR, GEORGE HERBERT, NYC (b/I–4–1821 Williston, Vt; d/XII–9–1896) MD NYMC 1852. *JAMA* 28:41, 1897. *K&B* III: 1188.

TAYLOR, GEORGE R , Waupaca, Wis (d/V–26–1897 @75) MD Cincinnati C M & S 1855. *JAMA* 28:1092, 1897. *Polk* 1886: 961.

TAYLOR, HORACE CLIFTON, Brockton, NY (d/XII–21–1903 @90) MD Ecl Med Inst Cinc 1849. *Bost m & s jour* 149: 748, 1903. *Polk* 1886: 643. Eclectic.

TAYLOR, ISAAC EBENEZER, NYC (b/IV–25–1812 Phila; d/X–30–1889) MD UPa 1834; AB Rutgers 1832. *Buff m&s j* :318, 1889 (Dec) *Med reg NY NJ Conn* 1890: 281. *Med s rep Phila* 15:355–61, 1866. *K&B* 1189.

TAYLOR, ISRAEL HOUSTON, Amherst, Mass (d/X–16–1890 @78) Lic Mass Med Soc 1842; <att Amherst> *Bost m & s jour* 123:408, 1890. *Polk* 1886: 453.

TAYLOR, J JUDSON, Syracuse, NY (d/VII–26–1897 @59) MD Castleton 1861. *JAMA* 29:297, 1897. *Polk* 1890: 853.

TAYLOR, JAMES, ?Philadelphia (d/X–28–1868 @22) MD ?Jefferson 1865. *Phila med reg & dir* 1871: 293.

TAYLOR, JAMES, W Fairfield, Pa (d/IV–30–1902 @85) MD Jefferson 1851. *Pa med jour* 6:262, 1902/03. *Flint* 1897: 839.

TAYLOR, JAMES BRAINERD, NYC; San Angelo, Tex (b/V–16–1846 Bristol, NY; d/VI–16–1896 @50) MD UCNY 1869. *Bost m & s jour* 134:653, 1896. *Atkinson* I: 278. *Polk* 1886: 695.

TAYLOR, JAMES L , St Joseph, Mo (d/VII–18–1901 @45) <MD NW M C St Joseph 1881> *JAMA* 37:342, 1901. *Polk* 1886: 560.

TAYLOR, JAMES M, Indiana Pa (d/II–21–1902 @82) MD Jeff'n 1848. *Pa m j* 6:262, 1902/03. *Flint* 1897:805.

TAYLOR, JAMES MARCUS, Corinth, Miss (b/1826 Jackson Co, Ga; d/XII–28–1895) MD Jefferson 1851. *JAMA* 26:93, 1896. *Atkinson* I:91. *Butler* 1874: 396.

TAYLOR, JAMES RIDLEY, NYC (b/Scotl'd; d/III–24 1895) MD Bellevue 1874. *Med reg NY NJ Conn* 1895: 241. *JAMA* 24:527, 1895. *Butler* 1878: 526.

TAYLOR, JAMES THEUS, NYC; New Orleans (b/Columbus, SC; d/IX–29–1878 @63?) MD UPa 1839. *Tr AMA* 30:885–6 1879. *Med reg NY NJ Conn* 1879: 201.

TAYLOR, JAMES WATT, Pittsburgh (d/III–18–1902 @ 72) MD [Pa] U Med & Surg 1865. *Pa med jour* 6:262, 1902/03. *Off'l Reg Pa phys* 1881–88: 14.

TAYLOR, JOHN BUNKER, E Cambridge, Mass (d/II–15–1889 @67) MD Harvard 1847. *Bost m&s j* 120:204, 228, 1889. *Butler* 1878: 344.

TAYLOR, JOHN E , Philadelphia (d/XI–27–1865 @49) MD ? *Med surg rep Phila* 13: 390, 1865.

TAYLOR, JOHN HOWARD, CW–USA;Philadelphia (b/ 1826 Kennett Sq; d/X–24–1905 @73) MD UPa 1852. *Pa m j* 9:127 1905/06 *Atkinson* I:703. *U Pa m alum CW*:1852.

TAYLOR, JOHN LANE HENDERSON,CW–CSA; Red Banks Miss (b/VII–17–1839 Oxford; d/IX–16–1880) MD UPa 1874. *U Pa m alum CW*: 1874.

TAYLOR, JOHN LEWIS, Pittsboro, NC (d/I–29–1829) MD ? AB UNC 1807; AM 1810. *UNC cat*: 611.

TAYLOR, JOHN LLOYD, Trenton, NJ (b/VI–8–1811 Middletown; d/III–2–1879) <MD UCNY> *Tr M S NJ* 1879: 207–08. *Butler* 1878: 476.

TAYLOR, JOHN SCOTT, CW–USA?; Chicago (b/Scotl; d/X–1–1893) MD Chic M C 1862. *JAMA* 21:746, 1893.

TAYLOR, JOHN TRAVIS, Richmond, Va (b/VII–7–1874 Bedford Co; d/VIII–31–1900) MD U M C Richm'd 1896; att Randolph–Macon. *Tr M S Va* 1900: 333–34.

TAYLOR, JOHN WINTHROP, USN 1838–79 (b/VIII–19–1817 NY; d/I–19–1880 Boston) MD UPa 1838; AB Princeton 1835. *Med surg rep Phila* 42:110, 1880. *Tr AMA* 33: 607, 1882. *Bost m & s jour* 99:569, 1878; 102:90, 1880. *K&B* II: 1920.

TAYLOR, JOSEPH, USA 1864–69; USN 1870– (b/E Marlborough Twp, Pa; d/VII–18–1890 Atlantic City) MD UPa 1862. *U Pa med alum CW*: 1862. *Polk* 1886: 419 (Shreveport, La).

TAYLOR, JOSEPH WRIGHT, Burlington, NJ (b/III–1–1810 Upper Freehold, NJ; d/I–18–1880 @69) MD UPa 1830. *Tr M S NJ* 1880–81: 124–26. *Med rec NY* 17: 164, 1880. *Med surg rep Phila* 42:110, 1880.

TAYLOR, LEROY M , Washington, DC (b/1838 NY; d/ IX–27–1904) MD Georgetown 1860. *Hist Med Soc DC:* 319. *Polk* 1893: 273.

TAYLOR, LEWIS, USA 1857– (b/Phila; d/I–66–1866 or 1868 Ft Wadsworth, Dakota) MD UPa 1853. *Phila m reg & dir* 1871:293. *Tr AMA* 21:491–92, 1870. *Med s rep Phila* 18:159, 1868. *U Pa m alum CW*: 1853.

TAYLOR, MARCUS L , Booneville, Miss (b/ca 1850; d/ I–25–1896 Phila) MD ? *JAMA* 26:286, 1896.

TAYLOR, MILTON N , Baltimore (d/II–25–1895 @ 68) MD Washington Med Coll 1848. *JAMA* 24: 370, 1895. *Butler* 1878: 323.

TAYLOR, MORSE KENT, USA 1847– (b/V–14–1823 Watertown, NY; d/X–20–1889 San Antonio) MD U Mich 1852. *JAMA* 13:685–86, 1889. *Daniel's Tex med jour* 5:194, 1889–90.

TAYLOR, OTHNIEL HART, Camden, NJ (b/V–4–1803 Phila; d/IX–5–1869) MD UPa 1825; Hon AM ? Princeton 1854. *Phila med reg & dir* 1871: 302. *Tr AMA* 21: 470–73, 1870. *Tr M S NJ* 1870: 90–93.

Spec. educ'l status abbrev. as: ***ng*** = college verified attendance without degree;

TAYLOR, PARRAN, Church Hill, Md (d/1832) MD UPa 1812. *Med annals Md:* 589.

TAYLOR, PAUL JOHN, Hoboken, NJ (d/VII-6-1895 @58) MD UCNY 1875. *JAMA* 25:123-24, 1895.

TAYLOR, RICHARD G , Philadelphia (d/XII-12-1871 @32) MD Hahnemann Phila 1862. *Phila med reg & dir* 1873: 304. ?Homeopath.

TAYLOR, ROBERT RANDOLPH, CW-USA; Philadelphia (b/II-14-1826 Hanover Co, Va; d/II-26-1895) MD UPa 1849. *Tr CPP* cent vol:29; 3s17:xliii ff, 1895. *JAMA* 24: 422, 1895. *U Pa med alum CW*: 1849.

TAYLOR, SAMUEL, Petersham, Mass (d/XII-31-1860 @50) MD UPa 1832. *Bost m&s j* 63: 528, 1861.

TAYLOR, SAMUEL W, Newark (d/VII-25-1884) MD ? *Med surg rep Phil* 51:168, 1884. *Butler* 1878: 452. Homeopath.

TAYLOR, THOMAS ARCHIBALD, Washington, DC (d/VI-30-1898) MD Georgetown 1885. *JAMA* 31:142, 1898. *Polk* 1896: 308.

TAYLOR, THOMAS L , Leedstown, Va (d/VII-2-1901 @67) MD M C Va 1874. *JAMA* 37:213, 1901.

TAYLOR, VERNON OTIS, Providence, RI (b/VIII-28 1847 Charleston, Mass; d/IX-10-1847) MD Harvard 1868. *Tr RI M S* 7:575, 1904-09. *Polk* 1896: 1354.

TAYLOR, WILLIAM, Manlius, NY (b/X-12-1791 Suffield, Conn; d/IX-16-1865) Lic Onondaga Co M S 1812; stud w/Dr Hezekiah L. Granger. *Tr M S St NY* 1867:431-438. *Tr AMA* 18:315, 1867. *Biogr dir Congr.*

TAYLOR, WILLIAM ADOLPHUS, Locksville, NC; CW-CSA (b/I-16-1838 Pittsboro; d/IX-9-1865) MD U Pa 1859; ng UNC 1855-57. *U Pa med alum CW*: 1859.

TAYLOR, WILLIAM BLACK, McKeesport, Pa (d/II-3 1900 @40) MD UPa 1887; AB Wooster 1883. *JAMA* 34: 446, 1900.

TAYLOR, WILLIAM GARDINER, Marietta Pa (d/VIII-29-1846 Darby; d/III-4-1904 Columbia) MD Hahnemann Phila 1870. *Tr Am Inst Hom* 1904: 965. *Polk* 1886: 796.

TAYLOR, WILLIAM HENRY, Washington, DC (b/I-26 1834 Pottsville, Pa; d/IX-5-1889) MD Columbian 1856. *Hist Med Soc DC:* 259. *Polk* 1886: 214.

TAYLOR, WILLIAM HENRY ODENHEIMER, Union Hill, NJ (b/VII-9-1858 Ridgefield, NJ; d/III-2-1891) MD UCNY 1881. *Med reg NY NJ Conn* 1892:289. *Tr M S NJ* 1891:230-31. *Polk* 1886: 612.

TAYLOR, WILLIAM HOWLAND, New Bedford, Mass (d/VII-20-1891 @37) MD UCNY 1876. *Bost m & s jour* 125:96, 1891. *Polk* 1890: 553.

TAYLOR, WILLIAM REMSEN, Long Isl City, NY (b/II-4-1840 Middletown, NJ; d/X-2-1896) MD LICH 1864; AB Rutgers 1860. *Bost m & s jour* 135:396, 1896. *JAMA* 27:215, 1896. *Polk* 1896: 1030.

TAYLOR, WILLIAM TERRY, Philadelphia (b/III-6-1822; d/III-2-1887) MD UPa 1848; AB 1842. *Med s rep Phila* 56:352, 1887? *Atkinson* I: 300-01. *Polk* 1886: 826.

TEACKLE, ST GEORGE WILLIAMSON Jr, Baltimore Co, Md (b/X-7-1849; d/VIII-30-1902) MD UMd 1870. *Med annals Md:* 590. *Polk* 1886: 439.

TEAL, NORMAN, Kendallville, Ind (b/1829 Preble Co [O?] d/II-11-1899) MD Rush 1866. *Tr Ind St M S* 1899: 403-04. *JAMA* 32:506, 1899. *Polk* 1896: 477.

TEARE, JOHN, Chicago (b/1818 Isle of Man; d/I-9-1889) <MRCP & S (London) 1845> *JAMA* 32:145, 1899. *Polk* 1896: 408.

TEBAULT, ALFRED GEORGE, Norfolk City, Va (b/II 23-1811 Charleston, SC; d/VIII-27-1895) <MD SC M C 1831> *Tr M S Va* 1895:215-17. *Polk* 1886: 922. *K&B* II: 1127-28.

TEBAULT, GEORGE, Madisonville, La (d/VIII-23-1897) MD Tulane 1859. *New Orl m&s j*50: 269, 1897. *Polk* 1896:618. *K&B* II:1127 [mention only].

TEBBETS, JEREMIAH EMERY, Cannon River Falls, Minn 1856- (b/X-13-1812 Berwick, Me; d/X-11-1882) ng Bowdoin 1847. *Tr Minn St M S* 1883:291-92.

TEBBETTS, CHARLES C , CW-CSA (d/V-19-1863 Greenfield, Mo) MD ? *Nat med jour* 1:303, 1870/71.

TEBBETTS, HIRAM BRADBURY, Concord, NH (b/II-2-1812 Northfield, NH; d/IV-8-1890) MD Harvard 1837. *Bost m & s jour* 122: 486, 1890. *Polk* 1886: 591.

TEBBS, THOMAS FOUSHEE, CW-CSA; Gainesville, Va (b/VIII-8-1828 Leesburg; d/1888) MD UPa 1850. *Polk* 1886:918. *U Pa med alum CW*: 1850.

TEELE, JONATHAN MERLE, Milton, Mass (d/XI-18-1890 @41) MD Harvard 1875; AB Tufts 1870. *New Engl med gaz* 26:52, 1891. *Polk* 1886:470. Homeopath.

TEEPLE, GEORGE M , Bridgeport, Conn (b/II-25-1825 Schoharie Co, NY; d/IX-6-1888) MD Albany 1849. *Proc Conn M S* ns4:259-60, 1889. *Polk* 1886: 191.

TEFFT [TEFT], ERASTUS, Topeka, Kans (b/1818 Lebanon, NY; d/I-8-1880) MD UCNY 1848. *Tr Kans St Med Soc* 1881:129-30. *Butler* 1878: 256.

TEFFT, LAKE I, Schuylersville, NY 1822-23; Marcellus to 1865; Syracuse (b/III-16-1797 Greenwich; d/V-10-1880) Lic Saratoga Co M S 1822. *Tr M S St NY* 1882: 350-54.

TEFFT, NATHAN R , Onondaga, NY (d/1890) Cert Exam Bd 1833. *Tr M S St NY* 1891:457. *Polk* 1886:700.

de TEJADA, ANTONIO GARCIA, NYC (d/1845 Colombia; d/XII-12-1880) MD Bellevue 1874; AB St Johns, Fordham. *Med reg NY NJ Conn* 1881:242. *Bost m & s jour* 103:623, 1880. *Butler* 1878: 526.

TELLER, SELIGMAN, NYC (b/XI-30-1830 Prague; d/III-13-1885) <MD U Vienna 1858> *Med reg NY NJ Conn* 1885:246. *Butler* 1878: 511.

TELLKAMPF, THEODORE A , NYC (b/IV-27-1812; d/IX-7-1883 Hanover, Gny) MD Vienna 1839. *Med reg NY NJ Conn* 1884:240. *Butler* 1878: 511.

TEMPLE, FRANCIS MARION, Fairview, Pa (d/VI-17 1896 @45) MD Cleveland M C 1880; MD UPa 1884. *JAMA* 27:52-53, 1896. *Polk* 1886: 807.

TEMPLE, JAMES D W , Kenton, Del (d/III-6-1885 @35) MD Jefferson 1874. *Med bull m&s* 7:225, 1885. *Med s rep Phila* 52:384, 1885.

TEMPLE, JOHN TAYLOR, Philadelphia to 1829; Washington, DC 4 yrs; Chicago 1833-42; St Louis 1843?- (b/V-5-1803 King Wm Co, Va; d/II-23-1877 @73) MD UMd 1824; att UPa. *US med invest* 5:406, 1877. *Ohio m&s rep* 11:202, 1877? *Cleave.* Homeopath.

TEMPLE, THERON, Waltham, Mass (b/Heath; d/XII-28 1890 @57) MD Berkshire 1856. *Bost m&s j* 124: 24, 52, 1891. *Polk* 1886: 475.

TEMPLE, THOMAS PRICE, Elizabeth City, Md (d/ 1830 Hanover Co, Va; d/V-2-1891) MD Jefferson 1850. *Med ann Md:* 590. *Polk* 1886: 442.

TEMPLETON, WILLIAM LAFAYETTE, Covington O (b/XI-3-1899) MD Miami 1882. *JAMA* 33:1441, 1899.

TEN BROECK, PETER G STUYVESANT, USA 1847- (d/XII-19-1867 or 1868 Portland Me) MD CPS NY 1847. *Tr AMA* 19:419, 454-55, 1868. *Bost m&s j* 77: 488, 1868. *Nat m j* 1:303, 1870/71. *Med s rep Phila* 18: 66, 1868.

TEN BROECK, STEPHEN PHILIP VAN RENSSE-LAER, Fairfield, Conn (b/XII-21-1802; d/VIII-1-1866 or 1868) MD CPSNY 1825. *Pr Conn M S* 1868: 19, 172.

TEN BROOK, JOHN, Paris, Ill (b/XII-21-1808 Turbotville, Pa; d/VIII-8-1885) MD Jefferson 1838; Hon MD Rush 1868; att Lafayette 1836. *Lafayette, Men of*: 140. *Butler* 1878: 176.

TENNEY [TENNY], CHARLES HARPER, Brattleboro, Vt (b/II-21-1830 Hartford, Vt; d/IV-23-1874) MD Dartmouth 1858; MD NYMC 1859. *Tr Vt M S* 1883:110.

TENNEY, JOHN WATERS, Webster, Mass (b/XII-25-1802 Sutton; d/IV-29-1849) MD ? AB Brown 1823; AM. *Brown hist cat* 1823. *Mass M S cat* 1894.

TENNEY, RICHARD PERLEY JEWETT, Pittsfield, Vt (b/VIII-18-1810 Loudon NH; d/VI-16-1876) MD Dartmouth 1832. *Tr NH M S* 1877: 109-110.

TERHUNE, ARCHIBALD ALEXANDER, CW-CSA; Jefferson Tx (b/I-3-1825 Monticello Ga; d/1891?) MD Jefferson 1848; att Oglethorpe. *Tex cour-rec med* 8:187, 1891. *Daniel's Tex m j* 6:362, 1890/91. *Polk* 1886: 888.

TERHUNE, GARRITT, Passaic, NJ (d/VII-2-1885 @ 84) MD Rutgers 1827. *Med reg NY NJ Conn* 1886: 254. *Tr M S NJ* 1886:153-55. *Butler* 1878: 476.

TERHUNE, GILLIAM C , Hackensack, NJ (b/I-19-1827 Spring Valley; d/XI-27-1880) MD NYMC 1854. *Tr M S NJ* 1880-81: 159-160. *Tr NH M S* 1881:145-46.

TERHUNE, RICHARD ALBERT, Passaic, NJ (d/II-5-1906 @77) MD CPSNY 1850. *Bost m & s jour* 154:200, 1906. *Polk* 1896: 946.

TERRELL, EARLY WALTON, Cullman, Ala (d/I-13-1900) MD Nashville Med Coll 1888. *JAMA* 34:251, 1900. *Polk* 1896: 158.

TERRELL, JOEL W , Navasota, Tx (d/X-21-1882 @77) MD ? *Tex med & surg rec* 3:551, 1883.

TERRELL, JOHN COLUMBUS, Philadelphia; NC (b/NC; d/III-28-1897 @80) MD UPa 1840. *NC m j* 39: 324, 1897. *Polk* 1886: 826.

TERRELL, WILLIS MONROE, Cedar Grove, NC (b/ XII-7-1830 Caswell Co; d/XII-15-1906) MD UPa 1860. *U Pa med alum CW*: 1860.

TERRETT, BURDETT A , Natchitoches, La (d/I-23 1903) MD Tulane 1900. *New Orl m&s j*55:524, 1903. *Polk* 1900: 1943.

TERRILL, GEORGE PARKER, Salem, Va (b/Covington; d/XI-4/5-1883/1884 @53) MD UPa 1853. *U Pa m alum CW*: 1853. *Med bull m&s* 7:59, 1885.

TERRILL, ROBERT MORTON, CW-CSA; Pitt Co, SC (b/XII-22 1838; d/II-5-1870) MD UPa 1860; att U Va. *U Pa med alum CW*: 1860.

TERRILL, WILLIAM, Lawrenceburg, Ind (b/II-25-1852 Moore's Hill; d/III-16-1887) MD Med Coll Ohio 1878. *Tr Ind St Med Soc* 1888: 200.

TERRILL, WILLIAM H , Petersburg, Ky (b/1829 Boone Co; d/XI- -1885) MD UVa 1850. *Tr Ind St MS* 1886: 210.

TERRY, A R , CW-USA (d/XII-2-1864) MD ? *Nat med jour* 1:303, 1870/71.

TERRY, CHARLES AUGUSTUS, Cleveland (b/X-9-1810 Hartford, Conn; d/II-5-1872) MD CPSNY 1833. *Bost m & s jour* ns9:113, 1872.

TERRY, CHARLES CHURCH, Fall River, Mass (d/VII 18-1892 @52) MD NYMC 1864; MD Harvard 1884. *Bost m&s j* 127: 76, 1892. *Polk* 1886: 466.

TERRY, CHARLES E , CW-USA (d/VIII-23-1865) MD ? *Nat med jour* 1:303, 1870/71.

TERRY [PERRY], JEREMIAH WADSWORTH, Englewood, NJ (d/IV-10-1905) MD Yale 1862. *Bost m & s jour* 152: 1905 (April). *Polk* 1896: 936.

TERRY, LOUIS W , Patchogue, NY (b/XII-19-1841 Sayville, NY; d/V-26-1894) MD Bellevue 1865. *Med reg NY NJ Conn* 1894: 250. *Butler* 1878: 577.

TERRY, ORMAN P , Bethel, Vt (d/IX-8-1880 @59) MD Castleton 1846. *Tr Vt M S* 1883:110.

TEST, ZACCHEUS, Richmond, Ind (b/IX-13-1828 Dunlapsville; d/XI-3-1905) MD UPa 1855; ng Haverford; AM Franklin & Marshall 1861. *Havfd biogr cat*: 43.

TETRICK, AMOS, DuQuoin, Ill (d/VIII-10-1901) Lic yrs pract. *Ill m j* ns3:189, 1901. *Polk* 1896: 417.

TEWKSBURY, SAMUEL HENRY, Portland, Me (b/III-22-1819; d/VII-28-1880) MD Bowdoin 1841; ng Harvard Med; ng CPSNY. *Tr AMA* 32:541-43, 1881. *K&B* III: 1195.

THACH, STEPHEN D , Decherd, Tenn (d/X-1-1900 @ 34) MD Vand'blt 1891. *Nashvl j m&s* 88:190-91, 1900.

THACHER, JAMES KINGSLEY, New Haven, Conn (b/ X-19-1847; d/IV-20-1891) MD Yale 1879; AB 1868. *Med reg NY NJ Conn* 1892: 289. *JAMA* 17:84, 1891. *Pr Conn M S* 1891:314-15. *K&B* III:1196-97.

THACKER, JOHN A , Cincinnati (b/I-1-1833 Goshen;

 Spec. educ'l status abbrev. as: *ng* = college verified attendance without degree;

d/XII-19-1891) MD Miami 1856; att Wittenberg. *Med bull m&s* 14:76, 1892. *Atkinson* I:15. *Polk* 1886: 745.

THACKER, LUDWELL GAINES, Defiance, O (d/VI-20-1901) MD Bellevue 1866. *JAMA* 37:43, 1901. *Polk* 1886: 753.

THACKER, WILLIAM HARRISON, Denver (d/VII-30 1876) MD U Mich 1862. *Tr Colo St M S* 1898-99:508. *Butler* 1874: 67.

THALLON, WILLIAM MORRISON, Brooklyn (d/X-1 1888 @29) MD CPSNY 1880 *Med reg NY NJ Conn* 1889: 288. *Bost m&s j* 119:370, 1888. *Polk* 1886:650.

THAXTER, DUNCAN McBEANE, Boston (d/XI-17-1873 @45) MD Harvard 1850; AB 1847. *Bost m&s j* ns 12: 548, 1873. *Mass Med Soc cat* 1894.

THAXTER, EZEKIEL, Abington, Mass (b/VII-22-1787; d/X-11-1856) MD Harvard 1815; AM 1812. *Bost m&s j* 55:255, 1857. Palmer's *Necrol Harv alum* 125.

THAXTER, ROBERT, Dorchester, Mass (b/X-21-1776 Hingham; d/II-9-1852) MD Harvard 1802; AB 1798. *Bost m&s j* 46:309-14, 1852. Palmer's *Necrol Harv alum*: 4.

THAYER, ALVIN, Erie, Pa (d/III-11-1906 @81) <MD Med Coll La 1839 or 1845> *Pa med jour* 9:524, 1905/06. *Off'l Reg Pa phys* 1881-88: 736. *Polk* 1886: 799.

THAYER, DAVID, Boston (b/VII-19-1813 Braintree, Mass; d/XII-14-1893) MD Berkshire 1843; att Harvard. *Tr Am Inst Hom* 1895: 234. *Polk* 1886: 462. *Cleave*. Homeopath.

THAYER, FREDERICK LYMAN, W Newton, Mass (d/III-4-1901 @53) MD Harvard 1871. *Bost m&s j* 144: 246, 269, 1901. *Polk* 1886: 475.

THAYER, HENRY WHITE, NYC (b/Providence, RI; d/V-20-1857) MD Harvard 1831; AB Brown 1826; AM. *Brown hist cat*: 1826.

THAYER, PROCTER, Cleveland (b/X-16-1823 Williamstown, Mass; d/X-1-1890 @66) MD Cleveland M C 1849. *JAMA* 15:879, 1890. *Bost m&s j* 123:360, 1890. *Atkinson* I: 622. *K&B* III: 1199.

THAYER, S B, Kalamazoo, Mich to 1846; Detroit; CW-USA; Battle Crk, Mich 1863- (b/II-12-1815 Canandaigua, NY; d/IX-1874) Hon MD Western Hom 1860. *Am j hom mat med* 8:80, 1874? *New Engl m gaz* 10:93, 1875. *Cleave*. Homeopath.

THAYER, SAMUEL EZRA, Wenham, Mass (d/II-5-1905) MD Buffalo 1869. *Bost m&s j* 152:178, 1905. *Polk* 1896: 725.

THAYER, SAMUEL WHITE, Burlington, Vt (b/V-21-1817 Braintree; d/XI-14-1882) MD Woodstock 1838; Hon AM Dartmouth 1866; LLD UVt 1877. *JAMA* 2:78-79, 1884. *Tr Minn St M S* 1884:181; 1902:307. *Tr Vt M S* 1883:110. *K&B* III:747 (mention only).

THAYER, WILLIAM HENRY, CW-USA; Lanesborough, Mass (b/ VI-18-1822 Milton; d/XII-22-1897) MD Harvard 1844; AB 1841. *Bost m&s j* 137:692, 1897; 138:94, 1898. *Harvard in CW*: 18. *Polk* 1896: 691.

THEBAUD, JULIUS STEPHEN, NYC (b/X-28-1827 Morristown, NJ; d/X-20-1876) MD CPSNY 1849. *Med reg NY NJ Conn* 1877:208. *Med surg rep Phila* 13:72-75, 1865; 35:414, 1876. *Med rec med & surg* 11:710, 1876. *Butler* 1878: 526.

THEOBALD, ELISHA WARFIELD, Baltimore (b/VII-11-1818; d/III-24-1851) MD Transylvania 1839. *Tr AMA* 31:1088, 1880. *Med annals Md:* 592.

THEOBALD, ELISHA WARFIELD Jr, Baltimore (b/VIII-12-1850; d/V-30-1877) MD UMd 1875. *Med annals Md:* 591.

THEOBALD, FREDERIC PAYSON, Gardiner Me (b/VI 23-1812 Wiscasset; d/I-18-1857) MD Bowdoin 1834; AB 1830. *Bowdoin cat*: 1830.

THEVENOT, JOHN BAPTIST ALEXANDER, Ala 1821? Mt Pleasant, Tenn (b/II-26-1793 France; d/1834) <MD Paris> *Tr M S Tenn* 1876: 87-88.

THEYSON, ROBERT H, NYC (d/1906 @49) MD UC NY 1891. *Bost m&s j* 155:106 1906. *Polk* 1896:1081.

THIGPEN, HENRY F, New Orleans (b/1871 Greenville, Ala; d/IX-8-1892) Med stud @ death. *New Orl m & s jour* ns20:287, 1892.

THOBURN, JOSEPH, Cookstown, Pa 1850-51; Wheeling, WVa; CW-USA (b/IV-29-1825 Belfast, Irel'd; d/X-19-1864 Shenandoah Valley, Va) MD Starling 1850. *Med s rep Phila* 12:195-96, 1864/65; 13:19-22, 1865. *Bost m&s j* 71:448, 1864. *Nat m j* 1:303, 1870/71.

THOM, J PEMBROKE, Baltimore (b/Culpeper Co, Va; d/VIII-21-1899 @71) MD Jefferson 1851. *JAMA* 33: 620, 1899. *Polk* 1896: 666.

THOM, WILLIAM ALEXANDER Jr, Norfolk, Va (b/III 20-1853 Northampton Co, Va; d/XI-2-1894) MD M C Va 1873. *Tr M S Va* 1895:213-14. *JAMA* 23:768, 1894.

THOMAS, ALEXANDER, Boston, Mass (d/I-2-1874) MD Harvard 1827; AB 1822. *Bost m&s j* 90:52, 1874. *Mass M S cat* 1894.

THOMAS, AMOS RUSSELL, CW-USA; Philadelphia (b/X-3-1826/1827 Watertown, NY; d/X-31-1895) <MD Syracuse M C (Ecl) 1854> Hon MD Pa Med Univ 1855; MD Hahnemann Phila 1886. *Hahn mo* 31:4-7, 105 (news & advt) 1896. *No Am j hom* 44:63, 1896. *K&B* III: 1199. *Cleave*. Homeopath.

THOMAS, BENJAMIN HARDIN, CW-CSA; Nashville (b/XI-5-1832 Montg'y Co; d/VI-27-1889) MD UPa 1859. *U Pa med alum CW*: 1859.

THOMAS, CALVIN, Tynesborough, Mass (b/XII-22-1765 Chesterfield, NH; d/X-23-1851) Hon MD Harvard 1824. *Bost m&s j* 48:19-21, 1853.

THOMAS, CHARLES HENRY, Baltimore (b/V-27-1847 Phila; d/V-13-1900) MD Hahnemann Phila 1873. *Tr Am Inst Hom* 1900: 842. *Polk* 1886: 439. Homeopath.

THOMAS, CHARLES K, CW-USA (d/I-18-1862 Fortress Monroe, Va @25) MD UPa 1860. *Med surg rep Phila* ns7: 576, 1861/62. *Nat med jour* 1:303, 1870/71.

THOMAS, CHARLES WIDGERY, Portland, Me (b/II-

14–1816; d/III–28–1868) MD Bowdoin 1837; AB 1834. *Tr Me M Assn* 1866–68: 64–68. *K&B* II: 1135.

THOMAS, D B, Dulles, Tex (d/1867) MD ? *Tr AMA* 19: 428, 1868.

THOMAS, D ERASTUS, Lacon, Ill (d/II–5–1903 @78) MD Evansville M C 1851. *Ill m j* ns4:470, 1903. *Polk* 1886: 285.

THOMAS, DANIEL GOLDEN, Utica, NY (b/X–24–1806 nr Poughkeepsie; d/III–27–1880 Troy) MD Jefferson 1837; ng Fairfield 1829. *Tr M S St NY* 1881:369–71. *Med surg rep Phila* 42:308, 1880. *Atkinson* I: 147.

THOMAS, FRANCIS A, NYC (d/IX–28–1899 @73) MD CPSNY 1853. *JAMA* 33:927, 1899. *Bost m&s j* 141: 352, 1899. *Polk* 1896: 1081.

THOMAS, FREDERICK SMITH, CW–USA; Council Bluffs Ia (b/IX–23–1845 Chatham NY; d/VIII–13–1899) MD CPS Keokuk 1870. *JAMA* 33:558 1899. *Tr Ia St M S* 18:394–95, 412, 1900. *Atkinson* I:432. *Polk* 1890: 411.

THOMAS, G D, Altoona Pa (d/X–26–1858 @43) MD ? *Tr AMA* 13:804, 1860. *Med s rep Phil* ns1:140, 1858/59.

THOMAS, GEORGE, Baltimore (d/VI–3 or X–1897 @ 38) MD CPS Balto 1882; AB Md Agric Coll. *Bost m&s j* 136:584, 1897. *JAMA* 28: 1156, 1897. *Med annals Md:* 591–92. *Polk* 1896: 666.

THOMAS, GEORGE WASHINGTON, Norristown, Pa (b/1790? d/IV–24–1848 @58) MD UPa 1813. *Tr Pa St M S* 1859:84; 1860:132–33. *Med reporter* (W Chester, Pa) 2:15, 1854.

THOMAS, GRIFFITH J, Pittsburgh (d/1891 @29) MD Medico–Chir Phil 1891 *Med bull m&s* 13:268, 1891.

THOMAS, ISAAC, W Chester, Pa (b/IX–16–1797 Chester Co; d/V–16–1879) MD UPa 1820. *Tr Pa St M S* 13: 261–68, 1880. *Atkinson* I: 309–10.

THOMAS, JAMES CAREY, Baltimore (b/VII–13–1833; d/XI–9–1897 @64) MD UMd 1854;AB Haverford 1851. *Med ann Md:* 392. *JAMA* 29:1081, 1129, 1897*Atkinson* I: 236–37. *K&B* III: 1200–01.

THOMAS, JAMES GRAY [GREY], CW–USA; Savannah; Washington, DC (b/VI–24–1835 Bloomfield, Ky; d/XII–6–1884) MD UCNY 1856. *JAMA* 4:222–24, 1885. *NC m j* 14:392, 1884. *Med bull m&s* 7:25, 1884. *K&B* III: 1201–02.

THOMAS, JAMES GREY, CW–CSA; Mobile, Ala (b/XII–15–1835 Cedar Rock; d/V–13–1904) MD UPa 1856. *U Pa med alum CW*: 1856. *Polk* 1886: 136.

THOMAS, JEFFERSON [JEFFREY] RANDALL, Bay City Mich (b/X–17–1827; d/IV–29–1883) MD Geneva 1850. *JAMA* 2:26, 1884. *Butler* 1878: 385.

THOMAS, JEROME E, Mexia, Tx (b/V–1–1852 Ala; d/IX–18–1897) <MD Mo M C 1886> *Tex m j* 13:248–49, 1897–98.

THOMAS, JESSE J, CW–USA (d/V–4–1862) MD ? *Nat med jour* 1:303, 1870/71.

THOMAS, JOHN GLOVER, Worcester, Mass (d/XI–29 1881 @35) MD Bowdoin 1879 *Bost m&s j* 106:24, 1882.

THOMAS, JOHN MOYLAN, Washington, DC (b/IX–29 1805; d/X–16–1853) MD UMd 1826. *Tr AMA* 31:1088–89, 1880. *Hist M S DC:* 229.

THOMAS, JOSEPH C, Cincinnati (d/XI–18–1890 @ 56) MD Bennett 1886. *JAMA* 27:1169, 1896.

THOMAS, JOSEPH DIO, Pittsburgh (d/I–10–1902) MD Bellevue 1869. *Pa med jour* 5:276,316, 1901/02; 6:262, 1902/03. *Flint* 1897: 831.

THOMAS, JOSEPH POTTS, Louisville (b/IX–9–1830 Clarksville, Tn; d/VI–26–1894) MD U Nashville 1871; <MD Ky Sch Med ad eundem> *JAMA* 23:86, 1894; 24:42, 1894. *Tr Ky St M S* ns3: , 1894. *Atkinson* I: 243.

THOMAS, KINSEY [KERSEY], G, Alliance, O (d/III–11–1869 @51) MD Cleveland M C 1851. *Med surg rep Phila* 20:256, 1869. *Tr O St M S* 1873:276. *Phila med reg & dir* 1871: 300.

THOMAS, LUTHER GOBLE, CW–USA (b/I–27–1830; d/V–1–1864) MD CPSNY 1852; AB Princeton 1849. *Tr M S NJ* 1865:69–70; 1867: 137.

THOMAS, MARY FRAME, Richmond, Ind (b/IX–25–1816 Berks Co, Pa; d/VIII–19–1888) Stud med Phil 1853–54; Cleveland 1854–55; Indianapolis 1869–70. *JAMA* 11:538–39, 1888. *Tr Ind St M S* 1889: 210. Kemper's *Indiana*: 348. *Butler* 1878: 222.

THOMAS, MOSES S, Leavenworth, Kans (d/VII–9–1896 @66) MD UMd 1853. *JAMA* 27:225, 1896.

THOMAS, RICHARD HENRY, Baltimore (b/VI–20–1805; d/I–15–1860. MD UPa 1827; AB 1822; AM 1825. *Tr AMA* 13:811–12, 1860. *Med ann Md:* 593. *Med s rep Phila* ns3:376, 1859/60. *Nashvl j m&s* 18:191, 1860.

THOMAS, RICHARD CURD, USA; Bowling Green, Ky (b/1838; d/XII–28–1879) MD Jefferson 1861. *Tr AMA* 31:1089–90, 1880. *Nashvl j m&s* ns25:137, 1880. *Med surg rep Phila* 42:66, 1880. *Med rec NY* 17:191, 1880.

THOMAS, ROBERT PENNELL, Philadelphia (b/V–29 1821; d/II–3–1864) MD UPa 1847. *Tr CPP* cent vol:264; ns4:159–62, 1863–64. *U Pa med alum CW*:1847. *Tr AMA* 18:326–27, 1867. *Tr Pa St M S* 1865:105–10. *K&B* III:1202–03.

THOMAS, THEODORE GAILLARD, NYC (b/XI–21–1831 Edisto Isl, SC; d/II–28–1903 Thomasville, Ga) MD M C SC 1852. *Chic m rec* 24:248–49, 1903. *Proc Conn Med Soc* 1903:395–96. *Bost m&s j* 148: 272–73, 455, 1903. *Atkinson* I: 23. *K&B* III: 1203.

THOMAS, THOMAS KEMBLE, Roxbury, Mass (d/XI–7–1863 S Barrington, Me) MD Harvard 1832; AB 1828. *Bost m&s j* 69:348, 1863.

THOMAS, TRISTRAM, Easton, Md (b/XII–25–1769 Talbot Co; d/VIII–5–1847) MD UPa 1792. *Med ann Md:* 593–94.

THOMAS, WILLIAM, Leonardtown, Md (b/III–8–1793 St Mary's Co; d/IX–30–1849) MD UPa 1814. *Med ann Md:* 594.

THOMAS, WILLIAM GEORGE, Tarboro, NC to 1850; Wilmington, NC (b/III–23–1818 Louisburg; d/II–18

Spec. educ'l status abbrev. as: ***ng*** = college verified attendance without degree;

1890) MD UPa 1840. *NC m j* 25:164–70, 1890. *Tr M S St NC* 1890:210–17. *K&B* III: 1204.

THOMASON, THOMAS J , Perrineville, NJ (b/1833 Phila; d/VIII–20–1880) MD Pa M C 1854? *Tr AMA* 33: 608, 1882. *Tr M S NJ* 1881:169.

THOMPSON, A W, Circleville O (d/IX–16–1895 @81) MD M C O 1841. *JAMA* 25:554, 1895. *Polk* 1890: 905.

THOMPSON, ABRAHAM GARDINER, Islip, NY (d/IX 26–1887 @71) MD CPSNY 1837; AB Columbia 1833; AM 1836. *Med reg NY NJ Conn* 1888:271. *Butler* 1878: 577.

THOMPSON, ABRAHAM RAND, Charlestown, Mass (b/V–20–1781; d/V–11–1866) Hon MD Dartm'th 1816; Hon MD Harvard 1826; lic c 1806. *Bost m&s j* 74: 328, 1866. *Med s rep Phila* 14:420, 1866. *K&B* III:1204.

THOMPSON, ALEXANDER, Aurora, NY (b/V–2–1809 Cambridge; d/IX–21–1869) MD CPSNY 1833; AB Union 1829. *Phila med reg & dir* 1871:302. *Tr M S St NY* 1871:362–68. *Tr AMA* 21:449, 1870.

THOMPSON, ALLEN L , Sandy Creek, NY (b/1811; d/ VIII– –1891) <MD Fairfield 1835> *Med reg NY NJ Conn* 1892:290. *Polk* 1886: 706.

THOMPSON, ALLEN R , Troy, NY (d/VIII–22–1903 Asbury Pk, NJ) MD Albany 1883. *Bost m&s j* 149:276, 1903. *Polk* 1896: 1108.

THOMPSON, ANDREW D , Philadelphia (d/IX– 1881) MD Jefferson 1877. *Med bull m&s* 3:247, 1881.

THOMPSON, ANDREW JACKSON, CW–USA; Salem, Mass (d/IV– –1879 @44) MD Harvard 1861. *Harvard in CW*: 268.

THOMPSON, AUSTIN WHITE, Northampton Mass (d/ VII–11–1889 @54) MD Harvard 1857; AB 1854. *Bost m&s j* 121: 75, 1889. *Butler* 1878: 358.

THOMPSON, BENEDICT, Washington, DC (b/IV– –1843; d/VII–22–1875) MD Columbian 1868. *Hist M S DC:* 290. *Tr AMA* 29:772–73, 1878. *Butler* 1874:95.

THOMPSON, BRADFORD SMITH, CW–USA; Salisbury, Conn (b/VI–13–1832 Thompson; d/I–1–1883) <MD UCNY 1861> MD Bellevue 1867; <Hon MD Yale 1872> *Proc Conn Med Soc* 1883: 177. *Atkinson* I:363.

THOMPSON, CHARLES A , Jefferson City, Mo (d/XII 15–1897 @74) <MD Indiana M C 1847> *JAMA* 30:48, 1898. *Butler* 1878: 440.

THOMPSON, DANIEL A , Indianapolis (b/1862 Rush Co; d/X–22–1904) MD M C Ind 1883. *Tr Ind St M S* 1905:460. *Polk* 1896: 476.

THOMPSON, EBEN, Newton Upper Falls, Mass (d/XII–7–1897 @49) MD Jefferson 1862. *Bost m&s j* 137:640, 1897. *Polk* 1896: 719.

THOMPSON, EDWIN B , CW–USA; Orange, NJ (d/III–24–1888 @57) MD UCNY 1857. *Med reg NY NJ Conn* 1888: 271. *Butler* 1878: 477.

THOMPSON, FOSTER HOCKETT, Preston, Miss (b/V 25–1816; d/I–31–1850) MD UPa 1840; stud U Ala 1836. *U Ala cat*: 58.

THOMPSON, FRANK L , Cleveland (d/IX–21–1897 @55) MD Ky Sch Med 1881. *JAMA* 29:761, 1897. *Polk* 1886: 749.

THOMPSON, FRANK P , St Louis (d/XI–5–1898) MD Ia St U 1882. *JAMA* 31:1257, 1898.

THOMPSON, FREDERICK, CW–CSA; Point Caswell, NC (d/1888) ng UCNY Med Sch 1861; MD U Nashville 1861. *NC m j* 21:128, 188. *Polk* 1886: 725.

THOMPSON, GEORGE, Sumner Co, Tn (b/V–2–1795 Albemarle Co, Va; d/IV–3–1874 Gallatin) Hon MD U Louisvl 1842; ng U Md Med Sch. *Tr M S Tenn* 1876:88.

THOMPSON, GEORGE, NYC (d/I–15–1877) MD UVt 1864. *Med reg NY NJ Conn* 1877:208. *Med rec NY* 12: 64, 1877. *Butler* 1878: 526.

THOMPSON, GEORGE ALBERT, Chicago (d/VI–1–1899 Shreveport, La) MD UCNY 1880. *JAMA* 32:1399, 1899. *Polk* 1896: 408.

THOMPSON [THOMSON], GEORGE NEWTON, Boston d/VII–13–1895 @82) MD Columbian 1843. *JAMA* 25:170, 1895. *Bost m&s j* 133:659, 1895. *Polk* 1890: 543.

THOMPSON, GEORGE W , Mt Union, Pa (d/I–4–1899 @85) MD Jefferson 1854. *JAMA* 32:196, 1899. *Polk* 1896:1293.

THOMPSON, GREEN HILL, Autaugaville, Ala (d/VIII 29–1886) <MD M C Atlanta 1860> *Tr M Assn St Ala* 1887:305. *Polk* 1886: 130.

THOMPSON, J KNOX, Petersburg & Dinwiddie CH, Va (b/VI–23–1824 Danville; d/III–19–1894) MD U Md 1868. *JAMA* 22:523, 1894. *Tr M S Va* 1894:190–91. *Butler* 1878: 837.

THOMPSON, JACOB ARTHUR, CW–CSA; Leasburg, NC (b/VI–24–1836; d/I–12–1903) MD UPa 1859. *U Pa med alum CW*: 1859.

THOMPSON, JAMES W , CW–USA (d/XI–25–1864 Wrightsville, Pa) MD ?Jefferson 1861. *Nat med jour* 1:303, 1870/71.

THOMPSON, JESSE C , S Bloomfield, O (b/I–9–1811 Heath, Mass; d/I–7–1879) MD Berkshire 1836. *Tr Ohio M S* 1889:8. *K&B* II:1140–11.

THOMPSON, JOHN ALEXANDER Jr, Wrightsville, Pa (d/I–13–1894 @35) MD Jefferson 1882. *JAMA* 22:122, 1894. *Off'l Reg Pa phys* 1881–88:416. *Polk* 1886: 840.

THOMPSON, JOHN B, Columbus (b/IX–15–1802 Cannonsburgh, Pa; d/V–12–1885) MD M C Ohio 1868. *Tr Ohio St M S* 1885: 203.

THOMPSON, JOHN CAMPBELL, So River, NJ (d/II–14–1895 @66) MD CPSNY 1856. *JAMA* 24:370, 1895. *Polk* 1886: 611.

THOMPSON, JOHN EMMET, Salem, Mo (d/I–19–1900 @75) Md Western Res 1888. *JAMA* 34:251, 1900.

THOMPSON, JOHN H , Otterbein, Ind (b/IV–16–1817 Cambridge, Md; d/XII–4–1883) MD UMd 1840. *Tr Ind St M S* 1884: 215.

THOMPSON, JOHN LELAND SHERMAN, Lancaster,

Mass (d/XII-25-1885 @74) MD Berkshire 1832. *Bost m&s j* 113:657, 1885.

THOMPSON, JOHN WESLEY, CW-USA (b/XI-4-1832 Phila; d/VII-1/4-1862/63 Coatesville, Pa) MD U Pa 1860. *U Pa med alum CW*:1860. *Nat med jour* 1:303, 1870/71. *Tr Ohio St M S* 1873:276.

THOMPSON, JOSEPH HEDGE, Salem, NJ (b/II-21-1815; d/XI-21-1886) MD UPa 1837. *Tr M S NJ* 1887: 296-97. *Butler* 1878: 477.

THOMPSON, JOSEPH WASHINGTON, CW-CSA; Paducah, Ky (b/VI-27-1838 Fancy Farm; d/III-30-1886) MD UPa 1859. *U Pa med alum CW*: 1859.

THOMPSON, LEVI H , Reading, Pa (b/Berks Co; d/X-23-1896 @73) MD Jefferson 1853. *JAMA* 27:1169, 1896. *Polk* 1886: 832.

THOMPSON, MARY HARRIS, Chicago (b/XI-15-1829 Ft Ann, NY; d/V-21-1895) MD New Engl Female Med Coll 1863; Hon MD Chic M C 1870. *Chic m rec* 8: 462, 1895. *JAMA* 24: 861, 1895. *Tr Ill St M S* 1896: 52-56. *Polk* 1886: 272.

THOMPSON, MATTHEW, Mt Vernon, O (b/Ireland; d/VI-19-1867 @51) MD UCNY 1844. *Tr Ohio St M S* 1868:197-98.

THOMPSON, NATHAN GRIER, Brandywine Manor, Pa (d/III-1-1894 Coatesville) MD Phila Coll M & S 1852. *JAMA* 22:391, 1894. *Butler* 1878: 743.

THOMPSON, NEWTON JASPER, CW-CSA; Graball, Tex (b/ VIII-29-1835; d/III-31-1897) <MD UPa> stud U Ala 1854. *U Ala cat*:124. *SHSP* 22:263, 1893.

THOMPSON, RALPH R , Mooresville, Ind (d/V-4-1906 @31) <MD M C Ind 1900> *Ill m j* 9:662, 1906.

THOMPSON, ROBERT, Columbus, O (b/1797 Pa; d/VIII-18-1865) MD M C Ohio 1834. *Tr AMA* 18:344-45, 1867. *Tr Ohio St M S* 1867:73-74. *Nashvl j m&s* ns1:319, 1866. *K&B* II:1142.

THOMPSON, SAMUEL M , Shelbyville, Tenn (d/V-28 1895 @58) MD U Nashville 1880. *JAMA* 24: 989, 1895. *Polk* 1890: 1061.

THOMPSON, SAMUEL Y , Danville, Pa (b/X-29-1843; d/X-28-1905) MD LICH 1866. *Pa med jour* 9: 147, 1905/06. *Ill m j* 1905:530. *Flint* 1897: 799.

THOMPSON, THOMAS C , CW-CSA; Galveston (b/IX-27 or 28-1839 Matagorda Co; d/IV-16/17-1898) MD Jefferson 1861; stud UNC 1857-59. *University medical* [U Galveston] 3(17):15, 1898. *Polk* 1890:1080.

THOMPSON, WILLIAM CLINTON, Indianapolis (d/IV 19-1897) MD Ohio M C 1839. *JAMA* 28:1091, 1897. *Polk* 1890: 376.

THOMPSON, WILLIAM ENOCH, CW-USA (d/V-31-1865 Indianapolis) MD U Mich 1858. *Nat med jour* 1:303, 1870/71.

THOMPSON, WILLIAM M MARSHALL, Opelousas, La (d/X-28-1906 @77) MD Tulane 1872. *New Orl m & s jour* 59:480, 1906. *Polk* 1896: 625.

THOMPSON, WILLIAM SEAL, CW-USA; Philadelphia (b/XI-29-1820 New Garden, Pa; d/VIII-10-1870) MD UPa 1857. *U Pa med alum CW*: 1857.

THOMPSON, WILLIAM Y , Luzerne, Pa (d/V-28-1903 @80) MD Castleton 1845. *Pa med jour* 7:280, 1903/04. *Flint* 1897: 808.

THOMSON, ARCHIBALD JOHN, Cadillac, Mich (d/I 27-1900 @59) MD U Mich 1879. *JAMA* 34:381, 1900. *Polk* 1890: 604.

THOMSON, CHARLES ROBERT, CW-CSA; ? (b/1825 Fort Motte, SC; d/1892) MD UPa 1848; AB SC 1845. *U Pa med alum CW*: 1848.

THOMSON [THOMPSON], CHARLES STEELE, New Haven, Conn (b/IV-6-1801 Tolland; d/VIII-15-1890) MD Yale 1822. *Med reg NY NJ Conn* 1892:290. *JAMA* 15: 626, 1890. *Proc Conn Med Soc* 1891: 298-99. *Bost m&s j* 123:192, 1890.

THOMSON, HORATIO, Belchertown, Conn (b/X-7-1803 Tolland; d/X-5-1860) MD Yale 1827. *Bost m&s j* 63:236-38, 1861.

THOMSON, I DAVIS, Baltimore (b/1832 Frederick Co; d/VI-14-1881) MD UMd 1861. *Med annals Md:* 595. *Butler* 1874: 316.

THOMSON, JOSEPH E , Delhi, La (d/XI-27-1905) MD Tulane 1901. *New Orl m&s j* 58:609, 682-83, 1906.

THOMSON, WILLIAM HENRY, New Haven, Conn (d/X-18-1893) MD Yale 1862. *Med reg NY NJ Conn* 1894: 250. *JAMA* 21:667, 1893. *Pr Conn M S* 1894: 245-47. *Butler* 1878: 83.

THORLEY, JOHN DAVID, Harrisburg, Pa (d/XI-13 1906 @58) MD Jefferson 1871. *Pa med jour* 10:295, 1906/07. *Off'l Reg Pa phys* 1881-88: 150.

THORN, ELIHU, Yellow Spr, O (b/I-11-1819 Oldtown; d/X-2-1876. <MD in Louisville 1848> MD Starling 1850. *Tr O St M S* 1877:65.

THORN, FRANK ARTHUR, Seattle (b/1860; d/XI-26-1904) MD CPS Chic 1891. *JAMA* 43:1983, 1904.

THORN, JAMES, London, Engl to 1832; Troy, NY 1832- (b/VII-20-1802 Colchester Engl; d/XI-27-1876) Hon MD Regents, U St NY 1850; <MRCS (L) 1824> *Tr M S St NY* 1877:365-67. *Med surg rep Phila* 35: 504. *Med rec* 12:408. *Butler* 1874: 562.

THORN, JAMES G , NYC (d/XI-18-1867 @57) MD ? *Med reg NY NJ Conn* 1867: 228.

THORN, JOHN S , Washington & Millbrook, NY (b/VIII-14-1821 Milan, NY; d/XI-11-1879) MD Castleton 1844. *Med s rep Phila* 41:528, 1879. *Tr M S NY* 1880: 464-65. *Butler* 1874: 562.

THORNBERRY, JOHN R , Crawfordsville Ind (d/IX-19 1894 @44) MD ? *JAMA* 23:561, 1894. *Polk* 1890: 367.

THORNDIKE [THORNDYKE], WILLIAM, CW-USA; Beverly, Mass; Milwaukee (d/I-29-1887 @51) MD Harvard 1857; AB 1854. *Bost m&s j* 116:122-23, 1887. *Harvard in CW*: 76. *Butler* 1878: 867.

THORNDIKE, WILLIAM HENRY, Boston (b/VI-5-1824 Salem; d/XII-26-1884) MD Harvard 1848; AB

 Spec. educ'l status abbrev. as: ***ng*** = college verified attendance without degree;

1845. *JAMA* 9:447–48, 1887. *Bost m&s j* 112:24, 69–70, 117, 1885; 113:656, 1885. *K&B* III: 1209–10.

THORNE, HENRY MARIANO, NYC (b/X–12–1852; d/III–9–1886) MD CPSNY 1874. *Med reg NY NJ Conn* 1886:255. *Butler* 1878: 526 [as Marianne Thorner!]

THORNE, JOHN SULLIVAN, Brooklyn (b/1807; d/IX–1–1880) MD CPSNY 1829. *Med reg NY NJ Conn* 1881: 242. *Butler* 1878: 535.

THORNE, MAX, Cincinnati (d/VIII–26–1899 @40) <MD U Munich 1884> *JAMA* 33:620, 1899. *Polk* 1896: 1168.

THORNLEY, JOHN, USN 1860–71; ? (b/VIII–27–1816 Bowling Green, Va; d/XI–8–1887) MD UPa 1838. *U Pa med alum CW*: 1848.

THORNTON, CHARLES, Cincinnati (d/VI–22–1868 @35) MD M C Ohio 1855. *Phila med reg & dir* 1871: 297. *Med surg rep Phila* 19:42, 1868.

THORNTON, GEORGE FRANCIS, CW–CSA; San Francisco (d/VIII–15–1893) <MD New Orl Med Sch> AB U Ala 1859. *JAMA* 21: 357, 1893.

THORNTON, JAMES B C , Snickersville, Va (b/1809! d/I–15–1839) MD UMd 1818. *Hist M S DC:* 229.

THORNTON, JOSEPH BACON, Eufaula, Ala; CW–CSA (b/VI–27–1840; d/1862 Manassas) <MD U La> AB U Ala 1858. *U Ala cat*: 130.

THORNTON, M Van B , CW–CSA; Hempstead, Tex (b/VIII–19–1840 Washington, DC; d/IX–28–1904) MD Columbian 1861; AB Madison Coll, Miss. *Tex st j m* 1: 245, 1905/06.

THORNTON, PATRICK H , Lakeport, Cal (d/III–24–1905 @69) MD U Louisville 1857. *So pract* 27:267, 1905. *Cal st j med* 3:198, 1905.

THORNTON, SAMUEL CARY, Moorestown, NJ (b/ 1791 Buckingham, Pa; d/III–19–1858) MD UPa 1816. *Tr AMA* 28:622, 1877. *Tr M S NJ* 1876: 140.

THORNTON, SAMUEL CARY Jr, Moorestown, NJ (b/ IV–26–1830; d/IV–10–1888) MD UPa 1852. *Tr M S NJ* 1888–89: 165–67. *Butler* 1878: 477.

THORNTON, THOMAS W , Kansas City, Mo (d/X–23 1899 @70) <MD U Louisville 1851> *JAMA* 33:1183, 1899. *Polk* 1886: 552.

THORNTON, WILLIAM, Washington, DC (b/V–27–1761 Tortola Isl, WI; d/III–27–1828) <MD Edinburgh> *Hist M S DC:* 221. *K&B* III: 1211.

THRAILKILL, JOHN W , St Louis, Mo (d/II–2–1883) MD Eclect Med Inst Cincinnati 1864. *Minn med mo* 1883: 66 (Mar). *Butler* 1874: 407. Eclectic.

THRALL, SENECA BROWN, CW–USA; Ottumwa, Ia 1856– (b/VIII–9–1832 Utica, O; d/I–20–1888) MD UCNY 1853; att Starling. *Atkinson* I: 67. *Tr Ia St M S* 7: 519–20, 1889. *Polk* 1886: 365.

THRASHER, MARTIN EDWARD, Vt; NYC (d/1858 Ft Wayne, Ind @26) MD U Vt 1857. *Med surg rep Phila* ns1:140, 1858/59.

THROCKMORTON, JOHN A , Houston, Tex (d/XII–28–1895 @75) <MD Transylvania 1844> *JAMA* 26:142, 1896. *Tex med jour* 11:395, 1895–96. *Polk* 1886: 888.

THROCKMORTON, JOHN B , Freehold, NJ (b/IV–3–1796; d/IX–19–1856) Lic 1822; att CPSNY. *Tr M S NJ* 1871: 81–82.

THROOP, BENJAMIN BADEN, Bourbon Co, Ky;CW–CSA; Lavaca Co & Anderson, Tex (b/1812; d/1874) Stud med Phila & Louisville, Ky. *Tr Tex St M Assn* 1875: 224.

THROOP, BENJAMIN H , Scranton, Pa (b/XI–9–1811 Oxford, NY; d/VI–26–1897) MD Fairfield 1833. *JAMA* 29:92, 1897. *Polk* 1896: 1336.

THROOP, JAMES MOTT, CW–USA; Lebanon, NY 1866–68 (b/VII–4–1838 Hamilton, NY; d/V–15–1889) MD UCNY 1862. *Tr M S NY* 1891:463–64.

THRUSH, THOMAS BENTON, Kansas City, Mo (d/II–11–1900 @38) MD Kansas City M C 1891. *JAMA* 34: 511, 1900.

THRUSTON, STEPHEN DOUGLAS [or DECATUR], CW–CSA; Dallas, Tex (b/XI–28–1833 Hickory Fork, Va; d/XI–15 1906) MD UPa 1854; att U Va 1851–53; stud law. *Tex st med jour* 2:223, 1906/07. *U Pa med alum CW*: 1854. *Polk* 1886: 884.

THUM, FREDERICK WILLIAM, Newark (b/IV–24 1865; d/VI–27–1902) MD CPSNY 1891; PhG NY Coll Pharm 1885. *Bost m&s j* 147:30, 1902. *Tr M S NJ* 1903: 386–87.

THURMAN, WILLIAM M , NYC (d/VII–21–1897) MD CPSNY 1864; AB UCNY 1860. *Bost m&s j* 137: 117, 1897. *JAMA* 29:297, 1897.

THURMOND, MILTON W , Lexington, Ky (b/SC; d/VI–26–1833 Carlisle) Stud med Transylv @ death. *Transylv jour med & assoc sci* 6:306, 1833.

THURSTON, ALFRED HENRY, CW–USA (b/1833? RI; d/VIII–2–1865 @32 Louisville) MD UCNY 1855. *Nat med jour* 1:303, 1870/71. *Med surg rep Phila* 13: 133, 1865. *Heitman*.

THURSTON, ARTHUR BURDETTE, Keene, NH (b/ IX–29–1958 Hartford, Vt; d/IX–17–1894) MD Dartmouth 1881. *JAMA* 23:593, 1894. *Polk* 1886: 709.

THWEATT, JOHN JAMES, Petersburg, Va (d/XII–13 1868) MD UPa 1836. *Phila med reg & dir* 1871: 299. *Med surg rep Phila* 20:40, 1869.

TIBBALS, WILLIAM F , Cincinnati (b/1843? d/IX–29–1879 @36) MD ? *Med surg rep Phila* 41:574, 1879.

TIBBETS, SAMUEL, Cincinnati (b/1777? d/VIII–12–1866 @91) MD ? *Med surg rep Phila* 15:208, 1866.

TIBO [TEBO], GEORGE HAYNES, Mt Sterling, Ill (b/VII–1–1838 Greensburgh, Ind; d/III–11–1888) MD Rush 1872. *Tr Ill St M S* 1890: 41.

TICE, LEWIS, CW–USA; Yorkville, NY (b/VIII–26–1827 Brockport; d/XII–23–1872) MD UCNY 1851; AB Union 1848. *Med reg NY NJ Conn* 1873: 353. *Med rec* 8: 185, 1873. *Med surg rep Phila* 28:52, 1873.

TICHENOR, HIRAM HALSEY, Newark, NJ (b/VIII–1 1828; d/V–2–1892) MD UCNY 1854. *Tr M S NJ* 1892:

296–97. *Med reg NY NJ Conn* 1892:290. *NW med jour* 20:128, 1892. *JAMA* 18:684, 1892.

TICHENOR, JACOB, Owensboro, Ky (b/1830; d/IX–12 1872 @42) MD U Louisville 1861. *Med surg rep Phila* 27:332, 1872.

TICKNOR, ALMON PEASE, ? (b/Lebanon NY; d/XII–25–1858 @36) MD Yale 1853. *Bost m&s j* 60:48, 1859.

TICKNOR, BENAJAH, USN (b/1786 Jericho, Vt; d/ XI–20–1858 Ann Arbor, Mich) Hon MD Berkshire 1838; Hon MD Yale 1836. *Pr Conn M S* 1864: 59–60. *Tr AMA* 13:823, 1860. *Bost m&s j* 59:248, 1859. *Med s rep Phila* ns1:44, 1858/59.

TICKNOR, LUTHER, Salisbury, Conn (b/III–9–1790 Jericho, Vt; d/IV–19–1846) Hon MD Berkshire 1827; Hon MD Yale 1829. *Tr AMA* 3:467–68, 1850. *Proc Conn Med Soc* 1863: 292–98.

TICKNOR [TINKER], MARTIN ANDERSON [AMOS], Brooklyn (b/IX–21–1821 Westfield, Mass; d/IX–11–1885) MD UCNY 1854; MD Berkshire 1856; ng Amherst 1848. *New Engl med times* 13:216, 1878[?]. Homeopath.

TIDBALL, LEANDER, Monticello, Ill (b/1847? d/V–19 1905 @58) MD U Mich 1874; MD UCNY 1883. *Ill med jour* 7:1611, 1905. *Polk* 1896: 430.

TIDD, EBENEZER, Clark, Pa (b/1845? d/III–17–1906 @ 61) MD U Mich 1870. *Pa med jour* 9: 523, 1905/06. *Polk* 1886: 795.

TIFFANY, RUSSELL H , Hartford, Conn (b/I–24–1812 Torrington; d/II–6–1892) MD Castleton 1837. *Proc Conn Med Soc* 1892: 843–44. *Butler* 1878: 83.

TIFFIN, CLAYTON, USA 1814–15; New Orleans (d/X–12–1859) MD ? *Med surg rep Phila* ns3:173, 1859/60. *Heitman*.

TILDEN, DANIEL, Sandusky, O (b/VIII–19–1788 Lebanon, NH; d/V–7–1870) MD Dartmouth 1812. *Tr Ohio St M S* 1870:245–49. *K&B* II: 1148–49.

TILDEN, JOHN NEWELL, Peekskill, NY (b/VI–16–1842 Onondaga, NY; d/VII–10–1902) MD LICH 1872. *Bost m&s j* 147: 88, 1902. *Polk* 1876: 1089.

TILFORD, JOHN H, Windom, Minn (d/IX–7–1899) MD Indiana M C 1873. *JAMA* 33:745, 1899. *Polk* 1886: 519.

TILGHMAN [TILMAN], FRISBY, Hagerstown, Md (d/ c1848) MD U Md 1829. *Med annals Md:* 597.

TILLEY, ROBERT, Chicago (b/1843? d/VI–1/2–1898 @55) MD Chicago M C 1876. *Chic m rec* 14:544, 1898. *JAMA* 30:1481, 1898. *Flint* 1897: 270.

TILLINGHAST, GEORGE HOPKINS, Providence, RI (b/III–19–1795; d/VIII–22–1858) MD ? AB Brown 1814. *Brown hist cat*: 1814.

TILLSON, HOSEA, CW–USA; Centerville, Ind (b/XII–15–1830 Darke Co, O; d/XI–21–1902) ng Miami M C. *Tr Ind St M S* 1903:356. Kemper's *Indiana*: 349.

TILTON, HENRY REMSEN, USA; Sacket's Harbor, NY (b/1836? d/VI–25–1906 @70) MD UPa 1859. *Bost m&s j* 155:26, 1906. *Polk* 1896: 1907.

TILTON, JAMES, RevWar–USA; Delaware (b/VI–1–1745 Kent Co [then in Pa] d/V–14–1822) MD UPa 1771. *Tr CPP* cent vol: 287. *Congr biogr dir*. *K&B* III: 1214.

TIMMONDS, GEORGE WASHINGTON, New Corydon, Ind (b/1842? d/X–8–1869 @27) nd U Mich Med Dept 1869. *Phila med reg & dir* 1871: 302.

TIMMS [TIMME], CHARLES WILLIAM, CW–CSA (b/V–21–1839 Red House, Va; d/X–22–1866 Buffalo, Va) MD U Pa 1861. *U Pa med alum CW*: 1861.

TINDALL, DANIEL WEBSTER, CW–USA; Taylor Mo (b/IX–19 1836 Phila; d/V–16–1904) MD U Mich 1864; BS Ill Coll 1859. *Rec AAS USA* 1891:96.

TINDLE, ROBERT McGREW, CW–USA; Pittsburgh (b/VIII–15 1830; d/XI–15–1895) MD UPa 1852. *U Pa med alum CW*: 1852. *Polk* 1886: 830.

TINEN, EDWARD HAROLD, Chicago (d/I–28–1896 @ 22) MD Rush 1893. *Chic m rec* 10:157, 1896. *JAMA* 26: 287, 1896.

TINGLEY, HENRY AUGUSTUS, Susquehanna, Pa (b/ Attleboro, Mass; d/X–28–1905 @85) MD Buffalo 1848. *Pa med jour* 9:220, 1905/06. *Flint* 1897: 830.

TINGLEY, HILBERT B , Rockaway Beach, NY (d/I–14 1903 @37) MD Balto U 1889. *Bost m&s j* 148:108 1903.

TINKER, CHARLES A , NYC (b/Mystic Bridge, Conn; d/VII–11–1906 @51) MD NY Hom 1879. *Bost m&s j* 155:78, 1906. *Polk* 1896: 1081. Homeopath.

TINSLAR, BENJAMIN RUSH, USN (d/XI–23–1864 Charlestown, Mass @64) MD ? *Nat med jour* 1:303, 1870/71.

TIPTON, JOSEPH S, CW–CSA, CSN; Hillsville Va (b/ 1837; d/III–V 1906 Roanoke) MD UCNY 1860. UCNY cat: 1860.

TITCOMB, BERIAH [BENIAH], Baltimore (b/1815 Vt; d/II–23–1882) MD U Md 1864. *Med annals Md:* 597.

TITSWORTH, JOHN, Sussex Co, NJ (b/IV–19–1793 Wantage, NJ; d/II–1–1873) MD Yale 1818; AB 1814; AM 1820. *Tr AMA* 24:366, 1873. *Tr M S NJ* 1873: 119. *Med surg rep Phila* 28: , 1873.

TITSWORTH, RANDOLPH, Plainfield, NJ (b/II–26–1821 Middlesex Co, NJ; d/III–18–1890) MD Hahnemann Phila 1853. *Med vis* 6:137, 1890. *Tr Am Inst Hom* 1890:151. *Polk* 1886: 610. *Cleave*. Homeopath.

TOBEY, JAMES EDWIN, Central Falls, RI (b/X–18–1848 Greenville; d/VII–28–1891) MD Harvard 1872. *Bost m&s j* 125:152, 1891. *Tr RI M S* 4:343 ff, 1889–93.

TOBEY, SAMUEL BOYD, Providence RI (b/Me; d/VI–23–1867 @ 61) MD UPa 1828. *Bost m&s j* 76:461–63, 1867.

TOBIE, PIERRE PHILIPPE EDWARD, Buffalo (b/V–1–1831 Forbach, Fr; d/V–12–1889) MD Geneva 1854; stud med Buffalo. *Buff m & s jour* 28:693, 1889. *Atkinson* I: 376. *Polk* 1886: 654.

TOBIEN, ALBERT SYLVESTER, Templeton, Mass (d/V 10–1890 @45) MD UCNY 1874. *Bost m&s j* 122:466, 1890. *Polk* 1886:474.

 Spec. educ'l status abbrev. as: ***ng*** = college verified attendance without degree;

TODD, FRANCIS WALTON, Springfield, Ill; Port Gibson, Miss; Auburn, Stockton, Capitola, Cal; Mex-War-USA (b/IV-17-18__ Bardstown, Ky; d/VIII-5-1898) MD Cincinnati Coll Med 1838. *JAMA* 31:551, 1898. *Atkinson* I: 519. *Polk* 1896: 213.

TODD, FRED ARTHUR, Toledo, O (d/IX-30-1898 @ 33 Chicago) MD U Mich 1886. *JAMA* 31:871-72, 1898.

TODD, GEORGE BRAINARD, USA & USN (b/1833 Onondaga Co, NY; d/IX-22-1874 Pensacola, Fl) <att UCNY> *Tr AMA* 26:466-67, 1875. *Med annals Md:* 597.

TODD, GEORGE R C, CW-CSA; Barnwell, SC (d/IV-25-1900) MD Transylvania 1848. *JAMA* 34:1210, 1900. *SHSP* 22:264, 1893. *Polk* 1886: 851.

TODD, HANFORD COMSTOCK, Dobbs Ferry, NY (b/II-17-1832 Norwalk, Conn; d/VIII-1-1870) MD CPS NY 1853. *Med reg NY NJ Conn* 1871:365; 1872:358.

TODD, JAMES R, Gridley, Cal (d/IV-21-1903) MD Kansas City M C 1883. *Cal st j m* 1:174, 1903. *Polk* 1896: 215.

TODD, JOHN R, CW-USA; Omaha, Nebr 1871-72; Lebanonville, NJ 1872- (b/Hunterdon Co, NJ; d/VII-12 1876 @35) MD CPSNY 1864. *Tr AMA* 28:625-26, 1877. *Tr M S NJ* 1877: 134. *Med s rep Phil* 35:120 1876.

TODD, LEVI LUTHER, Indianapolis (b/1830 Nicholasville, Ky; d/XI-16-1901) MD U Louisville 1856. *Tr Ind St M S* 1902:425. *Polk* 1896: 476.

TODD, LYMAN BEECHER, Lexington (b/IV-16-1832 Fayette Co, Ky; d/1902) MD Jefferson 1854; AB Centre Coll, Ky 1850. *Bost m&s j* 146:560, 1902. *Atkinson* I: 673. *Polk* 1896: 589.

TODD, ORRIN DERBY, Eminence, Ky (b/IV-28-1841 Shelby Co; d/V-4-1896 @55 Louisville) MD Jefferson 1865. *Buff m & s jour* 35:975, 1896. *Tr Ky St M S* 1897: 283-89. *JAMA* 26:995, 1896. *Polk* 1896: 583.

TODD, ROBERT NATHANIEL, CW-USA;Indianapolis (b/I-4 1827 Lexington, Ky; d/VI-13-1883) <MD Ind M C 1851; MD U Louisvl 1871> *Tr Ind St M S* 1884:209. *Atkinson* I: 522.

TODD, SETH JEWETT, Washington, DC (b/VIII-3-1842; d/III-13-1874) MD Columbian 1862. *Tr AMA* 25:525-26, 1874. *Hist M S DC:* 269.

TODD, SIMEON SEYMOUR, MexWar USA; Lawrenceburg, Ky to 1854; CW-USA; Calif to 1865; Kans City, Mo 1865- (b/VIII-10-1826 Vevay, Ind; d/X-19-1899) <MD Ind M C 1849> *JAMA* 33:1182, 1899. *Atkinson* I: 160.

TODD, VERNON [VERNER], L, Kansas City, Kans (b/1867? d/XII-22-1898 @31) <MD CPS Balto 1890> *JAMA* 32: 41, 1899.

TODD, WILLIAM ALLISON, Chariton, Ia (b/IV-4-1838 Danville, Ind; d/III-24-1897) MD M C Ind 1874. *Tr Ia St M S* 16:392, 1898. *JAMA* 28:1252, 1897. *Polk* 1896: 514.

TODD, WILLIAM SHERIDAN, Ridgefield, Conn (b/I-1 1840 Coleraine, Mass; d/II-19-1893) MD CPSNY 1869; AB Wesleyan 1864; AM 1867. *Med reg NY NJ Conn* 1893:316. *Pr Conn M S* 1893:254. *Butler* 1878: 83.

TOLAND, HUGH HUGER [HUGHES], San Francisco (b/IV-6-1806 Guilder's Crk, SC; d/II-28-1880) MD Transylv 1828. *Tr AMA* 31:1090-93, 1880. *Med s rep Phil* 42:242-308, 1880. *Waring* II:311. *K&B* III:1215-6.

TOLFORD, DANIEL MOUNTFORT, Portland, Me (b/VI-23-1844; d/I-12-1882) MD CPSNY 1874. *Tr Me Med Assoc* 1883:147. *Butler* 1878: 313.

TOLLES, NATHANIEL, Claremont, NH (b/IX-17-1805 Weathersfield, Vt; d/IV-24-1879) MD Dartmouth 1831. *Tr NH M S* 1880:117-20.

TOLMAN, HARVEY PUTNAM, E Onondaga, NY (d/XI 10-1901 @78) MD CPSNY 1848. *Bost m&s j* 145:582, 1901. *Polk* 1896: 1088.

TOLSON, BENJAMIN FRANKLIN, Chicago (d/IX-12 1901) MD Jefferson 1872. *Ill m j* ns3:295, 1901.

TOMBOEKEN [TOMBOKEN;TOMBREKEN] HENRY, Chicago (d/II-7-1903) MD Rush 1866. *Tr M S Ill* ns4: 665, 1903. *Polk* 1896: 408.

TOMLINSON, GEORGE, Shiloh, NJ (b/III-28-1808 Stow Crk, NJ; d/III-31-1892) MD Fairfield 1831. *Tr M S NJ* 1892: 205-06.

TOMLINSON, THOMAS PIERSON, CW-USA (b/VI-24-1844 Bristol, Pa; d/IX-7-1865 Nashville) MD UPa 1865. *U Pa m alum CW*:1865. *Nat m j* 1:303, 1870/71.

TOMPKINS, FRANK A, Sandy Pt, Tex; Galveston (b/Edgefield, SC; d/VII-26-1888 @59?) <MD Transylv 1852> *Daniel's Tex m j* 4:87, 1888.

TOMPKINS, FRED J, Lansingburgh, NY (d/VIII-12 1901) MD Albany 1885. *JAMA* 37:527, 1901.

TOMPKINS, JOHN EDWARD, Mobile, Ala (d/VI-30-1895) MD Vanderbilt 1880; att U Ala. *U Ala cat*: 251.

TOMPKINS, SILAS, New Bedford, Mass (b/X-8-1799 Little Compton, RI; d/XII-21-1853) MD Harvard 1828; AB Brown 1824;.AM. *Brown hist cat*: 1824.

[Le] TONELIER, JOHN STRINGER, NYC (b/VIII-25-1788 Schenectady; d/I-25-1873) MD CPSNY 1837. *Med reg NY NJ Conn* 1873:35. *Med rec NY* 8:144, 1873.

TONER, JOSEPH MEREDITH, Washington, DC 1855- (b/IV-30-1825 Pittsburgh; d/VIII-1-1896 Cresson Spr, Pa) MD Jefferson 1853; ng Woodstock 1850; att St Mary's Coll, Md. *JAMA* 27: 390, 1896. *Atkinson* I:166-67. *Hist M S DC:* 255-57. *Med annals Md:* 598. *K&B* III: 1218-19.

TOOKER, ROBERT NEWTON, CW-USA; Cincinnati 5 yrs; Chicago 1875- (b/III-28-1841 Rochester, NY; d/XI-9 1902) MD Bellevue 1865; att Rush 2 yrs; AB Genesee 1859. *Tr Am Inst Hom* 1903:728-29. *Polk* 1886: 272. Homeopath.

TOOLE, BARCKLEY WALLACE, CW-CSA; Marysville, Tenn; Talladega, Ala 1864- (b/II-17-1835; d/III-27-1898) MD U Nashville 1861. *Tr M S St Ala* 1898: 42-43, 241. *Polk* 1886: 140.

TOON, ALBERT, Louisville (d/V-9-1898 @58) MD M

C Ohio 1866. *JAMA* 30:1248, 1898. *Polk* 1896: 596.

TOOTHAKER, CHARLES EVERETT, Philadelphia (b/XI-30-1805 Dorchester, Mass; d/X-5-1890) MD Hahnemann 1851; AB Brown 1833. *Med vis* 7:48, 1891. *Polk* 1886: 826. *Cleave*. Homeopath.

TOPPING, GEORGE WASHINGTON, De Witt, Mich (b/XII-11-1827 Wentz, Pa; d/I-14-1895) MD U Mich 1854 *JAMA* 24:177 1895. *Atknsn* I:134 *Butler* 1878:384.

TOPPING, HENRY F, NYC (b/Unionville, NY; d/XI-15-1885 @61) MD CPSNY 1850. *Butler* 1878: 526. *Med reg NY NJ Conn* 1886: 255.

TOPPING, HENRY F Jr, NYC (d/VII-17-1890) MD UCNY 1884. *Med reg NY NJ Conn* 1891: 281. *Polk* 1886: 695.

TORRENCE, JAMES McNUTT, Jamestown, O (b/X-16 1819; d/VII-29-1899) ng Med Coll Ohio 1849-50, *Tr Ohio M S* 1890:7, 300. *Butler* 1878: 653.

TORREY, AUGUSTUS, Beverly, Mass (d/XI-1-1880) MD Harvard 1827; AB 1824; AM. *Tr AMA* 32:543, 1881. *Bost m&s j* 103:508, 1880.

TORREY, IRA A, CW-USA (d/IX-16-1863) MD ? *Nat med jour* 1:303, 1870/71.

TORREY, JOHN, NYC (b/VIII-15-1796; d/III-10-1873) MD CPSNY 1818; Hon AM Yale 1823. *Med reg NY NJ Conn* 1873: 355. *Med rec NY* 8:144, 1873. *K&B* III: 1219-20.

TORREY, NOAH, S Braintree, Mass (d/V-9-1897) MD Jefferson 1847. *JAMA* 28:1045, 1897. *Polk* 1896: 722.

TORREY, WILLIAM STONE, Brooklyn (d/III-4-1898 @35) MD UCNY 1884; att Lafayette. *JAMA* 30:624, 1898.

TOTTEN, GILBERT T, CW-USA (b/III-4-1840 Phila; d/V-29-1872 Quezaltenango, Guatemala) MD CPSNY 1861; AB Columbia 1858. *Med reg NY NJ Conn* 1873: 357. *Med surg rep Phila* 27: 94, 1872. *Med rec NY* 7: 448, 1872; 8:22, 1873.

TOTTEN, THOMAS HENRY, New Haven, Conn (b/III--1815; d/III-26-1874) MD Yale 1837. *Proc Conn Med Soc* 4:291, 1874.

TOUATRE, JUST CHARLES, New Orleans (b/IX-2-1838 Puycasquier, Fr; d/IX-21-1901) MD Paris 1865. *New Orl m&s j* 54:346, 408-09, 1901. *Polk* 1896:624. *K&B* III:1220-21.

TOURTELLOT, JOHN QUINCY ADAMS, Fall River, Mass (d/X-28-1892 @51) MD Bellevue 1873. *Bost m&s j* 127: 444, 1892. *Butler* 1878: 358.

TOURTELLOT, LOUIS A, Utica, NY (d/IV-4-1899 @67) MD UCNY 1854. *Tr M S St NY* 1900: 431. *Polk* 1886: 713.

TOURTELOT, FREEMAN, Greenfield, NY 36 yrs (b/VIII-4-1806 Corinth; d/XII-14-1868) MD Yale 1831. *Tr M S St NY* 1869:260-61. *Med rec NY* 3:558, 1868-69.

TOWARD, JOHN WILSON, Augusta, Me (b/X-15-1816 Vienna; d/1894?) MD Bowdoin 1847. *Tr Me M Assn* 12:186, 1895-97. *Bost m&s j* 133:195, 1895.

TOWER, CHARLES CARROLL, CW-USA; S Weymouth, Mass (d/V-29-1893 @59) MD Harvard 1856. *Bost m&s j* 128:583-84. *Harv in CW*:98. *Polk* 1886: 472.

TOWLE, JOSHUA J, Jamestown, NY (d/III-11-1898 @61) MD Berkshire 1862. *JAMA* 30:745, 1898. *Buff m & s jour* 37: 699, 1898. *Flint* 1897: 660.

TOWLE, SAMUEL KNAPP, CW-USA; Haverhill, Mass (d/VIII-16-1895 @66)MD Jefferson 1858; att Harvard 1858. *JAMA* 25:427, 1895. *Bost m&s j* 133:659, 1895. *Harvard in CW*: 251.

TOWLER, SAMUEL SMALLPAGE, Marionville Pa (b/VI-6-1843 Manchester, Engl; d/VI-19-1900) ng U Mich 1872-73; lic 1868. *Pa med jour* 4:85-86. 1900/01. *Polk* 1886: 806.

TOWLES, LEROY CROWNING, Accokee, Md (d/III-7 1900 @44) MD U Md 1878; AB Wash & Lee 1875. *JAMA* 34: 702, 1900.

TOWLES, WILLIAM BEVERLY, Missouri, Vt; Charlottesville, Va (b/III-2-1847 Fluvanna Co; d/IX-15 1893) MD U Va 1869. *Bost m&s j* 129:336, 1893. *JAMA* 21:746, 1893. *Tr M S Va* 1893: 219. *New Orl m&s j* 21: 398, 543, 1893-94. *K&B* III: 1221.

TOWNE, DEAN, Worcester, Mass (b/II-7-1810; d/III-4 1895) MD Castleton 1833. *JAMA* 24:422, 1895.

TOWNS, WILLIS U, Alvin, Tex (d/V-16-1906 McComb, Miss) MD ? *Tex st jour med* 2: 200, 1906.

TOWNSEND, ALBION PARRIS KEITH, Sidney, Me (b/1823; d/I-14-1873) MD Jefferson 1855; ng Bowdoin Med 1853. *Bowdoin cat*: 1853.

TOWNSEND, CLAYTON WILLIAM, Lanthal, O (b/XI 8-1847 Fredericktown; d/VI-30-1880) MD CPSNY 1870; ng Haverford. *Haverford biogr cat*: 148. *Butler* 1878: 631.

TOWNSEND, ELISHA, Philadelphia (d/X-3-1858) MD ? *Med s rep Phil* ns1:60, 1858/59. *Buff m j* 14:377, 1858.

TOWNSEND, FRANKLIN Jr, Albany, NY (d/X-31-1895 @ 41) MD CPSNY 1876. *Buff m&s j* 35: 424 ff, 1895. *JAMA* 25:911, 1895.

TOWNSEND, GEORGE DREW, CW-USA; Roxbury Mass (b/Providence, RI; d/VIII-20-1888 @46 Norfolk, Va) MD UPa 1865. *Bost m&s j* 119:240, 1888. *U Pa med alum CW*: 1865.

TOWNSEND, GEORGE JAMES, S Natick, Mass (d/XII 9-1894 @71) MD Harvard 1846; AB 1842. *Bost m&s j* 131: 600, 1894.

TOWNSEND, HOWARD, Albany, NY (b/XI-22-1823; d/I-16-1867) MD UPa 1847; ng Albany Med; pg Paris. *Tr AMA* 18:324, 1867. *Tr M S St NY* 1867:468-69. *Chic m j* 24:237, 1867.

TOWNSEND, JAMES C, Glen Cove NY (d/X-30-1883 @85) MD CPSNY 1820. *Med reg NY NJ Conn* 1883: 235. *Butler* 1878: 577.

TOWNSEND, JOHN FONDEY, NYC (d/I-8-1874 @ 64) MD UPa 1830; AB Union 1827. *Med reg NY NJ Conn* 1874: 292. *Med surg rep Phila* 30:88, 132, 1874.

    Spec. educ'l status abbrev. as: ***ng*** = college verified attendance without degree;

TOWNSEND, JUSTUS [JUSTICE], Springfield, Ill (d/XII–20–1900) MD Berkshire 1852. *Ill m j* ns2:533, 1901. *Polk* 1886: 298.

TOWNSEND, PETER SOLOMON, NYC (d/III–26–1849 @53) MD CPSNY 1816; AB Columbia 1812; AM 1816. *Tr AMA* 3:468–70, 1850. *South m&s j*:5:448, 1849.

TOWNSEND, RALPH MILBOURNE, Philadelphia (d/XII–12–1877) MD Jefferson 1866. *Tr CPP* cent vol:270.

TOWNSEND, RICHARD HAND, Philadelphia (b/II–10–1817; d/VIII–28–1898) MD UPa 1841. *Tr CPP* cent vol: 270. *JAMA* 31:618, 1898. *Butler* 1878: 698.

TOWNSEND, SOLOMON DAVIS, Boston (d/IX–19 1869 @76) MD Harvard 1815; AB 1811; AM 1815. *Phila med reg & dir* 1871:302. *Bost m&s j* 4:140, 144, 1869. *K&B* III: 1222.

TOWNSEND, STEPHEN, Philadelphia (b/VI–1804; d/VII–21–1881 @77) MD Jefferson 1865. *Med bull m&s* 3: 214, 1881.

TOWNSEND, TIMOTHY BEERS, New Haven Conn (d/III–31–1893 @57) MD Yale 1858. *Bost m&s j* 128:356, 1883.

TOWNSEND, WILLIAM EDWARD, Boston; CW–USA (d/XI–18–1866) MD Harvard 1844; AB 1839. *Nashvl j m&s* ns1:488, 1856. *Harvard in CW*: 14. *Med surg rep Phila* 15:445, 1866.

TOWNSEND, WILLIAM W , Chester Co, Pa; Philadelphia (d/III–5–1885 @77?) MD Jefferson 1844. *Med surg rep Phila* 52: 512, 1885. *Butler* 1878: 672.

TOWNSHEND, SMITH, Washington, DC (b/XII–13–1836 Pr Geo Co, Md; d/II–25–1896) MD Columbian 1870. *Hist M S DC:* 303. *Polk* 1893: 273.

TOWSEY, SAMUEL A , Galveston (b/1810 Engl; d/VII–11–1890) <MD in Engl> MD Galveston 1866. *Daniel's Texas m j* 6:37, 1890/91. *Polk* 1886: 886.

TOXEY, CALEB, CW–CSA; Mobile, Ala (b/I–30–1839 Tuscaloosa; d/III–11–1891) MD UPa 1860. *U Pa med alum CW*: 1860. *Atkinson* I:567.

TOXEY, WILLIAM SMITH, CW–CSA; Mobile, Ala (b/XI–21–1836 Tuscaloosa; d/X–15–1870) MD UPa 1860. *U Pa med alum CW*: 1860.

TRACEY, DENNIS J , Philadelphia (d/VI–20–1904 @ 60) <MD Jefferson 1867> *Pa med jour* 8:336, 1904/05.

TRACEY, STEPHEN, Siam 1836–39; Hudson, O 1840–48; Andover, Mass 1853– (b/II–25–1810 Hartford, Vt; d/I–13–1873) MD Dartmouth 1836. *Med surg rep Phila* 28:166, 1873. *Bost m&s j* ns11:96, 1873.

TRACY, ALBERT FRANCIS, Westfield, Mass (b/Aurora Ont; d/VII–18–1895 @32) <MD Victoria 1886> *Bost m&s j* 133:659, 1895. *JAMA* 25:208–09, 1895. *Polk* 1890: 559.

TRACY, RICHARD PROCTOR, Norwich, Conn (b/III–21–1791; d/III–17–1871) MD Yale 1816. *Med surg rep Phila* 24:344, 1871. *Pr Conn M S* 3:482–83, 503, 1871.

TRACY, ROBERT STORER, Plainfield, NJ (d/IV–13–1899 @27) MD CPSNY 1896; AB Yale 1893. *JAMA* 32: 1269, 1899. *Bost m&s j* 140:486, 1899.

TRACY, WILLIAM A , CW–USA; (d/III–15–1864 Nashua, NH) MD ? *Nat med jour* 1:303, 1870/71.

TRADER, JAMES LINDSAY, Connellsville, Pa (b/VI–9 1846 Uniontown; d/IV–23–1906) MD Jefferson 1871. *Pa m j* 9:608, 1905/06. *Atknsn* I:145. *Flint* 1897:799.

TRAFTON, CLARK CORNISH, CW–USA; Kennebunkport, Me (b/IV–19–1831; d/VIII–11–1864 Washington, DC) MD Bowdoin 1855. *Nat m j* 1:303, 1870/71.

TRAFTON, MARK, Poseyville, Ind; Mt Vernon, Ind (b/1817 Industry, Me; d/VI–9–1851) MD Bowdoin 1848. *Bowdoin cat*: 1848.

TRAIN, HORACE DWIGHT, CW–USA; Sheffield, Mass (b/I–6–1821 Boston; d/IV–24–1879) MD Harvard 1846; AB Amherst 1842. *Harvard in CW*: 233.

TRANSUE, ABSALOM, Bethlehem, Pa (b/VIII–28–1837; d/X–26–1880) MD UPa 1864. *U Pa med alum CW*: 1864.

TRAPNALL, PHILIP, Harrodsburg, Ky (b/I–4–1773; d/I–31–1853) MD UPa 1796. *Tr Ky M S* 1860:5–10. *Med annals Md:* 599.

TRAPP, ALBERT H , Lincoln, Ill (d/IX–22–1901) <MD Zurich 1836> *Ill m j* ns3:295, 1901. *Polk* 1886: 298.

TRASK, HOWARD PAYSON, NYC (d/V–19–1890) MD Rush 1888. *Bost m&s j* 122:534, 1890.

TRASK, JAMES DOWLING, Astoria, NY (b/1821 Beverly, Mass; d/IX–2–1883) MD UCNY 1844; AB Amherst 1839; AM 1842; Hon MD Buffalo. *Med reg NY NJ Conn* 1884:240. *Bost m&s j* 109:259, 1883. *Med surg rep Phila* 49:336, 364, 1883. *K&B* III: 1223.

TRAU, ADAM, Philadelphia; CW–USA; USN 1866–71 (b/XII–16–1840 Frankenthal, Bavaria; d/II–7–1902) MD UPa 1861 *Pa m j* 6:265 1902/03 *U Pa m alum CW*:1861.

TRAUB, CHRISTOPHER [CHRISTIAN] R , Chicago (d/VII–10–1899) Lic yrs pract. *Tr Ill St M S* 1899:287. *Polk* 1896: 408.

TRAUTMAN, BERTHOLD, Philadelphia (d/XII–19–1906 @62) MD Georgetown 1874. *Pa med jour* 10:295, 1906/07. *Flint* 1897: 826.

TRAVER, LORENZO, Providence, RI; USN 1861–68 (b/X–7–1834 Nassau, NY; d/X–24–1903) MD Albany 1857. *Tr RI M S* 6:679–80, 1899–1903. *Atkinson* I:677. *Polk* 1890: 1354.

TRAVER, RICHARD DUBOIS, Troy NY (d/V–17–1895 @56) <MD St Louis M C 1864> MD Bellevue 1867. *Med reg NY NJ Conn* 1895:242. *JAMA* 24:861, 1895.

TRAVERS, EDMUND ROCHE, Amboy, Ill (d/IV–13 1899 @67) MD U Mich 1861. *JAMA* 32:899, 1899. *Polk* 1886: 253.

TRAVERS, FRANK K , Seaford, Del; Matteawan, NJ (b/VI– –1840 Dorchester Co, Md; d/VII–24–1873) MD U Md 1860. *Tr M S NJ* 1874:99.

TREADWELL, JOHN GOODHUE, Salem, Mass (b/VIII 1–1805; d/VIII–6–1856) MD Harvard 1828; AB 1825.

Palmer, *Necrol alum Harv*:140. *K&B* III:1224 [mention].

TREADWELL, JOSHUA BRACKETT, CW–USA; Boston (d/V–6 1885 @44) MD Harvard 1862. *Bost m&s j* 112:492, 1885. *Harvard in CW*: 276. *Butler* 1878:344.

TREADWELL, OLIVER FERDINAND, New Haven, Conn (b/VI–25–1841 Balto; d/VIII–22–1898) MD Yale 1865. *Proc Conn Med Soc* 1899:357–58. *Atkinson* I: 387. *Butler* 1878: 83.

TREADWELL, SAMUEL, N Hempstead, NY (d/IX–25–1873) MD Rutgers 1827. *Med s rep Phila* 29:288, 1873.

TREADWELL, SAMUEL E , Havre-de-Grace, Md (d/IV–30–1860 @45? NYC) MD Rutgers 1827. *Med reg NY NJ Conn* 1862: 153. *Med s rep Phila* ns4:111 1860.

TREADWELL, WILLIAM E , Maple Park, Ill (d/III–17 1905 @54 Elgin, Ill) MD Bennett 1882. *Ill m j* 7:379, 1905. *Polk* 1886:287. Eclectic.

TREAT, CHARLES R , Sharon, Wis (d/V–8–1901) MD Chicago Hom 1888. *Ill m j* ns3:47, 1901. Homeopath.

TREBEL, GEORGE H , Hamilton, Ind (d/VI–9–1900 @ 35) <MD Miami 1887> AB Capital U, Columbus. *JAMA* 34:1645, 1900.

TREE, CHARLES MORGAN, Washington, DC (b/VII–17–1845; d/XII–4–1881) MD Georgetown 1867. *Hist M S DC:* 283. *Butler* 1874: 95.

TREGO, EDWIN HORACE, Philadelphia; CW–USA (b/II–18–1842 Alton, Ill; d/VI–5–1877) MD UPa 1865. *U Pa med alum CW*: 1865.

TREICHLER, JACOB FUNK, McKeansburg, Pa (b/XI–27–1806 Kimmelsville; d/VI–11–1878 or 1879) MD UPa 1852. *Tr AMA* 31:1093–94, 1880. *Tr Pa St M S* 1880:407–08. *Butler* 1878: 736.

TREICHLER, SAMUEL KNTEZ, Jonestown, Pa; CW–USA (b/VI–2–1831 Montgomery; d/X–13–1872) MD UPa 1854. *U Pa med alum CW*: 1854.

TREMAINE, WILLIAM HENRY, Hartford, Conn (b/VIII–26–1815 S Lee, Mass; d/IV–30–1883) MD Berkshire 1838. *Proc Conn M S* ns2:169, 1882–83. *Butler* 1878: 83.

TREMAINE, WILLIAM SCOTT, USA 1863–91; Buffalo (b/IX–13–1838 Pr Ed Isl, Can; d/I–9–1898 @59) MD UPa 1859. *Buff m&s j* 37:540–41, 1898. *JAMA* 30:166, 1898. *U Pa med alum CW*: 1859.

TREMBLAY, ADOLPH, Manchester, NH (b/Quebec; d/V–12–1879 @33) MD Albany 1867. *Tr NH M S* 1879: 167–68.

TREMBLEY, GEORGE D , Bippus, Ind (b/I–26–1846 Whitley Co, Ind; d/VI–17–1888) MD Cincinnati Coll Med & Surg 1875. *Tr Ind St M S* 1889:208. Kemper's *Indiana*: 351. *Polk* 1886: 311.

TRENCHARD, GEORGE O , Millington, Md (b/XI–9 1799; d/XI–28–1853) <MD UPa 1818> *Tr M S NJ* 1871: 179.

TRENCHARD, JOHN FRANKLIN, Philadelphia (d/VII 12–1901 @81) MD Jefferson 1847. *Pa med jour* 5:296, 1901/02. *Flint* 1897: 826.

TRENOR, JOHN Jr, CW–USA (d/VII–7–1867 abd USS Arizona) MD CPSNY 1856. *Nat m j* 1:303, 1870/ 71. *Tr AMA* 19:419, 1868.

TRENT, JOHN HENRY, Brooklyn (b/1846 Isle of Wight; d/XII–4–1906) MD LICH 1876. *Bost m&s j* 155: 734, 1906. *Polk* 1896: 1004.

TRENT, PETERFIELD, Va (b/X–24–1824 Richmond, Va; d/X–29–1875) MD Med Coll Ga 1849. *Tr M S Va*1877, 116. Blanton, *Va surgs CW*: 417.

TREXLER, JEREMIAH SAMUEL, Kutztown, Pa (b/1832 Trexlertown, Pa; d/IX–24–1901) MD UPa 1853. *Pa m j* 5:39, 101, 1901/02. *U Pa m alum CW*: 1853.

TREZEVANT, GEORGE T , Abilene, Tex (b/1846 Miss; d/II–7–1890) <MD New Orl Sch Med 1869> *JAMA* 14:518–19, 1890. *Polk* 1886:419 (Tallulah, Miss).

TRIBOU, GALEN JONES, Steuben, Me (b/III–5–1856 Hampden, Me; d/III–5–1889) MD U Vt 1883; pg stud NY. *Tr Me M Assn:* 1889: 167–68.

TRIBOU, NAHUM M Jr, Mystic, Conn (b/IX–1–1833 Middleboro, Mass; d/XI–28–1864) MD Jefferson 1858. *Proc Conn Med Soc* 1865: 158–59.

TRIMBLE, CYRUS WASHINGTON, Chillicothe, O (d/VIII– –1822) MD UPa 1819; AB Dickinson 1817. *Dickinson cat*: 1817.

TRIPLER, CHARLES STUART, USA 1827– (b/1806 NYC; d/1866 Cincinnati) MD CPSNY 1827; Hon AM Columbia 1860. *Nat med jour* 1:303, 1870/71. *Tr AMA* 18: 356, 1867. *Bost m&s j* 75:292, 1866. *Med surg rep Phila* 15:408, 1866. *K&B* III:1225.

TRIPLETT, WILLIAM HARRISON CW–USA;Woodstock, Va 1860?– ; Washington, DC 1873– ; Laurel Iron Wks, Monongalia Co, WVa (b/IX–15–1836 Mt Jackson, Va; d/III–27–1890 Woodstock, Va) MD Jefferson 1859. *Atkinson* I: 113–14. *Hist M S DC:*273. *Polk* 1886: 942. *K&B* II: 1161.

TRIPP, BENJAMIN HARLOCK, Rutland, Mass (d/II–3 1873) MD Bowdoin 1839. *Bost m&s j* ns11:176, 1873. *Mass M S cat* 1894.

TRIPP, ROBINSON, Chicago (d/VII–3–1900) Lic yrs pr. *Ill m j* ns2:141, 1900. McDonough's *Ill m dir* 1895: 155.

TRIST, HOAR BROWSE, USN 1857– ; CW–CSA; Washington, DC (b/II–20–1832; d/IV–5–1896) MD Jefferson 1857. *Hist M S DC:* 265. *Atkinson* I: 42–43.

TRITES, DAVID TRAINER, Sunbury Pa; Chesapeake City, Md; Manayunk Phil 1860– (b/III–8–1812 Ridley Twp;d/ V–29–1887) MD Jefferson 1842. *Hahn mo* 22: 447, 1887. *Med vis* 3:229, 1887. *Polk* 1886:826. Homeopath 1860– .

TRITES, WILLIAM BUDD, Manayunk, Phila (b/VIII–22–1847 Sunbury, Pa; d/I–19–1890) MD Hahnemann, Phila 1869. AB Central HS Phila. *Tr Hom M S Pa* 1890. *Hahn mo* 25:115, 1890. *Med vis* 6:71, 1890. *Polk* 1886: 826. *Cleave.* Homeopath.

TROJANA, GIOVANNI, Philadelphia (d/IX–26–1898 @ 35) <MD U Naples 1881> *JAMA* 31:871, 1898. *Polk*

 Spec. educ'l status abbrev. as: ***ng*** = college verified attendance without degree;

1896: 1320.

TROTH, SAMUEL N , Philadelphia (d/VI-11-1897 @ 72) MD Jefferson 1849. *JAMA* 28:1252, 1897. *Polk* 1896: 1320.

TROTT, THOMAS HENRY, Washington, DC (b/X-1-1843; d/IV-23-1896) MD Georgetown 1867; MD Bellevue 1869. *Hist M S DC:* 312. *Polk* 1893: 273.

TROTTER, JOHN H , Albany, NY (b/c1813; d/XII-30 1862) MD ? ng Amherst 1833. *Amherst cat*: 1833.

TROTTER, WILLIAM C, Daingerfield, Tex (d/IX-1-1885 @33) MD U Louisvl 1875. *Tex cour-rec med* 3:171 1885. *New Orl m&s j* ns13:578 1886. *Polk* 1886:883.

TROUBAT [TROUBALT], RAYMOND, Philadelphia (d/VII-6-1883 @77) MD Jefferson 1838. *Med surg rep Phila* 49:56, 1883. *Butler* 1878: 672.

TROUP, JAMES ROBERT, Darien, Ga; CW-CSA (b/VI 3-1835; d/1873) MD UPa 1858; att U Va. *U Pa med alum CW*: 1858.

TROUT, WILLIAM F , McConnellsburg, Pa (d/IX-7-1899 @66) MD Jefferson 1856. *JAMA* 33:745, 1899. *Polk* 1896: 1289.

TROUTMAN, SEYMOUR CARBRAY, Somerville, NJ (d/V-6-1905 @83) MD CPSNY 1854. *Bost m&s j* 152: 592, 1905. *Polk* 1896:949.

TROVINGER, M T , Hornelltown, O (d/I-23-1895 @35) MD ? *JAMA* 24: 177, 1895.

TROW, JOSIAH, Buckland, Mass (b/VII-15-1816 Wendell, NH; d/II-15-1890) MD Berkshire 1840. *Bost m&s j* 122:216, 1890. *Polk* 1886: 463.

TROW, NATHANIEL GILMAN, Sunderland, Mass (d/II-4-1888 @76) MD Berkshire 1837. *Bost m&s j* 119: 641, 1889.

TROWBRIDGE, GEORGE, NYC (d/IX-10-1898 @43) MD CPSNY 1881; AB Yale 1878. *Bost m&s j* 139: 354, 1898. *JAMA* 31:808, 1898.

TROWBRIDGE, RICHARD S , Philadelphia (d/VII-12 1904 @83) MD Phila Coll Med & Surg 1852. *Pa med jour* 8:336, 1904/05. *Flint* 1897: 826.

TROWBRIDGE, SILAS T , CW-USA; Decatur, Ill; Vera Cruz, Mex 1881- (d/1893 Napa, Cal @68) MD Rush 1851. *JAMA* 21: 94, 1893.

TROWBRIDGE, WILLIAM V , Burnett's Creek, Ind (b/1833 Owen Co, Ky; d/V-7-1897) <MD CPS Indianapolis 1878> *Tr Ind St M S* 1898: 374.

TROXELL, THOMAS S , Gallitzin, Pa (d/XII-15-1904 @50) MD Jefferson 1881. *Pa med jour* 8:336, 1904/05. *Flint* 1897: 802.

TRUAX, JOHN GILBERT, NYC (b/III-5-1848 Duramville, NY; d/II-16-1898) MD Rush 1872; <AB U Mich> *Bost m&s j* 138:198, 1898. *JAMA* 30:507, 1898. *Polk* 1896: 1081.

TRUDEAU, EDWARD LIVINGSTONE Jr, NYC (d/V-4-1904 @31) MD CPSNY 1900; AB Yale 1896. *Bost m&s j* 150:524, 1904.

TRUDEAU, JAMES de BERTY, New Orleans; CW-CSA (b/II-14-1817; d/V-25-1887) MD UPa 1837. *U Pa med alum CW*: 1837. *Polk* 1886: 418.

TRUE, NATHANIEL TUCKERMAN, Durham, Me 1846-48; NY; NH (b/III-15-1812 Pownal, Me; d/V-17 1887) MD Bowdoin 1846; AM Colby 1841; AM Bowdoin 1868. *Bowdoin cat*: 1837.

TRUESDALE, CALVIN, Rock Island, Ill (b/X-1822 Ohio; d/VI-9-1895) MD Western Res 1845. *JAMA* 24: 988-89, 1895. *Polk* 1890: 347.

TRUEX, STEPHEN PAUL, Brooklyn (b/VII-25-1855 Owego, NY; d/III-31-1904 @48) MD LICH 1891; att U Vt. *Bost m&s j* 150:390, 1904. *Polk* 1896: 1004.

TRULL, SAMUEL, Woburn, Mass (b/III-8-1815; d/V-26-1876) MD Harvard 1841; AB 1837; ng Amherst 1836. *Amherst, Men of*: 1836. *Mass M S cat* 1894.

TRULSON, THEODORE A, Stanton, Ia (d/XI-18-1903 @42) MD CPS Chicago 1885. *JAMA* 41:1423, 1903.

TRUMBO, GEORGE H, Linden Va (d/VIII-26-1899 @ 59) MD UMd 1862. *JAMA* 33:683, 1899. *Polk* 1886:920.

TRUMBULL, STEPHEN, Providence, RI (d/1886 at sea) MD Harv 1884;AB Yale 1880 *Bost m&s j* 114:628 1886.

TUBBS, A DEAN, CW-USN (d/I-6-1865 Cape Haytien, Haiti) MD ? *Nat med jour* 1:303, 1870/71.

TUCK, HENRY, NYC; CW-USA; (b/V-9-1842 Barnstable, Mass; d/ IX-2-1904) MD Harvard 1867; AB 1863. *Bost m&s j* 151:279, 1904. *Harvard in CW*: 201. *Atkinson* I: 184. *Polk* 1896: 1081.

TUCK, LORENZO WADSWORTH, Boston (b/VII-15-1860 S Weymouth, Mass; d/X-19-1888 @28) MD Harvard 1888; AB Amherst 1882. *Bost m&s j* 119: 419, 420, 1888.

TUCK, WILLIAM J EDMONDSON, Memphis (b/II-22 1814 Halifax Co, Va; d/VI-17-1859) MD UPa 1838; AB Kenyon 1834. *Nashvl j m&s* 17:190, 1859. *New Orl m&s j* 16:759, 1859.

TUCKER, BEVERLY ST GEORGE, CW-USA; Colorado Spr (d/III-30-1894 @55) MD UCNY 1860. *JAMA* 22:561, 1894. *Polk* 1890: 210.

TUCKER, DAVID HUNTER, Philadelphia (b/VI-18-1815; d/III-17-1871) MD UPa 1837; MD UVa 1836. *Tr AMA* 23:601-03, 1872. *Tr CPP* cent vol:270. *K&B* II: 1164.

TUCKER, ECHOL, Victoria, Ala (d/III- -1888) MD ? ; lic 1885. *Tr M Assn St Ala* 188: 315.

TUCKER, ELISHA GUSTAVUS, Boston (d/V-18-1895 @86) MD Berkshire 1837. *Bost m&s j* 133: 659, 1895. *Polk* 1886:462.

TUCKER, ERVIN ALDEN, NYC (b/II-2-1862 Attleboro, Mass; d/III-3-1902) MD CPSNY 1889; att Amherst. *Bost m&s j* 146: 297, 1902. *Polk* 1896: 1081.

TUCKER, GEORGE GRENVILLE, Westfield, Mass (b/1834; d/VIII-20-1883) MD Harvard 1855. *JAMA* 1: 407, 1883; 3:82, 1884. *Bost m&s j* 109:617, 1883. *Butler* 1878: 358.

TUCKER, GEORGE HERRIOT, CW-US San Comm;

NYC (b/XII-22-1828;d/I-25-1862) MD CPSNY 1851 *Tr AMA* 14:205 1864 *Med reg NYNJ Conn* 1865:209-10.

TUCKER, HERMAN, Sandgate, Vt (d/I-26-1862 @76 or I-6-1861 @72) Hon MD Castleton 1835. *Med surg rep Phila* ns7: 408, 1861/62.

TUCKER, JAMES IOANNES, Chicago (d/XI-12-1899 @59) MD Harvard 1867. *Tr Ill St M S* 1899:287. *JAMA* 33:1308 1899. *Bost m&s j* 141:504 1899. *Polk* 1896:409.

TUCKER, JOHN H , CW-CSA, CSN; Okolona, Miss 7 yrs; Henderson, NC 1874- (b/X-27-1842 Brunswick Co, Va; d/II-24-1900) MD Va Med Coll 1864; att Wm & Mary. *Tr M S St NC* 47:175-76, 1900. *Polk* 1886:723.

TUCKER, JOSEPH CLARENCE, CW-USA, USN; Oakland, Cal (b/IV-25-1828 NYC; d/XII-23-1891) MD UCNY 1848. *NW m j* 20:10, 1892. *Atkinson* I:592.

TUCKER, JOSEPH JOEL WASHINGTON, Raleigh, NC (b/1827; d/1856) MD UPa 1849; AB UNC 1847. *Tr NC M S* 1857: 12.

TUCKER, JOSHUA, Boston (b/VIII-7-1800 Winchendon, Mass; d/XI-7-1881) MD Geneva 1835; ng Woodstock 1835. *Bost m&s j* 105:634, 1881; 106:214, 1882.

TUCKER, NEWTON G , Nashville (b/III-29-1836; d/I-8-1899) MD U Nashvl 1861. *So pract* 21: 86-88, 1899. *JAMA* 32:145, 1899. *Nashvl j m&s* 85:44-47, 1899. *Flint* 1897: 885.

TUCKER, ROBERT MILTON, Helena, Ala (d/I-3-1900) MD ? *JAMA* 34:187, 1900. *Polk* 1893: 150.

TUCKER, SAMUEL GIBBS, New Shoreham, RI; Oakland, Cal (d/III-20-1897 @46) MD Hahnemann, Phila 1865. *Tr Am Inst Hom* 1898: 49. Homeopath.

TUCKER, SAMUEL SYDENHAM, Burlington, NJ c1810; Philadelphia (b/1789? d/XI-27-1863 @74) MD UPa 1806. *Med surg rep Phila* 10:440, 1863.

TUCKER, SIMEON, Stoughton, Mass (d/XI-20-1799 Canton; d/II-9-1878) MD Harvard 1825; AB Brown 1821; AM. *Brown hist cat*: 1821. *Mass M S cat*: 1894.

TUCKER, THOMAS M , Salem, Ind (b/VIII-25-1828 New Phila, Ind; d/X-19-1895) MD Ohio M C 1860. *Tr Ind St M S* 1896:257. *Butler* 1878: 223.

TUCKER, WILLIAM McKENDREE, Washington, DC (b/1821; d/I-31-1890) MD Columbian 1844. *Hist Med Soc DC:* 238.

TUELL, JOHN, Clarksburg, Ind (d/III-12-1873) MD ? *Med surg rep Phila* 28: 328, 1873.

TUFFS, EDWARD GILBERT, NYC (d/VII-20-1906 @55) MD UCNY 1879. *Bost m&s j* 155:106, 1906. *Polk* 1896: 1081.

TUFTS, CHARLES A , Dover, NH (d/1899 @77) MD Dartmouth 1872; PhG Mass Coll Pharm. *Bost m&s j* 140:200, 1899. *JAMA* 32:442, 1899. *Polk* 1896: 919.

TUKESBURY, ERVIN NOYES, Falmouth, Me (b/X-15 1812; d/VIII-27-1872) MD Bowdoin 1838. *Tr Me M Assn* 1871-73: 478.

TUKESBURY [TEWKSBURY], MONROE GEORGE JEWELL, Manchester, NH (b/X-8-1819 Amesbury, Mass; d/IX-2-1869) MD Woodstock 1840. *Phila med reg & dir* 1871: 302.

TULL, JOHN GRAHAM, Philadelphia (d/IV-29-1870 @53) MD UPa 1839; AB UNC 1836; AM 1839. *Phila med reg & dir* 1871: 294.

TULLER, EMERY R, Fairfield O; Newark O 1854-66; Vineland, NJ 1866- (b/X-1-1824 Rochester NY; d/ VIII 4-1891) <MD Cincinnati 1861> *Med vis* 7:330, 1891. *Tr Am Inst Hom* 1892: 218. *Polk* 1886:612. Homeopath.

TULLEY, ANDREW MELVILLE, Chicago (d/XI-5-1902 Hot Springs, NM) MD U Vt 1880. *Chic m rec* 23: 314, 1902. *Flint* 1897: 270.

TULLOSS, NATHAN H , Iowa City, Ia (b/III-24-1826 E Fairfield,O; d/IV-11-1882) MD Iowa St U 1871. *Tr Ia St M S* 6:459-60, 1883-85; 14:330, 1896.

TULLOSS, RICHARD H , CW-USA (d/IX-20-1864 Marietta, Ga) MD ? *Nat med jour* 1:303, 1870/71.

TULLY, MARCUS C , NYC (d/VII-30-1885 @68) MD UCNY 1847. *Med reg NY NJ Conn* 1886:255. *Butler* 1878: 526.

TULLY, WILLIAM, New Haven, Conn; Castleton, Vt (b/ XI-8-1785 Saybrook, Conn; d/II-28-1859 Springfield, Mass) <MD Yale 1819> AB 1806. *Tr AMA* 13:794-96, 1860. *Pr Conn M S* 1861: 109. *K&B* III: 1230-32.

TUNSTALL, ROBERT TAYLOR, Norfolk, Va (b/VIII-31-1818; d/IV-1-1883) MD UPa 1842. *JAMA* 2:27, 1884. *Tr M S Va* 1883: 187-88. *Atkinson* I:126. *K&B* III:1238 [mention].

TUPPER, CHARLES E , Ottawa, O (d/I-10-1894) MD Cleveland Med Coll 1854. *JAMA* 22:97 1894. *Butler* 1878:653.

TURLINGTON, WILLIS EDGAR, Benson, NC (b/X-22-1855 Johnston Co, NC; d/IX-21/22-1899) MD CPS Balto 1882; ng UNC 1879-80. *Tr M S NC* 1900:179-80. *Polk* 1886: 722.

TURNBULL, FREDERICK MONCRIEFF, Boston (d/ I-16-1897) MD Jefferson 1877. *JAMA* 28:328, 1897.

TURNBULL, JOHN FRANKLIN, CW-USA; Bellbrook, O (d/VII-19-1904 @64) MD Jefferson 1863. *JAMA* 43: 485, 1904. *Polk* 1886: 737.

TURNBULL, LAURENCE, CW-USA; Philadelphia (b/ IX-10-1821 Shotts, Scotl; d/X-24-1900) MD Jefferson 1845; PhG Phila Coll Pharm. *Bost m&s j* 143:465, 1900. *Atkinson* I: 218. *K&B* III: 1223.

TURNER, AGNES, S Bend, Ind (b/1862; d/XI-18-1901) MD U Ill 1901; att Hahnemann Chic 1897-98. *U Ill Coll Med alum*: 1901.

TURNER, ALEX, White Oak, Ala (d/XI-2-1899) MD M C SC 1851. *JAMA* 33:1441, 1891. *Polk* 1886: 141.

TURNER, BENJAMIN A , Owings Mills, Md (b/1849 Pr Geo Co, Md; d/V-7-1895) <MD CPS Balto 1881> *JAMA* 24:776, 1895. *Med ann Md:* 600. *Polk* 1886: 440.

TURNER, CHARLES E , Rising Sun, Md (d/IV-17-1900 @ c42) MD Jefferson 1877. *JAMA* 34:1084, 1900. *Polk* 1896: 674.

 Spec. educ'l status abbrev. as: ***ng*** = college verified attendance without degree;

TURNER, DANIEL, St Mary's, Ga (b/I-30-1782 E Greenwich, RI; d/1808) MD ? AB Brown 1799; AM. *Brown hist cat*: 1799.

TURNER, GEORGE FRANKLIN, USA 1833- (b/IV-22-1807 Boston; d/X-17-1854 Corpus Christi, Tex) MD Harvard 1830; AM 1826. Palmer's *Necrol Harv alum*: 55-56. *Heitman*.

TURNER, GEORGE W , Freedom, Ind (b/1864 Osawatombie, Kans; d/XII-17-1900) <MD CPS St Louis> *Tr Ind St M S* 1901: 501.

TURNER, HENRY EDWARD, Newport, RI (b/VI-15-1816 Greenwich; d/VI-4-1897) MD UPa 1836. *Bost m & s j* 136:581, 1897. *JAMA* 28:1202, 1897. *Tr RI M S* 5:489-92, 1894-98. *Rec AAS-USA* 1891:98. *U Pa med alum CW*: 1836.

TURNER, JARED, San Jose, Cal (d/I-14-1900 @75) MD Castleton 1846. *JAMA* 34:251, 1900. *Polk* 1886: 144 (Tucson, Ariz).

TURNER, JOHN, Mackall, Md (b/1812 Port Tobacco, Md; d/XI-9-1896) MD U Md 1834. *Med annals Md:* 600. *Polk* 1886: 444.

TURNER, JOHN J , CW-USA (d/X-27-1860 Freeburg, Ill) MD ? *Nat med jour* 1:303, 1870/71.

TURNER, JOHN MAXWELL, Gardiner, Me (d/XII-21 1899 @46) MD Dartmouth 1881. *JAMA* 34:187, 1900. *Polk* 1896: 636.

TURNER, JOSEPH M , Brooklyn (d/VII-2-1898 @82 Washington, Conn) MD Transylvania 1841. *JAMA* 31: 141, 1898. *Polk* 1886: 650.

TURNER, OBED CHESTER, N Cambridge, Mass (b/ Attleborough, Mass; d/X-31-1882) MD Georgetown 1864; AB Tufts 1859. *Bost m&s j* 107:456, 619, 1882.

TURNER, RICHARD G , CW-CSA; Houston (d/VI-8-1905 @65) MD U La 1860. *Texas st j m* 1:32, 1905/06. *Polk* 1886: 892.

TURNER, RUFUS, Middlesex Co, Conn (d/1852 @61) Hon MD Yale 1830. *Pr Conn M S* 1852:17; 1882:147.

TURNER, SAMUEL, Ky (d/VI-28-1901) MD Louisville M C 1894. *JAMA* 37: 126, 1901.

TURNER, SAMUEL F , CW-CSA; Robertson Co, Tex (b/1835 Talbot Co, Ga; d/1867) MD New Orl Sch Med 1859. *SHSP* 22:266, 1893.

TURNER, SAMUEL SIMPSON, USA 1876- ; Ft Columbia, Wash; Yankton, SD (b/VIII-12-1833 DeKalb Co Ga; d/XII-11-1904) MD Georgetown 1863. *Hist M S DC:* 286. *Rec AAS USA* 1891: 98-101. *Polk* 1893: 1162.

TURNER, SIMON, Brownsville, Tenn (d/XI-24-1858 @ 35) MD UPa 1847. *Bost m&s j* 59: 428, 1859.

TURNER, THEOPHILUS H, USA (d/VII-27-1869 Ft Wallace, Kans) MD Jefferson 1863. *Phila med reg & dir* 1871:301. *Tr AMA* 21:494 1870. *Nat m j* 1:303, 1870/71.

TURNER, THOMAS, CW-USA (b/Chester, Pa; d/VII-20-1868) MD UPa 1850. *U Pa med alum CW*: 1850.

TURNER, THOMAS J , Coldwater, Mich; USN 1853- (b/Pa; d/VIII-21-1901) MD Med Coll Pa 1851. *JAMA* 37:594, 1901. *Hamersly*: 199.

TURNER, WILLIAM, Newport, RI (b/IX-10-1775 Newark, NJ; d/IX-26-1837) Lic NJ Med Soc. *Tr RI M S* 1:10, 45-47, 1859-77.

TURNER, WILLIAM HAZLETT, Mantua, NJ (b/XI-18 1844; d/VIII-23-1876) MD UPa 1867. *Tr MS NJ* 1877: 131-32. *Tr AMA* 33:608-09, 1882.

TURNER, WILLIAM MASON, CW-CSA; Philadelphia (b/XII-15 1835 Petersburg, Va; d/X-13-1877) MD UPa 1858; PhB Brown 1855. *Phila m times* 8:72, 1877. *U Pa med alum CW*: 1858.

TURNEY, JOSEPH, Nevada, O (b/V-22-1825 Franklin Co, O; d/VII-1-1888) MD Starling 1851. *Tr Ohio St M S* 1889: 8, 266-667.

TURNEY, SAMUEL DENNY, Circleville, O; CW-USA (b/XII-26-1824 Columbus; d/I-18-1878 there) MD U Pa 1851. *U Pa m alum CW*: 1851. *Tr Ohio St M S* 1878: 190-91. *Tr AMA* 29:773-75, 1878. *K&B* III: 1233-34.

TURNIPSEED, EDWARD BERRIAM, CW-CSA; Columbia, SC (b/X-29-1829 Richland Co; d/IV-18-1883) MD M C SC 1853; AB M Zion Coll, SC. *JAMA* 1: 604, 1883. *Atkinson* I: 331-32. *K&B* III: 1234.

TURNPENNY, FREDERICK, Philadelphia (b/VIII-31-1809; d/VI-2-1840) MD UPa 1832. *Tr CPP* cent vol: 270. *Med exam* 3:365, 1840.

TURNURE, MILTON, Tenafly, NJ (b/VI-21-1851 NYC; d/IV-28-1891) MD Ky Sch Med 1876; MD UC NY 1878. *Tr M S NJ* 1891: *Med reg NY NJ Conn* 1892: 291.

TURPIN, CHARLES C , New Orleans (b/IX-17-1816; d/I-29-1886) <MD Paris 1843> *New Orl m&s j* ns13: 750-51, 1886. *Atkinson* I: 169. *Butler* 1878: 295.

TURPIN, THOMAS J , Madison Parish La (d/1879) MD U La 1871 *Tr La St M S* 19:27 1898.

TUTHILL, DANIEL HARMON STRONG, Chicago (b/ 1860? d/IV-18-1903 @43) MD Rush 1884. *Ill m j* ns4: 889, 1903. *Flint* 1897: 270.

TUTHILL, FRANKLIN, San Francisco (b/IV-3-1822 Greenport, NY; d/VIII-27-1865 Brooklyn) MD UCNY 1844; AB Amherst 1840. *Med s rep Phila* 13:166, 1865.

TUTHILL, JEROME KACKSON, Chicago (b/1864? d/V-12-1898 @34) MD Rush 1884. *JAMA* 30:1248, 1898. *Polk* 1896: 409.

TUTHILL, SAMUEL BURNET, CW-USA; Brooklyn (b/1838; d/II-3-1885) MD CPSNY 1859. *Med reg NY NJ Conn* 1885: 246.

TUTT, CHARLES PENDLETON, CW-USA; Philadelphia (b/XI-2 1832 Va; d/V-11-1866) MD UPa 1856. *Med surg rep Phila* 14:400, 420, 1866. *U Pa med alum CW*: 1856. *Tr CPP* cent vol:270; ns4:207-09, 1863-74. *Tr Pa St M S* 1867:289-90.

TUTT, SAMUEL J , Kirkwood, Mo (b/1819? d/IV-25-1900 @81) MD UPa 1841. *JAMA* 34:1146, 1900. *Polk* 1896: 851.

TUTTLE, FRANK BENJAMIN, Naugatuck, Conn (b/VI

–1840 Prospect; d/IV–21–1902) MD Yale 1863. *Proc Conn Med Soc* 1903:406–07. *Butler* 1878: 83.

TUTTLE, JOHN TODD, NYC (b/New Haven, Conn; d/I 27–1870 @68) MD Yale 1830. *Med reg NY NJ Conn* 1871: 366.

TUTTLE, LEVI W , Satartia, Miss (d/X–3–1886 @57) MD Jefferson 1850. *New Orl m&s j* ns14: 484, 1886. *Polk* 1886: 532.

TUTTLE, LYMAN MOORE, Holyoke, Mass (d/IV–26–1897 @60) MD Albany 1859. *JAMA* 28:1091, 1897. *Polk* 1890: 549.

TUTTLE, THERON, Brooklyn (d/IX–16–1897 @64) MD CPSNY 1854. *JAMA* 29:660, 1897. *Polk* 1896:1004.

TWITCHELL, AMOS, Keene, NH (b/IV–11–1781 Dublin; d/V–26–1850) MD Dartmouth 1805; BS 1802. *NH j m* 1:287–300, 1851. *Bost m&s j* 42:398, 1850; 44: 385–86, 1851. *K&B* III:1235–36.

TWITCHELL, GEORGE BROOKS, Keene NH; CW-USA (b/IX 20/25–1820 Petersburg, Va; d/III–30–1897) MD UPa 1843; Hon MD Dartmouth 1869. *Bost m&s j* 136:320, 342–43, 1897. *JAMA* 28:714, 1897. *Tr NH M S* 1897: 302–03. *Atkinson* I:348. *Polk* 1896:920.

TWITCHELL, WILLIAM LEANDER, Alameda, Cal (b/II–17–1825; d/XII–5–1886) MD Bowdoin 1850. *Tr Cal St M S* 1887:395–96. *Polk* 1886: 163.

TYDEMAN, WILLIAM WATSON, Knoxville; Jamaica, WI c20 yrs (b/1824 Engl; d/I–22–1898 Columbia, SC) Lic Tenn St Bd Exam 1890; stud w/Drs McKern & Kidd, London. *Tr Am Inst Hom* 1898: 49. *Polk* 1886:867. Homeopath.

TYLER, ABIGAIL CUTLER, Washington, DC (b/XI–11–1835 Warren, Mass; d/I–6–1906) MD New Engl Female MC 1868. *Hist M S DC:* 361. *Polk* 1893:273.

TYLER, DAVID ATWATER, New Haven, Conn (b/XI–10–1818 Northford; d/III–27–1885) MD Yale 1844. *Pr Conn M S* ns3:176–78, 1886. *Butler* 1878: 83.

TYLER, EDWIN HAWES, San Antonio, Tex (b/1851 Owensboro Ky; d/IV– –1890) MD Bellevue 1876. *Daniel's Tex m j* 6:76–77, 1890–91. *Polk* 1886: 894.

TYLER, GRAFTON, Georgetown DC (b/XI–21–1811 Pr Geo Co Md; d/VIII–26–1884) MD U Md 1833. *JAMA* 3: 307, 1884. *Med ann Md:*601. *Hist M S DC:*237. *Atkinson* I:238.

TYLER, GUSTAVUS B , Owensboro, Ky (d/XII–1–1896 @76) MD Jefferson 1845. *JAMA* 27:1260, 1896; 28:92, 1897. *Polk* 1890:474.

TYLER, JESSE HOPKINS, Albany, NY (b/V–4–1817 Rutland; d/III– –1860) MD ? ; ng Amherst 1839. *Amherst, Men of*: 1839.

TYLER, JOHN, Frederick City, Md (b/VI–29–1763 Pr Geo Co; d/X–15–1841) <Dipl St Bart's London 1784> *Med annals Md:* 601. *K&B* III: 1236–37.

TYLER, JOHN EUGENE, Boston (b/XII–9–1819; d/III 9–1878) MD UPa 1846; MD Dartmouth 1846; AB 1842. *Tr NH M S* 1878:197–98. *Atkinson* I: 701.

TYLER, LACHLAN [LACHLANS], NYC (b/XII–7–1851 Charles Co, Va; d/I–26–1902) MD CPSNY 1876. *Bost m&s j* 146: 156, 1902. *Hist M S DC:* 311. *Polk* 1896: 1086.

TYLER, SAMUEL, Frederick, Md (b/XII–10–1820; d/VII–26–1856) MD UPa 1842. *Med annals Md:* 601. *Tr AMA* 13:806, 1860.

TYLER, WALTER BOWIE, Washington, DC (b/IX–19 1846; d/III–6–1889 Summerville, SC) MD Columbian 1870. *Hist M S DC:* 296. *Polk* 1886: 214.

TYLER, WARREN, N Brookfield, Mass (d/IV–18 1891 @72) MD Berkshire 1850. *Bost m&s j* 124:444, 1891.

TYLER, WILLIAM Sr, Frederick, Md (b/V–7–1784 Pr Geo Co; d/IV–12–1872) MD UPa 1804. *M ann Md:* 602.

TYLER, WILLIAM BRADLEY, Frederick City, Md (b/V–31–1788 Pr Geo Co; d/IX–9–1863) MD UPa 1809. *Med ann Md:* 601. *Med surg rep Phila* 10:292, 1863.

TYRRELL, GERRARD GEORGE, Milwaukee; Grass Valley, Nev 1861– ; Sacramento 1868– (b/1831 Dalkey Irel'd; d/VI–8–1895) LRCS (Dublin) 1856; MD? King's & Queen's Coll 1859. *JAMA* 25:124, 1895. *Occidental m times* 9:576, 1895. *Atkinson* I: 24. *Polk* 1886: 170.

TYSON, JAMES LAWRENCE, Philadelphia 1838–43, 1851–58; Baltimore 1843–49; Calif 1849–51; Penllyn, Pa 1858– (b/XI–19–1813 Phila; d/XII–10–1898 Penllyn) MD UPa 1838. *Tr CPP* cent vol:271; 3s43:lxix–lxxv, 1921. *JAMA* 31:1584, 1898. *Atkinson* I:244–45.

TYSON, SAMUEL ELLICOTT, Washington, DC (b/XI–16–1809 Md; d/III–29–1883) <MD Washington M C Balto 1832> *Hist Med Soc DC:*239. *Med ann Md:* 602. *Butler* 1874.

TYSON, WILLIAM W, Fredonia Ala (d/XII –1890) MD M C Ga 1854 *Tr M Assn St Ala* 1891:260 *Butler* 1874:27.

UFFORD, EDWARD GOODRICH, Agawam, Mass (b/XI–1801 E Windsor, Conn; d/VIII–25–1889) MD Yale 1845. *Bost m&s j* 121:244, 1889. *Butler* 1878:359.

UGLOW, JAMES Jr, CW–USA (d/III–27–1865 Beaufort, SC) MD CPSNY 1851, AB UCNY 1847. *Nat med jour* 1:303, 1870/71. *Med reg NY NJ Conn* 1865: 236.

UHL, DAVID, Bolivar Venez; NYC (d/IX–17–1858 Bolivar) MD CPSNY 1850. *Med s rep Phil* ns1:76, 1858/59.

UHLER, ALGERNON SYDNEY, CW–USA; Philadelphia (b/VI–30 1838; d/X–15–1873) MD UPa 1863. *Med surg rep Phila* 29:324, 1873. *U Pa med alum CW*:1863.

UHLER, GEORGE, Philadelphia (b/X–9–1791; d/IV–21 1859) MD UPa 1815; AB 1812. *Med surg rep Phila* ns2: 105, 1859.

UHLER, HARRY NAGLEE, Manayunk, Phila (b/VIII–4 1834; d/III–25–1893) MD UPa 1894. *Tr M S NJ* 1893: 176. *Polk* 1886: 826.

UHLER, WILLIAM M , Germantown, Phila (d/XI–27–1865 @45) Hon MD Phila Coll M & S 1855? MD Pa M C 1859 ad eundem. *Med surg rep Phila* 13:390, 1865.

ULMER, CHARLES E , Atlantic City, NJ (d/I–15–1898

 Spec. educ'l status abbrev. as: ***ng*** = college verified attendance without degree;

@40) MD Jefferson 1890. *JAMA* 30:278, 279, 1898. *Polk* 1896: 933.

ULRICH, DANIEL A , Reading, Pa (b/IV-10-1819 Stroudsburg; d/I-6-1879) MD Jeff'n 1844; AB Princeton 1841; AM 1844. *Tr Pa St M S* 12:751-52, 1879.

ULRICH, RAIMOND C, Chicago (d/VIII-26-1901) <MD Würzburg 1871> *Ill med jour* ns3:295, 1901. *Polk* 1896: 409.

ULRICH, WILLIAM BAGGS, Fairview, La 1851-67; Galveston; Chester Pa 1868?- (b/V-4-1829 Phila; d/IV-24-1905) MD Phila Coll M & S 1850; MD New Orl Sch Med 1866. *Pa med jour* 8:543-44, 1904/05. *Atkinson* I:104. *Polk* 1896: 1272.

UNDERHILL, ALFRED, NYC (b/1809; d/XII-7-1873) MD CPSNY 1832. *Med reg NY NJ Conn* 1874:292. *Med rec NY* 9:46-47, 1874. *Med surg rep Phila* 30:22 1874.

UNDERHILL, GUSTAVE BREAUX, New Braunfels, Tex (b/VI-9-1853 New Orleans; d/1890) MD U La 1881. *New Orl m&s j* ns18:893-95, 1891. *Daniel's Tex m j* 6:301-02, 1890-91. *Polk* 1886: 418.

UNDERHILL, RICHARD TITUS, Croton Pt, NY (d/II-1-1871) MD CPSNY 1824. *Med reg NY NJ Conn* 1871: 366. *Med rec NY* 6:40, 94, 114, 1871-72.

UNDERWOOD, FRANCIS H , Swanzey, NH to 1859; Millbury, Mass 1863- ; Boston 1870- (b/VII-22-1830 Wales, Mass; d/II-16-1879) <MD Harvard 1866> MD Hahnemann, Phila 1867. *New Engl gaz* 14:95, 1879. Eclectic to 1859; homeopath 1859- .

UNDERWOOD, GIDEON, Pittston, Pa (b/XII-3-1819 Forty Fort; d/I-30-1896) <MD Geneva 1846> *Tr Luzerne Co* [Pa] *M S* 1896:172. *Polk* 1890: 1010.

UNDERWOOD, JOSEPH Jr, CW-USA; Quincy, Mass (d/IV-1-1881) MD Harvard 1847. *Harvard in CW*: 234.

UNDERWOOD, MYRON, Eldora, Ia (d/VIII-12-1894) MD Rush 1859. *Bost m & s jour* 131: 356, 1894. *Polk* 1890: 414.

UNDERWOOD, WARREN J , Akron, O (b/III-20-1840 Dillsburg, Pa; d/VI-9-1890) MD Jefferson 1864. *Tr O M S* 1891: 6, 343.

UNRUH, MARTIN L, Philadelphia (d/III-16-1899 @40) <MD CPS Balto> *JAMA* 32:787, 1899. *Polk* 1896:1320.

UPDEGRAFF, JONATHAN T , CW-USA; Mt Pleasant, O (b/Jefferson Co; d/XI-30-1882) MD UPa 1845. *U Pa med alum CW*: 1845.

UPDEGROVE, SILAS, CW-USA; Philadelphia (b/1829 Montgomery, Pa; d/X-1-1904) MD UPa 1854. *Pa med jour* 8:336, 1904/05. *U Pa med alum CW*: 1854. *Flint* 1897: 826.

UPFOLD [UPFORD], GEORGE Jr, Indiana (b/1796 Engl; d/VIII-26-1872) MD CPSNY 1816; AB Union 1814; STD Columbia 1831; DD, LLD Pittsburgh. *Med rec NY* 7:432. 1872.

UPHAM, ALBERT GALLATIN, Boston 1844- (b/VII-10-1819 Rochester, NH; d/VI-16-1847) MD Castleton 1842; AB Bowdoin 1840; AM 1845. *Bowdoin cat*: 1840.

UPHAM, ALFRED, NYC 1838- (b/VII-27-1804 Rochester, NH; d/XI-16-1878) MD Dartm'th 1834; AB Bowdoin 1825; AM 1848. *Bowd'n cat*:1825. *Butler* 1878:511.

UPHAM, EDWARD FISK, Randolph, Vt (b/I-29-1825 Warren; d/IV-15-1900) MD Castleton 1854. *JAMA* 34: 1356, 1900. *Polk* 1886: 907.

UPHAM, GEORGE BARNARD, Yonkers, NYC (b/III-29-1824; d/VIII-9-1889) MD Bowdoin 1850; AB 1846. *Bost m&s j* 121:169, 1889.

UPHAM, JABEZ BAXTER, CW-USA; Boston (b/ Claremont, NH; d/III-17-1902 @82 NYC) MD Harvard 1847; AB Dartmouth 1842. *Bost m&s j* 146: 318-19, 1902. *Harvard in CW*: 234.

UPSHUR, THOMAS HAROLD WILSON, CW-CSA (b/X-20-1829 East Shore, Va; d/IV-12-1902 Atlanta) MD UPa 1851. *U Pa med alum CW*: 1851.

UPSON, GEORGE C , Cuyahoga Falls, O (d/I-7-1895 @73) MD Cleveland M C 1882 [?] *JAMA* 24:101, 1895. *Polk* 1890: 912.

UPSON, HIRAM, NYC (b/IV-30-1803 New Canaan, NY; d/XI-17-1872 Bath, NY) MD ? *Med reg NY NJ Conn* 1873: 358. *Med surg rep Phila* 27: 488, 1872.

UPSON, SYLVESTER, CW-USA (d/X- -1865 Huron, NY) MD UCNY 1859. *UCNY cat*: 1859.

URIE, WILLIAM THOMAS, CW-USA; Kent Co, Md (b/XI-3-1842 Urieville; d/VII-17-1897 Chester, Pa) MD U Md 1863; MD Hahnemann, Phila 1867. *Hahn Coll Phila biogr cat*: 346. Homeopath.

URQUHART, DAVID COLIN, Philadelphia (d/I-6-1884 @72?) MD UPa 1879. *Med s rep Phila* 50:96 1884.

URQUHART, FRANCIS M , Southampton Co, Va (b/ XII-3-1857; d/II-14-1889) MD U Va 1878. *JAMA* 13: 179, 1889.

URQUHART, GEORGE, Wilkes-Barre, Pa (d/XII-10 1896 @68) MD Jefferson 1850. *JAMA* 28:140, 1897. *Polk* 1886: 840.

URWITZ, MAX, Houston c19 yrs (b/E Prussia; d/X-2-1905 @56) <MD Berlin> MD Tulane 1881. *Tex st j m* 1:184, 1905/06. *Polk* 1900: 1703.

USSERY, BENJAMIN WILLIAMS, CW-CSA; Orgain's Cross Roads, Tenn (b/VII-21-1829 Clarksville; d/XI-1-1894) MD UPa 1853. *U Pa med alum CW*: 1853. *SHSP* 22:266, 1893. *Polk* 1886: 871.

UTLEY, HENRY, Sterling, Ill (d/IV-27-1902 or 1905 @ 82) MD UCNY 1849. *Ill m j* 8:341, 1905. *Polk* 1896:409.

UTTER, FRANCIS ASBURY, NYC (d/XII-10-1901 @ 61) MD UCNY 1865. *Bost m&s j* 145:692, 1901. *Polk* 1896: 1082.

VAILLE, HENRY ROBERT, Springfield, Mass (d/VII-15-1885 @76) MD Berkshire 1838. *Bost m&s j* 113:96, 1885.

VALENTINE, JOHN FRANKLIN, Queens, NYC (b/ 1856 NY; d/II-5-1903) MD CPSNY 1879. *Bost m&s j* 148: 194, 1903. *Polk* 1896: 1093.

VALENTINE, PHILO G , CW–CSA; St Louis (b/Berkshire, NY; d/XII–22–1884 @52 Middletown, NY) <MD U Mich> AB Union 1854. *Hahn mo* 20:255, 1885. *Tr Am Inst Hom* 1885: 111. Homeopath.

VALENTINE, RICHARD KIRK, Brooklyn 1881– (b/V–7–1855 NYC; d/III–22–1901) MD NY Hom 1875; AB Swarthmore. *Tr Am Inst Hom* 1901: 920–21. *Polk* 1886: 650. Homeopath.

VALENTINE, SAMUEL M , NYC (d/VIII–7–1884 Switz) MD CPSNY 1838. *Med s rep Phila* 51: 280, 1884.

VALENTINY, CARL H , Brooklyn (b/Prussia; d/V–29–1882 @67) MD ? *Med reg NY NJ Conn* 1883:235. *Butler* 1878: 535.

VAN AERNAM, HENRY, Franklinville, NY (b/Marcellus; d/VI–1–1894) MD Willoughby 1845. *Med reg NY NJ Conn* 1894:250. *Buff m&s j* 33:744, 1894.

VAN ALLEN, THEODORE F C , Albany, NY (d/X–28 1902 @41) MD Albany 1883. *Tr MS St NY* 1903:[42] *Polk* 1886: 639.

VAN ALSTYNE, SYLVESTER M , Richmondville, NY (b/II–28–1833; d/X–28–1882) MD Albany 1854. *Tr MS St NY* 1883:283–86. *Butler* 1874: 563.

VAN ARNUM, JOHN WESLEY ?Washington, DC (b/1840 Manitou, Mich; d/XI–9–1884) MD Georgetown 1867. *Hist Med Soc DC:* 292. *Butler* 1874: 95.

VAN ARSDALE, HENRY Jr, (b/1814 New Brunswick, NJ; d/VIII–25–1888) MD UPa 1838; AB Rutgers 1835. *Med reg NY NJ Conn* 1889:288. *Butler* 1878: 526.

VAN ARSDALE, WILLIAM WALDO, NYC (d/III–17–1899 @43 Atlantic City, NJ) MD Leipzig 1883. *JAMA* 32: 733, 1956, 1899. *Nashvl j m&s* 85:194–95, 1899. *Polk* 1896: 1082.

VAN ARTSDALEN, FRANKLIN V , Philadelphia (b/Pa; d/XI–7–1903 @69) MD Jefferson 1857. *Pa med jour* 7:280, 1903/04. *Polk* 1886: 826.

VAN BIBBER, JOHN P , Baltimore (d/V–5–1892 @42) MD UMd 1871. *Chic m rec* 3:357, 1892 [?]. *Bost m&s j* 126: 484, 1892. *Med annals Md:* 602.

VAN BIBBER, WASHINGTON CHEW, Baltimore (b/VII–24–1824 Carroll Co; d/XII–14–1892) MD UMd 1845; AB Jefferson 1842. *Med annals Md:* 603. *Atkinson* I: 230–31.

VAN BLARCOM, HENRY, Perryville, NJ (b/IV–1–1831; d/VI–5–1869 Paterson, NJ) MD CPSNY 1854. *Phila med reg & dir* 1871:301. *Tr AMA* 21:470, 1870. *Tr M S NJ* 1870: 86–87. *Med surg rep Phila* 20:476, 1869.

VAN BUREN, HENRY, Chicago (d/X–28–1894 @59) MD Rush 1865. *JAMA* 23:735, 1894. *Butler* 1878:137.

VAN BUREN, PETER, Columbia Co & NYC (b/1802; d/XII–5–1873 @71) MD CPSNY 1823. *Med reg NY NJ Conn* 1874: 292. *Med surg rep Phila* 29:468, 1873. *Med rec NY* 9:71, 1874.

VAN BUREN, WILLIAM HOLME, NYC; CW–US San Comm (b/IV–5–1819 Phila; d/III–25–1883) MD UPa 1840; AB Yale 1838; AM 1864. *Med reg NY NJ Conn* 1883:236. *Bost m&s j* 108:305, 332, 1883; 109:615, 1883. *Nashvl j m&s* ns31:311–13, 1883. *Atkinson* I:471. *K&B* III:1239.

VAN BUSKIRK, AARON ELLIOTT, Ft Wayne, Ind (b/IX–27–1847 Harrisburg, O; d/I–22–1904) MD M C Ohio 1876. *Tr Ind St M S* 1904: 364. *Polk* 1896:468.

VAN BUSKIRK, JOSEPH T, Gorham, O (d/1868) MD Jefferson 1860. *Phila med reg & dir* 1871:296. *Med surg rep Phila* 18:398, 1868. *Med rec NY* 3:480, 1868–69.

VAN CAMP, JOSHUA EMANUEL, CW–USA; Carlisle, Pa (d/II–11–1904 @66) MD U Mich 1870. *Pa m j* 8: 336, 1904/05.

VANCE, DUNCAN M , Urbana, O (d/VIII–27–1878 @ 60) MD M C Ohio 1846. *Tr Ohio St M S* 1879: 187.

VANCE, REUBEN ALESHIRE, Cincinnati & Cleveland (b/VIII–18–1845 Gallipolis; d/III–19–1894) MD Bellevue 1867. *Tr Ohio St M S* 1884: 40. *Med reg NY NJ Conn* 1894: 251. *JAMA* 22:482, 1894. *K&B* III:1240.

VANCE, WILLIAM D , New Orleans (d/IV–25–1881 @ 27) MD ULa 1879. *New Orl m&s j* ns9:396, 1881.

VAN CLEEF, CHARLES EDWARD, Ithaca, NY (d/VIII 6–1896 @46) MD NY Hom 1874. *Tr Amer Inst Hom* 1898: 49. *No Am j hom* 44:600, 1896. *Polk* 1886: 644. Homeopath.

VAN DEN HEUVEL, CORNELIUS, Holland; France; Schenectady & Albany, NY (b/Vlaardingen, Holland; d/1800 Albany) <MD Leyden 1785> *NY med & phys j* 3:114–18, 1824.

VANDERBERGH [VANDENBURG], FEDERAL, Geneva, NY c20 yrs; NYC 1825?–48? (b/V–11–1788 Beekman; d/I–23–1868 Rhinebeck, NY) MD Yale 1826. *Bost m&s j* 1:32, 1868. *Med surg rep Phila* 18:112, 1868. *Tr Am Inst Hom* 1870:122. *Am hom obs* 5:157, 1868. *King* I–80–82. Homeopath.

VANDERGRIFF [VANDEGRIFFE], JOHN B , New Orleans (b/1827? d/XI–4–1898 @71) MD U La 1846. *JAMA* 32:41, 1899. *Polk* 1896: 624.

VANDERKEIFT, BERNARD A , Md; NY; CW–USA (b/Holland; d/IX–8–1866) MD ? *Tr AMA* 18:323, 1867. *Nat med jour* 1:303, 1870/71.

VANDER POEL, SAMUEL OAKLEY, Albany, NY; CW–USA (b/II–22–1824 Kinderhook; d/III–12–1886 Washington, DC) MD Jefferson 1845; AB UCNY 1842; AM 1845. *Bost m&s j* 114:260–64, 1886; 115:628, 1886. *Tr M S St NY* 1887:551–56. *K&B* III:1241.

VANDERPOOL, JAMES, Newark (b/XI–4–1841 NYC; d/I–14–1876 Yokohama, Japan) MD CPSNY 1866; AB Williams 1863. *Tr AMA* 28:623–24, 1877. *Tr M S NJ* 1876: 142–43.

VANDERSLOOT, FREDERICK W , York Pa (b/Windsor Twp; d/I–13–1904 @70) MD UMd 1855. *Pa med jour* 8:336, 1904/05. *Flint* 1897: 841.

VANDERVEER, CHARLES A , CW–USA (d/VII–16 1862 Carrollton, La) MD UCNY 1857. UCNY cat:1857.

VAN DERVEER, HENRY, Somerset Co, NJ (b/1792? d/

II–13–1874) MD ? AB Princeton 1811. *Tr AMA* 25: 528, 1874. *Tr M S NJ* 1874: 106.

VAN DERVEER, HENRY FERDINAND, CW–USA; Somerville, NJ (b/Hyde Park, NY; d/V–16–1885 @56) MD CPSNY 1851. *Tr MS NJ* 1884–85: .

VANDERVEER, JACOB H , NYC (b/1815 Freehold, NJ; d/VIII–20–1873 Long Branch) MD UCNY 1845. *Med s rep Phila* 29:198 1873. *Tr AMA* 25:527 1874. *Med reg NY NJ Conn* 1874: 293.

VANDERVOORT, JOHN LEDYARD, NYC (b/I–10–1809; d/VII–19–1891) MD CPSNY 1832; AB Columbia 1828; AM 1831. *Med reg NY NJ Conn* 1892:291. *NW m j* 19:118, 1891. *Bost m&s j* 125:96, 1891. *Atkinson* I:250. *Butler* 1878: 526.

VANDERVORT, IRA A , Bloomington, Ill (d/XI–1–1901) Lic by 24 yrs pract 1877. *Ill m j* ns3:346, 1901. *Polk* 1890: 351.

VAN DER WEYDE, PETER HENRI, NYC (b/1813 Holland; d/III–18–1895) MD UCNY 1857; <PhD Royal Acad Delft 1845> *Med reg NY NJ Conn* 1895:243. *K&B* III: 1242–43.

VAN DEURSEN [VAN DEUSEN], WILLIAM, New Brunswick, NJ (b/V–16–1791; d/II–16–1873) MD CPSNY 1813; AB Queens [Rutgers] 1809. *Tr AMA* 24: 366, 1873. *Tr M S NJ* 1873:120–21. *Med surg rep Phila* 28:220, 1873.

VANDEWATER, ALBERTUS LYMAN, Hackensack, NJ & NYC (b/1850 Brooklyn; d/III–2–1903) MD Bellevue 1870. *Bost m&s j* 148:300, 1903. *Tr M S NJ* 1903: 381–82.

VAN DOLSEN, HENRY CONE, NYC (b/IX–6–1856; d/V–8–1887) MD CPSNY 1882; AB Rutgers 1878; AM 1881. *Med reg NY NJ Conn* 1887: 276.

VAN DOREN, ABRAHAM TEN BROECK, Readington, Ringoes & Branchville, NJ (b/VI–15–1823; d/VI 30–1853) MD UCNY 1843; AB Rutgers 1840. *Tr M S NJ* 1872: 139.

VAN DOREN, J LIVINGSTONE, NYC (d/XII–7–1857 Charlotte, NC) MD ? *Bost m&s j* 57: 435, 1857.

VAN DOREN, MATTHEW DIKEMAN, NYC (b/V–14 1817; d/XI–2–1881) MD CPSNY 1841; AB Rutgers 1837; AM 1841. *Med reg NY NJ Conn* 1882: 235.

VAN DUSEN, ABRAM R , Humphreysville, NY (d/VIII 21–1901 @81) MD Albany 1841. *JAMA* 37:654, 1901. *Polk* 1886: 656.

VAN DUSEN, HARMON, Tully, NY 1826–47; Milwaukee; Mineral Pt 1847– (b/VII–23–1803 Salisbury Conn; d/VII–18–1885) Lic Onondaga Co M S 1826; MD Jefferson 1834. *Tr M S St NY* 1885:343–44. *Tr Wis St M S* 1891:357. *Butler* 1874: 834.

VAN DUSEN, MELVIN [MELVILLE] EDWARD, Angelica, NY (b/Wheeler; d/VI–15–1891) MD UCNY 1880. *Tr M S NY* 11:741 ff, 1894. *Polk* 1886:640.

VAN DUYN, STEPHEN WYNKOOP, CW–USA; Plainfield, NJ (d/ I–25–1898 @61) MD UCNY 1865; AB 1857. *JAMA* 30:507, 1898. *Polk* 1896: 944.

VAN DYCK, ANDREW, Oswego, NY (b/I–27–1801 Kinderhook; d/VIII– –1871) MD CPSNY 1822. *Tr M S NY* 1872: 336–45. *Med rec* 6:336, 553, 1871–72.

VAN DYCK [VANDYKE], EDWARD BOGART, CW–USA; Rocky Hill NJ (b/II–4–1832;d/VIII–31–1902) MD UPa 1856; AB Princeton 1853. *U Pa m alum CW*: 1856.

VANDYKE, FREDERICK AUGUSTUS, Abington, Pa (b/1788 New Brunswick; d/XI–18–1867 Phila) MD UPa 1810; AB Princeton 1807. *Med s rep Phila* 17:502, 1867.

VANDYKE, GEORGE M , W Newton, Pa (d/XII–13–1902 @44) MD Jefferson 1888. *Pa m j* 6:262, 1902/03. *Flint* 1897: 839.

VAN DYKE, GEORGE WILLIAM, Philadelphia (d/V 20–1864 @32) MD UPa 1852; AB Lafayette 1849? *Lafayette, Men of*: 162.

VAN DYKE, JOSEPH, Ashmore, Ill (d/X–12–1893 Charleston) Hon MD Rush 1868. *JAMA* 21:630, 1893. *Polk* 1886: 253.

VAN DYKE, RUSH, New Brunswick, NJ (b/IX–9–1813 Phila; d/IX–25–1882) MD UPa 1835; AB Rutgers 1830; AM 1833. *JAMA* 2:26–27, 1884. *Bost m&s j* 48:265, 1852. *Butler* 1878: 476.

VAN EMAN, W J , Leavenworth, Kans (d/XII– –1901) MD M C Ohio 1875. *Jour Kans M S* 1:219, 1901. *Polk* 1886: 386.

VAN EPPS, EVERT P , Schenectady (d/I–7–1899) MD Albany 1881. *JAMA* 32:92, 1889. *Polk* 1886: 707.

VAN ETTEN, SOLOMON, Port Jervis, NY (b/VII–30 1829; d/VII–7–1894) MD Albany 1855. *Med reg NY NJ Conn* 1895:243. *Tr M S St NY* 1895:374–76. *JAMA* 23: 164, 1894. *Butler* 1878: 578.

VAN HARLINGEN, JOHN, Brooklyn (b/Millstone, NJ; d/V–18–1903 @57) MD CPSNY 1869. *Bost m&s j* 148: 600, 1903. *Polk* 1896: 1004.

VAN HOEVENBERG, JAMES O , CW–USA; Staten Isl, NYC (b/VII–16–1823 Kingston; d/XII–9–1897) MD UCNY 1844. *Bost m&s j* 137: 637, 1897.

VAN HORN, A K , Yellow Creek, Ill (b/XII–7–1833 Athens, O; d/V–15–1889) Lic yrs pract; stud w/Dr G V Ewing, Rock City Ill 1861. *Tr Ill St M S* 1890: 42. *Polk* 1886: 302.

VAN HORN [VAN HORNE], JOHN, Readington, NJ (b/1766? d/1807 @41) MD ? *Tr M S NJ* 1872; 180–81. *Wickes*: 429.

VAN HORNE, ANDREW BRITTON, Orange, NJ (d/III 31–1888) MD CPSNY 1880; AB Yale 1877. *Med reg NY NJ Conn* 1888: 272.

VAN HOUTEN, JACOB ARTHUR, Ridgewood, NJ (b/XII–2–1853; d/XII–5–1880) MD CPSNY 1876. *Med reg NY NJ Conn* 1881: 242.

VAN KEUREN, CORNELIUS, NYC (d/I–21–1898 @ 60) MD CPSNY 1874. *Bost m&s j* 138:93, 1897. *JAMA* 30:278, 1898. *Polk* 1896: 1082.

VAN KIRK, BENNETT HUTCHINSON, W Newton, Pa

(b/VI-25-1844: d/I-24-1904) MD Jefferson 1869. *Pa m j* 7:448, 1903/04; 8:336, 1904/05. *Flint* 1897: 839.

VANKIRK, STEPHEN C , Grafton, WVa (d/VII-14-1901 @27) MD Jefferson 1901. *JAMA* 37:276, 1901.

VAN KLEECK, JOHN ROBERT, NYC (b/XI-12-1809; d/I-2-1876) MD CPSNY 1831. *Med reg NY NJ Conn* 1876: 258. *Med rec m & s* 11:62, 64, 420.

VAN KLEECK, RICHARD L , Brooklyn (b/1839 Berne, NY; d/XII-18-1895) MD UCNY 1863. *JAMA* 26:36, 1896. *Bost m&s j* 134:25, 1896. *Polk* 1890: 791.

VAN LEAR, MATTHEW SIMS, Sassafras Neck Md (d/1851) MD UPa 1811; AB Princ 1807. *Med ann Md:* 603.

VAN LEAR, WILLIAM, Williamsport, Md (b/I-29-1794 Mt Tamony; d/V-7-1838) MD UPa 1817; AB Washington Coll 1814. *Med ann Md:* 603.

VAN LEER, BERNHARDUS, ?Delaware Co, Pa (b/c1698 Gny; d/1790) <MD Gny & Italy> *Med reporter* (W Chester, Pa) 2:91-96, 1855.

VAN MATER, DANIEL G , Columbus, NJ (b/VI-27 1852 Holmdel; d/II-10/11-1895) MD Bellevue 1875; AB Rutgers 1873. *Tr M S NJ* 1894:202-03. *Atkinson* I: 426. *Butler* 1878: 479.

VAN NESS, JOHN, Brooklyn (b/Northville; d/1896) Lic Kings Co M S 1852; <att UCNY 1843-46> *JAMA* 26: 340-41, 1896. *Polk* 1886: 650.

VAN NETT, THOMAS MARTIN, Monticello, NY (d/VII-11-1894) MD UCNY 1890. *Med reg NY NJ Conn* 1895:244.

VAN NORMAN, HORACE BLACK, Cleveland (d/VII-9-1903) MD Cleveland Hom 1864. *Tr Am Inst Hom* 1904: 957. Homeopath.

VAN NUYS, WILLIAM, Anderson, Ind (d/VIII-28 1898) MD Rush 1855. *JAMA* 31:618, 1898. *Polk* 1886: 338.

VAN OLINDA, PETER, Albany, NY (b/XII-28-1797 Charleston; d/XI- -1872) Hon MD Reg SUNY 1844. *Tr M S St NY* 1873:178-79. *Tr AMA* 24:370, 1873.

VAN PEARSE, JAMES, Columbus (d/1857) MD UPa 1849. *Tr Ohio St M S* 1875: 196.

VAN PELT, MOSES D , NYC (d/IV-13-1895 @86) <MD SUNY 1835> *JAMA* 24:650, 1895. *Polk* 1886:697.

VAN PELT, WILLIAM, Williamsville, NY (d/X-12-1890 @75) MD Fairfield 1840. *Buff m&s j* 29:248, 1890. *Polk* 1886: 716.

VAN PRAAG, AARON S , NYC (d/I-16-1880 @73) MD Leyden 1826. *Med s rep Phila* 42:110, 132, 1880.

VAN RENSSELAER, JEREMIAH, NYC (b/VIII-4-1793; d/III-7-1871) MD Castleton 1823. *Med reg NY NJ Conn* 1871:366. *Med rec* 6:71, 1870-71. *K&B* II:1177.

VAN RENSSELAER, LEDYARD, Burlington, NJ (b/XI 20-1843; d/III-24-1892) MD UPa 1869; AB Princeton 1866; AM 1869. *Tr M S NJ* 1843; d/III-24-1892) *Med reg NY NJ Conn* 1892:291. *Bost m&s j* 126:328, 1892. *Atkinson* I:673. *Butler* 1878: 476.

VAN RIPER, MYRON HAWLEY, Kankakee, Ill (d/I-29 1900 @67) MD U Mich 1865. *Tr Ill St M S* 1899-1900: 463. *JAMA* 34:381, 1900. *Polk* 1886:284.

VANSANT, JOHN, USPHS (d/XII-12-1902) MD Jeff 1855 *Bost m&s j* 147:724 1901. *Polk* 1886:567 (St Louis)

VANSANT, JOSEPH B, Imlaystown, NJ (d/XI-10-1869 @25) MD Jefferson 1865. *Phila m reg & dir* 1871: 302.

VAN SAUN, JOHN DURYEE, Jersey City, NJ (b/III-21 1851; d/IV-9-1898) MD Bellevue 1873. *JAMA* 30:999, 1898. *Polk* 1896: 940.

VAN SYKEL [SICKLE], BENJAMIN MILLER, NYC (b/XII-7-1857 Newark; d/III-15-1903) MD Bellevue 1883; AB Rutgers 1880. *Bost m&s j* 148:356, 1903. *Polk* 1886: 696.

VAN TUYL, EDWARD A [or J], Riverside, Ill (d/X-26 1899) MD CPS Chicago 1883. *Tr Ill St M S* 1899: 287. *Polk* 1896: 438.

VAN VALZAH, FRANK H , Spring Mills, Pa (d/XI-26 1898 @60) MD ? *JAMA* 31:1490, 1898. *Polk* 1886:836.

VAN VALZAH, JOHN WILLIAM, CW-USA (d/VIII-10-1863 Freeport, Ill) MD UPa 1855; AB Princeton 1851. *Nat med jour* 1:303, 1870/71.

VAN VALZAH, SAMUEL B , Chicago (d/IV- -1900 @70) MD Jefferson 1854. *Tr Ill St M S* 1899-1900: 574. *Polk* 1896: 417.

VAN VALZAH, SHEPPARD LOWREY, Milton, Pa (d/VII-28-1895 @59) MD Pa Med Coll 1859. *JAMA* 25: 253, 1895. *Polk* 1890: 976.

VAN VLEEK, DANIEL P , CW-USA (d/XI-21-1862 abd US vessel) MD Albany M C 1842. *Nat med jour* 1: 303, 1870/71.

VAN VOAST, GEORGE [or GARRETT WILHELMUS VEEDER] CW-USA; Schenectady (d/VII-14-1892) MD CPSNY 1861. *Bost m&s j* 127:100, 1892. *Polk* 1886: 707.

VAN VOORHIES, HENRY, NYC (d/IV- -1861 @35?) MD Bellevue 1850. *Med reg NY NJ Conn* 1862: 154.

VAN VOORHIS, WALTER ALONZO, Philadelphia (d/IV-4-1906 @52) MD ? *Pa med jour* 9:607, 1905/06.

VAN VORST, JOHN Jr, Jersey City (b/X-18-1850; d/II 4-1887) MD Bellevue 1874; AB Princeton 1870; AM 1873. *Med reg NY NJ Conn* 1887:277. *Tr M S NJ* 1888-89: 153-54. *Med surg rep Phila* 56:256, 1887.

VAN VRANKEN, ADAM T , Watervliet, NY (d/I-19 1903 @52) MD Albany 1873. *Tr M S St NY* 1903:[412]. *Polk* 1886: 715.

VAN WAGNER, JAMES E , NYC (d/VI-9-1884 @52) MD UCNY 1857. *Med surg rep Phila* 51:28, 1884.

VAN WERDEN, H C , Leon, Iowa (b/IX-29-1854 Lee Co; d/VIII-5-1895) MD Keokuk M C 1878. *Tr Ia St M S* 1896:319. *Polk* 1890:419.

VAN WINKLE, EDWARD HENRY, NYC (d/XII-7-1894 @79) MD CPSNY 1836; AM Columbia 1865. *JAMA* 23:961, 1894. *Butler* 1878: 526.

VAN WINKLE, MARK, Little Falls, NJ (d/XI-29-1897 @73) MD CPSNY 1855. *JAMA* 29:1286, 1897. *Polk* 1896: 940.

VAN WYCK, EDWARD BUNTING, USN 1838–81 (d/IX–11–1887 Closter, NJ) MD UPa 1838. *U Pa med alum CW*: 1838.

VAN WYCK, JOHN C, Oakland Cal (b/1–1–1828 Balto; d/VIII–19–1877) MD U Md 1848. *Tr AMA* 31:1094–95, 1880. *Tr Cal St M S* 1877–78: 239.

VAN WYCK, PIERRE CORTLANDT, NYC (b/IX–24–1824; d/IV–23–1883 Ossining) MD CPSNY 1849; AB Princeton 1845. *Med reg NY NJ Conn* 1883: 237.

VAN WYCK, SAMUEL MAVERICK, CW–CSA (b/IV 24–Pendleton, SC; d/XI–24–1861 Marion, Ky) MD UCNY 1860; ng Amherst 1856. *Amherst, Men of*: 1856.

VAN WYCK, WILLIAM HARRISON, NYC (d/XI–16–1891) MD Bellevue 1865. *Med reg NY NJ Conn* 1892: 292. *Tr M S St NY* 1892: 495. *Bost m&s j* 125: 560, 1891.

VAN ZANDT, HENRY CLAY, Schenectady (d/I–16–1900 @56) *JAMA* 34:313, 1900. *Polk* 1896: 1099.

VARIAN, WILLIAM A , NYC (d/XII–23–1898) MD UCNY 1846. *JAMA* 32:41, 1899. *Polk* 1896: 1082.

VARICK, RICHARD, Poughkeepsie, NY (d/VIII–10 1871 @66) MD ? *Med rec NY* 6:310, 1871–72.

VARICK, THEODORE ROMEYN, Jersey City (b/VI–24–1825 Poughkeepsie, NY; d/XI–23–1887) MD UCNY 1846. *Bost m&s j* 117:636, 1887. *Tr M S NJ* 1888–89: 155–61. *Med reg NY NJ Conn* 1888: 272. *Atkinson* I:256. *Polk* 1886: 605.

VARLEY, CHRISTOPHER DIXON, NYC (b/Engl; d/XII–21–1887) MD UCNY 1844; AB Trinity 1841; AM 1844. *Med reg NY NJ Conn* 1888:272. *Butler* 1878: 526.

VARNEY, ALFRED EDMUND, Middleville, NY (b/XII 29–1807 Amenia, NY; d/II–24–1871) MD Fairfield 1831. *Tr M S St NY* 1872: 357–59.

VARONA [de VARONA], SERAPIO MANUEL de, NYC (b/XII– –1848 Cuba; d/XII–21–1873) MD Bellevue 1870. *Med reg NY NJ Conn* 1874: 272.

VASEY, WILSON P , Philadelphia (b/Bucks Co; d/XII–26–1838 @31) MD Jefferson 1852. *Tr AMA* 13: 804, 1860. *Med surg rep Phila* ns1:236, 1858/59.

VASSER, EDWARD MILHOUSE, Cahaba, Ala (b/III–12–1831 Lowndes Co; d/II–3–1879 Selma) <MD M C New Orl 1851> MD UCNY 1851. *Tr M Assn St Ala* 1879:169. *Butler* 1874: 27.

VASTINE, JACOB H , CW–USA; Catawissa, Pa (b/IV 2–1836 Northumberland Co; d/I–2–1904) MD Jefferson 1858. *Pa med jour* 8:336, 1904/05. *Atkinson* I: 518. *Flint* 1897: 798.

VATTIER, JOHN LORING, Cincinnati (b/X–31–1808; d/1881) MD M C Ohio 1830. *Tr AMA* 32:544–46, 1881. *Atkinson* I:283. *K&B* III: 1244–45.

VAUDAIN, ARNOLD, NYC (b/Dover, Del; d/1899 @70) <MD UPa 1852> *Bost m&s j* 140: 416, 1899.

VAUGHAN, BERNARD ELIAS, NYC (b/Worcester, Mass or Me; d/III–4–1895 @32) MD CPSNY 1889. *Med reg NY NJ Conn* 1895:244. *JAMA* 24:422, 1895. *Bost m&s j* 132:260, 1895.

VAUGHAN, CHARLES EVERETT, CW–USN; Cambridge, Mass; Santa Barbara, Cal (d/VI–24–1904 @68) MD Harvard 1863; AB 1856. *Harvard in CW*: 98. *Bost m&s j* 150:716, 1904. *Polk* 1896: 242.

VAUGHAN, HORACE, Middletown, Conn (b/1859 Del; d/I–22–1900) MD Jefferson 1888. *JAMA* 34:388, 1900. *Polk* 1896: 292.

VAUGHAN, THOMAS BRESSIE, Tuscaloosa, Ala (b/I–11–1826; d/V–1–1849) MD Jefferson 1848; att U Ala 1842. *U Ala cat*: 78.

VAUGHAN, THOMAS P , Brusly Landing, La (d/VIII–11–1905 @93) MD M C Ohio 1834. *New Orl m&s j* 58: 276, 1905. *Polk* 1886: 413.

VAUGHN, A , Amherst, ¦Va (d/III–3–1882) MD ? *Chic med rev* 5:181, 1882. *Butler* 1878: 837.

VAUGHN, BURTON D , Chicago (d/XII–3–1901) MD Bennett 1886. *Ill m j* ns3: 399, 1902.

VAUGHN, FRANK OWEN, Buffalo (d/III– –1891 @44) MD Buffalo 1880. *Buff m&s j* 30:570, 1891.

VAUGHN, WILLIAM M , Cherokee, Tex (d/VII–10 1901) MD ? *JAMA* 37: 276, 1901.

VAUGHT, ROBERT L , Chattanooga (b/V–24–1863; d/VIII–28–1895 Henderson, WVa) <MD U Nashville & Vanderbilt 1886> *JAMA* 25:427, 467, 1895. *Nashvl j m & s* 78:153–54, 1895. *Polk* 1890: 1048.

VEATCH, WILLIAM HENDRIX, Carthage, Ill (d/X–10 1897 @66) MD Rush 1867. *JAMA* 29:926, 1897. *Polk* 1886: 257.

VEAZEY, EDWARD, St Louis (b/III–26–1799 Cherry Grove, Md; d/XII–14–1870) MD U Md 1822. *Med annals Md:* 604.

VEAZEY, THOMAS REID, Pittsburgh (d/XII–10–1902 @45) MD Ky Sch Med 1885. *Pa m j* 6:262, 1902/03.

VEDDER, ALEXANDER MARSELIS, Schenectady; CW–USA (b/I–15–1814; d/XII–29–1878) MD UPa 1839; AB Union 1833; AM 1836. *Med reg NY NJ Conn* 1879: 201. *Tr M S St NY* 587–89. *Atkinson* I: 165. *Butler* 1878: 579.

VEDDER, JOSEPH HOLLAND, Flushing, NY (d/VII–18–1864 Schenectady) MD CPSNY 1853; AB Union 1851 *Tr AMA* 18:309 1867. *Med s rep Phil* 12:84 1864/5.

VEEDER, FREDERICK A , Utica NY (d/I–26–1899 @ 71) MD LICH 1874 *JAMA* 32:324 1899. *Polk* 1886:713.

VEEDER, LOUIS, Dansville, NY (b/1816; d/1877) <MD Vienna 1847> *Tr AMA* 31:1095, 1880.

VEES, CHARLES H , Baltimore (b/1859; d/V–27–1892) MD CPS Balto 1886. *Med ann Md:* 604. *Polk* 1890:516.

VEIRS, CHARLES OTHO, Jersey City (d/IV–5–1885 @44) MD Bellevue 1867. *Med surg rep Phila* 52:576, 1885. *Butler* 1878: 465.

VENABLE, HOWELL A , Prospect Depot, Va (d/VII–1871 @30) MD ? *Tr M S Va* 1872: 26, 154.

VENABLE, NATHANIEL HENRY, CW–CSA (b/XII–25–1828, Longwood, Pr Edw Co, Va; d/II–18–1868 Tuscaloosa, Ala) MD UPa 1849; AB Hampden Sidney

1845. *U Pa med alum CW*: 1849.

VERBRYCK, JAMES, CW-USA (d/VI-24-1864 Pt Hudson, La) MD ? *Nat med jour* 1:303, 1870/71.

VERDI, TULLIO SUZZARA, NYC 1850- ; Washington DC 1857-95 (b/1829 Mantua, It; d/XI-26-1902 Milan) MD Hahnemann Phila 1856. *Tr Am Inst Hom* 1903:703-04. *Hahn mo* : 1895 (Aug-Sept) *Polk* 1886: 214. Homeopath.

VERMEULE, FIELD, NYC (d/II-26-1877 @75) MD CPSNY 1825. *Med reg NY NJ Conn* 1877: 208.

VER MEULEN, EDMUND CARLYLE, CW-USN; Philadelphia (b/1833 NYC; d/I-21-1898) MD CPSNY 1860. *JAMA* 30:278, 1898.

VERMILYE, WILLIAM EDWARD, CW-USA; NYC (d/II-2-1888 @60 Flushing) MD CPSNY 1852; AB UCNY 1848; AB Williams 1848; hon AM. *Med reg NY NJ Conn* 1888: 273. *Polk* 1886: 471.

VERNON, JAMES BLACKWELL, Jacksonville, Ala (b/XII-31-1844; d/I-12-1873) MD Washington U, Balto 1868; att U Ala 1862. *U Ala cat*: 172.

VERNON, THOMAS, Providence, RI (b/XII-20-1797 Newport, RI; d/V-9-1876) <MD UPa> AB Brown 1816; AM. *Brown hist cat*: 1816.

VERRMYNE, JAN JOSEPH BASTIANUS, New Bedford, Mass (d/VIII-16-1898 @63 Francestown, NH) <MD Utrecht 1856> *Bost m&s j* 139:204, 1898. *Polk* 1886: 470.

VERTREES, WOODFORD M, Nashville (b/Ky; d/X-22 1902 @76) MD U Louisvl 1852. *So pract* 24:634 1902.

VIALLON, LOUIS H , Bayou Goula, Miss (d/III-14-1905) MD Tulane 1890. *New Orl m&s j* 57:787, 1905. *Polk* 1896: 614.

VIBBERT, WILLIAM WELSH, NYC (d/III-25-1900 @27) MD CPSNY 1898; AB Trinity 1894; AM 1897. *JAMA* 34:89, 1900.

VICK, THOMAS EUGENE, CW-CSA (b/IV-11-1831 Washington, Ky; d/II-2-1866 Mississippi River) MD UPa 1852; AB Centre 1851. *U Pa med alum CW*: 1852.

VICKERS, ALBERT, Brooklyn (d/VI-6-1877 @35) MD U Md 1866. *Med reg NY NJ Conn* 1877: 208.

VICKERS, E FRANK, CW-USA (d/VII-28-1865) MD ? *Nat med jour* 1:303, 1870/71.

VICKERY, ABSALOM M , Tipton, Ind (b/II-10-1822 Milton, Ind; d/II-11-1886) MD M C Ohio 1866; <MD Bellevue 1874> *Tr Ind St M S* 1886:212 *Butler* 1878:223.

VIELE, AUGUSTUS, NYC (d/II-12-1882 @66) MD Fairfield 1837. *Med reg NY NJ Conn* 1882: 236.

VIELE, FRANCIS, Elizabeth, NJ (d/IV- -1874) MD ? *Med surg rep Phila* 30:372, 1874.

VIGNERON, CHARLES ANTONIO, Newport, RI (b/c1722? d/1772 @50 NY) MD ? *Tr RI M S* 1:5, 1859-77.

VIGNERON, NORBERT FELICIEN, RI 1690- (b/Artois Fr; d/1764) MD ? *Tr RI M S* 1:5, 1859-77.

VILLANYI, EMIL J , NYC (b/VI-2-1828 Hungary; d/I-14-1885) <MD Pesth 1850; MD Karkov 1859> *Med reg NY NJ Conn* 1885: 246.

VINAL, LEONIDAS CURTIN [CURTIS], Middletown, Conn (b/VI-14-1838; d/VI-10-1884) MD Yale 1880. *Proc Conn Med Soc* 1886:187-88.

VINCELETTE, ARTHUR EDUARD ZEPHEREN, Lowell, Mass (d/VII-3-1891 @37 Quebec) <MD Laval U, Que> *Bost m&s j* 125:72, 1891. *Polk* 1886: 468.

VINCENT, CHARITY JANE, Allegheny, Pa (d/I-7-1902 @48) MD Woman's M C Pa 1882. *Pa med jour* 5: 276, 1901/02; 6:262, 1902/03. *Flint* 1897: 794.

VINCENT, EDWARD E , Detroit (d/V-4-1900) MD Hahnemann Chic 1887. *Ill m j* ns2:48, 1900.

VINCENT, FRANK LYON, Clifton Spr & Troy, NY (d/V-12-1889 @50) MD Hahnemann Chic 1861. *Bost m&s j* 120:520, 1889. *Tr Am Inst Hom* 1889:187. *Polk* 1886:712. Homeopath.

VINCENT, HENRY CLAY, Guildford, Ind; Cincinnati (b/X-26-1826; d/VII-11-1891) MD M C Ohio 1872. *Tr Ind St M S* 1891:287; 1892:280. *Atkinson* I:677.

VINSON, B C , Malden, WVa (b/Benton Co, Mo; d/VII 13-1888 @48?) MD St Louis M C 1867. *Tr M S WVa* 1889: 674. *Butler* 1878: 854.

VIRDIN, WILLIAM W Jr, Lapidum, Md (b/VIII-12 1829; d/V-20-1897 @68) MD UMd 1866. *JAMA* 28: 1092, 1897. *Med annals Md:* 604.

VIRGIN, SAMUEL HAHNEMANN, Macon, ? (d/X-28 1880) MD ? att U Ala 1864. *U Ala cat*: 211.

VISSMAN, WILLIAM, NYC (b/1865; d/III-29-1899 Morristown, NJ @33) MD Louisvl M C 1887; stud Berlin. *Bost m&s j* 140:364, 1899. *JAMA* 32:787, 1899.

VITTUM, STEPHEN, Laconia, NH (b/XI-9-1859 Sandwich, Mass? d/IV-13-1903) MD Dartmouth 1884. *Tr NH M S* 1903:241-42. *Polk* 1896:920.

VITZTHUM [VITZSTHRUN], CASPAR [de], Moline, Ill (d/II-24-1894 @71) MD Jena 1855. *JAMA* 22:391, 1894. *Polk* 1890: 340.

VIVIAN, GODFREY, Alexandria, Minn (d/VIII-26-1897) MD U Mich 1862; MD Bellevue 1876. *Tr Minn St M S* 1902:307. *Polk* 1896: 241.

VIXTRUM, JOHN A , Princeton, Ill (d/II-9-1905 Colorado Spr) MD Vanderbilt 1883. *Ill m j* 7:302, 1905.

VOELLER, HERMAN, Sacramento (d/XI-14-1898 @ 65) MD Cooper M C 1876. *JAMA* 31:1377, 1898. *Polk* 1886: 169.

VOGEL, FREDERICK WILLIAM, Roxbury, Mass (d/VII-16-1898 @52) <MD Halle 1868> *JAMA* 31:297, 1898. *Bost m&s j* 139:76, 1898. *Polk* 1886: 472.

VOGLER, CHARLES, Newark 1868- (b/Gny; d/I-7-1892) <MD U Berlin 1868> *Tr M S NJ* 1892:297. *Med reg NY NJ Conn* 1892: 292.

VOGLER, GEORGE WASHINGTON, Philadelphia (d/VIII-26-1897 @42 Estes Park, Col) MD UPa 1876; PhD 1876. *JAMA* 29:555, 1897. *Polk* 1896:1320.

VOGT, ARNOLD WILLIAM, Ft Madison, Ia (d/IX-2-1899 @90) MD Mo M C 1884. *JAMA* 33: 745, 1899.

Polk 1886: 301 (W Union, Ill).

VOGT, WILLIAM, Iowa City, Ia 1848– (b/Prussia; d/VIII–21–1873 @55) MD ? *Tr Ia St M S* 1872–76; 33, 221. Fairchild's *Iowa*: 32.

VOIGHT, LUDWIG G , Freeport, Ill (d/VIII–1–1900) MD UCNY 1866. *Ill m j* ns2:189, 1906. *Polk* 1896: 420.

VOLK, CARL AUGUSTUS, Claremont, NH (b/VI–18–1812 Hamburg, Gny; d/III–5–1883) MD Dartmouth 1860. *Tr NH M S* 1883: 175–76.

VOLKED, ANDREW J , Buffalo (d/XII–11–1899 @28) MD Buffalo 1892. *JAMA* 33:1632, 1899. *Buff m&s j* 39: 260, 1900. *Flint* 1897: 653.

VONDERSMITH, ELI W , CW–USA; NYC (d/III–18–1887) MD UCNY 1852. *Med reg NY NJ Conn* 1888:273. *Polk* 1886: 696.

VONDY, JOSEPH HARRISON, Jersey City, NJ (b/1829 New Brunswick, Can; d/IV–2–1900) MD UCNY 1851. *Bost m&s j* 142:396, 1900. *JAMA* 34: 957, 1900. *Polk* 1896: 940.

VON GOHREN, LUDWIG H , Bay St Louis, Miss; New Orleans (d/VIII–31–1906) <MD Charity Hosp NO 1876> *New Orl m&s j* 59:332, 1906. *Polk* 1890: 492.

VON SEYDEWITZ, PAUL, New Orleans (d/III–15–1901 @73) MD Heidelberg 1869 *New Orl m&s j* 53: 632–33, 1901. *Polk* 1890: 492.

VON URFF, CHARLES ADAM, Brooklyn (b/Gny; d/VII 16–1902 @35) MD LICH 1890. *Bost m&s j* 147:116, 1902. *Polk* 1896: 1004.

VOORHEES, CHARLES HOLBERT, CW–USA; New Brunswick, NJ (b/VIII–3–1824; d/V–13–1900) MD Jefferson 1850. *Bost m&s j* 142:556, 1900. *JAMA* 34:1356, 1431, 1900. *Atkinson* I: 84. *Polk* 1896: 945.

VOORHEES, GEORGE, NYC (d/IV–21–1887 @32) MD UCNY 1879. *Med reg NY NJ Conn* 1887: 277. *Polk* 1886: 696.

VOORHEES, JOSEPH, Brooklyn (d/VII–6–1865 @53 Red Bank, NJ) MD ? *Med surg rep Phila* 13:48, 1865.

VOORHEES, SYLVANUS R , Mason, O (b/X–31–1831 Warren Co; d/IV–23–1886) MD Miami 1868. *Tr Ohio M S* 1886:402–03. *Atkinson* I:363. *Butler* 1878: 654.

VOORHEES, WILLIAM, Spotsylvania, Va (d/XII–19–1897 @62) MD Geneva 1862. *JAMA* 30:48, 1898. *Polk* 1890: 1133.

VOORHIES, ALBERT, El Paso, Tex (d/III–16–1906) MD ? *New Orl m&s j* 58:862, 1906.

VOSBURG, JACOB, Erie, Pa (b/1788? d/I–1–1863 @75) MD ? *Med surg rep Phila* ns9:278, 1862/63.

VOSE, SAMUEL, New Portland, Me (b/VIII–2–1792 Antrim, NH; d/XI–14–1860 @68) MD Bowdoin 1823. *Bost m&s j* 63:426, 1861.

VOUGHT, JOHN, Monmouth, NJ (b/1816 Duanesburg, NY; d/III–21–1882) MD Albany 1839. *Tr M S NJ* 1882–83: 193–94. *Butler* 1878: 477.

VOUGHT, WALTER JOY, NYC (b/Buffalo; d/IX–24–1893 @31) MD CPSNY 1885; PhB Yale 1882. *Med reg NY NJ Conn* 1894:251. *JAMA* 21:546, 1893. *Buff m&s j* 33:171, 1893. *Bost m&s j* 129:336, 1893.

VREELAND, B , CW–USN (d/III–20–1866 abd Kearsarge at sea) MD ? *Nat med jour* 1:303, 1870/71.

VROOMAN, CHARLES W , Brooklyn (b/XI–7–1846 Canada; d/VIII–7–1881) MD U Mich 1868. *Med reg NY NJ Conn* 1882: 236.

WADDELL, JAMES ALEXANDER, CW–CSA; Staunton, Va (b/1818; d/VII–23–1883) MD UPa 1841; AB Wash & Lee 1837. *Tr M S Va* 1885:287–88. *Med s rep Phil* 49:392 1885. *UPa m al CW*:1841 *Butler* 1878:858.

WADDELL, LIVINGSTON, Lexington, Va (b/X–11–1799 Louisa Co; d/VIII–17–1881) MD UPa 1824. *UPa med alum CW*: 1824. Blanton *Va surgs CW*: 418.

WADDELL, THOMAS, Toledo, O (b/X–13–1843 Canada West; d/III–9–1879) MD Wooster 1871. *Tr AMA* 31:1095–96, 1880. *Tr Ohio St M S* 1879:188. *Buff m&s j* 18:394–95, 1879. *Atkinson* I: 169.

WADDILL, FRANK ALEXANDER, CW–CSA; Cheraw, SC (b/II–1–1849; d/V–22–1905) MD UPa 1876; att Wash & Lee. *U Pa med alum CW*: 1876. *Polk* 1886:853.

WADE, CHARLES H , NYC (b/IV–23–1836 Ulster Co; d/VI–23–1882) MD UCNY 1861. *Med reg NY NJ Conn* 1883: 238.

WADE, J TRIGG, Arlington, Nebr (d/IX–3–1899) MD CPS Balto 1884. *JAMA* 33:745, 1899. *Polk* 1886: 915 (Chatham Hill, Va).

WADE, JAMES D , Brooklyn (d/X–19–1902) MD UCNY 1866. *Bost m&s j* 147:504 1902. *Polk* 1896:1004.

WADE, JOSEPH L , CW–USA; Irvington, NJ (b/1829; d/IV–21 1895) MD UCNY 1850. *JAMA* 24:689, 1895. *Med reg NY NJ Conn* 1895: 245. *Butler* 1878: 477, as homeopath.

WADLEIGH, WALTER KENDALL, Hopkinton NH (b/IV–7–1865 Franklin; d/II–7–1905) MD Dartmouth 1887. *Tr NH M S* 1906:236–37. *Polk* 1896: 920.

WADSWORTH, FRANK L , Chicago (b/VI–18–1835 Hiram, Me; d/VIII–27–1891) MD Rush 1869. *Chic m rec* 2:79, 1891. *Atkinson* I: 621. *Butler* 1878: 138.

WADSWORTH, JOHN ATHERTON, Providence (b/XII–4–1793 Milton, Mass; d/IV–21–1866 @72) MD Brown 1818; AB 1814. *Bost m&s j* 74:268, 1866.

WADSWORTH, PELEG, Malden, Mass (d/IV–2–1904 @69) MD Columbian 1863; AB Dartmouth 1859. *Bost m&s j* 150:390, 1904. *Polk* 1896: 717.

WAGER, PETER, CW–USA (b/Montg'y Sq, Pa; d/XII 25–1868) MD UPa 1861. *U Pa med alum CW*: 1861.

WAGGONER, CALVIN C , Cedar Rapids, Ia 1861– (d/IX–24–1867 @c/32) MD ? *US m&s j* 3:231, 1868. *Med invest* 5:63, 1868. Homeopath.

WAGGONER, FIELDON R , Sacramento (d/IV–27–1903) MD Mo M C 1878. *Cal st j m* 1:174, 1903.

WAGGONER, JOSEPH, Ravenna, O (b/XII–30–1821 Richmond; d/VI–6–1897) MD Cleveland M C 1865.

JAMA 28:1203, 1897; 29:45, 1897. *Atkinson* I:646. *Polk* 1890: 931.

WAGLEY [MAGGLEY], JOHN L , Cleburne, Tex (d/XII-21-1893) MD Tulane 1873. *New Orl m&s j* ns 21: 550, 1894. *Daniel's Tex m j* 9:351-52, 358, 1893-94. *Polk* 1890: 1073.

WAGNER, ALBERT L , So Bend & La Paz, Ind (b/1860; d/IX-28-1901) MD CPS Chicago 1885. *JAMA* 36: 337, 1901.

WAGNER, ALBERT SCHMIDT, Baltimore (b/IX-20-1869; d/II-23-1893) MD CPS Balto 1892. *Med annals Md:* 605.

WAGNER, FRANCIS T R , Wilkesbarre, Pa (d/XI-1 1902 @68) MD Göttingen 1857. *Pa med jour* 6:262, 1902/03. *Polk* 1893: 1137.

WAGNER, FREDERICK, CW-USA (d/IX-25-1864 Sulphur Trustle, Ala) MD ? *Nat med jour* 1:303, 1870/71.

WAGNER, JOHN, Charleston (b/1791; d/V-22-1841) MD ? AB Yale 1812; AM 1815. *Am j m sci* ns2:526-27, 1841. *Waring* II: 313. *K&B* III: 1250.

WAGNER, LEWIS CLARK, Nicholasville, Ky (d/II-14 1895) MD Bellevue 1878. *JAMA* 24:294, 1895. *Polk* 1890: 474.

WAGNER, WILLIAM, Chicago (b/1825 Carlsruhe, Baden; d/VII-5-1872) <MD Gny> *Med reg* Chic 1872-73: 333-34.

WAGONER, HENRY G , Somerville, NJ (d/VII-2-1901 @78) MD UPa 1853. *Bost m&s j* 145:52, 1901. *Polk* 1896: 949.

WAGSTAFF, ALFRED, L I, NY (d/IV-26-1878 @74) MD CPSNY 1826; AB Columbia 1822. *Med reg NY NJ Conn* 1878: 192.

WAINWRIGHT, CHARLES H , CW-USN (d/VII-3-1862 Ship Island) MD ? *Tr AMA* 14:216, 1864. *Nat med jour* 1:303, 1870/71.

WAINWRIGHT, DANIEL WADSWORTH, CW-USN (d/VIII-5-1863 @31 New Orl abd US Blackhawk) MD ? *Med surg rep Phila* 10:240, 252, 1863. *Nat med jour* 1:303, 1870/71.

WAINWRIGHT, WILLIAM AUGUSTUS MUHLENBERG, Hartford, Conn (b/VIII-13-1844; d/IX-24-1894) MD CPSNY 1867; AB Trinity 1864. *Med reg NY NJ Conn* 1895:244. *Proc Conn Med Soc* 1895:356-60. *Bost m&s j* 131:328, 1894. *Butler* 1878: 83.

WAITE, DAVID VANDALIA, Rockton, Ill (d/I-26-1901) MD Geneva 1851. *Ill m j* ns2:533, 1901. *Polk* 1896: 296.

WAITE, EDWARD EVERETT, New Bedford, Mass (b/1857; d/VI-20-1901) MD Bellevue 1877. *JAMA* 37: 43, 1901.

WAITE [WAIT], PHOEBE JANE BABCOCK, NYC (b/IX-30-1838 Potter Hill, RI; d/I-30-1904) MD NY Coll & Hosp for Women 1871; AB Alfred U 1860. *Tr Am Inst Hom* 1904:957-58. *No Am j hom* 52:24 (curr events), 1904. *Polk* 1886: 696. Homeopath.

WAKEFIELD, ALLEY TALBOT, Cambridge, Mass (d/X-18-1886 @31) MD Harvard 1882; AB 1877. *Bost m&s j* 115: 416, 437, 1886.

WAKEFIELD, EDWARD BURTON, Brooklyn (d/III-12-1877 @28) MD UCNY 1873. *Med reg NY NJ Conn* 1879: 202. *Butler* 1878: 535.

WAKEFIELD, HORACE POOL, Reading & Leicester, Mass (b/I-4-1809; d/VIII-23 or 30-1883) MD Dartmouth 1837; AB Amherst 1832. *JAMA* 1:352, 1883. *Bost m&s j* 109:617, 1883. *Med bull m&s* 5:240, 1883. *Butler* 1878: 359.

WAKEFIELD, JONAS FRANKLIN, Everett Mass (b/VI-20-1825; d/I-14-1887) MD Phila Coll M & S 1853. *JAMA* 10:160, 1888. *Bost m&s j* 116:72, 1887.

WAKEFIELD, LUCIUS L , Summum, Ill (d/XII-23 1901) MD ? *Ill m j* ns3:399, 1902. *Flint* 1897: 289.

WAKEFIELD, MATTHEW F , CW-CSA; Ben Wheeler, Tex; Austin (b/c1846; d/VI-16-1905 @59?) MD Jefferson 1850. *Tex st j m* 1:84, 1905/06. *Polk* 1886: 881.

WAKEMAN, HARWOOD, NYC (b/VI-1-1848 Troy; d/VIII-15-1878/79 Adirondacks) MD Bel'vue 1872 *Med reg NY NJ Conn* 1879:202. *Med rec NY* 14:180, 1878.

WAKEMAN, MOSES H , Redding, Conn (b/XI-5-1829 Greenfield Hill, Conn; d/I- -1891/1892) MD Yale 1854. *Proc Conn Med Soc* 1892:858-59.

WALDO, ROSWELL [RUSSELL], Cairo, Ill (b/1846; d/1878) MD Columbian 1875. *Tr AMA* 30:886, 1879.

WALDOCK, JAMES, CW-USA; Roxbury Mass (d/1898) MD Harvard 1852; AB 1845. *Harvard in CW*: 30. *Polk* 1886: 472.

WALDRON, JESSE M , Porter, Mich (d/II-1-1896 @ 36) MD CPS Chicago 1886. *JAMA* 26:287, 1896. *Polk* 1893: 654.

WALES, BRADFORD LEONARD, Randolph, Mass (d/V-13-1890 @86) MD Harvard 1828; AB Middlebury 1824. *Bost m&s j* 122:514, 1890.

WALES, HENRY W , Boston (b/XII-11-1818; d/VI-8-1856 @37 Paris, Fr) MD Harvard 1841; AM 1838. *Bost m&s j* 54:447, 1856; 55:374, 1857. Palmer's *Necrol Harv alum*: 100.

WALES, PHILIP SKINNER, USN 1856-96; Washington, DC (b/II-27-1837 Annapolis, Md; d/IX-15-1906 Paris, Fr) MD UPa 1861. *U Pa med alum CW*: 1861. *Atkinson* I: 122. *K&B* III: 1251.

WALES, THOMAS BEALE, Randolph, Mass (d/1861 @38) MD Harvard 1847; AB Middlebury 1844. *Bost m&s j* 64:32, 1861.

WALKE, FRANK ANTHONY, Norfolk, Va; USN 1854-56; CW-CSA 1861-65 (b/X-1-1831 Pr Anne Co; d/VII-5-1904) MD UPa 1852. *So pract* 26:569, 1904; 28:166, 1906. *U Pa med alum CW*: 1852.

WALKE, JOHN WISTAR, CW-CSA; Manchester, Va (b/III-11-1824 Chesterfield Co; d/IX-11-1885) MD UPa 1848; MD Hampden Sidney 1844. *U Pa med alum*

 Spec. educ'l status abbrev. as: ***ng*** = college verified attendance without degree;

CW: 1848. Blanton, *Va surgs CW*: 418.

WALKE, SYDENHAM, Manchester, Va (b/VII–24–1816 Chesterfield, Va; d/VII– –1880) MD UPa 1843. *U Pa med alum CW*: 1843.

WALKER, AARON, Cranston, RI; Denver (b/VIII–20 1815 Belchertown, Mass; d/I–22–1899) MD NY Hom 1868; AB Amherst 1841. *Amherst, Men of*: 1841. *Polk* 1886: 184. Homeopath.

WALKER, ABEL W , Pontiac, Mich (d/XI–30–1865 @ 26) MD Homeop M C Mo 1861. *Am hom obs* 3:102, 1866. Homeopath.

WALKER, ALFRED EASTMAN, New Haven, Conn (b/I–5–1842; d/III–5–1873) MD Yale 1867. *Proc Conn Med Soc* 1873:225. *Med surg rep Phila* 28:256, 1873.

WALKER, AMOS, Bucks Co, Pa (b/1792? d/1889 @96) MD UPa 1846. *Bost m&s j* 120:176, 1889.

WALKER, BENJAMIN MAITLAND, CW–CSA; Danville Va (b/IV–10–1838 Plymouth NC; d/VIII–12–1902 Connelly's Spr NC) MD UPa 1858. *U Pa med alum CW*: 1858. *Polk* 1886: 916.

WALKER, CHARLES IRA, Powers, Mich (d/IX–11–1898 @35) MD Rush 1884. *JAMA* 31:808, 1898.

WALKER, CLEMENT ADAMS, So Boston (b/VII–3–1820 Fryeburg, Me; d/IV–26–1883) MD Harvard 1850; AB Dartmouth 1842. *JAMA* 3:107, 1884. *Atkinson* I:680. *K&B* III:1251–52. *Butler* 1878: 344.

WALKER, DAVID RUFUS, Lebanon, Ind (b/XII–16–1844 Henry Co; d/IV–16–1902) MD Indiana M C 1873. *Tr Ind St M S* 1902:426. *Polk* 1896: 488.

WALKER, DEKAVAN N , Ilion, NY (d/I–4–1891 @62) MD Jeff'n 1858. *Tr M S St NY* 1891:457. *Polk* 1886: 664.

WALKER, EDMUND RHETT, CW–CSA; Baltimore (b/VII–13–1836 Beaufort, SC; d/IX–30–1891) MD UVa 1857; MD UCNY 1858 *Med ann Md*:606 *Polk* 1886:440.

WALKER, EDWARD STAATS, CW–USA; Ilion NY (b/1824 Root; d/VII–12 or 17–1876) MD UCNY 1850; att U Vt. *Tr M S St NY* 1877:358–65.

WALKER, GEORGE BRINTON, Evansville, Ind (b/XII– –1807 Salem, NJ; d/IX–6–1887) MD M C Ohio 1830. *Tr Ind St M S* 1888:206. *Butler* 1878:223.

WALKER, HAMILTON BERRIEN, NYC (d/X–24–1876) MD CPSNY 1873. *Med reg NY NJ Conn* 1877: 209. *Med surg rep Phila* 35:414, 1876.

WALKER, J E , Georgetown, Tex (b/1831 Rockbridge Co, Va; d/III–31–1893) Stud med Chicago. *Tex cour-rec med* 10:292, 1893. *Daniel's Tex m j* 8:523–24, 1892–93. *Polk* 1886: 887.

WALKER, JAMES EDWIN, Brookline, Mass (b/V–8–1832 Fryeburg, Me; d/VI–15–1894) MD Bowdoin 1856. *Bost m&s j* 130:636, 1894.

WALKER, JAMES K, Waverly, Ky (b/1842 Taylorsville; d/IV–10–1887) MD Jeff'n 1870 *Tr Ind St M S* 1887: 197.

WALKER, JAMES PARKER, Manchester, NH (b/II–7–1828; d/V–6–1897) MD Harvard 1856; ng Amherst 1853. *Bost m&s j* 136:476, 1897; 137:263, 690, 1897.

WALKER, JAMES W H , Wildwood, NJ (d/VIII–1895 @23) MD Jefferson 1893. *Med bull m & s* 17:357, 1895.

WALKER, JAMES WISE, Los Gatos, Cal (d/1905) MD Harvard 1880; AB 1877; AM Capetown U, S Afr. *Cal st j m* 3:198, 1895.

WALKER, JOHN BAYLEY, Thomaston, Me (b/XII–12 1825 Union; d/IV–20–1888) MD Bowdoin 1847. *Tr Me M Assn* 1888:509–10.

WALKER, JOSHUA COCHRANE, Wilmington, NC; CW–CSA (b/IV–6–1833; d/XII–22–1882) MD UCNY 1858; AB UNC 1854. *NC m j* 10:416, 1882. *Tr NC M S* 1887:155–56. *Atkinson* I: 614.

WALKER, MAHLON MURPHY, Philadelphia (b/1845 Buck'm Twp, Pa; d/III–31–1896) MD Hahnemann Phil 1867; att U Vienna 1869. *Hahn mo* 31:51–53 (news & advt May)1896 *Tr Am Inst Hom* 1896:87. *Polk* 1886:923.

WALKER, MARK, N Barnstead NH (b/XII–18–1826; d/V–30–1879) MD Jeff'n 1854. *Tr NH M S* 1879:171–73.

WALKER, ROBERT C , Mobile, Ala (d/X–11–1896 @59) MD U Nashvl 1858. *JAMA* 27:1021, 1890. *Polk* 1896: 165.

WALKER, ROBERT J , Cottondale, Ala (d/II–7–1891) MD ? Lic 1878. *Tr M Assn St Ala* 1891:261.

WALKER, SEWALL, Dummerston, Vt (b/III–10–1796; d/VIII–14–1863) MD Castleton 1823. *Bost m&s j* 69: 108, 1863.

WALKER, SYDENHAM COSKERY, CW–USA; Fountaindale Pa (b/1826 Waynesboro; d/IX–26–1902) MD U Pa 1849; *Pa m j* 6:262, 1902/03. *UPa m alum CW*: 1849.

WALKER, U G MITCHELL, Tyler, Tex (b/III–4–1836 Dallas Co, Ala; d/I–20–1890 @53) MD U Nashvl 1857. *Nashvl j m&s* 45:84–85, 1890. *Daniel's Tex m j* 5: 316, 1889–90. *Polk* 1886: 891.

WALKER, WALTER, Rochester, NY; Chicago (d/IX–10 1868) MD Jefferson 1859. *Chic m j* 25:741, 1868. *Med surg rep Phila* 19:289, 1868.

WALKER, WILLIAM, NH (b/I–4–1828 Barnstead; d/VII–14–1855) MD Jefferson 1853; ng Bowdoin 1849–50. *Bowdoin cat*: 1853.

WALKER, WILLIAM, ?Tenn (b/V–8–1824 Nashville; d/IX–12–1860 Truxillo, Honduras) MD UPa 1843. *Tr M S Tenn* 1876: 88.

WALKER, WILLIAM JOHNSON, Newport, RI (b/1790 Charlestown, Mass; d/IV–2–1865) MD Harvard 1813; AB 1810. *Bost m&s j* 72:226–28.

WALKER, WILLIAM T , Dover Mills, Va (d/V– –1875) MD UVa 1867. *Med reg NY NJ Conn* 1875: 206. *Butler* 1874: 808.

WALKER, WILLIAM T , Lynchburg, Va (d/V–13–1898) MD Jefferson 1849. *JAMA* 30:1305, 1898. *Polk* 1896: 1493.

WALKER, WILLIAM WEIGHTMAN, Denver (d/V–4 1891) MD Medico–Chi Phila 1889. *Med bull m&s* 13: 231–32, 1891.

WALL, ANDREW, Cambridge, O (d/IV–17–1898) MD

M C Ohio 1862. *JAMA* 30:1061, 1898. *Polk* 1896: 1156.

WALL, ASA, USA 1856–61; CW–CSA –1865 (b/VI–2–1832 Winchester, Va; d/X–23–1903) MD UPa 1854. *U Pa med alum CW*: 1854.

WALL, JAMES OWEN, Huntington, WVa (b/XI–20–1845 or 1846 Greenbriar Co; d/X–20–1885) MD M C Ohio 1869; MD Bellevue 1875. *Tr M S WVa* 1886:338. *Atkinson* I: 171. *Butler* 1878: 854.

WALL, JOHN P, Tampa (b/IX–17–1836 Hamilton Co; d/IV–18–1895) MD U SC 1858. *Proc Fl M Assn* 1896: 41–45. *JAMA* 24:650, 689, 1895. *Butler* 1878: 102.

WALL, THOMAS WILLIAM CURLETTE, CW–CSA (b/I–31–1828 Winchester, Va; d/VIII–21–1900 Carthage, Mo) MD UPa 1851; MD Winchester 1850. *U Pa med alum CW*: 1851.

WALLACE, ALPHONSE MICHAEL, NYC (d/VI–7 1895 @27) MD CPSNY 1888. *Med reg NY NJ Conn* 1895:245. *JAMA* 24:989 1895. *Bost m&s j* 132:606 1895.

WALLACE, DAVID LYNDE, Newark, NJ (d/III–1 1904 @48) MD Bellevue 1875. *Bost m&s j* 150:254, 1904. *Polk* 1896: 944.

WALLACE, EDWARD, Philadelphia (b/III–28–1815 Lancaster Co; d/X–28–1875) MD UPa 1836; AB Princeton 1833; AM 1836. *Tr Pa St M S* 1876:303–06. *Phila m times* 6:168, 1875–76. *Med rec m & s* 11:388, 1876.

WALLACE, ELLERSLIE, Philadelphia (b/VI–15–1819; d/III–10–1885) MD Jefferson 1843; AB Bristol Coll. *Bost m&s j* 113:655, 1885. *Med surg rep Phila* 52:352, 1885. *Tr CPP* cent vol: 272. *K&B* III: 1254.

WALLACE, JAMES PAULDING, Greeley, Col (d/III–11–1894 @45) MD Bellevue 1875; MD Ohio M C 1874. *JAMA* 22:482, 1894.

WALLACE, JOHN BORLAND, Detroit (d/VIII–21–1898 @48) MD Detroit M C 1884. *JAMA* 31:551, 1898. *Polk* 1886: 668.

WALLACE, JOHN GORDON, Fredericksburg, Va (b/VII–24–1829; d/V–29–1878) MD UPa 1850. *U Pa med alum CW*: 1850.

WALLACE, JOHN S , Christiana, Pa (d/1903 @60) MD Jefferson 1865. *Pa med jour* 7:280, 1903/04.

WALLACE, JOSEPH D , Philadelphia (d/V–26–1899) MD ? *JAMA* 32: 1399, 1899.

WALLACE, JOSHUA MADDOX, Philadelphia (b/I––1815; d/XI–10–1851/1852) MD UPa 1836; AB Princeton 1833; AM 1836. *Tr CPP* cent vol: 272; ns1:315–20, 1850–53. *NW m&s j* 4:380, 1852. *NH j m* 2:167, 1852.

WALLACE, R BRUCE, Union, Nebr (b/Mo; d/IX–16 1901) MD Jefferson 1868. *JAMA* 37: 847, 1901.

WALLACE, ROBERT BENJAMIN, Harpersville, Ala (b/XI–1–1824; d/1859 Brattleboro, Vt) MD Jefferson 1848; ng U Ala 1842. *U Ala cat*: 80.

WALLACE, THEODORE CUNDALL, Cambridge, NY (d/III–12–1902 @72) MD Geneva 1850. *Tr M S St NY* 1903: [412]. *Polk* 1886: 655.

WALLACE, WILLIAM, Bristol Va (b/II–12–1834 Fredericksburg, Va; d/VI–24–1893) MD UPa 1857; <MD UVa 1855> *U Pa med alum CW*: 1857.

WALLACE, WILLIAM, Brooklyn (b/1835 Cork, Irel'd; d/XII–23–1896 @61) <MRCS (Edin) 1856; MRCP (Edin) 1860> *Bost m&s j* 136: 23, 1897. *JAMA* 28:92, 1897. *K&B* II: 1187.

WALLACE, WILLIAM BARRY, NYC (d/VI–7–1895 @53) MD CPSNY 1871. *Bost m&s j* 132:606, 1895. *Med reg NY NJ Conn* 1895:245. *JAMA* 24:989, 1895. *Butler* 1878: 527.

WALLACE-RUSSELL, JULIA EASTMAN, Concord, NH (b/III–24–1844 Hill, NH; d/VII–1–1906) MD Woman's M C & Inf NY 1877. *Tr NH M S* 1906:297–98. *Polk* 1890: 708 (as Julia W. Russell).

WALLACH, JOSEPH GABRIEL, NYC (d/XI–21–1899 @44) MD Bellevue 1877. *Bost m&s j* 141:564, 1899. *JAMA* 33:1441, 1899. *Polk* 1896: 1083.

WALLENS, MILES W , Woodstown, NJ 186_–70; Somerville 1870– (b/VII–15–1842 Phila; d/I–4–1874) MD Hahn'n Phila 1862. *Med s rep Phila* 30:88, 1874. *Am j hom mat med* 7:280, 1874? *Hahn mo* 9:428, 1873/75.

WALLER, MATTHEW PAGE, CW–CSA (b/VI–21–1823 Williamsburg Va; d/X–14–1861 Norfolk) MD UPa 1846. *U Pa med alum CW*: 1846.

WALLER, TRACY E , Burlington Co, NJ; Linwood Pa (d/XI–20–1872) MD Jefferson 1844. *Tr AMA* 24: 365, 1873. *Med surg rep Phila* 27:506, 1872.

WALLICK, FRANK, Williamsfield, Ill (d/III–27–1900) <MD Keokuk CPS 1896> *JAMA* 34: 891, 1900.

WALLING, GEORGE H , Louisville (d/VIII–21–1893) MD M Inst Louisvl 1846. *JAMA* 21:357, 1893. *Butler* 1878: 267.

WALLIS, JAMES MARSHALL, CW–USA; Philadelphia (b/X–14 1825 Mexico, Pa; d/XII–28–1901) MD U Pa 1847. *Pa m j* 5:296, 1901/02. *Butler* 1878:697.

WALLIS, ROBERT S, Dallas Tx (d/I–6–1903 @67) MD Jeff'n 1860. *So pract* 25:101–02, 1903. *Polk* 1896:1447.

WALLS, ENOCH GEORGE, NYC? Baltimore (b/IX–3–1850 Sudlersville, Md; d/X–5–1902) MD Wash U Balto 1872. *Med ann Md:* 606–07.

WALLS, J WILLIAM, Philadelphia (b/1835 Harpers Ferry, WVa; d/V–19–1881) <MD Winchester, Va> *Med ann Md:* 607.

WALSER, THEODORE, NYC (b/IV–25–1825 Switzerland; d/IV–23–1902) MD Jefferson 1851. *Bost m&s j* 146: 479, 1902. *Polk* 1896: 1033.

WALSH, EDMUND, E Cambridge, Mass (d/X–19–1898) MD Harvard 1873. *Bost m&s j* 139:432, 1898. *Polk* 1896:711.

WALSH, JOHN KEARNEY, Washington, DC (b/1845; d/I–15–1894) MD Georgetown 1865. *JAMA* 22:122, 1894. *Hist Med Soc DC:* 276. *Butler* 1878: 97.

WALSH, JOSEPH, Washington, DC (b/X–28–1806 Dublin, Irel'd; d/XI–9–1879) MD Columbian 1843; <Dipl Apothecaries' Hall Dubl> *Tr AMA* 31:1096–97,

1880. *Hist Med Soc DC:* 239–40.

WALSH, PETER DUGGAN, Boston (d/VIII–10–1902 @ 79) MD Harvard 1858. *Bost m&s j* 147: 196, 1902. *Polk* 1896: 707.

WALSH, VALENTINE, NYC (d/VII–29–1901) MD Dublin 1871. *JAMA* 37: 398, 1901.

WALTER, ALBERT P , Jersey City; Easton & New Berlin, Pa (b/1852? d/XII–18–1899 @47) MD CPS Balto 1884. *JAMA* 34:61, 1900. *Polk* 1886: 809.

WALTER, BARNET C, Farmersville Pa (d/VII–11 1906 @71) MD Jefferson 1859. *Pa med jour* 9:805, 1905/06.

WALTER, CARL G , Lawrenceburgh, Ind (b/1820 Gny; d/VI–2–1895) <MD Gny> *Tr Ind St M S* 1896:252. *Polk* 1886: 326.

WALTER, EDWARD ADOLPH, NYC (d/II–27–1904) MD Bellevue 1899. *Bost m&s j* 150:254, 1904.

WALTER, JOHN Jr, Washington, DC (b/IX–2–1844; d/XI–7–1906) MD Georgetown 1868. *Hist Med Soc DC:* 305. *Polk* 1893: 274.

WALTERS, A G , Pittsburgh 1836?– (b/Prussia; d/X–14–1876 @65) <MD Königsberg 1838> *Med rec NY* 11:710, 1876. *Med surg rep Phila* 35:370, 1876.

WALTERS, WALTER W , Johnstown, Pa (d/VII–23–1896 @73) MD Pa M C 1853. *JAMA* 27:337, 1896. *Polk* 1886: 803.

WALTERS, WILLIAM L , Richmond, Va (d/I–15–1895 @65) MD Jefferson 1854. *JAMA* 22:122, 1894. *Polk* 1886: 928.

WALTHALL, WILLIAM H , Roanoke, Va (d/X–18–1905 @70) MD M C Va 1865. *So pract* 28:167, 1906.

WALTON, EARLY WATKINS, NYC (d/IX–29–1888 @ 32) MD Bellevue 1882; MD U La 1878. *Bost m&s j* 119:370, 1888.

WALTON, JOHN, Pepperell, Mass (b/X–29–1770 Cambridge; d/XII–21–1862) MD Harvard 1811; AM 1791. Palmer's *Necrol alum Harvard*: 450–52.

WALTON, LUIS PUERTAS, NYC (b/England; d/IX–8 1903 London) MD CPSNY 1870; AB Columbia 1861. *Bost m&s j* 149:332, 1903. *Polk* 1896: 1083.

WALTON, MILTON W , Stephenson Co, Ill; Chicago; Beatrice, Nebr 1885– (b/V–5–1842 Thornton, Ind; d/VII–11–1895) MD Chicago M C 1868; stud Gny & Fr 2 yrs. *Proc Nebr St M S* 1896:20–21. *Polk* 1893: 755.

WALTON, RICHARD PEYTON, CW–CSA; Norfolk Va (b/III–31–1819 Cartersville; d/X–17–1892) MD UPa 1842. *U Pa med alum CW*: 1842. *Polk* 1886:923.

WALTON, THOMAS CAREY, Stroudsburg, Pa (d/VII–20–1903 @49) MD UPa 1878. *Pa med jour* 7:280, 1903/04. *Flint* 1897: 837.

WAMSLEY, WILLIAM EDWARD, Brooklyn (d/II–25 1900 @45) MD UCNY 1878. *Bost m&s j* 142:264 1900.

WARBURTON, H H , Santa Clara, Cal (b/1819 Engl; d/II–8–1903) Lic Exam Bd M S Cal; <Lic R S Apoth London> *Cal st j m* 1:125, 1903. *Polk* 1896: 242.

WARD, ANDREW JACKSON, MexWar–USA; CW–USA (b/III–1–1824 Milford, Pa; d/VII–10–1893 Hornellsville, NJ) MD UPa 1846. *U Pa med alum CW*:1846.

WARD, ARTHUR, Newark (b/XII–23–1823 Belleville, NJ; d/VII–6–1902) MD CPSNY 1847; AB Yale 1844. *Proc Conn Med Soc* 1904:511–12. *Bost m&s j* 147:88, 1902. *Tr M S NJ* 1903:385–86. *Atkinson* I: 677.

WARD, CHARLES SAMUEL, NYC (b/1843; d/VII–31–1898) MD Yale 1863. *Bost m&s j* 139:150, 1898. *JAMA* 31:366, 1898.

WARD, DANIEL O'C , Philadelphia d/III–22–1867 @30) MD Jefferson 1858. *Med s rep Phila* 16:272, 1867.

WARD, EDGAR BURT, Laingsburg, Mich (d/V–12–1899 @64) MD U Mich 1858. *JAMA* 32:1269, 1899. *Polk* 1886: 496.

WARD, ELEAZER D , NJ (b/II–23–1786; d/II–10–1868) MD ? *Tr M S NJ* 1868:116–17.

WARD, ELIAB [ELIJAH], ?Boston (d/1871 @48) MD Harvard 1848. *Phila med reg & dir* 1873:304. *Bost m&s j* 7:272, 1871.

WARD, ELIJAH J , Waxahachie, Tex (b/1842; d/XII–17 1892) MD Georgetown 1880. *Tex cour–rec med* 10:151, 1893. *Daniel's Tex m j* 8:334, 1892–93.

WARD, ERASTUS B , Chatham Hill, Va (b/III–13–1825 Tazewell Co; d/IV–21–1881) MD Jefferson 1851. *Tr M S Va* 1882: 518. *Butler* 1878: 838.

WARD, GEORGE AUGUSTUS, Corro de Pasco, Peru (d/IX–1882) MD Yale 1861. *Med bull m&s* 5:185, 1883.

WARD, GEORGE WHITFIELD, Upton, Mass (d/XII–11–1895 @79) MD Berkshire 1844; ng Woodstock 1843. *Bost m&s j* 134:100, 1896. *Polk* 1886: 474.

WARD, HENRY, Newark (b/1820 Northampton, Engl; d/V–6–1880) <MRCS (Engl) 1845> *Tr M S NJ* 1880–81: 128–29. *Butler* 1878: 464.

WARD, ISAAC MOREAU, Newark (b/1806 Bloomfield; d/II–24–1895) MD Rutgers 1829; AB Yale 1825. *No Am j hom* 43:256, 1895. Homeopath.

WARD, J M BROMWELL, Marcus Hook, Pa (d/I–22 1903 @36) MD Jefferson 1891. *Pa m j* 7:280, 1903/04. *Polk* 1896: 1272.

WARD, JAMES H , Brooklyn (d/IV–15–1891 @67) MD UCNY 1850. *Bost m&s j* 124:474, 1891.

WARD, JAMES ROBERT, Govanstown, Md (b/1807 Cecil Co; d/IV–29–1884) MD UMd 1828. *Med annals Md:* 607–08. *Butler* 1878: 331.

WARD, JOHN, Newark (b/IV–26–1774; d/VI–24–1836) MD ? *Tr M S NJ* 1867: 127–28.

WARD, JOHN, Bristol, Pa (b/IX–5–1838 Bath, Pa; d/III–26–1895) MD UPa 1864; PhG Phila Coll Pharm 1859. *U Pa med alum CW*: 1864. *Polk* 1886: 793.

WARD, JOHN A , NYC (d/III–4–1880) MD UCNY 1854. *Med surg rep Phila* 42:264, 1880. *Butler* 1878:512.

WARD, JOHN EDMUND, Coney Isl, NYC (b/1846 Epsom, Engl; d/II–25–1899) MRCS (Engl) 1868. *JAMA* 32:563, 1899. *Bost m&s j* 140:292, 1899. *Polk* 1886:697.

WARD, JOHN F , Newark (b/IX–28–1815 Bloomfield;

d/VII-11-1873) <MD Jefferson 1836> *Tr AMA* 25:527, 1874. *Tr M S NJ* 1874: 98-99.

WARD, MILO BUELL, Topeka, Kans 1886; Kansas City, Mo (d/VII-28-1901 @53) MD CPS Keokuk 1879. *JAMA* 37:397, 1901. *Polk* 1886: 385.

WARD, ORIN WARREN, Duncan Falls, O (d/IX-14-1896 @45) MD Bellevue 1877. *JAMA* 27:721, 1896. *Polk* 1896: 1186.

WARD, OWEN J ,NYC (d/VIII-17-1898 @58) MD UCNY 1865. *JAMA* 31:484, 1898. *Bost m&s j* 139:202, 1898. *Polk* 1896: 1083.

WARD, SAMUEL LAWRENCE, Belleville, NJ (b/V-6-1791 Bloomfield; d/VI-14-1869) <MD CPSNY 1847> *Med reg NY NJ Conn* 1869:326: 1870:334. *Tr M S NJ* 1870:87-88.

WARD, THOMAS, NYC (b/VI-8-1807 Newark; d/IV-13-1873) <MD Rutgers 1829> att Princeton. *Med reg NY NJ Conn* 1873: 358. *Med surg rep Phila* 28:346, 1874. *K&B* III:1256-57.

WARD, THOMAS BRYSON, CW-CSA; Norfolk Va (b/XII-6-1838; d/1884) MD UCNY 1860; att UVa 1857. *Tr M S Va* 1885:288-89. Blanton's *Va surgs CW*: 419. *Atkinson* I:424. *Polk* 1886: 923.

WARD, WALTER, Mt Holly, NJ (b/I-7-1816 Keene, NH; d/III-29-1888) MD Jefferson 1840; ng Woodstock. *Tr Am Inst Hom* 1888:211. *Med vis* 4:174, 1888. *Hahn mo* 23:256, 1888. *Cleave. King* I:245. Homeopath.

WARD, WILLIAM SMITH [SPENCER?], Newark (b/VI-12 or VII-13-1821 Bloomfield; d/IX-1-1900) MD CPSNY 1849; AB Princeton 1841. *Bost m&s j* 143:276, 1900. *Atkinson* I:671. *Polk* 1896: 944.

WARD, WILLIAM W , Plymouth, NC (d/V-9-1879 @62) MD ?UPa 1836. *NC m j* 3:444, 1879.

WARDEN, ALBERT WILLIAM, Union Hill, NJ (d/VIII-9-1904 @47) MD UVt 1878; MD UCNY 1880; LLB; BS. *Bost m&s j* 151:200, 1904. *Polk* 1886:612.

WARDEN, JONATHAN, Bradford, Vt (b/1796? d/VI-3 1868 @72) MD ? *Phila med reg & dir* 1871: 297.

WARDER, JOHN ASTON, No Bend, O (b/I-19-1812 Phila; d/VII-14-1883) MD Jefferson 1836. *JAMA* 1:96, 128, 1883. *Med s rep Phila* 49:196, 1883. *K&B* III:1357.

WARDER, WILLIAM HENRY, Chicago (d/XII-12-1904) MD Rush 1892. *Ill m j* 7:127 1904. *Polk* 1896:410.

WARDLE, JOHN KNIGHT, Hudson, NY (b/1825 Engl; d/III-4-1899) MD CPSNY 1851. *JAMA* 32:628, 1899.

WARDNER, HORACE, CW-USA; Laporte, Ind (b/VIII 25-1829 Perry, NY; d/III-18-1905) MD Rush 1856. *Tr Ind St M S* 1905:461. *Atkinson* I:29. *Polk* 1896: 478.

WARDWELL, WILLIAM TECUMSEH SHERMAN, Roslindale, Mass (d/VI-24-1893 @32) MD Harvard 1888. *Bost m&s j* 129:24, 1893.

WARE, CHARLES ELIOT, Winchendon, Mass (d/IX-3 1887 @73) MD Harvard 1837; AB 1834. *Bost m & s j* 117:244, 294-95, 1887. *Butler* 1878: 344.

WARE, CHARLES SEYMOUR, Niagara Falls, NY (d/IX-21-1872 @48) MD CPSNY 1849. *Med surg rep Phila* 27:380, 1872.

WARE, JOHN C , Boston (b/XII-19-1795 Hingham, Mass; d/IV-29-1864) MD Harvard 1816; AB 1813. *Bost m&s j* 70:284-87, 1864. *Nashvl j m&s* ns1:318, 1866. *Tr AMA* 16:611-12, 1865. *K&B* III:1257-58.

WARE, JOHN JAMES, CW-CSA; Brownsville, Tenn (b/VIII-23 1831; d/IX or X-8-1878) MD UPa 1861; stud UNC 1857-59. *Tr AMA* 30:886-87, 1879.

WARE, ROBERT, CW-US San Comm (b/IX-2-1833 Boston; d/IV-10-1863 Washington, NC) MD Harvard 1856; AM 1852. Palmer's *Necrol Harv alum* 495. *Harv in CW*: 62-63. *Nat med jour* 1:303, 1870/71.

WAREHEIM, EDWARD ARMACOST, Glen Rock, Pa (b/X-19-1844 Manchester, Md; d/VII-11-1898) MD NY Hom 1868. *Tr Am Inst Hom* 1899:936. *No Am j hom* 46:655, 1898. *Polk* 1886:800. Homeopath.

WARFIELD, PEREGRINE, Georgetown, Md (b/II--1779 Anne Arundel Co; d/VII-24-1856) Lic Med & Chir Fac Md 1817. *Hist M S DC:* 217. *Med ann Md:* 609.

WARING, EDMUND THOMAS, Newport, RI (b/XII-25 1779 Charleston, SC; d/I-21-1835) MD ? AB Brown 1799. *Tr RI M S* 1:10, 47-49, 1859-77.

WARING, JAMES JOHNSTON, CW-CSA; Washington, DC; Savannah (b/VIII-19-1830; d/I-8-1888) MD UPa 1852; AB Yale 1850. *Hist Med Soc DC:* 254. *U Pa med alum CW*: 1852. *Polk* 1886: 235.

WARING, WILLIAM RICHARD, CW-CSA; ?Atlanta (b/II-23-1827 Savannah; d/XII- -1892) MD UPa 1852. *U Pa med alum CW*: 1852 suppl.

WARMUTH [WARWORTH], HENRY JOSEPH, CW-CSA; Smyrna & Nashville, Tenn (b/I-19-1840; d/VIII-12 1904 Phila) MD Rush 1868. *So pract* 26:569-70, 1904. *JAMA* 43: 748, 1904.

WARN, WILLIAM HILTON, Denver; Lowell, Mass 1871-72 (b/IV-25-1845 Martin, Mich; d/I-7-1882) MD CPSNY 1871; AB Amherst 1869; stud Vienna 1872-73. *Tr Col St M S* 1898-99: 508.

WARNE, GEORGE, Independence, Ia (d/VII-5-1894 @ 70) MD Keokuk CPS 1872 ad eund. *JAMA* 23:164, 1894. *Tr Ia St M S* 1896:330; 1900:411. *Butler* 1878: 247.

WARNER, ABNER SPICER, CW-USA; Wethersfield, Conn (b/IX-7-1818 Manlius, NY; d/XI-2-1900) MD Dartmouth 1848; AB 1842. *Pr Conn M S* 1901: 280-81. *Atkinson* I:419. *Polk* 1896: 286.

WARNER, AUGUSTUS LOCKMAN, Richmond, Va (b/Balto; d/V-5-1847) MD UMd 1829; AM Princeton 1826. *So m&s j* ns3:191, 1847. *Med annals Md:* 610. *Ill & Ind m&s j* 2:191, 1847.

WARNER, ELI, Hartford Conn (b/III-24-1843 Ellington; d/V-28-1884) MD CPSNY 1867. *Pr Conn M S* ns3: 85, 211, 1885. *Butler* 1878: 83.

WARNER, EMERSON, Worcester, Mass (b/IV-30-1831 Braintree; d/XII-24-1905) MD Harvard 1863; AB Wesleyan 1856. *Bost m&s j* 154:116, 1906. *Polk* 1896: 728.

WARNER, ERASMUS DARWIN, New Haven Vt (b/VII 1-1806; d/II-22-1875) MD Castleton 1828. *Tr Vt M S* 1883: 110.

WARNER, EVERARDUS BROWER, NYC (d/XI-7-1885 @65) MD CPSNY 1845. *Med reg NY NJ Conn* 1886:256. *Butler* 1878: 527.

WARNER, FREDERICK MONTRESOR, NYC (b/ 1857; d/X-8-1895) MD CPSNY 1880; att Lehigh U 1877. *JAMA* 25: 726, 781, 1895. *Polk* 1886: 697.

WARNER, GEORGE OTIS, Leicester, Mass (d/XI-12-1885) MD Harvard 1870. *Bost m&s j* 113:504, 1885.

WARNER, JAMES EMERSON, Barre, NY; Volcano, Cal; Binghamton, NY; Sterling, Va 1869- (b/IX-24-1825 Plainfield, Mass; d/VI-6-1903) MD Berkshire 1853. *Tr M S Va* 1903:275-76. *Polk* 1900: 1776.

WARNER, JOHN TERRY, USA; Neosho Falls, Kans (b/1833; d/IX-26-1875) MD UCNY 1861. *UCNY cat*: 1861.

WARNER, LEVI FARR, St Louis; CW-USA; Boston 1868- (b/X 25-1822 Norwich, NY; d/X-12-1889) MD Chic M C 1863; att Geneva 1842-43. *JAMA* 13:720-21, 1889. *Bost m&s j* 121:448, 1889. *Atkinson* I:366. *Butler* 1878: 344.

WARNER, NEWELL PERRY, Syracuse (d/IX-16-1895) MD CPSNY 1875. *JAMA* 25:554, 1895.

WARNER, NOAH HULL, Van Dusenville, Mass; Buffalo 1836- (b/I-21-1808 Plymouth, Conn; d/VI-24-1860 Swampscott) MD Yale 1831. *Tr Am Inst Hom* 1893:158. *Tr NY Hom M S* 1863: . *US j hom* 2:216, 1861. Homeopath 1844- .

WARNER, RICHARD, Cromwell, Conn (b/X-19-1794 Hadlyne; d/IX-29-1853) MD Yale 1821. *Pr Conn M S* 1854:19, 58-60. *Med & s j* Phila 2:173-74, 1859. *Bost m&s j* 49:230, 1853.

WARNER, CLARK RIENZI, Chicago (d/I-2-1906 @ 65) MD Rush 1876. *Tr Ill M S* 9:228, 1906. *Polk* 1896: 410.

WARREN, DEWEY KELLOGG, Boston (d/X-11-1866 @45) MD Harvard 1863. *Bost m&s j* 75:252, 1866. *Mass M S cat* 1894.

WARREN, EDWARD, Boston (b/XII-19-1804; d/V-23 1878) MD Harvard 1829; AB 1826. *Bost m&s j* 99:320, 1878. *Atkinson* I: 57.

WARREN, EPHRAIM LEWIS, Melrose, Mass (d/IV-28 1901 @78) MD Berkshire 1848. *Bost m&s j* 144:540, 1901. *Polk* 1896: 718.

WARREN, FRANKLIN COOLEY Jr, Boston (d/I-2-1891 @37) MD Harvard 1879. *Bost m&s j* 125:718 1891.

WARREN, GEORGE AUGUSTUS, Hopkinton, Mass (d/ V-6-1887 @68) MD Berkshire 1845. *Bost m&s j* 116: , 1887.

WARREN, GEORGE WASHINGTON, W Boylston, Mass (b/I-6-1819 Lunenburg; d/IV-22-1900) MD Woodstock 1847; AB Amherst 1845. *Bost m&s j* 142: 528, 1900. *Polk* 1896: 725.

WARREN, JAMES J , Sharon, Tenn (d/VII-1-1898) MD U Nashvl 1871. *JAMA* 31:198, 1898. *Polk* 1886:860.

WARREN, JOEL ADDINGTON, Ellington, Conn (b/II 15-1834 Irisburg, Vt; d/XII-25-1890) MD CPSNY 1860; <MD Albany 1859> *Pr Conn M S* ns4:313, 1891. *Polk* 1886: 191.

WARREN, JOHN COLLINS, Boston (b/VIII-1-1778; d/V-4-1856) Hon MD Harvard 1819; AB 1797. *Am j m sci* ns32:288-91, 1856. *Bost m&s j* 54:286-87, 300-07, 1856. Palmer *Necrol Harv alum*:77-78. *K&B* III:1263-4.

WARREN, JOHN H , Palmyra, Wis (d/VIII-1-1901 @ 76) MD Rush 1849. *JAMA* 37:397, 1901.

WARREN, JONATHAN MASON, Boston (b/II-5-1811; d/1867) MD Harvard 1832; AM 1844. *Bost m&s j* 77:62, 66-68, 86, 1867? *Buff m&s j* 7:31-2, 1867. *Tr AMA* 19: 440-41, 1868. *K&B* III: 1264-65.

WARREN, JOSEPH EDWIN, Cumberland, RI (b/I-4-1813 Ashby, Mass; d/XI-8-1860) MD Woodstock 1840. *Tr RI M S* 1:138, 1859-77.

WARREN, JOSEPH HUCKINS, Boston (b/X-2-1831 Effingham, NH; d/III-24-1891) MD Bowdoin 1853; AM 1882. *Med bull m & s* 13:191, 272, 1891. *Bost m&s j* 124:348, 1891. *JAMA* 16:612, 1891. *Butler* 1878: 344.

WARREN, LEVI, Norwich, Conn (b/1831 Patterson, NY; d/II-22-1873) MD UCNY 1856 *Pr Conn MS* 1873:222.

WARREN, MARK W , Macon, Miss (d/VIII-13-1901) <MD So Med Coll Atlanta 1889> *JAMA* 37:527, 1901.

WARREN, ROYAL SIBLEY, Colorado Spr (d/II-13-1896 @73) MD Harvard 1846. *Bost m&s j* 134:204, 1896. *Polk* 1886: 475 (Waltham, Mass).

WARREN, WILLIAM BARNARD, Groton, Mass (b/ 1853 Leominster; d/IV-29-1905) MD UCNY 1881; ng Dartmouth 1879. *Bost m&s j* 152:535-36, 1905.

WARREN, WILLIAM C , CW-CSA; Edenton, NC (d/ 1871) MD UPa 1825. *Tr AMA* 24:386, 1873. *Tr M S Va* 1872: 154, 263.

WARREN, WINSLOW, Plymouth, Mass (b/1795? d/VI-10-1870 @75) MD UPa 1817; AB Harvard 1813. *Bost m&s j* 5:468, 1870.

WARREN-BEY [i.e.WARREN], EDWARD, Edenton, NC; Baltimore; Paris, Fr (b/I-22- ? Tyrrell Co, NC; d/IX 16-1893 Paris) MD Jefferson 1851; ng UVa 1846-49. *Bost m&s j* 129:312, 1893. *JAMA* 21:589-90, 1893; 21: 498, 1893. *NC m j* 2:113-29, 1878; 32:200, 1893. *Med annals Md:* 610. *K&B* III: 1259-60.

WARRINGTON, JOSEPH Jr, Philadelphia; Moorestown, NJ (d/X-11-1888 @83) MD UPa 1828. *Bost m&s j* 119:589, 1888.

WARRINGTON, JOSEPH H , Atlantic City (d/VI--1887 @54) MD Hahnemann, Phila 1877. *Hahn mo* 22: 384, 1887. *Med vis* 3:229, 1887. Homeopath.

WARTH, JOHN WILLIAM, Brooklyn (d/I-8-1899) MD CPSNY 1868; AB UCNY 1864; AM 1867. *JAMA* 32:145, 1899. *Polk* 1896: 1083.

WARWICK, BRADFUTE, CW-CSA (d/VI-27-1862 nr

Gaines Mill, ?) MD UCNY 1859. *UCNY cat*: 1859.

WASHBURN, CHARLES, ?Mexico City, Mex (b/Wilkesbarre, Pa; d/I–17–1873 Mex City) MD CPSNY 1866. *Med reg NY NJ Conn* 1873: 359.

WASHBURN, CHARLES ELLERY, Binghamton, NY 1849–51; Fredonia 1851–62; CW–USA (b/III–29–1816 Homer; d/IV–10–1865 Wilmington, NC) MD CPSNY 1845; AB Amherst 1838. *Buff m&s j* 4:507, 1865. *Nat med jour* 1:303, 1870/71.

WASHBURN, CYRUS, Vernon, Vt (b/177_? d/III–2–1860 @86) MD ? *Bost m&s j* 62:172, 1860.

WASHBURN, LEWIS, Weymouth, Mass (d/1834) MD Bowdoin 1833; AB Brown 1826. *Brown hist cat*: 1826.

WASHBURN, ROBERT RUSSELL, Waldron, Ind (b/III 12–1833 Laurel; d/XI–10–1900) MD Ind M Coll 1886. *Tr Ind St M S* 1901:502. *Polk* 1896:495.

WASHBURNE, DULANEY L , Louisville (b/1855 Jefferson Co, Ky; d/1897) MD U Louisvl 1883. *JAMA* 28: 906–07, 1897. *Polk* 1886: 401.

WASHINGTON, BAILEY, Washington, DC (b/V–12–1787 Westmoreland Co, Va; d/VIII–4–1854) MD UPa 1810. *Hist Med Soc DC:* 222. *JAMA* 28:431, 1897.

WASHINGTON, JAMES AUGUSTUS, NYC (b/VII–31 1803 Kinston, NC; d/VIII–30–1847) MD UPa 1826; AB UNC 1823. *UNC cat*: 648. *K&B* II: 1199–1200.

WASHINGTON, JAMES R , St Louis (b/1816; d/III–19 1875 Wayne Co, NC) MD U Pa 1841; att Randolph Macon. *Tr AMA* 26:469, 1875.

WASON, STEPHEN S , Black River Falls, Wis (d/VII–13–1901 @73) MD ? *JAMA* 37:276, 1901.

WASSON, HARMON, Amboy, Ill (d/VIII–20–1859) MD Rush 1850. *Chic m j* 2:643, 1859.

WASSON, JAMES E , Spruce Creek, Pa (d/IX–7–1894) MD Jefferson 1888. *JAMA* 23:440, 1894.

WATERHOUSE, BENJAMIN, Boston (b/III–4–1754 Newport, RI; d/X–2–1846) MD Leyden. *Tr RI M S* I: 9, 1859–77. *Buff m&s j* 2:316, 1846. *K&B* III:1266–69.

WATERHOUSE, MARVIN, CW–USA; Portage, Wis (b/IX–19–1827 Alden, NY; d/X–19–1878) MD Rush 1864. *Tr AMA* 31:1097–98, 1880. *Tr Wis St M S* 1879:289. *Atkinson* I: 182.

WATERMAN, JAMES HENRY, Westfield, Mass (d/XI–23–1887) MD Buffalo 1860. *Bost m&s j* 117:549, 1887.

WATERMAN, SIGISMOND, CW–USA; NYC (b/II–22 1819 Bruck, Bavaria; d/III–15–1899) MD Yale 1848; stud Erlangen. *Bost m&s j* 140:296, 1899. *JAMA* 32:732, 1899. *Atkinson* I:374. *K&B* II: 1204.

WATERMAN, THOMAS, Boston (b/1842; d/XII–14–1901) MD Harvard 1868; AB 1864. *Bost m&s j* 145:692, 1901; 146:27, 1902. *K&B* III: 1270.

WATERMAN, WILLIAM BENJAMIN, Brooklyn (d/VIII–21–1900 @38) MD UCNY 1887. *Bost m&s j* 143: 223, 1900. *Polk* 1887: 1005.

WATERS, JAMES W , Giles Co, Tenn (d/III–9–1896) <MD U Nashvl 1892> *Nashvl j m&s* 3:145–46, 1896.

WATERS, JOHN C , Indianapolis (b/1830 Ireland; d/VIII–23–1884) "MD in Europe" *Tr Ind St M S* 1885:222.

WATERS, JOHN W , Lexington, Ill (d/I–15–1898 @70) MD Starling 1855. *JAMA* 30:279, 1898. *Polk* 1886:286.

WATERS, WASHINGTON, Goshen, Md (b/1804 Brookeville; d/II–24–1882) MD U Md 1826. *Med annals Md:* 611–12. *Butler* 1878: 331.

WATERS, WILLIAM, Frederick City, Md (b/1800; d/VII–7–1862) MD UMd 1824. *Med annals Md:* 612.

WATERWORTH, WILLIAM, Brooklyn (b/1851 Salem, O; d/V–11–1904) MD Bellevue 1878; AB Adelbert 1878. *Bost m&s j* 150:552, 1904. *Polk* 1896: 1005.

WATKINS, ANDERSON, Augusta, Ga (b/1774? d/IX–16 1828 @54) MD ? *Transylv j m & assoc sci* 1:596, 1828.

WATKINS, BENJAMIN FRANKLIN, Prairieville, Tx; CW–CSA; (b/1831 Burnt Corn, Ala; d/XII–25–1905 Bryan Tx) MD UPa 1852. *U Pa med alum CW*: 1852. *Polk* 1886: 892.

WATKINS, EUSTACE VIRGIL, Newbury, Vt (b/V–11 1823 Stockbridge; d/XII–18–1888) MD Dartmouth 1850; ng Woodstock 1849. *Bost m&s j* 120:28, 1889. *Polk* 1886: 906.

WATKINS, FRANCIS BENJAMIN, Richmond, Va (d/VIII–3–1884 @69 Pamplins) MD UPa 1838;AM Hampden Sidney 1834. *Tr M S Va* 1884:8. *Butler* 1878:838.

WATKINS, JOHN M , New Orleans (b/Miss; d/IV–24–1898 @48) MD Tulane 1875. *New Orl m&s j* 50:669, 1898. *Polk* 1890: 492.

WATKINS, RALPH BRUCE, S Manchester, Conn (b/I–27–1861 Eastford; d/VI–19–1890) MD CPS Balto 1883. *Med reg NY NJ Conn* 1892:292. *Pr Conn M S* 1891:316–17. *Polk* 1886:440 (Balto).

WATKINS, THOMAS RICHARD, CW–CSA; ?Memphis (b/XI–20 1840 LaGrange, Tenn; d/V–31–1906) MD UPa 1868. *U Pa med alum CW*: 1868.

WATKINS, WILLIAM WOODBURY, Moscow, Idaho; W Plains, Mo (d/1901 @53) MD Wash U, St L 1871. *JAMA* 37:460, 1901. *Polk* 1886: 571.

WATSON, ABRAHAM ANDROS, Boston (d/VI–14–1868) MD Harvard 1828; AB 1823. *Bost m&s j* 1:324, 1868. *Mass M S cat* 1894.

WATSON, ARTHUR, Onancock, Va (d/II–25–1900 @ 82) MD UPa 1841. *JAMA* 34:639, 1900. *Polk* 1896:1497.

WATSON, BARRON CROWELL, Scituate, Mass (d/X–30–1894 @70) MD UPa 1846. *Bost m&s j* 131:476, 1894. *Mass M S cat* 1894.

WATSON, BERIAH ANDREW, CW–USA; Jersey City (b/III–26 1836; d/XII–22–1892) MC UCNY 1861. *Tr M S NJ* 1893:186–90. *Med reg NY NJ Conn* 1893:316. *Bost m&s j* 127:640, 1892. *K&B* III: 1271.

WATSON, COLON CHRISTOPHER, Nunda, Ill (d/III–28–1901) MD Rush 1878. *Ill m j* ns2:601, 1901. *Polk* 1896:432.

WATSON, DANIEL, Newport, RI (b/1799? d/V–17–1871 @72) MD UPa 1823. *Bost m&s j* 7: (May 25)1871.

 Spec. educ'l status abbrev. as: ***ng*** = college verified attendance without degree;

WATSON, DAVID, Bellefontaine, O (d/III-31-1894 @75) MD Cleveland M C 1852. *JAMA* 22:561, 1894. *Butler* 1878: 655.

WATSON, DAVID RINEHART, CW-USA; Donegal, Pa (b/I-16-1846; d/III-24-1869) MD UPa 1868. *Phila med reg & dir* 1871:300. *Med surg rep Phila* 20: 310, 1869. *U Pa med alum CW*: 1868.

WATSON, EDWARD H , Philadelphia (d/XII- -1853 at sea) MD Jefferson 1847. *Tr Pa St M S* 1856:185.

WATSON, EDWARD I , CW-USA (d/VII-19-1863 en route to Ft Craig, NM) MD ? *Nat m j* 1:304, 1870/71.

WATSON, GAVIN, Philadelphia (b/VI-20-1796 Scotland; d/X-28-1858) MD UPa 1852; stud surg Glasgow 1817. *Tr Pa St M S* 4:98-100, 1859. *Med surg rep Phila* ns1:108, 1858/59.

WATSON, HENRY PORTER, Manchester, NH (b/VI-8 1841 Guildhall, Vt; d/V-19-1905) MD Dartmouth 1867. *Tr NH M S* 1905:286-87. *Polk* 1896: 919.

WATSON, JAMES DAVIS, Hampden, Brooks & Waterville Me to 1875; Avoca, Ia 1875-84; Ewing, Nebr 1884- (b/III-24-1817 Newfield, Me; d/III-15-1899) MD Bowdoin 1849. *Bowdoin cat*: 1849.*Polk* 1886:580.

WATSON, JOHN, NYC (b/IV-16-1807 Ireland; d/VI-3 1863) MD CPSNY 1832. *Bost m&s j* 68:430, 1863. *Tr AMA* 14:206-07, 1864. *Med reg NY NJ Conn* 1865: 220. *K&B* III: 1272.

WATSON, JOHN McLARAN, BNashville (b/XI-20-1796 Wentworth, NC; d/IX-19-1866) MD CPSNY 1823. *Tr M S Tenn* 1876: 88. *So pract* 19:185, 1897. *Nashvl j m&s* ns1:316, 1866.

WATSON, K P [or T], Memphis (d/VIII-30-1878) MD ? *Tr AMA* 30:887, 1879. *Med rec NY* 14:220, 1878.

WATSON, LOTAN G , NC (d/1849) MD UPa 1823. *Tr AMA* 3:470, 1850.

WATSON, STUART S , Elgin, Tex (d/III-4-1906) MD U Louisvl 1873. *Tex st med jour* 1:352, 1905/06. *Polk* 1886: 882.

WATSON, WILLIAM, CW-USA; Bedford, Pa (b/IX-4-1837; d/III-13-1879) MD UPa 1861; AM Lafayette 1859. *U Pa med alum CW*: 1861. *Butler* 1878: 713.

WATSON, WILLIAM ARGYLE, CW-USA; NYC (b/ 1828 So Kingston, RI; d/VII-27-1901 Newport) MD UPa 1850. *U Pa med alum CW*: 1850. *Bost m&s j* 145: 139, 1901. *Polk* 1896: 1083.

WATT, JAMES, Brooklyn (b/VI-17-1843 Scotl'd; d/IX 11-1891) MD LICH 1866. *Med reg NY NJ Conn* 1892: 292. *JAMA* 17:979, 1891. *Bost m&s j* 125: 336, 1891. *Butler* 1878: 535.

WATTLES, GEORGE HAZZARD, Philadelphia (d/II-12-1884 @30) MD UPa 1882. *Med s rep Phila* 50: 288, 1884.

WATTLES, THOMAS P , N Stonington, Conn (d/IV-19 1855 @54?) Hon MD Yale 1845. *Bost m&s j* 52:227, 1855. *Pr Conn M S* 1855: 21.

WATTS, CHARLES JACKSON, Chicago (b/XI-27 1868 Racine, Wis; d/IX-21-1895) MD Hering, Chic 1893. *Tr Am Inst Hom* 1896: 87. Homeopath.

WATTS, EBER KINNEY, Richmond, Ind (b/XII-11-1854 Mich; d/I-3-1905) MD U Mich 1879. *Tr Ind St M S* 1905:462. *Polk* 1896: 489.

WATTS, EDWARD MAUPIN, CW-USA; Portsmouth, Va (b/IV-23-1835; d/VI-9-1890) MD UPa 1856. *U Pa med alum CW*: 1856. Blanton, *Va surgs CW*: 419. *Polk* 1886: 924.

WATTS, JOHN [JAMES?], Lafayette, Ore (d/VII-6-1901) MD Med Coll Ohio 1880. *JAMA* 37: 213, 1901.

WATTS, JOHN S , Millersburg, Ia (b/Amherst Co, Va; d/II-24-1900 @69) MD Jefferson 1867; MD Starling 1854. *JAMA* 34:702, 1900.

WATTS, NELSON, Chico, Cal (b/1830 Ohio; d/VI-14-1900) MD Cleveland Med Coll 1865. *JAMA* 34:1676, 1900. *Polk* 1886:164.

WATTS, ROBERT, NYC (b/VIII-31-1812; d/IX-8-1867) MD CPSNY 1837; AB Columbia 1831. *Tr AMA* 19:417-18, 1868. *Med reg NY NJ Conn* 1868: 337-38. *Med s rep Phila* 17:370, 480, 1867. *New Orl m&s j* 16: 205, 1868.

WAUGH, WILLIAM W , Faribault, Minn (d/I-8-1894 @47) MD NY Hom 1870. *JAMA* 22:158, 1894. *Butler* 1878: 396.

WAY, HENRY [HARVEY] ELLSWORTH, Bristol, Conn (b/I-17-1829 Meriden; d/VII-29-1893) MD UCNY 1849. *Pr Conn M S* 1894:236-7. *Butler* 1878:83.

WAY, JACOB HEALD, Nebraska City, Nebr; West Chester, Pa (b/III-22-1841 E Marlboro Twp; d/IX-3-1887 Ariz) MD Jefferson 1866; MD Hahnemann Phila 1872. *Tr Pa Hom S* 1887.

WAY, NICHOLAS, Delaware (d/IX-2-1797 @50) MD UPa 1771. *Tr CPP* cent vol: 287.

WAY, PALMER MARTIN, Ocean View, NJ (b/XI-18-1807; d/V-17-1893) MD Albany 1852. *Tr M S NJ* 1894: 278-79. *Polk* 1886: 611.

WAYSON, GEORGE W , Baltimore (b/XI-1819 Anne Arundel Co; d/IX-26-1899 @79) <MD Wash U Balto> *JAMA* 33:927, 1899. *Med ann Md:* 613. *Polk* 1886: 445.

WEAGLEY, SAMUEL G , Jacksonville, Ill (d/XII-7 1904) Lic yrs pract. *Ill m j* 7:127, 1905. *Polk* 1896: 433.

WEAN, CHARLES A , Chicago (d/V-28-1886 @40) MD Detroit M C 1885. *Ill m j* 8:80, 1905.

WEATHERBY, A S , Cardington, O (d/XI-23-1870 @ 33) MD Cinc Coll M & S 1862. *Tr O St M S* 1872:262. *Med surg rep Phila* 24:68, 1871.

WEATHERBY, JOSEPH C , Clarksboro, NJ (b/1812; d/ IV-20-1837) MD UPa 1837. *Tr M S NJ* 1884-85: 172-74. *Med surg rep Phila* 50:576, 1884.

WEATHERFORD, JAMES W , Portland, Ore (d/IX-20 1893) MD Willamette 1890. *JAMA* 21: 667, 1893. *Polk* 1893: 1048.

WEATHERRED [WESTHERED], ALONZO J , Waco, Tex (d/III-28-1906 @54) MD Vanderbilt 1882. *Tex st* *med jour* 2:36, 1906/07. *Polk* 1886: 891.

WEAVER, FRANCIS, CW–USA (d/III–29–1862) MD ? *Nat m j* 1:304, 1870/71.

WEAVER, JOHN D, Benton, Pa (d/VII–12–1901 @44) MD Jefferson 1885. *Pa med jour* 5:296, 1801/02. *JAMA* 37:276, 1901.

WEAVER, JOHN DERR, CW–USA (b/XII–19–1833 Berks Co, Pa; d/X–20–1872 Washingtonville) MD UPa 1861. *U Pa med alum CW*: 1861.

WEAVER, JOHN HENRY, Altoona, Pa (d/VIII–18 1906 @75 Greensboro, Md) MD UPa 1873. *Pa m j* 10: 53, 1906/07. *Off'l Reg Pa phys* 1881–88: 76.

WEAVER, SAMUEL J, Bethlehem, Pa (b/IX–2–1850 Weaversville; d/I–17–1905) MD Jefferson 1872. *Pa med jour* 8:726–27, 1904/05. *Polk* 1896: 1268.

WEBB, DANIEL MEIGS, Madison, Conn (b/IV–6–1822; d/I–1–1906) MD Yale 1849; AB 1846. *Pr Conn M S* 1906: 306–07. *Butler* 1873: 83.

WEBB, EDWIN, Hempstead, NY (b/1804 Engl; d/I–29–1890) MD CPSNY 1825. *Med reg NY NJ Conn* 1890: 283. *Bost m&s j* 122:144, 1890. *Butler* 1878:580.

WEBB, FRANCIS ROWAN, Chicago (d/XII–7–1905 @54) MD Chicago Med Coll 1875. *Ill m j* 9:130, 1906. *Polk* 1896: 410.

WEBB, J D, Cincinnati (d/VI–12–1873) MD Med Coll Ohio 1851. *Med surg rep Phila* 28:494, 1873.

WEBB, JAMES, Hillsboro, NC (b/II–22–1774; d/V– –1853) MD ? stud UNC 1795–96. *UNC cat*: 653.

WEBB, JAMES P, Bridgton, Me (d/1887 @64) MD LICH 1860. *Bost m&s j* 117: 296, 1887. *Butler* 1878:312.

WEBB, JOHN STAGG, NYC (d/V–5–1872 @23) MD CPSNY 1872. *Med reg NY NJ Conn* 1872: 358.

WEBB, LEWIS MUNSON, Ewing, Ill (d/III–9–1906 @59) MD St Louis Med Coll 1872. *Ill m j* 9:463, 1906. *Polk* 1886: 278.

WEBB, REYNOLDS, Madison, Conn (b/I–3–1791 Chester; d/VII–1–1856) MD Yale 1819. *Pr Conn M S* 1861: 129–32.

WEBB, SIDNEY VAUHAN, CW–CSA; Coffeeville, Ala (b/II–25–1832; d/1897) MD Jefferson 1858; att U Ala 1850. *U Ala cat*: 103. *Polk* 1886: 132.

WEBB, THOMAS HOPKINS, Quincy, Mass (b/IX–21–1801 Providence, RI; d/VIII–2–1866) MD Harvard 1825; AB Brown 1821; AM. *Brown hist cat*: 1821.

WEBB, WILLIAM H, Philadelphia (d/XII–20 or 23–1903) MD Jefferson 1866. *Pa med jour* 7: 280, 1903/04. *Flint* 1897: 827.

WEBB, WILLIAM KELSO, Baltimore (b/1850; d/VII–12–1895) MD UMd 1875. *Med annals Md:* 613. *Polk* 1886: 440.

WEBB, WILLIAM THOMAS, Calvert, Ala (b/X–24–1843; d/VIII–5–1878) MD Tulane 1867; AB U Ala 1864. *U Ala cat*: 190.

WEBBER, ALONZO CARTER, Cambridge, Mass (d/VIII–5–1904 @78) MD Harvard 1849. *Bost m&s j* 151:256, 1904. *Polk* 1896: 710.

WEBBER, ASHLEY ADAM, Brooklyn (b/Me; d/II–19–1903 @48) MD UCNY 1888. *Bost m&s j* 148:246, 1903. *Polk* 1896: 1005.

WEBBER, GEORGE CLARK, CW–USN; Millbury, Mass (b/XI–15 1837 Hallowell; d/VI–11–1895 @57) MD Harvard 1863; AB Wesleyan 1860. *Bost m&s j* 133: 659, 1895. *Harvard in CW*: 283.

WEBER, CHARLES, Pricetown, Pa 1849– (d/V–1–1899 Reading) <MD Tübingen 1848> *JAMA* 32: 1072, 1899. *Polk* 1896: 1330.

WEBER, HOWARD R, Chicago & Highland, Ill (d/IV–26–1906) MD U Md 1886. *Ill m j* 9:662, 1906.

WEBER, REINHARD [RICHARD] H, Philadelphia (b/Gny; d/III–29–1903 @59) MD Jefferson 1866. *Pa m j* 7:280, 1903/04. *Off'l Reg Pa phys* 1881–88:354.

WEBER, ROBERT LEWIS, CW–USN; Philadelphia (b/X–5–1837 Pottsville; d/XII–13–1884) MD UPa 1858. *U Pa med alum CW*: 1858.

WEBSTER, A W, St Louis (d/VII–30–1884 @76) MD ? *Med surg rep Phila* 51:280, 1884.

WEBSTER, AUGUSTINE JAMES, Killingworth, Conn (b/X–28–1835 Sandisfield, Mass; d/I–1–1864) MD Berkshire 1858. *Pr Conn M S* 1865: 152–53.

WEBSTER, CHARLES EDWIN, Portland, Me (b/II–9–1841 Durham?; d/XII–24–1892) MD Bowdoin 1869; AB 1866. *Tr Me M Assn* 1893:367–69. *Bost m&s j* 129: 44, 1893; 127:640, 1892. *Atkinson* I: 644. *Butler* 1878:312.

WEBSTER, CHARLES L, Chicago; Cleveland 1900– (b/VII–18–1863 Lyndonville, NY; d/XII–22–1905) MD CPS Chic 1894; MS Oberlin 1888; BD 1891. *JAMA* 46: 293, 1906.

WEBSTER, CLAUDIUS BUCHANAN, Concord, NH; CW–USA (b/XII–10–1815 Hampton; d/IX–7–1902) MD CPSNY 1844; AB Dartmouth 1836. *Bost m&s j* 147: 312, 1902. *Polk* 1896: 918.

WEBSTER, ELIPHALET KNIGHT, Pittsfield, NH (b/V 3–1802 Essex, Mass; d/XI–9–1881) Stud med w/Drs Farley, Ramsay, R D Mussey. *Tr AMA* 33:609–10, 1882. *Tr NH M S* 1882: 169–70.

WEBSTER, GEORGE WASHINGTON, Delaware City & Wilmington, Del (b/VIII–27–1824 Md; d/III–14–1870 NYC) MD UMd 1849. *Phila med reg & dir* 1871:304. *Tr AMA* 21:431–32, 1870. *Med reg NY NJ Conn* 1870/71: 335–36.

WEBSTER, HELEN BAKER WORTHING, CW–USA as nurse; New Bedford, Mass (b/1837 Boston; d/VII–19–1904) MD New Engl Fem Med Coll 1862. *JAMA* 43:486, 1904. *Bost m&s j* 151:525, 1904. *Polk* 1886: 470.

WEBSTER, HENRY WORTHINGTON, Baltimore (b/1795; d/X–23–1869) MD UMd 1822. *Med ann Md:* 614.

WEBSTER, HENRY WORTHINGTON Jr, Baltimore (b/II–23–1830; d/VIII–29–1894) MD UMd 1850. *JAMA* 23:440, 1894. *Med annals Md:* 614.

WEBSTER, HORACE F, Harrison Valley, Pa (d/V–2–

1905 @45) MD Bellevue 1888. *Pa med jour* 9:71, 1905/06. *Flint* 1897: 804.

WEBSTER, JAMES, Philadelphia; Rochester, NY 1839–52 (b/XII-12-1803 Washington or Warring, Lancs, Engl; d/VII-18-1854 Louisville, Ky) MD UPa 1824; att UMd Med Sch. *Tr M S St NY* 1855:165–69. *K&B* III: 1274.

WEBSTER, JAMES T , Emporia, Kans (d/XI-12-1898 @44) MD Keokuk CPS 1883. *JAMA* 31:1377, 1898. *Polk* 1886:584 (Vernon, Nebr).

WEBSTER, JOHN ORDWAY, San Diego, Cal (b/1842 Augusta, Me; d/IX-5-1896) MD Harvard 1868. *Tr Me M Assn* 1897:639–40. *Bost m&s j* 137:297, 1897. *Polk* 1886:423 (Augusta).

WEBSTER, STEPHEN HENRY, Troy, NY (d/I-6-1899 @ 33) MD Albany 1886. *JAMA* 32:195, 1899.

WEBSTER, WARREN, USA (b/III-7-1835 Gilmanton, NH; d/I-13-1896 Baltimore) MD Harvard 1861; ng Bowdoin. *Harvard in CW*: 268. *K&B* III: 1276–77.

WEBSTER, WILLIAM A , CW–USA; Manchester, NH (b/VI-13 1830 Rochester; d/II-7-1887) MD LICH 1862. Conn's *NH surgs CW*: 117–18. *Polk* 1886: 593.

WEDDINGTON, SAMUEL C , Union City, Ind 1856– ; CW–USA; Jonesboro 1866– (b/VII-15-1823 Rowan Co, NC; d/IV 25-1886) MD Med Coll Ind 1879. *Tr Ind St M S* 1886:217. *Atkinson* I: 592.

WEDEL, HENRY RUDOLPH, CW–USA; St Paul, Minn (b/IV-11 1839 Baltimore; d/IV-20-1887 Winona) MD UPa 1862. *U Pa med alum CW*:1862. *Polk* 1886: 518.

WEDERSTRANDT, JOHN CHARLES PERRY, New Orleans (b/1812 Balto; d/II-9-1864) MD UMd 1835. *New Orl m&s j* 19:569–74, 1867.

WEED, CHARLES L , Philadelphia (d/X-15-1889 @32) MD Jefferson 1883; AB Princeton 1880; AM 1883. *Med surg rep Phila* 61:476, 1889. *Polk* 1886:827.

WEED, FRANK J, Cleveland (d/III-27-1891 @46) MD W Res 1868. *Bost m&s j* 124:372, 1891. *Polk* 1890: 909.

WEED, SAMUEL, Portland, Me (b/VI-10-1774 Amesbury, Mass; d/XI-24-1857) Stud med w/Dr John Brooks; AM Harvard 1800. Palmer *Necr Harv alum*:172.

WEED, WILLIS EDWARD, Ridgefield, Conn (b/VII-9-1862 New Canaan; d/II-3-1901) MD CPSNY 1884. *Pr Conn M S* 1901: 313. *Polk* 1896: 284.

WEEDS, JAMES FOULKE, USA 1861– (d/X-1-1875 Nashville) MD U Mich 1857. *Tr AMA* 28:635–36, 1877. *Med rec NY* 10:687, 1875. Henry's *Milit rec civ appts USA*: 122.

WEEKS, ALBERT POLAND, Chelsea, Mass (d/IV-7-1893 @54) MD Bellevue 1868. *Bost m&s j* 128:380, 1893. *Butler* 1878: 344.

WEEKS, ALBION DEERING, Providence, RI (b/X-24 1845 Broomfield, Me; d/II-10-1887) MD UPa 1874. *Tr RI M S* 3:478, 1883–88. *Polk* 1886: 847.

WEEKS, CARLISLE B , Mantua, NJ (b/IX-4-1849 Vincentown, NJ; d/IX-19-1892) MD Jefferson 1880. *Tr M S NJ* 1893: 190.

WEEKS, CYRUS, Bloomfield, NJ (b/XI-16-1806 Sanbornton, NH; d/IX-29-1875)<MD Harvard 1829> *Med rec NY* 10:704, 1875.

WEEKS, FRANKLIN CHRISTOPHER, CW–USA (b/c1835; d/III-28-1864 NYC) MD Dartmouth 1858. *Nat m j* 1:304, 1870/71.

WEEKS, GEORGE W , NYC (d/II-15-1894 @29) MD Bellevue 1887. *Med reg NY NJ Conn* 1894: 251. *JAMA* 22:313, 1894.

WEEKS, WILLIAM JOSHUA, Malden, Mass (d/XII-23 1903) MD Harvard 1897. *Bost m&s j* 149: 748, 1903.

WEEMS, FRENCH, Louisville (b/1797 Pr Wm Co Va; d/XI- -1879) MD NY ? *Med s rep Phila* 41:506, 1879.

WEEMS, STEPHEN DECATUR [or H], Loch Eden, Md (b/II-14-1810 Calvert Co; d/VI- -1869) MD UMd 1833. *Med annals Md:* 614.

WEGEFARTH, J A W , El Paso, Tex (d/XII-9-1898 @35) MD CPS Balto 1886. *JAMA* 31:1542, 1898.

WEIDA, CHARLES BENJAMIN, Braddock, Pa (d/IV-27-1904 @37) MD Jefferson 1889. *Pa med jour* 8: 336, 1904/05. *Flint* 1897: 796.

WEIDLER, CARPENTER, Mechanicsburg, Pa (d/III-25 1898 @70) MD Pa Med Coll 1850, 1855. *JAMA* 30:874, 1898. *Polk* 1890: 979.

WEIDMAN, FELIX, Albany, NY (d/IX-10-1895 @70) MD Albany 1847. *JAMA* 25:510, 1895.

WEIDMAN, JOHN, Lebanon, Pa; CW–USA; (b/VIII-25 1814; d/IV 23-1863) MD UPa 1837; att? Dickinson. *U Pa med alum CW*: 1837, suppl.

WEIDMAN, WILLIAM MURRAY, CW–USA; Reading, Pa (b/V-8-1835 Lebanon; d/II-8-1902) MD UPa 1860; AB 1856; AB Gettysburg 1856. *Pa med jour* 5: 274–75, 292–94, 1901/02; 6:262, 1902/03. *U Pa med alum CW*: 1860.

WEIDMAN-HYNDS, FRANCES [FANNIE], Brooklyn (d/XII-5-1895) MD Buff 1891. *Buff m&s j* 35:597 1895.

WEIGEL, LOUIS A , Rochester, NY (d/V-31-1906 @52) MD UMd 1875. *Bost m&s j* 154:664, 1906. *Polk* 1886: 705.

WEIGHTMAN, RICHARD, USA; Washington, DC (b/c 1792 Alexandria, Va; d/X-30-1841 Ft Marion, Fla) MD UMd 1817. *Hist Med Soc DC:* 219.

WEIL, FRANK EDWARD, N Andover, Mass (d/I-6-1896 @35) MD Harvard 1882. *Bost m&s j* 134:52, 1896. *Polk* 1890: 554.

WEILL, MAX MILTON, NYC (b/VIII-21-1858; d/VII-27 or VIII-8-1896) MD LICH 1893; stud Bellevue 3 yrs. *Bost m&s j* 135:149, 1896. *Polk* 1896: 1083.

WEINHOLTZ, CHARLES HENRY, NYC (d/VIII-7 1896 @45) MD UCNY 1883. *JAMA* 27:449, 1896. *Bost m&s j* 135:174, 1896. *Polk* 1896: 1083.

WEIR, JOHN HENRY, Philadelphia (b/IX-1-1819; d/IX-12-1858) MD Jefferson 1842; AB Middlebury 1838. *Tr St M S [Pa?]* 1859: 98. *Tr AMA* 13:803–04, 1860. *Med surg rep Phila* ns1:28, 1858/59.

WEISER, HENRY KENLOCK, Philadelphia (d/XII-7-1906 @48) MD UPa 1881. *Pa med jour* 10:295, 1906/07.

WEISER, JOSIAH S , CW-USA (d/VII-24-1863) MD ? *Nat m j* 1:304, 1870/71.

WEISIGER, WILLIAM R , Manchester, Va (d/VII-28 1884) MD ? *Tr M S Va* 1884: 8. *Butler* 1878: 838.

WEISMANN, ADOLPH W , Keokuk, Ia (d/I-15-1899 @66) MD Keokuk CPS 1864. *JAMA* 32:263, 1899. *Polk* 1886: 361.

WEISS, LORENZO E , Miners Mills, Pa (b/II-12-1859 Nescopack; d/II-27-1897) MD Jefferson 1884. *Tr Luzerne Co [Pa] M S*: 1897: 204-05.

WEISSE, JOHN ADAM, NYC (b/XII-3-1810 Lorraine, Fr; d/I-12-1888) <MD Brussels> *Bost m&s j* 118:81, 1888. *Polk* 1886: 697.

WEISSELBURG, GUSTAV F , Austin, Tex (d/IX-19-1891 @67) <MD Berlin 1846> *Daniel's Tex m j* 7:150, 1891-92. *Polk* 1890: 1071.

WEIST, JACOB ROLLIN, CW-USA; Richmond, Ind (b/XI-26-1834 Preble Co; d/V-14-1900 @66) MD Jefferson 1861; att? Cleveland M C; att? Wesleyan, O. *JAMA* 34:1356, 1900. *Atkinson* I:111-12. *Polk* 1886: 334. *K&B* III: 1279.

WEIST, SAMUEL S , Schoeneck, Pa (d/IV-27-1902 @73) MD UCNY 1854. *Pa med jour* 6:262, 1902/03.

WELBORN, GEORGE WALKER, Stewardsville, Ind (b/III-17-1844 Evansville; d/III-23-1905 St Louis) MD Evansville M C 1877. *Tr Ind St M S* 1905: 463. *Polk* 1896: 492.

WELCH, ARCHIBALD, Hartford, Conn (b/III-13-1794 Mansfield; d/V-6-1853) Lic 1816 Bd Censors Windham Co; Hon MD Yale 1836. *Pr Conn M S* 1854: 19, 55-58. *Bost m&s j* 48:357, 1853; 50:189-97, 1854.

WELCH, BENJAMIN, Salisbury, Conn (b/V-24-1798 Norfolk; d/X-9-1873) MD Yale 1823; Hon MD Jefferson 1824. *Pr Conn M S* 1874:293 ff.

WELCH, EDWARD AUGUSTUS, Sutton, Mass (b/V-10-1862 Northfield; d/XI-9-1897) MD Harvard 1888; AB Wesleyan 1888. *Bost m&s j* 137:612, 1897. *Polk* 1896: 724.

WELCH, JAMES, Winsted, Conn (b/I-7-1807 Norfolk; d/XI-22-1886) MD Berkshire 1830. *Pr Conn M S* 1887:188-90. *Butler* 1878: 83.

WELCH, JOHN B , CW-USA (d/II-13-1862) MD ? *Nat m j* 1:304, 1870/71.

WELCH, LOUIS B, W Elizabeth, Pa (d/IV-27-1904 @ 68) MD UMd 1879 *Pa m j* 8:336 1904/5. *Polk* 1886:795.

WELCH, SELIM NEWELL, Sutton, NH (b/IX-6-1834/35 Burke, Vt; d/V-15-1896 Concord) MD Dartmouth 1877. *Tr NH M S* 1896:183-84. *Polk* 1890: 712.

WELCH, WILLIAM AMERICUS, Alpine, Ala (b/VII 24-1820; d/VII- -1900) MD Jefferson 1848; ng U Ala 1841-43. *Tr M Assn St Ala* 1902:130.

WELCH, WILLIAM J , NYC (d/I-14-1889 @42) MD UCNY 1866. *Med reg NY NJ Conn* 1889:289. *Butler* 1878: 527.

WELCH, WILLIAM WICKHAM, Norfolk, Conn (b/XII-10-1818; d/VII-30-1892) MD Yale 1839. *Pr Conn M S* 1893: 242-43. *Butler* 1878: 83.

WELD, EUGENE, New Iberia, La 1834- (b/VIII-10-1805 Boston; d/I-21-1849) MD CPSNY 1828; AB Bowdoin 1825. *Bowdoin cat*: 1825.

WELD, FRANCIS MINOT, CW-USA; USN; NYC; Jamaica Plain, Mass (b/1840 Dalton, NH; d/XII-31-1893) MD Harvard 1864; AB 1860. *Med reg NY NJ Conn* 1894: 251. *Bost m&s j* 130:52, 1894. *JAMA* 22:58,1894. *Harvard in CW*: 152.

WELD, MOSES WILLIAMS, Boston (d/I-16-1893 @75) MD Harvard 1843; AB 1840. *Bost m&s j* 128:76, 1893.

WELDON, ANDREW J , Paris Landing, Tenn (b/1831; d/III-7-1905) MD Jefferson 1860. *So pract* 27:201, 1805. *Butler* 1878: 779.

WELFLEY, DAVID PETER, Cumberland, Md (d/XII-21-1886) MD UPa 1863. *Med surg rep Phila* 56:32, 1887. *Polk* 1886: 441.

WELLER, FAYETTE MONTROSE, Chicago (d/IX-1-1895 @40) MD U Mich 1854) *JAMA* 25:427, 1895. *Chic m rec* 9:184, 1895. *Polk* 1886: 273.

WELLER [WELLES], FREDERICK S , CW-USA (d/I-15-1862 Hatteras Inlet, NC) MD CPSNY 1839. *Nat m j* 1:304, 1870/71.

WELLFORD, ARMISTEAD NELSON, CW-CSA (b/VIII-30-1826 Fredericksburg, Va; d/VII-1-1884 Richmond Co) MD UPa 1848. *U Pa med alum CW*:1848.

WELLFORD, BEVERLY RANDOLPH, Fredericksburg, Va (b/VII-29-1797; d/XII-27-1870) MD UMd 1816. *Med surg rep Phila* 24:22, 1871. *Phila m times* 1:1, 1870/71. *Tr AMA* 24:382-84, 1873. *K&B* III: 1280.

WELLFORD, FRANCIS PRESTON, CW-CSA; Fredericksburg, Va (b/IX-12-1829; d/X-18-1877 Fernandina, Fla) MD UPa 1852; AB Princeton 1848; AM 1851. *Bost m&s j* 112:514, 1885. *Med rec NY* 13:119, 1878. *U Pa med alum CW*: 1852.

WELLING, EDWARD LIVINGSTON, CW-USA; Pennington, NJ (b/VIII-24-1837; d/XI-29-1897 @63) MD UPa 1860; MD Rush 1859; AB Princeton 1857. *JAMA* 29:1234, 1897. *U Pa m alum CW*: 1860. *Polk* 1896: 947.

WELLINGTON, CHARLES BERWICK, Cambridgeport, Mass (d/II-17-1888 @28) MD Harvard 1885. *Bost m&s j* 118:212, 284, 1888.

WELLINGTON, TIMOTHY, W Cambridge, Mass (b/X-8-1781 Lexington, Mass; d/V-6-1853) MD Harvard 1811; AM 1806. Palmer *Necrol Harv alum*: 14-15.

WELLINGTON, WILLIAM WILLIAMSON, Cambridgeport, Mass (b/VII-29-1814; d/X-27-1896) MD Harvard 1838; AB 1832. *JAMA* 27:1169, 1896. *Bost m&s j* 135: 480, 610, 1896. *Atkinson* I: 30.

WELLMAN, GEORGE MARION, Dover Plains, NY (b/II-24-1837 Springfield, Mass; d/I-13-1902) MD

 Spec. educ'l status abbrev. as: ***ng*** = college verified attendance without degree;

Georgetown 1868; AB Amherst 1861. *Amherst, Men of*: 1861. *Polk* 1886: 658.

WELLS, CHARLES L , Minneapolis (b/Pompeii; d/I–20 1898 @56) <MD Geneva 1869> AM Hobart 1890 *JAMA* 30:335, 1898. *Tr Minn St M S* 1899:192. *Polk* 1886: 515.

WELLS, DANIEL, Newburgh, NY (d/VII–4–1890 @75) MD CPSNY 1835. *Med reg NY NJ Conn* 1891: 281. *JAMA* 15:232, 1890.

WELLS, DANIEL EATON, Hill, NH (b/X–21–1829 Woodstock, Vt; d/XII–30–1879 @52) MD Woodstock 1851. *Med s rep Phil* 42:88, 1880. *Tr NH M S* 1880: 117–22. Conn *NH surgs CW*: 304–05. *Butler* 1878: 458.

WELLS, EBENEZER, Freeport, Me 1826– (b/III–9–1801 Warren; d/X–23–1879) MD Bowdoin 1823. *Tr Me M Assn* 1880:204–05. *Atkinson* I:387–88. *K&B* II:1216.

WELLS, EDWARD D , Westminster, Md (d/IV–15–1898 @48) MD UMd 1867. *JAMA* 30:1061, 1898.

WELLS, ELMER HORTON, CW–USA; Meshoppen, Pa (d/XII–13–1904 @62) MD Bellevue 1867; BS & CE U Mich 1862; AM Lafayette 1869. *Pa med jour* 8:263, 336, 1904/05. *Flint* 1897: 809.

WELLS, GEORGE WILLIAM, Richmond Hill, NY (b/VI–5–1841 Tyrone; d/IX–2–1901) MD Bellevue 1868; AB Princeton 1865; AM 1868. *Bost m&s j* 145: 313, 1901. *Atkinson* I: 550. *Polk* 1896: 1084.

WELLS, HENRY MARTYN, USN 1861– (b/I–20–1835 Northampton, Mass; d/I–12–1905 Brooklyn) MD UPa 1860; ng Harvard Med 1859–60. *Bost m&s j* 152:89–90, 1905. *U Pa med alum CW*: 1860.

WELLS, JOHN ADAMS, Englewood, NJ (d/V–21–1901 @45) MD CPSNY 1879; AB Yale 1876. *Bost m&s j* 144: 540, 1901. *Polk* 1896: 936.

WELLS, JOHN B , Annapolis,Md; USA 1834– (d/VII–24–1853 Balto) MD UMd 1823. *Med annals Md:* 616. *Heitman*.

WELLS, JOHN EDMUND, Philippine Isl (b/II–24–1871 Scituate, RI; d/VI– –1902) Stud Jefferson 1900–01; PhB Brown 1898; AM 1900. *Brown hist cat*: 1898.

WELLS, JOHN FREME, Hartford, Conn (b/X–11–1810; d/V–4–1871) MD Yale 1844. *Pr Conn M S* 1871: 503 ff.

WELLS, JOHN H , Bellows Falls, Vt (b/1794? Rowe, Mass; d/I–1–1854 @60) <MD Castleton> *Tr Vt M S* 1883:111.

WELLS, OVID P , NYC (b/1805; d/VII–24–1891) MD Berkshire 1828. *Med reg NY NJ Conn* 1892:293. *Bost m&s j* 125: 124, 1891. *Polk* 1890: 838.

WELLS, PHINEAS PARKHURST, Brooklyn (b/1808 Hopkinton, NH; d/XI–22–1891 @83) MD Dartmouth 1834. *Med adv* 16:546, 1886. *Med vis* 8:13, 1892. *Polk* 1886: 650. Homeopath.

WELLS, WALTER SCOTT, NYC (d/III–4–1897) MD UCNY 1854. *Hist Med Soc DC:* 308. *Polk* 1893: 918.

WELLS, WILLIAM BENJAMIN, NYC (b/IV–30–1833; d/III–16–1870 Binghamton; MD CPSNY 1856; AB CCNY. *Med reg NY NJ Conn* 1870: 336.

WELLS, WILLIAM LEHMAN, Philadelphia (b/II–21–1834; d/IV–27–1883) MD UPa 1856. *Tr CPP* cent vol: 272. *Atkinson* I:90.

WELMAN, RICHMOND M , Jasper, Ind (b/XII–18–1824 Harrison Co, Ind; d/II–14–1884) MD Cincinnati M C 1861. *Tr Ind St M S* 1884:218. *Butler* 1878: 225.

WELSH, THOMAS, Huntington, WVa (d/III–21–1880) MD Harvard 1843; AB 1839. *Harvard in CW*: 14.

WELTON, HORATIO HACKETT, ?NYC (d/VIII–10–1888 @30) MD UCNY 1886. *Med reg NY NJ Conn* 1889: 289.

WEMPLE, DAVID FREDERICK, Sioux Falls, SD (d/XI–17–1883 @27) MD UCNY 1880. *Med surg rep Phila* 49:616, 1883.

WENDEL [WENDELL], JAMES E , Murfreesboro, Tenn (b/XI–29–1812; d/XII–21–1893) MD UPa 1839. *JAMA* 21: 1010, 1893. *Nashvl j m&s* 75:45–46, 95, 1894. *Butler* 1878: 779.

WENDELL, DANIEL A , Dover, NH (d/III–27–1871) MD Bowdoin 1866. *Bost m&s j* 7:240, 1871.

WENGER, ELIAS, Gilman, Ill (b/IV–17–1821 Augusta Co, Va; d/VIII–21–1887) MD Rush 1855. *Tr Ill St M S* 1888: 132–34. *Butler* 1878: 184.

WENNER, GEORGE V , Milford, NJ (d/VII–19–1904 @40) MD Medico–Chi Coll Phila 1896. *Bost m&s j* 151: 112, 1904. *Polk* 1900: 1142.

WENTWORTH, WILLIAM HANNAFORD, Sacramento (b/II–2–1864 Nevada City, Cal; d/IX–11–1901) MD Cooper 1895; AB . *Cal st j m* 1:229, 1903.

WENTWORTH, WILLIAM PARISH, New Rochelle, NY (b/Rochester, NY; d/XII–29–1897 @24) MD NY Hom 1896. *JAMA* 30:106, 1898. Homeopath.

WENTZ, CHARLES E , New Providence, RI (d/I–2 1906 @28) MD Medico–Chi Coll Phila 1903. *Pa med jour* 9:280, 360, 1905/06.

WENTZ, GEORGE SHRIVER, Drifton, Pa (d/VIII–29 1903 @75) MD UPa 1855. *Pa med jour* 7:280, 1903/04. *Flint* 1897: 800.

WENTZ, WILLIAM JAMES, New Providence, Pa (b/Lancaster Co; d/IX–5–1902 @64) MD Jeferson 1865. *Pa med jour* 6:262, 1902/03. *Polk* 1886: 810.

WENZEL, HENRY T , Milwaukee (b/VIII–20–1848; d/I 27–1897) MD Hosp Coll Med Central U Ky. *Tr Wis St M S* 31:636–38, 1897. *Polk* 1890: 1170.

WERMUTH, ADOLPH F , Fort Wayne, Ind (b/XII–8 1877 Saxony; d/XI–28–1901) <MD Med Coll Ft Wayne 1898> *Tr Ind St M S* 1902:427. Kemper's *Indiana*:354.

WERNER, HENRY E , Le Claire, Ia (d/VII–16–1898) MD Rush 1888. *JAMA* 31: 257, 1898.

WERSEL [WEISEL], SAMUEL, Williamsport, Md (b/V–16–1810; d/I–26–1872) MD UMd 1832. *Med annals Md:* 615.

WERT, JOHN M , Edge Hill, Pa (d/IX–13–1902 @52) MD Jefferson 1880. *Pa med jour* 6: 262, 1902/03. *Polk* 1886: 827 (Phila).

WERTMAN, AUSTIN G , Kunkletown, Pa (b/1872 Andreas, Pa; d/I–18–1905) MD U Balto 1898. *Pa med jour* 8:484, 1904/05.

WERTZ, PETER WEILER [WEISLER], CW–USA; Longswamp, Pa (b/II–19–1842; d/XI–14–1894) MD UPa 1864. *U Pa med alum CW*: 1864. *Polk* 1886: 807 (Mertztown, ?i.e. Wertztown, Pa).

WESCOTT, E SEYMOUR, Glassboro, NJ (b/VIII–27 1859; d/VI–17–1892) MD Jefferson 1883. *Tr M S NJ* 1893: 191–92.

WESCOTT, WILLIAM, Gorham, Me (b/VI– –1818 Standish; d/V–18–1876 or 1877) MD Bowdoin 1846. *Tr Me M Assn* 1877:244–46. *Butler* 1878: 312.

WESEMANN [WISEMAN], GEORGE THOMAS, Bainbridge, Pa (b/Hanover, Gny; d/VI–26–1894 @73) <MD Göttingen 1847> *JAMA* 23:42 1894 *Polk* 1886:791.

WESSELHOEFT, CONRAD, Boston (b/III–23–1834 Weimar, Gny; d/XII–17–1904) MD Harvard 1856. *Tr Am Inst Hom* 1905:837. *Polk* 1886. *K&B* III:1285. Homeopath.

WESSELHOEFT, WILLIAM, Bath, Pa 1824; Allen–town; Boston (b/1794 Saxe–Weimar; d/IX–1–1858) MD Jena 1820. *Tr Am Inst Hom* 1859:164. *Am hom rev* 1:96, 1858/59. *King* I:132–34. Homeopath.

WEST, A F , Casey, Ill (d/II–19–1901) Certif by Exam Bd. *Ill m j* ns2:533, 1901. *Polk* 1896: 369.

WEST, CALVIN, CW–USA; Hagerstown, Ind 18 yrs (d/VIII–25–1863) MD Fairfield 1831; MD Jefferson 1853 ad eundem. *Nat m j* 1:304, 1870/71. *Med surg rep Phila* 10:355, 1863. *Tr Ind St M S* 1870:162. *Nashvl j m&s* ns1: 317, 1866.

WEST, CHARLES W , Savannah (d/VI– –1860) MD M C Ga 1837. *So m&s j* 16:554, 1860. *Nashvl j m&s* 19: 192, 1860.

WEST, E M , CW–USA (d/IX–20–1865 Columbia, Tenn) MD ? *Nat m j* 1:304, 1870/71.

WEST, FRANCIS, Philadelphia (b/III–5–1810; d/IX–24 1868) MD UPa 1832; AB Dickinson 1827. *Tr CPP* cent vol:272–73; ns4:247–59, 1863–74. *Med surg rep Phila* 19:290, 1868. *Tr AMA* 21:459–60, 1870.

WEST, FRANK, Baltimore (b/III–20–1851; d/XI–18 1899 Asbury Park, NJ) MD UMd 1879. *JAMA* 33:1440, 1899.

WEST, GEORGE W , Richmond, Va; Washington, DC (b/1845 Buckingham Co; d/VII–24–1901) MD Rich–mond Med Coll 1868; stud London & Paris. *JAMA* 37: 398, 1901. *Atkinson* I:494. *Polk* 1886: 214.

WEST, GEORGE WASHINGTON, Petersville, Md (b/III–14–1803; d/VIII–18–1888) MD UMd 1825. *Med annals Md:* 616. *Polk* 1886: 444.

WEST, GEORGE WEBB, Newton, Mass (d/VIII–5–1897 @47) MD Harvard 1880; AB 1872. *Bost m&s j* 137:168, 1897. *Polk* 1896: 707.

WEST, GILLESPIE S , Palestine, Tex (d/XII–27–1904 @81) MD ? *So pract* 27:93–94, 1905. *Flint* 1897:911.

WEST, HAMILTON ATCHISON, CW–CSA; Galveston (b/III–30–1849 Russell's Cave Ky; d/XII–30–1903) MD U Louisvl 1872. *Tex st j m* 1:245–46, 1905–06. *Daniel's Tex m j* 8:33, 1892–93. *Atkinson* I:206. *K&B* III:1285–6.

WEST, HENRY SERGEANT, Binghamton, NY 1850–58; Sivas, Turkey 1859– (b/I–21–1827 Binghamton; d/IV–1–1876 Sivas) MD CPSNY 1850. *Tr M S St NY* 1877:354–57. *Med rec NY* 12:409, 1877. *K&B* III:1286.

WEST, JOSEPH EDWARD, CW–USA; Utica, NY (d/III–6–1897 @ 70) MD CPSNY 1852. *Tr M S St NY* 1898:403. *Polk* 1886:713.

WEST, JOSEPH THOMAS ODIORNE, Princeton, Mass (b/VI–21–1823 Barnstead, NH; d/I–28–1887) MD Harvard 1848; AB Dartmouth 1845. *JAMA* 10:128, 1888. *Bost m&s j* 116:124, 1887.

WEST, M CALVIN, Rome, NY (b/IX–11–1834; d/X–20–1891) MD U Mich 1860. *Bost m&s j* 125:480, 1891. *Atkinson* I:171. *Polk* 1886: 706.

WEST, SAMUEL, Tiverton, RI (b/VIII–9–1806; d/I–7 1879) MD Harvard 1831; AB 1828 Brown; AM. *Tr RI M S* 1:40, 1859–77. *Butler* 1878: 749.

WEST, SILAS, Binghamton, NY 1823– (b/III–11–1793 Watervliet; d/VIIII–27–1859) Lic Herkimer Co Med Soc; att Fairfield; Hon MD Regents U St NY 1856. *Tr MS St NY* 1860:168–71. *Buff m j* 15:633, 1860.

WEST, VINCENT T , Princeton, Ind (b/1812 Clermont Co, O; d/IV–28–1889) ng Med Coll Ohio 1836. *Tr Ind St M S* 1889: 217. *Butler* 1878: 224.

WEST, WILLIAM C , Geneseo, Ill (b/II–27–1835 Md; d/VII–10–1897) MD CPS Keokuk 1863. *JAMA* 29:251, 1897. *Ill m j* ns2:189, 1900.

WESTBROOK, BENJAMIN FRANKLIN, Brooklyn (b/II–4–1851 St Louis; d/IV–12–1895) MD LICH 1874. *Med reg NY NJ Conn* 1895:245. *Butler* 1878: 535.

WESTBROOK, GEORGE RANSOM, Brooklyn (b/II–1 1847 St Louis; d/IV–12–1895) MD LICH 1878. *JAMA* 24:650, 1895. *Polk* 1890:777.

WESTCOTT, ROBERT, CW–USA; Elizabeth, NJ (b/X 5–1832 Bethany, Pa; d/IV–30–1890) MD UPa 1853. *Med reg NY NJ Conn* 1890:283. *U Pa med alum CW*: 1853. *Butler* 1878: 478.

WESTERVELDT, J DOUGLAS, Corpus Christi, Tex (d/XII–10–1899) MD Atlanta MC 1875. *JAMA* 33: 1632, 1899. *Polk* 1886:854 (Gaffney City, SC)

WESTERVELT, JOHN S , New Brighton, NY (b/1799? d/VII–31–1869 @70) MD CPSNY 1820. *Phila med reg & dir* 1871:301. *Med surg rep Phila* 21:130, 1869.

WESTFALL, ALICE [ALMEDA] P , Dubuque, Ia (d/IV 29–1885) MD Hahnemann Chic 1881. *Med vis* 1:186, 1885. *Polk* 1886:357. Homeopath.

WESTFALL, LEWIS, Wantage, NJ (b/X–29–1839; d/V–29–1869) MD CPSNY 1863. *Tr M S NJ* 1870:85–86.

WESTLAKE, GEORGE WALKER, Red Bluff, Cal (b/V–28–1843 Mercer Co, Pa; d/IV–4–1903) MD Med Coll O 1866. *Cal st j m* 1:173, 1903. *Polk* 1896: 226.

 Spec. educ'l status abbrev. as: ***ng*** = college verified attendance without degree;

WESTMORELAND, JOHN GRAY, Atlanta (b/III-4-1816 Monticello, Ga; d/III-3-1887) <MD Med Coll Ga 1843> *Tex cour-rec med* 4:333, 1887. *New Orl m&s j* ns14: 693, 1887. *K&B* III: 1286.

WESTMORELAND, WILLIS FURMAN, CW-CSA; Atlanta (b/I-1-1828 Fayette Co; d/VI-27-1890) MD Jefferson 1850; ng Med Coll Ga. *JAMA* 15:158-59, 1890. *Atkinson* I: 467. *K&B* III: 1287-88.

WESTON, E EUGENE, Pittston, Pa (d/I-20-1900 @48) <MD CPS Balto 1881> *JAMA* 34:313, 1900. *Polk* 1890: 283.

WESTON, EDWARD HENRY, Somerville, Mass (d/III-28-1890 @70) MD Harvard 1865. *Bost m&s j* 123:629, 1890.

WESTON, HENRY O , Bay St Louis, Miss (d/XI-22-1906 @23) <MD Tulane> *New Orl m&s j* 59:481, 1906.

WESTON, JAMES CHASE, Bangor, Me (b/IX-18-1817 Bath; d/V-17-1877) MD Dartmouth 1844; AB 1842. *Tr Me M Assn* 1877:242, 244.

WETHERALL, GEORGE H , Baltimore (b/1802; d/III-6-1840) MD UMd 1826. *Med annals Md:* 616.

WETHERELL, GEORGE F , Chicago (d/III-20-1900) MD UCNY 1856. *JAMA* 34:766, 1900. *Tr Ill St M S* 1899-1900:509, 574. *Polk* 1896: 412.

WETHERELL, HENRY MAYER Jr, Philadelphia (d/VII-27-1904 @52) MD UPa 1877; PhG Phila Coll Pharm 1872. *Pa m j* 8:336, 1904/05. *Flint* 1897: 827.

WETHERILL, CHARLES MEYER, S Bethlehem Pa (d/III-5-1871) MD ? *Med surg rep Phila* 24:240, 1871.

WETHERILL, WILFRED HAWKE, Lambertville, NJ; CW-USN (b/III-26-1844 Wrightstown, Pa; d/IV-11-1866 @22) MD UPa 1865. *Med surg rep Phila* 14:320, 1866. *Nat m j* 1:304, 1870/71. *U Pa med alum CW*:1865.

WETHERILL, WILLIAM, Montgomery Co, Pa; CW-USA (b/I-31 1804 Phila; d/IV-28-1872) MD UPa 1825. *U Pa med alum CW*: 1825.

WETMORE, ADOLPHONSO, Waterloo, Ill (d/X-27-1900) <MD Washington U St Louis 1858> *Ill m j* ns2: 286, 1900. *Polk* 1886: 301.

WETMORE, CHARLES HENRY, War 1812-USA; Waterford, NY 1810- ; NYC 1816- ; Columbus 1819- (b/V-12-1784; d/X-10-1868) Lic Rensselaer Co M S; AB Yale 1804. *Med surg rep Phila* 19:368, 1868. *Phila med reg & dir* 1871: 298.

WETMORE, HOWARD GRAHAM, NYC (d/IV-27-1906) MD CPSNY 1879. *Bost m&s j* 154:538, 1906. *Polk* 1896: 1084.

WETZEL, WILLIAM, NYC (b/1822 Gny; d/II-25-1886) <MD Carlsruhe 1846> *Med reg NY NJ Conn* 1886: 257. *Polk* 1886: 697.

WEY, WILLIAM C , CW-USA; Elmira, NY (b/I-12 1829 Catskill; d/VI-30-1897) MD Albany 1849. *Bost m&s j* 137:44, 1897. *Buff m&s j* 37:54-58, 1897. *JAMA* 29:92, 1897. *Tr M S St NY* 1898: 404-06. *K&B* II: 1221.

WEYMOUTH, AURELIUS LANGDON, Boston 1835-77 (b/IX-15-1805 Newcastle, Me; d/IV-22-1878 Medford, Mass) MD Bowdoin 1835; AB 1831; AM 1863. *Bowdoin cat*: 1831.

WHALEY, BENTON HARRIS, Whaleysville, Md (b/X-11-1866; d/X-9-1896 @29) MD UPa 1889; att Lafayette. *JAMA* 27:1021, 1896.

WHALEY, EDWARD ARNOLD, Brooklyn (b/1827; d/V-13-1885) MD CPSNY 1851. *Med reg NY NJ Conn* 1885: 246. *Butler* 1878: 535.

WHARTENBY, JOHN A , Philadelphia (d/1872) MD Jefferson 1849. *Phila med reg & dir* 1873: 304.

WHARTON, RICHARD GOODE, Port Gibson, Miss (b/I-11-1815 Cartersville Va; d/VII-30-1896) MD UPa 1837 *JAMA* 27:503 1896. *Atkinson* I:537. *Polk* 1896:814.

WHARTON, SAMUEL L , Nashville (d/XII-2-1866) MD ? *Nashvl j m&s* ns1: 462, 488, 1866. *Med surg rep Phila* 15: 488, 1868.

WHARTON, WILLIAM HENRY, Nashville (b/VII-6-1796 Albemarle Co, Va; d/V-4-1872) MD UPa 1818. *Tr M S Tenn* 1876: 89.

WHEAT, LEWIS, Richmond, Va (d/XII-29-1902) <MD M C Va 1880> *Tr M S Va* 1903:276. *Polk* 1900: 1774.

WHEATLAND, HENRY, Salem Mass (d/II-27-1893 @ 81) MD Harvd 1837; AB 1832 *Bost m&s j* 128:228 1893.

WHEATLAND, RICHARD HENRY, Salem Mass (d/XII 21-1863 @33) MD Harvard 1853; AB 1850. *Bost m&s j* 69:428, 1863.

WHEATON, CHRISTOPHER COLUMBUS, Winchester, NH (b/VII-8-1802 Leicester, Mass; d/IX-24-1848) ng Dartmouth Med Sch 1832- ; AB Amherst 1828. *Amherst, Men of*: 1828.

WHEATON, FRANCIS LEVISON, Green Bay, Wis; Providence, RI; Mex War-USA; CW-USA (b/X-27-1804; d/XII-26-1895) MD Brown 1828; AB. *Tr RI M S* 5:248-50, 1894-98. *Polk* 1890: 1028.

WHEATON, HORATIO GATES, Charleston (d/X-8-1824) MD ? AB Brown 1820. *Brown hist cat*: 1820.

WHEATON, JOSEPH C , Millville, NJ (d/X-13-1897) MD Jefferson 1883. *JAMA* 29:926, 1897. *Polk* 1896:941.

WHEATON, LEVI, Providence (b/II-6-1761; d/VIII-28 1851) MD Brown 1812; AB 1782; AM. *Tr RI M S* 1: 19-25, 1859-77. *Bost m&s j* 45:126, 202, 213ff, 1851. *K&B* III:1288-89.

WHEATON, ROBERT ARCHIBALD, St Paul, Minn (b/Northfield; d/II-13 or 25-1898 @ 30 or 35) MD Harvard 1890. *Bost m&s j* 138:191, 1898. *Buff m&s j* 37:698, 1898. *JAMA* 30:624, 1898. *Tr Minn St M S* 1899: 192. *Flint* 1896: 521.

WHEATON, WALTER V , USA 1813- ; Philadelphia (b/1787? NY; d/IV-23-1860 @73) MD ? *Nashvl j m&s* 19:95, 1860.

WHEDON, ROBERT ALVIN, CW-USN (b/V-6-1839 Freedom, Mich; d/V-8-1876 Clinton; MD UPa 1866; MD U Mich 1863. *U Pa med alum CW*: 1866.

WHEEDEN, THOMAS J , Brooklyn (d/IV-16-1888)

MD UMd 1859. *Med reg NY NJ Conn* 1888:273. *Polk* 1886: 650.

WHEELAN, WILLIAM M , USN (b/1808; d/VI-11 1865) MD UPa 1828. *Tr AMA* 18:357–58, 1867. *Nat m j* 1:304, 1870/71. *Med surg rep Phila* 13:16, 1865.

WHEELER, CHARLES AUGUSTUS, Leominster, Mass (d/II-11-1904 @67) MD Worcester 1857? *Bost m&s j* 150:198, 1904. *Polk* 1896:715.

WHEELER, EDWARD A , Brooklyn (d/IX-19-1906) MD Bellevue 1879. *Bost m&s j* 155:364, 1906. *Polk* 1896:1005.

WHEELER, EDWARD REED, Spencer, Mass (b/VIII-1 1839 Paxton; d/IV-30-1904) MD UCNY 1864; AB Amherst 1860. *Bost m&s j* 150:496 1904. *Polk* 1896: 723.

WHEELER, ELBRIDGE GERRY, Middlefield, Mass (d/XII- -1893) MD Berkshire 1830. *Bost m&s j* 129: 632, 1893. *Mass M S cat* 1894.

WHEELER, ELIJAH D , NYC (b/XII-19-1818 Phila; d/II-12-1893) MD U Louisvl 1844. *Med reg NY NJ Conn* 1893:317. *Polk* 1886: 697.

WHEELER, ENOS S , Nicholson, Pa (b/I-7-1850 Waverly, Pa; d/X-31-1897) MD Jefferson 1873. *Pa med jour* 2:43, 1898. *Polk* 1896: 1295.

WHEELER, FRANCIS NELSON, Camden, Me (b/III-11-1844 Corinth; d/VI-12-1891) MD Bowdoin 1871. *Tr Me M Assn* 1892:197–98. *Bost m&s j* 124:618, 1891.

WHEELER, HENRY C , Carbondale, Pa (d/1904 @54) MD Jefferson 1877. *Pa med jour* 8:336, 1904/05. *Flint* 1897: 797.

WHEELER, HORACE KENNEDY, NYC (b/VIII-21-1835 Whitefield, Me; d/V-7-1868) MD Bowdoin 1858. *Med s rep Phil* 18:464 1868. *Phila m reg & dir*1871:296.

WHEELER, J M , ? (d/1878 Moscow, Tenn) MD ? *Tr AMA* 30: 887, 1879.

WHEELER, JAMES D, Decatur, Ill (d/IX-12-1900) MD Ecl Inst Cinc 1870. *Ill m j* ns2:237, 1900. *Polk* 1896:416.

WHEELER, JAMES HENRY, Dover, NH (b/IX-17-1831; d/I-26-1893) MD CPSNY 1862; att Brown. *Bost m&s j* 128:128, 1893. *Tr NH M S* 1893:154–55. *Atkinson* I:125. *Butler* 1878: 458.

WHEELER, JOHN, Pittsfield, NH Barnstead 1853–76; CW-USA (b/IX-5-1828; d/XII-20-1900) MD Berkshire 1852; AB Dartmouth 1850. *Tr NH M S* 1901:330. *Polk* 1896: 922.

WHEELER, JOHN H, Athens, NY (b/IV-4-1805; d/XI-3-1889) MD Fairfield 1827. *Med reg NY NJ Conn* 1890: 283. *Butler* 1878: 580.

WHEELER, JOHN HENRY, NYC (b/VIII-12-1829; d/VII-7-1897) MD LICH 1879. *JAMA* 29:201, 1897. *Polk* 1886: 697.

WHEELER, JOHN P , Hudson, NY (d/VI-28-1901 @34) MD UCNY 1843. *JAMA* 37:126, 1901.

WHEELER, WILLIAM GOODENOUGH, Chelsea, Mass (b/VIII-3-1821 Columbus, NY; d/IV-17-1897) MD Geneva 1846. *Bost m&s j* 136: 396, 419, 503, 1897.

WHEELOCK, ALBERT THOMPSON, Belfast, Me 1838–76 (b/XII-10-1813 Readfield; d/III-5-1876) MD Harvard 1838; AB Bowdoin 1834. *Bowdoin cat*: 1834.

WHEELWRIGHT, CHARLES HENRY, USN 1854–62 (d/VII-30-1862 @49 Pilotstown, La) MD Harvard 1837; AB 1834. *Bost m&s j* 67:48, 1862. *Harvard in CW*: 7. *Nat m j* 1:304, 1870/71.

WHEELWRIGHT, FRED D, Washington, DC (d/IX-12 1898 @81) MD UVa 1839. *JAMA* 31:808, 1898. *Polk* 1886:923 (Oak Grove, Va).

WHEELWRIGHT, JOSEPH, Heathsville, Va (b/XII-29 1791 Newburyport, Mass; d/VIII-24-1853) MD Harvard 1814; AB 1811. Palmer, *Necrol Harv alum*:31.

WHEET, THOMAS, Manchester, NH (d/III-25-1895 @ 74) MD Jeff 1847. *JAMA* 24:609, 1895. *Polk* 1890:710.

WHELAN, CHARLES, Greensboro Ala; Birmingham (b/V-26-1839; d/X-28-1897) MD ULa 1866; AB Georgetown. *Tr M Assn St Ala* 1898: 240; app:37–38. *Polk* 1886: 131.

WHIDDEN, PHILON CURRIER, CW-USA; Chicago (b/XI-21-1839 Rockford, Ill; d/III-7-1900) MD Harvard 1866; ng Amherst 1861. *Chic m rec* 18:323–24, 1900. *Tr Ill St M Assn* 1899–1900: 509. *JAMA* 34:702, 1900. *Butler* 1878: 138.

WHILLDIN, JOHN STITES, CW-USA; Erie, Pa 1861, 1866–67; St Paul Minn 1868– (b/V-28-1837 Phila; d/XI-23-1882) MD UPa 1861; AB Amherst 1859. *U Pa med alum CW*: 1861. *Tr Minn St M S* 1883:290–91.

WHINERY, EDWARD, Ft Madison, Ia (b/II-27-1812 Columbiana Co, O; d/II-25-1868) Stud med w/Dr Thos Carroll Cinc; <MD Transylvania 1840> *Med surg rep Phila* 18:270, 1868. *Phila med reg & dir* 1871:295. *Tr Ia St M S* 1867–71:262. Fairchild's *Iowa*: 38.

WHIPLEY, JEROME T , Cobden, Ill (d/XI-10-1904) Lic yrs pract. *Ill m j* 7:126, 1905.

WHIPPLE, ASHLEY COOPER, Ashland, NH (b/1852 New London; d/IV-4-1880) MD Dartmouth 1874. *Tr NH M S* 1880:129–31.

WHIPPLE, CHARLES KING, Newburyport, Mass (b/XI 17-1808; d/V-10-1900) MD ? AB Amherst 1831. *Amherst, Men of*: 1831.

WHIPPLE, GEORGE E , Essex Co, NY (d/1892) MD Albany 1883. *Tr M S St NY* 1892: 470.

WHIPPLE, JEREMIAH, Cumberland, RI (b/XII-2-1838; d/V-26-1871 Arcachon, Girone, Drand [?]) MD Harvard 1866; AB Brown 1859. *Bost m&s j* 7:424, 437, 1871.

WHIPPLE, SHELOMETH STOW, Boston (b/1795; d/IV-5-1859 @64) MD Brown 1818. *Bost m&s j* 60: 228, 1859.

WHIPPLE, SOLOMON MASON, New London, NH (b/VII-28-1820 Croydon; d/I-16-1884. MD Woodstock 1850; ng Dartmouth 1848. *Tr NH M S* 1884:195–97. *Butler* 1878: 458.

WHISTLER, SIMON MOWER, CW-USA; Harrisburg,

 Spec. educ'l status abbrev. as: ***ng*** = college verified attendance without degree;

Pa (b/III-8-1842 Franklin Co; d/VIII-17-1905) MD UPa 1866. *U Pa med alum CW*: 1866.

WHISTLER, WILLIAM McNEILL, CW-CSA; London, Engl (d/II-27-1900) MD UPa 1860. *Bost m&s j* 142: 316, 1900.

WHITAKER, BENJAMIN F , Enfield, NC (d/IV--1890) MD Jefferson 1848. *NC m j* 25:318, 1890. *Polk* 1886: 722.

WHITAKER, BENJAMIN REEVES, CW-USA; Phoenixville, Pa (b/III-28-1844; d/VIII-18-1897) MD UPa 1866. *U Pa med alum CW*: 1866. *JAMA* 29:555, 1897.

WHITAKER, CARY, Halifax Co, NC (b/XI-14-1782; d/VI-12-1858) MD ? AB UNC 1802. *UNC cat*: 660.

WHITAKER, JOHN BIRTWISTLE, Fall River, Mass (d/VIII-24-1893 @77) MD Harvard 1867. *Bost m&s j* 129:659, 1893.

WHITAKER, JONATHAN SHEPPARD, Millville, NJ (b/I-20-1823 Cedarville, NJ; d/II-14-1898) MD Jefferson 1845. *Tr M S NJ* 1898:366-68. *JAMA* 30:570, 1898. *Butler* 1878: 478.

WHITAKER, WILSON CURRY, Oswichee, Ala (b/IV-10-1830; d/III-15-1888) MD Jefferson 1853; AB UNC 1851? *Tr M Assn St Ala* 1888: 316.

WHITALL, SAMUEL, NYC (b/VIII-28-1840 Marlton, NJ; d/II-18-1882) MD CPSNY 1866. *Chic m rev* 5:128, 1882.*Med reg NY NJ Conn* 1882:236. *Butler* 1878:527.

WHITBECK, HENRY D , Syracuse, NY 4 yrs; Auburn (d/V-21-1901 Bath) <Lic Central NY Ecl M S 1874> *Bost m&s j* 144:540, 1901. *Polk* 1886: 641. Eclectic.

WHITCOMB, EDWIN E , Rochester, NY (d/VIII-1-1901 @50) MD Buffalo 1875. *JAMA* 37:461, 1901. *Polk* 1886: 705.

WHITCOMB, FIDELIA JANE MERRICK, Nunda, NY (d/IV-1-1888) MD Boston U 1876. *Tr Am Inst Hom* 1895:240. *Polk* 1886: 699.

WHITCOMB, FRANK W , Warren, Pa (b/Chandler's Valley; d/VI-30-1904 @46) MD Buffalo 1882. *Pa med jour* 8:336, 1904/05. *Flint* 1897: 838.

WHITCOMB, GEORGE HARRIS, Greenwich, NY (d/I 31-1900 @40) MD UCNY 1876. *Tr M S St NY* 1900: 431. *Polk* 1886: 662.

WHITCOMB, JAMES A , Indianapolis, Ind (b/I-12-1840 Lafayette; d/VII-13-1893) <MD Rush> *Tr Ind St M S* 1894: 217.

WHITCOMB, JAMES BARTON [or BIGELOW], CW-USA; Brooklyn (b/IX-1-1804 Boston; d/XII-22-1880) MD Bowdoin 1826. *Pr Conn M S* 1882: 170-71. *Atkinson* I: 362-63. *Butler* 1878: 83.

WHITE, A C , CW-CSA; Cuero, Tex (b/Va; d/XII-5-1888 @53) <MD New Orl M C> *Daniel's Tex m j* 4:278, 1888. *Polk* 1886: 882.

WHITE, ADONIJAH, Andover, Conn (b/IV-8-1784 or 1794? d/VI-8-1853) Hon MD Yale 1850. *Pr Conn M S* 1879:171; 1854:19.

WHITE, ALWARD M , El Paso, Tex (d/III-10-1898) MD UMd 1867. *JAMA* 30:745, 1898. *Polk* 1896: 1427. G. P. Red, *Med man in Texas*: 190-194.

WHITE, ALWARD McKEEL, Miles River Neck, Md (b/IX-29-1807 Cambridge; d/1884) MD UMd 1829. *Med annals Md:* 617.

WHITE, AMBROSE LIPSCOMBE, NYC;CW-USA (b/II-5-1804 Alexandria, DC; d/VI-2-1865) MD CPSNY 1831; AB Columbian 1825. *Med reg NY NJ Conn* 1866: 187. *Bost m&s j* 72:456, 1865. *Nat m j* 1:304, 1870/71.

WHITE, ANDREW MARION WILLIAM, Fall River, Mass (d/I-5-1885 @42) MD Bellevue 1881. *Bost m&s j* 112: 48, 1885.

WHITE, ASA JOHN, Cortland, NY (d/I-12-1897) MD Buffalo 1863. *JAMA* 28:236, 1897. *Polk* 1886: 658.

WHITE, BARTOW, Fishkill, NY (b/XI-7-1776 Yorktown; d/XII-10-1862) Lic 1799; Hon MD Regents U St 1845. *Tr M S St NY* 1863: 392.

WHITE, C E , Celeste, Tex (b/VII-12-1861 Mo; d/V 17-1904) <MD Memphis Hosp M C 1894> *Tex st jour med* 1:246, 1905/06. *Polk* 1900: 1685.

WHITE, CHARLES B , New Orleans (b/II-14-1826 Thetford, Vt; d/V- -1882) MD ULa 1852; AB Wabash Coll Ind 1846. *New Orl m&s j* ns9:873-74, 1882. *Butler* 1878: 295.

WHITE, CHARLES BELDEN, CW-USA; Georgetown & Columbus, O (b/IX-12-1837 NYC; d/VIII-10-1881 Wilton Conn) MD UCNY 1859;AB Free Acad NY 1854, AM 1857. *Med rec NY* 20:474, 1881. *Butler* 1878:633.

WHITE, CHARLES WARREN, Fairhaven, Mass (d/V 15-1904 @44) MD Bellevue 1885. *Bost m&s j* 150:578, 1904. *Polk* 1896: 711.

WHITE, DEVILLO, Sherburne, NY (b/II-11-1801; d/V-10-1882) Stud med w/Drs Squire White & Henry Mitchell, Norwich, NY. *Tr M S St NY* 1883:281-83. *Butler* 1874: 565.

WHITE, EDWARD HIRAM, Baltimore (b/X-20-1820 Somerset Co; d/VI-3-1897) MD UPa 1841. *Med annals Md:* 617. *Polk* 1886: 440.

WHITE, FRANCES EMILY, Jamaica Plain, Mass; Philadelphia (b/1832; d/XII-29-1903) MD Woman's M C Pa 1872. *Bost m&s j* 149:748, 1903. *Pa m j* 7:280, 1903/04. *Polk* 1896:1321. *K&B* III: 1290.

WHITE, FRANCIS VINTON [or VARIAN], NYC (b/X 10-1832; d/X-9-1889) MD UCNY 1855; AB 1852; AM 1855.*Med reg NY NJ Conn* 1890: 283. *Atkinson* I:227. *Butler* 1878: 527.

WHITE, FREDERICK ALLEN, Philadelphia (d/I-8 1895 @38) MD Jefferson 1888. *JAMA* 24:101, 1895.

WHITE, FREDERICK OLIN, New Haven, Conn (b/I-10-1852 Seymour; d/X-5-1899) MD Yale 1873. *Pr Conn M S* 1900:351-53. *Butler* 1878: 85.

WHITE, GEORGE, Lawrenceville, NJ (d/II-15-1877) MD UPa 1830. *Tr AMA* 28:627, 1877. *Tr M S NJ* 1877: [127].

WHITE, GEORGE WHARTON, Nashville (b/I-23-

1819; d/VII-4-1859) MD U Louisvl 1840. *Nashvl j m&s* ns12: 253, 1873.

WHITE, HENRY KIRKE, CW-USA (b/X-3-1843 Fairview, Va; d/XII-13-1865 Alleghany City, Pa) MD UPa 1865. *Med surg rep Phila* 14:80, 1866. *Nat m j* 1:304, 1870/71. *U Pa med alum CW*: 1865.

WHITE, HIRAM BINGHAM, Brooklyn(b/I-5-1822 Erving Mass; d/III-26-1883) MD Woodstock 1847. *Med reg NY NJ Conn* 1883:238; 1884:241. *Butler* 1878: 535.

WHITE, HORACE CARR, E Somerville, Mass (b/I-26-1836 Bowdoin, Me; d/XI-26-1903 @67) MD Bowdoin 1859. *Bost m&s j* 149:638, 1903. *Polk* 1896: 722.

WHITE, ISAAC, CW-CSA; Shawsville & Christiansburg, Va (d/VIII 3-1889 @52) MD Med Coll Va 1859. *Med surg rep Phila* 61:308, 1889. *Polk* 1886: 927.

WHITE, ISAIAH, Salt Lake City (b/1828; d/VII-23-1905) MD UCNY 1855. *UCNY cat*: 1855. *Polk* 1886: 899.

WHITE, J F, Oxford, O (b/V-3-1857 Kosciusko Co, Ind; d/III-3-1883) MD CPS Balto 1878. *Tr Ind St M S* 1883: 277. *Butler* 1878: 224.

WHITE, J F, Council Bluffs, Ia (d/1890) MD Med Coll Ind. *Tr Ia St M S* 18:412, 1900. *Polk* 1886: 354.

WHITE, J M, Austin, Miss (d/1878 Memphis) MD ? *Tr AMA* 30:887, 1879.

WHITE, J S, Macon, Ga (d/IX-30-1878 Memphis) MD ? *Tr AMA* 30:887, 1879.

WHITE, JAMES PLATT, Buffalo (b/III-11 or 14-1811 Austerlitz, NY; d/IX-28-1881) MD Jefferson 1834. *Buff m&s j* 21:137, 1881. *Bost m&s j* 105:383, 622, 1881; 106:253, 1882. *Tr M S St NY* 1882:337-46. *Atkinson* I:150-51. *K&B* III: 1292-93.

WHITE, JAMES W, Philadelphia (d/V-27-1891 @67) MD UPa 1873; DDS ? . *Bost m&s j* 124:570, 1891. *Med bull m&s* 13:266, 1891. *Butler* 1878: 697.

WHITE, JOHN BUEL, Saginaw, Mich (d/XI-21-1894) MD Phila Coll M & S 1852; MD Pa Med Coll 1859 ad eundem. *JAMA* 23:878, 1894. *Butler* 1878: 386.

WHITE, JOHN FLAVEL, Cincinnati; CW-USA (b/XII-3-1813 Snow Hill Md; d/V-3-1881) MD UPa 1837; AB Amherst 1833; ng Coll UPa 1833. *Amherst, Men of*: 1833. *Matrics cat Coll UPa*: 1833. *Butler* 1878: 592.

WHITE, JOHN LANE, Bloomington, Ill (b/XII-5-1832 Westminster, Mass; d/V-13-1902) MD Harvard 1854. *Ill m j* ns4:478-79, 1903. *Atkinson* I: 77. *Polk* 1896: 364.

WHITE, JOHN M, CW-USA (d/VIII-30-1863) MD ? *Nat m j* 1:304, 1870/71.

WHITE, JOHN PHILLIPS PAYSON, NYC (b/1838 Northampton, Mass; d/XII-3-1882) MD CPSNY 1861; AB Williams 1858; AM 1861. *Med reg NY NJ Conn* 1883:238. *Butler* 1878: 527.

WHITE, JOHN SPROUL, CW-USA (b/IX-10-1844 Lancaster, Pa; d/X-27-1868) MD UPa 1866. *U Pa med alum CW*: 1866.

WHITE, JONATHAN AMES, Brooklyn (b/II-28-1829 Erving, Mass; d/III-30-1884) MD Woodstock 1852. *Med reg NY NJ Conn* 1885: 247. *Med surg rep Phila* 50:512, 1884. *Butler* 1878: 536.

WHITE, JOSEPH RALSEY, Rochester, NY (d/III-5-1897) MD Albany 1855. *Tr Am Inst Hom* 1897: 64.

WHITE, LEONARD DARLING, Uxbridge, Mass (d/IX-18-1906) MD Harvard 1883. *Bost m&s j* 155:364, 1906. *Polk* 1896: 724.

WHITE, LEWIS H, Fishkill, NY (d/IX-24-1886 @79) Hon MD Bellevue 1858. *Med reg NY NJ Conn* 1887: 277. *Bost m&s j* 115:313, 1886. *Butler* 1878: 580.

WHITE, LORENZO, CW-CSA; Utica, Miss (d/II-16-1887) MD UPa 1854. *Tr Miss St M Assn* 1887: . *Polk* 1886: 533.

WHITE, LYSANDER T, Cortland, NY (d/I-16-1898 @55) MD Buffalo 1869. *JAMA* 30:279, 1898.

WHITE, MOSES CLARK, Fuh Chua, China 1845-53; New Haven, Conn 1854- (b/VII-24-1819 Paris, NY; d/X-24-1900) MD Yale 1854; AB Wesleyan 1845. *Pr Conn M S* 1901:291-93. *Bost m&s j* 143:463, 1900. *Atkinson* I: 61. *Butler* 1878: 83.

WHITE, NEWELL, Windham, O to 1840, 1845-50; Warren, O 1840-45; New Castle, Pa 1850- (b/XI-30-1807; d/1896) MD Berkshire 1834. *No Am j hom* 46:336, 1896. *Cleave*. Homeopath.

WHITE, OCTAVIUS A, Charleston 1848-65; NYC 1865- (b/II-8-1826; d/V-25-1903) MD Med Coll SC 1848; AB Charleston 1846. *Bost m&s j* 148:629, 1903. *Atkinson* I:89. *Polk* 1886:698.

WHITE, OLIVER, NYC (b/IV-9-1810 Somers, NY; d/XI-7-1879) Hon MD Bellevue 1875; <MD Yale 1831> *Med reg NY NJ Conn* 1880: 242. *Bost m&s j* 101: 746, 1879. *Med surg rep Phila* 41:484, 1879. *Med rec NY* 16:477, 1879, *Atkinson* I: 278.

WHITE, ORRIN CHESTER, Hebron, Conn (d/IX-13-1867 @64) Hon MD Yale 1847. *Bost m&s j* 77:200, 1867. *Pr Conn M S* 1870:441.

WHITE, ROBERT Jr, US Mar Hosp Serv (d/II-24-1880 Bedloe's Isl, NYC) MD Harvard 1867. *Med surg rep Phila* 42:242, 1880. *Bost m&s j* 102:234, 1880. *Med rec NY* 17: 274, 1880.

WHITE, RODERICK ADAMS, Simsbury, Conn (b/X-24-1809 Enfield; d/XII-3-1887) MD Yale 1832. *Pr Conn M S* 1893:236. *Butler* 1878: 83.

WHITE, SAMUEL POMEROY, NYC (b/XI-8-1801 Hudson, NJ; d/VI-6-1867) Dipl M S Columbia Co, NY 1823. *Med reg NY NJ Conn* 1869/70: 348-50. *Med & surg j Phila* 16:511, 1867. *Tr AMA* 19:419, 1868. *K&B* III: 1294.

WHITE, SARAH JANE (SMITH), NYC (b/1840 Whately, Mass; d/IV-9-1885) MD Women's Hom Med Coll 1873. *Am hom obs* 21:47, 1885. *Polk* 1886: 698. *Cleave*. Homeopath.

WHITE, SQUIRE, Canadaway, NY (b/XI-20-1785 Guilford, Vt; d/IV-2-1859 Fredonia, NY) Stud med w/

 Spec. educ'l status abbrev. as: ***ng*** = college verified attendance without degree;

Dr Asa White, Sherburne, NY; Lic Chenango Co M S 1808. *Tr M S St NY* 1865:274–75.

WHITE, STEPHEN B , Calvert Co, Md (b/Mass; d/ 1830) MD U Md 1823. *Med annals Md:* 618.

WHITE, STEPHEN STEWART, Sitka, Alaska (d/V–30 1899 @36!) <MD CPSNY 1855> *JAMA* 33:52, 1899.

WHITE, THOMAS JEFFERSON, Uniontown, Ala (d/ III–25–1887) MD Jefferson 1873. *Tr M Assn St Ala* 1887:306. *Polk* 1886: 140.

WHITE, THOMAS P , Cincinnati (d/VI–29–1901 @46) <MD Strasburg 1880> *JAMA* 37:125, 1901. *Polk* 1886:745.

WHITE, W EDWARD, CW–CSA (b/Raleigh, NC; d/ 1862 Wilmington) MD UCNY 1859. *UCNY cat*: 1859.

WHITE, WILLIAM DEE, Abbeville, La (b/Franklin, Tenn; d/II–24–1898 @61) MD U Nashvl 1860. *New Orl m&s j* 50:549, 1898. *Tr La St M S* 19:26, 1898. *Polk* 1890: 485.

WHITE, WILLIAM H , Brandon, Miss (d/X–17–1893) MD Tulane 1873. *New Orl m&s j* ns21:397, 1893. *Polk* 1886: 524.

WHITE, WILLIAM JAMES HAMILTON, USA 1852–62 (b/DC; d/IX–17–1862 Antietam) MD Columbian 1849. *Tr AMA* 14:214–15, 1864. *Med s rep Phil* ns9:242, 1862/3. *Bost m&s j* 67:248 1862. *Nat m j* 1:304, 1870/1. *Heitman*.

WHITE, WILLIAM M , New Haven, Conn (b/1823 Stockbridge, Mass; d/II–21–1879) MD Berkshire 1844. *Pr Conn M S* 1879–80: 163 ff. *Butler* 1878: 84.

WHITE, WILLIAM MAXWELL, Amsterdam, NY (d/ XII–29–1905 @49) MD Albany 1886; AB Union 1881. *Bost m&s j* 154:28, 1906.

WHITE, WILLIAM THOMAS, NYC (b/IV–7–1829 Richmond, Me; d/IX–17–1893) MD NYMC 1855. *Med reg NY NJ Conn* 1894:251. *JAMA* 21:498, 1893. *Bost m&s j* 129:312, 1893. *Atkinson* I:235. *Tr M S St NY* 11: 660–61. *Butler* 1878: 527.

WHITEFOOT, ROBERT MILLS, Bozeman, Mont (b/ 1840 Pa; d/VII–25–1906) MD Georgetown 1866. *Hist Med Soc DC:*280. *Polk* 1886: 573.

WHITEFORD, HUGH, Harford Co, Md (d/XI– –1814) MD UPa 1802. *Med annals Md:* 619.

WHITEFORD, HUGH CLAY, Darlington, Md (b/1846 Harford Co, Md; d/XI–12–1892) MD UMd 1868. *Med annals Md:* 619. *Polk* 1886: 441.

WHITEFORD, JAMES EDWIN, Baltimore (b/VI–24–1848 Harford Co, Md; d/XII–20–1898) MD CPS Balto 1877. *JAMA* 32:41, 1899. *Med annals Md:* 619. *Polk* 1886: 440.

WHITEHEAD, JOHN ELIAS [ELIAS JOHN], NYC (d/ II–22–1892 @67) MD CPSNY 1864; AB Rutgers 1844; AM 1846. *Med reg NY NJ Conn* 1892: 293. *Butler* 1878:527.

WHITEHEAD, JOHN G L , Crosswick & Bordentown, NJ (d/VI–29–1901) MD Phila Coll M & S 1852. *JAMA* 37:126, 1901. *Polk* 1886: 601.

WHITEHEAD, JOSEPH BOYKIN, Norfolk, Va; CW–CSA (b/XI–3–1838 Suffolk; d/IV–9–1878) MD UPa 1869. *U Pa med alum CW*: 1869. *Tr M S Va* 1878:509.

WHITEHEAD, MARCELLUS, Salisbury, NC (b/I–27–1821 Nelson Co, Va; d/I–2–1885 @63) MD Med Coll Va 1845. *NC m j* 15:48–51, 1885. *Med surg rep Phila* 52:128, 1885. *Tr NC M S* 1887:158. *Butler* 1878:599.

WHITEHEAD, N E , Greenwood, Miss (d/III–25–1905) MD Tulane 1867. *New Orl m&s j*57:861, 1905. *Polk* 1890: 630.

WHITEHEAD, PETER FLANAGAN, CW–CSA; Independence, Mo (b/VI–9–1838 Winchester, Ky; d/IX–5–1878 Vicksburg, Miss) MD Jefferson 1859. *Tr AMA* 30:837–38, 1879. *Tr Miss St M S* 1879:37, 48–51. *Med rec NY* 14:220, 1878.

WHITEHEAD, WILLIAM H , CW–CSA; Indian Spr, Ga (b/1823 Southampton Co, Va; d/1878) MD UCNY 1846. *UCNY cat*: 1846.

WHITEHEAD, WILLIAM MANLOVE, Elizabeth, NJ (d/I–28–1874 Woodbury) MD Hahnemann Phila 1872; AB UPa 1850; AB Union 1850; AM 1853; Hon AM Lewisburg (Bucknell) 1860. *Tr AMA* 27:652, 1876. *Tr M S NJ* 1875: [105]. *Med surg rep Phila* 30:204, 1874; 31:339, 1874. Homeopath.

WHITEHEAD, WILLIAM RIDDICK, Crimean War–Russ Army; CW–CSA; Denver (b/XI or XII–15–1831 Suffolk, Va; d/X–14–1902) MD U Paris 1860; gr Va Milit Inst 1851; MD UPa 1853. *Bost m&s j* 147:476, 1902. *U Pa med alum CW*: 1853. *Atkinson* I: 99. *K&B* III:1295–96.

WHITEHILL, JAMES CRAIG, CW–USA; Leadville, Col (b/Marietta, Pa; d/IX–10–1901 Los Angeles) MD UPa 1851. *U Pa med alum CW*: 1851.

WHITELY, ROBERT JOHN, Paterson, NJ 1846–49, 1853– ; Calif 1849–53 (b/I or II–16–1825; d/IV–10–1879) MD CPSNY 1846; att Rutgers. *Tr M S NJ* 1880–81: 126–27. *Atkinson* I: 492. *Butler* 1878: 478.

WHITERBEE, J J , CW–USN (d/VIII–30–1863 abd US ship off New Orleans) MD ? *Nat m j* 1:304, 1870/71.

WHITESELL, HALLIE W , Sewickley, Pa (d/III–27–1902 @28) MD W Pa U 1896. *Pa med jour* 6:262, 1902/03.

WHITESELL, PHILIP P , Clarksville & Noblesville Ind (b/XII–4–1823 Cincinnati; d/I–27–1896) MD ? *JAMA* 26:287 1896. *Tr Ind St MS* 1896:264. *Polk* 1886: 314.

WHITESIDE, JOHN E , Philadelphia (d/XI–25–1897 @74 Atlantic City, NJ) MD Pa Med Coll 1847. *JAMA* 29:1234, 1897. *Polk* 1896: 1321.

WHITFIELD [WHITEFIELD], ISAIAH J , Grand Rapids, Mich (b/1835? d/X–25–1891 @56) MD Cleveland Hom Hosp 1870. *Tr Am Inst Hom* 1896:87. *Polk* 1886: 494. Homeopath.

WHITFORD, BYRON, Providence (b/XI–13–1849

Oneco, Conn; d/II-8-1903) MD UCNY 1878. *Tr RI M S* 6:680, 1899-1903. *Polk* 1896:1354.

WHITING, ALEXANDER BACKUS, NYC (b/III-3-1814; d/V-2-1868) MD Yale 1838; AB 1833. *Tr AMA* 19:421, 1868; 21:433, 1870. *Med surg rep Phila* 18:442, 1868. *Med reg NY NJ Conn* 1869/70: 250-51.

WHITING, AUGUSTUS, Charlestown, Mass (b/1795? d/V-4-1867 @75) MD Harvard 1820; AB 1816. *Bost m&s j* 76:296, 1867.

WHITING, DANFORTH, Augusta, Me; Lunenburg, Mass (b/1830? d/XI-24-1867 @37) MD ? *Med surg rep Phila* 17:524, 1867. *No Am j hom* 18: 286, 1870. *New Engl med gaz* 3:43, 1868. Homeopath.

WHITING, ELLSWORTH D, Aurora, Ill (d/IV-26-1898) MD Rush 1897. *JAMA* 30:1125, 1898.

WHITING, HENRY, Lowell, Mass (b/II-19-1822; d/VI-23-1857 @35) MD Jefferson 1845; AB Harvard 1842. *Bost m&s j* 56:487, 1857. *Mass M S cat* 1894.

WHITING, HOWARD, Brooklyn (d/IV-16-1891 @44) MD CPSNY 1870. *Med reg NY NJ Conn* 1891: 281. *Butler* 1878: 536.

WHITING, JOHN M, CW-USN (d/VIII-16-1864 on US Steamer Norwich) MD ? *Nat m j* 1:304, 1870/71.

WHITING, LEWIS, Danvers, Mass (d/XII-29-1895 @64) MD NY Hom Med Coll 1865. *Tr Am Inst Hom* 1896: 87. *Polk* 1886: 465.

WHITMAN, ALMON CLARK, Fiskeville, RI (b/I-13-1805 Warwick; d/I-13-1879) MD Berkshire 1837. *Tr RI M S* 2:217, 1877-82.

WHITMAN, DANIEL, Bridgewater, Mass (b/IV-12-1784; d/IV-30-1879) MD ? AB Brown 1809. *Brown hist cat*: 1809.

WHITMAN, HENRY LYMAN, Des Moines, Ia (b/XII-30-1814 Hartford, Conn; d/1885) MD Jefferson 1845; AB Amherst 1839. *Tr Ia St M S* 18:412, 1900. *Polk* 1886:357.

WHITMAN, NOAH Jr, Bridgewater, Mass (b/III-3-1785; d/IV-24-1854) MD Dartmouth 1809; MB 1809; AB Brown 1806. *Brown hist cat*: 1806.

WHITMIRE, JAMES SMITH, CW-USA; Metamora, Ill (b/XII-13-1821 Sidney, O; d/VII-15-1897) MD Ill Coll 1847; MD Rush 1850 ad eundem; MD Jefferson 1856. *JAMA* 29:200, 251, 1897. *Atkinson* I: 28. *Polk* 1886:288.

WHITMIRE, ZACHARIAH LINCOLN, Urbana, Ill (d/XII-3-1899 @34) MD Rush 1890; BS. *Tr Ill St M S* 1899-1900: 352. *Polk* 1896: 444.

WHITMORE, CHADBOURNE WARREN, Gardiner, Me (b/X-4-1818 Bowdoinham; d/III-24-1884 Washington, DC) MD Bowdoin 1839. *Tr Me M Assn* 1884: 371-72. *Butler* 1878: 312.

WHITMORE, STEPHEN, Gardiner, Me (b/1814 Bowdoinham; d/II-9-1880) MD Bowdoin 1836. *Tr Me M Assn* 1881:392. *Butler* 1878: 312.

WHITNELL, JOSIAH, Vienna, Ill (d/VII-20-1900) MD U Louisvl 1855. *Ill m j* ns2:189, 1900. *Polk* 1890:341.

WHITNEY, ALLSTON WALDO, CW-USA; W Newton, Mass (d/XI-11-1881 @52) MD Harvard 1852. *Bost m&s j* 105:484, 622-24, 1881. *Harvard in CW*: 239.

WHITNEY, EDWARD J, CW-USA; Brooklyn (b/1839 NYC; d/VIII-7-1895) MD UCNY 1862. *Hahn mo* 30: 134 (news & advt, Oct) 1895. *Bost m&s j* 133:172, 1895. *Polk* 1885: 650.

WHITNEY, JAMES ORNE, Pawtucket, RI (b/III-2-1823 Attleboro, Mass; d/I-24-1895) MD Berkshire 1845. *Tr RI M S* 5:250-52, 1894-8. *JAMA* 24:250, 1895. *Atkinson* I: 652. *Polk* 1890: 1026.

WHITNEY, JOHN MARSHALL, CW-USN (b/VII-4-1842 Hopkinton, Mass; d/VIII-16-1864 Jacksonville, Fla) ng LICH; AB Amherst 1863. *Bost m&s j* 71:228, 1864. *Med surg rep Phila* 12:100, 1864/65. *Callahan.*

WHITNEY, SAMUEL STILLMAN, Dedham, Mass (b/I 6-1815 Natick, Mass; d/VI-30-1855) MD Harvard 1838; ng Amherst 1836. *Bost m&s j* 53:261-64, 1856.

WHITNEY, SIMON, Framingham, Mass (b/X-30-1798; d/IX-2-1861 @64) MD Harvard 1822; AM 1818. *Bost m&s j* 65:108, 1861. Palmer, *Necrol Harv alum*: 414-16. *Mass M S cat* 1894.

WHITNEY, WARREN JACOB, Dorchester, Mass (d/III 11-1891 @80) MD Harvard 1835; AB 1831. *Bost m&s j* 124:300, 1891. *Butler* 1878:345.

WHITRIDGE, JOHN, Baltimore (b/III-23-1793 Tiverton, RI; d/VII-23-1878 there) MD Harvard 1819; AB Union 1816; AM. *Tr AMA* 32:546, 1881. *Med annals Md:* 620.

WHITSITT [WHITSETT], THOMAS C S, Jonesboro, Ark (d/VIII-13-1887 @64) MD U Nashvl 1854. *New Orl m&s j* ns15:329, 1887. *Polk* 1886: 153.

WHITTAKER, DENNIS WARNER, Chattanooga (d/X-3-1898 @47) MD Columbus Med Coll 1883. *JAMA* 31: 942, 1898. *Polk* 1895: 1385.

WHITTAKER, JAMES THOMAS, Cincinnati; CW-USN (b/III-3-1843; d/VI-5-1900) MD UPa 1866; MD U Ohio 1867; AB Miami 1863; AM 1868. *Tr CPP* cent vol:287. *Buff m&s j* 39:933, 1900. *JAMA* 34:1504, 1900. *U Pa m alum CW*: 1866. *Atkinson* I: 182. *K&B* III:1298.

WHITTAKER, JOSIAS D, Baltimore (d/1876) MD U Md 1824. *Med annals Md:* 620. *Butler* 1878: 323.

WHITTELL, ALEXANDER POPE, San Francisco 1865?- (b/1850 Mt Vernon, NY; d/VII- -1893 Lake Tahoe) MD U Cal 1873; stud Fr & Gny. *Tr M S St Cal* 1894: 291-93.

WHITTEMORE, FRANCIS STOWELL, NYC (d/XI-24-1894 @30) MD Harvard 1890. *Bost m&s j* 131:548, 1894.

WHITTEMORE, FREDERICK WEBSTER, Cambridge, Mass (d/IV-14-1897 @45) MD Harvard 1878. *Bost m&s jour* 136:396, 1897; 137:263, 1897. *JAMA* 28:810, 1897.

WHITTEMORE, HORATIO HANCOCK FISKE, Marblehead, Mass (d/XI-25-1872 @42) MD Harvard

1855; AB 1852) *Bost m&s j* ns10:384, 1872.

WHITTEMORE, JAMES HENRY, Boston (b/VI-15-1839 Hillsboro, NH; d/I-6-1886) MD Dartmouth 1862. *Bost m&s j* 114:48, 69, 72, 96, 286, 1886.

WHITTEMORE, JOSEPH JAMES LLOYD, Scituate, Mass; Amiens, Fr (b/X-18-1811; d/X-14-1860 Paris) MD Heidelberg 1837; AB Harvard 1832. *Bost m&s j* 63:368, 1861. Palmer, *Necrol Harv alum*: 371.

WHITTEN, WILLIAM, Pilot's Point, Tex (d/XI-12-1899 @45 Chicago) MD Med Coll Va 1871. *JAMA* 33:1441, 1899. *Polk* 1886: 892.

WHITTIER, EDWARD NEWTON, Boston (b/VII-2-1840 or 1841; d/VI-14-1902 @60) MD Harvard 1869; AB Brown 1862. *Bost m&s j* 146:678, 704, 1902. *K&B* III: 1298-99.

WHITTIER, GARDNER MARK, Fairfield, Pa (d/I-30-1900 @52) MD Bellevue 1875. *JAMA* 34:381, 1900. *Polk* 1896: 1272.

WHITTIER, SAMUEL CROOK, CW-USA; Portsmouth NH (b/I-3-1837 Dover; d/II-1/2-1893) MD Harvard 1862. *Bost m&s j* 128:152, 1893. *Tr NH M S* 1893:156-57. *Harvard in CW*: 276.

WHITTING, JOSEPH BELLAMY Jr, Janesville, Wis; Span-Amer War-USA (b/1866; d/II-19-1905) MD CPS Chicago 1887. *JAMA* 43:729, 1905.

WHITTINGHAM, EDWARD THOMAS, CW-USA; Milburn, NJ (b/IV-2-1831; d/X-26-1886) MD UMd 1852; AB St James Coll 1849. *Med annals Md:* 621. *Atkinson* I:446. *Polk* 1886: 606.

WHITTLE, JOSHUA FOLSOM, Nashua, NH (b/VIII-5 1820 Deering; d/VIII-17-1888) MD Castleton 1843. *Med vis* 7:113 1891. *Polk* 1886:593. *Cleave.* Homeopath.

WHITTLESEY, HENRY N , NYC (d/VI-19-1869 @47) MD UCNY 1846. *Med reg NY NJ Conn* 1869: 326. *Phila med reg & dir* 1871:301. *Med surg rep Phila* 21: 68, 1869. *Tr AMA* 21:446, 1870.

WHITTRIDGE [WHITRIDGE], WILLIAM CUSHING, New Bedford, Mass (b/XI-25-1784; d/XII-28-1857 or 1859) Hon MD Harvard 1847; AB Union 1804; ng Brown. *Tr AMA* 13:790, 1860. *Bost m&s j* 57:475-6, 1857. *Tr RI M S* 1:40, 1859-77.

WHITWELL, BENJAMIN, Hanover, Mass (d/VIII-13 1857 @40) MD Harvard 1848. *Bost m&s j* 57:87, 1857.

WHITWELL, WILLIAM SCOLLAY, NYC (b/IV-14-1847 Keene, NH; d/1903?) MD Harvard 1872; AB 1869. *Bost m&s j* 148:456, 1903. *Polk* 1896:240.

WHITWORTH, DAVID M , Webb City, Mo (d/XI-26-1899 @70) MD U Nashville 1860. *JAMA* 33:1632, 1899. *Polk* 1890: 681.

WHYBREW, CHARLES THOMAS, NYC (d/III-8-1904) MD CPSNY 1870; att Coll UCNY, *Bost m&s j* 150:282, 1904. *Polk* 1896:1084.

WHYTE, THOMAS EDWARD, CW-CSA; Clarke Co, Ga (b/II-26 1827 Chapel Hill, NC; d/I-13-1901 or II-22-1900) MD UPa 1857; AB UNC 1845. *U Pa med alum CW*: 1857. *UNC cat*: 668.

WIBLE, BENJAMIN MILLER, Louisville (b/VIII-13 1814 Nelson Co, Ky; d/III-27-1877) MD Med Coll Ohio 1837. *Tr AMA* 32:546-47, 1881. *Tr Ky St M S* 1877: 205-08. *New Orl m&s j* ns4: 899, 1877.

WICK, DALLIS M , Cedar Falls, Ia (d/III-1-1904) MD Chic Med Coll 1874. *Tr Ia St M S* 22:342, 1904. *Polk* 1890: 514.

WICK, H M , New Bethlehem, Pa (d/III-15-1874 @58) MD ? *Med surg rep Phila* 30: 420, 1874.

WICK, WILLIAM W , Rimersburgh, Pa (d/XI-14-1861 @ c30) MD ? *Med surg rep Phila* ns7:240, 1861/62.

WICKERSHAM, NOAH LUDLOW, Anderson, Ind (b/I 7-1827 Clinton Co, O; d/IV-10-1897) MD Miami 1857. *Tr Ind St M S* 1897:356. *Polk* 1896: 458.

WICKERSHAM, SWAYNE, Chicago (d/IV-17-1895) MD UPa 1855. *Chic m rec* 8:394, 1895. *JAMA* 24:609, 1895. *Polk* 1886: 273.

WICKES, SIMON ALEXANDER, Philadelphia (d/1834 or V-14-1835 New Orleans) MD UPa 1831; AB Yale 1827. *Tr CPP* cent vol: 273.

WICKES, STEPHEN, Troy, NY; Orange, NJ (b/III-17-1813; d/VIII-8-1889) MD UPa 1834; AB Union 1831; AM 1834; AM Princeton 1868 ad eundem. *Tr M S NJ* 1890:335-39. *Med reg NY NJ Conn* 1890:284. *Atkinson* I: 26. *K&B* III:1299.

WICKS, EDMUND G , Denver (d/VIII-26-1892 @34) MD UMd 1888. *Tr Col St M S* 1898-99: 509.

WIDDIFIELD, CASPER SINGER, CW-USA (b/I-16-1829 Doylestown, Pa; d/IV-27-1862 Fortress Monroe, Va) MD UPa 1860. *U Pa med alum CW*: 1860. *Nat m j* 1:304, 1870/71.

WIEBER, GEORGE, CW-USA; Brooklyn (b/IV-15-1825 Weitzler, Gny; d/I-31-1896) <MD Giessen 1857> lic NY 1875. *JAMA* 26:890-91, 1896. *Tr NY M Assn* 13:523, 1896. *Polk* 1890: 777.

WIENER, JOSEPH, NYC (b/IV-5-1829 Bohemia; d/VIII-11-1904 @77) MD CPSNY 1874; <lic Prage 1848> *Bost m&s j* 151:197, 1904. *Polk* 1886: 698.

WIENGES [WEINGES], CONRAD, Jersey City, NJ (d/V-23-1901 @52) MD CPSNY 1883. *Bost m&s j* 144: 540, 1901. *Polk* 1896: 940.

WIESEL, HENRY JOSEPH, CW-USA; Wheeling, WVa (b/1840; d/VI-4-1873) MD Bellevue 1865. *Tr AMA* 25:535-36, 1874. *Tr M S WVa* 1873:630-32; 1884: 154.

WIESTLING, JACOB GROSS, CW-USA; Harrisburg, Pa (b/I-19-1827; d/I-10-1884) MD UPa 1849; AM Franklin & Marshall 1871. *U Pa med alum CW*: 1849. *Off'l Reg Pa phys* 1881-88:729.

WIESTLING, ROBERT ROSS, CW-USA; Middletown, Pa (b/VII-4-1837; d/VII-14-1889) MD UPa 1861; AB Washington & Jefferson 1857. *U Pa med alum CW*:1861.

WIGGIN, AUGUSTUS WISWALL, USA 1865-75 (b/1841 Wakefield, NH; d/III-7-1875 Ft Stevens, Ore) MD Georgt'n 1865; ng Bowdoin M C 1864; AB Dartmouth

1862. *Tr AMA* 28:635, 1877. *Med rec NY* 1875:248.

WIGGIN, CHARLES DEARBORN, Mystic, Conn (b/XII-7-1840 Meredith, NH; d/V-21-1904) MD Yale 1875; AB Brown 1868; AM. *Brown hist cat*: 1868.

WIGGIN, CHASE, Providence (b/XI-17-1812 Centre Harbor, NH: d/II-23-1891) MD Jefferson 1842; MD Dartmouth 1842; ng Bowdoin. *Bost m&s j* 124:248, 1891. *Tr RI M S* 4:338-40, 1889-93. *Butler* 1878:749.

WIGGIN, HENRY LOVE KEAG, Auburn, Me (b/IV-30 1820 Wolfeboro, NH; d/VIII-17-1875) MD CPSNY 1847. *Tr Me M Assn* 1874-76:432-34. *Butler* 1878:312.

WIGGIN, OLIVER CHASE, Kingston, RI (b/V-3-1839 Meredith, NH; d/II-2-1903 St Augustine, Fl) MD Harvard 1866; att Brown. *Tr RI M S* 6:676-78, 1899-1903. *Atkinson* I:267. *Polk* 1896: 1350.

WIGGINS, JOHN, St Louis (d/X-28-1894) MD CPSNY 1879;AB Harvd 1876 *JAMA* 23:735 1894 *Polk* 1890:904.

WIGGINS, LEVI OLMSTED, Newburgh, NY (d/XII-27 1891 @26) MD CPSNY 1888; AB Yale 1885. *Med reg NY NJ Conn* 1892:293. *JAMA* 18:30, 1892.

WIGGINS, LOUIS Y , Newburgh, NY (d/II-10-1896 @70) MD UCNY 1847. *JAMA* 26:391, 1896. *Polk* 1896:1034.

WIGGINTON, RICHARD MILES, Waukesha, Wis (b/II 21-1840 Usk, Engl; d/X-16-1898) MD Rush 1868. *JAMA* 31:1066, 1898. *Tr Wis St M S* 33:520-21, 1899. *Polk* 1886:962.

WIGGLESWORTH, EDWARD, CW-USA; Boston (b/XII-30-1840; d/I-23-1896) MD Harvard 1865; AB 1861. *Bost m&s j* 134:125, 126, 426, 1896. *Harvard in CW*: 177. *Med bull m&s* 18:114, 1896. *Atkinson* I: 668-69. *K&B* III: 1301-02.

WIGHT, JARVIS SHERMAN Sr, Brooklyn (b/I-4-1834 Centerville, NY; d/XI-16-1901) MD LICH 1864; AB Tufts 1861; AM 1882. *Bost m&s j* 145:582, 1901. *Tr M S St NY* 1902:[484]. *Atkinson* I: 262. *Polk* 1896: 1005.

WIGHT, NAHUM, Gilmanton, NH (b/XI-20-1807 Gilead, Me; d/V-4-1884) MD Bowdoin 1832. *Tr NH M S* 1884: 189-93. *Butler* 1878: 459.

WIGHT, ORLANDO WILLIAMS, Detroit (b/II-19-1824 Centerville, NY; d/XI- -1888) MD LICH 1865; Hon AM Yale 1859. *Bost m&s j* 119:640, 1888.

WIGHTMAN, JAMES, CW-USA (d/VI-15-1863 @22 Washington, DC) MD Harvard 1863. *Bost m&s j* 68:410, 1863. *Nat m j* 1:304, 1870/71. *Harvard in CW*: 284.

WIGTON, JACOB S , Spring Valley, NY (b/1828; d/IX-11-1888) MD UCNY 1850. *Med reg NY NJ Conn* 1889:289. *Butler* 1878:587.

WILBER, GEORGE DENSMORE, Silverton, Col; Mineral Pt, Wis (b/1828 Portland, NY; d/XII-11-1897 Pasadena, Cal) MD Ind Med Coll 1847. *Tr Wis St M S* 32:557, 1898. *Polk* 1890: 215.

WILBUR, GREENLEAF AUGUSTUS, Skowhegan, Me; CW-USA; (b/VIII-4-1820 Sidney; d/VII-19-1893) MD Jefferson 1850; ng Bowdoin Med 1849; AB Colby 1846. *Bowd'n cat*: 1849. *Atkinson* I: 620. *Polk* 1886: 429.

WILBUR, HERVEY BACKUS, Syracuse NY (b/VIII-18 1820 Wendell, Mass; d/V-1-1883) MD Berkshire 1842; AB Amherst 1838. *JAMA* 1:254, 1883. *Med reg NY NJ Conn* 1884:241 *Bost m&s j* 108:451 1883. *K&B* III:1302.

WILBUR, JOHN RICORD, Chicopee, Mass (b/1817 Leyden; d/IX-7-1878) MD Berkshire 1842. *Bost m&s j* 99:388, 481, 1878. *Mass M S cat* 1894.

WILBUR, JOSHUA GREEN, CW-USA; Brooklyn (b/IX-25-1825 Mass; d/VI-25-1895) MD Harvard 1862. *JAMA* 25:76, 1895. *Bost m&s j* 133:332, 1895. *Harvard in CW*: 277.

WILBUR, LLOYD, Hightstown, NJ (d/I-27-1900 @70) MD Jeff'n 1854. *JAMA* 34:381, 1900. *Polk* 1896: 937.

WILBUR, WILLIAM H , Westerly, RI (d/X-12-1879) MD UCNY 1847. *Med surg rep Phila* 41:374, 1879.

WILBUR, WILLIAM JOSEPH, Saxton's River, Vt (b/X 12-1861; d/1886?) MD U Vt 1884. *Med reg NY NJ Conn* 1887:277.

WILCOCKS, ALEXANDER, Philadelphia (b/1817; d/XI 10-1880) MD Jefferson 1844. *Tr CPP* cent vol: 273.

WILCOMB, WILLIAM WALLACE, Suncook, NH (b/X-15-1864 Chester; d/XII-1-1892) MD Bowdoin 1888. *Tr NH M S* 1893:160-61. *Bost m&s j* 127:564, 1892.

WILCOX, CHARLES H , CW-USA (d/XI-7-1862 Buffalo) MD ? *Nat m j* 1:304, 1870/71.

WILCOX, CHARLES K , Hico, La (d/XII-2-1894) MD Tulane 1875. *New Orl m&s j* ns22:558-59, 1898. *Polk* 1890: 487.

WILCOX, IRA, Franklin, NY (d/III- -1886) MD Bellevue 1867. *Med reg NY NJ Conn* 1886:257. *Butler* 1878:581.

WILCOX, JUSTUS DENSLOW, Granby, Conn (b/III-27-1800 Canton, Conn; d/III-27-1871) Hon MD Yale 1855; lic 1825. *Pr Conn M S* 1871: 503 ff.

WILCOX, LUCIAN SUMNER, Hartford, Conn (b/VII 17-1826 Granby; d/XII-26-1881) MD Yale 1855; AB 1850; AM 1855. *Tr AMA* 33:610, 1882. *Pr Conn M S* 1882:155-61. *Med rec NY* 20:643, 1881. *Atkinson* I:671.

WILCOX, MAJOR ALSTON, Halifax Co, NC (b/X-9-1797; d/III-30-1883) MD UPa 1822. *NC m j* 11:374, 1883. *Tr NC M S* 1887: 156.

WILCOX, WILLIAM LEROY, Irving Park, Ill (d/IX-22 1895 @35) MD Bennett 1883; MD Rush 1889. *JAMA* 25:554, 1895. *Chic m rec* 9:262, 1895. *Polk* 1895:335.

WILD, D M , Terre Haute, Ind (d/I-28-1868 @36) MD ? *Phila med reg & dir* 1871:295. *Med surg rep Phila* 18: 159, 1868.

WILD, EDWARD AUGUSTUS, USA (d/1891 Medalin, Colombia, SA) MD Jefferson 1846; AB Harvard 1844. *JAMA* 17:702, 1891. *Med bull m&s* 13:471, 1891.

WILD, JONATHAN, Braintree, Mass (b/IV-3-1784 S Weymouth; d/XII-7-1861) MD ? AB Harvard 1804; AM. Palmer, *Necrol Harv alum*: 399-400. *Bost m&s j* 65: 400, 1861.

 Spec. educ'l status abbrev. as: ***ng*** = college verified attendance without degree;

WILD, LEVI, Cincinnati (d/IX–25–1873 @30) MD Miami 1869. *Med surg rep Phila* 29:288, 1873.

WILDE, JAMES, Duxbury, Mass (d/X–15–1887 @75) MD Harvard 1835; AB 1832. *Bost m&s j* 117:396, 1887. *Polk* 1886:465.

WILDE, THOMAS, Brooklyn (d/X–6–1902) MD Bellevue 1866. *Bost m&s j* 147:448, 1902. *Polk* 1896: 1005.

WILDER, ABEL HERVEY, Bloomfield, NJ (b/VI–16–1801 Mass; d/I–2–1864) MD Dartmouth 1828. *Tr M S NJ* 1867:139–40.

WILDER, CHARLES WOODWARD, Leominster, Mass (b/XII–30–1790 Ashburnham; d/II–12–1851) MD Dartmouth 1817. *Bost m&s j* 44:86–87, 1851.

WILDER, FLAVIUS MYRON, Chicago (b/VI–24–1846 Oswego, NY; d/I–14–1892) MD U Mich 1868. *Chic m rec* 1:572, 1892. *Tr Ill St M S* 1892:34. *Polk* 1886:273.

WILDER, RUFUS LAWRENCE, NYC (b/VIII–31–1845 Leominster, Mass; d/XII–13–1888) MD Harvard 1867. *Med reg NY NJ Conn* 1889: 289. *Bost m&s j* 120: 28, 1889.

WILDING, ROBERT J , Malone, NY (d/III–2–1904 @67) Lic by Exam Bd 1855. *Tr M S St NY* 1904:[420]. *Polk* 1886: 656.

WILDMAN, ELIAS Sr, Philadelphia (d/VII–25–1876 @65) MD UPa 1834. *Med surg rep Phila* 35:180, 1876.

WILDMAN, ELIAS Jr, CW–USA; Fallsington, Pa (b/Yardleyville; d/XII–15–1877) MD UPa 1865. *U Pa med alum CW*: 1865.

WILDMAN, HENRY SMITH, Waterbury, Conn (b/II–16 1853 Brookfield; d/I–18–1894) MD LICH 1889. *Pr Conn M S* 1895: 363.

WILE, HENRY, Atlanta (d/IV–11–1887 en route to Denver) MD UPa 1882. *New Orl m&s j*ns14:986, 1887. *Polk* 1886: 225.

WILES, WILLAM V , Spencer, Ind (b/III–27–1827 Ripley, O; d/X–24–1892) MD Rush 1860. *Tr Ind St M S* 1893:252. *Butler* 1878: 225.

WILEY, ADAMS, Roxbury, Mass (b/XI–16–1826 Boston; d/IV–2–1860 Clifton, Mich) MD Harvard 1852; AB 1848. *Bost m&s j* 62:272, 1860. Palmer *Necrol Harv alum*: 331.

WILEY, ALFRED SOULE, Newton Highlands, Mass (b/V–12–1862 Kewanee, Ill; d/XII–20–1901) MD Dartmouth 1889. *Bost m&s j* 145:726, 1901. *Polk* 1896: 719.

WILEY, CHARLES R , Vineland, NJ (b/XI–2–1844 Goshen, NJ; d/IV–3–1897) MD Jefferson 1865. *Tr M S NJ* 1897: 297–99. *JAMA* 28:760, 1897. *Butler* 1878:478.

WILEY, JOHN, Cape May, NJ (b/VIII–6–1815; d/XII–24–1891) MD Jefferson 1837. *Tr M S NJ* 1892: . *Butler* 1878: 478.

WILEY, OSCAR, CW–CSA; Salem, Va (b/1830 Fincastle, Va; d/VIII–25–1904) <MD Randolph Macon 1851> MD Jefferson 1852. *Tr M S Va* 1904:326–28. *JAMA* 43: 748, 1904. *Polk* 1900: 1775.

WILEY, PHILANTHEUS CLEAVELAND, Bethel, Me (b/II–21–1840; d/IV–26–1877) MD Bowdoin 1864; AB 1861. *Tr Me M Assn* 1877:251–55. *Butler* 1878: 313.

WILEY, THOMAS ROYSTON, Gibson City, Ill (d/VI–30–1896 @52) MD Rush 1874. *JAMA* 27:109, 1896. *Polk* 1886: 280.

WILKERSON, BENJAMIN C , CW–CSA; Granville Co, NC (b/Blue Wing, NC; d/1870) MD UPa 1859; att Wake Forest. *U Pa med alum CW*: 1859.

WILKERSON, THOMAS BENTON, CW–CSA; Adoniram, NC (b/ VIII–14–1837; d/VII–12–1894) MD UPa 1859. *NC m j* 35:43, 1894. *U Pa med alum CW*: 1859.

WILKERSON, WILLIAM WASHINGTON, CW–CSA; Marion, Ala (b/VIII–15–1833 Tuscaloosa, Ala; d/III–7–1893) MD Jefferson 1855; att U Ala 1851. *U Ala cat*: 107. *Atkinson* I: 520. *Polk* 1886: 136.

WILKES, GEORGE, NYC (b/VIII–10–1801; d/XI–30–1876) MD CPSNY 1824; AB Columbia 1821. *Med reg NY NJ Conn* 1877:209. *Med rec NY* 12:15, 64, 1877; 15:47, 1879. *Med surg rep Phila* 35: 320, 1876.

WILKES, WILLIAM HENDERSON, Waco, Tex (b/IV–8–1833 Raymond, Miss; d/VIII–14–1896) MD U Nashvl 1855. *Tex m news* 5:516, 1895–96. *JAMA* 27:721–22, 1896. *Tex cour–rec med* 14:24, 1896. *Tex m j* 12:148–51, 1896–97. *Butler* 1878: 796.

WILKIE, MORTIMER VALLEAU, Cuddleback NY (d/VIII–31–1902 @45) MD CPSNY 1883. *Bost m&s j* 147: 312, 1902. *Polk* 1896: 1085.

WILKIN, CHARLES NORTON, NYC (b/1856 Middletown, NY; d/VI–6–1890) MD CPSNY 1878. *Bost m&s j* 122: 592, 1890. *Polk* 1886: 698.

WILKINS, ALEXANDER MARTIN, Pickensville, Ala (b/1817; d/III–15–1878) MD ? att U Ala 1835. *U Ala cat*: 58.

WILKINS, DAVID, Greenville, Ill (d/VII–23–1905 @76) MD U Mich 1853. *Ill m j* 8:185, 1905. *Polk* 1896: 422.

WILKINS, HENRY, Baltimore Co (b/1767 Annapolis; d/1847) MD UPa 1793. *Med annals Md:* 622.

WILKINS, JOSEPH, Baltimore (b/IX–21–1823; d/II–5 1902) MD UMd 1847. *Med annals Md:* 622.

WILKINS, WILLIAM WESLEY, Manchester, NH (b/VI–17–1829 DePeyster, NY; d/IX–1–1897) MD Woodstock 1856. *Bost m&s j* 127:252, 1892. *Tr NH M S* 1893:162– 63. *Polk* 1890: 710.

WILKINSON, J MARION, Dover, Del (d/VIII–25–1898 @48) MD UMd 1874. *JAMA* 31:618, 1898. *Polk* 1886: 206.

WILKINSON, JAMES, Jersey City, NJ (b/1837 Engl; d/II–18–1898) MD CPSNY 1858. *Bost m&s j* 138:190, 1898. *JAMA* 570, 1838.

WILKINSON, JOSEPH BIDDLE, New Orleans (b/1817; d/VII–21–1902) MD UPa 1839. *New Orl m&s j* 55:132, 1901. *Polk* 1886:531 (Pass Christian, Miss)

WILKINSON, THOMAS, Ann Arbor Mich (b/1799? d/V 26–1894 @95) MD Castleton 1824. *JAMA* 22:855, 1894.

WILKINSON, WALTER, Montgomery, Ala (d/II–9–

1905) MD Bellevue 1889. *New Orl m&s j* 57:704, 1905. *Polk* 1896: 940.

WILLARD, ALEXIS E , Friendship, NY (d/XI–20–1898 @67) MD Buffalo 1864. *Buff m&s j* 38:386–87, 1898. *JAMA* 31:1377, 1898.

WILLARD, ANDREW FULLER, Providence (b/Lancaster, Mass; d/VII–1–1885) <MD UPa 1860> AB Brown 1849. *Brown hist cat*: 1849.

WILLARD, AUGUSTUS, Greene, NY (b/VI–29–1799 Stafford, Conn; d/III–12–1868 Ellicottsville) MD Dartmouth 1824. *Tr M S St NY* 1869:264–66. *Med rec NY* 3:558, 1868–69.

WILLARD, DAVID, Chester, Conn 1861; Wilton (b/ 1789? d/II–9–1860 @71) MD ? *Med surg rep Phila* ns3:462, 1859/60. *Nashvl j m&s* 18:383, 1906. *Pr Conn M S* 1837:10. *K&B* III:305 (mention only).

WILLARD, FRANCIS ALEXANDER, Boston (d/I–27–1823 @64) MD Harvard 1832. *Bost m&s j* ns11:124, 1873. *Med surg rep Phila* 28:166.

WILLARD, GEORGE EDWIN, Chicago (b/1855; d/VI–9–1906 @51) MD Chic M C 1874. *Chic m rec* 28:412, 1906.

WILLARD, HENRY, Boston (b/V–18–1802 Holden, Mass; d/IX–24–1855) MD Harvard 1824. *Bost m&s j* 53: 214–15, 1856.

WILLARD, JOSIAH NEWELL, CW–USA; Philadelphia (d/V–1–1870 @34) MD Harvard 1860; AB 1857. *Bost m&s j* 5:344, 1870. *Harvard in CW*: 108–09.

WILLARD, MOSES THOMPSON, Concord, NH (b/VI–21–1806; d/V–31–1883) MD Dartmouth 1835. *JAMA* 1:254, 1883.

WILLARD, OLIVER AUGUSTUS, Lowell, Mass (d/I–7 1894 @28) MD Bellevue 1884. *JAMA* 22:97, 1894. *Bost m&s j* 130:52, 1894.

WILLARD, ROBERT, CW–USN; Boston (d/II–6–1892 @53) MD Harvard 1864; AB 1860. *Bost m&s j* 126:156, 1892. *Harvard in CW*:156. *Polk* 1890: 544.

WILLARD, S M , ?Indian Terr (d/XI–28–1873 @61 Choctaw Nation) MD ? *Med s rep Phila* 30:22, 1874.

WILLARD, SYLVESTER DAVID, CW–USA; Albany, NY (b/VI–19–1825 Wilton, Conn; d/IV–2–1865) MD Albany 1848. *Tr AMA* 18:311–13, 1867. *Buff m&s j* 4: 475, 1865. *Tr M S St NY* 1866:329–35. *K&B* III: 1305.

WILLENSKI, IRRANOFF, CW–USA (d/I–24–1865) MD ? *Nat m j* 1:304, 1870/71.

WILLETS, ANDREW JACKSON, CW–USA; Brooklyn (b/XI–30–1833; d/V–23–1870) MD CPSNY 1858; AB Yale 1855; AM 1858. *Med reg NY NJ Conn* 1871:366. *Med rec NY* 6:94, 1871/72.

WILLETT, E MILES Sr, Memphis (d/II–6–1888) MD Jefferson 1855. *New Orl m&s j* ns15:759, 1888. *Polk* 1886: 869.

WILLETT, JOHN EDWARD, Washington, DC (b/VI–23–1834 Rockville, Md; d/I–21–1887) MD Georgetown 1855. *Hist Med Soc DC:* 254.

WILLEY, SAMUEL, St Paul, Minn (d/X–21–1872 Bayfield, Wis @44) MD Cleveland Med Coll 1850. *Tr Minn St M S* 1873:114. *NW m&s j* 111:278–79, 1873.

WILLIAMS, ABRAHAM VALENTINE, Bloomingdale NY (b/VI–6–1802;d/II–28–1862) MD CPSNY 1824. *Tr AMA* 14:201–2 1864 *Med reg NY NJ Conn* 1865:210–12.

WILLIAMS, ADOLPHUS H , Nashville & Hendersonville, Tenn (d/IV–10 or 11–1896) MD U Nashvl & Vanderbilt 1875. *JAMA* 26:794, 843, 1896. *NC m j* 37: 277, 1896.

WILLIAMS, ALBERT, Boston (b/XI–14–1801 West Brookfield; d/III–13–1835) MD Bowdoin 1830; AB Amherst 1826. *Amherst, Men*: 1826.

WILLIAMS, ALBERT M , CW–USA; Bradford, Pa (b/ Meadville; d/1896) MD UPa 1867; AB Allegheny 1861. *U Pa med alum CW*: 1867. *Polk* 1886: 793.

WILLIAMS, AMOS LOOMIS, Brookfield, Conn (b/I–7 1811 Lebanon; d/IV–16–1896) MD Jefferson 1841. *Pr Conn M S* 1896: 322–26. *Butler* 1878: 84.

WILLIAMS, AUGUSTUS PURDY, CW–USA; Rutherford Park, NJ (b/1838 NYC; d/IV–11–1891) MD CPS NY 1860. *Med reg NY NJ Conn* 1891:282. *Bost m&s j* 124: 1891. *Butler* 1878: 478.

WILLIAMS, B BROWN, Meadville, Pa (d/II–15–1894 @79) MD Eclect M Inst Ohio 1847. *JAMA* 22: 313, 1894. *Polk* 1886: 807.

WILLIAMS, BODISCO, Washington, DC (b/1840; d/ XII–23–1873) MD Columbian 1863. *Tr AMA* 25:525, 1874. *Hist Med Soc DC:* 274–75.

WILLIAMS, CHARLES SMITH, Columbia City, Ind (b/VII–14–1842 NYC; d/VII–10–1905) No MD. *Tr Ind St M S* 1906: 489.

WILLIAMS, D BOONE, Philadelphia (d/XI–5–1873 Orange, Cal) MD ? *Med surg rep Phila* 28:345, 1873.

WILLIAMS, D J , Louisville (b/IV–17–1817; d/IX–20 1883) MD ? *Med surg rep Phila* 49: 420, 1883.

WILLIAMS, DATUS, E Haddam, Conn (b/II–25–1793 Norwich; d/XI–4–1867) Hon MD Yale 1843; lic 1823. *Pr Conn M S* 3:167–69, 1868. *Med surg rep Phila* 17: 436, 1867.

WILLIAMS, DAVID, Slatington, Pa (d/VI–1–1904 @42) MD Jefferson 1891. *Pa med jour* 8:330, 1904/05. *JAMA* 43:62, 1905. *Flint* 1897: 836.

WILLIAMS, DAVID B, Louisville (d/X–6–1895 @62) MD U Lsvl 1858. *JAMA* 25:682 1895. *Butler* 1878:267.

WILLIAMS, EDWARD NEWLIN, New Hope Pa (d/I–31–1902 @28 Me) MD UPa 1898 *Pa m j* 6:262 1902/03.

WILLIAMS, EDWARD PAYSON, Atlantic City, NJ (d/ IV–29–1900 @69) MD CPSNY 1875. *JAMA* 34:1211, 1900. *Polk* 1896: 933.

WILLIAMS, ELISHA, Hinsdale, Mass (d/1878 @53[!]) MD Castleton 1833. *Bost m&s j* 99: 777, 1878. *Mass M S* 1894.

WILLIAMS, ELKANAH, Cincinnati (b/XII–19–1822 Bedford, Ind; d/X–5–1888 Hazlewood, Pa) MD Lsvl M

Inst 1850. *Chic m j* 57:279, 1888. *Tr Ohio M S* 1889: 8, 265. *Med age* 6:494 1888. *Atksn* I:7–8 *K&B* III:1306–07.

WILLIAMS, FRANCKE, Aiken, SC (d/V–23–1871) MD ? *Bost m&s j* 7:376, 1871.

WILLIAMS, FREDERICK WILLIAM, CW–CSA; Laplace, Ala (b/XI–17–1830 Tuskegee; d/I–8–1890) MD UPa 1852; att U Ala 1849. *Tr M Assn St Ala* 1890:217. *U Pa med alum CW*: 1852. *Polk* 1886:135.

WILLIAMS, FREDERICK WILLIAM, NYC (d/XI–22 1899 @40 Colorado Spr) MD CPSNY 1885. *JAMA* 33: 1504, 1899. *Polk* 1896: 1085.

WILLIAMS, GEORGE CUSHMAN, Edgecombe, Me 1842–45; W Chester, Pa 1851–54, 1863–66; Philadelphia 1854–64; Coatesville, Pa 1866– (b/II–26–1818 Brewer, Me; d/III–10–1870 Coatesville) MD Bowdoin 1842; MD Hahnemann, Phila 1851. *Hahn mo* 7:180, 1871/72. Homeopath.

WILLIAMS, GEORGE MILTON, White Bluff, Ga (b/ XI– –1819 Savannah; d/X–19–1848) MD Jefferson 1847; AB Amherst 1840. *Amherst, Men of*: 1840.

WILLIAMS, GEORGE W , Aurora, Ill (d/III–23–1901) MD Northwestern 1873. *Ill m j* ns2:601, 1901.

WILLIAMS, HENRY E , CW–USA; E Haddam, Conn (d/XII–4–1870 @45) MD UCNY 1847. *Med reg NY NJ Conn* 1871: 368.

WILLIAMS, HENRY WILLARD, Boston (b/XII–11–1821; d/VI–14–1895 @73) MD Harvard 1849; Hon AM 1868; stud med Europe. *Bost m&s j* 132: 632, 654, 1895. *Buff m&s j* 35:177–78, 1895. *Tr RI M S* 5:243–44, 1894–98. *Atkinson* I: 649. *K&B* III: 1367.

WILLIAMS, HEZEKIAH, CW–USA; Alton, Ill 1854– (b/III–10–1827 Castine, Me; d/V–22–1872) MD Cleveland M C 1850; att Bowdoin 1844–47. *Bowd'n cat*: 1848.

WILLIAMS, HUGH TIMBERLAKE, Rising Sun Ind (b/ V–27–1812 Breckinridge Co, Ky; dXII–22–1879) MD Lsvl M Inst 1842. *Tr Ind St M S* 1880:244–45. Kemper's *Indiana*: 356. *Butler* 1878: 220.

WILLIAMS, J C , Bloomingdale, O (d/VI–8–1868) MD M C Ohio 1848. *Phila med reg & dir* 1871: 297.

WILLIAMS, JACOB LAFAYETTE, Boston (d/V–15–1906 @82) MD Harvard 1848. *Bost m&s j* 154:598, 1906. *Polk* 1896: 708.

WILLIAMS, JAMES ALEXANDER, NYC (b/Sinking Spr O; d/VIII–15–1901 @61) MD Rush 1863; MD Bellevue 1866. *Bost m&s j* 145:230, 1901. *Polk* 1896: 1085.

WILLIAMS, JAMES EDWARD, CW–CSA; Richmond, Va (b/X– –1828; d/VII– –1883) MD UPa 1846. *U Pa med alum CW*: 1846.

WILLIAMS, JEHIEL, New Milford, Conn (b/X–4–1781 Lebanon; d/VI–9–1862) Hon MD Yale 1822; lic 1807. *Pr Conn M S* 1863:299–303.

WILLIAMS, JOHN B, Brooklyn (b/Engl; d/X–13–1878/ 79?) MD UCNY 1855. *Med reg NY NJ Conn* 1879: 202.

WILLIAMS, JOHN D , Orange, NJ (b/XI–5–1765; d/I–25–1826) MD ? *Tr M S NJ* 1865–67: 132–34?

WILLIAMS, JOHN S, Gladys Va (d/IV–9–1905 @69) MD UCNY 1860 *So pract* 27:336 1905 *Butler* 1878:839.

WILLIAMS, JOSEPH B , Grafton, Ind (b/Cynthiana; d/I 6–1901) <MD Rush> *Tr Ind St M S* 1901: 503.

WILLIAMS, JOSEPH [or JAMES] MILLARD, Montgomery, Ala; CW–CSA (b/VIII–7–1832; d/X–15–1882) MD UPa 1853; att U Ala 1848. *Tr M Assn St Ala* 1883: 244. *U Pa med alum CW*: 1853. *Butler* 1874: 27.

WILLIAMS, LEROY B , Deedsville, Ind (b/IX–15–1847 Clermont Co, O; d/I–31–1880) MD Ind M C 1873. *Tr Ind St M S* 1881: 230.

WILLIAMS, LEWIS, Pomfret, Conn (b/VII–12–1815; d/VI–22–1881) MD Harvard 1842; ng Amherst 1838. *JAMA* 2:25, 1884. *Pr Conn M S* 1882:171–75. *Atkinson* I:341. *Butler* 1878: 84.

WILLIAMS, LEWIS, Marion, Ind (b/IV–17–1825 Clinton Co, O; d/III–5–1906) MD Miami 1857. *Tr Ind St M S* 1906: 494. *Polk* 1896: 481.

WILLIAMS, LEWIS JEFFERY, USN 1842–81 (b/X–14 1819 Havre de Grace, Md; d/IV–8–1888 Baltimore) MD UPa 1841; AB Princeton 1838. *U Pa m alum CW*: 1841.

WILLIAMS, MARTIN H Jr, Philadelphia (d/VI–30–1901 @39) MD Jefferson 1887. *Pa med jour* 5:296, 1901/02. *Flint* 1897: 827.

WILLIAMS, MATHEW WYATT, NC; CW–CSA (b/ 1818 Warren Co, NC; d/1888 NC) MD UPa 1845; att Wake Forest. *U Pa med alum CW*: 1845.

WILLIAMS, MERRILL WHITNEY, NYC (b/VII–14–1801 Colchester, Conn; d/XII–3–1873) Hon MD Yale 1850. *Med reg NY NJ Conn* 1874:293. *Med s rep Phila* 29:468, 1873; 30:132, 1874. *Med rec NY* 9:71, 1874.

WILLIAMS, OLIVER C , Muskegon, Mich (d/VII–8–1901 @65) <MD UCNY 1858> *JAMA* 37:213, 1901. *Polk* 1886: 499.

WILLIAMS, ORLANDO SILLS, Disputanta, Va (b/1828 Mecklenburg Co; d/I–12–1900) MD UVa 1851; MD Jefferson 1852. *Tr M S Va* 1900:320. *Polk* 1886: 916.

WILLIAMS, PHILIP CROUDSON, Baltimore (b/VIII–15–1828 Winchester, Va; d/XI–21–1896) MD UPa 1850; att UMd M Sch; stud Paris, Berlin, Vienna. *Med annals Md:* 623. *Atkinson* I:152. *Polk* 1886: 440.

WILLIAMS, PLATT, Albany, NY 1816–45; Alder Creek 1845–67; NYC (b/IX–17–1784 Huntington, NY; d/XII–8–1870) <MD CPSNY> AB Williams 1804. *Tr AMA* 24:368–69, 1873. *Tr M S St NY* 1873: 175–77.

WILLIAMS, R B , Woodburn, Ky (d/IX–8–1878 Memphis) MD ? *Med rec NY* 14:220, 1878. *Tr AMA* 30:888, 1879.

WILLIAMS, RICHARD, Milford, NH (b/c 1803; d/X–6–1842) MD Dartmouth 1830; ng Amherst 1829. *Amherst, Men of*: 1829.

WILLIAMS, RICHARD DALTON, Ireland; Mobile, Ala; Thibodeaux, La (b/1821/22? Co Tipperary; d/VIII–5 1862) MD ? att Carlow Coll. *Med surg rep Phila* ns8: 412, 1862.

WILLIAMS, ROBERT E , USA; San Francisco (d/XII 30-1902) MD Georgetown 1870. *Cal st j m* 1:70, 1903. *Polk* 1886: 175.

WILLIAMS, SAMUEL CLARENCE, CW-USA (b/XI-18-1834 Middlesex, Pa; d/II-25-1906 Hampton, Va) MD UPa 1858. *U Pa med alum CW*: 1858.

WILLIAMS, SETH WESTON, Portland, Me (d/IX-20-1879) MD Bellevue 1876. *Bost m&s j* 101:530-31, 1879. *Med rec NY* 16: 335-36, 1879.

WILLIAMS, STEPHEN WEST, Deerfield, Mass (b/III-27-1790; d/VII-7-1855 Laona Ill) Hon MD Berkshire 1824;att CPSNY 1812-3. *Bost m&s j* 62:507 1855; 53:29 -32, 1856. *Tr AMA* 29:775-77, 1878. *K&B* III: 1308-09.

WILLIAMS, THEODORE STRONG, Germantown, Pa 1847-57? Haddonfield, NJ (b/Me; d/VI-29-1899) MD Hahnemann Phila 1850; ng Bowdoin Med Sch 1842. *Bowdoin cat*: 1842. Homeopath.

WILLIAMS, THOMAS B , Delaware, O (b/1821 S Wales; d/VIII-20-1879) MD M C Ohio 1849. *Tr Ohio St M S* 1880: 116-17.

WILLIAMS, THOMAS CROCKER, Germantown Pa ca 1850; Philadelphia (b/1814 Bangor Me; d/X-1-1899) MD Hahnemann Phil 1853; ThB Bangor Theol Sem 1845. *Hahn mo* 1899 (news & advt, Nov) Homeopath.

WILLIAMS, THOMAS GEORGE, Watertown Wis (b/VIII-28-1844 Waukesha Co; d/I-18-1875 Cal) MD Chicago M C 1869; MD Bellevue 1872. *Tr Wis St M S* 1875: 95-96.

WILLIAMS, W H , Denver (d/III-15-1893 @53) MD ULa 1867. *Tr Col St M S* 1898-99: 509. *Polk* 1893:239.

WILLIAMS, WILLIAM CHAUNCEY, Hartford Co, Conn (b/1800 Lebanon; d/X-6-1857) Hon MD Yale 1842/ *Pr Conn M S* 1858: 113.

WILLIAMS, WILLIAM COOK, Cheshire, Conn (d/V-21-1894) MD Yale 1850. *JAMA* 22:855, 1894. *Polk* 1886: 191.

WILLIAMSON, A C , Kerens, Tex 1899- (b/X-28-1864 Newton Co, Miss; d/II-6-1905) <MD Barnes St Louis 1899> *Tex st jour med* 1:246, 1905/06.

WILLIAMSON, ABNER CRANE, Urbana, Ill (d/IV-8-1905 @65) MD Pulte 1879. *Ill m j* 7:379, 524, 1905. *Polk* 1896: 327 (Atlanta).

WILLIAMSON, AMOS P [or N], Washington, DC (b/1828 Fayetteville, NC; d/XII-22-1884) MD Columbian 1859. *Hist Med Soc DC:* 283. *Butler* 1874: 95.

WILLIAMSON, CHARLES HENRY, USN 1850-61; CSA 1861-65 (b/VIII-27-1826 Portsmouth, Va; d/IX-10-1894) MD UPa 1849. *Med reg NY NJ Conn* 1895: 246. *JAMA* 23:479, 1894. *U Pa med alum CW*:1849. *Polk* 1886: 650.

WILLIAMSON, GEORGE, NYC (d/XII-8-1889) MD UCNY 1875. *Med reg NY NJ Conn* 1890:284. *Polk* 1886: 698.

WILLIAMSON, GEORGE HENRY, Delphos, O (d/V-1 1899 @45) MD UMich 1895. *JAMA* 32:1074, 1899. *Polk* 1896: 753.

WILLIAMSON, GEORGE ROBERT, Nashville; CW-served wounded of both sides after battles (b/XII-13-1836 Salem, NC; d/II-18-1904) MD UPa 1860. *U Pa med alum CW*: 1860. *Polk* 1886: 871.

WILLIAMSON, J C , Honey Grove, Tex (d/VI-22-1896 @21) MD Ft Worth U 1896. *Texas cour-rec med* 14:1896.

WILLIAMSON, JACOB W , Somerville, NJ (b/V-12-1821; d/VIII-9-1852) MD UPa 1846 *Tr M S NJ* 1872:176.

WILLIAMSON, JAMES EDWARDS, Caswell Co, NC (d/I-23-1867) MD UPa 1825. *Tr NC M S* 1867: 39.

WILLIAMSON, JAMES GARDNER PAXTON, New Market, Va (b/V-19-1857; d/III-27-1894) MD UVa 1877. *Tr M S Va* 1894: 185-86.

WILLIAMSON, JEFFERSON, Ottumwa, Ia (b/III-31 1827 Adams Co, O; d/I-21-1904) MD West Res 1852; att Rush 1865-66. *Tr Ia St M S* 22:343, 1904. *Atkinson* I:133. *Polk* 1886: 365.

WILLIAMSON, NICHOLAS, New Brunswick, NJ (b/III-9-1845 NYC; d/VIII-15-1902) MD CPSNY 1872; MD UCNY 1871. *Bost m&s j* 147:224, 1902. *Tr M S NJ* 1903: 379. *Polk* 1896: 945.

WILLIAMSON, THOMAS, USN 1818- (b/1791; d/I-12-1859) MD ? *Tr AMA* 13:823-25, 1860. *Callahan*.

WILLIAMSON, THOMAS W C , CW-USA (d/V-24 1863 Champion, Miss) MD UCNY 1851. *Nat m j* 1:304, 1870/71.

WILLIAMSON, W L , CW-USA (d/I-20-1865) MD ? *Nat m j* 1:304, 1870/71.

WILLIAMSON, WALTER, Philadelphia (b/I-4-1811 Newtown, Pa; d/XII-19-1870) MD UPa 1833. *Tr Am Inst Hom* 1871:117. *Tr Hom M S Pa* 1873:158. *New Engl med gaz* 6:47, 1870. *Cleave*. Homeopath.

WILLIAMSON, WALTER MARTIN, Appleton, Wis 1858-61; Philadelphia 1861- (b/VII-3-1836 Newtown, Pa; d/V-5-1874) MD Hahnemann Phila 1857. *Am hom obs* 11:480, 1874. *Tr Hom M S St Pa* 2:83-84, 1874-78. *Hahn mo* 9:527, 1873/74. *Cleave*. Homeopath.

WILLIAMSON, WILLIAM BOSWELL, Edwards, Miss; Mex War-USA; CW-CSA (b/XI-23-1812 Sussex CH, Va; d/IX-27-1878) MD UPa 1835. *Tr AMA* 30:888, 1879. *Tr Miss St M Assn* 1879:39-40. *Atkinson* I: 571.

WILLING, CHARLES, Philadelphia (b/X-26-1805; d/IX-31-1887) MD UPa 1828; AB 1825. *Med bull m&s* 9:284, 1887.

WILLIS, ALEXANDER B , Johnsonville, NY (b/Coeymans, NY; d/V-10-1891) MD Albany 1870. *Tr M S St NY* 11:741 ff, 1894. *Polk* 1886: 665.

WILLIS, CHARLES NOTT, New Brunswick, NJ (b/IX-11-1858; d/IV-2-1883) MD CPSNY 1882. *Med reg NY NJ Conn* 1884: 242.

WILLIS, HARRISON, Brooklyn (b/VII-15-1836 Rehoboth, Mass; d/XII-2-1897) MD Cleveland Hom

1865; ng Berkshire 1862. *Tr Am Inst Hom* 1898: 49. *No Am j hom* 46:49, 1898. *Polk* 1886: 650.

WILLIS, JOEL SELMAN, Waco, Tex (b/X-6-1849 Barnesville, Ga; d/VII-6-1886) MD Bellevue 1872. *Tex cour-rec med* 3:527, 1886. *Atkinson* I: 489.

WILLIS, LATHROP A , Brooklyn (d/I-2-1885 @60) MD Albany 1849. *Med surg rep Phila* 52:159, 1885. *Butler* 1878: 521.

WILLIS [WILLS], WILLIAM S , USN (d/I-29-1869 or 1870 Port-au-Prince, Haiti or Key West, Fla) MD CPS NY 1864. *Tr AMA* 21:498, 1870. *Med rec* 6:94, 1871-72. *Nat m j* 1:304, 1870/71. *Phila m reg & dir* 1871: 303.

WILLITS, MARY, Norristown, Pa (b/X-16-1855; d/XII 16-1902 @47) MD Woman's Med Coll Pa 1881. *Pa med jour* 6:262, 1902/03. *Flint* 1897: 812.

WILLS, FRANCIS REED, Port Deposit, MD (b/IV-25-1803 Port Tobacco; d/VI-22-1872) MD UMd 1828. *Med annals Md:* 624.

WILLS, JESSE J , Camden, NJ (d/V-20-1894) MD Jefferson 1884. *Tr M S NJ* 1894: 263. *Polk* 1886: 602.

WILLS, SAMUEL E, Earlville, Md (b/1823 NJ; d/VII-10 1886) MD Jeff 1844. *Med ann Md:* 624. *Polk* 1886: 442.

WILLS, W S , ? (d/1878 Brownsville, Tenn) MD ? *Tr AMA* 30: 888, 1879.

WILLSON, ALEXANDER DUNCAN, Brooklyn; CW-USA (b/XII- -1836 Canandaigua, NY; d/III-10-1873) MD CPSNY 1859. *Med reg NY NJ Conn* 1873: 359.

WILLSON, HARRY GILBERT, Warrensville, Pa (d/I-21-1902) MD UPa 1895. *Pa med jour* 5: 314, 1901/02.

WILLSON, JOHN, Philadelphia (b/1840; d/IV-30-1870 Ft Scott, Kans) MD Jefferson 1861; AB UPa 1859. *Phila med reg & dir* 1871:305. *Tr AMA* 21:454-55, 1870.

WILLSON, WILLIAM GREENBURY GOLDSBOROUGH, Easton, Md (b/XI-26-1818; d/X-21-1894) MD UPa 1838. *Med annals Md:* 625. *Polk* 1886: 442.

WILMARTH, FRANK, Essex, NJ (b/III-28-1841 Smithfield, RI; d/VI-7-1881) MD CPSNY 1868; AB Rutgers 1867. *Tr M S NJ* 1882:183-84. *Butler* 1878:478. *Atkinson* I:451.

WILMARTH, JEROME, Milford, Mass (b/Montague; d/X-7-1890 @59) MD Harvard 1866. *Bost m&s j* 123: 360, 1890.

WILSEY, FERDINAND LITTLE, ?NYC (d/1862?) MD CPSNY 1844. *Med reg NY NJ Conn* 1862: 153.

WILSON, ABRAM DURYEA, NYC (d/VI-20-1864 @63) MD CPSNY 1821; AB Columbia 1818; AM 1821. *Am hom rev* 4:384, 1864. *Cleave.* Homeopath.

WILSON, ALFRED D , USA; Washington, DC (b/1839; d/1875 Camp McDowell, Ariz) MD UCNY 1863. *Med rec* 10:863, 1875. *Tr AMA* 28: 636, 1877.

WILSON, ALPHONSO S , Wilkesbarre, Pa (d/V-27-1902 @39) MD UPa 1892. *Pa med jour* 7:280, 1903/04. *Flint* 1897: 840. *Tr Luzerne Co (Pa) M S* 1903: 177.

WILSON, ANDREW C , Yazoo City, Miss (d/I-14-1860 @22 Philadelphia) Med stud UPa at death. *Med surg rep Phila* ns3:376, 1859/60.

WILSON, ARTHUR HERVEY, S Boston (b/VIII-18-1839 Paxton; d/V-11-1890) MD Dartmouth 1864. *Bost m&s j* 122:486-87, 536, 1890. *Polk* 1886: 473.

WILSON, ARTHUR MONTGOMERY, Philadelphia (d/III-31-1884 @21) MD UPa 1882. *Med surg rep Phila* 50: 512, 1884.

WILSON, CHARLES MEIGS, Knoxville (b/VII-29-1860 Phila; d/XII-29-1891) MD Jefferson 1883. *Med bull m&s* 14:77, 1892.

WILSON, CLAUDE [CLAUDIO], Waterville, NY (b/I-6 1850 Palmer, Mass; d/IV-22-1896) MD CPSNY 1876; AB Amherst 1871. *JAMA* 26:995, 1896. *Polk* 1886: 714.

WILSON, DAVID J , Baird, Tex (d/VI-19-1897) MD U Buffalo 1870. *Tex cour-rec med* 14:354, 1897. *Tex m news* 6:391, 1896-97. *Polk* 1896: 1070.

WILSON, DeWITT CLINTON, Painesville, O (d/IX-26 1894 @56) MD Bellevue 1870. *JAMA* 23:624, 1894. *Polk* 1890:920.

WILSON, ELLWOOD, Philadelphia (b/II-4-1822 Bucks Co, Pa; d/VII-14-1889 WaWa) MD Jefferson 1845. *Med bull m&s* 11:265, 1889. *Tr CPP* cent vol:274. *Med surg rep Phila* 61:112, 1889. *K&B* III: 1312.

WILSON, EZRA HERBERT, Brooklyn (b/Port Jefferson, NY; d/XII-19-1905 @47) MD CPSNY 1882. *Bost m&s j* 153:737, 1905. *Polk* 1896: 1005.

WILSON, GEORGE, NYC (b/VII-19-1822; d/II-25-1871) MD CPSNY 1845. *Med reg NY NJ Conn* 1871: 368. *Med surg rep Phila* 24:218, 1871.

WILSON, GEORGE, Dubois, Pa (d/XI-8-1894 @80) MD ? *JAMA* 23:802, 1894.

WILSON, GEORGE A , Peoria, Ill (d/IV-6-1900 @59) MD Rush 1866. *JAMA* 34:957, 1900. *Tr Ill St M S* 1899-1900: 574. *Polk* 1896: 435.

WILSON, GEORGE WARE, CW-USN (d/IV-24-1864 on US steamer Hetzel off NC) MD Chic M C 1864.*Nat m j* 1:304, 1870/71.

WILSON, GROVE HERRICK, W Meriden, Conn (d/I-10-1902) MD Berkshire 1849. *Tr Am Inst Hom* 1902: 850.)1886:193. Homeopath.

WILSON, HALL, Augusta, Tex (d/III-29-1906) MD Tulane 1888. *Tex st j m* 2:36, 1906. *Polk* 1896: 1415.

WILSON, HENRY, Oberlin O (d/IV-24-1897 @56) MD Buffalo 1872. *JAMA* 28:1045, 1897. *Polk* 1896:1206.

WILSON, HENRY PARKE CUSTIS, Baltimore (b/III-5 1827 Somerset Co; d/XII-27-1898) MD UMd 1851; AB Princeton 1848; AM 1851. *Med annals Md:* 625. *JAMA* 30:106, 1898. *Atkinson* I:73. *K&B* III: 1313.

WILSON, HUGH OSMUN, CW-USA; Slatington, Pa (b/XI-30-1823 Bath; d/II-24-1879) MD UPa 1845; att Lafayette. *Lafayette, Men of*: 153.

WILSON, JAMES, Plano Tex (d/V-4-1905) <MD Memphis M C 1848> *Tex st j m* 1:32, 1905/06.

WILSON, JAMES B , Creston, Ia (b/1836; d/1892) MD Mo M C 1872 *Tr Ia St M S* 18:412 1900. *Polk* 1890: 411.

WILSON, JAMES FOSTER, CW–USA; Philadelphia (b/VI– –1837 No Ireland; d/VII–18–1891) MD UPa 1864. *U Pa med alum CW*: 1864. *Polk* 1886: 827.

WILSON, JAMES FRANKLIN, Wilmington, Del (b/I–22–1818; d/IX–6–1868) MD ? *Phila m reg & dir* 1871: 298. *Hist M S DC:* 51. *Med s rep Phila* 19:330, 1868.

WILSON, JAMES HENRY, Philadelphia (d/VII–9–1865 @47) MD ? *Med surg rep Phila* 13:66, 1865.

WILSON, JAMES P , CW–USA (d/VII–5–1864 Harrisburg, Pa) MD Jefferson 1846 (?) *Nat m j* 1:304, 1870/71.

WILSON, JAMES W , Fremont, O (d/VII–21–1904 @ 88) MD Jefferson 1837. *JAMA* 32:485, 1904.

WILSON, JEREMIAH W , Contoocock, NH (b/I–11–1816 Salisbury, NH; d/IV–30–1846. *Tr NH M S* 1896: 183. *Polk* 1890: 708.

WILSON, JOB, Salisbury, NH 1813– (b/I–25–1776 Gilmanton, NH; d/IX– –1851 Franklin, NH) MD Dartmouth 1823; MB 1804. *NH j m* 2:55, 1851.

WILSON, JOHN BUTLER, CW–USA; Dexter, Me 1865– (b/II–24 1834 Portland; d/III–15–1866 Ft Gaines, Ala) MD Bowdoin 1858; MD Jefferson 1859; AB Colby 1854. *Bost m&s j* 74: 228, 1866. *Nat m j* 1:304, 1870/71.

WILSON, JOHN G , Martinsburg, WVa (b/VII–5–1819 Petersburg, Pa; d/III–1–1873) MD Jefferson 1841. *Tr AMA* 24:388–89, 1873. *Tr M S WVa* 1873: 472.

WILSON, JOHN HEWITT, NYC (b/Ireland; d/VII–17–1898 @80) <MD CPS Glasgow 1844> *Bost m&s j* 139, 74:1898. *JAMA* 31:257, 1898. *Polk* 1896: 1085.

WILSON, JOHN JOSEPH, Bristol, Conn (d/II–20–1905 @51) <MD CPS Balto 1886> *Pr Conn M S* 1905:515.

WILSON, JOHN ROBERTSON, Davidson Co, Tenn (b/IV–4–1799 SC; d/VIII–8–1854) MD Transylvania 1825. *Tr MS Tenn* 1876: 89.

WILSON, JOHN RUSSELL, Washington Co, Pa (b/IX–7–1822; d/III–15–1873) MD Jefferson 1850. *Tr M S Pa* 9:238–39, 1873.

WILSON, JOHN THEODORE, Galesburg, Ill (b/IX–10 1857 Sweden; d/XI–27–1896) MD Howard 1881. *JAMA* 27:1215, 1896. Black?

WILSON, JOSEPH, USN 1843–78 (b/Frankford, Pa I–5 1816; d/III–1–1887 Phila) MD UPa 1837. *Med surg rep Phila* 56:352, 1887. *U Pa med alum CW*: 1837.

WILSON, JOSHUA, Harford Co, Md (d/IV– –1885) MD UMd 1818. *Med bull m&s* 7:164, 1885.

WILSON, MILES ALEXANDER, Radford, Pa (b/1822 Brunswick Co, Va; d/II–4–1889) MD Jefferson 1846. *Tr M S Va* 1892:200–01. *Butler* 1878: 839.

WILSON, MILO A , Brooklyn; Denver (b/1845 Pittsburgh; d/VII–5–1882) MD M C Ohio 1866. *Med reg NY NJ Conn* 1883:239. *Bost m&s j* 107:68, 1882. *Tr Col St M S* 1898–99: 508. *Butler* 1878: 528.

WILSON, MOSES SWETT, Lincoln, Me (d/1900 @75) MD Castleton 1846. *JAMA* 34:703, 1900. *Polk* 1886:426.

WILSON, NEEDHAM M , Philadelphia (d/I–19–1904 @67) MD Jefferson 1866. *Pa med jour* 8:336, 1904/05. *Flint* 1897: 827.

WILSON, OSCAR EUGENE, Versailles, Ill (b/1858 Chambersburg, Ill; d/X–24–1882) MD CPS Keokuk 1881. *Chic m j* 45:559, 1882.

WILSON, ROBERT Q , Kokomo, Ind (b/XI–23–1822 Concord, Pa; d/III–30–1902) MD Rush 1853. *Tr Ind St M S* 1902:428. *Polk* 1896: 477.

WILSON, ROBERT VAN VALZAH, Clearfield, Pa (b/X– –1828 Spring Mills; d/II–13–1878) MD Jefferson 1849. *Tr M S Pa* 12:302–03, 1878.

WILSON, SAMUEL, White Hall, Pa; Quincy, Ill; CW–USA (b/IX–2–1822 Bath; d/V–4–1862 on ship at Pittsburg Landing, Tenn) MD UPa 1844; att Lafayette 184–. *Lafayette, Men of*: 153. *U Pa med alum CW*: 1844.

WILSON, SAMUEL ALLEN, Windsor, Conn (b/IX–9–1828; d/X–9–1904) MD Yale 1852. *Pr Conn M S* 1905: 79, 489 ff. *Butler* 1878: 84.

WILSON, THOMAS HOWARD, CW–USA; Lewisburg, Pa (b/V–17–1821; d/VIII–21–1903) MD UPa 1844. *Pa m j* 7:280 1903/4. *UPa m alum CW*:1844. *Flint* 1897:807.

WILSON, W FLETCHER, Denver (d/VI– –1889 @ c30) MD NY Ophthalmic & Aural Inst 1881. *Med surg rep Phila* 61:140, 1889.

WILSON, WILEY H , Lake Geneva, Wis (b/I–6–1842 La Grange, Ga; d/II–27–1898) MD Ky Sch Med 1880. *JAMA* 30:624, 1898.

WILSON, WILLIAM, Bethlehem, Pa (d/V–21–1866) MD UPa 1844. *Med surg rep Phila* 14:440, 1866.

WILSON, WILLIAM, NYC (d/1872 @67 Mendham, NJ) MD CPSNY 1829; AB Columbia 1825. *Med surg rep Phila* 27:524, 1872. *Tr AMA* 24:365, 1873.

WILSON, WILLIAM B , Philadelphia (b/1820; d/V–7 1851) MD UPa 1843; AM Emmetsburg, Md. *Tr CPP* cent vol:274; ns1:223–25, 1850–53.

WILSON, WILLIAM CHRISTY, New Orleans (b/1824 Pointe Coupee Parish, La; d/VI– –1902) MD U Lsvl 1848. *New Orl m&s j* 55:68, 1902. *Polk* 1886: 418.

WILSON, WILLIAM RANDOLPH, CW–CSA; Dixon, Mo (b/VIII–12–1838 Brierfield, Va; d/VI–6–1900 Rolla) MD UPa 1860. *U Pa med alum CW*: 1860.

WILSTACH, CHARLES FREDERICK, Lafayette, Ind (b/IX–3–1794 Phila; d/VII–1–1860) MD UPa 1820; PhM 1823. *Tr Ind St M S* 1870: 163.

WILTBANK, JOHN, Philadelphia (b/1806; d/IX–11–1860) MD UPa 1825; AB 1822. *Tr CPP* cent vol: 274. *Med s rep Phila* ns4:510, 1860. *Tr Pa St M S* 1862: 126.

WILTBANKS, ALFRED S , Lewes, Del (d/VIII–7–1860 @30) MD Med Dept Pa Coll 1850. *Med surg rep Phila* ns4: 427, 1860.

WILY, PENROSE, Leesport, Pa (b/IX–21–1815 Maidencreek; d/IV–19–1875) ng UPa 182– . *Tr Pa St M S* 1875:594.

WIMMER, JAMES MONROE, Richmond, Ind (b/X–19 1853 Grant Co; d/XII–28–1897) MD Howard 1890. *Tr Ind St M S* 1898: 383. *Polk* 1896: 481. Black?

 Spec. educ'l status abbrev. as: ***ng*** = college verified attendance without degree;

WINANS, CHARLES HARRISON, Bellville, NJ (d/XI-22-1899 Liberty, NJ) MD UCNY 1890. *JAMA* 33:1504, 1899. *Polk* 1896: 933.

WINBORNE, ROBERT HENRY, Barnitz[?], NC (b/VII 12-1826; d/XI-7-1898) MD UPa 1855; AB UNC 1847; AM 1850. *NC m j* 42:379, 1898. *Polk* 1886: 720.

WINBORNE, ROBERT W , Chowan Co, NC (d/X-11-1890 @25) MD UMd 1887. *NC m j*: 27:61, 1891.

WINCHELL, MARTIN EBENEZER, NYC (b/X--1829; d/V-1-1864) MD Yale 1853. *Med reg NY NJ Conn* 1865: 228.

WINCHESTER, WILLIAM, Elgin, Ill (d/XI-20-1893) <MD Rush 1859> *JAMA* 21:869, 1893. *Polk* 1890: 329.

WINDERS, JOHN K , Baltimore (d/XI-26-1886) MD UMd 1875. *New Orl m&s j* ns14:559. *Polk* 1886: 440.

WINDHAM, JAMES ALEXANDER, Memphis (b/II-23 1819; d/VIII-1854) MD ? att U Ala 1838. *U Ala cat*:61.

WINDSHIP, CHARLES MAY, Roxbury, Mass (d/VI-19 1865 @56) MD Harvard 1829. *Bost m&s j* 72:516, 1865.

WINDSHIP [WINSHIP], CHARLES WILLIAMS, Roxbury, Mass (b/VI-22-1774 Boston; d/VIII-27-1852) MD Glasgow 1797; AB Harvard 1793; AM 1797. Palmer *Necr Harv alum*: 11. *Bost m&s j* 47: 175 ff, 1852.

WINER, WILLIAM DICKINSON, Chicago (b/IX-3-1831 Hamilton, Ont; d/X-21-1872) <MD Kings Coll Toronto c1853> *Med reg Chic* 1872-73: 336-37.

WING, AUSTIN, NYC (b/IX-30-1818 Hinsdale, Mass; d/V-16-1856 Centr Amer) MD ? AB Amherst 1844. *Amherst, Men of*: 1844.

WING, HENRY, Collinsville, Ill (b/IV- -1822 Troy, Mo; d/II-18-1871) MD Ill Coll Med Dept 1846. *Tr Ill St M S* 1874: 158-59.

WING, JOEL A , Columbia Co, NY; Albany 1814- (b/VIII-13-1788 Hinsdale, Mass; d/IX-6-1852 Hartford, Conn) Lic Montg'y Co, NY M S 1811; Hon MD Berkshire 1825. *Tr M S St NY* 1853: [345]-349.

WING, THEODORE TYLER, CW-USA; Susquehanna, Pa (b/VI 1-1844 Phila; d/XI-8-1887) MD UPa 1873; AB Dickinson 1864; ThB Union Theol 1868. *U Pa med alum CW*: 1873. *Polk* 1886: 836.

WINGATE, WILLIAM L , Federalsburg, Md (d/IV-15 1851) MD UMd 1845. *Bost m&s j* 44:345, 1851. *Med annals Md:* 627.

WINGERT, HARVEY K , Knoxville (d/III-5-1900) MD Starling 1877. *JAMA* 34:702, 1900.

WINGFIELD [WINFIELD], THURMUR HAGGARD, CW-CSA; Towson Md (b/VIII-10-1826 Portsmouth Va; d/III-30 1885) MD UPa 1848. *Med s rep Phila* 52: 768, 1885. *U Pa med alum CW*:1848.*Butler* 1878:325.

WINLEY, JOHN W , Benton, Pa (d/V-9-1906) MD CPS Balto 1892. *Pa med jour* 9:672, 1905/06. *Flint* 1897: 796.

WINN, ALEXANDER MAXWELL, China, Me (b/I-8-1820 Wells, Me; d/I-5-1879) MD Dartmouth 1846. *Tr NH M S* 1879:165-66.

WINN, CHARLES W , Nashville (b/XI-25-1854 Woodford Co, Ky; d/I-15-1893 @39) MD U Nashville 1879. *So pract* 15:81-82, 1893. *Nashvl j m&s* 73:83 ff, 1893.

WINN, J M , Forest City, Ill (d/IX-5-1901 @71) Lic yrs pract. *Ill m j* ns3: 237, 1901. *JAMA* 37:790, 1901. *Polk* 1896: 420.

WINN, WILLIAM ADAMS, Arlington, Mass (b/XII-1-1848; d/I-20-1890) MD Harvard 1876; AB 1871. *Bost m&s j* 122:96, 1890. *Polk* 1886: 453.

WINNE, CHARLES, Buffalo (b/X-1811;d/V-9-1877) MD CPSNY 1833;AB Union 1828. *Buff m&s j* 16:315, 1877.

WINSHIP, CORNELIUS A , Rensselaer Co, NY (b/Litchfield, Conn; d/II-14-1888) MD Albany 1858. *Tr M S St NY* 11:741 ff, 1894. *Polk* 1886: 659.

WINSLOW, CALEB, Hertford, NC; Baltimore 1866- (b/I-24-1824 Perquimans Co,NC; d/VI-13-1895) MD UPa 1849; AB Haverford. *Med annals Md:* 627. *K&B* III: 1315.

WINSLOW, CAROLINE (BROWN), Washington, DC (b/XI-19-1832 Appledore, Engl; d/XII-7-1896) MD Cincinnati Ecl Med Inst 1853; MD W Coll Hom Cleveland 1882. *Tr Am Inst Hom* 1897:64. *So j hom* 1897 (Feb). *Polk* 1886: 214.

WINSLOW, CHARLES, CW-USA & San Comm;Guerrera Mx (b/VI-5-1839 Madras Ind; d/IX-30-1888) MD UPa 1866; AB Williams 1863. *UPa med alum CW*: 1866.

WINSLOW, FREDERICK C , Chicago (d/X-10-1901) MD NWU 1874. *Ill m j* ns3:295, 1901. *Polk* 1886: 284.

WINSLOW, JOHN, CW-USA; Ithaca; NYC (d/1900 @ 65) MD Bellevue 1866; MD CPSNY 1867; AB Harvard 1859. *Harvard in CW*: 134. *Polk* 1886: 664.

WINSLOW, JOHN RANDOLPH, Baltimore (b/NC? d/II 13-1886) MD UPa 1845; AB Haverford 1840. *Tr AMA* 18:338, 1867.

WINSLOW, JOSEPH WINSLOW, Easthampton, Mass (b/Enfield; d/II-24-1902 @81) MD Berkshire 1845. *Bost m&s j* 146:242, 1902. *Polk* 1896: 711.

WINSOR, FREDERICK, CW-USA; Winchester, Mass (b/1829 Boston; d/II-25-1889 Bermuda) MD Harv 1853 AB 1851. *Bost m&s j* 120:252, 1889. *Harv in CW*:54.

WINSOR, JOHN, Quidnick, RI (b/V-18-1843 Sterling, Conn; d/II-1-1906) MD Berkshire 1865. *Tr RI M S* 7: 573-74, 1904-09. *Polk* 1896: 1349.

WINSOR, LABIAN CLARK, San Josè, Cal (d/X-22-1903 @41) MD Bellevue 1885. *Cal st j m* 1:385, 1903. *Polk* 1890:325 (Denver).

WINSTON, CHARLES K , Nashville (b/VII-8-1811; d/III-29-1882) <MD Transylvania> *Nashvl j m&s* ns29: 184-85, 1882. *So pract* 19:184, 1897. *Butler* 1878: 780.

WINSTON, DICKERTON LYLE, Hanover CH, Va (b/II 8-1857; d/XII-11-1904) MD UCNY 1885. *Tr M S Va* 1905:453-54. *Polk* 1900: 1763.

WINSTON, GUSTAVUS STORRS, NYC (b/XI-15-1833 or II-15-1834; d/XII-29-1899) MD CPSNY 1863.

Bost m&s j 142:24, 1900. *JAMA* 34:61, 1900. *Atkinson* I: 633. *Polk* 1886: 1085.

WINSTON, JOSEPH SANDS, NYC (b/X-18-1844; d/V 10-1868 Vienna, Aust; MD CPSNY 1866. *Tr AMA* 21: 433-34, 1870. *Med reg NY NJ Conn* 1869/70: 251-53. *Med surg rep Phila* 18:464, 1868.

WINTER, ENOCH TENNEY, NYC (b/IX-19-1806 Danbury, NH; d/IV-27-1871) MD Yale 1845. *Med reg NY NJ Conn* 1872: 359.

WINTER, HARRISON R , Phoenicia, NY (d/1888) MD Albany 1864. *Tr M S St NY* 1889:364. *Polk* 1886: 701.

WINTER, JACOB CASTNER, Mt Pleasant, NJ (d/IX-17-1855 @25) MD UPa 1852; AB Union 1849; att Lafayette. *Lafayette, Men of*: 163.

WINTER, JOHN THOMAS, Washington, DC (b/IV-26-1842 Petersville Md; d/VI-22-1902) MD Georgt'n 1870. *Hist Med Soc DC*:297-98. *Polk* 1893:274.

WINTERMUTE, JAMES STINSON, Tacoma, Wash (b/IV-27-1860 St Paul, Minn; d/XI-10-1896) MD Rush 1883. *Chic m rec* 11:369, 1896. *JAMA* 27:1120, 1896. *Polk* 1896: 1516.

WINTERS, JACOB CASTNER, Mt Pleasant, NJ (d/IX-15-1855) MD UPa 1852. *Tr M S NJ* 1872: 192. Blane, *Hunterdon Co, NJ*: 104.

WINTERSTEEN, THOMAS BEAVER, ? Pa (d/IV-5-1906) MD UPa 1899. *Pa med jour* 9:638, 1905/06.

WINTHROP, HENRY, Charleston, SC (d/1890 @88) MD U Md 1825. *New Orl m&s j* ns20:332, 1890. *Waring* II:316. *Polk* 1886: 853.

WINTON, NELSON, Havana, NY; CW-USA (b/VIII--1800 Fairfield Co, Conn; d/VIII-27-1864) Hon MD Geneva 1844; att Fairfield; lic 1824. *Tr M S St NY* 1865: 299-301.

WINTON [WENTON], ROBERT, Muncie, Ind (b/XI-14 1820 Rossville,O; d/VII-30-1885) MD Rush 1856. *Tr Ind St M S* 1886:201. *Butler* 1878: 225.

WIRGMAN, CHARLES, Philadelphia (d/IV-10-1902 @55) MD Jefferson 1877. *Tr CPP* cent vol:275. *Pa med jour* 6:262, 1902/03. *Off'l Reg Pa phys* 1881-88: 316.

WIRTZ, HORACE RAGUET, USA 1846- (b/X-1-1823 Phila; d/I-24-1874 San Francisco) MD UPa 1846; AB 1842; AM 1845. *Tr AMA* 25:538, 1874. *Med rec NY* 14:103, 1874. C V Henry, *Milit rec*: 126.

WISDOM, FRANCIS LOUIS, CW-CSA; Buena Vista Ga; Texarkana Tex 1888- (b/X-22-1836 Ga; d/III-1-1906 @60) MD New Orl Sch Med 1860. *Tex st j m* 1: 352, 1905/06. *Polk* 1886: 227.

WISE, GEORGE GARRETT, CW-USA; Philadelphia (b/III-24-1844 Radnor; d/III-27-1906) MD UPa 1866. *U Pa med alum CW*: 1866. *Polk* 1886: 827.

WISE, HENRY A , Williamsburg, Va (b/XII-20-1873; d/V-6-1904 Richmond; MD Univ M C Richmd 1896;att Wm & Mary. *Tr M S Va* 1904:328-29. *Polk* 1900:1778.

WISE, JAMES HOSMER P , Morgan City, La (d/VII-9/10-1901 @56) MD New Orl Sch Med 1869. *New Orl m&s j* 54:121, 1901. *JAMA* 37:213, 1901. *Polk* 1886:415.

WISE, JOHN, Sherburne, Mass; War 1812-USN (b/I-20 1790; d/III-8-1829 Kennebunk, Me) MD Harvard 1816; AB Bowdoin 1810; AM 1813. *Bowdoin cat*: 1810.

WISE, JOHN BAILEY, CW-CSA; Franco-Pruss War (b/Greenwood, La; d/IX-22-1873 Shreveport) MD UPa 1868; att Hampden-Sidney. *U Pa med alum CW*: 1868.

WISE, JULIUS, Chicago (d/IV-19-1902 @49) MD U Mich 1872. *Bost m&s j* 146:450, 1902. *Polk* 1896: 413.

WISE, THOMAS WASHINGTON, Washington, DC (b/II-22-1846; d/II-17-1891) MD Georgetown 1866. *Hist Med Soc DC*:279. *Records AAS USA* 1891: 103 (served 1874). *Polk* 1886: 214.

WISEMAN, JAMES WASHINGTON, CW-CSA;Farmington, NC (b/I-20-1825 "Jersey Settlement," NC; d/VI-18-1899) MD UPa 1851. *U Pa med alum CW*: 1851. *Polk* 1886: 722.

WISHARD [WISHEAD], JOSEPH M , Greenwood, Ind (b/I-1-1838 Johnson Co; d/V-30-1905) MD Med Coll Ohio 1857. *Tr Ind St M S* 1905: 464. *Polk* 1896: 470.

WISHART, JAMES WILSON, CW-USA; Pittsburgh (b/IV-19-1829 Washington, Pa; d/VI-21-1902. MD U Pa 1851; AB Wash & Jeff 1846. *U Pa med alum CW*: 1851. *Polk* 1886: 831.

WISHART, JOHN, Washington, Pa (b/III-24-1781 Perthshire, Scotl; d/VI-16 or VII-19-1864) MD UPa 1808. *Med surg rep Phila* 12:52, 1864.

WISLIZENUS, FREDERICK ADOLPHUS, St Louis (b/V- -1810 Königsee, Gny; d/IX-22-1899) MD Zurich 1833. *Hist Med Soc DC*: 244-45. *Polk* 1886: 567. *K&B* III: 1317.

WISNER, BARNET NORTON, Pen Yan, NY (d/1843) MD Harvard 1831; ng Amherst. *Amherst, Men of*: 1830.

WISSLER, CHARLES H , Baltimore (b/XI-4-1863; d/IV-28-1894) MD Balto M C 1891. *Med annals Md*:629.

WISTAR, CASPAR Jr, Philadelphia (b/IX-13-1761; d/I-22-1818) MD UPa 1782; MD Edinburgh 1786. *Tr CPP* cent vol:275. *Am m recorder* 1: 1818. *K&B* III:1318-19.

WISTAR, CASPAR, Philadelphia (b/1801; d/IV-4-1867) MD UPa 1824. *Tr AMA* 19:424-25, 1868.

WISTAR, MIFFLIN, Philadelphia (b/1811; d/VIII-19-1872) MD UPa 1832. *Tr AMA* 24:379-80, 1873. *Phila med reg & dir* 1873: 304. *Med surg rep Phila* 27:260, 1872. *Med rec NY* 7:480, 1872.

WISTER, CASPAR, CW-USA; Philadelphia (b/IX-18 1818; d/XII-20-1888) MD UPa 1846. *Tr CPP* cent vol: 275; 3s12: lix ff, 1888. *U Pa med alum CW*: 1846.

WISTER, OWEN JONES, Philadelphia; USN 1848-52 (b/X-5-1825 Germantown, Pa; d/II-24-1896) MD UPa 1847. *Tr CPP* cent vol: 275; 3s18:xliii ff, 1896. *Polk* 1886: 827.

WITHERS, GEORGE WASHINGTON, CW-USA; W Lampeter Twp, Pa (b/VII-25-1831 Strasburg Twp; d/I-12-1870) MD UPa 1854. *U Pa med alum CW*: 1854.

WITHERS, HENRY DAVIS, Paterson, NJ (b/V-6-1860

 Spec. educ'l status abbrev. as: ***ng*** = college verified attendance without degree;

Cumberland, Md; d/VI-17-1895) MD UMd 1883. *Tr M S NJ* 1895: 209-10.

WITHERS, HOWARD HOPKINS, Lancaster, Pa (d/IX-15-1895) MD UPa 1874 *JAMA* 25:554 1895 as Winters.

WITHERS, THOMAS, Petersburg, Va (b/VII-30-1808 Dinwiddie Co; d/1879) MD UVa 1834. *Tr AMA* 30: 838-39, 1879. *Atkinson* I: 391.

WITHERSPOON, JOHN T , Lawrenceburg, Ky (d/X-12-1895 @25) MD U Lsvl 1892. *JAMA* 25:726, 1895.

WITHERSPOON, JUNIUS McQUIDE, CW-CSA; Columbus, Miss (b/VIII-14-1837; d/1869) MD U Nashville 1861; AB U Ala 1857. *U Ala cat*: 124.

WITHERWAX, JOHN MARTIN, Davenport, Ia; CW-USA (d/VI-15-1869) MD CPSNY 1848. *Med surg rep Phila* 21:224, 1869. *Tr Ia St M S* 1870:237-40. *Med rec* 4:430, 1869-70. *Nat m j* 1:304, 1870/71.

WITMAN, ALEXANDER HAMILTON, Reading, Pa; CW-USA (b/1800 Pa; d/1869) MD UPa 1826. *U Pa med alum CW*: 1826.

WITMER, ABRAHAM HARMON, Washington, DC (b/IV-10-1845 Lancaster, Pa; d/I-20-1900) MD Jefferson 1866. *JAMA* 34:251, 1900. *Hist Med Soc DC:* 337. *Polk* 1896, 308.

WITT, WILLIAM B , CW-USA (d/III-13-1864 Saluria Bayou, Tex) MD ? *Nat m j* 1:304, 1870/71.

WITTER, AMOS, CW-USA (d/III-13-1862 Mt Vernon, Tex) MD ? *Nat m j* 1:304, 1870/71.

WITTER, JOHN, Putnam, Conn (b/XII-30-1830 E Woodstock; d/V-19-1891) MD Yale 1857. *Pr Conn M S* 1892: 870. *Bost m&s j* 124:522, 1891. *Butler* 1878: 84.

WITTKAMP, ANDREW L VON, Philadelphia (b/Gny; d/II-2-1897) MD Jefferson 1876. *JAMA* 28:380, 1897. *Polk* 1896: 1322.

WITTWER, HERMAN ROBERT, Chicago (d/VII-26 1895) MD Rush 1888. *Chic m rec* 9:124, 1895. *JAMA* 25:209, 1895.

WOHLFARTH, AUGUSTUS, NYC (b/VIII-25-1838; d/VIII-26-1872 Obenhoff, Sax) MD CPSNY 1866. *Med reg NY NJ Conn* 1873:360. *Med rec NY* 8:24, 161, 1873.

WOHLGEMUTH, HENRY A , Springfield, Ill (d/XI-11-1905 @83) MD Ecl Med Inst Cincinnati 1854. *Ill m j* 8:530, 1905. *Polk* 1896: 442.

WOLCOTT, ERASTUS BRADLEY, Milwaukee (b/X-18-1804 Benton, NY; d/I-5-1880) MD Fairfield 1833; lic Yates Co, NY M S 1825. *Chic m j* 40:215, 1880. *JAMA* 2:391, 1884. *Tr Wis St M S* 1880:306; 1891:357. *K&B* III: 1322-23.

WOLCOTT, SAMUEL GARDNER, CW-USA; Utica, NY (b/1820 Hanover, Mass; d/VI-3-1883) MD Harvard 1847; AB Trinity, Hartford. *Tr M S St NY* 1883:286-88. *Med bull m & s* 5:166, 1883. *Butler* 1874: 566.

WOLF [WOLFE], FREDERICK, Austria; CW-USA (b/Austria; d/XI-11-1868) <MD Prague 1853> *Hist Med Soc DC:* 255. *Phila med reg & dir* 1871:298. *Med surg rep Phila* 19:468, 1868. *Nat m j* 1:304, 1870/71.

WOLFE, GEORGE, Philadelphia (d/VI-7-1869 @33) MD Hahnemann 1855. *Phila med reg & dir* 1871:294. *Med surg rep Phila* 21:24, 1869.

WOLFE, JOHN H R , Baltimore (d/V-14-1895 @65) MD UMd 1861. *JAMA* 24:810, 1895. *Butler* 1878: 332.

WOLFE, WILLIAM S , Fleetwood, Pa (d/VI-17-1903 @33) MD Jefferson 1897. *Pa m j* 7:280, 1903/04.

WOLFE, WILLIAM W , Milton, Del (d/III-27-1866) MD ? *Med surg rep Phila* 14:280, 1866.

WOLFERTZ, CHARLES WILLIAM, NYC (d/VI-19-1889 Orange, NJ) MD CPSNY 1886; BS CCNY 1883. *Med reg NY NJ Conn* 1890: 284.

WOLFF, ARTHUR S, Brownsville Tex; NYC; Tex (b/1819 Lyons Fr; d/X-30-1904) <MD Leyden; MD London> MD Acad med de Paris 1841. *Tex st j m* 1: 246, 1905/06.

WOLFF, LAURENCE, Philadelphia (d/VII-21-1901 @56) MD Jefferson 1880. *Pa med jour* 5:296, 1901/02. *Flint* 1897: 828.

WOLFLEY, WILLIAM IRVIN, ? CW-USA (b/I-6-1838 Lancaster, O; d/III-26-1892 Beltsville, Md) MD UPa 1861; AB Kenyon 1857. *U Pa med alum CW*: 1861.

WOLFSOHN, BENJAMIN, Alzey, Hesse, Gny; NYC 1856- (b/V-10-1796 Limbourg Nassau; d/IX-22-1865) <MD Giessen 1817> *Med reg NY NJ Conn* 1866:191.

WOLHAUPTER, DAVID PHILIP, Washington, DC (b/IV-6-1840 Woodstock, NB; d/VII-12-1900) MD Bowdoin 1862. *Hist Med Soc DC:* 285. *Polk* 1886: 214.

WOLHAUPTER, WILLIAM EDMUND, Washington, DC (b/IV-23-1869; d/I-21-1896) MD Georgetown 1890. *Hist Med Soc DC:* 356.

WOLLENS, JOSEPH Jr, Philadelphia (d/IV-7-1817 @ 34) MD UPa 1808. *Tr CPP* cent vol 1887: 275.

WOMACK, JAMES GREEN, CW-CSA; Jackson Tn (b/VII-25-1818 Pittsboro, NC; d/XII-26-1894) MD UPa 1840; AB UNC 1837; AM 1840. *UPa m alum CW*: 1840.

WOMERSLEY, THOMAS MELBOURNE, Watertown, Mass (d/III-7-1897 @81) MD Dartmouth 1842. *Bost m&s j* 136:244, 1897. *Polk* 1886: 467.

WOOD, ALFRED, Taunton, Mass (b/II-10-1797 Swansea, Mass; d/XII-28-1885) MD Brown 1822. *Bost m&s j* 115:630, 1886. *Butler* 1878: 360.

WOOD, CHARLES S, NYC (b/II-27-1825 Litchfield Conn; d/II-1-1890) MD Jeff 1851. *Bost m&s j* 29: 498, 1890. *Med reg NY NJ Conn* 1891:282. *JAMA* 14: 250, 1890. *Buff m&s j* 29:498, 1890.

WOOD, EDWARD STICKNEY, Boston (b/IV-28-1846; d/VII-11-1905 @59) MD Harvard 1871; AB 1867. *Bost m&s j* 153:94, 125, 1905. *Atkinson* I:676. *K&B* III: 1323-25.

WOOD, EDWIN MILLER, CW-USA; ?Cincinnati (b/I-30-1844 Smithfield, O; d/I-12-1878 Cincinnati) MD UPa 1868. *U Pa med alum CW*: 1868.

WOOD, EDWIN NEWTON, CW-CSA; Buchanan, Va (b/VIII-16-1826; d/XII-8-1899) MD UVa 1848; MD

Jefferson 1850. *Tr M S Va* 1900:316–19. *JAMA* 33:1632, 1899: 34:251, 1900. *Polk* 1896: 1487.

WOOD, ELI ALLEN, Pittsburgh (b/III–24–1834 Woods Run; d/VI–4–1894 Phila) MD W Res 1866. *Tr Pa St M S* 24:379–80, 1894. *JAMA* 22:967, 1894. *Butler* 1878: 701.

WOOD, ELIAS W , Northboro, Mass (b/IV– –1840 Middleboro; d/IX–6–1896) MD Geneva 1858. *JAMA* 27: 18, 1896. *Polk* 1886:291 (Oak Park, Ill as homeopath).

WOOD, FRED B , Garrett, Ind (d/III–1–1898) MD Rush 1871. *JAMA* 30:683, 1898. *Polk* 1886:958 (Milwaukee).

WOOD, G B , CW–USA (d/IV–14–1864) MD ? *Nat m j* 1:304, 1870/71.

WOOD, GEORGE BACON, Philadelphia (b/III–12–1797 Greenwich, NJ; d/III–30–1879) MD UPa 1818; AB 1815; AM 1818; LLD Princeton 1858. *Tr AMA* 30:839–44, 1879. *Tr Pa St M S* 12:852–55, 1879. *Bost m&s j* 100: , 1879; 41:236–40, 1849. *Tr CPP* cent vol:275; 3s5:xxv–lxxvi, 1881. *K&B* III: 1325.

WOOD, GEORGE LOUIS, Anthony, RI (b/VIII–6–1849; d/III–7–1890) MD UCNY 1880. *Bost m&s j* 122: 283, 1890. *Tr RI M S* 4:243, 1889–93. *Polk* 1886: 844.

WOOD, GEORGE WESTON, Minneapolis (d/I–6–1896 @53) MD McGill 1863 *JAMA* 26:142, 1896. *Atksn* I:571.

WOOD, ISAAC, NYC (b/VIII–21–1793 Clinton; d/III–25 1868) MD Rutgers 1816. *Tr AMA* 19:420–21, 1868. *Med reg NY NJ Conn* 1868: 339. *Med surg rep Phila* 15:454–58, 1866; 18:314, 1868. *Med rec NY* 3:71, 119, 1868–69. *K&B* III: 1327.

WOOD, JACOB ABBOTT, NYC (b/V–10–1810 Hancock, NH; d/III–21–1879) MD Vt M C 1836. *Med rec NY* 15:550, 1879.

WOOD, JAMES, USA; Newburgh, NY (d/III–3–1899 @30) MD Bellevue 1891. *JAMA* 32:628, 1899. *Bost m&s j* 140:291–92, 1899. *Polk* 1896: 1034.

WOOD, JAMES BAYARD, W Chester, Pa (b/XI–5–1817 Christiana, Del; d/IV–14–1889) MD Hahnemann Phila 1854. *Med vis* 5:222, 1889. *Hahn mo* 24:301, 1889. *Cleave.* Homeopath.

WOOD, JAMES RUSHMORE, NYC (b/IX–14–1813 Mamaroneck, NY; d/V–4–1882) MD Castleton 1834. *Med reg NY NJ Conn* 1882:236. *Bost m&s j* 106:451–52, 477, 493, 1882; 107:618–19, 1882. *Med surg rep Phila* 12:197–200, 1864/65. *Tr M S St NY* 1885:304–19. *K&B* III: 1327–28.

WOOD, JESSIE D , Topeka, Kans (d/II–2–1895) MD ? *JAMA* 24:250, 1895.

WOOD, JOHN PRESTON, Lamar Co, Tex (b/IV–4–1816 Amalia Co, Va; d/XI–12–1884) MD UPa 1839. *Med surg rep Phila* 52:128, 1885.

WOOD, LEE, Warsaw, Ark (d/VI–14–1901) MD U Tenn 1890. *JAMA* 37:43, 1901.

WOOD, ORLANDO S , Green Valley, Ill (d/III–28–1868) MD Rush 1864. *Chic m j* 25:474, 1868.

WOOD, ORSON, Somers, Conn (b/1791; d/VII–19–1874) Lic Conn St M S 1818; Hon MD Yale 1840. *Pr Conn M S* 1875:421–26, 442. *Butler* 1878: 84.

WOOD, PETER C , San Marcos, Tex (d/I–27–1898) MD U Lsvl 1842. *Tex m j* 13:420, 1897–98. *Polk* 1890:1092.

WOOD, ROBERT C , USA 1825–65 (b/IX– –1800 Newport, RI; d/III–28–1869) MD CPSNY 1821. *Phila med reg & dir* 1871:300. *Tr AMA* 21:493, 1870. *Med surg rep Phila* 20:275–76, 1869. *Nat m j* 1:304, 1870/71.

WOOD, ROBERT MITCHELL, Memphis (d/XI–2 1903 @71) MD Tulane 1856. *Nashvl j m&s* 94:280–81, 1903.

WOOD, STEPHEN, Flushing, NY (d/III–7–1884 @73) MD CPSNY 1833. *Med surg rep Phila* 50:448, 1884. *Butler* 1878: 513.

WOOD, STILLMAN GARDNER, Enfield, NH (b/c1824; d/II–8–1859) MD Dartmouth 1849. *Tr NH M S* 1859:5.

WOOD, THEOPHILUS EMMONS, E Randolph Mass (d/II–1–1871 @65) MD Yale 1826. *Bost m&s j* 7:104, 1871.

WOOD, THOMAS FANNING, CW–CSA; Wilmington, NC (b/II–23–1841 Nantucket, Mass or Wilm'tn; d/VIII 22–1892) Hon MD UMd 1868; att Med Coll Va. *JAMA* 19:325, 1892. *NC m j* 30:176–77, 1892. *Tr M S NC* 1893: 20–23. *Atkinson* I: 332–33. *K&B* III: 1329.

WOOD, WILLIAM, Cincinnati (d/VI–9–1857 @49) MD Transylvania 1834. *Bost m&s j* 56:467, 1857.

WOOD, WILLIAM, E Windsor Hill Conn (b/VII–7 1822 Waterbury; d/VIII–9–1885) MD UCNY 1847; att Berkshire. *Pr Conn M S* ns3:173–76, 1886. *Atkinson* I: 57–58.

WOOD, WILLIAM, Grand Rapids, Mich (d/I–14–1895 @ 56) MD U Mich 1862. *JAMA* 24:177, 1895. *Polk* 1886: 494.

WOOD, WILLIAM, Portland, Me (b/X–2–1810 Scarborough, Me; d/I–22–1899) MD Bowdoin 1833; AB 1829. *JAMA* 32:263, 1899. *K&B* III: 1330.

WOOD, WILLIAM GORDON, NYC (b/II–13–1813; d/V–6–1890) MD CPSNY 1839. *Med reg NY NJ Conn* 1890: 284. *Bost m&s j* 122: , 1890.

WOOD, WILLIAM MAXWELL, USN 1829–71? Owings Mills, Md (b/V–27–1809 Balto; d/III–1–1880) MD UMd 1829. *Med surg rep Phila* 42:242, 1880. *Tr AMA* 33:610–13, 1882. *Med annals Md:* 629. *K&B* III: 1330.

WOOD, WILLIAM RICHARD, CW–CSA; Scotland Neck, NC (b/ 1834 Washington Co; d/VII–12–1899 @75) MD UPa 1855. *Tr M S St NC* 47:176–77. *JAMA* 33:302, 1899. *Polk* 1896:1128.

WOOD, WILLOUGHBY ISRAEL, Brooklyn (d/II–20 1897 @28) MD Bellevue 1891. *Bost m&s j* 136:216, 1897. *JAMA* 28:476, 1897. *Polk* 1896: 1004.

WOODBRIDGE, JOHN ELIOT, Cleveland (d/VIII– –1901 in Europe) MD Charity Hosp M C Cleveland 1866. *Ill m j* ns3:237, 1901. *Chic m rec* 21:378, 1901.

WOODBRIDGE, LUTHER DANA, Williamstown, Mass (b/XII–27–1850 Amboy, NJ; d/XI–3 or 5 or23–1899) MD CPSNY 1877, *Bost m&s j* 141:484, 1899; 142:46–47, 1900. *JAMA* 33:1307, 1899. *Polk* 1896: 726.

WOODBURN, JAMES HANDY, Indianapolis (b/I–15–

 Spec. educ'l status abbrev. as: ***ng*** = college verified attendance without degree;

1822 Jefferson Co, Ind; d/IV-23-1901) MD U Lsvl 1847. *Tr Ind St M S* 1901:524. *Polk* 1896: 476.

WOODBURY, FREDERIC CLINTON, Boston (d/XII-4 1886 @25) MD Harvard 1886; AB 1882. *Bost m&s j* 115: 560, 1886.

WOODBURY, GEORGE FRANKLIN, Worcester, Mass (d/VI-18-1893 @42) MD Harvard 1882. *Bost m&s j* 128:636, 1893.

WOODBURY, HENRY ELISHA, Washington, DC (b/I-1-1827 Barrington, Vt; d/I-15-1905) MD Georgetown 1863. *Hist Med Soc DC:* 265-66.

WOODBURY, PETER PERKINS, Bedford, NH (b/VIII 8-1791 Francestown; d/XII-4-1860) ng Dartmouth 1814; hon MD 1846. *Bost m&s j* 63:408, 1861. *Tr NH M S* 1861: 6.

WOODBURY, SAMUEL IRA LAWRENCE, Warren, RI (b/XII-9-1852 Claremont, NH; d/XII-22-1893) MD Dartmouth 1889. *Tr RI M S* 4:627, 1889-93. *Polk* 1890: 1029.

WOODCOCK, ALLAN, NYC (d/X-31-1889) MD UC NY 1882 *Med reg NY NJ Conn* 1890:285 *Polk* 1886:698.

WOODEN, DAVID, Grayville, Ill (d/VIII-13-1901 @41) MD Lsvl M C 1885. *JAMA* 37:595, 1901. *Ill m j* ns3:237, 1901.

WOODEN, JOHN L , Greensburg, Ind (b/V-17-1826 Shelby Co, Ky; d/XI-20-1886) MD M C Ohio 1860. *Tr Ind St M S* 1887: 194. *Butler* 1878: 226.

WOODEN, WILLIAM HERSCHEL, Milford, Ind (b/ VIII-12-1857; d/IV-23-1903) MD M C Ohio 1879. *Tr Ind St M S* 1903: 357. *Polk* 1896: 470.

WOODEND, WILLIAM DUNN, Huntington, NY (b/V- -1832; d/III-8-1893) MD UPa 1855. *Med reg NY NJ Conn* 1894: 253.

WOODFERN [WOOLFOLK], GEORGE W , Paducah, Ky (d/IX-13-1878 Grenada, Miss) MD ? *Tr AMA* 30:889, 1879. *Med rec NY* 14:240, 1878.

WOODHOUSE, JAMES, Pa (b/XI-17-1770 Phila; d/VI-4-1809) MD UPa 1792; AB 1787. *NY med & philos jour* 1:299-300, 1809.

WOODHOUSE, SAMUEL WASHINGTON, Philadelphia (d/X-23-1904 @83) MD UPa 1847. *Pa med jour* 8:336, 1904/05. *Flint* 1897: 828.

WOODHULL, ADDISON WADDELL, Newark; CW-USA (b/1831 Monmouth Co, NJ; d/V-14-1876) MD UCNY 1856; AB Princeton 1854; AM 1857. *Tr AMA* 28: 624-25, 1877. *Tr M S NJ* 1876:[128]-129.

WOODHULL, GILBERT SMITH (b/I-11-1794; d/X-13-1830) MD CPSNY 1816. *Tr M S NJ* 1871:79-80.

WOODHULL, HENRY WILLIAM BECK, NYC (d/I-20-1894) MD CPSNY 1845; AB Princeton 1838; AM 1843. *Med reg NY NJ Conn* 1894:253. *Butler* 1878: 528.

WOODHULL, JOHN NEILSON, Princeton, NJ (b/VII-25-1807; d/I-12-1867) MD UPa 1832; AB Princeton 1828; AM 1831. *Tr M S NJ* 1867:211-12. *Tr AMA* 19: 430-31, 1868.

WOODHULL, JOHN TENNETT, Freehold, NJ (b/VIII-4-1786; d/XI-18-1869) MD UPa 1809. *Phila med reg & dir* 1871:302. *Tr M S NJ* 1870: 83; 1871:94-95.

WOODHULL, LAWRENCE SWAN, Brooklyn (b/1874 Huntington; d/VI-8-1899) MD LICH 1896. *JAMA* 32: 1460, 1899. *Bost m&s j* 140:596, 1899.

WOODMAN, GEORGE SULLIVAN, Cambridge, Mass (b/XI-22-1823 Boston; d/III-23-1906) MD Harvard 1849; AB Amherst 1846. *Polk* 1886: 470. *Amherst, Men of*: 1846.

WOODMAN, LUCIUS CAMPBELL DENMAN, Paw Paw, Mich (b/III-20-1828 Sutton, Vt; d/IV-12-1883) MD Woodstock 1850. *JAMA* 1:519-20, 1883. *Butler* 1878:387.

WOODRUFF, ELMER W , Columbus (b/VII-23-1863 Reynoldsburg, O; d/V-24-1900) MD Starling 1891. *JAMA* 34:1431, 1900. *Polk* 1896: 1182.

WOODRUFF, HENRY T , Harvard, Ill (d/XII-16-1900) MD NWU 1861. *Ill m j* ns2:533, 1901. *Polk* 1886: 282.

WOODRUFF, JULIAN SMITH, Reidville, NC; CW-CSA (b/II-9-1826 St Augustine, Fla; d/IX-9-1879) MD UPa 1847. *U Pa med alum CW*: 1847.

WOODRUFF, LOCKWOOD DE FOREST, NYC (b/II-1-1838; d/VII-9-1876) MD CPSNY 1863; AB UCNY 1859. *Med reg NY NJ Conn* 1877:209. *Med rec m&s* 11: 470, 517, 1876. *Butler* 1870: 528.

WOODRUFF, MOSES M , Elizabeth, NJ (b/1802; d/IV-11-1880) Lic M S NJ 1824. *Tr M S NJ* 1880-81:127-28.

WOODRUFF, WILLIAM H , Pine Bush, NY (d/XII-1-1869 @65) MD Albany 1854; AB Union 1851. *Bost m & s j* 135:610, 1896. *Polk* 1886: 701.

WOODRUFF, WILLIAM JESSUP, Los Angeles; Providence, RI (b/II-22-1870 Pine Bush, NY; d/VII-28 1900) MD Albany 1894. *Tr RI M S* 6:264-65, 1899-1903. *Polk* 1896: 221.

WOODRUFF, ZACHARY TAYLOR, Vicksburg, Miss (b/VI-22-1849 Tuscaloosa, Ala; d/VII-17-1878) MD ULa 1870; att U Ala. *Tr AMA* 30:888-89, 1879. *Tr Miss St M Assn* 1878: 38.

WOODS, BENJAMIN W , USA 1838-42; Govanstown, Md (d/VIII-19-1883) MD UMd 1836. *Med bull m&s* 5: 258, 1883. *Heitman*.

WOODS, JAMES SAMUEL, NYC (d/XI-21-1860 @ 29) MD NYMC 1857; AB Williams 1853. *Med reg NY NJ Conn* 1862: 153.

WOODS, MARSHALL, Providence, RI (b/XI-28-1824 Boston; d/VII-13 or 23-1899) MD UCNY 1849; AB Brown 1845. *Tr RI M S* 6:131-32, 1899-1903. *Polk* 1896: 1354.

WOODS, PETER N , Rome, O; Fairfield, Ia 1856- (b/IX-8-1829 Gremoille, O; d/III-19-1886) MD Ecl Med Inst Cincinnati 1854. *Tr Ia St M S* 18:412, 1900. Fairchild's *Iowa*: 232-33.

WOODS, ROBERT CALEB, Tenn; CW-CSA (b/IX-15 1830 Rocky Mount, Va; d/1873) MD UPa 1860. *U Pa* *med alum CW*: 1860.

WOODS, W S, CW–USA (d/IV– –1867 Monticello, Minn) MD *Nat m j* 1:304, 1870/71.

WOODSIDE, JOHN S, ?India; Chester, Ill (d/II–12 1901) MD Jefferson 1875. *Ill m j* ns2:533, 1901. *Polk* 1896: 425.

WOODVILLE, JAMES LEWIS Jr, CW–CSA; Sweet Springs, Va (b/I–8–1820 Fincastle; d/VIII–14–1904) MD UPa 1844; att Wash & Lee. *U Pa med alum CW*: 1844. *Polk* 1886: 944.

WOODVINE, DENTON GEORGE, Boston (b/V–3–1834 Little Meadley, Engl; d/XI–23–1894) MD UPa 1866. *Hahn mo* 30:5–6 (news & advt, no.1) 1895. *Tr Am Inst Hom* 1895:241. *Polk* 1886:463. Homeopath.

WOODWARD, ALVIN MAURICE, NYC (b/1836 Dresden Mills, Me; d/V– –1904) MD NY Hom 1862; ng Bowdoin Med Sch 1860–61. *Tr Am Inst Hom* 1904:959–60. Homeopath.

WOODWARD, ASHBEL, CW–USA; Franklin Conn (b/VI–26–1804 Willington; d/XII–20–1885) MD Bowdoin 1829; hon MD Yale 1855. *Pr Conn M S* ns3:179–81, 1886. *Tr RI M S* 2:221, 1877–82. *Atkinson* I:62. *Butler* 1878: 84.

WOODWARD, CHARLES, Middletown, Conn (b/IV–15 1798 Torringford; d/V–18–1870) Hon MD Yale 1837; lic 1821. *Pr Conn M S* 1871:414 473–7. *Butler* 1878:84.

WOODWARD, CHARLES, Cincinnati 1829– (d/VIII–1874) MD UPa 1826; AB Princeton 1823. *Med surg rep Phila* 31:200, 1874.

WOODWARD, CHARLES SAMUEL, NYC (b/Mich; d/VI–26–1904 @35) MD UCNY 1892. *Bost m&s j* 151: 28, 1904. *Polk* 1896: 1085.

WOODWARD, EBENEZER, Quincy, Mass (b/1798? d/V–21–1869 @71) MD Harvard; AB Dartmouth 1817. *Bost m&s j* 3:328, 1869.

WOODWARD, HENRY, Middletown, Conn (d/1832) Hon MD Yale 1828. *Pr Conn M S* ns2: 145, 1882–83.

WOODWARD, JAMES B, CW–USA; Montpelier, Vt (d/1879) MD UCNY 1851. *Tr Vt M S* 1883: 111.

WOODWARD, JAMES W, Bloomington, Ill (d/XI–24 1901) Lic 1885 by 35 yrs pract. *Ill m j* ns3:399, 1902.

WOODWARD, JOHN D, Memphis (d/1878) MD ? *Tr AMA* 30:889, 1879.

WOODWARD, JONATHAN DON Jr, Castleton, Vt (b/IV–28–1799 Hanover, NH; d/VI–20–1869) MD Castleton 1823. *Med surg rep Phila* 21:68, 1869. *Phila med reg & dir* 1871:301.

WOODWARD, JOSEPH JANVIER, USA 1861– ; Philadelphia (b/X–30–1833; d/VIII–18 or 26–1884 Delaware Co, Pa) MD UPa 1853. *Bost m&s j* 111:216, 237, 1884. *Med age* 2:264–65, 1884. *JAMA* 3:249–51, 279, 1884. *U Pa med alum CW*: 1853. *K&B* III:1332.

WOODWARD, ROLAND E, Chicago (d/VIII–6–1899) MD Georgetown 1864. *Tr Ill St M S* 1899: 287.

WOODWARD, ROLLIN CARLOS MALLORY, St Albans, Vt (b/II–10–1820 Castleton or Barre; d/XI–21–1873) MD Castl'n 1842. *Bost m&s j* 90:226, 252, 1874. *Med s rep Phil* 29:462, 1873. *Tr Vt M S* 1883: 110.

WOODWARD, RUFUS, CW–US San Comm; Worcester, Mass (b/X–3–1819 Wethersfield, Conn; d/XII–30–1885) MD Harvard 1845; AB 1841. *JAMA* 9:767, 1887. *Bost m &s j* 114:24, 46, 1886. *Atkinson* I:456. *K&B* II:1262–63.

WOODWARD, SAMUEL BAYARD, Northampton, Conn (b/VI–10–1787 Torringford; d/I–3–1850) Hon MD Yale 1822. *NW m&s j* 2:461, 1850. *K&B* III: 1332–33.

WOODWORTH, BENJAMIN STUDLEY, Ft Wayne, Ind (b/II–13–1816 Leicester, Mass; d/IX–10–1891) MD Berkshire 1837. *JAMA* 17:980, 1891. *Tr Ind St M S* 1892:294. *Med bull m&s* 14:38, 1892. *Atkinson* I:36. Kemper's *Indiana*: 357.

WOODWORTH, CARLOS C, E Berkshire, Vt (b/VI–28–1846; d/VIII–5–1878) MD Bellevue 1868. *Tr Vt M S* 1883: 110.

WOODWORTH, JOHN MAYNARD, Chicago; USA 1861– (b/VIII–15–1837 Big Flats, NY; d/III–14–1879) MD Chic M C 1862. *Bost m&s j* 100: 402–03, 1879. *New Orl m&s j* ns7:54–55, 1879. *Tr AMA* 30:845–47, 1879. *Chic m j* 38:664–71, 1879. *K&B* III: 1334.

WOODWORTH, ROBERT, USN 1835–67 (b/V– –1813 Albany, NY; d/III–17–1870) MD UPa 1834; AB Williams 1831. *Tr AMA* 21:498, 1870. *Phila med reg & dir* 1871: 304. *U Pa med alum CW*: 1834.

WOODYATT, WILLIAM H, Chicago (b/IX–12–1846 Brantford, Ont; d/I–31–1880) MD Cleveland Hom 1869. *US m inv* 11:177, 441, 1880. *Tr Am Inst Hom* 1880:157. *Med adv* 8:113, 154, 1880. *Cleave*. Homeopath.

WOOLF, THOMAS J, New Iberia, La (d/X–1–1900 @ 48 Denver) MD Tulane 1878. *New Orl m&s j* 53:297, 300. *Polk* 1890: 489.

WOOLLEY, CHARLES NATHAN, Newburgh, NY (b/X–8–1838 Southampton, NY; d/XII–11–1896 @58) MD LICH 1868; AB U Mich. *JAMA* 27:1360, 1896. *Bost m&s j* 135:633, 1896. *Polk* 1896: 1034.

WOOLLEY, GEORGE W, Williamsport, Md (b/Pa; d/XI–6–1893) MD M C Ohio 1836. *Hist Med Soc DC*: 294. *Polk* 1886: 214.

WOOLVERTON, JOHN, Trenton, NJ (b/X–27–1825 Stockton; d/IX–14–1888) MD UPa 1849. *Med reg NY NJ Conn* 1889:290. *Tr M S NJ* 1889:174–76. *Atkinson* I: 521. *Polk* 1886: 612.

WOOLVERTON, JOSEPH WOOD, CW–USA; ? NJ (b/X–6–1836 Stockton; d/VII–18–1887 Pr Anne, Md) MD UPa 1859. *U Pa med alum CW*: 1859 suppl.

WOOLWORTH, EARLE EUGENE, Brooklyn (b/Lyonsdale, NY; d/II–5–1903 @30) MD UCNY 1897. *Bost m&s j* 148:194, 1903.

WOOSTER, DAVID, Idaho Spr, Col (d/IV–8–1891 @37) MD U Cal 1885. *Tr Col St M S* 1898–99: 508.

WOOTEN, POWELL C, Lafayette, Ky (d/IV–23–1900 @75) MD U Lsvl 1853. *JAMA* 34:1146, 1900.

 Spec. educ'l status abbrev. as: ***ng*** = college verified attendance without degree;

WOOTEN, THOMAS DUDLEY, CW-CSA; Tompkinsville, Ky; Springfield, Mo 1856 & 65?; Paris, Tex; Austin, Tex 1876- (b/III-6-1829 Barren Co, Ky; d/VIII-1-1906 Eureka Spr, Ark) *Tex st j m* 2:144, 1906. Daniel's *Tex m j* 8:37-38, 1892-93. *Atkinson* I:536. *K&B* II:1265. *Polk* 1886: 880.

WOOTTON, RICHARD, Miss (b/IV-23-1807 Montgomery Co, Md; d/VI-20-1840) MD UPa 1831. *Med annals Md:* 631.

WOOTTON, WILLIAM TURNER, Frederick, Md (b/XI 21-1822 Montg'y Co; d/IX-14-1896) MD UPa 1846. *JAMA* 27:775-6 1896. *Med ann Md:*631. *Polk* 1896:670.

WORCESTER, CHARLES POMEROY, Newtonville, Mass (d/X-9-1898 @37) MD Harvard 1888; AB 1883. *Bost m&s j* 139:380, 1898. *Polk* 1896: 708.

WORCESTER, JONATHAN FOY, Salem, Mass (d/ 1869 @63) MD Harvard 1823; AB Dartmouth 1827. *Bost m&s j* 4:128, 1869.

WORCESTER, JOSEPH, NYC (b/XI-21-1803; d/VIII 7-1877) MD Berkshire 1835. *Med reg NY NJ Conn* 1878: 192. *Med rec NY* 13:119, 1878.

WORCESTER, SAMUEL HOWARD, Bridgewater, Mass (b/II-16-1824 Gloucester; d/XII-4-1891) MD NY Hom 1861; AB Brown 1845. *Brown hist cat*: 1845. *Polk* 1886: 463.

WORCESTER, WILLIAM LEONARD, Asylum Sta, Mass (b/1845 Chelsea, Vt; d/VI-5-1901) MD Columbian 1873. *Bost m&s j* 144:627, 1901. *Polk* 1886: 496.

WORDEN, THOMAS D, Wilkesbarre Pa (d/IV-19-1888 @34) MD Albany 1880. *Med reg NY NJ Conn* 1888:273.

WORK, ROBERT W , Bethlehem, Pa (d/VI-17-1902 @39) MD Jefferson 1892. *Pa med jour* 5:547, 1901/02; 6:262, 1902/03.

WORKMAN, JAMES CLARK, CW-CSA (b/I-10-1809 Philadelphia; d/1864) MD UPa 1830; att Coll UPa 1828. *U Pa med alum CW*: 1830.

WORKMAN, WILLIAM, Worcester, Mass (b/1798? Colerain; d/X-17-1885 @87) MD Harvard 1825. *JAMA* 9:543, 1887. *Bost m&s j* 113:408, 432, 1885. *Butler* 1878: 360.

WORLEY, GEORGE N , Williamsport, Md (d/XI-6 1893) MD Ft Wayne C M 1881. *JAMA* 21:784, 1893. *Polk* 1890: 385.

WORLEY, RICHARD T , Baton Rouge, La (d/XI-29-1897) MD Ky Sch Med 1876. *JAMA* 29: 1286, 1897.

WORMLEY, THEODORE GEORGE, Philadelphia (b/ IV-1-1826 Wormleysburg, Pa; d/I-3-1897) MD Pa Med Coll 1849; PhD Dickinson 1870; LLD. *Tr CPP* cent vol: 276; 3s19:lxxix-lxxxviii, 1897. *JAMA* 28:91, 1897. *Chic m rec* 12:154, 1897. *K&B* III:1335-36.

WORRELL, THOMAS F , Bloomington, Ill (b/1821 NC; d/IX-12-1887) <MD U Lsvl 1845> *Tr Ill St M S* 1888:135. *Polk* 1886: 255.

WORTH, JOHN MILTON, Asheboro, Md (d/IV-5-1900 @89) MD ? *JAMA* 34:957, 1900.

WORTHINGTON, ALBERT BROWNELL, Middle Haddam, Conn (b/V-23-1819 Colchester; d/IV-26-1898) MD Yale 1847. *Pr Conn M S* 1898:346-49. *JAMA* 30: 1192, 1898. *Atkinson* I:682. *Butler* 1878: 84.

WORTHINGTON, AMOS FRANCIS, Cincinnati (d/III-10-1898 @66) MD Cleveland Hom Hosp Coll 1870. *Tr Am Inst Hom* 1898: 49. *Polk* 1898:745. Homeopath.

WORTHINGTON, CHARLES, Georgetown, DC (b/X-9 1759 Anne Arundel Co, Md; d/IX-10-1836) MB UPa 1782. *Hist Med Soc DC:* 213. *Med annals Md:* 632.

WORTHINGTON, JAMES CHESTON, USA 1875- (b/ Md; d/VIII-11-1896 Louisville) MD UMd 1848. *Med annals Md:* 632. *JAMA* 27:555, 1896. *Polk* 1890: 70.

WORTHINGTON, JOHN, Byberry, Pa (b/I-21-1771 Bucks Co, Pa; d/XI-24-1831 Chester Co) Stud med w/Dr Jacob Ehrenzeller; att UPa. *Med reporter* (W Chester) 1:127-28, 1854.

WORTHINGTON, JOSHUA HUSBAND, Philadelphia (b/Harford Co, Md; d/XII-26-1885 @69) MD Jefferson 1838. *Med surg rep Phila* 54:32, 1886. *Atkinson* I:125. *Butler* 1878: 674.

WORTHINGTON, NICHOLAS WILLIAM, Brentwood, Md (b/1789; d/VII-24 or 30-1849) MD UPa 1815; AB Princeton 1808. *Hist Med Soc DC:* 217-18.

WORTHINGTON, R H , Denver (d/III-13-1892 @46) MD U Denver 1884. *Tr Col St M S* 1898-99:509. *Polk* 1886: 185.

WORTHINGTON, ROBERT HERBERT, Norfolk & Berkeley, Va; CW-CSA (b/X-27-1835; d/V-10-1886) MD UPa 1861. *U Pa med alum CW*:1861. *Polk* 1886: 914, 923.

WORTHINGTON, THOMAS, Laurel, Md (d/IX-15-1899 @80) MD UMd 1840. *JAMA* 33:807-08, 1899. *Polk* 1886: 440.

WORTHINGTON, WILLIAM HAMPHILL, CW-USA (b/VI-19-1827 W Chester, Pa; d/XI-24-1865 there) MD UPa 1849. *U Pa med alum CW*: 1849.

WORTHINGTON, WILMER, W Chester, Pa (b/I-22 1804 Chester Co; d/IX-11-1873) MD UPa 1825. *Med surg rep Phila* 29:216, 1873. *Tr Pa St M S* 1874:256-62. *Tr CPP* cent vol: 287.

WORTMAN, WILLIAM S , St Louis (d/VI-10-1884 @55) MD ? *Med surg rep Phila* 51:28, 1884.

WOTHERSPOON, ALEXANDER SOMERVILLE, Washington, DC (b/1817 NYC; d/V-4-1854) MD Columbian 1837. *Hist Med Soc DC:* 243.

WOTKYNS, ALFRED, Troy, NY (d/XII-23-1886) MD ? *Med rec NY* 12:408, 1877.

WOTRING, JONATHAN, CW-USA; Newark, O (b/IX-1-1828 Washington, Pa; d/XI-14-1890) MD UPa 1853; AB Wash & Jeff 1848. *U Pa med alum CW*: 1853. *Polk* 1886: 763.

WRAGG, JOHN ASHBY, Charleston, SC; CW-CSA (b/ 1805; d/X-9-1870) MD U Pa 1828. *U Pa med alum CW*:1828.

WRAY, JAMES H , Winterset, Ia (b/III-4-1853 Huntington, Pa; d/XI-12-1896) MD Jefferson 1877. *Tr Ia St M S* 15:368, 1897. *Polk* 1896: 429.

WRAY, JOSEPH JAMES, Dallas (d/X-21-1895 @36) MD Tulane 1888. *New Orl m&s j* ns23: 379, 1895. *Tex m news* 5:39, 1895. *Tex m j* 11:263-64. *Polk* 1890: 1075.

WREN, GEORGE WILLIAM CHRISTOPHER, NYC (d/III-23-1901 @27) MD UCNY & Bellevue 1899. *Bost m&s j* 144:318, 1901. *Polk* 1900: 1301.

WRIGHT, AARON [ARON], Brooklyn (d/XII-15-1885 @70) MD Yale 1836. *Med reg NY NJ Conn* 1886: 257.

WRIGHT, AARON B, Oshkosh, Wis (d/IV-2-1886) MD W Res 1845. *Tr Wis St M S* 1891: 357. *Polk* 1886:959.

WRIGHT, ADAM EMPIE, CW-CSA; Wilmington, NC (b/1833; d/1879) MD UCNY 1856; AB UNC 1853. *Tr NC M S* 1880:15. *NC m j* 4:69, 1879. *Med surg rep Phila* 41:176, 1879. *Butler* 1878: 600.

WRIGHT, ALBERT, Brooklyn (d/XII-10-1874 @70) MD ? *Med rec NY* 10: 8, 1875.

WRIGHT, ANDREW F , Sherman, Tex (d/VI-14-1901 @76) MD Ky Sch Med 1859. *JAMA* 37:43, 1901. *Polk* 1886: 894.

WRIGHT, ANDREW R , Buffalo (b/X-19-1825; d/II-24-1900 Chicago) <MD Cleveland U M & S 1858> *Buff m&s j* 39: 695, 1900. *Flint* 1897: 653.

WRIGHT, ARCHIBALD WESLEY, CW-USA; Philadelphia (b/1829; d/XII- -1891) MD UPa 1851; AB Dickinson 1848. *U Pa med alum CW*: 1851.

WRIGHT, AUGUSTUS S , Indianapolis 1850-62; Omaha, Neb 1862-74; Santa Rosa, Cal (d/1906) MD Hahnemann Phila 1850. *Cal st j m* 4:112, 1906. *Polk* 1896: 242. Homeopath.

WRIGHT, CHARLES, NYC (d/IX-2-1883 London, Engl) MD UCNY 1853. *Med reg NY NJ Conn* 1884: 242. *Bost m&s j* 109:259, 1883. *Med surg rep Phila* 49: 336, 364, 1883.

WRIGHT, CHARLES EDWARD, CW-USA; Indianapolis (b/XI-1 1843; d/II-22-1893) MD M C Ohio 1868. *Tr Ind St M S* 1893:255. *Atkinson* I:360. *Butler* 1878:226.

WRIGHT, CHARLES H , N Madison, Ind (b/XII-22 1839 Cincinnati; d/VIII-26-1889) MD M C Ohio 1870. *Tr Ind St M S* 1890: 154.

WRIGHT, CHARLOTTE E , Gilman, Ill (d/VIII-19-1900) Lic yrs pract. *Ill m j* ns2:237, 1900. Eclectic.

WRIGHT, CLARK, NYC (b/1859; d/III-17-1897) MD CPSNY 1885; AB Yale 1881. *Bost m&s j* 136:317, 1897. *JAMA* 28:620, 1897. *Polk* 1896: 1086.

WRIGHT, EDWARD [EDWIN], Carlinville, Ill (d/IX-11-1851) MD Rush 1851. *NW m&s j* 4:306, 1851. *Tr Ill St M S* 1895: 73.

WRIGHT, EMMA SCOTT, NYC (d/XI-17-1879 @31) MD NYMC & Hosp for Women 1872. *Med surg rep Phila* 41:528, 1879.

WRIGHT, FRANCIS MARKOE, Englewood, NJ; CW-USA (b/1830 NYC; d/III-16-1874 NYC) MD CPSNY 1854; AB CCNY 1848. *Tr M S NJ* 1874:106-08. *Tr AMA* 470, 1875. *Med rec NY* 9:191, 271, 1874. *Med reg NY NJ Conn* 1874: 295.

WRIGHT, GEORGE POWELL, NYC (d/VII-22-1876 @37) MD CPSNY 1865. *Med s rep Phila* 35:180, 1876.

WRIGHT, ISAAC H , Neenah, Wis (d/XI-29-1893 @ 80) MD Cleveland M C 1849. *JAMA* 21:907, 1893.

WRIGHT, J S , Newton, Ia (d/XI-24-1893) MD ? *JAMA* 21:907, 1893. *Polk* 1890: 422.

WRIGHT, JAMES A , Danville, Ia (b/Ohio; d/XII-19 1882 @38) MD Tulane 1879. *Tr Ia St M S* 6: 460, 1883-85. *Butler* 1878: 248.

WRIGHT, JAMES WILLIS, Fairmount, Ill (d/VII-17-1901) MD Med Coll Ind 1888. *JAMA* 37: 342, 1901.

WRIGHT, JOHN HARVEY, Brighton, Mass; USN 1839-71 (b/V-7-1815 Haverhill; d/XII-26-1879) MD Harvard 1838; ng Harvard Coll 1830-31; AB Amherst 1834. *Harvard in CW*: 8.

WRIGHT, JONATHAN J , Monrovia, Ind 1854- ; Emporia, Kans 1870- (b/X-7-1829 Fayette Co, Ind; d/V-13-1904) MD M C Ohio 1854. *J Kans M S* 4:458, 1904. *Kans St Bd Hlth* 4th Rept 1887: 226.

WRIGHT, JOSEPH JEFFERSON BURR, USA 1833- (b/V- 1801 Wilkesbarre, Pa; d/V-14-1878 Carlisle; MD Jeff'n 1836. *Phila m times* 8:456, 1878. *Tr AMA* 30: 847-48, 1879. G V Henry *Milit rec*: 128-29. *K&B* III: 1338.

WRIGHT, MARMADUKE BURR, Cincinnati (b/XI-15 1803 Pemberton, NJ; d/VIII-15-1879) MD UPa 1823. *Tr O St M S* 1880:112-15. *Tr AMA* 31:1098-1101, 1880. *Med surg rep Phila* 41:242, 1879. *K&B* III: 1338-39.

WRIGHT, NORMAN E , Berea, O (d/IX-10-1895 @61) MD Hom Hosp Cleveland 1874. *JAMA* 25:467, 1895. *Polk* 1890:894. Homeopath.

WRIGHT, OREN C , Pittsburgh (d/VII-26-1901 @55) MD W Pa M C 1894. *JAMA* 37: 398, 1901.

WRIGHT, R [?REGINALD] N, CW-USA (b/Md? d/VI -13-1865) MD ?Jefferson 1844. *Nat m j* 1:304, 1870/71.

WRIGHT, THOMAS H , Baltimore (b/NY; d/1856) MD CPSNY 1823; Hon MD UMd 1819. *Med ann Md:* 633.

WRIGHT, WALTER MELVIN, Orange, Mass (b/1846; d/VI-24-1899 @53) MD Dartmouth 1874; AB 1871; att Bowdoin. *JAMA* 33:53, 1899. *Bost m&s j* 140: 648, 1899. *Polk* 1890: 554.

WRIGHT, WILLARD ?R , CW-USA; Atlantic City (b/ VII-18-1832 Durham Co, NY;d/IX-8-1895) MD UPa 1867. *JAMA* 25:510, 1895. *U Pa med alum CW*: 1867. *Polk* 1886: 601.

WRIGHT, WILLIAM E , Knoxville, Ia (d/VI-19-1901 @50) MD CPS Keokuk 1866. *JAMA* 37:125, 1901. *Polk* 1886: 361.

WROTH, PEREGRINE, Eastern Md (b/IV-7-1786; d/VI-13-1879) Hon MD UMd 1841; att UPA Med Dept. *Med annals Md:* 633. *Tr AMA* 31:1101-02, 1880.

WROTH, THOMAS G , Baltimore (b/1814 Kent Co, Md; d/VI- -1888) MD UMd 1837. *Med annals Md:* 634.

Polk 1886: 440.

WÜLFINCH, MICHAEL W A , Reading, Pa (b/1846? d/II-17-1897 @51) <MD Amsterdam 1876> *JAMA* 28:523, 1897. *Polk* 1896: 1332.

WUNDERLICH, GERALD, ?NYC (d/IV-25-1864) <MD Würzburg 1828> *Med reg NY NJ Conn* 1865: 227.

WYATT, RICHARD OVERTON, Goochland Co, Va; CW-CSA (b/IV-18-1837; d/XII-16-1861) MD UMd 1861; att UVa Med Sch. Johnson, J L *U [Va] Memorial ... alum dec'd CW*: 613. Blanton's *Va surgs in CW*:420.

WYCHE, GEORGE A , Red Land, La (d/X-9-1887 @75) MD Tulane 1860. *New Orl m&s j* ns15:413, 1887.

WYCKOFF, CORNELIUS C , Buffalo (b/VIII-5-1822 Romulus; d/XI-6-1903) MD Buffalo 1848. *Tr M S St NY* 1904:[420]. *Atkinson* I: 404. *Polk* 1886: 654.

WYCKOFF, JAMES BARKLEY, NYC (d/XII-1862) MD CPSNY 1856. *Med reg NY NJ Conn* 1865:215.

WYCKOFF, SAMUEL STOUT, NYC (d/X-16-1888 @ 35) MD CPSNY 1877. *Med reg NY NJ Conn* 1889:291.

WYCKOFF, VAN BRUNT, Brooklyn (d/III-13-1889 @70) MD CPSNY 1845; AB Columbia 1840; AM 1844. *Med reg NY NJ Conn* 1889: 291.

WYMAN, GEORGE, Topeka, Kans (d/III-3-1894) <MD Harvard 1883> *JAMA* 22:391, 1894. *Polk* 1890: 449.

WYMAN, JEFFRIES, Cambridge, Mass (b/VIII-11-1814 Chelmsford; d/IX-4-1874 Bethlehem, NH) MD Harvard 1837; AB 1833. *Bost m&s j* 91:268, 283-84, 527, 1874. *Buff m&s j* 14: 76, 1874. *K&B* III:1341-44.

WYMAN, JOEL W , Brunson, SC (b/XII-6-1800 Westminster; d/VI-20-1883) MD M C SC 1831; AB Amherst 1825; AM 1828. *Amherst, Men of*: 1825.

WYMAN, MORRILL, Cambridge, Mass (b/VII-25 1812 Chelmsford; d/I-30-1903) MD Harvard 1837; AB 1833. *Bost m&s j* 149:195-203, 1903; 148:164-66, 1903. *Atkinson* I: 706. *K&B* III: 1344-45.

WYMAN, RUFUS H , Keokuk, Ia CW-USA; (b/III-24 1817 Oswego NY;d/II-11-1881) <MD UPa 1846> *Tr Ia St M S* 1881-82: 158-59; 1903:450. Fairchild's *Iowa*:36.

WYMAN, RUSSELL C , Maitland, Mo (d/VIII-14-1901) MD CPS Keokuk 1878. *JAMA* 37:654, 1901. *Polk* 1886: 554.

WYMAN, SAMUEL EDWIN, Cambridge, Mass (d/V-7-1896) MD Harvard 1879; AB 1874. *Bost m&s j* 134:500, 1896. *Polk* 1896: 709.

WYMAN, SAMUEL W , Boston (b/1792? d/1867 @75) MD Harvard 1818; AB 1814. *Bost m&s j* 76:28, 1867.

WYNNE, JAMES, Baltimore (b/1814 Utica, NY; d/II-11 1871 Guatemala) MD Fairfield 1835. *Med reg NY NJ Conn* 1871:368. *K&B* III: 1345-46.

WYNNE, WILLIAM B , CW-USA; Phoenixville Pa (b/ 1832; d/VIII-16-1902) MD UVt 1858. *Pa med jour* 6: 262, 1902/03. *Flint* 1897: 828.

WYTHE, JOSEPH HENRY, CW-USA; Oakland Cal (b/ III-19-1822 Manchester, Engl; d/VII-6-1901) MD Phila Coll M & S 1850. *Cal st j m* 1:228-29, 1903. *Atkinson* I: 692-93. *K&B* III:1346-47. *Polk* 1896: 225.

WYTHE, WILLIAM T , San Francisco (b/VI-9-1847 Pa; d/VI-27-1880) MD Willamette 1868. *Tr Cal M S* 1880: 328-29.

WYVILL, WALTER, Piscataway, Md (b/III-4-1781 Anne Arundel Co, Md; d/VIII-4-1860) <MD UPa 1802> *Med annals Md:* 635.

XANDER, WILLIAM OSCAR, Philadelphia (d/IX-7-1902 @35) MD UPa 1895 *Pa m j* 6:262,1902/3. *Flint* 1897: 828.

YALE, JOHN, Ware, Mass (b/IV-2-1820 New Hartford, Conn; d/II-25-1898 Beloit, Kans) MD Yale 1841. *Bost m&s j* 138:216 1898. *JAMA* 30:624 1898. *Polk* 1896:725.

YALE, LEROY MILTON, NYC (b/II-12-1841 Vineyard Haven, Mass; d/IX-12-1906) MD Bellevue 1866; AB Columbia 1862; AM 1865. *Bost m&s j* 155:322-23, 1906. *Atkinson* I:348. *K&B* III: 1347.

YANDELL, DAVID WENDEL, Louisville; CW-CSA (b/IX-4-1826 Cragg Bluff, Tenn; d/V-2-1898) MD U Lsvl 1846. *Tr CPP* cent vol: 287. *Buff m&s j* 37:854-55, 1898. *Nashvl j m&s* 83: 239-40, 1898. *JAMA* 30:1190-91, 1898. *K&B* III: 1347-48.

YANDELL, HENRY, Shelbyville, Tenn (d/IX-24-1835 @24) MD Transylvania 1833. *Transylv j m & assoc sci* 8:602, 1836.

YANDELL, LUNSFORD PITTS Sr, Louisville (b/VII-4 1803 Tenn; d/II-4-1878) MD U Md 1825; att Transylvania. *Tr AMA* 29:778-79, 1878. *New Orl m&s j* ns5: 737-38, 1878. *Chic m j* 36:442-43, 1878. *Atkinson* I: 469-70. *K&B* III: 1348.

YANDELL, LUNSFORD PITTS Jr, Louisville (b/VI-6-1837 Tenn; d/III-13-1884) MD U Lsvl 1857; <MD Memphia M C 1859> *JAMA* 2:360-62, 1884. *So pract* 6:188-89, 1884. *Nashvl j m&s* ns33:188-89, 1884. *Med age* 2:87-88, 1884.

YANDELL, WILLIAM N , El Paso, Tex (b/1842 Murfreesboro, Tenn; d/III-24-1900) MD Gross M C Denver 1888. *JAMA* 34:891, 1900. G P Red, *Med man in Tex*: 182-83.

YANDELL, WILSON, Murfreesboro, Tenn (b/XII-17-1774 Mecklenburg Co, NC; d/X-1-1827) Hon MD UMd 1823; stud w/Drs Wm Holt & Hamilton, Tenn. *Transylv j m & assoc sci* 1:[134]-46, 1828. *Tr M S Tenn* 1876: 89.

YARD, BENJAMIN F , CW-USA (d/XI-10-1865 @41) MD ? *Nat m j* 1:304, 1870/71.

YARDLEY, THOMAS HOWE, Philadelphia (b/XII-3 1800 Bucks Co, Pa; d/I-4-1860) MD UPa 1825. *Tr CPP* cent vol:276; ns3:335-44, 1856-62. *Med surg rep Phila* ns3:340, 1859/60.

YARROW, THOMAS JEFFERSON, CW-USA; Philadelphia (b/II-13-1840 Alloway, NJ; d/VIII-6-1903) MD UPa 1861. *Tr CPP* cent vol:276. *Pa med jour* 7:280, 1903/04. *U Pa med alum CW*: 1861. *Flint* 1897: 828.

YARROW, THOMAS JEFFERSON, Philadelphia (d/VI 27–1906 Cape May, NJ) MD UPa 1894. *Pa med jour* 9: 805, 1905/06.

YATES, EUGENE STEPHEN, Lawrence, Mass (d/VII–25–1886) MD Bellevue 1872. *Bost m&s j* 115:120, 1886.

YATES, ROBERT DAVID, Brooklyn (b/1857; d/1885?) MD UCNY 1881. *Med reg NY NJ Conn* 1886: 257.

YEAGER, GEORGE WASHINGTON, Mercer Pa; CW–USA (b/1824; d/IV–22–1898) MD UPa 1852. *Pa m j* 2: 164, 1898. *U Pa med alum CW*: 1852. *Flint* 1897: 809.

YEAGER, THEODORE CONRAD, Allentown Pa; CW–USA (b/IV–1–1838; d/I–14–1874) MD UPa 1860. *Tr Pa St M S* 1874:281–83. *U Pa med alum CW*: 1860.

YEATES, JOHN LLOYD, Baltimore (b/XII–27–1802; d/VII–24–1875) MD UMd 1822. *Tr AMA* 27:648–49, 1876. *Med annals Md:* 635.

YEMANS, CHARLES C , CW–USA; Detroit (d/VII–21 1901) MD Detroit M C 1872. *JAMA* 37:397, 1901. *Polk* 1886: 490.

YEOMANS, GEORGE, Ashland, Pa (b/II–25–1833; d/IV 18–1895 Philadelphia) MD Jefferson 1860; AB Williams 1856; att Lafayette. *Williams cat*: 1856. *Lafayette, Men of*: 159.

YETTER, FRANK PIERCE, Bowmansville, Pa (d/III–4 1894) MD Bellevue 1881. *JAMA* 22:482, 1894.

YOCKEY, DAVID HOOVER, Richmond, Ind (b/XI–17–1854 Delaware Co; d/X–7–1904) MD Med Coll Ind 1883. *Tr Ind St M S* 1905:465.

YOCUM, BENJAMIN B , Philadelphia (d/VII–21–1879) MD UPa 1872. *Phila m times* 9:540, 564, 1879. *Med surg rep Phila* 41:198, 1879.

YOCUM, JOSEPH JOHN, CW–USA; Ashland, Pa (b/III 21–1840 Catawissa; d/VII–10–1879) MD UPa 1866. *U Pa med alum CW*: 1866.

YOHN, EDWIN F , Valparaiso, Ind (b/1863 Logan Co; d/II–4–1906) MD U Lsvl 1894. *Tr Ind St M S* 1906: 499. *Polk* 1896: 471.

YOHN, WILLIAM A , Valparaiso, Ind (b/III–29–1850 Porter Co; d/VIII–12–1892) MD M C Ind 1879. *Tr Ind St M S* 1893:246. *Polk* 1890:391. Kemper's *Indiana*: 359.

YORK, JOHN COLBY, S Boston (d/VII–13–1855 @25) MD Harvard 1853. *Bost m&s j* 52:457, 1855.

YORK, JASPER HAZEN, Dover, NH (d/IV–7–1874) MD Harvard 1843. *Bost m&s j* 90:396, 1874. *Mass M S cat* 1894.

YORK, SHUBAL, CW–USA (d/III–28–1864 Charleston, Ill) MD ? *Nat m j* 1:304, 1870/71.

YOUKEY [YONKEY], WILLIAM P , Belleville, Ont; Lafayette, Ind (d/I–12–1899 @52) MD Ind Med Coll 1879. *JAMA* 32:196, 1899. *Polk* 1896: 478.

YOULIN, JOHN JUVENAL, Jersey City (b/XII–31–1821 Rupert, Vt; d/X–30–1881 @60) MD Western Coll Hom 1854. *Med rec NY* 20:529, 1881. *Hahn mo* 16:766, 1881. *Am obs* 19:63, 111, 1882. *Tr Am Inst Hom* 1882: 136. *King* I:251. Homeopath.

YOUMANS, HENRY AUGUSTUS, Mokwenga, Wis (b/III–22–1816 Coeymans, NY; d/X–4–1893) MD Geneva 1843. *JAMA* 21:630, 1893. *Tr Wis St M S* 1894: . *Butler* 1878: 868.

YOUMANS, JAMES, Davenport, Ia (b/Stillwater, NJ; d/III–16–1895 @69) MD Bennett 1878; att Lafayette. *JAMA* 24:497, 1895. *Polk* 1886: 353. Eclectic.

YOUMANS, JEREMIAH, Madison, Wis (b/Java, NY; d/X–7–1873) MD Rush 1852. *Tr Wis St M S* 1874: 111.

YOUMANS, WILLIAM JAY, Mt Vernon, NY (b/X–14–1838 Saratoga; d/IV–11–1901) MD UCNY 1865. *Bost m&s j* 144: 390, 1901. *Polk* 1896: 1086.

YOUNG, ALEXANDER, Goshen, NJ (b/III–27–1828 Beesley's Point; d/V–7–1887) MD Jefferson 1857. *Tr M S NJ* 1887:303–04. *Butler* 1878: 478.

YOUNG, CHARLES SAYWARD, Stoughton, Mass (d/V–16–1895 @43) MD LICH 1873. *Bost m&s j* 133: 659, 1895. *Polk* 1886: 474.

YOUNG, DELOS W , Aurora, Ill (b/1829; d/1874) MD CPS Keokuk 1851. *Tr AMA* 26:461–63, 1875. *Tr Ill St M S* 1875:228–29.

YOUNG, ELISHA, CW–CSA; Greensborough, Ala (b/IV 2–1837; d/XI–6–1898) MD Jefferson 1859. *Tr M Assn St Ala* 1899:232. *Polk* 1893: 156.

YOUNG, FENTON, Denison, Tex (d/VII–13–1893) MD Miami 1869. *Chic m rec* 5:136, 1893. *Polk* 1886: 884.

YOUNG, FRANCIS J , Bridgeport, Conn (b/II– –1843 Cornwall; d/I–4–1893) MD Yale 1866. *Pr Conn M S* 1893: 251–53. *Med reg NY NJ Conn* 1884–85: 162. *Bost m&s j* 128: 52, 1893.

YOUNG, FRANK N H , Danbury, Conn (b/VIII– –1831 Clifton, Engl; d/III–17–1868) MD Berkshire 1859. *Pr Conn M S* 1868: 170–71. *Phila med reg & dir* 1871:295. *Med surg rep Phila* 18:314, 1868.

YOUNG, FRANK RAYMOND, Smethport, Pa (d/1904 @27) MD UPa 1899. *Pa med jour* 8:336, 1904/05.

YOUNG, FRANKLIN A , W Charlton, NY (d/XII–17 1886) MD Albany 1860. *Med reg NY NJ Conn* 1887: 277. *Polk* 1886: 715.

YOUNG, HARRY, USA (d/II–5–1899 Philippines) MD ? *JAMA* 32:385, 1899.

YOUNG, ISRAEL GILBERT, Philadelphia (b/VI–21–1840 Chestnut Hill, Pa; d/IX–26–1899) MD UPa 1862. *JAMA* 33:927, 1899. *Atkinson* I: 631. *Polk* 1896: 1323.

YOUNG, JAMES THOMAS, Washington, DC (b/VI–2–1839; d/VII–3–1901) MD Bellevue 1864. *Hist Med Soc DC:* 272. *Polk* 1886: 214.

YOUNG, JOHN, Cold Spring, NY (b/IV–16–1822 Ireland; d/IX–2–1893) MD CPSNY 1844. *Med reg NY NJ Conn* 1894:253. *Tr M S St NY* 11:662, 1894.

YOUNG, JOHN HENRY WEIR, ?NYC (b/VI–19–1859 Phila; d/V–3–1882) MD UPa 1881; BS Cornell. *Med reg NY NJ Conn* 1882: 237.

YOUNG, JOHN SYLVESTER, Brooklyn (d/IX–23–1895 @63) MD CPSNY 1854; att Fordham. *JAMA* 25:

 Spec. educ'l status abbrev. as: ***ng*** = college verified attendance without degree;

682, 1895.

YOUNG, JOHN W, Bloomfield, Ia (b/1841 Indiana; d/III-17-1899) MD CPS Keokuk 1871. *JAMA* 32:787, 1899. *Polk* 1886: 351.

YOUNG, JOHN WATSON, Montague, NJ (b/I-1-1840; d/II-14-1864) MD UPa 1862. *Tr M S NJ* 1865:75-77; 1872: 186.

YOUNG, MATTHEW H, Ashland, Ky (d/VIII-26-1896) MD Jefferson 1859. *JAMA* 27: 661, 1896.

YOUNG, NICHOLAS D, Youngsville, La (d/II-8-1906 @64) MD Tulane 1867. *New Orl m&s j* 58:779, 1906. *Polk* 1896: 627.

YOUNG, NOBLE, Washington, DC (b/VI-26-1808 Baltimore; d/IV-11-1883) MD Columbian 1828. *JAMA* 1:520, 1883. *Hist Med Soc DC:* 227. *Atkinson* I:537.

YOUNG, OSCAR H, Sidney Centre, NY (b/Pa; d/I-21 1889) MD Jefferson 1876. *Tr MS St NY* 11:741 ff, 1894. *Polk* 1886: 708.

YOUNG, PARKE GEORGE, Washington, DC (b/II-21-1852; d/VII-30-1906) MD Georgetown 1872. *Hist Med Soc DC:* 304. *Polk* 1893: 274.

YOUNG, PETER W, CW-CSA; Wilmington, NC (d/IV 1884) MD UPa 1850. *NC m j* 13: 218, 1884.

YOUNG, SAMUEL, Hagerstown, Md (b/1739; d/1838) MD ? *Med annals Md:* 639.

YOUNG, SAMUEL DAVIS, CW-CSA; Vance Co, NC (b/1833 Granville Co; d/VI- -1885) MD UPa 1858. *U Pa med alum CW*: 1858 suppl.

YOUNG, SAMUEL LANE, Marblehead, Mass 1853-63; Bridgewater 1866-67; Gloucester 1868- (b/I-3-1813; d/IV-19-1893 Portland, Me) MD Harvard 1852; AB Bowdoin 1840. *Bowdn cat*: 1840. *Polk* 1886: 425.

YOUNG [JUNG], THEODORE JACOB, Titusville, Pa; CW-USA (b/XII-9-1834 Neustadt, Gny; d/XI-22-1900) MD UPa 1868. *U Pa med alum CW*: 1868.

YOUNG, THOMAS, ? (d/X-7-1878 Port Gibson, Miss) MD ? *Tr AMA* 30:889, 1879. *Med rec NY* 14:320, 1878.

YOUNG, THOMAS FRANCIS, Brooklyn (b/X-30-1865; d/X-26-1895) MD LICH 1891. *JAMA* 25: 911, 1895.

YOUNG, WILLIAM, Hingham, Mass (b/I-12-1809 Boston; d/VII-1-1863) MD Harvard 1834; AM 1829. Palmer, *Necrol alum Harvard*: 476.

YOUNG, WILLIAM, Cold Spring, NY (b/1820 Ireland; d/X-26-1902) <MD Glasgow 1842> *Bost m&s j* 147: 532, 1902. *Polk* 1896: 1016.

YOUNG, WILLIAM GAMBLE, S Easton, Pa (d/III-9 1894) MD UPa 1893; PhB Lafayette. *Lehigh Valley m mag* 5:169, 1893-94.

YOUNG, WILLIAM WALLACE, Nanticoke, Pa (b/VII 4-1872 Philadelphia; d/I-6-1902) MD UPa 1894. *Pa m j* 5:211, 1901/02. *Tr Luzerne Co* (Pa) *M S* 1902:154 ff. *Flint* 1897: 810.

YOUNG, ZACHARY T, Ville Platte, La (d/X-4-1905 @56) MD Tulane 1872. *New Orl m&s j* 58:430, 1905. *Polk* 1896: 627.

YOUNGBLOOD, WILLIAM S, Groveton, Tex (d/X-6 1895) MD Hosp M C Lsvl 1889. *JAMA* 25: 682, 1895. *Polk* 1890: 1094.

YOUNGLOVE, FRANK WARD, Wautoma, Wis (b/I-11 1860; d/XI-22-1890 Chicago) MD Rush 1882. *Tr Wis St M S* 1891: 328-29. *Polk* 1886: 962.

YOUNGMAN, DAVID, Boston (b/VIII-26-1817 Peterborough, NH; d/V-11-1895) MD Dartmouth 1846; AB 1839. *Bost m&s j* 133:659, 1895. *JAMA* 24:861, 1895. *Polk* 1890: 545.

YOUNKMAN, ANTHONY B, Bremen, Ind (d/V-16 1899) MD Ft Wayne Coll Med 1882. *JAMA* 32:1269, 1899. *Polk* 1896: 460.

ZABRISKIE, FRED TEMPLETON, NYC (d/XI-5-1905 @33) MD CPSNY 1895. *Bost m&s j* 153: 570, 1905. *Polk* 1896: 1086.

ZABRISKIE, GUILLIAM ARTHUR, NYC (b/X-24-1900) MD CPSNY 1882; att Rutgers 1876-77. *Bost m&s j* 143:490, 1900. *Polk* 1896: 1086.

ZABRISKIE, JOHN LLOYD, Flatbush, NY (b/VIII-26 1831; d/XI-11-1895) MD UCNY 1853. *JAMA* 25:912, 1895. *Bost m&s j* 133:528, 1895. *Polk* 1890: 789.

ZABRISKIE [LABRISKIE], LEMAIRE, NYC (d/III- -1866) MD Bellevue 1866. *Tr AMA* 18:317-18, 1867 *Med surg rep Phila* 14:280, 1866.

ZABRISKIE, PHILIP HAMILTON, Jersey City (d/1875 Cherry Hill) MD CPSNY 1836. *Tr AMA* 27: 654, 1876.

ZACHARIAS, JOHN FORNEY, CW-CSA; Cumberland, Md 1871- (d/VIII-16-1904 @63) MD Jefferson 1860. *JAMA* 43: 748, 1904.

ZAKRZEWSKA, MARIE ELISABETH, Jamaica Plain, Mass (b/1829 Berlin, Gny; d/V-12-1902) <MD Gny> att Cleveland Med Coll. *Bost m&s j* 146: 560, 1902. *K&B* III: 1353-54.

ZANTZINGER, ALFRED, Philadelphia (b/VI-27-1839; d/VIII-16-1873) MD Hahnemann 1862; AB UPa 1859. *Med surg rep Phila* 29:162, 1873. *Tr Am Inst Hom* 1874: 663. Homeopath.

ZANTZINGER, WILLIAM SHEAFF, Philadelphia, Canandaigua, NY (b/XI-22-1805; d/XII-11-1888) MD UPa 1828; AB 1823; AM 1828. *Tr CPP* cent vol: 277

ZEIGLER [ZIEGLER], JACOB L, Mt Joy, Pa (b/XI 17-1822 E Donegal Twp, Pa; d/XII-26-1906) MD Jefferson 1844. *Pa m j* 10:407, 1906/07. *Flint* 1897: 810.

ZEINER, LEVI S, Easton, Pa (d/VII-27-1895) MD Jefferson 1879. *JAMA* 25:253, 1895.

ZELLER, HENRY, Williamsport, Md (b/VIII-17-1810; d/VII- -1885) MD Jefferson 1837. *Med annals Md:* 636. *Polk* 1886: 446.

ZELLER, JOHN G, Spring Bay, Ill (b/XII-10-1828 Munich, Bavaria; d/VI-17-1893) MD St Louis Med Coll 1855; grad U Munich Polytechnic. *St Louis m & s j* 66: 65, 1894. *Tr Ill St M S* 1894: 50.

ZENZEN, LOUIS, CW–USN (d/XI–22–1868 abd US Arizona) MD ? *Nat m j* 1:304, 1870/71. *Tr AMA* 21: 495, 1870. *Med surg rep Phila* 19:487, 1868. *Phila med reg & dir* 1871: 298.

ZERNS, WILLIAM MAURICE, Philadelphia (b/Salem, NJ; d/IX–21–1887 Watertown, NY) MD Hahnemann Phila 1872. *Med vis* 3:350, 1887. *Hahn mo* 22:656, 1887. Homeopath.

ZEVELY, EDMUND A , CW–USA; Washington, DC (b/II–24–1845; d/III–1–1876) MD UPa 1865. *Hist Med Soc DC:* 305. *U Pa med alum CW*: 1865.

ZIEGENFUSS, AUGUSTUS A , Buck Mount, Pa (d/XII 7–1869 @43) MD Phila Coll Med & Surg 1852. *Phila med reg & dir* 1871: 303.

ZIEGLER, ELIJAH REMP, CW–USA; W Union, Iowa (b/III–9 1837 Rebersville, Pa; d/V–29–1873) MD UPa 1866. *U Pa med alum CW*: 1866.

ZILLIKEN, PAUL N , Evansville, Ill (d/III–18–1906) MD Hom Med Coll Mo 1892. *Ill m j* 9:463, 1906. *Polk* 1896: 369. Homeopath.

ZIMMERMAN, GEORGE M , Butler, Pa (d/VIII–6–1906 @61) MD Jefferson 1870. *Pa med jour* 9:894, 1905/06. *Flint* 1897: 797.

ZINK, WALTER, Branford, Conn (b/1841 Bavaria; d/1902) MD Würzburg 1862. *Pr Conn M S* 1902:425–26. *Polk* 1896: 274.

ZITZER, JOHN JACOB, Carlisle, Pa (b/II–20–1826 Prussia; d/X–30–1883) <MD Heidelberg> *JAMA* 1:548, 1883. *Butler* 1878: 715.

ZOLLICKOFFER, WILLIAM, Uniontown, Md (b/1793; d/1853 Carroll Co, Md) MD UMd 1818; MD Washington U Balto 1838. *Med annals Md:* 637.

ZOLNOWSKI, VINCENT Sr, NYC (d/X–21–1897 LI) MD UVt 1883. *JAMA* 29:925, 1897. *Polk* 1896: 1086.

ZOOK, ELI J, Newville Pa (d/VII–11–1904 @60) MD Jefferson 1878 *Pa m j* 8:336 1904/5. *JAMA* 43:621, 1904.

ZORNS, JACOB S , Philadelphia (d/XI–3–1869 @75) MD UPa 1827. *Phila med reg & dir* 1871: 294.

 Spec. educ'l status abbrev. as: ***ng*** = college verified attendance without degree;

For Product Safety Concerns and Information please contact our EU
representative GPSR@taylorandfrancis.com
Taylor & Francis Verlag GmbH, Kaufingerstraße 24, 80331 München, Germany

www.ingramcontent.com/pod-product-compliance
Lightning Source LLC
LaVergne TN
LVHW010524100826
845148LV00001B/86

* 9 7 8 0 3 6 7 0 2 7 4 9 0 *